Patterns of Economic Change by State and Area

INCOME, EMPLOYMENT, AND GROSS DOMESTIC PRODUCT

Eleventh Edition
2024

HANNAH ANDERSON KROG

Bernan Press
Lanham • Boulder • New York • London

Published by Bernan Press
An imprint of The Rowman & Littlefield Publishing Group, Inc.
4501 Forbes Boulevard, Suite 200, Lanham, Maryland 20706
www.rowman.com

86-90 Paul Street, London EC2A 4NE

ISBN 979-8-89205-042-5 (paperback) | ISBN 979-8-89205-043-2 (ebook)

Contents

PREFACE

Bernan Press is pleased to present the eleventh edition of *Patterns of Economic Change by State and Area.* It is a special edition of *Business Statistics of the United States: Patterns of Economic Change*, bringing together measurements for regions, states, and metropolitan areas of some of the time trends that are displayed at the national level in *Business Statistics.*

This volume also complements such titles as *State and Metropolitan Area Data Book* and *County and City Extra.* In contrast to their predominantly current and detailed cross-section data on states and metropolitan areas, this book contributes historical time-series measurements of key aggregates that show how the economies of regions, states, and metropolitan areas have responded over time to cyclical currents and long-term trends.

All these data are compiled and published by U.S. government professional statistical agencies—the Bureau of Economic Analysis and the Census Bureau. Specific references to publications and web sites, along with definitions of terms and other essential information, are detailed before each data series. With this information, the user can properly interpret and use the data and can update it, if desired, as the source agencies release new information over the course of the year.

The largest body of data included is "Part A: Personal Income and Employment by Region, State, and Area." These tables provide annual data, going as far back as 1960, for farm and nonfarm earnings of persons; payments to persons of dividends, interest, and rent; personal current transfer receipts, which are income sources such as Social Security; total personal income; population; per capita personal income and disposable (after income taxes) personal income (that is, total income divided by the size of the population); and the total number of jobs in the state or area. Using these data, the performance of any given state or area, whether at one moment in time or over a span of years, can be studied, compared, and contrasted with that of the nation and other states or areas.

Even more comprehensive than personal income is gross domestic product (GDP), the measure of total U.S. economic activity, available and published here in Part B at the state level both in current dollar values and in the form of an index of quantities produced (that is to say, change in real output, corrected to remove the effects of inflation).

Moving from indicators of aggregate economic trends to effects on individuals and households, Part C shows data on the poverty rate and median household incomes (the income of the "typical" household in the exact middle of the income distribution), corrected for inflation.

Part D, which was added in 2023, looks at consumer spending and pricing differences by area. Tables present data on historical per capital personal consumption expenditures on groceries, housing, and health care by region and state. Another table shows regional price parities by MSA.

Hannah Anderson Krog edited the past eight editions of *Patterns of Economic Change by State and Area.* Mary Meghan Ryan edited previous editions, and Cornelia J. Strawser provided assistance in planning the first edition.

PART A

PERSONAL INCOME AND EMPLOYMENT BY REGION, STATE, AND AREA

PART A: PERSONAL INCOME AND EMPLOYMENT BY REGION, STATE, AND AREA

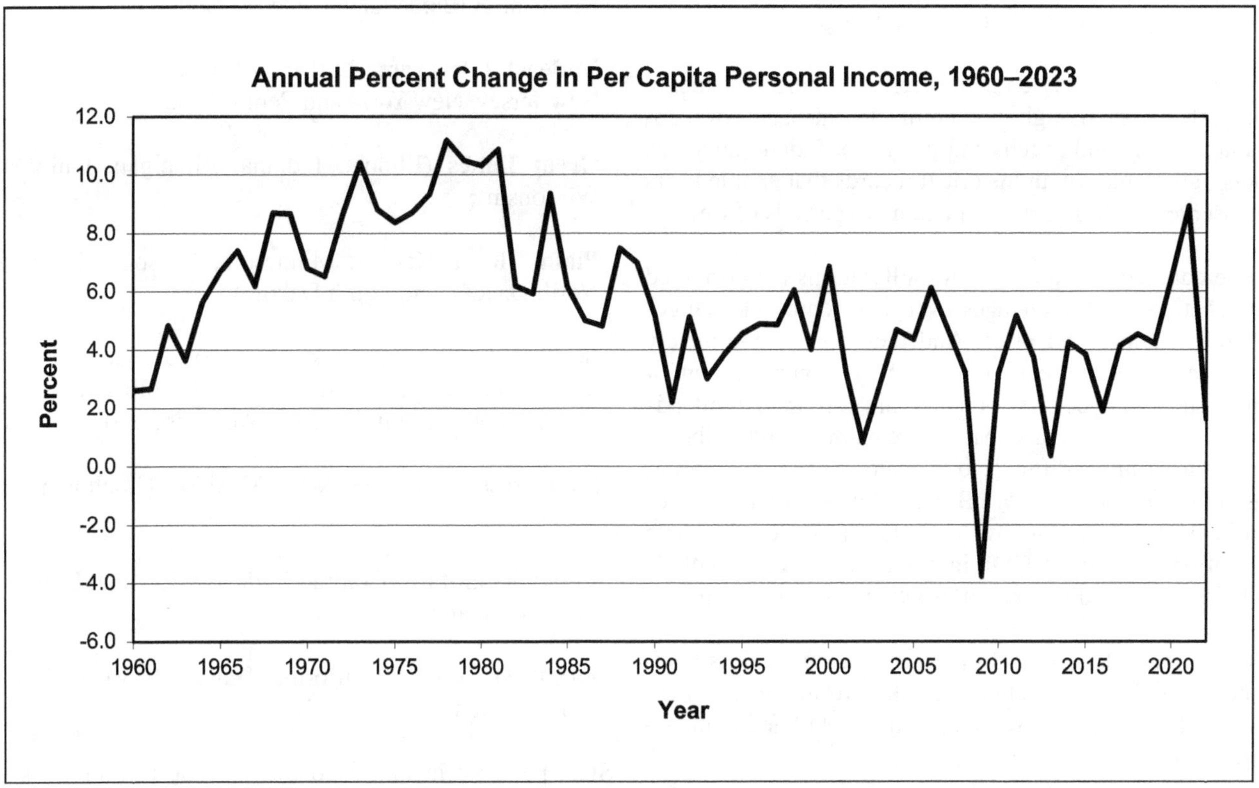

HIGHLIGHTS

- In 2023, nationwide per capita personal income increased 4.7 percent after increasing 1.6 percent in 2022 and 8.9 percent in 2021. From 1960 through 2020, per capita personal income only declined once, dropping from $40,854 in 2008 to $39,307 in 2009.

- Per capita personal income provides one measure of the affluence of the states and regions, and it varies widely. The District of Columbia had the highest per capita personal income in 2023, at $100,909, followed by Massachusetts ($87,812), and Connecticut ($87,447). Mississippi had the lowest per capita income at $48,110. The per capita personal income nationally was $68,531.

- As the economy continued to recover from the effects of the COVID-19 pandemic, total employment increased in all but 1 MSA in 2022. The areas that saw the largest growth in employment from 2021-2022 were: Midland, TX (9.5 percent), Las Vegas-Henderson-Paradise, NV (8.8 percent), Austin-Round Rock-Georgetown, TX (8.3 percent), Orlando-Kissimmee-Sanford, FL (8.1 percent), and Odessa, TX (7.5 percent). Kokomo, IN, saw no change in employment in 2022. The areas with the smallest growth in employment were: Columbus, GA-AL, Lake Charles, LA, and Sierra Vista-Douglas, AZ, which all saw growth of 0.3 percent.

- The value of total earnings by place of work in the United States increased 5.7 percent in 2023, after increasing 6.5 percent in 2022. These earnings include wages and salaries, supplements, and proprietors' income.

PART A NOTES AND DEFINITIONS: PERSONAL INCOME AND EMPLOYMENT BY REGION, STATE, AND AREA

Source: U.S. Department of Commerce, Bureau of Economic Analysis (BEA), https://www.bea.gov.

The personal income data set presented here provides a comprehensive, though not complete, measure of economic activity and purchasing power for individual states and smaller areas, with historical records that enable users to observe developments over extensive periods of time.

These data are stated in current-dollar terms not corrected for inflation, so that changes over time represent changes in both quantity and price. And they do not completely represent corporate economic activity: compensation of corporate employees is covered, as are corporate dividends received by individuals, but the remaining undistributed corporate profits—difficult to allocate to small geographical units—are not. See Part B that follows for measures of Gross Domestic Product by state, which provide a complete allocation to states of GDP in current dollars and include inflation-corrected indexes of growth in quantity terms.

The summary definitions of personal income and its components in the next section are taken from a BEA press release. In a following section, further detail and explanation of the concepts is provided.

BEA definitions

Personal income is the income received by persons from all sources. Personal income is the sum of net earnings by place of residence, property income, and personal current transfer receipts. **Property income** is rental income of persons, personal dividend income, and personal interest income. **Net earnings** is earnings by place of work (the sum of wage and salary disbursements, supplements to wages and salaries, and proprietors' income) less contributions for government social insurance, plus an adjustment to convert earnings by place of work to a place-of-residence basis. Personal income is measured before the deduction of personal income taxes and other personal taxes and is reported in current dollars (no adjustment is made for price changes).

The estimate of personal income in the United States is derived as the sum of the state estimates and the estimate for the District of Columbia; it differs from the estimate of personal income in the national income and product accounts (NIPAs) because of differences in coverage, in the methodologies used to prepare the estimates, and in the timing of the availability of source data.

BEA groups all 50 states and the District of Columbia into eight distinct regions for purposes of data collecting and analyses:

New England (Connecticut, Maine, Massachusetts, New Hampshire, Rhode Island, and Vermont);

Mideast (Delaware, District of Columbia, Maryland, New Jersey, New York, and Pennsylvania);

Great Lakes (Illinois, Indiana, Michigan, Ohio, and Wisconsin);

Plains (Iowa, Kansas, Minnesota, Missouri, Nebraska, North Dakota, and South Dakota);

Southeast (Alabama, Arkansas, Florida, Georgia, Kentucky, Louisiana, Mississippi, North Carolina, South Carolina, Tennessee, Virginia, and West Virginia);

Southwest (Arizona, New Mexico, Oklahoma, and Texas);

Rocky Mountain (Colorado, Idaho, Montana, Utah, and Wyoming); and

Far West (Alaska, California, Hawaii, Nevada, Oregon, and Washington).

State personal income statistics provide a framework for analyzing current economic conditions in each state and can serve as a basis for decision-making.

For example:

- Federal government agencies use the statistics as a basis for allocating funds and determining matching grants to states. The statistics are also used in forecasting models to project energy and water use.
- State governments use the statistics to project tax revenues and the need for public services.
- Academic regional economists use the statistics for applied research.
- Businesses, trade associations, and labor organizations use the statistics for market research.

BEA's national, international, regional, and industry estimates; the Survey of Current Business; and BEA news releases are available without charge at www.bea.gov. By visiting the site, you can also subscribe to receive free e-mail summaries of BEA releases and announcements.

More about income concepts

For the sake of simplicity, the following definitions and clarifications are written in terms of states, but all statements about "states" apply equally to regions and metropolitan areas.

The sum of state personal incomes for the United States (50 states and the District of Columbia) is somewhat smaller than U.S. personal income as shown in the national income and product accounts (NIPAs), due to slightly different definitions. The national total of the state estimates consists only of the income earned by persons who live in the United States and of foreign residents who work in the United States. The measure of personal income in the NIPAs is broader. It includes the earnings of federal civilian and military personnel stationed abroad and of U.S. residents on foreign assignment for less than a year. It also includes the investment income received by federal retirement plans for federal workers stationed abroad. NIPA personal income includes all income earned by U.S. citizens living abroad for less than a year; state personal income excludes the portion earned while the individual lives abroad. Earnings of foreign residents are included in the NIPAs only if they live and work in the United States for a year or more; state personal income, on the other hand, includes income paid to foreign nationals working in the United States regardless of length of residency. There are also statistical differences that reflect different timing of the availability of source data.

As in the NIPAs, personal income is defined to exclude capital gains.

Earnings by place of work consists of payments, to persons who work in the state, of wages and salaries; all supplements to wages and salaries (including employer contributions for government social insurance and all other benefits); and farm and nonfarm proprietors' income. Proprietor's income includes inventory valuation and capital consumption adjustments.

Contributions for government social insurance, which is subtracted from total earnings, includes both the employer and the employee contributions, on behalf of persons working in the state, for Social Security, Medicare, unemployment insurance, and other government social insurance, but does not include contributions to government employee retirement plans. Hence, personal income is defined as net of all contributions for government social insurance, which are commonly referred to as "Social Security taxes." Personal income is not net of other taxes on wages or other income such as Federal and state income taxes. These taxes are subtracted, however, to yield *"disposable personal income."*

Adjustment for residence. BEA adjusts earnings by place of work to a place-of-residence basis, to account for interstate and international commuting. The difference between earnings by place of residence and earnings by place of work is shown in the "Adjustment for residence" column. This adjustment is a net figure, equaling income received by state residents from employment outside the state minus income paid to persons residing outside the state but working in the state.

The effect of interstate commuting can be seen in its most extreme form in the District of Columbia. Its large negative adjustment for residence says that roughly half of total earnings by people working there are paid to persons living outside D.C. Compare with Maryland and Virginia, which have substantial positive adjustments, representing income flowing from the District of Columbia and other employment sources outside the state. There is also a large negative adjustment for New York, associated with positive adjustments for New Jersey and Connecticut.

Dividends, interest, and rent. The rental income component of personal income, like that in the NIPAs, includes imputed rent on owner-occupied homes, net of capital consumption with capital consumption adjustment.

Personal current transfer receipts are aggregates for state residents of benefits from Social Security, Medicare, Medicaid, unemployment insurance, veterans' benefits, and other government benefits including the earned income credit. It does not include payments from government employee retirement plans, which are accounted for in supplements to wages and salaries.

It should be noted that in both the personal income and the NIPA accounts, the value of Medicare and Medicaid spending, even though in practice it is usually paid directly from the government to the health care provider, is treated as if it were cash income to the consumer, which is then expended in personal consumption expenditures.

Population is the U.S. Census Bureau estimate for the middle of the year. Note that because Hurricane Katrina occurred in August 2005, the population decline in Louisiana caused by that event does not appear until the entry for 2006.

Total employment is the total number of jobs, full-time plus part-time; each job that any person holds is counted at full weight. The employment estimates are on a place-of-work basis. Both wage and salary employment and self-employment are included. The main source for the wage and salary employment estimates is Bureau of Labor Statistics (BLS) estimates from unemployment insurance data (the ES-202 data), which also provides benchmarks for the widely followed BLS payroll employment measures. Self-employment is estimated mainly from individual and partnership federal income tax returns. Therefore, this definition of employment is broader than BLS "total nonfarm payroll employment."

This concept of employment also differs from the concept of employment in the Current Population Survey (CPS), another BLS monthly survey, which is derived from a monthly count of persons employed; any individual will appear only once in the CPS in a given month, no matter how many different jobs he or she might hold. In addition, a self-employed individual who files more than one Schedule C income-tax filing will be counted more than once in the state figures. Finally, the state figures include members of the armed forces, who are not covered in the CPS. Due to these differences and other possible reporting inconsistencies, the BEA employment estimates are different from, and usually larger than, state employment estimates from the CPS.

The employment estimates correspond closely in coverage to the earnings estimates by place of work. However, the earnings estimates include the income of limited partnerships and of tax-exempt cooperatives, for which there are no corresponding employment estimates.

Per capita income is total income divided by the state's midyear population. This is an important tool for "scaling" income data to the size of the state, so that meaningful comparisons of economic performance among states can be made. Per capita income provides a useful gauge of economic strength, purchasing power, and fiscal capacity.

Users should not, however, assume that per capita income well represents the income of a typical state resident. Per capita incomes are averages—"means" in the technical language of statistics. Income of a typical person is better represented by the "median," which is the income of a person at the middle of the income distribution; half the population has higher income and half has lower. Where income is distributed so unequally that a relatively small number of persons have extremely high incomes, the mean will be higher than the median; and if the income distribution is becoming more unequal, the mean will rise faster than the median. Both of these conditions have been present for the U.S. economy as a whole in recent decades. Median household (not personal) incomes by state are presented in Part C.

UNITED STATES

Personal Income and Employment by Region and State: United States

(Millions of dollars, except as noted.)

Year	Personal income, total	Derivation of personal income: Earnings by place of work: Nonfarm	Earnings by place of work: Farm	Earnings by place of work: Total	Less: Contributions for government social insurance	Plus: Adjustment for residence	Equals: Net earnings by place of residence	Plus: Dividends, interest, and rent	Plus: Personal current transfer receipts	Per capita (dollars): Personal income	Per capita (dollars): Disposable personal income	Population (thousands)	Total employment (thousands)
1960	417,700	334,492	13,734	348,226	16,358	-260	331,608	60,352	25,740	2,321	2,066	179,972	...
1961	436,047	345,444	14,467	359,911	16,916	-250	342,745	63,852	29,450	2,383	2,126	182,976	...
1962	464,000	368,896	14,526	383,422	19,023	-202	364,197	69,411	30,392	2,498	2,221	185,739	...
1963	487,780	388,214	14,414	402,628	21,559	-173	380,896	74,675	32,209	2,589	2,300	188,434	...
1964	522,633	417,196	13,227	430,423	22,258	-170	407,995	81,134	33,504	2,735	2,463	191,085	...
1965	564,444	448,173	15,576	463,749	23,278	-111	440,360	87,906	36,178	2,918	2,620	193,460	...
1966	612,713	493,890	16,631	510,521	31,136	-99	479,286	93,810	39,617	3,134	2,796	195,499	...
1967	656,828	528,209	15,259	543,468	34,600	-96	508,772	100,042	48,014	3,328	2,959	197,375	...
1968	720,877	580,338	15,420	595,758	38,392	-119	557,247	107,536	56,094	3,617	3,183	199,312	...
1969	791,229	636,235	17,430	653,665	43,791	-107	609,767	119,140	62,322	3,931	3,415	201,298	91,053
1970	855,525	675,692	17,660	693,352	46,012	-112	647,228	133,564	74,733	4,198	3,695	203,799	91,278
1971	924,613	723,952	18,142	742,094	50,859	-122	691,113	145,252	88,248	4,471	3,981	206,818	91,581
1972	1,016,408	797,699	21,947	819,646	58,897	-145	760,604	157,674	98,130	4,857	4,269	209,275	94,312
1973	1,133,468	884,089	34,875	918,964	75,183	-153	843,628	176,992	112,848	5,363	4,739	211,349	98,428
1974	1,244,912	963,812	30,097	993,909	84,872	-163	908,874	202,399	133,639	5,836	5,130	213,334	100,112
1975	1,362,505	1,030,360	29,132	1,059,492	88,974	-199	970,319	221,762	170,424	6,324	5,641	215,457	98,901
1976	1,495,704	1,148,053	25,218	1,173,271	100,987	-211	1,072,073	238,786	184,845	6,875	6,083	217,554	101,591
1977	1,651,632	1,279,276	24,491	1,303,767	112,699	-235	1,190,833	265,688	195,111	7,516	6,618	219,761	105,042
1978	1,855,849	1,447,696	28,384	1,476,080	130,827	-257	1,344,996	300,292	210,561	8,356	7,324	222,098	109,687
1979	2,073,296	1,618,142	30,221	1,648,363	152,273	-231	1,495,859	341,061	236,376	9,232	8,038	224,569	113,147
1980	2,313,972	1,763,859	20,738	1,784,597	165,670	-255	1,618,672	414,426	280,874	10,184	8,869	227,225	113,983
1981	2,590,995	1,933,697	27,476	1,961,173	195,066	-208	1,765,899	505,334	319,762	11,291	9,788	229,466	114,914
1982	2,777,640	2,028,963	24,766	2,053,729	208,173	-255	1,845,301	576,198	356,141	11,990	10,463	231,664	114,163
1983	2,969,333	2,170,568	17,450	2,188,018	225,143	-212	1,962,663	621,999	384,671	12,701	11,195	233,792	115,646
1984	3,275,415	2,400,243	32,159	2,432,402	256,550	-254	2,175,598	698,585	401,232	13,889	12,291	235,825	120,528
1985	3,508,482	2,583,536	32,255	2,615,791	280,379	-257	2,335,155	747,566	425,761	14,746	12,995	237,924	123,797
1986	3,717,756	2,753,507	33,394	2,786,901	302,389	228	2,484,740	781,305	451,711	15,482	13,663	240,133	126,232
1987	3,931,800	2,956,412	39,588	2,996,000	322,006	259	2,674,253	789,453	468,094	16,228	14,212	242,289	129,548
1988	4,264,433	3,220,748	39,231	3,259,979	360,285	226	2,899,920	867,103	497,410	17,442	15,377	244,499	133,564
1989	4,605,107	3,420,858	46,169	3,467,027	384,001	236	3,083,262	977,659	544,186	18,658	16,363	246,819	136,178
1990	4,897,332	3,631,845	47,615	3,679,460	408,676	313	3,271,097	1,029,004	597,231	19,619	17,242	249,623	138,331
1991	5,072,291	3,746,947	42,481	3,789,428	428,555	367	3,361,240	1,043,003	668,048	20,050	17,728	252,981	137,613
1992	5,406,546	4,008,307	50,716	4,059,023	453,768	478	3,605,733	1,052,874	747,939	21,077	18,692	256,514	138,166
1993	5,643,648	4,189,837	47,600	4,237,437	476,331	493	3,761,599	1,089,143	792,906	21,713	19,221	259,919	140,774
1994	5,933,938	4,405,940	51,008	4,456,948	507,188	533	3,950,293	1,154,765	828,880	22,552	19,921	263,126	144,197
1995	6,278,125	4,635,040	39,809	4,674,849	531,874	703	4,143,678	1,251,073	883,374	23,577	20,770	266,278	147,916
1996	6,660,854	4,900,819	55,361	4,956,180	554,150	675	4,402,705	1,329,021	929,128	24,725	21,621	269,394	151,056
1997	7,068,422	5,236,736	51,311	5,288,047	586,295	672	4,702,424	1,411,201	954,797	25,925	22,511	272,647	154,541
1998	7,584,003	5,658,042	48,972	5,707,014	623,685	755	5,084,084	1,516,041	983,878	27,493	23,754	275,854	158,481
1999	7,978,449	6,048,481	49,561	6,098,042	660,310	2,515	5,440,247	1,512,058	1,026,144	28,592	24,611	279,040	161,531
2000	8,620,234	6,546,103	52,640	6,598,743	704,849	2,587	5,896,481	1,636,473	1,087,280	30,551	26,173	282,162	165,371
2001	8,990,104	6,810,126	55,165	6,865,291	732,117	2,692	6,135,866	1,661,673	1,192,565	31,548	27,204	284,969	165,522
2002	9,146,700	6,957,749	43,253	7,001,002	750,338	2,657	6,253,321	1,608,189	1,285,190	31,801	28,146	287,625	165,095
2003	9,474,684	7,184,365	59,012	7,243,377	777,906	2,679	6,468,150	1,659,306	1,347,228	32,659	29,204	290,108	165,922
2004	10,008,929	7,598,827	75,958	7,674,785	827,820	2,659	6,849,624	1,738,099	1,421,206	34,183	30,605	292,805	168,840
2005	10,540,800	7,967,309	71,929	8,039,238	871,941	2,614	7,169,911	1,854,178	1,516,711	35,669	31,571	295,517	172,338
2006	11,291,446	8,463,962	55,387	8,519,349	921,123	2,617	7,600,843	2,076,789	1,613,814	37,843	33,300	298,380	175,869
2007	11,925,044	8,798,471	67,790	8,866,261	960,011	2,596	7,908,846	2,288,133	1,728,065	39,588	34,639	301,231	179,544
2008	12,423,410	8,943,728	70,357	9,014,085	986,884	2,649	8,029,850	2,438,478	1,955,082	40,854	35,902	304,094	179,214
2009	12,058,253	8,630,453	58,460	8,688,913	962,826	3,019	7,729,106	2,182,454	2,146,693	39,307	35,555	306,772	173,637
2010	12,547,501	8,955,339	68,577	9,023,916	982,045	3,068	8,044,939	2,177,445	2,325,117	40,557	36,562	309,378	172,902
2011	13,299,818	9,350,011	94,376	9,444,387	915,062	3,201	8,532,526	2,408,638	2,358,654	42,649	37,994	311,842	176,092
2012	13,905,749	9,761,057	93,777	9,854,834	948,953	3,411	8,909,292	2,633,469	2,362,988	44,237	39,442	314,344	178,980
2013	14,063,283	10,054,599	125,971	10,180,570	1,102,460	3,651	9,081,761	2,557,205	2,424,317	44,401	39,109	316,735	182,328
2014	14,778,160	10,507,195	106,679	10,613,874	1,151,698	3,438	9,465,614	2,771,030	2,541,516	46,287	40,700	319,270	186,240
2015	15,467,113	10,950,175	89,646	11,039,821	1,202,909	3,403	9,840,315	2,941,428	2,685,370	48,060	42,034	321,829	190,326
2016	15,884,741	11,240,011	71,466	11,311,477	1,237,223	3,062	10,077,316	3,030,442	2,776,983	48,971	42,937	324,368	193,426
2017	16,658,962	11,770,561	77,644	11,848,205	1,297,292	2,980	10,553,893	3,249,424	2,855,645	51,004	44,735	326,623	196,394
2018	17,514,402	12,372,349	66,241	12,438,590	1,359,444	3,451	11,082,597	3,455,566	2,976,239	53,309	47,002	328,542	200,292
2019	18,343,601	12,920,869	68,228	12,989,097	1,422,193	3,438	11,570,342	3,628,959	3,144,300	55,547	48,894	330,233	201,635
2020	19,609,985	13,077,711	80,314	13,158,025	1,446,796	4,012	11,715,241	3,664,844	4,229,900	59,151	52,350	331,527	195,287
2021	21,392,812	14,169,739	108,304	14,278,043	1,555,569	4,209	12,726,683	4,024,286	4,641,843	64,427	56,172	332,049	202,752
2022	21,820,248	15,093,680	114,272	15,207,952	1,698,994	4,211	13,513,169	4,304,995	4,002,084	65,473	56,065	333,271	212,442
2023	22,952,028	15,986,423	88,144	16,074,567	1,802,156	4,095	14,276,505	4,574,822	4,100,702	68,531	60,299	334,915	...

... = Not available.

REGION

Personal Income and Employment by Region and State: Far West

(Millions of dollars, except as noted.)

Year	Personal income, total	Derivation of personal income: Earnings by place of work: Nonfarm	Farm	Total	Less: Contributions for government social insurance	Plus: Adjustment for residence	Equals: Net earnings by place of residence	Plus: Dividends, interest, and rent	Plus: Personal current transfer receipts	Per capita (dollars): Personal income	Disposable personal income	Population (thousands)	Total employment (thousands)
1960	61,279	48,132	1,965	50,097	2,357	-1	47,739	10,027	3,513	2,829	2,513	21,659	...
1961	64,770	50,820	1,866	52,687	2,496	-2	50,189	10,531	4,049	2,894	2,574	22,378	...
1962	69,808	55,159	1,975	57,134	2,979	-3	54,153	11,406	4,250	3,020	2,683	23,114	...
1963	74,242	58,967	1,914	60,881	3,461	-5	57,415	12,187	4,640	3,118	2,768	23,811	...
1964	80,068	63,360	2,018	65,379	3,582	-6	61,791	13,285	4,992	3,283	2,962	24,389	...
1965	85,799	67,585	2,009	69,594	3,732	-7	65,855	14,470	5,474	3,445	3,109	24,908	...
1966	93,565	74,686	2,259	76,945	4,927	-8	72,010	15,559	5,996	3,697	3,315	25,311	...
1967	100,755	80,087	2,125	82,211	5,452	-10	76,750	16,635	7,370	3,908	3,493	25,779	...
1968	110,716	88,310	2,383	90,692	6,123	-12	84,558	17,662	8,496	4,234	3,744	26,151	...
1969	121,725	96,417	2,481	98,898	6,626	-149	92,124	19,909	9,693	4,570	4,006	26,635	12,295
1970	131,576	101,828	2,440	104,267	6,894	-178	97,195	22,413	11,967	4,855	4,327	27,101	12,313
1971	140,637	107,701	2,470	110,171	7,516	-203	102,453	24,340	13,844	5,101	4,596	27,570	12,300
1972	154,353	118,742	3,114	121,856	8,729	-211	112,916	26,464	14,973	5,529	4,905	27,918	12,742
1973	170,589	131,079	4,254	135,333	11,058	-213	124,063	29,675	16,852	6,022	5,377	28,328	13,405
1974	191,194	144,766	5,389	150,155	12,600	-293	137,262	34,000	19,933	6,638	5,906	28,801	13,865
1975	212,899	159,546	4,811	164,358	13,656	-482	150,220	37,625	25,054	7,255	6,529	29,346	14,103
1976	236,675	179,946	4,813	184,759	15,727	-594	168,438	40,593	27,644	7,908	7,050	29,929	14,625
1977	262,401	201,508	4,684	206,192	17,862	-399	187,931	45,093	29,377	8,588	7,607	30,553	15,287
1978	298,986	231,858	4,757	236,615	21,059	-318	215,237	51,947	31,801	9,557	8,410	31,285	16,248
1979	339,287	263,608	5,909	269,516	25,060	-37	244,419	59,781	35,087	10,614	9,275	31,965	17,133
1980	385,164	291,682	7,355	299,037	27,354	-123	271,560	72,473	41,132	11,750	10,270	32,780	17,523
1981	430,453	320,814	5,852	326,665	32,526	-175	293,964	88,202	48,287	12,875	11,263	33,434	17,693
1982	460,352	338,206	5,929	344,136	34,875	-211	309,050	97,673	53,628	13,505	11,923	34,086	17,564
1983	496,622	364,642	5,969	370,611	38,249	-236	332,125	107,269	57,228	14,305	12,685	34,716	17,989
1984	546,427	403,662	6,614	410,276	43,877	-307	366,091	120,544	59,792	15,470	13,722	35,321	18,767
1985	588,724	437,078	6,383	443,461	48,006	-365	395,091	129,055	64,578	16,337	14,418	36,037	19,392
1986	630,006	471,785	7,290	479,075	52,251	-379	426,446	134,515	69,046	17,113	15,114	36,815	19,959
1987	672,948	513,537	8,487	522,024	56,781	-450	464,793	136,049	72,106	17,878	15,625	37,641	20,793
1988	734,351	563,551	8,996	572,547	64,107	-540	507,900	149,076	77,375	19,053	16,793	38,542	21,790
1989	795,728	602,481	9,003	611,484	69,060	-636	541,789	168,989	84,950	20,128	17,562	39,534	22,453
1990	857,541	649,865	9,490	659,355	74,731	-748	583,876	180,154	93,511	21,116	18,459	40,610	23,122
1991	895,025	677,754	8,641	686,395	78,399	-745	607,251	183,534	104,240	21,604	19,064	41,428	23,124
1992	948,260	716,768	9,397	726,165	82,247	-732	643,186	185,780	119,293	22,457	19,946	42,226	22,825
1993	979,463	735,050	10,709	745,759	84,534	-724	660,501	192,475	126,487	22,886	20,333	42,798	22,934
1994	1,017,352	762,545	10,055	772,600	88,382	-750	683,468	203,553	130,331	23,511	20,856	43,271	23,380
1995	1,072,422	797,148	9,667	806,815	91,651	-782	714,382	220,243	137,797	24,515	21,654	43,745	23,938
1996	1,141,299	846,798	11,191	857,989	95,355	-851	761,782	234,742	144,775	25,755	22,517	44,314	24,580
1997	1,210,811	910,066	11,489	921,555	101,059	-928	819,568	244,419	146,825	26,875	23,275	45,054	25,149
1998	1,314,333	995,053	11,103	1,006,155	108,701	-1,018	896,437	263,389	154,506	28,698	24,700	45,798	26,089
1999	1,403,240	1,078,866	11,608	1,090,475	116,480	-1,087	972,909	267,334	162,998	30,174	25,620	46,506	26,659
2000	1,536,590	1,193,146	11,786	1,204,932	127,413	-1,188	1,076,331	289,409	170,850	32,563	27,243	47,188	27,241
2001	1,592,908	1,230,263	11,209	1,241,472	132,590	-1,266	1,107,616	295,380	189,913	33,261	28,385	47,891	27,369
2002	1,620,546	1,255,006	11,813	1,266,819	136,502	-1,345	1,128,972	287,231	204,343	33,418	29,448	48,493	27,369
2003	1,693,126	1,308,038	13,773	1,321,811	143,038	-1,507	1,177,266	300,964	214,897	34,516	30,709	49,053	27,604
2004	1,800,779	1,396,676	16,077	1,412,753	155,498	-1,720	1,255,535	321,280	223,964	36,305	32,329	49,602	28,155
2005	1,901,853	1,471,457	15,895	1,487,352	163,438	-1,893	1,322,021	344,056	235,776	37,969	33,325	50,090	28,787
2006	2,050,381	1,566,061	13,861	1,579,922	170,372	-1,962	1,407,589	389,625	253,167	40,545	35,424	50,571	29,438
2007	2,155,173	1,618,942	16,867	1,635,810	174,760	-2,096	1,458,954	425,975	270,244	42,232	36,715	51,031	30,069
2008	2,207,775	1,614,677	15,027	1,629,704	177,517	-2,235	1,449,952	449,205	308,618	42,779	37,400	51,609	29,819
2009	2,137,487	1,551,637	16,144	1,567,781	172,542	-2,099	1,393,140	402,464	341,884	40,974	36,915	52,168	28,628
2010	2,226,135	1,612,184	17,169	1,629,352	174,524	-2,016	1,452,813	395,505	377,817	42,254	37,863	52,685	28,335
2011	2,362,927	1,690,526	20,268	1,710,795	164,046	-1,920	1,544,829	437,718	380,381	44,440	39,335	53,172	28,789
2012	2,501,102	1,781,306	22,597	1,803,903	170,677	-1,975	1,631,251	486,933	382,917	46,618	41,219	53,651	29,624
2013	2,536,152	1,844,455	26,126	1,870,581	199,349	-1,829	1,669,403	470,177	396,571	46,861	40,802	54,121	30,461
2014	2,697,505	1,938,355	27,775	1,966,130	210,370	-2,001	1,753,759	516,602	427,144	49,358	42,841	54,651	31,367
2015	2,886,097	2,061,473	27,900	2,089,372	222,574	-2,124	1,864,675	563,792	457,629	52,277	45,030	55,208	32,305
2016	3,016,423	2,156,259	24,404	2,180,663	231,945	-2,445	1,946,274	593,757	476,393	54,118	46,651	55,738	33,039
2017	3,169,741	2,277,057	25,376	2,302,434	244,871	-2,697	2,054,867	637,001	477,873	56,427	48,717	56,174	33,654
2018	3,339,907	2,408,725	20,063	2,428,788	259,122	-2,814	2,166,852	670,716	502,339	59,137	51,074	56,477	34,413
2019	3,524,620	2,538,759	21,014	2,559,774	273,212	-3,276	2,283,286	705,597	535,737	62,203	53,756	56,663	34,650
2020	3,828,495	2,599,728	23,043	2,622,772	278,251	-3,382	2,341,139	717,800	769,556	67,435	58,391	56,773	33,103
2021	4,179,488	2,857,253	21,050	2,878,303	304,456	-3,849	2,569,997	783,865	825,626	74,011	62,793	56,471	34,287
2022	4,193,955	2,984,618	21,913	3,006,530	330,996	-4,277	2,671,257	835,695	687,003	74,342	61,849	56,415	36,198
2023	4,387,201	3,149,456	18,013	3,167,470	350,210	-4,533	2,812,727	884,223	690,252	77,823	66,874	56,374	...

... = Not available.

Personal Income and Employment by Area: Great Lakes

(Millions of dollars, except as noted.)

Year	Personal income, total	Derivation of personal income: Earnings by place of work: Nonfarm	Farm	Total	Less: Contributions for government social insurance	Plus: Adjustment for residence	Equals: Net earnings by place of residence	Plus: Dividends, interest, and rent	Plus: Personal current transfer receipts	Per capita (dollars): Personal income	Disposable personal income	Population (thousands)	Total employment (thousands)
1960	88,934	73,742	2,014	75,757	3,657	-123	71,977	11,699	5,257	2,451	2,173	36,290	...
1961	91,139	73,915	2,446	76,361	3,618	-111	72,632	12,377	6,130	2,489	2,220	36,616	...
1962	96,685	78,906	2,352	81,259	4,044	-116	77,099	13,432	6,154	2,618	2,323	36,927	...
1963	101,231	82,828	2,365	85,193	4,562	-114	80,516	14,371	6,344	2,710	2,401	37,357	...
1964	108,770	89,549	2,045	91,594	4,763	-122	86,710	15,586	6,474	2,872	2,578	37,868	...
1965	118,706	97,360	2,631	99,992	4,947	-133	94,912	16,859	6,935	3,091	2,763	38,405	...
1966	129,096	107,454	2,972	110,426	6,742	-146	103,538	18,028	7,529	3,314	2,943	38,951	...
1967	135,847	112,657	2,535	115,192	7,274	-134	107,784	19,054	9,009	3,453	3,056	39,347	...
1968	148,258	123,088	2,431	125,519	7,989	-144	117,386	20,459	10,413	3,740	3,272	39,645	...
1969	162,017	134,868	2,870	137,737	9,311	262	128,688	21,994	11,334	4,060	3,495	39,904	17,785
1970	170,705	139,623	2,518	142,141	9,503	246	132,884	24,274	13,548	4,234	3,688	40,320	17,630
1971	183,695	148,678	2,899	151,577	10,424	319	141,472	26,120	16,102	4,522	3,992	40,622	17,549
1972	200,708	163,199	3,168	166,367	12,095	366	154,638	28,097	17,972	4,916	4,279	40,824	17,933
1973	224,429	182,057	5,213	187,271	15,631	417	172,057	31,434	20,938	5,481	4,794	40,947	18,710
1974	243,766	195,283	4,661	199,944	17,400	512	183,056	35,778	24,932	5,940	5,177	41,037	18,911
1975	263,253	203,397	5,818	209,215	17,669	588	192,134	39,088	32,031	6,404	5,658	41,105	18,399
1976	289,628	228,236	4,816	233,052	20,242	719	213,529	41,851	34,248	7,032	6,149	41,187	18,891
1977	321,434	256,353	4,818	261,171	22,758	899	239,311	46,353	35,769	7,773	6,760	41,353	19,508
1978	356,578	287,356	4,506	291,861	26,286	1,105	266,680	51,456	38,442	8,590	7,432	41,510	20,190
1979	392,789	314,968	5,223	320,191	29,932	1,269	291,528	57,797	43,465	9,440	8,131	41,611	20,491
1980	425,918	327,614	3,317	330,931	30,928	1,532	301,535	69,780	54,603	10,215	8,860	41,694	19,978
1981	464,510	349,522	3,683	353,205	35,439	1,340	319,107	84,700	60,703	11,153	9,632	41,648	19,795
1982	486,505	353,935	2,926	356,861	36,377	1,215	321,698	96,693	68,113	11,725	10,263	41,492	19,248
1983	512,332	374,045	-119	373,926	38,845	1,209	336,290	103,273	72,769	12,385	10,883	41,366	19,265
1984	564,805	413,823	4,409	418,232	44,260	1,335	375,307	114,965	74,532	13,645	12,043	41,393	20,028
1985	599,999	442,954	4,964	447,918	48,192	1,397	401,123	120,623	78,253	14,486	12,739	41,418	20,492
1986	632,186	470,521	4,488	475,008	51,647	1,472	424,833	125,419	81,934	15,250	13,431	41,455	20,934
1987	662,422	500,363	5,012	505,375	54,318	1,528	452,585	125,653	84,183	15,928	13,927	41,590	21,516
1988	712,256	543,351	3,363	546,714	60,614	1,647	487,747	136,595	87,914	17,072	15,001	41,721	22,070
1989	766,625	576,171	7,032	583,202	64,606	1,665	520,262	152,052	94,311	18,309	16,010	41,873	22,556
1990	810,261	608,229	6,005	614,234	68,951	1,923	547,206	159,996	103,058	19,250	16,864	42,091	22,928
1991	831,492	625,096	3,606	628,702	72,225	1,908	558,385	160,841	112,267	19,566	17,215	42,496	22,845
1992	890,190	670,955	6,123	677,078	76,663	2,021	602,436	163,757	123,997	20,749	18,333	42,903	22,971
1993	930,174	704,234	5,204	709,438	81,158	2,094	630,373	169,487	130,313	21,495	18,911	43,275	23,359
1994	986,856	748,980	6,083	755,063	87,642	2,271	669,692	182,800	134,363	22,640	19,855	43,590	24,060
1995	1,040,168	786,952	3,336	790,289	92,242	2,431	700,477	198,035	141,656	23,681	20,711	43,924	24,713
1996	1,097,451	824,326	6,936	831,263	95,306	2,677	738,635	210,635	148,182	24,807	21,563	44,239	25,105
1997	1,157,986	872,470	6,589	879,059	99,864	2,981	782,176	222,724	153,085	26,026	22,503	44,494	25,513
1998	1,231,449	933,009	5,575	938,584	104,854	3,020	836,750	239,160	155,539	27,532	23,698	44,728	25,953
1999	1,281,344	988,745	4,553	993,298	110,196	3,449	886,550	233,135	161,659	28,494	24,527	44,969	26,333
2000	1,365,620	1,049,572	5,392	1,054,964	114,559	3,792	944,197	250,194	171,230	30,202	26,037	45,216	26,830
2001	1,408,885	1,078,110	5,655	1,083,765	116,267	4,089	971,587	249,423	187,876	31,032	26,900	45,402	26,554
2002	1,426,200	1,097,661	3,724	1,101,385	118,065	4,148	987,468	239,081	199,651	31,310	27,692	45,550	26,272
2003	1,461,122	1,121,649	6,154	1,127,803	121,443	4,425	1,010,785	241,993	208,344	31,967	28,576	45,708	26,220
2004	1,517,095	1,164,290	10,141	1,174,431	127,769	4,929	1,051,591	248,367	217,137	33,092	29,676	45,844	26,440
2005	1,563,294	1,194,958	6,817	1,201,775	132,978	5,349	1,074,147	255,630	233,517	34,022	30,272	45,949	26,682
2006	1,642,386	1,242,556	6,502	1,249,058	138,375	5,657	1,116,340	280,584	245,462	35,649	31,559	46,072	26,875
2007	1,715,071	1,275,437	9,229	1,284,667	142,467	5,776	1,147,975	301,652	265,444	37,132	32,703	46,188	27,135
2008	1,775,399	1,283,740	11,362	1,295,102	145,177	6,358	1,156,283	320,324	298,791	38,366	33,900	46,275	26,872
2009	1,712,365	1,219,734	7,590	1,227,324	138,939	5,476	1,093,861	286,022	332,483	36,940	33,536	46,356	25,773
2010	1,768,446	1,256,552	9,086	1,265,638	140,999	5,349	1,129,988	282,462	355,996	38,071	34,436	46,451	25,659
2011	1,871,471	1,315,321	16,776	1,332,097	132,042	5,313	1,205,368	313,155	352,948	40,177	35,872	46,581	26,127
2012	1,948,109	1,373,756	11,775	1,385,531	137,182	5,635	1,253,984	341,073	353,052	41,713	37,245	46,702	26,417
2013	1,975,055	1,411,191	21,792	1,432,984	157,362	5,412	1,281,033	332,558	361,464	42,150	37,299	46,858	26,732
2014	2,053,532	1,461,886	13,449	1,475,335	162,459	5,841	1,318,717	358,635	376,181	43,709	38,702	46,982	27,124
2015	2,143,223	1,524,195	6,301	1,530,496	168,296	6,351	1,368,551	379,843	394,829	45,553	40,161	47,049	27,533
2016	2,185,988	1,552,686	7,924	1,560,610	172,699	6,498	1,394,409	389,706	401,873	46,376	40,907	47,136	27,817
2017	2,261,787	1,606,858	8,039	1,614,897	180,079	6,885	1,441,703	408,561	411,523	47,884	42,435	47,234	28,024
2018	2,368,542	1,675,262	9,167	1,684,428	187,187	7,979	1,505,221	436,703	426,618	50,068	44,576	47,307	28,348
2019	2,447,905	1,730,988	6,909	1,737,897	193,727	8,571	1,552,742	447,226	447,938	51,688	45,926	47,359	28,332
2020	2,620,797	1,739,560	13,291	1,752,851	195,578	8,114	1,565,387	451,800	603,610	55,355	49,545	47,345	27,185
2021	2,835,493	1,863,474	20,592	1,884,066	208,009	8,915	1,684,972	495,111	655,410	60,090	53,086	47,187	28,063
2022	2,863,569	1,968,959	21,912	1,990,871	226,813	9,815	1,773,874	530,573	559,122	60,800	52,814	47,098	29,223
2023	2,991,772	2,072,614	16,872	2,089,486	238,927	10,692	1,861,252	559,143	571,378	63,458	56,484	47,146	...

... = Not available.

Personal Income and Employment by Region and State: Mideast

(Millions of dollars, except as noted.)

Year	Personal income, total	Derivation of personal income: Earnings by place of work: Nonfarm	Farm	Total	Less: Contributions for government social insurance	Plus: Adjustment for residence	Equals: Net earnings by place of residence	Plus: Dividends, interest, and rent	Plus: Personal current transfer receipts	Per capita (dollars): Personal income	Disposable personal income	Population (thousands)	Total employment (thousands)
1960	102,030	85,593	901	86,495	4,355	-761	81,378	14,533	6,119	2,643	2,319	38,597	...
1961	106,262	88,420	906	89,326	4,582	-791	83,953	15,316	6,994	2,715	2,383	39,133	...
1962	112,437	93,612	733	94,345	5,118	-804	88,423	16,864	7,150	2,843	2,488	39,552	...
1963	117,654	97,361	799	98,160	5,644	-841	91,675	18,386	7,593	2,935	2,569	40,083	...
1964	126,000	103,790	802	104,592	5,693	-902	97,997	20,142	7,861	3,107	2,758	40,555	...
1965	134,825	110,543	896	111,439	5,940	-933	104,567	21,854	8,405	3,286	2,906	41,025	...
1966	145,317	120,725	917	121,642	7,891	-1,011	112,740	23,176	9,401	3,513	3,088	41,360	...
1967	156,524	129,069	972	130,040	8,614	-1,183	120,243	24,679	11,602	3,761	3,290	41,617	...
1968	171,747	140,938	920	141,859	9,400	-1,301	131,157	26,718	13,872	4,097	3,550	41,924	...
1969	184,917	153,081	1,105	154,186	11,072	-1,782	141,332	28,328	15,257	4,391	3,753	42,111	19,432
1970	199,975	163,311	1,063	164,374	11,658	-1,703	151,013	30,857	18,105	4,703	4,078	42,517	19,465
1971	214,652	173,493	970	174,464	12,772	-1,779	159,912	33,002	21,738	5,007	4,399	42,870	19,299
1972	232,153	188,066	966	189,032	14,535	-1,950	172,546	35,188	24,419	5,400	4,679	42,992	19,521
1973	251,007	203,906	1,387	205,293	18,195	-2,082	185,016	38,689	27,301	5,860	5,104	42,837	19,968
1974	272,562	218,491	1,292	219,783	20,160	-2,296	197,327	43,426	31,808	6,382	5,535	42,709	19,954
1975	295,272	230,686	1,198	231,884	20,837	-2,641	208,405	46,400	40,467	6,911	6,085	42,728	19,480
1976	317,632	249,080	1,278	250,359	22,890	-2,964	224,504	49,380	43,748	7,444	6,518	42,667	19,563
1977	345,171	271,848	1,097	272,946	24,858	-3,354	244,734	54,358	46,080	8,113	7,062	42,547	19,848
1978	378,978	301,100	1,311	302,412	28,208	-3,971	270,233	59,882	48,863	8,934	7,747	42,421	20,411
1979	416,720	331,582	1,523	333,105	32,254	-4,760	296,091	67,005	53,623	9,838	8,468	42,358	20,871
1980	462,955	360,298	1,140	361,438	35,164	-5,615	320,660	80,551	61,744	10,952	9,416	42,272	20,911
1981	514,142	392,584	1,499	394,083	40,993	-5,943	347,147	97,374	69,621	12,146	10,359	42,329	20,978
1982	555,305	415,170	1,458	416,628	43,999	-6,123	366,506	111,493	77,306	13,102	11,202	42,382	20,858
1983	594,510	445,111	1,092	446,202	47,849	-6,182	392,171	118,764	83,575	13,974	12,120	42,544	21,045
1984	652,851	490,129	1,904	492,033	54,383	-6,584	431,066	134,820	86,965	15,294	13,288	42,687	21,766
1985	698,661	528,536	2,016	530,552	59,564	-6,967	464,021	143,246	91,394	16,326	14,120	42,794	22,333
1986	744,511	567,698	2,200	569,898	64,798	-6,872	498,228	149,705	96,579	17,318	14,977	42,991	22,837
1987	792,765	616,451	2,286	618,737	69,479	-7,221	542,037	151,513	99,214	18,355	15,723	43,190	23,321
1988	870,128	679,111	2,187	681,298	77,653	-7,991	595,653	169,107	105,368	20,033	17,336	43,435	23,927
1989	939,516	719,726	2,579	722,305	81,572	-8,372	632,361	193,158	113,997	21,556	18,579	43,585	24,201
1990	998,496	761,626	2,519	764,145	84,116	-8,635	671,394	202,218	124,884	22,817	19,779	43,762	24,260
1991	1,018,867	767,150	2,052	769,202	86,917	-9,023	673,262	204,225	141,381	23,119	20,159	44,071	23,703
1992	1,077,163	816,603	2,646	819,250	91,293	-10,687	717,270	203,090	156,803	24,265	21,189	44,392	23,597
1993	1,112,544	842,950	2,516	845,467	94,558	-10,451	740,457	206,537	165,549	24,880	21,678	44,717	23,714
1994	1,151,105	871,502	2,305	873,807	99,384	-10,167	764,257	215,357	171,491	25,597	22,256	44,970	23,879
1995	1,210,390	908,644	1,759	910,403	102,991	-10,953	796,458	232,601	181,331	26,787	23,249	45,186	24,157
1996	1,273,656	952,756	2,698	955,454	106,056	-11,404	837,993	245,344	190,318	28,064	24,176	45,384	24,387
1997	1,345,023	1,012,597	1,845	1,014,442	110,906	-11,756	891,780	260,825	192,419	29,509	25,212	45,580	24,763
1998	1,428,589	1,079,778	2,312	1,082,090	116,433	-13,004	952,652	276,939	198,998	31,177	26,476	45,822	25,170
1999	1,503,323	1,154,584	2,304	1,156,888	122,348	-13,274	1,021,266	275,460	206,597	32,606	27,571	46,106	25,710
2000	1,625,348	1,249,144	2,767	1,251,911	130,693	-11,982	1,109,236	298,158	217,955	35,040	29,537	46,386	26,409
2001	1,692,957	1,306,543	2,840	1,309,383	136,829	-12,805	1,159,749	298,764	234,444	36,314	30,543	46,619	26,496
2002	1,712,114	1,328,895	1,955	1,330,850	140,121	-14,582	1,176,147	283,145	252,822	36,551	31,739	46,841	26,442
2003	1,754,023	1,360,832	2,893	1,363,725	144,166	-15,744	1,203,815	287,406	262,801	37,292	32,703	47,035	26,529
2004	1,842,805	1,433,972	3,660	1,437,631	151,842	-17,751	1,268,038	298,122	276,644	39,074	34,236	47,162	26,904
2005	1,915,930	1,488,091	3,439	1,491,530	159,284	-19,424	1,312,822	316,847	286,261	40,558	35,071	47,239	27,309
2006	2,040,721	1,569,422	2,970	1,572,392	168,427	-22,345	1,381,621	356,448	302,652	43,113	36,949	47,334	27,713
2007	2,173,520	1,653,137	3,554	1,656,690	177,137	-25,144	1,454,410	399,465	319,645	45,784	38,831	47,474	28,252
2008	2,243,335	1,677,680	3,916	1,681,595	183,301	-28,277	1,470,018	418,645	354,672	47,045	40,062	47,685	28,371
2009	2,204,552	1,643,591	3,003	1,646,594	179,773	-24,964	1,441,857	374,447	388,249	45,982	40,560	47,944	27,759
2010	2,290,212	1,714,777	3,856	1,718,633	184,332	-28,634	1,505,667	368,600	415,945	47,474	41,743	48,242	27,763
2011	2,412,405	1,782,441	4,699	1,787,139	170,182	-31,453	1,585,504	404,717	422,184	49,606	43,057	48,631	28,282
2012	2,502,397	1,841,595	5,232	1,846,827	174,491	-32,987	1,639,349	442,748	420,300	51,103	44,521	48,968	28,579
2013	2,523,331	1,890,878	6,183	1,897,061	203,122	-31,502	1,662,437	434,508	426,386	51,228	43,895	49,256	28,989
2014	2,618,310	1,952,942	6,403	1,959,345	211,454	-34,215	1,713,676	464,329	440,305	52,879	45,189	49,515	29,462
2015	2,730,528	2,030,704	4,434	2,035,139	220,362	-35,191	1,779,586	489,873	461,069	54,914	46,646	49,724	29,958
2016	2,817,599	2,089,132	3,204	2,092,336	225,057	-36,109	1,831,169	508,167	478,264	56,470	48,252	49,895	30,375
2017	2,952,031	2,179,695	4,775	2,184,470	236,296	-39,309	1,908,865	544,794	498,372	58,963	50,433	50,066	30,687
2018	3,073,000	2,274,447	3,184	2,277,632	245,100	-41,191	1,991,341	575,165	506,495	61,193	52,512	50,218	31,233
2019	3,187,604	2,350,480	4,718	2,355,198	254,658	-43,472	2,057,067	596,513	534,023	63,366	54,312	50,305	31,352
2020	3,362,442	2,343,684	3,677	2,347,361	253,014	-46,651	2,047,696	584,592	730,154	66,969	58,007	50,209	29,684
2021	3,597,298	2,502,411	5,197	2,507,609	271,645	-48,401	2,187,563	633,384	776,351	71,966	61,107	49,986	30,704
2022	3,597,384	2,629,278	6,906	2,636,184	294,090	-52,208	2,289,886	659,120	648,377	72,294	59,857	49,760	32,219
2023	3,779,199	2,773,322	4,385	2,777,706	309,615	-54,877	2,413,215	693,153	672,832	76,018	65,125	49,715	...

... = Not available.

Personal Income and Employment by Region and State: New England

(Millions of dollars, except as noted.)

Year	Personal income, total	Derivation of personal income: Earnings by place of work: Nonfarm	Farm	Total	Less: Contributions for government social insurance	Plus: Adjustment for residence	Equals: Net earnings by place of residence	Plus: Dividends, interest, and rent	Plus: Personal current transfer receipts	Per capita (dollars): Personal income	Disposable personal income	Population (thousands)	Total employment (thousands)
1960	26,543	21,356	318	21,674	1,025	27	20,676	4,106	1,761	2,520	2,219	10,532	...
1961	27,858	22,281	269	22,550	1,073	28	21,504	4,377	1,977	2,612	2,311	10,666	...
1962	29,543	23,651	259	23,910	1,216	32	22,726	4,810	2,007	2,735	2,414	10,800	...
1963	30,881	24,585	251	24,837	1,358	36	23,515	5,239	2,126	2,811	2,476	10,986	...
1964	33,063	26,134	289	26,423	1,400	42	25,064	5,792	2,207	2,956	2,646	11,186	...
1965	35,462	27,879	340	28,220	1,451	44	26,813	6,319	2,330	3,130	2,794	11,329	...
1966	38,500	30,746	345	31,090	1,937	51	29,204	6,785	2,512	3,368	2,982	11,430	...
1967	41,842	33,161	239	33,401	2,135	58	31,324	7,436	3,082	3,619	3,192	11,562	...
1968	45,291	35,993	266	36,260	2,370	71	33,961	7,649	3,682	3,892	3,382	11,637	...
1969	50,009	39,196	294	39,490	2,639	835	37,686	8,213	4,111	4,262	3,656	11,735	5,516
1970	53,915	41,706	306	42,012	2,775	843	40,080	8,932	4,903	4,539	3,961	11,878	5,518
1971	57,438	43,877	283	44,161	3,015	885	42,031	9,532	5,876	4,788	4,237	11,996	5,454
1972	62,243	47,830	288	48,118	3,456	951	45,613	10,223	6,408	5,149	4,491	12,088	5,573
1973	67,916	52,504	398	52,903	4,364	997	49,536	11,183	7,197	5,591	4,904	12,148	5,783
1974	73,639	55,983	430	56,413	4,833	1,083	52,663	12,445	8,531	6,058	5,303	12,157	5,843
1975	79,316	58,456	313	58,769	4,922	1,183	55,030	13,150	11,136	6,514	5,791	12,176	5,685
1976	86,257	64,298	428	64,727	5,524	1,286	60,488	14,078	11,690	7,066	6,227	12,207	5,811
1977	94,470	71,062	385	71,447	6,136	1,435	66,746	15,593	12,131	7,707	6,776	12,257	6,007
1978	104,955	79,969	397	80,366	7,103	1,626	74,890	17,244	12,821	8,531	7,451	12,303	6,276
1979	117,382	89,790	380	90,170	8,296	1,840	83,714	19,389	14,280	9,508	8,238	12,345	6,503
1980	132,761	99,350	368	99,718	9,177	2,158	92,700	23,622	16,439	10,731	9,264	12,372	6,623
1981	148,252	108,669	471	109,140	10,790	2,345	100,696	28,752	18,804	11,921	10,225	12,436	6,666
1982	161,497	116,202	513	116,715	11,780	2,514	107,449	33,496	20,552	12,953	11,175	12,468	6,667
1983	174,693	127,158	480	127,637	13,047	2,666	117,256	35,494	21,944	13,926	12,146	12,544	6,799
1984	195,509	143,581	568	144,149	15,176	2,859	131,832	40,685	22,992	15,465	13,548	12,642	7,159
1985	211,351	157,286	558	157,844	16,770	3,119	144,193	42,972	24,186	16,589	14,438	12,741	7,400
1986	228,205	171,426	576	172,002	18,495	3,237	156,744	46,064	25,396	17,783	15,397	12,833	7,638
1987	247,067	189,165	638	189,803	20,166	3,427	173,064	47,891	26,112	19,077	16,388	12,951	7,771
1988	272,988	208,760	653	209,413	22,629	3,693	190,477	54,427	28,085	20,863	18,140	13,085	8,018
1989	292,779	219,160	609	219,770	23,628	3,745	199,886	61,531	31,362	22,211	19,282	13,182	8,005
1990	301,686	223,211	702	223,912	24,142	3,436	203,207	63,410	35,069	22,804	19,836	13,230	7,853
1991	306,639	223,851	645	224,497	24,627	3,435	203,304	62,777	40,558	23,147	20,240	13,248	7,526
1992	323,631	236,864	794	237,658	25,840	4,688	216,507	63,145	43,980	24,386	21,300	13,271	7,566
1993	335,456	246,571	731	247,302	27,034	4,116	224,385	65,517	45,555	25,157	21,909	13,334	7,689
1994	349,814	257,843	678	258,521	28,609	3,910	233,821	68,126	47,866	26,113	22,698	13,396	7,782
1995	369,441	270,399	602	271,001	30,150	4,674	245,525	72,995	50,920	27,422	23,713	13,473	7,875
1996	389,889	285,779	688	286,468	31,550	5,430	260,348	77,115	52,426	28,764	24,584	13,555	8,004
1997	413,839	306,363	593	306,957	33,589	5,059	278,426	81,032	54,381	30,335	25,642	13,642	8,165
1998	443,846	330,053	656	330,708	35,668	6,550	301,591	87,159	55,096	32,318	27,076	13,734	8,361
1999	470,836	357,524	700	358,224	37,882	6,507	326,849	87,100	56,888	34,026	28,398	13,838	8,513
2000	518,807	396,459	774	397,233	41,129	6,760	362,864	95,897	60,046	37,191	30,601	13,950	8,740
2001	544,288	415,327	713	416,040	42,479	6,808	380,370	98,712	65,206	38,764	32,334	14,041	8,766
2002	546,839	418,581	658	419,239	43,000	6,906	383,144	93,505	70,190	38,721	33,511	14,122	8,712
2003	558,999	426,689	699	427,388	43,938	6,976	390,425	95,182	73,392	39,415	34,462	14,182	8,696
2004	588,011	450,332	798	451,130	46,970	8,008	412,168	98,511	77,332	41,390	36,201	14,207	8,809
2005	611,753	465,482	756	466,239	48,933	8,830	426,136	103,580	82,037	43,031	37,168	14,217	8,901
2006	655,755	490,637	659	491,296	51,094	9,952	450,155	119,203	86,397	46,032	39,574	14,246	8,998
2007	693,140	511,792	803	512,595	53,408	11,525	470,711	130,901	91,528	48,542	41,234	14,279	9,168
2008	726,656	525,807	910	526,717	55,036	12,575	484,257	137,967	104,433	50,673	43,482	14,340	9,173
2009	719,707	524,901	743	525,644	54,095	9,812	481,362	123,979	114,367	49,967	44,449	14,404	8,936
2010	749,402	548,805	909	549,714	55,116	11,714	506,312	122,530	120,560	51,768	45,806	14,476	8,892
2011	781,044	562,644	911	563,555	51,178	12,190	524,567	135,012	121,465	53,628	46,710	14,564	9,003
2012	802,748	570,725	1,117	571,842	52,752	13,881	532,970	147,524	122,253	54,794	47,828	14,650	9,113
2013	800,300	578,937	1,211	580,148	61,096	13,005	532,057	144,244	123,999	54,326	46,527	14,732	9,266
2014	833,957	597,947	1,067	599,014	63,561	13,407	548,861	156,453	128,643	56,285	48,068	14,817	9,411
2015	874,242	623,918	924	624,842	65,957	13,694	572,580	165,762	135,900	58,793	50,022	14,870	9,656
2016	900,401	641,572	724	642,296	67,869	13,011	587,437	172,481	140,482	60,324	51,554	14,926	9,778
2017	936,295	665,973	858	666,832	70,761	15,440	611,511	181,647	143,138	62,446	53,434	14,994	9,870
2018	981,390	693,631	670	694,301	73,841	17,154	637,614	193,253	150,522	65,195	56,094	15,053	9,992
2019	1,025,952	723,999	939	724,938	76,815	20,349	668,471	202,084	155,397	67,991	58,376	15,089	9,988
2020	1,089,449	732,925	824	733,749	77,395	23,601	679,955	196,075	213,419	72,351	62,518	15,058	9,514
2021	1,166,197	789,920	816	790,736	83,769	23,361	730,328	211,657	224,213	77,200	65,344	15,106	9,873
2022	1,188,528	833,066	1,040	834,106	89,682	26,344	770,767	223,201	194,560	78,603	65,110	15,121	10,310
2023	1,243,427	873,008	744	873,752	93,604	27,839	807,986	235,770	199,671	82,021	70,349	15,160	...

... = Not available.

Personal Income and Employment by Region and State: Plains

(Millions of dollars, except as noted.)

Year	Personal income, total	Derivation of personal income								Per capita (dollars)		Population (thousands)	Total employment (thousands)
		Earnings by place of work			Less: Contributions for government social insurance	Plus: Adjustment for residence	Equals: Net earnings by place of residence	Plus: Dividends, interest, and rent	Plus: Personal current transfer receipts	Personal income	Disposable personal income		
		Nonfarm	Farm	Total									
1960	33,349	24,119	3,122	27,240	1,157	8	26,091	5,040	2,218	2,162	1,942	15,424	...
1961	34,589	25,031	3,042	28,073	1,212	6	26,867	5,257	2,464	2,221	1,996	15,570	...
1962	36,922	26,543	3,542	30,085	1,318	7	28,774	5,589	2,560	2,358	2,117	15,657	...
1963	38,403	27,780	3,487	31,267	1,493	4	29,778	5,929	2,696	2,444	2,190	15,715	...
1964	40,038	29,687	2,795	32,482	1,555	5	30,932	6,317	2,788	2,536	2,303	15,787	...
1965	43,929	31,633	4,110	35,743	1,632	4	34,114	6,794	3,021	2,777	2,515	15,819	...
1966	47,250	34,720	4,310	39,030	2,197	-0	36,833	7,154	3,263	2,974	2,673	15,888	...
1967	49,583	37,182	3,678	40,860	2,551	-5	38,304	7,385	3,894	3,110	2,788	15,942	...
1968	54,099	40,694	3,670	44,364	2,839	-14	41,510	8,084	4,505	3,371	3,000	16,047	...
1969	59,316	44,699	4,220	48,918	3,160	-402	45,356	9,020	4,940	3,661	3,210	16,202	7,506
1970	64,334	47,663	4,443	52,106	3,338	-340	48,429	10,114	5,792	3,935	3,489	16,350	7,516
1971	69,267	51,030	4,611	55,640	3,693	-338	51,610	11,004	6,653	4,204	3,772	16,475	7,544
1972	76,510	55,663	6,161	61,824	4,221	-344	57,259	11,999	7,252	4,619	4,092	16,563	7,731
1973	89,249	61,651	11,294	72,944	5,396	-380	67,169	13,630	8,450	5,367	4,789	16,628	8,065
1974	94,449	67,832	7,686	75,518	6,185	-415	68,918	15,681	9,850	5,665	4,973	16,672	8,219
1975	103,645	73,512	7,499	81,012	6,595	-411	74,006	17,517	12,122	6,191	5,505	16,743	8,181
1976	111,098	82,629	4,408	87,037	7,513	-502	79,022	18,882	13,194	6,588	5,818	16,864	8,438
1977	122,799	91,373	5,192	96,565	8,271	-634	87,659	21,197	13,943	7,245	6,385	16,950	8,657
1978	138,981	102,717	7,837	110,554	9,610	-787	100,157	23,647	15,177	8,162	7,171	17,028	8,953
1979	153,330	115,180	6,613	121,793	11,215	-974	109,604	26,730	16,996	8,968	7,813	17,097	9,232
1980	165,796	124,093	1,879	125,973	12,037	-1,126	112,809	32,666	20,321	9,635	8,390	17,208	9,227
1981	187,414	133,902	5,447	139,348	13,886	-1,299	124,164	40,093	23,157	10,856	9,431	17,264	9,180
1982	199,623	138,806	4,004	142,811	14,670	-1,296	126,846	46,980	25,797	11,544	10,048	17,292	9,050
1983	209,273	147,580	1,577	149,157	15,669	-1,380	132,109	49,420	27,745	12,079	10,668	17,325	9,163
1984	233,033	162,450	6,545	168,995	17,707	-1,544	149,743	54,383	28,906	13,407	11,950	17,382	9,470
1985	246,057	171,852	7,464	179,317	19,108	-1,660	158,549	56,899	30,609	14,140	12,580	17,402	9,612
1986	257,493	180,991	8,061	189,052	20,469	-1,784	166,800	58,604	32,090	14,805	13,209	17,393	9,701
1987	270,365	193,085	9,777	202,861	21,691	-1,894	179,277	58,076	33,012	15,513	13,748	17,428	9,949
1988	284,713	206,938	7,383	214,321	24,080	-2,057	188,184	61,870	34,659	16,238	14,407	17,533	10,156
1989	307,031	220,563	9,207	229,771	25,698	-2,138	201,935	67,493	37,604	17,450	15,422	17,595	10,357
1990	325,127	233,385	10,544	243,929	27,917	-2,414	213,599	70,874	40,655	18,371	16,222	17,698	10,544
1991	336,693	243,055	8,117	251,171	29,420	-2,433	219,319	72,582	44,792	18,869	16,742	17,843	10,597
1992	360,198	261,004	10,635	271,639	31,222	-2,549	237,868	73,801	48,530	19,982	17,763	18,026	10,708
1993	372,185	273,681	6,237	279,918	32,831	-2,645	244,443	76,259	51,484	20,439	18,120	18,210	10,934
1994	397,337	290,478	10,482	300,960	35,227	-2,806	262,928	80,632	53,778	21,617	19,150	18,381	11,230
1995	416,676	306,991	5,742	312,733	37,055	-3,038	272,640	87,000	57,037	22,463	19,812	18,550	11,537
1996	448,058	324,702	13,572	338,274	38,591	-3,300	296,383	91,982	59,694	23,954	21,028	18,705	11,761
1997	471,188	345,600	9,882	355,482	41,154	-3,691	310,637	98,937	61,614	24,995	21,813	18,851	11,980
1998	501,896	371,105	9,199	380,303	43,759	-3,930	332,615	105,715	63,566	26,432	23,007	18,988	12,240
1999	521,547	393,034	7,938	400,972	46,129	-4,237	350,607	104,429	66,512	27,262	23,763	19,131	12,411
2000	558,113	418,180	9,609	427,788	48,646	-4,537	374,605	112,339	71,169	28,955	25,191	19,275	12,604
2001	578,785	432,831	9,072	441,903	50,180	-4,637	387,085	113,454	78,246	29,873	26,081	19,375	12,601
2002	590,337	446,152	6,191	452,343	51,466	-4,689	396,188	109,982	84,167	30,323	26,999	19,468	12,519
2003	615,429	460,351	12,389	472,740	53,399	-4,854	414,487	113,651	87,291	31,449	28,313	19,569	12,521
2004	649,065	486,047	16,614	502,662	56,023	-5,120	441,519	116,137	91,409	32,968	29,780	19,688	12,674
2005	672,324	504,086	15,836	519,922	58,713	-5,409	455,800	119,587	96,937	33,951	30,364	19,803	12,863
2006	713,140	532,755	10,687	543,442	62,042	-5,673	475,726	132,497	104,917	35,734	31,767	19,957	13,061
2007	759,018	556,111	15,648	571,759	64,816	-5,691	501,253	145,015	112,750	37,751	33,375	20,106	13,280
2008	808,863	576,782	20,702	597,484	67,566	-6,129	523,789	157,695	127,379	39,946	35,398	20,249	13,298
2009	787,291	563,567	15,070	578,637	66,208	-5,252	507,177	142,478	137,636	38,607	35,092	20,393	12,991
2010	816,746	582,004	17,862	599,867	67,461	-5,108	527,298	142,150	147,299	39,764	36,040	20,540	12,918
2011	875,496	607,472	29,737	637,210	62,817	-5,333	569,060	156,796	149,641	42,375	38,017	20,661	13,099
2012	920,626	639,121	27,881	667,002	65,078	-5,908	596,016	174,644	149,966	44,292	39,712	20,785	13,262
2013	929,356	656,780	33,914	690,694	75,751	-6,338	608,605	167,230	153,521	44,424	39,448	20,920	13,444
2014	966,354	685,591	24,595	710,186	78,655	-7,066	624,464	181,223	160,667	45,910	40,718	21,049	13,615
2015	997,298	711,483	17,866	729,349	81,594	-7,230	640,525	188,997	167,777	47,121	41,617	21,165	13,782
2016	1,010,852	720,417	13,259	733,677	83,183	-7,074	643,419	194,560	172,872	47,518	41,975	21,273	13,866
2017	1,043,303	745,722	12,198	757,920	86,277	-7,262	664,381	200,733	178,189	48,797	43,264	21,380	13,939
2018	1,093,520	775,600	13,002	788,603	90,007	-7,735	690,861	214,307	188,352	50,923	45,380	21,474	14,076
2019	1,133,999	802,662	12,315	814,978	93,503	-8,288	713,187	223,341	197,471	52,593	46,784	21,562	14,077
2020	1,211,726	813,320	19,317	832,637	96,345	-7,567	728,725	228,686	254,315	56,034	50,141	21,625	13,661
2021	1,318,413	864,281	30,292	894,573	101,249	-7,753	785,570	251,338	281,505	60,861	53,769	21,663	14,011
2022	1,364,311	927,492	32,080	959,573	110,022	-8,661	840,889	275,044	248,378	62,916	54,895	21,685	14,483
2023	1,435,873	981,736	29,751	1,011,487	116,527	-9,257	885,702	291,023	259,148	65,977	58,943	21,763	...

... = Not available.

Personal Income and Employment by Region and State: Rocky Mountain

(Millions of dollars, except as noted.)

		Derivation of personal income									Per capita (dollars)			
		Earnings by place of work												
Year	Personal income, total	Nonfarm	Farm	Total	Less: Contributions for government social insurance	Plus: Adjustment for residence	Equals: Net earnings by place of residence	Plus: Dividends, interest, and rent	Plus: Personal current transfer receipts	Personal income	Disposable personal income	Population (thousands)	Total employment (thousands)
1960	9,819	7,372	590	7,962	354	-3	7,605	1,591	624	2,257	2,021	4,350	...
1961	10,407	7,883	536	8,420	382	-3	8,035	1,682	690	2,314	2,072	4,497	...
1962	11,218	8,366	721	9,087	412	-3	8,673	1,825	721	2,449	2,201	4,580	...
1963	11,583	8,759	636	9,395	478	-2	8,915	1,911	758	2,501	2,241	4,632	...
1964	12,120	9,267	520	9,786	491	-2	9,294	2,049	777	2,594	2,364	4,673	...
1965	13,010	9,747	736	10,483	499	-2	9,982	2,187	840	2,766	2,518	4,703	...
1966	13,792	10,506	706	11,212	646	-1	10,565	2,326	902	2,913	2,637	4,735	...
1967	14,653	11,125	717	11,842	722	-1	11,119	2,465	1,069	3,064	2,762	4,783	...
1968	15,901	12,166	754	12,920	805	-1	12,115	2,572	1,215	3,267	2,921	4,868	...
1969	17,806	13,437	889	14,326	881	18	13,463	2,998	1,345	3,602	3,177	4,943	2,216
1970	19,931	14,797	1,003	15,800	962	20	14,858	3,473	1,601	3,956	3,530	5,038	2,271
1971	22,182	16,543	966	17,510	1,102	20	16,428	3,883	1,871	4,271	3,834	5,194	2,343
1972	25,137	18,788	1,269	20,057	1,320	23	18,759	4,288	2,090	4,682	4,174	5,368	2,482
1973	28,740	21,327	1,751	23,078	1,728	22	21,372	4,926	2,442	5,200	4,630	5,527	2,646
1974	32,390	23,981	1,836	25,818	2,002	24	23,840	5,713	2,838	5,733	5,079	5,650	2,740
1975	35,793	26,573	1,385	27,958	2,179	36	25,815	6,449	3,530	6,191	5,551	5,782	2,778
1976	39,578	30,110	1,026	31,136	2,512	40	28,665	7,024	3,889	6,690	5,957	5,916	2,912
1977	44,131	34,200	685	34,885	2,870	42	32,057	7,919	4,155	7,260	6,429	6,079	3,060
1978	51,079	39,772	956	40,728	3,411	52	37,370	9,168	4,542	8,164	7,217	6,257	3,257
1979	57,677	45,355	748	46,103	4,090	45	42,058	10,462	5,157	8,958	7,859	6,439	3,402
1980	65,490	50,410	964	51,374	4,596	68	46,846	12,588	6,056	9,934	8,724	6,592	3,474
1981	74,444	56,598	1,053	57,651	5,564	51	52,138	15,232	7,074	11,041	9,642	6,743	3,559
1982	80,465	60,191	824	61,015	6,033	52	55,034	17,383	8,048	11,655	10,206	6,904	3,596
1983	86,079	63,433	1,144	64,577	6,397	54	58,234	18,999	8,845	12,236	10,906	7,035	3,642
1984	93,102	69,070	1,042	70,113	7,175	75	63,012	20,859	9,231	13,096	11,716	7,109	3,801
1985	98,318	72,878	844	73,722	7,730	92	66,084	22,445	9,789	13,717	12,247	7,168	3,861
1986	101,841	74,974	1,242	76,216	8,019	113	68,309	23,023	10,508	14,145	12,682	7,200	3,854
1987	104,971	77,291	1,578	78,869	8,209	135	70,795	23,028	11,147	14,568	13,004	7,206	3,885
1988	111,214	82,283	1,625	83,908	9,123	174	74,959	24,500	11,755	15,441	13,801	7,203	4,021
1989	120,384	87,594	2,216	89,811	9,870	209	80,150	27,258	12,977	16,641	14,787	7,234	4,114
1990	128,561	94,193	2,514	96,707	10,976	245	85,976	28,553	14,032	17,599	15,572	7,305	4,230
1991	136,577	100,831	2,466	103,297	12,004	274	91,567	29,540	15,470	18,266	16,216	7,477	4,335
1992	147,631	110,190	2,543	112,733	12,992	306	100,047	30,363	17,221	19,182	17,017	7,696	4,434
1993	159,656	119,354	3,220	122,574	14,206	341	108,709	32,407	18,539	20,111	17,814	7,939	4,626
1994	170,764	128,625	2,094	130,719	15,410	393	115,701	35,571	19,492	20,898	18,450	8,171	4,886
1995	184,496	137,320	1,995	139,315	16,397	452	123,370	39,665	21,461	22,017	19,420	8,380	5,046
1996	198,139	147,253	2,190	149,443	17,263	525	132,704	42,971	22,464	23,132	20,273	8,565	5,249
1997	211,867	158,556	2,053	160,609	18,380	601	142,829	46,005	23,032	24,225	21,094	8,746	5,440
1998	230,915	173,756	2,393	176,149	19,327	699	157,520	49,645	23,750	25,893	22,474	8,918	5,621
1999	245,537	188,205	2,740	190,945	20,642	798	171,101	49,464	24,972	26,998	23,341	9,094	5,752
2000	268,774	206,935	2,383	209,318	22,510	857	187,664	54,312	26,798	28,997	24,944	9,269	5,953
2001	282,041	215,810	3,060	218,870	23,609	843	196,104	56,400	29,536	29,906	25,983	9,431	6,007
2002	286,470	219,933	2,314	222,246	24,443	835	198,639	55,576	32,256	29,943	26,645	9,567	6,002
2003	295,583	225,172	2,367	227,539	25,205	850	203,184	58,328	34,071	30,550	27,475	9,675	6,023
2004	312,110	236,978	3,372	240,350	27,024	881	214,207	61,995	35,908	31,824	28,649	9,808	6,166
2005	334,691	252,910	3,381	256,290	28,982	884	228,193	67,735	38,763	33,563	29,815	9,972	6,371
2006	365,904	275,802	2,310	278,112	31,437	858	247,533	76,555	41,817	35,908	31,626	10,190	6,589
2007	392,048	290,889	3,414	294,303	33,424	871	261,750	85,288	45,011	37,674	33,004	10,406	6,848
2008	411,924	297,994	3,381	301,376	34,539	929	267,766	91,857	52,301	38,826	34,304	10,610	6,896
2009	394,103	284,691	2,369	287,060	33,445	1,047	254,662	81,736	57,705	36,512	33,125	10,794	6,686
2010	407,052	291,413	3,355	294,767	34,008	1,225	261,984	80,758	64,310	37,175	33,621	10,950	6,635
2011	439,615	306,691	4,793	311,484	32,096	1,628	281,016	92,886	65,713	39,644	35,484	11,089	6,761
2012	464,962	323,622	4,534	328,156	33,559	2,254	296,851	102,028	66,083	41,403	36,988	11,230	6,882
2013	482,115	344,044	5,481	349,525	39,020	2,552	313,057	100,668	68,390	42,341	37,546	11,386	7,056
2014	515,988	366,245	5,603	371,848	41,461	2,825	333,212	110,254	72,522	44,714	39,567	11,540	7,253
2015	541,261	380,086	5,589	385,675	43,323	2,653	345,005	118,427	77,829	46,176	40,670	11,722	7,456
2016	553,887	388,016	4,500	392,516	44,701	2,455	350,270	122,137	81,480	46,483	40,843	11,916	7,642
2017	589,877	415,063	3,540	418,603	47,416	2,675	373,862	131,258	84,757	48,773	42,987	12,094	7,837
2018	633,665	446,193	3,803	449,996	50,260	2,834	402,570	140,306	90,789	51,651	45,781	12,268	8,058
2019	679,052	475,218	4,665	479,883	53,027	3,116	429,972	152,378	96,702	54,641	48,258	12,427	8,156
2020	733,062	495,702	4,987	500,689	55,552	2,972	448,109	157,996	126,957	58,256	51,522	12,583	8,121
2021	816,959	546,252	4,336	550,588	60,072	3,148	493,664	178,769	144,526	64,119	55,954	12,741	8,513
2022	864,062	594,792	5,524	600,316	66,937	3,560	536,939	198,434	128,689	67,160	57,784	12,866	8,929
2023	912,422	630,918	4,345	635,263	71,648	3,796	567,411	214,915	130,096	70,311	62,068	12,977	...

... = Not available.

Personal Income and Employment by Region and State: Southeast

(Millions of dollars, except as noted.)

Year	Personal income, total	Derivation of personal income: Earnings by place of work: Nonfarm	Farm	Total	Less: Contributions for government social insurance	Plus: Adjustment for residence	Equals: Net earnings by place of residence	Plus: Dividends, interest, and rent	Plus: Personal current transfer receipts	Per capita (dollars): Personal income	Disposable personal income	Population (thousands)	Total employment (thousands)
1960	66,930	51,896	3,350	55,246	2,447	589	53,388	8,939	4,603	1,721	1,565	38,885	...
1961	70,593	53,773	3,773	57,546	2,513	616	55,650	9,649	5,295	1,785	1,626	39,544	...
1962	75,390	57,877	3,533	61,410	2,806	676	59,281	10,554	5,556	1,876	1,700	40,179	...
1963	80,425	61,902	3,765	65,667	3,287	738	63,117	11,407	5,901	1,974	1,787	40,742	...
1964	86,835	67,360	3,625	70,985	3,444	801	68,343	12,335	6,157	2,100	1,920	41,349	...
1965	94,368	73,503	3,505	77,007	3,677	899	74,229	13,416	6,723	2,255	2,054	41,857	...
1966	103,487	81,959	3,714	85,673	4,914	1,000	81,759	14,388	7,340	2,449	2,214	42,257	...
1967	112,234	88,700	3,700	92,400	5,668	1,160	87,893	15,596	8,746	2,634	2,381	42,611	...
1968	124,348	98,752	3,572	102,324	6,410	1,258	97,173	17,075	10,100	2,889	2,585	43,042	...
1969	138,939	109,456	4,060	113,516	7,214	1,173	107,475	20,075	11,390	3,198	2,826	43,440	19,085
1970	152,550	117,976	4,050	122,026	7,779	1,084	115,332	23,440	13,778	3,469	3,095	43,974	19,254
1971	168,335	129,403	4,262	133,665	8,838	1,064	125,891	26,165	16,279	3,740	3,362	45,013	19,635
1972	189,159	146,065	4,964	151,029	10,455	1,127	141,702	29,037	18,420	4,110	3,653	46,019	20,523
1973	214,956	164,853	7,279	172,133	13,506	1,205	159,831	33,295	21,829	4,574	4,084	46,992	21,636
1974	239,478	181,787	6,663	188,450	15,479	1,305	174,276	38,811	26,391	4,994	4,439	47,955	22,069
1975	262,258	193,771	5,996	199,767	16,286	1,575	185,055	42,950	34,253	5,376	4,864	48,788	21,642
1976	291,460	217,654	6,366	224,020	18,675	1,779	207,124	46,883	37,453	5,886	5,281	49,514	22,351
1977	323,485	243,985	5,766	249,751	20,914	1,996	230,833	52,777	39,876	6,430	5,750	50,312	23,208
1978	367,595	278,118	6,931	285,048	24,375	2,393	263,066	60,877	43,652	7,192	6,399	51,113	24,305
1979	412,949	311,625	6,844	318,469	28,418	2,748	292,799	69,814	50,337	7,945	7,025	51,977	24,987
1980	465,607	343,617	4,173	347,791	31,420	3,314	319,685	85,824	60,098	8,805	7,775	52,881	25,324
1981	526,368	379,323	6,634	385,957	37,261	3,641	352,337	105,300	68,731	9,815	8,635	53,627	25,594
1982	564,136	399,041	6,759	405,799	39,941	3,822	369,680	118,202	76,254	10,399	9,193	54,249	25,499
1983	608,092	431,608	4,899	436,507	43,698	3,815	396,625	128,418	83,049	11,085	9,878	54,856	26,030
1984	674,730	479,757	8,400	488,156	49,934	4,070	442,293	144,929	87,508	12,154	10,896	55,515	27,280
1985	725,987	518,345	7,444	525,789	54,900	4,250	475,139	157,426	93,421	12,918	11,512	56,199	28,090
1986	773,596	555,092	6,952	562,043	59,997	4,449	506,496	167,489	99,611	13,605	12,133	56,861	28,826
1987	823,371	599,058	8,292	607,350	64,249	4,649	547,751	171,903	103,718	14,310	12,698	57,536	29,529
1988	898,157	651,929	10,868	662,797	72,102	5,120	595,815	191,043	111,298	15,453	13,788	58,120	30,527
1989	976,354	693,926	11,406	705,332	77,510	5,499	633,321	219,301	123,732	16,623	14,769	58,733	31,251
1990	1,039,795	737,578	10,875	748,453	83,397	6,148	671,205	232,765	135,825	17,471	15,559	59,516	31,840
1991	1,090,443	768,150	12,420	780,569	87,898	6,635	699,307	237,539	153,597	18,024	16,143	60,501	31,724
1992	1,168,700	829,036	13,206	842,242	94,074	7,073	755,241	240,112	173,347	19,001	17,048	61,508	32,180
1993	1,234,196	877,705	12,804	890,509	100,058	7,353	797,804	250,704	185,688	19,737	17,680	62,531	33,186
1994	1,308,801	931,123	14,006	945,129	107,408	7,255	844,975	266,563	197,262	20,587	18,391	63,574	34,135
1995	1,393,998	985,443	12,430	997,873	113,546	7,511	891,838	289,468	212,692	21,578	19,233	64,602	35,254
1996	1,478,652	1,042,682	14,181	1,056,863	118,968	7,178	945,073	308,226	225,352	22,537	19,962	65,611	36,087
1997	1,570,172	1,110,100	13,860	1,123,960	126,228	7,989	1,005,721	330,547	233,903	23,557	20,748	66,655	37,050
1998	1,687,081	1,203,741	12,928	1,216,669	135,202	8,011	1,089,478	357,013	240,590	24,947	21,883	67,627	38,014
1999	1,768,030	1,281,763	13,076	1,294,839	143,365	9,821	1,161,295	355,623	251,113	25,785	22,587	68,569	38,802
2000	1,894,415	1,371,739	14,403	1,386,143	151,844	8,281	1,242,580	383,638	268,197	27,259	23,857	69,497	39,694
2001	1,983,493	1,428,773	16,278	1,445,051	158,518	8,981	1,295,514	392,210	295,769	28,207	24,755	70,318	39,630
2002	2,039,761	1,478,038	10,337	1,488,375	163,764	10,641	1,335,252	385,293	319,216	28,668	25,695	71,152	39,667
2003	2,130,884	1,543,572	13,217	1,556,790	170,737	11,643	1,397,695	398,250	334,938	29,611	26,821	71,962	40,062
2004	2,277,223	1,648,207	16,814	1,665,021	182,216	12,373	1,495,178	423,040	359,005	31,187	28,277	73,019	41,037
2005	2,430,427	1,747,899	17,670	1,765,569	193,503	13,181	1,585,247	455,766	389,414	32,778	29,404	74,148	42,110
2006	2,603,706	1,857,855	13,150	1,871,006	206,555	15,101	1,679,551	510,703	413,453	34,686	30,966	75,066	43,150
2007	2,746,354	1,923,168	12,284	1,935,452	215,102	16,375	1,736,725	567,460	442,169	36,078	32,122	76,123	44,064
2008	2,846,347	1,940,431	11,664	1,952,095	220,556	18,548	1,750,088	594,264	501,996	36,938	33,061	77,058	43,725
2009	2,766,763	1,873,502	11,661	1,885,163	216,194	18,416	1,687,385	532,416	546,963	35,556	32,581	77,815	42,223
2010	2,882,037	1,935,400	10,695	1,946,096	220,637	20,188	1,745,646	543,267	593,124	36,681	33,548	78,570	42,066
2011	3,031,479	1,996,877	10,777	2,007,654	203,979	22,818	1,826,492	594,796	610,191	38,277	34,664	79,199	42,886
2012	3,152,000	2,076,687	14,358	2,091,044	211,166	22,825	1,902,704	637,103	612,193	39,455	35,763	79,889	43,433
2013	3,160,320	2,118,707	22,432	2,141,139	244,447	22,968	1,919,660	611,154	629,506	39,251	35,223	80,516	44,152
2014	3,326,261	2,218,761	18,753	2,237,514	255,032	25,237	2,007,719	660,666	657,876	40,962	36,707	81,204	45,200
2015	3,493,964	2,320,691	16,360	2,337,051	266,611	25,788	2,096,229	702,543	695,193	42,618	37,984	81,983	46,292
2016	3,598,072	2,393,574	11,677	2,405,251	274,574	26,819	2,157,497	723,684	716,892	43,437	38,802	82,835	47,201
2017	3,786,490	2,501,352	16,162	2,517,515	286,884	26,989	2,257,620	785,913	742,958	45,300	40,342	83,587	48,150
2018	3,978,127	2,626,475	10,895	2,637,370	301,382	27,052	2,363,041	837,808	777,278	47,228	42,399	84,233	49,285
2019	4,189,538	2,755,228	11,662	2,766,890	316,867	26,401	2,476,424	890,103	823,011	49,379	44,215	84,845	49,823
2020	4,480,458	2,809,505	9,077	2,818,583	326,472	26,606	2,518,717	904,976	1,056,765	52,446	47,126	85,429	49,062
2021	4,950,935	3,068,351	17,985	3,086,336	351,523	28,151	2,762,963	997,790	1,190,182	57,602	51,178	85,951	51,248
2022	5,102,324	3,310,114	19,166	3,329,279	387,091	29,065	2,971,254	1,071,624	1,059,446	58,784	51,335	86,799	53,608
2023	5,396,159	3,537,607	10,136	3,547,743	413,889	29,973	3,163,828	1,143,230	1,089,101	61,546	55,001	87,677	...

... = Not available.

Personal Income and Employment by Region and State: Southwest

(Millions of dollars, except as noted.)

Year	Personal income, total	Derivation of personal income: Earnings by place of work: Nonfarm	Farm	Total	Less: Contributions for government social insurance	Plus: Adjustment for residence	Equals: Net earnings by place of residence	Plus: Dividends, interest, and rent	Plus: Personal current transfer receipts	Per capita (dollars): Personal income	Disposable personal income	Population (thousands)	Total employment (thousands)
1960	28,817	22,282	1,474	23,756	1,006	5	22,755	4,417	1,645	2,024	1,826	14,235	...
1961	30,430	23,321	1,628	24,949	1,041	6	23,915	4,665	1,851	2,088	1,883	14,572	...
1962	31,996	24,782	1,411	26,192	1,132	9	25,069	4,932	1,995	2,143	1,928	14,930	...
1963	33,362	26,032	1,197	27,230	1,277	12	25,965	5,246	2,152	2,208	1,985	15,108	...
1964	35,741	28,050	1,132	29,182	1,330	14	27,865	5,629	2,247	2,339	2,134	15,278	...
1965	38,346	29,923	1,349	31,272	1,400	16	29,888	6,007	2,451	2,488	2,264	15,414	...
1966	41,706	33,093	1,409	34,503	1,882	17	32,638	6,394	2,674	2,679	2,420	15,567	...
1967	45,390	36,228	1,294	37,522	2,185	19	35,356	6,792	3,242	2,885	2,600	15,734	...
1968	50,518	40,397	1,423	41,820	2,456	24	39,388	7,318	3,812	3,158	2,817	15,998	...
1969	56,501	45,081	1,513	46,594	2,887	-62	43,645	8,604	4,252	3,460	3,052	16,328	7,219
1970	62,539	48,789	1,837	50,626	3,104	-84	47,438	10,062	5,038	3,763	3,356	16,621	7,311
1971	68,408	53,227	1,681	54,907	3,501	-90	51,317	11,206	5,885	4,006	3,615	17,077	7,457
1972	76,145	59,347	2,017	61,364	4,085	-107	57,171	12,379	6,594	4,350	3,884	17,503	7,807
1973	86,582	66,711	3,298	70,010	5,306	-121	64,583	14,160	7,839	4,825	4,325	17,943	8,215
1974	97,435	75,688	2,139	77,828	6,213	-83	71,532	16,547	9,357	5,309	4,712	18,354	8,511
1975	110,068	84,419	2,112	86,531	6,831	-46	79,653	18,584	11,831	5,858	5,276	18,789	8,633
1976	123,377	96,099	2,083	98,182	7,904	25	90,303	20,095	12,980	6,403	5,723	19,270	9,001
1977	137,741	108,947	1,864	110,811	9,030	-220	101,562	22,399	13,781	6,988	6,199	19,710	9,466
1978	158,697	126,806	1,689	128,496	10,776	-357	117,363	26,071	15,263	7,864	6,960	20,180	10,046
1979	183,163	146,035	2,982	149,017	13,007	-363	135,647	30,083	17,434	8,816	7,725	20,777	10,528
1980	210,281	166,795	1,542	168,336	14,995	-463	152,878	36,924	20,480	9,814	8,566	21,426	10,923
1981	245,412	192,286	2,837	195,123	18,608	-168	176,347	45,680	23,385	11,163	9,635	21,985	11,449
1982	269,759	207,412	2,353	209,765	20,499	-229	189,038	54,278	26,443	11,836	10,294	22,791	11,682
1983	287,733	216,992	2,409	219,401	21,389	-159	197,854	60,362	29,517	12,293	10,911	23,405	11,712
1984	314,958	237,772	2,677	240,449	24,038	-157	216,254	67,399	31,305	13,247	11,815	23,776	12,259
1985	339,385	254,606	2,582	257,188	26,109	-124	230,954	74,901	33,530	14,044	12,524	24,166	12,617
1986	349,919	261,020	2,586	263,606	26,713	-7	236,885	76,486	36,548	14,233	12,829	24,585	12,483
1987	357,892	267,461	3,519	270,980	27,114	84	243,951	75,339	38,602	14,462	12,963	24,748	12,785
1988	380,626	284,825	4,156	288,981	29,977	180	259,185	80,485	40,956	15,311	13,791	24,860	13,055
1989	406,690	301,237	4,117	305,354	32,059	264	273,559	87,877	45,253	16,214	14,522	25,083	13,241
1990	435,866	323,758	4,967	328,725	34,447	357	294,635	91,034	50,198	17,152	15,337	25,411	13,553
1991	456,555	341,059	4,535	345,594	37,065	316	308,845	91,966	55,744	17,616	15,831	25,917	13,759
1992	490,772	366,887	5,371	372,258	39,437	357	333,177	92,826	64,769	18,526	16,722	26,491	13,885
1993	519,975	390,291	6,179	396,470	41,953	410	354,927	95,756	69,292	19,176	17,290	27,116	14,332
1994	551,909	414,846	5,304	420,149	45,128	428	375,450	102,163	74,297	19,873	17,892	27,772	14,845
1995	590,534	442,143	4,279	446,422	47,841	408	398,988	111,067	80,480	20,779	18,679	28,420	15,396
1996	633,711	476,523	3,905	480,428	51,062	421	429,787	118,006	85,918	21,837	19,494	29,020	15,883
1997	687,536	520,983	5,000	525,984	55,115	417	471,285	126,712	89,539	23,208	20,590	29,625	16,482
1998	745,894	571,548	4,808	576,356	59,743	427	517,040	137,021	91,833	24,666	21,800	30,240	17,034
1999	784,591	605,760	6,642	612,403	63,268	537	549,671	139,514	95,406	25,451	22,490	30,827	17,353
2000	852,567	660,929	5,526	666,455	68,054	604	599,004	152,527	101,035	27,169	23,914	31,381	17,900
2001	906,746	702,469	6,338	708,808	71,645	678	637,841	157,330	111,575	28,432	25,163	31,892	18,099
2002	924,432	713,484	6,261	719,745	72,978	745	647,511	154,376	122,545	28,505	25,821	32,431	18,111
2003	965,519	738,061	7,522	745,583	75,981	890	670,492	163,533	131,494	29,326	26,814	32,924	18,266
2004	1,021,841	782,326	8,481	790,807	80,478	1,058	711,386	170,648	139,807	30,525	27,967	33,475	18,655
2005	1,110,529	842,426	8,135	850,561	86,111	1,096	765,546	190,977	154,006	32,569	29,485	34,098	19,317
2006	1,219,453	928,874	5,247	934,121	92,822	1,029	842,329	211,175	165,949	34,896	31,396	34,945	20,044
2007	1,290,719	968,995	5,990	974,985	98,897	980	877,069	232,377	181,274	36,232	32,510	35,624	20,727
2008	1,403,112	1,026,617	3,395	1,030,012	103,194	880	927,698	268,522	206,892	38,686	34,644	36,269	21,061
2009	1,335,984	968,829	1,880	970,710	101,631	584	869,663	238,913	227,408	36,206	33,434	36,899	20,640
2010	1,407,471	1,014,204	5,645	1,019,849	104,968	351	915,232	242,173	250,067	37,567	34,592	37,465	20,634
2011	1,525,381	1,088,039	6,415	1,094,454	98,722	-42	995,690	273,559	256,132	40,199	36,558	37,945	21,144
2012	1,613,805	1,154,246	6,283	1,160,529	104,048	-314	1,056,167	301,415	256,224	41,951	38,180	38,469	21,671
2013	1,656,654	1,209,606	8,832	1,218,438	122,313	-616	1,095,509	296,665	264,480	42,537	38,387	38,946	22,228
2014	1,766,253	1,285,467	9,035	1,294,502	128,707	-589	1,165,205	322,869	278,179	44,701	40,250	39,513	22,807
2015	1,800,501	1,297,624	10,272	1,307,897	134,192	-539	1,173,165	332,192	295,144	44,889	40,329	40,110	23,342
2016	1,801,519	1,298,356	5,774	1,304,130	137,195	-93	1,166,841	325,950	308,727	44,320	40,055	40,648	23,708
2017	1,919,437	1,378,840	6,696	1,385,536	144,709	258	1,241,085	359,516	318,836	46,709	42,039	41,094	24,233
2018	2,046,252	1,472,016	5,456	1,477,473	152,546	171	1,325,098	387,308	333,846	49,293	44,806	41,512	24,886
2019	2,154,932	1,543,535	6,005	1,549,539	160,384	38	1,389,194	411,717	354,021	51,330	46,508	41,982	25,259
2020	2,283,557	1,543,287	6,096	1,549,383	164,189	318	1,385,513	422,920	475,124	53,725	48,993	42,505	24,957
2021	2,528,030	1,677,797	8,037	1,685,834	174,845	638	1,511,627	472,373	544,031	58,870	53,157	42,942	26,053
2022	2,646,114	1,845,362	5,731	1,851,093	193,364	574	1,658,303	511,303	476,508	60,791	54,115	43,528	27,471
2023	2,805,975	1,967,761	3,899	1,971,659	207,736	462	1,764,385	553,365	488,225	63,623	57,762	44,103	...

... = Not available.

STATE

Personal Income and Employment by Region and State: Alabama

(Millions of dollars, except as noted.)

Year	Personal income, total	Derivation of personal income: Earnings by place of work: Nonfarm	Farm	Total	Less: Contributions for government social insurance	Plus: Adjustment for residence	Equals: Net earnings by place of residence	Plus: Dividends, interest, and rent	Plus: Personal current transfer receipts	Per capita (dollars): Personal income	Disposable personal income	Population (thousands)	Total employment (thousands)
1960	5,188	4,170	257	4,427	187	2	4,242	561	385	1,585	1,448	3,274	...
1961	5,360	4,279	247	4,526	194	3	4,335	596	429	1,616	1,484	3,316	...
1962	5,634	4,512	227	4,738	219	4	4,523	643	468	1,695	1,545	3,323	...
1963	5,984	4,779	275	5,054	260	7	4,801	687	496	1,782	1,625	3,358	...
1964	6,498	5,244	247	5,492	265	8	5,234	750	513	1,914	1,755	3,395	...
1965	7,052	5,704	257	5,961	273	11	5,699	803	551	2,048	1,874	3,443	...
1966	7,564	6,246	244	6,491	376	17	6,132	834	599	2,184	1,981	3,464	...
1967	7,992	6,613	209	6,822	429	23	6,415	886	691	2,311	2,096	3,458	...
1968	8,738	7,184	229	7,413	473	27	6,967	970	801	2,536	2,282	3,446	...
1969	9,738	7,833	280	8,112	551	130	7,692	1,154	892	2,831	2,515	3,440	1,411
1970	10,628	8,378	250	8,629	590	127	8,166	1,366	1,097	3,081	2,781	3,450	1,413
1971	11,699	9,124	279	9,403	655	133	8,881	1,534	1,285	3,345	3,032	3,497	1,423
1972	12,999	10,148	348	10,496	765	165	9,896	1,672	1,431	3,672	3,303	3,540	1,471
1973	14,639	11,327	535	11,862	983	183	11,062	1,896	1,681	4,088	3,677	3,581	1,526
1974	16,241	12,621	340	12,961	1,136	194	12,019	2,211	2,011	4,477	4,019	3,628	1,552
1975	18,100	13,631	414	14,046	1,222	200	13,024	2,476	2,601	4,918	4,460	3,681	1,543
1976	20,324	15,499	479	15,978	1,422	214	14,770	2,706	2,849	5,438	4,896	3,737	1,594
1977	22,395	17,332	383	17,716	1,596	246	16,365	3,024	3,005	5,920	5,324	3,783	1,651
1978	25,340	19,656	509	20,165	1,840	266	18,591	3,480	3,269	6,609	5,928	3,834	1,713
1979	28,151	21,682	521	22,204	2,103	291	20,392	3,950	3,809	7,275	6,491	3,869	1,736
1980	31,044	23,498	211	23,709	2,277	324	21,755	4,810	4,479	7,959	7,084	3,900	1,732
1981	34,454	25,323	490	25,813	2,644	421	23,589	5,840	5,025	8,793	7,808	3,919	1,719
1982	36,385	26,219	411	26,629	2,783	444	24,291	6,541	5,553	9,269	8,313	3,925	1,687
1983	38,979	28,289	293	28,582	3,053	436	25,965	7,002	6,012	9,908	8,886	3,934	1,717
1984	42,838	31,153	482	31,635	3,427	465	28,672	7,815	6,352	10,840	9,764	3,952	1,780
1985	46,086	33,713	467	34,180	3,739	473	30,914	8,464	6,708	11,601	10,384	3,973	1,822
1986	48,777	35,877	458	36,336	3,972	503	32,866	8,931	6,980	12,220	10,941	3,992	1,858
1987	51,514	38,286	541	38,827	4,195	513	35,145	9,236	7,133	12,830	11,419	4,015	1,912
1988	55,527	41,170	802	41,973	4,669	517	37,821	10,256	7,451	13,800	12,383	4,024	1,970
1989	60,351	43,679	941	44,619	4,970	539	40,188	11,741	8,422	14,975	13,366	4,030	2,006
1990	64,234	46,584	849	47,433	5,366	532	42,599	12,360	9,275	15,860	14,174	4,050	2,048
1991	67,983	48,981	1,124	50,105	5,681	563	44,987	12,739	10,257	16,585	14,880	4,099	2,060
1992	73,004	52,806	1,003	53,809	6,062	614	48,361	12,991	11,652	17,574	15,813	4,154	2,097
1993	76,346	55,246	1,018	56,264	6,419	665	50,509	13,470	12,366	18,116	16,281	4,214	2,159
1994	80,787	58,196	1,069	59,265	6,849	758	53,174	14,492	13,120	18,963	16,981	4,260	2,180
1995	85,394	60,931	788	61,720	7,217	839	55,342	15,858	14,194	19,874	17,754	4,297	2,242
1996	89,218	63,517	917	64,434	7,464	845	57,815	16,402	15,000	20,599	18,333	4,331	2,275
1997	93,852	66,557	954	67,511	7,830	949	60,630	17,545	15,678	21,487	19,057	4,368	2,321
1998	99,773	71,089	1,076	72,165	8,228	1,065	65,001	18,785	15,987	22,651	20,103	4,405	2,362
1999	103,204	74,185	1,244	75,429	8,593	1,131	67,968	18,584	16,653	23,296	20,648	4,430	2,378
2000	108,003	77,019	960	77,979	8,886	1,257	70,349	19,904	17,750	24,258	21,527	4,452	2,392
2001	111,894	78,918	1,391	80,309	9,189	1,315	72,435	20,253	19,207	25,046	22,243	4,468	2,376
2002	115,008	81,638	987	82,625	9,452	1,374	74,546	19,908	20,554	25,671	23,193	4,480	2,365
2003	120,241	84,577	1,307	85,884	9,794	1,454	77,544	20,884	21,812	26,700	24,330	4,503	2,371
2004	128,606	89,736	1,804	91,540	10,294	1,488	82,734	22,765	23,107	28,385	25,962	4,531	2,426
2005	136,088	95,124	1,675	96,799	10,951	1,554	87,403	23,834	24,851	29,780	26,961	4,570	2,487
2006	144,719	101,199	1,010	102,209	11,659	1,611	92,161	25,794	26,764	31,264	28,086	4,629	2,546
2007	151,943	104,755	828	105,583	12,221	1,727	95,089	28,043	28,812	32,516	29,148	4,673	2,604
2008	157,780	105,342	861	106,203	12,607	1,835	95,430	30,171	32,179	33,441	30,060	4,718	2,583
2009	155,667	103,327	915	104,242	12,336	1,804	93,709	27,281	34,677	32,717	30,104	4,758	2,480
2010	162,069	106,337	777	107,114	12,715	1,887	96,287	27,804	37,978	33,849	31,091	4,788	2,460
2011	167,882	109,407	382	109,788	11,651	2,033	100,170	28,992	38,720	34,887	31,760	4,812	2,498
2012	172,102	111,420	691	112,110	11,890	2,293	102,513	30,727	38,862	35,564	32,500	4,839	2,504
2013	173,721	113,380	1,978	115,358	13,676	2,375	104,057	29,948	39,715	35,713	32,399	4,864	2,523
2014	179,487	117,145	1,529	118,674	14,069	2,366	106,972	31,183	41,333	36,729	33,351	4,887	2,552
2015	187,475	121,000	1,547	122,547	14,542	2,353	110,358	32,795	44,322	38,197	34,538	4,908	2,588
2016	190,872	124,135	848	124,983	14,817	2,438	112,605	33,393	44,874	38,712	34,919	4,931	2,620
2017	197,964	128,479	1,262	129,741	15,394	2,392	116,739	35,474	45,751	39,975	36,173	4,952	2,649
2018	205,674	134,404	1,011	135,415	16,253	2,536	121,698	36,450	47,526	41,330	37,645	4,976	2,692
2019	215,166	140,119	766	140,885	16,863	2,640	126,662	38,340	50,164	43,004	39,015	5,003	2,712
2020	230,873	144,646	313	144,960	17,509	2,618	130,069	38,936	61,868	45,882	41,836	5,032	2,671
2021	252,792	154,425	1,427	155,853	18,631	2,836	140,058	42,534	70,200	50,054	45,186	5,050	2,769
2022	258,362	164,667	1,689	166,356	20,189	3,166	149,334	46,205	62,823	50,920	45,251	5,074	2,870
2023	271,640	176,199	476	176,674	21,572	3,328	158,431	48,878	64,332	53,175	48,163	5,108	...

... = Not available.

Personal Income and Employment by Region and State: Alaska

(Millions of dollars, except as noted.)

Year	Personal income, total	Derivation of personal income: Earnings by place of work: Nonfarm	Farm	Total	Less: Contributions for government social insurance	Plus: Adjustment for residence	Equals: Net earnings by place of residence	Plus: Dividends, interest, and rent	Plus: Personal current transfer receipts	Per capita (dollars): Personal income	Disposable personal income	Population (thousands)	Total employment (thousands)
1960	806	721	2	723	28	-2	694	91	22	3,521	3,162	229	...
1961	797	707	2	709	28	-3	678	92	27	3,347	3,026	238	...
1962	831	739	1	741	29	-5	707	98	26	3,378	3,030	246	...
1963	901	804	1	805	33	-9	763	110	27	3,518	3,146	256	...
1964	1,009	903	1	904	37	-13	854	126	29	3,835	3,497	263	...
1965	1,089	980	1	981	41	-18	922	135	31	4,016	3,612	271	...
1966	1,159	1,050	1	1,051	48	-23	980	145	34	4,276	3,853	271	...
1967	1,264	1,151	1	1,152	54	-31	1,067	158	39	4,545	4,091	278	...
1968	1,365	1,256	2	1,258	67	-39	1,152	166	48	4,790	4,293	285	...
1969	1,575	1,434	1	1,436	94	-25	1,317	206	53	5,322	4,624	296	144
1970	1,799	1,622	2	1,624	106	-46	1,472	255	72	5,911	5,222	304	149
1971	1,984	1,786	2	1,787	118	-60	1,609	284	91	6,269	5,569	316	153
1972	2,167	1,955	2	1,957	134	-75	1,748	314	104	6,636	5,822	326	158
1973	2,508	2,159	2	2,161	165	-93	1,902	359	246	7,525	6,681	333	167
1974	3,043	2,863	2	2,865	241	-209	2,415	419	208	8,827	7,643	345	189
1975	4,157	4,428	4	4,432	408	-610	3,414	506	237	11,205	9,577	371	227
1976	4,893	5,490	4	5,494	526	-879	4,088	571	234	12,447	10,600	393	243
1977	5,082	5,079	5	5,084	463	-452	4,169	635	278	12,789	10,937	397	237
1978	5,236	4,964	5	4,969	435	-324	4,210	727	299	13,018	11,335	402	238
1979	5,546	5,183	4	5,187	468	-274	4,445	809	293	13,744	11,816	404	241
1980	6,285	5,857	3	5,861	511	-329	5,021	921	344	15,507	13,587	405	244
1981	7,151	6,775	2	6,777	653	-457	5,667	1,077	407	17,086	14,642	418	252
1982	8,730	7,842	3	7,844	766	-548	6,530	1,336	864	19,417	16,928	450	277
1983	9,514	8,772	2	8,774	852	-606	7,316	1,564	633	19,479	17,172	488	297
1984	10,115	9,284	2	9,287	952	-620	7,714	1,718	683	19,690	17,562	514	309
1985	10,962	9,767	2	9,769	976	-616	8,177	1,898	887	20,586	18,448	532	316
1986	11,061	9,597	7	9,603	925	-561	8,118	1,945	998	20,322	18,452	544	310
1987	10,593	9,031	9	9,040	871	-526	7,643	1,910	1,039	19,642	17,656	539	310
1988	11,060	9,443	11	9,454	949	-552	7,953	1,989	1,118	20,406	18,469	542	317
1989	12,101	10,312	6	10,318	1,048	-618	8,652	2,210	1,239	22,117	19,715	547	329
1990	12,840	10,927	8	10,936	1,170	-625	9,142	2,328	1,371	23,207	20,544	553	339
1991	13,410	11,449	9	11,458	1,239	-669	9,551	2,386	1,473	23,518	21,016	570	347
1992	14,264	12,110	9	12,119	1,307	-705	10,107	2,522	1,635	24,227	21,754	589	351
1993	14,998	12,557	11	12,569	1,388	-726	10,455	2,722	1,821	25,020	22,498	599	358
1994	15,500	12,877	12	12,889	1,442	-741	10,706	2,928	1,866	25,691	23,037	603	363
1995	15,938	13,067	13	13,080	1,455	-746	10,880	3,102	1,956	26,369	23,675	604	365
1996	16,377	13,276	14	13,290	1,459	-769	11,062	3,209	2,105	26,910	24,094	609	369
1997	17,298	13,869	16	13,885	1,505	-777	11,604	3,421	2,273	28,219	25,210	613	374
1998	18,156	14,510	17	14,527	1,548	-822	12,157	3,528	2,471	29,287	26,112	620	382
1999	18,707	14,863	19	14,882	1,570	-827	12,485	3,506	2,716	29,941	26,760	625	381
2000	20,092	15,846	21	15,867	1,644	-878	13,345	3,670	3,077	31,996	28,557	628	390
2001	21,287	17,010	20	17,030	1,738	-863	14,429	3,639	3,220	33,591	29,933	634	395
2002	22,332	18,009	20	18,029	1,844	-791	15,394	3,630	3,307	34,766	31,592	642	402
2003	23,372	18,944	12	18,956	1,904	-700	16,353	3,774	3,246	36,045	33,081	648	406
2004	24,429	19,920	15	19,935	2,029	-607	17,299	3,922	3,208	37,054	34,194	659	414
2005	26,020	21,155	14	21,169	2,179	-512	18,478	4,137	3,405	39,013	35,787	667	421
2006	27,696	22,324	10	22,334	2,378	-420	19,536	4,545	3,616	41,013	37,430	675	431
2007	29,761	23,384	9	23,393	2,477	-308	20,609	5,069	4,084	43,747	39,647	680	440
2008	32,861	24,426	0	24,426	2,557	-173	21,696	5,704	5,461	47,800	43,193	687	444
2009	32,995	25,418	5	25,423	2,600	-179	22,645	5,603	4,748	47,211	43,684	699	443
2010	35,374	26,932	6	26,938	2,676	-180	24,082	5,956	5,336	49,543	45,803	714	444
2011	37,871	28,431	6	28,437	2,545	-194	25,698	6,634	5,539	52,415	48,150	723	450
2012	38,997	29,469	11	29,481	2,697	-205	26,578	7,017	5,402	53,340	49,166	731	459
2013	38,565	29,686	8	29,693	3,123	-206	26,364	6,784	5,417	52,252	47,672	738	461
2014	40,642	30,360	8	30,368	3,116	-220	27,032	7,130	6,480	55,098	50,262	738	461
2015	41,919	31,201	8	31,209	3,164	-224	27,822	7,459	6,638	56,714	51,514	739	462
2016	41,286	30,373	12	30,385	3,055	-195	27,136	7,558	6,592	55,535	50,718	743	457
2017	41,919	30,437	9	30,446	3,082	-182	27,182	7,727	7,011	56,499	51,925	742	456
2018	43,523	31,376	10	31,386	3,153	-192	28,042	7,875	7,606	58,997	54,641	738	455
2019	44,508	32,039	10	32,049	3,275	-197	28,578	7,919	8,011	60,569	55,857	735	455
2020	45,366	31,616	8	31,624	3,259	-190	28,176	7,806	9,385	61,894	57,337	733	431
2021	48,208	32,972	15	32,986	3,456	-189	29,341	8,445	10,422	65,596	60,065	735	443
2022	50,350	34,533	-7	34,526	3,724	-203	30,600	9,031	10,719	68,664	62,303	733	458
2023	52,524	37,480	-11	37,469	4,045	-222	33,203	9,556	9,765	71,616	65,899	733	...

... = Not available.

Personal Income and Employment by Region and State: Arizona

(Millions of dollars, except as noted.)

Year	Personal income, total	Derivation of personal income								Per capita (dollars)		Population (thousands)	Total employment (thousands)
		Earnings by place of work			Less: Contributions for government social insurance	Plus: Adjustment for residence	Equals: Net earnings by place of residence	Plus: Dividends, interest, and rent	Plus: Personal current transfer receipts				
		Nonfarm	Farm	Total						Personal income	Disposable personal income		
1960	2,856	2,205	128	2,333	118	-2	2,213	477	166	2,162	1,940	1,321	...
1961	3,110	2,370	135	2,505	125	-2	2,378	538	194	2,210	1,994	1,407	...
1962	3,350	2,567	138	2,705	139	-2	2,564	574	212	2,277	2,046	1,471	...
1963	3,522	2,724	113	2,837	162	-1	2,675	616	231	2,315	2,082	1,521	...
1964	3,777	2,898	130	3,029	167	(L)	2,861	666	250	2,427	2,219	1,556	...
1965	4,004	3,060	128	3,188	174	1	3,015	707	282	2,528	2,310	1,584	...
1966	4,360	3,425	121	3,547	232	0	3,315	740	305	2,701	2,456	1,614	...
1967	4,739	3,680	149	3,829	266	0	3,564	799	377	2,879	2,604	1,646	...
1968	5,437	4,161	192	4,353	313	3	4,043	959	435	3,233	2,902	1,682	...
1969	6,327	4,775	203	4,979	322	-26	4,631	1,204	492	3,643	3,218	1,737	711
1970	7,216	5,379	180	5,559	362	-30	5,168	1,456	592	4,020	3,570	1,795	747
1971	8,256	6,140	201	6,341	430	-29	5,882	1,664	710	4,354	3,912	1,896	786
1972	9,465	7,126	205	7,332	525	-32	6,775	1,874	816	4,711	4,192	2,009	850
1973	10,934	8,273	240	8,512	695	-31	7,786	2,165	983	5,145	4,624	2,125	925
1974	12,336	9,075	384	9,458	791	-41	8,627	2,522	1,188	5,546	4,956	2,224	955
1975	13,318	9,462	217	9,680	816	-47	8,816	2,841	1,660	5,825	5,324	2,286	935
1976	14,813	10,558	330	10,888	916	-48	9,924	3,061	1,828	6,309	5,723	2,348	976
1977	16,647	12,112	267	12,378	1,061	-57	11,261	3,459	1,928	6,858	6,175	2,427	1,048
1978	19,560	14,371	318	14,689	1,292	-70	13,328	4,059	2,173	7,768	6,935	2,518	1,150
1979	22,987	17,050	399	17,449	1,606	-72	15,771	4,743	2,472	8,712	7,722	2,639	1,240
1980	26,490	19,104	477	19,580	1,822	-81	17,678	5,836	2,976	9,676	8,606	2,738	1,283
1981	30,223	21,357	414	21,771	2,191	-16	19,564	7,164	3,496	10,755	9,480	2,810	1,313
1982	32,161	22,187	396	22,583	2,315	-9	20,259	8,001	3,902	11,129	9,860	2,890	1,315
1983	35,455	24,367	328	24,695	2,580	2	22,117	9,067	4,271	11,942	10,679	2,969	1,379
1984	39,989	27,746	526	28,272	3,018	5	25,259	10,152	4,578	13,038	11,674	3,067	1,504
1985	44,529	31,023	492	31,515	3,435	18	28,098	11,463	4,968	13,987	12,466	3,184	1,622
1986	48,698	34,175	472	34,646	3,805	38	30,880	12,368	5,450	14,720	13,141	3,308	1,701
1987	52,270	36,899	634	37,533	4,075	64	33,522	12,794	5,954	15,208	13,543	3,437	1,765
1988	56,653	39,995	760	40,755	4,563	106	36,298	13,820	6,536	16,025	14,364	3,535	1,833
1989	60,777	41,532	690	42,222	4,873	164	37,513	15,684	7,580	16,779	14,966	3,622	1,865
1990	63,798	43,722	642	44,364	5,269	223	39,319	16,076	8,403	17,317	15,434	3,684	1,894
1991	67,230	46,430	739	47,169	5,627	220	41,761	16,085	9,383	17,745	15,854	3,789	1,903
1992	71,608	50,011	673	50,683	6,016	247	44,914	16,010	10,684	18,287	16,407	3,916	1,925
1993	76,933	53,898	789	54,687	6,488	264	48,463	16,946	11,525	18,924	16,947	4,065	2,011
1994	84,206	59,449	577	60,026	7,169	275	53,131	18,768	12,306	19,836	17,718	4,245	2,141
1995	91,807	64,517	824	65,341	7,483	292	58,150	20,541	13,117	20,712	18,484	4,432	2,258
1996	99,450	70,756	737	71,493	8,374	322	63,442	22,038	13,969	21,681	19,145	4,587	2,388
1997	107,798	77,028	740	77,768	8,976	358	69,150	24,071	14,578	22,757	20,032	4,737	2,497
1998	117,835	85,265	870	86,136	9,786	406	76,756	25,949	15,130	24,130	21,147	4,883	2,616
1999	124,922	91,374	847	92,222	10,488	466	82,200	26,606	16,116	24,866	21,761	5,024	2,696
2000	135,574	99,984	807	100,790	11,419	525	89,896	28,650	17,028	26,271	22,931	5,161	2,802
2001	142,098	104,198	747	104,945	11,946	638	93,637	29,149	19,313	26,946	23,670	5,273	2,829
2002	147,455	107,776	765	108,541	12,362	698	96,876	29,065	21,514	27,325	24,572	5,396	2,847
2003	156,409	113,577	724	114,301	12,836	799	102,264	30,670	23,475	28,384	25,739	5,510	2,917
2004	170,443	123,959	1,024	124,983	13,906	949	112,026	32,642	25,775	30,154	27,300	5,652	3,041
2005	187,725	136,549	986	137,535	15,259	1,060	123,336	35,901	28,487	32,150	28,727	5,839	3,220
2006	207,763	151,859	713	152,572	16,715	1,094	136,950	39,680	31,132	34,460	30,674	6,029	3,375
2007	219,579	158,342	852	159,194	17,692	1,177	142,679	43,116	33,784	35,602	31,718	6,168	3,465
2008	223,495	156,103	634	156,736	17,899	1,216	140,053	44,082	39,360	35,586	32,036	6,280	3,403
2009	212,284	144,999	490	145,489	17,060	1,226	129,655	38,619	44,011	33,467	30,892	6,343	3,229
2010	216,224	145,544	671	146,216	17,240	1,250	130,226	38,112	47,886	33,774	31,055	6,402	3,182
2011	227,203	151,120	1,167	152,287	15,972	1,250	137,564	41,816	47,823	35,244	31,975	6,447	3,239
2012	236,431	157,954	881	158,835	16,516	1,350	143,669	44,911	47,852	36,333	33,019	6,507	3,296
2013	242,030	164,885	1,334	166,219	19,348	1,346	148,216	44,289	49,525	36,877	33,240	6,563	3,371
2014	253,712	171,736	975	172,712	19,980	1,455	154,186	47,336	52,189	38,220	34,441	6,638	3,448
2015	267,474	180,095	1,199	181,294	21,008	1,513	161,799	50,986	54,690	39,836	35,676	6,714	3,548
2016	279,697	188,317	1,347	189,664	21,883	1,594	169,375	52,957	57,365	41,122	36,850	6,802	3,645
2017	297,262	199,723	1,259	200,982	23,184	1,667	179,465	56,529	61,268	43,208	38,761	6,880	3,741
2018	315,459	213,283	984	214,267	24,907	1,720	191,080	60,061	64,319	45,260	40,703	6,970	3,855
2019	337,214	226,837	1,189	228,025	26,546	1,921	203,400	65,008	68,806	47,693	42,735	7,071	3,930
2020	374,312	239,573	808	240,382	28,141	1,896	214,136	67,132	93,043	52,084	46,930	7,187	3,920
2021	409,886	260,903	729	261,631	30,510	2,023	233,145	74,172	102,568	56,361	50,097	7,272	4,087
2022	430,084	284,876	965	285,841	33,562	2,394	254,673	83,131	92,280	58,390	51,203	7,366	4,288
2023	458,154	303,714	736	304,450	35,861	2,528	271,118	90,321	96,715	61,652	55,333	7,431	...

... = Not available.

Personal Income and Employment by Region and State: Arkansas

(Millions of dollars, except as noted.)

Year	Personal income, total	Derivation of personal income: Earnings by place of work: Nonfarm	Farm	Total	Less: Contributions for government social insurance	Plus: Adjustment for residence	Equals: Net earnings by place of residence	Plus: Dividends, interest, and rent	Plus: Personal current transfer receipts	Per capita (dollars): Personal income	Disposable personal income	Population (thousands)	Total employment (thousands)
1960	2,548	1,805	313	2,118	92	-2	2,025	283	240	1,424	1,314	1,789	...
1961	2,772	1,919	368	2,287	95	-2	2,190	313	269	1,535	1,418	1,806	...
1962	2,966	2,112	324	2,436	109	-3	2,324	354	288	1,600	1,464	1,853	...
1963	3,142	2,254	322	2,577	127	-4	2,446	386	310	1,676	1,533	1,875	...
1964	3,412	2,441	360	2,802	137	-4	2,661	425	326	1,799	1,668	1,897	...
1965	3,602	2,621	288	2,909	147	-6	2,756	488	357	1,902	1,755	1,894	...
1966	4,005	2,876	393	3,269	192	-4	3,074	540	391	2,109	1,925	1,899	...
1967	4,254	3,123	301	3,424	221	-5	3,198	588	468	2,238	2,043	1,901	...
1968	4,601	3,437	337	3,774	252	-7	3,516	560	525	2,419	2,184	1,902	...
1969	5,129	3,775	346	4,121	278	32	3,875	670	584	2,681	2,399	1,913	800
1970	5,627	4,026	415	4,441	296	24	4,168	775	684	2,915	2,623	1,930	805
1971	6,263	4,503	407	4,911	340	22	4,593	869	802	3,176	2,893	1,972	831
1972	7,071	5,123	482	5,605	405	22	5,222	956	893	3,504	3,178	2,018	867
1973	8,376	5,773	914	6,687	524	18	6,180	1,113	1,083	4,069	3,676	2,058	902
1974	9,354	6,468	833	7,301	609	11	6,704	1,335	1,315	4,453	3,993	2,100	927
1975	10,292	6,938	795	7,732	638	9	7,103	1,520	1,669	4,769	4,355	2,158	905
1976	11,379	7,991	641	8,632	745	-1	7,886	1,664	1,829	5,247	4,726	2,169	941
1977	12,662	8,968	725	9,693	847	-7	8,839	1,881	1,942	5,736	5,183	2,207	981
1978	14,669	10,203	1,176	11,379	987	-12	10,380	2,157	2,132	6,546	5,912	2,241	1,021
1979	16,089	11,320	995	12,315	1,134	-15	11,166	2,479	2,444	7,090	6,355	2,269	1,031
1980	17,396	12,275	372	12,647	1,220	-5	11,422	3,075	2,900	7,601	6,776	2,289	1,032
1981	19,703	13,193	851	14,044	1,422	-23	12,598	3,824	3,280	8,592	7,669	2,293	1,026
1982	20,697	13,647	642	14,289	1,498	-21	12,770	4,360	3,567	9,021	8,003	2,294	1,011
1983	21,947	14,819	417	15,237	1,638	-50	13,548	4,540	3,859	9,518	8,543	2,306	1,039
1984	24,447	16,424	883	17,307	1,869	-69	15,369	5,034	4,044	10,538	9,528	2,320	1,079
1985	25,982	17,435	865	18,300	2,005	-75	16,219	5,481	4,282	11,165	10,065	2,327	1,098
1986	27,303	18,534	805	19,338	2,141	-101	17,097	5,694	4,512	11,708	10,588	2,332	1,110
1987	28,357	19,594	935	20,529	2,251	-124	18,154	5,560	4,644	12,106	10,900	2,342	1,137
1988	30,490	20,919	1,344	22,264	2,507	-158	19,599	6,006	4,885	13,015	11,747	2,343	1,170
1989	32,695	22,240	1,238	23,477	2,675	-161	20,641	6,655	5,399	13,934	12,539	2,346	1,189
1990	34,456	23,756	1,048	24,803	2,965	-220	21,618	6,991	5,847	14,621	13,137	2,357	1,204
1991	36,494	25,240	1,128	26,368	3,149	-248	22,971	7,040	6,483	15,313	13,802	2,383	1,230
1992	39,698	27,564	1,430	28,994	3,409	-271	25,314	7,195	7,189	16,431	14,831	2,416	1,255
1993	41,623	29,115	1,336	30,450	3,619	-308	26,524	7,512	7,587	16,945	15,291	2,456	1,301
1994	44,252	31,067	1,466	32,533	3,908	-334	28,291	7,998	7,963	17,743	15,942	2,494	1,329
1995	47,112	32,823	1,481	34,305	4,110	-304	29,891	8,631	8,590	18,582	16,653	2,535	1,382
1996	49,970	34,261	1,922	36,183	4,252	-301	31,631	9,237	9,102	19,427	17,394	2,572	1,405
1997	52,481	36,076	1,811	37,887	4,460	-305	33,122	9,857	9,502	20,176	17,981	2,601	1,427
1998	55,686	38,815	1,596	40,410	4,734	-306	35,370	10,498	9,818	21,203	18,836	2,626	1,446
1999	57,922	40,849	1,807	42,655	4,962	-322	37,372	10,429	10,121	21,842	19,433	2,652	1,460
2000	60,886	43,005	1,704	44,709	5,196	-360	39,153	10,991	10,741	22,731	20,168	2,679	1,482
2001	64,169	44,768	2,010	46,778	5,350	-374	41,054	11,205	11,910	23,841	21,202	2,692	1,483
2002	65,699	46,561	1,271	47,832	5,539	-372	41,921	10,952	12,825	24,280	21,949	2,706	1,479
2003	69,656	48,618	2,403	51,021	5,746	-350	44,925	11,341	13,391	25,564	23,360	2,725	1,482
2004	74,309	51,523	2,763	54,286	6,030	-318	47,938	12,021	14,350	27,024	24,746	2,750	1,505
2005	77,990	54,273	1,866	56,138	6,387	-287	49,464	13,131	15,395	28,043	25,469	2,781	1,538
2006	82,892	56,814	1,506	58,320	6,815	-248	51,258	14,824	16,810	29,376	26,599	2,822	1,568
2007	88,411	58,683	1,900	60,583	7,095	-181	53,307	16,927	18,176	31,036	27,920	2,849	1,583
2008	92,436	59,196	1,613	60,809	7,391	-139	53,280	18,889	20,267	32,157	28,916	2,875	1,579
2009	90,992	58,418	943	59,362	7,392	-120	51,850	17,146	21,997	31,411	28,802	2,897	1,543
2010	94,127	60,489	679	61,168	7,603	-129	53,437	17,078	23,612	32,218	29,569	2,922	1,541
2011	100,450	62,849	724	63,573	7,115	-112	56,346	20,017	24,087	34,180	31,103	2,939	1,562
2012	107,007	65,537	1,127	66,664	7,258	-155	59,251	23,420	24,337	36,287	33,083	2,949	1,565
2013	107,209	66,773	2,538	69,311	8,240	-215	60,856	21,596	24,757	36,285	32,790	2,955	1,569
2014	113,172	68,863	2,293	71,156	8,599	-224	62,333	24,588	26,251	38,218	34,568	2,961	1,587
2015	116,632	70,753	1,341	72,094	8,866	-257	62,971	26,202	27,460	39,266	35,422	2,970	1,611
2016	119,759	71,957	965	72,922	8,981	-207	63,733	27,514	28,512	40,179	36,197	2,981	1,630
2017	123,825	74,349	1,615	75,964	9,312	-318	66,334	28,319	29,172	41,402	37,338	2,991	1,640
2018	128,971	76,629	1,367	77,996	9,586	-362	68,049	30,716	30,206	43,029	39,143	2,997	1,658
2019	131,439	80,156	765	80,921	10,071	-362	70,489	28,998	31,952	43,751	39,714	3,004	1,664
2020	142,112	82,881	670	83,551	10,618	-383	72,550	30,526	39,035	47,145	42,991	3,014	1,640
2021	156,362	89,096	2,341	91,438	11,200	-493	79,745	33,224	43,393	51,631	46,639	3,028	1,686
2022	160,254	94,803	2,721	97,524	12,121	-682	84,722	35,985	39,548	52,604	46,910	3,046	1,756
2023	166,722	100,666	1,027	101,693	12,824	-708	88,161	38,059	40,502	54,347	49,360	3,068	...

... = Not available.

Personal Income and Employment by Region and State: California

(Millions of dollars, except as noted.)

Year	Personal income, total	Derivation of personal income								Per capita (dollars)		Population (thousands)	Total employment (thousands)
		Earnings by place of work			Less: Contributions for government social insurance	Plus: Adjustment for residence	Equals: Net earnings by place of residence	Plus: Dividends, interest, and rent	Plus: Personal current transfer receipts				
		Nonfarm	Farm	Total						Personal income	Disposable personal income		
1960	46,521	36,478	1,437	37,915	1,720	-5	36,190	7,747	2,585	2,931	2,602	15,870	...
1961	49,267	38,626	1,369	39,996	1,832	-5	38,158	8,109	2,999	2,986	2,654	16,497	...
1962	53,086	41,937	1,433	43,370	2,249	-6	41,116	8,791	3,179	3,110	2,759	17,072	...
1963	56,740	45,049	1,367	46,416	2,625	-6	43,786	9,437	3,517	3,211	2,850	17,668	...
1964	61,405	48,481	1,517	49,997	2,731	-7	47,260	10,332	3,813	3,383	3,053	18,151	...
1965	65,618	51,529	1,464	52,993	2,846	-8	50,138	11,267	4,213	3,531	3,187	18,585	...
1966	71,356	56,763	1,583	58,346	3,740	-11	54,595	12,108	4,653	3,784	3,397	18,858	...
1967	76,732	60,732	1,496	62,227	4,100	-12	58,115	12,862	5,755	4,001	3,578	19,176	...
1968	84,056	66,766	1,720	68,486	4,587	-14	63,885	13,528	6,643	4,334	3,832	19,394	...
1969	92,160	72,625	1,705	74,329	4,827	-98	69,405	15,139	7,616	4,676	4,105	19,711	9,033
1970	99,418	76,644	1,709	78,352	5,018	-94	73,241	16,876	9,301	4,965	4,430	20,023	9,057
1971	105,987	80,876	1,707	82,583	5,449	-111	77,023	18,269	10,696	5,209	4,701	20,346	9,036
1972	116,351	89,229	2,173	91,402	6,333	-118	84,951	19,878	11,522	5,652	5,013	20,585	9,368
1973	127,777	97,953	2,931	100,884	7,973	-103	92,808	22,211	12,758	6,123	5,477	20,868	9,844
1974	142,507	107,472	3,645	111,117	9,013	-100	102,004	25,386	15,118	6,731	5,998	21,173	10,163
1975	157,640	117,020	3,273	120,293	9,600	17	110,710	27,936	18,994	7,320	6,602	21,537	10,286
1976	174,925	131,249	3,477	134,726	10,978	120	123,868	30,045	21,012	7,975	7,121	21,935	10,633
1977	194,033	147,538	3,543	151,081	12,560	-21	138,500	33,226	22,307	8,681	7,699	22,350	11,119
1978	220,640	169,787	3,489	173,277	14,806	-22	158,449	38,085	24,106	9,661	8,509	22,839	11,816
1979	250,182	192,947	4,573	197,520	17,663	62	179,919	43,777	26,486	10,758	9,410	23,255	12,461
1980	284,417	214,018	5,582	219,600	19,263	7	200,344	53,289	30,784	11,950	10,439	23,801	12,762
1981	319,357	236,420	4,354	240,774	23,093	286	217,967	65,179	36,211	13,150	11,510	24,286	12,935
1982	342,145	250,604	4,600	255,203	24,994	296	230,504	71,953	39,688	13,785	12,157	24,820	12,863
1983	369,926	271,683	4,235	275,917	27,641	300	248,577	78,974	42,376	14,587	12,901	25,360	13,182
1984	410,322	303,540	4,910	308,450	32,061	245	276,634	89,472	44,216	15,877	14,028	25,844	13,797
1985	443,889	330,520	4,950	335,470	35,323	195	300,342	95,744	47,803	16,788	14,748	26,441	14,285
1986	476,485	358,456	5,390	363,846	38,688	154	325,313	99,819	51,353	17,581	15,460	27,102	14,710
1987	511,613	392,750	6,591	399,341	42,355	76	357,062	100,972	53,579	18,418	16,009	27,777	15,300
1988	557,618	430,149	6,936	437,086	47,729	38	389,394	110,873	57,351	19,590	17,190	28,464	16,022
1989	600,194	456,298	6,839	463,137	51,065	25	412,098	125,282	62,814	20,542	17,850	29,218	16,426
1990	643,624	488,244	7,216	495,460	54,273	-47	441,140	133,311	69,173	21,483	18,709	29,960	16,835
1991	666,608	505,398	6,316	511,714	56,412	-38	455,264	134,618	76,725	21,877	19,273	30,471	16,750
1992	702,024	529,964	6,825	536,789	58,517	-43	478,229	135,159	88,636	22,664	20,121	30,975	16,391
1993	719,015	538,594	7,769	546,363	59,531	25	486,856	138,555	93,604	22,990	20,414	31,275	16,367
1994	741,652	554,983	7,547	562,530	61,692	36	500,874	144,954	95,824	23,556	20,888	31,484	16,541
1995	779,605	579,282	7,227	586,509	63,539	25	522,995	156,266	100,343	24,596	21,682	31,697	16,940
1996	828,147	614,255	8,129	622,384	65,645	14	556,752	166,131	105,264	25,864	22,544	32,019	17,342
1997	876,440	659,334	8,693	668,027	69,728	-68	598,231	172,384	105,825	26,979	23,262	32,486	17,667
1998	953,361	721,879	8,186	730,065	75,085	-74	654,906	186,729	111,725	28,901	24,763	32,988	18,433
1999	1,022,683	785,504	8,940	794,444	81,356	-79	713,009	192,289	117,386	30,529	25,769	33,499	18,852
2000	1,127,550	878,689	8,860	887,549	90,070	-254	797,226	208,147	122,178	33,175	27,424	33,988	19,229
2001	1,169,366	906,336	8,429	914,765	94,915	-314	819,536	214,146	135,685	33,915	28,677	34,479	19,341
2002	1,187,281	923,239	8,965	932,204	97,855	-432	833,917	207,319	146,045	34,047	29,843	34,872	19,358
2003	1,240,604	963,461	10,102	973,563	102,908	-597	870,058	216,304	154,242	35,191	31,148	35,253	19,479
2004	1,315,172	1,029,255	12,298	1,041,553	112,614	-791	928,148	225,573	161,452	36,969	32,732	35,575	19,784
2005	1,387,884	1,079,017	12,380	1,091,397	117,630	-981	972,787	245,797	169,301	38,737	33,772	35,828	20,127
2006	1,493,217	1,144,360	10,330	1,154,689	120,792	-1,236	1,032,661	278,703	181,853	41,454	35,966	36,021	20,505
2007	1,561,307	1,176,825	12,902	1,189,727	122,716	-1,508	1,065,503	303,009	192,795	43,070	37,131	36,250	20,889
2008	1,588,295	1,168,539	11,119	1,179,658	124,987	-1,757	1,052,914	317,313	218,067	43,391	37,601	36,604	20,654
2009	1,539,819	1,123,940	12,363	1,136,303	121,036	-1,517	1,013,750	285,017	241,051	41,660	37,290	36,961	19,838
2010	1,609,998	1,172,826	13,171	1,185,997	121,820	-1,455	1,062,722	280,368	266,907	43,138	38,364	37,322	19,643
2011	1,713,428	1,233,852	15,225	1,249,078	114,607	-1,402	1,133,069	311,856	268,504	45,509	39,963	37,651	19,986
2012	1,814,763	1,300,603	17,370	1,317,974	119,267	-1,308	1,197,398	346,265	271,101	47,794	41,888	37,970	20,667
2013	1,840,885	1,345,926	20,546	1,366,472	139,678	-1,161	1,225,633	333,250	282,002	48,076	41,448	38,291	21,319
2014	1,955,718	1,415,644	22,609	1,438,254	147,558	-1,250	1,289,445	364,839	301,434	50,619	43,467	38,636	21,997
2015	2,097,050	1,509,302	21,222	1,530,524	156,333	-1,457	1,372,734	398,095	326,220	53,817	45,854	38,966	22,687
2016	2,191,138	1,578,561	18,646	1,597,208	163,059	-1,630	1,432,518	419,577	339,043	55,863	47,721	39,223	23,178
2017	2,295,049	1,662,946	20,041	1,682,987	171,587	-1,850	1,509,550	449,925	335,573	58,214	49,754	39,424	23,549
2018	2,411,055	1,751,565	15,669	1,767,235	181,978	-1,905	1,583,352	475,097	352,606	60,984	52,048	39,536	24,077
2019	2,537,951	1,843,978	15,979	1,859,957	192,127	-2,079	1,665,750	495,482	376,719	64,174	54,852	39,548	24,225
2020	2,767,521	1,892,043	17,316	1,909,359	195,390	-2,212	1,711,757	504,027	551,738	70,058	59,964	39,503	23,154
2021	3,013,677	2,078,718	15,575	2,094,294	213,653	-2,619	1,878,021	549,839	585,816	76,987	64,382	39,145	23,935
2022	3,006,647	2,152,538	16,004	2,168,542	230,969	-2,562	1,935,012	588,271	483,365	77,013	63,115	39,041	25,301
2023	3,133,679	2,261,325	12,724	2,274,049	243,213	-2,619	2,028,217	623,202	482,260	80,423	68,267	38,965	...

... = Not available.

Personal Income and Employment by Region and State: Colorado

(Millions of dollars, except as noted.)

Year	Personal income, total	Derivation of personal income								Per capita (dollars)		Population (thousands)	Total employment (thousands)
		Earnings by place of work			Less: Contributions for government social insurance	Plus: Adjustment for residence	Equals: Net earnings by place of residence	Plus: Dividends, interest, and rent	Plus: Personal current transfer receipts	Personal income	Disposable personal income		
		Nonfarm	Farm	Total									
1960	4,353	3,287	174	3,462	133	1	3,330	748	276	2,461	2,184	1,769	...
1961	4,684	3,557	176	3,733	150	1	3,584	799	302	2,540	2,255	1,844	...
1962	4,942	3,755	156	3,911	164	1	3,748	875	319	2,602	2,314	1,899	...
1963	5,174	3,960	140	4,100	191	0	3,909	926	339	2,673	2,377	1,936	...
1964	5,474	4,206	137	4,343	197	(L)	4,146	985	344	2,779	2,520	1,970	...
1965	5,841	4,408	213	4,621	198	-0	4,423	1,043	375	2,942	2,664	1,985	...
1966	6,276	4,831	192	5,023	263	-1	4,759	1,110	407	3,127	2,812	2,007	...
1967	6,764	5,189	186	5,375	295	-1	5,079	1,201	483	3,294	2,951	2,053	...
1968	7,503	5,768	244	6,012	334	-2	5,676	1,278	549	3,539	3,137	2,120	...
1969	8,439	6,455	251	6,706	387	1	6,319	1,514	605	3,896	3,409	2,166	1,001
1970	9,540	7,184	289	7,473	427	3	7,049	1,761	730	4,290	3,800	2,224	1,032
1971	10,760	8,147	301	8,449	499	4	7,954	1,956	850	4,671	4,160	2,304	1,072
1972	12,176	9,340	333	9,673	606	5	9,072	2,162	943	5,064	4,452	2,405	1,149
1973	13,923	10,680	440	11,120	798	3	10,326	2,490	1,108	5,579	4,923	2,496	1,243
1974	15,609	11,815	535	12,350	906	4	11,449	2,877	1,283	6,142	5,396	2,541	1,276
1975	17,250	12,904	464	13,368	967	9	12,409	3,230	1,610	6,670	5,939	2,586	1,285
1976	18,981	14,483	336	14,820	1,105	9	13,723	3,496	1,762	7,211	6,385	2,632	1,340
1977	21,174	16,379	266	16,645	1,261	11	15,395	3,911	1,869	7,854	6,904	2,696	1,411
1978	24,414	19,130	209	19,339	1,507	19	17,852	4,529	2,033	8,824	7,733	2,767	1,506
1979	27,974	22,126	218	22,343	1,839	13	20,518	5,172	2,284	9,818	8,548	2,849	1,593
1980	32,053	24,945	290	25,235	2,106	20	23,149	6,251	2,653	11,019	9,590	2,909	1,651
1981	36,843	28,429	306	28,735	2,598	3	26,140	7,589	3,114	12,372	10,700	2,978	1,717
1982	40,469	31,059	185	31,244	2,908	0	28,336	8,604	3,529	13,218	11,417	3,062	1,760
1983	43,692	32,980	361	33,341	3,130	-2	30,209	9,580	3,903	13,943	12,352	3,134	1,788
1984	47,579	36,070	426	36,496	3,539	7	32,964	10,501	4,113	15,009	13,341	3,170	1,883
1985	50,442	38,164	396	38,559	3,835	16	34,741	11,397	4,305	15,720	13,941	3,209	1,915
1986	52,397	39,583	398	39,981	4,021	21	35,981	11,795	4,621	16,185	14,406	3,237	1,914
1987	54,179	40,935	477	41,413	4,121	32	37,323	11,875	4,981	16,617	14,732	3,260	1,903
1988	57,483	43,443	578	44,020	4,530	46	39,536	12,698	5,249	17,620	15,671	3,262	1,968
1989	61,922	45,962	621	46,582	4,888	63	41,757	14,315	5,850	18,903	16,688	3,276	2,003
1990	65,632	49,007	713	49,719	5,334	86	44,471	14,892	6,269	19,843	17,460	3,308	2,040
1991	69,633	52,468	640	53,107	5,856	97	47,348	15,322	6,963	20,558	18,130	3,387	2,087
1992	75,512	57,556	679	58,235	6,359	112	51,989	15,704	7,819	21,600	19,052	3,496	2,135
1993	81,699	62,492	815	63,307	6,987	124	56,444	16,873	8,382	22,608	19,891	3,614	2,234
1994	87,839	67,131	584	67,714	7,557	142	60,299	18,647	8,893	23,586	20,694	3,724	2,345
1995	95,469	72,072	544	72,616	8,075	163	64,704	20,790	9,975	24,948	21,883	3,827	2,425
1996	102,975	77,860	671	78,532	8,626	182	70,088	22,553	10,335	26,269	22,858	3,920	2,519
1997	110,722	84,530	676	85,206	9,300	205	76,111	24,110	10,501	27,554	23,760	4,018	2,629
1998	122,578	94,416	806	95,222	9,710	231	85,743	26,117	10,719	29,776	25,540	4,117	2,732
1999	131,713	103,813	937	104,750	10,549	261	94,462	25,848	11,404	31,167	26,610	4,226	2,808
2000	146,561	116,473	777	117,250	11,704	288	105,835	28,677	12,049	33,872	28,739	4,327	2,918
2001	154,067	121,840	1,074	122,915	12,314	309	110,910	29,802	13,355	34,812	29,944	4,426	2,942
2002	154,492	122,456	714	123,170	12,752	339	110,758	28,893	14,841	34,405	30,322	4,490	2,917
2003	157,405	124,000	754	124,754	12,982	364	112,135	29,687	15,583	34,757	31,014	4,529	2,909
2004	163,569	128,815	957	129,772	13,870	398	116,301	31,027	16,241	35,753	31,909	4,575	2,958
2005	174,248	136,348	1,115	137,464	14,724	429	123,169	33,530	17,549	37,619	33,187	4,632	3,037
2006	188,197	145,613	811	146,424	15,589	476	131,312	38,032	18,853	39,869	34,870	4,720	3,109
2007	200,611	152,389	1,106	153,495	16,428	505	137,573	42,846	20,193	41,760	36,275	4,804	3,218
2008	210,066	156,044	907	156,951	17,111	523	140,363	46,179	23,524	42,961	37,580	4,890	3,251
2009	200,170	147,579	766	148,345	16,484	563	132,424	41,616	26,130	40,258	36,237	4,972	3,164
2010	206,053	150,987	1,017	152,005	16,664	663	136,004	40,457	29,593	40,827	36,521	5,047	3,144
2011	223,874	159,634	1,326	160,960	15,793	827	145,994	47,330	30,551	43,732	38,645	5,119	3,204
2012	236,033	168,455	1,250	169,706	16,570	1,027	154,163	51,169	30,701	45,490	40,246	5,189	3,263
2013	247,817	181,787	1,378	183,165	19,242	1,183	165,107	50,846	31,864	47,082	41,353	5,264	3,357
2014	268,453	196,184	1,443	197,627	20,676	1,232	178,183	55,933	34,337	50,244	44,028	5,343	3,468
2015	279,696	200,968	1,637	202,605	21,822	1,232	182,014	60,292	37,389	51,394	44,766	5,442	3,574
2016	283,679	202,687	1,337	204,024	22,564	1,204	182,664	62,080	38,935	51,306	44,515	5,529	3,667
2017	303,367	218,559	1,017	219,577	23,932	1,319	196,964	66,363	40,040	54,171	47,187	5,600	3,761
2018	328,113	236,146	949	237,095	25,514	1,346	212,926	71,709	43,478	57,794	50,729	5,677	3,858
2019	351,373	251,739	1,124	252,863	26,929	1,387	227,321	78,324	45,729	61,258	53,644	5,736	3,895
2020	375,158	258,856	894	259,750	27,612	1,379	233,517	80,042	61,599	64,848	57,094	5,785	3,821
2021	417,968	285,772	1,400	287,172	29,840	1,553	258,886	90,178	68,904	71,920	62,483	5,812	3,989
2022	442,213	313,897	619	314,517	33,660	1,626	282,483	98,386	61,344	75,708	64,803	5,841	4,188
2023	463,852	330,558	515	331,073	35,985	1,729	296,817	106,482	60,554	78,918	69,353	5,878	...

... = Not available.

Personal Income and Employment by Region and State: Connecticut

(Millions of dollars, except as noted.)

Year	Personal income, total	Derivation of personal income: Earnings by place of work: Nonfarm	Farm	Total	Less: Contributions for government social insurance	Plus: Adjustment for residence	Equals: Net earnings by place of residence	Plus: Dividends, interest, and rent	Plus: Personal current transfer receipts	Per capita (dollars): Personal income	Disposable personal income	Population (thousands)	Total employment (thousands)
1960	7,276	5,829	63	5,892	278	3	5,617	1,270	389	2,860	2,499	2,544	...
1961	7,702	6,094	58	6,152	290	3	5,864	1,389	448	2,978	2,612	2,586	...
1962	8,227	6,517	59	6,576	320	3	6,259	1,528	441	3,108	2,722	2,647	...
1963	8,691	6,865	64	6,929	369	4	6,564	1,658	469	3,187	2,777	2,727	...
1964	9,335	7,337	62	7,399	379	5	7,025	1,815	495	3,336	2,963	2,798	...
1965	10,039	7,858	71	7,929	396	2	7,535	1,980	523	3,514	3,100	2,857	...
1966	11,024	8,795	73	8,868	553	-1	8,315	2,145	564	3,797	3,323	2,903	...
1967	12,086	9,505	58	9,563	602	1	8,961	2,424	702	4,118	3,575	2,935	...
1968	12,829	10,213	68	10,281	671	7	9,617	2,358	854	4,328	3,689	2,964	...
1969	14,693	11,149	67	11,216	753	723	11,187	2,559	948	4,898	4,144	3,000	1,417
1970	15,674	11,734	72	11,805	785	717	11,738	2,790	1,146	5,158	4,485	3,039	1,414
1971	16,514	12,145	69	12,215	841	749	12,122	2,968	1,424	5,394	4,764	3,061	1,388
1972	17,805	13,216	68	13,285	970	793	13,108	3,191	1,505	5,800	5,050	3,070	1,416
1973	19,393	14,633	81	14,714	1,236	804	14,283	3,481	1,630	6,319	5,537	3,069	1,480
1974	21,157	15,832	84	15,916	1,397	838	15,357	3,882	1,918	6,879	6,024	3,076	1,511
1975	22,726	16,487	75	16,563	1,424	929	16,068	4,112	2,546	7,367	6,547	3,085	1,468
1976	24,536	17,946	83	18,029	1,578	1,000	17,450	4,373	2,714	7,951	6,974	3,086	1,493
1977	27,033	19,979	84	20,062	1,779	1,105	19,389	4,807	2,837	8,752	7,678	3,089	1,546
1978	30,081	22,509	80	22,590	2,061	1,264	21,793	5,364	2,924	9,720	8,441	3,095	1,615
1979	33,817	25,390	79	25,469	2,421	1,439	24,487	6,076	3,254	10,909	9,398	3,100	1,673
1980	38,512	28,231	84	28,315	2,680	1,689	27,324	7,443	3,745	12,371	10,598	3,113	1,705
1981	43,179	30,953	82	31,035	3,155	1,893	29,772	9,087	4,320	13,800	11,767	3,129	1,727
1982	46,620	33,014	108	33,123	3,431	2,040	31,732	10,087	4,802	14,852	12,646	3,139	1,726
1983	49,957	35,629	106	35,735	3,737	2,178	34,176	10,597	5,185	15,797	13,799	3,162	1,743
1984	55,764	40,098	129	40,228	4,306	2,339	38,261	12,083	5,421	17,536	15,399	3,180	1,823
1985	59,934	43,677	128	43,805	4,742	2,577	41,640	12,546	5,748	18,723	16,298	3,201	1,879
1986	64,499	47,450	140	47,590	5,165	2,674	45,098	13,321	6,080	20,007	17,318	3,224	1,937
1987	70,110	52,742	142	52,884	5,653	2,823	50,054	13,772	6,284	21,590	18,491	3,247	1,984
1988	77,602	58,304	155	58,459	6,356	3,072	55,175	15,646	6,781	23,717	20,591	3,272	2,039
1989	84,162	61,502	141	61,642	6,676	3,087	58,053	18,506	7,602	25,633	22,273	3,283	2,032
1990	86,883	63,319	186	63,504	6,798	2,745	59,451	18,932	8,500	26,392	23,005	3,292	2,003
1991	87,908	64,201	165	64,366	7,011	2,709	60,065	18,322	9,521	26,615	23,226	3,303	1,923
1992	94,201	67,580	188	67,768	7,251	3,939	64,456	18,546	11,200	28,540	24,644	3,301	1,904
1993	97,258	70,246	210	70,456	7,516	3,346	66,286	19,289	11,683	29,390	25,270	3,309	1,925
1994	99,993	72,569	186	72,755	7,873	3,102	67,984	19,910	12,099	30,153	25,923	3,316	1,906
1995	105,484	75,853	173	76,026	8,269	3,827	71,584	20,946	12,954	31,733	27,096	3,324	1,944
1996	110,516	79,352	161	79,513	8,622	4,537	75,428	21,786	13,303	33,122	27,794	3,337	1,975
1997	117,285	86,018	158	86,175	9,146	4,072	81,102	22,516	13,668	35,017	28,981	3,349	2,000
1998	126,666	92,714	179	92,893	9,592	5,482	88,782	24,044	13,840	37,638	30,870	3,365	2,037
1999	133,690	99,841	192	100,033	10,054	5,362	95,341	24,178	14,171	39,479	32,285	3,386	2,070
2000	146,217	109,656	225	109,881	10,680	5,526	104,728	26,570	14,920	42,857	34,766	3,412	2,118
2001	154,586	116,759	200	116,959	11,047	5,563	111,474	27,275	15,836	45,032	36,660	3,433	2,125
2002	154,453	117,523	189	117,713	11,467	5,734	111,979	25,494	16,980	44,656	37,949	3,459	2,118
2003	156,439	118,798	189	118,987	11,710	5,837	113,114	26,000	17,325	44,898	38,568	3,484	2,112
2004	164,657	123,761	199	123,960	12,301	6,851	118,509	27,772	18,376	47,098	40,352	3,496	2,144
2005	173,329	128,992	189	129,181	12,720	7,660	124,121	30,250	18,958	49,424	41,636	3,507	2,172
2006	187,213	135,623	174	135,797	13,245	8,820	131,372	35,611	20,231	53,224	44,621	3,517	2,202
2007	201,450	142,901	200	143,101	13,840	10,344	139,605	40,379	21,466	57,112	47,307	3,527	2,246
2008	214,658	150,207	210	150,417	14,289	11,472	147,600	42,496	24,563	60,543	50,944	3,546	2,256
2009	212,234	152,557	204	152,761	13,922	8,864	147,703	37,287	27,244	59,586	52,338	3,562	2,196
2010	219,801	156,581	207	156,788	14,023	10,859	153,624	37,111	29,066	61,392	53,613	3,580	2,172
2011	226,306	158,523	192	158,716	12,978	11,371	157,109	40,044	29,153	62,964	54,084	3,594	2,206
2012	229,133	155,715	252	155,966	13,321	13,200	155,845	43,789	29,499	63,555	54,460	3,605	2,223
2013	223,834	154,544	303	154,846	15,458	12,524	151,912	42,093	29,829	61,999	51,844	3,610	2,247
2014	233,084	158,837	233	159,070	15,917	12,953	156,106	46,254	30,724	64,482	53,968	3,615	2,266
2015	239,185	162,158	251	162,410	16,408	13,274	159,276	48,192	31,717	66,220	55,282	3,612	2,288
2016	243,699	165,161	185	165,346	16,711	12,657	161,293	49,772	32,635	67,550	56,978	3,608	2,301
2017	249,451	167,261	235	167,496	17,159	15,096	165,433	50,861	33,157	69,146	58,241	3,608	2,300
2018	260,582	170,455	185	170,640	17,601	16,842	169,880	55,429	35,273	72,157	61,207	3,611	2,314
2019	267,553	172,918	233	173,151	18,102	20,157	175,205	56,219	36,129	74,173	62,937	3,607	2,298
2020	278,374	172,397	197	172,594	18,180	23,511	177,925	52,984	47,465	77,810	66,202	3,578	2,217
2021	292,371	181,168	190	181,358	19,097	23,342	185,603	56,059	50,709	81,131	67,378	3,604	2,290
2022	300,751	191,471	250	191,721	20,807	26,253	197,168	59,067	44,516	83,340	67,787	3,609	2,392
2023	316,311	202,130	208	202,338	21,938	27,673	208,073	62,391	45,848	87,447	73,888	3,617	...

... = Not available.

Personal Income and Employment by Region and State: Delaware

(Millions of dollars, except as noted.)

Year	Personal income, total	Derivation of personal income: Earnings by place of work: Nonfarm	Earnings by place of work: Farm	Earnings by place of work: Total	Less: Contributions for government social insurance	Plus: Adjustment for residence	Equals: Net earnings by place of residence	Plus: Dividends, interest, and rent	Plus: Personal current transfer receipts	Per capita (dollars): Personal income	Per capita (dollars): Disposable personal income	Population (thousands)	Total employment (thousands)
1960	1,290	1,035	34	1,069	53	-51	966	270	54	2,873	2,414	449	...
1961	1,331	1,062	30	1,092	51	-51	990	277	65	2,888	2,441	461	...
1962	1,414	1,127	33	1,160	58	-52	1,050	297	67	3,014	2,518	469	...
1963	1,517	1,223	26	1,249	69	-56	1,124	323	70	3,140	2,647	483	...
1964	1,641	1,322	26	1,348	68	-58	1,221	346	74	3,302	2,789	497	...
1965	1,806	1,459	35	1,494	69	-65	1,360	366	80	3,561	3,004	507	...
1966	1,903	1,599	26	1,625	99	-69	1,457	357	88	3,687	3,122	516	...
1967	2,031	1,701	32	1,733	117	-68	1,548	374	108	3,868	3,289	525	...
1968	2,215	1,860	29	1,890	119	-70	1,700	388	127	4,148	3,503	534	...
1969	2,441	2,000	55	2,055	139	-29	1,887	415	139	4,521	3,753	540	271
1970	2,600	2,136	35	2,171	147	-31	1,993	443	165	4,724	3,949	550	275
1971	2,844	2,360	38	2,398	168	-46	2,184	466	194	5,032	4,248	565	280
1972	3,125	2,616	49	2,665	196	-54	2,415	495	215	5,446	4,584	574	293
1973	3,462	2,912	96	3,008	253	-76	2,679	535	248	5,979	5,020	579	305
1974	3,747	3,129	82	3,211	282	-80	2,850	594	303	6,426	5,412	583	302
1975	4,029	3,316	92	3,408	293	-90	3,025	596	408	6,844	5,848	589	292
1976	4,404	3,643	84	3,727	325	-99	3,303	662	439	7,430	6,258	593	296
1977	4,741	3,934	56	3,990	351	-114	3,525	739	478	7,971	6,721	595	296
1978	5,202	4,368	61	4,429	401	-138	3,890	812	500	8,696	7,335	598	304
1979	5,718	4,798	54	4,853	460	-156	4,236	909	573	9,549	7,985	599	312
1980	6,434	5,318	13	5,331	510	-193	4,627	1,111	695	10,815	9,034	595	312
1981	7,084	5,714	43	5,756	591	-211	4,955	1,347	782	11,886	9,851	596	314
1982	7,621	6,145	65	6,211	648	-243	5,320	1,470	831	12,720	10,689	599	317
1983	8,132	6,622	79	6,700	703	-289	5,707	1,539	886	13,431	11,431	605	325
1984	8,955	7,280	96	7,376	779	-328	6,268	1,737	949	14,643	12,541	612	340
1985	9,724	7,963	104	8,068	865	-370	6,833	1,893	998	15,727	13,473	618	357
1986	10,350	8,434	144	8,578	933	-398	7,247	2,023	1,080	16,492	14,101	628	370
1987	11,140	9,270	114	9,384	1,016	-466	7,901	2,114	1,125	17,490	15,021	637	387
1988	12,248	10,126	181	10,307	1,149	-525	8,633	2,378	1,237	18,912	16,345	648	403
1989	13,621	11,092	192	11,284	1,262	-618	9,404	2,875	1,342	20,692	17,854	658	415
1990	14,370	11,762	141	11,903	1,312	-688	9,903	3,026	1,441	21,462	18,508	670	420
1991	15,216	12,294	133	12,427	1,378	-681	10,367	3,175	1,674	22,276	19,403	683	414
1992	15,850	12,884	117	13,001	1,421	-725	10,855	3,172	1,822	22,808	19,898	695	413
1993	16,458	13,255	108	13,363	1,476	-681	11,207	3,304	1,948	23,300	20,298	706	421
1994	17,158	13,863	121	13,985	1,571	-722	11,692	3,396	2,070	23,912	20,716	718	424
1995	18,157	14,617	87	14,704	1,656	-848	12,200	3,695	2,262	24,882	21,565	730	442
1996	19,406	15,554	120	15,675	1,735	-1,049	12,891	4,008	2,507	26,190	22,518	741	453
1997	20,307	16,633	95	16,728	1,843	-1,346	13,540	4,232	2,535	27,022	22,957	751	464
1998	22,476	18,456	142	18,597	1,997	-1,456	15,145	4,631	2,700	29,444	25,109	763	476
1999	24,117	20,474	140	20,613	2,134	-1,696	16,784	4,519	2,814	31,119	26,670	775	491
2000	26,587	22,371	147	22,519	2,237	-1,790	18,492	5,025	3,071	33,810	29,217	786	503
2001	29,375	24,863	212	25,074	2,295	-1,809	20,970	5,037	3,368	36,917	32,112	796	503
2002	30,360	25,680	88	25,768	2,390	-1,760	21,617	5,115	3,628	37,660	33,512	806	501
2003	31,072	26,085	175	26,260	2,490	-1,800	21,970	5,206	3,896	37,985	34,060	818	504
2004	32,271	26,886	254	27,141	2,679	-1,940	22,522	5,555	4,194	38,843	34,710	831	518
2005	33,073	27,483	291	27,775	2,808	-2,088	22,878	5,673	4,522	39,133	34,406	845	529
2006	35,003	28,898	207	29,105	3,001	-2,319	23,785	6,322	4,896	40,736	35,794	859	537
2007	36,211	29,255	210	29,465	3,085	-2,164	24,215	6,689	5,307	41,539	36,453	872	545
2008	36,463	28,458	229	28,687	3,191	-2,214	23,282	7,064	6,118	41,254	36,279	884	545
2009	36,611	27,900	295	28,195	3,120	-1,539	23,536	6,444	6,632	41,056	37,190	892	526
2010	36,981	28,276	262	28,539	3,143	-1,732	23,663	6,159	7,158	41,101	37,146	900	522
2011	39,761	30,257	231	30,489	2,845	-2,152	25,491	6,797	7,473	43,781	39,041	908	530
2012	40,123	30,201	290	30,491	2,979	-2,164	25,348	7,127	7,648	43,775	39,107	917	534
2013	40,678	30,610	441	31,051	3,483	-2,094	25,474	7,166	8,038	43,948	38,993	926	545
2014	42,423	31,888	513	32,401	3,676	-2,469	26,256	7,667	8,499	45,364	40,297	935	556
2015	44,626	33,525	396	33,921	3,825	-2,443	27,653	7,926	9,048	47,244	41,776	945	569
2016	45,928	33,826	319	34,145	3,863	-2,138	28,144	8,363	9,422	48,192	42,641	953	579
2017	48,077	35,112	510	35,622	4,017	-2,515	29,090	9,020	9,967	50,002	44,187	961	585
2018	51,150	37,427	406	37,833	4,220	-2,565	31,048	9,642	10,460	52,674	46,708	971	597
2019	52,741	38,116	423	38,539	4,373	-2,616	31,549	10,132	11,059	53,746	47,298	981	603
2020	55,338	38,180	183	38,363	4,481	-2,108	31,774	9,930	13,635	55,792	49,250	992	592
2021	59,172	40,145	401	40,546	4,827	-2,362	33,358	10,730	15,085	58,885	51,075	1,005	620
2022	64,407	45,237	769	46,006	5,403	-2,275	38,327	11,498	14,581	63,177	54,362	1,019	651
2023	67,478	47,532	459	47,991	5,694	-2,324	39,973	12,218	15,287	65,392	57,800	1,032	...

... = Not available.

Personal Income and Employment by Region and State: District of Columbia

(Millions of dollars, except as noted.)

Year	Personal income, total	Derivation of personal income: Earnings by place of work: Nonfarm	Farm	Total	Less: Contributions for government social insurance	Plus: Adjustment for residence	Equals: Net earnings by place of residence	Plus: Dividends, interest, and rent	Plus: Personal current transfer receipts	Per capita (dollars): Personal income	Disposable personal income	Population (thousands)	Total employment (thousands)
1960	2,390	3,255	0	3,255	102	-1,391	1,762	516	112	3,125	2,702	765	...
1961	2,517	3,454	0	3,454	108	-1,483	1,863	531	123	3,236	2,838	778	...
1962	2,709	3,718	0	3,718	115	-1,578	2,026	557	127	3,438	3,003	788	...
1963	2,877	4,005	0	4,005	139	-1,704	2,163	580	135	3,605	3,174	798	...
1964	3,054	4,294	0	4,294	136	-1,848	2,311	603	140	3,827	3,417	798	...
1965	3,291	4,631	0	4,631	141	-1,992	2,499	641	151	4,129	3,706	797	...
1966	3,436	4,995	0	4,995	186	-2,188	2,621	655	160	4,344	3,860	791	...
1967	3,682	5,651	0	5,651	215	-2,617	2,819	671	192	4,655	4,159	791	...
1968	3,865	6,079	0	6,079	237	-2,891	2,951	685	230	4,968	4,429	778	...
1969	3,764	6,459	0	6,459	254	-3,366	2,839	690	235	4,939	4,289	762	676
1970	4,174	7,066	0	7,066	276	-3,707	3,083	790	302	5,528	4,832	755	672
1971	4,647	7,747	0	7,747	302	-4,082	3,364	909	375	6,191	5,482	751	666
1972	5,044	8,391	0	8,391	346	-4,441	3,605	992	447	6,781	5,973	744	668
1973	5,316	8,916	0	8,916	417	-4,744	3,755	1,049	512	7,246	6,362	734	662
1974	5,769	9,625	0	9,625	475	-5,119	4,031	1,142	595	8,004	7,040	721	673
1975	6,275	10,598	0	10,598	524	-5,737	4,337	1,197	741	8,834	7,803	710	677
1976	6,648	11,463	0	11,463	576	-6,286	4,601	1,277	771	9,548	8,307	696	674
1977	7,138	12,407	0	12,407	612	-6,843	4,952	1,396	790	10,469	9,191	682	680
1978	7,604	13,579	0	13,579	674	-7,700	5,205	1,588	812	11,349	9,880	670	693
1979	8,001	14,711	0	14,711	777	-8,592	5,342	1,753	906	12,204	10,479	656	704
1980	8,447	16,000	0	16,000	866	-9,709	5,425	1,991	1,031	13,234	11,388	638	701
1981	9,074	17,115	0	17,115	1,010	-10,406	5,699	2,236	1,139	14,248	12,072	637	689
1982	9,673	18,049	0	18,049	1,077	-10,935	6,037	2,364	1,271	15,253	12,953	634	673
1983	10,187	18,929	0	18,929	1,298	-11,234	6,396	2,463	1,328	16,108	13,820	632	667
1984	11,099	20,642	0	20,642	1,472	-12,165	7,005	2,677	1,416	17,523	15,020	633	689
1985	11,764	22,068	0	22,068	1,687	-12,899	7,481	2,865	1,418	18,539	15,864	635	703
1986	12,381	23,269	0	23,269	1,867	-13,474	7,927	2,982	1,472	19,397	16,628	638	721
1987	13,015	24,768	0	24,768	2,031	-14,246	8,491	3,008	1,516	20,434	17,359	637	733
1988	14,289	27,404	0	27,404	2,320	-15,744	9,339	3,320	1,630	22,666	19,451	630	756
1989	15,132	29,005	0	29,005	2,556	-16,821	9,629	3,869	1,634	24,243	20,771	624	763
1990	15,809	30,998	0	30,998	2,759	-17,983	10,256	3,809	1,744	26,117	22,493	605	773
1991	16,540	32,678	0	32,678	2,940	-18,918	10,820	3,775	1,945	27,527	23,978	601	759
1992	17,351	34,522	0	34,522	3,124	-20,092	11,306	3,861	2,184	29,036	25,424	598	752
1993	18,044	35,643	0	35,643	3,273	-20,649	11,720	3,926	2,398	30,311	26,661	595	750
1994	18,458	36,434	0	36,434	3,415	-21,021	11,998	4,021	2,439	31,325	27,352	589	730
1995	18,589	36,700	0	36,700	3,484	-21,063	12,152	4,068	2,368	32,021	27,978	581	718
1996	19,346	37,294	0	37,294	3,521	-21,057	12,716	4,054	2,576	33,799	29,265	572	704
1997	20,244	38,590	0	38,590	3,666	-21,682	13,242	4,432	2,570	35,657	30,525	568	699
1998	21,515	40,635	0	40,635	3,742	-22,791	14,102	4,674	2,739	38,064	32,269	565	698
1999	22,625	44,067	0	44,067	4,084	-24,874	15,109	4,780	2,736	39,679	33,392	570	711
2000	24,828	46,750	0	46,750	4,310	-25,486	16,954	5,057	2,817	43,401	36,365	572	735
2001	25,743	50,026	0	50,026	4,922	-27,225	17,879	4,949	2,915	44,809	37,650	575	742
2002	25,863	52,635	0	52,635	5,204	-29,496	17,935	4,720	3,209	45,124	39,006	573	757
2003	26,139	55,152	0	55,152	5,423	-31,623	18,106	4,769	3,263	45,978	39,835	569	755
2004	28,380	59,948	0	59,948	5,814	-34,115	20,019	5,065	3,296	49,986	43,265	568	763
2005	29,880	63,289	0	63,289	6,133	-36,189	20,968	5,343	3,569	52,686	44,991	567	770
2006	31,607	65,683	0	65,683	6,516	-37,319	21,848	6,136	3,622	55,384	47,151	571	778
2007	34,096	69,568	0	69,568	6,876	-39,187	23,505	6,712	3,879	59,358	49,912	574	788
2008	35,168	71,861	0	71,861	7,394	-40,877	23,589	7,305	4,274	60,609	51,376	580	795
2009	35,540	73,183	0	73,183	7,619	-41,102	24,462	6,332	4,746	60,011	52,307	592	796
2010	38,212	77,992	0	77,992	8,033	-43,320	26,640	6,152	5,421	63,182	55,437	605	809
2011	41,361	81,559	0	81,559	7,359	-45,574	28,627	6,970	5,765	66,950	57,917	618	827
2012	42,582	82,182	0	82,182	7,601	-45,351	29,230	7,694	5,658	67,470	57,840	631	834
2013	43,214	83,456	0	83,456	8,852	-44,937	29,668	7,570	5,976	67,024	56,823	645	848
2014	46,124	87,637	0	87,637	9,282	-46,272	32,083	8,160	5,881	70,466	59,705	655	861
2015	49,742	91,991	0	91,991	9,666	-47,327	34,998	8,602	6,142	74,728	62,894	666	873
2016	52,191	96,041	0	96,041	9,962	-49,343	36,736	8,872	6,582	77,453	65,630	674	893
2017	54,159	98,979	0	98,979	10,378	-50,574	38,027	9,461	6,671	79,535	67,434	681	903
2018	56,396	102,845	0	102,845	10,871	-52,594	39,380	10,224	6,792	82,254	69,502	686	914
2019	57,492	104,552	0	104,552	11,141	-53,736	39,675	10,644	7,174	83,636	70,087	687	915
2020	60,179	106,412	0	106,412	11,364	-55,419	39,630	10,063	10,486	89,707	75,310	671	866
2021	65,206	112,716	0	112,716	11,713	-57,425	43,577	10,707	10,922	97,462	80,246	669	870
2022	64,473	116,955	0	116,955	12,388	-60,956	43,612	11,659	9,202	96,092	76,700	671	905
2023	68,515	123,091	0	123,091	12,978	-63,964	46,150	12,488	9,877	100,909	84,161	679	...

... = Not available.

Personal Income and Employment by Region and State: Florida

(Millions of dollars, except as noted.)

Year	Personal income, total	Derivation of personal income: Earnings by place of work: Nonfarm	Farm	Total	Less: Contributions for government social insurance	Plus: Adjustment for residence	Equals: Net earnings by place of residence	Plus: Dividends, interest, and rent	Plus: Personal current transfer receipts	Per capita (dollars): Personal income	Disposable personal income	Population (thousands)	Total employment (thousands)
1960	10,532	7,667	381	8,048	329	-1	7,718	2,099	715	2,105	1,911	5,004	...
1961	11,165	7,958	440	8,398	344	-1	8,053	2,284	829	2,130	1,934	5,243	...
1962	12,056	8,583	454	9,037	389	-1	8,647	2,481	929	2,209	2,004	5,458	...
1963	12,939	9,261	436	9,697	449	-1	9,247	2,681	1,011	2,299	2,087	5,628	...
1964	14,155	10,196	492	10,689	481	-1	10,206	2,895	1,055	2,449	2,238	5,781	...
1965	15,473	11,173	466	11,639	516	-1	11,122	3,180	1,171	2,599	2,369	5,954	...
1966	16,976	12,423	476	12,899	680	-2	12,217	3,453	1,306	2,781	2,530	6,104	...
1967	18,772	13,625	515	14,140	809	-3	13,327	3,816	1,628	3,007	2,711	6,242	...
1968	21,581	15,533	528	16,061	966	-5	15,091	4,555	1,936	3,355	2,989	6,433	...
1969	25,005	17,876	636	18,513	1,133	-19	17,361	5,450	2,195	3,765	3,326	6,641	2,857
1970	28,276	19,936	546	20,482	1,273	-22	19,188	6,443	2,646	4,131	3,692	6,845	2,966
1971	31,756	22,121	639	22,760	1,473	-17	21,270	7,299	3,188	4,433	3,987	7,163	3,082
1972	36,550	25,645	738	26,384	1,798	-14	24,572	8,223	3,755	4,860	4,302	7,520	3,338
1973	42,578	30,022	837	30,859	2,422	-12	28,425	9,593	4,561	5,371	4,778	7,927	3,666
1974	47,883	32,994	908	33,902	2,782	-3	31,117	11,268	5,498	5,757	5,139	8,317	3,766
1975	52,168	34,450	998	35,448	2,860	-11	32,577	12,408	7,183	6,107	5,558	8,542	3,676
1976	57,012	37,531	1,035	38,566	3,170	8	35,405	13,630	7,978	6,557	5,924	8,695	3,730
1977	63,844	42,079	1,033	43,113	3,572	19	39,560	15,555	8,730	7,182	6,471	8,889	3,929
1978	73,633	48,719	1,234	49,952	4,251	22	45,723	18,212	9,698	8,064	7,216	9,132	4,239
1979	84,679	55,770	1,312	57,082	5,112	13	51,982	21,460	11,237	8,941	7,944	9,471	4,454
1980	99,907	63,915	1,667	65,583	5,909	6	59,680	26,847	13,379	10,153	8,980	9,840	4,688
1981	115,555	72,211	1,402	73,613	7,183	117	66,547	33,378	15,630	11,337	10,005	10,193	4,865
1982	124,862	77,085	1,777	78,862	7,887	140	71,116	36,058	17,689	11,924	10,442	10,471	4,954
1983	138,140	85,333	2,465	87,798	8,778	166	79,187	39,612	19,341	12,850	11,524	10,750	5,167
1984	153,545	95,966	1,828	97,794	10,141	208	87,861	45,087	20,597	13,908	12,579	11,040	5,502
1985	168,155	105,471	1,835	107,306	11,348	254	96,212	49,720	22,224	14,814	13,244	11,351	5,772
1986	181,984	114,881	1,972	116,853	12,681	317	104,489	53,549	23,945	15,597	13,897	11,668	6,015
1987	195,918	126,439	2,135	128,573	13,789	378	115,162	55,370	25,387	16,330	14,514	11,997	6,094
1988	216,351	138,988	2,687	141,675	15,631	454	126,498	62,047	27,805	17,580	15,704	12,306	6,390
1989	240,835	148,914	2,484	151,397	16,945	534	134,986	74,479	31,370	19,057	17,004	12,638	6,596
1990	257,601	159,051	2,084	161,136	17,936	633	143,832	79,387	34,382	19,765	17,716	13,033	6,740
1991	268,849	165,646	2,458	168,104	18,806	677	149,975	80,239	38,635	20,109	18,160	13,370	6,718
1992	284,090	177,651	2,460	180,111	20,071	743	160,783	78,962	44,345	20,812	18,795	13,651	6,763
1993	301,152	189,871	2,535	192,406	21,337	793	171,862	81,808	47,482	21,623	19,505	13,927	7,002
1994	317,383	200,976	2,165	203,141	22,867	854	181,129	85,636	50,619	22,289	20,062	14,239	7,234
1995	341,123	214,077	2,211	216,287	24,235	922	192,974	93,477	54,673	23,464	21,075	14,538	7,494
1996	363,065	228,542	1,953	230,496	25,571	994	205,919	99,299	57,847	24,443	21,727	14,853	7,740
1997	385,679	242,218	2,167	244,385	27,135	1,095	218,344	107,330	60,005	25,397	22,383	15,186	8,005
1998	416,722	263,272	2,644	265,915	29,130	1,221	238,007	117,346	61,369	26,909	23,625	15,487	8,317
1999	435,930	282,203	2,703	284,906	30,996	1,353	255,264	116,870	63,797	27,662	24,256	15,759	8,578
2000	471,588	306,169	2,582	308,752	33,262	1,516	277,006	126,573	68,010	29,387	25,680	16,048	8,881
2001	497,335	324,422	2,582	327,004	35,634	1,618	292,988	130,209	74,139	30,405	26,726	16,357	8,939
2002	514,289	340,606	2,515	343,121	37,327	1,677	307,470	126,951	79,868	30,815	27,685	16,689	9,056
2003	540,366	359,867	2,200	362,067	39,327	1,773	324,513	130,588	85,265	31,779	28,968	17,004	9,283
2004	587,003	389,774	2,275	392,048	42,719	1,918	351,248	144,043	91,712	33,706	30,534	17,415	9,644
2005	637,603	422,527	2,689	425,217	46,628	2,081	380,669	158,448	98,486	35,736	31,839	17,842	10,067
2006	690,506	449,884	2,640	452,524	50,388	2,298	404,434	180,995	105,077	38,009	33,831	18,167	10,384
2007	719,734	457,355	2,266	459,621	51,890	2,597	410,328	197,600	111,807	39,184	34,886	18,368	10,531
2008	725,995	443,377	2,064	445,441	51,687	2,786	396,540	202,466	126,989	39,185	35,207	18,527	10,270
2009	685,983	418,249	2,186	420,434	49,965	2,644	373,113	174,386	138,483	36,777	33,879	18,653	9,842
2010	730,690	436,561	2,475	439,036	50,683	2,726	391,080	187,924	151,686	38,778	35,672	18,843	9,805
2011	769,798	448,514	2,184	450,698	46,678	2,932	406,952	205,089	157,758	40,433	36,766	19,039	10,037
2012	794,071	463,423	2,780	466,203	48,813	3,017	420,407	217,551	156,113	41,204	37,382	19,272	10,249
2013	794,604	478,012	2,812	480,824	56,738	3,052	427,137	206,566	160,901	40,733	36,526	19,508	10,540
2014	848,535	506,524	2,901	509,425	59,770	3,210	452,865	226,266	169,405	42,865	38,285	19,795	10,938
2015	905,451	537,556	3,622	541,178	62,921	3,342	481,599	244,841	179,011	44,945	39,849	20,146	11,367
2016	938,986	564,008	2,753	566,761	65,689	3,382	504,454	249,346	185,186	45,720	40,999	20,538	11,682
2017	1,011,002	597,547	3,101	600,648	69,211	3,458	534,895	282,105	194,002	48,439	42,650	20,872	12,098
2018	1,078,011	633,978	2,378	636,357	73,846	3,521	566,032	308,530	203,449	51,009	45,626	21,134	12,556
2019	1,145,461	668,323	2,557	670,880	78,919	3,600	595,561	333,075	216,825	53,640	47,907	21,355	12,761
2020	1,221,122	681,190	2,509	683,698	81,397	3,531	605,832	340,412	274,877	56,556	50,311	21,591	12,720
2021	1,376,880	765,730	2,669	768,399	88,822	3,670	683,247	379,614	314,019	63,071	55,476	21,831	13,458
2022	1,441,599	841,540	2,509	844,049	99,413	3,932	748,568	409,805	283,226	64,804	55,857	22,246	14,227
2023	1,543,132	908,536	2,233	910,769	107,533	4,098	807,335	442,118	293,680	68,248	60,397	22,611	...

... = Not available.

Personal Income and Employment by Region and State: Georgia

(Millions of dollars, except as noted.)

Year	Personal income, total	Derivation of personal income: Earnings by place of work: Nonfarm	Farm	Total	Less: Contributions for government social insurance	Plus: Adjustment for residence	Equals: Net earnings by place of residence	Plus: Dividends, interest, and rent	Plus: Personal current transfer receipts	Per capita (dollars): Personal income	Disposable personal income	Population (thousands)	Total employment (thousands)
1960	6,918	5,602	326	5,928	262	-15	5,651	849	418	1,749	1,587	3,956	...
1961	7,221	5,764	347	6,111	266	-17	5,828	920	473	1,799	1,636	4,015	...
1962	7,768	6,279	312	6,591	298	-21	6,272	1,008	488	1,901	1,719	4,086	...
1963	8,445	6,797	400	7,196	349	-25	6,822	1,101	522	2,024	1,829	4,172	...
1964	9,145	7,457	334	7,791	377	-30	7,385	1,213	547	2,148	1,954	4,258	...
1965	10,099	8,214	377	8,591	408	-36	8,148	1,351	601	2,331	2,116	4,332	...
1966	11,144	9,210	389	9,599	546	-45	9,008	1,479	656	2,545	2,296	4,379	...
1967	12,120	10,017	386	10,404	626	-54	9,723	1,616	781	2,750	2,490	4,408	...
1968	13,381	11,201	343	11,544	684	-64	10,796	1,655	930	2,986	2,671	4,482	...
1969	14,980	12,475	420	12,895	786	-93	12,015	1,902	1,063	3,292	2,889	4,551	2,119
1970	16,310	13,324	398	13,722	837	-78	12,807	2,204	1,299	3,542	3,153	4,605	2,121
1971	18,010	14,590	456	15,047	952	-78	14,017	2,447	1,546	3,823	3,439	4,710	2,167
1972	20,206	16,489	471	16,960	1,128	-71	15,761	2,705	1,741	4,203	3,730	4,807	2,253
1973	22,848	18,461	788	19,249	1,445	-70	17,734	3,104	2,010	4,656	4,159	4,907	2,356
1974	25,068	20,011	672	20,684	1,628	-70	18,986	3,570	2,511	5,019	4,479	4,995	2,374
1975	27,084	20,982	638	21,620	1,680	-58	19,883	3,874	3,327	5,354	4,869	5,059	2,313
1976	30,147	23,786	629	24,416	1,946	-88	22,381	4,204	3,562	5,881	5,297	5,126	2,400
1977	33,332	26,898	365	27,263	2,190	-105	24,968	4,670	3,694	6,396	5,726	5,212	2,503
1978	37,819	30,533	568	31,101	2,552	-86	28,463	5,343	4,013	7,154	6,365	5,286	2,621
1979	42,320	34,176	598	34,774	2,974	-106	31,693	6,056	4,571	7,850	6,900	5,391	2,700
1980	47,202	37,709	40	37,749	3,302	-115	34,332	7,389	5,481	8,604	7,588	5,486	2,741
1981	53,425	41,622	523	42,145	3,919	-36	38,190	8,992	6,243	9,594	8,426	5,568	2,776
1982	57,838	44,454	683	45,137	4,272	-77	40,788	10,233	6,817	10,237	9,046	5,650	2,793
1983	63,391	49,088	476	49,563	4,793	-120	44,651	11,343	7,398	11,066	9,763	5,728	2,877
1984	71,798	55,825	956	56,782	5,611	-155	51,015	12,882	7,901	12,305	10,907	5,835	3,068
1985	78,654	61,833	787	62,620	6,361	-169	56,090	14,092	8,472	13,191	11,612	5,963	3,207
1986	85,815	68,004	828	68,832	7,085	-218	61,529	15,260	9,026	14,104	12,435	6,085	3,335
1987	92,176	73,645	895	74,540	7,617	-227	66,696	16,014	9,467	14,847	13,017	6,208	3,433
1988	100,731	80,114	1,151	81,266	8,521	-229	72,516	17,997	10,218	15,948	14,065	6,316	3,545
1989	108,529	84,605	1,357	85,962	9,070	-192	76,699	20,476	11,354	16,928	14,867	6,411	3,608
1990	116,128	90,194	1,261	91,455	9,696	-113	81,646	21,851	12,631	17,831	15,682	6,513	3,664
1991	121,971	93,591	1,565	95,156	10,179	-132	84,845	22,500	14,626	18,333	16,236	6,653	3,622
1992	131,894	102,091	1,640	103,731	10,960	-178	92,594	22,978	16,323	19,347	17,170	6,817	3,698
1993	140,057	108,698	1,475	110,172	11,712	-182	98,279	24,318	17,460	20,070	17,742	6,978	3,866
1994	150,803	116,328	1,941	118,269	12,670	-237	105,362	26,619	18,823	21,070	18,599	7,157	4,020
1995	162,764	125,360	1,764	127,125	13,607	-340	113,178	29,242	20,344	22,210	19,555	7,328	4,188
1996	175,805	135,472	1,857	137,329	14,539	-375	122,415	31,734	21,655	23,437	20,497	7,501	4,333
1997	187,176	144,937	1,813	146,750	15,463	-448	130,839	34,179	22,158	24,356	21,165	7,685	4,449
1998	205,294	161,028	1,803	162,832	16,839	-585	145,408	37,225	22,661	26,107	22,597	7,864	4,608
1999	218,719	174,671	1,945	176,616	18,151	-600	157,865	36,945	23,909	27,184	23,501	8,046	4,729
2000	236,617	188,470	1,845	190,315	19,382	-732	170,201	40,493	25,924	28,760	24,815	8,227	4,861
2001	248,743	196,991	2,218	199,209	20,151	-777	178,282	41,962	28,499	29,693	25,745	8,377	4,872
2002	255,977	201,910	1,644	203,555	20,596	-822	182,137	41,590	32,250	30,086	26,745	8,508	4,858
2003	265,623	209,039	2,047	211,086	21,219	-840	189,027	43,754	32,841	30,805	27,670	8,623	4,895
2004	280,462	221,493	2,159	223,652	23,079	-799	199,774	45,296	35,393	31,982	28,812	8,769	5,022
2005	297,085	232,010	2,472	234,482	24,053	-782	209,647	48,816	38,622	33,283	29,696	8,926	5,196
2006	316,549	245,751	1,575	247,327	25,472	-788	221,067	54,002	41,480	34,574	30,641	9,156	5,358
2007	331,364	252,052	1,873	253,925	26,198	-778	226,949	59,761	44,654	35,440	31,299	9,350	5,491
2008	335,258	247,640	2,187	249,827	27,295	-694	221,838	61,993	51,427	35,272	31,329	9,505	5,451
2009	329,159	241,299	1,935	243,235	26,530	-924	215,781	56,847	56,531	34,213	31,160	9,621	5,247
2010	337,421	246,180	1,386	247,566	27,009	-948	219,610	55,836	61,975	34,741	31,536	9,713	5,211
2011	360,456	256,245	1,618	257,862	24,826	-1,182	231,854	63,688	64,914	36,761	33,093	9,805	5,326
2012	369,040	263,128	2,463	265,591	25,733	-1,338	238,521	66,229	64,291	37,251	33,558	9,907	5,385
2013	374,125	272,505	2,604	275,108	30,242	-1,513	243,353	64,147	66,624	37,486	33,414	9,981	5,497
2014	398,586	289,327	2,371	291,697	31,725	-1,602	258,371	70,329	69,886	39,551	35,234	10,078	5,671
2015	423,242	307,510	2,656	310,166	33,356	-1,624	275,186	75,056	73,000	41,529	36,840	10,191	5,833
2016	441,039	321,614	1,949	323,563	34,602	-1,837	287,124	78,228	75,688	42,744	38,004	10,318	5,974
2017	467,593	338,485	2,455	340,941	36,144	-1,702	303,094	86,204	78,294	44,838	39,783	10,428	6,128
2018	491,088	355,592	1,742	357,334	38,321	-1,607	317,406	91,285	82,397	46,626	41,667	10,533	6,287
2019	516,552	372,939	1,916	374,855	40,349	-1,463	333,044	96,294	87,215	48,535	43,253	10,643	6,399
2020	552,249	376,145	1,266	377,411	41,255	-1,575	334,580	97,808	119,860	51,456	46,065	10,732	6,327
2021	606,114	409,465	1,910	411,376	45,097	-1,842	364,436	109,239	132,438	56,172	49,587	10,790	6,640
2022	617,553	437,547	3,145	440,693	49,637	-1,943	389,113	114,584	113,856	56,588	48,919	10,913	6,971
2023	646,108	461,936	1,458	463,394	52,326	-1,965	409,103	121,198	115,808	58,581	51,921	11,029	...

... = Not available.

Personal Income and Employment by Region and State: Hawaii

(Millions of dollars, except as noted.)

Year	Personal income, total	Derivation of personal income: Earnings by place of work								Per capita (dollars)		Population (thousands)	Total employment (thousands)
		Nonfarm	Farm	Total	Less: Contributions for government social insurance	Plus: Adjustment for residence	Equals: Net earnings by place of residence	Plus: Dividends, interest, and rent	Plus: Personal current transfer receipts	Personal income	Disposable personal income		
1960	1,615	1,278	82	1,360	52	0	1,307	260	48	2,516	2,191	642	...
1961	1,754	1,383	75	1,458	57	0	1,401	294	59	2,661	2,316	659	...
1962	1,881	1,471	79	1,550	61	0	1,489	325	67	2,750	2,434	684	...
1963	2,011	1,579	88	1,667	76	0	1,591	350	70	2,949	2,614	682	...
1964	2,188	1,725	89	1,814	82	0	1,731	386	70	3,125	2,805	700	...
1965	2,402	1,887	91	1,978	86	0	1,893	428	81	3,412	3,076	704	...
1966	2,608	2,077	95	2,172	114	0	2,058	455	95	3,674	3,262	710	...
1967	2,831	2,239	98	2,338	131	0	2,206	504	121	3,915	3,468	723	...
1968	3,184	2,540	117	2,658	153	0	2,505	539	140	4,338	3,814	734	...
1969	3,643	2,922	119	3,041	182	0	2,859	624	160	4,903	4,254	743	416
1970	4,225	3,338	133	3,471	211	0	3,260	759	207	5,538	4,833	763	434
1971	4,584	3,579	131	3,709	236	0	3,474	840	270	5,791	5,131	792	437
1972	5,048	3,944	131	4,076	274	0	3,802	923	323	6,170	5,401	818	453
1973	5,593	4,378	138	4,517	348	0	4,168	1,055	370	6,643	5,828	842	473
1974	6,361	4,783	340	5,123	400	0	4,723	1,194	444	7,412	6,525	858	485
1975	6,919	5,288	202	5,489	442	0	5,047	1,295	577	7,907	7,111	875	499
1976	7,466	5,731	173	5,904	484	0	5,420	1,371	675	8,367	7,465	892	505
1977	8,084	6,219	184	6,403	522	0	5,881	1,495	708	8,828	7,840	916	509
1978	8,954	6,897	168	7,065	597	0	6,467	1,726	761	9,640	8,501	929	528
1979	10,044	7,752	193	7,945	701	0	7,245	1,959	840	10,572	9,282	950	556
1980	11,488	8,624	374	8,998	777	0	8,221	2,302	965	11,872	10,433	968	575
1981	12,428	9,318	199	9,517	896	0	8,620	2,674	1,134	12,705	11,168	978	568
1982	13,160	9,913	234	10,147	946	0	9,201	2,730	1,229	13,243	11,854	994	567
1983	14,447	10,665	338	11,003	1,036	0	9,967	3,129	1,351	14,265	12,765	1,013	577
1984	15,458	11,448	239	11,687	1,135	0	10,552	3,481	1,425	15,038	13,475	1,028	582
1985	16,447	12,245	222	12,467	1,237	0	11,230	3,706	1,511	15,819	14,119	1,040	598
1986	17,452	13,099	256	13,355	1,351	0	12,004	3,874	1,574	16,593	14,782	1,052	612
1987	18,561	14,206	239	14,445	1,477	0	12,969	3,963	1,629	17,380	15,267	1,068	643
1988	20,465	15,815	262	16,077	1,696	0	14,381	4,338	1,746	18,952	16,635	1,080	669
1989	22,856	17,595	248	17,843	1,887	0	15,956	4,963	1,937	20,880	18,143	1,095	696
1990	24,977	19,526	260	19,786	2,178	0	17,608	5,271	2,098	22,431	19,508	1,113	724
1991	26,455	20,771	232	21,003	2,345	0	18,658	5,493	2,304	23,272	20,138	1,137	745
1992	28,421	22,194	219	22,412	2,494	0	19,918	5,827	2,676	24,530	21,658	1,159	746
1993	29,456	22,716	216	22,932	2,543	0	20,389	6,136	2,930	25,115	22,208	1,173	742
1994	30,135	22,921	210	23,131	2,588	0	20,543	6,420	3,172	25,376	22,461	1,188	737
1995	30,826	22,936	199	23,136	2,586	0	20,550	6,689	3,587	25,756	22,930	1,197	734
1996	30,841	22,905	195	23,100	2,590	0	20,511	6,650	3,680	25,620	22,669	1,204	733
1997	31,736	23,537	205	23,742	2,630	0	21,112	6,930	3,694	26,192	23,156	1,212	734
1998	32,356	23,901	218	24,119	2,671	0	21,448	7,142	3,766	26,625	23,445	1,215	738
1999	33,426	24,831	245	25,076	2,740	0	22,336	7,167	3,922	27,618	24,284	1,210	738
2000	35,403	26,352	240	26,593	2,889	0	23,704	7,569	4,130	29,174	25,593	1,214	749
2001	36,997	27,826	237	28,063	3,048	0	25,015	7,531	4,450	30,178	26,532	1,226	753
2002	38,866	29,570	251	29,821	3,232	0	26,589	7,470	4,807	31,353	28,089	1,240	758
2003	40,734	31,493	250	31,743	3,478	0	28,265	7,506	4,963	32,557	29,360	1,251	774
2004	43,729	33,779	251	34,030	3,653	0	30,377	8,061	5,292	34,336	30,947	1,274	797
2005	46,898	36,243	260	36,503	3,920	0	32,583	8,588	5,727	36,278	32,320	1,293	820
2006	50,183	38,317	260	38,577	4,248	0	34,328	9,813	6,042	38,315	34,060	1,310	842
2007	53,023	39,642	247	39,889	4,450	0	35,439	10,947	6,637	40,301	35,809	1,316	865
2008	55,803	40,411	253	40,664	4,531	0	36,133	11,943	7,727	41,887	37,440	1,332	858
2009	55,409	39,877	294	40,171	4,472	0	35,699	11,417	8,294	41,144	37,599	1,347	830
2010	56,649	40,664	279	40,943	4,706	0	36,237	11,125	9,287	41,499	38,005	1,365	824
2011	59,226	42,142	306	42,448	4,476	0	37,972	11,601	9,653	42,765	38,835	1,385	835
2012	61,162	43,906	345	44,252	4,632	0	39,619	12,028	9,515	43,531	39,492	1,405	849
2013	61,983	45,248	339	45,588	5,414	0	40,174	11,943	9,866	43,553	39,073	1,423	868
2014	65,182	47,015	305	47,320	5,452	0	41,868	12,700	10,615	45,448	40,727	1,434	883
2015	68,201	49,354	338	49,692	5,700	0	43,992	13,177	11,032	47,150	41,904	1,446	901
2016	70,745	51,111	283	51,394	5,841	0	45,553	13,698	11,494	48,555	43,114	1,457	915
2017	73,646	53,110	287	53,397	6,074	0	47,324	14,363	11,960	50,499	44,867	1,458	921
2018	75,266	54,800	230	55,029	6,284	0	48,746	14,349	12,172	51,546	45,986	1,460	924
2019	78,552	56,713	206	56,919	6,534	0	50,386	15,415	12,751	53,912	47,926	1,457	914
2020	82,761	53,510	242	53,752	6,215	0	47,537	15,834	19,390	57,030	50,869	1,451	818
2021	88,948	58,181	265	58,446	6,668	0	51,779	16,782	20,387	61,481	53,877	1,447	861
2022	88,973	61,201	258	61,460	7,211	0	54,248	17,797	16,928	61,813	53,114	1,439	904
2023	93,501	64,903	266	65,169	7,659	0	57,510	18,952	17,040	65,151	57,427	1,435	...

... = Not available.

Personal Income and Employment by Region and State: Idaho

(Millions of dollars, except as noted.)

Year	Personal income, total	Derivation of personal income: Earnings by place of work: Nonfarm	Farm	Total	Less: Contributions for government social insurance	Plus: Adjustment for residence	Equals: Net earnings by place of residence	Plus: Dividends, interest, and rent	Plus: Personal current transfer receipts	Per capita (dollars): Personal income	Disposable personal income	Population (thousands)	Total employment (thousands)
1960	1,316	925	159	1,084	50	-3	1,031	195	90	1,961	1,762	671	...
1961	1,392	984	159	1,143	56	-3	1,084	206	102	2,035	1,841	684	...
1962	1,488	1,059	167	1,226	62	-3	1,161	221	106	2,150	1,949	692	...
1963	1,523	1,076	175	1,251	69	-2	1,180	234	109	2,230	2,013	683	...
1964	1,575	1,155	135	1,290	70	-2	1,218	245	112	2,316	2,117	680	...
1965	1,794	1,259	232	1,491	76	-2	1,414	260	120	2,615	2,392	686	...
1966	1,817	1,331	180	1,511	93	-1	1,417	271	129	2,638	2,401	689	...
1967	1,932	1,395	207	1,601	107	-1	1,494	283	155	2,808	2,547	688	...
1968	2,065	1,522	186	1,708	122	-0	1,586	305	174	2,971	2,682	695	...
1969	2,391	1,688	253	1,941	126	14	1,828	369	194	3,382	3,030	707	315
1970	2,648	1,843	267	2,110	136	15	1,988	431	229	3,691	3,336	717	324
1971	2,894	2,021	249	2,270	154	16	2,132	493	269	3,918	3,541	739	332
1972	3,304	2,302	320	2,622	182	17	2,457	541	306	4,329	3,938	763	347
1973	3,821	2,602	453	3,055	239	19	2,835	635	351	4,885	4,408	782	365
1974	4,497	2,966	628	3,595	281	23	3,336	740	422	5,566	4,983	808	381
1975	4,867	3,369	387	3,756	314	28	3,469	874	524	5,850	5,288	832	393
1976	5,436	3,895	343	4,237	368	35	3,904	940	593	6,343	5,719	857	419
1977	5,942	4,381	240	4,621	416	35	4,240	1,074	628	6,726	6,048	883	435
1978	6,830	5,069	308	5,377	485	42	4,935	1,225	670	7,497	6,722	911	460
1979	7,468	5,595	233	5,828	564	47	5,311	1,374	783	8,007	7,159	933	469
1980	8,396	5,969	408	6,376	606	60	5,830	1,628	937	8,857	7,925	948	464
1981	9,234	6,435	427	6,862	703	53	6,212	1,948	1,074	9,597	8,504	962	462
1982	9,694	6,450	393	6,844	720	62	6,186	2,276	1,233	9,956	8,922	974	452
1983	10,600	6,960	584	7,543	779	63	6,827	2,469	1,304	10,795	9,755	982	463
1984	11,280	7,546	501	8,047	870	76	7,253	2,679	1,349	11,385	10,310	991	472
1985	11,923	7,931	458	8,389	930	85	7,545	2,933	1,445	11,995	10,842	994	474
1986	12,166	8,066	479	8,545	955	100	7,690	2,950	1,525	12,286	11,160	990	474
1987	12,674	8,509	594	9,103	988	108	8,223	2,882	1,570	12,867	11,658	985	487
1988	13,748	9,340	670	10,010	1,128	126	9,008	3,054	1,686	13,948	12,622	986	508
1989	15,125	10,122	881	11,003	1,243	142	9,902	3,388	1,834	15,209	13,615	994	525
1990	16,343	11,071	1,000	12,071	1,435	157	10,794	3,571	1,979	16,143	14,399	1,012	548
1991	17,199	11,836	829	12,664	1,564	178	11,278	3,707	2,214	16,517	14,756	1,041	566
1992	18,882	13,141	875	14,016	1,701	196	12,510	3,894	2,478	17,619	15,651	1,072	586
1993	20,690	14,340	1,085	15,425	1,863	217	13,778	4,245	2,667	18,660	16,613	1,109	612
1994	22,134	15,699	779	16,478	2,051	246	14,673	4,632	2,829	19,329	17,204	1,145	647
1995	23,789	16,559	844	17,403	2,180	285	15,508	5,167	3,114	20,206	17,968	1,177	667
1996	25,264	17,375	952	18,327	2,242	331	16,416	5,519	3,330	20,999	18,628	1,203	689
1997	26,370	18,242	756	18,998	2,337	378	17,039	5,876	3,455	21,465	18,968	1,229	708
1998	28,498	19,713	956	20,669	2,483	446	18,632	6,268	3,599	22,756	20,140	1,252	733
1999	30,180	21,302	1,006	22,307	2,616	510	20,202	6,155	3,823	23,658	20,843	1,276	747
2000	32,667	23,290	1,013	24,304	2,847	524	21,981	6,542	4,145	25,139	22,016	1,299	777
2001	34,059	23,893	1,126	25,020	2,894	516	22,642	6,786	4,631	25,803	22,738	1,320	783
2002	35,214	24,868	1,100	25,968	2,991	501	23,477	6,711	5,026	26,272	23,788	1,340	791
2003	36,455	25,608	860	26,469	3,122	512	23,859	7,260	5,337	26,739	24,375	1,363	801
2004	39,387	27,152	1,372	28,524	3,332	520	25,712	7,957	5,718	28,299	25,803	1,392	825
2005	41,725	28,974	1,182	30,156	3,612	513	27,057	8,490	6,178	29,214	26,187	1,428	862
2006	45,888	32,014	1,092	33,105	3,998	489	29,596	9,585	6,707	31,244	27,785	1,469	900
2007	48,854	33,274	1,646	34,920	4,193	510	31,236	10,335	7,282	32,459	28,854	1,505	929
2008	50,157	33,010	1,652	34,662	4,226	561	30,997	10,683	8,477	32,690	29,349	1,534	921
2009	48,499	32,155	1,009	33,164	4,135	655	29,683	9,492	9,324	31,200	28,713	1,554	880
2010	50,202	32,618	1,432	34,050	4,317	724	30,456	9,496	10,249	31,950	29,405	1,571	869
2011	53,077	33,128	2,057	35,184	3,946	870	32,108	10,675	10,294	33,454	30,511	1,587	879
2012	55,720	34,134	2,066	36,200	4,047	1,098	33,252	12,038	10,431	34,825	31,736	1,600	883
2013	57,791	36,326	2,348	38,674	4,653	1,129	35,150	11,865	10,776	35,716	32,324	1,618	903
2014	60,897	38,003	2,461	40,464	4,856	1,233	36,842	12,710	11,345	37,128	33,567	1,640	926
2015	64,564	40,334	2,307	42,641	5,072	1,222	38,791	13,744	12,029	38,838	34,930	1,662	949
2016	67,294	42,220	2,082	44,301	5,326	1,285	40,260	14,465	12,569	39,676	35,568	1,696	977
2017	71,473	45,527	1,680	47,206	5,695	1,340	42,851	15,423	13,199	41,218	37,012	1,734	1,008
2018	76,530	49,089	1,738	50,826	6,057	1,385	46,155	16,321	14,054	43,270	39,082	1,769	1,041
2019	83,019	52,626	2,174	54,800	6,393	1,623	50,031	17,823	15,166	45,917	41,309	1,808	1,064
2020	91,889	56,477	2,486	58,964	6,967	1,680	53,677	18,928	19,284	49,687	44,520	1,849	1,078
2021	103,114	62,931	1,901	64,832	7,570	1,786	59,048	21,649	22,418	54,141	48,070	1,905	1,138
2022	109,776	67,852	2,740	70,592	8,370	2,049	64,272	24,874	20,630	56,615	49,693	1,939	1,191
2023	115,988	72,542	1,932	74,474	8,979	2,198	67,693	27,125	21,170	59,035	52,950	1,965	...

... = Not available.

Personal Income and Employment by Region and State: Illinois

(Millions of dollars, except as noted.)

Year	Personal income, total	Derivation of personal income: Earnings by place of work: Nonfarm	Farm	Total	Less: Contributions for government social insurance	Plus: Adjustment for residence	Equals: Net earnings by place of residence	Plus: Dividends, interest, and rent	Plus: Personal current transfer receipts	Per capita (dollars): Personal income	Disposable personal income	Population (thousands)	Total employment (thousands)
1960	27,210	22,630	647	23,277	1,073	-133	22,071	3,666	1,472	2,698	2,378	10,086	...
1961	28,282	23,063	814	23,877	1,089	-138	22,650	3,933	1,699	2,792	2,470	10,130	...
1962	29,885	24,344	798	25,142	1,196	-154	23,792	4,330	1,763	2,907	2,563	10,280	...
1963	31,096	25,257	821	26,079	1,329	-159	24,590	4,690	1,816	2,989	2,642	10,402	...
1964	33,241	27,105	665	27,771	1,337	-175	26,259	5,136	1,847	3,142	2,816	10,580	...
1965	36,068	29,103	903	30,006	1,356	-194	28,456	5,631	1,981	3,373	3,015	10,693	...
1966	39,099	32,041	976	33,018	1,821	-222	30,975	5,979	2,145	3,608	3,200	10,836	...
1967	41,606	34,021	936	34,957	1,988	-239	32,731	6,320	2,555	3,801	3,358	10,947	...
1968	44,582	36,706	691	37,397	2,194	-264	34,939	6,649	2,993	4,055	3,542	10,995	...
1969	48,485	40,069	913	40,982	2,715	64	38,330	6,918	3,236	4,392	3,765	11,039	5,179
1970	51,524	42,215	723	42,937	2,810	-16	40,111	7,576	3,837	4,632	3,992	11,125	5,144
1971	55,317	44,907	885	45,792	3,074	-59	42,659	8,068	4,590	4,936	4,321	11,206	5,104
1972	60,030	48,752	1,000	49,752	3,517	-83	46,152	8,711	5,167	5,332	4,608	11,258	5,155
1973	66,968	53,736	1,841	55,577	4,490	-100	50,987	9,833	6,147	5,947	5,172	11,260	5,351
1974	73,216	58,539	1,673	60,212	5,078	-117	55,016	11,192	7,009	6,494	5,622	11,274	5,441
1975	79,866	61,631	2,463	64,093	5,195	-141	58,758	12,125	8,984	7,064	6,202	11,306	5,342
1976	86,832	68,269	1,713	69,982	5,881	-132	63,969	12,936	9,927	7,644	6,642	11,360	5,458
1977	95,460	75,690	1,716	77,406	6,516	-70	70,819	14,256	10,384	8,369	7,252	11,406	5,587
1978	105,342	84,402	1,510	85,912	7,466	7	78,453	15,841	11,048	9,213	7,958	11,434	5,748
1979	115,574	92,288	1,838	94,126	8,484	74	85,716	17,826	12,032	10,118	8,674	11,423	5,803
1980	125,258	97,471	381	97,852	8,931	177	89,097	21,551	14,610	10,954	9,411	11,435	5,675
1981	138,771	104,307	1,522	105,829	10,249	116	95,696	26,293	16,782	12,127	10,399	11,443	5,664
1982	146,908	107,173	914	108,087	10,690	32	97,429	31,053	18,426	12,860	11,221	11,423	5,563
1983	153,073	112,268	-485	111,782	11,259	17	100,540	32,808	19,725	13,417	11,785	11,409	5,520
1984	168,503	123,383	1,227	124,610	12,810	-47	111,754	36,658	20,091	14,765	13,040	11,412	5,718
1985	177,117	130,498	1,718	132,216	13,763	-92	118,361	37,791	20,965	15,537	13,676	11,400	5,780
1986	186,323	138,918	1,426	140,344	14,681	-131	125,533	39,063	21,727	16,362	14,424	11,387	5,892
1987	196,408	149,490	1,431	150,921	15,562	-202	135,157	39,076	22,175	17,242	15,039	11,391	6,031
1988	212,485	163,793	856	164,649	17,396	-303	146,950	42,581	22,953	18,655	16,385	11,390	6,187
1989	226,700	172,648	2,174	174,822	18,513	-324	155,985	46,330	24,385	19,869	17,341	11,410	6,294
1990	240,792	183,408	1,763	185,172	19,273	-272	165,627	48,543	26,622	21,024	18,362	11,453	6,390
1991	246,146	187,719	977	188,696	20,215	-322	168,159	49,303	28,684	21,276	18,689	11,569	6,369
1992	265,620	201,962	2,056	204,018	21,320	-410	182,289	50,507	32,824	22,714	20,062	11,694	6,351
1993	275,148	210,352	1,712	212,063	22,492	-591	188,980	51,744	34,424	23,299	20,493	11,810	6,441
1994	289,798	221,487	2,306	223,794	24,002	-685	199,107	55,015	35,676	24,327	21,314	11,913	6,611
1995	307,442	234,255	604	234,860	25,277	-928	208,654	60,734	38,054	25,602	22,385	12,008	6,773
1996	326,998	246,538	2,501	249,040	26,332	-935	221,773	65,201	40,024	27,020	23,481	12,102	6,875
1997	345,582	261,993	2,135	264,128	27,787	-952	235,389	69,426	40,768	28,360	24,463	12,186	6,981
1998	366,594	279,080	1,537	280,617	29,384	-1,034	250,199	74,836	41,559	29,873	25,616	12,272	7,139
1999	382,605	297,355	1,083	298,437	30,782	-1,146	266,510	73,886	42,210	30,958	26,496	12,359	7,219
2000	411,221	317,609	1,810	319,419	32,338	-1,380	285,701	80,630	44,890	33,072	28,299	12,434	7,357
2001	427,182	331,258	1,691	332,949	33,140	-1,562	298,248	80,499	48,436	34,206	29,510	12,488	7,310
2002	432,382	337,882	981	338,863	33,713	-1,669	303,481	76,802	52,099	34,520	30,451	12,526	7,218
2003	440,480	343,319	1,860	345,179	34,580	-1,594	309,005	77,178	54,298	35,081	31,328	12,556	7,191
2004	457,834	356,119	3,626	359,745	36,631	-1,633	321,481	80,095	56,259	36,366	32,556	12,590	7,245
2005	475,646	368,452	1,730	370,182	38,708	-1,772	329,702	84,177	61,767	37,720	33,410	12,610	7,335
2006	506,022	388,839	1,923	390,762	40,464	-1,833	348,465	94,744	62,812	40,021	35,188	12,644	7,449
2007	535,103	404,624	3,145	407,770	42,291	-2,306	363,173	102,578	69,351	42,148	36,778	12,696	7,578
2008	551,160	406,902	4,568	411,470	43,044	-1,772	366,654	108,221	76,286	43,238	37,808	12,747	7,553
2009	525,794	385,878	2,625	388,504	41,140	-2,094	345,269	94,818	85,707	41,088	37,067	12,797	7,304
2010	540,881	396,064	2,652	398,716	41,807	-2,141	354,768	92,859	93,254	42,107	37,816	12,846	7,251
2011	568,230	412,367	5,490	417,857	39,298	-2,572	375,987	102,974	89,270	44,074	38,873	12,893	7,376
2012	593,814	432,484	3,122	435,607	41,012	-2,413	392,181	112,263	89,370	45,932	40,458	12,928	7,435
2013	605,682	445,350	7,964	453,314	47,076	-2,678	403,560	108,921	93,201	46,731	40,766	12,961	7,504
2014	629,465	462,309	3,682	465,991	48,529	-2,345	415,117	119,598	94,750	48,531	42,304	12,970	7,614
2015	657,080	481,885	386	482,271	49,996	-2,578	429,697	126,297	101,086	50,682	44,014	12,965	7,749
2016	664,687	485,805	2,710	488,515	50,991	-2,700	434,824	128,091	101,771	51,340	44,837	12,947	7,805
2017	685,633	499,081	2,378	501,459	52,661	-3,169	445,629	134,990	105,014	53,049	46,557	12,925	7,823
2018	722,687	522,288	3,107	525,396	55,089	-3,027	467,280	147,303	108,104	56,072	49,279	12,889	7,881
2019	741,717	539,274	2,112	541,386	56,773	-3,271	481,343	147,967	112,408	57,721	50,686	12,850	7,859
2020	787,488	537,598	3,868	541,466	56,843	-3,644	480,980	150,107	156,402	61,569	54,421	12,790	7,519
2021	853,521	574,553	7,860	582,413	60,179	-3,596	518,638	163,155	171,728	67,258	58,602	12,690	7,750
2022	851,243	597,532	9,030	606,562	65,794	-3,980	536,787	172,166	142,290	67,653	57,721	12,583	8,094
2023	890,438	626,258	8,279	634,537	68,881	-3,892	561,764	182,131	146,543	70,953	62,317	12,550	...

... = Not available.

Personal Income and Employment by Region and State: Indiana

(Millions of dollars, except as noted.)

Year	Personal income, total	Derivation of personal income: Earnings by place of work: Nonfarm	Farm	Total	Less: Contributions for government social insurance	Plus: Adjustment for residence	Equals: Net earnings by place of residence	Plus: Dividends, interest, and rent	Plus: Personal current transfer receipts	Per capita (dollars): Personal income	Disposable personal income	Population (thousands)	Total employment (thousands)
1960	10,390	8,573	366	8,939	415	41	8,564	1,222	604	2,223	1,986	4,674	...
1961	10,707	8,628	464	9,092	411	44	8,724	1,291	693	2,264	2,035	4,730	...
1962	11,464	9,328	452	9,780	461	49	9,367	1,400	697	2,421	2,163	4,736	...
1963	12,043	9,814	470	10,284	526	49	9,807	1,512	724	2,509	2,229	4,799	...
1964	12,817	10,637	301	10,938	545	47	10,440	1,629	749	2,639	2,368	4,856	...
1965	14,162	11,587	553	12,140	581	49	11,608	1,748	806	2,877	2,578	4,922	...
1966	15,288	12,835	480	13,315	818	56	12,553	1,869	866	3,058	2,715	4,999	...
1967	16,017	13,443	431	13,874	916	59	13,017	1,989	1,011	3,170	2,806	5,053	...
1968	17,413	14,645	379	15,024	993	69	14,100	2,133	1,180	3,419	3,001	5,093	...
1969	19,238	16,009	550	16,559	1,097	43	15,506	2,453	1,280	3,741	3,241	5,143	2,327
1970	20,029	16,441	381	16,821	1,115	78	15,785	2,744	1,501	3,849	3,377	5,204	2,291
1971	21,794	17,475	596	18,072	1,227	139	16,984	3,020	1,790	4,151	3,681	5,250	2,290
1972	23,847	19,381	507	19,888	1,441	178	18,625	3,252	1,970	4,503	3,950	5,296	2,367
1973	27,368	21,745	1,228	22,973	1,864	220	21,330	3,704	2,335	5,136	4,547	5,329	2,483
1974	29,274	23,332	735	24,067	2,089	280	22,258	4,260	2,757	5,472	4,769	5,350	2,493
1975	31,608	24,024	1,097	25,121	2,120	328	23,329	4,767	3,512	5,907	5,245	5,351	2,405
1976	35,132	27,285	1,076	28,362	2,438	385	26,309	5,149	3,674	6,540	5,742	5,372	2,489
1977	38,901	30,856	724	31,579	2,754	443	29,269	5,775	3,857	7,197	6,295	5,405	2,578
1978	43,398	34,726	731	35,457	3,190	498	32,765	6,392	4,242	7,968	6,938	5,446	2,670
1979	47,804	38,177	672	38,849	3,630	570	35,788	7,144	4,872	8,732	7,568	5,475	2,708
1980	51,435	39,292	379	39,671	3,714	682	36,639	8,696	6,099	9,368	8,179	5,491	2,626
1981	56,385	42,198	306	42,504	4,296	748	38,956	10,616	6,813	10,288	8,940	5,480	2,603
1982	58,406	42,247	307	42,555	4,390	811	38,975	11,839	7,592	10,682	9,366	5,468	2,522
1983	61,293	44,685	-260	44,425	4,660	839	40,603	12,518	8,172	11,246	9,931	5,450	2,542
1984	67,944	49,217	753	49,970	5,258	984	45,696	13,679	8,569	12,448	11,038	5,458	2,642
1985	71,782	52,223	682	52,905	5,686	1,058	48,277	14,486	9,019	13,149	11,619	5,459	2,695
1986	75,603	55,367	578	55,945	6,056	1,135	51,024	15,054	9,525	13,862	12,281	5,454	2,755
1987	79,994	59,677	763	60,440	6,434	1,185	55,191	15,094	9,709	14,616	12,897	5,473	2,849
1988	85,855	64,771	284	65,055	7,215	1,283	59,123	16,442	10,290	15,634	13,811	5,492	2,935
1989	93,484	69,194	965	70,158	7,737	1,349	63,770	18,526	11,188	16,924	14,879	5,524	3,010
1990	98,725	73,007	863	73,870	8,408	1,487	66,949	19,618	12,158	17,763	15,633	5,558	3,070
1991	101,845	76,121	242	76,363	8,884	1,495	68,973	19,493	13,378	18,134	16,008	5,616	3,072
1992	110,063	81,916	849	82,766	9,455	1,646	74,957	19,819	15,287	19,396	17,195	5,675	3,121
1993	115,996	86,578	866	87,444	10,062	1,866	79,247	20,611	16,138	20,212	17,871	5,739	3,197
1994	123,234	92,445	828	93,273	10,900	1,997	84,369	22,028	16,837	21,271	18,727	5,794	3,287
1995	128,817	96,459	349	96,808	11,416	2,278	87,671	23,995	17,151	22,014	19,349	5,851	3,379
1996	136,091	100,767	1,196	101,962	11,792	2,418	92,588	25,395	18,108	23,043	20,186	5,906	3,418
1997	143,320	106,429	1,161	107,590	12,409	2,547	97,728	27,002	18,590	24,066	20,989	5,955	3,476
1998	154,522	115,626	769	116,395	13,176	2,574	105,793	29,424	19,305	25,758	22,420	5,999	3,543
1999	160,466	122,398	473	122,871	13,815	2,826	111,882	28,382	20,202	26,545	23,124	6,045	3,597
2000	171,032	129,173	873	130,046	14,397	3,115	118,764	30,532	21,736	28,075	24,587	6,092	3,648
2001	175,230	130,784	1,068	131,852	14,582	3,360	120,629	30,572	24,028	28,596	25,065	6,128	3,589
2002	177,919	133,936	466	134,403	15,002	3,432	122,832	29,584	25,503	28,902	25,741	6,156	3,553
2003	182,458	136,987	1,242	138,229	15,523	3,516	126,222	29,723	26,513	29,445	26,467	6,197	3,552
2004	191,088	143,339	2,049	145,388	16,322	3,802	132,868	30,147	28,073	30,657	27,667	6,233	3,593
2005	196,999	147,931	1,321	149,251	17,067	4,106	136,290	30,141	30,568	31,376	28,126	6,279	3,635
2006	208,374	154,973	1,113	156,086	17,865	4,322	142,543	32,835	32,997	32,905	29,370	6,333	3,674
2007	215,920	158,275	1,550	159,825	18,378	4,695	146,142	35,166	34,612	33,845	30,029	6,380	3,720
2008	226,602	160,756	2,311	163,067	18,799	4,685	148,953	37,608	40,042	35,270	31,478	6,425	3,683
2009	220,909	154,117	1,564	155,681	18,033	4,600	142,248	34,410	44,251	34,200	31,242	6,459	3,523
2010	231,026	162,081	1,633	163,714	18,454	4,464	149,723	33,987	47,315	35,590	32,427	6,491	3,525
2011	245,731	170,846	2,816	173,662	17,096	4,722	161,288	37,084	47,359	37,682	33,995	6,521	3,590
2012	256,285	178,308	2,291	180,599	17,799	4,729	167,529	39,898	48,858	39,150	35,469	6,546	3,642
2013	259,535	181,053	5,335	186,389	20,648	5,232	170,973	39,325	49,237	39,436	35,452	6,581	3,684
2014	269,159	188,058	3,082	191,140	21,414	5,179	174,905	41,645	52,609	40,721	36,637	6,610	3,740
2015	279,386	196,062	1,340	197,403	22,313	5,761	180,850	43,902	54,633	42,149	37,717	6,629	3,796
2016	287,275	201,860	1,632	203,492	22,791	5,889	186,590	44,678	56,007	43,145	38,560	6,658	3,848
2017	297,991	209,263	1,610	210,873	23,707	6,285	193,451	46,982	57,558	44,570	40,066	6,686	3,903
2018	313,127	220,029	1,588	221,617	24,817	6,547	203,346	49,795	59,986	46,556	42,169	6,726	3,964
2019	326,387	228,969	1,219	230,188	25,915	7,249	211,523	51,226	63,638	48,270	43,460	6,762	3,970
2020	351,107	234,186	2,546	236,733	26,990	7,461	217,204	51,954	81,949	51,716	46,607	6,789	3,843
2021	387,919	255,466	4,083	259,550	29,088	7,198	237,660	57,077	93,183	56,931	50,801	6,814	3,978
2022	398,523	273,503	4,285	277,788	31,215	8,147	254,721	61,730	82,072	58,329	51,319	6,832	4,141
2023	411,993	285,739	3,294	289,033	32,534	8,654	265,153	65,095	81,744	60,038	53,943	6,862	...

... = Not available.

Personal Income and Employment by Region and State: Iowa

(Millions of dollars, except as noted.)

Year	Personal income, total	Derivation of personal income								Per capita (dollars)		Population (thousands)	Total employment (thousands)
		Earnings by place of work			Less: Contributions for government social insurance	Plus: Adjustment for residence	Equals: Net earnings by place of residence	Plus: Dividends, interest, and rent	Plus: Personal current transfer receipts	Personal income	Disposable personal income		
		Nonfarm	Farm	Total									
1960	5,745	3,908	732	4,640	186	35	4,489	872	385	2,085	1,876	2,756	...
1961	6,084	4,022	852	4,874	189	38	4,723	937	424	2,207	1,997	2,756	...
1962	6,345	4,203	883	5,086	203	41	4,924	977	444	2,307	2,086	2,750	...
1963	6,744	4,425	1,001	5,425	233	43	5,236	1,044	464	2,455	2,222	2,747	...
1964	7,059	4,742	921	5,663	247	47	5,463	1,117	479	2,571	2,346	2,746	...
1965	7,818	5,070	1,247	6,318	261	50	6,108	1,189	522	2,851	2,596	2,742	...
1966	8,513	5,640	1,346	6,986	352	55	6,689	1,258	566	3,082	2,777	2,762	...
1967	8,672	6,028	1,080	7,109	418	59	6,750	1,247	675	3,105	2,790	2,793	...
1968	9,347	6,490	1,021	7,511	457	63	7,117	1,448	782	3,335	2,974	2,803	...
1969	10,374	7,116	1,238	8,354	543	89	7,900	1,619	856	3,698	3,267	2,805	1,289
1970	11,095	7,540	1,215	8,756	567	97	8,285	1,818	992	3,923	3,493	2,829	1,295
1971	11,642	8,048	1,012	9,060	626	97	8,531	1,984	1,127	4,082	3,676	2,852	1,297
1972	13,040	8,770	1,485	10,255	719	103	9,640	2,185	1,216	4,559	4,039	2,861	1,316
1973	15,655	9,825	2,732	12,557	930	98	11,725	2,526	1,404	5,466	4,881	2,864	1,374
1974	16,225	11,001	1,721	12,722	1,092	91	11,721	2,878	1,626	5,657	4,920	2,868	1,407
1975	18,134	11,982	1,970	13,951	1,167	107	12,892	3,225	2,017	6,293	5,562	2,881	1,407
1976	19,280	13,552	1,227	14,779	1,322	100	13,557	3,504	2,219	6,640	5,815	2,904	1,455
1977	21,275	15,107	1,226	16,333	1,459	74	14,948	3,982	2,345	7,300	6,395	2,914	1,488
1978	24,537	16,681	2,441	19,122	1,671	73	17,524	4,430	2,584	8,406	7,387	2,919	1,513
1979	26,300	18,685	1,575	20,260	1,955	79	18,384	5,021	2,895	9,017	7,843	2,917	1,554
1980	28,010	19,755	717	20,473	2,058	98	18,513	6,085	3,412	9,612	8,346	2,914	1,537
1981	31,684	20,927	1,639	22,566	2,315	127	20,378	7,423	3,882	10,895	9,467	2,908	1,507
1982	32,545	20,949	816	21,765	2,344	200	19,621	8,498	4,426	11,268	9,892	2,888	1,471
1983	33,176	21,840	6	21,846	2,426	213	19,633	8,800	4,743	11,557	10,232	2,871	1,474
1984	36,916	23,534	1,463	24,997	2,684	242	22,555	9,502	4,859	12,914	11,606	2,859	1,499
1985	38,213	24,197	1,752	25,949	2,810	279	23,418	9,638	5,156	13,504	12,135	2,830	1,495
1986	39,474	24,982	2,128	27,110	2,966	274	24,418	9,705	5,351	14,139	12,735	2,792	1,494
1987	41,225	26,817	2,459	29,277	3,174	268	26,371	9,388	5,466	14,899	13,289	2,767	1,514
1988	42,727	28,845	1,646	30,491	3,527	311	27,276	9,738	5,714	15,434	13,744	2,768	1,557
1989	46,504	30,867	2,400	33,267	3,765	321	29,823	10,580	6,101	16,785	14,890	2,771	1,600
1990	49,020	32,666	2,504	35,170	4,079	319	31,410	10,980	6,630	17,627	15,601	2,781	1,635
1991	50,211	34,141	1,780	35,921	4,285	373	32,009	11,074	7,127	17,948	15,921	2,798	1,654
1992	53,763	36,441	2,700	39,141	4,529	411	35,023	11,042	7,698	19,076	17,003	2,818	1,669
1993	54,006	38,235	889	39,124	4,773	401	34,752	11,196	8,058	19,036	16,902	2,837	1,692
1994	58,889	40,747	2,861	43,608	5,142	423	38,889	11,625	8,376	20,657	18,390	2,851	1,725
1995	61,256	42,772	1,818	44,589	5,400	484	39,673	12,760	8,824	21,363	18,978	2,867	1,785
1996	66,725	44,925	3,724	48,649	5,382	529	43,796	13,660	9,269	23,168	20,594	2,880	1,815
1997	69,908	47,570	3,397	50,966	5,908	604	45,663	14,715	9,530	24,180	21,335	2,891	1,841
1998	73,148	51,278	2,161	53,438	6,289	695	47,844	15,535	9,769	25,198	22,207	2,903	1,877
1999	74,999	54,018	1,601	55,619	6,558	796	49,857	15,009	10,133	25,705	22,651	2,918	1,896
2000	80,083	56,758	2,462	59,219	6,806	881	53,295	15,936	10,853	27,341	24,173	2,929	1,915
2001	82,520	58,305	2,273	60,578	6,967	905	54,516	16,258	11,746	28,145	24,942	2,932	1,902
2002	84,518	59,778	2,128	61,906	7,093	942	55,754	15,832	12,932	28,804	26,001	2,934	1,880
2003	86,331	61,921	2,253	64,174	7,414	971	57,732	15,722	12,877	29,344	26,683	2,942	1,873
2004	93,378	65,899	4,787	70,686	7,802	988	63,872	16,165	13,341	31,615	28,871	2,954	1,902
2005	96,080	69,129	3,871	73,001	8,212	905	65,694	16,132	14,254	32,411	29,352	2,964	1,934
2006	101,999	73,664	2,848	76,513	8,680	841	68,674	17,605	15,720	34,197	30,791	2,983	1,966
2007	109,069	76,987	3,899	80,886	9,117	1,079	72,848	19,496	16,726	36,366	32,493	2,999	1,994
2008	116,113	79,669	4,807	84,476	9,546	1,149	76,080	20,979	19,054	38,490	34,511	3,017	1,998
2009	112,963	77,841	3,234	81,075	9,425	1,150	72,800	19,780	20,384	37,246	34,037	3,033	1,959
2010	116,536	80,127	3,653	83,780	9,738	1,187	75,229	19,586	21,721	38,190	34,811	3,051	1,950
2011	125,500	81,968	7,397	89,365	9,091	1,306	81,580	21,860	22,060	40,880	36,897	3,070	1,976
2012	131,137	86,592	6,739	93,331	9,384	1,229	85,177	23,977	21,984	42,541	38,305	3,083	1,993
2013	133,435	88,984	8,516	97,499	10,770	1,210	87,939	23,026	22,470	43,012	38,514	3,102	2,019
2014	137,734	93,875	5,858	99,733	11,113	1,048	89,667	24,409	23,657	44,123	39,522	3,122	2,039
2015	142,521	97,186	5,094	102,280	11,378	1,001	91,903	25,695	24,923	45,445	40,547	3,136	2,060
2016	143,840	99,393	2,801	102,195	11,873	1,049	91,371	26,953	25,516	45,672	40,723	3,149	2,067
2017	147,912	101,399	3,522	104,921	12,200	1,365	94,086	28,271	25,555	46,769	41,788	3,163	2,062
2018	154,686	105,277	4,035	109,312	12,726	1,358	97,943	28,979	27,764	48,775	43,895	3,171	2,077
2019	158,119	107,748	2,892	110,640	13,153	1,404	98,891	29,835	29,393	49,663	44,551	3,184	2,070
2020	167,779	109,598	2,425	112,023	13,754	1,699	99,968	30,248	37,563	52,580	47,433	3,191	2,010
2021	185,622	116,634	7,614	124,248	14,291	1,692	111,649	33,184	40,789	58,044	51,918	3,198	2,054
2022	192,742	125,358	9,845	135,203	15,529	1,704	121,378	35,252	36,112	60,238	53,238	3,200	2,114
2023	199,960	131,659	9,433	141,092	16,307	1,814	126,599	36,212	37,149	62,351	56,247	3,207	...

... = Not available.

Personal Income and Employment by Region and State: Kansas

(Millions of dollars, except as noted.)

Year	Personal income, total	Derivation of personal income: Earnings by place of work: Nonfarm	Farm	Total	Less: Contributions for government social insurance	Plus: Adjustment for residence	Equals: Net earnings by place of residence	Plus: Dividends, interest, and rent	Plus: Personal current transfer receipts	Per capita (dollars): Personal income	Disposable personal income	Population (thousands)	Total employment (thousands)
1960	4,827	3,295	443	3,737	161	175	3,752	773	302	2,211	1,991	2,183	...
1961	5,039	3,453	451	3,905	177	178	3,906	799	335	2,275	2,051	2,215	...
1962	5,244	3,635	422	4,057	183	194	4,068	831	345	2,351	2,110	2,231	...
1963	5,364	3,735	404	4,138	206	214	4,147	852	366	2,420	2,162	2,217	...
1964	5,650	3,980	368	4,349	213	236	4,371	900	379	2,558	2,330	2,209	...
1965	6,024	4,155	462	4,617	222	259	4,655	957	413	2,731	2,486	2,206	...
1966	6,452	4,550	478	5,029	293	294	5,030	979	444	2,933	2,633	2,200	...
1967	6,756	4,840	407	5,247	340	325	5,232	992	532	3,075	2,755	2,197	...
1968	7,360	5,311	400	5,711	377	355	5,689	1,055	616	3,321	2,948	2,216	...
1969	8,195	5,780	465	6,245	421	445	6,269	1,237	689	3,665	3,226	2,236	1,029
1970	8,893	6,084	606	6,690	442	445	6,693	1,396	803	3,956	3,510	2,248	1,017
1971	9,654	6,558	706	7,264	492	439	7,211	1,527	916	4,298	3,867	2,246	1,022
1972	10,763	7,252	963	8,215	573	458	8,101	1,678	985	4,772	4,252	2,256	1,048
1973	12,266	8,095	1,386	9,480	734	472	9,218	1,897	1,151	5,417	4,814	2,264	1,090
1974	13,262	9,028	1,060	10,088	853	485	9,720	2,219	1,324	5,848	5,138	2,268	1,122
1975	14,488	10,011	807	10,818	936	500	10,381	2,494	1,613	6,358	5,656	2,279	1,133
1976	15,746	11,265	584	11,848	1,069	510	11,290	2,673	1,784	6,850	6,082	2,299	1,169
1977	17,182	12,400	498	12,898	1,175	553	12,276	2,977	1,930	7,413	6,537	2,318	1,208
1978	19,014	14,055	285	14,340	1,374	599	13,565	3,345	2,104	8,151	7,161	2,333	1,252
1979	21,716	15,868	706	16,574	1,615	642	15,601	3,794	2,321	9,251	8,048	2,347	1,296
1980	23,880	17,382	101	17,483	1,757	716	16,442	4,676	2,761	10,080	8,755	2,369	1,309
1981	27,038	19,035	345	19,380	2,056	742	18,066	5,791	3,181	11,338	9,751	2,385	1,322
1982	29,314	19,733	577	20,310	2,180	764	18,893	6,851	3,569	12,208	10,547	2,401	1,306
1983	30,555	20,767	384	21,151	2,288	741	19,604	7,146	3,804	12,649	11,155	2,416	1,323
1984	33,489	22,750	751	23,500	2,567	800	21,734	7,834	3,922	13,815	12,303	2,424	1,365
1985	35,247	23,846	811	24,657	2,732	853	22,778	8,334	4,136	14,521	12,879	2,427	1,368
1986	36,950	25,183	938	26,121	2,885	843	24,079	8,531	4,340	15,189	13,582	2,433	1,368
1987	38,510	26,490	1,173	27,663	3,003	914	25,574	8,474	4,462	15,748	13,965	2,445	1,421
1988	40,671	28,096	1,141	29,237	3,318	918	26,838	9,152	4,682	16,520	14,662	2,462	1,432
1989	43,063	29,937	831	30,768	3,510	975	28,233	9,689	5,142	17,414	15,349	2,473	1,454
1990	45,745	31,587	1,383	32,970	3,887	968	30,051	10,113	5,582	18,436	16,315	2,481	1,474
1991	47,367	32,967	1,035	34,001	4,119	947	30,829	10,474	6,064	18,957	16,840	2,499	1,489
1992	50,913	35,562	1,408	36,970	4,382	1,027	33,614	10,576	6,723	20,105	17,960	2,532	1,502
1993	53,268	37,361	1,346	38,707	4,591	1,115	35,231	10,915	7,122	20,836	18,567	2,557	1,525
1994	55,684	39,217	1,436	40,653	4,897	1,066	36,822	11,506	7,357	21,579	19,190	2,581	1,551
1995	58,056	41,202	794	41,996	5,091	1,157	38,063	12,241	7,752	22,321	19,743	2,601	1,600
1996	61,821	43,512	1,508	45,020	5,327	1,147	40,840	12,967	8,015	23,645	20,820	2,615	1,632
1997	65,704	46,643	1,421	48,064	5,697	1,044	43,411	13,883	8,410	24,932	21,797	2,635	1,677
1998	69,711	49,938	1,309	51,248	6,069	1,065	46,244	14,923	8,544	26,201	22,874	2,661	1,724
1999	71,969	52,375	1,403	53,778	6,343	1,018	48,453	14,613	8,902	26,871	23,438	2,678	1,740
2000	75,871	55,059	1,014	56,073	6,656	1,121	50,538	15,682	9,651	28,166	24,519	2,694	1,760
2001	78,491	56,918	1,164	58,081	6,870	1,133	52,345	15,597	10,549	29,047	25,399	2,702	1,768
2002	79,285	58,378	493	58,871	7,046	1,199	53,024	15,053	11,209	29,218	26,072	2,714	1,746
2003	81,768	59,183	1,649	60,832	7,213	1,171	54,790	15,269	11,709	30,029	27,082	2,723	1,734
2004	84,077	61,365	1,566	62,931	7,595	1,120	56,456	15,581	12,041	30,748	27,766	2,734	1,751
2005	88,784	64,206	1,963	66,169	7,944	1,261	59,487	16,601	12,697	32,340	28,908	2,745	1,766
2006	97,839	70,756	1,133	71,889	8,409	1,370	64,850	19,347	13,643	35,411	31,484	2,763	1,795
2007	105,083	74,837	1,640	76,476	8,807	1,257	68,926	21,470	14,687	37,748	33,334	2,784	1,844
2008	115,298	80,018	2,083	82,101	9,212	1,414	74,304	24,442	16,553	41,060	36,471	2,808	1,858
2009	111,559	77,537	1,996	79,534	9,007	1,695	72,221	21,312	18,026	39,382	35,876	2,833	1,813
2010	113,843	79,261	2,537	81,798	9,243	1,675	74,230	20,423	19,190	39,822	36,135	2,859	1,802
2011	123,199	84,124	3,659	87,784	8,525	1,240	80,498	23,075	19,626	42,889	38,606	2,872	1,819
2012	129,850	89,440	3,052	92,492	8,826	1,641	85,307	25,188	19,355	44,914	40,542	2,891	1,841
2013	132,519	92,819	4,904	97,722	10,225	1,370	88,868	24,011	19,640	45,670	40,947	2,902	1,869
2014	134,774	94,804	2,755	97,559	10,609	1,188	88,138	26,250	20,385	46,290	41,502	2,912	1,896
2015	136,189	97,283	1,726	99,009	11,025	1,156	89,139	25,964	21,086	46,597	41,720	2,923	1,911
2016	136,754	96,404	2,165	98,570	10,910	1,275	88,935	25,979	21,840	46,718	41,867	2,927	1,916
2017	141,312	99,863	1,386	101,249	11,216	1,540	91,574	27,175	22,564	48,272	43,314	2,927	1,913
2018	147,407	103,483	1,682	105,165	11,748	1,551	94,967	28,740	23,700	50,283	45,114	2,932	1,926
2019	152,926	107,436	1,628	109,063	12,238	1,661	98,486	29,413	25,027	52,127	46,673	2,934	1,924
2020	161,705	108,387	2,841	111,229	12,618	1,547	100,158	29,497	32,049	55,037	49,426	2,938	1,879
2021	172,071	112,461	3,610	116,071	13,420	2,062	104,714	32,105	35,252	58,568	51,785	2,938	1,921
2022	177,475	123,283	898	124,181	14,710	2,398	111,869	34,513	31,093	60,433	52,742	2,937	1,982
2023	187,406	130,527	1,378	131,905	15,661	2,596	118,839	36,225	32,342	63,732	56,940	2,941	...

... = Not available.

Personal Income and Employment by Region and State: Kentucky

(Millions of dollars, except as noted.)

Year	Personal income, total	Derivation of personal income: Earnings by place of work: Nonfarm	Farm	Total	Less: Contributions for government social insurance	Plus: Adjustment for residence	Equals: Net earnings by place of residence	Plus: Dividends, interest, and rent	Plus: Personal current transfer receipts	Per capita (dollars): Personal income	Disposable personal income	Population (thousands)	Total employment (thousands)
1960	5,022	3,739	323	4,062	184	89	3,967	626	429	1,651	1,494	3,041	...
1961	5,346	3,838	396	4,235	185	81	4,131	661	555	1,750	1,593	3,054	...
1962	5,678	4,177	396	4,573	209	84	4,448	726	504	1,844	1,666	3,079	...
1963	5,968	4,445	405	4,850	240	84	4,693	771	504	1,928	1,745	3,096	...
1964	6,226	4,735	297	5,033	245	91	4,879	817	530	1,990	1,811	3,129	...
1965	6,750	5,119	366	5,485	258	96	5,323	848	579	2,150	1,953	3,140	...
1966	7,379	5,706	382	6,088	339	104	5,853	899	627	2,345	2,107	3,147	...
1967	7,988	6,206	383	6,589	400	79	6,268	974	746	2,518	2,274	3,172	...
1968	8,731	6,858	372	7,231	446	86	6,871	1,018	843	2,733	2,444	3,195	...
1969	9,712	7,494	428	7,922	509	162	7,575	1,193	944	3,037	2,669	3,198	1,332
1970	10,535	8,058	393	8,451	547	153	8,057	1,373	1,105	3,261	2,896	3,231	1,336
1971	11,466	8,773	408	9,180	615	97	8,662	1,506	1,298	3,476	3,116	3,298	1,360
1972	12,680	9,708	507	10,215	713	90	9,591	1,647	1,441	3,801	3,361	3,336	1,392
1973	14,253	10,966	579	11,545	919	45	10,670	1,863	1,720	4,227	3,780	3,372	1,461
1974	16,052	12,203	665	12,868	1,060	17	11,825	2,176	2,051	4,698	4,121	3,417	1,496
1975	17,479	13,107	482	13,589	1,122	10	12,478	2,418	2,584	5,039	4,517	3,469	1,465
1976	19,544	14,815	557	15,372	1,291	-18	14,063	2,650	2,831	5,536	4,938	3,530	1,523
1977	21,934	16,748	683	17,431	1,451	6	15,985	2,982	2,968	6,135	5,425	3,575	1,579
1978	24,444	18,942	605	19,547	1,686	28	17,890	3,377	3,178	6,769	5,962	3,611	1,645
1979	27,454	21,161	679	21,839	1,944	21	19,916	3,835	3,704	7,535	6,631	3,644	1,665
1980	29,880	22,189	561	22,750	2,059	52	20,743	4,669	4,469	8,154	7,211	3,664	1,642
1981	33,221	23,920	939	24,858	2,392	16	22,483	5,699	5,039	9,051	7,957	3,670	1,634
1982	35,387	24,786	902	25,689	2,526	10	23,173	6,715	5,499	9,607	8,471	3,683	1,616
1983	36,765	26,062	232	26,294	2,653	33	23,674	7,138	5,953	9,951	8,830	3,694	1,624
1984	41,024	28,742	1,121	29,863	3,000	3	26,866	7,930	6,229	11,101	9,944	3,695	1,676
1985	42,799	30,249	876	31,125	3,218	-4	27,903	8,380	6,517	11,584	10,330	3,695	1,698
1986	44,002	31,229	648	31,877	3,453	21	28,445	8,733	6,824	11,932	10,640	3,688	1,733
1987	46,347	33,475	731	34,207	3,682	4	30,529	8,761	7,057	12,583	11,162	3,683	1,765
1988	50,537	36,827	778	37,605	4,098	-7	33,500	9,542	7,495	13,733	12,237	3,680	1,816
1989	54,314	38,940	1,142	40,082	4,407	-43	35,632	10,447	8,235	14,770	13,071	3,677	1,865
1990	57,665	41,267	1,123	42,390	4,818	-32	37,540	11,115	9,010	15,610	13,786	3,694	1,906
1991	60,895	43,165	1,123	44,288	5,094	-38	39,157	11,493	10,245	16,359	14,535	3,722	1,903
1992	65,508	46,962	1,309	48,271	5,520	-255	42,496	11,764	11,248	17,397	15,463	3,765	1,949
1993	68,069	49,271	1,115	50,386	5,886	-245	44,255	12,111	11,702	17,855	15,853	3,812	1,993
1994	71,533	51,944	1,166	53,111	6,331	-328	46,452	12,807	12,274	18,584	16,458	3,849	2,035
1995	74,960	54,219	708	54,927	6,635	-330	47,963	13,796	13,202	19,283	17,011	3,887	2,110
1996	79,483	56,870	1,138	58,008	6,898	-314	50,796	14,705	13,982	20,279	17,847	3,920	2,141
1997	84,466	60,547	1,139	61,687	7,299	-315	54,073	15,617	14,777	21,369	18,710	3,953	2,189
1998	89,403	64,414	1,011	65,425	7,748	-188	57,490	16,742	15,171	22,433	19,587	3,985	2,224
1999	93,175	68,675	784	69,459	8,257	-272	60,930	16,509	15,736	23,189	20,243	4,018	2,264
2000	100,475	72,859	1,493	74,352	8,525	-295	65,533	18,034	16,908	24,815	21,739	4,049	2,306
2001	103,998	75,371	1,082	76,453	8,743	-444	67,267	18,304	18,427	25,564	22,379	4,068	2,284
2002	106,552	77,845	678	78,523	9,006	-507	69,011	17,808	19,733	26,053	23,224	4,090	2,263
2003	109,766	80,877	705	81,582	9,255	-733	71,594	17,825	20,347	26,661	23,938	4,117	2,273
2004	116,214	85,557	1,249	86,806	9,646	-925	76,235	18,079	21,900	28,030	25,319	4,146	2,301
2005	121,735	89,661	1,551	91,212	10,124	-1,310	79,777	18,750	23,207	29,104	26,110	4,183	2,338
2006	128,584	93,656	1,267	94,923	10,696	-1,355	82,872	20,712	25,001	30,476	27,316	4,219	2,375
2007	134,210	96,906	817	97,723	11,179	-1,498	85,046	22,267	26,897	31,529	28,111	4,257	2,415
2008	140,838	99,442	352	99,795	11,654	-1,789	86,351	24,158	30,329	32,830	29,309	4,290	2,402
2009	139,000	95,835	677	96,512	11,526	-1,850	83,136	22,398	33,466	32,198	29,360	4,317	2,325
2010	144,336	100,310	349	100,660	11,843	-2,137	86,680	22,201	35,454	33,187	30,208	4,349	2,326
2011	151,380	104,089	848	104,937	10,947	-2,341	91,649	23,801	35,930	34,607	31,243	4,374	2,368
2012	156,565	107,400	928	108,329	11,287	-2,394	94,647	25,942	35,976	35,631	32,257	4,394	2,389
2013	157,905	108,598	2,671	111,269	12,896	-2,038	96,335	24,725	36,846	35,759	32,121	4,416	2,408
2014	164,862	112,206	1,713	113,919	13,454	-1,977	98,488	26,164	40,210	37,226	33,399	4,429	2,440
2015	172,269	117,062	1,402	118,464	14,040	-2,057	102,367	27,577	42,326	38,768	34,605	4,444	2,474
2016	175,276	119,131	878	120,009	14,370	-2,014	103,625	28,987	42,663	39,321	35,055	4,458	2,499
2017	180,836	122,297	1,366	123,663	14,757	-2,141	106,766	29,979	44,092	40,404	36,142	4,476	2,520
2018	186,931	126,946	975	127,921	15,295	-2,406	110,220	31,333	45,379	41,658	37,433	4,487	2,546
2019	195,420	132,592	1,299	133,892	15,818	-2,704	115,370	32,681	47,369	43,445	38,989	4,498	2,550
2020	211,967	135,061	1,051	136,112	16,314	-3,089	116,709	32,872	62,386	47,019	42,597	4,508	2,472
2021	232,363	145,730	2,010	147,741	16,995	-3,650	127,095	36,068	69,200	51,549	46,296	4,508	2,558
2022	234,282	155,876	2,005	157,882	18,316	-4,008	135,558	38,158	60,567	51,929	45,890	4,512	2,659
2023	245,889	167,061	1,754	168,815	19,644	-4,485	144,686	39,701	61,502	54,326	48,937	4,526	...

... = Not available.

Personal Income and Employment by Region and State: Louisiana

(Millions of dollars, except as noted.)

Year	Personal income, total	Derivation of personal income: Earnings by place of work: Nonfarm	Farm	Total	Less: Contributions for government social insurance	Plus: Adjustment for residence	Equals: Net earnings by place of residence	Plus: Dividends, interest, and rent	Plus: Personal current transfer receipts	Per capita (dollars): Personal income	Disposable personal income	Population (thousands)	Total employment (thousands)
1960	5,591	4,382	186	4,567	185	-1	4,381	775	436	1,715	1,566	3,260	...
1961	5,819	4,499	218	4,717	188	-1	4,529	804	486	1,770	1,616	3,287	...
1962	6,158	4,790	204	4,995	208	-0	4,786	867	504	1,841	1,677	3,345	...
1963	6,564	5,086	261	5,347	246	-0	5,101	928	535	1,944	1,762	3,377	...
1964	7,016	5,530	226	5,756	262	-1	5,494	968	554	2,036	1,865	3,446	...
1965	7,602	6,052	198	6,250	286	-0	5,964	1,039	598	2,174	1,994	3,496	...
1966	8,410	6,812	239	7,051	389	3	6,665	1,103	642	2,369	2,140	3,550	...
1967	9,225	7,454	267	7,722	432	5	7,294	1,179	752	2,576	2,334	3,581	...
1968	10,106	8,199	299	8,498	489	4	8,012	1,243	850	2,805	2,521	3,603	...
1969	10,766	8,703	241	8,944	569	8	8,384	1,421	961	2,975	2,655	3,619	1,440
1970	11,663	9,199	283	9,482	592	6	8,897	1,612	1,154	3,195	2,893	3,650	1,429
1971	12,715	9,970	320	10,290	658	-7	9,625	1,772	1,318	3,427	3,107	3,711	1,445
1972	13,912	10,959	349	11,308	757	-20	10,531	1,931	1,450	3,698	3,330	3,762	1,488
1973	15,529	12,105	579	12,684	960	-37	11,687	2,156	1,686	4,098	3,701	3,789	1,550
1974	17,652	13,654	614	14,268	1,118	-54	13,096	2,581	1,975	4,620	4,135	3,821	1,598
1975	19,875	15,433	419	15,852	1,243	-83	14,526	2,909	2,440	5,113	4,627	3,887	1,641
1976	22,416	17,701	455	18,157	1,454	-112	16,591	3,126	2,698	5,672	5,077	3,952	1,702
1977	25,031	19,962	454	20,416	1,627	-138	18,651	3,477	2,903	6,234	5,563	4,016	1,756
1978	28,631	23,191	373	23,565	1,933	-184	21,448	4,026	3,157	7,029	6,227	4,073	1,849
1979	32,475	26,312	503	26,815	2,277	-234	24,304	4,579	3,592	7,846	6,895	4,139	1,897
1980	37,374	30,111	175	30,286	2,594	-337	27,356	5,726	4,292	8,850	7,749	4,223	1,964
1981	43,061	34,383	266	34,650	3,177	-352	31,121	7,150	4,790	10,053	8,730	4,283	2,030
1982	46,351	35,925	263	36,188	3,377	-331	32,481	8,346	5,525	10,649	9,393	4,353	2,023
1983	48,426	36,383	232	36,614	3,378	-312	32,924	9,217	6,285	11,018	9,834	4,395	1,984
1984	51,456	38,469	323	38,792	3,663	-302	34,827	10,085	6,544	11,693	10,488	4,400	2,023
1985	53,605	39,411	231	39,642	3,775	-273	35,594	10,963	7,048	12,161	10,897	4,408	2,009
1986	53,665	38,636	235	38,871	3,646	-219	35,006	10,922	7,737	12,177	11,056	4,407	1,928
1987	53,761	38,778	396	39,174	3,609	-185	35,380	10,546	7,834	12,376	11,213	4,344	1,904
1988	56,827	41,049	629	41,678	4,014	-166	37,498	11,108	8,221	13,250	12,055	4,289	1,935
1989	60,256	43,148	469	43,616	4,273	-133	39,210	12,055	8,991	14,168	12,805	4,253	1,953
1990	64,855	46,811	404	47,216	4,760	-111	42,345	12,604	9,905	15,363	13,869	4,222	2,005
1991	68,440	49,195	469	49,664	5,135	-127	44,403	12,712	11,325	16,091	14,561	4,253	2,030
1992	73,201	52,243	577	52,821	5,381	-125	47,315	12,891	12,995	17,051	15,502	4,293	2,038
1993	76,792	54,349	590	54,939	5,634	-129	49,176	13,309	14,307	17,791	16,155	4,316	2,086
1994	81,801	57,537	679	58,216	6,084	-148	51,984	13,992	15,824	18,816	17,059	4,347	2,126
1995	85,828	60,393	673	61,066	6,384	-176	54,505	15,318	16,005	19,601	17,729	4,379	2,194
1996	89,604	63,217	884	64,101	6,696	-204	57,202	16,110	16,292	20,370	18,247	4,399	2,239
1997	94,202	67,211	643	67,855	7,088	-219	60,549	17,066	16,587	21,307	18,972	4,421	2,290
1998	98,864	71,061	464	71,525	7,530	-236	63,759	18,292	16,813	22,265	19,854	4,440	2,336
1999	101,158	73,312	636	73,948	7,651	-217	66,080	17,827	17,251	22,677	20,293	4,461	2,353
2000	106,908	77,536	622	78,158	7,906	-230	70,022	19,197	17,688	23,907	21,391	4,472	2,389
2001	114,767	82,970	659	83,630	8,345	-272	75,013	19,471	20,284	25,630	22,933	4,478	2,398
2002	118,194	86,237	427	86,664	8,663	-299	77,702	19,120	21,373	26,281	23,928	4,497	2,399
2003	122,010	89,335	789	90,124	8,914	-349	80,861	19,727	21,422	26,987	24,818	4,521	2,419
2004	127,387	92,224	788	93,012	9,202	-383	83,427	20,310	23,650	27,983	25,835	4,552	2,434
2005	137,162	96,418	670	97,087	9,430	-362	87,296	22,147	27,720	29,970	27,607	4,577	2,397
2006	144,684	103,289	722	104,011	10,062	-425	93,523	25,601	25,560	33,627	30,569	4,303	2,414
2007	158,433	109,001	755	109,757	10,732	-453	98,571	33,269	26,594	36,208	32,616	4,376	2,501
2008	170,009	117,197	546	117,743	11,399	-498	105,847	33,875	30,287	38,328	34,439	4,436	2,551
2009	165,306	114,891	744	115,636	11,362	-486	103,789	29,406	32,111	36,803	33,867	4,492	2,530
2010	173,007	120,717	805	121,522	11,720	-516	109,286	29,231	34,490	38,067	35,121	4,545	2,537
2011	178,351	122,528	853	123,382	10,831	-416	112,135	31,270	34,947	38,966	35,738	4,577	2,565
2012	187,191	126,760	1,186	127,945	11,163	-350	116,433	35,045	35,713	40,662	37,095	4,604	2,601
2013	189,741	131,269	1,506	132,775	13,007	-410	119,357	33,426	36,958	40,997	37,138	4,628	2,642
2014	197,730	139,267	958	140,224	13,558	-562	126,105	35,016	36,609	42,533	38,502	4,649	2,685
2015	198,426	137,086	603	137,689	13,807	-580	123,302	34,694	40,430	42,484	38,554	4,671	2,697
2016	197,412	133,526	598	134,124	13,760	-736	119,628	35,080	42,704	42,132	38,154	4,686	2,691
2017	203,455	137,062	763	137,825	14,118	-954	122,753	36,492	44,210	43,486	39,587	4,679	2,693
2018	212,321	143,542	637	144,179	14,849	-891	128,439	37,844	46,038	45,464	41,611	4,670	2,725
2019	219,278	147,284	687	147,971	15,114	-712	132,145	38,850	48,283	47,009	42,867	4,665	2,718
2020	233,715	145,341	893	146,234	15,124	-614	130,496	39,278	63,941	50,239	46,488	4,652	2,593
2021	252,319	153,833	1,091	154,924	15,860	-813	138,251	43,418	70,650	54,531	50,057	4,627	2,695
2022	250,171	160,848	852	161,700	17,142	-740	143,819	44,385	61,967	54,527	49,364	4,588	2,785
2023	261,159	169,983	539	170,523	18,134	-766	151,622	46,214	63,322	57,100	52,557	4,574	...

... = Not available.

Personal Income and Employment by Region and State: Maine

(Millions of dollars, except as noted.)

Year	Personal income, total	Derivation of personal income: Earnings by place of work: Nonfarm	Farm	Total	Less: Contributions for government social insurance	Plus: Adjustment for residence	Equals: Net earnings by place of residence	Plus: Dividends, interest, and rent	Plus: Personal current transfer receipts	Per capita (dollars): Personal income	Disposable personal income	Population (thousands)	Total employment (thousands)
1960	1,952	1,507	103	1,610	70	-32	1,508	292	152	2,002	1,825	975	...
1961	1,977	1,548	67	1,615	73	-33	1,509	301	167	1,987	1,812	995	...
1962	2,054	1,609	66	1,675	78	-34	1,563	319	172	2,067	1,878	994	...
1963	2,122	1,660	59	1,719	87	-34	1,598	344	181	2,137	1,952	993	...
1964	2,293	1,766	90	1,856	92	-34	1,730	379	184	2,309	2,125	993	...
1965	2,474	1,864	126	1,989	93	-32	1,865	417	192	2,482	2,286	997	...
1966	2,630	2,031	107	2,138	119	-36	1,984	436	210	2,632	2,420	999	...
1967	2,761	2,175	55	2,230	138	-38	2,055	458	248	2,750	2,515	1,004	...
1968	2,940	2,352	55	2,408	157	-41	2,209	452	279	2,958	2,673	994	...
1969	3,236	2,534	74	2,608	181	-25	2,402	522	312	3,262	2,913	992	443
1970	3,557	2,733	78	2,810	193	-20	2,596	590	371	3,569	3,225	997	446
1971	3,823	2,903	66	2,969	211	-19	2,739	645	438	3,764	3,450	1,016	443
1972	4,188	3,190	65	3,255	242	-22	2,992	706	490	4,047	3,690	1,035	453
1973	4,707	3,513	148	3,661	302	-13	3,347	776	584	4,498	4,064	1,046	470
1974	5,229	3,795	195	3,991	338	-8	3,645	881	703	4,933	4,462	1,060	478
1975	5,652	4,076	82	4,157	357	-21	3,779	974	899	5,266	4,815	1,073	475
1976	6,447	4,705	163	4,869	422	-24	4,422	1,048	977	5,915	5,381	1,090	498
1977	7,008	5,144	129	5,273	461	-26	4,786	1,181	1,041	6,340	5,773	1,105	513
1978	7,741	5,772	90	5,862	531	-25	5,306	1,318	1,117	6,939	6,282	1,115	531
1979	8,589	6,412	76	6,488	607	-18	5,863	1,464	1,262	7,635	6,870	1,125	545
1980	9,655	7,073	49	7,122	668	-15	6,439	1,741	1,475	8,568	7,682	1,127	553
1981	10,639	7,583	118	7,701	771	-48	6,882	2,076	1,681	9,389	8,347	1,133	551
1982	11,563	8,044	104	8,148	831	-46	7,271	2,449	1,843	10,173	8,984	1,137	553
1983	12,471	8,737	72	8,810	910	-33	7,866	2,612	1,992	10,893	9,746	1,145	565
1984	13,761	9,668	118	9,786	1,043	-26	8,717	2,943	2,101	11,908	10,699	1,156	587
1985	14,877	10,525	103	10,628	1,132	-5	9,492	3,163	2,223	12,793	11,444	1,163	606
1986	16,108	11,477	93	11,570	1,239	35	10,366	3,435	2,306	13,766	12,246	1,170	630
1987	17,415	12,596	135	12,731	1,356	59	11,434	3,621	2,360	14,701	12,942	1,185	653
1988	19,257	14,036	117	14,153	1,543	73	12,683	4,067	2,507	15,996	14,134	1,204	686
1989	20,984	15,133	126	15,258	1,650	72	13,681	4,603	2,700	17,201	15,218	1,220	702
1990	21,861	15,631	173	15,804	1,788	71	14,086	4,761	3,014	17,748	15,751	1,232	701
1991	22,262	15,598	127	15,725	1,803	88	14,010	4,782	3,470	17,995	16,087	1,237	678
1992	23,295	16,247	178	16,424	1,905	132	14,651	4,811	3,832	18,809	16,890	1,239	681
1993	24,056	16,785	156	16,942	2,016	191	15,117	4,898	4,042	19,364	17,404	1,242	692
1994	25,037	17,450	148	17,598	2,130	251	15,719	5,088	4,229	20,148	18,042	1,243	703
1995	26,124	17,924	123	18,047	2,208	318	16,157	5,506	4,461	21,009	18,815	1,243	705
1996	27,578	18,705	151	18,856	2,273	371	16,954	5,851	4,772	22,079	19,655	1,249	714
1997	29,185	19,794	105	19,899	2,399	445	17,945	6,247	4,993	23,260	20,567	1,255	727
1998	31,264	21,291	178	21,468	2,544	519	19,443	6,680	5,141	24,830	21,790	1,259	749
1999	32,675	22,861	194	23,055	2,684	584	20,956	6,428	5,291	25,793	22,635	1,267	763
2000	35,091	24,454	207	24,662	2,815	701	22,548	6,922	5,622	27,478	23,993	1,277	784
2001	37,055	25,921	193	26,115	2,949	712	23,878	7,121	6,056	28,821	25,272	1,286	788
2002	38,291	27,016	157	27,173	2,990	677	24,860	6,970	6,461	29,546	26,448	1,296	791
2003	40,163	28,107	162	28,270	3,078	657	25,848	7,286	7,029	30,740	27,812	1,307	794
2004	42,165	29,567	178	29,745	3,237	683	27,191	7,484	7,489	32,096	29,098	1,314	808
2005	43,104	30,136	172	30,307	3,341	690	27,656	7,305	8,143	32,684	29,362	1,319	809
2006	45,226	31,681	170	31,851	3,540	722	29,033	7,854	8,339	34,168	30,595	1,324	818
2007	46,979	32,350	184	32,534	3,698	723	29,559	8,472	8,949	35,402	31,600	1,327	828
2008	49,176	32,827	192	33,019	3,802	706	29,923	8,929	10,324	36,960	33,073	1,331	824
2009	49,337	32,532	184	32,716	3,723	688	29,680	8,447	11,209	37,107	33,916	1,330	801
2010	50,487	33,511	264	33,775	3,830	729	30,674	8,482	11,331	38,018	34,735	1,328	791
2011	52,540	33,932	220	34,151	3,510	796	31,438	9,285	11,817	39,503	35,746	1,330	794
2012	53,227	34,410	268	34,678	3,611	832	31,899	9,575	11,753	39,993	36,214	1,331	797
2013	53,240	34,867	272	35,139	4,180	870	31,828	9,415	11,997	39,952	35,885	1,333	804
2014	54,985	35,969	222	36,192	4,271	928	32,849	9,795	12,341	41,140	36,988	1,337	811
2015	57,357	37,432	225	37,657	4,494	986	34,148	10,363	12,845	42,943	38,407	1,336	817
2016	59,287	38,514	163	38,677	4,618	1,003	35,062	11,032	13,193	44,238	39,446	1,340	827
2017	61,740	40,011	192	40,203	4,787	1,020	36,436	11,626	13,678	45,909	41,150	1,345	834
2018	64,463	41,836	155	41,991	5,056	1,069	38,004	12,005	14,454	47,732	43,024	1,351	844
2019	67,842	43,743	219	43,962	5,270	1,126	39,817	12,811	15,214	49,976	44,751	1,357	842
2020	74,042	45,595	201	45,796	5,483	1,138	41,452	13,092	19,499	54,263	48,782	1,365	813
2021	80,826	50,086	233	50,319	6,067	1,335	45,587	14,076	21,163	58,621	52,045	1,379	849
2022	83,951	53,830	308	54,138	6,590	1,320	48,869	15,150	19,932	60,425	52,858	1,389	877
2023	88,094	56,994	249	57,244	6,942	1,374	51,676	16,126	20,293	63,117	56,489	1,396	...

... = Not available.

Personal Income and Employment by Region and State: Maryland

(Millions of dollars, except as noted.)

Year	Personal income, total	Derivation of personal income: Earnings by place of work: Nonfarm	Farm	Total	Less: Contributions for government social insurance	Plus: Adjustment for residence	Equals: Net earnings by place of residence	Plus: Dividends, interest, and rent	Plus: Personal current transfer receipts	Per capita (dollars): Personal income	Disposable personal income	Population (thousands)	Total employment (thousands)
1960	7,739	5,743	94	5,838	289	627	6,176	1,222	341	2,486	2,178	3,113	...
1961	8,234	6,077	90	6,167	312	690	6,545	1,298	392	2,593	2,287	3,176	...
1962	8,897	6,552	85	6,638	351	774	7,061	1,420	416	2,727	2,377	3,263	...
1963	9,532	6,995	67	7,062	381	865	7,547	1,550	436	2,815	2,445	3,386	...
1964	10,386	7,593	86	7,679	397	953	8,235	1,692	460	2,974	2,622	3,492	...
1965	11,317	8,199	98	8,297	399	1,066	8,964	1,849	504	3,144	2,762	3,600	...
1966	12,477	9,210	79	9,289	526	1,187	9,950	1,970	557	3,377	2,926	3,695	...
1967	13,580	9,797	95	9,891	587	1,451	10,756	2,133	691	3,615	3,125	3,757	...
1968	15,000	10,868	87	10,955	643	1,619	11,930	2,244	826	3,932	3,310	3,815	...
1969	17,236	12,123	133	12,256	751	2,321	13,827	2,465	944	4,456	3,742	3,868	1,679
1970	19,167	13,216	122	13,338	815	2,717	15,240	2,801	1,126	4,867	4,165	3,938	1,702
1971	21,126	14,414	94	14,508	917	3,028	16,620	3,133	1,373	5,252	4,559	4,023	1,729
1972	23,176	15,835	128	15,964	1,060	3,285	18,189	3,414	1,574	5,679	4,854	4,081	1,781
1973	25,561	17,561	209	17,770	1,354	3,485	19,901	3,844	1,816	6,221	5,343	4,109	1,846
1974	27,903	19,131	165	19,296	1,533	3,687	21,450	4,348	2,105	6,751	5,749	4,133	1,868
1975	30,204	20,257	204	20,461	1,624	4,065	22,903	4,655	2,647	7,265	6,290	4,157	1,846
1976	32,907	22,268	175	22,443	1,808	4,359	24,995	5,057	2,855	7,887	6,823	4,172	1,866
1977	35,676	24,203	130	24,332	1,974	4,701	27,059	5,574	3,042	8,505	7,290	4,195	1,919
1978	39,617	26,948	184	27,132	2,262	5,074	29,944	6,319	3,354	9,407	8,050	4,212	2,004
1979	43,549	29,721	160	29,881	2,611	5,401	32,671	7,073	3,805	10,311	8,763	4,223	2,059
1980	48,519	32,476	58	32,534	2,866	5,863	35,531	8,453	4,535	11,477	9,798	4,228	2,070
1981	53,996	35,670	129	35,800	3,381	6,253	38,671	10,130	5,195	12,669	10,695	4,262	2,095
1982	58,547	37,520	144	37,664	3,617	6,771	40,819	11,946	5,783	13,670	11,618	4,283	2,084
1983	62,799	40,823	90	40,913	4,071	7,143	43,986	12,510	6,303	14,559	12,533	4,313	2,151
1984	69,587	45,375	266	45,641	4,673	7,820	48,789	14,155	6,644	15,941	13,695	4,365	2,243
1985	75,466	49,797	278	50,075	5,284	8,423	53,213	15,230	7,023	17,100	14,751	4,413	2,342
1986	81,514	54,136	288	54,424	5,837	9,033	57,620	16,400	7,494	18,167	15,690	4,487	2,428
1987	87,723	59,251	300	59,550	6,331	9,663	62,883	17,061	7,780	19,214	16,383	4,566	2,553
1988	96,685	65,472	365	65,837	7,214	10,709	69,331	19,049	8,304	20,757	17,937	4,658	2,647
1989	104,522	69,951	366	70,317	7,758	11,515	74,073	21,403	9,046	22,110	18,928	4,727	2,704
1990	110,892	74,155	357	74,512	8,395	12,115	78,232	22,751	9,910	23,104	19,835	4,800	2,737
1991	115,010	75,897	310	76,207	8,671	12,660	80,196	23,652	11,162	23,627	20,451	4,868	2,662
1992	120,582	79,300	343	79,643	9,016	13,419	84,045	24,022	12,514	24,492	21,295	4,923	2,636
1993	125,401	82,522	320	82,842	9,364	13,639	87,117	25,228	13,056	25,222	21,899	4,972	2,659
1994	131,301	86,487	308	86,796	9,916	14,036	90,915	26,743	13,642	26,140	22,629	5,023	2,706
1995	137,087	90,139	215	90,354	10,287	14,003	94,069	28,716	14,302	27,039	23,306	5,070	2,765
1996	143,495	93,888	395	94,283	10,645	14,376	98,014	30,186	15,296	28,070	24,055	5,112	2,806
1997	151,433	100,296	280	100,576	11,307	14,308	103,577	32,246	15,610	29,363	24,768	5,157	2,870
1998	163,509	108,959	325	109,284	11,980	15,668	112,972	34,250	16,288	31,417	26,691	5,204	2,935
1999	173,126	116,908	350	117,258	12,721	16,747	121,284	34,580	17,262	32,948	27,950	5,255	3,008
2000	188,437	126,761	416	127,177	13,591	18,990	132,576	37,615	18,246	35,480	30,019	5,311	3,092
2001	198,927	134,797	417	135,214	14,646	19,868	140,436	38,615	19,877	37,012	31,389	5,375	3,120
2002	206,707	142,178	225	142,403	15,442	20,239	147,200	38,158	21,350	37,995	32,956	5,440	3,157
2003	215,973	149,011	310	149,321	16,157	21,106	154,271	38,721	22,983	39,295	34,399	5,496	3,191
2004	230,279	159,369	444	159,813	17,306	22,552	165,059	41,226	23,995	41,515	36,402	5,547	3,248
2005	242,214	167,959	384	168,343	18,231	23,614	173,727	42,504	25,984	43,311	37,606	5,592	3,311
2006	254,883	176,187	315	176,503	19,381	22,952	180,074	47,772	27,037	45,293	39,102	5,627	3,378
2007	265,895	181,210	308	181,517	20,242	23,616	184,892	51,650	29,354	47,033	40,301	5,653	3,441
2008	278,708	188,043	429	188,471	21,009	23,080	190,542	54,734	33,432	49,026	42,392	5,685	3,431
2009	277,624	188,780	438	189,218	20,985	23,236	191,469	50,139	36,016	48,448	42,894	5,730	3,359
2010	287,359	196,458	387	196,844	21,770	23,637	198,712	49,453	39,194	49,617	43,934	5,792	3,345
2011	303,270	205,709	480	206,189	20,187	23,283	209,285	53,631	40,355	51,803	45,334	5,854	3,395
2012	310,420	210,707	628	211,335	20,768	22,946	213,513	56,140	40,768	52,490	45,986	5,914	3,439
2013	309,330	212,330	793	213,122	23,569	22,919	212,472	54,636	42,221	51,880	44,894	5,962	3,494
2014	318,983	217,905	640	218,545	24,139	22,086	216,492	57,733	44,758	53,084	45,875	6,009	3,538
2015	332,956	228,053	494	228,547	25,382	22,412	225,577	60,697	46,682	55,041	47,369	6,049	3,603
2016	344,195	236,885	395	237,280	25,965	22,575	233,891	61,269	49,036	56,614	48,740	6,080	3,659
2017	356,079	243,876	616	244,491	26,791	23,037	240,737	65,313	50,029	58,251	50,299	6,113	3,697
2018	367,831	250,490	375	250,865	28,085	24,569	247,350	68,048	52,433	59,919	51,868	6,139	3,753
2019	380,342	256,424	572	256,996	29,036	26,577	254,537	70,994	54,811	61,707	53,003	6,164	3,745
2020	400,176	257,977	266	258,243	29,466	27,754	256,530	70,024	73,622	64,820	56,137	6,174	3,622
2021	426,367	273,426	657	274,083	31,521	27,446	270,008	75,696	80,663	69,047	58,801	6,175	3,750
2022	432,933	287,059	865	287,924	33,510	29,924	284,338	79,742	68,854	70,236	58,648	6,164	3,887
2023	456,408	303,851	503	304,354	35,336	31,505	300,523	83,667	72,218	73,849	63,688	6,180	...

... = Not available.

Personal Income and Employment by Region and State: Massachusetts

(Millions of dollars, except as noted.)

Year	Personal income, total	Derivation of personal income: Earnings by place of work: Nonfarm	Farm	Total	Less: Contributions for government social insurance	Plus: Adjustment for residence	Equals: Net earnings by place of residence	Plus: Dividends, interest, and rent	Plus: Personal current transfer receipts	Per capita (dollars): Personal income	Disposable personal income	Population (thousands)	Total employment (thousands)
1960	13,147	10,795	68	10,864	499	-75	10,290	1,937	921	2,548	2,229	5,160	...
1961	13,814	11,303	60	11,363	528	-82	10,753	2,035	1,027	2,647	2,335	5,219	...
1962	14,597	11,957	61	12,017	617	-92	11,309	2,237	1,051	2,773	2,435	5,263	...
1963	15,203	12,363	61	12,424	680	-98	11,646	2,448	1,110	2,845	2,498	5,344	...
1964	16,233	13,084	63	13,147	698	-108	12,341	2,742	1,151	2,980	2,658	5,448	...
1965	17,320	13,887	69	13,956	714	-122	13,121	2,987	1,212	3,148	2,804	5,502	...
1966	18,650	15,162	72	15,234	942	-141	14,151	3,199	1,301	3,369	2,974	5,535	...
1967	20,261	16,325	56	16,381	1,033	-157	15,191	3,465	1,605	3,622	3,190	5,594	...
1968	22,127	17,783	65	17,848	1,139	-175	16,534	3,657	1,936	3,938	3,416	5,618	...
1969	24,042	19,391	66	19,458	1,262	-133	18,062	3,823	2,157	4,255	3,627	5,650	2,679
1970	25,961	20,692	69	20,761	1,327	-111	19,323	4,088	2,551	4,552	3,941	5,704	2,679
1971	27,742	21,885	63	21,948	1,448	-108	20,393	4,329	3,020	4,834	4,243	5,739	2,644
1972	29,978	23,764	63	23,827	1,651	-105	22,071	4,593	3,314	5,203	4,492	5,762	2,697
1973	32,574	25,968	71	26,039	2,075	-124	23,840	5,018	3,716	5,632	4,897	5,784	2,787
1974	35,182	27,560	70	27,630	2,275	-141	25,213	5,564	4,405	6,090	5,279	5,777	2,811
1975	37,802	28,677	69	28,746	2,296	-152	26,298	5,772	5,732	6,560	5,779	5,762	2,728
1976	40,689	31,218	76	31,295	2,556	-172	28,567	6,176	5,946	7,078	6,185	5,749	2,756
1977	44,298	34,335	79	34,414	2,817	-218	31,379	6,811	6,108	7,712	6,710	5,744	2,833
1978	48,939	38,438	104	38,542	3,248	-278	35,016	7,447	6,476	8,522	7,388	5,743	2,958
1979	54,486	43,061	91	43,152	3,796	-373	38,983	8,335	7,169	9,482	8,147	5,746	3,074
1980	61,412	47,684	106	47,789	4,215	-493	43,082	10,142	8,189	10,688	9,137	5,746	3,134
1981	68,412	52,262	116	52,378	4,981	-621	46,776	12,332	9,304	11,859	10,047	5,769	3,142
1982	75,002	56,170	132	56,301	5,484	-747	50,070	14,876	10,056	12,996	11,136	5,771	3,143
1983	81,459	61,918	164	62,082	6,141	-918	55,023	15,781	10,655	14,046	12,093	5,799	3,215
1984	91,789	70,529	183	70,711	7,225	-1,176	62,311	18,274	11,204	15,715	13,594	5,841	3,402
1985	99,275	77,403	160	77,564	8,002	-1,371	68,191	19,362	11,722	16,881	14,514	5,881	3,510
1986	107,092	84,175	175	84,350	8,883	-1,494	73,973	20,786	12,332	18,143	15,526	5,903	3,605
1987	115,602	92,452	153	92,605	9,651	-1,665	81,290	21,634	12,679	19,477	16,562	5,935	3,632
1988	127,634	101,838	172	102,010	10,787	-1,881	89,342	24,631	13,661	21,343	18,412	5,980	3,739
1989	135,076	106,030	153	106,183	11,166	-2,031	92,987	26,683	15,406	22,455	19,287	6,015	3,710
1990	139,213	107,297	153	107,451	11,186	-2,074	94,190	27,759	17,264	23,115	19,862	6,023	3,615
1991	141,495	107,264	173	107,436	11,384	-2,237	93,815	27,885	19,796	23,510	20,345	6,018	3,451
1992	148,384	113,789	171	113,960	11,985	-2,346	99,630	28,096	20,658	24,613	21,351	6,029	3,482
1993	154,232	118,617	164	118,782	12,586	-2,561	103,634	29,342	21,256	25,448	22,013	6,061	3,548
1994	162,008	124,844	150	124,994	13,380	-2,764	108,850	30,672	22,486	26,579	22,909	6,095	3,616
1995	171,516	131,467	146	131,613	14,168	-2,826	114,619	33,072	23,824	27,928	23,918	6,141	3,649
1996	182,244	140,289	166	140,455	14,935	-3,094	122,427	35,251	24,567	29,490	24,987	6,180	3,713
1997	193,169	149,916	168	150,084	15,992	-3,402	130,690	37,051	25,428	31,026	26,016	6,226	3,802
1998	205,509	160,461	108	160,568	17,060	-3,602	139,907	40,051	25,552	32,767	27,143	6,272	3,896
1999	219,633	175,059	108	175,167	18,309	-4,185	152,673	40,503	26,458	34,767	28,655	6,317	3,962
2000	244,147	196,523	131	196,654	20,253	-5,050	171,351	44,912	27,884	38,381	30,947	6,361	4,070
2001	254,058	203,031	110	203,141	20,769	-5,197	177,175	46,400	30,483	39,711	32,755	6,398	4,076
2002	252,960	201,807	131	201,938	20,650	-5,091	176,198	43,680	33,082	39,419	33,862	6,417	4,022
2003	257,918	204,690	130	204,821	20,858	-5,095	178,868	44,102	34,948	40,158	34,822	6,423	3,992
2004	270,866	217,868	146	218,014	22,643	-5,590	189,780	44,721	36,364	42,242	36,660	6,412	4,029
2005	282,138	224,294	124	224,419	23,700	-5,430	195,290	47,789	39,060	44,061	37,803	6,403	4,071
2006	303,265	236,927	131	237,059	24,662	-5,699	206,698	55,635	40,933	47,311	40,412	6,410	4,110
2007	319,407	248,603	132	248,735	25,858	-6,110	216,768	60,012	42,627	49,662	41,770	6,432	4,203
2008	333,451	254,315	193	254,508	26,685	-6,077	221,747	63,033	48,671	51,546	43,818	6,469	4,216
2009	330,773	252,534	165	252,699	26,299	-5,472	220,929	56,527	53,318	50,751	44,801	6,518	4,116
2010	346,270	267,076	166	267,241	26,852	-5,996	234,393	55,732	56,145	52,708	46,213	6,570	4,115
2011	363,076	276,225	165	276,390	25,041	-6,648	244,701	61,969	56,406	54,764	47,176	6,630	4,175
2012	376,591	284,498	231	284,730	25,909	-7,379	251,442	68,379	56,771	56,269	48,680	6,693	4,253
2013	379,250	291,705	214	291,919	30,063	-7,342	254,514	67,391	57,345	56,130	47,557	6,757	4,354
2014	396,489	302,263	168	302,432	31,528	-6,940	263,964	73,395	59,130	58,141	49,000	6,819	4,448
2015	422,548	320,136	142	320,278	32,704	-7,751	279,823	78,988	63,736	61,548	51,670	6,865	4,631
2016	438,599	331,104	136	331,241	33,825	-8,302	289,114	83,240	66,245	63,487	53,568	6,909	4,710
2017	459,779	348,072	136	348,207	35,532	-8,838	303,838	88,886	67,055	66,076	55,820	6,958	4,778
2018	483,954	366,159	125	366,283	37,419	-9,660	319,204	94,356	70,394	69,195	58,721	6,994	4,855
2019	507,713	387,026	177	387,204	39,233	-11,764	336,207	99,111	72,395	72,359	61,234	7,017	4,873
2020	541,421	391,814	158	391,972	39,261	-12,073	340,638	96,239	104,543	77,371	66,091	6,998	4,600
2021	583,363	422,647	137	422,784	43,042	-9,994	369,748	105,520	108,095	83,434	69,720	6,992	4,777
2022	590,400	444,915	165	445,080	45,397	-11,514	388,169	110,979	91,253	84,551	68,866	6,983	5,002
2023	614,807	463,221	146	463,367	46,871	-11,763	404,732	117,057	93,017	87,812	74,342	7,001	...

... = Not available.

Personal Income and Employment by Region and State: Michigan

(Millions of dollars, except as noted.)

Year	Personal income, total	Derivation of personal income: Earnings by place of work: Nonfarm	Farm	Total	Less: Contributions for government social insurance	Plus: Adjustment for residence	Equals: Net earnings by place of residence	Plus: Dividends, interest, and rent	Plus: Personal current transfer receipts	Per capita (dollars): Personal income	Disposable personal income	Population (thousands)	Total employment (thousands)
1960	18,884	15,838	240	16,078	824	37	15,290	2,482	1,112	2,411	2,148	7,834	...
1961	18,957	15,471	300	15,771	786	38	15,023	2,602	1,332	2,402	2,158	7,893	...
1962	20,319	16,771	275	17,047	888	42	16,200	2,815	1,304	2,561	2,280	7,933	...
1963	21,692	18,060	300	18,360	1,038	44	17,366	2,998	1,327	2,692	2,388	8,058	...
1964	23,774	19,843	295	20,139	1,077	49	19,111	3,298	1,366	2,904	2,608	8,187	...
1965	26,375	22,126	274	22,400	1,122	54	21,332	3,568	1,476	3,156	2,823	8,357	...
1966	28,764	24,429	349	24,778	1,572	63	23,270	3,877	1,617	3,379	3,006	8,512	...
1967	29,992	25,177	276	25,453	1,652	68	23,869	4,122	2,002	3,475	3,086	8,630	...
1968	33,161	27,965	304	28,269	1,854	76	26,491	4,357	2,312	3,813	3,325	8,696	...
1969	36,068	30,702	351	31,054	2,206	105	28,952	4,557	2,559	4,107	3,519	8,781	3,640
1970	37,362	30,875	341	31,216	2,196	113	29,132	5,014	3,216	4,200	3,656	8,897	3,558
1971	40,644	33,471	310	33,781	2,450	106	31,437	5,369	3,838	4,530	3,982	8,972	3,571
1972	45,132	37,389	427	37,816	2,905	114	35,024	5,790	4,318	5,001	4,319	9,025	3,687
1973	50,383	42,183	561	42,745	3,800	140	39,085	6,373	4,925	5,554	4,828	9,072	3,858
1974	53,913	43,801	649	44,450	4,082	140	40,507	7,253	6,153	5,918	5,170	9,109	3,854
1975	57,745	45,051	578	45,629	4,091	149	41,687	7,983	8,075	6,340	5,629	9,108	3,695
1976	64,458	51,691	478	52,169	4,794	191	47,566	8,569	8,323	7,070	6,176	9,117	3,844
1977	72,466	59,122	559	59,681	5,491	217	54,406	9,514	8,545	7,913	6,848	9,157	4,016
1978	80,773	66,736	510	67,245	6,391	260	61,115	10,575	9,083	8,778	7,527	9,202	4,186
1979	88,473	72,515	545	73,060	7,194	292	66,158	11,842	10,473	9,566	8,199	9,249	4,228
1980	94,702	73,189	536	73,725	7,174	337	66,888	13,988	13,826	10,232	8,900	9,256	4,030
1981	101,184	77,169	515	77,684	8,186	378	69,876	16,662	14,646	10,987	9,521	9,209	3,978
1982	104,754	76,677	410	77,087	8,241	381	69,227	19,178	16,349	11,492	10,098	9,115	3,823
1983	111,587	81,930	222	82,152	8,954	413	73,612	20,676	17,300	12,333	10,809	9,048	3,866
1984	123,022	91,555	551	92,106	10,356	479	82,229	23,303	17,491	13,594	11,941	9,049	4,040
1985	133,512	100,998	663	101,661	11,666	501	90,497	24,964	18,051	14,710	12,831	9,076	4,233
1986	141,960	108,387	493	108,879	12,551	488	96,817	26,214	18,930	15,553	13,586	9,128	4,349
1987	147,029	112,807	665	113,472	12,896	507	101,083	26,482	19,464	16,003	13,933	9,187	4,483
1988	157,390	121,619	585	122,204	14,305	515	108,413	28,674	20,302	17,074	14,945	9,218	4,582
1989	169,458	128,976	981	129,956	15,143	512	115,326	32,166	21,966	18,313	15,962	9,253	4,709
1990	177,358	134,521	776	135,297	16,053	458	119,702	33,853	23,803	19,048	16,691	9,311	4,791
1991	181,544	136,787	667	137,453	16,559	488	121,382	33,681	26,481	19,312	17,010	9,400	4,721
1992	192,090	146,116	757	146,873	17,547	552	129,879	34,161	28,051	20,265	17,960	9,479	4,751
1993	202,231	154,077	737	154,813	18,603	628	136,837	35,411	29,982	21,198	18,629	9,540	4,812
1994	217,482	165,969	563	166,532	20,421	754	146,865	40,341	30,276	22,660	19,847	9,598	4,985
1995	229,979	175,290	695	175,985	21,539	797	155,242	42,781	31,955	23,767	20,734	9,676	5,142
1996	241,755	183,671	618	184,289	22,020	823	163,092	45,107	33,557	24,773	21,495	9,759	5,247
1997	253,076	192,907	608	193,515	23,099	909	171,326	46,265	35,486	25,800	22,276	9,809	5,330
1998	268,712	206,810	628	207,438	24,260	993	184,171	49,295	35,247	27,286	23,429	9,848	5,384
1999	282,129	219,980	821	220,801	25,631	1,081	196,250	48,107	37,772	28,506	24,498	9,897	5,486
2000	301,060	235,341	607	235,949	26,849	1,098	210,197	51,820	39,043	30,250	26,131	9,952	5,621
2001	306,670	237,231	564	237,795	26,634	1,189	212,350	50,846	43,475	30,694	26,699	9,991	5,526
2002	306,427	237,558	601	238,158	26,848	1,216	212,526	48,838	45,063	30,595	27,173	10,016	5,466
2003	313,961	241,374	710	242,084	27,221	1,271	216,134	50,527	47,301	31,267	28,054	10,041	5,442
2004	322,698	246,894	1,152	248,046	28,187	1,367	221,226	52,156	49,317	32,092	28,939	10,055	5,468
2005	329,235	250,083	1,044	251,126	29,075	1,443	223,494	53,292	52,449	32,756	29,372	10,051	5,492
2006	336,843	252,220	1,144	253,364	29,870	1,630	225,124	55,726	55,993	33,563	30,012	10,036	5,457
2007	346,732	253,650	1,236	254,887	30,244	1,676	226,319	59,171	61,242	34,669	30,838	10,001	5,457
2008	356,356	250,575	1,383	251,958	30,261	1,682	223,378	63,266	69,712	35,826	31,942	9,947	5,338
2009	339,100	231,801	868	232,668	28,285	1,516	205,900	55,778	77,422	34,247	31,388	9,902	5,046
2010	352,074	239,124	1,421	240,546	28,656	1,579	213,469	55,921	82,685	35,635	32,498	9,880	5,038
2011	372,954	250,210	2,646	252,856	26,610	1,724	227,970	62,443	82,542	37,689	33,962	9,895	5,165
2012	387,339	261,443	1,653	263,096	27,744	1,908	237,261	67,950	82,129	39,043	35,104	9,921	5,234
2013	390,858	268,080	2,187	270,268	32,228	1,913	239,953	67,515	83,390	39,293	34,958	9,947	5,323
2014	407,267	277,902	1,379	279,281	33,296	2,068	248,054	72,756	86,458	40,830	36,348	9,975	5,412
2015	429,285	292,132	1,099	293,231	34,695	2,124	260,661	77,348	91,276	42,984	38,078	9,987	5,502
2016	441,557	300,939	930	301,869	35,680	2,265	268,453	79,868	93,236	44,081	38,882	10,017	5,576
2017	454,895	314,015	1,047	315,061	37,091	2,320	280,290	81,385	93,220	45,264	40,100	10,050	5,631
2018	474,208	326,137	1,059	327,196	39,019	2,531	290,709	86,249	97,250	47,088	41,962	10,071	5,715
2019	489,493	335,178	937	336,115	39,914	2,649	298,850	88,059	102,584	48,569	43,297	10,078	5,713
2020	531,530	333,540	1,929	335,469	39,485	2,588	298,572	88,654	144,304	52,780	47,545	10,071	5,388
2021	568,132	359,266	2,367	361,633	42,185	3,242	322,690	97,307	148,136	56,597	50,175	10,038	5,602
2022	572,325	384,584	2,383	386,966	46,547	3,409	343,828	105,143	123,354	57,043	49,696	10,033	5,864
2023	599,366	406,569	1,541	408,110	49,448	3,567	362,229	110,563	126,575	59,714	53,246	10,037	...

... = Not available.

Personal Income and Employment by Region and State: Minnesota

(Millions of dollars, except as noted.)

Year	Personal income, total	Derivation of personal income: Earnings by place of work: Nonfarm	Farm	Total	Less: Contributions for government social insurance	Plus: Adjustment for residence	Equals: Net earnings by place of residence	Plus: Dividends, interest, and rent	Plus: Personal current transfer receipts	Per capita (dollars): Personal income	Disposable personal income	Population (thousands)	Total employment (thousands)
1960	7,472	5,596	514	6,111	260	-1	5,849	1,116	507	2,182	1,948	3,425	...
1961	7,853	5,842	540	6,382	270	-3	6,110	1,172	571	2,263	2,023	3,470	...
1962	8,278	6,282	467	6,748	303	-3	6,443	1,245	590	2,356	2,096	3,513	...
1963	8,779	6,540	621	7,162	339	-4	6,819	1,336	625	2,486	2,220	3,531	...
1964	9,132	6,997	402	7,399	348	-4	7,048	1,433	651	2,566	2,317	3,558	...
1965	10,088	7,547	652	8,199	372	-7	7,821	1,559	708	2,808	2,526	3,592	...
1966	10,934	8,323	733	9,056	522	-13	8,521	1,652	761	3,023	2,701	3,617	...
1967	11,750	9,035	643	9,678	602	-17	9,059	1,766	925	3,211	2,859	3,659	...
1968	12,934	9,982	680	10,662	683	-24	9,955	1,921	1,058	3,493	3,092	3,703	...
1969	14,388	11,172	720	11,892	781	-33	11,079	2,147	1,162	3,829	3,331	3,758	1,691
1970	15,709	11,935	876	12,811	825	-26	11,959	2,376	1,373	4,117	3,632	3,815	1,699
1971	16,766	12,725	796	13,521	910	-27	12,585	2,588	1,594	4,353	3,880	3,852	1,706
1972	18,229	13,797	959	14,756	1,036	-29	13,691	2,776	1,762	4,714	4,139	3,867	1,780
1973	21,370	15,357	2,179	17,536	1,333	-35	16,168	3,137	2,066	5,500	4,891	3,885	1,878
1974	23,012	16,889	1,644	18,533	1,525	-31	16,977	3,611	2,424	5,903	5,146	3,898	1,921
1975	24,891	18,306	1,264	19,571	1,613	-32	17,925	4,042	2,924	6,340	5,571	3,926	1,920
1976	26,907	20,452	782	21,235	1,845	-40	19,350	4,343	3,214	6,801	5,936	3,957	1,977
1977	30,293	22,648	1,501	24,150	2,043	-54	22,052	4,860	3,380	7,612	6,630	3,980	2,034
1978	33,989	25,807	1,625	27,432	2,409	-69	24,954	5,407	3,628	8,487	7,354	4,005	2,122
1979	37,792	29,364	1,245	30,609	2,855	-94	27,661	6,076	4,056	9,359	8,029	4,038	2,218
1980	42,011	32,001	959	32,960	3,107	-101	29,752	7,392	4,866	10,284	8,864	4,085	2,248
1981	46,516	34,622	1,040	35,662	3,604	-132	31,926	9,007	5,583	11,313	9,717	4,112	2,233
1982	49,838	36,143	819	36,962	3,838	-155	32,969	10,592	6,277	12,063	10,426	4,131	2,192
1983	52,590	38,691	119	38,810	4,161	-183	34,465	11,359	6,766	12,698	11,023	4,141	2,219
1984	59,599	43,444	1,444	44,889	4,796	-240	39,852	12,651	7,097	14,335	12,570	4,158	2,324
1985	63,324	46,561	1,343	47,904	5,234	-288	42,382	13,402	7,540	15,134	13,274	4,184	2,385
1986	66,976	49,447	1,641	51,088	5,701	-326	45,061	14,036	7,879	15,927	14,016	4,205	2,417
1987	71,216	53,311	2,138	55,450	6,107	-376	48,967	14,120	8,128	16,815	14,666	4,235	2,509
1988	75,349	57,661	1,253	58,914	6,828	-452	51,633	15,127	8,588	17,539	15,335	4,296	2,580
1989	82,290	61,745	2,051	63,796	7,303	-439	56,054	16,886	9,351	18,969	16,562	4,338	2,634
1990	87,487	65,807	1,956	67,763	7,829	-471	59,463	17,974	10,051	19,929	17,336	4,390	2,692
1991	90,312	68,763	1,207	69,970	8,278	-476	61,216	18,291	10,805	20,337	17,791	4,441	2,717
1992	96,933	74,587	1,401	75,987	8,869	-509	66,609	18,575	11,748	21,562	18,819	4,496	2,762
1993	99,873	77,969	187	78,156	9,313	-515	68,328	19,150	12,395	21,921	19,069	4,556	2,817
1994	107,012	82,615	1,340	83,954	9,990	-561	73,403	20,571	13,037	23,211	20,182	4,610	2,904
1995	113,163	87,329	519	87,848	10,530	-610	76,708	22,638	13,817	24,283	21,006	4,660	2,995
1996	121,959	93,303	1,921	95,224	11,136	-685	83,403	24,091	14,464	25,878	22,135	4,713	3,056
1997	128,933	99,731	898	100,629	11,836	-767	88,026	26,216	14,692	27,067	23,094	4,763	3,109
1998	140,269	108,801	1,397	110,198	12,712	-847	96,639	28,424	15,206	29,141	24,783	4,813	3,189
1999	147,376	115,841	1,261	117,103	13,570	-951	102,582	28,807	15,988	30,240	25,906	4,873	3,257
2000	159,595	125,396	1,453	126,849	14,525	-1,037	111,288	31,180	17,128	32,348	27,520	4,934	3,331
2001	166,509	130,650	1,029	131,679	15,034	-1,084	115,561	31,726	19,222	33,417	28,635	4,983	3,347
2002	170,085	134,084	1,010	135,093	15,354	-1,113	118,627	30,589	20,870	33,889	29,564	5,019	3,338
2003	177,862	139,269	1,827	141,096	16,037	-1,181	123,878	32,101	21,884	35,195	31,084	5,054	3,347
2004	188,675	148,484	2,445	150,930	16,942	-1,259	132,729	32,938	23,009	37,084	32,902	5,088	3,390
2005	193,584	151,998	2,903	154,901	17,690	-1,322	135,889	33,583	24,112	37,812	33,137	5,120	3,448
2006	203,250	157,033	2,520	159,553	18,559	-1,276	139,718	36,978	26,553	39,362	34,321	5,164	3,496
2007	215,185	164,569	2,579	167,148	19,325	-1,393	146,430	39,678	29,078	41,325	35,867	5,207	3,540
2008	225,534	167,945	4,015	171,960	19,933	-1,422	150,605	41,969	32,960	42,983	37,341	5,247	3,526
2009	216,335	160,412	2,155	162,567	19,268	-1,148	142,151	38,002	36,183	40,963	36,641	5,281	3,424
2010	225,972	166,380	3,187	169,567	19,583	-1,106	148,878	38,067	39,027	42,539	37,886	5,312	3,408
2011	241,600	175,123	4,370	179,494	18,321	-1,143	160,030	42,229	39,340	45,137	39,699	5,353	3,469
2012	255,428	183,425	6,012	189,437	19,064	-927	169,446	46,626	39,356	47,404	41,715	5,388	3,505
2013	257,508	188,739	5,621	194,360	22,424	-890	171,046	45,693	40,768	47,419	41,138	5,430	3,556
2014	270,190	197,708	3,735	201,443	23,117	-920	177,406	49,539	43,245	49,365	42,759	5,473	3,604
2015	282,988	206,862	3,154	210,016	23,937	-1,024	185,055	53,228	44,706	51,362	44,169	5,510	3,663
2016	288,867	212,080	1,465	213,545	24,621	-1,197	187,726	55,027	46,113	51,990	44,693	5,556	3,698
2017	301,749	221,346	2,050	223,396	25,693	-1,336	196,367	57,275	48,107	53,832	46,529	5,605	3,736
2018	317,565	231,490	1,751	233,241	26,969	-1,320	204,953	61,389	51,223	56,205	48,872	5,650	3,777
2019	329,116	239,615	998	240,612	27,942	-1,495	211,176	64,750	53,190	57,874	50,263	5,687	3,783
2020	349,887	240,958	3,349	244,307	28,257	-1,511	214,539	64,239	71,109	61,270	53,609	5,711	3,607
2021	381,789	258,926	4,507	263,433	30,000	-1,703	231,730	71,747	78,313	66,770	57,585	5,718	3,712
2022	393,569	275,395	5,746	281,141	32,429	-1,833	246,879	78,843	67,847	68,874	58,638	5,714	3,845
2023	412,364	289,230	4,666	293,896	34,027	-1,836	258,033	83,575	70,756	71,866	62,963	5,738	...

... = Not available.

Personal Income and Employment by Region and State: Mississippi

(Millions of dollars, except as noted.)

Year	Personal income, total	Derivation of personal income: Earnings by place of work: Nonfarm	Farm	Total	Less: Contributions for government social insurance	Plus: Adjustment for residence	Equals: Net earnings by place of residence	Plus: Dividends, interest, and rent	Plus: Personal current transfer receipts	Per capita (dollars): Personal income	Disposable personal income	Population (thousands)	Total employment (thousands)
1960	2,764	2,031	281	2,312	101	12	2,224	308	233	1,267	1,174	2,182	...
1961	2,997	2,122	353	2,475	104	13	2,384	351	262	1,359	1,270	2,206	...
1962	3,133	2,277	297	2,574	115	15	2,474	385	273	1,397	1,294	2,243	...
1963	3,442	2,422	432	2,854	136	17	2,735	418	290	1,534	1,419	2,244	...
1964	3,563	2,588	370	2,958	143	20	2,834	427	303	1,590	1,482	2,241	...
1965	3,869	2,874	352	3,226	152	22	3,096	445	328	1,722	1,601	2,246	...
1966	4,217	3,219	347	3,566	197	23	3,392	465	360	1,879	1,732	2,245	...
1967	4,563	3,441	386	3,826	226	25	3,625	507	432	2,048	1,890	2,228	...
1968	4,993	3,823	364	4,187	253	31	3,966	539	489	2,250	2,065	2,219	...
1969	5,541	4,222	349	4,571	291	36	4,316	673	552	2,496	2,279	2,220	909
1970	6,077	4,487	394	4,881	310	37	4,608	780	689	2,736	2,488	2,221	917
1971	6,737	4,918	436	5,354	351	59	5,062	861	814	2,974	2,746	2,266	939
1972	7,677	5,655	494	6,148	421	74	5,801	958	918	3,327	3,029	2,307	979
1973	8,779	6,358	692	7,050	538	94	6,606	1,109	1,065	3,736	3,421	2,350	1,019
1974	9,648	7,017	515	7,532	616	123	7,039	1,297	1,312	4,056	3,677	2,379	1,031
1975	10,463	7,519	377	7,895	653	149	7,391	1,441	1,631	4,360	4,015	2,400	1,001
1976	11,878	8,537	576	9,112	757	179	8,535	1,557	1,786	4,887	4,461	2,430	1,039
1977	13,222	9,598	609	10,208	850	218	9,575	1,738	1,910	5,375	4,919	2,460	1,071
1978	14,722	10,879	455	11,334	982	272	10,624	1,998	2,100	5,917	5,355	2,488	1,101
1979	16,637	12,059	704	12,763	1,129	325	11,960	2,281	2,396	6,634	5,981	2,508	1,114
1980	18,103	13,012	185	13,198	1,210	410	12,398	2,826	2,879	7,168	6,460	2,525	1,111
1981	20,329	14,215	334	14,548	1,422	440	13,566	3,499	3,263	8,007	7,163	2,539	1,107
1982	21,462	14,610	425	15,035	1,497	457	13,995	3,879	3,588	8,394	7,644	2,557	1,079
1983	22,458	15,392	102	15,494	1,594	513	14,413	4,095	3,951	8,746	7,934	2,568	1,088
1984	24,514	16,655	480	17,135	1,773	572	15,934	4,495	4,086	9,509	8,668	2,578	1,117
1985	25,815	17,582	438	18,020	1,914	603	16,709	4,826	4,280	9,974	9,088	2,588	1,124
1986	26,776	18,498	204	18,702	2,032	592	17,261	4,980	4,535	10,324	9,448	2,594	1,131
1987	28,256	19,421	587	20,008	2,125	630	18,512	5,023	4,721	10,916	9,956	2,589	1,141
1988	30,286	20,790	733	21,523	2,374	672	19,821	5,436	5,029	11,737	10,747	2,580	1,169
1989	32,711	22,229	569	22,798	2,542	715	20,971	6,244	5,495	12,707	11,577	2,574	1,189
1990	34,437	23,665	493	24,158	2,803	749	22,103	6,371	5,962	13,353	12,163	2,579	1,203
1991	36,311	24,732	588	25,320	2,989	804	23,136	6,467	6,708	13,973	12,782	2,599	1,211
1992	39,043	26,698	671	27,369	3,192	823	25,000	6,528	7,515	14,881	13,626	2,624	1,234
1993	41,569	28,775	584	29,359	3,453	840	26,746	6,811	8,012	15,656	14,293	2,655	1,287
1994	44,970	31,222	844	32,066	3,779	838	29,125	7,345	8,500	16,724	15,218	2,689	1,335
1995	47,565	32,721	679	33,400	3,946	920	30,374	7,901	9,291	17,470	15,871	2,723	1,365
1996	50,455	34,139	1,078	35,217	4,069	962	32,110	8,387	9,959	18,360	16,630	2,748	1,389
1997	53,371	36,134	991	37,125	4,284	1,112	33,954	9,083	10,334	19,219	17,367	2,777	1,415
1998	56,581	38,719	967	39,686	4,579	1,188	36,294	9,868	10,419	20,173	18,195	2,805	1,445
1999	58,494	40,448	946	41,394	4,783	1,287	37,898	9,866	10,731	20,681	18,643	2,828	1,470
2000	61,605	42,172	792	42,964	4,926	1,478	39,516	10,563	11,526	21,628	19,541	2,848	1,476
2001	65,064	43,147	1,583	44,730	5,013	1,541	41,258	10,939	12,867	22,806	20,625	2,853	1,456
2002	66,326	44,734	639	45,373	5,238	1,585	41,720	10,791	13,815	23,202	21,303	2,859	1,455
2003	69,012	46,404	1,182	47,586	5,403	1,669	43,851	10,720	14,440	24,060	22,222	2,868	1,453
2004	73,055	48,872	1,801	50,673	5,726	1,780	46,727	10,805	15,523	25,287	23,561	2,889	1,464
2005	77,635	51,017	1,754	52,770	5,940	1,898	48,729	11,447	17,460	26,716	24,729	2,906	1,474
2006	80,836	53,794	816	54,610	6,398	2,114	50,326	12,926	17,583	27,827	25,499	2,905	1,508
2007	86,187	55,539	1,151	56,690	6,663	2,270	52,297	15,522	18,368	29,432	27,004	2,928	1,539
2008	90,603	57,756	742	58,498	6,890	2,411	54,020	15,791	20,791	30,736	28,099	2,948	1,537
2009	89,414	55,791	847	56,638	6,801	2,367	52,204	14,982	22,228	30,220	28,153	2,959	1,492
2010	92,714	57,552	892	58,444	6,894	2,429	53,980	14,645	24,090	31,213	28,902	2,970	1,491
2011	96,643	59,156	581	59,737	6,408	2,651	55,981	15,728	24,935	32,454	30,068	2,978	1,510
2012	99,733	61,267	815	62,082	6,622	2,853	58,313	16,505	24,915	33,441	30,924	2,982	1,520
2013	101,472	62,335	2,232	64,567	7,524	2,993	60,036	15,969	25,467	33,976	31,237	2,987	1,533
2014	103,443	63,847	1,621	65,468	7,739	3,054	60,783	16,446	26,214	34,624	31,849	2,988	1,557
2015	104,772	64,385	855	65,241	7,944	3,183	60,479	16,984	27,309	35,100	32,164	2,985	1,568
2016	106,356	65,196	659	65,856	8,120	3,224	60,960	17,180	28,216	35,638	32,620	2,984	1,581
2017	109,133	66,500	1,442	67,942	8,377	3,317	62,882	17,800	28,450	36,580	33,647	2,983	1,592
2018	111,918	68,507	1,143	69,651	8,585	3,510	64,575	17,920	29,423	37,624	34,785	2,975	1,603
2019	116,256	70,850	1,017	71,867	8,944	3,754	66,676	18,715	30,865	39,157	36,118	2,969	1,607
2020	125,761	72,734	604	73,338	9,256	3,770	67,852	19,105	38,804	42,510	39,421	2,958	1,573
2021	137,382	78,561	1,658	80,219	9,751	3,929	74,396	20,623	42,362	46,577	42,852	2,950	1,626
2022	136,330	82,484	1,202	83,687	10,570	4,317	77,433	22,142	36,756	46,388	42,186	2,939	1,674
2023	141,428	86,711	334	87,045	11,105	4,627	80,567	23,230	37,631	48,110	44,436	2,940	...

... = Not available.

Personal Income and Employment by Region and State: Missouri

(Millions of dollars, except as noted.)

Year	Personal income, total	Derivation of personal income: Earnings by place of work: Nonfarm	Earnings by place of work: Farm	Earnings by place of work: Total	Less: Contributions for government social insurance	Plus: Adjustment for residence	Equals: Net earnings by place of residence	Plus: Dividends, interest, and rent	Plus: Personal current transfer receipts	Per capita (dollars): Personal income	Per capita (dollars): Disposable personal income	Population (thousands)	Total employment (thousands)
1960	9,630	7,698	443	8,141	358	-180	7,603	1,356	671	2,226	1,984	4,326	...
1961	9,955	7,877	484	8,361	375	-185	7,801	1,409	745	2,289	2,040	4,349	...
1962	10,489	8,346	486	8,832	408	-202	8,222	1,496	771	2,407	2,138	4,357	...
1963	11,002	8,855	440	9,295	469	-227	8,599	1,595	808	2,505	2,219	4,392	...
1964	11,620	9,486	335	9,821	491	-250	9,079	1,710	830	2,616	2,354	4,442	...
1965	12,635	10,171	533	10,704	517	-275	9,911	1,835	888	2,828	2,528	4,467	...
1966	13,536	11,194	417	11,611	695	-314	10,602	1,974	960	2,993	2,666	4,523	...
1967	14,407	11,953	404	12,356	797	-351	11,209	2,078	1,120	3,174	2,825	4,539	...
1968	15,950	13,133	478	13,612	898	-387	12,326	2,310	1,313	3,492	3,086	4,568	...
1969	16,913	14,263	450	14,713	955	-752	13,006	2,478	1,428	3,645	3,163	4,640	2,216
1970	18,480	15,173	525	15,698	1,005	-694	13,999	2,788	1,692	3,945	3,471	4,685	2,203
1971	19,939	16,187	571	16,758	1,109	-680	14,970	3,018	1,951	4,222	3,750	4,723	2,200
1972	21,682	17,549	714	18,263	1,261	-698	16,304	3,266	2,112	4,562	4,003	4,753	2,242
1973	24,090	19,085	1,215	20,301	1,584	-729	17,987	3,653	2,450	5,045	4,473	4,775	2,325
1974	25,775	20,574	640	21,214	1,767	-756	18,691	4,192	2,892	5,386	4,737	4,785	2,341
1975	28,213	21,854	698	22,552	1,842	-771	19,939	4,618	3,655	5,883	5,248	4,795	2,291
1976	30,912	24,496	471	24,967	2,097	-839	22,032	4,976	3,904	6,409	5,667	4,824	2,365
1977	34,252	27,206	717	27,924	2,332	-969	24,623	5,555	4,075	7,070	6,250	4,845	2,424
1978	38,130	30,397	920	31,317	2,697	-1,121	27,499	6,202	4,428	7,828	6,869	4,871	2,512
1979	42,514	33,687	1,179	34,866	3,090	-1,287	30,489	7,017	5,008	8,695	7,592	4,889	2,576
1980	46,139	35,990	242	36,232	3,279	-1,495	31,458	8,582	6,099	9,374	8,190	4,922	2,549
1981	51,480	38,771	773	39,543	3,789	-1,629	34,125	10,502	6,852	10,438	9,075	4,932	2,540
1982	55,044	40,570	347	40,918	4,044	-1,685	35,189	12,385	7,470	11,166	9,664	4,929	2,516
1983	58,777	43,678	-103	43,575	4,389	-1,709	37,477	13,278	8,022	11,889	10,515	4,944	2,562
1984	65,105	48,321	426	48,746	4,997	-1,858	41,892	14,841	8,372	13,086	11,628	4,975	2,667
1985	69,704	51,821	798	52,619	5,479	-1,988	45,153	15,722	8,830	13,940	12,340	5,000	2,738
1986	73,379	55,042	584	55,626	5,879	-2,053	47,694	16,387	9,298	14,608	12,948	5,023	2,801
1987	77,026	58,668	739	59,407	6,196	-2,170	51,042	16,410	9,574	15,232	13,457	5,057	2,836
1988	82,057	62,711	658	63,369	6,836	-2,253	54,280	17,668	10,109	16,147	14,316	5,082	2,885
1989	87,942	66,534	912	67,446	7,299	-2,386	57,761	19,209	10,972	17,258	15,238	5,096	2,938
1990	91,897	69,600	708	70,308	7,872	-2,600	59,837	20,169	11,890	17,917	15,819	5,129	2,972
1991	96,075	71,629	589	72,218	8,214	-2,592	61,413	20,767	13,895	18,580	16,530	5,171	2,942
1992	102,078	76,312	862	77,174	8,666	-2,716	65,792	21,450	14,836	19,566	17,448	5,217	2,957
1993	106,723	79,824	500	80,324	9,093	-2,834	68,397	22,398	15,928	20,247	18,029	5,271	3,041
1994	113,257	84,809	725	85,534	9,774	-2,860	72,900	23,656	16,701	21,271	18,879	5,324	3,113
1995	119,400	90,015	219	90,234	10,357	-3,110	76,766	24,830	17,803	22,201	19,638	5,378	3,196
1996	126,394	94,801	1,052	95,854	10,779	-3,210	81,865	25,924	18,605	23,270	20,480	5,432	3,255
1997	134,118	100,826	1,059	101,886	11,410	-3,388	87,087	27,723	19,308	24,469	21,434	5,481	3,328
1998	140,840	106,686	545	107,230	12,010	-3,551	91,670	29,233	19,937	25,506	22,247	5,522	3,385
1999	146,173	113,122	241	113,363	12,637	-3,680	97,046	28,252	20,875	26,281	22,913	5,562	3,423
2000	156,202	120,047	788	120,835	13,301	-3,964	103,571	30,334	22,298	27,857	24,288	5,607	3,471
2001	161,531	123,503	836	124,340	13,689	-4,019	106,632	30,301	24,598	28,634	24,979	5,641	3,452
2002	165,390	127,641	401	128,042	14,054	-4,132	109,856	29,277	26,257	29,144	26,008	5,675	3,437
2003	171,593	131,186	1,038	132,224	14,486	-4,183	113,556	30,622	27,416	30,054	27,126	5,709	3,445
2004	180,454	137,279	2,270	139,549	15,022	-4,282	120,245	31,285	28,924	31,396	28,465	5,748	3,479
2005	186,771	142,579	1,429	144,008	15,775	-4,573	123,660	32,185	30,926	32,256	28,956	5,790	3,533
2006	197,834	149,795	1,254	151,049	16,689	-4,976	129,384	35,578	32,873	33,860	30,225	5,843	3,586
2007	207,411	154,485	1,401	155,886	17,396	-4,843	133,646	38,640	35,125	35,228	31,253	5,888	3,636
2008	219,922	160,206	2,045	162,251	18,248	-5,427	138,576	41,867	39,479	37,124	32,963	5,924	3,626
2009	216,425	157,426	1,637	159,063	17,716	-5,120	136,227	37,385	42,812	36,306	33,128	5,961	3,523
2010	221,760	160,045	1,481	161,526	17,697	-4,928	138,901	37,288	45,572	36,984	33,719	5,996	3,475
2011	230,858	163,114	2,185	165,299	16,297	-4,338	144,664	39,792	46,402	38,402	34,639	6,012	3,507
2012	240,968	168,960	1,401	170,361	16,733	-4,880	148,748	45,299	46,921	39,983	36,102	6,027	3,528
2013	242,493	173,871	2,894	176,765	19,427	-4,730	152,607	42,042	47,843	40,121	35,887	6,044	3,566
2014	250,784	177,272	3,273	180,545	20,010	-4,789	155,746	45,684	49,354	41,380	36,948	6,060	3,597
2015	259,350	184,753	781	185,534	21,073	-4,947	159,514	48,014	51,822	42,677	37,867	6,077	3,656
2016	267,049	188,864	1,086	189,950	21,470	-5,111	163,369	50,456	53,224	43,826	38,911	6,093	3,701
2017	273,774	195,477	1,078	196,555	22,210	-5,470	168,876	50,259	54,640	44,781	39,922	6,114	3,736
2018	286,084	202,350	605	202,956	23,159	-5,795	174,002	55,386	56,697	46,680	41,810	6,129	3,777
2019	297,349	210,297	1,106	211,403	24,154	-6,209	181,040	57,023	59,286	48,401	43,306	6,143	3,779
2020	320,593	214,911	1,649	216,560	24,950	-5,955	185,655	60,623	74,315	52,091	46,946	6,154	3,693
2021	345,961	227,692	2,292	229,985	25,930	-6,405	197,650	65,441	82,870	56,068	49,827	6,170	3,796
2022	357,195	243,373	2,636	246,009	28,230	-7,161	210,618	72,803	73,774	57,825	50,695	6,177	3,934
2023	379,838	259,868	1,976	261,844	30,164	-7,737	223,942	77,787	78,109	61,302	54,995	6,196	...

... = Not available.

Personal Income and Employment by Region and State: Montana

(Millions of dollars, except as noted.)

Year	Personal income, total	Derivation of personal income: Earnings by place of work: Nonfarm	Farm	Total	Less: Contributions for government social insurance	Plus: Adjustment for residence	Equals: Net earnings by place of residence	Plus: Dividends, interest, and rent	Plus: Personal current transfer receipts	Per capita (dollars): Personal income	Disposable personal income	Population (thousands)	Total employment (thousands)
1960	1,451	1,011	162	1,173	62	0	1,111	233	108	2,137	1,933	679	...
1961	1,455	1,059	110	1,169	63	(L)	1,106	231	117	2,090	1,878	696	...
1962	1,701	1,121	277	1,398	64	-0	1,334	248	119	2,437	2,223	698	...
1963	1,692	1,172	213	1,385	72	-0	1,313	258	121	2,406	2,181	703	...
1964	1,728	1,226	169	1,395	75	-0	1,321	281	126	2,447	2,245	706	...
1965	1,856	1,303	190	1,493	76	-0	1,417	305	134	2,629	2,398	706	...
1966	1,990	1,390	227	1,616	99	-0	1,517	330	143	2,814	2,556	707	...
1967	2,029	1,429	191	1,620	108	-0	1,511	349	169	2,895	2,620	701	...
1968	2,128	1,505	196	1,701	115	-1	1,585	352	191	3,040	2,750	700	...
1969	2,351	1,632	242	1,874	127	-1	1,747	394	210	3,387	2,980	694	298
1970	2,604	1,754	291	2,046	137	-1	1,908	455	241	3,735	3,339	697	301
1971	2,787	1,919	251	2,170	151	-1	2,018	489	280	3,920	3,549	711	307
1972	3,230	2,156	401	2,557	177	-0	2,380	541	310	4,492	4,022	719	319
1973	3,745	2,404	575	2,980	227	0	2,753	632	360	5,149	4,594	727	333
1974	4,070	2,705	466	3,171	262	1	2,909	738	423	5,521	4,909	737	344
1975	4,479	3,010	400	3,410	283	2	3,129	836	514	5,978	5,365	749	344
1976	4,807	3,419	225	3,644	324	3	3,323	913	570	6,337	5,639	759	359
1977	5,198	3,839	71	3,910	369	4	3,545	1,038	615	6,739	5,956	771	372
1978	6,091	4,361	303	4,664	433	3	4,235	1,182	675	7,768	6,908	784	390
1979	6,549	4,806	119	4,925	497	6	4,434	1,356	760	8,299	7,276	789	396
1980	7,216	5,108	120	5,228	542	13	4,699	1,622	895	9,148	8,043	789	393
1981	8,194	5,562	227	5,789	633	25	5,181	1,979	1,034	10,303	9,093	795	395
1982	8,633	5,714	172	5,886	664	17	5,239	2,236	1,158	10,737	9,583	804	391
1983	9,082	6,039	127	6,166	700	9	5,476	2,338	1,268	11,157	9,999	814	398
1984	9,594	6,392	44	6,436	758	6	5,684	2,557	1,353	11,687	10,508	821	408
1985	9,736	6,525	-84	6,441	790	3	5,655	2,651	1,431	11,840	10,647	822	406
1986	10,123	6,529	238	6,767	805	-2	5,960	2,635	1,528	12,440	11,298	814	402
1987	10,355	6,713	317	7,030	827	-3	6,200	2,555	1,601	12,862	11,582	805	406
1988	10,680	7,148	110	7,258	927	-1	6,331	2,656	1,693	13,346	11,962	800	416
1989	11,764	7,565	420	7,985	997	-3	6,985	2,923	1,856	14,711	13,106	800	424
1990	12,379	8,033	396	8,429	1,118	-4	7,306	3,041	2,033	15,470	13,808	800	433
1991	13,217	8,627	551	9,179	1,220	-11	7,948	3,129	2,140	16,323	14,650	810	444
1992	14,009	9,338	489	9,827	1,324	-2	8,501	3,187	2,321	16,965	15,203	826	456
1993	15,154	10,048	773	10,821	1,462	1	9,360	3,301	2,493	17,939	16,097	845	470
1994	15,574	10,634	390	11,024	1,547	5	9,482	3,504	2,589	18,082	16,149	861	494
1995	16,400	11,009	339	11,348	1,564	9	9,792	3,835	2,774	18,710	16,742	877	504
1996	17,174	11,496	310	11,806	1,563	11	10,255	4,039	2,880	19,378	17,292	886	519
1997	17,910	11,963	239	12,202	1,585	13	10,630	4,340	2,940	20,127	17,886	890	526
1998	19,126	12,772	299	13,071	1,643	18	11,446	4,627	3,052	21,431	19,018	892	536
1999	19,497	13,180	389	13,570	1,692	21	11,898	4,568	3,031	21,723	19,207	898	543
2000	20,771	13,996	261	14,256	1,793	26	12,490	4,891	3,390	22,982	20,277	904	553
2001	21,685	14,472	350	14,823	1,908	28	12,943	5,072	3,671	23,910	21,108	907	560
2002	22,350	15,308	198	15,505	2,013	26	13,519	5,023	3,808	24,516	22,052	912	565
2003	24,015	16,253	358	16,611	2,114	24	14,522	5,513	3,981	26,114	23,718	920	571
2004	26,072	17,542	555	18,097	2,249	23	15,871	5,958	4,243	28,034	25,527	930	586
2005	28,052	19,023	588	19,611	2,446	20	17,185	6,325	4,542	29,839	26,892	940	601
2006	30,363	20,726	162	20,888	2,653	15	18,250	7,196	4,917	31,870	28,551	953	617
2007	32,647	21,868	427	22,295	2,855	17	19,457	7,943	5,247	33,841	30,087	965	636
2008	34,731	22,473	522	22,995	2,930	27	20,093	8,673	5,965	35,569	31,812	976	636
2009	33,927	22,087	395	22,481	2,876	37	19,643	7,819	6,465	34,479	31,475	984	619
2010	35,671	22,955	565	23,520	2,943	74	20,651	7,961	7,059	36,000	32,947	991	616
2011	38,083	24,252	678	24,930	2,788	180	22,322	8,771	6,990	38,152	34,555	998	623
2012	40,437	25,443	750	26,193	2,871	358	23,681	9,569	7,187	40,220	36,295	1,005	633
2013	40,786	26,041	980	27,021	3,328	447	24,140	9,274	7,371	40,146	35,951	1,016	642
2014	42,901	27,035	724	27,759	3,485	547	24,822	10,325	7,755	41,855	37,306	1,025	649
2015	44,583	28,079	747	28,826	3,588	428	25,666	10,794	8,124	43,100	38,335	1,034	661
2016	45,283	28,411	547	28,957	3,554	269	25,672	10,833	8,779	43,306	38,587	1,046	668
2017	48,003	29,805	284	30,089	3,826	312	26,576	11,842	9,586	45,373	40,540	1,058	674
2018	50,352	30,899	542	31,441	4,045	381	27,776	12,647	9,929	47,211	42,374	1,067	684
2019	53,393	32,478	725	33,203	4,181	415	29,438	13,376	10,579	49,647	44,286	1,075	686
2020	58,209	34,106	878	34,984	4,473	294	30,806	13,920	13,483	53,540	47,769	1,087	684
2021	64,542	38,276	276	38,552	4,833	266	33,985	15,848	14,709	58,337	51,266	1,106	716
2022	68,477	41,511	1,017	42,528	5,390	338	37,476	17,891	13,111	60,984	52,822	1,123	746
2023	72,407	44,209	877	45,085	5,796	366	39,655	19,258	13,494	63,918	56,691	1,133	...

... = Not available.

Personal Income and Employment by Region and State: Nebraska

(Millions of dollars, except as noted.)

Year	Personal income, total	Derivation of personal income: Earnings by place of work: Nonfarm	Farm	Total	Less: Contributions for government social insurance	Plus: Adjustment for residence	Equals: Net earnings by place of residence	Plus: Dividends, interest, and rent	Plus: Personal current transfer receipts	Per capita (dollars): Personal income	Disposable personal income	Population (thousands)	Total employment (thousands)
1960	3,140	2,154	392	2,546	116	-11	2,419	536	185	2,216	2,005	1,417	...
1961	3,214	2,263	319	2,583	119	-11	2,452	557	205	2,223	1,996	1,446	...
1962	3,494	2,388	437	2,825	128	-10	2,687	591	216	2,386	2,165	1,464	...
1963	3,591	2,471	394	2,865	140	-10	2,716	646	229	2,433	2,201	1,476	...
1964	3,691	2,618	312	2,930	146	-9	2,775	680	236	2,491	2,282	1,482	...
1965	4,061	2,732	497	3,230	148	-8	3,074	730	258	2,761	2,537	1,471	...
1966	4,360	2,935	592	3,527	196	-8	3,323	757	280	2,995	2,729	1,456	...
1967	4,513	3,166	488	3,654	228	-8	3,418	754	341	3,097	2,809	1,457	...
1968	4,815	3,457	444	3,901	245	-8	3,648	774	394	3,282	2,952	1,467	...
1969	5,379	3,830	604	4,434	269	-103	4,062	888	429	3,649	3,220	1,474	704
1970	5,798	4,151	542	4,693	289	-110	4,294	1,007	498	3,897	3,468	1,488	715
1971	6,369	4,468	688	5,156	321	-113	4,722	1,084	562	4,234	3,833	1,504	728
1972	7,053	4,905	808	5,713	364	-122	5,227	1,206	620	4,645	4,131	1,518	748
1973	8,226	5,471	1,227	6,698	468	-125	6,105	1,379	741	5,382	4,798	1,529	775
1974	8,565	6,061	771	6,832	541	-133	6,158	1,561	847	5,570	4,906	1,538	793
1975	9,766	6,605	1,109	7,713	580	-142	6,992	1,739	1,036	6,336	5,693	1,541	790
1976	10,217	7,468	588	8,056	662	-149	7,246	1,867	1,105	6,597	5,901	1,549	811
1977	11,073	8,140	532	8,672	722	-148	7,801	2,095	1,177	7,123	6,291	1,554	831
1978	12,811	9,100	1,085	10,185	831	-171	9,184	2,323	1,305	8,208	7,287	1,561	854
1979	13,835	10,164	754	10,919	966	-199	9,753	2,629	1,453	8,844	7,751	1,564	876
1980	14,766	11,014	107	11,121	1,044	-216	9,861	3,208	1,697	9,392	8,244	1,572	877
1981	17,139	11,868	834	12,702	1,201	-254	11,247	3,937	1,956	10,858	9,614	1,579	871
1982	18,416	12,340	767	13,107	1,279	-262	11,566	4,695	2,154	11,643	10,160	1,582	861
1983	19,060	12,961	550	13,511	1,351	-276	11,884	4,845	2,331	12,031	10,768	1,584	867
1984	21,199	14,166	1,161	15,327	1,520	-316	13,491	5,263	2,444	13,344	12,079	1,589	886
1985	22,345	14,896	1,450	16,346	1,646	-342	14,359	5,390	2,596	14,101	12,757	1,585	898
1986	22,995	15,506	1,414	16,920	1,766	-344	14,810	5,470	2,715	14,606	13,213	1,574	898
1987	23,980	16,415	1,636	18,051	1,867	-343	15,841	5,362	2,777	15,307	13,794	1,567	925
1988	25,708	17,530	2,031	19,560	2,086	-379	17,095	5,717	2,896	16,359	14,741	1,571	947
1989	27,277	18,699	1,847	20,546	2,231	-392	17,924	6,234	3,119	17,320	15,511	1,575	965
1990	29,238	19,999	2,199	22,198	2,466	-391	19,341	6,514	3,383	18,486	16,525	1,582	988
1991	30,344	20,980	1,997	22,977	2,606	-427	19,945	6,760	3,640	19,014	17,046	1,596	992
1992	32,191	22,441	2,117	24,558	2,735	-471	21,352	6,888	3,952	19,974	17,946	1,612	999
1993	33,259	23,559	1,746	25,305	2,880	-487	21,938	7,101	4,220	20,460	18,357	1,626	1,021
1994	35,390	25,213	1,851	27,064	3,086	-502	23,476	7,512	4,401	21,592	19,346	1,639	1,061
1995	37,383	26,903	1,324	28,227	3,235	-548	24,444	8,251	4,688	22,561	20,105	1,657	1,071
1996	40,707	28,434	2,596	31,030	3,415	-599	27,016	8,703	4,988	24,321	21,654	1,674	1,097
1997	41,958	30,040	1,757	31,797	3,637	-677	27,484	9,304	5,171	24,880	21,933	1,686	1,111
1998	44,747	32,115	1,647	33,762	3,856	-714	29,192	10,044	5,511	26,387	23,220	1,696	1,138
1999	46,824	34,145	1,575	35,721	4,061	-800	30,860	10,138	5,826	27,467	24,164	1,705	1,157
2000	49,570	36,088	1,450	37,538	4,242	-868	32,428	11,032	6,110	28,924	25,384	1,714	1,174
2001	51,912	37,631	1,815	39,446	4,412	-875	34,159	11,033	6,720	30,184	26,657	1,720	1,175
2002	52,804	39,246	1,062	40,307	4,605	-901	34,802	10,857	7,146	30,553	27,510	1,728	1,166
2003	56,102	40,448	2,672	43,119	4,773	-937	37,410	11,239	7,454	32,268	29,397	1,739	1,169
2004	58,597	42,751	2,759	45,510	4,989	-943	39,578	11,210	7,810	33,496	30,527	1,749	1,180
2005	60,598	43,955	2,980	46,934	5,251	-940	40,743	11,587	8,268	34,401	31,085	1,761	1,192
2006	63,317	46,713	1,589	48,302	5,616	-856	41,829	12,555	8,933	35,718	31,989	1,773	1,208
2007	68,099	48,727	2,742	51,469	5,846	-947	44,676	14,002	9,421	38,184	34,040	1,783	1,231
2008	72,377	50,485	3,051	53,536	6,044	-980	46,513	15,283	10,582	40,291	36,096	1,796	1,237
2009	71,460	50,911	2,707	53,618	6,056	-957	46,605	13,802	11,053	39,422	36,123	1,813	1,223
2010	75,194	53,418	3,151	56,568	6,271	-898	49,399	13,926	11,868	41,086	37,521	1,830	1,220
2011	84,096	57,010	6,447	63,457	5,735	-963	56,759	15,244	12,093	45,611	41,496	1,844	1,233
2012	86,236	59,511	4,593	64,104	5,901	-999	57,205	16,848	12,184	46,391	41,958	1,859	1,251
2013	86,022	58,925	6,709	65,635	6,752	-969	57,914	15,774	12,335	45,918	41,185	1,873	1,266
2014	91,085	63,626	5,641	69,267	7,098	-937	61,233	16,933	12,918	48,195	43,154	1,890	1,283
2015	94,682	66,457	5,130	71,587	7,385	-1,020	63,182	17,900	13,600	49,716	44,548	1,904	1,303
2016	93,560	66,249	3,848	70,096	7,586	-1,067	61,443	18,031	14,086	48,695	43,546	1,921	1,311
2017	95,824	69,058	2,158	71,217	7,941	-1,167	62,110	18,905	14,809	49,538	44,427	1,934	1,318
2018	100,068	71,854	2,001	73,856	8,219	-1,123	64,514	19,844	15,710	51,439	46,401	1,945	1,330
2019	104,490	73,071	2,982	76,053	8,543	-1,138	66,373	21,530	16,587	53,450	48,044	1,955	1,328
2020	111,348	74,247	3,841	78,088	8,993	-1,190	67,904	22,400	21,043	56,715	51,096	1,963	1,306
2021	123,081	79,448	5,654	85,102	9,430	-1,257	74,415	24,747	23,919	62,660	55,923	1,964	1,334
2022	126,474	86,275	3,700	89,975	10,238	-1,349	78,388	26,950	21,135	64,263	56,647	1,968	1,372
2023	134,135	91,592	4,184	95,776	10,861	-1,445	83,470	28,637	22,028	67,800	61,114	1,978	...

... = Not available.

Personal Income and Employment by Region and State: Nevada

(Millions of dollars, except as noted.)

Year	Personal income, total	Derivation of personal income: Earnings by place of work: Nonfarm	Farm	Total	Less: Contributions for government social insurance	Plus: Adjustment for residence	Equals: Net earnings by place of residence	Plus: Dividends, interest, and rent	Plus: Personal current transfer receipts	Per capita (dollars): Personal income	Disposable personal income	Population (thousands)	Total employment (thousands)
1960	896	746	15	761	37	-2	722	134	41	3,079	2,730	291	...
1961	993	822	13	835	40	-3	792	152	49	3,153	2,771	315	...
1962	1,186	1,002	19	1,021	50	-4	966	168	51	3,369	2,975	352	...
1963	1,330	1,146	20	1,166	66	-6	1,094	178	58	3,350	2,941	397	...
1964	1,443	1,241	12	1,252	67	-6	1,180	198	65	3,388	3,040	426	...
1965	1,545	1,306	14	1,319	66	-5	1,249	225	72	3,480	3,130	444	...
1966	1,630	1,381	18	1,399	80	-4	1,316	237	78	3,656	3,279	446	...
1967	1,732	1,452	17	1,469	87	-3	1,379	258	95	3,857	3,451	449	...
1968	2,014	1,670	20	1,689	101	-4	1,585	316	113	4,340	3,802	464	...
1969	2,279	1,924	32	1,956	132	-33	1,791	363	125	4,747	4,068	480	244
1970	2,560	2,135	34	2,169	144	-39	1,986	427	148	5,191	4,615	493	256
1971	2,860	2,366	35	2,401	165	-41	2,195	481	184	5,501	4,945	520	267
1972	3,197	2,634	42	2,677	194	-44	2,439	540	218	5,847	5,225	547	280
1973	3,630	3,010	56	3,066	257	-54	2,756	621	254	6,381	5,703	569	304
1974	4,025	3,300	35	3,335	288	-56	2,992	718	315	6,746	6,006	597	317
1975	4,544	3,646	33	3,679	313	-58	3,308	798	438	7,331	6,692	620	326
1976	5,171	4,178	36	4,214	368	-68	3,778	902	490	7,994	7,184	647	349
1977	5,978	4,909	27	4,936	439	-84	4,413	1,030	535	8,815	7,873	678	384
1978	7,226	5,994	23	6,017	555	-116	5,346	1,276	604	10,045	8,883	719	432
1979	8,372	6,950	9	6,959	681	-132	6,147	1,513	713	10,942	9,593	765	468
1980	9,681	7,877	57	7,934	778	-160	6,996	1,820	866	11,949	10,545	810	489
1981	10,998	8,829	28	8,857	931	-167	7,759	2,184	1,055	12,975	11,411	848	500
1982	11,753	9,116	33	9,149	953	-168	8,027	2,550	1,175	13,332	11,828	882	494
1983	12,531	9,656	26	9,683	1,049	-177	8,457	2,789	1,285	13,893	12,426	902	499
1984	13,634	10,514	36	10,549	1,191	-190	9,168	3,090	1,376	14,741	13,200	925	523
1985	14,791	11,352	29	11,381	1,313	-200	9,868	3,412	1,512	15,553	13,845	951	545
1986	15,979	12,283	28	12,311	1,452	-217	10,642	3,652	1,685	16,295	14,468	981	570
1987	17,407	13,601	48	13,649	1,615	-240	11,794	3,815	1,798	17,009	15,021	1,023	616
1988	19,826	15,637	65	15,701	1,873	-281	13,547	4,305	1,975	18,443	16,235	1,075	662
1989	22,329	17,406	79	17,485	2,119	-326	15,040	5,009	2,280	19,632	17,276	1,137	710
1990	25,039	19,593	82	19,675	2,497	-377	16,802	5,629	2,609	20,512	18,023	1,221	756
1991	27,544	21,109	76	21,185	2,660	-346	18,179	6,144	3,221	21,250	18,862	1,296	769
1992	30,460	23,280	73	23,353	2,890	-305	20,158	6,657	3,645	22,540	19,972	1,351	776
1993	32,933	25,264	119	25,383	3,163	-344	21,876	7,207	3,849	23,337	20,604	1,411	819
1994	36,442	27,991	82	28,073	3,534	-354	24,186	8,220	4,037	24,306	21,541	1,499	898
1995	40,076	30,668	70	30,739	3,879	-349	26,510	9,186	4,379	25,339	22,447	1,582	953
1996	44,337	33,947	70	34,017	4,196	-368	29,453	10,169	4,714	26,608	23,308	1,666	1,024
1997	48,450	37,158	70	37,228	4,477	-328	32,423	11,002	5,025	27,464	24,114	1,764	1,089
1998	54,217	41,713	93	41,806	4,785	-350	36,671	12,195	5,352	29,256	25,555	1,853	1,131
1999	58,624	45,777	85	45,862	5,086	-382	40,395	12,646	5,583	30,301	26,453	1,935	1,189
2000	64,313	49,569	104	49,673	4,986	-338	44,348	13,963	6,001	31,858	27,743	2,019	1,254
2001	68,027	52,424	118	52,542	5,292	-354	46,896	14,342	6,789	32,418	28,441	2,098	1,285
2002	69,953	53,731	90	53,821	5,460	-364	47,997	14,304	7,651	32,180	28,757	2,174	1,300
2003	74,518	56,537	93	56,630	5,544	-410	50,676	15,624	8,219	33,136	29,853	2,249	1,353
2004	82,525	62,727	127	62,855	6,066	-495	56,294	17,355	8,876	35,173	31,486	2,346	1,441
2005	92,194	69,633	135	69,767	6,668	-549	62,551	20,066	9,577	37,907	33,539	2,432	1,534
2006	99,485	75,434	129	75,563	7,743	-474	67,346	21,790	10,349	39,437	34,940	2,523	1,604
2007	103,706	77,491	98	77,588	8,139	-400	69,050	23,342	11,314	39,870	35,362	2,601	1,644
2008	102,536	73,630	150	73,780	7,695	-320	65,765	23,409	13,362	38,640	34,684	2,654	1,619
2009	96,983	68,859	126	68,985	7,431	-307	61,247	20,471	15,265	36,125	33,092	2,685	1,513
2010	100,750	71,184	145	71,329	7,310	-252	63,767	20,157	16,827	37,288	34,193	2,702	1,478
2011	104,596	72,567	206	72,773	6,913	-145	65,714	21,831	17,051	38,589	35,178	2,711	1,502
2012	108,696	73,772	114	73,886	7,272	-157	66,457	25,044	17,195	39,671	36,048	2,740	1,519
2013	108,914	75,701	105	75,805	8,012	-136	67,658	23,685	17,571	39,319	35,212	2,770	1,561
2014	115,514	78,760	208	78,968	8,812	-177	69,979	26,265	19,270	41,112	36,986	2,810	1,609
2015	125,089	83,974	140	84,114	9,392	-128	74,595	29,406	21,089	43,783	39,224	2,857	1,665
2016	129,879	86,754	86	86,840	9,840	-201	76,798	30,777	22,304	44,700	39,679	2,906	1,725
2017	138,847	92,626	116	92,742	10,187	-195	82,360	33,053	23,434	46,977	42,025	2,956	1,781
2018	148,408	99,023	112	99,135	10,878	-207	88,051	35,421	24,937	49,278	44,133	3,012	1,849
2019	159,293	106,322	175	106,497	11,963	-282	94,252	38,318	26,723	51,905	46,713	3,069	1,884
2020	170,269	103,695	177	103,872	11,716	-187	91,970	38,976	39,324	54,646	49,061	3,116	1,771
2021	192,006	118,201	215	118,415	13,106	-222	105,088	43,739	43,179	61,020	54,219	3,147	1,913
2022	197,291	131,372	178	131,550	15,095	-533	115,921	47,365	34,005	62,092	53,876	3,177	2,062
2023	208,159	140,161	147	140,308	16,184	-604	123,520	49,803	34,837	65,168	57,934	3,194	...

... = Not available.

Personal Income and Employment by Region and State: New Hampshire

(Millions of dollars, except as noted.)

Year	Personal income, total	Derivation of personal income									Per capita (dollars)		Population (thousands)	Total employment (thousands)
		Earnings by place of work			Less: Contributions for government social insurance	Plus: Adjustment for residence	Equals: Net earnings by place of residence	Plus: Dividends, interest, and rent	Plus: Personal current transfer receipts		Personal income	Disposable personal income		
		Nonfarm	Farm	Total										
1960	1,383	1,037	20	1,056	56	82	1,083	210	90		2,271	2,036	609	...
1961	1,456	1,081	21	1,101	56	89	1,134	221	102		2,356	2,119	618	...
1962	1,557	1,153	19	1,172	62	98	1,208	244	105		2,464	2,210	632	...
1963	1,625	1,197	18	1,215	68	103	1,250	262	113		2,503	2,235	649	...
1964	1,747	1,283	18	1,301	71	112	1,342	290	116		2,635	2,401	663	...
1965	1,884	1,377	21	1,399	75	122	1,446	315	123		2,787	2,527	676	...
1966	2,064	1,528	24	1,552	103	142	1,591	341	132		3,031	2,716	681	...
1967	2,255	1,677	17	1,695	116	157	1,735	365	155		3,235	2,897	697	...
1968	2,491	1,846	20	1,866	128	175	1,913	399	180		3,513	3,124	709	...
1969	2,781	2,003	21	2,024	129	234	2,129	450	203		3,842	3,401	724	334
1970	2,966	2,125	17	2,141	136	220	2,226	499	241		3,997	3,520	742	334
1971	3,220	2,283	15	2,297	151	229	2,376	552	292		4,225	3,789	762	336
1972	3,562	2,536	16	2,553	177	252	2,628	611	322		4,557	4,025	782	350
1973	4,013	2,882	21	2,903	230	280	2,954	679	380		5,005	4,475	802	374
1974	4,417	3,114	14	3,128	258	323	3,193	769	456		5,406	4,812	817	381
1975	4,802	3,278	17	3,295	267	356	3,384	833	586		5,786	5,227	830	370
1976	5,436	3,779	19	3,798	310	400	3,888	922	626		6,418	5,748	847	394
1977	6,146	4,295	18	4,313	354	473	4,431	1,054	661		7,050	6,284	872	418
1978	7,091	5,008	19	5,027	421	564	5,170	1,196	725		7,932	7,008	894	446
1979	8,113	5,725	22	5,746	504	678	5,921	1,363	829		8,896	7,848	912	468
1980	9,282	6,347	14	6,361	560	840	6,642	1,668	972		10,043	8,888	924	482
1981	10,506	7,018	23	7,041	667	950	7,324	2,044	1,138		11,217	9,896	937	492
1982	11,562	7,573	19	7,592	740	1,036	7,889	2,425	1,248		12,199	10,885	948	498
1983	12,714	8,496	17	8,514	841	1,153	8,826	2,556	1,333		13,270	11,835	958	518
1984	14,353	9,593	22	9,614	977	1,362	9,999	2,944	1,410		14,693	13,142	977	553
1985	15,831	10,764	24	10,788	1,126	1,496	11,159	3,196	1,476		15,883	14,085	997	586
1986	17,500	12,099	25	12,124	1,276	1,571	12,419	3,532	1,548		17,072	15,046	1,025	617
1987	19,285	13,663	43	13,706	1,420	1,683	13,968	3,736	1,581		18,292	16,096	1,054	635
1988	21,308	15,081	45	15,126	1,606	1,823	15,343	4,252	1,713		19,682	17,451	1,083	660
1989	22,825	15,717	35	15,752	1,677	1,941	16,016	4,890	1,919		20,665	18,342	1,105	660
1990	23,005	15,582	44	15,627	1,710	1,972	15,889	4,966	2,150		20,681	18,455	1,112	643
1991	23,818	15,565	45	15,610	1,731	2,118	15,998	4,939	2,882		21,459	19,294	1,110	616
1992	24,952	16,677	51	16,728	1,839	2,177	17,067	4,815	3,070		22,323	20,090	1,118	629
1993	25,765	17,425	42	17,467	1,919	2,303	17,851	4,942	2,973		22,812	20,444	1,129	642
1994	27,503	18,583	40	18,623	2,075	2,399	18,947	5,180	3,376		24,071	21,597	1,143	666
1995	29,176	19,714	35	19,749	2,224	2,391	19,916	5,618	3,641		25,205	22,537	1,158	679
1996	30,893	21,039	41	21,080	2,347	2,566	21,298	5,995	3,599		26,298	23,289	1,175	696
1997	33,286	22,802	38	22,840	2,522	2,803	23,121	6,424	3,741		27,985	24,482	1,189	717
1998	36,598	25,535	40	25,575	2,734	2,904	25,745	6,973	3,880		30,348	26,587	1,206	743
1999	38,930	27,627	44	27,672	2,904	3,376	28,143	6,829	3,958		31,857	27,743	1,222	761
2000	43,796	31,066	44	31,111	3,190	4,021	31,941	7,594	4,261		35,323	30,496	1,240	784
2001	46,180	33,033	42	33,075	3,324	4,064	33,815	7,712	4,654		36,782	32,264	1,256	788
2002	46,972	33,915	43	33,957	3,371	3,936	34,522	7,383	5,067		37,013	33,313	1,269	788
2003	47,833	34,878	49	34,927	3,533	3,950	35,344	7,294	5,196		37,374	33,969	1,280	798
2004	50,733	36,819	58	36,877	3,792	4,230	37,315	7,736	5,682		39,324	35,869	1,290	813
2005	52,464	38,483	49	38,532	3,961	4,222	38,793	7,744	5,927		40,404	36,527	1,298	826
2006	56,085	40,908	41	40,949	4,149	4,376	41,176	8,581	6,329		42,866	38,576	1,308	836
2007	58,306	41,479	43	41,521	4,319	4,747	41,950	9,486	6,869		44,422	39,723	1,313	848
2008	60,154	41,591	60	41,651	4,459	4,878	42,070	10,131	7,953		45,713	41,027	1,316	845
2009	59,382	41,568	37	41,605	4,431	4,162	41,335	9,472	8,575		45,119	41,593	1,316	821
2010	61,881	43,423	53	43,475	4,557	4,768	43,686	9,059	9,136		46,983	43,139	1,317	814
2011	64,889	44,420	48	44,468	4,224	5,086	45,330	10,485	9,074		49,088	44,569	1,322	819
2012	67,318	45,052	85	45,136	4,328	5,493	46,301	11,801	9,216		50,719	46,249	1,327	824
2013	67,122	45,666	104	45,770	4,954	5,200	46,016	11,707	9,398		50,428	45,502	1,331	835
2014	69,631	47,350	80	47,430	5,128	4,942	47,244	12,362	10,024		51,993	46,713	1,339	845
2015	72,780	48,866	83	48,949	5,333	5,474	49,090	12,907	10,783		54,166	48,393	1,344	861
2016	75,229	50,578	55	50,633	5,520	5,854	50,968	12,824	11,438		55,681	49,571	1,351	873
2017	78,661	52,640	68	52,708	5,826	6,085	52,967	13,830	11,865		57,882	51,779	1,359	882
2018	82,354	55,177	49	55,226	6,075	6,412	55,563	14,198	12,593		60,338	54,334	1,365	893
2019	87,706	58,139	57	58,196	6,327	7,309	59,178	15,456	13,072		63,934	57,416	1,372	890
2020	93,582	60,391	46	60,437	6,534	7,367	61,270	15,264	17,048		67,877	61,072	1,379	858
2021	100,197	68,366	30	68,396	7,149	4,880	66,126	15,994	18,076		72,214	63,940	1,387	895
2022	103,122	70,817	-22	70,796	7,786	6,805	69,815	17,068	16,239		73,711	64,491	1,399	933
2023	108,323	74,713	-56	74,658	8,272	6,996	73,382	18,075	16,867		77,260	69,245	1,402	...

... = Not available.

Personal Income and Employment by Region and State: New Jersey

(Millions of dollars, except as noted.)

Year	Personal income, total	Derivation of personal income: Earnings by place of work: Nonfarm	Farm	Total	Less: Contributions for government social insurance	Plus: Adjustment for residence	Equals: Net earnings by place of residence	Plus: Dividends, interest, and rent	Plus: Personal current transfer receipts	Per capita (dollars): Personal income	Disposable personal income	Population (thousands)	Total employment (thousands)
1960	16,553	13,148	121	13,269	660	863	13,472	2,185	896	2,712	2,400	6,103	...
1961	17,396	13,698	120	13,818	695	920	14,044	2,328	1,024	2,777	2,457	6,265	...
1962	18,719	14,646	110	14,755	771	1,021	15,006	2,634	1,079	2,936	2,594	6,376	...
1963	19,647	15,280	108	15,388	870	1,097	15,615	2,873	1,159	3,008	2,655	6,531	...
1964	21,064	16,215	103	16,319	881	1,213	16,651	3,208	1,205	3,163	2,843	6,660	...
1965	22,629	17,351	119	17,471	935	1,324	17,860	3,484	1,286	3,344	2,983	6,767	...
1966	24,503	18,937	120	19,056	1,212	1,522	19,366	3,752	1,385	3,577	3,188	6,851	...
1967	26,394	20,281	105	20,386	1,346	1,687	20,726	4,025	1,642	3,810	3,372	6,928	...
1968	28,967	22,134	102	22,236	1,535	1,894	22,595	4,408	1,964	4,135	3,627	7,005	...
1969	32,504	24,069	105	24,175	1,829	3,165	25,510	4,782	2,213	4,581	3,982	7,095	3,061
1970	35,295	26,002	100	26,102	1,958	3,117	27,261	5,344	2,689	4,909	4,313	7,190	3,125
1971	38,078	27,808	93	27,902	2,170	3,213	28,944	5,857	3,277	5,229	4,658	7,282	3,119
1972	41,395	30,359	89	30,448	2,485	3,418	31,381	6,351	3,663	5,642	4,959	7,337	3,184
1973	45,063	33,412	127	33,538	3,131	3,513	33,921	7,011	4,131	6,143	5,442	7,335	3,288
1974	48,945	35,871	138	36,009	3,461	3,683	36,231	7,867	4,848	6,673	5,886	7,335	3,301
1975	52,878	37,649	97	37,746	3,544	3,887	38,090	8,451	6,338	7,203	6,445	7,341	3,191
1976	57,409	41,278	102	41,380	3,933	4,061	41,509	9,047	6,853	7,817	6,921	7,344	3,248
1977	62,802	45,429	112	45,541	4,316	4,420	45,645	9,929	7,229	8,554	7,490	7,342	3,325
1978	69,699	50,935	127	51,062	4,987	4,992	51,067	10,944	7,689	9,475	8,274	7,356	3,465
1979	77,369	56,448	127	56,575	5,748	5,707	56,534	12,285	8,550	10,493	9,069	7,373	3,552
1980	87,085	61,774	116	61,890	6,317	6,658	62,230	15,073	9,782	11,806	10,181	7,376	3,601
1981	97,168	67,613	150	67,763	7,369	7,275	67,669	18,519	10,980	13,118	11,279	7,407	3,631
1982	104,981	72,175	166	72,341	7,997	7,760	72,104	20,842	12,035	14,127	12,158	7,431	3,639
1983	113,461	78,787	192	78,979	8,983	8,101	78,097	22,372	12,992	15,193	13,224	7,468	3,739
1984	125,385	87,803	200	88,003	10,427	8,526	86,102	25,736	13,548	16,684	14,585	7,515	3,914
1985	134,485	95,257	227	95,484	11,395	8,952	93,040	27,246	14,199	17,776	15,395	7,566	4,026
1986	143,991	103,092	229	103,321	12,408	9,537	100,450	28,673	14,868	18,891	16,338	7,622	4,122
1987	154,711	113,024	258	113,282	13,525	10,071	109,828	29,523	15,360	20,169	17,270	7,671	4,220
1988	170,481	125,277	253	125,530	15,224	10,488	120,795	33,331	16,355	22,105	19,155	7,712	4,317
1989	182,884	132,044	246	132,290	15,871	10,338	126,757	38,600	17,527	23,671	20,533	7,726	4,351
1990	192,171	137,883	243	138,126	16,024	10,354	132,456	40,384	19,331	24,755	21,557	7,763	4,310
1991	196,170	139,450	228	139,678	16,533	10,312	133,457	40,464	22,249	25,103	21,949	7,815	4,172
1992	210,399	149,174	237	149,411	17,491	12,066	143,986	40,649	25,764	26,699	23,396	7,881	4,170
1993	217,404	155,154	265	155,419	18,116	12,251	149,554	40,928	26,922	27,350	23,880	7,949	4,197
1994	225,067	161,704	282	161,986	19,138	12,234	155,082	42,682	27,303	28,083	24,417	8,014	4,232
1995	238,902	169,469	277	169,746	19,894	13,366	163,218	46,513	29,170	29,555	25,762	8,083	4,296
1996	252,631	178,047	297	178,344	20,745	15,322	172,921	49,608	30,102	30,999	26,817	8,150	4,352
1997	268,793	188,565	247	188,812	21,524	18,082	185,369	52,559	30,865	32,705	28,054	8,219	4,412
1998	286,580	201,534	264	201,798	22,686	19,596	198,709	56,156	31,715	34,580	29,365	8,287	4,501
1999	299,724	213,127	230	213,357	23,766	21,496	211,088	55,597	33,039	35,854	30,230	8,360	4,571
2000	329,592	233,831	322	234,154	25,555	24,547	233,146	61,184	35,262	39,095	32,751	8,431	4,749
2001	341,309	241,842	269	242,111	26,593	25,181	240,700	61,411	39,198	40,189	33,807	8,493	4,777
2002	345,989	249,456	289	249,745	27,221	22,831	245,355	58,232	42,402	40,454	35,111	8,553	4,792
2003	354,098	256,883	307	257,189	27,670	23,085	252,603	58,616	42,878	41,167	36,146	8,601	4,825
2004	369,771	267,923	330	268,252	28,996	26,154	265,410	60,906	43,455	42,825	37,666	8,635	4,910
2005	382,749	276,921	337	277,258	30,462	28,606	275,401	61,588	45,760	44,238	38,347	8,652	4,991
2006	410,265	289,723	383	290,106	31,856	33,892	292,142	68,436	49,687	47,366	40,904	8,662	5,057
2007	435,049	300,059	397	300,457	33,670	40,311	307,097	75,897	52,055	50,133	42,774	8,678	5,130
2008	449,545	305,124	351	305,474	34,559	39,569	310,485	80,333	58,728	51,606	44,165	8,711	5,124
2009	436,271	300,440	358	300,798	33,745	31,131	298,185	72,822	65,264	49,828	44,210	8,756	4,992
2010	448,931	306,495	337	306,832	34,239	35,060	307,653	70,559	70,718	50,962	45,094	8,809	4,961
2011	469,253	312,678	358	313,037	31,429	39,121	320,729	77,070	71,454	52,862	46,115	8,877	5,019
2012	484,600	322,975	433	323,408	32,106	39,765	331,067	83,210	70,323	54,247	47,578	8,933	5,054
2013	488,591	332,779	438	333,217	37,404	40,789	336,602	80,999	70,990	54,380	46,907	8,985	5,133
2014	509,358	343,524	391	343,915	38,482	43,677	349,110	86,273	73,975	56,383	48,647	9,034	5,207
2015	530,303	356,179	464	356,644	39,790	45,673	362,527	91,345	76,431	58,425	50,093	9,077	5,303
2016	545,302	363,481	423	363,905	40,435	47,415	370,885	95,135	79,282	59,793	51,349	9,120	5,391
2017	566,237	376,070	427	376,497	42,191	50,578	384,883	100,808	80,546	61,716	53,145	9,175	5,449
2018	591,910	391,823	336	392,158	43,440	55,141	403,858	104,305	83,747	64,206	55,622	9,219	5,550
2019	624,820	408,233	530	408,763	45,014	61,756	425,505	111,904	87,411	67,484	58,428	9,259	5,571
2020	657,894	409,751	481	410,232	45,141	65,316	430,407	108,510	118,978	70,952	62,032	9,272	5,319
2021	705,095	436,031	471	436,501	49,067	68,872	456,306	118,071	130,718	76,069	65,282	9,269	5,585
2022	714,990	460,306	490	460,797	53,665	77,217	484,349	123,644	106,998	77,206	64,689	9,261	5,906
2023	749,993	483,111	446	483,557	56,206	81,754	509,106	129,925	110,962	80,724	69,883	9,291	...

... = Not available.

Personal Income and Employment by Region and State: New Mexico

(Millions of dollars, except as noted.)

Year	Personal income, total	Derivation of personal income: Earnings by place of work: Nonfarm	Farm	Total	Less: Contributions for government social insurance	Plus: Adjustment for residence	Equals: Net earnings by place of residence	Plus: Dividends, interest, and rent	Plus: Personal current transfer receipts	Per capita (dollars): Personal income	Disposable personal income	Population (thousands)	Total employment (thousands)
1960	1,912	1,535	86	1,622	61	-16	1,545	264	102	2,004	1,829	954	...
1961	2,000	1,573	102	1,675	61	-16	1,598	284	118	2,073	1,892	965	...
1962	2,079	1,662	83	1,745	66	-17	1,662	297	120	2,124	1,932	979	...
1963	2,150	1,714	87	1,801	74	-18	1,708	313	129	2,174	1,979	989	...
1964	2,273	1,828	66	1,894	78	-19	1,797	342	135	2,260	2,083	1,006	...
1965	2,412	1,924	78	2,002	81	-21	1,901	366	145	2,383	2,180	1,012	...
1966	2,535	2,014	100	2,115	104	-21	1,990	388	156	2,517	2,302	1,007	...
1967	2,620	2,084	90	2,174	121	-21	2,032	393	195	2,620	2,395	1,000	...
1968	2,837	2,228	102	2,330	125	-23	2,183	426	228	2,854	2,597	994	...
1969	3,144	2,456	107	2,564	152	-21	2,391	493	261	3,109	2,787	1,011	395
1970	3,500	2,653	131	2,784	163	-23	2,598	576	325	3,420	3,081	1,023	399
1971	3,872	2,926	130	3,056	188	-24	2,844	651	378	3,677	3,363	1,053	416
1972	4,353	3,302	137	3,439	220	-22	3,197	734	422	4,039	3,668	1,078	440
1973	4,882	3,673	180	3,853	282	-19	3,552	830	500	4,421	4,016	1,104	461
1974	5,487	4,119	147	4,266	328	-17	3,921	965	601	4,858	4,391	1,130	478
1975	6,268	4,626	177	4,803	366	-14	4,423	1,107	738	5,391	4,955	1,163	491
1976	6,987	5,255	124	5,379	420	-14	4,944	1,215	828	5,846	5,323	1,195	512
1977	7,820	5,942	135	6,077	481	-12	5,583	1,364	872	6,382	5,802	1,225	539
1978	8,948	6,813	168	6,980	565	-12	6,403	1,589	956	7,148	6,435	1,252	568
1979	10,087	7,655	207	7,862	667	-11	7,184	1,800	1,103	7,877	7,078	1,281	592
1980	11,325	8,418	180	8,598	737	-6	7,856	2,154	1,315	8,649	7,781	1,309	597
1981	12,790	9,461	129	9,591	889	-16	8,686	2,602	1,502	9,597	8,532	1,333	611
1982	14,011	10,094	116	10,210	966	-19	9,225	3,134	1,651	10,273	9,116	1,364	619
1983	15,087	10,729	127	10,856	1,035	-14	9,808	3,475	1,804	10,820	9,825	1,394	631
1984	16,451	11,720	147	11,867	1,164	-6	10,697	3,827	1,927	11,612	10,580	1,417	655
1985	17,812	12,558	208	12,766	1,271	1	11,496	4,252	2,064	12,384	11,258	1,438	674
1986	18,512	12,962	194	13,156	1,327	8	11,837	4,453	2,223	12,656	11,564	1,463	680
1987	19,236	13,505	241	13,746	1,371	22	12,398	4,488	2,350	13,010	11,756	1,479	699
1988	20,380	14,296	319	14,616	1,530	33	13,119	4,741	2,520	13,675	12,368	1,490	733
1989	21,827	15,180	383	15,563	1,648	42	13,956	5,076	2,796	14,514	13,063	1,504	749
1990	23,292	16,339	417	16,756	1,872	49	14,934	5,311	3,048	15,308	13,787	1,522	761
1991	24,954	17,558	403	17,961	2,032	61	15,990	5,547	3,417	16,044	14,495	1,555	784
1992	26,778	18,875	484	19,359	2,166	77	17,271	5,709	3,799	16,784	15,186	1,595	797
1993	28,793	20,373	530	20,903	2,341	96	18,658	6,017	4,118	17,595	15,879	1,636	825
1994	30,728	21,761	457	22,218	2,547	111	19,782	6,516	4,430	18,265	16,452	1,682	857
1995	33,017	23,209	391	23,600	2,718	122	21,004	7,134	4,878	19,191	17,310	1,720	898
1996	34,665	23,984	402	24,386	2,808	142	21,720	7,623	5,323	19,782	17,761	1,752	909
1997	36,400	25,169	543	25,713	2,931	163	22,945	8,017	5,437	20,509	18,313	1,775	923
1998	38,233	26,412	585	26,996	3,083	187	24,099	8,415	5,719	21,318	19,021	1,793	938
1999	38,915	27,183	679	27,862	3,203	215	24,874	7,991	6,051	21,523	19,142	1,808	942
2000	41,922	29,687	542	30,229	3,386	240	27,083	8,416	6,423	23,019	20,534	1,821	965
2001	44,959	31,502	789	32,291	3,624	212	28,878	8,912	7,169	24,545	21,832	1,832	977
2002	46,822	33,263	548	33,812	3,811	218	30,218	8,731	7,873	25,237	22,892	1,855	984
2003	49,020	34,971	570	35,542	4,003	206	31,745	8,845	8,430	26,108	23,883	1,878	1,003
2004	52,100	37,038	876	37,913	4,215	159	33,857	9,251	8,992	27,366	25,090	1,904	1,027
2005	55,541	39,323	878	40,201	4,485	92	35,808	10,029	9,704	28,744	26,117	1,932	1,050
2006	59,714	42,270	607	42,878	4,872	104	38,109	11,019	10,585	30,433	27,450	1,962	1,079
2007	63,244	43,882	872	44,754	5,131	96	39,719	12,004	11,521	31,780	28,578	1,990	1,103
2008	67,462	45,801	732	46,533	5,413	73	41,193	13,025	13,245	33,552	30,431	2,011	1,105
2009	67,012	45,126	413	45,540	5,359	87	40,267	12,078	14,667	32,901	30,295	2,037	1,072
2010	69,500	46,299	889	47,188	5,452	27	41,763	11,858	15,879	33,658	31,133	2,065	1,060
2011	73,018	47,821	1,133	48,954	5,032	-2	43,919	13,036	16,063	35,069	32,176	2,082	1,064
2012	74,611	48,471	1,024	49,495	5,143	3	44,355	14,238	16,018	35,695	32,806	2,090	1,067
2013	73,080	48,245	995	49,240	5,914	-39	43,287	13,612	16,180	34,858	31,691	2,097	1,076
2014	77,266	49,680	1,266	50,946	6,120	-47	44,780	14,741	17,745	36,880	33,558	2,095	1,084
2015	79,131	50,764	886	51,650	6,444	-40	45,167	14,787	19,177	37,753	34,305	2,096	1,092
2016	80,782	51,348	934	52,282	6,455	2	45,829	15,284	19,669	38,475	35,009	2,100	1,092
2017	82,354	52,527	941	53,468	6,563	34	46,939	15,716	19,699	39,197	35,740	2,101	1,095
2018	86,180	55,077	801	55,879	6,864	-29	48,986	16,343	20,850	40,977	37,528	2,103	1,111
2019	91,140	58,219	871	59,090	7,174	27	51,943	17,404	21,793	43,191	39,391	2,110	1,117
2020	98,783	58,279	927	59,206	7,304	129	52,030	17,820	28,933	46,629	43,092	2,118	1,070
2021	108,248	62,620	795	63,415	7,786	170	55,799	19,465	32,984	51,134	46,912	2,117	1,093
2022	110,303	67,442	885	68,326	8,504	173	59,995	20,071	30,238	52,190	47,271	2,113	1,139
2023	115,082	72,436	554	72,990	9,142	178	64,026	21,008	30,048	54,428	50,029	2,114	...

... = Not available.

Personal Income and Employment by Region and State: New York

(Millions of dollars, except as noted.)

Year	Personal income, total	Derivation of personal income: Earnings by place of work								Per capita (dollars)		Population (thousands)	Total employment (thousands)
		Nonfarm	Farm	Total	Less: Contributions for government social insurance	Plus: Adjustment for residence	Equals: Net earnings by place of residence	Plus: Dividends, interest, and rent	Plus: Personal current transfer receipts	Personal income	Disposable personal income		
1960	47,939	40,466	353	40,819	2,041	-729	38,050	7,096	2,794	2,847	2,478	16,838	...
1961	50,098	41,996	364	42,360	2,191	-781	39,387	7,504	3,207	2,936	2,543	17,061	...
1962	52,853	44,321	287	44,608	2,490	-866	41,251	8,307	3,295	3,055	2,649	17,301	...
1963	55,174	45,815	336	46,152	2,713	-930	42,509	9,116	3,549	3,160	2,742	17,461	...
1964	58,939	48,567	318	48,885	2,682	-1,026	45,177	10,039	3,723	3,351	2,948	17,589	...
1965	62,625	51,252	366	51,618	2,803	-1,110	47,705	10,904	4,016	3,531	3,097	17,734	...
1966	67,240	55,598	427	56,025	3,720	-1,263	51,042	11,563	4,636	3,768	3,284	17,843	...
1967	72,538	59,464	380	59,844	4,032	-1,404	54,407	12,231	5,900	4,044	3,496	17,935	...
1968	80,062	65,209	388	65,597	4,446	-1,584	59,568	13,281	7,213	4,435	3,807	18,051	...
1969	83,626	70,364	440	70,804	5,291	-3,437	62,076	13,815	7,735	4,619	3,896	18,105	8,494
1970	89,895	74,760	420	75,179	5,534	-3,395	66,251	14,736	8,909	4,920	4,228	18,272	8,466
1971	96,121	79,088	410	79,497	6,030	-3,518	69,949	15,428	10,744	5,234	4,564	18,365	8,345
1972	102,834	84,861	353	85,214	6,796	-3,786	74,633	16,208	11,994	5,603	4,833	18,352	8,348
1973	109,572	90,472	470	90,943	8,413	-3,919	78,611	17,672	13,289	6,022	5,217	18,195	8,465
1974	118,065	95,731	444	96,175	9,188	-4,120	82,867	19,780	15,418	6,533	5,640	18,073	8,392
1975	127,414	100,445	379	100,824	9,452	-4,406	86,966	20,942	19,506	7,066	6,194	18,032	8,172
1976	134,981	106,699	401	107,100	10,248	-4,663	92,189	21,992	20,800	7,510	6,550	17,975	8,125
1977	145,640	115,644	331	115,975	11,010	-5,198	99,767	24,115	21,759	8,158	7,088	17,852	8,199
1978	158,584	127,304	433	127,737	12,375	-5,879	109,483	26,314	22,786	8,949	7,741	17,720	8,384
1979	173,372	139,951	539	140,490	14,083	-6,758	119,649	29,386	24,337	9,832	8,442	17,634	8,581
1980	193,336	153,334	530	153,864	15,430	-7,854	130,580	34,765	27,991	11,006	9,414	17,567	8,602
1981	215,437	168,282	543	168,825	18,083	-8,521	142,221	41,628	31,588	12,263	10,386	17,568	8,666
1982	234,155	180,684	518	181,203	19,681	-9,315	152,207	47,393	34,555	13,312	11,253	17,590	8,673
1983	252,719	195,069	371	195,440	21,224	-9,879	164,337	51,005	37,377	14,288	12,292	17,687	8,730
1984	279,066	215,022	494	215,517	23,937	-10,582	180,997	58,510	39,559	15,726	13,564	17,746	9,003
1985	298,925	232,681	561	233,242	26,272	-11,352	195,618	61,552	41,755	16,801	14,396	17,792	9,227
1986	319,273	251,553	654	252,207	28,844	-11,969	211,394	63,633	44,246	17,903	15,326	17,833	9,424
1987	339,348	272,882	732	273,613	30,680	-12,771	230,163	63,798	45,387	18,991	16,087	17,869	9,472
1988	373,424	300,763	645	301,408	34,031	-13,698	253,679	71,451	48,295	20,814	17,852	17,941	9,684
1989	403,530	317,544	777	318,321	35,481	-13,758	269,082	81,425	53,023	22,439	19,135	17,983	9,752
1990	432,354	337,820	775	338,594	35,787	-13,471	289,337	84,852	58,165	23,992	20,646	18,021	9,727
1991	433,088	332,725	647	333,372	36,733	-13,448	283,190	85,154	64,744	23,898	20,675	18,123	9,483
1992	457,071	355,360	749	356,109	38,353	-16,580	301,176	83,531	72,364	25,050	21,700	18,247	9,410
1993	469,679	363,633	793	364,427	39,223	-16,351	308,852	83,973	76,854	25,561	22,059	18,375	9,431
1994	484,266	372,726	672	373,398	40,889	-16,345	316,164	87,501	80,601	26,234	22,636	18,459	9,465
1995	510,312	390,103	538	390,641	42,381	-18,578	329,683	94,854	85,775	27,549	23,718	18,524	9,511
1996	536,942	412,086	767	412,853	43,658	-21,430	347,765	99,743	89,435	28,886	24,655	18,588	9,595
1997	567,117	440,716	456	441,172	45,606	-23,990	371,576	106,203	89,338	30,398	25,765	18,657	9,732
1998	600,087	469,005	688	469,693	47,880	-27,293	394,521	112,239	93,328	31,995	26,876	18,756	9,901
1999	635,243	504,751	769	505,520	50,242	-28,503	426,775	112,301	96,167	33,641	28,101	18,883	10,165
2000	683,214	547,861	778	548,639	54,137	-32,299	462,203	120,365	100,646	35,955	29,930	19,002	10,425
2001	709,418	571,260	930	572,191	56,439	-33,137	482,615	119,590	107,213	37,176	30,598	19,083	10,439
2002	707,561	568,016	712	568,728	57,156	-30,983	480,589	110,386	116,586	36,972	31,703	19,138	10,348
2003	717,555	573,172	874	574,045	58,926	-31,588	483,531	112,521	121,503	37,420	32,400	19,176	10,378
2004	749,469	599,256	1,087	600,343	61,838	-36,268	502,236	116,359	130,874	39,093	33,663	19,172	10,513
2005	777,653	619,117	1,059	620,176	64,650	-40,255	515,271	132,057	130,326	40,645	34,473	19,133	10,655
2006	836,023	663,296	923	664,219	68,656	-46,885	548,678	149,851	137,493	43,760	36,589	19,105	10,810
2007	899,610	711,344	1,312	712,656	72,723	-55,941	583,992	171,935	143,683	47,020	38,820	19,132	11,083
2008	920,457	716,426	1,528	717,954	75,368	-56,406	586,180	177,205	157,071	47,909	39,676	19,212	11,198
2009	906,188	694,956	953	695,908	73,056	-44,018	578,834	155,292	172,062	46,936	40,661	19,307	10,985
2010	943,393	730,971	1,520	732,491	74,798	-50,278	607,415	153,506	182,471	48,579	41,863	19,420	11,006
2011	995,231	760,712	1,835	762,547	68,956	-53,995	639,596	170,002	185,633	50,775	43,137	19,601	11,294
2012	1,039,792	790,827	1,821	792,648	70,723	-56,409	665,516	189,987	184,288	52,628	44,941	19,757	11,433
2013	1,051,798	812,549	2,209	814,758	83,140	-56,318	675,300	190,664	185,834	52,875	44,154	19,892	11,619
2014	1,090,001	840,973	2,212	843,185	87,658	-60,207	695,320	204,651	190,029	54,495	45,274	20,002	11,866
2015	1,137,082	872,429	1,376	873,805	91,579	-62,456	719,770	217,282	200,031	56,603	46,705	20,089	12,099
2016	1,176,655	900,634	1,185	901,819	93,812	-64,053	743,954	227,645	205,055	58,392	48,765	20,151	12,259
2017	1,255,777	954,336	1,567	955,903	99,232	-69,829	786,842	247,801	221,134	62,196	51,946	20,190	12,391
2018	1,298,669	1,002,332	1,058	1,003,390	102,944	-76,617	823,830	260,837	214,002	64,218	53,635	20,223	12,655
2019	1,343,066	1,038,711	1,670	1,040,381	107,450	-87,092	845,840	267,147	230,080	66,415	55,577	20,222	12,746
2020	1,405,029	1,030,208	1,645	1,031,853	105,472	-94,765	831,616	255,157	318,256	69,886	59,243	20,105	11,872
2021	1,508,135	1,109,326	1,835	1,111,162	114,106	-98,309	898,746	275,772	333,617	75,959	62,900	19,855	12,228
2022	1,483,802	1,159,457	2,443	1,161,900	123,499	-110,161	928,240	281,339	274,224	75,423	60,463	19,673	12,892
2023	1,557,496	1,226,419	1,551	1,227,971	130,377	-116,604	980,989	293,499	283,008	79,581	66,393	19,571	...

... = Not available.

Personal Income and Employment by Region and State: North Carolina

(Millions of dollars, except as noted.)

Year	Personal income, total	Derivation of personal income								Per capita (dollars)		Population (thousands)	Total employment (thousands)
		Earnings by place of work			Less: Contributions for government social insurance	Plus: Adjustment for residence	Equals: Net earnings by place of residence	Plus: Dividends, interest, and rent	Plus: Personal current transfer receipts	Personal income	Disposable personal income		
		Nonfarm	Farm	Total									
1960	7,618	5,979	604	6,583	307	10	6,287	874	457	1,666	1,517	4,573	...
1961	8,064	6,250	645	6,895	314	10	6,591	950	524	1,729	1,576	4,663	...
1962	8,661	6,763	627	7,391	347	11	7,055	1,054	552	1,840	1,668	4,707	...
1963	9,110	7,182	606	7,788	412	11	7,387	1,128	595	1,921	1,737	4,742	...
1964	9,868	7,796	634	8,431	435	12	8,007	1,238	623	2,055	1,880	4,802	...
1965	10,671	8,580	532	9,113	467	11	8,656	1,336	679	2,194	1,989	4,863	...
1966	11,855	9,662	618	10,280	617	11	9,673	1,444	738	2,421	2,182	4,896	...
1967	12,817	10,510	607	11,117	716	10	10,412	1,546	859	2,588	2,335	4,952	...
1968	14,136	11,783	518	12,301	826	13	11,487	1,667	981	2,825	2,516	5,004	...
1969	15,858	13,023	673	13,695	900	19	12,814	1,937	1,107	3,152	2,772	5,031	2,458
1970	17,320	13,993	672	14,665	971	20	13,713	2,270	1,338	3,397	3,008	5,099	2,469
1971	18,857	15,279	627	15,906	1,102	15	14,819	2,469	1,569	3,626	3,238	5,201	2,490
1972	21,319	17,367	750	18,117	1,309	9	16,817	2,745	1,757	4,025	3,550	5,296	2,602
1973	24,175	19,497	1,162	20,659	1,678	7	18,988	3,148	2,038	4,491	3,986	5,382	2,720
1974	26,654	21,242	1,110	22,351	1,901	13	20,463	3,658	2,533	4,881	4,306	5,461	2,743
1975	28,943	22,287	1,066	23,353	1,978	15	21,390	4,030	3,523	5,229	4,723	5,535	2,647
1976	32,132	25,041	1,148	26,189	2,272	14	23,931	4,403	3,798	5,745	5,128	5,593	2,754
1977	35,208	27,878	857	28,734	2,513	19	26,240	4,961	4,007	6,211	5,520	5,668	2,851
1978	39,736	31,523	1,142	32,665	2,920	18	29,763	5,659	4,315	6,922	6,125	5,740	2,946
1979	43,907	35,226	757	35,983	3,390	8	32,601	6,374	4,933	7,568	6,638	5,802	3,046
1980	49,256	38,582	651	39,233	3,717	11	35,528	7,831	5,898	8,350	7,321	5,899	3,052
1981	55,448	42,422	1,049	43,472	4,380	-29	39,062	9,588	6,798	9,309	8,146	5,957	3,072
1982	59,375	44,527	1,064	45,591	4,635	-41	40,916	10,891	7,568	9,864	8,754	6,019	3,042
1983	64,652	49,212	635	49,847	5,173	-59	44,615	11,883	8,155	10,639	9,412	6,077	3,129
1984	73,043	55,475	1,292	56,767	5,969	-95	50,703	13,724	8,615	11,850	10,521	6,164	3,292
1985	78,976	60,390	1,161	61,550	6,589	-157	54,804	14,934	9,237	12,628	11,172	6,254	3,392
1986	85,149	65,521	1,145	66,666	7,294	-219	59,153	16,169	9,827	13,470	11,913	6,322	3,494
1987	91,579	71,603	1,141	72,744	7,869	-301	64,574	16,785	10,220	14,301	12,543	6,404	3,610
1988	100,512	78,140	1,477	79,618	8,838	-363	70,416	19,019	11,077	15,510	13,695	6,481	3,751
1989	109,592	83,798	1,722	85,519	9,490	-418	75,611	21,613	12,367	16,692	14,646	6,565	3,838
1990	116,495	88,317	2,135	90,452	10,257	-458	79,738	23,084	13,674	17,481	15,421	6,664	3,902
1991	121,969	91,320	2,394	93,715	10,747	-440	82,527	23,717	15,724	17,978	15,937	6,784	3,866
1992	132,578	100,252	2,340	102,592	11,649	-465	90,479	24,691	17,409	19,222	17,089	6,897	3,964
1993	141,327	106,326	2,613	108,939	12,435	-481	96,022	26,171	19,134	20,067	17,806	7,043	4,087
1994	150,420	113,462	2,826	116,288	13,399	-546	102,343	28,169	19,908	20,928	18,498	7,187	4,201
1995	161,279	120,481	2,710	123,191	14,228	-618	108,345	30,629	22,305	21,959	19,358	7,345	4,355
1996	172,516	127,553	2,996	130,549	14,926	-682	114,941	33,359	24,216	23,000	20,203	7,501	4,459
1997	185,209	137,434	3,064	140,498	15,978	-760	123,760	36,031	25,418	24,189	21,142	7,657	4,603
1998	198,232	148,217	2,409	150,625	17,207	-738	132,681	39,126	26,425	25,385	22,021	7,809	4,708
1999	207,943	157,709	2,240	159,949	18,335	-807	140,807	39,074	28,062	26,158	22,717	7,949	4,802
2000	221,516	167,496	2,965	170,462	19,428	-921	150,113	41,377	30,026	27,410	23,734	8,082	4,892
2001	228,091	170,991	3,122	174,113	20,100	-930	153,083	41,504	33,504	27,782	24,111	8,210	4,855
2002	231,931	174,727	1,513	176,240	20,457	-899	154,884	40,783	36,264	27,856	24,689	8,326	4,842
2003	241,805	181,814	1,592	183,407	21,459	-755	161,193	42,474	38,139	28,709	25,721	8,423	4,852
2004	261,603	195,645	2,371	198,016	22,560	-756	174,700	45,787	41,117	30,586	27,534	8,553	4,962
2005	280,392	208,349	3,206	211,555	24,119	-826	186,610	49,152	44,631	32,209	28,723	8,705	5,093
2006	304,873	226,950	2,607	229,558	25,771	-1,012	202,775	53,439	48,659	34,189	30,355	8,917	5,252
2007	327,887	242,619	2,296	244,915	27,508	-1,243	216,164	59,379	52,344	35,960	31,777	9,118	5,431
2008	351,638	255,919	2,239	258,158	28,285	-1,274	228,599	63,589	59,450	37,772	33,713	9,309	5,414
2009	339,442	241,090	2,268	243,358	27,493	-1,049	214,816	58,127	66,498	35,921	32,788	9,450	5,216
2010	343,104	242,128	2,399	244,527	27,829	-963	215,734	56,726	70,644	35,847	32,609	9,571	5,178
2011	355,002	245,424	2,066	247,491	25,944	-891	220,656	61,968	72,378	36,816	33,073	9,643	5,293
2012	377,867	263,141	2,892	266,033	26,976	-939	238,119	65,772	73,977	38,867	35,080	9,722	5,356
2013	373,141	262,001	3,416	265,417	31,279	-849	233,289	64,473	75,379	38,062	33,945	9,803	5,437
2014	393,886	275,346	3,808	279,154	32,937	-921	245,297	70,230	78,359	39,866	35,559	9,880	5,569
2015	414,760	289,078	3,252	292,330	34,560	-1,163	256,608	75,408	82,745	41,617	36,820	9,966	5,695
2016	429,055	300,408	2,575	302,983	35,544	-1,295	266,145	77,792	85,118	42,582	37,614	10,076	5,825
2017	449,818	314,167	3,219	317,386	36,885	-1,360	279,142	82,234	88,442	44,207	39,213	10,175	5,919
2018	473,093	331,519	1,485	333,004	38,385	-1,559	293,060	86,988	93,045	46,040	41,012	10,276	6,056
2019	501,587	351,029	1,994	353,023	40,570	-1,617	310,836	92,289	98,462	48,366	42,987	10,371	6,149
2020	541,078	364,126	1,574	365,700	42,201	-1,827	321,672	94,055	125,352	51,759	46,280	10,454	6,055
2021	599,134	396,098	3,183	399,281	45,600	-2,008	351,672	103,109	144,352	56,698	50,144	10,567	6,319
2022	621,706	431,252	3,415	434,667	50,417	-2,560	381,690	112,101	127,914	58,125	50,654	10,696	6,602
2023	655,369	459,882	1,914	461,797	53,927	-2,704	405,165	119,139	131,065	60,484	53,929	10,835	...

... = Not available.

Personal Income and Employment by Region and State: North Dakota

(Millions of dollars, except as noted.)

Year	Personal income, total	Derivation of personal income: Earnings by place of work: Nonfarm	Farm	Total	Less: Contributions for government social insurance	Plus: Adjustment for residence	Equals: Net earnings by place of residence	Plus: Dividends, interest, and rent	Plus: Personal current transfer receipts	Per capita (dollars): Personal income	Disposable personal income	Population (thousands)	Total employment (thousands)
1960	1,210	716	273	989	41	-12	937	190	83	1,909	1,764	634	...
1961	1,109	750	145	895	43	-12	840	179	90	1,730	1,593	641	...
1962	1,555	812	478	1,290	47	-14	1,229	232	94	2,441	2,268	637	...
1963	1,448	865	328	1,193	56	-14	1,123	228	98	2,249	2,072	644	...
1964	1,441	932	241	1,173	59	-17	1,097	239	104	2,220	2,051	649	...
1965	1,677	995	382	1,377	62	-17	1,298	265	114	2,584	2,402	649	...
1966	1,697	1,048	349	1,397	74	-16	1,307	267	123	2,623	2,422	647	...
1967	1,699	1,077	310	1,388	89	-16	1,282	270	147	2,714	2,489	626	...
1968	1,778	1,147	285	1,431	95	-16	1,320	294	164	2,864	2,624	621	...
1969	1,991	1,251	385	1,636	102	-55	1,478	330	183	3,205	2,889	621	274
1970	2,102	1,392	306	1,698	115	-58	1,525	365	212	3,397	3,088	619	281
1971	2,424	1,526	434	1,959	129	-60	1,770	406	248	3,868	3,573	627	284
1972	2,887	1,706	668	2,374	147	-64	2,162	449	276	4,576	4,215	631	288
1973	4,037	1,921	1,529	3,449	189	-68	3,193	534	310	6,383	5,880	632	300
1974	3,998	2,163	1,164	3,327	224	-79	3,024	619	356	6,304	5,635	634	308
1975	4,182	2,439	945	3,385	256	-83	3,045	716	420	6,549	5,881	638	314
1976	4,102	2,773	478	3,251	294	-97	2,860	777	465	6,357	5,704	645	326
1977	4,261	3,004	274	3,278	303	-103	2,873	882	507	6,564	5,918	649	331
1978	5,358	3,419	865	4,284	354	-113	3,818	987	553	8,235	7,398	651	345
1979	5,508	3,822	502	4,325	412	-130	3,783	1,112	613	8,446	7,566	652	353
1980	5,274	4,149	-383	3,766	450	-145	3,170	1,379	725	8,059	7,083	654	355
1981	6,904	4,637	372	5,009	533	-166	4,310	1,763	831	10,469	9,225	660	359
1982	7,455	4,903	306	5,209	576	-168	4,465	2,059	932	11,144	10,034	669	360
1983	7,838	5,163	366	5,529	613	-171	4,745	2,057	1,036	11,583	10,513	677	365
1984	8,457	5,361	612	5,973	652	-170	5,151	2,195	1,111	12,427	11,320	680	366
1985	8,743	5,453	699	6,152	678	-170	5,304	2,259	1,180	12,915	11,778	677	364
1986	8,871	5,510	693	6,203	698	-168	5,337	2,247	1,287	13,250	12,143	670	357
1987	9,106	5,736	789	6,525	727	-168	5,629	2,131	1,346	13,773	12,560	661	363
1988	8,461	5,984	-61	5,924	794	-175	4,954	2,153	1,353	12,911	11,660	655	366
1989	9,473	6,233	442	6,675	840	-180	5,655	2,343	1,474	14,656	13,277	646	370
1990	10,256	6,591	773	7,363	933	-184	6,246	2,432	1,578	16,084	14,590	638	374
1991	10,402	6,936	614	7,550	1,002	-191	6,357	2,439	1,605	16,362	14,817	636	382
1992	11,385	7,373	1,074	8,447	1,064	-206	7,176	2,437	1,772	17,839	16,246	638	388
1993	11,536	7,876	624	8,500	1,146	-225	7,129	2,541	1,867	17,991	16,286	641	397
1994	12,532	8,363	1,059	9,422	1,221	-241	7,961	2,670	1,901	19,435	17,663	645	411
1995	12,552	8,787	429	9,215	1,270	-262	7,684	2,858	2,010	19,376	17,502	648	418
1996	14,038	9,280	1,308	10,589	1,327	-294	8,967	2,978	2,093	21,584	19,582	650	426
1997	13,770	9,766	304	10,070	1,374	-321	8,375	3,214	2,182	21,194	19,050	650	430
1998	15,079	10,323	972	11,295	1,439	-344	9,513	3,357	2,209	23,286	21,017	648	435
1999	15,258	10,862	692	11,554	1,479	-370	9,705	3,248	2,304	23,683	21,352	644	436
2000	16,591	11,500	1,100	12,600	1,550	-404	10,646	3,473	2,472	25,842	23,329	642	441
2001	16,931	12,056	801	12,857	1,591	-432	10,833	3,561	2,537	26,493	23,824	639	445
2002	17,356	12,610	597	13,207	1,643	-447	11,118	3,550	2,689	27,197	24,881	638	443
2003	18,950	13,269	1,468	14,737	1,731	-470	12,536	3,626	2,788	29,663	27,410	639	444
2004	19,331	14,149	943	15,092	1,833	-522	12,737	3,647	2,948	29,984	27,684	645	453
2005	20,501	14,892	1,138	16,030	1,912	-570	13,548	3,847	3,107	31,731	29,101	646	462
2006	21,509	15,945	731	16,676	2,010	-635	14,031	4,163	3,314	33,120	30,086	649	471
2007	23,829	16,820	1,648	18,468	2,113	-704	15,652	4,624	3,552	36,501	32,976	653	482
2008	26,943	18,065	2,412	20,477	2,261	-762	17,454	5,471	4,018	40,973	36,851	658	492
2009	26,722	18,998	1,548	20,546	2,419	-803	17,324	5,198	4,200	40,186	36,878	665	492
2010	29,759	20,882	2,123	23,005	2,503	-967	19,535	5,680	4,543	44,084	40,263	675	504
2011	33,588	23,917	1,998	25,915	2,624	-1,321	21,970	6,968	4,650	48,886	43,889	687	530
2012	39,539	27,740	3,560	31,300	2,842	-1,901	26,557	8,290	4,692	56,077	50,147	705	567
2013	39,539	29,843	1,889	31,732	3,477	-2,291	25,963	8,715	4,860	54,358	48,039	727	587
2014	42,181	32,900	880	33,780	3,866	-2,635	27,279	9,731	5,171	56,665	50,106	744	607
2015	40,408	32,111	246	32,357	3,849	-2,384	26,124	8,920	5,364	52,981	47,201	763	598
2016	39,232	30,088	764	30,853	3,694	-1,969	25,190	8,504	5,538	51,307	46,162	765	577
2017	39,744	30,375	933	31,308	3,857	-2,083	25,369	8,714	5,661	51,839	46,796	767	573
2018	42,566	31,756	1,274	33,030	3,896	-2,281	26,853	9,644	6,069	55,180	50,267	771	578
2019	43,968	33,109	1,149	34,258	3,965	-2,372	27,921	9,678	6,369	56,622	51,310	777	581
2020	47,621	32,426	2,414	34,840	4,021	-2,014	28,805	10,273	8,543	61,087	56,029	780	560
2021	51,262	33,866	2,886	36,752	4,202	-1,959	30,592	11,484	9,185	65,891	59,804	778	568
2022	54,829	36,131	4,909	41,040	4,581	-2,261	34,198	12,500	8,131	70,391	63,367	779	588
2023	57,494	38,895	4,227	43,122	4,936	-2,473	35,713	13,432	8,349	73,341	67,093	784	...

... = Not available.

Personal Income and Employment by Region and State: Ohio

(Millions of dollars, except as noted.)

Year	Personal income, total	Derivation of personal income: Earnings by place of work: Nonfarm	Farm	Total	Less: Contributions for government social insurance	Plus: Adjustment for residence	Equals: Net earnings by place of residence	Plus: Dividends, interest, and rent	Plus: Personal current transfer receipts	Per capita (dollars): Personal income	Disposable personal income	Population (thousands)	Total employment (thousands)
1960	23,455	19,684	334	20,018	1,003	-131	18,884	3,060	1,512	2,410	2,139	9,734	...
1961	23,910	19,655	373	20,028	984	-122	18,922	3,227	1,760	2,426	2,167	9,854	...
1962	25,207	20,898	336	21,234	1,125	-126	19,983	3,493	1,731	2,539	2,258	9,929	...
1963	26,265	21,806	334	22,140	1,236	-129	20,775	3,708	1,782	2,630	2,336	9,986	...
1964	28,028	23,456	305	23,761	1,355	-134	22,272	3,967	1,789	2,781	2,505	10,080	...
1965	30,302	25,392	358	25,750	1,409	-147	24,195	4,214	1,893	2,970	2,659	10,201	...
1966	33,057	28,058	496	28,554	1,864	-166	26,524	4,495	2,039	3,200	2,850	10,330	...
1967	34,630	29,319	329	29,648	1,958	-160	27,529	4,722	2,379	3,325	2,959	10,414	...
1968	38,207	32,237	412	32,649	2,134	-183	30,332	5,186	2,690	3,633	3,194	10,516	...
1969	41,801	35,425	417	35,843	2,360	-200	33,284	5,617	2,900	3,957	3,432	10,563	4,695
1970	44,142	36,735	435	37,170	2,408	-183	34,579	6,168	3,396	4,137	3,640	10,669	4,683
1971	46,980	38,635	415	39,050	2,603	-134	36,313	6,654	4,014	4,376	3,911	10,735	4,627
1972	50,968	42,041	506	42,547	2,985	-133	39,429	7,101	4,438	4,743	4,173	10,747	4,710
1973	56,552	46,849	667	47,516	3,864	-158	43,494	7,893	5,166	5,252	4,626	10,767	4,902
1974	61,925	50,430	798	51,228	4,310	-134	46,784	8,939	6,203	5,752	5,051	10,766	4,964
1975	66,162	52,187	814	53,001	4,336	-93	48,572	9,658	7,933	6,143	5,444	10,770	4,809
1976	72,598	58,033	787	58,820	4,942	-108	53,770	10,325	8,502	6,752	5,945	10,753	4,889
1977	80,397	65,044	675	65,718	5,554	-114	60,050	11,417	8,930	7,464	6,530	10,771	5,034
1978	88,855	72,503	628	73,130	6,397	-136	66,598	12,662	9,594	8,231	7,180	10,795	5,206
1979	98,140	79,674	762	80,435	7,322	-172	72,942	14,245	10,953	9,088	7,872	10,799	5,291
1980	107,224	83,320	575	83,895	7,612	-194	76,089	17,325	13,811	9,928	8,650	10,801	5,204
1981	116,584	89,154	167	89,321	8,708	-483	80,130	21,107	15,348	10,807	9,359	10,788	5,135
1982	122,010	90,048	270	90,318	8,900	-609	80,810	23,390	17,810	11,342	9,945	10,757	4,967
1983	129,165	95,299	-69	95,230	9,613	-711	84,906	25,214	19,045	12,029	10,563	10,738	4,960
1984	142,496	105,804	874	106,678	10,932	-842	94,904	27,943	19,649	13,271	11,722	10,738	5,160
1985	151,345	113,033	870	113,904	11,870	-919	101,115	29,286	20,944	14,098	12,415	10,735	5,287
1986	158,418	118,945	684	119,629	12,856	-952	105,821	30,413	22,185	14,764	13,027	10,730	5,401
1987	165,484	125,890	734	126,624	13,614	-995	112,015	30,417	23,052	15,379	13,454	10,760	5,548
1988	178,137	136,113	783	136,896	15,149	-1,042	120,705	33,199	24,233	16,496	14,506	10,799	5,682
1989	191,537	144,483	1,171	145,654	16,209	-1,105	128,340	37,366	25,831	17,687	15,478	10,829	5,803
1990	202,968	152,071	1,205	153,276	17,415	-1,093	134,767	39,461	28,740	18,682	16,379	10,864	5,863
1991	207,868	156,084	702	156,786	18,308	-1,115	137,363	39,517	30,988	18,991	16,707	10,946	5,842
1992	221,075	166,674	1,184	167,858	19,470	-1,230	147,158	39,883	34,034	20,044	17,683	11,029	5,854
1993	230,184	174,334	933	175,267	20,592	-1,327	153,348	41,447	35,389	20,735	18,243	11,101	5,960
1994	243,075	185,104	1,162	186,265	22,172	-1,450	162,643	43,688	36,744	21,796	19,142	11,152	6,136
1995	254,778	192,988	891	193,879	23,353	-1,491	169,036	46,969	38,774	22,742	19,908	11,203	6,300
1996	266,670	201,099	1,250	202,349	24,062	-1,546	176,741	49,720	40,209	23,719	20,599	11,243	6,395
1997	282,199	212,537	1,684	214,221	24,790	-1,644	187,788	52,988	41,423	25,024	21,659	11,277	6,500
1998	298,491	226,220	1,270	227,491	25,558	-1,819	200,113	56,196	42,183	26,388	22,760	11,312	6,599
1999	307,407	237,388	851	238,238	26,717	-1,789	209,733	54,153	43,521	27,119	23,410	11,335	6,681
2000	323,813	248,750	1,208	249,958	27,074	-1,749	221,135	56,410	46,267	28,496	24,546	11,364	6,789
2001	333,209	254,539	1,139	255,679	27,710	-1,737	226,232	56,570	50,407	29,261	25,290	11,387	6,726
2002	338,463	259,500	581	260,081	27,845	-1,756	230,481	54,162	53,820	29,669	26,111	11,408	6,640
2003	348,429	267,452	786	268,238	28,971	-1,768	237,499	54,550	56,380	30,471	27,116	11,435	6,621
2004	361,753	278,739	1,412	280,151	30,670	-1,713	247,768	55,051	58,934	31,588	28,161	11,452	6,667
2005	371,634	284,895	1,066	285,960	31,521	-1,728	252,711	56,499	62,424	32,419	28,711	11,463	6,709
2006	390,090	296,192	932	297,124	32,776	-1,885	262,463	61,878	65,749	33,976	29,981	11,481	6,747
2007	406,787	304,146	1,181	305,327	33,575	-1,974	269,778	67,011	69,998	35,371	31,114	11,500	6,795
2008	422,086	307,593	1,282	308,875	34,522	-1,964	272,389	70,812	78,885	36,654	32,431	11,515	6,725
2009	410,350	294,123	1,591	295,714	33,456	-1,837	260,422	64,002	85,927	35,593	32,281	11,529	6,455
2010	422,204	302,398	1,604	304,003	33,669	-1,795	268,539	62,973	90,693	36,580	33,042	11,542	6,418
2011	449,924	317,898	2,890	320,789	31,803	-1,922	287,064	69,735	93,125	38,928	34,803	11,558	6,522
2012	466,162	331,305	1,941	333,246	32,860	-1,888	298,499	76,386	91,277	40,280	36,042	11,573	6,606
2013	473,219	342,104	3,096	345,200	36,883	-2,315	306,002	73,954	93,263	40,754	36,227	11,612	6,682
2014	492,476	353,735	2,049	355,784	38,048	-2,555	315,182	79,288	98,006	42,278	37,633	11,648	6,772
2015	511,340	367,059	663	367,722	39,385	-2,592	325,745	84,013	101,582	43,801	38,877	11,674	6,862
2016	521,623	373,444	666	374,109	40,914	-2,690	330,506	87,128	103,989	44,576	39,589	11,702	6,931
2017	541,289	387,276	1,063	388,339	43,316	-2,462	342,560	92,224	106,505	46,116	41,084	11,738	6,988
2018	562,523	400,181	1,609	401,791	44,177	-2,011	355,602	97,686	109,235	47,822	42,848	11,763	7,067
2019	582,400	413,641	685	414,325	46,071	-2,261	365,993	101,703	114,704	49,404	44,183	11,789	7,072
2020	623,836	417,085	1,973	419,058	46,700	-2,391	369,967	101,860	152,009	52,875	47,638	11,798	6,853
2021	670,873	442,886	3,284	446,170	49,538	-2,178	394,455	111,525	164,893	57,022	50,730	11,765	7,048
2022	679,233	468,399	2,846	471,245	53,913	-2,354	414,978	121,228	143,027	57,759	50,619	11,760	7,305
2023	711,895	495,842	2,072	497,914	57,129	-2,416	438,368	128,564	144,963	60,402	54,146	11,786	...

... = Not available.

Personal Income and Employment by Region and State: Oklahoma

(Millions of dollars, except as noted.)

Year	Personal income, total	Derivation of personal income: Earnings by place of work: Nonfarm	Farm	Total	Less: Contributions for government social insurance	Plus: Adjustment for residence	Equals: Net earnings by place of residence	Plus: Dividends, interest, and rent	Plus: Personal current transfer receipts	Per capita (dollars): Personal income	Disposable personal income	Population (thousands)	Total employment (thousands)
1960	4,612	3,359	335	3,694	150	7	3,550	684	378	1,974	1,789	2,336	...
1961	4,774	3,492	301	3,793	159	9	3,643	715	416	2,006	1,811	2,380	...
1962	4,985	3,723	240	3,963	178	11	3,796	749	441	2,054	1,853	2,427	...
1963	5,151	3,889	214	4,104	209	12	3,908	773	471	2,112	1,907	2,439	...
1964	5,519	4,180	208	4,388	208	14	4,195	833	491	2,256	2,056	2,446	...
1965	5,913	4,415	278	4,693	216	17	4,494	894	526	2,424	2,209	2,440	...
1966	6,343	4,812	267	5,079	286	21	4,814	946	584	2,585	2,343	2,454	...
1967	6,929	5,274	276	5,550	337	25	5,239	991	700	2,784	2,519	2,489	...
1968	7,589	5,856	219	6,076	385	31	5,721	1,080	789	3,032	2,726	2,503	...
1969	8,455	6,400	275	6,676	401	64	6,338	1,261	856	3,335	2,954	2,535	1,107
1970	9,326	6,897	359	7,256	431	65	6,890	1,454	981	3,634	3,257	2,566	1,120
1971	10,164	7,484	335	7,819	484	64	7,400	1,633	1,131	3,882	3,522	2,618	1,132
1972	11,153	8,246	417	8,664	558	73	8,179	1,735	1,240	4,197	3,754	2,657	1,183
1973	12,653	9,142	734	9,875	720	83	9,238	2,009	1,406	4,696	4,237	2,694	1,221
1974	14,080	10,379	452	10,831	845	106	10,092	2,324	1,664	5,153	4,576	2,732	1,256
1975	15,736	11,485	404	11,889	928	142	11,103	2,581	2,052	5,677	5,116	2,772	1,269
1976	17,349	12,810	338	13,148	1,054	177	12,270	2,828	2,251	6,145	5,503	2,823	1,305
1977	19,296	14,590	183	14,773	1,198	152	13,728	3,176	2,393	6,733	5,993	2,866	1,359
1978	21,896	16,739	174	16,913	1,418	149	15,644	3,678	2,575	7,517	6,623	2,913	1,428
1979	25,414	19,128	634	19,762	1,688	162	18,236	4,223	2,955	8,557	7,517	2,970	1,481
1980	29,287	22,149	265	22,413	1,971	170	20,612	5,256	3,419	9,631	8,401	3,041	1,547
1981	34,193	25,621	330	25,952	2,450	198	23,699	6,611	3,882	11,044	9,489	3,096	1,625
1982	38,159	28,022	487	28,509	2,748	204	25,965	7,818	4,376	11,902	10,152	3,206	1,673
1983	39,089	28,143	214	28,357	2,739	241	25,858	8,429	4,801	11,880	10,473	3,290	1,638
1984	41,897	29,974	376	30,351	2,969	289	27,671	9,245	4,982	12,752	11,345	3,286	1,665
1985	43,595	30,826	382	31,208	3,109	331	28,430	9,844	5,322	13,326	11,866	3,271	1,648
1986	43,868	30,715	645	31,360	3,161	382	28,580	9,630	5,658	13,486	12,275	3,253	1,588
1987	43,620	30,681	564	31,245	3,181	429	28,493	9,241	5,886	13,588	12,200	3,210	1,599
1988	45,585	31,950	765	32,715	3,498	478	29,694	9,659	6,231	14,393	12,925	3,167	1,608
1989	48,472	33,778	802	34,580	3,731	505	31,354	10,490	6,629	15,387	13,738	3,150	1,623
1990	51,112	35,735	862	36,597	4,066	568	33,099	10,880	7,133	16,232	14,316	3,149	1,655
1991	52,724	37,115	623	37,738	4,324	597	34,011	10,908	7,804	16,604	14,788	3,175	1,668
1992	56,001	39,331	844	40,175	4,550	618	36,244	11,028	8,730	17,389	15,556	3,221	1,680
1993	58,201	41,115	867	41,982	4,798	657	37,841	11,180	9,180	17,895	16,018	3,252	1,716
1994	60,763	42,739	826	43,565	5,058	714	39,221	11,790	9,753	18,520	16,545	3,281	1,748
1995	63,358	44,418	286	44,704	5,276	747	40,175	12,650	10,533	19,152	17,097	3,308	1,800
1996	67,111	47,018	359	47,377	5,474	780	42,682	13,375	11,055	20,092	17,850	3,340	1,850
1997	71,071	49,951	662	50,613	5,734	859	45,738	13,975	11,359	21,071	18,589	3,373	1,897
1998	74,944	52,879	518	53,397	6,033	893	48,257	15,098	11,589	22,009	19,382	3,405	1,939
1999	76,957	54,004	839	54,843	6,218	939	49,564	15,288	12,105	22,390	19,691	3,437	1,953
2000	83,332	58,212	831	59,044	6,600	1,019	53,463	17,073	12,797	24,124	21,224	3,454	1,994
2001	88,610	62,083	815	62,899	7,047	1,014	56,865	17,612	14,132	25,557	22,501	3,467	2,009
2002	90,712	63,618	977	64,595	7,297	986	58,284	17,330	15,098	25,999	23,399	3,489	1,988
2003	95,276	66,918	956	67,874	7,509	967	61,332	17,853	16,091	27,184	24,712	3,505	1,971
2004	102,917	72,810	1,260	74,070	8,031	949	66,988	18,930	16,999	29,194	26,624	3,525	1,998
2005	112,488	79,897	1,300	81,197	8,506	911	73,602	20,626	18,261	31,699	28,666	3,549	2,043
2006	124,537	88,928	681	89,609	9,110	883	81,382	23,151	20,004	34,650	31,151	3,594	2,096
2007	128,994	89,784	664	90,448	9,585	846	81,709	25,839	21,447	35,493	31,738	3,634	2,150
2008	143,655	99,887	800	100,686	10,040	791	91,437	28,160	24,058	39,154	35,169	3,669	2,187
2009	133,218	91,180	56	91,236	9,848	679	82,067	25,207	25,945	35,835	32,982	3,718	2,137
2010	139,695	94,871	815	95,686	10,095	612	86,203	25,805	27,688	37,157	34,211	3,760	2,130
2011	150,302	101,224	1,351	102,576	9,732	561	93,404	28,875	28,023	39,693	36,063	3,787	2,159
2012	159,875	108,019	1,760	109,779	10,324	551	100,006	31,227	28,642	41,903	38,111	3,815	2,212
2013	167,797	117,460	1,765	119,225	11,890	472	107,807	30,731	29,259	43,605	39,539	3,848	2,249
2014	177,636	124,028	2,192	126,220	12,225	462	114,456	33,003	30,177	45,882	41,612	3,872	2,274
2015	172,726	119,467	1,878	121,345	12,305	434	109,474	31,998	31,255	44,277	40,009	3,901	2,288
2016	164,709	111,816	993	112,809	12,060	456	101,205	31,206	32,298	42,052	38,057	3,917	2,287
2017	171,995	116,621	1,094	117,715	12,542	443	105,616	32,777	33,603	43,871	39,772	3,920	2,292
2018	180,824	122,987	940	123,928	13,259	475	111,144	34,889	34,792	46,029	41,993	3,928	2,312
2019	189,981	128,772	1,052	129,823	13,798	468	116,494	36,269	37,218	48,172	43,963	3,944	2,310
2020	199,233	128,142	808	128,951	14,034	459	115,376	37,049	46,809	50,245	46,276	3,965	2,267
2021	220,177	137,763	1,474	139,237	14,734	592	125,094	41,652	53,431	55,159	50,456	3,992	2,314
2022	226,308	149,271	560	149,831	15,999	652	134,483	43,114	48,711	56,306	50,965	4,019	2,413
2023	237,145	157,720	499	158,219	17,134	685	141,770	44,896	50,479	58,499	53,761	4,054	...

... = Not available.

Personal Income and Employment by Region and State: Oregon

(Millions of dollars, except as noted.)

Year	Personal income, total	Derivation of personal income								Per capita (dollars)		Population (thousands)	Total employment (thousands)
		Earnings by place of work			Less: Contributions for government social insurance	Plus: Adjustment for residence	Equals: Net earnings by place of residence	Plus: Dividends, interest, and rent	Plus: Personal current transfer receipts	Personal income	Disposable personal income		
		Nonfarm	Farm	Total									
1960	4,192	3,290	174	3,463	207	-18	3,238	650	304	2,366	2,083	1,772	...
1961	4,351	3,378	161	3,539	211	-19	3,309	690	352	2,435	2,163	1,787	...
1962	4,622	3,606	172	3,778	232	-23	3,524	739	359	2,542	2,249	1,818	...
1963	4,867	3,849	163	4,012	266	-27	3,718	778	371	2,626	2,304	1,853	...
1964	5,236	4,178	150	4,328	271	-33	4,025	828	384	2,773	2,451	1,888	...
1965	5,681	4,540	168	4,708	276	-39	4,394	872	414	2,933	2,610	1,937	...
1966	6,118	4,942	195	5,137	352	-42	4,742	929	447	3,107	2,747	1,969	...
1967	6,487	5,198	185	5,384	392	-47	4,945	1,010	533	3,278	2,899	1,979	...
1968	7,063	5,693	183	5,876	444	-54	5,378	1,085	601	3,524	3,085	2,004	...
1969	7,832	6,225	226	6,451	482	-82	5,887	1,283	662	3,798	3,273	2,062	920
1970	8,537	6,605	216	6,821	505	-63	6,254	1,479	805	4,065	3,564	2,100	926
1971	9,383	7,232	204	7,437	569	-52	6,817	1,634	932	4,364	3,861	2,150	951
1972	10,511	8,165	259	8,424	679	-45	7,700	1,789	1,022	4,788	4,197	2,195	1,001
1973	11,845	9,177	371	9,548	880	-50	8,618	2,015	1,213	5,291	4,653	2,239	1,058
1974	13,432	10,174	477	10,651	1,002	-58	9,590	2,346	1,496	5,889	5,144	2,281	1,089
1975	14,920	11,053	394	11,447	1,057	-31	10,359	2,660	1,901	6,418	5,699	2,325	1,105
1976	16,822	12,730	370	13,099	1,234	-15	11,850	2,901	2,071	7,091	6,233	2,372	1,156
1977	18,812	14,459	320	14,778	1,420	-74	13,284	3,290	2,239	7,712	6,683	2,439	1,223
1978	21,563	16,791	317	17,108	1,693	-128	15,288	3,831	2,444	8,592	7,418	2,510	1,296
1979	24,390	18,994	390	19,384	1,987	-178	17,220	4,430	2,740	9,460	8,134	2,578	1,350
1980	27,038	20,316	477	20,793	2,127	-218	18,449	5,333	3,256	10,237	8,853	2,641	1,350
1981	29,154	21,172	406	21,578	2,369	-269	18,941	6,446	3,767	10,927	9,488	2,668	1,319
1982	29,990	21,075	293	21,369	2,403	-258	18,708	7,036	4,247	11,254	9,803	2,665	1,270
1983	31,913	22,242	301	22,543	2,558	-246	19,739	7,610	4,564	12,029	10,588	2,653	1,295
1984	34,540	24,305	402	24,708	2,890	-286	21,532	8,295	4,713	12,953	11,450	2,667	1,342
1985	36,298	25,609	428	26,037	3,070	-315	22,652	8,715	4,931	13,581	11,959	2,673	1,370
1986	38,196	27,194	550	27,744	3,251	-371	24,123	9,053	5,020	14,233	12,470	2,684	1,406
1987	40,029	29,134	515	29,649	3,438	-433	25,778	9,054	5,197	14,820	12,975	2,701	1,455
1988	43,730	32,115	702	32,817	3,931	-501	28,385	9,814	5,531	15,952	14,144	2,741	1,522
1989	48,034	34,896	675	35,571	4,272	-562	30,738	11,213	6,083	17,213	14,990	2,791	1,574
1990	51,925	38,183	713	38,896	4,791	-618	33,487	11,824	6,615	18,153	15,959	2,860	1,626
1991	54,722	40,258	727	40,985	5,106	-683	35,196	12,201	7,325	18,686	16,365	2,929	1,636
1992	58,422	43,359	730	44,089	5,459	-780	37,850	12,422	8,151	19,528	17,098	2,992	1,654
1993	62,516	46,361	850	47,211	5,830	-875	40,506	13,306	8,704	20,428	17,844	3,060	1,698
1994	66,933	49,956	776	50,732	6,322	-941	43,469	14,428	9,037	21,444	18,660	3,121	1,781
1995	72,044	53,273	688	53,961	6,789	-1,119	46,053	15,980	10,011	22,624	19,709	3,184	1,845
1996	77,669	57,824	840	58,665	7,452	-1,355	49,858	17,158	10,652	23,919	20,737	3,247	1,920
1997	82,277	62,090	956	63,046	7,910	-1,540	53,596	17,718	10,963	24,900	21,399	3,304	1,986
1998	86,878	66,141	859	67,000	8,366	-1,664	56,971	18,508	11,399	25,915	22,307	3,352	2,022
1999	89,931	69,695	821	70,516	8,726	-1,757	60,033	17,492	12,406	26,498	22,660	3,394	2,051
2000	96,914	75,653	823	76,476	9,417	-1,999	65,060	18,804	13,049	28,257	24,061	3,430	2,092
2001	99,786	77,069	833	77,902	9,449	-2,111	66,342	18,792	14,652	28,774	24,830	3,468	2,079
2002	101,042	78,069	836	78,905	9,628	-2,189	67,088	18,133	15,821	28,759	25,326	3,513	2,062
2003	104,730	80,658	1,115	81,772	9,951	-2,366	69,455	19,015	16,259	29,523	26,203	3,547	2,077
2004	110,581	85,592	1,254	86,845	10,655	-2,592	73,598	20,253	16,730	30,980	27,506	3,569	2,133
2005	116,073	90,302	1,236	91,538	11,251	-2,883	77,404	21,000	17,669	32,125	28,091	3,613	2,197
2006	126,600	97,403	1,333	98,736	12,031	-3,274	83,431	24,165	19,004	34,488	30,073	3,671	2,256
2007	132,606	100,904	1,334	102,238	12,537	-3,545	86,156	26,029	20,421	35,624	31,245	3,722	2,307
2008	138,900	101,907	1,312	103,219	12,706	-3,667	86,846	28,343	23,711	36,856	32,286	3,769	2,289
2009	134,392	96,532	1,119	97,650	12,193	-3,490	81,968	25,343	27,081	35,286	31,784	3,809	2,189
2010	137,926	98,550	1,051	99,600	12,551	-3,370	83,679	24,966	29,282	35,941	32,252	3,838	2,174
2011	145,345	102,345	1,277	103,621	11,569	-3,702	88,350	27,309	29,687	37,531	33,246	3,873	2,202
2012	152,602	107,946	1,405	109,350	12,112	-3,913	93,325	29,618	29,659	39,128	34,724	3,900	2,220
2013	154,851	111,563	1,623	113,186	14,202	-3,906	95,078	29,022	30,752	39,462	34,501	3,924	2,260
2014	165,172	117,373	1,550	118,923	15,042	-3,887	99,994	31,535	33,643	41,653	36,391	3,965	2,323
2015	177,478	125,600	1,738	127,338	15,902	-4,140	107,296	34,296	35,886	44,166	38,284	4,018	2,391
2016	186,105	132,440	1,702	134,142	16,634	-4,527	112,981	36,144	36,980	45,467	39,294	4,093	2,450
2017	197,262	140,963	1,277	142,240	17,837	-4,732	119,672	39,436	38,155	47,565	41,260	4,147	2,516
2018	210,045	149,962	1,329	151,292	18,600	-5,114	127,578	42,022	40,446	50,209	43,771	4,183	2,570
2019	219,983	157,919	1,266	159,185	19,591	-5,468	134,126	43,015	42,842	52,178	45,336	4,216	2,579
2020	239,863	163,089	1,489	164,578	20,019	-5,990	138,569	44,336	56,957	56,504	49,658	4,245	2,493
2021	262,382	178,516	1,510	180,026	22,950	-6,351	150,725	48,852	62,806	61,643	53,447	4,256	2,560
2022	264,174	188,736	1,600	190,336	24,898	-7,168	158,270	50,824	55,080	62,314	53,089	4,239	2,658
2023	276,973	198,988	1,422	200,410	26,185	-7,533	166,693	53,137	57,144	65,426	57,306	4,233	...

... = Not available.

Personal Income and Employment by Region and State: Pennsylvania

(Millions of dollars, except as noted.)

Year	Personal income, total	Derivation of personal income: Earnings by place of work: Nonfarm	Farm	Total	Less: Contributions for government social insurance	Plus: Adjustment for residence	Equals: Net earnings by place of residence	Plus: Dividends, interest, and rent	Plus: Personal current transfer receipts	Per capita (dollars): Personal income	Disposable personal income	Population (thousands)	Total employment (thousands)
1960	26,119	21,947	298	22,245	1,211	-81	20,954	3,243	1,922	2,305	2,049	11,329	...
1961	26,686	22,134	302	22,436	1,225	-86	21,125	3,378	2,183	2,342	2,095	11,392	...
1962	27,845	23,248	219	23,467	1,334	-104	22,029	3,650	2,167	2,452	2,180	11,355	...
1963	28,908	24,044	261	24,305	1,474	-113	22,719	3,945	2,245	2,530	2,246	11,424	...
1964	30,915	25,799	269	26,068	1,530	-136	24,401	4,255	2,259	2,684	2,412	11,519	...
1965	33,159	27,650	278	27,928	1,594	-155	26,180	4,609	2,370	2,854	2,556	11,620	...
1966	35,757	30,386	266	30,652	2,148	-201	28,303	4,879	2,575	3,066	2,726	11,664	...
1967	38,299	32,176	359	32,535	2,317	-231	29,987	5,244	3,068	3,279	2,918	11,681	...
1968	41,638	34,789	314	35,102	2,421	-268	32,413	5,713	3,512	3,546	3,132	11,741	...
1969	45,346	38,065	372	38,437	2,809	-436	35,192	6,162	3,992	3,862	3,364	11,741	5,250
1970	48,844	40,132	387	40,519	2,928	-405	37,187	6,743	4,914	4,135	3,630	11,812	5,226
1971	51,836	42,076	335	42,411	3,186	-373	38,851	7,209	5,775	4,362	3,872	11,884	5,159
1972	56,580	46,003	347	46,350	3,654	-373	42,323	7,730	6,527	4,753	4,132	11,905	5,247
1973	62,033	50,635	485	51,119	4,627	-342	46,150	8,578	7,305	5,219	4,565	11,885	5,402
1974	68,133	55,005	463	55,468	5,222	-348	49,898	9,695	8,539	5,743	4,996	11,864	5,419
1975	74,473	58,422	425	58,847	5,400	-361	53,085	10,560	10,828	6,259	5,535	11,898	5,302
1976	81,283	63,729	517	64,246	6,000	-337	57,908	11,345	12,030	6,838	6,021	11,887	5,353
1977	89,174	70,233	469	70,701	6,595	-321	63,786	12,606	12,783	7,505	6,571	11,882	5,429
1978	98,272	77,966	506	78,472	7,508	-320	70,644	13,906	13,722	8,283	7,224	11,865	5,562
1979	108,710	85,953	642	86,595	8,576	-360	77,659	15,599	15,452	9,156	7,943	11,874	5,664
1980	119,134	91,396	424	91,820	9,175	-380	82,266	19,158	17,711	10,038	8,720	11,868	5,624
1981	131,384	98,190	635	98,825	10,559	-333	87,932	23,515	19,937	11,079	9,558	11,859	5,584
1982	140,328	100,597	564	101,160	10,980	-162	90,019	27,478	22,831	11,847	10,310	11,845	5,474
1983	147,212	104,882	361	105,242	11,571	-23	93,648	28,875	24,688	12,436	10,959	11,838	5,433
1984	158,759	114,007	848	114,855	13,095	145	101,905	32,005	24,849	13,437	11,843	11,815	5,577
1985	168,298	120,770	846	121,616	14,060	280	107,836	34,461	26,001	14,298	12,588	11,771	5,679
1986	177,003	127,213	886	128,098	14,908	399	113,589	35,995	27,420	15,022	13,252	11,783	5,772
1987	186,828	137,257	883	138,140	15,896	528	122,772	36,009	28,046	15,818	13,861	11,811	5,957
1988	203,002	150,069	743	150,812	17,715	779	133,876	39,578	29,547	17,137	15,076	11,846	6,120
1989	219,827	160,091	998	161,089	18,645	971	143,415	44,986	31,426	18,526	16,251	11,866	6,216
1990	232,900	169,009	1,002	170,011	19,839	1,039	151,211	47,396	34,293	19,566	17,218	11,903	6,293
1991	242,843	174,106	734	174,841	20,662	1,053	155,231	48,005	39,607	20,267	17,944	11,982	6,212
1992	255,912	185,362	1,202	186,565	21,889	1,226	165,902	47,855	42,155	21,238	18,792	12,049	6,216
1993	265,557	192,744	1,030	193,773	23,105	1,340	172,008	49,178	44,371	21,911	19,402	12,120	6,256
1994	274,856	200,288	921	201,209	24,456	1,652	178,405	51,015	45,436	22,592	19,946	12,166	6,323
1995	287,344	207,617	642	208,259	25,290	2,167	185,136	54,755	47,453	23,556	20,723	12,198	6,423
1996	301,836	215,888	1,118	217,006	25,752	2,433	193,687	57,746	50,402	24,699	21,599	12,220	6,477
1997	317,131	227,798	767	228,565	26,961	2,873	204,477	61,153	51,501	25,935	22,540	12,228	6,585
1998	334,422	241,189	893	242,082	28,148	3,271	217,204	64,989	52,229	27,309	23,633	12,246	6,658
1999	348,489	255,257	815	256,072	29,402	3,556	230,227	63,684	54,579	28,416	24,568	12,264	6,764
2000	372,691	271,569	1,103	272,673	30,864	4,056	245,865	68,912	57,914	30,339	26,217	12,284	6,905
2001	388,186	283,756	1,011	284,767	31,934	4,317	257,150	69,162	61,874	31,563	27,399	12,299	6,915
2002	395,633	290,930	641	291,571	32,708	4,588	263,451	66,535	65,647	32,084	28,464	12,331	6,887
2003	409,186	300,530	1,227	301,758	33,499	5,076	273,335	67,573	68,278	33,066	29,610	12,375	6,876
2004	432,635	320,589	1,545	322,135	35,209	5,866	292,792	69,011	70,831	34,860	31,322	12,411	6,952
2005	450,360	333,321	1,367	334,688	37,000	6,888	304,577	69,682	76,101	36,173	32,167	12,450	7,054
2006	472,941	345,635	1,142	346,777	39,017	7,335	315,094	77,930	79,916	37,803	33,405	12,511	7,153
2007	502,659	361,701	1,327	363,028	40,541	8,221	330,709	86,583	85,367	40,008	35,124	12,564	7,265
2008	522,994	367,768	1,380	369,148	41,780	8,572	335,940	92,005	95,049	41,467	36,510	12,612	7,279
2009	512,318	358,332	960	359,292	41,247	7,328	325,372	83,417	103,529	40,446	36,514	12,667	7,102
2010	535,336	374,584	1,351	375,935	42,349	7,999	341,584	82,770	110,982	42,098	37,915	12,717	7,120
2011	563,529	391,525	1,794	393,319	39,407	7,864	361,776	90,247	111,506	44,120	39,332	12,773	7,217
2012	584,880	404,704	2,059	406,763	40,314	8,225	374,674	98,592	111,615	45,638	40,796	12,816	7,285
2013	589,720	419,155	2,303	421,457	46,675	8,138	382,921	93,472	113,327	45,904	40,630	12,847	7,350
2014	611,422	431,015	2,647	433,662	48,217	8,970	394,415	99,844	117,163	47,469	41,929	12,880	7,435
2015	635,818	448,528	1,703	450,232	50,120	8,950	409,062	104,022	122,735	49,293	43,308	12,899	7,510
2016	653,329	458,264	882	459,146	51,022	9,435	417,559	106,883	128,887	50,574	44,545	12,918	7,594
2017	671,703	471,323	1,655	472,978	53,688	9,995	429,286	112,392	130,025	51,888	45,783	12,945	7,662
2018	707,043	489,531	1,009	490,541	55,541	10,874	445,874	122,109	139,060	54,468	48,397	12,981	7,763
2019	729,142	504,444	1,524	505,968	57,644	11,639	459,962	125,692	143,488	56,125	49,726	12,991	7,773
2020	783,826	501,157	1,102	502,259	57,090	12,571	457,740	130,909	195,177	60,315	53,885	12,995	7,413
2021	833,322	530,768	1,833	532,602	60,411	13,377	485,568	142,408	205,346	64,035	56,282	13,014	7,650
2022	836,778	560,264	2,339	562,603	65,627	14,044	511,020	151,239	174,520	64,506	55,624	12,972	7,978
2023	879,310	589,318	1,425	590,743	69,024	14,756	536,475	161,355	181,480	67,839	60,071	12,962	...

... = Not available.

Personal Income and Employment by Region and State: Rhode Island

(Millions of dollars, except as noted.)

Year	Personal income, total	Derivation of personal income: Earnings by place of work: Nonfarm	Farm	Total	Less: Contributions for government social insurance	Plus: Adjustment for residence	Equals: Net earnings by place of residence	Plus: Dividends, interest, and rent	Plus: Personal current transfer receipts	Per capita (dollars): Personal income	Disposable personal income	Population (thousands)	Total employment (thousands)
1960	2,016	1,615	8	1,622	96	54	1,580	285	151	2,358	2,107	855	...
1961	2,108	1,669	7	1,676	98	57	1,635	307	166	2,457	2,189	858	...
1962	2,267	1,788	7	1,796	108	62	1,750	348	169	2,603	2,328	871	...
1963	2,368	1,845	7	1,852	118	67	1,801	388	179	2,703	2,416	876	...
1964	2,522	1,969	8	1,977	122	73	1,928	410	184	2,849	2,580	885	...
1965	2,723	2,122	8	2,130	133	82	2,079	446	198	3,049	2,755	893	...
1966	2,973	2,344	9	2,353	162	95	2,286	469	218	3,307	2,966	899	...
1967	3,223	2,516	7	2,523	175	105	2,452	506	265	3,546	3,193	909	...
1968	3,522	2,748	8	2,757	200	115	2,672	543	308	3,820	3,403	922	...
1969	3,742	2,949	8	2,957	231	62	2,789	606	347	4,015	3,554	932	440
1970	4,093	3,164	9	3,174	245	63	2,992	678	423	4,306	3,854	951	440
1971	4,337	3,323	8	3,332	267	58	3,123	718	497	4,499	4,030	964	436
1972	4,722	3,656	8	3,664	307	53	3,410	766	546	4,836	4,283	976	447
1973	5,045	3,888	6	3,895	381	69	3,582	838	625	5,158	4,569	978	452
1974	5,289	3,956	9	3,965	410	88	3,642	913	734	5,547	4,898	954	439
1975	5,742	4,115	9	4,124	416	82	3,790	980	972	6,068	5,468	946	424
1976	6,272	4,606	9	4,615	473	88	4,229	1,049	995	6,600	5,890	950	442
1977	6,865	5,066	8	5,074	521	103	4,656	1,167	1,042	7,187	6,427	955	459
1978	7,531	5,628	9	5,637	597	101	5,141	1,278	1,112	7,868	6,937	957	474
1979	8,363	6,268	8	6,276	685	108	5,699	1,427	1,236	8,742	7,632	957	483
1980	9,393	6,823	8	6,831	745	122	6,208	1,755	1,431	9,901	8,699	949	484
1981	10,455	7,350	9	7,359	851	153	6,661	2,158	1,636	10,971	9,641	953	484
1982	11,259	7,701	27	7,728	902	207	7,034	2,429	1,796	11,799	10,428	954	475
1983	12,186	8,339	37	8,376	988	263	7,651	2,621	1,914	12,741	11,306	956	480
1984	13,361	9,223	32	9,256	1,136	331	8,451	2,943	1,967	13,890	12,367	962	504
1985	14,402	10,012	42	10,054	1,220	391	9,225	3,089	2,088	14,864	13,216	969	519
1986	15,441	10,873	43	10,917	1,330	417	10,003	3,266	2,172	15,799	13,969	977	537
1987	16,482	11,788	41	11,829	1,430	484	10,883	3,361	2,237	16,655	14,565	990	546
1988	18,223	12,997	42	13,039	1,595	559	12,003	3,822	2,398	18,289	16,106	996	560
1989	19,829	13,734	32	13,766	1,661	625	12,730	4,486	2,613	19,816	17,450	1,001	560
1990	20,430	14,076	31	14,107	1,790	671	12,987	4,553	2,890	20,309	17,936	1,006	550
1991	20,648	13,825	32	13,857	1,809	697	12,745	4,393	3,511	20,431	18,117	1,011	524
1992	21,573	14,684	29	14,713	1,923	718	13,508	4,403	3,661	21,305	18,973	1,013	529
1993	22,484	15,214	30	15,244	2,011	761	13,993	4,517	3,973	22,149	19,698	1,015	533
1994	23,051	15,747	25	15,772	2,109	830	14,492	4,608	3,951	22,689	20,137	1,016	533
1995	24,279	16,467	25	16,492	2,182	859	15,168	4,941	4,170	23,873	21,180	1,017	536
1996	25,113	16,958	23	16,982	2,229	929	15,681	5,179	4,253	24,599	21,693	1,021	540
1997	26,554	17,884	16	17,899	2,334	995	16,560	5,478	4,516	25,898	22,622	1,025	546
1998	28,350	19,354	15	19,370	2,472	1,074	17,971	5,813	4,566	27,493	23,920	1,031	555
1999	29,581	20,593	15	20,608	2,589	1,175	19,194	5,642	4,746	28,432	24,718	1,040	567
2000	31,875	22,225	16	22,241	2,756	1,335	20,820	6,133	4,922	30,350	26,192	1,050	583
2001	33,612	23,226	18	23,244	2,866	1,429	21,807	6,300	5,505	31,795	27,497	1,057	585
2002	34,966	24,468	22	24,491	2,975	1,415	22,931	6,291	5,744	32,801	29,059	1,066	588
2003	36,700	25,897	23	25,920	3,145	1,376	24,151	6,644	5,905	34,256	30,638	1,071	594
2004	38,542	27,198	25	27,223	3,295	1,599	25,527	6,716	6,298	35,867	32,121	1,075	602
2005	39,241	27,990	24	28,014	3,424	1,440	26,030	6,663	6,549	36,746	32,674	1,068	606
2006	41,162	29,344	23	29,367	3,615	1,452	27,205	7,171	6,786	38,719	34,275	1,063	611
2007	42,935	29,848	24	29,872	3,701	1,530	27,700	7,799	7,436	40,608	35,784	1,057	618
2008	43,769	29,744	27	29,771	3,748	1,311	27,334	8,173	8,262	41,487	36,711	1,055	609
2009	42,765	28,732	27	28,759	3,689	1,239	26,309	7,493	8,963	40,588	36,857	1,054	588
2010	44,974	30,611	27	30,638	3,789	1,024	27,872	7,568	9,534	42,631	38,651	1,055	586
2011	46,685	31,221	22	31,244	3,495	1,280	29,028	8,039	9,618	44,099	39,416	1,059	592
2012	48,187	32,330	26	32,356	3,579	1,423	30,200	8,497	9,490	45,305	40,690	1,064	593
2013	48,187	33,054	24	33,078	4,117	1,415	30,376	8,179	9,632	45,112	40,021	1,068	602
2014	50,045	34,203	20	34,223	4,290	1,154	31,087	8,595	10,364	46,639	41,287	1,073	613
2015	51,775	35,365	25	35,390	4,494	1,341	32,237	8,987	10,552	48,058	42,430	1,077	627
2016	52,515	35,892	17	35,910	4,616	1,421	32,714	9,228	10,573	48,523	42,753	1,082	633
2017	54,704	37,055	26	37,081	4,769	1,659	33,971	9,834	10,900	50,423	44,570	1,085	639
2018	56,919	38,297	20	38,317	4,934	2,061	35,444	10,315	11,161	52,135	46,371	1,092	649
2019	60,314	39,695	17	39,712	5,091	3,028	37,649	10,952	11,712	55,105	48,895	1,095	651
2020	64,757	39,960	17	39,978	5,084	3,186	38,079	10,981	15,696	59,061	52,707	1,096	616
2021	69,837	43,169	19	43,189	5,492	3,250	40,946	12,086	16,806	63,657	55,913	1,097	640
2022	69,514	45,844	26	45,871	5,909	2,962	42,924	12,506	14,085	63,551	54,687	1,094	669
2023	72,859	48,271	22	48,293	6,202	3,020	45,111	13,209	14,539	66,480	58,735	1,096	...

... = Not available.

Personal Income and Employment by Region and State: South Carolina

(Millions of dollars, except as noted.)

Year	Personal income, total	Derivation of personal income: Earnings by place of work: Nonfarm	Farm	Total	Less: Contributions for government social insurance	Plus: Adjustment for residence	Equals: Net earnings by place of residence	Plus: Dividends, interest, and rent	Plus: Personal current transfer receipts	Per capita (dollars): Personal income	Disposable personal income	Population (thousands)	Total employment (thousands)
1960	3,570	2,898	169	3,068	135	18	2,950	410	210	1,493	1,371	2,392	...
1961	3,748	2,990	196	3,186	138	19	3,067	443	238	1,556	1,427	2,409	...
1962	4,018	3,227	185	3,412	153	23	3,282	484	253	1,658	1,512	2,423	...
1963	4,252	3,433	189	3,621	189	26	3,458	522	272	1,728	1,577	2,460	...
1964	4,567	3,721	180	3,902	203	30	3,729	554	284	1,845	1,697	2,475	...
1965	5,048	4,125	182	4,307	221	35	4,122	616	310	2,024	1,853	2,494	...
1966	5,672	4,720	196	4,916	290	44	4,670	660	342	2,251	2,043	2,520	...
1967	6,121	5,099	197	5,296	342	50	5,004	715	401	2,416	2,193	2,533	...
1968	6,796	5,728	155	5,884	388	58	5,554	771	471	2,656	2,391	2,559	...
1969	7,604	6,260	188	6,448	417	128	6,159	909	537	2,959	2,641	2,570	1,170
1970	8,380	6,753	189	6,942	449	128	6,621	1,090	669	3,225	2,912	2,598	1,196
1971	9,181	7,360	204	7,564	509	138	7,193	1,209	779	3,449	3,120	2,662	1,215
1972	10,309	8,311	214	8,525	600	154	8,080	1,353	876	3,792	3,368	2,718	1,262
1973	11,692	9,405	303	9,708	773	167	9,101	1,547	1,044	4,213	3,758	2,775	1,328
1974	13,235	10,506	342	10,849	898	180	10,131	1,786	1,318	4,655	4,144	2,843	1,365
1975	14,394	11,040	277	11,317	928	191	10,580	2,000	1,814	4,963	4,529	2,900	1,326
1976	16,096	12,610	234	12,844	1,089	225	11,980	2,189	1,927	5,472	4,926	2,941	1,376
1977	17,593	13,900	188	14,088	1,199	247	13,135	2,444	2,013	5,886	5,280	2,989	1,411
1978	19,879	15,746	246	15,993	1,389	264	14,868	2,801	2,210	6,537	5,848	3,041	1,466
1979	22,283	17,625	260	17,885	1,608	286	16,563	3,171	2,549	7,219	6,387	3,087	1,507
1980	24,972	19,452	36	19,488	1,774	318	18,032	3,837	3,103	7,967	7,065	3,135	1,523
1981	28,102	21,429	172	21,601	2,091	348	19,857	4,661	3,584	8,839	7,800	3,179	1,536
1982	29,878	22,212	195	22,406	2,196	381	20,591	5,352	3,935	9,315	8,302	3,208	1,514
1983	32,452	24,358	51	24,408	2,470	392	22,330	5,926	4,196	10,034	8,941	3,234	1,547
1984	36,149	27,185	270	27,455	2,850	425	25,030	6,694	4,425	11,048	9,889	3,272	1,625
1985	38,692	29,037	197	29,233	3,096	477	26,614	7,283	4,794	11,713	10,452	3,303	1,655
1986	41,355	31,238	91	31,329	3,425	543	28,446	7,851	5,058	12,371	11,047	3,343	1,697
1987	44,240	33,735	250	33,985	3,665	586	30,906	8,135	5,199	13,087	11,633	3,381	1,738
1988	48,206	36,871	348	37,219	4,151	610	33,678	8,979	5,549	14,128	12,637	3,412	1,809
1989	52,467	39,458	367	39,825	4,513	571	35,883	10,161	6,423	15,178	13,477	3,457	1,858
1990	56,391	42,562	300	42,862	4,974	507	38,395	10,880	7,116	16,106	14,297	3,501	1,913
1991	58,931	43,801	399	44,200	5,192	494	39,502	11,270	8,159	16,505	14,775	3,570	1,886
1992	62,655	46,512	377	46,889	5,480	504	41,913	11,566	9,177	17,306	15,528	3,620	1,897
1993	65,852	48,866	337	49,204	5,824	520	43,900	12,118	9,835	17,976	16,115	3,663	1,931
1994	69,838	51,258	491	51,749	6,195	636	46,190	12,960	10,688	18,848	16,854	3,705	1,979
1995	73,997	54,047	384	54,431	6,555	767	48,644	13,924	11,430	19,740	17,575	3,749	2,038
1996	78,652	56,777	463	57,241	6,771	878	51,347	15,001	12,303	20,719	18,359	3,796	2,080
1997	83,697	60,342	472	60,814	7,187	1,036	54,663	16,146	12,888	21,685	19,143	3,860	2,141
1998	89,752	65,002	334	65,336	7,734	1,115	58,717	17,487	13,548	22,900	20,157	3,919	2,191
1999	94,149	69,147	403	69,550	8,169	1,203	62,585	17,189	14,374	23,687	20,831	3,975	2,241
2000	100,705	73,288	526	73,814	8,623	1,429	66,621	18,633	15,452	25,025	22,092	4,024	2,280
2001	104,242	74,810	650	75,460	8,877	1,519	68,102	18,895	17,245	25,644	22,689	4,065	2,257
2002	107,305	77,120	230	77,351	9,172	1,556	69,735	18,845	18,726	26,122	23,564	4,108	2,248
2003	111,197	80,038	524	80,562	9,561	1,591	72,591	18,923	19,682	26,792	24,360	4,150	2,264
2004	117,452	83,885	643	84,529	10,054	1,674	76,148	20,017	21,287	27,892	25,394	4,211	2,306
2005	124,417	88,078	639	88,718	10,526	1,869	80,061	21,472	22,885	29,136	26,271	4,270	2,356
2006	134,174	93,880	463	94,343	11,431	2,142	85,054	24,362	24,758	30,789	27,621	4,358	2,419
2007	143,055	98,725	306	99,031	11,951	2,514	89,595	27,107	26,354	32,190	28,805	4,444	2,482
2008	149,954	100,197	445	100,641	12,281	2,594	90,954	28,618	30,383	33,110	29,877	4,529	2,472
2009	146,754	95,851	490	96,341	11,925	2,583	87,000	26,176	33,578	31,973	29,460	4,590	2,368
2010	151,746	98,700	488	99,188	12,140	2,525	89,573	25,816	36,357	32,747	30,130	4,634	2,358
2011	160,391	103,604	367	103,971	11,410	2,561	95,123	28,520	36,749	34,398	31,353	4,663	2,427
2012	168,271	109,496	477	109,973	11,741	2,851	101,082	30,272	36,917	35,794	32,660	4,701	2,453
2013	170,205	112,416	750	113,166	13,574	2,953	102,545	29,738	37,921	35,906	32,432	4,740	2,501
2014	180,838	118,782	278	119,060	14,249	3,112	107,922	32,582	40,334	37,735	34,148	4,792	2,564
2015	192,055	125,602	222	125,823	15,009	3,486	114,300	34,906	42,849	39,577	35,575	4,853	2,636
2016	200,027	130,403	200	130,603	15,571	3,906	118,938	36,934	44,156	40,732	36,500	4,911	2,700
2017	210,388	137,181	320	137,502	16,412	4,075	125,165	39,518	45,706	42,368	38,061	4,966	2,759
2018	219,942	143,294	172	143,466	17,243	4,251	130,474	41,265	48,203	43,804	39,498	5,021	2,844
2019	234,324	151,144	153	151,297	18,238	4,516	137,575	45,329	51,420	46,149	41,386	5,078	2,882
2020	250,288	152,393	105	152,498	18,479	4,981	139,000	46,670	64,618	48,769	43,988	5,132	2,825
2021	274,348	164,310	448	164,758	19,833	5,521	150,446	51,186	72,716	52,822	47,125	5,194	2,938
2022	283,246	176,756	206	176,963	21,906	6,248	161,305	55,997	65,945	53,615	47,056	5,283	3,067
2023	301,581	190,182	-184	189,998	23,586	6,589	173,000	59,973	68,608	56,123	50,345	5,374	...

... = Not available.

Personal Income and Employment by Region and State: South Dakota

(Millions of dollars, except as noted.)

Year	Personal income, total	Derivation of personal income: Earnings by place of work: Nonfarm	Farm	Total	Less: Contributions for government social insurance	Plus: Adjustment for residence	Equals: Net earnings by place of residence	Plus: Dividends, interest, and rent	Plus: Personal current transfer receipts	Per capita (dollars): Personal income	Disposable personal income	Population (thousands)	Total employment (thousands)
1960	1,325	752	324	1,076	35	1	1,042	198	86	1,940	1,803	683	...
1961	1,333	823	251	1,074	39	0	1,035	203	94	1,924	1,774	693	...
1962	1,519	877	368	1,246	45	1	1,201	218	100	2,154	1,993	705	...
1963	1,473	889	299	1,188	51	1	1,138	229	106	2,081	1,916	708	...
1964	1,445	932	216	1,148	50	1	1,099	238	109	2,062	1,922	701	...
1965	1,626	963	334	1,298	51	2	1,248	259	119	2,350	2,198	692	...
1966	1,758	1,030	393	1,424	64	2	1,362	267	129	2,574	2,394	683	...
1967	1,786	1,084	344	1,429	77	3	1,354	278	154	2,662	2,472	671	...
1968	1,914	1,174	362	1,536	84	3	1,456	281	177	2,861	2,633	669	...
1969	2,076	1,288	357	1,645	90	6	1,561	321	194	3,108	2,838	668	303
1970	2,257	1,388	373	1,762	96	6	1,672	363	222	3,386	3,126	667	305
1971	2,473	1,518	404	1,921	106	6	1,821	396	255	3,684	3,441	671	306
1972	2,855	1,684	564	2,248	121	7	2,134	439	282	4,215	3,940	677	309
1973	3,605	1,897	1,027	2,924	158	7	2,773	505	327	5,310	4,928	679	323
1974	3,612	2,115	688	2,803	183	8	2,628	602	383	5,313	4,861	680	326
1975	3,972	2,315	707	3,022	200	10	2,832	684	456	5,829	5,411	681	326
1976	3,933	2,624	277	2,901	225	12	2,688	742	503	5,726	5,246	687	336
1977	4,463	2,867	445	3,312	238	13	3,087	846	530	6,477	6,011	689	342
1978	5,143	3,258	616	3,874	274	14	3,614	953	575	7,460	6,880	689	355
1979	5,665	3,590	652	4,242	322	15	3,935	1,082	649	8,222	7,561	689	359
1980	5,717	3,801	137	3,938	342	16	3,612	1,344	761	8,275	7,516	691	353
1981	6,653	4,042	444	4,486	388	13	4,111	1,671	872	9,648	8,792	690	348
1982	7,012	4,167	373	4,540	408	10	4,143	1,900	969	10,153	9,201	691	344
1983	7,277	4,480	255	4,736	441	4	4,299	1,936	1,042	10,501	9,679	693	353
1984	8,268	4,874	689	5,563	491	-2	5,069	2,097	1,102	11,858	11,042	697	362
1985	8,481	5,078	612	5,690	530	-5	5,155	2,155	1,171	12,144	11,285	698	365
1986	8,847	5,322	663	5,985	574	-12	5,400	2,228	1,220	12,711	11,822	696	366
1987	9,304	5,646	843	6,489	618	-19	5,852	2,192	1,260	13,366	12,364	696	381
1988	9,740	6,112	715	6,826	692	-27	6,108	2,315	1,318	13,952	12,899	698	388
1989	10,481	6,549	724	7,273	750	-37	6,485	2,552	1,445	15,044	13,848	697	396
1990	11,484	7,136	1,021	8,157	851	-54	7,252	2,692	1,540	16,474	15,114	697	409
1991	11,982	7,639	894	8,533	916	-68	7,549	2,777	1,656	17,028	15,639	704	420
1992	12,935	8,289	1,074	9,363	976	-85	8,301	2,834	1,800	18,147	16,666	713	431
1993	13,520	8,858	945	9,803	1,035	-100	8,668	2,958	1,895	18,722	17,105	722	442
1994	14,574	9,514	1,211	10,725	1,117	-130	9,477	3,092	2,005	19,943	18,315	731	464
1995	14,865	9,983	640	10,623	1,171	-150	9,302	3,421	2,142	20,144	18,401	738	472
1996	16,416	10,446	1,462	11,908	1,224	-189	10,494	3,659	2,262	22,117	20,270	742	479
1997	16,798	11,025	1,046	12,070	1,292	-186	10,593	3,884	2,321	22,571	20,449	744	485
1998	18,103	11,964	1,167	13,132	1,385	-233	11,514	4,200	2,389	24,265	22,009	746	491
1999	18,949	12,670	1,165	13,835	1,482	-249	12,104	4,362	2,483	25,251	22,780	750	502
2000	20,201	13,332	1,342	14,674	1,568	-267	12,840	4,704	2,658	26,727	24,167	756	512
2001	20,892	13,768	1,153	14,922	1,617	-265	13,040	4,979	2,874	27,563	24,934	758	512
2002	20,899	14,416	501	14,917	1,671	-237	13,009	4,824	3,065	27,497	25,237	760	510
2003	22,823	15,075	1,483	16,558	1,746	-225	14,586	5,072	3,165	29,883	27,819	764	510
2004	24,553	16,120	1,844	17,964	1,840	-221	15,904	5,312	3,338	31,871	29,673	770	518
2005	26,005	17,327	1,552	18,880	1,930	-171	16,779	5,653	3,573	33,534	31,002	775	528
2006	27,393	18,850	611	19,461	2,080	-141	17,240	6,271	3,882	34,983	32,046	783	539
2007	30,343	19,686	1,740	21,427	2,212	-139	19,076	7,106	4,161	38,330	35,074	792	552
2008	32,677	20,395	2,288	22,683	2,321	-104	20,258	7,684	4,735	40,891	37,495	799	561
2009	31,827	20,443	1,792	22,235	2,317	-69	19,849	7,000	4,978	39,435	36,885	807	556
2010	33,683	21,892	1,730	23,623	2,427	-71	21,125	7,180	5,378	41,274	38,533	816	558
2011	36,655	22,216	3,680	25,896	2,224	-113	23,558	7,626	5,470	44,530	41,184	823	566
2012	37,470	23,452	2,524	25,976	2,328	-72	23,576	8,418	5,476	44,992	41,364	833	575
2013	37,840	23,600	3,381	26,981	2,676	-38	24,267	7,968	5,605	44,983	41,102	841	581
2014	39,607	25,406	2,453	27,859	2,842	-22	24,995	8,676	5,936	46,727	42,538	848	589
2015	41,160	26,830	1,735	28,566	2,946	-12	25,608	9,276	6,276	48,302	43,893	852	593
2016	41,552	27,339	1,130	28,469	3,030	-53	25,386	9,610	6,555	48,279	43,853	861	597
2017	42,989	28,204	1,070	29,274	3,161	-112	26,002	10,135	6,853	49,404	45,200	870	601
2018	45,144	29,391	1,654	31,044	3,289	-126	27,629	10,324	7,191	51,575	47,527	875	610
2019	48,031	31,387	1,561	32,948	3,508	-140	29,300	11,112	7,620	54,426	50,221	883	610
2020	52,793	32,792	2,799	35,591	3,752	-143	31,696	11,407	9,691	59,462	54,796	888	606
2021	58,628	35,254	3,728	38,982	3,977	-184	34,821	12,629	11,179	65,411	59,725	896	626
2022	62,028	37,676	4,348	42,024	4,305	-160	37,558	14,183	10,287	68,173	61,638	910	648
2023	64,676	39,965	3,887	43,852	4,571	-176	39,105	15,156	10,416	70,353	64,656	919	...

... = Not available.

Personal Income and Employment by Region and State: Tennessee

(Millions of dollars, except as noted.)

Year	Personal income, total	Derivation of personal income: Earnings by place of work: Nonfarm	Farm	Total	Less: Contributions for government social insurance	Plus: Adjustment for residence	Equals: Net earnings by place of residence	Plus: Dividends, interest, and rent	Plus: Personal current transfer receipts	Per capita (dollars): Personal income	Disposable personal income	Population (thousands)	Total employment (thousands)
1960	5,931	4,826	246	5,072	243	31	4,861	666	404	1,659	1,512	3,575	...
1961	6,278	5,025	294	5,319	247	31	5,103	716	459	1,733	1,584	3,622	...
1962	6,668	5,395	254	5,649	273	31	5,406	784	477	1,815	1,633	3,673	...
1963	7,072	5,748	278	6,026	324	31	5,733	836	502	1,902	1,730	3,718	...
1964	7,604	6,251	238	6,490	339	30	6,181	899	525	2,016	1,853	3,771	...
1965	8,287	6,821	254	7,075	363	32	6,744	965	578	2,182	1,996	3,798	...
1966	9,123	7,675	258	7,933	502	34	7,465	1,023	636	2,387	2,164	3,822	...
1967	9,770	8,209	219	8,428	564	51	7,914	1,093	763	2,532	2,302	3,859	...
1968	10,894	9,124	225	9,349	635	50	8,764	1,255	875	2,809	2,523	3,878	...
1969	11,816	9,978	256	10,233	660	-146	9,428	1,410	978	3,032	2,692	3,897	1,789
1970	12,849	10,605	269	10,875	696	-144	10,035	1,618	1,197	3,264	2,920	3,937	1,785
1971	14,188	11,668	267	11,935	790	-155	10,990	1,801	1,397	3,538	3,190	4,010	1,817
1972	15,971	13,224	326	13,550	938	-183	12,429	2,003	1,539	3,906	3,518	4,088	1,924
1973	18,142	14,917	493	15,409	1,211	-166	14,032	2,293	1,817	4,384	3,946	4,138	2,025
1974	20,074	16,415	318	16,733	1,384	-176	15,173	2,680	2,221	4,778	4,299	4,202	2,055
1975	21,894	17,316	250	17,566	1,431	-180	15,955	3,005	2,934	5,138	4,671	4,261	1,983
1976	24,520	19,499	371	19,871	1,641	-173	18,057	3,256	3,207	5,664	5,123	4,329	2,052
1977	27,176	21,943	300	22,242	1,847	-230	20,165	3,644	3,367	6,174	5,586	4,402	2,135
1978	30,979	25,254	319	25,573	2,152	-294	23,127	4,179	3,673	6,943	6,248	4,462	2,227
1979	34,544	27,996	342	28,337	2,482	-348	25,508	4,761	4,276	7,620	6,843	4,533	2,279
1980	38,090	30,027	197	30,224	2,669	-416	27,139	5,792	5,159	8,280	7,422	4,600	2,259
1981	42,374	32,695	360	33,055	3,136	-446	29,473	7,055	5,846	9,157	8,205	4,628	2,255
1982	45,036	33,928	302	34,230	3,331	-404	30,495	8,127	6,415	9,693	8,730	4,646	2,217
1983	48,074	36,658	-33	36,625	3,652	-417	32,555	8,631	6,888	10,317	9,316	4,660	2,239
1984	53,445	40,665	412	41,078	4,190	-443	36,444	9,790	7,211	11,403	10,354	4,687	2,344
1985	57,198	43,854	335	44,190	4,590	-469	39,132	10,402	7,664	12,130	10,970	4,715	2,399
1986	61,207	47,325	241	47,567	5,066	-505	41,996	10,982	8,228	12,916	11,697	4,739	2,477
1987	65,770	51,556	305	51,861	5,474	-534	45,853	11,250	8,667	13,751	12,394	4,783	2,578
1988	71,613	56,016	389	56,405	6,108	-546	49,751	12,545	9,317	14,850	13,453	4,822	2,663
1989	76,876	59,415	443	59,858	6,569	-571	52,719	13,900	10,257	15,836	14,293	4,854	2,735
1990	81,787	62,856	443	63,299	7,002	-629	55,668	14,766	11,354	16,710	15,130	4,894	2,777
1991	86,093	65,826	510	66,336	7,455	-622	58,258	14,921	12,914	17,334	15,753	4,967	2,778
1992	94,022	72,205	665	72,871	8,067	-483	64,321	15,172	14,529	18,619	16,924	5,050	2,837
1993	100,042	77,302	593	77,895	8,654	-596	68,646	15,814	15,582	19,472	17,682	5,138	2,943
1994	106,434	82,665	655	83,320	9,401	-687	73,232	16,855	16,348	20,345	18,418	5,231	3,061
1995	114,276	88,262	441	88,703	10,015	-767	77,920	18,430	17,926	21,452	19,389	5,327	3,145
1996	120,649	93,021	393	93,414	10,377	-785	82,252	19,522	18,876	22,274	20,024	5,417	3,195
1997	127,785	99,351	381	99,732	11,008	-1,031	87,694	20,468	19,624	23,237	20,825	5,499	3,269
1998	139,760	110,098	205	110,304	11,708	-1,175	97,421	21,847	20,492	25,091	22,532	5,570	3,340
1999	145,232	115,549	57	115,607	12,361	-1,359	101,887	21,968	21,377	25,756	23,131	5,639	3,397
2000	153,990	121,594	328	121,922	12,928	-1,550	107,445	23,351	23,195	26,998	24,299	5,704	3,459
2001	158,125	123,577	461	124,038	13,337	-1,563	109,138	23,697	25,290	27,496	24,727	5,751	3,421
2002	162,879	128,440	89	128,529	13,906	-1,553	113,069	22,685	27,126	28,102	25,747	5,796	3,409
2003	169,930	133,318	198	133,515	14,403	-1,561	117,552	23,586	28,791	29,059	26,828	5,848	3,433
2004	179,893	141,682	383	142,065	15,201	-1,645	125,219	24,050	30,624	30,435	28,182	5,911	3,508
2005	188,178	147,057	545	147,602	15,833	-1,459	130,310	25,104	32,764	31,410	28,889	5,991	3,572
2006	200,189	155,875	276	156,151	16,751	-1,386	138,015	27,576	34,598	32,878	29,997	6,089	3,644
2007	209,747	160,612	-110	160,503	17,528	-1,486	141,489	30,218	38,040	33,963	30,900	6,176	3,702
2008	218,373	161,825	245	162,070	17,987	-1,387	142,696	32,905	42,772	34,954	32,022	6,247	3,677
2009	217,095	158,831	319	159,149	17,641	-972	140,536	30,539	46,020	34,427	32,241	6,306	3,524
2010	227,613	164,653	117	164,770	17,990	-750	146,030	31,172	50,411	35,809	33,456	6,356	3,516
2011	241,432	173,290	520	173,810	16,682	-764	156,365	33,681	51,386	37,698	34,934	6,404	3,589
2012	252,592	182,324	343	182,667	17,204	-1,077	164,386	36,318	51,889	39,082	36,227	6,463	3,635
2013	254,465	186,148	1,108	187,256	19,854	-1,242	166,160	34,875	53,429	39,102	35,965	6,508	3,690
2014	263,856	194,272	563	194,836	20,600	-1,203	173,033	36,741	54,082	40,230	36,895	6,559	3,773
2015	277,356	204,469	353	204,822	21,644	-1,323	181,856	38,608	56,893	41,942	38,283	6,613	3,859
2016	286,532	212,229	-4	212,225	22,443	-1,596	188,185	40,199	58,148	42,943	39,080	6,672	3,952
2017	299,308	221,502	65	221,568	23,714	-1,753	196,101	43,172	60,035	44,411	40,609	6,739	4,033
2018	316,177	233,596	-271	233,325	24,853	-1,976	206,496	46,751	62,930	46,452	42,725	6,807	4,120
2019	335,497	245,863	85	245,948	26,168	-2,329	217,451	51,082	66,965	48,889	44,966	6,862	4,169
2020	359,634	253,478	-60	253,418	27,321	-2,209	223,888	51,606	84,139	51,924	47,843	6,926	4,121
2021	396,986	279,118	647	279,765	29,500	-2,300	247,965	55,217	93,804	57,008	52,047	6,964	4,301
2022	411,035	303,438	284	303,722	33,057	-2,356	268,309	60,174	82,552	58,311	52,540	7,049	4,506
2023	435,067	323,580	18	323,597	35,242	-2,472	285,883	65,343	83,840	61,049	56,041	7,126	...

... = Not available.

Personal Income and Employment by Region and State: Texas

(Millions of dollars, except as noted.)

Year	Personal income, total	Derivation of personal income: Earnings by place of work: Nonfarm	Farm	Total	Less: Contributions for government social insurance	Plus: Adjustment for residence	Equals: Net earnings by place of residence	Plus: Dividends, interest, and rent	Plus: Personal current transfer receipts	Per capita (dollars): Personal income	Disposable personal income	Population (thousands)	Total employment (thousands)
1960	19,438	15,184	924	16,108	677	16	15,447	2,993	998	2,020	1,819	9,624	...
1961	20,546	15,886	1,090	16,976	696	16	16,296	3,127	1,122	2,092	1,884	9,820	...
1962	21,582	16,829	950	17,779	749	17	17,047	3,314	1,222	2,147	1,928	10,053	...
1963	22,539	17,705	783	18,488	832	18	17,674	3,544	1,321	2,219	1,990	10,159	...
1964	24,171	19,143	728	19,871	877	18	19,012	3,788	1,371	2,354	2,144	10,270	...
1965	26,017	20,524	865	21,389	930	19	20,478	4,040	1,498	2,507	2,278	10,378	...
1966	28,469	22,842	920	23,762	1,259	17	22,519	4,320	1,630	2,713	2,444	10,492	...
1967	31,101	25,190	778	25,969	1,462	15	24,522	4,610	1,969	2,934	2,637	10,599	...
1968	34,654	28,151	910	29,061	1,634	14	27,441	4,853	2,360	3,203	2,845	10,819	...
1969	38,575	31,449	927	32,376	2,012	-79	30,285	5,646	2,644	3,493	3,073	11,045	5,005
1970	42,497	33,860	1,168	35,027	2,149	-96	32,782	6,575	3,139	3,782	3,370	11,237	5,045
1971	46,116	36,677	1,015	37,692	2,399	-101	35,192	7,258	3,667	4,007	3,611	11,510	5,123
1972	51,173	40,672	1,257	41,929	2,783	-126	39,020	8,037	4,116	4,352	3,880	11,759	5,334
1973	58,113	45,624	2,145	47,769	3,608	-154	44,007	9,156	4,950	4,835	4,320	12,019	5,608
1974	65,532	52,116	1,157	53,272	4,249	-131	48,893	10,735	5,904	5,342	4,728	12,268	5,822
1975	74,747	58,845	1,314	60,159	4,721	-127	55,311	12,055	7,380	5,947	5,332	12,568	5,938
1976	84,228	67,476	1,292	68,768	5,513	-91	63,164	12,991	8,073	6,528	5,809	12,903	6,207
1977	93,979	76,304	1,280	77,584	6,290	-303	70,990	14,401	8,588	7,124	6,285	13,192	6,521
1978	108,293	88,884	1,030	89,914	7,501	-424	81,989	16,745	9,560	8,023	7,086	13,498	6,900
1979	124,675	102,202	1,741	103,943	9,047	-442	94,455	19,317	10,903	8,978	7,830	13,887	7,215
1980	143,179	117,125	620	117,744	10,466	-546	106,732	23,677	12,770	9,986	8,665	14,338	7,496
1981	168,206	135,846	1,963	137,810	13,078	-334	124,398	29,303	14,505	11,407	9,794	14,746	7,900
1982	185,427	147,110	1,354	148,464	14,470	-405	133,589	35,325	16,514	12,095	10,510	15,331	8,074
1983	198,102	153,753	1,741	155,493	15,035	-388	140,071	39,391	18,640	12,577	11,142	15,752	8,064
1984	216,621	168,331	1,628	169,959	16,887	-445	152,627	44,176	19,818	13,533	12,048	16,007	8,434
1985	233,449	180,199	1,500	181,698	18,295	-474	162,930	49,343	21,176	14,346	12,779	16,273	8,674
1986	238,841	183,168	1,275	184,443	18,420	-435	165,588	50,035	23,217	14,422	12,987	16,561	8,514
1987	242,766	186,375	2,081	188,456	18,487	-431	169,538	48,816	24,412	14,605	13,099	16,622	8,723
1988	258,008	198,583	2,312	200,896	20,385	-437	180,074	52,265	25,669	15,480	13,962	16,667	8,880
1989	275,613	210,747	2,242	212,989	21,806	-446	190,737	56,628	28,248	16,399	14,704	16,807	9,005
1990	297,664	227,961	3,047	231,008	23,240	-485	207,284	58,767	31,613	17,451	15,643	17,057	9,243
1991	311,649	239,956	2,770	242,726	25,081	-563	217,083	59,426	35,140	17,913	16,136	17,398	9,404
1992	336,385	258,670	3,370	262,040	26,705	-586	234,749	60,080	41,556	18,941	17,141	17,760	9,483
1993	356,048	274,904	3,993	278,898	28,326	-607	249,966	61,614	44,468	19,604	17,722	18,162	9,781
1994	376,213	290,896	3,444	294,340	30,353	-671	263,316	65,089	47,808	20,266	18,300	18,564	10,098
1995	402,353	309,999	2,778	312,777	32,365	-753	279,659	70,742	51,952	21,223	19,125	18,959	10,440
1996	432,485	334,765	2,408	337,172	34,406	-823	301,943	74,971	55,571	22,362	20,017	19,340	10,738
1997	472,268	368,835	3,055	371,890	37,474	-963	333,453	80,650	58,166	23,924	21,271	19,740	11,165
1998	514,883	406,992	2,835	409,827	40,840	-1,058	367,928	87,559	59,396	25,543	22,613	20,158	11,542
1999	543,798	433,199	4,277	437,477	43,360	-1,083	393,034	89,629	61,135	26,452	23,430	20,558	11,761
2000	591,738	473,046	3,347	476,393	46,650	-1,180	428,562	98,389	64,787	28,253	24,894	20,944	12,139
2001	631,080	504,687	3,987	508,674	49,028	-1,185	458,461	101,658	70,962	29,601	26,251	21,320	12,285
2002	639,443	508,827	3,970	512,797	49,508	-1,157	462,132	99,251	78,060	29,481	26,772	21,690	12,292
2003	664,815	522,595	5,272	527,867	51,634	-1,081	475,151	106,166	83,498	30,176	27,668	22,031	12,375
2004	696,381	548,519	5,321	553,840	54,327	-998	498,515	109,826	88,041	31,097	28,591	22,394	12,588
2005	754,776	586,657	4,971	591,629	57,861	-967	532,801	124,421	97,554	33,136	30,093	22,778	13,004
2006	827,440	645,817	3,246	649,063	62,124	-1,052	585,887	137,324	104,228	35,422	31,952	23,360	13,493
2007	878,902	676,988	3,601	680,589	66,489	-1,139	612,962	151,419	114,522	36,879	33,161	23,832	14,008
2008	968,499	724,827	1,229	726,056	69,841	-1,199	655,015	183,256	130,228	39,841	35,587	24,309	14,366
2009	923,471	687,524	922	688,446	69,364	-1,408	617,674	163,011	142,786	37,234	34,410	24,802	14,203
2010	982,053	727,490	3,270	730,760	72,181	-1,539	657,040	166,398	158,615	38,910	35,830	25,239	14,263
2011	1,074,858	787,874	2,764	790,638	67,985	-1,851	720,803	189,833	164,222	41,937	38,139	25,630	14,682
2012	1,142,888	839,802	2,618	842,420	72,065	-2,217	768,137	211,038	163,712	43,863	39,911	26,056	15,096
2013	1,173,747	879,016	4,739	883,755	85,161	-2,395	796,199	208,034	169,515	44,396	40,028	26,438	15,532
2014	1,257,640	940,022	4,602	944,625	90,383	-2,459	851,783	227,790	178,067	46,739	42,009	26,908	16,002
2015	1,281,170	947,298	6,310	953,608	94,435	-2,447	856,726	234,421	190,023	46,760	41,976	27,399	16,415
2016	1,276,331	946,875	2,499	949,374	96,797	-2,145	850,433	226,502	199,395	45,862	41,500	27,830	16,683
2017	1,367,826	1,009,970	3,402	1,013,371	102,419	-1,887	909,066	254,494	204,266	48,518	43,624	28,192	17,104
2018	1,463,790	1,080,669	2,731	1,083,400	107,516	-1,995	973,888	276,015	213,886	51,341	46,733	28,511	17,609
2019	1,536,597	1,129,707	2,894	1,132,601	112,866	-2,378	1,017,358	293,036	226,203	53,247	48,300	28,858	17,902
2020	1,611,228	1,117,292	3,554	1,120,845	114,709	-2,165	1,003,971	300,919	306,338	55,114	50,296	29,234	17,701
2021	1,789,719	1,216,511	5,039	1,221,551	121,816	-2,147	1,097,588	337,084	355,048	60,543	54,722	29,561	18,559
2022	1,879,420	1,343,773	3,322	1,347,095	135,298	-2,644	1,209,152	364,987	305,280	62,585	55,733	30,030	19,631
2023	1,995,594	1,433,890	2,110	1,436,000	145,600	-2,929	1,287,471	397,141	310,982	65,422	59,422	30,503	...

... = Not available.

Personal Income and Employment by Region and State: Utah

(Millions of dollars, except as noted.)

Year	Personal income, total	Derivation of personal income: Earnings by place of work: Nonfarm	Farm	Total	Less: Contributions for government social insurance	Plus: Adjustment for residence	Equals: Net earnings by place of residence	Plus: Dividends, interest, and rent	Plus: Personal current transfer receipts	Per capita (dollars): Personal income	Disposable personal income	Population (thousands)	Total employment (thousands)
1960	1,910	1,545	44	1,589	75	1	1,515	289	105	2,122	1,917	900	...
1961	2,047	1,665	35	1,700	79	1	1,621	309	117	2,187	1,972	936	...
1962	2,228	1,805	54	1,858	87	1	1,772	334	122	2,326	2,103	958	...
1963	2,315	1,904	41	1,945	105	1	1,841	343	132	2,377	2,146	974	...
1964	2,437	1,990	30	2,020	106	1	1,915	382	141	2,492	2,280	978	...
1965	2,583	2,079	47	2,127	109	1	2,019	412	152	2,599	2,381	994	...
1966	2,751	2,241	49	2,290	144	1	2,147	442	162	2,727	2,487	1,009	...
1967	2,904	2,356	63	2,419	159	1	2,262	451	191	2,849	2,592	1,019	...
1968	3,112	2,541	67	2,608	175	1	2,434	457	220	3,024	2,720	1,029	...
1969	3,407	2,751	74	2,825	175	4	2,654	505	248	3,254	2,895	1,047	444
1970	3,791	3,024	78	3,101	190	2	2,913	580	299	3,558	3,201	1,066	455
1971	4,243	3,363	77	3,440	218	2	3,224	666	352	3,855	3,495	1,101	467
1972	4,741	3,764	88	3,852	260	4	3,597	743	402	4,179	3,768	1,135	494
1973	5,283	4,198	130	4,328	338	7	3,997	814	472	4,520	4,070	1,169	523
1974	5,910	4,724	97	4,821	395	10	4,435	937	538	4,930	4,430	1,199	545
1975	6,591	5,232	67	5,299	432	13	4,880	1,037	673	5,341	4,854	1,234	553
1976	7,464	5,992	74	6,066	502	16	5,580	1,152	732	5,866	5,262	1,272	580
1977	8,441	6,842	64	6,906	575	21	6,351	1,301	788	6,412	5,733	1,316	613
1978	9,712	7,880	72	7,952	678	25	7,299	1,535	878	7,119	6,354	1,364	651
1979	10,970	8,911	82	8,993	810	33	8,216	1,755	999	7,747	6,876	1,416	678
1980	12,318	9,851	60	9,911	902	49	9,059	2,081	1,179	8,365	7,445	1,473	687
1981	13,878	11,026	42	11,067	1,089	53	10,032	2,466	1,381	9,158	8,107	1,515	697
1982	15,058	11,725	46	11,771	1,176	53	10,648	2,824	1,587	9,663	8,539	1,558	707
1983	16,136	12,479	36	12,515	1,267	43	11,291	3,116	1,729	10,117	9,048	1,595	719
1984	17,801	13,871	57	13,928	1,448	39	12,519	3,500	1,783	10,972	9,864	1,622	761
1985	19,060	14,844	57	14,901	1,578	41	13,364	3,760	1,936	11,601	10,400	1,643	789
1986	20,030	15,517	87	15,604	1,658	35	13,982	3,954	2,094	12,046	10,793	1,663	801
1987	20,928	16,182	130	16,313	1,723	26	14,616	4,069	2,244	12,471	11,132	1,678	830
1988	22,309	17,307	208	17,516	1,936	24	15,604	4,361	2,344	13,206	11,812	1,689	865
1989	23,942	18,536	205	18,741	2,115	22	16,648	4,706	2,588	14,035	12,570	1,706	897
1990	25,976	20,280	252	20,533	2,390	17	18,160	4,976	2,840	15,004	13,281	1,731	938
1991	27,878	21,905	233	22,138	2,619	12	19,530	5,211	3,137	15,663	13,949	1,780	961
1992	30,106	23,826	279	24,106	2,832	7	21,281	5,345	3,480	16,390	14,599	1,837	979
1993	32,467	25,763	300	26,063	3,077	7	22,993	5,699	3,775	17,102	15,195	1,898	1,026
1994	35,131	28,088	219	28,307	3,388	7	24,927	6,315	3,889	17,920	15,827	1,960	1,102
1995	38,275	30,417	166	30,583	3,687	0	26,896	7,160	4,219	19,003	16,721	2,014	1,150
1996	41,683	32,992	173	33,165	3,920	0	29,245	7,972	4,467	20,156	17,696	2,068	1,218
1997	45,001	35,831	198	36,029	4,202	-0	31,827	8,530	4,644	21,229	18,590	2,120	1,270
1998	48,099	38,426	232	38,658	4,484	-4	34,170	9,082	4,847	22,207	19,421	2,166	1,310
1999	50,670	40,937	240	41,177	4,730	-1	36,445	9,106	5,119	22,995	20,079	2,203	1,338
2000	54,231	43,537	207	43,744	5,046	5	38,703	10,029	5,499	24,162	21,088	2,245	1,381
2001	56,789	45,270	317	45,587	5,292	-0	40,295	10,462	6,031	24,867	21,841	2,284	1,392
2002	58,509	46,415	201	46,616	5,455	-2	41,159	10,749	6,601	25,167	22,575	2,325	1,395
2003	60,770	47,950	214	48,164	5,678	1	42,487	11,258	7,025	25,749	23,274	2,360	1,406
2004	64,795	51,581	307	51,887	6,169	2	45,720	11,636	7,439	26,980	24,429	2,402	1,453
2005	70,662	55,778	268	56,046	6,685	15	49,376	13,176	8,110	28,751	25,631	2,458	1,518
2006	78,561	62,503	147	62,650	7,284	20	55,386	14,365	8,811	31,107	27,532	2,526	1,593
2007	85,529	67,082	186	67,268	7,833	16	59,451	16,476	9,602	32,924	29,017	2,598	1,676
2008	89,968	68,380	193	68,573	8,022	34	60,585	18,169	11,214	33,784	30,139	2,663	1,688
2009	86,595	65,506	109	65,615	7,768	7	57,855	16,331	12,410	31,796	28,956	2,723	1,634
2010	88,941	66,649	218	66,867	7,864	1	59,004	16,170	13,767	32,038	29,220	2,776	1,621
2011	95,882	70,572	364	70,936	7,464	-1	63,471	18,191	14,220	34,022	30,763	2,818	1,664
2012	101,928	75,534	330	75,864	7,854	17	68,026	19,792	14,111	35,633	32,094	2,860	1,706
2013	105,028	79,305	537	79,843	9,301	28	70,569	19,865	14,593	36,116	32,239	2,908	1,753
2014	111,056	83,460	615	84,075	9,791	34	74,318	21,623	15,116	37,638	33,541	2,951	1,804
2015	119,662	89,191	609	89,799	10,233	8	79,574	24,031	16,056	39,899	35,392	2,999	1,866
2016	126,541	94,498	368	94,866	10,760	-28	84,079	25,687	16,775	41,312	36,528	3,063	1,933
2017	134,547	100,404	377	100,781	11,407	-33	89,340	27,878	17,328	43,044	38,201	3,126	1,995
2018	144,646	108,170	359	108,530	12,017	-31	96,482	29,707	18,457	45,473	40,399	3,181	2,070
2019	155,674	115,974	416	116,390	12,777	-49	103,564	31,998	20,112	48,156	42,586	3,233	2,103
2020	169,940	124,087	460	124,547	13,778	-96	110,673	33,236	26,031	51,748	45,643	3,284	2,136
2021	190,468	135,838	452	136,290	15,014	-135	121,141	38,085	31,243	57,039	49,587	3,339	2,250
2022	201,012	147,035	753	147,788	16,569	-137	131,082	42,896	27,034	59,449	50,999	3,381	2,368
2023	214,713	157,423	603	158,026	17,742	-155	140,129	46,602	27,982	62,823	55,371	3,418	...

... = Not available.

Personal Income and Employment by Region and State: Vermont

(Millions of dollars, except as noted.)

Year	Personal income, total	Derivation of personal income: Earnings by place of work: Nonfarm	Farm	Total	Less: Contributions for government social insurance	Plus: Adjustment for residence	Equals: Net earnings by place of residence	Plus: Dividends, interest, and rent	Plus: Personal current transfer receipts	Per capita (dollars): Personal income	Disposable personal income	Population (thousands)	Total employment (thousands)
1960	768	574	56	630	27	-6	597	112	59	1,975	1,781	389	...
1961	801	587	56	643	28	-5	609	124	67	2,053	1,855	390	...
1962	841	627	46	673	31	-5	637	134	70	2,139	1,933	393	...
1963	871	655	43	698	36	-5	657	140	75	2,195	1,963	397	...
1964	934	694	49	744	38	-5	700	156	77	2,340	2,110	399	...
1965	1,022	771	45	816	42	-8	767	174	81	2,530	2,297	404	...
1966	1,160	886	59	945	58	-10	877	196	87	2,808	2,513	413	...
1967	1,256	964	46	1,010	71	-10	929	219	107	2,969	2,654	423	...
1968	1,382	1,050	51	1,101	74	-11	1,016	240	126	3,215	2,844	430	...
1969	1,515	1,170	58	1,228	83	-27	1,118	254	144	3,468	3,019	437	203
1970	1,664	1,259	62	1,321	89	-26	1,205	287	172	3,728	3,265	446	205
1971	1,802	1,339	61	1,400	98	-24	1,278	319	205	3,967	3,570	454	206
1972	1,989	1,467	68	1,536	111	-21	1,404	355	230	4,294	3,797	463	211
1973	2,184	1,619	72	1,691	141	-20	1,531	391	262	4,661	4,168	469	220
1974	2,364	1,725	59	1,784	155	-16	1,613	436	315	4,996	4,469	473	222
1975	2,592	1,823	61	1,884	162	-11	1,711	479	401	5,401	4,857	480	220
1976	2,876	2,044	78	2,122	184	-5	1,933	511	432	5,928	5,356	485	228
1977	3,120	2,244	66	2,310	203	-1	2,105	572	442	6,339	5,679	492	236
1978	3,573	2,614	95	2,709	244	-1	2,464	642	467	7,171	6,417	498	252
1979	4,015	2,934	105	3,039	284	6	2,761	723	530	7,939	7,056	506	261
1980	4,507	3,191	108	3,299	309	15	3,005	873	629	8,793	7,785	513	266
1981	5,061	3,503	123	3,627	364	18	3,281	1,056	725	9,817	8,655	516	270
1982	5,491	3,699	123	3,822	392	24	3,454	1,231	807	10,578	9,427	519	271
1983	5,906	4,039	83	4,122	430	23	3,714	1,328	864	11,286	10,089	523	277
1984	6,480	4,469	84	4,553	490	29	4,092	1,498	890	12,305	11,023	527	289
1985	7,031	4,905	101	5,006	548	30	4,488	1,615	929	13,265	11,824	530	300
1986	7,565	5,352	99	5,452	602	34	4,884	1,724	957	14,165	12,566	534	311
1987	8,173	5,924	124	6,048	656	42	5,434	1,768	971	15,128	13,304	540	320
1988	8,965	6,505	121	6,626	742	47	5,931	2,009	1,025	16,307	14,420	550	334
1989	9,903	7,045	123	7,168	798	51	6,420	2,361	1,121	17,757	15,652	558	341
1990	10,294	7,306	115	7,421	870	52	6,603	2,440	1,251	18,226	16,101	565	341
1991	10,507	7,399	104	7,503	890	60	6,672	2,457	1,379	18,479	16,436	569	334
1992	11,227	7,887	177	8,064	937	68	7,195	2,473	1,560	19,602	17,492	573	342
1993	11,661	8,284	128	8,412	986	78	7,503	2,530	1,629	20,184	18,000	578	349
1994	12,223	8,650	129	8,780	1,043	93	7,829	2,669	1,725	20,936	18,698	584	359
1995	12,862	8,974	100	9,074	1,100	106	8,081	2,912	1,870	21,837	19,514	589	362
1996	13,546	9,436	147	9,583	1,144	122	8,561	3,053	1,932	22,816	20,251	594	367
1997	14,359	9,950	110	10,060	1,197	146	9,009	3,316	2,034	24,042	21,179	597	373
1998	15,459	10,699	136	10,835	1,266	174	9,743	3,599	2,117	25,747	22,612	600	381
1999	16,326	11,544	146	11,690	1,343	196	10,542	3,520	2,264	27,000	23,679	605	390
2000	17,680	12,534	150	12,685	1,435	227	11,477	3,766	2,437	29,002	25,326	610	401
2001	18,797	13,357	149	13,507	1,523	237	12,221	3,904	2,673	30,704	27,003	612	404
2002	19,198	13,852	115	13,967	1,547	234	12,654	3,688	2,856	31,194	27,918	615	406
2003	19,946	14,318	146	14,464	1,614	251	13,101	3,856	2,989	32,282	29,276	618	406
2004	21,049	15,118	194	15,312	1,702	237	13,846	4,080	3,123	33,955	30,854	620	413
2005	21,477	15,588	198	15,786	1,788	249	14,247	3,830	3,401	34,573	31,046	621	417
2006	22,804	16,154	121	16,275	1,884	281	14,672	4,352	3,780	36,609	32,677	623	421
2007	24,063	16,611	221	16,831	1,992	291	15,130	4,753	4,181	38,595	34,273	623	425
2008	25,449	17,124	229	17,352	2,054	285	15,584	5,205	4,661	40,774	36,434	624	424
2009	25,216	16,979	125	17,105	2,030	331	15,406	4,752	5,058	40,358	37,041	625	414
2010	25,989	17,604	193	17,797	2,065	330	16,062	4,579	5,348	41,492	38,043	626	413
2011	27,548	18,323	263	18,586	1,930	305	16,961	5,189	5,397	43,756	39,631	630	417
2012	28,292	18,720	255	18,976	2,004	313	17,284	5,483	5,525	44,861	40,751	631	422
2013	28,666	19,103	293	19,396	2,324	338	17,410	5,459	5,797	45,298	40,745	633	425
2014	29,725	19,326	342	19,668	2,427	371	17,611	6,052	6,061	46,897	42,100	634	429
2015	30,598	19,961	199	20,159	2,524	371	18,007	6,325	6,266	48,120	43,064	636	433
2016	31,073	20,321	168	20,490	2,581	378	18,287	6,387	6,399	48,831	43,616	636	434
2017	31,960	20,934	202	21,136	2,688	419	18,867	6,610	6,483	50,011	44,738	639	436
2018	33,117	21,708	136	21,844	2,756	431	19,519	6,951	6,647	51,692	46,469	641	438
2019	34,824	22,478	236	22,714	2,792	493	20,415	7,535	6,875	54,257	48,534	642	433
2020	37,274	22,767	205	22,973	2,853	471	20,591	7,515	9,168	57,974	52,111	643	409
2021	39,604	24,483	207	24,690	2,922	549	22,317	7,923	9,364	61,202	54,066	647	421
2022	40,790	26,188	313	26,501	3,195	518	23,823	8,431	8,536	63,035	54,918	647	436
2023	43,032	27,679	175	27,854	3,380	538	25,012	8,912	9,108	66,463	59,330	647	...

... = Not available.

Personal Income and Employment by Region and State: Virginia

(Millions of dollars, except as noted.)

Year	Personal income, total	Derivation of personal income: Earnings by place of work: Nonfarm	Farm	Total	Less: Contributions for government social insurance	Plus: Adjustment for residence	Equals: Net earnings by place of residence	Plus: Dividends, interest, and rent	Plus: Personal current transfer receipts	Per capita (dollars): Personal income	Disposable personal income	Population (thousands)	Total employment (thousands)
1960	8,173	6,217	214	6,432	268	467	6,631	1,170	373	2,050	1,837	3,986	...
1961	8,706	6,557	225	6,782	285	500	6,998	1,280	428	2,126	1,911	4,095	...
1962	9,396	7,075	222	7,297	318	553	7,532	1,411	452	2,248	2,010	4,180	...
1963	10,107	7,687	136	7,823	370	611	8,064	1,558	485	2,364	2,097	4,276	...
1964	11,151	8,410	222	8,632	384	664	8,912	1,728	512	2,559	2,312	4,357	...
1965	12,038	9,029	208	9,237	403	748	9,581	1,896	560	2,729	2,453	4,411	...
1966	13,027	9,948	156	10,104	544	827	10,387	2,029	610	2,923	2,608	4,456	...
1967	14,251	10,760	201	10,961	633	988	11,316	2,201	734	3,161	2,815	4,508	...
1968	15,768	12,027	178	12,205	700	1,064	12,569	2,344	855	3,459	3,057	4,558	...
1969	17,848	13,676	213	13,889	799	991	14,080	2,789	979	3,868	3,361	4,614	2,148
1970	19,372	14,675	213	14,889	869	909	14,928	3,264	1,180	4,157	3,633	4,660	2,158
1971	21,411	16,168	193	16,362	999	947	16,310	3,688	1,413	4,505	3,975	4,753	2,196
1972	23,764	17,994	254	18,248	1,166	1,003	18,085	4,058	1,622	4,922	4,286	4,828	2,263
1973	26,613	20,139	355	20,494	1,484	1,081	20,092	4,584	1,938	5,424	4,752	4,907	2,384
1974	29,490	22,172	316	22,488	1,701	1,189	21,976	5,212	2,302	5,924	5,150	4,978	2,451
1975	32,380	23,842	266	24,108	1,822	1,457	23,743	5,689	2,948	6,404	5,688	5,056	2,425
1976	35,771	26,494	237	26,731	2,071	1,684	26,344	6,198	3,229	6,969	6,147	5,133	2,501
1977	39,631	29,463	169	29,633	2,302	1,907	29,238	6,931	3,463	7,613	6,675	5,206	2,585
1978	44,990	33,182	291	33,473	2,624	2,313	33,162	8,005	3,824	8,514	7,427	5,284	2,698
1979	50,186	36,945	157	37,102	3,054	2,734	36,783	9,016	4,388	9,425	8,204	5,325	2,767
1980	56,746	40,771	69	40,840	3,380	3,317	40,776	10,746	5,224	10,571	9,193	5,368	2,797
1981	63,651	45,128	271	45,399	4,013	3,413	44,799	12,823	6,029	11,692	10,098	5,444	2,812
1982	68,805	48,523	122	48,645	4,369	3,433	47,709	14,510	6,586	12,526	10,891	5,493	2,824
1983	74,254	53,033	45	53,078	4,945	3,378	51,511	15,622	7,120	13,344	11,715	5,565	2,897
1984	82,550	59,187	328	59,516	5,702	3,575	57,388	17,630	7,531	14,626	12,916	5,644	3,041
1985	89,269	64,824	231	65,055	6,436	3,698	62,316	18,905	8,048	15,620	13,710	5,715	3,181
1986	96,310	70,638	277	70,915	7,279	3,821	67,457	20,322	8,531	16,572	14,553	5,812	3,316
1987	103,738	77,372	371	77,743	7,981	3,935	73,697	21,181	8,860	17,487	15,227	5,932	3,480
1988	113,856	84,771	523	85,293	9,002	4,328	80,620	23,762	9,474	18,860	16,532	6,037	3,558
1989	123,151	90,578	643	91,221	9,746	4,562	86,037	26,738	10,376	20,122	17,560	6,120	3,655
1990	129,562	94,416	687	95,103	10,317	5,196	89,982	28,317	11,263	20,840	18,256	6,217	3,700
1991	135,176	97,909	622	98,531	10,808	5,629	93,352	29,383	12,442	21,452	18,894	6,301	3,642
1992	143,617	104,131	672	104,803	11,444	6,032	99,391	30,232	13,994	22,390	19,772	6,414	3,657
1993	150,893	109,183	544	109,727	12,027	6,344	104,045	32,048	14,800	23,180	20,428	6,510	3,730
1994	158,793	114,674	644	115,318	12,719	6,269	108,867	34,253	15,673	24,085	21,160	6,593	3,813
1995	166,844	119,719	567	120,286	13,264	6,376	113,398	36,472	16,975	25,011	21,948	6,671	3,903
1996	175,084	126,233	570	126,802	13,952	5,925	118,776	38,369	17,940	25,935	22,646	6,751	3,983
1997	186,627	135,316	425	135,742	14,948	6,482	127,276	40,788	18,564	27,328	23,749	6,829	4,082
1998	199,884	147,092	419	147,511	16,045	6,211	137,677	42,993	19,213	28,965	24,829	6,901	4,168
1999	214,026	159,093	326	159,419	17,282	7,922	150,058	43,718	20,249	30,574	25,999	7,000	4,261
2000	231,870	174,742	568	175,310	18,641	6,063	162,731	47,449	21,690	32,631	27,760	7,106	4,399
2001	244,314	184,178	488	184,667	19,664	6,575	171,577	48,600	24,137	33,940	28,945	7,198	4,417
2002	251,358	188,774	377	189,152	20,357	8,084	176,879	48,883	25,596	34,495	30,199	7,287	4,422
2003	266,325	199,660	284	199,944	21,416	8,784	187,312	51,567	27,447	36,151	31,960	7,367	4,467
2004	284,687	216,302	548	216,850	23,337	9,249	202,762	52,943	28,983	38,082	33,753	7,476	4,587
2005	303,289	230,087	591	230,678	24,956	9,518	215,239	56,451	31,599	40,027	35,100	7,577	4,701
2006	323,554	241,476	293	241,769	26,489	10,812	226,091	62,901	34,561	42,164	36,802	7,674	4,782
2007	341,200	251,294	258	251,552	27,633	11,420	235,339	69,067	36,794	44,020	38,329	7,751	4,869
2008	355,506	255,351	400	255,751	28,536	13,262	240,478	72,695	42,334	45,383	39,567	7,833	4,870
2009	349,465	252,930	372	253,302	28,627	13,090	237,764	66,292	45,409	44,091	39,467	7,926	4,758
2010	364,678	263,619	356	263,975	29,511	14,603	249,066	66,028	49,584	45,443	40,560	8,025	4,743
2011	385,635	271,490	626	272,116	27,108	16,879	261,887	72,333	51,416	47,564	41,939	8,108	4,803
2012	402,072	281,435	661	282,096	27,983	16,850	270,963	79,203	51,906	49,052	43,459	8,197	4,857
2013	398,580	283,840	788	284,628	32,377	16,607	268,858	75,852	53,871	48,198	42,198	8,270	4,899
2014	414,710	291,240	701	291,940	33,130	18,513	277,324	80,791	56,596	49,764	43,526	8,334	4,953
2015	433,088	304,033	510	304,543	34,665	18,960	288,838	84,832	59,418	51,620	44,896	8,390	5,060
2016	444,691	309,843	283	310,126	35,398	19,841	294,569	88,432	61,691	52,659	45,811	8,445	5,157
2017	462,372	320,708	545	321,253	37,049	20,355	304,559	93,589	64,224	54,380	47,382	8,503	5,229
2018	479,767	332,124	307	332,431	38,328	20,803	314,906	97,264	67,597	56,133	49,077	8,547	5,299
2019	501,812	347,989	442	348,431	39,972	19,350	327,809	102,246	71,757	58,368	50,776	8,597	5,330
2020	530,920	355,975	211	356,186	41,104	19,238	334,321	101,328	95,271	61,469	53,854	8,637	5,225
2021	578,640	383,461	629	384,090	44,039	20,980	361,031	110,119	107,490	66,838	57,713	8,657	5,393
2022	599,042	409,796	1,087	410,883	47,747	20,909	384,045	117,276	97,721	69,021	58,609	8,679	5,600
2023	634,985	438,573	593	439,166	51,008	21,484	409,642	123,465	101,878	72,855	63,625	8,716	...

... = Not available.

Personal Income and Employment by Region and State: Washington

(Millions of dollars, except as noted.)

Year	Personal income, total	Derivation of personal income: Earnings by place of work: Nonfarm	Farm	Total	Less: Contributions for government social insurance	Plus: Adjustment for residence	Equals: Net earnings by place of residence	Plus: Dividends, interest, and rent	Plus: Personal current transfer receipts	Per capita (dollars): Personal income	Disposable personal income	Population (thousands)	Total employment (thousands)
1960	7,248	5,620	256	5,876	313	26	5,588	1,146	514	2,539	2,285	2,855	...
1961	7,609	5,904	247	6,150	328	29	5,852	1,194	563	2,640	2,374	2,882	...
1962	8,203	6,404	271	6,675	358	35	6,352	1,285	567	2,788	2,501	2,942	...
1963	8,394	6,541	275	6,815	395	42	6,463	1,333	598	2,841	2,544	2,955	...
1964	8,787	6,833	251	7,084	394	52	6,742	1,415	631	2,968	2,711	2,961	...
1965	9,465	7,343	271	7,614	418	63	7,259	1,543	663	3,190	2,905	2,967	...
1966	10,693	8,475	366	8,840	593	72	8,319	1,686	689	3,498	3,149	3,057	...
1967	11,710	9,314	327	9,642	688	83	9,037	1,845	829	3,689	3,307	3,174	...
1968	13,035	10,385	341	10,725	770	99	10,054	2,030	951	3,986	3,549	3,270	...
1969	14,236	11,287	398	11,685	909	89	10,865	2,294	1,077	4,258	3,755	3,343	1,539
1970	15,037	11,485	346	11,831	911	63	10,983	2,618	1,435	4,400	3,957	3,417	1,491
1971	15,839	11,863	391	12,254	979	61	11,336	2,831	1,671	4,595	4,171	3,447	1,457
1972	17,079	12,813	507	13,320	1,115	71	12,276	3,019	1,785	4,955	4,452	3,447	1,481
1973	19,236	14,402	756	15,158	1,435	87	13,810	3,415	2,011	5,532	4,953	3,477	1,558
1974	21,827	16,174	891	17,064	1,656	130	15,539	3,936	2,352	6,152	5,512	3,548	1,622
1975	24,720	18,112	906	19,018	1,837	200	17,381	4,431	2,907	6,831	6,145	3,619	1,659
1976	27,399	20,569	754	21,322	2,137	249	19,434	4,803	3,162	7,424	6,655	3,691	1,739
1977	30,412	23,305	604	23,909	2,457	232	21,684	5,418	3,310	8,062	7,206	3,772	1,815
1978	35,367	27,425	754	28,179	2,973	272	25,477	6,302	3,588	9,101	8,052	3,886	1,939
1979	40,753	31,782	740	32,521	3,561	484	29,444	7,294	4,015	10,156	8,909	4,013	2,058
1980	46,255	34,990	861	35,851	3,898	577	32,530	8,808	4,917	11,133	9,785	4,155	2,105
1981	51,365	38,301	863	39,163	4,585	431	35,009	10,644	5,712	12,127	10,624	4,236	2,119
1982	54,574	39,658	767	40,424	4,812	468	36,080	12,069	6,425	12,761	11,395	4,277	2,094
1983	58,292	41,624	1,066	42,690	5,114	494	38,070	13,203	7,019	13,555	12,236	4,300	2,140
1984	62,359	44,571	1,024	45,595	5,647	544	40,492	14,489	7,378	14,356	13,011	4,344	2,214
1985	66,337	47,585	753	48,337	6,087	572	42,823	15,580	7,935	15,076	13,636	4,400	2,277
1986	70,834	51,156	1,060	52,216	6,585	616	46,247	16,171	8,416	15,908	14,417	4,453	2,351
1987	74,746	54,816	1,084	55,900	7,025	672	49,547	16,336	8,862	16,493	14,827	4,532	2,470
1988	81,652	60,393	1,020	61,412	7,929	757	54,240	17,758	9,654	17,598	15,890	4,640	2,600
1989	90,214	65,974	1,156	67,129	8,669	845	59,305	20,312	10,596	19,007	16,985	4,746	2,718
1990	99,135	73,392	1,210	74,602	9,823	918	65,698	21,792	11,646	20,219	18,024	4,903	2,842
1991	106,288	78,770	1,281	80,051	10,638	990	70,404	22,693	13,192	21,149	18,955	5,026	2,877
1992	114,670	85,861	1,542	87,403	11,580	1,101	76,924	23,194	14,552	22,220	19,945	5,161	2,907
1993	120,546	89,558	1,744	91,302	12,079	1,196	80,419	24,550	15,578	22,836	20,561	5,279	2,951
1994	126,690	93,816	1,429	95,245	12,804	1,250	83,691	26,603	16,396	23,570	21,153	5,375	3,060
1995	133,935	97,921	1,468	99,389	13,404	1,407	87,393	29,021	17,521	24,436	21,897	5,481	3,101
1996	143,929	104,590	1,943	106,533	14,014	1,627	94,146	31,424	18,360	25,841	22,957	5,570	3,192
1997	154,611	114,078	1,549	115,627	14,810	1,786	102,602	32,964	19,044	27,245	24,000	5,675	3,298
1998	169,365	126,908	1,730	128,638	16,245	1,892	114,285	35,287	19,794	29,355	25,570	5,770	3,383
1999	179,870	138,196	1,498	139,694	17,002	1,958	124,651	34,234	20,986	30,786	26,365	5,843	3,447
2000	192,318	147,036	1,737	148,774	18,407	2,281	132,648	37,255	22,415	32,538	28,072	5,911	3,527
2001	197,446	149,599	1,573	151,171	18,149	2,376	135,399	36,930	25,117	32,986	28,962	5,986	3,516
2002	201,073	152,388	1,651	154,039	18,484	2,431	137,987	36,374	26,712	33,222	29,862	6,052	3,489
2003	209,168	156,945	2,201	159,146	19,254	2,566	142,459	38,741	27,968	34,267	31,129	6,104	3,516
2004	224,343	165,402	2,133	167,536	20,481	2,765	149,820	46,116	28,407	36,309	33,205	6,179	3,585
2005	232,784	175,107	1,871	176,978	21,792	3,033	158,219	44,468	30,097	37,202	33,652	6,257	3,688
2006	253,200	188,223	1,800	190,023	23,178	3,442	170,287	50,610	32,303	39,744	35,701	6,371	3,798
2007	274,770	200,696	2,278	202,974	24,442	3,665	182,198	57,579	34,994	42,524	37,954	6,462	3,925
2008	289,381	205,764	2,193	207,957	25,041	3,682	186,598	62,492	40,291	44,098	39,703	6,562	3,955
2009	277,890	197,012	2,237	199,249	24,811	3,394	177,832	54,613	45,445	41,679	38,458	6,667	3,816
2010	285,437	202,029	2,517	204,545	25,462	3,241	182,325	52,933	50,179	42,327	38,886	6,744	3,771
2011	302,461	211,189	3,248	214,438	23,936	3,525	194,026	58,487	49,948	44,281	40,145	6,830	3,814
2012	324,883	225,609	3,351	228,961	24,696	3,609	207,874	66,963	50,046	47,057	42,767	6,904	3,909
2013	330,953	236,331	3,506	239,838	28,921	3,580	214,497	65,493	50,963	47,454	42,643	6,974	3,992
2014	355,277	249,202	3,095	252,297	30,390	3,533	225,441	74,135	55,701	50,265	45,017	7,068	4,094
2015	376,361	262,041	4,453	266,494	32,083	3,825	238,236	81,360	56,765	52,415	46,604	7,180	4,199
2016	397,271	277,020	3,676	280,695	33,516	4,108	251,288	86,004	59,979	54,302	48,092	7,316	4,314
2017	423,017	296,975	3,645	300,621	36,104	4,262	268,779	92,499	61,740	56,805	50,470	7,447	4,432
2018	451,609	321,998	2,713	324,711	38,230	4,603	291,084	95,952	64,573	59,827	53,425	7,549	4,538
2019	484,334	341,790	3,377	345,167	39,722	4,750	310,194	105,449	68,691	63,405	56,469	7,639	4,592
2020	522,714	355,775	3,812	359,587	41,652	5,196	323,131	106,820	92,763	67,669	60,420	7,725	4,436
2021	574,267	390,665	3,470	394,135	44,622	5,531	355,043	116,207	103,016	74,181	65,310	7,741	4,576
2022	586,520	416,237	3,879	420,116	49,099	6,189	377,206	122,407	86,907	75,345	65,098	7,784	4,816
2023	622,365	446,600	3,465	450,065	52,924	6,445	403,585	129,574	89,206	79,659	70,589	7,813	...

... = Not available.

Personal Income and Employment by Region and State: West Virginia

(Millions of dollars, except as noted.)

Year	Personal income, total	Derivation of personal income: Earnings by place of work: Nonfarm	Farm	Total	Less: Contributions for government social insurance	Plus: Adjustment for residence	Equals: Net earnings by place of residence	Plus: Dividends, interest, and rent	Plus: Personal current transfer receipts	Per capita (dollars): Personal income	Disposable personal income	Population (thousands)	Total employment (thousands)
1960	3,076	2,579	50	2,629	155	-20	2,454	318	304	1,660	1,491	1,853	...
1961	3,117	2,572	43	2,615	153	-20	2,442	331	344	1,705	1,533	1,828	...
1962	3,256	2,687	32	2,719	168	-19	2,532	357	368	1,800	1,619	1,809	...
1963	3,400	2,809	25	2,834	186	-18	2,630	391	379	1,893	1,697	1,796	...
1964	3,628	2,988	23	3,011	173	-17	2,821	422	385	2,019	1,831	1,797	...
1965	3,878	3,190	25	3,215	184	-13	3,018	449	411	2,171	1,973	1,786	...
1966	4,115	3,463	15	3,478	244	-10	3,223	459	434	2,318	2,092	1,775	...
1967	4,361	3,642	29	3,671	268	-8	3,395	473	492	2,465	2,227	1,769	...
1968	4,623	3,855	23	3,877	298	2	3,581	498	544	2,622	2,344	1,763	...
1969	4,944	4,142	31	4,173	323	-73	3,777	569	599	2,832	2,487	1,746	652
1970	5,512	4,542	26	4,568	350	-75	4,143	647	722	3,156	2,800	1,747	660
1971	6,052	4,929	26	4,954	395	-90	4,469	712	871	3,418	3,049	1,770	670
1972	6,701	5,443	31	5,475	455	-103	4,917	786	998	3,729	3,312	1,797	684
1973	7,333	5,883	45	5,928	568	-105	5,255	892	1,186	4,062	3,631	1,805	700
1974	8,129	6,485	29	6,514	648	-120	5,747	1,038	1,344	4,481	3,959	1,814	711
1975	9,186	7,226	15	7,240	711	-124	6,405	1,180	1,601	4,991	4,423	1,841	717
1976	10,241	8,150	4	8,154	819	-153	7,183	1,300	1,758	5,455	4,805	1,877	739
1977	11,457	9,217	-1	9,215	918	-185	8,113	1,469	1,875	6,012	5,306	1,906	758
1978	12,753	10,288	13	10,301	1,058	-215	9,029	1,641	2,083	6,641	5,879	1,920	781
1979	14,223	11,352	18	11,370	1,212	-227	9,931	1,854	2,438	7,335	6,450	1,939	790
1980	15,638	12,076	9	12,086	1,311	-250	10,525	2,276	2,836	8,014	7,022	1,951	782
1981	17,045	12,783	-22	12,761	1,484	-227	11,051	2,791	3,203	8,723	7,658	1,954	762
1982	18,060	13,126	-28	13,098	1,572	-170	11,357	3,192	3,512	9,263	8,179	1,950	740
1983	18,554	12,983	-15	12,968	1,571	-145	11,252	3,411	3,891	9,539	8,477	1,945	722
1984	19,922	14,010	24	14,034	1,737	-112	12,185	3,763	3,975	10,335	9,227	1,928	732
1985	20,757	14,546	22	14,569	1,828	-107	12,633	3,975	4,149	10,885	9,717	1,907	732
1986	21,253	14,710	48	14,758	1,921	-86	12,751	4,096	4,406	11,291	10,117	1,882	731
1987	21,715	15,153	7	15,160	1,992	-26	13,142	4,044	4,528	11,690	10,463	1,858	738
1988	23,222	16,273	6	16,278	2,190	8	14,096	4,346	4,779	12,688	11,442	1,830	751
1989	24,579	16,923	34	16,957	2,310	95	14,743	4,794	5,043	13,606	12,179	1,807	757
1990	26,184	18,101	47	18,148	2,502	92	15,738	5,040	5,407	14,607	13,072	1,793	778
1991	27,332	18,745	37	18,782	2,663	74	16,194	5,058	6,079	15,195	13,645	1,799	779
1992	29,389	19,919	62	19,982	2,840	134	17,276	5,143	6,970	16,269	14,692	1,806	789
1993	30,476	20,703	65	20,768	3,059	132	17,840	5,215	7,420	16,767	15,147	1,818	801
1994	31,791	21,792	61	21,853	3,205	181	18,829	5,438	7,524	17,463	15,723	1,820	822
1995	32,856	22,410	24	22,434	3,352	224	19,306	5,790	7,759	18,016	16,197	1,824	838
1996	34,152	23,081	9	23,090	3,454	234	19,870	6,101	8,182	18,736	16,813	1,823	847
1997	35,628	23,976	-0	23,976	3,548	393	20,820	6,439	8,368	19,585	17,523	1,819	858
1998	37,131	24,934	1	24,935	3,721	439	21,653	6,805	8,673	20,451	18,276	1,816	868
1999	38,079	25,920	-13	25,907	3,826	501	22,582	6,644	8,853	21,017	18,782	1,812	868
2000	40,252	27,387	19	27,406	4,141	625	23,891	7,074	9,287	22,275	19,902	1,807	876
2001	42,750	28,630	30	28,660	4,115	772	25,317	7,172	10,261	23,731	21,181	1,801	873
2002	44,243	29,444	-33	29,412	4,050	816	26,178	6,978	11,087	24,506	22,254	1,805	871
2003	44,953	30,026	-14	30,012	4,240	960	26,732	6,860	11,361	24,804	22,681	1,812	868
2004	46,551	31,515	30	31,545	4,367	1,089	28,267	6,925	11,359	25,628	23,522	1,816	879
2005	48,854	33,301	11	33,312	4,556	1,288	30,044	7,016	11,795	26,836	24,407	1,820	891
2006	52,147	35,286	-24	35,262	4,624	1,337	31,975	7,572	12,601	28,528	25,892	1,828	903
2007	54,185	35,627	-57	35,569	4,503	1,486	32,552	8,302	13,331	29,544	26,681	1,834	916
2008	57,959	37,189	-30	37,159	4,544	1,441	34,056	9,114	14,789	31,494	28,305	1,840	918
2009	58,488	36,989	-35	36,954	4,596	1,329	33,686	8,836	15,965	31,653	28,992	1,848	899
2010	60,532	38,154	-29	38,125	4,701	1,460	34,883	8,808	16,841	32,642	29,891	1,854	900
2011	64,059	40,281	7	40,288	4,380	1,468	37,377	9,711	16,972	34,490	31,222	1,857	909
2012	65,488	41,355	-4	41,351	4,498	1,215	38,068	10,121	17,299	35,233	32,102	1,859	919
2013	65,153	41,430	30	41,461	5,040	1,255	37,676	9,838	17,639	35,092	31,766	1,857	914
2014	67,157	41,944	18	41,961	5,202	1,469	38,228	10,331	18,598	36,242	32,752	1,853	912
2015	68,438	42,158	-4	42,155	5,258	1,468	38,366	10,641	19,431	37,067	33,458	1,846	904
2016	68,068	41,123	-27	41,096	5,278	1,715	37,532	10,598	19,937	37,074	33,583	1,836	890
2017	70,798	43,073	10	43,083	5,512	1,619	39,191	11,028	20,579	38,840	35,261	1,823	889
2018	74,235	46,342	-50	46,292	5,839	1,233	41,687	11,463	21,085	41,000	37,448	1,811	898
2019	76,747	46,939	-18	46,921	5,842	1,727	42,807	12,204	21,736	42,627	38,835	1,800	882
2020	80,741	45,537	-59	45,478	5,895	2,165	41,748	12,380	26,614	45,067	41,413	1,792	841
2021	87,617	48,524	-29	48,494	6,194	2,320	44,621	13,439	29,558	49,079	44,722	1,785	865
2022	88,745	51,106	49	51,154	6,577	2,781	47,358	14,814	26,573	50,024	45,087	1,774	891
2023	93,080	54,299	-26	54,273	6,990	2,949	50,232	15,913	26,934	52,585	48,184	1,770	...

... = Not available.

Personal Income and Employment by Region and State: Wisconsin

(Millions of dollars, except as noted.)

Year	Personal income, total	Derivation of personal income: Earnings by place of work: Nonfarm	Farm	Total	Less: Contributions for government social insurance	Plus: Adjustment for residence	Equals: Net earnings by place of residence	Plus: Dividends, interest, and rent	Plus: Personal current transfer receipts	Per capita (dollars): Personal income	Disposable personal income	Population (thousands)	Total employment (thousands)
1960	8,994	7,017	428	7,445	341	64	7,167	1,269	558	2,270	2,003	3,962	...
1961	9,282	7,098	496	7,593	348	67	7,312	1,324	646	2,315	2,061	4,009	...
1962	9,810	7,565	492	8,056	374	75	7,757	1,395	658	2,423	2,146	4,049	...
1963	10,135	7,890	439	8,329	433	81	7,978	1,462	695	2,465	2,174	4,112	...
1964	10,909	8,508	478	8,986	449	92	8,628	1,557	724	2,619	2,336	4,165	...
1965	11,798	9,151	545	9,696	479	104	9,321	1,698	779	2,788	2,477	4,232	...
1966	12,888	10,092	670	10,762	668	124	10,217	1,809	863	3,016	2,654	4,274	...
1967	13,602	10,696	564	11,260	760	137	10,637	1,902	1,063	3,161	2,759	4,303	...
1968	14,896	11,536	645	12,181	815	158	11,524	2,135	1,237	3,428	2,991	4,345	...
1969	16,425	12,662	638	13,300	934	250	12,616	2,450	1,359	3,752	3,218	4,378	1,944
1970	17,649	13,357	639	13,997	974	255	13,277	2,773	1,599	3,988	3,469	4,426	1,954
1971	18,959	14,190	693	14,883	1,070	267	14,080	3,010	1,870	4,251	3,748	4,460	1,957
1972	20,732	15,635	729	16,365	1,248	291	15,408	3,244	2,079	4,609	4,019	4,498	2,014
1973	23,158	17,544	916	18,460	1,614	316	17,162	3,631	2,365	5,125	4,478	4,518	2,116
1974	25,437	19,183	806	19,989	1,840	343	18,491	4,135	2,811	5,605	4,870	4,538	2,159
1975	27,872	20,504	867	21,371	1,927	345	19,789	4,556	3,528	6,099	5,358	4,570	2,148
1976	30,609	22,957	762	23,720	2,188	383	21,915	4,872	3,823	6,676	5,828	4,585	2,211
1977	34,210	25,642	1,144	26,787	2,443	423	24,767	5,390	4,054	7,416	6,452	4,613	2,293
1978	38,210	28,989	1,128	30,117	2,843	475	27,749	5,986	4,475	8,249	7,117	4,632	2,380
1979	42,798	32,314	1,407	33,721	3,302	506	30,925	6,740	5,134	9,172	7,931	4,666	2,460
1980	47,299	34,342	1,446	35,788	3,497	530	32,822	8,220	6,257	10,038	8,716	4,712	2,443
1981	51,587	36,695	1,172	37,867	3,999	581	34,449	10,023	7,115	10,915	9,419	4,726	2,415
1982	54,426	37,789	1,024	38,814	4,157	601	35,258	11,232	7,936	11,509	10,026	4,729	2,373
1983	57,214	39,863	473	40,336	4,359	651	36,628	12,058	8,527	12,118	10,675	4,721	2,376
1984	62,839	43,864	1,003	44,868	4,904	761	40,725	13,383	8,732	13,270	11,723	4,736	2,467
1985	66,244	46,202	1,031	47,233	5,209	849	42,874	14,095	9,275	13,953	12,331	4,748	2,495
1986	69,881	48,904	1,307	50,211	5,503	930	45,638	14,675	9,568	14,694	12,987	4,756	2,537
1987	73,507	52,499	1,418	53,917	5,811	1,033	49,139	14,584	9,784	15,385	13,509	4,778	2,605
1988	78,390	57,055	855	57,910	6,549	1,194	52,555	15,699	10,136	16,255	14,298	4,822	2,684
1989	85,447	60,870	1,741	62,611	7,004	1,233	56,840	17,664	10,942	17,594	15,446	4,857	2,740
1990	90,418	65,223	1,397	66,620	7,801	1,343	60,161	18,521	11,735	18,435	16,159	4,905	2,814
1991	94,089	68,386	1,018	69,404	8,259	1,363	62,507	18,847	12,735	18,953	16,649	4,964	2,840
1992	101,342	74,287	1,276	75,563	8,872	1,462	68,153	19,387	13,802	20,166	17,729	5,025	2,894
1993	106,615	78,894	956	79,851	9,409	1,519	71,961	20,274	14,381	20,967	18,398	5,085	2,950
1994	113,267	83,975	1,224	85,199	10,146	1,656	76,709	21,727	14,830	22,063	19,309	5,134	3,040
1995	119,153	87,960	797	88,757	10,657	1,775	79,875	23,556	15,722	22,981	20,064	5,185	3,120
1996	125,937	92,251	1,372	93,623	11,100	1,918	84,442	25,212	16,283	24,080	20,884	5,230	3,171
1997	133,809	98,605	1,000	99,605	11,780	2,121	89,946	27,045	16,818	25,409	21,914	5,266	3,226
1998	143,130	105,273	1,370	106,643	12,476	2,306	96,473	29,410	17,247	27,018	23,210	5,298	3,288
1999	148,737	111,625	1,325	112,950	13,251	2,477	102,176	28,607	17,954	27,892	23,981	5,333	3,350
2000	158,494	118,698	894	119,592	13,901	2,707	108,399	30,801	19,294	29,493	25,421	5,374	3,414
2001	166,593	124,298	1,192	125,491	14,202	2,839	114,128	30,936	21,529	30,812	26,711	5,407	3,404
2002	171,010	128,784	1,095	129,880	14,657	2,925	118,148	29,696	23,166	31,406	27,822	5,445	3,395
2003	175,794	132,517	1,555	134,072	15,148	3,001	121,926	30,016	23,853	32,084	28,660	5,479	3,413
2004	183,721	139,199	1,903	141,101	15,959	3,107	128,250	30,918	24,554	33,319	29,863	5,514	3,468
2005	189,779	143,598	1,657	145,255	16,607	3,300	131,949	31,521	26,309	34,218	30,420	5,546	3,511
2006	201,058	150,333	1,389	151,722	17,400	3,423	137,746	35,401	27,912	36,047	31,848	5,578	3,547
2007	210,530	154,742	2,117	156,859	17,979	3,684	142,563	37,726	30,241	37,522	33,106	5,611	3,585
2008	219,195	157,915	1,818	159,733	18,551	3,728	144,910	40,418	33,867	38,857	34,281	5,641	3,573
2009	216,212	153,814	942	154,757	18,026	3,291	140,021	37,014	39,176	38,138	34,485	5,669	3,445
2010	222,261	156,884	1,775	158,659	18,413	3,243	143,489	36,723	42,049	39,048	35,286	5,692	3,426
2011	234,632	164,000	2,934	166,933	17,234	3,360	153,059	40,919	40,653	41,069	36,715	5,713	3,474
2012	244,508	170,216	2,767	172,983	17,767	3,299	158,515	44,576	41,418	42,641	38,166	5,734	3,499
2013	245,762	174,604	3,211	177,814	20,528	3,260	160,546	42,844	42,373	42,688	37,809	5,757	3,539
2014	255,165	179,882	3,257	183,139	21,173	3,494	165,460	45,349	44,357	44,159	39,202	5,778	3,586
2015	266,132	187,056	2,813	189,870	21,907	3,636	171,599	48,283	46,251	45,932	40,515	5,794	3,624
2016	270,847	190,638	1,986	192,624	22,323	3,735	174,035	49,941	46,870	46,598	40,988	5,812	3,658
2017	281,980	197,224	1,941	199,165	23,303	3,911	179,773	52,981	49,226	48,313	42,757	5,836	3,679
2018	295,997	206,626	1,803	208,429	24,085	3,939	188,283	55,671	52,043	50,522	44,957	5,859	3,721
2019	307,908	213,926	1,956	215,882	25,054	4,205	195,033	58,270	54,605	52,364	46,361	5,880	3,718
2020	326,837	217,151	2,975	220,126	25,561	4,101	198,666	59,226	68,945	55,427	49,583	5,897	3,582
2021	355,048	231,302	2,998	234,300	27,020	4,250	211,530	66,047	77,471	60,383	53,514	5,880	3,685
2022	362,245	244,942	3,368	248,310	29,343	4,593	223,560	70,307	68,379	61,496	53,759	5,891	3,819
2023	378,080	258,206	1,686	259,892	30,934	4,779	233,737	72,791	71,552	63,963	57,210	5,911	...

... = Not available.

Personal Income and Employment by Region and State: Wyoming

(Millions of dollars, except as noted.)

Year	Personal income, total	Derivation of personal income: Earnings by place of work: Nonfarm	Farm	Total	Less: Contributions for government social insurance	Plus: Adjustment for residence	Equals: Net earnings by place of residence	Plus: Dividends, interest, and rent	Plus: Personal current transfer receipts	Per capita (dollars): Personal income	Disposable personal income	Population (thousands)	Total employment (thousands)
1960	789	603	51	654	34	-2	618	125	45	2,382	2,138	331	...
1961	829	618	57	675	34	-1	640	137	53	2,461	2,223	337	...
1962	859	627	67	694	35	-1	658	147	55	2,580	2,319	333	...
1963	879	646	67	713	40	-1	672	151	56	2,616	2,327	336	...
1964	906	690	47	738	43	-1	694	158	55	2,673	2,445	339	...
1965	936	698	53	751	41	-1	710	168	58	2,818	2,574	332	...
1966	958	714	58	772	48	-0	724	173	62	2,967	2,692	323	...
1967	1,025	756	70	827	53	-0	773	181	72	3,184	2,871	322	...
1968	1,094	830	62	893	59	0	833	180	81	3,375	3,030	324	...
1969	1,219	911	70	981	66	(L)	915	215	89	3,704	3,285	329	158
1970	1,348	991	79	1,070	71	0	999	246	103	4,038	3,600	334	159
1971	1,498	1,093	88	1,181	81	-1	1,100	279	119	4,404	3,954	340	165
1972	1,685	1,226	126	1,352	95	-3	1,254	301	129	4,856	4,408	347	172
1973	1,969	1,443	153	1,596	127	-7	1,461	355	152	5,571	4,987	353	182
1974	2,303	1,771	111	1,882	158	-14	1,710	421	172	6,317	5,554	365	194
1975	2,607	2,058	67	2,125	181	-16	1,928	472	208	6,853	6,118	380	203
1976	2,890	2,322	48	2,369	213	-22	2,135	524	232	7,309	6,466	395	214
1977	3,376	2,759	45	2,804	249	-29	2,526	595	254	8,203	7,254	412	231
1978	4,034	3,331	65	3,396	309	-38	3,050	698	286	9,361	8,254	431	250
1979	4,716	3,917	96	4,014	380	-54	3,579	806	331	10,436	9,054	452	266
1980	5,507	4,538	86	4,623	441	-74	4,109	1,006	393	11,614	10,111	474	279
1981	6,294	5,146	51	5,197	541	-83	4,573	1,250	471	12,801	11,076	492	289
1982	6,612	5,242	29	5,271	565	-80	4,626	1,444	542	13,056	11,468	506	287
1983	6,569	4,976	36	5,012	522	-59	4,431	1,497	641	12,872	11,488	510	274
1984	6,848	5,193	14	5,207	560	-53	4,593	1,622	633	13,564	12,194	505	276
1985	7,156	5,414	18	5,432	599	-52	4,780	1,703	672	14,321	12,873	500	277
1986	7,125	5,279	40	5,319	581	-42	4,696	1,689	741	14,376	13,064	496	264
1987	6,834	4,951	59	5,010	550	-27	4,434	1,648	752	14,327	12,949	477	258
1988	6,994	5,045	59	5,105	602	-22	4,480	1,731	783	15,037	13,579	465	264
1989	7,632	5,410	90	5,500	628	-15	4,858	1,926	849	16,650	14,933	458	265
1990	8,231	5,802	153	5,955	699	-11	5,246	2,073	913	18,142	16,281	454	271
1991	8,651	5,996	213	6,209	745	-1	5,463	2,172	1,015	18,836	16,963	459	277
1992	9,122	6,328	221	6,549	777	-6	5,766	2,233	1,123	19,565	17,641	466	280
1993	9,647	6,712	247	6,959	817	-8	6,134	2,290	1,223	20,392	18,332	473	285
1994	10,086	7,073	122	7,195	866	-8	6,321	2,472	1,293	21,000	18,856	480	298
1995	10,563	7,263	102	7,365	891	-5	6,469	2,714	1,380	21,773	19,565	485	301
1996	11,043	7,530	83	7,614	913	0	6,702	2,889	1,453	22,622	19,889	488	304
1997	11,865	7,990	184	8,175	957	5	7,223	3,149	1,492	24,241	21,223	489	307
1998	12,615	8,429	99	8,528	1,007	8	7,529	3,552	1,534	25,704	22,463	491	310
1999	13,477	8,974	168	9,142	1,055	7	8,093	3,787	1,596	27,404	23,898	492	315
2000	14,545	9,639	124	9,764	1,121	14	8,656	4,173	1,716	29,426	25,465	494	325
2001	15,441	10,334	192	10,526	1,202	-9	9,315	4,277	1,849	31,215	27,252	495	330
2002	15,905	10,886	102	10,988	1,232	-29	9,726	4,199	1,980	31,810	28,577	500	334
2003	16,937	11,360	181	11,541	1,310	-50	10,182	4,611	2,145	33,642	30,592	503	337
2004	18,287	11,888	181	12,069	1,403	-63	10,603	5,417	2,267	35,921	32,744	509	344
2005	20,004	12,787	227	13,013	1,515	-93	11,406	6,214	2,385	38,907	34,859	514	354
2006	22,896	14,947	98	15,045	1,915	-141	12,990	7,376	2,530	43,805	38,507	523	370
2007	24,408	16,276	49	16,325	2,115	-177	14,032	7,689	2,687	45,634	39,925	535	388
2008	27,003	18,088	107	18,195	2,250	-216	15,728	8,154	3,121	49,451	43,653	546	399
2009	24,913	17,364	91	17,455	2,182	-216	15,057	6,479	3,377	44,499	40,914	560	387
2010	26,185	18,203	122	18,326	2,220	-238	15,869	6,675	3,642	46,395	42,254	564	385
2011	28,700	19,105	369	19,474	2,104	-247	17,122	7,920	3,658	50,630	45,972	567	390
2012	30,844	20,056	137	20,193	2,218	-246	17,729	9,461	3,654	53,596	47,751	575	397
2013	30,694	20,584	237	20,822	2,496	-234	18,091	8,818	3,786	52,836	46,956	581	401
2014	32,680	21,562	360	21,923	2,653	-222	19,048	9,664	3,968	56,252	50,073	581	406
2015	32,756	21,515	289	21,804	2,608	-237	18,959	9,565	4,231	56,122	50,085	584	406
2016	31,090	20,201	166	20,367	2,498	-275	17,594	9,073	4,423	53,421	48,096	582	398
2017	32,487	20,768	182	20,950	2,557	-263	18,130	9,753	4,605	56,377	50,609	576	399
2018	34,025	21,889	216	22,105	2,627	-247	19,231	9,922	4,872	59,195	53,615	575	405
2019	35,593	22,402	225	22,627	2,748	-260	19,618	10,858	5,117	61,863	55,699	575	408
2020	37,866	22,175	268	22,443	2,723	-284	19,437	11,870	6,560	65,551	58,622	578	402
2021	40,867	23,435	306	23,741	2,815	-322	20,605	13,010	7,252	70,515	62,015	580	420
2022	42,585	24,496	395	24,892	2,948	-316	21,627	14,387	6,571	73,216	63,301	582	437
2023	45,461	26,187	418	26,606	3,146	-342	23,118	15,448	6,896	77,837	69,039	584	...

... = Not available.

METROPOLITAN STATISTICAL AREA

Personal Income and Employment by Area: Abilene, TX

(Thousands of dollars, except as noted.)

		Derivation of personal income										
		Earnings by place of work										
Year	Personal income, total	Nonfarm	Farm	Total	Less: Contributions for government social insurance	Plus: Adjustment for residence	Equals: Net earnings by place of residence	Plus: Dividends, interest, and rent	Plus: Personal current transfer receipts	Per capita personal income (dollars)	Population (persons)	Total employment
1970	445,225	322,395	23,059	345,454	19,934	1,887	327,407	76,169	41,649	3,634	122,505	56,215
1971	476,061	346,964	20,798	367,762	22,303	2,011	347,470	81,400	47,191	3,813	124,841	56,614
1972	541,293	392,737	28,946	421,683	26,147	2,370	397,906	91,107	52,280	4,212	128,517	59,092
1973	581,519	418,998	27,728	446,726	31,846	2,456	417,336	101,206	62,977	4,560	127,533	60,359
1974	655,804	487,544	8,813	496,357	38,282	1,621	459,696	122,291	73,817	5,099	128,625	63,366
1975	771,668	561,861	21,367	583,228	44,278	1,693	540,643	142,335	88,690	5,889	131,031	65,822
1976	852,803	632,663	17,641	650,304	50,603	2,088	601,789	154,059	96,955	6,394	133,379	68,298
1977	926,754	695,027	12,946	707,973	55,793	2,168	654,348	169,472	102,934	6,965	133,052	69,994
1978	1,062,407	805,455	9,999	815,454	65,480	1,508	751,482	196,762	114,163	7,901	134,462	72,932
1979	1,210,008	915,614	20,602	936,216	78,599	1,030	858,647	224,507	126,854	8,858	136,601	75,773
1980	1,397,182	1,053,472	10,764	1,064,236	91,347	350	973,239	279,146	144,797	9,973	140,098	78,280
1981	1,681,458	1,246,899	46,280	1,293,179	116,795	-3,110	1,173,274	345,455	162,729	11,733	143,310	84,737
1982	1,804,667	1,317,942	23,155	1,341,097	125,452	-1,682	1,213,963	409,650	181,054	12,120	148,899	86,685
1983	1,890,846	1,371,204	8,428	1,379,632	129,737	-2,173	1,247,722	445,661	197,463	12,363	152,939	86,693
1984	2,009,206	1,447,398	10,327	1,457,725	140,379	-2,598	1,314,748	483,863	210,595	13,082	153,587	87,720
1985	2,138,379	1,530,638	308	1,530,946	150,084	-2,406	1,378,456	534,769	225,154	13,934	153,470	88,722
1986	2,128,401	1,495,841	10,951	1,506,792	144,782	-323	1,361,687	520,145	246,569	13,729	155,031	83,720
1987	2,090,408	1,429,973	28,279	1,458,252	138,648	1,501	1,321,105	509,020	260,283	13,605	153,655	82,965
1988	2,186,912	1,520,668	15,165	1,535,833	152,195	3,296	1,386,934	528,413	271,565	14,575	150,042	83,645
1989	2,271,782	1,521,562	18,571	1,540,133	154,717	7,412	1,392,828	588,603	290,351	15,214	149,324	82,367
1990	2,324,194	1,556,932	38,433	1,595,365	156,668	10,185	1,448,882	554,341	320,971	15,722	147,834	80,942
1991	2,385,186	1,624,567	14,310	1,638,877	168,263	4,971	1,475,585	551,741	357,860	16,182	147,400	82,259
1992	2,539,683	1,720,134	36,748	1,756,882	176,728	6,095	1,586,249	545,192	408,242	16,941	149,917	82,277
1993	2,664,760	1,800,905	30,802	1,831,707	184,214	6,165	1,653,658	581,997	429,105	17,427	152,909	84,362
1994	2,721,192	1,872,355	19,614	1,891,969	193,362	4,548	1,703,155	558,348	459,689	17,695	153,779	85,682
1995	2,911,786	1,974,194	17,649	1,991,843	203,788	3,487	1,791,542	619,095	501,149	18,654	156,097	88,181
1996	3,100,216	2,120,190	6,377	2,126,567	214,106	3,104	1,915,565	649,276	535,375	19,829	156,351	89,587
1997	3,324,250	2,298,130	22,943	2,321,073	227,051	4,368	2,098,390	664,780	561,080	21,119	157,405	91,934
1998	3,472,112	2,405,758	8,463	2,414,221	232,366	6,340	2,188,195	717,185	566,732	21,939	158,264	92,577
1999	3,609,231	2,511,768	30,364	2,542,132	240,232	7,570	2,309,470	713,779	585,982	22,592	159,755	91,417
2000	3,699,665	2,540,158	7,822	2,547,980	244,234	10,116	2,313,862	778,584	607,219	23,081	160,288	91,027
2001	3,781,370	2,555,473	37,105	2,592,578	251,060	10,981	2,352,499	772,685	656,186	23,795	158,917	89,511
2002	3,951,625	2,714,760	15,591	2,730,351	266,247	5,561	2,469,665	775,045	706,915	24,851	159,012	90,340
2003	4,201,840	2,874,011	32,464	2,906,475	282,845	3,889	2,627,519	820,813	753,508	26,458	158,810	91,133
2004	4,389,872	3,044,383	36,681	3,081,064	300,106	2,753	2,783,711	811,746	794,415	27,410	160,156	91,999
2005	4,626,074	3,187,770	30,714	3,218,484	313,539	1,838	2,906,783	856,585	862,706	28,776	160,761	92,938
2006	4,914,261	3,455,505	8,247	3,463,752	333,608	221	3,130,365	875,720	908,176	30,450	161,389	94,097
2007	5,173,944	3,543,134	30,011	3,573,145	354,043	-4,551	3,214,551	968,317	991,076	31,933	162,023	96,484
2008	5,724,861	3,865,246	-15,144	3,850,102	376,586	-4,638	3,468,878	1,170,368	1,085,615	35,228	162,508	99,264
2009	5,488,615	3,674,888	-12,614	3,662,274	376,274	-7,181	3,278,819	1,044,685	1,165,111	33,490	163,888	97,269
2010	5,787,829	3,833,241	22,493	3,855,734	385,671	-3,751	3,466,312	1,050,261	1,271,256	34,935	165,673	96,811
2011	6,150,171	3,991,156	11,209	4,002,365	356,942	3,294	3,648,717	1,198,556	1,302,898	36,812	167,069	98,200
2012	6,416,566	4,200,494	-7,152	4,193,342	375,422	12,427	3,830,347	1,284,804	1,301,415	38,138	168,246	99,848
2013	6,596,716	4,412,628	24,812	4,437,440	434,419	18,375	4,021,396	1,225,264	1,350,056	39,123	168,614	101,227
2014	7,042,550	4,727,748	4,248	4,731,996	457,864	25,781	4,299,913	1,330,681	1,411,956	41,461	169,859	102,335
2015	6,840,205	4,440,516	4,489	4,445,005	455,145	18,411	4,008,271	1,326,462	1,505,472	39,866	171,579	102,612
2016	6,745,585	4,329,665	-23,975	4,305,690	457,363	6,789	3,855,116	1,308,461	1,582,008	39,163	172,242	102,471
2017	6,982,977	4,421,569	-24,377	4,397,192	479,282	17,758	3,935,668	1,428,822	1,618,487	40,384	172,915	102,801
2018	7,444,071	4,768,086	-20,039	4,748,047	512,333	23,342	4,259,056	1,492,105	1,692,910	42,781	174,005	104,596
2019	7,894,120	5,133,050	-11,244	5,121,806	547,204	27,544	4,602,146	1,513,616	1,778,358	45,061	175,187	106,622
2020	8,524,002	5,241,311	-7,858	5,233,453	566,522	1,384	4,668,315	1,606,893	2,248,794	48,195	176,866	105,813
2021	9,342,567	5,497,778	-577	5,497,201	583,039	-2,613	4,911,549	1,752,259	2,678,759	52,537	177,829	108,498
2022	9,585,333	5,971,601	-17,357	5,954,244	645,467	1,813	5,310,590	1,889,469	2,385,274	53,457	179,308	112,812

Personal Income and Employment by Metropolitan Statistical Area: Akron, OH

(Thousands of dollars, except as noted.)

Year	Personal income, total	Derivation of personal income: Earnings by place of work: Nonfarm	Farm	Total	Less: Contributions for government social insurance	Plus: Adjustment for residence	Equals: Net earnings by place of residence	Plus: Dividends, interest, and rent	Plus: Personal current transfer receipts	Per capita personal income (dollars)	Population (persons)	Total employment
1970	2,838,776	2,326,281	6,504	2,332,785	158,576	98,246	2,272,455	358,765	207,556	4,180	679,077	279,931
1971	2,990,538	2,419,744	8,998	2,428,742	169,666	102,133	2,361,209	386,161	243,168	4,403	679,231	274,958
1972	3,263,561	2,662,679	9,046	2,671,725	197,372	105,272	2,579,625	412,531	271,405	4,820	677,046	283,207
1973	3,568,727	2,911,961	11,556	2,923,517	250,765	126,857	2,799,609	450,759	318,359	5,278	676,196	292,971
1974	3,882,656	3,113,113	14,191	3,127,304	276,803	144,555	2,995,056	508,902	378,698	5,793	670,284	296,332
1975	4,114,360	3,167,018	12,512	3,179,530	270,258	165,235	3,074,507	544,606	495,247	6,115	672,844	285,325
1976	4,425,010	3,391,701	11,154	3,402,855	295,638	209,112	3,316,329	578,749	529,932	6,625	667,910	284,907
1977	4,944,761	3,856,406	8,387	3,864,793	337,775	239,996	3,767,014	633,699	544,048	7,467	662,233	297,537
1978	5,471,768	4,283,010	2,354	4,285,364	387,518	290,804	4,188,650	702,735	580,383	8,309	658,517	305,459
1979	6,012,640	4,663,360	2,036	4,665,396	438,962	339,628	4,566,062	788,259	658,319	9,105	660,364	307,763
1980	6,610,014	4,904,761	136	4,904,897	458,075	379,799	4,826,621	956,705	826,688	10,010	660,334	300,754
1981	7,239,766	5,261,838	885	5,262,723	526,076	407,217	5,143,864	1,176,686	919,216	10,988	658,870	297,681
1982	7,571,663	5,343,818	3,026	5,346,844	538,767	396,010	5,204,087	1,323,149	1,044,427	11,540	656,126	289,691
1983	7,989,627	5,627,447	608	5,628,055	579,166	394,467	5,443,356	1,422,766	1,123,505	12,217	653,968	285,981
1984	8,692,790	6,154,095	10,113	6,164,208	647,822	435,915	5,952,301	1,584,105	1,156,384	13,334	651,917	296,150
1985	9,205,265	6,512,011	5,841	6,517,852	693,342	464,893	6,289,403	1,678,963	1,236,899	14,196	648,457	303,855
1986	9,631,902	6,863,252	5,499	6,868,751	748,895	462,711	6,582,567	1,742,085	1,307,250	14,895	646,647	308,919
1987	10,060,671	7,236,430	5,481	7,241,911	787,366	485,340	6,939,885	1,746,059	1,374,727	15,530	647,810	316,920
1988	10,763,469	7,723,140	3,746	7,726,886	868,903	530,037	7,388,020	1,922,111	1,453,338	16,488	652,814	325,266
1989	11,727,838	8,307,340	6,396	8,313,736	941,016	566,540	7,939,260	2,220,619	1,567,959	17,888	655,626	333,052
1990	12,392,348	8,699,694	5,510	8,705,204	1,005,923	627,937	8,327,218	2,302,800	1,762,330	18,815	658,654	337,124
1991	12,709,715	8,976,304	4,478	8,980,782	1,062,749	614,157	8,532,190	2,309,916	1,867,609	19,127	664,478	337,813
1992	13,565,559	9,637,314	9,294	9,646,608	1,140,106	644,341	9,150,843	2,367,265	2,047,451	20,255	669,752	341,070
1993	14,168,305	10,194,639	9,975	10,204,614	1,217,357	600,562	9,587,819	2,423,148	2,157,338	21,018	674,114	350,680
1994	15,051,438	10,847,749	12,657	10,860,406	1,316,336	662,179	10,206,249	2,579,693	2,265,496	22,198	678,063	364,299
1995	15,976,000	11,348,459	8,600	11,357,059	1,390,837	687,325	10,653,547	2,909,359	2,413,094	23,420	682,146	374,193
1996	16,791,980	11,972,235	14,035	11,986,270	1,454,194	734,339	11,266,415	3,026,498	2,499,067	24,433	687,264	380,965
1997	17,738,166	12,528,610	15,526	12,544,136	1,480,989	883,240	11,946,387	3,207,980	2,583,799	25,728	689,461	387,561
1998	18,868,855	13,369,513	11,111	13,380,624	1,527,802	973,513	12,826,335	3,447,375	2,595,145	27,305	691,039	385,717
1999	19,462,197	13,807,667	9,566	13,817,233	1,567,162	1,245,555	13,495,626	3,297,931	2,668,640	28,079	693,125	393,612
2000	20,616,520	14,486,445	7,362	14,493,807	1,585,455	1,355,831	14,264,183	3,500,987	2,851,350	29,624	695,946	397,340
2001	21,031,173	14,807,041	7,183	14,814,224	1,592,013	1,329,140	14,551,351	3,400,880	3,078,942	30,126	698,108	396,954
2002	21,350,531	15,334,841	6,875	15,341,716	1,627,016	1,143,466	14,858,166	3,192,841	3,299,524	30,521	699,533	396,663
2003	22,186,488	16,024,055	6,513	16,030,568	1,714,520	1,057,627	15,373,675	3,352,737	3,460,076	31,643	701,139	396,387
2004	23,032,227	16,889,158	7,470	16,896,628	1,844,217	1,134,683	16,187,094	3,245,519	3,599,614	32,818	701,811	404,590
2005	23,617,474	17,424,438	8,741	17,433,179	1,918,426	897,174	16,411,927	3,436,069	3,769,478	33,619	702,498	412,097
2006	24,551,474	17,967,328	5,465	17,972,793	1,987,955	828,866	16,813,704	3,780,009	3,957,761	34,952	702,433	417,595
2007	25,752,899	18,733,396	8,793	18,742,189	2,062,591	690,323	17,369,921	4,182,179	4,200,799	36,611	703,423	424,013
2008	26,977,431	19,510,217	5,314	19,515,531	2,162,524	447,573	17,800,580	4,430,192	4,746,659	38,358	703,300	424,081
2009	26,085,638	18,424,485	8,002	18,432,487	2,068,383	510,010	16,874,114	4,022,834	5,188,690	37,087	703,361	404,525
2010	26,772,180	18,859,519	6,774	18,866,293	2,082,726	514,535	17,298,102	3,963,099	5,510,979	38,080	703,057	402,554
2011	27,986,319	19,404,441	18,060	19,422,501	1,931,176	598,090	18,089,415	4,285,077	5,611,827	39,794	703,272	407,811
2012	28,861,419	19,885,340	12,463	19,897,803	1,984,186	803,162	18,716,779	4,685,799	5,458,841	41,099	702,245	412,050
2013	29,308,703	20,346,838	13,003	20,359,841	2,202,618	988,676	19,145,899	4,602,060	5,560,744	41,643	703,809	414,520
2014	30,554,060	21,234,357	5,183	21,239,540	2,288,198	856,483	19,807,825	4,916,789	5,829,446	43,331	705,134	421,228
2015	31,480,258	22,029,735	-154	22,029,581	2,378,180	647,744	20,299,145	5,146,898	6,034,215	44,674	704,664	426,047
2016	31,999,528	22,309,401	-3,988	22,305,413	2,460,815	636,673	20,481,271	5,382,669	6,135,588	45,463	703,862	427,371
2017	33,213,211	22,910,522	-4,530	22,905,992	2,582,204	902,638	21,226,426	5,706,054	6,280,731	47,163	704,229	427,974
2018	34,556,035	23,624,604	-3,193	23,621,411	2,619,611	962,446	21,964,246	6,130,783	6,461,006	49,091	703,925	430,278
2019	35,805,714	24,409,049	-7,074	24,401,975	2,719,829	1,111,841	22,793,987	6,266,299	6,745,428	50,907	703,361	428,441
2020	38,330,170	24,528,844	81	24,528,925	2,732,496	1,210,693	23,007,122	6,383,989	8,939,059	54,631	701,625	415,491
2021	41,309,189	26,023,090	3,638	26,026,728	2,908,449	1,437,435	24,555,714	7,029,493	9,723,982	59,333	696,225	425,497
2022	41,976,094	27,431,844	-5,564	27,426,280	3,162,734	1,618,971	25,882,517	7,700,848	8,392,729	60,170	697,627	442,746

Personal Income and Employment by Metropolitan Statistical Area: Albany, GA

(Thousands of dollars, except as noted.)

		Derivation of personal income										
		Earnings by place of work										
Year	Personal income, total	Nonfarm	Farm	Total	Less: Contributions for government social insurance	Plus: Adjustment for residence	Equals: Net earnings by place of residence	Plus: Dividends, interest, and rent	Plus: Personal current transfer receipts	Per capita personal income (dollars)	Population (persons)	Total employment
1970	372,190	297,814	16,248	314,062	17,905	-13,025	283,132	54,661	34,397	3,011	123,598	54,371
1971	424,311	334,108	21,618	355,726	21,157	-13,800	320,769	62,212	41,330	3,329	127,456	56,006
1972	480,038	387,614	19,613	407,227	25,893	-16,751	364,583	68,610	46,845	3,643	131,775	59,514
1973	555,071	441,621	35,085	476,706	33,669	-19,861	423,176	79,170	52,725	4,147	133,860	62,897
1974	572,953	448,536	33,039	481,575	35,971	-20,329	425,275	82,229	65,449	4,397	130,309	60,104
1975	601,973	464,312	25,674	489,986	36,839	-21,524	431,623	86,605	83,745	4,565	131,861	57,820
1976	669,194	523,930	24,987	548,917	41,877	-24,383	482,657	94,701	91,836	4,980	134,378	58,539
1977	731,117	595,304	13,054	608,358	47,319	-28,925	532,114	105,829	93,174	5,319	137,462	60,289
1978	843,252	690,899	20,594	711,493	56,417	-34,537	620,539	121,135	101,578	6,102	138,191	63,127
1979	944,315	789,019	14,233	803,252	67,674	-40,306	695,272	135,011	114,032	6,713	140,660	65,194
1980	1,053,833	870,234	-9,172	861,062	75,062	-37,395	748,605	166,920	138,308	7,370	142,986	64,930
1981	1,201,313	954,763	22,250	977,013	88,926	-45,455	842,632	200,463	158,218	8,298	144,771	65,616
1982	1,270,280	994,097	19,015	1,013,112	94,013	-47,982	871,117	227,664	171,499	8,716	145,744	64,644
1983	1,352,587	1,057,931	14,982	1,072,913	101,498	-50,449	920,966	244,205	187,416	9,274	145,846	64,805
1984	1,507,538	1,161,705	47,908	1,209,613	114,147	-54,826	1,040,640	268,348	198,550	10,288	146,534	68,104
1985	1,584,815	1,236,974	33,860	1,270,834	124,591	-56,815	1,089,428	284,144	211,243	10,764	147,235	69,838
1986	1,652,994	1,270,013	36,026	1,306,039	129,107	-54,495	1,122,437	302,212	228,345	11,275	146,612	69,663
1987	1,707,198	1,301,594	40,632	1,342,226	131,637	-54,290	1,156,299	312,082	238,817	11,707	145,828	69,817
1988	1,835,700	1,389,457	54,242	1,443,699	144,888	-55,301	1,243,510	334,608	257,582	12,663	144,961	69,309
1989	1,964,930	1,460,143	42,738	1,502,881	153,825	-56,211	1,292,845	386,792	285,293	13,640	144,058	69,849
1990	2,093,753	1,567,144	40,064	1,607,208	164,815	-60,434	1,381,959	398,202	313,592	14,639	143,025	71,183
1991	2,234,346	1,645,713	60,173	1,705,886	175,889	-69,175	1,460,822	413,863	359,661	15,498	144,169	70,695
1992	2,343,315	1,714,222	67,114	1,781,336	182,074	-70,376	1,528,886	413,390	401,039	16,012	146,343	70,547
1993	2,453,561	1,812,452	54,155	1,866,607	194,038	-80,150	1,592,419	433,762	427,380	16,564	148,122	72,265
1994	2,679,818	1,974,723	90,276	2,064,999	213,689	-91,613	1,759,697	462,767	457,354	17,942	149,356	75,195
1995	2,825,546	2,096,748	81,191	2,177,939	225,510	-93,929	1,858,500	486,716	480,330	18,824	150,100	77,353
1996	3,004,881	2,239,717	77,425	2,317,142	238,725	-104,922	1,973,495	522,241	509,145	19,822	151,596	79,382
1997	3,096,010	2,294,698	76,091	2,370,789	243,062	-107,720	2,020,007	549,589	526,414	20,276	152,692	79,818
1998	3,220,281	2,400,126	65,585	2,465,711	249,706	-109,947	2,106,058	579,011	535,212	20,986	153,449	79,360
1999	3,307,061	2,464,269	73,900	2,538,169	253,470	-109,693	2,175,006	570,420	561,635	21,537	153,555	78,769
2000	3,439,063	2,553,705	76,284	2,629,989	261,329	-119,936	2,248,724	583,106	607,233	22,392	153,585	79,557
2001	3,516,326	2,568,979	82,171	2,651,150	268,699	-117,191	2,265,260	593,854	657,212	22,873	153,730	78,011
2002	3,657,100	2,634,413	85,606	2,720,019	276,360	-114,182	2,329,477	592,629	734,994	23,899	153,024	76,898
2003	3,789,938	2,733,769	92,069	2,825,838	285,638	-115,575	2,424,625	626,324	738,989	24,805	152,790	78,081
2004	3,883,626	2,823,188	69,070	2,892,258	304,468	-115,500	2,472,290	622,515	788,821	25,402	152,887	77,925
2005	4,011,286	2,926,996	91,348	3,018,344	314,410	-116,718	2,587,216	594,139	829,931	26,231	152,919	79,976
2006	4,101,968	2,971,739	77,513	3,049,252	321,774	-111,957	2,615,521	608,688	877,759	26,717	153,535	80,420
2007	4,271,823	3,001,192	76,992	3,078,184	324,918	-110,320	2,642,946	704,362	924,515	27,800	153,661	80,951
2008	4,453,056	3,038,893	80,597	3,119,490	346,521	-105,986	2,666,983	747,537	1,038,536	28,949	153,823	80,471
2009	4,547,666	3,074,290	78,904	3,153,194	346,123	-104,956	2,702,115	706,725	1,138,826	29,452	154,409	78,504
2010	4,675,748	3,131,325	51,189	3,182,514	353,158	-107,139	2,722,217	719,646	1,233,885	30,317	154,227	77,588
2011	4,997,587	3,164,576	99,389	3,263,965	316,757	-102,275	2,844,933	861,653	1,291,001	32,256	154,933	78,989
2012	5,007,993	3,224,322	109,306	3,333,628	323,143	-86,893	2,923,592	824,126	1,260,275	32,379	154,669	79,184
2013	4,950,163	3,270,571	97,817	3,368,388	369,459	-92,663	2,906,266	752,374	1,291,523	32,211	153,680	79,505
2014	5,074,474	3,323,377	54,478	3,377,855	372,884	-80,078	2,924,893	797,889	1,351,692	33,110	153,263	80,587
2015	5,148,474	3,320,413	68,053	3,388,466	375,026	-67,542	2,945,898	820,950	1,381,626	33,868	152,018	81,426
2016	5,207,442	3,394,194	75,420	3,469,614	384,404	-92,506	2,992,704	817,288	1,397,450	34,476	151,044	81,659
2017	5,314,358	3,467,103	68,745	3,535,848	395,049	-100,695	3,040,104	829,980	1,444,274	35,338	150,387	81,924
2018	5,439,642	3,584,698	42,683	3,627,381	417,155	-112,028	3,098,198	849,982	1,491,462	36,158	150,440	82,473
2019	5,674,446	3,663,952	96,188	3,760,140	429,950	-112,514	3,217,676	880,817	1,575,953	37,949	149,530	82,646
2020	6,229,882	3,747,601	87,177	3,834,778	442,174	-124,829	3,267,775	908,288	2,053,819	42,025	148,244	81,189
2021	6,789,683	4,093,854	79,336	4,173,190	479,299	-126,483	3,567,408	932,054	2,290,221	46,851	144,922	85,812
2022	6,690,575	4,288,825	57,012	4,345,837	514,163	-131,884	3,699,790	972,871	2,017,914	45,893	145,786	88,654

Personal Income and Employment by Metropolitan Statistical Area: Albany-Lebanon, OR

(Thousands of dollars, except as noted.)

Year	Personal income, total	Derivation of personal income: Earnings by place of work: Nonfarm	Earnings by place of work: Farm	Earnings by place of work: Total	Less: Contributions for government social insurance	Plus: Adjustment for residence	Equals: Net earnings by place of residence	Plus: Dividends, interest, and rent	Plus: Personal current transfer receipts	Per capita personal income (dollars)	Population (persons)	Total employment
1970	242,957	197,621	9,156	206,777	16,044	-10,338	180,395	37,828	24,734	3,347	72,587	29,190
1971	268,934	219,603	9,305	228,908	18,472	-12,424	198,012	41,960	28,962	3,560	75,547	30,345
1972	298,356	246,218	9,966	256,184	21,770	-14,580	219,834	46,454	32,068	3,902	76,467	31,600
1973	345,781	279,172	20,904	300,076	28,275	-18,157	253,644	52,795	39,342	4,425	78,150	33,577
1974	396,139	315,326	24,904	340,230	32,806	-22,752	284,672	61,574	49,893	5,014	79,006	34,924
1975	430,189	345,304	10,517	355,821	34,806	-26,928	294,087	71,346	64,756	5,315	80,942	35,650
1976	496,928	405,812	18,081	423,893	41,288	-33,236	349,369	78,143	69,416	6,029	82,420	37,031
1977	561,977	464,701	17,381	482,082	47,606	-38,499	395,977	90,402	75,598	6,633	84,723	38,988
1978	626,200	530,514	8,533	539,047	55,649	-43,790	439,608	104,119	82,473	7,253	86,334	40,485
1979	692,148	580,794	7,402	588,196	62,649	-48,051	477,496	121,757	92,895	7,777	88,999	41,045
1980	763,606	621,534	8,106	629,640	67,047	-55,267	507,326	146,001	110,279	8,516	89,668	40,737
1981	833,954	639,605	21,633	661,238	73,921	-54,930	532,387	173,272	128,295	9,248	90,173	39,457
1982	857,929	626,513	17,560	644,073	73,527	-47,246	523,300	190,210	144,419	9,559	89,748	37,614
1983	904,701	665,038	11,243	676,281	79,247	-47,055	549,979	200,867	153,855	10,118	89,415	38,353
1984	970,857	712,679	13,701	726,380	88,384	-46,157	591,839	217,729	161,289	10,878	89,253	39,132
1985	1,012,539	732,336	20,176	752,512	91,647	-44,134	616,731	224,441	171,367	11,504	88,019	39,314
1986	1,055,277	749,081	27,446	776,527	93,033	-35,988	647,506	231,069	176,702	11,988	88,026	39,908
1987	1,117,016	801,795	35,590	837,385	98,036	-33,211	706,138	228,429	182,449	12,683	88,069	40,842
1988	1,246,927	886,310	65,344	951,654	111,697	-32,172	807,785	245,665	193,477	13,975	89,223	42,853
1989	1,342,550	949,388	46,701	996,089	119,410	-25,567	851,112	278,741	212,697	14,935	89,890	44,288
1990	1,415,247	994,709	47,858	1,042,567	128,354	-18,516	895,697	289,545	230,005	15,435	91,690	44,792
1991	1,494,771	1,040,462	49,302	1,089,764	136,171	-21,853	931,740	300,943	262,088	16,048	93,145	44,656
1992	1,587,733	1,103,699	56,730	1,160,429	143,269	-21,005	996,155	297,822	293,756	16,871	94,112	44,762
1993	1,698,486	1,169,018	60,085	1,229,103	153,941	-12,765	1,062,397	319,574	316,515	17,786	95,496	46,076
1994	1,797,356	1,277,105	57,032	1,334,137	168,314	-13,676	1,152,147	327,844	317,365	18,545	96,919	48,997
1995	1,917,693	1,381,992	31,183	1,413,175	183,023	-17,804	1,212,348	357,998	347,347	19,399	98,853	51,874
1996	2,088,151	1,494,822	60,586	1,555,408	200,735	-17,113	1,337,560	386,321	364,270	20,761	100,582	54,263
1997	2,156,851	1,583,734	35,554	1,619,288	209,543	-12,888	1,396,857	386,459	373,535	21,134	102,054	55,265
1998	2,216,809	1,609,166	28,929	1,638,095	212,715	-8,802	1,416,578	395,338	404,893	21,571	102,770	54,813
1999	2,264,510	1,633,202	35,709	1,668,911	214,179	-2,896	1,451,836	364,407	448,267	21,887	103,462	53,186
2000	2,351,714	1,678,360	24,495	1,702,855	218,515	14,037	1,498,377	385,186	468,151	22,828	103,020	52,649
2001	2,563,022	1,802,278	45,245	1,847,523	228,218	22,171	1,641,476	397,962	523,584	24,753	103,544	54,749
2002	2,642,147	1,838,944	56,978	1,895,922	232,243	36,708	1,700,387	383,827	557,933	25,269	104,561	54,137
2003	2,705,019	1,860,833	62,667	1,923,500	235,489	54,440	1,742,451	388,473	574,095	25,511	106,035	53,711
2004	2,888,589	1,952,349	85,826	2,038,175	249,557	77,050	1,865,668	418,350	604,571	27,047	106,799	54,698
2005	2,998,178	2,046,305	72,036	2,118,341	265,931	87,784	1,940,194	408,777	649,207	27,727	108,132	57,089
2006	3,270,997	2,189,166	92,766	2,281,932	284,112	103,015	2,100,835	466,977	703,185	29,531	110,764	58,163
2007	3,421,818	2,272,925	72,006	2,344,931	296,238	116,001	2,164,694	504,669	752,455	30,300	112,932	59,545
2008	3,554,002	2,294,904	45,560	2,340,464	303,589	99,948	2,136,823	573,584	843,595	30,913	114,967	59,479
2009	3,553,514	2,149,757	40,347	2,190,104	284,092	111,474	2,017,486	550,987	985,041	30,633	116,001	56,124
2010	3,693,143	2,205,462	35,238	2,240,700	291,492	119,893	2,069,101	551,323	1,072,719	31,609	116,840	55,560
2011	3,811,233	2,239,414	32,688	2,272,102	264,845	126,188	2,133,445	578,684	1,099,104	32,316	117,938	55,340
2012	3,920,700	2,348,932	42,145	2,391,077	276,729	128,247	2,242,595	573,085	1,105,020	33,264	117,865	55,669
2013	3,971,148	2,353,143	55,312	2,408,455	316,331	150,407	2,242,531	584,807	1,143,810	33,705	117,822	56,205
2014	4,245,071	2,422,678	60,108	2,482,786	331,933	149,620	2,300,473	678,809	1,265,789	35,888	118,285	57,684
2015	4,526,077	2,576,115	76,237	2,652,352	348,277	154,934	2,459,009	700,812	1,366,256	37,940	119,295	58,998
2016	4,743,153	2,752,124	70,926	2,823,050	369,823	176,471	2,629,698	704,948	1,408,507	38,991	121,648	59,657
2017	5,016,945	2,895,536	51,535	2,947,071	391,776	259,955	2,815,250	751,625	1,450,070	40,571	123,657	61,764
2018	5,415,982	3,153,426	59,354	3,212,780	417,993	265,058	3,059,845	809,473	1,546,664	43,056	125,788	63,424
2019	5,654,112	3,258,177	52,952	3,311,129	438,091	289,646	3,162,684	842,210	1,649,218	44,277	127,700	63,418
2020	6,142,058	3,293,802	57,514	3,351,316	445,665	309,865	3,215,516	832,462	2,094,080	47,621	128,978	61,876
2021	6,757,131	3,540,490	65,365	3,605,855	501,807	394,395	3,498,443	909,454	2,349,234	51,999	129,948	64,554
2022	6,845,480	3,827,271	68,003	3,895,274	552,418	412,469	3,755,325	946,334	2,143,821	52,469	130,467	66,620

Personal Income and Employment by Metropolitan Statistical Area: Albany-Schenectady-Troy, NY

(Thousands of dollars, except as noted.)

Year	Personal income, total	Derivation of personal income: Earnings by place of work: Nonfarm	Farm	Total	Less: Contributions for govewrnment social insurance	Plus: Adjustment for residence	Equals: Net earnings by place of residence	Plus: Dividends, interest, and rent	Plus: Personal current transfer receipts	Per capita personal income (dollars)	Population (persons)	Total employment
1970	3,299,252	2,800,707	18,008	2,818,715	218,154	-99,150	2,501,411	499,322	298,519	4,401	749,695	338,712
1971	3,648,157	3,097,958	17,331	3,115,289	248,053	-110,976	2,756,260	540,963	350,934	4,792	761,289	347,216
1972	3,926,002	3,331,968	16,643	3,348,611	278,178	-112,208	2,958,225	581,267	386,510	5,082	772,468	350,334
1973	4,229,899	3,586,099	19,914	3,606,013	345,098	-118,024	3,142,891	645,339	441,669	5,462	774,486	358,789
1974	4,588,365	3,834,657	18,043	3,852,700	380,223	-134,734	3,337,743	731,934	518,688	5,938	772,691	359,694
1975	4,962,911	3,999,876	16,565	4,016,441	390,931	-146,276	3,479,234	798,212	685,465	6,409	774,345	354,340
1976	5,302,714	4,294,760	19,204	4,313,964	432,721	-179,480	3,701,763	843,484	757,467	6,861	772,927	357,485
1977	5,731,221	4,641,126	14,406	4,655,532	466,785	-208,916	3,979,831	929,932	821,458	7,399	774,635	366,349
1978	6,268,119	5,157,580	17,638	5,175,218	532,454	-244,120	4,398,644	1,002,078	867,397	8,071	776,648	378,544
1979	6,893,898	5,657,652	22,512	5,680,164	604,006	-272,498	4,803,660	1,139,519	950,719	8,882	776,196	385,189
1980	7,706,948	6,118,178	22,965	6,141,143	639,168	-301,060	5,200,915	1,386,168	1,119,865	9,985	771,823	385,427
1981	8,541,421	6,637,413	22,763	6,660,176	733,697	-309,278	5,617,201	1,668,935	1,255,285	11,057	772,505	383,685
1982	9,360,265	7,134,458	22,347	7,156,805	787,805	-323,217	6,045,783	1,938,922	1,375,560	12,098	773,678	384,637
1983	10,091,016	7,659,313	17,273	7,676,586	848,981	-329,004	6,498,601	2,113,232	1,479,183	12,976	777,649	387,575
1984	11,154,998	8,560,738	20,518	8,581,256	966,547	-347,090	7,267,619	2,369,925	1,517,454	14,305	779,804	404,423
1985	11,982,631	9,303,284	21,973	9,325,257	1,069,592	-365,545	7,890,120	2,484,627	1,607,884	15,289	783,736	419,617
1986	12,897,621	10,094,951	26,337	10,121,288	1,174,343	-372,515	8,574,430	2,647,772	1,675,419	16,352	788,761	435,382
1987	13,647,830	10,838,435	26,652	10,865,087	1,244,257	-377,748	9,243,082	2,705,257	1,699,491	17,244	791,466	442,103
1988	14,860,037	11,884,885	23,341	11,908,226	1,399,086	-390,105	10,119,035	2,940,079	1,800,923	18,619	798,121	457,684
1989	16,396,531	12,842,634	28,838	12,871,472	1,481,657	-419,754	10,970,061	3,484,628	1,941,842	20,396	803,919	468,296
1990	17,346,457	13,640,429	27,860	13,668,289	1,509,964	-436,492	11,721,833	3,526,684	2,097,940	21,380	811,352	477,904
1991	17,941,174	14,006,763	22,539	14,029,302	1,595,895	-439,648	11,993,759	3,604,417	2,342,998	21,926	818,272	474,065
1992	18,983,818	14,855,342	27,212	14,882,554	1,662,870	-476,352	12,743,332	3,581,024	2,659,462	23,031	824,285	476,931
1993	19,583,059	15,378,083	27,362	15,405,445	1,725,843	-515,846	13,163,756	3,615,543	2,803,760	23,656	827,812	483,377
1994	20,221,703	15,887,306	22,765	15,910,071	1,809,582	-528,409	13,572,080	3,739,966	2,909,657	24,340	830,817	491,282
1995	20,876,789	16,098,700	19,459	16,118,159	1,830,759	-528,421	13,758,979	4,042,381	3,075,429	25,139	830,439	484,903
1996	21,516,307	16,572,119	27,042	16,599,161	1,844,696	-576,687	14,177,778	4,138,111	3,200,418	25,986	828,007	482,555
1997	22,745,449	17,552,800	6,249	17,559,049	1,923,586	-624,309	15,011,154	4,485,986	3,248,309	27,580	824,711	487,706
1998	23,891,176	18,413,682	21,201	18,434,883	2,013,354	-689,778	15,731,751	4,683,535	3,475,890	29,004	823,712	500,443
1999	25,080,928	19,682,457	25,279	19,707,736	2,098,294	-719,347	16,890,095	4,604,850	3,585,983	30,434	824,119	512,344
2000	26,898,468	21,461,551	28,751	21,490,302	2,271,840	-852,548	18,365,914	4,874,924	3,657,630	32,510	827,399	524,195
2001	28,087,576	22,599,727	33,873	22,633,600	2,404,546	-906,198	19,322,856	4,806,468	3,958,252	33,798	831,034	516,432
2002	28,336,896	23,156,227	25,165	23,181,392	2,478,932	-894,489	19,807,971	4,267,864	4,261,061	33,865	836,753	514,462
2003	29,334,792	23,909,476	30,860	23,940,336	2,587,689	-912,789	20,439,858	4,497,598	4,397,336	34,731	844,619	518,128
2004	30,614,179	24,772,521	35,046	24,807,567	2,683,612	-900,100	21,223,855	4,758,472	4,631,852	36,000	850,384	524,026
2005	31,541,783	25,231,662	31,046	25,262,708	2,768,918	-863,318	21,630,472	5,088,375	4,822,936	36,908	854,604	530,764
2006	33,231,091	26,437,728	25,125	26,462,853	2,900,931	-925,683	22,636,239	5,490,881	5,103,971	38,624	860,365	534,266
2007	34,703,367	27,175,340	33,202	27,208,542	2,966,744	-814,414	23,427,384	5,984,155	5,291,828	40,209	863,068	540,905
2008	36,766,707	28,195,974	48,821	28,244,795	3,114,746	-770,127	24,359,922	6,415,206	5,991,579	42,442	866,282	543,952
2009	37,056,662	28,671,668	36,220	28,707,888	3,126,150	-848,128	24,733,610	5,738,641	6,584,411	42,625	869,361	535,311
2010	38,478,206	29,470,347	60,332	29,530,679	3,151,102	-774,536	25,605,041	5,836,464	7,036,701	44,146	871,603	528,092
2011	39,880,474	29,921,284	72,245	29,993,529	2,889,053	-804,055	26,300,421	6,225,728	7,354,325	45,558	875,387	531,548
2012	41,075,100	30,672,870	80,507	30,753,377	2,954,054	-762,375	27,036,948	6,802,930	7,235,222	46,708	879,397	537,652
2013	41,925,141	31,966,812	95,935	32,062,747	3,473,451	-916,551	27,672,745	6,905,547	7,346,849	47,434	883,854	543,161
2014	43,250,532	32,554,021	90,723	32,644,744	3,614,567	-832,120	28,198,057	7,531,614	7,520,861	48,762	886,981	548,376
2015	45,477,656	33,967,675	58,973	34,026,648	3,788,186	-832,657	29,405,805	8,039,991	8,031,860	51,103	889,918	556,285
2016	46,420,368	34,830,722	48,871	34,879,593	3,883,523	-910,974	30,085,096	8,169,184	8,166,088	51,996	892,762	563,746
2017	49,061,892	36,248,258	69,400	36,317,658	4,061,039	-990,183	31,266,436	8,967,312	8,828,144	54,685	897,172	570,631
2018	50,521,025	37,406,237	48,928	37,455,165	4,133,255	-1,040,181	32,281,729	9,565,132	8,674,164	56,159	899,605	575,615
2019	52,388,271	38,428,716	82,420	38,511,136	4,256,181	-1,221,998	33,032,957	10,014,185	9,341,129	58,287	898,791	574,621
2020	56,502,674	39,267,452	67,652	39,335,104	4,313,821	-1,245,983	33,775,300	9,982,201	12,745,173	62,798	899,748	545,001
2021	60,629,206	42,330,031	74,063	42,404,094	4,729,801	-1,375,797	36,298,496	11,101,706	13,229,004	66,966	905,369	558,266
2022	60,594,702	44,683,469	101,784	44,785,253	5,116,567	-1,445,411	38,223,275	11,314,658	11,056,769	66,984	904,617	579,939

Personal Income and Employment by Metropolitan Statistical Area: Albuquerque, NM

(Thousands of dollars, except as noted.)

Year	Personal income, total	Derivation of personal income: Earnings by place of work: Nonfarm	Farm	Total	Less: Contributions for government social insurance	Plus: Adjustment for residence	Equals: Net earnings by place of residence	Plus: Dividends, interest, and rent	Plus: Personal current transfer receipts	Per capita personal income (dollars)	Population (persons)	Total employment
1970	1,414,627	1,099,938	8,526	1,108,464	69,248	14,663	1,053,879	237,800	122,948	3,702	382,076	152,994
1971	1,598,397	1,239,222	7,925	1,247,147	81,837	16,932	1,182,242	273,730	142,425	4,021	397,496	164,049
1972	1,834,590	1,433,302	9,518	1,442,820	98,796	19,045	1,363,069	311,896	159,625	4,499	407,732	177,980
1973	2,045,489	1,598,491	10,994	1,609,485	126,791	22,122	1,504,816	350,520	190,153	4,795	426,583	187,854
1974	2,292,455	1,754,689	11,608	1,766,297	142,552	32,265	1,656,010	408,348	228,097	5,203	440,633	193,502
1975	2,593,217	1,939,587	10,450	1,950,037	156,325	48,104	1,841,816	466,004	285,397	5,754	450,712	198,943
1976	2,935,369	2,205,178	8,613	2,213,791	180,604	66,231	2,099,418	514,117	321,834	6,318	464,570	210,271
1977	3,288,372	2,489,152	10,504	2,499,656	206,193	85,768	2,379,231	572,801	336,340	6,832	481,349	221,559
1978	3,809,512	2,895,245	16,512	2,911,757	247,261	107,888	2,772,384	672,595	364,533	7,729	492,914	237,762
1979	4,331,685	3,290,949	22,012	3,312,961	295,139	129,817	3,147,639	761,730	422,316	8,517	508,581	247,977
1980	4,860,081	3,607,732	25,181	3,632,913	322,760	127,562	3,437,715	909,693	512,673	9,247	525,593	248,765
1981	5,409,093	3,960,840	23,779	3,984,619	378,663	119,337	3,725,293	1,095,058	588,742	10,122	534,415	250,776
1982	5,718,373	4,126,812	21,598	4,148,410	400,925	60,614	3,808,099	1,292,818	617,456	11,187	511,169	248,041
1983	6,289,890	4,597,074	16,765	4,613,839	454,754	32,285	4,191,370	1,434,485	664,035	12,041	522,356	259,621
1984	6,981,247	5,122,781	22,804	5,145,585	522,520	33,113	4,656,178	1,600,461	724,608	13,085	533,544	275,851
1985	7,667,553	5,622,921	19,816	5,642,737	585,624	26,631	5,083,744	1,802,634	781,175	14,079	544,603	290,100
1986	8,168,901	5,990,074	17,588	6,007,662	631,203	27,506	5,403,965	1,924,442	840,494	14,617	558,859	300,497
1987	8,638,337	6,388,377	16,156	6,404,533	667,865	31,985	5,768,653	1,968,234	901,450	15,041	574,324	314,235
1988	9,210,625	6,832,863	22,915	6,855,778	739,904	31,959	6,147,833	2,090,604	972,188	15,772	583,976	330,259
1989	9,782,290	7,222,455	32,012	7,254,467	790,733	40,280	6,504,014	2,189,333	1,088,943	16,468	594,036	336,572
1990	10,478,433	7,735,466	31,253	7,766,719	899,468	49,046	6,916,297	2,367,896	1,194,240	17,389	602,588	341,067
1991	11,211,814	8,293,771	33,167	8,326,938	973,861	46,750	7,399,827	2,465,561	1,346,426	18,191	616,345	348,198
1992	12,025,572	8,977,563	26,268	9,003,831	1,045,197	41,967	8,000,601	2,537,403	1,487,568	18,997	633,032	355,488
1993	12,985,286	9,777,523	29,723	9,807,246	1,138,606	30,337	8,698,977	2,674,276	1,612,033	19,978	649,987	370,109
1994	14,111,389	10,695,020	23,835	10,718,855	1,270,717	30,222	9,478,360	2,933,936	1,699,093	21,070	669,734	389,822
1995	15,196,644	11,492,294	18,021	11,510,315	1,369,032	23,339	10,164,622	3,157,086	1,874,936	22,091	687,901	411,302
1996	16,010,836	11,983,379	24,087	12,007,466	1,425,874	9,135	10,590,727	3,379,809	2,040,300	22,867	700,161	418,022
1997	16,854,669	12,610,490	27,038	12,637,528	1,494,644	233	11,143,117	3,613,726	2,097,826	23,750	709,661	425,091
1998	17,595,601	13,235,479	27,424	13,262,903	1,568,638	3,629	11,697,894	3,754,697	2,143,010	24,527	717,406	431,253
1999	17,951,143	13,715,891	31,829	13,747,720	1,634,401	-6,493	12,106,826	3,555,990	2,288,327	24,839	722,692	433,808
2000	19,480,949	15,025,978	27,248	15,053,226	1,742,775	-16,452	13,293,999	3,739,111	2,447,839	26,605	732,220	446,700
2001	20,530,430	15,702,720	37,056	15,739,776	1,838,468	-27,041	13,874,267	3,903,990	2,752,173	27,672	741,932	448,753
2002	21,328,914	16,330,647	22,199	16,352,846	1,907,820	198	14,445,224	3,858,399	3,025,291	28,149	757,716	448,875
2003	22,362,921	17,161,167	35,287	17,196,454	1,997,849	24,964	15,223,569	3,877,764	3,261,588	28,963	772,128	454,372
2004	23,803,957	18,241,983	53,047	18,295,030	2,096,938	100,056	16,298,148	4,006,208	3,499,601	30,161	789,237	466,418
2005	25,301,580	19,201,189	43,282	19,244,471	2,215,638	174,288	17,203,121	4,310,209	3,788,250	31,254	809,551	476,219
2006	27,368,094	20,623,517	26,070	20,649,587	2,392,357	153,899	18,411,129	4,789,440	4,167,525	32,924	831,252	494,455
2007	28,692,068	21,241,056	46,252	21,287,308	2,489,337	194,224	18,992,195	5,166,885	4,532,988	33,770	849,641	503,922
2008	30,286,146	21,779,284	39,703	21,818,987	2,583,937	221,375	19,456,425	5,562,953	5,266,768	35,078	863,383	503,228
2009	30,239,770	21,635,579	16,833	21,652,412	2,571,897	168,034	19,248,549	5,177,798	5,813,423	34,503	876,448	486,485
2010	30,703,897	21,643,297	25,056	21,668,353	2,581,365	165,599	19,252,587	5,096,599	6,354,711	34,521	889,434	477,824
2011	32,053,994	22,134,235	49,909	22,184,144	2,361,678	173,511	19,995,977	5,605,471	6,452,546	35,720	897,378	476,862
2012	32,353,248	22,232,470	43,476	22,275,946	2,407,348	134,953	20,003,551	5,885,035	6,464,662	35,918	900,747	476,624
2013	31,909,267	22,014,774	36,159	22,050,933	2,761,547	148,927	19,438,313	5,894,653	6,576,301	35,330	903,185	479,183
2014	33,636,494	22,862,408	58,027	22,920,435	2,853,215	116,135	20,183,355	6,253,589	7,199,550	37,284	902,178	483,138
2015	34,898,581	23,662,299	44,409	23,706,708	3,054,063	135,721	20,788,366	6,348,482	7,761,733	38,644	903,085	489,374
2016	36,276,028	24,778,329	44,746	24,823,075	3,136,752	2,694	21,689,017	6,608,038	7,978,973	40,050	905,774	497,053
2017	37,056,685	25,301,950	41,894	25,343,844	3,159,633	5,649	22,189,860	6,863,591	8,003,234	40,802	908,217	502,369
2018	38,394,032	26,211,618	42,888	26,254,506	3,261,412	-25,461	22,967,633	6,967,770	8,458,629	42,178	910,284	508,987
2019	40,717,921	27,670,222	40,487	27,710,709	3,410,094	46,898	24,347,513	7,484,505	8,885,903	44,587	913,231	511,716
2020	44,640,471	28,233,879	47,826	28,281,705	3,528,057	69,393	24,823,041	7,930,485	11,886,945	48,654	917,502	493,238
2021	48,679,549	30,495,951	42,103	30,538,054	3,796,388	118,907	26,860,573	8,341,200	13,477,776	52,972	918,970	509,459
2022	49,612,727	32,785,028	41,160	32,826,188	4,130,006	120,575	28,816,757	8,604,011	12,191,959	53,954	919,543	532,840

Personal Income and Employment by Metropolitan Statistical Area: Alexandria, LA

(Thousands of dollars, except as noted.)

Year	Personal income, total	Derivation of personal income: Earnings by place of work: Nonfarm	Farm	Total	Less: Contributions for government social insurance	Plus: Adjustment for residence	Equals: Net earnings by place of residence	Plus: Dividends, interest, and rent	Plus: Personal current transfer receipts	Per capita personal income (dollars)	Population (persons)	Total employment
1970	398,474	293,678	7,270	300,948	17,442	2,398	285,904	62,613	49,957	3,012	132,287	50,427
1971	452,673	332,276	9,715	341,991	20,344	2,819	324,466	72,441	55,766	3,310	136,756	52,411
1972	494,074	363,553	10,548	374,101	22,986	2,898	354,013	79,113	60,948	3,595	137,425	52,809
1973	549,564	400,679	13,353	414,032	28,429	5,206	390,809	88,749	70,006	3,926	139,971	55,643
1974	596,522	430,241	9,874	440,115	31,787	4,381	412,709	100,669	83,144	4,256	140,176	55,277
1975	667,030	469,271	7,520	476,791	34,510	5,242	447,523	112,767	106,740	4,726	141,141	55,321
1976	750,300	526,745	15,920	542,665	39,761	7,174	510,078	122,768	117,454	5,218	143,786	57,332
1977	821,170	579,625	10,656	590,281	43,249	10,160	557,192	137,858	126,120	5,614	146,270	58,249
1978	932,091	654,535	14,608	669,143	49,095	15,216	635,264	159,792	137,035	6,314	147,614	60,432
1979	1,032,022	713,720	16,103	729,823	55,037	20,727	695,513	179,140	157,369	6,886	149,880	60,097
1980	1,177,483	809,564	3,030	812,594	62,753	24,091	773,932	217,803	185,748	7,737	152,197	61,010
1981	1,309,840	887,640	3,317	890,957	73,153	30,391	848,195	259,259	202,386	8,574	152,773	61,163
1982	1,409,394	926,121	2,289	928,410	76,196	25,654	877,868	294,010	237,516	9,219	152,877	61,401
1983	1,522,844	991,698	16,209	1,007,907	82,131	23,013	948,789	318,842	255,213	9,888	154,017	62,122
1984	1,612,424	1,059,657	8,389	1,068,046	90,312	19,160	996,894	342,278	273,252	10,435	154,515	63,636
1985	1,710,600	1,102,838	9,225	1,112,063	95,519	16,072	1,032,616	377,360	300,624	11,109	153,989	63,606
1986	1,774,798	1,144,184	8,769	1,152,953	99,624	7,976	1,061,305	390,836	322,657	11,500	154,335	63,566
1987	1,825,964	1,189,757	14,161	1,203,918	102,962	3,153	1,104,109	389,144	332,711	11,920	153,188	64,188
1988	1,930,855	1,257,149	22,823	1,279,972	113,970	1,237	1,167,239	413,603	350,013	12,755	151,377	64,413
1989	2,078,568	1,349,066	14,966	1,364,032	126,114	-8,031	1,229,887	462,457	386,224	13,841	150,180	65,261
1990	2,207,051	1,442,368	14,302	1,456,670	137,338	-8,714	1,310,618	464,635	431,798	14,814	148,982	65,706
1991	2,286,765	1,494,613	6,633	1,501,246	147,455	-7,307	1,346,484	458,992	481,289	15,343	149,046	65,863
1992	2,372,643	1,529,044	20,480	1,549,524	149,629	-3,450	1,396,445	443,135	533,063	16,073	147,621	64,337
1993	2,506,634	1,582,398	20,678	1,603,076	156,108	-5,674	1,441,294	451,630	613,710	17,624	142,225	65,441
1994	2,688,881	1,654,611	24,939	1,679,550	167,106	-6,194	1,506,250	483,147	699,484	18,792	143,086	66,500
1995	2,786,969	1,733,426	22,071	1,755,497	176,030	-5,574	1,573,893	525,303	687,773	19,332	144,162	69,293
1996	2,863,572	1,796,210	26,878	1,823,088	184,216	-5,173	1,633,699	547,849	682,024	19,890	143,970	69,670
1997	2,961,169	1,839,380	19,408	1,858,788	190,137	-3,261	1,665,390	585,284	710,495	20,566	143,986	70,362
1998	3,137,444	1,980,148	13,743	1,993,891	206,167	-7,698	1,780,026	630,575	726,843	21,738	144,330	72,287
1999	3,248,646	2,115,717	22,035	2,137,752	216,492	-12,790	1,908,470	614,865	725,311	22,435	144,803	74,507
2000	3,384,441	2,200,674	23,985	2,224,659	222,383	-12,528	1,989,748	653,847	740,846	23,312	145,179	75,003
2001	3,699,497	2,358,499	21,860	2,380,359	232,946	-16,286	2,131,127	667,621	900,749	25,496	145,102	74,686
2002	3,831,905	2,494,485	16,287	2,510,772	245,780	-25,240	2,239,752	660,394	931,759	26,351	145,416	75,251
2003	3,887,173	2,558,796	28,616	2,587,412	252,067	-30,184	2,305,161	676,901	905,111	26,621	146,017	75,321
2004	4,168,844	2,709,740	21,344	2,731,084	268,922	-45,409	2,416,753	712,741	1,039,350	28,365	146,973	77,127
2005	4,552,393	2,928,879	21,263	2,950,142	285,799	-53,922	2,610,421	799,371	1,142,601	30,774	147,930	79,635
2006	4,796,081	3,188,364	28,488	3,216,852	312,685	-73,178	2,830,989	792,464	1,172,628	31,732	151,142	83,037
2007	5,031,343	3,300,057	31,582	3,331,639	329,304	-79,574	2,922,761	881,988	1,226,594	33,209	151,506	84,411
2008	5,349,501	3,405,387	23,974	3,429,361	343,815	-87,846	2,997,700	1,012,138	1,339,663	35,092	152,442	84,915
2009	5,294,831	3,401,156	38,473	3,439,629	345,242	-96,867	2,997,520	895,954	1,401,357	34,570	153,164	82,890
2010	5,384,073	3,488,768	47,920	3,536,688	348,608	-90,883	3,097,197	834,293	1,452,583	34,936	154,112	81,413
2011	5,669,056	3,577,965	55,356	3,633,321	323,178	-94,751	3,215,392	980,111	1,473,553	36,684	154,538	81,797
2012	5,917,261	3,669,189	69,018	3,738,207	329,486	-102,493	3,306,228	1,077,352	1,533,681	38,264	154,643	81,052
2013	5,928,836	3,753,182	50,151	3,803,333	377,317	-116,280	3,309,736	1,016,823	1,602,277	38,257	154,972	80,896
2014	5,993,901	3,892,366	33,343	3,925,709	384,918	-112,777	3,428,014	1,021,896	1,543,991	38,665	155,021	81,634
2015	6,073,573	3,889,450	23,457	3,912,907	392,832	-114,477	3,405,598	990,746	1,677,229	39,271	154,658	81,926
2016	6,170,549	3,962,090	22,211	3,984,301	405,841	-129,432	3,449,028	1,000,240	1,721,281	39,871	154,763	81,656
2017	6,218,251	3,985,325	33,677	4,019,002	406,518	-131,358	3,481,126	982,169	1,754,956	40,302	154,292	80,944
2018	6,432,682	4,113,147	40,002	4,153,149	422,543	-130,932	3,599,674	1,025,153	1,807,855	41,876	153,614	80,919
2019	6,665,279	4,230,529	58,313	4,288,842	430,659	-131,846	3,726,337	1,033,301	1,905,641	43,559	153,019	80,054
2020	7,245,021	4,390,310	68,406	4,458,716	450,695	-148,172	3,859,849	1,017,425	2,367,747	47,730	151,792	78,959
2021	7,716,348	4,559,693	83,410	4,643,103	468,546	-160,429	4,014,128	1,099,014	2,603,206	51,115	150,960	82,294
2022	7,675,864	4,763,297	62,411	4,825,708	502,157	-159,212	4,164,339	1,110,789	2,400,736	51,451	149,189	84,307

Personal Income and Employment by Metropolitan Statistical Area: Allentown-Bethlehem-Easton, PA-NJ

(Thousands of dollars, except as noted.)

Year	Personal income, total	Derivation of personal income: Earnings by place of work: Nonfarm	Farm	Total	Less: Contributions for government social insurance	Plus: Adjustment for residence	Equals: Net earnings by place of residence	Plus: Dividends, interest, and rent	Plus: Personal current transfer receipts	Per capita personal income (dollars)	Population (persons)	Total employment
1970	2,470,715	2,045,622	15,931	2,061,553	156,077	22,192	1,927,668	326,336	216,711	4,148	595,577	272,973
1971	2,634,493	2,150,247	12,596	2,162,843	170,660	31,656	2,023,839	356,311	254,343	4,377	601,892	271,090
1972	2,921,986	2,392,436	13,758	2,406,194	199,397	39,217	2,246,014	388,667	287,305	4,828	605,156	277,879
1973	3,293,107	2,712,131	19,656	2,731,787	260,516	49,597	2,520,868	447,230	325,009	5,390	610,947	292,047
1974	3,695,845	3,016,404	21,975	3,038,379	300,799	56,673	2,794,253	517,312	384,280	5,983	617,690	297,119
1975	4,063,395	3,204,702	19,496	3,224,198	312,338	67,694	2,979,554	574,912	508,929	6,532	622,114	290,754
1976	4,421,259	3,450,069	21,927	3,471,996	339,840	92,278	3,224,434	615,702	581,123	7,076	624,814	291,781
1977	4,886,917	3,822,661	21,206	3,843,867	371,422	120,689	3,593,134	686,515	607,268	7,787	627,598	296,393
1978	5,432,118	4,270,480	23,713	4,294,193	426,495	152,251	4,019,949	756,715	655,454	8,626	629,719	304,849
1979	6,060,574	4,755,921	31,467	4,787,388	490,392	183,177	4,480,173	851,232	729,169	9,573	633,073	310,781
1980	6,688,734	5,061,136	16,665	5,077,801	527,711	227,997	4,778,087	1,057,591	853,056	10,510	636,389	310,670
1981	7,399,895	5,420,311	23,287	5,443,598	604,656	272,717	5,111,659	1,306,427	981,809	11,585	638,748	310,155
1982	7,930,465	5,533,041	20,473	5,553,514	626,695	325,890	5,252,709	1,540,820	1,136,936	12,376	640,790	302,259
1983	8,301,736	5,696,938	3,954	5,700,892	651,169	392,006	5,441,729	1,612,035	1,247,972	12,938	641,637	298,035
1984	9,094,132	6,311,417	26,639	6,338,056	750,312	454,017	6,041,761	1,804,189	1,248,182	14,103	644,843	309,576
1985	9,734,762	6,687,998	27,471	6,715,469	801,788	527,228	6,440,909	1,969,948	1,323,905	15,017	648,256	314,763
1986	10,254,857	6,957,755	22,123	6,979,878	829,533	614,509	6,764,854	2,071,912	1,418,091	15,671	654,365	317,329
1987	10,921,810	7,548,433	21,949	7,570,382	889,895	690,163	7,370,650	2,101,422	1,449,738	16,463	663,413	329,686
1988	11,886,809	8,212,969	26,781	8,239,750	988,633	800,418	8,051,535	2,290,905	1,544,369	17,616	674,767	339,830
1989	12,967,198	8,760,090	36,413	8,796,503	1,042,536	889,927	8,643,894	2,669,568	1,653,736	18,995	682,657	345,404
1990	13,678,792	9,185,091	33,673	9,218,764	1,088,667	984,129	9,114,226	2,731,011	1,833,555	19,859	688,801	349,846
1991	14,357,552	9,461,336	20,150	9,481,486	1,135,891	998,553	9,344,148	2,878,668	2,134,736	20,624	696,168	345,339
1992	15,186,343	10,179,798	35,527	10,215,325	1,211,040	1,077,087	10,081,372	2,814,739	2,290,232	21,604	702,948	345,658
1993	15,743,213	10,631,079	26,975	10,658,054	1,286,552	1,162,902	10,534,404	2,811,465	2,397,344	22,212	708,776	347,081
1994	16,318,825	11,053,320	21,304	11,074,624	1,360,581	1,207,430	10,921,473	2,933,255	2,464,097	22,855	714,019	351,274
1995	17,003,898	11,459,478	15,864	11,475,342	1,405,503	1,271,053	11,340,892	3,070,164	2,592,842	23,693	717,685	355,394
1996	17,916,540	11,906,128	33,545	11,939,673	1,420,267	1,395,872	11,915,278	3,232,907	2,768,355	24,813	722,063	357,386
1997	18,864,832	12,476,805	14,314	12,491,119	1,481,970	1,533,501	12,542,650	3,458,198	2,863,984	25,968	726,464	365,995
1998	19,796,301	13,062,238	16,069	13,078,307	1,539,031	1,712,513	13,251,789	3,632,755	2,911,757	27,089	730,779	369,703
1999	20,895,662	14,065,385	7,909	14,073,294	1,626,634	1,827,739	14,274,399	3,547,937	3,073,326	28,378	736,327	377,848
2000	22,524,409	14,900,759	27,725	14,928,484	1,702,769	2,172,147	15,397,862	3,852,078	3,274,469	30,364	741,817	388,803
2001	24,260,394	16,368,345	17,931	16,386,276	1,828,447	2,231,074	16,788,903	3,899,114	3,572,377	32,403	748,705	396,203
2002	25,027,250	16,927,154	11,046	16,938,200	1,883,433	2,305,073	17,359,840	3,826,369	3,841,041	33,077	756,628	395,668
2003	25,925,783	17,473,473	28,491	17,501,964	1,928,768	2,435,806	18,009,002	3,973,711	3,943,070	33,804	766,938	400,601
2004	27,361,830	18,567,317	38,700	18,606,017	2,023,655	2,809,357	19,391,719	3,863,882	4,106,229	35,202	777,277	408,169
2005	29,216,634	20,007,709	25,108	20,032,817	2,169,374	3,078,306	20,941,749	3,822,497	4,452,388	37,089	787,738	418,884
2006	30,649,013	20,593,968	22,710	20,616,678	2,294,894	3,432,076	21,753,860	4,174,950	4,720,203	38,379	798,586	428,103
2007	33,161,466	21,914,599	37,101	21,951,700	2,394,130	3,869,550	23,427,120	4,665,208	5,069,138	41,063	807,578	435,473
2008	34,493,147	22,238,879	36,429	22,275,308	2,442,729	3,716,040	23,548,619	5,202,674	5,741,854	42,372	814,050	435,262
2009	33,402,107	21,398,816	27,329	21,426,145	2,396,275	3,158,279	22,188,149	4,898,808	6,315,150	40,845	817,779	424,466
2010	34,755,032	22,133,947	33,408	22,167,355	2,456,966	3,423,156	23,133,545	4,806,819	6,814,668	42,274	822,144	425,820
2011	35,971,191	22,915,446	43,971	22,959,417	2,294,452	3,310,939	23,975,904	5,168,412	6,826,875	43,509	826,750	432,722
2012	36,448,990	23,353,795	56,842	23,410,637	2,345,153	3,078,219	24,143,703	5,436,991	6,868,296	43,937	829,566	438,774
2013	36,821,740	23,964,701	59,556	24,024,257	2,720,056	3,142,560	24,446,761	5,433,320	6,941,659	44,324	830,735	445,568
2014	38,242,249	24,779,961	56,112	24,836,073	2,821,326	3,175,144	25,189,891	5,851,626	7,200,732	45,795	835,077	452,890
2015	39,981,035	26,003,399	63,058	26,066,457	2,941,261	3,228,102	26,353,298	6,048,099	7,579,638	47,682	838,490	459,147
2016	41,228,221	26,696,851	36,299	26,733,150	3,035,065	3,328,509	27,026,594	6,195,900	8,005,727	48,896	843,181	466,968
2017	42,600,202	27,542,094	52,865	27,594,959	3,185,392	3,319,882	27,729,449	6,676,543	8,194,210	50,135	849,703	472,697
2018	44,618,559	28,308,355	35,536	28,343,891	3,270,768	3,739,698	28,812,821	7,049,251	8,756,487	52,126	855,983	480,499
2019	47,170,999	29,903,099	63,487	29,966,586	3,448,853	4,145,171	30,662,904	7,371,010	9,137,085	54,936	858,656	484,143
2020	51,179,548	29,414,604	53,109	29,467,713	3,424,908	4,914,285	30,957,090	7,649,749	12,572,709	59,407	861,508	462,632
2021	54,140,628	31,783,792	70,053	31,853,845	3,715,494	4,418,206	32,556,557	8,208,106	13,375,965	62,247	869,765	486,414
2022	54,810,693	33,526,937	67,666	33,594,603	4,034,909	5,320,738	34,880,432	8,715,837	11,214,424	62,912	871,229	507,693

Personal Income and Employment by Metropolitan Statistical Area: Altoona, PA

(Thousands of dollars, except as noted.)

Year	Personal income, total	Derivation of personal income: Earnings by place of work: Nonfarm	Earnings by place of work: Farm	Earnings by place of work: Total	Less: Contributions for government social insurance	Plus: Adjustment for residence	Equals: Net earnings by place of residence	Plus: Dividends, interest, and rent	Plus: Personal current transfer receipts	Per capita personal income (dollars)	Population (persons)	Total employment
1970	470,275	399,460	5,984	405,444	34,429	-18,697	352,318	49,266	68,691	3,470	135,538	57,438
1971	499,206	420,062	4,239	424,301	37,056	-19,261	367,984	52,867	78,355	3,644	136,999	56,621
1972	535,727	450,677	4,049	454,726	41,151	-21,087	392,488	56,584	86,655	3,891	137,687	57,144
1973	589,763	500,165	4,690	504,855	50,902	-24,338	429,615	63,530	96,618	4,319	136,556	59,254
1974	647,183	542,510	3,915	546,425	57,822	-26,668	461,935	72,020	113,228	4,725	136,956	58,969
1975	713,117	575,826	4,079	579,905	59,813	-27,735	492,357	79,630	141,130	5,220	136,611	57,981
1976	795,308	653,745	5,067	658,812	69,525	-33,229	556,058	86,372	152,878	5,847	136,023	59,523
1977	877,132	733,477	4,591	738,068	79,292	-39,330	619,446	96,830	160,856	6,402	137,015	60,379
1978	965,705	810,012	5,878	815,890	87,981	-45,210	682,699	106,910	176,096	7,013	137,705	61,616
1979	1,066,410	890,750	7,240	897,990	99,294	-50,634	748,062	119,198	199,150	7,730	137,966	61,945
1980	1,140,264	910,505	4,455	914,960	100,441	-53,620	760,899	151,555	227,810	8,357	136,443	60,840
1981	1,230,690	946,422	5,475	951,897	111,386	-53,458	787,053	187,334	256,303	9,085	135,457	59,371
1982	1,283,286	925,693	5,733	931,426	110,192	-46,927	774,307	219,333	289,646	9,464	135,600	56,566
1983	1,332,274	934,576	4,292	938,868	109,361	-44,964	784,543	232,174	315,557	9,913	134,397	55,220
1984	1,412,843	1,006,311	9,577	1,015,888	123,518	-48,291	844,079	256,431	312,333	10,629	132,925	56,874
1985	1,511,074	1,090,909	10,326	1,101,235	137,017	-57,124	907,094	276,004	327,976	11,426	132,253	58,346
1986	1,596,652	1,165,110	10,854	1,175,964	148,647	-62,355	964,962	293,208	338,482	12,137	131,556	59,616
1987	1,653,334	1,227,636	12,261	1,239,897	154,461	-63,570	1,021,866	290,098	341,370	12,553	131,712	60,857
1988	1,741,978	1,285,413	11,739	1,297,152	166,697	-60,752	1,069,703	313,492	358,783	13,256	131,408	62,323
1989	1,886,785	1,372,373	13,450	1,385,823	174,681	-61,465	1,149,677	360,672	376,436	14,453	130,546	63,201
1990	1,999,250	1,456,984	10,361	1,467,345	183,815	-65,532	1,217,998	364,949	416,303	15,309	130,593	64,824
1991	2,094,942	1,498,771	8,733	1,507,504	190,791	-68,366	1,248,347	372,492	474,103	15,972	131,160	63,975
1992	2,235,942	1,640,139	12,423	1,652,562	207,353	-80,663	1,364,546	373,699	497,697	17,033	131,270	65,472
1993	2,348,448	1,751,662	8,334	1,759,996	223,632	-91,553	1,444,811	384,166	519,471	17,837	131,661	67,208
1994	2,453,654	1,845,493	10,107	1,855,600	238,564	-99,031	1,518,005	403,399	532,250	18,571	132,124	68,011
1995	2,546,777	1,901,075	10,105	1,911,180	242,941	-103,166	1,565,073	430,488	551,216	19,323	131,802	69,263
1996	2,685,129	2,004,060	12,725	2,016,785	246,893	-112,103	1,657,789	443,717	583,623	20,485	131,080	70,018
1997	2,830,831	2,123,957	12,656	2,136,613	257,659	-118,624	1,760,330	472,320	598,181	21,621	130,931	70,970
1998	2,974,597	2,238,940	23,528	2,262,468	268,336	-132,051	1,862,081	492,762	619,754	22,792	130,509	71,039
1999	3,084,980	2,361,790	23,487	2,385,277	281,060	-144,847	1,959,370	481,843	643,767	23,775	129,757	72,406
2000	3,211,969	2,434,056	19,218	2,453,274	284,690	-151,027	2,017,557	512,660	681,752	24,903	128,981	72,331
2001	3,249,461	2,441,574	22,366	2,463,940	291,311	-152,562	2,020,067	498,421	730,973	25,293	128,471	72,750
2002	3,340,145	2,505,295	14,113	2,519,408	295,493	-154,549	2,069,366	494,850	775,929	26,170	127,631	72,973
2003	3,465,447	2,612,639	19,762	2,632,401	302,640	-165,896	2,163,865	500,251	801,331	27,211	127,353	73,402
2004	3,632,781	2,766,001	35,645	2,801,646	316,955	-175,431	2,309,260	482,488	841,033	28,561	127,194	74,356
2005	3,757,891	2,856,820	32,274	2,889,094	336,953	-186,637	2,365,504	498,292	894,095	29,653	126,730	75,270
2006	3,877,352	2,913,748	21,610	2,935,358	347,958	-179,827	2,407,573	530,785	938,994	30,530	127,002	75,416
2007	4,070,298	2,998,434	35,962	3,034,396	360,158	-189,813	2,484,425	589,769	996,104	32,037	127,048	76,071
2008	4,231,489	3,017,075	30,690	3,047,765	366,980	-184,249	2,496,536	636,542	1,098,411	33,289	127,112	75,331
2009	4,292,327	3,030,033	17,802	3,047,835	370,546	-186,550	2,490,739	626,022	1,175,566	33,755	127,161	74,053
2010	4,451,189	3,135,869	33,220	3,169,089	379,077	-179,497	2,610,515	624,637	1,216,037	35,024	127,089	73,705
2011	4,701,149	3,263,666	41,468	3,305,134	356,273	-187,092	2,761,769	697,299	1,242,081	36,961	127,192	74,408
2012	4,769,117	3,281,090	35,572	3,316,662	357,446	-192,849	2,766,367	742,859	1,259,891	37,573	126,931	74,543
2013	4,739,288	3,370,503	35,356	3,405,859	409,831	-196,982	2,799,046	668,117	1,272,125	37,498	126,389	75,177
2014	4,912,427	3,470,947	47,811	3,518,758	423,259	-200,279	2,895,220	707,626	1,309,581	38,992	125,986	75,211
2015	5,137,245	3,631,914	22,242	3,654,156	439,552	-209,608	3,004,996	751,086	1,381,163	40,944	125,469	75,540
2016	5,190,642	3,632,613	17,820	3,650,433	440,618	-202,194	3,007,621	743,457	1,439,564	41,604	124,764	75,257
2017	5,314,720	3,740,151	31,989	3,772,140	461,864	-213,096	3,097,180	760,003	1,457,537	42,754	124,310	75,498
2018	5,570,818	3,858,992	15,962	3,874,954	474,415	-217,650	3,182,889	843,655	1,544,274	44,979	123,854	75,521
2019	5,722,033	3,953,056	29,568	3,982,624	487,870	-228,725	3,266,029	862,196	1,593,808	46,379	123,376	75,089
2020	6,237,173	3,925,846	26,649	3,952,495	481,604	-230,059	3,240,832	941,825	2,054,516	50,853	122,651	71,772
2021	6,739,749	4,154,547	32,199	4,186,746	506,999	-241,212	3,438,535	1,093,918	2,207,296	55,162	122,181	73,707
2022	6,668,927	4,374,429	44,959	4,419,388	549,340	-261,663	3,608,385	1,153,309	1,907,233	55,101	121,032	75,696

Personal Income and Employment by Metropolitan Statistical Area: Amarillo, TX

(Thousands of dollars, except as noted.)

Year	Personal income, total	Derivation of personal income: Earnings by place of work: Nonfarm	Farm	Total	Less: Contributions for government social insurance	Plus: Adjustment for residence	Equals: Net earnings by place of residence	Plus: Dividends, interest, and rent	Plus: Personal current transfer receipts	Per capita personal income (dollars)	Population (persons)	Total employment
1970	603,484	462,240	34,855	497,095	30,161	-4,164	462,770	98,008	42,706	3,887	155,258	73,776
1971	657,441	503,098	35,705	538,803	33,600	-3,889	501,314	107,091	49,036	4,156	158,182	74,731
1972	702,455	545,465	26,606	572,071	38,300	-3,550	530,221	116,881	55,353	4,375	160,557	76,674
1973	819,510	610,516	61,278	671,794	49,703	-608	621,483	132,086	65,941	5,070	161,637	80,252
1974	891,605	718,026	5,605	723,631	60,173	-3,125	660,333	156,031	75,241	5,457	163,395	85,601
1975	1,100,596	847,704	57,335	905,039	69,359	-1,596	834,084	175,231	91,281	6,633	165,916	89,728
1976	1,204,978	969,914	30,894	1,000,808	80,048	-4,906	915,854	190,633	98,491	7,115	169,368	92,626
1977	1,330,264	1,072,517	33,243	1,105,760	89,765	-6,346	1,009,649	214,116	106,499	7,688	173,027	95,339
1978	1,505,057	1,221,268	28,581	1,249,849	104,114	-2,644	1,143,091	243,353	118,613	8,568	175,670	98,271
1979	1,692,935	1,366,620	38,566	1,405,186	122,572	-1,899	1,280,715	276,134	136,086	9,347	181,120	101,304
1980	1,856,015	1,501,915	-2,565	1,499,350	135,124	-1,471	1,362,755	336,022	157,238	10,003	185,546	102,188
1981	2,141,406	1,667,196	34,200	1,701,396	162,641	-795	1,537,960	422,962	180,484	11,354	188,598	104,700
1982	2,354,639	1,794,509	28,833	1,823,342	178,863	5,419	1,649,898	502,404	202,337	12,228	192,559	106,682
1983	2,629,202	1,943,123	113,847	2,056,970	192,822	-1,697	1,862,451	541,582	225,169	13,433	195,720	109,796
1984	2,789,468	2,083,090	74,321	2,157,411	213,771	2,274	1,945,914	599,212	244,342	14,024	198,910	113,248
1985	2,925,476	2,177,776	54,116	2,231,892	227,019	2,440	2,007,313	652,876	265,287	14,671	199,407	115,109
1986	2,960,403	2,192,953	62,145	2,255,098	226,562	-1,186	2,027,350	643,520	289,533	14,756	200,618	111,050
1987	3,002,155	2,248,365	39,110	2,287,475	227,335	-1,011	2,059,129	633,546	309,480	14,984	200,360	113,749
1988	3,051,742	2,216,356	49,748	2,266,104	234,504	27,341	2,058,941	658,365	334,436	15,178	201,069	112,617
1989	3,197,727	2,284,958	53,257	2,338,215	242,026	12,809	2,108,998	729,652	359,077	16,011	199,721	109,387
1990	3,337,861	2,388,468	81,987	2,470,455	246,417	17,061	2,241,099	705,969	390,793	16,816	198,488	110,406
1991	3,422,793	2,438,745	84,189	2,522,934	259,945	14,419	2,277,408	710,067	435,318	17,061	200,626	112,231
1992	3,674,818	2,650,568	90,477	2,741,045	277,660	7,537	2,470,922	697,817	506,079	18,070	203,371	113,046
1993	3,915,683	2,860,015	100,772	2,960,787	298,737	3,461	2,665,511	714,799	535,373	18,891	207,282	117,950
1994	4,145,759	3,078,651	58,101	3,136,752	325,510	-2,381	2,808,861	767,915	568,983	19,620	211,306	122,956
1995	4,394,475	3,289,609	49,618	3,339,227	346,914	-3,259	2,989,054	788,862	616,559	20,214	217,400	126,957
1996	4,590,838	3,421,890	49,137	3,471,027	355,720	-2,258	3,113,049	820,850	656,939	20,886	219,808	128,079
1997	4,899,374	3,644,809	63,534	3,708,343	374,066	-146	3,334,131	878,282	686,961	22,064	222,054	130,252
1998	5,136,616	3,803,670	67,524	3,871,194	390,246	2,469	3,483,417	958,149	695,050	22,978	223,545	141,013
1999	5,279,994	3,936,421	88,984	4,025,405	406,433	-3,044	3,615,928	948,119	715,947	23,299	226,621	141,705
2000	5,524,807	4,095,874	72,046	4,167,920	418,071	-4,561	3,745,288	1,026,083	753,436	24,103	229,215	144,574
2001	6,090,359	4,571,814	101,522	4,673,336	448,820	-9,830	4,214,686	1,051,960	823,713	26,439	230,351	136,232
2002	6,285,446	4,793,945	85,158	4,879,103	467,215	-15,317	4,396,571	1,005,419	883,456	27,054	232,326	137,021
2003	6,551,615	4,927,857	111,901	5,039,758	494,426	-21,131	4,524,201	1,086,765	940,649	27,863	235,138	139,781
2004	6,652,116	5,023,297	100,726	5,124,023	515,799	-18,605	4,589,619	1,069,548	992,949	28,001	237,566	142,938
2005	7,089,726	5,249,764	96,284	5,346,048	536,047	-9,773	4,800,228	1,213,231	1,076,267	29,494	240,380	144,958
2006	7,581,096	5,697,556	77,494	5,775,050	571,164	-6,625	5,197,261	1,241,672	1,142,163	31,242	242,656	148,349
2007	8,072,727	5,933,651	115,621	6,049,272	602,137	9,351	5,456,486	1,370,295	1,245,946	33,003	244,608	151,888
2008	9,041,151	6,514,950	78,728	6,593,678	642,401	49,154	6,000,431	1,646,604	1,394,116	36,684	246,458	154,940
2009	8,788,198	6,467,523	65,404	6,532,927	656,688	69,297	5,945,536	1,358,770	1,483,892	35,241	249,373	154,262
2010	9,613,137	6,917,542	158,831	7,076,373	679,220	90,510	6,487,663	1,487,899	1,637,575	38,036	252,739	152,812
2011	10,272,599	7,270,644	172,164	7,442,808	620,572	97,868	6,920,104	1,653,118	1,699,377	40,070	256,366	155,105
2012	10,513,292	7,468,783	125,437	7,594,220	638,446	111,229	7,067,003	1,766,297	1,679,992	40,669	258,511	156,757
2013	10,684,295	7,693,411	120,891	7,814,302	740,231	95,751	7,169,822	1,786,746	1,727,727	41,108	259,908	159,586
2014	11,199,233	7,939,742	173,372	8,113,114	764,703	107,768	7,456,179	1,933,065	1,809,989	42,723	262,135	160,752
2015	11,253,124	7,875,395	257,123	8,132,518	792,223	133,195	7,473,490	1,873,629	1,906,005	42,750	263,232	162,606
2016	11,254,737	7,936,697	135,177	8,071,874	820,065	138,401	7,390,210	1,870,887	1,993,640	42,505	264,785	164,583
2017	11,728,782	8,180,850	159,112	8,339,962	844,706	144,185	7,639,441	2,068,514	2,020,827	44,042	266,308	164,441
2018	12,196,143	8,509,026	141,452	8,650,478	877,299	125,220	7,898,399	2,175,643	2,122,101	45,765	266,497	165,432
2019	12,923,052	8,954,504	149,507	9,104,011	915,935	114,694	8,302,770	2,359,446	2,260,836	48,369	267,174	165,544
2020	14,021,833	9,469,233	147,290	9,616,523	966,618	120,753	8,770,658	2,366,119	2,885,056	52,122	269,018	164,101
2021	15,218,036	9,899,674	186,794	10,086,468	1,010,044	132,353	9,208,777	2,660,343	3,348,916	56,394	269,853	169,740
2022	15,490,467	10,491,771	140,700	10,632,471	1,082,501	152,596	9,702,566	2,866,970	2,920,931	57,124	271,171	176,343

Personal Income and Employment by Metropolitan Statistical Area: Ames, IA

(Thousands of dollars, except as noted.)

Year	Personal income, total	Derivation of personal income: Earnings by place of work: Nonfarm	Farm	Total	Less: Contributions for government social insurance	Plus: Adjustment for residence	Equals: Net earnings by place of residence	Plus: Dividends, interest, and rent	Plus: Personal current transfer receipts	Per capita personal income (dollars)	Population (persons)	Total employment
1970	325,305	211,582	32,799	244,381	15,583	10,227	239,025	60,212	26,068	3,637	89,447	38,973
1971	347,900	234,773	23,383	258,156	17,895	10,810	251,071	67,162	29,667	3,841	90,583	39,848
1972	389,057	255,002	36,094	291,096	20,614	11,361	281,843	75,066	32,148	4,224	92,099	40,902
1973	467,046	288,412	69,075	357,487	26,951	11,880	342,416	86,969	37,661	5,010	93,216	43,013
1974	497,093	324,253	48,584	372,837	31,996	13,086	353,927	99,835	43,331	5,281	94,131	44,432
1975	553,277	361,719	47,922	409,641	35,216	13,337	387,762	112,822	52,693	5,875	94,174	45,325
1976	594,919	410,740	29,365	440,105	39,986	13,044	413,163	123,513	58,243	6,241	95,325	47,494
1977	639,474	471,359	-3,317	468,042	45,134	13,439	436,347	141,542	61,585	6,637	96,351	49,421
1978	773,900	530,307	56,797	587,104	52,907	13,405	547,602	157,230	69,068	7,924	97,669	50,922
1979	839,189	596,338	35,709	632,047	62,126	13,428	583,349	178,376	77,464	8,582	97,790	52,477
1980	921,185	630,781	34,839	665,620	65,349	14,127	614,398	214,984	91,803	9,335	98,682	52,553
1981	1,017,589	666,676	46,720	713,396	73,808	15,830	655,418	258,334	103,837	10,264	99,140	50,935
1982	1,071,673	693,165	30,487	723,652	77,681	15,422	661,393	295,278	115,002	10,897	98,350	50,388
1983	1,130,680	731,572	26,182	757,754	81,226	16,889	693,417	310,423	126,840	11,396	99,213	51,078
1984	1,233,498	803,381	34,350	837,731	91,162	18,668	765,237	333,246	135,015	12,445	99,117	52,856
1985	1,308,192	854,490	36,964	891,454	99,016	18,876	811,314	345,538	151,340	13,140	99,559	53,889
1986	1,364,676	885,430	51,561	936,991	105,609	21,548	852,930	350,748	160,998	13,738	99,338	53,905
1987	1,430,014	937,388	56,251	993,639	111,653	24,837	906,823	347,333	175,858	14,523	98,466	54,195
1988	1,480,032	1,005,382	23,718	1,029,100	126,065	29,675	932,710	361,725	185,597	14,941	99,056	56,237
1989	1,625,923	1,090,540	56,261	1,146,801	135,694	31,351	1,042,458	387,307	196,158	16,453	98,820	57,863
1990	1,704,170	1,149,313	38,580	1,187,893	144,785	36,747	1,079,855	410,674	213,641	17,113	99,582	59,004
1991	1,783,564	1,202,747	35,172	1,237,919	149,842	38,123	1,126,200	429,317	228,047	17,866	99,832	59,379
1992	1,885,384	1,272,586	60,158	1,332,744	155,649	41,506	1,218,601	426,684	240,099	18,781	100,389	60,139
1993	1,928,367	1,345,326	10,329	1,355,655	163,171	41,215	1,233,699	437,030	257,638	19,066	101,141	60,384
1994	2,094,610	1,421,719	60,437	1,482,156	173,296	43,679	1,352,539	470,460	271,611	20,726	101,060	61,090
1995	2,189,046	1,481,440	54,198	1,535,638	180,334	45,847	1,401,151	519,263	268,632	21,520	101,721	62,763
1996	2,360,207	1,577,932	76,942	1,654,874	184,180	45,851	1,516,545	560,673	282,989	22,986	102,679	63,481
1997	2,501,748	1,675,884	70,349	1,746,233	202,578	48,791	1,592,446	609,538	299,764	24,089	103,856	63,650
1998	2,614,495	1,805,306	43,084	1,848,390	215,453	53,670	1,686,607	626,573	301,315	25,103	104,151	65,058
1999	2,706,400	1,921,798	31,087	1,952,885	227,888	56,108	1,781,105	614,757	310,538	25,644	105,536	66,585
2000	2,855,917	2,016,484	39,500	2,055,984	236,987	56,121	1,875,118	646,174	334,625	26,841	106,403	67,065
2001	2,929,393	2,070,111	33,238	2,103,349	239,914	59,687	1,923,122	641,852	364,419	27,504	106,509	69,062
2002	3,040,069	2,144,811	45,536	2,190,347	247,541	59,427	2,002,233	629,127	408,709	28,156	107,971	69,330
2003	3,160,493	2,258,869	47,606	2,306,475	261,642	51,230	2,096,063	665,719	398,711	29,183	108,300	69,904
2004	3,337,463	2,376,859	91,343	2,468,202	273,124	30,475	2,225,553	700,747	411,163	30,584	109,126	71,197
2005	3,421,296	2,478,087	78,588	2,556,675	283,811	19,548	2,292,412	704,883	424,001	31,278	109,384	71,911
2006	3,688,550	2,649,701	59,565	2,709,266	300,917	-5,052	2,403,297	792,836	492,417	33,167	111,210	72,878
2007	3,923,613	2,774,352	95,368	2,869,720	316,299	2,161	2,555,582	842,852	525,179	34,694	113,093	73,688
2008	4,112,888	2,932,927	76,286	3,009,213	334,415	-17,907	2,656,891	854,903	601,094	35,988	114,285	73,792
2009	4,021,042	2,889,853	76,301	2,966,154	330,334	-81,106	2,554,714	831,271	635,057	34,771	115,645	72,894
2010	4,028,327	2,922,280	53,732	2,976,012	334,379	-147,703	2,493,930	842,550	691,847	34,741	115,952	72,307
2011	4,334,943	2,977,619	123,382	3,101,001	308,025	-103,917	2,689,059	941,622	704,262	36,877	117,552	73,091
2012	4,700,021	3,310,620	125,644	3,436,264	329,416	-78,728	3,028,120	987,968	683,933	39,708	118,366	73,361
2013	4,590,972	3,290,174	163,471	3,453,645	373,027	-184,483	2,896,135	980,793	714,044	38,100	120,499	75,016
2014	4,785,977	3,522,344	111,691	3,634,035	395,829	-223,165	3,015,041	1,037,194	733,742	39,053	122,552	75,854
2015	4,923,545	3,701,886	90,476	3,792,362	408,835	-272,719	3,110,808	1,045,448	767,289	39,817	123,653	77,338
2016	4,956,035	3,728,113	47,585	3,775,698	414,813	-251,316	3,109,569	1,078,665	767,801	39,977	123,972	77,074
2017	5,065,587	3,852,037	24,768	3,876,805	432,436	-295,375	3,148,994	1,155,691	760,902	40,705	124,446	77,535
2018	5,303,438	3,992,252	34,162	4,026,414	450,577	-293,744	3,282,093	1,188,001	833,344	42,839	123,798	77,925
2019	5,486,985	4,097,078	32,574	4,129,652	467,273	-293,648	3,368,731	1,244,395	873,859	44,052	124,556	77,306
2020	5,748,390	4,086,384	38,082	4,124,466	483,674	-281,816	3,358,976	1,263,170	1,126,244	45,861	125,345	74,340
2021	6,258,947	4,366,687	135,067	4,501,754	511,731	-274,909	3,715,114	1,309,385	1,234,448	49,501	126,442	76,230
2022	6,397,069	4,586,691	143,427	4,730,118	547,277	-263,697	3,919,144	1,373,359	1,104,566	50,657	126,282	78,761

Personal Income and Employment by Area: Anchorage, AK

(Thousands of dollars, except as noted.)

Year	Personal income, total	Derivation of personal income: Earnings by place of work: Nonfarm	Farm	Total	Less: Contributions for government social insurance	Plus: Adjustment for residence	Equals: Net earnings by place of residence	Plus: Dividends, interest, and rent	Plus: Personal current transfer receipts	Per capita personal income (dollars)	Population (persons)	Total employment
1970	910,435	782,862	1,403	784,265	49,609	14,764	749,420	136,228	24,787	6,783	134,230	70,329
1971	1,004,489	870,955	1,236	872,191	56,795	4,983	820,379	152,187	31,923	7,080	141,875	73,124
1972	1,110,361	966,339	1,442	967,781	65,427	-3,500	898,854	172,734	38,773	7,353	151,010	77,502
1973	1,225,781	1,055,467	1,218	1,056,685	79,061	-10,972	966,652	199,536	59,593	7,871	155,729	81,822
1974	1,510,511	1,340,109	1,222	1,341,331	108,671	-16,019	1,216,641	232,101	61,769	9,361	161,355	92,715
1975	2,016,802	1,801,557	2,448	1,804,005	156,755	22,151	1,669,401	274,147	73,254	11,509	175,236	106,942
1976	2,407,760	2,155,068	2,892	2,157,960	195,289	55,863	2,018,534	306,719	82,507	12,936	186,127	113,300
1977	2,679,418	2,420,912	3,230	2,424,142	219,220	20,708	2,225,630	347,935	105,853	14,126	189,680	117,650
1978	2,727,115	2,416,737	3,226	2,419,963	213,574	4,834	2,211,223	400,681	115,211	14,052	194,074	119,090
1979	2,861,583	2,506,877	3,340	2,510,217	228,100	45,162	2,327,279	420,787	113,517	14,672	195,031	119,439
1980	3,211,748	2,795,046	3,111	2,798,157	246,621	54,739	2,606,275	471,698	133,775	16,569	193,839	119,735
1981	3,722,871	3,235,962	1,537	3,237,499	313,005	85,836	3,010,330	548,508	164,033	18,630	199,831	123,606
1982	4,630,928	3,836,987	2,413	3,839,400	380,164	94,389	3,553,625	681,586	395,717	21,354	216,861	139,054
1983	5,128,638	4,342,077	2,824	4,344,901	440,388	135,723	4,040,236	808,620	279,782	21,612	237,309	150,798
1984	5,580,641	4,781,737	4,136	4,785,873	510,278	107,272	4,382,867	894,075	303,699	22,122	252,265	158,830
1985	5,959,440	5,032,259	5,421	5,037,680	527,826	58,487	4,568,341	996,860	394,239	22,563	264,128	163,306
1986	5,976,461	5,009,371	8,802	5,018,173	505,305	-8,021	4,504,847	1,020,415	451,199	22,129	270,074	158,789
1987	5,648,003	4,688,726	10,913	4,699,639	466,304	-45,950	4,187,385	981,995	478,623	21,296	265,211	157,016
1988	5,714,178	4,714,736	11,517	4,726,253	486,333	-57,780	4,182,140	1,011,913	520,125	21,674	263,645	156,200
1989	6,216,429	5,048,301	8,453	5,056,754	524,312	-1,616	4,530,826	1,110,254	575,349	23,551	263,958	159,968
1990	6,667,050	5,512,466	8,855	5,521,321	605,982	-94,744	4,820,595	1,197,234	649,221	24,899	267,762	166,968
1991	7,010,576	5,826,891	8,567	5,835,458	646,249	-110,827	5,078,382	1,232,746	699,448	25,272	277,407	172,470
1992	7,523,421	6,197,631	6,855	6,204,486	680,640	-106,026	5,417,820	1,326,141	779,460	25,915	290,307	173,979
1993	7,957,854	6,507,768	8,900	6,516,668	728,971	-123,144	5,664,553	1,429,287	864,014	26,838	296,514	177,780
1994	8,276,362	6,707,187	10,960	6,718,147	763,899	-121,120	5,833,128	1,559,467	883,767	27,571	300,188	181,242
1995	8,433,538	6,718,610	11,250	6,729,860	759,813	-113,140	5,856,907	1,637,475	939,156	27,937	301,878	182,105
1996	8,696,018	6,836,109	11,873	6,847,982	762,965	-111,168	5,973,849	1,709,629	1,012,540	28,737	302,606	183,521
1997	9,317,321	7,278,480	13,771	7,292,251	801,936	-119,187	6,371,128	1,844,155	1,102,038	30,401	306,480	187,454
1998	9,893,646	7,698,396	11,040	7,709,436	834,620	-108,225	6,766,591	1,922,530	1,204,525	31,620	312,895	193,548
1999	10,245,634	7,952,096	11,946	7,964,042	855,896	-123,196	6,984,950	1,927,469	1,333,215	32,303	317,172	193,959
2000	10,952,169	8,402,434	11,862	8,414,296	890,910	-117,364	7,406,022	2,025,149	1,520,998	34,160	320,618	197,879
2001	11,834,041	9,201,434	11,047	9,212,481	962,532	-53,594	8,196,355	2,036,168	1,601,518	36,292	326,081	203,258
2002	12,524,289	9,833,891	11,631	9,845,522	1,033,483	-5,915	8,806,124	2,077,064	1,641,101	37,658	332,582	207,656
2003	13,093,843	10,386,957	8,859	10,395,816	1,072,203	26,502	9,350,115	2,137,956	1,605,772	38,770	337,730	211,662
2004	13,816,204	11,038,354	10,456	11,048,810	1,149,804	89,810	9,988,816	2,225,810	1,601,578	40,019	345,245	215,932
2005	14,744,647	11,723,637	9,865	11,733,502	1,231,884	170,231	10,671,849	2,379,167	1,693,631	42,019	350,903	220,731
2006	15,789,736	12,320,839	8,335	12,329,174	1,332,646	334,108	11,330,636	2,646,442	1,812,658	44,017	358,718	226,471
2007	17,085,504	12,938,528	7,453	12,945,981	1,386,565	524,083	12,083,499	2,935,498	2,066,507	47,434	360,194	231,101
2008	18,928,756	13,508,498	5,089	13,513,587	1,433,864	737,875	12,817,598	3,279,273	2,831,885	51,770	365,633	233,406
2009	18,929,242	14,049,829	6,633	14,056,462	1,458,923	724,307	13,321,846	3,186,490	2,420,906	50,537	374,562	233,611
2010	20,225,886	14,843,984	5,465	14,849,449	1,501,236	691,631	14,039,844	3,457,059	2,728,983	52,737	383,520	233,993
2011	21,391,927	15,521,447	4,099	15,525,546	1,412,689	724,624	14,837,481	3,725,374	2,829,072	55,052	388,580	236,747
2012	21,888,972	15,963,982	6,030	15,970,012	1,500,655	722,135	15,191,492	3,960,002	2,737,478	55,727	392,786	242,976
2013	21,586,515	16,018,673	5,555	16,024,228	1,737,327	682,879	14,969,780	3,850,693	2,766,042	54,223	398,109	244,447
2014	22,674,958	16,303,272	7,589	16,310,861	1,731,965	782,515	15,361,411	3,983,125	3,330,422	56,787	399,295	244,072
2015	23,525,428	16,849,216	7,192	16,856,408	1,759,462	775,459	15,872,405	4,219,404	3,433,619	58,808	400,037	245,161
2016	23,104,577	16,468,645	6,373	16,475,018	1,707,811	666,078	15,433,285	4,308,151	3,363,141	57,337	402,960	243,513
2017	23,373,457	16,509,259	8,072	16,517,331	1,725,698	622,111	15,413,744	4,357,950	3,601,763	58,110	402,227	243,023
2018	24,240,924	16,910,723	6,612	16,917,335	1,765,061	626,581	15,778,855	4,547,017	3,915,052	60,691	399,416	242,596
2019	24,716,096	17,172,426	6,828	17,179,254	1,822,717	667,412	16,023,949	4,541,599	4,150,548	62,080	398,135	242,218
2020	25,378,106	17,188,038	6,844	17,194,882	1,833,894	595,945	15,956,933	4,504,782	4,916,391	63,703	398,381	232,200
2021	26,995,646	17,985,474	7,985	17,993,459	1,943,168	552,784	16,603,075	4,978,525	5,414,046	67,529	399,761	240,342
2022	28,259,557	18,803,247	791	18,804,038	2,087,614	598,539	17,314,963	5,357,432	5,587,162	70,566	400,470	248,729

Personal Income and Employment by Area: Ann Arbor, MI

(Thousands of dollars, except as noted.)

Year	Personal income, total	Derivation of personal income								Per capita personal income (dollars)	Population (persons)	Total employment
		Earnings by place of work			Less: Contributions for government social insurance	Plus: Adjustment for residence	Equals: Net earnings by place of residence	Plus: Dividends, interest, and rent	Plus: Personal current transfer receipts			
		Nonfarm	Farm	Total								
1970	1,095,725	933,143	6,117	939,260	64,093	3,652	878,819	157,250	59,656	4,678	234,226	105,059
1971	1,212,039	1,060,056	5,067	1,065,123	74,950	-20,983	969,190	172,550	70,299	5,131	236,222	109,389
1972	1,349,916	1,186,555	9,904	1,196,459	89,223	-28,705	1,078,531	191,146	80,239	5,590	241,470	114,647
1973	1,518,740	1,373,322	12,572	1,385,894	120,110	-53,405	1,212,379	211,846	94,515	6,154	246,780	124,307
1974	1,638,400	1,431,938	6,577	1,438,515	129,203	-37,088	1,272,224	242,031	124,145	6,389	256,447	128,003
1975	1,805,963	1,518,701	12,638	1,531,339	133,228	-37,224	1,360,887	272,102	172,974	7,194	251,024	126,982
1976	2,038,347	1,835,426	7,804	1,843,230	164,904	-113,380	1,564,946	298,801	174,600	8,027	253,934	136,907
1977	2,297,921	2,151,919	9,577	2,161,496	192,960	-181,580	1,786,956	334,914	176,051	8,927	257,407	146,330
1978	2,616,066	2,545,115	4,964	2,550,079	236,617	-258,238	2,055,224	376,997	183,845	10,071	259,775	157,722
1979	2,903,535	2,852,435	5,136	2,857,571	272,261	-324,480	2,260,830	426,039	216,666	11,046	262,859	165,863
1980	3,192,512	2,989,418	3,921	2,993,339	277,809	-332,044	2,383,486	503,597	305,429	12,075	264,400	164,425
1981	3,432,768	3,203,486	7,135	3,210,621	322,787	-362,705	2,525,129	600,896	306,743	13,079	262,466	165,139
1982	3,636,617	3,267,964	3,102	3,271,066	334,386	-343,456	2,593,224	704,814	338,579	13,974	260,239	163,116
1983	3,925,635	3,567,477	-339	3,567,138	373,401	-397,982	2,795,755	772,325	357,555	15,086	260,212	167,452
1984	4,305,098	4,027,371	4,921	4,032,292	438,596	-498,030	3,095,666	856,440	352,992	16,511	260,737	174,759
1985	4,696,434	4,458,840	9,576	4,468,416	495,653	-567,117	3,405,646	929,000	361,788	17,887	262,568	181,371
1986	5,015,622	4,719,198	4,022	4,723,220	525,235	-543,793	3,654,192	992,402	369,028	18,850	266,087	187,119
1987	5,259,526	4,931,560	4,932	4,936,492	543,160	-546,194	3,847,138	1,031,832	380,556	19,500	269,717	195,094
1988	5,770,107	5,459,398	3,421	5,462,819	622,017	-627,286	4,213,516	1,159,464	397,127	21,109	273,346	202,667
1989	6,268,452	5,801,327	8,223	5,809,550	658,594	-659,477	4,491,479	1,341,209	435,764	22,441	279,329	207,606
1990	6,666,074	6,199,718	7,757	6,207,475	713,841	-697,952	4,795,682	1,392,698	477,694	23,473	283,987	213,654
1991	6,763,430	6,232,810	3,050	6,235,860	726,643	-689,658	4,819,559	1,413,866	530,005	23,556	287,126	210,795
1992	7,218,010	6,661,953	6,866	6,668,819	768,751	-707,095	5,192,973	1,463,365	561,672	24,862	290,323	213,642
1993	7,616,103	6,912,845	3,227	6,916,072	800,545	-663,691	5,451,836	1,560,645	603,622	26,117	291,617	217,534
1994	8,160,901	7,310,896	2,302	7,313,198	865,568	-667,420	5,780,210	1,762,025	618,666	27,789	293,671	220,460
1995	8,718,938	7,458,630	1,933	7,460,563	883,360	-439,452	6,137,751	1,883,235	697,952	29,265	297,926	221,177
1996	9,122,494	7,797,612	1,301	7,798,913	903,407	-457,241	6,438,265	1,928,692	755,537	30,094	303,133	224,214
1997	9,554,817	8,432,516	1,284	8,433,800	975,250	-659,409	6,799,141	2,008,225	747,451	30,982	308,398	228,650
1998	10,183,294	9,071,528	3,088	9,074,616	1,042,070	-730,986	7,301,560	2,139,457	742,277	32,576	312,601	230,049
1999	10,888,192	10,052,448	6,636	10,059,084	1,141,127	-1,008,574	7,909,383	2,146,602	832,207	34,211	318,270	238,824
2000	11,726,150	10,778,116	1,878	10,779,994	1,201,623	-1,027,237	8,551,134	2,304,826	870,190	36,150	324,372	244,514
2001	12,271,172	11,159,108	853	11,159,961	1,208,371	-967,782	8,983,808	2,323,860	963,504	37,327	328,749	244,933
2002	12,726,002	11,643,849	1,481	11,645,330	1,264,010	-1,020,056	9,361,264	2,340,468	1,024,270	38,243	332,763	245,399
2003	13,316,301	11,850,222	6,190	11,856,412	1,276,141	-887,209	9,693,062	2,523,769	1,099,470	39,614	336,154	243,625
2004	13,464,837	12,020,713	12,728	12,033,441	1,314,032	-1,091,866	9,627,543	2,696,669	1,140,625	39,670	339,422	245,362
2005	13,703,537	12,245,066	11,001	12,256,067	1,346,782	-1,091,669	9,817,616	2,661,087	1,224,834	40,041	342,234	247,806
2006	14,173,298	12,445,905	12,057	12,457,962	1,383,267	-1,167,503	9,907,192	2,950,575	1,315,531	41,199	344,018	247,692
2007	14,605,029	12,756,926	11,577	12,768,503	1,419,321	-1,157,404	10,191,778	2,964,055	1,449,196	42,295	345,310	247,694
2008	15,265,029	12,559,645	8,179	12,567,824	1,405,565	-691,780	10,470,479	3,078,263	1,716,287	44,688	341,595	242,929
2009	14,301,842	12,073,833	8,988	12,082,821	1,360,267	-1,025,356	9,697,198	2,729,564	1,875,080	41,633	343,520	238,350
2010	15,825,960	12,562,903	13,486	12,576,389	1,383,110	-307,441	10,885,838	2,882,039	2,058,083	45,727	346,099	241,928
2011	15,810,708	12,785,720	36,747	12,822,467	1,235,419	-935,928	10,651,120	3,075,386	2,084,202	45,086	350,678	245,232
2012	16,841,429	13,325,949	12,455	13,338,404	1,286,286	-825,682	11,226,436	3,553,943	2,061,050	47,603	353,787	246,722
2013	16,956,531	13,684,332	11,774	13,696,106	1,505,019	-948,581	11,242,506	3,567,015	2,147,010	47,353	358,086	250,461
2014	17,816,878	13,950,464	-3,185	13,947,279	1,551,177	-727,914	11,668,188	3,903,728	2,244,962	49,129	362,657	252,652
2015	18,869,915	14,905,144	724	14,905,868	1,634,878	-938,408	12,332,582	4,155,218	2,382,115	51,527	366,217	258,278
2016	19,714,573	15,364,273	608	15,364,881	1,683,626	-759,888	12,921,367	4,343,371	2,449,835	53,259	370,164	261,988
2017	20,722,255	16,199,411	1,854	16,201,265	1,776,400	-830,242	13,594,623	4,648,361	2,479,271	55,489	373,451	266,433
2018	21,650,159	16,966,776	3,635	16,970,411	1,878,473	-928,814	14,163,124	4,880,538	2,606,497	57,761	374,825	272,088
2019	22,653,609	17,793,109	5,534	17,798,643	1,965,275	-1,205,669	14,627,699	5,270,024	2,755,886	60,732	373,011	274,883
2020	24,021,472	18,034,459	13,131	18,047,590	1,982,023	-1,089,916	14,975,651	5,113,234	3,932,587	64,606	371,817	258,950
2021	25,510,478	19,310,604	19,655	19,330,259	2,102,494	-1,343,717	15,884,048	5,531,642	4,094,788	69,892	364,998	265,750
2022	26,147,662	20,216,259	13,715	20,229,974	2,263,050	-1,080,070	16,886,854	5,908,396	3,352,412	71,368	366,376	277,189

Personal Income and Employment by Area: Anniston-Oxford, AL

(Thousands of dollars, except as noted.)

Year	Personal income, total	Derivation of personal income: Earnings by place of work: Nonfarm	Farm	Total	Less: Contributions for government social insurance	Plus: Adjustment for residence	Equals: Net earnings by place of residence	Plus: Dividends, interest, and rent	Plus: Personal current transfer receipts	Per capita personal income (dollars)	Population (persons)	Total employment
1970	313,931	278,760	2,076	280,836	17,144	-27,477	236,215	46,648	31,068	3,044	103,125	46,650
1971	353,608	313,482	2,099	315,581	19,851	-31,130	264,600	52,488	36,520	3,412	103,622	47,036
1972	396,486	351,388	2,782	354,170	23,011	-33,457	297,702	58,462	40,322	3,818	103,846	48,347
1973	433,646	376,675	5,683	382,358	28,220	-33,219	320,919	65,440	47,287	4,129	105,027	49,305
1974	485,455	413,937	2,398	416,335	32,063	-35,241	349,031	78,368	58,056	4,583	105,917	50,224
1975	557,197	458,904	5,713	464,617	35,225	-39,070	390,322	90,919	75,956	5,207	107,005	50,663
1976	624,434	522,276	4,806	527,082	42,063	-41,648	443,371	100,489	80,574	5,537	112,768	53,001
1977	702,104	589,344	4,940	594,284	47,028	-45,335	501,921	115,115	85,068	6,224	112,801	55,396
1978	776,570	642,831	5,394	648,225	51,477	-44,892	551,856	132,970	91,744	6,667	116,474	56,359
1979	849,687	693,419	5,118	698,537	58,357	-43,210	596,970	147,270	105,447	7,278	116,742	56,639
1980	973,080	786,063	4,448	790,511	64,801	-52,911	672,799	175,060	125,221	8,108	120,016	57,453
1981	1,069,494	854,152	3,916	858,068	75,747	-58,267	724,054	203,915	141,525	8,852	120,814	55,980
1982	1,144,773	899,287	4,605	903,892	78,953	-66,489	758,450	230,150	156,173	9,375	122,109	55,531
1983	1,219,367	960,897	2,359	963,256	90,000	-70,040	803,216	248,073	168,078	10,057	121,249	56,216
1984	1,340,481	1,066,173	2,759	1,068,932	101,985	-78,926	888,021	275,549	176,911	11,011	121,739	58,552
1985	1,402,992	1,118,946	2,982	1,121,928	109,495	-86,890	925,543	289,932	187,517	11,825	118,644	58,483
1986	1,470,032	1,170,716	3,899	1,174,615	114,975	-90,548	969,092	306,516	194,424	12,490	117,700	59,039
1987	1,522,308	1,223,249	360	1,223,609	120,758	-93,560	1,009,291	315,314	197,703	12,891	118,092	59,851
1988	1,606,800	1,290,433	3,502	1,293,935	133,515	-97,178	1,063,242	336,574	206,984	13,703	117,260	61,561
1989	1,702,880	1,326,583	14,589	1,341,172	139,597	-102,966	1,098,609	368,287	235,984	14,632	116,381	61,654
1990	1,758,915	1,356,847	17,407	1,374,254	146,927	-103,935	1,123,392	377,317	258,206	15,148	116,118	61,400
1991	1,852,279	1,425,250	22,715	1,447,965	155,902	-112,350	1,179,713	384,335	288,231	16,072	115,247	60,775
1992	1,950,826	1,489,528	12,187	1,501,715	163,387	-108,720	1,229,608	396,499	324,719	16,846	115,804	61,360
1993	2,004,038	1,510,253	15,986	1,526,239	170,059	-105,947	1,250,233	409,569	344,236	17,228	116,324	61,935
1994	2,071,612	1,546,583	12,121	1,558,704	175,668	-98,566	1,284,470	426,050	361,092	17,834	116,161	60,986
1995	2,181,738	1,597,298	12,631	1,609,929	183,008	-99,088	1,327,833	462,181	391,724	18,681	116,790	61,993
1996	2,245,415	1,609,612	15,864	1,625,476	185,003	-92,483	1,347,990	480,576	416,849	19,244	116,684	62,273
1997	2,326,050	1,677,526	17,029	1,694,555	193,510	-90,749	1,410,296	481,780	433,974	19,838	117,254	63,984
1998	2,465,628	1,765,235	14,078	1,779,313	201,956	-98,262	1,479,095	535,378	451,155	21,042	117,179	64,336
1999	2,471,045	1,782,332	7,744	1,790,076	205,216	-93,841	1,491,019	506,052	473,974	21,504	114,910	63,078
2000	2,455,321	1,709,381	4,909	1,714,290	198,768	-68,390	1,447,132	502,170	506,019	22,104	111,081	60,846
2001	2,576,837	1,770,120	10,174	1,780,294	206,787	-77,911	1,495,596	528,305	552,936	23,159	111,266	59,639
2002	2,693,742	1,871,039	5,881	1,876,920	216,633	-88,375	1,571,912	525,276	596,554	24,132	111,625	60,125
2003	2,837,929	1,976,884	7,453	1,984,337	228,967	-106,639	1,648,731	555,540	633,658	25,180	112,705	60,523
2004	3,013,446	2,135,733	10,806	2,146,539	244,746	-131,881	1,769,912	588,750	654,784	26,559	113,462	62,606
2005	3,143,140	2,250,812	16,128	2,266,940	259,316	-142,249	1,865,375	578,657	699,108	27,457	114,477	63,110
2006	3,290,907	2,368,339	7,336	2,375,675	273,568	-168,605	1,933,502	612,038	745,367	28,520	115,388	63,819
2007	3,490,891	2,545,104	7,301	2,552,405	297,106	-220,358	2,034,941	663,068	792,882	30,039	116,211	65,678
2008	3,625,139	2,591,481	8,281	2,599,762	308,786	-254,005	2,036,971	704,763	883,405	30,912	117,274	64,696
2009	3,566,455	2,530,231	13,361	2,543,592	300,693	-257,064	1,985,835	623,109	957,511	30,132	118,363	61,553
2010	3,667,238	2,540,110	13,283	2,553,393	305,798	-237,224	2,010,371	623,287	1,033,580	30,949	118,493	60,192
2011	3,738,325	2,559,631	5,201	2,564,832	277,286	-232,211	2,055,335	638,589	1,044,401	31,645	118,132	60,615
2012	3,766,067	2,485,150	13,665	2,498,815	271,058	-177,941	2,049,816	665,844	1,050,407	31,948	117,880	59,995
2013	3,712,764	2,373,576	25,287	2,398,863	293,273	-107,920	1,997,670	654,645	1,060,449	31,607	117,465	58,405
2014	3,800,402	2,420,225	20,631	2,440,856	295,355	-91,083	2,054,418	668,987	1,076,997	32,424	117,209	58,098
2015	3,936,697	2,412,749	24,082	2,436,831	294,488	-63,665	2,078,678	696,083	1,161,936	33,633	117,048	58,066
2016	3,970,877	2,467,645	10,403	2,478,048	300,360	-68,617	2,109,071	689,873	1,171,933	33,994	116,810	57,696
2017	4,049,899	2,536,724	14,281	2,551,005	313,166	-84,025	2,153,814	707,879	1,188,206	34,675	116,796	58,547
2018	4,154,359	2,606,054	10,250	2,616,304	324,581	-78,298	2,213,425	719,234	1,221,700	35,622	116,622	58,808
2019	4,287,240	2,720,446	6,909	2,727,355	336,076	-96,403	2,294,876	717,150	1,275,214	36,747	116,669	58,469
2020	4,601,998	2,767,151	70	2,767,221	347,734	-96,504	2,322,983	709,050	1,569,965	39,591	116,239	57,268
2021	4,979,361	2,918,511	13,223	2,931,734	365,706	-98,377	2,467,651	754,199	1,757,511	43,045	115,677	58,569
2022	4,924,818	2,975,287	17,557	2,992,844	381,088	-66,812	2,544,944	784,728	1,595,146	42,533	115,788	59,633

Personal Income and Employment by Area: Appleton, WI

(Thousands of dollars, except as noted.)

Year	Personal income, total	Derivation of personal income: Earnings by place of work: Nonfarm	Farm	Total	Less: Contributions for government social insurance	Plus: Adjustment for residence	Equals: Net earnings by place of residence	Plus: Dividends, interest, and rent	Plus: Personal current transfer receipts	Per capita personal income (dollars)	Population (persons)	Total employment
1970	550,635	431,402	21,585	452,987	31,605	3,446	424,828	85,862	39,945	3,738	147,307	65,092
1971	581,862	450,163	24,127	474,290	34,056	2,602	442,836	92,757	46,269	3,923	148,324	64,945
1972	638,012	497,053	27,064	524,117	39,697	1,950	486,370	99,714	51,928	4,275	149,228	66,928
1973	723,046	573,426	31,917	605,343	53,011	-2,312	550,020	111,983	61,043	4,853	148,989	71,600
1974	800,861	642,544	27,607	670,151	61,582	-8,097	600,472	127,717	72,672	5,319	150,556	74,056
1975	877,279	676,090	32,698	708,788	63,425	-6,324	639,039	142,515	95,725	5,715	153,496	72,298
1976	977,626	777,488	30,329	807,817	74,164	-10,485	723,168	152,292	102,166	6,419	152,296	74,840
1977	1,092,940	865,519	48,117	913,636	82,671	-13,759	817,206	168,805	106,929	7,084	154,282	77,570
1978	1,211,224	975,152	42,134	1,017,286	95,932	-19,606	901,748	190,094	119,382	7,785	155,590	80,387
1979	1,398,101	1,146,008	59,161	1,205,169	117,583	-40,430	1,047,156	214,965	135,980	8,917	156,784	86,376
1980	1,543,867	1,232,348	57,885	1,290,233	126,106	-48,489	1,115,638	261,433	166,796	9,656	159,892	86,329
1981	1,684,084	1,325,034	40,137	1,365,171	144,820	-43,284	1,177,067	320,990	186,027	10,481	160,685	86,079
1982	1,780,220	1,377,941	30,510	1,408,451	152,278	-38,845	1,217,328	349,885	213,007	11,026	161,454	84,927
1983	1,908,620	1,471,855	19,134	1,490,989	162,367	-33,729	1,294,893	385,847	227,880	11,775	162,093	85,443
1984	2,130,040	1,646,098	36,915	1,683,013	185,940	-28,565	1,468,508	431,541	229,991	13,044	163,293	89,336
1985	2,282,389	1,768,288	39,811	1,808,099	201,469	-23,510	1,583,120	456,390	242,879	13,861	164,668	91,393
1986	2,447,555	1,899,329	50,700	1,950,029	215,930	-17,527	1,716,572	475,405	255,578	14,704	166,459	94,148
1987	2,598,178	2,063,562	57,328	2,120,890	230,837	-20,938	1,869,115	468,099	260,964	15,417	168,530	98,260
1988	2,774,792	2,246,891	33,449	2,280,340	259,451	-20,411	2,000,478	504,651	269,663	16,185	171,443	100,937
1989	3,023,753	2,393,085	64,510	2,457,595	274,877	-16,439	2,166,279	564,586	292,888	17,451	173,276	102,137
1990	3,206,142	2,533,011	51,740	2,584,751	303,945	10,546	2,291,352	600,231	314,559	18,286	175,333	105,276
1991	3,371,807	2,700,986	41,255	2,742,241	328,248	11,114	2,425,107	609,165	337,535	19,046	177,039	107,722
1992	3,692,809	2,957,411	62,295	3,019,706	354,871	18,120	2,682,955	646,011	363,843	20,569	179,533	109,626
1993	3,894,073	3,128,853	45,837	3,174,690	374,975	57,290	2,857,005	661,828	375,240	21,359	182,315	112,232
1994	4,184,160	3,361,225	66,530	3,427,755	407,322	62,392	3,082,825	711,897	389,438	22,518	185,813	116,611
1995	4,426,850	3,503,484	42,794	3,546,278	424,531	101,396	3,223,143	783,453	420,254	23,465	188,656	120,299
1996	4,706,436	3,725,578	61,312	3,786,890	448,721	87,188	3,425,357	838,772	442,307	24,566	191,586	124,832
1997	4,933,340	3,877,099	43,848	3,920,947	465,284	121,879	3,577,542	895,070	460,728	25,423	194,050	126,560
1998	5,219,350	3,988,543	64,275	4,052,818	475,235	188,751	3,766,334	977,928	475,088	26,524	196,776	125,341
1999	5,583,318	4,308,500	64,876	4,373,376	513,024	259,060	4,119,412	960,473	503,433	27,987	199,495	128,535
2000	6,040,192	4,637,123	43,974	4,681,097	545,383	303,560	4,439,274	1,054,846	546,072	29,811	202,618	132,249
2001	6,440,156	5,032,357	48,602	5,080,959	582,870	286,140	4,784,229	1,057,725	598,202	31,312	205,676	135,693
2002	6,688,495	5,195,482	43,894	5,239,376	595,015	347,247	4,991,608	1,032,151	664,736	32,041	208,747	136,556
2003	6,871,805	5,338,456	71,702	5,410,158	616,985	355,713	5,148,886	1,033,816	689,103	32,514	211,350	138,632
2004	7,129,341	5,670,563	73,694	5,744,257	658,562	285,384	5,371,079	1,043,559	714,703	33,378	213,592	142,539
2005	7,397,433	5,833,930	74,306	5,908,236	686,118	309,611	5,531,729	1,093,779	771,925	34,259	215,925	143,880
2006	7,776,102	6,037,929	55,441	6,093,370	712,443	325,364	5,706,291	1,231,555	838,256	35,598	218,441	145,291
2007	8,186,296	6,299,506	92,709	6,392,215	742,527	343,951	5,993,639	1,274,505	918,152	37,148	220,368	147,873
2008	8,574,198	6,381,052	80,625	6,461,677	759,946	401,868	6,103,599	1,412,667	1,057,932	38,553	222,402	146,875
2009	8,430,089	6,224,604	25,935	6,250,539	741,121	435,974	5,945,392	1,283,800	1,200,897	37,528	224,632	142,764
2010	8,684,516	6,323,707	59,999	6,383,706	758,957	468,466	6,093,215	1,291,413	1,299,888	38,429	225,987	141,907
2011	9,256,564	6,668,702	112,095	6,780,797	716,865	536,594	6,600,526	1,382,521	1,273,517	40,596	228,018	144,431
2012	9,628,086	6,965,296	120,226	7,085,522	743,595	526,406	6,868,333	1,486,104	1,273,649	41,943	229,551	146,017
2013	9,779,432	7,038,688	140,920	7,179,608	846,542	643,640	6,976,706	1,499,576	1,303,150	42,278	231,310	146,992
2014	10,260,723	7,345,278	169,339	7,514,617	879,214	621,386	7,256,789	1,619,090	1,384,844	43,963	233,393	150,017
2015	10,696,897	7,706,756	143,068	7,849,824	913,755	610,839	7,546,908	1,698,125	1,451,864	45,450	235,357	151,906
2016	11,052,559	7,979,143	95,828	8,074,971	943,565	646,736	7,778,142	1,783,385	1,491,032	46,662	236,862	154,725
2017	11,505,626	8,228,217	102,596	8,330,813	977,278	677,052	8,030,587	1,906,185	1,568,854	48,157	238,918	154,886
2018	12,024,941	8,595,780	90,372	8,686,152	1,008,754	652,831	8,330,229	2,011,967	1,682,745	49,967	240,660	157,202
2019	12,569,457	8,970,874	108,167	9,079,041	1,056,540	641,163	8,663,664	2,140,928	1,764,865	51,937	242,015	158,294
2020	13,374,503	9,124,012	142,800	9,266,812	1,075,287	659,521	8,851,046	2,178,189	2,345,268	54,943	243,423	153,423
2021	14,393,551	9,773,648	139,658	9,913,306	1,142,703	577,546	9,348,149	2,383,998	2,661,404	59,015	243,896	157,643
2022	14,705,451	10,437,611	150,646	10,588,257	1,246,621	579,982	9,921,618	2,529,013	2,254,820	60,060	244,845	163,652

Personal Income and Employment by Area: Asheville, NC

(Thousands of dollars, except as noted.)

		Derivation of personal income										
		Earnings by place of work										
Year	Personal income, total	Nonfarm	Farm	Total	Less: Contributions for government social insurance	Plus: Adjustment for residence	Equals: Net earnings by place of residence	Plus: Dividends, interest, and rent	Plus: Personal current transfer receipts	Per capita personal income (dollars)	Population (persons)	Total employment
1970	785,483	604,225	19,802	624,027	41,768	1,294	583,553	122,752	79,178	3,190	246,263	107,391
1971	861,652	664,748	17,192	681,940	47,442	916	635,414	135,111	91,127	3,431	251,104	108,988
1972	973,755	757,294	21,447	778,741	56,878	2,319	724,182	148,794	100,779	3,844	253,306	115,239
1973	1,111,269	875,051	20,034	895,085	75,821	2,068	821,332	171,493	118,444	4,319	257,291	122,493
1974	1,218,978	934,189	18,913	953,102	84,149	4,569	873,522	199,581	145,875	4,671	260,984	121,406
1975	1,318,910	950,469	23,361	973,830	84,222	8,332	897,940	219,298	201,672	4,981	264,807	115,701
1976	1,474,607	1,077,829	26,738	1,104,567	96,895	12,349	1,020,021	240,976	213,610	5,523	266,999	120,996
1977	1,653,861	1,210,375	37,511	1,247,886	108,165	15,775	1,155,496	273,240	225,125	6,108	270,770	126,497
1978	1,859,539	1,376,336	38,342	1,414,678	126,742	19,089	1,307,025	309,450	243,064	6,746	275,655	131,939
1979	2,064,242	1,516,845	38,992	1,555,837	144,801	25,828	1,436,864	350,287	277,091	7,381	279,654	134,546
1980	2,350,223	1,668,929	33,427	1,702,356	160,220	34,717	1,576,853	444,057	329,313	8,286	283,635	135,100
1981	2,646,310	1,810,736	49,471	1,860,207	186,898	38,174	1,711,483	550,936	383,891	9,253	285,988	136,135
1982	2,819,933	1,881,821	46,631	1,928,452	198,322	40,233	1,770,363	624,196	425,374	9,755	289,085	134,442
1983	3,096,586	2,063,902	54,479	2,118,381	219,368	41,075	1,940,088	692,782	463,716	10,684	289,822	138,779
1984	3,444,682	2,319,438	50,544	2,369,982	251,548	42,564	2,160,998	788,772	494,912	11,736	293,506	145,445
1985	3,682,878	2,486,906	41,163	2,528,069	274,382	39,411	2,293,098	857,946	531,834	12,418	296,586	149,776
1986	3,928,518	2,656,077	27,646	2,683,723	299,078	35,552	2,420,197	936,983	571,338	13,137	299,050	153,313
1987	4,204,254	2,873,920	36,167	2,910,087	319,888	37,108	2,627,307	973,737	603,210	14,003	300,229	156,232
1988	4,600,105	3,141,647	51,225	3,192,872	360,711	35,881	2,868,042	1,088,997	643,066	15,195	302,741	163,112
1989	5,033,844	3,339,472	38,993	3,378,465	386,395	34,969	3,027,039	1,291,411	715,394	16,478	305,480	167,964
1990	5,375,362	3,538,322	71,916	3,610,238	417,886	35,576	3,227,928	1,357,585	789,849	17,368	309,502	171,956
1991	5,666,820	3,714,616	70,075	3,784,691	443,852	32,881	3,373,720	1,391,022	902,078	17,981	315,160	172,486
1992	6,096,392	4,031,916	94,323	4,126,239	475,354	30,054	3,680,939	1,422,586	992,867	18,978	321,240	176,331
1993	6,515,105	4,299,374	112,821	4,412,195	510,769	22,600	3,924,026	1,502,695	1,088,384	19,850	328,220	181,752
1994	6,850,589	4,535,966	119,581	4,655,547	545,982	18,892	4,128,457	1,596,637	1,125,495	20,457	334,878	186,248
1995	7,375,343	4,772,356	123,208	4,895,564	576,466	16,742	4,335,840	1,781,334	1,258,169	21,582	341,739	191,577
1996	7,780,063	5,021,019	99,626	5,120,645	600,150	15,536	4,536,031	1,887,872	1,356,160	22,362	347,921	196,267
1997	8,395,978	5,440,362	96,290	5,536,652	642,957	14,820	4,908,515	2,064,650	1,422,813	23,714	354,052	203,879
1998	8,949,022	5,790,643	109,394	5,900,037	682,594	17,644	5,235,087	2,244,923	1,469,012	24,865	359,909	208,191
1999	9,247,214	6,081,178	129,993	6,211,171	718,055	15,146	5,508,262	2,174,547	1,564,405	25,324	365,159	211,901
2000	9,735,072	6,333,301	117,976	6,451,277	748,289	13,182	5,716,170	2,341,882	1,677,020	26,267	370,615	215,601
2001	10,167,434	6,709,701	94,007	6,803,708	782,811	-1,833	6,019,064	2,297,770	1,850,600	27,120	374,904	214,044
2002	10,302,600	6,844,892	57,881	6,902,773	798,750	-13,527	6,090,496	2,230,198	1,981,906	27,125	379,818	214,663
2003	10,566,509	7,103,965	66,597	7,170,562	843,579	-43,016	6,283,967	2,212,773	2,069,769	27,433	385,178	218,083
2004	11,376,805	7,528,574	75,212	7,603,786	884,511	-62,619	6,656,656	2,480,563	2,239,586	29,118	390,713	223,207
2005	12,018,802	7,892,374	116,491	8,008,865	938,566	-79,924	6,990,375	2,626,121	2,402,306	30,319	396,408	229,213
2006	13,080,082	8,514,056	113,002	8,627,058	999,764	-94,607	7,532,687	2,932,516	2,614,879	32,333	404,546	236,532
2007	13,899,253	8,925,005	56,473	8,981,478	1,060,234	-110,741	7,810,503	3,301,870	2,786,880	33,749	411,842	246,175
2008	14,414,593	8,997,687	71,048	9,068,735	1,071,351	-123,648	7,873,736	3,439,527	3,101,330	34,530	417,457	244,340
2009	14,037,094	8,571,473	76,567	8,648,040	1,040,407	-106,829	7,500,804	3,099,739	3,436,551	33,262	422,014	234,380
2010	14,312,533	8,786,138	65,223	8,851,361	1,055,963	-98,583	7,696,815	3,006,700	3,609,018	33,642	425,434	233,886
2011	14,901,072	8,902,651	65,555	8,968,206	985,633	-99,388	7,883,185	3,303,953	3,713,934	34,769	428,568	238,798
2012	15,732,240	9,368,373	59,512	9,427,885	1,018,252	-82,328	8,327,305	3,585,284	3,819,651	36,436	431,781	241,452
2013	15,753,289	9,606,671	59,593	9,666,264	1,194,132	-62,295	8,409,837	3,454,682	3,888,770	36,050	436,989	246,165
2014	16,809,316	10,218,659	67,195	10,285,854	1,265,376	-71,044	8,949,434	3,800,090	4,059,792	38,099	441,196	252,662
2015	17,834,583	10,775,927	69,076	10,845,003	1,334,986	-76,935	9,433,082	4,147,572	4,253,929	39,947	446,457	260,025
2016	18,695,414	11,404,909	61,101	11,466,010	1,398,239	-82,933	9,984,838	4,360,278	4,350,298	41,312	452,542	267,696
2017	19,615,716	11,879,279	66,705	11,945,984	1,446,623	-82,350	10,417,011	4,670,753	4,527,952	42,870	457,567	273,356
2018	20,800,118	12,648,257	36,374	12,684,631	1,524,840	-88,600	11,071,191	4,987,356	4,741,571	44,990	462,324	281,305
2019	22,254,952	13,406,394	46,873	13,453,267	1,613,321	-79,560	11,760,386	5,412,017	5,082,549	47,757	466,006	284,616
2020	23,530,332	13,446,189	56,235	13,502,424	1,635,693	-76,469	11,790,262	5,305,630	6,434,440	50,098	469,686	272,236
2021	26,267,444	14,846,543	49,464	14,896,007	1,781,826	-82,462	13,031,719	6,033,254	7,202,471	55,551	472,856	287,258
2022	27,521,654	16,426,487	35,762	16,462,249	1,992,828	-103,933	14,365,488	6,658,858	6,497,308	57,810	476,072	299,921

Personal Income and Employment by Area: Athens-Clarke County, GA

(Thousands of dollars, except as noted.)

Year	Personal income, total	Derivation of personal income								Per capita personal income (dollars)	Population (persons)	Total employment
		Earnings by place of work			Less: Contributions for government social insurance	Plus: Adjustment for residence	Equals: Net earnings by place of residence	Plus: Dividends, interest, and rent	Plus: Personal current transfer receipts			
		Nonfarm	Farm	Total								
1970	287,152	243,816	4,596	248,412	14,503	-10,546	223,363	42,106	21,683	3,033	94,672	42,435
1971	321,923	274,050	3,976	278,026	16,774	-11,825	249,427	47,055	25,441	3,311	97,214	44,721
1972	363,661	310,458	4,906	315,364	20,077	-13,930	281,357	53,011	29,293	3,601	100,987	47,189
1973	415,511	349,981	11,328	361,309	25,915	-16,563	318,831	61,879	34,801	3,936	105,560	48,552
1974	470,958	399,911	6,262	406,173	30,536	-20,689	354,948	72,985	43,025	4,374	107,666	50,427
1975	520,622	417,929	13,538	431,467	31,436	-18,723	381,308	81,556	57,758	4,811	108,211	49,988
1976	579,382	475,100	12,846	487,946	36,710	-23,136	428,100	89,810	61,472	5,460	106,120	51,555
1977	641,865	532,485	14,142	546,627	41,017	-28,419	477,191	100,468	64,206	5,981	107,309	54,049
1978	719,753	603,796	16,686	620,482	47,935	-35,789	536,758	112,296	70,699	6,637	108,452	56,422
1979	790,228	658,558	18,183	676,741	54,760	-36,548	585,433	124,373	80,422	7,240	109,148	57,722
1980	871,733	714,172	2,511	716,683	59,414	-38,926	618,343	155,853	97,537	7,625	114,324	57,313
1981	997,830	792,156	12,091	804,247	70,904	-39,355	693,988	192,349	111,493	8,528	117,011	58,812
1982	1,080,640	825,577	22,803	848,380	75,119	-38,765	734,496	223,033	123,111	9,136	118,289	58,163
1983	1,209,407	930,147	22,242	952,389	85,981	-42,326	824,082	250,092	135,233	10,048	120,365	60,122
1984	1,325,136	1,004,553	37,211	1,041,764	95,629	-41,377	904,758	275,497	144,881	10,820	122,473	63,350
1985	1,434,345	1,095,499	30,358	1,125,857	107,113	-42,511	976,233	300,512	157,600	11,537	124,327	65,645
1986	1,576,114	1,200,748	44,593	1,245,341	118,968	-44,402	1,081,971	324,923	169,220	12,565	125,434	68,018
1987	1,675,280	1,300,064	28,113	1,328,177	127,801	-44,317	1,156,059	340,009	179,212	13,088	128,002	70,290
1988	1,844,296	1,426,064	43,576	1,469,640	146,013	-44,020	1,279,607	373,990	190,699	14,123	130,586	72,042
1989	2,049,210	1,539,424	61,980	1,601,404	158,330	-45,100	1,397,974	440,864	210,372	15,305	133,894	73,601
1990	2,202,305	1,659,584	57,138	1,716,722	170,741	-46,416	1,499,565	464,899	237,841	16,085	136,914	74,955
1991	2,291,239	1,700,838	59,358	1,760,196	177,351	-45,552	1,537,293	480,797	273,149	16,441	139,359	73,882
1992	2,412,804	1,794,059	59,742	1,853,801	186,659	-38,696	1,628,446	481,071	303,287	17,004	141,899	74,262
1993	2,573,061	1,906,970	61,475	1,968,445	198,815	-32,637	1,736,993	514,627	321,441	17,756	144,916	78,030
1994	2,744,418	2,038,143	66,849	2,104,992	213,691	-39,481	1,851,820	552,837	339,761	18,425	148,953	80,774
1995	2,964,976	2,191,628	58,360	2,249,988	229,113	-37,209	1,983,666	611,648	369,662	19,543	151,718	85,085
1996	3,182,986	2,348,219	66,352	2,414,571	242,468	-38,754	2,133,349	656,165	393,472	20,538	154,977	88,923
1997	3,339,194	2,470,050	68,759	2,538,809	250,368	-49,553	2,238,888	704,203	396,103	21,095	158,291	90,120
1998	3,583,032	2,668,278	82,975	2,751,253	267,867	-49,059	2,434,327	746,410	402,295	22,348	160,330	92,124
1999	3,742,813	2,827,933	82,917	2,910,850	281,958	-58,411	2,570,481	743,227	429,105	22,898	163,456	93,748
2000	3,931,566	2,940,142	74,919	3,015,061	291,795	-62,125	2,661,141	795,679	474,746	23,576	166,763	95,550
2001	4,148,203	3,107,434	102,078	3,209,512	310,959	-81,430	2,817,123	810,584	520,496	24,550	168,973	95,547
2002	4,289,565	3,251,011	62,571	3,313,582	325,366	-96,992	2,891,224	815,235	583,106	25,109	170,838	96,119
2003	4,527,146	3,460,607	65,878	3,526,485	342,187	-137,022	3,047,276	891,490	588,380	26,041	173,847	97,796
2004	4,733,050	3,616,984	96,916	3,713,900	367,328	-141,151	3,205,421	894,567	633,062	26,574	178,106	99,781
2005	4,965,919	3,798,339	103,185	3,901,524	381,524	-170,142	3,349,858	919,378	696,683	27,747	178,974	103,690
2006	5,193,172	4,019,077	48,384	4,067,461	407,667	-224,703	3,435,091	1,020,687	737,394	28,351	183,171	107,236
2007	5,474,472	4,137,664	74,964	4,212,628	410,488	-284,199	3,517,941	1,156,095	800,436	29,310	186,781	111,041
2008	5,650,554	4,271,941	114,855	4,386,796	455,280	-396,148	3,535,368	1,183,633	931,553	29,748	189,948	111,944
2009	5,600,638	4,226,087	100,378	4,326,465	443,355	-462,299	3,420,811	1,166,317	1,013,510	29,167	192,021	109,044
2010	5,708,147	4,328,917	74,184	4,403,101	448,058	-515,203	3,439,840	1,146,817	1,121,490	29,506	193,456	108,272
2011	5,974,835	4,405,111	63,644	4,468,755	403,602	-515,402	3,549,751	1,229,066	1,196,018	30,723	194,477	108,825
2012	6,233,450	4,545,904	148,152	4,694,056	415,998	-516,496	3,761,562	1,293,012	1,178,876	31,773	196,186	110,116
2013	6,341,819	4,700,763	144,069	4,844,832	484,119	-497,718	3,862,995	1,259,405	1,219,419	32,048	197,886	112,568
2014	6,804,097	4,919,407	159,688	5,079,095	506,707	-419,257	4,153,131	1,380,792	1,270,174	34,235	198,748	114,105
2015	7,310,545	5,288,702	169,773	5,458,475	538,612	-475,450	4,444,413	1,526,193	1,339,939	36,004	203,049	117,386
2016	7,580,191	5,525,099	107,621	5,632,720	564,875	-487,836	4,580,009	1,619,960	1,380,222	36,824	205,850	121,919
2017	8,070,314	5,799,935	140,272	5,940,207	589,514	-519,291	4,831,402	1,814,223	1,424,689	38,520	209,508	125,945
2018	8,457,939	6,085,562	112,750	6,198,312	636,262	-497,865	5,064,185	1,891,588	1,502,166	39,882	212,076	128,901
2019	8,927,686	6,242,484	91,025	6,333,509	653,930	-250,608	5,428,971	1,917,652	1,581,063	41,624	214,486	129,814
2020	9,643,433	6,346,517	21,199	6,367,716	671,431	-223,255	5,473,030	2,029,629	2,140,774	44,708	215,699	125,840
2021	10,589,858	6,910,308	79,252	6,989,560	734,063	-245,872	6,009,625	2,228,173	2,352,060	48,525	218,235	131,319
2022	10,994,605	7,144,329	202,148	7,346,477	777,394	111,900	6,680,983	2,292,242	2,021,380	49,884	220,405	134,190

Personal Income and Employment by Area: Atlanta-Sandy Springs-Alpharetta, GA

(Thousands of dollars, except as noted.)

Year	Personal income, total	Derivation of personal income: Earnings by place of work: Nonfarm	Farm	Total	Less: Contributions for government social insurance	Plus: Adjustment for residence	Equals: Net earnings by place of residence	Plus: Dividends, interest, and rent	Plus: Personal current transfer receipts	Per capita personal income (dollars)	Population (persons)	Total employment
1970	7,695,760	6,697,987	32,676	6,730,663	424,490	-79,274	6,226,899	997,013	471,848	4,133	1,862,083	924,492
1971	8,534,310	7,385,975	28,231	7,414,206	485,358	-85,378	6,843,470	1,125,779	565,061	4,436	1,923,687	956,707
1972	9,754,566	8,498,897	36,008	8,534,905	587,731	-103,187	7,843,987	1,268,080	642,499	4,910	1,986,477	1,013,051
1973	11,042,213	9,652,707	67,946	9,720,653	767,896	-122,909	8,829,848	1,460,906	751,459	5,373	2,055,233	1,078,478
1974	12,157,534	10,475,353	33,695	10,509,048	862,290	-133,408	9,513,350	1,696,160	948,024	5,764	2,109,395	1,089,091
1975	13,096,935	10,934,479	63,265	10,997,744	880,136	-138,055	9,979,553	1,801,246	1,316,136	6,155	2,127,779	1,049,087
1976	14,504,859	12,264,616	71,420	12,336,036	1,009,289	-149,629	11,177,118	1,931,061	1,396,680	6,737	2,152,893	1,087,337
1977	16,314,364	14,013,062	63,099	14,076,161	1,148,484	-164,028	12,763,649	2,115,323	1,435,392	7,435	2,194,331	1,147,650
1978	18,510,403	16,006,272	68,900	16,075,172	1,351,575	-177,354	14,546,243	2,410,476	1,553,684	8,282	2,234,980	1,217,960
1979	20,855,840	18,059,329	72,610	18,131,939	1,586,598	-212,299	16,333,042	2,751,553	1,771,245	9,085	2,295,738	1,273,760
1980	23,760,348	20,259,773	27,771	20,287,544	1,788,440	-247,838	18,251,266	3,386,034	2,123,048	10,102	2,352,155	1,312,418
1981	26,806,318	22,567,671	57,878	22,625,549	2,148,708	-277,588	20,199,253	4,203,071	2,403,994	11,153	2,403,406	1,337,201
1982	29,049,824	24,236,859	95,879	24,332,738	2,366,061	-297,200	21,669,477	4,750,382	2,629,965	11,840	2,453,618	1,357,118
1983	32,386,589	27,101,118	69,657	27,170,775	2,681,241	-334,130	24,155,404	5,368,706	2,862,479	12,869	2,516,569	1,418,357
1984	37,225,090	31,372,930	106,421	31,479,351	3,192,267	-374,976	27,912,108	6,252,986	3,059,996	14,351	2,593,856	1,541,244
1985	41,697,695	35,461,380	84,875	35,546,255	3,691,992	-410,793	31,443,470	6,977,303	3,276,922	15,504	2,689,442	1,644,282
1986	46,092,096	39,467,364	101,677	39,569,041	4,155,215	-429,017	34,984,809	7,606,831	3,500,456	16,551	2,784,902	1,737,089
1987	50,203,091	43,416,808	57,437	43,474,245	4,528,976	-500,831	38,444,438	8,103,001	3,655,652	17,421	2,881,787	1,799,907
1988	55,333,147	47,539,042	100,323	47,639,365	5,075,484	-518,129	42,045,752	9,335,484	3,951,911	18,660	2,965,367	1,869,917
1989	59,463,113	50,102,768	153,761	50,256,529	5,379,911	-511,292	44,365,326	10,676,831	4,420,956	19,604	3,033,139	1,902,034
1990	64,022,794	53,655,678	144,832	53,800,510	5,790,472	-526,809	47,483,229	11,552,193	4,987,372	20,624	3,104,221	1,936,224
1991	67,012,511	55,810,627	160,299	55,970,926	6,085,729	-540,550	49,344,647	11,847,507	5,820,357	20,972	3,195,398	1,917,337
1992	72,916,504	61,307,423	172,661	61,480,084	6,580,558	-607,507	54,292,019	12,060,458	6,564,027	22,150	3,291,991	1,962,091
1993	78,283,418	65,856,736	167,381	66,024,117	7,086,996	-663,795	58,273,326	12,922,795	7,087,297	23,009	3,402,250	2,072,915
1994	84,701,551	70,877,072	192,293	71,069,365	7,724,387	-723,448	62,621,530	14,354,527	7,725,494	24,038	3,523,718	2,172,516
1995	92,679,227	77,202,240	156,150	77,358,390	8,385,323	-802,384	68,170,683	16,049,269	8,459,275	25,428	3,644,699	2,273,047
1996	101,449,693	84,644,509	175,481	84,819,990	9,078,334	-914,641	74,827,015	17,612,447	9,010,231	26,940	3,765,817	2,380,579
1997	109,387,619	91,523,953	178,862	91,702,815	9,784,315	-1,025,407	80,893,093	19,286,947	9,207,579	28,132	3,888,398	2,460,237
1998	122,287,094	103,542,136	213,859	103,755,995	10,810,080	-1,198,021	91,747,894	21,100,078	9,439,122	30,409	4,021,410	2,584,632
1999	131,902,543	113,892,335	203,708	114,096,043	11,840,565	-1,358,877	100,896,601	21,066,977	9,938,965	31,724	4,157,862	2,676,550
2000	145,380,280	125,267,913	164,511	125,432,424	12,836,545	-1,554,455	111,041,424	23,449,207	10,889,649	33,861	4,293,475	2,770,951
2001	153,811,599	131,982,805	228,703	132,211,508	13,367,097	-1,524,749	117,319,662	24,346,076	12,145,861	34,938	4,402,455	2,809,261
2002	157,161,260	134,050,035	135,124	134,185,159	13,516,708	-1,411,315	119,257,136	24,089,785	13,814,339	35,008	4,489,288	2,795,316
2003	162,294,514	137,575,824	146,064	137,721,888	13,829,536	-1,268,896	122,623,456	25,419,021	14,252,037	35,493	4,572,541	2,813,744
2004	171,999,951	146,202,431	228,425	146,430,856	15,037,216	-1,237,163	130,156,477	26,458,111	15,385,363	36,913	4,659,574	2,896,504
2005	183,419,060	153,326,417	233,096	153,559,513	15,675,533	-1,001,538	136,882,442	29,401,636	17,134,982	38,446	4,770,870	3,015,036
2006	197,581,252	163,148,017	111,702	163,259,719	16,612,796	-845,932	145,800,991	33,259,672	18,520,589	40,062	4,931,848	3,134,612
2007	206,619,036	167,959,276	167,294	168,126,570	17,214,136	-853,170	150,059,264	36,431,435	20,128,337	40,783	5,066,356	3,233,206
2008	206,236,089	162,641,585	225,698	162,867,283	17,699,773	-107,446	145,060,064	37,493,978	23,682,047	39,890	5,170,099	3,207,144
2009	200,658,053	157,429,577	193,247	157,622,824	17,100,349	278,430	140,800,905	33,550,026	26,307,122	38,287	5,240,828	3,087,489
2010	205,048,554	159,758,777	145,144	159,903,921	17,334,878	417,409	142,986,452	32,882,792	29,179,310	38,666	5,303,075	3,071,032
2011	220,609,538	167,595,314	107,999	167,703,313	15,945,082	322,388	152,080,619	37,884,401	30,644,518	41,092	5,368,727	3,151,613
2012	227,191,481	172,122,232	274,580	172,396,812	16,564,450	287,054	156,119,416	40,721,788	30,350,277	41,698	5,448,515	3,200,073
2013	230,846,272	179,190,551	260,110	179,450,661	19,694,205	280,753	160,037,209	39,207,156	31,601,907	41,847	5,516,376	3,285,695
2014	249,334,282	192,379,797	281,513	192,661,310	20,828,260	80,169	171,913,219	44,033,997	33,387,066	44,517	5,600,845	3,421,355
2015	266,188,019	205,838,174	283,316	206,121,490	22,011,697	92,995	184,202,788	46,881,182	35,104,049	46,735	5,695,632	3,540,979
2016	280,444,372	217,929,603	152,558	218,082,161	23,039,262	-406,030	194,636,869	49,240,411	36,567,092	48,350	5,800,316	3,653,542
2017	299,751,387	230,801,111	209,339	231,010,450	24,165,286	-217,437	206,627,727	55,273,764	37,849,896	50,920	5,886,680	3,762,137
2018	316,507,772	243,111,872	142,318	243,254,190	25,609,007	-307,967	217,337,216	59,180,834	39,989,722	53,081	5,962,727	3,879,721
2019	335,037,441	257,042,403	109,996	257,152,399	27,119,509	-711,653	229,321,237	63,150,536	42,565,668	55,471	6,039,848	3,962,817
2020	354,845,998	257,808,075	25,656	257,833,731	27,582,207	-817,560	229,433,964	63,605,959	61,806,075	58,140	6,103,261	3,911,819
2021	389,931,086	280,910,005	107,640	281,017,645	30,276,033	-1,116,023	249,625,589	72,815,177	67,490,320	63,474	6,143,138	4,125,495
2022	398,880,945	301,078,595	273,917	301,352,512	33,573,536	-2,245,354	265,533,622	76,831,266	56,516,057	64,107	6,222,106	4,368,266

Personal Income and Employment by Area: Atlantic City-Hammonton, NJ

(Thousands of dollars, except as noted.)

Year	Personal income, total	Derivation of personal income: Earnings by place of work: Nonfarm	Farm	Total	Less: Contributions for government social insurance	Plus: Adjustment for residence	Equals: Net earnings by place of residence	Plus: Dividends, interest, and rent	Plus: Personal current transfer receipts	Per capita personal income (dollars)	Population (persons)	Total employment
1970	782,866	555,691	6,342	562,033	39,518	35,867	558,382	124,240	100,244	4,450	175,908	79,885
1971	871,879	593,872	6,399	600,271	43,642	57,677	614,306	137,345	120,228	4,849	179,824	79,392
1972	964,555	651,292	5,316	656,608	50,285	74,206	680,529	149,736	134,290	5,214	184,987	82,297
1973	1,081,593	728,853	8,073	736,926	63,329	88,957	762,554	166,721	152,318	5,778	187,199	85,385
1974	1,173,626	763,744	8,991	772,735	68,812	104,358	808,281	186,919	178,426	6,206	189,113	84,867
1975	1,283,784	803,960	8,100	812,060	70,323	117,849	859,586	200,118	224,080	6,773	189,544	82,280
1976	1,421,862	901,015	8,936	909,951	77,981	129,498	961,468	213,516	246,878	7,499	189,613	84,161
1977	1,575,347	1,008,725	11,534	1,020,259	85,279	144,519	1,079,499	235,029	260,819	8,321	189,311	85,095
1978	1,779,776	1,180,610	11,718	1,192,328	103,083	149,616	1,238,861	265,544	275,371	9,312	191,121	90,253
1979	2,069,951	1,486,929	9,673	1,496,602	143,412	114,209	1,467,399	300,283	302,269	10,721	193,082	99,716
1980	2,387,058	1,792,440	11,740	1,804,180	180,700	65,015	1,688,495	367,931	330,632	12,269	194,566	109,410
1981	2,733,798	2,159,658	10,799	2,170,457	239,169	-2,231	1,929,057	448,228	356,513	13,949	195,984	118,656
1982	2,918,957	2,304,397	14,457	2,318,854	256,363	-34,785	2,027,706	515,024	376,227	14,851	196,548	119,783
1983	3,178,317	2,599,353	20,497	2,619,850	296,657	-86,287	2,236,906	541,407	400,004	15,958	199,168	124,824
1984	3,582,582	3,022,968	15,085	3,038,053	354,970	-143,070	2,540,013	630,324	412,245	17,670	202,752	133,475
1985	3,829,614	3,295,773	20,107	3,315,880	392,565	-198,372	2,724,943	668,307	436,364	18,586	206,045	139,336
1986	4,097,474	3,608,819	21,519	3,630,338	429,653	-269,689	2,930,996	707,288	459,190	19,569	209,388	141,884
1987	4,329,526	3,925,341	18,435	3,943,776	469,836	-349,855	3,124,085	729,262	476,179	20,366	212,581	148,142
1988	4,745,144	4,365,864	18,427	4,384,291	525,747	-450,998	3,407,546	825,042	512,556	21,822	217,445	152,703
1989	4,941,681	4,511,522	18,262	4,529,784	544,251	-548,976	3,436,557	952,010	553,114	22,301	221,589	155,641
1990	5,065,141	4,701,103	17,135	4,718,238	553,501	-679,996	3,484,741	973,960	606,440	22,469	225,431	159,479
1991	4,801,639	4,302,985	20,486	4,323,471	531,003	-647,708	3,144,760	943,886	712,993	20,990	228,763	152,342
1992	5,391,811	4,845,531	22,501	4,868,032	576,430	-672,976	3,618,626	932,255	840,930	23,279	231,612	152,205
1993	5,658,242	5,126,534	26,421	5,152,955	598,218	-705,633	3,849,104	925,769	883,369	24,151	234,288	153,047
1994	5,800,713	5,262,155	26,756	5,288,911	629,876	-704,206	3,954,829	967,847	878,037	24,518	236,589	154,444
1995	6,262,856	5,617,638	28,932	5,646,570	659,802	-708,400	4,278,368	1,037,993	946,495	26,181	239,212	157,855
1996	6,674,143	5,976,437	31,538	6,007,975	692,844	-713,318	4,601,813	1,094,900	977,430	27,562	242,152	159,704
1997	7,039,367	6,292,371	30,222	6,322,593	707,823	-746,039	4,868,731	1,168,422	1,002,214	28,759	244,771	162,668
1998	7,359,508	6,588,140	26,903	6,615,043	729,056	-780,184	5,105,803	1,226,568	1,027,137	29,692	247,863	167,700
1999	7,580,102	6,820,454	22,442	6,842,896	739,954	-781,138	5,321,804	1,207,923	1,050,375	30,268	250,432	170,052
2000	8,032,277	7,148,384	31,255	7,179,639	765,413	-793,178	5,621,048	1,287,155	1,124,074	31,664	253,674	173,765
2001	7,456,371	6,476,388	29,657	6,506,045	759,301	-839,103	4,907,641	1,288,073	1,260,657	29,156	255,737	171,600
2002	7,737,565	6,699,538	36,863	6,736,401	783,169	-811,846	5,141,386	1,214,725	1,381,454	29,844	259,263	171,666
2003	8,035,699	6,945,950	35,156	6,981,106	810,964	-789,387	5,380,755	1,224,463	1,430,481	30,521	263,285	174,183
2004	8,559,745	7,434,755	34,839	7,469,594	850,782	-785,091	5,833,721	1,301,333	1,424,691	31,972	267,723	177,412
2005	9,019,718	7,906,253	45,697	7,951,950	916,624	-792,158	6,243,168	1,217,600	1,558,950	33,365	270,332	183,113
2006	9,880,758	8,585,006	67,264	8,652,270	972,610	-739,933	6,939,727	1,234,443	1,706,588	36,359	271,759	184,525
2007	10,350,882	8,771,737	71,830	8,843,567	1,009,180	-697,288	7,137,099	1,400,446	1,813,337	38,012	272,303	183,098
2008	10,685,492	8,657,036	58,849	8,715,885	1,022,348	-692,191	7,001,346	1,630,002	2,054,144	39,139	273,014	181,294
2009	10,447,153	8,054,872	60,449	8,115,321	962,481	-592,722	6,560,118	1,591,702	2,295,333	38,121	274,049	172,713
2010	10,614,431	8,114,349	50,627	8,164,976	972,490	-631,875	6,560,611	1,562,766	2,491,054	38,606	274,943	171,007
2011	11,066,928	8,225,776	60,036	8,285,812	895,191	-537,537	6,853,084	1,681,316	2,532,528	40,085	276,084	170,763
2012	11,258,603	8,427,795	71,358	8,499,153	905,385	-585,768	7,008,000	1,752,497	2,498,106	40,605	277,274	171,855
2013	11,414,061	8,632,945	63,181	8,696,126	1,026,272	-528,123	7,141,731	1,734,551	2,537,779	41,037	278,140	171,411
2014	11,626,811	8,712,380	67,936	8,780,316	1,033,044	-595,072	7,152,200	1,822,329	2,652,282	41,890	277,553	168,470
2015	11,742,848	8,551,862	71,533	8,623,395	1,026,793	-505,018	7,091,584	1,914,604	2,736,660	42,510	276,237	164,856
2016	11,828,874	8,567,500	70,044	8,637,544	1,026,932	-457,640	7,152,972	1,857,328	2,818,574	43,120	274,324	165,300
2017	12,142,939	8,666,392	78,190	8,744,582	1,050,253	-350,601	7,343,728	1,930,136	2,869,075	44,374	273,651	163,859
2018	12,619,513	9,168,445	51,617	9,220,062	1,099,946	-455,212	7,664,904	1,982,544	2,972,065	46,175	273,295	168,110
2019	13,462,043	9,754,937	64,566	9,819,503	1,168,330	-386,126	8,265,047	2,061,800	3,135,196	49,116	274,085	169,841
2020	14,677,214	9,422,461	60,715	9,483,176	1,120,267	-271,351	8,091,558	2,100,819	4,484,837	53,533	274,172	150,987
2021	15,778,937	10,350,444	53,642	10,404,086	1,252,597	-309,757	8,841,732	2,224,048	4,713,157	57,351	275,130	163,200
2022	15,413,028	10,859,677	50,521	10,910,198	1,369,720	-290,314	9,250,164	2,308,087	3,854,777	55,918	275,638	171,816

Personal Income and Employment by Area: Auburn-Opelika, AL

(Thousands of dollars, except as noted.)

Year	Personal income, total	Derivation of personal income									Per capita personal income (dollars)	Population (persons)	Total employment
		Earnings by place of work			Less: Contributions for government social insurance	Plus: Adjustment for residence	Equals: Net earnings by place of residence	Plus: Dividends, interest, and rent	Plus: Personal current transfer receipts			
		Nonfarm	Farm	Total								
1970	169,722	135,029	2,208	137,237	10,502	7,656	134,391	22,021	13,310	2,770	61,262	25,031
1971	189,457	147,579	2,833	150,412	11,785	10,370	148,997	25,207	15,253	3,061	61,896	24,952
1972	214,225	168,266	3,307	171,573	14,043	11,540	169,070	28,048	17,107	3,446	62,158	26,173
1973	243,444	191,905	4,206	196,111	18,356	13,257	191,012	32,093	20,339	3,769	64,588	27,551
1974	273,005	212,386	1,937	214,323	20,983	16,472	209,812	37,967	25,226	3,967	68,823	27,763
1975	303,672	227,786	1,641	229,427	22,485	19,230	226,172	43,349	34,151	4,377	69,373	27,700
1976	344,275	257,209	3,543	260,752	25,931	23,778	258,599	49,023	36,653	4,920	69,980	28,875
1977	397,165	301,124	4,294	305,418	30,201	25,493	300,710	56,963	39,492	5,527	71,861	30,460
1978	457,487	346,744	6,677	353,421	35,224	29,437	347,634	66,941	42,912	6,176	74,069	32,087
1979	505,361	377,118	7,184	384,302	39,536	34,245	379,011	75,513	50,837	6,650	75,990	32,315
1980	571,558	421,296	6,441	427,737	44,769	36,674	419,642	90,198	61,718	7,461	76,610	32,917
1981	626,944	458,987	6,436	465,423	52,590	37,801	450,634	108,799	67,511	8,061	77,777	32,811
1982	665,044	473,717	6,100	479,817	54,906	41,196	466,107	125,109	73,828	8,418	79,001	32,816
1983	737,318	536,226	4,844	541,070	61,814	41,271	520,527	136,496	80,295	9,319	79,121	34,028
1984	817,874	609,253	3,601	612,854	71,016	41,928	583,766	150,646	83,462	10,187	80,289	36,719
1985	879,110	646,777	4,710	651,487	74,525	48,195	625,157	163,867	90,086	10,830	81,176	37,024
1986	932,329	678,665	3,796	682,461	77,162	54,313	659,612	177,247	95,470	11,263	82,776	37,444
1987	990,761	725,045	4,876	729,921	81,299	58,920	707,542	184,925	98,294	11,983	82,681	38,845
1988	1,074,282	794,060	5,176	799,236	92,555	58,536	765,217	204,841	104,224	12,698	84,601	40,675
1989	1,198,998	881,891	5,290	887,181	101,734	54,220	839,667	238,740	120,591	13,966	85,851	43,158
1990	1,263,639	923,878	6,036	929,914	107,168	61,294	884,040	244,372	135,227	14,403	87,735	43,140
1991	1,338,207	945,484	9,466	954,950	109,328	80,735	926,357	259,582	152,268	14,951	89,508	43,300
1992	1,460,605	1,031,334	6,649	1,037,983	117,463	98,903	1,019,423	269,411	171,771	15,950	91,572	44,434
1993	1,551,735	1,070,623	17,090	1,087,713	122,334	120,990	1,086,369	280,694	184,672	16,456	94,295	45,513
1994	1,656,065	1,133,461	8,893	1,142,354	130,330	143,858	1,155,882	300,339	199,844	17,240	96,057	46,095
1995	1,783,009	1,188,482	8,524	1,197,006	137,146	167,338	1,227,198	339,242	216,569	17,940	99,386	48,314
1996	1,869,848	1,225,957	5,676	1,231,633	140,354	196,688	1,287,967	351,857	230,024	18,299	102,185	49,880
1997	2,010,113	1,304,017	6,079	1,310,096	149,463	228,032	1,388,665	374,815	246,633	18,860	106,578	51,253
1998	2,163,539	1,383,142	5,148	1,388,290	154,724	266,300	1,499,866	406,941	256,732	19,680	109,936	51,944
1999	2,295,520	1,471,067	4,228	1,475,295	163,671	294,251	1,605,875	415,450	274,195	20,333	112,898	52,880
2000	2,417,194	1,515,212	3,701	1,518,913	169,746	322,128	1,671,295	449,161	296,738	20,941	115,430	54,697
2001	2,491,406	1,507,898	5,273	1,513,171	174,007	343,829	1,682,993	470,826	337,587	21,327	116,819	54,497
2002	2,625,724	1,603,853	7,272	1,611,125	184,100	350,478	1,777,503	489,466	358,755	22,178	118,392	56,379
2003	2,815,855	1,723,541	7,303	1,730,844	197,148	355,150	1,888,846	543,499	383,510	23,452	120,071	57,401
2004	3,075,137	1,936,071	9,592	1,945,663	218,208	344,827	2,072,282	591,265	411,590	25,150	122,274	61,406
2005	3,274,536	2,057,036	6,605	2,063,641	231,840	364,876	2,196,677	629,385	448,474	25,961	126,133	63,932
2006	3,529,062	2,206,339	8,005	2,214,344	250,148	375,869	2,340,065	698,108	490,889	27,305	129,247	67,107
2007	3,756,329	2,311,661	7,892	2,319,553	264,947	409,337	2,463,943	742,997	549,389	28,471	131,934	69,316
2008	4,040,618	2,333,921	4,350	2,338,271	275,045	464,659	2,527,885	876,608	636,125	30,036	134,524	68,619
2009	4,041,990	2,305,677	5,922	2,311,599	269,731	464,105	2,505,973	856,311	679,706	29,170	138,566	66,844
2010	4,223,395	2,330,741	4,142	2,334,883	273,838	527,946	2,588,991	863,182	771,222	29,958	140,975	66,717
2011	4,482,826	2,431,724	4,766	2,436,490	254,074	596,411	2,778,827	898,940	805,059	30,913	145,014	69,655
2012	4,789,381	2,551,087	14,316	2,565,403	264,501	676,076	2,976,978	995,228	817,175	31,888	150,195	71,760
2013	4,857,382	2,671,455	6,504	2,677,959	310,887	698,738	3,065,810	947,359	844,213	31,501	154,196	73,922
2014	5,153,727	2,848,552	4,261	2,852,813	330,307	695,400	3,217,906	1,034,114	901,707	32,684	157,684	76,545
2015	5,444,984	3,007,708	4,609	3,012,317	347,693	701,742	3,366,366	1,078,474	1,000,144	33,834	160,934	78,204
2016	5,704,763	3,167,373	8,085	3,175,458	363,481	770,374	3,582,351	1,091,910	1,030,502	34,783	164,008	80,754
2017	5,969,714	3,385,452	12,443	3,397,895	391,711	691,298	3,697,482	1,221,539	1,050,693	35,707	167,184	83,728
2018	6,230,684	3,490,186	9,759	3,499,945	409,308	800,188	3,890,825	1,231,060	1,108,799	36,560	170,423	85,740
2019	6,716,398	3,685,113	10,488	3,695,601	432,789	876,895	4,139,707	1,383,208	1,193,483	39,042	172,030	87,115
2020	7,221,431	3,849,125	10,595	3,859,720	458,416	883,506	4,284,810	1,381,666	1,554,955	41,326	174,742	86,012
2021	8,002,677	4,156,920	9,145	4,166,065	494,219	996,455	4,668,301	1,516,245	1,818,131	45,046	177,655	89,684
2022	8,440,449	4,515,508	2,308	4,517,816	546,191	1,202,679	5,174,304	1,674,658	1,591,487	46,691	180,773	94,182

Personal Income and Employment by Area: Augusta-Richmond County, GA-SC

(Thousands of dollars, except as noted.)

Year	Personal income, total	Derivation of personal income: Earnings by place of work								Per capita personal income (dollars)	Population (persons)	Total employment
		Nonfarm	Farm	Total	Less: Contributions for government social insurance	Plus: Adjustment for residence	Equals: Net earnings by place of residence	Plus: Dividends, interest, and rent	Plus: Personal current transfer receipts			
1970	1,151,713	947,281	12,844	960,125	59,380	-17,736	883,009	176,536	92,168	3,489	330,105	149,954
1971	1,243,591	1,019,335	17,231	1,036,566	67,016	-28,026	941,524	188,779	113,288	3,765	330,340	149,885
1972	1,347,080	1,104,590	16,681	1,121,271	75,514	-27,996	1,017,761	199,876	129,443	4,102	328,410	151,635
1973	1,500,532	1,213,557	34,737	1,248,294	94,054	-27,946	1,126,294	224,582	149,656	4,513	332,508	157,074
1974	1,683,378	1,353,556	22,469	1,376,025	109,140	-30,503	1,236,382	260,168	186,828	4,940	340,794	160,613
1975	1,813,963	1,419,381	20,486	1,439,867	114,385	-30,688	1,294,794	281,439	237,730	5,199	348,901	157,238
1976	2,080,859	1,663,727	24,825	1,688,552	136,281	-43,537	1,508,734	314,989	257,136	5,795	359,074	165,293
1977	2,283,948	1,844,119	22,400	1,866,519	150,578	-47,837	1,668,104	348,734	267,110	6,261	364,786	172,285
1978	2,550,572	2,059,940	20,102	2,080,042	171,732	-53,344	1,854,966	402,686	292,920	6,815	374,244	178,197
1979	2,884,499	2,309,983	41,217	2,351,200	199,677	-63,263	2,088,260	461,725	334,514	7,524	383,370	184,512
1980	3,192,040	2,534,164	5,825	2,539,989	219,943	-72,927	2,247,119	544,461	400,460	8,175	390,476	186,358
1981	3,571,836	2,777,968	25,099	2,803,067	259,245	-64,820	2,479,002	629,281	463,553	9,079	393,411	187,332
1982	3,987,594	3,126,131	22,811	3,148,942	297,024	-82,576	2,769,342	715,865	502,387	10,016	398,117	191,980
1983	4,320,277	3,400,961	-1,782	3,399,179	330,052	-85,013	2,984,114	792,678	543,485	10,718	403,081	192,244
1984	4,893,657	3,880,023	26,619	3,906,642	388,635	-91,864	3,426,143	889,049	578,465	11,939	409,893	205,007
1985	5,385,581	4,315,114	28,328	4,343,442	440,626	-102,968	3,799,848	960,363	625,370	12,861	418,761	214,148
1986	5,839,953	4,686,708	21,646	4,708,354	487,627	-102,569	4,118,158	1,051,060	670,735	13,657	427,630	221,104
1987	6,032,635	4,809,401	28,808	4,838,209	495,899	-95,359	4,246,951	1,070,581	715,103	14,049	429,399	221,744
1988	6,487,681	5,143,292	44,131	5,187,423	549,924	-97,053	4,540,446	1,172,518	774,717	15,016	432,054	227,226
1989	7,137,187	5,608,818	47,243	5,656,061	608,662	-111,217	4,936,182	1,327,784	873,221	16,361	436,235	235,072
1990	7,800,414	6,210,727	28,140	6,238,867	683,729	-133,955	5,421,183	1,413,727	965,504	17,482	446,200	247,348
1991	8,160,725	6,372,144	45,798	6,417,942	712,568	-122,362	5,583,012	1,458,302	1,119,411	17,749	459,773	243,584
1992	8,746,142	6,823,478	43,057	6,866,535	756,502	-117,741	5,992,292	1,519,715	1,234,135	18,436	474,398	243,360
1993	9,011,378	6,996,807	26,637	7,023,444	782,284	-111,450	6,129,710	1,559,223	1,322,445	18,899	476,818	247,474
1994	9,410,147	7,172,991	46,644	7,219,635	810,718	-93,362	6,315,555	1,699,832	1,394,760	19,469	483,333	251,197
1995	9,788,702	7,347,772	38,406	7,386,178	828,559	-75,545	6,482,074	1,797,294	1,509,334	20,014	489,089	253,558
1996	10,215,360	7,471,391	36,765	7,508,156	830,913	-46,035	6,631,208	1,968,206	1,615,946	20,814	490,788	254,613
1997	10,669,562	7,773,394	37,575	7,810,969	857,519	-25,107	6,928,343	2,078,350	1,662,869	21,510	496,030	260,000
1998	11,409,095	8,313,140	34,545	8,347,685	908,746	5,770	7,444,709	2,252,889	1,711,497	22,789	500,636	264,879
1999	11,889,480	8,768,146	38,979	8,807,125	957,095	8,189	7,858,219	2,221,231	1,810,030	23,548	504,895	270,712
2000	12,520,131	9,120,444	48,318	9,168,762	993,415	15,467	8,190,814	2,383,217	1,946,100	24,603	508,896	274,209
2001	12,880,054	9,277,824	72,270	9,350,094	1,021,886	-10,958	8,317,250	2,430,411	2,132,393	25,126	512,626	269,418
2002	13,481,540	9,667,039	54,668	9,721,707	1,071,978	-24,388	8,625,341	2,468,254	2,387,945	26,086	516,818	269,268
2003	14,133,837	10,286,603	62,390	10,348,993	1,120,561	-32,677	9,195,755	2,487,564	2,450,518	27,174	520,120	273,390
2004	14,898,574	10,901,665	86,622	10,988,287	1,203,911	-31,233	9,753,143	2,530,072	2,615,359	28,282	526,789	279,056
2005	15,471,184	11,245,002	97,180	11,342,182	1,236,837	-34,481	10,070,864	2,608,356	2,791,964	29,120	531,294	282,877
2006	16,291,709	11,666,396	71,227	11,737,623	1,295,316	-27,422	10,414,885	2,878,799	2,998,025	30,246	538,643	284,014
2007	17,077,388	12,019,098	56,295	12,075,393	1,324,319	-39,730	10,711,344	3,172,180	3,193,864	31,305	545,524	289,867
2008	17,822,517	12,420,605	54,757	12,475,362	1,423,400	-50,938	11,001,024	3,186,073	3,635,420	32,251	552,627	289,675
2009	18,101,732	12,503,058	64,287	12,567,345	1,427,043	-105,583	11,034,719	3,111,440	3,955,573	32,435	558,096	284,266
2010	18,843,494	13,054,037	59,403	13,113,440	1,482,673	-155,609	11,475,158	3,090,412	4,277,924	33,253	566,672	284,746
2011	19,960,037	13,543,909	37,705	13,581,614	1,376,294	-209,895	11,995,425	3,474,028	4,490,584	34,971	570,754	288,546
2012	20,117,850	13,815,885	54,142	13,870,027	1,407,923	-234,040	12,228,064	3,433,936	4,455,850	34,926	576,013	289,049
2013	20,222,504	13,937,084	93,248	14,030,332	1,591,915	-255,300	12,183,117	3,450,628	4,588,759	34,897	579,495	292,179
2014	21,168,252	14,572,162	62,407	14,634,569	1,657,079	-261,083	12,716,407	3,657,123	4,794,722	36,334	582,602	299,568
2015	22,451,235	15,441,298	62,553	15,503,851	1,744,834	-283,963	13,475,054	3,933,009	5,043,172	38,120	588,955	307,205
2016	23,070,860	15,848,937	45,318	15,894,255	1,781,549	-280,303	13,832,403	3,999,976	5,238,481	38,817	594,350	311,152
2017	24,182,977	16,597,194	69,891	16,667,085	1,859,120	-287,841	14,520,124	4,229,393	5,433,460	40,352	599,308	318,683
2018	25,074,060	17,227,227	28,880	17,256,107	1,951,024	-291,133	15,013,950	4,341,564	5,718,546	41,565	603,251	326,114
2019	26,415,050	18,158,776	48,114	18,206,890	2,068,502	-325,048	15,813,340	4,532,520	6,069,190	43,455	607,877	331,205
2020	28,684,772	18,577,011	54,159	18,631,170	2,135,187	-350,612	16,145,371	4,765,758	7,773,643	46,859	612,147	328,180
2021	30,789,040	19,687,823	72,651	19,760,474	2,264,168	-325,219	17,171,087	4,884,497	8,733,456	49,961	616,261	338,878
2022	30,889,357	20,605,128	60,666	20,665,794	2,418,345	-282,157	17,965,292	5,099,704	7,824,361	49,496	624,083	348,245

Personal Income and Employment by Area: Austin-Round Rock-Georgetown, TX

(Thousands of dollars, except as noted.)

Year	Personal income, total	Derivation of personal income: Earnings by place of work: Nonfarm	Farm	Total	Less: Contributions for government social insurance	Plus: Adjustment for residence	Equals: Net earnings by place of residence	Plus: Dividends, interest, and rent	Plus: Personal current transfer receipts	Per capita personal income (dollars)	Population (persons)	Total employment
1970	1,475,763	1,154,458	13,108	1,167,566	69,396	-1,049	1,097,121	273,548	105,094	3,672	401,871	184,371
1971	1,672,669	1,310,024	11,680	1,321,704	82,025	-126	1,239,553	311,934	121,182	3,990	419,249	195,537
1972	1,931,675	1,508,104	25,787	1,533,891	98,461	834	1,436,264	359,114	136,297	4,312	447,971	210,710
1973	2,213,246	1,716,806	45,885	1,762,691	128,968	1,944	1,635,667	408,966	168,613	4,676	473,351	226,304
1974	2,498,475	1,932,352	25,287	1,957,639	149,877	1,682	1,809,444	482,501	206,530	5,141	485,969	235,030
1975	2,874,184	2,192,861	18,666	2,211,527	167,560	3,940	2,047,907	560,196	266,081	5,779	497,356	240,694
1976	3,295,435	2,548,061	30,898	2,578,959	195,426	2,245	2,385,778	616,244	293,413	6,366	517,680	255,068
1977	3,657,562	2,880,709	6,674	2,887,383	224,831	-462	2,662,090	689,610	305,862	6,874	532,052	272,296
1978	4,258,129	3,352,895	15,778	3,368,673	269,208	-4,328	3,095,137	820,471	342,521	7,905	538,668	290,687
1979	4,927,971	3,869,012	28,186	3,897,198	326,104	-2,239	3,568,855	963,850	395,266	8,623	571,520	308,207
1980	5,678,599	4,419,614	2,256	4,421,870	373,621	382	4,048,631	1,162,508	467,460	9,632	589,582	322,221
1981	6,633,086	5,102,203	25,653	5,127,856	467,038	5,812	4,666,630	1,429,603	536,853	10,946	605,961	342,388
1982	7,615,413	5,760,113	28,665	5,788,778	532,851	6,331	5,262,258	1,748,381	604,774	12,022	633,452	362,756
1983	8,803,901	6,731,140	12,928	6,744,068	616,451	-8,127	6,119,490	2,017,133	667,278	13,174	668,303	388,622
1984	10,301,785	8,030,625	13,370	8,043,995	758,728	-23,084	7,262,183	2,319,172	720,430	14,558	707,646	431,932
1985	11,661,606	9,146,128	-6,662	9,139,466	877,555	-34,193	8,227,718	2,642,631	791,257	15,374	758,510	468,315
1986	12,183,165	9,532,708	-2,221	9,530,487	911,319	-34,431	8,584,737	2,713,562	884,866	15,361	793,109	471,436
1987	12,344,028	9,653,165	2,914	9,656,079	901,106	-22,248	8,732,725	2,655,568	955,735	15,289	807,392	481,326
1988	13,105,971	10,178,244	807	10,179,051	988,494	-11,237	9,179,320	2,902,984	1,023,667	16,039	817,153	484,629
1989	14,067,152	10,667,283	11,448	10,678,731	1,052,806	-1,386	9,624,539	3,299,444	1,143,169	16,911	831,848	490,138
1990	15,541,192	11,869,880	7,443	11,877,323	1,162,435	2,892	10,717,780	3,551,394	1,272,018	18,243	851,898	512,913
1991	16,520,239	12,992,033	12,737	13,004,770	1,301,884	-19,991	11,682,895	3,422,030	1,415,314	18,759	880,678	536,269
1992	18,117,965	14,340,745	19,923	14,360,668	1,432,140	-42,128	12,886,400	3,571,733	1,659,832	19,848	912,833	554,727
1993	19,830,743	15,873,548	30,278	15,903,826	1,589,251	-76,034	14,238,541	3,824,447	1,767,755	20,879	949,788	591,053
1994	21,687,492	17,465,266	20,938	17,486,204	1,777,162	-109,402	15,599,640	4,190,269	1,897,583	21,930	988,925	624,671
1995	23,970,743	19,454,834	21,924	19,476,758	1,994,940	-157,841	17,323,977	4,590,241	2,056,525	23,237	1,031,557	663,975
1996	26,268,417	21,522,017	-12,971	21,509,046	2,197,103	-212,794	19,099,149	4,959,488	2,209,780	24,480	1,073,037	692,327
1997	29,171,124	24,084,404	15,227	24,099,631	2,457,286	-280,329	21,362,016	5,466,499	2,342,609	26,250	1,111,264	725,886
1998	33,950,854	28,738,440	-5,486	28,732,954	2,884,186	-410,722	25,438,046	6,074,653	2,438,155	29,380	1,155,579	766,659
1999	38,224,824	32,838,693	28,249	32,866,942	3,276,563	-561,025	29,029,354	6,568,676	2,626,794	31,698	1,205,898	805,105
2000	41,841,154	36,152,559	13,534	36,166,093	3,638,499	-666,685	31,860,909	7,155,834	2,824,411	33,077	1,264,950	849,746
2001	46,767,324	40,358,290	14,131	40,372,421	3,785,399	-613,349	35,973,673	7,627,193	3,166,458	35,395	1,321,316	863,762
2002	46,467,797	39,574,287	15,431	39,589,718	3,677,790	-513,582	35,398,346	7,524,540	3,544,911	34,476	1,347,822	856,723
2003	47,316,860	39,750,276	42,553	39,792,829	3,811,147	-490,464	35,491,218	8,012,138	3,813,504	34,387	1,376,030	864,166
2004	48,355,797	39,946,231	67,393	40,013,624	3,948,908	-480,931	35,583,785	8,696,595	4,075,417	34,293	1,410,058	886,044
2005	52,969,867	43,075,652	48,994	43,124,646	4,239,146	-493,021	38,392,479	10,073,798	4,503,590	36,447	1,453,358	934,987
2006	59,055,683	47,783,479	43,351	47,826,830	4,564,191	-483,412	42,779,227	11,406,496	4,869,960	38,968	1,515,485	981,785
2007	62,858,535	50,584,711	43,868	50,628,579	4,903,021	-476,005	45,249,553	12,204,587	5,404,395	39,838	1,577,856	1,042,246
2008	68,698,333	52,216,705	-10,258	52,206,447	5,041,438	-414,842	46,750,167	15,534,156	6,414,010	42,046	1,633,870	1,072,083
2009	67,018,551	51,029,632	-12,453	51,017,179	5,067,389	-303,813	45,645,977	14,189,838	7,182,736	39,837	1,682,338	1,068,484
2010	71,526,109	54,522,367	561	54,522,928	5,340,091	-230,927	48,951,910	14,377,521	8,196,678	41,402	1,727,600	1,082,175
2011	79,393,393	59,508,799	-8,696	59,500,103	5,074,466	-115,111	54,310,526	16,491,924	8,590,943	44,576	1,781,093	1,116,592
2012	86,680,730	63,320,935	11,786	63,332,721	5,395,753	9,549	57,946,517	20,082,302	8,651,911	47,223	1,835,567	1,154,709
2013	90,605,620	67,948,265	40,409	67,988,674	6,506,869	116,445	61,598,250	19,889,185	9,118,185	48,072	1,884,778	1,211,305
2014	98,445,209	73,719,617	11,843	73,731,460	6,984,083	195,843	66,943,220	21,765,541	9,736,448	50,631	1,944,376	1,264,147
2015	104,002,582	78,250,599	45,555	78,296,154	7,620,357	157,617	70,833,414	22,655,411	10,513,757	51,884	2,004,539	1,324,648
2016	108,348,822	82,094,172	-3,959	82,090,213	8,174,686	63,584	73,979,111	23,309,725	11,059,986	52,471	2,064,915	1,382,313
2017	119,172,633	91,162,313	-4,635	91,157,678	8,948,621	6,135	82,215,192	25,497,889	11,459,552	56,253	2,118,521	1,441,856
2018	129,835,052	98,808,345	-20,457	98,787,888	9,542,396	-52,973	89,192,519	28,469,349	12,173,184	59,839	2,169,743	1,509,826
2019	139,297,033	105,514,246	-22,302	105,491,944	10,323,209	-130,593	95,038,142	31,158,664	13,100,227	62,426	2,231,398	1,557,122
2020	148,240,384	108,354,823	-15,385	108,339,438	10,967,919	-282,805	97,088,714	32,351,755	18,799,915	64,453	2,299,994	1,555,044
2021	169,417,418	123,565,971	-11,794	123,554,177	12,410,577	-432,341	110,711,259	37,109,273	21,596,886	71,844	2,358,130	1,674,840
2022	181,870,848	138,404,674	-56,390	138,348,284	14,157,408	-570,561	123,620,315	40,444,140	17,806,393	75,119	2,421,115	1,813,624

Personal Income and Employment by Area: Bakersfield, CA

(Thousands of dollars, except as noted.)

Year	Personal income, total	Derivation of personal income								Per capita personal income (dollars)	Population (persons)	Total employment
		Earnings by place of work			Less: Contributions for government social insurance	Plus: Adjustment for residence	Equals: Net earnings by place of residence	Plus: Dividends, interest, and rent	Plus: Personal current transfer receipts			
		Nonfarm	Farm	Total								
1970	1,357,079	1,005,293	118,613	1,123,906	62,497	-43,180	1,018,229	188,910	149,940	4,102	330,868	138,871
1971	1,464,866	1,078,629	130,600	1,209,229	69,145	-46,629	1,093,455	205,956	165,455	4,357	336,227	142,153
1972	1,593,327	1,166,044	149,304	1,315,348	77,970	-49,631	1,187,747	226,230	179,350	4,730	336,833	145,354
1973	1,818,667	1,307,130	203,198	1,510,328	99,741	-54,822	1,355,765	262,251	200,651	5,302	343,007	153,762
1974	2,156,400	1,485,631	316,347	1,801,978	118,147	-66,163	1,617,668	297,492	241,240	6,253	344,840	163,320
1975	2,343,300	1,671,625	255,472	1,927,097	130,242	-85,738	1,711,117	335,080	297,103	6,566	356,866	170,339
1976	2,763,966	1,890,159	418,562	2,308,721	150,213	-94,369	2,064,139	358,999	340,828	7,533	366,932	173,782
1977	2,921,259	2,097,594	334,713	2,432,307	170,352	-103,900	2,158,055	398,684	364,520	7,848	372,217	179,070
1978	3,216,417	2,384,974	276,117	2,661,091	196,120	-109,405	2,355,566	462,091	398,760	8,509	377,990	185,586
1979	3,830,222	2,728,872	473,541	3,202,413	233,331	-121,331	2,847,751	537,849	444,622	9,741	393,198	197,044
1980	4,499,771	3,072,783	641,573	3,714,356	260,094	-142,610	3,311,652	664,876	523,243	11,072	406,407	202,903
1981	4,818,599	3,457,147	398,604	3,855,751	321,575	-140,209	3,393,967	804,915	619,717	11,504	418,877	207,514
1982	5,251,641	3,730,040	447,822	4,177,862	358,328	-145,264	3,674,270	897,758	679,613	12,109	433,698	205,351
1983	5,469,058	3,922,694	346,178	4,268,872	388,348	-141,093	3,739,431	983,713	745,914	12,236	446,961	211,093
1984	6,023,448	4,347,523	367,679	4,715,202	447,857	-151,227	4,116,118	1,108,483	798,847	13,111	459,411	217,562
1985	6,465,055	4,731,854	335,570	5,067,424	495,995	-152,613	4,418,816	1,183,985	862,254	13,632	474,243	223,569
1986	6,901,112	4,975,803	428,057	5,403,860	528,616	-145,814	4,729,430	1,231,623	940,059	14,193	486,217	227,198
1987	7,142,678	5,140,302	464,962	5,605,264	547,258	-125,235	4,932,771	1,227,457	982,450	14,345	497,910	231,475
1988	7,846,773	5,707,273	503,156	6,210,429	629,888	-133,969	5,446,572	1,334,289	1,065,912	15,356	510,980	243,334
1989	8,359,689	5,987,471	483,707	6,471,178	667,124	-129,372	5,674,682	1,502,157	1,182,850	15,835	527,922	245,816
1990	9,088,299	6,519,468	567,906	7,087,374	724,774	-146,082	6,216,518	1,565,483	1,306,298	16,538	549,535	253,759
1991	9,712,261	7,128,741	440,670	7,569,411	796,668	-167,838	6,604,905	1,626,595	1,480,761	17,059	569,346	267,697
1992	10,185,890	7,301,971	502,880	7,804,851	810,003	-150,334	6,844,514	1,606,521	1,734,855	17,267	589,897	262,789
1993	10,674,838	7,465,810	695,604	8,161,414	832,911	-147,121	7,181,382	1,637,204	1,856,252	17,796	599,843	262,890
1994	10,918,343	7,607,304	650,492	8,257,796	846,041	-138,549	7,273,206	1,739,977	1,905,160	17,762	614,707	266,806
1995	11,312,751	7,931,250	566,500	8,497,750	871,572	-141,365	7,484,813	1,818,440	2,009,498	18,240	620,201	278,216
1996	11,922,153	8,247,029	647,960	8,894,989	875,197	-129,687	7,890,105	1,917,736	2,114,312	19,023	626,719	288,670
1997	12,275,494	8,594,613	560,139	9,154,752	900,356	-124,396	8,130,000	2,036,391	2,109,103	19,341	634,695	289,487
1998	13,023,767	9,332,739	425,385	9,758,124	958,485	-122,151	8,677,488	2,146,150	2,200,129	20,254	643,016	303,568
1999	13,436,155	9,554,119	402,941	9,957,060	980,461	-92,364	8,884,235	2,213,595	2,338,325	20,500	655,428	309,279
2000	14,247,370	10,219,431	503,584	10,723,015	1,049,406	-82,897	9,590,712	2,252,809	2,403,849	21,463	663,803	310,380
2001	15,112,815	10,919,007	510,950	11,429,957	1,194,181	-78,422	10,157,354	2,293,327	2,662,134	22,337	676,574	308,719
2002	16,043,891	11,535,765	725,679	12,261,444	1,279,914	-64,345	10,917,185	2,251,410	2,875,296	23,116	694,059	314,547
2003	17,124,257	12,407,362	633,532	13,040,894	1,387,238	-70,995	11,582,661	2,438,204	3,103,392	23,974	714,272	321,583
2004	18,395,999	13,171,217	1,076,135	14,247,352	1,520,446	-45,652	12,681,254	2,427,856	3,286,889	24,985	736,296	325,071
2005	19,804,585	14,397,201	1,166,554	15,563,755	1,654,630	-37,953	13,871,172	2,472,194	3,461,219	26,034	760,726	341,797
2006	21,411,340	15,969,612	887,207	16,856,819	1,754,844	-29,329	15,072,646	2,597,376	3,741,318	27,293	784,511	354,872
2007	23,183,294	16,720,506	1,260,786	17,981,292	1,812,319	-12,443	16,156,530	2,995,787	4,030,977	28,861	803,281	363,997
2008	23,890,508	17,269,497	772,346	18,041,843	1,894,653	-3,343	16,143,847	3,194,890	4,551,771	29,194	818,327	364,545
2009	23,733,721	16,771,099	900,474	17,671,573	1,867,468	-86,229	15,717,876	3,007,666	5,008,179	28,590	830,137	349,093
2010	25,809,681	18,137,630	1,244,548	19,382,178	1,906,377	-151,530	17,324,271	2,980,662	5,504,748	30,669	841,554	348,463
2011	27,307,412	19,220,897	1,354,098	20,574,995	1,846,041	-219,610	18,509,344	3,279,021	5,519,047	32,141	849,606	361,943
2012	28,877,595	20,356,630	1,601,525	21,958,155	1,961,264	-304,680	19,692,211	3,640,554	5,544,830	33,731	856,127	381,656
2013	29,679,549	21,006,705	1,984,898	22,991,603	2,259,585	-339,544	20,392,474	3,524,267	5,762,808	34,301	865,259	393,876
2014	31,577,551	22,076,466	2,079,930	24,156,396	2,361,027	-355,682	21,439,687	4,041,470	6,096,394	36,164	873,177	404,205
2015	32,173,940	21,982,279	1,960,197	23,942,476	2,341,216	-323,478	21,277,782	4,294,598	6,601,560	36,532	880,708	404,833
2016	32,048,150	21,758,745	1,848,962	23,607,707	2,357,231	-318,819	20,931,657	4,225,264	6,891,229	36,168	886,081	406,704
2017	32,666,174	22,265,250	2,062,238	24,327,488	2,428,224	-364,122	21,535,142	4,335,189	6,795,843	36,574	893,150	411,526
2018	33,813,117	23,609,887	1,671,510	25,281,397	2,581,122	-394,868	22,305,407	4,414,615	7,093,095	37,557	900,315	422,599
2019	35,596,941	24,863,023	1,677,828	26,540,851	2,748,724	-431,018	23,361,109	4,643,311	7,592,521	39,271	906,453	429,434
2020	40,300,516	25,433,630	1,780,341	27,213,971	2,803,635	-475,371	23,934,965	5,001,821	11,363,730	44,490	905,828	418,187
2021	42,561,996	27,034,919	1,539,361	28,574,280	2,984,922	-453,830	25,135,528	4,994,431	12,432,037	46,651	912,351	434,270
2022	41,098,858	28,428,896	1,410,481	29,839,377	3,262,388	-432,921	26,144,068	5,266,223	9,688,567	44,862	916,108	455,060

Personal Income and Employment by Area: Baltimore-Columbia-Towson, MD

(Thousands of dollars, except as noted.)

Year	Personal income, total	Derivation of personal income								Per capita personal income (dollars)	Population (persons)	Total employment
		Earnings by place of work			Less: Contributions for government social insurance	Plus: Adjustment for residence	Equals: Net earnings by place of residence	Plus: Dividends, interest, and rent	Plus: Personal current transfer receipts			
		Nonfarm	Farm	Total								
1970	9,420,898	7,783,621	31,091	7,814,712	496,727	65,121	7,383,106	1,329,181	708,611	4,497	2,094,838	991,821
1971	10,314,326	8,380,680	23,419	8,404,099	552,062	144,280	7,996,317	1,454,228	863,781	4,838	2,132,113	994,410
1972	11,336,168	9,114,000	32,179	9,146,179	629,686	236,439	8,752,932	1,586,680	996,556	5,267	2,152,232	1,011,325
1973	12,535,270	10,041,060	47,689	10,088,749	797,680	318,125	9,609,194	1,784,358	1,141,718	5,782	2,167,899	1,041,876
1974	13,835,894	10,987,901	44,100	11,032,001	907,009	393,552	10,518,544	2,014,321	1,303,029	6,349	2,179,392	1,056,134
1975	14,987,764	11,626,158	50,531	11,676,689	956,010	485,063	11,205,742	2,149,559	1,632,463	6,861	2,184,332	1,038,096
1976	16,344,005	12,660,144	42,381	12,702,525	1,058,328	611,567	12,255,764	2,329,451	1,758,790	7,467	2,188,964	1,040,323
1977	17,827,450	13,748,804	32,102	13,780,906	1,154,071	753,890	13,380,725	2,571,031	1,875,694	8,096	2,201,877	1,068,371
1978	19,889,912	15,288,294	47,166	15,335,460	1,319,784	910,339	14,926,015	2,895,953	2,067,944	9,023	2,204,362	1,108,082
1979	21,953,870	16,746,277	44,409	16,790,686	1,515,579	1,103,496	16,378,603	3,237,762	2,337,505	9,938	2,209,160	1,139,209
1980	24,637,014	18,238,156	25,118	18,263,274	1,651,213	1,320,361	17,932,422	3,904,739	2,799,853	11,181	2,203,385	1,139,485
1981	27,239,720	19,959,348	36,098	19,995,446	1,938,378	1,310,455	19,367,523	4,712,969	3,159,228	12,301	2,214,413	1,146,005
1982	29,307,084	20,849,242	36,616	20,885,858	2,050,386	1,384,754	20,220,226	5,586,618	3,500,240	13,197	2,220,748	1,137,050
1983	31,333,811	22,518,185	29,743	22,547,928	2,279,282	1,452,291	21,720,937	5,816,385	3,796,489	14,061	2,228,439	1,164,025
1984	34,376,123	24,765,818	69,673	24,835,491	2,588,034	1,613,921	23,861,378	6,550,005	3,964,740	15,314	2,244,735	1,202,935
1985	37,049,517	26,919,116	68,515	26,987,631	2,895,298	1,773,196	25,865,529	7,012,773	4,171,215	16,423	2,255,970	1,243,523
1986	39,758,908	28,898,196	55,037	28,953,233	3,148,149	1,927,138	27,732,222	7,521,529	4,505,157	17,395	2,285,633	1,276,452
1987	42,343,693	31,231,004	67,075	31,298,079	3,371,142	2,092,435	30,019,372	7,755,304	4,569,017	18,333	2,309,719	1,332,191
1988	46,410,956	34,334,191	78,740	34,412,931	3,819,265	2,264,376	32,858,042	8,703,497	4,849,417	19,826	2,340,870	1,366,737
1989	49,662,240	36,436,528	78,618	36,515,146	4,076,345	2,397,515	34,836,316	9,582,741	5,243,183	21,038	2,360,610	1,393,176
1990	52,649,423	38,575,462	90,099	38,665,561	4,397,515	2,495,792	36,763,838	10,182,550	5,703,035	22,024	2,390,543	1,404,128
1991	54,664,733	39,562,706	77,117	39,639,823	4,548,857	2,581,863	37,672,829	10,576,306	6,415,598	22,606	2,418,136	1,358,484
1992	57,173,222	41,152,714	94,402	41,247,116	4,706,278	2,767,040	39,307,878	10,709,812	7,155,532	23,431	2,440,078	1,339,950
1993	59,139,990	42,528,842	96,257	42,625,099	4,858,716	2,908,926	40,675,309	11,042,693	7,421,988	24,060	2,458,038	1,347,488
1994	61,720,885	44,198,785	88,186	44,286,971	5,092,663	3,072,885	42,267,193	11,690,232	7,763,460	24,934	2,475,364	1,371,332
1995	64,631,961	46,019,964	78,522	46,098,486	5,271,529	3,169,341	43,996,298	12,564,763	8,070,900	25,953	2,490,370	1,394,314
1996	67,769,588	47,942,214	112,173	48,054,387	5,437,437	3,334,711	45,951,661	13,159,727	8,658,200	27,092	2,501,453	1,409,343
1997	71,899,178	50,712,845	91,119	50,803,964	5,714,623	3,594,943	48,684,284	14,421,439	8,793,455	28,605	2,513,492	1,436,116
1998	77,245,101	54,763,917	106,533	54,870,450	6,024,788	3,866,286	52,711,948	15,467,810	9,065,343	30,589	2,525,266	1,466,512
1999	82,042,768	59,216,255	106,605	59,322,860	6,433,162	4,204,385	57,094,083	15,382,923	9,565,762	32,296	2,540,307	1,509,853
2000	88,326,131	63,612,480	131,510	63,743,990	6,818,698	4,661,709	61,587,001	16,718,845	10,020,285	34,530	2,557,958	1,543,762
2001	92,156,912	66,769,920	110,311	66,880,231	7,351,630	4,695,480	64,224,081	17,129,449	10,803,382	35,783	2,575,471	1,547,690
2002	95,693,391	70,357,946	89,626	70,447,572	7,757,904	4,608,052	67,297,720	16,893,482	11,502,189	36,855	2,596,501	1,558,792
2003	99,399,264	73,098,566	74,370	73,172,936	8,066,081	4,769,194	69,876,049	17,201,676	12,321,539	38,022	2,614,232	1,566,959
2004	104,994,782	77,489,328	94,317	77,583,645	8,617,934	4,844,195	73,809,906	18,351,505	12,833,371	39,908	2,630,946	1,593,877
2005	110,639,844	82,204,248	77,069	82,281,317	9,100,392	5,119,028	78,299,953	18,441,463	13,898,428	41,842	2,644,231	1,623,891
2006	117,510,767	87,167,568	66,005	87,233,573	9,729,826	4,635,593	82,139,340	20,966,860	14,404,567	44,208	2,658,162	1,658,553
2007	123,439,192	90,484,333	60,414	90,544,747	10,187,966	4,681,389	85,038,170	22,795,385	15,605,637	46,273	2,667,619	1,689,172
2008	128,344,198	93,151,320	92,861	93,244,181	10,545,066	3,973,359	86,672,474	24,113,790	17,557,934	47,893	2,679,819	1,686,082
2009	127,134,172	93,026,128	123,247	93,149,375	10,481,717	3,534,619	86,202,277	21,961,058	18,970,837	47,156	2,696,018	1,649,420
2010	130,958,127	96,226,636	108,238	96,334,874	10,866,610	3,509,418	88,977,682	21,535,403	20,445,042	48,203	2,716,811	1,645,073
2011	137,557,660	100,191,675	117,209	100,308,884	10,082,450	2,881,028	93,107,462	23,454,803	20,995,395	50,218	2,739,196	1,677,197
2012	141,264,855	104,131,972	159,357	104,291,329	10,499,878	1,796,329	95,587,780	24,450,187	21,226,888	51,100	2,764,471	1,707,303
2013	142,041,402	106,457,942	167,384	106,625,326	12,013,980	1,487,400	96,098,746	24,043,260	21,899,396	51,048	2,782,512	1,734,286
2014	147,299,825	109,956,340	128,604	110,084,944	12,334,089	942,217	98,693,072	25,411,061	23,195,692	52,631	2,798,729	1,755,299
2015	152,902,458	114,392,112	82,285	114,474,397	12,963,986	540,601	102,051,012	26,739,761	24,111,685	54,356	2,812,978	1,788,441
2016	157,209,112	118,277,863	82,079	118,359,942	13,237,381	88,192	105,210,753	26,743,507	25,254,852	55,720	2,821,424	1,814,636
2017	162,851,181	121,845,981	125,176	121,971,157	13,646,370	79,321	108,404,108	28,787,808	25,659,265	57,539	2,830,275	1,834,627
2018	168,643,491	126,383,363	72,067	126,455,430	14,371,165	10,690	112,094,955	29,804,824	26,743,712	59,432	2,837,598	1,864,180
2019	175,608,562	130,808,875	134,201	130,943,076	14,934,521	576,670	116,585,225	31,234,916	27,788,421	61,771	2,842,883	1,861,999
2020	186,680,910	133,038,362	95,379	133,133,741	15,213,221	977,166	118,897,686	31,316,865	36,466,359	65,676	2,842,463	1,798,543
2021	199,099,852	140,770,581	158,784	140,929,365	16,253,220	689,454	125,365,599	33,841,082	39,893,171	70,023	2,843,354	1,860,479
2022	202,523,076	148,242,625	136,870	148,379,495	17,339,671	1,097,006	132,136,830	35,701,420	34,684,826	71,420	2,835,672	1,929,613

Personal Income and Employment by Area: Bangor, ME

(Thousands of dollars, except as noted.)

Year	Personal income, total	Derivation of personal income: Earnings by place of work: Nonfarm	Farm	Total	Less: Contributions for government social insurance	Plus: Adjustment for residence	Equals: Net earnings by place of residence	Plus: Dividends, interest, and rent	Plus: Personal current transfer receipts	Per capita personal income (dollars)	Population (persons)	Total employment
1970	412,911	334,644	4,999	339,643	24,136	-2,996	312,511	57,990	42,410	3,282	125,812	53,058
1971	446,233	360,661	4,725	365,386	26,637	-5,384	333,365	62,468	50,400	3,488	127,935	53,213
1972	493,117	403,087	5,027	408,114	31,014	-8,233	368,867	67,583	56,667	3,822	129,035	54,697
1973	547,346	443,745	9,235	452,980	38,652	-9,060	405,268	75,253	66,825	4,185	130,797	57,117
1974	609,213	479,220	10,276	489,496	43,214	-4,829	441,453	86,528	81,232	4,614	132,038	58,222
1975	676,072	526,793	5,129	531,922	47,314	-8,272	476,336	96,199	103,537	5,067	133,434	59,000
1976	768,008	607,507	12,834	620,341	56,185	-10,571	553,585	102,596	111,827	5,666	135,542	61,770
1977	825,136	661,538	5,670	667,208	60,903	-14,938	591,367	114,349	119,420	6,061	136,134	63,665
1978	906,943	731,169	6,218	737,387	68,841	-18,780	649,766	128,697	128,480	6,624	136,912	65,596
1979	1,012,544	823,157	4,827	827,984	79,837	-23,430	724,717	143,057	144,770	7,382	137,157	67,939
1980	1,130,548	900,280	2,486	902,766	86,748	-27,548	788,470	170,581	171,497	8,238	137,228	68,884
1981	1,232,552	961,500	8,985	970,485	99,796	-34,106	836,583	201,520	194,449	8,935	137,952	68,180
1982	1,317,126	1,004,640	7,172	1,011,812	106,957	-35,775	869,080	236,268	211,778	9,543	138,020	67,853
1983	1,423,347	1,097,490	5,266	1,102,756	117,253	-41,548	943,955	250,908	228,484	10,307	138,101	69,290
1984	1,569,032	1,217,415	8,837	1,226,252	134,109	-45,212	1,046,931	280,855	241,246	11,330	138,488	71,880
1985	1,662,690	1,291,851	6,847	1,298,698	142,720	-46,503	1,109,475	299,593	253,622	11,992	138,654	73,522
1986	1,761,903	1,363,505	7,908	1,371,413	149,155	-46,070	1,176,188	322,532	263,183	12,660	139,169	74,368
1987	1,917,920	1,511,111	9,727	1,520,838	162,172	-53,500	1,305,166	342,638	270,116	13,679	140,207	76,675
1988	2,125,017	1,686,494	8,582	1,695,076	184,350	-61,776	1,448,950	388,942	287,125	14,898	142,639	80,867
1989	2,294,454	1,840,411	8,983	1,849,394	197,205	-66,925	1,585,264	398,778	310,412	15,780	145,402	82,915
1990	2,368,575	1,868,941	11,056	1,879,997	210,934	-62,442	1,606,621	413,199	348,755	16,108	147,046	82,886
1991	2,428,861	1,860,744	7,187	1,867,931	211,944	-65,701	1,590,286	439,669	398,906	16,488	147,315	80,019
1992	2,535,397	1,951,744	10,722	1,962,466	224,740	-70,779	1,666,947	431,188	437,262	17,314	146,435	80,228
1993	2,638,676	2,034,549	9,406	2,043,955	240,364	-74,733	1,728,858	439,522	470,296	17,981	146,752	82,174
1994	2,743,954	2,103,393	7,486	2,110,879	251,418	-77,337	1,782,124	469,925	491,905	18,666	147,000	82,635
1995	2,808,763	2,136,625	6,318	2,142,943	257,778	-79,564	1,805,601	485,183	517,979	19,275	145,724	82,741
1996	2,927,217	2,196,852	8,227	2,205,079	261,809	-79,117	1,864,153	510,281	552,783	20,138	145,356	83,203
1997	3,073,096	2,301,036	4,537	2,305,573	273,134	-83,599	1,948,840	545,305	578,951	21,207	144,910	83,642
1998	3,252,500	2,457,212	7,392	2,464,604	288,033	-92,875	2,083,696	569,394	599,410	22,497	144,574	85,931
1999	3,376,111	2,606,726	8,026	2,614,752	301,186	-101,797	2,211,769	546,106	618,236	23,299	144,902	86,803
2000	3,612,489	2,773,485	7,803	2,781,288	313,688	-107,485	2,360,115	599,250	653,124	24,925	144,937	89,410
2001	3,753,603	2,920,462	6,979	2,927,441	331,092	-127,140	2,469,209	586,956	697,438	25,690	146,110	90,067
2002	3,915,579	3,034,124	4,219	3,038,343	334,989	-134,413	2,568,941	603,878	742,760	26,583	147,298	90,461
2003	4,044,522	3,059,984	4,881	3,064,865	334,998	-128,166	2,601,701	626,721	816,100	27,188	148,759	89,794
2004	4,196,408	3,193,779	7,769	3,201,548	349,996	-138,813	2,712,739	604,731	878,938	28,199	148,814	90,965
2005	4,360,515	3,334,943	6,332	3,341,275	369,621	-150,909	2,820,745	587,574	952,196	29,123	149,726	92,336
2006	4,519,216	3,469,144	3,322	3,472,466	387,378	-160,302	2,924,786	615,693	978,737	29,840	151,446	93,311
2007	4,719,258	3,535,700	6,682	3,542,382	402,478	-167,279	2,972,625	691,228	1,055,405	31,000	152,232	94,138
2008	4,973,942	3,599,150	6,933	3,606,083	414,845	-172,219	3,019,019	739,501	1,215,422	32,431	153,372	93,708
2009	5,127,916	3,693,418	5,565	3,698,983	416,100	-177,860	3,105,023	707,706	1,315,187	33,348	153,770	91,486
2010	5,147,853	3,659,060	18,774	3,677,834	417,813	-161,913	3,098,108	721,460	1,328,285	33,454	153,877	89,460
2011	5,327,886	3,683,608	10,822	3,694,430	380,334	-157,906	3,156,190	785,000	1,386,696	34,632	153,842	89,531
2012	5,350,985	3,709,713	15,166	3,724,879	388,476	-152,163	3,184,240	787,911	1,378,834	34,860	153,501	89,682
2013	5,393,798	3,772,899	13,593	3,786,492	448,443	-142,094	3,195,955	791,759	1,406,084	35,152	153,444	90,214
2014	5,514,328	3,862,549	13,204	3,875,753	453,687	-140,933	3,281,133	801,031	1,432,164	35,927	153,487	90,517
2015	5,680,542	3,997,668	6,448	4,004,116	476,377	-154,008	3,373,731	815,378	1,491,433	37,305	152,271	90,457
2016	5,822,043	4,050,791	4,951	4,055,742	481,143	-156,880	3,417,719	868,096	1,536,228	38,378	151,703	90,403
2017	6,008,031	4,177,159	5,691	4,182,850	497,845	-159,144	3,525,861	906,674	1,575,496	39,497	152,112	90,591
2018	6,265,546	4,384,588	3,120	4,387,708	528,142	-178,990	3,680,576	932,964	1,652,006	41,176	152,166	91,895
2019	6,505,888	4,552,924	8,539	4,561,463	547,936	-201,722	3,811,805	962,878	1,731,205	42,736	152,234	92,418
2020	7,191,988	4,783,044	4,766	4,787,810	573,532	-212,129	4,002,149	996,854	2,192,985	47,264	152,165	89,214
2021	7,756,839	5,140,367	7,481	5,147,848	615,873	-193,039	4,338,936	1,061,963	2,355,940	50,753	152,834	92,232
2022	7,992,291	5,505,532	9,553	5,515,085	666,587	-208,803	4,639,695	1,130,522	2,222,074	51,998	153,704	96,022

Personal Income and Employment by Area: Barnstable Town, MA

(Thousands of dollars, except as noted.)

Year	Personal income, total	Derivation of personal income								Per capita personal income (dollars)	Population (persons)	Total employment
		Earnings by place of work			Less: Contributions for government social insurance	Plus: Adjustment for residence	Equals: Net earnings by place of residence	Plus: Dividends, interest, and rent	Plus: Personal current transfer receipts			
		Nonfarm	Farm	Total								
1970	467,126	295,491	1,016	296,507	17,483	-10,716	268,308	143,900	54,918	4,785	97,632	47,104
1971	537,720	331,593	942	332,535	20,635	-4,014	307,886	160,261	69,573	5,418	99,244	49,746
1972	614,361	371,515	1,042	372,557	24,040	3,759	352,276	178,694	83,391	6,191	99,237	52,776
1973	686,560	409,426	1,303	410,729	30,244	17,073	397,558	190,705	98,297	6,180	111,093	57,102
1974	756,444	429,015	1,271	430,286	32,765	29,222	426,743	210,591	119,110	6,109	123,816	57,828
1975	852,195	459,968	1,063	461,031	34,194	42,233	469,070	225,775	157,350	6,584	129,437	58,475
1976	966,532	529,904	1,205	531,109	39,344	54,757	546,522	251,143	168,867	7,259	133,142	61,244
1977	1,092,583	597,808	1,215	599,023	44,795	70,656	624,884	285,392	182,307	7,913	138,071	65,095
1978	1,240,807	685,664	1,853	687,517	52,316	90,647	725,848	315,846	199,113	8,802	140,966	69,572
1979	1,423,426	766,689	1,531	768,220	61,720	116,878	823,378	367,574	232,474	9,732	146,265	73,652
1980	1,651,175	846,968	2,161	849,129	69,045	147,756	927,840	449,564	273,771	11,093	148,847	76,419
1981	1,879,199	932,662	2,144	934,806	82,871	154,505	1,006,440	550,620	322,139	12,348	152,189	78,745
1982	2,104,036	996,095	2,902	998,997	91,500	165,848	1,073,345	674,174	356,517	13,622	154,460	81,237
1983	2,322,705	1,131,883	5,211	1,137,094	105,359	180,737	1,212,472	730,655	379,578	14,764	157,320	86,481
1984	2,663,707	1,334,972	4,481	1,339,453	128,140	202,418	1,413,731	840,601	409,375	16,429	162,135	92,174
1985	2,947,615	1,530,626	4,296	1,534,922	150,310	225,312	1,609,924	894,974	442,717	17,695	166,578	96,878
1986	3,245,177	1,718,921	4,405	1,723,326	174,084	248,003	1,797,245	970,473	477,459	18,908	171,633	101,045
1987	3,581,189	1,978,263	3,632	1,981,895	198,958	288,392	2,071,329	1,004,513	505,347	20,323	176,215	100,196
1988	3,924,102	2,162,931	4,838	2,167,769	221,023	321,312	2,268,058	1,121,581	534,463	21,664	181,137	104,357
1989	4,041,039	2,188,168	4,793	2,192,961	224,702	335,110	2,303,369	1,150,737	586,933	21,886	184,642	102,008
1990	4,324,096	2,167,716	4,460	2,172,176	219,873	390,739	2,343,042	1,313,295	667,759	23,082	187,335	100,006
1991	4,398,230	2,169,782	6,354	2,176,136	224,243	399,445	2,351,338	1,296,961	749,931	23,251	189,165	96,477
1992	4,690,688	2,324,864	6,365	2,331,229	237,615	424,900	2,518,514	1,360,289	811,885	24,482	191,595	99,683
1993	5,022,671	2,469,225	6,266	2,475,491	253,387	474,134	2,696,238	1,465,848	860,585	25,780	194,830	103,453
1994	5,340,640	2,641,858	5,500	2,647,358	273,854	528,302	2,901,806	1,535,199	903,635	26,901	198,533	107,427
1995	5,713,283	2,807,648	5,627	2,813,275	294,442	588,562	3,107,395	1,639,643	966,245	28,162	202,874	109,482
1996	6,136,634	2,998,292	9,896	3,008,188	308,868	625,068	3,324,388	1,785,904	1,026,342	29,667	206,852	112,108
1997	6,495,132	3,144,317	12,317	3,156,634	327,633	718,551	3,547,552	1,874,290	1,073,290	30,873	210,380	116,668
1998	7,061,199	3,452,014	3,014	3,455,028	355,236	806,527	3,906,319	2,052,011	1,102,869	32,920	214,497	121,308
1999	7,648,222	3,917,060	2,184	3,919,244	392,936	888,760	4,415,068	2,076,839	1,156,315	34,930	218,960	126,407
2000	8,069,562	4,058,090	3,581	4,061,671	408,383	1,011,313	4,664,601	2,173,958	1,231,003	36,181	223,031	131,099
2001	8,870,705	4,679,467	2,317	4,681,784	455,093	1,008,118	5,234,809	2,286,010	1,349,886	39,586	224,087	131,337
2002	8,921,528	4,954,247	3,135	4,957,382	484,998	963,775	5,436,159	2,055,854	1,429,515	39,577	225,421	133,340
2003	9,176,495	5,208,704	3,236	5,211,940	510,672	915,566	5,616,834	2,057,233	1,502,428	40,602	226,011	135,967
2004	9,794,989	5,560,404	4,216	5,564,620	561,406	930,200	5,933,414	2,299,632	1,561,943	43,676	224,264	138,761
2005	9,780,709	5,612,510	4,402	5,616,912	589,537	909,559	5,936,934	2,200,716	1,643,059	44,058	221,995	139,159
2006	10,163,094	5,728,237	4,621	5,732,858	601,340	900,473	6,031,991	2,380,641	1,750,462	46,188	220,037	138,664
2007	10,467,061	5,725,120	6,395	5,731,515	617,240	943,507	6,057,782	2,578,238	1,831,041	47,930	218,380	141,005
2008	10,773,876	5,697,997	8,762	5,706,759	622,074	861,175	5,945,860	2,795,969	2,032,047	49,634	217,066	139,833
2009	10,744,500	5,633,469	5,917	5,639,386	611,219	902,601	5,930,768	2,587,588	2,226,144	49,744	215,994	136,756
2010	11,143,892	5,866,277	7,074	5,873,351	613,349	893,762	6,153,764	2,658,113	2,332,015	51,523	216,289	136,167
2011	11,589,425	6,030,900	6,667	6,037,567	580,542	1,014,826	6,471,851	2,776,354	2,341,220	53,334	217,298	136,702
2012	12,063,951	6,285,860	8,464	6,294,324	602,567	1,043,290	6,735,047	2,958,207	2,370,697	55,263	218,300	139,344
2013	12,183,712	6,477,080	6,770	6,483,850	683,262	969,016	6,769,604	2,987,094	2,427,014	55,482	219,597	142,566
2014	12,805,698	6,695,130	3,091	6,698,221	715,421	866,198	6,848,998	3,455,106	2,501,594	57,961	220,938	145,008
2015	13,416,252	6,966,802	3,059	6,969,861	733,819	908,549	7,144,591	3,585,654	2,686,007	60,404	222,109	150,132
2016	13,942,986	7,183,482	2,252	7,185,734	765,448	1,042,281	7,462,567	3,684,682	2,795,737	62,393	223,471	151,450
2017	14,450,339	7,412,045	3,175	7,415,220	795,405	1,131,377	7,751,192	3,836,705	2,862,442	64,192	225,110	152,558
2018	15,199,571	7,771,240	3,943	7,775,183	840,993	1,128,190	8,062,380	4,118,455	3,018,736	67,070	226,622	153,912
2019	16,546,165	8,226,936	5,805	8,232,741	878,987	1,548,437	8,902,191	4,453,783	3,190,191	72,791	227,312	151,520
2020	18,218,342	8,043,984	6,084	8,050,068	860,538	2,169,272	9,358,802	4,598,529	4,261,011	79,606	228,856	141,669
2021	19,512,593	8,797,763	3,730	8,801,493	960,948	2,352,326	10,192,871	4,843,158	4,476,564	83,891	232,594	149,112
2022	19,832,524	9,200,810	3,134	9,203,944	1,019,794	2,591,049	10,775,199	5,143,110	3,914,215	85,317	232,457	155,665

Personal Income and Employment by Area: Baton Rouge, LA

(Thousands of dollars, except as noted.)

Year	Personal income, total	Derivation of personal income								Per capita personal income (dollars)	Population (persons)	Total employment
		Earnings by place of work			Less: Contributions for government social insurance	Plus: Adjustment for residence	Equals: Net earnings by place of residence	Plus: Dividends, interest, and rent	Plus: Personal current transfer receipts			
		Nonfarm	Farm	Total								
1970	1,576,705	1,257,251	33,303	1,290,554	79,389	26,654	1,237,819	204,337	134,549	3,238	486,888	180,490
1971	1,725,983	1,372,770	35,181	1,407,951	88,834	26,315	1,345,432	227,420	153,131	3,478	496,250	185,067
1972	1,908,876	1,516,551	41,705	1,558,256	102,910	32,542	1,487,888	251,134	169,854	3,749	509,145	193,801
1973	2,128,227	1,683,102	63,396	1,746,498	131,770	31,283	1,646,011	281,542	200,674	4,110	517,875	204,363
1974	2,510,325	1,982,009	82,087	2,064,096	161,028	32,465	1,935,533	338,282	236,510	4,754	528,099	217,634
1975	2,860,666	2,285,637	38,311	2,323,948	181,457	33,894	2,176,385	388,043	296,238	5,312	538,564	229,117
1976	3,361,442	2,744,189	56,290	2,800,479	223,906	30,987	2,607,560	425,844	328,038	6,073	553,502	245,478
1977	3,787,782	3,121,918	43,910	3,165,828	249,771	34,487	2,950,544	474,776	362,462	6,645	570,000	252,012
1978	4,310,005	3,583,647	38,770	3,622,417	294,735	41,112	3,368,794	549,746	391,465	7,400	582,400	268,051
1979	4,894,384	4,048,765	40,769	4,089,534	343,507	65,039	3,811,066	632,231	451,087	8,166	599,371	275,626
1980	5,794,804	4,763,787	24,042	4,787,829	402,058	52,445	4,438,216	819,583	537,005	9,394	616,887	289,611
1981	6,541,846	5,299,508	32,108	5,331,616	479,563	63,963	4,916,016	1,021,208	604,622	10,393	629,470	297,247
1982	7,017,073	5,560,143	29,322	5,589,465	506,015	48,302	5,131,752	1,191,762	693,559	10,931	641,928	299,016
1983	7,410,024	5,702,570	31,170	5,733,740	510,116	64,509	5,288,133	1,323,127	798,764	11,363	652,140	297,956
1984	7,927,684	6,081,620	15,474	6,097,094	557,103	68,114	5,608,105	1,478,952	840,627	12,067	656,970	308,997
1985	8,315,408	6,297,131	21,353	6,318,484	578,082	55,582	5,795,984	1,612,669	906,755	12,588	660,608	309,050
1986	8,278,216	6,151,571	31,010	6,182,581	553,007	43,150	5,672,724	1,603,382	1,002,110	12,537	660,308	301,582
1987	8,324,679	6,239,553	26,046	6,265,599	552,852	34,613	5,747,360	1,560,950	1,016,369	12,767	652,064	302,148
1988	8,936,338	6,817,980	53,778	6,871,758	641,558	15,661	6,245,861	1,619,793	1,070,684	13,792	647,939	309,761
1989	9,674,715	7,300,395	37,913	7,338,308	699,572	24,399	6,663,135	1,853,358	1,158,222	14,969	646,296	315,087
1990	10,501,923	8,026,787	35,919	8,062,706	793,284	34,574	7,303,996	1,913,229	1,284,698	16,206	648,009	327,540
1991	11,172,441	8,601,132	24,284	8,625,416	872,897	-5,624	7,746,895	1,959,614	1,465,932	16,983	657,862	336,736
1992	12,217,986	9,444,718	48,144	9,492,862	949,574	-29,932	8,513,356	2,008,305	1,696,325	18,241	669,807	346,882
1993	12,708,052	9,733,890	41,290	9,775,180	985,942	-17,676	8,771,562	2,074,080	1,862,410	18,692	679,884	354,288
1994	13,627,237	10,311,173	39,495	10,350,668	1,072,591	-19,300	9,258,777	2,273,132	2,095,328	19,832	687,147	362,657
1995	14,321,771	10,803,702	47,617	10,851,319	1,125,169	-14,669	9,711,481	2,467,324	2,142,966	20,633	694,120	374,802
1996	15,012,054	11,381,348	59,412	11,440,760	1,198,443	-19,459	10,222,858	2,600,808	2,188,388	21,406	701,312	384,506
1997	15,609,452	11,916,872	55,607	11,972,479	1,249,842	-12,018	10,710,619	2,674,625	2,224,208	22,016	709,007	389,227
1998	16,593,519	12,753,768	42,150	12,795,918	1,351,094	-16,896	11,427,928	2,918,803	2,246,788	23,167	716,245	402,809
1999	17,167,689	13,391,961	59,778	13,451,739	1,398,847	-39,359	12,013,533	2,856,401	2,297,755	23,708	724,139	412,481
2000	18,201,285	14,199,277	60,411	14,259,688	1,453,728	-48,147	12,757,813	3,055,486	2,387,986	24,902	730,913	422,692
2001	19,129,166	14,784,415	58,899	14,843,314	1,477,134	-59,232	13,306,948	3,086,899	2,735,319	26,064	733,925	419,933
2002	19,784,580	15,381,416	48,922	15,430,338	1,539,141	-80,897	13,810,300	3,046,019	2,928,261	26,787	738,589	421,115
2003	20,620,977	16,117,354	53,694	16,171,048	1,590,813	-102,420	14,477,815	3,178,345	2,964,817	27,659	745,536	427,179
2004	22,208,337	17,107,166	56,090	17,163,256	1,647,664	-70,178	15,445,414	3,438,410	3,324,513	29,490	753,093	430,923
2005	24,253,957	18,027,998	50,038	18,078,036	1,716,998	-93,415	16,267,623	3,695,052	4,291,282	31,968	758,706	446,999
2006	26,552,588	19,671,658	68,930	19,740,588	1,889,641	393,180	18,244,127	4,172,388	4,136,073	33,382	795,417	468,421
2007	28,762,615	21,060,654	60,271	21,120,925	2,037,788	449,180	19,532,317	4,953,982	4,276,316	35,804	803,339	479,779
2008	30,895,323	22,377,368	50,733	22,428,101	2,157,738	455,826	20,726,189	5,234,996	4,934,138	38,081	811,301	487,183
2009	30,648,566	22,716,221	54,682	22,770,903	2,191,237	47,531	20,627,197	4,841,185	5,180,184	37,403	819,405	486,015
2010	31,717,852	23,049,043	66,105	23,115,148	2,203,707	260,615	21,172,056	4,983,265	5,562,531	38,308	827,959	481,630
2011	33,540,431	23,774,461	72,925	23,847,386	2,048,094	473,355	22,272,647	5,603,220	5,664,564	40,262	833,044	486,893
2012	34,714,086	24,992,523	89,687	25,082,210	2,150,627	135,603	23,067,186	5,858,427	5,788,473	41,375	839,003	494,154
2013	35,368,503	26,151,043	95,659	26,246,702	2,565,281	-205,220	23,476,201	5,917,544	5,974,758	41,804	846,054	506,705
2014	36,547,035	27,189,233	52,592	27,241,825	2,657,884	-285,905	24,298,036	6,292,345	5,956,654	42,887	852,164	518,850
2015	37,270,858	28,059,988	36,466	28,096,454	2,800,416	-663,567	24,632,471	6,034,154	6,604,233	43,452	857,755	523,500
2016	38,105,971	28,214,605	18,797	28,233,402	2,858,040	-781,938	24,593,424	6,578,099	6,934,448	44,066	864,743	525,839
2017	39,167,846	29,103,420	27,751	29,131,171	2,947,715	-926,726	25,256,730	6,758,227	7,152,889	45,363	863,436	529,315
2018	41,046,161	30,692,722	24,190	30,716,912	3,122,411	-1,159,747	26,434,754	7,145,080	7,466,327	47,449	865,057	539,332
2019	42,617,759	31,440,761	42,616	31,483,377	3,176,855	-1,075,615	27,230,907	7,526,474	7,860,378	49,094	868,080	538,105
2020	45,803,762	31,464,340	55,540	31,519,880	3,177,320	-647,034	27,695,526	7,381,713	10,726,523	52,635	870,220	517,538
2021	49,601,855	33,216,139	79,395	33,295,534	3,345,999	-806,382	29,143,153	8,413,305	12,045,397	56,839	872,673	544,876
2022	49,674,323	35,117,332	31,653	35,148,985	3,643,573	-704,360	30,801,052	8,558,484	10,314,787	56,897	873,060	566,405

Personal Income and Employment by Area: Battle Creek, MI

(Thousands of dollars, except as noted.)

Year	Personal income, total	Derivation of personal income								Per capita personal income (dollars)	Population (persons)	Total employment
		Earnings by place of work			Less: Contributions for government social insurance	Plus: Adjustment for residence	Equals: Net earnings by place of residence	Plus: Dividends, interest, and rent	Plus: Personal current transfer receipts			
		Nonfarm	Farm	Total								
1970	576,982	500,248	7,173	507,421	36,214	-26,553	444,654	74,283	58,045	4,076	141,561	62,407
1971	628,950	546,341	6,267	552,608	40,854	-33,271	478,483	81,254	69,213	4,472	140,647	63,123
1972	692,203	604,719	9,419	614,138	47,211	-40,066	526,861	88,679	76,663	4,876	141,963	64,437
1973	761,421	672,120	15,821	687,941	60,903	-47,757	579,281	95,994	86,146	5,349	142,349	66,077
1974	806,447	708,617	7,321	715,938	66,185	-53,975	595,778	107,386	103,283	5,639	143,021	66,005
1975	895,883	762,360	12,747	775,107	69,442	-64,100	641,565	118,972	135,346	6,281	142,640	64,320
1976	980,447	857,529	9,566	867,095	80,024	-77,455	709,616	128,389	142,442	6,887	142,359	66,464
1977	1,061,283	943,955	8,157	952,112	88,510	-89,130	774,472	143,440	143,371	7,433	142,772	67,485
1978	1,163,902	1,047,678	6,575	1,054,253	100,211	-103,802	850,240	157,899	155,763	8,113	143,463	68,846
1979	1,263,039	1,130,988	6,581	1,137,569	112,584	-117,738	907,247	177,729	178,063	8,873	142,341	69,077
1980	1,340,174	1,142,470	4,081	1,146,551	112,244	-124,667	909,640	207,928	222,606	9,458	141,701	65,129
1981	1,451,028	1,202,812	10,190	1,213,002	127,255	-126,719	959,028	245,975	246,025	10,227	141,880	62,898
1982	1,515,673	1,199,419	2,563	1,201,982	127,081	-125,214	949,687	285,836	280,150	10,835	139,886	59,788
1983	1,554,100	1,221,002	-5,022	1,215,980	133,201	-121,649	961,130	300,460	292,510	11,292	137,629	59,063
1984	1,636,407	1,275,636	7,011	1,282,647	143,995	-122,003	1,016,649	328,042	291,716	12,061	135,682	59,859
1985	1,756,774	1,399,947	7,368	1,407,315	162,003	-134,740	1,110,572	347,740	298,462	13,059	134,523	61,694
1986	1,849,296	1,473,452	8,658	1,482,110	172,267	-139,362	1,170,481	365,805	313,010	13,768	134,316	62,869
1987	1,973,016	1,620,896	9,943	1,630,839	186,783	-159,302	1,284,754	368,128	320,134	14,631	134,849	66,233
1988	2,064,462	1,731,766	6,745	1,738,511	207,464	-169,553	1,361,494	371,253	331,715	15,354	134,459	66,844
1989	2,212,022	1,821,811	16,229	1,838,040	216,946	-171,425	1,449,669	407,756	354,597	16,330	135,457	67,838
1990	2,323,070	1,932,491	13,863	1,946,354	232,873	-180,538	1,532,943	412,526	377,601	17,053	136,226	69,258
1991	2,439,616	2,039,389	9,803	2,049,192	248,912	-197,954	1,602,326	420,613	416,677	17,832	136,814	71,364
1992	2,589,312	2,199,098	10,524	2,209,622	266,635	-221,296	1,721,691	427,387	440,234	18,859	137,298	72,964
1993	2,675,484	2,253,999	11,144	2,265,143	276,241	-221,768	1,767,134	438,432	469,918	19,419	137,775	73,362
1994	2,837,216	2,400,182	10,077	2,410,259	299,050	-238,393	1,872,816	487,384	477,016	20,573	137,910	75,666
1995	2,934,223	2,506,336	8,068	2,514,404	313,032	-250,736	1,950,636	484,702	498,885	21,356	137,393	78,757
1996	3,035,165	2,577,393	7,857	2,585,250	314,813	-252,279	2,018,158	498,790	518,217	22,214	136,630	77,972
1997	3,226,800	2,766,412	10,019	2,776,431	334,717	-274,919	2,166,795	507,598	552,407	23,582	136,834	80,495
1998	3,341,205	2,873,916	9,059	2,882,975	340,302	-278,926	2,263,747	532,885	544,573	24,250	137,783	78,310
1999	3,398,763	2,861,055	8,029	2,869,084	337,500	-259,013	2,272,571	543,773	582,419	24,625	138,021	75,611
2000	3,470,443	2,898,094	10,171	2,908,265	340,899	-265,474	2,301,892	564,545	604,006	25,146	138,014	75,174
2001	3,543,581	2,890,670	14,323	2,904,993	341,903	-257,764	2,305,326	560,969	677,286	25,649	138,158	77,978
2002	3,672,117	3,048,803	7,463	3,056,266	358,780	-286,590	2,410,896	561,476	699,745	26,498	138,580	77,979
2003	3,753,680	3,066,844	9,505	3,076,349	359,520	-271,482	2,445,347	569,841	738,492	27,012	138,962	76,412
2004	3,849,902	3,171,584	22,202	3,193,786	373,927	-308,034	2,511,825	571,178	766,899	27,609	139,443	76,705
2005	3,935,517	3,214,036	15,279	3,229,315	381,265	-318,831	2,529,219	595,013	811,285	28,324	138,946	75,647
2006	3,991,139	3,266,981	7,206	3,274,187	395,026	-327,148	2,552,013	568,172	870,954	28,860	138,291	74,705
2007	4,123,950	3,312,816	12,687	3,325,503	399,721	-348,565	2,577,217	601,289	945,444	29,974	137,582	74,217
2008	4,311,942	3,389,588	8,993	3,398,581	413,356	-403,943	2,581,282	668,025	1,062,635	31,402	137,313	72,222
2009	4,235,994	3,294,772	15,712	3,310,484	405,291	-440,524	2,464,669	615,022	1,156,303	31,078	136,301	68,940
2010	4,360,191	3,376,074	27,811	3,403,885	411,131	-496,021	2,496,733	619,723	1,243,735	32,068	135,967	68,650
2011	4,459,148	3,365,382	49,872	3,415,254	368,945	-488,416	2,557,893	665,495	1,235,760	32,987	135,180	69,081
2012	4,585,563	3,528,101	12,862	3,540,963	386,177	-529,221	2,625,565	735,569	1,224,429	33,998	134,878	68,489
2013	4,618,184	3,595,526	23,916	3,619,442	444,751	-539,240	2,635,451	736,108	1,246,625	34,219	134,960	69,536
2014	4,726,000	3,700,351	2,113	3,702,464	457,025	-583,782	2,661,657	771,303	1,293,040	34,987	135,079	70,344
2015	4,965,488	3,847,546	2,275	3,849,821	472,378	-610,497	2,766,946	823,655	1,374,887	36,873	134,665	71,328
2016	5,033,871	3,964,949	2,007	3,966,956	482,645	-650,469	2,833,842	800,118	1,399,911	37,374	134,688	71,215
2017	5,111,214	4,008,972	6,844	4,015,816	489,090	-633,532	2,893,194	832,503	1,385,517	37,994	134,526	70,753
2018	5,218,461	4,056,242	6,888	4,063,130	503,400	-635,508	2,924,222	852,916	1,441,323	38,854	134,311	69,922
2019	5,373,951	4,034,585	4,327	4,038,912	501,752	-532,329	3,004,831	852,515	1,516,605	40,010	134,314	68,695
2020	5,849,429	4,043,490	24,107	4,067,597	503,893	-612,124	2,951,580	833,574	2,064,275	43,593	134,184	64,858
2021	6,102,372	4,281,035	28,701	4,309,736	529,012	-662,109	3,118,615	851,431	2,132,326	45,582	133,878	66,469
2022	5,985,202	4,537,028	20,900	4,557,928	577,717	-683,241	3,296,970	896,708	1,791,524	44,904	133,289	68,808

Personal Income and Employment by Area: Bay City, MI

(Thousands of dollars, except as noted.)

Year	Personal income, total	Derivation of personal income: Earnings by place of work: Nonfarm	Farm	Total	Less: Contributions for government social insurance	Plus: Adjustment for residence	Equals: Net earnings by place of residence	Plus: Dividends, interest, and rent	Plus: Personal current transfer receipts	Per capita personal income (dollars)	Population (persons)	Total employment
1970	420,933	293,171	5,220	298,391	20,928	44,339	321,802	58,218	40,913	3,582	117,502	39,729
1971	464,555	319,945	4,167	324,112	23,426	52,885	353,571	62,993	47,991	3,920	118,513	39,422
1972	499,669	342,221	4,894	347,115	26,568	58,462	379,009	68,296	52,364	4,196	119,094	39,885
1973	561,721	385,948	11,092	397,040	34,621	65,470	427,889	75,372	58,460	4,688	119,824	41,851
1974	621,936	413,451	23,624	437,075	38,401	64,229	462,903	85,811	73,222	5,159	120,548	41,896
1975	662,994	428,891	10,222	439,113	39,024	70,387	470,476	97,405	95,113	5,505	120,441	40,211
1976	755,195	490,642	10,673	501,315	45,513	98,700	554,502	103,975	96,718	6,264	120,560	41,485
1977	862,681	562,104	10,968	573,072	52,335	124,738	645,475	116,510	100,696	7,100	121,500	43,222
1978	949,558	611,899	13,745	625,644	58,492	148,382	715,534	126,272	107,752	7,780	122,057	43,662
1979	1,037,642	653,386	17,957	671,343	64,790	164,777	771,330	141,709	124,603	8,570	121,074	43,509
1980	1,133,578	665,840	26,055	691,895	65,510	157,780	784,165	173,437	175,976	9,444	120,037	41,737
1981	1,220,242	734,563	4,991	739,554	78,205	170,925	832,274	209,754	178,214	10,135	120,401	42,279
1982	1,263,556	727,939	6,508	734,447	78,800	160,042	815,689	244,241	203,626	10,636	118,804	40,466
1983	1,329,237	753,758	5,011	758,769	82,139	174,651	851,281	259,985	217,971	11,329	117,330	40,371
1984	1,422,389	804,884	7,458	812,342	90,753	189,716	911,305	287,402	223,682	12,191	116,677	40,939
1985	1,498,834	847,921	13,314	861,235	98,160	207,748	970,823	299,134	228,877	13,031	115,017	41,442
1986	1,564,112	906,430	1,131	907,561	103,782	210,496	1,014,275	310,096	239,741	13,688	114,267	42,479
1987	1,616,716	935,297	10,654	945,951	105,920	220,599	1,060,630	305,890	250,196	14,187	113,959	43,197
1988	1,717,850	1,009,826	8,551	1,018,377	119,000	235,241	1,134,618	323,998	259,234	15,216	112,898	44,027
1989	1,798,169	1,028,296	16,004	1,044,300	121,084	252,792	1,176,008	339,104	283,057	16,046	112,061	44,282
1990	1,911,391	1,100,123	13,106	1,113,229	131,061	253,075	1,235,243	368,179	307,969	17,096	111,804	45,908
1991	1,977,009	1,132,904	11,929	1,144,833	137,290	264,235	1,271,778	370,307	334,924	17,683	111,803	45,846
1992	2,095,154	1,202,448	17,461	1,219,909	144,951	286,599	1,361,557	377,223	356,374	18,676	112,182	46,227
1993	2,180,972	1,280,894	14,293	1,295,187	155,429	273,025	1,412,783	387,903	380,286	19,404	112,397	46,432
1994	2,302,215	1,354,690	6,640	1,361,330	167,355	289,541	1,483,516	428,283	390,416	20,551	112,025	47,608
1995	2,384,630	1,432,599	17,518	1,450,117	177,855	274,341	1,546,603	433,294	404,733	21,352	111,680	49,673
1996	2,476,927	1,545,725	5,539	1,551,264	187,407	242,475	1,606,332	454,154	416,441	22,268	111,231	51,133
1997	2,584,026	1,608,401	7,438	1,615,839	194,336	249,806	1,671,309	473,847	438,870	23,271	111,040	52,171
1998	2,658,203	1,684,544	2,486	1,687,030	199,719	230,193	1,717,504	501,198	439,501	24,012	110,704	51,665
1999	2,764,996	1,741,541	8,506	1,750,047	204,049	270,226	1,816,224	475,519	473,253	25,069	110,295	52,077
2000	2,914,743	1,813,676	938	1,814,614	211,997	303,785	1,906,402	512,524	495,817	26,451	110,192	53,512
2001	2,967,792	1,812,489	-7,251	1,805,238	209,834	320,334	1,915,738	501,514	550,540	27,020	109,836	52,307
2002	2,961,291	1,823,046	8,389	1,831,435	211,875	292,784	1,912,344	480,761	568,186	26,955	109,861	51,737
2003	3,030,623	1,833,926	4,284	1,838,210	212,849	300,763	1,926,124	502,911	601,588	27,662	109,559	51,158
2004	3,095,016	1,855,650	12,238	1,867,888	218,792	326,516	1,975,612	488,528	630,876	28,277	109,453	51,482
2005	3,126,281	1,875,644	12,900	1,888,544	224,673	308,534	1,972,405	490,067	663,809	28,638	109,165	50,662
2006	3,233,720	1,940,173	15,321	1,955,494	236,359	315,339	2,034,474	487,211	712,035	29,746	108,711	50,202
2007	3,332,473	1,960,408	12,411	1,972,819	241,952	294,624	2,025,491	528,880	778,102	30,819	108,132	50,348
2008	3,490,785	1,985,175	21,254	2,006,429	248,031	259,324	2,017,722	596,450	876,613	32,227	108,320	49,859
2009	3,481,849	1,953,993	5,385	1,959,378	245,457	238,143	1,952,064	571,088	958,697	32,265	107,913	47,922
2010	3,617,623	1,978,353	12,849	1,991,202	244,655	273,700	2,020,247	556,661	1,040,715	33,587	107,710	47,475
2011	3,742,971	2,013,625	26,775	2,040,400	222,632	290,832	2,108,600	590,853	1,043,518	34,793	107,578	47,644
2012	3,786,703	2,061,604	18,956	2,080,560	229,676	277,027	2,127,911	625,258	1,033,534	35,304	107,260	48,002
2013	3,801,299	2,102,271	29,162	2,131,433	264,499	257,147	2,124,081	613,874	1,063,344	35,453	107,221	48,187
2014	3,876,118	2,102,510	4,443	2,106,953	266,834	281,000	2,121,119	643,441	1,111,558	36,362	106,599	48,034
2015	4,021,782	2,155,073	4,014	2,159,087	270,908	291,695	2,179,874	669,803	1,172,105	37,971	105,916	47,387
2016	4,106,448	2,163,631	1,071	2,164,702	272,697	331,218	2,223,223	691,071	1,192,154	39,041	105,184	47,529
2017	4,140,756	2,157,854	1,610	2,159,464	273,242	363,675	2,249,897	695,178	1,195,681	39,448	104,967	46,701
2018	4,366,150	2,204,297	-802	2,203,495	285,361	490,758	2,408,892	708,308	1,248,950	41,712	104,674	46,560
2019	4,440,787	2,246,657	-3,563	2,243,094	290,553	482,142	2,434,683	692,357	1,313,747	42,667	104,079	46,793
2020	4,878,569	2,368,390	23,439	2,391,829	302,971	381,263	2,470,121	692,198	1,716,250	47,030	103,733	44,540
2021	5,200,417	2,552,985	33,270	2,586,255	322,372	384,776	2,648,659	754,130	1,797,628	50,367	103,251	45,862
2022	5,106,814	2,702,750	26,535	2,729,285	353,505	386,116	2,761,896	806,910	1,538,008	49,667	102,821	47,472

Personal Income and Employment by Area: Beaumont-Port Arthur, TX

(Thousands of dollars, except as noted.)

Year	Personal income, total	Derivation of personal income: Earnings by place of work: Nonfarm	Farm	Total	Less: Contributions for government social insurance	Plus: Adjustment for residence	Equals: Net earnings by place of residence	Plus: Dividends, interest, and rent	Plus: Personal current transfer receipts	Per capita personal income (dollars)	Population (persons)	Total employment
1970	1,268,763	1,099,261	2,565	1,101,826	72,295	-23,841	1,005,690	161,984	101,089	3,649	347,694	137,330
1971	1,361,243	1,165,542	3,756	1,169,298	79,207	-23,492	1,066,599	176,104	118,540	3,891	349,841	138,305
1972	1,465,378	1,249,755	4,218	1,253,973	89,645	-23,714	1,140,614	191,393	133,371	4,171	351,292	139,671
1973	1,595,091	1,358,156	5,825	1,363,981	113,850	-24,160	1,225,971	211,115	158,005	4,610	345,976	144,491
1974	1,866,689	1,597,053	11,533	1,608,586	137,717	-33,430	1,437,439	245,849	183,401	5,387	346,501	151,143
1975	2,099,877	1,756,398	14,990	1,771,388	146,341	-30,465	1,594,582	277,495	227,800	5,971	351,699	151,237
1976	2,433,248	2,121,715	2,874	2,124,589	180,935	-57,841	1,885,813	301,956	245,479	6,811	357,229	161,151
1977	2,732,982	2,401,146	10,528	2,411,674	204,796	-70,866	2,136,012	335,701	261,269	7,527	363,114	167,362
1978	3,028,635	2,657,515	2,465	2,659,980	232,293	-73,015	2,354,672	383,112	290,851	8,304	364,725	171,119
1979	3,397,974	2,965,171	7,774	2,972,945	269,216	-77,497	2,626,232	440,521	331,221	9,161	370,911	176,281
1980	3,805,447	3,240,363	5,270	3,245,633	295,383	-75,959	2,874,291	546,297	384,859	10,153	374,797	174,519
1981	4,349,538	3,689,200	-2,198	3,687,002	360,367	-88,074	3,238,561	676,679	434,298	11,445	380,033	183,692
1982	4,605,091	3,759,275	-3,225	3,756,050	380,359	-90,669	3,285,022	811,585	508,484	11,934	385,895	176,744
1983	4,787,294	3,782,501	-739	3,781,762	377,250	-95,673	3,308,839	882,931	595,524	12,365	387,177	169,848
1984	4,952,985	3,825,326	-4,243	3,821,083	391,520	-94,509	3,335,054	984,783	633,148	12,864	385,029	169,565
1985	5,033,813	3,764,455	3,438	3,767,893	388,338	-90,240	3,289,315	1,084,104	660,394	13,233	380,408	165,698
1986	4,974,836	3,644,040	1,690	3,645,730	371,468	-85,913	3,188,349	1,069,376	717,111	13,525	367,831	157,807
1987	4,933,535	3,621,387	-1,940	3,619,447	367,542	-84,479	3,167,426	1,018,712	747,397	13,496	365,565	161,799
1988	5,225,925	3,870,150	13,670	3,883,820	409,705	-93,679	3,380,436	1,072,929	772,560	14,450	361,654	164,610
1989	5,540,873	3,996,677	10,997	4,007,674	426,792	-101,938	3,478,944	1,218,816	843,113	15,377	360,338	164,987
1990	5,846,040	4,337,108	11,217	4,348,325	455,697	-123,790	3,768,838	1,147,583	929,619	16,171	361,510	170,986
1991	6,321,199	4,798,714	16,513	4,815,227	513,578	-156,994	4,144,655	1,164,740	1,011,804	17,245	366,555	180,406
1992	6,776,276	5,121,478	13,966	5,135,444	544,103	-173,530	4,417,811	1,175,118	1,183,347	18,256	371,174	179,889
1993	6,776,047	5,109,717	13,495	5,123,212	543,230	-156,972	4,423,010	1,106,214	1,246,823	18,022	375,979	180,011
1994	7,051,394	5,301,456	10,297	5,311,753	571,809	-154,539	4,585,405	1,132,470	1,333,519	18,675	377,590	179,610
1995	7,356,464	5,420,877	10,410	5,431,287	591,605	-165,217	4,674,465	1,239,750	1,442,249	19,314	380,888	183,110
1996	7,547,459	5,506,792	6,342	5,513,134	596,115	-174,547	4,742,472	1,270,441	1,534,546	19,840	380,417	183,666
1997	8,205,801	6,131,262	6,795	6,138,057	653,412	-215,361	5,269,284	1,340,825	1,595,692	21,499	381,675	190,627
1998	8,709,600	6,645,111	6,272	6,651,383	697,109	-257,440	5,696,834	1,425,153	1,587,613	22,751	382,827	194,777
1999	8,699,928	6,630,003	6,005	6,636,008	691,860	-227,038	5,717,110	1,394,777	1,588,041	22,595	385,034	193,452
2000	9,174,515	6,980,261	3,477	6,983,738	708,536	-239,082	6,036,120	1,486,881	1,651,514	23,845	384,759	196,236
2001	9,554,678	7,233,341	2,348	7,235,689	725,149	-247,506	6,263,034	1,507,660	1,783,984	24,966	382,708	193,752
2002	9,712,419	7,346,757	2,482	7,349,239	740,355	-245,452	6,363,432	1,433,063	1,915,924	25,359	383,004	192,765
2003	10,117,480	7,613,184	13,464	7,626,648	779,905	-267,698	6,579,045	1,506,756	2,031,679	26,402	383,208	193,923
2004	10,276,209	7,768,136	20,567	7,788,703	794,666	-256,119	6,737,918	1,432,886	2,105,405	26,730	384,438	191,529
2005	10,906,326	8,120,904	27,771	8,148,675	842,587	-272,807	7,033,281	1,425,785	2,447,260	28,292	385,490	195,200
2006	11,640,817	8,962,811	33,601	8,996,412	922,756	-341,028	7,732,628	1,530,513	2,377,676	30,705	379,119	203,223
2007	12,225,373	9,301,482	33,168	9,334,650	975,779	-374,447	7,984,424	1,677,673	2,563,276	31,976	382,330	206,612
2008	13,262,493	9,933,857	577	9,934,434	1,031,819	-486,892	8,415,723	2,022,919	2,823,851	34,426	385,248	209,054
2009	13,115,783	9,739,646	861	9,740,507	1,022,706	-477,542	8,240,259	1,842,230	3,033,294	33,878	387,146	204,738
2010	13,839,868	10,139,150	-3,593	10,135,557	1,072,489	-523,011	8,540,057	2,006,564	3,293,247	35,542	389,399	203,245
2011	14,464,227	10,562,806	-8,617	10,554,189	996,743	-594,683	8,962,763	2,124,140	3,377,324	36,933	391,632	207,900
2012	15,126,908	10,989,327	-9,011	10,980,316	1,030,108	-618,835	9,331,373	2,439,195	3,356,340	38,695	390,922	207,819
2013	14,801,479	10,890,258	-8,987	10,881,271	1,149,905	-600,340	9,131,026	2,205,669	3,464,784	37,653	393,098	204,992
2014	15,971,469	11,786,437	-14,518	11,771,919	1,231,022	-525,705	10,015,192	2,363,535	3,592,742	40,524	394,119	210,607
2015	16,444,916	12,218,806	-8,279	12,210,527	1,283,489	-504,701	10,422,337	2,243,379	3,779,200	41,328	397,910	212,292
2016	16,426,333	12,086,782	-10,536	12,076,246	1,296,499	-395,728	10,384,019	2,114,164	3,928,150	41,042	400,237	208,905
2017	16,903,527	12,218,626	-13,514	12,205,112	1,329,932	-315,178	10,560,002	2,389,016	3,954,509	42,019	402,279	209,685
2018	17,232,201	12,572,121	-12,846	12,559,275	1,364,864	-326,358	10,868,053	2,320,845	4,043,303	43,334	397,657	213,538
2019	17,640,376	12,846,355	-11,643	12,834,712	1,393,731	-473,483	10,967,498	2,499,799	4,173,079	44,398	397,323	213,634
2020	18,476,504	12,245,623	-11,028	12,234,595	1,341,949	-458,143	10,434,503	2,556,552	5,485,449	46,516	397,209	206,088
2021	19,349,882	12,124,194	-12,338	12,111,856	1,336,877	-337,338	10,437,641	2,755,256	6,156,985	48,960	395,216	208,774
2022	19,492,325	13,076,237	-36,467	13,039,770	1,477,501	-550,505	11,011,764	2,985,276	5,495,285	49,526	393,575	218,716

Personal Income and Employment by Area: Beckley, WV

(Thousands of dollars, except as noted.)

Year	Personal income, total	Derivation of personal income: Earnings by place of work: Nonfarm	Farm	Total	Less: Contributions for government social insurance	Plus: Adjustment for residence	Equals: Net earnings by place of residence	Plus: Dividends, interest, and rent	Plus: Personal current transfer receipts	Per capita personal income (dollars)	Population (persons)	Total employment
1970	342,410	251,677	140	251,817	18,662	10,841	243,996	35,075	63,339	2,858	119,794	34,722
1971	383,565	272,329	278	272,607	21,177	11,565	262,995	39,343	81,227	3,134	122,399	35,712
1972	443,014	313,974	381	314,355	25,404	13,130	302,081	44,455	96,478	3,502	126,518	38,148
1973	494,158	337,210	651	337,861	31,511	13,764	320,114	51,802	122,242	3,839	128,707	39,217
1974	546,723	375,669	526	376,195	36,347	13,024	352,872	60,924	132,927	4,226	129,362	40,310
1975	645,359	451,517	488	452,005	43,395	16,415	425,025	70,688	149,646	4,867	132,602	43,351
1976	746,571	542,705	276	542,981	54,034	14,793	503,740	79,183	163,648	5,395	138,390	46,063
1977	810,403	592,080	288	592,368	57,770	15,216	549,814	88,826	171,763	5,697	142,246	46,317
1978	912,215	667,242	372	667,614	66,952	13,628	614,290	98,920	199,005	6,329	144,129	47,908
1979	1,002,764	695,943	837	696,780	72,995	23,404	647,189	112,354	243,221	6,913	145,047	46,987
1980	1,094,257	732,080	789	732,869	78,397	26,479	680,951	138,009	275,297	7,565	144,639	46,598
1981	1,191,283	790,176	-344	789,832	91,020	25,742	724,554	168,761	297,968	8,254	144,324	46,263
1982	1,276,142	820,539	-259	820,280	97,721	36,213	758,772	195,583	321,787	8,841	144,345	45,744
1983	1,281,795	781,388	-333	781,055	93,195	32,657	720,517	205,406	355,872	8,896	144,081	43,320
1984	1,374,516	862,166	100	862,266	105,675	36,121	792,712	227,694	354,110	9,667	142,180	44,190
1985	1,419,093	897,714	-292	897,422	112,018	35,997	821,401	239,353	358,339	10,120	140,228	44,214
1986	1,439,975	891,188	-411	890,777	114,608	44,867	821,036	239,251	379,688	10,448	137,822	43,044
1987	1,458,001	904,011	-346	903,665	117,441	54,278	840,502	234,169	383,330	10,903	133,725	42,517
1988	1,511,919	935,417	-553	934,864	124,629	52,249	862,484	247,503	401,932	11,652	129,757	42,630
1989	1,578,524	946,290	274	946,564	129,105	61,442	878,901	275,546	424,077	12,543	125,854	42,806
1990	1,664,113	999,207	-85	999,122	138,156	77,382	938,348	275,713	450,052	13,347	124,685	43,965
1991	1,767,453	1,051,158	-406	1,050,752	150,790	79,169	979,131	284,152	504,170	14,144	124,959	44,633
1992	1,880,439	1,101,416	53	1,101,469	160,399	86,581	1,027,651	282,567	570,221	15,017	125,222	45,282
1993	1,956,910	1,163,043	-51	1,162,992	176,515	71,683	1,058,160	289,758	608,992	15,489	126,345	46,344
1994	2,067,431	1,236,678	-316	1,236,362	187,441	83,729	1,132,650	306,048	628,733	16,333	126,577	48,415
1995	2,180,853	1,327,110	-576	1,326,534	205,287	86,741	1,207,988	329,680	643,185	17,095	127,571	50,747
1996	2,287,513	1,394,318	-958	1,393,360	215,541	89,176	1,266,995	347,532	672,986	17,812	128,425	52,378
1997	2,376,783	1,446,899	-635	1,446,264	220,495	93,424	1,319,193	371,889	685,701	18,529	128,275	53,304
1998	2,498,438	1,515,487	-917	1,514,570	232,045	96,184	1,378,709	396,683	723,046	19,536	127,892	54,760
1999	2,534,485	1,557,327	-1,396	1,555,931	236,771	99,162	1,418,322	386,427	729,736	19,889	127,431	54,481
2000	2,629,864	1,605,364	-978	1,604,386	250,295	107,593	1,461,684	412,710	755,470	20,785	126,525	54,322
2001	2,812,967	1,735,352	-1,087	1,734,265	253,180	95,904	1,576,989	413,971	822,007	22,447	125,318	54,716
2002	2,916,429	1,795,358	-1,843	1,793,515	250,410	85,007	1,628,112	405,874	882,443	23,207	125,672	54,883
2003	2,922,880	1,789,700	-1,970	1,787,730	256,432	79,053	1,610,351	399,872	912,657	23,286	125,519	54,029
2004	2,999,825	1,884,137	-1,467	1,882,670	267,116	67,750	1,683,304	396,459	920,062	23,971	125,145	55,171
2005	3,146,265	2,036,426	-1,955	2,034,471	284,441	57,084	1,807,114	389,201	949,950	25,257	124,570	56,028
2006	3,345,051	2,157,253	-2,080	2,155,173	289,892	56,032	1,921,313	418,142	1,005,596	26,894	124,378	56,871
2007	3,348,268	2,052,285	-2,583	2,049,702	283,059	41,193	1,807,836	473,470	1,066,962	26,879	124,566	57,277
2008	3,608,915	2,176,338	-1,433	2,174,905	287,726	27,773	1,914,952	535,833	1,158,130	28,976	124,550	57,763
2009	3,707,535	2,192,662	-1,371	2,191,291	297,870	33,749	1,927,170	550,193	1,230,172	29,704	124,816	56,339
2010	3,866,908	2,349,657	-1,196	2,348,461	305,729	43,210	2,085,942	502,365	1,278,601	30,949	124,943	56,750
2011	4,246,588	2,614,292	-907	2,613,385	291,525	72,477	2,394,337	572,603	1,279,648	33,904	125,252	58,011
2012	4,284,898	2,540,917	-563	2,540,354	294,358	86,788	2,332,784	638,603	1,313,511	34,255	125,089	58,218
2013	4,169,606	2,514,897	-542	2,514,355	317,845	87,023	2,283,533	561,211	1,324,862	33,540	124,316	56,936
2014	4,252,489	2,478,116	-682	2,477,434	318,586	86,709	2,245,557	595,473	1,411,459	34,492	123,289	56,260
2015	4,288,320	2,413,524	-463	2,413,061	312,775	89,617	2,189,903	619,466	1,478,951	35,151	121,997	55,287
2016	4,138,569	2,262,899	-768	2,262,131	304,328	67,827	2,025,630	601,499	1,511,440	34,392	120,335	53,370
2017	4,351,201	2,431,669	-277	2,431,392	323,870	54,145	2,161,667	625,723	1,563,811	36,708	118,537	53,649
2018	4,540,765	2,600,890	-756	2,600,134	340,861	67,685	2,326,958	618,499	1,595,308	38,771	117,118	53,879
2019	4,732,992	2,744,686	-85	2,744,601	353,495	51,198	2,442,304	650,367	1,640,321	40,822	115,943	53,796
2020	4,884,253	2,571,335	-318	2,571,017	349,797	44,272	2,265,492	663,320	1,955,441	42,542	114,811	51,218
2021	5,287,160	2,731,391	-776	2,730,615	367,008	46,091	2,409,698	711,028	2,166,434	46,426	113,884	52,496
2022	5,288,692	2,873,760	-944	2,872,816	387,903	49,987	2,534,900	771,939	1,981,853	47,065	112,369	53,899

Personal Income and Employment by Area: Bellingham, WA

(Thousands of dollars, except as noted.)

Year	Personal income, total	Derivation of personal income: Earnings by place of work: Nonfarm	Farm	Total	Less: Contributions for government social insurance	Plus: Adjustment for residence	Equals: Net earnings by place of residence	Plus: Dividends, interest, and rent	Plus: Personal current transfer receipts	Per capita personal income (dollars)	Population (persons)	Total employment
1970	321,153	236,478	15,801	252,279	19,139	-308	232,832	54,573	33,748	3,888	82,606	34,551
1971	369,028	278,308	17,662	295,970	23,859	-2,177	269,934	60,405	38,689	4,307	85,688	37,206
1972	389,183	287,246	20,011	307,257	25,342	-1,094	280,821	64,962	43,400	4,351	89,443	36,628
1973	434,564	318,446	24,205	342,651	32,310	-335	310,006	74,733	49,825	4,845	89,700	38,054
1974	490,746	355,963	25,038	381,001	37,079	-809	343,113	86,801	60,832	5,390	91,043	39,342
1975	557,944	402,445	25,466	427,911	41,778	-1,713	384,420	98,390	75,134	5,978	93,332	41,368
1976	635,961	464,202	32,419	496,621	48,448	-1,343	446,830	109,080	80,051	6,620	96,070	44,257
1977	703,824	522,154	29,485	551,639	55,259	-2,917	493,463	126,738	83,623	7,149	98,453	46,132
1978	799,446	603,850	26,584	630,434	65,007	-3,348	562,079	146,787	90,580	7,878	101,482	48,497
1979	911,718	683,912	32,817	716,729	76,119	-1,289	639,321	169,618	102,779	8,735	104,380	50,544
1980	997,048	722,336	24,518	746,854	80,749	312	666,417	204,453	126,178	9,299	107,222	50,074
1981	1,077,955	751,920	28,200	780,120	91,221	45	688,944	244,855	144,156	9,881	109,096	50,010
1982	1,132,608	773,910	26,531	800,441	96,332	951	705,060	267,454	160,094	10,307	109,885	49,658
1983	1,242,704	831,766	36,157	867,923	103,961	2,039	766,001	300,704	175,999	11,233	110,630	51,784
1984	1,325,788	881,058	35,699	916,757	113,542	2,930	806,145	332,143	187,500	11,912	111,294	52,881
1985	1,418,202	932,529	42,527	975,056	120,523	5,457	859,990	357,746	200,466	12,613	112,441	53,901
1986	1,521,647	1,013,620	53,521	1,067,141	131,482	6,433	942,092	368,232	211,323	13,435	113,262	56,022
1987	1,613,694	1,091,865	60,023	1,151,888	142,081	5,644	1,015,451	374,399	223,844	13,988	115,361	58,864
1988	1,752,644	1,186,058	57,470	1,243,528	157,061	11,123	1,097,590	414,242	240,812	14,728	119,002	62,798
1989	1,976,577	1,343,093	66,655	1,409,748	178,574	14,233	1,245,407	473,235	257,935	16,031	123,294	67,307
1990	2,261,852	1,591,920	75,914	1,667,834	213,535	14,172	1,468,471	508,088	285,293	17,519	129,111	73,036
1991	2,455,182	1,702,544	69,168	1,771,712	231,296	21,865	1,562,281	566,836	326,065	18,346	133,823	74,567
1992	2,605,234	1,815,695	89,406	1,905,101	246,567	29,336	1,687,870	562,385	354,979	18,748	138,957	77,046
1993	2,715,193	1,892,642	76,300	1,968,942	259,140	35,131	1,744,933	587,922	382,338	18,899	143,669	78,697
1994	2,896,828	2,013,979	75,184	2,089,163	277,226	41,244	1,853,181	631,195	412,452	19,627	147,593	82,327
1995	3,062,608	2,116,062	67,442	2,183,504	290,765	49,817	1,942,556	670,580	449,472	20,233	151,369	83,655
1996	3,310,010	2,241,436	95,281	2,336,717	300,369	57,166	2,093,514	737,890	478,606	21,336	155,134	86,113
1997	3,476,542	2,363,529	77,362	2,440,891	303,396	70,900	2,208,395	763,858	504,289	21,985	158,133	88,181
1998	3,750,283	2,520,536	104,978	2,625,514	320,373	85,804	2,390,945	829,295	530,043	23,295	160,988	89,503
1999	3,909,082	2,642,184	108,236	2,750,420	327,986	105,017	2,527,451	805,943	575,688	23,754	164,566	91,585
2000	4,131,943	2,751,660	89,497	2,841,157	347,087	122,266	2,616,336	885,372	630,235	24,639	167,696	93,409
2001	4,457,786	2,998,977	109,552	3,108,529	373,447	107,673	2,842,755	898,694	716,337	26,043	171,172	94,252
2002	4,537,386	3,151,852	91,078	3,242,930	391,060	104,910	2,956,780	822,429	758,177	25,942	174,904	96,467
2003	4,889,519	3,374,388	119,116	3,493,504	421,460	100,608	3,172,652	913,838	803,029	27,492	177,851	99,415
2004	5,294,136	3,676,625	124,623	3,801,248	457,917	96,880	3,440,211	1,018,552	835,373	29,128	181,756	102,984
2005	5,623,699	3,990,957	123,938	4,114,895	504,228	97,967	3,708,634	1,030,279	884,786	30,325	185,450	107,982
2006	6,085,213	4,235,574	85,639	4,321,213	528,352	117,161	3,910,022	1,224,200	950,991	32,210	188,926	110,383
2007	6,664,769	4,456,728	113,555	4,570,283	555,701	136,860	4,151,442	1,478,775	1,034,552	34,562	192,837	114,505
2008	7,151,388	4,650,407	86,351	4,736,758	579,483	145,068	4,302,343	1,648,376	1,200,669	36,355	196,708	115,003
2009	7,100,242	4,645,382	66,144	4,711,526	592,670	137,819	4,256,675	1,498,683	1,344,884	35,525	199,865	110,729
2010	7,347,345	4,772,744	104,339	4,877,083	602,746	134,225	4,408,562	1,447,340	1,491,443	36,468	201,471	109,082
2011	7,765,222	4,912,105	150,391	5,062,496	566,817	147,507	4,643,186	1,630,486	1,491,550	38,232	203,109	110,318
2012	8,223,205	5,214,394	145,548	5,359,942	582,370	155,906	4,933,478	1,798,055	1,491,672	40,273	204,189	112,809
2013	8,171,689	5,356,692	152,168	5,508,860	667,892	153,861	4,994,829	1,652,722	1,524,138	39,842	205,103	115,135
2014	8,610,703	5,410,193	186,941	5,597,134	681,851	175,578	5,090,861	1,849,570	1,670,272	41,623	206,873	117,197
2015	9,090,722	5,690,636	178,368	5,869,004	720,909	185,768	5,333,863	2,028,683	1,728,176	43,243	210,224	119,718
2016	9,427,108	5,953,781	152,858	6,106,639	750,817	201,889	5,557,711	2,036,448	1,832,949	43,970	214,400	123,422
2017	9,946,133	6,358,238	158,368	6,516,606	812,007	199,690	5,904,289	2,141,364	1,900,480	45,427	218,946	126,326
2018	10,698,779	6,889,731	124,840	7,014,571	859,112	237,518	6,392,977	2,296,617	2,009,185	48,140	222,242	129,212
2019	11,530,224	7,198,965	168,281	7,367,246	871,409	257,877	6,753,714	2,621,608	2,154,902	51,150	225,421	129,936
2020	12,250,878	7,255,302	184,057	7,439,359	890,560	261,456	6,810,255	2,527,228	2,913,395	53,867	227,430	123,963
2021	13,281,368	7,775,567	157,801	7,933,368	946,628	301,285	7,288,025	2,800,114	3,193,229	58,581	226,718	127,616
2022	13,608,269	8,491,277	209,091	8,700,368	1,067,243	295,634	7,928,759	2,973,470	2,706,040	58,993	230,677	134,622

Personal Income and Employment by Area: Bend, OR

(Thousands of dollars, except as noted.)

Year	Personal income, total	Derivation of personal income: Earnings by place of work: Nonfarm	Farm	Total	Less: Contributions for government social insurance	Plus: Adjustment for residence	Equals: Net earnings by place of residence	Plus: Dividends, interest, and rent	Plus: Personal current transfer receipts	Per capita personal income (dollars)	Population (persons)	Total employment
1970	124,676	90,412	1,419	91,831	6,623	2,318	87,526	24,821	12,329	4,037	30,882	13,667
1971	143,502	104,384	1,428	105,812	7,921	2,597	100,488	28,617	14,397	4,370	32,835	15,106
1972	168,880	123,271	3,740	127,011	9,891	2,933	120,053	32,392	16,435	4,852	34,804	16,767
1973	196,159	143,736	4,286	148,022	13,282	3,074	137,814	38,445	19,900	5,206	37,682	18,403
1974	221,209	156,821	3,468	160,289	14,878	3,635	149,046	46,476	25,687	5,509	40,155	18,902
1975	256,795	176,577	3,663	180,240	16,127	5,689	169,802	53,575	33,418	6,053	42,422	19,706
1976	308,998	221,349	3,277	224,626	20,214	4,372	208,784	62,484	37,730	6,915	44,686	22,354
1977	369,658	269,303	2,384	271,687	25,185	4,443	250,945	75,067	43,646	7,706	47,969	25,288
1978	443,826	328,928	132	329,060	31,690	4,307	301,677	92,920	49,229	8,319	53,349	28,444
1979	525,368	390,196	894	391,090	39,375	3,542	355,257	111,252	58,859	8,988	58,452	30,620
1980	574,147	402,570	1,159	403,729	40,276	4,173	367,626	132,838	73,683	9,206	62,365	30,066
1981	618,062	406,905	1,658	408,563	43,436	6,080	371,207	158,381	88,474	9,790	63,130	29,334
1982	640,382	400,660	901	401,561	43,503	6,727	364,785	172,793	102,804	10,160	63,031	27,771
1983	709,504	447,402	6,098	453,500	49,112	7,800	412,188	188,018	109,298	11,349	62,516	29,659
1984	790,024	508,790	6,702	515,492	57,380	9,011	467,123	207,709	115,192	12,375	63,839	31,566
1985	856,843	555,920	5,061	560,981	63,842	10,390	507,529	225,100	124,214	13,191	64,959	33,037
1986	913,580	596,503	1,660	598,163	68,210	12,448	542,401	243,261	127,918	13,809	66,160	34,685
1987	974,010	643,989	373	644,362	72,643	14,371	586,090	255,395	132,525	14,567	66,862	35,621
1988	1,090,057	728,980	2,340	731,320	85,024	17,310	663,606	280,613	145,838	15,825	68,882	38,234
1989	1,224,947	795,948	3,178	799,126	95,276	18,830	722,680	341,666	160,601	17,153	71,415	41,660
1990	1,391,902	940,480	1,483	941,963	114,536	17,956	845,383	371,489	175,030	18,302	76,053	45,455
1991	1,541,371	1,052,685	743	1,053,428	128,482	18,193	943,139	400,257	197,975	19,158	80,456	46,995
1992	1,678,787	1,145,013	-1,148	1,143,865	137,688	24,217	1,030,394	422,828	225,565	19,938	84,199	48,397
1993	1,845,471	1,264,066	-2,400	1,261,666	150,783	23,328	1,134,211	467,647	243,613	20,957	88,061	51,071
1994	1,979,023	1,359,337	-2,878	1,356,459	164,055	25,445	1,217,849	499,014	262,160	21,654	91,393	54,760
1995	2,145,676	1,426,925	-2,694	1,424,231	174,057	25,928	1,276,102	574,551	295,023	22,470	95,491	57,626
1996	2,346,751	1,555,263	-2,979	1,552,284	190,652	26,913	1,388,545	636,559	321,647	23,618	99,362	60,831
1997	2,502,187	1,653,885	-2,219	1,651,666	201,419	27,687	1,477,934	680,223	344,030	24,392	102,581	64,237
1998	2,743,578	1,807,304	176	1,807,480	219,272	27,725	1,615,933	767,038	360,607	25,684	106,820	66,592
1999	2,914,601	1,990,949	-4,365	1,986,584	240,501	26,447	1,772,530	738,960	403,111	26,039	111,933	70,590
2000	3,200,551	2,202,270	-5,976	2,196,294	266,207	26,246	1,956,333	810,702	433,516	27,457	116,566	74,782
2001	3,490,694	2,434,227	-4,569	2,429,658	284,014	19,196	2,164,840	830,455	495,399	28,962	120,526	76,099
2002	3,621,769	2,571,101	-4,726	2,566,375	302,687	13,608	2,277,296	790,872	553,601	28,917	125,247	77,415
2003	3,849,311	2,752,188	-3,137	2,749,051	325,811	3,959	2,427,199	841,681	580,431	29,818	129,094	80,404
2004	4,153,883	2,957,736	1,228	2,958,964	360,684	6,612	2,604,892	947,338	601,653	31,056	133,756	86,199
2005	4,617,933	3,326,370	-3,886	3,322,484	408,887	-776	2,912,821	1,053,367	651,745	32,852	140,567	92,847
2006	5,290,790	3,804,713	-5,093	3,799,620	462,263	-21,730	3,315,627	1,256,074	719,089	35,713	148,149	98,924
2007	5,600,115	3,914,143	-11,928	3,902,215	479,873	-18,991	3,403,351	1,406,082	790,682	36,690	152,633	102,261
2008	5,879,178	3,775,036	-13,685	3,761,351	467,601	-9,910	3,283,840	1,619,199	976,139	37,490	156,820	98,968
2009	5,449,981	3,333,253	-13,087	3,320,166	426,587	22,568	2,916,147	1,362,213	1,171,621	34,637	157,345	92,281
2010	5,492,507	3,263,609	-12,533	3,251,076	425,878	42,241	2,867,439	1,340,032	1,285,036	34,829	157,697	90,548
2011	5,897,179	3,373,974	-10,844	3,363,130	393,275	66,240	3,036,095	1,544,527	1,316,557	36,986	159,445	91,535
2012	6,316,066	3,690,759	-8,879	3,681,880	418,224	105,549	3,369,205	1,622,223	1,324,638	39,237	160,974	92,986
2013	6,775,338	4,043,594	-4,619	4,038,975	510,165	124,701	3,653,511	1,732,227	1,389,600	41,126	164,745	97,006
2014	7,294,926	4,549,190	-7,354	4,541,836	573,322	83,368	4,051,882	1,715,091	1,527,953	43,223	168,775	103,061
2015	8,189,375	5,080,343	-6,246	5,074,097	631,537	79,319	4,521,879	2,009,072	1,658,424	47,253	173,308	109,464
2016	8,921,964	5,589,025	-5,931	5,583,094	681,276	68,769	4,970,587	2,218,831	1,732,546	49,709	179,485	114,991
2017	9,744,419	6,126,461	-13,250	6,113,211	749,926	56,453	5,419,738	2,511,655	1,813,026	52,566	185,374	119,782
2018	10,529,174	6,590,161	-11,891	6,578,270	789,958	48,990	5,837,302	2,756,506	1,935,366	55,443	189,910	124,425
2019	11,265,156	7,122,345	-11,307	7,111,038	848,927	32,996	6,295,107	2,906,534	2,063,515	57,689	195,275	126,306
2020	12,781,035	7,620,678	-11,540	7,609,138	892,628	40,337	6,756,847	3,199,927	2,824,261	64,080	199,454	125,232
2021	14,408,123	8,723,643	-13,358	8,710,285	1,119,070	76,177	7,667,392	3,652,092	3,088,639	70,161	205,358	131,091
2022	14,794,468	9,358,110	-14,099	9,344,011	1,241,898	130,230	8,232,343	3,868,502	2,693,623	71,627	206,549	136,776

Personal Income and Employment by Area: Billings, MT

(Thousands of dollars, except as noted.)

Year	Personal income, total	Derivation of personal income: Earnings by place of work: Nonfarm	Farm	Total	Less: Contributions for government social insurance	Plus: Adjustment for residence	Equals: Net earnings by place of residence	Plus: Dividends, interest, and rent	Plus: Personal current transfer receipts	Per capita personal income (dollars)	Population (persons)	Total employment
1970	387,724	284,040	25,273	309,313	22,044	219	287,488	67,907	32,329	3,893	99,590	44,784
1971	428,239	317,371	23,533	340,904	24,982	587	316,509	73,886	37,844	4,188	102,264	46,384
1972	494,251	358,948	40,141	399,089	29,806	888	370,171	81,715	42,365	4,737	104,337	48,788
1973	546,169	401,977	37,640	439,617	38,623	1,093	402,087	94,450	49,632	5,157	105,903	51,919
1974	621,923	459,532	35,840	495,372	45,093	1,744	452,023	111,021	58,879	5,693	109,243	54,472
1975	696,796	519,275	20,842	540,117	49,148	4,907	495,876	129,001	71,919	6,232	111,813	55,366
1976	779,439	605,680	7,537	613,217	58,224	4,646	559,639	140,736	79,064	6,803	114,570	59,115
1977	884,007	695,055	5,241	700,296	67,464	5,806	638,638	159,576	85,793	7,553	117,033	61,995
1978	1,010,416	795,230	12,153	807,383	80,101	7,052	734,334	180,589	95,493	8,362	120,831	65,872
1979	1,127,295	892,552	4,934	897,486	93,988	8,112	811,610	208,810	106,875	9,227	122,169	67,269
1980	1,253,840	949,009	7,735	956,744	101,518	18,718	873,944	252,816	127,080	10,250	122,320	66,475
1981	1,418,748	1,051,733	4,372	1,056,105	120,677	16,362	951,790	320,511	146,447	11,416	124,281	68,012
1982	1,537,071	1,118,509	4,200	1,122,709	131,470	17,214	1,008,453	363,501	165,117	12,081	127,232	68,923
1983	1,633,963	1,189,966	6,512	1,196,478	140,262	14,034	1,070,250	379,361	184,352	12,523	130,476	70,459
1984	1,754,389	1,266,856	11,382	1,278,238	153,752	7,836	1,132,322	422,894	199,173	13,175	133,163	72,880
1985	1,806,630	1,297,923	11,244	1,309,167	160,565	6,817	1,155,419	438,452	212,759	13,496	133,865	72,543
1986	1,811,037	1,295,801	10,304	1,306,105	162,998	6,079	1,149,186	433,102	228,749	13,616	133,004	71,798
1987	1,848,550	1,315,945	22,267	1,338,212	164,011	6,393	1,180,594	425,160	242,796	14,127	130,848	71,895
1988	1,922,748	1,379,577	20,118	1,399,695	180,034	6,084	1,225,745	435,939	261,064	14,915	128,914	74,390
1989	2,081,660	1,463,468	27,432	1,490,900	192,229	6,706	1,305,377	489,531	286,752	16,232	128,242	75,800
1990	2,186,424	1,555,753	25,539	1,581,292	216,911	7,236	1,371,617	496,493	318,314	17,054	128,207	76,682
1991	2,332,576	1,687,084	31,846	1,718,930	239,290	9,239	1,488,879	508,522	335,175	17,930	130,091	78,682
1992	2,485,549	1,821,599	37,625	1,859,224	260,108	6,249	1,605,365	519,494	360,690	18,634	133,388	81,206
1993	2,643,395	1,965,266	43,642	2,008,908	287,419	4,836	1,726,325	526,874	390,196	19,335	136,715	83,114
1994	2,797,048	2,084,988	30,767	2,115,755	305,532	4,242	1,814,465	572,085	410,498	20,064	139,406	87,004
1995	2,942,983	2,163,465	15,387	2,178,852	309,148	3,361	1,873,065	631,216	438,702	20,775	141,662	88,139
1996	3,074,307	2,247,350	15,525	2,262,875	307,457	1,906	1,957,324	662,059	454,924	21,456	143,283	90,616
1997	3,228,650	2,347,354	11,127	2,358,481	311,315	1,245	2,048,411	713,943	466,296	22,370	144,327	91,387
1998	3,455,741	2,509,925	14,690	2,524,615	325,010	-703	2,198,902	772,071	484,768	23,850	144,892	94,168
1999	3,557,395	2,640,436	20,498	2,660,934	340,573	-3,032	2,317,329	758,615	481,451	24,311	146,331	96,026
2000	3,822,957	2,836,738	19,656	2,856,394	365,032	-6,217	2,485,145	802,340	535,472	25,940	147,378	97,833
2001	3,977,495	2,941,863	33,283	2,975,146	389,390	-6,671	2,579,085	817,020	581,390	26,720	148,858	99,701
2002	4,082,391	3,088,151	14,982	3,103,133	411,276	-9,740	2,682,117	798,956	601,318	27,158	150,320	100,722
2003	4,324,317	3,253,032	30,508	3,283,540	429,419	-10,967	2,843,154	852,956	628,207	28,466	151,913	101,670
2004	4,709,220	3,520,540	51,749	3,572,289	459,980	-13,998	3,098,311	935,845	675,064	30,645	153,672	104,542
2005	5,051,565	3,797,321	49,221	3,846,542	495,499	-15,299	3,335,744	991,659	724,162	32,377	156,025	106,964
2006	5,429,872	4,071,140	6,936	4,078,076	529,537	-18,865	3,529,674	1,106,327	793,871	34,332	158,157	108,830
2007	5,889,804	4,384,999	9,355	4,394,354	577,972	-22,726	3,793,656	1,243,782	852,366	36,729	160,358	112,641
2008	6,327,136	4,539,117	6,733	4,545,850	592,472	-23,915	3,929,463	1,426,565	971,108	38,778	163,165	113,501
2009	6,205,866	4,535,058	7,570	4,542,628	589,113	-5,222	3,948,293	1,222,683	1,034,890	37,481	165,575	111,298
2010	6,537,304	4,679,214	17,942	4,697,156	600,429	10,205	4,106,932	1,290,486	1,139,886	39,006	167,596	110,696
2011	6,995,353	4,952,110	41,469	4,993,579	569,780	47,417	4,471,216	1,398,573	1,125,564	41,360	169,134	112,646
2012	7,605,867	5,296,073	38,851	5,334,924	594,484	115,855	4,856,295	1,589,416	1,160,156	44,439	171,153	114,739
2013	7,667,342	5,528,051	60,439	5,588,490	694,310	154,162	5,048,342	1,434,593	1,184,407	44,147	173,677	115,025
2014	8,177,183	5,785,430	67,559	5,852,989	727,759	189,843	5,315,073	1,611,669	1,250,441	46,632	175,356	116,402
2015	8,397,531	6,001,272	81,562	6,082,834	754,547	146,458	5,474,745	1,619,670	1,303,116	47,480	176,865	119,111
2016	8,427,737	5,938,486	69,364	6,007,850	731,738	86,931	5,363,043	1,646,168	1,418,526	47,248	178,373	119,828
2017	8,914,122	6,225,588	37,057	6,262,645	782,132	92,064	5,572,577	1,795,974	1,545,571	49,499	180,087	120,257
2018	9,335,455	6,394,067	48,670	6,442,737	822,968	109,691	5,729,460	2,002,378	1,603,617	51,599	180,923	121,333
2019	9,643,567	6,653,935	61,671	6,715,606	846,003	111,538	5,981,141	1,970,002	1,692,424	52,852	182,465	121,342
2020	10,380,332	6,895,242	67,644	6,962,886	896,134	69,564	6,136,316	2,059,137	2,184,879	56,200	184,703	121,452
2021	11,578,761	7,644,692	17,200	7,661,892	955,106	51,381	6,758,167	2,424,568	2,396,026	61,824	187,285	126,541
2022	12,176,509	8,251,608	50,785	8,302,393	1,055,599	66,942	7,313,736	2,740,108	2,122,665	64,017	190,208	131,747

Personal Income and Employment by Area: Binghamton, NY

(Thousands of dollars, except as noted.)

Year	Personal income, total	Derivation of personal income: Earnings by place of work: Nonfarm	Farm	Total	Less: Contributions for government social insurance	Plus: Adjustment for residence	Equals: Net earnings by place of residence	Plus: Dividends, interest, and rent	Plus: Personal current transfer receipts	Per capita personal income (dollars)	Population (persons)	Total employment
1970	1,096,008	947,976	8,644	956,620	71,901	-32,537	852,182	139,431	104,395	4,077	268,851	117,119
1971	1,169,453	995,597	8,709	1,004,306	78,160	-35,921	890,225	150,584	128,644	4,319	270,746	116,349
1972	1,235,754	1,053,517	8,840	1,062,357	87,343	-36,472	938,542	162,556	134,656	4,619	267,509	117,444
1973	1,332,843	1,135,541	10,063	1,145,604	108,690	-37,418	999,496	181,261	152,086	4,982	267,518	120,927
1974	1,441,396	1,210,104	7,005	1,217,109	119,004	-38,143	1,059,962	204,081	177,353	5,426	265,630	121,541
1975	1,582,300	1,290,938	6,632	1,297,570	124,685	-44,596	1,128,289	224,056	229,955	5,890	268,656	119,091
1976	1,693,251	1,388,506	8,396	1,396,902	137,684	-48,956	1,210,262	238,667	244,322	6,293	269,063	120,675
1977	1,846,831	1,529,082	4,869	1,533,951	151,332	-59,543	1,323,076	263,691	260,064	6,874	268,668	124,414
1978	2,028,177	1,699,925	7,722	1,707,647	172,170	-67,866	1,467,611	280,747	279,819	7,576	267,705	128,940
1979	2,224,344	1,866,116	9,421	1,875,537	194,532	-76,784	1,604,221	317,753	302,370	8,331	266,989	130,555
1980	2,454,801	2,015,721	9,728	2,025,449	209,227	-85,762	1,730,460	378,863	345,478	9,311	263,639	129,633
1981	2,729,481	2,209,511	7,811	2,217,322	243,390	-96,836	1,877,096	457,305	395,080	10,344	263,859	129,925
1982	3,009,700	2,397,588	14,097	2,411,685	266,749	-110,602	2,034,334	531,610	443,756	11,400	264,005	129,662
1983	3,222,767	2,554,158	7,900	2,562,058	287,485	-113,789	2,160,784	586,857	475,126	12,232	263,473	128,801
1984	3,573,538	2,855,913	8,857	2,864,770	328,436	-125,157	2,411,177	668,312	494,049	13,578	263,182	135,188
1985	3,784,705	3,064,351	9,830	3,074,181	355,797	-136,692	2,581,692	685,628	517,385	14,297	264,719	139,580
1986	3,958,103	3,177,263	10,358	3,187,621	375,398	-133,264	2,678,959	727,478	551,666	15,013	263,651	140,401
1987	4,153,112	3,382,819	10,639	3,393,458	390,613	-136,720	2,866,125	723,429	563,558	15,835	262,266	140,900
1988	4,417,618	3,597,159	7,672	3,604,831	424,415	-138,516	3,041,900	777,922	597,796	16,746	263,797	145,553
1989	4,743,835	3,753,003	12,087	3,765,090	437,573	-135,423	3,192,094	904,388	647,353	17,943	264,388	143,469
1990	4,924,254	3,842,113	13,620	3,855,733	429,025	-137,304	3,289,404	930,302	704,548	18,601	264,731	142,457
1991	5,092,222	3,964,362	9,602	3,973,964	452,179	-142,050	3,379,735	943,940	768,547	19,170	265,632	139,936
1992	5,276,871	4,071,105	13,779	4,084,884	457,065	-148,880	3,478,939	934,323	863,609	19,795	266,571	138,396
1993	5,267,538	4,067,779	14,745	4,082,524	463,676	-152,952	3,465,896	886,351	915,291	19,803	265,993	137,687
1994	5,303,001	4,047,652	13,015	4,060,667	464,806	-145,663	3,450,198	899,189	953,614	20,081	264,082	136,661
1995	5,422,240	4,075,874	9,727	4,085,601	463,522	-145,195	3,476,884	941,845	1,003,511	20,848	260,079	134,001
1996	5,575,758	4,161,812	16,315	4,178,127	465,062	-139,323	3,573,742	959,903	1,042,113	21,721	256,702	132,577
1997	5,801,666	4,325,356	5,366	4,330,722	479,294	-135,514	3,715,914	1,048,417	1,037,335	22,822	254,213	134,726
1998	5,926,667	4,402,992	8,881	4,411,873	486,807	-141,432	3,783,634	1,065,731	1,077,302	23,404	253,235	134,427
1999	6,205,434	4,697,560	6,443	4,704,003	505,997	-152,591	4,045,415	1,054,645	1,105,374	24,549	252,773	138,052
2000	6,574,340	5,044,966	4,267	5,049,233	540,277	-172,029	4,336,927	1,103,453	1,133,960	26,069	252,189	141,139
2001	6,629,553	5,069,982	4,485	5,074,467	558,884	-153,972	4,361,611	1,053,446	1,214,496	26,247	252,580	139,580
2002	6,739,719	5,115,464	254	5,115,718	563,513	-137,287	4,414,918	1,004,433	1,320,368	26,594	253,430	136,480
2003	6,774,673	5,071,972	7,120	5,079,092	558,642	-109,092	4,411,358	996,945	1,366,370	26,785	252,932	134,839
2004	7,053,842	5,219,245	15,341	5,234,586	575,374	-99,226	4,559,986	1,061,728	1,432,128	27,924	252,605	134,829
2005	7,145,430	5,386,788	18,890	5,405,678	604,156	-99,970	4,701,552	945,111	1,498,767	28,345	252,088	135,174
2006	7,593,356	5,726,072	17,447	5,743,519	643,459	-100,369	4,999,691	1,000,143	1,593,522	30,080	252,441	136,660
2007	8,060,412	5,993,439	16,589	6,010,028	665,939	-96,996	5,247,093	1,127,968	1,685,351	31,930	252,442	139,311
2008	8,548,350	6,181,322	15,172	6,196,494	695,928	-84,751	5,415,815	1,256,206	1,876,329	33,851	252,527	139,392
2009	8,677,551	6,158,043	6,957	6,165,000	685,598	-72,184	5,407,218	1,184,130	2,086,203	34,411	252,171	135,658
2010	8,934,319	6,222,846	12,630	6,235,476	682,872	-11,370	5,541,234	1,167,617	2,225,468	35,492	251,728	133,187
2011	9,142,786	6,218,951	17,527	6,236,478	619,023	39,747	5,657,202	1,236,974	2,248,610	36,359	251,458	132,377
2012	9,316,721	6,297,033	13,571	6,310,604	619,524	88,046	5,779,126	1,303,753	2,233,842	37,097	251,144	131,868
2013	9,308,997	6,305,202	23,067	6,328,269	699,791	115,570	5,744,048	1,309,581	2,255,368	37,060	251,184	130,464
2014	9,390,755	6,282,982	24,629	6,307,611	711,354	132,577	5,728,834	1,361,308	2,300,613	37,385	251,193	129,531
2015	9,633,567	6,378,510	11,295	6,389,805	725,007	145,455	5,810,253	1,401,880	2,421,434	38,483	250,330	128,329
2016	9,698,986	6,439,990	10,993	6,450,983	737,409	118,385	5,831,959	1,420,093	2,446,934	38,905	249,300	128,162
2017	10,226,337	6,713,149	16,916	6,730,065	772,324	131,492	6,089,233	1,545,526	2,591,578	41,121	248,689	126,889
2018	10,454,457	6,962,705	10,906	6,973,611	793,501	131,512	6,311,622	1,595,478	2,547,357	42,083	248,426	127,507
2019	10,863,885	7,127,838	22,905	7,150,743	817,933	132,303	6,465,113	1,684,999	2,713,773	43,889	247,533	126,278
2020	11,802,922	7,160,047	18,741	7,178,788	823,435	118,882	6,474,235	1,692,640	3,636,047	47,886	246,478	117,715
2021	12,455,466	7,584,210	23,269	7,607,479	881,550	128,230	6,854,159	1,761,257	3,840,050	50,470	246,790	120,299
2022	12,052,532	7,826,683	31,202	7,857,885	941,400	155,915	7,072,400	1,774,849	3,205,283	49,216	244,889	124,184

Personal Income and Employment by Area: Birmingham-Hoover, AL

(Thousands of dollars, except as noted.)

Year	Personal income, total	Derivation of personal income: Earnings by place of work								Per capita personal income (dollars)	Population (persons)	Total employment
		Nonfarm	Farm	Total	Less: Contributions for government social insurance	Plus: Adjustment for residence	Equals: Net earnings by place of residence	Plus: Dividends, interest, and rent	Plus: Personal current transfer receipts			
1970	2,696,770	2,292,742	15,875	2,308,617	167,237	-42,869	2,098,511	332,809	265,450	3,468	777,652	339,189
1971	2,956,117	2,490,152	18,097	2,508,249	185,128	-55,765	2,267,356	369,487	319,274	3,757	786,842	342,771
1972	3,278,494	2,784,032	23,698	2,807,730	217,447	-74,304	2,515,979	403,287	359,228	4,145	790,951	354,810
1973	3,685,599	3,128,966	38,675	3,167,641	282,192	-84,350	2,801,099	454,380	430,120	4,600	801,240	369,708
1974	4,155,513	3,534,577	17,556	3,552,133	328,882	-93,665	3,129,586	527,867	498,060	5,154	806,250	379,432
1975	4,647,467	3,854,766	31,546	3,886,312	354,271	-100,201	3,431,840	586,045	629,582	5,686	817,389	379,941
1976	5,167,650	4,294,513	34,168	4,328,681	403,262	-98,175	3,827,244	637,234	703,172	6,234	828,889	387,167
1977	5,701,076	4,771,808	38,173	4,809,981	449,330	-101,261	4,259,390	704,153	737,533	6,782	840,643	400,462
1978	6,415,085	5,403,610	34,934	5,438,544	518,666	-104,445	4,815,433	796,512	803,140	7,544	850,344	414,839
1979	7,158,416	5,990,398	42,077	6,032,475	595,998	-113,477	5,323,000	906,309	929,107	8,337	858,633	423,566
1980	7,866,833	6,387,566	27,662	6,415,228	633,427	-111,280	5,670,521	1,102,220	1,094,092	9,125	862,076	416,301
1981	8,552,641	6,788,105	31,544	6,819,649	726,177	-121,415	5,972,057	1,362,877	1,217,707	9,922	861,973	409,432
1982	9,023,268	7,027,802	32,578	7,060,380	765,711	-127,945	6,166,724	1,521,883	1,334,661	10,514	858,219	401,491
1983	9,594,324	7,460,116	28,672	7,488,788	821,853	-132,615	6,534,320	1,620,567	1,439,437	11,165	859,337	403,462
1984	10,525,396	8,217,284	32,167	8,249,451	921,888	-140,755	7,186,808	1,822,811	1,515,777	12,187	863,666	419,281
1985	11,374,618	8,939,126	37,937	8,977,063	1,011,168	-153,391	7,812,504	1,989,932	1,572,182	13,088	869,074	433,876
1986	12,052,546	9,540,589	21,521	9,562,110	1,077,828	-163,442	8,320,840	2,106,298	1,625,408	13,806	872,990	448,044
1987	12,742,097	10,147,143	35,596	10,182,739	1,134,041	-185,838	8,862,860	2,212,743	1,666,494	14,483	879,812	460,819
1988	13,834,553	10,985,174	57,981	11,043,155	1,264,597	-226,165	9,552,393	2,561,927	1,720,233	15,670	882,893	475,038
1989	15,119,629	11,715,265	82,148	11,797,413	1,344,390	-237,798	10,215,225	2,975,234	1,929,170	17,054	886,556	481,695
1990	16,246,612	12,629,851	80,103	12,709,954	1,465,483	-261,542	10,982,929	3,159,314	2,104,369	18,233	891,067	492,088
1991	17,067,293	13,247,148	100,033	13,347,181	1,548,615	-284,398	11,514,168	3,258,193	2,294,932	18,932	901,517	494,712
1992	18,279,962	14,286,209	85,194	14,371,403	1,647,827	-300,530	12,423,046	3,263,896	2,593,020	20,048	911,803	503,007
1993	19,145,409	14,923,968	96,800	15,020,768	1,736,227	-324,216	12,960,325	3,454,785	2,730,299	20,735	923,335	516,698
1994	20,463,897	15,880,631	77,740	15,958,371	1,871,245	-348,649	13,738,477	3,827,379	2,898,041	21,900	934,428	524,531
1995	21,841,987	16,875,596	76,587	16,952,183	1,998,208	-373,048	14,580,927	4,138,597	3,122,463	23,129	944,372	540,012
1996	23,048,005	17,916,822	68,860	17,985,682	2,098,304	-382,901	15,504,477	4,258,974	3,284,554	24,197	952,500	549,878
1997	24,327,527	18,776,496	77,762	18,854,258	2,203,146	-413,637	16,237,475	4,682,252	3,407,800	25,340	960,026	563,132
1998	25,984,696	20,292,537	83,508	20,376,045	2,338,478	-472,270	17,565,297	5,023,328	3,396,071	26,819	968,885	576,169
1999	27,119,231	21,531,704	79,306	21,611,010	2,477,863	-502,877	18,630,270	4,967,728	3,521,233	27,767	976,656	584,344
2000	28,989,058	22,948,891	57,090	23,005,981	2,605,907	-521,380	19,878,694	5,365,229	3,745,135	29,499	982,704	590,606
2001	29,819,378	23,573,428	84,818	23,658,246	2,704,349	-542,293	20,411,604	5,457,141	3,950,633	30,160	988,718	591,371
2002	30,743,801	24,463,181	60,210	24,523,391	2,795,657	-549,402	21,178,332	5,336,531	4,228,938	30,954	993,201	589,362
2003	31,992,628	25,134,748	81,106	25,215,854	2,875,121	-525,417	21,815,316	5,698,645	4,478,667	31,936	1,001,781	589,752
2004	34,533,680	26,643,523	98,160	26,741,683	3,005,165	-570,046	23,166,472	6,647,239	4,719,969	34,206	1,009,575	600,384
2005	36,532,522	27,977,399	76,883	28,054,282	3,153,215	-514,869	24,386,198	7,089,796	5,056,528	35,893	1,017,818	613,933
2006	38,976,440	29,450,193	36,910	29,487,103	3,310,174	-450,017	25,726,912	7,786,697	5,462,831	37,820	1,030,584	626,822
2007	40,679,206	30,607,025	31,421	30,638,446	3,476,768	-437,931	26,723,747	8,096,471	5,858,988	39,131	1,039,561	640,597
2008	41,913,535	30,634,055	26,230	30,660,285	3,571,513	-369,710	26,719,062	8,568,356	6,626,117	39,946	1,049,266	634,805
2009	40,288,476	29,728,062	39,210	29,767,272	3,443,339	-336,052	25,987,881	7,265,919	7,034,676	38,083	1,057,924	606,604
2010	41,878,145	30,326,282	35,482	30,361,764	3,491,267	-269,289	26,601,208	7,557,323	7,719,614	39,422	1,062,299	600,866
2011	43,485,183	31,276,827	2,707	31,279,534	3,188,399	-323,162	27,767,973	7,698,286	8,018,924	40,756	1,066,967	608,248
2012	45,477,417	32,583,176	22,992	32,606,168	3,325,882	-365,332	28,914,954	8,529,416	8,033,047	42,389	1,072,868	616,877
2013	45,417,850	33,108,984	96,121	33,205,105	3,838,258	-355,721	29,011,126	8,159,314	8,247,410	42,032	1,080,550	622,893
2014	47,199,423	34,258,261	73,159	34,331,420	3,956,837	-293,374	30,081,209	8,515,917	8,602,297	43,457	1,086,106	631,057
2015	49,627,782	35,511,197	82,445	35,593,642	4,111,761	-242,231	31,239,650	9,229,620	9,158,512	45,440	1,092,150	639,565
2016	50,504,342	36,190,952	35,702	36,226,654	4,159,931	-293,853	31,772,870	9,446,512	9,284,960	46,011	1,097,647	649,475
2017	53,065,467	37,905,171	63,875	37,969,046	4,337,183	-312,888	33,318,975	10,245,599	9,500,893	48,120	1,102,770	656,451
2018	55,474,303	39,903,873	55,563	39,959,436	4,595,084	-431,037	34,933,315	10,720,051	9,820,937	50,091	1,107,463	671,282
2019	57,720,290	41,330,535	31,589	41,362,124	4,743,256	-452,230	36,166,638	11,209,886	10,343,766	51,901	1,112,118	676,791
2020	61,205,207	42,035,651	5,509	42,041,160	4,832,809	-516,047	36,692,304	11,698,890	12,814,013	54,817	1,116,544	663,670
2021	67,197,478	45,200,998	69,501	45,270,499	5,165,780	-692,885	39,411,834	13,213,399	14,572,245	60,157	1,117,042	690,926
2022	69,537,997	48,424,497	98,848	48,523,345	5,630,934	-806,941	42,085,470	14,563,748	12,888,779	62,262	1,116,857	719,813

Personal Income and Employment by Area: Bismarck, ND

(Thousands of dollars, except as noted.)

Year	Personal income, total	Derivation of personal income								Per capita personal income (dollars)	Population (persons)	Total employment
		Earnings by place of work			Less: Contributions for government social insurance	Plus: Adjustment for residence	Equals: Net earnings by place of residence	Plus: Dividends, interest, and rent	Plus: Personal current transfer receipts			
		Nonfarm	Farm	Total								
1970	226,639	169,949	16,707	186,656	13,738	-1,315	171,603	36,491	18,545	3,571	63,474	29,430
1971	255,405	185,393	23,060	208,453	15,300	-948	192,205	40,844	22,356	3,968	64,359	29,583
1972	296,070	207,926	35,403	243,329	17,781	-367	225,181	45,248	25,641	4,530	65,363	30,687
1973	350,444	238,567	53,430	291,997	23,844	4	268,157	52,877	29,410	5,200	67,396	32,567
1974	386,378	277,015	38,862	315,877	29,187	2,784	289,474	62,680	34,224	5,587	69,160	34,151
1975	438,879	322,462	32,369	354,831	34,024	5,778	326,585	70,627	41,667	6,127	71,634	36,105
1976	491,869	385,787	20,103	405,890	40,989	1,056	365,957	79,381	46,531	6,629	74,201	38,696
1977	554,001	434,659	14,667	449,326	44,034	5,340	410,632	92,023	51,346	7,265	76,261	40,678
1978	650,694	487,219	35,149	522,368	50,507	14,737	486,598	107,200	56,896	8,359	77,840	42,642
1979	731,168	559,620	24,842	584,462	60,522	18,203	542,143	124,867	64,158	9,078	80,547	45,083
1980	788,134	616,275	-11,077	605,198	67,425	18,664	556,437	152,902	78,795	9,531	82,690	45,600
1981	922,165	657,295	33,608	690,903	75,618	21,232	636,517	193,746	91,902	11,066	83,333	45,187
1982	1,001,554	700,087	20,202	720,289	81,866	32,173	670,596	229,213	101,745	11,841	84,582	45,360
1983	1,070,112	739,703	15,260	754,963	86,640	57,917	726,240	228,534	115,338	12,388	86,386	46,326
1984	1,114,938	782,592	19,061	801,653	94,501	37,610	744,762	242,090	128,086	12,707	87,741	47,239
1985	1,139,099	809,726	16,619	826,345	100,685	23,461	749,121	252,969	137,009	12,955	87,927	47,538
1986	1,183,620	829,934	32,128	862,062	105,331	16,923	773,654	257,026	152,940	13,490	87,741	47,595
1987	1,229,127	873,109	40,329	913,438	110,597	18,442	821,283	247,602	160,242	14,177	86,699	48,852
1988	1,232,417	919,411	2,723	922,134	121,660	15,717	816,191	251,871	164,355	14,283	86,285	49,781
1989	1,342,351	974,554	18,269	992,823	130,168	15,076	877,731	279,798	184,822	15,564	86,247	51,555
1990	1,425,843	1,044,433	18,352	1,062,785	147,504	15,607	930,888	295,177	199,778	16,516	86,329	52,908
1991	1,484,878	1,106,376	17,774	1,124,150	159,031	14,647	979,766	298,432	206,680	17,046	87,112	54,515
1992	1,624,657	1,197,990	38,840	1,236,830	171,845	15,141	1,080,126	310,587	233,944	18,336	88,603	55,770
1993	1,724,646	1,281,884	37,132	1,319,016	185,099	16,041	1,149,958	325,994	248,694	19,136	90,124	57,442
1994	1,806,866	1,360,425	26,799	1,387,224	198,671	18,391	1,206,944	347,294	252,628	19,829	91,123	59,882
1995	1,896,494	1,430,933	7,865	1,438,798	208,280	20,691	1,251,209	375,223	270,062	20,516	92,442	60,725
1996	2,013,055	1,488,791	25,466	1,514,257	214,817	26,735	1,326,175	399,565	287,315	21,465	93,781	61,687
1997	2,089,886	1,573,374	-9,379	1,563,995	224,526	19,992	1,359,461	424,416	306,009	22,067	94,705	63,083
1998	2,254,434	1,679,740	26,304	1,706,044	237,727	20,078	1,488,395	451,269	314,770	23,537	95,784	64,969
1999	2,343,692	1,779,370	23,233	1,802,603	246,108	21,807	1,578,302	439,533	325,857	24,332	96,321	66,643
2000	2,535,074	1,892,666	48,741	1,941,407	259,464	21,156	1,703,099	475,952	356,023	26,157	96,917	67,825
2001	2,733,800	2,078,714	40,254	2,118,968	273,230	26,153	1,871,891	491,711	370,198	28,110	97,253	68,045
2002	2,797,469	2,168,644	8,595	2,177,239	281,650	29,346	1,924,935	481,377	391,157	28,472	98,254	68,454
2003	2,997,390	2,298,481	41,288	2,339,769	300,773	31,321	2,070,317	515,588	411,485	30,238	99,128	69,558
2004	3,183,112	2,420,659	43,529	2,464,188	315,690	38,838	2,187,336	553,120	442,656	31,789	100,134	71,512
2005	3,389,180	2,565,024	61,741	2,626,765	330,057	41,649	2,338,357	578,512	472,311	33,274	101,858	73,523
2006	3,615,286	2,733,724	23,548	2,757,272	347,639	51,755	2,461,388	646,919	506,979	34,859	103,713	76,119
2007	3,941,503	2,926,297	55,224	2,981,521	367,009	58,505	2,673,017	718,138	550,348	37,308	105,648	78,215
2008	4,278,561	3,094,324	57,342	3,151,666	385,667	72,322	2,838,321	809,928	630,312	39,908	107,210	79,897
2009	4,452,404	3,271,335	51,951	3,323,286	417,292	98,949	3,004,943	787,920	659,541	40,844	109,009	80,760
2010	4,820,187	3,494,978	59,926	3,554,904	420,874	112,981	3,247,011	844,810	728,366	43,345	111,206	82,269
2011	5,397,963	3,793,788	58,103	3,851,891	419,086	154,918	3,587,723	1,058,838	751,402	47,632	113,327	84,543
2012	6,120,201	4,082,622	157,162	4,239,784	423,787	220,854	4,036,851	1,319,118	764,232	52,516	116,539	88,016
2013	6,390,543	4,395,603	66,858	4,462,461	519,698	282,070	4,224,833	1,369,214	796,496	53,030	120,508	91,022
2014	6,988,155	4,771,107	48,770	4,819,877	569,913	332,322	4,582,286	1,549,219	856,650	56,424	123,850	93,413
2015	6,988,305	4,953,306	24,587	4,977,893	603,093	304,926	4,679,726	1,416,436	892,143	54,827	127,462	95,088
2016	7,023,434	4,991,087	18,749	5,009,836	611,208	264,765	4,663,393	1,436,023	924,018	54,116	129,785	94,904
2017	7,037,485	4,968,379	36,176	5,004,555	631,186	268,863	4,642,232	1,446,852	948,401	53,664	131,140	93,892
2018	7,372,979	5,094,169	34,165	5,128,334	627,699	281,521	4,782,156	1,572,674	1,018,149	55,936	131,811	93,440
2019	7,649,126	5,223,880	24,788	5,248,668	632,869	306,639	4,922,438	1,646,983	1,079,705	57,610	132,775	93,658
2020	8,169,343	5,324,532	79,555	5,404,087	668,980	259,515	4,994,622	1,749,287	1,425,434	61,067	133,776	92,062
2021	9,024,570	5,687,284	140,213	5,827,497	709,526	242,334	5,360,305	2,100,666	1,563,599	67,147	134,400	94,473
2022	9,263,708	5,963,838	126,558	6,090,396	759,604	262,126	5,592,918	2,296,310	1,374,480	68,698	134,846	96,906

Personal Income and Employment by Area: Blacksburg-Christiansburg, VA

(Thousands of dollars, except as noted.)

Year	Personal income, total	Derivation of personal income: Earnings by place of work: Nonfarm	Farm	Total	Less: Contributions for government social insurance	Plus: Adjustment for residence	Equals: Net earnings by place of residence	Plus: Dividends, interest, and rent	Plus: Personal current transfer receipts	Per capita personal income (dollars)	Population (persons)	Total employment
1970	308,501	281,169	2,441	283,610	18,040	-20,056	245,514	36,092	26,895	2,930	105,279	46,819
1971	330,774	293,491	2,794	296,285	19,675	-18,553	258,057	40,252	32,465	3,061	108,059	46,502
1972	372,444	330,742	3,746	334,488	23,392	-19,918	291,178	44,712	36,554	3,361	110,811	48,518
1973	426,571	375,630	4,564	380,194	30,532	-20,455	329,207	52,480	44,884	3,726	114,478	51,301
1974	471,225	408,247	2,077	410,324	34,567	-19,788	355,969	61,269	53,987	3,961	118,956	52,570
1975	521,040	430,024	1,760	431,784	35,711	-17,716	378,357	69,518	73,165	4,274	121,908	51,584
1976	581,487	479,927	3,187	483,114	40,458	-18,496	424,160	77,062	80,265	4,704	123,619	52,797
1977	651,281	545,071	1,824	546,895	46,047	-21,445	479,403	86,874	85,004	5,169	126,002	54,971
1978	742,546	623,108	3,328	626,436	54,020	-24,011	548,405	100,211	93,930	5,780	128,476	58,079
1979	831,866	691,122	5,259	696,381	62,279	-28,541	605,561	116,406	109,899	6,406	129,849	60,025
1980	932,496	747,200	4,426	751,626	67,913	-27,702	656,011	145,585	130,900	7,161	130,226	60,742
1981	1,026,906	804,748	3,307	808,055	78,578	-28,852	700,625	174,764	151,517	7,793	131,772	59,482
1982	1,108,901	851,858	1,331	853,189	84,817	-31,358	737,014	207,882	164,005	8,388	132,202	59,192
1983	1,214,258	943,451	3,695	947,146	95,336	-40,219	811,591	224,571	178,096	9,176	132,324	60,531
1984	1,353,809	1,075,750	3,369	1,079,119	112,257	-51,786	915,076	253,162	185,571	10,142	133,483	64,176
1985	1,449,113	1,159,298	1,858	1,161,156	122,931	-57,785	980,440	271,120	197,553	10,795	134,236	66,227
1986	1,540,350	1,234,965	2,887	1,237,852	134,873	-62,585	1,040,394	291,398	208,558	11,378	135,376	67,178
1987	1,639,200	1,336,155	8,801	1,344,956	144,375	-70,978	1,129,603	297,238	212,359	12,025	136,318	69,528
1988	1,782,654	1,467,475	11,202	1,478,677	163,275	-83,416	1,231,986	325,246	225,422	12,878	138,426	72,202
1989	1,910,730	1,545,965	12,718	1,558,683	171,706	-89,794	1,297,183	371,065	242,482	13,700	139,471	73,017
1990	1,988,472	1,596,591	12,931	1,609,522	177,156	-89,363	1,343,003	378,328	267,141	14,084	141,184	73,301
1991	2,016,804	1,577,755	10,498	1,588,253	177,079	-81,159	1,330,015	397,668	289,121	14,225	141,780	71,029
1992	2,126,006	1,670,843	8,761	1,679,604	186,274	-86,659	1,406,671	399,983	319,352	14,891	142,774	70,976
1993	2,209,776	1,736,967	6,892	1,743,859	193,484	-87,587	1,462,788	412,726	334,262	15,389	143,594	72,196
1994	2,334,166	1,847,414	6,495	1,853,909	203,701	-92,513	1,557,695	428,408	348,063	16,106	144,923	73,606
1995	2,456,114	1,907,586	5,707	1,913,293	209,502	-90,407	1,613,384	466,494	376,236	16,881	145,498	76,033
1996	2,536,187	1,961,666	4,861	1,966,527	213,248	-92,077	1,661,202	480,462	394,523	17,361	146,082	76,685
1997	2,708,727	2,108,844	2,664	2,111,508	227,588	-100,687	1,783,233	516,082	409,412	18,434	146,943	77,680
1998	2,848,538	2,228,590	5,012	2,233,602	236,411	-103,390	1,893,801	528,823	425,914	19,109	149,066	77,742
1999	3,022,929	2,422,161	3,918	2,426,079	255,810	-120,780	2,049,489	531,447	441,993	20,056	150,727	81,341
2000	3,190,876	2,517,489	10,937	2,528,426	264,386	-119,052	2,144,988	575,876	470,012	21,055	151,553	82,109
2001	3,322,962	2,600,273	9,104	2,609,377	285,975	-120,142	2,203,260	596,890	522,812	21,669	153,348	81,027
2002	3,430,288	2,726,995	7,908	2,734,903	300,686	-124,927	2,309,290	577,026	543,972	22,373	153,326	81,464
2003	3,601,908	2,864,568	4,220	2,868,788	312,960	-139,296	2,416,532	594,417	590,959	23,388	154,009	82,176
2004	3,781,845	3,009,506	8,789	3,018,295	331,831	-151,926	2,534,538	620,553	626,754	24,455	154,647	82,908
2005	3,986,634	3,163,176	9,418	3,172,594	356,030	-165,233	2,651,331	654,590	680,713	25,490	156,402	84,230
2006	4,222,282	3,297,687	2,115	3,299,802	375,167	-175,220	2,749,415	731,818	741,049	26,677	158,277	84,952
2007	4,475,005	3,413,425	-1,795	3,411,630	387,638	-171,676	2,852,316	829,824	792,865	27,954	160,085	85,709
2008	4,618,186	3,387,074	-1,242	3,385,832	391,780	-152,954	2,841,098	875,603	901,485	28,640	161,247	85,802
2009	4,653,518	3,305,582	79	3,305,661	384,252	-136,365	2,785,044	905,973	962,501	28,657	162,385	83,094
2010	4,678,344	3,322,131	953	3,323,084	384,620	-138,072	2,800,392	842,263	1,035,689	28,681	163,115	81,267
2011	4,863,463	3,412,952	6,585	3,419,537	355,606	-154,553	2,909,378	905,250	1,048,835	29,775	163,343	82,726
2012	5,052,844	3,578,421	8,303	3,586,724	371,517	-168,076	3,047,131	954,199	1,051,514	30,818	163,956	84,057
2013	5,117,992	3,702,184	9,377	3,711,561	428,977	-175,163	3,107,421	934,486	1,076,085	31,018	165,000	85,037
2014	5,379,412	3,871,638	12,214	3,883,852	446,966	-195,731	3,241,155	1,016,340	1,121,917	32,533	165,353	85,937
2015	5,602,124	4,055,863	8,041	4,063,904	465,909	-193,262	3,404,733	1,047,150	1,150,241	33,884	165,333	87,436
2016	5,721,310	4,114,415	810	4,115,225	471,667	-207,941	3,435,617	1,089,844	1,195,849	34,437	166,139	87,651
2017	5,942,721	4,223,984	5,298	4,229,282	489,496	-212,561	3,527,225	1,178,407	1,237,089	35,798	166,007	87,763
2018	6,238,130	4,469,648	1,903	4,471,551	517,929	-248,828	3,704,794	1,241,533	1,291,803	37,403	166,780	88,929
2019	6,406,993	4,586,151	4,325	4,590,476	538,348	-264,633	3,787,495	1,267,836	1,351,662	38,426	166,737	89,517
2020	6,797,500	4,573,915	3,475	4,577,390	544,266	-262,900	3,770,224	1,282,556	1,744,720	40,883	166,269	85,756
2021	7,414,890	5,087,892	3,813	5,091,705	605,550	-317,313	4,168,842	1,337,990	1,908,058	44,730	165,769	90,629
2022	7,684,525	5,510,249	3,585	5,513,834	665,528	-352,465	4,495,841	1,410,335	1,778,349	46,345	165,812	95,460

Personal Income and Employment by Area: Bloomington, IL

(Thousands of dollars, except as noted.)

Year	Personal income, total	Derivation of personal income: Earnings by place of work: Nonfarm	Farm	Total	Less: Contributions for government social insurance	Plus: Adjustment for residence	Equals: Net earnings by place of residence	Plus: Dividends, interest, and rent	Plus: Personal current transfer receipts	Per capita personal income (dollars)	Population (persons)	Total employment
1970	426,195	332,491	23,261	355,752	21,170	-4,889	329,693	67,030	29,472	4,056	105,073	49,339
1971	474,637	367,846	29,824	397,670	24,157	-4,945	368,568	72,577	33,492	4,398	107,920	50,699
1972	516,881	409,471	21,790	431,261	28,456	-5,690	397,115	82,043	37,723	4,573	113,024	53,021
1973	608,697	454,090	54,319	508,409	36,488	-5,048	466,873	97,490	44,334	5,329	114,221	55,892
1974	679,627	505,814	59,286	565,100	42,644	-4,031	518,425	110,009	51,193	5,913	114,945	57,470
1975	796,858	566,848	86,561	653,409	46,090	-3,066	604,253	126,038	66,567	6,988	114,040	57,543
1976	851,569	622,074	71,940	694,014	51,424	-562	642,028	136,407	73,134	7,377	115,432	58,560
1977	926,750	686,703	65,112	751,815	57,099	1,228	695,944	154,027	76,779	7,931	116,848	60,239
1978	996,868	769,640	37,906	807,546	65,664	3,361	745,243	168,551	83,074	8,481	117,535	63,110
1979	1,118,683	849,751	55,877	905,628	75,895	6,313	836,046	190,844	91,793	9,466	118,173	64,509
1980	1,200,025	913,322	15,274	928,596	81,388	11,434	858,642	226,948	114,435	10,054	119,354	63,288
1981	1,366,691	1,013,302	40,866	1,054,168	98,143	6,889	962,914	272,540	131,237	11,393	119,963	64,442
1982	1,465,988	1,063,887	22,888	1,086,775	103,420	2,627	985,982	334,786	145,220	12,178	120,379	64,190
1983	1,500,259	1,129,085	-24,867	1,104,218	109,498	-2,456	992,264	350,261	157,734	12,335	121,622	65,014
1984	1,670,439	1,210,266	33,477	1,243,743	121,233	3,445	1,125,955	382,102	162,382	13,659	122,295	65,763
1985	1,746,870	1,269,176	47,934	1,317,110	129,550	3,443	1,191,003	381,469	174,398	14,212	122,918	65,433
1986	1,810,124	1,350,026	42,745	1,392,771	138,673	-24,376	1,229,722	400,528	179,874	14,760	122,638	66,812
1987	1,895,091	1,478,265	31,059	1,509,324	150,954	-36,864	1,321,506	386,532	187,053	15,244	124,317	69,500
1988	2,031,658	1,619,207	15,109	1,634,316	169,063	-35,141	1,430,112	403,418	198,128	16,122	126,021	72,765
1989	2,294,667	1,822,237	44,286	1,866,523	192,957	-63,661	1,609,905	476,105	208,657	17,980	127,624	77,151
1990	2,472,437	2,038,610	46,980	2,085,590	211,629	-86,942	1,787,019	460,834	224,584	19,061	129,715	79,934
1991	2,542,695	2,131,264	17,294	2,148,558	227,497	-94,266	1,826,795	477,003	238,897	19,234	132,200	81,260
1992	2,786,285	2,340,326	46,539	2,386,865	246,234	-110,822	2,029,809	490,126	266,350	20,762	134,198	83,752
1993	2,886,013	2,449,412	32,013	2,481,425	259,093	-121,202	2,101,130	505,062	279,821	21,092	136,831	84,448
1994	3,124,437	2,690,847	58,658	2,749,505	286,774	-146,066	2,316,665	522,054	285,718	22,541	138,613	88,268
1995	3,281,695	2,865,618	-2,048	2,863,570	302,332	-164,723	2,396,515	576,639	308,541	23,284	140,945	90,575
1996	3,522,796	2,998,624	70,409	3,069,033	310,936	-180,232	2,577,865	616,228	328,703	24,745	142,363	92,403
1997	3,712,831	3,175,483	60,142	3,235,625	325,106	-198,324	2,712,195	660,037	340,599	25,722	144,342	96,023
1998	3,936,559	3,441,991	19,716	3,461,707	346,448	-226,302	2,888,957	692,508	355,094	26,866	146,526	100,753
1999	4,254,559	3,830,848	24,808	3,855,656	377,888	-277,500	3,200,268	688,950	365,341	28,528	149,135	106,179
2000	4,521,501	4,060,709	55,570	4,116,279	396,157	-314,850	3,405,272	729,885	386,344	29,975	150,844	108,052
2001	4,893,877	4,461,950	58,547	4,520,497	442,049	-343,258	3,735,190	742,148	416,539	32,046	152,713	109,029
2002	5,042,894	4,745,856	47,167	4,793,023	470,769	-384,301	3,937,953	659,838	445,103	32,351	155,882	110,524
2003	5,223,299	4,904,307	57,310	4,961,617	487,495	-412,912	4,061,210	695,971	466,118	33,102	157,795	110,089
2004	5,396,002	4,968,719	104,248	5,072,967	505,171	-422,081	4,145,715	756,412	493,875	33,917	159,096	109,226
2005	5,473,204	5,083,723	52,634	5,136,357	514,960	-416,472	4,204,925	720,864	547,415	34,144	160,299	109,997
2006	5,939,674	5,425,347	70,791	5,496,138	545,470	-435,625	4,515,043	849,840	574,791	36,456	162,925	110,933
2007	6,203,018	5,532,894	126,666	5,659,560	560,744	-422,082	4,676,734	896,658	629,626	37,543	165,223	112,618
2008	6,575,432	5,755,275	172,186	5,927,461	587,762	-436,527	4,903,172	954,646	717,614	39,415	166,825	113,557
2009	6,567,243	5,782,607	97,262	5,879,869	588,212	-455,276	4,836,381	935,434	795,428	38,922	168,727	111,831
2010	6,837,846	5,998,894	99,954	6,098,848	602,388	-500,666	4,995,794	957,446	884,606	40,268	169,808	111,407
2011	7,227,139	6,168,834	197,499	6,366,333	553,183	-487,341	5,325,809	1,027,445	873,885	42,288	170,902	112,016
2012	7,375,802	6,356,463	122,624	6,479,087	575,936	-524,714	5,378,437	1,127,395	869,970	42,710	172,693	113,167
2013	7,571,709	6,554,860	265,623	6,820,483	668,705	-583,867	5,567,911	1,102,624	901,174	43,271	174,985	111,479
2014	7,522,657	6,467,014	135,609	6,602,623	657,537	-512,660	5,432,426	1,167,757	922,474	43,226	174,031	110,677
2015	7,870,184	6,668,641	16,606	6,685,247	666,023	-362,650	5,656,574	1,225,475	988,135	45,478	173,055	112,408
2016	8,004,176	6,676,083	92,000	6,768,083	672,318	-375,881	5,719,884	1,272,630	1,011,662	46,278	172,957	111,468
2017	8,101,355	6,679,386	81,570	6,760,956	673,222	-361,997	5,725,737	1,324,714	1,050,904	46,955	172,536	111,869
2018	8,425,764	6,913,998	112,510	7,026,508	694,490	-379,329	5,952,689	1,371,735	1,101,340	48,958	172,103	111,548
2019	8,515,404	6,892,992	69,748	6,962,740	694,180	-366,451	5,902,109	1,440,134	1,173,161	49,805	170,976	110,658
2020	9,392,021	7,426,218	125,075	7,551,293	753,299	-453,887	6,344,107	1,426,092	1,621,822	54,939	170,954	107,170
2021	10,141,996	7,732,778	255,467	7,988,245	782,114	-465,614	6,740,517	1,559,942	1,841,537	59,244	171,190	109,966
2022	9,956,632	7,725,703	310,643	8,036,346	810,657	-382,950	6,842,739	1,625,641	1,488,252	58,178	171,141	111,463

Personal Income and Employment by Area: Bloomington, IN

(Thousands of dollars, except as noted.)

Year	Personal income, total	Derivation of personal income: Earnings by place of work: Nonfarm	Farm	Total	Less: Contributions for government social insurance	Plus: Adjustment for residence	Equals: Net earnings by place of residence	Plus: Dividends, interest, and rent	Plus: Personal current transfer receipts	Per capita personal income (dollars)	Population (persons)	Total employment
1970	295,962	245,530	1,772	247,302	16,732	-2,338	228,232	46,647	21,083	3,031	97,656	40,115
1971	339,662	284,719	2,718	287,437	20,166	-4,207	263,064	52,579	24,019	3,406	99,712	43,719
1972	372,513	307,737	3,263	311,000	23,115	-682	287,203	57,952	27,358	3,597	103,553	45,422
1973	417,304	339,642	6,908	346,550	29,379	1,126	318,297	65,496	33,511	4,001	104,311	47,027
1974	449,449	357,808	4,027	361,835	32,425	4,273	333,683	75,322	40,444	4,231	106,218	46,825
1975	486,091	360,750	3,663	364,413	32,416	12,169	344,166	86,349	55,576	4,676	103,965	44,564
1976	551,508	419,148	5,377	424,525	37,758	13,308	400,075	95,585	55,848	5,206	105,944	47,509
1977	620,179	471,357	3,593	474,950	42,021	18,067	450,996	108,966	60,217	5,647	109,821	48,817
1978	707,249	535,610	3,150	538,760	49,020	24,014	513,754	125,161	68,334	6,302	112,226	50,475
1979	778,364	578,870	2,958	581,828	54,893	33,960	560,895	138,768	78,701	6,886	113,041	51,520
1980	875,868	634,954	-424	634,530	59,704	37,379	612,205	171,401	92,262	7,612	115,057	53,462
1981	982,972	700,631	3	700,634	71,211	38,864	668,287	209,393	105,292	8,435	116,537	54,013
1982	1,049,032	737,043	27	737,070	76,225	36,206	697,051	234,780	117,201	8,926	117,520	54,716
1983	1,125,088	802,262	-6,533	795,729	82,352	31,933	745,310	253,755	126,023	9,532	118,037	55,528
1984	1,233,730	880,014	-150	879,864	91,264	36,295	824,895	275,913	132,922	10,460	117,945	57,620
1985	1,321,606	947,634	-1,712	945,922	99,460	38,674	885,136	295,151	141,319	11,186	118,146	59,678
1986	1,431,650	1,045,555	-2,662	1,042,893	110,086	35,283	968,090	317,117	146,443	12,026	119,043	61,907
1987	1,534,845	1,151,256	-1,707	1,149,549	118,969	28,128	1,058,708	321,868	154,269	12,738	120,497	65,078
1988	1,661,003	1,251,405	-4,104	1,247,301	135,487	25,857	1,137,671	356,611	166,721	13,602	122,111	67,474
1989	1,829,954	1,353,762	1,960	1,355,722	146,849	26,440	1,235,313	410,318	184,323	14,657	124,856	68,835
1990	1,962,975	1,450,795	6	1,450,801	161,910	28,689	1,317,580	443,267	202,128	15,484	126,773	70,276
1991	2,072,150	1,543,240	-1,831	1,541,409	173,933	27,578	1,395,054	451,994	225,102	16,191	127,983	70,628
1992	2,231,993	1,674,679	2,602	1,677,281	187,554	19,265	1,508,992	470,581	252,420	17,152	130,131	72,264
1993	2,331,457	1,762,577	2,007	1,764,584	198,452	7,109	1,573,241	490,116	268,100	17,610	132,395	74,141
1994	2,444,982	1,856,263	2,090	1,858,353	213,630	-9,161	1,635,562	531,056	278,364	18,154	134,678	75,988
1995	2,575,898	1,950,252	50	1,950,302	224,497	-13,051	1,712,754	574,615	288,529	18,902	136,275	78,167
1996	2,736,168	2,061,017	2,885	2,063,902	235,628	-23,395	1,804,879	615,627	315,662	19,857	137,794	80,732
1997	2,916,630	2,208,500	2,638	2,211,138	251,722	-36,313	1,923,103	663,832	329,695	20,942	139,271	82,095
1998	3,112,436	2,343,880	-566	2,343,314	262,697	-43,185	2,037,432	712,990	362,014	22,148	140,527	82,583
1999	3,253,162	2,480,930	-1,511	2,479,419	275,245	-51,496	2,152,678	712,218	388,266	22,947	141,770	84,309
2000	3,461,648	2,633,042	792	2,633,834	289,429	-61,788	2,282,617	761,988	417,043	24,257	142,709	85,477
2001	3,526,618	2,639,104	1,579	2,640,683	285,517	-67,074	2,288,092	780,512	458,014	24,550	143,650	86,472
2002	3,589,414	2,743,241	-356	2,742,885	297,396	-72,935	2,372,554	733,237	483,623	24,805	144,707	86,444
2003	3,766,459	2,889,701	3,461	2,893,162	315,117	-90,245	2,487,800	773,390	505,269	25,651	146,835	88,849
2004	3,984,365	3,003,442	7,656	3,011,098	328,728	-98,303	2,584,067	865,861	534,437	26,822	148,549	90,037
2005	4,112,198	3,112,590	5,211	3,117,801	346,283	-99,751	2,671,767	855,363	585,068	27,397	150,096	90,894
2006	4,358,846	3,228,452	2,643	3,231,095	361,491	-103,538	2,766,066	955,429	637,351	28,574	152,548	92,079
2007	4,521,736	3,337,082	4,539	3,341,621	377,795	-112,543	2,851,283	997,736	672,717	29,295	154,352	94,396
2008	4,857,914	3,445,175	7,899	3,453,074	391,968	-121,382	2,939,724	1,131,697	786,493	31,108	156,164	94,460
2009	4,844,013	3,475,497	8,256	3,483,753	395,869	-116,058	2,971,826	1,022,526	849,661	30,689	157,840	94,187
2010	4,948,102	3,519,410	10,533	3,529,943	395,667	-103,803	3,030,473	988,413	929,216	30,935	159,950	93,006
2011	5,236,675	3,654,766	13,108	3,667,874	358,753	-93,023	3,216,098	1,087,764	932,813	32,564	160,810	93,292
2012	5,451,650	3,793,687	3,075	3,796,762	371,013	-77,083	3,348,666	1,141,181	961,803	33,820	161,197	92,914
2013	5,456,252	3,813,346	19,624	3,832,970	428,107	-73,177	3,331,686	1,162,003	962,563	33,928	160,817	92,751
2014	5,717,597	3,964,327	4,368	3,968,695	443,562	-80,547	3,444,586	1,226,687	1,046,324	35,458	161,248	93,831
2015	6,011,540	4,198,472	-3,796	4,194,676	467,384	-96,189	3,631,103	1,291,308	1,089,129	37,307	161,138	94,442
2016	6,321,060	4,389,531	1,683	4,391,214	481,505	-88,224	3,821,485	1,364,743	1,134,832	39,045	161,893	95,319
2017	6,666,749	4,655,088	2,302	4,657,390	509,344	-92,679	4,055,367	1,449,230	1,162,152	41,187	161,864	97,282
2018	6,977,382	4,859,673	2,765	4,862,438	526,207	-82,722	4,253,509	1,506,020	1,217,853	43,141	161,733	99,305
2019	7,261,483	5,087,966	845	5,088,811	555,287	-104,226	4,429,298	1,542,157	1,290,028	44,911	161,687	100,275
2020	7,717,017	5,246,161	8,859	5,255,020	591,071	-130,555	4,533,394	1,535,313	1,648,310	47,966	160,885	97,553
2021	8,429,079	5,658,564	15,625	5,674,189	636,860	-186,486	4,850,843	1,699,904	1,878,332	52,171	161,567	100,002
2022	8,663,477	6,067,649	10,243	6,077,892	684,499	-197,411	5,195,982	1,798,836	1,668,659	53,735	161,227	104,511

Personal Income and Employment by Area: Bloomsberg-Berwick, PA

(Thousands of dollars, except as noted.)

		Derivation of personal income										
		Earnings by place of work										
Year	Personal income, total	Nonfarm	Farm	Total	Less: Contributions for government social insurance	Plus: Adjustment for residence	Equals: Net earnings by place of residence	Plus: Dividends, interest, and rent	Plus: Personal current transfer receipts	Per capita personal income (dollars)	Population (persons)	Total employment
1970	250,744	206,101	6,163	212,264	15,627	-11,192	185,445	30,231	35,068	3,488	71,882	33,766
1971	267,673	218,976	4,975	223,951	17,361	-8,829	197,761	32,696	37,216	3,655	73,233	33,943
1972	303,979	249,270	4,873	254,143	20,463	-9,182	224,498	36,461	43,020	4,080	74,511	35,339
1973	344,214	282,155	7,632	289,787	26,299	-9,585	253,903	42,002	48,309	4,577	75,213	37,183
1974	382,390	313,792	7,241	321,033	30,729	-14,991	275,313	48,051	59,026	5,021	76,162	37,830
1975	412,614	309,436	7,075	316,511	28,978	-5,749	281,784	52,710	78,120	5,364	76,926	35,596
1976	450,624	332,725	8,236	340,961	31,763	-3,376	305,822	56,924	87,878	5,847	77,069	35,569
1977	489,756	369,040	7,012	376,052	35,346	-5,216	335,490	64,086	90,180	6,323	77,452	36,182
1978	546,098	421,502	7,769	429,271	41,398	-8,244	379,629	70,805	95,664	7,020	77,789	37,911
1979	611,147	476,008	10,442	486,450	48,245	-14,956	423,249	78,681	109,217	7,796	78,394	38,953
1980	659,629	502,503	5,215	507,718	51,415	-19,705	436,598	97,208	125,823	8,372	78,787	38,905
1981	733,980	542,114	9,826	551,940	59,321	-20,012	472,607	118,397	142,976	9,266	79,211	38,916
1982	785,535	559,300	8,196	567,496	61,708	-20,217	485,571	138,044	161,920	9,915	79,223	37,763
1983	837,176	607,619	-1,411	606,208	67,718	-28,282	510,208	153,679	173,289	10,508	79,674	38,203
1984	901,512	663,927	7,281	671,208	76,996	-37,327	556,885	168,953	175,674	11,392	79,135	39,057
1985	965,499	725,646	8,420	734,066	85,560	-48,209	600,297	183,425	181,777	12,271	78,679	40,396
1986	1,015,478	758,597	6,188	764,785	89,567	-46,058	629,160	194,634	191,684	12,898	78,729	40,797
1987	1,068,517	814,135	7,788	821,923	94,966	-49,643	677,314	196,427	194,776	13,574	78,718	41,605
1988	1,155,541	887,567	9,295	896,862	106,285	-51,226	739,351	210,409	205,781	14,545	79,446	43,282
1989	1,261,659	952,530	12,390	964,920	112,265	-57,291	795,364	240,043	226,252	15,726	80,226	44,433
1990	1,318,526	1,018,861	11,032	1,029,893	120,234	-68,356	841,303	242,884	234,339	16,255	81,113	45,090
1991	1,387,812	1,063,339	3,361	1,066,700	126,958	-77,757	861,985	252,367	273,460	16,993	81,669	44,976
1992	1,474,157	1,154,012	18,069	1,172,081	137,573	-100,202	934,306	253,056	286,795	17,894	82,381	45,346
1993	1,526,188	1,211,594	15,083	1,226,677	146,651	-111,035	968,991	260,546	296,651	18,432	82,802	45,742
1994	1,565,395	1,291,421	15,604	1,307,025	159,541	-134,793	1,012,691	262,969	289,735	18,906	82,801	46,889
1995	1,617,133	1,256,991	5,784	1,262,775	154,393	-83,180	1,025,202	289,105	302,826	19,481	83,012	46,421
1996	1,673,982	1,263,296	15,878	1,279,174	151,946	-66,384	1,060,844	291,862	321,276	20,165	83,013	45,448
1997	1,728,509	1,347,040	14,226	1,361,266	161,202	-108,159	1,091,905	309,273	327,331	20,847	82,914	45,712
1998	1,804,413	1,480,203	12,366	1,492,569	173,093	-163,352	1,156,124	323,009	325,280	21,839	82,623	47,654
1999	1,846,598	1,546,587	8,392	1,554,979	177,329	-174,267	1,203,383	305,361	337,854	22,397	82,449	47,905
2000	1,970,005	1,593,669	15,455	1,609,124	180,255	-141,578	1,287,291	321,503	361,211	23,963	82,211	48,593
2001	2,049,371	1,596,968	10,948	1,607,916	180,680	-102,868	1,324,368	336,266	388,737	24,813	82,592	46,782
2002	2,172,460	1,706,799	5,975	1,712,774	190,174	-105,272	1,417,328	336,606	418,526	26,225	82,838	47,452
2003	2,264,653	1,742,958	15,517	1,758,475	192,009	-76,440	1,490,026	333,816	440,811	27,206	83,240	47,102
2004	2,341,845	1,863,950	23,544	1,887,494	204,948	-124,591	1,557,955	323,970	459,920	28,042	83,511	48,146
2005	2,407,674	1,954,292	17,722	1,972,014	217,580	-146,948	1,607,486	305,428	494,760	28,759	83,718	49,455
2006	2,524,613	2,064,748	16,258	2,081,006	230,685	-166,923	1,683,398	325,673	515,542	30,056	83,996	50,636
2007	2,701,919	2,204,221	14,849	2,219,070	246,860	-193,238	1,778,972	369,217	553,730	32,050	84,303	51,635
2008	2,850,249	2,278,403	10,492	2,288,895	258,353	-230,647	1,799,895	427,013	623,341	33,637	84,735	51,999
2009	2,822,620	2,284,822	8,421	2,293,243	260,920	-301,665	1,730,658	405,313	686,649	33,058	85,385	51,226
2010	2,977,802	2,401,598	16,403	2,418,001	271,939	-288,239	1,857,823	412,381	707,598	34,766	85,652	51,588
2011	3,123,537	2,541,112	14,811	2,555,923	254,810	-335,403	1,965,710	435,893	721,934	36,558	85,441	52,579
2012	3,186,975	2,616,766	22,117	2,638,883	260,509	-354,334	2,024,040	445,218	717,717	37,291	85,462	53,554
2013	3,261,835	2,774,568	25,783	2,800,351	307,640	-417,792	2,074,919	457,045	729,871	38,113	85,584	54,458
2014	3,319,155	2,719,208	24,721	2,743,929	308,544	-354,945	2,080,440	477,218	761,497	38,806	85,531	53,087
2015	3,423,518	2,816,965	17,061	2,834,026	318,923	-371,694	2,143,409	489,360	790,749	40,289	84,973	52,720
2016	3,522,775	2,884,028	5,625	2,889,653	325,154	-350,692	2,213,807	496,564	812,404	41,749	84,379	52,704
2017	3,622,061	2,974,517	14,871	2,989,388	343,537	-366,497	2,279,354	521,390	821,317	43,194	83,855	52,893
2018	3,743,675	3,038,642	8,571	3,047,213	348,144	-374,919	2,324,150	547,158	872,367	44,885	83,405	52,816
2019	3,840,730	3,139,460	16,869	3,156,329	360,007	-425,385	2,370,937	554,744	915,049	46,190	83,150	53,052
2020	4,170,300	3,159,884	12,064	3,171,948	362,350	-432,767	2,376,831	573,578	1,219,891	50,359	82,811	51,240
2021	4,445,489	3,343,927	27,635	3,371,562	383,029	-441,745	2,546,788	587,698	1,311,003	53,507	83,083	52,250
2022	4,433,004	3,555,308	25,817	3,581,125	419,006	-472,691	2,689,428	618,671	1,124,905	53,399	83,017	53,876

Personal Income and Employment by Area: Boise City, ID

(Thousands of dollars, except as noted.)

Year	Personal income, total	Derivation of personal income: Earnings by place of work: Nonfarm	Farm	Total	Less: Contributions for government social insurance	Plus: Adjustment for residence	Equals: Net earnings by place of residence	Plus: Dividends, interest, and rent	Plus: Personal current transfer receipts	Per capita personal income (dollars)	Population (persons)	Total employment
1970	779,735	574,503	42,703	617,206	40,945	4,147	580,408	133,624	65,703	4,042	192,885	93,530
1971	875,459	645,302	42,222	687,524	47,174	4,019	644,369	153,300	77,790	4,322	202,549	97,869
1972	996,230	744,039	49,919	793,958	57,213	3,496	740,241	167,099	88,890	4,709	211,579	103,513
1973	1,146,673	849,734	74,955	924,689	76,192	3,112	851,609	192,729	102,335	5,214	219,916	110,066
1974	1,319,146	965,328	87,151	1,052,479	88,942	3,533	967,070	226,367	125,709	5,733	230,081	114,790
1975	1,511,201	1,118,116	64,001	1,182,117	101,179	6,646	1,087,584	269,165	154,452	6,382	236,798	119,885
1976	1,703,255	1,302,391	52,111	1,354,502	120,033	7,997	1,242,466	292,150	168,639	6,915	246,322	128,647
1977	1,919,604	1,490,477	39,297	1,529,774	138,147	10,256	1,401,883	337,244	180,477	7,499	255,984	136,175
1978	2,225,440	1,746,071	47,195	1,793,266	163,952	12,028	1,641,342	384,840	199,258	8,330	267,147	146,795
1979	2,448,323	1,913,838	42,590	1,956,428	190,026	15,110	1,781,512	429,590	237,221	8,872	275,953	150,083
1980	2,715,476	2,045,709	62,521	2,108,230	205,087	15,438	1,918,581	508,301	288,594	9,651	281,376	148,453
1981	2,991,147	2,207,009	64,806	2,271,815	239,179	18,793	2,051,429	609,608	330,110	10,462	285,918	146,355
1982	3,199,747	2,280,504	66,400	2,346,904	252,351	15,708	2,110,261	713,799	375,687	11,058	289,363	145,330
1983	3,471,509	2,449,761	93,734	2,543,495	271,882	16,562	2,288,175	781,287	402,047	11,873	292,391	148,415
1984	3,762,288	2,701,653	84,064	2,785,717	307,614	14,476	2,492,579	854,550	415,159	12,665	297,051	154,103
1985	4,033,929	2,886,607	76,445	2,963,052	334,317	12,063	2,640,798	946,455	446,676	13,395	301,145	156,609
1986	4,159,844	2,979,838	77,450	3,057,288	347,902	12,836	2,722,222	965,696	471,926	13,740	302,755	158,446
1987	4,362,806	3,175,513	89,486	3,264,999	361,845	12,405	2,915,559	959,881	487,366	14,364	303,727	163,218
1988	4,803,712	3,561,184	100,905	3,662,089	422,204	9,423	3,249,308	1,032,995	521,409	15,675	306,455	172,597
1989	5,285,391	3,897,915	135,821	4,033,736	468,796	6,977	3,571,917	1,148,189	565,285	16,888	312,962	181,032
1990	5,754,164	4,272,798	145,370	4,418,168	543,905	11,592	3,885,855	1,260,572	607,737	17,853	322,316	190,433
1991	6,189,857	4,654,453	149,546	4,803,999	605,818	9,628	4,207,809	1,297,060	684,988	18,456	335,378	198,902
1992	6,926,853	5,296,795	143,780	5,440,575	674,563	9,581	4,775,593	1,382,319	768,941	19,925	347,646	207,984
1993	7,739,854	5,953,007	192,678	6,145,685	758,923	5,427	5,392,189	1,519,489	828,176	21,256	364,123	220,250
1994	8,587,689	6,676,807	134,865	6,811,672	855,552	10,394	5,966,514	1,740,207	880,968	22,590	380,160	236,337
1995	9,343,961	7,217,877	132,566	7,350,443	931,138	15,141	6,434,446	1,936,695	972,820	23,633	395,382	245,882
1996	9,874,367	7,562,474	135,754	7,698,228	957,172	15,618	6,756,674	2,068,974	1,048,719	24,115	409,471	255,743
1997	10,424,332	7,949,378	121,237	8,070,615	999,287	19,051	7,090,379	2,243,809	1,090,144	24,656	422,797	266,539
1998	11,423,731	8,679,243	155,169	8,834,412	1,075,034	20,059	7,779,437	2,466,551	1,177,743	26,057	438,421	279,851
1999	12,395,238	9,626,878	150,283	9,777,161	1,159,224	23,671	8,641,608	2,491,461	1,262,169	27,372	452,837	287,846
2000	13,878,251	10,991,436	147,349	11,138,785	1,317,635	25,516	9,846,666	2,663,528	1,368,057	29,590	469,017	304,508
2001	14,203,941	11,030,879	181,107	11,211,986	1,326,071	30,618	9,916,533	2,761,717	1,525,691	29,222	486,078	311,229
2002	14,796,143	11,406,665	168,084	11,574,749	1,349,390	42,565	10,267,924	2,837,500	1,690,719	29,593	499,994	313,223
2003	15,314,168	11,696,620	139,377	11,835,997	1,398,338	45,861	10,483,520	3,020,113	1,810,535	29,882	512,491	317,238
2004	16,498,329	12,456,322	214,950	12,671,272	1,501,075	46,374	11,216,571	3,344,797	1,936,961	31,367	525,975	328,238
2005	17,585,595	13,352,657	190,427	13,543,084	1,637,243	64,310	11,970,151	3,490,656	2,124,788	32,150	546,980	346,499
2006	19,727,611	14,888,433	164,888	15,053,321	1,833,259	33,398	13,253,460	4,166,069	2,308,082	34,574	570,583	367,712
2007	20,697,447	15,365,137	241,629	15,606,766	1,897,402	57,248	13,766,612	4,384,509	2,546,326	35,061	590,330	379,151
2008	20,832,071	15,049,119	228,444	15,277,563	1,876,262	84,716	13,486,017	4,288,503	3,057,551	34,535	603,218	373,383
2009	20,190,302	14,586,212	103,545	14,689,757	1,820,560	159,461	13,028,658	3,713,731	3,447,913	33,026	611,341	353,831
2010	20,774,150	14,680,146	222,399	14,902,545	1,899,119	193,706	13,197,132	3,752,590	3,824,428	33,621	617,891	350,377
2011	21,902,063	15,076,930	299,623	15,376,553	1,746,187	238,764	13,869,130	4,200,140	3,832,793	34,889	627,764	356,786
2012	23,121,732	15,500,792	318,282	15,819,074	1,793,997	290,827	14,315,904	4,881,573	3,924,255	36,264	637,590	361,967
2013	24,240,997	16,822,075	325,613	17,147,688	2,099,631	326,024	15,374,081	4,772,938	4,093,978	37,326	649,437	372,452
2014	25,832,678	17,910,138	357,233	18,267,371	2,218,325	343,654	16,392,700	5,127,473	4,312,505	38,969	662,904	383,138
2015	27,467,646	19,014,274	324,479	19,338,753	2,333,938	314,063	17,318,878	5,573,418	4,575,350	40,694	674,981	395,850
2016	28,746,083	19,899,979	281,742	20,181,721	2,458,189	332,258	18,055,790	5,888,606	4,801,687	41,559	691,695	411,130
2017	30,769,845	21,488,720	238,637	21,727,357	2,638,510	336,358	19,425,205	6,290,168	5,054,472	43,335	710,044	427,378
2018	33,251,293	23,235,616	249,210	23,484,826	2,844,627	333,149	20,973,348	6,871,395	5,406,550	45,595	729,282	448,988
2019	35,951,884	24,905,139	303,252	25,208,391	3,032,240	321,162	22,497,313	7,602,840	5,851,731	47,963	749,581	463,970
2020	39,823,601	27,005,669	344,183	27,349,852	3,322,256	337,001	24,364,597	7,823,848	7,635,156	51,706	770,188	472,505
2021	45,398,952	30,465,535	270,894	30,736,429	3,649,375	287,353	27,374,407	9,194,841	8,829,704	56,963	796,989	502,931
2022	48,468,791	33,267,296	369,963	33,637,259	4,065,921	267,751	29,839,089	10,567,919	8,061,783	59,739	811,336	529,557

Personal Income and Employment by Area: Boston-Cambridge-Newton, MA-NH

(Thousands of dollars, except as noted.)

Year	Personal income, total	Derivation of personal income: Earnings by place of work								Per capita personal income (dollars)	Population (persons)	Total employment
		Nonfarm	Farm	Total	Less: Contributions for government social insurance	Plus: Adjustment for residence	Equals: Net earnings by place of residence	Plus: Dividends, interest, and rent	Plus: Personal current transfer receipts			
1970	18,740,176	15,238,914	28,963	15,267,877	969,109	-250,943	14,047,825	2,956,834	1,735,517	4,770	3,928,508	1,906,572
1971	20,020,412	16,180,918	27,487	16,208,405	1,061,528	-306,074	14,840,803	3,132,887	2,046,722	5,064	3,953,760	1,880,515
1972	21,594,282	17,579,606	29,773	17,609,379	1,211,526	-373,090	16,024,763	3,322,375	2,247,144	5,425	3,980,347	1,918,584
1973	23,369,418	19,146,754	32,016	19,178,770	1,515,854	-461,314	17,201,602	3,645,133	2,522,683	5,867	3,982,918	1,976,758
1974	25,216,971	20,325,075	30,843	20,355,918	1,663,210	-547,831	18,144,877	4,065,765	3,006,329	6,352	3,969,705	1,995,376
1975	26,958,682	21,255,778	32,501	21,288,279	1,692,392	-632,845	18,963,042	4,199,728	3,795,912	6,819	3,953,504	1,943,843
1976	28,988,024	23,089,919	36,941	23,126,860	1,878,742	-743,612	20,504,506	4,507,373	3,976,145	7,345	3,946,719	1,961,507
1977	31,575,637	25,498,977	39,821	25,538,798	2,078,220	-930,894	22,529,684	4,980,850	4,065,103	7,999	3,947,472	2,021,580
1978	34,874,102	28,644,337	50,711	28,695,048	2,404,024	-1,179,412	25,111,612	5,467,860	4,294,630	8,842	3,944,294	2,118,025
1979	38,846,972	32,274,276	49,871	32,324,147	2,826,669	-1,457,149	28,040,329	6,109,426	4,697,217	9,853	3,942,625	2,213,716
1980	43,938,589	36,087,528	59,301	36,146,829	3,172,323	-1,787,547	31,186,959	7,407,271	5,344,359	11,135	3,946,114	2,271,006
1981	49,207,615	39,821,372	61,881	39,883,253	3,786,086	-1,980,790	34,116,377	9,021,182	6,070,056	12,405	3,966,836	2,288,684
1982	54,212,994	43,175,506	71,846	43,247,352	4,217,874	-2,182,492	36,846,986	10,862,232	6,503,776	13,631	3,977,211	2,304,308
1983	59,207,829	47,930,787	93,378	48,024,165	4,762,616	-2,450,105	40,811,444	11,506,608	6,889,777	14,777	4,006,648	2,364,109
1984	66,908,876	54,621,754	96,576	54,718,330	5,601,867	-2,806,856	46,309,607	13,349,854	7,249,415	16,567	4,038,686	2,509,018
1985	72,633,936	60,146,142	83,269	60,229,411	6,241,202	-3,102,538	50,885,671	14,200,968	7,547,297	17,838	4,071,845	2,591,649
1986	78,447,514	65,421,072	88,426	65,509,498	6,932,105	-3,314,520	55,262,873	15,285,637	7,899,004	19,187	4,088,650	2,660,368
1987	84,717,533	71,704,507	79,340	71,783,847	7,518,153	-3,591,271	60,674,423	15,971,773	8,071,337	20,639	4,104,797	2,682,717
1988	93,906,531	79,054,496	94,044	79,148,540	8,407,372	-3,948,663	66,792,505	18,384,298	8,729,728	22,764	4,125,293	2,758,108
1989	99,203,701	82,231,809	80,238	82,312,047	8,689,863	-4,062,384	69,559,800	19,821,018	9,822,883	23,965	4,139,484	2,735,161
1990	102,249,341	83,295,942	78,374	83,374,316	8,743,141	-4,220,117	70,411,058	20,825,053	11,013,230	24,714	4,137,302	2,665,144
1991	104,084,577	83,460,145	95,748	83,555,893	8,918,557	-4,176,836	70,460,500	20,971,510	12,652,567	25,213	4,128,150	2,541,026
1992	109,638,274	88,716,165	97,012	88,813,177	9,416,088	-4,306,428	75,090,661	21,307,725	13,239,888	26,497	4,137,692	2,555,157
1993	113,991,770	92,389,532	96,751	92,486,283	9,866,980	-4,450,400	78,168,903	22,221,943	13,600,924	27,378	4,163,698	2,603,207
1994	119,698,740	97,285,822	85,358	97,371,180	10,519,475	-4,828,291	82,023,414	23,262,661	14,412,665	28,573	4,189,180	2,655,650
1995	127,262,472	103,307,414	89,064	103,396,478	11,225,962	-5,320,083	86,850,433	25,093,254	15,318,785	30,080	4,230,795	2,685,848
1996	135,630,775	110,564,610	93,865	110,658,475	11,888,420	-5,660,085	93,109,970	26,749,496	15,771,309	31,797	4,265,564	2,740,663
1997	144,078,788	118,842,425	91,918	118,934,343	12,809,869	-6,630,096	99,494,378	28,270,186	16,314,224	33,486	4,302,696	2,813,151
1998	154,298,288	128,057,917	60,552	128,118,469	13,741,716	-7,301,778	107,074,975	30,833,779	16,389,534	35,571	4,337,751	2,889,492
1999	165,662,513	140,634,220	53,847	140,688,067	14,842,772	-8,453,737	117,391,558	31,336,496	16,934,459	37,911	4,369,743	2,941,149
2000	186,312,248	159,789,607	64,743	159,854,350	16,565,380	-10,018,985	133,269,985	35,187,506	17,854,757	42,332	4,401,256	3,027,183
2001	192,526,409	163,740,905	54,833	163,795,738	16,817,846	-10,386,385	136,591,507	36,414,146	19,520,756	43,439	4,432,132	3,031,090
2002	190,539,807	161,214,885	69,146	161,284,031	16,574,675	-10,072,805	134,636,551	34,754,794	21,148,462	42,914	4,440,034	2,977,796
2003	193,399,030	162,708,632	72,388	162,781,020	16,669,001	-10,036,760	136,075,259	35,076,294	22,247,477	43,610	4,434,723	2,947,087
2004	203,469,231	173,950,754	78,518	174,029,272	18,108,479	-11,012,574	144,908,219	35,370,023	23,190,989	45,982	4,424,956	2,973,045
2005	212,751,933	179,479,932	63,246	179,543,178	18,913,863	-11,306,859	149,322,456	38,634,458	24,795,019	48,155	4,418,046	3,013,683
2006	230,095,948	190,553,106	75,782	190,628,888	19,748,381	-12,122,059	158,758,448	45,354,064	25,983,436	51,971	4,427,356	3,051,159
2007	242,837,680	200,751,426	78,306	200,829,732	20,807,135	-12,795,473	167,227,124	48,462,361	27,148,195	54,597	4,447,838	3,131,645
2008	252,918,720	204,959,379	122,812	205,082,191	21,499,754	-12,581,437	171,001,000	50,775,341	31,142,379	56,416	4,483,141	3,150,404
2009	250,696,876	204,702,275	100,632	204,802,907	21,254,464	-11,842,259	171,706,184	45,004,100	33,986,592	55,375	4,527,220	3,081,336
2010	263,768,646	217,441,983	98,707	217,540,690	21,805,428	-12,443,583	183,291,679	44,605,869	35,871,098	57,744	4,567,869	3,085,607
2011	277,073,397	224,390,863	121,091	224,511,954	20,230,688	-13,024,726	191,256,540	49,804,118	36,012,739	60,005	4,617,467	3,132,898
2012	287,269,558	230,645,411	174,808	230,820,219	20,961,318	-14,119,433	195,739,468	55,429,052	36,101,038	61,505	4,670,666	3,190,680
2013	289,338,446	236,877,281	160,471	237,037,752	24,429,623	-13,883,673	198,724,456	54,128,473	36,485,517	61,256	4,723,453	3,268,009
2014	303,557,723	246,118,085	131,569	246,249,654	25,662,405	-13,813,733	206,773,516	59,078,518	37,705,689	63,585	4,774,046	3,344,619
2015	324,860,055	261,629,154	119,038	261,748,192	26,755,680	-14,731,817	220,260,695	64,039,943	40,559,417	67,506	4,812,312	3,490,821
2016	338,199,582	271,444,870	129,358	271,574,228	27,691,330	-15,792,401	228,090,497	67,886,752	42,222,333	69,736	4,849,741	3,557,016
2017	356,543,141	286,054,369	114,614	286,168,983	29,155,911	-16,330,512	240,682,560	72,993,897	42,866,684	72,924	4,889,220	3,611,318
2018	376,271,938	301,680,189	98,494	301,778,683	30,741,597	-17,292,556	253,744,530	77,467,408	45,060,000	76,594	4,912,542	3,673,915
2019	394,943,226	319,942,623	114,855	320,057,478	32,324,232	-20,328,088	267,405,158	81,228,936	46,309,132	80,065	4,932,771	3,695,663
2020	417,539,000	325,126,333	111,585	325,237,918	32,395,924	-21,140,574	271,701,420	78,130,549	67,707,031	84,684	4,930,567	3,494,314
2021	453,110,104	353,147,599	84,388	353,231,987	35,607,631	-21,027,813	296,596,543	87,050,725	69,462,836	92,402	4,903,708	3,624,906
2022	461,055,126	370,471,468	91,933	370,563,401	37,626,370	-22,019,674	310,917,357	91,712,032	58,425,737	94,082	4,900,550	3,799,363

Personal Income and Employment by Area: Boulder, CO

(Thousands of dollars, except as noted.)

Year	Personal income, total	Derivation of personal income: Earnings by place of work: Nonfarm	Farm	Total	Less: Contributions for government social insurance	Plus: Adjustment for residence	Equals: Net earnings by place of residence	Plus: Dividends, interest, and rent	Plus: Personal current transfer receipts	Per capita personal income (dollars)	Population (persons)	Total employment
1970	600,343	394,155	5,052	399,207	21,172	78,885	456,920	110,838	32,585	4,502	133,342	55,395
1971	680,907	452,090	474	452,564	24,881	88,777	516,460	125,725	38,722	4,836	140,808	59,121
1972	768,819	512,284	4,041	516,325	30,157	100,009	586,177	138,854	43,788	5,081	151,309	64,116
1973	864,808	574,054	2,914	576,968	39,837	115,077	652,208	157,983	54,617	5,422	159,509	69,942
1974	979,831	660,914	2,695	663,609	46,970	115,564	732,203	184,486	63,142	5,887	166,449	75,635
1975	1,109,846	749,498	6,510	756,008	52,425	114,065	817,648	211,485	80,713	6,659	166,670	78,961
1976	1,245,164	859,746	7,921	867,667	61,907	116,065	921,825	234,964	88,375	7,363	169,117	85,236
1977	1,434,420	1,020,741	7,292	1,028,033	74,657	119,529	1,072,905	265,788	95,727	8,053	178,121	92,627
1978	1,683,852	1,223,210	6,797	1,230,007	92,236	130,401	1,268,172	310,863	104,817	9,180	183,432	102,720
1979	1,958,786	1,429,615	5,149	1,434,764	114,316	162,073	1,482,521	357,269	118,996	10,468	187,125	110,002
1980	2,217,986	1,557,263	9,224	1,566,487	127,270	209,267	1,648,484	432,465	137,037	11,616	190,935	112,861
1981	2,552,506	1,774,431	12,943	1,787,374	156,444	227,322	1,858,252	534,150	160,104	13,043	195,705	117,528
1982	2,818,906	1,988,313	8,662	1,996,975	181,654	226,234	2,041,555	600,047	177,304	14,036	200,827	121,300
1983	3,094,908	2,223,219	9,338	2,232,557	208,132	212,014	2,236,439	664,746	193,723	14,992	206,440	128,223
1984	3,446,563	2,530,218	10,185	2,540,403	247,455	202,813	2,495,761	749,588	201,214	16,318	211,206	141,199
1985	3,617,751	2,597,339	5,064	2,602,403	258,111	241,883	2,586,175	817,258	214,318	16,910	213,942	140,650
1986	3,789,442	2,725,919	4,846	2,730,765	273,381	244,942	2,702,326	854,337	232,779	17,546	215,971	141,908
1987	4,003,997	2,957,351	5,572	2,962,923	294,035	210,790	2,879,678	872,493	251,826	18,365	218,024	143,586
1988	4,333,526	3,217,085	8,427	3,225,512	332,840	224,968	3,117,640	949,622	266,264	19,705	219,915	152,086
1989	4,733,834	3,423,711	10,222	3,433,933	361,914	224,851	3,296,870	1,129,872	307,092	21,180	223,507	155,495
1990	5,071,772	3,724,890	11,309	3,736,199	403,647	217,693	3,550,245	1,197,306	324,221	22,404	226,374	160,076
1991	5,392,946	4,074,399	12,648	4,087,047	452,876	166,419	3,800,590	1,240,233	352,123	23,161	232,846	164,862
1992	5,952,683	4,587,347	7,319	4,594,666	503,546	142,533	4,233,653	1,328,866	390,164	24,758	240,430	169,291
1993	6,419,291	5,016,126	9,237	5,025,363	555,170	93,209	4,563,402	1,438,741	417,148	25,946	247,405	178,775
1994	6,954,563	5,446,358	9,281	5,455,639	609,705	-20,036	4,825,898	1,687,315	441,350	27,345	254,324	186,270
1995	7,529,966	5,868,502	9,403	5,877,905	658,239	-72,238	5,147,428	1,898,955	483,583	29,015	259,520	192,888
1996	8,135,336	6,352,059	11,385	6,363,444	707,621	-78,666	5,577,157	2,049,971	508,208	30,742	264,630	198,754
1997	8,807,740	6,998,726	11,363	7,010,089	779,674	-133,779	6,096,636	2,200,857	510,247	32,532	270,744	207,295
1998	9,696,056	8,176,368	10,361	8,186,729	867,531	-516,243	6,802,955	2,384,867	508,234	34,933	277,562	213,453
1999	10,545,077	8,983,948	9,179	8,993,127	944,613	-451,240	7,597,274	2,410,353	537,450	36,884	285,901	221,120
2000	12,100,049	11,068,542	8,218	11,076,760	1,144,858	-1,144,908	8,786,994	2,736,746	576,309	41,247	293,358	237,310
2001	12,647,917	11,318,053	10,105	11,328,158	1,165,776	-992,797	9,169,585	2,823,637	654,695	42,140	300,137	243,644
2002	11,542,437	9,852,558	9,449	9,862,007	1,022,732	-556,099	8,283,176	2,582,748	676,513	41,301	279,468	215,528
2003	11,756,992	9,890,460	6,004	9,896,464	1,030,000	-475,253	8,391,211	2,633,741	732,040	42,175	278,768	210,508
2004	12,074,002	10,278,583	10,390	10,288,973	1,099,663	-692,175	8,497,135	2,829,208	747,659	43,163	279,728	214,504
2005	12,859,256	10,653,457	8,622	10,662,079	1,137,802	-755,798	8,768,479	3,247,313	843,464	45,886	280,241	218,031
2006	13,804,847	11,185,035	7,018	11,192,053	1,186,954	-756,432	9,248,667	3,711,940	844,240	48,567	284,243	221,740
2007	14,494,686	11,726,200	7,082	11,733,282	1,251,973	-930,159	9,551,150	4,015,288	928,248	50,429	287,428	228,949
2008	15,214,729	11,951,860	6,911	11,958,771	1,286,184	-907,331	9,765,256	4,289,322	1,160,151	52,310	290,859	235,185
2009	13,808,407	11,348,315	10,396	11,358,711	1,219,184	-1,324,986	8,814,541	3,742,010	1,251,856	47,097	293,190	228,868
2010	14,861,552	11,696,209	9,111	11,705,320	1,242,127	-786,540	9,676,653	3,754,263	1,430,636	50,356	295,131	227,792
2011	15,739,217	12,210,346	16,679	12,227,025	1,176,512	-939,919	10,110,594	4,164,198	1,464,425	52,388	300,434	234,428
2012	16,629,822	12,903,850	9,944	12,913,794	1,233,176	-985,371	10,695,247	4,467,938	1,466,637	54,447	305,430	239,470
2013	17,381,687	13,559,317	10,914	13,570,231	1,439,267	-951,299	11,179,665	4,660,588	1,541,434	55,964	310,586	245,023
2014	18,682,169	14,415,431	10,588	14,426,019	1,529,802	-1,002,387	11,893,830	5,132,243	1,656,096	59,514	313,911	252,707
2015	20,257,478	15,191,536	13,220	15,204,756	1,621,129	-824,421	12,759,206	5,698,444	1,799,828	63,274	320,154	258,599
2016	20,790,581	15,613,078	10,300	15,623,378	1,675,860	-939,917	13,007,601	5,903,834	1,879,146	64,195	323,865	263,942
2017	22,267,272	16,516,337	11,037	16,527,374	1,764,210	-837,485	13,925,679	6,396,718	1,944,875	68,415	325,475	269,048
2018	23,504,502	17,498,310	11,794	17,510,104	1,878,673	-1,190,197	14,441,234	6,939,531	2,123,737	71,604	328,259	274,068
2019	25,878,040	19,398,556	10,616	19,409,172	2,045,384	-1,476,299	15,887,489	7,726,951	2,263,600	78,610	329,194	275,774
2020	27,027,395	19,740,823	11,570	19,752,393	2,080,112	-1,520,613	16,151,668	7,785,881	3,089,846	81,673	330,922	269,099
2021	30,572,385	21,765,296	10,467	21,775,763	2,266,440	-1,837,179	17,672,144	9,479,357	3,420,884	93,472	327,075	280,028
2022	32,273,001	23,280,276	9,238	23,289,514	2,524,059	-1,972,004	18,793,451	10,417,356	3,062,194	98,553	327,468	294,092

Personal Income and Employment by Area: Bowling Green, KY

(Thousands of dollars, except as noted.)

		Derivation of personal income										
		Earnings by place of work										
Year	Personal income, total	Nonfarm	Farm	Total	Less: Contributions for government social insurance	Plus: Adjustment for residence	Equals: Net earnings by place of residence	Plus: Dividends, interest, and rent	Plus: Personal current transfer receipts	Per capita personal income (dollars)	Population (persons)	Total employment
1970	238,044	175,431	15,726	191,157	11,945	710	179,922	29,864	28,258	2,655	89,652	37,297
1971	265,227	195,047	17,127	212,174	13,712	744	199,206	33,690	32,331	2,836	93,520	38,393
1972	303,342	224,576	21,037	245,613	16,575	766	229,804	38,107	35,431	3,183	95,307	40,228
1973	350,258	259,340	25,936	285,276	21,794	2,357	265,839	42,966	41,453	3,669	95,464	42,648
1974	387,810	286,550	22,853	309,403	25,070	3,170	287,503	50,095	50,212	4,002	96,904	43,625
1975	427,934	311,056	15,600	326,656	26,799	3,162	303,019	58,089	66,826	4,351	98,351	43,179
1976	485,803	358,953	14,572	373,525	31,446	5,009	347,088	64,516	74,199	4,832	100,546	45,371
1977	541,776	397,195	22,342	419,537	34,784	7,967	392,720	73,739	75,317	5,294	102,335	46,883
1978	620,309	465,232	21,200	486,432	41,834	8,768	453,366	85,380	81,563	5,953	104,207	50,148
1979	707,101	522,879	26,878	549,757	48,699	12,358	513,416	98,457	95,228	6,693	105,640	50,732
1980	776,569	551,391	16,764	568,155	51,615	13,489	530,029	125,571	120,969	7,220	107,557	49,865
1981	902,724	629,693	27,548	657,241	63,699	15,670	609,212	156,069	137,443	8,237	109,593	50,960
1982	963,036	649,035	23,333	672,368	66,817	23,721	629,272	180,744	153,020	8,383	114,875	50,359
1983	999,915	696,520	-5,907	690,613	71,491	21,752	640,874	195,056	163,985	8,557	116,854	51,861
1984	1,134,471	780,102	26,201	806,303	81,520	19,740	744,523	219,138	170,810	9,969	113,805	53,904
1985	1,195,151	847,991	13,813	861,804	90,459	20,072	791,417	225,391	178,343	10,561	113,170	54,825
1986	1,207,738	846,391	13,792	860,183	93,862	22,487	788,808	230,052	188,878	10,733	112,523	55,198
1987	1,272,248	894,216	21,528	915,744	98,646	25,649	842,747	231,812	197,689	11,336	112,227	55,910
1988	1,403,965	995,269	24,017	1,019,286	110,514	23,971	932,743	259,136	212,086	12,499	112,325	57,594
1989	1,534,525	1,069,756	36,531	1,106,287	121,280	19,333	1,004,340	294,582	235,603	13,619	112,679	59,974
1990	1,608,181	1,114,048	36,270	1,150,318	129,977	20,252	1,040,593	304,402	263,186	14,074	114,270	61,201
1991	1,725,334	1,197,080	37,618	1,234,698	141,901	18,917	1,111,714	315,428	298,192	14,927	115,583	62,846
1992	1,880,380	1,338,490	43,313	1,381,803	158,802	16,766	1,239,767	317,770	322,843	16,003	117,502	65,051
1993	1,991,220	1,430,073	37,730	1,467,803	172,045	20,304	1,316,062	334,747	340,411	16,548	120,327	66,995
1994	2,136,074	1,573,545	34,123	1,607,668	192,986	16,269	1,430,951	348,195	356,928	17,411	122,686	69,464
1995	2,246,905	1,669,832	14,256	1,684,088	205,612	13,615	1,492,091	370,874	383,940	17,926	125,345	72,461
1996	2,411,079	1,767,588	31,371	1,798,959	215,456	9,334	1,592,837	401,407	416,835	18,874	127,749	73,893
1997	2,585,929	1,903,766	32,931	1,936,697	229,465	10,223	1,717,455	425,465	443,009	19,878	130,090	75,666
1998	2,703,551	2,010,486	12,190	2,022,676	240,271	13,702	1,796,107	450,225	457,219	20,445	132,238	75,648
1999	2,840,427	2,165,497	3,828	2,169,325	257,540	12,565	1,924,350	442,487	473,590	21,237	133,747	77,333
2000	3,076,916	2,293,106	34,044	2,327,150	263,296	14,898	2,078,752	490,249	507,915	22,730	135,367	78,805
2001	3,205,604	2,364,156	31,734	2,395,890	267,659	18,233	2,146,464	497,272	561,868	23,415	136,901	79,048
2002	3,315,951	2,480,287	22,188	2,502,475	279,540	23,347	2,246,282	461,849	607,820	23,940	138,510	78,926
2003	3,451,448	2,598,341	24,321	2,622,662	290,172	30,356	2,362,846	462,313	626,289	24,492	140,921	80,185
2004	3,697,808	2,743,585	46,468	2,790,053	303,136	24,982	2,511,899	508,632	677,277	25,851	143,044	82,085
2005	3,921,993	2,925,416	60,734	2,986,150	327,079	24,569	2,683,640	517,984	720,369	26,878	145,918	84,828
2006	4,107,464	3,041,320	55,565	3,096,885	345,551	20,032	2,771,366	554,250	781,848	27,507	149,324	86,881
2007	4,321,311	3,175,283	25,799	3,201,082	362,624	13,346	2,851,804	617,777	851,730	28,484	151,710	89,662
2008	4,588,513	3,276,024	16,672	3,292,696	380,494	15,349	2,927,551	684,141	976,821	29,697	154,513	89,148
2009	4,494,429	3,075,038	24,190	3,099,228	372,377	-4,316	2,722,535	669,092	1,102,802	28,631	156,978	85,546
2010	4,761,857	3,264,912	28,177	3,293,089	380,412	-1,055	2,911,622	673,486	1,176,749	29,886	159,333	86,244
2011	4,998,155	3,408,083	53,020	3,461,103	352,358	-19,244	3,089,501	709,104	1,199,550	31,058	160,929	89,439
2012	5,164,640	3,565,807	56,821	3,622,628	366,726	-19,838	3,236,064	732,402	1,196,174	31,814	162,341	90,984
2013	5,278,346	3,668,742	114,944	3,783,686	426,803	-43,202	3,313,681	741,448	1,223,217	32,088	164,495	92,283
2014	5,534,975	3,825,596	86,255	3,911,851	451,779	-55,880	3,404,192	776,654	1,354,129	33,260	166,417	94,241
2015	5,823,659	4,047,295	64,281	4,111,576	475,930	-60,165	3,575,481	820,097	1,428,081	34,408	169,252	96,190
2016	5,969,875	4,180,352	43,960	4,224,312	501,170	-71,836	3,651,306	882,127	1,436,442	34,748	171,804	99,922
2017	6,205,745	4,313,334	53,000	4,366,334	516,480	-59,870	3,789,984	915,049	1,500,712	35,532	174,654	101,391
2018	6,349,503	4,447,744	29,847	4,477,591	533,673	-55,891	3,888,027	904,209	1,557,267	35,988	176,436	102,928
2019	6,687,528	4,646,562	42,895	4,689,457	550,737	-51,724	4,086,996	972,116	1,628,416	37,476	178,450	103,231
2020	7,275,581	4,675,107	38,742	4,713,849	565,872	-78,215	4,069,762	1,008,043	2,197,776	40,407	180,057	100,414
2021	8,032,880	5,079,792	81,282	5,161,074	588,775	-78,992	4,493,307	1,092,283	2,447,290	44,024	182,468	104,544
2022	8,337,429	5,738,182	86,917	5,825,099	649,363	-100,673	5,075,063	1,162,016	2,100,350	44,902	185,682	109,923

Personal Income and Employment by Area: Bremerton-Silverdale-Port Orchard, WA

(Thousands of dollars, except as noted.)

Year	Personal income, total	Derivation of personal income: Earnings by place of work: Nonfarm	Farm	Total	Less: Contributions for government social insurance	Plus: Adjustment for residence	Equals: Net earnings by place of residence	Plus: Dividends, interest, and rent	Plus: Personal current transfer receipts	Per capita personal income (dollars)	Population (persons)	Total employment
1970	486,434	391,738	1,502	393,240	17,268	-42,165	333,807	117,933	34,694	4,787	101,617	45,195
1971	507,925	401,290	1,060	402,350	18,254	-46,638	337,458	128,587	41,880	4,999	101,606	41,911
1972	550,509	432,237	1,156	433,393	20,733	-47,840	364,820	138,859	46,830	5,385	102,225	41,798
1973	629,457	489,297	2,012	491,309	26,640	-49,714	414,955	160,827	53,675	5,607	112,257	45,114
1974	742,964	582,283	1,568	583,851	32,475	-59,689	491,687	189,692	61,585	6,636	111,965	49,047
1975	858,418	673,210	1,237	674,447	40,020	-65,973	568,454	213,532	76,432	7,207	119,117	51,652
1976	955,374	751,785	1,182	752,967	47,753	-66,976	638,238	231,812	85,324	7,897	120,976	54,063
1977	1,101,571	868,973	1,259	870,232	56,003	-73,202	741,027	267,355	93,189	8,749	125,902	58,694
1978	1,260,302	970,341	1,744	972,085	63,907	-65,994	842,184	316,688	101,430	9,502	132,640	61,793
1979	1,449,583	1,098,866	1,980	1,100,846	74,979	-53,386	972,481	364,240	112,862	10,300	140,733	65,222
1980	1,625,620	1,180,646	1,577	1,182,223	82,672	-31,881	1,067,670	416,364	141,586	10,928	148,762	67,650
1981	1,785,374	1,275,129	1,644	1,276,773	97,426	-40,319	1,139,028	477,833	168,513	11,525	154,907	68,860
1982	1,980,528	1,411,352	1,663	1,413,015	105,653	-59,487	1,247,875	547,620	185,033	12,773	155,059	70,104
1983	2,208,615	1,600,922	1,159	1,602,081	131,219	-65,729	1,405,133	607,079	196,403	13,760	160,515	73,806
1984	2,321,239	1,658,720	406	1,659,126	141,762	-54,598	1,462,766	646,424	212,049	14,351	161,742	75,920
1985	2,449,093	1,708,620	133	1,708,753	155,676	-30,562	1,522,515	697,062	229,516	14,975	163,546	77,990
1986	2,519,857	1,708,605	-354	1,708,251	162,310	3,016	1,548,957	724,912	245,988	15,338	164,293	77,909
1987	2,700,692	1,844,068	1,287	1,845,355	179,383	27,602	1,693,574	744,957	262,161	15,909	169,760	83,191
1988	2,996,012	2,085,596	577	2,086,173	211,614	24,680	1,899,239	817,420	279,353	16,744	178,929	90,373
1989	3,257,683	2,206,752	3,607	2,210,359	231,970	55,871	2,034,260	913,271	310,152	17,854	182,461	92,716
1990	3,783,695	2,518,561	2,237	2,520,798	274,093	217,275	2,463,980	975,145	344,570	19,719	191,879	99,487
1991	4,160,523	2,789,438	3,826	2,793,264	308,907	220,130	2,704,487	1,054,507	401,529	20,841	199,636	103,816
1992	4,498,651	3,008,567	3,536	3,012,103	340,130	266,715	2,938,688	1,108,511	451,452	21,467	209,562	105,396
1993	4,738,832	3,010,174	3,068	3,013,242	347,167	391,393	3,057,468	1,180,923	500,441	22,431	211,262	103,073
1994	4,952,725	3,104,821	3,211	3,108,032	362,329	418,926	3,164,629	1,256,970	531,126	23,098	214,422	106,538
1995	5,222,378	3,220,839	1,691	3,222,530	377,135	430,611	3,276,006	1,370,653	575,719	23,378	223,391	108,268
1996	5,484,428	3,332,704	1,399	3,334,103	385,052	420,946	3,369,997	1,506,560	607,871	24,205	226,584	112,627
1997	5,918,965	3,493,289	2,134	3,495,423	396,145	598,614	3,697,892	1,577,186	643,887	25,802	229,403	111,977
1998	6,179,200	3,537,432	720	3,538,152	401,458	746,110	3,882,804	1,625,428	670,968	26,998	228,878	110,034
1999	6,437,092	3,699,802	918	3,700,720	414,137	834,946	4,121,529	1,607,557	708,006	28,061	229,393	110,431
2000	7,043,621	3,943,478	1,281	3,944,759	444,603	1,068,776	4,568,932	1,695,027	779,662	30,267	232,720	112,566
2001	7,293,601	4,138,066	890	4,138,956	467,175	1,047,814	4,719,595	1,699,088	874,918	31,101	234,513	113,167
2002	7,667,227	4,617,023	1,080	4,618,103	524,890	962,359	5,055,572	1,674,037	937,618	32,198	238,129	117,075
2003	8,094,983	4,926,246	2,693	4,928,939	560,867	918,666	5,286,738	1,817,510	990,735	33,763	239,758	119,296
2004	8,629,298	5,291,835	1,914	5,293,749	607,972	925,995	5,611,772	1,993,072	1,024,454	35,664	241,960	121,921
2005	9,050,679	5,597,390	810	5,598,200	645,405	920,930	5,873,725	2,073,871	1,103,083	37,742	239,806	124,982
2006	9,492,531	5,846,452	2,126	5,848,578	681,180	875,678	6,043,076	2,252,021	1,197,434	38,736	245,054	127,064
2007	9,934,701	5,964,890	1,580	5,966,470	699,158	927,276	6,194,588	2,448,945	1,291,168	40,698	244,105	127,591
2008	10,506,212	6,163,620	-709	6,162,911	722,999	873,846	6,313,758	2,699,180	1,493,274	42,550	246,912	127,474
2009	10,346,027	6,205,181	424	6,205,605	748,641	805,779	6,262,743	2,420,523	1,662,761	41,584	248,800	123,188
2010	10,622,561	6,399,858	-1,235	6,398,623	764,468	767,373	6,401,528	2,375,835	1,845,198	42,193	251,762	120,814
2011	10,942,562	6,469,429	339	6,469,768	707,619	713,596	6,475,745	2,612,391	1,854,426	42,965	254,685	120,715
2012	11,323,302	6,580,669	-462	6,580,207	712,254	738,564	6,606,517	2,844,250	1,872,535	44,402	255,017	121,381
2013	11,284,209	6,560,063	-1,395	6,558,668	796,167	861,051	6,623,552	2,755,395	1,905,262	44,531	253,403	121,568
2014	11,908,967	6,812,787	-659	6,812,128	830,094	963,420	6,945,454	2,892,316	2,071,197	46,756	254,705	124,397
2015	12,465,030	7,163,262	2,159	7,165,421	877,341	977,986	7,266,066	3,068,364	2,130,600	47,776	260,904	127,315
2016	13,091,767	7,557,094	-355	7,556,739	909,824	1,025,675	7,672,590	3,172,586	2,246,591	49,373	265,159	131,352
2017	13,799,592	7,798,037	3,801	7,801,838	949,239	1,236,688	8,089,287	3,381,272	2,329,033	51,361	268,681	132,189
2018	14,671,540	7,998,924	2,257	8,001,181	968,779	1,637,374	8,669,776	3,542,607	2,459,157	53,952	271,938	131,634
2019	15,857,731	8,335,889	4,518	8,340,407	993,680	2,044,283	9,391,010	3,837,285	2,629,436	57,672	274,963	131,632
2020	17,152,713	8,834,210	8,924	8,843,134	1,064,580	1,951,520	9,730,074	4,003,810	3,418,829	62,192	275,802	128,028
2021	18,509,168	9,318,070	9,036	9,327,106	1,106,756	2,183,282	10,403,632	4,295,580	3,809,956	66,919	276,591	131,253
2022	18,936,661	9,979,316	6,872	9,986,188	1,203,798	2,332,993	11,115,383	4,479,177	3,342,101	68,198	277,673	136,669

Personal Income and Employment by Area: Bridgeport-Stamford-Norwalk, CT

(Thousands of dollars, except as noted.)

Year	Personal income, total	Derivation of personal income: Earnings by place of work: Nonfarm	Farm	Total	Less: Contributions for government social insurance	Plus: Adjustment for residence	Equals: Net earnings by place of residence	Plus: Dividends, interest, and rent	Plus: Personal current transfer receipts	Per capita personal income (dollars)	Population (persons)	Total employment
1970	4,860,504	3,147,197	3,681	3,150,878	208,962	665,217	3,607,133	969,894	283,477	6,130	792,934	366,252
1971	5,101,426	3,251,071	3,673	3,254,744	223,363	679,467	3,710,848	1,039,763	350,815	6,435	792,758	358,267
1972	5,483,660	3,537,389	3,649	3,541,038	258,000	702,508	3,985,546	1,124,024	374,090	6,959	788,034	364,054
1973	5,883,424	3,911,903	4,252	3,916,155	330,354	698,151	4,283,952	1,192,810	406,662	7,480	786,524	379,191
1974	6,352,715	4,229,786	4,041	4,233,827	374,258	717,665	4,577,234	1,300,388	475,093	8,059	788,324	383,909
1975	6,814,123	4,464,601	3,695	4,468,296	386,283	775,075	4,857,088	1,334,125	622,910	8,576	794,554	374,936
1976	7,449,088	4,970,834	3,072	4,973,906	437,127	811,283	5,348,062	1,430,568	670,458	9,341	797,444	385,892
1977	8,289,329	5,643,127	3,313	5,646,440	498,579	872,536	6,020,397	1,566,193	702,739	10,228	810,423	403,360
1978	9,308,626	6,427,273	3,316	6,430,589	585,428	966,337	6,811,498	1,758,611	738,517	11,597	802,642	425,460
1979	10,523,535	7,296,754	2,917	7,299,671	692,806	1,082,157	7,689,022	2,013,647	820,866	13,111	802,656	442,700
1980	12,120,829	8,285,890	2,688	8,288,578	789,350	1,234,151	8,733,379	2,437,459	949,991	14,988	808,703	455,859
1981	13,746,592	9,249,786	2,181	9,251,967	949,492	1,354,594	9,657,069	3,015,928	1,073,595	16,905	813,186	470,540
1982	14,853,676	9,924,754	3,067	9,927,821	1,048,044	1,444,001	10,323,778	3,336,518	1,193,380	18,160	817,943	474,803
1983	15,787,053	10,612,277	2,425	10,614,702	1,128,848	1,557,939	11,043,793	3,456,747	1,286,513	19,209	821,854	476,184
1984	17,697,312	12,032,503	2,881	12,035,384	1,308,932	1,661,584	12,388,036	3,964,504	1,344,772	21,449	825,107	495,194
1985	19,094,996	13,146,476	2,624	13,149,100	1,448,341	1,845,563	13,546,322	4,118,832	1,429,842	22,995	830,396	509,468
1986	20,466,773	14,290,306	2,965	14,293,271	1,579,604	1,884,766	14,598,433	4,352,983	1,515,357	24,605	831,797	519,808
1987	22,193,860	15,825,783	3,085	15,828,868	1,717,306	2,004,167	16,115,729	4,512,168	1,565,963	26,795	828,277	525,397
1988	24,954,495	17,752,236	2,656	17,754,892	1,932,958	2,175,903	17,997,837	5,266,216	1,690,442	30,189	826,605	537,634
1989	27,082,171	18,556,240	2,065	18,558,305	2,015,062	2,193,847	18,737,090	6,459,736	1,885,345	32,727	827,517	532,086
1990	27,932,347	19,191,242	3,099	19,194,341	2,057,938	1,815,410	18,951,813	6,872,135	2,108,399	33,700	828,860	521,951
1991	28,283,912	19,492,459	3,962	19,496,421	2,126,970	1,795,318	19,164,769	6,763,520	2,355,623	33,950	833,094	503,321
1992	31,661,069	21,065,940	5,910	21,071,850	2,232,533	2,923,827	21,763,144	7,122,475	2,775,450	37,946	834,372	501,927
1993	32,590,562	22,181,213	8,461	22,189,674	2,333,814	2,285,973	22,141,833	7,542,457	2,906,272	38,847	838,945	512,679
1994	33,419,908	22,923,375	9,607	22,932,982	2,452,079	2,033,100	22,514,003	7,902,315	3,003,590	39,668	842,482	508,287
1995	36,351,941	24,736,400	10,395	24,746,795	2,636,559	2,592,670	24,702,906	8,424,597	3,224,438	42,865	848,057	518,746
1996	38,898,298	26,343,803	5,162	26,348,965	2,785,707	3,161,417	26,724,675	8,863,532	3,310,091	45,526	854,421	528,175
1997	41,567,619	29,305,153	4,646	29,309,799	3,007,275	2,478,555	28,781,079	9,383,597	3,402,943	48,277	861,020	537,529
1998	46,205,749	32,008,342	6,901	32,015,243	3,184,139	3,677,052	32,508,156	10,285,028	3,412,565	53,193	868,651	551,305
1999	49,125,247	34,919,382	10,098	34,929,480	3,371,946	3,364,443	34,921,977	10,703,789	3,499,481	56,012	877,043	563,031
2000	54,531,487	39,248,422	11,380	39,259,802	3,622,577	3,214,954	38,852,179	11,979,740	3,699,568	61,662	884,364	577,741
2001	58,851,329	42,880,869	11,820	42,892,689	3,734,864	3,100,931	42,258,756	12,670,869	3,921,704	66,195	889,063	576,192
2002	57,719,330	41,940,323	11,781	41,952,104	3,782,678	3,490,463	41,659,889	11,869,796	4,189,645	64,643	892,900	574,091
2003	57,801,486	42,132,570	11,379	42,143,949	3,870,648	3,522,269	41,795,570	11,754,371	4,251,545	64,486	896,342	575,371
2004	61,229,957	42,608,184	12,626	42,620,810	4,011,321	4,424,441	43,033,930	13,632,995	4,563,032	68,225	897,472	583,532
2005	66,038,195	44,832,032	14,839	44,846,871	4,156,944	4,863,388	45,553,315	15,865,608	4,619,272	73,568	897,653	591,243
2006	72,843,264	47,270,020	16,258	47,286,278	4,358,494	5,579,177	48,506,961	19,440,849	4,895,454	81,275	896,254	600,690
2007	80,559,629	51,647,142	19,327	51,666,469	4,650,998	6,854,339	53,869,810	21,537,113	5,152,706	89,760	897,498	617,952
2008	89,447,911	58,058,999	17,853	58,076,852	4,888,134	8,212,098	61,400,816	22,162,951	5,884,144	98,966	903,824	621,965
2009	89,204,697	62,178,643	18,613	62,197,256	4,708,989	6,578,770	64,067,037	18,634,425	6,503,235	97,982	910,421	608,206
2010	94,335,493	64,102,204	17,608	64,119,812	4,762,381	8,452,687	67,810,118	19,610,174	6,915,201	102,572	919,702	605,634
2011	95,763,724	63,461,226	14,288	63,475,514	4,351,990	8,691,758	67,815,282	21,032,117	6,916,325	102,997	929,775	621,729
2012	95,456,676	59,288,167	19,784	59,307,951	4,413,058	10,507,819	65,402,712	23,053,096	7,000,868	101,729	938,339	628,393
2013	89,816,686	56,298,347	27,638	56,325,985	5,101,686	9,861,426	61,085,725	21,649,413	7,081,548	95,083	944,612	639,197
2014	94,765,954	57,887,850	19,717	57,907,567	5,268,445	10,044,886	62,684,008	24,758,411	7,323,535	99,718	950,338	646,565
2015	96,431,968	57,785,147	21,270	57,806,417	5,419,063	10,665,516	63,052,870	25,807,949	7,571,149	101,239	952,518	657,037
2016	98,903,423	59,012,385	17,611	59,029,996	5,493,450	10,064,306	63,600,852	27,460,492	7,842,079	103,708	953,669	663,787
2017	102,056,991	59,139,960	25,533	59,165,493	5,560,282	12,618,709	66,223,920	27,901,110	7,931,961	106,972	954,050	658,198
2018	108,026,996	59,205,605	19,240	59,224,845	5,636,413	13,757,946	67,346,378	32,234,274	8,446,344	112,898	956,852	663,335
2019	108,758,938	58,649,049	26,411	58,675,460	5,710,646	15,730,611	68,695,425	31,522,290	8,541,223	113,634	957,097	653,822
2020	110,675,438	58,219,084	17,334	58,236,418	5,680,257	18,430,056	70,986,217	28,366,142	11,323,079	115,859	955,261	633,880
2021	115,548,981	61,049,973	14,063	61,064,036	6,004,786	18,271,902	73,331,152	30,245,451	11,972,378	119,982	963,050	660,242
2022	120,546,115	64,263,338	20,396	64,283,734	6,610,154	20,345,181	78,018,761	32,009,483	10,517,871	125,185	962,946	697,773

Personal Income and Employment by Area: Brownsville-Harlingen, TX

(Thousands of dollars, except as noted.)

		Derivation of personal income										
		Earnings by place of work										
Year	Personal income, total	Nonfarm	Farm	Total	Less: Contributions for government social insurance	Plus: Adjustment for residence	Equals: Net earnings by place of residence	Plus: Dividends, interest, and rent	Plus: Personal current transfer receipts	Per capita personal income (dollars)	Population (persons)	Total employment
1970	313,753	235,891	12,535	248,426	15,000	-8,878	224,548	50,419	38,786	2,222	141,196	48,384
1971	365,169	265,273	24,210	289,483	17,408	-9,731	262,344	57,081	45,744	2,471	147,753	50,443
1972	413,943	311,343	20,676	332,019	21,566	-12,223	298,230	64,453	51,260	2,628	157,489	54,936
1973	485,003	367,116	15,921	383,037	29,725	-15,229	338,083	75,667	71,253	2,905	166,939	59,244
1974	571,166	422,375	25,565	447,940	35,323	-17,547	395,070	90,871	85,225	3,317	172,211	62,830
1975	653,609	486,103	17,041	503,144	40,246	-21,223	441,675	106,211	105,723	3,575	182,806	64,977
1976	729,412	547,870	16,964	564,834	45,664	-23,177	495,993	115,036	118,383	3,851	189,415	67,457
1977	800,019	593,551	25,495	619,046	49,589	-24,873	544,584	129,059	126,376	4,109	194,722	69,508
1978	943,986	707,392	33,308	740,700	60,254	-27,499	652,947	150,912	140,127	4,745	198,941	74,442
1979	1,075,922	816,103	13,414	829,517	72,680	-27,998	728,839	179,276	167,807	5,235	205,544	77,871
1980	1,235,886	921,222	3,944	925,166	82,787	-27,631	814,748	218,670	202,468	5,831	211,944	81,655
1981	1,454,896	1,048,635	39,017	1,087,652	101,802	-22,495	963,355	265,855	225,686	6,608	220,184	84,935
1982	1,560,838	1,108,240	15,480	1,123,720	108,940	-23,753	991,027	318,388	251,423	6,765	230,718	85,599
1983	1,673,194	1,122,637	30,554	1,153,191	107,925	-22,308	1,022,958	355,541	294,695	7,004	238,878	83,585
1984	1,773,134	1,170,093	28,770	1,198,863	114,124	-22,305	1,062,434	389,535	321,165	7,316	242,355	83,931
1985	1,925,649	1,251,313	43,113	1,294,426	122,365	-22,590	1,149,471	430,635	345,543	7,831	245,894	85,022
1986	1,982,515	1,295,455	15,734	1,311,189	124,438	-22,434	1,164,317	443,254	374,944	7,899	250,996	83,543
1987	2,036,532	1,318,754	41,152	1,359,906	125,588	-22,625	1,211,693	434,488	390,351	8,027	253,714	85,358
1988	2,203,595	1,436,577	50,888	1,487,465	143,188	-21,344	1,322,933	465,141	415,521	8,662	254,410	88,741
1989	2,377,664	1,558,053	28,628	1,586,681	160,254	-22,753	1,403,674	509,089	464,901	9,269	256,512	93,483
1990	2,649,631	1,756,567	39,592	1,796,159	177,535	-26,635	1,591,989	516,447	541,195	10,124	261,728	98,639
1991	2,860,011	1,881,741	30,741	1,912,482	194,117	-26,856	1,691,509	538,109	630,393	10,622	269,261	101,267
1992	3,200,857	2,065,785	38,156	2,103,941	211,567	-30,382	1,861,992	562,985	775,880	11,542	277,322	104,646
1993	3,472,993	2,254,178	57,997	2,312,175	232,090	-32,174	2,047,911	572,000	853,082	12,047	288,297	109,851
1994	3,696,490	2,405,663	51,942	2,457,605	251,640	-33,139	2,172,826	594,469	929,195	12,433	297,316	115,588
1995	3,865,960	2,480,523	25,422	2,505,945	260,821	-31,483	2,213,641	649,329	1,002,990	12,678	304,928	117,889
1996	4,080,770	2,583,709	48,255	2,631,964	269,176	-27,407	2,335,381	657,147	1,088,242	13,076	312,086	121,253
1997	4,386,051	2,811,319	44,581	2,855,900	289,749	-26,725	2,539,426	706,951	1,139,674	13,780	318,281	124,620
1998	4,682,744	3,039,491	69,786	3,109,277	308,587	-27,514	2,773,176	762,052	1,147,516	14,428	324,556	127,625
1999	4,860,932	3,183,321	73,284	3,256,605	320,998	-22,899	2,912,708	772,585	1,175,639	14,718	330,277	132,109
2000	5,229,497	3,417,713	67,296	3,485,009	342,345	-21,320	3,121,344	841,434	1,266,719	15,558	336,123	139,353
2001	5,755,875	3,871,867	62,748	3,934,615	370,866	-69,123	3,494,626	870,346	1,390,903	16,812	342,368	142,995
2002	6,147,498	4,143,788	55,222	4,199,010	396,537	-78,273	3,724,200	864,503	1,558,795	17,555	350,194	148,214
2003	6,480,306	4,272,173	93,272	4,365,445	416,660	-71,797	3,876,988	940,425	1,662,893	18,077	358,492	150,342
2004	6,680,126	4,440,453	81,499	4,521,952	435,713	-64,236	4,022,003	912,707	1,745,416	18,237	366,299	154,156
2005	7,049,699	4,566,404	80,994	4,647,398	457,676	-44,613	4,145,109	956,046	1,948,544	18,878	373,429	156,331
2006	7,528,719	4,921,895	65,117	4,987,012	490,118	-36,523	4,460,371	996,270	2,072,078	19,804	380,169	162,681
2007	8,036,544	5,111,058	63,096	5,174,154	522,686	-21,078	4,630,390	1,089,336	2,316,818	20,804	386,306	167,174
2008	8,638,749	5,314,836	41,071	5,355,907	544,155	-4,620	4,807,132	1,247,367	2,584,250	21,982	393,000	169,861
2009	8,984,042	5,473,285	32,798	5,506,083	562,404	-14,658	4,929,021	1,190,643	2,864,378	22,443	400,303	170,022
2010	9,622,957	5,850,452	47,639	5,898,091	597,237	-25,979	5,274,875	1,196,450	3,151,632	23,612	407,541	171,918
2011	10,100,398	6,093,127	42,559	6,135,686	550,486	-33,726	5,551,474	1,323,576	3,225,348	24,470	412,772	178,639
2012	10,294,980	6,275,714	36,614	6,312,328	571,477	-33,979	5,706,872	1,412,008	3,176,100	24,801	415,102	181,220
2013	10,528,940	6,434,884	65,967	6,500,851	655,512	-24,361	5,820,978	1,442,554	3,265,408	25,297	416,219	185,495
2014	10,907,188	6,647,980	33,857	6,681,837	678,971	-16,383	5,986,483	1,537,985	3,382,720	26,125	417,498	187,620
2015	11,163,559	6,821,734	37,902	6,859,636	706,697	-26,535	6,126,404	1,472,910	3,564,245	26,734	417,572	188,761
2016	11,467,671	6,954,596	28,652	6,983,248	735,215	-47,313	6,200,720	1,514,849	3,752,102	27,362	419,104	191,137
2017	11,628,649	7,001,785	38,840	7,040,625	752,157	-38,801	6,249,667	1,587,890	3,791,092	27,726	419,418	192,455
2018	12,117,617	7,290,053	31,417	7,321,470	784,261	-28,607	6,508,602	1,656,511	3,952,504	28,916	419,064	196,298
2019	12,674,326	7,688,932	24,763	7,713,695	824,389	-24,597	6,864,709	1,711,583	4,098,034	30,180	419,958	197,865
2020	14,204,344	8,010,202	36,875	8,047,077	886,140	-16,095	7,144,842	1,688,453	5,371,049	33,704	421,445	196,814
2021	16,079,007	8,722,173	65,978	8,788,151	949,881	-16,640	7,821,630	1,883,526	6,373,851	38,001	423,124	206,176
2022	15,870,893	9,379,655	-2,575	9,377,080	1,042,629	-25,975	8,308,476	1,977,697	5,584,720	37,325	425,208	216,083

Personal Income and Employment by Area: Brunswick, GA

(Thousands of dollars, except as noted.)

		Derivation of personal income										
		Earnings by place of work										
Year	Personal income, total	Nonfarm	Farm	Total	Less: Contributions for government social insurance	Plus: Adjustment for residence	Equals: Net earnings by place of residence	Plus: Dividends, interest, and rent	Plus: Personal current transfer receipts	Per capita personal income (dollars)	Population (persons)	Total employment
1970	217,294	170,827	2,545	173,372	10,952	2,535	164,955	34,841	17,498	3,390	64,102	27,191
1971	248,873	196,850	2,304	199,154	13,264	2,749	188,639	39,534	20,700	3,782	65,809	28,897
1972	275,680	217,472	2,732	220,204	15,250	3,828	208,782	43,607	23,291	4,082	67,537	29,346
1973	297,353	229,832	4,341	234,173	18,125	4,829	220,877	48,693	27,783	4,344	68,446	29,715
1974	314,290	235,988	4,817	240,805	19,641	6,201	227,365	52,381	34,544	4,638	67,760	29,309
1975	320,878	227,190	5,782	232,972	18,695	7,249	221,526	52,935	46,417	4,840	66,301	27,827
1976	367,868	266,859	5,543	272,402	22,053	7,772	258,121	59,975	49,772	5,504	66,832	29,663
1977	412,371	302,830	4,017	306,847	24,900	8,840	290,787	68,329	53,255	6,041	68,260	31,063
1978	469,980	342,739	5,484	348,223	28,580	10,391	330,034	81,261	58,685	6,865	68,464	32,995
1979	531,710	385,094	3,838	388,932	33,403	12,738	368,267	96,248	67,195	7,565	70,289	33,871
1980	601,185	425,002	2,186	427,188	37,008	16,925	407,105	114,142	79,938	8,355	71,952	34,773
1981	666,223	454,115	3,723	457,838	42,747	19,961	435,052	139,311	91,860	9,162	72,718	34,166
1982	705,193	464,925	4,853	469,778	44,653	21,601	446,726	157,127	101,340	9,578	73,627	33,888
1983	756,299	497,565	3,778	501,343	48,038	22,239	475,544	170,992	109,763	10,163	74,420	34,276
1984	837,597	552,992	5,345	558,337	54,688	25,732	529,381	189,030	119,186	11,092	75,513	35,831
1985	919,297	618,061	4,013	622,074	62,484	24,486	584,076	207,794	127,427	12,014	76,517	37,907
1986	992,670	666,243	4,978	671,221	68,210	27,883	630,894	225,230	136,546	12,747	77,877	38,823
1987	1,049,451	707,612	3,121	710,733	72,101	29,283	667,915	236,431	145,105	13,276	79,049	39,594
1988	1,149,670	772,898	5,119	778,017	81,220	28,963	725,760	264,612	159,298	14,323	80,269	41,522
1989	1,269,556	823,750	8,088	831,838	87,379	30,895	775,354	322,635	171,567	15,594	81,414	42,364
1990	1,355,957	871,336	6,950	878,286	91,814	33,871	820,343	345,601	190,013	16,448	82,437	42,569
1991	1,427,816	900,538	7,553	908,091	96,001	43,029	855,119	351,509	221,188	17,140	83,303	42,130
1992	1,537,165	973,310	8,274	981,584	102,507	43,025	922,102	369,788	245,275	18,243	84,259	42,703
1993	1,622,955	1,026,748	7,183	1,033,931	109,033	42,316	967,214	390,798	264,943	18,954	85,624	44,165
1994	1,729,043	1,079,618	6,499	1,086,117	116,267	47,788	1,017,638	422,893	288,512	19,992	86,487	45,056
1995	1,867,963	1,160,986	5,703	1,166,689	124,503	50,984	1,093,170	463,776	311,017	21,343	87,522	47,089
1996	2,020,052	1,241,338	5,420	1,246,758	131,581	53,320	1,168,497	516,566	334,989	22,815	88,541	48,188
1997	2,130,921	1,304,075	4,864	1,308,939	135,852	58,135	1,231,222	553,122	346,577	23,670	90,027	48,883
1998	2,279,702	1,408,496	5,060	1,413,556	143,870	68,851	1,338,537	588,372	352,793	25,008	91,160	50,359
1999	2,349,775	1,468,638	5,340	1,473,978	148,574	73,638	1,399,042	584,426	366,307	25,425	92,420	50,905
2000	2,485,639	1,544,424	4,867	1,549,291	155,640	65,682	1,459,333	636,631	389,675	26,629	93,344	52,025
2001	2,570,933	1,596,451	5,619	1,602,070	164,136	59,104	1,497,038	658,066	415,829	27,048	95,052	52,363
2002	2,670,093	1,681,698	3,544	1,685,242	172,956	54,330	1,566,616	638,495	464,982	27,637	96,612	52,598
2003	2,830,863	1,821,834	3,677	1,825,511	186,123	45,768	1,685,156	671,070	474,637	28,833	98,180	52,537
2004	3,085,670	1,984,275	3,910	1,988,185	207,798	33,523	1,813,910	753,084	518,676	30,894	99,879	54,372
2005	3,277,626	2,123,565	3,707	2,127,272	216,866	30,572	1,940,978	794,465	542,183	32,282	101,532	56,366
2006	3,545,787	2,312,188	1,129	2,313,317	238,894	18,556	2,092,979	873,922	578,886	33,861	104,715	58,123
2007	3,660,789	2,329,038	1,674	2,330,712	239,549	9,774	2,100,937	940,577	619,275	34,107	107,334	59,413
2008	3,631,752	2,252,618	1,282	2,253,900	252,543	-5,492	1,995,865	935,755	700,132	33,143	109,579	59,055
2009	3,481,286	2,132,204	1,218	2,133,422	239,789	952	1,894,585	827,316	759,385	31,266	111,343	55,724
2010	3,599,446	2,211,187	1,244	2,212,431	241,710	7,166	1,977,887	799,350	822,209	32,030	112,378	53,853
2011	3,757,057	2,190,022	1,299	2,191,321	215,698	8,127	1,983,750	912,484	860,823	33,492	112,178	53,754
2012	3,802,997	2,212,188	2,956	2,215,144	222,169	4,077	1,997,052	944,172	861,773	33,947	112,026	54,199
2013	3,852,302	2,258,313	2,960	2,261,273	255,852	4,221	2,009,642	953,060	889,600	34,400	111,984	54,750
2014	4,026,761	2,304,877	870	2,305,747	259,133	11,822	2,058,436	1,026,608	941,717	35,870	112,260	55,993
2015	4,278,756	2,441,233	2,049	2,443,282	273,263	11,408	2,181,427	1,097,843	999,486	37,894	112,915	56,949
2016	4,375,005	2,498,953	1,059	2,500,012	284,166	22,816	2,238,662	1,102,079	1,034,264	38,638	113,230	57,834
2017	4,609,949	2,578,741	2,773	2,581,514	293,943	19,449	2,307,020	1,215,942	1,086,987	40,526	113,753	59,055
2018	4,894,375	2,748,955	-410	2,748,545	318,065	10,793	2,441,273	1,316,354	1,136,748	43,016	113,781	60,401
2019	5,011,768	2,798,508	-287	2,798,221	326,444	17,390	2,489,167	1,340,841	1,181,760	44,106	113,629	60,586
2020	5,525,602	2,849,984	760	2,850,744	333,873	16,643	2,533,514	1,443,857	1,548,231	48,683	113,501	59,506
2021	6,120,176	3,152,760	-252	3,152,508	367,441	19,275	2,804,342	1,637,167	1,678,667	53,744	113,877	62,488
2022	6,274,455	3,480,239	-199	3,480,040	414,679	14,703	3,080,064	1,693,724	1,500,667	54,827	114,442	66,123

Personal Income and Employment by Area: Buffalo-Cheektowaga, NY

(Thousands of dollars, except as noted.)

		Derivation of personal income										
		Earnings by place of work										
Year	Personal income, total	Nonfarm	Farm	Total	Less: Contributions for government social insurance	Plus: Adjustment for residence	Equals: Net earnings by place of residence	Plus: Dividends, interest, and rent	Plus: Personal current transfer receipts	Per capita personal income (dollars)	Population (persons)	Total employment
1970	5,668,577	4,726,169	22,870	4,749,039	357,861	-65,438	4,325,740	793,271	549,566	4,194	1,351,513	568,934
1971	6,108,318	5,045,253	22,715	5,067,968	392,449	-72,100	4,603,419	831,633	673,266	4,509	1,354,743	567,469
1972	6,463,718	5,358,152	18,241	5,376,393	439,976	-75,416	4,861,001	869,349	733,368	4,796	1,347,603	566,533
1973	7,018,358	5,874,983	26,612	5,901,595	559,600	-79,245	5,262,750	956,667	798,941	5,262	1,333,861	585,656
1974	7,575,057	6,237,591	25,992	6,263,583	613,643	-78,942	5,570,998	1,082,439	921,620	5,744	1,318,687	586,402
1975	8,181,205	6,467,022	23,307	6,490,329	623,846	-79,680	5,786,803	1,181,521	1,212,881	6,231	1,312,980	568,364
1976	8,816,270	7,026,697	23,390	7,050,087	691,508	-87,641	6,270,938	1,242,949	1,302,383	6,766	1,303,095	569,298
1977	9,606,553	7,699,188	22,196	7,721,384	753,883	-97,786	6,869,715	1,365,810	1,371,028	7,448	1,289,794	577,315
1978	10,367,645	8,389,444	27,648	8,417,092	840,374	-104,683	7,472,035	1,469,604	1,426,006	8,125	1,276,092	585,744
1979	11,384,626	9,203,500	31,775	9,235,275	949,644	-111,376	8,174,255	1,656,175	1,554,196	9,010	1,263,570	597,758
1980	12,365,785	9,593,044	31,575	9,624,619	985,941	-110,055	8,528,623	1,989,069	1,848,093	9,962	1,241,275	583,672
1981	13,480,459	10,277,495	34,392	10,311,887	1,125,826	-112,834	9,073,227	2,364,778	2,042,454	10,936	1,232,720	575,313
1982	14,196,724	10,360,665	32,821	10,393,486	1,144,119	-104,891	9,144,476	2,706,451	2,345,797	11,603	1,223,579	552,973
1983	14,903,127	10,730,086	24,781	10,754,867	1,191,178	-101,940	9,461,749	2,903,659	2,537,719	12,312	1,210,449	542,712
1984	16,268,279	11,788,276	31,688	11,819,964	1,329,736	-103,711	10,386,517	3,240,996	2,640,766	13,585	1,197,531	560,459
1985	17,206,362	12,622,536	34,497	12,657,033	1,447,002	-108,043	11,101,988	3,372,063	2,732,311	14,437	1,191,856	572,233
1986	18,108,432	13,354,940	39,283	13,394,223	1,548,370	-106,435	11,739,418	3,480,153	2,888,861	15,287	1,184,555	585,218
1987	18,796,127	14,049,820	45,235	14,095,055	1,606,660	-101,381	12,387,014	3,451,210	2,957,903	15,932	1,179,756	593,226
1988	20,196,508	15,274,567	39,417	15,313,984	1,777,758	-105,557	13,430,669	3,619,586	3,146,253	17,099	1,181,174	611,066
1989	21,635,759	16,189,409	43,670	16,233,079	1,869,984	-104,205	14,258,890	4,015,578	3,361,291	18,243	1,185,954	623,408
1990	23,062,710	17,086,455	42,119	17,128,574	1,890,005	-107,287	15,131,282	4,278,567	3,652,861	19,365	1,190,943	630,513
1991	23,567,108	17,404,398	35,470	17,439,868	1,994,519	-109,638	15,335,711	4,247,982	3,983,415	19,722	1,194,992	622,358
1992	24,686,825	18,336,720	36,249	18,372,969	2,068,492	-114,500	16,189,977	4,123,568	4,373,280	20,598	1,198,490	619,834
1993	25,181,027	18,683,220	37,038	18,720,258	2,125,441	-117,044	16,477,773	4,124,951	4,578,303	20,971	1,200,744	620,260
1994	26,098,159	19,353,292	31,806	19,385,098	2,223,142	-120,362	17,041,594	4,230,562	4,826,003	21,740	1,200,479	633,711
1995	27,213,268	19,965,145	26,445	19,991,590	2,294,800	-129,294	17,567,496	4,589,421	5,056,351	22,718	1,197,885	626,083
1996	28,012,006	20,504,777	31,638	20,536,415	2,313,895	-144,685	18,077,835	4,687,068	5,247,103	23,457	1,194,167	626,699
1997	29,177,058	21,277,274	26,443	21,303,717	2,362,260	-150,298	18,791,159	5,094,575	5,291,324	24,598	1,186,175	631,833
1998	30,168,850	21,995,986	33,540	22,029,526	2,421,097	-171,229	19,437,200	5,266,909	5,464,741	25,600	1,178,462	627,096
1999	31,374,685	23,311,324	43,617	23,354,941	2,509,677	-186,096	20,659,168	5,135,896	5,579,621	26,745	1,173,102	638,318
2000	32,998,931	24,628,699	47,912	24,676,611	2,628,277	-204,560	21,843,774	5,410,029	5,745,128	28,227	1,169,060	646,437
2001	32,936,539	24,366,486	52,046	24,418,532	2,695,014	-184,030	21,539,488	5,277,787	6,119,264	28,270	1,165,067	634,355
2002	33,464,951	24,945,436	46,347	24,991,783	2,785,258	-180,942	22,025,583	4,977,188	6,462,180	28,807	1,161,678	630,522
2003	34,542,921	25,746,493	52,594	25,799,087	2,882,178	-175,820	22,741,089	5,163,057	6,638,775	29,780	1,159,918	631,295
2004	35,855,180	27,106,191	57,583	27,163,774	3,031,922	-186,187	23,945,665	4,896,093	7,013,422	31,015	1,156,070	635,993
2005	36,253,746	27,323,148	52,883	27,376,031	3,108,263	-165,608	24,102,160	4,862,584	7,289,002	31,564	1,148,563	636,774
2006	38,005,361	28,600,439	49,363	28,649,802	3,245,596	-164,311	25,239,895	5,063,763	7,701,703	33,288	1,141,712	636,531
2007	39,941,176	29,614,171	71,477	29,685,648	3,332,393	-140,517	26,212,738	5,680,519	8,047,919	35,108	1,137,678	643,426
2008	41,790,779	30,287,955	91,581	30,379,536	3,451,091	-109,727	26,818,718	6,064,200	8,907,861	36,776	1,136,364	648,231
2009	42,221,657	30,273,071	62,131	30,335,202	3,420,066	-107,431	26,807,705	5,719,239	9,694,713	37,187	1,135,377	635,328
2010	43,640,114	31,366,702	88,967	31,455,669	3,486,885	-141,184	27,827,600	5,582,726	10,229,788	38,394	1,136,632	634,457
2011	45,404,827	32,399,073	96,969	32,496,042	3,254,122	-214,686	29,027,234	6,019,336	10,358,257	39,807	1,140,622	642,234
2012	46,748,183	33,407,565	102,078	33,509,643	3,319,077	-298,320	29,892,246	6,517,228	10,338,709	40,874	1,143,708	646,727
2013	47,180,146	34,273,726	109,805	34,383,531	3,830,302	-361,382	30,191,847	6,488,268	10,500,031	41,094	1,148,113	651,222
2014	48,310,092	34,934,571	91,687	35,026,258	3,986,510	-398,918	30,640,830	6,913,267	10,755,995	41,928	1,152,225	656,960
2015	50,313,813	36,252,403	59,018	36,311,421	4,137,059	-426,197	31,748,165	7,285,345	11,280,303	43,594	1,154,153	663,515
2016	51,288,577	36,984,713	44,623	37,029,336	4,236,350	-451,742	32,341,244	7,460,039	11,487,294	44,390	1,155,397	667,541
2017	53,863,781	38,585,327	55,951	38,641,278	4,408,599	-480,526	33,752,153	7,887,689	12,223,939	46,468	1,159,165	670,084
2018	55,270,064	40,122,115	35,290	40,157,405	4,516,774	-510,273	35,130,358	8,089,822	12,049,884	47,516	1,163,185	678,072
2019	57,603,032	41,498,615	59,483	41,558,098	4,667,194	-548,034	36,342,870	8,393,671	12,866,491	49,430	1,165,340	679,024
2020	63,137,098	41,600,825	63,420	41,664,245	4,628,538	-490,350	36,545,357	8,551,272	18,040,469	54,208	1,164,723	631,874
2021	66,296,864	44,144,428	67,921	44,212,349	5,005,673	-461,048	38,745,628	9,146,497	18,404,739	56,847	1,166,241	649,870
2022	65,507,279	46,714,514	79,828	46,794,342	5,427,083	-534,689	40,832,570	9,324,357	15,350,352	56,414	1,161,192	678,533

Personal Income and Employment by Area: Burlington, NC

(Thousands of dollars, except as noted.)

Year	Personal income, total	Derivation of personal income: Earnings by place of work: Nonfarm	Farm	Total	Less: Contributions for government social insurance	Plus: Adjustment for residence	Equals: Net earnings by place of residence	Plus: Dividends, interest, and rent	Plus: Personal current transfer receipts	Per capita personal income (dollars)	Population (persons)	Total employment
1970	350,273	292,866	6,208	299,074	21,451	8,984	286,607	40,056	23,610	3,617	96,843	51,242
1971	381,007	314,564	5,430	319,994	24,016	12,575	308,553	43,718	28,736	3,868	98,499	51,105
1972	424,017	348,621	6,033	354,654	27,936	17,226	343,944	47,873	32,200	4,251	99,740	52,100
1973	469,926	383,222	9,782	393,004	35,009	21,217	379,212	53,137	37,577	4,702	99,940	53,563
1974	504,551	397,986	9,484	407,470	37,926	27,630	397,174	60,448	46,929	5,083	99,272	52,836
1975	536,960	402,929	6,373	409,302	37,596	32,948	404,654	66,561	65,745	5,466	98,243	49,823
1976	590,057	433,619	11,436	445,055	41,198	40,692	444,549	72,477	73,031	5,977	98,721	49,923
1977	628,721	453,265	9,621	462,886	42,848	52,776	472,814	80,789	75,118	6,383	98,505	49,601
1978	697,983	496,298	8,532	504,830	48,507	72,615	528,938	90,053	78,992	7,083	98,540	50,016
1979	781,923	552,483	6,792	559,275	55,701	88,374	591,948	100,152	89,823	7,894	99,048	53,068
1980	871,973	592,943	4,996	597,939	60,008	101,791	639,722	125,118	107,133	8,761	99,532	52,664
1981	979,181	662,094	9,242	671,336	71,609	100,131	699,858	155,582	123,741	9,784	100,083	53,335
1982	1,049,182	686,110	9,436	695,546	74,489	99,631	720,688	185,473	143,021	10,388	101,000	52,891
1983	1,133,579	760,024	4,830	764,854	82,845	100,760	782,769	200,567	150,243	11,162	101,559	53,988
1984	1,252,503	848,649	10,577	859,226	94,675	103,009	867,560	230,419	154,524	12,315	101,706	56,603
1985	1,333,916	908,102	6,762	914,864	102,634	104,358	916,588	250,074	167,254	13,011	102,524	57,844
1986	1,447,711	1,004,694	7,089	1,011,783	116,026	98,867	994,624	274,722	178,365	13,986	103,515	59,960
1987	1,543,043	1,104,383	5,294	1,109,677	125,289	95,262	1,079,650	275,264	188,129	14,686	105,072	62,866
1988	1,681,431	1,215,900	8,774	1,224,674	140,611	89,085	1,173,148	303,697	204,586	15,814	106,327	66,241
1989	1,827,615	1,295,831	14,869	1,310,700	150,086	82,898	1,243,512	357,682	226,421	17,013	107,425	67,397
1990	1,900,981	1,351,755	19,328	1,371,083	160,375	74,882	1,285,590	370,197	245,194	17,489	108,695	68,152
1991	1,983,233	1,408,424	18,350	1,426,774	170,158	70,134	1,326,750	376,579	279,904	17,905	110,762	66,347
1992	2,109,796	1,499,798	18,130	1,517,928	178,542	80,636	1,420,022	383,266	306,508	18,700	112,825	67,347
1993	2,242,999	1,600,013	16,625	1,616,638	192,222	80,759	1,505,175	408,807	329,017	19,559	114,678	68,752
1994	2,376,695	1,696,634	15,536	1,712,170	206,111	87,961	1,594,020	435,074	347,601	20,351	116,788	69,706
1995	2,541,804	1,780,465	10,378	1,790,843	216,596	100,358	1,674,605	481,365	385,834	21,396	118,796	71,463
1996	2,690,364	1,871,189	10,954	1,882,143	226,641	103,465	1,758,967	516,687	414,710	22,186	121,263	73,122
1997	2,888,267	2,031,817	10,023	2,041,840	242,913	107,055	1,905,982	548,853	433,432	23,316	123,877	74,821
1998	3,109,442	2,178,210	9,317	2,187,527	260,532	134,533	2,061,528	601,496	446,418	24,633	126,232	78,580
1999	3,270,188	2,361,889	12,115	2,374,004	282,326	126,220	2,217,898	583,446	468,844	25,401	128,743	80,175
2000	3,438,877	2,447,515	16,135	2,463,650	292,749	140,918	2,311,819	624,707	502,351	26,166	131,423	81,244
2001	3,585,860	2,482,777	16,481	2,499,258	296,194	182,235	2,385,299	633,826	566,735	26,891	133,346	77,847
2002	3,661,043	2,503,041	5,156	2,508,197	295,297	215,684	2,428,584	625,617	606,842	27,071	135,239	76,385
2003	3,791,842	2,499,030	10,705	2,509,735	300,811	287,847	2,496,771	654,447	640,624	27,879	136,009	75,173
2004	3,873,962	2,624,702	11,166	2,635,868	312,879	211,771	2,534,760	650,095	689,107	28,150	137,619	75,967
2005	4,027,474	2,697,080	14,689	2,711,769	327,177	238,103	2,622,695	663,976	740,803	28,910	139,311	76,703
2006	4,376,096	2,847,635	12,569	2,860,204	342,380	279,112	2,796,936	750,718	828,442	30,935	141,462	77,138
2007	4,671,246	2,940,715	11,613	2,952,328	355,136	344,782	2,941,974	851,725	877,547	32,280	144,712	80,082
2008	4,871,361	2,994,978	5,653	3,000,631	361,796	379,645	3,018,480	849,573	1,003,308	32,981	147,704	78,756
2009	4,754,710	2,766,220	2,957	2,769,177	337,757	440,693	2,872,113	782,020	1,100,577	31,708	149,954	74,926
2010	4,845,905	2,850,663	2,642	2,853,305	342,921	440,462	2,950,846	739,098	1,155,961	31,996	151,452	74,327
2011	5,058,491	2,946,145	-486	2,945,659	325,042	438,927	3,059,544	834,901	1,164,046	33,109	152,782	76,420
2012	5,219,274	3,119,592	5,722	3,125,314	337,556	403,850	3,191,608	832,681	1,194,985	34,019	153,421	77,709
2013	5,286,774	3,130,275	5,161	3,135,436	389,661	451,547	3,197,322	876,038	1,213,414	34,245	154,381	77,880
2014	5,514,086	3,201,253	7,796	3,209,049	399,555	532,614	3,342,108	929,584	1,242,394	35,424	155,658	78,967
2015	5,701,062	3,265,569	5,960	3,271,529	408,967	594,265	3,456,827	926,808	1,317,427	36,228	157,367	79,320
2016	5,927,766	3,454,852	393	3,455,245	430,347	598,921	3,623,819	947,601	1,356,346	36,896	160,663	81,190
2017	6,204,277	3,566,635	1,332	3,567,967	442,604	653,016	3,778,379	1,015,554	1,410,344	37,907	163,671	82,383
2018	6,562,167	3,723,940	-5,835	3,718,105	456,764	750,890	4,012,231	1,066,011	1,483,925	39,318	166,901	84,193
2019	6,984,074	3,965,936	-3,842	3,962,094	484,935	788,233	4,265,392	1,136,979	1,581,703	41,182	169,590	85,908
2020	7,604,373	4,189,328	-4,988	4,184,340	514,688	765,647	4,435,299	1,145,958	2,023,116	44,223	171,954	83,920
2021	8,383,946	4,634,280	-505	4,633,775	562,916	754,378	4,825,237	1,214,811	2,343,898	48,218	173,876	88,322
2022	8,637,798	4,924,015	-3,408	4,920,607	607,457	939,521	5,252,671	1,314,101	2,071,026	48,980	176,353	90,941

Personal Income and Employment by Area: Burlington-South Burlington, VT

(Thousands of dollars, except as noted.)

		Derivation of personal income										
		Earnings by place of work										
Year	Personal income, total	Nonfarm	Farm	Total	Less: Contributions for government social insurance	Plus: Adjustment for residence	Equals: Net earnings by place of residence	Plus: Dividends, interest, and rent	Plus: Personal current transfer receipts	Per capita personal income (dollars)	Population (persons)	Total employment
1970	516,335	422,616	17,722	440,338	29,444	-13,527	397,367	72,287	46,681	3,834	134,673	62,022
1971	556,777	447,386	17,720	465,106	31,994	-12,818	420,294	80,023	56,460	4,048	137,553	62,103
1972	606,443	484,457	19,304	503,761	36,122	-13,220	454,419	87,894	64,130	4,314	140,585	62,800
1973	654,967	521,330	20,573	541,903	44,911	-12,976	484,016	97,541	73,410	4,650	140,865	64,201
1974	706,184	553,004	16,913	569,917	49,146	-12,374	508,397	109,757	88,030	4,985	141,657	64,786
1975	791,194	604,097	17,982	622,079	52,565	-13,623	555,891	125,097	110,206	5,509	143,608	64,467
1976	880,961	681,928	22,301	704,229	60,602	-15,170	628,457	134,176	118,328	6,067	145,209	67,585
1977	960,758	755,626	18,942	774,568	67,583	-16,735	690,250	150,250	120,258	6,513	147,509	70,446
1978	1,114,324	893,339	27,525	920,864	82,639	-21,653	816,572	171,296	126,456	7,478	149,023	76,185
1979	1,265,422	1,023,961	29,838	1,053,799	98,499	-26,303	928,997	192,905	143,520	8,350	151,554	80,057
1980	1,428,785	1,134,802	30,079	1,164,881	109,727	-29,188	1,025,966	233,891	168,928	9,192	155,430	82,463
1981	1,620,671	1,283,722	32,918	1,316,640	133,162	-36,152	1,147,326	281,670	191,675	10,322	157,017	85,578
1982	1,766,130	1,389,929	31,780	1,421,709	147,354	-42,601	1,231,754	326,784	207,592	11,131	158,663	87,158
1983	1,912,933	1,523,752	21,355	1,545,107	163,393	-49,561	1,332,153	359,948	220,832	11,934	160,287	89,680
1984	2,102,712	1,687,829	22,047	1,709,876	186,031	-56,226	1,467,619	408,187	226,906	13,002	161,724	94,035
1985	2,311,147	1,866,984	27,639	1,894,623	209,699	-64,958	1,619,966	452,678	238,503	14,114	163,751	98,992
1986	2,493,263	2,029,452	27,935	2,057,387	228,907	-71,776	1,756,704	490,869	245,690	15,035	165,834	103,108
1987	2,697,040	2,233,000	36,515	2,269,515	247,883	-80,470	1,941,162	504,536	251,342	16,077	167,755	107,321
1988	2,987,948	2,490,757	34,060	2,524,817	284,100	-97,568	2,143,149	577,586	267,213	17,425	171,477	113,250
1989	3,342,992	2,739,025	35,548	2,774,573	309,471	-108,811	2,356,291	690,175	296,526	19,105	174,979	117,499
1990	3,520,753	2,895,469	33,930	2,929,399	346,095	-117,385	2,465,919	725,287	329,547	19,807	177,757	117,930
1991	3,616,538	2,964,492	28,614	2,993,106	357,372	-118,632	2,517,102	736,698	362,738	20,154	179,447	115,960
1992	3,847,738	3,133,575	49,875	3,183,450	373,108	-123,622	2,686,720	751,041	409,977	21,237	181,178	117,796
1993	4,017,423	3,296,137	39,987	3,336,124	394,254	-129,512	2,812,358	771,923	433,142	21,845	183,909	120,276
1994	4,177,047	3,388,569	40,336	3,428,905	409,134	-129,998	2,889,773	833,102	454,172	22,315	187,186	123,280
1995	4,452,188	3,560,273	31,957	3,592,230	434,510	-142,111	3,015,609	941,257	495,322	23,519	189,300	125,287
1996	4,728,961	3,810,527	46,011	3,856,538	460,096	-159,377	3,237,065	979,238	512,658	24,753	191,043	128,300
1997	4,995,346	4,007,208	34,235	4,041,443	480,696	-169,545	3,391,202	1,061,191	542,953	25,877	193,040	130,011
1998	5,402,569	4,352,659	44,123	4,396,782	513,716	-185,351	3,697,715	1,141,487	563,367	27,749	194,691	133,049
1999	5,776,229	4,757,783	47,902	4,805,685	552,638	-201,416	4,051,631	1,118,267	606,331	29,317	197,026	136,879
2000	6,298,280	5,207,839	51,158	5,258,997	595,562	-223,176	4,440,259	1,196,289	661,732	31,555	199,600	142,039
2001	6,624,238	5,460,384	52,174	5,512,558	630,201	-231,906	4,650,451	1,247,626	726,161	32,897	201,361	144,163
2002	6,783,169	5,604,072	39,718	5,643,790	632,245	-231,135	4,780,410	1,224,850	777,909	33,406	203,052	143,704
2003	7,111,723	5,815,077	48,319	5,863,396	657,883	-236,222	4,969,291	1,327,166	815,266	34,827	204,201	144,042
2004	7,476,747	6,130,050	65,327	6,195,377	692,713	-241,891	5,260,773	1,368,435	847,539	36,356	205,652	147,050
2005	7,654,992	6,308,664	66,593	6,375,257	721,408	-248,392	5,405,457	1,324,594	924,941	37,046	206,637	147,963
2006	8,127,892	6,535,722	41,219	6,576,941	758,390	-241,031	5,577,520	1,532,964	1,017,408	39,185	207,426	149,068
2007	8,572,251	6,756,281	72,418	6,828,699	800,363	-252,180	5,776,156	1,655,998	1,140,097	41,167	208,232	151,290
2008	9,140,576	7,049,473	71,475	7,120,948	833,235	-254,437	6,033,276	1,817,184	1,290,116	43,665	209,332	151,593
2009	9,044,380	7,044,085	40,120	7,084,205	832,095	-245,817	6,006,293	1,641,563	1,396,524	42,979	210,435	149,157
2010	9,296,377	7,285,857	62,146	7,348,003	852,277	-256,482	6,239,244	1,567,566	1,489,567	43,924	211,648	150,323
2011	10,010,073	7,605,310	84,549	7,689,859	795,801	-241,075	6,652,983	1,837,242	1,519,848	46,815	213,820	153,437
2012	10,329,236	7,852,546	79,629	7,932,175	834,789	-266,739	6,830,647	1,944,763	1,553,826	48,036	215,032	156,053
2013	10,552,623	8,106,490	99,232	8,205,722	974,955	-264,814	6,965,953	1,961,909	1,624,761	48,769	216,378	157,594
2014	10,990,317	8,239,827	117,352	8,357,179	1,017,251	-244,609	7,095,319	2,187,084	1,707,914	50,481	217,712	159,924
2015	11,336,618	8,549,671	70,645	8,620,316	1,061,999	-250,083	7,308,234	2,277,451	1,750,933	51,600	219,701	162,253
2016	11,606,747	8,756,685	62,593	8,819,278	1,088,876	-248,937	7,481,465	2,338,227	1,787,055	52,640	220,494	163,804
2017	11,979,491	8,995,891	73,331	9,069,222	1,128,372	-223,631	7,717,219	2,444,446	1,817,826	53,857	222,432	164,711
2018	12,411,362	9,377,706	52,905	9,430,611	1,159,176	-231,415	8,040,020	2,496,747	1,874,595	55,447	223,841	165,595
2019	13,066,681	9,749,068	86,293	9,835,361	1,176,677	-231,379	8,427,305	2,760,026	1,879,350	58,165	224,648	165,398
2020	13,814,516	9,903,070	77,515	9,980,585	1,204,952	-244,700	8,530,933	2,668,543	2,615,040	61,207	225,702	156,884
2021	14,767,711	10,615,901	78,230	10,694,131	1,239,592	-275,634	9,178,905	2,884,982	2,703,824	65,021	227,122	162,297
2022	15,321,655	11,410,350	113,301	11,523,651	1,356,260	-301,552	9,865,839	3,077,145	2,378,671	67,342	227,521	168,152

Personal Income and Employment by Area: California-Lexington Park, MD

(Thousands of dollars, except as noted.)

		Derivation of personal income										
		Earnings by place of work			Less: Contributions for government social insurance	Plus: Adjustment for residence	Equals: Net earnings by place of residence	Plus: Dividends, interest, and rent	Plus: Personal current transfer receipts			
Year	Personal income, total	Nonfarm	Farm	Total						Per capita personal income (dollars)	Population (persons)	Total employment
1970	205,033	147,579	5,694	153,273	7,478	9,180	154,975	40,708	9,350	4,286	47,840	19,164
1971	230,307	162,424	4,453	166,877	8,459	16,464	174,882	44,176	11,249	4,594	50,127	19,026
1972	259,542	180,400	5,240	185,640	9,625	21,320	197,335	49,277	12,930	5,109	50,805	19,653
1973	278,652	184,440	8,012	192,452	10,637	28,303	210,118	53,378	15,156	5,581	49,928	19,221
1974	314,963	206,087	7,933	214,020	12,701	34,066	235,385	61,333	18,245	6,096	51,667	20,064
1975	313,494	194,757	6,410	201,167	12,572	40,585	229,180	61,405	22,909	5,944	52,738	18,610
1976	347,827	213,201	7,717	220,918	14,073	48,689	255,534	67,077	25,216	6,474	53,724	18,852
1977	383,723	229,288	7,698	236,986	15,214	58,547	280,319	75,729	27,675	7,038	54,522	19,582
1978	429,820	247,819	10,702	258,521	16,768	70,747	312,500	86,780	30,540	7,575	56,744	20,556
1979	464,979	265,540	7,430	272,970	19,870	83,876	336,976	92,917	35,086	7,943	58,541	20,935
1980	527,930	299,399	3,785	303,184	22,922	97,923	378,185	107,168	42,577	8,773	60,176	21,211
1981	637,072	360,097	11,537	371,634	26,509	114,503	459,628	127,619	49,825	10,413	61,182	22,032
1982	694,982	388,632	18,623	407,255	29,106	116,780	494,929	144,657	55,396	11,264	61,697	22,268
1983	736,268	422,493	9,533	432,026	34,543	123,654	521,137	154,976	60,155	11,790	62,450	23,501
1984	807,054	465,867	8,430	474,297	39,891	133,613	568,019	173,506	65,529	12,761	63,245	24,650
1985	880,022	508,956	12,874	521,830	45,530	146,604	622,904	186,836	70,282	13,619	64,618	25,721
1986	950,679	563,958	4,446	568,404	52,568	159,571	675,407	201,424	73,848	14,281	66,570	27,230
1987	1,040,520	628,687	5,201	633,888	59,506	169,875	744,257	214,075	82,188	15,062	69,083	29,457
1988	1,177,759	736,180	6,935	743,115	73,916	182,863	852,062	236,450	89,247	16,407	71,785	32,351
1989	1,293,098	809,524	3,530	813,054	83,119	195,682	925,617	265,363	102,118	17,444	74,130	34,042
1990	1,395,131	882,991	5,634	888,625	93,090	206,199	1,001,734	278,998	114,399	18,270	76,361	35,990
1991	1,476,688	946,457	6,380	952,837	101,081	194,623	1,046,379	298,264	132,045	18,944	77,952	36,785
1992	1,554,265	994,877	4,799	999,676	106,975	195,047	1,087,748	312,065	154,452	19,720	78,815	36,686
1993	1,584,624	1,004,048	4,259	1,008,307	108,684	201,152	1,100,775	322,163	161,686	20,317	77,994	35,928
1994	1,637,268	1,039,231	5,236	1,044,467	114,623	200,746	1,130,590	339,988	166,690	20,794	78,737	36,940
1995	1,711,885	1,091,329	-5,492	1,085,837	119,644	196,155	1,162,348	371,062	178,475	21,609	79,222	38,098
1996	1,840,633	1,192,243	14,510	1,206,753	130,378	184,227	1,260,602	391,447	188,584	22,827	80,633	40,147
1997	2,102,100	1,460,019	7,330	1,467,349	159,123	149,108	1,457,334	447,664	197,102	25,276	83,165	44,464
1998	2,343,633	1,709,910	1,114	1,711,024	183,865	116,209	1,643,368	497,510	202,755	27,583	84,967	47,377
1999	2,424,389	1,772,182	2,619	1,774,801	190,597	120,945	1,705,149	502,712	216,528	28,313	85,627	48,147
2000	2,614,703	1,941,485	10,795	1,952,280	206,222	105,661	1,851,719	529,286	233,698	30,228	86,498	49,501
2001	2,681,023	1,957,713	10,929	1,968,642	210,328	135,972	1,894,286	525,653	261,084	30,656	87,455	47,090
2002	2,918,847	2,177,603	-4,722	2,172,881	234,611	142,956	2,081,226	546,439	291,182	32,497	89,819	49,309
2003	3,174,349	2,405,148	6,115	2,411,263	259,356	139,477	2,291,384	573,356	309,609	34,379	92,333	51,658
2004	3,417,742	2,582,878	8,146	2,591,024	281,161	190,778	2,500,641	582,399	334,702	36,014	94,900	52,799
2005	3,641,646	2,685,351	5,064	2,690,415	290,983	274,146	2,673,578	599,333	368,735	37,593	96,871	53,233
2006	3,904,482	2,898,705	3,289	2,901,994	318,381	272,616	2,856,229	656,027	392,226	39,499	98,849	54,952
2007	4,193,998	3,052,540	2,443	3,054,983	339,736	295,640	3,010,887	750,413	432,698	41,690	100,599	56,575
2008	4,498,772	3,116,101	3,087	3,119,188	352,335	367,445	3,134,298	857,454	507,020	44,140	101,921	56,062
2009	4,683,933	3,371,897	3,069	3,374,966	379,712	310,130	3,305,384	837,590	540,959	45,355	103,273	56,278
2010	4,967,118	3,722,608	-278	3,722,330	422,198	218,060	3,518,192	851,171	597,755	46,967	105,758	57,620
2011	5,273,037	3,996,075	2,846	3,998,921	402,634	118,912	3,715,199	927,772	630,066	49,043	107,518	58,338
2012	5,356,441	4,022,720	102	4,022,822	408,267	127,411	3,741,966	963,579	650,896	49,270	108,717	58,503
2013	5,366,153	4,037,686	-26	4,037,660	463,329	120,848	3,695,179	995,539	675,435	49,188	109,094	59,095
2014	5,526,188	4,139,571	-2,075	4,137,496	473,337	130,183	3,794,342	1,016,253	715,593	50,355	109,745	59,500
2015	5,780,643	4,263,996	-4,047	4,259,949	490,294	178,250	3,947,905	1,074,413	758,325	52,185	110,772	60,302
2016	5,936,011	4,408,971	-2,670	4,406,301	499,891	164,009	4,070,419	1,067,726	797,866	53,238	111,500	61,230
2017	6,074,389	4,550,192	1,170	4,551,362	518,317	150,780	4,183,825	1,070,628	819,936	54,151	112,174	62,076
2018	6,320,851	4,667,515	-1,833	4,665,682	535,353	221,664	4,351,993	1,104,012	864,846	56,222	112,427	62,614
2019	6,607,788	4,920,006	4,961	4,924,967	564,796	184,128	4,544,299	1,155,881	907,608	58,387	113,172	63,558
2020	7,119,548	5,287,198	1,693	5,288,891	610,631	37,778	4,716,038	1,191,324	1,212,186	62,459	113,987	64,038
2021	7,466,688	5,484,690	6,770	5,491,460	637,341	29,687	4,883,806	1,210,240	1,372,642	65,118	114,664	66,487
2022	7,598,680	5,665,223	-1,012	5,664,211	660,444	176,782	5,180,549	1,253,003	1,165,128	66,146	114,877	66,988

Personal Income and Employment by Area: Canton-Massillon, OH

(Thousands of dollars, except as noted.)

Year	Personal income, total	Derivation of personal income: Earnings by place of work: Nonfarm	Farm	Total	Less: Contributions for government social insurance	Plus: Adjustment for residence	Equals: Net earnings by place of residence	Plus: Dividends, interest, and rent	Plus: Personal current transfer receipts	Per capita personal income (dollars)	Population (persons)	Total employment
1970	1,539,014	1,257,308	6,263	1,263,571	86,403	32,588	1,209,756	204,466	124,792	3,902	394,389	166,024
1971	1,594,880	1,266,119	7,849	1,273,968	89,495	43,474	1,227,947	218,615	148,318	4,019	396,830	160,591
1972	1,767,736	1,416,355	7,807	1,424,162	105,412	52,319	1,371,069	232,722	163,945	4,480	394,589	163,820
1973	1,991,029	1,613,297	9,499	1,622,796	139,857	59,081	1,542,020	258,597	190,412	4,919	404,798	173,392
1974	2,228,143	1,791,284	10,639	1,801,923	161,136	65,845	1,706,632	296,003	225,508	5,483	406,348	179,109
1975	2,393,365	1,852,965	14,869	1,867,834	162,465	73,265	1,778,634	320,367	294,364	5,947	402,470	173,184
1976	2,607,650	2,026,060	15,741	2,041,801	180,923	82,159	1,943,037	342,940	321,673	6,510	400,573	173,726
1977	2,889,951	2,249,265	13,768	2,263,033	200,669	112,452	2,174,816	380,708	334,427	7,201	401,304	177,260
1978	3,219,758	2,529,202	8,722	2,537,924	233,670	133,927	2,438,181	425,251	356,326	7,967	404,117	184,559
1979	3,618,881	2,836,297	7,293	2,843,590	272,784	154,282	2,725,088	484,741	409,052	8,982	402,887	189,646
1980	3,961,900	2,948,295	297	2,948,592	282,431	174,671	2,840,832	599,209	521,859	9,798	404,365	186,051
1981	4,375,593	3,211,721	2,760	3,214,481	329,515	176,999	3,061,965	735,153	578,475	10,851	403,233	184,686
1982	4,518,169	3,144,256	4,582	3,148,838	326,647	188,297	3,010,488	816,446	691,235	11,250	401,616	177,193
1983	4,674,523	3,194,008	-311	3,193,697	334,666	204,919	3,063,950	870,147	740,426	11,694	399,727	172,450
1984	5,077,556	3,513,085	10,183	3,523,268	378,965	220,889	3,365,192	957,786	754,578	12,722	399,131	179,713
1985	5,306,476	3,659,949	12,457	3,672,406	400,955	235,901	3,507,352	999,422	799,702	13,382	396,527	183,119
1986	5,452,664	3,703,347	12,327	3,715,674	417,024	263,292	3,561,942	1,031,375	859,347	13,854	393,569	185,112
1987	5,695,822	3,940,389	14,925	3,955,314	443,742	265,131	3,776,703	1,021,755	897,364	14,525	392,135	191,292
1988	6,111,423	4,259,918	14,230	4,274,148	494,459	278,247	4,057,936	1,113,840	939,647	15,521	393,752	194,561
1989	6,550,904	4,483,325	19,738	4,503,063	522,312	303,825	4,284,576	1,264,021	1,002,307	16,606	394,481	198,003
1990	6,931,530	4,723,907	17,440	4,741,347	560,477	311,808	4,492,678	1,312,781	1,126,071	17,566	394,606	201,081
1991	7,048,683	4,813,851	9,328	4,823,179	582,378	322,021	4,562,822	1,294,008	1,191,853	17,754	397,025	200,722
1992	7,526,150	5,160,203	20,514	5,180,717	617,528	340,888	4,904,077	1,313,575	1,308,498	18,844	399,399	199,451
1993	7,855,381	5,424,606	16,229	5,440,835	661,054	364,750	5,144,531	1,359,221	1,351,629	19,536	402,098	202,448
1994	8,285,313	5,766,366	25,708	5,792,074	711,120	391,221	5,472,175	1,448,926	1,364,212	20,528	403,612	207,012
1995	8,670,922	5,995,431	27,036	6,022,467	749,400	416,943	5,690,010	1,547,858	1,433,054	21,414	404,924	212,418
1996	9,032,919	6,186,992	26,678	6,213,670	762,440	452,524	5,903,754	1,627,552	1,501,613	22,253	405,915	215,591
1997	9,404,950	6,412,641	27,659	6,440,300	772,726	476,334	6,143,908	1,721,507	1,539,535	23,152	406,235	218,984
1998	10,098,078	6,956,008	54,885	7,010,893	807,271	500,235	6,703,857	1,796,215	1,598,006	24,861	406,189	224,798
1999	10,360,583	7,180,885	46,529	7,227,414	824,802	532,880	6,935,492	1,770,542	1,654,549	25,457	406,983	226,886
2000	10,931,651	7,560,069	35,204	7,595,273	837,972	560,094	7,317,395	1,846,920	1,767,336	26,867	406,887	232,230
2001	11,058,751	7,564,434	33,110	7,597,544	853,492	606,301	7,350,353	1,797,822	1,910,576	27,221	406,256	225,330
2002	11,222,477	7,631,423	26,076	7,657,499	845,794	676,234	7,487,939	1,692,976	2,041,562	27,639	406,039	221,373
2003	11,552,419	7,766,145	25,282	7,791,427	871,669	768,007	7,687,765	1,721,850	2,142,804	28,451	406,046	217,705
2004	11,914,640	8,097,344	29,738	8,127,082	919,180	817,944	8,025,846	1,696,614	2,192,180	29,349	405,960	218,626
2005	12,266,960	8,257,072	31,614	8,288,686	952,195	911,875	8,248,366	1,684,658	2,333,936	30,276	405,168	220,178
2006	12,762,398	8,321,307	25,162	8,346,469	962,305	1,081,277	8,465,441	1,829,950	2,467,007	31,485	405,343	216,107
2007	13,397,229	8,475,628	31,855	8,507,483	980,828	1,164,664	8,691,319	2,071,529	2,634,381	33,003	405,939	217,395
2008	13,858,693	8,599,094	33,555	8,632,649	1,011,615	1,132,353	8,753,387	2,155,035	2,950,271	34,123	406,140	215,548
2009	13,376,170	8,111,327	39,978	8,151,305	972,828	1,021,651	8,200,128	1,946,719	3,229,323	33,017	405,127	205,926
2010	13,792,905	8,275,252	44,704	8,319,956	972,002	1,100,630	8,448,584	1,938,191	3,406,130	34,114	404,317	203,979
2011	14,692,386	8,814,414	58,998	8,873,412	938,977	1,127,341	9,061,776	2,148,865	3,481,745	36,377	403,896	209,438
2012	15,232,320	9,159,703	47,596	9,207,299	967,347	1,206,991	9,446,943	2,361,096	3,424,281	37,661	404,461	213,735
2013	15,410,793	9,586,878	50,465	9,637,343	1,090,036	1,074,338	9,621,645	2,245,132	3,544,016	38,064	404,867	217,150
2014	15,966,113	9,937,992	44,091	9,982,083	1,120,716	1,070,224	9,931,591	2,395,879	3,638,643	39,360	405,644	220,103
2015	16,483,778	9,987,609	18,797	10,006,406	1,128,929	1,272,055	10,149,532	2,562,939	3,771,307	40,714	404,863	219,328
2016	16,429,765	9,906,573	9,574	9,916,147	1,149,099	1,269,222	10,036,270	2,549,459	3,844,036	40,672	403,961	220,205
2017	17,010,289	10,340,983	11,148	10,352,131	1,232,065	1,244,328	10,364,394	2,725,256	3,920,639	42,244	402,666	221,474
2018	17,545,649	10,582,118	17,861	10,599,979	1,246,587	1,326,881	10,680,273	2,846,039	4,019,337	43,624	402,202	222,209
2019	18,105,853	10,863,544	3,369	10,866,913	1,286,849	1,357,408	10,937,472	2,982,847	4,185,534	45,061	401,805	220,281
2020	19,526,085	10,879,167	20,590	10,899,757	1,299,833	1,430,282	11,030,206	2,998,713	5,497,166	48,671	401,183	214,410
2021	21,082,381	11,543,952	37,013	11,580,965	1,377,186	1,575,941	11,779,720	3,347,563	5,955,098	52,663	400,330	220,568
2022	21,233,562	12,182,734	25,091	12,207,825	1,497,220	1,680,898	12,391,503	3,646,846	5,195,213	53,175	399,316	227,027

Personal Income and Employment by Area: Cape Coral-Fort Myers, FL

(Thousands of dollars, except as noted.)

Year	Personal income, total	Derivation of personal income: Earnings by place of work: Nonfarm	Farm	Total	Less: Contributions for government social insurance	Plus: Adjustment for residence	Equals: Net earnings by place of residence	Plus: Dividends, interest, and rent	Plus: Personal current transfer receipts	Per capita personal income (dollars)	Population (persons)	Total employment
1970	424,777	255,307	7,788	263,095	16,301	5,688	252,482	122,719	49,576	3,954	107,430	42,485
1971	481,303	281,710	8,448	290,158	18,792	5,892	277,258	141,942	62,103	4,116	116,946	44,589
1972	566,888	337,228	9,099	346,327	23,700	6,875	329,502	161,431	75,955	4,440	127,672	49,836
1973	700,122	418,684	10,076	428,760	33,844	9,862	404,778	199,141	96,203	5,100	137,276	58,032
1974	822,773	483,494	9,569	493,063	41,155	10,583	462,491	243,677	116,605	5,604	146,825	61,830
1975	916,640	503,421	15,192	518,613	42,100	8,456	484,969	277,494	154,177	5,917	154,905	61,397
1976	1,045,610	577,994	17,346	595,340	48,458	8,386	555,268	316,668	173,674	6,550	159,632	65,373
1977	1,224,202	680,308	18,233	698,541	57,763	10,705	651,483	376,352	196,367	7,036	173,998	73,310
1978	1,483,214	833,626	23,175	856,801	72,566	14,151	798,386	456,106	228,722	8,109	182,920	83,121
1979	1,761,801	986,198	24,644	1,010,842	90,397	14,876	935,321	554,067	272,413	9,148	192,597	90,770
1980	2,152,377	1,146,092	25,998	1,172,090	106,373	17,288	1,083,005	735,870	333,502	10,345	208,050	96,755
1981	2,565,646	1,313,646	22,103	1,335,749	131,787	18,978	1,222,940	939,166	403,540	11,726	218,795	103,581
1982	2,740,348	1,363,942	27,149	1,391,091	142,832	16,969	1,265,228	1,002,347	472,773	11,866	230,932	106,186
1983	3,094,785	1,542,321	39,899	1,582,220	160,655	14,593	1,436,158	1,135,429	523,198	12,812	241,554	113,430
1984	3,521,595	1,774,399	39,545	1,813,944	189,367	16,479	1,641,056	1,310,888	569,651	13,794	255,299	121,575
1985	3,982,393	2,003,597	43,315	2,046,912	218,359	18,900	1,847,453	1,496,621	638,319	14,909	267,107	129,854
1986	4,436,817	2,253,269	50,847	2,304,116	252,185	18,722	2,070,653	1,660,132	706,032	15,818	280,483	136,443
1987	4,876,760	2,556,640	58,630	2,615,270	282,950	19,805	2,352,125	1,759,717	764,918	16,517	295,262	138,260
1988	5,477,747	2,881,768	58,449	2,940,217	329,695	23,554	2,634,076	2,002,624	841,047	17,852	306,842	149,455
1989	6,375,258	3,197,310	61,650	3,258,960	372,326	24,713	2,911,347	2,507,259	956,652	19,783	322,253	159,512
1990	6,808,624	3,426,826	41,827	3,468,653	394,898	30,003	3,103,758	2,652,521	1,052,345	20,084	339,012	164,024
1991	6,949,532	3,616,892	48,490	3,665,382	417,708	-93,352	3,154,322	2,623,224	1,171,986	19,795	351,069	163,361
1992	7,301,909	3,871,763	46,252	3,918,015	445,103	-147,040	3,325,872	2,638,797	1,337,240	20,301	359,679	162,757
1993	7,773,792	4,134,713	49,101	4,183,814	472,610	-79,233	3,631,971	2,712,238	1,429,583	21,071	368,938	170,194
1994	8,320,610	4,468,729	39,826	4,508,555	518,294	-69,540	3,920,721	2,869,298	1,530,591	21,843	380,928	178,317
1995	9,077,143	4,768,774	41,282	4,810,056	549,600	-75,801	4,184,655	3,237,320	1,655,168	23,166	391,823	186,043
1996	9,507,322	5,136,363	30,688	5,167,051	582,228	-150,179	4,434,644	3,310,771	1,761,907	23,725	400,723	191,718
1997	10,163,808	5,292,558	33,445	5,326,003	604,113	-57,310	4,664,580	3,658,437	1,840,791	24,739	410,841	196,507
1998	11,007,245	5,885,618	43,275	5,928,893	656,736	-145,508	5,126,649	4,019,761	1,860,835	26,090	421,889	205,733
1999	11,548,822	6,446,621	45,651	6,492,272	710,017	-147,080	5,635,175	3,962,812	1,950,835	26,735	431,981	211,109
2000	12,731,525	6,961,704	43,776	7,005,480	764,422	-7,656	6,233,402	4,399,473	2,098,650	28,655	444,311	219,932
2001	14,392,541	8,167,560	42,924	8,210,484	886,105	-9,902	7,314,477	4,795,586	2,282,478	31,218	461,037	232,767
2002	14,922,278	8,751,039	45,612	8,796,651	947,432	-21,890	7,827,329	4,631,936	2,463,013	31,160	478,889	240,328
2003	16,157,022	9,743,146	43,847	9,786,993	1,053,410	-22,861	8,710,722	4,801,276	2,645,024	32,466	497,662	258,604
2004	18,684,037	11,286,361	42,380	11,328,741	1,214,359	-74,350	10,040,032	5,771,799	2,872,206	35,764	522,431	276,152
2005	20,736,680	12,527,554	45,660	12,573,214	1,366,179	-52,891	11,154,144	6,486,168	3,096,368	37,361	555,029	300,560
2006	23,879,781	14,477,957	35,410	14,513,367	1,549,387	-91,076	12,872,904	7,632,721	3,374,156	40,983	582,678	316,333
2007	24,546,605	14,244,623	25,761	14,270,384	1,562,566	37,534	12,745,352	8,126,707	3,674,546	40,592	604,716	315,784
2008	25,105,243	13,360,701	25,750	13,386,451	1,508,874	-16,133	11,861,444	8,992,800	4,250,999	41,090	610,984	298,699
2009	24,394,442	12,466,280	30,718	12,496,998	1,442,504	8,967	11,063,461	8,620,853	4,710,128	39,841	612,297	284,895
2010	24,495,250	12,717,631	41,158	12,758,789	1,429,920	-148,525	11,180,344	8,131,104	5,183,802	39,510	619,982	284,635
2011	26,354,773	13,054,459	41,120	13,095,579	1,330,074	-21,837	11,743,668	9,151,702	5,459,403	41,922	628,655	292,607
2012	26,937,586	13,389,815	56,641	13,446,456	1,394,857	-209,301	11,842,298	9,523,437	5,571,851	42,105	639,773	301,977
2013	27,361,388	13,739,221	51,119	13,790,340	1,628,095	-113,875	12,048,370	9,493,205	5,819,813	41,883	653,285	314,680
2014	29,875,071	14,928,722	41,975	14,970,697	1,760,937	-291,770	12,917,990	10,751,246	6,205,835	44,693	668,448	334,645
2015	32,065,038	16,164,584	53,230	16,217,814	1,895,525	-505,550	13,816,739	11,581,600	6,666,699	46,576	688,440	353,160
2016	34,451,376	17,365,722	49,137	17,414,859	2,021,062	-604,689	14,789,108	12,675,017	6,987,251	48,594	708,970	364,215
2017	36,717,764	18,435,088	49,443	18,484,531	2,136,548	-734,419	15,613,564	13,698,972	7,405,228	50,716	723,989	378,078
2018	38,954,271	19,334,292	55,482	19,389,774	2,280,480	-752,357	16,356,937	14,730,532	7,866,802	52,981	735,249	391,906
2019	41,426,102	19,797,167	53,050	19,850,217	2,405,684	-765,775	16,678,758	16,261,297	8,486,047	55,271	749,512	398,523
2020	44,505,846	20,708,430	54,618	20,763,048	2,536,719	-1,139,091	17,087,238	16,735,184	10,683,424	58,139	765,504	402,942
2021	49,641,402	22,804,686	51,435	22,856,121	2,751,129	-1,087,129	19,017,863	18,320,401	12,303,138	62,783	790,676	428,164
2022	52,281,287	25,377,425	50,889	25,428,314	3,107,398	-1,193,101	21,127,815	19,778,655	11,374,817	63,568	822,453	450,880

Personal Income and Employment by Area: Cape Girardeau, MO-IL

(Thousands of dollars, except as noted.)

Year	Personal income, total	Derivation of personal income: Earnings by place of work: Nonfarm	Farm	Total	Less: Contributions for government social insurance	Plus: Adjustment for residence	Equals: Net earnings by place of residence	Plus: Dividends, interest, and rent	Plus: Personal current transfer receipts	Per capita personal income (dollars)	Population (persons)	Total employment
1970	222,083	169,627	9,171	178,798	11,405	-6,509	160,884	33,039	28,160	3,153	70,436	30,842
1971	242,481	185,875	8,250	194,125	12,963	-7,055	174,107	36,531	31,843	3,373	71,899	31,125
1972	262,465	198,524	10,466	208,990	14,450	-6,576	187,964	40,310	34,191	3,564	73,647	31,770
1973	296,723	217,718	18,539	236,257	18,254	-6,082	211,921	45,786	39,016	4,048	73,297	33,247
1974	330,521	250,830	10,119	260,949	21,944	-7,705	231,300	52,907	46,314	4,431	74,588	34,420
1975	379,546	274,221	17,405	291,626	23,478	-8,765	259,383	60,443	59,720	5,087	74,605	34,141
1976	422,961	317,320	15,432	332,752	27,451	-10,990	294,311	66,143	62,507	5,506	76,817	36,445
1977	463,456	349,977	14,501	364,478	30,208	-11,215	323,055	75,134	65,267	5,973	77,598	37,517
1978	526,451	401,003	19,953	420,956	35,866	-12,988	372,102	83,560	70,789	6,678	78,829	39,115
1979	589,979	444,672	24,964	469,636	41,160	-14,618	413,858	95,677	80,444	7,380	79,941	39,912
1980	633,041	466,106	2,883	468,989	43,073	-11,193	414,723	120,397	97,921	7,761	81,562	39,014
1981	720,416	496,981	16,547	513,528	49,323	-11,267	452,938	147,149	120,329	8,781	82,038	39,055
1982	755,832	513,919	10,882	524,801	51,882	-12,557	460,362	176,029	119,441	9,265	81,576	39,480
1983	802,936	561,348	-1,820	559,528	56,354	-16,825	486,349	187,815	128,772	9,846	81,546	40,586
1984	892,347	616,270	13,170	629,440	63,602	-17,580	548,258	210,320	133,769	10,918	81,732	41,905
1985	948,660	656,136	16,431	672,567	68,883	-18,391	585,293	221,718	141,649	11,539	82,211	43,356
1986	996,766	714,065	2,341	716,406	75,566	-22,000	618,840	229,942	147,984	12,101	82,368	44,845
1987	1,060,519	775,813	9,625	785,438	81,133	-23,305	681,000	227,665	151,854	12,851	82,524	46,098
1988	1,114,580	826,657	4,319	830,976	89,028	-23,958	717,990	236,987	159,603	13,465	82,775	46,557
1989	1,202,829	877,513	12,982	890,495	95,487	-25,682	769,326	257,383	176,120	14,539	82,734	47,610
1990	1,237,845	911,743	9,411	921,154	102,290	-30,307	788,557	259,637	189,651	14,907	83,037	49,146
1991	1,303,281	947,215	6,612	953,827	108,025	-33,450	812,352	275,690	215,239	15,535	83,892	48,247
1992	1,402,587	1,030,767	14,305	1,045,072	116,490	-44,219	884,363	284,983	233,241	16,478	85,118	49,450
1993	1,473,374	1,084,704	10,172	1,094,876	123,263	-49,132	922,481	303,013	247,880	17,172	85,803	50,713
1994	1,558,158	1,165,094	8,418	1,173,512	133,147	-53,235	987,130	312,080	258,948	18,062	86,267	52,387
1995	1,660,127	1,248,750	3,121	1,251,871	142,368	-62,958	1,046,545	336,110	277,472	19,064	87,084	54,098
1996	1,732,537	1,286,209	9,210	1,295,419	144,810	-67,070	1,083,539	356,222	292,776	19,694	87,975	54,280
1997	1,821,753	1,351,047	8,961	1,360,008	150,825	-71,907	1,137,276	377,194	307,283	20,638	88,270	54,484
1998	1,925,846	1,449,492	3,270	1,452,762	161,180	-81,892	1,209,690	393,376	322,780	21,716	88,682	56,838
1999	2,026,818	1,586,002	2,332	1,588,334	175,468	-100,140	1,312,726	384,464	329,628	22,516	90,016	58,769
2000	2,164,967	1,670,686	10,129	1,680,815	181,444	-107,855	1,391,516	417,705	355,746	23,915	90,527	59,512
2001	2,251,674	1,715,256	13,124	1,728,380	186,856	-110,703	1,430,821	425,025	395,828	24,682	91,226	57,816
2002	2,341,151	1,803,684	7,252	1,810,936	195,966	-118,018	1,496,952	412,558	431,641	25,532	91,694	57,782
2003	2,449,206	1,871,475	21,867	1,893,342	202,984	-120,202	1,570,156	426,321	452,729	26,668	91,840	58,151
2004	2,618,206	1,985,383	37,677	2,023,060	211,869	-115,014	1,696,177	439,619	482,410	28,234	92,734	58,284
2005	2,704,519	2,094,434	19,044	2,113,478	224,679	-118,833	1,769,966	413,872	520,681	29,027	93,173	59,722
2006	2,848,749	2,211,314	11,786	2,223,100	238,866	-131,531	1,852,703	445,807	550,239	30,252	94,167	61,011
2007	3,042,173	2,323,487	5,856	2,329,343	254,271	-143,915	1,931,157	518,948	592,068	32,153	94,616	62,376
2008	3,128,190	2,273,414	30,233	2,303,647	255,133	-137,064	1,911,450	561,187	655,553	32,918	95,031	61,854
2009	3,114,999	2,278,816	13,566	2,292,382	256,038	-144,044	1,892,300	515,540	707,159	32,572	95,634	60,384
2010	3,202,205	2,329,281	20,351	2,349,632	256,244	-140,585	1,952,803	495,806	753,596	33,198	96,458	59,225
2011	3,341,791	2,369,610	23,889	2,393,499	234,440	-121,623	2,037,436	540,557	763,798	34,450	97,003	59,164
2012	3,544,507	2,483,807	17,970	2,501,777	242,434	-108,852	2,150,491	622,318	771,698	36,447	97,251	59,667
2013	3,580,422	2,558,625	42,032	2,600,657	279,920	-108,066	2,212,671	578,832	788,919	36,817	97,250	60,565
2014	3,624,455	2,552,191	45,053	2,597,244	283,453	-92,800	2,220,991	599,129	804,335	37,173	97,502	60,083
2015	3,766,353	2,660,600	1,766	2,662,366	294,594	-75,092	2,292,680	619,458	854,215	38,641	97,470	60,168
2016	3,848,689	2,678,219	16,403	2,694,622	298,503	-81,219	2,314,900	661,107	872,682	39,543	97,330	60,496
2017	3,933,938	2,729,635	17,748	2,747,383	304,801	-78,915	2,363,667	671,247	899,024	40,532	97,058	60,470
2018	4,094,990	2,846,523	2,874	2,849,397	321,836	-88,610	2,438,951	722,650	933,389	42,108	97,249	61,493
2019	4,133,324	2,881,310	12,834	2,894,144	330,743	-91,821	2,471,580	695,925	965,819	42,527	97,193	61,605
2020	4,464,064	2,939,733	23,198	2,962,931	342,912	-102,296	2,517,723	727,190	1,219,151	45,765	97,543	60,664
2021	4,700,656	3,039,255	33,937	3,073,192	350,870	-80,894	2,641,428	725,155	1,334,073	48,085	97,757	61,819
2022	4,832,152	3,260,391	32,001	3,292,392	383,421	-85,342	2,823,629	795,349	1,213,174	49,170	98,275	63,579

Personal Income and Employment by Area: Carbondale-Marion, IL

(Thousands of dollars, except as noted.)

Year	Personal income, total	Derivation of personal income: Earnings by place of work								Per capita personal income (dollars)	Population (persons)	Total employment
		Nonfarm	Farm	Total	Less: Contributions for government social insurance	Plus: Adjustment for residence	Equals: Net earnings by place of residence	Plus: Dividends, interest, and rent	Plus: Personal current transfer receipts			
1970	347,017	271,293	3,458	274,751	15,808	154	259,097	45,643	42,277	3,100	111,942	42,531
1971	390,087	301,308	5,083	306,391	18,033	-354	288,004	50,342	51,741	3,411	114,352	43,896
1972	428,740	327,202	5,373	332,575	20,385	1,239	313,429	55,943	59,368	3,692	116,113	44,940
1973	487,959	358,699	12,662	371,361	25,441	2,110	348,030	64,773	75,156	4,237	115,162	45,845
1974	528,866	381,886	11,570	393,456	28,281	4,894	370,069	74,585	84,212	4,561	115,944	46,928
1975	628,826	436,948	16,349	453,297	31,017	7,056	429,336	87,708	111,782	5,271	119,299	47,628
1976	705,697	506,308	13,334	519,642	37,612	6,834	488,864	95,884	120,949	5,727	123,226	50,771
1977	766,969	552,135	14,354	566,489	41,623	11,014	535,880	107,684	123,405	6,126	125,206	52,204
1978	835,300	609,703	10,043	619,746	46,868	11,603	584,481	119,645	131,174	6,630	125,985	53,029
1979	940,553	668,852	13,044	681,896	53,490	23,623	652,029	137,802	150,722	7,358	127,835	54,460
1980	1,032,196	710,643	2,828	713,471	56,404	27,732	684,799	168,503	178,894	8,040	128,383	54,137
1981	1,143,297	756,758	9,393	766,151	63,496	28,223	730,878	205,960	206,459	8,764	130,453	54,100
1982	1,256,741	810,061	4,763	814,824	68,914	35,932	781,842	256,898	218,001	9,646	130,280	54,033
1983	1,335,023	871,389	-142	871,247	74,500	27,732	824,479	274,569	235,975	10,208	130,778	55,161
1984	1,451,408	949,073	3,337	952,410	83,786	28,748	897,372	310,906	243,130	11,153	130,139	56,323
1985	1,511,779	966,168	14,097	980,265	86,439	40,117	933,943	326,440	251,396	11,541	130,992	56,447
1986	1,549,758	1,005,044	-3,955	1,001,089	89,765	40,261	951,585	342,376	255,797	11,849	130,792	58,154
1987	1,616,755	1,056,945	9,416	1,066,361	92,711	35,318	1,008,968	340,458	267,329	12,325	131,172	58,609
1988	1,678,429	1,098,156	9,873	1,108,029	100,865	39,875	1,047,039	349,983	281,407	12,855	130,569	58,595
1989	1,810,558	1,153,133	25,533	1,178,666	107,675	44,572	1,115,563	394,095	300,900	13,901	130,245	59,587
1990	1,882,905	1,243,266	10,158	1,253,424	114,035	43,457	1,182,846	381,641	318,418	14,473	130,094	61,514
1991	1,950,331	1,302,824	5,835	1,308,659	124,227	31,775	1,216,207	394,400	339,724	14,998	130,041	61,999
1992	2,104,977	1,399,221	14,417	1,413,638	131,528	31,335	1,313,445	401,367	390,165	16,027	131,336	62,930
1993	2,154,695	1,432,866	16,417	1,449,283	136,815	26,196	1,338,664	410,072	405,959	16,280	132,350	63,450
1994	2,279,770	1,538,175	18,098	1,556,273	150,515	32,269	1,438,027	429,042	412,701	17,104	133,285	66,521
1995	2,403,811	1,606,131	10,146	1,616,277	157,687	28,600	1,487,190	476,501	440,120	17,954	133,889	67,208
1996	2,500,256	1,646,768	16,661	1,663,429	160,060	28,942	1,532,311	505,042	462,903	18,645	134,097	67,252
1997	2,607,237	1,712,179	16,235	1,728,414	164,415	28,739	1,592,738	535,802	478,697	19,394	134,438	68,160
1998	2,732,349	1,790,486	17,908	1,808,394	171,964	27,870	1,664,300	572,091	495,958	20,299	134,607	69,232
1999	2,849,378	1,935,175	9,825	1,945,000	181,240	20,873	1,784,633	563,604	501,141	21,220	134,280	71,824
2000	2,986,147	2,035,732	13,587	2,049,319	187,218	19,808	1,881,909	577,667	526,571	22,327	133,748	73,462
2001	3,218,449	2,233,162	8,894	2,242,056	199,667	9,261	2,051,650	604,955	561,844	24,007	134,061	73,611
2002	3,346,834	2,395,858	197	2,396,055	215,432	-5,087	2,175,536	570,271	601,027	25,062	133,540	73,591
2003	3,431,702	2,425,757	10,695	2,436,452	221,476	-7,757	2,207,219	599,303	625,180	25,465	134,761	73,375
2004	3,543,925	2,495,098	25,894	2,520,992	230,283	-13,991	2,276,718	604,559	662,648	26,107	135,744	73,634
2005	3,678,508	2,638,091	11,930	2,650,021	253,021	-32,341	2,364,659	582,102	731,747	26,910	136,697	75,313
2006	3,833,593	2,785,469	12,508	2,797,977	265,753	-48,215	2,484,009	603,349	746,235	27,884	137,483	76,446
2007	3,979,573	2,860,228	7,046	2,867,274	275,377	-55,138	2,536,759	623,601	819,213	28,940	137,511	76,737
2008	4,203,942	2,943,835	18,765	2,962,600	284,875	-78,325	2,599,400	710,683	893,859	30,474	137,950	76,310
2009	4,367,239	3,016,942	2,051	3,018,993	290,158	-85,726	2,643,109	734,239	989,891	31,533	138,497	75,981
2010	4,646,880	3,238,105	10,302	3,248,407	306,355	-84,841	2,857,211	715,902	1,073,767	33,347	139,349	76,007
2011	4,792,421	3,307,769	21,449	3,329,218	286,129	-77,224	2,965,865	779,977	1,046,579	34,311	139,675	76,531
2012	4,852,858	3,343,553	9,689	3,353,242	293,569	-68,881	2,990,792	818,882	1,043,184	35,112	138,209	76,246
2013	4,895,979	3,368,512	19,513	3,388,025	327,494	-71,064	2,989,467	813,883	1,092,629	35,132	139,360	75,114
2014	4,962,730	3,403,757	227	3,403,984	332,962	-72,947	2,998,075	854,195	1,110,460	35,770	138,740	75,590
2015	5,154,453	3,503,907	-14,390	3,489,517	340,454	-83,818	3,065,245	880,894	1,208,314	37,273	138,289	76,612
2016	5,180,052	3,514,044	-469	3,513,575	348,145	-99,993	3,065,437	907,644	1,206,971	37,723	137,319	76,750
2017	5,299,601	3,577,648	6,148	3,583,796	358,627	-109,392	3,115,777	924,956	1,258,868	39,006	135,866	76,469
2018	5,460,546	3,768,770	13,489	3,782,259	377,827	-141,450	3,262,982	902,250	1,295,314	40,456	134,976	76,618
2019	5,608,211	3,836,553	5,851	3,842,404	389,597	-126,979	3,325,828	943,679	1,338,704	41,873	133,935	76,598
2020	6,041,921	3,853,394	11,492	3,864,886	397,497	-149,008	3,318,381	955,681	1,767,859	45,312	133,341	73,501
2021	6,511,741	4,084,328	50,602	4,134,930	417,670	-161,698	3,555,562	981,888	1,974,291	48,931	133,080	74,632
2022	6,417,486	4,316,094	48,988	4,365,082	461,692	-176,474	3,726,916	1,001,215	1,689,355	48,363	132,693	77,141

Personal Income and Employment by Area: Carson City, NV

(Thousands of dollars, except as noted.)

Year	Personal income, total	Derivation of personal income: Earnings by place of work: Nonfarm	Farm	Total	Less: Contributions for government social insurance	Plus: Adjustment for residence	Equals: Net earnings by place of residence	Plus: Dividends, interest, and rent	Plus: Personal current transfer receipts	Per capita personal income (dollars)	Population (persons)	Total employment
1970	86,094	65,872	47	65,919	2,301	842	64,460	16,519	5,115	5,367	16,041	8,194
1971	104,264	78,136	305	78,441	2,907	2,438	77,972	19,716	6,576	5,655	18,439	9,095
1972	122,082	90,520	155	90,675	3,824	4,421	91,272	22,899	7,911	6,107	19,991	9,860
1973	142,199	105,907	460	106,367	5,579	6,513	107,301	25,575	9,323	6,418	22,158	11,152
1974	163,239	121,672	96	121,768	6,755	7,175	122,188	29,322	11,729	6,856	23,808	12,036
1975	189,435	138,032	137	138,169	7,117	7,685	138,737	33,800	16,898	7,433	25,484	12,528
1976	220,730	162,807	143	162,950	8,899	7,350	161,401	40,294	19,035	8,459	26,094	13,820
1977	256,190	190,877	134	191,011	11,001	6,348	186,358	47,840	21,992	9,374	27,331	15,384
1978	311,643	237,818	116	237,934	14,851	2,251	225,334	60,625	25,684	10,398	29,972	17,838
1979	352,459	271,089	122	271,211	18,744	-2,476	249,991	72,891	29,577	11,090	31,782	19,081
1980	397,841	295,960	234	296,194	20,592	4	275,606	85,474	36,761	12,308	32,323	19,360
1981	451,678	338,030	153	338,183	24,862	-7,787	305,534	101,921	44,223	13,493	33,475	19,536
1982	475,372	341,380	164	341,544	25,085	-6,997	309,462	118,727	47,183	13,850	34,324	18,960
1983	503,617	362,389	163	362,552	29,896	-12,149	320,507	129,665	53,445	14,533	34,654	19,392
1984	551,720	397,542	274	397,816	35,190	-13,078	349,548	145,302	56,870	15,647	35,260	20,535
1985	600,723	438,202	115	438,317	41,267	-21,131	375,919	161,908	62,896	16,508	36,389	21,622
1986	646,000	470,487	104	470,591	45,552	-26,442	398,597	178,065	69,338	17,419	37,086	22,495
1987	670,119	509,136	221	509,357	49,982	-35,743	423,632	172,214	74,273	17,916	37,403	24,244
1988	736,123	564,654	116	564,770	57,172	-41,237	466,361	189,780	79,982	19,180	38,379	25,165
1989	807,680	606,056	153	606,209	62,183	-49,839	494,187	220,709	92,784	20,367	39,657	25,785
1990	872,064	658,267	190	658,457	69,064	-41,374	548,019	221,784	102,261	21,419	40,714	26,766
1991	942,492	705,768	152	705,920	73,328	-50,234	582,358	237,201	122,933	22,480	41,926	27,173
1992	1,024,950	777,146	140	777,286	79,210	-58,763	639,313	250,661	134,976	23,709	43,231	27,073
1993	1,079,543	834,535	176	834,711	86,047	-80,502	668,162	269,978	141,403	24,220	44,572	28,566
1994	1,161,953	916,896	79	916,975	96,962	-99,375	720,638	298,113	143,202	25,201	46,108	30,498
1995	1,258,367	1,002,315	-8	1,002,307	106,936	-119,214	776,157	325,693	156,517	26,343	47,768	32,941
1996	1,335,846	1,076,306	-105	1,076,201	110,691	-146,982	818,528	354,221	163,097	27,102	49,290	34,369
1997	1,426,123	1,171,737	-179	1,171,558	116,711	-172,289	882,558	372,294	171,271	28,261	50,463	35,519
1998	1,518,197	1,274,413	-6	1,274,407	122,451	-183,328	968,628	370,253	179,316	29,848	50,864	36,263
1999	1,582,397	1,369,872	117	1,369,989	128,616	-211,838	1,029,535	371,782	181,080	30,458	51,953	37,564
2000	1,742,328	1,484,649	139	1,484,788	122,044	-220,960	1,141,784	405,291	195,253	33,144	52,568	39,240
2001	1,251,711	997,010	315	997,325	127,172	-231,773	638,380	397,229	216,102	23,409	53,472	41,635
2002	1,096,365	879,874	564	880,438	130,904	-256,809	492,725	364,193	239,447	20,116	54,503	41,775
2003	1,167,505	918,110	302	918,412	133,997	-281,162	503,253	411,350	252,902	21,137	55,234	41,912
2004	1,176,875	934,978	300	935,278	138,269	-320,943	476,066	437,153	263,656	21,018	55,995	43,061
2005	1,367,137	1,155,446	297	1,155,743	146,413	-364,517	644,813	442,372	279,952	24,421	55,982	43,881
2006	1,674,470	1,489,795	320	1,490,115	156,077	-390,657	943,381	440,625	290,464	30,220	55,410	43,922
2007	1,601,776	1,444,942	193	1,445,135	177,484	-448,678	818,973	473,801	309,002	28,971	55,288	42,267
2008	1,641,687	1,498,606	1,167	1,499,773	181,927	-486,305	831,541	462,649	347,497	29,552	55,552	41,157
2009	2,273,614	2,109,140	1,442	2,110,582	167,569	-508,356	1,434,657	447,726	391,231	41,039	55,401	39,406
2010	2,449,154	2,292,851	2,439	2,295,290	166,010	-531,115	1,598,165	423,989	427,000	44,494	55,044	38,434
2011	2,350,263	2,136,774	3,390	2,140,164	151,716	-529,739	1,458,709	459,011	432,543	42,738	54,992	38,072
2012	2,304,701	2,097,495	3,584	2,101,079	157,391	-522,489	1,421,199	442,584	440,918	41,997	54,878	37,408
2013	2,227,264	2,032,082	1,936	2,034,018	167,114	-534,756	1,332,148	447,352	447,764	40,844	54,531	37,528
2014	2,267,624	1,998,124	2,433	2,000,557	174,990	-553,993	1,271,574	490,099	505,951	41,117	55,150	37,518
2015	2,397,386	2,130,518	1,398	2,131,916	182,717	-589,393	1,359,806	492,456	545,124	43,244	55,439	37,671
2016	2,404,344	2,081,895	1,380	2,083,275	185,884	-573,341	1,324,050	515,740	564,554	43,038	55,866	38,257
2017	2,587,337	2,284,502	1,407	2,285,909	203,075	-629,045	1,453,789	551,233	582,315	45,801	56,491	39,440
2018	2,757,916	2,370,637	1,324	2,371,961	209,520	-593,533	1,568,908	570,310	618,698	48,072	57,370	39,505
2019	2,912,610	2,516,876	1,038	2,517,914	225,911	-649,805	1,642,198	609,039	661,373	49,993	58,260	39,690
2020	3,214,408	2,581,815	1,592	2,583,407	236,959	-689,597	1,656,851	727,294	830,263	54,776	58,683	39,158
2021	3,503,024	2,666,334	1,643	2,667,977	247,270	-693,883	1,726,824	826,420	949,780	59,579	58,796	40,618
2022	3,547,426	2,857,133	1,233	2,858,366	279,186	-708,058	1,871,122	875,468	800,836	61,026	58,130	41,748

Personal Income and Employment by Area: Casper, WY

(Thousands of dollars, except as noted.)

Year	Personal income, total	Derivation of personal income: Earnings by place of work: Nonfarm	Farm	Total	Less: Contributions for government social insurance	Plus: Adjustment for residence	Equals: Net earnings by place of residence	Plus: Dividends, interest, and rent	Plus: Personal current transfer receipts	Per capita personal income (dollars)	Population (persons)	Total employment
1970	241,410	188,187	4,641	192,828	12,904	6,633	186,557	39,276	15,577	4,698	51,381	25,733
1971	259,416	201,896	2,614	204,510	14,304	7,402	197,608	44,035	17,773	4,977	52,121	26,453
1972	276,780	215,571	4,135	219,706	16,194	7,371	210,883	46,949	18,948	5,212	53,106	27,009
1973	317,814	247,875	7,885	255,760	21,425	6,133	240,468	55,207	22,139	6,018	52,814	28,431
1974	389,544	312,607	5,375	317,982	26,848	6,833	297,967	66,489	25,088	7,281	53,504	30,410
1975	468,746	389,022	2,302	391,324	32,946	7,283	365,661	72,880	30,205	8,357	56,088	33,334
1976	517,903	434,447	1,994	436,441	39,067	5,594	402,968	82,115	32,820	8,843	58,567	35,183
1977	632,083	544,927	1,847	546,774	47,380	3,957	503,351	93,416	35,316	10,273	61,526	39,229
1978	769,151	678,521	1,662	680,183	61,393	-603	618,187	111,199	39,765	11,740	65,515	44,060
1979	883,564	786,350	2,593	788,943	75,562	-5,854	707,527	129,442	46,595	12,926	68,354	46,821
1980	1,016,267	896,573	1,898	898,471	86,058	-13,176	799,237	161,914	55,116	14,013	72,523	48,294
1981	1,179,696	1,026,343	1,174	1,027,517	106,676	-10,562	910,279	203,713	65,704	15,720	75,042	51,043
1982	1,205,461	1,003,390	3,855	1,007,245	107,639	-7,792	891,814	236,813	76,834	15,636	77,094	49,117
1983	1,122,090	878,412	7,597	886,009	92,206	-3,794	790,009	241,053	91,028	14,708	76,292	44,001
1984	1,147,550	899,112	3,260	902,372	97,199	-1,058	804,115	254,064	89,371	15,684	73,166	44,094
1985	1,134,276	864,391	2,436	866,827	95,245	2,316	773,898	261,642	98,736	15,849	71,569	42,169
1986	1,031,851	748,539	839	749,378	83,057	5,496	671,817	252,359	107,675	14,916	69,177	37,710
1987	1,032,042	752,602	1,434	754,036	80,841	6,040	679,235	243,382	109,425	15,988	64,552	36,574
1988	1,047,729	750,229	988	751,217	87,737	8,298	671,778	261,244	114,707	16,762	62,507	37,519
1989	1,176,160	844,153	-123	844,030	91,643	11,744	764,131	285,445	126,584	19,056	61,722	37,111
1990	1,300,267	934,077	-415	933,662	105,507	13,547	841,702	318,616	139,949	21,213	61,296	38,058
1991	1,309,392	883,181	3,403	886,584	107,684	12,180	791,080	365,302	153,010	21,013	62,312	38,809
1992	1,383,246	924,194	2,646	926,840	110,741	12,014	828,113	382,971	172,162	21,926	63,087	38,045
1993	1,456,356	972,736	2,716	975,452	115,007	11,615	872,060	393,988	190,308	22,762	63,981	38,759
1994	1,496,845	1,000,710	1,633	1,002,343	119,060	11,880	895,163	409,333	192,349	22,917	65,316	39,738
1995	1,521,989	1,024,082	1,098	1,025,180	121,354	10,863	914,689	400,727	206,573	23,170	65,687	40,383
1996	1,584,165	1,070,284	782	1,071,066	123,361	10,381	958,086	409,235	216,844	24,054	65,859	40,551
1997	1,729,119	1,194,660	2,625	1,197,285	131,861	10,045	1,075,469	431,782	221,868	26,076	66,311	41,280
1998	1,800,934	1,230,220	1,420	1,231,640	137,166	8,824	1,103,298	468,034	229,602	27,227	66,146	41,582
1999	1,906,749	1,323,556	2,592	1,326,148	144,108	7,132	1,189,172	481,590	235,987	28,767	66,282	42,325
2000	2,164,754	1,535,293	2,137	1,537,430	164,005	2,549	1,375,974	533,834	254,946	32,502	66,603	43,624
2001	2,129,799	1,489,692	3,642	1,493,334	169,590	3,509	1,327,253	532,610	269,936	31,798	66,978	44,539
2002	2,179,049	1,548,940	3,261	1,552,201	172,335	2,940	1,382,806	504,500	291,743	32,256	67,554	44,732
2003	2,321,611	1,652,989	5,489	1,658,478	184,879	289	1,473,888	530,047	317,676	34,018	68,246	45,555
2004	2,482,673	1,770,775	4,539	1,775,314	205,125	-3,292	1,566,897	583,357	332,419	35,963	69,035	47,197
2005	2,814,156	1,982,795	7,469	1,990,264	225,970	-6,198	1,758,096	711,117	344,943	40,247	69,922	48,828
2006	3,276,873	2,397,832	1,245	2,399,077	287,515	-9,993	2,101,569	822,661	352,643	46,280	70,806	50,904
2007	3,402,834	2,539,349	-431	2,538,918	313,016	-6,081	2,219,821	809,565	373,448	47,023	72,365	52,729
2008	3,964,477	2,988,479	-1,029	2,987,450	339,976	54	2,647,528	876,674	440,275	53,805	73,682	53,986
2009	3,430,796	2,585,645	336	2,585,981	313,901	-2,057	2,270,023	685,694	475,079	45,599	75,238	51,712
2010	3,782,497	2,847,073	1,321	2,848,394	327,250	-13,477	2,507,667	765,508	509,322	50,124	75,463	51,840
2011	4,130,136	3,093,429	8,998	3,102,427	320,840	-32,175	2,749,412	873,960	506,764	54,087	76,361	53,363
2012	4,721,799	3,575,666	1,463	3,577,129	356,513	-42,926	3,177,690	1,045,089	499,020	60,159	78,489	55,502
2013	4,976,309	3,726,294	4,031	3,730,325	406,093	-45,326	3,278,906	1,175,226	522,177	61,453	80,978	56,650
2014	5,546,021	4,097,561	9,922	4,107,483	443,834	-50,298	3,613,351	1,387,599	545,071	68,305	81,195	57,793
2015	5,723,789	4,047,934	6,002	4,053,936	427,153	-28,385	3,598,398	1,531,155	594,236	69,893	81,894	57,144
2016	4,930,290	3,564,563	898	3,565,461	380,423	-2,980	3,182,058	1,138,737	609,495	61,137	80,643	53,913
2017	4,978,320	3,754,801	487	3,755,288	396,152	-6,739	3,352,397	997,004	628,919	62,866	79,190	53,760
2018	5,305,323	4,036,635	1,785	4,038,420	411,184	-8,662	3,618,574	1,026,625	660,124	67,452	78,653	54,093
2019	5,108,412	3,901,844	2,166	3,904,010	425,406	14,777	3,493,381	917,561	697,470	64,514	79,183	54,308
2020	5,117,034	3,580,001	4,249	3,584,250	396,630	20,169	3,207,789	977,936	931,309	63,738	80,282	52,309
2021	5,336,085	3,592,990	4,135	3,597,125	392,566	21,496	3,226,055	1,110,290	999,740	66,986	79,660	54,154
2022	5,450,408	3,750,302	7,628	3,757,930	419,412	7,573	3,346,091	1,215,484	888,833	68,472	79,601	56,808

Personal Income and Employment by Area: Cedar Rapids, IA

(Thousands of dollars, except as noted.)

Year	Personal income, total	Derivation of personal income: Earnings by place of work: Nonfarm	Farm	Total	Less: Contributions for government social insurance	Plus: Adjustment for residence	Equals: Net earnings by place of residence	Plus: Dividends, interest, and rent	Plus: Personal current transfer receipts	Per capita personal income (dollars)	Population (persons)	Total employment
1970	867,743	679,218	45,908	725,126	51,334	-2,882	670,910	134,314	62,519	4,209	206,165	96,649
1971	907,248	707,397	41,325	748,722	55,651	-4,373	688,698	145,349	73,201	4,372	207,532	94,803
1972	981,866	759,844	52,935	812,779	63,501	-5,226	744,052	157,433	80,381	4,721	207,990	96,324
1973	1,117,635	853,889	84,216	938,105	82,738	-7,020	848,347	177,093	92,195	5,400	206,982	100,990
1974	1,220,471	954,387	61,195	1,015,582	95,619	-8,229	911,734	201,519	107,218	5,871	207,881	104,894
1975	1,361,320	1,043,807	68,297	1,112,104	102,083	-8,965	1,001,056	226,327	133,937	6,481	210,055	105,550
1976	1,485,204	1,178,599	42,148	1,220,747	116,619	-11,145	1,092,983	244,575	147,646	7,023	211,491	108,639
1977	1,624,848	1,297,383	39,153	1,336,536	127,413	-13,161	1,195,962	274,570	154,316	7,706	210,846	110,943
1978	1,842,812	1,460,396	77,545	1,537,941	148,920	-18,597	1,370,424	305,064	167,324	8,732	211,033	114,026
1979	2,051,637	1,679,912	40,486	1,720,398	178,273	-26,118	1,516,007	347,137	188,493	9,680	211,937	121,050
1980	2,208,240	1,766,082	4,504	1,770,586	185,620	-26,026	1,558,940	420,131	229,169	10,335	213,666	119,634
1981	2,434,117	1,850,059	45,517	1,895,576	206,607	-29,124	1,659,845	516,056	258,216	11,453	212,534	116,231
1982	2,519,763	1,832,522	14,324	1,846,846	206,424	-30,294	1,610,128	607,848	301,787	11,978	210,374	111,314
1983	2,572,169	1,895,554	-19,506	1,876,048	213,291	-26,154	1,636,603	614,992	320,574	12,352	208,238	110,835
1984	2,824,928	2,036,395	51,007	2,087,402	234,825	-24,354	1,828,223	675,268	321,437	13,583	207,969	113,084
1985	2,965,820	2,185,531	35,174	2,220,705	255,289	-32,133	1,933,283	694,302	338,235	14,328	206,995	115,476
1986	3,117,609	2,311,408	59,524	2,370,932	274,778	-35,343	2,060,811	702,374	354,424	15,144	205,865	117,488
1987	3,301,168	2,507,122	71,887	2,579,009	296,097	-38,284	2,244,628	694,507	362,033	16,058	205,577	119,721
1988	3,482,229	2,712,436	22,352	2,734,788	329,956	-40,599	2,364,233	736,628	381,368	16,789	207,415	125,116
1989	3,852,602	2,934,587	81,773	3,016,360	354,020	-42,079	2,620,261	824,408	407,933	18,387	209,528	129,901
1990	4,038,907	3,113,667	83,721	3,197,388	386,919	-47,345	2,763,124	825,980	449,803	19,124	211,200	131,540
1991	4,167,505	3,237,493	48,500	3,285,993	405,898	-46,218	2,833,877	851,908	481,720	19,524	213,453	132,831
1992	4,409,844	3,433,228	87,268	3,520,496	427,000	-50,178	3,043,318	842,698	523,828	20,339	216,818	133,978
1993	4,581,436	3,646,243	35,798	3,682,041	457,550	-56,146	3,168,345	867,754	545,337	20,830	219,948	136,563
1994	4,928,596	3,927,887	85,138	4,013,025	498,316	-63,500	3,451,209	903,784	573,603	22,130	222,711	140,427
1995	5,218,079	4,165,021	44,740	4,209,761	528,393	-77,691	3,603,677	1,004,149	610,253	23,052	226,357	146,630
1996	5,576,754	4,352,447	115,314	4,467,761	532,629	-87,329	3,847,803	1,083,511	645,440	24,466	227,938	149,382
1997	5,906,488	4,620,115	100,181	4,720,296	580,125	-99,070	4,041,101	1,195,857	669,530	25,626	230,490	152,680
1998	6,448,972	5,216,993	67,573	5,284,566	645,874	-133,066	4,505,626	1,254,338	689,008	27,749	232,402	157,170
1999	6,782,581	5,607,686	60,402	5,668,088	684,543	-150,861	4,832,684	1,224,973	724,924	28,817	235,365	161,738
2000	7,241,887	5,972,706	78,402	6,051,108	721,437	-181,137	5,148,534	1,316,277	777,076	30,434	237,950	164,865
2001	7,410,000	5,981,819	93,973	6,075,792	720,710	-156,157	5,198,925	1,349,464	861,611	30,856	240,145	163,779
2002	7,543,848	5,946,859	87,246	6,034,105	710,942	-127,597	5,195,566	1,379,508	968,774	31,160	242,099	160,452
2003	7,694,269	6,102,925	84,190	6,187,115	735,947	-116,275	5,334,893	1,380,275	979,101	31,628	243,272	159,067
2004	8,097,603	6,446,511	138,449	6,584,960	767,868	-96,626	5,720,466	1,362,262	1,014,875	33,037	245,108	161,777
2005	8,399,775	6,731,548	91,743	6,823,291	806,732	-91,250	5,925,309	1,374,866	1,099,600	33,971	247,265	164,720
2006	8,895,053	7,048,437	69,435	7,117,872	847,490	-94,479	6,175,903	1,514,630	1,204,520	35,648	249,524	168,373
2007	9,586,753	7,543,980	103,605	7,647,585	908,091	-105,681	6,633,813	1,663,944	1,288,996	37,936	252,709	172,468
2008	10,267,033	7,928,167	112,525	8,040,692	962,933	-129,138	6,948,621	1,836,855	1,481,557	40,184	255,503	174,570
2009	10,208,669	7,829,877	78,051	7,907,928	953,266	-92,719	6,861,943	1,744,206	1,602,520	39,739	256,896	172,879
2010	10,614,984	8,130,002	86,928	8,216,930	991,945	-58,619	7,166,366	1,736,997	1,711,621	41,062	258,511	173,026
2011	11,169,841	8,384,562	192,983	8,577,545	926,257	-128,492	7,522,796	1,902,553	1,744,492	42,735	261,375	175,501
2012	11,714,235	8,719,181	140,962	8,860,143	943,510	-114,266	7,802,367	2,162,462	1,749,406	44,619	262,537	176,558
2013	11,743,881	8,864,682	196,783	9,061,465	1,074,751	-35,569	7,951,145	2,012,569	1,780,167	44,551	263,606	177,268
2014	12,271,547	9,297,100	87,510	9,384,610	1,110,567	-88,957	8,185,086	2,184,053	1,902,408	46,225	265,477	178,997
2015	12,787,985	9,558,479	102,814	9,661,293	1,136,122	-51,361	8,473,810	2,278,789	2,035,386	47,754	267,786	181,131
2016	13,102,490	9,734,350	78,963	9,813,313	1,176,684	-38,663	8,597,966	2,410,489	2,094,035	48,539	269,939	181,357
2017	13,471,795	9,993,467	75,962	10,069,429	1,213,155	-32,328	8,823,946	2,532,697	2,115,152	49,399	272,715	181,242
2018	14,030,906	10,485,853	78,860	10,564,713	1,276,671	-230,922	9,057,120	2,662,078	2,311,708	51,131	274,409	182,283
2019	14,371,616	10,480,613	72,416	10,553,029	1,295,425	-120,070	9,137,534	2,781,349	2,452,733	52,096	275,868	182,809
2020	15,148,760	10,532,379	94,682	10,627,061	1,336,852	-139,916	9,150,293	2,813,324	3,185,143	54,768	276,598	175,741
2021	16,416,754	11,140,998	292,235	11,433,233	1,379,549	-203,542	9,850,142	3,142,494	3,424,118	59,478	276,016	179,583
2022	16,856,661	12,004,895	320,658	12,325,553	1,483,156	-370,230	10,472,167	3,383,996	3,000,498	61,165	275,592	184,740

Personal Income and Employment by Area: Chambersburg-Waynesboro, PA

(Thousands of dollars, except as noted.)

Year	Personal income, total	Derivation of personal income								Per capita personal income (dollars)	Population (persons)	Total employment
		Earnings by place of work			Less: Contributions for government social insurance	Plus: Adjustment for residence	Equals: Net earnings by place of residence	Plus: Dividends, interest, and rent	Plus: Personal current transfer receipts			
		Nonfarm	Farm	Total								
1970	402,056	309,060	16,046	325,106	18,784	5,766	312,088	56,053	33,915	3,976	101,127	45,763
1971	425,498	324,248	13,591	337,839	20,346	5,906	323,399	62,672	39,427	4,128	103,082	44,890
1972	477,416	365,265	15,581	380,846	24,028	6,773	363,591	69,487	44,338	4,630	103,103	46,239
1973	536,494	412,697	17,730	430,427	31,392	7,042	406,077	81,097	49,320	5,144	104,285	48,655
1974	598,323	454,468	20,778	475,246	36,378	8,300	447,168	92,240	58,915	5,611	106,640	50,542
1975	657,255	498,091	13,610	511,701	38,922	5,461	478,240	102,310	76,705	6,083	108,052	50,373
1976	715,956	534,221	17,185	551,406	42,775	8,489	517,120	111,164	87,672	6,498	110,183	50,555
1977	779,494	572,139	15,349	587,488	45,380	18,131	560,239	125,589	93,666	7,072	110,218	50,537
1978	878,988	646,979	19,434	666,413	52,338	21,139	635,214	144,298	99,476	7,907	111,166	51,634
1979	964,007	698,445	23,399	721,844	59,353	30,962	693,453	160,715	109,839	8,594	112,172	52,438
1980	1,060,325	768,492	15,522	784,014	66,285	20,079	737,808	196,829	125,688	9,317	113,810	53,620
1981	1,179,897	829,800	24,183	853,983	76,659	21,831	799,155	235,205	145,537	10,323	114,302	53,452
1982	1,245,178	812,820	25,195	838,015	75,731	28,294	790,578	275,375	179,225	10,857	114,688	52,664
1983	1,300,510	826,574	21,758	848,332	79,810	37,685	806,207	294,226	200,077	11,280	115,293	51,891
1984	1,414,477	899,524	40,751	940,275	91,648	54,666	903,293	321,609	189,575	12,143	116,482	52,342
1985	1,523,830	969,709	43,945	1,013,654	100,315	59,405	972,744	352,173	198,913	13,037	116,882	53,479
1986	1,606,966	1,003,965	52,853	1,056,818	106,556	71,896	1,022,158	373,125	211,683	13,680	117,464	54,682
1987	1,695,254	1,085,071	40,582	1,125,653	114,902	83,772	1,094,523	384,042	216,689	14,389	117,819	56,100
1988	1,819,660	1,170,801	40,010	1,210,811	128,795	99,761	1,181,777	408,958	228,925	15,297	118,953	58,222
1989	1,961,816	1,267,849	46,972	1,314,821	139,385	113,546	1,288,982	428,382	244,452	16,378	119,780	60,503
1990	2,106,091	1,337,049	39,001	1,376,050	148,842	130,521	1,357,729	476,646	271,716	17,334	121,503	62,343
1991	2,198,024	1,381,189	29,346	1,410,535	156,037	134,849	1,389,347	489,407	319,270	17,864	123,039	61,587
1992	2,313,603	1,445,747	53,088	1,498,835	165,136	151,350	1,485,049	493,064	335,490	18,644	124,095	61,679
1993	2,412,581	1,508,199	44,271	1,552,470	176,823	163,469	1,539,116	520,875	352,590	19,292	125,056	62,013
1994	2,504,744	1,584,387	39,805	1,624,192	188,917	181,351	1,616,626	526,162	361,956	19,879	126,002	62,399
1995	2,592,443	1,633,690	27,916	1,661,606	194,707	202,646	1,669,545	545,122	377,776	20,497	126,479	63,732
1996	2,771,035	1,723,243	47,791	1,771,034	200,937	217,740	1,787,837	578,685	404,513	21,837	126,897	65,054
1997	2,871,126	1,775,823	42,297	1,818,120	207,474	241,628	1,852,274	598,110	420,742	22,484	127,696	66,252
1998	3,053,102	1,874,924	54,958	1,929,882	215,656	267,058	1,981,284	632,289	439,529	23,761	128,492	65,520
1999	3,149,680	1,905,835	57,776	1,963,611	217,466	305,872	2,052,017	626,778	470,885	24,440	128,875	64,503
2000	3,328,320	1,982,095	61,459	2,043,554	224,819	335,075	2,153,810	671,914	502,596	25,653	129,745	65,163
2001	3,527,055	2,060,147	71,433	2,131,580	232,527	390,571	2,289,624	683,102	554,329	27,006	130,604	64,999
2002	3,633,258	2,151,738	32,176	2,183,914	242,574	424,582	2,365,922	679,712	587,624	27,525	131,998	65,382
2003	3,854,747	2,270,718	64,983	2,335,701	254,336	468,258	2,549,623	690,081	615,043	28,857	133,583	66,731
2004	4,208,953	2,512,466	95,718	2,608,184	279,500	534,727	2,863,411	689,918	655,624	31,007	135,742	69,437
2005	4,557,472	2,740,411	93,513	2,833,924	309,182	631,351	3,156,093	689,077	712,302	32,805	138,927	72,375
2006	4,868,264	2,909,913	72,431	2,982,344	334,000	689,490	3,337,834	756,079	774,351	34,182	142,421	74,676
2007	5,186,350	3,031,859	107,444	3,139,303	349,526	702,090	3,491,867	863,247	831,236	35,807	144,840	76,581
2008	5,357,293	3,072,512	113,352	3,185,864	356,321	679,476	3,509,019	928,587	919,687	36,436	147,032	77,398
2009	5,258,845	2,940,783	70,584	3,011,367	351,093	641,138	3,301,412	890,810	1,066,623	35,375	148,662	73,879
2010	5,442,670	3,042,401	91,830	3,134,231	362,428	680,380	3,452,183	863,676	1,126,811	36,301	149,933	73,834
2011	5,744,648	3,145,346	123,906	3,269,252	340,052	762,644	3,691,844	910,034	1,142,770	38,047	150,989	74,712
2012	5,831,851	3,221,019	124,666	3,345,685	346,889	764,262	3,763,058	913,213	1,155,580	38,471	151,590	75,354
2013	5,940,588	3,327,736	130,685	3,458,421	399,975	748,024	3,806,470	933,623	1,200,495	39,055	152,107	76,268
2014	6,203,864	3,427,520	162,115	3,589,635	413,866	771,772	3,947,541	994,071	1,262,252	40,596	152,819	77,155
2015	6,379,568	3,595,098	98,257	3,693,355	432,423	744,063	4,004,995	1,035,783	1,338,790	41,616	153,297	78,838
2016	6,487,839	3,651,535	43,726	3,695,261	441,915	790,560	4,043,906	1,029,161	1,414,772	42,092	154,136	79,390
2017	6,763,142	3,783,065	96,326	3,879,391	463,113	828,010	4,244,288	1,072,034	1,446,820	43,644	154,962	79,403
2018	7,114,690	3,982,886	57,981	4,040,867	485,175	862,697	4,418,389	1,145,746	1,550,555	45,841	155,205	80,988
2019	7,388,087	4,134,421	89,238	4,223,659	505,814	915,606	4,633,451	1,146,346	1,608,290	47,416	155,814	80,769
2020	7,999,119	4,143,209	60,139	4,203,348	504,168	988,574	4,687,754	1,177,428	2,133,937	51,296	155,939	77,917
2021	8,632,012	4,331,011	110,437	4,441,448	525,987	1,113,631	5,029,092	1,274,102	2,328,818	55,125	156,589	79,503
2022	8,662,802	4,574,034	158,215	4,732,249	570,979	1,184,533	5,345,803	1,344,930	1,972,069	55,212	156,902	82,313

Personal Income and Employment by Area: Champaign-Urbana, IL

(Thousands of dollars, except as noted.)

Year	Personal income, total	Derivation of personal income								Per capita personal income (dollars)	Population (persons)	Total employment
		Earnings by place of work			Less: Contributions for government social insurance	Plus: Adjustment for residence	Equals: Net earnings by place of residence	Plus: Dividends, interest, and rent	Plus: Personal current transfer receipts			
		Nonfarm	Farm	Total								
1970	726,344	569,088	29,521	598,609	30,378	-16,095	552,136	134,798	39,410	4,062	178,800	84,921
1971	811,945	626,647	45,318	671,965	34,998	-17,313	619,654	145,449	46,842	4,510	180,014	87,413
1972	865,313	671,603	34,932	706,535	39,167	-16,860	650,508	160,898	53,907	4,818	179,585	88,459
1973	988,309	725,965	76,189	802,154	48,143	-16,341	737,670	186,731	63,908	5,394	183,233	92,485
1974	1,068,777	785,947	76,000	861,947	55,161	-16,648	790,138	205,378	73,261	5,807	184,061	93,736
1975	1,256,855	900,180	112,755	1,012,935	61,838	-18,787	932,310	231,517	93,028	6,886	182,530	95,734
1976	1,327,481	979,179	87,890	1,067,069	69,834	-16,367	980,868	245,980	100,633	7,155	185,536	97,061
1977	1,423,545	1,047,025	90,582	1,137,607	75,136	-12,235	1,050,236	269,047	104,262	7,605	187,177	98,444
1978	1,528,483	1,144,951	68,622	1,213,573	84,192	-10,642	1,118,739	297,059	112,685	8,129	188,020	99,780
1979	1,678,218	1,237,486	84,981	1,322,467	95,499	-6,651	1,220,317	334,073	123,828	9,097	184,480	101,628
1980	1,775,203	1,306,045	31,810	1,337,855	99,349	-800	1,237,706	387,481	150,016	9,570	185,490	101,208
1981	1,996,702	1,417,384	63,482	1,480,866	115,730	-1,240	1,363,896	455,658	177,148	10,664	187,231	101,155
1982	2,141,245	1,505,149	40,485	1,545,634	123,728	-8,583	1,413,323	536,801	191,121	11,385	188,079	101,614
1983	2,224,293	1,600,418	-6,736	1,593,682	133,322	-12,024	1,448,336	563,926	212,031	11,913	186,715	101,002
1984	2,491,231	1,738,905	68,381	1,807,286	149,930	-5,354	1,652,002	618,748	220,481	13,312	187,144	103,920
1985	2,618,571	1,845,175	85,077	1,930,252	162,638	-13,415	1,754,199	637,287	227,085	13,962	187,547	106,269
1986	2,749,445	2,002,423	68,244	2,070,667	177,558	-44,908	1,848,201	668,355	232,889	14,532	189,193	111,207
1987	2,877,805	2,153,629	51,519	2,205,148	188,822	-60,397	1,955,929	679,337	242,539	15,171	189,687	113,863
1988	3,039,463	2,328,994	23,289	2,352,283	215,127	-67,675	2,069,481	718,771	251,211	15,981	190,188	116,968
1989	3,283,292	2,410,926	76,257	2,487,183	225,180	-73,330	2,188,673	823,122	271,497	17,412	188,564	116,540
1990	3,447,664	2,628,149	66,242	2,694,391	244,583	-89,000	2,360,808	795,019	291,837	18,252	188,891	118,855
1991	3,503,004	2,691,758	31,948	2,723,706	257,782	-88,557	2,377,367	809,368	316,269	18,334	191,070	117,580
1992	3,748,903	2,865,261	71,962	2,937,223	271,600	-100,812	2,564,811	827,135	356,957	19,342	193,825	117,614
1993	3,754,274	2,833,505	77,277	2,910,782	271,629	-96,947	2,542,206	834,411	377,657	19,706	190,519	113,982
1994	3,883,757	2,933,333	105,111	3,038,444	286,942	-101,936	2,649,566	850,116	384,075	20,589	188,635	116,082
1995	4,035,405	3,072,865	22,289	3,095,154	301,813	-110,426	2,682,915	942,470	410,020	21,363	188,896	118,170
1996	4,286,572	3,190,533	96,591	3,287,124	312,060	-118,938	2,856,126	995,892	434,554	22,424	191,162	119,770
1997	4,509,645	3,339,581	80,246	3,419,827	323,716	-134,259	2,961,852	1,095,585	452,208	23,374	192,937	121,130
1998	4,716,506	3,528,494	40,226	3,568,720	339,068	-139,354	3,090,298	1,159,808	466,400	24,408	193,235	123,316
1999	4,955,051	3,806,203	32,532	3,838,735	358,735	-157,042	3,322,958	1,144,730	487,363	25,405	195,040	126,090
2000	5,349,589	4,095,238	63,767	4,159,005	377,806	-182,344	3,598,855	1,239,875	510,859	27,234	196,428	128,979
2001	5,691,230	4,456,259	66,335	4,522,594	398,790	-225,801	3,898,003	1,236,493	556,734	28,698	198,313	129,448
2002	5,841,022	4,735,239	51,853	4,787,092	424,128	-281,615	4,081,349	1,158,948	600,725	29,145	200,414	128,910
2003	6,039,371	4,839,957	66,278	4,906,235	438,033	-302,228	4,165,974	1,242,806	630,591	29,694	203,388	128,837
2004	6,327,274	5,007,205	133,361	5,140,566	452,730	-342,619	4,345,217	1,318,305	663,752	30,853	205,080	130,049
2005	6,396,893	5,129,767	55,760	5,185,527	472,793	-347,247	4,365,487	1,297,953	733,453	30,857	207,308	129,850
2006	6,711,080	5,359,615	83,509	5,443,124	487,294	-376,703	4,579,127	1,372,866	759,087	31,878	210,526	130,923
2007	7,130,784	5,616,967	141,521	5,758,488	514,073	-398,417	4,845,998	1,456,171	828,615	33,433	213,285	133,054
2008	7,611,194	5,869,887	212,858	6,082,745	540,340	-450,381	5,092,024	1,574,111	945,059	35,519	214,286	134,029
2009	8,041,306	5,992,990	122,065	6,115,055	540,459	-374,272	5,200,324	1,789,725	1,051,257	37,101	216,742	131,699
2010	8,348,115	6,394,785	130,467	6,525,252	560,425	-375,800	5,589,027	1,598,731	1,160,357	38,261	218,190	130,030
2011	8,709,116	6,490,419	233,362	6,723,781	514,485	-323,025	5,886,271	1,698,528	1,124,317	39,672	219,528	129,468
2012	8,849,869	6,700,698	123,939	6,824,637	535,013	-306,128	5,983,496	1,753,261	1,113,112	40,138	220,485	129,603
2013	9,268,700	7,052,459	313,494	7,365,953	611,484	-331,921	6,422,548	1,681,094	1,165,058	41,767	221,916	130,359
2014	9,538,636	7,351,937	161,617	7,513,554	634,264	-321,296	6,557,994	1,760,704	1,219,938	42,755	223,099	131,721
2015	9,833,877	7,584,136	21,535	7,605,671	650,096	-309,432	6,646,143	1,884,201	1,303,533	43,869	224,166	133,584
2016	9,751,561	7,359,719	105,777	7,465,496	648,767	-298,697	6,518,032	1,897,468	1,336,061	43,371	224,840	133,434
2017	9,879,287	7,334,249	103,853	7,438,102	660,938	-310,170	6,466,994	2,048,326	1,363,967	43,973	224,667	134,689
2018	10,092,530	7,505,662	145,206	7,650,868	683,423	-316,076	6,651,369	2,018,639	1,422,522	45,083	223,868	135,217
2019	10,423,191	7,751,302	84,717	7,836,019	711,387	-328,653	6,795,979	2,131,242	1,495,970	46,747	222,972	135,907
2020	11,281,129	8,066,351	165,295	8,231,646	750,469	-377,447	7,103,730	2,098,422	2,078,977	50,747	222,303	132,808
2021	12,394,436	8,587,934	321,793	8,909,727	796,344	-406,500	7,706,883	2,306,417	2,381,136	55,459	223,489	136,700
2022	12,405,012	8,933,001	383,215	9,316,216	867,806	-325,968	8,122,442	2,365,511	1,917,059	55,562	223,265	142,198

Personal Income and Employment by Area: Charleston, WV

(Thousands of dollars, except as noted.)

Year	Personal income, total	Derivation of personal income: Earnings by place of work									Per capita personal income (dollars)	Population (persons)	Total employment
		Nonfarm	Farm	Total	Less: Contributions for government social insurance	Plus: Adjustment for residence	Equals: Net earnings by place of residence	Plus: Dividends, interest, and rent	Plus: Personal current transfer receipts			
1970	1,095,925	947,223	1,150	948,373	70,859	-28,835	848,679	129,697	117,549	3,607	303,824	123,426
1971	1,186,393	1,014,059	1,052	1,015,111	78,903	-31,460	904,748	141,506	140,139	3,884	305,473	124,223
1972	1,297,245	1,114,031	1,559	1,115,590	91,108	-42,165	982,317	154,290	160,638	4,237	306,144	126,920
1973	1,421,893	1,234,647	1,648	1,236,295	117,529	-59,703	1,059,063	174,128	188,702	4,671	304,424	131,311
1974	1,576,062	1,376,985	1,157	1,378,142	135,719	-83,841	1,158,582	203,794	213,686	5,192	303,574	134,891
1975	1,768,759	1,537,617	878	1,538,495	149,874	-102,037	1,286,584	229,142	253,033	5,729	308,748	137,433
1976	1,968,379	1,732,841	941	1,733,782	172,142	-122,850	1,438,790	251,084	278,505	6,314	311,754	141,841
1977	2,189,257	1,950,639	926	1,951,565	192,318	-145,862	1,613,385	281,176	294,696	6,936	315,639	146,084
1978	2,439,245	2,209,494	880	2,210,374	224,933	-182,648	1,802,793	311,202	325,250	7,648	318,947	152,494
1979	2,730,303	2,489,692	1,457	2,491,149	264,215	-228,597	1,998,337	350,282	381,684	8,506	320,992	156,276
1980	2,958,672	2,639,111	451	2,639,562	285,644	-256,474	2,097,444	420,156	441,072	9,165	322,812	152,464
1981	3,218,980	2,771,994	-476	2,771,518	320,927	-264,701	2,185,890	514,088	519,002	9,959	323,232	145,666
1982	3,421,292	2,875,365	-1,260	2,874,105	342,562	-273,208	2,258,335	586,346	576,611	10,629	321,893	141,138
1983	3,498,559	2,842,962	-299	2,842,663	341,230	-268,890	2,232,543	624,538	641,478	10,943	319,711	136,608
1984	3,728,300	3,022,819	1,783	3,024,602	369,504	-279,149	2,375,949	688,341	664,010	11,777	316,565	137,842
1985	3,889,197	3,145,776	878	3,146,654	387,633	-286,600	2,472,421	727,612	689,164	12,464	312,026	138,153
1986	3,950,702	3,177,230	1,313	3,178,543	408,688	-299,137	2,470,718	745,210	734,774	12,839	307,701	138,108
1987	3,981,566	3,200,235	-1,047	3,199,188	415,022	-297,367	2,486,799	734,765	760,002	13,082	304,351	137,617
1988	4,315,312	3,447,736	-989	3,446,747	451,491	-281,577	2,713,679	795,676	805,957	14,464	298,341	139,362
1989	4,543,526	3,581,776	-682	3,581,094	476,138	-292,522	2,812,434	886,388	844,704	15,460	293,891	140,383
1990	4,839,309	3,836,868	90	3,836,958	518,648	-324,175	2,994,135	943,453	901,721	16,662	290,435	144,191
1991	5,046,316	4,004,425	-588	4,003,837	556,808	-342,795	3,104,234	921,213	1,020,869	17,375	290,435	144,766
1992	5,393,301	4,273,763	940	4,274,703	597,729	-400,396	3,276,578	942,044	1,174,679	18,497	291,582	147,343
1993	5,601,692	4,441,426	58	4,441,484	641,466	-410,308	3,389,710	959,747	1,252,235	19,174	292,148	149,778
1994	5,888,859	4,714,137	178	4,714,315	677,571	-441,880	3,594,864	1,020,808	1,273,187	20,219	291,252	154,304
1995	6,067,749	4,884,545	-1,772	4,882,773	713,038	-478,269	3,691,466	1,073,417	1,302,866	20,811	291,561	157,425
1996	6,280,011	5,052,474	-3,399	5,049,075	738,641	-527,176	3,783,258	1,127,203	1,369,550	21,566	291,197	158,902
1997	6,492,299	5,249,749	-4,033	5,245,716	759,589	-564,364	3,921,763	1,170,780	1,399,756	22,367	290,266	161,195
1998	6,847,743	5,534,265	-3,919	5,530,346	804,457	-572,673	4,153,216	1,257,300	1,437,227	23,720	288,693	162,819
1999	6,997,298	5,775,376	-4,522	5,770,854	831,439	-600,769	4,338,646	1,199,633	1,459,019	24,362	287,226	164,269
2000	7,387,411	6,080,645	-1,440	6,079,205	895,804	-635,534	4,547,867	1,302,911	1,536,633	25,858	285,694	165,406
2001	7,619,024	6,159,076	-944	6,158,132	873,693	-664,936	4,619,503	1,305,637	1,693,884	26,867	283,588	163,753
2002	7,824,911	6,239,725	-3,383	6,236,342	845,102	-688,955	4,702,285	1,278,178	1,844,448	27,701	282,476	162,133
2003	7,898,629	6,293,928	-4,507	6,289,421	875,632	-693,563	4,720,226	1,293,845	1,884,558	27,995	282,146	160,493
2004	7,960,292	6,521,356	-1,360	6,519,996	891,289	-742,522	4,886,185	1,213,602	1,860,505	28,256	281,718	160,423
2005	8,362,662	6,922,578	-2,473	6,920,105	926,642	-839,256	5,154,207	1,280,537	1,927,918	29,886	279,823	161,216
2006	8,864,239	7,293,172	-6,469	7,286,703	934,995	-951,528	5,400,180	1,411,969	2,052,090	31,807	278,691	162,752
2007	9,200,850	7,409,431	-8,398	7,401,033	908,680	-960,417	5,531,936	1,495,792	2,173,122	33,072	278,207	164,083
2008	9,805,413	7,713,803	-5,326	7,708,477	909,029	-982,640	5,816,808	1,584,773	2,403,832	35,298	277,793	163,925
2009	9,828,748	7,725,362	-4,377	7,720,985	922,047	-1,060,152	5,738,786	1,492,453	2,597,509	35,308	278,370	160,806
2010	10,041,269	7,854,666	-4,301	7,850,365	930,687	-1,092,755	5,826,923	1,502,597	2,711,749	36,130	277,921	159,707
2011	10,561,934	8,176,844	-1,573	8,175,271	855,909	-1,089,460	6,229,902	1,633,542	2,698,490	38,080	277,361	160,245
2012	10,744,069	8,282,580	1,077	8,283,657	865,832	-1,116,207	6,301,618	1,681,753	2,760,698	38,693	277,677	160,454
2013	10,549,852	8,142,932	-764	8,142,168	955,083	-1,061,635	6,125,450	1,599,776	2,824,626	38,110	276,823	158,546
2014	10,796,410	8,164,036	-3,134	8,160,902	977,842	-1,027,760	6,155,300	1,646,790	2,994,320	39,199	275,423	156,903
2015	10,883,311	8,148,134	-4,572	8,143,562	984,523	-1,066,277	6,092,762	1,685,874	3,104,675	39,855	273,071	154,413
2016	10,751,689	7,950,537	-6,731	7,943,806	985,613	-1,064,549	5,893,644	1,699,207	3,158,838	39,705	270,787	151,246
2017	10,948,652	8,064,413	-7,516	8,056,897	1,002,160	-1,127,268	5,927,469	1,757,546	3,263,637	40,975	267,206	148,792
2018	11,440,931	8,966,612	-8,412	8,958,200	1,094,892	-1,552,084	6,311,224	1,802,315	3,327,392	43,425	263,466	152,479
2019	11,680,341	8,602,953	-6,249	8,596,704	1,041,526	-1,191,871	6,363,307	1,897,665	3,419,369	44,782	260,828	145,349
2020	12,222,781	8,394,276	-7,404	8,386,872	1,051,934	-1,104,147	6,230,791	1,827,295	4,164,695	47,367	258,046	137,307
2021	13,139,824	8,838,406	-8,481	8,829,925	1,096,260	-1,174,530	6,559,135	1,981,835	4,598,854	51,487	255,207	140,278
2022	13,192,547	9,222,171	-10,437	9,211,734	1,154,052	-1,167,797	6,889,885	2,134,344	4,168,318	52,369	251,914	144,204

Personal Income and Employment by Area: Charleston-North Charleston, SC

(Thousands of dollars, except as noted.)

		Derivation of personal income										
		Earnings by place of work										
Year	Personal income, total	Nonfarm	Farm	Total	Less: Contributions for government social insurance	Plus: Adjustment for residence	Equals: Net earnings by place of residence	Plus: Dividends, interest, and rent	Plus: Personal current transfer receipts	Per capita personal income (dollars)	Population (persons)	Total employment
1970	1,279,669	1,056,968	7,639	1,064,607	59,898	-11,367	993,342	216,524	69,803	3,801	336,669	152,101
1971	1,383,879	1,130,473	7,446	1,137,919	66,798	-11,343	1,059,778	238,548	85,553	4,011	345,034	151,142
1972	1,517,813	1,232,701	9,813	1,242,514	75,438	-10,819	1,156,257	263,516	98,040	4,286	354,123	153,558
1973	1,680,008	1,364,230	10,318	1,374,548	94,055	-12,543	1,267,950	294,968	117,090	4,634	362,524	162,266
1974	1,959,389	1,576,872	15,077	1,591,949	113,060	-14,022	1,464,867	346,905	147,617	5,189	377,614	172,300
1975	2,213,586	1,756,358	19,661	1,776,019	128,328	-16,947	1,630,744	388,448	194,394	5,691	388,945	176,227
1976	2,459,268	1,977,834	12,311	1,990,145	148,863	-21,212	1,820,070	424,015	215,183	6,111	402,464	183,691
1977	2,651,205	2,136,753	8,786	2,145,539	159,554	-24,348	1,961,637	463,506	226,062	6,511	407,216	188,099
1978	3,009,689	2,408,891	15,418	2,424,309	181,834	-28,414	2,214,061	545,654	249,974	7,209	417,483	197,797
1979	3,372,578	2,698,623	20,159	2,718,782	212,054	-34,732	2,471,996	612,934	287,648	7,933	425,158	204,605
1980	3,810,509	3,020,853	6,976	3,027,829	237,871	-41,007	2,748,951	708,238	353,320	8,788	433,615	209,543
1981	4,323,308	3,408,083	10,642	3,418,725	287,607	-45,365	3,085,753	830,612	406,943	9,709	445,278	217,214
1982	4,674,382	3,626,698	23,524	3,650,222	308,623	-46,431	3,295,168	934,839	444,375	10,312	453,298	217,116
1983	5,039,969	3,909,629	10,127	3,919,756	349,967	-40,132	3,529,657	1,034,439	475,873	10,935	460,906	222,685
1984	5,569,292	4,339,955	19,015	4,358,970	403,264	-50,105	3,905,601	1,154,173	509,518	11,917	467,325	236,807
1985	5,932,352	4,635,729	8,199	4,643,928	444,899	-56,914	4,142,115	1,243,726	546,511	12,639	469,353	246,759
1986	6,358,999	4,964,353	7,302	4,971,655	493,245	-59,917	4,418,493	1,357,256	583,250	13,222	480,947	255,473
1987	6,780,629	5,323,389	11,954	5,335,343	528,764	-62,639	4,743,940	1,434,489	602,200	13,827	490,378	263,378
1988	7,325,546	5,787,906	17,965	5,805,871	601,080	-69,612	5,135,179	1,548,010	642,357	14,866	492,783	270,818
1989	7,951,267	6,149,175	13,890	6,163,065	653,838	-75,414	5,433,813	1,718,032	799,422	15,813	502,823	275,672
1990	8,657,719	6,731,605	12,967	6,744,572	739,637	-85,291	5,919,644	1,863,762	874,313	17,014	508,851	289,036
1991	9,039,264	6,961,780	19,060	6,980,840	777,915	-77,665	6,125,260	1,959,348	954,656	17,255	523,852	287,878
1992	9,490,068	7,237,437	16,418	7,253,855	813,485	-64,278	6,376,092	2,013,761	1,100,215	17,893	530,382	283,152
1993	9,852,438	7,402,313	23,960	7,426,273	843,836	-58,346	6,524,091	2,130,231	1,198,116	18,523	531,913	282,830
1994	10,079,104	7,417,182	34,106	7,451,288	861,532	-42,789	6,546,967	2,230,599	1,301,538	19,040	529,376	280,828
1995	10,297,497	7,435,391	31,774	7,467,165	869,583	-27,616	6,569,966	2,317,606	1,409,925	19,720	522,192	281,375
1996	10,793,922	7,691,660	27,846	7,719,506	889,684	-19,559	6,810,263	2,465,143	1,518,516	20,839	517,970	282,824
1997	11,570,726	8,250,086	28,077	8,278,163	958,508	-16,237	7,303,418	2,671,001	1,596,307	21,900	528,354	293,859
1998	12,578,326	9,068,067	20,573	9,088,640	1,053,237	-12,938	8,022,465	2,887,105	1,668,756	23,481	535,674	304,992
1999	13,425,134	9,889,082	24,118	9,913,200	1,142,910	-10,635	8,759,655	2,900,523	1,764,956	24,581	546,169	316,969
2000	14,522,152	10,713,020	25,266	10,738,286	1,227,919	-1,877	9,508,490	3,120,902	1,892,760	26,360	550,916	323,851
2001	14,916,979	10,896,374	26,859	10,923,233	1,271,569	-8,593	9,643,071	3,174,300	2,099,608	26,786	556,901	327,147
2002	15,671,020	11,566,923	16,070	11,582,993	1,358,443	-18,166	10,206,384	3,185,574	2,279,062	27,728	565,179	333,496
2003	16,480,792	12,253,155	25,889	12,279,044	1,445,852	-26,127	10,807,065	3,268,267	2,405,460	28,743	573,376	341,026
2004	17,838,784	13,232,628	21,899	13,254,527	1,554,812	-33,461	11,666,254	3,576,257	2,596,273	30,378	587,231	353,799
2005	19,460,128	14,313,907	23,744	14,337,651	1,663,886	-45,923	12,627,842	4,025,892	2,806,394	32,525	598,313	364,419
2006	21,130,658	15,393,477	15,704	15,409,181	1,818,228	-48,041	13,542,912	4,582,276	3,005,470	34,389	614,463	374,768
2007	22,882,685	16,693,357	15,356	16,708,713	1,956,632	-61,081	14,691,000	5,009,584	3,182,101	36,415	628,384	391,791
2008	23,571,834	16,723,860	10,193	16,734,053	2,017,021	-62,360	14,654,672	5,196,723	3,720,439	36,624	643,613	394,811
2009	22,955,625	16,109,637	16,333	16,125,970	1,972,511	-41,062	14,112,397	4,719,497	4,123,731	35,023	655,447	381,962
2010	24,632,081	17,197,613	17,848	17,215,461	2,050,245	-28,214	15,137,002	4,982,021	4,513,058	36,922	667,147	384,813
2011	26,828,092	18,673,333	15,018	18,688,351	1,952,512	-19,415	16,716,424	5,487,305	4,624,363	39,472	679,672	399,867
2012	29,301,754	20,673,212	18,576	20,691,788	2,054,060	-7,922	18,629,806	5,999,115	4,672,833	42,223	693,984	408,509
2013	29,022,028	20,584,770	23,795	20,608,565	2,364,189	-7,794	18,236,582	5,932,141	4,853,305	41,047	707,045	418,721
2014	31,340,654	22,050,101	10,883	22,060,984	2,518,315	2,764	19,545,433	6,604,070	5,191,151	43,458	721,173	432,464
2015	33,667,886	23,628,942	7,412	23,636,354	2,685,393	-14,084	20,936,877	7,168,362	5,562,647	45,617	738,057	448,886
2016	35,523,246	24,845,411	7,047	24,852,458	2,820,669	-40,694	21,991,095	7,753,729	5,778,422	47,186	752,834	468,545
2017	37,621,109	26,190,157	8,773	26,198,930	2,981,938	-48,633	23,168,359	8,431,490	6,021,260	49,138	765,626	480,407
2018	39,612,251	27,436,938	5,225	27,442,163	3,147,670	-67,076	24,227,417	9,025,320	6,359,514	50,996	776,775	497,816
2019	43,068,189	29,645,645	6,429	29,652,074	3,388,556	-81,616	26,181,902	10,096,125	6,790,162	54,527	789,852	505,352
2020	45,603,804	29,682,641	10,505	29,693,146	3,415,199	-80,796	26,197,151	10,600,041	8,806,612	56,763	803,413	494,412
2021	50,004,845	31,941,955	14,330	31,956,285	3,682,193	-101,930	28,172,162	11,928,634	9,904,049	61,372	814,782	517,997
2022	52,455,190	34,746,238	3,474	34,749,712	4,129,643	-118,081	30,501,988	13,124,732	8,828,470	63,159	830,529	548,488

Personal Income and Employment by Area: Charlotte-Concord-Gastonia, NC-SC

(Thousands of dollars, except as noted.)

Year	Personal income, total	Derivation of personal income: Earnings by place of work: Nonfarm	Farm	Total	Less: Contributions for government social insurance	Plus: Adjustment for residence	Equals: Net earnings by place of residence	Plus: Dividends, interest, and rent	Plus: Personal current transfer receipts	Per capita personal income (dollars)	Population (persons)	Total employment
1970	3,627,824	3,218,606	25,315	3,243,921	228,486	-43,484	2,971,951	403,618	252,255	3,585	1,011,955	511,572
1971	3,966,969	3,499,387	29,240	3,528,627	257,750	-47,715	3,223,162	446,575	297,232	3,846	1,031,374	519,318
1972	4,475,750	3,972,712	36,128	4,008,840	307,100	-56,178	3,645,562	495,841	334,347	4,254	1,052,081	543,510
1973	4,996,034	4,422,231	72,475	4,494,706	392,737	-61,123	4,040,846	560,111	395,077	4,680	1,067,459	566,399
1974	5,433,819	4,735,796	57,152	4,792,948	435,551	-64,291	4,293,106	645,573	495,140	5,039	1,078,395	566,214
1975	5,847,774	4,893,475	48,240	4,941,715	439,796	-70,395	4,431,524	708,596	707,654	5,398	1,083,225	540,283
1976	6,537,250	5,551,935	57,383	5,609,318	511,168	-79,110	5,019,040	775,368	742,842	5,995	1,090,448	562,341
1977	7,243,233	6,215,418	52,170	6,267,588	570,134	-92,114	5,605,340	866,738	771,155	6,578	1,101,205	585,960
1978	8,208,654	7,104,873	65,786	7,170,659	671,249	-111,489	6,387,921	990,685	830,048	7,330	1,119,946	614,689
1979	9,274,210	8,057,233	72,170	8,129,403	788,562	-137,679	7,203,162	1,131,604	939,444	8,132	1,140,515	642,177
1980	10,431,628	8,894,020	39,016	8,933,036	870,353	-164,157	7,898,526	1,414,018	1,119,084	8,929	1,168,323	647,215
1981	11,720,167	9,853,945	43,788	9,897,733	1,034,266	-196,782	8,666,685	1,763,689	1,289,793	9,889	1,185,227	654,480
1982	12,551,282	10,311,373	59,087	10,370,460	1,094,343	-211,483	9,064,634	2,034,395	1,452,253	10,441	1,202,085	644,062
1983	13,755,155	11,372,475	42,952	11,415,427	1,217,468	-230,214	9,967,745	2,223,765	1,563,645	11,351	1,211,827	658,173
1984	15,593,392	12,905,430	139,171	13,044,601	1,415,906	-259,884	11,368,811	2,583,138	1,641,443	12,660	1,231,696	698,059
1985	16,916,099	13,997,205	157,412	14,154,617	1,555,296	-284,118	12,315,203	2,826,390	1,774,506	13,482	1,254,725	721,856
1986	18,341,370	15,293,777	153,819	15,447,596	1,735,606	-314,872	13,397,118	3,064,071	1,880,181	14,416	1,272,319	748,162
1987	19,983,311	16,990,352	91,484	17,081,836	1,901,388	-360,097	14,820,351	3,211,142	1,951,818	15,413	1,296,549	778,947
1988	22,147,703	18,733,361	133,679	18,867,040	2,137,446	-398,524	16,331,070	3,701,103	2,115,530	16,763	1,321,246	814,091
1989	24,187,292	20,264,237	174,394	20,438,631	2,310,189	-438,868	17,689,574	4,130,590	2,367,128	17,992	1,344,353	836,798
1990	25,983,776	21,769,020	224,419	21,993,439	2,546,132	-480,717	18,966,590	4,398,193	2,618,993	18,920	1,373,345	855,907
1991	26,980,388	22,242,872	262,154	22,505,026	2,636,538	-477,089	19,391,399	4,557,095	3,031,894	19,210	1,404,496	841,597
1992	29,180,125	24,135,008	258,476	24,393,484	2,820,300	-501,602	21,071,582	4,745,965	3,362,578	20,419	1,429,067	854,956
1993	31,236,393	25,757,149	281,849	26,038,998	3,023,921	-525,521	22,489,556	5,084,152	3,662,685	21,392	1,460,199	884,610
1994	33,745,081	27,894,547	280,824	28,175,371	3,308,794	-565,850	24,300,727	5,605,448	3,838,906	22,571	1,495,064	920,169
1995	36,678,380	30,171,068	310,887	30,481,955	3,572,559	-613,322	26,296,074	6,148,644	4,233,662	23,916	1,533,653	959,858
1996	39,605,972	32,332,660	295,206	32,627,866	3,782,826	-645,291	28,199,749	6,809,911	4,596,312	25,136	1,575,674	986,357
1997	42,679,540	35,027,548	265,938	35,293,486	4,075,342	-698,955	30,519,189	7,357,544	4,802,807	26,346	1,619,972	1,025,865
1998	46,784,296	38,543,631	315,066	38,858,697	4,459,525	-759,400	33,639,772	8,109,024	5,035,500	28,094	1,665,276	1,056,196
1999	49,842,226	41,531,700	356,253	41,887,953	4,812,048	-838,212	36,237,693	8,270,949	5,333,584	29,115	1,711,905	1,094,733
2000	53,453,831	44,492,894	348,315	44,841,209	5,133,767	-901,601	38,805,841	8,885,888	5,762,102	30,476	1,753,958	1,126,455
2001	52,648,769	43,146,367	380,186	43,526,553	5,352,451	-967,272	37,206,830	8,957,298	6,484,641	29,330	1,795,029	1,131,782
2002	54,194,888	44,714,783	223,713	44,938,496	5,524,691	-1,003,906	38,409,899	8,699,168	7,085,821	29,577	1,832,361	1,134,688
2003	57,539,211	47,514,932	258,723	47,773,655	5,776,003	-1,000,759	40,996,893	9,041,427	7,500,891	30,815	1,867,238	1,137,800
2004	63,958,784	52,873,511	304,480	53,177,991	6,091,345	-1,087,481	45,999,165	9,877,820	8,081,799	33,550	1,906,396	1,166,392
2005	70,534,997	58,419,490	339,661	58,759,151	6,627,695	-1,164,131	50,967,325	10,821,066	8,746,606	35,973	1,960,753	1,209,694
2006	79,752,658	66,365,326	312,105	66,677,431	7,243,946	-1,184,320	58,249,165	11,904,571	9,598,922	39,174	2,035,838	1,263,384
2007	88,884,355	74,103,948	261,299	74,365,247	7,874,455	-1,178,248	65,312,544	13,157,621	10,414,190	42,069	2,112,817	1,320,243
2008	100,484,416	82,865,290	176,347	83,041,637	8,176,082	-1,136,747	73,728,808	14,666,511	12,089,097	46,124	2,178,593	1,322,588
2009	91,424,691	72,871,155	183,818	73,054,973	7,713,923	-875,004	64,466,046	13,121,705	13,836,940	41,131	2,222,773	1,269,805
2010	87,281,854	67,674,401	191,051	67,865,452	7,590,618	-727,967	59,546,867	12,803,763	14,931,224	38,793	2,249,938	1,263,142
2011	92,096,332	70,470,484	195,311	70,665,795	7,206,128	-608,593	62,851,074	14,111,001	15,134,257	40,387	2,280,323	1,318,071
2012	103,528,310	80,752,149	313,623	81,065,772	7,723,568	-495,996	72,846,208	15,316,062	15,366,040	44,685	2,316,865	1,347,244
2013	99,055,912	77,353,966	344,731	77,698,697	8,974,420	-322,684	68,401,593	14,970,007	15,684,312	42,046	2,355,919	1,383,040
2014	105,452,225	82,166,318	371,390	82,537,708	9,570,712	-461,853	72,505,143	16,463,343	16,483,739	43,999	2,396,711	1,437,677
2015	113,375,600	88,023,519	461,978	88,485,497	10,232,383	-527,366	77,725,748	18,038,259	17,611,593	46,408	2,443,016	1,490,961
2016	119,034,090	93,020,716	339,819	93,360,535	10,676,049	-546,524	82,137,962	18,758,950	18,137,178	47,733	2,493,738	1,541,284
2017	127,187,134	99,067,730	409,787	99,477,517	11,207,951	-610,601	87,658,965	20,635,842	18,892,327	50,016	2,542,910	1,589,260
2018	134,583,610	105,063,293	230,497	105,293,790	11,708,435	-703,084	92,882,271	21,782,013	19,919,326	52,070	2,584,646	1,637,131
2019	143,236,333	111,946,998	269,666	112,216,664	12,446,443	-787,156	98,983,065	23,203,502	21,049,766	54,531	2,626,694	1,675,715
2020	155,195,936	116,327,527	241,355	116,568,882	12,963,258	-948,888	102,656,736	24,751,389	27,787,811	58,149	2,668,915	1,668,732
2021	170,310,551	125,538,801	374,222	125,913,023	13,972,733	-1,133,303	110,806,987	27,573,507	31,930,057	62,906	2,707,369	1,749,830
2022	179,574,730	138,027,803	510,492	138,538,295	15,601,282	-1,243,338	121,693,675	30,286,804	27,594,251	65,156	2,756,069	1,842,427

Personal Income and Employment by Area: Charlottesville, VA

(Thousands of dollars, except as noted.)

Year	Personal income, total	Derivation of personal income: Earnings by place of work: Nonfarm	Farm	Total	Less: Contributions for government social insurance	Plus: Adjustment for residence	Equals: Net earnings by place of residence	Plus: Dividends, interest, and rent	Plus: Personal current transfer receipts	Per capita personal income (dollars)	Population (persons)	Total employment
1970	359,223	293,993	6,272	300,265	18,380	-23,996	257,889	74,522	26,812	3,549	101,224	48,991
1971	393,550	319,557	5,742	325,299	20,791	-24,472	280,036	81,662	31,852	3,827	102,848	49,650
1972	450,137	352,008	6,204	358,212	24,190	-10,239	323,783	90,026	36,328	4,160	108,206	51,866
1973	518,261	403,968	9,787	413,755	31,528	-12,049	370,178	104,543	43,540	4,649	111,489	55,555
1974	579,070	446,059	9,892	455,951	36,315	-13,729	405,907	120,209	52,954	5,057	114,500	57,668
1975	639,537	482,110	5,572	487,682	38,499	-8,903	440,280	129,110	70,147	5,352	119,504	57,046
1976	714,579	535,698	4,192	539,890	43,261	-3,098	493,531	143,924	77,124	5,893	121,254	59,262
1977	783,820	589,738	3,350	593,088	48,145	-4,682	540,261	161,370	82,189	6,411	122,257	61,126
1978	895,580	682,289	8,834	691,123	56,620	-13,235	621,268	185,722	88,590	7,254	123,463	64,812
1979	991,454	779,860	9,066	788,926	67,527	-30,908	690,491	199,879	101,084	7,923	125,144	68,600
1980	1,130,717	880,245	5,015	885,260	77,491	-43,434	764,335	246,340	120,042	8,952	126,303	71,221
1981	1,284,463	959,563	2,995	962,558	90,861	-38,058	833,639	311,884	138,940	10,019	128,197	71,535
1982	1,412,358	1,033,489	1,983	1,035,472	99,219	-41,595	894,658	364,680	153,020	10,931	129,201	72,117
1983	1,537,137	1,145,606	572	1,146,178	112,303	-49,644	984,231	385,948	166,958	11,812	130,129	73,962
1984	1,705,493	1,265,796	3,212	1,269,008	127,665	-50,269	1,091,074	437,152	177,267	13,002	131,176	76,494
1985	1,851,842	1,376,761	2,197	1,378,958	141,719	-53,183	1,184,056	478,825	188,961	13,864	133,568	78,570
1986	2,000,247	1,497,596	2,451	1,500,047	159,506	-54,733	1,285,808	516,367	198,072	14,977	133,555	82,260
1987	2,155,238	1,625,707	6,435	1,632,142	172,042	-54,444	1,405,656	543,920	205,662	15,836	136,096	86,597
1988	2,459,899	1,853,895	6,756	1,860,651	199,728	-57,151	1,603,772	637,896	218,231	17,747	138,612	87,779
1989	2,695,963	1,991,031	9,369	2,000,400	216,016	-57,542	1,726,842	724,586	244,535	19,045	141,561	90,725
1990	2,912,900	2,121,623	11,555	2,133,178	232,943	-56,756	1,843,479	806,605	262,816	20,091	144,984	92,037
1991	3,087,684	2,224,353	11,645	2,235,998	245,067	-55,184	1,935,747	859,702	292,235	20,938	147,465	91,325
1992	3,316,148	2,358,807	10,581	2,369,388	259,010	-58,313	2,052,065	926,876	337,207	22,110	149,981	92,199
1993	3,558,798	2,528,588	8,441	2,537,029	275,367	-65,112	2,196,550	999,022	363,226	23,209	153,337	95,594
1994	3,744,784	2,656,147	8,068	2,664,215	289,365	-68,458	2,306,392	1,061,795	376,597	24,001	156,024	97,549
1995	4,014,616	2,772,206	9,563	2,781,769	300,304	-73,079	2,408,386	1,192,501	413,729	25,317	158,577	100,210
1996	4,251,062	2,949,539	8,219	2,957,758	318,600	-84,190	2,554,968	1,255,724	440,370	26,310	161,576	103,087
1997	4,574,415	3,186,333	5,911	3,192,244	340,557	-89,169	2,762,518	1,350,051	461,846	27,788	164,621	106,329
1998	4,944,514	3,486,975	6,382	3,493,357	369,879	-108,672	3,014,806	1,460,639	469,069	29,446	167,916	110,257
1999	5,204,620	3,715,652	6,658	3,722,310	393,824	-118,560	3,209,926	1,499,674	495,020	30,319	171,662	113,129
2000	5,664,243	4,063,842	10,249	4,074,091	423,552	-138,277	3,512,262	1,611,135	540,846	32,371	174,979	116,535
2001	5,971,881	4,273,600	4,581	4,278,181	451,927	-150,070	3,676,184	1,698,881	596,816	33,596	177,754	117,073
2002	6,109,678	4,471,329	4,594	4,475,923	473,706	-168,721	3,833,496	1,650,133	626,049	33,860	180,442	118,126
2003	6,511,321	4,675,302	-509	4,674,793	494,383	-182,902	3,997,508	1,845,652	668,161	35,670	182,545	118,613
2004	6,959,664	5,028,260	1,473	5,029,733	533,001	-202,321	4,294,411	1,965,138	700,115	37,657	184,817	122,141
2005	7,465,698	5,385,751	-1,892	5,383,859	576,270	-236,024	4,571,565	2,125,270	768,863	39,590	188,574	125,998
2006	8,184,107	5,739,050	-11,897	5,727,153	617,320	-265,043	4,844,790	2,496,068	843,249	42,632	191,972	130,610
2007	8,705,352	6,057,704	-14,081	6,043,623	657,279	-296,950	5,089,394	2,720,242	895,716	44,724	194,646	134,172
2008	9,149,356	6,300,798	1,078	6,301,876	687,770	-329,382	5,284,724	2,847,163	1,017,469	46,243	197,853	135,568
2009	8,837,901	6,285,391	3,895	6,289,286	690,380	-315,677	5,283,229	2,464,643	1,090,029	44,183	200,028	132,992
2010	9,287,244	6,583,150	2,700	6,585,850	706,337	-286,797	5,592,716	2,512,912	1,181,616	45,988	201,949	132,303
2011	9,777,251	6,668,953	5,072	6,674,025	640,663	-282,494	5,750,868	2,810,779	1,215,604	47,958	203,871	134,026
2012	10,572,605	7,048,819	14,912	7,063,731	664,895	-269,843	6,128,993	3,203,868	1,239,744	51,329	205,979	135,975
2013	10,464,633	7,093,444	6,490	7,099,934	774,980	-251,317	6,073,637	3,098,844	1,292,152	50,460	207,384	137,571
2014	11,028,783	7,418,540	253	7,418,793	812,327	-270,416	6,336,050	3,325,719	1,367,014	52,516	210,010	141,027
2015	11,723,179	7,923,036	-1,859	7,921,177	872,359	-311,610	6,737,208	3,544,995	1,440,976	55,164	212,514	145,787
2016	12,394,979	8,216,485	-3,368	8,213,117	900,970	-324,673	6,987,474	3,908,935	1,498,570	57,658	214,974	149,412
2017	13,446,923	8,714,634	7,259	8,721,893	965,072	-367,567	7,389,254	4,490,977	1,566,692	61,779	217,661	152,848
2018	14,213,892	9,086,195	-4,706	9,081,489	1,007,223	-398,299	7,675,967	4,830,353	1,707,572	64,878	219,086	155,690
2019	14,929,703	9,328,536	2,637	9,331,173	1,034,936	-405,380	7,890,857	5,250,004	1,788,842	67,651	220,686	157,802
2020	15,195,857	9,401,577	-2,463	9,399,114	1,054,268	-408,308	7,936,538	4,874,124	2,385,195	68,575	221,595	151,079
2021	17,521,669	10,573,795	-4,273	10,569,522	1,178,616	-459,347	8,931,559	5,862,907	2,727,203	78,538	223,097	157,751
2022	18,122,821	11,206,580	-477	11,206,103	1,276,475	-471,031	9,458,597	6,260,401	2,403,823	80,969	223,825	164,934

Personal Income and Employment by Area: Chattanooga, TN-GA

(Thousands of dollars, except as noted.)

Year	Personal income, total	Derivation of personal income								Per capita personal income (dollars)	Population (persons)	Total employment
		Earnings by place of work			Less: Contributions for government social insurance	Plus: Adjustment for residence	Equals: Net earnings by place of residence	Plus: Dividends, interest, and rent	Plus: Personal current transfer receipts			
		Nonfarm	Farm	Total								
1970	1,330,318	1,169,675	4,311	1,173,986	76,760	-43,113	1,054,113	163,961	112,244	3,575	372,113	172,095
1971	1,474,581	1,286,539	3,807	1,290,346	86,418	-46,757	1,157,171	185,424	131,986	3,876	380,419	174,934
1972	1,674,323	1,471,219	5,289	1,476,508	103,374	-52,526	1,320,608	206,648	147,067	4,326	387,034	186,173
1973	1,872,144	1,645,219	9,097	1,654,316	133,722	-55,932	1,464,662	232,672	174,810	4,739	395,063	196,966
1974	2,054,698	1,779,157	4,370	1,783,527	149,824	-59,310	1,574,393	269,803	210,502	5,154	398,683	197,405
1975	2,230,144	1,866,010	7,212	1,873,222	152,748	-54,890	1,665,584	291,987	272,573	5,554	401,552	190,016
1976	2,492,020	2,092,790	9,431	2,102,221	174,051	-51,873	1,876,297	317,315	298,408	6,140	405,890	196,745
1977	2,755,079	2,327,332	6,532	2,333,864	191,994	-62,047	2,079,823	356,215	319,041	6,703	411,025	201,417
1978	3,145,986	2,683,708	5,564	2,689,272	222,836	-75,066	2,391,370	408,219	346,397	7,563	415,992	211,442
1979	3,430,232	2,893,475	7,112	2,900,587	250,372	-80,228	2,569,987	459,065	401,180	8,097	423,664	214,637
1980	3,724,773	3,037,880	5,674	3,043,554	263,229	-80,633	2,699,692	540,524	484,557	8,714	427,429	208,292
1981	4,083,136	3,251,775	8,296	3,260,071	304,253	-83,778	2,872,040	658,994	552,102	9,484	430,519	206,190
1982	4,326,395	3,351,053	9,992	3,361,045	319,349	-79,210	2,962,486	765,326	598,583	10,127	427,203	199,884
1983	4,558,743	3,516,322	4,627	3,520,949	343,115	-71,071	3,106,763	811,647	640,333	10,771	423,243	199,125
1984	4,948,046	3,815,634	10,868	3,826,502	385,049	-72,288	3,369,165	906,267	672,614	11,666	424,137	206,887
1985	5,273,672	4,064,629	9,024	4,073,653	420,743	-69,584	3,583,326	974,077	716,269	12,422	424,535	211,855
1986	5,636,665	4,383,968	9,036	4,393,004	464,410	-85,131	3,843,463	1,031,699	761,503	13,268	424,816	218,811
1987	6,096,483	4,829,699	6,719	4,836,418	507,109	-89,610	4,239,699	1,059,932	796,852	14,200	429,335	229,011
1988	6,664,845	5,256,800	9,993	5,266,793	566,692	-94,921	4,605,180	1,207,181	852,484	15,385	433,218	235,200
1989	7,070,818	5,448,067	15,959	5,464,026	598,981	-98,410	4,766,635	1,361,754	942,429	16,292	434,018	240,365
1990	7,499,064	5,750,245	15,581	5,765,826	637,022	-89,725	5,039,079	1,434,690	1,025,295	17,290	433,718	243,572
1991	7,755,239	5,893,734	18,198	5,911,932	664,466	-91,520	5,155,946	1,431,150	1,168,143	17,710	437,902	243,018
1992	8,332,899	6,284,235	19,817	6,304,052	701,306	-64,594	5,538,152	1,472,941	1,321,806	18,871	441,576	245,510
1993	8,915,667	6,763,107	20,399	6,783,506	757,314	-68,373	5,957,819	1,543,716	1,414,132	19,927	447,416	254,759
1994	9,335,900	7,123,340	22,557	7,145,897	810,876	-92,961	6,242,060	1,606,523	1,487,317	20,616	452,845	261,969
1995	9,913,486	7,519,582	14,640	7,534,222	857,439	-105,977	6,570,806	1,737,089	1,605,591	21,641	458,090	266,963
1996	10,490,148	7,945,480	16,684	7,962,164	893,109	-93,577	6,975,478	1,835,679	1,678,991	22,702	462,090	273,762
1997	11,056,183	8,511,578	17,224	8,528,802	943,645	-113,277	7,471,880	1,840,419	1,743,884	23,687	466,756	276,491
1998	11,821,355	9,153,506	21,914	9,175,420	983,559	-101,354	8,090,507	1,974,411	1,756,437	25,145	470,131	282,947
1999	12,536,832	9,860,405	19,584	9,879,989	1,058,967	-118,792	8,702,230	1,993,647	1,840,955	26,459	473,820	291,583
2000	13,278,328	10,430,505	16,622	10,447,127	1,113,624	-134,478	9,199,025	2,100,317	1,978,986	27,800	477,630	298,758
2001	13,339,725	10,321,957	30,395	10,352,352	1,129,226	-135,925	9,087,201	2,099,302	2,153,222	27,687	481,798	295,485
2002	13,620,980	10,540,566	12,803	10,553,369	1,156,447	-119,037	9,277,885	2,018,102	2,324,993	28,029	485,957	292,897
2003	14,232,324	11,047,484	12,475	11,059,959	1,207,298	-124,166	9,728,495	2,081,692	2,422,137	29,040	490,089	294,809
2004	14,930,439	11,565,180	24,814	11,589,994	1,253,774	-88,289	10,247,931	2,102,112	2,580,396	30,180	494,709	297,319
2005	15,571,490	12,030,243	29,597	12,059,840	1,309,176	-103,944	10,646,720	2,172,748	2,752,022	31,170	499,564	302,468
2006	16,572,699	12,660,407	8,312	12,668,719	1,380,570	-132,908	11,155,241	2,474,460	2,942,998	32,722	506,473	308,302
2007	17,359,494	13,016,260	11,383	13,027,643	1,436,460	-121,471	11,469,712	2,674,991	3,214,791	33,833	513,100	313,706
2008	18,116,423	13,401,841	29,530	13,431,371	1,497,891	-200,238	11,733,242	2,788,679	3,594,502	34,921	518,778	309,632
2009	17,891,584	13,051,088	26,637	13,077,725	1,456,485	-140,821	11,480,419	2,595,545	3,815,620	34,139	524,082	291,430
2010	18,898,364	13,766,862	16,387	13,783,249	1,514,801	-196,938	12,071,510	2,669,968	4,156,886	35,722	529,033	290,398
2011	19,942,906	14,482,318	7,528	14,489,846	1,401,894	-215,032	12,872,920	2,810,267	4,259,719	37,411	533,078	297,164
2012	21,027,161	15,253,501	44,714	15,298,215	1,447,194	-257,314	13,593,707	3,146,900	4,286,554	39,151	537,077	299,766
2013	20,953,373	15,355,591	55,943	15,411,534	1,653,728	-260,399	13,497,407	3,020,743	4,435,223	38,755	540,656	303,126
2014	21,534,180	15,610,641	60,535	15,671,176	1,686,369	-116,043	13,868,764	3,131,492	4,533,924	39,720	542,153	303,657
2015	22,694,573	16,416,545	65,180	16,481,725	1,768,562	-184,411	14,528,752	3,412,737	4,753,084	41,668	544,658	310,840
2016	23,271,763	16,909,697	33,165	16,942,862	1,823,553	-141,648	14,977,661	3,427,531	4,866,571	42,406	548,785	318,295
2017	24,377,323	17,720,921	50,630	17,771,551	1,931,260	-295,984	15,544,307	3,786,656	5,046,360	44,142	552,242	326,612
2018	25,488,734	18,541,524	38,040	18,579,564	2,020,728	-423,173	16,135,663	4,069,335	5,283,736	45,809	556,415	335,384
2019	26,656,206	19,306,012	27,594	19,333,606	2,117,386	-492,004	16,724,216	4,378,582	5,553,408	47,628	559,673	339,151
2020	28,360,543	19,646,174	-5,843	19,640,331	2,210,517	-537,651	16,892,163	4,532,502	6,935,878	50,290	563,940	334,337
2021	30,411,054	20,916,175	30,682	20,946,857	2,341,478	-633,713	17,971,666	4,667,196	7,772,192	53,592	567,454	345,784
2022	31,405,623	22,823,002	91,959	22,914,961	2,627,895	-865,460	19,421,606	5,056,335	6,927,682	54,665	574,507	361,800

Personal Income and Employment by Area: Cheyenne, WY

(Thousands of dollars, except as noted.)

Year	Personal income, total	Derivation of personal income: Earnings by place of work: Nonfarm	Farm	Total	Less: Contributions for government social insurance	Plus: Adjustment for residence	Equals: Net earnings by place of residence	Plus: Dividends, interest, and rent	Plus: Personal current transfer receipts	Per capita personal income (dollars)	Population (persons)	Total employment
1970	252,643	194,127	4,016	198,143	14,212	-933	182,998	50,776	18,869	4,462	56,619	28,563
1971	278,822	214,779	3,692	218,471	16,164	-1,574	200,733	56,613	21,476	4,812	57,944	29,358
1972	316,308	248,403	5,405	253,808	19,435	-2,894	231,479	61,832	22,997	5,272	59,997	31,164
1973	368,918	299,024	2,699	301,723	26,358	-4,924	270,441	71,862	26,615	5,907	62,458	33,858
1974	421,372	339,216	5,972	345,188	30,392	-6,058	308,738	82,317	30,317	6,504	64,789	34,558
1975	460,198	369,276	3,179	372,455	32,738	-7,183	332,534	91,017	36,647	7,118	64,656	34,715
1976	499,110	401,915	2,462	404,377	37,177	-8,805	358,395	99,945	40,770	7,608	65,603	35,707
1977	545,964	439,633	1,956	441,589	40,521	-10,254	390,814	110,483	44,667	8,233	66,313	36,652
1978	633,865	513,924	3,702	517,626	48,371	-13,259	455,996	128,116	49,753	9,461	67,001	39,071
1979	714,060	582,650	3,925	586,575	57,616	-16,372	512,587	143,824	57,649	10,324	69,168	41,258
1980	815,908	654,505	5,503	660,008	63,994	-19,446	576,568	172,212	67,128	11,826	68,994	42,593
1981	912,596	720,837	4,130	724,967	75,197	-19,777	629,993	203,307	79,296	13,004	70,176	42,834
1982	986,088	763,875	2,479	766,354	80,704	-20,797	664,853	232,568	88,667	13,863	71,129	43,159
1983	1,017,581	770,854	3,502	774,356	80,500	-20,521	673,335	242,228	102,018	13,957	72,907	41,915
1984	1,078,496	819,217	1,091	820,308	87,568	-21,390	711,350	262,080	105,066	14,704	73,345	42,415
1985	1,126,737	852,893	828	853,721	92,828	-22,115	738,778	277,055	110,904	15,413	73,102	42,570
1986	1,171,806	878,550	4,623	883,173	96,753	-21,676	764,744	286,955	120,107	15,748	74,411	42,461
1987	1,185,622	881,608	8,265	889,873	98,059	-20,752	771,062	290,068	124,492	15,787	75,101	43,181
1988	1,222,390	907,476	7,579	915,055	107,833	-21,294	785,928	305,875	130,587	16,403	74,523	43,939
1989	1,306,497	954,078	8,791	962,869	112,896	-21,744	828,229	335,200	143,068	17,735	73,667	44,287
1990	1,399,985	997,700	14,182	1,011,882	122,599	-22,116	867,167	378,793	154,025	19,132	73,175	44,257
1991	1,464,546	1,053,903	14,714	1,068,617	130,928	-21,637	916,052	377,698	170,796	19,797	73,978	45,286
1992	1,548,134	1,129,599	16,041	1,145,640	139,826	-22,010	983,804	374,761	189,569	20,417	75,826	46,097
1993	1,629,399	1,199,571	19,740	1,219,311	147,894	-20,663	1,050,754	373,756	204,889	21,026	77,495	47,556
1994	1,719,636	1,259,646	9,595	1,269,241	155,020	-17,720	1,096,501	403,802	219,333	21,799	78,885	48,911
1995	1,804,126	1,286,473	15,818	1,302,291	157,386	-14,328	1,130,577	444,279	229,270	22,690	79,513	49,370
1996	1,863,624	1,305,018	12,029	1,317,047	159,500	-11,386	1,146,161	478,046	239,417	23,241	80,186	49,791
1997	1,960,826	1,337,613	24,662	1,362,275	165,561	-9,471	1,187,243	526,694	246,889	24,410	80,328	50,275
1998	2,111,197	1,442,052	16,567	1,458,619	176,008	-8,275	1,274,336	585,497	251,364	26,219	80,522	50,884
1999	2,229,846	1,536,445	13,621	1,550,066	186,812	-6,981	1,356,273	610,673	262,900	27,526	81,009	51,821
2000	2,389,438	1,635,750	15,282	1,651,032	195,864	-2,791	1,452,377	650,910	286,151	29,202	81,825	53,509
2001	2,507,090	1,737,212	19,801	1,757,013	207,338	-7,773	1,541,902	650,713	314,475	30,369	82,554	52,757
2002	2,680,487	1,889,550	5,629	1,895,179	219,825	-17,577	1,657,777	681,751	340,959	32,207	83,226	54,637
2003	2,871,785	2,012,685	12,995	2,025,680	237,564	-24,972	1,763,144	738,009	370,632	34,154	84,084	55,782
2004	3,057,401	2,132,864	13,465	2,146,329	254,113	-31,236	1,860,980	795,934	400,487	35,790	85,427	56,604
2005	3,199,528	2,240,406	18,228	2,258,634	264,660	-37,317	1,956,657	817,113	425,758	37,320	85,732	57,730
2006	3,464,434	2,500,419	13,013	2,513,432	324,262	-47,321	2,141,849	863,421	459,164	39,904	86,819	58,709
2007	3,634,553	2,604,794	19,309	2,624,103	341,456	-51,033	2,231,614	911,960	490,979	41,465	87,654	61,105
2008	4,039,261	2,790,999	30,373	2,821,372	354,346	-58,581	2,408,445	1,057,813	573,003	45,346	89,077	62,259
2009	3,819,467	2,750,781	25,317	2,776,098	358,119	-77,258	2,340,721	855,003	623,743	42,237	90,430	61,619
2010	3,996,095	2,843,796	32,978	2,876,774	363,052	-89,767	2,423,955	892,990	679,150	43,320	92,247	61,451
2011	4,458,735	3,033,594	70,644	3,104,238	345,760	-109,529	2,648,949	1,119,563	690,223	48,141	92,619	62,839
2012	4,579,579	3,215,558	38,397	3,253,955	370,887	-133,587	2,749,481	1,139,367	690,731	48,325	94,766	63,572
2013	4,604,769	3,380,201	34,064	3,414,265	424,611	-153,773	2,835,881	1,063,621	705,267	48,065	95,803	65,598
2014	4,743,224	3,444,185	36,164	3,480,349	443,508	-155,444	2,881,397	1,119,924	741,903	49,334	96,145	66,344
2015	4,813,116	3,518,311	17,157	3,535,468	446,806	-157,970	2,930,692	1,097,262	785,162	49,560	97,116	67,099
2016	4,712,581	3,486,673	14,465	3,501,138	445,495	-159,731	2,895,912	1,002,575	814,094	48,055	98,067	67,489
2017	4,867,408	3,594,073	13,308	3,607,381	458,628	-163,559	2,985,194	1,031,483	850,731	49,347	98,636	68,812
2018	5,158,900	3,775,017	12,030	3,787,047	468,080	-172,651	3,146,316	1,119,243	893,341	51,948	99,308	70,824
2019	5,255,466	3,935,318	16,393	3,951,711	497,358	-185,110	3,269,243	1,054,836	931,387	52,600	99,914	72,208
2020	5,624,265	3,981,764	8,796	3,990,560	509,939	-189,901	3,290,720	1,181,481	1,152,064	55,842	100,718	73,372
2021	5,919,055	4,202,207	35,502	4,237,709	529,348	-210,212	3,498,149	1,137,049	1,283,857	58,724	100,794	78,578
2022	5,957,582	4,309,883	28,199	4,338,082	538,836	-209,506	3,589,740	1,202,184	1,165,658	59,148	100,723	81,027

Personal Income and Employment by Area: Chicago-Naperville-Elgin, IL-IN-WI

(Thousands of dollars, except as noted.)

Year	Personal income, total	Derivation of personal income: Earnings by place of work: Nonfarm	Farm	Total	Less: Contributions for government social insurance	Plus: Adjustment for residence	Equals: Net earnings by place of residence	Plus: Dividends, interest, and rent	Plus: Personal current transfer receipts	Per capita personal income (dollars)	Population (persons)	Total employment
1970	39,042,067	33,236,351	86,734	33,323,085	2,242,085	-220,877	30,860,123	5,547,563	2,634,381	4,945	7,895,845	3,748,330
1971	41,693,277	35,164,992	126,592	35,291,584	2,443,040	-244,656	32,603,888	5,907,509	3,181,880	5,241	7,955,398	3,702,932
1972	45,123,683	38,201,968	88,392	38,290,360	2,799,518	-282,518	35,208,324	6,315,266	3,600,093	5,660	7,972,491	3,731,149
1973	49,732,970	42,130,409	182,890	42,313,299	3,579,992	-323,899	38,409,408	7,039,001	4,284,561	6,243	7,966,188	3,874,673
1974	54,553,129	45,828,588	148,968	45,977,556	4,034,979	-355,799	41,586,778	8,058,457	4,907,894	6,842	7,973,418	3,934,993
1975	58,433,668	47,799,792	229,126	48,028,918	4,091,563	-373,026	43,564,329	8,592,841	6,276,498	7,315	7,988,641	3,831,128
1976	64,192,731	52,906,047	158,417	53,064,464	4,622,553	-385,479	48,056,432	9,175,117	6,961,182	8,009	8,014,978	3,918,359
1977	71,017,879	59,068,433	161,840	59,230,273	5,147,532	-420,169	53,662,572	10,062,019	7,293,288	8,825	8,047,518	4,032,483
1978	78,718,037	65,965,004	168,100	66,133,104	5,908,887	-471,484	59,752,733	11,183,394	7,781,910	9,757	8,067,880	4,165,078
1979	86,310,936	72,420,326	198,815	72,619,141	6,739,277	-549,764	65,330,100	12,552,801	8,428,035	10,715	8,055,256	4,212,288
1980	94,204,059	76,333,919	73,393	76,407,312	7,075,545	-549,110	68,782,657	15,158,076	10,263,326	11,698	8,052,943	4,122,105
1981	103,527,771	81,715,572	171,801	81,887,373	8,119,333	-532,929	73,235,111	18,580,544	11,712,116	12,880	8,038,127	4,108,351
1982	109,443,065	83,822,464	126,959	83,949,423	8,481,571	-536,551	74,931,301	21,729,689	12,782,075	13,600	8,047,477	4,025,482
1983	115,057,533	87,965,256	-55,778	87,909,478	8,964,223	-522,985	78,422,270	22,991,648	13,643,615	14,302	8,044,580	3,992,825
1984	125,899,633	96,611,498	128,843	96,740,341	10,162,988	-549,846	86,027,507	25,872,775	13,999,351	15,605	8,067,923	4,150,208
1985	132,851,377	102,665,752	184,891	102,850,643	10,958,616	-559,835	91,332,192	26,934,053	14,585,132	16,458	8,072,070	4,206,304
1986	140,607,559	109,791,496	169,806	109,961,302	11,741,284	-592,810	97,627,208	27,845,344	15,135,007	17,406	8,078,098	4,297,096
1987	149,436,079	118,922,940	208,759	119,131,699	12,511,093	-687,125	105,933,481	28,138,127	15,364,471	18,451	8,099,059	4,429,471
1988	163,512,367	130,986,934	127,766	131,114,700	14,014,942	-769,460	116,330,298	31,299,810	15,882,259	20,145	8,116,756	4,560,934
1989	173,412,739	138,222,041	323,630	138,545,671	14,916,130	-824,615	122,804,926	33,702,646	16,905,167	21,269	8,153,134	4,646,403
1990	185,611,128	146,689,250	253,715	146,942,965	15,585,480	-888,115	130,469,370	36,616,019	18,525,739	22,627	8,203,210	4,719,223
1991	190,376,562	150,385,797	96,837	150,482,634	16,335,975	-929,968	133,216,691	37,175,619	19,984,252	22,924	8,304,560	4,690,670
1992	205,045,813	162,159,225	181,171	162,340,396	17,251,406	-1,051,239	144,037,751	38,059,629	22,948,433	24,373	8,412,788	4,668,331
1993	213,158,832	168,909,187	167,898	169,077,085	18,167,401	-1,147,986	149,761,698	39,205,178	24,191,956	25,039	8,512,911	4,745,984
1994	224,568,150	177,411,966	258,907	177,670,873	19,346,697	-1,259,920	157,064,256	42,197,004	25,306,890	26,095	8,605,735	4,860,416
1995	240,184,377	188,258,913	115,890	188,374,803	20,441,215	-1,377,373	166,556,215	46,770,801	26,857,361	27,628	8,693,383	4,989,418
1996	255,091,922	199,112,850	251,170	199,364,020	21,398,761	-1,524,040	176,441,219	50,340,806	28,309,897	29,046	8,782,253	5,072,565
1997	270,809,517	212,456,555	226,612	212,683,167	22,676,284	-1,679,736	188,327,147	53,715,838	28,766,532	30,556	8,862,719	5,159,787
1998	289,283,576	227,396,945	164,548	227,561,493	24,078,958	-1,891,667	201,590,868	58,444,041	29,248,667	32,325	8,949,190	5,291,308
1999	303,352,868	242,852,778	137,640	242,990,418	25,310,222	-2,081,340	215,598,856	57,988,959	29,765,053	33,573	9,035,654	5,357,397
2000	327,581,114	260,611,635	171,115	260,782,750	26,717,579	-2,294,321	231,770,850	63,946,924	31,863,340	35,946	9,113,234	5,462,648
2001	338,721,691	269,996,256	186,933	270,183,189	27,152,182	-2,482,647	240,548,360	63,681,353	34,491,978	36,940	9,169,580	5,450,274
2002	342,365,336	273,814,319	138,948	273,953,267	27,486,715	-2,609,873	243,856,679	61,342,120	37,166,537	37,189	9,206,032	5,386,970
2003	347,769,595	278,625,431	186,128	278,811,559	28,241,430	-2,713,726	247,856,403	61,256,612	38,656,580	37,665	9,233,303	5,387,036
2004	360,792,039	289,267,911	381,473	289,649,384	29,935,534	-2,899,935	256,813,915	64,020,287	39,957,837	38,960	9,260,676	5,446,236
2005	377,509,533	299,036,050	233,194	299,269,244	31,538,196	-3,150,483	264,580,565	69,007,377	43,921,591	40,696	9,276,302	5,528,271
2006	402,634,914	315,484,068	228,649	315,712,717	32,965,085	-3,408,703	279,338,929	78,773,688	44,522,297	43,305	9,297,749	5,627,640
2007	426,510,807	329,043,637	435,723	329,479,360	34,468,692	-3,548,065	291,462,603	85,895,391	49,152,813	45,679	9,337,140	5,733,943
2008	435,635,411	329,668,689	448,598	330,117,287	34,987,844	-3,552,535	291,576,908	89,654,959	54,403,544	46,420	9,384,555	5,715,115
2009	409,770,413	308,710,653	209,246	308,919,899	33,132,693	-2,999,146	272,788,060	75,607,008	61,375,345	43,456	9,429,498	5,515,295
2010	419,943,511	315,190,276	241,443	315,431,719	33,514,802	-3,002,149	278,914,768	74,054,910	66,973,833	44,319	9,475,529	5,470,741
2011	440,835,363	328,061,089	535,711	328,596,800	31,422,075	-3,131,511	294,043,214	82,656,037	64,136,112	46,280	9,525,380	5,581,961
2012	466,821,937	347,659,580	352,541	348,012,121	32,997,306	-3,275,236	311,739,579	90,684,689	64,397,669	48,768	9,572,335	5,643,174
2013	474,491,577	360,279,666	875,026	361,154,692	38,178,322	-3,293,269	319,683,101	87,852,460	66,956,016	49,353	9,614,209	5,730,604
2014	499,083,844	375,564,220	466,947	376,031,167	39,448,928	-3,275,002	333,307,237	97,518,952	68,257,655	51,751	9,643,982	5,831,946
2015	524,857,900	392,971,734	126,002	393,097,736	40,814,254	-3,581,176	348,702,306	103,551,404	72,604,190	54,358	9,655,619	5,963,824
2016	531,362,317	398,422,847	256,039	398,678,886	41,790,818	-3,669,004	353,219,064	104,985,539	73,157,714	55,027	9,656,432	6,044,064
2017	550,041,825	410,552,801	162,412	410,715,213	43,277,527	-3,914,747	363,522,939	111,110,774	75,408,112	56,964	9,655,887	6,077,118
2018	582,796,558	430,895,609	189,026	431,084,635	45,332,393	-4,112,406	381,639,836	123,493,042	77,663,680	60,416	9,646,352	6,136,370
2019	599,384,264	446,040,158	167,843	446,208,001	46,835,174	-4,250,531	395,122,296	123,476,890	80,785,078	62,215	9,634,076	6,136,139
2020	632,332,447	443,310,054	347,130	443,657,184	46,766,162	-4,113,427	392,777,595	125,731,990	113,822,862	65,862	9,600,822	5,862,023
2021	684,435,276	476,427,005	656,837	477,083,842	49,756,894	-4,432,862	422,894,086	136,861,983	124,679,207	71,898	9,519,538	6,068,361
2022	684,652,105	495,684,027	664,710	496,348,737	54,367,387	-4,960,266	437,021,084	144,876,750	102,754,271	72,512	9,441,957	6,358,080

Personal Income and Employment by Area: Chico, CA

(Thousands of dollars, except as noted.)

Year	Personal income, total	Derivation of personal income: Earnings by place of work: Nonfarm	Farm	Total	Less: Contributions for government social insurance	Plus: Adjustment for residence	Equals: Net earnings by place of residence	Plus: Dividends, interest, and rent	Plus: Personal current transfer receipts	Per capita personal income (dollars)	Population (persons)	Total employment
1970	381,579	226,169	24,434	250,603	14,475	6,603	242,731	75,745	63,103	3,716	102,682	36,830
1971	415,603	245,668	24,962	270,630	16,360	7,415	261,685	83,366	70,552	3,924	105,916	38,010
1972	461,533	273,571	28,920	302,491	19,113	8,632	292,010	92,503	77,020	4,093	112,775	40,361
1973	536,861	308,483	46,152	354,635	24,717	10,218	340,136	107,837	88,888	4,742	113,223	42,508
1974	630,119	341,944	70,657	412,601	28,409	12,178	396,370	125,323	108,426	5,372	117,295	44,300
1975	699,800	385,750	52,089	437,839	31,333	15,044	421,550	144,403	133,847	5,754	121,626	45,985
1976	766,349	448,738	29,862	478,600	36,886	17,894	459,608	157,418	149,323	6,112	125,377	48,998
1977	861,046	504,728	38,057	542,785	42,231	21,127	521,681	179,095	160,270	6,651	129,470	51,665
1978	974,489	579,081	31,548	610,629	49,225	25,708	587,112	210,537	176,840	7,394	131,797	54,807
1979	1,130,623	653,895	56,369	710,264	58,625	29,538	681,177	247,474	201,972	8,162	138,531	58,299
1980	1,321,327	741,991	61,407	803,398	65,175	32,436	770,659	310,512	240,156	9,123	144,828	60,482
1981	1,467,012	789,069	56,521	845,590	75,524	33,286	803,352	375,834	287,826	9,882	148,451	61,097
1982	1,532,373	803,809	42,256	846,065	78,860	34,777	801,982	408,146	322,245	10,087	151,913	59,921
1983	1,647,991	875,651	16,628	892,279	87,126	34,913	840,066	457,176	350,749	10,683	154,263	62,688
1984	1,801,550	965,397	31,211	996,608	99,960	37,453	934,101	494,746	372,703	11,490	156,791	64,197
1985	1,945,601	1,056,120	33,846	1,089,966	111,319	39,682	1,018,329	526,129	401,143	12,109	160,680	66,863
1986	2,078,259	1,150,414	27,616	1,178,030	122,664	44,484	1,099,850	545,655	432,754	12,732	163,233	68,099
1987	2,247,596	1,271,158	64,147	1,335,305	137,044	47,262	1,245,523	545,396	456,677	13,461	166,970	71,391
1988	2,466,028	1,411,174	80,281	1,491,455	157,578	51,066	1,384,943	589,178	491,907	14,345	171,909	76,545
1989	2,660,747	1,525,321	43,753	1,569,074	174,453	54,397	1,449,018	668,802	542,927	15,068	176,583	79,880
1990	2,872,522	1,672,337	63,550	1,735,887	187,601	59,937	1,608,223	683,061	581,238	15,641	183,652	84,276
1991	3,056,106	1,774,585	64,187	1,838,772	200,253	63,722	1,702,241	704,209	649,656	16,284	187,678	85,153
1992	3,237,077	1,859,396	80,716	1,940,112	209,022	67,796	1,798,886	704,577	733,614	17,001	190,409	84,849
1993	3,336,713	1,905,387	83,170	1,988,557	214,257	71,090	1,845,390	723,412	767,911	17,304	192,831	84,708
1994	3,476,118	2,041,969	64,102	2,106,071	228,399	73,431	1,951,103	736,107	788,908	17,858	194,648	88,262
1995	3,584,303	2,075,376	46,513	2,121,889	230,371	81,829	1,973,347	785,477	825,479	18,280	196,083	89,235
1996	3,790,496	2,194,163	58,420	2,252,583	234,610	86,177	2,104,150	826,068	860,278	19,307	196,327	91,583
1997	4,008,690	2,353,526	75,495	2,429,021	245,932	93,018	2,276,107	868,061	864,522	20,247	197,994	93,148
1998	4,195,559	2,499,915	14,212	2,514,127	256,909	101,508	2,358,726	926,526	910,307	20,979	199,993	94,625
1999	4,388,974	2,658,288	44,542	2,702,830	272,895	110,869	2,540,804	909,501	938,669	21,805	201,282	97,199
2000	4,708,483	2,890,524	59,537	2,950,061	292,111	123,407	2,781,357	951,117	976,009	23,103	203,807	98,639
2001	5,102,640	3,214,580	59,442	3,274,022	333,459	132,905	3,073,468	959,823	1,069,349	24,747	206,193	99,172
2002	5,243,959	3,426,217	65,900	3,492,117	360,907	134,230	3,265,440	854,877	1,123,642	25,076	209,120	101,094
2003	5,481,124	3,552,637	91,099	3,643,736	376,712	143,829	3,410,853	883,226	1,187,045	25,918	211,481	100,790
2004	5,827,903	3,752,243	101,965	3,854,208	414,686	151,381	3,590,903	977,524	1,259,476	27,353	213,065	101,811
2005	6,028,351	3,899,998	115,424	4,015,422	438,141	158,560	3,735,841	970,610	1,321,900	28,071	214,752	103,948
2006	6,459,357	4,105,600	77,841	4,183,441	446,594	168,029	3,904,876	1,122,490	1,431,991	29,791	216,824	105,269
2007	6,807,003	4,203,778	104,705	4,308,483	452,381	178,632	4,034,734	1,253,540	1,518,729	31,301	217,469	106,782
2008	6,966,490	4,101,684	151,537	4,253,221	455,681	186,897	3,984,437	1,287,292	1,694,761	31,806	219,034	103,872
2009	7,003,765	4,058,414	212,293	4,270,707	455,160	157,271	3,972,818	1,184,204	1,846,743	31,868	219,777	99,077
2010	7,254,896	4,216,245	201,860	4,418,105	453,040	146,938	4,112,003	1,137,782	2,005,111	32,994	219,882	97,798
2011	7,394,936	4,259,858	217,257	4,477,115	422,456	130,716	4,185,375	1,198,976	2,010,585	33,669	219,638	97,750
2012	7,606,689	4,335,685	236,477	4,572,162	434,134	118,984	4,257,012	1,302,498	2,047,179	34,536	220,253	100,632
2013	7,807,319	4,512,137	293,314	4,805,451	502,987	110,406	4,412,870	1,268,020	2,126,429	35,368	220,746	104,299
2014	8,138,129	4,679,772	186,811	4,866,583	523,792	113,292	4,456,083	1,400,989	2,281,057	36,603	222,335	107,432
2015	8,782,120	4,992,026	187,364	5,179,390	552,505	117,108	4,743,993	1,566,567	2,471,560	39,352	223,167	110,042
2016	9,126,674	5,219,876	207,316	5,427,192	582,027	116,176	4,961,341	1,610,615	2,554,718	40,662	224,454	112,493
2017	9,423,550	5,508,171	211,267	5,719,438	616,819	122,156	5,224,775	1,652,908	2,545,867	41,581	226,630	114,487
2018	9,718,118	5,797,720	188,273	5,985,993	657,328	114,985	5,443,650	1,625,838	2,648,630	42,630	227,962	114,493
2019	9,927,494	5,955,511	158,778	6,114,289	671,520	136,142	5,578,911	1,660,963	2,687,620	45,917	216,206	111,203
2020	10,781,637	5,977,127	182,078	6,159,205	673,381	160,460	5,646,284	1,686,879	3,448,474	51,308	210,135	105,087
2021	11,548,920	6,373,297	182,136	6,555,433	715,849	177,930	6,017,514	1,843,430	3,687,976	56,011	206,190	107,682
2022	11,396,345	6,675,355	142,150	6,817,505	774,438	181,922	6,224,989	1,934,794	3,236,562	54,974	207,303	111,904

Personal Income and Employment by Area: Cincinnati, OH-KY-IN

(Thousands of dollars, except as noted.)

Year	Personal income, total	Derivation of personal income: Earnings by place of work: Nonfarm	Farm	Total	Less: Contributions for government social insurance	Plus: Adjustment for residence	Equals: Net earnings by place of residence	Plus: Dividends, interest, and rent	Plus: Personal current transfer receipts	Per capita personal income (dollars)	Population (persons)	Total employment
1970	6,962,971	5,646,840	45,212	5,692,052	377,042	66,544	5,381,554	1,048,443	532,974	4,095	1,700,386	722,168
1971	7,282,265	5,827,200	39,033	5,866,233	400,201	62,832	5,528,864	1,122,811	630,590	4,263	1,708,315	710,549
1972	7,918,571	6,361,043	46,428	6,407,471	460,695	77,233	6,024,009	1,195,199	699,363	4,639	1,706,802	723,783
1973	8,776,113	7,083,326	60,756	7,144,082	592,264	86,603	6,638,421	1,323,581	814,111	5,111	1,717,232	753,831
1974	9,635,550	7,660,888	74,777	7,735,665	664,150	86,260	7,157,775	1,502,391	975,384	5,617	1,715,321	762,200
1975	10,377,321	8,058,247	77,220	8,135,467	681,367	86,177	7,540,277	1,621,240	1,215,804	6,058	1,713,012	746,270
1976	11,475,193	9,004,220	77,004	9,081,224	778,667	102,654	8,405,211	1,742,613	1,327,369	6,660	1,723,002	763,920
1977	12,757,286	10,107,282	69,823	10,177,105	875,638	117,625	9,419,092	1,932,663	1,405,531	7,359	1,733,497	791,799
1978	14,243,878	11,447,266	53,030	11,500,296	1,023,808	126,352	10,602,840	2,142,362	1,498,676	8,153	1,747,118	829,320
1979	15,857,630	12,734,028	47,722	12,781,750	1,190,240	135,243	11,726,753	2,418,191	1,712,686	9,036	1,754,927	848,775
1980	17,580,243	13,590,548	43,134	13,633,682	1,263,902	134,662	12,504,442	2,958,601	2,117,200	9,973	1,762,711	845,165
1981	19,293,598	14,510,897	44,997	14,555,894	1,440,928	148,910	13,263,876	3,667,200	2,362,522	10,919	1,766,939	834,439
1982	20,418,099	14,929,790	75,591	15,005,381	1,508,300	160,976	13,658,057	4,054,744	2,705,298	11,530	1,770,840	816,914
1983	21,722,342	15,887,675	-3,341	15,884,334	1,632,959	176,828	14,428,203	4,385,184	2,908,955	12,262	1,771,586	820,948
1984	23,897,695	17,549,929	65,888	17,615,817	1,838,330	208,902	15,986,389	4,857,961	3,053,345	13,429	1,779,589	855,071
1985	25,576,483	18,933,627	60,729	18,994,356	2,014,778	233,871	17,213,449	5,103,861	3,259,173	14,293	1,789,470	885,819
1986	27,150,405	20,312,563	19,882	20,332,445	2,231,345	245,879	18,346,979	5,379,815	3,423,611	15,063	1,802,446	914,135
1987	28,772,815	21,896,842	25,715	21,922,557	2,406,721	251,983	19,767,819	5,455,068	3,549,928	15,808	1,820,093	944,766
1988	31,089,586	23,531,339	26,770	23,558,109	2,658,623	293,451	21,192,937	6,131,253	3,765,396	16,977	1,831,240	975,835
1989	33,670,087	25,178,192	58,975	25,237,167	2,861,455	309,683	22,685,395	6,975,759	4,008,933	18,295	1,840,429	1,000,796
1990	36,311,819	27,088,683	57,260	27,145,943	3,141,930	313,856	24,317,869	7,550,651	4,443,299	19,556	1,856,819	1,020,680
1991	37,418,468	28,111,239	46,011	28,157,250	3,339,346	337,679	25,155,583	7,413,007	4,849,878	19,918	1,878,636	1,022,045
1992	40,151,478	30,350,198	76,293	30,426,491	3,586,154	352,199	27,192,536	7,631,559	5,327,383	21,150	1,898,372	1,032,358
1993	41,927,238	31,674,711	52,672	31,727,383	3,767,354	395,809	28,355,838	7,993,922	5,577,478	21,837	1,920,041	1,048,976
1994	44,134,636	33,389,413	64,820	33,454,233	4,041,262	434,941	29,847,912	8,494,152	5,792,572	22,825	1,933,569	1,077,549
1995	46,514,385	35,067,619	14,168	35,081,787	4,281,425	456,788	31,257,150	9,109,607	6,147,628	23,882	1,947,676	1,108,193
1996	49,486,770	37,198,680	44,221	37,242,901	4,490,799	464,228	33,216,330	9,874,842	6,395,598	25,236	1,960,948	1,137,723
1997	52,870,157	39,930,358	68,314	39,998,672	4,724,582	489,145	35,763,235	10,510,224	6,596,698	26,735	1,977,566	1,165,732
1998	56,914,237	43,304,226	47,151	43,351,377	4,984,849	490,273	38,856,801	11,379,982	6,677,454	28,560	1,992,781	1,201,335
1999	59,106,895	46,046,251	19,700	46,065,951	5,301,303	506,938	41,271,586	10,939,365	6,895,944	29,458	2,006,474	1,221,846
2000	62,459,722	48,369,062	87,037	48,456,099	5,424,065	527,228	43,559,262	11,518,700	7,381,760	30,893	2,021,806	1,242,902
2001	65,340,911	50,511,601	71,377	50,582,978	5,577,960	532,370	45,537,388	11,702,327	8,101,196	32,116	2,034,543	1,235,548
2002	66,886,328	51,896,506	15,309	51,911,815	5,680,052	538,741	46,770,504	11,433,969	8,681,855	32,741	2,042,871	1,226,692
2003	68,936,272	53,552,372	37,207	53,589,579	5,900,204	522,802	48,212,177	11,703,461	9,020,634	33,558	2,054,229	1,233,872
2004	72,560,326	56,153,311	94,396	56,247,707	6,229,567	495,314	50,513,454	12,544,863	9,502,009	35,128	2,065,605	1,249,240
2005	75,325,576	58,230,000	66,169	58,296,169	6,461,046	471,467	52,306,590	12,899,933	10,119,053	36,250	2,077,928	1,266,615
2006	79,545,959	60,234,350	52,988	60,287,338	6,691,484	585,249	54,181,103	14,613,685	10,751,171	38,004	2,093,082	1,276,807
2007	82,222,322	62,155,241	33,811	62,189,052	6,923,391	534,271	55,799,932	14,954,000	11,468,390	39,018	2,107,318	1,292,054
2008	85,294,938	62,867,269	30,060	62,897,329	7,152,015	521,830	56,267,144	15,934,460	13,093,334	40,264	2,118,370	1,287,559
2009	82,320,725	60,860,002	60,710	60,920,712	7,011,617	432,766	54,341,861	13,756,141	14,222,723	38,633	2,130,844	1,246,637
2010	85,410,916	63,302,649	39,339	63,341,988	7,111,628	401,354	56,631,714	13,627,599	15,151,603	39,883	2,141,549	1,236,569
2011	91,190,138	66,398,472	84,802	66,483,274	6,627,515	425,008	60,280,767	15,395,704	15,513,667	42,417	2,149,841	1,251,350
2012	94,746,532	69,068,844	58,895	69,127,739	6,845,320	433,800	62,716,219	16,765,487	15,264,826	43,888	2,158,821	1,262,587
2013	96,109,433	70,891,602	118,506	71,010,108	7,783,256	462,624	63,689,476	16,738,064	15,681,893	44,271	2,170,953	1,277,022
2014	100,490,828	73,503,626	27,052	73,530,678	8,082,720	464,248	65,912,206	17,990,155	16,588,467	46,017	2,183,787	1,298,608
2015	105,192,744	76,414,414	-23,080	76,391,334	8,404,073	460,601	68,447,862	19,417,134	17,327,748	47,906	2,195,796	1,322,790
2016	108,762,610	79,123,316	-3,434	79,119,882	8,816,800	419,309	70,722,391	20,257,472	17,782,747	49,237	2,208,942	1,345,122
2017	113,469,550	82,249,722	9,627	82,259,349	9,306,259	455,731	73,408,821	21,808,220	18,252,509	51,044	2,222,957	1,367,675
2018	118,192,689	85,650,066	13,707	85,663,773	9,561,362	477,078	76,579,489	22,817,774	18,795,426	52,888	2,234,793	1,392,364
2019	124,439,604	90,335,215	1,494	90,336,709	10,097,399	444,125	80,683,435	23,851,905	19,904,264	55,348	2,248,317	1,400,976
2020	132,831,175	91,701,916	62,328	91,764,244	10,281,695	484,177	81,966,726	24,153,758	26,710,691	58,803	2,258,932	1,359,528
2021	143,935,561	97,089,680	115,322	97,205,002	10,859,601	457,578	86,802,979	27,906,846	29,225,736	63,690	2,259,955	1,409,350
2022	147,802,274	103,370,015	69,650	103,439,665	11,832,172	441,541	92,049,034	30,550,871	25,202,369	65,253	2,265,051	1,471,537

Personal Income and Employment by Area: Clarksville, TN-KY

(Thousands of dollars, except as noted.)

Year	Personal income, total	Derivation of personal income								Per capita personal income (dollars)	Population (persons)	Total employment
		Earnings by place of work			Less: Contributions for government social insurance	Plus: Adjustment for residence	Equals: Net earnings by place of residence	Plus: Dividends, interest, and rent	Plus: Personal current transfer receipts			
		Nonfarm	Farm	Total								
1970	490,355	396,561	17,358	413,919	22,597	-20,244	371,078	82,034	37,243	3,614	135,674	67,161
1971	551,612	445,845	21,793	467,638	26,814	-23,505	417,319	90,834	43,459	3,949	139,678	67,997
1972	586,784	462,886	25,457	488,343	29,742	-15,595	443,006	95,873	47,905	4,241	138,363	66,676
1973	762,901	592,782	34,029	626,811	41,942	-10,739	574,130	132,165	56,606	4,985	153,046	77,311
1974	851,095	659,535	28,370	687,905	49,080	-10,269	628,556	154,342	68,197	5,381	158,160	78,459
1975	891,122	684,068	18,662	702,730	53,625	-10,271	638,834	166,243	86,045	5,706	156,167	76,095
1976	1,033,050	800,006	23,647	823,653	65,092	-10,748	747,813	192,767	92,470	6,457	159,985	82,730
1977	1,111,165	850,533	39,789	890,322	67,259	-15,425	807,638	204,656	98,871	6,722	165,292	81,993
1978	1,219,358	932,507	29,927	962,434	73,193	-15,600	873,641	237,965	107,752	7,340	166,124	83,177
1979	1,357,546	1,033,497	44,176	1,077,673	83,190	-23,804	970,679	262,365	124,502	8,050	168,638	83,604
1980	1,429,605	1,072,324	19,361	1,091,685	87,532	-21,065	983,088	295,492	151,025	8,476	168,672	82,777
1981	1,613,564	1,215,999	35,984	1,251,983	103,864	-47,761	1,100,358	340,848	172,358	9,496	169,914	83,529
1982	1,726,486	1,255,284	31,224	1,286,508	106,381	-27,534	1,152,593	381,629	192,264	9,876	174,812	82,011
1983	1,787,557	1,331,715	-15,170	1,316,545	118,027	-17,565	1,180,953	403,036	203,568	10,197	175,305	82,330
1984	1,962,179	1,424,681	33,356	1,458,037	131,157	-13,251	1,313,629	434,349	214,201	11,132	176,266	84,660
1985	2,096,563	1,510,911	31,026	1,541,937	141,721	1,895	1,402,111	466,171	228,281	11,602	180,704	85,825
1986	2,211,499	1,602,265	22,264	1,624,529	154,413	7,549	1,477,665	492,161	241,673	12,277	180,129	87,288
1987	2,367,296	1,725,968	25,947	1,751,915	167,303	12,394	1,597,006	517,365	252,925	13,063	181,228	90,662
1988	2,538,197	1,848,768	24,489	1,873,257	187,297	22,209	1,708,169	555,555	274,473	13,843	183,356	92,050
1989	2,700,768	1,905,236	37,793	1,943,029	198,673	35,585	1,779,941	615,444	305,383	14,519	186,014	93,715
1990	2,708,187	1,891,844	32,573	1,924,417	203,146	46,620	1,767,891	598,893	341,403	14,227	190,352	91,116
1991	2,910,209	2,039,778	28,348	2,068,126	222,477	45,887	1,891,536	625,903	392,770	15,336	189,761	91,608
1992	3,444,631	2,468,517	44,790	2,513,307	273,085	49,202	2,289,424	717,866	437,341	17,210	200,158	100,787
1993	3,594,345	2,576,450	35,578	2,612,028	289,812	48,832	2,371,048	764,370	458,927	17,799	201,941	103,964
1994	3,787,684	2,693,182	45,407	2,738,589	301,995	51,518	2,488,112	815,202	484,370	18,283	207,171	106,901
1995	4,072,655	2,860,925	32,587	2,893,512	315,640	65,031	2,642,903	890,419	539,333	19,225	211,843	111,466
1996	4,322,593	3,013,238	49,109	3,062,347	330,141	73,958	2,806,164	945,997	570,432	19,696	219,461	113,678
1997	4,485,931	3,142,792	45,364	3,188,156	344,017	90,886	2,935,025	944,503	606,403	20,029	223,972	116,127
1998	4,773,690	3,311,998	23,236	3,335,234	357,207	105,281	3,083,308	1,054,454	635,928	21,051	226,773	116,885
1999	5,065,470	3,577,627	3,879	3,581,506	386,471	108,128	3,303,163	1,087,509	674,798	22,084	229,368	121,792
2000	5,574,462	3,931,621	49,123	3,980,744	416,483	114,900	3,679,161	1,156,227	739,074	23,887	233,367	124,843
2001	5,621,782	3,959,206	46,793	4,005,999	433,231	96,449	3,669,217	1,131,617	820,948	23,867	235,549	125,242
2002	6,041,409	4,276,716	29,266	4,305,982	466,796	82,469	3,921,655	1,228,847	890,907	25,517	236,758	126,537
2003	6,480,838	4,623,466	39,321	4,662,787	495,887	67,266	4,234,166	1,289,618	957,054	27,395	236,569	127,605
2004	6,969,733	5,068,746	70,898	5,139,644	537,648	56,077	4,658,073	1,279,401	1,032,259	28,855	241,543	131,330
2005	7,843,916	5,865,043	92,639	5,957,682	614,371	3,997	5,347,308	1,380,702	1,115,906	31,316	250,476	138,276
2006	8,410,081	6,332,930	69,334	6,402,264	669,256	-14,474	5,718,534	1,481,532	1,210,015	33,601	250,292	141,083
2007	8,717,020	6,498,597	30,986	6,529,583	692,274	-16,323	5,820,986	1,578,399	1,317,635	33,418	260,846	143,448
2008	9,342,041	6,876,285	46,219	6,922,504	741,342	-52,064	6,129,098	1,685,502	1,527,441	35,721	261,530	143,774
2009	9,539,382	6,938,116	53,175	6,991,291	763,770	-33,035	6,194,486	1,685,626	1,659,270	35,357	269,798	141,680
2010	10,089,745	7,345,812	22,542	7,368,354	805,430	-53,645	6,509,279	1,746,780	1,833,686	36,671	275,142	143,637
2011	10,972,507	7,886,710	68,051	7,954,761	780,886	-72,659	7,101,216	1,937,196	1,934,095	39,425	278,310	147,222
2012	11,096,790	7,936,859	72,698	8,009,557	787,249	-44,778	7,177,530	1,961,530	1,957,730	38,389	289,063	147,356
2013	10,863,359	7,689,301	162,801	7,852,102	849,541	-15,821	6,986,740	1,840,818	2,035,801	37,742	287,831	147,259
2014	10,953,312	7,709,780	76,907	7,786,687	862,734	-5,515	6,918,438	1,885,726	2,149,148	37,408	292,807	148,730
2015	11,320,766	7,881,719	59,804	7,941,523	883,812	19,861	7,077,572	1,907,640	2,335,554	38,138	296,839	151,147
2016	11,472,230	7,842,518	36,229	7,878,747	869,161	40,676	7,050,262	1,966,491	2,455,477	38,445	298,403	150,243
2017	11,898,240	8,144,088	59,070	8,203,158	909,745	60,669	7,354,082	1,933,529	2,610,629	39,106	304,258	154,817
2018	12,353,236	8,485,399	25,837	8,511,236	940,582	58,101	7,628,755	1,986,593	2,737,888	39,741	310,842	157,941
2019	12,993,469	8,887,950	52,206	8,940,156	973,369	64,059	8,030,846	2,022,225	2,940,398	41,084	316,267	160,903
2020	14,345,838	9,356,658	57,794	9,414,452	1,026,771	74,741	8,462,422	2,110,516	3,772,900	44,577	321,824	163,004
2021	15,815,286	10,231,667	120,535	10,352,202	1,092,087	101,295	9,361,410	2,099,644	4,354,232	48,057	329,094	170,434
2022	15,962,151	10,899,952	78,129	10,978,081	1,182,450	143,088	9,938,719	2,204,922	3,818,510	47,421	336,605	177,615

Personal Income and Employment by Area: Cleveland, TN

(Thousands of dollars, except as noted.)

Year	Personal income, total	Derivation of personal income: Earnings by place of work: Nonfarm	Farm	Total	Less: Contributions for government social insurance	Plus: Adjustment for residence	Equals: Net earnings by place of residence	Plus: Dividends, interest, and rent	Plus: Personal current transfer receipts	Per capita personal income (dollars)	Population (persons)	Total employment
1970	194,832	162,070	1,834	163,904	10,907	2,891	155,888	21,776	17,168	3,100	62,840	28,344
1971	219,046	182,333	1,642	183,975	12,691	3,605	174,889	24,270	19,887	3,352	65,350	29,244
1972	250,052	209,708	2,478	212,186	15,388	4,579	201,377	26,910	21,765	3,719	67,241	31,705
1973	289,286	241,832	4,671	246,503	20,176	5,569	231,896	31,443	25,947	4,154	69,648	34,135
1974	306,477	248,205	1,718	249,923	21,519	7,385	235,789	36,749	33,939	4,275	71,692	32,962
1975	328,845	256,727	1,754	258,481	21,615	5,185	242,051	42,087	44,707	4,542	72,406	30,714
1976	373,202	293,661	2,363	296,024	25,427	10,653	281,250	44,653	47,299	5,048	73,937	32,387
1977	405,364	307,285	3,381	310,666	26,937	20,899	304,628	49,130	51,606	5,342	75,881	33,401
1978	463,234	361,237	1,083	362,320	32,219	21,888	351,989	55,502	55,743	5,966	77,652	35,414
1979	524,550	404,388	2,423	406,811	37,619	26,497	395,689	62,883	65,978	6,587	79,631	36,135
1980	600,596	451,872	4,438	456,310	41,941	26,364	440,733	77,210	82,653	7,382	81,363	36,047
1981	679,663	507,718	7,806	515,524	50,809	27,805	492,520	95,593	91,550	8,282	82,061	36,618
1982	724,701	528,431	7,029	535,460	53,899	29,804	511,365	112,085	101,251	8,823	82,139	36,932
1983	798,337	594,647	3,427	598,074	60,906	29,205	566,373	123,700	108,264	9,683	82,449	37,384
1984	884,974	654,245	11,349	665,594	69,126	33,524	629,992	139,834	115,148	10,579	83,652	39,385
1985	947,130	704,741	7,979	712,720	75,125	35,663	673,258	151,471	122,401	11,210	84,486	39,808
1986	1,011,388	736,719	12,234	748,953	80,203	47,574	716,324	163,264	131,800	11,918	84,865	40,542
1987	1,095,529	809,196	6,728	815,924	86,928	54,090	783,086	174,614	137,829	12,837	85,340	42,402
1988	1,182,692	859,208	7,790	866,998	94,423	71,293	843,868	189,151	149,673	13,672	86,505	43,780
1989	1,295,862	916,032	18,674	934,706	100,873	80,223	914,056	216,246	165,560	14,912	86,902	44,308
1990	1,361,814	962,812	16,411	979,223	106,456	81,257	954,024	222,714	185,076	15,531	87,684	43,815
1991	1,436,697	1,013,578	20,118	1,033,696	114,229	77,395	996,862	224,052	215,783	16,151	88,954	43,128
1992	1,585,145	1,123,040	19,717	1,142,757	124,999	82,863	1,100,621	230,849	253,675	17,551	90,317	44,380
1993	1,645,973	1,150,811	20,987	1,171,798	129,003	97,991	1,140,786	234,133	271,054	17,895	91,979	45,808
1994	1,755,368	1,238,505	17,079	1,255,584	140,271	98,985	1,214,298	260,130	280,940	18,842	93,161	46,481
1995	1,851,035	1,300,093	10,124	1,310,217	146,305	101,286	1,265,198	278,671	307,166	19,457	95,133	48,418
1996	1,991,162	1,406,596	13,214	1,419,810	154,757	100,678	1,365,731	297,843	327,588	20,560	96,848	50,123
1997	2,150,512	1,557,220	5,690	1,562,910	166,490	97,664	1,494,084	311,907	344,521	21,501	100,019	51,829
1998	2,320,903	1,688,769	10,176	1,698,945	173,033	107,919	1,633,831	332,669	354,403	22,809	101,755	51,846
1999	2,385,248	1,740,269	8,715	1,748,984	182,631	111,191	1,677,544	337,765	369,939	23,162	102,982	52,450
2000	2,432,166	1,722,547	6,423	1,728,970	182,997	128,758	1,674,731	358,604	398,831	23,310	104,338	52,528
2001	2,454,637	1,655,376	25,895	1,681,271	185,478	140,352	1,636,145	372,847	445,645	23,312	105,295	53,704
2002	2,514,246	1,720,472	4,486	1,724,958	192,977	155,151	1,687,132	350,737	476,377	23,724	105,979	53,650
2003	2,661,845	1,790,288	6,119	1,796,407	200,262	186,227	1,782,372	370,263	509,210	24,934	106,754	54,089
2004	2,837,346	1,937,329	19,793	1,957,122	215,198	176,819	1,918,743	369,833	548,770	26,248	108,099	55,469
2005	2,941,603	1,962,357	21,960	1,984,317	218,539	205,077	1,970,855	380,062	590,686	26,886	109,410	55,736
2006	3,142,598	2,043,492	6,323	2,049,815	226,713	272,910	2,096,012	405,107	641,479	28,267	111,177	56,348
2007	3,334,065	2,105,510	3,833	2,109,343	234,819	296,565	2,171,089	455,338	707,638	29,522	112,935	56,070
2008	3,531,494	2,112,729	12,530	2,125,259	239,437	330,801	2,216,623	514,814	800,057	30,895	114,306	55,211
2009	3,452,901	2,013,269	19,158	2,032,427	236,872	298,299	2,093,854	497,805	861,242	30,002	115,090	53,670
2010	3,580,997	2,097,918	26,812	2,124,730	241,511	299,957	2,183,176	443,110	954,711	30,894	115,911	53,272
2011	3,794,590	2,228,961	25,800	2,254,761	230,373	301,588	2,325,976	502,389	966,225	32,530	116,648	54,836
2012	4,007,197	2,457,711	27,371	2,485,082	245,603	255,892	2,495,371	537,615	974,211	34,013	117,815	56,878
2013	4,032,657	2,525,704	47,108	2,572,812	287,572	199,708	2,484,948	554,147	993,562	33,998	118,613	60,403
2014	4,141,700	2,634,587	43,748	2,678,335	298,037	170,914	2,551,212	565,041	1,025,447	34,594	119,723	62,289
2015	4,304,664	2,669,027	33,687	2,702,714	303,768	231,905	2,630,851	597,780	1,076,033	35,614	120,870	61,958
2016	4,378,042	2,703,362	14,306	2,717,668	311,200	253,311	2,659,779	598,817	1,119,446	36,020	121,546	62,671
2017	4,499,654	2,728,472	17,261	2,745,733	317,409	293,666	2,721,990	612,603	1,165,061	36,680	122,674	62,330
2018	4,735,750	2,871,909	14,460	2,886,369	331,786	323,085	2,877,668	627,683	1,230,399	38,031	124,524	62,665
2019	4,905,017	3,036,588	6,366	3,042,954	352,297	277,612	2,968,269	641,796	1,294,952	39,113	125,405	64,466
2020	5,349,006	3,241,733	-8,284	3,233,449	380,196	264,030	3,117,283	655,911	1,575,812	42,322	126,388	65,230
2021	5,804,959	3,363,830	30,660	3,394,490	388,277	375,728	3,381,941	644,361	1,778,657	45,510	127,553	65,238
2022	5,940,846	3,521,232	78,959	3,600,191	418,145	506,326	3,688,372	689,684	1,562,790	46,240	128,479	66,999

Personal Income and Employment by Area: Cleveland-Elyria, OH

(Thousands of dollars, except as noted.)

Year	Personal income, total	Derivation of personal income: Earnings by place of work: Nonfarm	Farm	Total	Less: Contributions for government social insurance	Plus: Adjustment for residence	Equals: Net earnings by place of residence	Plus: Dividends, interest, and rent	Plus: Personal current transfer receipts	Per capita personal income (dollars)	Population (persons)	Total employment
1970	10,739,310	9,265,524	19,843	9,285,367	615,025	-286,840	8,383,502	1,563,124	792,684	4,631	2,318,811	1,076,814
1971	11,259,149	9,579,995	26,837	9,606,832	653,378	-305,674	8,647,780	1,662,229	949,140	4,869	2,312,528	1,044,149
1972	12,122,234	10,377,214	28,586	10,405,800	747,243	-333,289	9,325,268	1,751,339	1,045,627	5,322	2,277,630	1,053,824
1973	13,319,112	11,511,398	20,630	11,532,028	964,373	-386,076	10,181,579	1,933,610	1,203,923	5,878	2,266,062	1,095,299
1974	14,613,538	12,493,333	27,215	12,520,548	1,082,844	-437,928	10,999,776	2,199,298	1,414,464	6,502	2,247,641	1,114,246
1975	15,457,357	12,922,717	37,515	12,960,232	1,088,512	-478,207	11,393,513	2,321,621	1,742,223	6,908	2,237,565	1,077,447
1976	16,767,087	14,216,214	39,604	14,255,818	1,227,678	-556,120	12,472,020	2,447,461	1,847,606	7,553	2,219,936	1,088,064
1977	18,581,102	15,973,198	35,760	16,008,958	1,377,706	-655,152	13,976,100	2,664,318	1,940,684	8,394	2,213,651	1,114,106
1978	20,527,552	17,785,247	35,968	17,821,215	1,585,566	-765,894	15,469,755	2,964,130	2,093,667	9,302	2,206,866	1,148,501
1979	22,410,000	19,369,101	28,215	19,397,316	1,799,238	-879,608	16,718,470	3,323,898	2,367,632	10,258	2,184,615	1,159,618
1980	24,320,163	20,080,895	27,342	20,108,237	1,851,713	-945,404	17,311,120	3,984,354	3,024,689	11,195	2,172,438	1,133,733
1981	26,476,300	21,402,715	31,574	21,434,289	2,110,018	-1,026,226	18,298,045	4,857,442	3,320,813	12,245	2,162,129	1,112,891
1982	27,688,069	21,587,658	29,419	21,617,077	2,157,804	-1,021,570	18,437,703	5,392,690	3,857,676	12,874	2,150,690	1,072,341
1983	29,114,715	22,541,029	29,722	22,570,751	2,293,980	-1,053,273	19,223,498	5,740,592	4,150,625	13,563	2,146,550	1,058,826
1984	31,870,274	24,857,262	34,010	24,891,272	2,586,673	-1,156,170	21,148,429	6,401,735	4,320,110	14,884	2,141,290	1,090,297
1985	33,837,047	26,504,152	30,694	26,534,846	2,793,441	-1,228,522	22,512,883	6,743,300	4,580,864	15,877	2,131,240	1,106,952
1986	35,166,520	27,642,351	28,348	27,670,699	2,998,393	-1,261,039	23,411,267	6,883,462	4,871,791	16,583	2,120,606	1,123,074
1987	36,751,458	29,256,843	43,283	29,300,126	3,175,125	-1,319,711	24,805,290	6,897,834	5,048,334	17,386	2,113,892	1,145,205
1988	39,840,171	31,881,886	72,163	31,954,049	3,540,963	-1,427,920	26,985,166	7,576,651	5,278,354	18,953	2,102,075	1,171,445
1989	42,372,820	33,661,202	92,851	33,754,053	3,777,616	-1,526,393	28,450,044	8,295,704	5,627,072	20,142	2,103,702	1,194,435
1990	45,292,614	35,534,500	91,401	35,625,901	4,077,758	-1,658,953	29,889,190	9,208,212	6,195,212	21,524	2,104,288	1,206,598
1991	45,912,309	35,967,900	64,799	36,032,699	4,222,480	-1,660,691	30,149,528	9,103,330	6,659,451	21,682	2,117,512	1,192,489
1992	48,079,095	37,974,810	120,349	38,095,159	4,431,334	-1,781,332	31,882,493	8,965,889	7,230,713	22,561	2,131,036	1,181,133
1993	49,946,804	39,298,637	115,739	39,414,376	4,636,173	-1,807,043	32,971,160	9,420,027	7,555,617	23,335	2,140,398	1,195,585
1994	52,445,085	41,807,523	110,591	41,918,114	4,994,766	-1,965,583	34,957,765	9,685,351	7,801,969	24,435	2,146,303	1,223,705
1995	54,996,370	43,425,785	111,046	43,536,831	5,246,490	-2,075,032	36,215,309	10,535,877	8,245,184	25,577	2,150,203	1,251,048
1996	57,199,234	44,919,621	110,572	45,030,193	5,370,277	-2,208,654	37,451,262	11,250,011	8,497,961	26,560	2,153,598	1,268,542
1997	60,153,642	47,458,441	111,744	47,570,185	5,550,527	-2,497,579	39,522,079	11,875,439	8,756,124	27,944	2,152,676	1,290,060
1998	63,385,302	49,987,166	118,657	50,105,823	5,695,634	-2,704,627	41,705,562	12,898,071	8,781,669	29,460	2,151,568	1,305,773
1999	64,930,938	52,420,534	123,577	52,544,111	5,938,787	-3,063,285	43,542,039	12,371,767	9,017,132	30,201	2,149,943	1,324,094
2000	68,179,619	54,993,962	97,698	55,091,660	6,021,111	-3,318,379	45,752,170	12,891,504	9,535,945	31,748	2,147,532	1,341,671
2001	68,275,975	54,501,337	103,652	54,604,989	6,010,848	-3,400,755	45,193,386	12,855,977	10,226,612	31,878	2,141,787	1,322,201
2002	68,429,031	54,470,111	94,179	54,564,290	5,921,884	-3,328,347	45,314,059	12,308,578	10,806,394	32,033	2,136,201	1,294,120
2003	69,850,981	56,309,861	71,326	56,381,187	6,173,895	-3,415,938	46,791,354	11,715,634	11,343,993	32,776	2,131,150	1,291,759
2004	72,511,212	58,613,951	116,004	58,729,955	6,527,212	-3,630,983	48,571,760	12,145,235	11,794,217	34,156	2,122,934	1,296,313
2005	74,596,288	59,576,029	125,297	59,701,326	6,674,337	-3,622,100	49,404,889	12,844,000	12,347,399	35,325	2,111,699	1,299,446
2006	78,748,078	62,421,683	85,721	62,507,404	6,958,954	-3,847,747	51,700,703	14,198,776	12,848,599	37,510	2,099,415	1,309,410
2007	82,385,479	64,334,031	101,949	64,435,980	7,125,739	-3,868,563	53,441,678	15,340,586	13,603,215	39,389	2,091,596	1,316,312
2008	85,254,771	65,011,829	92,038	65,103,867	7,289,132	-3,622,716	54,192,019	15,946,739	15,116,013	40,887	2,085,110	1,302,328
2009	81,233,592	61,229,902	102,605	61,332,507	6,984,719	-3,330,091	51,017,697	14,070,558	16,145,337	39,035	2,081,063	1,251,116
2010	82,441,651	62,116,826	103,667	62,220,493	7,008,143	-3,382,228	51,830,122	13,666,420	16,945,109	39,702	2,076,521	1,243,053
2011	87,601,039	65,312,554	115,500	65,428,054	6,621,426	-3,617,292	55,189,336	15,084,150	17,327,553	42,231	2,074,333	1,260,054
2012	91,344,067	68,266,885	129,544	68,396,429	6,872,132	-3,917,405	57,606,892	16,695,599	17,041,576	44,034	2,074,413	1,277,761
2013	92,275,125	70,527,343	119,561	70,646,904	7,742,517	-3,993,295	58,911,092	15,933,259	17,430,774	44,341	2,081,047	1,290,737
2014	96,305,282	72,418,993	94,139	72,513,132	7,904,376	-3,901,242	60,707,514	17,305,665	18,292,103	46,177	2,085,571	1,299,891
2015	99,383,124	74,494,746	85,723	74,580,469	8,113,960	-3,848,065	62,618,444	17,948,323	18,816,357	47,631	2,086,509	1,313,567
2016	101,756,151	75,783,593	87,112	75,870,705	8,400,530	-3,797,970	63,672,205	18,835,939	19,248,007	48,746	2,087,456	1,323,995
2017	105,253,943	78,585,374	81,208	78,666,582	8,867,546	-3,951,115	65,847,921	19,689,339	19,716,683	50,412	2,087,871	1,329,843
2018	109,128,922	80,738,753	78,881	80,817,634	9,026,542	-4,284,138	67,506,954	21,427,016	20,194,952	52,261	2,088,149	1,349,051
2019	112,881,734	83,119,357	76,829	83,196,186	9,417,797	-4,534,745	69,243,644	22,558,354	21,079,736	54,078	2,087,392	1,351,461
2020	118,688,354	82,816,990	87,262	82,904,252	9,440,199	-4,753,714	68,710,339	21,865,395	28,112,620	56,884	2,086,509	1,300,695
2021	127,944,315	88,659,839	105,431	88,765,270	10,064,567	-5,190,641	73,510,062	24,358,385	30,075,868	61,714	2,073,183	1,340,432
2022	129,815,209	93,567,663	76,387	93,644,050	10,913,672	-5,574,438	77,155,940	26,584,572	26,074,697	62,921	2,063,132	1,390,752

Personal Income and Employment by Area: Coeur d'Alene, ID

(Thousands of dollars, except as noted.)

		Derivation of personal income										
		Earnings by place of work										
Year	Personal income, total	Nonfarm	Farm	Total	Less: Contributions for government social insurance	Plus: Adjustment for residence	Equals: Net earnings by place of residence	Plus: Dividends, interest, and rent	Plus: Personal current transfer receipts	Per capita personal income (dollars)	Population (persons)	Total employment
1970	128,305	73,697	2,621	76,318	5,381	19,416	90,353	23,733	14,219	3,606	35,579	12,625
1971	144,854	83,293	2,309	85,602	6,311	21,534	100,825	27,061	16,968	3,953	36,644	13,312
1972	167,854	99,844	3,474	103,318	7,992	23,533	118,859	29,712	19,283	4,283	39,195	14,772
1973	189,600	119,658	-2,546	117,112	11,145	26,406	132,373	34,293	22,934	4,459	42,519	16,223
1974	226,270	132,897	5,892	138,789	12,506	31,147	157,430	40,687	28,153	5,073	44,600	17,126
1975	258,825	146,483	4,059	150,542	13,391	36,093	173,244	49,070	36,511	5,464	47,365	17,382
1976	299,824	175,897	4,336	180,233	16,255	41,164	205,142	54,520	40,162	6,140	48,828	19,043
1977	345,686	209,355	2,752	212,107	19,534	45,764	238,337	64,401	42,948	6,704	51,565	20,572
1978	414,419	253,716	4,235	257,951	23,770	55,165	289,346	77,393	47,680	7,482	55,386	22,466
1979	475,270	289,101	3,523	292,624	28,596	64,247	328,275	90,174	56,821	8,093	58,728	24,047
1980	527,946	302,354	3,992	306,346	29,744	73,117	349,719	108,936	69,291	8,800	59,996	23,469
1981	575,627	315,204	2,922	318,126	33,338	79,541	364,329	131,263	80,035	9,463	60,827	23,099
1982	600,132	310,392	2,918	313,310	33,498	71,656	351,468	152,492	96,172	9,612	62,436	22,576
1983	679,315	362,177	5,631	367,808	39,518	76,449	404,739	173,483	101,093	10,785	62,987	24,041
1984	747,335	407,933	4,995	412,928	46,351	83,776	450,353	193,221	103,761	11,411	65,494	26,144
1985	793,045	426,584	3,827	430,411	49,274	85,468	466,605	214,207	112,233	11,875	66,783	26,831
1986	826,426	446,205	3,458	449,663	52,293	87,858	485,228	221,920	119,278	12,379	66,761	27,960
1987	852,239	475,753	147	475,900	54,613	94,272	515,559	213,063	123,617	12,881	66,160	29,674
1988	940,485	527,218	3,150	530,368	63,210	106,935	574,093	231,820	134,572	14,067	66,859	31,474
1989	1,047,408	591,079	3,829	594,908	72,137	117,228	639,999	259,183	148,226	15,463	67,738	33,071
1990	1,149,314	667,785	5,524	673,309	85,508	127,284	715,085	271,426	162,803	16,316	70,443	35,431
1991	1,248,152	737,398	2,405	739,803	96,752	127,420	770,471	291,924	185,757	16,879	73,946	38,117
1992	1,419,768	860,885	4,753	865,638	110,936	138,587	893,289	318,311	208,168	18,301	77,577	41,164
1993	1,574,843	968,572	5,297	973,869	125,377	143,321	991,813	353,947	229,083	19,053	82,654	44,016
1994	1,733,307	1,088,379	570	1,088,949	141,171	157,630	1,105,408	384,422	243,477	19,686	88,046	48,249
1995	1,862,878	1,132,332	339	1,132,671	148,654	170,330	1,154,347	438,163	270,368	20,101	92,677	50,172
1996	2,004,172	1,206,336	1,380	1,207,716	154,829	192,665	1,245,552	464,865	293,755	20,749	96,590	51,999
1997	2,122,697	1,275,589	-898	1,274,691	163,795	214,740	1,325,636	487,049	310,012	21,204	100,108	54,341
1998	2,313,805	1,401,944	1,090	1,403,034	175,767	244,964	1,472,231	514,827	326,747	22,526	102,717	55,676
1999	2,436,545	1,507,297	1,902	1,509,199	183,862	267,873	1,593,210	491,805	351,530	22,911	106,346	57,772
2000	2,625,426	1,659,765	2,872	1,662,637	198,607	240,520	1,704,550	534,648	386,228	23,979	109,487	59,995
2001	2,816,828	1,796,108	3,530	1,799,638	210,469	227,309	1,816,478	555,027	445,323	25,254	111,542	61,217
2002	2,911,908	1,892,911	4,042	1,896,953	223,627	222,316	1,895,642	532,959	483,307	25,618	113,667	62,925
2003	3,082,430	1,976,515	3,167	1,979,682	238,945	231,102	1,971,839	596,037	514,554	26,456	116,512	64,170
2004	3,367,638	2,160,346	4,144	2,164,490	264,732	239,476	2,139,234	669,939	558,465	27,831	121,002	68,872
2005	3,697,923	2,375,331	3,240	2,378,571	296,552	228,420	2,310,439	777,951	609,533	29,355	125,972	73,508
2006	4,012,075	2,653,944	1,703	2,655,647	332,856	208,244	2,531,035	827,051	653,989	30,979	129,510	77,157
2007	4,287,499	2,774,604	2,008	2,776,612	352,920	226,913	2,650,605	925,829	711,065	32,283	132,811	80,539
2008	4,436,177	2,725,477	-1,491	2,723,986	353,949	264,131	2,634,168	972,750	829,259	32,709	135,627	80,342
2009	4,346,267	2,558,709	314	2,559,023	341,996	313,562	2,530,589	901,136	914,542	31,631	137,407	76,282
2010	4,485,713	2,602,465	-2,181	2,600,284	360,044	336,176	2,576,416	900,304	1,008,993	32,294	138,902	75,106
2011	4,770,239	2,638,352	3,463	2,641,815	329,749	414,878	2,726,944	1,020,553	1,022,742	33,784	141,197	75,833
2012	5,045,131	2,674,209	4,160	2,678,369	333,354	547,286	2,892,301	1,106,526	1,046,304	35,391	142,556	75,147
2013	5,279,971	2,875,644	2,715	2,878,359	385,665	531,744	3,024,438	1,175,251	1,080,282	36,519	144,581	77,748
2014	5,629,670	3,017,228	1,758	3,018,986	402,400	563,298	3,179,884	1,284,794	1,164,992	38,185	147,432	80,319
2015	6,019,691	3,215,269	2,036	3,217,305	424,902	571,714	3,364,117	1,415,856	1,239,718	39,997	150,504	82,700
2016	6,309,928	3,414,836	2,000	3,416,836	450,311	608,569	3,575,094	1,433,165	1,301,669	40,880	154,354	85,111
2017	6,763,553	3,713,455	43	3,713,498	484,913	613,840	3,842,425	1,539,299	1,381,829	42,553	158,944	88,108
2018	7,295,195	4,058,877	186	4,059,063	522,324	673,291	4,210,030	1,610,695	1,474,470	44,794	162,860	91,565
2019	8,002,439	4,376,557	60	4,376,617	554,756	785,178	4,607,039	1,778,516	1,616,884	47,785	167,469	93,471
2020	8,982,647	4,805,504	2,982	4,808,486	611,607	817,511	5,014,390	1,903,084	2,065,173	51,986	172,790	95,356
2021	10,385,723	5,450,647	774	5,451,421	673,927	888,358	5,665,852	2,373,532	2,346,339	57,652	180,146	101,710
2022	11,101,780	5,809,527	1,553	5,811,080	734,174	1,107,563	6,184,469	2,738,469	2,178,842	60,474	183,578	105,602

Personal Income and Employment by Area: College Station-Bryan, TX

(Thousands of dollars, except as noted.)

Year	Personal income, total	Derivation of personal income: Earnings by place of work: Nonfarm	Farm	Total	Less: Contributions for government social insurance	Plus: Adjustment for residence	Equals: Net earnings by place of residence	Plus: Dividends, interest, and rent	Plus: Personal current transfer receipts	Per capita personal income (dollars)	Population (persons)	Total employment
1970	239,328	175,727	9,198	184,925	11,227	67	173,765	40,225	25,338	2,901	82,495	33,470
1971	273,855	204,457	8,439	212,896	13,554	-418	198,924	45,721	29,210	3,229	84,820	35,764
1972	313,756	228,045	17,136	245,181	15,656	-159	229,366	52,246	32,144	3,483	90,094	37,801
1973	349,995	253,478	14,939	268,417	19,832	889	249,474	62,083	38,438	3,687	94,934	39,127
1974	384,608	276,825	7,244	284,069	22,472	2,363	263,960	74,108	46,540	3,861	99,612	39,846
1975	439,121	317,036	-2,657	314,379	25,202	3,532	292,709	87,888	58,524	4,449	98,699	41,325
1976	508,891	370,375	3,632	374,007	29,612	4,330	348,725	96,480	63,686	4,983	102,118	44,451
1977	579,396	424,639	6,122	430,761	34,291	5,755	402,225	109,327	67,844	5,486	105,615	48,208
1978	671,254	496,345	7,202	503,547	40,972	6,793	469,368	126,102	75,784	5,992	112,021	51,286
1979	763,458	565,527	7,896	573,423	48,901	9,181	533,703	144,030	85,725	6,520	117,089	53,353
1980	903,261	667,756	194	667,950	57,432	11,575	622,093	181,352	99,816	7,362	122,685	57,181
1981	1,142,976	871,905	14,397	886,302	81,533	-5,411	799,358	230,587	113,031	8,735	130,852	63,834
1982	1,295,885	957,990	9,929	967,919	90,480	-3,472	873,967	293,544	128,374	9,096	142,471	66,877
1983	1,410,376	1,031,014	5,877	1,036,891	94,658	-5,074	937,159	332,528	140,689	9,594	147,011	68,500
1984	1,550,981	1,123,356	4,258	1,127,614	103,557	-795	1,023,262	377,550	150,169	10,357	149,749	70,778
1985	1,621,529	1,149,608	2,369	1,151,977	105,487	2,815	1,049,305	412,024	160,200	10,617	152,724	71,201
1986	1,625,091	1,154,713	-8,884	1,145,829	104,172	4,815	1,046,472	405,208	173,411	10,557	153,931	69,985
1987	1,661,053	1,171,910	5,750	1,177,660	103,761	6,139	1,080,038	398,513	182,502	10,909	152,259	71,753
1988	1,766,651	1,272,115	3,305	1,275,420	119,754	2,524	1,158,190	416,464	191,997	11,709	150,882	74,831
1989	1,925,288	1,374,458	11,017	1,385,475	131,463	-3,105	1,250,907	460,435	213,946	12,803	150,375	77,282
1990	2,042,920	1,480,269	13,272	1,493,541	139,619	-1,242	1,352,680	454,293	235,947	13,485	151,495	79,083
1991	2,165,635	1,570,220	14,666	1,584,886	152,142	1,780	1,434,524	472,944	258,167	14,057	154,062	81,933
1992	2,315,937	1,691,121	20,737	1,711,858	163,031	147	1,548,974	470,119	296,844	14,629	158,308	83,359
1993	2,484,768	1,819,336	18,552	1,837,888	175,008	-4,050	1,658,830	514,735	311,203	15,083	164,742	87,560
1994	2,598,504	1,925,310	18,169	1,943,479	188,508	-6,590	1,748,381	524,226	325,897	15,475	167,911	90,558
1995	2,738,593	1,990,436	11,857	2,002,293	195,985	-7,923	1,798,385	578,012	362,196	16,052	170,608	92,132
1996	2,883,520	2,093,838	-883	2,092,955	204,183	-9,269	1,879,503	615,814	388,203	16,731	172,341	93,646
1997	3,155,470	2,321,249	8,985	2,330,234	224,079	-10,138	2,096,017	650,394	409,059	17,919	176,098	97,342
1998	3,348,430	2,503,138	-1,658	2,501,480	240,604	-14,063	2,246,813	677,537	424,080	18,654	179,498	100,944
1999	3,524,249	2,652,241	27,165	2,679,406	252,813	-16,569	2,410,024	678,723	435,502	19,329	182,327	100,840
2000	3,789,486	2,847,417	11,517	2,858,934	269,367	-19,758	2,569,809	754,809	464,868	20,400	185,760	104,085
2001	4,077,962	3,086,973	26,826	3,113,799	284,046	-24,635	2,805,118	766,209	506,635	21,655	188,315	107,288
2002	4,225,549	3,181,198	45,586	3,226,784	291,566	-31,571	2,903,647	766,986	554,916	22,006	192,016	108,136
2003	4,585,694	3,396,878	62,901	3,459,779	316,055	-49,014	3,094,710	884,220	606,764	23,368	196,234	109,796
2004	4,792,105	3,567,974	60,344	3,628,318	332,750	-40,677	3,254,891	900,334	636,880	24,036	199,374	111,766
2005	5,116,460	3,789,215	48,937	3,838,152	353,131	-32,985	3,452,036	966,745	697,679	25,142	203,500	115,731
2006	5,547,894	4,115,583	29,259	4,144,842	376,527	-41,037	3,727,278	1,077,955	742,661	26,543	209,014	119,923
2007	5,873,120	4,286,787	26,720	4,313,507	399,409	-40,020	3,874,078	1,179,784	819,258	27,573	213,000	120,075
2008	6,557,550	4,561,219	-12,605	4,548,614	421,183	-25,389	4,102,042	1,510,341	945,167	29,990	218,658	123,007
2009	6,644,278	4,770,614	-9,713	4,760,901	444,084	-44,738	4,272,079	1,341,381	1,030,818	29,515	225,114	127,083
2010	7,122,667	5,025,616	14,327	5,039,943	461,690	-28,788	4,549,465	1,423,464	1,149,738	31,040	229,471	128,060
2011	7,433,207	5,141,675	-3,774	5,137,901	422,489	11,494	4,726,906	1,522,425	1,183,876	32,106	231,518	128,354
2012	7,884,338	5,390,452	986	5,391,438	441,621	36,230	4,986,047	1,712,735	1,185,556	33,652	234,291	131,844
2013	8,230,728	5,710,621	40,547	5,751,168	519,399	36,238	5,268,007	1,735,316	1,227,405	34,581	238,015	137,269
2014	8,828,267	6,107,670	40,398	6,148,068	554,791	60,673	5,653,950	1,886,481	1,287,836	36,314	243,106	141,754
2015	9,119,239	6,342,075	75,077	6,417,152	584,067	39,773	5,872,858	1,860,482	1,385,899	36,341	250,932	146,044
2016	9,213,987	6,438,473	16,524	6,454,997	599,680	7,744	5,863,061	1,895,738	1,455,188	36,145	254,919	149,633
2017	9,830,936	6,825,806	16,354	6,842,160	639,994	-18,672	6,183,494	2,141,133	1,506,309	37,868	259,613	152,738
2018	10,620,870	7,255,229	12,854	7,268,083	681,234	-18,213	6,568,636	2,476,769	1,575,465	40,529	262,055	158,637
2019	11,067,502	7,511,629	7,673	7,519,302	713,177	-21,464	6,784,661	2,583,932	1,698,909	41,685	265,501	161,662
2020	11,974,233	7,749,891	10,815	7,760,706	752,988	-39,260	6,968,458	2,726,762	2,279,013	44,524	268,937	159,430
2021	12,979,560	8,370,276	26,877	8,397,153	813,661	-65,634	7,517,858	2,781,284	2,680,418	47,607	272,641	167,316
2022	13,478,398	9,234,053	23,660	9,257,713	925,210	-86,741	8,245,762	2,935,094	2,297,542	48,514	277,824	179,298

Personal Income and Employment by Area: Colorado Springs, CO

(Thousands of dollars, except as noted.)

Year	Personal income, total	Derivation of personal income: Earnings by place of work: Nonfarm	Farm	Total	Less: Contributions for government social insurance	Plus: Adjustment for residence	Equals: Net earnings by place of residence	Plus: Dividends, interest, and rent	Plus: Personal current transfer receipts	Per capita personal income (dollars)	Population (persons)	Total employment
1970	1,072,245	797,479	2,787	800,266	44,176	-1,431	754,659	256,190	61,396	4,439	241,543	116,502
1971	1,171,605	873,849	2,542	876,391	50,659	720	826,452	270,050	75,103	4,614	253,897	117,553
1972	1,372,920	1,036,652	2,983	1,039,635	63,176	3,817	980,276	304,806	87,838	5,020	273,474	128,822
1973	1,580,510	1,192,341	5,401	1,197,742	80,698	10,160	1,127,204	348,639	104,667	5,358	294,996	140,951
1974	1,736,052	1,294,218	3,687	1,297,905	91,168	15,798	1,222,535	393,970	119,547	5,793	299,705	142,577
1975	1,868,907	1,357,894	4,571	1,362,465	97,001	21,608	1,287,072	430,007	151,828	6,234	299,777	139,515
1976	2,016,953	1,464,140	5,370	1,469,510	106,204	29,776	1,393,082	460,611	163,260	6,777	297,633	143,093
1977	2,188,790	1,573,271	5,306	1,578,577	114,467	39,738	1,503,848	512,179	172,763	7,119	307,449	147,428
1978	2,528,015	1,809,887	4,390	1,814,277	132,674	50,253	1,731,856	606,473	189,686	8,101	312,072	154,227
1979	2,887,629	2,083,521	1,307	2,084,828	161,856	63,743	1,986,715	686,601	214,313	9,105	317,132	164,283
1980	3,281,952	2,336,633	2,454	2,339,087	185,717	81,271	2,234,641	793,400	253,911	10,250	320,180	170,287
1981	3,844,213	2,738,309	471	2,738,780	233,888	85,164	2,590,056	950,819	303,338	11,639	330,278	178,535
1982	4,255,060	3,016,989	2,944	3,019,933	259,813	88,409	2,848,529	1,064,751	341,780	12,463	341,418	185,178
1983	4,674,156	3,317,823	2,039	3,319,862	295,714	87,858	3,112,006	1,180,566	381,584	13,221	353,551	192,322
1984	5,286,947	3,804,454	1,309	3,805,763	353,241	86,829	3,539,351	1,328,733	418,863	14,495	364,735	209,639
1985	5,817,522	4,205,563	70	4,205,633	402,736	86,991	3,889,888	1,477,345	450,289	15,264	381,127	220,895
1986	6,267,680	4,557,466	-280	4,557,186	442,102	85,509	4,200,593	1,579,108	487,979	15,899	394,224	226,673
1987	6,634,098	4,838,504	1,600	4,840,104	467,635	85,321	4,457,790	1,642,418	533,890	16,308	406,810	229,718
1988	7,044,682	5,185,712	289	5,186,001	520,170	87,236	4,753,067	1,721,815	569,800	17,254	408,302	236,180
1989	7,400,104	5,327,103	467	5,327,570	551,517	90,538	4,866,591	1,895,494	638,019	18,060	409,747	238,697
1990	7,605,226	5,437,106	-297	5,436,809	578,739	104,702	4,962,772	1,945,611	696,843	18,549	410,017	235,412
1991	8,094,395	5,851,287	380	5,851,667	637,897	106,627	5,320,397	1,986,031	787,967	19,400	417,227	241,791
1992	8,824,372	6,426,039	2,367	6,428,406	703,765	108,413	5,833,054	2,102,370	888,948	20,254	435,686	250,936
1993	9,381,148	6,838,459	1,656	6,840,115	760,643	111,913	6,191,385	2,238,339	951,424	20,761	451,855	262,001
1994	10,163,361	7,428,476	-983	7,427,493	830,835	109,639	6,706,297	2,439,284	1,017,780	21,489	472,965	279,017
1995	11,123,600	8,038,681	-1,140	8,037,541	890,427	109,933	7,257,047	2,721,788	1,144,765	22,847	486,869	291,270
1996	11,977,078	8,705,752	-1,053	8,704,699	958,233	112,962	7,859,428	2,926,625	1,191,025	24,121	496,543	303,895
1997	12,683,649	9,328,054	-285	9,327,769	1,023,592	123,854	8,428,031	3,024,063	1,231,555	25,061	506,107	315,465
1998	14,124,997	10,509,130	301	10,509,431	1,084,615	136,164	9,560,980	3,286,658	1,277,359	27,279	517,799	326,466
1999	15,173,712	11,521,836	1,521	11,523,357	1,170,527	156,118	10,508,948	3,291,110	1,373,654	28,665	529,338	334,576
2000	16,599,934	12,695,641	3,994	12,699,635	1,280,838	177,419	11,596,216	3,546,431	1,457,287	30,707	540,593	345,217
2001	17,312,456	13,233,676	5,866	13,239,542	1,350,375	184,267	12,073,434	3,610,238	1,628,784	31,078	557,057	349,511
2002	17,761,843	13,556,622	3,869	13,560,491	1,418,650	175,832	12,317,673	3,613,717	1,830,453	31,399	565,688	347,097
2003	18,232,804	13,854,215	1,052	13,855,267	1,458,453	183,317	12,580,131	3,704,430	1,948,243	32,031	569,231	347,806
2004	19,004,959	14,470,542	8,390	14,478,932	1,567,261	193,898	13,105,569	3,851,865	2,047,525	32,861	578,345	353,754
2005	20,192,162	15,435,223	4,803	15,440,026	1,679,016	204,547	13,965,557	3,989,615	2,236,990	34,353	587,778	365,035
2006	21,341,639	16,070,574	1,045	16,071,619	1,753,998	229,807	14,547,428	4,361,077	2,433,134	35,420	602,532	371,145
2007	22,537,162	16,554,789	-2,044	16,552,745	1,807,612	259,995	15,005,128	4,886,621	2,645,413	36,977	609,490	378,800
2008	23,530,196	16,770,534	-3,627	16,766,907	1,856,809	280,220	15,190,318	5,161,239	3,178,639	37,913	620,644	378,136
2009	23,857,217	16,990,831	-1,198	16,989,633	1,885,891	309,858	15,413,600	4,839,670	3,603,947	37,809	630,998	371,587
2010	24,934,929	17,636,609	-769	17,635,840	1,957,845	358,117	16,036,112	4,734,718	4,164,099	38,325	650,611	372,158
2011	26,632,570	18,381,427	3,867	18,385,294	1,862,563	424,927	16,947,658	5,331,516	4,353,396	40,291	661,004	378,177
2012	27,559,009	18,866,404	1,810	18,868,214	1,914,285	673,020	17,626,949	5,527,281	4,404,779	41,144	669,817	379,519
2013	27,826,785	19,296,410	1,529	19,297,939	2,146,431	559,654	17,711,162	5,563,221	4,552,402	40,968	679,233	386,438
2014	29,442,931	20,170,894	2,127	20,173,021	2,251,075	667,670	18,589,616	5,964,979	4,888,336	42,836	687,337	394,873
2015	30,905,918	20,935,926	3,447	20,939,373	2,355,880	700,506	19,283,999	6,208,371	5,413,548	44,235	698,671	404,635
2016	31,861,007	21,648,106	1,419	21,649,525	2,425,072	623,048	19,847,501	6,320,832	5,692,674	44,612	714,179	412,280
2017	33,639,551	22,883,023	587	22,883,610	2,554,516	717,193	21,046,287	6,667,748	5,925,516	46,258	727,221	426,162
2018	35,576,506	24,126,104	-124	24,125,980	2,683,831	694,120	22,136,269	6,988,921	6,451,316	48,086	739,845	437,436
2019	37,926,070	25,648,047	-2,031	25,646,016	2,834,535	857,755	23,669,236	7,431,695	6,825,139	50,598	749,558	444,787
2020	41,321,608	27,105,436	275	27,105,711	2,993,249	738,932	24,851,394	7,590,638	8,879,576	54,580	757,089	446,468
2021	45,590,937	29,244,388	-2,111	29,242,277	3,187,559	785,747	26,840,465	8,657,284	10,093,188	59,818	762,167	466,031
2022	46,856,609	31,053,074	-7,994	31,045,080	3,487,712	839,169	28,396,537	9,292,866	9,167,206	61,217	765,424	485,700

Personal Income and Employment by Area: Columbia, MO

(Thousands of dollars, except as noted.)

Year	Personal income, total	Derivation of personal income: Earnings by place of work: Nonfarm	Farm	Total	Less: Contributions for government social insurance	Plus: Adjustment for residence	Equals: Net earnings by place of residence	Plus: Dividends, interest, and rent	Plus: Personal current transfer receipts	Per capita personal income (dollars)	Population (persons)	Total employment
1970	372,582	289,515	17,633	307,148	18,280	-3,143	285,725	59,463	27,394	3,503	106,363	51,070
1971	409,586	316,546	18,442	334,988	20,516	-2,317	312,155	65,885	31,546	3,801	107,760	51,755
1972	453,446	348,229	21,115	369,344	23,057	-1,735	344,552	74,082	34,812	4,137	109,595	53,453
1973	523,785	386,185	40,090	426,275	29,454	-1,080	395,741	86,082	41,962	4,607	113,695	56,242
1974	575,620	432,328	26,936	459,264	34,177	-346	424,741	101,418	49,461	4,976	115,683	57,270
1975	641,361	486,958	11,013	497,971	37,971	-277	459,723	118,232	63,406	5,670	113,108	58,308
1976	719,394	551,630	8,787	560,417	43,201	1,706	518,922	130,004	70,468	6,139	117,187	60,696
1977	798,231	603,784	16,402	620,186	47,198	5,701	578,689	145,284	74,258	6,727	118,666	62,147
1978	902,522	682,226	21,676	703,902	55,263	10,603	659,242	162,468	80,812	7,454	121,087	64,735
1979	1,025,866	765,288	34,601	799,889	64,256	13,563	749,196	184,709	91,961	8,414	121,926	68,159
1980	1,128,649	840,981	2,165	843,146	69,630	16,740	790,256	227,323	111,070	8,998	125,427	68,940
1981	1,247,804	884,280	20,318	904,598	78,316	19,263	845,545	274,562	127,697	9,843	126,768	68,247
1982	1,345,836	931,620	7,953	939,573	83,382	19,987	876,178	329,609	140,049	10,559	127,455	67,981
1983	1,472,198	1,038,527	-6,336	1,032,191	93,299	16,831	955,723	361,211	155,264	11,514	127,859	71,185
1984	1,600,493	1,117,794	12,130	1,129,924	103,312	12,939	1,039,551	397,424	163,518	12,382	129,258	73,590
1985	1,711,380	1,203,927	26,258	1,230,185	113,729	5,776	1,122,232	416,411	172,737	13,224	129,412	76,138
1986	1,812,475	1,294,529	13,671	1,308,200	124,116	5,170	1,189,254	440,807	182,414	13,851	130,855	79,181
1987	1,922,933	1,395,315	18,601	1,413,916	132,670	2,290	1,283,536	448,418	190,979	14,566	132,014	80,778
1988	2,042,164	1,506,770	17,511	1,524,281	151,673	-2,425	1,370,183	469,949	202,032	15,232	134,072	83,504
1989	2,198,565	1,613,586	31,283	1,644,869	163,831	-2,299	1,478,739	494,746	225,080	16,184	135,850	85,249
1990	2,345,513	1,746,646	16,904	1,763,550	182,343	-7,931	1,573,276	526,246	245,991	17,082	137,307	88,163
1991	2,545,180	1,896,404	19,218	1,915,622	200,400	-14,886	1,700,336	555,280	289,564	18,209	139,776	90,220
1992	2,751,418	2,087,276	18,549	2,105,825	218,588	-22,250	1,864,987	576,678	309,753	19,291	142,630	92,518
1993	2,920,011	2,191,490	11,028	2,202,518	230,377	-24,432	1,947,709	628,894	343,408	20,030	145,785	95,607
1994	3,123,174	2,370,201	9,766	2,379,967	250,655	-33,659	2,095,653	668,382	359,139	21,020	148,579	98,838
1995	3,299,770	2,486,625	-6,107	2,480,518	262,393	-34,358	2,183,767	727,512	388,491	21,760	151,643	102,111
1996	3,550,655	2,664,726	24,557	2,689,283	276,884	-40,298	2,372,101	773,192	405,362	22,952	154,701	105,629
1997	3,791,568	2,797,663	18,153	2,815,816	289,133	-41,279	2,485,404	884,290	421,874	24,082	157,447	108,004
1998	3,961,412	2,990,932	12,278	3,003,210	307,797	-47,091	2,648,322	872,750	440,340	24,891	159,149	109,260
1999	4,114,139	3,183,320	-7,019	3,176,301	322,969	-49,699	2,803,633	849,029	461,477	25,589	160,778	110,017
2000	4,396,229	3,374,216	17,740	3,391,956	339,597	-58,341	2,994,018	897,504	504,707	26,990	162,886	113,660
2001	4,619,748	3,562,806	16,631	3,579,437	359,748	-59,023	3,160,666	891,565	567,517	27,990	165,050	114,547
2002	4,763,487	3,758,427	9,533	3,767,960	377,284	-72,979	3,317,697	841,038	604,752	28,394	167,766	115,743
2003	4,978,179	3,865,876	20,842	3,886,718	387,741	-67,042	3,431,935	911,852	634,392	29,270	170,077	116,242
2004	5,368,642	4,085,297	63,520	4,148,817	409,583	-75,469	3,663,765	1,033,572	671,305	31,111	172,563	118,990
2005	5,554,604	4,272,991	16,253	4,289,244	435,066	-78,853	3,775,325	1,051,749	727,530	31,514	176,257	122,425
2006	5,907,053	4,484,082	18,588	4,502,670	461,057	-82,686	3,958,927	1,167,420	780,706	32,741	180,420	124,970
2007	6,207,007	4,596,192	32,422	4,628,614	478,667	-66,475	4,083,472	1,284,518	839,017	33,837	183,438	126,689
2008	6,701,632	4,734,615	45,304	4,779,919	498,803	-30,022	4,251,094	1,464,909	985,629	36,083	185,729	126,577
2009	6,981,202	4,847,415	40,284	4,887,699	500,897	-33,046	4,353,756	1,557,482	1,069,964	37,075	188,301	124,029
2010	6,986,297	5,052,517	40,010	5,092,527	512,587	-53,719	4,526,221	1,284,940	1,175,136	36,582	190,975	125,017
2011	7,343,620	5,277,810	53,728	5,331,538	480,883	-60,907	4,789,748	1,332,803	1,221,069	37,817	194,186	128,177
2012	7,735,207	5,580,623	25,589	5,606,212	505,565	-91,364	5,009,283	1,484,371	1,241,553	39,298	196,836	131,552
2013	7,980,797	5,896,542	54,283	5,950,825	597,661	-99,496	5,253,668	1,458,829	1,268,300	40,055	199,246	134,754
2014	8,215,355	6,026,760	63,471	6,090,231	617,984	-106,293	5,365,954	1,538,893	1,310,508	40,862	201,050	136,039
2015	8,567,659	6,267,474	7,878	6,275,352	650,416	-101,637	5,523,299	1,666,749	1,377,611	42,237	202,849	138,318
2016	8,774,238	6,410,407	27,913	6,438,320	667,157	-110,789	5,660,374	1,670,298	1,443,566	42,812	204,946	139,930
2017	9,121,004	6,586,559	31,490	6,618,049	691,455	-136,690	5,789,904	1,840,932	1,490,168	44,117	206,747	142,230
2018	9,330,879	6,756,187	15,173	6,771,360	712,422	-141,804	5,917,134	1,860,627	1,553,118	44,852	208,039	143,679
2019	9,948,755	7,182,359	33,102	7,215,461	761,769	-169,838	6,283,854	2,027,944	1,636,957	47,472	209,569	143,861
2020	10,563,467	7,406,583	49,155	7,455,738	813,229	-174,790	6,467,719	2,011,939	2,083,809	50,103	210,834	141,268
2021	11,406,675	7,911,314	69,039	7,980,353	861,118	-233,209	6,886,026	2,204,701	2,315,948	53,584	212,875	146,137
2022	11,722,762	8,325,116	73,316	8,398,432	913,229	-205,652	7,279,551	2,389,111	2,054,100	54,618	214,630	151,335

Personal Income and Employment by Area: Columbia, SC

(Thousands of dollars, except as noted.)

Year	Personal income, total	Derivation of personal income: Earnings by place of work: Nonfarm	Farm	Total	Less: Contributions for government social insurance	Plus: Adjustment for residence	Equals: Net earnings by place of residence	Plus: Dividends, interest, and rent	Plus: Personal current transfer receipts	Per capita personal income (dollars)	Population (persons)	Total employment
1970	1,458,229	1,201,538	16,335	1,217,873	75,700	3,781	1,145,954	214,869	97,406	3,598	405,343	198,370
1971	1,616,213	1,329,307	18,059	1,347,366	87,312	59	1,260,113	241,138	114,962	3,842	420,632	204,042
1972	1,823,762	1,504,783	19,471	1,524,254	102,692	-2,007	1,419,555	271,112	133,095	4,265	427,654	213,386
1973	2,066,739	1,709,134	30,056	1,739,190	133,028	-7,773	1,598,389	307,624	160,726	4,713	438,518	225,415
1974	2,366,539	1,953,031	27,300	1,980,331	157,478	-17,789	1,805,064	360,780	200,695	5,198	455,302	237,022
1975	2,609,730	2,107,240	20,220	2,127,460	168,366	-23,138	1,935,956	401,503	272,271	5,651	461,809	235,356
1976	2,864,484	2,340,665	22,657	2,363,322	192,250	-31,126	2,139,946	431,774	292,764	6,131	467,203	240,094
1977	3,126,547	2,575,393	17,681	2,593,074	210,735	-37,931	2,344,408	477,280	304,859	6,547	477,566	247,405
1978	3,486,845	2,881,165	22,598	2,903,763	240,838	-46,195	2,616,730	535,739	334,376	7,215	483,307	255,079
1979	3,918,398	3,234,514	38,056	3,272,570	280,476	-59,818	2,932,276	601,435	384,687	7,968	491,796	263,946
1980	4,365,243	3,550,356	11,064	3,561,420	308,873	-68,581	3,183,966	715,401	465,876	8,734	499,796	267,308
1981	4,880,923	3,892,115	20,223	3,912,338	362,580	-67,307	3,482,451	860,551	537,921	9,660	505,283	268,434
1982	5,226,561	4,104,020	23,009	4,127,029	389,853	-66,546	3,670,630	977,268	578,663	10,296	507,615	268,213
1983	5,719,692	4,536,553	5,736	4,542,289	445,301	-72,302	4,024,686	1,073,501	621,505	11,142	513,337	276,269
1984	6,342,605	5,050,832	39,351	5,090,183	513,530	-75,959	4,500,694	1,186,434	655,477	12,228	518,709	289,340
1985	6,841,697	5,465,683	24,303	5,489,986	567,218	-75,135	4,847,633	1,287,885	706,179	13,124	521,313	298,320
1986	7,367,051	5,921,990	22,745	5,944,735	633,376	-77,944	5,233,415	1,389,997	743,639	13,943	528,371	308,968
1987	7,867,345	6,391,718	22,246	6,413,964	679,178	-76,109	5,658,677	1,442,736	765,932	14,765	532,846	314,930
1988	8,525,056	6,944,769	30,612	6,975,381	773,397	-82,102	6,119,882	1,585,514	819,660	15,860	537,516	327,808
1989	9,236,535	7,403,954	36,732	7,440,686	833,624	-75,081	6,531,981	1,764,427	940,127	16,982	543,917	335,359
1990	9,823,521	7,847,709	30,645	7,878,354	906,993	-101,390	6,869,971	1,904,127	1,049,423	17,808	551,633	341,316
1991	10,313,414	8,091,255	49,811	8,141,066	945,457	-75,699	7,119,910	1,975,847	1,217,657	18,311	563,238	336,460
1992	10,904,786	8,577,220	44,069	8,621,289	995,843	-92,263	7,533,183	2,015,547	1,356,056	19,054	572,323	340,420
1993	11,419,868	8,933,708	34,259	8,967,967	1,046,068	-55,597	7,866,302	2,102,328	1,451,238	19,623	581,956	344,577
1994	12,148,573	9,459,480	53,843	9,513,323	1,124,681	-77,629	8,311,013	2,269,012	1,568,548	20,595	589,879	356,921
1995	12,956,871	10,040,859	48,331	10,089,190	1,195,160	-73,669	8,820,361	2,463,160	1,673,350	21,625	599,158	369,402
1996	13,907,951	10,742,757	60,899	10,803,656	1,257,023	-85,793	9,460,840	2,649,322	1,797,789	22,839	608,946	382,266
1997	14,766,437	11,442,836	64,606	11,507,442	1,338,110	-84,631	10,084,701	2,805,543	1,876,193	23,826	619,752	393,077
1998	16,064,208	12,490,556	78,087	12,568,643	1,454,543	-87,387	11,026,713	3,063,129	1,974,366	25,460	630,966	405,382
1999	16,802,123	13,268,852	73,988	13,342,840	1,534,020	-115,584	11,693,236	3,013,943	2,094,944	26,248	640,126	413,431
2000	17,997,954	14,149,775	69,282	14,219,057	1,623,335	-99,471	12,496,251	3,243,085	2,258,618	27,708	649,567	422,563
2001	18,419,488	14,375,388	86,135	14,461,523	1,663,788	-125,806	12,671,929	3,211,405	2,536,154	27,945	659,125	416,234
2002	19,039,874	14,876,411	48,429	14,924,840	1,722,806	-153,493	13,048,541	3,228,835	2,762,498	28,585	666,087	415,120
2003	19,793,261	15,519,169	83,983	15,603,152	1,806,104	-189,715	13,607,333	3,274,702	2,911,226	29,276	676,083	418,241
2004	20,899,349	16,385,583	115,669	16,501,252	1,912,875	-236,343	14,352,034	3,400,804	3,146,511	30,270	690,421	424,595
2005	22,006,291	17,213,491	100,267	17,313,758	1,996,877	-292,383	15,024,498	3,591,465	3,390,328	31,475	699,160	433,129
2006	23,799,078	18,541,022	86,184	18,627,206	2,180,262	-359,236	16,087,708	4,040,229	3,671,141	33,281	715,091	446,639
2007	25,187,874	19,442,269	56,893	19,499,162	2,273,143	-388,992	16,837,027	4,428,978	3,921,869	34,478	730,546	459,370
2008	26,520,171	20,112,938	59,578	20,172,516	2,366,703	-396,867	17,408,946	4,552,159	4,559,066	35,562	745,740	459,029
2009	26,141,812	19,526,146	72,524	19,598,670	2,324,045	-355,821	16,918,804	4,286,858	4,936,150	34,424	759,400	443,165
2010	26,729,738	19,615,594	85,498	19,701,092	2,321,925	-339,253	17,039,914	4,252,473	5,437,351	34,746	769,294	438,962
2011	27,916,986	20,280,258	42,992	20,323,250	2,144,216	-364,323	17,814,711	4,596,124	5,506,151	36,050	774,398	446,239
2012	28,989,335	21,132,244	77,538	21,209,782	2,197,561	-363,160	18,649,061	4,847,722	5,492,552	37,167	779,984	453,371
2013	29,629,029	21,933,965	141,715	22,075,680	2,562,985	-402,026	19,110,669	4,847,081	5,671,279	37,691	786,096	463,161
2014	31,114,782	23,082,248	53,017	23,135,265	2,694,366	-493,756	19,947,143	5,086,955	6,080,684	39,254	792,645	473,799
2015	33,030,513	24,388,462	88,464	24,476,926	2,845,966	-560,402	21,070,558	5,458,631	6,501,324	41,217	801,380	489,365
2016	33,963,249	25,232,920	58,511	25,291,431	2,934,334	-603,066	21,754,031	5,545,260	6,663,958	42,039	807,908	498,415
2017	35,597,983	26,186,545	85,848	26,272,393	3,044,832	-523,549	22,704,012	5,990,878	6,903,093	43,733	813,987	504,539
2018	36,624,945	26,836,348	72,031	26,908,379	3,120,315	-429,911	23,358,153	5,964,858	7,301,934	44,691	819,515	511,463
2019	38,559,758	28,099,806	46,123	28,145,929	3,286,438	-463,649	24,395,842	6,370,882	7,793,034	46,732	825,129	513,664
2020	41,124,052	28,695,618	25,696	28,721,314	3,356,811	-460,842	24,903,661	6,417,655	9,802,736	49,542	830,082	504,809
2021	45,036,643	30,849,553	104,586	30,954,139	3,586,063	-497,469	26,870,607	6,964,800	11,201,236	53,782	837,388	520,372
2022	46,280,839	33,069,956	89,102	33,159,058	3,936,277	-506,265	28,716,516	7,534,690	10,029,633	54,597	847,686	542,041

Personal Income and Employment by Area: Columbus, GA-AL

(Thousands of dollars, except as noted.)

Year	Personal income, total	Derivation of personal income: Earnings by place of work: Nonfarm	Farm	Total	Less: Contributions for government social insurance	Plus: Adjustment for residence	Equals: Net earnings by place of residence	Plus: Dividends, interest, and rent	Plus: Personal current transfer receipts	Per capita personal income (dollars)	Population (persons)	Total employment
1970	997,883	789,701	6,274	795,975	49,103	-1,159	745,713	178,641	73,529	3,727	267,760	126,207
1971	1,054,760	834,924	6,633	841,557	54,714	-2,283	784,560	183,789	86,411	3,956	266,637	123,613
1972	1,097,129	864,889	7,196	872,085	58,651	-2,166	811,268	187,236	98,625	4,229	259,408	118,732
1973	1,188,217	929,089	10,062	939,151	70,076	-2,639	866,436	206,605	115,176	4,749	250,185	119,925
1974	1,300,484	1,000,775	8,246	1,009,021	78,966	-6,415	923,640	233,900	142,944	5,061	256,975	120,321
1975	1,389,281	1,056,485	6,422	1,062,907	84,355	-12,901	965,651	246,877	176,753	5,298	262,218	118,250
1976	1,536,069	1,182,556	9,953	1,192,509	96,895	-21,617	1,073,997	269,330	192,742	5,736	267,778	123,223
1977	1,677,630	1,314,062	5,093	1,319,155	107,117	-31,073	1,180,965	296,759	199,906	6,301	266,240	127,936
1978	1,868,015	1,456,736	8,753	1,465,489	119,668	-40,688	1,305,133	345,120	217,762	6,861	272,274	130,940
1979	1,995,858	1,540,401	10,967	1,551,368	132,510	-42,452	1,376,406	371,678	247,774	7,317	272,778	129,478
1980	2,190,346	1,653,999	7,141	1,661,140	143,103	-42,702	1,475,335	425,427	289,584	8,041	272,394	128,948
1981	2,442,884	1,791,438	14,616	1,806,054	164,344	-14,865	1,626,845	486,019	330,020	8,984	271,914	126,852
1982	2,668,554	1,931,003	15,288	1,946,291	175,406	-18,240	1,752,645	558,148	357,761	9,675	275,828	129,275
1983	2,825,296	2,058,587	9,302	2,067,889	194,068	-21,862	1,851,959	590,913	382,424	10,300	274,304	129,429
1984	3,139,821	2,314,997	12,793	2,327,790	224,495	-30,164	2,073,131	662,589	404,101	11,402	275,369	137,077
1985	3,369,532	2,498,262	7,825	2,506,087	246,562	-39,838	2,219,687	719,223	430,622	12,169	276,891	140,079
1986	3,599,359	2,684,464	6,534	2,690,998	268,457	-43,884	2,378,657	771,339	449,363	12,918	278,633	142,461
1987	3,804,357	2,873,219	9,367	2,882,586	288,101	-48,619	2,545,866	797,263	461,228	13,601	279,713	144,940
1988	4,059,078	3,042,731	12,637	3,055,368	316,889	-49,403	2,689,076	884,458	485,544	14,562	278,750	147,275
1989	4,204,841	3,115,595	12,810	3,128,405	330,452	-54,625	2,743,328	920,395	541,118	15,134	277,832	145,771
1990	4,443,980	3,281,237	12,229	3,293,466	350,789	-53,798	2,888,879	959,066	596,035	15,922	279,107	144,921
1991	4,651,409	3,404,281	16,920	3,421,201	368,045	-66,027	2,987,129	997,931	666,349	16,709	278,370	141,412
1992	5,045,446	3,697,380	15,785	3,713,165	400,527	-88,640	3,223,998	1,082,045	739,403	17,533	287,768	144,865
1993	5,198,214	3,800,921	15,846	3,816,767	415,393	-106,197	3,295,177	1,127,073	775,964	17,943	289,712	147,349
1994	5,434,723	3,951,726	19,989	3,971,715	432,870	-124,628	3,414,217	1,187,251	833,255	18,566	292,731	148,784
1995	5,661,871	4,100,729	12,306	4,113,035	446,693	-134,710	3,531,632	1,236,302	893,937	19,428	291,424	150,714
1996	5,874,547	4,297,923	17,478	4,315,401	465,778	-168,346	3,681,277	1,251,207	942,063	20,148	291,572	155,925
1997	6,255,043	4,624,706	15,851	4,640,557	497,154	-203,994	3,939,409	1,344,980	970,654	21,366	292,760	160,463
1998	6,726,470	4,991,538	18,908	5,010,446	529,087	-237,111	4,244,248	1,488,664	993,558	22,993	292,548	165,506
1999	6,995,013	5,261,308	26,325	5,287,633	556,450	-261,779	4,469,404	1,481,353	1,044,256	23,903	292,647	166,756
2000	7,352,919	5,499,529	19,386	5,518,915	577,251	-286,901	4,654,763	1,589,847	1,108,309	24,986	294,278	169,412
2001	7,699,711	5,750,451	25,487	5,775,938	602,745	-327,785	4,845,408	1,637,770	1,216,533	26,041	295,679	166,770
2002	8,047,556	5,947,394	22,852	5,970,246	620,170	-371,024	4,979,052	1,735,267	1,333,237	27,044	297,571	164,749
2003	8,297,545	6,170,853	25,919	6,196,772	640,382	-443,829	5,112,561	1,815,290	1,369,694	28,500	291,137	163,792
2004	8,618,804	6,378,094	23,704	6,401,798	679,448	-518,331	5,204,019	1,949,032	1,465,753	29,000	297,196	165,954
2005	9,015,642	6,709,565	25,059	6,734,624	715,411	-695,286	5,323,927	2,111,189	1,580,526	30,167	298,859	168,742
2006	9,407,053	7,011,486	18,276	7,029,762	755,750	-839,341	5,434,671	2,300,509	1,671,873	31,179	301,715	171,425
2007	9,576,803	7,200,692	13,254	7,213,946	776,860	-995,035	5,442,051	2,337,305	1,797,447	32,030	298,991	171,820
2008	9,852,179	7,532,601	19,286	7,551,887	838,975	-1,267,571	5,445,341	2,376,065	2,030,773	32,874	299,698	175,499
2009	9,702,211	7,645,174	17,882	7,663,056	856,683	-1,449,127	5,357,246	2,163,429	2,181,536	31,726	305,809	175,494
2010	10,193,666	8,004,540	13,409	8,017,949	894,898	-1,453,513	5,669,538	2,140,231	2,383,897	32,920	309,646	177,564
2011	10,967,092	8,316,894	12,134	8,329,028	834,925	-1,439,657	6,054,446	2,395,470	2,517,176	34,688	316,160	182,899
2012	11,190,928	8,628,599	21,665	8,650,264	869,916	-1,569,736	6,210,612	2,464,016	2,516,300	34,509	324,289	183,586
2013	11,083,535	8,617,114	29,826	8,646,940	976,566	-1,649,200	6,021,174	2,449,777	2,612,584	33,564	330,220	184,178
2014	11,324,383	8,638,543	18,819	8,657,362	978,819	-1,605,811	6,072,732	2,532,093	2,719,558	34,492	328,321	182,972
2015	11,828,777	8,847,290	16,031	8,863,321	1,000,493	-1,598,247	6,264,581	2,723,795	2,840,401	36,228	326,506	182,260
2016	12,003,633	8,800,468	10,229	8,810,697	987,364	-1,494,825	6,328,508	2,775,783	2,899,342	37,127	323,312	180,279
2017	12,332,477	9,068,132	12,208	9,080,340	1,018,418	-1,558,189	6,503,733	2,838,598	2,990,146	38,455	320,695	181,462
2018	12,725,526	9,347,177	7,207	9,354,384	1,061,484	-1,611,730	6,681,170	2,915,710	3,128,646	39,315	323,682	184,204
2019	13,102,843	9,648,126	8,527	9,656,653	1,102,034	-1,660,409	6,894,210	2,922,007	3,286,626	40,017	327,435	186,288
2020	14,102,092	9,888,160	7,010	9,895,170	1,133,638	-1,755,336	7,006,196	2,877,148	4,218,748	42,838	329,194	184,193
2021	15,273,759	10,583,753	10,738	10,594,491	1,205,935	-2,014,804	7,373,752	3,162,520	4,737,487	46,791	326,427	188,955
2022	15,151,456	10,606,149	10,897	10,617,046	1,239,163	-1,712,254	7,665,629	3,248,742	4,237,085	46,748	324,110	189,454

Personal Income and Employment by Area: Columbus, IN

(Thousands of dollars, except as noted.)

Year	Personal income, total	Derivation of personal income: Earnings by place of work: Nonfarm	Farm	Total	Less: Contributions for government social insurance	Plus: Adjustment for residence	Equals: Net earnings by place of residence	Plus: Dividends, interest, and rent	Plus: Personal current transfer receipts	Per capita personal income (dollars)	Population (persons)	Total employment
1970	238,843	265,039	3,416	268,455	17,850	-58,896	191,709	33,176	13,958	4,184	57,080	32,082
1971	261,594	282,359	5,698	288,057	19,784	-60,499	207,774	37,204	16,616	4,537	57,662	32,179
1972	285,134	307,801	4,624	312,425	22,947	-63,887	225,591	40,728	18,815	4,845	58,851	32,600
1973	332,282	356,150	12,215	368,365	30,828	-73,882	263,655	46,444	22,183	5,564	59,716	35,298
1974	373,571	403,896	10,806	414,702	36,163	-84,379	294,160	53,609	25,802	6,200	60,249	36,323
1975	380,739	390,507	7,833	398,340	34,116	-76,970	287,254	58,974	34,511	6,258	60,844	33,996
1976	437,420	462,798	12,561	475,359	41,400	-96,326	337,633	64,082	35,705	7,134	61,316	35,623
1977	495,850	539,452	7,900	547,352	47,605	-113,660	386,087	71,939	37,824	7,950	62,371	37,582
1978	550,984	609,589	7,443	617,032	55,638	-130,820	430,574	78,504	41,906	8,711	63,254	39,086
1979	608,112	687,200	4,795	691,995	65,182	-152,334	474,479	86,159	47,474	9,485	64,113	40,753
1980	623,363	658,768	1,774	660,542	62,493	-143,579	454,470	108,434	60,459	9,596	64,960	37,946
1981	703,140	728,834	4,143	732,977	74,793	-159,201	498,983	136,401	67,756	10,935	64,301	38,067
1982	712,438	695,270	3,942	699,212	72,517	-141,961	484,734	147,452	80,252	11,133	63,992	35,323
1983	759,976	743,070	-1,617	741,453	78,199	-145,820	517,434	157,795	84,747	11,918	63,765	35,344
1984	916,444	911,817	13,083	924,900	98,989	-182,858	643,053	186,051	87,340	14,417	63,567	37,712
1985	932,226	898,158	9,932	908,090	98,711	-163,978	645,401	193,896	92,929	14,704	63,398	37,442
1986	923,394	879,346	6,887	886,233	97,528	-150,726	637,979	187,719	97,696	14,671	62,940	37,657
1987	1,016,570	1,002,494	5,872	1,008,366	108,090	-171,116	729,160	187,740	99,670	16,027	63,427	38,972
1988	1,077,854	1,051,930	1,467	1,053,397	115,962	-166,340	771,095	200,794	105,965	17,002	63,395	40,195
1989	1,149,214	1,060,263	8,580	1,068,843	116,697	-148,862	803,284	230,808	115,122	18,134	63,375	40,871
1990	1,203,707	1,095,690	7,761	1,103,451	124,521	-140,685	838,245	240,983	124,479	18,851	63,855	42,137
1991	1,224,269	1,128,809	400	1,129,209	131,024	-151,044	847,141	241,782	135,346	18,881	64,843	42,105
1992	1,358,083	1,276,994	8,547	1,285,541	147,202	-184,484	953,855	247,509	156,719	20,745	65,467	44,050
1993	1,471,008	1,420,880	7,836	1,428,716	165,337	-223,872	1,039,507	266,071	165,430	22,168	66,357	46,277
1994	1,568,825	1,524,128	4,260	1,528,388	178,444	-238,573	1,111,371	285,745	171,709	23,320	67,273	48,419
1995	1,693,948	1,614,573	2,103	1,616,676	189,198	-252,260	1,175,218	339,003	179,727	24,762	68,410	49,868
1996	1,767,766	1,656,196	15,960	1,672,156	191,464	-267,226	1,213,466	359,246	195,054	25,608	69,031	50,171
1997	1,853,357	1,753,770	9,042	1,762,812	201,100	-285,052	1,276,660	377,582	199,115	26,641	69,568	51,045
1998	2,016,347	1,909,550	4,959	1,914,509	213,218	-312,028	1,389,263	416,255	210,829	28,692	70,275	52,869
1999	2,083,658	2,009,145	720	2,009,865	223,325	-318,862	1,467,678	397,378	218,602	29,497	70,639	52,944
2000	2,225,399	2,126,433	10,554	2,136,987	231,664	-342,622	1,562,701	427,282	235,416	31,010	71,763	52,846
2001	2,151,788	1,952,872	11,863	1,964,735	218,591	-283,116	1,463,028	423,505	265,255	29,840	72,110	50,295
2002	2,198,369	1,976,037	1,348	1,977,385	222,208	-257,656	1,497,521	416,558	284,290	30,580	71,890	49,163
2003	2,286,318	2,032,903	12,906	2,045,809	232,445	-257,698	1,555,666	432,260	298,392	31,623	72,299	48,781
2004	2,405,332	2,178,039	22,170	2,200,209	251,099	-289,963	1,659,147	427,562	318,623	33,003	72,882	50,425
2005	2,459,271	2,274,106	12,674	2,286,780	262,393	-323,290	1,701,097	410,101	348,073	33,387	73,660	51,642
2006	2,650,358	2,424,154	9,967	2,434,121	281,795	-346,279	1,806,047	468,131	376,180	35,571	74,508	52,458
2007	2,755,277	2,531,369	10,714	2,542,083	294,247	-384,057	1,863,779	493,729	397,769	36,608	75,265	53,866
2008	2,908,965	2,654,585	21,859	2,676,444	309,139	-436,212	1,931,093	517,422	460,450	38,236	76,080	54,449
2009	2,764,046	2,410,726	28,414	2,439,140	285,591	-367,893	1,785,656	467,565	510,825	36,100	76,566	50,968
2010	2,911,353	2,551,579	7,584	2,559,163	297,804	-355,046	1,906,313	462,419	542,621	37,922	76,773	50,846
2011	3,168,991	2,853,857	22,543	2,876,400	295,349	-456,217	2,124,834	501,767	542,390	40,951	77,385	54,102
2012	3,436,636	3,194,784	25,052	3,219,836	327,431	-591,288	2,301,117	572,010	563,509	43,742	78,566	57,390
2013	3,412,352	3,169,854	50,231	3,220,085	369,682	-564,660	2,285,743	557,118	569,491	43,186	79,016	57,341
2014	3,594,516	3,352,683	21,657	3,374,340	389,286	-591,717	2,393,337	600,186	600,993	45,127	79,654	59,038
2015	3,772,199	3,612,687	2,463	3,615,150	415,790	-671,521	2,527,839	610,203	634,157	46,916	80,403	60,063
2016	3,844,983	3,668,790	16,765	3,685,555	412,422	-694,321	2,578,812	613,141	653,030	47,448	81,035	60,669
2017	4,011,815	3,817,570	19,413	3,836,983	424,047	-713,661	2,699,275	645,125	667,415	49,589	80,902	61,246
2018	4,323,240	4,112,493	18,927	4,131,420	457,386	-790,862	2,883,172	748,707	691,361	53,188	81,282	61,983
2019	4,455,624	4,241,333	19,986	4,261,319	479,993	-804,766	2,976,560	751,637	727,427	54,307	82,045	61,913
2020	4,590,932	4,085,342	33,770	4,119,112	475,222	-733,861	2,910,029	737,591	943,312	55,840	82,216	58,403
2021	4,956,752	4,318,102	46,350	4,364,452	499,253	-783,476	3,081,723	810,367	1,064,662	59,915	82,730	59,219
2022	5,172,771	4,760,045	41,080	4,801,125	543,484	-891,225	3,366,416	868,718	937,637	61,920	83,540	62,201

Personal Income and Employment by Area: Columbus, OH

(Thousands of dollars, except as noted.)

Year	Personal income, total	Derivation of personal income: Earnings by place of work: Nonfarm	Earnings by place of work: Farm	Earnings by place of work: Total	Less: Contributions for government social insurance	Plus: Adjustment for residence	Equals: Net earnings by place of residence	Plus: Dividends, interest, and rent	Plus: Personal current transfer receipts	Per capita personal income (dollars)	Population (persons)	Total employment
1970	4,968,990	4,158,986	53,117	4,212,103	255,499	-13,377	3,943,227	676,637	349,126	4,061	1,223,517	547,892
1971	5,458,636	4,557,086	45,568	4,602,654	286,905	-18,713	4,297,036	750,203	411,397	4,378	1,246,879	559,807
1972	5,989,818	5,012,476	58,579	5,071,055	332,507	-23,089	4,715,459	814,676	459,683	4,759	1,258,508	585,094
1973	6,652,006	5,574,927	69,628	5,644,555	427,157	-25,458	5,191,940	914,853	545,213	5,232	1,271,417	610,863
1974	7,312,298	6,007,561	100,605	6,108,166	477,150	-26,863	5,604,153	1,042,202	665,943	5,682	1,286,905	619,395
1975	7,847,629	6,277,019	95,947	6,372,966	487,253	-30,747	5,854,966	1,128,666	863,997	6,038	1,299,613	608,330
1976	8,620,957	6,961,090	91,912	7,053,002	554,547	-33,276	6,465,179	1,215,221	940,557	6,619	1,302,532	620,404
1977	9,594,795	7,827,893	90,878	7,918,771	625,734	-39,334	7,253,703	1,350,317	990,775	7,292	1,315,830	642,252
1978	10,614,320	8,728,771	85,091	8,813,862	721,267	-45,812	8,046,783	1,507,739	1,059,798	8,018	1,323,883	669,335
1979	11,803,381	9,686,036	123,960	9,809,996	837,183	-52,602	8,920,211	1,686,902	1,196,268	8,872	1,330,412	687,708
1980	12,979,750	10,378,815	66,247	10,445,062	900,504	-63,572	9,480,986	2,039,226	1,459,538	9,765	1,329,236	695,825
1981	14,226,535	11,194,518	6,487	11,201,005	1,037,963	-67,261	10,095,781	2,457,642	1,673,112	10,612	1,340,612	689,230
1982	15,244,367	11,726,956	25,071	11,752,027	1,093,306	-88,359	10,570,362	2,760,209	1,913,796	11,343	1,343,981	680,904
1983	16,481,492	12,727,787	-10,765	12,717,022	1,220,698	-109,713	11,386,611	3,026,104	2,068,777	12,191	1,351,988	690,537
1984	18,329,115	14,248,862	107,378	14,356,240	1,398,990	-140,536	12,816,714	3,361,860	2,150,541	13,456	1,362,111	726,332
1985	19,836,983	15,606,512	114,542	15,721,054	1,565,680	-184,658	13,970,716	3,560,061	2,306,206	14,433	1,374,432	760,496
1986	21,088,829	16,780,235	93,278	16,873,513	1,734,416	-224,227	14,914,870	3,740,967	2,432,992	15,193	1,388,054	787,782
1987	22,326,440	18,059,786	71,251	18,131,037	1,872,917	-262,106	15,996,014	3,799,065	2,531,361	15,884	1,405,633	823,595
1988	24,314,913	19,774,678	86,205	19,860,883	2,098,442	-331,281	17,431,160	4,189,145	2,694,608	17,002	1,430,091	848,911
1989	26,575,755	21,362,530	99,899	21,462,429	2,280,710	-399,247	18,782,472	4,900,425	2,892,858	18,355	1,447,914	876,674
1990	28,250,461	22,788,408	104,717	22,893,125	2,493,677	-450,009	19,949,439	5,104,072	3,196,950	19,241	1,468,263	894,479
1991	29,409,808	23,755,872	42,654	23,798,526	2,670,032	-462,922	20,665,572	5,197,724	3,546,512	19,704	1,492,559	898,033
1992	31,731,133	25,693,055	118,915	25,811,970	2,899,512	-507,699	22,404,759	5,391,620	3,934,754	20,909	1,517,612	909,049
1993	33,496,537	27,102,667	111,147	27,213,814	3,083,895	-536,334	23,593,585	5,780,173	4,122,779	21,742	1,540,611	930,524
1994	35,782,720	28,958,344	141,493	29,099,837	3,359,274	-576,201	25,164,362	6,313,670	4,304,688	22,934	1,560,222	964,490
1995	37,549,331	30,531,351	104,343	30,635,694	3,583,732	-629,522	26,422,440	6,545,355	4,581,536	23,774	1,579,412	1,001,985
1996	39,402,271	32,171,506	147,669	32,319,175	3,743,954	-677,696	27,897,525	6,815,605	4,689,141	24,733	1,593,111	1,023,195
1997	42,374,673	34,509,309	204,551	34,713,860	3,916,245	-763,713	30,033,902	7,506,774	4,833,997	26,269	1,613,135	1,044,212
1998	45,556,292	37,692,726	142,351	37,835,077	4,130,792	-861,347	32,842,938	7,731,655	4,981,699	27,834	1,636,690	1,074,387
1999	47,941,582	40,285,312	106,766	40,392,078	4,419,902	-940,715	35,031,461	7,648,677	5,261,444	28,912	1,658,194	1,096,790
2000	51,914,406	43,775,730	156,430	43,932,160	4,623,523	-1,045,656	38,262,981	7,997,376	5,654,049	30,863	1,682,068	1,132,103
2001	53,025,200	44,279,579	150,075	44,429,654	4,741,456	-1,121,142	38,567,056	8,205,133	6,253,011	31,067	1,706,779	1,142,117
2002	54,580,702	45,641,513	79,958	45,721,471	4,820,925	-1,162,826	39,737,720	8,027,411	6,815,571	31,616	1,726,352	1,136,087
2003	56,528,466	47,114,741	100,258	47,214,999	4,998,432	-1,213,508	41,003,059	8,310,908	7,214,499	32,316	1,749,262	1,137,226
2004	59,232,349	49,664,425	178,725	49,843,150	5,329,120	-1,332,002	43,182,028	8,392,594	7,657,727	33,473	1,769,572	1,151,481
2005	61,683,035	51,369,712	95,230	51,464,942	5,499,280	-1,396,779	44,568,883	8,841,546	8,272,606	34,438	1,791,126	1,166,767
2006	65,187,685	53,790,011	91,746	53,881,757	5,761,084	-1,456,637	46,664,036	9,679,241	8,844,408	35,877	1,816,992	1,181,266
2007	68,859,093	56,325,573	130,466	56,456,039	5,990,043	-1,476,336	48,989,660	10,372,690	9,496,743	37,392	1,841,539	1,205,621
2008	71,888,511	57,432,197	131,413	57,563,610	6,211,495	-1,446,365	49,905,750	11,048,840	10,933,921	38,533	1,865,647	1,204,011
2009	71,034,278	56,145,902	193,242	56,339,144	6,146,786	-1,366,537	48,825,821	10,288,731	11,919,726	37,633	1,887,548	1,174,262
2010	73,745,427	58,075,419	193,378	58,268,797	6,194,167	-1,393,090	50,681,540	10,250,836	12,813,051	38,682	1,906,456	1,173,142
2011	79,612,065	61,708,238	348,744	62,056,982	5,884,763	-1,471,557	54,700,662	11,550,892	13,360,511	41,318	1,926,815	1,200,554
2012	84,795,007	65,857,495	222,633	66,080,128	6,158,499	-1,668,436	58,253,193	13,478,111	13,063,703	43,528	1,948,076	1,228,211
2013	86,534,576	68,721,663	360,699	69,082,362	7,005,767	-1,749,941	60,326,654	12,827,280	13,380,642	43,807	1,975,360	1,256,919
2014	90,513,779	71,274,304	192,349	71,466,653	7,264,866	-1,823,819	62,377,968	13,978,930	14,156,881	45,181	2,003,354	1,285,656
2015	95,257,047	74,611,354	45,329	74,656,683	7,606,186	-1,887,221	65,163,276	15,318,593	14,775,178	46,931	2,029,729	1,314,368
2016	98,107,074	76,698,293	61,233	76,759,526	7,952,237	-2,007,771	66,799,518	16,122,845	15,184,711	47,740	2,055,047	1,343,688
2017	102,377,841	80,410,904	103,258	80,514,162	8,509,407	-2,199,294	69,805,461	16,951,403	15,620,977	49,080	2,085,945	1,369,738
2018	106,583,823	83,242,812	159,703	83,402,515	8,698,608	-2,348,934	72,354,973	18,162,114	16,066,736	50,564	2,107,893	1,395,403
2019	110,697,628	86,419,897	38,724	86,458,621	9,121,985	-2,446,702	74,889,934	18,855,783	16,951,911	52,018	2,128,071	1,407,593
2020	119,727,813	89,149,701	245,686	89,395,387	9,428,046	-2,429,693	77,537,648	18,906,685	23,283,480	55,902	2,141,756	1,383,016
2021	130,059,487	96,133,204	399,631	96,532,835	10,145,226	-2,626,587	83,761,022	20,667,888	25,630,577	60,579	2,146,951	1,436,498
2022	132,344,114	101,849,221	325,554	102,174,775	11,058,345	-2,648,140	88,468,290	22,352,673	21,523,151	61,228	2,161,511	1,489,955

Personal Income and Employment by Area: Corpus Christi, TX

(Thousands of dollars, except as noted.)

Year	Personal income, total	Derivation of personal income: Earnings by place of work: Nonfarm	Farm	Total	Less: Contributions for government social insurance	Plus: Adjustment for residence	Equals: Net earnings by place of residence	Plus: Dividends, interest, and rent	Plus: Personal current transfer receipts	Per capita personal income (dollars)	Population (persons)	Total employment
1970	1,038,764	861,156	14,451	875,607	50,211	-14,854	810,542	158,479	69,743	3,631	286,066	122,301
1971	1,133,351	936,736	14,560	951,296	56,310	-16,201	878,785	171,782	82,784	3,855	294,016	124,623
1972	1,232,582	1,013,209	19,930	1,033,139	63,422	-19,415	950,302	186,138	96,142	4,080	302,081	125,345
1973	1,372,439	1,112,805	40,620	1,153,425	80,558	-22,927	1,049,940	204,895	117,604	4,556	301,233	129,910
1974	1,560,106	1,261,402	40,207	1,301,609	94,044	-28,265	1,179,300	237,396	143,410	5,200	300,039	132,848
1975	1,765,119	1,433,156	29,292	1,462,448	104,821	-33,285	1,324,342	264,316	176,461	5,775	305,639	133,817
1976	2,013,643	1,665,559	33,365	1,698,924	121,769	-41,228	1,535,927	283,291	194,425	6,468	311,341	137,601
1977	2,121,636	1,754,591	21,657	1,776,248	130,881	-41,446	1,603,921	310,454	207,261	6,785	312,679	140,264
1978	2,449,604	2,056,850	18,416	2,075,266	156,868	-53,733	1,864,665	358,184	226,755	7,790	314,437	148,764
1979	2,816,594	2,386,480	21,241	2,407,721	192,413	-66,320	2,148,988	409,220	258,386	8,779	320,820	156,588
1980	3,153,465	2,675,171	-14,766	2,660,405	219,866	-76,334	2,364,205	488,786	300,474	9,620	327,815	160,530
1981	3,667,325	3,033,509	44,768	3,078,277	273,038	-79,296	2,725,943	609,116	332,266	11,007	333,196	169,585
1982	3,938,049	3,210,910	12,058	3,222,968	299,676	-86,681	2,836,611	728,444	372,994	11,452	343,883	173,200
1983	4,089,258	3,208,455	17,958	3,226,413	298,028	-81,271	2,847,114	804,347	437,797	11,644	351,176	169,136
1984	4,316,905	3,356,929	24,581	3,381,510	320,754	-83,843	2,976,913	877,466	462,526	12,242	352,620	171,916
1985	4,552,143	3,489,054	32,506	3,521,560	338,785	-83,272	3,099,503	969,611	483,029	12,901	352,862	173,253
1986	4,516,308	3,385,441	14,100	3,399,541	323,747	-81,026	2,994,768	981,194	540,346	12,675	356,314	163,669
1987	4,471,456	3,296,791	40,803	3,337,594	311,095	-67,205	2,959,294	937,628	574,534	12,714	351,700	164,126
1988	4,692,367	3,476,286	36,663	3,512,949	343,209	-73,199	3,096,541	995,036	600,790	13,449	348,913	166,215
1989	4,928,084	3,602,301	-887	3,601,414	362,201	-75,138	3,164,075	1,107,694	656,315	14,146	348,374	166,506
1990	5,340,500	3,990,780	3,055	3,993,835	397,080	-78,055	3,518,700	1,100,131	721,669	15,242	350,392	171,492
1991	5,691,969	4,227,525	43,596	4,271,121	431,904	-88,213	3,751,004	1,119,480	821,485	16,037	354,923	174,811
1992	6,153,958	4,514,314	30,871	4,545,185	458,243	-96,137	3,990,805	1,193,029	970,124	17,136	359,135	176,073
1993	6,417,285	4,799,020	39,481	4,838,501	488,875	-105,518	4,244,108	1,162,808	1,010,369	17,515	366,390	181,625
1994	6,793,784	5,059,611	54,153	5,113,764	520,185	-113,246	4,480,333	1,223,994	1,089,457	18,281	371,637	185,899
1995	7,082,045	5,188,497	72,420	5,260,917	537,034	-130,218	4,593,665	1,304,154	1,184,226	18,934	374,037	189,560
1996	7,538,631	5,618,532	5,485	5,624,017	574,990	-150,740	4,898,287	1,372,502	1,267,842	19,981	377,290	195,734
1997	8,015,715	5,954,365	41,431	5,995,796	604,764	-156,604	5,234,428	1,464,067	1,317,220	21,060	380,616	200,842
1998	8,444,311	6,309,961	34,458	6,344,419	636,963	-177,118	5,530,338	1,557,331	1,356,642	22,124	381,683	204,098
1999	8,702,102	6,537,649	103,570	6,641,219	651,074	-180,490	5,809,655	1,529,741	1,362,706	22,796	381,738	203,469
2000	9,039,836	6,767,338	72,949	6,840,287	674,582	-201,054	5,964,651	1,651,599	1,423,586	23,726	381,006	206,855
2001	9,768,954	7,463,876	16,287	7,480,163	720,713	-235,902	6,523,548	1,707,482	1,537,924	25,683	380,360	209,256
2002	10,083,028	7,725,163	17,780	7,742,943	749,482	-271,412	6,722,049	1,687,234	1,673,745	26,321	383,076	210,085
2003	10,650,902	8,130,608	98,256	8,228,864	797,859	-319,464	7,111,541	1,756,634	1,782,727	27,732	384,072	212,756
2004	11,149,702	8,607,011	122,759	8,729,770	836,551	-381,739	7,511,480	1,757,848	1,880,374	28,672	388,869	213,607
2005	11,978,159	9,183,291	52,311	9,235,602	891,744	-391,636	7,952,222	1,966,647	2,059,290	30,498	392,747	217,363
2006	12,769,261	10,036,639	2,285	10,038,924	957,111	-553,553	8,528,260	2,050,838	2,190,163	32,235	396,135	221,336
2007	13,210,053	10,177,251	64,469	10,241,720	1,009,314	-656,735	8,575,671	2,228,815	2,405,567	33,255	397,235	228,299
2008	14,664,311	11,335,545	27,584	11,363,129	1,085,948	-824,006	9,453,175	2,540,411	2,670,725	36,666	399,943	233,321
2009	13,924,180	10,458,112	27,718	10,485,830	1,055,960	-682,067	8,747,803	2,288,152	2,888,225	34,468	403,971	229,572
2010	14,904,861	10,831,304	174,475	11,005,779	1,095,375	-573,273	9,337,131	2,378,142	3,189,588	36,849	404,486	228,461
2011	16,149,609	11,479,032	217,966	11,696,998	1,020,762	-435,095	10,241,141	2,633,649	3,274,819	39,702	406,770	231,634
2012	16,883,904	12,130,564	42,911	12,173,475	1,089,811	-372,334	10,711,330	2,933,651	3,238,923	41,034	411,466	238,350
2013	17,634,122	12,750,253	180,981	12,931,234	1,272,049	-295,389	11,363,796	2,941,544	3,328,782	42,335	416,542	243,336
2014	18,414,237	13,378,811	16,976	13,395,787	1,340,059	-321,342	11,734,386	3,203,558	3,476,293	43,847	419,964	248,237
2015	18,124,202	13,112,496	18,882	13,131,378	1,350,146	-357,723	11,423,509	3,015,047	3,685,646	42,801	423,451	248,920
2016	17,306,234	12,555,631	5,784	12,561,415	1,343,559	-458,444	10,759,412	2,695,336	3,851,486	40,817	423,993	246,837
2017	18,114,539	12,970,749	46,240	13,016,989	1,395,172	-475,913	11,145,904	3,028,320	3,940,315	42,859	422,659	250,843
2018	18,548,158	13,090,510	39,253	13,129,763	1,409,678	-422,815	11,297,270	3,176,533	4,074,355	43,950	422,025	252,103
2019	19,645,110	13,985,165	46,537	14,031,702	1,457,820	-367,069	12,206,813	3,170,025	4,268,272	46,612	421,457	250,527
2020	20,546,865	13,619,158	-28,516	13,590,642	1,443,467	-380,989	11,766,186	3,178,806	5,601,873	48,665	422,214	240,311
2021	22,692,011	14,599,266	126,693	14,725,959	1,493,051	-434,811	12,798,097	3,505,298	6,388,616	53,654	422,931	244,621
2022	23,154,024	15,782,158	-24,578	15,757,580	1,615,977	-459,977	13,681,626	3,773,174	5,699,224	54,916	421,628	254,623

Personal Income and Employment by Area: Corvallis, OR

(Thousands of dollars, except as noted.)

Year	Personal income, total	Derivation of personal income: Earnings by place of work: Nonfarm	Farm	Total	Less: Contributions for government social insurance	Plus: Adjustment for residence	Equals: Net earnings by place of residence	Plus: Dividends, interest, and rent	Plus: Personal current transfer receipts	Per capita personal income (dollars)	Population (persons)	Total employment
1970	183,578	134,535	3,433	137,968	9,350	3,667	132,285	38,670	12,623	3,403	53,943	19,498
1971	205,429	149,891	3,253	153,144	10,653	4,572	147,063	43,658	14,708	3,740	54,929	20,207
1972	232,456	169,342	4,151	173,493	12,614	6,328	167,207	48,778	16,471	3,866	60,135	21,016
1973	263,806	188,695	7,172	195,867	16,164	8,837	188,540	55,152	20,114	4,448	59,313	22,257
1974	299,249	208,349	8,217	216,566	18,409	11,940	210,097	64,254	24,898	4,887	61,230	23,381
1975	338,181	234,630	4,033	238,663	20,124	14,727	233,266	73,162	31,753	5,488	61,618	24,344
1976	389,271	272,697	5,906	278,603	23,621	18,516	273,498	80,894	34,879	6,248	62,299	25,929
1977	446,823	319,660	5,389	325,049	28,481	20,496	317,064	91,855	37,904	6,815	65,569	28,314
1978	514,888	372,914	5,090	378,004	34,732	23,441	366,713	106,666	41,509	7,690	66,955	30,807
1979	569,902	407,035	6,139	413,174	39,681	28,321	401,814	120,680	47,408	8,360	68,171	30,922
1980	629,988	436,130	6,890	443,020	43,078	32,430	432,372	142,169	55,447	9,201	68,471	30,495
1981	706,338	480,849	9,536	490,385	51,101	33,438	472,722	171,689	61,927	10,182	69,369	30,876
1982	744,966	510,570	8,591	519,161	55,909	26,470	489,722	184,907	70,337	10,725	69,461	31,071
1983	798,497	542,406	10,905	553,311	60,004	26,286	519,593	202,931	75,973	11,700	68,245	31,395
1984	857,647	580,422	14,585	595,007	65,980	27,920	556,947	220,768	79,932	12,711	67,474	32,566
1985	887,616	590,442	15,656	606,098	66,999	30,460	569,559	232,822	85,235	13,194	67,275	33,707
1986	936,492	635,723	19,477	655,200	72,524	26,593	609,269	243,966	83,257	13,990	66,940	35,204
1987	985,679	684,582	16,704	701,286	76,909	26,063	650,440	246,849	88,390	14,583	67,590	36,280
1988	1,062,218	752,431	23,404	775,835	89,034	25,898	712,699	257,080	92,439	15,649	67,876	37,645
1989	1,169,259	820,494	18,932	839,426	96,679	23,954	766,701	303,294	99,264	16,733	69,879	38,457
1990	1,226,137	868,393	17,570	885,963	104,845	25,074	806,192	311,296	108,649	17,255	71,059	39,188
1991	1,281,174	909,801	15,276	925,077	110,006	25,743	840,814	324,368	115,992	17,917	71,507	39,115
1992	1,366,958	987,886	12,485	1,000,371	118,561	22,193	904,003	335,963	126,992	18,824	72,618	39,372
1993	1,477,829	1,093,560	17,297	1,110,857	131,750	8,954	988,061	356,785	132,983	19,971	73,997	41,016
1994	1,589,481	1,200,624	21,742	1,222,366	146,441	1,459	1,077,384	368,466	143,631	21,058	75,481	42,864
1995	1,741,541	1,299,198	18,212	1,317,410	159,999	-7,508	1,149,903	430,397	161,241	22,760	76,517	44,979
1996	1,924,220	1,442,262	25,420	1,467,682	180,491	-21,546	1,265,645	486,670	171,905	24,741	77,776	48,096
1997	2,061,053	1,577,311	25,086	1,602,397	194,761	-34,854	1,372,782	511,443	176,828	26,235	78,560	49,568
1998	2,156,755	1,644,178	24,245	1,668,423	201,579	-33,501	1,433,343	536,331	187,081	27,320	78,943	50,743
1999	2,161,030	1,652,069	30,850	1,682,919	199,773	-29,732	1,453,414	502,689	204,927	27,616	78,254	50,485
2000	2,269,002	1,745,987	28,512	1,774,499	212,636	-45,008	1,516,855	539,169	212,978	29,002	78,236	51,408
2001	2,364,604	1,822,814	38,241	1,861,055	210,891	-45,090	1,605,074	525,745	233,785	30,126	78,491	48,298
2002	2,403,152	1,847,173	38,259	1,885,432	213,974	-34,520	1,636,938	516,926	249,288	29,963	80,203	45,829
2003	2,540,988	1,907,239	42,869	1,950,108	220,773	-39,396	1,689,939	587,662	263,387	31,635	80,322	45,885
2004	2,591,428	1,971,398	45,092	2,016,490	229,041	-83,076	1,704,373	618,340	268,715	32,333	80,149	47,618
2005	2,644,453	2,056,587	35,430	2,092,017	240,682	-84,233	1,767,102	585,002	292,349	32,671	80,943	48,101
2006	2,793,965	2,141,062	37,796	2,178,858	251,987	-80,963	1,845,908	631,468	316,589	34,091	81,957	48,809
2007	2,900,331	2,185,155	29,138	2,214,293	260,166	-65,483	1,888,644	673,084	338,603	34,644	83,718	48,374
2008	3,074,943	2,210,124	25,614	2,235,738	265,103	-48,226	1,922,409	755,500	397,034	36,541	84,150	48,204
2009	2,950,799	2,204,740	24,383	2,229,123	262,758	-137,015	1,829,350	681,662	439,787	34,557	85,390	47,485
2010	3,059,405	2,278,029	21,208	2,299,237	271,757	-139,486	1,887,994	691,645	479,766	35,733	85,619	47,450
2011	3,234,454	2,313,912	27,747	2,341,659	244,844	-150,269	1,946,546	807,332	480,576	37,395	86,494	48,578
2012	3,252,247	2,395,204	32,455	2,427,659	253,760	-170,678	2,003,221	779,662	469,364	37,341	87,095	48,476
2013	3,234,109	2,410,272	28,806	2,439,078	290,334	-155,158	1,993,586	751,181	489,342	37,266	86,784	48,191
2014	3,429,054	2,472,869	23,335	2,496,204	301,563	-131,440	2,063,201	849,994	515,859	38,951	88,034	49,280
2015	3,582,335	2,584,086	23,884	2,607,970	312,458	-156,039	2,139,473	894,722	548,140	40,085	89,368	50,426
2016	3,784,693	2,695,984	25,933	2,721,917	326,691	-119,375	2,275,851	938,525	570,317	41,509	91,178	50,754
2017	3,943,228	2,845,950	21,500	2,867,450	346,442	-154,018	2,366,990	989,942	586,296	42,283	93,257	52,221
2018	4,205,820	3,014,796	22,013	3,036,809	361,018	-161,554	2,514,237	1,072,461	619,122	44,723	94,042	52,765
2019	4,431,794	3,129,658	18,787	3,148,445	372,902	-151,925	2,623,618	1,144,046	664,130	46,727	94,844	52,530
2020	4,759,412	3,242,063	25,582	3,267,645	379,416	-143,781	2,744,448	1,143,422	871,542	49,990	95,208	50,788
2021	5,258,868	3,529,959	24,309	3,554,268	431,415	-99,014	3,023,839	1,258,784	976,245	54,622	96,277	51,714
2022	5,401,411	3,636,045	22,999	3,659,044	459,439	68,972	3,268,577	1,297,216	835,618	55,325	97,630	53,625

Personal Income and Employment by Area: Crestview-Fort Walton Beach-Destin, FL

(Thousands of dollars, except as noted.)

Year	Personal income, total	Derivation of personal income: Earnings by place of work: Nonfarm	Farm	Total	Less: Contributions for government social insurance	Plus: Adjustment for residence	Equals: Net earnings by place of residence	Plus: Dividends, interest, and rent	Plus: Personal current transfer receipts	Per capita personal income (dollars)	Population (persons)	Total employment
1970	397,526	320,410	1,010	321,420	17,638	-22,403	281,379	92,961	23,186	3,797	104,708	43,341
1971	451,674	365,524	2,955	368,479	21,210	-25,032	322,237	102,043	27,394	4,194	107,706	45,369
1972	512,479	413,090	3,357	416,447	24,411	-27,783	364,253	115,408	32,818	4,547	112,702	46,894
1973	559,571	440,551	7,473	448,024	28,184	-27,264	392,576	127,077	39,918	4,872	114,864	49,238
1974	617,777	478,596	9,103	487,699	32,799	-26,278	428,622	141,985	47,170	5,302	116,509	51,718
1975	691,636	520,856	9,441	530,297	36,987	-27,385	465,925	161,890	63,821	5,583	123,878	51,954
1976	757,512	573,751	5,722	579,473	41,822	-31,306	506,345	180,898	70,269	6,100	124,190	53,408
1977	830,796	626,811	2,592	629,403	45,680	-32,180	551,543	203,270	75,983	6,522	127,380	55,208
1978	949,826	702,757	6,354	709,111	51,189	-33,630	624,292	242,590	82,944	7,374	128,807	58,497
1979	1,042,919	762,910	8,298	771,208	58,529	-35,615	677,064	268,592	97,263	7,920	131,677	60,253
1980	1,158,715	827,984	3,131	831,115	62,925	-36,598	731,592	310,779	116,344	8,771	132,104	60,453
1981	1,355,493	974,409	1,404	975,813	79,429	-43,819	852,565	364,805	138,123	10,011	135,394	63,432
1982	1,482,886	1,060,369	2,488	1,062,857	87,829	-46,562	928,466	395,602	158,818	10,647	139,276	65,789
1983	1,633,472	1,164,725	1,356	1,166,081	102,149	-46,609	1,017,323	439,589	176,560	11,301	144,536	69,831
1984	1,833,880	1,305,357	3,932	1,309,289	118,650	-50,444	1,140,195	500,847	192,838	12,273	149,428	75,701
1985	1,987,628	1,400,002	2,645	1,402,647	131,934	-47,872	1,222,841	551,060	213,727	12,847	154,718	79,525
1986	2,163,426	1,531,459	3,898	1,535,357	149,316	-51,256	1,334,785	597,871	230,770	13,568	159,450	84,261
1987	2,346,915	1,673,457	3,871	1,677,328	163,337	-53,044	1,460,947	640,465	245,503	14,307	164,034	86,072
1988	2,556,147	1,802,928	7,717	1,810,645	183,804	-65,426	1,561,415	725,113	269,619	15,301	167,059	88,777
1989	2,798,993	1,931,770	8,849	1,940,619	200,434	-62,308	1,677,877	816,695	304,421	16,481	169,832	91,122
1990	3,048,527	2,047,442	7,352	2,054,794	216,146	-14,630	1,824,018	887,792	336,717	17,694	172,290	91,622
1991	3,261,616	2,191,957	7,569	2,199,526	234,359	-33,655	1,931,512	945,833	384,271	18,343	177,811	94,263
1992	3,552,561	2,359,319	8,806	2,368,125	254,874	-3,601	2,109,650	1,006,470	436,441	19,381	183,299	96,788
1993	3,789,829	2,505,998	7,412	2,513,410	272,059	-31,395	2,209,956	1,108,701	471,172	20,079	188,744	100,240
1994	3,978,803	2,605,404	7,325	2,612,729	285,679	-31,456	2,295,594	1,179,491	503,718	20,546	193,649	105,827
1995	4,305,052	2,817,684	7,071	2,824,755	304,730	-99,185	2,420,840	1,309,417	574,795	21,799	197,484	109,725
1996	4,580,781	3,040,468	10,114	3,050,582	327,754	-133,987	2,588,841	1,402,189	589,751	22,770	201,172	114,103
1997	4,895,778	3,197,909	9,292	3,207,201	347,886	-120,858	2,738,457	1,530,121	627,200	23,904	204,814	118,905
1998	5,195,060	3,395,559	4,895	3,400,454	368,075	-163,154	2,869,225	1,678,401	647,434	25,132	206,708	122,256
1999	5,513,457	3,590,191	7,235	3,597,426	386,769	-158,668	3,051,989	1,764,910	696,558	26,391	208,918	124,906
2000	5,821,101	3,855,011	3,353	3,858,364	413,892	-215,937	3,228,535	1,827,930	764,636	27,464	211,955	129,035
2001	6,176,835	4,150,979	3,174	4,154,153	439,687	-229,929	3,484,537	1,834,471	857,827	28,735	214,955	123,262
2002	6,683,174	4,623,239	-4,639	4,618,600	487,887	-285,516	3,845,197	1,900,825	937,152	30,352	220,192	128,005
2003	7,338,598	5,206,340	488	5,206,828	543,417	-343,042	4,320,369	2,006,819	1,011,410	32,875	223,227	134,488
2004	7,980,415	5,851,536	2,231	5,853,767	612,212	-396,713	4,844,842	2,047,164	1,088,409	34,694	230,024	145,294
2005	8,559,605	6,357,856	2,257	6,360,113	667,602	-447,123	5,245,388	2,169,681	1,144,536	36,668	233,437	150,540
2006	9,074,221	6,619,991	4,349	6,624,340	718,266	-481,515	5,424,559	2,434,675	1,214,987	38,578	235,216	155,237
2007	9,310,450	6,594,067	3,564	6,597,631	727,138	-516,431	5,354,062	2,673,831	1,282,557	39,614	235,032	155,604
2008	9,374,592	6,395,582	2,423	6,398,005	720,202	-532,973	5,144,830	2,760,142	1,469,620	39,838	235,315	150,967
2009	9,107,875	6,237,312	1,181	6,238,493	727,589	-548,607	4,962,297	2,538,751	1,606,827	38,644	235,687	146,832
2010	9,643,020	6,453,103	2,569	6,455,672	742,281	-571,364	5,142,027	2,676,520	1,824,473	40,876	235,907	144,416
2011	10,012,047	6,673,208	4,056	6,677,264	699,336	-618,679	5,359,249	2,756,008	1,896,790	41,952	238,654	148,400
2012	10,761,041	7,257,256	6,668	7,263,924	761,446	-704,374	5,798,104	3,105,359	1,857,578	43,591	246,864	151,339
2013	10,818,843	7,457,796	7,192	7,464,988	868,809	-731,732	5,864,447	3,011,371	1,943,025	42,976	251,744	155,619
2014	11,403,847	7,670,011	17,195	7,687,206	895,303	-732,323	6,059,580	3,287,744	2,056,523	44,597	255,707	158,397
2015	12,032,038	8,022,699	23,318	8,046,017	930,464	-743,486	6,372,067	3,479,610	2,180,361	46,156	260,683	163,184
2016	12,652,693	8,490,022	10,610	8,500,632	969,771	-782,881	6,747,980	3,627,213	2,277,500	47,663	265,460	167,549
2017	13,550,123	9,002,327	16,563	9,018,890	1,021,029	-817,629	7,180,232	3,927,948	2,441,943	49,951	271,267	173,637
2018	14,582,344	9,494,668	11,500	9,506,168	1,080,236	-846,863	7,579,069	4,408,912	2,594,363	52,588	277,296	179,238
2019	15,891,481	10,404,593	10,073	10,414,666	1,187,602	-951,680	8,275,384	4,838,673	2,777,424	55,948	284,042	183,066
2020	16,968,227	11,028,843	9,498	11,038,341	1,270,926	-1,052,558	8,714,857	4,770,574	3,482,796	58,916	288,008	186,850
2021	19,470,875	12,328,077	17,045	12,345,122	1,380,152	-1,151,780	9,813,190	5,615,409	4,042,276	66,310	293,635	198,555
2022	20,331,372	13,333,200	18,511	13,351,711	1,512,406	-1,212,941	10,626,364	6,058,489	3,646,519	67,820	299,786	207,548

Personal Income and Employment by Area: Cumberland, MD-WV

(Thousands of dollars, except as noted.)

Year	Personal income, total	Derivation of personal income: Earnings by place of work: Nonfarm	Farm	Total	Less: Contributions for government social insurance	Plus: Adjustment for residence	Equals: Net earnings by place of residence	Plus: Dividends, interest, and rent	Plus: Personal current transfer receipts	Per capita personal income (dollars)	Population (persons)	Total employment
1970	356,715	312,900	927	313,827	24,342	-16,997	272,488	37,925	46,302	3,329	107,140	42,280
1971	385,369	330,253	911	331,164	26,475	-15,047	289,642	40,826	54,901	3,577	107,735	41,720
1972	416,815	352,062	1,034	353,096	29,385	-13,265	310,446	43,942	62,427	3,807	109,483	41,890
1973	454,127	382,041	1,507	383,548	36,229	-13,120	334,199	49,681	70,247	4,186	108,476	42,897
1974	492,609	408,275	1,269	409,544	40,100	-16,764	352,680	57,331	82,598	4,516	109,091	42,044
1975	530,985	412,802	1,056	413,858	39,740	-14,308	359,810	63,995	107,180	4,903	108,304	40,012
1976	572,138	448,160	568	448,728	43,766	-15,627	389,335	70,221	112,582	5,290	108,148	39,976
1977	635,602	506,203	561	506,764	49,281	-18,480	439,003	78,999	117,600	5,892	107,873	40,722
1978	698,318	560,358	1,506	561,864	56,213	-19,548	486,103	86,768	125,447	6,518	107,138	42,694
1979	773,296	612,568	1,558	614,126	63,670	-17,884	532,572	96,309	144,415	7,163	107,955	42,382
1980	861,370	654,571	1,299	655,870	68,487	-16,712	570,671	120,999	169,700	7,985	107,868	42,213
1981	939,727	687,247	590	687,837	77,975	-11,664	598,198	147,168	194,361	8,699	108,027	41,782
1982	998,357	693,114	703	693,817	80,802	-7,662	605,353	176,387	216,617	9,305	107,298	40,498
1983	1,053,796	718,611	2,040	720,651	84,752	-4,970	630,929	187,220	235,647	9,928	106,147	40,484
1984	1,115,420	759,600	2,909	762,509	93,196	-5,439	663,874	206,443	245,103	10,674	104,497	40,688
1985	1,172,861	794,867	2,419	797,286	99,367	-4,048	693,871	219,822	259,168	11,343	103,396	41,264
1986	1,197,892	802,512	2,684	805,196	103,360	-143	701,693	231,639	264,560	11,668	102,668	40,906
1987	1,263,266	854,754	1,439	856,193	108,253	-78	747,862	229,671	285,733	12,352	102,270	42,300
1988	1,343,220	928,205	1,185	929,390	123,070	-1,823	804,497	237,832	300,891	13,145	102,187	43,808
1989	1,434,459	967,968	1,388	969,356	128,927	-1,033	839,396	273,786	321,277	14,051	102,086	44,253
1990	1,509,084	1,007,002	1,622	1,008,624	132,333	8,436	884,727	279,514	344,843	14,848	101,634	44,793
1991	1,561,642	1,016,568	967	1,017,535	133,761	10,177	893,951	288,086	379,605	15,295	102,101	44,400
1992	1,608,410	1,024,395	1,954	1,026,349	134,115	13,211	905,445	279,723	423,242	15,721	102,312	43,742
1993	1,660,649	1,066,450	2,083	1,068,533	139,819	11,659	940,373	283,279	436,997	16,224	102,359	43,705
1994	1,724,806	1,107,793	2,166	1,109,959	144,814	9,941	975,086	301,824	447,896	16,826	102,508	44,034
1995	1,778,859	1,132,264	823	1,133,087	148,127	9,550	994,510	314,063	470,286	17,320	102,704	44,466
1996	1,843,667	1,172,719	992	1,173,711	153,051	7,442	1,028,102	328,344	487,221	18,000	102,424	45,200
1997	1,935,041	1,228,414	-525	1,227,889	158,815	3,270	1,072,344	365,593	497,104	18,886	102,457	45,957
1998	1,991,935	1,266,304	108	1,266,412	160,072	3,955	1,110,295	378,176	503,464	19,392	102,718	46,271
1999	2,054,922	1,320,591	126	1,320,717	165,147	5,968	1,161,538	365,605	527,779	20,056	102,458	46,460
2000	2,156,106	1,386,992	1,054	1,388,046	172,771	7,132	1,222,407	386,668	547,031	21,168	101,858	47,376
2001	2,514,340	1,717,190	273	1,717,463	195,246	14,263	1,536,480	386,007	591,853	24,748	101,596	47,090
2002	2,627,012	1,837,393	319	1,837,712	204,965	9,322	1,642,069	358,335	626,608	25,892	101,462	46,956
2003	2,718,154	1,902,348	1,987	1,904,335	212,426	10,372	1,702,281	350,705	665,168	26,791	101,457	46,791
2004	2,803,969	1,970,341	3,929	1,974,270	219,536	8,202	1,762,936	363,302	677,731	27,582	101,658	47,692
2005	2,750,491	1,888,709	3,214	1,891,923	224,516	13,436	1,680,843	345,504	724,144	27,186	101,172	48,482
2006	2,729,911	1,842,416	1,060	1,843,476	229,260	16,095	1,630,311	348,853	750,747	26,948	101,304	48,718
2007	2,806,670	1,806,448	-783	1,805,665	229,201	26,102	1,602,566	405,489	798,615	27,521	101,981	48,387
2008	3,010,627	1,875,623	16	1,875,639	236,007	25,039	1,664,671	461,007	884,949	29,383	102,462	48,375
2009	3,104,368	1,928,792	-143	1,928,649	242,346	6,177	1,692,480	453,916	957,972	30,087	103,181	48,070
2010	3,226,948	2,026,709	-184	2,026,525	253,606	-12,156	1,760,763	445,517	1,020,668	31,291	103,126	48,281
2011	3,314,462	2,074,654	98	2,074,752	232,587	-24,887	1,817,278	464,975	1,032,209	32,368	102,399	48,579
2012	3,349,795	2,076,724	-2,143	2,074,581	232,652	-31,089	1,810,840	490,708	1,048,247	33,029	101,419	48,374
2013	3,354,015	2,109,026	-348	2,108,678	262,040	-37,318	1,809,320	463,986	1,080,709	33,318	100,666	48,065
2014	3,466,359	2,120,584	-645	2,119,939	266,168	-33,212	1,820,559	508,848	1,136,952	34,731	99,805	47,980
2015	3,550,182	2,194,717	-1,528	2,193,189	278,597	-37,605	1,876,987	513,668	1,159,527	35,889	98,920	48,359
2016	3,685,858	2,255,955	-2,003	2,253,952	286,407	-39,625	1,927,920	552,115	1,205,823	37,500	98,290	48,301
2017	3,758,365	2,325,832	-829	2,325,003	294,733	-37,254	1,993,016	540,851	1,224,498	38,660	97,217	48,096
2018	3,882,783	2,399,692	-2,077	2,397,615	306,514	-39,237	2,051,864	561,689	1,269,230	40,277	96,403	48,357
2019	4,004,076	2,467,462	-661	2,466,801	315,642	-38,354	2,112,805	575,516	1,315,755	41,839	95,701	48,023
2020	4,318,718	2,452,328	-2,839	2,449,489	320,779	-30,847	2,097,863	597,643	1,623,212	45,534	94,845	45,408
2021	4,538,997	2,537,025	-592	2,536,433	333,955	-27,560	2,174,918	592,176	1,771,903	48,003	94,557	46,475
2022	4,424,972	2,589,449	1,497	2,590,946	347,398	-29,451	2,214,097	601,398	1,609,477	47,013	94,122	47,584

Personal Income and Employment by Area: Dallas-Fort Worth-Arlington, TX

(Thousands of dollars, except as noted.)

Year	Personal income, total	Derivation of personal income: Earnings by place of work: Nonfarm	Farm	Total	Less: Contributions for government social insurance	Plus: Adjustment for residence	Equals: Net earnings by place of residence	Plus: Dividends, interest, and rent	Plus: Personal current transfer receipts	Per capita personal income (dollars)	Population (persons)	Total employment
1970	10,510,767	8,968,070	37,283	9,005,353	587,380	-30,336	8,387,637	1,509,443	613,687	4,335	2,424,838	1,189,575
1971	11,236,654	9,436,080	33,853	9,469,933	633,441	-2,773	8,833,719	1,668,351	734,584	4,552	2,468,331	1,190,262
1972	12,446,130	10,465,361	44,402	10,509,763	738,077	12,731	9,784,417	1,837,314	824,399	5,012	2,483,389	1,247,681
1973	13,956,811	11,756,735	78,387	11,835,122	958,681	18,941	10,895,382	2,083,338	978,091	5,501	2,537,114	1,324,793
1974	15,795,060	13,213,247	27,519	13,240,766	1,101,958	32,494	12,171,302	2,460,333	1,163,425	6,056	2,608,035	1,368,901
1975	17,609,865	14,508,196	32,042	14,540,238	1,179,331	54,527	13,415,434	2,693,256	1,501,175	6,634	2,654,603	1,366,632
1976	19,663,563	16,466,493	55,797	16,522,290	1,371,019	42,141	15,193,412	2,860,273	1,609,878	7,220	2,723,580	1,424,689
1977	22,002,447	18,838,743	15,979	18,854,722	1,587,787	-77,915	17,189,020	3,127,331	1,686,096	7,928	2,775,384	1,505,789
1978	25,560,202	22,017,132	36,438	22,053,570	1,900,497	-133,549	20,019,524	3,660,786	1,879,892	8,995	2,841,618	1,610,676
1979	29,642,299	25,722,823	39,842	25,762,665	2,323,714	-167,692	23,271,259	4,255,022	2,116,018	10,137	2,924,299	1,710,438
1980	34,466,684	29,728,686	-285	29,728,401	2,704,023	-227,965	26,796,413	5,204,907	2,465,364	11,355	3,035,483	1,783,735
1981	39,715,033	34,009,282	47,073	34,056,355	3,327,457	-241,537	30,487,361	6,411,827	2,815,845	12,734	3,118,847	1,866,469
1982	44,203,045	37,156,569	48,979	37,205,548	3,713,490	-277,546	33,214,512	7,775,357	3,213,176	13,680	3,231,253	1,913,919
1983	49,053,773	41,212,210	47,889	41,260,099	4,128,435	-339,566	36,792,098	8,748,295	3,513,380	14,684	3,340,555	1,983,208
1984	55,845,336	47,358,611	43,586	47,402,197	4,877,285	-426,916	42,097,996	10,022,001	3,725,339	16,158	3,456,129	2,154,576
1985	62,051,908	52,555,739	22,211	52,577,950	5,494,278	-503,766	46,579,906	11,442,466	4,029,536	17,255	3,596,198	2,282,704
1986	65,657,632	55,648,484	-530	55,647,954	5,765,175	-542,009	49,340,770	11,919,793	4,397,069	17,594	3,731,895	2,310,171
1987	67,783,254	57,744,955	7,712	57,752,667	5,885,821	-544,534	51,322,312	11,808,238	4,652,704	17,769	3,814,627	2,383,007
1988	71,828,222	61,088,388	10,397	61,098,785	6,375,729	-563,379	54,159,677	12,735,001	4,933,544	18,613	3,858,983	2,414,222
1989	76,563,523	64,811,907	37,094	64,849,001	6,773,014	-567,711	57,508,276	13,608,011	5,447,236	19,542	3,917,872	2,445,797
1990	82,850,652	69,997,610	45,267	70,042,877	7,208,998	-745,637	62,088,242	14,681,529	6,080,881	20,663	4,009,530	2,507,837
1991	86,004,421	72,700,053	41,700	72,741,753	7,673,749	-786,016	64,281,988	14,909,867	6,812,566	20,929	4,109,324	2,529,960
1992	92,292,889	77,944,612	64,057	78,008,669	8,150,800	-835,424	69,022,445	15,213,812	8,056,632	22,004	4,194,301	2,542,635
1993	97,974,920	83,411,792	58,600	83,470,392	8,696,100	-1,004,278	73,770,014	15,541,303	8,663,603	22,865	4,284,857	2,616,854
1994	104,504,762	88,985,050	69,938	89,054,988	9,410,925	-1,138,441	78,505,622	16,660,450	9,338,690	23,816	4,388,097	2,708,936
1995	112,396,555	95,565,592	29,438	95,595,030	10,122,255	-1,255,898	84,216,877	18,051,117	10,128,561	24,998	4,496,174	2,814,870
1996	122,460,876	104,437,852	23,291	104,461,143	10,925,437	-1,416,698	92,119,008	19,510,048	10,831,820	26,492	4,622,564	2,923,393
1997	134,454,461	115,655,041	60,331	115,715,372	12,041,273	-1,689,674	101,984,425	21,119,114	11,350,922	28,216	4,765,255	3,057,914
1998	149,008,094	129,370,634	36,899	129,407,533	13,297,916	-1,953,563	114,156,054	23,089,014	11,763,026	30,331	4,912,807	3,176,906
1999	158,425,067	139,008,780	91,109	139,099,889	14,342,833	-2,192,533	122,564,523	23,808,711	12,051,833	31,342	5,054,705	3,284,237
2000	175,314,330	154,028,523	38,113	154,066,636	15,627,779	-2,534,723	135,904,134	26,488,313	12,921,883	33,798	5,187,122	3,417,830
2001	184,082,671	160,954,791	63,369	161,018,160	16,143,727	-2,571,751	142,302,682	27,466,694	14,313,295	34,557	5,326,971	3,463,068
2002	185,695,972	161,744,183	58,533	161,802,716	16,107,402	-2,492,509	143,202,805	26,571,092	15,922,075	34,183	5,432,371	3,424,893
2003	189,811,224	163,146,523	120,715	163,267,238	16,594,428	-2,392,276	144,280,534	28,611,963	16,918,727	34,362	5,523,937	3,432,679
2004	197,376,153	169,529,970	129,416	169,659,386	17,393,780	-2,482,061	149,783,545	29,738,535	17,854,073	35,161	5,613,420	3,499,340
2005	214,665,761	181,224,304	111,779	181,336,083	18,410,955	-2,505,214	160,419,914	34,364,417	19,881,430	37,513	5,722,444	3,621,892
2006	236,045,160	198,492,051	107,228	198,599,279	19,567,632	-2,679,907	176,351,740	38,180,088	21,513,332	40,096	5,886,950	3,766,955
2007	249,760,355	206,290,977	96,587	206,387,564	20,661,784	-2,645,090	183,080,690	42,963,559	23,716,106	41,454	6,025,041	3,914,003
2008	270,537,123	214,663,177	24,902	214,688,079	21,310,932	-2,472,241	190,904,906	51,942,072	27,690,145	43,970	6,152,770	3,993,668
2009	252,729,530	200,598,053	8,048	200,606,101	20,890,542	-2,215,420	177,500,139	44,632,090	30,597,301	40,228	6,282,484	3,914,537
2010	266,251,045	210,264,370	25,952	210,290,322	21,622,905	-2,094,145	186,573,272	45,450,409	34,227,364	41,657	6,391,451	3,929,902
2011	296,886,888	228,571,305	11,643	228,582,948	20,185,998	-2,073,890	206,323,060	55,052,250	35,511,578	45,624	6,507,200	4,069,108
2012	312,085,846	242,542,052	88,241	242,630,293	21,299,863	-2,147,101	219,183,329	57,272,369	35,630,148	47,013	6,638,289	4,191,362
2013	321,023,808	255,724,864	34,453	255,759,317	25,296,170	-2,087,767	228,375,380	55,684,473	36,963,955	47,597	6,744,646	4,319,431
2014	344,877,113	272,918,245	-18,918	272,899,327	26,778,306	-2,209,556	243,911,465	61,907,293	39,058,355	50,147	6,877,353	4,464,858
2015	357,111,400	282,429,018	42,533	282,471,551	28,618,317	-2,602,077	251,251,157	64,056,593	41,803,650	50,821	7,026,835	4,634,309
2016	369,242,759	291,324,080	-104,445	291,219,635	30,117,605	-3,104,256	257,997,774	67,380,130	43,864,855	51,451	7,176,620	4,794,803
2017	395,002,697	313,374,753	-155,518	313,219,235	32,090,484	-3,493,748	277,635,003	72,707,122	44,660,572	53,996	7,315,457	4,930,541
2018	424,650,728	333,989,049	-191,916	333,797,133	33,465,521	-3,588,357	296,743,255	80,898,870	47,008,603	57,137	7,432,101	5,085,293
2019	448,305,608	353,583,367	-171,860	353,411,507	35,366,685	-4,175,542	313,869,280	84,474,891	49,961,437	59,413	7,545,583	5,184,758
2020	472,842,214	354,508,034	-156,594	354,351,440	36,442,329	-4,560,161	313,348,950	89,446,377	70,046,887	61,681	7,665,875	5,170,447
2021	528,153,891	392,862,390	-161,310	392,701,080	39,395,077	-5,186,100	348,119,903	99,063,657	80,970,331	67,945	7,773,289	5,492,350
2022	559,970,576	435,331,296	-370,116	434,961,180	43,814,068	-6,093,827	385,053,285	107,703,585	67,213,706	70,493	7,943,685	5,845,180

Personal Income and Employment by Area: Dalton, GA

(Thousands of dollars, except as noted.)

Year	Personal income, total	Derivation of personal income: Earnings by place of work			Less: Contributions for government social insurance	Plus: Adjustment for residence	Equals: Net earnings by place of residence	Plus: Dividends, interest, and rent	Plus: Personal current transfer receipts	Per capita personal income (dollars)	Population (persons)	Total employment
		Nonfarm	Farm	Total								
1970	226,414	216,086	1,961	218,047	14,777	-17,244	186,026	23,412	16,976	3,302	68,569	35,168
1971	261,434	250,526	1,661	252,187	17,866	-19,826	214,495	27,731	19,208	3,668	71,282	37,695
1972	308,176	298,195	2,312	300,507	22,166	-23,763	254,578	32,270	21,328	4,181	73,703	41,452
1973	352,394	338,969	6,935	345,904	28,752	-26,394	290,758	36,323	25,313	4,572	77,080	43,738
1974	368,916	350,741	2,108	352,849	30,881	-27,036	294,932	41,509	32,475	4,641	79,491	42,486
1975	390,877	345,986	7,050	353,036	29,680	-25,210	298,146	45,394	47,337	4,936	79,193	39,069
1976	449,453	413,024	6,373	419,397	36,331	-30,444	352,622	49,729	47,102	5,630	79,835	42,562
1977	507,878	477,596	5,544	483,140	41,985	-36,857	404,298	55,433	48,147	6,203	81,872	45,560
1978	569,576	535,049	7,840	542,889	48,285	-40,370	454,234	63,446	51,896	6,826	83,444	47,923
1979	637,590	597,910	6,303	604,213	55,821	-44,599	503,793	73,638	60,159	7,512	84,874	49,185
1980	687,230	633,071	1,856	634,927	59,510	-49,270	526,147	88,122	72,961	8,014	85,754	48,891
1981	752,674	683,023	3,224	686,247	68,680	-56,357	561,210	107,448	84,016	8,674	86,771	48,672
1982	787,715	698,261	4,025	702,286	70,769	-61,810	569,707	124,950	93,058	9,036	87,177	46,909
1983	894,059	817,804	3,407	821,211	84,276	-78,978	657,957	137,116	98,986	10,200	87,649	50,744
1984	998,592	928,458	6,665	935,123	98,633	-94,550	741,940	150,844	105,808	11,182	89,307	54,398
1985	1,075,904	1,005,792	5,828	1,011,620	108,630	-108,117	794,873	167,271	113,760	11,867	90,663	56,119
1986	1,182,029	1,125,642	7,744	1,133,386	123,034	-128,881	881,471	179,712	120,846	12,824	92,171	58,945
1987	1,296,060	1,263,199	4,010	1,267,209	136,072	-153,868	977,269	193,340	125,451	13,736	94,353	62,232
1988	1,405,846	1,369,835	8,831	1,378,666	150,179	-172,975	1,055,512	216,444	133,890	14,598	96,302	65,112
1989	1,521,926	1,447,870	13,693	1,461,563	159,680	-189,612	1,112,271	259,033	150,622	15,557	97,831	66,708
1990	1,594,500	1,517,577	12,135	1,529,712	167,188	-205,558	1,156,966	268,972	168,562	16,113	98,957	67,995
1991	1,653,378	1,551,461	13,775	1,565,236	173,148	-216,677	1,175,411	282,073	195,894	16,470	100,385	66,329
1992	1,807,970	1,739,010	13,431	1,752,441	190,828	-254,775	1,306,838	280,633	220,499	17,758	101,814	69,845
1993	1,940,230	1,898,056	15,688	1,913,744	209,087	-289,727	1,414,930	290,811	234,489	18,739	103,540	73,741
1994	2,080,749	2,027,206	18,282	2,045,488	224,844	-318,611	1,502,033	321,781	256,935	19,597	106,177	76,724
1995	2,186,468	2,099,390	16,696	2,116,086	231,754	-334,129	1,550,203	354,339	281,926	20,102	108,771	78,552
1996	2,340,822	2,229,592	21,771	2,251,363	243,654	-363,782	1,643,927	390,364	306,531	21,075	111,071	80,144
1997	2,445,264	2,355,967	21,618	2,377,585	254,299	-389,889	1,733,397	399,447	312,420	21,514	113,661	81,060
1998	2,626,253	2,544,839	28,777	2,573,616	272,825	-426,690	1,874,101	433,811	318,341	22,754	115,417	82,126
1999	2,706,560	2,652,304	28,180	2,680,484	283,031	-447,055	1,950,398	415,493	340,669	22,937	118,000	83,196
2000	2,886,049	2,859,875	23,481	2,883,356	305,756	-506,969	2,070,631	445,824	369,594	23,860	120,959	87,006
2001	3,201,686	3,134,462	32,936	3,167,398	324,501	-533,712	2,309,185	477,252	415,249	25,817	124,015	85,876
2002	3,298,781	3,220,765	22,658	3,243,423	332,726	-566,394	2,344,303	478,659	475,819	26,138	126,208	86,499
2003	3,434,303	3,369,542	19,089	3,388,631	348,968	-612,562	2,427,101	520,929	486,273	26,731	128,476	86,672
2004	3,554,282	3,518,108	24,635	3,542,743	387,184	-647,189	2,508,370	524,842	521,070	27,068	131,307	88,307
2005	3,546,256	3,535,469	22,486	3,557,955	390,707	-676,734	2,490,514	495,253	560,489	26,487	133,885	89,189
2006	3,632,411	3,595,752	-555	3,595,197	394,004	-711,312	2,489,881	529,952	612,578	26,595	136,581	90,339
2007	3,741,263	3,611,387	8,193	3,619,580	394,813	-741,382	2,483,385	591,043	666,835	26,956	138,792	89,952
2008	3,756,153	3,404,319	19,527	3,423,846	388,638	-695,963	2,339,245	648,614	768,294	26,750	140,415	84,981
2009	3,558,858	3,173,560	15,620	3,189,180	364,501	-674,703	2,149,976	555,640	853,242	25,259	140,897	77,652
2010	3,675,157	3,208,233	9,855	3,218,088	364,981	-658,095	2,195,012	550,618	929,527	25,837	142,245	76,814
2011	3,802,318	3,247,803	3,114	3,250,917	339,848	-699,130	2,211,939	630,738	959,641	26,752	142,133	77,690
2012	3,930,758	3,375,775	34,770	3,410,545	351,046	-678,854	2,380,645	603,710	946,403	27,684	141,985	76,683
2013	4,102,354	3,552,096	46,251	3,598,347	410,022	-699,033	2,489,292	640,044	973,018	28,992	141,499	76,808
2014	4,393,561	3,858,812	56,352	3,915,164	439,570	-806,184	2,669,410	715,515	1,008,636	30,991	141,769	80,181
2015	4,704,355	4,054,686	69,743	4,124,429	456,799	-820,200	2,847,430	827,199	1,029,726	33,026	142,446	81,983
2016	4,814,489	4,187,495	39,478	4,226,973	471,729	-875,125	2,880,119	875,280	1,059,090	33,688	142,913	81,889
2017	4,913,443	4,126,586	56,779	4,183,365	464,882	-773,394	2,945,089	871,094	1,097,260	34,358	143,008	79,931
2018	5,183,536	4,222,467	45,783	4,268,250	475,739	-748,519	3,043,992	991,665	1,147,879	36,252	142,988	81,621
2019	5,397,346	4,260,647	29,303	4,289,950	479,852	-665,325	3,144,773	1,055,671	1,196,902	37,695	143,183	79,981
2020	5,744,697	4,275,445	-6,757	4,268,688	485,626	-634,304	3,148,758	989,391	1,606,548	40,232	142,788	78,007
2021	6,099,153	4,619,254	22,579	4,641,833	526,726	-704,685	3,410,422	910,133	1,778,598	42,735	142,720	80,861
2022	6,187,734	4,946,518	92,013	5,038,531	570,428	-766,289	3,701,814	962,435	1,523,485	43,089	143,604	83,272

Personal Income and Employment by Area: Danville, IL

(Thousands of dollars, except as noted.)

Year	Personal income, total	Derivation of personal income: Earnings by place of work: Nonfarm	Farm	Total	Less: Contributions for government social insurance	Plus: Adjustment for residence	Equals: Net earnings by place of residence	Plus: Dividends, interest, and rent	Plus: Personal current transfer receipts	Per capita personal income (dollars)	Population (persons)	Total employment
1970	373,467	304,412	13,951	318,363	20,397	-10,243	287,723	48,330	37,414	3,846	97,100	43,790
1971	414,577	333,407	21,318	354,725	22,802	-14,798	317,125	52,163	45,289	4,255	97,441	43,260
1972	449,098	370,566	17,581	388,147	26,546	-19,719	341,882	57,540	49,676	4,591	97,815	44,707
1973	529,893	426,433	39,440	465,873	35,525	-26,151	404,197	67,439	58,257	5,404	98,058	46,897
1974	558,284	445,175	38,951	484,126	38,523	-29,029	416,574	75,557	66,153	5,713	97,719	46,993
1975	623,023	472,955	54,161	527,116	39,974	-32,495	454,647	82,867	85,509	6,382	97,623	45,416
1976	674,821	537,858	44,156	582,014	46,452	-40,496	495,066	88,503	91,252	6,874	98,166	46,632
1977	720,640	584,000	41,993	625,993	50,321	-47,384	528,288	98,484	93,868	7,365	97,842	46,973
1978	779,928	650,821	31,194	682,015	57,774	-56,369	567,872	112,597	99,459	7,977	97,772	47,926
1979	841,488	681,808	48,559	730,367	62,548	-62,406	605,413	126,397	109,678	8,682	96,928	47,142
1980	865,850	687,293	14,957	702,250	62,509	-65,522	574,219	155,860	135,771	9,102	95,130	44,925
1981	964,659	726,477	30,391	756,868	71,108	-69,179	616,581	189,361	158,717	10,198	94,596	44,283
1982	1,001,509	724,682	18,848	743,530	72,098	-62,866	608,566	220,606	172,337	10,769	92,998	42,605
1983	1,009,314	753,304	-1,949	751,355	75,918	-61,656	613,781	215,323	180,210	10,881	92,758	42,368
1984	1,130,878	828,630	34,545	863,175	87,063	-66,032	710,080	240,122	180,676	12,273	92,141	42,881
1985	1,161,086	841,809	39,563	881,372	89,976	-63,658	727,738	244,079	189,269	12,678	91,584	42,021
1986	1,186,155	858,317	33,487	891,804	92,516	-59,737	739,551	249,324	197,280	12,956	91,551	42,054
1987	1,219,280	903,088	21,977	925,065	95,654	-58,103	771,308	244,562	203,410	13,412	90,909	42,017
1988	1,268,872	941,167	16,305	957,472	102,026	-53,168	802,278	254,678	211,916	14,125	89,831	42,051
1989	1,358,100	960,779	44,448	1,005,227	105,252	-48,630	851,345	285,739	221,016	15,304	88,740	41,546
1990	1,380,483	968,231	39,532	1,007,763	103,486	-36,920	867,357	270,736	242,390	15,660	88,155	41,527
1991	1,405,739	1,000,442	18,429	1,018,871	109,806	-37,298	871,767	273,067	260,905	15,977	87,986	41,296
1992	1,523,280	1,062,372	42,431	1,104,803	114,270	-39,303	951,230	276,183	295,867	17,321	87,944	41,311
1993	1,553,461	1,077,925	48,604	1,126,529	118,952	-37,074	970,503	277,059	305,899	17,706	87,738	40,834
1994	1,645,664	1,151,333	60,617	1,211,950	128,418	-39,610	1,043,922	289,409	312,333	18,717	87,922	42,042
1995	1,620,001	1,128,310	18,415	1,146,725	126,039	-30,257	990,429	301,815	327,757	18,713	86,570	41,796
1996	1,703,545	1,147,025	47,654	1,194,679	127,040	-27,277	1,040,362	321,962	341,221	19,972	85,298	42,425
1997	1,725,032	1,170,655	32,364	1,203,019	129,080	-23,568	1,050,371	329,396	345,265	20,229	85,274	42,515
1998	1,778,225	1,219,685	15,118	1,234,803	133,571	-25,432	1,075,800	348,530	353,895	20,921	84,996	42,324
1999	1,810,426	1,260,848	10,270	1,271,118	134,904	-19,156	1,117,058	336,148	357,220	21,482	84,276	42,214
2000	1,879,767	1,275,179	29,716	1,304,895	133,817	-9,630	1,161,448	345,493	372,826	22,426	83,821	42,344
2001	1,964,419	1,320,447	30,901	1,351,348	137,411	-2,108	1,211,829	355,230	397,360	23,485	83,646	40,683
2002	2,000,110	1,355,180	18,824	1,374,004	139,683	3,772	1,238,093	337,656	424,361	24,011	83,299	40,062
2003	2,126,056	1,443,497	35,520	1,479,017	149,305	-446	1,329,266	348,354	448,436	25,616	82,996	40,636
2004	2,185,781	1,488,190	60,329	1,548,519	156,437	2,122	1,394,204	324,009	467,568	26,349	82,955	40,029
2005	2,181,251	1,520,095	21,046	1,541,141	167,022	5,103	1,379,222	298,331	503,698	26,367	82,728	40,189
2006	2,267,762	1,572,265	39,951	1,612,216	171,143	9,165	1,450,238	294,190	523,334	27,417	82,715	39,863
2007	2,348,054	1,565,363	59,759	1,625,122	171,668	23,137	1,476,591	305,068	566,395	28,545	82,258	39,719
2008	2,516,291	1,587,460	101,924	1,689,384	176,033	30,520	1,543,871	367,647	604,773	30,713	81,930	39,184
2009	2,509,185	1,561,036	61,794	1,622,830	172,782	22,420	1,472,468	356,975	679,742	30,708	81,710	37,824
2010	2,621,348	1,637,510	78,361	1,715,871	178,604	21,940	1,559,207	339,319	722,822	32,118	81,617	37,284
2011	2,754,570	1,718,373	127,600	1,845,973	169,541	12,074	1,688,506	362,842	703,222	33,881	81,302	38,009
2012	2,736,505	1,742,326	84,428	1,826,754	174,091	11,922	1,664,585	378,120	693,800	33,928	80,657	38,163
2013	2,822,925	1,733,570	159,552	1,893,122	192,185	7,607	1,708,544	388,097	726,284	35,161	80,285	37,346
2014	2,786,326	1,765,367	77,911	1,843,278	196,536	10,063	1,656,805	387,014	742,507	35,095	79,393	37,667
2015	2,810,855	1,805,443	10,468	1,815,911	198,792	11,232	1,628,351	394,044	788,460	35,718	78,696	37,771
2016	2,813,563	1,772,373	55,262	1,827,635	198,036	11,830	1,641,429	384,969	787,165	36,119	77,897	36,630
2017	2,878,687	1,776,604	43,945	1,820,549	199,927	20,591	1,641,213	419,962	817,512	37,373	77,026	35,994
2018	2,932,340	1,802,433	62,908	1,865,341	204,237	25,364	1,686,468	408,948	836,924	38,624	75,921	35,447
2019	2,979,949	1,848,611	41,324	1,889,935	209,756	27,878	1,708,057	414,070	857,822	39,801	74,871	35,079
2020	3,276,479	1,869,370	84,646	1,954,016	213,427	38,888	1,779,477	397,126	1,099,876	44,276	74,001	33,958
2021	3,586,194	1,955,181	152,160	2,107,341	219,868	58,513	1,945,986	402,443	1,237,765	48,950	73,263	34,245
2022	3,552,142	2,077,138	175,389	2,252,527	244,033	59,083	2,067,577	415,921	1,068,644	49,105	72,337	35,416

Personal Income and Employment by Area: Daphne-Fairhope-Foley, AL

(Thousands of dollars, except as noted.)

Year	Personal income, total	Derivation of personal income: Earnings by place of work: Nonfarm	Farm	Total	Less: Contributions for government social insurance	Plus: Adjustment for residence	Equals: Net earnings by place of residence	Plus: Dividends, interest, and rent	Plus: Personal current transfer receipts	Per capita personal income (dollars)	Population (persons)	Total employment
1970	172,745	79,248	5,789	85,037	6,071	47,185	126,151	28,828	17,766	2,905	59,474	19,749
1971	196,684	89,196	8,786	97,982	6,919	51,482	142,545	33,364	20,775	3,270	60,142	20,505
1972	223,797	104,139	9,606	113,745	8,432	57,438	162,751	37,514	23,532	3,584	62,435	21,727
1973	268,069	121,106	20,473	141,579	11,236	63,826	194,169	45,617	28,283	4,176	64,196	23,015
1974	305,794	137,576	17,877	155,453	13,293	73,014	215,174	55,843	34,777	4,628	66,072	23,738
1975	345,248	151,882	16,280	168,162	14,678	83,503	236,987	63,422	44,839	5,088	67,861	24,458
1976	406,080	180,248	27,854	208,102	17,557	94,603	285,148	71,220	49,712	5,781	70,244	25,750
1977	435,048	202,296	9,603	211,899	19,860	107,108	299,147	82,483	53,418	6,009	72,399	26,965
1978	496,475	218,663	20,914	239,577	21,592	124,081	342,066	95,253	59,156	6,660	74,550	27,291
1979	542,295	244,352	4,309	248,661	24,913	138,082	361,830	109,266	71,199	7,080	76,594	27,875
1980	615,985	263,431	1,749	265,180	26,777	159,044	397,447	134,805	83,733	7,804	78,931	27,777
1981	717,375	291,361	10,495	301,856	32,333	184,421	453,944	167,588	95,843	8,935	80,287	28,722
1982	759,092	306,308	438	306,746	34,707	192,619	464,658	187,712	106,722	9,220	82,331	29,388
1983	844,681	349,814	6,907	356,721	39,188	203,122	520,655	205,875	118,151	10,058	83,978	31,306
1984	939,753	395,399	4,842	400,241	45,369	224,335	579,207	231,774	128,772	10,833	86,752	33,057
1985	1,047,779	437,883	14,040	451,923	49,964	250,708	652,667	255,276	139,836	11,720	89,401	33,969
1986	1,114,801	469,386	9,187	478,573	53,058	270,666	696,181	270,936	147,684	12,209	91,311	34,674
1987	1,177,163	499,048	14,112	513,160	56,032	289,608	746,736	278,607	151,820	12,629	93,214	36,081
1988	1,280,441	528,899	14,640	543,539	61,784	315,329	797,084	314,966	168,391	13,528	94,649	37,654
1989	1,435,313	568,898	18,028	586,926	67,236	347,393	867,083	375,686	192,544	14,920	96,198	38,889
1990	1,566,377	631,608	11,511	643,119	74,864	390,110	958,365	397,768	210,244	15,829	98,955	40,545
1991	1,738,285	697,625	17,516	715,141	82,626	448,657	1,081,172	416,839	240,274	16,972	102,420	42,388
1992	1,928,823	773,910	20,742	794,652	90,355	506,108	1,210,405	440,577	277,841	18,095	106,595	44,246
1993	2,126,732	860,852	26,233	887,085	101,563	564,261	1,349,783	476,269	300,680	19,088	111,416	47,280
1994	2,343,978	965,130	21,661	986,791	116,178	601,469	1,472,082	536,454	335,442	20,109	116,565	50,770
1995	2,554,178	1,073,129	22,922	1,096,051	129,352	621,992	1,588,691	596,980	368,507	21,127	120,896	54,511
1996	2,796,479	1,194,516	23,839	1,218,355	140,649	669,688	1,747,394	647,165	401,920	22,298	125,412	56,932
1997	3,053,744	1,299,527	23,367	1,322,894	154,451	740,059	1,908,502	717,674	427,568	23,461	130,164	60,806
1998	3,310,043	1,498,614	4,949	1,503,563	171,529	745,606	2,077,640	783,027	449,376	24,620	134,444	64,758
1999	3,487,304	1,625,770	20,689	1,646,459	187,352	760,813	2,219,920	795,867	471,517	25,352	137,555	67,472
2000	3,771,417	1,746,938	15,186	1,762,124	199,875	816,514	2,378,763	871,670	520,984	26,683	141,342	69,423
2001	3,943,845	1,808,269	10,662	1,818,931	211,491	828,822	2,436,262	916,998	590,585	27,222	144,875	70,661
2002	4,085,695	1,922,226	3,453	1,925,679	224,085	823,475	2,525,069	910,056	650,570	27,614	147,957	71,895
2003	4,297,587	2,047,090	16,654	2,063,744	239,158	846,765	2,671,351	916,167	710,069	28,365	151,509	73,848
2004	4,792,805	2,264,567	19,135	2,283,702	262,099	884,723	2,906,326	1,103,996	782,483	30,671	156,266	77,693
2005	5,272,521	2,575,615	9,487	2,585,102	297,640	927,652	3,215,114	1,209,022	848,385	32,510	162,183	82,614
2006	5,880,129	2,887,868	17,331	2,905,199	333,320	976,340	3,548,219	1,403,294	928,616	34,976	168,121	87,769
2007	6,243,633	2,996,449	15,845	3,012,294	354,822	1,049,626	3,707,098	1,528,754	1,007,781	36,215	172,404	92,730
2008	6,368,395	2,862,289	10,238	2,872,527	360,174	1,151,001	3,663,354	1,563,087	1,141,954	36,220	175,827	92,682
2009	6,344,357	2,706,405	15,567	2,721,972	344,065	1,247,767	3,625,674	1,462,695	1,255,988	35,363	179,406	89,326
2010	6,741,297	2,794,590	5,419	2,800,009	353,144	1,367,520	3,814,385	1,485,734	1,441,178	36,797	183,200	89,247
2011	7,113,915	2,897,614	8,153	2,905,767	328,220	1,530,010	4,107,557	1,521,531	1,484,827	38,046	186,981	91,996
2012	7,314,284	2,981,883	14,452	2,996,335	337,472	1,567,797	4,226,660	1,584,177	1,503,447	38,307	190,941	93,218
2013	7,534,558	3,175,079	18,849	3,193,928	400,561	1,552,059	4,345,426	1,616,277	1,572,855	38,428	196,067	96,460
2014	7,949,643	3,388,139	11,966	3,400,105	424,702	1,596,069	4,571,472	1,704,465	1,673,706	39,598	200,759	99,818
2015	8,504,769	3,621,295	11,627	3,632,922	451,377	1,690,645	4,872,190	1,822,393	1,810,186	41,502	204,925	103,921
2016	9,032,772	3,852,712	11,340	3,864,052	476,792	1,853,356	5,240,616	1,904,665	1,887,491	43,012	210,004	107,817
2017	9,583,207	4,018,153	16,901	4,035,054	503,855	1,944,881	5,476,080	2,125,439	1,981,688	44,498	215,365	111,634
2018	10,139,295	4,313,549	16,026	4,329,575	547,867	2,044,584	5,826,292	2,181,653	2,131,350	45,852	221,132	115,698
2019	10,879,470	4,579,830	14,525	4,594,355	578,961	2,107,263	6,122,657	2,417,862	2,338,951	47,911	227,079	116,997
2020	11,947,762	4,856,455	20,988	4,877,443	614,773	2,281,205	6,543,875	2,470,650	2,933,237	51,230	233,219	117,238
2021	13,371,784	5,351,472	26,268	5,377,740	675,650	2,496,618	7,198,708	2,809,209	3,363,867	55,865	239,361	124,924
2022	13,984,484	5,797,630	-3,322	5,794,308	747,968	2,834,506	7,880,846	3,063,649	3,039,989	56,747	246,435	131,489

Personal Income and Employment by Area: Davenport-Moline-Rock Island, IA-IL

(Thousands of dollars, except as noted.)

Year	Personal income, total	Derivation of personal income: Earnings by place of work: Nonfarm	Farm	Total	Less: Contributions for government social insurance	Plus: Adjustment for residence	Equals: Net earnings by place of residence	Plus: Dividends, interest, and rent	Plus: Personal current transfer receipts	Per capita personal income (dollars)	Population (persons)	Total employment
1970	1,622,020	1,314,949	48,364	1,363,313	86,009	-23,965	1,253,339	247,937	120,744	4,271	379,817	169,173
1971	1,717,581	1,386,972	39,893	1,426,865	93,458	-24,620	1,308,787	267,879	140,915	4,505	381,302	167,145
1972	1,887,827	1,523,131	59,947	1,583,078	108,874	-27,326	1,446,878	288,283	152,666	4,942	382,010	171,157
1973	2,171,907	1,743,142	100,802	1,843,944	145,158	-34,572	1,664,214	329,699	177,994	5,648	384,562	183,158
1974	2,433,004	1,994,591	80,378	2,074,969	173,786	-45,473	1,855,710	376,985	200,309	6,229	390,568	193,442
1975	2,697,281	2,135,977	126,030	2,262,007	182,626	-50,025	2,029,356	417,038	250,887	6,809	396,120	192,380
1976	2,898,322	2,358,686	83,964	2,442,650	206,986	-61,919	2,173,745	443,408	281,169	7,267	398,850	194,882
1977	3,188,957	2,644,316	69,582	2,713,898	233,113	-79,809	2,400,976	489,416	298,565	7,967	400,292	199,126
1978	3,503,443	2,903,381	91,583	2,994,964	265,345	-93,679	2,635,940	544,638	322,865	8,709	402,294	202,184
1979	3,914,712	3,293,948	77,154	3,371,102	315,315	-111,632	2,944,155	610,862	359,695	9,699	403,603	207,010
1980	4,258,571	3,540,230	-3,913	3,536,317	335,077	-124,393	3,076,847	747,999	433,725	10,530	404,420	202,488
1981	4,739,795	3,758,083	68,794	3,826,877	380,316	-124,569	3,321,992	909,027	508,776	11,699	405,162	201,299
1982	4,902,042	3,642,553	38,353	3,680,906	362,166	-108,850	3,209,890	1,086,543	605,609	12,193	402,024	190,760
1983	4,881,766	3,610,918	-51,993	3,558,925	361,772	-102,481	3,094,672	1,120,548	666,546	12,297	396,986	186,120
1984	5,372,072	3,914,382	80,114	3,994,496	403,808	-110,539	3,480,149	1,233,900	658,023	13,673	392,904	190,977
1985	5,567,005	4,057,419	106,178	4,163,597	426,120	-111,729	3,625,748	1,256,349	684,908	14,392	386,807	191,204
1986	5,573,722	4,037,613	73,382	4,110,995	428,583	-101,697	3,580,715	1,283,697	709,310	14,666	380,036	188,955
1987	5,827,588	4,329,220	95,775	4,424,995	455,506	-108,218	3,861,271	1,249,060	717,257	15,567	374,353	191,033
1988	6,025,685	4,507,399	53,648	4,561,047	489,638	-103,667	3,967,742	1,307,295	750,648	16,265	370,464	194,882
1989	6,466,798	4,767,320	78,925	4,846,245	524,236	-105,354	4,216,655	1,457,131	793,012	17,532	368,854	199,096
1990	6,793,630	5,089,042	80,068	5,169,110	563,270	-110,837	4,495,003	1,441,865	856,762	18,445	368,316	203,953
1991	6,978,994	5,230,028	66,233	5,296,261	591,533	-114,757	4,589,971	1,469,037	919,986	18,813	370,975	207,790
1992	7,415,398	5,539,152	105,292	5,644,444	618,884	-119,908	4,905,652	1,482,723	1,027,023	19,850	373,565	207,908
1993	7,515,393	5,620,413	65,738	5,686,151	641,015	-114,245	4,930,891	1,514,578	1,069,924	20,084	374,198	206,295
1994	7,841,310	5,932,866	92,223	6,025,089	686,342	-124,994	5,213,753	1,543,542	1,084,015	20,942	374,425	209,569
1995	8,262,093	6,231,860	16,812	6,248,672	720,540	-130,454	5,397,678	1,702,885	1,161,530	22,033	374,979	214,131
1996	8,828,912	6,549,229	117,691	6,666,920	739,237	-128,012	5,799,671	1,829,737	1,199,504	23,562	374,708	218,500
1997	9,309,851	6,968,091	96,402	7,064,493	794,612	-147,431	6,122,450	1,978,759	1,208,642	24,826	375,006	223,429
1998	9,828,067	7,364,741	70,613	7,435,354	836,377	-148,741	6,450,236	2,116,293	1,261,538	26,170	375,549	229,670
1999	9,920,637	7,513,258	36,182	7,549,440	844,388	-140,449	6,564,603	2,040,885	1,315,149	26,337	376,678	229,932
2000	10,423,799	7,836,990	69,660	7,906,650	871,865	-141,403	6,893,382	2,133,313	1,397,104	27,740	375,763	231,704
2001	10,789,058	8,135,379	59,323	8,194,702	894,376	-153,147	7,147,179	2,126,982	1,514,897	28,805	374,561	228,307
2002	10,982,041	8,343,953	45,070	8,389,023	912,170	-168,631	7,308,222	2,031,794	1,642,025	29,384	373,740	224,714
2003	11,368,323	8,629,632	123,781	8,753,413	944,027	-176,327	7,633,059	2,057,776	1,677,488	30,480	372,975	223,503
2004	12,300,651	9,444,774	166,503	9,611,277	1,019,877	-189,603	8,401,797	2,148,785	1,750,069	33,001	372,740	226,897
2005	12,653,962	9,871,730	71,519	9,943,249	1,084,500	-204,608	8,654,141	2,105,373	1,894,448	33,936	372,876	231,282
2006	13,335,525	10,337,590	68,135	10,405,725	1,126,838	-212,662	9,066,225	2,242,618	2,026,682	35,679	373,762	231,779
2007	14,128,831	10,760,598	136,289	10,896,887	1,183,013	-162,108	9,551,766	2,386,713	2,190,352	37,665	375,121	233,980
2008	15,075,554	11,163,266	196,389	11,359,655	1,239,240	-155,404	9,965,011	2,637,744	2,472,799	40,045	376,467	234,378
2009	14,718,653	10,895,173	88,303	10,983,476	1,214,432	-179,436	9,589,608	2,363,187	2,765,858	38,927	378,108	225,858
2010	15,205,603	11,185,289	70,053	11,255,342	1,253,543	-226,987	9,774,812	2,384,521	3,046,270	40,023	379,921	223,981
2011	16,132,975	11,693,423	249,864	11,943,287	1,185,106	-261,361	10,496,820	2,663,922	2,972,233	42,287	381,514	227,453
2012	16,460,644	12,024,714	157,208	12,181,922	1,213,264	-279,982	10,688,676	2,851,809	2,920,159	42,878	383,897	228,827
2013	16,637,901	12,016,973	402,545	12,419,518	1,366,177	-282,535	10,770,806	2,850,404	3,016,691	43,109	385,950	228,839
2014	16,738,002	12,002,837	215,745	12,218,582	1,361,722	-253,668	10,603,192	3,009,927	3,124,883	43,271	386,816	230,115
2015	17,026,346	12,191,071	38,923	12,229,994	1,376,786	-242,747	10,610,461	3,118,136	3,297,749	44,025	386,743	229,883
2016	17,325,510	12,295,089	106,373	12,401,462	1,406,146	-198,490	10,796,826	3,197,202	3,331,482	44,868	386,144	228,280
2017	17,935,600	12,777,308	82,589	12,859,897	1,468,491	-253,581	11,137,825	3,418,172	3,379,603	46,512	385,612	229,912
2018	18,391,380	13,092,302	113,131	13,205,433	1,514,514	-270,463	11,420,456	3,420,242	3,550,682	47,768	385,016	230,160
2019	18,645,407	13,307,842	79,320	13,387,162	1,553,670	-328,542	11,504,950	3,499,192	3,641,265	48,432	384,985	229,663
2020	19,894,186	13,476,914	155,496	13,632,410	1,593,584	-356,126	11,682,700	3,427,678	4,783,808	51,841	383,754	219,074
2021	21,408,524	14,119,662	367,555	14,487,217	1,652,736	-357,053	12,477,428	3,732,152	5,198,944	56,086	381,706	224,042
2022	21,506,836	14,821,304	435,078	15,256,382	1,793,841	-393,484	13,069,057	3,951,514	4,486,265	56,690	379,374	231,742

Personal Income and Employment by Area: Dayton-Kettering, OH

(Thousands of dollars, except as noted.)

Year	Personal income, total	Derivation of personal income: Earnings by place of work: Nonfarm	Farm	Total	Less: Contributions for government social insurance	Plus: Adjustment for residence	Equals: Net earnings by place of residence	Plus: Dividends, interest, and rent	Plus: Personal current transfer receipts	Per capita personal income (dollars)	Population (persons)	Total employment
1970	3,724,442	3,390,457	19,936	3,410,393	206,990	-242,805	2,960,598	543,195	220,649	4,556	817,533	388,647
1971	3,850,553	3,424,747	18,705	3,443,452	213,624	-233,979	2,995,849	585,702	269,002	4,717	816,329	370,912
1972	4,198,442	3,763,377	22,439	3,785,816	249,182	-252,601	3,284,033	616,987	297,422	5,158	813,964	380,981
1973	4,556,792	4,086,845	38,039	4,124,884	313,612	-271,616	3,539,656	671,252	345,884	5,652	806,273	389,418
1974	4,879,893	4,261,889	41,241	4,303,130	335,862	-267,085	3,700,183	748,201	431,509	6,109	798,827	389,620
1975	5,259,095	4,445,463	35,020	4,480,483	342,172	-252,970	3,885,341	818,851	554,903	6,593	797,720	377,791
1976	5,777,472	4,971,522	30,386	5,001,908	397,541	-287,581	4,316,786	876,501	584,185	7,276	794,070	386,876
1977	6,352,071	5,511,820	24,938	5,536,758	443,501	-321,804	4,771,453	971,897	608,721	8,056	788,517	399,513
1978	6,966,972	6,061,433	24,825	6,086,258	502,416	-354,280	5,229,562	1,082,236	655,174	8,835	788,528	414,200
1979	7,679,718	6,636,020	42,521	6,678,541	573,379	-397,072	5,708,090	1,207,885	763,743	9,706	791,260	421,805
1980	8,300,940	6,896,544	27,641	6,924,185	592,645	-405,543	5,925,997	1,427,560	947,383	10,481	792,002	412,506
1981	8,919,574	7,464,360	2,936	7,467,296	684,596	-624,734	6,157,966	1,708,044	1,053,564	11,279	790,829	408,425
1982	9,316,562	7,536,479	14,243	7,550,722	698,140	-622,600	6,229,982	1,863,848	1,222,732	11,851	786,167	394,889
1983	9,946,597	8,060,817	-10,541	8,050,276	778,279	-648,339	6,623,658	2,026,058	1,296,881	12,697	783,366	397,786
1984	11,003,490	9,009,710	36,095	9,045,805	897,233	-720,736	7,427,836	2,236,885	1,338,769	14,003	785,813	418,017
1985	11,789,043	9,735,177	49,998	9,785,175	998,701	-773,045	8,013,429	2,347,871	1,427,743	14,945	788,847	431,975
1986	12,427,687	10,281,818	35,647	10,317,465	1,092,539	-796,345	8,428,581	2,478,573	1,520,533	15,710	791,049	443,823
1987	12,869,214	10,672,036	29,137	10,701,173	1,134,955	-798,189	8,768,029	2,517,327	1,583,858	16,164	796,181	455,751
1988	13,940,953	11,648,723	35,824	11,684,547	1,283,792	-867,320	9,533,435	2,733,877	1,673,641	17,369	802,640	464,150
1989	14,948,215	12,273,783	47,404	12,321,187	1,363,771	-887,701	10,069,715	3,114,265	1,764,235	18,630	802,358	471,695
1990	15,592,080	12,712,259	45,026	12,757,285	1,450,064	-914,708	10,392,513	3,213,187	1,986,380	19,385	804,335	473,295
1991	16,211,193	13,084,446	27,917	13,112,363	1,529,416	-940,617	10,642,330	3,446,521	2,122,342	20,019	809,809	470,098
1992	16,884,981	13,721,775	53,109	13,774,884	1,603,407	-951,356	11,220,121	3,329,610	2,335,250	20,731	814,480	464,432
1993	17,542,786	14,359,306	41,646	14,400,952	1,695,609	-1,043,833	11,661,510	3,477,578	2,403,698	21,474	816,922	469,215
1994	18,379,188	15,117,514	45,918	15,163,432	1,812,080	-1,139,751	12,211,601	3,658,836	2,508,751	22,554	814,885	481,730
1995	19,469,407	15,864,914	30,974	15,895,888	1,915,624	-1,230,619	12,749,645	4,070,087	2,649,675	23,871	815,608	491,268
1996	20,186,193	16,405,037	44,535	16,449,572	1,962,614	-1,282,642	13,204,316	4,240,136	2,741,741	24,793	814,188	492,909
1997	21,185,478	17,230,660	66,260	17,296,920	2,022,001	-1,395,764	13,879,155	4,472,507	2,833,816	26,115	811,250	499,170
1998	22,034,808	17,840,225	46,723	17,886,948	2,030,387	-1,355,259	14,501,302	4,650,706	2,882,800	27,164	811,168	502,538
1999	22,449,211	18,413,785	26,549	18,440,334	2,092,884	-1,391,137	14,956,313	4,525,588	2,967,310	27,783	808,010	497,259
2000	23,575,275	19,185,952	42,182	19,228,134	2,113,710	-1,480,499	15,633,925	4,762,645	3,178,705	29,252	805,938	503,030
2001	24,191,992	19,566,553	48,764	19,615,317	2,150,185	-1,478,645	15,986,487	4,700,274	3,505,231	30,072	804,479	497,721
2002	24,515,720	19,846,250	25,474	19,871,724	2,154,560	-1,479,081	16,238,083	4,531,095	3,746,542	30,481	804,286	488,979
2003	25,010,411	20,326,376	38,325	20,364,701	2,229,161	-1,493,513	16,642,027	4,448,399	3,919,985	31,072	804,926	484,368
2004	25,638,878	21,131,525	53,633	21,185,158	2,340,387	-1,544,728	17,300,043	4,239,143	4,099,692	31,813	805,930	484,033
2005	26,076,495	21,340,977	40,938	21,381,915	2,380,347	-1,579,217	17,422,351	4,313,906	4,340,238	32,403	804,766	482,762
2006	27,452,234	22,099,502	39,182	22,138,684	2,472,600	-1,589,280	18,076,804	4,749,491	4,625,939	34,166	803,498	481,809
2007	28,195,295	22,055,971	45,898	22,101,869	2,465,195	-1,515,463	18,121,211	5,124,843	4,949,241	35,163	801,852	481,031
2008	28,917,955	21,870,317	31,044	21,901,361	2,495,710	-1,426,232	17,979,419	5,323,642	5,614,894	36,138	800,209	471,120
2009	28,354,230	20,976,538	53,882	21,030,420	2,413,709	-1,334,272	17,282,439	4,948,425	6,123,366	35,492	798,895	450,118
2010	29,064,292	21,460,546	44,596	21,505,142	2,435,262	-1,456,195	17,613,685	4,918,340	6,532,267	36,339	799,815	447,819
2011	30,764,179	22,442,273	67,986	22,510,259	2,293,797	-1,540,844	18,675,618	5,403,501	6,685,060	38,382	801,527	454,620
2012	31,459,670	23,096,727	46,807	23,143,534	2,352,203	-1,538,504	19,252,827	5,659,478	6,547,365	39,187	802,802	457,498
2013	31,750,265	23,622,535	89,062	23,711,597	2,607,139	-1,454,635	19,649,823	5,449,372	6,651,070	39,534	803,112	457,993
2014	33,005,190	24,340,836	23,461	24,364,297	2,679,560	-1,450,449	20,234,288	5,806,346	6,964,556	41,090	803,249	463,450
2015	34,218,800	25,123,720	-2,905	25,120,815	2,776,538	-1,405,321	20,938,956	6,062,520	7,217,324	42,619	802,897	470,131
2016	34,981,536	25,651,241	16,797	25,668,038	2,887,010	-1,408,925	21,372,103	6,209,178	7,400,255	43,451	805,086	474,316
2017	36,558,265	26,671,463	28,915	26,700,378	3,056,308	-1,449,959	22,194,111	6,800,622	7,563,532	45,295	807,112	481,854
2018	37,931,583	27,877,708	34,238	27,911,946	3,139,125	-1,476,868	23,295,953	6,873,453	7,762,177	46,867	809,348	487,410
2019	39,329,247	28,988,945	4,154	28,993,099	3,287,674	-1,590,757	24,114,668	7,080,857	8,133,722	48,400	812,591	488,572
2020	42,528,818	29,733,002	68,055	29,801,057	3,374,802	-1,682,535	24,743,720	7,139,038	10,646,060	52,236	814,162	475,227
2021	45,380,361	31,311,040	106,349	31,417,389	3,541,111	-1,649,063	26,227,215	7,556,195	11,596,951	55,806	813,183	482,732
2022	45,885,237	32,945,550	79,417	33,024,967	3,817,949	-1,639,937	27,567,081	8,183,152	10,135,004	56,468	812,595	498,430

Personal Income and Employment by Area: Decatur, AL

(Thousands of dollars, except as noted.)

Year	Personal income, total	Derivation of personal income: Earnings by place of work: Nonfarm	Farm	Total	Less: Contributions for government social insurance	Plus: Adjustment for residence	Equals: Net earnings by place of residence	Plus: Dividends, interest, and rent	Plus: Personal current transfer receipts	Per capita personal income (dollars)	Population (persons)	Total employment
1970	350,823	250,850	13,280	264,130	18,331	38,890	284,689	34,748	31,386	3,341	105,018	41,444
1971	375,836	259,423	13,605	273,028	19,308	44,382	298,102	39,856	37,878	3,491	107,661	41,034
1972	407,614	285,521	15,993	301,514	22,367	43,641	322,788	43,186	41,640	3,716	109,678	42,354
1973	453,561	322,270	25,527	347,797	29,339	39,651	358,109	48,194	47,258	4,106	110,455	44,291
1974	492,008	371,689	10,504	382,193	35,236	34,359	381,316	55,450	55,242	4,359	112,864	46,325
1975	564,046	417,398	22,106	439,504	39,305	28,271	428,470	61,781	73,795	4,943	114,103	46,956
1976	623,154	457,488	28,380	485,868	43,614	31,851	474,105	67,845	81,204	5,387	115,667	47,493
1977	691,124	514,088	27,274	541,362	48,987	38,188	530,563	76,445	84,116	5,901	117,115	49,637
1978	781,117	600,536	21,239	621,775	58,622	39,714	602,867	88,721	89,529	6,548	119,287	52,721
1979	892,044	681,679	26,101	707,780	68,697	48,524	687,607	101,174	103,263	7,383	120,822	53,931
1980	958,090	694,627	10,421	705,048	69,838	69,996	705,206	125,780	127,104	7,955	120,435	51,505
1981	1,074,354	752,569	20,057	772,626	81,113	85,280	776,793	154,495	143,066	8,927	120,351	51,147
1982	1,132,185	771,157	14,944	786,101	85,213	92,499	793,387	177,481	161,317	9,350	121,091	49,815
1983	1,222,968	831,192	5,425	836,617	92,272	114,380	858,725	189,494	174,749	10,030	121,928	50,679
1984	1,396,928	927,618	26,803	954,421	104,560	144,518	994,379	215,360	187,189	11,309	123,522	53,337
1985	1,528,858	999,951	19,773	1,019,724	112,814	185,141	1,092,051	236,975	199,832	12,223	125,076	54,919
1986	1,629,822	1,054,073	25,274	1,079,347	118,461	207,277	1,168,163	251,389	210,270	12,881	126,532	56,295
1987	1,718,645	1,131,996	27,374	1,159,370	125,489	211,141	1,245,022	258,711	214,912	13,412	128,146	58,491
1988	1,875,691	1,209,923	41,230	1,251,153	138,353	249,350	1,362,150	288,265	225,276	14,538	129,017	60,490
1989	2,036,601	1,300,380	45,530	1,345,910	149,201	254,361	1,451,070	324,430	261,101	15,647	130,162	62,258
1990	2,174,256	1,404,547	33,469	1,438,016	163,235	260,888	1,535,669	347,831	290,756	16,457	132,118	65,211
1991	2,305,915	1,504,415	46,433	1,550,848	176,515	245,307	1,619,640	363,224	323,051	17,180	134,218	65,427
1992	2,472,354	1,597,818	43,713	1,641,531	184,643	293,168	1,750,056	357,424	364,874	18,185	135,959	65,640
1993	2,563,279	1,682,309	36,775	1,719,084	197,412	288,543	1,810,215	368,578	384,486	18,573	138,014	67,205
1994	2,727,382	1,741,331	51,368	1,792,699	205,850	323,328	1,910,177	407,446	409,759	19,629	138,947	67,605
1995	2,854,475	1,823,949	25,330	1,849,279	217,009	334,812	1,967,082	444,561	442,832	20,330	140,404	69,872
1996	2,965,662	1,911,547	40,469	1,952,016	224,534	300,111	2,027,593	469,844	468,225	20,946	141,587	71,005
1997	3,083,991	2,018,406	42,605	2,061,011	235,839	274,345	2,099,517	490,343	494,131	21,573	142,959	72,474
1998	3,292,413	2,178,344	57,964	2,236,308	251,529	275,818	2,260,597	522,953	508,863	22,834	144,192	74,066
1999	3,399,657	2,286,978	61,927	2,348,905	265,258	259,700	2,343,347	518,182	538,128	23,412	145,207	75,040
2000	3,491,108	2,318,222	43,601	2,361,823	269,729	265,431	2,357,525	553,060	580,523	23,896	146,095	75,786
2001	3,590,576	2,383,860	64,564	2,448,424	281,825	267,944	2,434,543	557,295	598,738	24,500	146,552	75,846
2002	3,596,926	2,328,605	33,728	2,362,333	273,687	316,932	2,405,578	554,472	636,876	24,558	146,464	73,530
2003	3,789,717	2,388,851	53,739	2,442,590	280,094	353,158	2,515,654	594,239	679,824	25,713	147,386	72,559
2004	4,008,940	2,566,201	87,416	2,653,617	296,995	337,457	2,694,079	608,213	706,648	27,212	147,324	74,240
2005	4,167,252	2,645,615	71,149	2,716,764	309,202	372,017	2,779,579	622,969	764,704	28,081	148,399	74,953
2006	4,370,944	2,749,686	17,581	2,767,267	323,517	421,586	2,865,336	668,254	837,354	29,233	149,519	75,304
2007	4,586,125	2,859,539	33,770	2,893,309	340,518	405,835	2,958,626	721,364	906,135	30,434	150,690	77,105
2008	4,758,022	2,873,859	45,725	2,919,584	347,845	370,092	2,941,831	804,960	1,011,231	31,325	151,890	76,559
2009	4,677,975	2,744,670	41,498	2,786,168	332,566	392,157	2,845,759	719,087	1,113,129	30,521	153,269	72,447
2010	4,824,525	2,838,794	29,352	2,868,146	348,017	364,940	2,885,069	737,304	1,202,152	31,318	154,048	71,654
2011	4,915,138	2,928,116	-3,104	2,925,012	321,786	359,760	2,962,986	743,500	1,208,652	31,804	154,545	73,436
2012	5,025,034	2,998,246	14,827	3,013,073	328,462	362,231	3,046,842	754,620	1,223,572	32,470	154,760	73,505
2013	5,123,513	3,034,221	78,792	3,113,013	375,131	366,016	3,103,898	762,189	1,257,426	33,189	154,372	73,752
2014	5,325,147	3,119,850	51,170	3,171,020	380,179	402,040	3,192,881	834,275	1,297,991	34,473	154,475	73,346
2015	5,403,452	3,097,957	39,430	3,137,387	382,078	421,698	3,177,007	830,347	1,396,098	35,008	154,349	72,998
2016	5,415,853	3,176,213	-3,324	3,172,889	391,193	399,932	3,181,628	810,655	1,423,570	35,040	154,563	73,269
2017	5,596,575	3,240,707	15,527	3,256,234	401,975	432,132	3,286,391	866,106	1,444,078	36,198	154,610	73,930
2018	5,841,962	3,451,813	3,190	3,455,003	431,781	410,450	3,433,672	909,497	1,498,793	37,659	155,126	75,712
2019	6,149,126	3,725,538	-10,258	3,715,280	460,826	363,925	3,618,379	966,142	1,564,605	39,453	155,859	77,113
2020	6,501,090	3,942,901	-32,735	3,910,166	489,284	277,137	3,698,019	906,299	1,896,772	41,573	156,377	76,596
2021	7,100,947	4,104,887	41,540	4,146,427	511,954	320,327	3,954,800	987,701	2,158,446	45,366	156,526	78,024
2022	7,118,013	4,424,961	37,675	4,462,636	558,616	230,406	4,134,426	1,060,835	1,922,752	45,215	157,425	80,635

Personal Income and Employment by Area: Decatur, IL

(Thousands of dollars, except as noted.)

Year	Personal income, total	Derivation of personal income: Earnings by place of work: Nonfarm	Farm	Total	Less: Contributions for government social insurance	Plus: Adjustment for residence	Equals: Net earnings by place of residence	Plus: Dividends, interest, and rent	Plus: Personal current transfer receipts	Per capita personal income (dollars)	Population (persons)	Total employment
1970	534,200	488,789	10,288	499,077	34,906	-46,430	417,741	72,420	44,039	4,277	124,905	61,590
1971	572,760	516,740	12,685	529,425	37,852	-49,155	442,418	77,520	52,822	4,572	125,278	60,980
1972	620,388	568,459	10,017	578,476	43,869	-56,878	477,729	84,808	57,851	4,954	125,241	62,469
1973	694,282	625,380	23,435	648,815	55,686	-63,795	529,334	95,765	69,183	5,471	126,910	65,047
1974	769,313	698,627	25,338	723,965	64,811	-74,750	584,404	107,382	77,527	6,022	127,752	66,355
1975	841,296	730,642	37,107	767,749	66,126	-78,732	622,891	118,966	99,439	6,511	129,218	65,268
1976	919,355	820,774	28,793	849,567	75,820	-90,491	683,256	126,297	109,802	7,088	129,701	66,311
1977	1,002,082	904,795	28,199	932,994	83,754	-101,449	747,791	139,167	115,124	7,628	131,366	68,395
1978	1,101,786	1,018,082	21,022	1,039,104	96,485	-117,748	824,871	155,806	121,109	8,321	132,404	69,932
1979	1,176,548	1,073,949	26,143	1,100,092	105,044	-122,398	872,650	171,217	132,681	8,889	132,364	69,000
1980	1,292,815	1,153,101	7,733	1,160,834	112,300	-137,072	911,462	217,918	163,435	9,853	131,205	67,250
1981	1,444,689	1,231,812	25,701	1,257,513	128,901	-143,184	985,428	270,601	188,660	11,088	130,295	67,071
1982	1,488,242	1,199,761	17,011	1,216,772	126,890	-127,184	962,698	310,278	215,266	11,583	128,485	63,475
1983	1,480,416	1,195,349	-9,713	1,185,636	127,257	-116,645	941,734	310,801	227,881	11,663	126,932	60,376
1984	1,646,102	1,339,794	19,603	1,359,397	148,894	-127,377	1,083,126	342,159	220,817	13,061	126,033	62,722
1985	1,723,211	1,400,256	24,463	1,424,719	158,147	-130,489	1,136,083	355,019	232,109	13,789	124,970	62,271
1986	1,765,408	1,440,701	21,468	1,462,169	163,100	-147,547	1,151,522	367,341	246,545	14,379	122,775	62,625
1987	1,833,126	1,523,430	18,364	1,541,794	169,262	-158,174	1,214,358	366,555	252,213	15,209	120,527	62,642
1988	1,917,262	1,601,787	11,177	1,612,964	183,047	-152,525	1,277,392	378,197	261,673	16,108	119,024	63,093
1989	2,076,853	1,680,742	25,595	1,706,337	192,223	-159,311	1,354,803	441,464	280,586	17,642	117,723	64,147
1990	2,151,754	1,773,585	18,461	1,792,046	197,032	-159,738	1,435,276	412,100	304,378	18,349	117,271	64,900
1991	2,192,070	1,806,697	10,554	1,817,251	206,416	-158,589	1,452,246	410,534	329,290	18,579	117,984	65,857
1992	2,350,044	1,879,588	30,313	1,909,901	209,510	-161,039	1,539,352	439,916	370,776	19,866	118,297	65,119
1993	2,394,117	1,943,611	21,164	1,964,775	220,566	-169,068	1,575,141	428,634	390,342	20,301	117,933	65,228
1994	2,465,144	2,005,041	35,406	2,040,447	229,876	-175,665	1,634,906	435,435	394,803	20,982	117,490	65,479
1995	2,539,672	2,032,617	4,948	2,037,565	232,692	-173,821	1,631,052	490,925	417,695	21,653	117,289	65,836
1996	2,714,912	2,195,898	35,233	2,231,131	248,948	-199,862	1,782,321	493,874	438,717	23,289	116,573	68,553
1997	2,781,074	2,245,218	30,525	2,275,743	253,983	-206,579	1,815,181	516,324	449,569	24,036	115,706	68,850
1998	2,929,744	2,386,526	12,501	2,399,027	267,200	-221,328	1,910,499	556,661	462,584	25,376	115,453	68,933
1999	3,104,080	2,614,091	13,372	2,627,463	285,856	-247,578	2,094,029	538,391	471,660	26,959	115,142	71,554
2000	3,183,878	2,631,495	22,768	2,654,263	285,957	-251,727	2,116,579	574,467	492,832	27,807	114,499	71,803
2001	3,423,795	2,814,876	24,597	2,839,473	294,524	-223,745	2,321,204	571,249	531,342	30,138	113,604	68,070
2002	3,426,927	2,820,070	17,532	2,837,602	288,422	-192,242	2,356,938	489,893	580,096	30,444	112,564	65,474
2003	3,382,992	2,767,323	20,436	2,787,759	293,636	-195,746	2,298,377	485,508	599,107	30,321	111,572	64,829
2004	3,530,251	2,837,410	49,960	2,887,370	312,932	-191,523	2,382,915	531,218	616,118	31,752	111,181	65,064
2005	3,610,012	2,962,758	23,611	2,986,369	332,831	-215,771	2,437,767	510,631	661,614	32,498	111,083	65,140
2006	3,806,999	3,098,831	30,660	3,129,491	342,678	-200,566	2,586,247	540,782	679,970	34,357	110,808	65,743
2007	4,053,203	3,267,107	51,210	3,318,317	363,677	-214,052	2,740,588	568,239	744,376	36,597	110,751	66,943
2008	4,279,420	3,327,846	69,384	3,397,230	372,713	-190,779	2,833,738	642,537	803,145	38,697	110,588	66,553
2009	4,276,276	3,219,281	49,791	3,269,072	359,894	-170,148	2,739,030	639,689	897,557	38,618	110,732	64,188
2010	4,326,883	3,268,196	47,053	3,315,249	361,838	-190,175	2,763,236	598,991	964,656	39,050	110,803	63,820
2011	4,568,326	3,422,728	84,198	3,506,926	342,398	-196,776	2,967,752	673,295	927,279	41,235	110,788	65,205
2012	4,552,566	3,463,943	36,223	3,500,166	347,859	-257,311	2,894,996	717,141	940,429	41,267	110,321	64,628
2013	4,646,224	3,443,012	118,835	3,561,847	386,148	-210,724	2,964,975	697,189	984,060	42,306	109,823	63,058
2014	4,750,670	3,677,313	43,464	3,720,777	405,290	-268,843	3,046,644	705,824	998,202	43,642	108,855	63,089
2015	4,685,162	3,758,779	183	3,758,962	414,355	-423,510	2,921,097	715,896	1,048,169	43,480	107,755	63,016
2016	4,679,690	3,672,006	29,111	3,701,117	411,936	-413,543	2,875,638	746,947	1,057,105	43,804	106,832	62,580
2017	4,740,806	3,700,141	32,147	3,732,288	417,817	-425,022	2,889,449	758,909	1,092,448	44,742	105,958	62,136
2018	4,958,670	3,880,355	43,894	3,924,249	438,857	-444,320	3,041,072	794,417	1,123,181	47,192	105,075	62,225
2019	4,947,426	3,858,865	24,673	3,883,538	435,689	-418,098	3,029,751	752,675	1,165,000	47,289	104,620	60,482
2020	5,340,725	3,823,245	48,072	3,871,317	430,337	-407,490	3,033,490	785,953	1,521,282	51,474	103,756	57,282
2021	5,793,197	4,072,126	94,276	4,166,402	452,842	-448,150	3,265,410	839,359	1,688,428	56,437	102,649	57,969
2022	5,761,622	4,343,660	111,651	4,455,311	505,596	-510,502	3,439,213	895,127	1,427,282	56,774	101,483	59,709

Personal Income and Employment by Area: Deltona-Daytona Beach-Ormond Beach, FL

(Thousands of dollars, except as noted.)

Year	Personal income, total	Derivation of personal income: Earnings by place of work								Per capita personal income (dollars)	Population (persons)	Total employment
		Nonfarm	Farm	Total	Less: Contributions for government social insurance	Plus: Adjustment for residence	Equals: Net earnings by place of residence	Plus: Dividends, interest, and rent	Plus: Personal current transfer receipts			
1970	639,900	359,669	9,803	369,472	23,287	19,725	365,910	176,934	97,056	3,659	174,894	64,013
1971	714,677	399,988	11,223	411,211	27,196	20,456	404,471	196,772	113,434	3,928	181,923	67,875
1972	817,755	468,530	13,503	482,033	33,731	21,860	470,162	217,774	129,819	4,311	189,672	74,167
1973	968,502	563,638	17,467	581,105	46,286	24,516	559,335	252,842	156,325	4,748	203,993	82,359
1974	1,098,055	630,594	16,556	647,150	54,411	24,871	617,610	296,592	183,853	5,058	217,106	86,169
1975	1,220,491	667,839	21,824	689,663	56,789	26,874	659,748	328,800	231,943	5,424	225,008	85,659
1976	1,339,947	731,492	21,117	752,609	62,502	29,616	719,723	364,031	256,193	5,820	230,241	86,843
1977	1,500,427	811,580	19,171	830,751	69,862	33,186	794,075	420,703	285,649	6,309	237,833	91,275
1978	1,738,599	949,251	21,542	970,793	83,901	41,409	928,301	494,354	315,944	7,044	246,836	98,192
1979	2,026,469	1,099,207	20,979	1,120,186	102,201	48,652	1,066,637	590,843	368,989	7,769	260,852	104,567
1980	2,430,692	1,247,869	27,051	1,274,920	117,822	57,387	1,214,485	770,683	445,524	8,915	272,648	110,011
1981	2,853,886	1,397,086	27,496	1,424,582	142,423	77,320	1,359,479	968,918	525,489	10,048	284,026	114,209
1982	3,110,206	1,482,872	40,034	1,522,906	156,730	98,522	1,464,698	1,049,257	596,251	10,545	294,958	117,353
1983	3,495,654	1,657,339	44,242	1,701,581	174,334	122,416	1,649,663	1,183,366	662,625	11,448	305,348	123,065
1984	3,906,443	1,897,103	42,595	1,939,698	204,642	151,886	1,886,942	1,320,297	699,204	12,363	315,969	131,569
1985	4,323,400	2,124,848	40,643	2,165,491	233,859	180,917	2,112,549	1,451,711	759,140	13,187	327,855	140,900
1986	4,724,200	2,333,911	44,216	2,378,127	263,237	216,896	2,331,786	1,569,583	822,831	13,883	340,285	148,201
1987	5,087,055	2,596,306	41,088	2,637,394	288,771	257,582	2,606,205	1,602,936	877,914	14,348	354,554	149,553
1988	5,653,951	2,839,151	48,483	2,887,634	327,682	305,066	2,865,018	1,804,053	984,880	15,293	369,706	156,611
1989	6,220,965	2,983,452	47,893	3,031,345	355,332	356,069	3,032,082	2,100,367	1,088,516	16,184	384,379	156,972
1990	6,653,276	3,154,811	47,618	3,202,429	369,846	415,168	3,247,751	2,210,495	1,195,030	16,482	403,674	155,591
1991	6,887,047	3,272,734	56,995	3,329,729	387,560	429,510	3,371,679	2,179,125	1,336,243	16,572	415,595	155,691
1992	7,278,767	3,494,452	64,726	3,559,178	412,271	472,100	3,619,007	2,144,654	1,515,106	17,097	425,733	156,162
1993	7,699,272	3,738,673	61,361	3,800,034	440,756	509,667	3,868,945	2,196,036	1,634,291	17,680	435,486	162,045
1994	8,164,368	3,947,259	62,090	4,009,349	474,971	547,248	4,081,626	2,329,870	1,752,872	18,333	445,335	166,426
1995	8,769,942	4,221,394	59,703	4,281,097	508,047	583,368	4,356,418	2,520,040	1,893,484	19,341	453,432	173,778
1996	9,334,092	4,469,265	59,170	4,528,435	529,476	643,166	4,642,125	2,688,712	2,003,255	20,267	460,565	177,992
1997	9,915,766	4,680,035	67,347	4,747,382	554,799	724,253	4,916,836	2,902,202	2,096,728	21,058	470,889	180,114
1998	10,504,398	4,883,458	64,760	4,948,218	575,459	819,196	5,191,955	3,147,429	2,165,014	21,930	478,995	183,443
1999	10,967,817	5,256,778	67,523	5,324,301	610,568	906,693	5,620,426	3,100,153	2,247,238	22,535	486,692	187,376
2000	11,793,614	5,592,601	65,783	5,658,384	646,447	1,018,547	6,030,484	3,384,862	2,378,268	23,801	495,514	192,200
2001	12,987,235	6,385,296	66,948	6,452,244	718,318	1,152,404	6,886,330	3,485,431	2,615,474	25,715	505,047	214,468
2002	13,655,870	6,870,387	61,795	6,932,182	770,957	1,266,983	7,428,208	3,427,590	2,800,072	26,457	516,153	220,860
2003	14,588,604	7,429,827	56,442	7,486,269	833,165	1,401,849	8,054,953	3,554,542	2,979,109	27,577	529,021	229,416
2004	15,924,993	8,049,230	62,350	8,111,580	914,919	1,589,018	8,785,679	3,883,977	3,255,337	29,154	546,232	239,563
2005	17,172,785	8,585,707	75,173	8,660,880	995,430	1,947,942	9,613,392	4,002,621	3,556,772	30,486	563,305	253,526
2006	18,563,819	9,192,066	66,248	9,258,314	1,086,902	2,186,289	10,357,701	4,347,339	3,858,779	32,057	579,087	263,122
2007	19,596,541	9,244,029	69,172	9,313,201	1,115,727	2,390,211	10,587,685	4,913,501	4,095,355	33,245	589,451	265,560
2008	19,992,778	8,926,088	62,592	8,988,680	1,109,895	2,467,354	10,346,139	5,067,300	4,579,339	33,834	590,912	256,907
2009	18,899,577	8,325,161	67,032	8,392,193	1,062,501	2,251,829	9,581,521	4,329,363	4,988,693	32,066	589,388	244,592
2010	19,862,801	8,635,324	66,529	8,701,853	1,084,614	2,231,985	9,849,224	4,609,189	5,404,388	33,646	590,342	241,577
2011	20,475,745	8,769,236	58,183	8,827,419	997,883	2,196,837	10,026,373	4,862,761	5,586,611	34,640	591,098	245,677
2012	21,195,116	9,202,901	71,384	9,274,285	1,051,704	2,333,176	10,555,757	5,023,817	5,615,542	35,714	593,476	249,422
2013	21,371,693	9,366,824	55,368	9,422,192	1,201,590	2,377,218	10,597,820	4,946,491	5,827,382	35,734	598,074	254,059
2014	22,537,034	9,784,811	58,029	9,842,840	1,258,304	2,467,494	11,052,030	5,343,142	6,141,862	37,206	605,730	261,490
2015	23,764,283	10,268,657	83,183	10,351,840	1,315,730	2,642,803	11,678,913	5,536,982	6,548,388	38,482	617,539	269,029
2016	25,151,076	10,851,226	76,697	10,927,923	1,393,868	2,967,847	12,501,902	5,803,623	6,845,551	39,817	631,664	278,027
2017	26,838,568	11,405,265	97,485	11,502,750	1,467,828	3,203,026	13,237,948	6,399,013	7,201,607	41,733	643,106	287,043
2018	28,436,066	12,047,084	88,286	12,135,370	1,569,378	3,439,203	14,005,195	6,882,382	7,548,489	43,571	652,635	296,310
2019	30,832,010	12,623,635	87,331	12,710,966	1,668,827	3,900,609	14,942,748	7,825,644	8,063,618	46,594	661,722	299,733
2020	32,971,162	12,870,605	85,354	12,955,959	1,734,263	4,127,116	15,348,812	7,676,825	9,945,525	49,079	671,794	300,206
2021	36,719,224	14,353,775	80,013	14,433,788	1,883,953	4,918,753	17,468,588	7,883,957	11,366,679	53,457	686,892	316,930
2022	38,660,345	15,602,421	84,463	15,686,884	2,095,556	6,066,681	19,658,009	8,487,792	10,514,544	54,768	705,897	332,120

Personal Income and Employment by Area: Denver-Aurora-Lakewood, CO

(Thousands of dollars, except as noted.)

Year	Personal income, total	Derivation of personal income: Earnings by place of work: Nonfarm	Farm	Total	Less: Contributions for government social insurance	Plus: Adjustment for residence	Equals: Net earnings by place of residence	Plus: Dividends, interest, and rent	Plus: Personal current transfer receipts	Per capita personal income (dollars)	Population (persons)	Total employment
1970	5,351,690	4,403,071	26,626	4,429,697	270,949	-109,466	4,049,282	932,879	369,529	4,756	1,125,162	567,136
1971	6,094,357	5,053,265	23,366	5,076,631	320,688	-131,908	4,624,035	1,042,520	427,802	5,241	1,162,772	597,433
1972	6,853,290	5,762,156	25,378	5,787,534	387,316	-157,136	5,243,082	1,139,174	471,034	5,684	1,205,736	638,174
1973	7,737,318	6,568,662	24,903	6,593,565	508,353	-191,006	5,894,206	1,294,503	548,609	6,200	1,247,871	688,969
1974	8,578,515	7,183,300	32,259	7,215,559	566,765	-208,214	6,440,580	1,498,373	639,562	6,793	1,262,795	697,029
1975	9,496,789	7,791,838	37,955	7,829,793	597,161	-223,994	7,008,638	1,672,380	815,771	7,387	1,285,565	696,348
1976	10,499,533	8,708,263	20,824	8,729,087	680,395	-253,921	7,794,771	1,810,821	893,941	7,975	1,316,528	721,876
1977	11,794,472	9,896,069	23,133	9,919,202	779,024	-298,472	8,841,706	2,012,975	939,791	8,778	1,343,631	763,237
1978	13,650,331	11,591,379	23,197	11,614,576	936,019	-357,878	10,320,679	2,313,138	1,016,514	9,819	1,390,221	821,600
1979	15,558,567	13,377,621	13,171	13,390,792	1,137,696	-454,110	11,798,986	2,625,873	1,133,708	10,864	1,432,057	870,090
1980	17,850,992	15,219,049	25,601	15,244,650	1,310,693	-561,062	13,372,895	3,178,943	1,299,154	12,219	1,460,960	901,316
1981	20,549,478	17,376,595	11,188	17,387,783	1,620,340	-624,457	15,142,986	3,883,555	1,522,937	13,718	1,497,985	939,574
1982	22,810,973	19,151,580	6,212	19,157,792	1,831,815	-650,748	16,675,229	4,416,291	1,719,453	14,800	1,541,261	968,403
1983	24,590,403	20,348,236	26,176	20,374,412	1,974,064	-642,135	17,758,213	4,943,428	1,888,762	15,576	1,578,689	980,047
1984	26,794,822	22,248,352	14,552	22,262,904	2,229,228	-642,135	19,391,541	5,416,484	1,986,797	16,744	1,600,224	1,034,156
1985	28,507,234	23,602,827	19,681	23,622,508	2,418,292	-672,310	20,531,906	5,896,912	2,078,416	17,563	1,623,121	1,054,857
1986	29,474,213	24,316,255	19,923	24,336,178	2,515,287	-662,969	21,157,922	6,083,901	2,232,390	18,002	1,637,259	1,047,201
1987	30,179,377	24,797,776	29,466	24,827,242	2,545,953	-614,437	21,666,852	6,092,281	2,420,244	18,351	1,644,586	1,033,523
1988	31,784,766	26,000,447	28,334	26,028,781	2,755,193	-606,011	22,667,577	6,558,003	2,559,186	19,401	1,638,280	1,053,281
1989	34,322,241	27,507,728	22,435	27,530,163	2,951,815	-592,139	23,986,209	7,481,782	2,854,250	20,936	1,639,407	1,065,789
1990	36,429,405	29,346,793	14,816	29,361,609	3,221,649	-583,435	25,556,525	7,805,251	3,067,629	21,972	1,658,024	1,084,091
1991	38,697,020	31,355,518	10,303	31,365,821	3,524,055	-567,243	27,274,523	8,037,477	3,385,020	22,732	1,702,298	1,108,061
1992	41,729,440	34,248,653	29,343	34,277,996	3,808,347	-593,442	29,876,207	8,057,015	3,796,218	23,697	1,760,945	1,129,013
1993	45,201,907	37,206,046	43,203	37,249,249	4,179,058	-586,670	32,483,521	8,637,270	4,081,116	24,846	1,819,298	1,174,291
1994	48,449,497	39,521,899	16,130	39,538,029	4,464,304	-495,940	34,577,785	9,543,380	4,328,332	26,007	1,862,948	1,223,582
1995	52,640,051	42,410,544	30,701	42,441,245	4,763,892	-484,530	37,192,823	10,602,562	4,844,666	27,550	1,910,680	1,259,599
1996	56,798,142	45,859,517	20,003	45,879,520	5,092,702	-533,473	40,253,345	11,519,147	5,025,650	28,985	1,959,552	1,304,522
1997	61,171,607	49,757,078	27,672	49,784,750	5,494,671	-566,941	43,723,138	12,384,633	5,063,836	30,400	2,012,227	1,362,615
1998	68,020,564	55,481,178	24,582	55,505,760	5,730,471	-321,911	49,453,378	13,465,908	5,101,278	33,002	2,061,091	1,421,735
1999	73,319,344	61,510,032	28,850	61,538,882	6,276,909	-523,419	54,738,554	13,191,666	5,389,124	34,608	2,118,555	1,465,962
2000	82,320,405	68,859,102	24,780	68,883,882	6,951,624	-58,794	61,873,464	14,754,138	5,692,803	37,919	2,170,977	1,523,011
2001	85,854,010	71,556,760	36,317	71,593,077	7,264,826	-212,803	64,115,448	15,423,708	6,314,854	38,695	2,218,759	1,518,724
2002	86,432,927	72,215,328	32,856	72,248,184	7,569,339	-469,222	64,209,623	15,122,956	7,100,348	38,130	2,266,781	1,521,827
2003	87,515,872	72,923,911	19,830	72,943,741	7,676,774	-577,846	64,689,121	15,381,024	7,445,727	38,302	2,284,876	1,510,968
2004	90,485,298	75,641,580	49,809	75,691,389	8,167,555	-543,790	66,980,044	15,784,852	7,720,402	39,259	2,304,818	1,533,283
2005	96,256,625	80,109,984	51,162	80,161,146	8,643,806	-599,498	70,917,842	17,076,658	8,262,125	41,263	2,332,749	1,571,107
2006	104,509,321	85,709,100	39,026	85,748,126	9,140,261	-744,871	75,862,994	19,742,669	8,903,658	44,019	2,374,194	1,607,028
2007	110,449,522	89,190,077	56,272	89,246,349	9,578,483	-728,854	78,939,012	21,974,339	9,536,171	45,665	2,418,686	1,664,565
2008	115,535,611	91,866,997	42,545	91,909,542	10,038,906	-856,505	81,014,131	23,178,099	11,343,381	46,890	2,463,971	1,683,608
2009	108,894,477	85,720,784	52,534	85,773,318	9,650,876	-546,125	75,576,317	20,665,897	12,652,263	43,394	2,509,417	1,643,671
2010	112,248,937	88,323,662	46,177	88,369,839	9,764,992	-1,000,862	77,603,985	20,262,727	14,382,225	43,948	2,554,106	1,637,504
2011	123,884,133	94,501,861	83,325	94,585,186	9,232,635	-858,897	84,493,654	24,570,215	14,820,264	47,633	2,600,806	1,672,970
2012	131,655,328	100,427,589	55,855	100,483,444	9,746,718	-999,754	89,736,972	27,059,238	14,859,118	49,749	2,646,393	1,715,523
2013	139,340,191	110,244,792	48,994	110,293,786	11,467,928	-935,880	97,889,978	26,013,502	15,436,711	51,706	2,694,842	1,776,658
2014	151,950,098	120,012,094	48,141	120,060,235	12,387,269	-936,681	106,736,285	28,610,037	16,603,776	55,328	2,746,356	1,844,025
2015	156,148,546	121,473,094	51,871	121,524,965	13,116,087	-1,328,962	107,079,916	31,064,609	18,004,021	55,702	2,803,288	1,917,038
2016	156,778,699	120,742,413	37,171	120,779,584	13,572,797	-1,524,494	105,682,293	32,472,538	18,623,868	55,105	2,845,074	1,981,833
2017	169,647,839	132,371,650	26,915	132,398,565	14,472,684	-1,730,314	116,195,567	34,444,846	19,007,426	58,947	2,877,961	2,030,502
2018	185,257,197	144,535,137	25,785	144,560,922	15,449,636	-1,677,476	127,433,810	37,277,365	20,546,022	63,534	2,915,881	2,088,775
2019	198,942,183	154,662,930	29,836	154,692,766	16,303,895	-1,964,829	136,424,042	41,006,108	21,512,033	67,568	2,944,333	2,114,530
2020	212,394,700	158,874,358	24,540	158,898,898	16,662,606	-2,259,151	139,977,141	42,657,994	29,759,565	71,515	2,969,922	2,065,814
2021	236,552,364	177,729,220	45,367	177,774,587	18,159,461	-2,620,052	156,995,074	46,582,700	32,974,590	79,438	2,977,833	2,161,089
2022	253,165,841	197,437,223	6,473	197,443,696	20,631,304	-3,445,133	173,367,259	50,930,434	28,868,148	84,788	2,985,871	2,279,515

Personal Income and Employment by Area: Des Moines-West Des Moines, IA

(Thousands of dollars, except as noted.)

Year	Personal income, total	Derivation of personal income: Earnings by place of work: Nonfarm	Farm	Total	Less: Contributions for government social insurance	Plus: Adjustment for residence	Equals: Net earnings by place of residence	Plus: Dividends, interest, and rent	Plus: Personal current transfer receipts	Per capita personal income (dollars)	Population (persons)	Total employment
1970	1,748,807	1,417,683	68,395	1,486,078	104,249	-40,636	1,341,193	268,853	138,761	4,373	399,921	203,253
1971	1,876,257	1,523,572	54,798	1,578,370	115,890	-41,882	1,420,598	295,823	159,836	4,627	405,521	205,016
1972	2,088,606	1,691,765	81,224	1,772,989	135,971	-46,825	1,590,193	324,225	174,188	5,110	408,769	211,629
1973	2,371,928	1,874,528	152,880	2,027,408	174,827	-50,132	1,802,449	365,981	203,498	5,706	415,714	220,372
1974	2,579,363	2,091,561	88,982	2,180,543	203,140	-55,323	1,922,080	419,685	237,598	6,145	419,776	225,213
1975	2,885,291	2,297,502	101,113	2,398,615	217,763	-58,768	2,122,084	462,839	300,368	6,824	422,837	227,934
1976	3,167,353	2,546,816	88,557	2,635,373	242,483	-60,658	2,332,232	502,014	333,107	7,443	425,568	235,165
1977	3,478,689	2,856,519	44,649	2,901,168	269,588	-66,220	2,565,360	564,157	349,172	8,186	424,930	243,317
1978	3,930,348	3,177,016	118,222	3,295,238	310,454	-70,099	2,914,685	631,826	383,837	9,208	426,848	251,488
1979	4,374,909	3,594,809	74,407	3,669,216	366,858	-76,076	3,226,282	719,541	429,086	10,241	427,184	258,763
1980	4,731,999	3,791,602	30,323	3,821,925	384,362	-78,614	3,358,949	863,966	509,084	11,030	429,024	258,231
1981	5,249,709	4,043,846	88,034	4,131,880	436,615	-83,515	3,611,750	1,053,837	584,122	12,220	429,608	253,385
1982	5,566,164	4,170,806	53,651	4,224,457	453,038	-85,352	3,686,067	1,217,124	662,973	12,995	428,333	250,128
1983	5,834,957	4,437,241	6,581	4,443,822	481,886	-92,568	3,869,368	1,257,193	708,396	13,606	428,866	253,236
1984	6,362,210	4,845,155	64,814	4,909,969	540,532	-101,414	4,268,023	1,373,097	721,090	14,799	429,899	261,699
1985	6,661,149	5,093,269	72,107	5,165,376	576,626	-108,022	4,480,728	1,415,128	765,293	15,466	430,709	265,912
1986	6,960,370	5,357,703	92,897	5,450,600	620,805	-115,327	4,714,468	1,451,543	794,359	16,125	431,642	268,852
1987	7,361,268	5,774,329	115,811	5,890,140	666,415	-127,300	5,096,425	1,458,459	806,384	16,939	434,565	276,740
1988	7,941,598	6,351,260	58,201	6,409,461	752,450	-144,430	5,512,581	1,578,343	850,674	18,066	439,587	287,292
1989	8,628,853	6,828,853	124,038	6,952,891	805,657	-154,797	5,992,437	1,738,558	897,858	19,368	445,514	296,645
1990	9,317,854	7,343,175	106,771	7,449,946	893,318	-171,899	6,384,729	1,946,655	986,470	20,574	452,891	308,022
1991	9,616,344	7,720,265	81,247	7,801,512	946,830	-179,778	6,674,904	1,870,469	1,070,971	20,943	459,159	312,787
1992	10,271,402	8,302,600	124,488	8,427,088	1,011,906	-194,913	7,220,269	1,889,538	1,161,595	21,997	466,939	317,445
1993	10,645,013	8,725,396	34,967	8,760,363	1,066,021	-204,687	7,489,655	1,935,711	1,219,647	22,446	474,241	322,612
1994	11,414,742	9,304,546	135,762	9,440,308	1,151,306	-217,533	8,071,469	2,077,107	1,266,166	23,780	480,013	331,027
1995	12,148,226	9,872,311	86,200	9,958,511	1,219,032	-233,886	8,505,593	2,304,632	1,338,001	24,956	486,778	344,792
1996	12,992,811	10,456,123	175,880	10,632,003	1,248,633	-250,540	9,132,830	2,441,601	1,418,380	26,354	493,009	352,418
1997	13,770,660	11,117,284	159,360	11,276,644	1,354,590	-268,380	9,653,674	2,664,626	1,452,360	27,633	498,350	357,578
1998	14,844,205	12,077,511	102,190	12,179,701	1,449,079	-292,358	10,438,264	2,900,852	1,505,089	29,390	505,070	366,381
1999	15,556,766	12,982,788	69,901	13,052,689	1,550,281	-315,768	11,186,640	2,816,163	1,553,963	30,324	513,020	373,463
2000	16,506,822	13,651,157	95,291	13,746,448	1,607,242	-325,510	11,813,696	3,017,889	1,675,237	31,714	520,495	378,721
2001	17,372,457	14,430,966	80,993	14,511,959	1,691,234	-348,081	12,472,644	3,065,481	1,834,332	32,956	527,138	380,712
2002	17,941,276	14,938,625	93,468	15,032,093	1,747,396	-361,368	12,923,329	3,001,837	2,016,110	33,609	533,828	379,714
2003	18,539,714	15,606,481	98,773	15,705,254	1,838,834	-365,892	13,500,528	3,026,287	2,012,899	34,262	541,109	381,348
2004	20,064,308	16,739,683	241,380	16,981,063	1,947,573	-367,941	14,665,549	3,319,271	2,079,488	36,554	548,902	391,753
2005	21,001,924	17,567,972	188,906	17,756,878	2,041,403	-366,506	15,348,969	3,409,152	2,243,803	37,566	559,060	399,663
2006	22,542,999	18,640,314	145,407	18,785,721	2,159,402	-364,664	16,261,655	3,798,149	2,483,195	39,547	570,026	410,368
2007	23,790,921	19,402,987	241,482	19,644,469	2,275,811	-387,413	16,981,245	4,135,926	2,673,750	40,965	580,757	421,369
2008	25,044,079	20,020,231	278,449	20,298,680	2,371,264	-365,853	17,561,563	4,328,065	3,154,451	42,394	590,747	424,054
2009	24,704,929	19,821,521	202,913	20,024,434	2,374,771	-305,091	17,344,572	3,978,408	3,381,949	41,211	599,480	419,239
2010	25,703,695	20,493,452	130,956	20,624,408	2,444,828	-241,236	17,938,344	4,074,427	3,690,924	42,207	608,998	417,406
2011	26,907,031	20,748,519	342,773	21,091,292	2,256,930	-298,523	18,535,839	4,592,881	3,778,311	43,493	618,648	423,436
2012	28,673,827	22,036,101	280,528	22,316,629	2,344,121	-339,827	19,632,681	5,232,302	3,808,844	45,700	627,432	431,045
2013	29,095,581	22,797,539	343,697	23,141,236	2,733,362	-238,292	20,169,582	4,989,577	3,936,422	45,546	638,819	440,936
2014	31,043,466	24,344,677	212,129	24,556,806	2,852,111	-240,195	21,464,500	5,386,498	4,192,468	47,688	650,974	451,463
2015	32,760,666	25,443,769	153,744	25,597,513	2,945,960	-197,460	22,454,093	5,860,988	4,445,585	49,546	661,212	459,050
2016	34,071,867	26,514,567	89,639	26,604,206	3,129,777	-238,422	23,236,007	6,252,386	4,583,474	50,612	673,194	470,104
2017	35,401,572	27,549,377	107,094	27,656,471	3,262,599	-223,117	24,170,755	6,593,778	4,637,039	51,754	684,038	477,086
2018	36,928,112	28,634,511	133,097	28,767,608	3,414,042	-247,039	25,106,527	6,724,706	5,096,879	53,230	693,742	484,443
2019	38,480,372	29,624,376	105,116	29,729,492	3,552,357	-254,448	25,922,687	7,058,430	5,499,255	54,714	703,296	487,324
2020	41,434,836	30,908,598	104,988	31,013,586	3,774,139	-288,523	26,950,924	7,039,464	7,444,448	58,268	711,109	477,033
2021	45,535,466	33,133,582	356,200	33,489,782	3,957,490	-344,531	29,187,761	8,148,022	8,199,683	63,202	720,480	495,070
2022	46,951,654	35,551,891	410,649	35,962,540	4,321,017	-396,196	31,245,327	8,718,878	6,987,449	64,401	729,053	514,839

Personal Income and Employment by Area: Detroit-Warren-Dearborn, MI

(Thousands of dollars, except as noted.)

		Derivation of personal income										
		Earnings by place of work										
Year	Personal income, total	Nonfarm	Farm	Total	Less: Contributions for government social insurance	Plus: Adjustment for residence	Equals: Net earnings by place of residence	Plus: Dividends, interest, and rent	Plus: Personal current transfer receipts	Per capita personal income (dollars)	Population (persons)	Total employment
1970	20,473,778	17,605,595	34,095	17,639,690	1,256,732	-159,525	16,223,433	2,652,970	1,597,375	4,612	4,439,498	1,819,813
1971	22,059,058	18,836,787	31,718	18,868,505	1,384,176	-163,954	17,320,375	2,817,309	1,921,374	4,946	4,459,793	1,803,088
1972	24,440,594	21,041,099	41,104	21,082,203	1,647,001	-194,485	19,240,717	3,002,171	2,197,706	5,488	4,453,517	1,854,501
1973	27,254,747	23,795,186	46,739	23,841,925	2,162,977	-205,465	21,473,483	3,271,605	2,509,659	6,144	4,435,796	1,939,903
1974	28,883,744	24,572,344	46,143	24,618,487	2,307,355	-272,983	22,038,149	3,724,458	3,121,137	6,532	4,422,090	1,926,974
1975	30,323,450	24,691,187	48,695	24,739,882	2,257,459	-276,919	22,205,504	4,022,648	4,095,298	6,900	4,394,458	1,808,270
1976	33,800,030	28,193,834	46,030	28,239,864	2,634,598	-247,928	25,357,338	4,297,514	4,145,178	7,750	4,361,574	1,876,295
1977	38,051,495	32,337,048	54,020	32,391,068	3,025,529	-259,649	29,105,890	4,714,191	4,231,414	8,744	4,351,973	1,960,763
1978	42,389,221	36,367,129	37,866	36,404,995	3,511,594	-272,371	32,621,030	5,251,067	4,517,124	9,730	4,356,619	2,043,005
1979	46,117,667	39,215,984	42,807	39,258,791	3,917,301	-295,693	35,045,797	5,837,108	5,234,762	10,585	4,356,811	2,045,908
1980	48,831,844	39,109,989	42,303	39,152,292	3,863,007	-295,440	34,993,845	6,833,435	7,004,564	11,252	4,339,778	1,921,891
1981	51,354,836	40,433,542	42,368	40,475,910	4,317,843	-219,346	35,938,721	8,114,319	7,301,796	12,011	4,275,732	1,876,138
1982	52,886,764	40,006,836	38,997	40,045,833	4,330,097	-214,096	35,501,640	9,300,525	8,084,599	12,523	4,223,098	1,789,482
1983	56,204,513	42,406,862	28,272	42,435,134	4,666,625	-160,427	37,608,082	10,013,229	8,583,202	13,430	4,185,050	1,798,974
1984	62,373,484	47,915,976	43,472	47,959,448	5,454,814	-172,234	42,332,400	11,384,768	8,656,316	14,912	4,182,763	1,897,635
1985	68,542,977	53,790,970	47,716	53,838,686	6,254,816	-203,195	47,380,675	12,305,984	8,856,318	16,335	4,195,986	2,012,186
1986	73,081,158	57,955,880	32,547	57,988,427	6,757,969	-269,732	50,960,726	12,860,752	9,259,680	17,319	4,219,771	2,067,378
1987	75,267,492	60,063,155	43,870	60,107,025	6,922,493	-322,849	52,861,683	12,962,027	9,443,782	17,746	4,241,494	2,118,647
1988	80,923,393	64,885,558	43,872	64,929,430	7,645,413	-370,301	56,913,716	14,178,119	9,831,558	19,112	4,234,083	2,168,474
1989	86,859,550	68,592,022	58,979	68,651,001	8,080,678	-361,934	60,208,389	16,099,434	10,551,727	20,496	4,237,904	2,227,089
1990	90,526,489	71,050,389	53,028	71,103,417	8,530,456	-373,478	62,199,483	16,966,498	11,360,508	21,295	4,250,986	2,244,909
1991	91,263,322	71,286,205	52,748	71,338,953	8,683,405	-387,980	62,267,568	16,469,050	12,526,704	21,295	4,285,663	2,181,991
1992	96,241,721	76,355,416	50,528	76,405,944	9,228,885	-555,608	66,621,451	16,360,059	13,260,211	22,279	4,319,806	2,182,305
1993	101,356,066	80,702,199	49,252	80,751,451	9,788,207	-775,673	70,187,571	16,999,013	14,169,482	23,329	4,344,712	2,209,546
1994	108,985,578	86,839,370	47,119	86,886,489	10,725,780	-938,142	75,222,567	19,478,518	14,284,493	24,966	4,365,423	2,279,342
1995	115,603,019	92,219,112	50,486	92,269,598	11,339,603	-1,317,006	79,612,989	20,929,980	15,060,050	26,275	4,399,746	2,339,032
1996	121,621,638	96,737,305	44,670	96,781,975	11,578,418	-1,524,152	83,679,405	22,156,804	15,785,429	27,435	4,433,102	2,391,801
1997	127,234,115	101,384,059	46,255	101,430,314	12,118,956	-1,579,550	87,731,808	22,622,236	16,880,071	28,654	4,440,400	2,425,583
1998	136,162,306	109,829,810	45,202	109,875,012	12,817,546	-1,894,327	95,163,139	24,384,784	16,614,383	30,655	4,441,717	2,463,358
1999	142,613,366	116,860,796	55,365	116,916,161	13,571,475	-1,982,089	101,362,597	23,667,256	17,583,513	32,065	4,447,649	2,511,959
2000	153,825,307	126,766,959	36,107	126,803,066	14,321,259	-2,449,788	110,032,019	25,816,541	17,976,747	34,525	4,455,503	2,580,828
2001	155,695,849	127,540,579	32,098	127,572,677	14,283,779	-2,502,466	110,786,432	25,040,357	19,869,060	34,895	4,461,855	2,536,678
2002	153,788,936	125,706,092	32,990	125,739,082	14,236,292	-2,408,703	109,094,087	24,218,463	20,476,386	34,509	4,456,433	2,500,119
2003	156,836,404	127,838,942	40,208	127,879,150	14,433,918	-2,682,794	110,762,438	24,706,353	21,367,613	35,217	4,453,371	2,486,055
2004	159,721,026	130,451,519	64,133	130,515,652	14,876,759	-2,725,199	112,913,694	24,614,129	22,193,203	35,926	4,445,887	2,487,083
2005	162,804,632	132,075,172	64,360	132,139,532	15,319,118	-3,049,457	113,770,957	25,424,799	23,608,876	36,742	4,431,048	2,503,796
2006	164,441,185	131,064,150	78,586	131,142,736	15,496,441	-2,813,910	112,832,385	26,598,146	25,010,654	37,291	4,409,697	2,475,008
2007	168,857,946	131,799,452	66,479	131,865,931	15,659,157	-2,801,356	113,405,418	28,161,327	27,291,201	38,577	4,377,116	2,471,009
2008	170,174,642	128,801,054	71,795	128,872,849	15,526,114	-3,020,186	110,326,549	28,822,764	31,025,329	39,215	4,339,504	2,413,782
2009	160,012,432	115,942,360	50,253	115,992,613	14,155,340	-1,884,137	99,953,136	25,293,289	34,766,007	37,111	4,311,728	2,255,804
2010	164,173,409	118,980,309	61,596	119,041,905	14,299,995	-2,425,045	102,316,865	24,867,658	36,988,886	38,240	4,293,284	2,258,033
2011	175,623,403	126,693,706	109,795	126,803,501	13,419,995	-2,116,395	111,267,111	27,494,161	36,862,131	40,827	4,301,641	2,329,532
2012	183,212,138	133,129,447	96,388	133,225,835	14,042,367	-2,437,960	116,745,508	29,805,517	36,661,113	42,420	4,319,028	2,372,887
2013	184,356,582	136,276,836	101,103	136,377,939	16,319,973	-2,218,317	117,839,649	29,744,832	36,772,101	42,558	4,331,922	2,415,138
2014	192,940,091	141,866,079	56,261	141,922,340	16,840,399	-2,559,374	122,522,567	32,425,458	37,992,066	44,398	4,345,692	2,458,033
2015	204,834,629	150,291,901	68,878	150,360,779	17,636,825	-2,582,821	130,141,133	34,699,140	39,994,356	47,063	4,352,394	2,508,363
2016	210,038,500	154,348,658	58,716	154,407,374	18,119,718	-2,986,262	133,301,394	35,978,191	40,758,915	48,092	4,367,436	2,547,259
2017	216,025,432	161,135,890	58,094	161,193,984	18,849,958	-3,282,083	139,061,943	36,432,406	40,531,083	49,309	4,381,076	2,581,898
2018	225,800,056	166,943,092	63,798	167,006,890	19,743,501	-3,422,586	143,840,803	39,738,641	42,220,612	51,429	4,390,557	2,628,720
2019	232,250,927	171,484,599	67,931	171,552,530	20,153,275	-3,416,925	147,982,330	39,891,286	44,377,311	52,855	4,394,145	2,637,284
2020	249,491,912	168,970,116	101,418	169,071,534	19,721,954	-3,534,686	145,814,894	39,444,110	64,232,908	56,901	4,384,636	2,480,476
2021	264,131,093	181,800,820	125,126	181,925,946	21,052,093	-3,683,268	157,190,585	43,017,458	63,923,050	60,488	4,366,696	2,591,102
2022	266,491,825	194,700,605	113,402	194,814,007	23,256,153	-4,359,541	167,198,313	46,574,308	52,719,204	61,322	4,345,761	2,717,041

Personal Income and Employment by Area: Dothan, AL

(Thousands of dollars, except as noted.)

Year	Personal income, total	Derivation of personal income: Earnings by place of work: Nonfarm	Farm	Total	Less: Contributions for government social insurance	Plus: Adjustment for residence	Equals: Net earnings by place of residence	Plus: Dividends, interest, and rent	Plus: Personal current transfer receipts	Per capita personal income (dollars)	Population (persons)	Total employment
1970	278,801	176,422	18,077	194,499	13,404	33,743	214,838	34,597	29,366	3,026	92,122	41,593
1971	309,458	202,576	18,535	221,111	15,620	30,304	235,795	39,747	33,916	3,287	94,147	43,039
1972	349,141	236,764	26,184	262,948	19,290	24,201	267,859	43,535	37,747	3,567	97,881	45,497
1973	427,476	299,282	42,225	341,507	28,113	18,936	332,330	51,235	43,911	4,257	100,409	49,519
1974	477,002	343,152	34,200	377,352	33,309	18,523	362,566	61,501	52,935	4,526	105,391	51,163
1975	519,787	350,060	40,273	390,333	33,496	21,286	378,123	71,999	69,665	4,811	108,046	49,593
1976	598,322	425,514	38,312	463,826	41,836	21,820	443,810	78,332	76,180	5,450	109,777	51,727
1977	642,890	473,313	24,878	498,191	46,582	22,871	474,480	87,443	80,967	5,794	110,966	53,046
1978	728,189	537,027	33,225	570,252	53,830	22,535	538,957	100,998	88,234	6,457	112,772	54,447
1979	792,678	572,646	31,322	603,968	59,219	30,298	575,047	114,772	102,859	6,976	113,631	54,259
1980	870,596	655,750	-14,240	641,510	68,002	32,645	606,153	143,803	120,640	7,603	114,505	55,050
1981	1,038,661	691,486	44,870	736,356	77,054	64,388	723,690	176,966	138,005	8,987	115,576	54,328
1982	1,064,585	700,654	24,051	724,705	79,005	73,451	719,151	192,609	152,825	9,173	116,060	52,319
1983	1,121,484	749,082	9,441	758,523	84,617	76,092	749,998	205,164	166,322	9,670	115,974	52,832
1984	1,266,394	820,164	55,594	875,758	94,794	78,841	859,805	230,644	175,945	10,870	116,501	54,538
1985	1,329,839	883,993	28,328	912,321	102,348	81,062	891,035	249,585	189,219	11,335	117,318	55,398
1986	1,415,940	956,258	22,117	978,375	109,452	82,499	951,422	264,957	199,561	12,037	117,628	56,956
1987	1,513,921	1,037,794	35,133	1,072,927	117,653	82,672	1,037,946	268,439	207,536	12,724	118,980	59,215
1988	1,655,987	1,127,224	59,962	1,187,186	131,995	80,068	1,135,259	298,003	222,725	13,881	119,302	61,390
1989	1,838,516	1,234,438	75,457	1,309,895	144,223	71,898	1,237,570	349,798	251,148	15,391	119,455	64,645
1990	1,887,149	1,319,482	53,615	1,373,097	155,000	29,317	1,247,414	371,856	267,879	15,619	120,826	66,534
1991	1,984,800	1,376,551	82,868	1,459,419	163,317	19,532	1,315,634	379,792	289,374	16,202	122,507	67,078
1992	2,153,905	1,506,764	76,357	1,583,121	176,485	35,014	1,441,650	383,353	328,902	17,421	123,636	68,384
1993	2,193,525	1,555,054	62,167	1,617,221	184,224	23,562	1,456,559	391,665	345,301	17,552	124,976	69,447
1994	2,326,517	1,623,796	79,605	1,703,401	194,602	20,669	1,529,468	426,766	370,283	18,607	125,036	69,704
1995	2,475,189	1,718,817	76,707	1,795,524	207,125	19,157	1,607,556	463,784	403,849	19,664	125,872	71,949
1996	2,543,169	1,777,315	63,168	1,840,483	211,223	11,889	1,641,149	472,845	429,175	20,015	127,060	72,959
1997	2,658,270	1,855,721	46,335	1,902,056	220,356	26,823	1,708,523	499,322	450,425	20,758	128,062	74,932
1998	2,837,163	1,983,475	55,439	2,038,914	231,918	41,493	1,848,489	535,558	453,116	22,006	128,927	75,252
1999	2,962,984	2,045,876	78,733	2,124,609	239,342	64,556	1,949,823	535,004	478,157	22,797	129,970	75,357
2000	3,046,926	2,103,806	38,648	2,142,454	247,014	70,657	1,966,097	569,797	511,032	23,255	131,024	75,270
2001	3,308,158	2,212,312	94,751	2,307,063	256,021	79,644	2,130,686	597,725	579,747	25,174	131,413	74,332
2002	3,418,114	2,283,088	94,590	2,377,678	263,838	102,633	2,216,473	578,555	623,086	25,901	131,967	73,974
2003	3,539,733	2,369,448	85,700	2,455,148	274,718	118,575	2,299,005	573,898	666,830	26,498	133,586	74,709
2004	3,798,015	2,523,015	85,842	2,608,857	291,749	132,258	2,449,366	621,172	727,477	28,122	135,057	77,192
2005	4,045,977	2,660,072	89,104	2,749,176	307,827	148,083	2,589,432	673,602	782,943	29,610	136,643	78,856
2006	4,301,103	2,812,573	57,596	2,870,169	329,788	195,125	2,735,506	713,452	852,145	30,928	139,070	80,330
2007	4,571,596	2,881,144	55,870	2,937,014	342,319	225,806	2,820,501	826,339	924,756	32,387	141,157	82,337
2008	4,688,316	2,832,568	58,018	2,890,586	344,645	247,468	2,793,409	868,570	1,026,337	32,795	142,958	80,563
2009	4,672,270	2,773,101	39,023	2,812,124	338,688	304,400	2,777,836	778,847	1,115,587	32,357	144,396	77,267
2010	4,913,770	2,842,345	35,949	2,878,294	349,082	343,201	2,872,413	815,198	1,226,159	33,680	145,895	76,394
2011	5,093,426	2,886,796	31,276	2,918,072	316,521	349,008	2,950,559	883,700	1,259,167	34,706	146,758	76,926
2012	5,142,963	2,934,183	25,505	2,959,688	320,567	363,284	3,002,405	868,157	1,272,401	34,821	147,699	76,756
2013	5,188,731	3,011,605	92,137	3,103,742	369,514	308,472	3,042,700	844,214	1,301,817	35,105	147,804	76,921
2014	5,359,275	3,076,652	94,101	3,170,753	376,029	290,358	3,085,082	895,005	1,379,188	36,143	148,281	77,264
2015	5,558,074	3,174,855	89,906	3,264,761	388,404	282,306	3,158,663	922,225	1,477,186	37,418	148,542	77,984
2016	5,674,231	3,249,776	93,042	3,342,818	395,774	290,900	3,237,944	953,878	1,482,409	38,218	148,472	77,731
2017	5,813,795	3,329,267	92,057	3,421,324	410,008	320,162	3,331,478	969,268	1,513,049	39,117	148,624	78,392
2018	6,060,488	3,506,267	73,590	3,579,857	436,180	302,771	3,446,448	1,020,732	1,593,308	40,656	149,067	79,735
2019	6,402,071	3,673,148	86,614	3,759,762	452,576	297,397	3,604,583	1,100,383	1,697,105	42,540	150,494	80,610
2020	6,913,336	3,831,376	51,085	3,882,461	475,644	321,575	3,728,392	1,125,216	2,059,728	45,736	151,157	80,401
2021	7,514,788	4,068,544	105,072	4,173,616	504,230	321,063	3,990,449	1,161,571	2,362,768	49,585	151,554	82,522
2022	7,546,912	4,306,757	86,055	4,392,812	544,746	292,326	4,140,392	1,249,215	2,157,305	49,482	152,517	85,672

Personal Income and Employment by Area: Dover, DE

(Thousands of dollars, except as noted.)

Year	Personal income, total	Derivation of personal income: Earnings by place of work: Nonfarm	Farm	Total	Less: Contributions for government social insurance	Plus: Adjustment for residence	Equals: Net earnings by place of residence	Plus: Dividends, interest, and rent	Plus: Personal current transfer receipts	Per capita personal income (dollars)	Population (persons)	Total employment
1970	329,298	278,854	9,441	288,295	18,575	-15,601	254,119	53,737	21,442	3,985	82,633	42,223
1971	366,988	310,011	9,377	319,388	21,322	-15,923	282,143	59,234	25,611	4,236	86,628	43,110
1972	408,579	343,571	11,098	354,669	24,323	-15,582	314,764	65,369	28,446	4,565	89,512	45,268
1973	456,659	370,705	24,117	394,822	29,554	-14,087	351,181	72,425	33,053	5,058	90,286	46,076
1974	510,034	406,440	29,191	435,631	33,776	-14,561	387,294	82,590	40,150	5,603	91,026	45,692
1975	562,531	442,630	21,485	464,115	37,052	-14,248	412,815	92,126	57,590	6,080	92,521	44,751
1976	607,527	477,290	20,993	498,283	41,024	-12,981	444,278	100,515	62,734	6,431	94,465	44,883
1977	649,026	515,906	11,058	526,964	43,991	-13,072	469,901	111,225	67,900	6,742	96,264	45,851
1978	716,082	553,939	18,542	572,481	48,484	-7,114	516,883	125,887	73,312	7,288	98,251	45,902
1979	771,112	587,704	14,983	602,687	53,413	-2,193	547,081	139,806	84,225	7,776	99,166	46,424
1980	843,044	631,423	-63	631,360	58,556	4,109	576,913	165,975	100,156	8,578	98,280	46,321
1981	949,366	696,007	10,271	706,278	69,248	7,624	644,654	191,298	113,414	9,656	98,317	46,451
1982	1,025,966	747,928	9,497	757,425	74,883	11,834	694,376	209,685	121,905	10,340	99,225	47,096
1983	1,090,969	785,065	10,206	795,271	79,384	20,652	736,539	223,201	131,229	10,807	100,953	47,036
1984	1,192,633	859,394	15,794	875,188	87,901	24,726	812,013	244,805	135,815	11,778	101,261	48,525
1985	1,286,658	931,003	12,394	943,397	95,516	31,182	879,063	263,595	144,000	12,514	102,818	51,069
1986	1,388,507	1,010,584	12,461	1,023,045	105,128	32,184	950,101	283,854	154,552	13,260	104,713	52,893
1987	1,491,993	1,093,487	9,590	1,103,077	112,217	38,754	1,029,614	300,667	161,712	14,041	106,263	54,198
1988	1,637,695	1,185,429	26,827	1,212,256	128,408	45,280	1,129,128	329,777	178,790	15,311	106,965	55,677
1989	1,798,834	1,291,494	25,551	1,317,045	140,250	48,822	1,225,617	378,256	194,961	16,495	109,052	57,099
1990	1,913,241	1,403,891	21,541	1,425,432	150,359	50,540	1,325,613	374,703	212,925	17,138	111,638	58,224
1991	2,034,052	1,467,999	24,819	1,492,818	159,055	42,593	1,376,356	409,239	248,457	17,798	114,288	59,918
1992	2,143,458	1,559,597	28,902	1,588,499	168,611	33,120	1,453,008	414,516	275,934	18,529	115,682	61,604
1993	2,208,424	1,625,135	20,250	1,645,385	177,808	22,458	1,490,035	418,813	299,576	18,718	117,987	62,713
1994	2,312,117	1,709,259	24,506	1,733,765	188,586	14,551	1,559,730	451,744	300,643	19,423	119,039	63,944
1995	2,465,177	1,821,555	13,066	1,834,621	202,186	256	1,632,691	491,270	341,216	20,421	120,715	65,999
1996	2,641,639	1,914,314	25,237	1,939,551	209,957	-5,152	1,724,442	527,839	389,358	21,751	121,447	67,066
1997	2,696,741	1,941,933	15,958	1,957,891	211,276	6,399	1,753,014	545,920	397,807	22,029	122,419	66,499
1998	2,935,981	2,136,507	25,618	2,162,125	224,793	3,728	1,941,060	561,793	433,128	23,667	124,056	67,593
1999	3,149,408	2,357,061	25,467	2,382,528	236,636	-1,564	2,144,328	564,976	440,104	25,073	125,611	70,155
2000	3,449,867	2,602,664	30,733	2,633,397	245,923	-3,311	2,384,163	588,410	477,294	27,115	127,229	71,832
2001	3,480,655	2,577,598	33,580	2,611,178	247,663	-7,454	2,356,061	604,460	520,134	26,934	129,228	72,004
2002	3,707,342	2,812,675	12,677	2,825,352	284,155	-30,253	2,510,944	629,807	566,591	28,123	131,824	73,666
2003	3,963,100	2,969,185	24,081	2,993,266	298,929	-25,063	2,669,274	674,274	619,552	29,442	134,605	75,127
2004	4,298,527	3,247,052	45,504	3,292,556	327,550	-33,308	2,931,698	689,712	677,117	30,849	139,342	78,243
2005	4,504,720	3,381,064	52,868	3,433,932	350,007	-29,027	3,054,898	700,939	748,883	31,156	144,585	81,732
2006	4,862,907	3,583,693	45,961	3,629,654	374,654	27,560	3,282,560	759,229	821,118	32,483	149,704	83,358
2007	5,107,447	3,665,313	52,145	3,717,458	394,248	35,069	3,358,279	844,898	904,270	33,172	153,969	84,924
2008	5,291,088	3,574,472	49,073	3,623,545	404,953	65,483	3,284,075	948,614	1,058,399	33,504	157,925	84,610
2009	5,545,302	3,636,542	72,627	3,709,169	405,541	120,717	3,424,345	956,583	1,164,374	34,641	160,081	81,630
2010	5,576,528	3,681,775	67,804	3,749,579	407,367	33,182	3,375,394	933,550	1,267,584	34,224	162,940	81,677
2011	5,866,771	3,779,088	79,915	3,859,003	370,622	29,612	3,517,993	1,012,837	1,335,941	35,557	164,997	83,870
2012	5,944,793	3,839,911	97,398	3,937,309	391,122	16,466	3,562,653	1,007,292	1,374,848	35,582	167,072	84,777
2013	6,151,281	3,924,922	127,236	4,052,158	453,936	49,892	3,648,114	1,055,912	1,447,255	36,460	168,711	86,581
2014	6,376,046	4,071,992	143,344	4,215,336	479,220	11,708	3,747,824	1,068,522	1,559,700	37,280	171,031	87,631
2015	6,519,354	4,134,876	96,816	4,231,692	490,804	60,863	3,801,751	1,077,112	1,640,491	37,770	172,605	88,470
2016	6,845,986	4,344,914	82,720	4,427,634	505,943	40,004	3,961,695	1,165,975	1,718,316	39,358	173,940	90,381
2017	7,182,594	4,497,317	136,915	4,634,232	524,319	47,474	4,157,387	1,214,070	1,811,137	40,860	175,786	91,843
2018	7,543,351	4,775,094	114,589	4,889,683	547,135	7,385	4,349,933	1,289,799	1,903,619	42,413	177,853	94,122
2019	7,971,491	5,074,895	127,757	5,202,652	576,619	2,389	4,628,422	1,336,658	2,006,411	44,223	180,255	95,276
2020	8,398,176	5,224,866	60,870	5,285,736	613,006	18,250	4,690,980	1,234,626	2,472,570	46,052	182,362	95,060
2021	9,092,417	5,616,739	124,133	5,740,872	653,130	-12,113	5,075,629	1,251,939	2,764,849	49,316	184,371	100,564
2022	9,569,448	5,906,249	221,683	6,127,932	698,411	221,147	5,650,668	1,302,525	2,616,255	51,188	186,946	104,668

Personal Income and Employment by Area: Dubuque, IA

(Thousands of dollars, except as noted.)

Year	Personal income, total	Derivation of personal income								Per capita personal income (dollars)	Population (persons)	Total employment
		Earnings by place of work			Less: Contributions for government social insurance	Plus: Adjustment for residence	Equals: Net earnings by place of residence	Plus: Dividends, interest, and rent	Plus: Personal current transfer receipts			
		Nonfarm	Farm	Total								
1970	337,786	307,536	17,404	324,940	23,291	-44,302	257,347	53,394	27,045	3,721	90,790	43,244
1971	359,129	331,103	14,793	345,896	26,066	-49,402	270,428	57,715	30,986	3,915	91,739	42,981
1972	395,076	371,627	15,811	387,438	30,892	-57,756	298,790	62,315	33,971	4,260	92,731	44,134
1973	447,182	422,366	22,897	445,263	40,709	-67,567	336,987	70,607	39,588	4,772	93,700	47,239
1974	496,919	486,881	13,798	500,679	48,829	-83,056	368,794	81,629	46,496	5,299	93,779	48,892
1975	546,504	516,800	20,357	537,157	50,614	-88,482	398,061	88,916	59,527	5,774	94,655	48,652
1976	595,507	573,928	13,839	587,767	57,048	-99,337	431,382	97,669	66,456	6,223	95,687	49,568
1977	672,610	665,079	12,712	677,791	65,783	-121,728	490,280	111,401	70,929	7,135	94,270	51,642
1978	748,022	731,010	27,794	758,804	74,826	-137,240	546,738	123,429	77,855	7,982	93,716	52,499
1979	807,761	808,131	15,871	824,002	85,847	-156,094	582,061	138,762	86,938	8,646	93,425	53,560
1980	857,200	846,784	-3,233	843,551	89,565	-169,579	584,407	167,810	104,983	9,148	93,701	52,948
1981	944,683	862,351	16,276	878,627	96,839	-161,420	620,368	205,453	118,862	10,124	93,307	50,728
1982	954,962	794,332	5,392	799,724	90,003	-131,970	577,751	234,490	142,721	10,381	91,992	47,472
1983	982,249	817,102	-12,104	804,998	92,792	-127,843	584,363	246,449	151,437	10,878	90,296	47,693
1984	1,103,495	898,295	30,820	929,115	105,242	-138,338	685,535	268,842	149,118	12,314	89,616	49,513
1985	1,144,173	932,711	27,501	960,212	110,615	-139,541	710,056	279,906	154,211	12,842	89,096	49,643
1986	1,169,835	924,084	38,284	962,368	111,192	-127,164	724,012	288,702	157,121	13,328	87,771	49,358
1987	1,260,517	1,040,545	46,379	1,086,924	123,784	-144,570	818,570	283,527	158,420	14,468	87,125	51,309
1988	1,303,044	1,082,791	29,898	1,112,689	132,632	-144,506	835,551	301,591	165,902	14,917	87,351	52,579
1989	1,404,250	1,130,826	50,926	1,181,752	137,134	-144,691	899,927	324,917	179,406	16,207	86,644	53,836
1990	1,466,923	1,189,145	49,245	1,238,390	148,355	-151,890	938,145	334,827	193,951	16,966	86,462	55,086
1991	1,516,439	1,245,508	35,645	1,281,153	156,991	-156,853	967,309	342,218	206,912	17,433	86,988	56,048
1992	1,641,838	1,353,425	55,414	1,408,839	169,294	-169,792	1,069,753	348,657	223,428	18,727	87,672	56,773
1993	1,693,886	1,418,303	36,742	1,455,045	178,349	-171,571	1,105,125	352,659	236,102	19,192	88,261	57,566
1994	1,816,683	1,543,263	48,326	1,591,589	196,176	-182,267	1,213,146	358,993	244,544	20,492	88,654	58,805
1995	1,920,862	1,634,454	29,762	1,664,216	207,539	-195,227	1,261,450	401,864	257,548	21,598	88,938	60,614
1996	2,002,826	1,622,889	58,676	1,681,565	198,749	-197,429	1,285,387	440,468	276,971	22,479	89,097	60,234
1997	2,076,042	1,703,508	48,299	1,751,807	214,751	-209,668	1,327,388	463,669	284,985	23,327	88,996	61,363
1998	2,203,826	1,779,884	41,126	1,821,010	223,409	-217,955	1,379,646	519,268	304,912	24,825	88,775	61,304
1999	2,216,538	1,829,015	29,371	1,858,386	227,345	-218,595	1,412,446	488,624	315,468	24,923	88,934	61,845
2000	2,345,715	1,896,204	48,391	1,944,595	232,991	-225,429	1,486,175	525,237	334,303	26,297	89,201	62,242
2001	2,394,867	1,900,513	43,056	1,943,569	231,545	-216,138	1,495,886	535,095	363,886	26,929	88,932	61,990
2002	2,456,301	1,969,179	31,449	2,000,628	238,521	-212,833	1,549,274	512,124	394,903	27,558	89,132	61,810
2003	2,532,654	2,064,269	35,101	2,099,370	253,668	-217,628	1,628,074	507,501	397,079	28,137	90,012	62,350
2004	2,621,622	2,141,797	56,407	2,198,204	267,748	-242,608	1,687,848	520,965	412,809	28,980	90,462	63,652
2005	2,714,907	2,233,508	44,572	2,278,080	282,286	-252,900	1,742,894	534,324	437,689	29,910	90,769	65,289
2006	2,960,663	2,389,134	29,150	2,418,284	296,035	-258,203	1,864,046	608,364	488,253	32,443	91,258	67,156
2007	3,225,745	2,523,763	40,805	2,564,568	305,896	-257,964	2,000,708	693,515	531,522	35,013	92,130	67,775
2008	3,376,643	2,609,556	32,078	2,641,634	320,433	-251,801	2,069,400	708,546	598,697	36,497	92,519	67,407
2009	3,307,663	2,593,053	7,288	2,600,341	321,033	-247,881	2,031,427	661,152	615,084	35,586	92,948	66,390
2010	3,469,303	2,774,044	25,960	2,800,004	349,151	-282,379	2,168,474	642,221	658,608	36,918	93,972	67,901
2011	3,707,324	2,908,675	62,115	2,970,790	331,864	-317,711	2,321,215	723,783	662,326	39,085	94,854	69,908
2012	3,891,673	3,116,538	69,918	3,186,456	346,497	-375,707	2,464,252	765,282	662,139	40,732	95,544	71,137
2013	3,940,687	3,148,581	81,247	3,229,828	391,672	-365,048	2,473,108	774,072	693,507	40,830	96,515	71,677
2014	4,108,228	3,275,861	69,220	3,345,081	397,798	-387,453	2,559,830	817,427	730,971	42,250	97,237	72,517
2015	4,277,631	3,354,348	76,692	3,431,040	402,574	-410,337	2,618,129	879,162	780,340	43,741	97,794	73,527
2016	4,359,993	3,386,811	50,377	3,437,188	414,124	-411,294	2,611,770	943,877	804,346	44,561	97,843	72,785
2017	4,492,228	3,500,552	66,553	3,567,105	432,023	-430,752	2,704,330	979,671	808,227	45,674	98,355	72,838
2018	4,763,024	3,678,265	59,658	3,737,923	456,105	-457,287	2,824,531	1,061,722	876,771	48,446	98,316	73,465
2019	4,900,508	3,840,388	43,076	3,883,464	477,725	-495,273	2,910,466	1,067,933	922,109	49,521	98,959	73,328
2020	5,243,002	3,883,156	67,145	3,950,301	493,326	-486,669	2,970,306	1,071,449	1,201,247	52,804	99,291	70,875
2021	5,733,915	4,142,137	92,981	4,235,118	517,048	-505,314	3,212,756	1,248,018	1,273,141	58,027	98,815	72,422
2022	5,929,463	4,451,878	137,752	4,589,630	562,125	-557,834	3,469,671	1,337,834	1,121,958	60,090	98,677	75,042

Personal Income and Employment by Area: Duluth, MN-WI

(Thousands of dollars, except as noted.)

Year	Personal income, total	Derivation of personal income: Earnings by place of work: Nonfarm	Farm	Total	Less: Contributions for government social insurance	Plus: Adjustment for residence	Equals: Net earnings by place of residence	Plus: Dividends, interest, and rent	Plus: Personal current transfer receipts	Per capita personal income (dollars)	Population (persons)	Total employment
1970	1,091,237	861,529	3,960	865,489	62,543	-3,828	799,118	160,430	131,689	3,550	307,354	119,718
1971	1,176,718	924,744	3,527	928,271	69,564	-4,789	853,918	172,161	150,639	3,800	309,676	120,390
1972	1,272,078	1,001,072	4,021	1,005,093	79,071	-5,850	920,172	182,456	169,450	4,122	308,615	122,633
1973	1,392,187	1,094,420	6,488	1,100,908	98,795	-6,432	995,681	204,227	192,279	4,559	305,360	126,022
1974	1,529,535	1,183,875	4,806	1,188,681	112,233	-6,106	1,070,342	234,967	224,226	5,074	301,462	127,627
1975	1,779,868	1,379,913	3,645	1,383,558	129,710	-1,685	1,252,163	262,743	264,962	5,859	303,795	130,902
1976	2,000,382	1,564,594	4,452	1,569,046	147,819	2,625	1,423,852	281,643	294,887	6,492	308,153	135,198
1977	2,071,046	1,587,916	6,686	1,594,602	150,369	-6,668	1,437,565	311,068	322,413	6,719	308,252	132,970
1978	2,390,958	1,895,574	7,208	1,902,782	182,475	-11,671	1,708,636	340,139	342,183	7,777	307,442	139,886
1979	2,653,492	2,118,619	7,991	2,126,610	211,915	-18,940	1,895,755	377,933	379,804	8,586	309,061	144,237
1980	2,883,742	2,184,923	7,569	2,192,492	216,386	-19,528	1,956,578	460,213	466,951	9,321	309,366	141,582
1981	3,177,715	2,362,649	8,737	2,371,386	253,438	-21,646	2,096,302	562,532	518,881	10,330	307,609	138,410
1982	3,150,638	2,143,417	6,911	2,150,328	235,791	-19,256	1,895,281	630,239	625,118	10,341	304,672	127,076
1983	3,167,216	2,065,226	4,774	2,070,000	228,977	-12,458	1,828,565	667,769	670,882	10,604	298,685	121,717
1984	3,380,017	2,238,297	4,923	2,243,220	256,152	-12,547	1,974,521	729,844	675,652	11,550	292,640	124,494
1985	3,479,511	2,281,710	6,284	2,287,994	265,804	-13,170	2,009,020	761,498	708,993	12,109	287,347	124,629
1986	3,590,996	2,349,266	11,924	2,361,190	280,165	-15,904	2,065,121	796,023	729,852	12,704	282,661	125,531
1987	3,692,016	2,473,277	3,576	2,476,853	291,421	-18,016	2,167,416	781,820	742,780	13,187	279,965	127,961
1988	3,888,856	2,668,350	2,390	2,670,740	329,953	-16,841	2,323,946	814,796	750,114	13,987	278,026	131,312
1989	4,268,540	2,922,574	5,954	2,928,528	363,503	-15,452	2,549,573	917,392	801,575	15,318	278,668	136,028
1990	4,551,006	3,150,307	3,684	3,153,991	390,287	16,013	2,779,717	925,119	846,170	16,243	280,185	138,971
1991	4,737,606	3,346,767	1,550	3,348,317	417,996	-35,011	2,895,310	942,244	900,052	16,817	281,710	142,162
1992	5,017,988	3,575,296	4,661	3,579,957	439,062	-38,788	3,102,107	939,258	976,623	17,700	283,508	144,448
1993	5,134,753	3,667,768	4,558	3,672,326	454,548	-44,005	3,173,773	952,878	1,008,102	18,077	284,052	143,999
1994	5,375,316	3,845,824	5,279	3,851,103	481,456	-49,020	3,320,627	1,004,034	1,050,655	18,893	284,517	147,115
1995	5,701,813	4,046,803	2,748	4,049,551	504,938	-48,308	3,496,305	1,106,772	1,098,736	20,179	282,567	150,759
1996	6,007,462	4,255,520	2,827	4,258,347	525,061	-51,580	3,681,706	1,182,849	1,142,907	21,204	283,317	153,572
1997	6,251,320	4,443,539	1,870	4,445,409	549,926	-55,461	3,840,022	1,249,044	1,162,254	21,970	284,541	155,848
1998	6,716,126	4,802,703	3,394	4,806,097	584,617	-61,516	4,159,964	1,349,883	1,206,279	23,605	284,526	159,178
1999	6,981,837	5,084,830	3,181	5,088,011	617,074	-67,573	4,403,364	1,336,432	1,242,041	24,436	285,719	162,282
2000	7,431,708	5,407,240	2,252	5,409,492	647,086	-71,594	4,690,812	1,430,154	1,310,742	25,907	286,858	165,422
2001	7,551,806	5,365,702	2,628	5,368,330	647,895	-65,682	4,654,753	1,419,779	1,477,274	26,213	288,091	163,056
2002	7,848,490	5,592,440	1,718	5,594,158	668,977	-66,942	4,858,239	1,396,214	1,594,037	27,254	287,980	162,990
2003	8,077,740	5,708,381	4,189	5,712,570	685,368	-64,629	4,962,573	1,462,530	1,652,637	28,012	288,371	162,550
2004	8,375,144	5,999,236	4,470	6,003,706	714,880	-64,704	5,224,122	1,414,979	1,736,043	29,061	288,187	163,214
2005	8,409,845	6,077,097	3,088	6,080,185	743,418	-64,572	5,272,195	1,328,649	1,809,001	29,232	287,696	164,995
2006	8,835,983	6,311,399	4,118	6,315,517	781,782	-64,934	5,468,801	1,418,176	1,949,006	30,715	287,672	166,985
2007	9,374,505	6,606,036	5,330	6,611,366	815,254	-67,339	5,728,773	1,544,756	2,100,976	32,534	288,147	169,325
2008	10,006,946	7,017,225	505	7,017,730	862,973	-71,921	6,082,836	1,627,489	2,296,621	34,574	289,433	169,023
2009	9,936,799	6,769,188	-1,599	6,767,589	837,260	-77,078	5,853,251	1,538,801	2,544,747	34,225	290,337	163,380
2010	10,548,034	7,306,589	3,709	7,310,298	876,025	-85,557	6,348,716	1,523,748	2,675,570	36,296	290,614	163,260
2011	11,143,091	7,721,389	4,031	7,725,420	829,590	-102,938	6,792,892	1,673,127	2,677,072	38,298	290,956	164,451
2012	11,313,717	7,806,109	1,989	7,808,098	836,762	-107,236	6,864,100	1,769,871	2,679,746	38,902	290,825	165,099
2013	11,289,187	7,838,130	2,694	7,840,824	966,536	-119,555	6,754,733	1,759,917	2,774,537	38,776	291,136	167,087
2014	11,717,392	8,030,564	6,033	8,036,597	985,093	-124,265	6,927,239	1,881,189	2,908,964	40,196	291,503	168,551
2015	12,069,397	8,146,905	2,579	8,149,484	999,600	-122,639	7,027,245	2,015,351	3,026,801	41,436	291,279	169,223
2016	12,017,225	8,054,609	696	8,055,305	995,453	-129,770	6,930,082	2,006,132	3,081,011	41,266	291,213	168,542
2017	12,446,918	8,364,258	986	8,365,244	1,044,754	-137,264	7,183,226	2,070,990	3,192,702	42,738	291,236	170,326
2018	13,203,020	8,872,241	224	8,872,465	1,111,576	-145,704	7,615,185	2,201,506	3,386,329	45,242	291,834	170,733
2019	13,586,913	9,155,500	-1,317	9,154,183	1,156,218	-149,136	7,848,829	2,219,448	3,518,636	46,574	291,727	169,632
2020	14,362,976	9,016,621	2,662	9,019,283	1,149,278	-147,688	7,722,317	2,190,438	4,450,221	49,270	291,518	158,889
2021	15,667,705	9,689,331	262	9,689,593	1,223,405	-159,778	8,306,410	2,526,739	4,834,556	53,874	290,822	163,884
2022	15,896,183	10,286,279	2,935	10,289,214	1,311,114	-183,464	8,794,636	2,722,271	4,379,276	54,565	291,323	168,350

Personal Income and Employment by Area: Durham-Chapel Hill, NC

(Thousands of dollars, except as noted.)

Year	Personal income, total	Derivation of personal income: Earnings by place of work: Nonfarm	Farm	Total	Less: Contributions for government social insurance	Plus: Adjustment for residence	Equals: Net earnings by place of residence	Plus: Dividends, interest, and rent	Plus: Personal current transfer receipts	Per capita personal income (dollars)	Population (persons)	Total employment
1970	981,085	817,544	33,203	850,747	54,337	-20,683	775,727	128,893	76,465	3,512	279,347	135,231
1971	1,105,333	929,862	35,568	965,430	63,978	-31,054	870,398	144,366	90,569	3,864	286,042	140,386
1972	1,222,566	1,033,971	37,716	1,071,687	74,226	-37,691	959,770	161,740	101,056	4,150	294,596	145,675
1973	1,352,372	1,129,589	60,805	1,190,394	93,981	-44,178	1,052,235	184,049	116,088	4,503	300,358	149,120
1974	1,493,363	1,248,530	52,306	1,300,836	107,986	-55,974	1,136,876	213,507	142,980	4,892	305,263	151,751
1975	1,665,544	1,375,386	55,175	1,430,561	118,591	-74,614	1,237,356	240,385	187,803	5,473	304,340	150,060
1976	1,855,362	1,532,566	70,000	1,602,566	134,414	-86,625	1,381,527	264,877	208,958	6,011	308,683	155,071
1977	2,046,775	1,722,241	60,755	1,782,996	149,747	-108,621	1,524,628	298,666	223,481	6,501	314,854	161,572
1978	2,308,274	1,975,810	67,190	2,043,000	178,419	-134,524	1,730,057	339,537	238,680	7,258	318,017	168,794
1979	2,561,869	2,223,915	48,516	2,272,431	209,271	-159,980	1,903,180	387,071	271,618	7,927	323,182	176,228
1980	2,874,741	2,446,112	40,539	2,486,651	231,132	-182,330	2,073,189	478,903	322,649	8,792	326,966	177,188
1981	3,270,299	2,729,708	77,300	2,807,008	278,716	-216,744	2,311,548	591,531	367,220	9,904	330,198	180,527
1982	3,568,041	2,992,069	67,125	3,059,194	307,096	-262,691	2,489,407	682,236	396,398	10,698	333,520	181,952
1983	3,866,128	3,314,191	37,093	3,351,284	344,335	-307,848	2,699,101	739,805	427,222	11,453	337,571	186,655
1984	4,411,949	3,815,653	72,095	3,887,748	403,506	-387,430	3,096,812	862,913	452,224	12,877	342,627	199,427
1985	4,863,887	4,314,039	49,252	4,363,291	464,299	-472,310	3,426,682	956,346	480,859	13,944	348,815	212,331
1986	5,255,801	4,705,470	49,777	4,755,247	518,252	-535,403	3,701,592	1,048,960	505,249	14,689	357,810	220,948
1987	5,657,629	5,165,967	45,528	5,211,495	559,701	-623,025	4,028,769	1,098,871	529,989	15,512	364,725	228,908
1988	6,205,051	5,654,593	53,403	5,707,996	633,670	-693,449	4,380,877	1,248,188	575,986	16,710	371,330	238,296
1989	6,909,456	6,213,669	77,758	6,291,427	695,673	-818,323	4,777,431	1,494,781	637,244	18,276	378,059	246,727
1990	7,434,448	6,777,567	87,012	6,864,579	778,501	-930,654	5,155,424	1,570,677	708,347	19,292	385,372	252,950
1991	7,885,551	7,341,322	93,658	7,434,980	853,864	-1,136,602	5,444,514	1,626,273	814,764	20,038	393,526	258,426
1992	8,597,265	8,134,152	82,994	8,217,146	931,250	-1,321,855	5,964,041	1,734,736	898,488	21,358	402,525	265,991
1993	9,145,888	8,633,434	88,713	8,722,147	990,031	-1,424,163	6,307,953	1,844,592	993,343	22,153	412,857	274,063
1994	9,646,519	9,107,939	82,898	9,190,837	1,062,206	-1,525,021	6,603,610	1,997,615	1,045,294	22,899	421,262	280,283
1995	10,265,157	9,771,087	83,626	9,854,713	1,141,369	-1,733,264	6,980,080	2,122,334	1,162,743	23,847	430,468	290,732
1996	10,968,667	10,460,562	83,755	10,544,317	1,216,470	-1,911,520	7,416,327	2,300,505	1,251,835	24,971	439,255	301,154
1997	11,694,975	11,357,710	87,370	11,445,080	1,313,428	-2,246,943	7,884,709	2,499,207	1,311,059	26,026	449,362	311,495
1998	12,511,964	12,323,937	97,087	12,421,024	1,423,321	-2,508,066	8,489,637	2,683,922	1,338,405	27,239	459,340	323,476
1999	13,247,213	13,508,901	93,206	13,602,107	1,555,195	-2,887,562	9,159,350	2,692,867	1,394,996	28,323	467,724	332,170
2000	14,215,135	15,042,125	99,737	15,141,862	1,712,365	-3,560,578	9,868,919	2,839,306	1,506,910	29,930	474,940	339,445
2001	14,784,277	15,464,420	115,865	15,580,285	1,761,358	-3,577,117	10,241,810	2,868,087	1,674,380	30,460	485,366	335,490
2002	14,874,082	15,533,574	48,339	15,581,913	1,761,709	-3,581,561	10,238,643	2,811,180	1,824,259	30,124	493,757	335,487
2003	15,370,761	15,970,337	58,336	16,028,673	1,832,539	-3,638,361	10,557,773	2,898,825	1,914,163	30,788	499,238	335,953
2004	17,148,123	17,227,499	85,956	17,313,455	1,932,593	-3,599,593	11,781,269	3,315,079	2,051,775	33,982	504,619	344,705
2005	18,276,790	17,945,512	87,170	18,032,682	2,014,591	-3,557,786	12,460,305	3,573,053	2,243,432	35,669	512,402	349,810
2006	19,809,187	19,498,648	86,063	19,584,711	2,170,258	-3,920,310	13,494,143	3,905,269	2,409,775	37,847	523,405	361,730
2007	21,495,980	21,067,980	72,480	21,140,460	2,355,135	-4,264,974	14,520,351	4,352,721	2,622,908	40,100	536,055	375,670
2008	22,702,071	21,776,673	67,968	21,844,641	2,444,477	-4,311,932	15,088,232	4,597,602	3,016,237	41,406	548,275	377,738
2009	22,428,321	21,644,538	65,924	21,710,462	2,448,247	-4,379,807	14,882,408	4,206,752	3,339,161	40,110	559,164	371,996
2010	23,221,645	22,640,775	67,617	22,708,392	2,502,263	-4,622,359	15,583,770	4,047,770	3,590,105	41,008	566,275	369,995
2011	24,246,096	22,248,945	37,129	22,286,074	2,223,950	-4,099,547	15,962,577	4,564,586	3,718,933	42,349	572,531	372,118
2012	25,430,042	23,436,365	71,983	23,508,348	2,311,763	-4,491,043	16,705,542	4,914,800	3,809,700	43,712	581,763	380,007
2013	25,434,106	23,955,137	80,723	24,035,860	2,729,156	-4,702,608	16,604,096	4,921,286	3,908,724	43,082	590,363	385,891
2014	27,084,810	25,378,062	100,138	25,478,200	2,907,282	-5,099,645	17,471,273	5,514,717	4,098,820	45,200	599,215	401,174
2015	28,489,929	25,840,882	102,723	25,943,605	2,963,171	-4,791,466	18,188,968	6,016,737	4,284,224	46,887	607,634	407,819
2016	29,861,915	26,681,397	73,077	26,754,474	3,045,347	-4,727,482	18,981,645	6,429,459	4,450,811	48,324	617,947	426,373
2017	31,478,055	27,829,528	83,339	27,912,867	3,171,567	-4,830,778	19,910,522	6,938,568	4,628,965	50,340	625,313	434,161
2018	33,108,772	29,527,780	30,178	29,557,958	3,317,480	-5,277,004	20,963,474	7,253,897	4,891,401	51,957	637,232	446,159
2019	35,386,715	31,322,284	38,702	31,360,986	3,523,675	-5,560,899	22,276,412	7,958,707	5,151,596	54,926	644,257	453,870
2020	37,601,472	33,691,689	42,544	33,734,233	3,787,904	-6,821,720	23,124,609	7,827,835	6,649,028	58,201	646,061	452,476
2021	40,893,497	36,438,664	53,686	36,492,350	4,112,894	-7,712,002	24,667,454	8,604,216	7,621,827	62,243	657,000	471,588
2022	42,382,080	39,035,454	58,955	39,094,409	4,468,918	-8,246,028	26,379,463	9,347,033	6,655,584	63,799	664,310	490,381

Personal Income and Employment by Area: East Stroudsburg, PA

(Thousands of dollars, except as noted.)

Year	Personal income, total	Derivation of personal income: Earnings by place of work: Nonfarm	Farm	Total	Less: Contributions for government social insurance	Plus: Adjustment for residence	Equals: Net earnings by place of residence	Plus: Dividends, interest, and rent	Plus: Personal current transfer receipts	Per capita personal income (dollars)	Population (persons)	Total employment
1970	194,209	182,295	827	183,122	10,715	-31,752	140,655	35,461	18,093	4,274	45,441	25,965
1971	213,335	196,699	428	197,127	12,257	-32,102	152,768	39,287	21,280	4,607	46,302	26,505
1972	248,897	225,488	371	225,859	14,780	-30,103	180,976	43,302	24,619	5,088	48,917	27,900
1973	288,633	255,839	1,253	257,092	19,290	-27,452	210,350	49,387	28,896	5,582	51,711	30,353
1974	332,565	284,289	444	284,733	22,923	-21,738	240,072	57,013	35,480	6,060	54,877	31,305
1975	376,892	310,120	1,209	311,329	24,286	-21,927	265,116	63,225	48,551	6,539	57,637	31,147
1976	419,438	340,807	1,441	342,248	27,013	-20,304	294,931	69,090	55,417	6,948	60,370	31,868
1977	466,232	374,938	1,261	376,199	29,933	-18,455	327,811	78,578	59,843	7,418	62,848	33,116
1978	527,126	428,874	605	429,479	34,743	-20,408	374,328	87,436	65,362	8,043	65,535	34,888
1979	594,116	464,086	1,693	465,779	39,493	-7,479	418,807	100,794	74,515	8,748	67,911	35,265
1980	671,701	502,881	847	503,728	43,763	-1,091	458,874	124,358	88,469	9,644	69,649	35,960
1981	747,968	543,688	1,354	545,042	50,517	-2,152	492,373	153,482	102,113	10,614	70,470	36,945
1982	819,642	575,935	628	576,563	53,316	-3,409	519,838	183,009	116,795	11,433	71,688	37,363
1983	886,653	621,275	-703	620,572	60,457	3,873	563,988	193,080	129,585	12,237	72,455	38,614
1984	995,797	705,394	127	705,521	71,441	12,221	646,301	214,928	134,568	13,538	73,556	41,607
1985	1,101,448	772,694	490	773,184	80,655	20,504	713,033	243,409	145,006	14,637	75,250	43,899
1986	1,224,793	858,957	-310	858,647	91,421	34,923	802,149	266,498	156,146	15,677	78,127	46,679
1987	1,353,307	975,575	-184	975,391	104,863	38,173	908,701	281,830	162,776	16,575	81,647	49,932
1988	1,519,586	1,077,847	258	1,078,105	119,941	64,965	1,023,129	318,550	177,907	17,433	87,169	52,588
1989	1,660,255	1,172,745	307	1,173,052	129,279	80,753	1,124,526	342,567	193,162	17,958	92,452	54,322
1990	1,753,002	1,198,259	1,230	1,199,489	134,266	91,776	1,156,999	374,302	221,701	18,093	96,889	54,242
1991	1,826,966	1,191,145	805	1,191,950	134,807	142,673	1,199,816	364,976	262,174	18,005	101,469	51,670
1992	1,952,960	1,223,833	652	1,224,485	139,601	219,505	1,304,389	358,453	290,118	18,485	105,649	51,456
1993	2,097,332	1,272,615	376	1,272,991	148,043	274,122	1,399,070	388,556	309,706	19,056	110,062	52,129
1994	2,238,989	1,342,685	813	1,343,498	159,585	308,249	1,492,162	408,208	338,619	19,512	114,752	54,504
1995	2,384,605	1,412,106	221	1,412,327	167,964	333,079	1,577,442	446,014	361,149	20,027	119,070	55,406
1996	2,549,330	1,485,514	874	1,486,388	172,585	377,439	1,691,242	466,517	391,571	20,675	123,307	56,753
1997	2,734,207	1,556,759	300	1,557,059	179,586	449,521	1,826,994	492,711	414,502	21,450	127,470	58,180
1998	2,958,901	1,664,753	67	1,664,820	189,520	514,905	1,990,205	528,100	440,596	22,586	131,007	59,561
1999	3,164,483	1,795,717	-421	1,795,296	202,208	590,379	2,183,467	514,019	466,997	23,452	134,936	61,565
2000	3,531,504	2,006,772	945	2,007,717	222,797	677,943	2,462,863	561,747	506,894	25,277	139,710	65,634
2001	3,810,181	2,176,915	-112	2,176,803	239,633	695,600	2,632,770	621,734	555,677	26,501	143,775	67,036
2002	4,008,840	2,342,594	-558	2,342,036	258,828	704,887	2,788,095	607,458	613,287	26,935	148,833	68,785
2003	4,226,958	2,491,717	826	2,492,543	273,844	732,805	2,951,504	620,195	655,259	27,443	154,027	70,437
2004	4,526,411	2,745,409	2,174	2,747,583	299,466	764,123	3,212,240	606,256	707,915	28,615	158,181	72,676
2005	4,784,610	2,913,150	1,270	2,914,420	322,849	819,403	3,410,974	624,923	748,713	29,526	162,045	74,894
2006	5,048,114	3,109,192	1,121	3,110,313	347,438	852,862	3,615,737	634,906	797,471	30,560	165,185	77,434
2007	5,374,846	3,246,422	-592	3,245,830	365,899	908,910	3,788,841	723,854	862,151	32,117	167,352	79,619
2008	5,617,034	3,336,705	1,380	3,338,085	380,110	827,973	3,785,948	818,436	1,012,650	33,320	168,576	80,002
2009	5,503,090	3,245,852	2,346	3,248,198	374,975	709,576	3,582,799	812,388	1,107,903	32,488	169,390	77,120
2010	5,507,966	3,366,699	2,746	3,369,445	385,958	525,700	3,509,187	799,968	1,198,811	32,436	169,809	76,354
2011	5,773,317	3,394,475	2,454	3,396,929	353,201	619,390	3,663,118	886,943	1,223,256	34,021	169,701	75,724
2012	5,685,427	3,387,546	4,018	3,391,564	351,781	561,699	3,601,482	870,028	1,213,917	33,785	168,281	75,096
2013	5,969,483	3,368,185	3,574	3,371,759	390,961	827,442	3,808,240	908,017	1,253,226	35,773	166,870	74,387
2014	6,217,394	3,376,709	3,470	3,380,179	392,668	929,717	3,917,228	987,197	1,312,969	37,308	166,649	73,895
2015	6,415,040	3,560,602	1,839	3,562,441	411,062	912,125	4,063,504	971,926	1,379,610	38,716	165,695	75,420
2016	6,578,464	3,656,290	1,203	3,657,493	423,683	930,975	4,164,785	936,054	1,477,625	39,811	165,244	76,876
2017	6,827,296	3,760,752	2,021	3,762,773	443,876	945,756	4,264,653	1,029,397	1,533,246	40,939	166,769	77,757
2018	7,149,916	3,834,581	713	3,835,294	452,166	1,066,582	4,449,710	1,051,053	1,649,153	42,541	168,072	78,493
2019	7,566,193	4,011,518	2,062	4,013,580	477,751	1,167,169	4,702,998	1,142,548	1,720,647	44,917	168,447	79,504
2020	8,225,972	4,015,881	1,254	4,017,135	476,075	1,233,662	4,774,722	1,089,717	2,361,533	48,872	168,316	74,797
2021	8,757,149	4,297,759	1,464	4,299,223	509,638	1,210,811	5,000,396	1,263,636	2,493,117	51,931	168,629	78,109
2022	8,801,847	4,403,500	995	4,404,495	540,276	1,460,705	5,324,924	1,374,214	2,102,709	52,643	167,198	80,872

Personal Income and Employment by Area: Eau Claire, WI

(Thousands of dollars, except as noted.)

Year	Personal income, total	Derivation of personal income: Earnings by place of work: Nonfarm	Farm	Total	Less: Contributions for government social insurance	Plus: Adjustment for residence	Equals: Net earnings by place of residence	Plus: Dividends, interest, and rent	Plus: Personal current transfer receipts	Per capita personal income (dollars)	Population (persons)	Total employment
1970	419,956	338,337	18,916	357,253	24,606	-15,205	317,442	60,574	41,940	3,634	115,555	51,672
1971	458,788	366,348	19,437	385,785	27,578	-15,059	343,148	66,738	48,902	3,868	118,617	52,507
1972	498,973	396,468	21,232	417,700	31,497	-14,966	371,237	72,549	55,187	4,117	121,204	53,066
1973	544,971	421,461	27,307	448,768	38,435	-13,749	396,584	82,783	65,604	4,532	120,238	53,548
1974	593,854	448,670	23,743	472,413	42,635	-12,378	417,400	95,445	81,009	4,900	121,193	53,903
1975	654,586	478,280	23,005	501,285	44,802	-10,849	445,634	105,868	103,084	5,278	124,012	54,581
1976	718,124	522,433	22,471	544,904	49,332	-8,453	487,119	114,646	116,359	5,768	124,496	55,598
1977	809,882	591,713	33,334	625,047	55,755	-8,927	560,365	128,716	120,801	6,376	127,012	58,235
1978	903,140	663,937	32,358	696,295	64,252	-8,085	623,958	145,308	133,874	7,006	128,912	60,913
1979	1,001,521	721,254	39,869	761,123	73,061	-5,310	682,752	163,387	155,382	7,746	129,293	62,962
1980	1,135,415	788,012	38,953	826,965	80,069	-3,752	743,144	204,353	187,918	8,641	131,405	63,315
1981	1,257,540	867,406	28,946	896,352	94,693	-6,369	795,290	252,788	209,462	9,456	132,986	63,776
1982	1,334,956	897,855	31,085	928,940	98,771	-5,587	824,582	283,407	226,967	9,982	133,738	63,651
1983	1,418,568	962,471	17,044	979,515	104,736	-6,070	868,709	304,316	245,543	10,624	133,527	63,838
1984	1,539,319	1,036,771	36,546	1,073,317	114,793	-6,756	951,768	331,729	255,822	11,471	134,188	65,777
1985	1,624,292	1,091,947	38,545	1,130,492	121,819	-6,865	1,001,808	348,331	274,153	12,111	134,120	66,855
1986	1,738,038	1,188,545	46,202	1,234,747	132,621	-9,456	1,092,670	365,134	280,234	12,946	134,252	69,351
1987	1,829,864	1,280,738	46,161	1,326,899	140,459	-8,519	1,177,921	361,042	290,901	13,531	135,233	71,536
1988	1,930,929	1,382,778	35,469	1,418,247	158,022	-8,101	1,252,124	378,419	300,386	14,185	136,125	73,958
1989	2,101,091	1,458,885	58,235	1,517,120	168,017	-6,236	1,342,867	436,509	321,715	15,316	137,187	74,933
1990	2,210,052	1,549,512	45,879	1,595,391	184,659	-3,909	1,406,823	457,020	346,209	16,041	137,771	75,588
1991	2,293,108	1,634,203	29,109	1,663,312	196,411	-5,928	1,460,973	459,752	372,383	16,459	139,325	77,150
1992	2,472,371	1,770,557	39,166	1,809,723	210,432	-6,098	1,593,193	476,784	402,394	17,583	140,614	78,688
1993	2,554,491	1,849,389	28,959	1,878,348	219,142	-4,464	1,654,742	494,088	405,661	17,991	141,985	79,787
1994	2,728,553	1,993,723	39,188	2,032,911	238,979	-8,667	1,785,265	528,492	414,796	19,081	142,998	83,136
1995	2,886,449	2,122,856	23,168	2,146,024	256,322	-13,876	1,875,826	574,309	436,314	20,052	143,950	87,319
1996	3,067,265	2,260,603	48,049	2,308,652	271,154	-19,616	2,017,882	598,638	450,745	21,177	144,842	90,392
1997	3,288,806	2,463,325	27,624	2,490,949	293,360	-29,143	2,168,446	656,664	463,696	22,552	145,834	92,863
1998	3,559,373	2,683,325	41,695	2,725,020	316,442	-34,822	2,373,756	706,850	478,767	24,301	146,470	95,170
1999	3,718,918	2,878,236	40,283	2,918,519	339,429	-36,658	2,542,432	684,792	491,694	25,234	147,378	98,899
2000	3,979,225	3,086,019	23,291	3,109,310	358,894	-42,184	2,708,232	740,432	530,561	26,768	148,656	99,914
2001	4,117,581	3,097,389	30,283	3,127,672	349,893	-40,232	2,737,547	785,739	594,295	27,514	149,655	95,828
2002	4,247,360	3,247,685	26,906	3,274,591	364,782	-46,556	2,863,253	745,854	638,253	28,157	150,846	95,803
2003	4,370,910	3,350,244	39,142	3,389,386	377,593	-45,347	2,966,446	746,469	657,995	28,791	151,816	96,728
2004	4,542,439	3,516,761	56,976	3,573,737	398,216	-28,299	3,147,222	715,928	679,289	29,608	153,419	98,735
2005	4,713,858	3,644,683	43,810	3,688,493	421,823	-30,958	3,235,712	745,149	732,997	30,450	154,809	100,611
2006	5,040,522	3,903,135	31,468	3,934,603	450,122	-43,318	3,441,163	831,155	768,204	32,276	156,167	103,407
2007	5,387,947	4,125,137	50,974	4,176,111	473,679	-54,795	3,647,637	902,050	838,260	34,176	157,654	105,098
2008	5,642,870	4,207,545	54,337	4,261,882	488,605	-61,397	3,711,880	993,344	937,646	35,557	158,700	104,838
2009	5,758,398	4,238,584	17,745	4,256,329	488,369	-50,521	3,717,439	966,664	1,074,295	35,929	160,271	101,941
2010	5,960,671	4,400,987	54,944	4,455,931	505,224	-57,014	3,893,693	910,348	1,156,630	36,860	161,709	102,787
2011	6,311,944	4,558,014	96,764	4,654,778	467,928	-58,506	4,128,344	1,049,298	1,134,302	38,684	163,165	104,739
2012	6,575,010	4,738,758	81,167	4,819,925	485,985	-71,074	4,262,866	1,150,389	1,161,755	39,997	164,387	106,084
2013	6,604,602	4,772,635	101,431	4,874,066	551,798	-72,540	4,249,728	1,151,947	1,202,927	39,896	165,547	106,164
2014	6,903,817	4,962,851	94,200	5,057,051	577,477	-60,628	4,418,946	1,229,103	1,255,768	41,596	165,972	107,736
2015	7,044,669	5,083,369	75,553	5,158,922	593,310	-83,923	4,481,689	1,246,216	1,316,764	42,268	166,668	108,522
2016	7,073,393	5,101,939	49,143	5,151,082	598,448	-90,250	4,462,384	1,278,753	1,332,256	42,137	167,865	109,144
2017	7,465,787	5,385,318	41,727	5,427,045	637,287	-111,078	4,678,680	1,397,377	1,389,730	44,188	168,956	110,393
2018	7,913,242	5,730,384	45,972	5,776,356	665,062	-122,772	4,988,522	1,458,279	1,466,441	46,522	170,097	111,755
2019	8,231,733	5,929,962	43,692	5,973,654	692,106	-156,381	5,125,167	1,530,886	1,575,680	48,109	171,106	111,708
2020	8,797,345	6,054,049	78,121	6,132,170	713,917	-166,412	5,251,841	1,554,950	1,990,554	51,085	172,211	107,900
2021	9,558,117	6,412,618	89,376	6,501,994	754,954	-191,261	5,555,779	1,767,352	2,234,986	55,372	172,616	111,698
2022	9,763,179	6,851,745	98,824	6,950,569	826,921	-232,328	5,891,320	1,887,526	1,984,333	56,225	173,644	116,411

Personal Income and Employment by Area: El Centro, CA

(Thousands of dollars, except as noted.)

Year	Personal income, total	Derivation of personal income: Earnings by place of work: Nonfarm	Farm	Total	Less: Contributions for government social insurance	Plus: Adjustment for residence	Equals: Net earnings by place of residence	Plus: Dividends, interest, and rent	Plus: Personal current transfer receipts	Per capita personal income (dollars)	Population (persons)	Total employment
1970	299,115	175,395	102,809	278,204	12,340	-39,358	226,506	35,112	37,497	3,999	74,795	34,273
1971	301,362	187,379	88,107	275,486	13,656	-38,450	223,380	37,989	39,993	4,022	74,931	34,377
1972	384,220	203,216	148,542	351,758	15,533	-37,939	298,286	42,324	43,610	5,064	75,869	35,499
1973	425,947	232,410	155,052	387,462	20,286	-39,142	328,034	50,959	46,954	5,348	79,648	37,260
1974	488,692	268,810	177,654	446,464	24,223	-47,271	374,970	57,885	55,837	5,994	81,526	39,718
1975	523,162	305,287	168,146	473,433	26,376	-57,783	389,274	65,016	68,872	6,304	82,989	42,553
1976	581,199	343,522	181,160	524,682	30,301	-65,269	429,112	67,212	84,875	6,816	85,264	44,782
1977	603,258	373,672	166,362	540,034	32,857	-71,274	435,903	73,034	94,321	6,936	86,981	44,503
1978	656,466	414,805	168,076	582,881	36,740	-77,911	468,230	84,373	103,863	7,420	88,474	44,679
1979	929,247	466,456	371,339	837,795	43,714	-76,661	717,420	97,390	114,437	10,315	90,086	46,745
1980	892,750	501,697	271,261	772,958	46,460	-87,007	639,491	119,893	133,366	9,643	92,584	45,523
1981	937,763	534,114	203,896	738,010	52,687	-53,920	631,403	147,685	158,675	9,944	94,301	43,663
1982	1,039,080	549,167	267,565	816,732	54,739	-61,416	700,577	164,295	174,208	10,859	95,688	43,260
1983	1,100,685	550,956	290,123	841,079	56,053	-60,135	724,891	184,422	191,372	11,360	96,890	42,970
1984	1,126,580	600,390	255,088	855,478	63,262	-65,130	727,086	188,552	210,942	11,558	97,475	42,308
1985	1,123,275	635,816	200,804	836,620	66,587	-64,735	705,298	190,395	227,582	11,323	99,199	41,051
1986	1,161,130	700,264	174,015	874,279	74,683	-63,037	736,559	194,563	230,008	11,742	98,885	42,325
1987	1,361,218	768,105	303,976	1,072,081	81,927	-62,779	927,375	195,217	238,626	13,602	100,077	43,579
1988	1,567,808	881,931	393,506	1,275,437	98,187	-65,519	1,111,731	203,858	252,219	15,389	101,881	47,530
1989	1,688,119	966,360	385,739	1,352,099	110,979	-67,273	1,173,847	233,892	280,380	16,052	105,166	52,145
1990	1,788,952	1,045,624	369,225	1,414,849	118,763	-64,759	1,231,327	241,305	316,320	16,140	110,839	52,121
1991	1,875,359	1,094,401	359,154	1,453,555	123,658	-57,914	1,271,983	245,683	357,693	16,009	117,143	51,265
1992	2,014,568	1,232,205	297,403	1,529,608	135,611	-63,856	1,330,141	249,126	435,301	16,270	123,823	52,634
1993	2,261,329	1,315,565	431,050	1,746,615	144,367	-62,945	1,539,303	261,887	460,139	17,033	132,758	55,335
1994	2,283,722	1,371,806	382,693	1,754,499	150,955	-65,039	1,538,505	281,552	463,665	17,003	134,315	56,933
1995	2,359,013	1,372,800	396,911	1,769,711	149,162	-60,419	1,560,130	305,946	492,937	17,221	136,986	58,101
1996	2,343,970	1,406,497	306,694	1,713,191	146,736	-56,152	1,510,303	314,326	519,341	16,987	137,987	58,050
1997	2,438,612	1,492,990	312,060	1,805,050	151,731	-53,773	1,599,546	329,022	510,044	17,592	138,624	59,914
1998	2,618,686	1,601,412	352,679	1,954,091	159,715	-49,135	1,745,241	334,342	539,103	18,756	139,615	61,395
1999	2,713,480	1,679,382	336,057	2,015,439	169,696	-42,253	1,803,490	343,078	566,912	19,237	141,056	63,093
2000	2,721,238	1,760,164	256,305	2,016,469	176,722	-33,083	1,806,664	341,703	572,871	19,108	142,410	60,311
2001	2,977,969	1,940,927	263,770	2,204,697	201,616	-1,292	2,001,789	353,875	622,305	20,723	143,707	59,479
2002	3,349,019	2,117,419	420,878	2,538,297	224,189	-21,638	2,292,470	363,922	692,627	22,995	145,640	63,153
2003	3,483,389	2,291,849	330,728	2,622,577	246,704	-32,834	2,343,039	405,479	734,871	23,381	148,984	65,357
2004	3,582,583	2,400,669	337,700	2,738,369	264,495	-38,429	2,435,445	392,313	754,825	23,530	152,259	65,538
2005	3,761,791	2,551,013	359,551	2,910,564	281,975	-57,043	2,571,546	392,577	797,668	24,097	156,113	67,023
2006	4,066,254	2,764,176	359,156	3,123,332	297,092	-75,271	2,750,969	426,930	888,355	25,334	160,505	71,937
2007	4,323,904	2,921,836	367,926	3,289,762	306,893	-110,146	2,872,723	472,730	978,451	26,270	164,596	74,213
2008	4,719,809	3,019,191	570,998	3,590,189	323,867	-146,253	3,120,069	514,717	1,085,023	28,108	167,917	74,053
2009	4,793,296	3,035,855	488,183	3,524,038	329,095	-151,346	3,043,597	519,597	1,230,102	27,867	172,008	72,575
2010	5,087,461	3,185,065	468,738	3,653,803	327,686	-153,708	3,172,409	537,078	1,377,974	29,124	174,685	72,569
2011	5,484,146	3,311,606	693,338	4,004,944	310,408	-157,443	3,537,093	570,413	1,376,640	31,225	175,632	73,795
2012	5,541,036	3,377,169	636,808	4,013,977	319,726	-161,508	3,532,743	623,289	1,385,004	31,428	176,308	75,283
2013	5,743,731	3,433,034	796,230	4,229,264	359,319	-164,724	3,705,221	607,206	1,431,304	32,627	176,043	77,661
2014	5,990,271	3,502,269	917,703	4,419,972	373,727	-168,684	3,877,561	599,327	1,513,383	33,758	177,447	80,237
2015	6,439,648	3,655,106	1,088,745	4,743,851	384,056	-180,343	4,179,452	617,793	1,642,403	36,121	178,280	81,474
2016	6,323,414	3,708,429	810,378	4,518,807	395,765	-172,944	3,950,098	661,892	1,711,424	35,252	179,377	79,772
2017	6,428,926	3,826,327	812,494	4,638,821	414,147	-182,621	4,042,053	676,826	1,710,047	35,585	180,662	80,045
2018	6,353,010	3,951,809	517,688	4,469,497	430,602	-179,758	3,859,137	687,016	1,806,857	35,217	180,396	80,930
2019	6,740,447	4,127,992	596,294	4,724,286	456,644	-184,123	4,083,519	727,518	1,929,410	37,511	179,694	80,938
2020	8,183,274	4,350,213	620,881	4,971,094	478,458	-188,998	4,303,638	803,183	3,076,453	45,565	179,595	78,410
2021	8,643,247	4,678,509	476,431	5,154,940	517,154	-199,941	4,437,845	807,632	3,397,770	48,228	179,215	82,010
2022	8,075,656	4,963,496	582,341	5,545,837	572,904	-217,000	4,755,933	831,480	2,488,243	45,188	178,713	84,886

Personal Income and Employment by Area: Elizabethtown-Fort Knox, KY

(Thousands of dollars, except as noted.)

Year	Personal income, total	Derivation of personal income: Earnings by place of work								Per capita personal income (dollars)	Population (persons)	Total employment
		Nonfarm	Farm	Total	Less: Contributions for government social insurance	Plus: Adjustment for residence	Equals: Net earnings by place of residence	Plus: Dividends, interest, and rent	Plus: Personal current transfer receipts			
1970	491,984	398,423	12,529	410,952	23,039	-14,461	373,452	98,882	19,650	4,570	107,652	63,118
1971	506,089	410,110	12,972	423,082	25,386	-13,153	384,543	98,997	22,549	4,693	107,830	58,437
1972	542,596	436,669	15,160	451,829	27,167	-11,239	413,423	104,010	25,163	5,120	105,967	55,176
1973	560,221	437,445	20,332	457,777	28,728	-7,041	422,008	107,957	30,256	5,651	99,133	53,229
1974	652,568	507,481	21,922	529,403	35,205	-8,168	486,030	128,841	37,697	6,222	104,885	56,273
1975	671,920	527,785	8,542	536,327	39,119	-9,799	487,409	135,350	49,161	6,085	110,417	55,211
1976	706,293	550,417	11,074	561,491	41,609	-7,908	511,974	139,162	55,157	5,984	118,037	54,863
1977	813,909	630,775	15,044	645,819	47,522	-5,233	593,064	164,089	56,756	6,840	118,999	58,950
1978	870,028	663,260	13,202	676,462	49,187	-891	626,384	183,007	60,637	7,440	116,940	58,530
1979	963,365	726,754	18,573	745,327	55,912	1,808	691,223	200,689	71,453	8,099	118,949	58,857
1980	1,043,735	774,609	12,994	787,603	60,353	6,490	733,740	222,920	87,075	8,468	123,258	59,302
1981	1,120,070	824,555	23,285	847,840	67,596	-1,735	778,509	239,002	102,559	9,239	121,230	55,951
1982	1,225,019	902,266	19,247	921,513	73,092	-6,467	841,954	270,674	112,391	10,140	120,805	57,731
1983	1,302,057	970,267	-4,977	965,290	82,238	-4,472	878,580	301,471	122,006	10,689	121,809	59,250
1984	1,419,578	1,040,392	20,621	1,061,013	89,965	-6,182	964,866	322,753	131,959	11,614	122,225	59,602
1985	1,507,280	1,115,054	13,121	1,128,175	98,762	-7,492	1,021,921	343,850	141,509	12,272	122,818	61,588
1986	1,570,433	1,159,048	10,639	1,169,687	107,212	-4,045	1,058,430	360,931	151,072	12,745	123,219	62,886
1987	1,644,122	1,216,479	15,614	1,232,093	114,431	-1,060	1,116,602	370,213	157,307	13,361	123,053	63,165
1988	1,739,853	1,287,933	13,949	1,301,882	127,116	3,614	1,178,380	388,609	172,864	13,933	124,869	64,064
1989	1,866,550	1,356,676	27,634	1,384,310	137,220	1,961	1,249,051	420,390	197,109	14,996	124,472	65,539
1990	1,952,649	1,417,728	27,448	1,445,176	149,829	-1,596	1,293,751	441,181	217,717	15,563	125,466	66,277
1991	2,027,249	1,465,668	26,767	1,492,435	157,434	3,573	1,338,574	438,720	249,955	16,686	121,495	63,642
1992	2,220,347	1,601,058	31,941	1,632,999	174,927	12,968	1,471,040	469,050	280,257	18,494	120,059	64,628
1993	2,260,542	1,616,181	28,089	1,644,270	179,628	26,923	1,491,565	478,915	290,062	17,869	126,505	64,846
1994	2,351,260	1,650,695	29,606	1,680,301	185,251	42,886	1,537,936	510,186	303,138	18,323	128,321	65,357
1995	2,424,763	1,676,822	12,002	1,688,824	187,469	58,150	1,559,505	535,529	329,729	18,735	129,423	66,847
1996	2,547,787	1,737,716	25,435	1,763,151	193,965	70,444	1,639,630	555,281	352,876	19,766	128,895	67,246
1997	2,655,752	1,821,853	13,987	1,835,840	203,643	87,851	1,720,048	556,319	379,385	20,400	130,182	67,884
1998	2,843,843	1,918,497	2,078	1,920,575	213,770	112,510	1,819,315	626,148	398,380	21,638	131,428	69,443
1999	2,969,592	2,028,470	-17,686	2,010,784	226,410	138,522	1,922,896	632,829	413,867	22,402	132,558	70,620
2000	3,284,289	2,218,645	10,401	2,229,046	241,336	158,738	2,146,448	685,997	451,844	24,417	134,506	72,649
2001	3,413,598	2,316,789	12,327	2,329,116	253,373	150,293	2,226,036	686,584	500,978	25,163	135,657	73,306
2002	3,507,750	2,403,756	-8,285	2,395,471	262,922	134,684	2,267,233	690,622	549,895	25,681	136,591	72,028
2003	3,670,469	2,583,823	-395	2,583,428	280,532	95,259	2,398,155	699,762	572,552	26,923	136,333	73,744
2004	3,860,984	2,742,840	12,133	2,754,973	295,868	79,527	2,538,632	696,725	625,627	27,932	138,230	74,802
2005	4,010,721	2,841,096	28,565	2,869,661	305,840	68,429	2,632,250	709,106	669,365	28,612	140,177	73,789
2006	4,207,218	3,057,065	19,473	3,076,538	333,732	-5,677	2,737,129	736,765	733,324	29,866	140,870	76,302
2007	4,393,646	3,125,770	7,363	3,133,133	343,205	-13,571	2,776,357	820,504	796,785	30,975	141,844	76,952
2008	4,608,515	3,284,959	-2,310	3,282,649	365,324	-114,290	2,803,035	890,329	915,151	32,230	142,988	76,796
2009	4,768,462	3,356,293	3,851	3,360,144	385,016	-121,847	2,853,281	891,391	1,023,790	33,154	143,829	75,095
2010	5,054,471	3,813,413	-5,024	3,808,389	426,652	-369,188	3,012,549	932,669	1,109,253	33,723	149,882	78,857
2011	5,316,493	4,121,590	13,722	4,135,312	415,901	-581,701	3,137,710	1,049,223	1,129,560	35,087	151,525	80,815
2012	5,434,541	3,997,455	15,997	4,013,452	406,564	-346,326	3,260,562	1,032,274	1,141,705	35,784	151,871	78,596
2013	5,398,180	3,967,892	61,971	4,029,863	450,405	-346,785	3,232,673	989,645	1,175,862	35,341	152,744	78,185
2014	5,561,353	3,885,127	6,465	3,891,592	444,777	-160,625	3,286,190	1,009,641	1,265,522	36,502	152,356	76,916
2015	5,711,949	3,854,626	833	3,855,459	447,014	-16,168	3,392,277	982,165	1,337,507	38,360	148,904	76,581
2016	5,925,712	3,916,466	-14,726	3,901,740	453,024	75,362	3,524,078	1,031,890	1,369,744	39,547	149,841	77,452
2017	6,117,340	3,997,747	-7,218	3,990,529	461,671	137,316	3,666,174	1,014,128	1,437,038	40,392	151,451	77,456
2018	6,323,296	4,064,054	-21,776	4,042,278	470,601	227,171	3,798,848	1,030,082	1,494,366	40,953	154,405	78,151
2019	6,642,434	4,226,803	2,093	4,228,896	484,095	241,184	3,985,985	1,077,759	1,578,690	42,820	155,123	78,422
2020	7,213,687	4,327,924	9,243	4,337,167	504,610	232,569	4,065,126	1,060,381	2,088,180	46,324	155,723	76,135
2021	7,929,259	4,673,767	32,994	4,706,761	527,729	278,583	4,457,615	1,136,773	2,334,871	50,530	156,922	77,470
2022	7,945,829	4,992,345	806	4,993,151	570,876	310,253	4,732,528	1,182,120	2,031,181	50,602	157,026	80,408

Personal Income and Employment by Area: Elkhart-Goshen, IN

(Thousands of dollars, except as noted.)

Year	Personal income, total	Derivation of personal income: Earnings by place of work: Nonfarm	Farm	Total	Less: Contributions for government social insurance	Plus: Adjustment for residence	Equals: Net earnings by place of residence	Plus: Dividends, interest, and rent	Plus: Personal current transfer receipts	Per capita personal income (dollars)	Population (persons)	Total employment
1970	552,330	558,921	6,678	565,599	39,107	-84,845	441,647	75,883	34,800	4,362	126,624	71,287
1971	601,971	610,634	8,364	618,998	44,415	-97,279	477,304	83,731	40,936	4,739	127,025	73,110
1972	683,157	714,024	8,090	722,114	55,043	-119,974	547,097	90,643	45,417	5,271	129,596	80,429
1973	759,373	796,745	15,797	812,542	70,119	-137,515	604,908	101,066	53,399	5,740	132,290	84,783
1974	749,526	758,336	8,299	766,635	69,608	-128,774	568,253	114,582	66,691	5,656	132,510	77,343
1975	785,862	762,915	14,151	777,066	68,709	-132,132	576,225	122,928	86,709	5,977	131,484	73,077
1976	908,745	942,599	15,240	957,839	86,525	-176,615	694,699	132,572	81,474	6,916	131,402	82,175
1977	1,021,030	1,088,803	10,433	1,099,236	101,518	-211,138	786,580	147,905	86,545	7,644	133,567	87,444
1978	1,141,941	1,247,694	4,913	1,252,607	119,592	-251,937	881,078	166,552	94,311	8,428	135,493	93,129
1979	1,203,213	1,286,651	3,826	1,290,477	126,331	-260,684	903,462	186,864	112,887	8,803	136,687	89,398
1980	1,226,626	1,224,092	8,290	1,232,382	118,426	-245,510	868,446	216,552	141,628	8,934	137,292	80,021
1981	1,352,901	1,332,543	6,274	1,338,817	137,810	-264,066	936,941	260,775	155,185	9,887	136,836	81,375
1982	1,442,204	1,403,536	2,142	1,405,678	148,234	-281,887	975,557	294,608	172,039	10,437	138,179	82,288
1983	1,645,910	1,695,142	-736	1,694,406	179,196	-355,256	1,159,954	311,591	174,365	11,733	140,286	91,798
1984	1,883,457	1,950,161	14,866	1,965,027	212,635	-409,292	1,343,100	355,604	184,753	13,016	144,701	100,401
1985	1,992,955	2,050,682	14,229	2,064,911	228,276	-427,103	1,409,532	380,553	202,870	13,531	147,287	101,827
1986	2,159,186	2,242,074	14,300	2,256,374	250,771	-465,717	1,539,886	402,139	217,161	14,492	148,990	106,079
1987	2,346,869	2,476,699	17,339	2,494,038	273,523	-514,418	1,706,097	418,150	222,622	15,525	151,167	112,993
1988	2,540,723	2,706,767	9,082	2,715,849	306,591	-562,980	1,846,278	455,775	238,670	16,507	153,917	118,921
1989	2,729,616	2,807,367	24,021	2,831,388	319,493	-572,219	1,939,676	536,323	253,617	17,519	155,813	119,871
1990	2,802,938	2,822,729	20,457	2,843,186	330,838	-558,262	1,954,086	568,633	280,219	17,908	156,517	117,792
1991	2,856,749	2,854,635	11,015	2,865,650	336,297	-557,371	1,971,982	569,651	315,116	18,065	158,141	113,810
1992	3,138,262	3,178,927	18,894	3,197,821	369,889	-627,461	2,200,471	574,834	362,957	19,559	160,454	117,964
1993	3,346,637	3,431,207	18,421	3,449,628	399,069	-673,830	2,376,729	589,974	379,934	20,467	163,510	123,339
1994	3,614,824	3,765,878	16,011	3,781,889	444,647	-743,793	2,593,449	624,458	396,917	21,711	166,498	129,440
1995	3,806,201	3,942,977	10,087	3,953,064	468,165	-765,387	2,719,512	675,303	411,386	22,407	169,869	134,046
1996	3,968,421	4,047,205	21,687	4,068,892	480,126	-779,650	2,809,116	715,364	443,941	22,994	172,582	133,328
1997	4,127,808	4,180,777	26,012	4,206,789	495,175	-799,408	2,912,206	759,144	456,458	23,551	175,274	134,160
1998	4,489,040	4,584,103	25,812	4,609,915	534,681	-880,246	3,194,988	806,053	487,999	25,236	177,885	140,573
1999	4,776,251	5,000,052	12,762	5,012,814	576,084	-968,374	3,468,356	794,603	513,292	26,440	180,645	146,242
2000	5,023,469	5,215,659	16,832	5,232,491	593,743	-1,011,425	3,627,323	843,377	552,769	27,389	183,412	147,774
2001	4,932,185	4,933,784	27,500	4,961,284	558,095	-953,677	3,449,512	857,356	625,317	26,703	184,708	137,494
2002	5,120,918	5,239,508	21,523	5,261,031	595,357	-1,032,916	3,632,758	829,076	659,084	27,749	184,543	137,559
2003	5,326,199	5,484,951	37,248	5,522,199	627,984	-1,116,958	3,777,257	864,399	684,543	28,460	187,149	140,019
2004	5,637,967	6,081,948	50,735	6,132,683	694,627	-1,353,053	4,085,003	825,642	727,322	29,781	189,316	148,000
2005	5,902,837	6,398,538	35,677	6,434,215	736,645	-1,458,639	4,238,931	863,288	800,618	30,705	192,242	150,927
2006	6,132,063	6,634,718	25,931	6,660,649	762,377	-1,589,565	4,308,707	951,407	871,949	31,439	195,047	153,411
2007	6,299,068	6,628,646	36,147	6,664,793	762,035	-1,572,066	4,330,692	1,049,061	919,315	32,088	196,304	152,218
2008	6,172,690	6,006,261	37,192	6,043,453	704,073	-1,359,567	3,979,813	1,094,389	1,098,488	31,213	197,762	140,894
2009	5,644,125	4,925,439	11,965	4,937,404	595,806	-918,009	3,423,589	931,616	1,288,920	28,576	197,514	120,624
2010	6,038,797	5,475,739	36,227	5,511,966	654,089	-1,083,426	3,774,451	947,785	1,316,561	30,581	197,472	126,838
2011	6,424,889	5,713,733	66,753	5,780,486	616,234	-1,119,784	4,044,468	1,070,162	1,310,259	32,386	198,387	130,770
2012	6,921,230	6,446,066	63,695	6,509,761	675,221	-1,311,067	4,523,473	1,054,664	1,343,093	34,752	199,160	136,435
2013	7,174,727	6,867,120	115,285	6,982,405	815,978	-1,454,197	4,712,230	1,120,507	1,341,990	35,789	200,474	142,367
2014	7,728,708	7,532,331	119,241	7,651,572	878,659	-1,649,077	5,123,836	1,170,678	1,434,194	38,304	201,774	148,040
2015	8,096,897	8,022,491	105,535	8,128,026	933,968	-1,777,083	5,416,975	1,218,463	1,461,459	39,802	203,430	151,729
2016	8,436,448	8,632,149	66,609	8,698,758	985,768	-1,974,732	5,738,258	1,209,718	1,488,472	41,332	204,114	154,715
2017	9,114,688	9,689,866	84,974	9,774,840	1,092,724	-2,430,581	6,251,535	1,337,904	1,525,249	44,496	204,843	162,365
2018	9,449,457	9,992,783	77,373	10,070,156	1,115,986	-2,564,825	6,389,345	1,481,772	1,578,340	45,820	206,230	166,165
2019	9,438,978	9,576,475	55,433	9,631,908	1,087,636	-2,350,395	6,193,877	1,520,736	1,724,365	45,602	206,985	161,305
2020	10,211,653	9,749,363	94,199	9,843,562	1,156,963	-2,355,997	6,330,602	1,575,002	2,306,049	49,336	206,983	153,511
2021	11,692,033	12,052,076	133,305	12,185,381	1,436,551	-3,374,793	7,374,037	1,740,496	2,577,500	56,465	207,066	167,144
2022	12,117,622	12,829,374	200,667	13,030,041	1,472,238	-3,567,370	7,990,433	1,908,227	2,218,962	58,570	206,890	173,324

Personal Income and Employment by Area: Elmira, NY

(Thousands of dollars, except as noted.)

Year	Personal income, total	Derivation of personal income: Earnings by place of work: Nonfarm	Farm	Total	Less: Contributions for government social insurance	Plus: Adjustment for residence	Equals: Net earnings by place of residence	Plus: Dividends, interest, and rent	Plus: Personal current transfer receipts	Per capita personal income (dollars)	Population (persons)	Total employment
1970	396,780	335,313	2,368	337,681	25,373	-12,399	299,909	53,299	43,572	3,911	101,457	45,446
1971	417,926	347,540	2,230	349,770	27,192	-12,258	310,320	55,746	51,860	4,135	101,080	44,720
1972	450,654	375,041	2,196	377,237	30,787	-12,053	334,397	60,356	55,901	4,433	101,665	44,763
1973	493,677	413,405	2,892	416,297	39,391	-11,728	365,178	66,953	61,546	4,915	100,452	47,207
1974	534,102	431,076	2,210	433,286	42,454	-7,486	383,346	76,704	74,052	5,344	99,936	46,263
1975	573,579	441,164	1,974	443,138	42,399	-4,851	395,888	82,717	94,974	5,707	100,497	44,186
1976	619,058	479,784	2,702	482,486	47,320	-5,821	429,345	87,803	101,910	6,190	100,008	44,018
1977	663,650	500,579	2,167	502,746	49,351	695	454,090	96,318	113,242	6,681	99,335	43,206
1978	714,037	546,455	2,186	548,641	55,145	3,982	497,478	101,245	115,314	7,235	98,689	43,898
1979	774,193	585,742	2,967	588,709	60,779	8,535	536,465	110,385	127,343	7,793	99,339	44,018
1980	866,699	638,179	3,316	641,495	65,977	11,908	587,426	133,003	146,270	8,894	97,443	43,155
1981	948,605	687,973	3,108	691,081	75,556	7,810	623,335	159,307	165,963	9,840	96,406	43,073
1982	996,832	684,350	3,010	687,360	75,753	10,379	621,986	186,032	188,814	10,380	96,032	40,676
1983	1,045,699	706,479	2,736	709,215	78,723	11,496	641,988	195,821	207,890	11,047	94,659	39,693
1984	1,127,876	766,289	3,740	770,029	86,977	11,202	694,254	213,028	220,594	12,103	93,190	40,900
1985	1,158,326	778,630	4,238	782,868	89,739	18,782	711,911	220,592	225,823	12,563	92,200	41,191
1986	1,219,736	820,878	5,105	825,983	96,525	21,794	751,252	233,111	235,373	13,377	91,179	42,328
1987	1,294,493	913,947	5,771	919,718	105,457	10,338	824,599	232,802	237,092	14,098	91,819	44,422
1988	1,394,077	1,001,625	4,398	1,006,023	118,303	11,924	899,644	245,947	248,486	14,967	93,142	46,262
1989	1,534,661	1,094,119	4,544	1,098,663	127,681	9,090	980,072	293,050	261,539	16,205	94,701	47,884
1990	1,612,371	1,147,490	4,132	1,151,622	127,221	10,605	1,035,006	297,070	280,295	16,920	95,292	48,188
1991	1,667,329	1,178,931	3,035	1,181,966	133,598	8,796	1,057,164	302,929	307,236	17,551	95,001	47,118
1992	1,727,858	1,225,409	3,014	1,228,423	136,941	-230	1,091,252	296,394	340,212	18,197	94,954	46,818
1993	1,755,996	1,252,064	3,197	1,255,261	142,315	-8,945	1,104,001	299,114	352,881	18,541	94,711	46,964
1994	1,819,429	1,307,149	2,784	1,309,933	150,604	-19,537	1,139,792	308,808	370,829	19,328	94,132	47,823
1995	1,888,701	1,356,925	2,175	1,359,100	156,193	-23,720	1,179,187	323,189	386,325	20,162	93,675	47,762
1996	1,955,304	1,405,460	3,161	1,408,621	160,241	-27,928	1,220,452	332,280	402,572	21,031	92,972	48,771
1997	2,029,494	1,474,302	1,506	1,475,808	165,208	-41,805	1,268,795	350,721	409,978	22,021	92,162	49,516
1998	2,103,704	1,547,533	2,626	1,550,159	172,207	-50,812	1,327,140	357,250	419,314	22,918	91,791	50,968
1999	2,188,910	1,618,285	2,624	1,620,909	175,117	-45,224	1,400,568	349,343	438,999	23,979	91,284	51,569
2000	2,316,402	1,672,978	2,705	1,675,683	180,729	8,745	1,503,699	369,347	443,356	25,429	91,094	51,377
2001	2,316,148	1,668,533	3,073	1,671,606	185,828	-3,329	1,482,449	357,638	476,061	25,514	90,780	49,776
2002	2,302,988	1,667,557	1,242	1,668,799	187,375	-16,451	1,464,973	316,761	521,254	25,416	90,613	48,142
2003	2,344,917	1,700,433	2,124	1,702,557	191,359	-20,996	1,490,202	315,632	539,083	26,010	90,154	47,039
2004	2,423,254	1,750,244	2,754	1,752,998	198,027	-29,206	1,525,765	323,773	573,716	26,992	89,777	46,334
2005	2,518,074	1,838,829	2,304	1,841,133	213,363	-30,879	1,596,891	324,378	596,805	28,338	88,860	46,499
2006	2,644,565	1,914,413	1,410	1,915,823	223,776	5,759	1,697,806	321,265	625,494	29,804	88,732	47,091
2007	2,763,408	1,988,774	1,961	1,990,735	229,936	-14,105	1,746,694	361,281	655,433	31,178	88,634	47,912
2008	2,967,848	2,096,913	1,900	2,098,813	244,109	-21,191	1,833,513	412,659	721,676	33,534	88,503	47,836
2009	2,987,353	2,054,577	103	2,054,680	235,818	-14,949	1,803,913	392,543	790,897	33,623	88,849	45,893
2010	3,122,248	2,211,674	1,726	2,213,400	249,648	-42,077	1,921,675	367,981	832,592	35,109	88,931	45,940
2011	3,272,918	2,289,679	2,756	2,292,435	234,503	-27,142	2,030,790	412,612	829,516	36,735	89,095	46,424
2012	3,313,337	2,339,244	2,871	2,342,115	236,025	-32,374	2,073,716	411,012	828,609	37,028	89,483	45,983
2013	3,345,388	2,352,002	5,342	2,357,344	267,965	-20,360	2,069,019	428,331	848,038	37,722	88,686	45,278
2014	3,408,518	2,379,139	4,263	2,383,402	276,451	-12,555	2,094,396	447,605	866,517	38,810	87,826	45,289
2015	3,434,299	2,377,026	1,635	2,378,661	276,067	-21,814	2,080,780	448,700	904,819	39,254	87,489	45,076
2016	3,421,413	2,329,990	1,981	2,331,971	274,189	-6,478	2,051,304	446,813	923,296	39,538	86,535	44,004
2017	3,569,951	2,358,208	3,450	2,361,658	279,538	25,567	2,107,687	478,055	984,209	41,611	85,793	43,545
2018	3,670,532	2,449,474	2,333	2,451,807	286,460	40,594	2,205,941	501,867	962,724	43,119	85,126	43,692
2019	3,820,604	2,487,459	4,112	2,491,571	292,067	62,086	2,261,590	525,543	1,033,471	45,149	84,622	43,375
2020	4,118,178	2,480,315	4,094	2,484,409	290,531	9,206	2,203,084	555,807	1,359,287	49,058	83,945	41,187
2021	4,290,383	2,644,377	6,522	2,650,899	315,573	-1,447	2,333,879	556,466	1,400,038	51,797	82,830	41,395
2022	4,204,007	2,729,037	6,983	2,736,020	334,556	40,183	2,441,647	556,933	1,205,427	51,630	81,426	42,692

Personal Income and Employment by Area: El Paso, TX

(Thousands of dollars, except as noted.)

Year	Personal income, total	Derivation of personal income: Earnings by place of work: Nonfarm	Farm	Total	Less: Contributions for government social insurance	Plus: Adjustment for residence	Equals: Net earnings by place of residence	Plus: Dividends, interest, and rent	Plus: Personal current transfer receipts	Per capita personal income (dollars)	Population (persons)	Total employment
1970	1,203,259	973,527	9,345	982,872	62,026	-22,756	898,090	218,760	86,409	3,316	362,854	150,442
1971	1,316,139	1,072,835	7,844	1,080,679	71,639	-32,199	976,841	236,278	103,020	3,542	371,562	155,024
1972	1,427,111	1,168,213	13,411	1,181,624	81,214	-48,817	1,051,593	255,821	119,697	3,748	380,771	158,645
1973	1,630,778	1,347,813	10,984	1,358,797	105,969	-63,759	1,189,069	298,364	143,345	4,069	400,736	172,265
1974	1,831,322	1,504,699	11,675	1,516,374	122,106	-76,391	1,317,877	344,888	168,557	4,422	414,149	178,186
1975	1,939,079	1,650,839	11,999	1,662,838	135,057	-180,306	1,347,475	376,772	214,832	4,509	430,008	183,213
1976	2,161,399	1,845,061	16,226	1,861,287	153,446	-198,826	1,509,015	408,068	244,316	4,879	443,031	189,986
1977	2,380,879	2,036,842	20,615	2,057,457	168,057	-224,304	1,665,096	452,808	262,975	5,260	452,639	194,248
1978	2,668,601	2,290,265	12,779	2,303,044	192,179	-249,540	1,861,325	514,473	292,803	5,762	463,126	200,883
1979	3,036,699	2,583,433	10,812	2,594,245	227,863	-248,753	2,117,629	576,302	342,768	6,394	474,925	208,458
1980	3,372,775	2,851,352	6,588	2,857,940	253,028	-311,008	2,293,904	672,078	406,793	6,933	486,485	214,832
1981	4,061,441	3,239,015	20,461	3,259,476	308,726	-128,327	2,822,423	787,498	451,520	8,115	500,476	223,237
1982	4,386,695	3,442,956	6,794	3,449,750	326,341	-157,921	2,965,488	916,327	504,880	8,519	514,949	222,683
1983	4,727,998	3,635,297	17,879	3,653,176	343,899	-152,590	3,156,687	1,003,231	568,080	9,023	523,973	219,571
1984	5,091,935	3,935,097	15,534	3,950,631	383,119	-181,848	3,385,664	1,091,290	614,981	9,564	532,385	227,764
1985	5,499,966	4,238,111	17,161	4,255,272	416,452	-198,636	3,640,184	1,203,095	656,687	10,156	541,534	232,617
1986	5,804,278	4,470,682	8,031	4,478,713	438,314	-195,351	3,845,048	1,245,989	713,241	10,510	552,279	235,285
1987	6,013,634	4,645,236	19,333	4,664,569	453,731	-214,745	3,996,093	1,260,492	757,049	10,697	562,186	245,513
1988	6,450,577	5,017,373	18,127	5,035,500	508,260	-231,511	4,295,729	1,343,877	810,971	11,285	571,624	254,501
1989	7,061,537	5,375,779	16,492	5,392,271	554,062	-242,817	4,595,392	1,530,868	935,277	12,095	583,850	264,114
1990	7,632,214	5,714,230	12,285	5,726,515	581,941	-267,853	4,876,721	1,693,064	1,062,429	12,757	598,255	269,064
1991	7,949,648	6,040,646	7,748	6,048,394	624,970	-296,909	5,126,515	1,606,275	1,216,858	13,009	611,092	271,145
1992	8,766,477	6,659,925	26,917	6,686,842	688,724	-318,195	5,679,923	1,616,367	1,470,187	14,093	622,040	281,367
1993	9,235,574	7,005,752	23,325	7,029,077	731,023	-330,787	5,967,267	1,675,569	1,592,738	14,500	636,952	288,491
1994	9,741,476	7,426,708	31,411	7,458,119	774,093	-367,066	6,316,960	1,721,779	1,702,737	15,008	649,075	295,015
1995	10,225,510	7,715,170	27,551	7,742,721	802,130	-381,764	6,558,827	1,814,676	1,852,007	15,555	657,359	299,334
1996	10,618,555	7,885,941	25,758	7,911,699	813,916	-393,012	6,704,771	1,880,563	2,033,221	16,097	659,655	298,829
1997	11,395,959	8,455,018	31,215	8,486,233	865,889	-433,301	7,187,043	2,072,271	2,136,645	17,052	668,300	307,305
1998	12,033,959	8,983,520	37,465	9,020,985	913,758	-461,794	7,645,433	2,262,584	2,125,942	17,842	674,484	313,506
1999	12,336,468	9,318,037	32,288	9,350,325	942,936	-476,669	7,930,720	2,239,932	2,165,816	18,176	678,720	317,940
2000	13,131,054	9,963,918	28,706	9,992,624	984,600	-497,230	8,510,794	2,337,248	2,283,012	19,167	685,086	325,078
2001	13,741,821	10,347,298	29,458	10,376,756	1,019,086	-367,751	8,989,919	2,270,965	2,480,937	19,842	692,568	324,108
2002	14,497,091	10,838,172	31,405	10,869,577	1,062,840	-402,611	9,404,126	2,348,111	2,744,854	20,715	699,844	331,534
2003	15,063,129	11,314,065	41,980	11,356,045	1,120,431	-397,128	9,838,486	2,290,378	2,934,265	21,259	708,545	336,127
2004	15,882,466	11,965,957	36,514	12,002,471	1,183,753	-363,371	10,455,347	2,397,536	3,029,583	22,028	720,997	342,442
2005	16,885,388	12,521,206	36,324	12,557,530	1,247,427	-312,170	10,997,933	2,555,793	3,331,662	23,083	731,511	351,156
2006	17,902,134	13,195,631	20,194	13,215,825	1,316,319	-337,084	11,562,422	2,802,432	3,537,280	23,925	748,254	363,341
2007	19,013,134	13,735,906	23,047	13,758,953	1,398,910	-363,638	11,996,405	3,117,167	3,899,562	25,049	759,040	375,533
2008	20,107,393	14,077,120	12,211	14,089,331	1,453,157	-363,849	12,272,325	3,429,211	4,405,857	26,002	773,304	382,010
2009	21,131,622	14,709,757	9,959	14,719,716	1,529,346	-403,369	12,787,001	3,477,082	4,867,539	26,743	790,182	382,247
2010	23,232,993	16,167,404	18,344	16,185,748	1,659,593	-369,268	14,156,887	3,637,458	5,438,648	28,769	807,558	389,862
2011	24,792,804	17,028,344	13,030	17,041,374	1,566,967	-328,032	15,146,375	4,013,776	5,632,653	30,017	825,963	402,644
2012	25,902,729	17,635,572	7,487	17,643,059	1,642,184	-289,657	15,711,218	4,612,254	5,579,257	30,817	840,532	406,486
2013	25,473,733	17,554,022	12,118	17,566,140	1,839,225	-193,482	15,533,433	4,198,750	5,741,550	30,281	841,232	411,105
2014	26,701,108	18,135,589	17,366	18,152,955	1,899,882	-162,972	16,090,101	4,588,592	6,022,415	31,551	846,285	415,539
2015	27,505,066	18,798,585	17,925	18,816,510	1,988,849	-204,649	16,623,012	4,516,625	6,365,429	32,484	846,733	424,010
2016	28,033,251	19,181,700	13,321	19,195,021	2,035,435	-259,135	16,900,451	4,522,987	6,609,813	32,889	852,347	431,491
2017	29,047,586	19,883,512	16,532	19,900,044	2,119,639	-248,368	17,532,037	4,740,804	6,774,745	33,899	856,887	438,402
2018	30,343,116	20,730,231	12,675	20,742,906	2,192,904	-122,247	18,427,755	4,826,936	7,088,425	35,333	858,769	450,470
2019	31,852,524	21,859,241	11,483	21,870,724	2,303,255	-146,449	19,421,020	4,982,179	7,449,325	36,907	863,056	459,313
2020	34,939,529	22,652,435	11,515	22,663,950	2,420,889	-193,758	20,049,303	5,105,189	9,785,037	40,172	869,750	452,923
2021	38,421,177	23,895,013	16,474	23,911,487	2,534,864	-266,952	21,109,671	5,693,900	11,617,606	44,093	871,375	465,529
2022	38,519,049	25,359,010	-2,399	25,356,611	2,717,702	-259,964	22,378,945	6,118,262	10,021,842	44,163	872,195	484,280

Personal Income and Employment by Area: Enid, OK

(Thousands of dollars, except as noted.)

Year	Personal income, total	Derivation of personal income: Earnings by place of work: Nonfarm	Farm	Total	Less: Contributions for government social insurance	Plus: Adjustment for residence	Equals: Net earnings by place of residence	Plus: Dividends, interest, and rent	Plus: Personal current transfer receipts	Per capita personal income (dollars)	Population (persons)	Total employment
1970	220,525	166,678	8,631	175,309	11,088	-2,899	161,322	39,804	19,399	3,901	56,532	27,435
1971	240,055	178,534	10,934	189,468	12,299	-3,212	173,957	43,734	22,364	4,166	57,616	27,233
1972	259,831	196,276	11,158	207,434	13,972	-3,625	189,837	45,394	24,600	4,511	57,604	27,881
1973	289,212	214,464	16,047	230,511	17,570	-3,914	209,027	51,890	28,295	5,115	56,540	28,388
1974	320,536	240,903	12,184	253,087	20,314	-4,312	228,461	58,966	33,109	5,568	57,571	29,130
1975	359,151	270,396	9,176	279,572	22,654	-4,663	252,255	66,454	40,442	6,115	58,729	29,368
1976	398,849	300,179	11,996	312,175	25,466	-5,485	281,224	72,464	45,161	6,633	60,129	29,733
1977	451,706	346,053	10,672	356,725	29,242	-5,644	321,839	81,213	48,654	7,393	61,098	31,156
1978	505,892	397,053	2,592	399,645	34,472	-6,976	358,197	94,515	53,180	8,169	61,926	32,482
1979	594,685	454,123	19,567	473,690	40,859	-7,145	425,686	108,010	60,989	9,551	62,264	33,792
1980	695,080	529,905	12,190	542,095	47,952	-7,285	486,858	137,851	70,371	11,002	63,179	35,874
1981	825,532	634,097	-2,412	631,685	61,671	-5,745	564,269	180,090	81,173	12,799	64,500	38,599
1982	908,467	658,696	20,290	678,986	65,953	-5,431	607,602	205,778	95,087	13,439	67,597	38,596
1983	889,362	641,599	-1,483	640,116	63,240	-9,440	567,436	217,156	104,770	13,230	67,225	36,727
1984	950,720	660,272	25,158	685,430	66,602	-10,526	608,302	232,353	110,065	14,458	65,759	36,862
1985	936,923	643,775	12,083	655,858	66,345	-8,527	580,986	235,929	120,008	14,605	64,151	35,121
1986	912,140	613,712	21,029	634,741	64,342	-6,325	564,074	217,631	130,435	14,583	62,550	32,271
1987	878,072	587,530	18,944	606,474	62,250	-3,540	540,684	206,149	131,239	14,669	59,858	31,523
1988	917,814	599,302	33,457	632,759	67,383	-3,391	561,985	216,993	138,836	15,909	57,691	31,608
1989	953,248	613,127	35,200	648,327	69,388	-686	578,253	227,282	147,713	16,672	57,178	31,302
1990	982,125	639,771	30,832	670,603	74,187	-783	595,633	226,496	159,996	17,326	56,686	31,722
1991	989,772	658,766	7,459	666,225	78,644	-4,160	583,421	227,943	178,408	17,522	56,486	32,187
1992	1,049,351	682,126	18,974	701,100	81,154	-6,919	613,027	241,763	194,561	18,481	56,780	31,861
1993	1,080,308	717,264	19,081	736,345	86,160	-7,870	642,315	229,370	208,623	18,993	56,879	32,707
1994	1,131,894	748,281	20,343	768,624	90,287	-8,893	669,444	245,923	216,527	19,755	57,296	33,416
1995	1,149,512	760,362	3,273	763,635	91,903	-8,459	663,273	254,303	231,936	19,840	57,939	33,519
1996	1,192,142	775,439	7,042	782,481	92,905	-9,612	679,964	271,688	240,490	20,627	57,794	33,499
1997	1,293,837	844,995	23,345	868,340	98,343	-11,154	758,843	283,825	251,169	22,373	57,831	34,343
1998	1,337,321	860,952	21,705	882,657	99,713	-11,914	771,030	305,972	260,319	23,009	58,122	34,609
1999	1,328,581	862,383	18,653	881,036	100,653	-13,548	766,835	306,903	254,843	22,829	58,197	34,232
2000	1,398,332	891,784	24,460	916,244	102,943	-13,372	799,929	334,431	263,972	24,226	57,721	34,319
2001	1,461,768	948,756	15,557	964,313	109,627	-14,280	840,406	335,243	286,119	25,520	57,279	33,369
2002	1,519,004	994,910	20,046	1,014,956	116,330	-18,388	880,238	333,270	305,496	26,533	57,249	33,258
2003	1,619,583	1,051,156	43,860	1,095,016	121,392	-20,312	953,312	347,111	319,160	28,300	57,230	33,991
2004	1,737,727	1,124,577	52,558	1,177,135	129,892	-21,783	1,025,460	365,378	346,889	30,243	57,459	34,451
2005	1,824,339	1,216,507	39,461	1,255,968	136,709	-21,696	1,097,563	372,764	354,012	31,806	57,358	34,822
2006	2,030,779	1,314,412	43,894	1,358,306	144,899	-20,173	1,193,234	448,796	388,749	35,181	57,723	35,565
2007	2,113,758	1,349,874	17,589	1,367,463	153,788	-25,037	1,188,638	510,817	414,303	36,348	58,153	36,830
2008	2,275,854	1,464,728	22,127	1,486,855	160,966	-31,593	1,294,296	528,358	453,200	38,675	58,845	38,099
2009	2,195,581	1,454,947	2,670	1,457,617	164,264	-39,520	1,253,833	465,526	476,222	36,600	59,989	37,696
2010	2,403,141	1,597,012	10,005	1,607,017	172,827	-46,222	1,387,968	516,088	499,085	39,516	60,815	37,994
2011	2,551,838	1,655,995	30,321	1,686,316	165,362	-46,326	1,474,628	575,609	501,601	41,842	60,987	38,073
2012	2,754,096	1,785,098	48,532	1,833,630	179,884	-60,502	1,593,244	652,265	508,587	44,592	61,762	39,159
2013	2,704,700	1,879,678	25,539	1,905,217	209,542	-63,490	1,632,185	566,675	505,840	42,967	62,948	39,624
2014	2,895,567	2,008,752	29,877	2,038,629	220,857	-68,967	1,748,805	641,775	504,987	45,554	63,563	40,239
2015	2,792,889	1,976,677	24,035	2,000,712	220,212	-72,851	1,707,649	568,212	517,028	43,509	64,191	39,831
2016	2,747,417	1,962,111	11,068	1,973,179	222,982	-85,513	1,664,684	549,685	533,048	43,133	63,696	39,657
2017	2,652,119	1,763,152	8,870	1,772,022	201,373	-34,180	1,536,469	563,334	552,316	42,104	62,990	37,546
2018	2,692,538	1,763,079	3,053	1,766,132	204,755	-25,032	1,536,345	594,614	561,579	42,941	62,703	37,260
2019	2,730,653	1,766,933	15,377	1,782,310	207,025	-21,317	1,553,968	591,311	585,374	43,388	62,936	36,804
2020	2,792,550	1,700,078	21,549	1,721,627	206,367	-37,887	1,477,373	587,950	727,227	44,544	62,692	36,148
2021	3,036,214	1,756,889	38,718	1,795,607	215,603	-37,753	1,542,251	653,053	840,910	49,013	61,947	36,283
2022	3,026,153	1,856,766	-1,789	1,854,977	230,919	-34,361	1,589,697	676,436	760,020	48,872	61,920	37,174

Personal Income and Employment by Area: Erie, PA

(Thousands of dollars, except as noted.)

Year	Personal income, total	Derivation of personal income: Earnings by place of work: Nonfarm	Farm	Total	Less: Contributions for government social insurance	Plus: Adjustment for residence	Equals: Net earnings by place of residence	Plus: Dividends, interest, and rent	Plus: Personal current transfer receipts	Per capita personal income (dollars)	Population (persons)	Total employment
1970	1,032,554	874,070	9,693	883,763	65,451	-14,813	803,499	129,382	99,673	3,907	264,315	117,410
1971	1,114,365	945,500	7,669	953,169	73,696	-17,222	862,251	137,096	115,018	4,148	268,634	118,885
1972	1,215,863	1,040,511	6,961	1,047,472	85,357	-19,558	942,557	144,961	128,345	4,464	272,384	121,771
1973	1,356,689	1,172,171	13,611	1,185,782	110,177	-22,308	1,053,297	161,374	142,018	4,942	274,509	128,972
1974	1,518,598	1,310,640	13,040	1,323,680	128,119	-26,417	1,169,144	182,506	166,948	5,516	275,306	133,424
1975	1,650,464	1,377,633	12,089	1,389,722	130,633	-28,723	1,230,366	199,742	220,356	5,910	279,275	131,019
1976	1,762,065	1,452,937	13,712	1,466,649	140,390	-28,375	1,297,884	212,574	251,607	6,262	281,390	128,968
1977	1,926,260	1,603,342	15,839	1,619,181	157,429	-31,394	1,430,358	234,711	261,191	6,879	280,019	131,617
1978	2,133,750	1,794,375	19,266	1,813,641	181,303	-35,723	1,596,615	257,994	279,141	7,664	278,420	136,329
1979	2,351,094	1,976,366	15,477	1,991,843	205,530	-39,030	1,747,283	290,700	313,111	8,433	278,792	137,775
1980	2,573,272	2,091,398	10,104	2,101,502	214,290	-41,132	1,846,080	358,488	368,704	9,189	280,043	134,200
1981	2,826,169	2,239,417	16,432	2,255,849	244,875	-45,621	1,965,353	440,967	419,849	10,074	280,529	131,270
1982	2,982,658	2,289,517	10,085	2,299,602	254,517	-49,390	1,995,695	504,663	482,300	10,602	281,320	128,148
1983	3,080,963	2,318,991	7,358	2,326,349	260,836	-49,879	2,015,634	532,778	532,551	10,938	281,683	124,998
1984	3,307,197	2,537,766	10,711	2,548,477	298,687	-56,030	2,193,760	591,318	522,119	11,772	280,928	128,793
1985	3,477,913	2,668,220	13,588	2,681,808	317,654	-61,846	2,302,308	630,375	545,230	12,529	277,584	130,880
1986	3,605,208	2,741,417	15,076	2,756,493	325,801	-66,196	2,364,496	659,378	581,334	13,009	277,123	131,407
1987	3,743,060	2,878,186	21,354	2,899,540	336,665	-70,451	2,492,424	657,178	593,458	13,574	275,759	133,889
1988	4,016,581	3,129,085	14,988	3,144,073	373,075	-78,674	2,692,324	701,364	622,893	14,620	274,732	138,424
1989	4,400,979	3,379,005	21,128	3,400,133	393,719	-87,655	2,918,759	819,031	663,189	15,976	275,474	141,704
1990	4,658,401	3,605,066	23,708	3,628,774	423,356	-97,078	3,108,340	821,785	728,276	16,884	275,911	145,501
1991	4,915,909	3,779,019	23,928	3,802,947	449,018	-104,717	3,249,212	834,453	832,244	17,685	277,973	145,836
1992	5,229,168	4,031,863	36,226	4,068,089	477,472	-115,153	3,475,464	862,611	891,093	18,706	279,548	146,388
1993	5,479,441	4,230,493	25,935	4,256,428	508,745	-122,734	3,624,949	914,031	940,461	19,514	280,796	148,918
1994	5,705,276	4,369,077	21,488	4,390,565	537,160	-125,821	3,727,584	1,014,926	962,766	20,257	281,649	149,803
1995	5,870,252	4,527,431	15,063	4,542,494	557,374	-133,657	3,851,463	1,009,656	1,009,133	20,807	282,127	153,226
1996	6,168,098	4,639,289	28,540	4,667,829	562,161	-138,863	3,966,805	1,124,447	1,076,846	21,828	282,582	154,003
1997	6,450,102	4,845,324	19,469	4,864,793	582,948	-146,456	4,135,389	1,213,213	1,101,500	22,823	282,609	155,708
1998	6,616,991	4,991,938	23,396	5,015,334	594,444	-152,531	4,268,359	1,235,818	1,112,814	23,484	281,764	156,304
1999	6,812,291	5,268,700	31,915	5,300,615	617,585	-165,525	4,517,505	1,137,867	1,156,919	24,218	281,294	160,400
2000	7,109,479	5,426,173	29,401	5,455,574	629,898	-174,993	4,650,683	1,234,543	1,224,253	25,318	280,803	163,440
2001	7,285,595	5,548,634	25,505	5,574,139	635,251	-186,510	4,752,378	1,206,187	1,327,030	25,960	280,647	161,055
2002	7,443,355	5,605,562	17,123	5,622,685	636,851	-190,822	4,795,012	1,219,662	1,428,681	26,547	280,379	158,746
2003	7,547,192	5,643,949	26,202	5,670,151	636,358	-196,841	4,836,952	1,201,972	1,508,268	26,940	280,153	157,206
2004	7,868,786	5,959,472	19,706	5,979,178	668,905	-201,824	5,108,449	1,203,345	1,556,992	28,319	277,864	159,167
2005	8,102,044	6,195,506	19,089	6,214,595	712,943	-210,635	5,291,017	1,145,777	1,665,250	29,227	277,211	161,236
2006	8,531,785	6,425,607	16,815	6,442,422	744,121	-216,483	5,481,818	1,296,236	1,753,731	30,647	278,389	161,895
2007	9,033,939	6,640,310	16,094	6,656,404	767,062	-225,733	5,663,609	1,492,335	1,877,995	32,429	278,573	163,253
2008	9,479,677	6,762,335	13,437	6,775,772	781,426	-218,296	5,776,050	1,576,391	2,127,236	34,016	278,686	162,484
2009	9,350,128	6,470,647	7,830	6,478,477	760,283	-189,318	5,528,876	1,391,473	2,429,779	33,413	279,838	156,492
2010	9,725,313	6,685,681	11,334	6,697,015	779,731	-188,702	5,728,582	1,403,891	2,592,840	34,626	280,864	156,243
2011	10,359,215	7,190,199	18,709	7,208,908	750,876	-213,472	6,244,560	1,517,257	2,597,398	36,797	281,521	159,171
2012	10,649,045	7,287,857	27,111	7,314,968	757,689	-212,802	6,344,477	1,801,876	2,502,692	37,774	281,914	160,351
2013	10,612,044	7,422,428	26,891	7,449,319	861,131	-199,458	6,388,730	1,590,238	2,633,076	37,682	281,621	160,518
2014	10,831,616	7,506,814	26,478	7,533,292	872,742	-198,349	6,462,201	1,700,222	2,669,193	38,603	280,592	161,036
2015	11,116,226	7,758,418	22,145	7,780,563	904,081	-191,759	6,684,723	1,662,626	2,768,877	39,758	279,599	161,268
2016	11,237,980	7,632,346	14,561	7,646,907	899,281	-188,873	6,558,753	1,775,835	2,903,392	40,425	277,995	158,748
2017	11,395,495	7,642,597	25,286	7,667,883	916,752	-157,568	6,593,563	1,888,742	2,913,190	41,376	275,410	157,829
2018	11,990,733	7,882,615	12,536	7,895,151	943,027	-172,862	6,779,262	2,105,119	3,106,352	43,836	273,535	158,403
2019	12,285,482	8,112,705	21,307	8,134,012	972,396	-183,424	6,978,192	2,101,941	3,205,349	45,254	271,476	157,504
2020	13,575,479	8,062,095	18,890	8,080,985	962,729	-181,356	6,936,900	2,298,469	4,340,110	50,179	270,539	148,929
2021	14,016,506	8,371,293	24,188	8,395,481	996,053	-171,031	7,228,397	2,159,335	4,628,774	52,048	269,300	152,615
2022	13,758,095	8,821,885	16,313	8,838,198	1,080,685	-180,170	7,577,343	2,268,529	3,912,223	51,396	267,689	158,140

Personal Income and Employment by Area: Eugene-Springfield, OR

(Thousands of dollars, except as noted.)

Year	Personal income, total	Derivation of personal income: Earnings by place of work: Nonfarm	Farm	Total	Less: Contributions for government social insurance	Plus: Adjustment for residence	Equals: Net earnings by place of residence	Plus: Dividends, interest, and rent	Plus: Personal current transfer receipts	Per capita personal income (dollars)	Population (persons)	Total employment
1970	790,124	621,254	6,452	627,706	49,259	8,542	586,989	131,403	71,732	3,651	216,409	85,936
1971	879,451	692,758	5,215	697,973	56,290	9,497	651,180	145,222	83,049	3,983	220,797	90,186
1972	997,847	798,153	6,534	804,687	68,255	10,105	746,537	158,553	92,757	4,395	227,016	96,964
1973	1,130,280	906,120	11,626	917,746	88,722	10,947	839,971	179,716	110,593	4,898	230,743	103,424
1974	1,260,360	978,382	15,718	994,100	98,024	12,657	908,733	210,351	141,276	5,328	236,565	105,876
1975	1,401,281	1,053,462	9,081	1,062,543	101,333	14,525	975,735	241,064	184,482	5,831	240,324	106,648
1976	1,623,286	1,251,885	12,309	1,264,194	122,087	16,756	1,158,863	267,512	196,911	6,601	245,932	114,312
1977	1,861,298	1,455,925	9,812	1,465,737	144,512	18,971	1,340,196	305,464	215,638	7,388	251,925	122,378
1978	2,139,948	1,684,533	7,703	1,692,236	170,596	21,750	1,543,390	360,246	236,312	8,223	260,240	130,003
1979	2,403,225	1,874,776	10,665	1,885,441	195,854	27,639	1,717,226	419,439	266,560	8,973	267,827	133,161
1980	2,603,052	1,946,630	5,590	1,952,220	203,446	33,881	1,782,655	499,175	321,222	9,441	275,708	131,154
1981	2,774,074	1,983,381	13,181	1,996,562	222,567	24,719	1,798,714	602,279	373,081	10,012	277,068	126,204
1982	2,774,228	1,900,988	9,777	1,910,765	217,298	24,260	1,717,727	640,288	416,213	10,186	272,346	118,130
1983	2,959,061	2,028,661	4,847	2,033,508	233,172	26,017	1,826,353	688,825	443,883	11,023	268,453	121,237
1984	3,195,495	2,220,843	14,399	2,235,242	263,752	25,668	1,997,158	741,305	457,032	11,929	267,878	127,016
1985	3,344,098	2,325,967	15,078	2,341,045	278,457	25,767	2,088,355	773,075	482,668	12,522	267,051	129,177
1986	3,492,058	2,442,536	20,513	2,463,049	292,120	25,690	2,196,619	803,305	492,134	13,116	266,239	132,737
1987	3,714,089	2,662,080	18,942	2,681,022	315,104	25,038	2,390,956	811,984	511,149	13,826	268,636	139,567
1988	4,086,926	2,933,454	31,426	2,964,880	361,121	26,120	2,629,879	912,016	545,031	14,970	273,014	146,319
1989	4,491,454	3,159,084	30,636	3,189,720	390,738	24,929	2,823,911	1,070,732	596,811	16,118	278,665	151,322
1990	4,747,690	3,362,480	33,135	3,395,615	422,888	27,283	3,000,010	1,097,631	650,049	16,702	284,261	154,526
1991	4,947,109	3,475,986	25,783	3,501,769	440,054	29,390	3,091,105	1,135,768	720,236	17,148	288,490	152,184
1992	5,247,278	3,704,663	26,624	3,731,287	466,027	29,869	3,295,129	1,145,265	806,884	17,941	292,482	153,541
1993	5,617,304	3,950,642	39,806	3,990,448	494,180	28,868	3,525,136	1,226,229	865,939	18,896	297,281	156,357
1994	6,027,315	4,293,508	35,161	4,328,669	538,188	29,209	3,819,690	1,300,582	907,043	19,970	301,819	164,297
1995	6,440,909	4,466,458	27,241	4,493,699	562,765	34,489	3,965,423	1,464,433	1,011,053	21,000	306,704	167,644
1996	6,853,363	4,733,782	25,572	4,759,354	605,433	37,165	4,191,086	1,592,772	1,069,505	22,036	311,004	173,379
1997	7,240,457	5,078,260	25,440	5,103,700	640,341	37,429	4,500,788	1,636,446	1,103,223	22,871	316,579	177,912
1998	7,680,385	5,397,826	15,137	5,412,963	677,272	32,764	4,768,455	1,711,589	1,200,341	24,028	319,646	181,115
1999	7,848,721	5,606,560	15,656	5,622,216	697,280	30,168	4,955,104	1,595,000	1,298,617	24,392	321,778	184,549
2000	8,318,796	5,934,551	15,178	5,949,729	732,125	29,534	5,247,138	1,707,507	1,364,151	25,716	323,492	186,789
2001	8,712,577	6,166,390	18,503	6,184,893	748,825	14,083	5,450,151	1,742,125	1,520,301	26,820	324,855	185,129
2002	8,790,974	6,315,454	18,066	6,333,520	775,133	627	5,559,014	1,659,301	1,572,659	26,842	327,506	184,589
2003	9,001,688	6,547,112	29,257	6,576,369	803,680	-14,500	5,758,189	1,609,181	1,634,318	27,208	330,845	185,157
2004	9,564,433	6,965,987	31,849	6,997,836	863,842	-32,886	6,101,108	1,758,430	1,704,895	28,780	332,327	191,074
2005	10,185,897	7,443,930	29,145	7,473,075	927,508	-54,328	6,491,239	1,892,157	1,802,501	30,330	335,831	196,412
2006	11,147,007	7,973,924	39,288	8,013,212	983,156	-72,045	6,958,011	2,251,744	1,937,252	32,792	339,926	201,135
2007	11,435,692	8,098,763	38,442	8,137,205	1,011,782	-89,100	7,036,323	2,334,383	2,064,986	33,162	344,844	205,429
2008	11,778,776	8,062,654	40,618	8,103,272	1,017,528	-99,814	6,985,930	2,463,280	2,329,566	33,830	348,176	201,543
2009	11,455,951	7,530,691	38,477	7,569,168	958,453	-75,279	6,535,436	2,214,470	2,706,045	32,652	350,850	189,703
2010	11,809,631	7,713,328	33,545	7,746,873	984,302	-70,874	6,691,697	2,234,748	2,883,186	33,555	351,945	187,145
2011	12,201,496	7,874,301	39,236	7,913,537	898,108	-70,024	6,945,405	2,340,936	2,915,155	34,457	354,104	189,057
2012	12,702,759	8,228,873	46,270	8,275,143	933,331	-68,752	7,273,060	2,516,322	2,913,377	35,763	355,191	189,499
2013	12,743,333	8,372,510	56,966	8,429,476	1,079,361	-65,716	7,284,399	2,446,300	3,012,634	35,834	355,618	191,251
2014	13,535,495	8,753,177	54,121	8,807,298	1,138,467	-67,958	7,600,873	2,617,128	3,317,494	37,784	358,230	195,902
2015	14,485,437	9,370,793	64,463	9,435,256	1,203,257	-75,844	8,156,155	2,806,794	3,522,488	39,992	362,208	201,107
2016	15,172,554	9,826,575	69,396	9,895,971	1,252,247	-68,667	8,575,057	2,946,373	3,651,124	41,101	369,149	204,870
2017	16,123,295	10,392,994	57,372	10,450,366	1,332,298	-71,775	9,046,293	3,274,307	3,802,695	42,923	375,633	209,419
2018	16,924,089	10,920,665	53,413	10,974,078	1,379,466	-66,744	9,527,868	3,350,222	4,045,999	44,684	378,749	213,472
2019	17,686,726	11,347,045	49,558	11,396,603	1,439,652	-66,411	9,890,540	3,540,537	4,255,649	46,300	382,003	213,113
2020	19,432,684	11,798,706	59,162	11,857,868	1,485,195	-70,513	10,302,160	3,575,443	5,555,081	50,701	383,279	205,382
2021	21,485,107	12,971,079	58,317	13,029,396	1,719,757	-65,306	11,244,333	4,125,644	6,115,130	55,942	384,063	210,711
2022	21,483,599	13,620,388	55,772	13,676,160	1,849,687	-63,065	11,763,408	4,304,674	5,415,517	56,188	382,353	217,874

Personal Income and Employment by Area: Evansville, IN-KY

(Thousands of dollars, except as noted.)

Year	Personal income, total	Derivation of personal income: Earnings by place of work: Nonfarm	Farm	Total	Less: Contributions for government social insurance	Plus: Adjustment for residence	Equals: Net earnings by place of residence	Plus: Dividends, interest, and rent	Plus: Personal current transfer receipts	Per capita personal income (dollars)	Population (persons)	Total employment
1970	949,474	831,356	6,874	838,230	57,264	-57,900	723,066	140,278	86,130	3,725	254,890	118,647
1971	1,042,382	897,264	16,810	914,074	64,130	-61,476	788,468	154,108	99,806	4,044	257,776	121,245
1972	1,131,669	983,940	15,568	999,508	74,477	-69,189	855,842	165,904	109,923	4,384	258,125	124,254
1973	1,292,367	1,108,139	33,292	1,141,431	96,499	-73,780	971,152	188,286	132,929	4,969	260,065	130,416
1974	1,415,870	1,200,170	25,662	1,225,832	108,186	-77,528	1,040,118	218,779	156,973	5,434	260,547	129,898
1975	1,557,836	1,281,996	24,500	1,306,496	113,155	-72,907	1,120,434	241,653	195,749	5,970	260,965	127,384
1976	1,744,746	1,460,432	29,192	1,489,624	131,133	-86,889	1,271,602	265,907	207,237	6,647	262,498	133,259
1977	2,012,432	1,713,916	26,138	1,740,054	151,081	-100,161	1,488,812	302,808	220,812	7,564	266,046	139,775
1978	2,252,233	1,949,581	16,816	1,966,397	177,541	-118,834	1,670,022	342,175	240,036	8,331	270,348	146,579
1979	2,500,695	2,152,238	26,957	2,179,195	203,196	-132,555	1,843,444	382,616	274,635	9,165	272,865	148,866
1980	2,734,286	2,266,959	18,288	2,285,247	215,759	-140,803	1,928,685	479,435	326,166	9,890	276,466	146,600
1981	3,015,161	2,417,357	14,470	2,431,827	248,251	-140,233	2,043,343	596,450	375,368	10,897	276,701	145,853
1982	3,198,345	2,500,387	11,966	2,512,353	263,673	-136,868	2,111,812	672,610	413,923	11,513	277,792	144,080
1983	3,338,785	2,622,082	-24,714	2,597,368	275,498	-139,789	2,182,081	710,398	446,306	11,996	278,314	143,145
1984	3,729,244	2,924,062	22,230	2,946,292	315,667	-155,717	2,474,908	782,952	471,384	13,345	279,451	148,687
1985	3,920,457	3,058,474	15,490	3,073,964	337,196	-156,070	2,580,698	840,809	498,950	13,991	280,221	149,820
1986	4,062,311	3,153,899	16,298	3,170,197	352,470	-153,517	2,664,210	867,800	530,301	14,519	279,786	150,742
1987	4,179,929	3,281,954	11,856	3,293,810	360,659	-147,745	2,785,406	851,308	543,215	14,963	279,347	152,301
1988	4,496,390	3,535,865	10,569	3,546,434	398,862	-160,263	2,987,309	933,941	575,140	16,121	278,923	155,991
1989	4,821,502	3,687,445	33,366	3,720,811	419,194	-160,296	3,141,321	1,051,091	629,090	17,286	278,930	158,985
1990	5,113,620	3,922,661	10,152	3,932,813	457,802	-168,193	3,306,818	1,118,124	688,678	18,303	279,384	161,461
1991	5,272,587	4,105,751	-6,760	4,098,991	484,657	-174,894	3,439,440	1,078,168	754,979	18,746	281,270	161,774
1992	5,689,437	4,427,157	28,439	4,455,596	515,557	-198,143	3,741,896	1,099,757	847,784	20,021	284,179	164,642
1993	5,972,425	4,674,717	16,998	4,691,715	550,692	-217,135	3,923,888	1,150,063	898,474	20,830	286,723	169,312
1994	6,233,120	4,878,218	18,122	4,896,340	584,389	-238,672	4,073,279	1,228,193	931,648	21,592	288,681	174,356
1995	6,438,743	5,010,893	6,702	5,017,595	602,783	-245,369	4,169,443	1,307,819	961,481	22,206	289,950	177,218
1996	6,852,255	5,313,183	52,924	5,366,107	633,377	-278,699	4,454,031	1,382,432	1,015,792	23,456	292,136	179,775
1997	7,184,919	5,657,704	23,574	5,681,278	670,544	-310,124	4,700,610	1,450,647	1,033,662	24,447	293,894	182,816
1998	7,741,837	6,091,662	12,250	6,103,912	710,749	-299,669	5,093,494	1,578,326	1,070,017	26,287	294,517	183,227
1999	7,918,552	6,346,737	4,679	6,351,416	741,752	-315,197	5,294,467	1,511,927	1,112,158	26,787	295,610	185,640
2000	8,393,645	6,635,421	41,242	6,676,663	763,431	-314,978	5,598,254	1,607,378	1,188,013	28,311	296,480	188,367
2001	8,755,522	6,947,248	45,299	6,992,547	781,347	-346,605	5,864,595	1,596,291	1,294,636	29,477	297,027	189,688
2002	8,963,218	7,197,714	14,821	7,212,535	810,774	-360,762	6,040,999	1,548,121	1,374,098	30,039	298,383	188,927
2003	9,203,415	7,347,655	48,576	7,396,231	833,583	-356,878	6,205,770	1,578,124	1,419,521	30,614	300,628	188,809
2004	9,527,265	7,549,476	78,217	7,627,693	857,640	-339,863	6,430,190	1,592,478	1,504,597	31,515	302,310	187,452
2005	9,907,487	7,863,703	76,614	7,940,317	902,896	-360,325	6,677,096	1,610,705	1,619,686	32,607	303,844	188,584
2006	10,522,276	8,312,031	62,663	8,374,694	951,292	-380,455	7,042,947	1,722,489	1,756,840	34,437	305,549	189,348
2007	10,630,877	8,256,931	53,200	8,310,131	954,415	-390,615	6,965,101	1,818,806	1,846,970	34,576	307,468	189,397
2008	11,300,451	8,568,570	93,838	8,662,408	1,000,348	-426,972	7,235,088	1,961,162	2,104,201	36,617	308,614	189,167
2009	11,146,572	8,344,802	88,101	8,432,903	974,931	-349,788	7,108,184	1,785,251	2,253,137	35,937	310,170	183,632
2010	11,859,282	8,934,066	35,594	8,969,660	1,007,613	-312,793	7,649,254	1,815,229	2,394,799	38,039	311,769	184,470
2011	12,662,235	9,391,103	114,636	9,505,739	922,749	-279,302	8,303,688	1,966,829	2,391,718	40,514	312,540	188,284
2012	13,064,361	9,405,516	54,226	9,459,742	927,764	-190,364	8,341,614	2,256,242	2,466,505	41,721	313,133	188,272
2013	12,585,089	9,072,879	188,749	9,261,628	1,046,819	-116,947	8,097,862	1,990,898	2,496,329	40,091	313,912	186,884
2014	13,110,187	9,388,307	58,761	9,447,068	1,094,044	-117,526	8,235,498	2,176,252	2,698,437	41,710	314,315	189,262
2015	13,510,826	9,642,980	18,187	9,661,167	1,135,056	-131,279	8,394,832	2,274,505	2,841,489	42,984	314,320	191,197
2016	13,643,868	9,663,487	49,806	9,713,293	1,133,427	-115,120	8,464,746	2,271,580	2,907,542	43,387	314,468	191,997
2017	14,156,712	9,982,460	51,974	10,034,434	1,177,733	-145,189	8,711,512	2,431,474	3,013,726	45,115	313,795	193,488
2018	14,589,494	10,354,558	34,822	10,389,380	1,224,525	-160,011	9,004,844	2,455,918	3,128,732	46,553	313,392	195,582
2019	15,366,152	10,843,996	52,307	10,896,303	1,282,083	-153,732	9,460,488	2,588,711	3,316,953	48,995	313,624	194,815
2020	16,484,322	10,926,348	84,688	11,011,036	1,303,278	-126,570	9,581,188	2,678,405	4,224,729	52,470	314,168	186,797
2021	17,942,692	11,599,063	136,565	11,735,628	1,364,756	-139,085	10,231,787	2,954,407	4,756,498	57,063	314,436	191,934
2022	18,257,592	12,307,280	111,581	12,418,861	1,446,266	-162,592	10,810,003	3,210,880	4,236,709	58,138	314,038	197,900

Personal Income and Employment by Area: Fairbanks, AK

(Thousands of dollars, except as noted.)

Year	Personal income, total	Derivation of personal income: Earnings by place of work: Nonfarm	Farm	Total	Less: Contributions for government social insurance	Plus: Adjustment for residence	Equals: Net earnings by place of residence	Plus: Dividends, interest, and rent	Plus: Personal current transfer receipts	Per capita personal income (dollars)	Population (persons)	Total employment
1970	278,000	251,770	204	251,974	16,197	-10,816	224,961	45,117	7,922	6,051	45,940	23,571
1971	290,765	270,347	203	270,550	17,661	-20,842	232,047	48,301	10,417	6,152	47,260	23,042
1972	310,392	296,147	334	296,481	19,878	-30,049	246,554	51,911	11,927	6,509	47,690	23,612
1973	328,225	312,778	325	313,103	23,188	-35,913	254,002	56,336	17,887	6,888	47,654	23,221
1974	453,568	509,522	560	510,082	45,652	-94,118	370,312	66,370	16,886	9,356	48,480	28,366
1975	808,224	934,522	905	935,427	92,818	-136,400	706,209	81,971	20,044	15,613	51,765	38,163
1976	853,100	945,688	943	946,631	95,099	-114,199	737,333	91,765	24,002	15,239	55,983	36,768
1977	765,561	819,917	704	820,621	77,007	-117,926	625,688	102,826	37,047	13,811	55,433	34,246
1978	737,979	707,912	884	708,796	62,669	-65,693	580,434	116,434	41,111	13,339	55,325	31,953
1979	756,718	729,717	438	730,155	66,245	-65,855	598,055	122,099	36,564	13,781	54,910	32,015
1980	826,635	788,250	272	788,522	67,972	-72,008	648,542	138,729	39,364	15,162	54,520	31,780
1981	941,109	895,633	30	895,663	82,597	-81,623	731,443	160,439	49,227	16,634	56,576	33,124
1982	1,193,835	1,070,101	5	1,070,106	99,139	-91,359	879,608	199,616	114,611	19,929	59,905	36,850
1983	1,271,592	1,170,511	-237	1,170,274	108,703	-102,343	959,228	227,247	85,117	19,356	65,695	38,748
1984	1,327,430	1,247,388	-879	1,246,509	122,340	-135,328	988,841	247,637	90,952	19,435	68,300	41,113
1985	1,425,267	1,323,381	-1,903	1,321,478	129,256	-152,881	1,039,341	273,169	112,757	19,953	71,433	42,878
1986	1,398,076	1,245,323	-943	1,244,380	115,724	-139,393	989,263	278,942	129,871	19,016	73,520	41,269
1987	1,364,692	1,185,755	527	1,186,282	109,801	-129,908	946,573	282,497	135,622	18,560	73,528	42,080
1988	1,405,748	1,200,925	848	1,201,773	117,071	-128,112	956,590	302,479	146,679	18,653	75,364	42,911
1989	1,533,883	1,253,789	-338	1,253,451	122,923	-88,941	1,041,587	329,264	163,032	19,889	77,121	43,488
1990	1,586,460	1,318,497	777	1,319,274	134,191	-123,168	1,061,915	339,012	185,533	20,322	78,067	43,739
1991	1,654,218	1,379,678	1,557	1,381,235	142,481	-132,571	1,106,183	350,349	197,686	20,555	80,479	44,917
1992	1,783,702	1,493,547	2,452	1,495,999	156,612	-149,132	1,190,255	372,905	220,542	21,619	82,506	45,630
1993	1,862,352	1,524,482	1,486	1,525,968	161,877	-151,533	1,212,558	406,650	243,144	22,444	82,979	46,493
1994	1,877,759	1,527,702	312	1,528,014	164,413	-145,660	1,217,941	412,694	247,124	22,485	83,512	46,423
1995	1,957,225	1,585,299	1,216	1,586,515	170,479	-156,030	1,260,006	441,098	256,121	23,886	81,941	46,681
1996	2,008,648	1,620,618	111	1,620,729	173,795	-164,431	1,282,503	452,466	273,679	24,236	82,880	47,330
1997	2,104,486	1,696,642	271	1,696,913	182,291	-177,090	1,337,532	471,714	295,240	25,514	82,483	48,611
1998	2,220,098	1,780,539	641	1,781,180	189,355	-181,737	1,410,088	488,404	321,606	26,652	83,299	49,469
1999	2,291,739	1,828,744	567	1,829,311	191,633	-190,440	1,447,238	497,299	347,202	27,482	83,390	49,335
2000	2,458,545	1,951,993	399	1,952,392	201,949	-207,277	1,543,166	524,472	390,907	29,619	83,005	50,450
2001	2,539,350	2,021,037	2,036	2,023,073	208,023	-183,774	1,631,276	495,697	412,377	29,940	84,814	51,232
2002	2,723,718	2,189,118	2,280	2,191,398	226,587	-166,896	1,797,915	506,753	419,050	31,636	86,095	52,610
2003	2,901,731	2,346,938	3,946	2,350,884	239,544	-147,653	1,963,687	531,118	406,926	33,397	86,885	52,966
2004	3,053,953	2,479,488	3,971	2,483,459	257,304	-119,303	2,106,852	549,392	397,709	34,298	89,043	54,099
2005	3,346,212	2,692,153	5,617	2,697,770	281,493	-84,651	2,331,626	591,244	423,342	37,003	90,431	55,118
2006	3,669,257	2,919,735	4,800	2,924,535	314,669	-36,528	2,573,338	645,556	450,363	40,524	90,545	56,727
2007	3,947,315	3,000,517	4,937	3,005,454	319,523	23,640	2,709,571	727,498	510,246	42,197	93,545	57,965
2008	4,371,859	3,118,204	1,281	3,119,485	330,645	88,460	2,877,300	798,840	695,719	46,238	94,552	58,052
2009	4,398,194	3,241,955	3,425	3,245,380	337,948	86,565	2,993,997	804,903	599,294	46,181	95,238	57,507
2010	4,600,079	3,363,077	3,642	3,366,719	343,783	79,219	3,102,155	821,357	676,567	46,814	98,262	57,321
2011	5,048,355	3,643,759	3,369	3,647,128	336,067	77,576	3,388,637	956,856	702,862	51,461	98,101	58,908
2012	5,104,024	3,719,801	5,794	3,725,595	350,296	67,118	3,442,417	984,099	677,508	50,889	100,297	59,378
2013	4,923,446	3,633,601	1,788	3,635,389	382,773	64,751	3,317,367	935,136	670,943	48,789	100,913	58,167
2014	5,127,407	3,663,099	3,013	3,666,112	377,395	74,385	3,363,102	960,975	803,330	51,669	99,236	57,194
2015	5,281,037	3,785,585	1,786	3,787,371	389,360	78,538	3,476,549	977,720	826,768	53,019	99,607	58,123
2016	5,247,243	3,737,442	3,536	3,740,978	380,744	70,585	3,430,819	1,001,916	814,508	52,139	100,639	57,743
2017	5,322,940	3,738,344	1,658	3,740,002	387,279	69,976	3,422,699	1,028,570	871,671	53,421	99,641	58,016
2018	5,544,411	3,888,198	2,433	3,890,631	400,481	70,654	3,560,804	1,025,792	957,815	56,321	98,443	58,175
2019	5,647,682	3,944,489	2,614	3,947,103	409,786	72,842	3,610,159	1,039,146	998,377	58,371	96,755	57,795
2020	5,758,789	4,017,043	945	4,017,988	420,956	60,807	3,657,839	958,224	1,142,726	60,410	95,328	56,489
2021	6,232,535	4,243,052	1,532	4,244,584	450,417	68,012	3,862,179	1,071,758	1,298,598	65,243	95,528	58,119
2022	6,464,225	4,413,438	722	4,414,160	476,944	73,151	4,010,367	1,133,318	1,320,540	67,790	95,356	59,518

Personal Income and Employment by Area: Fargo, ND-MN

(Thousands of dollars, except as noted.)

Year	Personal income, total	Derivation of personal income: Earnings by place of work: Nonfarm	Farm	Total	Less: Contributions for government social insurance	Plus: Adjustment for residence	Equals: Net earnings by place of residence	Plus: Dividends, interest, and rent	Plus: Personal current transfer receipts	Per capita personal income (dollars)	Population (persons)	Total employment
1970	462,348	361,915	26,901	388,816	28,348	-5,513	354,955	71,315	36,078	3,831	120,690	57,963
1971	509,069	392,060	32,997	425,057	31,523	-6,368	387,166	78,783	43,120	4,123	123,471	58,638
1972	565,942	432,614	43,016	475,630	36,305	-7,404	431,921	85,331	48,690	4,511	125,464	60,388
1973	740,158	493,239	148,456	641,695	47,657	-8,724	585,314	98,645	56,199	5,863	126,247	64,939
1974	775,821	552,470	107,712	660,182	55,300	-10,016	594,866	115,532	65,423	6,084	127,527	66,730
1975	804,871	613,867	53,703	667,570	60,545	-11,089	595,936	131,978	76,957	6,242	128,935	68,868
1976	954,422	711,829	100,034	811,863	71,960	-13,660	726,243	143,295	84,884	7,244	131,761	72,986
1977	966,351	792,758	13,485	806,243	78,082	-16,702	711,459	162,641	92,251	7,239	133,484	75,490
1978	1,164,667	899,988	90,175	990,163	91,267	-20,479	878,417	183,566	102,684	8,549	136,239	78,760
1979	1,241,704	996,539	47,748	1,044,287	105,121	-23,809	915,357	209,604	116,743	9,063	137,013	80,905
1980	1,283,483	1,031,439	-10,742	1,020,697	108,371	-25,814	886,512	258,331	138,640	9,302	137,979	78,475
1981	1,480,308	1,110,942	34,643	1,145,585	123,868	-27,913	993,804	328,110	158,394	10,639	139,144	77,415
1982	1,590,294	1,159,755	29,562	1,189,317	131,226	-27,365	1,030,726	382,986	176,582	11,341	140,221	76,983
1983	1,689,814	1,240,660	37,578	1,278,238	142,297	-27,895	1,108,046	386,266	195,502	11,868	142,387	79,004
1984	1,843,989	1,354,008	55,770	1,409,778	160,412	-29,543	1,219,823	414,480	209,686	12,790	144,178	82,450
1985	1,926,112	1,433,338	39,665	1,473,003	174,605	-30,232	1,268,166	434,213	223,733	13,181	146,132	84,299
1986	2,052,564	1,525,323	65,203	1,590,526	190,012	-29,970	1,370,544	442,442	239,578	13,939	147,258	85,952
1987	2,167,613	1,624,747	87,881	1,712,628	202,064	-30,064	1,480,500	430,296	256,817	14,589	148,578	89,329
1988	2,236,337	1,727,719	43,833	1,771,552	222,884	-30,925	1,517,743	451,248	267,346	14,862	150,478	92,213
1989	2,415,535	1,843,034	40,085	1,883,119	240,368	-31,437	1,611,314	507,077	297,144	15,910	151,829	94,155
1990	2,609,418	1,981,888	80,174	2,062,062	271,881	-32,461	1,757,720	524,912	326,786	16,972	153,752	96,333
1991	2,713,540	2,100,563	64,604	2,165,167	294,377	-36,981	1,833,809	546,519	333,212	17,447	155,533	100,109
1992	2,942,192	2,252,448	97,922	2,350,370	313,892	-40,252	1,996,226	577,719	368,247	18,600	158,182	102,535
1993	3,043,356	2,393,887	30,961	2,424,848	336,103	-43,728	2,045,017	604,957	393,382	18,965	160,472	104,841
1994	3,294,880	2,572,735	91,129	2,663,864	362,866	-48,204	2,252,794	641,578	400,508	20,224	162,919	109,730
1995	3,469,113	2,706,890	51,556	2,758,446	378,920	-53,013	2,326,513	720,186	422,414	21,015	165,081	113,090
1996	3,763,297	2,890,201	136,773	3,026,974	400,545	-57,562	2,568,867	753,531	440,899	22,576	166,691	115,991
1997	3,952,661	3,087,997	65,393	3,153,390	421,829	-64,461	2,667,100	828,753	456,808	23,424	168,747	118,867
1998	4,282,162	3,376,136	71,915	3,448,051	453,932	-74,523	2,919,596	880,667	481,899	25,058	170,893	121,710
1999	4,530,217	3,606,690	96,598	3,703,288	476,985	-81,307	3,144,996	871,974	513,247	26,203	172,892	123,691
2000	4,959,024	3,946,395	98,584	4,044,979	512,075	-89,308	3,443,596	961,891	553,537	28,342	174,970	126,440
2001	5,007,098	3,982,345	90,341	4,072,686	516,223	-94,605	3,461,858	965,822	579,418	28,283	177,033	128,846
2002	5,255,268	4,185,597	89,618	4,275,215	538,185	-96,865	3,640,165	993,093	622,010	29,377	178,891	129,742
2003	5,550,842	4,416,066	138,790	4,554,856	569,751	-103,039	3,882,066	1,014,393	654,383	30,577	181,539	131,636
2004	5,910,091	4,779,331	118,423	4,897,754	608,687	-111,517	4,177,550	1,036,317	696,224	31,698	186,448	135,321
2005	6,254,097	5,044,097	111,989	5,156,086	636,782	-120,064	4,399,240	1,119,709	735,148	33,037	189,303	139,305
2006	6,787,510	5,427,817	122,112	5,549,929	674,004	-134,301	4,741,624	1,248,234	797,652	35,094	193,412	144,062
2007	7,277,560	5,740,008	143,259	5,883,267	708,060	-140,451	5,034,756	1,372,526	870,278	36,919	197,121	148,942
2008	8,044,921	6,089,814	181,519	6,271,333	746,395	-146,082	5,378,856	1,650,081	1,015,984	39,956	201,346	151,713
2009	7,971,703	6,246,073	54,265	6,300,338	782,043	-162,906	5,355,389	1,524,199	1,092,115	38,656	206,223	151,415
2010	8,501,156	6,419,095	137,681	6,556,776	769,989	-169,196	5,617,591	1,688,195	1,195,370	40,577	209,505	152,290
2011	9,298,049	6,938,731	136,193	7,074,924	758,017	-195,064	6,121,843	1,943,746	1,232,460	43,550	213,501	156,416
2012	10,307,332	7,555,878	268,088	7,823,966	775,113	-209,067	6,839,786	2,218,385	1,249,161	47,253	218,133	161,517
2013	10,512,400	8,004,067	129,688	8,133,755	928,306	-231,579	6,973,870	2,230,138	1,308,392	46,902	224,134	166,028
2014	11,226,338	8,733,577	29,149	8,762,726	1,009,857	-251,913	7,500,956	2,330,916	1,394,466	49,066	228,801	171,360
2015	11,642,577	9,060,557	20,515	9,081,072	1,071,719	-278,233	7,731,120	2,462,065	1,449,392	49,723	234,149	174,363
2016	11,775,313	9,203,578	62,483	9,266,061	1,110,632	-281,206	7,874,223	2,391,065	1,510,025	49,325	238,729	176,297
2017	12,192,568	9,385,332	56,407	9,441,739	1,157,774	-305,186	7,978,779	2,640,599	1,573,190	50,126	243,239	177,989
2018	13,045,682	9,788,495	56,402	9,844,897	1,182,691	-308,307	8,353,899	3,002,669	1,689,114	52,949	246,383	180,093
2019	13,363,536	10,257,738	75,728	10,333,466	1,219,548	-316,395	8,797,523	2,794,782	1,771,231	53,821	248,298	182,251
2020	14,469,916	10,608,207	176,017	10,784,224	1,301,113	-325,253	9,157,858	2,905,470	2,406,588	57,832	250,206	178,542
2021	16,035,951	11,490,618	243,664	11,734,282	1,406,412	-337,560	9,990,310	3,350,679	2,694,962	62,896	254,958	185,081
2022	16,675,390	12,270,189	319,770	12,589,959	1,528,340	-384,245	10,677,374	3,712,896	2,285,120	64,468	258,663	192,974

Personal Income and Employment by Area: Farmington, NM

(Thousands of dollars, except as noted.)

Year	Personal income, total	Derivation of personal income								Per capita personal income (dollars)	Population (persons)	Total employment
		Earnings by place of work			Less: Contributions for government social insurance	Plus: Adjustment for residence	Equals: Net earnings by place of residence	Plus: Dividends, interest, and rent	Plus: Personal current transfer receipts			
		Nonfarm	Farm	Total								
1970	142,881	114,267	1,940	116,207	7,015	1,483	110,675	16,931	15,275	2,707	52,779	16,564
1971	169,166	138,014	1,434	139,448	8,874	1,095	131,669	19,602	17,895	3,138	53,916	17,929
1972	196,092	159,271	1,861	161,132	10,557	1,102	151,677	22,671	21,744	3,517	55,756	18,919
1973	231,880	190,934	2,493	193,427	14,961	625	179,091	26,211	26,578	3,949	58,722	21,634
1974	281,735	231,832	2,617	234,449	18,932	-95	215,422	31,952	34,361	4,609	61,123	24,337
1975	330,766	269,538	2,067	271,605	21,833	-476	249,296	39,869	41,601	5,117	64,638	26,037
1976	388,734	322,765	1,509	324,274	26,842	-1,819	295,613	45,593	47,528	5,703	68,161	27,389
1977	464,962	398,173	2,605	400,778	33,905	-6,503	360,370	53,296	51,296	6,514	71,376	30,699
1978	547,021	484,735	-835	483,900	42,910	-11,789	429,201	61,858	55,962	7,281	75,134	33,028
1979	603,422	534,884	-1,030	533,854	48,919	-17,273	467,662	70,736	65,024	7,646	78,915	34,065
1980	705,484	633,084	-2,554	630,530	57,992	-27,037	545,501	86,314	73,669	8,570	82,318	36,207
1981	826,646	744,103	-277	743,826	73,413	-33,574	636,839	108,654	81,153	9,635	85,794	38,634
1982	863,958	756,826	-2,089	754,737	75,962	-33,125	645,650	133,213	85,095	9,726	88,833	37,760
1983	852,814	706,122	2,322	708,444	70,334	-27,335	610,775	143,887	98,152	9,402	90,708	35,488
1984	887,975	727,078	2,359	729,437	74,216	-24,925	630,296	155,074	102,605	9,722	91,339	35,364
1985	943,908	767,645	4,056	771,701	79,346	-26,175	666,180	170,476	107,252	10,300	91,644	36,677
1986	948,772	753,247	5,969	759,216	78,176	-24,865	656,175	174,662	117,935	10,139	93,577	35,730
1987	924,954	716,349	13,662	730,011	72,747	-21,284	635,980	168,431	120,543	10,022	92,289	34,608
1988	977,176	759,373	23,430	782,803	81,894	-22,870	678,039	172,941	126,196	10,618	92,031	36,149
1989	1,077,662	834,745	29,476	864,221	91,184	-25,552	747,485	188,064	142,113	11,661	92,413	37,919
1990	1,194,288	961,062	29,246	990,308	111,589	-29,917	848,802	194,421	151,065	13,043	91,567	40,164
1991	1,295,133	1,036,456	25,319	1,061,775	121,371	-31,740	908,664	212,474	173,995	13,814	93,755	42,648
1992	1,381,889	1,101,192	31,061	1,132,253	127,329	-32,119	972,805	216,196	192,888	14,511	95,233	43,061
1993	1,496,464	1,188,491	38,632	1,227,123	137,673	-34,399	1,055,051	230,189	211,224	15,298	97,821	44,491
1994	1,607,565	1,269,470	38,871	1,308,341	148,593	-36,437	1,123,311	247,599	236,655	16,059	100,106	46,604
1995	1,724,343	1,354,505	42,618	1,397,123	157,750	-38,218	1,201,155	268,117	255,071	17,007	101,390	49,846
1996	1,800,506	1,380,975	37,394	1,418,369	159,973	-35,828	1,222,568	287,300	290,638	17,327	103,911	50,807
1997	1,904,570	1,438,097	70,613	1,508,710	165,344	-36,747	1,306,619	304,027	293,924	18,053	105,501	52,569
1998	1,990,530	1,507,873	54,905	1,562,778	173,867	-37,617	1,351,294	317,992	321,244	18,335	108,565	53,560
1999	2,038,857	1,568,884	44,525	1,613,409	181,862	-35,726	1,395,821	299,245	343,791	18,111	112,574	54,235
2000	2,174,839	1,696,172	31,985	1,728,157	188,995	-33,991	1,505,171	305,762	363,906	19,056	114,131	54,446
2001	2,364,429	1,856,583	18,884	1,875,467	214,303	-34,674	1,626,490	333,367	404,572	20,428	115,745	56,802
2002	2,453,552	1,911,196	9,185	1,920,381	220,287	-27,061	1,673,033	336,750	443,769	20,544	119,430	57,349
2003	2,590,701	2,002,415	7,736	2,010,151	229,434	-20,227	1,760,490	355,579	474,632	21,313	121,553	58,045
2004	2,813,621	2,194,579	7,212	2,201,791	249,344	-15,629	1,936,818	380,196	496,607	22,842	123,179	60,226
2005	3,098,510	2,391,888	6,696	2,398,584	268,234	-7,338	2,123,012	436,836	538,662	24,826	124,809	62,060
2006	3,422,749	2,664,608	175	2,664,783	299,445	3,712	2,369,050	478,325	575,374	27,376	125,028	64,094
2007	3,728,747	2,845,974	10,473	2,856,447	324,274	23,392	2,555,565	550,666	622,516	29,558	126,149	65,733
2008	4,151,613	3,135,299	13,133	3,148,432	358,260	31,590	2,821,762	614,032	715,819	32,714	126,905	67,357
2009	3,933,739	2,891,324	16,555	2,907,879	335,884	11,312	2,583,307	557,444	792,988	30,409	129,359	64,355
2010	3,993,577	2,911,601	14,186	2,925,787	334,005	-9,041	2,582,741	546,003	864,833	30,682	130,161	62,506
2011	4,233,330	3,104,747	31,601	3,136,348	317,919	-34,858	2,783,571	576,399	873,360	32,691	129,495	63,441
2012	4,304,593	3,158,129	25,119	3,183,248	325,266	-58,514	2,799,468	641,395	863,730	33,275	129,365	64,470
2013	4,165,501	3,135,116	19,484	3,154,600	372,039	-76,289	2,706,272	598,541	860,688	32,318	128,892	64,554
2014	4,376,102	3,206,499	23,776	3,230,275	385,211	-76,150	2,768,914	666,972	940,216	34,099	128,335	65,458
2015	4,392,183	3,192,402	26,424	3,218,826	395,457	-81,367	2,742,002	634,112	1,016,069	34,494	127,330	65,138
2016	4,245,197	2,980,482	25,455	3,005,937	370,004	-67,801	2,568,132	628,362	1,048,703	33,471	126,832	62,577
2017	4,309,611	3,033,160	19,648	3,052,808	379,074	-73,549	2,600,185	652,016	1,057,410	34,288	125,687	62,156
2018	4,442,751	3,089,395	18,715	3,108,110	386,897	-73,078	2,648,135	678,398	1,116,218	35,791	124,131	61,267
2019	4,470,844	3,087,236	19,685	3,106,921	381,660	-74,308	2,650,953	663,002	1,156,889	36,545	122,339	60,277
2020	4,739,467	2,881,819	26,547	2,908,366	362,004	-57,887	2,488,475	658,892	1,592,100	39,050	121,368	55,804
2021	5,200,944	3,069,618	22,746	3,092,364	382,834	-64,283	2,645,247	727,722	1,827,975	43,031	120,866	56,136
2022	5,236,874	3,304,769	15,931	3,320,700	417,706	-73,855	2,829,139	739,321	1,668,414	43,489	120,418	58,849

Personal Income and Employment by Area: Fayetteville, NC

(Thousands of dollars, except as noted.)

Year	Personal income, total	Derivation of personal income: Earnings by place of work: Nonfarm	Farm	Total	Less: Contributions for government social insurance	Plus: Adjustment for residence	Equals: Net earnings by place of residence	Plus: Dividends, interest, and rent	Plus: Personal current transfer receipts	Per capita personal income (dollars)	Population (persons)	Total employment
1970	1,029,361	826,663	26,153	852,816	51,809	-16,932	784,075	191,333	53,953	3,700	278,220	130,821
1971	1,090,006	881,061	25,787	906,848	58,920	-17,686	830,242	194,872	64,892	3,866	281,976	127,663
1972	1,245,518	1,013,664	29,145	1,042,809	69,025	-21,110	952,674	217,748	75,096	4,361	285,636	131,695
1973	1,404,978	1,140,614	33,029	1,173,643	84,280	-22,383	1,066,980	250,884	87,114	4,805	292,377	138,451
1974	1,619,882	1,298,796	39,210	1,338,006	100,448	-22,594	1,214,964	296,529	108,389	5,294	306,006	143,834
1975	1,750,260	1,374,932	34,984	1,409,916	111,405	-20,598	1,277,913	324,399	147,948	5,669	308,733	141,825
1976	1,876,865	1,470,246	36,764	1,507,010	122,719	-19,323	1,364,968	343,085	168,812	5,981	313,826	143,016
1977	2,000,032	1,556,905	27,324	1,584,229	128,070	-12,824	1,443,335	377,515	179,182	6,250	320,009	143,995
1978	2,194,689	1,673,778	30,440	1,704,218	137,434	-3,363	1,563,421	437,312	193,956	6,781	323,646	144,058
1979	2,369,507	1,822,851	15,572	1,838,423	156,636	-127	1,681,660	470,574	217,273	7,334	323,079	147,650
1980	2,730,931	2,067,876	19,336	2,087,212	176,034	6,671	1,917,849	552,044	261,038	8,322	328,174	152,971
1981	3,026,209	2,277,584	26,049	2,303,633	204,580	14,909	2,113,962	612,223	300,024	9,131	331,428	151,340
1982	3,265,516	2,432,671	31,555	2,464,226	214,689	18,519	2,268,056	668,736	328,724	9,787	333,647	150,336
1983	3,572,300	2,681,853	14,441	2,696,294	246,275	24,082	2,474,101	739,934	358,265	10,571	337,949	155,153
1984	3,935,876	2,939,493	27,951	2,967,444	276,697	36,644	2,727,391	823,468	385,017	11,484	342,731	162,137
1985	4,195,569	3,122,567	25,030	3,147,597	299,722	49,569	2,897,444	884,681	413,444	12,097	346,823	165,023
1986	4,454,608	3,312,391	23,633	3,336,024	325,190	56,402	3,067,236	955,609	431,763	12,779	348,596	167,147
1987	4,702,715	3,519,253	31,466	3,550,719	347,573	57,530	3,260,676	996,935	445,104	13,294	353,741	171,800
1988	5,029,445	3,775,782	47,019	3,822,801	391,833	64,108	3,495,076	1,046,819	487,550	14,213	353,863	175,086
1989	5,385,799	3,974,716	53,855	4,028,571	418,500	74,667	3,684,738	1,148,564	552,497	14,859	362,468	179,646
1990	5,613,441	4,108,646	74,317	4,182,963	446,888	83,102	3,819,177	1,178,561	615,703	15,303	366,814	179,045
1991	5,909,883	4,318,224	65,079	4,383,303	477,059	78,512	3,984,756	1,223,105	702,022	15,881	372,145	177,020
1992	6,997,127	5,225,605	63,964	5,289,569	581,278	69,915	4,778,206	1,436,345	782,576	18,582	376,549	194,280
1993	7,328,084	5,395,565	63,142	5,458,707	612,129	84,586	4,931,164	1,530,932	865,988	18,858	388,588	198,606
1994	7,545,764	5,507,994	72,365	5,580,359	618,295	100,588	5,062,652	1,581,977	901,135	19,138	394,281	201,676
1995	7,990,190	5,730,112	50,783	5,780,895	634,758	106,319	5,252,456	1,719,495	1,018,239	19,931	400,896	207,596
1996	8,372,797	5,909,720	72,068	5,981,788	652,348	122,138	5,451,578	1,812,076	1,109,143	20,596	406,521	209,134
1997	8,753,918	6,215,347	81,448	6,296,795	683,456	146,697	5,760,036	1,822,849	1,171,033	21,153	413,831	213,228
1998	9,285,858	6,545,363	48,987	6,594,350	718,439	175,085	6,050,996	2,016,084	1,218,778	22,236	417,599	220,834
1999	9,701,186	6,815,755	46,389	6,862,144	750,233	207,757	6,319,668	2,063,544	1,317,974	22,903	423,568	223,872
2000	10,243,601	7,135,895	99,232	7,235,127	785,625	235,411	6,684,913	2,145,694	1,412,994	23,874	429,071	226,368
2001	10,441,288	7,283,152	98,094	7,381,246	806,105	190,580	6,765,721	2,088,274	1,587,293	24,158	432,206	215,091
2002	11,086,075	7,900,108	31,228	7,931,336	873,497	13,645	7,071,484	2,273,633	1,740,958	25,358	437,190	219,285
2003	11,608,405	8,550,572	18,576	8,569,148	948,447	-248,677	7,372,024	2,381,993	1,854,388	26,588	436,610	223,188
2004	12,228,617	9,138,440	83,012	9,221,452	1,011,540	-416,901	7,793,011	2,413,709	2,021,897	27,524	444,293	228,131
2005	12,957,485	10,023,792	123,327	10,147,119	1,107,470	-862,113	8,177,536	2,537,965	2,241,984	29,169	444,221	234,807
2006	13,496,623	10,674,890	128,911	10,803,801	1,181,390	-1,180,045	8,442,366	2,618,733	2,435,524	29,876	451,761	239,265
2007	14,001,693	11,439,484	58,276	11,497,760	1,268,696	-1,776,125	8,452,939	2,899,832	2,648,922	30,668	456,550	246,450
2008	14,739,828	12,214,331	93,711	12,308,042	1,353,331	-2,169,175	8,785,536	2,936,131	3,018,161	31,735	464,464	249,487
2009	14,946,802	12,619,855	77,538	12,697,393	1,419,720	-2,612,611	8,665,062	2,977,011	3,304,729	31,499	474,524	248,686
2010	15,609,160	13,231,607	74,749	13,306,356	1,484,335	-2,815,307	9,006,714	3,023,149	3,579,297	31,835	490,322	248,914
2011	16,155,922	13,501,960	57,560	13,559,520	1,398,973	-2,998,894	9,161,653	3,219,668	3,774,601	32,418	498,360	250,825
2012	16,529,731	13,610,010	89,105	13,699,115	1,409,790	-2,888,237	9,401,088	3,237,219	3,891,424	32,982	501,175	249,542
2013	16,513,438	13,363,819	117,809	13,481,628	1,552,923	-2,632,545	9,296,160	3,240,925	3,976,353	32,573	506,974	248,767
2014	16,967,336	13,273,533	131,793	13,405,326	1,555,905	-2,381,109	9,468,312	3,350,051	4,148,973	33,421	507,688	248,260
2015	17,421,922	13,522,534	94,678	13,617,212	1,598,033	-2,459,143	9,560,036	3,383,631	4,478,255	34,277	508,274	249,093
2016	17,552,603	13,568,556	87,009	13,655,565	1,609,916	-2,500,246	9,545,403	3,381,376	4,625,824	34,253	512,445	252,096
2017	18,057,191	13,937,090	112,962	14,050,052	1,626,464	-2,613,009	9,810,579	3,380,486	4,866,126	35,242	512,370	255,693
2018	18,863,941	14,376,375	69,212	14,445,587	1,664,607	-2,533,305	10,247,675	3,457,428	5,158,838	36,507	516,726	260,271
2019	19,763,773	15,048,533	78,325	15,126,858	1,737,639	-2,664,595	10,724,624	3,532,085	5,507,064	38,022	519,801	264,069
2020	21,499,121	15,556,393	58,161	15,614,554	1,803,430	-2,779,854	11,031,270	3,515,404	6,952,447	41,312	520,410	262,762
2021	23,714,483	16,715,826	118,947	16,834,773	1,915,085	-2,919,328	12,000,360	3,632,522	8,081,601	45,071	526,153	272,783
2022	23,846,488	17,575,488	118,282	17,693,770	2,037,012	-2,858,762	12,797,996	3,792,621	7,255,871	45,051	529,318	280,413

Personal Income and Employment by Area: Fayetteville-Springdale-Rogers, AR

(Thousands of dollars, except as noted.)

Year	Personal income, total	Derivation of personal income: Earnings by place of work: Nonfarm	Farm	Total	Less: Contributions for government social insurance	Plus: Adjustment for residence	Equals: Net earnings by place of residence	Plus: Dividends, interest, and rent	Plus: Personal current transfer receipts	Per capita personal income (dollars)	Population (persons)	Total employment
1970	382,774	298,435	9,165	307,600	21,711	-12,864	273,025	64,498	45,251	2,774	137,964	65,779
1971	435,716	329,195	16,275	345,470	24,461	-12,612	308,397	73,673	53,646	3,058	142,504	66,670
1972	515,342	378,099	37,294	415,393	29,458	-13,289	372,646	82,604	60,092	3,423	150,554	70,232
1973	617,952	433,498	65,317	498,815	38,813	-14,469	445,533	100,311	72,108	3,976	155,437	73,064
1974	656,463	487,323	17,714	505,037	45,226	-15,891	443,920	123,504	89,039	4,083	160,788	75,574
1975	785,217	517,807	72,088	589,895	47,033	-16,923	525,939	142,783	116,495	4,820	162,918	73,995
1976	886,431	616,371	57,495	673,866	56,583	-20,077	597,206	160,036	129,189	5,265	168,357	78,993
1977	996,163	710,154	50,323	760,477	66,051	-23,316	671,110	186,367	138,686	5,683	175,276	83,957
1978	1,153,753	820,184	69,384	889,568	78,275	-27,933	783,360	216,946	153,447	6,406	180,094	88,497
1979	1,286,565	922,116	56,147	978,263	90,904	-32,809	854,550	255,431	176,584	6,927	185,731	91,510
1980	1,447,722	1,018,326	33,185	1,051,511	100,388	-38,844	912,279	323,806	211,637	7,603	190,423	93,690
1981	1,662,165	1,127,070	53,403	1,180,473	121,044	-48,065	1,011,364	405,052	245,749	8,668	191,769	95,863
1982	1,775,280	1,167,977	58,654	1,226,631	127,344	-50,115	1,049,172	457,120	268,988	9,199	192,984	95,526
1983	1,956,768	1,304,012	68,607	1,372,619	143,557	-57,674	1,171,388	490,631	294,749	10,013	195,422	98,815
1984	2,240,413	1,495,620	129,469	1,625,089	168,684	-68,569	1,387,836	540,991	311,586	11,246	199,226	104,541
1985	2,451,773	1,627,405	155,856	1,783,261	184,856	-75,877	1,522,528	596,674	332,571	12,099	202,649	108,540
1986	2,706,932	1,796,821	213,157	2,009,978	204,891	-85,077	1,720,010	634,694	352,228	13,155	205,768	112,719
1987	2,844,630	1,998,195	160,541	2,158,736	226,171	-93,709	1,838,856	635,946	369,828	13,498	210,744	119,406
1988	3,110,349	2,218,315	156,519	2,374,834	261,080	-108,300	2,005,454	714,206	390,689	14,515	214,286	125,414
1989	3,425,102	2,418,567	193,799	2,612,366	284,404	-120,635	2,207,327	786,654	431,121	15,735	217,677	129,607
1990	3,658,400	2,621,354	148,901	2,770,255	322,130	-145,010	2,303,115	885,802	469,483	16,296	224,503	132,377
1991	3,953,857	2,838,093	141,565	2,979,658	349,846	-151,640	2,478,172	957,791	517,894	16,936	233,465	139,455
1992	4,431,098	3,198,322	175,503	3,373,825	391,911	-157,605	2,824,309	1,033,811	572,978	18,273	242,497	145,845
1993	4,799,754	3,483,039	157,410	3,640,449	428,351	-175,032	3,037,066	1,150,574	612,114	18,831	254,890	155,806
1994	5,278,163	3,855,546	172,360	4,027,906	479,685	-203,026	3,345,195	1,277,560	655,408	19,778	266,871	164,425
1995	5,801,279	4,186,616	172,786	4,359,402	517,610	-211,169	3,630,623	1,456,153	714,503	20,690	280,387	174,737
1996	6,258,450	4,415,181	207,682	4,622,863	542,436	-230,807	3,849,620	1,643,582	765,248	21,428	292,072	180,230
1997	6,751,588	4,717,303	214,716	4,932,019	579,870	-259,573	4,092,576	1,841,935	817,077	22,434	300,947	184,366
1998	7,409,119	5,204,145	216,424	5,420,569	634,212	-266,596	4,519,761	2,020,732	868,626	24,037	308,242	187,561
1999	7,964,222	5,714,097	249,331	5,963,428	696,033	-288,728	4,978,667	2,080,750	904,805	25,103	317,266	193,627
2000	8,624,901	6,215,188	206,038	6,421,226	753,958	-313,891	5,353,377	2,298,183	973,341	26,306	327,867	200,211
2001	9,310,134	6,688,601	246,378	6,934,979	792,881	-333,507	5,808,591	2,409,982	1,091,561	27,654	336,662	208,886
2002	9,878,554	7,292,491	174,386	7,466,877	863,468	-343,176	6,260,233	2,444,414	1,173,907	28,557	345,922	216,344
2003	10,639,060	7,809,873	189,913	7,999,786	918,716	-341,606	6,739,464	2,661,398	1,238,198	29,772	357,352	222,184
2004	12,019,610	8,603,253	304,531	8,907,784	992,986	-337,115	7,577,683	3,110,657	1,331,270	32,461	370,284	230,621
2005	13,263,659	9,314,583	223,685	9,538,268	1,079,610	-327,725	8,130,933	3,678,504	1,454,222	34,427	385,269	244,033
2006	14,757,242	9,929,998	114,561	10,044,559	1,169,157	-301,912	8,573,490	4,559,179	1,624,573	36,798	401,039	253,466
2007	16,056,606	10,161,163	170,469	10,331,632	1,209,633	-262,257	8,859,742	5,406,143	1,790,721	38,827	413,543	257,517
2008	17,274,308	10,319,998	146,580	10,466,578	1,271,716	-226,362	8,968,500	6,231,660	2,074,148	40,775	423,649	256,013
2009	16,449,875	10,182,387	23,657	10,206,044	1,268,599	-204,702	8,732,743	5,411,552	2,305,580	38,073	432,067	248,536
2010	17,252,243	10,735,419	16,730	10,752,149	1,321,740	-191,334	9,239,075	5,464,291	2,548,877	39,003	442,335	249,955
2011	19,788,152	11,326,086	-39,025	11,287,061	1,257,022	-196,566	9,833,473	7,313,201	2,641,478	43,674	453,091	256,844
2012	22,986,386	12,198,848	83,101	12,281,949	1,308,714	-222,460	10,750,775	9,536,185	2,699,426	49,682	462,670	263,200
2013	22,897,542	13,174,621	183,089	13,357,710	1,569,112	-263,141	11,525,457	8,560,527	2,811,558	48,544	471,687	269,951
2014	26,023,654	14,017,418	315,797	14,333,215	1,681,944	-283,232	12,368,039	10,638,415	3,017,200	54,080	481,205	281,219
2015	28,253,908	14,953,454	218,110	15,171,564	1,790,097	-314,458	13,067,009	11,979,883	3,207,016	57,357	492,594	292,314
2016	29,981,677	15,645,321	107,779	15,753,100	1,865,423	-325,209	13,562,468	13,052,198	3,367,011	59,389	504,839	304,654
2017	31,629,291	16,661,917	196,022	16,857,939	1,988,722	-369,637	14,499,580	13,649,041	3,480,670	61,204	516,787	312,711
2018	34,356,316	17,264,738	194,584	17,459,322	2,054,738	-387,589	15,016,995	15,676,570	3,662,751	65,248	526,546	321,570
2019	33,410,959	18,498,117	30,978	18,529,095	2,214,161	-422,690	15,892,244	13,619,057	3,899,658	62,267	536,574	327,239
2020	35,494,255	19,779,692	-92,695	19,686,997	2,411,730	-474,992	16,800,275	13,612,898	5,081,082	64,548	549,888	330,510
2021	40,752,206	21,937,525	219,302	22,156,827	2,626,745	-536,804	18,993,278	15,885,419	5,873,509	72,389	562,965	345,458
2022	43,197,558	23,628,557	451,271	24,079,828	2,882,218	-597,828	20,599,782	17,524,284	5,073,492	74,943	576,403	367,291

Personal Income and Employment by Area: Flagstaff, AZ

(Thousands of dollars, except as noted.)

Year	Personal income, total	Derivation of personal income: Earnings by place of work: Nonfarm	Farm	Total	Less: Contributions for government social insurance	Plus: Adjustment for residence	Equals: Net earnings by place of residence	Plus: Dividends, interest, and rent	Plus: Personal current transfer receipts	Per capita personal income (dollars)	Population (persons)	Total employment
1970	161,686	132,931	2,083	135,014	7,929	-8,930	118,155	27,929	15,602	3,288	49,180	20,148
1971	191,445	162,410	2,268	164,678	10,419	-13,511	140,748	31,211	19,486	3,590	53,330	21,705
1972	232,114	207,239	3,051	210,290	14,192	-21,420	174,678	35,213	22,223	3,988	58,203	24,041
1973	274,482	248,659	4,013	252,672	19,668	-25,647	207,357	41,102	26,023	4,452	61,654	26,189
1974	296,520	262,069	150	262,219	21,044	-21,542	219,633	46,865	30,022	4,574	64,831	26,719
1975	335,707	276,024	5,866	281,890	21,637	-16,201	244,052	51,260	40,395	4,808	69,825	26,902
1976	361,820	292,722	1,493	294,215	22,768	-10,177	261,270	55,485	45,065	5,449	66,403	27,565
1977	397,913	321,980	1,148	323,128	25,138	-5,960	292,030	63,450	42,433	5,772	68,939	29,570
1978	470,375	379,802	6,516	386,318	30,620	-6,757	348,941	74,313	47,121	6,642	70,815	32,397
1979	520,707	420,865	646	421,511	35,957	-6,140	379,414	86,371	54,922	7,098	73,357	33,879
1980	600,593	474,627	2,285	476,912	41,461	-5,742	429,709	104,481	66,403	7,947	75,579	35,165
1981	665,561	513,603	666	514,269	48,110	-2,137	464,022	127,353	74,186	8,555	77,794	35,739
1982	712,812	530,367	3,444	533,811	50,961	169	483,019	149,087	80,706	9,005	79,156	35,849
1983	783,231	573,780	3,431	577,211	57,080	-871	519,260	173,145	90,826	9,655	81,118	37,242
1984	871,849	642,102	5,768	647,870	64,982	-4,049	578,839	195,346	97,664	10,424	83,640	39,790
1985	955,877	707,414	935	708,349	73,183	-5,919	629,247	218,550	108,080	11,321	84,431	41,603
1986	1,054,216	788,879	3,307	792,186	82,627	-8,346	701,213	238,507	114,496	12,038	87,575	43,483
1987	1,120,960	844,065	1,538	845,603	88,022	-9,829	747,752	247,340	125,868	12,403	90,380	45,220
1988	1,206,853	911,094	678	911,772	99,815	-14,652	797,305	272,138	137,410	12,928	93,355	46,586
1989	1,280,053	928,295	-305	927,990	104,398	-15,740	807,852	308,332	163,869	13,447	95,194	47,115
1990	1,388,177	1,006,709	775	1,007,484	116,587	-20,241	870,656	335,039	182,482	14,295	97,106	48,543
1991	1,486,189	1,078,998	1,751	1,080,749	126,058	-22,486	932,205	350,982	203,002	14,915	99,647	49,766
1992	1,628,372	1,184,719	2,163	1,186,882	138,436	-25,497	1,022,949	373,672	231,751	15,887	102,498	51,643
1993	1,721,764	1,252,786	107	1,252,893	147,040	-24,798	1,081,055	394,101	246,608	16,309	105,570	53,787
1994	1,869,825	1,347,781	-1,110	1,346,671	157,844	-23,859	1,164,968	443,959	260,898	17,205	108,680	56,507
1995	1,998,096	1,416,351	-1,248	1,415,103	158,661	-23,422	1,233,020	500,677	264,399	18,008	110,954	58,867
1996	2,144,561	1,522,068	899	1,522,967	174,577	-23,145	1,325,245	534,803	284,513	19,031	112,686	61,574
1997	2,284,900	1,618,796	734	1,619,530	181,721	-18,896	1,418,913	571,501	294,486	19,965	114,444	62,567
1998	2,445,925	1,718,819	4,577	1,723,396	190,811	-15,932	1,516,653	618,931	310,341	21,292	114,874	65,405
1999	2,573,841	1,813,712	9,544	1,823,256	200,315	-13,820	1,609,121	633,581	331,139	22,322	115,307	66,761
2000	2,758,501	1,944,066	4,261	1,948,327	213,779	-11,272	1,723,276	686,250	348,975	23,623	116,773	69,832
2001	2,943,490	2,038,508	9,119	2,047,627	226,594	-4,873	1,816,160	716,820	410,510	24,885	118,283	66,819
2002	3,084,623	2,153,397	424	2,153,821	240,040	2,433	1,916,214	712,174	456,235	25,428	121,308	67,694
2003	3,238,459	2,288,122	-120	2,288,002	250,817	9,274	2,046,459	688,991	503,009	26,354	122,882	69,157
2004	3,484,527	2,464,920	1,732	2,466,652	268,880	17,552	2,215,324	746,803	522,400	27,850	125,117	72,519
2005	3,724,854	2,612,612	29	2,612,641	288,189	32,348	2,356,800	793,997	574,057	29,324	127,025	74,558
2006	4,085,582	2,835,340	-18	2,835,322	306,983	43,499	2,571,838	901,262	612,482	31,746	128,695	76,553
2007	4,391,868	3,074,903	18,019	3,092,922	336,571	43,923	2,800,274	927,885	663,709	33,669	130,442	79,192
2008	4,723,132	3,183,698	9,916	3,193,614	350,617	42,960	2,885,957	1,064,088	773,087	35,821	131,853	78,695
2009	4,550,095	3,039,042	5,392	3,044,434	341,979	52,021	2,754,476	932,897	862,722	34,089	133,477	76,108
2010	4,650,693	3,116,238	5,765	3,122,003	349,198	63,383	2,836,188	866,194	948,311	34,531	134,680	76,339
2011	4,901,006	3,226,523	6,708	3,233,231	318,950	86,565	3,000,846	958,276	941,884	36,414	134,590	76,953
2012	5,043,930	3,209,156	1,005	3,210,161	320,771	109,128	2,998,518	1,124,877	920,535	36,893	136,717	78,067
2013	5,270,807	3,425,214	3,240	3,428,454	382,488	129,070	3,175,036	1,150,862	944,909	38,325	137,531	80,078
2014	5,546,207	3,589,490	5,801	3,595,291	399,714	125,799	3,321,376	1,204,829	1,020,002	40,000	138,656	81,605
2015	5,919,742	3,803,566	8,995	3,812,561	423,180	130,937	3,520,318	1,319,988	1,079,436	42,186	140,326	83,443
2016	6,137,865	3,940,546	6,221	3,946,767	433,363	141,936	3,655,340	1,347,166	1,135,359	43,197	142,091	84,993
2017	6,584,272	4,195,333	12,471	4,207,804	458,908	148,779	3,897,675	1,475,875	1,210,722	46,032	143,036	86,618
2018	6,919,869	4,396,062	28,585	4,424,647	481,466	155,861	4,099,042	1,558,057	1,262,770	47,749	144,921	87,247
2019	7,150,200	4,399,025	7,871	4,406,896	487,894	172,482	4,091,484	1,718,347	1,340,369	48,892	146,244	86,432
2020	7,678,620	4,363,578	23,734	4,387,312	489,822	202,656	4,100,146	1,681,592	1,896,882	52,890	145,180	81,635
2021	8,067,791	4,594,491	33,712	4,628,203	519,347	238,660	4,347,516	1,694,818	2,025,457	56,505	142,780	84,722
2022	8,489,905	5,085,923	18,221	5,104,144	568,856	251,093	4,786,381	1,875,614	1,827,910	58,933	144,060	88,910

Personal Income and Employment by Area: Flint, MI

(Thousands of dollars, except as noted.)

Year	Personal income, total	Derivation of personal income: Earnings by place of work: Nonfarm	Farm	Total	Less: Contributions for government social insurance	Plus: Adjustment for residence	Equals: Net earnings by place of residence	Plus: Dividends, interest, and rent	Plus: Personal current transfer receipts	Per capita personal income (dollars)	Population (persons)	Total employment
1970	1,771,022	1,618,255	3,749	1,622,004	113,439	-119,282	1,389,283	218,119	163,620	3,970	446,058	169,418
1971	2,050,637	1,926,510	3,188	1,929,698	138,409	-154,672	1,636,617	232,021	181,999	4,574	448,310	180,597
1972	2,232,036	2,115,753	5,044	2,120,797	164,610	-174,935	1,781,252	246,822	203,962	4,975	448,656	181,540
1973	2,452,316	2,368,810	6,331	2,375,141	213,069	-199,956	1,962,116	263,227	226,973	5,428	451,762	190,536
1974	2,474,702	2,265,756	6,992	2,272,748	211,254	-185,181	1,876,313	291,930	306,459	5,497	450,155	181,085
1975	2,695,600	2,418,511	7,264	2,425,775	222,103	-204,701	1,998,971	311,066	385,563	6,032	446,850	172,646
1976	3,205,305	3,025,601	6,365	3,031,966	283,603	-283,283	2,465,080	346,210	394,015	7,205	444,880	184,610
1977	3,692,290	3,590,047	5,861	3,595,908	336,765	-356,096	2,903,047	391,656	397,587	8,269	446,546	197,459
1978	4,042,108	3,975,603	1,933	3,977,536	387,416	-396,187	3,193,933	431,999	416,176	8,990	449,607	205,560
1979	4,413,788	4,291,343	4,071	4,295,414	427,340	-427,461	3,440,613	485,406	487,769	9,785	451,082	209,373
1980	4,645,161	4,176,568	3,704	4,180,272	408,258	-413,108	3,358,906	563,675	722,580	10,343	449,131	193,291
1981	5,060,798	4,628,517	4,682	4,633,199	493,230	-463,852	3,676,117	671,665	713,016	11,427	442,878	196,257
1982	5,036,785	4,339,488	-159	4,339,329	468,809	-408,904	3,461,616	773,821	801,348	11,523	437,115	180,848
1983	5,492,216	4,828,984	2,642	4,831,626	531,404	-466,921	3,833,301	830,731	828,184	12,696	432,600	184,486
1984	6,102,931	5,469,115	5,904	5,475,019	624,808	-524,443	4,325,768	940,609	836,554	14,184	430,254	194,055
1985	6,633,197	6,008,042	4,895	6,012,937	705,066	-561,600	4,746,271	1,016,551	870,375	15,381	431,268	202,416
1986	6,958,376	6,236,728	3,838	6,240,566	732,763	-554,803	4,953,000	1,086,745	918,631	16,069	433,037	205,863
1987	6,640,058	5,698,352	4,050	5,702,402	661,344	-421,645	4,619,413	1,054,475	966,170	15,323	433,335	202,507
1988	6,889,105	5,769,787	3,977	5,773,764	685,436	-378,341	4,709,987	1,140,521	1,038,597	16,018	430,096	194,226
1989	7,218,880	5,982,754	6,405	5,989,159	714,198	-370,688	4,904,273	1,179,038	1,135,569	16,829	428,946	198,317
1990	7,557,547	6,128,473	5,372	6,133,845	741,866	-353,885	5,038,094	1,297,904	1,221,549	17,537	430,938	201,117
1991	7,934,033	6,395,000	1,817	6,396,817	786,256	-356,856	5,253,705	1,290,027	1,390,301	18,401	431,184	196,856
1992	8,176,954	6,499,758	1,331	6,501,089	789,813	-291,065	5,420,211	1,291,299	1,465,444	18,975	430,944	195,695
1993	8,532,297	6,717,044	1,467	6,718,511	823,066	-248,481	5,646,964	1,329,896	1,555,437	19,810	430,702	195,165
1994	9,411,826	7,556,622	-1,445	7,555,177	930,484	-287,550	6,337,143	1,512,069	1,562,614	21,850	430,742	205,760
1995	9,920,031	7,821,296	1,510	7,822,806	957,530	-235,380	6,629,896	1,605,995	1,684,140	22,949	432,261	214,744
1996	10,345,821	7,855,211	-1,952	7,853,259	933,462	-128,532	6,791,265	1,673,665	1,880,891	23,877	433,302	218,418
1997	10,457,145	7,909,096	-2,213	7,906,883	937,396	-17,786	6,951,701	1,719,305	1,786,139	24,152	432,978	218,542
1998	10,809,231	8,131,759	-2,760	8,128,999	942,670	120,122	7,306,451	1,760,884	1,741,896	24,954	433,160	217,360
1999	11,128,068	8,222,323	2,631	8,224,954	956,751	248,024	7,516,227	1,742,704	1,869,137	25,617	434,409	214,621
2000	11,696,861	8,496,090	-2,081	8,494,009	970,839	391,559	7,914,729	1,825,158	1,956,974	26,768	436,965	215,500
2001	11,646,797	8,213,631	-5,569	8,208,062	953,701	505,479	7,759,840	1,730,834	2,156,123	26,555	438,584	208,522
2002	11,741,147	8,254,048	-899	8,253,149	959,906	512,661	7,805,904	1,694,120	2,241,123	26,681	440,062	206,220
2003	12,106,770	8,310,735	2,261	8,312,996	961,058	614,488	7,966,426	1,761,862	2,378,482	27,410	441,689	204,038
2004	12,325,730	8,487,999	6,580	8,494,579	998,853	723,870	8,219,596	1,637,561	2,468,573	27,853	442,534	205,081
2005	12,500,021	8,205,454	7,689	8,213,143	975,550	981,663	8,219,256	1,663,307	2,617,458	28,248	442,508	199,146
2006	12,867,985	8,411,995	8,496	8,420,491	1,025,891	973,118	8,367,718	1,729,471	2,770,796	29,168	441,164	199,337
2007	13,013,729	8,166,657	8,310	8,174,967	1,004,752	973,880	8,144,095	1,821,727	3,047,907	29,704	438,109	197,347
2008	13,189,568	7,738,541	12,062	7,750,603	968,551	1,013,182	7,795,234	1,904,899	3,489,435	30,455	433,082	189,371
2009	12,672,806	7,295,122	5,203	7,300,325	923,251	689,443	7,066,517	1,717,973	3,888,316	29,610	427,989	181,516
2010	13,001,099	7,421,874	10,107	7,431,981	917,940	542,694	7,056,735	1,736,240	4,208,124	30,592	424,983	179,304
2011	13,551,613	7,730,053	22,279	7,752,332	851,047	633,575	7,534,860	1,844,123	4,172,630	32,099	422,179	182,697
2012	13,895,202	7,891,122	22,228	7,913,350	870,350	790,939	7,833,939	1,944,857	4,116,406	33,206	418,453	182,460
2013	14,076,201	8,012,502	21,039	8,033,541	1,005,293	808,626	7,836,874	1,979,587	4,259,740	33,836	416,016	185,550
2014	14,442,336	8,180,028	10,313	8,190,341	1,024,640	817,870	7,983,571	2,090,577	4,368,188	34,940	413,344	187,614
2015	15,112,837	8,559,946	12,340	8,572,286	1,061,822	853,693	8,364,157	2,172,094	4,576,586	36,766	411,060	187,290
2016	15,445,475	8,632,454	9,914	8,642,368	1,076,304	979,138	8,545,202	2,291,343	4,608,930	37,706	409,634	186,024
2017	15,814,955	8,895,238	9,874	8,905,112	1,111,189	1,116,901	8,910,824	2,341,412	4,562,719	38,729	408,345	187,276
2018	16,359,898	9,170,930	10,283	9,181,213	1,167,580	1,195,615	9,209,248	2,426,002	4,724,648	40,158	407,386	188,371
2019	16,931,601	9,473,602	11,412	9,485,014	1,200,388	1,232,341	9,516,967	2,510,865	4,903,769	41,647	406,554	188,194
2020	18,414,693	9,136,632	17,986	9,154,618	1,164,699	1,383,159	9,373,078	2,426,866	6,614,749	45,384	405,757	175,059
2021	19,488,910	9,718,686	23,001	9,741,687	1,226,441	1,609,532	10,124,778	2,514,263	6,849,869	48,161	404,662	181,043
2022	19,119,944	10,204,654	18,730	10,223,384	1,333,525	1,798,237	10,688,096	2,653,478	5,778,370	47,564	401,983	189,253

Personal Income and Employment by Area: Florence, SC

(Thousands of dollars, except as noted.)

Year	Personal income, total	Derivation of personal income: Earnings by place of work: Nonfarm	Farm	Total	Less: Contributions for government social insurance	Plus: Adjustment for residence	Equals: Net earnings by place of residence	Plus: Dividends, interest, and rent	Plus: Personal current transfer receipts	Per capita personal income (dollars)	Population (persons)	Total employment
1970	406,157	335,541	23,087	358,628	23,637	-14,584	320,407	44,564	41,186	2,838	143,122	68,218
1971	445,235	367,395	23,811	391,206	26,699	-15,648	348,859	49,311	47,065	3,058	145,616	69,457
1972	501,497	419,930	24,895	444,825	31,941	-18,444	394,440	54,827	52,230	3,411	147,002	72,381
1973	576,880	485,934	30,377	516,311	42,491	-22,080	451,740	63,233	61,907	3,797	151,937	76,728
1974	674,759	556,988	43,467	600,455	50,584	-27,202	522,669	71,430	80,660	4,281	157,632	78,964
1975	713,992	562,197	31,022	593,219	49,699	-24,181	519,339	81,545	113,108	4,438	160,899	74,439
1976	792,398	647,423	23,012	670,435	58,461	-27,504	584,470	88,827	119,101	4,881	162,337	76,550
1977	870,486	719,410	20,706	740,116	65,020	-29,942	645,154	99,658	125,674	5,230	166,445	77,460
1978	994,242	816,651	32,603	849,254	75,495	-32,210	741,549	111,762	140,931	5,879	169,123	79,149
1979	1,099,485	915,714	21,030	936,744	87,479	-37,987	811,278	125,789	162,418	6,400	171,805	80,572
1980	1,223,399	1,014,044	1,734	1,015,778	96,820	-44,287	874,671	156,222	192,506	7,062	173,231	81,883
1981	1,399,586	1,127,787	25,746	1,153,533	115,644	-52,448	985,441	195,236	218,909	8,040	174,072	82,700
1982	1,462,221	1,133,795	33,593	1,167,388	119,110	-48,188	1,000,090	225,348	236,783	8,384	174,401	79,678
1983	1,557,680	1,220,378	11,315	1,231,693	130,065	-45,508	1,056,120	249,279	252,281	8,961	173,824	80,119
1984	1,736,060	1,371,216	23,390	1,394,606	151,219	-53,936	1,189,451	281,012	265,597	9,926	174,898	83,677
1985	1,831,527	1,422,115	22,453	1,444,568	158,687	-51,826	1,234,055	306,069	291,403	10,440	175,430	82,212
1986	1,927,414	1,527,243	-3,836	1,523,407	174,548	-49,323	1,299,536	322,954	304,924	11,001	175,210	83,463
1987	2,061,719	1,621,557	28,369	1,649,926	182,753	-46,687	1,420,486	329,266	311,967	11,794	174,806	84,803
1988	2,253,416	1,773,409	39,132	1,812,541	207,128	-50,803	1,554,610	366,228	332,578	12,896	174,734	88,568
1989	2,479,739	1,897,413	37,198	1,934,611	225,135	-51,146	1,658,330	436,529	384,880	14,117	175,658	91,566
1990	2,655,604	2,058,136	23,238	2,081,374	247,476	-52,701	1,781,197	446,265	428,142	15,028	176,706	93,814
1991	2,831,493	2,166,822	33,573	2,200,395	262,966	-60,015	1,877,414	460,326	493,753	15,773	179,519	94,063
1992	3,022,578	2,304,152	36,008	2,340,160	277,060	-61,101	2,001,999	461,924	558,655	16,604	182,044	95,003
1993	3,184,739	2,439,147	29,036	2,468,183	296,509	-64,948	2,106,726	481,321	596,692	17,291	184,186	96,466
1994	3,362,306	2,541,304	43,427	2,584,731	312,172	-64,294	2,208,265	518,302	635,739	18,102	185,744	98,121
1995	3,526,397	2,689,484	23,097	2,712,581	329,940	-72,024	2,310,617	543,171	672,609	18,780	187,778	100,459
1996	3,773,169	2,857,197	44,991	2,902,188	344,323	-82,434	2,475,431	578,825	718,913	19,971	188,929	102,855
1997	3,942,833	3,005,831	40,799	3,046,630	360,923	-88,509	2,597,198	601,188	744,447	20,678	190,674	106,126
1998	4,177,460	3,210,444	17,350	3,227,794	384,709	-94,785	2,748,300	651,314	777,846	21,794	191,680	107,187
1999	4,317,882	3,333,481	20,786	3,354,267	395,262	-94,334	2,864,671	629,329	823,882	22,414	192,641	107,966
2000	4,599,034	3,521,866	50,162	3,572,028	416,543	-101,366	3,054,119	679,761	865,154	23,793	193,290	108,664
2001	4,773,663	3,591,338	67,434	3,658,772	427,543	-106,652	3,124,577	698,713	950,373	24,576	194,240	106,048
2002	4,905,498	3,728,555	-7,340	3,721,215	443,420	-110,623	3,167,172	698,469	1,039,857	25,081	195,590	106,520
2003	5,075,355	3,803,526	47,197	3,850,723	453,260	-106,870	3,290,593	701,919	1,082,843	25,756	197,053	105,212
2004	5,324,497	3,951,544	37,849	3,989,393	472,772	-107,850	3,408,771	742,245	1,173,481	26,890	198,010	105,334
2005	5,502,796	4,042,133	24,231	4,066,364	483,650	-105,214	3,477,500	773,177	1,252,119	27,629	199,167	105,677
2006	5,888,209	4,283,106	22,526	4,305,632	521,533	-116,167	3,667,932	887,362	1,332,915	29,307	200,913	107,464
2007	6,173,789	4,456,413	8,266	4,464,679	540,846	-121,831	3,802,002	968,875	1,402,912	30,526	202,246	109,513
2008	6,432,710	4,503,518	14,546	4,518,064	550,798	-128,427	3,838,839	1,000,400	1,593,471	31,563	203,805	109,124
2009	6,306,477	4,336,254	11,300	4,347,554	538,105	-149,845	3,659,604	921,449	1,725,424	30,790	204,825	104,992
2010	6,429,859	4,409,925	8,744	4,418,669	543,486	-167,785	3,707,398	873,789	1,848,672	31,280	205,556	104,416
2011	6,713,140	4,558,600	17,989	4,576,589	503,152	-189,356	3,884,081	979,427	1,849,632	32,708	205,247	106,933
2012	6,820,654	4,714,340	24,809	4,739,149	513,794	-218,825	4,006,530	968,761	1,845,363	33,266	205,034	107,474
2013	6,944,666	4,907,509	47,177	4,954,686	598,819	-254,334	4,101,533	979,221	1,863,912	33,954	204,533	108,536
2014	7,185,326	5,042,462	11,428	5,053,890	611,394	-264,918	4,177,578	1,039,775	1,967,973	35,130	204,537	109,045
2015	7,427,577	5,227,311	-15,946	5,211,365	636,451	-277,380	4,297,534	1,056,860	2,073,183	36,425	203,913	110,721
2016	7,626,929	5,280,360	13,907	5,294,267	644,242	-269,544	4,380,481	1,141,956	2,104,492	37,547	203,128	111,487
2017	7,857,404	5,482,814	13,902	5,496,716	670,544	-274,284	4,551,888	1,170,731	2,134,785	38,849	202,254	112,406
2018	8,181,781	5,729,747	1,241	5,730,988	702,700	-283,257	4,745,031	1,211,524	2,225,226	40,629	201,378	116,319
2019	8,656,239	6,003,893	23,923	6,027,816	738,172	-296,416	4,993,228	1,353,060	2,309,951	43,142	200,647	116,533
2020	9,134,800	6,057,283	21,230	6,078,513	745,048	-292,522	5,040,943	1,271,587	2,822,270	45,753	199,654	113,709
2021	9,929,789	6,445,782	39,569	6,485,351	788,077	-307,883	5,389,391	1,378,588	3,161,810	49,862	199,147	116,251
2022	10,091,118	6,928,292	15,216	6,943,508	867,447	-352,587	5,723,474	1,480,142	2,887,502	50,679	199,119	120,558

Personal Income and Employment by Area: Florence-Muscle Shoals, AL

(Thousands of dollars, except as noted.)

Year	Personal income, total	Derivation of personal income								Per capita personal income (dollars)	Population (persons)	Total employment
		Earnings by place of work			Less: Contributions for government social insurance	Plus: Adjustment for residence	Equals: Net earnings by place of residence	Plus: Dividends, interest, and rent	Plus: Personal current transfer receipts			
		Nonfarm	Farm	Total								
1970	364,774	287,164	11,269	298,433	19,076	2,687	282,044	46,066	36,664	3,089	118,093	45,574
1971	407,840	318,621	13,503	332,124	21,253	1,580	312,451	52,655	42,734	3,383	120,545	46,466
1972	445,489	358,547	14,600	373,147	25,604	-4,397	343,146	55,976	46,367	3,664	121,579	48,921
1973	491,305	395,681	19,485	415,166	33,191	-7,031	374,944	62,878	53,483	3,976	123,562	50,449
1974	546,775	444,839	13,243	458,082	38,994	-9,088	410,000	72,785	63,990	4,405	124,134	51,771
1975	599,466	470,334	11,781	482,115	40,917	-9,315	431,883	82,063	85,520	4,741	126,431	50,742
1976	692,149	554,355	23,631	577,986	48,689	-22,388	506,909	91,098	94,142	5,413	127,873	53,503
1977	763,431	630,581	17,434	648,015	55,060	-32,363	560,592	104,147	98,692	5,863	130,206	55,877
1978	875,787	733,682	18,412	752,094	64,530	-39,858	647,706	121,832	106,249	6,641	131,868	59,286
1979	975,455	791,588	28,891	820,479	72,305	-34,423	713,751	139,693	122,011	7,249	134,560	59,603
1980	1,078,589	855,949	12,059	868,008	77,974	-37,922	752,112	175,431	151,046	7,971	135,322	58,791
1981	1,195,198	902,580	22,282	924,862	89,305	-20,524	815,033	212,768	167,397	8,782	136,104	57,118
1982	1,241,775	911,897	22,328	934,225	92,173	-18,223	823,829	231,994	185,952	9,189	135,139	55,778
1983	1,290,448	943,668	1,285	944,953	98,913	-6,182	839,858	244,366	206,224	9,627	134,050	56,395
1984	1,394,868	993,222	13,187	1,006,409	106,894	4,489	904,004	270,828	220,036	10,449	133,488	57,561
1985	1,475,093	1,029,173	12,687	1,041,860	112,866	24,358	953,352	289,871	231,870	11,062	133,350	57,338
1986	1,554,339	1,077,852	7,737	1,085,589	118,286	40,267	1,007,570	304,459	242,310	11,717	132,653	57,115
1987	1,631,317	1,124,151	13,778	1,137,929	122,477	57,339	1,072,791	309,699	248,827	12,374	131,839	58,321
1988	1,776,374	1,216,672	18,618	1,235,290	137,899	80,045	1,177,436	342,387	256,551	13,546	131,132	60,565
1989	1,892,301	1,276,150	14,515	1,290,665	147,401	82,228	1,225,492	379,400	287,409	14,471	130,762	62,347
1990	2,078,313	1,396,662	9,946	1,406,608	161,988	111,392	1,356,012	408,068	314,233	15,764	131,838	64,761
1991	2,175,518	1,460,542	19,772	1,480,314	170,877	107,923	1,417,360	409,401	348,757	16,268	133,733	66,343
1992	2,320,500	1,565,121	23,991	1,589,112	180,401	112,866	1,521,577	409,206	389,717	17,167	135,174	67,141
1993	2,412,264	1,633,439	16,628	1,650,067	192,102	120,224	1,578,189	423,381	410,694	17,611	136,971	68,977
1994	2,552,944	1,724,956	32,016	1,756,972	204,809	117,419	1,669,582	446,589	436,773	18,528	137,786	69,508
1995	2,699,109	1,806,876	3,344	1,810,220	217,006	129,057	1,722,271	503,898	472,940	19,423	138,962	72,519
1996	2,814,275	1,865,923	25,920	1,891,843	221,563	124,747	1,795,027	519,149	500,099	20,056	140,318	73,172
1997	2,902,199	1,912,989	15,974	1,928,963	226,908	129,863	1,831,918	543,623	526,658	20,534	141,339	73,294
1998	2,959,843	1,894,596	15,560	1,910,156	222,525	147,908	1,835,539	575,017	549,287	20,838	142,041	71,742
1999	3,025,698	1,950,726	11,379	1,962,105	229,243	157,117	1,889,979	566,047	569,672	21,262	142,305	71,492
2000	3,138,585	1,979,834	18,250	1,998,084	231,976	163,177	1,929,285	606,517	602,783	21,943	143,036	71,922
2001	3,238,424	1,998,908	20,577	2,019,485	237,371	171,354	1,953,468	615,402	669,554	22,712	142,584	70,339
2002	3,271,198	2,006,112	6,630	2,012,742	235,601	173,143	1,950,284	604,244	716,670	23,010	142,163	67,795
2003	3,430,081	2,086,840	32,598	2,119,438	244,453	191,494	2,066,479	608,143	755,459	24,091	142,382	67,532
2004	3,645,674	2,233,844	49,806	2,283,650	259,504	201,167	2,225,313	608,172	812,189	25,474	143,112	68,950
2005	3,861,764	2,363,213	48,392	2,411,605	278,474	217,499	2,350,630	646,026	865,108	26,871	143,717	71,143
2006	4,073,300	2,516,131	38,672	2,554,803	298,372	232,955	2,489,386	650,984	932,930	28,149	144,707	73,602
2007	4,304,315	2,565,237	30,004	2,595,241	310,415	243,345	2,528,171	781,563	994,581	29,564	145,593	74,996
2008	4,422,516	2,538,306	32,597	2,570,903	318,593	252,164	2,504,474	826,121	1,091,921	30,152	146,675	74,033
2009	4,388,008	2,537,486	26,418	2,563,904	316,870	221,292	2,468,326	745,114	1,174,568	29,860	146,952	72,410
2010	4,601,409	2,684,584	1,427	2,686,011	335,348	220,400	2,571,063	758,429	1,271,917	31,234	147,319	72,494
2011	4,724,009	2,737,345	1,541	2,738,886	308,244	219,593	2,650,235	806,794	1,266,980	32,044	147,424	73,882
2012	4,773,690	2,750,622	4,175	2,754,797	309,510	225,838	2,671,125	831,148	1,271,417	32,311	147,740	73,574
2013	4,799,482	2,809,892	48,629	2,858,521	353,475	204,439	2,709,485	799,122	1,290,875	32,437	147,964	73,873
2014	4,998,592	2,932,592	24,079	2,956,671	366,067	203,342	2,793,946	867,321	1,337,325	33,678	148,422	74,894
2015	5,114,506	3,015,060	1,054	3,016,114	375,057	187,211	2,828,268	860,912	1,425,326	34,544	148,058	75,155
2016	5,182,335	3,038,832	-7,591	3,031,241	379,931	198,047	2,849,357	902,951	1,430,027	34,944	148,304	75,450
2017	5,270,723	3,074,583	597	3,075,180	389,957	206,878	2,892,101	928,452	1,450,170	35,399	148,895	75,476
2018	5,435,056	3,156,050	-9,120	3,146,930	406,715	234,907	2,975,122	953,235	1,506,699	36,373	149,427	76,496
2019	5,714,108	3,251,943	-7,354	3,244,589	414,957	256,342	3,085,974	1,042,619	1,585,515	38,041	150,210	76,821
2020	6,262,688	3,357,153	-6,650	3,350,503	432,285	281,705	3,199,923	1,125,612	1,937,153	41,386	151,324	75,194
2021	6,746,945	3,558,071	28,840	3,586,911	456,524	292,252	3,422,639	1,141,934	2,182,372	44,248	152,481	76,820
2022	6,881,779	3,875,799	-7,478	3,868,321	502,737	309,064	3,674,648	1,247,378	1,959,753	44,713	153,911	79,987

Personal Income and Employment by Area: Fond du Lac, WI

(Thousands of dollars, except as noted.)

Year	Personal income, total	Derivation of personal income: Earnings by place of work: Nonfarm	Farm	Total	Less: Contributions for government social insurance	Plus: Adjustment for residence	Equals: Net earnings by place of residence	Plus: Dividends, interest, and rent	Plus: Personal current transfer receipts	Per capita personal income (dollars)	Population (persons)	Total employment
1970	322,337	245,447	18,456	263,903	18,807	-2,948	242,148	51,698	28,491	3,820	84,380	39,020
1971	344,029	256,193	21,497	277,690	20,238	-439	257,013	54,692	32,324	4,117	83,569	38,765
1972	375,685	283,304	20,008	303,312	23,510	2,230	282,032	57,881	35,772	4,406	85,264	40,118
1973	423,011	320,486	21,909	342,395	30,581	4,070	315,884	65,629	41,498	4,889	86,518	41,920
1974	463,052	342,328	21,018	363,346	33,885	9,154	338,615	74,774	49,663	5,349	86,561	42,694
1975	510,326	358,433	25,368	383,801	34,687	14,014	363,128	82,665	64,533	5,857	87,138	41,961
1976	565,686	406,292	22,955	429,247	39,852	17,934	407,329	88,011	70,346	6,515	86,830	42,917
1977	637,421	447,527	39,691	487,218	44,127	23,397	466,488	97,760	73,173	7,271	87,670	44,071
1978	702,220	499,994	32,151	532,145	50,575	32,239	513,809	107,829	80,582	8,005	87,720	44,857
1979	794,374	561,380	40,505	601,885	59,087	40,462	583,260	119,368	91,746	9,009	88,172	46,299
1980	864,471	584,669	35,167	619,836	61,496	45,419	603,759	147,352	113,360	9,721	88,924	45,661
1981	949,111	648,281	24,762	673,043	73,081	43,431	643,393	180,783	124,935	10,718	88,556	46,334
1982	1,000,288	663,058	21,333	684,391	75,710	43,957	652,638	205,418	142,232	11,320	88,361	45,665
1983	1,041,909	698,402	6,129	704,531	79,161	49,116	674,486	217,485	149,938	11,801	88,289	45,170
1984	1,160,497	779,539	23,085	802,624	90,274	52,567	764,917	244,189	151,391	13,105	88,552	46,517
1985	1,215,156	812,202	25,336	837,538	94,159	55,589	798,968	253,937	162,251	13,662	88,942	46,739
1986	1,277,463	847,996	33,960	881,956	98,070	65,577	849,463	261,178	166,822	14,368	88,909	45,908
1987	1,360,715	929,495	41,385	970,880	105,180	70,435	936,135	256,126	168,454	15,282	89,038	46,598
1988	1,427,613	1,005,506	20,739	1,026,245	117,347	76,933	985,831	266,939	174,843	15,900	89,787	47,180
1989	1,605,786	1,142,789	45,809	1,188,598	132,902	66,671	1,122,367	292,398	191,021	17,892	89,748	50,119
1990	1,688,352	1,205,476	39,054	1,244,530	145,119	81,364	1,180,775	301,727	205,850	18,698	90,296	51,402
1991	1,726,711	1,235,946	34,829	1,270,775	151,298	80,649	1,200,126	306,878	219,707	18,920	91,265	51,910
1992	1,854,783	1,348,197	37,534	1,385,731	163,385	84,970	1,307,316	308,386	239,081	20,150	92,049	52,863
1993	1,957,789	1,441,595	27,400	1,468,995	175,227	86,871	1,380,639	328,202	248,948	21,080	92,876	54,466
1994	2,101,685	1,549,146	42,564	1,591,710	189,851	93,629	1,495,488	348,906	257,291	22,426	93,717	55,863
1995	2,194,680	1,599,473	26,664	1,626,137	196,601	100,715	1,530,251	393,369	271,060	23,222	94,509	56,839
1996	2,312,708	1,659,296	43,435	1,702,731	202,376	106,941	1,607,296	421,002	284,410	24,209	95,529	57,633
1997	2,418,784	1,733,499	27,387	1,760,886	211,527	111,298	1,660,657	464,491	293,636	25,196	95,998	57,950
1998	2,563,791	1,847,042	41,761	1,888,803	224,813	115,714	1,779,704	479,056	305,031	26,564	96,512	59,514
1999	2,621,975	1,903,914	36,959	1,940,873	232,476	126,455	1,834,852	473,709	313,414	27,035	96,985	59,881
2000	2,775,528	2,020,475	22,116	2,042,591	241,625	133,365	1,934,331	499,135	342,062	28,499	97,390	60,814
2001	2,819,412	1,994,474	29,469	2,023,943	235,571	160,123	1,948,495	489,724	381,193	28,812	97,856	58,683
2002	2,923,216	2,083,319	23,906	2,107,225	243,692	160,984	2,024,517	486,918	411,781	29,799	98,097	59,001
2003	2,990,125	2,103,649	42,383	2,146,032	249,207	176,784	2,073,609	491,020	425,496	30,366	98,470	58,355
2004	3,089,579	2,195,011	48,949	2,243,960	261,405	195,928	2,178,483	478,486	432,610	31,230	98,929	58,532
2005	3,180,604	2,258,197	45,457	2,303,654	272,214	207,834	2,239,274	478,007	463,323	32,031	99,297	58,971
2006	3,315,059	2,328,040	34,752	2,362,792	280,974	221,986	2,303,804	519,418	491,837	33,177	99,920	59,306
2007	3,520,607	2,403,774	66,217	2,469,991	291,583	242,314	2,420,722	566,737	533,148	35,024	100,520	59,937
2008	3,718,242	2,493,881	64,677	2,558,558	305,357	249,402	2,502,603	621,210	594,429	36,770	101,122	59,768
2009	3,605,345	2,375,943	19,752	2,395,695	291,962	230,970	2,334,703	570,945	699,697	35,566	101,370	56,804
2010	3,738,093	2,439,720	63,761	2,503,481	297,997	229,367	2,434,851	550,045	753,197	36,789	101,608	56,463
2011	3,885,770	2,507,384	109,318	2,616,702	279,781	230,926	2,567,847	599,835	718,088	38,107	101,969	57,212
2012	4,047,674	2,638,165	104,693	2,742,858	292,593	210,024	2,660,289	659,597	727,788	39,657	102,067	57,437
2013	4,068,339	2,693,488	116,860	2,810,348	334,665	188,359	2,664,042	653,679	750,618	39,811	102,191	58,957
2014	4,262,163	2,803,248	137,073	2,940,321	346,295	195,956	2,789,982	684,482	787,699	41,584	102,495	59,849
2015	4,423,992	2,933,057	101,619	3,034,676	358,606	199,059	2,875,129	729,999	818,864	43,123	102,590	60,012
2016	4,476,635	2,996,851	73,697	3,070,548	363,994	194,668	2,901,222	736,422	838,991	43,493	102,927	60,069
2017	4,663,355	3,105,634	81,847	3,187,481	380,162	212,930	3,020,249	758,325	884,781	45,196	103,180	59,985
2018	4,930,665	3,301,665	68,387	3,370,052	399,943	199,216	3,169,325	822,998	938,342	47,523	103,754	61,266
2019	5,156,295	3,414,465	82,039	3,496,504	415,871	206,350	3,286,983	885,358	983,954	49,496	104,175	61,566
2020	5,459,482	3,417,515	115,415	3,532,930	419,649	224,893	3,338,174	878,356	1,242,952	52,419	104,150	58,485
2021	5,902,723	3,612,762	111,817	3,724,579	441,229	241,025	3,524,375	981,645	1,396,703	56,667	104,166	59,910
2022	6,043,639	3,855,868	127,795	3,983,663	484,389	263,177	3,762,451	1,038,667	1,242,521	58,204	103,836	61,561

Personal Income and Employment by Area: Fort Collins, CO

(Thousands of dollars, except as noted.)

Year	Personal income, total	Derivation of personal income: Earnings by place of work: Nonfarm	Farm	Total	Less: Contributions for government social insurance	Plus: Adjustment for residence	Equals: Net earnings by place of residence	Plus: Dividends, interest, and rent	Plus: Personal current transfer receipts	Per capita personal income (dollars)	Population (persons)	Total employment
1970	313,677	208,982	6,352	215,334	10,780	10,531	215,085	71,132	27,460	3,443	91,095	35,982
1971	368,477	241,027	11,168	252,195	12,652	15,147	254,690	81,986	31,801	3,794	97,125	37,219
1972	428,182	287,685	8,067	295,752	16,568	20,953	300,137	92,060	35,985	4,002	106,999	41,926
1973	500,034	333,401	9,374	342,775	22,325	28,122	348,572	108,156	43,306	4,447	112,441	45,809
1974	577,813	378,997	8,603	387,600	26,294	37,079	398,385	128,229	51,199	4,817	119,945	48,576
1975	676,045	432,904	12,393	445,297	29,156	45,535	461,676	149,076	65,293	5,606	120,593	51,021
1976	782,016	513,053	9,461	522,514	35,067	57,830	545,277	165,255	71,484	6,348	123,187	55,630
1977	898,522	601,869	5,331	607,200	42,418	68,661	633,443	188,208	76,871	6,808	131,973	60,594
1978	1,065,075	723,405	6,673	730,078	52,744	84,224	761,558	218,268	85,249	7,730	137,780	66,489
1979	1,254,849	864,441	399	864,840	66,507	101,647	899,980	257,917	96,952	8,626	145,474	71,512
1980	1,436,951	958,536	127	958,663	75,088	119,479	1,003,054	317,571	116,326	9,574	150,091	73,957
1981	1,629,655	1,054,111	7,402	1,061,513	88,905	131,876	1,104,484	384,305	140,866	10,627	153,347	74,913
1982	1,785,262	1,136,352	5,147	1,141,499	97,245	151,874	1,196,128	428,280	160,854	11,341	157,410	76,547
1983	1,976,345	1,249,884	10,291	1,260,175	109,134	166,883	1,317,924	481,768	176,653	12,214	161,816	80,642
1984	2,168,313	1,394,294	8,358	1,402,652	126,427	181,030	1,457,255	524,275	186,783	13,135	165,073	86,194
1985	2,334,397	1,495,821	6,159	1,501,980	139,172	194,165	1,556,973	576,809	200,615	13,757	169,687	88,750
1986	2,497,768	1,618,044	5,133	1,623,177	153,186	201,889	1,671,880	607,504	218,384	14,333	174,271	91,424
1987	2,660,566	1,739,402	4,839	1,744,241	162,522	213,223	1,794,942	625,537	240,087	14,980	177,612	92,603
1988	2,852,567	1,875,881	8,116	1,883,997	184,099	232,046	1,931,944	667,354	253,269	15,794	180,610	98,006
1989	3,129,089	2,036,601	13,274	2,049,875	205,906	249,525	2,093,494	751,113	284,482	17,052	183,507	101,762
1990	3,365,468	2,227,547	13,687	2,241,234	232,183	267,881	2,276,932	782,430	306,106	17,968	187,299	105,353
1991	3,591,020	2,397,691	13,097	2,410,788	256,406	291,957	2,446,339	806,181	338,500	18,591	193,154	110,094
1992	3,915,873	2,653,828	17,321	2,671,149	280,347	307,507	2,698,309	835,538	382,026	19,559	200,212	113,837
1993	4,282,864	2,924,534	21,225	2,945,759	314,947	321,978	2,952,790	921,071	409,003	20,577	208,143	121,231
1994	4,643,005	3,224,557	16,963	3,241,520	352,302	333,719	3,222,937	986,128	433,940	21,409	216,868	128,209
1995	5,059,300	3,464,978	13,973	3,478,951	378,997	352,543	3,452,497	1,120,126	486,677	22,713	222,750	134,280
1996	5,541,840	3,858,405	22,078	3,880,483	417,305	363,199	3,826,377	1,207,300	508,163	24,269	228,350	143,321
1997	5,985,189	4,170,154	22,625	4,192,779	445,415	395,887	4,143,251	1,324,040	517,898	25,606	233,746	148,781
1998	6,490,324	4,538,775	21,216	4,559,991	454,298	452,499	4,558,192	1,398,582	533,550	26,957	240,765	154,951
1999	6,902,614	4,888,876	17,691	4,906,567	485,220	503,442	4,924,789	1,407,319	570,506	27,959	246,884	159,167
2000	7,776,157	5,546,268	13,743	5,560,011	547,163	592,449	5,605,297	1,562,340	608,520	30,727	253,072	166,868
2001	8,354,451	6,052,944	17,855	6,070,799	592,762	592,491	6,070,528	1,600,851	683,072	32,066	260,541	170,194
2002	8,449,666	6,273,093	7,465	6,280,558	635,518	514,197	6,159,237	1,529,656	760,773	31,841	265,372	171,106
2003	8,525,283	6,332,193	2,445	6,334,638	646,544	517,084	6,205,178	1,525,203	794,902	31,758	268,448	171,668
2004	8,883,582	6,521,295	18,501	6,539,796	688,866	531,563	6,382,493	1,669,320	831,769	32,719	271,510	176,182
2005	9,346,231	6,814,647	19,771	6,834,418	728,843	537,421	6,642,996	1,788,493	914,742	33,972	275,116	180,850
2006	10,032,283	7,173,242	14,420	7,187,662	764,790	563,213	6,986,085	2,041,529	1,004,669	35,739	280,713	184,620
2007	10,776,675	7,503,388	25,068	7,528,456	802,501	588,870	7,314,825	2,369,442	1,092,408	37,666	286,112	190,983
2008	11,170,474	7,494,055	21,425	7,515,480	817,325	613,260	7,311,415	2,536,001	1,323,058	38,301	291,650	192,607
2009	10,985,633	7,384,304	19,362	7,403,666	802,744	551,731	7,152,653	2,343,229	1,489,751	37,027	296,696	188,962
2010	11,258,594	7,563,052	27,770	7,590,822	821,438	540,165	7,309,549	2,275,621	1,673,424	37,474	300,434	189,257
2011	11,937,108	7,837,875	30,474	7,868,349	783,122	569,267	7,654,494	2,552,819	1,729,795	39,109	305,227	193,371
2012	12,671,282	8,326,281	33,180	8,359,461	826,203	600,430	8,133,688	2,794,425	1,743,169	40,768	310,813	196,972
2013	13,372,320	8,813,247	33,847	8,847,094	932,055	637,422	8,552,461	2,992,340	1,827,519	42,294	316,178	203,447
2014	14,466,510	9,406,248	38,048	9,444,296	1,008,784	703,115	9,138,627	3,347,545	1,980,338	44,658	323,942	210,484
2015	15,478,499	10,072,814	37,382	10,110,196	1,082,480	710,055	9,737,771	3,588,440	2,152,288	46,451	333,219	217,266
2016	16,293,556	10,753,015	27,287	10,780,302	1,155,711	658,492	10,283,083	3,734,988	2,275,485	48,079	338,891	226,392
2017	17,688,537	11,651,266	26,121	11,677,387	1,235,707	710,800	11,152,480	4,151,301	2,384,756	51,432	343,920	233,079
2018	18,810,826	12,259,463	28,460	12,287,923	1,314,859	781,368	11,754,432	4,456,213	2,600,181	53,689	350,367	240,198
2019	20,041,008	12,984,534	34,174	13,018,708	1,387,896	868,017	12,498,829	4,776,590	2,765,589	56,220	356,472	241,771
2020	21,508,425	13,464,230	30,436	13,494,666	1,439,555	831,885	12,886,996	4,935,347	3,686,082	59,762	359,899	238,096
2021	23,757,935	14,627,529	36,306	14,663,835	1,547,549	843,704	13,959,990	5,656,454	4,141,491	65,501	362,713	249,138
2022	24,885,632	15,844,781	25,744	15,870,525	1,739,393	914,068	15,045,200	6,139,675	3,700,757	67,849	366,778	261,704

Personal Income and Employment by Area: Fort Smith, AR-OK

(Thousands of dollars, except as noted.)

Year	Personal income, total	Derivation of personal income: Earnings by place of work: Nonfarm	Farm	Total	Less: Contributions for government social insurance	Plus: Adjustment for residence	Equals: Net earnings by place of residence	Plus: Dividends, interest, and rent	Plus: Personal current transfer receipts	Per capita personal income (dollars)	Population (persons)	Total employment
1970	414,509	336,316	11,232	347,548	24,611	-18,860	304,077	59,556	50,876	2,955	140,273	59,847
1971	466,663	373,529	13,660	387,189	28,172	-18,687	340,330	66,022	60,311	3,227	144,622	62,199
1972	524,973	422,955	18,043	440,998	33,519	-22,214	385,265	71,823	67,885	3,535	148,492	65,034
1973	602,115	479,695	26,938	506,633	43,920	-25,757	436,956	83,612	81,547	3,991	150,863	68,917
1974	687,121	553,212	18,924	572,136	52,271	-29,962	489,903	100,160	97,058	4,408	155,863	72,576
1975	768,624	599,063	22,728	621,791	54,970	-32,394	534,427	110,634	123,563	4,168	184,406	71,516
1976	863,725	687,210	21,385	708,595	64,918	-36,159	607,518	120,450	135,757	5,258	164,261	75,059
1977	973,632	794,870	17,686	812,556	76,174	-43,288	693,094	136,613	143,925	5,730	169,925	79,659
1978	1,107,095	910,810	20,950	931,760	89,715	-52,300	789,745	159,625	157,725	6,376	173,623	83,746
1979	1,230,709	996,767	24,878	1,021,645	101,403	-57,309	862,933	183,934	183,842	6,985	176,196	84,470
1980	1,380,455	1,087,965	12,161	1,100,126	108,467	-61,979	929,680	229,756	221,019	7,765	177,783	84,480
1981	1,558,507	1,202,632	21,873	1,224,505	129,298	-70,891	1,024,316	286,859	247,332	8,733	178,468	86,667
1982	1,625,730	1,218,481	17,774	1,236,255	133,873	-71,681	1,030,701	325,363	269,666	9,117	178,319	83,788
1983	1,745,746	1,343,796	13,723	1,357,519	149,918	-83,393	1,124,208	336,081	285,457	9,647	180,957	87,516
1984	1,943,976	1,522,841	17,733	1,540,574	174,934	-94,306	1,271,334	377,774	294,868	10,577	183,801	92,236
1985	2,088,172	1,629,086	21,957	1,651,043	188,278	-100,219	1,362,546	411,410	314,216	11,260	185,446	94,951
1986	2,232,147	1,756,598	28,390	1,784,988	202,781	-107,418	1,474,789	425,007	332,351	11,926	187,172	97,625
1987	2,365,539	1,911,286	22,966	1,934,252	217,881	-119,161	1,597,210	422,607	345,722	12,507	189,134	101,790
1988	2,531,046	2,033,805	29,879	2,063,684	239,821	-125,744	1,698,119	462,023	370,904	13,324	189,964	104,805
1989	2,662,543	2,089,101	38,279	2,127,380	245,177	-122,380	1,759,823	493,823	408,897	13,949	190,880	104,234
1990	2,788,540	2,191,921	28,600	2,220,521	268,227	-128,413	1,823,881	515,219	449,440	14,576	191,316	105,059
1991	2,943,411	2,333,030	30,728	2,363,758	285,879	-141,061	1,936,818	507,058	499,535	15,152	194,262	107,737
1992	3,242,232	2,586,378	42,083	2,628,461	313,926	-154,355	2,160,180	520,389	561,663	16,383	197,898	110,073
1993	3,357,613	2,689,786	42,145	2,731,931	330,864	-158,956	2,242,111	522,459	593,043	16,614	202,092	115,420
1994	3,615,366	2,908,418	49,758	2,958,176	362,317	-168,697	2,427,162	563,591	624,613	17,656	204,772	118,989
1995	3,837,170	3,051,745	40,681	3,092,426	376,909	-164,978	2,550,539	609,477	677,154	18,292	209,771	123,379
1996	4,029,481	3,175,050	50,046	3,225,096	387,875	-167,231	2,669,990	641,566	717,925	18,837	213,913	125,863
1997	4,246,400	3,347,957	58,176	3,406,133	406,134	-184,351	2,815,648	685,946	744,806	19,584	216,833	127,286
1998	4,525,504	3,595,756	53,280	3,649,036	430,791	-187,829	3,030,416	731,165	763,923	20,618	219,494	129,066
1999	4,705,427	3,769,537	64,028	3,833,565	452,252	-187,529	3,193,784	716,306	795,337	21,153	222,450	131,182
2000	5,032,132	4,053,396	59,895	4,113,291	480,186	-202,464	3,430,641	760,176	841,315	22,290	225,759	133,529
2001	5,101,312	4,000,545	67,259	4,067,804	481,031	-209,223	3,377,550	784,012	939,750	22,384	227,899	133,586
2002	5,191,067	4,053,152	53,278	4,106,430	485,808	-206,874	3,413,748	755,983	1,021,336	22,604	229,652	132,472
2003	5,463,183	4,269,634	56,891	4,326,525	504,543	-210,319	3,611,663	773,927	1,077,593	23,611	231,379	132,610
2004	5,911,189	4,615,097	87,841	4,702,938	533,278	-213,763	3,955,897	785,310	1,169,982	25,330	233,367	134,160
2005	6,196,557	4,834,366	72,484	4,906,850	564,522	-221,119	4,121,209	828,875	1,246,473	26,266	235,912	137,292
2006	6,647,278	5,156,531	46,027	5,202,558	610,026	-235,851	4,356,681	918,254	1,372,343	27,695	240,017	140,458
2007	6,919,278	5,192,720	51,206	5,243,926	620,837	-230,875	4,392,214	1,049,162	1,477,902	28,480	242,953	142,475
2008	7,323,200	5,258,888	34,525	5,293,413	645,655	-218,170	4,429,588	1,225,019	1,668,593	29,921	244,749	141,884
2009	7,227,808	5,005,707	10,877	5,016,584	624,674	-178,287	4,213,623	1,179,625	1,834,560	29,255	247,064	136,489
2010	7,468,164	5,196,556	5,828	5,202,384	649,967	-153,339	4,399,078	1,107,086	1,962,000	30,084	248,243	134,608
2011	7,968,234	5,428,197	-4,691	5,423,506	602,318	-124,728	4,696,460	1,261,323	2,010,451	32,058	248,560	132,420
2012	8,226,757	5,536,749	32,786	5,569,535	603,548	-105,677	4,860,310	1,329,393	2,037,054	33,140	248,245	132,227
2013	8,208,738	5,505,273	47,492	5,552,765	669,336	-62,612	4,820,817	1,297,543	2,090,378	33,265	246,769	130,907
2014	8,544,305	5,623,556	83,320	5,706,876	693,394	-41,597	4,971,885	1,377,172	2,195,248	34,754	245,849	131,699
2015	8,748,146	5,717,650	50,216	5,767,866	709,543	-35,087	5,023,236	1,434,958	2,289,952	35,581	245,866	133,293
2016	8,822,983	5,802,758	12,756	5,815,514	716,677	-48,163	5,050,674	1,405,312	2,366,997	35,914	245,667	134,893
2017	9,024,494	5,883,080	31,629	5,914,709	731,590	-58,758	5,124,361	1,474,752	2,425,381	36,673	246,078	134,171
2018	9,215,823	6,006,997	28,321	6,035,318	746,059	-62,472	5,226,787	1,483,373	2,505,663	37,544	245,468	134,775
2019	9,597,038	6,292,609	-8,738	6,283,871	789,243	-64,828	5,429,800	1,516,831	2,650,407	39,202	244,808	134,202
2020	10,254,852	6,339,131	-33,876	6,305,255	818,723	-58,537	5,427,995	1,578,708	3,248,149	41,972	244,328	130,835
2021	11,040,411	6,698,955	45,365	6,744,320	853,884	-85,591	5,804,845	1,572,905	3,662,661	44,979	245,456	133,468
2022	11,252,518	7,185,323	73,293	7,258,616	930,176	-108,283	6,220,157	1,674,119	3,358,242	45,543	247,072	138,296

Personal Income and Employment by Area: Fort Wayne, IN

(Thousands of dollars, except as noted.)

		Derivation of personal income										
		Earnings by place of work										
Year	Personal income, total	Nonfarm	Farm	Total	Less: Contributions for government social insurance	Plus: Adjustment for residence	Equals: Net earnings by place of residence	Plus: Dividends, interest, and rent	Plus: Personal current transfer receipts	Per capita personal income (dollars)	Population (persons)	Total employment
1970	1,251,254	1,178,506	11,708	1,190,214	81,043	-126,843	982,328	188,065	80,861	4,106	304,766	152,382
1971	1,354,873	1,257,945	17,794	1,275,739	89,462	-132,775	1,053,502	204,104	97,267	4,387	308,823	152,765
1972	1,497,105	1,410,354	14,889	1,425,243	106,847	-147,726	1,170,670	218,138	108,297	4,806	311,532	159,477
1973	1,679,408	1,569,140	32,600	1,601,740	137,402	-159,473	1,304,865	245,757	128,786	5,360	313,308	167,366
1974	1,828,313	1,708,204	18,081	1,726,285	155,494	-172,484	1,398,307	282,912	147,094	5,810	314,699	170,701
1975	1,915,448	1,710,079	24,075	1,734,154	153,150	-165,222	1,415,782	308,967	190,699	6,096	314,214	161,615
1976	2,144,531	1,948,741	24,212	1,972,953	177,179	-184,406	1,611,368	334,714	198,449	6,844	313,330	167,876
1977	2,415,644	2,222,315	24,996	2,247,311	201,940	-209,431	1,835,940	374,493	205,211	7,691	314,068	175,898
1978	2,699,790	2,519,197	12,337	2,531,534	235,690	-234,012	2,061,832	412,620	225,338	8,489	318,033	183,656
1979	3,003,770	2,797,653	18,519	2,816,172	270,657	-258,256	2,287,259	459,007	257,504	9,386	320,027	187,190
1980	3,197,327	2,833,664	16,204	2,849,868	272,481	-247,742	2,329,645	548,684	318,998	9,990	320,067	177,732
1981	3,482,869	3,011,049	1,418	3,012,467	311,348	-258,863	2,442,256	672,007	368,606	10,972	317,424	176,502
1982	3,557,101	2,948,232	5,277	2,953,509	309,870	-244,278	2,399,361	746,084	411,656	11,283	315,257	169,040
1983	3,689,959	3,060,397	-6,933	3,053,464	323,535	-241,766	2,488,163	761,389	440,407	11,794	312,857	168,483
1984	4,096,320	3,420,647	11,609	3,432,256	370,944	-260,669	2,800,643	839,633	456,044	13,100	312,693	176,940
1985	4,434,625	3,750,253	4,185	3,754,438	414,439	-287,931	3,052,068	904,445	478,112	14,032	316,042	184,637
1986	4,854,272	4,159,584	8,227	4,167,811	461,788	-322,765	3,383,258	965,764	505,250	15,152	320,376	193,672
1987	5,204,271	4,545,430	12,002	4,557,432	498,513	-352,386	3,706,533	986,277	511,461	15,997	325,330	202,368
1988	5,723,178	4,958,427	6,484	4,964,911	557,815	-384,652	4,022,444	1,136,995	563,739	17,501	327,022	209,654
1989	6,235,070	5,336,787	14,567	5,351,354	600,376	-406,446	4,344,532	1,284,619	605,919	19,003	328,102	216,802
1990	6,513,700	5,561,963	26,190	5,588,153	644,478	-427,193	4,516,482	1,347,954	649,264	19,775	329,394	217,786
1991	6,575,354	5,627,804	11,666	5,639,470	664,875	-443,324	4,531,271	1,320,796	723,287	19,778	332,450	216,692
1992	7,144,203	6,085,998	17,761	6,103,759	709,009	-463,646	4,931,104	1,362,540	850,559	21,294	335,501	220,647
1993	7,417,456	6,390,930	19,618	6,410,548	747,848	-487,882	5,174,818	1,365,918	876,720	21,901	338,686	223,960
1994	7,858,738	6,754,606	17,302	6,771,908	800,883	-496,866	5,474,159	1,457,441	927,138	23,033	341,199	228,361
1995	8,311,316	7,075,979	9,957	7,085,936	837,936	-486,251	5,761,749	1,600,528	949,039	24,156	344,066	233,165
1996	8,705,614	7,351,380	23,893	7,375,273	859,755	-507,382	6,008,136	1,707,271	990,207	25,034	347,757	235,092
1997	9,143,435	7,733,340	38,330	7,771,670	901,064	-557,354	6,313,252	1,823,114	1,007,069	26,024	351,342	239,764
1998	9,878,179	8,330,216	17,345	8,347,561	950,813	-549,857	6,846,891	1,969,044	1,062,244	27,771	355,706	244,426
1999	10,240,337	8,812,920	-3,065	8,809,855	994,717	-574,017	7,241,121	1,896,516	1,102,700	28,500	359,306	244,700
2000	10,778,871	9,174,804	6,689	9,181,493	1,024,677	-632,835	7,523,981	2,037,357	1,217,533	29,660	363,420	247,124
2001	10,769,169	9,032,200	13,199	9,045,399	1,028,352	-600,065	7,416,982	2,002,467	1,349,720	29,428	365,954	243,280
2002	11,001,414	9,170,386	23	9,170,409	1,050,921	-564,126	7,555,362	2,013,144	1,432,908	29,863	368,402	240,691
2003	11,006,940	9,146,418	26,499	9,172,917	1,063,960	-497,825	7,611,132	1,908,388	1,487,420	29,653	371,190	237,016
2004	11,469,235	9,394,671	42,245	9,436,916	1,101,861	-468,762	7,866,293	2,024,583	1,578,359	30,769	372,757	239,514
2005	11,844,187	9,733,044	21,543	9,754,587	1,151,067	-456,920	8,146,600	1,966,622	1,730,965	31,549	375,420	242,117
2006	12,728,782	10,335,577	24,687	10,360,264	1,209,308	-488,302	8,662,654	2,198,320	1,867,808	33,593	378,911	246,950
2007	13,232,748	10,637,707	30,204	10,667,911	1,246,997	-496,001	8,924,913	2,353,617	1,954,218	34,606	382,387	250,314
2008	13,547,307	10,575,743	47,443	10,623,186	1,250,374	-489,871	8,882,941	2,381,595	2,282,771	35,251	384,311	247,720
2009	13,029,171	9,964,127	49,892	10,014,019	1,199,777	-455,701	8,358,541	2,139,583	2,531,047	33,683	386,818	236,247
2010	13,457,252	10,330,335	22,073	10,352,408	1,222,271	-461,216	8,668,921	2,074,823	2,713,508	34,559	389,395	235,588
2011	14,385,390	10,881,559	47,827	10,929,386	1,136,708	-476,185	9,316,493	2,342,387	2,726,510	36,621	392,816	240,880
2012	15,081,679	11,271,946	77,824	11,349,770	1,164,351	-463,663	9,721,756	2,532,488	2,827,435	38,173	395,090	243,332
2013	15,140,209	11,365,152	151,849	11,517,001	1,330,736	-390,149	9,796,116	2,490,728	2,853,365	38,051	397,892	243,320
2014	15,963,859	11,926,340	85,455	12,011,795	1,385,752	-362,797	10,263,246	2,646,726	3,053,887	39,885	400,246	247,289
2015	16,782,312	12,555,578	24,537	12,580,115	1,458,136	-339,497	10,782,482	2,801,756	3,198,074	41,656	402,877	252,464
2016	17,199,955	12,865,764	51,346	12,917,110	1,478,578	-416,828	11,021,704	2,892,051	3,286,200	42,437	405,304	254,720
2017	17,732,850	13,308,946	45,509	13,354,455	1,532,713	-461,171	11,360,571	2,979,933	3,392,346	43,440	408,212	258,281
2018	18,797,298	14,120,878	46,003	14,166,881	1,622,743	-459,655	12,084,483	3,177,548	3,535,267	45,605	412,177	264,027
2019	19,517,598	14,730,009	36,696	14,766,705	1,708,631	-508,029	12,550,045	3,257,002	3,710,551	46,879	416,338	266,445
2020	21,053,482	15,159,505	62,424	15,221,929	1,781,199	-580,646	12,860,084	3,257,562	4,935,836	50,077	420,420	258,667
2021	23,568,331	16,520,131	114,651	16,634,782	1,913,494	-600,773	14,120,515	3,803,201	5,644,615	55,638	423,604	268,120
2022	24,319,839	17,913,570	102,627	18,016,197	2,062,877	-667,977	15,285,343	4,123,107	4,911,389	57,079	426,076	280,994

Personal Income and Employment by Area: Fresno, CA

(Thousands of dollars, except as noted.)

Year	Personal income, total	Derivation of personal income: Earnings by place of work: Nonfarm	Farm	Total	Less: Contributions for government social insurance	Plus: Adjustment for residence	Equals: Net earnings by place of residence	Plus: Dividends, interest, and rent	Plus: Personal current transfer receipts	Per capita personal income (dollars)	Population (persons)	Total employment
1970	1,653,102	1,109,998	163,187	1,273,185	75,618	-4,476	1,193,091	232,777	227,234	3,984	414,886	180,330
1971	1,799,992	1,225,503	164,215	1,389,718	85,514	-7,487	1,296,717	255,099	248,176	4,238	424,697	185,808
1972	2,036,193	1,390,133	213,278	1,603,411	100,608	-11,442	1,491,361	285,236	259,596	4,714	431,918	198,065
1973	2,339,957	1,570,947	293,372	1,864,319	129,483	-16,508	1,718,328	336,201	285,428	5,320	439,865	206,954
1974	2,740,807	1,763,526	430,003	2,193,529	149,994	-23,959	2,019,576	389,487	331,744	6,092	449,886	216,106
1975	2,963,789	1,964,177	335,593	2,299,770	162,430	-33,144	2,104,196	445,799	413,794	6,385	464,183	222,296
1976	3,397,744	2,227,009	456,376	2,683,385	187,712	-43,594	2,452,079	485,010	460,655	7,121	477,162	231,059
1977	3,628,639	2,495,762	367,290	2,863,052	214,584	-54,572	2,593,896	546,221	488,522	7,420	489,016	239,078
1978	4,040,140	2,864,223	324,389	3,188,612	250,027	-68,567	2,870,018	632,586	537,536	8,120	497,564	249,946
1979	4,792,411	3,311,998	539,229	3,851,227	303,647	-88,968	3,458,612	740,793	593,006	9,465	506,332	267,295
1980	5,542,361	3,628,152	717,272	4,345,424	326,936	-107,200	3,911,288	928,120	702,953	10,706	517,679	275,120
1981	5,807,285	3,879,272	444,440	4,323,712	379,992	-93,593	3,850,127	1,117,969	839,189	10,980	528,891	275,530
1982	6,123,544	4,010,237	471,836	4,482,073	401,117	-100,053	3,980,903	1,206,259	936,382	11,308	541,500	277,400
1983	6,445,527	4,302,610	347,771	4,650,381	437,230	-102,263	4,110,888	1,308,784	1,025,855	11,595	555,873	284,985
1984	7,113,502	4,687,867	487,089	5,174,956	495,426	-109,563	4,569,967	1,438,541	1,104,994	12,434	572,091	289,156
1985	7,643,191	4,986,147	583,227	5,569,374	532,729	-114,982	4,921,663	1,512,238	1,209,290	13,086	584,070	292,647
1986	8,157,589	5,335,201	634,627	5,969,828	579,005	-117,592	5,273,231	1,573,394	1,310,964	13,742	593,621	296,092
1987	8,884,599	5,873,438	806,603	6,680,041	641,395	-126,559	5,912,087	1,602,469	1,370,043	14,593	608,831	308,325
1988	9,566,290	6,374,272	855,872	7,230,144	718,300	-138,381	6,373,463	1,707,308	1,485,519	15,241	627,658	320,730
1989	10,370,017	6,867,247	832,276	7,699,523	785,036	-157,434	6,757,053	1,974,657	1,638,307	15,935	650,755	328,682
1990	11,303,948	7,597,429	880,645	8,478,074	861,373	-181,107	7,435,594	2,011,737	1,856,617	16,814	672,302	342,583
1991	11,862,727	8,138,502	690,165	8,828,667	924,760	-184,097	7,719,810	2,053,860	2,089,057	17,153	691,569	351,296
1992	12,608,219	8,519,837	743,824	9,263,661	961,799	-178,295	8,123,567	2,037,744	2,446,908	17,751	710,263	347,643
1993	13,348,277	8,957,593	890,254	9,847,847	1,007,233	-189,181	8,651,433	2,105,511	2,591,333	18,364	726,859	356,938
1994	13,661,123	9,296,839	828,600	10,125,439	1,043,404	-190,868	8,891,167	2,191,282	2,578,674	18,465	739,835	364,559
1995	14,205,895	9,619,847	725,940	10,345,787	1,062,270	-189,176	9,094,341	2,421,152	2,690,402	18,953	749,534	377,757
1996	14,842,295	9,940,951	834,813	10,775,764	1,063,581	-186,490	9,525,693	2,494,520	2,822,082	19,493	761,409	384,048
1997	15,261,271	10,297,980	829,925	11,127,905	1,082,842	-168,788	9,876,275	2,582,766	2,802,230	19,784	771,391	379,588
1998	16,165,777	11,076,614	705,103	11,781,717	1,136,945	-164,956	10,479,816	2,662,143	3,023,818	20,762	778,615	392,386
1999	17,127,818	11,660,991	897,326	12,558,317	1,195,780	-159,393	11,203,144	2,741,207	3,183,467	21,697	789,405	395,669
2000	18,484,717	13,044,566	807,023	13,851,589	1,302,738	-151,134	12,397,717	2,813,820	3,273,180	23,069	801,288	400,136
2001	19,073,727	13,553,352	610,836	14,164,188	1,459,012	-170,559	12,534,617	2,846,715	3,692,395	23,460	813,021	399,740
2002	20,421,046	14,609,200	823,322	15,432,522	1,595,683	-204,210	13,632,629	2,844,125	3,944,292	24,611	829,762	410,519
2003	21,910,996	15,465,833	1,178,664	16,644,497	1,705,909	-206,142	14,732,446	2,957,950	4,220,600	25,863	847,193	411,429
2004	23,181,267	16,608,672	1,363,577	17,972,249	1,889,248	-232,293	15,850,708	2,887,479	4,443,080	26,923	861,035	416,395
2005	24,077,832	17,368,855	1,282,863	18,651,718	1,984,224	-237,614	16,429,880	2,984,879	4,663,073	27,597	872,470	424,619
2006	25,753,508	18,644,299	1,196,371	19,840,670	2,044,601	-213,735	17,582,334	3,178,696	4,992,478	29,137	883,862	435,405
2007	27,140,658	19,247,759	1,227,120	20,474,879	2,080,231	-231,707	18,162,941	3,609,113	5,368,604	30,293	895,933	445,269
2008	27,702,269	19,151,507	844,357	19,995,864	2,124,973	-212,818	17,658,073	4,030,188	6,014,008	30,454	909,630	441,478
2009	27,806,136	18,475,104	1,294,765	19,769,869	2,076,967	-228,230	17,464,672	3,686,099	6,655,365	30,176	921,478	424,085
2010	29,066,562	18,985,472	1,404,635	20,390,107	2,059,165	-246,499	18,084,443	3,581,251	7,400,868	31,181	932,185	420,803
2011	30,713,635	19,726,945	1,760,772	21,487,717	1,935,997	-255,150	19,296,570	3,972,545	7,444,520	32,669	940,133	426,274
2012	31,502,991	20,131,049	1,687,737	21,818,786	1,984,421	-206,942	19,627,423	4,285,833	7,589,735	33,288	946,381	439,614
2013	32,824,378	20,868,782	2,237,087	23,105,869	2,306,955	-208,624	20,590,290	4,283,737	7,950,351	34,426	953,473	455,369
2014	35,044,607	21,858,350	2,433,036	24,291,386	2,407,632	-209,702	21,674,052	4,851,698	8,518,857	36,385	963,149	465,006
2015	37,251,040	23,174,199	2,279,580	25,453,779	2,531,633	-283,212	22,638,934	5,313,625	9,298,481	38,296	972,726	475,907
2016	38,323,050	24,290,972	1,930,734	26,221,706	2,672,460	-283,372	23,265,874	5,405,176	9,652,000	39,072	980,843	486,869
2017	39,208,890	25,398,645	1,994,839	27,393,484	2,790,214	-293,662	24,309,608	5,511,729	9,387,553	39,600	990,130	496,577
2018	40,504,743	26,722,719	1,550,770	28,273,489	2,948,319	-327,087	24,998,083	5,655,216	9,851,444	40,606	997,501	508,659
2019	42,828,739	28,455,232	1,409,401	29,864,633	3,149,898	-396,212	26,318,523	6,007,044	10,503,172	42,622	1,004,849	519,760
2020	48,552,515	29,587,196	1,533,125	31,120,321	3,250,655	-375,897	27,493,769	6,145,912	14,912,834	48,095	1,009,503	505,885
2021	52,363,942	31,974,060	1,420,187	33,394,247	3,511,241	-525,250	29,357,756	6,450,753	16,555,433	51,692	1,012,992	524,611
2022	51,316,407	33,973,579	1,342,946	35,316,525	3,865,419	-658,122	30,792,984	6,845,221	13,678,202	50,549	1,015,190	551,760

Personal Income and Employment by Area: Gadsden, AL

(Thousands of dollars, except as noted.)

Year	Personal income, total	Derivation of personal income: Earnings by place of work: Nonfarm	Farm	Total	Less: Contributions for government social insurance	Plus: Adjustment for residence	Equals: Net earnings by place of residence	Plus: Dividends, interest, and rent	Plus: Personal current transfer receipts	Per capita personal income (dollars)	Population (persons)	Total employment
1970	283,339	229,243	2,232	231,475	16,770	6,374	221,079	29,382	32,878	3,010	94,134	35,044
1971	311,494	242,333	2,771	245,104	18,185	11,363	238,282	32,903	40,309	3,283	94,887	35,388
1972	349,727	274,756	3,487	278,243	21,681	13,044	269,606	36,166	43,955	3,652	95,758	36,119
1973	387,651	304,307	5,490	309,797	27,982	14,122	295,937	41,468	50,246	4,035	96,072	37,400
1974	425,798	329,803	2,314	332,117	31,337	16,052	316,832	49,118	59,848	4,409	96,579	37,366
1975	471,815	346,616	5,355	351,971	32,685	19,206	338,492	56,235	77,088	4,818	97,936	36,837
1976	515,075	378,681	5,050	383,731	36,323	23,586	370,994	61,110	82,971	5,204	98,984	36,805
1977	589,445	448,970	5,004	453,974	43,210	23,590	434,354	68,414	86,677	5,884	100,171	39,116
1978	670,912	519,574	6,142	525,716	51,079	25,699	500,336	78,024	92,552	6,595	101,731	41,070
1979	752,535	584,238	5,449	589,687	59,354	27,393	557,726	88,334	106,475	7,311	102,937	42,239
1980	822,089	614,799	-41	614,758	62,117	35,288	587,929	107,735	126,425	7,973	103,112	41,418
1981	915,339	664,594	8,550	673,144	72,394	40,580	641,330	130,156	143,853	8,874	103,143	40,735
1982	928,146	638,288	4,786	643,074	71,414	46,895	618,555	146,189	163,402	9,053	102,524	38,726
1983	986,443	677,930	5,322	683,252	77,162	46,113	652,203	157,999	176,241	9,604	102,707	38,722
1984	1,077,646	744,516	4,324	748,840	86,808	50,694	712,726	178,449	186,471	10,533	102,307	40,376
1985	1,130,735	771,669	6,044	777,713	90,103	57,510	745,120	191,042	194,573	11,054	102,291	40,925
1986	1,177,240	789,320	8,419	797,739	91,110	62,145	768,774	204,468	203,998	11,580	101,664	40,944
1987	1,246,697	866,238	3,147	869,385	98,401	64,708	835,692	203,203	207,802	12,305	101,314	41,863
1988	1,329,026	920,953	8,917	929,870	107,870	73,322	895,322	219,327	214,377	13,194	100,728	42,754
1989	1,411,511	934,795	13,807	948,602	109,714	82,360	921,248	246,121	244,142	14,069	100,327	43,434
1990	1,457,860	947,542	12,087	959,629	111,742	86,859	934,746	257,702	265,412	14,606	99,809	43,565
1991	1,501,111	962,533	12,656	975,189	114,402	91,643	952,430	252,462	296,219	14,957	100,365	43,913
1992	1,613,768	1,050,939	13,248	1,064,187	123,013	92,086	1,033,260	250,681	329,827	15,986	100,950	44,463
1993	1,691,500	1,101,830	13,949	1,115,779	131,091	99,478	1,084,166	262,303	345,031	16,696	101,310	46,081
1994	1,792,329	1,182,869	17,652	1,200,521	141,431	87,771	1,146,861	273,218	372,250	17,535	102,213	46,709
1995	1,854,557	1,232,100	9,837	1,241,937	149,036	81,420	1,174,321	289,244	390,992	18,121	102,342	47,735
1996	1,941,762	1,229,260	16,302	1,245,562	147,524	128,938	1,226,976	297,971	416,815	18,841	103,063	48,513
1997	2,041,367	1,280,513	20,697	1,301,210	153,033	138,860	1,287,037	321,386	432,944	19,604	104,129	49,701
1998	2,121,317	1,334,617	20,001	1,354,618	157,471	141,853	1,339,000	333,304	449,013	20,326	104,367	49,727
1999	2,165,964	1,344,520	21,306	1,365,826	157,854	161,326	1,369,298	328,697	467,969	20,826	104,002	49,023
2000	2,243,729	1,377,546	17,878	1,395,424	160,962	167,009	1,401,471	346,427	495,831	21,723	103,286	49,443
2001	2,294,582	1,356,832	23,460	1,380,292	162,238	172,714	1,390,768	360,200	543,614	22,283	102,976	48,338
2002	2,370,659	1,411,975	16,869	1,428,844	169,052	175,594	1,435,386	356,362	578,911	23,019	102,988	49,062
2003	2,455,666	1,436,093	20,140	1,456,233	172,621	189,229	1,472,841	377,855	604,970	23,836	103,025	48,001
2004	2,586,601	1,526,186	31,030	1,557,216	182,586	204,384	1,579,014	380,386	627,201	25,093	103,080	49,326
2005	2,675,577	1,588,921	12,341	1,601,262	191,453	218,085	1,627,894	376,444	671,239	25,933	103,174	50,113
2006	2,764,680	1,638,189	-4,338	1,633,851	198,620	231,098	1,666,329	378,922	719,429	26,705	103,528	49,827
2007	2,940,430	1,676,159	2,942	1,679,101	205,189	249,046	1,722,958	441,857	775,615	28,302	103,893	49,836
2008	3,038,482	1,677,938	4,786	1,682,724	211,696	251,955	1,722,983	467,338	848,161	29,158	104,206	49,618
2009	3,031,828	1,651,780	4,698	1,656,478	207,648	225,111	1,673,941	439,299	918,588	29,085	104,239	46,997
2010	3,153,919	1,716,034	4,231	1,720,265	216,883	216,939	1,720,321	443,395	990,203	30,190	104,468	46,791
2011	3,200,276	1,751,984	-7,976	1,744,008	198,850	209,507	1,754,665	459,403	986,208	30,626	104,495	48,418
2012	3,237,697	1,767,854	-3,004	1,764,850	200,997	211,554	1,775,407	468,281	994,009	30,977	104,521	48,497
2013	3,247,727	1,774,371	18,050	1,792,421	226,800	208,203	1,773,824	453,891	1,020,012	31,154	104,249	48,595
2014	3,349,630	1,833,072	16,405	1,849,477	232,709	215,923	1,832,691	461,645	1,055,294	32,245	103,880	49,579
2015	3,491,980	1,884,394	19,451	1,903,845	239,623	221,250	1,885,472	498,331	1,108,177	33,706	103,601	49,738
2016	3,543,313	1,933,240	5,247	1,938,487	244,703	231,555	1,925,339	485,762	1,132,212	34,201	103,603	50,609
2017	3,648,847	1,972,030	13,776	1,985,806	251,755	240,716	1,974,767	506,519	1,167,561	35,134	103,854	50,445
2018	3,745,235	2,022,666	11,930	2,034,596	262,493	253,976	2,026,079	502,966	1,216,190	36,135	103,646	50,729
2019	3,855,996	2,058,412	5,253	2,063,665	263,508	276,614	2,076,771	512,707	1,266,518	37,278	103,440	49,726
2020	4,097,213	2,043,174	-4,149	2,039,025	269,434	292,810	2,062,401	511,422	1,523,390	39,607	103,447	46,511
2021	4,390,748	2,064,949	16,106	2,081,055	270,277	337,081	2,147,859	542,990	1,699,899	42,571	103,139	46,310
2022	4,427,730	2,178,688	24,776	2,203,464	289,896	366,938	2,280,506	585,425	1,561,799	42,951	103,088	47,489

Personal Income and Employment by Area: Gainesville, FL

(Thousands of dollars, except as noted.)

Year	Personal income, total	Derivation of personal income: Earnings by place of work: Nonfarm	Farm	Total	Less: Contributions for government social insurance	Plus: Adjustment for residence	Equals: Net earnings by place of residence	Plus: Dividends, interest, and rent	Plus: Personal current transfer receipts	Per capita personal income (dollars)	Population (persons)	Total employment
1970	396,092	319,005	9,953	328,958	18,398	-11,375	299,185	65,401	31,506	3,259	121,523	54,958
1971	452,791	360,215	12,364	372,579	21,920	-13,104	337,555	75,938	39,298	3,600	125,771	57,404
1972	538,804	434,223	13,202	447,425	27,662	-16,356	403,407	89,489	45,908	3,891	138,486	63,264
1973	638,408	513,894	19,483	533,377	38,046	-18,475	476,856	107,075	54,477	4,378	145,835	68,634
1974	714,188	572,052	15,593	587,645	44,690	-20,812	522,143	126,094	65,951	4,702	151,894	71,126
1975	794,165	618,885	14,930	633,815	48,432	-20,427	564,956	142,584	86,625	5,146	154,323	71,919
1976	863,239	669,751	15,419	685,170	54,539	-21,703	608,928	155,316	98,995	5,566	155,080	71,990
1977	950,893	746,590	8,853	755,443	61,739	-24,356	669,348	173,016	108,529	5,923	160,544	75,621
1978	1,091,052	851,433	15,553	866,986	73,493	-26,123	767,370	201,727	121,955	6,558	166,359	80,598
1979	1,238,232	951,846	25,618	977,464	86,763	-26,338	864,363	229,672	144,197	7,240	171,015	84,268
1980	1,426,641	1,068,586	22,778	1,091,364	95,899	-28,203	967,262	286,674	172,705	8,007	178,181	87,702
1981	1,626,614	1,188,562	23,343	1,211,905	115,566	-24,132	1,072,207	352,783	201,624	8,910	182,554	89,459
1982	1,796,581	1,299,988	32,222	1,332,210	129,679	-28,423	1,174,108	398,517	223,956	9,574	187,659	92,371
1983	1,991,623	1,441,615	28,874	1,470,489	143,658	-34,281	1,292,550	449,560	249,513	10,428	190,981	95,019
1984	2,237,125	1,643,088	26,223	1,669,311	166,942	-43,929	1,458,440	509,386	269,299	11,446	195,442	100,960
1985	2,471,377	1,834,208	22,544	1,856,752	189,549	-50,563	1,616,640	560,678	294,059	12,334	200,365	106,901
1986	2,645,867	1,963,346	21,275	1,984,621	206,651	-58,322	1,719,648	609,382	316,837	13,008	203,408	111,952
1987	2,831,791	2,111,233	19,524	2,130,757	217,410	-63,429	1,849,918	643,100	338,773	13,695	206,776	112,989
1988	3,106,938	2,317,538	28,069	2,345,607	248,939	-75,699	2,020,969	716,088	369,881	14,787	210,108	117,564
1989	3,427,935	2,511,806	33,835	2,545,641	270,615	-87,515	2,187,511	814,721	425,703	16,018	214,001	120,751
1990	3,677,064	2,695,484	36,644	2,732,128	287,709	-98,993	2,345,426	858,986	472,652	16,821	218,597	124,697
1991	3,882,497	2,838,750	44,006	2,882,756	305,118	-106,009	2,471,629	877,192	533,676	17,232	225,313	125,671
1992	4,119,806	3,022,310	62,326	3,084,636	324,930	-117,038	2,642,668	869,659	607,479	17,804	231,403	126,156
1993	4,370,320	3,222,947	62,155	3,285,102	343,709	-127,572	2,813,821	902,765	653,734	18,430	237,132	131,965
1994	4,599,587	3,412,550	59,474	3,472,024	367,876	-149,841	2,954,307	952,935	692,345	19,136	240,362	136,299
1995	4,902,110	3,578,550	52,550	3,631,100	385,808	-159,007	3,086,285	1,068,512	747,313	19,883	246,551	140,765
1996	5,148,435	3,768,211	56,788	3,824,999	404,052	-185,149	3,235,798	1,122,060	790,577	20,524	250,845	144,926
1997	5,456,940	3,977,666	66,937	4,044,603	427,976	-206,583	3,410,044	1,229,252	817,644	21,348	255,618	146,908
1998	5,818,400	4,297,882	70,920	4,368,802	460,320	-236,830	3,671,652	1,318,236	828,512	22,411	259,624	152,389
1999	6,059,087	4,526,172	77,583	4,603,755	482,434	-212,167	3,909,154	1,293,743	856,190	22,968	263,802	155,906
2000	6,429,405	4,791,405	67,219	4,858,624	508,786	-237,074	4,112,764	1,377,440	939,201	24,017	267,698	160,520
2001	6,861,196	5,112,522	79,957	5,192,479	543,138	-251,381	4,397,960	1,419,554	1,043,682	25,307	271,119	165,423
2002	7,052,130	5,372,620	51,395	5,424,015	570,467	-261,315	4,592,233	1,330,904	1,128,993	25,637	275,080	167,114
2003	7,326,439	5,532,747	52,119	5,584,866	589,090	-247,943	4,747,833	1,365,579	1,213,027	26,301	278,563	168,430
2004	8,101,349	6,216,476	65,174	6,281,650	662,904	-312,252	5,306,494	1,573,010	1,221,845	28,662	282,648	172,983
2005	8,697,787	6,626,725	65,680	6,692,405	711,756	-319,007	5,661,642	1,675,334	1,360,811	30,210	287,912	176,107
2006	9,337,386	7,032,069	54,540	7,086,609	763,660	-331,958	5,990,991	1,926,908	1,419,487	31,633	295,176	179,852
2007	9,806,940	7,292,156	33,717	7,325,873	799,537	-337,833	6,188,503	2,106,060	1,512,377	32,744	299,499	181,975
2008	10,197,715	7,340,773	30,139	7,370,912	816,783	-346,587	6,207,542	2,245,964	1,744,209	33,712	302,494	179,826
2009	9,917,804	7,194,417	23,995	7,218,412	811,302	-348,752	6,058,358	1,982,615	1,876,831	32,585	304,366	172,803
2010	10,378,357	7,376,532	53,291	7,429,823	819,419	-375,766	6,234,638	2,072,150	2,071,569	33,969	305,521	170,947
2011	10,768,138	7,398,171	49,182	7,447,353	736,727	-397,383	6,313,243	2,280,141	2,174,754	34,975	307,878	171,746
2012	10,803,441	7,557,166	95,515	7,652,681	764,429	-438,851	6,449,401	2,222,051	2,131,989	34,867	309,848	172,918
2013	10,856,204	7,738,604	90,716	7,829,320	886,230	-465,489	6,477,601	2,168,220	2,210,383	34,886	311,192	174,949
2014	11,468,358	8,038,531	140,798	8,179,329	922,456	-457,060	6,799,813	2,339,766	2,328,779	36,427	314,827	179,714
2015	11,971,451	8,402,327	156,192	8,558,519	955,123	-473,092	7,130,304	2,392,691	2,448,456	37,426	319,868	184,354
2016	12,412,244	8,750,243	123,167	8,873,410	992,977	-499,245	7,381,188	2,491,286	2,539,770	38,071	326,030	187,741
2017	13,254,250	9,243,170	159,309	9,402,479	1,048,633	-557,863	7,795,983	2,779,508	2,678,759	40,176	329,906	193,958
2018	14,000,453	9,836,374	117,525	9,953,899	1,122,621	-596,520	8,234,758	2,958,146	2,807,549	41,888	334,234	198,963
2019	14,745,153	10,268,424	126,774	10,395,198	1,188,644	-621,804	8,584,750	3,165,375	2,995,028	43,835	336,378	202,201
2020	15,809,345	10,749,052	125,218	10,874,270	1,258,268	-682,958	8,933,044	3,129,636	3,746,665	46,405	340,684	200,198
2021	17,388,795	11,636,074	133,695	11,769,769	1,337,861	-798,215	9,633,693	3,464,835	4,290,267	50,508	344,281	207,637
2022	17,724,889	12,352,427	122,321	12,474,748	1,446,032	-837,180	10,191,536	3,646,760	3,886,593	50,892	348,282	214,690

Personal Income and Employment by Area: Gainesville, GA

(Thousands of dollars, except as noted.)

Year	Personal income, total	Derivation of personal income: Earnings by place of work: Nonfarm	Farm	Total	Less: Contributions for government social insurance	Plus: Adjustment for residence	Equals: Net earnings by place of residence	Plus: Dividends, interest, and rent	Plus: Personal current transfer receipts	Per capita personal income (dollars)	Population (persons)	Total employment
1970	196,115	166,060	3,899	169,959	10,560	-984	158,415	22,573	15,127	3,279	59,814	29,685
1971	211,988	176,451	3,140	179,591	11,564	239	168,266	25,655	18,067	3,419	62,007	30,211
1972	241,760	199,657	4,894	204,551	13,765	1,616	192,402	28,815	20,543	3,813	63,406	30,977
1973	275,604	217,549	12,623	230,172	17,172	3,451	216,451	34,675	24,478	4,187	65,831	31,482
1974	300,115	237,747	5,711	243,458	19,557	3,811	227,712	41,882	30,521	4,494	66,786	32,098
1975	337,306	245,702	15,535	261,237	19,800	5,242	246,679	47,460	43,167	4,884	69,063	31,241
1976	381,368	286,568	16,659	303,227	23,544	6,513	286,196	50,643	44,529	5,477	69,626	33,292
1977	431,665	331,720	15,914	347,634	27,087	8,017	328,564	55,649	47,452	6,064	71,185	35,486
1978	497,468	386,312	17,534	403,846	32,505	9,659	381,000	64,226	52,242	6,858	72,534	37,509
1979	559,805	444,692	9,311	454,003	39,116	11,140	426,027	74,484	59,294	7,537	74,275	39,816
1980	637,199	487,502	2,974	490,476	42,989	19,235	466,722	97,052	73,425	8,376	76,074	39,846
1981	716,166	533,787	5,942	539,729	50,546	20,331	509,514	123,038	83,614	9,225	77,629	40,631
1982	769,892	557,933	10,285	568,218	53,837	24,027	538,408	137,625	93,859	9,766	78,832	40,711
1983	845,135	614,201	9,698	623,899	59,650	26,538	590,787	153,022	101,326	10,528	80,278	42,095
1984	986,283	711,590	29,324	740,914	71,046	28,735	698,603	180,552	107,128	12,024	82,024	45,932
1985	1,084,768	799,866	24,107	823,973	81,984	29,615	771,604	199,705	113,459	12,887	84,174	48,216
1986	1,203,978	880,117	40,447	920,564	91,438	30,729	859,855	223,557	120,566	13,830	87,054	49,668
1987	1,276,014	974,783	25,526	1,000,309	101,462	25,453	924,300	225,622	126,092	14,322	89,092	51,538
1988	1,396,858	1,058,771	35,774	1,094,545	113,502	23,561	1,004,604	253,099	139,155	15,252	91,583	53,765
1989	1,520,809	1,123,222	49,850	1,173,072	121,110	17,584	1,069,546	297,626	153,637	16,202	93,865	55,176
1990	1,613,312	1,199,398	41,786	1,241,184	129,249	9,654	1,121,589	318,605	173,118	16,768	96,215	55,485
1991	1,693,433	1,239,543	41,418	1,280,961	135,421	16,961	1,162,501	328,875	202,057	17,015	99,525	55,068
1992	1,836,882	1,357,096	38,613	1,395,709	145,832	21,789	1,271,666	332,551	232,665	17,976	102,186	56,420
1993	1,991,007	1,497,728	40,924	1,538,652	161,353	10,821	1,388,120	352,780	250,107	18,800	105,903	60,311
1994	2,183,013	1,650,342	37,617	1,687,959	178,913	6,591	1,515,637	393,732	273,644	19,840	110,029	64,802
1995	2,334,543	1,761,205	33,533	1,794,738	190,092	13,408	1,618,054	414,728	301,761	20,395	114,464	67,737
1996	2,538,002	1,882,168	39,090	1,921,258	200,645	29,986	1,750,599	462,014	325,389	21,301	119,147	69,621
1997	2,688,503	2,016,335	34,976	2,051,311	212,011	30,223	1,869,523	484,359	334,621	21,643	124,219	71,817
1998	2,998,716	2,245,116	48,776	2,293,892	230,680	42,724	2,105,936	548,287	344,493	23,213	129,182	74,904
1999	3,286,428	2,510,516	46,581	2,557,097	254,113	50,162	2,353,146	569,094	364,188	24,383	134,781	77,324
2000	3,569,281	2,711,986	37,046	2,749,032	274,545	47,380	2,521,867	639,641	407,773	25,315	140,993	81,590
2001	3,774,259	2,812,035	53,698	2,865,733	290,758	72,104	2,647,079	675,451	451,729	25,825	146,148	81,018
2002	3,962,122	2,951,112	32,710	2,983,822	304,070	75,800	2,755,552	688,447	518,123	26,374	150,229	81,385
2003	4,257,713	3,190,519	32,565	3,223,084	321,804	84,388	2,985,668	741,603	530,442	27,727	153,561	83,282
2004	4,600,613	3,375,690	49,591	3,425,281	351,857	190,708	3,264,132	745,116	591,365	29,419	156,385	85,879
2005	4,958,198	3,610,846	46,660	3,657,506	373,833	151,015	3,434,688	864,590	658,920	30,800	160,979	89,025
2006	5,268,703	3,795,048	16,373	3,811,421	399,304	200,797	3,612,914	933,249	722,540	31,639	166,524	92,746
2007	5,558,505	3,916,568	15,469	3,932,037	413,942	264,711	3,782,806	993,278	782,421	32,233	172,446	97,307
2008	5,573,024	3,936,173	20,042	3,956,215	440,314	58,833	3,574,734	1,088,300	909,990	31,437	177,277	97,751
2009	5,467,205	3,736,781	12,360	3,749,141	413,832	63,160	3,398,469	1,049,689	1,019,047	30,628	178,503	92,173
2010	5,563,350	3,835,725	4,380	3,840,105	423,979	57,157	3,473,283	963,426	1,126,641	30,906	180,008	92,865
2011	6,022,774	4,192,635	-7,150	4,185,485	403,320	-48,005	3,734,160	1,104,793	1,183,821	33,095	181,983	95,937
2012	6,217,654	4,247,003	18,172	4,265,175	411,275	62,865	3,916,765	1,115,512	1,185,377	33,873	183,559	96,178
2013	6,413,370	4,519,215	21,997	4,541,212	494,402	36,574	4,083,384	1,088,323	1,241,663	34,552	185,613	99,870
2014	6,872,113	4,855,158	27,317	4,882,475	524,300	35,506	4,393,681	1,201,391	1,277,041	36,548	188,031	102,352
2015	7,477,842	5,324,125	31,246	5,355,371	568,453	-22,074	4,764,844	1,336,096	1,376,902	39,185	190,834	107,559
2016	7,851,741	5,565,324	11,563	5,576,887	594,218	51,179	5,033,848	1,382,702	1,435,191	40,379	194,452	111,532
2017	8,412,543	6,028,041	16,932	6,044,973	637,103	-33,248	5,374,622	1,550,994	1,486,927	42,741	196,827	116,266
2018	8,979,337	6,400,531	10,926	6,411,457	686,427	-61,271	5,663,759	1,732,292	1,583,286	45,109	199,059	119,642
2019	9,341,548	6,616,857	2,614	6,619,471	732,156	24,878	5,912,193	1,782,198	1,647,157	46,326	201,647	121,182
2020	10,188,484	6,850,127	-15,049	6,835,078	760,454	51,521	6,126,145	1,882,970	2,179,369	50,009	203,735	121,919
2021	11,442,825	7,578,432	691	7,579,123	846,786	222,917	6,955,254	2,015,327	2,472,244	55,175	207,393	128,673
2022	12,211,909	8,623,580	34,144	8,657,724	967,051	283,169	7,973,842	2,116,595	2,121,472	57,416	212,692	136,460

Personal Income and Employment by Area: Gettysburg, PA

(Thousands of dollars, except as noted.)

Year	Personal income, total	Derivation of personal income: Earnings by place of work: Nonfarm	Earnings by place of work: Farm	Earnings by place of work: Total	Less: Contributions for government social insurance	Plus: Adjustment for residence	Equals: Net earnings by place of residence	Plus: Dividends, interest, and rent	Plus: Personal current transfer receipts	Per capita personal income (dollars)	Population (persons)	Total employment
1970	220,477	127,784	8,495	136,279	9,340	45,619	172,558	30,080	17,839	3,857	57,165	24,009
1971	237,257	135,820	6,958	142,778	10,344	51,401	183,835	32,904	20,518	4,047	58,628	23,992
1972	267,285	148,867	7,988	156,855	11,787	61,140	206,208	36,362	24,715	4,395	60,815	24,380
1973	301,015	164,296	11,039	175,335	14,854	70,682	231,163	42,540	27,312	4,806	62,627	25,256
1974	335,085	175,629	15,221	190,850	16,536	80,121	254,435	48,094	32,556	5,275	63,523	24,999
1975	363,640	184,376	9,788	194,164	16,850	87,465	264,779	55,566	43,295	5,697	63,834	24,443
1976	414,886	211,826	16,688	228,514	19,568	98,477	307,423	59,358	48,105	6,439	64,435	25,654
1977	458,548	230,076	18,720	248,796	21,206	114,087	341,677	66,439	50,432	7,012	65,398	26,298
1978	511,846	264,210	10,236	274,446	24,871	133,925	383,500	74,873	53,473	7,728	66,235	27,477
1979	574,468	289,874	10,133	300,007	28,216	155,522	427,313	87,780	59,375	8,522	67,409	28,152
1980	644,015	316,371	5,865	322,236	31,259	173,845	464,822	110,201	68,992	9,400	68,513	28,790
1981	710,624	345,427	6,185	351,612	36,658	182,038	496,992	133,737	79,895	10,224	69,506	28,581
1982	767,382	361,305	15,662	376,967	38,529	181,085	519,523	154,568	93,291	10,897	70,422	28,659
1983	805,023	394,083	8,998	403,081	42,342	185,341	546,080	157,456	101,487	11,390	70,679	29,204
1984	885,695	436,075	18,378	454,453	48,502	203,780	609,731	176,132	99,832	12,601	70,290	30,229
1985	950,181	472,516	17,063	489,579	53,468	217,442	653,553	189,883	106,745	13,375	71,043	31,718
1986	1,026,077	511,426	27,130	538,556	58,291	228,438	708,703	203,679	113,695	14,154	72,492	32,650
1987	1,094,292	567,064	21,028	588,092	64,203	246,419	770,308	205,924	118,060	14,793	73,976	34,638
1988	1,201,246	630,820	22,895	653,715	72,596	266,978	848,097	224,063	129,086	15,947	75,326	35,985
1989	1,306,854	691,461	19,197	710,658	78,200	279,016	911,474	254,921	140,459	17,059	76,609	36,964
1990	1,397,769	737,450	29,588	767,038	83,836	295,928	979,130	261,588	157,051	17,739	78,797	37,551
1991	1,450,555	753,256	31,501	784,757	87,711	297,569	994,615	272,749	183,191	18,012	80,531	37,987
1992	1,540,246	816,671	40,966	857,637	94,768	298,829	1,061,698	277,178	201,370	18,836	81,771	38,543
1993	1,589,506	860,235	33,922	894,157	101,617	302,232	1,094,772	282,949	211,785	19,148	83,013	38,395
1994	1,628,413	896,407	19,829	916,236	108,842	302,310	1,109,704	293,875	224,834	19,343	84,186	39,636
1995	1,727,050	918,521	29,863	948,384	112,176	311,242	1,147,450	341,902	237,698	20,303	85,063	40,120
1996	1,833,759	941,005	41,584	982,589	112,157	334,327	1,204,759	371,286	257,714	21,260	86,252	40,211
1997	1,959,225	977,396	33,758	1,011,154	114,458	394,644	1,291,340	401,297	266,588	22,327	87,751	40,491
1998	2,067,521	1,057,905	25,231	1,083,136	120,725	397,152	1,359,563	430,645	277,313	23,211	89,074	43,308
1999	2,208,179	1,173,198	32,651	1,205,849	129,700	411,820	1,487,969	424,441	295,769	24,437	90,363	44,773
2000	2,388,674	1,249,309	19,880	1,269,189	137,388	469,514	1,601,315	464,898	322,461	26,118	91,457	46,362
2001	2,601,522	1,331,603	32,258	1,363,861	146,441	523,107	1,740,527	501,830	359,165	28,097	92,591	42,614
2002	2,709,957	1,406,468	19,216	1,425,684	153,369	563,985	1,836,300	492,003	381,654	28,850	93,934	43,293
2003	2,888,714	1,495,132	32,800	1,527,932	161,106	623,792	1,990,618	498,255	399,841	30,247	95,503	43,866
2004	3,023,016	1,588,901	22,265	1,611,166	171,716	675,168	2,114,618	479,130	429,268	31,069	97,300	44,833
2005	3,181,133	1,686,814	18,730	1,705,544	184,822	736,524	2,257,246	457,406	466,481	32,261	98,606	46,439
2006	3,327,644	1,747,745	8,824	1,756,569	199,618	773,645	2,330,596	494,480	502,568	33,310	99,899	47,900
2007	3,525,804	1,776,883	30,566	1,807,449	205,011	820,485	2,422,923	557,931	544,950	35,082	100,502	48,288
2008	3,731,300	1,732,500	66,495	1,798,995	205,993	894,182	2,487,184	622,055	622,061	36,923	101,056	47,540
2009	3,726,646	1,658,534	59,537	1,718,071	201,765	873,468	2,389,774	568,887	767,985	36,806	101,252	45,689
2010	3,812,958	1,723,875	56,894	1,780,769	205,077	900,763	2,476,455	575,332	761,171	37,567	101,498	45,039
2011	3,968,960	1,780,000	57,158	1,837,158	191,085	941,062	2,587,135	634,579	747,246	39,061	101,610	44,673
2012	4,052,496	1,815,272	78,927	1,894,199	195,301	945,270	2,644,168	657,816	750,512	39,924	101,506	45,139
2013	4,132,615	1,914,703	73,336	1,988,039	230,409	930,991	2,688,621	674,786	769,208	40,714	101,504	47,103
2014	4,332,931	1,977,507	68,712	2,046,219	238,799	1,007,774	2,815,194	709,589	808,148	42,551	101,830	47,513
2015	4,525,454	2,034,462	47,481	2,081,943	244,535	1,033,437	2,870,845	784,582	870,027	44,189	102,411	47,604
2016	4,590,593	2,085,000	28,334	2,113,334	252,199	992,321	2,853,456	826,106	911,031	44,732	102,625	48,548
2017	4,744,217	2,182,007	59,422	2,241,429	269,107	1,000,534	2,972,856	840,704	930,657	45,876	103,414	48,900
2018	4,968,932	2,261,448	23,603	2,285,051	277,567	1,060,573	3,068,057	897,545	1,003,330	47,809	103,932	49,096
2019	5,069,573	2,360,113	37,433	2,397,546	289,960	1,071,045	3,178,631	833,373	1,057,569	48,850	103,778	48,706
2020	5,527,061	2,351,545	27,491	2,379,036	286,032	1,107,711	3,200,715	903,988	1,422,358	53,258	103,779	46,418
2021	5,896,214	2,491,327	58,790	2,550,117	303,455	1,188,041	3,434,703	938,695	1,522,816	55,818	105,632	48,162
2022	5,894,792	2,600,515	52,380	2,652,895	328,717	1,268,353	3,592,531	992,692	1,309,569	55,597	106,027	49,147

Personal Income and Employment by Area: Glens Falls, NY

(Thousands of dollars, except as noted.)

Year	Personal income, total	Derivation of personal income: Earnings by place of work: Nonfarm	Farm	Total	Less: Contributions for government social insurance	Plus: Adjustment for residence	Equals: Net earnings by place of residence	Plus: Dividends, interest, and rent	Plus: Personal current transfer receipts	Per capita personal income (dollars)	Population (persons)	Total employment
1970	370,853	296,401	9,468	305,869	22,577	-2,946	280,346	49,620	40,887	3,614	102,612	43,236
1971	398,502	313,681	9,831	323,512	24,786	-5,209	293,517	55,570	49,415	3,807	104,666	43,913
1972	426,819	335,677	10,127	345,804	27,754	-7,268	310,782	62,395	53,642	4,030	105,917	44,230
1973	465,658	365,632	11,125	376,757	34,816	-8,843	333,098	71,137	61,423	4,378	106,354	45,768
1974	507,356	392,985	9,488	402,473	38,663	-10,694	353,116	80,230	74,010	4,753	106,739	46,106
1975	550,664	405,548	7,154	412,702	39,089	-10,840	362,773	88,338	99,553	5,081	108,378	44,892
1976	600,360	451,064	9,186	460,250	44,431	-12,579	403,240	93,763	103,357	5,513	108,894	46,339
1977	647,233	492,063	6,145	498,208	48,256	-17,165	432,787	104,268	110,178	5,893	109,831	47,327
1978	711,564	551,820	10,298	562,118	55,170	-24,050	482,898	110,443	118,223	6,449	110,335	48,379
1979	779,738	605,743	14,680	620,423	62,393	-31,440	526,590	125,373	127,775	7,059	110,464	49,743
1980	870,071	652,921	15,690	668,611	67,336	-36,254	565,021	154,428	150,622	7,930	109,725	49,896
1981	964,162	705,103	15,255	720,358	77,390	-37,415	605,553	186,745	171,864	8,779	109,830	50,090
1982	1,047,808	746,098	16,038	762,136	82,735	-35,763	643,638	211,543	192,627	9,546	109,768	50,097
1983	1,129,054	797,043	14,578	811,621	88,645	-33,967	689,009	236,544	203,501	10,260	110,046	50,967
1984	1,261,635	906,295	14,725	921,020	102,388	-35,462	783,170	266,660	211,805	11,414	110,536	52,557
1985	1,352,156	965,146	15,939	981,085	110,118	-28,379	842,588	285,884	223,684	12,134	111,433	53,905
1986	1,471,288	1,070,654	17,836	1,088,490	123,438	-30,789	934,263	304,860	232,165	13,106	112,257	56,468
1987	1,594,687	1,183,461	18,413	1,201,874	134,970	-30,310	1,036,594	321,135	236,958	13,983	114,046	57,673
1988	1,755,113	1,317,205	14,952	1,332,157	153,030	-29,409	1,149,718	351,300	254,095	15,176	115,651	60,396
1989	1,904,941	1,370,907	19,982	1,390,889	158,086	-16,979	1,215,824	418,396	270,721	16,279	117,016	60,320
1990	1,998,240	1,418,909	22,262	1,441,171	157,428	-8,934	1,274,809	426,262	297,169	16,788	119,027	60,604
1991	2,056,772	1,447,568	16,786	1,464,354	164,915	-41	1,299,398	425,893	331,481	17,099	120,286	59,605
1992	2,213,596	1,551,649	22,557	1,574,206	172,985	6,686	1,407,907	426,913	378,776	18,250	121,290	59,655
1993	2,266,585	1,589,942	22,127	1,612,069	178,490	15,201	1,448,780	424,823	392,982	18,492	122,572	60,889
1994	2,351,400	1,654,966	17,571	1,672,537	188,805	17,416	1,501,148	432,064	418,188	19,151	122,783	63,236
1995	2,470,258	1,714,967	13,731	1,728,698	193,808	25,277	1,560,167	467,092	442,999	20,003	123,496	64,371
1996	2,566,188	1,754,698	23,186	1,777,884	194,754	37,117	1,620,247	480,516	465,425	20,760	123,615	63,799
1997	2,690,302	1,838,420	9,380	1,847,800	199,577	53,437	1,701,660	517,831	470,811	21,800	123,410	63,862
1998	2,823,255	1,890,558	24,182	1,914,740	204,778	70,462	1,780,424	546,835	495,996	22,872	123,436	62,144
1999	2,929,977	1,966,985	23,760	1,990,745	206,746	93,592	1,877,591	536,567	515,819	23,615	124,074	63,464
2000	3,157,499	2,150,218	20,324	2,170,542	222,553	114,458	2,062,447	559,566	535,486	25,412	124,250	64,595
2001	3,165,558	2,089,308	25,354	2,114,662	228,593	147,006	2,033,075	555,314	577,169	25,416	124,548	65,139
2002	3,227,944	2,157,768	16,178	2,173,946	240,157	150,285	2,084,074	520,066	623,804	25,839	124,926	65,406
2003	3,388,092	2,286,584	20,441	2,307,025	253,701	159,038	2,212,362	521,107	654,623	26,902	125,944	66,493
2004	3,649,618	2,467,928	29,186	2,497,114	272,417	191,633	2,416,330	533,556	699,732	28,770	126,854	68,545
2005	3,747,156	2,560,778	28,434	2,589,212	289,546	181,132	2,480,798	530,082	736,276	29,349	127,674	69,450
2006	3,905,813	2,657,110	17,700	2,674,810	303,222	218,509	2,590,097	523,851	791,865	30,437	128,325	70,193
2007	4,042,991	2,710,925	20,908	2,731,833	307,799	229,196	2,653,230	551,506	838,255	31,391	128,794	71,097
2008	4,345,448	2,827,478	21,644	2,849,122	325,349	187,790	2,711,563	697,621	936,264	33,660	129,100	72,898
2009	4,481,827	2,865,524	12,948	2,878,472	325,666	208,520	2,761,326	678,705	1,041,796	34,805	128,771	71,229
2010	4,670,829	2,983,965	31,564	3,015,529	333,389	187,180	2,869,320	689,345	1,112,164	36,182	129,091	70,232
2011	4,842,571	3,024,753	47,273	3,072,026	309,795	214,266	2,976,497	736,184	1,129,890	37,489	129,172	70,771
2012	4,956,682	3,134,426	47,229	3,181,655	318,659	175,611	3,038,607	784,941	1,133,134	38,415	129,030	70,840
2013	5,031,310	3,152,757	58,932	3,211,689	361,744	254,145	3,104,090	787,327	1,139,893	39,087	128,721	70,559
2014	5,065,638	3,223,692	63,860	3,287,552	378,826	180,719	3,089,445	780,794	1,195,399	39,431	128,468	71,316
2015	5,228,822	3,329,179	30,993	3,360,172	391,389	149,633	3,118,416	868,296	1,242,110	40,838	128,038	71,756
2016	5,333,412	3,381,756	26,015	3,407,771	398,927	186,945	3,195,789	864,125	1,273,498	41,701	127,895	71,322
2017	5,647,599	3,534,352	32,381	3,566,733	417,001	208,328	3,358,060	943,429	1,346,110	44,187	127,812	71,630
2018	5,778,882	3,621,142	20,641	3,641,783	421,222	250,876	3,471,437	971,345	1,336,100	45,268	127,658	71,723
2019	6,075,735	3,729,552	37,196	3,766,748	433,682	286,185	3,619,251	1,019,201	1,437,283	47,673	127,446	70,906
2020	6,621,292	3,748,602	36,113	3,784,715	431,432	256,260	3,609,543	1,087,164	1,924,585	52,210	126,820	66,487
2021	6,974,276	4,021,124	37,274	4,058,398	474,938	279,986	3,863,446	1,066,961	2,043,869	55,025	126,748	68,458
2022	6,885,146	4,185,402	53,116	4,238,518	508,432	334,790	4,064,876	1,090,781	1,729,489	54,454	126,440	70,255

Personal Income and Employment by Area: Goldsboro, NC

(Thousands of dollars, except as noted.)

Year	Personal income, total	Derivation of personal income								Per capita personal income (dollars)	Population (persons)	Total employment
		Earnings by place of work			Less: Contributions for government social insurance	Plus: Adjustment for residence	Equals: Net earnings by place of residence	Plus: Dividends, interest, and rent	Plus: Personal current transfer receipts			
		Nonfarm	Farm	Total								
1970	287,524	231,276	16,522	247,798	15,680	-13,255	218,863	45,911	22,750	3,353	85,747	42,648
1971	314,929	253,442	17,910	271,352	17,999	-14,972	238,381	49,683	26,865	3,581	87,943	43,039
1972	355,430	282,502	23,683	306,185	20,513	-15,628	270,044	54,623	30,763	3,943	90,151	43,682
1973	393,421	303,687	35,177	338,864	24,689	-14,463	299,712	59,977	33,732	4,355	90,338	44,400
1974	446,433	340,317	40,079	380,396	28,817	-16,734	334,845	70,375	41,213	4,863	91,807	45,687
1975	479,207	357,004	36,633	393,637	31,216	-14,561	347,860	77,419	53,928	5,181	92,498	44,628
1976	521,085	390,154	35,703	425,857	35,037	-13,861	376,959	84,659	59,467	5,582	93,352	45,876
1977	551,523	421,116	21,812	442,928	37,333	-12,618	392,977	95,911	62,635	5,825	94,674	46,344
1978	618,738	464,609	33,578	498,187	41,876	-12,063	444,248	107,345	67,145	6,393	96,788	46,994
1979	671,168	519,193	18,240	537,433	48,700	-11,014	477,719	117,293	76,156	6,910	97,135	48,534
1980	739,643	561,213	13,743	574,956	52,559	-10,891	511,506	136,886	91,251	7,601	97,314	48,041
1981	814,766	600,252	26,141	626,393	60,103	-14,058	552,232	156,916	105,618	8,308	98,066	47,291
1982	875,661	635,369	28,662	664,031	63,595	-17,091	583,345	176,876	115,440	8,881	98,603	46,959
1983	935,893	690,958	16,564	707,522	70,066	-17,294	620,162	190,752	124,979	9,416	99,391	47,490
1984	1,061,421	751,523	61,483	813,006	78,344	-16,233	718,429	211,245	131,747	10,573	100,393	48,551
1985	1,107,443	786,648	55,857	842,505	83,299	-13,452	745,754	220,471	141,218	10,944	101,193	48,845
1986	1,154,090	821,094	53,196	874,290	88,997	-11,929	773,364	230,624	150,102	11,517	100,205	48,493
1987	1,198,960	882,543	28,753	911,296	95,038	-10,412	805,846	237,823	155,291	11,836	101,296	49,782
1988	1,300,742	960,115	30,270	990,385	107,845	-15,596	866,944	265,022	168,776	12,719	102,269	52,540
1989	1,427,014	1,018,678	46,259	1,064,937	114,807	-12,413	937,717	303,360	185,937	13,729	103,938	52,694
1990	1,542,212	1,074,164	56,241	1,130,405	123,204	17,181	1,024,382	309,678	208,152	14,702	104,896	53,244
1991	1,629,428	1,105,557	73,633	1,179,190	128,107	20,249	1,071,332	318,602	239,494	15,293	106,545	51,973
1992	1,767,885	1,186,551	69,324	1,255,875	136,880	50,575	1,169,570	333,623	264,692	16,428	107,614	52,502
1993	1,865,745	1,256,753	73,468	1,330,221	146,115	45,901	1,230,007	341,604	294,134	17,216	108,374	53,661
1994	1,981,342	1,309,248	79,421	1,388,669	152,634	71,720	1,307,755	366,091	307,496	18,101	109,459	55,617
1995	2,100,507	1,385,452	73,618	1,459,070	161,288	60,401	1,358,183	398,479	343,845	18,825	111,578	57,476
1996	2,210,025	1,437,978	82,389	1,520,367	165,815	62,704	1,417,256	420,867	371,902	19,575	112,898	57,498
1997	2,315,416	1,511,699	82,324	1,594,023	173,536	49,655	1,470,142	449,952	395,322	20,424	113,366	59,127
1998	2,389,421	1,584,247	59,431	1,643,678	182,322	35,955	1,497,311	486,852	405,258	21,065	113,429	58,373
1999	2,474,834	1,642,987	43,209	1,686,196	190,142	63,705	1,559,759	483,699	431,376	21,867	113,176	58,682
2000	2,606,132	1,717,943	50,595	1,768,538	198,294	72,444	1,642,688	507,797	455,647	22,932	113,648	59,844
2001	2,748,284	1,828,022	56,717	1,884,739	209,699	75,818	1,750,858	503,170	494,256	24,122	113,934	59,739
2002	2,842,320	1,905,916	36,652	1,942,568	219,202	72,109	1,795,475	513,919	532,926	24,866	114,305	59,788
2003	2,899,249	1,923,869	16,009	1,939,878	224,143	83,674	1,799,409	532,359	567,481	25,300	114,595	58,554
2004	3,089,193	2,050,363	34,089	2,084,452	236,978	88,848	1,936,322	544,753	608,118	26,520	116,484	58,829
2005	3,228,646	2,113,642	56,634	2,170,276	246,117	96,222	2,020,381	549,406	658,859	27,593	117,009	58,870
2006	3,391,370	2,220,230	37,197	2,257,427	258,564	97,978	2,096,841	572,760	721,769	28,854	117,534	59,751
2007	3,636,361	2,303,258	69,665	2,372,923	272,092	117,088	2,217,919	650,478	767,964	30,573	118,942	61,541
2008	3,771,911	2,336,094	107,066	2,443,160	276,222	115,597	2,282,535	640,167	849,209	31,456	119,910	60,725
2009	3,794,742	2,339,323	94,156	2,433,479	279,590	86,740	2,240,629	622,010	932,103	31,305	121,217	59,759
2010	3,898,084	2,390,326	111,696	2,502,022	282,402	77,318	2,296,938	622,679	978,467	31,762	122,727	58,748
2011	4,023,498	2,472,494	102,442	2,574,936	268,665	59,618	2,365,889	649,534	1,008,075	32,651	123,226	60,037
2012	4,201,963	2,570,071	141,308	2,711,379	275,164	39,987	2,476,202	693,178	1,032,583	34,138	123,087	59,949
2013	4,130,812	2,542,569	170,551	2,713,120	308,895	34,928	2,439,153	637,013	1,054,646	33,732	122,459	59,385
2014	4,258,517	2,548,762	192,496	2,741,258	311,110	67,116	2,497,264	673,752	1,087,501	34,962	121,805	59,131
2015	4,317,276	2,555,930	147,749	2,703,679	316,688	76,974	2,463,965	727,367	1,125,944	35,706	120,912	58,965
2016	4,349,653	2,597,948	110,014	2,707,962	321,278	84,781	2,471,465	729,924	1,148,264	36,182	120,215	58,743
2017	4,517,298	2,665,720	134,906	2,800,626	325,521	92,090	2,567,195	757,657	1,192,446	38,143	118,432	59,131
2018	4,648,856	2,765,457	66,672	2,832,129	333,240	114,846	2,613,735	795,886	1,239,235	39,381	118,048	59,748
2019	4,861,021	2,917,100	83,668	3,000,768	350,298	127,679	2,778,149	795,723	1,287,149	41,268	117,792	59,793
2020	5,181,855	3,039,602	48,223	3,087,825	366,655	124,318	2,845,488	763,098	1,573,269	44,189	117,266	58,861
2021	5,741,810	3,198,476	154,902	3,353,378	380,986	143,452	3,115,844	777,630	1,848,336	49,132	116,866	59,741
2022	5,790,425	3,390,052	156,973	3,547,025	408,613	181,087	3,319,499	810,871	1,660,055	49,370	117,286	60,610

Personal Income and Employment by Area: Grand Forks, ND-MN

(Thousands of dollars, except as noted.)

Year	Personal income, total	Derivation of personal income: Earnings by place of work: Nonfarm	Farm	Total	Less: Contributions for government social insurance	Plus: Adjustment for residence	Equals: Net earnings by place of residence	Plus: Dividends, interest, and rent	Plus: Personal current transfer receipts	Per capita personal income (dollars)	Population (persons)	Total employment
1970	358,608	247,966	33,965	281,931	18,853	4,879	267,957	61,147	29,504	3,738	95,935	43,052
1971	392,498	269,553	34,767	304,320	21,288	7,785	290,817	67,120	34,561	4,010	97,885	43,405
1972	442,727	300,299	47,267	347,566	24,388	7,675	330,853	73,963	37,911	4,490	98,607	44,636
1973	580,655	339,134	142,350	481,484	30,746	1,052	451,790	86,188	42,677	5,818	99,795	46,958
1974	604,087	376,816	119,775	496,591	36,013	-4,430	456,148	97,751	50,188	6,035	100,100	48,256
1975	644,297	414,932	102,682	517,614	40,614	-4,337	472,663	111,422	60,212	6,561	98,203	48,980
1976	683,917	485,209	67,380	552,589	48,357	-7,470	496,762	121,311	65,844	6,797	100,617	51,544
1977	679,040	500,791	29,499	530,290	48,635	-7,202	474,453	133,621	70,966	6,661	101,935	51,571
1978	819,219	549,210	105,612	654,822	54,218	-8,021	592,583	147,963	78,673	8,093	101,225	52,678
1979	851,656	599,987	72,976	672,963	61,546	-9,252	602,165	162,478	87,013	8,400	101,383	52,989
1980	886,174	643,622	19,371	662,993	66,540	-10,034	586,419	196,110	103,645	8,768	101,074	53,483
1981	1,002,555	698,397	30,374	728,771	75,838	-9,498	643,435	240,168	118,952	9,890	101,367	52,972
1982	1,095,925	741,001	37,012	778,013	80,770	-9,023	688,220	275,936	131,769	10,760	101,851	53,099
1983	1,169,353	783,530	47,597	831,127	86,799	-7,839	736,489	284,262	148,602	11,341	103,104	54,018
1984	1,303,205	830,392	111,083	941,475	94,693	-8,065	838,717	304,356	160,132	12,562	103,741	54,465
1985	1,317,248	875,412	62,395	937,807	102,024	-8,259	827,524	318,142	171,582	12,701	103,712	55,684
1986	1,419,007	920,225	110,567	1,030,792	110,241	-8,929	911,622	327,692	179,693	13,730	103,349	55,969
1987	1,467,574	975,157	110,250	1,085,407	117,601	-9,350	958,456	319,276	189,842	14,190	103,422	57,658
1988	1,473,521	1,018,897	63,615	1,082,512	128,680	-8,138	945,694	331,356	196,471	14,122	104,341	58,645
1989	1,560,121	1,074,278	56,876	1,131,154	137,303	-7,758	986,093	361,167	212,861	14,988	104,094	59,627
1990	1,653,945	1,119,893	89,844	1,209,737	148,093	-7,858	1,053,786	371,744	228,415	16,030	103,177	59,698
1991	1,688,312	1,184,404	64,659	1,249,063	159,621	-10,696	1,078,746	376,702	232,864	16,386	103,034	61,249
1992	1,823,321	1,252,808	121,728	1,374,536	169,609	-14,019	1,190,908	373,189	259,224	17,501	104,181	61,836
1993	1,821,732	1,326,213	29,754	1,355,967	181,395	-17,530	1,157,042	393,824	270,866	17,442	104,443	63,139
1994	1,948,621	1,399,164	63,520	1,462,684	191,770	-20,806	1,250,108	425,813	272,700	18,453	105,601	65,108
1995	2,023,008	1,467,099	42,450	1,509,549	199,214	-25,651	1,284,684	450,513	287,811	19,148	105,650	66,896
1996	2,173,931	1,526,145	129,960	1,656,105	206,135	-28,969	1,421,001	455,812	297,118	20,617	105,443	67,548
1997	2,150,208	1,586,608	31,905	1,618,513	212,440	-33,015	1,373,058	478,827	298,323	20,746	103,643	65,519
1998	2,267,080	1,643,083	96,213	1,739,296	219,425	-36,686	1,483,185	488,868	295,027	22,685	99,938	65,303
1999	2,258,909	1,678,306	61,419	1,739,725	222,496	-38,384	1,478,845	468,909	311,155	23,069	97,919	64,607
2000	2,384,300	1,724,420	107,074	1,831,494	228,382	-41,347	1,561,765	486,954	335,581	24,478	97,405	64,457
2001	2,418,320	1,794,739	60,123	1,854,862	230,233	-44,746	1,579,883	481,558	356,879	25,018	96,663	65,352
2002	2,538,468	1,896,181	56,463	1,952,644	239,572	-49,766	1,663,306	492,963	382,199	26,342	96,367	65,616
2003	2,746,025	2,011,918	144,655	2,156,573	253,073	-57,318	1,846,182	500,143	399,700	28,525	96,267	66,488
2004	2,802,496	2,136,094	62,141	2,198,235	266,696	-63,241	1,868,298	511,817	422,381	28,549	98,164	67,726
2005	2,921,140	2,225,728	76,934	2,302,662	277,879	-67,975	1,956,808	514,843	449,489	29,876	97,777	69,038
2006	3,097,596	2,329,122	107,748	2,436,870	288,186	-73,201	2,075,483	543,156	478,957	31,523	98,266	69,865
2007	3,307,806	2,418,861	146,083	2,564,944	298,525	-78,380	2,188,039	604,953	514,814	33,889	97,606	70,623
2008	3,619,467	2,494,716	240,135	2,734,851	307,052	-82,142	2,345,657	693,925	579,885	36,899	98,092	69,993
2009	3,526,157	2,560,618	103,553	2,664,171	322,805	-83,475	2,257,891	650,222	618,044	36,003	97,941	69,547
2010	3,728,294	2,662,740	152,261	2,815,001	318,566	-82,557	2,413,878	651,153	663,263	37,766	98,721	69,223
2011	4,000,881	2,763,029	146,504	2,909,533	306,184	-68,985	2,534,364	785,409	681,108	40,562	98,637	69,280
2012	4,398,366	2,931,607	283,644	3,215,251	310,280	-46,664	2,858,307	855,373	684,686	43,991	99,984	71,403
2013	4,482,660	3,032,902	258,908	3,291,810	362,630	-39,038	2,890,142	886,664	705,854	43,929	102,043	71,739
2014	4,559,497	3,190,632	104,907	3,295,539	386,246	-42,751	2,866,542	942,273	750,682	44,288	102,951	72,214
2015	4,669,667	3,333,562	48,584	3,382,146	408,012	-40,647	2,933,487	958,591	777,589	44,933	103,926	72,815
2016	4,721,813	3,446,145	76,440	3,522,585	421,124	-50,750	3,050,711	875,739	795,363	45,096	104,705	72,534
2017	4,830,523	3,512,525	75,779	3,588,304	435,586	-50,721	3,101,997	907,641	820,885	45,966	105,090	72,406
2018	5,047,543	3,599,864	69,911	3,669,775	438,581	-54,993	3,176,201	993,997	877,345	48,006	105,143	72,205
2019	5,156,053	3,669,058	57,885	3,726,943	445,443	-57,038	3,224,462	1,023,493	908,098	49,370	104,436	71,643
2020	5,679,600	3,710,978	240,660	3,951,638	462,102	-58,926	3,430,610	1,046,299	1,202,691	54,502	104,209	69,193
2021	6,091,822	3,893,340	268,898	4,162,238	482,284	-32,627	3,647,327	1,145,881	1,298,614	58,956	103,329	69,777
2022	6,236,262	4,068,725	338,403	4,407,128	515,214	-45,196	3,846,718	1,234,853	1,154,691	60,462	103,144	71,450

Personal Income and Employment by Area: Grand Island, NE

(Thousands of dollars, except as noted.)

Year	Personal income, total	Derivation of personal income: Earnings by place of work: Nonfarm	Farm	Total	Less: Contributions for government social insurance	Plus: Adjustment for residence	Equals: Net earnings by place of residence	Plus: Dividends, interest, and rent	Plus: Personal current transfer receipts	Per capita personal income (dollars)	Population (persons)	Total employment
1970	222,563	157,417	25,919	183,336	10,930	-7,538	164,868	37,743	19,952	3,812	58,389	28,332
1971	235,467	164,276	26,847	191,123	11,690	-7,170	172,263	40,896	22,308	4,016	58,638	27,856
1972	259,159	182,120	27,486	209,606	13,308	-7,743	188,555	46,068	24,536	4,387	59,072	29,194
1973	297,673	206,510	35,715	242,225	17,483	-8,589	216,153	52,377	29,143	4,987	59,686	30,771
1974	322,820	224,629	33,481	258,110	19,763	-8,731	229,616	59,541	33,663	5,389	59,908	31,219
1975	368,729	246,097	45,230	291,327	21,151	-9,582	260,594	67,943	40,192	6,044	61,010	31,074
1976	381,322	279,656	20,747	300,403	24,317	-10,239	265,847	73,045	42,430	6,248	61,032	32,202
1977	403,307	308,776	3,271	312,047	26,703	-11,300	274,044	83,130	46,133	6,502	62,026	33,268
1978	482,838	342,825	40,087	382,912	30,517	-12,260	340,135	91,954	50,749	7,751	62,295	34,529
1979	511,621	386,127	15,066	401,193	35,811	-14,187	351,195	103,244	57,182	8,092	63,224	34,949
1980	542,511	425,136	-21,376	403,760	39,521	-17,041	347,198	128,299	67,014	8,526	63,633	35,544
1981	657,843	462,435	21,242	483,677	45,719	-17,600	420,358	159,113	78,372	10,217	64,390	35,806
1982	676,789	464,755	737	465,492	46,970	-17,172	401,350	187,280	88,159	10,419	64,956	34,680
1983	702,022	478,354	603	478,957	48,596	-17,111	413,250	192,298	96,474	10,827	64,838	34,857
1984	802,082	513,386	54,310	567,696	53,770	-17,955	495,971	204,393	101,718	12,341	64,995	35,094
1985	812,740	520,976	52,105	573,081	56,216	-17,962	498,903	206,609	107,228	12,588	64,563	34,679
1986	844,499	546,859	60,198	607,057	60,755	-20,008	526,294	205,523	112,682	13,307	63,463	34,669
1987	876,283	570,411	73,474	643,885	63,395	-19,551	560,939	199,533	115,811	13,895	63,063	35,138
1988	932,802	599,748	91,514	691,262	69,559	-18,819	602,884	207,889	122,029	14,816	62,960	36,148
1989	997,983	632,888	90,075	722,963	73,638	-19,080	630,245	237,785	129,953	15,882	62,837	36,957
1990	1,048,175	684,660	96,777	781,437	82,209	-20,871	678,357	230,336	139,482	16,580	63,218	37,838
1991	1,107,770	727,887	98,728	826,615	88,116	-23,705	714,794	242,753	150,223	17,357	63,821	38,722
1992	1,156,121	777,439	87,858	865,297	92,650	-24,987	747,660	244,344	164,117	17,918	64,522	39,668
1993	1,194,059	832,450	62,976	895,426	99,666	-27,211	768,549	253,428	172,082	18,255	65,409	40,429
1994	1,290,127	901,848	78,189	980,037	108,139	-28,785	843,113	264,799	182,215	19,541	66,020	42,642
1995	1,347,179	951,411	62,312	1,013,723	112,512	-32,182	869,029	287,056	191,094	20,163	66,814	42,693
1996	1,463,473	1,000,799	104,330	1,105,129	117,931	-34,510	952,688	306,145	204,640	21,739	67,320	43,958
1997	1,491,328	1,054,869	67,128	1,121,997	125,347	-36,475	960,175	316,808	214,345	22,042	67,658	44,482
1998	1,573,440	1,105,471	62,388	1,167,859	130,199	-37,197	1,000,463	345,690	227,287	23,081	68,171	45,183
1999	1,627,457	1,158,878	52,503	1,211,381	135,135	-39,283	1,036,963	347,152	243,342	23,783	68,430	45,980
2000	1,705,604	1,202,665	56,105	1,258,770	139,264	-41,044	1,078,462	374,218	252,924	24,993	68,244	46,005
2001	1,809,890	1,278,677	59,050	1,337,727	146,404	-44,022	1,147,301	382,248	280,341	26,616	68,001	45,317
2002	1,844,092	1,337,823	38,373	1,376,196	153,125	-50,537	1,172,534	370,299	301,259	27,038	68,203	44,653
2003	1,960,176	1,375,944	89,046	1,464,990	158,367	-58,991	1,247,632	394,118	318,426	28,577	68,592	44,911
2004	1,969,204	1,421,162	80,871	1,502,033	163,299	-64,811	1,273,923	361,896	333,385	28,582	68,896	45,230
2005	2,047,051	1,485,123	104,380	1,589,503	174,826	-71,142	1,343,535	351,885	351,631	29,723	68,871	46,169
2006	2,134,760	1,585,489	60,978	1,646,467	189,253	-78,548	1,378,666	381,995	374,099	30,778	69,360	47,293
2007	2,316,809	1,691,013	95,317	1,786,330	201,433	-90,352	1,494,545	428,752	393,512	33,200	69,784	48,157
2008	2,479,916	1,720,470	85,787	1,806,257	205,888	-88,246	1,512,123	526,758	441,035	35,032	70,790	48,904
2009	2,437,223	1,734,724	97,002	1,831,726	208,353	-109,340	1,514,033	463,703	459,487	33,824	72,056	48,934
2010	2,518,813	1,798,636	98,370	1,897,006	218,912	-114,157	1,563,937	463,050	491,826	34,514	72,980	48,651
2011	2,767,243	1,866,697	197,633	2,064,330	198,835	-128,003	1,737,492	535,836	493,915	37,519	73,755	49,692
2012	2,833,929	1,975,587	163,075	2,138,662	204,337	-144,140	1,790,185	544,625	499,119	37,992	74,593	50,694
2013	2,889,335	2,014,784	247,661	2,262,445	235,445	-152,425	1,874,575	512,278	502,482	38,439	75,166	51,313
2014	2,965,870	2,145,960	184,401	2,330,361	248,008	-162,898	1,919,455	517,069	529,346	39,073	75,906	51,590
2015	3,121,813	2,198,744	188,875	2,387,619	250,078	-144,803	1,992,738	572,721	556,354	41,003	76,136	51,138
2016	3,111,783	2,220,720	157,597	2,378,317	257,016	-143,830	1,977,471	566,312	568,000	40,608	76,629	51,380
2017	3,153,149	2,321,205	80,532	2,401,737	270,407	-152,802	1,978,528	579,311	595,310	41,112	76,696	51,513
2018	3,228,742	2,379,664	62,370	2,442,034	276,402	-154,351	2,011,281	593,206	624,255	41,918	77,026	51,708
2019	3,389,041	2,424,196	111,565	2,535,761	286,212	-161,957	2,087,592	644,391	657,058	43,930	77,146	50,988
2020	3,661,514	2,489,710	133,968	2,623,678	306,685	-159,358	2,157,635	658,693	845,186	47,615	76,899	49,762
2021	4,116,208	2,770,097	174,736	2,944,833	334,666	-181,066	2,429,101	730,866	956,241	53,961	76,281	51,530
2022	4,147,592	2,973,793	106,603	3,080,396	358,167	-198,555	2,523,674	786,635	837,283	54,336	76,333	52,945

Personal Income and Employment by Area: Grand Junction, CO

(Thousands of dollars, except as noted.)

Year	Personal income, total	Derivation of personal income: Earnings by place of work: Nonfarm	Farm	Total	Less: Contributions for government social insurance	Plus: Adjustment for residence	Equals: Net earnings by place of residence	Plus: Dividends, interest, and rent	Plus: Personal current transfer receipts	Per capita personal income (dollars)	Population (persons)	Total employment
1970	193,533	138,826	3,993	142,819	8,195	121	134,745	35,603	23,185	3,552	54,479	23,121
1971	214,485	149,183	7,157	156,340	8,932	453	147,861	39,596	27,028	3,878	55,311	23,077
1972	236,705	168,812	4,600	173,412	10,758	1,085	163,739	43,570	29,396	4,159	56,912	24,258
1973	275,667	193,357	8,130	201,487	14,205	2,062	189,344	51,947	34,376	4,756	57,962	26,242
1974	326,263	232,044	6,702	238,746	17,459	3,077	224,364	62,191	39,708	5,532	58,973	28,069
1975	383,882	275,267	7,304	282,571	20,538	3,683	265,716	70,980	47,186	6,068	63,261	30,541
1976	429,725	311,045	5,577	316,622	23,291	5,450	298,781	79,703	51,241	6,450	66,628	32,111
1977	516,171	386,961	3,986	390,947	28,908	6,548	368,587	92,818	54,766	7,526	68,585	35,299
1978	600,883	456,683	827	457,510	35,274	8,449	430,685	110,150	60,048	8,320	72,223	37,820
1979	693,282	524,270	4,395	528,665	43,288	10,824	496,201	128,771	68,310	9,010	76,946	40,671
1980	815,682	609,596	2,580	612,176	51,893	13,732	574,015	160,565	81,102	9,852	82,796	43,710
1981	986,825	743,970	2,350	746,320	69,526	15,786	692,580	198,717	95,528	11,258	87,659	48,937
1982	1,092,710	798,516	-1,789	796,727	76,842	21,073	740,958	237,839	113,913	11,606	94,152	50,531
1983	1,108,526	768,535	1,206	769,741	73,346	23,077	719,472	255,261	133,793	11,546	96,012	48,319
1984	1,104,529	749,044	1,610	750,654	72,847	21,440	699,247	263,677	141,605	11,689	94,496	46,669
1985	1,101,299	730,827	-854	729,973	73,140	21,662	678,495	274,957	147,847	12,323	89,368	44,600
1986	1,080,915	688,008	-4,408	683,600	71,250	22,458	634,808	283,036	163,071	12,369	87,386	42,603
1987	1,163,143	752,858	-1,131	751,727	75,766	22,254	698,215	285,833	179,095	13,302	87,443	42,211
1988	1,275,102	839,702	433	840,135	87,270	22,207	775,072	310,180	189,850	14,348	88,872	45,112
1989	1,367,769	881,899	2,537	884,436	96,136	23,659	811,959	344,641	211,169	14,992	91,231	47,556
1990	1,469,368	958,419	2,293	960,712	107,105	28,304	881,911	360,615	226,842	15,672	93,757	49,479
1991	1,569,648	1,034,550	4,680	1,039,230	119,169	26,522	946,583	369,844	253,221	16,291	96,348	50,610
1992	1,707,461	1,131,597	8,463	1,140,060	128,847	23,770	1,034,983	389,275	283,203	17,427	97,977	51,414
1993	1,822,367	1,211,686	10,155	1,221,841	139,318	25,404	1,107,927	406,752	307,688	18,119	100,579	53,284
1994	1,936,370	1,286,510	7,041	1,293,551	149,380	30,782	1,174,953	435,515	325,902	18,732	103,373	55,648
1995	2,109,647	1,365,684	6,204	1,371,888	158,716	32,017	1,245,189	498,911	365,547	19,908	105,968	58,004
1996	2,238,691	1,462,006	8,137	1,470,143	167,445	33,633	1,336,331	522,966	379,394	20,704	108,131	61,078
1997	2,432,216	1,613,502	8,572	1,622,074	181,526	36,097	1,476,645	566,152	389,419	21,998	110,566	63,850
1998	2,667,264	1,764,478	12,211	1,776,689	183,059	39,817	1,633,447	603,681	430,136	23,670	112,686	66,443
1999	2,787,012	1,884,287	8,016	1,892,303	193,575	42,442	1,741,170	588,670	457,172	24,271	114,827	68,110
2000	3,013,126	2,033,166	8,630	2,041,796	204,229	47,355	1,884,922	649,593	478,611	25,615	117,631	69,890
2001	3,258,466	2,239,100	12,979	2,252,079	225,828	51,528	2,077,779	656,840	523,847	27,268	119,496	71,083
2002	3,378,966	2,379,869	13,499	2,393,368	250,714	53,858	2,196,512	605,291	577,163	27,597	122,440	72,724
2003	3,478,868	2,444,664	9,124	2,453,788	260,754	60,167	2,253,201	630,410	595,257	27,832	124,994	73,952
2004	3,663,724	2,541,769	14,581	2,556,350	283,655	71,126	2,343,821	686,856	633,047	28,695	127,678	76,251
2005	3,966,993	2,749,711	17,844	2,767,555	311,209	98,239	2,554,585	725,087	687,321	30,470	130,194	79,068
2006	4,399,319	3,051,504	11,871	3,063,375	342,067	144,960	2,866,268	793,802	739,249	32,669	134,665	82,251
2007	4,942,435	3,405,520	10,886	3,416,406	383,092	186,737	3,220,051	942,256	780,128	35,446	139,434	87,488
2008	5,550,866	3,705,701	7,862	3,713,563	423,930	223,043	3,512,676	1,162,642	875,548	38,775	143,155	90,891
2009	5,147,972	3,455,549	6,523	3,462,072	395,219	177,460	3,244,313	992,968	910,691	34,819	147,851	86,305
2010	5,023,372	3,264,723	7,441	3,272,164	373,489	186,554	3,085,229	935,726	1,002,417	34,343	146,272	83,207
2011	5,248,190	3,337,561	14,250	3,351,811	352,672	218,563	3,217,702	1,012,175	1,018,313	35,645	147,236	83,893
2012	5,448,678	3,459,473	14,188	3,473,661	363,241	254,485	3,364,905	1,065,206	1,018,567	36,961	147,416	84,752
2013	5,516,467	3,544,783	7,863	3,552,646	403,511	281,984	3,431,119	1,035,836	1,049,512	37,443	147,331	84,977
2014	5,832,309	3,670,958	19,688	3,690,646	419,670	308,944	3,579,920	1,121,170	1,131,219	39,589	147,323	86,749
2015	5,976,511	3,700,767	20,910	3,721,677	428,250	270,553	3,563,980	1,131,813	1,280,718	40,302	148,294	86,505
2016	5,978,899	3,670,006	11,632	3,681,638	428,785	226,288	3,479,141	1,135,552	1,364,206	39,847	150,045	86,750
2017	6,387,317	3,958,164	7,660	3,965,824	459,526	232,008	3,738,306	1,241,275	1,407,736	42,125	151,628	88,780
2018	6,820,162	4,241,020	11,292	4,252,312	494,964	249,882	4,007,230	1,268,787	1,544,145	44,413	153,563	90,782
2019	7,118,150	4,372,160	10,941	4,383,101	511,620	257,576	4,129,057	1,362,810	1,626,283	45,981	154,807	90,926
2020	7,573,662	4,427,965	10,995	4,438,960	520,476	229,008	4,147,492	1,367,160	2,059,010	48,548	156,005	89,429
2021	8,374,551	4,756,057	19,084	4,775,141	553,847	224,376	4,445,670	1,601,279	2,327,602	53,194	157,434	94,079
2022	8,670,085	5,140,900	8,222	5,149,122	616,608	252,343	4,784,857	1,732,500	2,152,728	54,654	158,636	97,302

Personal Income and Employment by Area: Grand Rapids-Kentwood, MI

(Thousands of dollars, except as noted.)

Year	Personal income, total	Derivation of personal income: Earnings by place of work: Nonfarm	Farm	Total	Less: Contributions for government social insurance	Plus: Adjustment for residence	Equals: Net earnings by place of residence	Plus: Dividends, interest, and rent	Plus: Personal current transfer receipts	Per capita personal income (dollars)	Population (persons)	Total employment
1970	2,434,527	2,010,531	38,888	2,049,419	145,463	-27,539	1,876,417	341,254	216,856	3,893	625,388	263,744
1971	2,634,403	2,167,064	35,876	2,202,940	161,915	-29,371	2,011,654	365,600	257,149	4,191	628,659	268,073
1972	2,934,004	2,436,703	45,863	2,482,566	191,604	-36,086	2,254,876	395,040	284,088	4,623	634,587	280,748
1973	3,272,644	2,757,567	56,373	2,813,940	251,592	-44,520	2,517,828	433,059	321,757	5,076	644,786	297,296
1974	3,580,211	2,964,981	65,928	3,030,909	280,282	-56,369	2,694,258	491,905	394,048	5,510	649,816	302,969
1975	3,866,422	3,065,933	56,711	3,122,644	280,304	-55,722	2,786,618	553,976	525,828	5,910	654,227	293,895
1976	4,308,318	3,518,721	54,200	3,572,921	330,887	-68,205	3,173,829	591,763	542,726	6,522	660,598	309,789
1977	4,862,998	4,059,003	67,968	4,126,971	383,179	-91,249	3,652,543	658,614	551,841	7,265	669,380	328,391
1978	5,543,857	4,724,910	79,522	4,804,432	459,910	-121,272	4,223,250	738,659	581,948	8,168	678,766	351,149
1979	6,190,414	5,312,394	81,968	5,394,362	541,334	-148,788	4,704,240	831,222	654,952	8,955	691,273	362,233
1980	6,754,107	5,556,256	82,831	5,639,087	563,662	-153,076	4,922,349	1,005,031	826,727	9,605	703,150	354,253
1981	7,392,446	5,995,250	78,741	6,073,991	654,629	-162,030	5,257,332	1,222,740	912,374	10,412	710,020	355,077
1982	7,832,683	6,119,124	91,551	6,210,675	676,435	-172,046	5,362,194	1,432,179	1,038,310	11,001	712,009	348,630
1983	8,463,577	6,702,719	57,125	6,759,844	754,450	-195,629	5,809,765	1,562,178	1,091,634	11,838	714,973	361,159
1984	9,486,443	7,655,855	97,088	7,752,943	892,419	-250,032	6,610,492	1,775,547	1,100,404	13,084	725,043	382,900
1985	10,286,231	8,349,716	130,313	8,480,029	983,892	-280,299	7,215,838	1,909,679	1,160,714	13,973	736,142	401,299
1986	10,962,294	8,949,480	96,010	9,045,490	1,052,315	-279,393	7,713,782	2,021,492	1,227,020	14,684	746,557	410,214
1987	11,725,293	9,698,320	117,068	9,815,388	1,118,618	-336,355	8,360,415	2,090,266	1,274,612	15,438	759,505	428,279
1988	12,715,311	10,671,547	100,160	10,771,707	1,272,420	-400,452	9,098,835	2,284,978	1,331,498	16,392	775,721	447,755
1989	13,819,280	11,500,687	160,768	11,661,455	1,355,231	-436,451	9,869,773	2,472,792	1,476,715	17,517	788,902	463,568
1990	14,822,846	12,218,535	141,959	12,360,494	1,467,756	-478,411	10,414,327	2,783,640	1,624,879	18,477	802,244	479,198
1991	15,450,474	12,541,681	151,393	12,693,074	1,525,468	-470,050	10,697,556	2,915,262	1,837,656	18,805	821,606	477,564
1992	16,691,219	13,557,938	145,802	13,703,740	1,635,891	-543,560	11,524,289	3,203,598	1,963,332	20,032	833,220	484,587
1993	17,561,737	14,512,507	134,581	14,647,088	1,764,796	-607,750	12,274,542	3,191,371	2,095,824	20,780	845,126	496,825
1994	19,124,174	15,918,494	116,300	16,034,794	1,980,119	-710,342	13,344,333	3,662,295	2,117,546	22,288	858,061	523,152
1995	20,346,977	17,122,328	123,097	17,245,425	2,135,840	-834,134	14,275,451	3,887,599	2,183,927	23,326	872,287	550,074
1996	21,606,467	18,193,800	128,336	18,322,136	2,230,267	-952,501	15,139,368	4,175,912	2,291,187	24,370	886,603	564,463
1997	22,902,940	19,335,581	127,589	19,463,170	2,379,265	-1,055,106	16,028,799	4,389,799	2,484,342	25,441	900,230	579,262
1998	24,625,088	20,894,136	135,664	21,029,800	2,525,095	-1,142,604	17,362,101	4,744,948	2,518,039	26,990	912,389	583,457
1999	25,827,328	22,197,283	156,719	22,354,002	2,662,582	-1,293,595	18,397,825	4,716,209	2,713,294	27,891	926,004	594,828
2000	27,709,711	23,896,814	128,484	24,025,298	2,803,105	-1,461,189	19,761,004	5,068,113	2,880,594	29,512	938,933	613,988
2001	28,439,845	24,141,237	135,027	24,276,264	2,715,861	-1,462,557	20,097,846	5,098,277	3,243,722	29,966	949,059	611,718
2002	28,539,724	24,439,896	142,447	24,582,343	2,745,656	-1,395,729	20,440,958	4,667,132	3,431,634	29,810	957,389	603,735
2003	29,454,833	24,725,317	156,054	24,881,371	2,781,364	-1,374,459	20,725,548	5,109,391	3,619,894	30,543	964,358	602,518
2004	31,210,626	25,393,056	206,052	25,599,108	2,910,341	-1,474,116	21,214,651	6,208,437	3,787,538	32,154	970,646	613,666
2005	32,092,483	26,176,637	183,108	26,359,745	3,044,314	-1,586,346	21,729,085	6,330,970	4,032,428	32,887	975,837	622,742
2006	33,778,255	26,872,045	212,394	27,084,439	3,171,297	-1,580,231	22,332,911	7,059,677	4,385,667	34,392	982,157	621,181
2007	34,883,686	27,003,748	233,789	27,237,537	3,208,019	-1,484,978	22,544,540	7,532,577	4,806,569	35,348	986,863	622,431
2008	36,991,655	27,108,952	261,942	27,370,894	3,242,634	-1,285,992	22,842,268	8,581,743	5,567,644	37,367	989,942	612,257
2009	34,185,025	25,456,589	210,720	25,667,309	3,065,778	-1,039,453	21,562,078	6,460,836	6,162,111	34,472	991,670	578,876
2010	36,174,583	26,344,805	289,951	26,634,756	3,121,793	-906,276	22,606,687	6,904,201	6,663,695	36,377	994,432	580,542
2011	39,394,565	27,611,573	433,504	28,045,077	2,914,758	-941,406	24,188,913	8,536,374	6,669,278	39,261	1,003,408	605,110
2012	42,189,733	29,423,139	297,424	29,720,563	3,096,204	-965,363	25,658,996	9,904,948	6,625,789	41,558	1,015,208	623,504
2013	42,522,189	30,632,739	393,774	31,026,513	3,634,421	-1,007,625	26,384,467	9,396,852	6,740,870	41,374	1,027,754	642,071
2014	44,636,646	32,492,570	288,307	32,780,877	3,829,352	-1,134,171	27,817,354	9,826,143	6,993,149	42,951	1,039,241	661,229
2015	47,441,258	34,587,347	251,312	34,838,659	4,034,032	-1,230,975	29,573,652	10,458,568	7,409,038	45,242	1,048,602	681,566
2016	48,876,121	35,945,846	212,340	36,158,186	4,184,664	-1,531,186	30,442,336	10,863,655	7,570,130	46,139	1,059,323	703,098
2017	50,096,526	37,761,594	207,295	37,968,889	4,363,093	-1,651,313	31,954,483	10,524,358	7,617,685	46,865	1,068,952	715,855
2018	52,350,845	39,746,317	229,011	39,975,328	4,642,450	-1,760,876	33,572,002	10,803,598	7,975,245	48,608	1,077,003	732,885
2019	54,311,694	41,187,482	167,515	41,354,997	4,794,340	-2,020,489	34,540,168	11,263,299	8,508,227	50,150	1,082,982	735,682
2020	59,953,115	41,669,560	298,742	41,968,302	4,789,336	-1,944,341	35,234,625	12,116,681	12,601,809	55,061	1,088,852	692,159
2021	66,142,128	45,084,183	344,897	45,429,080	5,146,018	-2,146,829	38,136,233	14,765,371	13,240,524	60,593	1,091,572	722,460
2022	67,983,934	48,937,051	403,241	49,340,292	5,754,813	-2,486,402	41,099,077	16,264,340	10,620,517	62,131	1,094,198	761,403

Personal Income and Employment by Area: Grants Pass, OR

(Thousands of dollars, except as noted.)

Year	Personal income, total	Derivation of personal income: Earnings by place of work: Nonfarm	Farm	Total	Less: Contributions for government social insurance	Plus: Adjustment for residence	Equals: Net earnings by place of residence	Plus: Dividends, interest, and rent	Plus: Personal current transfer receipts	Per capita personal income (dollars)	Population (persons)	Total employment
1970	127,591	84,708	1,526	86,234	6,304	439	80,369	27,610	19,612	3,515	36,304	12,674
1971	145,879	97,541	756	98,297	7,507	763	91,553	31,251	23,075	3,755	38,848	13,786
1972	164,653	112,117	246	112,363	9,217	1,163	104,309	34,611	25,733	4,085	40,305	14,944
1973	189,515	128,229	688	128,917	11,930	1,500	118,487	39,534	31,494	4,392	43,151	16,085
1974	210,775	131,836	2,143	133,979	12,576	2,481	123,884	46,312	40,579	4,603	45,787	15,850
1975	244,329	148,887	2,164	151,051	13,613	2,464	139,902	53,550	50,877	5,087	48,032	16,628
1976	288,436	184,198	2,857	187,055	17,001	2,488	172,542	60,980	54,914	5,688	50,710	18,506
1977	328,896	211,863	2,509	214,372	20,079	2,836	197,129	71,580	60,187	6,259	52,549	19,980
1978	378,846	247,264	1,869	249,133	23,949	3,295	228,479	84,367	66,000	6,794	55,762	21,235
1979	422,644	269,795	2,398	272,193	27,102	4,392	249,483	98,459	74,702	7,300	57,893	22,222
1980	470,418	277,918	3,929	281,847	28,014	5,255	259,088	121,130	90,200	7,980	58,948	22,300
1981	509,072	281,703	2,732	284,435	30,389	4,082	258,128	146,417	104,527	8,599	59,202	21,755
1982	526,348	273,541	2,478	276,019	30,290	3,901	249,630	161,076	115,642	9,051	58,154	21,089
1983	586,156	302,726	2,473	305,199	33,996	5,462	276,665	185,794	123,697	10,186	57,548	21,796
1984	637,123	332,766	2,819	335,585	38,447	7,612	304,750	202,546	129,827	10,784	59,083	22,691
1985	682,224	354,174	2,161	356,335	41,573	7,614	322,376	222,322	137,526	11,246	60,666	23,251
1986	717,211	373,838	1,591	375,429	43,644	9,298	341,083	233,834	142,294	11,815	60,702	23,778
1987	743,204	404,470	1,206	405,676	47,005	10,745	369,416	225,330	148,458	12,136	61,238	24,388
1988	803,287	448,091	1,426	449,517	54,412	11,923	407,028	235,641	160,618	13,015	61,721	25,684
1989	889,260	482,737	2,335	485,072	59,498	11,803	437,377	271,734	180,149	14,374	61,865	26,508
1990	936,023	511,815	2,100	513,915	63,479	14,406	464,842	272,551	198,630	14,861	62,985	26,838
1991	981,513	516,620	2,494	519,114	65,289	16,434	470,259	287,858	223,396	15,200	64,575	26,716
1992	1,036,548	544,658	1,564	546,222	68,861	20,249	497,610	292,486	246,452	15,823	65,507	27,206
1993	1,115,124	586,946	4,314	591,260	73,697	22,483	540,046	309,722	265,356	16,520	67,500	27,970
1994	1,193,242	626,934	5,559	632,493	79,320	27,199	580,372	323,976	288,894	17,192	69,406	29,344
1995	1,283,048	645,406	5,102	650,508	83,051	30,847	598,304	355,983	328,761	17,992	71,313	29,760
1996	1,365,472	692,375	3,890	696,265	88,809	35,021	642,477	373,882	349,113	18,884	72,310	30,589
1997	1,434,489	741,202	3,505	744,707	93,532	39,940	691,115	378,874	364,500	19,532	73,442	31,808
1998	1,525,482	797,896	4,311	802,207	99,068	45,096	748,235	388,871	388,376	20,489	74,455	32,339
1999	1,577,660	845,805	1,351	847,156	104,471	50,794	793,479	359,650	424,531	20,977	75,209	33,340
2000	1,663,140	878,821	684	879,505	108,782	60,684	831,407	387,687	444,046	21,926	75,851	33,734
2001	1,753,312	920,955	1,903	922,858	111,719	68,112	879,251	377,796	496,265	22,934	76,452	33,417
2002	1,799,923	976,650	954	977,604	120,339	73,671	930,936	350,013	518,974	23,161	77,712	33,915
2003	1,894,140	1,061,649	2,635	1,064,284	130,538	77,884	1,011,630	355,240	527,270	24,044	78,779	35,229
2004	2,050,666	1,174,872	4,667	1,179,539	145,266	84,691	1,118,964	392,030	539,672	25,720	79,729	36,698
2005	2,172,201	1,254,520	4,323	1,258,843	158,833	90,522	1,190,532	419,321	562,348	26,930	80,660	37,990
2006	2,306,884	1,319,773	2,315	1,322,088	167,237	90,279	1,245,130	462,967	598,787	28,270	81,601	38,787
2007	2,410,524	1,293,410	-138	1,293,272	168,958	110,442	1,234,756	537,523	638,245	29,488	81,746	38,855
2008	2,410,172	1,233,087	-2,363	1,230,724	165,888	96,231	1,161,067	536,684	712,421	29,254	82,389	37,744
2009	2,408,164	1,187,597	-1,139	1,186,458	163,122	89,728	1,113,064	482,162	812,938	29,255	82,315	35,860
2010	2,477,006	1,216,770	-682	1,216,088	166,948	86,803	1,135,943	460,335	880,728	29,887	82,880	34,892
2011	2,541,105	1,228,518	1,847	1,230,365	153,005	79,087	1,156,447	482,448	902,210	30,717	82,726	35,005
2012	2,645,267	1,265,085	4,073	1,269,158	156,448	103,093	1,215,803	521,354	908,110	31,949	82,796	34,952
2013	2,693,172	1,261,140	4,952	1,266,092	176,283	134,040	1,223,849	525,146	944,177	32,375	83,186	35,041
2014	2,843,856	1,342,938	4,365	1,347,303	188,992	110,012	1,268,323	542,971	1,032,562	34,079	83,449	36,115
2015	3,043,153	1,454,384	3,642	1,458,026	200,794	100,458	1,357,690	575,775	1,109,688	35,960	84,626	37,118
2016	3,149,721	1,543,373	4,252	1,547,625	210,046	103,729	1,441,308	577,852	1,130,561	36,785	85,624	37,757
2017	3,359,027	1,682,750	2,638	1,685,388	227,218	109,067	1,567,237	622,339	1,169,451	38,715	86,762	38,764
2018	3,578,986	1,832,521	2,637	1,835,158	242,437	110,636	1,703,357	640,267	1,235,362	40,924	87,455	39,780
2019	3,833,958	2,022,119	1,423	2,023,542	262,192	85,283	1,846,633	687,860	1,299,465	43,706	87,721	40,186
2020	4,231,297	2,156,948	3,551	2,160,499	278,816	80,744	1,962,427	682,070	1,586,800	47,955	88,235	40,258
2021	4,604,845	2,337,152	2,888	2,340,040	330,616	91,627	2,101,051	723,758	1,780,036	51,979	88,590	41,743
2022	4,576,508	2,419,777	1,012	2,420,789	356,751	107,440	2,171,478	777,613	1,627,417	52,166	87,730	43,365

Personal Income and Employment by Area: Great Falls, MT

(Thousands of dollars, except as noted.)

Year	Personal income, total	Derivation of personal income: Earnings by place of work: Nonfarm	Earnings by place of work: Farm	Earnings by place of work: Total	Less: Contributions for government social insurance	Plus: Adjustment for residence	Equals: Net earnings by place of residence	Plus: Dividends, interest, and rent	Plus: Personal current transfer receipts	Per capita personal income (dollars)	Population (persons)	Total employment
1970	357,739	274,671	13,037	287,708	20,138	-2,111	265,459	65,329	26,951	4,349	82,258	37,297
1971	384,731	293,892	13,295	307,187	21,982	-2,088	283,117	69,545	32,069	4,556	84,453	37,626
1972	429,950	328,497	17,116	345,613	25,407	-2,093	318,113	75,876	35,961	5,068	84,842	38,689
1973	468,382	355,573	17,888	373,461	30,802	-1,945	340,714	86,205	41,463	5,528	84,728	39,742
1974	516,168	389,822	17,376	407,198	34,694	-1,442	371,062	97,763	47,343	6,064	85,126	40,285
1975	558,424	417,570	16,120	433,690	37,319	420	396,791	105,311	56,322	6,594	84,693	39,860
1976	619,187	476,800	10,105	486,905	43,737	1,464	444,632	113,283	61,272	7,296	84,869	42,084
1977	670,908	523,517	3,862	527,379	48,578	3,160	481,961	124,099	64,848	7,779	86,247	43,274
1978	740,513	571,385	7,251	578,636	54,438	6,830	531,028	137,934	71,551	8,550	86,611	44,429
1979	798,648	609,316	5,506	614,822	60,509	10,180	564,493	152,657	81,498	9,454	84,475	44,026
1980	848,176	620,563	6,544	627,107	62,439	16,247	580,915	173,537	93,724	10,520	80,627	42,836
1981	910,885	654,362	4,250	658,612	70,056	9,533	598,089	205,706	107,090	11,360	80,183	42,087
1982	956,058	670,222	4,248	674,470	72,419	8,405	610,456	227,576	118,026	11,982	79,791	41,059
1983	1,019,747	710,399	10,537	720,936	77,767	7,234	650,403	238,733	130,611	12,649	80,621	41,553
1984	1,074,409	741,781	8,905	750,686	84,046	6,851	673,491	261,363	139,555	13,377	80,318	41,719
1985	1,084,177	742,958	1,261	744,219	85,621	6,025	664,623	273,004	146,550	13,622	79,591	40,524
1986	1,118,085	757,102	9,147	766,249	89,223	4,320	681,346	278,932	157,807	14,302	78,179	40,276
1987	1,146,159	777,522	9,394	786,916	91,849	3,831	698,898	279,413	167,848	14,745	77,733	40,260
1988	1,214,698	830,277	5,527	835,804	103,647	2,181	734,338	302,309	178,051	15,637	77,681	42,046
1989	1,302,335	875,469	20,390	895,859	109,806	2,000	788,053	325,036	189,246	16,676	78,098	42,690
1990	1,353,003	920,421	12,318	932,739	122,123	2,415	813,031	334,466	205,506	17,393	77,788	43,160
1991	1,423,557	978,542	18,455	996,997	132,082	948	865,863	339,886	217,808	18,100	78,651	44,293
1992	1,479,012	1,029,610	16,016	1,045,626	141,655	291	904,262	342,632	232,118	18,551	79,727	44,595
1993	1,571,807	1,079,972	35,116	1,115,088	151,703	-738	962,647	359,870	249,290	19,398	81,028	44,940
1994	1,593,921	1,107,873	12,336	1,120,209	155,313	-1,055	963,841	373,082	256,998	19,406	82,134	46,791
1995	1,675,201	1,142,382	15,472	1,157,854	156,308	-2,638	998,908	403,231	273,062	20,379	82,201	47,358
1996	1,727,694	1,183,971	7,935	1,191,906	156,317	-3,493	1,032,096	413,540	282,058	20,960	82,429	47,981
1997	1,775,883	1,199,096	9,215	1,208,311	154,218	-4,108	1,049,985	435,919	289,979	21,962	80,861	47,438
1998	1,868,985	1,265,147	8,516	1,273,663	159,070	-6,373	1,108,220	460,917	299,848	23,157	80,709	48,102
1999	1,884,929	1,291,078	9,690	1,300,768	161,459	-7,906	1,131,403	457,505	296,021	23,387	80,596	47,682
2000	1,968,791	1,331,049	2,228	1,333,277	166,538	-9,304	1,157,435	480,587	330,769	24,512	80,318	47,944
2001	2,048,679	1,395,999	4,962	1,400,961	175,485	-10,347	1,215,129	480,576	352,974	25,591	80,055	47,844
2002	2,142,241	1,484,221	1,753	1,485,974	185,295	-11,931	1,288,748	491,191	362,302	26,829	79,848	47,693
2003	2,233,220	1,559,786	4,941	1,564,727	193,857	-12,117	1,358,753	498,353	376,114	28,044	79,633	47,643
2004	2,367,383	1,651,474	16,473	1,667,947	205,463	-14,092	1,448,392	520,369	398,622	29,519	80,198	48,326
2005	2,464,798	1,725,684	18,073	1,743,757	216,030	-16,089	1,511,638	523,780	429,380	30,794	80,041	48,759
2006	2,662,738	1,840,380	9,947	1,850,327	232,558	-19,367	1,598,402	604,531	459,805	33,291	79,984	49,920
2007	2,791,935	1,904,303	14,720	1,919,023	243,494	-21,275	1,654,254	654,945	482,736	34,856	80,099	50,128
2008	2,921,269	1,974,944	16,526	1,991,470	253,360	-20,899	1,717,211	657,335	546,723	36,276	80,529	50,813
2009	2,962,953	2,038,241	10,339	2,048,580	259,996	-22,520	1,766,064	605,384	591,505	36,725	80,680	50,231
2010	3,136,507	2,147,546	15,840	2,163,386	269,238	-20,805	1,873,343	625,134	638,030	38,445	81,585	49,974
2011	3,227,297	2,177,254	21,592	2,198,846	248,583	-11,940	1,938,323	658,619	630,355	39,311	82,097	49,736
2012	3,297,071	2,176,939	19,353	2,196,292	248,176	5,029	1,953,145	707,608	636,318	40,057	82,310	49,763
2013	3,261,145	2,149,013	27,748	2,176,761	276,370	11,001	1,911,392	700,170	649,583	39,201	83,191	50,039
2014	3,391,468	2,240,841	19,581	2,260,422	290,673	14,300	1,984,049	728,012	679,407	40,685	83,359	50,094
2015	3,491,093	2,309,236	17,902	2,327,138	296,942	7,093	2,037,289	744,935	708,869	41,814	83,491	50,311
2016	3,545,502	2,338,121	13,493	2,351,614	292,718	-2,034	2,056,862	735,754	752,886	42,472	83,478	50,077
2017	3,689,900	2,422,970	3,751	2,426,721	311,754	810	2,115,777	765,814	808,309	44,005	83,852	50,334
2018	3,853,259	2,486,086	18,151	2,504,237	325,854	6,340	2,184,723	840,546	827,990	45,776	84,177	50,626
2019	3,944,548	2,566,499	29,541	2,596,040	332,583	7,746	2,271,203	799,211	874,134	46,902	84,102	50,623
2020	4,258,036	2,656,861	33,951	2,690,812	350,336	-271	2,340,205	838,593	1,079,238	50,449	84,402	49,458
2021	4,609,262	2,885,529	4,506	2,890,035	369,713	-2,785	2,517,537	899,738	1,191,987	54,549	84,498	51,031
2022	4,838,950	3,162,868	40,544	3,203,412	414,380	-4,424	2,784,608	990,125	1,064,217	57,020	84,864	53,176

Personal Income and Employment by Area: Greeley, CO

(Thousands of dollars, except as noted.)

Year	Personal income, total	Derivation of personal income: Earnings by place of work: Nonfarm	Farm	Total	Less: Contributions for government social insurance	Plus: Adjustment for residence	Equals: Net earnings by place of residence	Plus: Dividends, interest, and rent	Plus: Personal current transfer receipts	Per capita personal income (dollars)	Population (persons)	Total employment
1970	331,691	170,975	74,032	245,007	10,272	17,255	251,990	50,900	28,801	3,685	90,012	34,611
1971	368,062	197,135	70,784	267,919	12,225	21,518	277,212	57,097	33,753	3,925	93,779	35,647
1972	431,460	244,014	77,292	321,306	16,200	24,968	330,074	64,144	37,242	4,332	99,597	39,546
1973	513,873	293,321	93,932	387,253	22,619	28,633	393,267	76,129	44,477	4,922	104,411	44,129
1974	613,721	344,588	127,349	471,937	27,829	30,523	474,631	87,798	51,292	5,679	108,059	47,670
1975	670,486	376,142	120,928	497,070	29,231	38,025	505,864	102,237	62,385	6,181	108,479	47,671
1976	726,285	439,870	100,074	539,944	34,841	43,656	548,759	109,805	67,721	6,599	110,052	49,788
1977	745,537	478,520	49,520	528,040	38,072	58,979	548,947	123,442	73,148	6,624	112,555	51,346
1978	871,664	536,035	72,424	608,459	42,909	80,550	646,100	142,967	82,597	7,585	114,919	52,739
1979	978,025	604,891	59,800	664,691	50,846	102,936	716,781	168,514	92,730	8,137	120,194	53,520
1980	1,065,321	655,293	16,013	671,306	55,380	129,636	745,562	206,902	112,857	8,607	123,767	54,564
1981	1,232,142	709,558	68,999	778,557	63,899	140,449	855,107	246,502	130,533	9,875	124,780	55,002
1982	1,294,841	769,127	33,936	803,063	70,895	140,138	872,306	276,362	146,173	10,298	125,733	55,718
1983	1,405,541	845,887	40,986	886,873	78,878	131,316	939,311	305,316	160,914	10,850	129,542	58,126
1984	1,548,344	916,915	85,385	1,002,300	88,737	134,174	1,047,737	329,935	170,672	11,841	130,764	59,839
1985	1,604,734	996,896	56,504	1,053,400	99,499	117,776	1,071,677	354,394	178,663	12,212	131,402	60,864
1986	1,641,922	1,036,242	69,237	1,105,479	106,056	107,015	1,106,438	345,175	190,309	12,466	131,715	60,862
1987	1,709,585	1,075,134	93,869	1,169,003	108,873	96,737	1,156,867	350,933	201,785	12,980	131,713	61,351
1988	1,814,990	1,162,629	119,612	1,282,241	123,424	73,192	1,232,009	367,879	215,102	13,766	131,842	65,219
1989	1,978,076	1,260,501	150,496	1,410,997	136,556	61,342	1,335,783	408,763	233,530	14,963	132,202	66,292
1990	2,051,767	1,332,867	158,672	1,491,539	146,974	58,020	1,402,585	400,939	248,243	15,525	132,161	66,690
1991	2,159,327	1,427,706	140,126	1,567,832	163,701	70,484	1,474,615	412,119	272,593	16,083	134,262	68,491
1992	2,334,427	1,540,781	133,374	1,674,155	173,718	108,144	1,608,581	418,982	306,864	16,970	137,560	69,676
1993	2,587,430	1,688,187	180,102	1,868,289	193,207	133,523	1,808,605	450,314	328,511	18,146	142,586	73,905
1994	2,763,804	1,836,512	142,257	1,978,769	211,562	157,873	1,925,080	488,317	350,407	18,760	147,328	77,289
1995	2,935,290	1,942,759	114,611	2,057,370	221,986	184,968	2,020,352	516,983	397,955	19,293	152,140	79,705
1996	3,201,610	2,076,067	152,216	2,228,283	231,869	228,382	2,224,796	567,088	409,726	20,505	156,140	82,605
1997	3,455,518	2,218,265	188,080	2,406,345	243,969	280,704	2,443,080	593,723	418,715	21,393	161,525	86,239
1998	3,840,093	2,479,772	185,670	2,665,442	247,932	348,822	2,766,332	646,503	427,258	23,057	166,547	89,357
1999	4,208,126	2,749,869	208,377	2,958,246	271,280	415,698	3,102,664	643,938	461,524	24,137	174,342	92,082
2000	4,640,463	3,025,098	176,691	3,201,789	294,496	526,439	3,433,732	714,344	492,387	25,377	182,861	95,735
2001	5,004,179	3,201,258	270,794	3,472,052	325,591	555,525	3,701,986	752,433	549,760	26,015	192,360	103,132
2002	5,021,000	3,388,995	146,890	3,535,885	358,006	524,215	3,702,094	712,589	606,317	24,828	202,234	104,924
2003	5,268,056	3,505,890	145,363	3,651,253	372,744	585,889	3,864,398	760,850	642,808	25,223	208,858	108,332
2004	5,826,468	3,727,097	190,522	3,917,619	407,161	799,190	4,309,648	834,332	682,488	27,059	215,322	112,357
2005	6,394,054	3,958,171	235,805	4,193,976	433,568	962,656	4,723,064	922,003	748,987	28,688	222,879	116,670
2006	6,915,948	4,281,804	179,281	4,461,085	466,157	1,146,408	5,141,336	964,711	809,901	29,978	230,703	121,487
2007	7,672,542	4,571,102	243,474	4,814,576	502,327	1,335,282	5,647,531	1,155,260	869,751	32,279	237,692	126,303
2008	8,283,671	4,740,371	238,183	4,978,554	526,654	1,465,409	5,917,309	1,337,554	1,028,808	34,027	243,442	125,726
2009	8,137,164	4,460,026	184,903	4,644,929	496,411	1,586,691	5,735,209	1,232,240	1,169,715	32,786	248,193	122,018
2010	8,504,144	4,613,047	271,746	4,884,793	511,813	1,509,869	5,882,849	1,269,342	1,351,953	33,458	254,172	121,407
2011	9,187,200	5,054,036	289,748	5,343,784	504,330	1,528,755	6,368,209	1,411,622	1,407,369	35,526	258,604	126,412
2012	9,801,325	5,588,981	340,657	5,929,638	550,242	1,535,449	6,914,845	1,463,981	1,422,499	37,191	263,543	129,877
2013	10,481,395	6,153,676	392,016	6,545,692	659,137	1,606,323	7,492,878	1,511,012	1,477,505	38,907	269,395	136,888
2014	11,726,005	7,115,689	472,637	7,588,326	754,959	1,518,883	8,352,250	1,771,216	1,602,539	42,404	276,529	146,133
2015	12,516,198	7,409,182	597,932	8,007,114	793,016	1,712,279	8,926,377	1,851,536	1,738,285	43,873	285,282	150,061
2016	12,938,222	7,401,612	509,168	7,910,780	794,238	2,163,855	9,280,397	1,828,052	1,829,773	43,882	294,841	148,519
2017	13,517,947	7,786,645	461,520	8,248,165	859,313	2,188,100	9,576,952	2,040,764	1,900,231	44,352	304,788	156,081
2018	14,980,012	8,656,385	409,427	9,065,812	945,069	2,487,671	10,608,414	2,295,507	2,076,091	47,817	313,278	162,390
2019	16,021,244	9,110,215	454,842	9,565,057	1,002,501	2,844,680	11,407,236	2,416,258	2,197,750	49,708	322,305	166,305
2020	17,207,773	8,913,730	406,270	9,320,000	985,525	3,363,684	11,698,159	2,456,978	3,052,636	51,920	331,427	163,062
2021	19,230,730	9,180,933	470,548	9,651,481	1,007,920	4,148,079	12,791,640	2,863,852	3,575,238	56,592	339,811	167,685
2022	20,611,438	10,112,998	398,120	10,511,118	1,150,276	5,019,208	14,380,050	3,121,161	3,110,227	58,860	350,176	176,574

Personal Income and Employment by Area: Green Bay, WI

(Thousands of dollars, except as noted.)

Year	Personal income, total	Derivation of personal income: Earnings by place of work: Nonfarm	Farm	Total	Less: Contributions for government social insurance	Plus: Adjustment for residence	Equals: Net earnings by place of residence	Plus: Dividends, interest, and rent	Plus: Personal current transfer receipts	Per capita personal income (dollars)	Population (persons)	Total employment
1970	723,595	568,772	26,951	595,723	42,146	-2,902	550,675	113,239	59,681	3,554	203,616	84,132
1971	787,959	616,445	28,725	645,170	47,141	-3,678	594,351	124,304	69,304	3,814	206,593	84,910
1972	872,204	690,828	29,312	720,140	55,645	-4,683	659,812	135,357	77,035	4,184	208,479	89,459
1973	972,298	770,852	33,593	804,445	71,346	-3,882	729,217	153,938	89,143	4,609	210,941	94,338
1974	1,097,809	868,232	31,139	899,371	83,458	-4,612	811,301	177,764	108,744	5,172	212,277	98,309
1975	1,222,330	950,818	32,090	982,908	89,570	-4,320	889,018	196,751	136,561	5,675	215,386	100,255
1976	1,361,715	1,063,775	36,830	1,100,605	101,874	-2,297	996,434	211,575	153,706	6,257	217,622	103,497
1977	1,542,093	1,207,214	52,286	1,259,500	114,792	-859	1,143,849	236,141	162,103	7,053	218,655	107,283
1978	1,736,528	1,372,594	48,825	1,421,419	133,934	1,719	1,289,204	266,289	181,035	7,884	220,260	112,205
1979	1,942,551	1,508,557	67,284	1,575,841	153,374	8,535	1,431,002	299,311	212,238	8,798	220,801	114,982
1980	2,166,565	1,624,828	70,215	1,695,043	165,303	9,919	1,539,659	371,131	255,775	9,657	224,345	115,673
1981	2,368,987	1,751,084	53,614	1,804,698	190,829	7,175	1,621,044	455,304	292,639	10,476	226,129	114,829
1982	2,530,678	1,851,639	49,943	1,901,582	204,176	-1,303	1,696,103	510,915	323,660	11,135	227,271	115,900
1983	2,707,042	2,013,353	28,352	2,041,705	221,114	-11,241	1,809,350	547,461	350,231	11,860	228,249	117,407
1984	3,003,498	2,253,006	46,873	2,299,879	254,312	-18,931	2,026,636	615,574	361,288	13,005	230,950	122,659
1985	3,227,818	2,435,652	56,057	2,491,709	277,836	-26,487	2,187,386	660,237	380,195	13,896	232,292	126,109
1986	3,430,134	2,633,306	55,903	2,689,209	299,488	-33,444	2,356,277	681,913	391,944	14,614	234,712	131,147
1987	3,578,227	2,796,453	62,502	2,858,955	312,667	-40,046	2,506,242	666,381	405,604	15,101	236,959	132,768
1988	3,789,233	2,988,209	38,158	3,026,367	344,451	-50,500	2,631,416	736,470	421,347	15,824	239,462	136,000
1989	4,172,294	3,187,002	96,220	3,283,222	364,293	-58,638	2,860,291	857,461	454,542	17,296	241,229	138,858
1990	4,473,256	3,530,005	76,628	3,606,633	420,243	-79,617	3,106,773	878,731	487,752	18,279	244,716	145,741
1991	4,697,014	3,718,119	56,536	3,774,655	447,195	-62,196	3,265,264	895,652	536,098	18,862	249,019	147,990
1992	5,077,521	4,062,741	73,858	4,136,599	482,357	-65,812	3,588,430	910,216	578,875	20,063	253,077	152,470
1993	5,396,449	4,373,207	57,581	4,430,788	517,199	-91,534	3,822,055	966,784	607,610	20,925	257,897	157,686
1994	5,764,574	4,716,105	72,490	4,788,595	565,259	-128,942	4,094,394	1,041,281	628,899	21,997	262,056	164,348
1995	6,111,756	4,979,922	46,735	5,026,657	601,021	-160,361	4,265,275	1,177,311	669,170	22,911	266,765	170,096
1996	6,532,638	5,271,944	72,413	5,344,357	631,804	-179,216	4,533,337	1,299,334	699,967	24,116	270,879	174,894
1997	7,056,250	5,758,015	54,416	5,812,431	685,183	-220,022	4,907,226	1,424,951	724,073	25,736	274,177	179,143
1998	7,541,147	6,143,632	90,304	6,233,936	725,345	-238,480	5,270,111	1,526,202	744,834	27,231	276,931	183,607
1999	7,874,533	6,634,854	94,194	6,729,048	784,256	-323,117	5,621,675	1,480,918	771,940	28,113	280,100	190,780
2000	8,422,802	7,138,862	68,234	7,207,096	833,331	-400,819	5,972,946	1,622,100	827,756	29,733	283,282	196,203
2001	8,629,956	7,176,226	87,080	7,263,306	822,957	-392,524	6,047,825	1,658,604	923,527	30,198	285,783	195,881
2002	8,952,128	7,483,956	80,052	7,564,008	859,624	-394,226	6,310,158	1,632,400	1,009,570	31,007	288,713	195,989
2003	9,313,791	7,837,562	119,140	7,956,702	896,480	-393,126	6,667,096	1,597,977	1,048,718	31,988	291,169	199,253
2004	9,790,534	8,286,008	138,742	8,424,750	947,900	-429,207	7,047,643	1,654,630	1,088,261	33,237	294,570	204,051
2005	10,090,225	8,517,706	121,586	8,639,292	984,280	-410,862	7,244,150	1,662,359	1,183,716	33,997	296,800	205,767
2006	10,653,440	8,850,634	99,627	8,950,261	1,025,484	-429,912	7,494,865	1,876,964	1,281,611	35,666	298,702	206,836
2007	11,185,419	9,128,465	162,106	9,290,571	1,059,510	-429,442	7,801,619	1,987,441	1,396,359	37,137	301,190	209,194
2008	11,749,015	9,382,344	162,297	9,544,641	1,099,932	-424,758	8,019,951	2,137,763	1,591,301	38,844	302,468	207,786
2009	11,590,302	9,247,306	67,467	9,314,773	1,084,242	-416,354	7,814,177	1,944,467	1,831,658	38,040	304,686	202,059
2010	12,080,369	9,454,529	142,518	9,597,047	1,111,236	-437,323	8,048,488	2,045,212	1,986,669	39,367	306,867	201,969
2011	12,765,893	9,932,672	225,229	10,157,901	1,036,493	-465,299	8,656,109	2,163,806	1,945,978	41,285	309,212	204,711
2012	13,421,294	10,385,281	243,197	10,628,478	1,074,110	-457,861	9,096,507	2,358,443	1,966,344	43,060	311,691	206,577
2013	13,583,781	10,735,878	257,494	10,993,372	1,244,621	-500,987	9,247,764	2,316,402	2,019,615	43,324	313,540	208,615
2014	14,063,168	10,965,829	321,755	11,287,584	1,275,349	-465,685	9,546,550	2,413,476	2,103,142	44,489	316,105	210,999
2015	14,585,335	11,452,414	248,109	11,700,523	1,326,509	-521,928	9,852,086	2,539,272	2,193,977	45,829	318,259	213,895
2016	14,813,098	11,600,879	178,675	11,779,554	1,343,832	-524,956	9,910,766	2,632,549	2,269,783	46,221	320,483	215,854
2017	15,486,153	12,021,214	198,706	12,219,920	1,406,061	-538,463	10,275,396	2,829,911	2,380,846	47,916	323,196	218,142
2018	16,421,451	12,702,171	169,996	12,872,167	1,462,702	-604,495	10,804,970	3,049,484	2,566,997	50,480	325,306	221,641
2019	16,949,145	13,010,252	202,773	13,213,025	1,511,668	-617,350	11,084,007	3,185,183	2,679,955	51,838	326,962	220,727
2020	18,338,937	13,265,826	259,647	13,525,473	1,545,459	-629,613	11,350,401	3,556,339	3,432,197	55,818	328,551	212,993
2021	19,605,125	13,932,421	240,352	14,172,773	1,614,661	-639,875	11,918,237	3,771,609	3,915,279	59,629	328,784	218,718
2022	20,206,881	14,859,812	263,734	15,123,546	1,759,008	-704,163	12,660,375	4,164,729	3,381,777	61,179	330,292	226,695

Personal Income and Employment by Area: Greensboro-High Point, NC

(Thousands of dollars, except as noted.)

Year	Personal income, total	Derivation of personal income: Earnings by place of work: Nonfarm	Earnings by place of work: Farm	Earnings by place of work: Total	Less: Contributions for government social insurance	Plus: Adjustment for residence	Equals: Net earnings by place of residence	Plus: Dividends, interest, and rent	Plus: Personal current transfer receipts	Per capita personal income (dollars)	Population (persons)	Total employment
1970	1,732,134	1,582,881	25,267	1,608,148	112,594	-84,167	1,411,387	208,940	111,807	3,948	438,730	247,290
1971	1,898,502	1,735,432	29,467	1,764,899	128,225	-98,959	1,537,715	228,812	131,975	4,237	448,079	251,788
1972	2,112,332	1,951,088	29,637	1,980,725	151,619	-114,907	1,714,199	251,481	146,652	4,637	455,577	262,903
1973	2,343,880	2,161,142	48,538	2,209,680	192,675	-128,401	1,888,604	283,978	171,298	5,087	460,732	272,867
1974	2,552,770	2,331,214	42,217	2,373,431	215,681	-143,080	2,014,670	327,723	210,377	5,501	464,097	272,067
1975	2,729,702	2,391,914	46,541	2,438,455	216,506	-149,287	2,072,662	356,806	300,234	5,851	466,520	258,218
1976	2,998,783	2,651,047	47,890	2,698,937	245,749	-166,917	2,286,271	390,453	322,059	6,362	471,352	268,292
1977	3,321,180	2,960,163	46,006	3,006,169	273,013	-188,910	2,544,246	438,513	338,421	6,959	477,233	278,421
1978	3,780,639	3,433,254	49,194	3,482,448	326,691	-237,130	2,918,627	494,830	367,182	7,836	482,440	291,685
1979	4,169,559	3,803,078	32,284	3,835,362	375,104	-268,693	3,191,565	560,147	417,847	8,558	487,216	298,117
1980	4,620,320	4,112,067	23,149	4,135,216	406,218	-298,967	3,430,031	689,798	500,491	9,368	493,196	296,162
1981	5,162,364	4,491,894	43,888	4,535,782	475,054	-334,560	3,726,168	859,177	577,019	10,388	496,975	298,011
1982	5,482,338	4,688,531	47,363	4,735,894	500,111	-354,412	3,881,371	958,278	642,689	10,950	500,656	295,265
1983	5,969,261	5,146,874	33,403	5,180,277	552,305	-395,415	4,232,557	1,050,980	685,724	11,838	504,241	302,975
1984	6,695,755	5,798,995	32,881	5,831,876	639,045	-448,454	4,744,377	1,232,233	719,145	13,170	508,397	320,355
1985	7,173,579	6,206,659	32,460	6,239,119	692,214	-476,702	5,070,203	1,335,574	767,802	14,004	512,256	327,294
1986	7,692,716	6,666,345	37,953	6,704,298	757,438	-511,721	5,435,139	1,442,558	815,019	14,886	516,765	338,297
1987	8,343,757	7,387,134	34,186	7,421,320	825,923	-575,556	6,019,841	1,473,377	850,539	15,947	523,217	351,897
1988	9,137,740	7,991,259	51,903	8,043,162	914,104	-624,503	6,504,555	1,711,467	921,718	17,241	530,011	364,650
1989	9,802,802	8,471,197	81,424	8,552,621	967,586	-658,708	6,926,327	1,852,702	1,023,773	18,311	535,336	368,711
1990	10,458,082	8,869,060	94,276	8,963,336	1,040,295	-689,531	7,233,510	2,108,826	1,115,746	19,274	542,612	373,827
1991	10,766,171	8,986,075	100,492	9,086,567	1,067,433	-654,972	7,364,162	2,137,737	1,264,272	19,476	552,787	365,866
1992	11,572,263	9,750,456	100,651	9,851,107	1,141,837	-696,522	8,012,748	2,173,292	1,386,223	20,606	561,591	368,982
1993	12,262,801	10,302,681	113,315	10,415,996	1,216,308	-775,697	8,423,991	2,328,289	1,510,521	21,465	571,281	381,473
1994	13,033,323	11,015,725	120,599	11,136,324	1,313,291	-825,774	8,997,259	2,460,315	1,575,749	22,398	581,897	391,593
1995	13,822,283	11,705,459	118,868	11,824,327	1,397,498	-940,721	9,486,108	2,578,283	1,757,892	23,255	594,390	405,535
1996	14,731,894	12,350,650	137,178	12,487,828	1,458,882	-1,023,858	10,005,088	2,814,470	1,912,336	24,343	605,175	414,861
1997	15,774,387	13,136,041	139,871	13,275,912	1,537,512	-1,056,843	10,681,557	3,089,517	2,003,313	25,627	615,526	423,430
1998	16,878,409	14,084,198	140,740	14,224,938	1,645,589	-1,099,608	11,479,741	3,310,464	2,088,204	26,924	626,891	427,270
1999	17,436,433	14,897,603	146,895	15,044,498	1,741,108	-1,192,187	12,111,203	3,136,807	2,188,423	27,372	637,026	434,398
2000	18,238,628	15,419,731	129,924	15,549,655	1,798,470	-1,183,164	12,568,021	3,327,719	2,342,888	28,259	645,409	437,861
2001	18,731,388	15,792,348	136,387	15,928,735	1,838,663	-1,224,241	12,865,831	3,257,664	2,607,893	28,697	652,741	436,712
2002	18,858,398	15,915,671	63,891	15,979,562	1,842,298	-1,258,463	12,878,801	3,170,281	2,809,316	28,666	657,855	431,444
2003	19,267,655	16,310,798	72,375	16,383,173	1,928,270	-1,338,198	13,116,705	3,226,949	2,924,001	29,055	663,140	430,124
2004	20,458,588	17,047,366	99,600	17,146,966	1,993,577	-1,294,915	13,858,474	3,438,200	3,161,914	30,640	667,711	437,754
2005	21,514,262	17,791,183	113,918	17,905,101	2,099,155	-1,368,735	14,437,211	3,675,319	3,401,732	31,775	677,080	445,613
2006	23,112,660	18,882,636	109,869	18,992,505	2,198,281	-1,425,902	15,368,322	4,050,752	3,693,586	33,514	689,637	455,391
2007	24,155,220	19,501,996	79,181	19,581,177	2,287,070	-1,529,738	15,764,369	4,439,000	3,951,851	34,484	700,485	464,615
2008	25,067,774	19,788,421	59,885	19,848,306	2,320,111	-1,535,351	15,992,844	4,552,375	4,522,555	35,237	711,405	460,754
2009	24,215,816	18,637,107	70,294	18,707,401	2,210,241	-1,376,073	15,121,087	3,992,182	5,102,547	33,684	718,902	437,298
2010	24,857,343	19,064,038	75,894	19,139,932	2,235,973	-1,375,739	15,528,220	3,905,149	5,423,974	34,271	725,316	434,447
2011	25,649,617	19,323,084	36,301	19,359,385	2,080,339	-1,356,128	15,922,918	4,188,211	5,538,488	35,122	730,309	442,997
2012	26,941,521	20,293,127	77,218	20,370,345	2,146,786	-1,399,355	16,824,204	4,501,206	5,616,111	36,615	735,810	445,751
2013	26,813,695	20,705,461	90,460	20,795,921	2,511,299	-1,465,577	16,819,045	4,295,962	5,698,688	36,184	741,036	450,674
2014	28,294,355	21,568,618	122,080	21,690,698	2,610,976	-1,394,159	17,685,563	4,686,812	5,921,980	37,877	747,011	457,315
2015	29,783,421	22,562,918	121,496	22,684,414	2,725,017	-1,421,474	18,537,923	4,982,035	6,263,463	39,613	751,869	466,170
2016	30,144,799	22,780,139	81,647	22,861,786	2,729,653	-1,474,759	18,657,374	5,109,010	6,378,415	39,704	759,247	470,832
2017	31,290,353	23,590,926	101,902	23,692,828	2,804,003	-1,564,425	19,324,400	5,373,522	6,592,431	41,021	762,787	472,698
2018	32,584,865	24,388,373	46,745	24,435,118	2,853,934	-1,551,185	20,029,999	5,619,271	6,935,595	42,461	767,401	478,618
2019	34,428,215	25,600,053	53,377	25,653,430	2,991,653	-1,571,330	21,090,447	5,973,142	7,364,626	44,554	772,730	483,280
2020	36,708,286	26,043,082	49,876	26,092,958	3,054,737	-1,514,933	21,523,288	5,837,010	9,347,988	47,359	775,104	468,339
2021	40,197,375	27,681,211	78,907	27,760,118	3,252,674	-1,511,161	22,996,283	6,401,882	10,799,210	51,593	779,125	483,456
2022	41,035,771	29,585,470	113,128	29,698,598	3,529,397	-1,624,644	24,544,557	6,999,136	9,492,078	52,335	784,101	499,419

Personal Income and Employment by Area: Greenville, NC

(Thousands of dollars, except as noted.)

Year	Personal income, total	Derivation of personal income: Earnings by place of work: Nonfarm	Farm	Total	Less: Contributions for government social insurance	Plus: Adjustment for residence	Equals: Net earnings by place of residence	Plus: Dividends, interest, and rent	Plus: Personal current transfer receipts	Per capita personal income (dollars)	Population (persons)	Total employment
1970	217,915	137,288	31,833	169,121	9,442	7,107	166,786	30,911	20,218	2,941	74,101	32,746
1971	236,862	158,056	25,375	183,431	11,293	7,848	179,986	33,751	23,125	3,145	75,306	33,622
1972	265,316	177,025	28,590	205,615	13,155	10,292	202,752	37,703	24,861	3,539	74,977	34,854
1973	310,619	199,898	42,623	242,521	17,074	12,152	237,599	44,363	28,657	4,099	75,787	36,126
1974	352,192	224,206	44,966	269,172	19,969	15,769	264,972	51,862	35,358	4,636	75,977	37,100
1975	405,664	258,569	47,129	305,698	23,147	17,238	299,789	59,383	46,492	5,142	78,887	37,475
1976	462,176	296,537	51,297	347,834	27,161	21,331	342,004	66,428	53,744	5,767	80,147	39,729
1977	486,896	334,443	24,155	358,598	30,283	24,331	352,646	75,954	58,296	6,015	80,948	40,727
1978	566,804	379,836	47,162	426,998	35,460	27,257	418,795	84,327	63,682	6,915	81,969	41,601
1979	604,560	426,208	20,821	447,029	41,457	30,469	436,041	94,676	73,843	7,300	82,819	43,563
1980	700,731	475,032	28,325	503,357	46,473	35,653	492,537	118,561	89,633	7,736	90,580	43,433
1981	794,024	525,309	35,185	560,494	55,352	38,079	543,221	147,912	102,891	8,626	92,047	44,149
1982	866,505	566,857	41,688	608,545	60,823	37,344	585,066	168,607	112,832	9,277	93,400	44,824
1983	927,766	629,339	21,149	650,488	67,871	40,284	622,901	182,319	122,546	9,792	94,750	46,159
1984	1,058,658	730,122	35,167	765,289	80,509	40,104	724,884	205,200	128,574	11,009	96,164	48,581
1985	1,128,495	781,517	34,765	816,282	86,971	43,464	772,775	218,671	137,049	11,547	97,730	49,206
1986	1,218,865	861,438	31,169	892,607	97,342	43,334	838,599	235,251	145,015	12,234	99,626	51,663
1987	1,320,854	952,467	32,498	984,965	105,837	46,019	925,147	245,672	150,035	12,949	102,001	53,714
1988	1,473,099	1,063,172	43,205	1,106,377	122,968	48,572	1,031,981	280,122	160,996	14,123	104,306	57,254
1989	1,662,971	1,195,880	47,865	1,243,745	137,500	43,883	1,150,128	330,493	182,350	15,619	106,474	59,652
1990	1,815,946	1,322,371	54,999	1,377,370	153,437	34,813	1,258,746	344,714	212,486	16,652	109,054	62,264
1991	1,927,098	1,371,088	56,497	1,427,585	160,932	53,890	1,320,543	359,432	247,123	17,212	111,965	61,864
1992	2,065,267	1,500,945	42,116	1,543,061	173,496	48,821	1,418,386	370,636	276,245	18,066	114,318	62,509
1993	2,216,282	1,618,738	41,781	1,660,519	186,632	42,996	1,516,883	392,108	307,291	18,987	116,728	64,747
1994	2,347,207	1,739,749	43,301	1,783,050	202,221	13,487	1,594,316	431,635	321,256	19,610	119,694	67,248
1995	2,533,273	1,847,686	28,171	1,875,857	214,195	31,276	1,692,938	472,575	367,760	20,676	122,525	71,899
1996	2,679,519	1,951,259	51,852	2,003,111	223,116	-18,914	1,761,081	516,664	401,774	21,460	124,861	72,840
1997	2,913,713	2,099,700	61,051	2,160,751	238,592	-1,329	1,920,830	571,795	421,088	22,797	127,812	73,994
1998	3,007,328	2,207,378	25,190	2,232,568	252,510	6,117	1,986,175	610,491	410,662	23,041	130,519	74,574
1999	3,132,758	2,373,472	16,643	2,390,115	272,347	-43,849	2,073,919	601,354	457,485	23,634	132,554	77,601
2000	3,362,596	2,577,602	36,589	2,614,191	293,428	-62,513	2,258,250	627,222	477,124	25,038	134,298	79,638
2001	3,452,720	2,669,431	29,737	2,699,168	298,481	-73,790	2,326,897	606,858	518,965	25,275	136,605	80,176
2002	3,561,812	2,751,746	16,506	2,768,252	307,452	-93,217	2,367,583	623,403	570,826	25,601	139,128	80,734
2003	3,702,344	2,838,999	20,720	2,859,719	323,958	-110,380	2,425,381	669,365	607,598	26,145	141,610	81,221
2004	3,933,913	2,979,309	27,675	3,006,984	337,787	-108,037	2,561,160	714,599	658,154	27,227	144,486	83,743
2005	4,243,022	3,193,809	25,556	3,219,365	365,724	-101,118	2,752,523	761,710	728,789	28,683	147,929	86,277
2006	4,625,286	3,451,204	26,138	3,477,342	389,377	-114,956	2,973,009	834,918	817,359	30,244	152,934	89,253
2007	4,979,346	3,688,281	33,386	3,721,667	420,597	-114,111	3,186,959	898,610	893,777	31,619	157,479	93,878
2008	5,323,899	3,806,195	41,971	3,848,166	431,893	-107,888	3,308,385	993,289	1,022,225	32,840	162,116	94,591
2009	5,294,905	3,749,914	45,397	3,795,311	428,743	-104,534	3,262,034	927,122	1,105,749	31,978	165,581	91,734
2010	5,472,483	3,922,289	41,051	3,963,340	441,922	-122,979	3,398,439	895,296	1,178,748	32,462	168,582	91,865
2011	5,640,831	3,955,110	43,241	3,998,351	405,087	-109,589	3,483,675	937,235	1,219,921	33,302	169,382	93,856
2012	6,077,608	4,263,736	64,312	4,328,048	429,448	-136,003	3,762,597	1,050,734	1,264,277	35,664	170,413	95,591
2013	6,091,755	4,341,072	72,080	4,413,152	500,141	-133,707	3,779,304	1,017,785	1,294,666	35,697	170,652	96,303
2014	6,328,339	4,513,712	79,243	4,592,955	522,534	-156,807	3,913,614	1,082,438	1,332,287	37,206	170,087	97,882
2015	6,512,982	4,678,646	44,342	4,722,988	539,251	-181,496	4,002,241	1,143,233	1,367,508	38,308	170,015	98,469
2016	6,704,218	4,819,024	44,044	4,863,068	554,074	-182,229	4,126,765	1,159,104	1,418,349	39,457	169,913	99,322
2017	6,951,839	5,031,608	51,656	5,083,264	572,464	-194,029	4,316,771	1,163,156	1,471,912	40,881	170,051	100,282
2018	7,331,644	5,305,497	18,759	5,324,256	594,660	-219,288	4,510,308	1,264,021	1,557,315	43,168	169,839	102,500
2019	7,731,083	5,613,810	29,278	5,643,088	626,674	-254,440	4,761,974	1,329,644	1,639,465	45,437	170,150	103,798
2020	8,334,899	5,779,200	19,794	5,798,994	650,641	-247,078	4,901,275	1,342,365	2,091,259	48,920	170,378	101,697
2021	9,081,502	6,139,061	52,669	6,191,730	692,390	-261,656	5,237,684	1,399,523	2,444,295	52,716	172,273	104,870
2022	9,283,701	6,602,403	41,997	6,644,400	754,282	-254,659	5,635,459	1,466,304	2,181,938	53,495	173,542	108,707

Personal Income and Employment by Area: Greenville-Anderson, SC

(Thousands of dollars, except as noted.)

Year	Personal income, total	Derivation of personal income: Earnings by place of work: Nonfarm	Farm	Total	Less: Contributions for government social insurance	Plus: Adjustment for residence	Equals: Net earnings by place of residence	Plus: Dividends, interest, and rent	Plus: Personal current transfer receipts	Per capita personal income (dollars)	Population (persons)	Total employment
1970	1,517,638	1,293,717	8,982	1,302,699	91,249	15,671	1,227,121	173,462	117,055	3,326	456,342	218,306
1971	1,662,943	1,412,959	11,057	1,424,016	103,491	14,053	1,334,578	192,023	136,342	3,556	467,592	222,013
1972	1,881,594	1,623,546	9,444	1,632,990	124,784	8,914	1,517,120	212,529	151,945	3,918	480,222	236,053
1973	2,156,975	1,876,081	15,114	1,891,195	165,193	3,580	1,729,582	245,943	181,450	4,389	491,446	252,272
1974	2,430,522	2,103,600	12,242	2,115,842	191,998	-5,886	1,917,958	285,791	226,773	4,811	505,159	260,780
1975	2,583,672	2,127,910	10,248	2,138,158	188,404	-2,358	1,947,396	315,266	321,010	5,048	511,828	245,959
1976	2,908,608	2,441,789	11,286	2,453,075	222,212	-1,082	2,229,781	343,912	334,915	5,683	511,833	258,160
1977	3,222,013	2,729,079	11,405	2,740,484	248,827	-8,633	2,483,024	386,767	352,222	6,135	525,157	267,903
1978	3,629,476	3,102,405	14,667	3,117,072	290,594	-15,926	2,810,552	434,931	383,993	6,795	534,157	279,956
1979	4,091,553	3,497,367	18,593	3,515,960	338,065	-24,405	3,153,490	494,803	443,260	7,533	543,173	288,304
1980	4,631,302	3,866,445	4,404	3,870,849	372,658	-26,156	3,472,035	620,288	538,979	8,340	555,331	291,377
1981	5,162,331	4,219,502	5,059	4,224,561	436,152	-29,495	3,758,914	772,405	631,012	9,150	564,171	292,183
1982	5,454,750	4,304,405	10,036	4,314,441	451,197	-26,750	3,836,494	913,935	704,321	9,590	568,779	286,688
1983	5,916,973	4,670,057	4,206	4,674,263	497,912	-27,013	4,149,338	1,015,938	751,697	10,351	571,626	291,548
1984	6,542,552	5,179,946	11,794	5,191,740	569,765	-26,911	4,595,064	1,157,867	789,621	11,361	575,900	304,398
1985	7,027,653	5,553,548	8,695	5,562,243	618,437	-28,007	4,915,799	1,250,659	861,195	12,085	581,502	310,248
1986	7,546,962	6,009,604	6,087	6,015,691	686,336	-35,717	5,293,638	1,340,482	912,842	12,868	586,510	318,643
1987	8,126,007	6,568,268	13,879	6,582,147	739,784	-36,905	5,805,458	1,378,944	941,605	13,712	592,638	328,469
1988	8,987,084	7,308,389	18,862	7,327,251	844,693	-50,015	6,432,543	1,548,991	1,005,550	14,933	601,817	345,744
1989	9,715,834	7,810,300	21,905	7,832,205	913,491	-63,625	6,855,089	1,730,944	1,129,801	15,914	610,505	356,698
1990	10,500,122	8,415,151	22,059	8,437,210	1,001,801	-87,539	7,347,870	1,894,585	1,257,667	16,928	620,288	364,023
1991	10,861,349	8,599,197	21,967	8,621,164	1,038,668	-79,447	7,503,049	1,916,241	1,442,059	17,279	628,575	358,319
1992	11,546,205	9,021,057	28,135	9,049,192	1,079,692	10,735	7,980,235	1,958,203	1,607,767	18,116	637,366	358,466
1993	12,284,129	9,686,658	31,473	9,718,131	1,169,456	-29,883	8,518,792	2,050,485	1,714,852	18,980	647,208	372,522
1994	13,150,942	10,332,964	33,321	10,366,285	1,262,494	-5,713	9,098,078	2,192,285	1,860,579	20,010	657,228	383,788
1995	14,206,773	11,116,545	22,907	11,139,452	1,364,194	13,361	9,788,619	2,447,993	1,970,161	21,250	668,549	398,851
1996	15,118,435	11,779,574	10,759	11,790,333	1,420,055	-7,333	10,362,945	2,646,716	2,108,774	22,192	681,257	409,377
1997	16,021,123	12,433,582	18,703	12,452,285	1,498,581	20,076	10,973,780	2,848,606	2,198,737	23,100	693,566	418,744
1998	17,287,082	13,357,101	19,993	13,377,094	1,608,087	72,280	11,841,287	3,129,616	2,316,179	24,476	706,300	427,192
1999	17,973,654	14,157,217	27,821	14,185,038	1,692,276	15,120	12,507,882	3,014,348	2,451,424	25,050	717,514	437,552
2000	19,267,125	15,124,937	31,760	15,156,697	1,796,844	-46,857	13,312,996	3,299,891	2,654,238	26,475	727,743	448,598
2001	20,130,367	15,713,625	29,280	15,742,905	1,859,079	-43,509	13,840,317	3,309,281	2,980,769	27,363	735,668	440,664
2002	20,383,846	15,727,103	20,991	15,748,094	1,862,440	-21,252	13,864,402	3,280,999	3,238,445	27,504	741,131	428,784
2003	20,729,771	16,044,340	14,418	16,058,758	1,917,735	-43,024	14,097,999	3,251,096	3,380,676	27,740	747,276	430,609
2004	21,303,325	16,177,681	26,281	16,203,962	1,959,414	43,206	14,287,754	3,338,924	3,676,647	28,246	754,196	435,726
2005	22,322,915	16,865,818	32,847	16,898,665	2,045,369	20,792	14,874,088	3,486,414	3,962,413	29,255	763,048	446,434
2006	24,036,168	17,830,780	10,949	17,841,729	2,207,759	71,718	15,705,688	4,016,036	4,314,444	30,915	777,494	457,280
2007	25,812,910	18,837,299	4,977	18,842,276	2,316,535	147,018	16,672,759	4,550,339	4,589,812	32,530	793,500	470,193
2008	26,996,113	19,232,584	-1,745	19,230,839	2,391,137	135,885	16,975,587	4,724,885	5,295,641	33,379	808,765	470,324
2009	26,056,693	18,141,481	16,319	18,157,800	2,287,268	147,673	16,018,205	4,135,991	5,902,497	31,804	819,279	445,318
2010	27,260,888	18,885,237	23,126	18,908,363	2,348,373	187,315	16,747,305	4,144,340	6,369,243	33,020	825,582	444,341
2011	28,728,131	20,048,148	6,327	20,054,475	2,241,121	103,414	17,916,768	4,420,234	6,391,129	34,486	833,026	462,597
2012	30,264,710	21,314,618	15,121	21,329,739	2,302,893	184,757	19,211,603	4,630,111	6,422,996	36,006	840,536	466,241
2013	30,770,628	21,964,529	32,836	21,997,365	2,675,397	270,393	19,592,361	4,627,658	6,550,609	36,291	847,897	476,323
2014	32,806,305	23,322,815	18,316	23,341,131	2,808,781	312,640	20,844,990	5,005,254	6,956,061	38,165	859,587	491,133
2015	34,847,658	24,752,387	15,137	24,767,524	2,960,099	280,820	22,088,245	5,444,105	7,315,308	39,978	871,665	507,351
2016	35,950,910	25,484,341	-598	25,483,743	3,057,272	269,732	22,696,203	5,754,871	7,499,836	40,698	883,360	516,736
2017	37,947,994	26,771,181	6,974	26,778,155	3,214,160	273,685	23,837,680	6,350,866	7,759,448	42,441	894,137	528,424
2018	39,609,797	27,958,157	-352	27,957,805	3,376,829	239,809	24,820,785	6,648,129	8,140,883	43,746	905,447	545,714
2019	41,892,555	29,217,411	-5,217	29,212,194	3,534,504	337,624	26,015,314	7,220,774	8,656,467	45,589	918,912	552,798
2020	44,462,751	29,238,849	-6,626	29,232,223	3,559,315	435,821	26,108,729	7,432,683	10,921,339	47,775	930,676	540,275
2021	48,410,344	31,423,613	6,246	31,429,859	3,812,112	266,668	27,884,415	8,219,426	12,306,503	51,431	941,269	566,108
2022	50,059,655	34,198,115	-8,876	34,189,239	4,248,095	2,028	29,943,172	9,006,056	11,110,427	52,202	958,958	595,340

Personal Income and Employment by Area: Gulfport-Biloxi, MS

(Thousands of dollars, except as noted.)

Year	Personal income, total	Derivation of personal income: Earnings by place of work: Nonfarm	Farm	Total	Less: Contributions for government social insurance	Plus: Adjustment for residence	Equals: Net earnings by place of residence	Plus: Dividends, interest, and rent	Plus: Personal current transfer receipts	Per capita personal income (dollars)	Population (persons)	Total employment
1970	866,191	762,721	2,947	765,668	49,039	-53,731	662,898	145,451	57,842	3,470	249,647	112,864
1971	932,032	806,394	3,507	809,901	53,760	-48,271	707,870	155,160	69,002	3,587	259,846	115,030
1972	1,097,641	970,455	3,238	973,693	67,550	-59,948	846,195	172,766	78,680	4,108	267,166	124,008
1973	1,249,133	1,097,965	4,992	1,102,957	84,531	-64,109	954,317	200,330	94,486	4,459	280,155	131,843
1974	1,366,895	1,180,337	3,822	1,184,159	94,269	-66,116	1,023,774	225,907	117,214	4,804	284,551	132,344
1975	1,540,743	1,332,397	2,532	1,334,929	108,495	-78,799	1,147,635	247,857	145,251	5,389	285,918	135,234
1976	1,721,514	1,498,512	3,277	1,501,789	124,614	-87,461	1,289,714	267,921	163,879	5,850	294,260	141,736
1977	1,886,035	1,652,065	4,237	1,656,302	141,335	-101,055	1,413,912	293,339	178,784	6,270	300,806	146,752
1978	2,079,969	1,798,506	4,939	1,803,445	155,536	-105,571	1,542,338	337,229	200,402	6,794	306,127	146,760
1979	2,246,122	1,885,058	6,605	1,891,663	167,829	-93,223	1,630,611	375,121	240,390	7,287	308,249	143,536
1980	2,540,465	2,075,736	2,717	2,078,453	180,226	-90,887	1,807,340	448,514	284,611	8,170	310,937	146,515
1981	2,920,336	2,373,587	2,695	2,376,282	220,499	-109,389	2,046,394	542,706	331,236	9,284	314,558	148,729
1982	3,205,292	2,638,445	6,091	2,644,536	251,084	-148,362	2,245,090	592,334	367,868	9,978	321,223	152,498
1983	3,257,980	2,570,265	2,780	2,573,045	248,106	-117,738	2,207,201	627,435	423,344	10,014	325,332	144,840
1984	3,422,230	2,673,255	3,343	2,676,598	264,214	-117,345	2,295,039	686,435	440,756	10,549	324,401	146,949
1985	3,638,788	2,852,704	3,350	2,856,054	288,979	-138,006	2,429,069	743,313	466,406	11,086	328,245	151,218
1986	3,884,736	3,064,948	1,209	3,066,157	314,395	-161,106	2,590,656	797,454	496,626	11,646	333,567	157,309
1987	3,985,846	3,146,914	3,035	3,149,949	322,765	-173,269	2,653,915	808,892	523,039	11,991	332,404	156,002
1988	4,221,337	3,316,789	3,662	3,320,451	356,020	-185,033	2,779,398	880,360	561,579	12,844	328,651	157,632
1989	4,478,854	3,431,556	4,031	3,435,587	369,963	-184,975	2,880,649	973,505	624,700	13,776	325,114	157,735
1990	4,692,550	3,610,817	3,037	3,613,854	408,085	-194,883	3,010,886	994,419	687,245	14,518	323,228	158,430
1991	4,983,012	3,858,484	3,151	3,861,635	443,767	-212,289	3,205,579	1,002,532	774,901	15,289	325,925	162,063
1992	5,402,641	4,197,347	5,126	4,202,473	481,498	-230,685	3,490,290	1,034,268	878,083	16,154	334,452	166,982
1993	5,996,966	4,735,104	2,894	4,737,998	546,756	-264,466	3,926,776	1,128,786	941,404	17,464	343,381	182,116
1994	6,483,948	5,135,499	877	5,136,376	608,520	-265,190	4,262,666	1,228,033	993,249	18,380	352,763	191,732
1995	6,785,626	5,247,317	131	5,247,448	619,182	-258,820	4,369,446	1,314,397	1,101,783	18,935	358,359	190,748
1996	7,060,865	5,330,498	-1,777	5,328,721	629,795	-240,036	4,458,890	1,402,650	1,199,325	19,636	359,587	193,142
1997	7,469,014	5,637,590	-1,456	5,636,134	669,297	-260,146	4,706,691	1,499,110	1,263,213	20,525	363,897	199,274
1998	8,250,501	6,426,347	-1,093	6,425,254	767,772	-342,831	5,314,651	1,667,187	1,268,663	22,373	368,769	209,623
1999	8,647,784	6,807,360	639	6,807,999	813,073	-348,738	5,646,188	1,685,686	1,315,910	23,090	374,519	216,805
2000	9,170,833	7,120,464	1,503	7,121,967	837,826	-352,587	5,931,554	1,807,900	1,431,379	24,194	379,061	215,671
2001	9,312,610	7,025,913	3,944	7,029,857	800,869	-378,292	5,850,696	1,867,214	1,594,700	24,360	382,293	213,234
2002	9,567,501	7,184,088	1,695	7,185,783	826,489	-406,885	5,952,409	1,910,448	1,704,644	24,847	385,054	212,987
2003	9,992,244	7,603,694	2,537	7,606,231	870,404	-481,781	6,254,046	1,930,396	1,807,802	25,904	385,735	215,160
2004	10,361,309	7,956,070	4,017	7,960,087	913,032	-537,527	6,509,528	1,886,512	1,965,269	26,301	393,947	215,065
2005	11,364,160	8,236,865	2,507	8,239,372	947,235	-637,748	6,654,389	1,758,549	2,951,222	28,510	398,601	205,247
2006	10,928,698	8,401,480	3,592	8,405,072	984,750	-685,102	6,735,220	1,966,723	2,226,755	30,088	363,221	201,735
2007	12,896,356	9,063,624	-3,958	9,059,666	1,071,337	-795,236	7,193,093	3,577,913	2,125,350	34,570	373,053	214,716
2008	12,835,668	9,598,860	-5,457	9,593,403	1,124,185	-925,656	7,543,562	2,862,225	2,429,881	33,745	380,374	217,793
2009	12,929,521	9,600,769	-4,438	9,596,331	1,135,725	-922,927	7,537,679	2,790,813	2,601,029	33,584	384,985	213,019
2010	13,373,297	9,868,143	-7,472	9,860,671	1,147,787	-920,791	7,792,093	2,677,607	2,903,597	34,352	389,297	213,871
2011	13,451,030	9,729,431	-5,200	9,724,231	1,029,810	-863,459	7,830,962	2,573,679	3,046,389	34,178	393,556	212,494
2012	13,544,754	9,780,779	-3,899	9,776,880	1,047,194	-815,973	7,913,713	2,592,689	3,038,352	34,167	396,431	212,576
2013	13,541,986	9,892,827	342	9,893,169	1,196,401	-820,417	7,876,351	2,534,256	3,131,379	33,908	399,375	214,910
2014	13,880,764	10,063,951	-1,620	10,062,331	1,214,258	-790,224	8,057,849	2,574,090	3,248,825	34,437	403,078	215,171
2015	14,034,285	10,084,104	-3,175	10,080,929	1,234,287	-811,866	8,034,776	2,583,895	3,415,614	34,598	405,634	214,594
2016	14,387,726	10,324,015	-5,732	10,318,283	1,269,135	-838,807	8,210,341	2,613,905	3,563,480	35,288	407,720	217,130
2017	14,742,803	10,503,849	-452	10,503,397	1,304,159	-823,922	8,375,316	2,700,357	3,667,130	35,852	411,212	219,254
2018	15,088,583	10,759,007	-5,798	10,753,209	1,332,066	-863,819	8,557,324	2,692,257	3,839,002	36,569	412,609	221,081
2019	15,790,148	11,102,233	-3,923	11,098,310	1,380,221	-862,468	8,855,621	2,857,094	4,077,433	38,067	414,800	222,773
2020	17,236,532	11,438,619	-616	11,438,003	1,425,564	-903,013	9,109,426	2,883,816	5,243,290	41,371	416,637	218,962
2021	19,141,575	12,630,326	-2,313	12,628,013	1,529,585	-981,065	10,117,363	3,307,783	5,716,429	45,715	418,715	229,222
2022	19,189,201	13,300,404	-14,830	13,285,574	1,653,483	-1,020,761	10,611,330	3,609,069	4,968,802	45,604	420,782	235,743

Personal Income and Employment by Area: Hagerstown-Martinsburg, MD-WV

(Thousands of dollars, except as noted.)

Year	Personal income, total	Derivation of personal income								Per capita personal income (dollars)	Population (persons)	Total employment
		Earnings by place of work			Less: Contributions for government social insurance	Plus: Adjustment for residence	Equals: Net earnings by place of residence	Plus: Dividends, interest, and rent	Plus: Personal current transfer receipts			
		Nonfarm	Farm	Total								
1970	552,688	429,228	11,925	441,153	31,025	26,150	436,278	66,507	49,903	3,712	148,883	63,787
1971	604,683	454,366	10,847	465,213	33,649	36,615	468,179	73,444	63,060	4,008	150,879	63,139
1972	671,247	509,964	13,199	523,163	39,806	41,578	524,935	81,074	65,238	4,375	153,440	65,229
1973	745,555	567,170	16,234	583,404	50,527	47,012	579,889	92,592	73,074	4,779	156,013	67,813
1974	836,865	632,612	17,658	650,270	58,435	51,449	643,284	107,937	85,644	5,275	158,650	69,232
1975	923,367	679,184	14,213	693,397	61,591	58,445	690,251	121,079	112,037	5,732	161,085	68,440
1976	1,007,847	738,142	10,900	749,042	67,651	70,712	752,103	131,860	123,884	6,165	163,470	69,285
1977	1,122,092	839,305	9,660	848,965	77,762	73,532	844,735	147,653	129,704	6,798	165,050	71,627
1978	1,268,129	948,496	20,278	968,774	88,878	83,878	963,774	166,982	137,373	7,595	166,974	74,563
1979	1,418,262	1,066,775	19,211	1,085,986	104,119	88,198	1,070,065	190,865	157,332	8,369	169,470	76,992
1980	1,529,830	1,097,167	10,718	1,107,885	107,092	108,491	1,109,284	229,755	190,791	8,959	170,768	75,012
1981	1,677,554	1,179,495	9,694	1,189,189	122,698	115,338	1,181,829	276,829	218,896	9,795	171,271	74,580
1982	1,783,662	1,187,000	9,638	1,196,638	125,507	125,033	1,196,164	331,432	256,066	10,385	171,761	72,648
1983	1,878,339	1,255,289	9,635	1,264,924	136,604	120,248	1,248,568	351,380	278,391	10,801	173,911	74,170
1984	2,100,618	1,426,976	17,358	1,444,334	160,260	128,197	1,412,271	399,751	288,596	11,937	175,968	77,433
1985	2,239,419	1,519,071	18,951	1,538,022	173,433	139,766	1,504,355	425,539	309,525	12,584	177,953	79,572
1986	2,383,191	1,602,521	25,692	1,628,213	185,699	165,217	1,607,731	453,176	322,284	13,243	179,954	82,410
1987	2,553,931	1,741,657	22,377	1,764,034	200,529	183,802	1,747,307	461,640	344,984	13,968	182,847	86,730
1988	2,764,336	1,880,933	22,604	1,903,537	222,750	212,974	1,893,761	499,348	371,227	14,904	185,478	90,771
1989	3,005,580	2,017,309	19,751	2,037,060	240,159	235,182	2,032,083	571,097	402,400	15,901	189,013	93,713
1990	3,143,270	2,140,635	23,438	2,164,073	259,291	215,693	2,120,475	588,084	434,711	16,204	193,986	96,039
1991	3,250,988	2,250,877	21,925	2,272,802	278,697	154,897	2,149,002	606,015	495,971	16,402	198,209	96,187
1992	3,423,324	2,369,140	32,524	2,401,664	293,856	142,516	2,250,324	605,313	567,687	16,946	202,010	95,973
1993	3,563,948	2,456,890	20,585	2,477,475	308,283	158,096	2,327,288	634,746	601,914	17,442	204,329	97,861
1994	3,800,603	2,612,420	17,732	2,630,152	329,044	186,909	2,488,017	684,940	627,646	18,385	206,723	99,511
1995	3,977,967	2,761,915	8,994	2,770,909	348,388	181,054	2,603,575	727,512	646,880	18,991	209,468	103,577
1996	4,223,605	2,888,758	14,643	2,903,401	362,169	216,006	2,757,238	772,646	693,721	19,930	211,921	105,519
1997	4,593,560	3,098,371	10,157	3,108,528	382,935	321,378	3,046,971	838,642	707,947	21,452	214,131	107,820
1998	4,793,955	3,293,045	14,994	3,308,039	401,042	256,981	3,163,978	886,009	743,968	22,075	217,168	109,543
1999	5,002,374	3,537,500	15,490	3,552,990	425,463	222,529	3,350,056	866,230	786,088	22,717	220,200	111,434
2000	5,472,117	3,753,385	16,001	3,769,386	452,027	392,475	3,709,834	930,003	832,280	24,492	223,429	113,751
2001	5,990,356	4,050,167	19,277	4,069,444	485,079	481,751	4,066,116	989,817	934,423	26,414	226,791	118,685
2002	6,270,668	4,168,962	8,650	4,177,612	495,619	568,972	4,250,965	986,537	1,033,166	27,126	231,167	118,965
2003	6,637,509	4,385,762	21,456	4,407,218	524,937	696,453	4,578,734	957,378	1,101,397	27,987	237,168	120,743
2004	7,168,650	4,698,835	31,689	4,730,524	559,391	848,665	5,019,798	1,024,571	1,124,281	29,404	243,798	123,474
2005	7,695,950	4,989,973	30,224	5,020,197	595,506	1,051,646	5,476,337	1,014,789	1,204,824	30,703	250,660	127,900
2006	8,276,112	5,276,869	26,042	5,302,911	626,404	1,194,077	5,870,584	1,114,733	1,290,795	32,123	257,642	130,837
2007	8,774,326	5,342,082	26,538	5,368,620	630,451	1,343,580	6,081,749	1,285,917	1,406,660	33,399	262,715	132,392
2008	9,127,695	5,326,386	29,769	5,356,155	633,886	1,397,376	6,119,645	1,380,181	1,627,869	34,337	265,823	131,020
2009	9,094,562	5,205,600	25,807	5,231,407	620,724	1,368,380	5,979,063	1,340,725	1,774,774	34,016	267,363	127,126
2010	9,430,307	5,373,851	27,948	5,401,799	643,799	1,432,094	6,190,094	1,302,111	1,938,102	34,936	269,934	126,566
2011	9,885,879	5,649,508	45,913	5,695,421	603,571	1,393,782	6,485,632	1,405,283	1,994,964	36,286	272,442	129,310
2012	10,191,920	5,891,455	60,437	5,951,892	631,748	1,363,304	6,683,448	1,479,955	2,028,517	37,163	274,246	132,922
2013	10,266,117	6,004,365	59,738	6,064,103	713,720	1,326,838	6,677,221	1,465,731	2,123,165	37,182	276,101	134,192
2014	10,626,810	6,158,903	67,084	6,225,987	730,726	1,355,621	6,850,882	1,544,250	2,231,678	38,185	278,295	135,350
2015	11,012,582	6,328,030	27,474	6,355,504	756,375	1,462,525	7,061,654	1,609,453	2,341,475	39,312	280,131	136,182
2016	11,459,695	6,433,901	23,239	6,457,140	770,995	1,642,599	7,328,744	1,674,223	2,456,728	40,500	282,952	136,998
2017	11,831,729	6,629,997	39,570	6,669,567	797,340	1,713,493	7,585,720	1,712,791	2,533,218	41,442	285,504	138,436
2018	12,389,254	6,959,880	38,123	6,998,003	845,145	1,808,881	7,961,739	1,766,869	2,660,646	42,924	288,635	140,412
2019	13,017,924	7,079,586	68,071	7,147,657	865,746	2,117,631	8,399,542	1,839,343	2,779,039	44,657	291,510	139,237
2020	14,172,756	7,142,476	48,869	7,191,345	892,139	2,383,276	8,682,482	1,851,263	3,639,011	48,132	294,455	134,781
2021	15,488,380	7,777,678	64,104	7,841,782	969,683	2,531,826	9,403,925	1,983,017	4,101,438	51,858	298,671	140,978
2022	15,859,501	8,122,177	51,427	8,173,604	1,019,753	3,041,272	10,195,123	2,107,964	3,556,414	52,426	302,510	145,196

Personal Income and Employment by Area: Hammond, LA

(Thousands of dollars, except as noted.)

Year	Personal income, total	Derivation of personal income								Per capita personal income (dollars)	Population (persons)	Total employment
		Earnings by place of work			Less: Contributions for government social insurance	Plus: Adjustment for residence	Equals: Net earnings by place of residence	Plus: Dividends, interest, and rent	Plus: Personal current transfer receipts			
		Nonfarm	Farm	Total								
1970	155,386	92,684	9,962	102,646	5,808	12,770	109,608	19,447	26,331	2,346	66,244	20,955
1971	172,304	99,361	12,708	112,069	6,320	14,793	120,542	21,298	30,464	2,518	68,421	21,042
1972	191,624	111,771	13,297	125,068	7,388	17,725	135,405	23,458	32,761	2,803	68,368	22,132
1973	221,073	127,091	17,087	144,178	9,546	20,763	155,395	27,758	37,920	3,207	68,944	23,356
1974	246,895	139,869	12,603	152,472	10,737	26,110	167,845	34,186	44,864	3,527	70,000	23,840
1975	287,159	151,486	16,710	168,196	11,233	34,234	191,197	39,119	56,843	3,987	72,031	23,535
1976	326,518	171,822	15,038	186,860	12,930	45,232	219,162	43,822	63,534	4,400	74,202	24,397
1977	368,182	193,437	15,626	209,063	14,430	53,638	248,271	50,386	69,525	4,826	76,299	24,835
1978	417,571	225,679	11,984	237,663	17,242	64,465	284,886	57,144	75,541	5,349	78,065	26,739
1979	476,031	251,175	9,122	260,297	19,426	83,092	323,963	64,736	87,332	5,967	79,771	26,121
1980	550,471	275,442	7,470	282,912	21,049	100,702	362,565	80,697	107,209	6,794	81,026	27,010
1981	622,925	306,832	7,413	314,245	24,519	114,797	404,523	98,739	119,663	7,579	82,194	27,882
1982	688,886	325,855	6,516	332,371	25,612	119,746	426,505	117,959	144,422	8,137	84,663	28,300
1983	746,979	349,457	7,721	357,178	26,796	116,784	447,166	138,150	161,663	8,629	86,562	28,974
1984	797,440	384,254	8,146	392,400	30,162	117,027	479,265	148,789	169,386	9,058	88,037	29,761
1985	844,772	407,758	13,146	420,904	32,175	111,116	499,845	162,059	182,868	9,505	88,876	30,136
1986	866,533	423,075	16,492	439,567	33,353	103,401	509,615	165,211	191,707	9,710	89,239	30,240
1987	868,704	424,920	20,654	445,574	33,584	100,001	511,991	157,489	199,224	9,875	87,971	29,887
1988	902,853	435,394	20,048	455,442	37,054	111,084	529,472	164,426	208,955	10,375	87,019	30,165
1989	964,378	462,187	22,992	485,179	41,367	115,890	559,702	173,200	231,476	11,158	86,429	30,880
1990	1,038,599	504,404	18,542	522,946	45,965	128,229	605,210	174,535	258,854	12,111	85,754	31,266
1991	1,134,661	565,490	15,416	580,906	52,909	133,241	661,238	181,294	292,129	13,120	86,485	32,005
1992	1,256,225	635,286	21,559	656,845	58,929	141,865	739,781	182,156	334,288	14,255	88,124	33,722
1993	1,368,946	696,338	21,192	717,530	64,390	143,434	796,574	192,881	379,491	15,230	89,885	35,685
1994	1,489,564	752,348	23,940	776,288	71,411	155,376	860,253	210,838	418,473	16,239	91,726	37,632
1995	1,562,578	800,723	25,547	826,270	76,855	165,856	915,271	224,164	423,143	16,663	93,775	39,337
1996	1,628,182	842,588	28,427	871,015	81,835	175,604	964,784	236,054	427,344	17,166	94,851	40,716
1997	1,717,607	896,674	20,373	917,047	86,394	194,278	1,024,931	246,996	445,680	17,796	96,515	41,476
1998	1,806,517	946,882	24,539	971,421	90,979	218,644	1,099,086	264,565	442,866	18,388	98,246	41,204
1999	1,869,080	1,014,851	25,309	1,040,160	96,629	222,633	1,166,164	262,544	440,372	18,758	99,643	42,758
2000	1,987,449	1,101,390	21,034	1,122,424	102,926	231,556	1,251,054	274,802	461,593	19,733	100,716	44,352
2001	2,164,229	1,166,515	21,916	1,188,431	110,355	244,223	1,322,299	283,642	558,288	21,290	101,657	46,530
2002	2,244,807	1,226,307	13,545	1,239,852	116,592	260,470	1,383,730	289,064	572,013	21,898	102,511	46,881
2003	2,348,540	1,324,882	11,619	1,336,501	124,511	263,098	1,475,088	307,679	565,773	22,630	103,782	48,699
2004	2,555,577	1,465,539	19,015	1,484,554	134,945	253,834	1,603,443	308,959	643,175	24,261	105,335	50,296
2005	2,825,604	1,621,011	12,275	1,633,286	146,862	267,438	1,753,862	329,902	741,840	26,411	106,987	52,422
2006	3,289,640	1,907,305	16,267	1,923,572	174,147	350,768	2,100,193	412,742	776,705	28,831	114,102	57,422
2007	3,583,263	1,991,095	15,741	2,006,836	183,454	383,926	2,207,308	556,778	819,177	30,681	116,792	59,680
2008	3,848,742	2,110,402	12,106	2,122,508	195,695	425,297	2,352,110	574,485	922,147	32,446	118,621	60,153
2009	3,840,483	2,080,431	6,592	2,087,023	192,273	384,277	2,279,027	578,779	982,677	32,002	120,009	59,765
2010	4,057,424	2,348,489	11,153	2,359,642	213,034	302,104	2,448,712	559,856	1,048,856	33,424	121,394	60,129
2011	4,191,829	2,451,788	13,354	2,465,142	204,078	288,330	2,549,394	568,117	1,074,318	34,263	122,344	60,297
2012	4,278,050	2,375,005	14,000	2,389,005	197,469	396,329	2,587,865	578,488	1,111,697	34,775	123,022	60,282
2013	4,330,383	2,331,625	8,462	2,340,087	221,182	467,600	2,586,505	590,272	1,153,606	34,748	124,622	60,214
2014	4,469,399	2,435,654	7,982	2,443,636	229,258	500,366	2,714,744	608,085	1,146,570	35,519	125,831	60,861
2015	4,535,206	2,315,444	5,789	2,321,233	225,447	671,021	2,766,807	564,580	1,203,819	35,643	127,239	60,778
2016	4,706,535	2,389,572	2,097	2,391,669	236,745	656,013	2,810,937	631,998	1,263,600	36,513	128,900	62,736
2017	4,882,470	2,517,827	4,845	2,522,672	246,627	614,470	2,890,515	674,733	1,317,222	37,483	130,259	64,743
2018	5,031,470	2,552,849	3,803	2,556,652	253,420	670,151	2,973,383	678,232	1,379,855	38,280	131,438	65,220
2019	5,345,348	2,651,392	5,170	2,656,562	262,892	775,865	3,169,535	701,157	1,474,656	40,492	132,009	66,073
2020	5,864,115	2,786,395	9,858	2,796,253	288,179	651,308	3,159,382	730,320	1,974,413	43,882	133,635	65,490
2021	6,470,262	3,031,494	9,933	3,041,427	309,166	735,310	3,467,571	795,297	2,207,394	47,748	135,508	69,595
2022	6,511,396	3,130,249	2,839	3,133,088	334,369	938,596	3,737,315	808,127	1,965,954	47,512	137,048	72,328

Personal Income and Employment by Area: Hanford-Corcoran, CA

(Thousands of dollars, except as noted.)

Year	Personal income, total	Derivation of personal income: Earnings by place of work: Nonfarm	Farm	Total	Less: Contributions for government social insurance	Plus: Adjustment for residence	Equals: Net earnings by place of residence	Plus: Dividends, interest, and rent	Plus: Personal current transfer receipts	Per capita personal income (dollars)	Population (persons)	Total employment
1970	265,191	175,825	37,589	213,414	11,865	-8,679	192,870	43,833	28,488	3,984	66,570	28,533
1971	278,879	191,990	32,327	224,317	13,714	-8,561	202,042	46,309	30,528	4,197	66,450	29,151
1972	314,305	208,843	45,745	254,588	15,460	-8,092	231,036	50,634	32,635	4,611	68,161	29,839
1973	345,342	229,881	49,406	279,287	18,610	-7,992	252,685	58,022	34,635	5,056	68,308	30,582
1974	437,143	254,002	108,358	362,360	21,533	-7,783	333,044	63,756	40,343	6,329	69,067	31,905
1975	445,741	273,562	83,520	357,082	23,364	-8,100	325,618	69,573	50,550	6,315	70,590	32,738
1976	532,959	285,581	150,747	436,328	25,188	-6,386	404,754	71,307	56,898	7,432	71,708	32,207
1977	531,403	315,464	110,503	425,967	28,226	-6,872	390,869	79,788	60,746	7,333	72,467	33,077
1978	525,109	351,796	48,869	400,665	31,315	-6,554	362,796	93,740	68,573	7,139	73,556	33,605
1979	684,405	394,720	147,861	542,581	36,572	-5,747	500,262	107,800	76,343	9,304	73,562	35,517
1980	847,075	419,904	246,478	666,382	37,787	-4,077	624,518	129,197	93,360	11,406	74,265	35,016
1981	828,481	486,981	126,860	613,841	46,727	-3,357	563,757	156,119	108,605	10,868	76,229	35,983
1982	892,023	519,191	139,665	658,856	49,548	-2,700	606,608	170,010	115,405	11,405	78,213	34,679
1983	859,217	550,976	51,580	602,556	53,930	-3,003	545,623	191,857	121,737	10,590	81,138	35,641
1984	998,903	608,023	125,454	733,477	62,251	-6,245	664,981	206,273	127,649	12,034	83,004	36,754
1985	1,006,381	622,559	107,477	730,036	64,022	-5,716	660,298	208,794	137,289	11,811	85,205	36,258
1986	1,007,409	632,734	82,972	715,706	66,238	-4,883	644,585	212,575	150,249	11,664	86,372	36,047
1987	1,155,634	691,427	170,505	861,932	72,961	-12,208	776,763	222,218	156,653	13,127	88,032	36,612
1988	1,243,284	800,009	149,802	949,811	87,444	-24,926	837,441	236,867	168,976	13,155	94,510	39,367
1989	1,381,336	917,990	150,800	1,068,790	99,417	-40,996	928,377	267,722	185,237	13,834	99,850	41,267
1990	1,393,415	938,368	117,547	1,055,915	102,318	-37,194	916,403	271,085	205,927	13,676	101,885	40,087
1991	1,496,715	995,724	157,140	1,152,864	111,478	-44,469	996,917	267,104	232,694	14,345	104,334	41,203
1992	1,629,712	1,035,715	207,796	1,243,511	116,239	-42,021	1,085,251	268,646	275,815	15,172	107,414	41,535
1993	1,718,643	1,098,392	208,763	1,307,155	124,648	-42,907	1,139,600	284,536	294,507	15,744	109,161	43,577
1994	1,781,393	1,149,491	201,742	1,351,233	128,725	-44,300	1,178,208	309,510	293,675	15,967	111,565	44,229
1995	1,801,184	1,187,253	165,464	1,352,717	130,220	-44,008	1,178,489	315,693	307,002	15,822	113,840	45,163
1996	1,927,687	1,228,973	219,171	1,448,144	131,371	-40,775	1,275,998	329,243	322,446	16,703	115,411	47,583
1997	1,971,334	1,303,109	173,915	1,477,024	136,100	-40,667	1,300,257	349,954	321,123	16,882	116,769	48,573
1998	1,999,312	1,333,866	119,950	1,453,816	135,158	-24,769	1,293,889	355,021	350,402	16,461	121,457	47,999
1999	2,137,468	1,412,665	157,289	1,569,954	143,528	-23,215	1,403,211	364,598	369,659	16,910	126,402	48,316
2000	2,256,782	1,516,274	153,947	1,670,221	153,816	-24,455	1,491,950	383,512	381,320	17,382	129,835	49,518
2001	2,454,775	1,610,764	207,143	1,817,907	171,804	-8,638	1,637,465	389,639	427,671	18,473	132,881	48,875
2002	2,728,925	1,902,204	183,324	2,085,528	200,292	-50,723	1,834,513	432,436	461,976	20,159	135,369	53,296
2003	3,081,153	2,117,081	298,467	2,415,548	224,858	-90,256	2,100,434	475,715	505,004	22,104	139,393	55,629
2004	3,331,631	2,279,515	417,367	2,696,882	250,397	-118,796	2,327,689	466,759	537,183	23,201	143,601	56,225
2005	3,434,580	2,374,810	390,553	2,765,363	259,321	-116,432	2,389,610	475,572	569,398	23,663	145,147	57,082
2006	3,473,368	2,548,647	191,887	2,740,534	271,308	-108,039	2,361,187	502,675	609,506	23,514	147,712	57,126
2007	3,995,536	2,679,561	507,795	3,187,356	276,609	-130,604	2,780,143	557,122	658,271	26,563	150,420	58,764
2008	3,873,560	2,780,365	237,674	3,018,039	292,393	-174,151	2,551,495	574,599	747,466	25,479	152,027	58,720
2009	3,729,952	2,717,189	95,853	2,813,042	292,119	-175,369	2,345,554	571,626	812,772	24,494	152,278	56,881
2010	4,013,295	2,808,561	224,777	3,033,338	292,389	-213,501	2,527,448	579,484	906,363	26,345	152,339	56,178
2011	4,447,898	2,863,330	575,368	3,438,698	274,847	-243,019	2,920,832	616,091	910,975	29,308	151,765	56,157
2012	4,318,502	2,853,055	445,832	3,298,887	275,986	-249,188	2,773,713	623,793	920,996	28,626	150,860	56,741
2013	4,452,325	2,902,284	536,277	3,438,561	306,498	-232,501	2,899,562	589,010	963,753	29,642	150,203	57,503
2014	4,899,529	3,066,437	752,772	3,819,209	320,290	-258,873	3,240,046	641,464	1,018,019	32,810	149,329	59,719
2015	4,906,911	3,159,770	516,108	3,675,878	332,562	-211,521	3,131,795	674,436	1,100,680	32,733	149,905	60,554
2016	5,097,044	3,381,333	449,007	3,830,340	361,492	-262,599	3,206,249	753,968	1,136,827	34,161	149,205	63,262
2017	5,290,349	3,558,819	548,919	4,107,738	384,319	-328,412	3,395,007	782,782	1,112,560	35,395	149,468	65,225
2018	5,296,250	3,599,486	416,345	4,015,831	388,936	-282,552	3,344,343	788,547	1,163,360	35,042	151,138	65,187
2019	5,548,160	3,803,913	449,295	4,253,208	416,679	-333,911	3,502,618	793,081	1,252,461	36,350	152,633	66,432
2020	6,292,586	3,984,628	509,701	4,494,329	433,999	-397,975	3,662,355	827,668	1,802,563	41,185	152,790	65,221
2021	6,690,054	4,207,886	442,734	4,650,620	457,300	-428,868	3,764,452	896,632	2,028,970	43,818	152,679	66,600
2022	6,505,590	4,337,925	476,092	4,814,017	496,280	-339,495	3,978,242	906,811	1,620,537	42,525	152,981	69,086

Personal Income and Employment by Area: Harrisburg-Carlisle, PA

(Thousands of dollars, except as noted.)

Year	Personal income, total	Derivation of personal income: Earnings by place of work: Nonfarm	Farm	Total	Less: Contributions for government social insurance	Plus: Adjustment for residence	Equals: Net earnings by place of residence	Plus: Dividends, interest, and rent	Plus: Personal current transfer receipts	Per capita personal income (dollars)	Population (persons)	Total employment
1970	1,758,789	1,560,954	20,955	1,581,909	110,101	-106,855	1,364,953	245,001	148,835	4,275	411,421	212,257
1971	1,917,418	1,706,275	14,838	1,721,113	124,668	-126,574	1,469,871	272,500	175,047	4,599	416,883	214,199
1972	2,121,103	1,910,446	14,822	1,925,268	145,631	-157,035	1,622,602	301,387	197,114	5,030	421,671	223,174
1973	2,356,228	2,156,395	22,403	2,178,798	187,977	-190,961	1,799,860	339,716	216,652	5,519	426,925	233,699
1974	2,599,131	2,383,862	22,150	2,406,012	215,859	-234,788	1,955,365	388,242	255,524	6,067	428,390	239,598
1975	2,821,295	2,521,931	17,999	2,539,930	222,482	-256,242	2,061,206	432,620	327,469	6,575	429,067	235,721
1976	3,088,512	2,789,215	22,334	2,811,549	253,182	-301,773	2,256,594	472,452	359,466	7,174	430,488	239,343
1977	3,368,794	3,083,367	15,433	3,098,800	281,710	-358,783	2,458,307	530,428	380,059	7,746	434,923	244,658
1978	3,691,961	3,419,471	16,109	3,435,580	320,415	-420,237	2,694,928	589,596	407,437	8,454	436,716	251,930
1979	4,054,310	3,787,793	21,438	3,809,231	368,646	-502,307	2,938,278	657,111	458,921	9,178	441,734	257,914
1980	4,474,635	4,119,103	3,739	4,122,842	400,551	-589,267	3,133,024	810,845	530,766	9,972	448,717	260,074
1981	4,959,046	4,448,631	13,774	4,462,405	462,945	-625,109	3,374,351	980,692	604,003	10,970	452,040	259,996
1982	5,428,250	4,709,298	18,666	4,727,964	493,249	-649,964	3,584,751	1,156,013	687,486	12,038	450,941	259,191
1983	5,796,619	5,028,179	10,726	5,038,905	535,159	-678,339	3,825,407	1,232,600	738,612	12,794	453,087	260,817
1984	6,333,344	5,541,161	39,001	5,580,162	615,633	-737,641	4,226,888	1,360,100	746,356	13,912	455,244	271,598
1985	6,804,675	5,932,606	38,270	5,970,876	670,934	-761,516	4,538,426	1,465,952	800,297	14,907	456,461	279,915
1986	7,313,764	6,410,164	39,315	6,449,479	733,678	-821,765	4,894,036	1,563,657	856,071	15,907	459,787	288,050
1987	7,766,630	6,906,025	35,700	6,941,725	783,928	-859,359	5,298,438	1,588,802	879,390	16,791	462,555	299,738
1988	8,433,262	7,552,283	22,946	7,575,229	887,071	-912,004	5,776,154	1,718,748	938,360	18,088	466,243	310,881
1989	9,271,334	8,155,649	40,703	8,196,352	941,695	-962,377	6,292,280	1,973,044	1,006,010	19,700	470,638	320,922
1990	9,904,948	8,739,119	38,935	8,778,054	1,015,958	-994,629	6,767,467	2,011,978	1,125,503	20,815	475,860	327,398
1991	10,448,035	9,218,616	23,514	9,242,130	1,082,773	-1,092,637	7,066,720	2,088,109	1,293,206	21,678	481,975	329,899
1992	11,016,787	9,848,115	49,123	9,897,238	1,150,845	-1,201,056	7,545,337	2,100,164	1,371,286	22,646	486,480	332,619
1993	11,455,753	10,313,123	42,620	10,355,743	1,220,846	-1,293,108	7,841,789	2,174,612	1,439,352	23,291	491,859	336,584
1994	11,927,480	10,821,713	44,246	10,865,959	1,306,071	-1,383,393	8,176,495	2,270,367	1,480,618	24,040	496,159	345,672
1995	12,477,768	11,282,037	26,713	11,308,750	1,359,786	-1,502,117	8,446,847	2,474,718	1,556,203	25,015	498,803	353,789
1996	13,172,026	11,873,357	53,202	11,926,559	1,401,137	-1,638,746	8,886,676	2,627,076	1,658,274	26,240	501,990	360,378
1997	13,819,841	12,531,392	27,454	12,558,846	1,467,197	-1,732,115	9,359,534	2,751,579	1,708,728	27,441	503,624	364,360
1998	14,553,386	13,347,757	37,548	13,385,305	1,541,738	-1,899,027	9,944,540	2,852,028	1,756,818	28,733	506,506	370,887
1999	15,091,483	13,979,510	34,938	14,014,448	1,600,680	-1,986,138	10,427,630	2,806,778	1,857,075	29,697	508,176	373,847
2000	15,790,310	14,514,089	51,106	14,565,195	1,639,948	-2,042,311	10,882,936	2,941,754	1,965,620	30,995	509,451	377,751
2001	16,653,736	15,323,664	49,032	15,372,696	1,720,160	-2,113,951	11,538,585	2,965,654	2,149,497	32,566	511,391	374,212
2002	17,237,985	15,977,677	23,148	16,000,825	1,795,542	-2,220,339	11,984,944	2,948,145	2,304,896	33,436	515,553	376,385
2003	17,877,158	16,530,365	57,227	16,587,592	1,846,431	-2,286,394	12,454,767	3,017,280	2,405,111	34,435	519,152	377,870
2004	18,577,701	17,507,899	87,520	17,595,419	1,943,890	-2,528,068	13,123,461	2,959,840	2,494,400	35,598	521,882	382,829
2005	19,211,721	18,051,809	76,729	18,128,538	2,015,070	-2,583,859	13,529,609	2,956,589	2,725,523	36,540	525,775	386,122
2006	19,902,513	18,701,009	61,130	18,762,139	2,103,220	-2,768,683	13,890,236	3,112,758	2,899,519	37,392	532,268	393,448
2007	21,023,973	19,394,450	100,779	19,495,229	2,167,790	-2,852,848	14,474,591	3,491,990	3,057,392	39,131	537,268	397,214
2008	21,845,167	19,657,139	111,837	19,768,976	2,215,432	-2,937,235	14,616,309	3,741,072	3,487,786	40,282	542,301	397,578
2009	21,652,738	19,371,921	69,282	19,441,203	2,212,294	-2,995,518	14,233,391	3,525,315	3,894,032	39,594	546,874	389,701
2010	22,389,548	19,841,293	82,934	19,924,227	2,258,725	-3,044,221	14,621,281	3,531,394	4,236,873	40,682	550,358	387,037
2011	23,471,249	20,558,732	128,334	20,687,066	2,088,379	-3,223,542	15,375,145	3,786,798	4,309,306	42,399	553,586	391,075
2012	24,291,725	21,108,361	135,250	21,243,611	2,132,270	-3,258,687	15,852,654	4,077,884	4,361,187	43,579	557,416	393,309
2013	24,602,088	22,049,133	141,862	22,190,995	2,498,731	-3,532,162	16,160,102	3,961,773	4,480,213	43,811	561,554	398,085
2014	25,565,874	22,789,670	169,248	22,958,918	2,586,504	-3,665,294	16,707,120	4,221,482	4,637,272	45,197	565,650	402,888
2015	26,765,482	23,931,806	98,677	24,030,483	2,710,933	-3,843,370	17,476,180	4,380,858	4,908,444	46,936	570,255	409,330
2016	27,152,997	24,194,240	38,375	24,232,615	2,741,587	-3,891,303	17,599,725	4,389,092	5,164,180	47,285	574,247	412,489
2017	28,322,220	25,157,579	92,197	25,249,776	2,899,400	-3,990,671	18,359,705	4,686,275	5,276,240	48,949	578,608	416,802
2018	29,823,213	26,314,726	54,758	26,369,484	3,002,241	-4,148,586	19,218,657	4,964,478	5,640,078	51,145	583,108	423,381
2019	31,289,799	27,620,729	94,422	27,715,151	3,157,364	-4,360,787	20,197,000	5,151,323	5,941,476	53,260	587,497	427,261
2020	33,903,386	28,182,694	56,531	28,239,225	3,191,269	-4,480,573	20,567,383	5,170,266	8,165,737	57,198	592,736	410,934
2021	36,449,052	29,670,215	120,873	29,791,088	3,372,956	-4,572,373	21,845,759	5,807,020	8,796,273	60,777	599,721	424,762
2022	36,646,022	31,306,516	178,736	31,485,252	3,644,852	-4,711,490	23,128,910	6,126,400	7,390,712	60,723	603,493	440,571

Personal Income and Employment by Area: Harrisonburg, VA

(Thousands of dollars, except as noted.)

Year	Personal income, total	Derivation of personal income: Earnings by place of work: Nonfarm	Farm	Total	Less: Contributions for government social insurance	Plus: Adjustment for residence	Equals: Net earnings by place of residence	Plus: Dividends, interest, and rent	Plus: Personal current transfer receipts	Per capita personal income (dollars)	Population (persons)	Total employment
1970	210,184	159,308	12,492	171,800	10,339	8,817	170,278	25,491	14,415	3,347	62,807	31,524
1971	229,751	176,658	12,350	189,008	11,932	7,283	184,359	28,595	16,797	3,529	65,099	32,660
1972	253,679	193,377	15,843	209,220	13,760	7,118	202,578	31,893	19,208	3,721	68,174	33,531
1973	294,399	222,196	23,025	245,221	18,182	6,335	233,374	38,404	22,621	4,248	69,311	35,796
1974	303,767	236,044	7,781	243,825	20,082	6,971	230,714	45,086	27,967	4,237	71,687	35,967
1975	333,756	249,944	11,408	261,352	20,724	2,530	243,158	49,898	40,700	4,543	73,459	35,112
1976	372,627	287,316	10,015	297,331	24,226	2,083	275,188	55,956	41,483	5,023	74,179	36,872
1977	413,003	319,000	11,996	330,996	26,990	544	304,550	64,616	43,837	5,498	75,123	37,960
1978	462,426	359,285	14,429	373,714	30,889	-1,674	341,151	72,758	48,517	6,038	76,581	38,530
1979	520,349	409,958	12,404	422,362	36,745	-7,855	377,762	87,769	54,818	6,770	76,866	40,432
1980	589,846	456,943	6,669	463,612	41,118	-9,633	412,861	111,394	65,591	7,651	77,093	41,367
1981	652,889	488,353	9,645	497,998	47,159	-12,103	438,736	135,806	78,347	8,319	78,483	40,603
1982	707,637	534,390	6,509	540,899	52,748	-16,796	471,355	152,739	83,543	8,948	79,086	41,535
1983	767,919	582,123	7,545	589,668	57,810	-18,349	513,509	162,786	91,624	9,650	79,575	43,301
1984	878,226	644,472	39,436	683,908	65,629	-18,823	599,456	181,512	97,258	11,016	79,725	44,841
1985	950,445	698,847	45,043	743,890	72,863	-22,617	648,410	195,209	106,826	11,819	80,416	46,105
1986	1,070,346	804,368	62,602	866,970	86,474	-32,815	747,681	211,255	111,410	13,145	81,428	48,414
1987	1,118,831	880,142	33,168	913,310	94,127	-33,757	785,426	217,822	115,583	13,501	82,868	49,974
1988	1,251,579	967,379	47,932	1,015,311	106,028	-38,916	870,367	251,119	130,093	14,737	84,927	51,531
1989	1,379,787	1,040,573	73,416	1,113,989	115,263	-43,427	955,299	286,219	138,269	15,943	86,545	52,875
1990	1,445,705	1,102,078	71,671	1,173,749	122,934	-50,622	1,000,193	290,096	155,416	16,270	88,857	54,138
1991	1,517,434	1,157,523	72,910	1,230,433	130,379	-60,434	1,039,620	305,897	171,917	16,690	90,921	54,601
1992	1,641,540	1,266,277	91,635	1,357,912	141,737	-73,959	1,142,216	308,187	191,137	17,634	93,087	56,747
1993	1,743,295	1,359,286	93,859	1,453,145	151,741	-85,787	1,215,617	325,928	201,750	18,286	95,333	58,861
1994	1,835,425	1,454,191	91,837	1,546,028	161,951	-96,375	1,287,702	338,994	208,729	18,800	97,631	60,901
1995	1,906,037	1,512,773	85,100	1,597,873	168,027	-106,463	1,323,383	355,715	226,939	19,058	100,011	62,815
1996	1,982,218	1,563,057	82,479	1,645,536	171,045	-109,937	1,364,554	377,457	240,207	19,310	102,652	63,643
1997	2,090,109	1,687,792	67,985	1,755,777	182,829	-123,374	1,449,574	393,968	246,567	20,055	104,218	65,073
1998	2,233,705	1,798,793	85,944	1,884,737	191,849	-136,888	1,556,000	420,941	256,764	21,170	105,512	65,511
1999	2,335,720	1,928,816	81,427	2,010,243	205,633	-157,027	1,647,583	417,076	271,061	21,766	107,311	68,004
2000	2,505,995	2,053,095	95,406	2,148,501	215,833	-173,068	1,759,600	455,066	291,329	23,115	108,414	69,394
2001	2,737,398	2,229,623	153,535	2,383,158	240,341	-198,151	1,944,666	469,171	323,561	24,814	110,317	71,676
2002	2,684,806	2,301,635	51,649	2,353,284	249,692	-219,935	1,883,657	452,894	348,255	23,939	112,152	72,153
2003	2,863,919	2,438,877	64,765	2,503,642	262,735	-254,686	1,986,221	508,129	369,569	25,311	113,151	72,915
2004	3,030,183	2,542,431	113,527	2,655,958	276,487	-247,798	2,131,673	494,366	404,144	26,455	114,542	74,111
2005	3,192,026	2,657,787	144,880	2,802,667	291,179	-264,830	2,246,658	498,511	446,857	27,375	116,602	74,980
2006	3,324,365	2,831,878	76,352	2,908,230	316,258	-311,314	2,280,658	553,131	490,576	27,969	118,858	77,387
2007	3,517,807	2,932,045	106,407	3,038,452	328,442	-342,540	2,367,470	628,475	521,862	29,115	120,825	79,008
2008	3,704,953	3,014,917	104,520	3,119,437	341,836	-355,277	2,422,324	690,110	592,519	30,279	122,361	79,040
2009	3,641,877	2,993,275	67,017	3,060,292	341,053	-364,836	2,354,403	654,237	633,237	29,336	124,144	77,215
2010	3,833,545	3,085,319	115,375	3,200,694	347,335	-353,637	2,499,722	650,772	683,051	30,568	125,411	77,302
2011	4,024,944	3,146,248	132,712	3,278,960	317,919	-367,812	2,593,229	714,319	717,396	31,740	126,808	78,822
2012	4,189,508	3,285,870	112,110	3,397,980	329,412	-372,639	2,695,929	762,061	731,518	32,613	128,461	79,296
2013	4,262,197	3,347,443	178,127	3,525,570	381,170	-357,799	2,786,601	737,269	738,327	33,047	128,974	79,923
2014	4,519,285	3,474,014	204,984	3,678,998	392,861	-346,161	2,939,976	789,536	789,773	34,648	130,433	80,903
2015	4,804,934	3,744,347	184,375	3,928,722	417,957	-341,755	3,169,010	812,827	823,097	36,638	131,145	82,111
2016	4,752,225	3,712,893	128,587	3,841,480	425,055	-365,619	3,050,806	850,166	851,253	35,729	133,007	84,317
2017	5,049,725	3,895,125	157,820	4,052,945	445,688	-364,906	3,242,351	909,243	898,131	37,635	134,178	85,242
2018	5,287,036	4,079,021	121,245	4,200,266	464,597	-379,752	3,355,917	966,281	964,838	39,164	134,997	86,366
2019	5,490,958	4,292,482	113,871	4,406,353	491,185	-450,294	3,464,874	1,010,141	1,015,943	40,536	135,460	87,213
2020	5,872,485	4,470,493	34,586	4,505,079	517,724	-423,614	3,563,741	983,184	1,325,560	43,349	135,471	84,069
2021	6,535,463	4,742,915	176,972	4,919,887	552,542	-489,539	3,877,806	1,160,794	1,496,863	48,056	135,996	86,924
2022	7,027,979	5,100,974	431,737	5,532,711	602,664	-502,380	4,427,667	1,245,872	1,354,440	51,466	136,555	90,030

Personal Income and Employment by Area: Hartford-East Hartford-Middletown, CT

(Thousands of dollars, except as noted.)

Year	Personal income, total	Derivation of personal income: Earnings by place of work: Nonfarm	Farm	Total	Less: Contributions for government social insurance	Plus: Adjustment for residence	Equals: Net earnings by place of residence	Plus: Dividends, interest, and rent	Plus: Personal current transfer receipts	Per capita personal income (dollars)	Population (persons)	Total employment
1970	5,171,164	4,382,190	37,659	4,419,849	293,222	-178,390	3,948,237	837,241	385,686	4,983	1,037,762	515,814
1971	5,395,535	4,476,209	34,903	4,511,112	309,310	-172,558	4,029,244	879,270	487,021	5,155	1,046,710	504,925
1972	5,783,030	4,851,833	32,162	4,883,995	356,062	-185,231	4,342,702	930,871	509,457	5,503	1,050,940	514,795
1973	6,343,191	5,387,507	38,187	5,425,694	455,426	-210,705	4,759,563	1,037,071	546,557	6,031	1,051,711	538,925
1974	6,962,111	5,840,648	53,090	5,893,738	515,034	-238,519	5,140,185	1,178,313	643,613	6,602	1,054,609	551,581
1975	7,500,799	6,140,389	40,568	6,180,957	528,872	-267,332	5,384,753	1,267,437	848,609	7,139	1,050,706	539,442
1976	8,014,376	6,582,807	43,958	6,626,765	579,288	-286,404	5,761,073	1,344,305	908,998	7,649	1,047,780	544,412
1977	8,754,771	7,252,770	43,950	7,296,720	650,126	-315,200	6,331,394	1,477,326	946,051	8,409	1,041,160	560,291
1978	9,761,716	8,269,703	39,082	8,308,785	764,832	-378,481	7,165,472	1,636,876	959,368	9,325	1,046,844	589,554
1979	11,040,886	9,452,555	39,097	9,491,652	909,025	-476,857	8,105,770	1,854,382	1,080,734	10,532	1,048,331	614,832
1980	12,569,924	10,559,925	46,358	10,606,283	1,004,620	-574,712	9,026,951	2,294,812	1,248,161	11,932	1,053,458	629,793
1981	13,944,880	11,475,731	41,916	11,517,647	1,172,453	-633,163	9,712,031	2,792,399	1,440,450	13,173	1,058,562	632,664
1982	15,068,656	12,238,619	47,685	12,286,304	1,267,473	-688,284	10,330,547	3,137,807	1,600,302	14,214	1,060,120	629,064
1983	16,157,272	13,197,026	50,346	13,247,372	1,378,411	-757,302	11,111,659	3,312,340	1,733,273	15,127	1,068,101	636,326
1984	17,959,112	14,777,920	53,766	14,831,686	1,579,981	-880,412	12,371,293	3,768,002	1,819,817	16,718	1,074,268	666,698
1985	19,331,114	16,206,894	58,141	16,265,035	1,750,056	-1,026,210	13,488,769	3,905,200	1,937,145	17,873	1,081,595	692,320
1986	21,027,000	17,892,877	64,897	17,957,774	1,939,613	-1,198,652	14,819,509	4,156,014	2,051,477	19,249	1,092,348	723,469
1987	22,926,375	19,938,607	66,046	20,004,653	2,126,561	-1,376,167	16,501,925	4,297,915	2,126,535	20,721	1,106,430	745,697
1988	25,214,783	21,868,359	84,760	21,953,119	2,387,606	-1,530,090	18,035,423	4,879,820	2,299,540	22,489	1,121,183	767,174
1989	27,392,469	23,219,803	77,794	23,297,597	2,517,746	-1,692,058	19,087,793	5,712,746	2,591,930	24,386	1,123,307	766,227
1990	28,310,935	24,047,525	102,455	24,149,980	2,579,643	-1,913,925	19,656,412	5,758,136	2,896,387	25,164	1,125,047	758,360
1991	28,605,130	24,265,381	88,972	24,354,353	2,641,821	-1,872,015	19,840,517	5,512,478	3,252,135	25,371	1,127,479	724,845
1992	29,821,671	25,028,753	93,327	25,122,080	2,694,450	-1,886,543	20,541,087	5,466,148	3,814,436	26,506	1,125,083	709,988
1993	30,674,873	25,702,048	97,715	25,799,763	2,765,965	-1,903,408	21,130,390	5,573,262	3,971,221	27,251	1,125,634	710,405
1994	31,373,615	26,294,783	79,656	26,374,439	2,867,030	-1,891,772	21,615,637	5,649,502	4,108,476	27,864	1,125,949	698,042
1995	32,370,064	26,836,961	81,929	26,918,890	2,952,749	-1,781,485	22,184,656	5,787,411	4,397,997	28,785	1,124,531	708,359
1996	33,591,914	27,697,988	68,047	27,766,035	3,044,154	-1,619,123	23,102,758	5,978,127	4,511,029	29,822	1,126,396	715,650
1997	35,545,700	29,605,234	62,968	29,668,202	3,199,897	-1,608,984	24,859,321	6,055,419	4,630,960	31,484	1,128,992	722,220
1998	37,997,059	31,962,098	71,910	32,034,008	3,362,301	-1,723,468	26,948,239	6,340,355	4,708,465	33,497	1,134,353	733,474
1999	39,949,209	34,401,456	72,652	34,474,108	3,536,467	-1,950,035	28,987,606	6,154,835	4,806,768	35,003	1,141,318	745,821
2000	43,614,906	37,524,738	88,871	37,613,609	3,753,931	-1,947,231	31,912,447	6,650,393	5,052,066	37,897	1,150,872	762,284
2001	45,003,170	38,692,120	81,841	38,773,961	3,855,347	-1,993,367	32,925,247	6,723,967	5,353,956	38,846	1,158,513	765,606
2002	45,265,225	39,177,967	73,389	39,251,356	4,014,105	-1,865,967	33,371,284	6,153,011	5,740,930	38,721	1,169,000	757,707
2003	46,222,401	39,640,822	73,071	39,713,893	4,075,513	-1,752,406	33,885,974	6,472,247	5,864,180	39,192	1,179,394	752,249
2004	48,857,438	42,461,789	74,132	42,535,921	4,341,186	-1,933,932	36,260,803	6,428,346	6,168,289	41,313	1,182,605	763,536
2005	50,879,000	44,354,883	66,197	44,421,080	4,515,650	-1,972,460	37,932,970	6,550,425	6,395,605	42,830	1,187,929	775,258
2006	54,485,171	46,770,446	63,721	46,834,167	4,697,207	-1,918,783	40,218,177	7,413,729	6,853,265	45,643	1,193,725	786,918
2007	57,769,409	48,725,369	79,869	48,805,238	4,883,280	-2,110,622	41,811,336	8,660,688	7,297,385	48,206	1,198,395	801,933
2008	60,144,431	49,201,608	76,596	49,278,204	4,992,828	-1,901,238	42,384,138	9,401,851	8,358,442	49,936	1,204,436	807,420
2009	59,458,716	48,241,272	74,868	48,316,140	4,885,446	-1,753,867	41,676,827	8,503,840	9,278,049	49,156	1,209,604	785,193
2010	60,826,879	49,483,822	80,738	49,564,560	4,918,476	-1,737,685	42,908,399	8,012,524	9,905,956	50,090	1,214,343	774,624
2011	63,318,724	51,260,785	75,931	51,336,716	4,594,457	-1,942,002	44,800,257	8,589,334	9,929,133	52,008	1,217,487	786,137
2012	64,937,931	52,092,244	95,191	52,187,435	4,751,685	-2,007,727	45,428,023	9,467,774	10,042,134	53,321	1,217,861	791,454
2013	65,255,235	53,319,971	117,762	53,437,733	5,560,659	-2,137,021	45,740,053	9,335,981	10,179,201	53,554	1,218,502	798,553
2014	67,692,834	55,246,430	100,743	55,347,173	5,749,746	-2,359,723	47,237,704	9,984,049	10,471,081	55,543	1,218,741	806,912
2015	69,871,006	57,215,060	94,183	57,309,243	5,942,933	-2,514,753	48,851,557	10,255,474	10,763,975	57,378	1,217,737	813,786
2016	70,859,687	57,792,074	64,340	57,856,414	6,036,158	-2,339,791	49,480,465	10,345,389	11,033,833	58,296	1,215,505	816,205
2017	72,131,334	58,749,336	77,682	58,827,018	6,229,925	-2,388,361	50,208,732	10,675,231	11,247,371	59,368	1,214,984	818,381
2018	74,663,026	60,789,147	61,060	60,850,207	6,444,904	-2,468,076	51,937,227	10,752,167	11,973,632	61,429	1,215,440	824,016
2019	76,904,415	62,388,255	78,629	62,466,884	6,675,951	-2,677,320	53,113,613	11,481,714	12,309,088	63,322	1,214,503	821,499
2020	80,129,738	61,973,667	65,595	62,039,262	6,669,513	-2,755,480	52,614,269	11,365,267	16,150,202	66,219	1,210,079	789,946
2021	83,958,118	63,868,679	69,004	63,937,683	6,886,249	-2,390,228	54,661,206	11,961,740	17,335,172	68,802	1,220,287	808,329
2022	85,260,262	67,432,064	82,597	67,514,661	7,435,367	-2,570,496	57,508,798	12,576,864	15,174,600	69,787	1,221,725	837,262

Personal Income and Employment by Area: Hattiesburg, MS

(Thousands of dollars, except as noted.)

Year	Personal income, total	Derivation of personal income								Per capita personal income (dollars)	Population (persons)	Total employment
		Earnings by place of work			Less: Contributions for government social insurance	Plus: Adjustment for residence	Equals: Net earnings by place of residence	Plus: Dividends, interest, and rent	Plus: Personal current transfer receipts			
		Nonfarm	Farm	Total								
1970	257,751	195,511	7,332	202,843	13,696	3,677	192,824	32,716	32,211	2,674	96,397	38,332
1971	286,004	214,926	7,546	222,472	15,420	4,267	211,319	37,208	37,477	2,897	98,710	39,775
1972	323,399	243,743	8,621	252,364	18,232	4,914	239,046	41,884	42,469	3,186	101,513	42,209
1973	366,815	271,095	14,110	285,205	23,122	5,905	267,988	49,079	49,748	3,539	103,641	43,891
1974	415,101	303,776	11,402	315,178	26,854	6,547	294,871	58,730	61,500	3,936	105,464	44,997
1975	459,032	331,666	9,330	340,996	28,893	7,566	319,669	63,707	75,656	4,297	106,832	44,859
1976	521,127	380,217	10,638	390,855	33,573	9,349	366,631	70,185	84,311	4,795	108,675	46,592
1977	586,995	432,452	11,936	444,388	37,913	11,213	417,688	78,775	90,532	5,299	110,785	48,693
1978	655,096	481,082	13,039	494,121	43,128	14,158	465,151	89,379	100,566	5,843	112,108	50,195
1979	729,233	528,921	15,675	544,596	49,212	17,457	512,841	100,213	116,179	6,406	113,837	50,641
1980	818,511	579,741	6,991	586,732	54,047	19,374	552,059	128,076	138,376	7,042	116,240	51,040
1981	916,770	632,731	7,916	640,647	63,756	19,446	596,337	162,399	158,034	7,738	118,481	50,917
1982	969,432	651,337	14,669	666,006	67,527	19,227	617,706	179,116	172,610	8,056	120,340	50,012
1983	1,044,826	734,654	8,096	742,750	76,928	-1,373	664,449	190,086	190,291	8,497	122,962	52,206
1984	1,128,054	778,217	11,884	790,101	83,232	6,957	713,826	214,165	200,063	9,109	123,842	52,688
1985	1,182,393	791,605	12,888	804,493	86,187	23,973	742,279	232,626	207,488	9,536	123,994	52,503
1986	1,239,651	841,387	13,616	855,003	92,614	19,733	782,122	242,974	214,555	9,934	124,783	53,370
1987	1,310,549	906,297	13,824	920,121	99,545	16,184	836,760	246,624	227,165	10,499	124,828	55,016
1988	1,399,480	971,169	17,393	988,562	111,458	16,916	894,020	262,151	243,309	11,215	124,783	56,082
1989	1,539,607	1,058,881	20,729	1,079,610	121,064	15,693	974,239	299,025	266,343	12,236	125,825	57,582
1990	1,629,866	1,144,426	12,116	1,156,542	135,058	15,976	1,037,460	302,107	290,299	12,918	126,171	57,977
1991	1,699,499	1,173,433	13,696	1,187,129	141,630	19,019	1,064,518	309,789	325,192	13,366	127,154	58,506
1992	1,832,712	1,261,031	18,791	1,279,822	150,421	16,724	1,146,125	322,919	363,668	14,319	127,993	59,352
1993	1,955,185	1,347,643	19,677	1,367,320	160,302	19,912	1,226,930	343,073	385,182	15,092	129,550	61,920
1994	2,114,360	1,481,404	22,593	1,503,997	176,937	16,898	1,343,958	366,032	404,370	16,096	131,356	65,097
1995	2,276,334	1,579,259	22,067	1,601,326	187,750	13,422	1,426,998	404,856	444,480	16,989	133,991	68,046
1996	2,413,715	1,668,948	26,728	1,695,676	195,176	15,209	1,515,709	423,544	474,462	17,710	136,289	69,009
1997	2,592,239	1,790,728	28,244	1,818,972	207,944	18,234	1,629,262	468,896	494,081	18,780	138,032	71,101
1998	2,731,957	1,879,848	37,276	1,917,124	217,896	24,419	1,723,647	513,391	494,919	19,498	140,118	73,886
1999	2,843,624	1,976,248	38,139	2,014,387	228,785	21,799	1,807,401	522,033	514,190	20,065	141,723	76,332
2000	2,975,832	2,026,629	35,748	2,062,377	232,737	23,459	1,853,099	570,828	551,905	20,699	143,768	77,033
2001	3,194,740	2,167,927	51,780	2,219,707	246,714	16,392	1,989,385	579,861	625,494	22,119	144,434	76,420
2002	3,336,431	2,284,950	39,827	2,324,777	261,041	10,328	2,074,064	578,295	684,072	22,907	145,651	77,226
2003	3,413,951	2,377,579	39,205	2,416,784	271,062	8,474	2,154,196	546,303	713,452	23,219	147,031	78,101
2004	3,659,699	2,537,157	74,125	2,611,282	291,107	2,878	2,323,053	570,393	766,253	24,630	148,587	78,714
2005	3,914,064	2,694,045	74,294	2,768,339	305,859	3,932	2,466,412	580,324	867,328	26,043	150,295	80,556
2006	4,224,259	2,997,512	37,078	3,034,590	345,487	-1,115	2,687,988	666,803	869,468	27,480	153,722	85,806
2007	4,469,012	3,109,764	43,101	3,152,865	361,897	-8,136	2,782,832	768,519	917,661	28,501	156,803	88,488
2008	4,748,489	3,160,279	31,630	3,191,909	367,093	19,361	2,844,177	860,771	1,043,541	29,884	158,899	87,811
2009	4,803,647	3,165,895	32,834	3,198,729	372,778	24,628	2,850,579	829,664	1,123,404	29,877	160,782	86,217
2010	5,011,981	3,266,197	25,440	3,291,637	376,718	52,346	2,967,265	816,144	1,228,572	30,761	162,931	86,357
2011	5,237,772	3,325,214	-4,499	3,320,715	346,010	86,696	3,061,401	892,050	1,284,321	31,714	165,157	87,338
2012	5,511,749	3,479,870	16,631	3,496,501	361,739	109,860	3,244,622	988,775	1,278,352	33,074	166,647	88,408
2013	5,646,537	3,534,251	95,297	3,629,548	410,967	148,475	3,367,056	977,176	1,302,305	33,626	167,923	89,279
2014	5,854,584	3,700,066	104,120	3,804,186	430,663	153,835	3,527,358	982,831	1,344,395	34,762	168,418	91,557
2015	6,062,963	3,847,831	75,362	3,923,193	454,385	131,888	3,600,696	1,056,652	1,405,615	35,792	169,393	93,164
2016	6,072,054	3,891,281	36,796	3,928,077	465,063	107,249	3,570,263	1,047,897	1,453,894	35,729	169,946	93,486
2017	6,258,421	3,994,253	99,982	4,094,235	484,486	94,378	3,704,127	1,084,304	1,469,990	36,860	169,789	95,414
2018	6,413,827	4,066,463	88,883	4,155,346	492,950	110,092	3,772,488	1,112,852	1,528,487	37,592	170,615	96,162
2019	6,560,817	4,155,415	68,104	4,223,519	509,738	115,394	3,829,175	1,135,679	1,595,963	38,259	171,485	96,360
2020	7,085,174	4,309,411	12,864	4,322,275	532,676	99,496	3,889,095	1,167,223	2,028,856	41,115	172,325	94,934
2021	7,728,604	4,684,581	76,443	4,761,024	568,992	81,050	4,273,082	1,216,449	2,239,073	44,669	173,018	97,989
2022	7,715,620	4,907,551	101,768	5,009,319	614,346	97,954	4,492,927	1,293,764	1,928,929	44,507	173,359	101,082

Personal Income and Employment by Area: Hickory-Lenoir-Morganton, NC

(Thousands of dollars, except as noted.)

Year	Personal income, total	Derivation of personal income: Earnings by place of work: Nonfarm	Earnings by place of work: Farm	Earnings by place of work: Total	Less: Contributions for government social insurance	Plus: Adjustment for residence	Equals: Net earnings by place of residence	Plus: Dividends, interest, and rent	Plus: Personal current transfer receipts	Per capita personal income (dollars)	Population (persons)	Total employment
1970	784,523	713,459	5,822	719,281	51,357	-23,029	644,895	86,257	53,371	3,436	228,324	123,300
1971	866,297	785,457	7,418	792,875	58,880	-25,108	708,887	95,199	62,211	3,695	234,432	126,489
1972	980,621	901,560	4,440	906,000	70,924	-28,007	807,069	105,342	68,210	4,078	240,460	133,573
1973	1,106,372	1,008,941	17,369	1,026,310	90,692	-30,299	905,319	119,939	81,114	4,476	247,184	139,492
1974	1,187,079	1,063,524	12,392	1,075,916	99,690	-30,382	945,844	139,272	101,963	4,722	251,418	138,142
1975	1,257,076	1,056,724	12,323	1,069,047	97,494	-26,341	945,212	151,529	160,335	4,962	253,359	129,718
1976	1,414,855	1,225,822	15,129	1,240,951	116,385	-32,821	1,091,745	165,410	157,700	5,553	254,783	137,473
1977	1,593,399	1,395,622	18,542	1,414,164	132,099	-37,335	1,244,730	185,145	163,524	6,187	257,538	143,921
1978	1,760,066	1,551,002	15,989	1,566,991	151,127	-39,311	1,376,553	208,652	174,861	6,710	262,291	148,852
1979	1,936,402	1,693,762	15,718	1,709,480	170,929	-40,681	1,497,870	236,962	201,570	7,287	265,722	150,985
1980	2,158,477	1,830,125	11,711	1,841,836	183,352	-41,466	1,617,018	295,002	246,457	7,963	271,068	151,175
1981	2,428,746	2,028,459	20,220	2,048,679	217,563	-48,764	1,782,352	365,501	280,893	8,906	272,705	153,144
1982	2,573,364	2,089,696	17,859	2,107,555	224,665	-50,410	1,832,480	415,153	325,731	9,359	274,966	150,999
1983	2,852,695	2,354,136	16,805	2,370,941	255,634	-59,225	2,056,082	452,657	343,956	10,349	275,660	156,262
1984	3,193,587	2,641,839	30,453	2,672,292	295,026	-68,055	2,309,211	523,611	360,765	11,449	278,940	164,550
1985	3,387,049	2,794,099	29,010	2,823,109	315,256	-68,794	2,439,059	560,497	387,493	11,976	282,830	167,043
1986	3,684,786	3,051,532	33,545	3,085,077	350,071	-75,541	2,659,465	610,756	414,565	12,971	284,074	172,324
1987	3,968,506	3,348,547	22,195	3,370,742	377,613	-82,637	2,910,492	629,357	428,657	13,865	286,235	178,889
1988	4,356,509	3,653,979	23,866	3,677,845	420,871	-90,229	3,166,745	723,753	466,011	15,049	289,487	185,685
1989	4,737,747	3,861,043	44,579	3,905,622	443,266	-92,308	3,370,048	848,041	519,658	16,274	291,125	189,029
1990	4,964,060	4,031,894	54,256	4,086,150	474,202	-93,216	3,518,732	874,137	571,191	16,914	293,489	191,322
1991	5,125,459	4,081,079	64,011	4,145,090	485,908	-90,920	3,568,262	892,324	664,873	17,256	297,026	187,870
1992	5,553,833	4,492,475	71,782	4,564,257	526,798	-104,012	3,933,447	900,911	719,475	18,452	300,989	193,366
1993	5,906,886	4,780,030	77,439	4,857,469	566,701	-109,425	4,181,343	936,474	789,069	19,315	305,812	198,101
1994	6,288,828	5,096,740	78,139	5,174,879	610,972	-113,116	4,450,791	1,018,940	819,097	20,222	310,993	201,756
1995	6,607,553	5,225,176	75,032	5,300,208	628,501	-100,268	4,571,439	1,111,044	925,070	20,873	316,556	206,522
1996	6,974,723	5,437,075	80,034	5,517,109	648,959	-101,226	4,766,924	1,199,475	1,008,324	21,667	321,905	208,510
1997	7,411,258	5,766,804	83,910	5,850,714	681,434	-97,363	5,071,917	1,273,969	1,065,372	22,629	327,516	211,062
1998	7,912,305	6,149,800	92,049	6,241,849	730,047	-99,149	5,412,653	1,386,390	1,113,262	23,771	332,861	213,060
1999	8,296,849	6,504,145	96,133	6,600,278	768,441	-96,545	5,735,292	1,389,314	1,172,243	24,550	337,955	216,340
2000	8,695,541	6,803,751	89,654	6,893,405	802,122	-99,426	5,991,857	1,447,421	1,256,263	25,333	343,247	221,379
2001	8,943,543	6,829,102	92,276	6,921,378	808,511	-74,891	6,037,976	1,479,108	1,426,459	25,777	346,952	215,026
2002	8,921,980	6,749,798	54,215	6,804,013	790,422	-58,356	5,955,235	1,418,661	1,548,084	25,616	348,299	206,902
2003	9,038,797	6,693,651	56,295	6,749,946	800,722	-35,356	5,913,868	1,498,234	1,626,695	25,864	349,472	201,094
2004	9,466,846	7,040,898	65,434	7,106,332	831,967	-19,899	6,254,466	1,475,801	1,736,579	26,954	351,224	203,391
2005	9,923,371	7,171,415	100,228	7,271,643	863,923	19,882	6,427,602	1,603,605	1,892,164	28,020	354,159	203,029
2006	10,459,687	7,552,025	89,036	7,641,061	900,721	-9,857	6,730,483	1,658,076	2,071,128	29,259	357,492	205,213
2007	10,862,659	7,667,785	58,143	7,725,928	920,481	11,218	6,816,665	1,824,589	2,221,405	30,108	360,791	205,454
2008	11,124,441	7,612,664	24,294	7,636,958	915,643	39,865	6,761,180	1,857,971	2,505,290	30,561	364,003	200,168
2009	10,891,366	6,985,262	48,914	7,034,176	848,891	73,677	6,258,962	1,740,084	2,892,320	29,787	365,639	185,663
2010	11,083,925	7,165,197	52,056	7,217,253	863,734	72,475	6,425,994	1,654,201	3,003,730	30,328	365,466	182,842
2011	11,296,114	7,251,735	20,299	7,272,034	815,450	70,142	6,526,726	1,761,468	3,007,920	31,038	363,941	185,633
2012	11,691,878	7,475,552	41,165	7,516,717	822,823	91,258	6,785,152	1,848,836	3,057,890	32,238	362,671	185,886
2013	11,567,642	7,525,915	56,763	7,582,678	949,316	87,862	6,721,224	1,773,363	3,073,055	31,961	361,925	187,059
2014	12,105,608	7,820,472	84,998	7,905,470	986,135	128,392	7,047,727	1,902,799	3,155,082	33,521	361,130	188,556
2015	12,755,744	8,186,015	120,154	8,306,169	1,032,888	137,325	7,410,606	1,998,906	3,346,232	35,339	360,956	191,535
2016	13,149,253	8,446,948	77,290	8,524,238	1,057,661	148,366	7,614,943	2,113,192	3,421,118	36,334	361,895	194,841
2017	13,860,989	8,943,805	94,537	9,038,342	1,106,938	135,955	8,067,359	2,261,876	3,531,754	38,133	363,490	198,198
2018	14,339,037	9,308,443	55,380	9,363,823	1,134,811	157,633	8,386,645	2,275,576	3,676,816	39,377	364,152	199,656
2019	15,047,277	9,653,925	57,082	9,711,007	1,183,595	174,433	8,701,845	2,420,372	3,925,060	41,239	364,876	200,504
2020	16,238,993	9,822,015	46,438	9,868,453	1,211,079	184,163	8,841,537	2,459,159	4,938,297	44,419	365,583	194,733
2021	17,791,676	10,610,423	94,598	10,705,021	1,295,293	189,680	9,599,408	2,597,589	5,594,679	48,547	366,483	200,456
2022	18,305,764	11,559,207	154,549	11,713,756	1,431,614	206,164	10,488,306	2,798,972	5,018,486	49,697	368,347	207,649

Personal Income and Employment by Area: Hilton Head Island-Bluffton, SC

(Thousands of dollars, except as noted.)

		Derivation of personal income										
		Earnings by place of work										
Year	Personal income, total	Nonfarm	Farm	Total	Less: Contributions for government social insurance	Plus: Adjustment for residence	Equals: Net earnings by place of residence	Plus: Dividends, interest, and rent	Plus: Personal current transfer receipts	Per capita personal income (dollars)	Population (persons)	Total employment
1970	266,573	199,240	4,221	203,461	12,006	4,872	196,327	56,914	13,332	4,224	63,110	34,783
1971	270,191	202,275	4,282	206,557	13,002	4,711	198,266	56,195	15,730	4,179	64,658	32,961
1972	326,122	248,954	4,614	253,568	16,252	3,954	241,270	66,636	18,216	4,743	68,755	35,347
1973	365,162	280,043	3,754	283,797	20,026	2,965	266,736	76,815	21,611	5,321	68,623	37,134
1974	393,386	293,067	5,248	298,315	22,034	3,859	280,140	85,961	27,285	5,933	66,303	36,514
1975	434,814	312,863	6,507	319,370	24,645	5,268	299,993	96,610	38,211	5,791	75,090	36,956
1976	512,916	369,939	4,328	374,267	29,810	6,623	351,080	117,781	44,055	6,570	78,071	40,575
1977	557,655	401,628	3,417	405,045	32,099	6,390	379,336	132,675	45,644	7,274	76,668	41,908
1978	620,329	440,125	2,761	442,886	35,133	5,554	413,307	155,924	51,098	7,899	78,535	43,150
1979	698,820	495,328	3,202	498,530	41,307	3,591	460,814	176,416	61,590	8,765	79,724	44,712
1980	796,261	557,774	396	558,170	46,426	2,366	514,110	206,420	75,731	9,888	80,532	46,210
1981	954,880	663,141	579	663,720	58,587	6,585	611,718	254,608	88,554	11,515	82,926	46,448
1982	1,010,761	690,976	3,044	694,020	61,621	7,778	640,177	275,306	95,278	11,818	85,527	46,606
1983	1,068,160	729,606	6	729,612	67,731	8,013	669,894	294,529	103,737	12,225	87,375	47,483
1984	1,230,245	851,902	-714	851,188	82,141	4,762	773,809	342,270	114,166	13,630	90,263	51,207
1985	1,350,759	937,203	-1,446	935,757	93,582	2,551	844,726	382,194	123,839	14,670	92,077	54,742
1986	1,473,414	1,018,037	508	1,018,545	104,259	4,790	919,076	421,287	133,051	15,643	94,192	56,562
1987	1,549,199	1,055,800	2,219	1,058,019	108,382	9,401	959,038	450,155	140,006	16,101	96,218	57,567
1988	1,674,593	1,119,053	3,149	1,122,202	119,791	15,898	1,018,309	506,728	149,556	17,014	98,423	58,897
1989	1,836,022	1,181,398	3,522	1,184,920	128,926	18,814	1,074,808	587,963	173,251	18,333	100,147	60,252
1990	2,031,611	1,279,139	3,677	1,282,816	143,710	16,965	1,156,071	681,778	193,762	19,772	102,754	61,850
1991	2,122,109	1,309,073	5,364	1,314,437	149,813	18,060	1,182,684	714,456	224,969	20,027	105,964	60,325
1992	2,333,107	1,425,795	3,751	1,429,546	163,687	17,969	1,283,828	791,369	257,910	21,313	109,469	61,579
1993	2,489,636	1,498,321	13,358	1,511,679	174,901	19,813	1,356,591	849,587	283,458	21,918	113,587	63,720
1994	2,738,108	1,642,656	9,740	1,652,396	194,233	18,933	1,477,096	944,470	316,542	23,206	117,989	66,792
1995	2,937,634	1,804,789	8,815	1,813,604	213,245	8,319	1,608,678	982,847	346,109	24,037	122,214	71,135
1996	3,226,910	1,948,874	5,183	1,954,057	227,817	17,956	1,744,196	1,100,576	382,138	25,392	127,083	74,453
1997	3,542,230	2,116,373	5,582	2,121,955	247,887	8,334	1,882,402	1,247,403	412,425	26,836	131,994	78,311
1998	3,896,097	2,316,514	6,592	2,323,106	271,066	3,717	2,055,757	1,394,162	446,178	28,640	136,035	81,074
1999	4,141,310	2,545,248	9,812	2,555,060	294,660	-12,247	2,248,153	1,412,287	480,870	29,918	138,422	84,993
2000	4,432,796	2,706,826	8,601	2,715,427	314,195	-18,944	2,382,288	1,523,043	527,465	30,993	143,027	88,583
2001	4,765,768	2,926,818	9,910	2,936,728	335,758	-19,084	2,581,886	1,582,709	601,173	32,514	146,574	92,982
2002	4,918,192	3,025,084	10,842	3,035,926	350,283	-15,687	2,669,956	1,588,611	659,625	32,702	150,392	94,863
2003	5,213,173	3,241,754	21,298	3,263,052	378,655	-15,547	2,868,850	1,627,558	716,765	34,244	152,234	97,377
2004	5,757,335	3,501,333	28,207	3,529,540	412,402	-12,054	3,105,084	1,877,770	774,481	36,488	157,787	101,290
2005	6,266,447	3,773,940	24,890	3,798,830	441,897	-8,233	3,348,700	2,068,226	849,521	38,364	163,343	105,262
2006	6,998,841	4,095,431	28,605	4,124,036	491,872	2,943	3,635,107	2,419,873	943,861	41,262	169,619	109,637
2007	7,494,048	4,329,357	12,892	4,342,249	518,726	21,199	3,844,722	2,621,037	1,028,289	42,975	174,382	112,988
2008	7,686,484	4,279,418	23,387	4,302,805	519,929	38,418	3,821,294	2,673,440	1,191,750	42,698	180,019	110,948
2009	7,511,840	3,998,825	22,119	4,020,944	496,655	43,875	3,568,164	2,600,142	1,343,534	40,832	183,971	105,853
2010	7,349,263	3,953,442	26,044	3,979,486	489,435	49,698	3,539,749	2,345,548	1,463,966	39,180	187,575	103,814
2011	7,817,507	4,051,044	22,190	4,073,234	453,088	62,531	3,682,677	2,604,002	1,530,828	41,567	188,069	104,380
2012	8,236,841	4,282,702	16,132	4,298,834	470,993	64,231	3,892,072	2,771,870	1,572,899	43,091	191,149	106,100
2013	8,463,365	4,467,763	13,490	4,481,253	542,247	65,672	4,004,678	2,795,046	1,663,641	43,519	194,476	108,053
2014	9,181,914	4,746,645	6,225	4,752,870	573,247	72,294	4,251,917	3,144,449	1,785,548	46,355	198,078	111,522
2015	9,869,374	5,060,841	8,948	5,069,789	611,010	66,503	4,525,282	3,415,246	1,928,846	48,722	202,563	115,571
2016	10,437,019	5,254,251	6,467	5,260,718	625,855	61,488	4,696,351	3,712,858	2,027,810	50,697	205,872	118,535
2017	10,833,775	5,363,815	8,310	5,372,125	661,532	68,499	4,779,092	3,927,314	2,127,369	51,979	208,425	122,676
2018	11,470,204	5,572,988	6,741	5,579,729	696,880	84,398	4,967,247	4,240,096	2,262,861	54,471	210,576	127,455
2019	12,498,121	5,990,424	4,667	5,995,091	747,639	69,402	5,316,854	4,718,023	2,463,244	58,524	213,556	129,511
2020	13,346,693	6,225,027	6,172	6,231,199	776,567	59,026	5,513,658	4,821,753	3,011,282	61,516	216,962	127,516
2021	14,818,977	6,858,055	9,325	6,867,380	844,826	77,338	6,099,892	5,331,866	3,387,219	66,613	222,463	134,358
2022	15,484,879	7,203,696	2,167	7,205,863	915,888	96,998	6,386,973	5,918,900	3,179,006	67,794	228,410	138,339

Personal Income and Employment by Area: Hinesville, GA

(Thousands of dollars, except as noted.)

Year	Personal income, total	Derivation of personal income: Earnings by place of work: Nonfarm	Farm	Total	Less: Contributions for government social insurance	Plus: Adjustment for residence	Equals: Net earnings by place of residence	Plus: Dividends, interest, and rent	Plus: Personal current transfer receipts	Per capita personal income (dollars)	Population (persons)	Total employment
1970	76,182	69,871	971	70,842	3,612	-15,192	52,038	18,977	5,167	3,576	21,303	9,248
1971	81,026	73,877	1,172	75,049	4,095	-15,067	55,887	18,749	6,390	3,753	21,587	9,029
1972	88,560	79,395	1,184	80,579	4,411	-14,059	62,109	19,458	6,993	4,045	21,894	8,729
1973	95,721	83,692	1,648	85,340	4,854	-14,302	66,184	21,462	8,075	4,516	21,198	8,747
1974	106,241	92,488	1,473	93,961	5,503	-15,517	72,941	23,150	10,150	5,014	21,188	9,148
1975	124,820	103,795	1,017	104,812	6,553	-12,661	85,598	26,095	13,127	5,005	24,937	9,529
1976	172,775	188,499	734	189,233	13,903	-64,524	110,806	47,879	14,090	5,980	28,894	15,280
1977	228,210	266,272	-512	265,760	19,864	-102,625	143,271	70,274	14,665	6,787	33,625	20,349
1978	267,881	304,939	1,463	306,402	21,728	-120,805	163,869	87,554	16,458	7,042	38,038	21,446
1979	309,228	352,061	1,416	353,477	25,705	-138,622	189,150	101,048	19,030	7,856	39,364	22,895
1980	356,744	398,492	986	399,478	29,189	-148,494	221,795	111,903	23,046	8,298	42,989	24,553
1981	398,257	443,478	940	444,418	33,385	-155,526	255,507	116,099	26,651	8,575	46,444	26,045
1982	449,519	490,269	1,455	491,724	36,015	-161,725	293,984	125,953	29,582	9,257	48,561	26,948
1983	454,815	487,866	1,604	489,470	38,682	-156,903	293,885	128,551	32,379	9,546	47,647	25,701
1984	488,771	517,505	1,431	518,936	41,864	-160,001	317,071	135,606	36,094	9,769	50,034	25,809
1985	528,736	557,970	599	558,569	46,189	-168,505	343,875	145,887	38,974	10,313	51,268	26,658
1986	558,532	584,465	770	585,235	49,627	-176,841	358,767	158,222	41,543	10,764	51,890	27,196
1987	592,806	612,650	366	613,016	53,134	-178,405	381,477	167,664	43,665	10,932	54,228	28,028
1988	616,787	642,680	800	643,480	59,925	-188,242	395,313	174,033	47,441	11,057	55,780	27,945
1989	657,880	666,133	1,200	667,333	63,613	-186,668	417,052	187,521	53,307	11,426	57,578	28,135
1990	661,645	596,900	743	597,643	58,718	-109,372	429,553	169,521	62,571	11,168	59,247	24,410
1991	722,991	688,479	1,200	689,679	69,660	-161,302	458,717	191,896	72,378	12,018	60,158	25,608
1992	864,256	871,334	1,504	872,838	92,266	-243,358	537,214	241,568	85,474	13,282	65,072	29,828
1993	907,259	849,496	1,405	850,901	91,634	-193,799	565,468	248,309	93,482	14,003	64,792	29,680
1994	954,019	876,294	1,744	878,038	91,285	-198,157	588,596	263,951	101,472	14,069	67,809	30,543
1995	1,026,375	930,826	1,482	932,308	93,857	-211,560	626,891	287,634	111,850	14,991	68,468	32,025
1996	1,079,424	953,228	1,722	954,950	95,815	-201,751	657,384	299,553	122,487	15,472	69,766	32,488
1997	1,123,009	1,009,225	1,817	1,011,042	100,400	-203,774	706,868	287,669	128,472	15,711	71,477	32,627
1998	1,168,979	1,036,761	2,480	1,039,241	102,701	-223,067	713,473	322,934	132,572	16,456	71,035	32,828
1999	1,241,344	1,068,254	3,138	1,071,392	105,026	-192,882	773,484	325,246	142,614	17,218	72,095	32,807
2000	1,303,113	1,159,678	3,118	1,162,796	114,134	-239,751	808,911	337,101	157,101	18,053	72,181	34,607
2001	1,365,804	1,233,903	4,471	1,238,374	123,958	-256,574	857,842	329,715	178,247	18,986	71,939	34,716
2002	1,489,312	1,321,837	3,432	1,325,269	132,234	-287,333	905,702	378,873	204,737	20,291	73,399	34,713
2003	1,655,145	1,528,732	3,827	1,532,559	151,016	-358,164	1,023,379	421,641	210,125	23,229	71,252	35,795
2004	1,755,059	1,642,438	4,236	1,646,674	167,210	-396,555	1,082,909	435,888	236,262	23,523	74,609	37,375
2005	1,832,172	1,850,236	3,889	1,854,125	184,692	-572,731	1,096,702	470,508	264,962	23,983	76,395	37,291
2006	1,939,242	1,951,914	2,419	1,954,333	197,726	-567,056	1,189,551	467,033	282,658	25,788	75,199	37,607
2007	1,988,666	2,079,094	2,989	2,082,083	208,335	-705,477	1,168,271	513,514	306,881	26,136	76,089	38,875
2008	2,087,604	2,348,410	3,629	2,352,039	242,297	-894,187	1,215,555	521,302	350,747	27,695	75,379	41,575
2009	2,171,244	2,367,304	2,892	2,370,196	249,029	-842,147	1,279,020	512,957	379,267	26,856	80,848	41,168
2010	2,247,536	2,567,861	2,757	2,570,618	273,322	-1,015,367	1,281,929	539,270	426,337	29,066	77,325	42,511
2011	2,439,957	2,707,435	3,018	2,710,453	265,505	-1,055,212	1,389,736	588,239	461,982	30,424	80,198	44,252
2012	2,395,933	2,658,329	4,264	2,662,593	264,589	-996,171	1,401,833	545,878	448,222	29,853	80,257	43,431
2013	2,401,575	2,616,562	5,733	2,622,295	285,664	-942,489	1,394,142	534,253	473,180	30,570	78,561	43,179
2014	2,468,452	2,546,068	4,855	2,550,923	279,208	-834,238	1,437,477	527,618	503,357	30,564	80,764	42,010
2015	2,524,338	2,545,620	4,611	2,550,231	280,463	-806,924	1,462,844	525,133	536,361	32,062	78,734	41,525
2016	2,526,637	2,461,984	3,108	2,465,092	265,548	-751,921	1,447,623	512,639	566,375	31,927	79,137	40,493
2017	2,629,355	2,524,134	3,555	2,527,689	273,590	-763,499	1,490,600	537,787	600,968	33,058	79,538	42,122
2018	2,749,622	2,592,568	2,696	2,595,264	282,158	-736,500	1,576,606	535,243	637,773	34,923	78,734	43,053
2019	2,830,559	2,670,192	2,498	2,672,690	290,132	-771,938	1,610,620	538,669	681,270	34,941	81,009	43,887
2020	3,069,905	2,728,914	1,778	2,730,692	299,022	-805,209	1,626,461	507,716	935,728	37,628	81,586	43,962
2021	3,405,125	2,989,205	2,880	2,992,085	325,059	-881,948	1,785,078	531,975	1,088,072	40,570	83,933	46,206
2022	3,421,958	3,096,020	4,606	3,100,626	339,520	-820,103	1,941,003	538,946	942,009	39,616	86,378	47,426

Personal Income and Employment by Area: Homosassa Springs, FL

(Thousands of dollars, except as noted.)

Year	Personal income, total	Derivation of personal income: Earnings by place of work: Nonfarm	Farm	Total	Less: Contributions for government social insurance	Plus: Adjustment for residence	Equals: Net earnings by place of residence	Plus: Dividends, interest, and rent	Plus: Personal current transfer receipts	Per capita personal income (dollars)	Population (persons)	Total employment
1970	63,421	35,041	678	35,719	2,186	-1,249	32,284	19,180	11,957	3,203	19,799	6,020
1971	76,322	40,929	795	41,724	2,741	-1,234	37,749	23,066	15,507	3,365	22,680	6,864
1972	95,300	53,382	1,015	54,397	3,804	-2,118	48,475	26,951	19,874	3,542	26,906	8,318
1973	128,831	77,449	1,403	78,852	6,375	-4,742	67,735	35,003	26,093	3,829	33,646	10,406
1974	143,423	73,420	1,064	74,484	6,439	-1,982	66,063	43,948	33,412	3,851	37,239	10,038
1975	166,390	75,222	1,144	76,366	6,531	-1,571	68,264	49,888	48,238	4,175	39,855	9,797
1976	184,511	85,307	1,259	86,566	7,386	-1,648	77,532	56,670	50,309	4,472	41,261	10,225
1977	214,481	96,935	1,277	98,212	8,587	-737	88,888	67,976	57,617	4,721	45,432	11,298
1978	259,922	116,001	1,533	117,534	10,487	324	107,371	85,459	67,092	5,375	48,361	12,617
1979	317,450	140,283	1,520	141,803	13,412	-16	128,375	107,200	81,875	6,154	51,586	14,045
1980	396,146	171,115	1,412	172,527	16,575	-1,208	154,744	140,902	100,500	7,110	55,719	15,605
1981	484,741	208,787	669	209,456	21,753	-1,676	186,027	176,821	121,893	8,123	59,678	17,682
1982	546,553	239,393	1,306	240,699	26,216	-4,893	209,590	192,327	144,636	8,684	62,938	18,878
1983	619,395	255,254	743	255,997	27,762	1,709	229,944	220,666	168,785	9,265	66,850	19,846
1984	758,396	304,519	901	305,420	33,645	3,346	275,121	290,971	192,304	10,674	71,051	21,909
1985	891,501	381,495	223	381,718	43,101	-1,079	337,538	341,821	212,142	11,931	74,724	24,290
1986	964,530	377,798	266	378,064	44,255	10,193	344,002	386,754	233,774	12,193	79,104	25,542
1987	1,054,454	443,599	-472	443,127	50,824	13,832	406,135	395,800	252,519	12,687	83,112	26,811
1988	1,173,437	467,778	39	467,817	56,724	23,189	434,282	451,337	287,818	13,641	86,021	27,981
1989	1,330,522	519,534	242	519,776	65,527	27,136	481,385	533,329	315,808	14,848	89,607	29,039
1990	1,429,451	547,819	129	547,948	68,280	30,514	510,182	569,195	350,074	15,103	94,645	29,942
1991	1,517,186	606,784	692	607,476	75,406	32,426	564,496	554,480	398,210	15,550	97,569	30,207
1992	1,608,444	663,014	1,314	664,328	81,939	36,770	619,159	534,793	454,492	16,051	100,210	30,105
1993	1,696,549	711,859	999	712,858	87,648	43,854	669,064	543,643	483,842	16,636	101,978	31,764
1994	1,815,813	755,961	977	756,938	95,342	51,934	713,530	582,509	519,774	17,388	104,429	33,496
1995	1,896,356	778,770	617	779,387	99,307	62,224	742,304	587,958	566,094	17,627	107,581	34,117
1996	2,013,981	818,976	626	819,602	102,910	72,172	788,864	620,648	604,469	18,317	109,954	35,859
1997	2,163,034	889,315	1,288	890,603	111,376	77,935	857,162	673,663	632,209	19,318	111,972	36,610
1998	2,315,838	935,509	1,638	937,147	116,114	90,667	911,700	751,246	652,892	20,253	114,344	38,580
1999	2,462,793	1,024,157	2,957	1,027,114	123,987	99,394	1,002,521	783,324	676,948	21,116	116,634	40,133
2000	2,662,103	1,079,942	2,660	1,082,602	130,395	110,746	1,062,953	874,063	725,087	22,437	118,649	41,747
2001	2,829,759	1,189,915	2,970	1,192,885	141,404	118,580	1,170,061	873,849	785,849	23,348	121,197	41,251
2002	2,932,489	1,233,872	2,375	1,236,247	146,655	132,301	1,221,893	872,425	838,171	23,747	123,491	41,904
2003	3,104,508	1,325,335	1,744	1,327,079	157,786	151,088	1,320,381	892,367	891,760	24,597	126,215	42,828
2004	3,295,172	1,410,237	1,723	1,411,960	171,389	170,410	1,410,981	906,923	977,268	25,379	129,840	44,819
2005	3,619,586	1,589,572	1,673	1,591,245	196,001	193,679	1,588,923	953,291	1,077,372	27,054	133,791	47,675
2006	3,938,101	1,751,778	2,162	1,753,940	222,448	212,928	1,744,420	1,012,485	1,181,196	28,573	137,826	50,649
2007	4,194,839	1,759,163	1,752	1,760,915	230,283	224,560	1,755,192	1,168,748	1,270,899	29,756	140,974	51,288
2008	4,311,935	1,683,165	1,642	1,684,807	228,545	232,944	1,689,206	1,207,263	1,415,466	30,340	142,122	49,577
2009	4,255,161	1,662,627	1,803	1,664,430	231,057	207,064	1,640,437	1,091,578	1,523,146	30,097	141,381	47,290
2010	4,432,186	1,736,379	1,626	1,738,005	238,949	196,569	1,695,625	1,114,643	1,621,918	31,387	141,210	46,763
2011	4,522,086	1,728,937	1,137	1,730,074	219,580	203,733	1,714,227	1,132,436	1,675,423	32,314	139,943	46,580
2012	4,564,074	1,778,153	2,628	1,780,781	228,285	214,963	1,767,459	1,110,300	1,686,315	32,717	139,503	46,872
2013	4,624,117	1,767,044	2,214	1,769,258	253,311	220,642	1,736,589	1,165,120	1,722,408	33,194	139,304	46,811
2014	4,757,839	1,768,428	2,225	1,770,653	254,922	244,795	1,760,526	1,181,182	1,816,131	34,119	139,450	47,083
2015	4,993,995	1,837,435	1,972	1,839,407	262,838	271,027	1,847,596	1,250,809	1,895,590	35,400	141,075	47,836
2016	5,119,969	1,870,422	1,609	1,872,031	271,173	293,574	1,894,432	1,272,993	1,952,544	35,602	143,811	48,738
2017	5,330,024	1,927,338	1,553	1,928,891	283,509	315,031	1,960,413	1,328,603	2,041,008	36,360	146,591	49,668
2018	5,598,283	1,984,162	13	1,984,175	300,837	339,619	2,022,957	1,427,388	2,147,938	37,561	149,044	50,962
2019	5,913,372	2,054,344	253	2,054,597	318,464	364,529	2,100,662	1,500,495	2,312,215	39,048	151,440	51,016
2020	6,430,151	2,096,031	-517	2,095,514	333,337	392,149	2,154,326	1,515,248	2,760,577	41,602	154,565	50,927
2021	7,179,333	2,363,585	-1,147	2,362,438	359,049	439,738	2,443,127	1,644,964	3,091,242	45,406	158,113	53,717
2022	7,367,510	2,568,181	-1,480	2,566,701	400,694	486,384	2,652,391	1,761,468	2,953,651	45,330	162,529	56,458

Personal Income and Employment by Area: Hot Springs, AR

(Thousands of dollars, except as noted.)

Year	Personal income, total	Derivation of personal income: Earnings by place of work: Nonfarm	Farm	Total	Less: Contributions for government social insurance	Plus: Adjustment for residence	Equals: Net earnings by place of residence	Plus: Dividends, interest, and rent	Plus: Personal current transfer receipts	Per capita personal income (dollars)	Population (persons)	Total employment
1970	173,467	119,289	641	119,930	8,762	-1,571	109,597	37,543	26,327	3,176	54,620	23,344
1971	200,806	139,363	719	140,082	10,589	-1,719	127,774	42,337	30,695	3,510	57,207	25,542
1972	227,659	159,222	1,156	160,378	12,631	-1,443	146,304	46,817	34,538	3,845	59,206	26,849
1973	260,759	180,998	2,534	183,532	16,531	-1,700	165,301	53,861	41,597	4,251	61,347	28,786
1974	298,775	204,407	1,321	205,728	19,377	-938	185,413	63,626	49,736	4,691	63,691	29,920
1975	325,437	209,333	2,726	212,059	19,256	-2,398	190,405	71,302	63,730	5,080	64,058	27,808
1976	370,291	242,384	2,507	244,891	22,333	-949	221,609	80,088	68,594	5,634	65,728	29,099
1977	417,981	275,434	1,754	277,188	25,723	-280	251,185	92,960	73,836	6,190	67,520	30,813
1978	470,699	307,926	2,692	310,618	29,330	545	281,833	107,601	81,265	6,872	68,495	31,529
1979	525,802	337,778	2,588	340,366	33,365	714	307,715	124,855	93,232	7,509	70,026	31,939
1980	604,324	369,045	2,229	371,274	36,186	2,563	337,651	157,701	108,972	8,567	70,545	31,739
1981	680,681	391,403	2,699	394,102	41,789	1,359	353,672	199,307	127,702	9,663	70,445	31,654
1982	731,343	413,381	2,682	416,063	45,082	-3,473	367,508	223,581	140,254	10,369	70,534	31,979
1983	766,248	438,565	1,524	440,089	48,177	-277	391,635	222,880	151,733	10,724	71,455	32,719
1984	835,872	473,557	1,806	475,363	53,759	2,854	424,458	251,255	160,159	11,582	72,172	33,519
1985	891,096	497,825	1,429	499,254	57,652	2,247	443,849	276,683	170,564	12,341	72,209	34,063
1986	937,135	519,566	2,412	521,978	60,434	1,635	463,179	290,609	183,347	12,928	72,487	34,160
1987	968,852	546,713	863	547,576	63,590	1,967	485,953	288,912	193,987	13,228	73,244	34,459
1988	1,027,032	571,580	1,125	572,705	69,363	4,117	507,459	311,196	208,377	14,104	72,821	34,781
1989	1,136,054	604,959	2,193	607,152	74,204	6,208	539,156	367,696	229,202	15,521	73,195	35,525
1990	1,202,761	638,633	1,272	639,905	81,091	9,261	568,075	384,912	249,774	16,350	73,563	35,662
1991	1,273,321	682,663	1,532	684,195	86,841	6,726	604,080	386,651	282,590	17,013	74,844	36,928
1992	1,381,902	745,386	1,842	747,228	94,627	6,072	658,673	406,465	316,764	18,052	76,553	38,245
1993	1,487,189	809,422	4,640	814,062	103,034	3,742	714,770	436,184	336,235	18,929	78,568	40,364
1994	1,575,321	871,695	5,867	877,562	113,501	2,184	766,245	459,270	349,806	19,527	80,673	41,171
1995	1,677,542	937,569	7,341	944,910	121,724	420	823,606	477,722	376,214	20,454	82,015	43,164
1996	1,760,684	972,955	7,369	980,324	125,848	786	855,262	509,156	396,266	21,057	83,615	43,870
1997	1,857,676	1,019,293	8,089	1,027,382	132,076	-500	894,806	542,980	419,890	21,850	85,021	45,357
1998	1,969,476	1,099,347	7,695	1,107,042	140,574	-1,689	964,779	567,786	436,911	22,855	86,172	45,848
1999	2,001,037	1,152,918	6,924	1,159,842	147,049	-3,476	1,009,317	545,936	445,784	22,954	87,177	46,295
2000	2,088,793	1,208,787	3,928	1,212,715	153,070	-3,617	1,056,028	562,151	470,614	23,653	88,311	47,186
2001	2,173,070	1,259,323	3,438	1,262,761	156,158	7,077	1,113,680	540,315	519,075	24,408	89,032	48,005
2002	2,214,682	1,305,950	1,613	1,307,563	161,832	19,259	1,164,990	503,413	546,279	24,709	89,630	47,860
2003	2,316,928	1,379,821	2,413	1,382,234	170,474	30,652	1,242,412	506,907	567,609	25,606	90,483	48,610
2004	2,450,693	1,446,658	3,586	1,450,244	178,305	32,739	1,304,678	546,681	599,334	26,906	91,084	49,726
2005	2,614,239	1,520,161	3,740	1,523,901	189,879	42,775	1,376,797	593,922	643,520	28,386	92,096	51,052
2006	2,835,110	1,599,092	4,435	1,603,527	202,321	67,357	1,468,563	658,076	708,471	30,136	94,077	52,168
2007	2,969,117	1,627,703	7,444	1,635,147	209,676	87,646	1,513,117	700,925	755,075	31,335	94,753	52,987
2008	3,018,387	1,621,682	6,108	1,627,790	215,133	95,545	1,508,202	676,951	833,234	31,561	95,636	52,337
2009	3,029,486	1,610,594	3,208	1,613,802	216,410	85,284	1,482,676	637,698	909,112	31,610	95,840	51,467
2010	3,096,678	1,665,974	2,321	1,668,295	221,205	69,269	1,516,359	622,862	957,457	32,227	96,090	50,915
2011	3,255,301	1,746,491	1,353	1,747,844	209,318	67,402	1,605,928	673,438	975,935	33,583	96,932	51,183
2012	3,375,609	1,827,034	2,291	1,829,325	213,759	51,479	1,667,045	719,761	988,803	34,754	97,129	51,562
2013	3,316,253	1,837,868	3,067	1,840,935	239,447	21,546	1,623,034	683,944	1,009,275	33,889	97,857	51,634
2014	3,487,179	1,870,777	3,225	1,874,002	247,836	25,514	1,651,680	763,008	1,072,491	35,581	98,008	52,143
2015	3,579,457	1,924,280	1,882	1,926,162	255,086	33,517	1,704,593	747,308	1,127,556	36,480	98,121	52,088
2016	3,688,123	1,972,551	1,090	1,973,641	259,645	37,212	1,751,208	764,880	1,172,035	37,412	98,582	52,159
2017	3,786,811	2,076,604	1,820	2,078,424	274,020	33,281	1,837,685	740,643	1,208,483	38,353	98,737	52,340
2018	3,913,245	2,133,446	870	2,134,316	283,498	22,547	1,873,365	786,958	1,252,922	39,362	99,417	53,322
2019	4,130,036	2,234,026	964	2,234,990	296,445	24,482	1,963,027	810,797	1,356,212	41,382	99,802	53,703
2020	4,524,202	2,304,377	1,547	2,305,924	320,486	29,955	2,015,393	874,726	1,634,083	45,130	100,249	52,171
2021	4,794,647	2,417,638	1,921	2,419,559	331,547	26,764	2,114,776	906,414	1,773,457	47,762	100,386	53,552
2022	4,855,065	2,560,205	591	2,560,796	358,332	18,252	2,220,716	960,850	1,673,499	48,507	100,089	55,781

Personal Income and Employment by Area: Houma-Thibodaux, LA

(Thousands of dollars, except as noted.)

		Derivation of personal income										
		Earnings by place of work										
Year	Personal income, total	Nonfarm	Farm	Total	Less: Contributions for government social insurance	Plus: Adjustment for residence	Equals: Net earnings by place of residence	Plus: Dividends, interest, and rent	Plus: Personal current transfer receipts	Per capita personal income (dollars)	Population (persons)	Total employment
1970	423,303	328,870	9,719	338,589	21,274	29,133	346,448	47,657	29,198	2,910	145,445	50,412
1971	468,085	363,406	10,296	373,702	24,071	30,669	380,300	53,522	34,263	3,163	147,993	51,619
1972	516,657	402,699	11,561	414,260	28,022	32,663	418,901	59,174	38,582	3,413	151,395	53,708
1973	583,587	456,134	20,999	477,133	36,898	31,238	471,473	66,501	45,613	3,816	152,931	56,711
1974	685,979	525,971	34,047	560,018	43,757	35,480	551,741	80,827	53,411	4,432	154,770	59,281
1975	791,965	624,045	15,974	640,019	51,256	41,742	630,505	96,568	64,892	4,984	158,910	62,632
1976	922,987	735,221	24,000	759,221	61,058	44,598	742,761	106,845	73,381	5,671	162,751	66,030
1977	1,044,855	840,102	26,866	866,968	70,733	47,446	843,681	120,779	80,395	6,283	166,289	69,860
1978	1,229,617	1,022,063	11,096	1,033,159	88,373	57,282	1,002,068	137,090	90,459	7,248	169,656	75,915
1979	1,417,621	1,194,781	10,196	1,204,977	107,246	60,569	1,158,300	155,827	103,494	8,147	173,998	79,997
1980	1,686,763	1,402,591	7,637	1,410,228	124,425	69,867	1,355,670	205,264	125,829	9,459	178,317	84,311
1981	1,981,923	1,621,737	12,222	1,633,959	154,750	91,968	1,571,177	264,526	146,220	10,785	183,763	88,068
1982	2,100,397	1,648,024	12,443	1,660,467	160,941	101,437	1,600,963	324,673	174,761	11,150	188,371	87,004
1983	2,026,759	1,477,704	7,082	1,484,786	140,742	104,600	1,448,644	356,132	221,983	10,676	189,850	78,980
1984	2,110,892	1,528,496	1,389	1,529,885	150,224	114,505	1,494,166	390,416	226,310	11,138	189,525	79,729
1985	2,161,067	1,541,748	1,402	1,543,150	151,877	120,042	1,511,315	407,162	242,590	11,394	189,669	79,101
1986	2,042,556	1,372,901	2,912	1,375,813	131,002	112,971	1,357,782	395,760	289,014	10,826	188,665	71,653
1987	1,977,192	1,319,396	5,552	1,324,948	124,085	108,649	1,309,512	376,144	291,536	10,691	184,936	70,421
1988	2,104,850	1,405,752	8,702	1,414,454	140,681	126,961	1,400,734	404,881	299,235	11,445	183,916	71,686
1989	2,242,319	1,459,834	9,953	1,469,787	147,345	140,830	1,463,272	449,760	329,287	12,238	183,230	71,631
1990	2,448,608	1,638,318	5,470	1,643,788	170,148	161,035	1,634,675	451,416	362,517	13,391	182,852	75,007
1991	2,592,749	1,719,511	6,979	1,726,490	182,082	166,839	1,711,247	457,528	423,974	14,056	184,458	75,913
1992	2,705,681	1,742,531	9,646	1,752,177	180,380	164,456	1,736,253	468,361	501,067	14,581	185,561	73,772
1993	2,856,797	1,861,746	11,240	1,872,986	196,269	154,328	1,831,045	473,862	551,890	15,352	186,083	77,661
1994	3,059,769	1,995,190	9,383	2,004,573	215,175	158,227	1,947,625	497,773	614,371	16,356	187,077	79,935
1995	3,204,518	2,074,168	10,704	2,084,872	223,948	166,285	2,027,209	552,294	625,015	17,048	187,973	82,540
1996	3,429,799	2,261,051	8,758	2,269,809	243,694	166,024	2,192,139	596,848	640,812	18,120	189,283	86,114
1997	3,806,166	2,606,894	9,871	2,616,765	278,714	165,980	2,504,031	652,430	649,705	19,892	191,339	92,368
1998	4,039,707	2,819,076	8,663	2,827,739	301,210	169,977	2,696,506	704,483	638,718	20,859	193,664	97,205
1999	3,974,877	2,766,418	10,281	2,776,699	291,840	153,362	2,638,221	679,391	657,265	20,429	194,569	95,887
2000	4,313,377	3,039,474	9,093	3,048,567	311,883	138,158	2,874,842	755,828	682,707	22,173	194,531	98,985
2001	4,758,126	3,407,810	9,210	3,417,020	358,268	141,195	3,199,947	771,516	786,663	24,356	195,360	99,867
2002	4,925,974	3,556,680	8,204	3,564,884	374,899	141,386	3,331,371	770,555	824,048	25,044	196,692	102,116
2003	5,080,316	3,677,768	8,064	3,685,832	387,384	147,051	3,445,499	787,650	847,167	25,638	198,156	103,899
2004	5,244,003	3,755,154	8,740	3,763,894	392,504	151,517	3,522,907	782,004	939,092	26,304	199,363	104,126
2005	5,881,492	4,195,202	10,967	4,206,169	423,927	118,327	3,900,569	935,374	1,045,549	29,339	200,467	108,051
2006	6,978,520	5,199,365	28,266	5,227,631	515,766	61,610	4,773,475	1,119,870	1,085,175	34,145	204,379	115,417
2007	7,837,502	5,926,552	12,657	5,939,209	586,338	3,707	5,356,578	1,336,952	1,143,972	38,157	205,401	120,804
2008	8,495,445	6,253,228	30,281	6,283,509	621,799	-21,792	5,639,918	1,560,806	1,294,721	41,030	207,056	123,092
2009	8,130,289	5,984,481	30,116	6,014,597	605,014	-88,512	5,321,071	1,456,009	1,353,209	39,131	207,769	119,745
2010	8,344,179	6,368,055	40,244	6,408,299	627,650	-165,302	5,615,347	1,258,078	1,470,754	40,072	208,232	119,410
2011	8,328,862	6,359,030	40,638	6,399,668	566,707	-229,137	5,603,824	1,251,515	1,473,523	39,918	208,651	118,234
2012	8,812,107	6,761,044	37,365	6,798,409	602,998	-390,510	5,804,901	1,523,081	1,484,125	42,210	208,767	121,799
2013	9,065,316	7,267,955	34,971	7,302,926	748,053	-624,530	5,930,343	1,583,816	1,551,157	43,204	209,826	126,526
2014	9,514,672	7,646,675	27,899	7,674,574	779,223	-678,808	6,216,543	1,768,459	1,529,670	45,059	211,162	129,174
2015	9,200,373	7,030,700	31,236	7,061,936	734,789	-585,296	5,741,851	1,780,383	1,678,139	43,424	211,874	124,483
2016	8,505,493	6,053,023	23,265	6,076,288	645,672	-403,509	5,027,107	1,679,031	1,799,355	40,272	211,203	116,726
2017	8,585,158	6,022,570	22,194	6,044,764	637,058	-360,671	5,047,035	1,642,786	1,895,337	40,972	209,536	113,699
2018	8,746,619	6,216,558	23,232	6,239,790	670,249	-425,322	5,144,219	1,606,663	1,995,737	41,910	208,698	115,331
2019	9,066,343	6,389,128	33,434	6,422,562	684,672	-446,192	5,291,698	1,667,274	2,107,371	43,652	207,696	114,679
2020	9,429,635	6,267,090	33,962	6,301,052	684,739	-430,461	5,185,852	1,497,818	2,745,965	45,589	206,839	109,890
2021	10,262,441	6,522,632	39,745	6,562,377	703,934	-422,791	5,435,652	1,716,165	3,110,624	49,685	206,550	110,641
2022	10,111,929	6,909,900	27,702	6,937,602	770,158	-511,209	5,656,235	1,753,261	2,702,433	50,394	200,656	113,513

Personal Income and Employment by Area: Houston-The Woodlands-Sugar Land, TX

(Thousands of dollars, except as noted.)

Year	Personal income, total	Derivation of personal income								Per capita personal income (dollars)	Population (persons)	Total employment
		Earnings by place of work			Less: Contributions for government social insurance	Plus: Adjustment for residence	Equals: Net earnings by place of residence	Plus: Dividends, interest, and rent	Plus: Personal current transfer receipts			
		Nonfarm	Farm	Total								
1970	9,359,224	8,128,677	28,654	8,157,331	527,413	-74,349	7,555,569	1,305,406	498,249	4,240	2,207,116	1,022,725
1971	10,267,131	8,894,756	28,463	8,923,219	594,467	-117,671	8,211,081	1,458,027	598,023	4,513	2,275,020	1,053,329
1972	11,387,434	9,901,050	32,560	9,933,610	697,119	-153,914	9,082,577	1,620,638	684,219	4,881	2,333,148	1,105,219
1973	12,901,143	11,326,510	64,053	11,390,563	931,233	-205,257	10,254,073	1,831,342	815,728	5,371	2,401,849	1,187,670
1974	15,333,368	13,502,750	60,173	13,562,923	1,140,478	-216,332	12,206,113	2,164,938	962,317	6,183	2,479,921	1,264,423
1975	18,149,058	15,962,486	60,526	16,023,012	1,320,396	-165,827	14,536,789	2,416,939	1,195,330	7,014	2,587,627	1,336,396
1976	20,806,358	18,545,698	27,670	18,573,368	1,570,081	-118,601	16,884,686	2,594,763	1,326,909	7,717	2,696,239	1,417,454
1977	23,738,842	21,411,387	67,965	21,479,352	1,816,811	-185,043	19,477,498	2,848,120	1,413,224	8,477	2,800,536	1,511,549
1978	28,053,834	25,502,679	32,374	25,535,053	2,223,125	-231,447	23,080,481	3,386,542	1,586,811	9,622	2,915,493	1,631,614
1979	32,753,231	29,880,688	67,348	29,948,036	2,726,076	-285,482	26,936,478	4,007,740	1,809,013	10,800	3,032,641	1,734,505
1980	38,350,559	34,806,575	44,589	34,851,164	3,205,119	-344,911	31,301,134	4,909,936	2,139,489	12,087	3,172,859	1,823,264
1981	45,571,768	41,379,084	37,608	41,416,692	4,104,376	-364,642	36,947,674	6,164,464	2,459,630	13,770	3,309,381	1,961,475
1982	50,561,122	45,112,034	17,728	45,129,762	4,584,155	-387,445	40,158,162	7,495,379	2,907,581	14,426	3,504,930	2,009,330
1983	51,614,247	44,694,129	43,932	44,738,061	4,497,421	-366,729	39,873,911	8,278,300	3,462,036	14,316	3,605,388	1,927,450
1984	54,921,002	47,258,042	21,480	47,279,522	4,858,734	-382,208	42,038,580	9,245,772	3,636,650	15,161	3,622,633	1,979,788
1985	57,756,657	48,932,715	91,236	49,023,951	5,058,357	-308,419	43,657,175	10,233,664	3,865,818	15,917	3,628,588	1,979,670
1986	57,596,273	48,113,481	49,160	48,162,641	4,916,134	-272,658	42,973,849	10,255,410	4,367,014	15,702	3,668,133	1,894,904
1987	58,217,645	48,745,125	42,192	48,787,317	4,881,212	-224,470	43,681,635	9,984,721	4,551,289	16,055	3,626,052	1,925,079
1988	62,956,886	52,787,551	112,518	52,900,069	5,486,529	-289,877	47,123,663	11,105,938	4,727,285	17,414	3,615,294	2,000,883
1989	68,608,624	57,955,088	87,195	58,042,283	6,026,368	-345,623	51,670,292	11,791,954	5,146,378	18,694	3,670,089	2,075,840
1990	75,800,625	64,229,024	70,910	64,299,934	6,578,646	-431,247	57,290,041	12,753,298	5,757,286	20,076	3,775,620	2,171,989
1991	80,253,304	68,217,795	95,407	68,313,202	7,166,962	-488,862	60,657,378	13,123,070	6,472,856	20,658	3,884,885	2,231,824
1992	86,925,456	73,858,873	86,891	73,945,764	7,594,953	-517,876	65,832,935	13,284,524	7,807,997	21,787	3,989,770	2,228,085
1993	91,159,271	77,380,665	80,701	77,461,366	7,899,739	-540,777	69,020,850	13,587,512	8,550,909	22,367	4,075,564	2,271,445
1994	95,124,021	80,350,595	100,474	80,451,069	8,337,138	-572,265	71,541,666	14,345,756	9,236,599	22,903	4,153,355	2,333,616
1995	102,454,139	85,862,865	109,662	85,972,527	8,851,912	-622,251	76,498,364	15,879,827	10,075,948	24,235	4,227,574	2,402,453
1996	111,533,720	94,023,956	86,489	94,110,445	9,450,817	-699,915	83,959,713	16,884,478	10,689,529	25,850	4,314,589	2,471,047
1997	123,599,934	105,106,474	103,190	105,209,664	10,346,003	-813,227	94,050,434	18,391,826	11,157,674	28,045	4,407,210	2,579,858
1998	135,891,150	116,187,125	96,728	116,283,853	11,307,087	-915,769	104,060,997	20,430,535	11,399,618	30,105	4,513,913	2,704,046
1999	142,897,404	122,882,811	119,355	123,002,166	11,887,878	-966,359	110,147,929	20,889,393	11,860,082	30,911	4,622,857	2,735,747
2000	156,875,243	134,785,426	86,633	134,872,059	12,816,910	-1,116,483	120,938,666	23,334,397	12,602,180	33,254	4,717,507	2,817,971
2001	166,217,893	143,046,975	91,011	143,137,986	13,603,411	-1,277,626	128,256,949	24,100,098	13,860,846	34,501	4,817,815	2,877,532
2002	165,481,070	141,216,997	98,344	141,315,341	13,687,828	-1,307,170	126,320,343	23,796,555	15,364,172	33,518	4,937,081	2,900,992
2003	172,573,887	145,759,767	142,427	145,902,194	14,192,476	-1,315,053	130,394,665	25,776,397	16,402,825	34,265	5,036,393	2,921,574
2004	185,551,051	157,557,735	158,762	157,716,497	15,039,943	-1,493,344	141,183,210	27,058,446	17,309,395	36,151	5,132,602	2,974,126
2005	202,687,324	169,525,658	149,901	169,675,559	16,093,176	-1,738,334	151,844,049	31,413,950	19,429,325	38,727	5,233,729	3,078,424
2006	226,891,971	189,308,077	154,987	189,463,064	17,471,752	-2,086,428	169,904,884	36,245,919	20,741,168	41,834	5,423,615	3,209,386
2007	242,755,190	202,076,142	115,097	202,191,239	19,068,141	-2,514,560	180,608,538	39,380,010	22,766,642	43,812	5,540,882	3,331,863
2008	271,971,248	219,852,094	95,073	219,947,167	20,212,876	-2,731,035	197,003,256	48,674,728	26,293,264	47,913	5,676,381	3,456,219
2009	256,035,894	206,116,667	69,618	206,186,285	19,985,709	-2,493,151	183,707,425	43,407,456	28,921,013	43,946	5,826,108	3,431,310
2010	271,340,509	217,649,804	56,872	217,706,676	20,543,084	-2,413,198	194,750,394	43,839,178	32,750,937	45,627	5,946,920	3,435,234
2011	294,719,024	235,743,585	35,702	235,779,287	19,417,391	-2,800,843	213,561,053	47,002,211	34,155,760	48,677	6,054,602	3,546,924
2012	323,242,524	256,992,428	77,881	257,070,309	20,882,156	-3,256,337	232,931,816	56,322,674	33,988,034	52,301	6,180,465	3,675,600
2013	329,038,636	266,547,487	61,886	266,609,373	25,013,918	-3,499,781	238,095,674	55,698,192	35,244,770	52,033	6,323,626	3,809,433
2014	355,206,208	287,950,465	13,093	287,963,558	26,758,331	-3,878,697	257,326,530	60,696,783	37,182,895	54,699	6,493,835	3,950,712
2015	361,231,296	287,448,034	60,511	287,508,545	27,694,509	-3,870,709	255,943,327	65,347,925	39,940,044	54,210	6,663,596	4,049,986
2016	345,583,499	278,423,576	16,002	278,439,578	27,611,575	-3,673,388	247,154,615	56,153,590	42,275,294	50,841	6,797,324	4,043,225
2017	371,957,658	291,105,061	7,705	291,112,766	28,654,188	-3,305,885	259,152,693	68,936,015	43,868,950	54,000	6,888,064	4,165,315
2018	397,446,898	312,086,349	-19,946	312,066,403	30,006,792	-3,586,343	278,473,268	73,226,342	45,747,288	57,086	6,962,207	4,297,969
2019	415,072,385	320,442,470	-23,700	320,418,770	31,168,891	-3,869,946	285,379,933	81,050,281	48,642,171	58,887	7,048,589	4,385,858
2020	426,115,174	312,616,862	1,908	312,618,770	31,008,024	-3,588,940	278,021,806	79,311,575	68,781,793	59,674	7,140,749	4,329,116
2021	472,473,159	337,476,218	23,765	337,499,983	32,123,279	-3,534,521	301,842,183	90,989,938	79,641,038	65,477	7,215,837	4,520,411
2022	501,652,678	375,875,209	-152,031	375,723,178	35,770,461	-4,002,558	335,950,159	98,576,873	67,125,646	68,344	7,340,118	4,783,219

Personal Income and Employment by Area: Huntington-Ashland, WV-KY-OH

(Thousands of dollars, except as noted.)

Year	Personal income, total	Derivation of personal income: Earnings by place of work: Nonfarm	Farm	Total	Less: Contributions for government social insurance	Plus: Adjustment for residence	Equals: Net earnings by place of residence	Plus: Dividends, interest, and rent	Plus: Personal current transfer receipts	Per capita personal income (dollars)	Population (persons)	Total employment
1970	1,066,477	870,150	7,114	877,264	67,861	174	809,577	127,423	129,477	3,181	335,277	122,361
1971	1,162,932	935,566	5,808	941,374	74,755	3,928	870,547	139,866	152,519	3,409	341,152	123,796
1972	1,247,856	990,509	8,699	999,208	82,431	10,540	927,317	151,410	169,129	3,624	344,285	122,761
1973	1,379,621	1,092,708	10,732	1,103,440	103,826	14,863	1,014,477	170,649	194,495	4,008	344,204	126,424
1974	1,556,635	1,209,013	10,745	1,219,758	118,192	29,072	1,130,638	198,860	227,137	4,504	345,630	129,188
1975	1,737,393	1,312,619	10,342	1,322,961	126,952	39,229	1,235,238	223,829	278,326	4,977	349,106	129,649
1976	1,966,189	1,510,328	9,660	1,519,988	148,853	43,814	1,414,949	247,684	303,556	5,516	356,426	134,051
1977	2,205,649	1,706,593	8,576	1,715,169	167,088	55,476	1,603,557	281,918	320,174	6,087	362,372	139,786
1978	2,479,513	1,942,248	7,784	1,950,032	196,703	69,535	1,822,864	309,513	347,136	6,772	366,117	144,993
1979	2,789,177	2,180,491	5,729	2,186,220	227,902	86,702	2,045,020	346,658	397,499	7,512	371,303	146,790
1980	3,062,989	2,291,430	4,088	2,295,518	240,288	96,560	2,151,790	423,335	487,864	8,176	374,638	144,563
1981	3,324,256	2,430,818	8,364	2,439,182	273,943	93,364	2,258,603	515,610	550,043	8,884	374,204	142,210
1982	3,468,022	2,434,486	9,897	2,444,383	282,797	109,209	2,270,795	589,992	607,235	9,315	372,325	136,377
1983	3,572,973	2,442,713	366	2,443,079	286,256	120,185	2,277,008	627,121	668,844	9,567	373,461	132,940
1984	3,849,239	2,620,790	10,324	2,631,114	314,369	142,321	2,459,066	695,922	694,251	10,381	370,813	135,238
1985	4,051,537	2,751,882	5,340	2,757,222	334,968	161,520	2,583,774	726,903	740,860	11,016	367,777	136,293
1986	4,163,246	2,813,553	1,479	2,815,032	356,425	172,227	2,630,834	753,578	778,834	11,468	363,025	137,258
1987	4,328,405	2,976,081	-419	2,975,662	373,894	176,937	2,778,705	738,453	811,247	12,014	360,272	139,588
1988	4,608,313	3,199,373	249	3,199,622	416,927	183,917	2,966,612	787,445	854,256	12,890	357,514	143,129
1989	4,927,469	3,374,594	3,735	3,378,329	443,308	198,657	3,133,678	876,801	916,990	13,839	356,066	146,522
1990	5,257,773	3,623,298	6,683	3,629,981	484,227	218,360	3,364,114	895,010	998,649	14,787	355,563	151,850
1991	5,496,423	3,732,856	9,714	3,742,570	505,672	228,669	3,465,567	912,451	1,118,405	15,345	358,201	151,926
1992	5,952,814	4,051,468	11,012	4,062,480	540,762	256,003	3,777,721	922,356	1,252,737	16,518	360,389	155,062
1993	6,159,198	4,163,601	6,206	4,169,807	573,010	284,181	3,880,978	951,011	1,327,209	16,932	363,756	156,624
1994	6,403,667	4,354,754	7,179	4,361,933	601,210	284,403	4,045,126	985,932	1,372,609	17,521	365,475	160,099
1995	6,610,345	4,407,226	387	4,407,613	617,803	317,445	4,107,255	1,047,862	1,455,228	18,027	366,691	164,290
1996	6,869,525	4,507,285	-406	4,506,879	635,080	354,662	4,226,461	1,114,321	1,528,743	18,703	367,286	165,723
1997	7,244,361	4,747,105	2,827	4,749,932	659,954	379,937	4,469,915	1,184,536	1,589,910	19,700	367,728	168,689
1998	7,507,318	4,905,959	2,222	4,908,181	686,548	382,341	4,603,974	1,260,144	1,643,200	20,421	367,621	171,051
1999	7,666,196	5,056,626	-3,163	5,053,463	706,841	404,423	4,751,045	1,212,911	1,702,240	20,878	367,182	172,069
2000	8,044,486	5,275,115	3,479	5,278,594	745,464	419,546	4,952,676	1,288,219	1,803,591	21,923	366,942	172,735
2001	8,482,401	5,496,742	-1,508	5,495,234	751,470	434,541	5,178,305	1,313,942	1,990,154	23,189	365,792	170,396
2002	8,797,161	5,690,147	-4,827	5,685,320	760,019	441,463	5,366,764	1,289,110	2,141,287	24,052	365,758	169,970
2003	9,021,616	5,903,821	-1,507	5,902,314	796,951	425,778	5,531,141	1,280,122	2,210,353	24,568	367,208	171,327
2004	9,220,433	6,158,851	543	6,159,394	822,885	393,292	5,729,801	1,218,325	2,272,307	25,115	367,134	173,527
2005	9,551,094	6,363,109	-1,591	6,361,518	851,461	419,864	5,929,921	1,224,099	2,397,074	25,991	367,471	174,508
2006	10,162,998	6,718,240	-4,507	6,713,733	873,766	453,190	6,293,157	1,322,515	2,547,326	27,563	368,725	176,389
2007	10,725,904	7,032,388	-8,215	7,024,173	888,562	414,452	6,550,063	1,469,800	2,706,041	29,046	369,267	180,396
2008	11,483,893	7,392,493	-9,612	7,382,881	914,871	370,508	6,838,518	1,636,869	3,008,506	31,057	369,769	180,446
2009	11,699,679	7,329,104	-6,008	7,323,096	918,404	445,478	6,850,170	1,596,326	3,253,183	31,559	370,722	174,357
2010	12,010,248	7,555,932	-7,958	7,547,974	937,260	469,173	7,079,887	1,527,384	3,402,977	32,356	371,189	173,774
2011	12,517,717	7,787,959	-6,107	7,781,852	855,788	417,009	7,343,073	1,724,925	3,449,719	33,667	371,807	174,010
2012	12,710,889	7,925,580	-3,806	7,921,774	878,143	418,075	7,461,706	1,768,078	3,481,105	34,149	372,219	174,885
2013	12,610,260	7,954,782	-4,229	7,950,553	981,413	399,565	7,368,705	1,697,311	3,544,244	33,898	372,004	173,903
2014	13,015,722	8,139,815	-7,339	8,132,476	1,020,257	382,841	7,495,060	1,759,977	3,760,685	35,053	371,320	174,354
2015	13,385,524	8,265,980	-5,756	8,260,224	1,035,814	453,660	7,678,070	1,814,600	3,892,854	36,160	370,178	173,643
2016	13,313,761	8,061,545	-8,688	8,052,857	1,038,014	530,795	7,545,638	1,805,369	3,962,754	36,124	368,557	171,957
2017	13,704,048	8,289,556	-8,089	8,281,467	1,061,314	535,856	7,756,009	1,856,413	4,091,626	37,440	366,030	172,715
2018	14,366,020	8,733,273	-8,501	8,724,772	1,106,210	628,917	8,247,479	1,926,266	4,192,275	39,514	363,565	172,761
2019	14,785,016	9,038,699	-6,139	9,032,560	1,131,097	466,839	8,368,302	2,042,480	4,374,234	40,962	360,946	172,320
2020	15,845,411	9,051,771	-4,919	9,046,852	1,162,690	479,084	8,363,246	2,098,232	5,383,933	44,094	359,357	166,047
2021	16,971,558	9,466,044	-4,153	9,461,891	1,203,142	586,747	8,845,496	2,202,112	5,923,950	47,584	356,663	170,449
2022	17,116,838	10,134,267	-8,555	10,125,712	1,297,371	563,709	9,392,050	2,406,259	5,318,529	48,311	354,304	176,071

Personal Income and Employment by Area: Huntsville, AL

(Thousands of dollars, except as noted.)

Year	Personal income, total	Derivation of personal income: Earnings by place of work: Nonfarm	Farm	Total	Less: Contributions for government social insurance	Plus: Adjustment for residence	Equals: Net earnings by place of residence	Plus: Dividends, interest, and rent	Plus: Personal current transfer receipts	Per capita personal income (dollars)	Population (persons)	Total employment
1970	904,666	873,867	19,625	893,492	43,750	-126,294	723,448	133,007	48,211	3,962	228,314	107,133
1971	999,215	955,338	26,234	981,572	48,042	-144,472	789,058	154,603	55,554	4,335	230,509	106,235
1972	1,083,376	1,029,043	26,466	1,055,509	55,275	-147,449	852,785	168,389	62,202	4,663	232,339	109,439
1973	1,167,328	1,086,939	35,145	1,122,084	68,262	-147,250	906,572	186,355	74,401	5,005	233,247	111,439
1974	1,257,789	1,154,541	29,060	1,183,601	76,269	-150,845	956,487	209,969	91,333	5,424	231,872	112,513
1975	1,339,700	1,205,924	21,649	1,227,573	81,776	-154,615	991,182	226,889	121,629	5,770	232,194	110,559
1976	1,487,058	1,332,981	31,163	1,364,144	95,385	-159,128	1,109,631	245,271	132,156	6,337	234,646	113,836
1977	1,626,884	1,482,801	18,543	1,501,344	109,274	-172,591	1,219,479	271,369	136,036	6,866	236,952	119,368
1978	1,830,708	1,662,427	24,866	1,687,293	126,390	-187,817	1,373,086	311,502	146,120	7,689	238,094	125,751
1979	2,019,672	1,831,386	33,993	1,865,379	145,226	-216,300	1,503,853	345,800	170,019	8,417	239,958	126,654
1980	2,232,470	2,012,098	6,819	2,018,917	157,763	-251,689	1,609,465	413,003	210,002	9,164	243,620	126,604
1981	2,506,663	2,237,668	29,027	2,266,695	190,810	-291,987	1,783,898	490,061	232,704	10,199	245,771	128,803
1982	2,743,209	2,442,661	28,965	2,471,626	213,585	-323,357	1,934,684	551,368	257,157	11,010	249,166	131,353
1983	3,025,446	2,809,057	-7,338	2,801,719	263,464	-384,785	2,153,470	592,591	279,385	11,917	253,867	139,295
1984	3,461,132	3,244,000	23,922	3,267,922	312,351	-460,090	2,495,481	670,513	295,138	13,394	258,407	149,177
1985	3,843,903	3,677,065	18,660	3,695,725	365,035	-545,450	2,785,240	740,297	318,366	14,528	264,588	158,683
1986	4,172,025	4,038,312	10,465	4,048,777	407,722	-603,322	3,037,733	796,582	337,710	15,438	270,237	166,030
1987	4,543,004	4,420,443	13,831	4,434,274	445,998	-646,247	3,342,029	855,707	345,268	16,419	276,697	174,660
1988	4,985,477	4,878,755	28,462	4,907,217	508,593	-740,551	3,658,073	961,208	366,196	17,569	283,769	182,016
1989	5,410,807	5,178,900	20,431	5,199,331	546,312	-765,364	3,887,655	1,102,300	420,852	18,685	289,588	186,585
1990	5,788,120	5,560,434	14,241	5,574,675	604,328	-829,780	4,140,567	1,180,595	466,958	19,664	294,353	191,461
1991	6,158,363	5,840,931	30,927	5,871,858	640,791	-832,534	4,398,533	1,225,750	534,080	20,388	302,052	192,008
1992	6,691,424	6,378,932	32,797	6,411,729	699,801	-918,549	4,793,379	1,291,010	607,035	21,504	311,170	195,615
1993	6,869,650	6,538,408	18,591	6,556,999	726,486	-941,644	4,888,869	1,330,312	650,469	21,401	320,998	200,042
1994	7,101,701	6,691,189	42,729	6,733,918	762,922	-985,929	4,985,067	1,436,436	680,198	21,810	325,620	196,887
1995	7,440,427	6,941,009	6,460	6,947,469	796,018	-1,037,016	5,114,435	1,582,965	743,027	22,853	325,571	200,903
1996	7,748,718	7,047,168	37,511	7,084,679	811,714	-989,520	5,283,445	1,668,600	796,673	23,658	327,532	204,454
1997	8,265,163	7,431,943	8,422	7,440,365	861,785	-949,176	5,629,404	1,796,408	839,351	25,025	330,281	209,852
1998	8,840,066	7,954,029	24,699	7,978,728	917,217	-988,959	6,072,552	1,901,756	865,758	26,269	336,527	216,761
1999	9,053,439	8,172,540	27,566	8,200,106	952,310	-999,169	6,248,627	1,884,169	920,643	26,661	339,572	218,936
2000	9,740,573	8,740,684	31,325	8,772,009	1,015,421	-1,059,724	6,696,864	2,038,241	1,005,468	28,318	343,972	224,393
2001	10,035,592	8,995,422	26,206	9,021,628	1,034,389	-1,099,829	6,887,410	2,015,941	1,132,241	28,800	348,453	226,046
2002	10,392,633	9,418,272	-4,581	9,413,691	1,078,989	-1,164,557	7,170,145	1,984,784	1,237,704	29,348	354,116	225,574
2003	11,043,302	10,007,000	55,126	10,062,126	1,147,060	-1,250,648	7,664,418	2,039,432	1,339,452	30,683	359,920	230,522
2004	11,797,075	10,540,064	78,134	10,618,198	1,199,457	-1,268,741	8,150,000	2,209,106	1,437,969	32,299	365,248	237,470
2005	12,670,097	11,250,797	61,034	11,311,831	1,284,220	-1,349,747	8,677,864	2,418,712	1,573,521	33,988	372,777	244,687
2006	13,692,101	12,121,605	54,221	12,175,826	1,387,533	-1,475,256	9,313,037	2,647,051	1,732,013	35,766	382,821	252,343
2007	14,723,232	12,824,969	35,478	12,860,447	1,477,711	-1,491,623	9,891,113	2,926,027	1,906,092	37,567	391,922	263,134
2008	15,890,969	13,396,550	56,103	13,452,653	1,566,674	-1,475,268	10,410,711	3,285,880	2,194,378	39,494	402,361	267,111
2009	16,058,119	13,749,572	35,274	13,784,846	1,601,073	-1,511,306	10,672,467	2,993,284	2,392,368	38,959	412,182	262,892
2010	16,914,656	14,213,188	1,112	14,214,300	1,670,314	-1,471,371	11,072,615	3,153,523	2,688,518	40,316	419,552	262,774
2011	17,873,974	14,662,562	34,234	14,696,796	1,525,714	-1,485,867	11,685,215	3,377,157	2,811,602	41,904	426,545	266,700
2012	18,332,698	14,878,551	39,038	14,917,589	1,558,365	-1,456,687	11,902,537	3,580,433	2,849,728	42,373	432,653	267,883
2013	18,510,626	15,173,847	96,057	15,269,904	1,811,934	-1,438,615	12,019,355	3,531,866	2,959,405	42,133	439,336	271,671
2014	19,158,625	15,684,063	49,869	15,733,932	1,871,128	-1,499,899	12,362,905	3,673,566	3,122,154	43,014	445,402	274,632
2015	20,016,250	16,269,610	16,601	16,286,211	1,944,720	-1,530,141	12,811,350	3,835,108	3,369,792	44,403	450,781	280,666
2016	20,781,173	16,836,477	3,547	16,840,024	1,989,479	-1,507,879	13,342,666	3,961,876	3,476,631	45,464	457,090	287,075
2017	21,750,050	17,585,677	16,326	17,602,003	2,082,290	-1,549,287	13,970,426	4,169,572	3,610,052	46,807	464,678	294,038
2018	23,023,200	18,644,338	6,211	18,650,549	2,217,153	-1,581,464	14,851,932	4,335,272	3,835,996	48,636	473,379	302,020
2019	24,601,542	19,925,263	13,068	19,938,331	2,360,115	-1,617,413	15,960,803	4,550,206	4,090,533	50,951	482,846	308,995
2020	26,955,036	21,337,513	12,003	21,349,516	2,531,787	-1,654,898	17,162,831	4,616,503	5,175,702	54,489	494,692	309,923
2021	29,552,158	22,753,097	61,006	22,814,103	2,701,015	-1,793,559	18,319,529	5,208,573	6,024,056	58,638	503,974	325,939
2022	30,701,534	24,302,370	9,178	24,311,548	2,910,293	-1,716,192	19,685,063	5,689,060	5,327,411	59,677	514,465	340,185

Personal Income and Employment by Area: Idaho Falls, ID

(Thousands of dollars, except as noted.)

Year	Personal income, total	Derivation of personal income: Earnings by place of work: Nonfarm	Farm	Total	Less: Contributions for government social insurance	Plus: Adjustment for residence	Equals: Net earnings by place of residence	Plus: Dividends, interest, and rent	Plus: Personal current transfer receipts	Per capita personal income (dollars)	Population (persons)	Total employment
1970	249,121	198,596	24,705	223,301	14,927	-10,811	197,563	34,689	16,869	3,705	67,248	31,286
1971	269,269	212,764	23,431	236,195	16,559	-10,097	209,539	39,780	19,950	4,001	67,297	31,832
1972	304,063	241,079	26,886	267,965	19,582	-10,943	237,440	43,715	22,908	4,370	69,575	33,559
1973	351,493	266,228	44,126	310,354	24,925	-11,685	273,744	51,777	25,972	5,006	70,208	34,784
1974	410,130	302,807	57,679	360,486	29,228	-11,978	319,280	60,750	30,100	5,605	73,174	36,116
1975	444,191	347,607	34,227	381,834	33,247	-13,891	334,696	71,791	37,704	5,906	75,210	37,509
1976	500,212	408,781	27,596	436,377	39,932	-18,324	378,121	77,337	44,754	6,487	77,106	40,884
1977	553,282	469,082	20,883	489,965	46,295	-23,854	419,816	87,235	46,231	6,943	79,685	43,056
1978	616,679	536,043	21,740	557,783	53,797	-32,363	471,623	97,935	47,121	7,444	82,839	45,361
1979	664,861	583,963	15,097	599,060	61,177	-37,303	500,580	108,532	55,749	7,901	84,150	44,826
1980	748,443	627,866	31,508	659,374	65,989	-37,807	555,578	126,834	66,031	8,808	84,969	44,180
1981	818,693	667,660	40,290	707,950	74,874	-41,904	591,172	151,141	76,380	9,492	86,247	42,968
1982	861,083	687,115	38,654	725,769	78,757	-45,064	601,948	176,604	82,531	10,018	85,951	42,575
1983	934,566	741,751	50,722	792,473	85,383	-53,762	653,328	191,591	89,647	10,764	86,820	43,606
1984	1,012,491	817,070	41,824	858,894	96,249	-53,399	709,246	209,055	94,190	11,545	87,700	44,662
1985	1,104,330	897,409	41,031	938,440	107,543	-58,347	772,550	230,325	101,455	12,531	88,130	46,059
1986	1,147,989	949,246	40,198	989,444	114,285	-67,189	807,970	231,215	108,804	12,939	88,724	46,656
1987	1,202,525	1,003,024	46,630	1,049,654	118,797	-71,136	859,721	228,735	114,069	13,378	89,885	47,643
1988	1,283,459	1,066,947	41,180	1,108,127	125,814	-66,438	915,875	243,017	124,567	14,211	90,313	49,146
1989	1,409,548	1,139,087	62,426	1,201,513	136,728	-67,336	997,449	276,348	135,751	15,549	90,651	50,522
1990	1,525,432	1,256,424	76,906	1,333,330	162,007	-79,336	1,091,987	283,592	149,853	16,561	92,109	53,055
1991	1,595,326	1,345,490	56,415	1,401,905	176,974	-94,526	1,130,405	297,405	167,516	16,833	94,772	55,402
1992	1,728,860	1,444,051	65,525	1,509,576	187,529	-98,697	1,223,350	314,757	190,753	17,751	97,397	56,340
1993	1,829,746	1,520,859	76,074	1,596,933	197,824	-106,344	1,292,765	328,901	208,080	18,490	98,961	58,099
1994	1,894,057	1,576,824	49,431	1,626,255	209,700	-100,477	1,316,078	356,166	221,813	18,878	100,332	59,318
1995	1,973,624	1,601,801	59,956	1,661,757	217,304	-99,172	1,345,281	384,063	244,280	19,582	100,789	58,985
1996	2,031,061	1,661,754	64,420	1,726,174	224,566	-139,057	1,362,551	407,515	260,995	20,148	100,809	60,883
1997	2,121,406	1,743,803	48,598	1,792,401	234,734	-143,215	1,414,452	434,239	272,715	20,900	101,505	62,038
1998	2,251,198	1,859,080	62,680	1,921,760	248,314	-151,122	1,522,324	451,544	277,330	21,979	102,425	63,214
1999	2,370,349	1,954,862	72,803	2,027,665	258,050	-146,309	1,623,306	448,434	298,609	22,913	103,450	64,963
2000	2,533,006	2,080,952	80,240	2,161,192	274,220	-158,336	1,728,636	475,277	329,093	24,111	105,055	66,613
2001	2,723,593	2,239,280	76,805	2,316,085	267,143	-193,621	1,855,321	504,037	364,235	25,674	106,082	67,441
2002	2,851,821	2,341,780	110,099	2,451,879	280,370	-194,469	1,977,040	484,516	390,265	26,463	107,768	68,159
2003	2,988,680	2,446,862	62,030	2,508,892	296,765	-194,967	2,017,160	555,709	415,811	27,185	109,937	70,441
2004	3,256,746	2,582,383	102,479	2,684,862	313,376	-179,049	2,192,437	609,338	454,971	28,778	113,168	72,824
2005	3,518,656	2,753,907	71,676	2,825,583	335,597	-184,340	2,305,646	716,136	496,874	30,279	116,208	76,233
2006	3,913,184	3,066,111	90,193	3,156,304	368,722	-195,769	2,591,813	771,193	550,178	32,615	119,981	79,150
2007	4,201,773	3,207,289	134,896	3,342,185	390,191	-199,329	2,752,665	864,586	584,522	33,830	124,203	82,921
2008	4,351,948	3,180,790	137,574	3,318,364	401,825	-172,306	2,744,233	932,132	675,583	33,906	128,353	82,655
2009	4,235,510	3,271,103	98,234	3,369,337	410,069	-163,248	2,796,020	715,885	723,605	32,180	131,621	80,100
2010	4,387,762	3,395,512	89,471	3,484,983	435,419	-193,215	2,856,349	739,329	792,084	32,774	133,880	80,052
2011	4,588,010	3,345,516	125,101	3,470,617	388,732	-198,627	2,883,258	905,035	799,717	33,912	135,290	80,141
2012	4,866,958	3,450,331	102,153	3,552,484	391,402	-159,997	3,001,085	1,042,138	823,735	35,590	136,752	79,833
2013	4,864,905	3,565,520	122,987	3,688,507	440,285	-153,262	3,094,960	916,598	853,347	35,329	137,702	81,105
2014	5,023,145	3,686,296	109,619	3,795,915	452,475	-142,839	3,200,601	941,050	881,494	36,146	138,970	82,818
2015	5,519,379	4,014,019	118,026	4,132,045	482,028	-175,851	3,474,166	1,095,112	950,101	39,153	140,971	85,566
2016	6,073,487	4,355,087	108,576	4,463,663	513,412	-195,511	3,754,740	1,323,466	995,281	42,118	144,201	88,738
2017	6,714,063	4,992,698	59,796	5,052,494	562,436	-237,627	4,252,431	1,423,424	1,038,208	45,494	147,582	91,231
2018	7,426,649	5,702,467	82,963	5,785,430	610,792	-266,474	4,908,164	1,409,367	1,109,118	49,203	150,939	94,391
2019	8,115,685	6,408,873	110,086	6,518,959	655,492	-319,652	5,543,815	1,379,738	1,192,132	52,557	154,417	96,593
2020	8,860,885	6,627,299	133,220	6,760,519	707,257	-370,457	5,682,805	1,661,408	1,516,672	55,948	158,376	99,413
2021	9,448,695	7,056,256	74,538	7,130,794	748,144	-413,808	5,968,842	1,665,232	1,814,621	57,986	162,948	105,230
2022	9,817,179	7,334,760	147,382	7,482,142	812,652	-467,676	6,201,814	1,965,693	1,649,672	59,280	165,608	110,290

Personal Income and Employment by Area: Indianapolis-Carmel-Anderson, IN

(Thousands of dollars, except as noted.)

Year	Personal income, total	Derivation of personal income								Per capita personal income (dollars)	Population (persons)	Total employment
		Earnings by place of work			Less: Contributions for government social insurance	Plus: Adjustment for residence	Equals: Net earnings by place of residence	Plus: Dividends, interest, and rent	Plus: Personal current transfer receipts			
		Nonfarm	Farm	Total								
1970	5,360,907	4,622,519	39,661	4,662,180	310,573	-84,768	4,266,839	739,463	354,605	4,164	1,287,512	599,216
1971	5,839,732	4,978,349	70,109	5,048,458	346,518	-95,670	4,606,270	812,287	421,175	4,506	1,295,884	600,061
1972	6,365,329	5,482,566	56,661	5,539,227	404,591	-106,019	5,028,617	870,883	465,829	4,872	1,306,519	616,990
1973	7,184,781	6,138,364	152,176	6,290,540	522,040	-121,213	5,647,287	979,685	557,809	5,478	1,311,545	646,904
1974	7,780,405	6,615,844	91,430	6,707,274	584,815	-131,081	5,991,378	1,125,819	663,208	5,892	1,320,524	656,064
1975	8,387,294	6,899,935	137,348	7,037,283	599,376	-139,061	6,298,846	1,243,125	845,323	6,362	1,318,435	637,432
1976	9,268,165	7,728,948	139,556	7,868,504	683,115	-153,850	7,031,539	1,336,461	900,165	7,010	1,322,178	654,608
1977	10,288,075	8,706,575	91,621	8,798,196	771,125	-171,716	7,855,355	1,484,625	948,095	7,749	1,327,653	676,374
1978	11,464,111	9,736,240	100,568	9,836,808	887,910	-191,630	8,757,268	1,664,203	1,042,640	8,574	1,337,003	701,877
1979	12,664,332	10,755,794	91,570	10,847,364	1,017,331	-212,498	9,617,535	1,851,947	1,194,850	9,435	1,342,252	718,694
1980	13,867,721	11,281,584	71,980	11,353,564	1,059,244	-217,028	10,077,292	2,264,353	1,526,076	10,282	1,348,738	706,615
1981	15,181,212	12,131,363	55,427	12,186,790	1,227,322	-225,997	10,733,471	2,774,338	1,673,403	11,240	1,350,644	699,352
1982	15,710,173	12,254,495	47,358	12,301,853	1,262,594	-208,770	10,830,489	3,036,907	1,842,777	11,625	1,351,396	681,888
1983	16,748,266	13,091,688	-12,281	13,079,407	1,354,195	-201,043	11,524,169	3,232,698	1,991,399	12,383	1,352,538	690,577
1984	18,574,249	14,633,969	91,586	14,725,555	1,547,881	-260,579	12,917,095	3,566,333	2,090,821	13,648	1,360,966	724,435
1985	19,966,615	15,837,763	91,139	15,928,902	1,707,527	-284,544	13,936,831	3,821,895	2,207,889	14,604	1,367,229	748,013
1986	21,276,150	17,030,091	52,965	17,083,056	1,846,264	-312,443	14,924,349	4,011,063	2,340,738	15,470	1,375,291	774,534
1987	22,651,451	18,361,542	78,028	18,439,570	1,969,893	-321,382	16,148,295	4,113,089	2,390,067	16,314	1,388,481	801,322
1988	24,581,228	19,975,913	34,077	20,009,990	2,210,822	-334,944	17,464,224	4,568,135	2,548,869	17,580	1,398,243	826,484
1989	26,867,260	21,482,143	107,608	21,589,751	2,383,415	-369,621	18,836,715	5,253,398	2,777,147	19,029	1,411,888	856,717
1990	28,812,255	22,980,471	102,593	23,083,064	2,636,267	-397,893	20,048,904	5,741,964	3,021,387	20,130	1,431,307	881,268
1991	30,144,043	24,337,484	23,006	24,360,490	2,823,491	-409,169	21,127,830	5,656,920	3,359,293	20,683	1,457,442	887,840
1992	32,581,770	26,165,767	93,135	26,258,902	3,012,842	-360,895	22,885,165	5,832,180	3,864,425	22,000	1,481,005	898,464
1993	34,535,029	27,711,309	120,286	27,831,595	3,201,070	-359,879	24,270,646	6,163,988	4,100,395	22,939	1,505,485	922,306
1994	36,923,002	29,621,276	94,716	29,715,992	3,476,896	-356,744	25,882,352	6,744,347	4,296,303	24,142	1,529,405	948,056
1995	38,631,202	30,873,402	43,899	30,917,301	3,642,370	-346,062	26,928,869	7,340,915	4,361,418	24,899	1,551,504	975,060
1996	40,878,821	32,614,207	137,691	32,751,898	3,801,785	-371,019	28,579,094	7,762,982	4,536,745	25,977	1,573,626	992,151
1997	43,278,660	34,702,931	135,600	34,838,531	4,032,517	-395,362	30,410,652	8,170,438	4,697,570	27,137	1,594,815	1,015,309
1998	47,614,675	38,270,405	82,284	38,352,689	4,339,653	-478,054	33,534,982	9,242,708	4,836,985	29,475	1,615,438	1,044,041
1999	49,963,139	40,931,923	52,781	40,984,704	4,606,376	-510,985	35,867,343	8,995,913	5,099,883	30,474	1,639,509	1,070,835
2000	54,461,001	44,493,137	99,289	44,592,426	4,924,340	-560,648	39,107,438	9,803,608	5,549,955	32,729	1,663,995	1,099,383
2001	56,421,997	45,999,363	116,763	46,116,126	5,039,789	-644,793	40,431,544	9,845,235	6,145,218	33,441	1,687,209	1,095,475
2002	57,265,022	46,830,991	55,033	46,886,024	5,163,384	-667,369	41,055,271	9,630,519	6,579,232	33,527	1,708,018	1,089,130
2003	58,417,779	47,650,120	139,141	47,789,261	5,330,523	-686,111	41,772,627	9,749,040	6,896,112	33,781	1,729,297	1,096,054
2004	61,265,219	50,094,546	233,312	50,327,858	5,633,648	-766,605	43,927,605	10,042,401	7,295,213	34,996	1,750,639	1,114,587
2005	63,564,837	51,999,960	145,905	52,145,865	5,913,766	-805,163	45,426,936	10,188,541	7,949,360	35,852	1,772,959	1,133,884
2006	67,884,354	55,021,060	125,043	55,146,103	6,244,201	-835,616	48,066,286	11,249,041	8,569,027	37,698	1,800,724	1,153,300
2007	69,980,207	56,370,669	165,386	56,536,055	6,438,677	-811,262	49,286,116	11,633,791	9,060,300	38,314	1,826,515	1,176,672
2008	74,228,422	58,449,165	268,002	58,717,167	6,675,822	-767,366	51,273,979	12,304,107	10,650,336	40,117	1,850,321	1,180,110
2009	74,357,114	58,364,239	294,493	58,658,732	6,542,330	-813,721	51,302,681	11,204,584	11,849,849	39,690	1,873,460	1,141,321
2010	78,742,553	61,855,693	215,787	62,071,480	6,655,944	-856,445	54,559,091	11,253,672	12,929,790	41,593	1,893,178	1,141,371
2011	84,408,662	65,683,801	322,770	66,006,571	6,144,629	-756,801	59,105,141	12,248,216	13,055,305	44,112	1,913,506	1,165,452
2012	88,082,212	68,381,990	183,066	68,565,056	6,433,729	-626,133	61,505,194	13,237,332	13,339,686	45,526	1,934,783	1,190,472
2013	89,311,141	70,093,650	576,398	70,670,048	7,554,959	-606,860	62,508,229	13,230,660	13,572,252	45,542	1,961,091	1,214,338
2014	92,569,683	72,275,363	185,371	72,460,734	7,820,816	-591,324	64,048,594	14,009,549	14,511,540	46,732	1,980,873	1,239,192
2015	97,110,898	75,827,212	-8,117	75,819,095	8,198,372	-534,078	67,086,645	15,001,102	15,023,151	48,593	1,998,456	1,269,270
2016	101,167,705	79,252,328	117,475	79,369,803	8,480,227	-584,704	70,304,872	15,500,866	15,361,967	50,039	2,021,771	1,299,021
2017	104,694,751	81,997,457	90,160	82,087,617	8,840,700	-597,366	72,649,551	16,328,559	15,716,641	51,188	2,045,301	1,328,752
2018	111,036,232	86,632,456	93,277	86,725,733	9,267,309	-566,264	76,892,160	17,680,235	16,463,837	53,582	2,072,279	1,355,130
2019	118,171,650	92,647,573	74,232	92,721,805	9,824,872	-691,790	82,205,143	18,454,015	17,512,492	56,417	2,094,610	1,369,607
2020	127,709,967	97,124,525	198,912	97,323,437	10,351,866	-682,876	86,288,695	18,539,071	22,882,201	60,412	2,113,979	1,337,862
2021	142,170,827	106,588,476	318,293	106,906,769	11,194,672	-923,908	94,788,189	21,062,583	26,320,055	66,789	2,128,664	1,399,054
2022	147,180,567	114,404,283	259,322	114,663,605	12,179,438	-1,075,685	101,408,482	22,992,690	22,779,395	68,719	2,141,779	1,470,519

Personal Income and Employment by Area: Iowa City, IA

(Thousands of dollars, except as noted.)

Year	Personal income, total	Derivation of personal income								Per capita personal income (dollars)	Population (persons)	Total employment
		Earnings by place of work			Less: Contributions for government social insurance	Plus: Adjustment for residence	Equals: Net earnings by place of residence	Plus: Dividends, interest, and rent	Plus: Personal current transfer receipts			
		Nonfarm	Farm	Total								
1970	344,368	252,377	28,880	281,257	18,405	-4,060	258,792	63,584	21,992	3,774	91,237	44,389
1971	373,977	278,994	25,278	304,272	21,175	-4,434	278,663	69,347	25,967	4,039	92,581	45,252
1972	408,804	295,816	35,247	331,063	23,487	-1,627	305,949	75,610	27,245	4,417	92,551	45,759
1973	475,914	331,842	55,593	387,435	30,370	-63	357,002	87,063	31,849	5,049	94,258	48,094
1974	510,072	374,099	33,921	408,020	36,076	699	372,643	100,138	37,291	5,339	95,544	50,462
1975	603,951	420,639	61,549	482,188	40,020	2,621	444,789	113,544	45,618	6,293	95,973	52,099
1976	658,636	482,778	39,319	522,097	45,784	4,516	480,829	127,411	50,396	6,667	98,784	54,408
1977	742,509	555,447	33,628	589,075	51,730	3,831	541,176	147,932	53,401	7,485	99,194	56,853
1978	857,185	628,384	60,378	688,762	61,179	4,806	632,389	165,812	58,984	8,604	99,624	59,367
1979	939,363	696,009	47,130	743,139	70,908	9,314	681,545	191,048	66,770	9,233	101,738	60,040
1980	1,026,286	762,195	19,130	781,325	77,533	12,160	715,952	231,532	78,802	10,031	102,308	61,267
1981	1,171,274	819,717	52,002	871,719	88,949	17,524	800,294	279,811	91,169	11,276	103,873	60,386
1982	1,252,232	871,463	39,792	911,255	95,657	13,743	829,341	321,238	101,653	11,961	104,697	61,469
1983	1,330,229	955,722	15,720	971,442	104,077	8,346	875,711	344,490	110,028	12,564	105,874	62,017
1984	1,482,147	1,034,760	63,644	1,098,404	115,033	5,829	989,200	379,111	113,836	13,835	107,132	64,839
1985	1,545,879	1,089,623	53,494	1,143,117	123,179	7,948	1,027,886	393,652	124,341	14,274	108,304	65,524
1986	1,624,693	1,159,225	51,982	1,211,207	134,748	6,884	1,083,343	411,308	130,042	14,902	109,024	66,717
1987	1,707,381	1,240,814	58,387	1,299,201	143,026	8,453	1,164,628	406,339	136,414	15,520	110,013	67,957
1988	1,811,104	1,366,548	28,662	1,395,210	163,850	6,309	1,237,669	427,652	145,783	16,142	112,201	70,554
1989	2,037,114	1,513,547	54,196	1,567,743	179,342	-75	1,388,326	489,299	159,489	17,875	113,962	73,114
1990	2,156,330	1,618,888	58,582	1,677,470	194,937	-1,045	1,481,488	501,123	173,719	18,555	116,212	75,272
1991	2,264,665	1,722,505	43,157	1,765,662	206,707	-5,743	1,553,212	524,870	186,583	19,305	117,311	77,243
1992	2,420,981	1,841,677	58,207	1,899,884	217,347	-5,799	1,676,738	543,965	200,278	20,270	119,436	78,669
1993	2,542,021	1,944,021	32,319	1,976,340	227,463	-10,078	1,738,799	589,326	213,896	21,002	121,037	81,316
1994	2,757,248	2,106,782	63,227	2,170,009	249,094	-19,265	1,901,650	629,842	225,756	22,401	123,084	84,043
1995	2,881,596	2,212,381	27,996	2,240,377	260,281	-23,981	1,956,115	684,212	241,269	23,102	124,733	87,281
1996	3,084,296	2,321,242	72,285	2,393,527	263,873	-27,391	2,102,263	724,206	257,827	24,536	125,704	88,742
1997	3,258,877	2,448,788	77,451	2,526,239	285,923	-28,400	2,211,916	776,795	270,166	25,650	127,050	90,147
1998	3,459,413	2,660,824	38,181	2,699,005	308,010	-26,951	2,364,044	818,014	277,355	26,958	128,325	93,857
1999	3,661,684	2,896,256	24,210	2,920,466	331,844	-35,371	2,553,251	813,894	294,539	28,082	130,392	95,422
2000	4,010,902	3,211,957	43,068	3,255,025	361,484	-51,433	2,842,108	844,284	324,510	30,346	132,173	97,843
2001	4,170,948	3,365,797	46,197	3,411,994	376,231	-98,373	2,937,390	880,378	353,180	30,985	134,610	101,247
2002	4,322,127	3,539,296	34,653	3,573,949	391,969	-136,506	3,045,474	884,871	391,782	31,767	136,056	103,312
2003	4,460,504	3,705,472	36,487	3,741,959	412,437	-167,464	3,162,058	908,005	390,441	32,355	137,863	105,124
2004	4,728,915	3,904,340	91,080	3,995,420	431,399	-214,201	3,349,820	965,309	413,786	33,742	140,149	107,198
2005	4,847,760	4,060,509	66,314	4,126,823	449,002	-251,294	3,426,527	969,306	451,927	34,224	141,650	109,141
2006	5,187,884	4,280,188	71,060	4,351,248	473,726	-284,265	3,593,257	1,096,975	497,652	36,103	143,698	111,735
2007	5,554,102	4,558,002	81,684	4,639,686	508,235	-321,850	3,809,601	1,193,185	551,316	38,008	146,129	114,834
2008	5,976,376	4,792,987	95,498	4,888,485	538,470	-321,712	4,028,303	1,288,242	659,831	40,164	148,799	116,134
2009	5,994,973	4,886,350	60,456	4,946,806	545,031	-360,362	4,041,413	1,265,809	687,751	39,556	151,556	116,039
2010	6,160,414	5,038,431	64,427	5,102,858	561,724	-386,549	4,154,585	1,256,901	748,928	40,256	153,030	115,902
2011	6,736,023	5,205,136	168,758	5,373,894	520,749	-336,911	4,516,234	1,440,707	779,082	43,196	155,941	118,992
2012	7,088,285	5,486,503	154,627	5,641,130	542,736	-347,126	4,751,268	1,546,456	790,561	44,560	159,074	121,266
2013	7,373,782	5,807,668	227,988	6,035,656	636,164	-416,335	4,983,157	1,569,963	820,662	45,463	162,193	123,969
2014	7,803,163	6,130,355	194,740	6,325,095	659,713	-390,566	5,274,816	1,657,318	871,029	47,327	164,876	124,898
2015	8,015,827	6,336,776	127,082	6,463,858	678,967	-436,672	5,348,219	1,729,132	938,476	47,934	167,226	126,643
2016	8,287,696	6,553,944	85,838	6,639,782	706,291	-463,014	5,470,477	1,837,452	979,767	48,967	169,251	129,620
2017	8,755,191	6,800,624	143,194	6,943,818	738,145	-483,835	5,721,838	2,028,457	1,004,896	50,943	171,862	130,919
2018	9,302,699	7,057,474	159,379	7,216,853	760,951	-340,228	6,115,674	2,085,968	1,101,057	53,772	173,002	131,050
2019	9,532,258	7,284,585	108,904	7,393,489	786,658	-434,995	6,171,836	2,167,774	1,192,648	54,659	174,394	130,703
2020	9,958,928	7,348,079	64,642	7,412,721	821,527	-438,060	6,153,134	2,205,030	1,600,764	56,720	175,582	126,164
2021	11,050,033	7,795,890	211,115	8,007,005	855,003	-398,995	6,753,007	2,545,261	1,751,765	62,250	177,510	127,926
2022	11,526,759	8,255,969	272,954	8,528,923	918,101	-270,648	7,340,174	2,645,150	1,541,435	64,399	178,991	132,366

Personal Income and Employment by Area: Ithaca, NY

(Thousands of dollars, except as noted.)

Year	Personal income, total	Derivation of personal income: Earnings by place of work: Nonfarm	Farm	Total	Less: Contributions for government social insurance	Plus: Adjustment for residence	Equals: Net earnings by place of residence	Plus: Dividends, interest, and rent	Plus: Personal current transfer receipts	Per capita personal income (dollars)	Population (persons)	Total employment
1970	271,269	236,134	4,196	240,330	16,309	-20,643	203,378	45,649	22,242	3,523	77,008	31,858
1971	294,050	251,453	4,118	255,571	17,878	-20,846	216,847	49,515	27,688	3,805	77,277	32,074
1972	322,700	277,365	4,935	282,300	20,756	-23,888	237,656	54,134	30,910	4,029	80,102	33,322
1973	362,411	313,742	9,405	323,147	27,404	-28,274	267,469	60,705	34,237	4,349	83,324	35,318
1974	403,237	352,450	6,680	359,130	32,015	-33,404	293,711	68,707	40,819	4,712	85,580	37,573
1975	431,758	362,864	7,334	370,198	33,070	-34,553	302,575	74,270	54,913	5,052	85,471	36,913
1976	455,987	383,542	7,249	390,791	35,377	-35,343	320,071	78,517	57,399	5,298	86,067	37,712
1977	473,732	390,126	6,288	396,414	36,238	-34,468	325,708	86,784	61,240	5,490	86,287	38,255
1978	518,008	433,202	7,527	440,729	42,019	-38,273	360,437	92,078	65,493	5,992	86,457	39,942
1979	567,270	475,124	9,980	485,104	47,948	-43,727	393,429	102,566	71,275	6,508	87,161	41,218
1980	652,424	540,195	8,416	548,611	54,902	-51,772	441,937	126,677	83,810	7,471	87,331	41,835
1981	753,270	616,279	9,996	626,275	66,918	-57,250	502,107	156,280	94,883	8,545	88,150	43,881
1982	839,507	695,191	9,818	705,009	73,620	-66,837	564,552	170,670	104,285	9,490	88,458	45,648
1983	950,262	795,641	8,255	803,896	83,920	-78,166	641,810	194,353	114,099	10,698	88,828	48,064
1984	1,060,974	900,504	10,705	911,209	95,917	-86,543	728,749	212,396	119,829	11,910	89,080	50,756
1985	1,136,144	973,550	13,415	986,965	105,424	-96,482	785,059	223,793	127,292	12,653	89,791	52,407
1986	1,216,237	1,048,076	12,947	1,061,023	115,514	-102,515	842,994	239,723	133,520	13,561	89,687	54,502
1987	1,290,536	1,136,011	10,312	1,146,323	123,762	-111,024	911,537	243,096	135,903	14,297	90,264	55,893
1988	1,388,076	1,226,604	11,747	1,238,351	138,425	-121,893	978,033	265,491	144,552	15,106	91,888	58,258
1989	1,554,875	1,346,359	15,043	1,361,402	150,636	-133,080	1,077,686	322,227	154,962	16,672	93,262	60,237
1990	1,618,654	1,395,401	16,417	1,411,818	149,888	-141,085	1,120,845	328,954	168,855	17,176	94,241	60,340
1991	1,664,339	1,435,577	16,652	1,452,229	158,268	-150,020	1,143,941	332,649	187,749	17,467	95,283	60,526
1992	1,743,729	1,488,179	25,689	1,513,868	160,008	-156,245	1,197,615	335,107	211,007	18,224	95,685	59,647
1993	1,774,559	1,502,659	33,802	1,536,461	162,169	-164,510	1,209,782	345,430	219,347	18,462	96,122	59,660
1994	1,843,346	1,586,272	24,187	1,610,459	175,117	-181,222	1,254,120	361,913	227,313	19,120	96,409	60,253
1995	1,926,468	1,635,949	23,837	1,659,786	181,551	-193,555	1,284,680	391,968	249,820	19,887	96,870	60,082
1996	1,951,199	1,634,953	25,893	1,660,846	181,412	-196,039	1,283,395	411,489	256,315	20,262	96,298	58,651
1997	2,028,086	1,737,912	10,029	1,747,941	192,824	-215,993	1,339,124	428,086	260,876	21,078	96,216	58,558
1998	2,116,024	1,797,884	13,350	1,811,234	200,197	-235,942	1,375,095	464,212	276,717	22,034	96,036	57,896
1999	2,253,174	1,984,828	13,566	1,998,394	216,490	-275,376	1,506,528	461,328	285,318	23,311	96,656	61,479
2000	2,373,780	2,077,015	17,245	2,094,260	226,797	-290,858	1,576,605	497,618	299,557	24,571	96,608	62,504
2001	2,498,834	2,203,643	18,594	2,222,237	244,051	-304,997	1,673,189	499,580	326,065	25,640	97,458	64,225
2002	2,564,264	2,331,083	10,079	2,341,162	261,941	-332,416	1,746,805	462,507	354,952	26,105	98,227	64,594
2003	2,692,021	2,481,333	12,503	2,493,836	282,086	-364,126	1,847,624	475,956	368,441	27,179	99,049	66,031
2004	2,844,040	2,604,485	16,096	2,620,581	292,064	-373,990	1,954,527	497,627	391,886	28,574	99,531	67,459
2005	2,851,530	2,643,450	14,527	2,657,977	300,873	-389,071	1,968,033	476,905	406,592	28,678	99,433	68,246
2006	2,997,684	2,776,634	10,279	2,786,913	316,326	-407,074	2,063,513	504,872	429,299	30,082	99,651	68,278
2007	3,170,768	2,889,239	18,706	2,907,945	324,970	-413,158	2,169,817	548,091	452,860	31,736	99,910	69,486
2008	3,428,662	3,057,852	20,050	3,077,902	350,987	-434,784	2,292,131	626,347	510,184	34,156	100,383	70,254
2009	3,477,801	3,131,489	10,729	3,142,218	354,955	-466,533	2,320,730	596,917	560,154	34,265	101,497	68,617
2010	3,554,343	3,196,952	18,477	3,215,429	355,807	-476,621	2,383,001	566,865	604,477	34,897	101,851	67,608
2011	3,733,496	3,267,904	22,896	3,290,800	327,490	-489,293	2,474,017	645,455	614,024	36,459	102,402	67,422
2012	3,880,411	3,432,473	20,940	3,453,413	339,375	-531,117	2,582,921	696,515	600,975	37,390	103,783	68,184
2013	3,874,439	3,475,674	26,137	3,501,811	386,409	-524,258	2,591,144	669,218	614,077	36,865	105,099	68,888
2014	3,968,579	3,500,237	28,550	3,528,787	396,082	-528,886	2,603,819	732,616	632,144	37,653	105,398	67,814
2015	4,174,692	3,657,710	14,701	3,672,411	418,298	-532,257	2,721,856	783,753	669,083	39,575	105,487	69,690
2016	4,154,775	3,713,001	13,181	3,726,182	423,215	-605,477	2,697,490	779,809	677,476	39,278	105,780	69,916
2017	4,400,962	3,843,325	18,527	3,861,852	438,291	-602,458	2,821,103	849,471	730,388	41,557	105,903	69,894
2018	4,520,920	3,991,266	11,990	4,003,256	457,563	-622,796	2,922,897	866,510	731,513	42,655	105,989	70,090
2019	4,733,413	3,991,651	22,231	4,013,882	455,224	-587,562	2,971,096	968,792	793,525	44,651	106,008	68,204
2020	5,036,291	3,989,412	19,195	4,008,607	459,115	-596,823	2,952,669	959,287	1,124,335	50,472	99,784	64,959
2021	5,358,130	4,258,019	21,388	4,279,407	490,547	-623,389	3,165,471	1,018,367	1,174,292	50,527	106,044	65,432
2022	5,361,286	4,495,872	30,840	4,526,712	530,715	-654,562	3,341,435	1,049,733	970,118	51,169	104,777	67,347

Personal Income and Employment by Area: Jackson, MI

(Thousands of dollars, except as noted.)

Year	Personal income, total	Derivation of personal income: Earnings by place of work: Nonfarm	Farm	Total	Less: Contributions for government social insurance	Plus: Adjustment for residence	Equals: Net earnings by place of residence	Plus: Dividends, interest, and rent	Plus: Personal current transfer receipts	Per capita personal income (dollars)	Population (persons)	Total employment
1970	584,669	480,910	6,320	487,230	34,559	7,225	459,896	74,513	50,260	4,082	143,227	58,293
1971	610,313	488,957	5,032	493,989	36,270	12,886	470,605	78,483	61,225	4,250	143,589	56,632
1972	686,460	560,197	6,598	566,795	44,160	15,317	537,952	84,046	64,462	4,755	144,372	59,352
1973	772,999	634,747	9,711	644,458	58,182	20,765	607,041	93,496	72,462	5,313	145,481	62,549
1974	828,625	672,318	3,531	675,849	63,956	21,257	633,150	106,901	88,574	5,641	146,903	62,188
1975	907,391	703,745	8,532	712,277	65,210	22,433	669,500	119,346	118,545	6,135	147,902	60,080
1976	981,361	750,851	6,588	757,439	70,800	38,279	724,918	127,665	128,778	6,609	148,498	60,290
1977	1,091,243	841,405	6,622	848,027	79,826	51,413	819,614	142,471	129,158	7,260	150,313	62,569
1978	1,229,816	962,270	4,487	966,757	93,660	64,487	937,584	155,861	136,371	8,117	151,502	65,436
1979	1,347,998	1,042,928	3,241	1,046,169	105,633	77,711	1,018,247	174,010	155,741	8,881	151,789	65,967
1980	1,436,670	1,058,381	1,934	1,060,315	105,607	81,281	1,035,989	206,421	194,260	9,480	151,554	62,760
1981	1,549,003	1,119,591	5,662	1,125,253	120,698	80,832	1,085,387	246,502	217,114	10,227	151,459	62,048
1982	1,589,230	1,099,663	3,562	1,103,225	120,194	76,595	1,059,626	281,822	247,782	10,581	150,195	58,972
1983	1,651,167	1,119,695	-6,602	1,113,093	123,429	85,070	1,074,734	310,897	265,536	11,162	147,930	57,854
1984	1,762,412	1,182,823	5,205	1,188,028	135,043	99,092	1,152,077	345,592	264,743	12,123	145,374	58,403
1985	1,842,477	1,223,763	7,805	1,231,568	142,157	113,853	1,203,264	363,339	275,874	12,742	144,602	59,140
1986	1,943,042	1,296,592	5,415	1,302,007	150,672	113,037	1,264,372	384,822	293,848	13,368	145,355	60,642
1987	2,080,256	1,437,206	11,410	1,448,616	164,651	102,930	1,386,895	389,512	303,849	14,079	147,758	62,691
1988	2,194,452	1,513,779	7,773	1,521,552	180,075	116,534	1,458,011	414,923	321,518	14,792	148,357	63,018
1989	2,377,853	1,625,741	15,571	1,641,312	191,220	112,710	1,562,802	469,523	345,528	15,978	148,816	65,309
1990	2,456,212	1,686,143	9,843	1,695,986	200,410	113,644	1,609,220	472,621	374,371	16,361	150,128	65,679
1991	2,509,884	1,699,562	5,075	1,704,637	204,988	118,715	1,618,364	470,925	420,595	16,617	151,039	64,640
1992	2,650,654	1,795,129	4,868	1,799,997	214,691	136,774	1,722,080	477,733	450,841	17,500	151,465	65,537
1993	2,798,677	1,895,789	2,106	1,897,895	228,257	142,608	1,812,246	503,265	483,166	18,359	152,445	66,378
1994	2,972,928	2,019,463	1,032	2,020,495	248,591	161,288	1,933,192	553,729	486,007	19,522	152,288	68,008
1995	3,150,741	2,136,255	1,839	2,138,094	264,250	166,847	2,040,691	601,940	508,110	20,551	153,313	70,813
1996	3,289,972	2,231,711	1,558	2,233,269	269,764	181,293	2,144,798	616,227	528,947	21,323	154,289	72,489
1997	3,443,264	2,330,312	471	2,330,783	282,425	205,748	2,254,106	632,600	556,558	22;167	155,331	73,186
1998	3,583,896	2,424,176	1,044	2,425,220	290,915	238,333	2,372,638	651,030	560,228	22,975	155,991	72,741
1999	3,823,314	2,643,432	4,576	2,648,008	314,985	260,178	2,593,201	624,520	605,593	24,339	157,085	75,602
2000	4,032,390	2,765,447	4,304	2,769,751	326,581	289,834	2,733,004	675,098	624,288	25,412	158,679	77,800
2001	4,117,114	2,793,374	880	2,794,254	320,100	282,016	2,756,170	664,009	696,935	25,769	159,772	76,959
2002	4,155,644	2,820,464	136	2,820,600	324,059	295,251	2,791,792	636,599	727,253	25,829	160,893	76,541
2003	4,228,029	2,816,335	-1,025	2,815,310	322,126	309,595	2,802,779	657,741	767,509	26,080	162,119	75,906
2004	4,364,645	2,988,303	7,247	2,995,550	342,489	288,971	2,942,032	630,755	791,858	26,919	162,140	77,087
2005	4,464,005	3,062,104	5,796	3,067,900	358,529	277,323	2,986,694	635,159	842,152	27,379	163,047	77,182
2006	4,559,146	3,088,973	8,168	3,097,141	366,052	272,220	3,003,309	648,782	907,055	27,904	163,387	75,803
2007	4,672,231	3,103,090	7,334	3,110,424	371,740	264,832	3,003,516	678,674	990,041	28,609	163,316	75,170
2008	4,850,812	3,112,498	-768	3,111,730	376,488	241,647	2,976,889	756,127	1,117,796	30,162	160,825	74,167
2009	4,727,437	2,936,960	1,440	2,938,400	358,365	186,183	2,766,218	712,217	1,249,002	29,525	160,114	70,412
2010	4,880,972	3,050,669	12,935	3,063,604	363,421	160,555	2,860,738	683,032	1,337,202	30,470	160,191	69,183
2011	5,050,301	3,167,446	25,804	3,193,250	343,973	126,342	2,975,619	739,914	1,334,768	31,550	160,072	72,194
2012	5,169,973	3,297,404	4,676	3,302,080	357,067	95,852	3,040,865	787,690	1,341,418	32,167	160,722	72,244
2013	5,222,513	3,448,498	12,919	3,461,417	421,137	27,859	3,068,139	783,098	1,371,276	32,492	160,733	73,835
2014	5,402,747	3,513,344	-5,283	3,508,061	428,731	44,874	3,124,204	849,464	1,429,079	33,589	160,850	74,187
2015	5,643,023	3,637,887	-5,452	3,632,435	440,797	54,806	3,246,444	898,352	1,498,227	35,041	161,039	74,817
2016	5,852,971	3,796,187	-3,814	3,792,373	458,313	46,595	3,380,655	930,762	1,541,554	36,495	160,376	75,581
2017	5,975,328	3,903,832	-889	3,902,943	471,222	52,379	3,484,100	955,622	1,535,606	37,110	161,016	75,242
2018	6,215,612	4,051,561	-867	4,050,694	496,279	57,707	3,612,122	1,005,605	1,597,885	38,538	161,284	76,067
2019	6,359,277	4,143,921	-2,121	4,141,800	505,512	58,072	3,694,360	965,345	1,699,572	39,408	161,372	74,760
2020	6,957,521	4,155,384	7,626	4,163,010	502,545	42,274	3,702,739	962,685	2,292,097	43,423	160,225	70,810
2021	7,514,270	4,512,766	13,506	4,526,272	542,634	35,378	4,019,016	1,078,275	2,416,979	46,886	160,266	74,248
2022	7,428,423	4,781,282	6,141	4,787,423	596,615	40,565	4,231,373	1,159,109	2,037,941	46,409	160,066	77,241

Personal Income and Employment by Area: Jackson, MS

(Thousands of dollars, except as noted.)

Year	Personal income, total	Derivation of personal income: Earnings by place of work: Nonfarm	Farm	Total	Less: Contributions for government social insurance	Plus: Adjustment for residence	Equals: Net earnings by place of residence	Plus: Dividends, interest, and rent	Plus: Personal current transfer receipts	Per capita personal income (dollars)	Population (persons)	Total employment
1970	1,212,074	961,865	57,415	1,019,280	65,640	-12,048	941,592	155,320	115,162	3,151	384,724	177,513
1971	1,350,740	1,063,222	66,093	1,129,315	75,002	-13,256	1,041,057	173,065	136,618	3,430	393,789	182,920
1972	1,518,480	1,204,235	71,824	1,276,059	88,932	-15,513	1,171,614	191,217	155,649	3,784	401,287	190,068
1973	1,747,650	1,378,772	102,798	1,481,570	117,257	-19,749	1,344,564	221,478	181,608	4,280	408,337	202,175
1974	1,980,302	1,557,768	88,680	1,646,448	136,941	-15,863	1,493,644	262,645	224,013	4,713	420,198	208,233
1975	2,123,601	1,643,700	51,107	1,694,807	142,399	-4,099	1,548,309	294,870	280,422	4,961	428,072	200,935
1976	2,396,019	1,838,972	82,468	1,921,440	162,594	3,292	1,762,138	319,091	314,790	5,514	434,534	205,578
1977	2,690,131	2,101,928	71,620	2,173,548	184,780	6,919	1,995,687	356,210	338,234	6,102	440,858	214,237
1978	3,081,061	2,425,321	72,361	2,497,682	219,380	17,939	2,296,241	412,266	372,554	6,842	450,296	226,940
1979	3,531,645	2,746,162	106,306	2,852,468	258,696	39,363	2,633,135	478,931	419,579	7,721	457,391	234,028
1980	3,843,590	2,984,586	26,410	3,010,996	280,272	16,100	2,746,824	596,311	500,455	8,291	463,566	232,944
1981	4,278,615	3,216,145	41,122	3,257,267	325,102	29,840	2,962,005	742,809	573,801	9,150	467,583	231,320
1982	4,508,766	3,312,356	71,037	3,383,393	341,926	21,559	3,063,026	826,552	619,188	9,571	471,062	225,940
1983	4,779,953	3,554,119	16,065	3,570,184	369,824	28,450	3,228,810	870,290	680,853	10,056	475,352	229,233
1984	5,250,843	3,900,117	98,268	3,998,385	416,935	13,145	3,594,595	954,330	701,918	10,938	480,048	237,038
1985	5,526,137	4,161,650	49,026	4,210,676	455,485	-939	3,754,252	1,032,608	739,277	11,330	487,729	241,634
1986	5,784,674	4,387,152	39,686	4,426,838	485,117	-14,752	3,926,969	1,069,657	788,048	11,804	490,055	244,657
1987	6,138,065	4,645,489	90,487	4,735,976	510,084	-21,039	4,204,853	1,098,528	834,684	12,489	491,476	247,923
1988	6,587,867	4,975,742	103,082	5,078,824	567,412	-19,149	4,492,263	1,201,296	894,308	13,428	490,609	254,403
1989	7,218,169	5,343,970	92,223	5,436,193	605,803	-24,460	4,805,930	1,438,507	973,732	14,680	491,697	259,523
1990	7,591,333	5,678,808	82,125	5,760,933	668,476	-24,552	5,067,905	1,458,182	1,065,246	15,330	495,183	261,550
1991	8,005,649	5,964,035	94,037	6,058,072	716,976	-31,184	5,309,912	1,498,962	1,196,775	16,047	498,888	264,256
1992	8,571,236	6,415,227	79,670	6,494,897	761,973	-33,096	5,699,828	1,530,042	1,341,366	17,015	503,746	269,229
1993	9,106,932	6,839,649	81,902	6,921,551	811,388	-40,273	6,069,890	1,593,559	1,443,483	17,928	507,981	279,205
1994	9,851,933	7,377,457	119,580	7,497,037	881,347	-48,131	6,567,559	1,731,635	1,552,739	19,169	513,948	288,125
1995	10,564,385	7,915,982	82,751	7,998,733	939,380	-58,309	7,001,044	1,876,242	1,687,099	20,335	519,525	296,821
1996	11,188,951	8,300,410	136,163	8,436,573	972,144	-67,808	7,396,621	1,999,056	1,793,274	21,242	526,742	303,153
1997	11,935,154	8,827,257	114,879	8,942,136	1,028,503	-83,217	7,830,416	2,247,231	1,857,507	22,410	532,588	309,800
1998	12,680,136	9,491,240	125,251	9,616,491	1,096,164	-91,682	8,428,645	2,392,599	1,858,892	23,510	539,345	316,636
1999	13,063,588	9,914,428	118,142	10,032,570	1,147,161	-101,359	8,784,050	2,370,412	1,909,126	24,051	543,159	319,753
2000	13,832,436	10,434,923	86,941	10,521,864	1,192,489	-115,367	9,214,008	2,561,706	2,056,722	25,246	547,903	322,368
2001	14,609,230	10,882,728	151,534	11,034,262	1,232,812	-119,336	9,682,114	2,606,089	2,321,027	26,592	549,383	324,028
2002	14,951,537	11,219,832	43,004	11,262,836	1,281,539	-108,226	9,873,071	2,573,868	2,504,598	27,098	551,767	324,336
2003	15,634,271	11,759,857	128,416	11,888,273	1,336,741	-128,815	10,422,717	2,595,560	2,615,994	28,119	555,999	329,235
2004	16,620,862	12,502,023	214,015	12,716,038	1,430,241	-165,199	11,120,598	2,701,123	2,799,141	29,553	562,401	334,956
2005	17,735,033	13,131,137	212,159	13,343,296	1,475,054	-176,136	11,692,106	3,061,151	2,981,776	31,251	567,496	340,105
2006	19,058,862	13,988,489	96,970	14,085,459	1,602,960	-204,748	12,277,751	3,614,206	3,166,905	33,042	576,809	350,996
2007	19,683,750	14,276,233	129,754	14,405,987	1,655,691	-217,692	12,532,604	3,794,953	3,356,193	34,004	578,863	357,685
2008	21,238,212	15,287,885	78,433	15,366,318	1,743,770	-192,514	13,430,034	3,972,089	3,836,089	36,519	581,567	359,785
2009	20,455,768	14,497,633	102,306	14,599,939	1,706,738	-219,882	12,673,319	3,655,906	4,126,543	35,037	583,837	354,343
2010	21,325,727	15,010,901	110,950	15,121,851	1,726,236	-225,749	13,169,866	3,662,322	4,493,539	36,249	588,315	353,874
2011	22,682,107	15,692,699	72,567	15,765,266	1,603,223	-278,895	13,883,148	4,131,870	4,667,089	38,211	593,598	359,846
2012	23,370,767	16,210,937	68,140	16,279,077	1,651,324	-282,686	14,345,067	4,374,558	4,651,142	39,216	595,954	361,099
2013	23,724,100	16,857,970	237,232	17,095,202	1,917,430	-394,039	14,783,733	4,178,335	4,762,032	39,748	596,870	366,131
2014	24,513,914	17,442,104	157,200	17,599,304	1,995,335	-402,851	15,201,118	4,387,759	4,925,037	40,989	598,060	373,058
2015	24,803,859	17,406,370	82,984	17,489,354	2,050,494	-420,591	15,018,269	4,642,703	5,142,887	41,421	598,827	378,482
2016	24,924,387	17,449,489	62,474	17,511,963	2,078,623	-407,086	15,026,254	4,591,102	5,307,031	41,489	600,752	381,114
2017	25,197,057	17,538,057	122,437	17,660,494	2,122,210	-385,682	15,152,602	4,715,255	5,329,200	41,960	600,507	382,227
2018	25,724,952	17,901,561	85,539	17,987,100	2,154,802	-375,111	15,457,187	4,758,760	5,509,005	42,966	598,726	383,061
2019	26,625,206	18,359,520	97,254	18,456,774	2,233,675	-377,931	15,845,168	4,986,350	5,793,688	44,635	596,513	383,741
2020	28,752,144	18,815,738	26,357	18,842,095	2,294,097	-306,119	16,241,879	5,103,024	7,407,241	48,660	590,873	371,264
2021	31,118,382	20,110,251	130,937	20,241,188	2,405,642	-311,537	17,524,009	5,550,473	8,043,900	53,001	587,131	379,223
2022	31,263,100	21,214,171	62,189	21,276,360	2,630,126	-290,164	18,356,070	5,998,833	6,908,197	53,606	583,197	393,160

Personal Income and Employment by Area: Jackson, TN

(Thousands of dollars, except as noted.)

Year	Personal income, total	Derivation of personal income: Earnings by place of work			Less: Contributions for government social insurance	Plus: Adjustment for residence	Equals: Net earnings by place of residence	Plus: Dividends, interest, and rent	Plus: Personal current transfer receipts	Per capita personal income (dollars)	Population (persons)	Total employment
		Nonfarm	Farm	Total								
1970	417,041	339,912	24,385	364,297	23,524	-15,049	325,724	45,655	45,662	3,016	138,282	68,717
1971	460,982	367,866	31,191	399,057	26,044	-15,677	357,336	51,552	52,094	3,282	140,474	68,920
1972	509,917	417,327	26,046	443,373	30,857	-17,821	394,695	57,781	57,441	3,544	143,877	73,324
1973	578,841	459,588	41,257	500,845	38,470	-17,647	444,728	66,264	67,849	3,998	144,788	75,102
1974	621,956	510,949	15,269	526,218	44,713	-20,231	461,274	76,869	83,813	4,271	145,635	75,640
1975	689,053	545,453	16,552	562,005	46,791	-22,873	492,341	87,837	108,875	4,718	146,061	72,402
1976	758,706	602,331	18,167	620,498	52,551	-24,014	543,933	94,966	119,807	5,141	147,576	71,778
1977	833,153	672,506	14,942	687,448	59,026	-27,499	600,923	106,883	125,347	5,605	148,649	72,763
1978	922,096	742,622	17,708	760,330	66,297	-29,414	664,619	121,337	136,140	6,193	148,899	73,065
1979	1,010,167	806,634	17,554	824,188	74,692	-34,052	715,444	137,600	157,123	6,728	150,149	73,297
1980	1,081,252	839,303	-5,908	833,395	77,879	-36,001	719,515	172,426	189,311	7,123	151,801	71,388
1981	1,193,708	887,917	7,902	895,819	87,912	-36,731	771,176	211,410	211,122	7,854	151,980	69,450
1982	1,260,640	905,086	2,448	907,534	90,743	-38,931	777,860	250,865	231,915	8,319	151,536	67,349
1983	1,359,634	1,009,532	-17,184	992,348	102,114	-42,093	848,141	264,769	246,724	9,037	150,448	69,373
1984	1,552,186	1,143,829	24,484	1,168,313	120,449	-48,343	999,521	298,755	253,910	10,271	151,124	74,151
1985	1,621,485	1,195,666	12,787	1,208,453	127,339	-47,309	1,033,805	316,198	271,482	10,672	151,937	72,807
1986	1,715,229	1,276,984	11,472	1,288,456	138,552	-49,399	1,100,505	322,974	291,750	11,328	151,419	73,798
1987	1,852,635	1,379,239	44,832	1,424,071	148,330	-53,498	1,222,243	323,179	307,213	12,283	150,834	75,907
1988	2,003,302	1,513,818	41,226	1,555,044	168,038	-56,120	1,330,886	344,565	327,851	13,310	150,511	79,463
1989	2,135,069	1,622,950	32,490	1,655,440	182,833	-62,919	1,409,688	368,509	356,872	14,190	150,460	82,337
1990	2,277,149	1,718,795	30,342	1,749,137	193,975	-67,752	1,487,410	400,283	389,456	15,082	150,984	83,215
1991	2,391,146	1,793,480	46,106	1,839,586	206,068	-74,878	1,558,640	394,904	437,602	15,672	152,576	83,604
1992	2,652,742	2,009,998	74,200	2,084,198	227,116	-88,816	1,768,266	394,617	489,859	17,170	154,503	87,107
1993	2,772,038	2,144,941	42,076	2,187,017	243,749	-99,305	1,843,963	402,309	525,766	17,690	156,701	89,911
1994	3,016,072	2,344,402	80,901	2,425,303	269,753	-116,520	2,039,030	424,921	552,121	19,010	158,657	94,970
1995	3,183,991	2,482,916	53,679	2,536,595	285,635	-128,236	2,122,724	454,747	606,520	19,744	161,265	96,749
1996	3,342,596	2,585,000	70,157	2,655,157	291,859	-136,921	2,226,377	486,257	629,962	20,475	163,253	96,688
1997	3,554,902	2,816,642	47,739	2,864,381	315,295	-160,389	2,388,697	513,933	652,272	21,521	165,185	100,971
1998	3,810,650	3,073,768	19,498	3,093,266	331,532	-171,798	2,589,936	544,344	676,370	22,791	167,199	102,040
1999	3,937,364	3,222,909	1,492	3,224,401	348,793	-187,182	2,688,426	548,857	700,081	23,295	169,023	103,784
2000	4,177,095	3,373,283	33,123	3,406,406	361,878	-200,785	2,843,743	575,422	757,930	24,533	170,267	105,147
2001	4,038,994	3,139,400	35,344	3,174,744	354,886	-191,515	2,628,343	588,405	822,246	23,570	171,360	101,082
2002	4,135,223	3,214,416	10,792	3,225,208	365,656	-178,369	2,681,183	567,947	886,093	24,072	171,787	99,419
2003	4,402,584	3,345,940	46,997	3,392,937	376,271	-175,198	2,841,468	587,983	973,133	25,655	171,605	99,409
2004	4,651,475	3,593,467	52,261	3,645,728	397,687	-192,379	3,055,662	565,128	1,030,685	26,858	173,185	100,997
2005	4,812,301	3,677,186	74,083	3,751,269	410,445	-192,866	3,147,958	566,070	1,098,273	27,638	174,116	100,991
2006	4,969,211	3,795,689	73,294	3,868,983	426,247	-199,594	3,243,142	577,867	1,148,202	28,282	175,703	102,285
2007	5,235,237	3,955,104	28,417	3,983,521	444,700	-213,545	3,325,276	642,531	1,267,430	29,643	176,608	103,600
2008	5,453,979	3,955,677	61,517	4,017,194	454,760	-218,199	3,344,235	716,347	1,393,397	30,700	177,654	103,303
2009	5,549,109	3,862,076	70,490	3,932,566	448,158	-162,541	3,321,867	730,204	1,497,038	31,046	178,739	98,680
2010	5,769,308	4,048,763	24,353	4,073,116	457,760	-174,579	3,440,777	692,780	1,635,751	32,087	179,801	98,885
2011	6,234,729	4,321,206	112,709	4,433,915	424,507	-203,136	3,806,272	765,524	1,662,933	34,661	179,878	101,124
2012	6,275,007	4,477,736	-3,749	4,473,987	432,716	-223,295	3,817,976	790,554	1,666,477	34,823	180,198	102,028
2013	6,335,019	4,487,505	127,666	4,615,171	489,390	-250,020	3,875,761	758,708	1,700,550	35,134	180,310	102,133
2014	6,318,423	4,559,172	20,096	4,579,268	497,544	-266,393	3,815,331	804,132	1,698,960	35,109	179,967	103,056
2015	6,489,789	4,689,909	-11,380	4,678,529	512,423	-263,272	3,902,834	816,466	1,770,489	36,186	179,345	103,834
2016	6,582,629	4,817,746	-12,486	4,805,260	532,150	-285,016	3,988,094	825,840	1,768,695	36,734	179,197	105,757
2017	6,820,120	4,992,455	-17,398	4,975,057	557,787	-307,817	4,109,453	875,616	1,835,051	38,030	179,335	106,339
2018	7,033,590	5,178,677	-48,158	5,130,519	577,258	-322,291	4,230,970	883,903	1,918,717	39,183	179,507	107,662
2019	7,484,866	5,401,320	16,171	5,417,491	599,916	-336,129	4,481,446	959,114	2,044,306	41,618	179,846	108,422
2020	8,048,629	5,657,140	-3,990	5,653,150	639,098	-364,505	4,649,547	958,218	2,440,864	44,579	180,549	106,931
2021	8,868,284	6,086,061	81,130	6,167,191	676,281	-404,099	5,086,811	1,060,388	2,721,085	49,106	180,594	110,745
2022	8,902,447	6,527,185	-21,130	6,506,055	751,359	-422,585	5,332,111	1,131,018	2,439,318	49,028	181,579	114,664

Personal Income and Employment by Area: Jacksonville, FL

(Thousands of dollars, except as noted.)

Year	Personal income, total	Derivation of personal income: Earnings by place of work: Nonfarm	Farm	Total	Less: Contributions for government social insurance	Plus: Adjustment for residence	Equals: Net earnings by place of residence	Plus: Dividends, interest, and rent	Plus: Personal current transfer receipts	Per capita personal income (dollars)	Population (persons)	Total employment
1970	2,567,000	2,114,878	13,021	2,127,899	135,388	-12,090	1,980,421	409,149	177,430	4,118	623,388	295,684
1971	2,840,266	2,332,698	15,481	2,348,179	155,780	-13,747	2,178,652	452,843	208,771	4,475	634,713	301,891
1972	3,189,179	2,625,387	17,939	2,643,326	183,196	-15,387	2,444,743	498,579	245,857	4,935	646,275	313,941
1973	3,576,714	2,951,238	22,872	2,974,110	235,105	-17,600	2,721,405	560,453	294,856	5,421	659,829	332,075
1974	4,037,450	3,303,980	26,398	3,330,378	272,986	-20,804	3,036,588	657,261	343,601	5,871	687,746	345,616
1975	4,422,511	3,540,411	33,133	3,573,544	290,668	-22,670	3,260,206	721,995	440,310	6,403	690,714	341,634
1976	4,737,665	3,786,512	32,329	3,818,841	319,292	-25,046	3,474,503	767,905	495,257	6,782	698,553	340,298
1977	5,172,586	4,145,695	25,448	4,171,143	350,583	-29,579	3,790,981	846,601	535,004	7,338	704,888	349,448
1978	5,780,316	4,638,128	17,301	4,655,429	401,184	-31,398	4,222,847	972,313	585,156	8,076	715,770	368,161
1979	6,357,394	5,078,857	14,875	5,093,732	460,712	-32,343	4,600,677	1,089,232	667,485	8,808	721,782	371,167
1980	7,258,173	5,688,556	20,702	5,709,258	517,785	-33,196	5,158,277	1,315,063	784,833	9,790	741,394	381,950
1981	8,269,881	6,405,018	34,314	6,439,332	624,302	-36,377	5,778,653	1,585,941	905,287	10,947	755,420	390,199
1982	9,055,021	6,947,284	53,584	7,000,868	690,891	-24,581	6,285,396	1,757,462	1,012,163	11,784	768,427	397,586
1983	9,890,149	7,612,807	48,983	7,661,790	769,182	-31,186	6,861,422	1,922,033	1,106,694	12,625	783,354	411,897
1984	11,132,267	8,642,815	45,034	8,687,849	897,080	-35,688	7,755,081	2,208,103	1,169,083	13,843	804,178	442,276
1985	12,235,368	9,543,628	41,498	9,585,126	1,005,112	-37,216	8,542,798	2,443,355	1,249,215	14,782	827,746	470,849
1986	13,300,609	10,427,117	46,883	10,474,000	1,129,350	-32,231	9,312,419	2,661,326	1,326,864	15,589	853,211	493,439
1987	14,320,570	11,296,748	48,872	11,345,620	1,211,438	-10,755	10,123,427	2,802,837	1,394,306	16,371	874,757	503,658
1988	15,533,803	12,191,677	55,776	12,247,453	1,355,028	-4,925	10,887,500	3,118,627	1,527,676	17,329	896,417	519,933
1989	16,993,755	12,973,452	51,174	13,024,626	1,448,341	10,052	11,586,337	3,675,760	1,731,658	18,792	904,284	536,809
1990	18,328,960	13,916,376	59,205	13,975,581	1,553,282	32,226	12,454,525	3,972,943	1,901,492	19,663	932,169	555,661
1991	19,043,445	14,449,029	60,202	14,509,231	1,627,259	36,270	12,918,242	3,982,612	2,142,591	19,929	955,572	555,630
1992	20,149,070	15,363,270	56,741	15,420,011	1,733,723	44,234	13,730,522	3,954,023	2,464,525	20,609	977,699	555,070
1993	21,328,841	16,253,606	55,119	16,308,725	1,823,866	43,100	14,527,959	4,151,058	2,649,824	21,533	990,520	568,743
1994	22,501,212	17,124,875	51,594	17,176,469	1,928,864	41,921	15,289,526	4,436,053	2,775,633	22,401	1,004,478	582,196
1995	24,195,496	18,259,675	48,373	18,308,048	2,042,844	34,463	16,299,667	4,893,732	3,002,097	23,706	1,020,631	603,371
1996	25,982,099	19,617,974	54,202	19,672,176	2,176,148	20,583	17,516,611	5,291,513	3,173,975	24,689	1,052,363	630,841
1997	27,722,603	20,976,000	61,165	21,037,165	2,327,388	5,447	18,715,224	5,708,282	3,299,097	25,739	1,077,069	648,513
1998	30,116,109	22,790,872	69,420	22,860,292	2,491,426	-5,807	20,363,059	6,412,032	3,341,018	27,506	1,094,889	671,238
1999	31,344,909	23,841,114	71,207	23,912,321	2,602,713	-655	21,308,953	6,550,224	3,485,732	28,240	1,109,951	687,819
2000	34,180,490	26,097,668	71,479	26,169,147	2,809,077	-19,811	23,340,259	7,078,780	3,761,451	30,348	1,126,282	715,920
2001	35,387,722	26,796,632	85,413	26,882,045	2,938,300	-38,467	23,905,278	7,341,217	4,141,227	30,823	1,148,091	682,257
2002	36,759,658	28,008,651	72,630	28,081,281	3,074,909	-68,661	24,937,711	7,265,598	4,556,349	31,382	1,171,363	685,894
2003	39,132,886	30,020,444	62,836	30,083,280	3,280,724	-82,953	26,719,603	7,520,567	4,892,716	32,801	1,193,042	706,047
2004	41,943,940	31,999,755	71,382	32,071,137	3,507,331	-145,904	28,417,902	8,236,933	5,289,105	34,300	1,222,866	728,214
2005	45,301,497	34,253,734	71,668	34,325,402	3,762,319	-172,062	30,391,021	9,166,455	5,744,021	36,268	1,249,072	752,278
2006	49,299,759	36,797,124	61,328	36,858,452	4,130,488	-218,067	32,509,897	10,532,341	6,257,521	38,446	1,282,311	781,234
2007	51,618,451	37,934,050	63,886	37,997,936	4,268,241	-231,936	33,497,759	11,376,410	6,744,282	39,500	1,306,788	794,724
2008	52,497,210	37,075,735	52,186	37,127,921	4,251,891	-188,048	32,687,982	11,980,584	7,828,644	39,689	1,322,728	783,525
2009	49,952,660	35,158,514	43,097	35,201,611	4,105,067	-77,147	31,019,397	10,240,448	8,692,815	37,419	1,334,972	750,537
2010	52,611,117	36,482,103	48,657	36,530,760	4,197,794	7,176	32,340,142	10,554,993	9,715,982	38,986	1,349,493	746,887
2011	55,299,868	37,033,186	30,783	37,063,969	3,856,172	64,496	33,272,293	11,885,658	10,141,917	40,517	1,364,861	762,030
2012	57,401,409	38,634,689	32,677	38,667,366	4,062,915	72,310	34,676,761	12,677,007	10,047,641	41,509	1,382,855	771,158
2013	58,008,923	39,778,455	36,708	39,815,163	4,690,796	106,313	35,230,680	12,345,364	10,432,879	41,404	1,401,041	787,568
2014	60,784,355	41,785,118	34,861	41,819,979	4,920,248	53,077	36,952,808	12,769,300	11,062,247	42,610	1,426,514	810,710
2015	64,508,091	43,986,940	47,836	44,034,776	5,137,189	44,343	38,941,930	13,854,667	11,711,494	44,266	1,457,278	839,191
2016	67,391,488	46,322,466	32,976	46,355,442	5,378,294	32,435	41,009,583	14,269,811	12,112,094	45,174	1,491,834	869,038
2017	72,709,127	49,876,639	49,775	49,926,414	5,752,922	-11,020	44,162,472	15,738,295	12,808,360	47,725	1,523,486	913,156
2018	76,695,891	52,878,533	41,013	52,919,546	6,097,301	-101,192	46,721,053	16,524,739	13,450,099	49,361	1,553,781	941,970
2019	81,607,498	55,952,131	41,386	55,993,517	6,516,024	-161,609	49,315,884	17,836,707	14,454,907	51,537	1,583,466	960,363
2020	88,458,579	58,345,769	50,005	58,395,774	6,827,546	-154,241	51,413,987	18,367,770	18,676,822	54,849	1,612,764	965,537
2021	99,770,861	64,418,394	58,288	64,476,682	7,340,397	-181,191	56,955,094	21,251,595	21,564,172	60,798	1,641,026	1,013,493
2022	105,112,904	71,429,477	41,851	71,471,328	8,273,442	-301,540	62,896,346	23,053,924	19,162,634	62,729	1,675,668	1,066,580

Personal Income and Employment by Area: Jacksonville, NC

(Thousands of dollars, except as noted.)

Year	Personal income, total	Derivation of personal income								Per capita personal income (dollars)	Population (persons)	Total employment
		Earnings by place of work			Less: Contributions for government social insurance	Plus: Adjustment for residence	Equals: Net earnings by place of residence	Plus: Dividends, interest, and rent	Plus: Personal current transfer receipts			
		Nonfarm	Farm	Total								
1970	469,455	387,871	6,832	394,703	23,178	-10,622	360,903	96,734	11,818	4,576	102,582	63,781
1971	454,696	381,011	5,501	386,512	24,401	-11,196	350,915	89,706	14,075	4,509	100,831	56,615
1972	504,609	422,174	6,898	429,072	27,138	-11,986	389,948	98,491	16,170	5,330	94,669	55,778
1973	548,029	451,825	12,176	464,001	30,157	-12,840	421,004	108,671	18,354	5,881	93,193	55,913
1974	638,970	525,931	11,996	537,927	37,150	-14,725	486,052	130,787	22,131	6,631	96,362	59,332
1975	717,056	586,542	14,622	601,164	45,481	-15,531	540,152	146,977	29,927	6,361	112,734	62,166
1976	758,046	619,248	11,994	631,242	49,730	-15,706	565,806	157,783	34,457	6,576	115,272	62,032
1977	800,311	651,778	6,364	658,142	51,230	-16,926	589,986	173,609	36,716	6,877	116,382	62,822
1978	882,656	703,220	8,889	712,109	54,031	-18,155	639,923	203,192	39,541	7,451	118,455	63,952
1979	906,494	724,563	4,673	729,236	57,850	-18,387	652,999	207,460	46,035	8,011	113,156	61,681
1980	956,772	757,109	7,614	764,723	60,076	-18,985	685,662	214,765	56,345	8,429	113,515	60,235
1981	1,231,182	987,034	7,606	994,640	81,794	-17,691	895,155	270,491	65,536	10,604	116,100	62,778
1982	1,333,918	1,059,261	11,799	1,071,060	85,350	-16,697	969,013	290,445	74,460	11,221	118,881	62,899
1983	1,434,731	1,145,114	4,867	1,149,981	97,164	-17,228	1,035,589	317,450	81,692	11,550	124,216	66,943
1984	1,606,495	1,283,199	3,660	1,286,859	112,447	-16,632	1,157,780	359,342	89,373	12,522	128,297	69,653
1985	1,771,351	1,418,385	1,713	1,420,098	125,829	-17,746	1,276,523	397,582	97,246	13,294	133,240	72,992
1986	1,858,660	1,474,006	2,639	1,476,645	134,088	-15,520	1,327,037	426,270	105,353	13,455	138,143	73,307
1987	1,987,291	1,570,567	7,133	1,577,700	144,848	-15,119	1,417,733	459,342	110,216	14,078	141,166	77,154
1988	2,074,611	1,643,768	4,219	1,647,987	161,757	-12,476	1,473,754	478,880	121,977	14,539	142,695	77,449
1989	2,237,154	1,751,909	4,745	1,756,654	175,342	-11,933	1,569,379	529,293	138,482	14,997	149,174	80,413
1990	2,108,677	1,624,641	18,608	1,643,249	169,454	-16,633	1,457,162	498,404	153,111	14,049	150,098	73,735
1991	2,159,771	1,642,416	27,745	1,670,161	174,542	-11,292	1,484,327	499,672	175,772	14,271	151,342	71,053
1992	2,542,865	1,963,168	24,415	1,987,583	214,925	-21,223	1,751,435	597,000	194,430	17,373	146,370	78,921
1993	2,543,574	1,912,752	32,473	1,945,225	214,636	-15,069	1,715,520	610,865	217,189	17,211	147,789	79,122
1994	2,734,947	2,041,898	32,768	2,074,666	222,585	-14,988	1,837,093	665,087	232,767	18,636	146,760	80,724
1995	2,864,961	2,101,260	31,653	2,132,913	222,558	-11,550	1,898,805	699,460	266,696	19,455	147,258	83,029
1996	2,992,843	2,164,203	35,414	2,199,617	229,257	-5,315	1,965,045	731,813	295,985	20,132	148,658	84,330
1997	3,201,819	2,298,137	35,197	2,333,334	243,953	-4,131	2,085,250	804,244	312,325	21,640	147,955	86,093
1998	3,341,019	2,411,819	13,744	2,425,563	255,504	1,376	2,171,435	836,589	332,995	22,159	150,773	86,108
1999	3,508,762	2,527,615	16,338	2,543,953	268,261	4,483	2,280,175	869,648	358,939	23,450	149,628	87,777
2000	3,624,519	2,581,409	33,097	2,614,506	275,415	9,829	2,348,920	891,974	383,625	24,055	150,678	87,507
2001	3,762,739	2,736,528	35,247	2,771,775	291,416	2,089	2,482,448	850,794	429,497	24,908	151,068	88,590
2002	3,885,867	2,777,335	12,960	2,790,295	294,880	-3,074	2,492,341	925,815	467,711	25,332	153,397	90,614
2003	4,276,538	3,117,332	6,944	3,124,276	329,432	-25,192	2,769,652	1,005,359	501,527	28,419	150,481	92,409
2004	4,772,016	3,561,844	11,407	3,573,251	378,484	-48,650	3,146,117	1,067,919	557,980	30,043	158,837	95,729
2005	5,219,274	3,914,116	27,341	3,941,457	413,018	-68,067	3,460,372	1,140,317	618,585	33,200	157,205	99,290
2006	5,501,281	4,177,672	8,505	4,186,177	447,666	-83,681	3,654,830	1,163,756	682,695	34,130	161,185	102,153
2007	6,121,988	4,667,935	22,758	4,690,693	498,043	-116,387	4,076,263	1,306,406	739,319	37,499	163,256	104,596
2008	6,842,741	5,254,620	38,732	5,293,352	558,294	-164,767	4,570,291	1,419,735	852,715	40,475	169,059	109,720
2009	7,452,832	5,790,200	34,911	5,825,111	628,923	-215,204	4,980,984	1,535,784	936,064	43,064	173,064	113,560
2010	8,013,123	6,232,985	56,883	6,289,868	677,135	-247,408	5,365,325	1,609,940	1,037,858	42,865	186,940	114,633
2011	8,289,284	6,309,231	49,944	6,359,175	637,968	-257,527	5,463,680	1,734,320	1,091,284	44,765	185,175	114,457
2012	8,305,638	6,289,707	67,433	6,357,140	644,108	-254,119	5,458,913	1,714,845	1,131,880	43,483	191,007	113,432
2013	8,017,001	6,148,489	76,581	6,225,070	692,927	-244,166	5,287,977	1,551,115	1,177,909	41,582	192,798	113,476
2014	8,112,075	6,127,403	79,787	6,207,190	695,505	-235,244	5,276,441	1,590,139	1,245,495	42,160	192,411	112,788
2015	8,240,359	6,082,783	62,378	6,145,161	697,512	-219,085	5,228,564	1,607,723	1,404,072	42,515	193,823	110,288
2016	8,411,372	6,142,077	50,193	6,192,270	656,282	-215,879	5,320,109	1,616,051	1,475,212	43,531	193,227	109,295
2017	8,234,789	5,946,273	62,013	6,008,286	671,595	-199,872	5,136,819	1,528,097	1,569,873	42,040	195,881	110,878
2018	8,604,445	6,258,434	39,758	6,298,192	700,354	-206,593	5,391,245	1,543,896	1,669,304	43,527	197,682	110,612
2019	8,953,015	6,501,043	45,614	6,546,657	723,063	-207,928	5,615,666	1,552,652	1,784,697	44,001	203,475	111,791
2020	9,587,104	6,733,074	39,121	6,772,195	750,927	-217,987	5,803,281	1,554,579	2,229,244	46,781	204,937	110,361
2021	10,537,886	7,291,517	64,200	7,355,717	803,429	-240,914	6,311,374	1,572,567	2,653,945	51,490	204,660	115,094
2022	10,693,469	7,715,697	72,915	7,788,612	857,679	-253,371	6,677,562	1,660,538	2,355,369	51,585	207,298	118,459

Personal Income and Employment by Area: Janesville-Beloit, WI

(Thousands of dollars, except as noted.)

Year	Personal income, total	Derivation of personal income: Earnings by place of work								Per capita personal income (dollars)	Population (persons)	Total employment
		Nonfarm	Farm	Total	Less: Contributions for government social insurance	Plus: Adjustment for residence	Equals: Net earnings by place of residence	Plus: Dividends, interest, and rent	Plus: Personal current transfer receipts			
1970	508,949	375,550	15,862	391,412	27,547	26,750	390,615	73,909	44,425	3,859	131,872	53,249
1971	554,306	405,743	18,858	424,601	30,633	26,140	420,108	80,143	54,055	4,191	132,257	53,167
1972	597,945	438,445	18,644	457,089	35,424	29,198	450,863	86,080	61,002	4,487	133,253	53,902
1973	675,634	502,648	27,163	529,811	46,955	30,845	513,701	95,047	66,886	5,019	134,603	57,505
1974	732,589	543,377	20,932	564,309	52,883	31,782	543,208	106,539	82,842	5,387	135,984	59,092
1975	789,143	564,013	24,949	588,962	53,851	29,997	565,108	116,622	107,413	5,732	137,680	58,336
1976	886,974	673,086	11,494	684,580	64,971	26,211	645,820	125,638	115,516	6,455	137,402	60,119
1977	1,002,959	776,744	22,736	799,480	74,572	24,746	749,654	139,568	113,737	7,275	137,859	62,999
1978	1,113,290	868,548	21,388	889,936	86,392	32,246	835,790	153,315	124,185	8,064	138,065	64,619
1979	1,234,619	955,810	28,106	983,916	98,137	33,792	919,571	168,696	146,352	8,831	139,809	66,458
1980	1,320,747	932,825	28,814	961,639	94,885	41,361	908,115	203,348	209,284	9,483	139,269	63,602
1981	1,468,580	1,042,565	26,676	1,069,241	113,731	40,377	995,887	247,747	224,946	10,616	138,336	64,284
1982	1,484,552	1,014,534	13,209	1,027,743	112,561	41,601	956,783	283,158	244,611	10,766	137,893	61,023
1983	1,606,320	1,144,744	-1,542	1,143,202	126,634	39,358	1,055,926	306,140	244,254	11,678	137,549	62,519
1984	1,787,664	1,280,520	12,983	1,293,503	145,659	52,690	1,200,534	337,283	249,847	12,999	137,523	65,192
1985	1,887,842	1,350,155	18,198	1,368,353	156,866	62,931	1,274,418	348,525	264,899	13,709	137,713	65,868
1986	1,957,442	1,359,842	23,452	1,383,294	156,925	85,072	1,311,441	368,345	277,656	14,230	137,555	66,699
1987	2,027,104	1,400,451	36,795	1,437,246	158,400	99,535	1,378,381	360,460	288,263	14,945	135,641	68,104
1988	2,204,837	1,582,383	16,307	1,598,690	184,087	115,125	1,529,728	381,785	293,324	16,142	136,588	70,857
1989	2,353,586	1,649,706	35,354	1,685,060	193,402	130,629	1,622,287	418,497	312,802	17,035	138,161	71,522
1990	2,493,982	1,764,660	30,483	1,795,143	214,277	140,084	1,720,950	436,485	336,547	17,832	139,859	73,269
1991	2,552,105	1,760,612	22,044	1,782,656	215,679	145,160	1,712,137	456,756	383,212	18,072	141,219	71,991
1992	2,816,774	2,027,663	31,349	2,059,012	245,807	128,273	1,941,478	469,970	405,326	19,711	142,904	75,226
1993	2,941,405	2,132,308	19,344	2,151,652	258,685	135,774	2,028,741	496,469	416,195	20,374	144,372	76,394
1994	3,121,061	2,286,242	29,048	2,315,290	277,868	151,810	2,189,232	511,906	419,923	21,380	145,982	78,980
1995	3,311,306	2,435,468	23,590	2,459,058	295,923	152,581	2,315,716	551,778	443,812	22,347	148,179	82,349
1996	3,438,440	2,501,199	34,925	2,536,124	299,102	159,787	2,396,809	582,403	459,228	22,933	149,937	82,642
1997	3,625,302	2,656,207	22,985	2,679,192	313,931	166,044	2,531,305	625,686	468,311	24,145	150,145	84,076
1998	3,807,460	2,763,896	27,031	2,790,927	323,369	184,816	2,652,374	678,357	476,729	25,244	150,827	83,619
1999	3,898,703	2,857,959	28,459	2,886,418	334,925	202,514	2,754,007	647,415	497,281	25,727	151,541	84,649
2000	4,071,129	2,937,423	21,376	2,958,799	340,681	225,805	2,843,923	682,214	544,992	26,702	152,464	84,977
2001	4,201,795	2,979,790	27,152	3,006,942	350,877	231,875	2,887,940	704,294	609,561	27,432	153,174	83,958
2002	4,335,663	3,106,368	19,682	3,126,050	363,212	230,815	2,993,653	687,021	654,989	28,222	153,628	83,124
2003	4,489,772	3,241,736	33,732	3,275,468	378,933	229,129	3,125,664	688,516	675,592	29,104	154,268	83,551
2004	4,648,076	3,314,829	49,064	3,363,893	388,709	287,602	3,262,786	687,530	697,760	29,856	155,685	84,841
2005	4,787,552	3,391,387	37,510	3,428,897	403,924	319,738	3,344,711	692,160	750,681	30,540	156,761	85,936
2006	5,111,745	3,674,798	32,317	3,707,115	440,022	311,371	3,578,464	742,346	790,935	32,243	158,538	87,119
2007	5,270,478	3,645,466	44,589	3,690,055	438,883	333,258	3,584,430	833,034	853,014	32,959	159,912	87,009
2008	5,395,000	3,561,170	31,103	3,592,273	434,230	353,929	3,511,972	899,337	983,691	33,583	160,647	84,577
2009	5,291,722	3,276,232	26,474	3,302,706	398,859	398,129	3,301,976	844,440	1,145,306	32,989	160,411	78,106
2010	5,431,790	3,268,329	39,383	3,307,712	399,266	374,104	3,282,550	937,264	1,211,976	33,890	160,276	77,419
2011	5,706,193	3,428,679	72,364	3,501,043	374,852	453,148	3,579,339	964,786	1,162,068	35,669	159,976	77,874
2012	5,961,101	3,657,421	37,395	3,694,816	396,750	391,873	3,689,939	1,081,693	1,189,469	37,199	160,251	79,449
2013	6,083,922	3,956,715	53,932	4,010,647	474,685	283,262	3,819,224	1,044,730	1,219,968	37,882	160,602	80,879
2014	6,158,784	3,867,286	24,288	3,891,574	473,314	359,998	3,778,258	1,103,866	1,276,660	38,191	161,261	82,043
2015	6,388,810	4,052,979	36,289	4,089,268	492,013	351,832	3,949,087	1,108,991	1,330,732	39,580	161,417	83,321
2016	6,529,348	4,162,727	34,318	4,197,045	505,823	363,131	4,054,353	1,132,284	1,342,711	40,368	161,746	84,034
2017	6,756,430	4,311,080	25,356	4,336,436	530,489	339,885	4,145,832	1,212,648	1,397,950	41,522	162,721	85,170
2018	7,085,148	4,582,418	28,757	4,611,175	557,569	320,028	4,373,634	1,247,771	1,463,743	43,382	163,319	86,325
2019	7,447,418	4,807,275	21,889	4,829,164	589,361	387,040	4,626,843	1,281,129	1,539,446	45,500	163,681	86,901
2020	7,845,226	4,853,630	48,014	4,901,644	597,905	392,154	4,695,893	1,220,735	1,928,598	47,909	163,751	83,465
2021	8,530,579	5,108,897	63,993	5,172,890	625,045	427,491	4,975,336	1,367,422	2,187,821	51,955	164,192	86,025
2022	8,615,932	5,404,192	72,862	5,477,054	675,933	449,217	5,250,338	1,453,126	1,912,468	52,517	164,060	89,092

Personal Income and Employment by Area: Jefferson City, MO

(Thousands of dollars, except as noted.)

Year	Personal income, total	Derivation of personal income: Earnings by place of work: Nonfarm	Earnings by place of work: Farm	Earnings by place of work: Total	Less: Contributions for government social insurance	Plus: Adjustment for residence	Equals: Net earnings by place of residence	Plus: Dividends, interest, and rent	Plus: Personal current transfer receipts	Per capita personal income (dollars)	Population (persons)	Total employment
1970	342,121	265,871	17,635	283,506	16,832	-8,684	257,990	52,799	31,332	3,639	94,027	47,791
1971	371,341	291,732	14,825	306,557	19,137	-10,723	276,697	58,903	35,741	3,926	94,588	48,879
1972	406,798	316,119	19,926	336,045	21,652	-11,969	302,424	65,672	38,702	4,166	97,637	50,046
1973	465,525	350,251	35,029	385,280	27,702	-13,646	343,932	76,362	45,231	4,726	98,495	52,912
1974	514,010	393,519	25,828	419,347	32,363	-15,738	371,246	89,718	53,046	5,143	99,942	54,087
1975	560,744	421,875	19,171	441,046	33,845	-17,562	389,639	102,264	68,841	5,495	102,037	53,159
1976	628,573	491,201	14,904	506,105	39,834	-24,515	441,756	112,340	74,477	6,060	103,718	55,939
1977	702,792	560,481	19,949	580,430	45,955	-35,386	499,089	126,394	77,309	6,689	105,067	59,122
1978	809,163	664,645	27,687	692,332	57,196	-50,724	584,412	140,490	84,261	7,477	108,217	63,595
1979	896,598	738,510	30,741	769,251	66,049	-60,044	643,158	157,999	95,441	8,172	109,714	64,788
1980	992,992	815,622	3,830	819,452	71,753	-71,472	676,227	200,423	116,342	8,762	113,330	65,774
1981	1,129,716	897,104	16,658	913,762	85,063	-77,297	751,402	245,056	133,258	9,873	114,422	66,216
1982	1,235,770	966,390	12,608	978,998	93,981	-86,028	798,989	288,561	148,220	10,726	115,211	65,896
1983	1,327,002	1,032,427	3,568	1,035,995	100,137	-84,266	851,592	314,614	160,796	11,395	116,456	67,159
1984	1,440,275	1,085,083	19,960	1,105,043	106,525	-74,361	924,157	347,969	168,149	12,274	117,342	68,046
1985	1,495,099	1,094,732	22,559	1,117,291	107,857	-61,483	947,951	369,535	177,613	12,779	117,000	67,660
1986	1,608,549	1,196,428	21,281	1,217,709	119,473	-67,254	1,030,982	390,429	187,138	13,590	118,360	69,180
1987	1,673,090	1,260,239	23,077	1,283,316	124,791	-69,140	1,089,385	393,992	189,713	14,032	119,231	69,132
1988	1,752,156	1,341,431	15,683	1,357,114	140,418	-67,557	1,149,139	405,280	197,737	14,645	119,646	70,870
1989	1,918,615	1,446,941	23,913	1,470,854	152,246	-72,008	1,246,600	454,851	217,164	15,955	120,250	73,463
1990	2,018,173	1,559,467	21,113	1,580,580	167,205	-83,079	1,330,296	449,500	238,377	16,664	121,107	75,568
1991	2,146,525	1,644,181	18,083	1,662,264	178,156	-88,557	1,395,551	474,216	276,758	17,437	123,100	76,650
1992	2,288,188	1,773,417	17,008	1,790,425	190,254	-95,943	1,504,228	480,586	303,374	18,335	124,802	77,896
1993	2,403,830	1,856,797	16,679	1,873,476	199,701	-100,530	1,573,245	507,383	323,202	18,978	126,662	79,861
1994	2,545,538	1,983,027	4,921	1,987,948	214,580	-106,865	1,666,503	534,362	344,673	19,811	128,490	82,641
1995	2,704,440	2,118,785	-4,155	2,114,630	229,148	-118,395	1,767,087	569,524	367,829	20,621	131,148	85,679
1996	2,893,341	2,259,849	19,850	2,279,699	240,978	-130,198	1,908,523	604,297	380,521	21,657	133,601	88,188
1997	3,087,925	2,425,120	21,067	2,446,187	256,540	-144,513	2,045,134	645,475	397,316	22,754	135,707	90,574
1998	3,222,134	2,548,816	8,891	2,557,707	268,657	-152,478	2,136,572	671,308	414,254	23,473	137,268	92,096
1999	3,383,576	2,763,728	-4,584	2,759,144	287,921	-173,270	2,297,953	652,109	433,514	24,389	138,736	93,723
2000	3,580,155	2,903,311	10,394	2,913,705	301,096	-184,985	2,427,624	693,376	459,155	25,521	140,285	95,500
2001	3,722,722	3,015,686	13,394	3,029,080	313,499	-201,145	2,514,436	697,255	511,031	26,404	140,991	96,794
2002	3,779,059	3,089,309	4,397	3,093,706	320,424	-203,455	2,569,827	663,948	545,284	26,578	142,190	95,949
2003	3,975,962	3,253,056	16,797	3,269,853	335,928	-229,495	2,704,430	700,771	570,761	27,771	143,171	97,940
2004	4,245,228	3,439,182	80,498	3,519,680	351,449	-235,270	2,932,961	700,034	612,233	29,762	142,637	98,618
2005	4,385,190	3,560,513	57,036	3,617,549	368,276	-242,190	3,007,083	719,071	659,036	30,358	144,450	99,230
2006	4,621,331	3,750,660	48,847	3,799,507	385,054	-240,510	3,173,943	745,993	701,395	31,728	145,654	99,543
2007	4,862,754	3,849,001	52,135	3,901,136	399,560	-251,376	3,250,200	854,724	757,830	33,203	146,455	100,714
2008	5,191,623	4,016,491	80,010	4,096,501	421,527	-273,157	3,401,817	929,967	859,839	35,128	147,792	101,620
2009	5,138,194	3,976,430	48,558	4,024,988	415,040	-294,367	3,315,581	890,466	932,147	34,512	148,880	100,051
2010	5,246,379	4,067,938	65,599	4,133,537	421,366	-311,638	3,400,533	841,916	1,003,930	34,977	149,996	99,164
2011	5,375,509	4,092,769	80,020	4,172,789	381,172	-322,456	3,469,161	888,482	1,017,866	35,734	150,430	98,434
2012	5,565,398	4,151,808	52,219	4,204,027	382,743	-316,241	3,505,043	1,025,377	1,034,978	36,997	150,428	97,657
2013	5,650,230	4,380,190	69,656	4,449,846	447,313	-344,517	3,658,016	927,543	1,064,671	37,487	150,725	98,066
2014	5,801,176	4,421,751	124,104	4,545,855	457,863	-348,820	3,739,172	968,968	1,093,036	38,474	150,782	98,221
2015	5,936,629	4,534,365	50,093	4,584,458	475,846	-362,167	3,746,445	1,028,835	1,161,349	39,315	151,000	98,969
2016	6,009,500	4,595,336	13,469	4,608,805	488,906	-369,583	3,750,316	1,051,194	1,207,990	39,680	151,449	100,786
2017	6,221,412	4,716,368	6,224	4,722,592	504,298	-373,085	3,845,209	1,134,753	1,241,450	41,090	151,408	101,347
2018	6,326,577	4,811,134	4,229	4,815,363	515,971	-388,873	3,910,519	1,128,404	1,287,654	41,762	151,493	101,603
2019	6,708,896	5,039,166	9,318	5,048,484	543,519	-406,915	4,098,050	1,234,725	1,376,121	44,433	150,990	102,010
2020	7,225,296	5,260,118	24,108	5,284,226	574,666	-425,771	4,283,789	1,227,286	1,714,221	48,353	149,429	101,092
2021	7,600,504	5,423,002	33,716	5,456,718	586,443	-397,967	4,472,308	1,226,389	1,901,807	50,673	149,991	102,076
2022	7,808,633	5,797,828	61,744	5,859,572	640,695	-422,937	4,795,940	1,323,067	1,689,626	51,936	150,350	105,118

Personal Income and Employment by Area: Johnson City, TN

(Thousands of dollars, except as noted.)

Year	Personal income, total	Derivation of personal income: Earnings by place of work: Nonfarm	Earnings by place of work: Farm	Earnings by place of work: Total	Less: Contributions for government social insurance	Plus: Adjustment for residence	Equals: Net earnings by place of residence	Plus: Dividends, interest, and rent	Plus: Personal current transfer receipts	Per capita personal income (dollars)	Population (persons)	Total employment
1970	399,260	283,219	7,417	290,636	18,568	36,480	308,548	46,788	43,924	3,002	132,997	51,412
1971	442,056	317,167	6,578	323,745	21,424	36,652	338,973	52,757	50,326	3,241	136,401	53,402
1972	494,553	355,301	10,656	365,957	25,215	39,926	380,668	58,854	55,031	3,529	140,121	56,559
1973	561,016	409,661	13,635	423,296	33,261	40,407	430,442	66,783	63,791	3,980	140,947	60,518
1974	618,936	445,610	10,492	456,102	37,493	44,492	463,101	77,246	78,589	4,320	143,257	60,850
1975	656,423	437,761	7,022	444,783	35,459	51,423	460,747	87,020	108,656	4,511	145,524	55,431
1976	728,393	491,869	11,555	503,424	40,948	59,464	521,940	92,739	113,714	4,867	149,645	57,109
1977	802,321	546,191	9,283	555,474	45,671	71,439	581,242	103,325	117,754	5,371	149,374	59,709
1978	918,853	629,814	9,013	638,827	53,515	88,273	673,585	118,985	126,283	6,094	150,780	62,719
1979	1,033,023	707,064	4,474	711,538	63,248	101,892	750,182	137,510	145,331	6,727	153,562	64,552
1980	1,172,642	783,979	7,798	791,777	70,751	109,669	830,695	170,249	171,698	7,521	155,925	66,128
1981	1,316,508	858,016	14,605	872,621	83,424	121,557	910,754	206,907	198,847	8,331	158,024	65,685
1982	1,377,912	878,357	13,403	891,760	86,848	118,993	923,905	232,303	221,704	8,698	158,424	64,173
1983	1,472,476	945,994	4,682	950,676	94,516	124,980	981,140	251,992	239,344	9,261	158,995	64,560
1984	1,603,475	1,036,645	10,254	1,046,899	107,358	127,354	1,066,895	285,135	251,445	10,038	159,742	67,109
1985	1,689,866	1,089,982	10,028	1,100,010	114,429	142,887	1,128,468	296,973	264,425	10,600	159,422	67,936
1986	1,808,264	1,176,558	5,215	1,181,773	126,535	152,564	1,207,802	318,704	281,758	11,349	159,326	69,445
1987	1,914,400	1,271,104	7,170	1,278,274	136,009	155,758	1,298,023	319,970	296,407	12,015	159,337	72,376
1988	2,058,730	1,361,853	10,211	1,372,064	152,084	169,513	1,389,493	351,254	317,983	12,933	159,181	75,181
1989	2,225,711	1,436,197	11,320	1,447,517	162,954	193,774	1,478,337	395,024	352,350	13,960	159,430	77,238
1990	2,402,094	1,567,238	17,634	1,584,872	178,343	207,179	1,613,708	400,366	388,020	14,925	160,942	80,870
1991	2,534,049	1,646,317	19,679	1,665,996	190,435	208,654	1,684,215	412,260	437,574	15,539	163,079	80,820
1992	2,743,643	1,819,474	22,254	1,841,728	208,268	207,427	1,840,887	413,295	489,461	16,645	164,834	83,910
1993	2,868,464	1,883,846	22,440	1,906,286	215,761	230,210	1,920,735	421,395	526,334	17,166	167,100	85,376
1994	2,975,489	1,995,543	21,143	2,016,686	233,661	194,648	1,977,673	446,705	551,111	17,573	169,319	88,631
1995	3,168,054	2,104,697	14,908	2,119,605	248,129	206,493	2,077,969	487,051	603,034	18,456	171,654	91,968
1996	3,351,021	2,208,066	7,894	2,215,960	257,747	230,464	2,188,677	523,224	639,120	19,226	174,296	93,587
1997	3,544,038	2,376,632	12,082	2,388,714	273,736	219,192	2,334,170	538,711	671,157	20,039	176,853	95,673
1998	3,764,479	2,547,861	10,984	2,558,845	287,385	213,403	2,484,863	567,936	711,680	21,080	178,581	96,099
1999	3,824,279	2,651,017	7,567	2,658,584	298,780	155,243	2,515,047	569,430	739,802	21,229	180,145	97,479
2000	4,075,185	2,856,665	13,316	2,869,981	318,515	106,503	2,657,969	601,876	815,340	22,398	181,944	99,329
2001	4,231,862	2,916,257	7,002	2,923,259	327,879	127,902	2,723,282	627,083	881,497	23,228	182,187	98,166
2002	4,356,206	2,987,038	3,079	2,990,117	337,187	135,434	2,788,364	599,717	968,125	23,679	183,973	96,242
2003	4,543,486	3,104,332	3,843	3,108,175	347,737	144,617	2,905,055	625,621	1,012,810	24,422	186,040	97,299
2004	4,921,046	3,391,066	5,198	3,396,264	375,476	147,851	3,168,639	663,254	1,089,153	26,271	187,317	100,019
2005	5,081,250	3,519,306	6,785	3,526,091	393,843	131,702	3,263,950	654,211	1,163,089	26,859	189,182	102,267
2006	5,385,895	3,677,793	2,550	3,680,343	414,506	177,890	3,443,727	706,739	1,235,429	28,060	191,943	103,421
2007	5,734,641	3,843,119	-2,994	3,840,125	437,387	173,241	3,575,979	800,075	1,358,587	29,588	193,819	106,089
2008	6,041,506	3,918,821	-2,409	3,916,412	454,578	179,350	3,641,184	886,427	1,513,895	30,786	196,242	105,554
2009	6,074,871	3,886,499	5,962	3,892,461	455,675	144,022	3,580,808	875,903	1,618,160	30,728	197,698	101,330
2010	6,354,277	3,961,878	887	3,962,765	459,048	205,260	3,708,977	875,393	1,769,907	31,917	199,085	100,754
2011	6,752,905	4,178,617	-852	4,177,765	428,914	257,721	4,006,572	933,804	1,812,529	33,776	199,934	103,421
2012	6,944,547	4,346,594	2,848	4,349,442	435,000	234,888	4,149,330	973,668	1,821,549	34,528	201,130	103,612
2013	6,898,399	4,313,446	5,284	4,318,730	488,080	267,826	4,098,476	948,719	1,851,204	34,250	201,415	101,683
2014	7,039,046	4,357,456	7,517	4,364,973	493,592	280,625	4,152,006	993,459	1,893,581	34,976	201,252	102,079
2015	7,338,491	4,577,210	7,682	4,584,892	515,601	273,485	4,342,776	1,028,388	1,967,327	36,355	201,857	103,396
2016	7,446,385	4,647,875	-781	4,647,094	526,126	264,265	4,385,233	1,059,547	2,001,605	36,621	203,338	104,238
2017	7,724,993	4,871,894	743	4,872,637	557,637	249,377	4,564,377	1,096,859	2,063,757	37,834	204,179	106,070
2018	8,058,783	5,067,758	-2,555	5,065,203	579,660	255,756	4,741,299	1,151,693	2,165,791	39,203	205,565	106,840
2019	8,541,192	5,278,353	-1,214	5,277,139	596,752	234,239	4,914,626	1,314,518	2,312,048	41,363	206,496	106,654
2020	9,185,747	5,547,753	-1,424	5,546,329	627,600	207,301	5,126,030	1,310,587	2,749,130	44,278	207,458	105,992
2021	10,036,019	6,084,144	1,501	6,085,645	676,079	201,967	5,611,533	1,347,292	3,077,194	48,424	207,252	110,921
2022	10,298,001	6,537,388	-1,852	6,535,536	749,187	252,704	6,039,053	1,458,090	2,800,858	48,978	210,256	115,151

Personal Income and Employment by Area: Johnstown, PA

(Thousands of dollars, except as noted.)

Year	Personal income, total	Derivation of personal income: Earnings by place of work: Nonfarm	Farm	Total	Less: Contributions for government social insurance	Plus: Adjustment for residence	Equals: Net earnings by place of residence	Plus: Dividends, interest, and rent	Plus: Personal current transfer receipts	Per capita personal income (dollars)	Population (persons)	Total employment
1970	607,109	520,299	2,913	523,212	39,131	-33,390	450,691	64,614	91,804	3,246	187,061	70,524
1971	652,058	546,212	2,272	548,484	42,709	-35,117	470,658	68,879	112,521	3,453	188,837	70,619
1972	729,191	618,943	1,235	620,178	50,029	-41,017	529,132	73,513	126,546	3,848	189,521	71,565
1973	810,449	686,485	4,001	690,486	63,793	-45,292	581,401	83,154	145,894	4,282	189,286	73,454
1974	915,701	781,170	3,920	785,090	75,704	-54,371	655,015	96,054	164,632	4,858	188,475	74,173
1975	1,052,072	887,051	3,081	890,132	83,580	-63,706	742,846	111,633	197,593	5,572	188,819	76,041
1976	1,149,286	958,304	3,689	961,993	91,481	-65,987	804,525	120,748	224,013	6,046	190,087	76,121
1977	1,262,593	1,041,240	3,134	1,044,374	98,398	-69,171	876,805	135,930	249,858	6,635	190,302	76,013
1978	1,361,707	1,099,172	6,242	1,105,414	105,791	-68,354	931,269	153,374	277,064	7,237	188,155	74,653
1979	1,521,023	1,239,482	7,715	1,247,197	122,559	-85,132	1,039,506	176,424	305,093	8,161	186,373	76,327
1980	1,595,476	1,210,659	9,740	1,220,399	120,236	-78,987	1,021,176	222,662	351,638	8,719	182,986	71,866
1981	1,716,418	1,246,443	13,143	1,259,586	133,237	-73,017	1,053,332	273,104	389,982	9,456	181,509	69,018
1982	1,764,091	1,189,815	4,771	1,194,586	129,013	-53,757	1,011,816	310,730	441,545	9,877	178,601	65,149
1983	1,796,823	1,146,506	2,825	1,149,331	124,334	-42,414	982,583	339,387	474,853	10,152	176,996	62,516
1984	1,899,968	1,229,874	6,383	1,236,257	140,633	-40,069	1,055,555	375,158	469,255	10,812	175,730	63,475
1985	1,937,442	1,244,431	4,915	1,249,346	144,362	-35,815	1,069,169	390,377	477,896	11,212	172,797	64,019
1986	1,956,775	1,226,039	4,333	1,230,372	145,986	-31,281	1,053,105	403,868	499,802	11,483	170,400	64,855
1987	2,012,180	1,288,327	3,779	1,292,106	151,505	-24,581	1,116,020	388,808	507,352	11,939	168,535	66,371
1988	2,207,778	1,482,240	574	1,482,814	173,230	-27,356	1,282,228	402,751	522,799	13,299	166,006	68,288
1989	2,358,623	1,570,265	3,398	1,573,663	183,133	-31,027	1,359,503	454,962	544,158	14,384	163,970	69,263
1990	2,485,505	1,655,592	5,587	1,661,179	193,552	-26,802	1,440,825	453,099	591,581	15,254	162,938	71,269
1991	2,632,619	1,717,959	5,359	1,723,318	202,554	-22,261	1,498,503	451,988	682,128	16,203	162,473	70,635
1992	2,728,077	1,778,494	8,837	1,787,331	209,030	-6,225	1,572,076	446,007	709,994	16,814	162,247	70,141
1993	2,797,643	1,814,365	8,520	1,822,885	218,475	5,337	1,609,747	447,405	740,491	17,294	161,770	70,383
1994	2,884,858	1,883,497	7,006	1,890,503	232,805	12,598	1,670,296	464,320	750,242	17,944	160,766	71,846
1995	2,991,965	1,939,322	5,389	1,944,711	240,731	10,014	1,713,994	507,583	770,388	18,712	159,892	73,380
1996	3,068,255	1,940,042	8,967	1,949,009	237,144	20,471	1,732,336	523,537	812,382	19,347	158,588	73,457
1997	3,174,250	1,992,758	2,679	1,995,437	243,537	26,392	1,778,292	568,564	827,394	20,167	157,396	73,397
1998	3,309,560	2,118,843	2,245	2,121,088	251,288	27,903	1,897,703	581,913	829,944	21,259	155,677	74,169
1999	3,436,591	2,235,900	625	2,236,525	262,887	29,888	2,003,526	568,643	864,422	22,328	153,911	75,076
2000	3,526,858	2,232,539	3,120	2,235,659	260,881	46,805	2,021,583	599,840	905,435	23,187	152,107	75,088
2001	3,714,737	2,327,849	-1,257	2,326,592	267,609	60,928	2,119,911	623,274	971,552	24,617	150,902	72,951
2002	3,775,469	2,362,253	-2,518	2,359,735	270,892	74,533	2,163,376	586,028	1,026,065	25,198	149,831	71,795
2003	3,895,121	2,444,433	4,066	2,448,499	277,905	83,797	2,254,391	589,909	1,050,821	26,171	148,836	71,476
2004	4,006,492	2,556,024	2,501	2,558,525	290,373	88,843	2,356,995	553,079	1,096,418	27,092	147,886	72,180
2005	4,119,565	2,634,460	5,314	2,639,774	310,612	95,524	2,424,686	533,838	1,161,041	28,029	146,975	72,655
2006	4,252,812	2,724,011	7,126	2,731,137	324,553	77,624	2,484,208	556,823	1,211,781	29,110	146,093	74,221
2007	4,484,107	2,794,792	8,234	2,803,026	336,266	81,010	2,547,770	645,686	1,290,651	30,865	145,283	74,950
2008	4,706,930	2,864,914	12,687	2,877,601	347,738	86,845	2,616,708	685,357	1,404,865	32,541	144,646	75,028
2009	4,689,846	2,817,698	6,770	2,824,468	347,138	100,869	2,578,199	667,407	1,444,240	32,526	144,186	72,740
2010	4,684,564	2,917,878	5,866	2,923,744	356,378	-21,055	2,546,311	631,674	1,506,579	32,628	143,574	72,283
2011	5,007,373	2,981,212	16,006	2,997,218	328,326	147,660	2,816,552	678,049	1,512,772	34,975	143,171	72,198
2012	5,040,356	2,967,513	17,106	2,984,619	325,360	178,878	2,838,137	704,080	1,498,139	35,345	142,604	71,680
2013	5,011,276	2,967,146	11,855	2,979,001	362,535	206,007	2,822,473	663,158	1,525,645	35,709	140,335	70,667
2014	5,125,254	2,974,466	10,372	2,984,838	375,174	225,354	2,835,018	719,634	1,570,602	36,739	139,503	69,882
2015	5,214,783	3,006,614	5,207	3,011,821	373,788	232,919	2,870,952	707,611	1,636,220	37,672	138,427	69,153
2016	5,220,861	2,965,403	2,450	2,967,853	373,232	224,050	2,818,671	710,139	1,692,051	38,031	137,280	68,018
2017	5,304,376	2,990,995	5,048	2,996,043	383,712	242,243	2,854,574	757,917	1,691,885	38,943	136,209	66,666
2018	5,592,595	3,091,547	1,492	3,093,039	395,386	276,188	2,973,841	809,729	1,809,025	41,411	135,052	66,027
2019	5,739,807	3,183,130	6,577	3,189,707	406,278	277,802	3,061,231	794,858	1,883,718	42,810	134,077	65,092
2020	6,160,474	3,094,420	5,180	3,099,600	400,162	276,046	2,975,484	815,313	2,369,677	46,250	133,199	61,333
2021	6,476,552	3,132,047	9,657	3,141,704	405,923	291,792	3,027,573	856,331	2,592,648	48,961	132,281	62,429
2022	6,305,307	3,262,299	3,817	3,266,116	435,644	308,795	3,139,267	897,760	2,268,280	47,971	131,441	63,943

Personal Income and Employment by Area: Jonesboro, AR

(Thousands of dollars, except as noted.)

Year	Personal income, total	Derivation of personal income: Earnings by place of work: Nonfarm	Farm	Total	Less: Contributions for government social insurance	Plus: Adjustment for residence	Equals: Net earnings by place of residence	Plus: Dividends, interest, and rent	Plus: Personal current transfer receipts	Per capita personal income (dollars)	Population (persons)	Total employment
1970	232,177	146,372	43,150	189,522	11,136	3,789	182,175	25,548	24,454	2,919	79,540	34,569
1971	251,604	164,558	38,960	203,518	12,866	3,752	194,404	28,764	28,436	3,050	82,495	35,576
1972	278,732	188,955	37,116	226,071	15,373	3,709	214,407	31,858	32,467	3,330	83,698	36,928
1973	340,701	207,580	72,099	279,679	19,394	3,969	264,254	37,607	38,840	4,010	84,953	37,486
1974	382,837	227,529	78,869	306,398	21,956	4,146	288,588	46,024	48,225	4,465	85,734	37,982
1975	408,780	257,744	54,099	311,843	24,362	3,836	291,317	55,182	62,281	4,735	86,332	38,045
1976	438,467	300,452	36,526	336,978	28,746	3,042	311,274	59,555	67,638	4,971	88,200	39,374
1977	491,063	337,792	44,679	382,471	32,614	1,791	351,648	66,348	73,067	5,478	89,644	41,014
1978	630,210	386,681	126,999	513,680	38,343	1,378	476,715	74,094	79,401	6,981	90,272	42,812
1979	629,581	431,483	67,534	499,017	44,209	280	455,088	84,828	89,665	6,931	90,835	42,949
1980	650,641	455,975	28,711	484,686	46,459	148	438,375	103,464	108,802	7,207	90,274	42,267
1981	739,062	474,473	67,706	542,179	52,321	-315	489,543	128,535	120,984	8,203	90,094	40,797
1982	768,155	490,565	51,517	542,082	54,932	183	487,333	149,840	130,982	8,602	89,303	40,231
1983	787,822	527,441	25,220	552,661	59,214	93	493,540	151,113	143,169	8,845	89,065	40,737
1984	907,418	594,052	64,617	658,669	68,381	223	590,511	165,800	151,107	10,148	89,417	42,557
1985	948,852	630,009	51,211	681,220	73,061	512	608,671	180,450	159,731	10,573	89,745	43,490
1986	967,494	677,597	17,228	694,825	78,652	135	616,308	186,184	165,002	10,770	89,832	44,766
1987	1,057,696	745,089	50,416	795,505	85,954	-737	708,814	179,015	169,867	11,617	91,051	46,963
1988	1,158,540	805,294	78,456	883,750	96,410	580	787,920	192,512	178,108	12,601	91,939	48,776
1989	1,220,466	863,127	46,661	909,788	103,622	1,084	807,250	214,120	199,096	13,164	92,714	49,447
1990	1,288,853	906,721	43,599	950,320	112,976	4,871	842,215	228,058	218,580	13,711	93,999	49,752
1991	1,379,165	951,822	67,661	1,019,483	118,918	7,372	907,937	226,837	244,391	14,639	94,210	49,788
1992	1,514,268	1,048,408	89,017	1,137,425	130,022	6,749	1,014,152	230,900	269,216	15,775	95,994	51,479
1993	1,576,878	1,115,099	74,143	1,189,242	138,930	5,848	1,056,160	239,292	281,426	16,101	97,939	52,981
1994	1,655,578	1,182,789	81,584	1,264,373	148,863	6,386	1,121,896	246,433	287,249	16,745	98,872	53,314
1995	1,794,289	1,263,900	98,035	1,361,935	158,288	4,583	1,208,230	275,058	311,001	17,795	100,831	56,015
1996	1,899,818	1,321,408	113,473	1,434,881	164,198	5,299	1,275,982	295,533	328,303	18,507	102,652	56,986
1997	1,990,502	1,398,162	108,787	1,506,949	172,907	5,343	1,339,385	308,925	342,192	19,116	104,130	57,997
1998	2,100,448	1,508,926	90,009	1,598,935	182,681	5,668	1,421,922	321,260	357,266	19,889	105,607	59,098
1999	2,208,853	1,625,636	79,814	1,705,450	194,296	2,149	1,513,303	321,676	373,874	20,728	106,563	60,455
2000	2,327,390	1,701,763	90,537	1,792,300	202,406	2,084	1,591,978	339,506	395,906	21,523	108,136	61,241
2001	2,393,686	1,695,634	93,165	1,788,799	201,817	-2,814	1,584,168	357,604	451,914	22,006	108,774	61,014
2002	2,456,996	1,776,014	43,622	1,819,636	209,896	-13,815	1,595,925	356,144	504,927	22,502	109,191	61,135
2003	2,698,792	1,863,746	184,100	2,047,846	219,185	-24,505	1,804,156	366,148	528,488	24,495	110,177	61,583
2004	2,796,549	1,994,755	165,866	2,160,621	231,997	-35,251	1,893,373	328,068	575,108	25,110	111,370	62,827
2005	2,878,303	2,089,534	102,011	2,191,545	245,867	-38,517	1,907,161	349,433	621,709	25,569	112,570	63,512
2006	3,013,925	2,153,450	113,817	2,267,267	259,024	-44,662	1,963,581	375,592	674,752	26,293	114,629	64,962
2007	3,184,300	2,208,651	108,634	2,317,285	268,013	-41,163	2,008,109	442,119	734,072	27,412	116,163	64,737
2008	3,367,723	2,293,072	109,956	2,403,028	286,341	-64,316	2,052,371	482,715	832,637	28,561	117,915	64,977
2009	3,426,358	2,297,414	100,470	2,397,884	290,631	-60,092	2,047,161	463,090	916,107	28,526	120,114	64,438
2010	3,620,810	2,463,917	95,189	2,559,106	305,382	-60,782	2,192,942	443,859	984,009	29,865	121,238	65,199
2011	3,881,668	2,585,620	123,647	2,709,267	289,098	-48,109	2,372,060	494,217	1,015,391	31,623	122,748	67,911
2012	4,058,082	2,724,629	79,988	2,804,617	296,989	-30,730	2,476,898	549,272	1,031,912	32,700	124,099	68,058
2013	4,170,447	2,797,071	196,622	2,993,693	338,159	-32,992	2,622,542	498,297	1,049,608	33,217	125,553	69,147
2014	4,266,122	2,894,465	87,016	2,981,481	355,540	-31,260	2,594,681	553,738	1,117,703	33,740	126,442	70,413
2015	4,358,768	3,007,670	27,988	3,035,658	370,651	-39,473	2,625,534	559,859	1,173,375	34,055	127,992	72,438
2016	4,483,226	3,088,496	39,677	3,128,173	379,246	-61,599	2,687,328	572,196	1,223,702	34,645	129,403	74,468
2017	4,627,127	3,203,832	66,910	3,270,742	396,675	-89,143	2,784,924	596,911	1,245,292	35,425	130,618	76,750
2018	4,776,543	3,353,203	39,958	3,393,161	411,901	-105,082	2,876,178	608,023	1,292,342	36,158	132,103	78,194
2019	5,051,139	3,538,244	65,944	3,604,188	438,350	-119,173	3,046,665	638,507	1,365,967	37,888	133,316	79,656
2020	5,620,896	3,774,210	78,414	3,852,624	474,754	-146,357	3,231,513	715,848	1,673,535	41,774	134,555	79,140
2021	6,208,299	4,128,755	137,788	4,266,543	505,843	-158,319	3,602,381	735,817	1,870,101	46,152	134,518	81,779
2022	6,197,834	4,318,271	81,211	4,399,482	540,406	-161,390	3,697,686	786,317	1,713,831	45,736	135,512	84,468

Personal Income and Employment by Area: Joplin, MO

(Thousands of dollars, except as noted.)

Year	Personal income, total	Derivation of personal income: Earnings by place of work: Nonfarm	Farm	Total	Less: Contributions for government social insurance	Plus: Adjustment for residence	Equals: Net earnings by place of residence	Plus: Dividends, interest, and rent	Plus: Personal current transfer receipts	Per capita personal income (dollars)	Population (persons)	Total employment
1970	354,813	273,450	10,341	283,791	18,399	-6,324	259,068	50,657	45,088	3,139	113,028	48,807
1971	379,110	291,191	9,671	300,862	20,308	-8,264	272,290	55,148	51,672	3,314	114,407	49,252
1972	428,365	331,460	15,571	347,031	24,322	-9,849	312,860	60,360	55,145	3,650	117,364	52,210
1973	485,292	368,637	26,756	395,393	31,341	-10,957	353,095	68,326	63,871	4,064	119,399	55,584
1974	523,487	407,601	9,893	417,494	35,911	-12,970	368,613	79,832	75,042	4,328	120,962	55,905
1975	568,447	423,422	10,444	433,866	36,445	-12,682	384,739	88,212	95,496	4,693	121,126	53,422
1976	632,272	474,540	14,454	488,994	41,337	-14,227	433,430	97,416	101,426	5,192	121,777	55,436
1977	702,099	534,084	13,728	547,812	46,634	-15,924	485,254	111,778	105,067	5,675	123,716	57,532
1978	786,186	607,725	14,860	622,585	54,953	-19,920	547,712	124,480	113,994	6,294	124,905	59,753
1979	879,673	678,401	16,617	695,018	63,378	-21,304	610,336	141,122	128,215	6,940	126,753	61,872
1980	980,325	724,351	17,943	742,294	67,466	-23,754	651,074	174,508	154,743	7,668	127,845	61,478
1981	1,099,757	801,562	15,893	817,455	79,874	-27,315	710,266	212,650	176,841	8,532	128,894	62,909
1982	1,178,087	838,831	6,326	845,157	84,985	-32,243	727,929	251,501	198,657	9,116	129,226	62,312
1983	1,269,677	905,250	6,240	911,490	91,712	-35,713	784,065	273,901	211,711	9,794	129,634	64,321
1984	1,402,602	1,013,969	5,248	1,019,217	105,788	-41,985	871,444	311,330	219,828	10,733	130,678	67,177
1985	1,493,539	1,092,186	7,212	1,099,398	116,190	-47,730	935,478	325,135	232,926	11,357	131,504	69,624
1986	1,589,855	1,169,757	14,388	1,184,145	124,873	-55,234	1,004,038	338,979	246,838	12,029	132,165	71,862
1987	1,666,412	1,263,879	7,274	1,271,153	132,982	-61,637	1,076,534	332,779	257,099	12,503	133,284	73,545
1988	1,782,575	1,340,886	12,251	1,353,137	145,718	-64,608	1,142,811	360,814	278,950	13,336	133,670	74,700
1989	1,896,368	1,415,771	20,801	1,436,572	155,491	-66,999	1,214,082	387,973	294,313	14,109	134,404	75,726
1990	1,999,813	1,499,680	14,731	1,514,411	169,119	-74,123	1,271,169	409,792	318,852	14,789	135,219	77,595
1991	2,118,067	1,589,294	12,284	1,601,578	181,051	-79,848	1,340,679	407,617	369,771	15,494	136,705	78,870
1992	2,311,681	1,731,192	14,248	1,745,440	195,106	-87,409	1,462,925	447,853	400,903	16,647	138,865	81,177
1993	2,454,162	1,845,759	13,136	1,858,895	209,232	-95,612	1,554,051	465,993	434,118	17,337	141,558	84,247
1994	2,642,613	2,014,517	11,926	2,026,443	230,112	-109,248	1,687,083	500,179	455,351	18,325	144,212	88,024
1995	2,797,736	2,142,519	7,933	2,150,452	245,997	-116,625	1,787,830	519,189	490,717	19,064	146,755	90,789
1996	2,960,104	2,258,581	21,944	2,280,525	256,494	-123,538	1,900,493	533,719	525,892	19,806	149,456	93,362
1997	3,153,221	2,414,215	22,213	2,436,428	274,230	-136,764	2,025,434	570,185	557,602	20,765	151,852	95,844
1998	3,312,203	2,548,530	22,394	2,570,924	289,694	-144,713	2,136,517	599,369	576,317	21,499	154,066	98,516
1999	3,453,584	2,691,431	15,778	2,707,209	303,575	-148,092	2,255,542	589,360	608,682	22,164	155,822	99,452
2000	3,644,622	2,814,860	8,374	2,823,234	313,644	-151,922	2,357,668	635,951	651,003	23,116	157,665	100,269
2001	3,868,582	2,990,232	21,161	3,011,393	329,644	-159,064	2,522,685	613,772	732,125	24,397	158,567	99,129
2002	3,952,846	3,093,119	15,217	3,108,336	337,557	-171,277	2,599,502	566,260	787,084	24,691	160,092	97,882
2003	4,079,369	3,184,352	29,189	3,213,541	349,490	-185,667	2,678,384	573,919	827,066	25,176	162,037	97,822
2004	4,355,831	3,334,132	67,733	3,401,865	365,690	-192,326	2,843,849	647,174	864,808	26,560	163,997	98,482
2005	4,449,738	3,390,422	64,671	3,455,093	379,033	-194,224	2,881,836	635,750	932,152	26,780	166,160	99,545
2006	4,683,422	3,583,209	41,478	3,624,687	404,934	-211,640	3,008,113	698,387	976,922	27,762	168,701	102,127
2007	4,919,754	3,700,049	40,873	3,740,922	424,129	-210,079	3,106,714	760,655	1,052,385	28,733	171,224	105,109
2008	5,285,192	3,823,413	84,755	3,908,168	448,359	-203,106	3,256,703	853,474	1,175,015	30,596	172,744	105,168
2009	5,301,400	3,802,188	49,960	3,852,148	442,032	-186,561	3,223,555	802,051	1,275,794	30,399	174,394	101,995
2010	5,404,894	3,858,842	62,301	3,921,143	442,593	-181,803	3,296,747	758,318	1,349,829	30,733	175,867	100,018
2011	5,728,045	4,011,746	56,888	4,068,634	414,515	-181,436	3,472,683	870,115	1,385,247	32,913	174,037	101,069
2012	6,005,735	4,198,346	59,075	4,257,421	422,429	-173,119	3,661,873	1,000,485	1,343,377	34,367	174,751	102,070
2013	5,934,011	4,268,957	83,666	4,352,623	482,662	-171,531	3,698,430	874,236	1,361,345	33,789	175,622	101,939
2014	6,149,392	4,313,709	125,034	4,438,743	490,214	-135,247	3,813,282	928,380	1,407,730	34,843	176,489	101,464
2015	6,424,783	4,544,672	91,281	4,635,953	516,745	-124,921	3,994,287	956,438	1,474,058	36,206	177,452	101,631
2016	6,559,755	4,616,647	44,404	4,661,051	523,497	-101,973	4,035,581	994,365	1,529,809	36,788	178,314	101,838
2017	6,756,497	4,792,790	34,894	4,827,684	542,487	-112,572	4,172,625	1,011,277	1,572,595	37,696	179,235	102,400
2018	7,091,434	4,918,901	43,458	4,962,359	560,682	-114,998	4,286,679	1,172,343	1,632,412	39,480	179,620	103,643
2019	7,124,655	4,975,229	35,057	5,010,286	581,462	-99,967	4,328,857	1,091,688	1,704,110	39,423	180,723	103,997
2020	7,493,614	4,923,445	52,027	4,975,472	592,170	-74,624	4,308,678	1,070,800	2,114,136	41,273	181,562	100,876
2021	8,021,356	5,196,868	71,813	5,268,681	614,910	-112,766	4,541,005	1,118,686	2,361,665	43,890	182,762	104,525
2022	8,265,543	5,527,055	168,253	5,695,308	669,546	-111,582	4,914,180	1,227,955	2,123,408	44,900	184,086	107,946

Personal Income and Employment by Area: Kahului-Wailuku-Lahaina, HI

(Thousands of dollars, except as noted.)

Year	Personal income, total	Derivation of personal income: Earnings by place of work: Nonfarm	Farm	Total	Less: Contributions for government social insurance	Plus: Adjustment for residence	Equals: Net earnings by place of residence	Plus: Dividends, interest, and rent	Plus: Personal current transfer receipts	Per capita personal income (dollars)	Population (persons)	Total employment
1970	199,508	124,379	37,343	161,722	9,259	33	152,496	31,550	15,462	4,338	45,995	22,016
1971	220,100	135,780	37,904	173,684	10,635	-55	162,994	36,754	20,352	4,250	51,784	22,664
1972	242,138	148,307	39,733	188,040	12,183	-104	175,753	41,218	25,167	4,703	51,488	23,264
1973	268,541	165,033	38,686	203,719	15,878	-219	187,622	50,240	30,679	5,096	52,693	24,568
1974	357,443	191,969	89,294	281,263	19,580	-722	260,961	58,908	37,574	6,661	53,661	26,464
1975	379,559	233,660	54,923	288,583	21,968	-2,371	264,244	66,618	48,697	6,698	56,669	29,157
1976	423,121	269,325	54,157	323,482	25,324	-3,083	295,075	72,317	55,729	7,032	60,173	31,192
1977	475,251	315,645	55,733	371,378	29,810	-4,017	337,551	81,038	56,662	7,572	62,763	33,058
1978	529,548	365,868	47,483	413,351	36,293	-4,767	372,291	95,966	61,291	8,030	65,950	35,880
1979	612,140	424,955	53,938	478,893	43,393	-5,641	429,859	114,847	67,434	8,803	69,537	37,847
1980	733,858	469,621	97,238	566,859	47,270	-6,073	513,516	139,253	81,089	10,246	71,624	39,255
1981	769,352	515,529	51,457	566,986	55,584	-4,128	507,274	166,339	95,739	10,391	74,043	38,790
1982	837,663	569,940	58,659	628,599	62,351	-4,242	562,006	168,868	106,789	10,864	77,103	40,711
1983	979,940	634,055	103,443	737,498	68,462	-3,693	665,343	196,709	117,888	12,240	80,060	43,194
1984	1,037,669	705,774	69,577	775,351	77,922	-3,750	693,679	221,203	122,787	12,507	82,969	44,749
1985	1,126,860	788,252	63,316	851,568	88,160	-4,534	758,874	238,550	129,436	13,234	85,147	48,048
1986	1,227,781	865,151	73,511	938,662	97,650	-4,753	836,259	256,681	134,841	14,050	87,389	50,149
1987	1,324,850	961,975	73,277	1,035,252	108,359	-4,900	921,993	263,901	138,956	14,634	90,532	53,953
1988	1,499,372	1,124,023	66,870	1,190,893	128,164	-5,472	1,057,257	294,201	147,914	15,990	93,767	58,381
1989	1,746,424	1,324,148	60,850	1,384,998	149,806	-8,235	1,226,957	355,532	163,935	18,038	96,819	62,829
1990	1,953,516	1,503,118	67,682	1,570,800	177,004	-9,771	1,384,025	389,076	180,415	19,207	101,709	66,255
1991	2,082,536	1,618,460	67,274	1,685,734	192,438	-10,153	1,483,143	396,309	203,084	19,721	105,599	69,643
1992	2,301,765	1,760,085	97,223	1,857,308	208,876	-9,965	1,638,467	417,662	245,636	21,198	108,585	72,764
1993	2,439,272	1,861,638	57,066	1,918,704	215,201	-9,403	1,694,100	482,999	262,173	21,790	111,944	72,912
1994	2,536,551	1,942,678	58,477	2,001,155	228,246	-10,547	1,762,362	493,331	280,858	22,104	114,754	73,468
1995	2,616,843	1,972,859	59,511	2,032,370	229,713	-9,454	1,793,203	502,258	321,382	22,196	117,895	73,984
1996	2,647,995	1,988,076	56,091	2,044,167	233,397	-10,586	1,800,184	506,095	341,716	21,941	120,689	74,645
1997	2,719,377	2,043,023	57,536	2,100,559	238,101	-10,989	1,851,469	530,159	337,749	22,150	122,772	75,979
1998	2,841,573	2,124,904	65,049	2,189,953	245,746	-12,084	1,932,123	556,194	353,256	22,797	124,648	78,154
1999	3,057,295	2,318,242	70,622	2,388,864	264,067	-14,833	2,109,964	569,164	378,167	24,233	126,160	80,371
2000	3,270,211	2,481,256	62,275	2,543,531	281,362	-16,679	2,245,490	626,151	398,570	25,335	129,078	82,260
2001	3,496,187	2,675,614	66,466	2,742,080	298,538	-14,901	2,428,641	646,487	421,059	26,401	132,428	85,069
2002	3,698,263	2,848,561	72,148	2,920,709	316,633	-12,852	2,591,224	648,054	458,985	27,479	134,583	85,815
2003	3,933,897	3,091,158	73,624	3,164,782	344,379	-10,436	2,809,967	644,724	479,206	28,590	137,596	87,997
2004	4,275,480	3,330,435	78,711	3,409,146	360,486	-8,331	3,040,329	714,613	520,538	30,403	140,625	91,839
2005	4,619,810	3,615,812	85,014	3,700,826	393,405	-7,143	3,300,278	754,840	564,692	32,205	143,448	96,095
2006	4,973,678	3,816,901	95,125	3,912,026	430,725	-4,681	3,476,620	903,811	593,247	34,119	145,776	98,708
2007	5,302,680	3,988,095	94,224	4,082,319	456,965	-2,704	3,622,650	1,022,317	657,713	35,801	148,117	102,898
2008	5,566,786	3,981,191	77,586	4,058,777	453,791	2,028	3,607,014	1,178,338	781,434	36,763	151,424	101,177
2009	5,270,442	3,725,605	76,734	3,802,339	422,418	8,208	3,388,129	1,015,931	866,382	34,359	153,393	94,943
2010	5,478,115	3,745,842	78,758	3,824,600	441,007	13,066	3,396,659	1,099,329	982,127	35,333	155,041	93,937
2011	5,752,810	3,915,205	84,141	3,999,346	422,886	17,763	3,594,223	1,136,941	1,021,646	36,717	156,681	95,095
2012	6,130,493	4,205,537	103,188	4,308,725	444,673	20,948	3,885,000	1,245,962	999,531	38,717	158,340	97,165
2013	6,199,047	4,316,972	104,497	4,421,469	525,446	25,570	3,921,593	1,247,054	1,030,400	38,707	160,153	100,058
2014	6,535,165	4,533,710	88,424	4,622,134	528,654	27,124	4,120,604	1,299,370	1,115,191	40,369	161,887	102,726
2015	6,901,861	4,840,064	73,414	4,913,478	557,575	28,210	4,384,113	1,370,064	1,147,684	42,487	162,447	104,667
2016	7,182,558	5,016,813	58,504	5,075,317	576,551	30,158	4,528,924	1,436,114	1,217,520	43,868	163,731	106,853
2017	7,560,684	5,319,613	33,012	5,352,625	610,176	30,023	4,772,472	1,514,158	1,274,054	46,020	164,291	108,607
2018	7,848,988	5,607,925	20,943	5,628,868	647,826	30,726	5,011,768	1,544,029	1,293,191	47,597	164,904	110,298
2019	8,451,472	6,033,948	16,630	6,050,578	694,158	30,284	5,386,704	1,683,614	1,381,154	51,253	164,897	112,651
2020	8,723,779	5,131,853	23,511	5,155,364	594,772	30,320	4,590,912	1,684,399	2,448,468	52,923	164,840	93,358
2021	9,941,138	6,165,213	28,363	6,193,576	634,103	28,616	5,588,089	1,985,423	2,367,626	60,287	164,898	103,995
2022	9,927,886	6,601,535	26,899	6,628,434	709,097	30,781	5,950,118	2,122,812	1,854,956	60,376	164,433	110,277

Personal Income and Employment by Area: Kalamazoo-Portage, MI

(Thousands of dollars, except as noted.)

Year	Personal income, total	Derivation of personal income: Earnings by place of work: Nonfarm	Farm	Total	Less: Contributions for government social insurance	Plus: Adjustment for residence	Equals: Net earnings by place of residence	Plus: Dividends, interest, and rent	Plus: Personal current transfer receipts	Per capita personal income (dollars)	Population (persons)	Total employment
1970	823,998	730,419	5,429	735,848	52,369	-43,323	640,156	124,293	59,549	4,091	201,415	88,509
1971	867,108	761,462	5,340	766,802	56,310	-44,736	665,756	130,020	71,332	4,302	201,573	87,326
1972	943,128	833,128	7,664	840,792	64,888	-49,728	726,176	137,810	79,142	4,649	202,874	90,162
1973	1,051,739	933,121	12,673	945,794	84,408	-57,810	803,576	155,775	92,388	5,229	201,125	94,661
1974	1,162,709	1,023,040	7,947	1,030,987	95,988	-68,986	866,013	181,472	115,224	5,738	202,616	97,083
1975	1,288,708	1,107,563	12,359	1,119,922	100,960	-78,354	940,608	195,809	152,291	6,326	203,707	97,955
1976	1,414,496	1,238,352	7,263	1,245,615	115,253	-88,729	1,041,633	211,648	161,215	6,869	205,925	100,731
1977	1,583,390	1,410,422	8,886	1,419,308	130,302	-106,182	1,182,824	235,634	164,932	7,631	207,490	105,885
1978	1,758,350	1,581,942	7,670	1,589,612	150,066	-122,135	1,317,411	261,410	179,529	8,411	209,043	110,283
1979	1,950,581	1,775,296	6,316	1,781,612	175,855	-149,002	1,456,755	290,664	203,162	9,276	210,292	112,779
1980	2,133,377	1,880,659	5,990	1,886,649	185,526	-166,177	1,534,946	346,074	252,357	10,034	212,606	111,333
1981	2,356,798	2,037,591	9,662	2,047,253	216,215	-173,717	1,657,321	421,676	277,801	11,062	213,055	110,831
1982	2,473,277	2,076,791	7,539	2,084,330	224,498	-170,316	1,689,516	476,250	307,511	11,588	213,434	108,429
1983	2,657,990	2,225,698	6,374	2,232,072	244,357	-177,903	1,809,812	517,216	330,962	12,512	212,440	108,176
1984	2,891,132	2,420,197	11,785	2,431,982	275,428	-189,922	1,966,632	579,936	344,564	13,574	212,995	111,299
1985	3,086,601	2,594,915	13,327	2,608,242	299,529	-200,514	2,108,199	610,162	368,240	14,407	214,247	114,469
1986	3,317,447	2,783,130	14,946	2,798,076	321,616	-197,399	2,279,061	651,599	386,787	15,343	216,220	118,200
1987	3,532,702	2,984,887	22,244	3,007,131	339,450	-200,785	2,466,896	669,520	396,286	16,154	218,687	123,581
1988	3,840,242	3,289,426	19,283	3,308,709	383,211	-214,767	2,710,731	716,064	413,447	17,346	221,394	128,967
1989	4,217,741	3,523,230	26,437	3,549,667	406,345	-229,909	2,913,413	851,455	452,873	18,944	222,646	134,437
1990	4,349,319	3,629,891	24,855	3,654,746	428,189	-228,764	2,997,793	859,771	491,755	19,421	223,951	135,706
1991	4,568,102	3,816,735	25,014	3,841,749	454,883	-236,881	3,149,985	872,965	545,152	20,301	225,015	137,208
1992	4,802,024	4,025,746	24,293	4,050,039	476,836	-234,231	3,338,972	882,303	580,749	21,132	227,238	138,198
1993	5,054,315	4,230,283	20,747	4,251,030	503,412	-251,440	3,496,178	932,311	625,826	22,024	229,489	141,216
1994	5,326,268	4,410,592	22,327	4,432,919	535,818	-253,155	3,643,946	1,055,054	627,268	23,102	230,556	143,279
1995	5,612,188	4,616,963	27,131	4,644,094	562,645	-268,045	3,813,404	1,097,466	701,318	24,171	232,184	147,040
1996	5,881,616	4,872,611	25,431	4,898,042	581,493	-314,861	4,001,688	1,166,664	713,264	25,143	233,923	148,677
1997	6,067,915	4,979,537	28,534	5,008,071	595,709	-271,189	4,141,173	1,178,526	748,216	25,811	235,090	149,366
1998	6,432,084	5,243,335	30,258	5,273,593	619,032	-244,441	4,410,120	1,278,682	743,282	27,219	236,312	148,671
1999	6,568,728	5,396,176	33,010	5,429,186	632,509	-242,094	4,554,583	1,200,335	813,810	27,648	237,581	149,974
2000	6,837,667	5,546,696	36,657	5,583,353	644,803	-244,327	4,694,223	1,299,795	843,649	28,609	239,008	151,273
2001	7,261,612	5,954,478	37,022	5,991,500	649,242	-270,333	5,071,925	1,241,434	948,253	30,247	240,080	148,422
2002	7,402,574	6,122,915	41,508	6,164,423	671,473	-314,152	5,178,798	1,240,356	983,420	30,597	241,937	147,622
2003	7,572,736	6,333,714	33,477	6,367,191	695,027	-400,363	5,271,801	1,267,475	1,033,460	31,057	243,834	146,658
2004	7,699,846	6,251,400	43,318	6,294,718	704,438	-348,686	5,241,594	1,362,614	1,095,638	31,751	242,505	147,671
2005	7,841,076	6,275,645	37,580	6,313,225	721,649	-349,358	5,242,218	1,431,751	1,167,107	32,233	243,259	148,848
2006	8,251,508	6,459,678	44,379	6,504,057	754,375	-276,143	5,473,539	1,524,038	1,253,931	33,793	244,178	149,362
2007	8,522,092	6,623,114	43,330	6,666,444	779,569	-276,583	5,610,292	1,537,920	1,373,880	34,723	245,431	150,994
2008	9,099,660	6,819,698	43,986	6,863,684	809,606	-207,277	5,846,801	1,679,728	1,573,131	36,861	246,862	148,548
2009	8,954,467	6,571,473	47,091	6,618,564	784,158	-212,131	5,622,275	1,608,906	1,723,286	35,958	249,023	143,336
2010	9,171,016	6,689,094	62,691	6,751,785	782,834	-187,646	5,781,305	1,529,170	1,860,541	36,588	250,654	140,774
2011	9,771,583	6,894,194	81,583	6,975,777	716,025	-188,724	6,071,028	1,818,813	1,881,742	38,756	252,131	141,485
2012	10,154,478	7,187,380	61,980	7,249,360	747,184	-206,441	6,295,735	2,009,838	1,848,905	39,900	254,498	143,342
2013	10,397,710	7,439,392	63,346	7,502,738	878,818	-201,431	6,422,489	2,085,277	1,889,944	40,605	256,069	145,780
2014	10,693,687	7,552,335	46,715	7,599,050	895,468	-171,666	6,531,916	2,205,397	1,956,374	41,559	257,316	147,919
2015	11,329,402	8,002,142	51,332	8,053,474	939,453	-196,030	6,917,991	2,323,730	2,087,681	43,971	257,654	150,357
2016	11,776,346	8,322,238	54,165	8,376,403	973,285	-150,977	7,252,141	2,383,671	2,140,534	45,469	258,996	153,182
2017	12,088,777	8,786,563	59,322	8,845,885	1,018,582	-252,189	7,575,114	2,369,298	2,144,365	46,430	260,368	155,474
2018	12,650,367	9,178,822	58,295	9,237,117	1,075,948	-283,469	7,877,700	2,526,080	2,246,587	48,346	261,663	158,154
2019	13,117,606	9,612,186	58,736	9,670,922	1,117,458	-443,459	8,110,005	2,640,585	2,367,016	50,134	261,653	158,218
2020	14,349,521	9,633,055	81,463	9,714,518	1,103,783	-368,854	8,241,881	2,804,267	3,303,373	54,818	261,767	150,793
2021	15,326,372	10,480,164	86,057	10,566,221	1,193,259	-417,147	8,955,815	2,898,622	3,471,935	58,792	260,688	155,514
2022	15,570,936	11,238,510	84,124	11,322,634	1,315,941	-438,617	9,568,076	3,144,298	2,858,562	59,619	261,173	162,853

Personal Income and Employment by Area: Kankakee, IL

(Thousands of dollars, except as noted.)

Year	Personal income, total	Derivation of personal income: Earnings by place of work: Nonfarm	Farm	Total	Less: Contributions for government social insurance	Plus: Adjustment for residence	Equals: Net earnings by place of residence	Plus: Dividends, interest, and rent	Plus: Personal current transfer receipts	Per capita personal income (dollars)	Population (persons)	Total employment
1970	374,165	287,108	11,263	298,371	19,044	13,017	292,344	50,444	31,377	3,844	97,342	39,706
1971	414,326	310,688	18,119	328,807	21,318	14,675	322,164	54,359	37,803	4,200	98,659	40,376
1972	449,044	341,706	12,309	354,015	24,795	16,894	346,114	60,005	42,925	4,504	99,695	40,906
1973	513,219	373,462	30,151	403,613	31,456	19,694	391,851	68,386	52,982	5,166	99,351	42,692
1974	553,924	405,097	23,455	428,552	35,238	22,246	415,560	77,069	61,295	5,551	99,787	43,581
1975	607,935	412,224	36,404	448,628	34,949	26,458	440,137	87,154	80,644	6,080	99,990	42,589
1976	653,633	445,681	30,555	476,236	38,528	32,936	470,644	92,157	90,832	6,507	100,458	42,763
1977	719,099	491,423	30,958	522,381	42,611	39,799	519,569	101,895	97,635	7,076	101,619	44,000
1978	791,542	545,425	27,246	572,671	48,497	49,309	573,483	112,909	105,150	7,683	103,025	45,063
1979	865,013	584,871	33,924	618,795	54,028	58,966	623,733	125,832	115,448	8,298	104,238	44,868
1980	924,781	607,234	10,574	617,808	55,847	64,991	626,952	157,870	139,959	8,988	102,886	43,027
1981	1,038,357	651,774	27,418	679,192	64,401	66,403	681,194	194,484	162,679	10,126	102,544	43,280
1982	1,082,194	654,843	18,876	673,719	65,026	67,399	676,092	224,990	181,112	10,692	101,218	41,632
1983	1,093,474	667,295	-1,245	666,050	66,316	68,982	668,716	226,406	198,352	10,983	99,560	40,857
1984	1,181,576	698,087	24,129	722,216	71,530	79,457	730,143	251,124	200,309	11,994	98,513	41,023
1985	1,219,050	723,948	29,777	753,725	75,637	83,448	761,536	252,018	205,496	12,562	97,039	41,045
1986	1,266,287	758,244	28,807	787,051	79,429	87,192	794,814	259,465	212,008	13,201	95,926	41,221
1987	1,323,239	815,370	25,452	840,822	84,303	91,790	848,309	258,549	216,381	13,828	95,692	42,154
1988	1,405,980	867,158	33,595	900,753	92,654	99,526	907,625	270,253	228,102	14,725	95,481	42,337
1989	1,507,492	911,043	43,751	954,794	98,324	105,489	961,959	302,776	242,757	15,767	95,611	42,756
1990	1,641,199	1,012,318	60,016	1,072,334	106,983	103,992	1,069,343	306,821	265,035	16,997	96,560	45,566
1991	1,666,431	1,055,434	38,170	1,093,604	114,440	107,255	1,086,419	295,043	284,969	17,074	97,598	47,700
1992	1,789,267	1,122,429	42,895	1,165,324	119,928	115,052	1,160,448	303,766	325,053	18,034	99,215	45,999
1993	1,895,584	1,215,709	50,451	1,266,160	131,719	114,605	1,249,046	308,726	337,812	18,812	100,766	47,610
1994	1,995,066	1,294,961	53,546	1,348,507	142,625	120,356	1,326,238	322,567	346,261	19,610	101,736	50,134
1995	2,126,410	1,387,561	35,545	1,423,106	153,522	120,890	1,390,474	362,307	373,629	20,863	101,923	52,190
1996	2,225,382	1,418,261	52,412	1,470,673	154,895	133,964	1,449,742	384,042	391,598	21,754	102,296	51,612
1997	2,285,900	1,465,262	30,408	1,495,670	159,395	148,634	1,484,909	399,538	401,453	22,204	102,951	52,245
1998	2,366,327	1,512,696	21,850	1,534,546	163,146	169,291	1,540,691	416,505	409,131	22,925	103,222	53,006
1999	2,447,290	1,592,738	18,531	1,611,269	168,868	189,759	1,632,160	399,492	415,638	23,605	103,675	53,241
2000	2,611,906	1,687,502	28,639	1,716,141	175,943	208,469	1,748,667	427,426	435,813	25,153	103,842	54,118
2001	2,737,896	1,751,718	23,880	1,775,598	182,946	237,350	1,830,002	439,432	468,462	26,202	104,490	53,784
2002	2,813,172	1,820,724	15,438	1,836,162	189,726	247,973	1,894,409	412,054	506,709	26,809	104,932	52,858
2003	2,887,129	1,826,215	15,862	1,842,077	191,727	268,528	1,918,878	433,872	534,379	27,290	105,794	52,114
2004	2,976,896	1,876,822	49,132	1,925,954	201,095	295,713	2,020,572	399,629	556,695	27,888	106,744	52,381
2005	3,103,864	1,945,361	34,536	1,979,897	214,497	337,633	2,103,033	382,309	618,522	28,762	107,917	53,554
2006	3,288,763	2,045,348	37,872	2,083,220	225,313	366,978	2,224,885	420,736	643,142	29,970	109,735	54,878
2007	3,491,279	2,106,133	75,198	2,181,331	234,870	384,807	2,331,268	454,671	705,340	31,312	111,499	55,454
2008	3,683,079	2,150,577	102,822	2,253,399	240,695	374,008	2,386,712	523,232	773,135	32,693	112,658	55,182
2009	3,625,673	2,134,984	69,549	2,204,533	236,167	293,261	2,261,627	492,262	871,784	32,055	113,107	54,090
2010	3,715,019	2,168,937	55,745	2,224,682	238,600	320,112	2,306,194	471,142	937,683	32,764	113,387	53,687
2011	3,829,690	2,238,478	88,672	2,327,150	223,702	323,003	2,426,451	500,072	903,167	33,782	113,365	53,600
2012	3,877,978	2,358,386	53,342	2,411,728	237,239	268,961	2,443,450	532,416	902,112	34,412	112,694	54,821
2013	4,010,059	2,431,878	117,347	2,549,225	270,057	275,787	2,554,955	527,898	927,206	35,699	112,329	55,127
2014	4,025,549	2,499,434	62,585	2,562,019	277,949	252,896	2,536,966	549,427	939,156	36,152	111,352	55,372
2015	4,155,491	2,585,645	29,798	2,615,443	284,475	265,533	2,596,501	555,025	1,003,965	37,407	111,089	55,580
2016	4,239,464	2,607,029	57,684	2,664,713	289,959	261,900	2,636,654	595,852	1,006,958	38,456	110,241	55,166
2017	4,335,776	2,723,613	25,425	2,749,038	305,194	257,612	2,701,456	587,766	1,046,554	39,568	109,578	56,551
2018	4,504,357	2,814,286	39,528	2,853,814	316,034	281,028	2,818,808	612,840	1,072,709	41,405	108,787	56,318
2019	4,673,932	2,952,354	36,624	2,988,978	331,157	259,165	2,916,986	644,937	1,112,009	43,131	108,365	56,394
2020	5,085,534	2,988,259	52,803	3,041,062	335,212	248,260	2,954,110	643,305	1,488,119	47,418	107,250	54,495
2021	5,513,016	3,115,904	104,050	3,219,954	343,519	294,199	3,170,634	678,892	1,663,490	51,692	106,652	54,557
2022	5,414,861	3,140,765	113,422	3,254,187	366,777	395,070	3,282,480	728,319	1,404,062	51,048	106,074	55,949

Personal Income and Employment by Area: Kansas City, MO-KS

(Thousands of dollars, except as noted.)

Year	Personal income, total	Derivation of personal income								Per capita personal income (dollars)	Population (persons)	Total employment
		Earnings by place of work			Less: Contributions for government social insurance	Plus: Adjustment for residence	Equals: Net earnings by place of residence	Plus: Dividends, interest, and rent	Plus: Personal current transfer receipts			
		Nonfarm	Farm	Total								
1970	6,169,809	5,158,197	69,514	5,227,711	347,962	-33,526	4,846,223	879,775	443,811	4,346	1,419,593	674,424
1971	6,725,331	5,595,335	73,673	5,669,008	390,806	-34,424	5,243,778	965,919	515,634	4,695	1,432,356	679,124
1972	7,371,520	6,140,083	96,596	6,236,679	452,442	-35,334	5,748,903	1,054,654	567,963	5,120	1,439,848	697,223
1973	8,099,191	6,738,317	139,328	6,877,645	574,782	-36,305	6,266,558	1,168,589	664,044	5,568	1,454,634	727,985
1974	8,769,756	7,240,121	70,030	7,310,151	637,906	-33,670	6,638,575	1,352,257	778,924	6,044	1,450,974	734,327
1975	9,649,950	7,825,073	73,351	7,898,424	677,428	-37,882	7,183,114	1,474,431	992,405	6,684	1,443,816	727,345
1976	10,609,345	8,742,798	50,836	8,793,634	772,971	-44,874	7,975,789	1,575,007	1,058,549	7,306	1,452,126	751,366
1977	11,816,254	9,797,017	83,989	9,881,006	861,914	-55,016	8,964,076	1,738,988	1,113,190	8,120	1,455,117	776,160
1978	13,124,062	10,954,612	94,470	11,049,082	996,230	-61,952	9,990,900	1,941,426	1,191,736	8,935	1,468,792	807,453
1979	14,672,650	12,193,464	153,550	12,347,014	1,149,435	-70,298	11,127,281	2,198,870	1,346,499	9,943	1,475,676	828,859
1980	16,050,773	13,021,290	7,307	13,028,597	1,224,137	-76,412	11,728,048	2,686,140	1,636,585	10,814	1,484,234	821,393
1981	17,639,346	13,876,092	99,884	13,975,976	1,399,849	-83,329	12,492,798	3,268,427	1,878,121	11,840	1,489,775	814,405
1982	18,914,734	14,519,770	34,995	14,554,765	1,495,497	-87,283	12,971,985	3,879,220	2,063,529	12,656	1,494,551	808,137
1983	20,017,009	15,482,528	-19,609	15,462,919	1,612,417	-92,196	13,758,306	4,096,603	2,162,100	13,321	1,502,652	812,620
1984	22,207,470	17,270,105	12,963	17,283,068	1,846,369	-93,130	15,343,569	4,605,825	2,258,076	14,622	1,518,797	856,338
1985	24,055,955	18,816,530	107,515	18,924,045	2,056,544	-137,357	16,730,144	4,929,000	2,396,811	15,658	1,536,347	889,683
1986	25,593,015	20,192,538	68,334	20,260,872	2,220,942	-159,229	17,880,701	5,160,329	2,551,985	16,464	1,554,473	916,814
1987	27,096,706	21,620,669	75,366	21,696,035	2,345,522	-174,089	19,176,424	5,256,506	2,663,776	17,187	1,576,591	941,024
1988	28,900,759	22,922,233	69,250	22,991,483	2,566,560	-181,644	20,243,279	5,791,611	2,865,869	18,131	1,593,958	960,486
1989	30,743,294	24,223,330	103,879	24,327,209	2,711,475	-182,651	21,433,083	6,223,723	3,086,488	19,182	1,602,744	975,387
1990	32,208,701	25,380,669	55,057	25,435,726	2,964,632	-225,927	22,245,167	6,612,442	3,351,092	19,895	1,618,905	985,056
1991	33,783,750	26,428,389	23,415	26,451,804	3,126,474	-242,345	23,082,985	6,896,505	3,804,260	20,644	1,636,516	981,595
1992	36,216,216	28,549,610	103,864	28,653,474	3,342,084	-286,900	25,024,490	7,035,569	4,156,157	21,905	1,653,327	988,989
1993	38,045,424	30,125,270	34,715	30,159,985	3,523,700	-308,698	26,327,587	7,267,302	4,450,535	22,728	1,673,964	1,013,149
1994	40,303,315	31,940,776	89,670	32,030,446	3,772,849	-361,296	27,896,301	7,727,821	4,679,193	23,792	1,693,952	1,037,813
1995	42,618,344	33,740,224	7,622	33,747,846	3,955,817	-392,203	29,399,826	8,208,225	5,010,293	24,914	1,710,587	1,069,637
1996	45,217,679	35,806,521	121,449	35,927,970	4,151,627	-442,821	31,333,522	8,617,057	5,267,100	26,086	1,733,398	1,093,386
1997	48,024,726	38,174,909	111,615	38,286,524	4,413,127	-498,104	33,375,293	9,268,160	5,381,273	27,341	1,756,537	1,131,838
1998	51,522,608	41,143,594	64,375	41,207,969	4,716,704	-557,056	35,934,209	10,049,126	5,539,273	28,995	1,776,976	1,162,276
1999	54,251,638	44,255,862	36,660	44,292,522	5,060,339	-635,431	38,596,752	9,858,607	5,796,279	30,195	1,796,711	1,182,542
2000	58,228,713	47,485,220	61,218	47,546,438	5,395,456	-719,949	41,431,033	10,584,195	6,213,485	32,030	1,817,929	1,202,207
2001	58,591,252	47,439,060	91,953	47,531,013	5,572,852	-733,621	41,224,540	10,528,211	6,838,501	31,886	1,837,551	1,208,113
2002	60,034,692	48,925,164	20,077	48,945,241	5,714,888	-742,120	42,488,233	10,263,503	7,282,956	32,298	1,858,778	1,200,016
2003	61,403,773	49,820,471	75,208	49,895,679	5,866,579	-755,741	43,273,359	10,513,040	7,617,374	32,746	1,875,142	1,198,511
2004	63,202,425	51,332,440	240,333	51,572,773	6,121,423	-743,627	44,707,723	10,518,530	7,976,172	33,403	1,892,097	1,214,816
2005	66,276,649	53,869,913	134,124	54,004,037	6,378,843	-769,127	46,856,067	10,924,126	8,496,456	34,710	1,909,428	1,233,750
2006	72,887,542	58,764,047	80,356	58,844,403	6,749,546	-788,947	51,305,910	12,448,125	9,133,507	37,731	1,931,764	1,255,242
2007	78,129,396	62,280,656	117,115	62,397,771	7,086,207	-830,415	54,481,149	13,785,627	9,862,620	39,970	1,954,688	1,286,688
2008	84,059,131	65,110,764	167,668	65,278,432	7,406,398	-840,534	57,031,500	15,682,895	11,344,736	42,586	1,973,888	1,288,954
2009	82,541,908	64,394,998	172,830	64,567,828	7,271,080	-645,469	56,651,279	13,601,858	12,288,771	41,378	1,994,834	1,254,505
2010	83,317,606	64,172,768	121,846	64,294,614	7,303,861	-569,241	56,421,512	13,644,694	13,251,400	41,371	2,013,908	1,237,307
2011	87,740,509	66,200,654	205,163	66,405,817	6,701,438	-488,879	59,215,500	15,046,121	13,478,888	43,258	2,028,300	1,254,964
2012	93,075,136	70,986,617	119,286	71,105,903	6,975,573	-394,001	63,736,329	15,797,496	13,541,311	45,545	2,043,597	1,269,582
2013	94,735,433	73,729,478	249,521	73,978,999	8,132,209	-289,361	65,557,429	15,299,197	13,878,807	45,963	2,061,129	1,288,921
2014	97,979,650	75,689,127	211,102	75,900,229	8,458,120	-310,961	67,131,148	16,386,402	14,462,100	47,134	2,078,737	1,313,945
2015	103,085,433	79,620,510	-7,117	79,613,393	8,989,027	-373,240	70,251,126	17,617,436	15,216,871	49,140	2,097,773	1,342,615
2016	105,207,114	80,405,740	84,429	80,490,169	9,064,136	-295,338	71,130,695	18,270,813	15,805,606	49,597	2,121,223	1,367,858
2017	109,564,331	83,988,333	99,792	84,088,125	9,396,376	-332,575	74,359,174	18,882,609	16,322,548	51,103	2,143,999	1,386,138
2018	114,270,273	87,259,339	51,979	87,311,318	9,835,823	-408,883	77,066,612	20,122,439	17,081,222	52,798	2,164,286	1,406,699
2019	118,942,322	90,830,708	121,816	90,952,524	10,255,649	-466,312	80,230,563	20,746,419	17,965,340	54,550	2,180,431	1,411,457
2020	126,055,304	91,984,379	215,218	92,199,597	10,568,981	-370,929	81,259,687	21,504,178	23,291,439	57,427	2,195,043	1,378,941
2021	133,739,172	96,258,817	282,813	96,541,630	11,109,030	-389,226	85,043,374	22,607,789	26,088,009	60,710	2,202,933	1,419,489
2022	140,119,784	105,377,659	191,797	105,569,456	12,213,865	-460,838	92,894,753	24,682,746	22,542,285	63,417	2,209,494	1,475,718

Personal Income and Employment by Area: Kennewick-Richland, WA

(Thousands of dollars, except as noted.)

Year	Personal income, total	Derivation of personal income: Earnings by place of work: Nonfarm	Farm	Total	Less: Contributions for government social insurance	Plus: Adjustment for residence	Equals: Net earnings by place of residence	Plus: Dividends, interest, and rent	Plus: Personal current transfer receipts	Per capita personal income (dollars)	Population (persons)	Total employment
1970	382,393	297,502	25,178	322,680	24,115	553	299,118	49,341	33,934	4,090	93,499	40,817
1971	403,538	308,377	26,738	335,115	26,085	119	309,149	54,984	39,405	4,289	94,080	40,315
1972	451,875	341,910	38,957	380,867	30,826	-1,475	348,566	61,045	42,264	4,753	95,067	41,832
1973	523,780	392,533	57,633	450,166	41,352	-4,858	403,956	73,021	46,803	5,501	95,211	44,867
1974	634,502	471,785	84,601	556,386	51,670	-8,891	495,825	84,289	54,388	6,431	98,666	49,005
1975	764,899	594,964	84,272	679,236	65,038	-16,353	597,845	100,652	66,402	7,282	105,045	54,232
1976	857,709	684,978	79,488	764,466	75,583	-18,344	670,539	112,492	74,678	7,601	112,838	58,982
1977	1,001,877	868,960	50,060	919,020	96,883	-33,539	788,598	134,023	79,256	8,375	119,629	64,042
1978	1,228,865	1,084,451	72,695	1,157,146	124,589	-49,876	982,681	160,140	86,044	9,510	129,214	71,236
1979	1,418,632	1,281,988	58,472	1,340,460	152,526	-59,727	1,128,207	191,301	99,124	10,285	137,929	77,504
1980	1,594,758	1,349,092	107,312	1,456,404	159,895	-62,359	1,234,150	232,324	128,284	10,959	145,515	78,001
1981	1,881,374	1,675,968	95,127	1,771,095	217,248	-104,700	1,449,147	283,356	148,871	12,591	149,418	82,905
1982	1,950,590	1,663,589	87,982	1,751,571	216,889	-89,311	1,445,371	322,441	182,778	12,742	153,079	77,676
1983	1,990,312	1,632,158	93,703	1,725,861	210,908	-68,500	1,446,453	342,902	200,957	13,325	149,371	74,772
1984	1,976,987	1,513,389	126,040	1,639,429	199,586	-45,382	1,394,461	369,697	212,829	13,410	147,429	71,264
1985	2,006,096	1,578,698	71,484	1,650,182	210,827	-47,764	1,391,591	390,515	223,990	13,703	146,400	72,013
1986	2,102,247	1,629,793	98,519	1,728,312	218,866	-45,946	1,463,500	401,047	237,700	14,345	146,551	72,890
1987	2,170,881	1,681,752	105,728	1,787,480	225,286	-45,205	1,516,989	403,369	250,523	14,713	147,547	76,282
1988	2,241,009	1,711,011	123,261	1,834,272	236,351	-44,705	1,553,216	411,305	276,488	15,271	146,750	76,763
1989	2,394,583	1,785,798	123,374	1,909,172	246,957	-40,653	1,621,562	474,220	298,801	16,388	146,117	78,677
1990	2,632,662	2,030,622	127,930	2,158,552	286,225	-48,263	1,824,064	479,999	328,599	17,397	151,331	84,264
1991	2,881,150	2,210,477	116,961	2,327,438	315,115	-22,007	1,990,316	509,461	381,373	18,470	155,993	86,871
1992	3,203,273	2,469,799	144,861	2,614,660	349,838	-23,399	2,241,423	541,391	420,459	19,812	161,680	89,400
1993	3,555,991	2,714,808	217,013	2,931,821	377,536	-24,295	2,529,990	575,615	450,386	21,157	168,075	93,769
1994	3,823,435	3,008,774	186,200	3,194,974	429,446	-30,291	2,735,237	612,996	475,202	21,854	174,957	100,015
1995	3,904,963	2,971,296	215,708	3,187,004	428,019	-22,365	2,736,620	652,165	516,178	21,634	180,501	97,934
1996	4,045,974	2,948,025	281,136	3,229,161	416,240	-14,156	2,798,765	691,770	555,439	22,279	181,605	97,910
1997	4,142,014	3,025,474	226,829	3,252,303	411,766	-10,146	2,830,391	732,362	579,261	22,522	183,909	98,810
1998	4,351,583	3,185,984	244,470	3,430,454	433,364	870	2,997,960	747,153	606,470	23,359	186,290	98,097
1999	4,548,943	3,392,668	221,052	3,613,720	446,774	8,716	3,175,662	718,541	654,740	24,065	189,025	101,094
2000	4,890,529	3,585,883	263,398	3,849,281	481,824	15,860	3,383,317	770,531	736,681	25,380	192,696	102,447
2001	5,278,590	3,919,513	252,573	4,172,086	509,989	16,490	3,678,587	774,771	825,232	26,874	196,420	106,138
2002	5,581,107	4,261,385	279,452	4,540,837	561,755	16,934	3,996,016	732,903	852,188	27,535	202,688	109,060
2003	5,983,903	4,514,280	358,271	4,872,551	593,046	24,403	4,303,908	761,260	918,735	28,625	209,043	111,933
2004	6,322,975	4,863,863	313,785	5,177,648	640,369	26,147	4,563,426	814,997	944,552	29,567	213,854	113,664
2005	6,563,549	5,047,923	319,340	5,367,263	667,941	29,302	4,728,624	813,368	1,021,557	29,959	219,086	116,263
2006	6,794,094	5,097,079	352,451	5,449,530	671,020	46,573	4,825,083	867,552	1,101,459	30,311	224,149	117,442
2007	7,513,634	5,529,159	403,746	5,932,905	728,068	46,527	5,251,364	1,056,842	1,205,428	32,774	229,255	123,033
2008	8,240,444	5,946,073	330,036	6,276,109	778,606	51,403	5,548,906	1,278,524	1,413,014	34,719	237,348	127,072
2009	8,771,182	6,397,318	359,206	6,756,524	848,164	43,543	5,951,903	1,252,767	1,566,512	35,713	245,600	129,449
2010	9,598,473	7,123,554	384,500	7,508,054	912,294	34,274	6,630,034	1,235,153	1,733,286	37,558	255,562	134,759
2011	10,275,917	7,381,474	494,505	7,875,979	855,530	29,508	7,049,957	1,458,607	1,767,353	38,984	263,591	137,298
2012	10,164,960	7,037,065	510,503	7,547,568	809,073	72,315	6,810,810	1,529,981	1,824,169	37,891	268,265	138637
2013	10,129,944	7,069,037	564,943	7,633,980	924,754	83,075	6,792,301	1,484,034	1,853,609	37,372	271,056	139,042
2014	10,510,853	7,287,176	474,029	7,761,205	962,551	91,262	6,889,916	1,569,247	2,051,690	38,289	274,511	141,351
2015	11,343,008	7,808,475	720,400	8,528,875	1,018,656	75,657	7,585,876	1,661,590	2,095,542	40,600	279,386	145,217
2016	11,724,423	8,119,442	587,979	8,707,421	1,055,993	83,288	7,734,716	1,768,539	2,221,168	41,251	284,221	148,489
2017	12,150,686	8,504,407	527,607	9,032,014	1,120,062	68,755	7,980,707	1,865,615	2,304,364	41,806	290,646	151,721
2018	12,613,510	8,990,902	360,808	9,351,710	1,165,410	77,030	8,263,330	1,930,480	2,419,700	42,637	295,833	155,999
2019	13,537,299	9,518,597	487,586	10,006,183	1,198,524	68,808	8,876,467	2,078,085	2,582,747	45,061	300,422	159,710
2020	14,647,817	9,895,419	472,420	10,367,839	1,255,608	82,446	9,194,677	2,048,359	3,404,781	48,096	304,556	155,166
2021	16,101,713	10,606,549	422,462	11,029,011	1,329,042	81,786	9,781,755	2,318,427	4,001,531	52,158	308,711	161,440
2022	16,133,676	11,238,198	466,798	11,704,996	1,465,461	110,001	10,349,536	2,449,143	3,334,997	51,799	311,469	168,918

Personal Income and Employment by Area: Killeen-Temple, TX

(Thousands of dollars, except as noted.)

Year	Personal income, total	Derivation of personal income								Per capita personal income (dollars)	Population (persons)	Total employment
		Earnings by place of work			Less: Contributions for government social insurance	Plus: Adjustment for residence	Equals: Net earnings by place of residence	Plus: Dividends, interest, and rent	Plus: Personal current transfer receipts			
		Nonfarm	Farm	Total								
1970	748,345	597,282	6,948	604,230	36,662	-13,348	554,220	153,901	40,224	4,410	169,695	89,828
1971	809,895	650,281	5,616	655,897	42,553	-12,151	601,193	161,896	46,806	4,644	174,387	90,083
1972	983,904	790,808	10,687	801,495	51,897	-13,039	736,559	193,728	53,617	5,081	193,630	97,294
1973	1,137,414	888,878	26,109	914,987	62,086	-3,559	849,342	224,455	63,617	5,248	216,716	102,623
1974	1,257,555	989,954	5,656	995,610	72,599	819	923,830	259,042	74,683	5,669	221,833	106,605
1975	1,410,652	1,101,052	6,746	1,107,798	85,600	-2,353	1,019,845	297,248	93,559	6,380	221,119	110,740
1976	1,567,438	1,225,124	4,861	1,229,985	97,634	4,614	1,136,965	326,238	104,235	6,819	229,880	115,223
1977	1,669,358	1,299,360	-4,065	1,295,295	102,590	5,241	1,197,946	358,650	112,762	7,180	232,517	117,302
1978	1,862,386	1,427,039	2,093	1,429,132	111,551	-204	1,317,377	419,298	125,711	7,859	236,961	120,403
1979	1,899,492	1,442,481	2,644	1,445,125	118,080	3,477	1,330,522	422,017	146,953	8,162	232,714	114,795
1980	2,157,297	1,621,366	-3,352	1,618,014	132,995	8,282	1,493,301	489,234	174,762	9,464	227,951	117,723
1981	2,450,737	1,858,642	8,900	1,867,542	159,975	-13,481	1,694,086	558,225	198,426	10,531	232,715	121,283
1982	2,678,055	2,018,611	6,046	2,024,657	170,762	-14,745	1,839,150	620,225	218,680	11,203	239,048	121,716
1983	2,888,459	2,163,268	-2,144	2,161,124	188,938	-13,979	1,958,207	689,296	240,956	11,923	242,252	122,761
1984	3,122,281	2,335,619	439	2,336,058	209,963	-11,974	2,114,121	749,831	258,329	12,760	244,697	126,897
1985	3,359,034	2,498,086	-5,052	2,493,034	228,543	-12,639	2,251,852	823,862	283,320	13,295	252,645	131,716
1986	3,539,625	2,633,785	-6,190	2,627,595	243,038	-18,992	2,365,565	866,538	307,522	13,969	253,385	133,296
1987	3,655,275	2,713,229	2,846	2,716,075	250,254	-23,820	2,442,001	883,844	329,430	14,075	259,706	137,444
1988	3,888,299	2,903,587	442	2,904,029	283,667	-28,334	2,592,028	938,787	357,484	14,820	262,373	139,949
1989	4,048,603	2,965,417	7,253	2,972,670	296,528	-28,094	2,648,048	1,003,981	396,574	15,194	266,463	140,155
1990	4,169,303	3,070,759	4,510	3,075,269	310,506	-32,843	2,731,920	990,139	447,244	15,470	269,515	139,118
1991	4,068,039	2,944,663	9,484	2,954,147	303,482	-21,645	2,629,020	950,486	488,533	15,313	265,657	128,838
1992	4,715,687	3,450,897	9,043	3,459,940	361,663	-27,040	3,071,237	1,059,977	584,473	17,419	270,722	139,350
1993	5,245,305	3,874,091	9,453	3,883,544	411,515	-31,496	3,440,533	1,182,403	622,369	18,302	286,593	151,294
1994	5,701,932	4,238,387	7,485	4,245,872	444,099	-32,735	3,769,038	1,287,859	645,035	18,520	307,884	162,733
1995	6,034,992	4,453,068	-73	4,452,995	458,481	-26,274	3,968,240	1,365,388	701,364	19,267	313,222	169,153
1996	6,310,586	4,600,007	2,812	4,602,819	473,084	-10,976	4,118,759	1,439,552	752,275	19,806	318,613	170,885
1997	6,480,295	4,776,377	2,363	4,778,740	487,424	13,395	4,304,711	1,378,460	797,124	20,136	321,821	172,991
1998	6,949,414	5,016,445	-5,193	5,011,252	506,799	47,122	4,551,575	1,559,290	838,549	21,361	325,335	176,092
1999	7,439,656	5,343,100	10,188	5,353,288	535,396	90,303	4,908,195	1,647,583	883,878	22,858	325,473	179,581
2000	7,858,623	5,625,492	5,480	5,630,972	561,098	117,911	5,187,785	1,694,089	976,749	23,600	332,989	182,507
2001	8,378,706	6,092,130	4,920	6,097,050	602,166	95,123	5,590,007	1,701,072	1,087,627	24,906	336,409	181,905
2002	8,982,426	6,534,185	8,839	6,543,024	644,479	50,034	5,948,579	1,842,074	1,191,773	26,324	341,231	184,094
2003	9,662,647	7,083,775	24,499	7,108,274	701,288	28,910	6,435,896	1,897,613	1,329,138	28,182	342,865	185,272
2004	10,172,282	7,466,787	27,503	7,494,290	746,224	20,243	6,768,309	1,992,282	1,411,691	29,085	349,745	187,503
2005	11,162,044	8,251,624	23,348	8,274,972	821,553	4,312	7,457,731	2,154,480	1,549,833	31,220	357,533	194,938
2006	12,291,303	9,243,700	20,136	9,263,836	916,704	-21,941	8,325,191	2,297,220	1,668,892	33,632	365,460	203,768
2007	13,509,113	10,083,435	2,717	10,086,152	1,003,190	-38,241	9,044,721	2,605,986	1,858,406	35,475	380,804	214,008
2008	14,733,344	10,936,605	-33,981	10,902,624	1,094,524	-82,267	9,725,833	2,862,830	2,144,681	37,562	392,237	222,204
2009	15,147,019	11,307,830	-41,034	11,266,796	1,163,757	-127,872	9,975,167	2,905,677	2,266,175	38,311	395,375	220,672
2010	15,517,098	11,365,741	-26,490	11,339,251	1,178,620	-140,604	10,020,027	2,882,226	2,614,845	37,987	408,489	216,552
2011	16,326,169	11,693,412	-29,472	11,663,940	1,105,882	-174,059	10,383,999	3,156,653	2,785,517	39,487	413,454	219,858
2012	16,476,532	11,653,993	-5,852	11,648,141	1,110,608	-176,562	10,360,971	3,279,186	2,836,375	38,724	425,485	219,552
2013	16,110,316	11,468,400	-1,468	11,466,932	1,209,693	-202,764	10,054,475	3,059,133	2,996,708	37,750	426,759	218,869
2014	16,534,277	11,614,318	-4,097	11,610,221	1,225,995	-211,652	10,172,574	3,176,105	3,185,598	38,443	430,099	219,268
2015	17,282,057	12,093,202	5,893	12,099,095	1,294,211	-221,563	10,583,321	3,195,996	3,502,740	39,533	437,152	224,810
2016	17,386,496	12,103,189	-22,770	12,080,419	1,300,237	-206,348	10,573,834	3,129,000	3,683,662	39,355	441,790	225,402
2017	18,298,056	12,642,146	-31,956	12,610,190	1,362,499	-202,427	11,045,264	3,354,687	3,898,105	40,744	449,098	230,613
2018	18,860,188	12,987,431	-34,250	12,953,181	1,389,404	-181,811	11,381,966	3,326,126	4,152,096	41,167	458,143	232,799
2019	19,622,175	13,516,208	-32,096	13,484,112	1,434,310	-162,970	11,886,832	3,313,716	4,421,627	41,829	469,109	235,542
2020	21,456,685	14,017,089	-20,299	13,996,790	1,506,998	-160,330	12,329,462	3,469,306	5,657,917	44,975	477,082	238,021
2021	23,598,554	14,983,966	-27,179	14,956,787	1,577,540	-159,141	13,220,106	3,651,949	6,726,499	48,471	486,860	246,389
2022	23,660,068	15,713,401	-56,142	15,657,259	1,678,772	-144,797	13,833,690	3,847,765	5,978,613	47,680	496,228	254,618

Personal Income and Employment by Area: Kingsport-Bristol, TN-VA

(Thousands of dollars, except as noted.)

Year	Personal income, total	Derivation of personal income: Earnings by place of work: Nonfarm	Farm	Total	Less: Contributions for government social insurance	Plus: Adjustment for residence	Equals: Net earnings by place of residence	Plus: Dividends, interest, and rent	Plus: Personal current transfer receipts	Per capita personal income (dollars)	Population (persons)	Total employment
1970	756,289	657,355	19,281	676,636	43,978	-29,013	603,645	83,145	69,499	3,128	241,800	103,480
1971	815,430	699,806	16,521	716,327	48,661	-25,377	642,289	92,330	80,811	3,301	247,013	103,817
1972	905,205	769,693	23,320	793,013	56,042	-24,552	712,419	102,083	90,703	3,625	249,683	106,749
1973	1,020,110	863,873	27,630	891,503	72,613	-23,459	795,431	116,176	108,503	4,028	253,233	112,348
1974	1,142,412	967,469	21,652	989,121	84,923	-27,950	876,248	134,502	131,662	4,439	257,350	115,905
1975	1,245,816	1,037,484	12,733	1,050,217	88,947	-41,942	919,328	154,390	172,098	4,779	260,702	114,222
1976	1,397,018	1,171,544	19,217	1,190,761	101,998	-48,104	1,040,659	169,393	186,966	5,282	264,479	119,484
1977	1,556,484	1,329,485	13,402	1,342,887	115,508	-60,005	1,167,374	192,127	196,983	5,819	267,499	124,891
1978	1,765,212	1,532,092	16,489	1,548,581	133,630	-86,041	1,328,910	219,250	217,052	6,497	271,688	131,666
1979	1,942,789	1,692,646	6,596	1,699,242	151,086	-110,267	1,437,889	251,060	253,840	7,065	275,007	133,425
1980	2,125,715	1,779,746	9,212	1,788,958	159,005	-117,623	1,512,330	312,585	300,800	7,626	278,763	130,586
1981	2,418,683	1,986,809	23,148	2,009,957	191,421	-133,767	1,684,769	385,428	348,486	8,638	279,993	131,108
1982	2,563,837	2,035,633	19,381	2,055,014	206,451	-100,961	1,747,602	433,967	382,268	9,143	280,418	128,310
1983	2,708,314	2,131,874	7,064	2,138,938	218,001	-98,156	1,822,781	472,172	413,361	9,703	279,113	127,756
1984	2,911,892	2,246,681	13,856	2,260,537	235,450	-87,676	1,937,411	535,710	438,771	10,456	278,485	129,086
1985	3,139,496	2,456,970	14,105	2,471,075	261,926	-97,035	2,112,114	561,760	465,622	11,298	277,884	132,126
1986	3,316,668	2,604,902	4,864	2,609,766	285,255	-97,743	2,226,768	593,170	496,730	11,979	276,878	133,598
1987	3,480,163	2,745,119	14,931	2,760,050	298,286	-93,670	2,368,094	590,523	521,546	12,554	277,217	136,288
1988	3,761,719	2,961,603	18,197	2,979,800	330,066	-104,253	2,545,481	657,283	558,955	13,638	275,824	139,584
1989	4,037,045	3,176,435	21,918	3,198,353	358,458	-117,313	2,722,582	699,092	615,371	14,645	275,656	143,467
1990	4,356,273	3,379,242	28,262	3,407,504	383,983	-117,090	2,906,431	775,498	674,344	15,772	276,205	147,539
1991	4,609,857	3,565,438	29,767	3,595,205	410,767	-125,344	3,059,094	796,427	754,336	16,532	278,847	148,554
1992	4,905,212	3,789,679	39,437	3,829,116	431,847	-120,006	3,277,263	781,663	846,286	17,376	282,292	151,184
1993	5,059,547	3,910,474	31,123	3,941,597	448,578	-132,514	3,360,505	797,161	901,881	17,744	285,142	153,439
1994	5,217,592	3,959,881	27,311	3,987,192	458,289	-95,866	3,433,037	835,910	948,645	18,204	286,625	153,499
1995	5,549,231	4,183,207	15,043	4,198,250	483,661	-110,917	3,603,672	912,394	1,033,165	19,151	289,762	158,102
1996	5,848,571	4,414,634	2,027	4,416,661	500,828	-139,533	3,776,300	987,424	1,084,847	20,019	292,153	158,808
1997	6,065,901	4,505,090	6,655	4,511,745	505,902	-111,564	3,894,279	1,029,160	1,142,462	20,615	294,250	160,258
1998	6,356,041	4,650,940	8,213	4,659,153	512,556	-92,894	4,053,703	1,114,018	1,188,320	21,449	296,333	158,389
1999	6,642,753	4,825,182	9,366	4,834,548	527,387	-21,954	4,285,207	1,124,800	1,232,746	22,301	297,863	159,345
2000	7,006,517	4,927,108	24,280	4,951,388	537,426	28,269	4,442,231	1,234,228	1,330,058	23,470	298,534	158,601
2001	7,202,124	5,074,232	17,871	5,092,103	575,413	-8,782	4,507,908	1,240,355	1,453,861	24,116	298,648	158,986
2002	7,380,582	5,193,008	10,985	5,203,993	593,495	-11,200	4,599,298	1,217,846	1,563,438	24,662	299,267	158,936
2003	7,676,321	5,437,458	-2,085	5,435,373	618,912	-31,240	4,785,221	1,255,884	1,635,216	25,556	300,370	158,847
2004	8,046,885	5,725,893	8,338	5,734,231	645,497	-27,230	5,061,504	1,237,435	1,747,946	26,763	300,668	157,428
2005	8,343,664	5,900,653	8,378	5,909,031	669,967	-16,937	5,222,127	1,231,058	1,890,479	27,581	302,519	159,091
2006	8,967,372	6,289,643	-9,449	6,280,194	722,171	-80,624	5,477,399	1,439,993	2,049,980	29,446	304,535	161,832
2007	9,478,854	6,517,338	-18,293	6,499,045	750,593	-86,284	5,662,168	1,592,747	2,223,939	30,895	306,805	162,866
2008	10,047,810	6,743,579	-14,110	6,729,469	783,523	-108,606	5,837,340	1,727,752	2,482,718	32,615	308,069	163,311
2009	9,820,083	6,469,198	-11,400	6,457,798	762,342	-73,517	5,621,939	1,518,622	2,679,522	31,750	309,293	157,047
2010	9,977,133	6,588,940	-10,641	6,578,299	777,079	-115,948	5,685,272	1,424,432	2,867,429	32,239	309,475	154,852
2011	10,596,888	7,020,782	-6,611	7,014,171	735,402	-175,099	6,103,670	1,571,240	2,921,978	34,285	309,081	158,094
2012	10,984,669	7,249,317	-8,483	7,240,834	743,213	-156,861	6,340,760	1,706,530	2,937,379	35,596	308,594	157,066
2013	10,749,755	7,169,395	-3,864	7,165,531	830,064	-170,590	6,164,877	1,579,854	3,005,024	34,927	307,782	156,894
2014	10,858,107	7,110,917	6,739	7,117,656	832,420	-176,034	6,109,202	1,690,205	3,058,700	35,351	307,154	157,366
2015	11,075,674	7,195,307	4,310	7,199,617	851,661	-160,509	6,187,447	1,705,656	3,182,571	36,169	306,220	156,755
2016	11,177,052	7,184,266	-15,025	7,169,241	861,922	-143,652	6,163,667	1,762,059	3,251,326	36,528	305,989	157,812
2017	11,553,217	7,433,956	-7,459	7,426,497	896,677	-132,203	6,397,617	1,820,033	3,335,567	37,701	306,443	158,096
2018	12,060,194	7,787,949	-17,012	7,770,937	931,826	-145,832	6,693,279	1,894,268	3,472,647	39,333	306,618	158,657
2019	12,484,956	7,882,737	-14,908	7,867,829	945,623	-125,556	6,796,650	2,018,750	3,669,556	40,640	307,208	156,915
2020	13,342,431	7,995,601	-16,024	7,979,577	966,078	-98,929	6,914,570	2,037,182	4,390,679	43,360	307,716	153,826
2021	14,467,191	8,726,812	-13,877	8,712,935	1,039,248	-92,607	7,581,080	1,959,453	4,926,658	46,851	308,794	157,302
2022	14,767,408	9,409,718	-10,686	9,399,032	1,149,007	-139,014	8,111,011	2,104,366	4,552,031	47,442	311,272	163,870

Personal Income and Employment by Area: Kingston, NY

(Thousands of dollars, except as noted.)

Year	Personal income, total	Derivation of personal income: Earnings by place of work: Nonfarm	Farm	Total	Less: Contributions for government social insurance	Plus: Adjustment for residence	Equals: Net earnings by place of residence	Plus: Dividends, interest, and rent	Plus: Personal current transfer receipts	Per capita personal income (dollars)	Population (persons)	Total employment
1970	574,715	408,659	6,869	415,528	31,226	42,656	426,958	92,490	55,267	4,040	142,242	52,414
1971	623,694	434,425	6,704	441,129	34,452	51,529	458,206	99,732	65,756	4,251	146,705	53,640
1972	675,172	463,921	4,043	467,964	38,536	62,140	491,568	107,667	75,937	4,498	150,111	54,890
1973	754,760	514,178	7,123	521,301	49,347	70,847	542,801	123,627	88,332	4,934	152,980	57,237
1974	828,152	543,464	8,995	552,459	53,684	81,243	580,018	142,095	106,039	5,376	154,057	57,453
1975	913,241	564,474	9,644	574,118	54,755	92,992	612,355	156,217	144,669	5,853	156,022	55,738
1976	967,361	593,541	8,456	601,997	58,960	103,865	646,902	162,711	157,748	6,131	157,793	55,635
1977	1,038,576	634,078	9,387	643,465	62,659	120,240	701,046	176,929	160,601	6,592	157,559	56,665
1978	1,143,405	708,103	10,910	719,013	71,437	139,471	787,047	188,084	168,274	7,209	158,617	58,794
1979	1,271,321	792,499	13,556	806,055	82,280	160,972	884,747	204,474	182,100	7,965	159,606	61,376
1980	1,421,272	855,033	12,069	867,102	89,455	185,478	963,125	245,416	212,731	8,989	158,111	61,668
1981	1,573,292	924,422	10,227	934,649	102,508	203,748	1,035,889	294,271	243,132	9,981	157,625	61,536
1982	1,767,594	1,045,447	12,650	1,058,097	116,493	219,266	1,160,870	340,190	266,534	11,204	157,770	63,222
1983	1,944,078	1,193,234	6,514	1,199,748	134,108	222,073	1,287,713	373,596	282,769	12,272	158,414	66,330
1984	2,182,454	1,365,290	8,563	1,373,853	156,527	242,039	1,459,365	428,493	294,596	13,678	159,557	69,296
1985	2,346,042	1,468,029	11,961	1,479,990	170,522	266,506	1,575,974	460,431	309,637	14,674	159,880	71,174
1986	2,524,907	1,627,393	12,194	1,639,587	191,321	275,582	1,723,848	480,722	320,337	15,804	159,760	74,612
1987	2,640,481	1,704,139	15,992	1,720,131	196,061	300,025	1,824,095	489,651	326,735	16,313	161,865	73,866
1988	2,823,345	1,795,549	18,746	1,814,295	211,745	333,553	1,936,103	536,775	350,467	17,333	162,889	76,380
1989	3,079,919	1,904,405	19,024	1,923,429	220,621	354,067	2,056,875	638,229	384,815	18,739	164,359	76,774
1990	3,207,986	1,978,148	18,161	1,996,309	219,512	376,801	2,153,598	630,601	423,787	19,320	166,049	77,348
1991	3,381,949	2,098,553	23,424	2,121,977	238,891	376,771	2,259,857	649,701	472,391	20,027	168,869	77,826
1992	3,583,260	2,192,767	18,949	2,211,716	244,835	403,842	2,370,723	671,825	540,712	20,970	170,872	78,504
1993	3,516,833	2,073,378	18,762	2,092,140	232,371	443,940	2,303,709	642,427	570,697	20,376	172,594	76,404
1994	3,525,370	2,006,115	16,512	2,022,627	226,596	466,460	2,262,491	649,341	613,538	20,466	172,252	76,405
1995	3,602,022	1,944,036	16,993	1,961,029	219,587	518,840	2,260,282	695,585	646,155	20,898	172,362	74,331
1996	3,701,295	1,942,217	14,804	1,957,021	215,026	573,216	2,315,211	707,352	678,732	21,369	173,205	74,388
1997	3,900,151	2,051,499	13,923	2,065,422	222,365	606,784	2,449,841	758,079	692,231	22,396	174,148	75,635
1998	4,209,659	2,212,794	12,085	2,224,879	238,236	673,725	2,660,368	809,929	739,362	24,044	175,085	77,766
1999	4,449,573	2,388,061	19,247	2,407,308	250,908	745,784	2,902,184	793,364	754,025	25,206	176,526	80,901
2000	4,763,272	2,551,539	18,365	2,569,904	268,289	827,780	3,129,395	839,957	793,920	26,789	177,810	83,102
2001	4,897,788	2,576,336	19,102	2,595,438	275,273	886,434	3,206,599	835,381	855,808	27,448	178,440	84,862
2002	4,943,176	2,681,812	7,966	2,689,778	290,065	887,721	3,287,434	742,973	912,769	27,443	180,128	85,463
2003	5,116,468	2,808,689	15,130	2,823,819	303,566	899,899	3,420,152	744,966	951,350	28,277	180,942	86,619
2004	5,588,043	2,980,723	12,611	2,993,334	319,161	1,095,441	3,769,614	816,547	1,001,882	30,729	181,847	86,993
2005	5,844,523	3,075,856	8,175	3,084,031	336,215	1,168,670	3,916,486	880,424	1,047,613	32,036	182,438	87,643
2006	6,184,842	3,359,842	13,307	3,373,149	372,909	1,152,091	4,152,331	919,107	1,113,404	33,826	182,845	88,733
2007	6,488,365	3,462,821	26,234	3,489,055	384,631	1,221,402	4,325,826	981,906	1,180,633	35,491	182,818	89,800
2008	6,828,145	3,511,094	28,594	3,539,688	396,089	1,173,057	4,316,656	1,195,880	1,315,609	37,277	183,174	89,276
2009	6,799,538	3,510,928	23,538	3,534,466	390,181	1,039,932	4,184,217	1,160,005	1,455,316	37,230	182,638	87,248
2010	7,014,378	3,668,055	27,335	3,695,390	395,353	1,040,737	4,340,774	1,111,890	1,561,714	38,429	182,526	86,537
2011	7,264,513	3,684,450	22,657	3,707,107	360,711	1,099,520	4,445,916	1,213,627	1,604,970	39,701	182,980	86,148
2012	7,455,865	3,774,841	24,454	3,799,295	365,139	1,063,161	4,497,317	1,320,960	1,637,588	40,857	182,487	85,984
2013	7,470,674	3,844,445	28,712	3,873,157	418,238	1,060,023	4,514,942	1,297,020	1,658,712	41,035	182,058	86,819
2014	7,707,562	3,885,611	21,083	3,906,694	434,687	1,092,629	4,564,636	1,405,065	1,737,861	42,309	182,173	88,654
2015	7,960,319	4,016,618	19,823	4,036,441	452,191	1,118,447	4,702,697	1,421,692	1,835,930	43,779	181,830	89,294
2016	8,186,051	4,119,895	20,491	4,140,386	466,535	1,185,037	4,858,888	1,463,611	1,863,552	45,084	181,574	90,311
2017	8,581,973	4,266,746	29,279	4,296,025	485,672	1,214,970	5,025,323	1,559,839	1,996,811	47,263	181,579	90,945
2018	8,897,244	4,478,209	11,437	4,489,646	503,960	1,290,742	5,276,428	1,655,558	1,965,258	48,927	181,848	92,064
2019	9,636,341	4,600,565	18,311	4,618,876	518,983	1,624,380	5,724,273	1,799,507	2,112,561	53,043	181,669	91,135
2020	10,586,115	4,565,397	18,598	4,583,995	519,212	1,866,899	5,931,682	1,837,354	2,817,079	58,285	181,627	86,525
2021	11,247,096	4,943,214	20,399	4,963,613	568,156	1,933,392	6,328,849	1,959,963	2,958,284	61,224	183,704	88,910
2022	11,353,095	5,315,678	20,050	5,335,728	626,938	2,086,422	6,795,212	2,002,259	2,555,624	62,270	182,319	92,516

Personal Income and Employment by Area: Knoxville, TN

(Thousands of dollars, except as noted.)

Year	Personal income, total	Derivation of personal income: Earnings by place of work: Nonfarm	Earnings by place of work: Farm	Earnings by place of work: Total	Less: Contributions for government social insurance	Plus: Adjustment for residence	Equals: Net earnings by place of residence	Plus: Dividends, interest, and rent	Plus: Personal current transfer receipts	Per capita personal income (dollars)	Population (persons)	Total employment
1970	1,650,630	1,377,853	7,611	1,385,464	88,530	-23,558	1,273,376	209,468	167,786	3,209	514,357	211,769
1971	1,819,300	1,506,962	7,215	1,514,177	100,002	-24,272	1,389,903	232,141	197,256	3,455	526,504	215,593
1972	2,013,061	1,668,820	11,644	1,680,464	116,249	-23,176	1,541,039	254,735	217,287	3,773	533,511	224,162
1973	2,265,844	1,869,790	17,704	1,887,494	149,103	-26,386	1,712,005	293,420	260,419	4,206	538,759	235,844
1974	2,544,948	2,077,147	13,030	2,090,177	170,758	-29,967	1,889,452	345,645	309,851	4,670	544,906	239,259
1975	2,865,986	2,268,025	9,667	2,277,692	182,970	-27,744	2,066,978	403,953	395,055	5,161	555,290	239,174
1976	3,242,139	2,585,156	18,935	2,604,091	211,600	-30,502	2,361,989	444,299	435,851	5,714	567,394	251,742
1977	3,636,186	2,941,570	14,083	2,955,653	239,734	-38,215	2,677,704	501,798	456,684	6,296	577,558	262,613
1978	4,155,693	3,384,320	12,148	3,396,468	278,783	-38,709	3,078,976	572,698	504,019	7,101	585,187	275,258
1979	4,668,273	3,786,728	10,214	3,796,942	325,237	-48,103	3,423,602	653,840	590,831	7,837	595,675	286,163
1980	5,194,400	4,082,827	16,510	4,099,337	351,044	-55,504	3,692,789	802,597	699,014	8,558	606,956	286,768
1981	5,800,974	4,472,319	22,649	4,494,968	417,320	-50,787	4,026,861	978,025	796,088	9,456	613,462	291,001
1982	6,234,835	4,752,706	19,371	4,772,077	458,050	-60,646	4,253,381	1,119,431	862,023	10,065	619,485	294,311
1983	6,586,673	4,998,301	9,845	5,008,146	489,969	-56,850	4,461,327	1,184,406	940,940	10,602	621,248	286,934
1984	7,181,947	5,446,350	19,030	5,465,380	556,366	-66,072	4,842,942	1,353,555	985,450	11,594	619,469	296,374
1985	7,598,277	5,779,698	12,394	5,792,092	602,655	-66,479	5,122,958	1,431,113	1,044,206	12,263	619,633	301,662
1986	8,025,319	6,129,865	12,165	6,142,030	656,738	-81,181	5,404,111	1,496,061	1,125,147	13,017	616,527	310,059
1987	8,650,229	6,709,066	12,760	6,721,826	709,499	-88,422	5,923,905	1,536,243	1,190,081	13,961	619,620	322,676
1988	9,518,076	7,443,086	12,480	7,455,566	808,653	-106,996	6,539,917	1,707,140	1,271,019	15,219	625,415	338,618
1989	10,055,663	7,831,147	18,370	7,849,517	866,851	-110,894	6,871,772	1,774,778	1,409,113	15,942	630,777	345,872
1990	10,827,666	8,295,749	19,599	8,315,348	926,049	-100,186	7,289,113	1,985,123	1,553,430	17,014	636,386	352,518
1991	11,411,866	8,732,311	21,004	8,753,315	994,752	-141,734	7,616,829	2,039,084	1,755,953	17,620	647,671	355,057
1992	12,335,692	9,577,714	23,640	9,601,354	1,078,206	-185,596	8,337,552	2,027,970	1,970,170	18,686	660,168	365,916
1993	13,149,200	10,251,136	24,342	10,275,478	1,157,556	-205,139	8,912,783	2,129,214	2,107,203	19,596	671,010	379,540
1994	13,794,284	10,748,394	19,863	10,768,257	1,245,797	-221,891	9,300,569	2,285,214	2,208,501	20,187	683,318	391,671
1995	14,669,243	11,305,565	17,313	11,322,878	1,314,840	-240,513	9,767,525	2,500,036	2,401,682	21,086	695,685	400,565
1996	15,326,312	11,785,605	9,862	11,795,467	1,350,898	-271,576	10,172,993	2,640,347	2,512,972	21,722	705,564	404,060
1997	16,156,765	12,435,811	11,050	12,446,861	1,417,214	-321,808	10,707,839	2,839,942	2,608,984	22,675	712,532	407,962
1998	17,573,518	13,682,890	12,666	13,695,556	1,507,663	-325,525	11,862,368	3,007,924	2,703,226	24,497	717,379	417,918
1999	18,001,665	14,055,207	19,363	14,074,570	1,566,871	-302,253	12,205,446	2,975,484	2,820,735	24,897	723,054	423,353
2000	19,409,083	15,080,288	22,683	15,102,971	1,658,686	-327,567	13,116,718	3,194,498	3,097,867	26,617	729,194	433,435
2001	19,671,728	15,072,548	34,613	15,107,161	1,676,524	-347,722	13,082,915	3,251,754	3,337,059	26,737	735,744	429,902
2002	20,469,790	15,885,062	33,815	15,918,877	1,775,104	-377,923	13,765,850	3,120,350	3,583,590	27,572	742,420	433,350
2003	21,350,271	16,575,341	20,380	16,595,721	1,851,016	-386,119	14,358,586	3,260,877	3,730,808	28,434	750,863	438,827
2004	22,599,141	17,733,759	17,138	17,750,897	1,962,051	-415,959	15,372,887	3,270,453	3,955,801	29,790	758,622	452,228
2005	23,707,398	18,603,127	13,939	18,617,066	2,049,037	-463,723	16,104,306	3,385,849	4,217,243	30,837	768,798	460,995
2006	25,199,548	19,679,638	3,768	19,683,406	2,169,747	-517,984	16,995,675	3,700,165	4,503,708	32,196	782,685	471,894
2007	26,457,427	20,389,179	-6,350	20,382,829	2,275,246	-571,890	17,535,693	4,013,406	4,908,328	33,315	794,171	480,589
2008	27,722,328	20,685,169	-5,514	20,679,655	2,354,122	-625,726	17,699,807	4,512,876	5,509,645	34,450	804,719	483,344
2009	27,228,225	20,144,241	833	20,145,074	2,323,298	-662,594	17,159,182	4,144,243	5,924,800	33,559	811,349	463,608
2010	28,473,890	20,932,376	3,794	20,936,170	2,388,984	-633,006	17,914,180	4,144,034	6,415,676	34,890	816,113	462,484
2011	30,237,234	21,973,815	1,393	21,975,208	2,222,398	-771,149	18,981,661	4,723,741	6,531,832	36,817	821,279	470,981
2012	31,749,943	22,855,694	13,469	22,869,163	2,249,879	-644,149	19,975,135	5,133,897	6,640,911	38,436	826,042	470,593
2013	31,747,244	23,362,781	23,269	23,386,050	2,594,536	-666,124	20,125,390	4,787,237	6,834,617	38,226	830,506	473,633
2014	32,946,345	24,235,922	22,507	24,258,429	2,675,643	-668,099	20,914,687	5,111,483	6,920,175	39,462	834,896	482,128
2015	34,562,270	25,363,739	22,319	25,386,058	2,795,715	-684,080	21,906,263	5,291,718	7,364,289	41,134	840,236	491,126
2016	35,726,507	26,266,113	6,561	26,272,674	2,896,706	-678,402	22,697,566	5,417,135	7,611,806	42,139	847,835	500,839
2017	37,312,982	27,298,985	9,227	27,308,212	3,045,154	-652,165	23,610,893	5,859,559	7,842,530	43,539	857,009	507,621
2018	39,700,033	28,958,847	-1,944	28,956,903	3,188,583	-684,938	25,083,382	6,342,625	8,274,026	45,883	865,239	516,253
2019	42,237,838	30,169,201	1,517	30,170,718	3,309,225	-637,637	26,223,856	7,231,139	8,782,843	48,406	872,567	520,104
2020	45,680,306	31,880,461	5,222	31,885,683	3,514,145	-704,597	27,666,941	7,204,951	10,808,414	51,776	882,268	519,538
2021	50,967,019	35,459,206	9,168	35,468,374	3,819,953	-778,785	30,869,636	7,941,856	12,155,527	57,057	893,262	541,707
2022	52,879,219	38,526,128	-10,445	38,515,683	4,287,887	-854,975	33,372,821	8,675,149	10,831,249	58,239	907,968	569,166

Personal Income and Employment by Area: Kokomo, IN

(Thousands of dollars, except as noted.)

Year	Personal income, total	Derivation of personal income: Earnings by place of work: Nonfarm	Farm	Total	Less: Contributions for government social insurance	Plus: Adjustment for residence	Equals: Net earnings by place of residence	Plus: Dividends, interest, and rent	Plus: Personal current transfer receipts	Per capita personal income (dollars)	Population (persons)	Total employment
1970	331,938	339,172	5,101	344,273	22,733	-52,896	268,644	41,170	22,124	3,982	83,353	42,282
1971	384,616	400,068	7,664	407,732	27,903	-65,921	313,908	45,197	25,511	4,584	83,904	44,735
1972	429,095	460,468	5,807	466,275	34,537	-78,852	352,886	48,118	28,091	5,058	84,832	46,840
1973	498,639	535,902	17,916	553,818	46,926	-94,878	412,014	54,917	31,708	5,815	85,745	50,105
1974	506,802	533,449	9,731	543,180	48,464	-94,141	400,575	62,950	43,277	5,811	87,215	47,441
1975	529,985	520,790	17,570	538,360	46,757	-92,491	399,112	70,449	60,424	6,098	86,906	43,959
1976	603,238	646,150	10,822	656,972	58,907	-124,706	473,359	77,332	52,547	6,958	86,700	47,377
1977	672,470	746,027	5,793	751,820	67,991	-152,531	531,298	87,137	54,035	7,719	87,123	49,509
1978	739,370	827,340	9,483	836,823	77,815	-174,283	584,725	94,161	60,484	8,474	87,248	50,886
1979	782,926	868,097	7,452	875,549	84,319	-185,636	605,594	102,400	74,932	8,968	87,305	49,709
1980	839,818	862,252	1,444	863,696	83,180	-187,632	592,884	123,720	123,214	9,678	86,774	45,809
1981	887,814	921,843	85	921,928	95,940	-197,215	628,773	149,813	109,228	10,312	86,098	46,275
1982	883,158	865,791	2,790	868,581	91,592	-176,894	600,095	161,674	121,389	10,390	85,004	42,641
1983	974,902	993,201	-1,920	991,281	106,423	-208,022	676,836	172,690	125,376	11,533	84,532	43,455
1984	1,113,513	1,164,886	7,157	1,172,043	128,577	-250,029	793,437	192,089	127,987	13,151	84,671	47,020
1985	1,209,608	1,285,017	8,624	1,293,641	143,969	-278,525	871,147	205,398	133,063	14,322	84,459	47,707
1986	1,233,443	1,289,057	6,711	1,295,768	143,515	-271,605	880,648	212,340	140,455	14,725	83,768	47,674
1987	1,253,311	1,302,142	9,828	1,311,970	143,223	-267,045	901,702	206,544	145,065	15,227	82,308	48,068
1988	1,366,317	1,450,340	5,576	1,455,916	163,395	-302,451	990,070	220,631	155,616	16,869	80,994	48,902
1989	1,471,323	1,534,112	10,431	1,544,543	173,296	-317,319	1,053,928	246,190	171,205	18,220	80,751	49,968
1990	1,515,587	1,541,538	13,107	1,554,645	180,308	-304,114	1,070,223	255,533	189,831	18,716	80,976	50,562
1991	1,552,191	1,587,854	8,786	1,596,640	187,804	-319,740	1,089,096	253,120	209,975	18,947	81,924	50,375
1992	1,661,647	1,715,362	12,379	1,727,741	199,092	-359,591	1,169,058	251,811	240,778	20,132	82,537	52,015
1993	1,769,267	1,857,559	15,884	1,873,443	218,365	-404,640	1,250,438	267,068	251,761	21,247	83,271	53,683
1994	1,882,652	2,043,334	16,630	2,059,964	240,029	-467,548	1,352,387	272,532	257,733	22,524	83,584	53,788
1995	1,976,484	2,129,197	8,025	2,137,222	236,695	-505,926	1,394,601	317,705	264,178	23,556	83,905	56,546
1996	2,039,310	2,162,744	21,936	2,184,680	229,036	-525,716	1,429,928	327,592	281,790	24,089	84,656	56,874
1997	2,078,446	2,175,566	20,605	2,196,171	227,438	-528,344	1,440,389	348,834	289,223	24,548	84,669	56,082
1998	2,204,366	2,327,553	11,951	2,339,504	232,284	-568,732	1,538,488	368,647	297,231	26,130	84,361	56,595
1999	2,308,768	2,500,430	7,155	2,507,585	245,559	-627,794	1,634,232	358,631	315,905	27,235	84,772	57,213
2000	2,400,913	2,558,018	13,580	2,571,598	248,837	-648,040	1,674,721	385,757	340,435	28,266	84,940	57,398
2001	2,349,385	2,448,629	15,228	2,463,857	281,622	-594,994	1,587,241	377,490	384,654	27,669	84,909	54,466
2002	2,390,772	2,505,490	9,637	2,515,127	288,975	-599,341	1,626,811	360,718	403,243	28,272	84,563	53,874
2003	2,446,933	2,531,056	14,733	2,545,789	293,301	-596,494	1,655,994	368,893	422,046	28,945	84,538	52,400
2004	2,518,996	2,628,195	24,688	2,652,883	301,613	-619,465	1,731,805	335,704	451,487	29,885	84,291	51,985
2005	2,557,356	2,616,128	15,350	2,631,478	301,859	-604,357	1,725,262	339,454	492,640	30,307	84,382	51,577
2006	2,637,853	2,662,643	10,263	2,672,906	311,050	-613,805	1,748,051	351,744	538,058	31,424	83,943	51,183
2007	2,755,872	2,684,610	11,820	2,696,430	314,759	-593,371	1,788,300	402,083	565,489	32,909	83,743	50,586
2008	2,708,825	2,390,048	25,075	2,415,123	286,416	-467,475	1,661,232	404,424	643,169	32,452	83,472	48,135
2009	2,527,979	1,998,087	10,866	2,008,953	246,960	-323,174	1,438,819	381,966	707,194	30,568	82,701	43,131
2010	2,582,551	2,027,447	3,774	2,031,221	246,773	-321,120	1,463,328	378,791	740,432	31,200	82,775	44,467
2011	2,733,026	2,161,911	20,913	2,182,824	234,507	-361,812	1,586,505	402,052	744,469	32,960	82,919	45,454
2012	2,849,175	2,252,539	26,260	2,278,799	242,322	-379,039	1,657,438	422,822	768,915	34,303	83,059	46,385
2013	2,895,357	2,343,215	61,934	2,405,149	290,561	-418,004	1,696,584	413,140	785,633	34,860	83,057	47,549
2014	3,020,715	2,460,835	34,729	2,495,564	302,791	-427,875	1,764,898	427,829	827,988	36,385	83,020	48,287
2015	3,109,118	2,535,594	4,189	2,539,783	313,018	-428,239	1,798,526	451,018	859,574	37,525	82,855	48,491
2016	3,160,214	2,582,025	15,425	2,597,450	314,801	-439,771	1,842,878	443,588	873,748	38,091	82,965	49,709
2017	3,241,632	2,633,762	10,514	2,644,276	314,743	-444,905	1,884,628	456,784	900,220	39,075	82,960	49,764
2018	3,401,685	2,668,040	13,966	2,682,006	321,853	-359,724	2,000,429	467,353	933,903	40,941	83,087	48,917
2019	3,479,246	2,711,075	6,970	2,718,045	336,697	-375,459	2,005,889	491,041	982,316	41,668	83,500	47,870
2020	3,661,971	2,526,018	19,939	2,545,957	332,955	-284,826	1,928,176	494,829	1,238,966	43,810	83,588	45,863
2021	3,963,612	2,575,087	35,124	2,610,211	337,480	-232,375	2,040,356	533,381	1,389,875	47,388	83,642	45,316
2022	3,960,413	2,713,038	28,822	2,741,860	345,542	-249,200	2,147,118	580,350	1,232,945	47,388	83,574	45,315

Personal Income and Employment by Area: La Crosse-Onalaska, WI-MN

(Thousands of dollars, except as noted.)

Year	Personal income, total	Derivation of personal income: Earnings by place of work: Nonfarm	Farm	Total	Less: Contributions for government social insurance	Plus: Adjustment for residence	Equals: Net earnings by place of residence	Plus: Dividends, interest, and rent	Plus: Personal current transfer receipts	Per capita personal income (dollars)	Population (persons)	Total employment
1970	351,917	265,134	18,975	284,109	19,719	-6,989	257,401	58,922	35,594	3,581	98,260	42,995
1971	379,780	284,348	19,289	303,637	21,845	-7,215	274,577	63,301	41,902	3,825	99,301	43,907
1972	413,433	312,253	21,855	334,108	25,281	-8,400	300,427	67,254	45,752	4,187	98,738	45,533
1973	468,010	352,671	31,478	384,149	32,705	-9,942	341,502	73,946	52,562	4,672	100,165	48,430
1974	514,132	391,540	24,873	416,413	37,822	-11,753	366,838	83,326	63,968	5,050	101,810	49,921
1975	566,448	428,642	19,890	448,532	40,610	-13,097	394,825	93,088	78,535	5,414	104,618	50,747
1976	637,150	492,901	19,442	512,343	47,636	-16,096	448,611	103,081	85,458	6,143	103,720	53,331
1977	718,376	552,252	30,107	582,359	53,355	-19,477	509,527	117,690	91,159	6,757	106,314	55,192
1978	803,419	632,290	28,734	661,024	62,648	-24,020	574,356	128,712	100,351	7,337	109,509	57,889
1979	898,800	712,223	27,666	739,889	73,651	-26,480	639,758	141,639	117,403	8,072	111,346	60,200
1980	1,021,782	791,881	25,165	817,046	81,539	-31,203	704,304	177,462	140,016	9,315	109,696	61,582
1981	1,139,236	868,894	25,271	894,165	95,804	-38,062	760,299	219,660	159,277	10,312	110,473	62,428
1982	1,217,306	903,873	24,697	928,570	100,726	-38,787	789,057	252,757	175,492	10,967	111,000	61,655
1983	1,293,903	972,405	9,211	981,616	107,946	-42,044	831,626	270,854	191,423	11,644	111,122	62,200
1984	1,415,143	1,059,573	25,696	1,085,269	120,446	-45,464	919,359	298,104	197,680	12,610	112,222	64,086
1985	1,491,701	1,110,621	30,350	1,140,971	127,277	-47,789	965,905	312,588	213,208	13,208	112,937	64,642
1986	1,568,742	1,161,748	41,491	1,203,239	133,262	-49,390	1,020,587	329,950	218,205	13,869	113,108	65,626
1987	1,667,990	1,254,420	46,390	1,300,810	141,399	-53,645	1,105,766	337,832	224,392	14,609	114,178	67,341
1988	1,769,609	1,375,472	26,650	1,402,122	161,277	-60,672	1,180,173	355,696	233,740	15,390	114,981	70,751
1989	1,941,193	1,479,517	45,117	1,524,634	174,225	-64,302	1,286,107	401,539	253,547	16,779	115,693	70,706
1990	2,091,932	1,562,487	47,337	1,609,824	190,348	-65,650	1,353,826	467,417	270,689	17,915	116,769	72,019
1991	2,143,936	1,634,282	34,342	1,668,624	201,250	-69,287	1,398,087	458,491	287,358	18,215	117,700	73,440
1992	2,279,682	1,761,316	33,911	1,795,227	213,581	-74,424	1,507,222	460,132	312,328	19,124	119,207	75,248
1993	2,417,739	1,878,634	23,131	1,901,765	226,964	-79,069	1,595,732	499,581	322,426	20,048	120,597	77,177
1994	2,559,688	2,004,817	25,708	2,030,525	244,263	-83,919	1,702,343	528,138	329,207	21,006	121,856	79,874
1995	2,635,471	2,052,175	12,051	2,064,226	251,076	-83,820	1,729,330	554,130	352,011	21,442	122,910	81,628
1996	2,786,511	2,193,133	26,283	2,219,416	266,816	-90,450	1,862,150	564,961	359,400	22,486	123,920	83,209
1997	2,943,157	2,350,771	19,722	2,370,493	283,334	-98,561	1,988,598	583,784	370,775	23,636	124,521	85,030
1998	3,166,492	2,514,344	29,424	2,543,768	300,088	-103,770	2,139,910	648,551	378,031	25,257	125,371	86,896
1999	3,269,380	2,617,847	24,211	2,642,058	311,887	-97,344	2,232,827	638,884	397,669	25,939	126,041	87,257
2000	3,445,728	2,732,021	14,949	2,746,970	322,952	-99,162	2,324,856	687,242	433,630	27,127	127,021	88,620
2001	3,594,789	2,834,617	17,959	2,852,576	331,754	-113,360	2,407,462	701,197	486,130	28,167	127,624	88,333
2002	3,685,704	2,922,648	14,382	2,937,030	341,137	-105,889	2,490,004	661,431	534,269	28,736	128,261	87,530
2003	3,839,434	3,050,870	26,484	3,077,354	354,964	-110,761	2,611,629	678,462	549,343	29,814	128,780	88,468
2004	3,991,112	3,175,551	38,063	3,213,614	366,913	-125,055	2,721,646	703,811	565,655	30,941	128,992	88,135
2005	4,142,730	3,294,633	36,430	3,331,063	384,134	-131,250	2,815,679	725,999	601,052	31,978	129,549	89,428
2006	4,363,348	3,457,514	27,261	3,484,775	404,462	-144,464	2,935,849	791,927	635,572	33,526	130,147	91,456
2007	4,600,709	3,573,083	27,117	3,600,200	421,489	-154,766	3,023,945	887,302	689,462	35,069	131,190	92,485
2008	4,916,739	3,724,945	32,204	3,757,149	441,311	-171,415	3,144,423	1,001,527	770,789	37,271	131,920	92,629
2009	4,977,645	3,776,642	13,682	3,790,324	444,228	-189,394	3,156,702	938,019	882,924	37,406	133,072	90,820
2010	5,085,946	3,909,701	28,986	3,938,687	462,171	-207,157	3,269,359	857,505	959,082	37,964	133,967	91,104
2011	5,373,651	4,028,599	53,718	4,082,317	428,123	-227,980	3,426,214	1,020,066	927,371	39,971	134,439	92,208
2012	5,658,991	4,207,961	57,914	4,265,875	442,581	-255,457	3,567,837	1,140,145	951,009	41,639	135,907	93,975
2013	5,610,861	4,326,412	57,933	4,384,345	513,706	-276,256	3,594,383	1,036,751	979,727	41,097	136,528	95,044
2014	5,941,526	4,540,266	57,317	4,597,583	535,429	-287,977	3,774,177	1,121,805	1,045,544	43,281	137,279	95,398
2015	6,136,724	4,679,589	42,348	4,721,937	549,188	-290,369	3,882,380	1,178,847	1,075,497	44,535	137,795	95,854
2016	6,256,537	4,790,450	29,218	4,819,668	560,471	-325,060	3,934,137	1,223,323	1,099,077	45,299	138,115	96,684
2017	6,483,211	4,911,452	31,748	4,943,200	584,352	-332,314	4,026,534	1,295,986	1,160,691	46,745	138,693	97,114
2018	6,770,021	5,148,865	27,556	5,176,421	605,694	-346,940	4,223,787	1,317,267	1,228,967	48,739	138,904	97,909
2019	7,058,157	5,392,123	23,288	5,415,411	634,060	-374,017	4,407,334	1,376,632	1,274,191	50,725	139,146	97,320
2020	7,543,968	5,498,423	52,030	5,550,453	646,916	-382,789	4,520,748	1,412,178	1,611,042	53,970	139,781	93,436
2021	8,225,268	5,789,814	49,632	5,839,446	685,501	-411,567	4,742,378	1,672,400	1,810,490	59,519	138,196	96,567
2022	8,401,530	6,130,695	62,820	6,193,515	739,862	-461,619	4,992,034	1,791,994	1,617,502	60,402	139,094	99,505

Personal Income and Employment by Area: Lafayette, LA

(Thousands of dollars, except as noted.)

Year	Personal income, total	Derivation of personal income: Earnings by place of work: Nonfarm	Earnings by place of work: Farm	Earnings by place of work: Total	Less: Contributions for government social insurance	Plus: Adjustment for residence	Equals: Net earnings by place of residence	Plus: Dividends, interest, and rent	Plus: Personal current transfer receipts	Per capita personal income (dollars)	Population (persons)	Total employment
1970	805,165	584,621	39,652	624,273	36,957	24,925	612,241	109,467	83,457	2,707	297,437	106,400
1971	884,670	645,894	38,897	684,791	41,721	23,475	666,545	122,172	95,953	2,932	301,678	108,662
1972	985,311	729,548	45,181	774,729	49,714	21,077	746,092	134,920	104,299	3,201	307,819	113,843
1973	1,152,474	825,043	101,536	926,579	65,085	17,213	878,707	152,911	120,856	3,689	312,430	119,859
1974	1,347,267	952,477	122,915	1,075,392	77,644	17,866	1,015,614	187,384	144,269	4,248	317,134	124,542
1975	1,562,706	1,128,221	105,665	1,233,886	91,074	18,513	1,161,325	224,040	177,341	4,844	322,597	130,569
1976	1,724,255	1,333,387	42,940	1,376,327	109,380	13,869	1,280,816	246,297	197,142	5,211	330,873	137,893
1977	1,992,514	1,574,370	50,850	1,625,220	128,516	6,313	1,503,017	279,570	209,927	5,899	337,770	147,120
1978	2,381,562	1,960,774	35,423	1,996,197	164,968	-2,722	1,828,507	324,157	228,898	6,917	344,306	161,185
1979	2,787,440	2,320,543	53,177	2,373,720	204,852	-15,882	2,152,986	374,121	260,333	7,924	351,776	170,540
1980	3,335,049	2,773,721	27,202	2,800,923	244,515	-32,872	2,523,536	501,468	310,045	9,227	361,450	181,105
1981	4,094,191	3,456,825	16,031	3,472,856	329,428	-61,617	3,081,811	669,081	343,299	11,032	371,133	199,253
1982	4,570,931	3,752,185	42,429	3,794,614	370,924	-77,237	3,346,453	821,437	403,041	11,851	385,710	205,964
1983	4,550,904	3,528,606	27,416	3,556,022	341,351	-63,472	3,151,199	896,648	503,057	11,558	393,737	193,845
1984	4,696,713	3,651,637	12,044	3,663,681	364,278	-57,348	3,242,055	950,095	504,563	11,952	392,956	193,564
1985	4,912,014	3,748,245	28,171	3,776,416	379,562	-57,444	3,339,410	1,039,269	533,335	12,420	395,505	192,643
1986	4,643,375	3,370,084	16,568	3,386,652	334,428	-35,476	3,016,748	992,018	634,609	11,695	397,056	174,850
1987	4,387,648	3,143,569	22,222	3,165,791	306,254	-15,162	2,844,375	910,675	632,598	11,276	389,109	164,848
1988	4,752,047	3,434,996	79,750	3,514,746	352,178	-16,763	3,145,805	959,996	646,246	12,380	383,841	171,932
1989	5,105,040	3,646,308	65,716	3,712,024	376,285	-11,263	3,324,476	1,068,275	712,289	13,301	383,800	177,407
1990	5,548,269	4,079,953	36,132	4,116,085	432,146	-18,684	3,665,255	1,102,609	780,405	14,471	383,397	186,879
1991	5,840,198	4,272,778	43,202	4,315,980	464,821	-21,801	3,829,358	1,114,186	896,654	15,040	388,299	191,220
1992	6,130,431	4,406,144	61,344	4,467,488	470,247	-2,034	3,995,207	1,106,521	1,028,703	15,618	392,531	188,119
1993	6,516,646	4,676,688	72,349	4,749,037	503,980	-5,552	4,239,505	1,155,962	1,121,179	16,377	397,922	195,210
1994	7,003,188	5,037,096	54,811	5,091,907	554,587	-24,162	4,513,158	1,231,269	1,258,761	17,404	402,385	201,325
1995	7,409,095	5,295,005	89,238	5,384,243	582,134	-47,360	4,754,749	1,354,699	1,299,647	18,219	406,658	208,746
1996	7,992,948	5,806,145	99,344	5,905,489	636,479	-76,643	5,192,367	1,474,775	1,325,806	19,437	411,228	217,292
1997	8,771,354	6,521,408	85,973	6,607,381	707,931	-100,298	5,799,152	1,609,369	1,362,833	21,057	416,562	228,667
1998	9,333,454	6,991,300	78,049	7,069,349	751,691	-126,093	6,191,565	1,739,716	1,402,173	22,165	421,081	237,170
1999	9,293,537	6,831,560	72,812	6,904,372	723,676	-93,214	6,087,482	1,734,214	1,471,841	21,913	424,114	232,472
2000	9,909,105	7,309,973	71,407	7,381,380	761,358	-116,591	6,503,431	1,889,428	1,516,246	23,307	425,158	236,014
2001	10,845,248	8,058,627	76,068	8,134,695	861,628	-154,234	7,118,833	1,973,107	1,753,308	25,414	426,750	241,219
2002	11,043,008	8,263,915	44,949	8,308,864	881,508	-148,833	7,278,523	1,906,460	1,858,025	25,660	430,358	241,715
2003	11,480,217	8,595,868	89,341	8,685,209	901,765	-129,866	7,653,578	1,967,377	1,859,262	26,519	432,900	243,518
2004	11,899,758	8,904,797	75,309	8,980,106	930,631	-171,100	7,878,375	1,978,144	2,043,239	27,292	436,018	244,290
2005	13,367,624	9,906,667	54,594	9,961,261	1,003,741	-238,913	8,718,607	2,374,812	2,274,205	30,385	439,936	252,867
2006	15,274,584	11,407,019	65,584	11,472,603	1,140,683	-301,627	10,030,293	2,860,822	2,383,469	33,888	450,740	266,579
2007	16,276,011	12,108,687	68,047	12,176,734	1,227,998	-361,797	10,586,939	3,193,551	2,495,521	35,825	454,315	274,645
2008	18,276,896	13,110,862	134,199	13,245,061	1,312,265	-408,173	11,524,623	3,880,067	2,872,206	39,809	459,111	281,712
2009	17,162,860	12,452,135	126,464	12,578,599	1,272,043	-323,270	10,983,286	3,168,338	3,011,236	36,989	463,998	277,481
2010	18,196,334	13,075,699	139,306	13,215,005	1,308,227	-256,301	11,650,477	3,333,610	3,212,247	38,935	467,346	278,001
2011	18,936,767	13,653,199	115,166	13,768,365	1,228,427	-197,284	12,342,654	3,322,266	3,271,847	40,324	469,617	284,505
2012	20,789,822	14,676,337	145,813	14,822,150	1,306,368	-154,748	13,361,034	4,107,084	3,321,704	44,062	471,829	292,878
2013	21,056,293	15,557,981	162,497	15,720,478	1,547,419	-22,257	14,150,802	3,458,357	3,447,134	44,206	476,323	299,554
2014	21,837,304	16,021,611	101,788	16,123,399	1,588,995	34,328	14,568,732	3,822,061	3,446,511	45,467	480,285	303,431
2015	20,874,750	14,708,351	81,453	14,789,804	1,510,476	137,579	13,416,907	3,629,151	3,828,692	43,148	483,798	295,373
2016	19,743,813	13,011,045	82,713	13,093,758	1,368,646	294,188	12,019,300	3,620,111	4,104,402	40,788	484,056	286,638
2017	20,374,088	13,182,126	99,861	13,281,987	1,387,431	300,096	12,194,652	3,865,792	4,313,644	42,246	482,268	285,232
2018	21,147,312	13,698,597	87,560	13,786,157	1,463,844	322,367	12,644,680	3,986,737	4,515,895	43,997	480,655	289,369
2019	21,572,990	13,925,552	96,348	14,021,900	1,486,833	307,091	12,842,158	3,986,464	4,744,368	45,014	479,248	288,739
2020	23,275,557	14,034,823	172,253	14,207,076	1,499,389	301,439	13,009,126	3,927,076	6,339,355	48,671	478,220	280,594
2021	25,489,720	14,776,446	152,086	14,928,532	1,563,060	330,378	13,695,850	4,651,216	7,142,654	53,114	479,909	291,311
2022	25,260,366	15,540,514	101,974	15,642,488	1,705,182	351,620	14,288,926	4,717,488	6,253,952	52,503	481,125	302,626

Personal Income and Employment by Area: Lafayette-West Lafayette, IN

(Thousands of dollars, except as noted.)

Year	Personal income, total	Derivation of personal income: Earnings by place of work: Nonfarm	Farm	Total	Less: Contributions for government social insurance	Plus: Adjustment for residence	Equals: Net earnings by place of residence	Plus: Dividends, interest, and rent	Plus: Personal current transfer receipts	Per capita personal income (dollars)	Population (persons)	Total employment
1970	535,609	425,705	24,706	450,411	28,902	-8,674	412,835	87,082	35,692	3,637	147,278	65,646
1971	597,007	451,883	43,949	495,832	31,773	-7,073	456,986	97,396	42,625	3,996	149,406	66,040
1972	637,933	493,458	32,908	526,366	36,675	-6,530	483,161	106,308	48,464	4,168	153,040	67,817
1973	765,802	546,383	91,749	638,132	46,769	-5,875	585,488	123,099	57,215	5,044	151,818	70,373
1974	802,481	598,445	60,827	659,272	54,021	-8,320	596,931	140,599	64,951	5,215	153,879	71,774
1975	909,362	629,579	104,173	733,752	56,348	-8,505	668,899	157,986	82,477	5,916	153,713	70,943
1976	966,945	700,093	78,180	778,273	63,079	-5,992	709,202	170,935	86,808	6,209	155,735	73,131
1977	1,046,637	792,839	48,258	841,097	70,720	-8,108	762,269	193,280	91,088	6,648	157,441	75,810
1978	1,188,042	904,886	59,906	964,792	82,830	-9,964	871,998	214,599	101,445	7,458	159,298	78,628
1979	1,321,453	1,002,904	68,076	1,070,980	95,208	-12,143	963,629	242,491	115,333	8,221	160,741	78,968
1980	1,411,891	1,066,033	28,660	1,094,693	100,615	-13,587	980,491	293,987	137,413	8,775	160,894	79,248
1981	1,580,168	1,140,626	48,658	1,189,284	116,394	-9,969	1,062,921	358,181	159,066	9,775	161,650	78,644
1982	1,661,617	1,172,077	46,139	1,218,216	122,156	-14,888	1,081,172	401,193	179,252	10,216	162,646	77,641
1983	1,702,450	1,221,198	-3,009	1,218,189	126,688	-12,835	1,078,666	428,002	195,782	10,462	162,734	77,761
1984	1,894,470	1,334,332	57,195	1,391,527	141,088	-11,514	1,238,925	450,189	205,356	11,689	162,068	80,489
1985	2,001,365	1,408,016	64,396	1,472,412	151,149	-15,246	1,306,017	478,710	216,638	12,312	162,555	81,813
1986	2,092,909	1,512,118	42,473	1,554,591	163,006	-23,765	1,367,820	496,496	228,593	12,877	162,531	83,535
1987	2,206,383	1,627,485	55,245	1,682,730	171,998	-31,579	1,479,153	495,135	232,095	13,529	163,087	85,981
1988	2,317,015	1,763,846	16,520	1,780,366	194,806	-29,342	1,556,218	516,742	244,055	14,064	164,744	88,375
1989	2,590,385	1,919,995	73,306	1,993,301	212,638	-35,666	1,744,997	581,237	264,151	15,495	167,174	90,804
1990	2,746,964	2,082,574	64,180	2,146,754	236,532	-50,578	1,859,644	602,999	284,321	16,425	167,246	93,753
1991	2,816,607	2,227,569	-7,900	2,219,669	256,124	-62,786	1,900,759	609,196	306,652	16,591	169,771	95,184
1992	3,056,312	2,380,573	51,252	2,431,825	270,673	-72,733	2,088,419	622,196	345,697	17,760	172,094	96,586
1993	3,209,520	2,497,189	55,367	2,552,556	285,612	-75,998	2,190,946	655,098	363,476	18,339	175,012	98,559
1994	3,406,702	2,653,969	70,472	2,724,441	306,722	-87,032	2,330,687	696,698	379,317	19,255	176,930	100,883
1995	3,574,962	2,835,623	5,981	2,841,604	327,179	-106,207	2,408,218	776,722	390,022	19,922	179,451	104,651
1996	3,799,269	2,951,672	100,272	3,051,944	335,439	-118,546	2,597,959	790,484	410,826	20,931	181,510	106,321
1997	4,029,053	3,157,260	83,698	3,240,958	357,628	-140,395	2,742,935	859,975	426,143	22,053	182,700	108,955
1998	4,291,277	3,414,183	39,039	3,453,222	375,728	-147,738	2,929,756	901,260	460,261	23,308	184,114	112,548
1999	4,424,197	3,580,025	30,716	3,610,741	390,929	-151,121	3,068,691	870,905	484,601	23,825	185,692	115,035
2000	4,762,483	3,843,493	39,265	3,882,758	411,728	-168,618	3,302,412	934,413	525,658	25,419	187,356	116,546
2001	4,807,815	3,847,952	54,025	3,901,977	424,143	-181,181	3,296,653	938,545	572,617	25,403	189,259	112,123
2002	4,859,981	3,913,425	39,750	3,953,175	430,755	-193,407	3,329,013	918,692	612,276	25,528	190,379	111,403
2003	4,904,567	3,954,654	59,337	4,013,991	439,333	-198,219	3,376,439	887,845	640,283	25,517	192,210	108,774
2004	5,180,386	4,139,773	113,389	4,253,162	462,645	-188,332	3,602,185	896,211	681,990	26,758	193,605	109,752
2005	5,392,199	4,358,100	76,506	4,434,606	491,412	-206,036	3,737,158	909,208	745,833	27,420	196,649	111,845
2006	5,657,158	4,481,795	71,699	4,553,494	508,596	-188,395	3,856,503	991,786	808,869	28,189	200,685	114,330
2007	5,957,099	4,660,986	114,728	4,775,714	529,374	-204,523	4,041,817	1,058,513	856,769	29,244	203,703	116,313
2008	6,447,599	4,851,182	185,614	5,036,796	553,324	-195,633	4,287,839	1,152,791	1,006,969	31,215	206,556	116,386
2009	6,311,729	4,708,316	111,734	4,820,050	540,101	-198,750	4,081,199	1,128,847	1,101,683	30,155	209,308	112,418
2010	6,570,265	4,862,878	123,479	4,986,357	548,849	-193,294	4,244,214	1,115,866	1,210,185	31,215	210,481	112,283
2011	7,034,257	5,158,872	227,709	5,386,581	514,048	-216,162	4,656,371	1,187,891	1,189,995	33,147	212,213	116,137
2012	7,351,609	5,452,595	147,724	5,600,319	538,326	-238,894	4,823,099	1,310,139	1,218,371	34,260	214,580	119,311
2013	7,468,534	5,460,483	379,800	5,840,283	616,316	-227,782	4,996,185	1,245,791	1,226,558	34,504	216,457	119,779
2014	7,712,357	5,773,408	191,257	5,964,665	648,108	-230,400	5,086,157	1,317,903	1,308,297	35,406	217,825	122,069
2015	7,840,883	5,989,480	22,999	6,012,479	677,108	-248,040	5,087,331	1,396,460	1,357,092	35,795	219,051	123,157
2016	8,120,936	6,163,262	95,622	6,258,884	688,948	-268,302	5,301,634	1,424,492	1,394,810	36,645	221,610	125,221
2017	8,468,487	6,418,581	75,031	6,493,612	719,175	-283,939	5,490,498	1,541,441	1,436,548	38,203	221,673	127,509
2018	9,022,903	6,965,014	78,784	7,043,798	774,717	-341,328	5,927,753	1,593,321	1,501,829	40,408	223,295	130,979
2019	9,214,518	7,043,436	60,952	7,104,388	798,579	-343,573	5,962,236	1,668,833	1,583,449	41,209	223,602	132,310
2020	9,698,755	6,928,432	146,219	7,074,651	816,532	-297,430	5,960,689	1,646,899	2,091,167	43,329	223,840	126,815
2021	10,628,137	7,305,537	253,394	7,558,931	855,459	-283,961	6,419,511	1,815,700	2,392,926	47,186	225,241	131,448
2022	10,905,414	7,889,894	218,947	8,108,841	918,248	-295,519	6,895,074	1,955,706	2,054,634	48,158	226,452	137,933

Personal Income and Employment by Area: Lake Charles, LA

(Thousands of dollars, except as noted.)

		Derivation of personal income										
		Earnings by place of work										
Year	Personal income, total	Nonfarm	Farm	Total	Less: Contributions for government social insurance	Plus: Adjustment for residence	Equals: Net earnings by place of residence	Plus: Dividends, interest, and rent	Plus: Personal current transfer receipts	Per capita personal income (dollars)	Population (persons)	Total employment
1970	491,476	408,068	8,433	416,501	26,515	-3,039	386,947	59,370	45,159	3,200	153,590	57,589
1971	529,251	439,671	8,758	448,429	29,222	-5,714	413,493	65,351	50,407	3,422	154,666	57,881
1972	556,300	457,816	8,903	466,719	31,780	-5,935	429,004	70,912	56,384	3,540	157,151	57,794
1973	626,807	515,599	18,047	533,646	41,616	-10,313	481,717	78,029	67,061	3,945	158,870	60,991
1974	712,607	590,165	16,504	606,669	49,209	-15,434	542,026	93,025	77,556	4,472	159,343	62,986
1975	811,538	669,467	15,228	684,695	54,433	-21,300	608,962	106,385	96,191	5,060	160,391	65,067
1976	919,711	790,080	2,070	792,150	65,168	-28,884	698,098	115,252	106,361	5,652	162,731	68,125
1977	1,036,821	894,285	8,560	902,845	73,112	-36,865	792,868	127,998	115,955	6,263	165,539	71,271
1978	1,224,395	1,090,022	10,762	1,100,784	91,950	-59,417	949,417	151,283	123,695	7,304	167,630	78,314
1979	1,407,724	1,283,800	11,753	1,295,553	112,962	-85,509	1,097,082	174,061	136,581	8,189	171,913	82,909
1980	1,641,290	1,492,938	8,637	1,501,575	130,913	-112,164	1,258,498	215,878	166,914	9,249	177,456	86,336
1981	1,897,278	1,722,383	3,871	1,726,254	162,348	-127,778	1,436,128	275,618	185,532	10,498	180,724	89,401
1982	1,941,631	1,644,337	5,670	1,650,007	157,870	-105,339	1,386,798	325,749	229,084	10,560	183,865	82,812
1983	2,038,350	1,661,668	4,750	1,666,418	157,302	-108,239	1,400,877	364,764	272,709	11,037	184,681	80,277
1984	2,056,836	1,630,558	2,356	1,632,914	156,757	-94,455	1,381,702	400,291	274,843	11,161	184,287	78,899
1985	2,121,225	1,659,056	4,615	1,663,671	160,808	-95,607	1,407,256	432,788	281,181	11,589	183,031	78,558
1986	2,128,043	1,643,559	61	1,643,620	158,069	-95,019	1,390,532	428,523	308,988	11,738	181,297	76,259
1987	2,186,689	1,712,486	1,930	1,714,416	162,760	-95,225	1,456,431	416,093	314,165	12,134	180,214	77,853
1988	2,325,136	1,796,623	13,651	1,810,274	179,495	-95,490	1,535,289	463,222	326,625	12,993	178,955	79,865
1989	2,464,911	1,920,278	2,519	1,922,797	195,459	-106,515	1,620,823	476,325	367,763	13,865	177,773	82,655
1990	2,747,959	2,170,146	4,960	2,175,106	227,865	-125,659	1,821,582	518,765	407,612	15,479	177,524	87,736
1991	2,909,501	2,306,447	2,286	2,308,733	247,094	-131,832	1,929,807	525,355	454,339	16,214	179,439	89,353
1992	3,053,269	2,404,060	4,581	2,408,641	254,461	-133,887	2,020,293	526,656	506,320	16,894	180,736	88,809
1993	3,200,811	2,483,285	5,344	2,488,629	264,065	-143,262	2,081,302	563,030	556,479	17,578	182,093	89,641
1994	3,451,251	2,665,015	1,629	2,666,644	287,657	-157,124	2,221,863	607,401	621,987	18,738	184,181	93,804
1995	3,669,419	2,832,378	6,465	2,838,843	305,109	-169,093	2,364,641	662,370	642,408	19,664	186,607	97,914
1996	3,889,759	3,061,153	2,306	3,063,459	330,253	-187,238	2,545,968	690,626	653,165	20,544	189,335	102,120
1997	4,093,878	3,286,609	3,640	3,290,249	353,288	-199,666	2,737,295	684,025	672,558	21,425	191,076	105,423
1998	4,234,663	3,377,266	6,882	3,384,148	369,902	-214,006	2,800,240	758,541	675,882	22,002	192,470	107,839
1999	4,302,314	3,432,825	6,198	3,439,023	370,431	-216,882	2,851,710	739,039	711,565	22,245	193,408	107,766
2000	4,471,145	3,547,016	5,291	3,552,307	374,473	-217,516	2,960,318	778,513	732,314	23,108	193,491	108,617
2001	4,709,978	3,671,268	11,315	3,682,583	382,945	-238,312	3,061,326	817,751	830,901	24,382	193,171	108,198
2002	4,802,713	3,751,844	5,371	3,757,215	395,074	-236,548	3,125,593	809,256	867,864	24,843	193,321	108,037
2003	4,853,991	3,792,859	10,549	3,803,408	396,488	-228,946	3,177,974	788,791	887,226	24,950	194,552	107,587
2004	5,105,771	4,006,040	11,106	4,017,146	411,579	-253,883	3,351,684	785,600	968,487	26,124	195,444	106,569
2005	5,584,336	4,311,501	4,233	4,315,734	432,942	-292,281	3,590,511	843,663	1,150,162	28,453	196,263	108,682
2006	6,023,436	4,635,420	13,460	4,648,880	459,802	-305,342	3,883,736	1,056,150	1,083,550	31,198	193,069	110,932
2007	6,673,249	4,891,995	3,261	4,895,256	488,913	-327,772	4,078,571	1,472,953	1,121,725	34,292	194,598	113,093
2008	7,137,010	5,262,300	2,405	5,264,705	522,060	-377,869	4,364,776	1,486,527	1,285,707	36,346	196,362	115,652
2009	6,784,998	5,070,997	6,188	5,077,185	507,048	-315,874	4,254,263	1,179,095	1,351,640	34,266	198,010	112,608
2010	6,982,222	5,143,313	8,721	5,152,034	505,409	-288,145	4,358,480	1,169,712	1,454,030	34,877	200,196	110,785
2011	7,269,862	5,312,835	8,284	5,321,119	475,284	-306,076	4,539,759	1,248,526	1,481,577	36,013	201,866	112,346
2012	7,688,193	5,581,209	16,021	5,597,230	494,928	-315,842	4,786,460	1,371,163	1,530,570	37,773	203,535	114,551
2013	7,795,508	5,872,769	24,078	5,896,847	586,136	-368,717	4,941,994	1,271,001	1,582,513	37,889	205,746	117,178
2014	8,336,366	6,732,599	13,929	6,746,528	666,583	-634,710	5,445,235	1,328,388	1,562,743	40,084	207,970	123,687
2015	8,884,548	7,232,133	2,703	7,234,836	728,047	-759,988	5,746,801	1,408,970	1,728,777	42,081	211,129	129,088
2016	9,130,125	7,827,046	-370	7,826,676	805,686	-1,054,933	5,966,057	1,340,494	1,823,574	42,537	214,640	135,687
2017	9,639,307	8,454,205	-327	8,453,878	877,830	-1,306,560	6,269,488	1,474,021	1,895,798	44,261	217,783	143,037
2018	10,115,604	8,991,567	-5,489	8,986,078	941,636	-1,397,365	6,647,077	1,491,291	1,977,236	45,998	219,916	145,921
2019	10,116,817	8,883,640	-6,780	8,876,860	924,071	-1,259,975	6,692,814	1,359,393	2,064,610	45,645	221,639	141,960
2020	10,444,322	8,001,651	770	8,002,421	841,106	-1,015,403	6,145,912	1,472,033	2,826,377	47,028	222,088	124,256
2021	10,883,994	8,286,023	-5,488	8,280,535	875,841	-1,120,356	6,284,338	1,689,631	2,910,025	51,781	210,194	126,250
2022	10,739,017	8,441,656	-7,882	8,433,774	905,286	-1,032,076	6,496,412	1,716,043	2,526,562	51,799	207,320	126,590

Personal Income and Employment by Area: Lake Havasu City-Kingman, AZ

(Thousands of dollars, except as noted.)

Year	Personal income, total	Derivation of personal income: Earnings by place of work: Nonfarm	Farm	Total	Less: Contributions for government social insurance	Plus: Adjustment for residence	Equals: Net earnings by place of residence	Plus: Dividends, interest, and rent	Plus: Personal current transfer receipts	Per capita personal income (dollars)	Population (persons)	Total employment
1970	102,490	66,091	1,274	67,365	4,225	11,209	74,349	18,445	9,696	3,891	26,338	9,297
1971	118,683	73,925	2,040	75,965	4,937	13,553	84,581	21,589	12,513	4,130	28,736	9,969
1972	135,971	83,329	3,489	86,818	5,873	14,746	95,691	24,804	15,476	4,374	31,084	10,832
1973	163,490	97,737	5,483	103,220	7,882	18,447	113,785	30,171	19,534	4,804	34,030	11,853
1974	182,255	115,194	686	115,880	9,800	16,123	122,203	36,302	23,750	4,983	36,572	13,269
1975	211,573	125,660	9,382	135,042	10,576	15,944	140,410	42,053	29,110	5,372	39,388	13,882
1976	230,847	141,398	54	141,452	11,874	18,049	147,627	47,091	36,129	5,437	42,458	14,593
1977	269,381	160,553	2,912	163,465	13,812	21,870	171,523	55,967	41,891	6,220	43,312	15,773
1978	328,934	196,295	3,876	200,171	17,289	26,737	209,619	69,182	50,133	7,148	46,017	17,606
1979	397,469	247,144	1,930	249,074	23,306	27,618	253,386	83,817	60,266	7,676	51,783	20,022
1980	461,141	268,553	4,924	273,477	25,668	31,928	279,737	105,486	75,918	8,173	56,423	21,285
1981	515,797	282,505	3,578	286,083	29,311	36,741	293,513	128,461	93,823	8,801	58,607	21,566
1982	548,781	270,741	4,562	275,303	28,949	42,111	288,465	149,885	110,431	8,775	62,539	20,609
1983	614,985	289,999	7,597	297,596	31,045	49,929	316,480	175,209	123,296	9,608	64,005	21,081
1984	715,472	341,804	5,857	347,661	37,252	56,842	367,251	211,388	136,833	10,621	67,364	23,340
1985	815,089	389,168	2,387	391,555	43,430	66,435	414,560	244,422	156,107	11,518	70,769	25,423
1986	910,001	432,044	1,266	433,310	48,416	77,985	462,879	272,703	174,419	12,074	75,366	26,881
1987	997,436	485,900	1,456	487,356	54,319	92,319	525,356	276,495	195,585	12,901	77,314	29,243
1988	1,118,879	536,321	3,910	540,231	62,328	112,478	590,381	307,706	220,792	13,582	82,381	31,315
1989	1,256,458	595,501	6,951	602,452	72,849	136,044	665,647	341,098	249,713	14,435	87,040	33,410
1990	1,444,414	702,053	8,192	710,245	86,995	164,857	788,107	373,506	282,801	15,126	95,491	36,930
1991	1,547,521	759,732	7,829	767,561	94,310	170,535	843,786	380,663	323,072	15,133	102,263	38,893
1992	1,651,322	811,377	7,696	819,073	100,658	182,942	901,357	383,627	366,338	15,199	108,644	39,206
1993	1,795,029	875,755	6,157	881,912	109,043	198,515	971,384	422,173	401,472	15,514	115,706	40,507
1994	1,984,667	957,454	5,223	962,677	120,219	216,911	1,059,369	482,001	443,297	16,148	122,906	43,326
1995	2,037,024	982,316	1,863	984,179	120,797	234,062	1,097,444	455,782	483,798	15,636	130,274	43,977
1996	2,190,433	1,046,698	3,450	1,050,148	131,001	255,698	1,174,845	488,553	527,035	16,055	136,436	46,030
1997	2,360,860	1,158,289	2,951	1,161,240	139,899	277,141	1,298,482	502,582	559,796	16,753	140,922	47,793
1998	2,574,969	1,250,558	4,018	1,254,576	149,045	302,842	1,408,373	555,083	611,513	17,739	145,155	49,316
1999	2,748,992	1,351,280	6,174	1,357,454	160,454	332,622	1,529,622	567,364	652,006	18,284	150,351	51,247
2000	2,969,409	1,472,338	7,868	1,480,206	174,489	355,097	1,660,814	606,120	702,475	19,008	156,215	54,312
2001	3,258,541	1,630,318	7,331	1,637,649	193,606	389,455	1,833,498	641,638	783,405	20,326	160,312	57,796
2002	3,474,253	1,778,416	5,176	1,783,592	211,626	418,967	1,990,933	620,339	862,981	20,910	166,155	59,875
2003	3,746,038	1,905,589	8,565	1,914,154	226,818	472,429	2,159,765	646,706	939,567	21,699	172,633	63,760
2004	4,135,804	2,093,547	11,858	2,105,405	249,270	564,275	2,420,410	691,926	1,023,468	22,910	180,521	67,457
2005	4,516,172	2,281,964	11,241	2,293,205	279,031	622,368	2,636,542	755,591	1,124,039	23,924	188,773	72,539
2006	4,811,080	2,490,996	9,552	2,500,548	305,628	601,693	2,796,613	774,643	1,239,824	24,525	196,168	75,361
2007	4,995,016	2,472,137	6,371	2,478,508	313,303	593,883	2,759,088	892,571	1,343,357	25,005	199,760	74,679
2008	5,123,377	2,438,525	5,703	2,444,228	316,540	547,268	2,674,956	940,230	1,508,191	25,607	200,078	70,532
2009	5,125,877	2,277,800	3,936	2,281,736	302,211	572,136	2,551,661	891,958	1,682,258	25,668	199,696	65,566
2010	5,179,503	2,281,004	3,493	2,284,497	308,325	562,997	2,539,169	859,414	1,780,920	25,864	200,260	64,093
2011	5,239,740	2,274,047	17,789	2,291,836	283,840	496,640	2,504,636	923,874	1,811,230	25,875	202,500	64,080
2012	5,338,669	2,298,025	2,792	2,300,817	286,453	521,135	2,535,499	951,942	1,851,228	26,327	202,781	63,232
2013	5,493,504	2,425,001	18,438	2,443,439	330,623	492,751	2,605,567	964,021	1,923,916	27,154	202,308	63,996
2014	5,778,545	2,525,574	13,784	2,539,358	340,951	538,370	2,736,777	1,026,651	2,015,117	28,558	202,345	65,381
2015	5,977,569	2,619,566	17,552	2,637,118	354,997	537,460	2,819,581	1,038,766	2,119,222	29,410	203,247	66,864
2016	6,240,157	2,667,663	17,904	2,685,567	368,363	605,961	2,923,165	1,093,117	2,223,875	30,598	203,940	67,872
2017	6,625,763	2,841,013	24,576	2,865,589	394,784	630,284	3,101,089	1,140,820	2,383,854	32,260	205,389	69,882
2018	6,992,432	3,001,176	27,024	3,028,200	427,887	642,925	3,243,238	1,220,180	2,529,014	33,657	207,757	71,866
2019	7,477,170	3,152,508	23,699	3,176,207	451,214	767,609	3,492,602	1,274,586	2,709,982	35,457	210,880	72,854
2020	8,616,065	3,447,843	32,311	3,480,154	491,385	757,447	3,746,216	1,364,722	3,505,127	40,229	214,176	73,806
2021	9,280,769	3,782,616	28,332	3,810,948	538,874	776,566	4,048,640	1,477,914	3,754,215	42,777	216,957	79,117
2022	9,858,399	4,234,979	29,302	4,264,281	597,911	1,072,507	4,738,877	1,629,701	3,489,821	44,645	220,816	81,675

Personal Income and Employment by Area: Lakeland-Winter Haven, FL

(Thousands of dollars, except as noted.)

Year	Personal income, total	Derivation of personal income: Earnings by place of work: Nonfarm	Farm	Total	Less: Contributions for government social insurance	Plus: Adjustment for residence	Equals: Net earnings by place of residence	Plus: Dividends, interest, and rent	Plus: Personal current transfer receipts	Per capita personal income (dollars)	Population (persons)	Total employment
1970	804,411	584,104	54,769	638,873	38,981	-22,544	577,348	145,461	81,602	3,492	230,334	97,281
1971	895,766	644,399	62,637	707,036	44,615	-23,517	638,904	159,356	97,506	3,709	241,479	100,888
1972	1,029,634	746,353	76,593	822,946	54,268	-27,489	741,189	175,690	112,755	4,079	252,394	107,814
1973	1,199,202	891,703	73,763	965,466	74,503	-34,508	856,455	208,355	134,392	4,576	262,049	118,069
1974	1,383,145	1,044,138	75,436	1,119,574	91,301	-44,243	984,030	244,445	154,670	5,047	274,042	125,364
1975	1,564,674	1,170,262	79,911	1,250,173	100,928	-56,828	1,092,417	273,124	199,133	5,501	284,417	128,059
1976	1,690,740	1,244,502	91,047	1,335,549	108,871	-57,797	1,168,881	297,710	224,149	5,839	289,562	128,195
1977	1,904,825	1,395,553	116,831	1,512,384	122,456	-68,148	1,321,780	337,426	245,619	6,434	296,048	134,567
1978	2,198,857	1,599,310	156,694	1,756,004	143,986	-80,311	1,531,707	396,279	270,871	7,301	301,183	142,680
1979	2,512,240	1,842,204	154,007	1,996,211	173,781	-98,243	1,724,187	470,314	317,739	8,033	312,723	149,427
1980	2,987,387	2,132,894	203,370	2,336,264	202,950	-117,504	2,015,810	594,397	377,180	9,219	324,038	156,846
1981	3,305,852	2,358,635	135,209	2,493,844	241,458	-125,421	2,126,965	736,196	442,691	9,928	332,973	160,268
1982	3,449,438	2,358,083	132,440	2,490,523	247,168	-111,860	2,131,495	805,797	512,146	10,147	339,930	155,026
1983	3,753,755	2,508,403	171,774	2,680,177	263,157	-99,305	2,317,715	879,704	556,336	10,846	346,080	157,947
1984	4,104,910	2,805,097	122,032	2,927,129	301,586	-90,952	2,534,591	991,182	579,137	11,582	354,414	165,687
1985	4,438,915	3,010,169	127,755	3,137,924	329,542	-83,599	2,724,783	1,082,570	631,562	12,201	363,802	173,302
1986	4,741,082	3,178,503	117,296	3,295,799	356,930	-68,405	2,870,464	1,180,597	690,021	12,743	372,057	176,446
1987	5,119,746	3,483,511	136,969	3,620,480	383,942	-65,200	3,171,338	1,220,984	727,424	13,469	380,106	178,789
1988	5,683,411	3,820,099	190,740	4,010,839	434,129	-59,470	3,517,240	1,344,885	821,286	14,604	389,160	188,505
1989	6,246,147	4,131,686	148,850	4,280,536	475,193	-61,495	3,743,848	1,594,881	907,418	15,685	398,231	195,457
1990	6,557,135	4,303,229	120,957	4,424,186	489,615	-25,670	3,908,901	1,642,847	1,005,387	16,081	407,756	194,693
1991	6,824,475	4,398,968	134,981	4,533,949	504,114	61,879	4,091,714	1,607,976	1,124,785	16,439	415,136	191,941
1992	7,200,589	4,648,776	78,279	4,727,055	530,097	99,681	4,296,639	1,609,133	1,294,817	17,016	423,171	188,240
1993	7,594,186	4,888,768	84,171	4,972,939	553,994	183,094	4,602,039	1,587,158	1,404,989	17,693	429,224	192,484
1994	8,216,209	5,279,642	87,382	5,367,024	604,922	234,620	4,996,722	1,711,171	1,508,316	18,738	438,480	199,641
1995	8,845,079	5,584,518	96,626	5,681,144	636,279	339,012	5,383,877	1,841,720	1,619,482	19,780	447,182	205,287
1996	9,381,943	5,976,920	80,402	6,057,322	670,561	338,439	5,725,200	1,934,921	1,721,822	20,642	454,512	210,699
1997	9,719,838	6,128,069	89,533	6,217,602	692,674	440,210	5,965,138	1,959,989	1,794,711	20,970	463,519	214,741
1998	10,678,217	6,693,894	132,364	6,826,258	746,304	506,341	6,586,295	2,219,698	1,872,224	22,650	471,450	223,190
1999	11,198,085	7,116,170	115,792	7,231,962	781,582	674,472	7,124,852	2,139,293	1,933,940	23,425	478,047	227,091
2000	11,713,269	7,269,959	120,892	7,390,851	808,731	760,536	7,342,656	2,316,969	2,053,644	24,125	485,515	234,576
2001	12,679,253	8,098,941	102,568	8,201,509	886,154	710,179	8,025,534	2,422,783	2,230,936	25,723	492,917	232,840
2002	12,952,374	8,349,136	118,585	8,467,721	912,066	724,928	8,280,583	2,256,782	2,415,009	25,829	501,469	235,386
2003	13,651,479	8,793,525	94,544	8,888,069	959,424	713,019	8,641,664	2,400,872	2,608,943	26,608	513,058	238,685
2004	14,721,796	9,352,071	92,689	9,444,760	1,031,819	726,395	9,139,336	2,715,880	2,866,580	27,899	527,685	249,749
2005	16,004,826	10,208,825	134,776	10,343,601	1,143,060	716,632	9,917,173	3,003,999	3,083,654	29,239	547,373	266,191
2006	16,733,970	10,540,361	150,622	10,690,983	1,227,269	695,479	10,159,193	3,232,865	3,341,912	29,444	568,324	275,018
2007	17,514,273	10,690,971	90,920	10,781,891	1,253,518	686,477	10,214,850	3,627,154	3,672,269	29,889	585,982	276,632
2008	18,102,452	10,598,612	80,769	10,679,381	1,264,782	617,174	10,031,773	3,875,968	4,194,711	30,434	594,801	268,508
2009	17,443,242	10,225,808	106,799	10,332,607	1,250,201	485,513	9,567,919	3,357,203	4,518,120	29,136	598,683	258,200
2010	18,610,582	10,474,307	125,789	10,600,096	1,250,593	437,751	9,787,254	3,916,740	4,906,588	30,873	602,820	255,712
2011	19,611,331	10,636,427	132,975	10,769,402	1,144,032	416,138	10,041,508	4,439,932	5,129,891	32,228	608,513	258,253
2012	19,660,903	11,069,456	147,101	11,216,557	1,197,440	398,259	10,417,376	4,099,614	5,143,913	32,082	612,827	261,791
2013	19,768,545	11,475,059	147,864	11,622,923	1,393,700	325,857	10,555,080	3,883,852	5,329,613	31,947	618,786	267,005
2014	20,676,962	11,832,409	132,792	11,965,201	1,441,540	402,235	10,925,896	4,145,348	5,605,718	32,859	629,269	273,868
2015	21,680,805	12,295,248	151,906	12,447,154	1,489,913	450,880	11,408,121	4,357,069	5,915,615	33,767	642,067	281,071
2016	22,176,518	12,719,379	112,792	12,832,171	1,550,357	484,208	11,766,022	4,305,821	6,104,675	33,702	658,019	287,241
2017	23,852,470	13,477,135	119,274	13,596,409	1,637,477	488,819	12,447,751	4,964,674	6,440,045	35,287	675,948	300,183
2018	25,178,791	14,352,925	82,465	14,435,390	1,756,164	497,752	13,176,978	5,267,136	6,734,677	36,200	695,556	312,758
2019	26,883,856	15,278,148	99,538	15,377,686	1,905,264	542,509	14,014,931	5,683,643	7,185,282	37,771	711,750	323,517
2020	29,793,992	16,289,944	73,918	16,363,862	2,056,696	286,264	14,593,430	5,845,500	9,355,062	40,807	730,111	336,051
2021	33,163,312	18,033,635	61,378	18,095,013	2,211,680	376,406	16,259,739	6,061,712	10,841,861	43,915	755,179	362,866
2022	34,033,970	19,781,989	70,771	19,852,760	2,470,207	533,112	17,915,665	6,500,243	9,618,062	43,223	787,404	379,656

Personal Income and Employment by Area: Lancaster, PA

(Thousands of dollars, except as noted.)

Year	Personal income, total	Derivation of personal income: Earnings by place of work: Nonfarm	Farm	Total	Less: Contributions for government social insurance	Plus: Adjustment for residence	Equals: Net earnings by place of residence	Plus: Dividends, interest, and rent	Plus: Personal current transfer receipts	Per capita personal income (dollars)	Population (persons)	Total employment
1970	1,391,393	1,059,372	84,767	1,144,139	78,563	42,606	1,108,182	182,577	100,634	4,331	321,290	156,017
1971	1,454,953	1,116,689	66,208	1,182,897	86,287	48,751	1,145,361	193,890	115,702	4,447	327,155	156,834
1972	1,616,518	1,258,627	65,432	1,324,059	102,540	56,771	1,278,290	208,956	129,272	4,867	332,160	163,540
1973	1,831,295	1,428,735	87,805	1,516,540	134,168	65,280	1,447,652	240,102	143,541	5,437	336,819	172,896
1974	1,976,296	1,532,955	68,078	1,601,033	149,336	78,236	1,529,933	271,772	174,591	5,810	340,170	173,356
1975	2,128,090	1,595,007	62,793	1,657,800	150,550	88,929	1,596,179	300,811	231,100	6,172	344,814	168,983
1976	2,345,672	1,790,272	51,857	1,842,129	172,580	101,587	1,771,136	326,352	248,184	6,752	347,407	173,386
1977	2,594,683	2,012,731	28,510	2,041,241	193,513	116,154	1,963,882	368,503	262,298	7,390	351,084	179,617
1978	2,972,383	2,299,560	70,842	2,370,402	226,062	133,832	2,278,172	410,765	283,446	8,381	354,667	187,604
1979	3,337,948	2,563,110	90,470	2,653,580	261,659	155,987	2,547,908	465,059	324,981	9,289	359,329	192,732
1980	3,612,090	2,707,502	46,456	2,753,958	279,918	181,615	2,655,655	578,339	378,096	9,939	363,420	194,330
1981	3,998,713	2,902,309	83,261	2,985,570	320,438	195,278	2,860,410	705,102	433,201	10,896	366,979	193,300
1982	4,299,980	3,025,906	69,015	3,094,921	338,229	198,595	2,955,287	838,835	505,858	11,590	370,992	191,675
1983	4,604,793	3,282,674	52,440	3,335,114	370,797	199,558	3,163,875	897,364	543,554	12,239	376,234	194,960
1984	5,148,808	3,662,780	147,665	3,810,445	431,253	211,263	3,590,455	1,006,182	552,171	13,518	380,892	203,704
1985	5,544,247	3,975,471	116,493	4,091,964	472,106	216,995	3,836,853	1,108,674	598,720	14,391	385,245	210,863
1986	6,043,677	4,345,460	167,565	4,513,025	516,025	219,696	4,216,696	1,185,590	641,391	15,404	392,339	218,827
1987	6,506,164	4,774,976	168,649	4,943,625	560,536	231,498	4,614,587	1,220,122	671,455	16,194	401,773	228,379
1988	7,047,197	5,282,181	81,846	5,364,027	627,239	244,879	4,981,667	1,336,032	729,498	17,182	410,152	237,036
1989	7,880,450	5,727,587	178,115	5,905,702	666,534	259,862	5,499,030	1,585,611	795,809	18,871	417,585	244,037
1990	8,253,473	6,099,780	110,193	6,209,973	717,200	264,732	5,757,505	1,632,241	863,727	19,422	424,947	250,269
1991	8,503,264	6,235,028	83,396	6,318,424	740,612	275,491	5,853,303	1,654,158	995,803	19,719	431,229	247,396
1992	9,077,864	6,670,842	146,879	6,817,721	787,280	288,418	6,318,859	1,693,962	1,065,043	20,826	435,886	249,064
1993	9,642,426	7,049,622	148,174	7,197,796	845,373	288,318	6,640,741	1,881,150	1,120,535	21,862	441,056	251,472
1994	9,865,231	7,343,425	123,479	7,466,904	895,352	298,940	6,870,492	1,825,722	1,169,017	22,107	446,254	255,573
1995	10,263,191	7,668,162	77,836	7,745,998	929,798	306,171	7,122,371	1,901,875	1,238,945	22,715	451,817	263,269
1996	10,897,733	7,994,597	183,834	8,178,431	946,195	320,010	7,552,246	2,012,595	1,332,892	23,910	455,783	266,835
1997	11,536,973	8,547,278	149,084	8,696,362	996,179	337,155	8,037,338	2,119,333	1,380,302	25,076	460,085	273,421
1998	12,080,724	8,929,601	140,947	9,070,548	1,035,042	359,356	8,394,862	2,236,607	1,449,255	26,021	464,272	272,593
1999	12,585,873	9,426,029	114,586	9,540,615	1,078,043	376,553	8,839,125	2,208,348	1,538,400	26,900	467,879	276,989
2000	13,652,371	10,188,376	167,337	10,355,713	1,146,931	393,303	9,602,085	2,398,919	1,651,367	28,927	471,955	282,826
2001	14,493,590	10,846,497	179,171	11,025,668	1,201,685	422,900	10,246,883	2,424,563	1,822,144	30,482	475,483	287,532
2002	14,676,442	11,221,178	97,545	11,318,723	1,236,596	425,571	10,507,698	2,204,474	1,964,270	30,568	480,118	287,525
2003	15,325,145	11,592,907	177,982	11,770,889	1,271,398	434,101	10,933,592	2,298,443	2,093,110	31,590	485,119	287,565
2004	16,378,292	12,356,893	265,552	12,622,445	1,337,534	463,869	11,748,780	2,440,527	2,188,985	33,427	489,977	294,484
2005	17,153,152	12,963,478	262,121	13,225,599	1,406,529	477,787	12,296,857	2,437,220	2,419,075	34,672	494,722	300,351
2006	17,715,625	13,298,872	205,690	13,504,562	1,469,459	533,055	12,568,158	2,557,798	2,589,669	35,366	500,922	303,191
2007	18,530,968	13,414,962	308,081	13,723,043	1,480,850	573,107	12,815,300	2,935,922	2,779,746	36,576	506,639	307,738
2008	19,314,644	13,508,189	229,957	13,738,146	1,512,874	571,930	12,797,202	3,334,009	3,183,433	37,727	511,957	308,125
2009	18,921,543	12,992,124	126,221	13,118,345	1,477,670	645,773	12,286,448	3,086,907	3,548,188	36,629	516,577	299,349
2010	19,840,901	13,532,069	265,399	13,797,468	1,513,764	751,370	13,035,074	2,997,436	3,808,391	38,120	520,480	298,772
2011	20,852,903	13,861,719	324,736	14,186,455	1,395,089	892,549	13,683,915	3,318,305	3,850,683	39,736	524,782	300,903
2012	21,529,443	14,219,106	331,176	14,550,282	1,423,028	961,342	14,088,596	3,545,318	3,895,529	40,747	528,372	305,700
2013	22,164,867	14,806,965	428,437	15,235,402	1,644,583	1,044,016	14,634,835	3,539,513	3,990,519	41,650	532,174	309,653
2014	23,277,739	15,552,281	512,511	16,064,792	1,722,209	1,049,482	15,392,065	3,749,261	4,136,413	43,418	536,132	316,777
2015	24,540,270	16,713,022	339,946	17,052,968	1,828,349	1,046,277	16,270,896	3,926,066	4,343,308	45,501	539,334	323,988
2016	25,221,184	17,311,511	120,069	17,431,580	1,893,764	1,056,568	16,594,384	4,104,857	4,521,943	46,505	542,338	330,634
2017	26,546,133	18,175,193	268,265	18,443,458	2,005,585	1,103,621	17,541,494	4,392,618	4,612,021	48,614	546,058	334,600
2018	28,078,893	19,280,154	213,089	19,493,243	2,096,364	1,093,068	18,489,947	4,652,809	4,936,137	51,114	549,342	341,675
2019	29,367,764	20,236,439	230,345	20,466,784	2,201,562	1,119,410	19,384,632	4,828,806	5,154,326	53,252	551,484	342,459
2020	31,958,383	20,666,331	136,348	20,802,679	2,222,674	1,113,613	19,693,618	5,014,252	7,250,513	57,816	552,761	328,900
2021	34,350,132	21,978,826	317,520	22,296,346	2,386,624	1,155,166	21,064,888	5,665,592	7,619,652	61,775	556,049	342,308
2022	35,091,885	23,484,689	576,578	24,061,267	2,629,922	1,223,412	22,654,757	6,064,563	6,372,565	63,044	556,629	357,866

Personal Income and Employment by Area: Lansing-East Lansing, MI

(Thousands of dollars, except as noted.)

Year	Personal income, total	Derivation of personal income: Earnings by place of work: Nonfarm	Farm	Total	Less: Contributions for government social insurance	Plus: Adjustment for residence	Equals: Net earnings by place of residence	Plus: Dividends, interest, and rent	Plus: Personal current transfer receipts	Per capita personal income (dollars)	Population (persons)	Total employment
1970	1,730,118	1,400,021	28,376	1,428,397	95,947	19,560	1,352,010	240,173	137,935	3,910	442,507	178,895
1971	1,957,067	1,604,116	25,335	1,629,451	112,787	16,043	1,532,707	262,264	162,096	4,372	447,595	183,933
1972	2,163,837	1,777,111	34,212	1,811,323	132,742	17,293	1,695,874	288,983	178,980	4,788	451,948	189,758
1973	2,404,261	1,998,424	39,069	2,037,493	172,536	19,900	1,884,857	319,813	199,591	5,227	459,983	197,773
1974	2,538,285	2,004,263	47,524	2,051,787	178,400	37,650	1,911,037	362,440	264,808	5,453	465,472	197,353
1975	2,831,820	2,190,592	42,828	2,233,420	191,650	34,631	2,076,401	411,386	344,033	6,056	467,615	198,704
1976	3,168,428	2,540,245	32,061	2,572,306	226,610	24,647	2,370,343	445,295	352,790	6,749	469,498	205,673
1977	3,565,355	2,870,805	37,609	2,908,414	255,610	31,054	2,683,858	498,521	382,976	7,524	473,839	212,578
1978	3,941,808	3,246,767	28,288	3,275,055	298,282	32,001	3,008,774	556,303	376,731	8,206	480,378	222,263
1979	4,400,127	3,627,240	37,264	3,664,504	343,948	23,101	3,343,657	629,015	427,455	9,072	485,040	229,673
1980	4,803,968	3,789,906	33,580	3,823,486	350,610	12,879	3,485,755	745,880	572,333	9,777	491,349	226,162
1981	5,251,713	4,140,433	41,068	4,181,501	418,280	6,584	3,769,805	874,875	607,033	10,672	492,122	224,497
1982	5,435,319	4,163,962	14,764	4,178,726	423,791	-4,193	3,750,742	1,004,412	680,165	11,202	485,223	216,037
1983	5,918,887	4,599,849	7,697	4,607,546	478,411	-16,177	4,112,958	1,096,611	709,318	12,281	481,941	220,586
1984	6,412,386	4,954,331	31,618	4,985,949	529,528	5,371	4,461,792	1,220,983	729,611	13,303	482,037	225,220
1985	6,906,493	5,416,599	34,179	5,450,778	599,136	10,238	4,861,880	1,297,893	746,720	14,250	484,662	237,012
1986	7,338,603	5,770,262	24,777	5,795,039	641,267	16,302	5,170,074	1,376,431	792,098	14,923	491,775	244,872
1987	7,520,179	5,889,148	35,219	5,924,367	647,156	14,387	5,291,598	1,394,981	833,600	15,144	496,579	254,928
1988	7,993,000	6,321,466	31,672	6,353,138	723,664	9,027	5,638,501	1,487,192	867,307	15,994	499,754	260,357
1989	8,629,046	6,750,616	61,832	6,812,448	769,562	16,905	6,059,791	1,625,008	944,247	17,250	500,232	268,054
1990	9,012,056	7,037,143	44,759	7,081,902	811,621	20,792	6,291,073	1,696,554	1,024,429	17,906	503,291	272,882
1991	9,435,555	7,355,133	28,341	7,383,474	861,178	20,628	6,542,924	1,743,044	1,149,587	18,602	507,226	273,360
1992	9,910,768	7,781,891	32,909	7,814,800	903,438	20,237	6,931,599	1,775,532	1,203,637	19,444	509,714	274,660
1993	10,235,532	7,931,622	36,301	7,967,923	922,868	56,260	7,101,315	1,835,302	1,298,915	19,980	512,279	274,370
1994	10,954,677	8,488,537	27,384	8,515,921	1,007,180	79,830	7,588,571	2,045,538	1,320,568	21,313	513,997	282,017
1995	11,408,773	8,874,827	31,413	8,906,240	1,054,771	91,775	7,943,244	2,086,689	1,378,840	22,155	514,962	294,433
1996	11,951,126	9,253,401	37,201	9,290,602	1,072,412	99,189	8,317,379	2,191,657	1,442,090	23,035	518,831	299,015
1997	12,461,486	9,607,658	37,622	9,645,280	1,113,419	109,226	8,641,087	2,278,362	1,542,037	23,979	519,679	298,372
1998	12,846,949	9,945,998	35,490	9,981,488	1,137,314	140,947	8,985,121	2,310,178	1,551,650	24,740	519,274	297,865
1999	13,571,768	10,683,129	56,482	10,739,611	1,218,168	145,480	9,666,923	2,245,628	1,659,217	26,161	518,786	302,774
2000	14,244,321	11,221,512	27,636	11,249,148	1,264,231	165,347	10,150,264	2,363,735	1,730,322	27,369	520,449	306,462
2001	14,702,225	11,555,547	26,688	11,582,235	1,277,633	133,992	10,438,594	2,334,197	1,929,434	28,054	524,067	305,758
2002	14,793,509	11,794,331	25,238	11,819,569	1,311,273	108,521	10,616,817	2,173,889	2,002,803	28,040	527,582	303,962
2003	15,102,011	11,901,461	38,900	11,940,361	1,322,073	90,673	10,708,961	2,281,988	2,111,062	28,450	530,834	304,310
2004	15,434,707	12,048,422	80,556	12,128,978	1,344,685	116,286	10,900,579	2,325,083	2,209,045	28,863	534,758	302,520
2005	15,662,798	12,140,146	58,217	12,198,363	1,378,218	96,478	10,916,623	2,379,537	2,366,638	29,249	535,500	299,189
2006	16,160,734	12,507,755	66,816	12,574,571	1,446,785	44,705	11,172,491	2,441,191	2,547,052	30,140	536,188	300,246
2007	16,675,137	12,609,979	77,706	12,687,685	1,473,051	-727	11,213,907	2,658,916	2,802,314	31,097	536,230	301,630
2008	17,327,837	12,706,398	88,954	12,795,352	1,501,806	-67,532	11,226,014	2,869,240	3,232,583	32,379	535,161	296,411
2009	16,963,912	12,164,536	43,613	12,208,149	1,438,571	-105,947	10,663,631	2,706,795	3,593,486	31,776	533,857	282,680
2010	17,789,968	12,802,266	92,807	12,895,073	1,484,652	-176,722	11,233,699	2,705,094	3,851,175	33,269	534,726	282,864
2011	18,317,428	12,869,710	215,964	13,085,674	1,325,932	-143,410	11,616,332	2,851,406	3,849,690	34,188	535,779	285,875
2012	18,545,907	12,955,584	134,426	13,090,010	1,346,263	-137,626	11,606,121	3,102,585	3,837,201	34,631	535,526	284,701
2013	18,694,331	13,298,130	154,746	13,452,876	1,569,441	-168,771	11,714,664	3,043,129	3,936,538	34,880	535,954	286,871
2014	19,393,095	13,631,039	84,271	13,715,310	1,613,098	-168,464	11,933,748	3,334,650	4,124,697	36,099	537,214	290,486
2015	20,208,391	14,249,128	39,500	14,288,628	1,667,828	-134,814	12,485,986	3,363,454	4,358,951	37,578	537,777	293,679
2016	20,925,648	14,786,161	21,236	14,807,397	1,732,080	-147,790	12,927,527	3,525,406	4,472,715	38,709	540,583	296,909
2017	21,614,934	15,299,959	35,333	15,335,292	1,794,188	-134,436	13,406,668	3,690,430	4,517,836	39,815	542,883	299,452
2018	22,414,761	15,860,675	39,059	15,899,734	1,885,196	-129,390	13,885,148	3,811,602	4,718,011	41,334	542,279	300,879
2019	23,252,944	16,320,676	59,424	16,380,100	1,935,362	-135,083	14,309,655	3,955,722	4,987,567	42,860	542,535	298,739
2020	25,474,045	16,509,006	115,355	16,624,361	1,957,075	-162,306	14,504,980	3,976,822	6,992,243	47,089	540,979	283,423
2021	27,212,637	17,721,957	152,776	17,874,733	2,084,085	-184,950	15,605,698	4,187,741	7,419,198	51,544	527,954	291,641
2022	27,393,461	19,197,893	146,242	19,344,135	2,318,791	-225,918	16,799,426	4,474,365	6,119,670	50,647	540,870	305,654

Personal Income and Employment by Area: Laredo, TX

(Thousands of dollars, except as noted.)

Year	Personal income, total	Derivation of personal income: Earnings by place of work: Nonfarm	Farm	Total	Less: Contributions for government social insurance	Plus: Adjustment for residence	Equals: Net earnings by place of residence	Plus: Dividends, interest, and rent	Plus: Personal current transfer receipts	Per capita personal income (dollars)	Population (persons)	Total employment
1970	182,339	148,940	3,057	151,997	9,355	-6,614	136,028	26,908	19,403	2,480	73,536	27,042
1971	197,620	160,158	4,055	164,213	10,408	-7,881	145,924	29,265	22,431	2,548	77,556	26,710
1972	220,806	180,117	3,804	183,921	12,054	-9,644	162,223	33,058	25,525	2,725	81,025	27,421
1973	236,894	193,246	4,793	198,039	14,681	-11,745	171,613	34,890	30,391	2,851	83,080	28,534
1974	242,858	195,468	3,075	198,543	16,009	-13,392	169,142	31,894	41,822	3,141	77,327	28,206
1975	280,802	225,483	2,604	228,087	18,440	-16,652	192,995	34,875	52,932	3,383	83,006	29,172
1976	315,306	257,838	1,274	259,112	21,264	-18,238	219,610	37,659	58,037	3,564	88,481	30,810
1977	353,652	293,594	895	294,489	24,151	-20,362	249,976	41,780	61,896	3,864	91,535	32,558
1978	404,598	335,136	753	335,889	27,980	-21,926	285,983	50,368	68,247	4,315	93,776	34,251
1979	471,385	385,312	4,058	389,370	33,811	-23,487	332,072	60,372	78,941	4,867	96,844	36,084
1980	558,866	461,411	-189	461,222	41,358	-29,385	390,479	74,518	93,869	5,562	100,481	38,920
1981	673,298	549,253	82	549,335	53,540	-21,138	474,657	94,818	103,823	6,408	105,077	42,261
1982	728,022	571,934	3,387	575,321	56,014	-23,214	496,093	112,516	119,413	6,552	111,106	42,033
1983	723,032	527,107	-2,178	524,929	49,979	-21,025	453,925	122,099	147,008	6,264	115,419	37,681
1984	780,213	578,509	-2,660	575,849	56,077	-24,618	495,154	136,136	148,923	6,693	116,566	39,429
1985	846,515	644,650	-6,055	638,595	63,528	-28,700	546,367	146,948	153,200	7,164	118,164	42,213
1986	883,066	662,819	-5,409	657,410	64,312	-27,396	565,702	149,899	167,465	7,238	122,011	41,857
1987	927,335	700,009	-1,422	698,587	66,954	-28,954	602,679	149,616	175,040	7,447	124,528	43,947
1988	1,030,658	792,458	-1,595	790,863	78,923	-30,282	681,658	163,575	185,425	8,143	126,575	46,882
1989	1,164,348	886,758	-482	886,276	89,321	-32,409	764,546	182,623	217,179	8,960	129,943	50,230
1990	1,314,693	1,011,975	1,399	1,013,374	99,842	-35,655	877,877	187,691	249,125	9,780	134,430	53,910
1991	1,482,192	1,147,790	1,924	1,149,714	116,074	-40,331	993,309	201,190	287,693	10,581	140,082	57,729
1992	1,712,036	1,304,340	1,666	1,306,006	130,193	-44,505	1,131,308	228,738	351,990	11,644	147,026	60,857
1993	1,884,793	1,455,104	-406	1,454,698	144,729	-49,309	1,260,660	250,161	373,972	12,196	154,536	65,418
1994	2,069,491	1,614,502	-1,622	1,612,880	162,665	-54,234	1,395,981	256,538	416,972	12,845	161,107	69,329
1995	2,161,524	1,616,084	-803	1,615,281	162,391	-51,570	1,401,320	292,147	468,057	12,907	167,466	68,700
1996	2,330,510	1,730,822	-2,648	1,728,174	172,940	-54,560	1,500,674	312,297	517,539	13,582	171,583	70,431
1997	2,557,777	1,924,038	-390	1,923,648	193,219	-60,237	1,670,192	342,960	544,625	14,439	177,140	75,384
1998	2,712,271	2,049,169	2,566	2,051,735	206,035	-60,021	1,785,679	379,123	547,469	14,822	182,994	78,704
1999	2,833,710	2,151,340	8,200	2,159,540	218,126	-62,139	1,879,275	396,214	558,221	14,992	189,014	81,214
2000	3,097,481	2,347,214	9,208	2,356,422	235,889	-67,012	2,053,521	450,918	593,042	15,919	194,576	85,583
2001	3,798,754	2,965,545	14,027	2,979,572	265,924	-83,565	2,630,083	517,573	651,098	18,961	200,347	90,442
2002	4,019,554	3,159,988	14,802	3,174,790	284,671	-95,285	2,794,834	487,863	736,857	19,512	206,001	95,634
2003	4,250,244	3,267,671	23,183	3,290,854	304,073	-99,575	2,887,206	568,898	794,140	20,069	211,786	98,786
2004	4,355,031	3,369,210	20,699	3,389,909	320,540	-104,636	2,964,733	562,031	828,267	19,990	217,858	103,896
2005	4,861,914	3,714,955	9,998	3,724,953	350,497	-111,748	3,262,708	660,449	938,757	21,734	223,703	108,662
2006	5,279,013	3,991,738	12,563	4,004,301	368,222	-112,492	3,523,587	751,709	1,003,717	23,022	229,307	113,280
2007	5,504,087	4,085,694	2,388	4,088,082	388,411	-114,992	3,584,679	793,974	1,125,434	23,462	234,594	117,868
2008	6,300,702	4,531,516	-1,971	4,529,545	409,161	-110,882	4,009,502	996,946	1,294,254	26,222	240,287	119,897
2009	6,095,402	4,249,882	-4,221	4,245,661	403,780	-108,102	3,733,779	903,574	1,458,049	24,787	245,908	118,450
2010	6,586,709	4,629,115	-5,409	4,623,706	433,862	-109,268	4,080,576	887,458	1,618,675	26,229	251,126	119,890
2011	7,212,334	5,077,105	1,639	5,078,744	416,773	-108,029	4,553,942	1,000,703	1,657,689	28,318	254,692	126,850
2012	7,473,407	5,243,373	1,733	5,245,106	437,156	-101,358	4,706,592	1,118,742	1,648,073	28,931	258,314	128,759
2013	7,658,868	5,332,661	8,111	5,340,772	501,207	-78,437	4,761,128	1,206,543	1,691,197	29,333	261,101	132,183
2014	7,897,146	5,521,678	9,099	5,530,777	520,066	-71,923	4,938,788	1,199,381	1,758,977	30,020	263,059	135,969
2015	8,001,402	5,559,406	12,503	5,571,909	541,281	-97,721	4,932,907	1,199,440	1,869,055	30,266	264,372	139,279
2016	8,081,065	5,560,377	-1,501	5,558,876	553,216	-125,615	4,880,045	1,242,760	1,958,260	30,405	265,778	140,051
2017	8,288,862	5,745,425	964	5,746,389	573,189	-111,224	5,061,976	1,250,745	1,976,141	31,153	266,072	141,350
2018	8,672,165	5,997,528	3,820	6,001,348	597,680	-92,183	5,311,485	1,319,092	2,041,588	32,554	266,391	144,030
2019	9,194,983	6,410,962	2,813	6,413,775	628,745	-106,227	5,678,803	1,409,702	2,106,478	34,440	266,986	147,681
2020	9,895,846	6,373,534	1,411	6,374,945	641,659	-130,907	5,602,379	1,442,617	2,850,850	37,015	267,345	142,757
2021	10,986,536	6,697,467	3,128	6,700,595	670,108	-141,823	5,888,664	1,628,171	3,469,701	41,051	267,633	146,885
2022	10,945,018	7,174,488	-2,558	7,171,930	719,208	-129,883	6,322,839	1,724,344	2,897,835	40,873	267,780	152,645

Personal Income and Employment by Area: Las Cruces, NM

(Thousands of dollars, except as noted.)

Year	Personal income, total	Derivation of personal income: Earnings by place of work: Nonfarm	Farm	Total	Less: Contributions for government social insurance	Plus: Adjustment for residence	Equals: Net earnings by place of residence	Plus: Dividends, interest, and rent	Plus: Personal current transfer receipts	Per capita personal income (dollars)	Population (persons)	Total employment
1970	228,654	179,992	12,396	192,388	8,393	-7,128	176,867	33,883	17,904	3,255	70,254	27,080
1971	258,499	201,793	14,117	215,910	9,841	-9,006	197,063	39,537	21,899	3,554	72,726	28,316
1972	282,005	216,482	15,179	231,661	11,044	-7,422	213,195	44,161	24,649	3,684	76,553	29,477
1973	311,428	236,988	16,334	253,322	14,266	-6,964	232,092	50,351	28,985	4,049	76,909	30,621
1974	358,809	258,971	28,036	287,007	16,312	-6,599	264,096	59,152	35,561	4,548	78,888	31,045
1975	392,408	277,990	16,500	294,490	17,752	1,175	277,913	70,047	44,448	4,787	81,979	31,211
1976	444,278	315,981	22,899	338,880	20,374	-1,548	316,958	77,039	50,281	5,211	85,259	32,448
1977	494,883	362,914	20,042	382,956	24,369	-3,966	354,621	86,662	53,600	5,604	88,302	35,175
1978	568,285	414,060	24,856	438,916	28,803	-4,403	405,710	102,735	59,840	6,164	92,193	37,771
1979	621,445	455,273	14,132	469,405	33,333	-3,067	433,005	117,915	70,525	6,629	93,741	39,643
1980	702,654	486,953	21,677	508,630	35,824	1,380	474,186	142,122	86,346	7,243	97,012	39,628
1981	811,303	544,423	35,568	579,991	43,145	4,760	541,606	171,111	98,586	8,144	99,623	40,165
1982	903,802	596,421	32,691	629,112	48,468	8,417	589,061	204,246	110,495	8,737	103,448	41,829
1983	1,026,727	673,980	46,103	720,083	57,163	9,322	672,242	230,983	123,502	9,540	107,627	44,305
1984	1,125,610	740,969	41,180	782,149	64,306	12,808	730,651	257,849	137,110	10,008	112,474	46,879
1985	1,233,182	798,558	49,585	848,143	71,816	18,442	794,769	290,903	147,510	10,602	116,321	48,564
1986	1,331,557	846,845	67,614	914,459	78,524	26,879	862,814	311,090	157,653	11,053	120,474	49,986
1987	1,418,875	903,131	65,169	968,300	84,078	35,159	919,381	327,321	172,173	11,348	125,032	52,506
1988	1,498,297	946,044	66,638	1,012,682	94,931	44,420	962,171	348,453	187,673	11,524	130,016	55,774
1989	1,660,942	1,021,714	93,269	1,114,983	104,886	45,867	1,055,964	392,924	212,054	12,492	132,957	57,095
1990	1,783,955	1,098,787	103,630	1,202,417	118,717	54,573	1,138,273	403,810	241,872	13,060	136,593	57,771
1991	1,912,118	1,189,970	87,239	1,277,209	130,352	66,502	1,213,359	423,210	275,549	13,539	141,228	59,961
1992	2,097,816	1,301,388	102,692	1,404,080	141,765	81,056	1,343,371	442,027	312,418	14,271	146,995	60,744
1993	2,237,054	1,384,856	86,376	1,471,232	151,673	95,860	1,415,419	473,643	347,992	14,617	153,049	61,738
1994	2,326,622	1,415,925	75,878	1,491,803	159,767	110,897	1,442,933	501,916	381,773	14,769	157,530	62,238
1995	2,535,404	1,511,295	100,397	1,611,692	170,318	120,042	1,561,416	542,939	431,049	15,746	161,014	65,557
1996	2,649,301	1,568,447	76,986	1,645,433	177,394	129,003	1,597,042	582,753	469,506	15,996	165,618	67,010
1997	2,784,146	1,632,149	104,121	1,736,270	185,515	144,038	1,694,793	606,240	483,113	16,466	169,081	68,290
1998	2,981,917	1,760,777	112,492	1,873,269	201,388	156,247	1,828,128	636,891	516,898	17,331	172,057	69,944
1999	3,051,135	1,829,059	112,265	1,941,324	213,429	174,051	1,901,946	599,104	550,085	17,546	173,889	72,267
2000	3,225,465	1,975,603	80,172	2,055,775	223,570	188,888	2,021,093	611,869	592,503	18,421	175,098	74,836
2001	3,610,193	2,221,309	112,816	2,334,125	243,433	169,986	2,260,678	669,428	680,087	20,455	176,496	78,825
2002	3,856,658	2,436,152	94,733	2,530,885	265,012	175,198	2,441,071	654,498	761,089	21,610	178,464	80,982
2003	4,110,046	2,645,353	115,943	2,761,296	287,502	162,355	2,636,149	657,303	816,594	22,577	182,045	83,346
2004	4,366,755	2,828,686	152,375	2,981,061	306,947	119,754	2,793,868	699,323	873,564	23,612	184,939	86,094
2005	4,710,739	3,096,974	172,058	3,269,032	337,983	57,481	2,988,530	772,374	949,835	24,898	189,199	89,624
2006	5,008,658	3,312,330	123,121	3,435,451	366,353	64,062	3,133,160	835,619	1,039,879	25,858	193,701	91,990
2007	5,369,499	3,441,931	177,270	3,619,201	389,795	56,495	3,285,901	934,449	1,149,149	27,139	197,853	94,727
2008	5,646,275	3,569,093	108,784	3,677,877	413,674	39,586	3,303,789	1,015,169	1,327,317	28,111	200,855	95,893
2009	5,998,286	3,731,422	127,540	3,858,962	429,403	97,529	3,527,088	972,110	1,499,088	29,203	205,401	94,897
2010	6,412,335	3,922,807	222,335	4,145,142	443,292	103,224	3,805,074	979,845	1,627,416	30,525	210,066	95,637
2011	6,604,691	3,965,189	197,008	4,162,197	403,231	128,316	3,887,282	1,064,626	1,652,783	31,012	212,973	97,248
2012	6,688,302	3,940,898	129,693	4,070,591	407,176	187,961	3,851,376	1,196,436	1,640,490	31,228	214,179	97,099
2013	6,515,500	3,924,346	134,514	4,058,860	467,837	170,417	3,761,440	1,109,373	1,644,687	30,462	213,887	98,970
2014	6,768,371	4,002,441	141,952	4,144,393	482,508	164,364	3,826,249	1,129,515	1,812,607	31,715	213,413	99,342
2015	7,084,337	4,146,921	146,441	4,293,362	516,498	173,258	3,950,122	1,158,236	1,975,979	33,202	213,373	99,925
2016	7,322,279	4,291,462	158,708	4,450,170	529,387	174,421	4,095,204	1,201,258	2,025,817	34,235	213,885	100,744
2017	7,515,865	4,384,449	161,171	4,545,620	536,233	197,060	4,206,447	1,261,840	2,047,578	34,906	215,315	100,124
2018	7,740,464	4,613,626	115,204	4,728,830	564,768	143,378	4,307,440	1,244,111	2,188,913	35,764	216,434	102,593
2019	8,225,505	4,853,579	119,121	4,972,700	587,523	211,000	4,596,177	1,345,748	2,283,580	37,786	217,687	103,245
2020	8,993,528	4,940,727	106,315	5,047,042	612,126	272,083	4,706,999	1,238,234	3,048,295	40,871	220,047	100,328
2021	10,118,335	5,351,844	121,170	5,473,014	649,977	315,912	5,138,949	1,434,598	3,544,788	45,649	221,655	103,346
2022	10,130,839	5,668,965	90,581	5,759,546	708,585	340,929	5,391,890	1,479,430	3,259,519	45,361	223,337	107,767

Personal Income and Employment by Area: Las Vegas-Henderson-Paradise, NV

(Thousands of dollars, except as noted.)

Year	Personal income, total	Derivation of personal income: Earnings by place of work: Nonfarm	Farm	Total	Less: Contributions for government social insurance	Plus: Adjustment for residence	Equals: Net earnings by place of residence	Plus: Dividends, interest, and rent	Plus: Personal current transfer receipts	Per capita personal income (dollars)	Population (persons)	Total employment
1970	1,429,017	1,180,655	1,732	1,182,387	82,314	41,419	1,141,492	211,557	75,968	5,176	276,079	134,095
1971	1,582,762	1,301,670	1,334	1,303,004	93,505	37,347	1,246,846	238,405	97,511	5,402	293,008	138,801
1972	1,747,451	1,447,250	1,318	1,448,568	109,842	26,181	1,364,907	265,291	117,253	5,684	307,426	145,742
1973	1,984,224	1,677,474	1,418	1,678,892	146,925	12,703	1,544,670	302,171	137,383	6,212	319,399	160,282
1974	2,221,573	1,845,898	2,006	1,847,904	164,868	13,850	1,696,886	350,892	173,795	6,594	336,930	168,726
1975	2,515,704	2,038,508	2,074	2,040,582	180,969	15,006	1,874,619	398,951	242,134	7,160	351,339	174,218
1976	2,863,774	2,335,534	2,783	2,338,317	213,203	9,012	2,134,126	454,439	275,209	7,750	369,529	186,546
1977	3,296,192	2,723,422	2,580	2,726,002	251,966	931	2,474,967	517,855	303,370	8,453	389,965	204,806
1978	3,959,777	3,293,521	2,496	3,296,017	314,392	-2,960	2,978,665	642,527	338,585	9,590	412,913	228,609
1979	4,630,517	3,856,001	1,518	3,857,519	388,226	-10,567	3,458,726	763,926	407,865	10,492	441,358	251,535
1980	5,358,883	4,367,073	3,213	4,370,286	443,251	-3,508	3,923,527	932,196	503,160	11,422	469,185	265,076
1981	6,156,325	4,920,769	1,887	4,922,656	530,878	19,508	4,411,286	1,122,732	622,307	12,494	492,747	272,538
1982	6,625,066	5,103,473	2,477	5,105,950	541,265	40,724	4,605,409	1,322,896	696,761	12,897	513,708	269,949
1983	7,093,052	5,443,056	926	5,443,982	597,931	43,564	4,889,615	1,446,661	756,776	13,378	530,195	274,043
1984	7,677,223	5,869,268	2,951	5,872,219	670,344	52,388	5,254,263	1,604,941	818,019	14,089	544,893	286,101
1985	8,372,251	6,356,946	2,478	6,359,424	739,665	69,681	5,689,440	1,776,383	906,428	14,922	561,081	300,096
1986	9,138,380	6,937,323	1,535	6,938,858	825,195	64,130	6,177,793	1,936,822	1,023,765	15,735	580,775	316,982
1987	10,033,816	7,766,744	2,128	7,768,872	930,044	46,213	6,885,041	2,044,829	1,103,946	16,401	611,763	345,999
1988	11,495,419	8,971,169	2,161	8,973,330	1,086,946	42,522	7,928,906	2,335,090	1,231,423	17,756	647,410	375,496
1989	13,183,129	10,218,492	2,945	10,221,437	1,263,165	13,806	8,972,078	2,783,329	1,427,722	19,065	691,467	412,843
1990	15,090,973	11,841,257	3,280	11,844,537	1,541,960	-15,835	10,286,742	3,144,621	1,659,610	19,957	756,170	452,016
1991	16,742,593	12,877,528	3,501	12,881,029	1,653,818	-2,894	11,224,317	3,448,738	2,069,538	20,516	816,085	465,549
1992	18,660,123	14,327,433	4,769	14,332,202	1,812,173	-11,810	12,508,219	3,786,034	2,365,870	21,765	857,357	472,519
1993	20,530,800	15,885,082	5,733	15,890,815	2,021,746	-83,001	13,786,068	4,216,350	2,528,382	22,753	902,338	504,060
1994	23,017,431	17,922,081	5,450	17,927,531	2,295,749	-143,308	15,488,474	4,831,975	2,696,982	23,665	972,624	567,840
1995	25,550,577	19,882,711	5,574	19,888,285	2,551,332	-189,245	17,147,708	5,481,381	2,921,488	24,666	1,035,847	606,312
1996	28,589,960	22,357,483	6,320	22,363,803	2,809,592	-279,104	19,275,107	6,145,846	3,169,007	25,993	1,099,894	662,190
1997	31,629,874	24,752,452	6,527	24,758,979	3,033,850	-302,979	21,422,150	6,805,772	3,401,952	26,868	1,177,230	713,369
1998	35,921,375	28,188,695	6,871	28,195,566	3,280,705	-317,567	24,597,294	7,676,595	3,647,486	28,708	1,251,258	749,408
1999	39,226,327	31,281,166	6,434	31,287,600	3,531,451	-350,779	27,405,370	7,994,155	3,826,802	29,689	1,321,254	803,146
2000	43,220,927	34,131,998	5,112	34,137,110	3,489,358	-371,878	30,275,874	8,824,021	4,121,032	31,007	1,393,909	853,137
2001	46,417,362	36,905,547	5,103	36,910,650	3,741,988	-414,649	32,754,013	8,975,951	4,687,398	31,782	1,460,500	882,073
2002	48,327,299	38,219,544	3,951	38,223,495	3,893,403	-423,468	33,906,624	9,113,425	5,307,250	31,732	1,522,962	896,533
2003	51,607,812	40,216,786	3,434	40,220,220	3,948,210	-461,495	35,810,515	10,082,616	5,714,681	32,577	1,584,166	941,659
2004	57,552,364	45,184,526	3,455	45,187,981	4,373,524	-555,461	40,258,996	11,142,805	6,150,563	34,612	1,662,773	1,011,910
2005	65,174,906	50,636,512	3,115	50,639,627	4,857,742	-616,724	45,165,161	13,362,925	6,646,820	37,684	1,729,522	1,087,086
2006	70,658,033	54,945,980	3,874	54,949,854	5,704,081	-578,014	48,667,759	14,810,109	7,180,165	39,172	1,803,774	1,145,471
2007	74,098,045	56,929,171	2,609	56,931,780	6,001,486	-547,371	50,382,923	15,847,323	7,867,799	39,671	1,867,817	1,174,115
2008	73,157,227	54,072,378	4,288	54,076,666	5,656,204	-484,672	47,935,790	15,855,322	9,366,115	38,255	1,912,349	1,160,284
2009	67,741,924	49,207,919	4,333	49,212,252	5,429,236	-449,690	43,333,326	13,688,079	10,720,519	34,929	1,939,407	1,081,908
2010	69,690,053	49,899,487	3,738	49,903,225	5,287,575	-377,588	44,238,062	13,586,028	11,865,963	35,707	1,951,737	1,057,024
2011	72,486,084	51,555,017	4,291	51,559,308	4,999,138	-278,533	46,281,637	14,212,695	11,991,752	37,028	1,957,626	1,076,791
2012	77,122,169	53,190,554	1,881	53,192,435	5,286,234	-316,648	47,589,553	17,444,149	12,088,467	38,923	1,981,384	1,093,018
2013	77,179,892	55,121,602	1,220	55,122,822	5,814,287	-327,309	48,981,226	15,869,509	12,329,157	38,479	2,005,757	1,125,664
2014	82,308,254	57,694,768	1,391	57,696,159	6,449,710	-363,339	50,883,110	17,906,261	13,518,883	40,388	2,037,960	1,168,840
2015	88,989,148	61,235,100	162	61,235,262	6,904,471	-364,731	53,966,060	20,189,783	14,833,305	42,829	2,077,790	1,216,009
2016	92,300,696	63,196,657	-365	63,196,292	7,224,163	-462,085	55,510,044	21,022,529	15,768,123	43,621	2,115,963	1,263,383
2017	98,136,446	66,904,634	482	66,905,116	7,391,489	-483,173	59,030,454	22,471,653	16,634,339	45,547	2,154,616	1,303,257
2018	104,221,369	71,183,888	-452	71,183,436	7,877,704	-509,886	62,795,846	23,720,954	17,704,569	47,466	2,195,698	1,355,054
2019	112,745,711	76,928,866	1,219	76,930,085	8,720,327	-625,502	67,584,256	26,153,180	19,008,275	50,382	2,237,815	1,387,803
2020	119,563,676	73,363,400	560	73,363,960	8,338,999	-535,508	64,489,453	25,921,745	29,152,478	52,562	2,274,734	1,283,836
2021	134,011,250	84,260,223	1,033	84,261,256	9,380,575	-587,330	74,293,351	28,119,825	31,598,074	58,388	2,295,194	1,400,541
2022	137,403,632	94,377,503	491	94,377,994	10,903,483	-970,359	82,504,152	30,499,392	24,400,088	59,150	2,322,985	1,523,197

Personal Income and Employment by Area: Lawrence, KS

(Thousands of dollars, except as noted.)

Year	Personal income, total	Derivation of personal income: Earnings by place of work: Nonfarm	Farm	Total	Less: Contributions for government social insurance	Plus: Adjustment for residence	Equals: Net earnings by place of residence	Plus: Dividends, interest, and rent	Plus: Personal current transfer receipts	Per capita personal income (dollars)	Population (persons)	Total employment
1970	189,361	142,025	2,913	144,938	10,193	8,576	143,321	32,485	13,555	3,252	58,233	23,010
1971	213,246	161,457	4,306	165,763	12,103	7,864	161,524	36,144	15,578	3,577	59,621	24,197
1972	229,915	168,765	5,104	173,869	13,315	11,364	171,918	39,849	18,148	3,784	60,767	24,524
1973	254,888	186,789	6,280	193,069	17,182	12,738	188,625	44,338	21,925	4,121	61,848	25,994
1974	284,949	214,048	2,360	216,408	20,658	11,429	207,179	51,485	26,285	4,534	62,844	27,633
1975	323,561	237,196	4,435	241,631	22,712	12,337	231,256	60,123	32,182	5,341	60,580	27,762
1976	364,929	274,812	3,491	278,303	26,556	12,679	264,426	64,704	35,799	5,934	61,498	29,598
1977	418,143	316,234	7,089	323,323	30,394	13,500	306,429	71,205	40,509	6,644	62,932	31,544
1978	465,468	355,024	4,192	359,216	35,431	16,802	340,587	80,154	44,727	7,086	65,685	33,135
1979	518,698	396,388	4,206	400,594	41,165	19,444	378,873	92,072	47,753	7,775	66,710	34,211
1980	572,150	419,356	-20	419,336	43,725	23,859	399,470	114,768	57,912	8,408	68,045	34,501
1981	642,735	451,328	2,407	453,735	50,291	30,125	433,569	142,238	66,928	9,239	69,569	33,622
1982	673,912	460,947	353	461,300	51,836	35,502	444,966	159,529	69,417	9,634	69,948	33,433
1983	724,484	492,959	-3,135	489,824	54,363	40,770	476,231	173,210	75,043	10,358	69,947	33,914
1984	798,355	537,198	1,966	539,164	59,561	48,678	528,281	193,347	76,727	11,305	70,618	35,192
1985	864,660	569,561	7,741	577,302	63,298	56,939	570,943	210,904	82,813	11,984	72,151	36,131
1986	933,660	626,540	5,794	632,334	69,329	62,871	625,876	224,882	82,902	12,526	74,538	37,149
1987	979,306	657,993	8,028	666,021	72,255	69,053	662,819	227,846	88,641	12,861	76,148	39,566
1988	1,068,053	721,227	10,187	731,414	83,155	76,146	724,405	246,292	97,356	13,558	78,779	42,190
1989	1,180,101	794,481	8,100	802,581	90,618	82,085	794,048	277,299	108,754	14,734	80,092	43,552
1990	1,242,501	849,239	5,626	854,865	102,000	88,542	841,407	278,671	122,423	15,110	82,229	44,906
1991	1,320,841	900,019	4,465	904,484	109,468	98,469	893,485	289,576	137,780	15,784	83,683	46,550
1992	1,436,892	974,359	11,483	985,842	117,094	110,528	979,276	302,477	155,139	16,830	85,379	47,328
1993	1,527,248	1,038,426	2,834	1,041,260	124,409	124,739	1,041,590	318,268	167,390	17,370	87,926	48,723
1994	1,647,567	1,109,372	5,717	1,115,089	135,054	137,113	1,117,148	357,710	172,709	18,371	89,683	49,946
1995	1,748,676	1,173,731	1,989	1,175,720	141,405	151,082	1,185,397	379,708	183,571	19,130	91,408	53,006
1996	1,857,092	1,232,841	9,201	1,242,042	146,670	168,413	1,263,785	402,770	190,537	19,887	93,381	54,732
1997	2,036,752	1,355,899	8,054	1,363,953	161,080	182,491	1,385,364	448,752	202,636	21,281	95,706	57,637
1998	2,212,386	1,478,444	504	1,478,948	173,287	206,192	1,511,853	485,679	214,854	22,676	97,566	59,943
1999	2,307,475	1,556,298	-2,401	1,553,897	182,295	234,450	1,606,052	475,678	225,745	23,193	99,490	62,118
2000	2,492,392	1,671,754	-5,718	1,666,036	196,728	260,619	1,729,927	513,860	248,605	24,863	100,247	63,729
2001	2,693,565	1,861,995	-3,140	1,858,855	214,525	257,261	1,901,591	517,887	274,087	26,598	101,269	67,353
2002	2,770,667	1,911,436	-7,119	1,904,317	220,041	263,224	1,947,500	530,572	292,595	27,017	102,552	65,799
2003	2,855,052	1,941,132	-1,972	1,939,160	225,317	263,716	1,977,559	570,195	307,298	27,566	103,570	66,160
2004	2,916,520	2,021,435	7,815	2,029,250	235,629	249,291	2,042,912	553,714	319,894	27,822	104,826	67,329
2005	3,058,719	2,087,414	1,779	2,089,193	244,582	274,269	2,118,880	602,270	337,569	28,943	105,681	67,573
2006	3,279,413	2,174,715	-3,085	2,171,630	253,334	297,241	2,215,537	705,259	358,617	30,595	107,187	68,146
2007	3,444,796	2,220,802	1,667	2,222,469	256,453	337,350	2,303,366	746,473	394,957	31,928	107,892	69,119
2008	3,686,657	2,360,156	4,311	2,364,467	266,278	348,529	2,446,718	767,668	472,271	33,819	109,010	67,972
2009	3,747,170	2,367,427	13,378	2,380,805	270,209	346,070	2,456,666	778,202	512,302	34,053	110,039	67,410
2010	3,804,506	2,385,262	6,269	2,391,531	272,864	392,036	2,510,703	730,911	562,892	34,237	111,122	66,700
2011	4,003,647	2,426,928	14,881	2,441,809	242,562	396,744	2,595,991	824,236	583,420	35,720	112,084	66,323
2012	4,100,594	2,455,930	9,825	2,465,755	246,548	474,371	2,693,578	829,395	577,621	36,417	112,602	66,193
2013	4,193,891	2,567,410	13,602	2,581,012	289,187	471,536	2,763,361	834,114	596,416	36,894	113,674	67,794
2014	4,387,303	2,687,796	3,368	2,691,164	303,187	483,033	2,871,010	897,478	618,815	38,126	115,075	69,517
2015	4,613,120	2,845,802	1,686	2,847,488	318,980	517,338	3,045,846	927,328	639,946	39,621	116,431	70,432
2016	4,751,072	2,950,885	3,759	2,954,644	326,711	477,200	3,105,133	972,162	673,777	40,376	117,670	71,535
2017	5,008,346	3,062,033	6,621	3,068,654	340,371	527,211	3,255,494	1,049,872	702,980	42,462	117,950	73,543
2018	5,261,764	3,159,426	12,421	3,171,847	352,745	590,736	3,409,838	1,101,706	750,220	44,441	118,398	74,333
2019	5,478,757	3,309,840	12,611	3,322,451	371,047	604,657	3,556,061	1,125,250	797,446	46,052	118,968	74,668
2020	5,781,592	3,336,852	18,670	3,355,522	382,722	595,455	3,568,255	1,147,431	1,065,906	48,676	118,777	70,989
2021	6,195,233	3,548,254	30,532	3,578,786	414,793	643,846	3,807,839	1,225,443	1,161,951	51,852	119,480	72,257
2022	6,334,017	3,780,017	3,557	3,783,574	448,512	698,826	4,033,888	1,294,753	1,005,376	52,799	119,964	75,214

Personal Income and Employment by Area: Lawton, OK

(Thousands of dollars, except as noted.)

Year	Personal income, total	Derivation of personal income								Per capita personal income (dollars)	Population (persons)	Total employment
		Earnings by place of work			Less: Contributions for government social insurance	Plus: Adjustment for residence	Equals: Net earnings by place of residence	Plus: Dividends, interest, and rent	Plus: Personal current transfer receipts			
		Nonfarm	Farm	Total								
1970	474,227	374,178	6,559	380,737	21,692	-8,085	350,960	98,035	25,232	4,130	114,835	57,235
1971	477,877	376,915	5,259	382,174	23,342	-8,435	350,397	98,092	29,388	4,166	114,717	53,368
1972	488,467	382,516	7,874	390,390	23,936	-8,844	357,610	98,147	32,710	4,561	107,106	50,475
1973	547,261	417,401	18,630	436,031	28,238	-9,675	398,118	111,374	37,769	5,005	109,334	51,921
1974	601,813	461,535	11,260	472,795	32,850	-10,389	429,556	126,662	45,595	5,431	110,808	53,070
1975	644,183	489,898	9,177	499,075	37,042	-10,527	451,506	136,542	56,135	5,721	112,591	53,108
1976	746,867	571,485	10,070	581,555	44,720	-10,773	526,062	158,260	62,545	6,164	121,157	56,963
1977	793,076	611,743	1,099	612,842	47,460	-11,188	554,194	172,660	66,222	6,476	122,462	57,631
1978	877,968	678,582	1,598	680,180	53,308	-15,422	611,450	196,142	70,376	7,057	124,413	58,416
1979	974,044	729,988	18,862	748,850	59,447	-11,862	677,541	214,528	81,975	7,971	122,200	58,783
1980	1,063,931	793,776	5,723	799,499	64,973	-8,850	725,676	242,633	95,622	8,849	120,234	59,943
1981	1,226,711	905,657	13,931	919,588	77,698	-6,092	835,798	283,073	107,840	10,073	121,777	60,159
1982	1,388,501	1,035,816	9,655	1,045,471	87,837	-10,703	946,931	321,214	120,356	10,983	126,418	63,838
1983	1,462,225	1,075,200	8,504	1,083,704	93,866	-10,191	979,647	351,675	130,903	11,328	129,084	63,134
1984	1,554,084	1,149,242	4,486	1,153,728	102,427	-11,491	1,039,810	376,364	137,910	12,137	128,046	64,339
1985	1,658,395	1,224,058	12,685	1,236,743	111,421	-13,857	1,111,465	400,010	146,920	13,031	127,261	65,425
1986	1,722,463	1,272,786	24,740	1,297,526	118,538	-16,188	1,162,800	406,098	153,565	13,682	125,897	64,430
1987	1,774,465	1,331,655	12,310	1,343,965	125,431	-19,141	1,199,393	412,040	163,032	14,162	125,301	65,717
1988	1,793,957	1,334,787	22,196	1,356,983	134,684	-16,025	1,206,274	411,179	176,504	14,551	123,289	64,438
1989	1,828,409	1,343,760	17,241	1,361,001	138,495	-14,968	1,207,538	429,962	190,909	15,359	119,044	63,133
1990	1,900,700	1,386,326	27,272	1,413,598	147,994	-14,148	1,251,456	438,581	210,663	16,092	118,112	62,529
1991	1,953,616	1,436,876	13,199	1,450,075	157,106	-15,065	1,277,904	443,177	232,535	16,571	117,896	60,909
1992	2,205,320	1,641,892	20,012	1,661,904	181,848	-22,261	1,457,795	485,529	261,996	17,308	127,413	65,370
1993	2,196,845	1,611,894	19,351	1,631,245	182,537	-18,488	1,430,220	494,204	272,421	17,507	125,485	64,545
1994	2,223,892	1,623,666	11,813	1,635,479	183,414	-16,913	1,435,152	498,526	290,214	17,745	125,323	63,353
1995	2,298,625	1,646,448	2,162	1,648,610	185,112	-16,592	1,446,906	534,820	316,899	18,626	123,412	64,135
1996	2,358,388	1,664,511	9,673	1,674,184	185,858	-13,949	1,474,377	551,336	332,675	19,118	123,357	64,864
1997	2,392,368	1,702,736	12,275	1,715,011	189,191	-10,752	1,515,068	536,897	340,403	19,530	122,497	64,740
1998	2,500,268	1,766,176	11,404	1,777,580	195,291	-11,733	1,570,556	582,725	346,987	20,481	122,076	64,171
1999	2,566,783	1,794,498	17,240	1,811,738	199,703	-11,159	1,600,876	593,161	372,746	20,946	122,542	64,417
2000	2,688,402	1,865,730	19,278	1,885,008	206,075	-8,451	1,670,482	623,461	394,459	22,091	121,695	64,749
2001	2,895,096	2,039,629	10,597	2,050,226	221,370	-17,673	1,811,183	642,393	441,520	24,135	119,955	64,488
2002	3,052,934	2,157,273	18,577	2,175,850	235,221	-28,478	1,912,151	668,564	472,219	25,465	119,889	64,633
2003	3,247,805	2,328,178	19,711	2,347,889	251,868	-43,899	2,052,122	679,142	516,541	27,645	117,484	64,921
2004	3,356,214	2,439,748	31,667	2,471,415	268,544	-57,079	2,145,792	671,633	538,789	27,433	122,341	66,046
2005	3,512,976	2,549,965	35,723	2,585,688	276,325	-67,907	2,241,456	684,402	587,118	28,919	121,475	64,461
2006	3,836,501	2,838,315	13,925	2,852,240	306,014	-87,935	2,458,291	743,157	635,053	31,196	122,980	67,139
2007	4,024,450	2,931,197	3,469	2,934,666	318,480	-99,074	2,517,112	819,020	688,318	31,987	125,814	68,757
2008	4,308,851	3,105,939	21,320	3,127,259	335,649	-114,730	2,676,880	858,966	773,005	34,702	124,166	69,390
2009	4,413,437	3,232,945	-12,102	3,220,843	357,779	-120,852	2,742,212	839,997	831,228	34,991	126,131	69,555
2010	4,777,088	3,523,223	-5,428	3,517,795	385,856	-130,459	3,001,480	877,552	898,056	36,309	131,569	71,528
2011	4,920,908	3,511,531	10,691	3,522,222	354,231	-113,389	3,054,602	938,439	927,867	37,196	132,297	69,614
2012	4,888,769	3,427,448	26,003	3,453,451	348,674	-92,984	3,011,793	922,737	954,239	36,872	132,587	68,302
2013	4,890,910	3,447,066	25,626	3,472,692	390,441	-84,711	2,997,540	915,305	978,065	37,391	130,805	68,868
2014	4,969,592	3,446,299	51,559	3,497,858	389,595	-80,048	3,028,215	926,532	1,014,845	38,011	130,742	68,611
2015	5,050,307	3,544,882	24,928	3,569,810	399,475	-87,162	3,083,173	909,404	1,057,730	38,947	129,671	68,975
2016	4,999,729	3,487,592	15,185	3,502,777	387,061	-98,790	3,016,926	887,764	1,095,039	39,233	127,438	68,430
2017	5,116,372	3,533,159	13,618	3,546,777	399,415	-95,094	3,052,268	922,311	1,141,793	40,031	127,809	68,928
2018	5,198,141	3,590,935	8,036	3,598,971	410,894	-94,949	3,093,128	918,953	1,186,060	41,016	126,734	68,769
2019	5,385,086	3,708,029	10,798	3,718,827	423,546	-96,213	3,199,068	896,520	1,289,498	42,471	126,793	69,666
2020	5,787,176	3,818,963	14,153	3,833,116	440,774	-94,666	3,297,676	900,693	1,588,807	45,691	126,660	68,526
2021	6,189,665	4,012,096	7,993	4,020,089	458,504	-96,911	3,464,674	921,472	1,803,519	48,393	127,905	68,752
2022	6,132,959	4,109,448	-10,056	4,099,392	477,158	-95,347	3,526,887	943,463	1,662,609	47,719	128,523	69,301

Personal Income and Employment by Area: Lebanon, PA

(Thousands of dollars, except as noted.)

Year	Personal income, total	Derivation of personal income: Earnings by place of work								Per capita personal income (dollars)	Population (persons)	Total employment
		Nonfarm	Farm	Total	Less: Contributions for government social insurance	Plus: Adjustment for residence	Equals: Net earnings by place of residence	Plus: Dividends, interest, and rent	Plus: Personal current transfer receipts			
1970	391,453	298,815	11,617	310,432	20,759	19,833	309,506	47,907	34,040	3,907	100,193	44,662
1971	404,211	306,448	9,638	316,086	21,967	18,236	312,355	52,181	39,675	3,928	102,907	43,469
1972	447,121	342,576	9,890	352,466	25,787	19,329	346,008	56,886	44,227	4,324	103,414	44,721
1973	496,917	379,209	12,642	391,851	33,035	23,374	382,190	65,090	49,637	4,729	105,069	45,978
1974	552,795	420,008	10,251	430,259	38,229	26,580	418,610	74,675	59,510	5,249	105,311	46,696
1975	608,263	453,233	8,655	461,888	39,642	20,145	442,391	83,740	82,132	4,894	124,289	46,734
1976	663,856	494,491	9,602	504,093	43,853	26,255	486,495	90,724	86,637	6,135	108,206	46,955
1977	736,809	549,915	8,027	557,942	48,559	33,321	542,704	102,161	91,944	6,819	108,055	47,783
1978	815,150	603,635	10,665	614,300	54,533	42,959	602,726	115,077	97,347	7,457	109,308	48,272
1979	917,866	671,491	14,272	685,763	62,616	56,864	680,011	129,288	108,567	8,337	110,096	49,036
1980	1,003,613	704,701	8,178	712,879	66,213	70,289	716,955	162,064	124,594	9,221	108,839	48,871
1981	1,108,507	739,817	12,109	751,926	74,753	90,543	767,716	196,746	144,045	10,110	109,645	48,150
1982	1,172,768	727,547	10,790	738,337	74,059	110,562	774,840	229,491	168,437	10,606	110,574	46,129
1983	1,241,142	757,908	10,838	768,746	79,392	123,749	813,103	246,335	181,704	11,263	110,199	45,813
1984	1,344,134	802,345	24,989	827,334	88,124	152,585	891,795	271,634	180,705	12,192	110,250	46,912
1985	1,425,270	840,161	25,334	865,495	93,751	167,294	939,038	293,550	192,682	12,912	110,382	47,415
1986	1,514,776	874,113	32,066	906,179	97,923	191,796	1,000,052	308,369	206,355	13,676	110,764	47,688
1987	1,606,990	950,214	28,399	978,613	106,467	215,662	1,087,808	310,113	209,069	14,394	111,646	50,000
1988	1,748,810	1,055,604	14,420	1,070,024	120,929	241,298	1,190,393	332,322	226,095	15,525	112,643	52,423
1989	1,923,843	1,129,960	23,680	1,153,640	127,606	275,678	1,301,712	378,674	243,457	17,024	113,009	52,792
1990	2,027,628	1,170,877	31,606	1,202,483	133,393	289,932	1,359,022	397,636	270,970	17,769	114,109	52,552
1991	2,131,967	1,195,964	26,362	1,222,326	138,596	323,655	1,407,385	409,119	315,463	18,499	115,248	52,326
1992	2,246,691	1,277,068	28,901	1,305,969	147,783	351,273	1,509,459	406,114	331,118	19,357	116,066	52,293
1993	2,340,570	1,314,541	24,837	1,339,378	155,620	387,085	1,570,843	416,833	352,894	20,045	116,764	51,088
1994	2,450,766	1,400,028	23,340	1,423,368	166,279	409,686	1,666,775	424,579	359,412	20,873	117,415	51,472
1995	2,528,011	1,381,406	16,045	1,397,451	166,169	469,945	1,701,227	446,109	380,675	21,459	117,809	52,277
1996	2,660,549	1,398,455	28,451	1,426,906	164,900	525,979	1,787,985	464,624	407,940	22,473	118,391	52,193
1997	2,794,930	1,473,706	26,696	1,500,402	172,786	556,098	1,883,714	490,689	420,527	23,536	118,753	53,347
1998	2,967,497	1,544,604	29,248	1,573,852	179,237	609,017	2,003,632	527,182	436,683	24,814	119,590	51,923
1999	3,074,751	1,641,066	20,649	1,661,715	187,998	613,924	2,087,641	519,926	467,184	25,635	119,944	52,886
2000	3,228,503	1,737,945	38,391	1,776,336	198,705	605,962	2,183,593	550,107	494,803	26,835	120,309	54,561
2001	3,460,574	1,928,060	40,987	1,969,047	215,421	623,154	2,376,780	549,058	534,736	28,611	120,954	58,544
2002	3,544,735	1,992,863	21,049	2,013,912	220,804	659,319	2,452,427	517,588	574,720	29,127	121,698	58,829
2003	3,672,562	2,083,429	47,453	2,130,882	229,526	665,331	2,566,687	506,474	599,401	29,821	123,154	59,506
2004	3,982,226	2,224,367	73,684	2,298,051	244,445	723,421	2,777,027	566,154	639,045	31,949	124,644	60,914
2005	4,167,768	2,322,297	67,623	2,389,920	258,779	775,350	2,906,491	558,987	702,290	33,026	126,197	62,303
2006	4,358,398	2,470,688	44,494	2,515,182	280,148	783,043	3,018,077	599,294	741,027	33,970	128,302	64,152
2007	4,582,693	2,535,425	64,630	2,600,055	287,667	791,994	3,104,382	691,985	786,326	35,202	130,182	65,331
2008	4,800,770	2,556,340	66,717	2,623,057	294,977	805,215	3,133,295	765,999	901,476	36,487	131,574	64,941
2009	4,752,730	2,520,794	52,255	2,573,049	295,906	734,067	3,011,210	728,426	1,013,094	35,746	132,959	64,006
2010	4,939,452	2,677,300	60,280	2,737,580	311,422	741,746	3,167,904	698,820	1,072,728	36,943	133,705	64,609
2011	5,149,723	2,807,355	87,827	2,895,182	294,569	727,140	3,327,753	733,967	1,088,003	38,225	134,722	66,017
2012	5,261,530	2,893,003	93,524	2,986,527	302,349	679,941	3,364,119	800,420	1,096,991	38,722	135,880	67,511
2013	5,316,406	2,942,438	105,814	3,048,252	341,439	715,963	3,422,776	761,509	1,132,121	39,003	136,307	67,410
2014	5,521,526	2,967,736	119,098	3,086,834	346,643	773,009	3,513,200	836,026	1,172,300	40,244	137,201	67,180
2015	5,785,678	3,076,652	76,780	3,153,432	357,078	855,027	3,651,381	891,605	1,242,692	41,829	138,317	66,949
2016	6,014,035	3,170,636	19,498	3,190,134	369,724	905,224	3,725,634	971,326	1,317,075	43,121	139,470	67,314
2017	6,295,746	3,314,966	50,381	3,365,347	390,855	958,055	3,932,547	1,017,375	1,345,824	44,768	140,629	67,360
2018	6,620,981	3,463,195	41,185	3,504,380	407,195	993,050	4,090,235	1,091,850	1,438,896	46,481	142,446	68,448
2019	6,884,361	3,674,988	42,160	3,717,148	433,972	984,140	4,267,316	1,113,570	1,503,475	48,207	142,809	69,187
2020	7,502,472	3,684,286	19,494	3,703,780	436,030	1,000,152	4,267,902	1,182,692	2,051,878	52,362	143,282	66,500
2021	8,044,252	3,975,105	72,029	4,047,134	469,683	1,011,131	4,588,582	1,243,857	2,211,813	55,937	143,809	69,535
2022	8,094,389	4,201,490	147,298	4,348,788	511,372	1,038,959	4,876,375	1,343,149	1,874,865	56,207	144,011	71,855

Personal Income and Employment by Area: Lewiston, ID-WA

(Thousands of dollars, except as noted.)

Year	Personal income, total	Derivation of personal income: Earnings by place of work: Nonfarm	Farm	Total	Less: Contributions for government social insurance	Plus: Adjustment for residence	Equals: Net earnings by place of residence	Plus: Dividends, interest, and rent	Plus: Personal current transfer receipts	Per capita personal income (dollars)	Population (persons)	Total employment
1970	166,225	115,690	8,313	124,003	9,095	4,896	119,804	28,181	18,240	3,760	44,211	17,980
1971	181,691	127,026	8,214	135,240	10,329	4,341	129,252	31,868	20,571	4,056	44,792	18,651
1972	203,450	142,757	11,849	154,606	12,020	3,283	145,869	34,459	23,122	4,384	46,404	18,905
1973	228,028	161,996	15,283	177,279	15,830	877	162,326	39,323	26,379	4,909	46,454	20,121
1974	264,950	182,986	25,104	208,090	18,365	-1,615	188,110	45,392	31,448	5,679	46,658	20,911
1975	290,248	206,659	13,662	220,321	20,154	-1,031	199,136	52,835	38,277	6,209	46,744	21,367
1976	317,152	232,783	12,210	244,993	23,000	-1,725	220,268	55,180	41,704	6,660	47,617	22,040
1977	345,508	259,594	10,087	269,681	25,749	-4,144	239,788	61,530	44,190	7,213	47,898	22,824
1978	387,945	295,864	10,330	306,194	29,545	-5,900	270,749	68,503	48,693	7,992	48,543	23,861
1979	428,607	333,801	8,658	342,459	35,020	-11,042	296,397	76,441	55,769	8,742	49,026	24,620
1980	480,383	358,439	15,518	373,957	37,639	-13,004	323,314	91,112	65,957	9,592	50,082	24,405
1981	520,042	372,463	18,414	390,877	42,011	-12,380	336,486	109,052	74,504	10,366	50,169	23,670
1982	546,566	368,653	19,741	388,394	42,465	-10,409	335,520	127,401	83,645	10,963	49,856	22,989
1983	601,182	399,246	27,815	427,061	46,124	-9,347	371,590	141,215	88,377	12,103	49,673	23,660
1984	625,676	419,818	16,212	436,030	50,195	-8,228	377,607	155,194	92,875	12,448	50,264	23,775
1985	638,964	423,522	4,636	428,158	51,026	-6,531	370,601	167,448	100,915	12,714	50,257	23,403
1986	661,775	434,370	11,266	445,636	52,988	-4,807	387,841	168,205	105,729	13,264	49,891	23,465
1987	678,920	457,146	8,254	465,400	55,791	-4,977	404,632	163,162	111,126	13,561	50,063	24,138
1988	729,003	494,108	12,478	506,586	62,664	-2,210	441,712	168,370	118,921	14,582	49,995	25,462
1989	794,472	529,533	18,246	547,779	67,867	-393	479,519	188,395	126,558	15,589	50,964	26,044
1990	853,351	578,610	21,540	600,150	77,582	1,310	523,878	191,731	137,742	16,562	51,526	26,983
1991	902,435	616,733	10,877	627,610	83,610	364	544,364	200,239	157,832	17,193	52,487	27,518
1992	984,529	689,699	9,824	699,523	92,283	-1,673	605,567	207,319	171,643	18,358	53,629	28,639
1993	1,065,420	742,210	23,147	765,357	99,583	-2,502	663,272	219,116	183,032	19,460	54,750	29,620
1994	1,115,309	796,689	7,128	803,817	107,177	-3,639	693,001	227,088	195,220	19,921	55,987	31,132
1995	1,159,965	796,278	10,704	806,982	107,804	-2,827	696,351	252,042	211,572	20,451	56,718	31,384
1996	1,228,664	838,195	13,468	851,663	111,092	-5,414	735,157	269,841	223,666	21,431	57,332	32,113
1997	1,284,592	894,615	426	895,041	116,075	-7,940	771,026	282,349	231,217	22,196	57,874	33,058
1998	1,364,618	954,521	6,457	960,978	121,624	-9,839	829,515	290,479	244,624	23,481	58,116	33,458
1999	1,413,901	1,012,036	8,571	1,020,607	124,741	-11,683	884,183	275,687	254,031	24,360	58,042	33,588
2000	1,477,082	1,041,145	19,696	1,060,841	129,407	-12,685	918,749	285,015	273,318	25,492	57,944	34,320
2001	1,524,817	1,062,263	19,933	1,082,196	132,703	-13,731	935,762	289,262	299,793	26,543	57,446	33,539
2002	1,537,935	1,090,963	16,574	1,107,537	136,401	-12,714	958,422	265,417	314,096	26,700	57,601	33,447
2003	1,599,803	1,125,876	18,567	1,144,443	141,816	-13,306	989,321	280,164	330,318	27,496	58,183	33,601
2004	1,673,630	1,162,070	23,439	1,185,509	145,927	-12,445	1,027,137	296,141	350,352	28,570	58,581	33,584
2005	1,701,345	1,182,143	21,822	1,203,965	151,582	-13,591	1,038,792	294,972	367,581	28,847	58,979	33,984
2006	1,814,816	1,262,390	16,318	1,278,708	161,535	-12,565	1,104,608	312,886	397,322	30,426	59,646	34,469
2007	1,950,651	1,321,765	21,217	1,342,982	169,745	-11,067	1,162,170	357,919	430,562	32,561	59,908	35,179
2008	2,055,467	1,348,461	24,405	1,372,866	174,130	-12,434	1,186,302	396,793	472,372	34,142	60,203	34,972
2009	2,037,101	1,323,715	17,931	1,341,646	173,139	-11,677	1,156,830	372,953	507,318	33,691	60,464	33,927
2010	2,128,404	1,384,648	22,622	1,407,270	182,329	-12,525	1,212,416	369,953	546,035	34,856	61,062	33,986
2011	2,192,063	1,388,520	25,248	1,413,768	164,326	-13,668	1,235,774	409,223	547,066	35,629	61,524	33,983
2012	2,227,328	1,408,510	22,302	1,430,812	165,209	-12,516	1,253,087	430,484	543,757	36,146	61,620	33,500
2013	2,288,966	1,487,725	29,741	1,517,466	190,529	-18,874	1,308,063	418,201	562,702	36,778	62,238	34,443
2014	2,363,903	1,517,047	6,887	1,523,934	197,386	-18,611	1,307,937	452,405	603,561	37,859	62,439	34,882
2015	2,451,195	1,587,345	17,715	1,605,060	205,555	-19,095	1,380,410	461,642	609,143	39,145	62,618	35,298
2016	2,535,202	1,654,805	7,990	1,662,795	214,614	-19,962	1,428,219	469,802	637,181	40,207	63,053	35,918
2017	2,658,874	1,742,230	4,506	1,746,736	225,995	-22,202	1,498,539	493,987	666,348	41,833	63,559	36,464
2018	2,768,756	1,779,603	7,573	1,787,176	228,963	-19,186	1,539,027	530,506	699,223	43,425	63,760	36,152
2019	2,888,910	1,840,808	15,817	1,856,625	236,908	-17,742	1,601,975	557,498	729,437	45,121	64,026	36,083
2020	3,111,541	1,945,366	24,664	1,970,030	255,398	-21,653	1,692,979	535,822	882,740	48,266	64,466	35,626
2021	3,402,708	2,059,640	25,380	2,085,020	262,353	-21,303	1,801,364	598,405	1,002,939	52,368	64,977	36,525
2022	3,563,419	2,233,065	34,575	2,267,640	288,624	-24,099	1,954,917	664,136	944,366	54,393	65,512	38,083

Personal Income and Employment by Area: Lewiston-Auburn, ME

(Thousands of dollars, except as noted.)

Year	Personal income, total	Derivation of personal income: Earnings by place of work: Nonfarm	Farm	Total	Less: Contributions for government social insurance	Plus: Adjustment for residence	Equals: Net earnings by place of residence	Plus: Dividends, interest, and rent	Plus: Personal current transfer receipts	Per capita personal income (dollars)	Population (persons)	Total employment
1970	339,559	245,390	6,907	252,297	19,291	21,803	254,809	46,393	38,357	3,713	91,463	42,844
1971	350,474	240,860	7,099	247,959	19,477	25,854	254,336	49,865	46,273	3,773	92,881	40,634
1972	373,641	255,844	9,495	265,339	21,738	27,410	271,011	53,438	49,192	3,985	93,756	40,343
1973	423,220	288,072	18,096	306,168	27,820	29,065	307,413	58,582	57,225	4,451	95,076	42,562
1974	459,977	308,823	13,975	322,798	30,844	32,348	324,302	67,275	68,400	4,798	95,870	43,143
1975	506,117	329,092	14,041	343,133	32,268	35,036	345,901	74,436	85,780	5,298	95,535	42,320
1976	579,076	381,103	23,386	404,489	38,489	43,097	409,097	78,590	91,389	5,962	97,130	44,591
1977	622,266	416,443	18,291	434,734	42,096	46,293	438,931	87,384	95,951	6,338	98,181	46,014
1978	683,401	465,446	15,016	480,462	48,555	54,180	486,087	95,442	101,872	6,914	98,837	47,120
1979	750,788	509,826	12,901	522,727	54,493	63,221	531,455	103,248	116,085	7,534	99,656	47,810
1980	843,623	553,477	11,128	564,605	59,010	77,759	583,354	123,883	136,386	8,476	99,531	47,774
1981	920,210	583,782	13,423	597,205	66,270	85,622	616,557	147,288	156,365	9,246	99,522	47,298
1982	993,450	600,158	15,140	615,298	68,408	100,216	647,106	175,531	170,813	10,049	98,860	45,953
1983	1,075,385	655,243	13,366	668,609	74,858	107,146	700,897	189,195	185,293	10,834	99,262	46,577
1984	1,179,074	729,743	20,067	749,810	85,417	111,488	775,881	209,450	193,743	11,789	100,018	48,103
1985	1,241,551	773,236	17,568	790,804	90,215	112,663	813,252	223,508	204,791	12,401	100,114	48,570
1986	1,335,908	837,104	14,671	851,775	97,136	127,450	882,089	241,694	212,125	13,332	100,204	50,078
1987	1,450,932	939,048	14,137	953,185	107,058	138,865	984,992	250,010	215,930	14,312	101,378	51,603
1988	1,594,504	1,028,427	12,437	1,040,864	119,791	163,975	1,085,048	278,890	230,566	15,397	103,559	53,611
1989	1,731,878	1,097,709	10,731	1,108,440	126,141	184,319	1,166,618	319,121	246,139	16,451	105,276	54,122
1990	1,784,715	1,113,528	17,088	1,130,616	134,139	195,162	1,191,639	315,162	277,914	16,931	105,412	53,181
1991	1,789,029	1,115,132	16,841	1,131,973	136,424	167,018	1,162,567	307,584	318,878	17,043	104,973	50,918
1992	1,859,232	1,155,416	16,732	1,172,148	142,774	180,542	1,209,916	296,802	352,514	17,820	104,335	50,835
1993	1,922,814	1,217,047	22,212	1,239,259	154,004	172,019	1,257,274	296,470	369,070	18,406	104,464	52,166
1994	2,012,204	1,287,349	27,361	1,314,710	164,818	168,189	1,318,081	306,913	387,210	19,327	104,112	53,466
1995	2,066,583	1,327,018	10,621	1,337,639	171,013	162,335	1,328,961	333,013	404,609	19,915	103,769	53,265
1996	2,161,012	1,378,531	21,502	1,400,033	174,536	153,081	1,378,578	350,333	432,101	20,988	102,966	53,134
1997	2,267,249	1,448,483	14,203	1,462,686	182,904	174,217	1,453,999	364,131	449,119	22,116	102,518	53,271
1998	2,375,589	1,557,054	13,637	1,570,691	194,455	161,145	1,537,381	378,460	459,748	23,037	103,120	55,697
1999	2,487,806	1,702,606	23,816	1,726,422	208,786	145,825	1,663,461	358,523	465,822	24,059	103,403	58,684
2000	2,639,007	1,828,505	23,546	1,852,051	220,048	130,307	1,762,310	386,563	490,134	25,411	103,852	60,420
2001	2,724,274	1,874,917	24,369	1,899,286	226,267	138,779	1,811,798	384,919	527,557	26,130	104,260	59,480
2002	2,868,950	2,013,609	23,319	2,036,928	237,225	113,494	1,913,197	392,470	563,283	27,307	105,063	60,213
2003	3,018,729	2,088,293	30,885	2,119,178	243,796	122,968	1,998,350	402,259	618,120	28,441	106,140	60,114
2004	3,099,207	2,163,744	23,172	2,186,916	250,214	145,393	2,082,095	365,394	651,718	29,001	106,867	60,631
2005	3,164,615	2,203,035	8,922	2,211,957	257,161	137,051	2,091,847	355,286	717,482	29,479	107,352	60,554
2006	3,313,151	2,344,184	10,657	2,354,841	274,277	123,163	2,203,727	387,276	722,148	30,697	107,932	61,323
2007	3,466,084	2,427,154	17,514	2,444,668	288,428	103,440	2,259,680	437,214	769,190	32,171	107,739	62,999
2008	3,623,256	2,472,373	29,372	2,501,745	296,307	78,393	2,283,831	451,520	887,905	33,461	108,284	62,504
2009	3,645,144	2,419,946	21,321	2,441,267	289,523	61,824	2,213,568	458,059	973,517	33,805	107,830	60,519
2010	3,682,036	2,473,955	21,029	2,494,984	298,807	27,984	2,224,161	489,123	968,752	34,165	107,773	60,263
2011	3,767,576	2,496,108	22,896	2,519,004	272,586	5,933	2,252,351	501,555	1,013,670	34,960	107,767	60,365
2012	3,818,287	2,553,109	37,614	2,590,723	280,799	-3,308	2,306,616	511,634	1,000,037	35,330	108,075	60,352
2013	3,754,929	2,572,925	46,120	2,619,045	323,573	-6,298	2,289,174	456,278	1,009,477	34,745	108,072	60,396
2014	3,846,236	2,688,661	30,487	2,719,148	333,545	-46,352	2,339,251	481,726	1,025,259	35,461	108,463	61,260
2015	4,036,729	2,780,954	56,316	2,837,270	348,450	-34,402	2,454,418	518,702	1,063,609	37,210	108,485	61,713
2016	4,069,714	2,849,206	23,543	2,872,749	353,961	-63,249	2,455,539	527,889	1,086,286	37,359	108,936	62,432
2017	4,215,288	2,932,471	27,775	2,960,246	363,580	-58,845	2,537,821	560,552	1,116,915	38,565	109,303	62,617
2018	4,383,681	3,063,370	24,684	3,088,054	382,146	-55,217	2,650,691	562,597	1,170,393	39,837	110,040	63,266
2019	4,613,312	3,226,409	25,506	3,251,915	401,352	-80,411	2,770,152	618,177	1,224,983	41,685	110,670	63,266
2020	5,099,252	3,375,396	25,228	3,400,624	419,455	-125,693	2,855,476	664,355	1,579,421	45,865	111,180	61,611
2021	5,428,031	3,625,348	23,815	3,649,163	455,540	-70,653	3,122,970	583,119	1,721,942	48,186	112,648	63,099
2022	5,544,341	3,824,246	49,572	3,873,818	482,601	-61,274	3,329,943	612,749	1,601,649	49,055	113,023	64,228

Personal Income and Employment by Area: Lexington-Fayette, KY

(Thousands of dollars, except as noted.)

Year	Personal income, total	Derivation of personal income								Per capita personal income (dollars)	Population (persons)	Total employment
		Earnings by place of work			Less: Contributions for government social insurance	Plus: Adjustment for residence	Equals: Net earnings by place of residence	Plus: Dividends, interest, and rent	Plus: Personal current transfer receipts			
		Nonfarm	Farm	Total								
1970	1,017,530	857,895	42,124	900,019	54,163	-49,882	795,974	147,327	74,229	3,804	267,481	140,584
1971	1,127,053	949,712	39,006	988,718	61,436	-52,159	875,123	165,006	86,924	4,118	273,697	143,669
1972	1,251,564	1,055,175	51,243	1,106,418	72,088	-61,923	972,407	182,977	96,180	4,440	281,894	148,727
1973	1,400,290	1,196,803	54,506	1,251,309	94,851	-71,630	1,084,828	204,737	110,725	4,868	287,662	158,535
1974	1,560,999	1,325,589	56,972	1,382,561	108,738	-83,358	1,190,465	236,865	133,669	5,270	296,218	162,910
1975	1,710,621	1,417,655	60,952	1,478,607	115,190	-84,944	1,278,473	257,114	175,034	5,747	297,670	157,519
1976	1,934,689	1,627,457	71,845	1,699,302	135,761	-104,743	1,458,798	285,649	190,242	6,377	303,393	166,412
1977	2,150,870	1,802,950	94,260	1,897,210	150,367	-118,230	1,628,613	318,572	203,685	6,973	308,473	170,538
1978	2,444,284	2,029,243	148,323	2,177,566	175,832	-139,295	1,862,439	362,713	219,132	7,841	311,728	180,152
1979	2,731,737	2,297,636	141,902	2,439,538	206,600	-166,088	2,066,850	417,561	247,326	8,622	316,817	184,649
1980	3,035,302	2,437,328	193,405	2,630,733	221,253	-173,540	2,235,940	502,732	296,630	9,540	318,175	183,059
1981	3,435,147	2,664,961	258,179	2,923,140	260,843	-186,483	2,475,814	622,472	336,861	10,739	319,884	183,889
1982	3,692,636	2,822,928	231,382	3,054,310	281,232	-195,340	2,577,738	751,961	362,937	11,458	322,286	185,181
1983	4,025,075	3,083,752	280,225	3,363,977	310,274	-218,600	2,835,103	795,875	394,097	12,414	324,231	191,185
1984	4,551,103	3,502,078	364,345	3,866,423	359,216	-258,001	3,249,206	886,727	415,170	13,998	325,133	200,185
1985	4,848,558	3,792,516	341,328	4,133,844	396,859	-285,048	3,451,937	952,211	444,410	14,671	330,485	205,232
1986	4,989,003	3,988,198	253,497	4,241,695	433,192	-295,642	3,512,861	1,009,123	467,019	14,885	335,169	212,210
1987	5,265,038	4,279,590	238,901	4,518,491	463,752	-322,510	3,732,229	1,041,441	491,368	15,531	339,008	216,098
1988	5,876,892	4,827,944	245,711	5,073,655	520,277	-352,113	4,201,265	1,142,368	533,259	17,125	343,186	223,962
1989	6,315,551	5,208,599	233,857	5,442,456	570,760	-400,890	4,470,806	1,248,095	596,650	18,312	344,891	230,602
1990	6,893,146	5,737,963	242,676	5,980,639	652,399	-465,640	4,862,600	1,373,674	656,872	19,686	350,161	235,619
1991	7,327,218	6,058,058	248,903	6,306,961	692,106	-469,386	5,145,469	1,435,649	746,100	20,590	355,861	237,345
1992	7,832,879	6,483,642	314,329	6,797,971	739,905	-507,662	5,550,404	1,458,735	823,740	21,567	363,195	242,428
1993	8,142,973	6,757,974	281,970	7,039,944	778,884	-510,742	5,750,318	1,516,309	876,346	22,018	369,839	248,440
1994	8,462,521	6,998,601	278,514	7,277,115	825,454	-546,720	5,904,941	1,644,470	913,110	22,538	375,478	251,588
1995	9,016,202	7,412,527	279,784	7,692,311	878,581	-602,243	6,211,487	1,820,652	984,063	23,721	380,096	264,124
1996	9,644,243	7,992,998	321,845	8,314,843	937,877	-698,997	6,677,969	1,917,805	1,048,469	24,978	386,117	272,024
1997	10,318,606	8,544,408	387,127	8,931,535	999,011	-776,624	7,155,900	2,053,695	1,109,011	26,386	391,065	279,832
1998	11,068,070	9,158,863	448,361	9,607,224	1,069,447	-811,958	7,725,819	2,201,220	1,141,031	27,825	397,775	286,606
1999	11,722,113	9,783,837	547,130	10,330,967	1,148,367	-846,332	8,336,268	2,211,310	1,174,535	28,987	404,393	293,947
2000	12,643,669	10,402,017	643,031	11,045,048	1,192,481	-920,499	8,932,068	2,417,789	1,293,812	30,844	409,924	300,557
2001	12,740,689	10,585,664	402,456	10,988,120	1,215,144	-956,318	8,816,658	2,474,246	1,449,785	30,736	414,520	297,666
2002	12,991,561	10,938,726	390,176	11,328,902	1,253,956	-993,649	9,081,297	2,334,535	1,575,729	31,047	418,448	293,683
2003	13,381,826	11,392,772	285,935	11,678,707	1,289,480	-1,039,729	9,349,498	2,401,894	1,630,434	31,490	424,953	296,940
2004	14,212,115	12,046,062	340,598	12,386,660	1,337,406	-1,080,004	9,969,250	2,494,364	1,748,501	33,034	430,229	301,324
2005	14,913,919	12,606,209	292,086	12,898,295	1,389,671	-1,154,963	10,353,661	2,697,358	1,862,900	34,136	436,898	307,891
2006	16,015,295	13,300,632	301,621	13,602,253	1,478,051	-1,219,581	10,904,621	3,097,588	2,013,086	35,934	445,685	316,787
2007	16,836,948	13,978,279	243,639	14,221,918	1,558,285	-1,288,141	11,375,492	3,276,905	2,184,551	37,239	452,138	324,487
2008	17,460,565	14,390,666	-43,634	14,347,032	1,623,886	-1,252,420	11,470,726	3,437,075	2,552,764	37,949	460,112	322,849
2009	17,033,502	13,675,121	5,743	13,680,864	1,581,983	-1,130,321	10,968,560	3,231,144	2,833,798	36,449	467,328	312,512
2010	17,620,244	14,034,371	41,189	14,075,560	1,596,272	-1,056,908	11,422,380	3,064,351	3,133,513	37,224	473,358	312,867
2011	18,635,734	14,507,537	57,893	14,565,430	1,460,466	-1,083,816	12,021,148	3,428,601	3,185,985	38,933	478,659	317,115
2012	19,488,692	15,102,557	146,800	15,249,357	1,514,714	-1,117,350	12,617,293	3,683,778	3,187,621	40,205	484,729	321,704
2013	20,105,945	15,517,226	603,320	16,120,546	1,769,395	-1,126,238	13,224,913	3,585,852	3,295,180	41,020	490,155	327,531
2014	21,020,828	16,174,611	495,832	16,670,443	1,855,722	-1,208,059	13,606,662	3,868,231	3,545,935	42,540	494,144	335,615
2015	22,135,669	17,083,351	531,153	17,614,504	1,974,978	-1,284,796	14,354,730	4,070,006	3,710,933	44,251	500,235	345,921
2016	22,612,304	17,341,530	469,482	17,811,012	2,031,437	-1,438,012	14,341,563	4,581,504	3,689,237	44,849	504,186	352,146
2017	23,443,693	17,763,599	578,997	18,342,596	2,078,376	-1,558,013	14,706,207	4,982,443	3,755,043	45,980	509,867	356,648
2018	24,347,623	18,222,669	539,620	18,762,289	2,105,020	-1,502,524	15,154,745	5,295,426	3,897,452	47,493	512,657	357,814
2019	25,658,345	19,167,936	599,067	19,767,003	2,191,019	-1,622,426	15,953,558	5,606,536	4,098,251	49,832	514,901	357,932
2020	27,562,813	19,669,479	444,837	20,114,316	2,264,203	-1,686,367	16,163,746	5,687,048	5,712,019	53,274	517,378	346,791
2021	29,392,808	21,040,684	535,466	21,576,150	2,342,110	-1,784,468	17,449,572	5,698,173	6,245,063	56,894	516,627	357,592
2022	29,974,372	22,553,189	619,972	23,173,161	2,527,217	-1,963,398	18,682,546	6,009,807	5,282,019	57,875	517,916	373,377

Personal Income and Employment by Area: Lima, OH

(Thousands of dollars, except as noted.)

Year	Personal income, total	Derivation of personal income									Per capita personal income (dollars)	Population (persons)	Total employment
		Earnings by place of work			Less: Contributions for government social insurance	Plus: Adjustment for residence	Equals: Net earnings by place of residence	Plus: Dividends, interest, and rent	Plus: Personal current transfer receipts				
		Nonfarm	Farm	Total									
1970	439,385	419,832	4,748	424,580	28,588	-51,050	344,942	59,351	35,092		3,955	111,084	56,153
1971	465,872	433,323	4,889	438,212	30,076	-47,402	360,734	62,791	42,347		4,181	111,437	54,945
1972	489,289	452,316	6,580	458,896	33,227	-47,821	377,848	66,074	45,367		4,422	110,643	54,610
1973	554,243	523,367	9,359	532,726	44,576	-59,143	429,007	73,044	52,192		5,027	110,245	57,847
1974	607,835	571,175	10,743	581,918	50,375	-67,191	464,352	81,822	61,661		5,494	110,637	58,786
1975	647,153	592,884	8,751	601,635	50,985	-71,164	479,486	88,010	79,657		5,840	110,806	56,340
1976	699,455	642,001	10,327	652,328	56,239	-76,457	519,632	94,956	84,867		6,367	109,853	56,613
1977	775,298	733,388	6,671	740,059	64,248	-95,838	579,973	106,674	88,651		7,018	110,465	58,352
1978	861,705	837,741	6,315	844,056	76,299	-116,955	650,802	117,121	93,782		7,846	109,828	60,165
1979	953,508	931,402	7,214	938,616	88,075	-137,447	713,094	131,455	108,959		8,571	111,247	61,611
1980	1,035,392	954,363	7,039	961,402	88,646	-145,698	727,058	164,163	144,171		9,229	112,188	58,688
1981	1,097,890	980,401	-194	980,207	97,348	-146,869	735,990	200,621	161,279		9,827	111,726	57,444
1982	1,147,231	1,007,272	-1,951	1,005,321	101,638	-155,678	748,005	219,282	179,944		10,446	109,826	55,345
1983	1,224,202	1,080,158	-5,489	1,074,669	110,331	-169,124	795,214	235,910	193,078		11,238	108,936	55,927
1984	1,384,845	1,237,251	14,176	1,251,427	129,461	-199,519	922,447	264,079	198,319		12,631	109,642	58,993
1985	1,466,200	1,341,397	12,473	1,353,870	142,609	-222,020	989,241	272,916	204,043		13,378	109,601	61,057
1986	1,547,640	1,449,376	10,201	1,459,577	158,698	-246,519	1,054,360	281,149	212,131		14,101	109,755	62,105
1987	1,580,497	1,494,184	10,926	1,505,110	164,129	-250,705	1,090,276	276,279	213,942		14,352	110,123	62,506
1988	1,666,276	1,563,857	12,609	1,576,466	176,828	-258,948	1,140,690	293,694	231,892		15,077	110,518	64,316
1989	1,748,877	1,597,140	22,643	1,619,783	182,532	-261,467	1,175,784	325,205	247,888		15,860	110,270	65,527
1990	1,815,215	1,635,960	26,710	1,662,670	190,919	-265,352	1,206,399	332,177	276,639		16,526	109,841	65,107
1991	1,853,854	1,676,769	16,968	1,693,737	199,575	-269,672	1,224,490	333,464	295,900		16,866	109,916	64,909
1992	1,978,732	1,750,331	18,530	1,768,861	207,498	-263,603	1,297,760	339,619	341,353		17,949	110,242	63,879
1993	1,992,481	1,790,955	12,010	1,802,965	213,805	-273,608	1,315,552	342,761	334,168		18,070	110,262	64,648
1994	2,111,086	1,883,849	14,207	1,898,056	227,168	-285,339	1,385,549	370,107	355,430		19,168	110,138	65,381
1995	2,164,957	1,877,951	4,325	1,882,276	227,671	-263,976	1,390,629	399,252	375,076		19,710	109,841	66,147
1996	2,220,759	1,895,983	6,756	1,902,739	226,168	-259,872	1,416,699	418,246	385,814		20,267	109,573	66,212
1997	2,294,809	1,933,167	20,069	1,953,236	224,798	-269,304	1,459,134	440,491	395,184		21,024	109,150	66,563
1998	2,438,526	2,057,428	7,448	2,064,876	230,519	-287,615	1,546,742	481,548	410,236		22,454	108,599	67,726
1999	2,551,630	2,250,359	875	2,251,234	249,302	-350,157	1,651,775	475,549	424,306		23,584	108,192	71,158
2000	2,681,099	2,375,739	13,401	2,389,140	252,349	-379,848	1,756,943	477,439	446,717		24,690	108,589	72,973
2001	2,722,876	2,382,326	12,328	2,394,654	259,990	-369,227	1,765,437	472,514	484,925		25,090	108,523	69,825
2002	2,781,077	2,435,067	-2,090	2,432,977	262,433	-359,427	1,811,117	462,102	507,858		25,628	108,518	69,132
2003	2,861,863	2,509,135	3,641	2,512,776	273,327	-351,980	1,887,469	442,132	532,262		26,642	107,418	68,371
2004	2,929,571	2,606,067	19,221	2,625,288	290,243	-374,040	1,961,005	411,874	556,692		27,424	106,826	68,614
2005	2,995,795	2,655,756	12,819	2,668,575	300,377	-366,774	2,001,424	399,956	594,415		28,035	106,861	68,551
2006	3,139,303	2,736,631	14,500	2,751,131	307,113	-354,445	2,089,573	415,350	634,380		29,417	106,716	67,906
2007	3,299,915	2,774,730	14,487	2,789,217	310,342	-323,840	2,155,035	467,410	677,470		30,922	106,717	66,741
2008	3,398,905	2,747,750	14,733	2,762,483	311,823	-296,581	2,154,079	497,783	747,043		31,833	106,773	65,414
2009	3,408,781	2,742,197	20,182	2,762,379	312,740	-338,891	2,110,748	472,048	825,985		32,002	106,518	62,898
2010	3,506,072	2,812,448	32,733	2,845,181	313,126	-367,603	2,164,452	469,477	872,143		32,969	106,345	62,428
2011	3,635,585	2,885,602	47,431	2,933,033	291,164	-399,632	2,242,237	494,152	899,196		34,300	105,995	62,951
2012	3,720,653	2,940,605	27,851	2,968,456	299,370	-393,049	2,276,037	557,736	886,880		35,342	105,277	63,340
2013	3,708,589	3,000,247	48,592	3,048,839	331,396	-406,116	2,311,327	492,297	904,965		35,284	105,108	63,605
2014	3,844,389	3,056,798	22,806	3,079,604	335,598	-388,833	2,355,173	549,616	939,600		36,636	104,935	63,373
2015	3,948,314	3,109,714	1,173	3,110,887	340,053	-352,230	2,418,604	548,487	981,223		37,891	104,201	63,572
2016	4,025,272	3,202,752	7,713	3,210,465	359,352	-388,807	2,462,306	565,081	997,885		38,793	103,763	63,440
2017	4,145,841	3,328,359	11,289	3,339,648	381,298	-418,262	2,540,088	580,196	1,025,557		40,150	103,258	63,903
2018	4,306,723	3,420,907	17,951	3,438,858	386,660	-412,460	2,639,738	620,423	1,046,562		41,877	102,843	63,649
2019	4,419,491	3,447,462	7,068	3,454,530	393,843	-379,403	2,681,284	644,271	1,093,936		43,093	102,558	62,945
2020	4,794,131	3,497,921	24,644	3,522,565	404,490	-421,147	2,696,928	648,359	1,448,844		46,952	102,107	61,140
2021	5,079,044	3,669,087	52,492	3,721,579	422,507	-434,605	2,864,467	651,390	1,563,187		49,896	101,792	62,453
2022	5,075,440	3,891,800	38,588	3,930,388	460,210	-473,499	2,996,679	705,120	1,373,641		50,195	101,115	64,238

Personal Income and Employment by Area: Lincoln, NE

(Thousands of dollars, except as noted.)

Year	Personal income, total	Derivation of personal income: Earnings by place of work: Nonfarm	Farm	Total	Less: Contributions for government social insurance	Plus: Adjustment for residence	Equals: Net earnings by place of residence	Plus: Dividends, interest, and rent	Plus: Personal current transfer receipts	Per capita personal income (dollars)	Population (persons)	Total employment
1970	761,119	608,314	15,182	623,496	40,790	-6,171	576,535	129,698	54,886	4,153	183,265	94,866
1971	834,654	664,518	18,341	682,859	45,895	-7,420	629,544	142,287	62,823	4,446	187,741	98,445
1972	918,081	733,434	19,078	752,512	52,849	-8,983	690,680	157,073	70,328	4,705	195,133	102,842
1973	1,035,680	824,266	30,980	855,246	69,063	-11,138	775,045	176,253	84,382	5,280	196,134	107,748
1974	1,148,954	925,745	21,704	947,449	81,359	-14,011	852,079	200,984	95,891	5,756	199,608	111,765
1975	1,303,224	1,018,528	45,582	1,064,110	87,628	-16,032	960,450	223,085	119,689	6,552	198,905	112,328
1976	1,421,987	1,151,154	19,752	1,170,906	100,169	-18,503	1,052,234	241,615	128,138	7,145	199,025	116,047
1977	1,554,224	1,264,079	14,912	1,278,991	110,723	-19,926	1,148,342	270,128	135,754	7,743	200,719	119,912
1978	1,768,411	1,415,813	55,099	1,470,912	128,277	-23,080	1,319,555	297,763	151,093	8,711	203,010	123,341
1979	1,932,111	1,570,522	26,032	1,596,554	147,910	-26,869	1,421,775	341,340	168,996	9,453	204,382	127,203
1980	2,096,196	1,689,474	-10,358	1,679,116	158,154	-29,388	1,491,574	405,272	199,350	10,012	209,378	127,424
1981	2,367,047	1,830,003	23,553	1,853,556	184,336	-33,852	1,635,368	499,132	232,547	11,180	211,713	125,565
1982	2,571,557	1,908,397	44,769	1,953,166	196,722	-35,309	1,721,135	594,838	255,584	12,082	212,839	123,845
1983	2,688,692	2,025,454	18,131	2,043,585	209,412	-38,474	1,795,699	615,854	277,139	12,552	214,209	124,320
1984	2,921,476	2,223,999	22,541	2,246,540	236,591	-43,916	1,966,033	669,130	286,313	13,511	216,231	128,322
1985	3,122,361	2,375,135	36,630	2,411,765	259,391	-46,389	2,105,985	704,548	311,828	14,346	217,648	132,780
1986	3,260,209	2,504,488	45,520	2,550,008	283,776	-51,466	2,214,766	721,675	323,768	14,891	218,934	134,997
1987	3,439,775	2,703,200	41,939	2,745,139	306,228	-57,545	2,381,366	724,722	333,687	15,606	220,410	140,194
1988	3,721,804	2,900,111	61,759	2,961,870	343,753	-62,871	2,555,246	812,175	354,383	16,681	223,119	146,113
1989	3,988,297	3,121,506	59,010	3,180,516	368,854	-69,400	2,742,262	860,422	385,613	17,615	226,420	149,477
1990	4,302,436	3,379,562	63,057	3,442,619	412,491	-77,428	2,952,700	928,996	420,740	18,695	230,144	155,589
1991	4,519,066	3,547,152	45,534	3,592,686	434,956	-83,056	3,074,674	988,036	456,356	19,360	233,419	156,858
1992	4,834,458	3,802,221	59,416	3,861,637	456,948	-92,375	3,312,314	1,023,563	498,581	20,328	237,827	158,269
1993	5,077,507	4,029,718	31,059	4,060,777	484,027	-102,357	3,474,393	1,063,628	539,486	20,914	242,779	162,253
1994	5,474,575	4,314,357	58,159	4,372,516	520,710	-112,431	3,739,375	1,175,282	559,918	22,260	245,933	169,247
1995	5,872,120	4,613,025	17,899	4,630,924	546,447	-119,231	3,965,246	1,304,985	601,889	23,442	250,498	172,577
1996	6,273,820	4,851,905	94,383	4,946,288	577,489	-128,618	4,240,181	1,388,383	645,256	24,709	253,904	177,454
1997	6,573,737	5,122,993	53,369	5,176,362	615,519	-139,184	4,421,659	1,482,937	669,141	25,539	257,404	180,195
1998	7,132,318	5,579,685	54,298	5,633,983	663,623	-157,927	4,812,433	1,585,448	734,437	27,325	261,021	184,836
1999	7,511,638	5,927,873	47,648	5,975,521	698,063	-170,234	5,107,224	1,631,926	772,488	28,466	263,880	189,577
2000	8,163,173	6,436,624	43,775	6,480,399	741,392	-186,868	5,552,139	1,791,868	819,166	30,455	268,042	193,410
2001	8,373,254	6,681,116	45,303	6,726,419	767,732	-202,813	5,755,874	1,698,872	918,508	30,871	271,237	196,992
2002	8,739,579	7,056,998	14,274	7,071,272	811,185	-212,975	6,047,112	1,699,650	992,817	31,784	274,972	198,178
2003	9,107,237	7,250,969	61,202	7,312,171	837,269	-221,168	6,253,734	1,806,828	1,046,675	32,620	279,194	200,972
2004	9,456,271	7,575,963	87,739	7,663,702	871,366	-220,308	6,572,028	1,776,416	1,107,827	33,560	281,768	203,838
2005	9,799,022	7,888,416	57,738	7,946,154	917,154	-229,448	6,799,552	1,816,429	1,183,041	34,326	285,469	206,855
2006	10,336,721	8,245,688	28,707	8,274,395	969,707	-227,526	7,077,162	1,996,480	1,263,079	35,775	288,940	209,579
2007	10,926,863	8,566,353	68,362	8,634,715	1,002,215	-210,081	7,422,419	2,154,813	1,349,631	37,357	292,502	213,469
2008	11,502,427	8,763,792	99,012	8,862,804	1,023,756	-220,554	7,618,494	2,347,638	1,536,295	38,826	296,258	212,955
2009	11,349,662	8,768,821	88,005	8,856,826	1,020,277	-232,797	7,603,752	2,132,787	1,613,123	37,879	299,633	209,802
2010	11,725,538	9,026,531	92,296	9,118,827	1,056,596	-258,232	7,803,999	2,168,449	1,753,090	38,693	303,041	208,794
2011	12,399,251	9,227,503	183,203	9,410,706	958,300	-307,317	8,145,089	2,465,090	1,789,072	40,389	306,993	210,616
2012	13,077,123	9,798,587	94,030	9,892,617	988,966	-341,449	8,562,202	2,698,194	1,816,727	42,048	311,004	215,163
2013	13,128,268	10,023,289	146,449	10,169,738	1,151,310	-369,148	8,649,280	2,624,641	1,854,347	41,666	315,086	218,776
2014	13,731,279	10,533,275	81,886	10,615,161	1,205,423	-386,515	9,023,223	2,759,574	1,948,482	42,786	320,926	221,999
2015	14,463,603	11,022,909	83,518	11,106,427	1,257,126	-401,015	9,448,286	2,949,888	2,065,429	44,544	324,704	226,767
2016	14,758,016	11,299,231	49,636	11,348,867	1,301,672	-400,021	9,647,174	2,944,094	2,166,748	44,808	329,359	229,368
2017	15,495,773	11,754,061	47,634	11,801,695	1,363,217	-434,363	10,004,115	3,211,603	2,280,055	46,522	333,088	230,622
2018	16,287,940	12,360,614	53,330	12,413,944	1,428,788	-472,983	10,512,173	3,344,840	2,430,927	48,487	335,926	235,689
2019	17,052,542	12,699,938	71,384	12,771,322	1,490,352	-503,274	10,777,696	3,692,520	2,582,326	50,410	338,279	236,410
2020	18,212,160	12,981,802	85,038	13,066,840	1,560,230	-498,692	11,007,918	3,859,461	3,344,781	53,446	340,758	230,900
2021	20,183,629	13,841,985	162,326	14,004,311	1,642,921	-521,257	11,840,133	4,539,314	3,804,182	59,189	341,004	235,483
2022	20,649,415	14,576,411	110,833	14,687,244	1,752,889	-534,859	12,399,496	4,930,167	3,319,752	60,299	342,448	241,706

Personal Income and Employment by Area: Little Rock-North Little Rock-Conway, AR

(Thousands of dollars, except as noted.)

Year	Personal income, total	Derivation of personal income: Earnings by place of work: Nonfarm	Derivation of personal income: Earnings by place of work: Farm	Derivation of personal income: Earnings by place of work: Total	Less: Contributions for government social insurance	Plus: Adjustment for residence	Equals: Net earnings by place of residence	Plus: Dividends, interest, and rent	Plus: Personal current transfer receipts	Per capita personal income (dollars)	Population (persons)	Total employment
1970	1,450,105	1,195,466	28,284	1,223,750	85,462	-22,602	1,115,686	212,105	122,314	3,635	398,923	189,395
1971	1,637,474	1,351,485	29,033	1,380,518	99,363	-27,327	1,253,828	238,788	144,858	3,989	410,511	196,544
1972	1,855,105	1,542,392	36,863	1,579,255	119,038	-29,083	1,431,134	261,792	162,179	4,397	421,948	209,206
1973	2,127,721	1,751,201	68,368	1,819,569	155,333	-35,216	1,629,020	295,990	202,711	4,901	434,101	221,631
1974	2,415,090	1,963,866	72,021	2,035,887	180,073	-35,516	1,820,298	346,681	248,111	5,364	450,208	229,229
1975	2,686,035	2,144,029	53,257	2,197,286	192,768	-35,115	1,969,403	396,535	320,097	5,906	454,800	226,577
1976	2,986,826	2,424,519	40,363	2,464,882	221,591	-36,549	2,206,742	429,553	350,531	6,451	463,036	234,682
1977	3,296,427	2,702,565	41,072	2,743,637	249,469	-37,769	2,456,399	473,904	366,124	7,000	470,916	243,509
1978	3,760,823	3,065,938	70,406	3,136,344	290,242	-36,380	2,809,722	544,482	406,619	7,845	479,418	254,644
1979	4,186,268	3,405,122	49,201	3,454,323	334,368	-14,005	3,105,950	614,661	465,657	8,624	485,427	260,249
1980	4,661,439	3,718,187	28,470	3,746,657	364,058	-20,345	3,362,254	744,123	555,062	9,403	495,743	259,470
1981	5,128,890	4,005,442	38,154	4,043,596	423,958	-34,267	3,585,371	913,848	629,671	10,289	498,489	257,023
1982	5,488,216	4,248,231	21,921	4,270,152	457,671	-47,239	3,765,242	1,037,996	684,978	10,948	501,306	256,891
1983	5,925,251	4,626,428	18,750	4,645,178	504,405	-54,245	4,086,528	1,091,347	747,376	11,729	505,195	264,519
1984	6,475,712	5,064,971	35,275	5,100,246	567,820	-60,883	4,471,543	1,219,223	784,946	12,681	510,658	275,936
1985	7,003,948	5,492,804	35,424	5,528,228	623,358	-72,796	4,832,074	1,331,853	840,021	13,565	516,324	284,898
1986	7,453,592	5,854,297	26,615	5,880,912	669,379	-72,437	5,139,096	1,419,469	895,027	14,276	522,119	289,743
1987	7,742,635	6,149,972	45,518	6,195,490	700,160	-87,015	5,408,315	1,408,173	926,147	14,675	527,622	295,390
1988	8,215,017	6,494,406	75,779	6,570,185	770,332	-94,651	5,705,202	1,534,649	975,166	15,537	528,733	304,689
1989	8,871,826	6,900,422	63,311	6,963,733	818,996	-105,848	6,038,889	1,740,103	1,092,834	16,663	532,436	312,014
1990	9,435,097	7,417,202	50,965	7,468,167	917,204	-122,068	6,428,895	1,819,143	1,187,059	17,588	536,444	317,357
1991	10,020,595	7,934,088	49,661	7,983,749	980,039	-148,948	6,854,762	1,840,454	1,325,379	18,457	542,913	324,532
1992	10,855,675	8,656,144	64,548	8,720,692	1,060,472	-173,689	7,486,531	1,904,455	1,464,689	19,655	552,311	331,121
1993	11,380,250	9,096,830	57,578	9,154,408	1,111,552	-194,986	7,847,870	1,982,490	1,549,890	20,254	561,887	341,004
1994	11,996,438	9,606,281	63,673	9,669,954	1,191,713	-221,502	8,256,739	2,115,554	1,624,145	21,087	568,889	347,270
1995	12,785,740	10,202,122	59,899	10,262,021	1,260,003	-252,130	8,749,888	2,276,473	1,759,379	22,184	576,345	361,633
1996	13,607,050	10,773,247	83,088	10,856,335	1,319,934	-281,281	9,255,120	2,435,144	1,916,786	23,265	584,861	370,043
1997	14,288,110	11,358,757	73,912	11,432,669	1,388,622	-310,118	9,733,929	2,579,816	1,974,365	24,147	591,707	376,359
1998	15,261,747	12,223,870	60,985	12,284,855	1,476,276	-347,229	10,461,350	2,789,105	2,011,292	25,529	597,826	382,432
1999	15,880,014	12,838,448	66,956	12,905,404	1,542,730	-383,706	10,978,968	2,797,384	2,103,662	26,235	605,291	387,438
2000	16,769,555	13,541,813	71,602	13,613,415	1,612,187	-418,570	11,582,658	2,900,844	2,286,053	27,387	612,313	392,022
2001	17,830,764	14,445,131	76,119	14,521,250	1,680,385	-465,424	12,375,441	2,909,239	2,546,084	28,846	618,126	395,201
2002	18,422,157	14,880,054	50,667	14,930,721	1,725,033	-487,190	12,718,498	2,952,075	2,751,584	29,515	624,166	393,404
2003	19,493,869	15,706,561	104,485	15,811,046	1,808,476	-518,705	13,483,865	3,106,484	2,903,520	30,892	631,032	397,415
2004	20,553,111	16,545,788	108,773	16,654,561	1,886,143	-555,142	14,213,276	3,212,948	3,126,887	32,136	639,558	403,987
2005	21,968,229	17,563,343	56,773	17,620,116	1,985,955	-580,247	15,053,914	3,533,479	3,380,836	33,861	648,784	412,770
2006	23,211,287	18,299,901	66,688	18,366,589	2,116,918	-631,401	15,618,270	3,906,312	3,686,705	35,077	661,719	423,915
2007	24,881,972	19,503,604	77,627	19,581,231	2,248,898	-769,111	16,563,222	4,295,844	4,022,906	37,058	671,441	432,622
2008	25,568,989	19,199,034	61,938	19,260,972	2,307,089	-697,859	16,256,024	4,785,754	4,527,211	37,497	681,888	433,698
2009	25,586,170	19,304,851	39,321	19,344,172	2,331,930	-648,572	16,363,670	4,321,009	4,901,491	36,979	691,903	426,970
2010	26,221,024	19,409,031	25,888	19,434,919	2,346,988	-611,611	16,476,320	4,411,028	5,333,676	37,332	702,382	427,392
2011	27,475,599	19,960,035	15,403	19,975,438	2,183,920	-643,973	17,147,545	4,850,648	5,477,406	38,639	711,086	435,026
2012	29,162,933	20,855,301	34,414	20,889,715	2,236,525	-592,206	18,060,984	5,515,333	5,586,616	40,594	718,398	435,677
2013	28,786,275	21,141,167	100,718	21,241,885	2,543,914	-671,592	18,026,379	5,037,035	5,722,861	39,748	724,220	438,776
2014	29,968,544	21,779,663	57,656	21,837,319	2,641,131	-690,842	18,505,346	5,346,939	6,116,259	41,082	729,485	441,886
2015	30,968,655	22,365,542	21,273	22,386,815	2,725,496	-736,137	18,925,182	5,613,743	6,429,730	42,283	732,417	448,777
2016	31,748,597	22,773,659	19,487	22,793,146	2,745,567	-744,289	19,303,290	5,751,612	6,693,695	43,156	735,662	453,733
2017	32,443,654	23,224,938	34,627	23,259,565	2,813,751	-802,694	19,643,120	5,935,961	6,864,573	43,870	739,545	458,935
2018	33,365,462	23,858,492	20,129	23,878,621	2,899,910	-839,062	20,139,649	6,088,509	7,137,304	44,948	742,305	463,921
2019	34,807,501	24,845,844	7,260	24,853,104	3,026,950	-840,393	20,985,761	6,272,715	7,549,025	46,740	744,708	463,621
2020	38,129,575	25,660,163	36,173	25,696,336	3,157,498	-846,236	21,692,602	6,998,457	9,438,516	50,911	748,940	453,784
2021	41,280,969	27,193,920	51,531	27,245,451	3,303,509	-877,109	23,064,833	7,790,453	10,425,683	54,900	751,937	469,798
2022	42,311,618	29,057,634	16,578	29,074,212	3,577,564	-975,810	24,520,838	8,345,516	9,445,264	55,848	757,615	492,139

Personal Income and Employment by Area: Logan, UT-ID

(Thousands of dollars, except as noted.)

		Derivation of personal income										
		Earnings by place of work										
Year	Personal income, total	Nonfarm	Farm	Total	Less: Contributions for government social insurance	Plus: Adjustment for residence	Equals: Net earnings by place of residence	Plus: Dividends, interest, and rent	Plus: Personal current transfer receipts	Per capita personal income (dollars)	Population (persons)	Total employment
1970	142,719	86,078	14,685	100,763	5,819	10,307	105,251	24,791	12,677	2,865	49,811	19,220
1971	159,132	94,999	15,313	110,312	6,628	11,930	115,614	28,571	14,947	3,133	50,796	19,811
1972	180,672	108,052	18,233	126,285	7,903	13,271	131,653	32,203	16,816	3,416	52,893	20,828
1973	202,208	122,470	21,084	143,554	10,481	13,859	146,932	35,522	19,754	3,716	54,413	22,111
1974	227,739	137,895	23,551	161,446	12,370	15,826	164,902	40,522	22,315	4,082	55,792	23,183
1975	252,002	156,895	17,379	174,274	13,729	18,489	179,034	45,642	27,326	4,384	57,480	23,664
1976	289,615	186,124	17,899	204,023	16,419	20,959	208,563	50,696	30,356	4,911	58,974	25,332
1977	318,071	207,964	13,463	221,427	18,121	24,211	227,517	57,793	32,761	5,228	60,841	26,351
1978	363,517	239,975	14,333	254,308	21,308	28,234	261,234	66,372	35,911	5,823	62,424	27,771
1979	412,818	275,882	11,630	287,512	25,753	33,639	295,398	76,519	40,901	6,438	64,124	29,228
1980	467,824	304,979	12,162	317,141	29,480	39,020	326,681	92,674	48,469	7,010	66,734	30,090
1981	516,718	331,033	7,358	338,391	34,407	44,931	348,915	109,722	58,081	7,462	69,244	29,973
1982	556,131	340,354	11,617	351,971	35,436	49,524	366,059	125,893	64,179	7,780	71,482	29,880
1983	608,540	376,033	9,287	385,320	38,861	54,243	400,702	138,731	69,107	8,266	73,620	30,808
1984	666,707	413,702	12,819	426,521	43,782	59,899	442,638	150,499	73,570	8,917	74,772	31,754
1985	716,312	440,197	15,646	455,843	47,165	67,155	475,833	160,209	80,270	9,518	75,261	32,227
1986	777,515	485,805	21,073	506,878	52,725	71,217	525,370	169,019	83,126	10,278	75,651	33,320
1987	843,573	522,209	33,077	555,286	56,726	78,944	577,504	174,498	91,571	11,034	76,454	34,995
1988	896,565	567,102	34,688	601,790	65,303	83,469	619,956	182,322	94,287	11,547	77,643	36,896
1989	984,572	625,543	40,451	665,994	73,152	87,105	679,947	199,205	105,420	12,482	78,881	39,229
1990	1,049,557	684,099	45,831	729,930	81,411	89,104	737,623	197,092	114,842	13,166	79,719	40,769
1991	1,118,909	743,145	42,607	785,752	89,444	91,446	787,754	206,136	125,019	13,585	82,362	41,907
1992	1,212,123	813,171	50,395	863,566	96,617	96,825	863,774	208,160	140,189	14,210	85,299	42,939
1993	1,311,093	884,289	51,483	935,772	105,471	98,462	928,763	229,139	153,191	14,869	88,175	44,894
1994	1,394,871	970,935	44,482	1,015,417	116,911	99,594	998,100	240,741	156,030	15,294	91,202	48,049
1995	1,489,099	1,022,994	39,471	1,062,465	123,620	104,255	1,043,100	273,917	172,082	15,808	94,198	50,269
1996	1,601,997	1,092,675	47,950	1,140,625	128,601	108,655	1,120,679	301,619	179,699	16,548	96,807	52,531
1997	1,726,009	1,185,898	46,597	1,232,495	137,296	116,770	1,211,969	327,952	186,088	17,474	98,774	54,389
1998	1,839,220	1,250,095	65,862	1,315,957	145,350	125,130	1,295,737	348,210	195,273	18,225	100,916	55,955
1999	1,904,498	1,313,066	64,843	1,377,909	152,513	122,288	1,347,684	349,095	207,719	18,758	101,532	57,125
2000	1,977,805	1,355,812	43,170	1,398,982	157,431	131,273	1,372,824	378,435	226,546	19,163	103,211	58,582
2001	2,131,713	1,453,528	68,348	1,521,876	167,909	128,528	1,482,495	398,023	251,195	20,439	104,294	59,183
2002	2,186,054	1,541,739	35,024	1,576,763	178,771	123,895	1,521,887	393,295	270,872	20,396	107,180	60,142
2003	2,333,143	1,676,044	34,787	1,710,831	194,774	121,240	1,637,297	410,746	285,100	21,441	108,819	62,061
2004	2,528,360	1,802,376	59,977	1,862,353	212,850	122,499	1,772,002	448,599	307,759	22,816	110,813	64,374
2005	2,596,146	1,864,316	38,242	1,902,558	221,940	130,525	1,811,143	451,368	333,635	23,060	112,580	65,731
2006	2,747,241	1,987,422	23,506	2,010,928	232,624	141,655	1,919,959	465,937	361,345	24,243	113,321	68,176
2007	2,992,347	2,117,719	46,521	2,164,240	249,073	146,221	2,061,388	531,306	399,653	25,818	115,901	71,641
2008	3,313,881	2,288,368	51,542	2,339,910	266,386	148,949	2,222,473	619,550	471,858	27,756	119,394	72,978
2009	3,328,064	2,310,499	28,659	2,339,158	265,819	140,818	2,214,157	597,313	516,594	27,047	123,048	71,798
2010	3,536,532	2,461,798	48,922	2,510,720	280,220	134,663	2,365,163	595,554	575,815	28,013	126,246	71,845
2011	3,788,432	2,603,827	65,825	2,669,652	260,963	135,890	2,544,579	652,678	591,175	29,597	128,000	73,552
2012	3,953,862	2,640,871	65,847	2,706,718	260,663	149,951	2,596,006	776,632	581,224	30,548	129,431	74,287
2013	3,980,071	2,739,586	86,957	2,826,543	307,459	171,828	2,690,912	695,082	594,077	30,404	130,906	75,291
2014	4,185,871	2,821,663	97,844	2,919,507	322,848	182,757	2,779,416	773,346	633,109	31,655	132,234	77,432
2015	4,510,492	3,010,672	98,140	3,108,812	333,130	193,411	2,969,093	861,742	679,657	33,547	134,451	79,600
2016	4,754,677	3,256,955	68,240	3,325,195	352,768	202,493	3,174,920	865,919	713,838	34,514	137,759	81,220
2017	5,150,413	3,565,871	63,352	3,629,223	376,810	214,563	3,466,976	940,303	743,134	36,686	140,390	83,605
2018	5,558,621	3,855,625	64,309	3,919,934	394,160	236,501	3,762,275	1,003,485	792,861	38,838	143,123	85,704
2019	5,921,124	4,093,354	73,391	4,166,745	417,044	254,242	4,003,943	1,059,626	857,555	40,714	145,431	87,440
2020	6,321,665	4,259,391	81,953	4,341,344	456,143	255,825	4,141,026	1,096,241	1,084,398	42,741	147,908	90,485
2021	7,301,189	4,763,807	75,495	4,839,302	515,564	282,735	4,606,473	1,334,711	1,360,005	48,001	152,105	95,566
2022	7,466,543	4,925,064	110,312	5,035,376	543,759	319,433	4,811,050	1,487,824	1,167,669	48,059	155,362	99,593

Personal Income and Employment by Area: Longview, TX

(Thousands of dollars, except as noted.)

Year	Personal income, total	Derivation of personal income: Earnings by place of work: Nonfarm	Earnings by place of work: Farm	Earnings by place of work: Total	Less: Contributions for government social insurance	Plus: Adjustment for residence	Equals: Net earnings by place of residence	Plus: Dividends, interest, and rent	Plus: Personal current transfer receipts	Per capita personal income (dollars)	Population (persons)	Total employment
1970	565,808	437,458	5,622	443,080	28,461	1,807	416,426	83,881	65,501	3,217	175,877	71,996
1971	614,183	471,943	4,231	476,174	31,597	3,307	447,884	91,438	74,861	3,426	179,278	72,724
1972	678,748	517,311	8,473	525,784	36,241	5,893	495,436	100,163	83,149	3,701	183,388	75,103
1973	767,182	579,264	15,974	595,238	47,308	7,826	555,756	112,990	98,436	4,136	185,487	77,765
1974	893,993	675,650	15,660	691,310	56,964	9,230	643,576	133,788	116,629	4,730	189,013	81,290
1975	1,025,800	772,889	4,940	777,829	63,489	9,422	723,762	158,441	143,597	5,275	194,459	84,238
1976	1,179,519	907,689	5,438	913,127	75,645	11,421	848,903	173,390	157,226	5,948	198,315	88,921
1977	1,307,719	1,009,035	876	1,009,911	84,541	17,073	942,443	195,933	169,343	6,413	203,922	92,775
1978	1,520,224	1,182,741	5,351	1,188,092	101,260	19,842	1,106,674	225,227	188,323	7,254	209,570	98,704
1979	1,732,677	1,358,967	3,642	1,362,609	121,901	19,358	1,260,066	259,234	213,377	7,985	216,996	102,647
1980	2,005,958	1,545,964	-1,047	1,544,917	140,228	18,493	1,423,182	333,966	248,810	8,984	223,273	106,274
1981	2,370,853	1,811,471	460	1,811,931	177,722	23,301	1,657,510	429,649	283,694	10,364	228,764	114,008
1982	2,634,982	1,938,066	13,209	1,951,275	195,402	16,905	1,772,778	534,582	327,622	10,996	239,639	116,366
1983	2,746,802	1,962,742	3,221	1,965,963	195,571	-1,012	1,769,380	609,309	368,113	11,274	243,631	112,871
1984	2,929,368	2,075,586	4,025	2,079,611	212,290	20,294	1,887,615	659,360	382,393	12,025	243,602	115,340
1985	3,115,579	2,155,782	1,218	2,157,000	222,913	38,407	1,972,494	739,383	403,702	12,858	242,312	116,461
1986	3,135,654	2,143,140	1,595	2,144,735	218,747	30,219	1,956,207	738,970	440,477	13,001	241,187	112,508
1987	3,118,482	2,148,427	-4,679	2,143,748	216,680	34,794	1,961,862	698,147	458,473	13,042	239,119	115,689
1988	3,309,506	2,296,283	-4,425	2,291,858	240,343	40,614	2,092,129	741,302	476,075	13,903	238,036	117,162
1989	3,525,417	2,371,897	12,097	2,383,994	250,969	38,619	2,171,644	837,940	515,833	14,880	236,919	115,969
1990	3,723,104	2,560,225	15,283	2,575,508	265,111	38,769	2,349,166	805,772	568,166	15,663	237,693	119,174
1991	3,889,816	2,673,127	19,217	2,692,344	284,038	43,627	2,451,933	815,268	622,615	16,213	239,922	121,039
1992	4,163,154	2,854,749	30,720	2,885,469	299,234	44,668	2,630,903	813,249	719,002	17,242	241,456	121,601
1993	4,258,026	2,923,608	26,929	2,950,537	306,518	59,206	2,703,225	787,719	767,082	17,481	243,576	123,960
1994	4,460,523	3,060,606	24,918	3,085,524	324,328	63,283	2,824,479	824,298	811,746	18,185	245,290	127,332
1995	4,703,261	3,197,540	12,732	3,210,272	342,556	65,224	2,932,940	894,306	876,015	18,930	248,452	130,308
1996	4,991,903	3,417,387	9,412	3,426,799	361,119	68,832	3,134,512	930,857	926,534	19,878	251,124	133,351
1997	5,335,524	3,690,598	25,037	3,715,635	384,245	77,770	3,409,160	959,627	966,737	21,071	253,216	137,649
1998	5,633,477	3,913,548	26,650	3,940,198	404,423	82,949	3,618,724	1,027,333	987,420	22,107	254,823	140,025
1999	5,794,284	4,031,555	42,491	4,074,046	414,217	89,532	3,749,361	1,044,916	1,000,007	22,620	256,162	140,452
2000	6,209,643	4,291,395	31,814	4,323,209	432,635	103,191	3,993,765	1,166,680	1,049,198	24,242	256,153	143,195
2001	6,553,817	4,497,331	49,045	4,546,376	454,452	93,669	4,185,593	1,225,129	1,143,095	25,439	257,630	143,402
2002	6,672,261	4,577,712	54,394	4,632,106	460,209	78,037	4,249,934	1,178,213	1,244,114	25,681	259,812	142,651
2003	6,988,410	4,782,623	57,250	4,839,873	489,006	61,723	4,412,590	1,262,018	1,313,802	26,718	261,565	143,489
2004	7,194,293	4,990,995	49,735	5,040,730	515,158	54,643	4,580,215	1,229,280	1,384,798	27,270	263,814	144,631
2005	7,854,280	5,513,231	36,298	5,549,529	563,992	31,791	5,017,328	1,336,704	1,500,248	29,541	265,873	149,154
2006	8,716,102	6,271,329	17,040	6,288,369	617,575	-11,910	5,658,884	1,466,667	1,590,551	32,373	269,236	153,909
2007	9,254,718	6,589,928	18,265	6,608,193	665,597	-58,238	5,884,358	1,648,004	1,722,356	34,091	271,474	160,756
2008	10,716,579	7,573,203	-9,843	7,563,360	725,319	-124,856	6,713,185	2,088,910	1,914,484	39,088	274,165	165,638
2009	10,018,849	6,884,203	-12,391	6,871,812	704,910	-153,253	6,013,649	1,915,349	2,089,851	35,999	278,306	161,788
2010	10,400,729	7,395,210	4,594	7,399,804	756,503	-185,069	6,458,232	1,678,238	2,264,259	37,083	280,474	163,910
2011	11,415,107	7,949,724	-3,396	7,946,328	720,734	-246,487	6,979,107	2,122,143	2,313,857	40,431	282,336	166,708
2012	11,539,299	8,362,180	21,635	8,383,815	769,076	-322,905	7,291,834	1,945,978	2,301,487	40,791	282,887	172,060
2013	11,444,582	8,475,642	34,894	8,510,536	885,386	-358,525	7,266,625	1,806,331	2,371,626	40,531	282,364	174,096
2014	12,004,035	8,754,499	35,633	8,790,132	906,093	-353,782	7,530,257	2,006,837	2,466,941	42,429	282,920	175,462
2015	11,547,635	8,204,526	54,283	8,258,809	882,254	-331,158	7,045,397	1,887,992	2,614,246	40,747	283,400	174,375
2016	11,126,920	7,676,459	4,247	7,680,706	853,847	-273,097	6,553,762	1,833,413	2,739,745	39,281	283,267	171,379
2017	11,389,522	7,746,395	6,790	7,753,185	878,911	-270,929	6,603,345	2,007,529	2,778,648	40,090	284,096	170,228
2018	11,972,276	8,237,198	14,136	8,251,334	926,345	-304,972	7,020,017	2,053,963	2,898,296	42,051	284,711	173,137
2019	12,512,236	8,613,384	-3,212	8,610,172	953,009	-334,691	7,322,472	2,164,272	3,025,492	43,777	285,815	173,796
2020	13,276,426	8,245,748	1,480	8,247,228	917,728	-253,231	7,076,269	2,332,440	3,867,717	46,367	286,334	168,852
2021	14,292,152	8,623,962	10,865	8,634,827	944,583	-229,721	7,460,523	2,403,667	4,427,962	49,559	288,388	175,738
2022	14,772,522	9,463,235	42,311	9,505,546	1,055,231	-304,543	8,145,772	2,612,312	4,014,438	50,727	291,219	184,045

Personal Income and Employment by Area: Longview, WA

(Thousands of dollars, except as noted.)

Year	Personal income, total	Derivation of personal income: Earnings by place of work: Nonfarm	Farm	Total	Less: Contributions for government social insurance	Plus: Adjustment for residence	Equals: Net earnings by place of residence	Plus: Dividends, interest, and rent	Plus: Personal current transfer receipts	Per capita personal income (dollars)	Population (persons)	Total employment
1970	274,017	243,870	2,108	245,978	22,330	-12,156	211,492	35,172	27,353	3,983	68,799	29,467
1971	285,111	247,004	2,301	249,305	23,414	-11,683	214,208	38,153	32,750	4,083	69,830	28,695
1972	322,011	286,469	3,030	289,499	28,573	-14,451	246,475	41,290	34,246	4,660	69,102	30,465
1973	364,830	325,522	6,572	332,094	37,278	-17,067	277,749	47,421	39,660	5,126	71,174	32,414
1974	415,761	370,547	6,439	376,986	43,530	-21,077	312,379	56,157	47,225	5,774	72,006	33,292
1975	476,003	422,291	5,023	427,314	48,366	-24,976	353,972	63,974	58,057	6,394	74,445	34,143
1976	538,891	498,857	5,355	504,212	58,514	-39,452	406,246	69,345	63,300	7,249	74,340	35,416
1977	579,382	529,984	3,537	533,521	61,768	-39,331	432,422	77,622	69,338	7,760	74,659	35,411
1978	641,679	581,592	6,920	588,512	69,021	-42,967	476,524	88,945	76,210	8,495	75,532	35,985
1979	715,425	639,634	8,125	647,759	77,342	-47,517	522,900	103,228	89,297	9,158	78,118	36,487
1980	801,444	706,760	4,568	711,328	85,927	-58,814	566,587	123,871	110,986	10,068	79,601	37,129
1981	855,846	731,944	6,468	738,412	95,066	-56,299	587,047	147,046	121,753	10,744	79,657	36,029
1982	877,173	706,263	7,424	713,687	93,703	-49,030	570,954	165,056	141,163	11,103	79,006	34,093
1983	947,734	758,964	7,525	766,489	102,389	-53,278	610,822	184,960	151,952	12,011	78,908	34,630
1984	998,542	795,732	7,438	803,170	111,335	-49,979	641,856	196,829	159,857	12,618	79,138	35,602
1985	1,020,677	788,948	8,431	797,379	110,318	-43,725	643,336	207,874	169,467	12,981	78,627	35,058
1986	1,063,197	817,574	8,571	826,145	114,439	-40,562	671,144	214,972	177,081	13,695	77,632	35,534
1987	1,107,639	872,300	5,495	877,795	121,803	-43,108	712,884	210,065	184,690	14,123	78,428	37,670
1988	1,196,966	955,100	6,574	961,674	136,437	-43,348	781,889	225,749	189,328	15,050	79,531	39,451
1989	1,311,473	1,026,077	9,732	1,035,809	145,867	-43,866	846,076	260,086	205,311	16,195	80,982	40,985
1990	1,410,606	1,118,843	10,582	1,129,425	161,250	-44,735	923,440	261,340	225,826	17,103	82,478	42,731
1991	1,531,388	1,210,750	12,040	1,222,790	176,574	-56,409	989,807	283,378	258,203	18,186	84,207	43,637
1992	1,573,217	1,204,947	13,060	1,218,007	172,426	-41,090	1,004,491	283,875	284,851	18,440	85,316	42,176
1993	1,639,168	1,251,714	13,214	1,264,928	181,554	-43,207	1,040,167	287,999	311,002	18,949	86,506	42,678
1994	1,722,765	1,328,882	11,345	1,340,227	192,804	-54,152	1,093,271	301,510	327,984	19,623	87,791	44,279
1995	1,793,360	1,372,206	10,264	1,382,470	198,976	-52,115	1,131,379	316,847	345,134	20,086	89,284	45,260
1996	1,865,466	1,411,803	8,959	1,420,762	197,846	-47,190	1,175,726	337,664	352,076	20,653	90,325	46,179
1997	1,930,410	1,438,446	7,117	1,445,563	192,889	-40,751	1,211,923	353,690	364,797	21,128	91,367	46,315
1998	2,035,127	1,507,223	7,488	1,514,711	200,348	-38,655	1,275,708	372,576	386,843	22,049	92,301	46,458
1999	2,116,190	1,589,674	7,662	1,597,336	205,288	-42,231	1,349,817	356,022	410,351	22,799	92,820	47,768
2000	2,202,590	1,645,205	4,851	1,650,056	218,063	-38,015	1,393,978	374,647	433,965	23,688	92,984	48,330
2001	2,319,600	1,691,118	4,953	1,696,071	226,888	-21,765	1,447,418	378,669	493,513	24,780	93,608	47,910
2002	2,330,110	1,676,368	3,632	1,680,000	222,056	4,992	1,462,936	343,725	523,449	24,703	94,325	46,430
2003	2,410,887	1,703,875	7,748	1,711,623	226,634	37,345	1,522,334	344,692	543,861	25,508	94,516	46,147
2004	2,538,527	1,770,684	7,277	1,777,961	238,560	86,621	1,626,022	353,251	559,254	26,570	95,541	46,412
2005	2,721,030	1,884,335	2,038	1,886,373	256,016	142,520	1,772,877	353,646	594,507	28,187	96,536	47,467
2006	2,913,981	1,961,374	-50	1,961,324	264,110	207,969	1,905,183	359,486	649,312	29,386	99,162	48,319
2007	3,219,402	2,120,080	-616	2,119,464	278,554	214,067	2,054,977	458,557	705,868	31,956	100,744	49,380
2008	3,395,846	2,137,719	1,225	2,138,944	278,142	206,379	2,067,181	519,167	809,498	33,395	101,688	48,588
2009	3,381,170	2,043,993	2,831	2,046,824	275,946	173,978	1,944,856	511,742	924,572	33,108	102,126	46,239
2010	3,568,574	2,289,688	4,348	2,294,036	297,604	89,352	2,085,784	485,586	997,204	34,867	102,349	45,873
2011	3,608,903	2,252,695	7,530	2,260,225	272,188	113,932	2,101,969	526,363	980,571	35,289	102,267	45,875
2012	3,740,315	2,385,708	6,924	2,392,632	278,344	90,218	2,204,506	540,051	995,758	36,819	101,586	45,860
2013	3,782,436	2,492,909	6,027	2,498,936	323,647	50,605	2,225,894	540,585	1,015,957	37,310	101,378	46,459
2014	3,944,984	2,593,042	6,414	2,599,456	339,418	9,408	2,269,446	583,151	1,092,387	38,808	101,654	48,213
2015	4,098,681	2,684,609	14,908	2,699,517	349,523	42,259	2,392,253	591,148	1,115,280	39,857	102,835	48,554
2016	4,246,927	2,668,382	15,552	2,683,934	352,521	128,119	2,459,532	617,324	1,170,071	40,632	104,523	48,787
2017	4,440,167	2,779,876	43,990	2,823,866	376,064	149,572	2,597,374	637,629	1,205,164	41,683	106,522	50,345
2018	4,689,148	2,910,722	41,124	2,951,846	389,307	196,939	2,759,478	668,147	1,261,523	43,277	108,351	50,948
2019	5,041,323	3,096,619	39,371	3,135,990	401,783	233,696	2,967,903	726,507	1,346,913	45,822	110,020	51,776
2020	5,550,791	3,264,766	52,324	3,317,090	428,416	233,796	3,122,470	766,976	1,661,345	49,999	111,019	50,696
2021	6,043,590	3,516,364	49,882	3,566,246	454,292	266,809	3,378,763	770,567	1,894,260	54,131	111,648	52,448
2022	6,116,134	3,789,981	31,446	3,821,427	499,682	305,686	3,627,431	810,103	1,678,600	54,630	111,956	54,192

Personal Income and Employment by Area: Los Angeles-Long Beach-Anaheim, CA

(Thousands of dollars, except as noted.)

Year	Personal income, total	Derivation of personal income: Earnings by place of work								Per capita personal income (dollars)	Population (persons)	Total employment
		Nonfarm	Farm	Total	Less: Contributions for government social insurance	Plus: Adjustment for residence	Equals: Net earnings by place of residence	Plus: Dividends, interest, and rent	Plus: Personal current transfer receipts			
1970	42,898,309	35,477,189	66,565	35,543,754	2,395,587	-780,077	32,368,090	6,588,317	3,941,902	5,062	8,475,377	3,938,904
1971	44,962,023	36,759,101	64,606	36,823,707	2,548,382	-971,593	33,303,732	7,066,371	4,591,920	5,236	8,587,868	3,890,306
1972	48,982,924	40,567,852	78,966	40,646,818	2,973,135	-1,207,361	36,466,322	7,597,646	4,918,956	5,700	8,593,421	4,034,431
1973	53,179,424	44,483,547	94,016	44,577,563	3,757,828	-1,409,001	39,410,734	8,379,692	5,388,998	6,150	8,647,592	4,258,523
1974	58,755,856	48,584,652	111,613	48,696,265	4,214,122	-1,628,292	42,853,851	9,556,937	6,345,068	6,711	8,754,864	4,372,383
1975	64,589,683	52,389,382	102,827	52,492,209	4,418,812	-1,799,274	46,274,123	10,404,577	7,910,983	7,304	8,842,499	4,367,984
1976	71,531,619	58,791,328	124,366	58,915,694	5,066,226	-2,010,333	51,839,135	11,024,916	8,667,568	7,962	8,984,368	4,520,496
1977	79,408,612	66,386,922	139,889	66,526,811	5,818,748	-2,417,011	58,291,052	11,993,009	9,124,551	8,761	9,063,784	4,733,736
1978	90,398,475	76,611,969	133,347	76,745,316	6,892,751	-2,864,364	66,988,201	13,620,952	9,789,322	9,821	9,204,893	5,044,872
1979	102,138,228	87,340,061	187,217	87,527,278	8,234,187	-3,332,339	75,960,752	15,657,790	10,519,686	10,991	9,292,983	5,314,599
1980	115,334,975	96,965,793	267,554	97,233,347	8,975,819	-4,027,096	84,230,432	19,084,053	12,020,490	12,199	9,454,611	5,404,030
1981	129,912,948	107,551,171	228,530	107,779,701	10,795,659	-4,596,711	92,387,331	23,495,765	14,029,852	13,513	9,613,602	5,490,043
1982	138,243,504	112,998,736	253,341	113,252,077	11,580,792	-5,010,937	96,660,348	26,170,270	15,412,886	14,087	9,813,347	5,398,676
1983	148,511,373	121,526,229	310,139	121,836,368	12,641,973	-5,613,165	103,581,230	28,532,808	16,397,335	14,837	10,009,841	5,496,333
1984	164,049,585	135,345,465	318,906	135,664,371	14,595,207	-6,471,654	114,597,510	32,549,111	16,902,964	16,139	10,165,047	5,772,337
1985	177,186,608	147,249,103	316,614	147,565,717	16,037,576	-7,382,219	124,145,922	34,830,009	18,210,677	17,111	10,354,836	5,967,933
1986	189,665,877	159,613,704	301,198	159,914,902	17,526,767	-8,322,840	134,065,295	36,163,730	19,436,852	17,855	10,622,535	6,154,066
1987	204,161,730	176,172,958	299,373	176,472,331	19,283,345	-9,568,987	147,619,999	36,433,529	20,108,202	18,842	10,835,330	6,389,935
1988	220,252,238	191,114,270	325,423	191,439,693	21,470,922	-10,671,083	159,297,688	39,796,043	21,158,507	20,022	11,000,781	6,660,585
1989	233,781,539	200,934,238	345,310	201,279,548	22,709,207	-11,806,804	166,763,537	44,110,409	22,907,593	20,915	11,177,630	6,773,734
1990	251,202,315	214,141,690	377,725	214,519,415	23,982,890	-13,665,422	176,871,103	49,165,970	25,165,242	22,236	11,297,143	6,881,721
1991	255,829,680	216,050,544	310,597	216,361,141	24,281,688	-13,199,420	178,880,033	49,118,668	27,830,979	22,440	11,400,816	6,700,497
1992	267,626,682	223,782,190	277,269	224,059,459	24,789,754	-12,911,995	186,357,710	48,922,537	32,346,435	23,166	11,552,438	6,471,123
1993	270,295,963	224,582,107	282,541	224,864,648	24,834,589	-13,017,954	187,012,105	49,134,173	34,149,685	23,236	11,632,798	6,397,429
1994	277,161,172	228,868,687	274,942	229,143,629	25,480,488	-12,819,200	190,843,941	50,966,074	35,351,157	23,764	11,663,207	6,402,534
1995	289,008,833	235,778,197	319,223	236,097,420	25,913,590	-12,865,864	197,317,966	54,856,361	36,834,506	24,717	11,692,693	6,550,063
1996	305,468,733	247,567,022	323,988	247,891,010	26,499,315	-12,764,236	208,627,459	58,184,953	38,656,321	25,951	11,771,038	6,656,417
1997	321,442,388	262,890,272	364,919	263,255,191	27,831,330	-13,905,135	221,518,726	61,155,413	38,768,249	26,976	11,915,815	6,736,278
1998	349,689,724	285,689,526	411,870	286,101,396	29,795,724	-14,126,996	242,178,676	66,502,635	41,008,413	28,932	12,086,776	7,020,536
1999	368,890,334	303,490,236	441,804	303,932,040	31,532,370	-14,210,576	258,189,094	67,498,242	43,202,998	30,106	12,253,223	7,121,223
2000	393,795,590	324,205,955	463,293	324,669,248	33,580,848	-14,915,022	276,173,378	72,682,781	44,939,431	31,776	12,392,704	7,216,670
2001	409,130,058	335,106,592	393,286	335,499,878	35,406,470	-15,732,824	284,360,584	74,563,369	50,206,105	32,700	12,511,491	7,247,391
2002	419,605,470	345,741,350	410,589	346,151,939	36,954,588	-16,228,835	292,968,516	72,758,187	53,878,767	33,265	12,614,158	7,236,748
2003	440,960,966	363,653,649	459,079	364,112,728	39,079,013	-16,783,888	308,249,827	75,890,715	56,820,424	34,731	12,696,521	7,270,603
2004	467,094,158	391,615,250	418,838	392,034,088	42,861,273	-17,812,377	331,360,438	76,309,435	59,424,285	36,678	12,734,974	7,374,040
2005	495,979,739	409,529,792	420,981	409,950,773	44,607,493	-18,359,279	346,984,001	87,084,244	61,911,494	38,972	12,726,428	7,475,697
2006	535,081,832	433,866,495	461,394	434,327,889	45,745,487	-19,660,764	368,921,638	100,323,046	65,837,148	42,231	12,670,216	7,603,483
2007	553,677,946	442,629,386	389,930	443,019,316	46,285,184	-20,196,184	376,537,948	108,011,439	69,128,559	43,831	12,631,988	7,727,201
2008	562,615,480	438,012,553	382,564	438,395,117	46,937,922	-19,718,673	371,738,522	113,250,897	77,626,061	44,326	12,692,740	7,623,456
2009	541,507,704	416,876,455	355,869	417,232,324	44,949,136	-18,356,501	353,926,687	102,124,270	85,456,747	42,389	12,774,577	7,303,670
2010	567,108,646	435,002,851	304,211	435,307,062	45,240,548	-17,787,782	372,278,732	100,285,104	94,544,810	44,169	12,839,428	7,244,659
2011	605,354,050	461,733,668	259,303	461,992,971	42,614,202	-18,621,453	400,757,316	109,451,219	95,145,515	46,814	12,931,008	7,398,752
2012	645,335,739	487,060,612	312,283	487,372,895	44,152,466	-19,142,688	424,077,741	125,184,722	96,073,276	49,553	13,023,028	7,684,580
2013	641,995,627	497,121,763	267,160	497,388,923	51,176,685	-19,080,545	427,131,693	115,045,416	99,818,518	48,965	13,111,248	7,926,197
2014	676,869,349	516,933,406	245,299	517,178,705	53,649,262	-19,247,613	444,281,830	125,906,182	106,681,337	51,337	13,184,705	8,163,917
2015	723,002,680	544,017,876	271,228	544,289,104	56,311,183	-19,143,598	468,834,323	138,414,584	115,753,773	54,538	13,256,931	8,403,128
2016	748,381,829	562,169,500	255,505	562,425,005	58,206,405	-20,942,829	483,275,771	144,523,859	120,582,199	56,287	13,295,906	8,564,100
2017	775,685,639	584,570,564	305,785	584,876,349	60,535,760	-21,329,914	503,010,675	153,838,364	118,836,600	58,282	13,309,287	8,655,977
2018	806,414,541	606,590,794	186,776	606,777,570	63,651,551	-22,932,402	520,193,617	161,246,776	124,974,148	60,697	13,285,814	8,850,828
2019	850,624,522	637,773,653	229,634	638,003,287	66,859,601	-24,856,365	546,287,321	170,584,046	133,753,155	64,262	13,236,839	8,889,564
2020	914,040,421	634,717,181	251,602	634,968,783	66,252,083	-25,342,106	543,374,594	173,182,968	197,482,859	69,362	13,177,752	8,404,421
2021	977,881,120	678,325,446	239,080	678,564,526	71,571,362	-24,620,491	582,372,673	188,226,373	207,282,074	75,379	12,972,847	8,687,265
2022	984,030,663	717,164,764	288,533	717,453,297	78,264,913	-29,410,878	609,777,506	202,470,681	171,782,476	76,445	12,872,322	9,191,840

Personal Income and Employment by Area: Louisville/Jefferson County, KY-IN

(Thousands of dollars, except as noted.)

Year	Personal income, total	Derivation of personal income								Per capita personal income (dollars)	Population (persons)	Total employment
		Earnings by place of work			Less: Contributions for government social insurance	Plus: Adjustment for residence	Equals: Net earnings by place of residence	Plus: Dividends, interest, and rent	Plus: Personal current transfer receipts			
		Nonfarm	Farm	Total								
1970	3,750,987	3,177,946	37,570	3,215,516	221,121	-36,303	2,958,092	507,336	285,559	3,972	944,381	439,474
1971	4,025,374	3,373,151	39,102	3,412,253	242,337	-40,197	3,129,719	552,899	342,756	4,201	958,302	440,568
1972	4,428,492	3,743,589	43,722	3,787,311	284,759	-51,661	3,450,891	595,029	382,572	4,608	960,977	452,694
1973	4,940,461	4,200,784	53,671	4,254,455	368,123	-65,737	3,820,595	665,805	454,061	5,079	972,713	474,154
1974	5,411,762	4,518,382	60,028	4,578,410	409,612	-71,547	4,097,251	769,085	545,426	5,517	980,860	482,140
1975	5,779,903	4,666,980	49,170	4,716,150	413,293	-68,521	4,234,336	837,074	708,493	5,877	983,510	462,783
1976	6,352,019	5,175,942	54,036	5,229,978	466,591	-76,101	4,687,286	902,033	762,700	6,428	988,211	470,309
1977	7,066,169	5,830,837	58,424	5,889,261	524,938	-86,701	5,277,622	1,005,337	783,210	7,141	989,554	486,870
1978	7,873,591	6,573,795	46,929	6,620,724	606,049	-96,964	5,917,711	1,118,615	837,265	7,903	996,252	508,829
1979	8,674,791	7,196,883	47,012	7,243,895	686,837	-111,958	6,445,100	1,267,086	962,605	8,673	1,000,248	513,721
1980	9,505,380	7,583,425	45,493	7,628,918	722,935	-117,457	6,788,526	1,539,803	1,177,051	9,529	997,538	504,651
1981	10,519,382	8,175,422	70,913	8,246,335	838,791	-122,954	7,284,590	1,904,787	1,330,005	10,553	996,787	500,731
1982	11,129,186	8,303,545	83,941	8,387,486	866,732	-103,116	7,417,638	2,237,725	1,473,823	11,145	998,540	484,418
1983	11,790,271	8,838,256	37,107	8,875,363	928,853	-108,672	7,837,838	2,381,739	1,570,694	11,816	997,786	485,350
1984	12,927,808	9,709,275	112,793	9,822,068	1,043,959	-134,664	8,643,445	2,648,748	1,635,615	12,979	996,037	501,259
1985	13,627,253	10,233,950	106,989	10,340,939	1,116,335	-142,403	9,082,201	2,815,852	1,729,200	13,706	994,276	509,997
1986	14,281,285	10,736,034	100,189	10,836,223	1,207,285	-149,562	9,479,376	2,976,932	1,824,977	14,378	993,281	523,128
1987	15,022,626	11,444,334	114,855	11,559,189	1,280,832	-156,853	10,121,504	3,017,306	1,883,816	15,120	993,543	534,484
1988	16,490,372	12,586,514	115,194	12,701,708	1,423,906	-163,262	11,114,540	3,373,717	2,002,115	16,610	992,777	554,912
1989	17,787,149	13,379,670	190,734	13,570,404	1,519,033	-162,211	11,889,160	3,699,084	2,198,905	17,895	993,963	567,446
1990	18,875,841	14,145,299	166,599	14,311,898	1,658,125	-160,645	12,493,128	3,992,321	2,390,392	18,907	998,334	582,395
1991	19,676,381	14,684,928	149,742	14,834,670	1,745,773	-173,939	12,914,958	4,100,761	2,660,662	19,517	1,008,144	580,133
1992	21,147,704	15,965,603	105,950	16,071,553	1,886,168	-218,363	13,967,022	4,263,932	2,916,750	20,768	1,018,303	590,254
1993	22,110,993	16,847,557	91,468	16,939,025	2,009,200	-258,230	14,671,595	4,398,629	3,040,769	21,496	1,028,593	606,018
1994	23,271,057	17,834,458	81,061	17,915,519	2,166,236	-304,857	15,444,426	4,642,942	3,183,689	22,419	1,038,000	623,373
1995	24,581,184	18,738,050	43,015	18,781,065	2,278,547	-332,300	16,170,218	5,021,582	3,389,384	23,464	1,047,610	644,754
1996	25,913,430	19,584,474	64,958	19,649,432	2,360,805	-352,203	16,936,424	5,390,955	3,586,051	24,545	1,055,733	654,083
1997	27,374,620	20,715,997	54,560	20,770,557	2,487,111	-389,366	17,894,080	5,706,964	3,773,576	25,721	1,064,309	669,931
1998	29,557,970	22,580,603	56,772	22,637,375	2,685,645	-449,097	19,502,633	6,193,746	3,861,591	27,556	1,072,659	684,771
1999	30,821,828	24,159,266	25,682	24,184,948	2,875,422	-524,368	20,785,158	6,086,722	3,949,948	28,456	1,083,137	698,297
2000	33,061,203	25,745,719	81,159	25,826,878	2,979,378	-588,667	22,258,833	6,564,456	4,237,914	30,253	1,092,810	712,388
2001	34,098,614	26,574,134	65,900	26,640,034	3,075,407	-625,778	22,938,849	6,543,129	4,616,636	30,987	1,100,423	705,441
2002	34,752,855	27,026,839	27,188	27,054,027	3,135,298	-631,453	23,287,276	6,511,342	4,954,237	31,356	1,108,339	696,599
2003	35,693,727	27,863,727	53,506	27,917,233	3,203,484	-630,032	24,083,717	6,487,073	5,122,937	31,885	1,119,435	695,615
2004	37,689,499	29,588,014	75,671	29,663,685	3,350,603	-667,893	25,645,189	6,579,074	5,465,236	33,370	1,129,452	703,461
2005	39,025,867	30,452,268	43,579	30,495,847	3,456,073	-693,877	26,345,897	6,843,873	5,836,097	34,235	1,139,934	715,551
2006	41,600,251	31,806,629	43,732	31,850,361	3,650,184	-672,483	27,527,694	7,814,699	6,257,858	36,038	1,154,352	729,837
2007	43,355,160	32,998,502	41,247	33,039,749	3,824,981	-694,860	28,519,908	8,114,202	6,721,050	37,066	1,169,680	744,073
2008	44,787,692	32,957,460	38,193	32,995,653	3,904,179	-566,327	28,525,147	8,629,704	7,632,841	37,833	1,183,814	739,775
2009	43,756,049	31,885,878	29,292	31,915,170	3,836,729	-459,690	27,618,751	7,692,889	8,444,409	36,618	1,194,945	715,470
2010	45,581,611	33,068,543	23,940	33,092,483	3,914,522	-361,731	28,816,230	7,737,345	9,028,036	37,825	1,205,068	713,469
2011	47,902,076	34,497,768	59,792	34,557,560	3,601,891	-231,485	30,724,184	8,021,736	9,156,156	39,460	1,213,944	723,659
2012	51,016,755	36,469,544	58,958	36,528,502	3,790,330	-475,605	32,262,567	9,537,727	9,216,461	41,682	1,223,959	737,969
2013	50,651,706	37,323,370	151,988	37,475,358	4,411,841	-517,909	32,545,608	8,721,931	9,384,167	40,925	1,237,673	752,527
2014	53,161,422	38,985,297	86,965	39,072,262	4,640,151	-650,784	33,781,327	9,214,190	10,165,905	42,646	1,246,579	769,610
2015	56,303,572	41,502,383	73,864	41,576,247	4,941,462	-864,069	35,770,716	9,885,994	10,646,862	44,856	1,255,214	788,140
2016	57,948,744	43,124,844	37,537	43,162,381	5,115,301	-1,061,131	36,985,949	10,174,361	10,788,434	45,876	1,263,150	805,286
2017	60,231,249	44,749,604	62,007	44,811,611	5,287,900	-1,104,358	38,419,353	10,669,148	11,142,748	47,348	1,272,088	816,855
2018	62,961,946	46,672,973	48,191	46,721,164	5,503,031	-1,201,685	40,016,448	11,410,616	11,534,882	49,337	1,276,167	828,856
2019	65,575,369	48,800,282	47,390	48,847,672	5,742,335	-1,281,940	41,823,397	11,671,018	12,080,954	51,183	1,281,193	830,069
2020	70,258,469	49,445,568	82,856	49,528,424	5,909,503	-1,242,941	42,375,980	11,649,872	16,232,617	54,631	1,286,046	802,877
2021	77,536,608	53,210,226	141,463	53,351,689	6,186,932	-1,359,184	45,805,573	13,784,448	17,946,587	60,373	1,284,286	835,030
2022	78,987,798	56,606,374	173,740	56,780,114	6,653,800	-1,430,311	48,696,003	14,788,150	15,503,645	61,490	1,284,553	870,840

Personal Income and Employment by Area: Lubbock, TX

(Thousands of dollars, except as noted.)

		Derivation of personal income										
		Earnings by place of work										
Year	Personal income, total	Nonfarm	Farm	Total	Less: Contributions for government social insurance	Plus: Adjustment for residence	Equals: Net earnings by place of residence	Plus: Dividends, interest, and rent	Plus: Personal current transfer receipts	Per capita personal income (dollars)	Population (persons)	Total employment
1970	727,087	533,818	72,755	606,573	32,937	-1,711	571,925	109,849	45,313	3,665	198,372	89,704
1971	744,276	572,888	36,994	609,882	36,625	-1,626	571,631	119,421	53,224	3,657	203,502	90,946
1972	836,301	646,093	42,473	688,566	43,026	-2,402	643,138	132,929	60,234	3,980	210,117	96,524
1973	1,017,162	726,950	128,140	855,090	56,164	-3,917	795,009	149,038	73,115	4,840	210,167	102,204
1974	1,062,522	835,745	39,322	875,067	66,753	-5,234	803,080	174,571	84,871	4,970	213,786	106,461
1975	1,163,883	919,912	16,898	936,810	72,294	-5,652	858,864	200,995	104,024	5,385	216,123	107,353
1976	1,353,581	1,049,798	64,733	1,114,531	84,120	-6,996	1,023,415	217,755	112,411	6,204	218,179	112,458
1977	1,533,010	1,183,170	91,656	1,274,826	95,619	-9,115	1,170,092	243,382	119,536	6,923	221,434	118,015
1978	1,686,400	1,336,251	61,042	1,397,293	110,060	-10,588	1,276,645	275,371	134,384	7,496	224,976	121,963
1979	1,900,030	1,497,212	76,650	1,573,862	129,659	-13,776	1,430,427	313,120	156,483	8,365	227,137	122,321
1980	2,085,847	1,661,255	23,238	1,684,493	145,428	-13,303	1,525,762	378,185	181,900	9,086	229,562	124,241
1981	2,415,770	1,793,157	128,361	1,921,518	168,020	-12,483	1,741,015	466,987	207,768	10,473	230,672	124,379
1982	2,573,831	1,919,228	53,595	1,972,823	181,998	-9,493	1,781,332	559,323	233,176	11,071	232,493	125,658
1983	2,844,779	2,101,300	79,715	2,181,015	197,026	-13,552	1,970,437	612,606	261,736	12,061	235,862	126,896
1984	2,963,600	2,170,234	66,769	2,237,003	205,249	-7,688	2,024,066	654,094	285,440	12,489	237,294	126,165
1985	3,141,081	2,295,354	59,799	2,355,153	219,087	-7,907	2,128,159	703,308	309,614	13,338	235,499	127,720
1986	3,188,288	2,348,151	34,368	2,382,519	222,947	-12,273	2,147,299	703,029	337,960	13,514	235,917	125,110
1987	3,312,431	2,343,976	142,163	2,486,139	222,187	-1,761	2,262,191	684,623	365,617	14,069	235,440	129,492
1988	3,508,507	2,519,661	145,844	2,665,505	247,887	-3,960	2,413,658	704,468	390,381	14,842	236,385	131,935
1989	3,640,899	2,625,134	79,322	2,704,456	262,524	-9,791	2,432,141	776,745	432,013	15,351	237,184	131,633
1990	3,911,045	2,825,466	131,118	2,956,584	277,252	-2,107	2,677,225	750,564	483,256	16,489	237,193	134,323
1991	3,990,491	2,957,733	47,069	3,004,802	296,464	-2,744	2,705,594	750,474	534,423	16,656	239,584	135,650
1992	4,272,120	3,105,408	115,664	3,221,072	308,706	-13,049	2,899,317	737,838	634,965	17,713	241,180	134,968
1993	4,540,786	3,288,856	169,934	3,458,790	326,178	-15,083	3,117,529	752,897	670,360	18,526	245,109	139,393
1994	4,776,216	3,489,819	134,153	3,623,972	349,420	-19,007	3,255,545	791,819	728,852	19,142	249,516	141,802
1995	4,975,085	3,614,435	91,851	3,706,286	364,715	-24,753	3,316,818	870,920	787,347	19,727	252,199	146,373
1996	5,280,898	3,790,123	139,585	3,929,708	378,064	-29,956	3,521,688	911,808	847,402	20,827	253,555	147,374
1997	5,504,516	3,981,279	128,863	4,110,142	393,844	-32,856	3,683,442	935,264	885,810	21,656	254,178	150,419
1998	5,746,662	4,295,901	74,900	4,370,801	416,963	-41,369	3,912,469	999,312	834,881	22,669	253,502	151,104
1999	5,899,776	4,421,911	90,276	4,512,187	423,366	-45,919	4,042,902	988,534	868,340	23,181	254,507	151,946
2000	6,251,056	4,727,713	41,836	4,769,549	448,345	-55,290	4,265,914	1,065,777	919,365	24,356	256,651	155,675
2001	6,426,953	4,786,222	56,871	4,843,093	462,169	-55,594	4,325,330	1,105,318	996,305	24,718	260,015	157,772
2002	6,653,876	5,003,794	54,829	5,058,623	482,586	-69,966	4,506,071	1,073,911	1,073,894	25,331	262,680	157,230
2003	7,042,539	5,100,023	122,437	5,222,460	501,872	-70,089	4,650,499	1,241,663	1,150,377	26,442	266,338	156,115
2004	7,216,321	5,296,375	188,658	5,485,033	522,162	-67,983	4,894,888	1,124,697	1,196,736	26,880	268,466	158,611
2005	7,653,478	5,527,905	207,998	5,735,903	546,882	-81,138	5,107,883	1,236,068	1,309,527	28,296	270,478	161,147
2006	8,045,107	5,949,188	74,540	6,023,728	579,377	-81,241	5,363,110	1,270,159	1,411,838	29,317	274,419	164,126
2007	8,550,741	6,038,027	174,709	6,212,736	597,263	-73,031	5,542,442	1,477,415	1,530,884	30,817	277,466	166,208
2008	9,132,425	6,336,005	20,262	6,356,267	626,334	-34,322	5,695,611	1,739,570	1,697,244	32,578	280,321	170,038
2009	9,312,129	6,463,862	62,804	6,526,666	646,473	-24,041	5,856,152	1,623,174	1,832,803	32,533	286,236	170,815
2010	9,989,909	6,810,986	168,660	6,979,646	671,640	18,224	6,326,230	1,660,802	2,002,877	34,192	292,175	170,477
2011	10,392,472	7,002,675	-10,755	6,991,920	611,335	97,048	6,477,633	1,834,825	2,080,014	35,238	294,923	174,025
2012	10,980,105	7,309,550	-31,631	7,277,919	639,175	192,724	6,831,468	2,096,143	2,052,494	36,967	297,022	176,441
2013	11,394,482	7,688,157	195,598	7,883,755	752,548	237,401	7,368,608	1,914,543	2,111,331	37,977	300,038	181,127
2014	11,881,754	8,108,940	3,509	8,112,449	792,580	279,424	7,599,293	2,088,870	2,193,591	39,014	304,548	184,486
2015	12,196,792	8,404,974	-12,126	8,392,848	834,630	229,259	7,787,477	2,092,508	2,316,807	39,588	308,090	188,348
2016	12,442,014	8,575,794	-37,416	8,538,378	868,047	146,905	7,817,236	2,204,283	2,420,495	39,943	311,496	194,053
2017	12,896,286	8,850,665	31,933	8,882,598	908,303	183,523	8,157,818	2,263,582	2,474,886	41,015	314,428	198,588
2018	13,647,263	9,271,381	11,645	9,283,026	944,252	245,311	8,584,085	2,472,608	2,590,570	43,145	316,314	200,909
2019	14,380,623	9,708,875	43,193	9,752,068	985,743	266,533	9,032,858	2,628,929	2,718,836	45,089	318,941	203,019
2020	15,472,051	10,005,946	-17,045	9,988,901	1,030,383	167,790	9,126,308	2,783,368	3,562,375	48,010	322,267	201,261
2021	16,928,252	10,480,939	136,308	10,617,247	1,067,887	181,860	9,731,220	3,060,337	4,136,695	52,033	325,334	208,970
2022	17,167,677	11,138,639	-23,538	11,115,101	1,154,600	274,493	10,234,994	3,277,343	3,655,340	52,295	328,283	217,590

Personal Income and Employment by Area: Lynchburg, VA

(Thousands of dollars, except as noted.)

Year	Personal income, total	Derivation of personal income								Per capita personal income (dollars)	Population (persons)	Total employment
		Earnings by place of work			Less: Contributions for government social insurance	Plus: Adjustment for residence	Equals: Net earnings by place of residence	Plus: Dividends, interest, and rent	Plus: Personal current transfer receipts			
		Nonfarm	Farm	Total								
1970	547,509	472,206	9,319	481,525	31,116	-26,330	424,079	75,244	48,186	3,289	166,469	79,441
1971	587,464	504,460	8,535	512,995	34,589	-30,739	447,667	82,670	57,127	3,428	171,359	79,326
1972	657,724	575,398	9,656	585,054	41,585	-40,432	503,037	90,628	64,059	3,764	174,732	82,093
1973	737,153	644,213	13,386	657,599	53,726	-45,041	558,832	103,314	75,007	4,177	176,483	86,237
1974	823,007	714,378	13,987	728,365	61,975	-51,373	615,017	119,232	88,758	4,617	178,257	88,455
1975	894,903	745,675	7,790	753,465	62,991	-42,580	647,894	128,750	118,259	4,856	184,275	85,436
1976	1,004,788	846,797	6,035	852,832	72,634	-45,667	734,531	141,546	128,711	5,418	185,470	89,082
1977	1,121,386	945,660	3,417	949,077	81,181	-47,207	820,689	159,905	140,792	6,006	186,723	91,298
1978	1,275,770	1,083,347	4,841	1,088,188	95,045	-55,066	938,077	180,566	157,127	6,672	191,211	95,509
1979	1,443,930	1,223,282	5,991	1,229,273	111,791	-61,112	1,056,370	207,690	179,870	7,449	193,855	99,044
1980	1,607,807	1,308,883	1,023	1,309,906	119,808	-63,517	1,126,581	260,747	220,479	8,261	194,636	97,473
1981	1,781,131	1,400,922	3,913	1,404,835	138,455	-64,800	1,201,580	322,534	257,017	9,083	196,102	96,671
1982	1,899,521	1,440,062	-3,295	1,436,767	144,672	-54,140	1,237,955	373,846	287,720	9,635	197,158	95,302
1983	2,071,451	1,552,528	953	1,553,481	158,174	-45,584	1,349,723	408,030	313,698	10,508	197,122	95,745
1984	2,295,200	1,720,334	3,257	1,723,591	180,864	-38,718	1,504,009	461,421	329,770	11,577	198,260	99,984
1985	2,454,455	1,816,934	803	1,817,737	194,439	-22,129	1,601,169	491,723	361,563	12,329	199,074	102,302
1986	2,621,417	1,938,447	916	1,939,363	213,488	-9,377	1,716,498	513,752	391,167	13,082	200,383	103,804
1987	2,831,989	2,088,859	7,842	2,096,701	227,523	5,716	1,874,894	539,797	417,298	14,055	201,487	108,094
1988	3,059,398	2,221,508	8,971	2,230,479	248,829	20,049	2,001,699	610,216	447,483	15,059	203,166	109,641
1989	3,344,611	2,371,309	13,715	2,385,024	268,223	37,284	2,154,085	712,718	477,808	16,331	204,803	112,967
1990	3,502,221	2,499,655	14,603	2,514,258	284,313	57,530	2,287,475	703,929	510,817	16,926	206,913	115,259
1991	3,611,587	2,569,006	11,071	2,580,077	295,244	62,796	2,347,629	720,011	543,947	17,283	208,971	114,238
1992	3,826,001	2,704,000	12,641	2,716,641	306,734	77,106	2,487,013	730,807	608,181	17,972	212,888	114,404
1993	4,048,658	2,899,911	5,357	2,905,268	329,660	87,355	2,662,963	762,224	623,471	18,841	214,890	117,353
1994	4,254,958	3,049,551	9,034	3,058,585	346,479	98,953	2,811,059	788,837	655,062	19,543	217,728	120,192
1995	4,438,512	3,134,649	4,530	3,139,179	355,677	115,837	2,899,339	834,410	704,763	20,211	219,612	122,217
1996	4,630,700	3,237,784	3,755	3,241,539	365,273	128,260	3,004,526	885,514	740,660	20,871	221,872	123,775
1997	4,849,825	3,419,938	685	3,420,623	382,495	141,842	3,179,970	903,914	765,941	21,636	224,156	125,140
1998	5,177,164	3,632,268	3,828	3,636,096	400,557	164,647	3,400,186	974,144	802,834	22,941	225,675	125,567
1999	5,448,458	3,888,300	-1,754	3,886,546	426,803	178,118	3,637,861	956,288	854,309	23,966	227,337	128,961
2000	5,801,234	4,082,567	10,769	4,093,336	440,851	201,019	3,853,504	1,033,057	914,673	25,349	228,855	131,133
2001	5,931,658	4,076,674	2,414	4,079,088	459,821	205,875	3,825,142	1,080,828	1,025,688	25,846	229,499	127,137
2002	6,005,672	4,094,419	-775	4,093,644	465,575	213,244	3,841,313	1,076,226	1,088,133	26,071	230,356	124,539
2003	6,229,826	4,248,319	-9,238	4,239,081	481,179	210,319	3,968,221	1,096,359	1,165,246	26,780	232,634	124,270
2004	6,524,937	4,463,107	-3,194	4,459,913	513,375	216,679	4,163,217	1,138,633	1,223,087	27,816	234,574	126,424
2005	6,838,349	4,722,230	-3,950	4,718,280	550,773	220,714	4,388,221	1,139,929	1,310,199	28,671	238,515	129,816
2006	7,313,259	4,982,370	-22,519	4,959,851	586,377	221,835	4,595,309	1,259,800	1,458,150	30,069	243,213	132,759
2007	7,717,943	5,197,533	-24,613	5,172,920	611,668	226,057	4,787,309	1,379,035	1,551,599	31,269	246,827	135,950
2008	8,163,775	5,324,193	-18,538	5,305,655	633,117	228,319	4,900,857	1,485,527	1,777,391	32,747	249,299	137,060
2009	8,056,072	5,231,973	-13,979	5,217,994	627,324	225,713	4,816,383	1,316,716	1,922,973	32,040	251,441	133,023
2010	8,278,944	5,343,984	-12,744	5,331,240	639,322	223,505	4,915,423	1,272,770	2,090,751	32,735	252,910	131,508
2011	8,593,937	5,388,289	-5,263	5,383,026	581,024	242,871	5,044,873	1,346,029	2,203,035	33,847	253,902	131,580
2012	8,899,276	5,532,156	121	5,532,277	591,898	257,408	5,197,787	1,519,633	2,181,856	34,871	255,203	132,219
2013	8,897,965	5,619,383	-4,577	5,614,806	684,904	258,685	5,188,587	1,451,417	2,257,961	34,749	256,066	132,791
2014	9,243,995	5,786,724	-798	5,785,926	703,881	260,251	5,342,296	1,560,847	2,340,852	35,975	256,953	134,242
2015	9,513,498	5,903,387	-7,263	5,896,124	720,965	286,121	5,461,280	1,629,404	2,422,814	36,846	258,199	135,054
2016	9,608,806	5,910,002	-15,461	5,894,541	728,066	283,982	5,450,457	1,635,493	2,522,856	37,098	259,012	135,123
2017	9,950,354	6,110,107	-8,406	6,101,701	760,968	277,248	5,617,981	1,720,032	2,612,341	38,262	260,059	136,758
2018	10,349,294	6,341,619	-16,077	6,325,542	791,353	288,870	5,823,059	1,803,776	2,722,459	39,638	261,098	138,944
2019	10,725,561	6,511,051	-9,038	6,502,013	815,096	297,125	5,984,042	1,876,370	2,865,149	41,008	261,549	138,667
2020	11,554,573	6,648,429	-10,987	6,637,442	832,491	302,184	6,107,135	1,864,617	3,582,821	44,166	261,614	135,763
2021	12,460,478	6,975,267	-9,423	6,965,844	874,509	322,204	6,413,539	1,975,405	4,071,534	47,456	262,569	138,462
2022	12,720,528	7,364,241	-15,435	7,348,806	940,052	346,452	6,755,206	2,121,114	3,844,208	48,255	263,613	140,360

Personal Income and Employment by Area: Macon-Bibb County, GA

(Thousands of dollars, except as noted.)

Year	Personal income, total	Derivation of personal income: Earnings by place of work								Per capita personal income (dollars)	Population (persons)	Total employment
		Nonfarm	Farm	Total	Less: Contributions for government social insurance	Plus: Adjustment for residence	Equals: Net earnings by place of residence	Plus: Dividends, interest, and rent	Plus: Personal current transfer receipts			
1970	664,522	453,972	5,480	459,452	29,751	92,391	522,092	84,817	57,613	3,667	181,228	78,317
1971	732,150	495,189	6,314	501,503	33,500	98,912	566,915	96,346	68,889	3,940	185,839	79,907
1972	795,018	545,837	6,403	552,240	38,739	98,209	611,710	104,987	78,321	4,219	188,436	81,664
1973	856,424	596,161	9,270	605,431	48,637	95,145	651,939	116,182	88,303	4,539	188,667	83,070
1974	945,818	663,483	6,565	670,048	56,266	92,922	706,704	131,618	107,496	4,996	189,318	85,187
1975	1,047,179	726,728	6,406	733,134	60,628	92,610	765,116	146,321	135,742	5,458	191,852	85,941
1976	1,138,426	803,285	7,557	810,842	68,332	90,120	832,630	157,814	147,982	5,921	192,268	87,195
1977	1,231,221	870,916	5,885	876,801	73,582	98,538	901,757	175,529	153,935	6,292	195,693	87,585
1978	1,341,220	959,621	7,626	967,247	83,090	95,486	979,643	195,696	165,881	6,790	197,518	88,125
1979	1,488,317	1,082,640	8,213	1,090,853	97,897	89,177	1,082,133	218,623	187,561	7,497	198,531	89,341
1980	1,660,695	1,211,020	3,215	1,214,235	109,783	73,345	1,177,797	262,140	220,758	8,353	198,810	91,031
1981	1,875,526	1,335,345	4,189	1,339,534	130,634	97,210	1,306,110	319,006	250,410	9,390	199,746	91,575
1982	2,011,988	1,414,743	6,712	1,421,455	140,826	100,751	1,381,380	360,076	270,532	10,016	200,885	91,762
1983	2,166,338	1,528,127	4,380	1,532,507	152,985	94,033	1,473,555	397,206	295,577	10,701	202,440	92,018
1984	2,375,306	1,699,389	7,142	1,706,531	175,195	89,478	1,620,814	441,287	313,205	11,673	203,490	95,941
1985	2,527,544	1,826,714	7,939	1,834,653	192,199	82,643	1,725,097	465,126	337,321	12,372	204,300	97,593
1986	2,693,223	1,981,740	8,443	1,990,183	210,655	58,584	1,838,112	496,842	358,269	13,178	204,377	99,644
1987	2,866,531	2,151,765	11,064	2,162,829	226,332	24,200	1,960,697	528,058	377,776	13,980	205,043	101,989
1988	3,104,022	2,330,908	15,057	2,345,965	253,819	10,072	2,102,218	586,138	415,666	15,061	206,097	105,223
1989	3,340,775	2,457,819	17,966	2,475,785	268,615	7,373	2,214,543	677,805	448,427	16,154	206,803	106,740
1990	3,482,129	2,596,757	19,002	2,615,759	282,424	-43,720	2,289,615	702,164	490,350	16,806	207,190	108,636
1991	3,657,271	2,687,702	20,952	2,708,654	296,447	-50,100	2,362,107	727,581	567,583	17,469	209,358	106,541
1992	3,887,517	2,877,444	20,696	2,898,140	313,038	-39,517	2,545,585	716,113	625,819	18,449	210,716	107,456
1993	4,053,915	2,987,869	23,445	3,011,314	326,647	-48,346	2,636,321	749,219	668,375	18,988	213,497	111,132
1994	4,293,135	3,162,059	24,655	3,186,714	347,432	-63,202	2,776,080	798,832	718,223	19,930	215,416	113,744
1995	4,595,311	3,375,736	19,344	3,395,080	370,203	-54,567	2,970,310	871,661	753,340	21,179	216,979	118,082
1996	4,912,556	3,544,448	16,840	3,561,288	389,881	21,561	3,192,968	920,019	799,569	22,462	218,702	121,131
1997	5,077,657	3,728,143	17,764	3,745,907	408,023	-41,540	3,296,344	958,669	822,644	22,990	220,860	122,871
1998	5,388,583	3,943,828	20,479	3,964,307	424,429	-15,330	3,524,548	1,037,158	826,877	24,302	221,736	123,933
1999	5,561,553	4,124,315	26,541	4,150,856	439,740	-5,875	3,705,241	994,264	862,048	25,048	222,038	125,300
2000	5,821,526	4,202,019	23,909	4,225,928	446,287	39,601	3,819,242	1,085,813	916,471	26,175	222,407	126,496
2001	5,931,369	4,254,559	30,298	4,284,857	453,101	31,819	3,863,575	1,088,374	979,420	26,614	222,869	123,568
2002	6,203,409	4,383,158	21,422	4,404,580	468,994	44,129	3,979,715	1,096,765	1,126,929	27,612	224,661	123,272
2003	6,296,883	4,500,207	23,439	4,523,646	478,399	50,193	4,095,440	1,067,854	1,133,589	27,864	225,987	124,394
2004	6,517,131	4,731,789	26,604	4,758,393	514,333	538	4,244,598	1,078,704	1,193,829	28,660	227,394	126,767
2005	6,725,064	4,819,907	29,042	4,848,949	523,041	16,664	4,342,572	1,083,177	1,299,315	29,480	228,125	127,959
2006	6,999,469	4,988,518	14,187	5,002,705	541,686	-12,850	4,448,169	1,167,964	1,383,336	30,478	229,655	128,865
2007	7,231,829	4,921,424	18,177	4,939,601	535,350	43,485	4,447,736	1,298,480	1,485,613	31,381	230,452	129,861
2008	7,476,594	5,058,206	23,873	5,082,079	576,767	-27,632	4,477,680	1,337,952	1,660,962	32,322	231,314	131,919
2009	7,384,752	5,015,102	22,394	5,037,496	569,008	-89,649	4,378,839	1,223,502	1,782,411	31,822	232,065	126,731
2010	7,560,973	5,121,238	22,651	5,143,889	577,280	-108,834	4,457,775	1,166,002	1,937,196	32,549	232,293	126,188
2011	7,935,783	5,247,407	30,189	5,277,596	523,381	-152,935	4,601,280	1,335,843	1,998,660	34,030	233,198	128,200
2012	7,849,477	5,341,350	40,591	5,381,941	534,915	-242,453	4,604,573	1,273,687	1,971,217	33,600	233,614	129,504
2013	7,879,541	5,540,470	41,338	5,581,808	628,916	-324,946	4,627,946	1,249,104	2,002,491	33,894	232,479	130,179
2014	8,207,173	5,780,043	43,421	5,823,464	649,301	-382,448	4,791,715	1,334,389	2,081,069	35,364	232,076	133,012
2015	8,483,335	6,025,866	43,657	6,069,523	672,196	-467,872	4,929,455	1,415,572	2,138,308	36,597	231,805	134,819
2016	8,571,907	6,034,441	29,562	6,064,003	672,875	-426,357	4,964,771	1,405,294	2,201,842	37,037	231,443	134,393
2017	8,887,866	6,192,975	34,827	6,227,802	692,014	-467,281	5,068,507	1,552,761	2,266,598	38,365	231,664	136,515
2018	9,164,440	6,415,286	23,778	6,439,064	730,097	-492,408	5,216,559	1,584,294	2,363,587	39,393	232,641	137,960
2019	9,392,904	6,500,261	19,520	6,519,781	748,044	-485,909	5,285,828	1,647,689	2,459,387	40,240	233,424	139,436
2020	10,077,125	6,532,850	7,229	6,540,079	756,776	-503,596	5,279,707	1,609,184	3,188,234	43,140	233,591	137,035
2021	11,072,043	7,075,256	19,328	7,094,584	819,084	-540,391	5,735,109	1,814,801	3,522,133	47,487	233,161	142,071
2022	10,870,089	7,219,551	48,070	7,267,621	859,870	-566,952	5,840,799	1,896,905	3,132,385	46,470	233,916	145,303

Personal Income and Employment by Area: Madera, CA

(Thousands of dollars, except as noted.)

Year	Personal income, total	Derivation of personal income								Per capita personal income (dollars)	Population (persons)	Total employment
		Earnings by place of work			Less: Contributions for government social insurance	Plus: Adjustment for residence	Equals: Net earnings by place of residence	Plus: Dividends, interest, and rent	Plus: Personal current transfer receipts			
		Nonfarm	Farm	Total								
1970	157,504	77,600	31,793	109,393	5,536	4,117	107,974	24,016	25,514	3,776	41,707	16,486
1971	172,911	87,734	31,328	119,062	6,478	5,925	118,509	26,382	28,020	4,044	42,754	17,136
1972	203,344	101,333	42,466	143,799	7,799	8,456	144,456	30,122	28,766	4,705	43,223	18,531
1973	252,612	114,738	67,670	182,408	10,095	11,556	183,869	36,730	32,013	5,682	44,458	19,251
1974	288,523	129,786	76,193	205,979	11,862	14,683	208,800	41,798	37,925	6,263	46,071	20,413
1975	303,984	147,138	57,037	204,175	13,043	16,991	208,123	48,018	47,843	6,344	47,917	21,108
1976	351,479	169,492	69,799	239,291	15,238	21,020	245,073	52,088	54,318	7,072	49,699	22,320
1977	404,651	192,466	84,098	276,564	17,549	26,612	285,627	59,394	59,630	7,667	52,777	23,161
1978	443,859	224,422	68,117	292,539	20,658	34,823	306,704	71,974	65,181	7,963	55,741	24,123
1979	599,779	271,185	149,895	421,080	25,567	43,401	438,914	88,134	72,731	9,968	60,169	26,794
1980	679,437	296,759	158,035	454,794	27,387	51,617	479,024	112,550	87,863	10,623	63,961	27,854
1981	666,134	318,383	81,551	399,934	31,941	56,724	424,717	136,135	105,282	9,911	67,214	28,249
1982	687,563	324,111	77,066	401,177	33,232	59,124	427,069	147,237	113,257	9,930	69,240	28,791
1983	699,726	351,466	40,329	391,795	36,685	63,411	418,521	156,688	124,517	9,786	71,504	30,018
1984	779,800	394,232	59,288	453,520	42,339	69,856	481,037	169,356	129,407	10,683	72,996	29,837
1985	830,338	423,961	53,885	477,846	46,061	74,742	506,527	175,265	148,546	11,054	75,118	30,233
1986	922,016	471,010	78,828	549,838	51,630	78,322	576,530	183,152	162,334	11,980	76,960	30,149
1987	1,046,436	540,669	125,140	665,809	59,764	81,084	687,129	190,393	168,914	13,246	79,003	32,257
1988	1,133,167	585,973	120,682	706,655	67,278	89,250	728,627	211,452	193,088	13,859	81,762	33,655
1989	1,220,935	615,483	111,293	726,776	71,317	109,158	764,617	246,349	209,969	14,398	84,797	34,542
1990	1,330,429	679,841	111,716	791,557	77,542	121,671	835,686	262,927	231,816	14,928	89,125	35,423
1991	1,419,620	762,409	90,776	853,185	87,066	120,407	886,526	266,305	266,789	14,948	94,973	38,461
1992	1,602,125	826,780	164,280	991,060	94,001	121,154	1,018,213	269,990	313,922	16,096	99,536	38,949
1993	1,663,578	886,417	129,811	1,016,228	99,760	124,899	1,041,367	282,568	339,643	15,990	104,039	39,682
1994	1,698,345	940,685	94,313	1,034,998	105,318	125,166	1,054,846	298,450	345,049	15,814	107,396	41,256
1995	1,726,961	955,518	66,891	1,022,409	108,669	124,663	1,038,403	321,402	367,156	15,800	109,300	44,780
1996	1,883,944	998,930	136,248	1,135,178	109,957	122,880	1,148,101	341,121	394,722	16,651	113,143	46,793
1997	2,018,407	1,091,316	176,901	1,268,217	116,813	116,193	1,267,597	351,208	399,602	17,334	116,442	48,055
1998	2,102,992	1,240,423	91,598	1,332,021	128,752	109,005	1,312,274	364,588	426,130	17,651	119,143	52,112
1999	2,229,722	1,303,914	131,265	1,435,179	137,399	113,086	1,410,866	366,819	452,037	18,294	121,883	52,404
2000	2,332,803	1,344,791	151,869	1,496,660	142,081	129,054	1,483,633	384,315	464,855	18,876	123,587	51,446
2001	2,524,143	1,550,605	105,360	1,655,965	165,852	138,005	1,628,118	382,372	513,653	20,100	125,581	50,566
2002	2,729,631	1,672,638	149,658	1,822,296	182,244	157,661	1,797,713	380,589	551,329	21,264	128,369	51,999
2003	2,924,881	1,821,958	150,365	1,972,323	201,170	147,770	1,918,923	419,066	586,892	22,035	132,738	54,042
2004	3,244,606	1,945,794	353,971	2,299,765	222,644	156,902	2,234,023	402,393	608,190	23,665	137,106	56,155
2005	3,385,176	2,079,927	345,182	2,425,109	238,845	149,392	2,335,656	408,945	640,575	24,126	140,313	57,801
2006	3,576,915	2,314,716	249,120	2,563,836	253,221	111,083	2,421,698	459,966	695,251	24,905	143,622	60,055
2007	3,914,631	2,408,757	360,829	2,769,586	258,751	117,157	2,627,992	540,463	746,176	26,800	146,067	60,961
2008	3,928,264	2,393,405	298,022	2,691,427	262,076	90,436	2,519,787	566,537	841,940	26,478	148,359	59,935
2009	3,819,644	2,380,618	138,304	2,518,922	265,492	96,899	2,350,329	540,821	928,494	25,595	149,234	58,444
2010	4,245,578	2,452,550	382,505	2,835,055	259,767	115,170	2,690,458	533,131	1,021,989	28,121	150,978	57,486
2011	4,446,463	2,500,375	492,068	2,992,443	244,230	108,386	2,856,599	559,772	1,030,092	29,341	151,545	57,252
2012	4,674,829	2,597,470	677,337	3,274,807	256,509	40,529	3,058,827	570,075	1,045,927	30,904	151,269	59,608
2013	4,840,670	2,681,211	777,447	3,458,658	295,942	22,549	3,185,265	582,091	1,073,314	32,072	150,933	61,040
2014	5,167,474	2,777,423	882,827	3,660,250	306,372	17,213	3,371,091	661,409	1,134,974	33,801	152,878	62,791
2015	5,246,433	2,846,856	660,126	3,506,982	312,458	93,665	3,288,189	720,685	1,237,559	34,323	152,856	61,466
2016	5,497,117	3,057,579	640,535	3,698,114	335,735	74,111	3,436,490	786,463	1,274,164	35,931	152,989	63,716
2017	5,687,523	3,200,884	669,883	3,870,767	355,680	81,114	3,596,201	842,150	1,249,172	36,871	154,256	64,516
2018	5,815,299	3,363,750	618,426	3,982,176	370,974	101,448	3,712,650	800,508	1,302,141	37,414	155,430	66,032
2019	6,076,859	3,563,120	562,586	4,125,706	395,643	153,289	3,883,352	808,448	1,385,059	39,040	155,658	67,005
2020	6,940,713	3,833,086	591,181	4,424,267	421,347	108,697	4,111,617	860,529	1,968,567	44,394	156,343	66,481
2021	7,553,475	4,115,706	591,445	4,707,151	448,812	240,376	4,498,715	867,880	2,186,880	47,533	158,910	69,048
2022	7,436,909	4,356,794	528,801	4,885,595	495,513	337,121	4,727,203	927,441	1,782,265	46,406	160,256	72,617

Personal Income and Employment by Area: Madison, WI

(Thousands of dollars, except as noted.)

Year	Personal income, total	Derivation of personal income: Earnings by place of work: Nonfarm	Farm	Total	Less: Contributions for government social insurance	Plus: Adjustment for residence	Equals: Net earnings by place of residence	Plus: Dividends, interest, and rent	Plus: Personal current transfer receipts	Per capita personal income (dollars)	Population (persons)	Total employment
1970	1,708,448	1,316,440	87,386	1,403,826	90,597	-18,928	1,294,301	293,796	120,351	4,524	377,631	191,581
1971	1,854,242	1,421,354	91,918	1,513,272	101,500	-19,685	1,392,087	323,086	139,069	4,846	382,627	194,234
1972	1,997,037	1,529,585	94,778	1,624,363	115,366	-18,198	1,490,799	351,273	154,965	5,219	382,656	200,459
1973	2,225,349	1,693,667	119,509	1,813,176	147,243	-16,418	1,649,515	394,456	181,378	5,766	385,942	208,252
1974	2,423,637	1,852,574	97,909	1,950,483	169,979	-16,747	1,763,757	446,644	213,236	6,172	392,653	212,493
1975	2,710,063	2,030,435	115,196	2,145,631	184,359	-17,051	1,944,221	497,860	267,982	6,920	391,644	216,816
1976	2,970,088	2,279,797	90,258	2,370,055	209,710	-13,796	2,146,549	541,772	281,767	7,488	396,665	227,364
1977	3,305,419	2,525,419	116,541	2,641,960	232,485	-8,929	2,400,546	604,477	300,396	8,234	401,437	235,127
1978	3,713,483	2,855,398	123,377	2,978,775	270,539	-5,121	2,703,115	681,225	329,143	9,141	406,224	243,149
1979	4,110,395	3,132,711	146,018	3,278,729	311,040	1,637	2,969,326	760,599	380,470	10,037	409,524	250,720
1980	4,586,175	3,413,658	147,235	3,560,893	341,201	-2,230	3,217,462	914,316	454,397	10,981	417,638	255,057
1981	4,989,464	3,646,271	135,612	3,781,883	391,202	-6	3,390,675	1,093,404	505,385	11,855	420,874	253,625
1982	5,381,135	3,897,883	109,991	4,007,874	417,110	-11,063	3,579,701	1,250,127	551,307	12,730	422,726	253,833
1983	5,718,223	4,168,577	31,920	4,200,497	438,106	-12,197	3,750,194	1,362,277	605,752	13,441	425,420	257,282
1984	6,253,991	4,558,053	92,057	4,650,110	482,639	-13,984	4,153,487	1,477,307	623,197	14,550	429,829	267,580
1985	6,718,370	4,938,119	104,018	5,042,137	525,882	-26,352	4,489,903	1,560,892	667,575	15,464	434,452	276,651
1986	7,185,824	5,312,413	144,315	5,456,728	565,268	-39,449	4,852,011	1,637,315	696,498	16,357	439,308	283,663
1987	7,686,009	5,801,217	168,547	5,969,764	607,559	-53,341	5,308,864	1,659,049	718,096	17,281	444,766	295,146
1988	8,077,474	6,250,324	76,938	6,327,262	688,813	-61,951	5,576,498	1,749,938	751,038	17,874	451,906	305,036
1989	8,971,197	6,802,542	178,065	6,980,607	753,182	-76,401	6,151,024	1,999,033	821,140	19,656	456,408	315,061
1990	9,636,573	7,421,863	140,059	7,561,922	855,604	-93,280	6,613,038	2,134,013	889,522	20,760	464,185	326,175
1991	10,167,776	7,921,260	105,479	8,026,739	923,289	-119,696	6,983,754	2,210,325	973,697	21,445	474,124	332,549
1992	11,077,121	8,657,116	140,284	8,797,400	996,869	-141,416	7,659,115	2,344,339	1,073,667	22,901	483,693	340,984
1993	11,732,442	9,279,813	94,381	9,374,194	1,061,193	-162,896	8,150,105	2,454,081	1,128,256	23,730	494,411	349,725
1994	12,490,793	9,895,627	121,567	10,017,194	1,149,866	-183,307	8,684,021	2,643,257	1,163,515	24,864	502,367	359,601
1995	13,252,261	10,407,456	76,177	10,483,633	1,211,728	-200,827	9,071,078	2,932,853	1,248,330	26,000	509,694	367,663
1996	13,968,384	10,859,504	133,845	10,993,349	1,263,846	-224,362	9,505,141	3,146,565	1,316,678	27,058	516,235	374,687
1997	14,880,282	11,677,144	87,598	11,764,742	1,351,134	-259,272	10,154,336	3,347,067	1,378,879	28,409	523,795	381,856
1998	15,991,409	12,554,806	127,719	12,682,525	1,441,825	-299,083	10,941,617	3,677,401	1,372,391	30,340	527,073	390,131
1999	16,706,449	13,430,633	141,874	13,572,507	1,549,306	-350,075	11,673,126	3,594,215	1,439,108	31,440	531,380	399,716
2000	18,109,059	14,628,035	99,766	14,727,801	1,664,914	-412,186	12,650,701	3,895,417	1,562,941	33,692	537,485	409,450
2001	19,330,229	15,837,257	138,054	15,975,311	1,745,886	-483,566	13,745,859	3,855,903	1,728,467	35,483	544,773	414,371
2002	20,100,176	16,773,388	118,414	16,891,802	1,848,253	-562,986	14,480,563	3,757,966	1,861,647	36,393	552,305	417,984
2003	20,811,539	17,359,859	159,734	17,519,593	1,922,799	-609,962	14,986,832	3,886,395	1,938,312	37,221	559,138	422,518
2004	21,744,147	18,285,034	221,076	18,506,110	2,031,398	-718,888	15,755,824	3,979,568	2,008,755	38,393	566,363	432,840
2005	22,615,573	19,022,595	191,367	19,213,962	2,119,832	-797,062	16,297,068	4,144,435	2,174,070	39,466	573,036	442,100
2006	24,128,110	19,906,317	169,774	20,076,091	2,222,119	-839,304	17,014,668	4,788,160	2,325,282	41,579	580,296	447,314
2007	25,256,744	20,564,216	238,490	20,802,706	2,307,038	-905,887	17,589,781	5,061,413	2,605,550	42,975	587,711	454,822
2008	26,054,675	20,915,844	190,209	21,106,053	2,374,439	-921,210	17,810,404	5,301,535	2,942,736	43,830	594,452	454,582
2009	25,682,119	20,574,795	124,734	20,699,529	2,327,019	-962,489	17,410,021	5,007,880	3,264,218	42,682	601,715	444,111
2010	26,374,914	20,931,712	205,613	21,137,325	2,376,494	-971,117	17,789,714	5,001,278	3,583,922	43,458	606,899	444,526
2011	28,304,069	22,274,203	326,363	22,600,566	2,241,768	-1,112,746	19,246,052	5,549,578	3,508,439	46,059	614,521	454,126
2012	29,591,168	23,223,457	245,421	23,468,878	2,322,206	-1,093,820	20,052,852	5,948,986	3,589,330	47,560	622,190	462,169
2013	30,436,792	24,508,572	265,864	24,774,436	2,778,156	-1,159,879	20,836,401	5,894,787	3,705,604	48,279	630,440	468,341
2014	31,762,742	25,414,340	241,650	25,655,990	2,868,281	-1,254,006	21,533,703	6,364,107	3,864,932	49,776	638,114	477,941
2015	33,660,186	26,941,476	215,921	27,157,397	3,025,286	-1,325,310	22,806,801	6,778,874	4,074,511	52,095	646,126	488,690
2016	34,965,753	28,005,388	170,722	28,176,110	3,138,140	-1,468,970	23,569,000	7,232,249	4,164,504	53,334	655,599	501,909
2017	36,538,238	29,157,018	153,301	29,310,319	3,298,986	-1,527,017	24,484,316	7,685,199	4,368,723	55,068	663,510	505,690
2018	38,837,144	30,786,203	149,476	30,935,679	3,423,344	-1,614,585	25,897,750	8,304,894	4,634,500	58,032	669,240	512,141
2019	41,147,949	32,682,816	148,558	32,831,374	3,646,444	-1,754,763	27,430,167	8,841,763	4,876,019	60,890	675,780	516,457
2020	43,494,885	33,628,576	276,307	33,904,883	3,767,284	-1,894,506	28,243,093	8,859,857	6,391,935	63,791	681,838	499,081
2021	47,902,122	36,345,512	294,197	36,639,709	4,030,040	-2,063,488	30,546,181	10,177,835	7,178,106	70,349	680,923	513,947
2022	49,137,180	38,442,271	338,554	38,780,825	4,381,132	-2,152,745	32,246,948	10,745,742	6,144,490	71,516	687,077	537,663

Personal Income and Employment by Area: Manchester-Nashua, NH

(Thousands of dollars, except as noted.)

Year	Personal income, total	Derivation of personal income: Earnings by place of work: Nonfarm	Farm	Total	Less: Contributions for government social insurance	Plus: Adjustment for residence	Equals: Net earnings by place of residence	Plus: Dividends, interest, and rent	Plus: Personal current transfer receipts	Per capita personal income (dollars)	Population (persons)	Total employment
1970	961,049	790,738	3,474	794,212	51,606	679	743,285	144,957	72,807	4,245	226,390	115,787
1971	1,027,801	829,329	3,064	832,393	56,139	5,277	781,531	158,168	88,102	4,328	237,461	114,427
1972	1,119,971	899,311	3,113	902,424	64,221	13,875	852,078	172,363	95,530	4,748	235,887	115,341
1973	1,257,989	1,015,714	4,381	1,020,095	83,627	20,612	957,080	188,675	112,234	5,251	239,589	122,872
1974	1,385,255	1,097,185	2,685	1,099,870	93,381	31,323	1,037,812	212,725	134,718	5,686	243,605	125,196
1975	1,509,213	1,158,130	3,301	1,161,431	96,173	38,495	1,103,753	231,058	174,402	6,080	248,215	121,735
1976	1,718,541	1,330,041	3,868	1,333,909	111,678	55,789	1,278,020	254,812	185,709	6,718	255,826	129,826
1977	1,965,431	1,514,419	4,452	1,518,871	127,409	89,041	1,480,503	290,200	194,728	7,475	262,922	137,799
1978	2,299,436	1,760,599	5,581	1,766,180	151,020	141,574	1,756,734	329,780	212,922	8,559	268,671	147,386
1979	2,640,859	2,027,604	4,870	2,032,474	181,677	172,350	2,023,147	376,092	241,620	9,596	275,208	155,080
1980	3,042,085	2,277,113	2,559	2,279,672	204,182	217,796	2,293,286	466,074	282,725	10,935	278,189	159,785
1981	3,434,286	2,529,616	3,425	2,533,041	243,930	241,265	2,530,376	574,264	329,646	12,100	283,833	162,816
1982	3,797,952	2,774,331	4,012	2,778,343	274,341	252,767	2,756,769	683,771	357,412	13,218	287,334	166,065
1983	4,212,857	3,161,244	3,488	3,164,732	317,734	261,831	3,108,829	722,989	381,039	14,486	290,819	174,012
1984	4,814,106	3,665,172	3,817	3,668,989	380,778	286,526	3,574,737	840,137	399,232	16,150	298,089	189,171
1985	5,312,321	4,092,400	5,022	4,097,422	435,028	309,996	3,972,390	921,243	418,688	17,276	307,490	199,943
1986	5,858,794	4,567,324	5,080	4,572,404	489,177	310,582	4,393,809	1,023,273	441,712	18,525	316,260	208,594
1987	6,411,052	5,123,463	9,013	5,132,476	541,236	296,319	4,887,559	1,073,309	450,184	19,774	324,218	214,561
1988	6,976,501	5,554,163	10,442	5,564,605	600,714	323,415	5,287,306	1,199,041	490,154	21,185	329,319	220,131
1989	7,360,440	5,697,606	6,849	5,704,455	617,690	353,846	5,440,611	1,364,544	555,285	21,968	335,057	215,952
1990	7,348,024	5,663,611	7,989	5,671,600	631,768	303,373	5,343,205	1,380,659	624,160	21,819	336,768	208,783
1991	7,635,314	5,685,850	8,088	5,693,938	642,201	341,752	5,393,489	1,403,096	838,729	22,652	337,066	199,944
1992	7,965,140	6,104,347	7,564	6,111,911	684,290	295,866	5,723,487	1,350,650	891,003	23,353	341,078	202,042
1993	8,204,226	6,220,447	6,256	6,226,703	696,541	410,964	5,941,126	1,398,899	864,201	23,784	344,944	204,282
1994	8,752,565	6,532,366	5,723	6,538,089	740,156	500,159	6,298,092	1,495,588	958,885	25,065	349,190	209,544
1995	9,331,472	6,898,603	5,160	6,903,763	785,395	557,951	6,676,319	1,620,364	1,034,789	26,386	353,651	212,713
1996	10,026,191	7,486,169	5,126	7,491,295	841,908	585,806	7,235,193	1,760,466	1,030,532	27,957	358,624	218,719
1997	10,914,054	8,125,875	4,700	8,130,575	903,787	679,363	7,906,151	1,937,207	1,070,696	29,962	364,261	225,406
1998	12,032,706	9,069,530	3,949	9,073,479	978,970	699,800	8,794,309	2,122,552	1,115,845	32,469	370,595	233,399
1999	12,975,208	9,891,345	6,394	9,897,739	1,049,913	873,650	9,721,476	2,112,027	1,141,705	34,471	376,407	238,338
2000	14,704,314	11,130,903	6,002	11,136,905	1,162,891	1,135,191	11,109,205	2,376,385	1,218,724	38,477	382,162	246,068
2001	14,759,491	10,965,049	5,176	10,970,225	1,162,758	1,190,780	10,998,247	2,432,552	1,328,692	38,097	387,414	245,028
2002	14,825,658	11,093,367	5,735	11,099,102	1,157,374	1,113,485	11,055,213	2,325,323	1,445,122	38,047	389,665	242,387
2003	15,213,543	11,647,502	5,873	11,653,375	1,228,964	999,341	11,423,752	2,313,100	1,476,691	38,863	391,461	246,091
2004	16,207,843	12,342,188	5,880	12,348,068	1,317,693	1,064,302	12,094,677	2,514,883	1,598,283	41,092	394,428	250,596
2005	16,581,889	12,915,674	3,269	12,918,943	1,372,499	954,931	12,501,375	2,416,620	1,663,894	41,833	396,381	255,100
2006	17,693,884	13,526,994	2,847	13,529,841	1,423,798	1,103,960	13,210,003	2,711,029	1,772,852	44,438	398,169	256,756
2007	18,570,133	14,092,244	774	14,093,018	1,500,628	1,012,453	13,604,843	3,038,895	1,926,395	46,560	398,843	260,419
2008	19,216,189	14,295,202	1,201	14,296,403	1,549,606	985,778	13,732,575	3,241,140	2,242,474	48,094	399,556	258,237
2009	18,654,699	13,867,024	-975	13,866,049	1,514,570	773,318	13,124,797	3,093,564	2,436,338	46,619	400,148	250,781
2010	19,066,109	14,195,566	-1,067	14,194,499	1,543,423	1,105,678	13,756,754	2,695,350	2,614,005	47,527	401,162	247,075
2011	20,105,642	14,843,843	-2,744	14,841,099	1,441,551	940,714	14,340,262	3,195,450	2,569,930	49,850	403,323	249,488
2012	20,922,251	15,078,642	1,140	15,079,782	1,473,926	1,033,912	14,639,768	3,674,809	2,607,674	51,618	405,328	250,660
2013	20,763,451	15,338,646	9,121	15,347,767	1,693,195	978,751	14,633,323	3,476,446	2,653,682	51,053	406,704	254,371
2014	21,484,828	16,246,949	3,538	16,250,487	1,771,100	745,882	15,225,269	3,430,897	2,828,662	52,511	409,149	258,589
2015	22,240,561	16,755,108	4,119	16,759,227	1,830,374	879,723	15,808,576	3,399,445	3,032,540	54,070	411,330	264,867
2016	22,965,825	17,389,116	2,670	17,391,786	1,895,288	935,170	16,431,668	3,325,664	3,208,493	55,459	414,107	269,069
2017	23,893,774	18,033,408	4,889	18,038,297	1,992,315	1,043,017	17,088,999	3,480,304	3,324,471	57,371	416,477	271,987
2018	24,993,383	18,905,676	2,510	18,908,186	2,077,706	1,054,575	17,885,055	3,597,128	3,511,200	59,755	418,261	276,134
2019	26,414,949	19,750,872	5,915	19,756,787	2,162,635	1,311,110	18,905,262	3,893,650	3,616,037	62,667	421,513	276,458
2020	28,018,649	20,727,543	691	20,728,234	2,246,679	1,030,872	19,512,427	3,708,302	4,797,920	66,256	422,883	266,918
2021	29,643,657	23,333,183	-1,866	23,331,317	2,458,604	-191,790	20,680,923	3,891,273	5,071,461	69,833	424,496	277,851
2022	30,613,013	24,545,101	-10,898	24,534,203	2,701,163	138,838	21,971,878	4,173,209	4,467,926	71,761	426,594	291,340

Personal Income and Employment by Area: Manhattan, KS

(Thousands of dollars, except as noted.)

Year	Personal income, total	Derivation of personal income: Earnings by place of work: Nonfarm	Farm	Total	Less: Contributions for government social insurance	Plus: Adjustment for residence	Equals: Net earnings by place of residence	Plus: Dividends, interest, and rent	Plus: Personal current transfer receipts	Per capita personal income (dollars)	Population (persons)	Total employment
1970	450,472	348,108	7,591	355,699	22,078	5,911	339,532	90,026	20,914	4,626	97,383	55,028
1971	500,378	394,207	8,206	402,413	26,796	3,771	379,388	97,246	23,744	4,970	100,682	56,351
1972	520,484	408,324	11,586	419,910	28,189	994	392,715	100,883	26,886	5,173	100,610	53,279
1973	568,980	440,661	17,188	457,849	32,601	-1,133	424,115	113,411	31,454	5,448	104,436	54,202
1974	632,299	494,668	13,738	508,406	38,807	-5,016	464,583	130,625	37,091	5,943	106,397	55,304
1975	671,533	529,596	12,948	542,544	44,328	-10,890	487,326	138,967	45,240	6,275	107,019	55,567
1976	707,568	565,550	9,902	575,452	48,284	-16,366	510,802	145,519	51,247	6,509	108,713	56,205
1977	765,830	617,617	4,519	622,136	52,233	-24,331	545,572	163,663	56,595	7,178	106,696	58,638
1978	833,631	664,407	10,668	675,075	56,607	-32,721	585,747	186,141	61,743	7,706	108,173	59,172
1979	909,257	721,636	8,956	730,592	63,718	-35,825	631,049	209,958	68,250	8,425	107,926	60,127
1980	1,003,949	799,704	158	799,862	70,093	-46,948	682,821	240,242	80,886	9,233	108,729	61,047
1981	1,146,207	912,752	16,297	929,049	83,897	-70,969	774,183	280,083	91,941	10,332	110,942	62,723
1982	1,232,179	965,738	14,009	979,747	87,515	-72,776	819,456	312,908	99,815	11,019	111,825	62,416
1983	1,291,625	999,128	9,833	1,008,961	92,698	-64,321	851,942	329,834	109,849	11,315	114,155	61,991
1984	1,361,528	1,049,181	10,715	1,059,896	99,337	-64,022	896,537	351,012	113,979	12,076	112,745	62,052
1985	1,467,336	1,118,504	20,281	1,138,785	107,333	-65,070	966,382	376,844	124,110	13,056	112,388	63,482
1986	1,533,351	1,167,525	18,277	1,185,802	113,276	-61,366	1,011,160	398,360	123,831	13,698	111,943	63,967
1987	1,584,237	1,208,972	19,621	1,228,593	118,215	-58,487	1,051,891	404,194	128,152	14,103	112,334	65,659
1988	1,638,606	1,257,923	17,623	1,275,546	131,361	-54,287	1,089,898	413,808	134,900	14,492	113,069	66,363
1989	1,744,964	1,322,932	12,183	1,335,115	138,831	-51,054	1,145,230	450,122	149,612	15,440	113,013	66,962
1990	1,775,550	1,353,890	18,637	1,372,527	149,113	-53,113	1,170,301	443,363	161,886	15,589	113,901	67,440
1991	1,809,030	1,377,433	10,793	1,388,226	154,678	-54,304	1,179,244	452,491	177,295	16,274	111,164	65,324
1992	2,081,814	1,602,423	22,688	1,625,111	181,821	-64,745	1,378,545	506,621	196,648	17,550	118,624	69,278
1993	2,075,680	1,590,393	15,757	1,606,150	181,726	-63,475	1,360,949	509,955	204,776	17,804	116,586	69,313
1994	2,177,099	1,666,628	19,208	1,685,836	189,836	-66,412	1,429,588	540,874	206,637	18,409	118,263	70,287
1995	2,174,322	1,656,137	4,803	1,660,940	186,080	-62,764	1,412,096	542,717	219,509	18,498	117,544	70,774
1996	2,159,912	1,608,475	25,607	1,634,082	181,405	-54,638	1,398,039	535,650	226,223	19,409	111,286	68,200
1997	2,207,121	1,656,001	16,439	1,672,440	187,893	-55,481	1,429,066	540,455	237,600	20,185	109,343	68,923
1998	2,314,923	1,725,061	10,064	1,735,125	194,511	-55,871	1,484,743	587,847	242,333	21,182	109,287	69,961
1999	2,430,464	1,829,494	13,389	1,842,883	205,316	-58,977	1,578,590	595,849	256,025	22,273	109,123	70,983
2000	2,604,704	1,963,909	13,000	1,976,909	221,809	-64,491	1,690,609	636,810	277,285	23,812	109,384	72,177
2001	2,743,932	2,132,191	18,443	2,150,634	237,055	-84,994	1,828,585	611,516	303,831	25,129	109,195	72,131
2002	2,834,136	2,229,552	5,867	2,235,419	247,977	-107,414	1,880,028	629,902	324,206	26,029	108,884	70,545
2003	3,016,874	2,396,051	18,563	2,414,614	265,451	-150,592	1,998,571	674,556	343,747	27,582	109,379	71,508
2004	3,173,775	2,569,285	26,616	2,595,901	286,251	-172,250	2,137,400	680,132	356,243	28,706	110,560	73,399
2005	3,297,000	2,702,621	21,992	2,724,613	301,068	-207,740	2,215,805	703,832	377,363	29,624	111,294	73,628
2006	3,705,744	3,080,583	8,602	3,089,185	341,593	-266,981	2,480,611	823,334	401,799	32,405	114,356	77,815
2007	4,148,209	3,498,206	12,958	3,511,164	383,000	-362,480	2,765,684	947,239	435,286	35,861	115,675	83,386
2008	4,607,363	3,916,606	10,429	3,927,035	425,535	-441,398	3,060,102	1,036,277	510,984	38,202	120,604	86,707
2009	4,763,346	3,997,498	20,836	4,018,334	440,418	-407,275	3,170,641	1,041,088	551,617	38,809	122,738	87,482
2010	5,179,486	4,330,999	15,079	4,346,078	479,283	-399,588	3,467,207	1,097,850	614,429	40,267	128,627	89,283
2011	5,527,465	4,481,373	40,775	4,522,148	445,303	-361,556	3,715,289	1,169,540	642,636	42,101	131,291	88,982
2012	5,658,489	4,517,510	33,056	4,550,566	452,348	-311,175	3,787,043	1,233,066	638,380	40,768	138,799	89,090
2013	5,499,934	4,391,656	51,364	4,443,020	486,444	-250,808	3,705,768	1,139,343	654,823	39,910	137,807	88,191
2014	5,632,280	4,480,161	25,286	4,505,447	499,356	-252,391	3,753,700	1,196,322	682,258	40,918	137,647	88,908
2015	5,765,524	4,617,668	12,724	4,630,392	517,253	-263,167	3,849,972	1,210,954	704,598	41,339	139,468	89,215
2016	5,776,670	4,593,116	12,398	4,605,514	502,913	-266,750	3,835,851	1,206,753	734,066	42,155	137,034	87,738
2017	5,863,784	4,636,705	10,815	4,647,520	511,442	-268,637	3,867,441	1,239,087	757,256	43,456	134,937	90,132
2018	5,974,340	4,725,528	23,377	4,748,905	521,515	-272,177	3,955,213	1,223,124	796,003	44,146	135,332	90,788
2019	6,058,105	4,736,269	22,225	4,758,494	526,703	-278,230	3,953,561	1,252,861	851,683	45,610	132,825	91,351
2020	6,491,154	4,934,541	36,762	4,971,303	553,479	-292,202	4,125,622	1,238,285	1,127,247	48,378	134,175	89,099
2021	6,904,015	5,209,069	45,060	5,254,129	583,713	-299,164	4,371,252	1,264,712	1,268,051	51,591	133,821	89,900
2022	6,992,099	5,530,883	1,255	5,532,138	624,948	-316,568	4,590,622	1,323,139	1,078,338	52,544	133,072	92,229

Personal Income and Employment by Area: Mankato, MN

(Thousands of dollars, except as noted.)

Year	Personal income, total	Derivation of personal income: Earnings by place of work: Nonfarm	Farm	Total	Less: Contributions for government social insurance	Plus: Adjustment for residence	Equals: Net earnings by place of residence	Plus: Dividends, interest, and rent	Plus: Personal current transfer receipts	Per capita personal income (dollars)	Population (persons)	Total employment
1970	264,523	181,093	29,959	211,052	12,252	-954	197,846	45,102	21,575	3,434	77,037	32,324
1971	280,227	199,226	23,124	222,350	14,015	-2,141	206,194	49,222	24,811	3,592	78,012	32,665
1972	305,079	213,266	29,059	242,325	15,686	-2,016	224,623	52,926	27,530	3,937	77,494	34,258
1973	379,991	240,844	69,116	309,960	20,598	-3,140	286,222	61,588	32,181	4,944	76,854	36,352
1974	406,071	271,570	53,774	325,344	24,431	-4,673	296,240	71,574	38,257	5,240	77,488	37,064
1975	438,278	298,401	44,128	342,529	26,495	-6,458	309,576	81,837	46,865	5,668	77,328	37,194
1976	452,057	330,594	19,745	350,339	29,938	-8,012	312,389	87,667	52,001	5,809	77,818	37,739
1977	538,793	364,602	62,841	427,443	33,056	-9,703	384,684	98,636	55,473	6,901	78,073	39,224
1978	598,122	414,191	65,510	479,701	38,944	-12,069	428,688	109,183	60,251	7,677	77,906	40,917
1979	639,266	461,106	47,155	508,261	45,017	-14,614	448,630	122,566	68,070	8,147	78,471	42,687
1980	689,301	489,996	32,905	522,901	47,553	-16,386	458,962	148,472	81,867	8,683	79,381	42,871
1981	764,633	529,639	34,659	564,298	55,025	-16,468	492,805	179,424	92,404	9,588	79,753	43,218
1982	810,348	552,547	19,326	571,873	58,109	-16,479	497,285	210,100	102,963	10,135	79,958	43,012
1983	839,949	589,845	-6,280	583,565	62,631	-16,743	504,191	224,402	111,356	10,526	79,795	43,112
1984	959,740	636,944	42,219	679,163	69,110	-13,609	596,444	247,133	116,163	12,029	79,784	43,684
1985	999,659	657,324	47,123	704,447	72,838	-10,972	620,637	254,419	124,603	12,465	80,198	44,449
1986	1,041,100	690,146	45,184	735,330	78,541	-9,726	647,063	263,216	130,821	12,967	80,288	44,537
1987	1,140,297	748,250	80,606	828,856	84,844	-10,632	733,380	268,744	138,173	14,187	80,379	45,846
1988	1,158,552	809,357	42,856	852,213	95,148	-9,481	747,584	266,655	144,313	14,239	81,366	47,128
1989	1,286,372	864,863	73,909	938,772	101,569	-6,927	830,276	302,548	153,548	15,773	81,555	47,596
1990	1,354,710	931,697	59,515	991,212	109,677	-4,752	876,783	313,890	164,037	16,464	82,283	48,587
1991	1,390,457	989,991	29,459	1,019,450	118,050	-11,133	890,267	326,425	173,765	16,801	82,758	49,463
1992	1,502,760	1,095,190	44,590	1,139,780	128,820	-16,600	994,360	322,305	186,095	18,116	82,954	51,307
1993	1,539,373	1,158,705	-331	1,158,374	136,851	-22,569	998,954	345,220	195,199	18,484	83,283	52,620
1994	1,676,911	1,239,692	51,008	1,290,700	148,154	-26,556	1,115,990	356,264	204,657	20,031	83,717	54,719
1995	1,743,478	1,295,081	22,553	1,317,634	154,359	-29,089	1,134,186	391,935	217,357	20,622	84,545	55,982
1996	1,878,768	1,360,297	81,129	1,441,426	160,183	-31,249	1,249,994	404,524	224,250	22,126	84,912	56,419
1997	1,919,789	1,414,337	51,682	1,466,019	166,294	-34,530	1,265,195	426,583	228,011	22,613	84,897	56,660
1998	2,098,301	1,582,272	53,040	1,635,312	182,558	-47,075	1,405,679	461,011	231,611	24,753	84,771	60,139
1999	2,167,579	1,652,269	43,173	1,695,442	192,115	-52,584	1,450,743	472,896	243,940	25,469	85,105	61,312
2000	2,269,897	1,739,647	59,137	1,798,784	200,945	-58,597	1,539,242	468,262	262,393	26,427	85,892	61,984
2001	2,482,496	1,915,843	48,419	1,964,262	214,998	-65,880	1,683,384	499,300	299,812	28,500	87,105	61,726
2002	2,567,208	2,041,341	41,512	2,082,853	225,791	-75,991	1,781,071	462,143	323,994	29,137	88,107	62,348
2003	2,698,357	2,107,016	60,311	2,167,327	236,271	-86,868	1,844,188	508,954	345,215	30,205	89,336	62,584
2004	2,837,198	2,210,911	125,001	2,335,912	247,181	-93,541	1,995,190	481,117	360,891	31,471	90,152	63,322
2005	2,922,531	2,318,870	145,096	2,463,966	264,797	-114,618	2,084,551	460,115	377,865	32,077	91,111	65,186
2006	3,149,568	2,513,717	130,816	2,644,533	289,600	-133,275	2,221,658	506,764	421,146	33,910	92,879	67,009
2007	3,221,242	2,532,719	96,520	2,629,239	293,180	-138,865	2,197,194	564,068	459,980	34,282	93,963	67,768
2008	3,345,289	2,485,550	165,377	2,650,927	295,817	-147,665	2,207,445	611,185	526,659	35,169	95,121	67,299
2009	3,218,864	2,406,768	104,142	2,510,910	288,899	-144,447	2,077,564	556,270	585,030	33,491	96,111	65,731
2010	3,365,863	2,455,025	147,540	2,602,565	290,736	-157,255	2,154,574	567,990	643,299	34,746	96,871	65,592
2011	3,652,366	2,600,099	223,978	2,824,077	275,427	-177,279	2,371,371	642,966	638,029	37,481	97,447	66,923
2012	3,908,773	2,754,531	263,404	3,017,935	288,081	-190,956	2,538,898	731,097	638,778	39,799	98,213	67,084
2013	3,929,677	2,842,883	214,886	3,057,769	338,754	-177,143	2,541,872	729,197	658,608	40,083	98,038	68,247
2014	4,086,515	3,014,417	181,703	3,196,120	352,787	-190,414	2,652,919	728,424	705,172	41,237	99,098	68,726
2015	4,270,394	3,146,477	136,361	3,282,838	363,976	-189,095	2,729,767	820,293	720,334	42,821	99,726	70,060
2016	4,243,704	3,207,187	46,717	3,253,904	374,958	-200,233	2,678,713	816,249	748,742	42,124	100,742	70,618
2017	4,422,367	3,343,766	100,852	3,444,618	396,162	-223,897	2,824,559	806,589	791,219	43,489	101,689	71,526
2018	4,651,920	3,493,273	82,823	3,576,096	415,121	-231,772	2,929,203	885,038	837,679	45,426	102,407	72,200
2019	4,802,049	3,641,488	44,883	3,686,371	433,321	-242,613	3,010,437	922,950	868,662	46,594	103,062	72,634
2020	5,166,290	3,675,313	106,302	3,781,615	438,717	-256,650	3,086,248	899,312	1,180,730	49,812	103,715	69,081
2021	5,509,242	3,849,959	164,979	4,014,938	455,629	-280,296	3,279,013	931,805	1,298,424	53,109	103,734	70,596
2022	5,675,775	4,147,042	205,789	4,352,831	498,387	-289,659	3,564,785	1,000,069	1,110,921	54,537	104,072	73,024

Personal Income and Employment by Area: Mansfield, OH

(Thousands of dollars, except as noted.)

Year	Personal income, total	Derivation of personal income: Earnings by place of work: Nonfarm	Farm	Total	Less: Contributions for government social insurance	Plus: Adjustment for residence	Equals: Net earnings by place of residence	Plus: Dividends, interest, and rent	Plus: Personal current transfer receipts	Per capita personal income (dollars)	Population (persons)	Total employment
1970	516,298	469,915	2,941	472,856	31,347	-27,267	414,242	65,513	36,543	3,976	129,838	60,931
1971	567,752	518,416	1,989	520,405	36,010	-30,507	453,888	70,589	43,275	4,387	129,411	63,089
1972	606,042	554,492	3,572	558,064	40,680	-33,389	483,995	74,974	47,073	4,632	130,847	63,607
1973	670,311	618,207	4,793	623,000	53,147	-37,425	532,428	83,357	54,526	5,120	130,923	66,236
1974	707,235	629,762	5,918	635,680	56,036	-34,472	545,172	94,271	67,792	5,425	130,356	64,297
1975	746,455	636,939	7,033	643,972	55,070	-33,286	555,616	100,804	90,035	5,703	130,887	60,904
1976	822,879	716,878	8,277	725,155	63,706	-39,105	622,344	107,710	92,825	6,274	131,160	61,493
1977	924,472	823,791	6,640	830,431	74,107	-48,160	708,164	119,352	96,956	7,083	130,524	64,527
1978	1,002,098	893,232	4,947	898,179	82,483	-49,941	765,755	131,348	104,995	7,657	130,866	65,594
1979	1,097,088	969,585	4,548	974,133	92,464	-52,503	829,166	148,624	119,298	8,428	130,178	65,972
1980	1,190,591	1,009,230	153	1,009,383	95,333	-55,893	858,157	184,148	148,286	9,080	131,116	65,230
1981	1,326,343	1,113,393	327	1,113,720	112,650	-69,082	931,988	226,192	168,163	10,166	130,465	65,158
1982	1,347,602	1,066,001	3,203	1,069,204	107,859	-64,687	896,658	247,683	203,261	10,435	129,141	61,624
1983	1,482,392	1,208,763	-2,432	1,206,331	126,327	-83,038	996,966	270,907	214,519	11,575	128,066	63,435
1984	1,613,503	1,320,629	6,262	1,326,891	141,117	-89,481	1,096,293	299,333	217,877	12,558	128,485	66,715
1985	1,714,886	1,421,297	7,323	1,428,620	154,326	-101,702	1,172,592	309,147	233,147	13,379	128,181	67,043
1986	1,788,061	1,476,521	5,310	1,481,831	164,713	-104,322	1,212,796	321,862	253,403	14,033	127,418	68,043
1987	1,835,362	1,531,199	6,927	1,538,126	170,131	-105,948	1,262,047	315,989	257,326	14,413	127,345	69,183
1988	1,937,640	1,636,096	6,640	1,642,736	187,832	-113,146	1,341,758	329,060	266,822	15,237	127,167	70,397
1989	2,049,003	1,702,809	10,767	1,713,576	196,549	-118,077	1,398,950	362,666	287,387	16,186	126,590	71,654
1990	2,110,292	1,720,229	9,376	1,729,605	201,886	-114,084	1,413,635	374,208	322,449	16,727	126,160	70,803
1991	2,114,000	1,704,297	1,482	1,705,779	202,509	-103,217	1,400,053	365,654	348,293	16,640	127,040	68,169
1992	2,210,885	1,751,265	14,244	1,765,509	204,693	-95,621	1,465,195	367,216	378,474	17,344	127,475	68,884
1993	2,336,654	1,886,585	5,787	1,892,372	225,177	-101,956	1,565,239	376,647	394,768	18,285	127,792	71,627
1994	2,449,623	1,960,444	11,829	1,972,273	236,861	-88,755	1,646,657	390,266	412,700	19,096	128,281	72,358
1995	2,527,862	2,024,062	14,140	2,038,202	246,504	-93,381	1,698,317	395,844	433,701	19,715	128,217	74,128
1996	2,647,514	2,110,894	16,478	2,127,372	253,674	-99,849	1,773,849	418,674	454,991	20,540	128,894	74,963
1997	2,789,024	2,214,945	17,427	2,232,372	258,857	-102,710	1,870,805	450,070	468,149	21,642	128,868	75,038
1998	2,870,451	2,254,415	14,627	2,269,042	256,895	-93,857	1,918,290	471,900	480,261	22,331	128,540	72,778
1999	2,950,630	2,347,402	9,902	2,357,304	264,069	-96,541	1,996,694	452,066	501,870	22,832	129,233	73,336
2000	3,078,560	2,430,549	10,520	2,441,069	264,559	-95,106	2,081,404	472,885	524,271	23,892	128,853	73,985
2001	3,230,622	2,532,755	11,061	2,543,816	277,173	-91,688	2,174,955	471,238	584,429	25,202	128,187	74,473
2002	3,343,789	2,627,844	3,760	2,631,604	281,815	-85,753	2,264,036	456,715	623,038	26,049	128,363	73,892
2003	3,449,539	2,685,542	4,142	2,689,684	291,329	-80,031	2,318,324	469,035	662,180	26,884	128,312	72,844
2004	3,493,566	2,750,197	9,653	2,759,850	305,720	-104,067	2,350,063	451,347	692,156	27,273	128,094	72,728
2005	3,515,729	2,742,033	6,593	2,748,626	307,140	-100,668	2,340,818	450,172	724,739	27,526	127,724	72,385
2006	3,611,010	2,810,140	6,689	2,816,829	317,366	-117,950	2,381,513	459,877	769,620	28,368	127,292	72,402
2007	3,713,590	2,752,335	7,645	2,759,980	309,102	-88,180	2,362,698	530,626	820,266	29,242	126,995	71,445
2008	3,864,741	2,751,253	8,643	2,759,896	317,841	-74,627	2,367,428	585,293	912,020	30,641	126,128	70,018
2009	3,732,933	2,539,444	9,876	2,549,320	298,568	-63,914	2,186,838	543,215	1,002,880	29,790	125,308	65,882
2010	3,764,316	2,538,004	21,584	2,559,588	293,791	-61,191	2,204,606	519,710	1,040,000	30,295	124,254	64,779
2011	3,956,085	2,615,960	35,021	2,650,981	275,094	-59,749	2,316,138	572,149	1,067,798	31,997	123,639	66,091
2012	4,014,900	2,647,649	22,173	2,669,822	277,119	-30,733	2,361,970	593,474	1,059,456	32,503	123,523	64,819
2013	4,069,503	2,676,113	42,946	2,719,059	301,574	17,536	2,435,021	564,449	1,070,033	32,923	123,605	64,774
2014	4,252,184	2,761,264	39,026	2,800,290	311,213	19,213	2,508,290	614,231	1,129,663	34,379	123,685	65,567
2015	4,374,678	2,797,464	10,755	2,808,219	313,081	55,542	2,550,680	649,779	1,174,219	35,347	123,763	65,093
2016	4,381,363	2,807,549	7,244	2,814,793	322,318	46,892	2,539,367	646,393	1,195,603	35,404	123,753	65,020
2017	4,514,797	2,920,347	15,946	2,936,293	342,736	59,004	2,652,561	651,510	1,210,726	36,615	123,305	64,555
2018	4,699,237	3,047,791	21,598	3,069,389	353,064	23,543	2,739,868	717,472	1,241,897	37,796	124,330	65,431
2019	4,947,858	3,092,754	8,618	3,101,372	360,987	171,290	2,911,675	718,991	1,317,192	39,583	125,000	64,786
2020	5,334,007	3,090,048	21,997	3,112,045	364,072	88,250	2,836,223	763,154	1,734,630	42,685	124,962	61,973
2021	5,665,390	3,281,548	47,135	3,328,683	385,438	72,536	3,015,781	752,589	1,897,020	45,205	125,327	63,644
2022	5,639,149	3,430,189	40,719	3,470,908	415,342	103,741	3,159,307	810,607	1,669,235	44,998	125,319	65,127

Personal Income and Employment by Area: McAllen-Edinburg-Mission, TX

(Thousands of dollars, except as noted.)

Year	Personal income, total	Derivation of personal income: Earnings by place of work: Nonfarm	Farm	Total	Less: Contributions for government social insurance	Plus: Adjustment for residence	Equals: Net earnings by place of residence	Plus: Dividends, interest, and rent	Plus: Personal current transfer receipts	Per capita personal income (dollars)	Population (persons)	Total employment
1970	364,139	260,864	22,601	283,465	15,860	-9,141	258,464	59,886	45,789	1,989	183,040	55,167
1971	428,483	296,938	37,595	334,533	18,581	-8,638	307,314	67,788	53,381	2,216	193,397	58,147
1972	479,788	346,602	25,965	372,567	22,664	-8,990	340,913	77,030	61,845	2,342	204,904	64,427
1973	571,221	405,838	26,895	432,733	31,119	-9,421	392,193	91,716	87,312	2,632	217,004	69,841
1974	671,642	475,413	30,438	505,851	37,482	-11,518	456,851	110,674	104,117	3,001	223,800	74,338
1975	791,763	555,034	34,284	589,318	42,731	-12,780	533,807	130,410	127,546	3,316	238,746	77,588
1976	903,307	658,565	22,947	681,512	51,002	-14,133	616,377	145,074	141,856	3,628	249,003	82,908
1977	1,051,173	734,940	70,547	805,487	57,494	-15,582	732,411	166,181	152,581	4,063	258,732	87,780
1978	1,185,172	831,701	64,062	895,763	66,294	-14,859	814,610	194,956	175,606	4,454	266,103	90,869
1979	1,326,907	934,978	39,547	974,525	78,510	-13,656	882,359	227,941	216,607	4,817	275,488	93,698
1980	1,551,168	1,078,146	28,323	1,106,469	92,606	-14,859	999,004	284,015	268,149	5,413	286,540	99,240
1981	1,847,587	1,234,897	86,461	1,321,358	116,678	-8,014	1,196,666	350,208	300,713	6,188	298,559	106,048
1982	2,022,291	1,336,876	67,723	1,404,599	128,049	-9,088	1,267,462	419,873	334,956	6,456	313,256	110,680
1983	2,160,384	1,387,666	48,611	1,436,277	129,299	-9,757	1,297,221	462,723	400,440	6,618	326,453	108,973
1984	2,352,603	1,502,659	52,377	1,555,036	142,003	-9,061	1,403,972	509,477	439,154	7,032	334,571	110,090
1985	2,586,213	1,648,875	44,532	1,693,407	156,625	-8,546	1,528,236	569,853	488,124	7,581	341,145	113,109
1986	2,684,973	1,714,213	30,958	1,745,171	160,769	-8,836	1,575,566	585,278	524,129	7,660	350,514	112,319
1987	2,786,850	1,781,761	53,465	1,835,226	166,031	-9,065	1,660,130	580,000	546,720	7,778	358,307	117,858
1988	3,071,976	2,001,417	65,415	2,066,832	193,315	-8,300	1,865,217	611,001	595,758	8,405	365,499	124,638
1989	3,366,319	2,152,316	46,903	2,199,219	214,557	-5,100	1,979,562	700,795	685,962	8,927	377,106	131,460
1990	3,685,011	2,343,101	60,723	2,403,824	229,546	-3,836	2,170,442	712,536	802,033	9,517	387,200	134,822
1991	4,069,353	2,564,273	81,093	2,645,366	256,872	-4,084	2,384,410	763,480	921,463	10,083	403,571	138,175
1992	4,508,910	2,788,544	83,404	2,871,948	276,611	-1,656	2,593,681	763,525	1,151,704	10,626	424,312	142,423
1993	4,886,008	3,055,318	113,222	3,168,540	304,283	-2,325	2,861,932	782,361	1,241,715	10,918	447,508	148,166
1994	5,308,347	3,335,923	100,392	3,436,315	337,829	-6,002	3,092,484	831,620	1,384,243	11,321	468,906	155,816
1995	5,640,088	3,494,633	83,306	3,577,939	355,901	-6,263	3,215,775	893,553	1,530,760	11,567	487,593	163,571
1996	6,077,550	3,771,188	60,367	3,831,555	378,066	-8,099	3,445,390	943,965	1,688,195	12,073	503,411	171,626
1997	6,604,824	4,186,474	60,429	4,246,903	413,115	-11,486	3,822,302	1,009,373	1,773,149	12,704	519,903	182,919
1998	7,124,955	4,558,472	111,074	4,669,546	443,519	-11,719	4,214,308	1,076,106	1,834,541	13,245	537,929	188,244
1999	7,485,341	4,857,744	122,054	4,979,798	472,252	-16,449	4,491,097	1,110,580	1,883,664	13,466	555,875	199,684
2000	8,185,980	5,393,201	111,147	5,504,348	512,439	-18,981	4,972,928	1,208,351	2,004,701	14,281	573,216	212,033
2001	8,814,159	5,883,660	126,783	6,010,443	552,375	-96,632	5,361,436	1,248,362	2,204,361	14,938	590,067	220,968
2002	9,530,104	6,352,025	110,823	6,462,848	595,149	-99,531	5,768,168	1,247,416	2,514,520	15,610	610,520	230,572
2003	10,318,908	6,874,141	154,823	7,028,964	652,306	-91,091	6,285,567	1,293,970	2,739,371	16,315	632,475	242,798
2004	11,196,170	7,592,047	140,307	7,732,354	714,374	-77,945	6,940,035	1,367,731	2,888,404	17,125	653,779	256,673
2005	12,194,103	8,095,548	158,625	8,254,173	779,427	-68,424	7,406,322	1,508,821	3,278,960	18,066	674,982	270,974
2006	13,160,233	8,808,915	105,987	8,914,902	840,979	-30,454	8,043,469	1,582,073	3,534,691	18,926	695,352	283,005
2007	14,034,310	9,188,888	93,461	9,282,349	905,201	-14,642	8,362,506	1,711,675	3,960,129	19,621	715,264	302,765
2008	15,331,528	9,576,262	39,810	9,616,072	946,270	22,477	8,692,279	2,139,719	4,499,530	20,811	736,694	308,239
2009	16,177,160	10,054,641	33,713	10,088,354	997,746	62,262	9,152,870	2,022,753	5,001,537	21,357	757,468	310,587
2010	17,306,518	10,716,733	66,942	10,783,675	1,049,454	89,280	9,823,501	2,022,951	5,460,066	22,215	779,032	316,445
2011	18,296,373	11,302,062	36,628	11,338,690	980,248	153,295	10,511,737	2,197,278	5,587,358	23,014	794,996	329,914
2012	18,831,078	11,660,907	54,914	11,715,821	1,012,586	244,983	10,948,218	2,413,399	5,469,461	23,324	807,357	335,376
2013	19,546,259	12,231,191	151,167	12,382,358	1,175,492	323,254	11,530,120	2,427,833	5,588,306	23,918	817,205	342,990
2014	20,335,192	12,822,352	93,871	12,916,223	1,233,736	363,910	12,046,397	2,508,109	5,780,686	24,561	827,938	354,064
2015	21,044,291	13,193,606	127,204	13,320,810	1,291,798	335,394	12,364,406	2,556,694	6,123,191	25,133	837,320	361,842
2016	21,410,649	13,431,900	110,782	13,542,682	1,342,380	255,488	12,455,790	2,580,250	6,374,609	25,307	846,030	368,341
2017	21,994,898	13,877,709	134,720	14,012,429	1,399,523	244,894	12,857,800	2,708,920	6,428,178	25,794	852,699	374,852
2018	23,024,927	14,517,640	95,905	14,613,545	1,461,255	273,696	13,425,986	2,916,460	6,682,481	26,823	858,413	387,906
2019	24,277,037	15,461,016	61,771	15,522,787	1,537,736	293,607	14,278,658	2,985,131	7,013,248	28,081	864,536	393,890
2020	27,327,410	15,702,182	92,249	15,794,431	1,614,862	302,670	14,482,239	3,120,792	9,724,379	31,310	872,806	393,745
2021	30,481,804	16,575,656	230,328	16,805,984	1,683,231	288,938	15,411,691	3,465,381	11,604,732	34,614	880,633	412,086
2022	29,782,422	17,778,099	50,834	17,828,933	1,826,199	337,288	16,340,022	3,651,682	9,790,718	33,525	888,367	432,360

Personal Income and Employment by Area: Medford, OR

(Thousands of dollars, except as noted.)

Year	Personal income, total	Derivation of personal income: Earnings by place of work: Nonfarm	Farm	Total	Less: Contributions for government social insurance	Plus: Adjustment for residence	Equals: Net earnings by place of residence	Plus: Dividends, interest, and rent	Plus: Personal current transfer receipts	Per capita personal income (dollars)	Population (persons)	Total employment
1970	332,495	235,360	5,186	240,546	18,016	4,488	227,018	66,784	38,693	3,486	95,374	36,133
1971	380,955	270,822	8,211	279,033	21,443	4,906	262,496	74,284	44,175	3,829	99,487	39,058
1972	431,925	315,140	6,464	321,604	26,338	5,515	300,781	81,932	49,212	4,260	101,396	41,785
1973	493,284	357,936	9,492	367,428	34,228	5,701	338,901	94,253	60,130	4,600	107,245	44,421
1974	558,936	392,826	10,847	403,673	38,393	5,140	370,420	110,978	77,538	5,039	110,926	45,606
1975	631,982	431,477	9,193	440,670	40,680	5,661	405,651	126,796	99,535	5,499	114,924	46,756
1976	720,268	503,909	10,334	514,243	47,733	7,192	473,702	137,426	109,140	6,120	117,683	49,250
1977	821,643	585,794	8,841	594,635	56,268	8,152	546,519	155,328	119,796	6,717	122,329	52,964
1978	954,398	685,593	11,085	696,678	67,432	8,997	638,243	185,293	130,862	7,549	126,435	57,334
1979	1,073,367	761,390	16,388	777,778	77,611	9,066	709,233	216,368	147,766	8,262	129,918	58,937
1980	1,197,303	810,659	20,498	831,157	83,028	9,296	757,425	263,507	176,371	9,007	132,929	58,583
1981	1,282,151	824,827	12,612	837,439	90,124	11,231	758,546	319,948	203,657	9,529	134,546	57,391
1982	1,316,595	808,493	10,891	819,384	90,009	11,801	741,176	347,444	227,975	9,837	133,847	54,859
1983	1,432,821	890,677	5,080	895,757	100,092	12,197	807,862	384,596	240,363	10,763	133,130	57,463
1984	1,593,651	1,018,091	11,081	1,029,172	117,621	11,714	923,265	421,832	248,554	11,820	134,830	60,553
1985	1,686,273	1,075,541	12,473	1,088,014	125,208	12,434	975,240	444,786	266,247	12,359	136,444	61,517
1986	1,780,509	1,149,334	13,786	1,163,120	133,867	11,846	1,041,099	469,461	269,949	12,959	137,397	63,925
1987	1,891,004	1,263,653	6,955	1,270,608	146,275	11,682	1,136,015	471,662	283,327	13,543	139,626	67,656
1988	2,073,138	1,380,746	9,246	1,389,992	165,594	12,519	1,236,917	531,194	305,027	14,718	140,860	71,400
1989	2,277,498	1,473,649	13,546	1,487,195	176,766	14,277	1,324,706	613,279	339,513	15,866	143,549	72,786
1990	2,430,953	1,597,449	10,885	1,608,334	195,763	13,899	1,426,470	633,494	370,989	16,493	147,392	75,872
1991	2,573,309	1,654,405	16,701	1,671,106	205,922	13,418	1,478,602	675,346	419,361	17,047	150,956	76,214
1992	2,758,780	1,808,225	16,851	1,825,076	224,257	11,803	1,612,622	688,625	457,533	17,801	154,975	78,291
1993	2,972,386	1,957,182	19,986	1,977,168	240,025	11,393	1,748,536	734,015	489,835	18,688	159,054	80,714
1994	3,230,889	2,155,409	15,642	2,171,051	264,507	9,377	1,915,921	792,780	522,188	19,758	163,527	85,896
1995	3,436,398	2,225,294	14,502	2,239,796	276,436	9,649	1,973,009	882,347	581,042	20,531	167,378	88,260
1996	3,657,311	2,348,369	20,101	2,368,470	295,222	9,815	2,083,063	951,472	622,776	21,423	170,715	91,601
1997	3,802,798	2,470,427	19,388	2,489,815	309,399	9,581	2,189,997	972,800	640,001	21,915	173,523	95,490
1998	4,066,000	2,657,190	14,939	2,672,129	329,882	9,032	2,351,279	1,026,137	688,584	23,018	176,645	97,290
1999	4,297,098	2,896,065	14,277	2,910,342	352,882	8,565	2,566,025	977,990	753,083	23,971	179,264	100,050
2000	4,574,065	3,068,911	10,209	3,079,120	376,502	7,217	2,709,835	1,063,789	800,441	25,163	181,775	103,307
2001	4,913,350	3,314,083	12,986	3,327,069	393,415	1,141	2,934,795	1,079,662	898,893	26,727	183,835	103,859
2002	5,042,823	3,482,686	11,090	3,493,776	417,666	-4,283	3,071,827	1,017,097	953,899	27,010	186,704	103,966
2003	5,393,769	3,685,422	16,230	3,701,652	444,116	-7,523	3,250,013	1,135,360	1,008,396	28,412	189,838	107,560
2004	5,699,486	3,937,479	18,338	3,955,817	480,858	-11,063	3,463,896	1,192,959	1,042,631	29,656	192,185	111,965
2005	5,963,520	4,069,367	17,670	4,087,037	508,610	-14,007	3,564,420	1,288,107	1,110,993	30,629	194,701	115,393
2006	6,468,187	4,309,637	17,075	4,326,712	533,734	-9,480	3,783,498	1,488,397	1,196,292	32,857	196,858	117,400
2007	6,703,554	4,387,571	18,232	4,405,803	553,232	-26,308	3,826,263	1,599,355	1,277,936	33,660	199,152	119,397
2008	6,859,054	4,316,098	16,557	4,332,655	548,934	-13,105	3,770,616	1,641,388	1,447,050	34,097	201,162	116,119
2009	6,618,463	4,076,154	20,225	4,096,379	528,972	-25,261	3,542,146	1,429,503	1,646,814	32,716	202,301	110,154
2010	6,803,217	4,125,123	17,809	4,142,932	539,819	-32,027	3,571,086	1,455,766	1,776,365	33,449	203,390	109,129
2011	7,160,803	4,226,122	21,150	4,247,272	491,883	-32,123	3,723,266	1,618,779	1,818,758	34,937	204,966	109,020
2012	7,390,090	4,439,657	23,136	4,462,793	513,674	-65,674	3,883,445	1,656,743	1,849,902	35,832	206,244	109,922
2013	7,527,112	4,635,158	25,686	4,660,844	605,690	-107,842	3,947,312	1,651,366	1,928,434	36,230	207,758	112,539
2014	8,112,673	4,863,409	23,501	4,886,910	641,916	-82,740	4,162,254	1,815,901	2,134,518	38,643	209,941	114,849
2015	8,681,852	5,197,974	20,764	5,218,738	675,692	-70,220	4,472,826	1,926,780	2,282,246	40,889	212,327	117,907
2016	9,098,875	5,490,593	22,148	5,512,741	707,595	-73,026	4,732,120	2,015,506	2,351,249	42,223	215,498	120,468
2017	9,572,301	5,792,449	18,140	5,810,589	755,116	-77,247	4,978,226	2,141,820	2,452,255	43,892	218,087	122,917
2018	10,016,020	6,108,574	9,951	6,118,525	785,922	-78,713	5,253,890	2,163,725	2,598,405	45,355	220,838	126,190
2019	10,484,815	6,424,064	7,418	6,431,482	827,683	-57,130	5,546,669	2,199,063	2,739,083	47,187	222,195	125,190
2020	11,594,427	6,754,086	12,432	6,766,518	861,737	-50,801	5,853,980	2,230,071	3,510,376	51,850	223,614	123,833
2021	12,770,524	7,440,929	12,165	7,453,094	1,006,308	-63,739	6,383,047	2,515,069	3,872,408	56,928	224,327	126,109
2022	12,755,983	7,849,069	8,040	7,857,109	1,086,722	-81,274	6,689,113	2,615,053	3,451,817	57,552	221,644	130,009

Personal Income and Employment by Area: Memphis, TN-MS-AR

(Thousands of dollars, except as noted.)

Year	Personal income, total	Derivation of personal income: Earnings by place of work: Nonfarm	Farm	Total	Less: Contributions for government social insurance	Plus: Adjustment for residence	Equals: Net earnings by place of residence	Plus: Dividends, interest, and rent	Plus: Personal current transfer receipts	Per capita personal income (dollars)	Population (persons)	Total employment
1970	3,213,665	2,672,872	58,659	2,731,531	175,515	-22,352	2,533,664	424,434	255,567	3,521	912,644	411,985
1971	3,605,837	3,008,254	58,281	3,066,535	204,541	-30,881	2,831,113	470,434	304,290	3,909	922,397	426,703
1972	4,090,721	3,447,759	61,650	3,509,409	243,837	-39,962	3,225,610	524,408	340,703	4,366	936,928	452,953
1973	4,553,737	3,838,825	90,020	3,928,845	311,587	-47,983	3,569,275	584,659	399,803	4,841	940,699	470,113
1974	5,044,573	4,213,496	58,136	4,271,632	353,302	-52,338	3,865,992	682,320	496,261	5,294	952,945	477,695
1975	5,472,305	4,431,947	54,426	4,486,373	366,409	-54,740	4,065,224	745,985	661,096	5,724	956,022	461,803
1976	5,953,927	4,819,437	70,334	4,889,771	408,094	-55,202	4,426,475	785,996	741,456	6,191	961,749	464,794
1977	6,541,807	5,346,667	85,108	5,431,775	454,216	-58,456	4,919,103	852,835	769,869	6,762	967,472	479,162
1978	7,387,855	6,081,898	85,248	6,167,146	524,938	-60,924	5,581,284	966,497	840,074	7,573	975,489	498,978
1979	8,258,188	6,788,620	91,607	6,880,227	610,824	-73,442	6,195,961	1,094,195	968,032	8,356	988,272	511,941
1980	9,142,643	7,418,453	12,849	7,431,302	666,675	-85,732	6,678,895	1,309,472	1,154,276	9,165	997,527	512,669
1981	9,994,709	7,931,788	50,836	7,982,624	766,908	-95,433	7,120,283	1,576,774	1,297,652	10,055	994,005	501,492
1982	10,548,475	8,231,061	40,587	8,271,648	810,702	-118,508	7,342,438	1,817,589	1,388,448	10,578	997,175	489,460
1983	11,327,033	8,912,693	-477	8,912,216	887,948	-136,617	7,887,651	1,934,870	1,504,512	11,308	1,001,648	499,210
1984	12,546,319	9,903,418	53,335	9,956,753	1,017,625	-151,156	8,787,972	2,190,866	1,567,481	12,483	1,005,067	520,437
1985	13,423,544	10,673,018	54,162	10,727,180	1,113,189	-161,988	9,452,003	2,321,680	1,649,861	13,213	1,015,899	531,906
1986	14,274,977	11,454,308	17,664	11,471,972	1,220,635	-173,491	10,077,846	2,436,585	1,760,546	13,915	1,025,882	549,849
1987	15,398,375	12,470,757	76,261	12,547,018	1,321,834	-171,644	11,053,540	2,505,945	1,838,890	14,822	1,038,870	571,384
1988	16,708,915	13,472,857	100,826	13,573,683	1,472,482	-160,949	11,940,252	2,811,207	1,957,456	15,864	1,053,270	593,608
1989	18,158,182	14,484,154	62,797	14,546,951	1,594,289	-196,433	12,756,229	3,285,341	2,116,612	17,082	1,063,001	614,507
1990	19,252,345	15,454,322	66,726	15,521,048	1,722,615	-229,191	13,569,242	3,383,868	2,299,235	17,983	1,070,570	621,984
1991	20,105,815	16,150,029	71,844	16,221,873	1,825,890	-244,079	14,151,904	3,389,585	2,564,326	18,552	1,083,757	617,028
1992	21,679,287	17,509,675	99,405	17,609,080	1,950,743	-269,659	15,388,678	3,439,578	2,851,031	19,774	1,096,360	618,985
1993	23,050,627	18,688,199	72,431	18,760,630	2,077,522	-301,602	16,381,506	3,581,755	3,087,366	20,778	1,109,384	635,969
1994	24,823,475	20,250,108	114,944	20,365,052	2,278,693	-351,771	17,734,588	3,836,433	3,252,454	22,066	1,124,952	668,943
1995	26,678,835	21,678,957	74,704	21,753,661	2,428,341	-395,673	18,929,647	4,163,034	3,586,154	23,398	1,140,221	686,110
1996	28,303,164	22,957,917	137,842	23,095,759	2,532,047	-442,319	20,121,393	4,397,067	3,784,704	24,536	1,153,559	699,961
1997	29,929,414	24,400,726	92,110	24,492,836	2,685,493	-494,025	21,313,318	4,740,953	3,875,143	25,703	1,164,412	719,012
1998	33,358,224	27,716,139	47,931	27,764,070	2,923,313	-569,128	24,271,629	5,013,433	4,073,162	28,296	1,178,903	738,335
1999	34,369,393	28,832,831	53,015	28,885,846	3,074,465	-622,913	25,188,468	4,977,401	4,203,524	28,767	1,194,756	748,678
2000	35,675,051	29,743,496	47,476	29,790,972	3,167,245	-675,105	25,948,622	5,254,154	4,472,275	29,527	1,208,223	761,155
2001	37,800,887	31,584,290	144,786	31,729,076	3,373,708	-708,576	27,646,792	5,275,792	4,878,303	31,070	1,216,621	758,173
2002	38,737,521	32,607,028	33,675	32,640,703	3,513,981	-729,192	28,397,530	5,110,177	5,229,814	31,568	1,227,121	754,849
2003	40,088,477	33,455,515	157,954	33,613,469	3,603,908	-756,532	29,253,029	5,281,807	5,553,641	32,347	1,239,341	757,117
2004	41,850,048	35,071,190	177,338	35,248,528	3,759,307	-805,929	30,683,292	5,368,693	5,798,063	33,459	1,250,802	765,890
2005	43,323,143	35,991,629	148,771	36,140,400	3,850,599	-826,450	31,463,351	5,657,537	6,202,255	34,284	1,263,658	777,461
2006	46,072,882	38,084,166	122,462	38,206,628	4,078,538	-863,339	33,264,751	6,325,385	6,482,746	35,899	1,283,389	796,540
2007	47,983,656	39,258,964	112,513	39,371,477	4,259,467	-911,050	34,200,960	6,701,262	7,081,434	37,091	1,293,670	811,934
2008	48,536,679	38,616,837	105,947	38,722,784	4,279,701	-904,244	33,538,839	7,004,003	7,993,837	37,277	1,302,060	808,603
2009	47,034,850	36,869,325	108,868	36,978,193	4,150,222	-820,277	32,007,694	6,463,639	8,563,517	35,931	1,309,030	780,257
2010	48,755,187	37,658,868	38,877	37,697,745	4,174,413	-803,586	32,719,746	6,555,374	9,480,067	37,012	1,317,291	778,368
2011	51,178,549	39,010,435	117,232	39,127,667	3,820,912	-832,744	34,474,011	7,010,361	9,694,177	38,692	1,322,717	792,401
2012	53,436,161	40,780,302	44,847	40,825,149	3,898,883	-868,946	36,057,320	7,569,496	9,809,345	40,194	1,329,469	797,282
2013	53,253,488	41,011,439	288,734	41,300,173	4,463,622	-843,270	35,993,281	7,193,691	10,066,516	40,062	1,329,277	801,307
2014	54,368,204	41,984,331	105,728	42,090,059	4,571,547	-853,743	36,664,769	7,552,159	10,151,276	40,888	1,329,687	814,204
2015	56,138,598	43,371,667	11,593	43,383,260	4,706,669	-880,771	37,795,820	7,687,566	10,655,212	42,206	1,330,099	826,859
2016	57,406,703	44,416,915	21,466	44,438,381	4,841,875	-924,101	38,672,405	7,892,016	10,842,282	43,143	1,330,625	841,725
2017	59,352,029	45,667,094	60,165	45,727,259	5,048,994	-943,582	39,734,683	8,531,491	11,085,855	44,557	1,332,047	849,394
2018	61,707,859	47,371,427	16,766	47,388,193	5,239,054	-979,234	41,169,905	8,987,758	11,550,196	46,218	1,335,134	863,138
2019	64,505,044	48,993,739	80,989	49,074,728	5,523,454	-1,011,644	42,539,630	9,682,259	12,283,155	48,265	1,336,471	868,871
2020	68,692,532	50,356,844	78,540	50,435,384	5,762,930	-1,070,418	43,602,036	9,319,903	15,770,593	51,325	1,338,391	853,511
2021	75,555,773	55,012,608	184,477	55,197,085	6,072,799	-1,192,448	47,931,838	9,984,384	17,639,551	56,579	1,335,407	889,192
2022	75,194,683	57,134,872	40,950	57,175,822	6,536,842	-1,238,364	49,400,616	10,846,208	14,947,859	56,440	1,332,305	921,733

Personal Income and Employment by Area: Merced, CA

(Thousands of dollars, except as noted.)

Year	Personal income, total	Derivation of personal income								Per capita personal income (dollars)	Population (persons)	Total employment
		Earnings by place of work			Less: Contributions for government social insurance	Plus: Adjustment for residence	Equals: Net earnings by place of residence	Plus: Dividends, interest, and rent	Plus: Personal current transfer receipts			
		Nonfarm	Farm	Total								
1970	434,859	250,899	78,531	329,430	17,297	3,889	316,022	69,432	49,405	4,131	105,275	45,456
1971	460,187	276,214	69,534	345,748	20,013	4,009	329,744	75,213	55,230	4,260	108,032	47,188
1972	517,524	305,479	88,135	393,614	22,997	4,804	375,421	83,926	58,177	4,681	110,548	49,741
1973	612,840	341,807	130,956	472,763	28,522	4,907	449,148	99,070	64,622	5,355	114,436	51,449
1974	685,840	385,206	137,450	522,656	33,496	5,443	494,603	113,996	77,241	5,815	117,949	54,411
1975	783,346	426,877	167,674	594,551	37,128	4,103	561,526	126,213	95,607	6,450	121,456	56,336
1976	878,577	486,963	186,623	673,586	43,470	3,221	633,337	135,638	109,602	6,953	126,358	58,502
1977	964,456	545,897	191,997	737,894	49,215	3,848	692,527	151,964	119,965	7,619	126,591	60,515
1978	1,017,192	620,943	134,596	755,539	55,799	5,790	705,530	177,983	133,679	7,920	128,435	61,473
1979	1,170,253	693,339	179,664	873,003	63,665	9,295	818,633	202,307	149,313	8,881	131,775	64,328
1980	1,332,247	747,337	223,498	970,835	67,547	10,589	913,877	239,977	178,393	9,823	135,625	64,044
1981	1,362,863	802,049	127,573	929,622	77,661	16,004	867,965	282,793	212,105	9,760	139,632	62,729
1982	1,461,819	861,647	118,986	980,633	84,178	18,868	915,323	310,061	236,435	10,239	142,766	62,096
1983	1,529,580	916,685	83,605	1,000,290	91,329	22,110	931,071	336,496	262,013	10,359	147,657	62,975
1984	1,772,736	1,030,951	167,318	1,198,269	106,646	26,559	1,118,182	369,999	284,555	11,712	151,357	64,798
1985	1,911,485	1,118,344	171,155	1,289,499	116,771	32,444	1,205,172	387,787	318,526	12,258	155,939	66,196
1986	2,059,788	1,194,808	202,346	1,397,154	126,063	40,180	1,311,271	404,575	343,942	12,956	158,988	67,501
1987	2,280,758	1,318,563	271,136	1,589,699	137,528	53,453	1,505,624	417,383	357,751	13,996	162,956	70,309
1988	2,394,464	1,409,767	258,992	1,668,759	154,488	66,018	1,580,289	429,327	384,848	14,274	167,749	73,220
1989	2,608,681	1,497,751	283,848	1,781,599	166,916	76,733	1,691,416	492,979	424,286	15,080	172,988	74,815
1990	2,786,273	1,607,353	285,166	1,892,519	178,913	90,856	1,804,462	510,627	471,184	15,483	179,953	76,728
1991	2,913,132	1,679,683	275,569	1,955,252	190,027	96,776	1,862,001	519,715	531,416	15,654	186,091	78,038
1992	3,107,591	1,751,785	298,703	2,050,488	197,766	106,911	1,959,633	516,630	631,328	16,400	189,489	76,943
1993	3,205,001	1,796,353	308,550	2,104,903	204,979	117,898	2,017,822	521,818	665,361	16,594	193,137	78,232
1994	3,281,429	1,819,611	326,879	2,146,490	206,089	132,272	2,072,673	529,883	678,873	16,590	197,798	77,678
1995	3,168,188	1,752,652	218,588	1,971,240	197,363	157,534	1,931,411	524,904	711,873	16,223	195,291	77,043
1996	3,479,676	1,799,133	399,358	2,198,491	194,827	184,826	2,188,490	543,549	747,637	17,861	194,819	77,229
1997	3,582,169	1,922,956	358,554	2,281,510	203,560	210,706	2,297,047	547,998	736,524	18,063	198,312	77,931
1998	3,789,839	2,098,350	299,252	2,397,602	215,286	255,929	2,438,245	575,199	776,395	18,737	202,264	82,507
1999	3,991,450	2,211,430	291,519	2,502,949	229,183	304,963	2,578,729	593,056	819,665	19,307	206,734	83,851
2000	4,213,632	2,352,118	246,546	2,598,664	243,538	385,739	2,740,865	626,863	845,904	19,851	212,258	83,061
2001	4,554,256	2,523,778	298,821	2,822,599	269,346	394,953	2,948,206	648,384	957,666	20,813	218,816	82,590
2002	4,852,311	2,790,668	315,234	3,105,902	303,301	375,349	3,177,950	639,270	1,035,091	21,532	225,351	87,070
2003	5,309,025	3,037,677	432,323	3,470,000	332,907	395,292	3,532,385	674,066	1,102,574	22,910	231,735	87,523
2004	5,803,155	3,224,858	682,611	3,907,469	364,012	435,819	3,979,276	656,310	1,167,569	24,467	237,180	87,877
2005	6,024,774	3,421,652	612,095	4,033,747	381,804	496,975	4,148,918	649,068	1,226,788	24,839	242,554	87,575
2006	6,196,043	3,658,110	400,704	4,058,814	392,680	497,936	4,164,070	704,318	1,327,655	25,255	245,338	90,188
2007	6,951,831	3,696,018	873,753	4,569,771	396,783	535,140	4,708,128	816,803	1,426,900	27,971	248,540	92,970
2008	6,716,600	3,568,312	562,681	4,130,993	401,169	530,057	4,259,881	847,284	1,609,435	26,809	250,538	90,759
2009	6,775,527	3,643,076	464,276	4,107,352	409,141	470,350	4,168,561	818,896	1,788,070	26,855	252,302	88,877
2010	7,185,521	3,738,905	588,630	4,327,535	399,331	455,479	4,383,683	810,992	1,990,846	27,985	256,762	88,614
2011	7,738,146	3,779,901	962,128	4,742,029	371,444	521,389	4,891,974	851,551	1,994,621	29,817	259,518	88,470
2012	7,902,641	3,928,435	915,347	4,843,782	390,416	470,224	4,923,590	946,175	2,032,876	30,248	261,264	92,114
2013	8,269,597	4,051,604	1,074,120	5,125,724	446,609	478,077	5,157,192	983,255	2,129,150	31,492	262,597	94,631
2014	9,079,656	4,233,797	1,465,639	5,699,436	462,484	510,115	5,747,067	1,044,034	2,288,555	34,240	265,177	97,893
2015	9,400,054	4,496,552	1,132,787	5,629,339	483,988	553,719	5,699,070	1,205,353	2,495,631	35,167	267,299	100,020
2016	9,575,058	4,691,298	940,089	5,631,387	518,150	630,292	5,743,529	1,246,939	2,584,590	35,626	268,766	100,914
2017	9,919,653	4,938,270	1,096,169	6,034,439	550,550	651,095	6,134,984	1,258,850	2,525,819	36,405	272,480	103,767
2018	10,148,451	5,083,171	839,352	5,922,523	574,491	867,252	6,215,284	1,281,309	2,651,858	36,820	275,626	106,081
2019	10,711,229	5,379,100	766,924	6,146,024	616,127	974,725	6,504,622	1,381,310	2,825,297	38,355	279,263	106,551
2020	12,445,651	5,540,598	949,078	6,489,676	633,174	1,106,101	6,962,603	1,440,815	4,042,233	44,163	281,814	105,222
2021	13,532,782	5,941,936	852,640	6,794,576	673,277	1,371,170	7,492,469	1,472,719	4,567,594	47,574	284,458	108,777
2022	13,395,227	6,242,737	1,029,015	7,271,752	746,419	1,582,355	8,107,688	1,541,387	3,746,152	46,188	290,014	113,738

Personal Income and Employment by Area: Miami-Fort Lauderdale-Pompano Beach, FL

(Thousands of dollars, except as noted.)

Year	Personal income, total	Derivation of personal income: Earnings by place of work: Nonfarm	Farm	Total	Less: Contributions for government social insurance	Plus: Adjustment for residence	Equals: Net earnings by place of residence	Plus: Dividends, interest, and rent	Plus: Personal current transfer receipts	Per capita personal income (dollars)	Population (persons)	Total employment
1970	10,723,332	7,570,402	105,059	7,675,461	490,761	-12,205	7,172,495	2,659,151	891,686	4,755	2,255,202	1,054,067
1971	11,973,429	8,308,995	122,138	8,431,133	560,807	-16,498	7,853,828	3,031,972	1,087,629	5,063	2,364,750	1,087,984
1972	13,740,830	9,599,126	131,527	9,730,653	685,284	-20,550	9,024,819	3,421,480	1,294,531	5,543	2,478,824	1,178,470
1973	16,065,434	11,326,691	139,634	11,466,325	933,948	-29,219	10,503,158	3,990,093	1,572,183	6,168	2,604,637	1,304,027
1974	18,109,416	12,365,697	201,117	12,566,814	1,064,125	-29,226	11,473,463	4,697,119	1,938,834	6,595	2,745,960	1,330,500
1975	19,421,822	12,579,507	226,346	12,805,853	1,059,036	-29,180	11,717,637	5,107,965	2,596,220	6,845	2,837,578	1,275,484
1976	21,171,455	13,680,499	233,926	13,914,425	1,168,205	-26,213	12,720,007	5,586,433	2,865,015	7,341	2,884,080	1,292,596
1977	23,699,865	15,373,859	208,539	15,582,398	1,322,007	-32,310	14,228,081	6,362,645	3,109,139	8,068	2,937,632	1,367,587
1978	27,264,542	17,882,167	195,555	18,077,722	1,585,493	-48,109	16,444,120	7,376,673	3,443,749	9,079	3,002,966	1,485,993
1979	31,540,463	20,620,971	210,600	20,831,571	1,919,378	-69,043	18,843,150	8,743,580	3,953,733	10,103	3,121,950	1,567,870
1980	37,310,762	23,914,041	291,109	24,205,150	2,247,862	-92,270	21,865,018	10,783,689	4,662,055	11,463	3,254,936	1,663,461
1981	43,235,051	26,903,058	323,739	27,226,797	2,720,704	-39,422	24,466,671	13,376,164	5,392,216	12,768	3,386,317	1,715,798
1982	45,998,854	28,320,823	422,817	28,743,640	2,943,142	-48,518	25,751,980	14,214,845	6,032,029	13,334	3,449,745	1,720,145
1983	50,365,902	31,038,118	715,874	31,753,992	3,233,549	-70,133	28,450,310	15,363,230	6,552,362	14,363	3,506,541	1,771,008
1984	55,446,687	34,386,680	450,907	34,837,587	3,677,992	-90,906	31,068,689	17,360,109	7,017,889	15,574	3,560,292	1,862,036
1985	60,214,771	37,502,274	454,282	37,956,556	4,075,773	-111,884	33,768,899	18,982,197	7,463,675	16,575	3,632,834	1,921,376
1986	64,542,786	40,538,030	537,808	41,075,838	4,520,079	-120,123	36,435,636	20,138,309	7,968,841	17,400	3,709,283	1,976,279
1987	69,501,409	44,844,978	590,313	45,435,291	4,932,983	-140,525	40,361,783	20,761,462	8,378,164	18,304	3,797,118	1,983,981
1988	76,235,138	49,129,398	621,712	49,751,110	5,554,394	-157,717	44,038,999	23,107,931	9,088,208	19,589	3,891,758	2,077,107
1989	84,488,304	51,724,493	555,191	52,279,684	5,905,326	-157,569	46,216,789	28,038,826	10,232,689	21,207	3,984,047	2,124,442
1990	90,442,645	54,865,738	431,771	55,297,509	6,200,007	-183,751	48,913,751	30,387,124	11,141,770	22,175	4,078,578	2,151,815
1991	94,609,609	56,931,782	512,637	57,444,419	6,462,509	-177,290	50,804,620	31,206,884	12,598,105	22,652	4,176,731	2,129,237
1992	99,448,500	60,974,711	600,067	61,574,778	6,856,548	-166,722	54,551,508	30,305,110	14,591,882	23,328	4,262,995	2,133,944
1993	105,518,862	65,856,904	661,304	66,518,208	7,360,272	-169,949	58,987,987	31,070,013	15,460,862	24,312	4,340,175	2,221,343
1994	110,498,396	69,319,487	484,294	69,803,781	7,836,300	-175,188	61,792,293	32,340,834	16,365,269	24,858	4,445,162	2,289,282
1995	118,666,281	73,641,770	516,285	74,158,055	8,275,297	-174,552	65,708,206	35,207,050	17,751,025	26,097	4,547,191	2,367,458
1996	126,153,127	78,465,201	417,206	78,882,407	8,695,324	-179,933	70,007,150	37,340,619	18,805,358	27,116	4,652,414	2,423,829
1997	132,797,064	82,220,890	450,641	82,671,531	9,113,267	-167,907	73,390,357	40,103,287	19,303,420	27,956	4,750,249	2,495,838
1998	143,482,413	89,430,354	548,389	89,978,743	9,749,850	-173,540	80,055,353	43,776,689	19,650,371	29,664	4,836,853	2,580,377
1999	149,622,286	95,628,247	630,980	96,259,227	10,377,349	-177,720	85,704,158	43,555,933	20,362,195	30,337	4,932,004	2,668,615
2000	162,787,705	104,880,353	574,363	105,454,716	11,201,074	-196,716	94,056,926	47,063,750	21,667,029	32,390	5,025,895	2,759,068
2001	171,606,065	112,291,613	629,770	112,921,383	12,206,605	-427,793	100,286,985	47,844,234	23,474,846	33,577	5,110,780	2,854,679
2002	176,751,226	117,327,533	617,713	117,945,246	12,685,793	-641,160	104,618,293	47,042,009	25,090,924	34,009	5,197,205	2,884,752
2003	182,627,477	122,085,773	549,922	122,635,695	13,165,743	-857,055	108,612,897	47,281,048	26,733,532	34,709	5,261,713	2,947,089
2004	197,437,158	131,283,048	521,933	131,804,981	14,136,554	-1,037,565	116,630,862	52,265,730	28,540,566	36,998	5,336,368	3,033,206
2005	214,685,638	141,946,826	594,369	142,541,195	15,397,519	-1,490,659	125,653,017	58,466,055	30,566,566	39,675	5,411,148	3,153,336
2006	232,059,032	150,322,634	593,433	150,916,067	16,490,229	-1,721,016	132,704,822	67,521,443	31,832,767	42,738	5,429,748	3,234,619
2007	241,589,209	152,652,292	560,854	153,213,146	17,012,044	-1,758,407	134,442,695	73,913,899	33,232,615	44,549	5,422,987	3,292,482
2008	239,830,603	146,377,595	504,242	146,881,837	16,905,368	-1,863,718	128,112,751	74,208,647	37,509,205	43,968	5,454,633	3,238,713
2009	221,175,723	135,589,376	550,900	136,140,276	16,209,876	-1,692,228	118,238,172	62,273,881	40,663,670	40,180	5,504,624	3,113,069
2010	240,570,248	145,429,505	552,413	145,981,918	16,565,731	-1,214,569	128,201,618	68,089,451	44,279,179	43,094	5,582,496	3,125,041
2011	252,533,684	150,585,569	456,949	151,042,518	15,282,507	-1,410,007	134,350,004	72,522,584	45,661,096	44,589	5,663,565	3,232,132
2012	263,674,223	153,881,026	529,461	154,410,487	15,842,667	-2,012,161	136,555,659	82,626,868	44,491,696	45,960	5,737,057	3,317,135
2013	261,258,507	159,870,619	621,487	160,492,106	18,588,583	-2,233,121	139,670,402	76,097,375	45,490,730	44,967	5,809,981	3,435,057
2014	281,171,012	171,453,689	537,436	171,991,125	19,700,148	-2,285,913	150,005,064	83,706,049	47,459,899	47,844	5,876,841	3,586,431
2015	301,933,983	181,889,249	731,976	182,621,225	20,756,288	-2,431,437	159,433,500	92,926,197	49,574,286	50,764	5,947,797	3,752,370
2016	308,009,959	189,967,281	657,113	190,624,394	21,487,240	-3,117,265	166,019,889	90,988,838	51,001,232	51,091	6,028,626	3,836,806
2017	336,146,426	202,668,598	668,126	203,336,724	22,647,794	-3,182,383	177,506,547	105,999,452	52,640,427	55,246	6,084,581	3,948,385
2018	361,398,797	214,840,354	536,718	215,377,072	24,099,771	-3,473,473	187,803,828	118,637,754	54,957,215	59,197	6,105,049	4,108,900
2019	382,311,129	224,854,581	596,251	225,450,832	25,566,648	-3,777,433	196,106,751	127,966,760	58,237,618	62,417	6,125,139	4,152,255
2020	398,325,578	223,769,286	594,995	224,364,281	25,888,757	-3,842,308	194,633,216	129,256,773	74,435,589	64,949	6,132,940	4,140,444
2021	454,919,916	255,365,335	591,998	255,957,333	28,477,226	-5,111,797	222,368,310	147,007,614	85,543,992	74,463	6,109,373	4,392,117
2022	477,224,463	280,030,366	553,224	280,583,590	31,864,255	-6,762,013	241,957,322	158,815,366	76,451,775	77,732	6,139,340	4,649,526

Personal Income and Employment by Area: Michigan City-La Porte, IN

(Thousands of dollars, except as noted.)

Year	Personal income, total	Derivation of personal income: Earnings by place of work: Nonfarm	Farm	Total	Less: Contributions for government social insurance	Plus: Adjustment for residence	Equals: Net earnings by place of residence	Plus: Dividends, interest, and rent	Plus: Personal current transfer receipts	Per capita personal income (dollars)	Population (persons)	Total employment
1970	405,753	319,798	5,729	325,527	22,456	20,794	323,865	52,362	29,526	3,847	105,461	45,672
1971	430,233	326,695	10,528	337,223	23,782	24,105	337,546	57,107	35,580	4,047	106,310	44,103
1972	472,811	362,812	7,144	369,956	27,838	31,250	373,368	61,092	38,351	4,429	106,744	45,366
1973	539,615	403,999	16,325	420,324	35,558	40,068	424,834	70,270	44,511	5,037	107,134	47,958
1974	588,706	436,701	8,392	445,093	40,261	50,675	455,507	81,867	51,332	5,493	107,180	48,730
1975	640,124	444,936	17,067	462,003	40,208	59,369	481,164	91,172	67,788	5,963	107,353	46,388
1976	706,083	493,075	16,159	509,234	45,038	71,727	535,923	98,545	71,615	6,562	107,604	47,203
1977	783,754	551,728	8,926	560,654	50,054	88,834	599,434	110,281	74,039	7,224	108,496	48,332
1978	889,401	624,138	13,976	638,114	58,176	106,904	686,842	121,496	81,063	8,174	108,807	50,502
1979	980,689	678,623	9,852	688,475	65,577	128,351	751,249	135,847	93,593	8,985	109,142	50,703
1980	1,062,854	718,909	4,803	723,712	69,332	126,985	781,365	166,784	114,705	9,782	108,657	49,332
1981	1,153,295	751,346	5,889	757,235	77,837	135,856	815,254	203,993	134,048	10,628	108,515	48,011
1982	1,165,358	748,457	886	749,343	79,295	125,490	795,538	216,469	153,351	10,776	108,140	46,152
1983	1,181,509	766,599	-8,369	758,230	81,529	108,903	785,604	226,401	169,504	11,018	107,230	45,219
1984	1,276,027	820,235	10,149	830,384	89,348	111,613	852,649	251,421	171,957	11,928	106,976	46,096
1985	1,334,552	870,773	8,641	879,414	96,368	111,823	894,869	260,553	179,130	12,510	106,680	47,280
1986	1,388,251	917,291	7,760	925,051	102,005	103,385	926,431	269,651	192,169	13,134	105,696	48,106
1987	1,462,539	981,898	14,118	996,016	107,304	108,724	997,436	267,914	197,189	13,823	105,806	49,835
1988	1,564,484	1,074,771	4,993	1,079,764	123,643	113,211	1,069,332	289,872	205,280	14,768	105,941	51,945
1989	1,705,269	1,139,715	22,362	1,162,077	131,127	119,488	1,150,438	333,449	221,382	16,012	106,502	53,294
1990	1,778,428	1,193,902	20,991	1,214,893	139,609	119,409	1,194,693	345,227	238,508	16,581	107,257	53,683
1991	1,818,156	1,236,959	2,954	1,239,913	146,180	118,611	1,212,344	347,170	258,642	16,811	108,151	53,728
1992	1,956,071	1,319,951	19,383	1,339,334	154,983	126,091	1,310,442	348,895	296,734	17,957	108,928	53,920
1993	2,028,405	1,374,752	14,238	1,388,990	162,404	128,006	1,354,592	358,009	315,804	18,531	109,461	54,837
1994	2,132,943	1,446,160	19,164	1,465,324	172,869	142,006	1,434,461	373,466	325,016	19,458	109,620	55,637
1995	2,225,093	1,493,922	13,892	1,507,814	179,301	144,695	1,473,208	421,014	330,871	20,307	109,571	57,043
1996	2,327,193	1,532,927	22,259	1,555,186	182,094	154,641	1,527,733	448,289	351,171	21,198	109,783	56,722
1997	2,465,392	1,632,939	23,965	1,656,904	192,651	154,283	1,618,536	485,347	361,509	22,459	109,774	57,371
1998	2,591,524	1,740,085	18,884	1,758,969	200,631	164,043	1,722,381	498,480	370,663	23,569	109,954	58,248
1999	2,617,574	1,789,742	9,345	1,799,087	206,167	163,766	1,756,686	476,515	384,373	23,790	110,028	58,957
2000	2,772,164	1,896,580	13,320	1,909,900	216,581	156,338	1,849,657	516,620	405,887	25,174	110,121	59,904
2001	2,842,732	1,921,488	19,422	1,940,910	220,586	171,118	1,891,442	506,684	444,606	25,825	110,077	58,597
2002	2,886,660	1,947,472	10,653	1,958,125	225,364	191,571	1,924,332	490,358	471,970	26,349	109,555	57,873
2003	2,968,025	1,945,473	23,002	1,968,475	226,940	225,802	1,967,337	510,332	490,356	27,223	109,027	56,936
2004	3,033,914	2,010,229	41,129	2,051,358	236,104	225,436	2,040,690	475,172	518,052	27,856	108,914	56,940
2005	3,140,806	2,083,681	22,117	2,105,798	248,550	260,518	2,117,766	460,239	562,801	28,672	109,541	57,596
2006	3,305,548	2,149,482	25,759	2,175,241	256,478	296,171	2,214,934	488,881	601,733	30,149	109,641	57,499
2007	3,452,769	2,218,438	26,060	2,244,498	266,812	316,575	2,294,261	527,319	631,189	31,149	110,846	57,995
2008	3,649,785	2,247,270	30,643	2,277,913	272,192	340,268	2,345,989	582,069	721,727	32,802	111,267	57,095
2009	3,454,449	2,133,529	15,076	2,148,605	260,421	242,039	2,130,223	520,998	803,228	30,991	111,465	54,442
2010	3,572,824	2,161,725	32,698	2,194,423	260,177	294,357	2,228,603	488,167	856,054	32,037	111,523	53,241
2011	3,799,757	2,239,394	50,965	2,290,359	239,064	347,560	2,398,855	553,445	847,457	34,033	111,650	53,919
2012	3,993,382	2,305,120	54,660	2,359,780	243,383	383,838	2,500,235	621,128	872,019	35,686	111,902	53,671
2013	4,028,068	2,324,137	120,604	2,444,741	279,392	389,094	2,554,443	589,443	884,182	35,871	112,292	53,437
2014	4,110,092	2,390,010	72,729	2,462,739	286,425	379,320	2,555,634	612,735	941,723	36,412	112,877	53,506
2015	4,174,462	2,396,633	26,699	2,423,332	288,776	444,196	2,578,752	621,503	974,207	37,193	112,237	53,301
2016	4,292,650	2,423,504	40,029	2,463,533	290,850	476,369	2,649,052	643,394	1,000,204	38,349	111,937	53,133
2017	4,424,111	2,473,359	29,659	2,503,018	299,175	512,617	2,716,460	677,374	1,030,277	39,566	111,815	53,194
2018	4,611,182	2,572,841	24,902	2,597,743	311,935	522,624	2,808,432	727,454	1,075,296	41,080	112,250	53,329
2019	4,707,917	2,562,449	22,064	2,584,513	319,215	588,597	2,853,895	700,527	1,153,495	41,880	112,414	53,240
2020	5,050,741	2,597,815	50,153	2,647,968	331,980	525,779	2,841,767	723,767	1,485,207	44,985	112,276	51,421
2021	5,528,009	2,807,423	69,317	2,876,740	354,148	570,349	3,092,941	758,170	1,676,898	49,144	112,486	52,792
2022	5,582,895	2,928,199	63,782	2,991,981	374,692	670,563	3,287,852	812,727	1,482,316	49,992	111,675	54,682

Personal Income and Employment by Area: Midland, MI

(Thousands of dollars, except as noted.)

Year	Personal income, total	Derivation of personal income: Earnings by place of work: Nonfarm	Farm	Total	Less: Contributions for government social insurance	Plus: Adjustment for residence	Equals: Net earnings by place of residence	Plus: Dividends, interest, and rent	Plus: Personal current transfer receipts	Per capita personal income (dollars)	Population (persons)	Total employment
1970	277,325	285,670	1,613	287,283	20,219	-51,018	216,046	46,103	15,176	4,336	63,956	28,920
1971	299,208	301,232	1,394	302,626	22,121	-49,458	231,047	48,866	19,295	4,600	65,050	27,915
1972	321,559	317,665	2,621	320,286	24,578	-48,235	247,473	52,486	21,600	4,925	65,286	27,970
1973	352,547	350,732	3,187	353,919	31,828	-50,754	271,337	56,352	24,858	5,310	66,390	29,341
1974	410,969	406,363	7,733	414,096	38,416	-61,308	314,372	62,574	34,023	6,119	67,168	28,737
1975	449,291	438,157	4,214	442,371	40,362	-64,940	337,069	70,659	41,563	6,547	68,626	30,639
1976	511,778	508,866	2,797	511,663	47,602	-73,031	391,030	77,753	42,995	7,382	69,324	32,404
1977	594,681	603,469	4,500	607,969	56,695	-89,582	461,692	87,179	45,810	8,389	70,888	35,226
1978	663,859	672,619	3,989	676,608	64,444	-92,878	519,286	95,591	48,982	9,233	71,900	35,972
1979	730,843	738,168	3,508	741,676	74,550	-99,421	567,705	108,133	55,005	9,990	73,158	36,279
1980	773,731	735,259	2,014	737,273	73,494	-89,820	573,959	127,105	72,667	10,473	73,882	34,846
1981	852,902	791,988	2,026	794,014	85,842	-91,281	616,891	158,953	77,058	11,382	74,936	34,356
1982	902,591	823,353	1,165	824,518	92,225	-99,958	632,335	183,297	86,959	12,069	74,784	33,960
1983	953,142	841,331	-235	841,096	94,247	-89,066	657,783	200,605	94,754	12,675	75,198	33,798
1984	1,019,195	851,133	2,194	853,327	96,306	-62,394	694,627	221,964	102,604	13,440	75,835	33,330
1985	1,090,883	881,598	2,030	883,628	100,225	-41,815	741,588	241,506	107,789	15,048	72,492	33,734
1986	1,172,967	959,534	1,050	960,584	108,944	-43,366	808,274	248,886	115,807	16,157	72,598	34,691
1987	1,263,395	1,036,999	2,758	1,039,757	115,912	-47,231	876,614	265,329	121,452	17,294	73,054	36,329
1988	1,398,622	1,154,807	4,046	1,158,853	132,013	-48,428	978,412	293,616	126,594	18,884	74,065	37,224
1989	1,549,762	1,231,158	7,238	1,238,396	141,271	-52,154	1,044,971	364,260	140,531	20,728	74,767	39,737
1990	1,644,755	1,306,722	2,919	1,309,641	153,520	-48,783	1,107,338	383,260	154,157	21,641	76,002	41,424
1991	1,700,165	1,330,532	2,997	1,333,529	157,915	-28,573	1,147,041	381,449	171,675	22,157	76,733	41,784
1992	1,824,693	1,469,540	3,582	1,473,122	173,186	-49,563	1,250,373	390,018	184,302	23,438	77,853	43,653
1993	1,910,549	1,505,679	4,413	1,510,092	178,711	-25,394	1,305,987	402,342	202,220	24,303	78,614	43,354
1994	1,991,907	1,525,778	1,693	1,527,471	185,902	-4,758	1,336,811	448,189	206,907	25,102	79,352	43,013
1995	2,108,942	1,629,057	2,723	1,631,780	197,828	-12,731	1,421,221	471,729	215,992	26,414	79,841	43,166
1996	2,246,968	1,736,784	1,452	1,738,236	206,769	10,999	1,542,466	481,654	222,848	27,776	80,897	44,035
1997	2,298,127	1,798,138	1,115	1,799,253	212,924	-6,371	1,579,958	471,830	246,339	28,147	81,648	44,500
1998	2,474,516	1,879,423	859	1,880,282	219,695	31,880	1,692,467	530,538	251,511	30,147	82,081	44,439
1999	2,509,561	1,904,508	2,739	1,907,247	222,736	43,789	1,728,300	506,192	275,069	30,382	82,599	45,798
2000	2,629,591	2,088,256	2,099	2,090,355	244,437	-31,238	1,814,680	520,332	294,579	31,715	82,913	47,165
2001	2,796,146	2,236,470	1,332	2,237,802	233,432	-46,886	1,957,484	510,241	328,421	33,456	83,576	45,811
2002	2,785,943	2,190,215	1,639	2,191,854	230,962	-17,555	1,943,337	497,683	344,923	33,299	83,664	45,387
2003	2,892,262	2,269,881	1,391	2,271,272	235,583	-6,377	2,029,312	501,152	361,798	34,427	84,012	44,687
2004	3,121,270	2,433,428	4,465	2,437,893	258,130	-48,257	2,131,506	608,388	381,376	37,132	84,058	44,371
2005	3,103,528	2,376,138	5,552	2,381,690	257,953	6,734	2,130,471	563,014	410,043	36,978	83,930	44,862
2006	3,230,104	2,425,826	2,930	2,428,756	270,214	21,168	2,179,710	616,348	434,046	38,595	83,693	45,446
2007	3,329,444	2,490,872	5,395	2,496,267	282,575	21,848	2,235,540	616,493	477,411	39,826	83,600	46,417
2008	3,618,382	2,668,666	9,319	2,677,985	302,524	-16,912	2,358,549	714,548	545,285	43,279	83,605	46,547
2009	3,514,866	2,577,061	2,673	2,579,734	295,269	55,316	2,339,781	584,842	590,243	42,024	83,639	45,168
2010	3,592,356	2,698,126	6,734	2,704,860	299,396	14,091	2,419,555	541,337	631,464	42,939	83,661	45,044
2011	3,837,110	2,826,153	18,655	2,844,808	278,178	42,527	2,609,157	596,614	631,339	45,772	83,831	45,974
2012	3,916,181	2,792,947	13,756	2,806,703	276,594	68,441	2,598,550	683,206	634,425	46,758	83,754	45,865
2013	3,860,843	2,773,881	15,978	2,789,859	318,445	65,293	2,536,707	675,402	648,734	46,128	83,699	46,558
2014	4,097,372	2,891,314	7,456	2,898,770	341,084	98,139	2,655,825	760,661	680,886	49,037	83,556	47,547
2015	3,465,465	2,191,003	3,698	2,194,701	341,483	76,786	1,930,004	812,805	722,656	41,387	83,733	47,789
2016	4,256,621	2,946,994	1,617	2,948,611	341,332	61,766	2,669,045	841,872	745,704	50,967	83,517	47,565
2017	4,775,896	3,401,110	1,840	3,402,950	373,095	104,856	3,134,711	885,682	755,503	57,210	83,480	47,231
2018	4,424,672	3,289,450	1,745	3,291,195	379,202	-147,017	2,764,976	868,989	790,707	52,997	83,489	47,764
2019	4,516,065	3,287,413	446	3,287,859	382,416	-171,401	2,734,042	943,572	838,451	54,111	83,460	47,691
2020	4,724,096	3,190,311	8,025	3,198,336	371,208	-154,282	2,672,846	914,953	1,136,297	56,589	83,481	45,714
2021	5,018,053	3,371,208	8,491	3,379,699	390,070	-135,779	2,853,850	954,994	1,209,209	60,150	83,426	47,877
2022	5,090,894	3,527,704	7,787	3,535,491	419,373	-85,182	3,030,936	1,037,230	1,022,728	60,842	83,674	49,292

Personal Income and Employment by Area: Midland, TX

(Thousands of dollars, except as noted.)

		Derivation of personal income										
		Earnings by place of work										
Year	Personal income, total	Nonfarm	Farm	Total	Less: Contributions for government social insurance	Plus: Adjustment for residence	Equals: Net earnings by place of residence	Plus: Dividends, interest, and rent	Plus: Personal current transfer receipts	Per capita personal income (dollars)	Population (persons)	Total employment
1970	328,929	277,558	8,502	286,060	16,115	-7,782	262,163	53,050	13,716	4,679	70,297	34,454
1971	355,615	301,824	7,968	309,792	17,843	-8,549	283,400	56,237	15,978	4,987	71,302	35,324
1972	384,016	326,266	7,542	333,808	19,843	-8,860	305,105	60,738	18,173	5,373	71,477	35,958
1973	437,833	360,467	20,683	381,150	25,760	-10,138	345,252	70,440	22,141	6,144	71,259	37,635
1974	491,237	417,190	2,960	420,150	30,516	-11,597	378,037	86,365	26,835	6,701	73,313	39,497
1975	595,384	522,571	-1,933	520,638	37,720	-17,134	465,784	97,785	31,815	7,872	75,637	43,247
1976	688,235	593,053	13,799	606,852	42,464	-18,467	545,921	106,781	35,533	8,830	77,943	43,997
1977	776,522	677,281	17,684	694,965	50,590	-25,750	618,625	120,021	37,876	9,803	79,216	48,808
1978	928,623	828,981	7,603	836,584	62,781	-34,602	739,201	146,086	43,336	11,474	80,934	52,831
1979	1,084,263	941,549	32,756	974,305	74,353	-39,898	860,054	174,695	49,514	12,978	83,546	54,875
1980	1,287,089	1,177,604	-11,224	1,166,380	96,272	-59,704	1,010,404	219,042	57,643	14,511	88,700	61,483
1981	1,654,524	1,453,620	33,403	1,487,023	131,837	-69,448	1,285,738	304,196	64,590	17,608	93,964	71,676
1982	1,867,022	1,634,787	21,385	1,656,172	157,802	-75,718	1,422,652	370,357	74,013	17,959	103,959	77,759
1983	1,813,057	1,526,316	3,763	1,530,079	148,806	-64,716	1,316,557	403,620	92,880	16,160	112,195	73,906
1984	1,888,394	1,562,175	-6,629	1,555,546	157,124	-57,698	1,340,724	446,568	101,102	16,873	111,919	74,561
1985	2,052,833	1,660,032	1,141	1,661,173	171,287	-54,549	1,435,337	506,572	110,924	18,008	113,997	76,826
1986	1,963,879	1,537,951	6,383	1,544,334	154,851	-49,153	1,340,330	491,047	132,502	16,747	117,265	68,942
1987	1,897,569	1,456,826	30,395	1,487,221	145,530	-37,450	1,304,241	454,416	138,912	16,899	112,287	69,786
1988	2,096,719	1,600,115	26,466	1,626,581	164,594	-37,719	1,424,268	527,207	145,244	18,815	111,439	71,380
1989	2,211,497	1,667,737	4,013	1,671,750	167,598	-27,531	1,476,621	571,455	163,421	19,835	111,494	68,991
1990	2,416,843	1,732,693	20,527	1,753,220	170,704	-18,709	1,563,807	673,181	179,855	21,652	111,624	68,901
1991	2,409,691	1,704,105	2,682	1,706,787	178,546	-15,811	1,512,430	692,860	204,401	21,244	113,427	70,299
1992	2,581,027	1,824,349	20,668	1,845,017	185,283	-14,069	1,645,665	688,388	246,974	22,380	115,325	68,743
1993	2,750,316	1,951,608	28,854	1,980,462	195,575	-9,093	1,775,794	708,698	265,824	23,617	116,456	71,541
1994	2,810,328	1,942,231	11,153	1,953,384	195,530	4	1,757,858	760,569	291,901	23,871	117,728	72,932
1995	2,881,618	2,043,332	8,911	2,052,243	202,016	3,397	1,853,624	713,458	314,536	24,319	118,493	73,505
1996	3,133,648	2,253,914	170	2,254,084	212,205	5,456	2,047,335	748,517	337,796	26,291	119,192	74,051
1997	3,566,350	2,641,052	21,220	2,662,272	237,930	1,291	2,425,633	787,386	353,331	29,307	121,691	78,960
1998	3,643,494	2,679,311	-6,554	2,672,757	238,763	15,913	2,449,907	836,875	356,712	29,575	123,197	79,647
1999	3,537,890	2,493,359	19,973	2,513,332	223,788	17,602	2,307,146	859,178	371,566	28,895	122,440	76,928
2000	3,907,857	2,719,902	-1,135	2,718,767	237,610	30,912	2,512,069	1,004,480	391,308	32,490	120,280	77,716
2001	5,867,314	4,749,730	5,752	4,755,482	326,231	23,940	4,453,191	994,707	419,416	48,540	120,877	78,340
2002	5,908,182	4,833,871	593	4,834,464	329,100	29,684	4,535,048	914,752	458,382	48,281	122,371	78,440
2003	6,497,194	5,301,142	34,926	5,336,068	357,435	24,885	5,003,518	1,008,265	485,411	52,517	123,717	81,467
2004	6,731,586	5,445,911	23,788	5,469,699	381,150	19,933	5,108,482	1,112,260	510,844	53,791	125,144	82,559
2005	7,695,970	6,214,469	34,166	6,248,635	435,305	-17,918	5,795,412	1,353,120	547,438	60,616	126,963	86,941
2006	8,367,765	6,679,173	13,318	6,692,491	474,182	-24,146	6,194,163	1,588,168	585,434	64,226	130,287	92,734
2007	8,193,535	6,332,991	45,437	6,378,428	505,180	11,457	5,884,705	1,649,831	658,999	61,399	133,448	97,252
2008	12,012,456	9,862,553	-24,563	9,837,990	652,172	-45,946	9,139,872	2,149,663	722,921	87,644	137,060	105,811
2009	8,857,605	6,979,613	7,841	6,987,454	559,456	-12,215	6,415,783	1,672,186	769,636	62,843	140,948	102,537
2010	10,515,954	8,522,207	40,577	8,562,784	637,127	-118,442	7,807,215	1,869,884	838,855	74,245	141,639	108,115
2011	14,462,235	12,401,840	4,220	12,406,060	708,500	-175,682	11,521,878	2,089,715	850,642	100,205	144,327	113,600
2012	16,493,406	14,113,579	472	14,114,051	806,976	-348,819	12,958,256	2,699,763	835,387	109,357	150,822	126,593
2013	17,748,417	15,747,923	39,303	15,787,226	1,001,219	-470,494	14,315,513	2,582,080	850,824	114,219	155,389	134,099
2014	19,246,368	17,185,002	-2,089	17,182,913	1,131,390	-699,402	15,352,121	3,011,442	882,805	120,911	159,178	142,639
2015	14,762,473	12,646,184	-2,906	12,643,278	1,001,505	-586,832	11,054,941	2,777,670	929,862	89,944	164,130	143,409
2016	12,416,932	10,197,054	-3,482	10,193,572	898,351	-494,139	8,801,082	2,636,119	979,731	75,304	164,890	141,981
2017	18,047,078	15,532,308	17,351	15,549,659	1,150,669	-696,823	13,702,167	3,348,651	996,260	109,043	165,504	147,259
2018	22,420,528	19,940,921	28,793	19,969,714	1,419,583	-1,027,183	17,522,948	3,878,316	1,019,264	130,526	171,770	159,247
2019	23,522,564	21,243,464	-7,675	21,235,789	1,522,912	-1,158,026	18,554,851	3,903,748	1,063,965	134,550	174,824	160,957
2020	18,651,780	15,017,350	10,637	15,027,987	1,222,226	-829,931	12,975,830	4,088,385	1,587,565	106,217	175,600	145,803
2021	21,448,241	16,735,017	12,961	16,747,978	1,230,128	-999,812	14,518,038	5,105,424	1,824,779	123,682	173,414	153,396
2022	25,470,876	20,938,417	-8,674	20,929,743	1,512,776	-1,098,091	18,318,876	5,683,653	1,468,347	143,728	177,216	167,939

Personal Income and Employment by Area: Milwaukee-Waukesha, WI

(Thousands of dollars, except as noted.)

		Derivation of personal income										
		Earnings by place of work										
Year	Personal income, total	Nonfarm	Farm	Total	Less: Contributions for government social insurance	Plus: Adjustment for residence	Equals: Net earnings by place of residence	Plus: Dividends, interest, and rent	Plus: Personal current transfer receipts	Per capita personal income (dollars)	Population (persons)	Total employment
1970	6,418,920	5,365,616	22,593	5,388,209	393,284	-108,182	4,886,743	995,361	536,816	4,570	1,404,488	659,946
1971	6,824,581	5,640,215	26,072	5,666,287	428,350	-119,326	5,118,611	1,071,160	634,810	4,857	1,405,231	655,077
1972	7,440,734	6,206,286	23,554	6,229,840	499,766	-138,434	5,591,640	1,143,239	705,855	5,255	1,416,024	671,565
1973	8,211,703	6,947,193	28,048	6,975,241	648,379	-162,233	6,164,629	1,256,193	790,881	5,827	1,409,344	707,070
1974	9,017,395	7,565,349	23,235	7,588,584	731,201	-187,190	6,670,193	1,432,008	915,194	6,398	1,409,473	721,019
1975	9,729,832	7,980,681	29,193	8,009,874	752,534	-201,553	7,055,787	1,540,515	1,133,530	6,974	1,395,236	705,141
1976	10,579,079	8,789,971	27,862	8,817,833	844,519	-233,015	7,740,299	1,628,018	1,210,762	7,558	1,399,726	718,806
1977	11,669,454	9,793,781	40,202	9,833,983	940,487	-273,294	8,620,202	1,770,268	1,278,984	8,371	1,394,089	744,641
1978	12,981,107	10,993,424	39,093	11,032,517	1,087,913	-319,901	9,624,703	1,933,345	1,423,059	9,344	1,389,196	773,376
1979	14,416,821	12,205,380	47,736	12,253,116	1,256,825	-375,138	10,621,153	2,179,427	1,616,241	10,333	1,395,212	794,684
1980	15,866,684	12,943,741	52,592	12,996,333	1,324,228	-414,992	11,257,113	2,655,793	1,953,778	11,360	1,396,659	783,371
1981	17,366,511	13,753,251	46,335	13,799,586	1,504,611	-441,360	11,853,615	3,263,145	2,249,751	12,479	1,391,672	769,054
1982	18,358,185	14,150,386	39,592	14,189,978	1,561,049	-441,702	12,187,227	3,637,037	2,533,921	13,192	1,391,628	746,855
1983	19,058,341	14,536,177	21,344	14,557,521	1,603,592	-437,376	12,516,553	3,807,400	2,734,388	13,738	1,387,307	735,233
1984	20,846,197	16,058,439	30,560	16,088,999	1,816,823	-480,804	13,791,372	4,280,365	2,774,460	15,053	1,384,897	771,524
1985	21,953,796	16,913,597	34,538	16,948,135	1,928,278	-502,368	14,517,489	4,503,522	2,932,785	15,801	1,389,361	782,599
1986	23,046,728	17,833,942	38,849	17,872,791	2,031,939	-524,424	15,316,428	4,666,965	3,063,335	16,564	1,391,362	794,602
1987	24,267,300	19,082,113	40,547	19,122,660	2,134,088	-545,886	16,442,686	4,691,782	3,132,832	17,357	1,398,088	815,518
1988	26,314,025	20,805,707	28,981	20,834,688	2,401,141	-585,526	17,848,021	5,204,708	3,261,296	18,668	1,409,602	847,896
1989	28,469,319	22,180,765	54,825	22,235,590	2,557,497	-617,951	19,060,142	5,916,521	3,492,656	20,026	1,421,621	867,258
1990	30,021,572	23,538,894	38,823	23,577,717	2,830,199	-638,247	20,109,271	6,170,632	3,741,669	20,917	1,435,303	881,288
1991	31,050,043	24,344,100	35,545	24,379,645	2,955,609	-672,422	20,751,614	6,245,162	4,053,267	21,417	1,449,760	874,176
1992	33,173,950	26,240,001	47,706	26,287,707	3,155,661	-765,859	22,366,187	6,408,696	4,399,067	22,680	1,462,728	882,783
1993	34,761,203	27,630,930	37,627	27,668,557	3,318,792	-851,404	23,498,361	6,656,481	4,606,361	23,635	1,470,728	893,226
1994	36,609,814	29,114,093	38,932	29,153,025	3,551,456	-951,836	24,649,733	7,175,367	4,784,714	24,799	1,476,272	915,146
1995	38,474,898	30,465,172	30,041	30,495,213	3,723,666	-1,047,814	25,723,733	7,716,311	5,034,854	25,973	1,481,347	932,863
1996	40,420,714	31,983,353	36,415	32,019,768	3,875,309	-1,127,016	27,017,443	8,261,379	5,141,892	27,200	1,486,045	942,951
1997	42,896,734	34,110,390	26,294	34,136,684	4,114,381	-1,253,473	28,768,830	8,818,499	5,309,405	28,839	1,487,435	959,068
1998	45,910,927	36,523,291	34,555	36,557,846	4,363,496	-1,362,762	30,831,588	9,645,321	5,434,018	30,794	1,490,926	978,150
1999	47,636,434	38,551,066	35,752	38,586,818	4,618,169	-1,376,654	32,591,995	9,373,256	5,671,183	31,837	1,496,255	989,784
2000	50,496,774	40,621,551	30,404	40,651,955	4,803,281	-1,558,219	34,290,455	10,139,143	6,067,176	33,610	1,502,420	1,004,465
2001	53,263,716	43,113,840	42,544	43,156,384	4,923,487	-1,737,109	36,495,788	9,975,619	6,792,309	35,338	1,507,257	1,007,270
2002	53,958,041	43,973,505	43,783	44,017,288	5,019,238	-1,847,503	37,150,547	9,548,796	7,258,698	35,633	1,514,251	993,684
2003	54,610,833	44,759,421	61,459	44,820,880	5,135,011	-1,970,269	37,715,600	9,470,675	7,424,558	35,934	1,519,746	991,383
2004	56,754,503	46,657,313	66,699	46,724,012	5,366,158	-1,994,135	39,363,719	9,840,843	7,549,941	37,282	1,522,302	1,000,346
2005	58,760,515	48,123,629	51,351	48,174,980	5,557,601	-2,158,533	40,458,846	10,300,492	8,001,177	38,598	1,522,391	1,008,174
2006	63,104,391	51,057,179	47,340	51,104,519	5,864,033	-2,371,726	42,868,760	11,859,209	8,376,422	41,410	1,523,907	1,019,498
2007	65,491,950	52,661,846	57,899	52,719,745	6,051,683	-2,508,646	44,159,416	12,353,310	8,979,224	42,791	1,530,492	1,032,274
2008	67,623,107	53,829,025	53,122	53,882,147	6,239,384	-2,629,117	45,013,646	12,678,368	9,931,093	43,962	1,538,232	1,031,655
2009	66,533,401	51,989,372	43,712	52,033,084	6,016,417	-2,422,053	43,594,614	11,251,857	11,686,930	42,935	1,549,613	990,272
2010	67,942,335	52,645,846	59,617	52,705,463	6,115,797	-2,299,921	44,289,745	11,081,202	12,571,388	43,647	1,556,625	981,202
2011	71,552,574	55,081,124	78,562	55,159,686	5,718,893	-2,447,001	46,993,792	12,535,897	12,022,885	45,838	1,561,000	994,366
2012	74,627,315	56,642,626	77,505	56,720,131	5,846,150	-2,291,663	48,582,318	13,789,877	12,255,120	47,634	1,566,683	1,000,518
2013	74,247,257	57,827,008	74,725	57,901,733	6,734,844	-2,367,191	48,799,698	12,974,076	12,473,483	47,264	1,570,896	1,014,533
2014	76,535,666	58,996,359	70,194	59,066,553	6,909,020	-2,303,947	49,853,586	13,683,461	12,998,619	48,627	1,573,940	1,025,463
2015	79,834,420	61,065,427	66,301	61,131,728	7,119,707	-2,407,757	51,604,264	14,754,835	13,475,321	50,685	1,575,104	1,037,374
2016	81,175,227	61,981,550	45,238	62,026,788	7,218,510	-2,490,191	52,318,087	15,381,670	13,475,470	51,560	1,574,396	1,044,293
2017	83,904,150	63,703,197	47,934	63,751,131	7,473,370	-2,576,489	53,701,272	16,039,631	14,163,247	53,341	1,572,978	1,050,989
2018	87,915,167	66,481,038	41,702	66,522,740	7,682,868	-2,643,749	56,196,123	16,864,021	14,855,023	55,900	1,572,723	1,063,974
2019	90,633,374	68,454,149	47,610	68,501,759	7,931,110	-2,821,493	57,749,156	17,464,559	15,419,659	57,571	1,574,296	1,063,339
2020	95,297,152	68,949,788	68,079	69,017,867	8,023,049	-2,736,124	58,258,694	17,401,055	19,637,403	60,530	1,574,391	1,017,743
2021	104,078,976	73,371,285	72,108	73,443,393	8,447,529	-2,690,245	62,305,619	19,975,339	21,798,018	66,586	1,563,075	1,046,554
2022	106,308,070	77,683,338	78,229	77,761,567	9,134,337	-2,933,273	65,693,957	21,400,335	19,213,778	68,155	1,559,792	1,086,034

Personal Income and Employment by Area: Minneapolis-St. Paul-Bloomington, MN-WI

(Thousands of dollars, except as noted.)

Year	Personal income, total	Derivation of personal income: Earnings by place of work: Nonfarm	Farm	Total	Less: Contributions for government social insurance	Plus: Adjustment for residence	Equals: Net earnings by place of residence	Plus: Dividends, interest, and rent	Plus: Personal current transfer receipts	Per capita personal income (dollars)	Population (persons)	Total employment
1970	9,744,716	8,094,681	104,516	8,199,197	561,513	-60,037	7,577,647	1,430,622	736,447	4,711	2,068,705	995,308
1971	10,403,873	8,561,320	96,910	8,658,230	614,103	-58,621	7,985,506	1,555,720	862,647	4,982	2,088,348	992,091
1972	11,198,796	9,230,563	109,433	9,339,996	696,347	-62,283	8,581,366	1,664,841	952,589	5,354	2,091,790	1,031,875
1973	12,471,355	10,283,969	184,682	10,468,651	899,156	-70,184	9,499,311	1,843,967	1,128,077	5,911	2,109,880	1,091,273
1974	13,740,086	11,269,276	146,185	11,415,461	1,018,599	-75,141	10,321,721	2,112,290	1,306,075	6,452	2,129,481	1,116,872
1975	14,938,866	12,044,353	129,237	12,173,590	1,059,148	-80,976	11,033,466	2,315,382	1,590,018	6,985	2,138,738	1,109,090
1976	16,381,692	13,388,306	87,768	13,476,074	1,209,815	-92,906	12,173,353	2,469,896	1,738,443	7,611	2,152,425	1,141,084
1977	18,305,786	15,073,616	190,112	15,263,728	1,361,129	-114,461	13,788,138	2,730,861	1,786,787	8,460	2,163,785	1,191,937
1978	20,560,147	17,142,948	177,584	17,320,532	1,601,813	-133,716	15,585,003	3,062,084	1,913,060	9,411	2,184,787	1,252,108
1979	23,339,440	19,702,420	166,566	19,868,986	1,917,954	-166,457	17,784,575	3,432,666	2,122,199	10,564	2,209,422	1,323,747
1980	26,262,707	21,771,823	129,087	21,900,910	2,118,736	-184,331	19,597,843	4,147,870	2,516,994	11,680	2,248,444	1,353,773
1981	29,106,177	23,658,547	132,465	23,791,012	2,465,080	-204,119	21,121,813	5,092,215	2,892,149	12,785	2,276,602	1,351,057
1982	31,510,144	25,018,644	119,152	25,137,796	2,658,365	-210,343	22,269,088	6,019,871	3,221,185	13,689	2,301,875	1,330,443
1983	33,811,141	27,041,511	26,740	27,068,251	2,912,211	-227,796	23,928,244	6,419,336	3,463,561	14,596	2,316,538	1,349,781
1984	38,028,559	30,660,926	145,677	30,806,603	3,388,880	-268,487	27,149,236	7,260,533	3,618,790	16,253	2,339,846	1,438,623
1985	41,128,408	33,302,495	141,135	33,443,630	3,738,596	-300,174	29,404,860	7,830,478	3,893,070	17,310	2,375,997	1,491,140
1986	43,830,505	35,640,049	157,883	35,797,932	4,102,617	-318,520	31,376,795	8,352,597	4,101,113	18,162	2,413,349	1,526,757
1987	46,957,977	38,671,869	200,469	38,872,338	4,412,814	-344,416	34,115,108	8,581,145	4,261,724	19,133	2,454,248	1,596,460
1988	50,761,482	41,885,487	114,677	42,000,164	4,922,328	-375,575	36,702,261	9,491,625	4,567,596	20,232	2,508,985	1,647,950
1989	54,935,418	44,706,084	230,828	44,936,912	5,237,153	-375,658	39,324,101	10,633,751	4,977,566	21,561	2,547,922	1,683,813
1990	58,547,187	47,352,391	198,341	47,550,732	5,602,527	-367,684	41,580,521	11,565,332	5,401,334	22,589	2,591,808	1,715,543
1991	60,833,544	49,373,051	139,171	49,512,222	5,907,276	-393,074	43,211,872	11,756,534	5,865,138	23,113	2,631,964	1,722,420
1992	65,388,550	53,639,600	157,157	53,796,757	6,342,576	-455,491	46,998,690	11,995,790	6,394,070	24,451	2,674,248	1,750,362
1993	68,210,655	56,048,965	90,783	56,139,748	6,651,484	-494,243	48,994,021	12,427,828	6,788,806	25,081	2,719,621	1,788,522
1994	72,639,698	59,438,602	150,558	59,589,160	7,145,181	-562,707	51,881,272	13,612,735	7,145,691	26,300	2,761,929	1,846,637
1995	77,634,396	63,106,569	87,232	63,193,801	7,558,520	-629,015	55,006,266	15,027,750	7,600,380	27,685	2,804,246	1,905,175
1996	82,884,069	67,440,157	161,325	67,601,482	8,008,707	-713,508	58,879,267	16,028,485	7,976,317	29,118	2,846,496	1,945,109
1997	89,025,468	72,447,471	110,423	72,557,894	8,549,780	-802,188	63,205,926	17,716,002	8,103,540	30,826	2,888,020	1,983,236
1998	97,143,739	79,294,748	171,529	79,466,277	9,213,741	-911,319	69,341,217	19,397,235	8,405,287	33,139	2,931,378	2,041,242
1999	102,619,468	84,821,069	157,645	84,978,714	9,883,330	-1,078,680	74,016,704	19,761,605	8,841,159	34,443	2,979,405	2,089,976
2000	112,037,432	92,710,053	149,363	92,859,416	10,672,159	-1,267,089	80,920,168	21,577,685	9,539,579	36,987	3,029,064	2,145,458
2001	116,510,241	96,326,968	131,836	96,458,804	11,021,946	-1,387,037	84,049,821	21,770,730	10,689,690	37,936	3,071,250	2,160,572
2002	118,359,361	97,921,530	143,819	98,065,349	11,165,994	-1,417,994	85,481,361	21,217,909	11,660,091	38,170	3,100,852	2,149,706
2003	123,244,450	101,635,999	198,543	101,834,542	11,659,430	-1,489,752	88,685,360	22,375,959	12,183,131	39,398	3,128,159	2,159,268
2004	131,161,989	108,538,855	264,579	108,803,434	12,331,176	-1,658,303	94,813,955	23,557,747	12,790,287	41,550	3,156,700	2,193,069
2005	135,296,573	111,510,408	265,440	111,775,848	12,893,491	-1,751,492	97,130,865	24,693,102	13,472,606	42,494	3,183,920	2,236,097
2006	142,592,386	115,305,461	239,050	115,544,511	13,500,346	-1,771,987	100,272,178	27,471,240	14,848,968	44,294	3,219,203	2,271,773
2007	151,162,057	121,491,241	242,350	121,733,591	14,070,383	-1,840,903	105,822,305	28,942,128	16,397,624	46,449	3,254,350	2,303,940
2008	156,397,435	123,386,894	309,470	123,696,364	14,441,120	-1,801,323	107,453,921	30,114,676	18,828,838	47,596	3,285,969	2,295,674
2009	148,600,896	116,375,342	215,595	116,590,937	13,816,195	-1,405,131	101,369,611	26,655,082	20,576,203	44,822	3,315,368	2,220,596
2010	154,433,594	120,307,011	271,843	120,578,854	14,030,415	-1,387,539	105,160,900	26,897,980	22,374,714	46,226	3,340,873	2,213,662
2011	165,333,937	127,287,568	359,656	127,647,224	13,157,593	-1,490,690	112,998,941	29,792,440	22,542,556	48,947	3,377,834	2,264,925
2012	174,956,521	133,911,134	462,724	134,373,858	13,743,021	-1,467,360	119,163,477	33,160,539	22,632,505	51,247	3,413,964	2,294,026
2013	176,943,126	138,328,786	455,700	138,784,486	16,245,544	-1,463,542	121,075,400	32,363,673	23,504,053	51,251	3,452,486	2,334,972
2014	187,792,672	145,365,381	362,647	145,728,028	16,813,942	-1,514,583	127,399,503	35,408,296	24,984,873	53,784	3,491,595	2,376,034
2015	197,583,458	152,286,000	293,206	152,579,206	17,431,219	-1,525,682	133,622,305	38,121,142	25,840,011	56,085	3,522,901	2,424,192
2016	203,633,462	156,575,352	170,959	156,746,311	17,938,115	-1,545,083	137,263,113	39,683,312	26,687,037	57,172	3,561,786	2,460,122
2017	213,046,166	164,022,508	201,298	164,223,806	18,738,988	-1,668,429	143,816,389	41,421,970	27,807,807	59,132	3,602,878	2,495,856
2018	224,925,166	171,526,416	163,664	171,690,080	19,639,323	-1,736,882	150,313,875	44,960,120	29,651,171	61,785	3,640,447	2,533,448
2019	234,285,102	177,556,249	119,337	177,675,586	20,353,289	-1,798,138	155,524,159	47,802,155	30,958,788	63,795	3,672,456	2,540,567
2020	245,388,286	178,342,950	292,625	178,635,575	20,512,645	-1,928,752	156,194,178	46,806,625	42,387,483	66,431	3,693,860	2,416,591
2021	268,164,110	191,481,530	402,156	191,883,686	21,800,360	-2,141,392	167,941,934	53,704,970	46,517,206	72,654	3,690,987	2,494,190
2022	277,634,965	204,122,968	440,226	204,563,194	23,617,825	-2,338,992	178,606,377	59,352,872	39,675,716	75,164	3,693,729	2,599,455

Personal Income and Employment by Area: Missoula, MT

(Thousands of dollars, except as noted.)

Year	Personal income, total	Derivation of personal income: Earnings by place of work: Nonfarm	Farm	Total	Less: Contributions for government social insurance	Plus: Adjustment for residence	Equals: Net earnings by place of residence	Plus: Dividends, interest, and rent	Plus: Personal current transfer receipts	Per capita personal income (dollars)	Population (persons)	Total employment
1970	208,980	173,995	696	174,691	13,535	-5,092	156,064	34,810	18,106	3,574	58,472	25,139
1971	233,708	194,017	977	194,994	15,269	-5,764	173,961	38,324	21,423	3,896	59,990	26,508
1972	263,307	221,506	1,412	222,918	18,329	-8,015	196,574	42,382	24,351	4,253	61,918	28,195
1973	290,502	243,366	2,012	245,378	23,012	-9,280	213,086	48,531	28,885	4,509	64,424	29,798
1974	329,287	272,000	1,830	273,830	26,113	-10,928	236,789	57,230	35,268	4,914	67,007	30,952
1975	367,339	295,014	1,130	296,144	26,809	-11,672	257,663	66,425	43,251	5,478	67,056	31,090
1976	421,544	346,931	1,104	348,035	32,426	-14,908	300,701	73,432	47,411	6,062	69,539	33,780
1977	491,819	415,461	176	415,637	39,930	-20,077	355,630	84,894	51,295	6,930	70,970	36,648
1978	572,589	490,751	1,716	492,467	48,972	-25,212	418,283	98,461	55,845	7,928	72,226	40,008
1979	639,203	544,983	1,559	546,542	56,986	-30,859	458,697	114,648	65,858	8,628	74,088	40,389
1980	694,817	572,923	1,393	574,316	61,324	-33,542	479,450	135,925	79,442	9,129	76,115	39,442
1981	736,851	576,096	435	576,531	65,004	-22,824	488,703	156,457	91,691	9,651	76,352	37,592
1982	770,629	586,216	309	586,525	67,402	-25,984	493,139	179,419	98,071	10,242	75,242	36,696
1983	827,637	645,419	1,154	646,573	75,130	-29,372	542,071	180,252	105,314	10,952	75,571	38,399
1984	907,129	710,418	155	710,573	84,485	-31,930	594,158	201,366	111,605	11,800	76,875	40,726
1985	951,777	743,286	-522	742,764	89,956	-32,139	620,669	210,652	120,456	12,238	77,774	41,567
1986	985,202	766,659	955	767,614	94,262	-31,563	641,789	213,067	130,346	12,639	77,949	41,942
1987	1,021,377	797,419	-243	797,176	97,936	-31,731	667,509	214,397	139,471	13,149	77,680	43,048
1988	1,085,118	844,354	-516	843,838	109,213	-33,722	700,903	234,387	149,828	13,990	77,564	44,555
1989	1,161,529	902,230	369	902,599	118,659	-36,861	747,079	247,338	167,112	14,892	77,995	45,814
1990	1,254,739	980,021	197	980,218	137,269	-40,329	802,620	266,847	185,272	15,867	79,080	47,616
1991	1,334,910	1,045,332	284	1,045,616	148,125	-43,356	854,135	285,850	194,925	16,460	81,098	49,299
1992	1,463,457	1,168,467	293	1,168,760	165,648	-51,008	952,104	299,772	211,581	17,516	83,549	51,852
1993	1,571,072	1,268,176	700	1,268,876	184,306	-56,127	1,028,443	318,698	223,931	18,217	86,243	54,021
1994	1,664,757	1,332,212	-1,778	1,330,434	191,727	-58,399	1,080,308	353,956	230,493	18,910	88,037	56,003
1995	1,778,196	1,400,291	-2,871	1,397,420	196,342	-64,169	1,136,909	391,575	249,712	19,667	90,413	58,094
1996	1,883,174	1,480,167	-4,343	1,475,824	198,806	-71,175	1,205,843	418,116	259,215	20,481	91,947	60,152
1997	1,989,456	1,551,695	-4,406	1,547,289	202,649	-75,323	1,269,317	456,834	263,305	21,357	93,151	61,250
1998	2,128,375	1,655,481	-2,582	1,652,899	210,240	-83,013	1,359,646	496,198	272,531	22,679	93,847	62,905
1999	2,195,500	1,745,093	-1,462	1,743,631	220,943	-92,443	1,430,245	498,379	266,876	23,161	94,791	64,766
2000	2,390,388	1,880,192	-1,758	1,878,434	238,255	-103,029	1,537,150	550,513	302,725	24,854	96,178	66,193
2001	2,448,105	1,923,211	632	1,923,843	251,331	-114,615	1,557,897	551,164	339,044	25,126	97,435	68,296
2002	2,586,915	2,055,607	3,088	2,058,695	269,136	-128,132	1,661,427	573,599	351,889	26,139	98,968	69,237
2003	2,755,362	2,188,560	158	2,188,718	283,675	-141,356	1,763,687	624,982	366,693	27,560	99,976	70,825
2004	2,938,318	2,325,167	753	2,325,920	296,527	-162,065	1,867,328	686,634	384,356	29,111	100,934	72,120
2005	3,086,823	2,428,303	390	2,428,693	313,500	-183,059	1,932,134	739,913	414,776	30,175	102,298	73,459
2006	3,374,020	2,573,468	-1,640	2,571,828	333,259	-195,918	2,042,651	882,291	449,078	32,327	104,372	75,242
2007	3,582,220	2,713,394	-772	2,712,622	356,092	-216,279	2,140,251	960,943	481,026	33,759	106,110	77,706
2008	3,831,446	2,797,305	-4,177	2,793,128	365,758	-233,423	2,193,947	1,071,339	566,160	35,560	107,747	76,961
2009	3,918,320	2,795,464	-1,517	2,793,947	364,261	-235,564	2,194,122	1,104,017	620,181	36,041	108,717	75,732
2010	3,819,128	2,820,355	-1,676	2,818,679	364,661	-218,583	2,235,435	894,006	689,687	34,911	109,397	75,060
2011	4,075,649	2,937,924	5,518	2,943,442	340,465	-232,883	2,370,094	1,020,851	684,704	37,086	109,896	76,129
2012	4,344,170	3,011,644	-3,286	3,008,358	344,597	-216,554	2,447,207	1,193,219	703,744	39,341	110,423	76,745
2013	4,322,745	3,095,086	-781	3,094,305	399,076	-201,702	2,493,527	1,107,722	721,496	38,945	110,996	77,716
2014	4,632,529	3,232,598	-1,180	3,231,418	419,088	-196,677	2,615,653	1,251,768	765,108	41,504	111,616	78,868
2015	5,113,177	3,435,071	909	3,435,980	438,251	-207,651	2,790,078	1,517,010	806,089	45,391	112,647	80,149
2016	5,182,221	3,562,953	2,516	3,565,469	442,621	-248,957	2,873,891	1,434,503	873,827	45,217	114,608	82,177
2017	5,617,529	3,794,393	2,659	3,797,052	483,064	-268,790	3,045,198	1,620,125	952,206	48,532	115,750	83,756
2018	5,810,701	3,983,798	1,836	3,985,634	515,304	-276,094	3,194,236	1,622,159	994,306	49,960	116,307	85,950
2019	6,215,725	4,223,952	1,860	4,225,812	536,884	-314,939	3,373,989	1,800,755	1,040,981	53,093	117,072	86,811
2020	6,814,562	4,402,133	4,758	4,406,891	571,923	-352,987	3,481,981	1,963,412	1,369,169	57,586	118,337	85,607
2021	7,405,590	5,037,268	1,614	5,038,882	626,240	-406,847	4,005,795	1,926,616	1,473,179	61,813	119,806	90,006
2022	7,721,261	5,389,463	-201	5,389,262	690,191	-465,801	4,233,270	2,203,451	1,284,540	63,790	121,041	93,228

Personal Income and Employment by Area: Montgomery, AL

(Thousands of dollars, except as noted.)

Year	Personal income, total	Derivation of personal income: Earnings by place of work: Nonfarm	Farm	Total	Less: Contributions for government social insurance	Plus: Adjustment for residence	Equals: Net earnings by place of residence	Plus: Dividends, interest, and rent	Plus: Personal current transfer receipts	Per capita personal income (dollars)	Population (persons)	Total employment
1970	821,743	648,601	20,376	668,977	45,411	-2,883	620,683	129,782	71,278	3,435	239,239	109,720
1971	932,728	734,677	23,155	757,832	52,137	-3,781	701,914	147,823	82,991	3,846	242,500	112,842
1972	1,082,001	854,494	32,191	886,685	63,004	-4,927	818,754	170,200	93,047	4,288	252,309	119,422
1973	1,224,140	962,843	42,950	1,005,793	80,874	-6,957	917,962	195,847	110,331	4,744	258,064	124,450
1974	1,359,239	1,072,465	25,326	1,097,791	93,246	-10,014	994,531	228,732	135,976	5,151	263,893	126,242
1975	1,469,402	1,137,036	21,515	1,158,551	100,379	-11,539	1,046,633	248,750	174,019	5,524	265,984	124,938
1976	1,646,376	1,271,461	42,584	1,314,045	115,289	-15,561	1,183,195	269,571	193,610	6,094	270,156	127,870
1977	1,792,684	1,413,534	19,548	1,433,082	128,629	-21,154	1,283,299	300,436	208,949	6,570	272,860	132,672
1978	2,041,480	1,606,309	33,859	1,640,168	148,010	-29,809	1,462,349	347,640	231,491	7,376	276,789	139,055
1979	2,270,347	1,785,676	40,331	1,826,007	171,725	-41,172	1,613,110	387,076	270,161	8,056	281,831	142,495
1980	2,508,143	1,946,081	18,150	1,964,231	188,418	-43,970	1,731,843	459,299	317,001	8,753	286,531	142,176
1981	2,759,312	2,074,007	17,490	2,091,497	215,256	-29,463	1,846,778	555,059	357,475	9,568	288,378	139,589
1982	2,943,900	2,165,214	27,443	2,192,657	227,512	-31,417	1,933,728	611,409	398,763	10,177	289,284	137,511
1983	3,218,011	2,402,691	19,706	2,422,397	256,127	-42,377	2,123,893	666,169	427,949	11,106	289,744	141,881
1984	3,534,105	2,661,352	21,969	2,683,321	287,780	-51,895	2,343,646	737,078	453,381	12,087	292,394	147,345
1985	3,821,043	2,899,209	29,648	2,928,857	315,600	-62,721	2,550,536	793,833	476,674	12,978	294,421	150,916
1986	4,082,425	3,135,792	23,556	3,159,348	339,756	-71,924	2,747,668	838,007	496,750	13,703	297,919	156,125
1987	4,358,955	3,366,284	43,316	3,409,600	359,967	-83,824	2,965,809	884,124	509,022	14,464	301,371	160,694
1988	4,698,847	3,611,645	53,144	3,664,789	403,537	-95,245	3,166,007	993,868	538,972	15,522	302,729	166,464
1989	5,099,680	3,807,685	49,481	3,857,166	426,323	-104,099	3,326,744	1,159,991	612,945	16,720	305,003	169,489
1990	5,364,284	4,003,332	50,701	4,054,033	455,455	-111,635	3,486,943	1,191,217	686,124	17,528	306,042	170,900
1991	5,659,887	4,207,688	63,503	4,271,191	481,977	-116,986	3,672,228	1,231,217	756,442	18,191	311,129	171,043
1992	6,080,232	4,523,547	43,101	4,566,648	513,121	-126,539	3,926,988	1,294,120	859,124	19,182	316,981	175,249
1993	6,365,326	4,760,072	29,227	4,789,299	541,797	-134,807	4,112,695	1,330,222	922,409	19,725	322,707	179,984
1994	6,786,590	5,091,592	29,287	5,120,879	583,257	-144,367	4,393,255	1,421,727	971,608	20,713	327,654	183,466
1995	7,182,035	5,302,616	13,297	5,315,913	609,465	-153,064	4,553,384	1,572,740	1,055,911	21,656	331,647	189,986
1996	7,512,921	5,554,393	23,807	5,578,200	634,896	-165,318	4,777,986	1,621,220	1,113,715	22,426	335,014	194,046
1997	7,935,346	5,816,476	38,983	5,855,459	667,339	-179,617	5,008,503	1,759,345	1,167,498	23,415	338,906	197,762
1998	8,398,175	6,239,652	34,635	6,274,287	703,270	-197,355	5,373,662	1,830,523	1,193,990	24,547	342,120	201,452
1999	8,751,830	6,596,901	50,102	6,647,003	741,330	-217,042	5,688,631	1,817,795	1,245,404	25,401	344,540	205,388
2000	9,191,869	6,875,011	42,499	6,917,510	770,641	-230,656	5,916,213	1,953,628	1,322,028	26,483	347,080	206,869
2001	9,299,144	6,941,495	53,726	6,995,221	798,430	-258,064	5,938,727	1,962,970	1,397,447	26,666	348,725	209,312
2002	9,737,805	7,305,328	34,755	7,340,083	837,922	-284,235	6,217,926	1,990,750	1,529,129	27,744	350,984	210,019
2003	10,241,990	7,645,456	61,396	7,706,852	874,983	-309,606	6,522,263	2,081,521	1,638,206	29,063	352,411	212,974
2004	10,928,634	8,073,196	103,205	8,176,401	913,772	-322,521	6,940,108	2,266,856	1,721,670	30,784	355,009	216,887
2005	11,435,384	8,486,945	106,550	8,593,495	961,560	-350,153	7,281,782	2,301,096	1,852,506	31,884	358,659	222,864
2006	12,104,297	8,988,491	95,825	9,084,316	1,024,522	-387,795	7,671,999	2,427,235	2,005,063	33,073	365,989	227,675
2007	12,535,611	9,253,731	60,871	9,314,602	1,064,871	-422,286	7,827,445	2,536,212	2,171,954	33,936	369,390	234,199
2008	12,843,806	9,296,451	54,070	9,350,521	1,110,255	-452,979	7,787,287	2,631,588	2,424,931	34,690	370,249	231,515
2009	12,759,452	9,246,537	64,171	9,310,708	1,098,422	-466,567	7,745,719	2,412,489	2,601,244	34,313	371,860	223,840
2010	13,112,957	9,399,655	61,030	9,460,685	1,116,630	-481,606	7,862,449	2,370,063	2,880,445	34,928	375,431	220,617
2011	13,656,857	9,579,132	55,030	9,634,162	1,011,053	-514,843	8,108,266	2,578,467	2,970,124	36,205	377,209	221,798
2012	13,742,787	9,539,169	81,004	9,620,173	1,012,763	-528,090	8,079,320	2,715,145	2,948,322	36,370	377,864	218,630
2013	13,815,323	9,733,525	124,460	9,857,985	1,159,955	-539,066	8,158,964	2,635,676	3,020,683	36,508	378,424	219,374
2014	14,166,808	9,931,118	103,108	10,034,226	1,178,932	-546,168	8,309,126	2,731,098	3,126,584	37,369	379,109	221,222
2015	14,790,033	10,277,468	69,122	10,346,590	1,215,569	-568,770	8,562,251	2,832,906	3,394,876	38,885	380,358	222,822
2016	15,219,512	10,735,650	46,070	10,781,720	1,254,019	-597,512	8,930,189	2,866,676	3,422,647	39,809	382,309	225,521
2017	15,646,324	10,952,201	69,860	11,022,061	1,287,131	-593,543	9,141,387	3,004,815	3,500,122	40,753	383,935	228,046
2018	15,979,817	11,185,804	59,985	11,245,789	1,328,799	-598,393	9,318,597	3,015,835	3,645,385	41,611	384,025	228,032
2019	16,457,262	11,498,312	48,125	11,546,437	1,369,813	-627,742	9,548,882	3,096,930	3,811,450	42,727	385,174	227,372
2020	17,543,754	11,791,138	41,138	11,832,276	1,413,198	-642,875	9,776,203	2,968,958	4,798,593	45,527	385,350	222,880
2021	18,822,212	12,254,794	61,727	12,316,521	1,489,167	-683,401	10,143,953	3,239,674	5,438,585	48,911	384,826	229,567
2022	18,939,164	12,915,391	56,674	12,972,065	1,597,761	-725,305	10,648,999	3,470,543	4,819,622	49,134	385,460	235,938

Personal Income and Employment by Area: Morgantown, WV

(Thousands of dollars, except as noted.)

Year	Personal income, total	Derivation of personal income: Earnings by place of work: Nonfarm	Farm	Total	Less: Contributions for government social insurance	Plus: Adjustment for residence	Equals: Net earnings by place of residence	Plus: Dividends, interest, and rent	Plus: Personal current transfer receipts	Per capita personal income (dollars)	Population (persons)	Total employment
1970	266,124	213,095	847	213,942	14,864	4,512	203,590	34,199	28,335	2,983	89,219	34,394
1971	296,621	236,461	952	237,413	17,315	3,306	223,404	38,242	34,975	3,271	90,684	35,273
1972	340,664	276,990	870	277,860	21,296	-358	256,206	43,192	41,266	3,622	94,067	37,872
1973	364,176	293,102	1,016	294,118	25,961	-3,432	264,725	49,168	50,283	3,791	96,069	38,107
1974	403,584	326,114	47	326,161	29,918	-7,206	289,037	57,364	57,183	4,106	98,296	38,804
1975	458,241	370,883	-100	370,783	33,555	-11,189	326,039	64,298	67,904	4,685	97,808	40,252
1976	511,329	419,851	-102	419,749	38,650	-18,190	362,909	72,906	75,514	5,135	99,573	42,073
1977	574,724	472,629	-184	472,445	42,227	-19,927	410,291	83,603	80,830	5,659	101,553	43,083
1978	645,097	532,986	905	533,891	48,968	-27,495	457,428	95,938	91,731	6,255	103,131	44,710
1979	695,828	570,263	312	570,575	55,473	-32,905	482,197	106,853	106,778	6,669	104,338	43,728
1980	775,793	623,361	32	623,393	63,757	-41,419	518,217	134,473	123,103	7,331	105,829	43,877
1981	871,730	679,195	-2,339	676,856	73,808	-38,063	564,985	165,060	141,685	8,138	107,115	43,092
1982	952,634	754,738	-2,007	752,731	85,550	-49,347	617,834	185,428	149,372	8,874	107,348	43,856
1983	1,018,735	786,567	-461	786,106	90,595	-51,575	643,936	208,175	166,624	9,438	107,934	44,249
1984	1,096,590	854,460	1,748	856,208	100,426	-54,576	701,206	222,082	173,302	10,132	108,233	45,127
1985	1,153,960	899,735	1,867	901,602	107,846	-58,776	734,980	236,064	182,916	10,806	106,785	46,436
1986	1,194,172	927,208	2,476	929,684	117,075	-66,016	746,593	250,363	197,216	11,250	106,152	47,850
1987	1,245,924	985,257	-576	984,681	125,455	-71,385	787,841	253,817	204,266	11,774	105,816	49,184
1988	1,390,296	1,097,171	-372	1,096,799	140,715	-64,059	892,025	277,512	220,759	13,186	105,441	50,388
1989	1,460,573	1,129,622	1,329	1,130,951	148,822	-56,605	925,524	297,838	237,211	13,911	104,993	51,305
1990	1,573,104	1,221,234	178	1,221,412	162,961	-58,103	1,000,348	317,806	254,950	15,025	104,696	53,460
1991	1,669,997	1,287,530	-1,523	1,286,007	175,060	-59,758	1,051,189	328,008	290,800	15,721	106,229	54,423
1992	1,824,596	1,384,288	638	1,384,926	191,376	-69,566	1,123,984	353,987	346,625	16,978	107,468	56,208
1993	1,878,920	1,421,435	814	1,422,249	202,955	-71,936	1,147,358	362,099	369,463	17,304	108,582	56,446
1994	1,976,296	1,522,433	1,007	1,523,440	217,818	-80,263	1,225,359	378,216	372,721	18,049	109,494	58,961
1995	2,035,832	1,532,728	-1,598	1,531,130	223,573	-76,227	1,231,330	418,847	385,655	18,466	110,247	59,587
1996	2,108,187	1,553,855	48	1,553,903	224,494	-73,527	1,255,882	441,192	411,113	19,069	110,553	59,610
1997	2,166,317	1,566,618	-2,136	1,564,482	223,570	-63,502	1,277,410	464,701	424,206	19,555	110,781	59,184
1998	2,257,793	1,651,870	-2,359	1,649,511	238,968	-78,661	1,331,882	491,283	434,628	20,356	110,918	59,873
1999	2,347,829	1,761,749	-3,454	1,758,295	252,997	-88,580	1,416,718	487,916	443,195	21,173	110,888	60,730
2000	2,541,664	1,952,745	-603	1,952,142	285,711	-106,902	1,559,529	512,839	469,296	22,828	111,338	62,298
2001	2,714,850	2,071,511	-1,146	2,070,365	287,987	-120,849	1,661,529	526,425	526,896	24,076	112,764	63,393
2002	2,872,674	2,194,689	-4,384	2,190,305	284,864	-133,499	1,771,942	525,044	575,688	25,123	114,343	64,323
2003	2,934,034	2,277,625	-6,934	2,270,691	308,032	-145,697	1,816,962	528,998	588,074	25,192	116,466	64,978
2004	3,156,427	2,507,227	-4,109	2,503,118	324,193	-141,888	2,037,037	537,894	581,496	26,735	118,062	67,251
2005	3,404,114	2,711,821	-4,824	2,706,997	344,001	-144,912	2,218,084	580,489	605,541	28,383	119,937	69,269
2006	3,587,328	2,820,838	-5,411	2,815,427	352,755	-158,657	2,304,015	639,990	643,323	29,430	121,894	70,365
2007	3,752,741	2,922,714	-6,700	2,916,014	349,900	-177,546	2,388,568	678,357	685,816	30,385	123,507	73,420
2008	4,010,254	3,100,755	-4,954	3,095,801	358,547	-211,163	2,526,091	722,205	761,958	32,014	125,267	75,370
2009	4,162,307	3,309,728	-6,421	3,303,307	385,492	-259,336	2,658,479	687,640	816,188	32,646	127,498	76,172
2010	4,563,040	3,584,504	-7,469	3,577,035	414,160	-285,492	2,877,383	788,116	897,541	35,016	130,314	77,844
2011	4,824,562	3,678,745	-4,577	3,674,168	373,873	-240,375	3,059,920	853,803	910,839	36,349	132,730	78,364
2012	4,938,587	3,811,386	-5,681	3,805,705	387,763	-277,351	3,140,591	877,163	920,833	36,607	134,910	80,642
2013	5,022,967	3,938,694	-2,746	3,935,948	452,347	-315,113	3,168,488	910,164	944,315	36,913	136,074	81,776
2014	5,270,451	4,133,253	-2,779	4,130,474	477,545	-313,371	3,339,558	917,154	1,013,739	38,319	137,542	82,948
2015	5,550,134	4,377,630	-2,712	4,374,918	504,432	-381,627	3,488,859	1,000,956	1,060,319	40,015	138,703	84,295
2016	5,512,597	4,336,715	-3,725	4,332,990	513,033	-419,928	3,400,029	1,008,340	1,104,228	39,478	139,638	84,210
2017	5,781,502	4,616,724	-2,620	4,614,104	550,254	-477,898	3,585,952	1,048,637	1,146,913	41,325	139,902	85,896
2018	6,068,442	4,743,677	-3,960	4,739,717	555,970	-453,585	3,730,162	1,152,118	1,186,162	43,521	139,436	86,965
2019	6,285,560	4,949,816	-676	4,949,140	572,782	-463,538	3,912,820	1,161,645	1,211,095	44,988	139,717	86,336
2020	6,639,271	5,041,920	-1,906	5,040,014	596,809	-534,871	3,908,334	1,189,785	1,541,152	47,392	140,092	83,300
2021	7,237,589	5,352,033	-3,250	5,348,783	629,860	-566,171	4,152,752	1,358,208	1,726,629	51,419	140,757	86,613
2022	7,350,275	5,619,058	-5,410	5,613,648	666,434	-586,743	4,360,471	1,478,484	1,511,320	52,114	141,041	89,214

Personal Income and Employment by Area: Morristown, TN

(Thousands of dollars, except as noted.)

Year	Personal income, total	Derivation of personal income: Earnings by place of work: Nonfarm	Farm	Total	Less: Contributions for government social insurance	Plus: Adjustment for residence	Equals: Net earnings by place of residence	Plus: Dividends, interest, and rent	Plus: Personal current transfer receipts	Per capita personal income (dollars)	Population (persons)	Total employment
1970	208,793	182,208	7,757	189,965	11,955	-13,334	164,676	22,370	21,747	2,672	78,134	36,402
1971	237,203	210,398	7,496	217,894	14,416	-16,293	187,185	25,470	24,548	2,923	81,139	38,187
1972	276,190	246,908	10,638	257,546	17,883	-19,963	219,700	29,050	27,440	3,289	83,966	42,059
1973	314,502	276,578	14,380	290,958	22,887	-20,958	247,113	33,629	33,760	3,681	85,437	43,481
1974	341,662	296,235	11,235	307,470	25,536	-21,519	260,415	39,157	42,090	3,880	88,058	42,570
1975	359,314	292,459	5,817	298,276	24,933	-18,196	255,147	43,388	60,779	4,058	88,539	38,529
1976	408,717	336,163	13,992	350,155	29,264	-21,033	299,858	47,488	61,371	4,507	90,679	41,244
1977	453,425	386,164	7,660	393,824	34,003	-25,706	334,115	54,010	65,300	4,848	93,534	44,214
1978	520,585	445,497	9,258	454,755	39,851	-27,731	387,173	62,585	70,827	5,455	95,428	46,708
1979	580,614	488,738	7,157	495,895	45,210	-25,584	425,101	71,700	83,813	6,027	96,337	46,840
1980	635,815	502,986	6,330	509,316	46,239	-22,077	441,000	90,342	104,473	6,510	97,668	44,699
1981	704,166	532,581	11,372	543,953	52,897	-15,947	475,109	111,432	117,625	7,126	98,812	43,722
1982	751,253	555,918	9,480	565,398	56,001	-19,864	489,533	130,409	131,311	7,475	100,501	43,089
1983	809,990	611,551	-189	611,362	62,098	-22,019	527,245	140,944	141,801	7,817	103,613	44,764
1984	905,506	689,654	7,101	696,755	72,576	-24,058	600,121	156,561	148,824	8,753	103,446	46,639
1985	948,680	712,664	7,728	720,392	75,783	-18,013	626,596	164,636	157,448	9,416	100,755	46,550
1986	1,005,870	754,251	3,911	758,162	81,852	-12,713	663,597	171,007	171,266	10,024	100,345	47,431
1987	1,082,739	820,996	4,429	825,425	88,784	-10,241	726,400	175,871	180,468	10,875	99,561	49,087
1988	1,191,946	906,767	3,556	910,323	101,124	-6,510	802,689	193,725	195,532	11,904	100,133	51,617
1989	1,321,456	1,003,009	6,330	1,009,339	112,740	-12,691	883,908	223,040	214,508	13,209	100,041	54,507
1990	1,431,566	1,084,780	7,974	1,092,754	122,237	-3,237	967,280	224,716	239,570	14,182	100,942	56,431
1991	1,506,063	1,117,567	9,224	1,126,791	127,805	-6,856	992,130	229,680	284,253	14,730	102,245	55,722
1992	1,665,932	1,231,267	13,989	1,245,256	139,090	3,728	1,109,894	228,401	327,637	16,004	104,094	57,641
1993	1,778,778	1,320,009	12,091	1,332,100	150,729	5,404	1,186,775	238,142	353,861	16,707	106,466	59,658
1994	1,862,292	1,367,888	10,414	1,378,302	159,655	21,376	1,240,023	253,620	368,649	17,180	108,399	60,298
1995	1,995,905	1,454,419	5,625	1,460,044	169,775	29,363	1,319,632	280,825	395,448	17,926	111,344	62,073
1996	2,113,640	1,527,998	-1,665	1,526,333	176,363	40,003	1,389,973	301,581	422,086	18,483	114,358	63,041
1997	2,290,798	1,641,182	6,096	1,647,278	186,377	65,470	1,526,371	315,552	448,875	19,541	117,228	64,050
1998	2,495,692	1,800,181	10,166	1,810,347	197,918	84,491	1,696,920	333,848	464,924	20,888	119,479	65,468
1999	2,589,668	1,911,802	8,525	1,920,327	210,847	54,635	1,764,115	338,220	487,333	21,255	121,840	67,470
2000	2,711,613	1,973,460	16,320	1,989,780	219,574	43,177	1,813,383	359,521	538,709	21,965	123,449	68,923
2001	2,771,303	1,952,667	14,734	1,967,401	221,882	53,891	1,799,410	377,297	594,596	22,253	124,536	64,956
2002	2,869,037	2,003,710	12,782	2,016,492	227,856	62,390	1,851,026	364,389	653,622	22,980	124,851	63,885
2003	2,987,439	2,102,189	12,126	2,114,315	239,105	56,713	1,931,923	377,994	677,522	23,609	126,539	64,461
2004	3,147,213	2,269,902	11,054	2,280,956	255,262	48,542	2,074,236	362,736	710,241	24,623	127,816	66,063
2005	3,240,571	2,263,425	11,945	2,275,370	256,384	92,281	2,111,267	360,683	768,621	25,009	129,574	65,689
2006	3,380,654	2,311,564	6,501	2,318,065	263,221	126,803	2,181,647	378,780	820,227	25,634	131,883	66,399
2007	3,546,509	2,341,025	-3,148	2,337,877	271,559	132,903	2,199,221	441,388	905,900	26,450	134,085	66,738
2008	3,730,127	2,341,972	-5,609	2,336,363	276,996	135,242	2,194,609	508,333	1,027,185	27,530	135,495	65,920
2009	3,722,407	2,180,735	-1,282	2,179,453	263,742	183,474	2,099,185	502,797	1,120,425	27,344	136,131	61,241
2010	3,871,213	2,294,768	4,101	2,298,869	274,574	153,021	2,177,316	488,745	1,205,152	28,273	136,923	60,941
2011	4,129,329	2,360,492	-359	2,360,133	252,783	251,772	2,359,122	543,771	1,226,436	30,043	137,447	61,372
2012	4,192,772	2,495,853	2,095	2,497,948	259,208	179,563	2,418,303	541,042	1,233,427	30,480	137,557	61,621
2013	4,232,605	2,524,715	8,965	2,533,680	293,565	206,321	2,446,436	521,589	1,264,580	30,751	137,640	62,113
2014	4,367,077	2,623,325	9,598	2,632,923	301,891	203,968	2,535,000	545,639	1,286,438	31,668	137,903	63,111
2015	4,599,597	2,756,423	6,956	2,763,379	314,026	214,698	2,664,051	577,015	1,358,531	33,151	138,745	64,163
2016	4,681,083	2,812,298	-2,588	2,809,710	324,961	211,618	2,696,367	577,341	1,407,375	33,600	139,319	65,340
2017	4,867,996	2,938,657	-1,345	2,937,312	344,317	194,234	2,787,229	631,022	1,449,745	34,719	140,211	66,823
2018	5,121,959	3,061,667	-6,507	3,055,160	359,105	241,142	2,937,197	658,724	1,526,038	36,342	140,937	67,502
2019	5,379,491	3,208,476	-5,625	3,202,851	376,399	219,711	3,046,163	723,538	1,609,790	37,921	141,861	68,391
2020	5,792,314	3,309,239	-3,133	3,306,106	396,831	227,772	3,137,047	708,106	1,947,161	40,503	143,008	68,428
2021	6,482,898	3,660,387	-455	3,659,932	419,591	353,543	3,593,884	722,379	2,166,635	45,087	143,785	70,555
2022	6,619,518	3,943,681	-5,736	3,937,945	471,017	417,079	3,884,007	777,773	1,957,738	45,286	146,172	73,259

Personal Income and Employment by Area: Mount Vernon-Anacortes, WA

(Thousands of dollars, except as noted.)

Year	Personal income, total	Derivation of personal income: Earnings by place of work: Nonfarm	Farm	Total	Less: Contributions for government social insurance	Plus: Adjustment for residence	Equals: Net earnings by place of residence	Plus: Dividends, interest, and rent	Plus: Personal current transfer receipts	Per capita personal income (dollars)	Population (persons)	Total employment
1970	210,795	141,229	11,282	152,511	11,412	7,281	148,380	37,494	24,921	4,021	52,419	21,242
1971	230,211	153,460	13,347	166,807	12,966	6,666	160,507	41,403	28,301	4,369	52,694	21,537
1972	252,938	172,325	14,626	186,951	15,490	5,487	176,948	45,513	30,477	4,759	53,145	22,736
1973	295,178	204,667	21,565	226,232	21,484	3,742	208,490	51,704	34,984	5,544	53,244	24,711
1974	326,194	215,809	26,573	242,382	22,871	4,979	224,490	58,799	42,905	6,024	54,151	24,990
1975	364,169	238,472	25,179	263,651	24,749	4,920	243,822	68,001	52,346	6,816	53,431	25,161
1976	415,084	288,481	23,491	311,972	30,573	1,063	282,462	75,232	57,390	7,351	56,468	26,771
1977	445,393	303,666	20,725	324,391	32,150	4,190	296,431	87,078	61,884	7,716	57,722	26,893
1978	506,036	352,263	18,807	371,070	37,624	5,526	338,972	100,852	66,212	8,503	59,516	28,633
1979	583,952	399,018	26,152	425,170	43,649	8,588	390,109	118,378	75,465	9,504	61,443	29,681
1980	659,360	429,456	24,671	454,127	47,239	8,273	415,161	148,356	95,843	10,224	64,491	29,998
1981	729,938	465,388	21,994	487,382	56,258	7,366	438,490	180,632	110,816	11,097	65,779	30,968
1982	783,971	482,315	22,382	504,697	59,947	7,341	452,091	206,291	125,589	11,734	66,812	30,991
1983	862,121	528,545	31,270	559,815	66,188	4,978	498,605	225,383	138,133	12,661	68,094	32,337
1984	904,565	538,015	28,703	566,718	69,957	8,803	505,564	251,681	147,320	13,149	68,795	32,176
1985	959,049	564,778	28,368	593,146	72,868	12,611	532,889	271,319	154,841	13,871	69,139	32,600
1986	1,018,589	601,228	35,546	636,774	78,055	18,410	577,129	278,440	163,020	14,478	70,353	33,374
1987	1,044,965	606,607	47,568	654,175	78,676	26,374	601,873	272,275	170,817	14,675	71,206	34,918
1988	1,166,476	688,936	53,987	742,923	91,067	30,689	682,545	300,104	183,827	15,875	73,477	37,811
1989	1,336,342	791,395	55,908	847,303	106,387	33,532	774,448	362,984	198,910	17,571	76,054	40,078
1990	1,462,349	895,756	55,632	951,388	122,256	39,460	868,592	377,787	215,970	18,176	80,457	42,865
1991	1,585,496	984,040	55,087	1,039,127	135,814	38,954	942,267	400,058	243,171	18,929	83,761	44,137
1992	1,710,682	1,056,331	66,374	1,122,705	145,824	45,697	1,022,578	408,902	279,202	19,789	86,445	44,728
1993	1,813,115	1,111,181	76,876	1,188,057	152,711	51,776	1,087,122	424,236	301,757	20,251	89,530	45,889
1994	1,938,412	1,196,398	74,805	1,271,203	166,432	45,221	1,149,992	463,566	324,854	21,109	91,829	48,619
1995	2,075,792	1,260,151	81,677	1,341,828	176,352	45,561	1,211,037	512,938	351,817	22,070	94,053	49,832
1996	2,220,468	1,301,820	84,985	1,386,805	175,792	57,486	1,268,499	575,271	376,698	23,192	95,743	51,671
1997	2,347,131	1,400,126	82,817	1,482,943	180,821	72,963	1,375,085	586,240	385,806	24,064	97,539	52,910
1998	2,561,144	1,540,170	87,614	1,627,784	193,760	89,126	1,523,150	633,281	404,713	25,635	99,909	53,846
1999	2,711,063	1,715,720	92,672	1,808,392	210,679	78,617	1,676,330	604,075	430,658	26,657	101,701	56,204
2000	2,890,140	1,853,748	83,347	1,937,095	231,506	69,827	1,775,416	652,794	461,930	27,946	103,420	58,486
2001	2,958,139	1,847,470	93,837	1,941,307	235,388	81,016	1,786,935	657,515	513,689	28,298	104,534	58,680
2002	3,043,817	1,936,137	80,226	2,016,363	246,449	110,567	1,880,481	619,831	543,505	28,834	105,563	58,711
2003	3,218,217	2,030,451	101,100	2,131,551	259,419	138,658	2,010,790	641,993	565,434	29,973	107,369	59,855
2004	3,377,424	2,161,836	84,017	2,245,853	274,162	121,989	2,093,680	697,063	586,681	30,977	109,030	60,780
2005	3,576,953	2,347,073	87,206	2,434,279	302,198	126,221	2,258,302	693,509	625,142	32,317	110,683	63,203
2006	3,925,281	2,485,325	90,102	2,575,427	317,644	156,985	2,414,768	841,904	668,609	34,854	112,621	64,923
2007	4,230,085	2,583,163	94,380	2,677,543	334,230	211,214	2,554,527	956,919	718,639	37,085	114,066	66,686
2008	4,480,235	2,652,892	107,503	2,760,395	344,001	180,029	2,596,423	1,059,865	823,947	38,687	115,808	66,356
2009	4,388,437	2,489,075	125,239	2,614,314	337,199	187,814	2,464,929	995,153	928,355	37,651	116,557	63,179
2010	4,451,490	2,580,271	114,000	2,694,271	341,698	158,784	2,511,357	920,328	1,019,805	38,073	116,920	62,294
2011	4,667,550	2,635,623	113,082	2,748,705	317,013	204,500	2,636,192	1,006,589	1,024,769	39,731	117,479	62,391
2012	4,915,673	2,781,669	115,916	2,897,585	325,453	197,674	2,769,806	1,115,798	1,030,069	41,822	117,538	62,621
2013	4,987,202	2,948,295	116,427	3,064,722	383,969	163,106	2,843,859	1,090,534	1,052,809	42,260	118,013	64,899
2014	5,197,293	3,090,305	117,253	3,207,558	402,353	126,847	2,932,052	1,120,058	1,145,183	43,438	119,648	66,276
2015	5,480,387	3,224,169	145,491	3,369,660	420,248	121,115	3,070,527	1,224,137	1,185,723	45,232	121,161	66,731
2016	5,750,677	3,346,490	122,738	3,469,228	430,945	169,354	3,207,637	1,291,620	1,251,420	46,699	123,144	67,698
2017	6,095,349	3,600,657	127,739	3,728,396	468,719	138,102	3,397,779	1,402,362	1,295,208	48,668	125,243	69,103
2018	6,436,934	3,911,294	110,636	4,021,930	499,773	66,666	3,588,823	1,482,874	1,365,237	50,675	127,025	70,900
2019	6,931,076	4,136,047	136,416	4,272,463	517,298	92,207	3,847,372	1,625,637	1,458,067	53,987	128,383	71,277
2020	7,519,006	4,063,730	136,669	4,200,399	518,710	273,669	3,955,358	1,678,287	1,885,361	57,890	129,884	67,788
2021	8,171,766	4,384,945	133,993	4,518,938	550,923	268,394	4,236,409	1,819,293	2,116,064	62,412	130,933	69,614
2022	8,253,187	4,665,814	154,180	4,819,994	607,913	302,670	4,514,751	1,908,011	1,830,425	62,915	131,179	72,502

Personal Income and Employment by Area: Muncie, IN

(Thousands of dollars, except as noted.)

Year	Personal income, total	Derivation of personal income: Earnings by place of work: Nonfarm	Farm	Total	Less: Contributions for government social insurance	Plus: Adjustment for residence	Equals: Net earnings by place of residence	Plus: Dividends, interest, and rent	Plus: Personal current transfer receipts	Per capita personal income (dollars)	Population (persons)	Total employment
1970	453,679	398,132	4,642	402,774	26,965	-19,063	356,746	64,129	32,804	3,506	129,415	54,161
1971	495,858	422,022	8,306	430,328	29,576	-15,021	385,731	70,305	39,822	3,799	130,524	53,900
1972	525,032	444,527	5,567	450,094	33,280	-11,531	405,283	75,122	44,627	3,937	133,342	54,086
1973	596,151	496,955	14,805	511,760	42,844	-8,954	459,962	83,914	52,275	4,482	133,005	55,918
1974	647,781	541,518	7,282	548,800	48,890	-9,909	490,001	95,856	61,924	4,935	131,273	56,276
1975	686,269	538,737	12,836	551,573	48,237	-6,185	497,151	106,361	82,757	5,266	130,324	53,413
1976	752,516	598,265	9,773	608,038	53,908	-1,661	552,469	115,032	85,015	5,766	130,508	54,644
1977	841,773	678,215	6,761	684,976	60,869	-1,438	622,669	128,705	90,399	6,467	130,160	57,114
1978	930,089	745,110	8,060	753,170	68,838	2,496	686,828	143,156	100,105	7,170	129,712	57,799
1979	1,026,330	822,227	6,886	829,113	78,526	-370	750,217	161,463	114,650	7,980	128,611	59,035
1980	1,125,537	858,189	2,578	860,767	81,171	-3,111	776,485	198,232	150,820	8,766	128,394	57,729
1981	1,217,873	900,763	1,571	902,334	92,243	540	810,631	243,909	163,333	9,564	127,338	56,902
1982	1,233,095	874,294	4,049	878,343	91,568	5,878	792,653	259,792	180,650	9,795	125,887	54,123
1983	1,310,328	938,943	-4,074	934,869	98,405	9,087	845,551	271,972	192,805	10,561	124,068	54,000
1984	1,428,704	1,025,955	8,332	1,034,287	109,770	15,135	939,652	288,505	200,547	11,562	123,569	55,565
1985	1,492,402	1,072,384	5,784	1,078,168	116,765	18,346	979,749	304,946	207,707	12,228	122,044	56,476
1986	1,571,252	1,145,382	5,656	1,151,038	125,155	13,460	1,039,343	314,736	217,173	13,010	120,770	57,543
1987	1,630,992	1,208,244	9,926	1,218,170	130,697	11,162	1,098,635	310,475	221,882	13,470	121,082	58,948
1988	1,748,091	1,306,406	4,447	1,310,853	145,694	16,740	1,181,899	332,521	233,671	14,488	120,662	60,820
1989	1,882,518	1,373,438	9,547	1,382,985	154,616	23,517	1,251,886	375,477	255,155	15,693	119,962	61,574
1990	2,002,936	1,461,454	9,279	1,470,733	168,665	21,441	1,323,509	397,072	282,355	16,723	119,774	62,976
1991	2,076,296	1,537,656	4,990	1,542,646	179,242	10,114	1,373,518	396,653	306,125	17,306	119,973	62,840
1992	2,167,845	1,664,256	8,886	1,673,142	191,084	-47,599	1,434,459	391,018	342,368	18,013	120,352	65,363
1993	2,239,115	1,721,570	11,760	1,733,330	199,661	-52,524	1,481,145	395,678	362,292	18,515	120,935	65,781
1994	2,363,044	1,837,554	15,737	1,853,291	215,603	-72,259	1,565,429	419,736	377,879	19,608	120,514	67,867
1995	2,458,734	1,914,997	8,157	1,923,154	224,657	-83,797	1,614,700	464,105	379,929	20,369	120,707	69,973
1996	2,531,237	1,918,513	11,212	1,929,725	222,557	-58,073	1,649,095	481,436	400,706	20,992	120,582	68,253
1997	2,613,133	2,008,351	16,568	2,024,919	232,241	-71,144	1,721,534	483,900	407,699	21,679	120,539	68,126
1998	2,756,342	2,051,152	13,413	2,064,565	232,569	-31,882	1,800,114	530,613	425,615	23,067	119,495	68,306
1999	2,828,203	2,097,870	10,358	2,108,228	236,184	-9,952	1,862,092	512,569	453,542	23,812	118,772	68,754
2000	2,991,026	2,201,452	12,916	2,214,368	245,065	-5,754	1,963,549	544,096	483,381	25,182	118,776	69,098
2001	3,053,709	2,208,034	14,706	2,222,740	250,885	-14,889	1,956,966	559,020	537,723	25,388	120,281	68,548
2002	3,050,121	2,209,817	4,624	2,214,441	251,698	-6,100	1,956,643	533,592	559,886	25,428	119,949	65,879
2003	3,116,173	2,249,675	12,752	2,262,427	257,695	-17,203	1,987,529	551,801	576,843	25,982	119,935	64,628
2004	3,141,455	2,282,365	22,948	2,305,313	261,122	6,625	2,050,816	485,225	605,414	26,413	118,938	63,454
2005	3,172,857	2,285,035	14,533	2,299,568	267,469	22,322	2,054,421	459,801	658,635	26,850	118,170	62,538
2006	3,181,041	2,294,887	10,442	2,305,329	271,224	-27,930	2,006,175	468,012	706,854	27,113	117,326	63,300
2007	3,209,792	2,310,264	9,084	2,319,348	275,618	-68,797	1,974,933	507,009	727,850	27,381	117,229	63,377
2008	3,324,113	2,307,537	18,025	2,325,562	278,172	-111,696	1,935,694	558,304	830,115	28,410	117,007	62,096
2009	3,259,142	2,200,625	12,223	2,212,848	270,206	-121,082	1,821,560	518,512	919,070	27,740	117,490	59,145
2010	3,311,711	2,188,801	10,256	2,199,057	265,150	-107,751	1,826,156	501,433	984,122	28,154	117,628	57,769
2011	3,469,715	2,274,079	24,472	2,298,551	243,704	-118,973	1,935,874	554,136	979,705	29,481	117,695	58,554
2012	3,602,710	2,391,927	20,694	2,412,621	254,686	-143,503	2,014,432	569,556	1,018,722	30,881	116,663	58,937
2013	3,651,098	2,430,977	57,493	2,488,470	294,678	-154,336	2,039,456	585,659	1,025,983	31,393	116,304	58,990
2014	3,771,431	2,503,971	26,531	2,530,502	302,584	-148,044	2,079,874	594,036	1,097,521	32,570	115,794	58,580
2015	3,872,188	2,603,570	4,062	2,607,632	314,887	-171,972	2,120,773	610,832	1,140,583	33,696	114,914	59,590
2016	3,936,721	2,624,697	15,089	2,639,786	314,379	-154,595	2,170,812	596,680	1,169,229	34,344	114,627	60,289
2017	4,061,398	2,700,742	8,467	2,709,209	324,995	-175,545	2,208,669	640,823	1,211,906	35,617	114,031	60,392
2018	4,153,955	2,748,040	9,484	2,757,524	332,945	-169,604	2,254,975	650,443	1,248,537	36,851	112,723	60,241
2019	4,328,406	2,862,512	8,525	2,871,037	350,695	-166,669	2,353,673	658,701	1,316,032	38,575	112,208	60,061
2020	4,658,228	2,943,087	17,274	2,960,361	366,483	-232,611	2,361,267	682,919	1,614,042	41,680	111,763	57,878
2021	5,048,854	3,080,309	30,986	3,111,295	380,420	-188,727	2,542,148	698,500	1,808,206	45,087	111,981	58,143
2022	5,093,482	3,278,724	24,190	3,302,914	405,585	-186,826	2,710,503	740,255	1,642,724	45,465	112,031	59,783

Personal Income and Employment by Area: Muskegon, MI

(Thousands of dollars, except as noted.)

Year	Personal income, total	Derivation of personal income: Earnings by place of work: Nonfarm	Farm	Total	Less: Contributions for government social insurance	Plus: Adjustment for residence	Equals: Net earnings by place of residence	Plus: Dividends, interest, and rent	Plus: Personal current transfer receipts	Per capita personal income (dollars)	Population (persons)	Total employment
1970	580,833	502,485	3,319	505,804	36,139	-23,834	445,831	67,863	67,139	3,686	157,595	61,851
1971	601,588	499,296	3,304	502,600	37,037	-19,104	446,459	72,066	83,063	3,799	158,338	59,280
1972	668,217	562,195	3,743	565,938	44,138	-22,281	499,519	77,269	91,429	4,226	158,137	61,124
1973	727,752	621,504	3,694	625,198	56,776	-26,740	541,682	84,338	101,732	4,631	157,135	63,037
1974	805,200	679,210	5,755	684,965	63,978	-31,455	589,532	96,443	119,225	5,151	156,315	64,536
1975	880,409	712,195	4,593	716,788	65,004	-33,296	618,488	107,755	154,166	5,634	156,266	63,935
1976	959,264	787,449	4,627	792,076	73,762	-34,110	684,204	113,032	162,028	6,095	157,395	65,187
1977	1,051,818	872,209	5,573	877,782	81,465	-33,802	762,515	123,098	166,205	6,678	157,496	66,515
1978	1,179,804	982,422	7,285	989,707	95,122	-35,263	859,322	138,824	181,658	7,502	157,258	68,481
1979	1,295,220	1,072,957	5,242	1,078,199	108,592	-35,326	934,281	156,971	203,968	8,194	158,067	68,649
1980	1,395,487	1,108,549	5,379	1,113,928	110,521	-38,716	964,691	188,076	242,720	8,841	157,850	66,135
1981	1,504,371	1,162,622	7,758	1,170,380	125,075	-41,412	1,003,893	224,909	275,569	9,488	158,550	64,362
1982	1,574,292	1,154,252	9,653	1,163,905	125,615	-34,949	1,003,341	260,043	310,908	10,084	156,114	61,143
1983	1,639,926	1,192,327	7,477	1,199,804	131,908	-27,090	1,040,806	269,853	329,267	10,615	154,496	60,591
1984	1,807,207	1,335,798	8,729	1,344,527	154,387	-25,795	1,164,345	310,577	332,285	11,671	154,844	64,284
1985	1,915,590	1,420,334	12,683	1,433,017	166,241	-23,985	1,242,791	324,005	348,794	12,307	155,654	66,520
1986	1,983,867	1,474,821	8,086	1,482,907	172,581	-30,062	1,280,264	337,707	365,896	12,732	155,812	67,445
1987	2,067,854	1,511,736	8,319	1,520,055	173,494	-14,652	1,331,909	360,456	375,489	13,226	156,345	67,252
1988	2,164,125	1,587,473	7,751	1,595,224	188,961	-586	1,405,677	368,228	390,220	13,728	157,643	68,222
1989	2,311,415	1,669,433	10,877	1,680,310	197,412	6,304	1,489,202	401,109	421,104	14,595	158,365	69,448
1990	2,430,918	1,738,463	7,588	1,746,051	208,189	8,270	1,546,132	425,280	459,506	15,252	159,384	70,361
1991	2,501,272	1,746,604	9,589	1,756,193	211,795	17,735	1,562,133	428,812	510,327	15,547	160,885	68,332
1992	2,638,782	1,856,422	10,002	1,866,424	223,688	36,027	1,678,763	430,344	529,675	16,275	162,135	68,157
1993	2,749,405	1,917,508	8,785	1,926,293	233,846	54,267	1,746,714	447,863	554,828	16,859	163,082	67,576
1994	2,935,050	2,033,507	8,135	2,041,642	254,701	86,535	1,873,476	506,188	555,386	17,932	163,678	69,480
1995	3,078,188	2,131,597	9,654	2,141,251	270,894	98,905	1,969,262	528,305	580,621	18,717	164,457	71,863
1996	3,241,603	2,230,168	8,884	2,239,052	279,187	121,891	2,081,756	548,652	611,195	19,556	165,763	73,599
1997	3,447,262	2,378,999	9,540	2,388,539	297,185	144,462	2,235,816	569,286	642,160	20,633	167,077	75,236
1998	3,659,727	2,570,631	11,277	2,581,908	317,126	159,168	2,423,950	589,184	646,593	21,765	168,147	77,667
1999	3,882,070	2,744,430	11,905	2,756,335	335,486	171,223	2,592,072	583,313	706,685	22,926	169,331	81,008
2000	4,087,313	2,872,463	7,757	2,880,220	350,599	198,559	2,728,180	624,504	734,629	23,987	170,396	83,059
2001	4,149,355	2,824,957	8,372	2,833,329	329,755	206,920	2,710,494	610,875	827,986	24,257	171,055	79,334
2002	4,182,700	2,838,027	6,190	2,844,217	331,033	208,308	2,721,492	593,817	867,391	24,380	171,563	78,856
2003	4,285,584	2,876,999	9,459	2,886,458	336,897	198,482	2,748,043	624,497	913,044	24,877	172,269	79,852
2004	4,377,584	2,975,367	13,939	2,989,306	354,823	196,668	2,831,151	607,163	939,270	25,337	172,771	81,911
2005	4,513,102	3,037,675	13,668	3,051,343	372,552	234,915	2,913,706	601,538	997,858	25,996	173,608	82,259
2006	4,673,302	3,133,792	14,776	3,148,568	390,206	238,013	2,996,375	607,414	1,069,513	26,903	173,710	82,619
2007	4,851,540	3,144,047	19,646	3,163,693	394,224	247,786	3,017,255	665,880	1,168,405	27,924	173,738	81,968
2008	4,954,693	3,152,474	20,407	3,172,881	398,968	153,813	2,927,726	712,490	1,314,477	28,500	173,846	80,355
2009	4,807,947	2,933,796	14,753	2,948,549	372,796	109,648	2,685,401	661,805	1,460,741	27,831	172,755	75,603
2010	4,996,117	3,039,000	24,015	3,063,015	380,315	90,119	2,772,819	666,489	1,556,809	29,052	171,970	74,816
2011	5,250,621	3,156,517	40,214	3,196,731	354,809	99,169	2,941,091	775,069	1,534,461	30,834	170,289	76,748
2012	5,417,363	3,315,300	20,708	3,336,008	371,381	113,056	3,077,683	809,781	1,529,899	31,753	170,612	77,716
2013	5,478,992	3,363,469	37,745	3,401,214	424,808	132,794	3,109,200	800,105	1,569,687	31,684	172,927	78,223
2014	5,759,125	3,490,009	27,412	3,517,421	439,836	189,907	3,267,492	864,102	1,627,531	33,269	173,110	79,808
2015	6,028,784	3,639,535	20,806	3,660,341	452,745	203,796	3,411,392	899,509	1,717,883	34,747	173,504	80,448
2016	6,170,875	3,667,887	22,498	3,690,385	457,117	300,052	3,533,320	879,848	1,757,707	35,355	174,538	79,877
2017	6,370,064	3,820,867	18,005	3,838,872	474,395	301,331	3,665,808	939,922	1,764,334	36,360	175,196	81,178
2018	6,594,984	3,937,915	16,833	3,954,748	496,953	335,065	3,792,860	959,627	1,842,497	37,621	175,302	81,417
2019	6,883,580	3,973,753	15,062	3,988,815	500,131	442,585	3,931,269	1,012,691	1,939,620	39,240	175,421	80,302
2020	7,627,568	3,870,814	23,335	3,894,149	486,675	423,985	3,831,459	1,061,154	2,734,955	43,376	175,848	74,994
2021	8,127,512	4,280,096	22,723	4,302,819	528,119	395,640	4,170,340	1,083,331	2,873,841	46,019	176,612	78,640
2022	8,046,286	4,613,383	28,867	4,642,250	586,235	418,978	4,474,993	1,162,555	2,408,738	45,571	176,565	82,589

Personal Income and Employment by Area: Myrtle Beach-Conway-North Myrtle Beach, SC-NC

(Thousands of dollars, except as noted.)

Year	Personal income, total	Derivation of personal income: Earnings by place of work: Nonfarm	Farm	Total	Less: Contributions for government social insurance	Plus: Adjustment for residence	Equals: Net earnings by place of residence	Plus: Dividends, interest, and rent	Plus: Personal current transfer receipts	Per capita personal income (dollars)	Population (persons)	Total employment
1970	285,259	204,494	19,298	223,792	13,478	6,039	216,353	42,169	26,737	2,993	95,303	42,155
1971	335,024	240,583	18,453	259,036	16,402	9,073	251,707	52,169	31,148	3,312	101,165	45,218
1972	391,975	288,747	22,502	311,249	20,303	6,150	297,096	59,818	35,061	3,652	107,339	48,709
1973	450,877	333,232	27,197	360,429	26,458	5,982	339,953	69,526	41,398	3,977	113,376	52,009
1974	513,110	372,614	36,788	409,402	31,109	2,325	380,618	79,473	53,019	4,337	118,307	53,860
1975	578,653	422,534	28,498	451,032	35,517	-2,511	413,004	91,816	73,833	4,743	121,997	55,574
1976	641,890	479,653	22,519	502,172	40,806	-4,428	456,938	101,264	83,688	5,035	127,490	58,366
1977	708,269	540,277	17,141	557,418	45,663	-8,564	503,191	117,371	87,707	5,532	128,032	62,138
1978	829,350	619,934	36,238	656,172	53,200	-11,309	591,663	140,742	96,945	6,277	132,125	66,349
1979	914,684	697,988	15,134	713,122	62,065	-15,805	635,252	164,864	114,568	6,798	134,546	68,739
1980	1,042,716	771,768	12,589	784,357	68,908	-20,136	695,313	204,939	142,464	7,526	138,543	70,280
1981	1,206,475	864,210	27,210	891,420	83,236	-22,806	785,378	251,720	169,377	8,408	143,488	72,021
1982	1,335,311	945,094	17,925	963,019	93,370	-24,540	845,109	296,047	194,155	9,024	147,977	75,532
1983	1,541,702	1,102,138	14,018	1,116,156	109,956	-18,355	987,845	340,674	213,183	9,929	155,270	80,547
1984	1,757,949	1,266,857	10,611	1,277,468	131,306	-20,986	1,125,176	402,472	230,301	10,746	163,585	88,239
1985	1,955,916	1,391,938	18,514	1,410,452	147,079	-21,673	1,241,700	457,924	256,292	11,416	171,336	91,199
1986	2,113,793	1,487,991	-2,657	1,485,334	161,192	1,164	1,325,306	507,888	280,599	11,906	177,546	93,765
1987	2,308,475	1,621,672	21,732	1,643,404	173,473	11,217	1,481,148	530,593	296,734	12,590	183,363	95,855
1988	2,537,784	1,762,174	24,547	1,786,721	195,414	24,720	1,616,027	597,873	323,884	13,564	187,091	100,892
1989	2,809,010	1,887,664	27,082	1,914,746	213,944	39,742	1,740,544	681,939	386,527	14,726	190,746	103,297
1990	3,024,832	2,031,032	28,366	2,059,398	235,653	56,799	1,880,544	707,868	436,420	15,398	196,448	107,397
1991	3,212,738	2,168,175	37,160	2,205,335	256,757	31,685	1,980,263	737,096	495,379	15,859	202,583	108,714
1992	3,422,206	2,282,384	39,524	2,321,908	268,812	46,847	2,099,943	751,524	570,739	16,429	208,302	109,888
1993	3,579,932	2,359,916	36,261	2,396,177	281,331	45,682	2,160,528	793,920	625,484	17,177	208,415	111,547
1994	3,908,949	2,577,562	35,349	2,612,911	313,926	41,679	2,340,664	866,602	701,683	18,124	215,675	118,839
1995	4,341,632	2,872,774	23,808	2,896,582	349,625	37,615	2,584,572	980,256	776,804	19,316	224,765	128,781
1996	4,795,777	3,147,288	33,975	3,181,263	373,954	52,001	2,859,310	1,085,155	851,312	20,404	235,041	135,319
1997	5,276,552	3,469,655	39,667	3,509,322	411,646	63,604	3,161,280	1,204,527	910,745	21,529	245,090	144,171
1998	5,723,238	3,803,526	1,544	3,805,070	451,428	84,939	3,438,581	1,301,163	983,494	22,477	254,627	149,824
1999	6,116,556	4,155,680	13,674	4,169,354	490,065	94,428	3,773,717	1,291,674	1,051,165	23,239	263,200	155,162
2000	6,550,449	4,364,716	42,355	4,407,071	518,334	100,589	3,989,326	1,417,421	1,143,702	24,106	271,736	158,299
2001	6,830,318	4,480,149	60,989	4,541,138	537,167	69,926	4,073,897	1,472,135	1,284,286	24,571	277,987	161,326
2002	7,007,204	4,632,041	-10,734	4,621,307	559,314	75,471	4,137,464	1,455,999	1,413,741	24,599	284,862	163,519
2003	7,469,816	4,989,880	22,314	5,012,194	609,125	25,780	4,428,849	1,507,254	1,533,713	25,555	292,309	168,878
2004	8,244,252	5,524,003	24,121	5,548,124	669,412	21,878	4,900,590	1,631,759	1,711,903	27,261	302,421	178,125
2005	9,081,282	6,060,252	22,870	6,083,122	731,237	46,924	5,398,809	1,789,915	1,892,558	28,580	317,745	189,672
2006	10,049,149	6,635,317	12,016	6,647,333	822,020	87,857	5,913,170	2,028,959	2,107,020	29,896	336,132	202,103
2007	10,773,915	6,787,476	7,315	6,794,791	846,664	187,065	6,135,192	2,348,568	2,290,155	30,654	351,472	208,187
2008	11,277,169	6,591,011	30,314	6,621,325	836,632	212,716	5,997,409	2,606,417	2,673,343	30,993	363,866	204,746
2009	11,295,408	6,161,178	35,989	6,197,167	803,169	345,837	5,739,835	2,498,936	3,056,637	30,412	371,417	194,537
2010	11,534,364	6,211,332	37,005	6,248,337	813,424	382,537	5,817,450	2,371,799	3,345,115	30,519	377,945	192,090
2011	12,082,793	6,368,829	30,169	6,398,998	762,509	382,059	6,018,548	2,597,480	3,466,765	31,499	383,594	197,164
2012	12,634,176	6,643,833	39,186	6,683,019	784,562	376,269	6,274,726	2,760,357	3,599,093	32,433	389,544	200,127
2013	13,222,104	7,067,241	48,191	7,115,432	922,454	425,785	6,618,763	2,784,321	3,819,020	33,208	398,162	205,957
2014	14,214,416	7,505,206	36,404	7,541,610	976,132	422,431	6,987,909	3,058,973	4,167,534	34,788	408,600	211,144
2015	15,452,993	7,998,472	5,981	8,004,453	1,033,662	474,712	7,445,503	3,446,850	4,560,640	36,645	421,689	216,868
2016	16,602,675	8,442,011	11,329	8,453,340	1,094,785	631,892	7,990,447	3,743,185	4,869,043	38,109	435,666	224,552
2017	17,694,062	9,077,656	14,978	9,092,634	1,185,096	608,515	8,516,053	3,951,957	5,226,052	39,364	449,494	231,019
2018	19,010,479	9,626,108	-1,580	9,624,528	1,264,613	695,255	9,055,170	4,243,185	5,712,124	40,941	464,335	240,745
2019	20,682,433	10,231,528	-1,586	10,229,942	1,347,499	801,769	9,684,212	4,713,634	6,284,587	43,338	477,232	245,385
2020	23,007,900	10,398,250	-4,273	10,393,977	1,390,319	1,014,184	10,017,842	5,049,411	7,940,647	46,773	491,902	238,795
2021	25,761,940	12,080,063	9,665	12,089,728	1,580,842	1,049,329	11,558,215	5,217,613	8,986,112	50,432	510,825	256,150
2022	26,924,445	13,194,627	-19,971	13,174,656	1,780,331	1,352,938	12,747,263	5,710,622	8,466,560	50,217	536,165	271,144

Personal Income and Employment by Area: Napa, CA

(Thousands of dollars, except as noted.)

Year	Personal income, total	Derivation of personal income: Earnings by place of work: Nonfarm	Farm	Total	Less: Contributions for government social insurance	Plus: Adjustment for residence	Equals: Net earnings by place of residence	Plus: Dividends, interest, and rent	Plus: Personal current transfer receipts	Per capita personal income (dollars)	Population (persons)	Total employment
1970	381,497	200,291	6,511	206,802	11,903	65,775	260,674	82,224	38,599	4,795	79,562	27,680
1971	416,801	217,607	6,258	223,865	13,468	70,994	281,391	92,646	42,764	5,097	81,771	28,531
1972	448,277	232,249	7,762	240,011	15,010	75,874	300,875	101,594	45,808	5,387	83,208	29,297
1973	508,478	267,159	13,400	280,559	19,876	80,542	341,225	114,786	52,467	5,797	87,718	31,552
1974	578,763	302,113	9,589	311,702	23,560	95,826	383,968	132,347	62,448	6,377	90,759	33,495
1975	674,732	346,569	15,444	362,013	26,750	111,299	446,562	149,514	78,656	7,207	93,627	35,667
1976	745,064	379,543	16,148	395,691	29,226	126,868	493,333	162,843	88,888	7,846	94,964	36,033
1977	827,296	412,087	21,533	433,620	32,188	144,783	546,215	183,287	97,794	8,571	96,521	36,858
1978	943,170	471,624	26,011	497,635	37,931	166,309	626,013	212,576	104,581	9,780	96,437	38,852
1979	1,055,739	542,121	20,588	562,709	46,332	175,840	692,217	242,326	121,196	10,687	98,789	41,207
1980	1,166,558	582,073	20,909	602,982	49,794	187,810	740,998	286,915	138,645	11,744	99,331	43,047
1981	1,325,634	662,298	22,664	684,962	62,311	197,520	820,171	345,400	160,063	13,301	99,662	44,376
1982	1,426,311	690,523	37,653	728,176	66,593	215,123	876,706	375,369	174,236	14,097	101,178	44,528
1983	1,519,714	733,184	19,871	753,055	72,031	235,458	916,482	414,524	188,708	14,965	101,549	45,542
1984	1,655,563	829,270	19,956	849,226	84,904	245,371	1,009,693	451,368	194,502	16,247	101,902	47,379
1985	1,786,951	900,721	21,142	921,863	93,809	261,734	1,089,788	486,620	210,543	17,347	103,014	49,000
1986	1,919,001	995,525	30,221	1,025,746	105,436	270,878	1,191,188	504,509	223,304	18,410	104,237	51,024
1987	1,998,411	1,069,171	23,722	1,092,893	113,218	281,208	1,260,883	507,468	230,060	19,031	105,010	52,434
1988	2,181,917	1,195,782	28,504	1,224,286	132,032	293,245	1,385,499	551,223	245,195	20,559	106,130	54,863
1989	2,413,073	1,265,289	59,217	1,324,506	141,886	308,321	1,490,941	651,862	270,270	22,207	108,662	56,480
1990	2,568,332	1,390,694	45,325	1,436,019	155,675	339,481	1,619,825	659,198	289,309	23,079	111,284	59,343
1991	2,719,113	1,488,245	54,906	1,543,151	167,013	345,002	1,721,140	678,968	319,005	24,227	112,233	60,173
1992	2,840,028	1,594,834	44,668	1,639,502	177,659	326,086	1,787,929	689,000	363,099	24,842	114,322	60,221
1993	2,955,061	1,665,021	33,636	1,698,657	185,461	320,854	1,834,050	737,290	383,721	25,702	114,972	60,849
1994	3,085,763	1,755,620	35,649	1,791,269	194,629	333,985	1,930,625	765,393	389,745	26,584	116,077	62,499
1995	3,219,652	1,863,604	40,338	1,903,942	205,052	301,113	2,000,003	812,947	406,702	27,590	116,697	64,022
1996	3,452,240	2,010,971	53,432	2,064,403	214,396	289,237	2,139,244	885,171	427,825	29,257	117,996	67,250
1997	3,669,433	2,194,095	98,409	2,292,504	233,144	253,070	2,312,430	919,328	437,675	30,628	119,808	70,898
1998	3,945,710	2,440,831	63,703	2,504,534	254,403	249,485	2,499,616	980,973	465,121	32,453	121,583	77,036
1999	4,305,906	2,803,319	76,809	2,880,128	289,604	229,023	2,819,547	1,021,765	464,594	35,000	123,026	81,319
2000	4,739,145	3,084,190	139,774	3,223,964	318,179	232,753	3,138,538	1,113,358	487,249	38,046	124,565	82,348
2001	5,185,732	3,660,354	136,466	3,796,820	378,150	132,526	3,551,196	1,111,345	523,191	40,891	126,818	83,462
2002	5,274,411	3,865,113	149,310	4,014,423	404,711	53,933	3,663,645	1,055,323	555,443	40,968	128,744	85,106
2003	5,339,221	3,964,581	116,944	4,081,525	427,823	-30,396	3,623,306	1,129,983	585,932	41,027	130,138	85,768
2004	5,408,459	4,049,607	95,311	4,144,918	463,737	-95,486	3,585,695	1,206,381	616,383	41,480	130,387	87,005
2005	5,708,247	4,174,139	151,742	4,325,881	475,848	-74,016	3,776,017	1,280,768	651,462	43,781	130,381	87,729
2006	6,035,436	4,391,074	88,488	4,479,562	479,925	-80,916	3,918,721	1,412,559	704,156	45,918	131,440	88,028
2007	6,283,049	4,599,928	67,017	4,666,945	499,458	-159,527	4,007,960	1,529,010	746,079	47,390	132,583	91,175
2008	6,330,818	4,641,936	44,966	4,686,902	514,093	-268,940	3,903,869	1,587,860	839,089	47,212	134,093	91,679
2009	6,228,367	4,507,099	107,686	4,614,785	499,330	-230,401	3,885,054	1,437,556	905,757	46,041	135,280	88,603
2010	6,390,918	4,654,966	85,623	4,740,589	491,464	-258,957	3,990,168	1,411,262	989,488	46,720	136,791	87,944
2011	6,644,810	4,690,469	60,224	4,750,693	452,159	-244,115	4,054,419	1,584,233	1,006,158	48,198	137,865	89,319
2012	7,334,742	5,057,089	206,572	5,263,661	477,312	-279,580	4,506,769	1,813,203	1,014,770	52,821	138,861	92,265
2013	7,603,966	5,487,163	234,846	5,722,009	573,014	-294,664	4,854,331	1,705,153	1,044,482	54,298	140,041	96,097
2014	8,212,768	5,996,132	213,123	6,209,255	616,358	-404,118	5,188,779	1,925,599	1,098,390	58,241	141,014	99,860
2015	8,890,655	6,533,300	174,852	6,708,152	662,782	-377,415	5,667,955	2,052,787	1,169,913	62,781	141,613	103,116
2016	9,415,486	6,865,672	181,764	7,047,436	693,274	-278,675	6,075,487	2,128,741	1,211,258	66,405	141,789	103,107
2017	9,595,776	6,997,738	200,621	7,198,359	717,357	-420,047	6,060,955	2,330,300	1,204,521	68,063	140,984	104,686
2018	9,657,020	6,990,944	157,966	7,148,910	745,723	-475,450	5,927,737	2,468,539	1,260,744	69,010	139,937	107,561
2019	10,184,848	7,262,287	144,751	7,407,038	782,275	-407,732	6,217,031	2,617,223	1,350,594	73,195	139,146	106,557
2020	11,260,752	7,091,230	158,686	7,249,916	746,683	-27,410	6,475,823	2,826,273	1,958,656	81,905	137,485	98,244
2021	11,907,435	7,807,768	177,489	7,985,257	819,248	-162,572	7,003,437	2,882,427	2,021,571	87,422	136,206	100,928
2022	11,665,710	8,273,558	142,611	8,416,169	911,855	-610,050	6,894,264	3,082,814	1,688,632	86,863	134,300	107,782

Personal Income and Employment by Area: Naples-Marco Island, FL

(Thousands of dollars, except as noted.)

Year	Personal income, total	Derivation of personal income: Earnings by place of work: Nonfarm	Farm	Total	Less: Contributions for government social insurance	Plus: Adjustment for residence	Equals: Net earnings by place of residence	Plus: Dividends, interest, and rent	Plus: Personal current transfer receipts	Per capita personal income (dollars)	Population (persons)	Total employment
1970	208,518	126,251	9,560	135,811	7,829	-11,869	116,113	77,669	14,736	5,364	38,874	19,784
1971	248,158	142,417	12,446	154,863	9,157	-11,225	134,481	93,439	20,238	5,814	42,683	21,385
1972	290,752	162,864	15,182	178,046	11,053	-11,510	155,483	110,868	24,401	5,916	49,144	22,959
1973	368,203	214,688	16,135	230,823	16,968	-14,942	198,913	138,061	31,229	6,724	54,757	28,113
1974	426,924	236,006	18,908	254,914	19,697	-15,257	219,960	168,112	38,852	7,311	58,396	30,121
1975	456,499	232,806	21,777	254,583	18,884	-10,919	224,780	178,930	52,789	7,177	63,602	28,974
1976	523,920	264,984	22,891	287,875	20,883	-9,240	257,752	206,728	59,440	7,923	66,125	29,334
1977	620,590	324,165	21,698	345,863	26,089	-10,612	309,162	243,861	67,567	8,942	69,404	34,304
1978	756,148	404,583	25,432	430,015	33,747	-13,342	382,926	294,875	78,347	10,103	74,844	40,053
1979	893,339	476,453	35,609	512,062	41,994	-13,099	456,969	342,716	93,654	10,909	81,890	44,215
1980	1,083,586	555,386	37,864	593,250	49,835	-13,171	530,244	438,816	114,526	12,383	87,504	46,868
1981	1,332,445	645,952	37,397	683,349	63,122	-13,292	606,935	586,435	139,075	14,255	93,473	50,278
1982	1,437,053	657,479	49,704	707,183	67,559	-8,947	630,677	638,810	167,566	14,385	99,902	51,225
1983	1,646,721	722,358	84,208	806,566	73,794	-6,628	726,144	732,636	187,941	15,794	104,265	55,623
1984	1,889,666	832,272	78,778	911,050	87,495	-9,320	814,235	867,805	207,626	17,162	110,105	61,169
1985	2,109,939	948,845	88,742	1,037,587	102,725	-11,856	923,006	956,850	230,083	18,255	115,584	65,543
1986	2,389,939	1,069,544	104,993	1,174,537	119,764	-11,800	1,042,973	1,089,754	257,212	19,701	121,311	71,756
1987	2,731,214	1,285,247	122,892	1,408,139	141,862	-15,835	1,250,442	1,200,109	280,663	21,351	127,921	74,893
1988	3,373,068	1,491,305	142,264	1,633,569	169,085	-21,502	1,442,982	1,607,422	322,664	24,909	135,413	83,812
1989	3,852,124	1,697,170	177,436	1,874,606	196,272	-25,905	1,652,429	1,836,917	362,778	26,605	144,790	89,342
1990	4,153,976	1,835,917	114,906	1,950,823	211,501	-29,203	1,710,119	2,029,305	414,552	26,875	154,568	92,101
1991	4,657,039	1,966,306	163,669	2,129,975	226,354	100,981	2,004,602	2,175,378	477,059	28,399	163,988	94,434
1992	5,237,628	2,135,932	207,357	2,343,289	243,320	161,865	2,261,834	2,412,619	563,175	30,438	172,077	96,093
1993	5,673,488	2,337,418	204,490	2,541,908	264,512	97,714	2,375,110	2,684,321	614,057	31,295	181,288	101,102
1994	6,246,230	2,583,059	154,108	2,737,167	295,029	92,194	2,534,332	3,038,163	673,735	32,680	191,132	104,131
1995	6,778,920	2,821,678	147,719	2,969,397	316,757	106,301	2,758,941	3,287,597	732,382	33,956	199,639	107,407
1996	7,467,388	3,092,576	134,526	3,227,102	342,643	184,819	3,069,278	3,608,809	789,301	35,694	209,205	113,188
1997	8,341,083	3,500,077	142,932	3,643,009	386,804	100,338	3,356,543	4,145,385	839,155	37,756	220,923	119,660
1998	9,323,994	3,821,332	164,529	3,985,861	417,181	195,648	3,764,328	4,682,550	877,116	39,954	233,371	128,002
1999	9,981,131	4,252,919	154,215	4,407,134	457,397	202,008	4,151,745	4,885,202	944,184	40,724	245,094	133,485
2000	10,777,335	4,724,567	156,123	4,880,690	507,357	67,461	4,440,794	5,299,233	1,037,308	42,428	254,015	143,309
2001	12,212,766	5,621,460	147,768	5,769,228	592,234	80,670	5,257,664	5,805,717	1,149,385	46,218	264,240	151,622
2002	12,757,520	6,001,815	164,406	6,166,221	633,765	108,019	5,640,475	5,877,890	1,239,155	46,308	275,490	157,774
2003	13,563,750	6,529,045	142,774	6,671,819	695,348	110,534	6,087,005	6,141,872	1,334,873	47,539	285,321	168,141
2004	15,591,751	6,916,018	144,726	7,060,744	759,339	176,582	6,477,987	7,665,233	1,448,531	52,671	296,021	177,641
2005	17,741,863	7,763,165	178,014	7,941,179	846,342	166,214	7,261,051	8,874,136	1,606,676	57,706	307,452	182,757
2006	20,309,693	8,393,661	166,763	8,560,424	927,871	231,128	7,863,681	10,712,445	1,733,567	64,966	312,621	190,180
2007	21,220,889	8,290,465	155,976	8,446,441	934,073	163,987	7,676,355	11,684,860	1,859,674	67,489	314,437	186,382
2008	21,343,560	7,416,215	143,479	7,559,694	882,040	299,491	6,977,145	12,236,346	2,130,069	67,406	316,641	178,682
2009	18,368,991	6,775,285	150,231	6,925,516	834,051	311,387	6,402,852	9,594,654	2,371,485	57,676	318,485	169,939
2010	20,306,964	7,387,255	137,359	7,524,614	855,008	515,720	7,185,326	10,524,199	2,597,439	63,015	322,255	170,286
2011	21,255,653	7,647,816	116,608	7,764,424	791,034	445,512	7,418,902	11,128,175	2,708,576	65,193	326,042	176,894
2012	23,729,762	7,723,685	132,663	7,856,348	823,924	689,757	7,722,181	13,282,589	2,724,992	72,049	329,357	183,067
2013	23,286,392	7,984,857	141,727	8,126,584	959,515	640,889	7,807,958	12,664,921	2,813,513	69,561	334,760	190,510
2014	26,246,129	8,975,156	106,646	9,081,802	1,056,769	825,141	8,850,174	14,439,122	2,956,833	76,843	341,555	200,954
2015	28,935,924	9,701,981	113,755	9,815,736	1,130,213	1,058,999	9,744,522	16,031,171	3,160,231	82,935	348,897	210,278
2016	30,423,335	10,284,819	96,536	10,381,355	1,191,588	1,161,727	10,351,494	16,780,291	3,291,550	85,250	356,874	217,148
2017	33,281,822	10,658,917	98,828	10,757,745	1,233,933	1,308,585	10,832,397	18,954,554	3,494,871	91,778	362,634	222,426
2018	37,355,366	11,423,979	86,664	11,510,643	1,342,200	1,349,869	11,518,312	22,108,131	3,728,923	101,957	366,385	231,608
2019	39,600,011	12,338,180	79,434	12,417,614	1,455,726	1,382,962	12,344,850	23,172,213	4,082,948	106,469	371,939	234,709
2020	41,877,033	12,786,660	88,009	12,874,669	1,524,849	1,747,545	13,097,365	23,705,331	5,074,337	110,993	377,293	236,432
2021	48,804,286	14,761,160	89,649	14,850,809	1,700,254	1,746,231	14,896,786	28,070,406	5,837,094	126,031	387,241	250,927
2022	52,200,912	16,273,456	87,820	16,361,276	1,906,699	1,895,993	16,350,570	30,418,110	5,432,232	131,160	397,994	266,851

Personal Income and Employment by Area: Nashville-Davidson—Murfreesboro—Franklin, TN

(Thousands of dollars, except as noted.)

Year	Personal income, total	Derivation of personal income: Earnings by place of work: Nonfarm	Farm	Total	Less: Contributions for government social insurance	Plus: Adjustment for residence	Equals: Net earnings by place of residence	Plus: Dividends, interest, and rent	Plus: Personal current transfer receipts	Per capita personal income (dollars)	Population (persons)	Total employment
1970	2,840,901	2,361,689	51,747	2,413,436	154,062	-9,633	2,249,741	374,530	216,630	3,629	782,791	384,087
1971	3,093,374	2,560,271	47,692	2,607,963	171,780	-9,515	2,426,668	411,821	254,885	3,895	794,123	386,662
1972	3,478,182	2,906,610	56,917	2,963,527	205,806	-15,816	2,741,905	455,459	280,818	4,253	817,813	410,060
1973	3,967,896	3,325,306	80,413	3,405,719	270,427	-20,244	3,115,048	521,139	331,709	4,787	828,842	437,018
1974	4,425,026	3,692,380	60,977	3,753,357	313,130	-25,744	3,414,483	608,731	401,812	5,227	846,500	449,628
1975	4,784,715	3,891,990	35,850	3,927,840	323,237	-27,166	3,577,437	674,207	533,071	5,526	865,829	432,989
1976	5,402,069	4,438,200	59,985	4,498,185	374,543	-37,893	4,085,749	732,615	583,705	6,157	877,324	452,961
1977	6,080,300	5,050,358	64,741	5,115,099	424,545	-50,150	4,640,404	827,577	612,319	6,788	895,688	476,503
1978	6,965,307	5,847,123	65,976	5,913,099	499,077	-68,750	5,345,272	949,303	670,732	7,607	915,701	498,198
1979	7,821,088	6,552,091	61,234	6,613,325	583,933	-76,562	5,952,830	1,087,514	780,744	8,374	934,008	515,771
1980	8,643,918	7,030,649	45,529	7,076,178	628,480	-84,178	6,363,520	1,319,045	961,353	9,088	951,182	511,396
1981	9,740,921	7,829,940	71,788	7,901,728	756,690	-120,497	7,024,541	1,621,847	1,094,533	10,152	959,546	518,546
1982	10,423,901	8,201,133	69,722	8,270,855	813,636	-99,791	7,357,428	1,851,329	1,215,144	10,795	965,628	514,563
1983	11,244,756	9,002,336	-2,954	8,999,382	906,685	-104,154	7,988,543	1,959,970	1,296,243	11,538	974,554	525,924
1984	12,710,102	10,205,451	70,663	10,276,114	1,058,268	-131,299	9,086,547	2,258,517	1,365,038	12,844	989,602	561,634
1985	13,952,121	11,364,324	53,023	11,417,347	1,194,680	-169,351	10,053,316	2,438,605	1,460,200	13,886	1,004,758	591,924
1986	15,262,249	12,601,480	16,601	12,618,081	1,352,180	-205,577	11,060,324	2,630,877	1,571,048	14,888	1,025,161	623,352
1987	16,509,027	13,801,349	14,938	13,816,287	1,467,551	-251,819	12,096,917	2,746,659	1,665,451	15,728	1,049,634	651,734
1988	17,924,247	14,885,817	17,335	14,903,152	1,613,355	-273,295	13,016,502	3,096,946	1,810,799	16,842	1,064,279	667,168
1989	19,100,065	15,787,845	30,514	15,818,359	1,731,417	-323,870	13,763,072	3,340,521	1,996,472	17,724	1,077,625	678,985
1990	20,289,437	16,540,515	36,298	16,576,813	1,831,964	-368,037	14,376,812	3,676,682	2,235,943	18,586	1,091,656	686,367
1991	21,547,450	17,630,659	49,762	17,680,421	1,980,741	-429,475	15,270,205	3,720,908	2,556,337	19,352	1,113,436	693,187
1992	23,837,445	19,732,924	67,727	19,800,651	2,181,266	-500,159	17,119,226	3,850,762	2,867,457	20,944	1,138,170	709,895
1993	25,679,800	21,417,391	64,294	21,481,685	2,364,769	-562,171	18,554,745	4,068,947	3,056,108	21,989	1,167,842	746,416
1994	27,758,287	23,348,186	61,214	23,409,400	2,617,088	-626,204	20,166,108	4,385,809	3,206,370	23,126	1,200,308	789,780
1995	30,324,209	25,414,970	44,718	25,459,688	2,834,414	-704,941	21,920,333	4,878,034	3,525,842	24,623	1,231,557	818,516
1996	32,230,044	27,072,022	-10,099	27,061,923	2,963,672	-749,855	23,348,396	5,172,778	3,708,870	25,531	1,262,391	842,907
1997	34,375,494	29,106,597	28,742	29,135,339	3,187,397	-825,461	25,122,481	5,396,213	3,856,800	26,595	1,292,550	873,293
1998	38,215,773	32,559,548	-3,291	32,556,257	3,403,433	-871,895	28,280,929	5,874,870	4,059,974	28,999	1,317,819	904,136
1999	40,229,592	34,634,384	-35,714	34,598,670	3,629,424	-959,337	30,009,909	5,976,589	4,243,094	30,005	1,340,742	924,626
2000	43,566,655	37,422,175	24,620	37,446,795	3,872,844	-1,053,375	32,520,576	6,420,273	4,625,806	31,918	1,364,950	947,537
2001	44,675,201	38,111,079	5,204	38,116,283	3,992,997	-1,026,571	33,096,715	6,477,018	5,101,468	32,224	1,386,403	943,611
2002	46,171,270	39,756,889	-37,459	39,719,430	4,156,840	-1,030,957	34,531,633	6,156,933	5,482,704	32,870	1,404,664	942,466
2003	48,296,942	41,377,131	-45,278	41,331,853	4,315,486	-1,051,554	35,964,813	6,475,402	5,856,727	33,852	1,426,723	953,300
2004	51,396,944	44,036,689	-6,826	44,029,863	4,580,809	-1,086,925	38,362,129	6,763,125	6,271,690	35,330	1,454,773	985,288
2005	54,168,676	46,126,828	-4,481	46,122,347	4,817,676	-1,106,074	40,198,597	7,220,751	6,749,328	36,419	1,487,370	1,017,379
2006	58,854,017	50,061,911	-29,171	50,032,740	5,176,878	-1,189,552	43,666,310	8,045,882	7,141,825	38,486	1,529,238	1,047,441
2007	61,790,623	51,697,749	-74,789	51,622,960	5,453,919	-1,174,018	44,995,023	8,909,905	7,885,695	39,410	1,567,875	1,072,266
2008	64,996,909	52,856,745	-10,778	52,845,967	5,654,397	-1,155,320	46,036,250	9,919,120	9,041,539	40,565	1,602,302	1,066,282
2009	65,564,176	53,690,728	-31,377	53,659,351	5,584,831	-986,812	47,087,708	8,739,793	9,736,675	40,232	1,629,646	1,027,894
2010	69,486,307	55,978,040	-34,238	55,943,802	5,697,001	-943,378	49,303,423	9,354,772	10,828,112	42,071	1,651,630	1,028,988
2011	74,160,472	59,416,241	-8,695	59,407,546	5,295,536	-965,471	53,146,539	9,965,690	11,048,243	44,180	1,678,600	1,057,165
2012	78,815,237	63,288,081	69,157	63,357,238	5,594,355	-1,100,223	56,662,660	11,034,961	11,117,616	46,062	1,711,079	1,090,888
2013	80,449,125	65,972,116	77,745	66,049,861	6,588,732	-1,198,682	58,262,447	10,661,028	11,525,650	46,077	1,745,958	1,126,978
2014	85,879,156	70,949,985	49,006	70,998,991	7,007,178	-1,262,064	62,729,749	11,367,867	11,781,540	48,169	1,782,857	1,174,296
2015	92,440,800	76,435,652	44,788	76,480,440	7,564,777	-1,371,244	67,544,419	12,387,775	12,508,606	50,712	1,822,874	1,222,648
2016	97,654,553	80,812,815	-23,751	80,789,064	7,923,054	-1,548,824	71,317,186	13,404,615	12,932,752	52,406	1,863,407	1,273,375
2017	103,119,727	85,410,635	-12,788	85,397,847	8,480,817	-1,708,124	75,208,906	14,544,800	13,366,021	54,263	1,900,375	1,323,787
2018	110,913,555	91,265,594	-59,767	91,205,827	8,984,369	-1,814,004	80,407,454	16,463,030	14,043,071	57,340	1,934,319	1,370,254
2019	119,201,680	97,732,316	-34,415	97,697,901	9,596,618	-1,956,838	86,144,445	17,956,472	15,100,763	60,675	1,964,602	1,402,256
2020	127,569,449	100,478,145	-38,035	100,440,110	9,951,870	-1,934,754	88,553,486	18,654,672	20,361,291	63,891	1,996,681	1,384,861
2021	141,803,946	111,837,302	13,236	111,850,538	10,995,834	-2,214,884	98,639,820	20,797,312	22,366,814	70,507	2,011,204	1,465,657
2022	151,537,735	124,651,525	-48,680	124,602,845	12,607,191	-2,535,958	109,459,696	23,008,596	19,069,443	74,035	2,046,828	1,554,201

Personal Income and Employment by Area: New Bern, NC

(Thousands of dollars, except as noted.)

Year	Personal income, total	Derivation of personal income								Per capita personal income (dollars)	Population (persons)	Total employment
		Earnings by place of work			Less: Contributions for government social insurance	Plus: Adjustment for residence	Equals: Net earnings by place of residence	Plus: Dividends, interest, and rent	Plus: Personal current transfer receipts			
		Nonfarm	Farm	Total								
1970	286,284	229,469	15,138	244,607	12,390	-13,232	218,985	47,616	19,683	3,488	82,081	40,058
1971	300,887	247,778	11,597	259,375	13,749	-16,696	228,930	49,119	22,838	3,587	83,889	38,574
1972	334,128	269,626	18,626	288,252	15,358	-18,796	254,098	53,366	26,664	3,925	85,129	38,318
1973	394,009	312,781	26,311	339,092	19,658	-21,141	298,293	65,748	29,968	4,502	87,526	40,884
1974	434,747	344,290	26,683	370,973	23,207	-22,831	324,935	73,667	36,145	5,020	86,605	41,460
1975	474,739	370,115	25,448	395,563	26,471	-23,745	345,347	82,400	46,992	5,344	88,837	41,185
1976	463,825	357,054	24,001	381,055	25,898	-21,912	333,245	77,350	53,230	5,094	91,051	37,864
1977	517,429	404,858	14,147	419,005	29,647	-22,907	366,451	93,006	57,972	5,685	91,010	40,592
1978	617,906	479,328	24,300	503,628	35,161	-29,375	439,092	115,841	62,973	6,751	91,529	43,032
1979	674,654	533,663	10,629	544,292	41,013	-30,258	473,021	130,365	71,268	7,442	90,650	44,787
1980	786,830	604,323	16,815	621,138	46,284	-32,283	542,571	158,729	85,530	8,604	91,445	46,872
1981	837,752	644,322	16,948	661,270	51,043	-49,501	560,726	179,012	98,014	9,070	92,365	43,576
1982	941,832	717,127	26,122	743,249	56,875	-56,953	629,421	202,764	109,647	10,007	94,122	45,190
1983	989,806	770,861	6,322	777,183	65,449	-58,565	653,169	218,664	117,973	10,383	95,328	46,894
1984	1,135,648	878,967	20,643	899,610	76,938	-63,452	759,220	249,925	126,503	11,677	97,256	49,839
1985	1,226,161	958,230	13,553	971,783	86,660	-70,552	814,571	273,786	137,804	12,279	99,860	51,285
1986	1,314,461	1,021,827	15,701	1,037,528	95,177	-74,935	867,416	298,904	148,141	13,105	100,306	52,168
1987	1,370,941	1,052,231	23,782	1,076,013	100,713	-70,135	905,165	308,226	157,550	13,710	99,999	52,819
1988	1,470,096	1,127,392	25,509	1,152,901	113,405	-77,603	961,893	334,932	173,271	14,513	101,292	53,217
1989	1,598,220	1,190,726	25,672	1,216,398	122,442	-81,110	1,012,846	390,105	195,269	15,706	101,757	54,451
1990	1,650,489	1,212,698	26,557	1,239,255	129,664	-73,156	1,036,435	397,982	216,072	16,037	102,918	54,413
1991	1,744,974	1,260,166	35,313	1,295,479	136,845	-80,120	1,078,514	414,477	251,983	16,737	104,258	53,677
1992	1,926,956	1,414,134	29,937	1,444,071	154,766	-91,728	1,197,577	451,263	278,116	18,238	105,655	55,701
1993	1,982,842	1,415,588	31,525	1,447,113	157,550	-86,760	1,202,803	471,552	308,487	18,729	105,871	55,763
1994	2,085,237	1,484,901	31,139	1,516,040	165,790	-92,204	1,258,046	504,491	322,700	19,590	106,443	56,340
1995	2,221,108	1,557,251	29,094	1,586,345	173,313	-96,514	1,316,518	541,611	362,979	20,538	108,147	58,223
1996	2,394,278	1,658,302	44,778	1,703,080	184,524	-102,302	1,416,254	586,473	391,551	21,796	109,848	60,554
1997	2,557,975	1,744,128	52,150	1,796,278	193,807	-97,973	1,504,498	643,868	409,609	22,945	111,484	62,242
1998	2,678,736	1,872,841	21,825	1,894,666	208,638	-106,051	1,579,977	673,282	425,477	23,792	112,591	64,020
1999	2,797,115	1,963,534	20,620	1,984,154	219,899	-108,319	1,655,936	680,488	460,691	24,517	114,091	64,804
2000	2,989,209	2,078,516	66,499	2,145,015	232,725	-113,909	1,798,381	702,992	487,836	25,958	115,156	65,818
2001	3,056,600	2,104,473	80,082	2,184,555	235,425	-121,240	1,827,890	690,492	538,218	26,262	116,388	64,919
2002	3,066,793	2,133,125	28,698	2,161,823	239,669	-117,568	1,804,586	689,491	572,716	26,515	115,664	64,574
2003	3,261,812	2,303,998	28,660	2,332,658	261,061	-138,836	1,932,761	724,487	604,564	28,173	115,776	65,373
2004	3,516,487	2,491,555	55,605	2,547,160	281,181	-154,723	2,111,256	755,181	650,050	30,179	116,520	67,058
2005	3,770,750	2,653,549	92,384	2,745,933	300,450	-171,155	2,274,328	794,328	702,094	32,013	117,787	68,387
2006	3,962,565	2,788,723	63,994	2,852,717	316,735	-173,050	2,362,932	841,603	758,030	33,045	119,915	69,503
2007	4,247,685	2,968,557	41,454	3,010,011	338,947	-197,789	2,473,275	957,646	816,764	35,142	120,873	70,191
2008	4,448,586	3,026,165	43,438	3,069,603	346,139	-186,834	2,536,630	998,062	913,894	36,318	122,491	69,701
2009	4,485,546	3,057,716	42,654	3,100,370	354,255	-232,669	2,513,446	971,303	1,000,797	35,826	125,202	67,937
2010	4,619,083	3,155,512	53,481	3,208,993	364,209	-251,770	2,593,014	960,730	1,065,339	36,257	127,398	67,084
2011	4,746,580	3,174,933	57,369	3,232,302	338,466	-281,565	2,612,271	1,036,287	1,098,022	37,076	128,022	66,550
2012	4,893,186	3,264,273	78,607	3,342,880	348,395	-304,786	2,689,699	1,072,957	1,130,530	38,167	128,206	66,849
2013	4,788,833	3,188,815	92,879	3,281,694	384,970	-288,620	2,608,104	1,023,675	1,157,054	37,745	126,873	66,949
2014	4,925,681	3,257,289	84,846	3,342,135	395,455	-300,930	2,645,750	1,085,591	1,194,340	38,972	126,389	67,106
2015	5,025,072	3,334,760	35,144	3,369,904	405,814	-304,950	2,659,140	1,121,225	1,244,707	40,236	124,890	67,395
2016	5,076,592	3,370,639	37,645	3,408,284	399,267	-314,810	2,694,207	1,105,124	1,277,261	40,811	124,394	68,053
2017	5,169,736	3,348,800	54,811	3,403,611	403,489	-259,902	2,740,220	1,104,741	1,324,775	41,670	124,065	67,319
2018	5,314,157	3,465,634	13,960	3,479,594	415,377	-264,921	2,799,296	1,121,337	1,393,524	42,913	123,836	67,285
2019	5,628,885	3,622,738	43,405	3,666,143	432,499	-280,124	2,953,520	1,187,456	1,487,909	45,798	122,906	67,685
2020	5,969,191	3,769,599	22,586	3,792,185	451,008	-331,929	3,009,248	1,156,394	1,803,549	48,889	122,096	66,683
2021	6,524,335	3,945,830	85,616	4,031,446	469,145	-319,104	3,243,197	1,216,318	2,064,820	53,548	121,841	68,402
2022	6,576,349	4,145,963	57,054	4,203,017	500,498	-325,498	3,377,021	1,303,912	1,895,416	53,690	122,488	69,803

Personal Income and Employment by Area: New Haven-Milford, CT

(Thousands of dollars, except as noted.)

Year	Personal income, total	Derivation of personal income: Earnings by place of work: Nonfarm	Farm	Total	Less: Contributions for government social insurance	Plus: Adjustment for residence	Equals: Net earnings by place of residence	Plus: Dividends, interest, and rent	Plus: Personal current transfer receipts	Per capita personal income (dollars)	Population (persons)	Total employment
1970	3,590,216	2,760,353	7,183	2,767,536	188,141	96,473	2,675,868	594,547	319,801	4,803	747,435	341,697
1971	3,810,156	2,882,319	7,292	2,889,611	203,266	99,169	2,785,514	629,329	395,313	5,033	757,031	335,504
1972	4,112,415	3,138,423	7,069	3,145,492	234,151	114,248	3,025,589	670,534	416,292	5,424	758,131	342,677
1973	4,482,966	3,443,164	8,267	3,451,431	296,384	134,906	3,289,953	742,518	450,495	5,924	756,777	357,175
1974	4,889,082	3,684,913	7,802	3,692,715	330,304	158,023	3,520,434	839,886	528,762	6,439	759,277	364,298
1975	5,244,296	3,764,841	8,099	3,772,940	329,632	190,058	3,633,366	900,869	710,061	6,904	759,648	349,425
1976	5,615,847	4,039,411	7,787	4,047,198	359,127	222,825	3,910,896	954,001	750,950	7,406	758,263	351,258
1977	6,151,807	4,438,053	9,735	4,447,788	396,063	264,928	4,316,653	1,049,528	785,626	8,117	757,917	361,753
1978	6,799,915	4,939,406	11,701	4,951,107	452,783	327,551	4,825,875	1,168,388	805,652	8,981	757,121	374,218
1979	7,572,308	5,478,014	10,419	5,488,433	524,191	404,746	5,368,988	1,314,039	889,281	9,961	760,219	385,300
1980	8,489,012	5,890,414	11,139	5,901,553	563,729	519,787	5,857,611	1,627,643	1,003,758	11,139	762,066	386,193
1981	9,458,988	6,318,965	8,176	6,327,141	648,154	622,376	6,301,363	1,975,004	1,182,621	12,391	763,373	385,348
1982	10,131,107	6,640,676	12,366	6,653,042	692,012	696,675	6,657,705	2,159,447	1,313,955	13,245	764,877	381,104
1983	10,922,442	7,217,360	12,025	7,229,385	757,949	742,720	7,214,156	2,291,163	1,417,123	14,167	770,970	385,388
1984	12,194,549	8,147,769	12,890	8,160,659	877,892	835,865	8,118,632	2,604,261	1,471,656	15,709	776,264	406,456
1985	13,058,131	8,816,021	12,253	8,828,274	961,245	935,065	8,802,094	2,705,699	1,550,338	16,675	783,092	416,819
1986	14,057,954	9,534,083	13,458	9,547,541	1,042,786	1,038,690	9,543,445	2,880,993	1,633,516	17,806	789,528	428,205
1987	15,270,474	10,654,077	12,641	10,666,718	1,151,944	1,120,314	10,635,088	2,951,665	1,683,721	19,172	796,486	441,230
1988	16,908,277	11,854,486	13,924	11,868,410	1,306,442	1,229,962	11,791,930	3,303,656	1,812,691	21,100	801,339	455,617
1989	18,222,898	12,455,333	11,670	12,467,003	1,368,849	1,329,074	12,427,228	3,762,742	2,032,928	22,665	804,000	453,175
1990	18,765,228	12,731,771	13,039	12,744,810	1,381,440	1,382,171	12,745,541	3,749,086	2,270,601	23,300	805,366	445,131
1991	18,995,091	12,984,378	11,418	12,995,796	1,436,140	1,335,227	12,894,883	3,564,002	2,536,206	23,524	807,490	426,841
1992	19,956,442	13,639,580	13,825	13,653,405	1,486,998	1,314,011	13,480,418	3,478,388	2,997,636	24,678	808,659	424,565
1993	20,724,909	14,144,222	17,019	14,161,241	1,540,077	1,374,035	13,995,199	3,603,562	3,126,148	25,619	808,977	429,976
1994	21,340,122	14,527,521	15,310	14,542,831	1,597,601	1,453,729	14,398,959	3,681,329	3,259,834	26,373	809,178	425,475
1995	22,293,080	14,995,960	16,502	15,012,462	1,665,622	1,549,737	14,896,577	3,912,937	3,483,566	27,551	809,157	432,879
1996	22,987,109	15,670,023	13,890	15,683,913	1,738,809	1,467,156	15,412,260	4,010,863	3,563,986	28,344	811,000	442,172
1997	24,200,722	16,725,898	13,178	16,739,076	1,831,397	1,524,483	16,432,162	4,109,005	3,659,555	29,749	813,505	446,766
1998	25,588,879	17,945,626	15,391	17,961,017	1,916,099	1,593,836	17,638,754	4,249,372	3,700,753	31,309	817,313	455,111
1999	26,910,554	18,998,882	17,509	19,016,391	1,982,874	1,873,298	18,906,815	4,215,834	3,787,905	32,802	820,396	460,583
2000	29,132,362	20,724,489	20,168	20,744,657	2,098,394	1,876,552	20,522,815	4,612,669	3,996,878	35,316	824,911	470,567
2001	30,501,592	21,989,599	20,368	22,009,967	2,192,188	1,982,639	21,800,418	4,465,768	4,235,406	36,754	829,875	474,576
2002	30,849,486	22,727,587	23,687	22,751,274	2,327,359	1,706,558	22,130,473	4,175,200	4,543,813	36,941	835,099	474,529
2003	31,159,984	22,914,599	23,333	22,937,932	2,379,233	1,669,251	22,227,950	4,309,671	4,622,363	37,010	841,939	472,080
2004	32,238,092	23,888,983	25,708	23,914,691	2,498,239	1,694,849	23,111,301	4,209,248	4,917,543	38,174	844,505	482,149
2005	33,366,437	24,498,622	27,769	24,526,391	2,551,708	1,984,229	23,958,912	4,311,553	5,095,972	39,386	847,162	485,556
2006	35,508,910	25,641,918	27,519	25,669,437	2,638,764	2,198,936	25,229,609	4,864,335	5,414,966	41,765	850,207	491,430
2007	37,428,292	26,328,265	31,163	26,359,428	2,718,904	2,313,352	25,953,876	5,751,566	5,722,850	43,848	853,598	498,329
2008	38,550,914	26,644,838	32,958	26,677,796	2,785,974	2,064,061	25,955,883	6,061,041	6,533,990	45,003	856,622	496,830
2009	37,564,909	26,020,791	34,749	26,055,540	2,727,528	1,365,793	24,693,805	5,636,002	7,235,102	43,679	860,025	483,312
2010	38,258,599	26,571,203	34,577	26,605,780	2,744,530	1,437,672	25,298,922	5,259,145	7,700,532	44,296	863,694	477,548
2011	39,765,111	27,041,496	26,503	27,067,999	2,547,802	1,709,678	26,229,875	5,795,006	7,740,230	45,947	865,458	482,732
2012	40,677,916	27,541,621	34,008	27,575,629	2,638,783	1,635,248	26,572,094	6,254,762	7,851,060	46,896	867,409	487,949
2013	40,911,228	28,105,396	43,081	28,148,477	3,062,691	1,616,601	26,702,387	6,316,227	7,892,614	47,193	866,896	492,770
2014	42,155,161	28,751,482	37,523	28,789,005	3,130,904	1,905,282	27,563,383	6,484,541	8,107,237	48,555	868,202	496,762
2015	43,407,412	29,728,792	45,307	29,774,099	3,228,066	1,626,005	28,172,038	6,873,069	8,362,305	50,082	866,734	501,019
2016	43,905,396	30,356,163	39,622	30,395,785	3,303,393	1,480,795	28,573,187	6,733,190	8,599,019	50,725	865,560	504,365
2017	44,624,504	31,002,029	41,982	31,044,011	3,422,362	1,404,618	29,026,267	6,885,263	8,712,974	51,504	866,435	506,204
2018	46,564,739	31,784,556	32,986	31,817,542	3,527,039	1,932,902	30,223,405	7,067,052	9,274,282	53,729	866,667	510,921
2019	48,806,770	32,826,590	37,461	32,864,051	3,657,099	2,779,352	31,986,304	7,369,961	9,450,505	56,441	864,743	511,012
2020	52,231,213	33,279,790	36,947	33,316,737	3,755,971	3,026,714	32,587,480	7,330,833	12,312,900	60,506	863,234	499,399
2021	55,275,981	35,728,439	36,038	35,764,477	3,987,627	2,711,151	34,488,001	7,641,719	13,146,261	63,599	869,138	515,302
2022	56,370,422	37,781,582	27,557	37,809,139	4,326,735	3,268,814	36,751,218	7,991,879	11,627,325	64,829	869,527	538,440

Personal Income and Employment by Area: New Orleans-Metairie, LA

(Thousands of dollars, except as noted.)

Year	Personal income, total	Derivation of personal income: Earnings by place of work: Nonfarm	Farm	Total	Less: Contributions for government social insurance	Plus: Adjustment for residence	Equals: Net earnings by place of residence	Plus: Dividends, interest, and rent	Plus: Personal current transfer receipts	Per capita personal income (dollars)	Population (persons)	Total employment
1970	4,300,405	3,687,179	10,681	3,697,860	241,315	-111,456	3,345,089	600,296	355,020	3,750	1,146,894	504,994
1971	4,646,375	3,963,952	11,797	3,975,749	266,323	-132,441	3,576,985	658,144	411,246	3,983	1,166,467	508,631
1972	5,077,018	4,355,333	14,514	4,369,847	307,439	-154,871	3,907,537	711,210	458,271	4,276	1,187,285	526,614
1973	5,591,596	4,802,185	22,938	4,825,123	390,737	-172,319	4,262,067	789,363	540,166	4,670	1,197,218	548,458
1974	6,302,891	5,347,613	31,416	5,379,029	446,765	-203,708	4,728,556	943,799	630,536	5,240	1,202,899	563,281
1975	7,101,589	6,018,452	13,862	6,032,314	493,477	-243,251	5,295,586	1,033,246	772,757	5,835	1,217,164	581,071
1976	7,969,835	6,848,418	15,927	6,864,345	572,554	-289,431	6,002,360	1,108,962	858,513	6,427	1,239,970	600,729
1977	8,844,129	7,649,764	14,610	7,664,374	636,449	-329,431	6,698,494	1,217,885	927,750	7,045	1,255,289	617,879
1978	10,030,800	8,731,336	11,747	8,743,083	740,630	-387,270	7,615,183	1,404,702	1,010,915	7,897	1,270,252	640,835
1979	11,304,384	9,895,502	11,342	9,906,844	872,300	-472,185	8,562,359	1,596,746	1,145,279	8,793	1,285,635	657,374
1980	12,974,472	11,253,188	9,160	11,262,348	985,674	-587,254	9,689,420	1,929,093	1,355,959	9,916	1,308,411	679,099
1981	14,859,989	12,772,706	12,294	12,785,000	1,201,115	-622,317	10,961,568	2,377,731	1,520,690	11,235	1,322,669	695,393
1982	16,010,058	13,467,443	13,603	13,481,046	1,291,861	-645,369	11,543,816	2,743,291	1,722,951	11,939	1,340,939	692,756
1983	16,765,722	13,745,419	14,467	13,759,886	1,312,453	-659,576	11,787,857	3,037,198	1,940,667	12,407	1,351,273	679,426
1984	17,855,422	14,545,801	8,367	14,554,168	1,420,914	-676,923	12,456,331	3,366,330	2,032,761	13,222	1,350,467	693,125
1985	18,562,915	14,744,956	11,223	14,756,179	1,445,102	-638,592	12,672,485	3,691,951	2,198,479	13,751	1,349,897	681,199
1986	18,879,516	14,771,492	12,490	14,783,982	1,430,585	-577,817	12,775,580	3,722,131	2,381,805	14,012	1,347,337	660,295
1987	19,010,986	14,919,564	11,818	14,931,382	1,421,105	-560,103	12,950,174	3,640,418	2,420,394	14,322	1,327,369	650,890
1988	19,940,710	15,641,137	17,881	15,659,018	1,557,720	-571,016	13,530,282	3,842,789	2,567,639	15,218	1,310,318	664,408
1989	21,075,244	16,364,374	17,963	16,382,337	1,638,471	-581,261	14,162,605	4,117,770	2,794,869	16,250	1,296,918	668,800
1990	22,538,696	17,560,423	8,413	17,568,836	1,807,204	-640,125	15,121,507	4,343,254	3,073,935	17,540	1,285,014	681,627
1991	23,678,218	18,369,775	9,733	18,379,508	1,937,658	-646,168	15,795,682	4,345,029	3,537,507	18,285	1,294,966	685,564
1992	25,279,892	19,390,972	14,708	19,405,680	2,014,170	-647,112	16,744,398	4,461,397	4,074,097	19,341	1,307,069	683,945
1993	26,394,494	20,052,448	19,104	20,071,552	2,088,595	-639,201	17,343,756	4,596,040	4,454,698	20,068	1,315,265	695,199
1994	27,887,142	21,172,538	14,246	21,186,784	2,243,430	-664,756	18,278,598	4,737,912	4,870,632	21,072	1,323,418	705,084
1995	29,443,568	22,293,618	15,692	22,309,310	2,357,522	-705,890	19,245,898	5,250,867	4,946,803	22,135	1,330,188	724,157
1996	30,400,654	22,974,303	13,828	22,988,131	2,427,218	-725,063	19,835,850	5,531,881	5,032,923	22,838	1,331,131	732,972
1997	32,118,041	24,329,973	15,079	24,345,052	2,564,260	-766,006	21,014,786	5,989,388	5,113,867	24,085	1,333,525	747,596
1998	33,642,958	25,711,172	16,509	25,727,681	2,723,496	-802,998	22,201,187	6,316,670	5,125,101	25,191	1,335,520	756,651
1999	34,391,661	26,588,208	17,049	26,605,257	2,776,012	-780,058	23,049,187	6,105,547	5,236,927	25,697	1,338,370	760,569
2000	36,373,110	27,958,350	15,318	27,973,668	2,840,824	-785,920	24,346,924	6,657,462	5,368,724	27,159	1,339,280	770,060
2001	39,004,444	30,083,144	15,637	30,098,781	2,979,655	-843,767	26,275,359	6,637,016	6,092,069	29,010	1,344,528	775,759
2002	40,218,275	31,241,078	14,848	31,255,926	3,085,636	-898,873	27,271,417	6,585,400	6,361,458	29,689	1,354,638	774,900
2003	41,323,581	32,362,701	16,072	32,378,773	3,179,810	-948,204	28,250,759	6,765,998	6,306,824	30,270	1,365,146	779,312
2004	42,106,160	32,632,169	16,519	32,648,688	3,254,615	-1,051,853	28,342,220	6,884,614	6,879,326	30,563	1,377,699	783,021
2005	43,826,459	32,355,202	17,098	32,372,300	3,155,567	-1,012,844	28,203,889	7,004,158	8,618,412	31,611	1,386,429	699,846
2006	42,368,500	32,416,182	36,775	32,452,957	3,128,577	-1,664,974	27,659,406	8,621,239	6,087,855	40,731	1,040,195	648,231
2007	48,925,099	34,210,469	21,606	34,232,075	3,341,170	-1,840,081	29,050,824	13,657,795	6,216,480	44,625	1,096,365	691,842
2008	50,647,148	37,157,957	27,333	37,185,290	3,552,770	-2,015,937	31,616,583	11,784,593	7,245,972	44,590	1,135,831	715,201
2009	48,586,283	36,205,887	28,524	36,234,411	3,556,073	-1,496,702	31,181,636	9,621,459	7,783,188	41,603	1,167,842	715,351
2010	51,311,434	38,388,075	36,758	38,424,833	3,692,203	-1,616,282	33,116,348	9,494,965	8,700,121	42,926	1,195,359	725,363
2011	51,897,919	38,618,980	37,012	38,655,992	3,383,236	-1,808,794	33,463,962	9,582,491	8,851,466	42,745	1,214,121	730,892
2012	55,244,814	39,619,908	31,002	39,650,910	3,447,079	-1,517,175	34,686,656	11,542,225	9,015,933	45,023	1,227,049	745,948
2013	56,098,521	40,781,700	30,495	40,812,195	3,996,073	-1,249,764	35,566,358	11,156,390	9,375,773	45,251	1,239,715	762,254
2014	60,332,420	44,923,050	17,187	44,940,237	4,222,613	-1,256,057	39,461,567	11,488,677	9,382,176	48,305	1,248,997	776,591
2015	60,808,243	44,228,544	17,640	44,246,184	4,364,625	-1,140,954	38,740,605	11,642,365	10,425,273	48,248	1,260,322	791,504
2016	60,493,893	43,115,883	7,650	43,123,533	4,395,771	-1,075,580	37,652,182	11,799,710	11,042,001	47,719	1,267,717	797,215
2017	62,833,316	44,395,961	8,183	44,404,144	4,509,507	-1,012,643	38,881,994	12,432,309	11,519,013	49,461	1,270,372	798,019
2018	65,921,595	46,691,986	5,020	46,697,006	4,714,625	-819,759	41,162,622	12,742,858	12,016,115	51,880	1,270,659	809,667
2019	68,829,947	48,648,153	13,011	48,661,164	4,856,394	-1,032,262	42,772,508	13,474,062	12,583,377	54,089	1,272,533	813,982
2020	71,446,160	46,853,723	13,545	46,867,268	4,798,794	-1,251,322	40,817,152	13,385,272	17,243,736	56,248	1,270,206	761,617
2021	78,123,142	50,293,077	16,944	50,310,021	5,059,950	-1,244,558	44,005,513	15,258,689	18,858,940	61,860	1,262,909	794,029
2022	77,014,753	52,277,098	8,174	52,285,272	5,471,265	-1,664,930	45,149,077	15,664,457	16,201,219	61,801	1,246,176	825,017

Personal Income and Employment by Area: New York-Newark-Jersey City, NY-NJ-PA

(Thousands of dollars, except as noted.)

Year	Personal income, total	Derivation of personal income: Earnings by place of work: Nonfarm	Farm	Total	Less: Contributions for government social insurance	Plus: Adjustment for residence	Equals: Net earnings by place of residence	Plus: Dividends, interest, and rent	Plus: Personal current transfer receipts	Per capita personal income (dollars)	Population (persons)	Total employment
1970	90,396,327	73,430,900	57,133	73,488,033	5,439,016	-1,021,953	67,027,064	15,042,767	8,326,496	5,290	17,089,280	8,073,922
1971	96,410,189	77,495,385	53,070	77,548,455	5,921,565	-1,137,523	70,489,367	15,854,269	10,066,553	5,617	17,162,560	7,922,322
1972	103,427,115	83,413,031	45,973	83,459,004	6,692,402	-1,346,955	75,419,647	16,706,039	11,301,429	6,039	17,125,818	7,943,751
1973	110,001,431	89,090,638	70,364	89,161,002	8,282,485	-1,555,808	79,322,709	18,149,572	12,529,150	6,480	16,974,851	8,045,221
1974	118,338,536	94,209,409	75,187	94,284,596	9,026,239	-1,764,662	83,493,695	20,294,458	14,550,383	7,020	16,857,193	7,950,778
1975	127,505,633	99,088,523	62,680	99,151,203	9,286,653	-2,019,246	87,845,304	21,405,185	18,255,144	7,599	16,778,386	7,718,680
1976	135,572,917	105,752,343	61,703	105,814,046	10,084,830	-2,291,086	93,438,130	22,595,218	19,539,569	8,112	16,712,756	7,696,630
1977	146,764,176	115,017,156	74,852	115,092,008	10,869,973	-2,664,934	101,557,101	24,774,428	20,432,647	8,850	16,584,115	7,778,853
1978	160,679,003	127,241,291	89,369	127,330,660	12,303,380	-3,054,267	111,973,013	27,284,928	21,421,062	9,757	16,468,444	7,991,342
1979	175,881,909	139,949,863	97,822	140,047,685	14,032,271	-3,513,876	122,501,538	30,401,644	22,978,727	10,724	16,400,125	8,177,740
1980	196,872,322	153,900,426	117,607	154,018,033	15,480,830	-4,025,024	134,512,179	36,174,988	26,185,155	12,021	16,377,893	8,250,921
1981	219,969,929	169,142,717	131,119	169,273,836	18,179,113	-4,312,846	146,781,877	43,670,425	29,517,627	13,410	16,403,191	8,336,160
1982	238,801,778	182,007,499	131,327	182,138,826	19,905,658	-4,729,503	157,503,665	49,301,822	31,996,291	14,526	16,439,430	8,370,456
1983	258,934,528	198,141,379	138,530	198,279,909	21,808,259	-5,088,414	171,383,236	52,913,137	34,638,155	15,632	16,564,621	8,492,281
1984	286,343,259	218,701,574	156,128	218,857,702	24,806,010	-5,574,227	188,477,465	61,205,014	36,660,780	17,189	16,658,685	8,785,468
1985	307,214,653	237,081,923	158,471	237,240,394	27,207,944	-6,105,132	203,927,318	64,570,458	38,716,877	18,362	16,730,929	8,994,880
1986	329,099,170	257,546,464	161,049	257,707,513	29,941,921	-6,338,617	221,426,975	66,773,520	40,898,675	19,577	16,810,158	9,183,635
1987	352,855,629	282,202,824	188,978	282,391,802	32,261,772	-6,817,359	243,312,671	67,439,060	42,103,898	20,931	16,858,269	9,264,870
1988	390,830,588	312,493,879	189,308	312,683,187	35,900,009	-7,473,120	269,310,058	76,755,514	44,765,016	23,130	16,896,865	9,423,421
1989	420,150,065	328,575,082	180,884	328,755,966	37,268,626	-7,664,727	283,822,613	87,257,775	49,069,677	24,890	16,880,387	9,446,416
1990	449,477,478	348,752,681	171,778	348,924,459	37,600,715	-7,607,723	303,716,021	91,694,684	54,066,773	26,614	16,888,902	9,344,755
1991	449,279,177	342,637,956	149,252	342,787,208	38,386,930	-7,747,481	296,652,797	91,797,790	60,828,590	26,461	16,979,004	9,029,995
1992	477,166,233	367,583,448	153,589	367,737,037	40,355,169	-9,414,298	317,967,570	90,627,689	68,570,974	27,880	17,114,713	8,955,065
1993	492,403,625	378,664,862	156,804	378,821,666	41,431,938	-9,285,921	328,103,807	91,494,528	72,805,290	28,507	17,273,224	8,981,162
1994	509,035,597	390,278,388	152,559	390,430,947	43,437,061	-9,389,853	337,604,033	95,863,839	75,567,725	29,243	17,407,324	8,987,008
1995	540,990,250	411,304,564	153,526	411,458,090	45,240,843	-10,585,115	355,632,132	104,612,685	80,745,433	30,835	17,544,499	9,117,756
1996	573,714,718	437,444,765	152,767	437,597,532	47,073,060	-12,098,296	378,426,176	111,269,187	84,019,355	32,447	17,681,708	9,249,305
1997	609,393,957	469,304,849	135,990	469,440,839	49,278,444	-12,652,655	407,509,740	117,690,773	84,193,444	34,167	17,835,528	9,400,699
1998	649,399,883	503,497,594	151,684	503,649,278	52,101,921	-14,956,723	436,590,634	125,481,895	87,327,354	36,062	18,007,924	9,607,048
1999	686,920,732	540,521,144	153,448	540,674,592	54,860,805	-14,900,907	470,912,880	125,555,153	90,452,699	37,759	18,192,429	9,842,948
2000	748,937,663	592,734,249	191,148	592,925,397	59,450,226	-16,700,995	516,774,176	136,786,756	95,376,731	40,800	18,356,204	10,175,147
2001	780,502,633	619,780,455	166,952	619,947,407	61,773,537	-17,299,870	540,874,000	136,976,120	102,652,513	42,242	18,476,764	10,250,875
2002	777,842,350	618,330,483	191,528	618,522,011	62,387,014	-17,558,413	538,576,584	127,648,160	111,617,606	41,922	18,554,586	10,187,690
2003	786,367,631	623,473,479	195,409	623,668,888	63,791,741	-18,213,248	541,663,899	129,043,540	115,660,192	42,281	18,598,803	10,217,649
2004	821,370,845	650,730,341	195,131	650,925,472	66,920,982	-20,454,832	563,549,658	134,451,625	123,369,562	44,165	18,597,871	10,371,721
2005	854,408,884	673,399,190	196,409	673,595,599	70,076,564	-22,442,218	581,076,817	150,627,221	122,704,846	46,013	18,568,830	10,533,756
2006	923,821,308	719,565,976	216,700	719,782,676	74,227,097	-25,159,246	620,396,333	173,209,274	130,215,701	49,832	18,538,752	10,720,979
2007	996,114,280	770,162,314	213,432	770,375,746	79,212,278	-29,094,656	662,068,812	198,076,055	135,969,413	53,634	18,572,325	11,017,810
2008	1,014,236,047	774,157,905	292,993	774,450,898	81,701,535	-29,726,772	663,022,591	202,314,694	148,898,762	54,318	18,672,355	11,117,189
2009	986,006,316	748,983,717	304,729	749,288,446	78,928,564	-24,013,669	646,346,213	176,105,290	163,554,813	52,447	18,800,157	10,893,604
2010	1,024,294,911	783,325,525	280,972	783,606,497	80,668,378	-25,897,481	677,040,638	173,004,761	174,249,512	54,062	18,946,836	10,924,466
2011	1,082,325,329	814,870,201	250,061	815,120,262	74,251,140	-26,953,821	713,915,301	191,617,108	176,792,920	56,455	19,171,388	11,240,293
2012	1,131,808,291	848,285,466	299,797	848,585,263	76,203,360	-28,622,849	743,759,054	213,573,276	174,475,961	58,446	19,365,133	11,396,888
2013	1,145,228,463	873,769,800	288,069	874,057,869	89,907,943	-27,474,469	756,675,457	213,055,767	175,497,239	58,611	19,539,317	11,635,122
2014	1,193,930,370	908,938,989	222,338	909,161,327	94,548,390	-28,916,896	785,696,041	228,264,424	179,969,905	60,631	19,691,851	11,920,163
2015	1,246,867,312	943,668,830	227,129	943,895,959	98,659,586	-29,700,494	815,535,879	242,988,934	188,342,499	62,877	19,830,288	12,210,615
2016	1,294,032,721	974,033,809	203,999	974,237,808	100,937,375	-29,230,441	844,069,992	255,570,767	194,391,962	64,886	19,943,198	12,417,920
2017	1,374,463,338	1,029,624,620	208,270	1,029,832,890	106,742,111	-32,405,692	890,685,087	277,039,411	206,738,840	68,621	20,029,850	12,579,054
2018	1,429,963,983	1,081,824,475	177,354	1,082,001,829	110,815,264	-35,150,595	936,035,970	290,785,631	203,142,382	71,172	20,091,554	12,888,349
2019	1,485,635,270	1,122,694,463	264,660	1,122,959,123	115,623,049	-39,559,887	967,776,187	301,381,974	216,477,109	73,798	20,131,062	12,996,562
2020	1,541,127,648	1,113,171,879	239,544	1,113,411,423	113,583,905	-44,024,906	955,802,612	285,165,430	300,159,606	76,868	20,048,886	12,168,041
2021	1,660,301,585	1,195,838,467	227,925	1,196,066,392	122,903,406	-43,611,777	1,029,551,209	311,023,800	319,726,576	83,962	19,774,386	12,628,604
2022	1,649,539,506	1,251,996,651	280,059	1,252,276,710	133,511,682	-49,510,176	1,069,254,852	320,493,292	259,791,362	84,084	19,617,869	13,395,511

Personal Income and Employment by Area: Niles, MI

(Thousands of dollars, except as noted.)

Year	Personal income, total	Derivation of personal income: Earnings by place of work: Nonfarm	Earnings by place of work: Farm	Earnings by place of work: Total	Less: Contributions for government social insurance	Plus: Adjustment for residence	Equals: Net earnings by place of residence	Plus: Dividends, interest, and rent	Plus: Personal current transfer receipts	Per capita personal income (dollars)	Population (persons)	Total employment
1970	666,696	546,019	13,052	559,071	39,687	-10,848	508,536	93,336	64,824	4,066	163,981	74,168
1971	717,542	586,702	12,290	598,992	43,922	-12,948	542,122	98,540	76,880	4,343	165,230	73,938
1972	808,588	679,053	11,695	690,748	53,707	-17,187	619,854	105,678	83,056	4,810	168,102	78,406
1973	895,502	754,205	15,564	769,769	69,060	-17,940	682,769	116,362	96,371	5,248	170,653	81,115
1974	974,624	796,330	22,494	818,824	75,629	-18,182	725,013	132,310	117,301	5,666	172,002	80,618
1975	1,031,937	804,883	15,667	820,550	74,539	-15,095	730,916	143,838	157,183	5,951	173,395	76,020
1976	1,102,463	859,801	13,170	872,971	80,940	-9,851	782,180	153,215	167,068	6,304	174,881	77,131
1977	1,228,915	973,031	20,099	993,130	91,954	-12,492	888,684	170,555	169,676	7,028	174,870	80,061
1978	1,344,483	1,062,997	22,766	1,085,763	103,327	-8,030	974,406	186,530	183,547	7,752	173,427	81,369
1979	1,434,694	1,121,221	10,930	1,132,151	113,332	-3,241	1,015,578	207,234	211,882	8,263	173,635	80,344
1980	1,525,568	1,127,396	10,910	1,138,306	113,486	-540	1,024,280	247,323	253,965	8,906	171,288	75,636
1981	1,657,921	1,191,069	14,545	1,205,614	129,067	574	1,077,121	298,331	282,469	9,698	170,961	73,651
1982	1,724,442	1,189,713	16,173	1,205,886	130,946	2,382	1,077,322	339,200	307,920	10,336	166,840	70,908
1983	1,790,114	1,232,584	10,889	1,243,473	137,640	5,089	1,110,922	352,688	326,504	10,894	164,326	70,184
1984	1,931,707	1,342,440	15,670	1,358,110	155,332	8,530	1,211,308	391,364	329,035	11,829	163,308	71,984
1985	2,034,800	1,415,625	24,911	1,440,536	165,932	8,940	1,283,544	406,789	344,467	12,488	162,945	73,946
1986	2,157,499	1,536,716	16,730	1,553,446	180,070	4,415	1,377,791	418,718	360,990	13,284	162,415	75,938
1987	2,301,081	1,666,538	28,463	1,695,001	191,830	5,731	1,508,902	420,319	371,860	14,119	162,973	78,673
1988	2,426,715	1,754,125	20,933	1,775,058	208,736	13,657	1,579,979	459,872	386,864	14,888	163,001	80,352
1989	2,589,698	1,845,320	30,772	1,876,092	218,200	14,224	1,672,116	508,988	408,594	15,972	162,143	81,954
1990	2,678,277	1,923,656	18,952	1,942,608	231,038	13,325	1,724,895	510,921	442,461	16,592	161,415	82,670
1991	2,758,543	1,962,365	22,914	1,985,279	238,957	16,890	1,763,212	507,337	487,994	17,068	161,622	81,364
1992	2,959,486	2,120,627	24,690	2,145,317	255,654	18,768	1,908,431	530,395	520,660	18,270	161,982	81,260
1993	3,136,218	2,284,249	19,862	2,304,111	278,217	19,983	2,045,877	533,934	556,407	19,328	162,266	81,681
1994	3,313,086	2,402,562	20,202	2,422,764	300,932	25,096	2,146,928	606,898	559,260	20,407	162,353	85,310
1995	3,485,879	2,516,923	22,834	2,539,757	314,856	34,909	2,259,810	650,786	575,283	21,383	163,022	88,048
1996	3,599,816	2,578,165	19,748	2,597,913	316,430	42,537	2,324,020	681,361	594,435	22,102	162,873	88,373
1997	3,813,742	2,734,934	24,180	2,759,114	334,147	42,472	2,467,439	701,090	645,213	23,483	162,407	88,512
1998	3,956,912	2,845,060	24,055	2,869,115	340,598	61,709	2,590,226	732,493	634,193	24,418	162,046	90,479
1999	4,182,245	3,063,067	29,509	3,092,576	360,311	63,699	2,795,964	698,570	687,711	25,812	162,028	89,527
2000	4,380,495	3,195,502	25,938	3,221,440	370,470	73,171	2,924,141	743,573	712,781	26,962	162,471	90,418
2001	4,532,683	3,218,339	33,411	3,251,750	355,894	91,834	2,987,690	736,523	808,470	28,127	161,153	87,082
2002	4,573,582	3,304,019	26,109	3,330,128	363,917	78,670	3,044,881	704,718	823,983	28,477	160,604	85,405
2003	4,669,914	3,297,338	34,574	3,331,912	364,554	97,751	3,065,109	737,658	867,147	29,130	160,314	84,105
2004	4,859,686	3,444,063	47,016	3,491,079	382,318	104,389	3,213,150	750,931	895,605	30,422	159,742	84,378
2005	4,863,412	3,428,047	39,220	3,467,267	393,131	111,568	3,185,704	735,946	941,762	30,682	158,510	84,910
2006	5,119,625	3,539,856	48,234	3,588,090	409,620	159,506	3,337,976	773,966	1,007,683	32,498	157,537	84,497
2007	5,368,980	3,666,731	59,075	3,725,806	428,617	137,904	3,435,093	839,767	1,094,120	34,115	157,378	86,794
2008	5,668,244	3,656,289	46,475	3,702,764	437,373	178,728	3,444,119	986,210	1,237,915	36,016	157,380	85,425
2009	5,400,859	3,483,707	36,397	3,520,104	418,316	98,699	3,200,487	858,292	1,342,080	34,387	157,059	80,369
2010	5,685,164	3,647,537	45,704	3,693,241	427,972	101,998	3,367,267	883,144	1,434,753	36,265	156,768	80,304
2011	5,914,552	3,607,129	69,657	3,676,786	383,051	135,229	3,428,964	1,056,405	1,429,183	37,661	157,047	80,616
2012	5,905,226	3,613,950	56,372	3,670,322	387,609	200,191	3,482,904	1,001,634	1,420,688	37,633	156,915	80,624
2013	5,983,904	3,797,128	65,537	3,862,665	457,555	146,973	3,552,083	997,688	1,434,133	38,221	156,559	80,930
2014	6,222,512	3,911,584	42,246	3,953,830	475,806	174,116	3,652,140	1,082,794	1,487,578	39,751	156,538	82,473
2015	6,585,954	4,100,183	45,327	4,145,510	493,374	139,630	3,791,766	1,228,714	1,565,474	42,297	155,706	83,445
2016	6,774,644	4,168,079	56,047	4,224,126	504,858	231,347	3,950,615	1,219,720	1,604,309	43,671	155,129	82,713
2017	6,920,793	4,302,917	54,390	4,357,307	519,882	219,921	4,057,346	1,283,152	1,580,295	44,636	155,050	83,564
2018	7,256,430	4,425,184	48,332	4,473,516	540,289	324,615	4,257,842	1,352,955	1,645,633	46,881	154,784	83,445
2019	7,601,580	4,490,160	50,404	4,540,564	547,369	448,477	4,441,672	1,422,544	1,737,364	49,249	154,349	82,730
2020	8,271,146	4,526,615	82,465	4,609,080	548,826	430,236	4,490,490	1,437,676	2,342,980	53,645	154,183	77,689
2021	9,159,537	4,765,580	85,247	4,850,827	573,156	802,491	5,080,162	1,591,067	2,488,308	59,719	153,377	80,014
2022	9,221,598	5,131,293	86,604	5,217,897	637,941	790,615	5,370,571	1,722,022	2,129,005	60,311	152,900	83,837

Personal Income and Employment by Area: North Port-Sarasota-Bradenton, FL

(Thousands of dollars, except as noted.)

Year	Personal income, total	Derivation of personal income: Earnings by place of work: Nonfarm	Farm	Total	Less: Contributions for government social insurance	Plus: Adjustment for residence	Equals: Net earnings by place of residence	Plus: Dividends, interest, and rent	Plus: Personal current transfer receipts	Per capita personal income (dollars)	Population (persons)	Total employment
1970	980,330	504,474	18,012	522,486	33,169	-5,753	483,564	363,853	132,913	4,457	219,936	86,898
1971	1,112,894	566,278	21,641	587,919	38,956	-5,054	543,909	407,924	161,061	4,786	232,523	91,869
1972	1,283,455	666,653	25,314	691,967	48,314	-4,779	638,874	454,839	189,742	5,245	244,710	99,827
1973	1,532,026	813,255	27,042	840,297	67,612	-7,418	765,267	533,683	233,076	5,787	264,738	113,242
1974	1,747,243	902,560	28,319	930,879	79,394	-8,017	843,468	628,415	275,360	6,192	282,181	117,686
1975	1,907,301	924,571	30,883	955,454	79,931	-6,189	869,334	690,820	347,147	6,602	288,894	114,242
1976	2,152,544	1,047,108	33,441	1,080,549	89,893	-5,415	985,241	784,879	382,424	7,256	296,666	119,612
1977	2,489,070	1,214,865	32,209	1,247,074	105,433	-6,511	1,135,130	926,606	427,334	8,116	306,701	130,788
1978	2,950,698	1,466,006	37,440	1,503,446	130,343	-8,201	1,364,902	1,103,473	482,323	9,161	322,092	144,674
1979	3,451,922	1,690,972	51,405	1,742,377	157,614	-11,360	1,573,403	1,313,344	565,175	10,194	338,608	153,849
1980	4,143,353	1,916,918	71,451	1,988,369	180,928	-12,157	1,795,284	1,672,613	675,456	11,680	354,724	160,146
1981	4,920,613	2,152,201	62,577	2,214,778	218,919	8,750	2,004,609	2,118,968	797,036	13,293	370,172	166,835
1982	5,276,296	2,263,193	91,159	2,354,352	241,096	28,554	2,141,810	2,226,278	908,208	13,715	384,723	172,913
1983	5,972,163	2,567,549	140,496	2,708,045	272,030	53,104	2,489,119	2,484,034	999,010	14,947	399,556	183,463
1984	6,667,668	2,927,954	94,846	3,022,800	319,317	85,995	2,789,478	2,819,891	1,058,299	16,122	413,582	196,895
1985	7,351,583	3,167,307	94,367	3,261,674	353,652	126,462	3,034,484	3,162,445	1,154,654	17,232	426,636	204,184
1986	8,004,732	3,455,183	102,700	3,557,883	396,180	171,110	3,332,813	3,417,412	1,254,507	18,253	438,539	213,336
1987	8,625,324	3,904,690	111,600	4,016,290	441,934	221,358	3,795,714	3,488,865	1,340,745	19,157	450,241	215,825
1988	9,559,884	4,250,039	129,257	4,379,296	499,472	285,029	4,164,853	3,925,153	1,469,878	20,655	462,830	227,771
1989	11,159,592	4,620,544	127,372	4,747,916	554,788	348,031	4,541,159	5,013,219	1,605,214	23,433	476,235	237,209
1990	11,919,097	5,020,773	100,338	5,121,111	589,888	408,588	4,939,811	5,240,543	1,738,743	24,161	493,311	246,876
1991	12,185,684	5,334,006	120,688	5,454,694	630,499	337,313	5,161,508	5,131,258	1,892,918	24,125	505,103	251,512
1992	12,885,989	5,820,568	136,436	5,957,004	680,413	381,087	5,657,678	5,128,826	2,099,485	25,207	511,201	257,502
1993	13,418,586	6,273,631	139,204	6,412,835	728,539	295,151	5,979,447	5,210,005	2,229,134	25,761	520,892	269,675
1994	14,379,967	6,790,615	117,265	6,907,880	802,290	285,672	6,391,262	5,611,395	2,377,310	27,018	532,241	286,866
1995	15,317,065	7,581,935	117,902	7,699,837	892,232	122,623	6,930,228	5,860,069	2,526,768	28,273	541,758	309,665
1996	16,247,988	7,767,724	107,746	7,875,470	898,128	410,581	7,387,923	6,196,984	2,663,081	29,488	551,004	304,542
1997	17,323,923	8,308,507	132,073	8,440,580	962,960	450,745	7,928,365	6,635,997	2,759,561	30,863	561,309	317,015
1998	18,984,054	8,954,953	158,915	9,113,868	1,025,285	652,933	8,741,516	7,377,521	2,865,017	33,131	573,004	321,983
1999	19,744,232	9,631,197	159,969	9,791,166	1,085,400	880,898	9,586,664	7,195,268	2,962,300	33,931	581,892	329,161
2000	21,349,182	10,627,431	163,214	10,790,645	1,180,689	700,840	10,310,796	7,917,930	3,120,456	36,014	592,809	353,692
2001	21,488,147	10,391,700	169,717	10,561,417	1,184,832	709,952	10,086,537	8,044,156	3,357,454	35,460	605,988	324,277
2002	22,161,245	11,429,927	178,801	11,608,728	1,297,814	589,203	10,900,117	7,696,734	3,564,394	35,713	620,540	343,089
2003	23,267,196	12,198,209	162,456	12,360,665	1,363,847	516,137	11,512,955	8,005,085	3,749,156	36,649	634,862	348,498
2004	25,830,142	13,759,144	166,924	13,926,068	1,532,413	499,740	12,893,395	8,953,521	3,983,226	39,500	653,934	367,127
2005	28,344,723	15,347,469	216,194	15,563,663	1,717,496	378,223	14,224,390	9,864,981	4,255,352	42,007	674,757	387,812
2006	30,641,321	16,372,708	203,900	16,576,608	1,858,050	313,807	15,032,365	11,009,315	4,599,641	44,723	685,132	399,382
2007	31,174,775	15,740,769	187,784	15,928,553	1,844,694	295,020	14,378,879	11,894,746	4,901,150	45,068	691,735	397,908
2008	30,589,469	14,262,757	162,607	14,425,364	1,738,683	343,789	13,030,470	12,042,175	5,516,824	43,954	695,944	372,081
2009	28,228,152	13,144,926	169,870	13,314,796	1,659,075	375,982	12,031,703	10,162,150	6,034,299	40,443	697,973	355,548
2010	29,651,966	13,400,530	174,680	13,575,210	1,651,463	472,271	12,396,018	10,784,471	6,471,477	42,177	703,038	346,050
2011	31,484,054	13,874,877	139,497	14,014,374	1,533,903	547,011	13,027,482	11,743,238	6,713,334	44,458	708,168	352,491
2012	32,069,084	14,096,131	153,984	14,250,115	1,590,470	565,919	13,225,564	12,082,277	6,761,243	44,705	717,345	361,761
2013	32,901,935	14,785,239	168,090	14,953,329	1,867,129	576,310	13,662,510	12,219,048	7,020,377	45,228	727,470	375,448
2014	35,998,578	16,108,768	154,510	16,263,278	2,004,633	576,407	14,835,052	13,734,507	7,429,019	48,553	741,432	394,097
2015	39,012,337	17,639,054	180,183	17,819,237	2,153,682	592,663	16,258,218	14,801,318	7,952,801	51,336	759,948	411,470
2016	40,742,676	18,571,097	159,306	18,730,403	2,256,340	585,798	17,059,861	15,384,026	8,298,789	52,289	779,181	419,613
2017	44,048,643	19,646,922	175,667	19,822,589	2,385,328	654,814	18,092,075	17,244,746	8,711,822	55,478	793,984	434,199
2018	46,978,310	21,054,386	152,984	21,207,370	2,581,889	609,438	19,234,919	18,527,409	9,215,982	58,174	807,547	449,870
2019	50,812,226	22,167,240	153,560	22,320,800	2,763,837	624,595	20,181,558	20,621,750	10,008,918	61,762	822,713	456,278
2020	53,946,588	22,785,928	132,032	22,917,960	2,881,345	707,630	20,744,245	21,030,671	12,171,672	64,391	837,800	457,584
2021	61,098,171	25,577,495	114,799	25,692,294	3,157,198	764,988	23,300,084	23,985,149	13,812,938	70,878	862,024	483,751
2022	64,463,112	28,319,589	123,630	28,443,219	3,550,481	732,702	25,625,440	25,933,892	12,903,780	72,316	891,411	507,472

Personal Income and Employment by Area: Norwich-New London, CT

(Thousands of dollars, except as noted.)

		Derivation of personal income										
		Earnings by place of work										
Year	Personal income, total	Nonfarm	Farm	Total	Less: Contributions for government social insurance	Plus: Adjustment for residence	Equals: Net earnings by place of residence	Plus: Dividends, interest, and rent	Plus: Personal current transfer receipts	Per capita personal income (dollars)	Population (persons)	Total employment
1970	1,008,957	824,578	8,094	832,672	52,910	-39,085	740,677	196,971	71,309	4,360	231,405	102,499
1971	1,089,406	889,425	8,046	897,471	60,164	-44,709	792,598	211,530	85,278	4,656	233,975	103,331
1972	1,198,510	975,833	8,926	984,759	69,019	-48,262	867,478	235,528	95,504	5,018	238,857	104,979
1973	1,323,721	1,094,458	11,330	1,105,788	86,485	-57,752	961,551	257,823	104,347	5,559	238,138	109,925
1974	1,476,722	1,237,671	6,002	1,243,673	102,790	-73,596	1,067,287	286,834	122,601	6,195	238,362	115,819
1975	1,577,780	1,272,595	10,476	1,283,071	105,536	-71,607	1,105,928	312,521	159,331	6,530	241,627	112,930
1976	1,709,395	1,394,392	11,625	1,406,017	118,516	-77,840	1,209,661	326,218	173,516	7,065	241,968	116,012
1977	1,896,632	1,569,033	13,141	1,582,174	138,790	-91,808	1,351,576	362,075	182,981	7,861	241,265	122,050
1978	2,049,957	1,656,323	8,360	1,664,683	147,775	-81,593	1,435,315	415,903	198,739	8,445	242,732	121,499
1979	2,260,763	1,826,902	9,990	1,836,892	168,617	-83,669	1,584,606	460,464	215,693	9,388	240,812	123,476
1980	2,567,144	2,032,729	11,647	2,044,376	183,291	-90,734	1,770,351	549,041	247,752	10,731	239,228	126,114
1981	2,923,529	2,309,541	18,060	2,327,601	223,217	-115,386	1,988,998	648,731	285,800	12,081	241,985	129,103
1982	3,209,244	2,549,499	22,255	2,571,754	251,097	-141,363	2,179,294	715,536	314,414	13,204	243,051	131,160
1983	3,531,083	2,856,192	24,081	2,880,273	288,556	-163,766	2,427,951	764,669	338,463	14,307	246,802	135,782
1984	3,916,459	3,145,076	38,287	3,183,363	326,082	-166,590	2,690,691	864,925	360,843	15,729	248,990	140,610
1985	4,153,836	3,332,122	37,036	3,369,158	348,267	-155,280	2,865,611	902,987	385,238	16,736	248,201	143,521
1986	4,301,431	3,353,329	38,619	3,391,948	346,231	-110,581	2,935,136	955,751	410,544	17,291	248,765	144,825
1987	4,636,200	3,636,935	43,265	3,680,200	372,044	-92,885	3,215,271	995,356	425,573	18,504	250,549	149,270
1988	4,941,057	3,860,267	38,843	3,899,110	407,836	-77,896	3,413,378	1,068,648	459,031	19,538	252,893	151,325
1989	5,371,142	4,107,397	36,125	4,143,522	433,533	-86,475	3,623,514	1,230,673	516,955	21,162	253,805	152,415
1990	5,596,843	4,123,638	44,215	4,167,853	433,970	52,655	3,786,538	1,228,757	581,548	21,908	255,474	149,439
1991	5,693,950	4,242,618	40,538	4,283,156	454,987	10,904	3,839,073	1,200,958	653,919	22,263	255,761	143,950
1992	6,033,337	4,411,978	42,499	4,454,477	470,077	83,420	4,067,820	1,197,120	768,397	23,913	252,306	141,923
1993	6,262,084	4,614,692	54,397	4,669,089	491,002	28,971	4,207,058	1,249,523	805,503	24,665	253,886	143,783
1994	6,579,643	5,002,731	48,516	5,051,247	542,941	-77,498	4,430,808	1,320,951	827,884	25,740	255,618	145,989
1995	6,873,836	5,321,951	34,773	5,356,724	581,631	-195,648	4,579,445	1,407,946	886,445	26,661	257,828	151,338
1996	7,115,775	5,534,907	37,243	5,572,150	604,401	-236,645	4,731,104	1,467,270	917,401	27,502	258,741	153,594
1997	7,538,931	5,964,492	35,484	5,999,976	636,423	-277,513	5,086,040	1,506,601	946,290	29,146	258,662	157,056
1998	7,978,644	6,219,907	37,409	6,257,316	649,285	-199,519	5,408,512	1,593,827	976,305	31,091	256,626	157,246
1999	8,324,717	6,587,785	38,018	6,625,803	664,632	-203,273	5,757,898	1,565,428	1,001,391	32,320	257,568	158,947
2000	8,798,273	6,884,984	41,753	6,926,737	682,769	-131,672	6,112,296	1,638,406	1,047,571	33,859	259,848	162,098
2001	9,175,193	7,194,670	45,596	7,240,266	704,213	-125,311	6,410,742	1,644,001	1,120,450	35,101	261,396	163,919
2002	9,505,230	7,527,184	51,616	7,578,800	758,515	-176,101	6,644,184	1,654,162	1,206,884	35,910	264,698	167,601
2003	9,923,754	7,884,096	48,376	7,932,472	784,179	-236,872	6,911,421	1,768,679	1,243,654	37,226	266,584	168,575
2004	10,603,642	8,477,928	46,252	8,524,180	829,585	-175,831	7,518,764	1,773,046	1,311,832	39,478	268,595	169,466
2005	10,911,172	8,801,376	41,486	8,842,862	856,071	-206,402	7,780,389	1,762,471	1,368,312	40,462	269,664	172,254
2006	11,429,803	9,080,107	38,138	9,118,245	882,758	-195,648	8,039,839	1,915,342	1,474,622	42,205	270,814	172,894
2007	12,076,664	9,312,499	42,884	9,355,383	909,968	-75,142	8,370,273	2,119,365	1,587,026	44,618	270,669	174,719
2008	12,561,837	9,508,083	54,051	9,562,134	943,705	-199,383	8,419,046	2,319,871	1,822,920	46,076	272,634	176,186
2009	12,487,966	9,457,527	53,552	9,511,079	941,648	-295,527	8,273,904	2,179,938	2,034,124	45,638	273,630	171,181
2010	12,588,969	9,525,310	46,920	9,572,230	936,869	-307,217	8,328,144	2,062,642	2,198,183	45,928	274,104	168,285
2011	13,071,673	9,598,073	45,294	9,643,367	858,631	-197,787	8,586,949	2,271,129	2,213,595	47,792	273,513	168,026
2012	13,310,126	9,548,164	62,625	9,610,789	871,148	-144,172	8,595,469	2,485,347	2,229,310	48,410	274,945	166,646
2013	13,216,227	9,517,199	75,920	9,593,119	988,700	20,896	8,625,315	2,324,103	2,266,809	48,199	274,204	165,934
2014	13,546,462	9,605,928	54,651	9,660,579	1,004,366	142,471	8,798,684	2,409,913	2,337,865	49,614	273,038	164,515
2015	14,146,886	9,844,283	79,556	9,923,839	1,029,363	261,049	9,155,525	2,565,260	2,426,101	52,089	271,593	164,721
2016	14,449,565	10,355,480	57,932	10,413,412	1,077,744	84,819	9,420,487	2,536,855	2,492,223	53,370	270,745	166,953
2017	14,772,421	10,643,510	74,624	10,718,134	1,123,082	52,864	9,647,916	2,590,665	2,533,840	54,659	270,266	168,381
2018	15,017,232	10,757,373	62,281	10,819,654	1,134,674	116,077	9,801,057	2,525,599	2,690,576	55,649	269,857	166,335
2019	15,596,073	10,817,838	67,438	10,885,276	1,161,852	342,482	10,065,906	2,714,790	2,815,377	58,005	268,874	163,508
2020	16,360,343	10,432,122	63,796	10,495,918	1,149,296	564,627	9,911,249	2,706,979	3,742,115	61,119	267,680	150,870
2021	17,220,107	11,260,187	57,481	11,317,668	1,227,213	340,101	10,430,556	2,814,047	3,975,504	64,182	268,300	157,094
2022	17,423,249	11,876,143	90,754	11,966,897	1,325,873	388,861	11,029,885	2,915,138	3,478,226	64,847	268,681	163,717

Personal Income and Employment by Area: Ocala, FL

(Thousands of dollars, except as noted.)

Year	Personal income, total	Derivation of personal income: Earnings by place of work: Nonfarm	Farm	Total	Less: Contributions for government social insurance	Plus: Adjustment for residence	Equals: Net earnings by place of residence	Plus: Dividends, interest, and rent	Plus: Personal current transfer receipts	Per capita personal income (dollars)	Population (persons)	Total employment
1970	228,020	151,527	10,838	162,365	9,942	5,163	157,586	43,619	26,815	3,243	70,320	28,119
1971	264,761	174,869	11,581	186,450	12,020	6,115	180,545	51,201	33,015	3,452	76,690	30,308
1972	314,537	208,462	13,638	222,100	15,029	8,338	215,409	59,517	39,611	3,880	81,072	32,968
1973	382,637	252,427	15,795	268,222	20,854	10,472	257,840	74,699	50,098	4,265	89,718	36,754
1974	424,854	271,214	9,833	281,047	23,546	11,828	269,329	90,753	64,772	4,361	97,426	37,392
1975	463,166	280,611	8,011	288,622	24,147	14,187	278,662	101,142	83,362	4,644	99,728	36,675
1976	514,585	308,808	6,790	315,598	27,176	16,915	305,337	110,296	98,952	4,889	105,252	37,671
1977	576,504	344,768	6,406	351,174	30,542	19,304	339,936	125,714	110,854	5,252	109,765	39,712
1978	668,831	401,363	6,772	408,135	36,357	21,981	393,759	150,969	124,103	5,938	112,629	43,276
1979	786,041	472,472	5,470	477,942	44,930	23,639	456,651	182,227	147,163	6,673	117,793	46,365
1980	959,624	547,299	9,789	557,088	52,422	27,503	532,169	245,587	181,868	7,725	124,218	50,295
1981	1,132,993	623,975	1,985	625,960	64,198	39,039	600,801	314,521	217,671	8,655	130,907	52,796
1982	1,275,909	676,871	14,606	691,477	71,612	50,664	670,529	351,179	254,201	9,287	137,381	54,974
1983	1,445,556	767,700	17,815	785,515	80,556	58,896	763,855	399,153	282,548	9,965	145,069	58,774
1984	1,639,074	886,544	20,324	906,868	95,426	72,250	883,692	455,730	299,652	10,817	151,521	63,433
1985	1,864,448	998,809	25,105	1,023,914	109,924	89,753	1,003,743	520,869	339,836	11,692	159,464	68,511
1986	2,080,417	1,122,175	30,358	1,152,533	126,021	102,930	1,129,442	572,552	378,423	12,445	167,170	73,388
1987	2,276,157	1,247,957	27,728	1,275,685	138,434	121,210	1,258,461	602,658	415,038	13,054	174,370	74,876
1988	2,534,103	1,373,285	33,223	1,406,508	157,498	144,799	1,393,809	675,564	464,730	14,057	180,277	77,900
1989	2,839,283	1,487,741	32,666	1,520,407	174,992	169,026	1,514,441	788,318	536,524	15,138	187,560	79,822
1990	3,089,219	1,584,235	33,303	1,617,538	184,262	199,936	1,633,212	851,660	604,347	15,674	197,095	81,784
1991	3,183,625	1,651,947	32,379	1,684,326	193,640	133,289	1,623,975	864,053	695,597	15,623	203,775	81,874
1992	3,406,622	1,771,490	45,330	1,816,820	207,277	139,488	1,749,031	862,582	795,009	16,269	209,388	82,420
1993	3,663,299	1,926,896	53,045	1,979,941	225,314	154,397	1,909,024	897,676	856,599	17,053	214,818	86,980
1994	3,956,404	2,068,885	54,190	2,123,075	245,865	182,789	2,059,999	963,280	933,125	17,700	223,523	89,626
1995	4,272,667	2,218,703	55,084	2,273,787	261,688	173,431	2,185,530	1,077,316	1,009,821	18,528	230,611	92,766
1996	4,608,135	2,429,561	55,140	2,484,701	280,098	156,461	2,361,064	1,171,464	1,075,607	19,473	236,637	98,351
1997	4,905,365	2,554,042	66,722	2,620,764	295,990	198,880	2,523,654	1,244,248	1,137,463	20,165	243,264	102,369
1998	5,366,884	2,771,134	63,007	2,834,141	317,260	245,523	2,762,404	1,387,960	1,216,520	21,460	250,086	107,202
1999	5,656,498	2,974,559	56,858	3,031,417	336,418	284,985	2,979,984	1,398,716	1,277,798	22,185	254,964	110,338
2000	6,070,437	3,110,302	32,989	3,143,291	350,230	387,444	3,180,505	1,527,431	1,362,501	23,328	260,221	113,425
2001	6,422,226	3,337,243	36,351	3,373,594	381,846	370,412	3,362,160	1,568,487	1,491,579	24,276	264,553	111,456
2002	6,592,940	3,553,335	37,325	3,590,660	405,370	345,718	3,531,008	1,456,875	1,605,057	24,264	271,716	114,395
2003	7,016,486	3,853,274	21,145	3,874,419	441,065	326,594	3,759,948	1,536,934	1,719,604	25,051	280,091	119,810
2004	7,631,071	4,141,356	23,586	4,164,942	485,171	324,478	4,004,249	1,731,505	1,895,317	26,209	291,164	126,040
2005	8,466,986	4,578,078	13,061	4,591,139	542,056	318,023	4,367,106	1,982,427	2,117,453	27,892	303,558	134,599
2006	9,368,566	5,044,845	17,654	5,062,499	615,018	286,734	4,734,215	2,304,006	2,330,345	29,618	316,310	143,129
2007	9,825,874	5,080,160	-17,309	5,062,851	628,152	266,292	4,700,991	2,607,701	2,517,182	30,175	325,634	145,871
2008	9,996,953	4,923,064	-41,146	4,881,918	624,664	219,679	4,476,933	2,671,517	2,848,503	30,289	330,052	140,816
2009	9,764,824	4,522,904	-39,507	4,483,397	594,315	236,632	4,125,714	2,504,578	3,134,532	29,512	330,880	131,469
2010	10,106,495	4,571,972	-21,974	4,549,998	594,246	249,979	4,205,731	2,524,165	3,376,599	30,494	331,428	128,573
2011	10,574,046	4,619,421	-59,778	4,559,643	549,336	264,897	4,275,204	2,796,640	3,502,202	31,777	332,757	129,807
2012	10,690,897	4,781,381	26,968	4,808,349	573,007	252,167	4,487,509	2,668,438	3,534,950	31,939	334,726	132,021
2013	10,535,061	4,880,175	-2,046	4,878,129	654,221	249,811	4,473,719	2,438,661	3,622,681	31,324	336,328	134,635
2014	10,958,819	5,058,828	16,184	5,075,012	679,218	261,533	4,657,327	2,539,477	3,762,015	32,264	339,657	138,719
2015	11,419,005	5,288,829	20,173	5,309,002	703,160	285,890	4,891,732	2,591,179	3,936,094	33,170	344,255	141,992
2016	12,031,413	5,668,487	14,576	5,683,063	746,688	295,363	5,231,738	2,733,384	4,066,291	34,354	350,220	146,349
2017	12,725,247	5,823,633	31,653	5,855,286	773,787	341,788	5,423,287	3,014,324	4,287,636	35,683	356,623	150,216
2018	13,361,441	6,111,880	8,882	6,120,762	828,453	372,847	5,665,156	3,210,029	4,486,256	36,837	362,717	155,560
2019	14,197,537	6,420,869	6,513	6,427,382	887,941	406,398	5,945,839	3,460,951	4,790,747	38,420	369,537	157,617
2020	15,436,434	6,802,795	-492	6,802,303	939,001	424,339	6,287,641	3,388,363	5,760,430	40,896	377,459	162,246
2021	17,332,265	7,593,842	29,656	7,623,498	1,017,255	484,795	7,091,038	3,640,450	6,600,777	45,009	385,084	171,193
2022	17,648,907	8,233,257	2,443	8,235,700	1,131,217	549,660	7,654,143	3,886,660	6,108,104	44,521	396,415	178,963

Personal Income and Employment by Area: Ocean City, NJ

(Thousands of dollars, except as noted.)

Year	Personal income, total	Derivation of personal income: Earnings by place of work: Nonfarm	Farm	Total	Less: Contributions for government social insurance	Plus: Adjustment for residence	Equals: Net earnings by place of residence	Plus: Dividends, interest, and rent	Plus: Personal current transfer receipts	Per capita personal income (dollars)	Population (persons)	Total employment
1970	261,323	151,397	1,101	152,498	11,075	25,634	167,057	60,153	34,113	4,337	60,259	25,672
1971	292,415	168,190	962	169,152	12,787	26,784	183,149	67,702	41,564	4,606	63,485	26,985
1972	333,999	190,401	1,019	191,420	15,084	33,244	209,580	75,505	48,914	5,036	66,321	28,236
1973	393,430	227,699	1,460	229,159	20,299	39,212	248,072	87,912	57,446	5,769	68,194	30,935
1974	441,926	246,154	1,582	247,736	22,708	46,879	271,907	101,901	68,118	6,144	71,929	30,751
1975	503,624	270,699	1,387	272,086	24,926	55,495	302,655	113,843	87,126	6,804	74,014	31,385
1976	568,484	305,685	1,313	306,998	27,963	65,176	344,211	124,376	99,897	7,398	76,838	32,553
1977	631,487	338,815	883	339,698	31,255	75,048	383,491	140,519	107,477	8,070	78,248	34,569
1978	710,744	383,200	1,093	384,293	35,993	89,114	437,414	156,072	117,258	8,900	79,862	36,393
1979	790,271	413,999	981	414,980	40,783	111,040	485,237	173,929	131,105	9,670	81,725	37,189
1980	915,940	453,260	557	453,817	44,694	137,946	547,069	218,537	150,334	11,068	82,754	38,264
1981	1,036,444	485,257	1,037	486,294	51,461	167,294	602,127	263,119	171,198	12,258	84,550	39,013
1982	1,120,981	509,761	1,647	511,408	54,472	178,275	635,211	295,247	190,523	13,172	85,104	39,669
1983	1,215,915	565,725	2,287	568,012	62,140	191,757	697,629	312,396	205,890	14,194	85,665	42,138
1984	1,333,052	626,495	2,308	628,803	71,701	208,607	765,709	352,908	214,435	15,306	87,092	43,146
1985	1,437,825	689,826	2,381	692,207	79,433	222,972	835,746	382,070	220,009	16,220	88,647	43,532
1986	1,548,809	755,144	2,461	757,605	88,217	234,715	904,103	414,201	230,505	17,184	90,130	44,391
1987	1,646,870	826,555	1,996	828,551	97,329	250,322	981,544	425,770	239,556	17,893	92,038	44,431
1988	1,804,463	928,587	2,216	930,803	112,132	267,562	1,086,233	462,722	255,508	19,411	92,961	46,515
1989	1,941,413	980,201	2,274	982,475	118,262	279,156	1,143,369	523,735	274,309	20,473	94,830	47,087
1990	2,040,585	1,015,630	2,425	1,018,055	118,685	309,461	1,208,831	531,921	299,833	21,397	95,368	47,010
1991	2,093,902	1,031,464	2,088	1,033,552	123,706	313,807	1,223,653	522,395	347,854	21,585	97,006	46,586
1992	2,238,636	1,106,230	2,240	1,108,470	131,728	328,195	1,304,937	522,793	410,906	22,815	98,121	47,721
1993	2,344,107	1,147,829	2,833	1,150,662	135,222	358,326	1,373,766	534,282	436,059	23,797	98,504	47,462
1994	2,415,040	1,195,960	3,379	1,199,339	143,375	360,307	1,416,271	550,783	447,986	24,257	99,561	47,835
1995	2,550,345	1,243,912	2,923	1,246,835	148,403	376,241	1,474,673	596,210	479,462	25,401	100,405	48,319
1996	2,669,541	1,293,094	2,485	1,295,579	154,359	390,421	1,531,641	635,076	502,824	26,468	100,861	49,078
1997	2,905,131	1,397,775	2,297	1,400,072	160,756	441,200	1,680,516	702,486	522,129	28,656	101,380	50,322
1998	3,069,509	1,449,669	3,604	1,453,273	165,875	497,999	1,785,397	747,643	536,469	30,128	101,883	51,329
1999	3,185,505	1,548,811	4,309	1,553,120	173,335	510,252	1,890,037	742,386	553,082	31,189	102,135	52,030
2000	3,397,068	1,641,421	5,603	1,647,024	181,897	542,592	2,007,719	808,123	581,226	33,202	102,314	54,163
2001	3,604,499	1,825,266	5,651	1,830,917	198,948	539,637	2,171,606	803,193	629,700	35,330	102,023	55,135
2002	3,717,086	1,945,123	6,236	1,951,359	211,968	518,292	2,257,683	750,301	709,102	36,552	101,694	55,664
2003	3,761,689	2,062,549	6,032	2,068,581	221,814	484,479	2,331,246	745,376	685,067	36,984	101,710	56,474
2004	3,935,872	2,222,981	6,109	2,229,090	240,080	459,143	2,448,153	804,087	683,632	39,170	100,482	58,376
2005	4,009,633	2,354,071	6,379	2,360,450	264,159	417,097	2,513,388	766,555	729,690	40,392	99,269	60,457
2006	4,088,670	2,382,858	7,135	2,389,993	271,045	398,378	2,517,326	772,540	798,804	41,427	98,695	60,130
2007	4,141,079	2,286,174	7,419	2,293,593	272,929	412,094	2,432,758	863,707	844,614	42,392	97,686	59,742
2008	4,174,679	2,242,858	7,057	2,249,915	275,683	307,035	2,281,267	969,227	924,185	42,795	97,550	59,284
2009	4,128,764	2,202,605	6,354	2,208,959	273,343	249,253	2,184,869	916,657	1,027,238	42,460	97,238	58,523
2010	4,335,612	2,259,584	5,770	2,265,354	278,423	249,106	2,236,037	1,008,159	1,091,416	44,553	97,314	58,090
2011	4,448,837	2,252,123	4,883	2,257,006	255,874	292,536	2,293,668	1,047,832	1,107,337	45,872	96,984	58,109
2012	4,568,742	2,325,636	5,486	2,331,122	259,957	322,184	2,393,349	1,074,072	1,101,321	47,053	97,098	58,054
2013	4,617,833	2,418,347	6,183	2,424,530	297,660	290,035	2,416,905	1,091,658	1,109,270	47,738	96,732	58,723
2014	4,763,802	2,534,125	5,641	2,539,766	309,670	235,673	2,465,769	1,152,806	1,145,227	49,359	96,513	59,771
2015	4,929,704	2,639,829	5,728	2,645,557	320,860	223,899	2,548,596	1,192,932	1,188,176	51,225	96,236	60,317
2016	5,071,537	2,720,853	6,324	2,727,177	328,161	276,071	2,675,087	1,175,570	1,220,880	52,782	96,085	60,593
2017	5,316,888	2,812,476	6,827	2,819,303	341,474	285,166	2,762,995	1,308,234	1,245,659	55,446	95,893	61,555
2018	5,542,473	2,949,242	6,381	2,955,623	353,092	296,951	2,899,482	1,350,623	1,292,368	58,002	95,556	62,090
2019	5,933,687	3,212,932	8,234	3,221,166	376,539	386,437	3,231,064	1,342,636	1,359,987	62,102	95,548	62,088
2020	6,542,215	3,210,223	9,221	3,219,444	375,150	488,276	3,332,570	1,443,149	1,766,496	68,836	95,040	58,229
2021	7,034,972	3,619,818	8,340	3,628,158	428,497	410,192	3,609,853	1,505,278	1,919,841	73,458	95,768	62,884
2022	6,846,399	3,612,419	8,763	3,621,182	460,394	502,505	3,663,293	1,533,894	1,649,212	71,590	95,634	65,393

Personal Income and Employment by Area: Odessa, TX

(Thousands of dollars, except as noted.)

Year	Personal income, total	Derivation of personal income: Earnings by place of work: Nonfarm	Farm	Total	Less: Contributions for government social insurance	Plus: Adjustment for residence	Equals: Net earnings by place of residence	Plus: Dividends, interest, and rent	Plus: Personal current transfer receipts	Per capita personal income (dollars)	Population (persons)	Total employment
1970	342,782	301,150	460	301,610	18,409	7,072	290,273	35,455	17,054	3,698	92,704	38,555
1971	367,519	321,697	99	321,796	20,093	7,271	308,974	38,512	20,033	3,926	93,609	39,295
1972	405,464	356,961	-680	356,281	23,239	7,691	340,733	42,015	22,716	4,291	94,500	40,684
1973	451,399	397,916	225	398,141	30,713	8,140	375,568	48,411	27,420	4,840	93,264	43,432
1974	542,855	479,145	610	479,755	37,996	9,519	451,278	58,976	32,601	5,616	96,667	46,851
1975	653,641	571,871	55	571,926	44,309	15,237	542,854	71,025	39,762	6,562	99,614	49,230
1976	795,881	709,582	298	709,880	52,843	16,327	673,364	78,591	43,926	7,773	102,392	51,191
1977	897,303	801,150	74	801,224	61,468	21,501	761,257	88,971	47,075	8,570	104,702	54,572
1978	1,031,873	920,635	743	921,378	73,925	29,019	876,472	102,072	53,329	9,538	108,189	58,659
1979	1,126,888	998,173	221	998,394	85,385	34,562	947,571	117,099	62,218	10,114	111,422	59,768
1980	1,349,505	1,174,121	72	1,174,193	102,391	54,480	1,126,282	150,889	72,334	11,529	117,052	64,450
1981	1,751,099	1,546,000	1,095	1,547,095	144,618	59,842	1,462,319	206,272	82,508	14,188	123,418	73,670
1982	1,890,177	1,620,139	1,234	1,621,373	158,107	64,563	1,527,829	265,711	96,637	13,950	135,501	74,922
1983	1,754,641	1,431,154	383	1,431,537	139,207	52,217	1,344,547	287,256	122,838	12,711	138,041	67,260
1984	1,758,572	1,407,125	475	1,407,600	142,278	51,889	1,317,211	312,665	128,696	13,123	134,006	66,031
1985	1,811,732	1,444,681	696	1,445,377	150,025	46,565	1,341,917	334,008	135,807	13,599	133,225	67,259
1986	1,616,328	1,215,730	509	1,216,239	123,137	44,198	1,137,300	314,257	164,771	12,099	133,588	57,894
1987	1,541,058	1,154,249	598	1,154,847	116,067	33,551	1,072,331	301,820	166,907	12,311	125,180	55,809
1988	1,600,374	1,200,397	232	1,200,629	126,055	33,441	1,108,015	322,340	170,019	13,111	122,067	57,518
1989	1,662,633	1,221,551	127	1,221,678	127,452	27,279	1,121,505	344,773	196,355	13,887	119,722	55,919
1990	1,707,770	1,268,409	-158	1,268,251	131,684	23,840	1,160,407	328,806	218,557	14,393	118,652	57,211
1991	1,812,284	1,357,487	-590	1,356,897	143,785	17,958	1,231,070	327,888	253,326	15,108	119,955	58,006
1992	1,860,156	1,364,858	-233	1,364,625	142,361	15,820	1,238,084	319,742	302,330	15,370	121,027	56,475
1993	1,928,220	1,424,822	-532	1,424,290	149,040	9,580	1,284,830	316,713	326,677	15,933	121,018	56,906
1994	1,991,115	1,473,181	-185	1,472,996	155,738	667	1,317,925	321,849	351,341	16,420	121,258	58,224
1995	2,053,468	1,499,812	-1,185	1,498,627	158,991	-1,990	1,337,646	341,585	374,237	16,968	121,017	58,734
1996	2,139,275	1,565,046	-2,232	1,562,814	163,408	-6,811	1,392,595	352,464	394,216	17,604	121,519	59,531
1997	2,344,978	1,753,101	-1,810	1,751,291	179,062	-9,729	1,562,500	375,570	406,908	19,261	121,749	61,867
1998	2,524,100	1,945,227	-1,614	1,943,613	196,917	-30,423	1,716,273	402,432	405,395	20,431	123,544	64,989
1999	2,400,337	1,795,910	-1,469	1,794,441	177,728	-24,985	1,591,728	383,424	425,185	19,603	122,450	60,926
2000	2,586,976	1,965,182	-852	1,964,330	190,295	-38,711	1,735,324	412,892	438,760	21,434	120,694	62,662
2001	2,806,702	2,164,186	-575	2,163,611	215,174	-38,117	1,910,320	424,033	472,349	23,234	120,802	64,327
2002	2,873,757	2,196,323	443	2,196,766	217,705	-46,213	1,932,848	417,904	523,005	23,517	122,199	64,275
2003	2,939,974	2,201,663	1,001	2,202,664	225,789	-41,783	1,935,092	447,081	557,801	23,953	122,739	64,164
2004	3,022,294	2,292,849	988	2,293,837	237,328	-35,306	2,021,203	426,197	574,894	24,341	124,163	65,347
2005	3,368,146	2,534,669	837	2,535,506	265,495	-4,971	2,265,040	479,116	623,990	26,864	125,378	67,944
2006	3,906,258	3,053,991	550	3,054,541	308,733	-6,310	2,739,498	519,064	647,696	30,643	127,476	72,761
2007	4,331,374	3,472,956	835	3,473,791	351,209	-51,997	3,070,585	565,816	694,973	33,201	130,459	76,576
2008	5,045,410	3,990,969	-1,809	3,989,160	394,909	-7,023	3,587,228	701,517	756,665	37,917	133,064	81,244
2009	4,559,014	3,570,859	-2,006	3,568,853	361,542	-111,094	3,096,217	643,424	819,373	33,294	136,930	77,130
2010	4,876,508	3,850,721	-2,397	3,848,324	389,002	-120,868	3,338,454	627,496	910,558	35,591	137,016	78,567
2011	5,632,503	4,656,177	-2,337	4,653,840	421,056	-274,895	3,957,889	776,109	898,505	40,403	139,407	85,463
2012	6,541,131	5,627,806	-2,294	5,625,512	489,740	-378,017	4,757,755	910,556	872,820	45,408	144,053	92,095
2013	6,704,974	6,075,142	309	6,075,451	590,233	-476,269	5,008,949	818,007	878,018	44,999	149,003	94,683
2014	7,484,946	6,725,392	504	6,725,896	654,063	-420,875	5,650,958	926,994	906,994	48,697	153,705	100,794
2015	6,812,933	5,888,510	5,336	5,893,846	593,400	-384,134	4,916,312	924,654	971,967	42,910	158,774	97,162
2016	5,994,736	4,991,912	-153	4,991,759	524,245	-354,715	4,112,799	843,933	1,038,004	38,312	156,471	90,238
2017	6,733,629	5,775,019	1,089	5,776,108	604,410	-356,103	4,815,595	878,407	1,039,627	43,345	155,348	95,521
2018	7,942,585	6,974,222	975	6,975,197	723,684	-349,816	5,901,697	973,990	1,066,898	49,602	160,126	104,623
2019	8,654,622	7,625,481	-377	7,625,104	768,705	-303,573	6,552,826	996,016	1,105,780	52,707	164,204	107,396
2020	7,961,725	6,166,908	-478	6,166,430	631,686	-271,441	5,263,303	1,022,923	1,675,499	48,111	165,485	95,625
2021	8,472,763	6,188,534	682	6,189,216	630,901	-174,563	5,383,752	1,158,782	1,930,229	52,703	160,764	95,387
2022	8,919,825	7,219,192	472	7,219,664	749,401	-379,174	6,091,089	1,262,305	1,566,431	55,448	160,869	102,551

Personal Income and Employment by Area: Ogden-Clearfield, UT

(Thousands of dollars, except as noted.)

		Derivation of personal income										
		Earnings by place of work										
Year	Personal income, total	Nonfarm	Farm	Total	Less: Contributions for government social insurance	Plus: Adjustment for residence	Equals: Net earnings by place of residence	Plus: Dividends, interest, and rent	Plus: Personal current transfer receipts	Per capita personal income (dollars)	Population (persons)	Total employment
1970	969,165	736,060	19,328	755,388	36,595	24,125	742,918	161,646	64,601	3,747	258,652	101,375
1971	1,105,674	848,798	18,875	867,673	42,032	9,697	835,338	194,041	76,295	4,165	265,466	102,505
1972	1,187,967	897,136	21,518	918,654	49,285	22,305	891,674	210,639	85,654	4,379	271,286	106,947
1973	1,288,341	956,805	29,967	986,772	61,191	32,578	958,159	228,315	101,867	4,675	275,564	109,681
1974	1,428,952	1,058,738	25,577	1,084,315	71,464	41,988	1,054,839	258,192	115,921	5,109	279,691	112,270
1975	1,572,838	1,167,556	15,280	1,182,836	79,865	45,407	1,148,378	282,220	142,240	5,487	286,672	114,043
1976	1,763,256	1,318,691	15,401	1,334,092	92,699	54,155	1,295,548	313,031	154,677	6,012	293,292	118,620
1977	1,955,618	1,458,309	10,038	1,468,347	104,226	72,824	1,436,945	351,641	167,032	6,489	301,368	123,292
1978	2,244,010	1,656,985	13,471	1,670,456	121,620	93,536	1,642,372	415,834	185,804	7,217	310,926	130,121
1979	2,522,605	1,853,976	15,558	1,869,534	145,163	115,748	1,840,119	470,210	212,276	7,865	320,746	136,040
1980	2,833,195	2,032,680	12,117	2,044,797	159,248	149,395	2,034,944	548,572	249,679	8,542	331,666	137,885
1981	3,177,266	2,273,345	6,066	2,279,411	190,343	157,393	2,246,461	637,761	293,044	9,334	340,400	140,230
1982	3,465,321	2,433,209	7,952	2,441,161	206,927	178,716	2,412,950	718,801	333,570	9,936	348,770	141,296
1983	3,740,499	2,596,199	5,019	2,601,218	232,532	221,385	2,590,071	788,731	361,697	10,512	355,842	143,806
1984	4,128,117	2,895,050	7,831	2,902,881	269,072	240,057	2,873,866	879,641	374,610	11,419	361,527	152,784
1985	4,503,242	3,193,429	5,909	3,199,338	310,562	253,156	3,141,932	949,757	411,553	12,267	367,103	161,151
1986	4,764,667	3,374,296	12,637	3,386,933	334,104	267,333	3,320,162	1,004,950	439,555	12,786	372,647	166,082
1987	4,952,857	3,452,378	35,064	3,487,442	343,673	317,093	3,460,862	1,032,739	459,256	13,059	379,274	171,824
1988	5,257,876	3,664,639	52,004	3,716,643	384,819	346,550	3,678,374	1,093,001	486,501	13,792	381,216	178,142
1989	5,631,267	3,922,772	47,140	3,969,912	421,983	374,148	3,922,077	1,174,258	534,932	14,622	385,120	184,178
1990	6,110,022	4,215,190	60,135	4,275,325	471,422	497,683	4,301,586	1,218,604	589,832	15,674	389,815	190,389
1991	6,479,842	4,497,255	54,339	4,551,594	511,109	521,926	4,562,411	1,274,800	642,631	16,263	398,436	192,203
1992	6,953,545	4,779,187	73,622	4,852,809	544,894	629,575	4,937,490	1,303,249	712,806	17,011	408,757	193,998
1993	7,416,916	5,055,433	75,662	5,131,095	583,898	719,306	5,266,503	1,370,148	780,265	17,664	419,888	199,000
1994	7,908,845	5,360,880	55,777	5,416,657	630,691	810,357	5,596,323	1,506,459	806,063	18,350	430,988	213,802
1995	8,556,185	5,749,554	44,342	5,793,896	679,335	886,761	6,001,322	1,683,890	870,973	19,414	440,732	220,335
1996	9,242,855	6,161,854	49,938	6,211,792	723,711	993,911	6,481,992	1,834,562	926,301	20,506	450,737	233,975
1997	9,956,786	6,597,480	53,417	6,650,897	766,366	1,157,574	7,042,105	1,946,462	968,219	21,612	460,703	244,207
1998	10,622,824	6,951,991	54,154	7,006,145	806,334	1,316,458	7,516,269	2,090,594	1,015,961	22,592	470,206	248,177
1999	11,102,590	7,234,177	48,133	7,282,310	836,286	1,494,242	7,940,266	2,088,081	1,074,243	23,180	478,978	251,600
2000	11,837,536	7,645,893	34,947	7,680,840	884,895	1,614,349	8,410,294	2,279,159	1,148,083	24,262	487,906	257,400
2001	12,647,910	8,219,151	46,865	8,266,016	946,366	1,697,407	9,017,057	2,361,601	1,269,252	25,528	495,459	259,182
2002	13,121,613	8,647,933	23,662	8,671,595	999,799	1,701,529	9,373,325	2,361,419	1,386,869	26,022	504,247	263,452
2003	13,739,482	9,087,112	28,708	9,115,820	1,060,734	1,699,664	9,754,750	2,500,019	1,484,713	26,782	513,021	266,982
2004	14,423,569	9,589,377	41,873	9,631,250	1,139,929	1,844,286	10,335,607	2,534,572	1,553,390	27,612	522,374	276,021
2005	15,395,053	10,085,965	38,599	10,124,564	1,201,559	2,030,590	10,953,595	2,761,667	1,679,791	28,915	532,425	283,618
2006	16,888,180	11,133,791	30,917	11,164,708	1,298,659	2,305,399	12,171,448	2,896,232	1,820,500	30,945	545,746	294,827
2007	18,493,905	11,725,644	39,780	11,765,424	1,369,982	2,652,611	13,048,053	3,451,192	1,994,660	32,921	561,767	308,356
2008	19,335,320	11,924,904	37,977	11,962,881	1,403,479	2,758,892	13,318,294	3,656,450	2,360,576	33,508	577,040	309,965
2009	18,888,442	11,542,633	28,123	11,570,756	1,370,367	2,703,767	12,904,156	3,397,681	2,586,605	32,081	588,773	301,208
2010	19,363,932	11,774,172	38,517	11,812,689	1,388,413	2,763,926	13,188,202	3,287,900	2,887,830	32,280	599,873	297,161
2011	20,701,049	12,306,264	78,695	12,384,959	1,308,111	2,994,925	14,071,773	3,652,555	2,976,721	34,147	606,239	304,012
2012	21,680,993	12,884,045	66,585	12,950,630	1,353,053	3,228,077	14,825,654	3,892,567	2,962,772	35,347	613,373	308,447
2013	22,045,456	13,245,229	97,771	13,343,000	1,576,883	3,392,878	15,158,995	3,844,138	3,042,323	35,388	622,956	315,424
2014	23,156,829	13,915,624	101,574	14,017,198	1,659,425	3,484,647	15,842,420	4,148,333	3,166,076	36,579	633,070	324,251
2015	24,592,866	14,783,125	82,432	14,865,557	1,731,463	3,666,243	16,800,337	4,424,514	3,368,015	38,234	643,219	335,509
2016	26,011,534	15,615,781	54,298	15,670,079	1,820,323	3,917,953	17,767,709	4,734,222	3,509,603	39,657	655,918	346,448
2017	27,351,039	16,525,980	59,797	16,585,777	1,922,778	3,991,200	18,654,199	5,079,272	3,617,568	40,952	667,881	357,795
2018	29,115,212	17,629,457	36,537	17,665,994	2,014,539	4,287,885	19,939,340	5,330,475	3,845,397	42,963	677,677	369,549
2019	30,948,480	18,643,396	67,154	18,710,550	2,119,926	4,609,051	21,199,675	5,563,084	4,185,721	44,987	687,948	374,318
2020	33,584,427	20,006,992	79,281	20,086,273	2,299,736	4,720,126	22,506,663	5,676,899	5,400,865	48,181	697,045	380,136
2021	37,206,295	21,373,121	38,149	21,411,270	2,439,381	5,317,711	24,289,600	6,435,441	6,481,254	52,671	706,394	394,770
2022	39,026,330	22,859,784	80,301	22,940,085	2,643,090	6,103,601	26,400,596	7,122,090	5,503,644	54,671	713,839	410,765

Personal Income and Employment by Area: Oklahoma City, OK

(Thousands of dollars, except as noted.)

Year	Personal income, total	Derivation of personal income: Earnings by place of work: Nonfarm	Farm	Total	Less: Contributions for government social insurance	Plus: Adjustment for residence	Equals: Net earnings by place of residence	Plus: Dividends, interest, and rent	Plus: Personal current transfer receipts	Per capita personal income (dollars)	Population (persons)	Total employment
1970	3,017,627	2,484,654	27,488	2,512,142	143,758	-51,610	2,316,774	464,939	235,914	4,144	728,165	354,356
1971	3,364,882	2,741,764	26,904	2,768,668	164,431	-50,514	2,553,723	534,130	277,029	4,479	751,178	364,970
1972	3,694,011	3,051,263	24,884	3,076,147	194,150	-70,361	2,811,636	572,407	309,968	4,796	770,165	385,385
1973	4,089,347	3,349,156	61,343	3,410,499	249,832	-77,259	3,083,408	649,403	356,536	5,210	784,927	398,352
1974	4,571,230	3,727,100	40,620	3,767,720	288,038	-76,960	3,402,722	746,500	422,008	5,766	792,748	407,075
1975	5,025,160	4,021,527	34,624	4,056,151	309,340	-64,598	3,682,213	811,597	531,350	6,296	798,210	406,103
1976	5,510,871	4,415,814	30,336	4,446,150	347,102	-60,130	4,038,918	890,986	580,967	6,818	808,238	411,197
1977	6,194,095	5,057,117	17,862	5,074,979	398,459	-95,441	4,581,079	1,004,204	608,812	7,547	820,775	432,760
1978	7,111,495	5,879,414	13,197	5,892,611	480,958	-126,266	5,285,387	1,173,766	652,342	8,495	837,101	465,144
1979	8,191,205	6,780,232	37,811	6,818,043	580,145	-146,557	6,091,341	1,350,642	749,222	9,615	851,930	488,083
1980	9,605,913	7,950,111	23,121	7,973,232	688,884	-183,866	7,100,482	1,641,654	863,777	10,949	877,354	513,837
1981	11,186,820	9,218,441	5,797	9,224,238	861,510	-181,364	8,181,364	2,028,026	977,430	12,462	897,677	543,150
1982	12,607,330	10,246,235	16,888	10,263,123	981,046	-173,809	9,108,268	2,407,536	1,091,526	13,450	937,318	568,698
1983	13,054,378	10,446,756	4,078	10,450,834	1,000,019	-203,821	9,246,994	2,619,166	1,188,218	13,431	971,970	562,358
1984	14,008,920	11,171,586	10,990	11,182,576	1,089,785	-213,296	9,879,495	2,891,275	1,238,150	14,242	983,657	574,026
1985	14,532,602	11,400,213	26,215	11,426,428	1,130,774	-200,088	10,095,566	3,090,328	1,346,708	14,711	987,888	562,905
1986	14,533,255	11,313,973	49,383	11,363,356	1,144,357	-185,922	10,033,077	3,051,607	1,448,571	14,770	983,997	542,698
1987	14,510,479	11,325,693	42,464	11,368,157	1,153,140	-171,629	10,043,388	2,946,445	1,520,646	14,959	970,003	543,299
1988	15,209,708	11,850,729	57,831	11,908,560	1,271,501	-181,277	10,455,782	3,116,695	1,637,231	15,738	966,423	549,865
1989	16,333,837	12,568,148	64,905	12,633,053	1,357,679	-166,664	11,108,710	3,481,465	1,743,662	16,839	969,976	557,627
1990	17,022,879	13,126,286	51,645	13,177,931	1,467,296	-181,919	11,528,716	3,602,183	1,891,980	17,504	972,512	567,554
1991	17,581,522	13,569,205	41,302	13,610,507	1,554,084	-183,099	11,873,324	3,618,638	2,089,560	17,868	983,942	568,264
1992	18,677,802	14,426,436	61,647	14,488,083	1,644,894	-197,307	12,645,882	3,670,918	2,361,002	18,708	998,407	574,498
1993	19,580,146	15,197,954	54,227	15,252,181	1,749,775	-212,283	13,290,123	3,824,990	2,465,033	19,291	1,014,998	586,259
1994	20,562,984	15,830,712	63,012	15,893,724	1,853,382	-225,995	13,814,347	4,086,745	2,661,892	19,977	1,029,338	599,649
1995	21,531,982	16,526,980	7,759	16,534,739	1,943,716	-242,302	14,348,721	4,308,863	2,874,398	20,717	1,039,343	621,260
1996	22,876,782	17,561,956	19,233	17,581,189	2,028,027	-240,728	15,312,434	4,549,518	3,014,830	21,748	1,051,886	640,572
1997	23,947,601	18,386,764	27,930	18,414,694	2,099,330	-250,415	16,064,949	4,763,712	3,118,940	22,479	1,065,333	652,676
1998	25,474,414	19,522,769	13,887	19,536,656	2,209,087	-258,424	17,069,145	5,166,498	3,238,771	23,692	1,075,233	667,154
1999	26,482,114	20,350,961	36,648	20,387,609	2,314,528	-300,054	17,773,027	5,295,445	3,413,642	24,332	1,088,347	679,360
2000	29,211,916	22,374,597	34,232	22,408,829	2,498,503	-343,523	19,566,803	5,927,984	3,717,129	26,601	1,098,132	698,058
2001	31,570,889	24,231,233	42,071	24,273,304	2,660,654	-344,329	21,268,321	6,149,852	4,152,716	28,471	1,108,860	707,782
2002	32,483,199	25,071,517	60,875	25,132,392	2,784,059	-356,382	21,991,951	6,241,029	4,250,219	28,945	1,122,241	703,499
2003	34,678,474	26,969,997	48,043	27,018,040	2,925,568	-358,834	23,733,638	6,405,514	4,539,322	30,569	1,134,419	703,624
2004	36,651,378	28,438,671	86,110	28,524,781	3,102,698	-395,134	25,026,949	6,855,118	4,769,311	31,995	1,145,524	718,954
2005	39,882,058	30,630,544	97,620	30,728,164	3,227,288	-397,308	27,103,568	7,520,047	5,258,443	34,342	1,161,308	733,069
2006	43,769,599	33,152,039	44,091	33,196,130	3,423,585	-412,211	29,360,334	8,627,757	5,781,508	37,009	1,182,668	749,102
2007	45,021,268	33,338,072	57,505	33,395,577	3,575,831	-353,861	29,465,885	9,324,800	6,230,583	37,528	1,199,665	764,891
2008	49,705,231	36,802,982	66,739	36,869,721	3,756,857	-375,376	32,737,488	9,855,196	7,112,547	40,854	1,216,645	780,102
2009	47,688,232	35,128,267	-10,308	35,117,959	3,744,590	-386,142	30,987,227	8,999,778	7,701,227	38,527	1,237,780	766,952
2010	49,574,385	36,212,026	30,220	36,242,246	3,846,564	-413,185	31,982,497	9,288,042	8,303,846	39,411	1,257,896	771,474
2011	52,977,126	38,307,569	66,960	38,374,529	3,710,011	-466,408	34,198,110	10,315,885	8,463,131	41,465	1,277,632	790,646
2012	55,612,977	40,222,903	108,355	40,331,258	3,927,621	-482,289	35,921,348	11,012,468	8,679,161	42,818	1,298,832	814,000
2013	57,234,856	42,171,714	55,292	42,227,006	4,547,305	-513,419	37,166,282	11,098,088	8,970,486	43,310	1,321,527	832,946
2014	60,780,754	44,532,210	91,799	44,624,009	4,694,184	-497,351	39,432,474	12,037,904	9,310,376	45,429	1,337,930	846,371
2015	61,824,236	45,587,522	42,010	45,629,532	4,799,332	-521,692	40,308,508	11,809,505	9,706,223	45,486	1,359,199	857,655
2016	61,605,369	44,948,993	-12,466	44,936,527	4,786,546	-515,887	39,634,094	11,913,392	10,057,883	44,787	1,375,508	862,803
2017	63,697,425	46,321,139	-14,815	46,306,324	4,986,989	-593,982	40,725,353	12,465,983	10,506,089	46,015	1,384,267	868,885
2018	66,709,085	48,553,220	-25,645	48,527,575	5,263,843	-675,107	42,588,625	13,139,284	10,981,176	47,746	1,397,154	883,591
2019	72,114,045	52,716,594	-23,422	52,693,172	5,536,811	-673,238	46,483,123	13,924,391	11,706,531	51,036	1,413,004	886,099
2020	76,700,735	53,167,246	-20,526	53,146,720	5,647,399	-618,455	46,880,866	14,665,609	15,154,260	53,642	1,429,854	871,085
2021	85,256,270	57,121,460	10,417	57,131,877	5,974,068	-626,184	50,531,625	17,348,796	17,375,849	59,059	1,443,587	898,822
2022	88,564,986	62,310,068	-105,577	62,204,491	6,507,815	-708,372	54,988,304	18,027,682	15,549,000	60,687	1,459,380	943,288

Personal Income and Employment by Area: Olympia-Lacey-Tumwater, WA

(Thousands of dollars, except as noted.)

Year	Personal income, total	Derivation of personal income: Earnings by place of work: Nonfarm	Farm	Total	Less: Contributions for government social insurance	Plus: Adjustment for residence	Equals: Net earnings by place of residence	Plus: Dividends, interest, and rent	Plus: Personal current transfer receipts	Per capita personal income (dollars)	Population (persons)	Total employment
1970	357,422	257,443	5,347	262,790	19,590	9,066	252,266	74,654	30,502	4,612	77,498	34,767
1971	395,612	282,099	4,690	286,789	22,570	12,001	276,220	82,623	36,769	4,950	79,920	35,873
1972	427,521	302,358	6,506	308,864	25,336	12,561	296,089	89,073	42,359	5,216	81,970	36,700
1973	487,701	336,283	15,247	351,530	32,489	19,457	338,498	100,428	48,775	5,742	84,930	37,999
1974	554,735	378,724	14,107	392,831	38,280	24,275	378,826	116,368	59,541	6,201	89,466	39,450
1975	633,132	428,183	11,846	440,029	42,959	27,113	424,183	135,535	73,414	6,753	93,760	41,096
1976	726,738	494,329	12,270	506,599	50,440	35,592	491,751	152,802	82,185	7,431	97,798	43,594
1977	823,320	558,826	11,627	570,453	57,128	46,068	559,393	175,852	88,075	7,729	106,529	45,440
1978	981,445	671,900	17,035	688,935	71,083	57,249	675,101	208,296	98,048	8,702	112,782	49,562
1979	1,127,945	756,875	18,956	775,831	81,440	76,925	771,316	244,632	111,997	9,465	119,176	53,380
1980	1,300,822	833,419	19,121	852,540	92,880	103,080	862,740	295,197	142,885	10,380	125,325	55,242
1981	1,467,204	904,824	19,848	924,672	108,596	134,400	950,476	351,240	165,488	11,345	129,326	55,939
1982	1,553,410	916,616	21,445	938,061	112,255	151,499	977,305	392,325	183,780	11,759	132,109	55,768
1983	1,681,671	1,000,683	19,571	1,020,254	124,859	140,246	1,035,641	444,123	201,907	12,559	133,899	58,575
1984	1,843,809	1,123,256	17,246	1,140,502	142,948	139,820	1,137,374	492,181	214,254	13,585	135,721	61,228
1985	2,023,627	1,231,413	17,362	1,248,775	158,993	155,616	1,245,398	539,822	238,407	14,597	138,632	63,934
1986	2,189,217	1,339,786	16,932	1,356,718	176,564	173,805	1,353,959	574,369	260,889	15,417	141,998	67,550
1987	2,327,726	1,445,632	12,531	1,458,163	189,590	195,022	1,463,595	584,436	279,695	15,964	145,813	71,492
1988	2,540,942	1,575,925	12,051	1,587,976	215,743	225,336	1,597,569	635,055	308,318	16,890	150,439	75,337
1989	2,848,585	1,742,739	19,838	1,762,577	236,833	241,308	1,767,052	734,402	347,131	18,335	155,365	79,332
1990	3,159,883	1,961,185	19,785	1,980,970	265,618	309,793	2,025,145	757,569	377,169	19,384	163,014	83,933
1991	3,514,585	2,215,612	21,606	2,237,218	299,051	325,281	2,263,448	821,838	429,299	20,749	169,388	87,571
1992	3,863,956	2,449,048	25,923	2,474,971	326,309	380,674	2,529,336	848,997	485,623	21,904	176,407	90,233
1993	4,139,566	2,635,703	26,964	2,662,667	348,416	395,367	2,709,618	903,270	526,678	22,614	183,054	92,374
1994	4,342,173	2,745,385	28,357	2,773,742	368,276	415,392	2,820,858	962,567	558,748	23,221	186,997	96,701
1995	4,587,970	2,864,437	26,118	2,890,555	384,235	448,991	2,955,311	1,024,765	607,894	23,894	192,013	97,945
1996	4,847,820	2,986,163	28,790	3,014,953	386,722	490,570	3,118,801	1,089,692	639,327	24,703	196,247	101,394
1997	5,174,478	3,172,363	29,377	3,201,740	394,405	591,031	3,398,366	1,116,887	659,225	25,936	199,512	103,918
1998	5,542,307	3,437,166	34,681	3,471,847	428,253	620,857	3,664,451	1,188,059	689,797	27,430	202,050	106,533
1999	5,764,164	3,694,592	33,051	3,727,643	447,239	588,434	3,868,838	1,157,054	738,272	28,135	204,873	108,667
2000	6,374,883	4,017,070	22,702	4,039,772	489,668	784,277	4,334,381	1,237,696	802,806	30,606	208,287	110,972
2001	6,771,206	4,335,305	24,902	4,360,207	510,946	769,992	4,619,253	1,255,585	896,368	31,876	212,421	111,844
2002	6,976,894	4,572,405	19,012	4,591,417	543,203	758,517	4,806,731	1,217,046	953,117	32,254	216,313	114,989
2003	7,296,712	4,771,248	33,291	4,804,539	571,569	731,281	4,964,251	1,325,803	1,006,658	33,243	219,499	118,085
2004	7,672,282	4,969,410	29,611	4,999,021	599,730	787,730	5,187,021	1,432,856	1,052,405	34,407	222,985	120,664
2005	8,054,512	5,261,144	22,280	5,283,424	641,084	805,996	5,448,336	1,477,364	1,128,812	35,479	227,023	124,220
2006	8,638,607	5,596,824	22,701	5,619,525	684,077	823,561	5,759,009	1,646,753	1,232,845	37,125	232,688	128,591
2007	9,367,287	6,006,442	23,627	6,030,069	729,117	847,012	6,147,964	1,872,441	1,346,882	39,396	237,772	133,304
2008	10,066,246	6,282,721	37,515	6,320,236	751,599	843,548	6,412,185	2,102,814	1,551,247	41,199	244,332	134,596
2009	9,998,954	6,183,531	40,584	6,224,115	765,168	816,687	6,275,634	1,983,155	1,740,165	40,006	249,936	130,605
2010	10,253,008	6,272,102	41,160	6,313,262	770,480	761,997	6,304,779	2,015,376	1,932,853	40,518	253,048	128,663
2011	10,530,342	6,269,959	45,170	6,315,129	702,746	769,684	6,382,067	2,190,084	1,958,191	41,034	256,623	128,333
2012	10,942,198	6,505,622	55,841	6,561,463	709,382	808,722	6,660,803	2,311,606	1,969,789	42,256	258,949	130,349
2013	11,028,683	6,826,525	57,397	6,883,922	834,880	697,746	6,746,788	2,244,933	2,036,962	42,019	262,469	133,689
2014	11,530,249	7,086,739	63,821	7,150,560	876,868	647,029	6,920,721	2,389,342	2,220,186	43,392	265,722	137,142
2015	12,040,697	7,323,756	107,970	7,431,726	915,435	694,661	7,210,952	2,523,205	2,306,540	44,763	268,989	140,197
2016	12,719,723	7,771,331	68,810	7,840,141	963,364	744,391	7,621,168	2,650,558	2,447,997	46,284	274,820	144,622
2017	13,379,926	8,330,182	82,001	8,412,183	1,052,956	628,484	7,987,711	2,834,086	2,558,129	47,542	281,435	150,034
2018	14,052,605	9,049,996	71,026	9,121,022	1,130,295	413,973	8,404,700	2,942,148	2,705,757	48,957	287,041	154,932
2019	15,092,620	9,588,711	83,932	9,672,643	1,169,338	474,365	8,977,670	3,209,761	2,905,189	51,827	291,214	156,204
2020	16,229,187	9,966,449	95,672	10,062,121	1,239,086	477,324	9,300,359	3,074,530	3,854,298	54,831	295,988	151,619
2021	17,586,890	10,915,231	78,170	10,993,401	1,336,032	323,899	9,981,268	3,374,300	4,231,322	59,001	298,078	157,423
2022	17,835,065	11,847,422	89,265	11,936,687	1,485,195	254,939	10,706,431	3,480,325	3,648,309	59,697	298,758	166,328

Personal Income and Employment by Area: Omaha-Council Bluffs, NE-IA

(Thousands of dollars, except as noted.)

		Derivation of personal income										
		Earnings by place of work										
Year	Personal income, total	Nonfarm	Farm	Total	Less: Contributions for government social insurance	Plus: Adjustment for residence	Equals: Net earnings by place of residence	Plus: Dividends, interest, and rent	Plus: Personal current transfer receipts	Per capita personal income (dollars)	Population (persons)	Total employment
1970	2,658,127	2,116,323	83,142	2,199,465	148,476	-19,851	2,031,138	421,134	205,855	4,275	621,778	297,197
1971	2,865,198	2,278,984	85,385	2,364,369	165,260	-20,673	2,178,436	452,896	233,866	4,521	633,774	301,792
1972	3,145,062	2,492,519	111,595	2,604,114	188,058	-20,522	2,395,534	491,936	257,592	4,886	643,739	308,000
1973	3,540,683	2,757,779	180,756	2,938,535	237,937	-19,679	2,680,919	551,880	307,884	5,461	648,329	318,343
1974	3,807,732	3,019,017	96,778	3,115,795	270,557	-15,226	2,830,012	622,810	354,910	5,832	652,850	324,237
1975	4,208,664	3,248,219	128,980	3,377,199	285,951	-9,372	3,081,876	680,934	445,854	6,484	649,131	321,665
1976	4,587,524	3,627,621	80,493	3,708,114	324,424	-5,899	3,377,791	735,142	474,591	6,989	656,376	330,324
1977	5,033,558	3,976,861	103,766	4,080,627	355,442	-3,453	3,721,732	816,588	495,238	7,683	655,126	339,330
1978	5,651,599	4,422,594	172,349	4,594,943	405,439	1,217	4,190,721	910,036	550,842	8,584	658,391	350,508
1979	6,192,345	4,917,955	97,417	5,015,372	469,203	3,890	4,550,059	1,024,334	617,952	9,415	657,736	359,581
1980	6,838,947	5,344,448	41,975	5,386,423	507,665	12,439	4,891,197	1,224,803	722,947	10,442	654,969	356,972
1981	7,647,434	5,791,831	125,271	5,917,102	586,703	-5,105	5,325,294	1,498,815	823,325	11,630	657,562	357,821
1982	8,293,299	6,153,201	105,617	6,258,818	635,310	-10,353	5,613,155	1,779,038	901,106	12,552	660,724	356,924
1983	8,701,153	6,553,252	44,620	6,597,872	685,649	-13,209	5,899,014	1,833,914	968,225	13,113	663,573	363,321
1984	9,602,794	7,210,488	122,261	7,332,749	774,541	-16,021	6,542,187	2,035,894	1,024,713	14,362	668,605	375,618
1985	10,242,185	7,681,521	209,689	7,891,210	844,222	-17,304	7,029,684	2,118,916	1,093,585	15,257	671,289	386,904
1986	10,663,807	8,085,405	163,430	8,248,835	913,550	-19,646	7,315,639	2,204,091	1,144,077	15,859	672,408	392,455
1987	11,166,106	8,573,341	156,780	8,730,121	961,734	-18,557	7,749,830	2,239,808	1,176,468	16,604	672,505	405,568
1988	11,886,700	9,150,158	145,083	9,295,241	1,067,328	-20,736	8,207,177	2,441,959	1,237,564	17,558	677,009	416,931
1989	12,659,827	9,747,638	149,828	9,897,466	1,136,374	-23,078	8,738,014	2,603,337	1,318,476	18,593	680,885	428,864
1990	13,701,695	10,481,838	161,014	10,642,852	1,272,819	-24,871	9,345,162	2,911,855	1,444,678	19,918	687,913	439,366
1991	14,327,749	10,972,034	159,207	11,131,241	1,344,446	-31,476	9,755,319	3,001,585	1,570,845	20,573	696,443	440,334
1992	15,213,020	11,682,087	200,167	11,882,254	1,412,508	-38,352	10,431,394	3,071,053	1,710,573	21,598	704,360	442,339
1993	15,720,902	12,162,962	87,622	12,250,584	1,473,216	-39,351	10,738,017	3,162,025	1,820,860	22,202	708,077	450,793
1994	16,872,928	13,022,545	185,663	13,208,208	1,581,812	-45,886	11,580,510	3,380,198	1,912,220	23,595	715,120	466,628
1995	18,174,677	14,101,757	62,935	14,164,692	1,687,153	-60,089	12,417,450	3,729,721	2,027,506	25,072	724,894	477,507
1996	19,617,754	15,125,447	249,890	15,375,337	1,798,568	-77,564	13,499,205	3,976,937	2,141,612	26,621	736,937	491,378
1997	20,720,641	16,040,743	188,442	16,229,185	1,935,009	-96,453	14,197,723	4,295,242	2,227,676	27,762	746,356	499,983
1998	22,212,239	17,165,317	127,937	17,293,254	2,053,627	-107,923	15,131,704	4,749,056	2,331,479	29,465	753,844	516,047
1999	23,604,858	18,473,195	120,821	18,594,016	2,193,107	-131,089	16,269,820	4,864,865	2,470,173	30,994	761,603	527,810
2000	25,199,387	19,566,422	151,266	19,717,688	2,296,117	-148,151	17,273,420	5,319,591	2,606,376	32,757	769,291	538,603
2001	26,223,765	20,350,850	154,642	20,505,492	2,366,596	-154,841	17,984,055	5,380,207	2,859,503	33,786	776,165	538,485
2002	27,116,312	21,119,400	110,763	21,230,163	2,462,783	-170,158	18,597,222	5,437,504	3,081,586	34,606	783,567	534,303
2003	28,063,587	21,884,123	172,768	22,056,891	2,569,675	-186,224	19,300,992	5,554,031	3,208,564	35,430	792,086	536,732
2004	30,098,713	23,452,975	325,872	23,778,847	2,704,684	-198,279	20,875,884	5,861,371	3,361,458	37,473	803,214	544,751
2005	31,092,827	23,982,841	248,743	24,231,584	2,848,854	-222,853	21,159,877	6,332,569	3,600,381	38,183	814,309	552,645
2006	33,441,311	25,803,496	154,060	25,957,556	3,070,267	-259,703	22,627,586	6,903,423	3,910,302	40,537	824,961	564,068
2007	35,311,101	26,658,557	226,543	26,885,100	3,149,987	-270,255	23,464,858	7,697,055	4,149,188	42,311	834,554	574,931
2008	37,396,871	27,881,852	319,062	28,200,914	3,277,143	-271,573	24,652,198	7,982,112	4,762,561	44,250	845,119	580,755
2009	37,019,028	28,117,927	374,835	28,492,762	3,282,875	-223,008	24,986,879	7,043,310	4,988,839	43,235	856,233	572,112
2010	39,222,736	29,624,088	291,421	29,915,509	3,386,182	-163,210	26,366,117	7,435,343	5,421,276	45,186	868,031	568,946
2011	43,007,464	32,456,059	524,073	32,980,132	3,117,714	-131,913	29,730,505	7,695,573	5,581,386	48,994	877,809	574,968
2012	44,802,292	33,491,283	379,111	33,870,394	3,213,922	-81,790	30,574,682	8,613,071	5,614,539	50,465	887,787	583,921
2013	43,125,321	32,435,237	486,704	32,921,941	3,657,171	-41,263	29,223,507	8,174,563	5,727,251	47,994	898,559	593,006
2014	46,716,786	35,463,499	228,542	35,692,041	3,838,953	-22,937	31,830,151	8,887,309	5,999,326	51,365	909,504	603,947
2015	48,753,150	36,918,582	272,584	37,191,166	4,025,682	-32,350	33,133,134	9,280,325	6,339,691	52,947	920,790	615,882
2016	48,714,647	36,817,574	143,308	36,960,882	4,142,797	-25,701	32,792,384	9,394,011	6,528,252	52,237	932,571	623,087
2017	50,884,473	38,542,824	127,944	38,670,768	4,335,801	-2,974	34,331,993	9,814,917	6,737,563	53,974	942,758	631,269
2018	53,507,023	40,195,278	134,681	40,329,959	4,497,017	22,059	35,855,001	10,458,234	7,193,788	56,148	952,958	639,462
2019	55,260,318	40,715,776	208,633	40,924,409	4,682,874	5,006	36,246,541	11,436,502	7,577,275	57,448	961,926	642,093
2020	58,045,226	40,978,586	175,129	41,153,715	4,904,363	39,698	36,289,050	12,068,829	9,687,347	59,897	969,077	629,171
2021	63,493,824	43,564,586	492,983	44,057,569	5,119,238	50,366	38,988,697	13,518,807	10,986,320	65,275	972,708	647,242
2022	66,986,349	47,717,496	411,395	48,128,891	5,600,977	56,190	42,584,104	14,782,959	9,619,286	68,586	976,671	669,816

Personal Income and Employment by Area: Orlando-Kissimmee-Sanford, FL

(Thousands of dollars, except as noted.)

Year	Personal income, total	Derivation of personal income: Earnings by place of work								Per capita personal income (dollars)	Population (persons)	Total employment
		Nonfarm	Farm	Total	Less: Contributions for government social insurance	Plus: Adjustment for residence	Equals: Net earnings by place of residence	Plus: Dividends, interest, and rent	Plus: Personal current transfer receipts			
1970	2,090,897	1,475,800	96,216	1,572,016	95,062	21,012	1,497,966	409,705	183,226	3,959	528,201	232,835
1971	2,437,079	1,741,054	108,392	1,849,446	117,558	18,945	1,750,833	464,677	221,569	4,362	558,715	252,062
1972	2,891,041	2,104,942	129,052	2,233,994	149,361	18,016	2,102,649	534,268	254,124	4,820	599,794	289,075
1973	3,413,913	2,562,815	130,585	2,693,400	208,780	12,732	2,497,352	613,688	302,873	5,300	644,122	323,363
1974	3,739,141	2,759,499	128,252	2,887,751	233,515	11,735	2,665,971	705,075	368,095	5,495	680,514	326,248
1975	4,010,805	2,825,531	150,953	2,976,484	235,913	6,317	2,746,888	771,442	492,475	5,816	689,597	315,687
1976	4,430,995	3,137,586	168,736	3,306,322	268,006	-2,942	3,035,374	849,409	546,212	6,286	704,932	327,025
1977	4,932,360	3,498,088	193,055	3,691,143	301,156	-6,855	3,383,132	958,454	590,774	6,797	725,644	344,104
1978	5,766,388	4,115,821	248,997	4,364,818	363,424	-17,613	3,983,781	1,132,571	650,036	7,698	749,095	375,240
1979	6,653,545	4,784,260	244,634	5,028,894	441,872	-25,285	4,561,737	1,329,228	762,580	8,520	780,907	396,668
1980	7,923,342	5,556,322	327,856	5,884,178	516,163	-37,826	5,330,189	1,673,654	919,499	9,743	813,225	418,551
1981	9,152,750	6,441,513	237,729	6,679,242	640,439	-53,329	5,985,474	2,088,328	1,078,948	10,825	845,498	441,015
1982	10,199,147	7,244,703	280,905	7,525,608	736,135	-95,159	6,694,314	2,279,598	1,225,235	11,625	877,348	463,274
1983	11,474,131	8,263,247	351,236	8,614,483	845,668	-136,517	7,632,298	2,504,275	1,337,558	12,524	916,199	494,692
1984	12,893,289	9,562,360	229,751	9,792,111	1,004,967	-189,229	8,597,915	2,875,945	1,419,429	13,464	957,644	537,857
1985	14,292,742	10,763,771	210,047	10,973,818	1,151,298	-247,651	9,574,869	3,177,320	1,540,553	14,345	996,347	573,928
1986	15,730,636	12,065,859	202,627	12,268,486	1,323,854	-324,095	10,620,537	3,448,984	1,661,115	15,148	1,038,445	615,381
1987	17,082,991	13,361,815	188,910	13,550,725	1,451,403	-416,091	11,683,231	3,630,247	1,769,513	15,786	1,082,164	636,135
1988	19,118,917	15,031,321	217,068	15,248,389	1,671,735	-502,114	13,074,540	4,082,227	1,962,150	17,071	1,119,977	672,874
1989	21,316,461	16,525,533	193,250	16,718,783	1,850,633	-604,232	14,263,918	4,797,832	2,254,711	18,197	1,171,413	713,886
1990	23,035,686	17,978,789	163,502	18,142,291	2,002,469	-715,400	15,424,422	5,093,907	2,517,357	18,566	1,240,724	739,630
1991	24,115,129	18,653,927	199,941	18,853,868	2,093,957	-655,956	16,103,955	5,155,130	2,856,044	18,791	1,283,301	737,044
1992	25,668,988	20,103,559	184,609	20,288,168	2,247,476	-718,926	17,321,766	5,002,936	3,344,286	19,462	1,318,902	755,421
1993	27,373,023	21,526,255	184,234	21,710,489	2,389,448	-795,098	18,525,943	5,183,448	3,663,632	20,170	1,357,101	788,146
1994	28,879,730	22,778,146	164,982	22,943,128	2,568,550	-881,051	19,493,527	5,450,205	3,935,998	20,712	1,394,315	813,296
1995	31,040,652	24,346,099	177,566	24,523,665	2,723,278	-924,260	20,876,127	5,893,503	4,271,022	21,731	1,428,415	840,455
1996	33,466,140	26,340,074	159,583	26,499,657	2,922,086	-1,002,497	22,575,074	6,326,069	4,564,997	22,772	1,469,619	885,718
1997	36,122,528	28,601,905	186,603	28,788,508	3,176,978	-1,156,342	24,455,188	6,870,225	4,797,115	23,763	1,520,145	935,200
1998	39,462,182	31,675,530	197,641	31,873,171	3,493,768	-1,353,022	27,026,381	7,503,168	4,932,633	25,169	1,567,910	987,408
1999	42,187,397	34,580,251	197,969	34,778,220	3,771,177	-1,523,649	29,483,394	7,566,654	5,137,349	26,236	1,607,993	1,032,530
2000	45,781,670	37,588,649	197,064	37,785,713	4,065,800	-1,766,325	31,953,588	8,274,367	5,553,715	27,631	1,656,890	1,071,873
2001	47,257,566	38,554,189	195,950	38,750,139	4,293,386	-1,885,195	32,571,558	8,529,379	6,156,629	27,630	1,710,359	1,083,195
2002	49,066,143	40,211,234	181,033	40,392,267	4,471,566	-1,990,967	33,929,734	8,306,412	6,829,997	27,873	1,760,345	1,082,815
2003	52,125,836	42,788,421	151,529	42,939,950	4,742,647	-2,127,568	36,069,735	8,652,439	7,403,662	28,774	1,811,544	1,121,193
2004	56,623,754	47,026,616	173,809	47,200,425	5,222,310	-2,405,041	39,573,074	9,042,287	8,008,393	30,150	1,878,077	1,179,821
2005	61,864,331	51,849,317	191,197	52,040,514	5,796,391	-2,824,093	43,420,030	9,786,811	8,657,490	31,631	1,955,794	1,250,735
2006	67,317,692	55,676,281	186,890	55,863,171	6,277,433	-3,067,138	46,518,600	11,465,761	9,333,331	33,325	2,020,057	1,303,551
2007	70,486,956	57,482,655	172,312	57,654,967	6,526,249	-3,228,552	47,900,166	12,561,891	10,024,899	34,252	2,057,865	1,340,655
2008	71,523,439	56,509,258	169,766	56,679,024	6,573,144	-3,255,130	46,850,750	13,045,055	11,627,634	34,263	2,087,489	1,316,014
2009	68,197,478	52,704,678	191,230	52,895,908	6,235,386	-2,975,209	43,685,313	11,647,335	12,864,830	32,292	2,111,917	1,253,734
2010	71,902,882	54,048,024	207,722	54,255,746	6,305,281	-2,971,125	44,979,340	12,397,143	14,526,399	33,600	2,139,975	1,254,295
2011	76,026,728	55,682,885	191,600	55,874,485	5,791,298	-3,008,982	47,074,205	13,666,561	15,285,962	34,873	2,180,117	1,295,430
2012	79,027,502	59,130,712	241,422	59,372,134	6,178,491	-3,339,599	49,854,044	13,989,851	15,183,607	35,389	2,233,131	1,335,405
2013	81,162,751	62,029,425	201,100	62,230,525	7,274,328	-3,478,518	51,477,679	13,952,603	15,732,469	35,579	2,281,217	1,374,942
2014	86,703,496	66,330,509	206,541	66,537,050	7,737,292	-3,622,512	55,177,246	14,751,596	16,774,654	37,065	2,339,238	1,438,244
2015	93,609,935	71,480,829	272,245	71,753,074	8,241,407	-3,887,211	59,624,456	16,090,113	17,895,366	38,884	2,407,405	1,504,935
2016	98,001,882	76,029,465	215,754	76,245,219	8,699,211	-4,406,668	63,139,340	16,301,882	18,560,660	39,527	2,479,365	1,567,895
2017	105,664,055	80,865,647	241,412	81,107,059	9,215,618	-4,753,872	67,137,569	18,834,980	19,691,506	41,500	2,546,121	1,645,405
2018	112,491,127	86,949,123	182,452	87,131,575	9,956,562	-5,153,229	72,021,784	19,754,016	20,715,327	43,151	2,606,900	1,727,972
2019	119,287,514	91,906,247	208,886	92,115,133	10,691,220	-5,698,697	75,725,216	21,456,814	22,105,484	45,129	2,643,259	1,772,507
2020	127,863,111	91,746,448	215,355	91,961,803	10,707,012	-5,768,621	75,486,170	22,162,868	30,214,073	47,705	2,680,313	1,704,259
2021	143,550,328	104,348,736	210,852	104,559,588	11,893,106	-7,030,814	85,635,668	23,784,410	34,130,250	53,183	2,699,199	1,827,457
2022	149,152,213	115,879,811	198,285	116,078,096	13,456,088	-8,739,873	93,882,135	25,772,637	29,497,441	53,959	2,764,182	1,975,455

Personal Income and Employment by Area: Oshkosh-Neenah, WI

(Thousands of dollars, except as noted.)

Year	Personal income, total	Derivation of personal income: Earnings by place of work: Nonfarm	Earnings by place of work: Farm	Earnings by place of work: Total	Less: Contributions for government social insurance	Plus: Adjustment for residence	Equals: Net earnings by place of residence	Plus: Dividends, interest, and rent	Plus: Personal current transfer receipts	Per capita personal income (dollars)	Population (persons)	Total employment
1970	507,667	426,630	8,094	434,724	31,107	-23,835	379,782	86,312	41,573	3,899	130,213	58,052
1971	532,948	441,404	8,734	450,138	33,318	-24,933	391,887	91,773	49,288	4,061	131,228	57,187
1972	575,795	483,646	9,278	492,924	38,654	-29,932	424,338	97,177	54,280	4,375	131,616	58,727
1973	639,027	543,038	10,572	553,610	50,124	-34,170	469,316	106,937	62,774	4,896	130,530	61,323
1974	705,292	592,502	11,118	603,620	56,715	-38,572	508,333	120,816	76,143	5,462	129,132	62,563
1975	778,467	645,338	11,649	656,987	60,727	-44,291	551,969	131,687	94,811	5,969	130,425	62,538
1976	856,350	723,404	8,554	731,958	69,024	-50,845	612,089	141,797	102,464	6,559	130,569	64,799
1977	959,040	814,165	15,525	829,690	76,947	-59,724	693,019	157,453	108,568	7,342	130,632	66,556
1978	1,064,165	917,622	12,376	929,998	89,300	-69,056	771,642	173,338	119,185	8,190	129,936	68,792
1979	1,189,670	1,022,195	16,827	1,039,022	103,272	-74,109	861,641	193,831	134,198	9,092	130,845	71,146
1980	1,310,752	1,082,976	17,305	1,100,281	109,167	-77,430	913,684	233,897	163,171	9,949	131,746	69,583
1981	1,428,904	1,157,088	12,466	1,169,554	124,390	-83,999	961,165	285,309	182,430	10,880	131,335	68,777
1982	1,520,280	1,206,581	10,160	1,216,741	131,822	-88,737	996,182	318,181	205,917	11,576	131,330	68,279
1983	1,632,808	1,303,772	1,762	1,305,534	142,548	-99,589	1,063,397	346,696	222,715	12,413	131,539	68,795
1984	1,787,645	1,441,315	8,571	1,449,886	161,739	-112,060	1,176,087	383,610	227,948	13,430	133,106	72,636
1985	1,901,838	1,541,980	7,785	1,549,765	174,897	-120,610	1,254,258	407,543	240,037	14,170	134,219	74,641
1986	2,005,572	1,642,673	9,520	1,652,193	186,159	-131,553	1,334,481	423,794	247,297	14,815	135,372	76,626
1987	2,111,339	1,763,203	11,760	1,774,963	197,085	-142,325	1,435,553	421,786	254,000	15,488	136,319	78,525
1988	2,249,480	1,896,669	5,323	1,901,992	218,356	-153,409	1,530,227	454,723	264,530	16,282	138,161	80,578
1989	2,449,066	1,990,637	14,624	2,005,261	228,125	-145,417	1,631,719	531,507	285,840	17,619	139,004	81,836
1990	2,634,244	2,184,047	12,963	2,197,010	261,182	-166,885	1,768,943	557,973	307,328	18,700	140,871	86,195
1991	2,757,246	2,332,957	9,998	2,342,955	280,841	-194,163	1,867,951	558,761	330,534	19,246	143,263	88,504
1992	2,999,771	2,579,159	13,232	2,592,391	306,477	-233,981	2,051,933	589,554	358,284	20,624	145,449	90,993
1993	3,102,539	2,706,721	5,775	2,712,496	323,819	-260,812	2,127,865	600,175	374,499	20,959	148,031	92,431
1994	3,313,352	2,856,093	15,263	2,871,356	343,770	-266,661	2,260,925	663,283	389,144	22,257	148,867	94,352
1995	3,512,813	3,058,483	6,186	3,064,669	367,889	-301,646	2,395,134	706,100	411,579	23,306	150,725	97,363
1996	3,680,840	3,156,890	12,232	3,169,122	377,150	-290,469	2,501,503	753,773	425,564	24,183	152,206	98,410
1997	3,867,058	3,337,565	7,138	3,344,703	396,056	-317,706	2,630,941	796,818	439,299	25,188	153,525	99,045
1998	4,150,806	3,639,227	12,837	3,652,064	429,602	-409,274	2,813,188	888,559	449,059	26,876	154,444	101,732
1999	4,294,678	3,890,440	12,225	3,902,665	455,407	-478,738	2,968,520	861,980	464,178	27,565	155,801	103,893
2000	4,553,854	4,120,342	7,322	4,127,664	478,865	-475,679	3,173,120	883,068	497,666	28,986	157,103	106,300
2001	4,718,735	4,253,394	6,496	4,259,890	493,270	-493,772	3,272,848	895,612	550,275	29,835	158,163	106,369
2002	4,825,984	4,404,006	8,767	4,412,773	509,010	-550,767	3,352,996	877,501	595,487	30,327	159,134	107,053
2003	4,980,522	4,498,572	15,809	4,514,381	519,851	-571,908	3,422,622	948,620	609,280	31,238	159,440	106,192
2004	5,270,838	4,766,429	16,172	4,782,601	549,565	-525,505	3,707,531	934,908	628,399	32,916	160,130	107,037
2005	5,406,721	4,908,187	17,172	4,925,359	569,064	-562,070	3,794,225	940,183	672,313	33,488	161,451	108,306
2006	5,742,038	5,056,849	12,050	5,068,899	587,719	-582,678	3,898,502	1,124,603	718,933	35,286	162,727	109,149
2007	5,964,496	5,274,937	21,646	5,296,583	608,177	-612,486	4,075,920	1,117,639	770,937	36,361	164,037	110,164
2008	6,159,129	5,427,510	27,861	5,455,371	634,564	-685,567	4,135,240	1,140,513	883,376	37,348	164,910	111,414
2009	5,996,247	5,244,252	8,860	5,253,112	615,861	-689,534	3,947,717	1,029,536	1,018,994	36,029	166,429	107,965
2010	6,224,537	5,461,139	14,407	5,475,546	648,673	-737,383	4,089,490	1,049,011	1,086,036	37,240	167,146	108,915
2011	6,578,743	5,673,012	28,849	5,701,861	599,092	-814,207	4,288,562	1,234,727	1,055,454	39,255	167,591	111,006
2012	6,732,743	5,816,037	26,624	5,842,661	609,945	-798,051	4,434,665	1,230,111	1,067,967	39,923	168,645	110,633
2013	6,691,544	5,982,111	29,250	6,011,361	709,195	-883,975	4,418,191	1,174,273	1,099,080	39,497	169,420	111,741
2014	6,952,107	6,126,727	28,415	6,155,142	723,947	-870,996	4,560,199	1,248,891	1,143,017	41,019	169,486	112,448
2015	7,252,755	6,327,835	24,127	6,351,962	745,421	-881,076	4,725,465	1,325,357	1,201,933	42,806	169,433	113,080
2016	7,483,491	6,531,023	18,259	6,549,282	765,997	-934,327	4,848,958	1,418,863	1,215,670	44,055	169,866	115,449
2017	7,731,580	6,745,928	18,452	6,764,380	801,969	-985,067	4,977,344	1,469,705	1,284,531	45,311	170,632	116,126
2018	8,088,702	6,947,564	16,329	6,963,893	808,565	-972,382	5,182,946	1,542,722	1,363,034	47,336	170,879	116,243
2019	8,361,927	7,214,184	21,570	7,235,754	845,967	-994,311	5,395,476	1,528,645	1,437,806	48,651	171,875	115,550
2020	8,908,632	7,176,264	29,912	7,206,176	841,647	-1,008,292	5,356,237	1,719,725	1,832,670	51,855	171,800	112,244
2021	9,594,164	7,558,440	36,251	7,594,691	883,889	-965,109	5,745,693	1,776,090	2,072,381	56,253	170,554	114,705
2022	9,710,157	7,954,950	37,957	7,992,907	955,215	-1,016,136	6,021,556	1,883,462	1,805,139	56,878	170,718	119,175

Personal Income and Employment by Area: Owensboro, KY

(Thousands of dollars, except as noted.)

Year	Personal income, total	Derivation of personal income: Earnings by place of work: Nonfarm	Farm	Total	Less: Contributions for government social insurance	Plus: Adjustment for residence	Equals: Net earnings by place of residence	Plus: Dividends, interest, and rent	Plus: Personal current transfer receipts	Per capita personal income (dollars)	Population (persons)	Total employment
1970	320,584	255,753	11,629	267,382	17,575	-1,232	248,575	41,388	30,621	3,348	95,768	42,800
1971	346,680	270,549	12,931	283,480	19,049	751	265,182	45,118	36,380	3,575	96,960	42,627
1972	385,742	296,311	15,826	312,137	22,120	6,029	296,046	49,231	40,465	3,968	97,215	43,642
1973	428,085	325,627	25,247	350,874	28,023	3,235	326,086	54,150	47,849	4,364	98,090	45,008
1974	476,524	359,775	24,164	383,939	32,271	3,164	354,832	62,435	59,257	4,814	98,996	46,164
1975	518,329	385,142	16,717	401,859	34,050	5,519	373,328	70,276	74,725	5,193	99,816	44,188
1976	577,142	433,257	18,542	451,799	38,732	8,008	421,075	77,790	78,277	5,749	100,389	45,399
1977	648,219	481,530	26,841	508,371	42,776	13,433	479,028	88,556	80,635	6,433	100,759	46,935
1978	726,593	560,633	15,482	576,115	51,356	14,556	539,315	101,407	85,871	7,125	101,985	49,522
1979	822,435	625,831	19,612	645,443	59,521	21,366	607,288	116,513	98,634	7,969	103,209	49,610
1980	913,904	691,076	3,400	694,476	66,050	19,807	648,233	148,389	117,282	8,794	103,927	49,868
1981	1,026,541	748,621	22,733	771,354	76,964	15,095	709,485	183,846	133,210	9,847	104,247	49,877
1982	1,081,186	764,057	15,520	779,577	79,631	19,445	719,391	215,233	146,562	10,323	104,731	49,194
1983	1,122,789	830,883	-22,117	808,766	86,159	17,917	740,524	225,212	157,053	10,650	105,422	50,297
1984	1,253,616	876,692	34,038	910,730	93,698	20,473	837,505	247,634	168,477	11,768	106,527	51,708
1985	1,283,981	897,363	21,806	919,169	97,176	20,509	842,502	262,182	179,297	12,091	106,197	51,751
1986	1,310,431	923,335	17,374	940,709	103,153	16,489	854,045	266,618	189,768	12,392	105,746	52,395
1987	1,348,687	963,108	15,413	978,521	106,507	15,735	887,749	264,098	196,840	12,838	105,054	52,141
1988	1,447,609	1,047,980	17,796	1,065,776	116,803	14,206	963,179	275,820	208,610	13,849	104,527	52,711
1989	1,565,976	1,095,825	47,480	1,143,305	124,637	14,288	1,032,956	302,206	230,814	14,977	104,559	54,131
1990	1,650,483	1,158,564	42,261	1,200,825	136,171	14,063	1,078,717	321,256	250,510	15,762	104,716	54,954
1991	1,714,997	1,198,480	33,325	1,231,805	142,422	11,556	1,100,939	331,345	282,713	16,303	105,194	54,878
1992	1,836,456	1,278,481	56,361	1,334,842	149,956	7,763	1,192,649	336,388	307,419	17,322	106,017	55,861
1993	1,899,972	1,355,874	45,428	1,401,302	162,107	4,918	1,244,113	341,346	314,513	17,816	106,646	57,276
1994	2,022,775	1,444,381	53,978	1,498,359	176,059	1,540	1,323,840	365,846	333,089	18,810	107,539	59,266
1995	2,090,505	1,502,993	31,868	1,534,861	184,350	-1,103	1,349,408	382,885	358,212	19,315	108,234	60,800
1996	2,193,215	1,534,198	64,763	1,598,961	187,131	-1,830	1,410,000	406,676	376,539	20,200	108,573	60,962
1997	2,335,968	1,673,182	43,614	1,716,796	202,595	-10,643	1,503,558	434,358	398,052	21,460	108,851	62,246
1998	2,410,746	1,740,643	29,201	1,769,844	211,952	-7,994	1,549,898	453,890	406,958	22,102	109,075	62,960
1999	2,491,532	1,836,875	26,715	1,863,590	222,740	-6,958	1,633,892	431,145	426,495	22,747	109,533	63,701
2000	2,678,140	1,923,184	62,272	1,985,456	226,118	-9,334	1,750,004	472,732	455,404	24,333	110,064	64,172
2001	2,746,548	1,962,014	63,219	2,025,233	229,522	-7,224	1,788,487	462,982	495,079	24,971	109,991	62,827
2002	2,808,745	2,031,053	19,607	2,050,660	236,521	4,463	1,818,602	456,925	533,218	25,490	110,190	62,108
2003	2,902,587	2,084,300	36,108	2,120,408	240,333	12,323	1,892,398	462,330	547,859	26,212	110,735	62,425
2004	3,074,446	2,188,236	81,850	2,270,086	247,636	20,162	2,042,612	443,709	588,125	27,698	110,999	62,786
2005	3,226,010	2,267,319	111,209	2,378,528	258,201	25,857	2,146,184	449,976	629,850	28,941	111,469	62,986
2006	3,435,965	2,414,582	88,584	2,503,166	275,682	30,340	2,257,824	494,303	683,838	30,637	112,152	64,130
2007	3,659,171	2,562,872	67,477	2,630,349	292,797	39,272	2,376,824	543,013	739,334	32,411	112,900	65,383
2008	4,076,223	2,815,687	81,031	2,896,718	317,874	40,396	2,619,240	621,083	835,900	35,866	113,651	65,106
2009	3,894,858	2,566,238	110,232	2,676,470	304,117	20,519	2,392,872	575,779	926,207	34,050	114,385	63,030
2010	3,988,195	2,684,972	62,628	2,747,600	311,680	13,713	2,449,633	554,675	983,887	34,736	114,815	63,216
2011	4,150,068	2,688,668	121,282	2,809,950	281,388	-1,954	2,526,608	627,677	995,783	35,940	115,473	64,637
2012	4,224,547	2,757,174	95,223	2,852,397	293,755	-42,563	2,516,079	718,198	990,270	36,306	116,360	66,233
2013	4,325,870	2,822,839	222,218	3,045,057	340,166	-62,684	2,642,207	670,537	1,013,126	36,993	116,938	66,029
2014	4,473,700	2,914,280	142,412	3,056,692	353,827	-60,214	2,642,651	724,895	1,106,154	38,149	117,270	66,082
2015	4,631,509	3,055,328	87,175	3,142,503	371,304	-81,254	2,689,945	772,091	1,169,473	39,101	118,451	67,071
2016	4,583,795	3,023,406	63,228	3,086,634	374,862	-79,712	2,632,060	771,244	1,180,491	38,454	119,201	67,740
2017	4,726,157	3,056,826	91,792	3,148,618	381,110	-67,979	2,699,529	806,198	1,220,430	39,478	119,716	67,823
2018	4,817,494	3,161,996	75,306	3,237,302	394,189	-73,081	2,770,032	790,734	1,256,728	40,056	120,268	67,884
2019	5,064,390	3,313,996	82,568	3,396,564	405,457	-84,969	2,906,138	835,940	1,322,312	41,852	121,008	67,394
2020	5,541,360	3,383,028	69,728	3,452,756	420,347	-87,660	2,944,749	884,985	1,711,626	45,559	121,630	65,127
2021	6,033,837	3,620,598	151,511	3,772,109	437,623	-90,536	3,243,950	880,853	1,909,034	49,723	121,350	67,075
2022	6,031,071	3,812,509	157,583	3,970,092	459,038	-90,964	3,420,090	933,008	1,677,973	49,701	121,348	68,977

Personal Income and Employment by Area: Oxnard-Thousand Oaks-Ventura, CA

(Thousands of dollars, except as noted.)

Year	Personal income, total	Derivation of personal income: Earnings by place of work: Nonfarm	Farm	Total	Less: Contributions for government social insurance	Plus: Adjustment for residence	Equals: Net earnings by place of residence	Plus: Dividends, interest, and rent	Plus: Personal current transfer receipts	Per capita personal income (dollars)	Population (persons)	Total employment
1970	1,675,029	993,450	70,144	1,063,594	59,659	266,591	1,270,526	276,675	127,828	4,394	381,174	135,394
1971	1,846,661	1,087,352	77,954	1,165,306	66,834	287,697	1,386,169	309,432	151,060	4,667	395,691	140,085
1972	2,086,155	1,221,184	91,278	1,312,462	79,079	340,746	1,574,129	342,236	169,790	5,107	408,523	147,656
1973	2,368,468	1,352,274	129,273	1,481,547	99,113	401,405	1,783,839	391,554	193,075	5,646	419,461	155,861
1974	2,697,313	1,508,134	139,016	1,647,150	114,703	473,033	2,005,480	454,295	237,538	6,217	433,885	164,301
1975	3,067,325	1,696,502	143,245	1,839,747	128,038	534,204	2,245,913	512,953	308,459	6,833	448,918	171,738
1976	3,415,649	1,894,313	110,060	2,004,373	145,545	635,485	2,494,313	565,057	356,279	7,418	460,485	176,285
1977	3,925,078	2,169,151	148,233	2,317,384	171,933	764,228	2,909,679	637,153	378,246	8,200	478,695	188,053
1978	4,631,103	2,530,991	191,946	2,722,937	206,263	940,953	3,457,627	755,761	417,715	9,373	494,086	202,771
1979	5,233,232	2,859,840	153,355	3,013,195	245,491	1,153,980	3,921,684	847,845	463,703	10,217	512,189	213,342
1980	6,077,616	3,212,435	161,842	3,374,277	270,790	1,379,112	4,482,599	1,047,603	547,414	11,406	532,827	221,151
1981	6,887,707	3,585,011	155,419	3,740,430	327,718	1,547,680	4,960,392	1,276,445	650,870	12,606	546,389	225,479
1982	7,500,064	3,908,134	206,124	4,114,258	366,910	1,616,401	5,363,749	1,418,398	717,917	13,342	562,142	229,893
1983	8,137,498	4,256,520	213,837	4,470,357	413,523	1,741,025	5,797,859	1,580,744	758,895	14,138	575,586	237,557
1984	9,069,533	4,810,054	238,127	5,048,181	488,379	1,915,735	6,475,537	1,785,952	808,044	15,404	588,790	248,225
1985	9,877,759	5,326,172	217,602	5,543,774	551,106	2,083,634	7,076,302	1,920,117	881,340	16,386	602,819	260,105
1986	10,814,424	5,881,893	317,243	6,199,136	616,305	2,255,143	7,837,974	2,024,467	951,983	17,572	615,422	270,559
1987	11,764,391	6,527,630	387,110	6,914,740	694,225	2,491,653	8,712,168	2,065,799	986,424	18,613	632,062	287,425
1988	12,936,019	7,317,836	445,607	7,763,443	804,748	2,646,744	9,605,439	2,274,501	1,056,079	19,876	650,851	305,846
1989	13,955,933	7,805,015	427,647	8,232,662	870,346	2,809,535	10,171,851	2,634,914	1,149,168	20,996	664,692	317,976
1990	14,969,214	8,453,809	465,101	8,918,910	938,783	3,079,208	11,059,335	2,663,226	1,246,653	22,338	670,117	327,267
1991	15,632,575	8,925,682	438,537	9,364,219	993,420	3,157,377	11,528,176	2,707,944	1,396,455	23,135	675,706	332,915
1992	16,199,633	9,482,041	285,341	9,767,382	1,048,851	3,190,239	11,908,770	2,699,627	1,591,236	23,679	684,143	332,193
1993	16,970,471	9,803,744	414,090	10,217,834	1,084,064	3,310,079	12,443,849	2,842,540	1,684,082	24,597	689,943	335,316
1994	17,651,243	10,297,146	358,400	10,655,546	1,145,221	3,373,256	12,883,581	3,055,472	1,712,190	25,270	698,509	344,984
1995	18,814,025	10,587,326	441,879	11,029,205	1,164,919	3,642,324	13,506,610	3,504,720	1,802,695	26,744	703,486	352,089
1996	19,570,276	11,124,804	332,740	11,457,544	1,195,213	3,721,707	13,984,038	3,682,263	1,903,975	27,555	710,215	358,399
1997	20,825,239	11,784,445	413,120	12,197,565	1,254,224	4,153,317	15,096,658	3,784,475	1,944,106	28,880	721,107	357,142
1998	21,786,403	12,631,099	406,776	13,037,875	1,339,466	4,085,732	15,784,141	3,957,818	2,044,444	29,813	730,779	371,587
1999	23,407,986	13,854,545	461,734	14,316,279	1,451,002	4,191,007	17,056,284	4,191,092	2,160,610	31,490	743,357	385,759
2000	25,583,483	15,580,589	424,619	16,005,208	1,609,561	4,375,904	18,771,551	4,526,247	2,285,685	33,818	756,506	395,387
2001	27,275,956	17,130,336	305,730	17,436,066	1,802,749	4,511,675	20,144,992	4,594,827	2,536,137	35,576	766,689	407,454
2002	28,078,272	17,886,747	370,082	18,256,829	1,907,188	4,559,587	20,909,228	4,447,691	2,721,353	36,021	779,489	415,673
2003	29,702,009	19,217,794	366,180	19,583,974	2,070,801	4,497,308	22,010,481	4,797,217	2,894,311	37,690	788,070	423,002
2004	31,719,741	20,625,853	523,308	21,149,161	2,300,183	4,833,884	23,682,862	5,024,638	3,012,241	39,950	793,994	428,592
2005	32,871,529	21,525,191	509,086	22,034,277	2,414,730	4,688,683	24,308,230	5,379,336	3,183,963	41,390	794,197	435,423
2006	35,153,237	22,300,570	648,558	22,949,128	2,450,396	5,002,244	25,500,976	6,224,108	3,428,153	44,042	798,183	441,026
2007	36,590,158	22,962,292	623,320	23,585,612	2,478,451	4,988,891	26,096,052	6,844,210	3,649,896	45,736	800,027	447,562
2008	36,911,153	22,239,065	666,966	22,906,031	2,459,225	5,217,909	25,664,715	7,027,939	4,218,499	45,775	806,353	441,331
2009	36,220,079	22,109,411	848,191	22,957,602	2,452,136	4,579,157	25,084,623	6,448,305	4,687,151	44,435	815,130	427,317
2010	37,914,623	23,333,493	930,830	24,264,323	2,469,487	4,585,385	26,380,221	6,327,334	5,207,068	45,947	825,175	424,880
2011	39,733,578	23,928,124	824,605	24,752,729	2,296,558	4,729,496	27,185,667	7,278,079	5,269,832	47,868	830,061	430,081
2012	41,338,513	24,268,259	1,054,116	25,322,375	2,327,966	5,284,037	28,278,446	7,778,012	5,282,055	49,592	833,566	438,477
2013	41,728,534	24,644,816	1,221,758	25,866,574	2,668,087	5,262,823	28,461,310	7,779,614	5,487,610	49,787	838,135	446,545
2014	43,769,630	25,513,353	1,198,476	26,711,829	2,765,584	5,572,682	29,518,927	8,406,998	5,843,705	51,943	842,648	456,369
2015	45,901,737	26,499,558	1,232,036	27,731,594	2,845,631	6,188,570	31,074,533	8,537,221	6,289,983	54,241	846,263	460,902
2016	47,265,014	26,905,976	1,088,597	27,994,573	2,915,978	6,437,520	31,516,115	9,202,321	6,546,578	55,756	847,718	464,957
2017	48,791,042	27,683,011	1,135,970	28,818,981	3,008,620	6,445,352	32,255,713	9,946,646	6,588,683	57,456	849,196	467,595
2018	50,711,842	28,280,887	881,412	29,162,299	3,115,586	7,142,380	33,189,093	10,586,021	6,936,728	59,781	848,290	474,203
2019	53,163,902	29,656,519	1,025,120	30,681,639	3,295,638	7,312,718	34,698,719	10,972,565	7,492,618	62,886	845,396	474,857
2020	57,575,258	30,615,398	1,041,036	31,656,434	3,356,621	7,427,794	35,727,607	11,037,131	10,810,520	68,273	843,310	457,453
2021	62,554,527	32,708,586	866,745	33,575,331	3,570,351	8,182,956	38,187,936	12,838,222	11,528,369	74,527	839,358	468,293
2022	63,589,878	34,081,291	915,597	34,996,888	3,873,539	9,223,766	40,347,115	13,732,911	9,509,852	76,375	832,605	492,048

Personal Income and Employment by Area: Palm Bay-Melbourne-Titusville, FL

(Thousands of dollars, except as noted.)

Year	Personal income, total	Derivation of personal income: Earnings by place of work: Nonfarm	Farm	Total	Less: Contributions for government social insurance	Plus: Adjustment for residence	Equals: Net earnings by place of residence	Plus: Dividends, interest, and rent	Plus: Personal current transfer receipts	Per capita personal income (dollars)	Population (persons)	Total employment
1970	960,656	824,515	3,649	828,164	48,418	-25,113	754,633	150,345	55,678	4,183	229,660	96,024
1971	997,539	816,909	5,158	822,067	49,360	-19,279	753,428	173,574	70,537	4,305	231,701	92,542
1972	1,098,130	882,554	7,339	889,893	56,797	-17,371	815,725	196,562	85,843	4,764	230,503	95,402
1973	1,214,884	957,791	9,272	967,063	71,295	-13,390	882,378	228,012	104,494	5,100	238,222	101,054
1974	1,288,875	973,540	8,879	982,419	75,325	-11,004	896,090	263,759	129,026	5,405	238,464	99,316
1975	1,425,801	1,047,870	6,844	1,054,714	80,238	-13,507	960,969	297,553	167,279	5,910	241,241	97,287
1976	1,545,551	1,120,597	6,191	1,126,788	87,661	-10,513	1,028,614	331,243	185,694	6,419	240,791	98,836
1977	1,722,462	1,250,238	6,385	1,256,623	100,298	-9,675	1,146,650	375,662	200,150	7,134	241,451	103,907
1978	2,011,797	1,458,540	7,983	1,466,523	120,935	-9,244	1,336,344	450,487	224,966	8,014	251,031	113,104
1979	2,363,064	1,724,273	10,283	1,734,556	150,984	-10,221	1,573,351	528,727	260,986	8,984	263,038	121,837
1980	2,825,225	2,014,927	13,200	2,028,127	178,073	-8,382	1,841,672	671,181	312,372	10,249	275,664	129,188
1981	3,257,048	2,273,293	9,240	2,282,533	216,346	-8,218	2,057,969	828,360	370,719	11,390	285,963	133,908
1982	3,577,651	2,479,572	12,079	2,491,651	243,013	-9,954	2,238,684	914,484	424,483	11,961	299,098	138,412
1983	3,983,783	2,772,922	13,416	2,786,338	277,932	-13,214	2,495,192	1,019,629	468,962	12,851	310,006	147,424
1984	4,524,963	3,187,974	10,245	3,198,219	330,120	-16,119	2,851,980	1,162,444	510,539	14,019	322,780	159,722
1985	5,013,003	3,545,117	10,256	3,555,373	375,182	-15,706	3,164,485	1,286,446	562,072	14,878	336,935	170,814
1986	5,345,421	3,734,718	9,107	3,743,825	407,335	-9,341	3,327,149	1,395,846	622,426	15,308	349,183	175,694
1987	5,740,106	4,048,894	9,653	4,058,547	437,498	-5,669	3,615,380	1,455,950	668,776	15,961	359,628	176,540
1988	6,365,615	4,501,813	15,615	4,517,428	500,038	-4,057	4,013,333	1,611,381	740,901	17,133	371,547	187,777
1989	7,143,726	4,916,005	14,347	4,930,352	551,202	-599	4,378,551	1,907,363	857,812	18,583	384,423	196,440
1990	7,626,878	5,236,681	14,051	5,250,732	585,860	749	4,665,621	1,995,741	965,516	18,915	403,209	202,232
1991	8,031,831	5,533,472	16,213	5,549,685	624,172	-2,683	4,922,830	2,005,890	1,103,111	19,330	415,512	203,022
1992	8,557,784	5,919,345	14,610	5,933,955	666,016	5,229	5,273,168	2,003,090	1,281,526	20,108	425,584	203,939
1993	8,918,792	6,109,457	13,347	6,122,804	685,358	23,368	5,460,814	2,073,087	1,384,891	20,443	436,282	206,630
1994	9,289,346	6,252,356	12,453	6,264,809	725,784	44,783	5,583,808	2,202,649	1,502,889	20,913	444,198	209,999
1995	9,779,448	6,407,829	11,076	6,418,905	745,828	68,157	5,741,234	2,408,359	1,629,855	21,669	451,310	211,373
1996	10,202,518	6,551,493	8,958	6,560,451	766,054	98,717	5,893,114	2,561,921	1,747,483	22,379	455,889	215,068
1997	10,952,087	6,982,652	10,210	6,992,862	816,791	123,097	6,299,168	2,810,121	1,842,798	23,722	461,686	223,138
1998	11,589,494	7,393,662	14,001	7,407,663	859,734	163,082	6,711,011	2,969,127	1,909,356	24,784	467,624	230,763
1999	12,028,794	7,753,218	15,783	7,769,001	894,939	205,353	7,079,415	2,930,219	2,019,160	25,477	472,138	234,135
2000	13,245,501	8,632,969	16,542	8,649,511	983,084	232,838	7,899,265	3,193,953	2,152,283	27,721	477,819	242,259
2001	13,869,100	8,990,141	16,267	9,006,408	1,008,906	244,642	8,242,144	3,263,647	2,363,309	28,512	486,429	244,989
2002	14,323,236	9,351,898	17,682	9,369,580	1,050,000	259,971	8,579,551	3,182,488	2,561,197	28,911	495,425	244,586
2003	15,257,255	9,985,475	14,820	10,000,295	1,125,016	280,606	9,155,885	3,349,629	2,751,741	30,222	504,847	252,213
2004	16,389,627	10,966,530	14,119	10,980,649	1,240,429	302,110	10,042,330	3,348,332	2,998,965	31,596	518,722	261,983
2005	17,546,494	11,898,351	18,427	11,916,778	1,347,008	332,061	10,901,831	3,462,910	3,181,753	33,112	529,907	272,269
2006	18,750,372	12,543,645	16,275	12,559,920	1,438,100	374,020	11,495,840	3,823,765	3,430,767	35,038	535,138	278,455
2007	19,504,937	12,594,554	11,583	12,606,137	1,461,694	430,663	11,575,106	4,277,819	3,652,012	36,139	539,719	277,304
2008	20,123,786	12,579,379	9,069	12,588,448	1,483,329	446,790	11,551,909	4,448,547	4,123,330	37,103	542,378	269,408
2009	19,373,090	12,130,142	9,963	12,140,105	1,454,832	387,955	11,073,228	3,881,292	4,418,570	35,737	542,109	258,626
2010	20,183,284	12,489,077	16,955	12,506,032	1,477,805	374,643	11,402,870	4,033,380	4,747,034	37,102	543,996	256,561
2011	20,957,599	12,546,674	15,487	12,562,161	1,338,106	378,980	11,603,035	4,381,497	4,973,067	38,495	544,420	257,436
2012	20,908,217	12,451,887	23,138	12,475,025	1,355,062	416,776	11,536,739	4,382,315	4,989,163	38,218	547,074	258,429
2013	20,869,883	12,430,823	15,968	12,446,791	1,526,741	430,609	11,350,659	4,386,791	5,132,433	37,917	550,410	260,574
2014	21,684,068	12,599,090	17,712	12,616,802	1,551,695	479,573	11,544,680	4,738,302	5,401,086	39,018	555,747	265,372
2015	23,078,249	13,315,040	24,644	13,339,684	1,624,908	499,200	12,213,976	5,103,467	5,760,806	40,773	566,018	272,815
2016	23,952,989	13,923,862	17,894	13,941,756	1,698,748	526,020	12,769,028	5,217,434	5,966,527	41,496	577,242	279,767
2017	25,556,036	14,887,072	18,301	14,905,373	1,808,436	561,555	13,658,492	5,689,749	6,207,795	43,462	588,002	291,657
2018	27,177,629	15,907,500	12,356	15,919,856	1,940,640	610,129	14,589,345	6,125,395	6,462,889	45,693	594,787	303,830
2019	28,921,629	17,150,417	11,951	17,162,368	2,111,103	617,685	15,668,950	6,375,192	6,877,487	48,136	600,836	310,799
2020	31,173,262	17,833,868	11,556	17,845,424	2,215,481	574,407	16,204,350	6,467,949	8,500,963	51,212	608,713	310,575
2021	34,552,679	19,568,047	11,976	19,580,023	2,372,878	665,115	17,872,260	7,096,067	9,584,352	55,934	617,742	326,616
2022	35,833,890	21,239,170	13,080	21,252,250	2,631,191	758,784	19,379,843	7,640,732	8,813,315	56,817	630,693	339,006

Personal Income and Employment by Area: Panama City, FL

(Thousands of dollars, except as noted.)

Year	Personal income, total	Derivation of personal income: Earnings by place of work: Nonfarm	Farm	Total	Less: Contributions for government social insurance	Plus: Adjustment for residence	Equals: Net earnings by place of residence	Plus: Dividends, interest, and rent	Plus: Personal current transfer receipts	Per capita personal income (dollars)	Population (persons)	Total employment
1970	266,684	211,683	174	211,857	12,184	-4	199,669	47,388	19,627	3,524	75,685	31,565
1971	296,150	233,485	210	233,695	14,076	-794	218,825	53,827	23,498	3,794	78,060	32,183
1972	328,489	257,455	210	257,665	16,149	-866	240,650	59,651	28,188	4,119	79,749	33,112
1973	375,372	293,280	439	293,719	20,861	-967	271,891	68,888	34,593	4,587	81,835	36,083
1974	428,739	332,352	796	333,148	25,023	-1,500	306,625	80,116	41,998	4,953	86,559	38,372
1975	480,586	362,110	793	362,903	27,383	-1,822	333,698	91,542	55,346	5,390	89,167	38,786
1976	541,800	410,905	656	411,561	31,745	-2,198	377,618	102,242	61,940	5,899	91,847	40,643
1977	588,134	442,353	448	442,801	34,444	-3,288	405,069	114,599	68,466	6,296	93,418	42,085
1978	676,419	504,367	341	504,708	39,627	-3,771	461,310	139,774	75,335	7,138	94,759	44,224
1979	745,777	546,634	277	546,911	45,687	-4,439	496,785	161,796	87,196	7,648	97,516	44,727
1980	856,035	618,242	301	618,543	51,940	-9,245	557,358	194,421	104,256	8,707	98,318	46,220
1981	980,542	705,311	170	705,481	63,836	-10,117	631,528	228,659	120,355	9,762	100,445	48,026
1982	1,076,598	759,045	304	759,349	69,892	-10,814	678,643	259,960	137,995	10,361	103,904	49,844
1983	1,182,641	836,952	275	837,227	78,592	-12,369	746,266	284,531	151,844	11,154	106,027	51,945
1984	1,336,541	961,646	321	961,967	92,643	-16,229	853,095	320,777	162,669	12,233	109,256	56,846
1985	1,462,185	1,055,202	375	1,055,577	104,172	-17,633	933,772	352,331	176,082	12,859	113,707	61,163
1986	1,580,779	1,137,831	537	1,138,368	115,410	-17,338	1,005,620	384,184	190,975	13,380	118,149	63,669
1987	1,650,964	1,187,548	621	1,188,169	119,566	-16,003	1,052,600	394,604	203,760	13,597	121,417	63,235
1988	1,794,539	1,289,951	565	1,290,516	134,598	-14,687	1,141,231	430,021	223,287	14,489	123,857	64,784
1989	1,941,628	1,346,327	279	1,346,606	143,135	-13,352	1,190,119	493,012	258,497	15,446	125,703	66,197
1990	2,110,885	1,465,537	138	1,465,675	156,715	-16,089	1,292,871	529,285	288,729	16,579	127,323	68,858
1991	2,274,339	1,591,747	-25	1,591,722	171,165	-20,748	1,399,809	546,950	327,580	17,495	130,000	70,705
1992	2,425,504	1,691,654	-263	1,691,391	182,875	-23,955	1,484,561	567,806	373,137	18,178	133,432	71,810
1993	2,594,090	1,791,743	-32	1,791,711	193,767	-26,896	1,571,048	621,568	401,474	18,917	137,127	73,794
1994	2,694,946	1,868,055	372	1,868,427	204,026	-30,727	1,633,674	628,030	433,242	19,300	139,636	75,035
1995	2,920,040	1,979,137	653	1,979,790	213,855	-34,157	1,731,778	701,655	486,607	20,549	142,101	76,802
1996	3,073,069	2,098,886	1,170	2,100,056	225,890	-40,231	1,833,935	745,696	493,438	21,219	144,826	79,624
1997	3,234,386	2,207,277	1,766	2,209,043	238,524	-45,115	1,925,404	790,099	518,883	22,055	146,651	80,779
1998	3,400,183	2,326,446	1,461	2,327,907	252,707	-52,204	2,022,996	848,150	529,037	23,129	147,011	82,258
1999	3,511,871	2,425,229	1,359	2,426,588	261,453	-56,781	2,108,354	841,855	561,662	23,705	148,149	82,839
2000	3,654,873	2,472,597	1,070	2,473,667	266,155	-57,835	2,149,677	900,183	605,013	24,630	148,393	83,228
2001	4,016,435	2,766,561	1,064	2,767,625	295,457	-65,096	2,407,072	938,393	670,970	26,739	150,207	84,003
2002	4,261,354	2,998,367	861	2,999,228	318,451	-73,696	2,607,081	914,457	739,816	27,899	152,741	85,802
2003	4,570,655	3,239,569	584	3,240,153	343,506	-76,965	2,819,682	956,723	794,250	29,480	155,044	87,916
2004	4,910,340	3,497,545	724	3,498,269	375,766	-89,485	3,033,018	1,027,345	849,977	30,921	158,804	93,083
2005	5,305,347	3,834,578	822	3,835,400	415,096	-111,417	3,308,887	1,086,256	910,204	32,565	162,917	97,039
2006	5,681,931	4,117,551	753	4,118,304	452,582	-111,944	3,553,778	1,166,771	961,382	34,302	165,644	100,144
2007	5,915,870	4,088,470	688	4,089,158	456,710	-101,937	3,530,511	1,367,836	1,017,523	35,779	165,345	100,800
2008	6,118,020	4,108,882	651	4,109,533	465,660	-95,544	3,548,329	1,410,471	1,159,220	36,796	166,267	99,121
2009	5,968,923	3,988,195	576	3,988,771	463,775	-91,231	3,433,765	1,271,736	1,263,422	35,643	167,464	96,106
2010	6,288,567	4,109,395	640	4,110,035	474,038	-98,722	3,537,275	1,326,374	1,424,918	37,148	169,286	95,626
2011	6,453,325	4,083,018	771	4,083,789	427,544	-81,825	3,574,420	1,405,830	1,473,075	37,967	169,970	96,595
2012	6,489,950	4,114,816	741	4,115,557	438,617	-68,107	3,608,833	1,439,149	1,441,968	37,619	172,518	96,984
2013	6,546,238	4,213,706	849	4,214,555	502,579	-46,990	3,664,986	1,395,761	1,485,491	37,251	175,733	98,853
2014	6,890,938	4,464,276	941	4,465,217	532,590	-61,624	3,871,003	1,463,692	1,556,243	38,324	179,809	102,770
2015	7,278,242	4,686,713	867	4,687,580	553,542	-69,861	4,064,177	1,584,761	1,629,304	39,683	183,408	105,242
2016	7,494,033	4,851,832	1,028	4,852,860	569,903	-101,612	4,181,345	1,622,739	1,689,949	40,323	185,851	107,234
2017	7,614,967	4,922,679	6,358	4,929,037	578,777	-102,337	4,247,923	1,589,077	1,777,967	40,662	187,276	108,669
2018	7,938,513	5,100,376	5,196	5,105,572	603,958	-134,876	4,366,738	1,690,451	1,881,324	41,924	189,354	110,067
2019	8,115,966	5,232,241	7,067	5,239,308	624,783	-111,972	4,502,553	1,766,867	1,846,546	45,897	176,830	104,795
2020	8,737,281	5,353,274	8,002	5,361,276	642,370	-95,719	4,623,187	1,821,007	2,293,087	50,069	174,506	105,211
2021	9,807,417	6,019,240	9,986	6,029,226	701,000	-115,222	5,213,004	1,971,208	2,623,205	54,638	179,498	112,818
2022	10,046,785	6,419,023	1,836	6,420,859	759,417	-103,652	5,557,790	2,118,859	2,370,136	54,268	185,134	117,455

Personal Income and Employment by Area: Parkersburg-Vienna, WV

(Thousands of dollars, except as noted.)

Year	Personal income, total	Derivation of personal income: Earnings by place of work: Nonfarm	Farm	Total	Less: Contributions for government social insurance	Plus: Adjustment for residence	Equals: Net earnings by place of residence	Plus: Dividends, interest, and rent	Plus: Personal current transfer receipts	Per capita personal income (dollars)	Population (persons)	Total employment
1970	318,216	265,753	716	266,469	20,162	1,957	248,264	39,781	30,171	3,509	90,698	37,759
1971	337,191	281,115	831	281,946	22,081	-935	258,930	42,875	35,386	3,742	90,111	38,352
1972	369,651	314,547	1,037	315,584	26,269	-5,806	283,509	46,904	39,238	4,062	91,003	39,746
1973	406,901	349,601	1,456	351,057	33,776	-7,880	309,401	52,316	45,184	4,429	91,866	42,037
1974	463,093	397,299	819	398,118	40,232	-10,347	347,539	60,887	54,667	5,024	92,182	43,648
1975	495,791	401,490	280	401,770	39,454	-7,941	354,375	68,177	73,239	5,322	93,160	41,134
1976	547,765	449,447	-144	449,303	44,953	-8,070	396,280	73,983	77,502	5,820	94,121	42,127
1977	622,084	514,767	-243	514,524	51,319	-8,240	454,965	82,680	84,439	6,551	94,964	44,102
1978	701,671	585,813	151	585,964	60,451	-5,687	519,826	91,768	90,077	7,255	96,719	46,028
1979	772,372	648,676	219	648,895	69,301	-14,120	565,474	103,977	102,921	7,928	97,422	46,895
1980	849,783	696,324	344	696,668	75,171	-22,970	598,527	126,133	125,123	8,623	98,551	46,059
1981	931,513	757,522	-821	756,701	87,222	-31,702	637,777	153,556	140,180	9,458	98,486	45,220
1982	966,178	776,733	-1,633	775,100	91,943	-41,391	641,766	169,584	154,828	9,910	97,500	44,032
1983	1,023,628	814,630	-1,352	813,278	97,825	-47,167	668,286	186,902	168,440	10,513	97,368	44,220
1984	1,105,007	880,315	-197	880,118	108,095	-48,810	723,213	206,170	175,624	11,397	96,959	45,190
1985	1,170,981	930,261	103	930,364	115,381	-53,259	761,724	219,926	189,331	12,144	96,427	45,545
1986	1,200,311	953,390	-393	952,997	122,683	-55,034	775,280	223,743	201,288	12,510	95,949	45,461
1987	1,234,811	998,037	-848	997,189	130,717	-66,039	800,433	224,453	209,925	13,070	94,480	47,158
1988	1,341,797	1,101,076	-690	1,100,386	147,160	-76,351	876,875	240,204	224,718	14,291	93,892	47,850
1989	1,408,650	1,123,379	-473	1,122,906	152,118	-70,857	899,931	269,606	239,113	15,203	92,654	48,408
1990	1,495,095	1,183,029	109	1,183,138	162,087	-77,527	943,524	292,121	259,450	16,224	92,156	48,937
1991	1,540,285	1,208,214	-631	1,207,583	170,145	-81,763	955,675	293,199	291,411	16,643	92,547	48,290
1992	1,646,001	1,299,458	-114	1,299,344	183,199	-86,378	1,029,767	280,363	335,871	17,671	93,148	49,325
1993	1,720,794	1,359,514	-88	1,359,426	195,216	-89,645	1,074,565	286,322	359,907	18,352	93,766	50,279
1994	1,779,427	1,412,973	48	1,413,021	201,174	-91,617	1,120,230	298,342	360,855	18,892	94,190	51,179
1995	1,845,772	1,457,850	-335	1,457,515	208,383	-95,613	1,153,519	320,460	371,793	19,547	94,428	51,896
1996	1,919,562	1,525,764	-135	1,525,629	218,300	-116,681	1,190,648	332,958	395,956	20,354	94,308	52,966
1997	1,987,014	1,583,280	-543	1,582,737	224,583	-118,738	1,239,416	339,564	408,034	21,087	94,229	53,811
1998	2,042,654	1,601,616	-1,698	1,599,918	228,663	-104,996	1,266,259	354,557	421,838	21,722	94,035	53,323
1999	2,123,095	1,665,102	-2,112	1,662,990	235,228	-112,907	1,314,855	377,089	431,151	22,596	93,958	53,370
2000	2,212,155	1,761,423	-1,867	1,759,556	255,487	-133,765	1,370,304	387,181	454,670	23,606	93,711	54,205
2001	2,291,371	1,774,623	-2,470	1,772,153	249,284	-108,907	1,413,962	373,844	503,565	24,497	93,536	53,714
2002	2,390,541	1,798,454	-3,628	1,794,826	247,873	-79,018	1,467,935	371,721	550,885	25,588	93,424	52,637
2003	2,417,196	1,814,320	-2,598	1,811,722	254,923	-76,411	1,480,388	374,357	562,451	25,999	92,974	52,170
2004	2,484,141	1,900,784	-2,116	1,898,668	263,620	-99,295	1,535,753	386,820	561,568	26,796	92,705	52,523
2005	2,500,168	1,903,859	-2,953	1,900,906	261,598	-91,021	1,548,287	361,162	590,719	26,984	92,655	52,251
2006	2,679,235	2,016,033	-4,152	2,011,881	265,485	-97,578	1,648,818	393,655	636,762	29,014	92,343	52,839
2007	2,798,482	2,009,058	-5,183	2,003,875	253,334	-65,665	1,684,876	435,305	678,301	30,321	92,295	52,703
2008	2,944,343	2,023,404	-3,775	2,019,629	247,137	-50,637	1,721,855	469,633	752,855	31,821	92,528	51,863
2009	2,954,394	1,993,118	-4,162	1,988,956	247,196	-72,475	1,669,285	453,070	832,039	31,924	92,544	50,389
2010	3,020,317	2,037,045	-4,198	2,032,847	250,110	-86,567	1,696,170	445,690	878,457	32,577	92,712	50,090
2011	3,182,062	2,121,597	-3,067	2,118,530	231,739	-90,334	1,796,457	491,611	893,994	34,314	92,734	50,713
2012	3,291,447	2,198,444	-3,561	2,194,883	238,800	-91,938	1,864,145	525,806	901,496	35,564	92,551	51,028
2013	3,283,669	2,202,541	-3,047	2,199,494	267,881	-52,601	1,879,012	488,397	916,260	35,464	92,592	50,569
2014	3,498,865	2,290,485	-4,105	2,286,380	280,923	-2,810	2,002,647	531,152	965,066	37,801	92,559	50,451
2015	3,521,429	2,273,736	-4,647	2,269,089	282,841	-7,496	1,978,752	533,519	1,009,158	38,067	92,507	49,806
2016	3,463,978	2,167,904	-5,873	2,162,031	278,303	19,770	1,903,498	534,222	1,026,258	37,677	91,940	48,586
2017	3,565,832	2,260,608	-6,148	2,254,460	289,453	8,961	1,973,968	543,038	1,048,826	39,033	91,355	47,463
2018	3,960,356	2,475,217	-7,005	2,468,212	302,759	114,820	2,280,273	606,393	1,073,690	43,713	90,599	46,837
2019	4,131,097	2,686,893	-5,715	2,681,178	315,739	42,910	2,408,349	608,745	1,114,003	45,919	89,964	46,565
2020	4,258,813	2,569,812	-6,400	2,563,412	318,694	4,656	2,249,374	644,472	1,364,967	47,676	89,328	44,105
2021	4,860,826	3,009,466	-6,918	3,002,548	350,440	-36,237	2,615,871	729,205	1,515,750	54,708	88,850	45,845
2022	5,062,767	3,317,590	-9,422	3,308,168	383,429	-22,166	2,902,573	799,823	1,360,371	57,251	88,431	47,107

Personal Income and Employment by Area: Pensacola-Ferry Pass-Brent, FL

(Thousands of dollars, except as noted.)

Year	Personal income, total	Derivation of personal income								Per capita personal income (dollars)	Population (persons)	Total employment
		Earnings by place of work										
		Nonfarm	Farm	Total	Less: Contributions for government social insurance	Plus: Adjustment for residence	Equals: Net earnings by place of residence	Plus: Dividends, interest, and rent	Plus: Personal current transfer receipts			
1970	972,357	794,688	3,947	798,635	44,344	-2,881	751,410	162,500	58,447	3,983	244,134	104,526
1971	1,100,934	895,132	5,392	900,524	52,591	-2,529	845,404	187,255	68,275	4,384	251,153	107,815
1972	1,233,579	1,002,625	5,444	1,008,069	61,568	-186	946,315	207,360	79,904	4,725	261,051	111,779
1973	1,323,451	1,059,444	12,847	1,072,291	73,602	1,476	1,000,165	225,422	97,864	5,005	264,441	114,005
1974	1,479,983	1,172,003	15,565	1,187,568	85,207	857	1,103,218	259,423	117,342	5,532	267,551	117,846
1975	1,639,777	1,275,812	16,176	1,291,988	93,858	702	1,198,832	288,913	152,032	5,948	275,666	119,341
1976	1,738,312	1,347,341	9,495	1,356,836	101,929	7,883	1,262,790	303,945	171,577	6,158	282,287	118,547
1977	1,897,906	1,467,712	5,051	1,472,763	111,237	10,067	1,371,593	341,027	185,286	6,650	285,381	121,814
1978	2,131,332	1,618,448	11,976	1,630,424	124,900	13,710	1,519,234	405,824	206,274	7,441	286,428	126,124
1979	2,378,490	1,802,495	9,538	1,812,033	146,096	14,948	1,680,885	459,370	238,235	8,225	289,161	128,844
1980	2,629,150	1,944,806	2,698	1,947,504	160,743	22,367	1,809,128	538,871	281,151	9,009	291,830	131,667
1981	3,009,496	2,213,251	4,358	2,217,609	195,341	26,237	2,048,505	632,520	328,471	10,049	299,477	135,907
1982	3,274,799	2,386,495	3,212	2,389,707	215,098	32,554	2,207,163	702,136	365,500	10,776	303,905	136,941
1983	3,553,442	2,586,381	3,495	2,589,876	241,151	32,475	2,381,200	770,893	401,349	11,379	312,280	140,353
1984	3,896,751	2,813,639	9,967	2,823,606	269,943	38,773	2,592,436	873,875	430,440	12,361	315,257	148,279
1985	4,151,176	2,978,060	8,145	2,986,205	292,900	41,407	2,734,712	952,487	463,977	12,942	320,743	154,423
1986	4,441,502	3,180,697	7,457	3,188,154	322,615	48,517	2,914,056	1,031,666	495,780	13,561	327,528	161,370
1987	4,689,805	3,356,802	12,090	3,368,892	338,530	56,194	3,086,556	1,076,232	527,017	14,005	334,873	161,606
1988	5,015,467	3,554,814	15,904	3,570,718	373,388	76,587	3,273,917	1,166,928	574,622	15,021	333,905	162,727
1989	5,427,864	3,740,755	13,018	3,753,773	399,157	81,778	3,436,394	1,325,655	665,815	15,887	341,654	165,545
1990	5,771,297	3,979,135	16,662	3,995,797	426,961	50,140	3,618,976	1,419,059	733,262	16,694	345,706	167,249
1991	6,088,705	4,156,584	17,949	4,174,533	451,021	82,930	3,806,442	1,452,306	829,957	17,249	352,981	168,899
1992	6,482,733	4,476,474	22,207	4,498,681	489,554	55,126	4,064,253	1,466,615	951,865	17,909	361,975	172,885
1993	6,767,522	4,613,137	23,817	4,636,954	505,620	94,647	4,225,981	1,523,298	1,018,243	18,406	367,689	174,170
1994	7,075,529	4,786,058	21,746	4,807,804	529,859	108,091	4,386,036	1,600,059	1,089,434	18,929	373,790	178,056
1995	7,518,289	4,946,295	12,332	4,958,627	546,166	189,476	4,601,937	1,732,652	1,183,700	19,774	380,205	183,511
1996	8,106,518	5,302,499	21,581	5,324,080	579,626	234,978	4,979,432	1,887,581	1,239,505	20,867	388,477	190,014
1997	8,613,909	5,629,591	15,609	5,645,200	616,172	238,705	5,267,733	2,050,739	1,295,437	21,539	399,925	198,535
1998	9,158,526	5,959,463	10,244	5,969,707	647,224	298,998	5,621,481	2,234,720	1,302,325	22,396	408,930	204,939
1999	9,482,365	6,192,478	16,158	6,208,636	670,496	311,066	5,849,206	2,244,336	1,388,823	23,126	410,026	207,920
2000	10,117,249	6,519,689	21,790	6,541,479	704,176	387,591	6,224,894	2,388,196	1,504,159	24,492	413,085	212,573
2001	10,913,263	7,031,146	16,454	7,047,600	756,938	399,008	6,689,670	2,539,086	1,684,507	26,044	419,037	209,983
2002	11,309,700	7,228,805	13,087	7,241,892	781,432	448,451	6,908,911	2,553,284	1,847,505	26,611	425,006	209,429
2003	11,907,706	7,636,797	23,844	7,660,641	822,979	498,312	7,335,974	2,566,011	2,005,721	27,817	428,066	213,125
2004	12,632,481	8,160,245	15,793	8,176,038	891,049	547,958	7,832,947	2,596,812	2,202,722	29,009	435,466	219,670
2005	13,328,807	8,697,415	18,089	8,715,504	955,071	596,441	8,356,874	2,689,882	2,282,051	30,329	439,471	223,705
2006	14,282,249	9,291,110	24,151	9,315,261	1,044,256	632,407	8,903,412	2,948,949	2,429,888	32,212	443,378	229,442
2007	14,922,563	9,447,127	9,982	9,457,109	1,068,774	691,652	9,079,987	3,230,124	2,612,452	33,643	443,551	232,031
2008	15,306,262	9,387,137	10,663	9,397,800	1,079,071	726,114	9,044,843	3,286,612	2,974,807	34,366	445,392	225,918
2009	15,198,912	9,228,353	1,191	9,229,544	1,079,808	722,020	8,871,756	3,099,859	3,227,297	34,036	446,559	217,881
2010	15,916,033	9,504,879	8,477	9,513,356	1,098,787	746,564	9,161,133	3,200,533	3,554,367	35,291	450,999	217,740
2011	16,743,276	9,802,126	19,992	9,822,118	1,028,389	792,681	9,586,410	3,455,888	3,700,978	36,774	455,303	220,466
2012	17,117,794	10,072,156	893	10,073,049	1,068,365	873,110	9,877,794	3,581,621	3,658,379	37,060	461,889	221,304
2013	17,066,474	10,134,316	14,877	10,149,193	1,206,984	903,928	9,846,137	3,441,643	3,778,694	36,508	467,466	225,232
2014	17,785,943	10,457,528	10,636	10,468,164	1,245,700	949,393	10,171,857	3,650,636	3,963,450	37,752	471,131	229,485
2015	18,632,491	10,962,712	19,263	10,981,975	1,298,997	962,232	10,645,210	3,794,933	4,192,348	39,128	476,193	233,491
2016	19,604,608	11,714,888	17,183	11,732,071	1,373,214	958,186	11,317,043	3,956,882	4,330,683	40,645	482,334	243,674
2017	20,720,079	12,398,381	19,696	12,418,077	1,456,886	968,151	11,929,342	4,203,343	4,587,394	42,420	488,453	253,386
2018	21,496,401	12,800,374	15,366	12,815,740	1,513,914	1,030,362	12,332,188	4,346,140	4,818,073	43,374	495,610	257,523
2019	22,836,993	13,665,398	19,388	13,684,786	1,630,494	1,130,058	13,184,350	4,512,933	5,139,710	45,294	504,196	261,912
2020	24,863,739	14,205,720	13,552	14,219,272	1,709,065	1,189,925	13,700,132	4,717,748	6,445,859	48,606	511,540	263,036
2021	27,616,001	15,620,892	20,183	15,641,075	1,832,697	1,288,495	15,096,873	5,160,008	7,359,120	53,389	517,263	275,051
2022	28,365,532	16,804,431	18,159	16,822,590	2,005,427	1,379,770	16,196,933	5,525,217	6,643,382	54,221	523,146	284,991

Personal Income and Employment by Area: Peoria, IL

(Thousands of dollars, except as noted.)

Year	Personal income, total	Derivation of personal income: Earnings by place of work: Nonfarm	Farm	Total	Less: Contributions for government social insurance	Plus: Adjustment for residence	Equals: Net earnings by place of residence	Plus: Dividends, interest, and rent	Plus: Personal current transfer receipts	Per capita personal income (dollars)	Population (persons)	Total employment
1970	1,721,287	1,395,805	48,701	1,444,506	94,307	-8,418	1,341,781	248,275	131,231	4,240	405,961	179,333
1971	1,876,463	1,513,946	57,120	1,571,066	105,778	-9,885	1,455,403	266,005	155,055	4,556	411,910	179,647
1972	2,027,148	1,638,804	53,673	1,692,477	120,871	-10,599	1,561,007	290,114	176,027	4,869	416,337	180,275
1973	2,344,586	1,871,348	109,827	1,981,175	160,917	-15,328	1,804,930	333,850	205,806	5,617	417,402	191,054
1974	2,621,964	2,122,150	102,244	2,224,394	189,281	-22,649	2,012,464	379,817	229,683	6,251	419,469	197,814
1975	3,009,756	2,363,544	161,722	2,525,266	206,194	-30,881	2,288,191	432,501	289,064	7,138	421,670	202,638
1976	3,236,367	2,593,290	122,875	2,716,165	231,412	-34,998	2,449,755	462,188	324,424	7,615	424,983	207,320
1977	3,511,394	2,826,162	114,343	2,940,505	251,072	-40,895	2,648,538	516,566	346,290	8,246	425,828	207,941
1978	3,892,295	3,201,442	95,297	3,296,739	294,382	-51,237	2,951,120	570,131	371,044	9,101	427,665	213,255
1979	4,186,702	3,378,842	119,576	3,498,418	321,880	-53,265	3,123,273	644,151	419,278	9,792	427,585	209,956
1980	4,553,499	3,668,475	25,011	3,693,486	351,179	-70,965	3,271,342	770,853	511,304	10,552	431,519	207,205
1981	5,036,814	3,850,890	125,585	3,976,475	396,051	-68,912	3,511,512	931,061	594,241	11,682	431,170	203,884
1982	5,096,378	3,641,919	86,772	3,728,691	377,891	-50,080	3,300,720	1,097,913	697,745	11,945	426,671	190,562
1983	4,902,689	3,399,726	-38,987	3,360,739	351,733	-24,281	2,984,725	1,146,351	771,613	11,654	420,685	180,636
1984	5,348,555	3,677,568	81,697	3,759,265	394,975	-18,398	3,345,892	1,259,643	743,020	12,946	413,134	186,024
1985	5,500,901	3,751,463	133,995	3,885,458	407,181	-9,171	3,469,106	1,262,785	769,010	13,608	404,250	184,325
1986	5,642,128	3,871,759	96,247	3,968,006	420,188	-11,425	3,536,393	1,300,979	804,756	14,230	396,484	185,434
1987	5,824,704	4,105,153	77,238	4,182,391	438,131	-10,645	3,733,615	1,260,609	830,480	14,812	393,240	188,176
1988	6,307,130	4,615,847	28,250	4,644,097	506,882	-15,343	4,121,872	1,324,947	860,311	16,056	392,830	195,520
1989	6,844,489	4,933,439	81,920	5,015,359	545,036	-2,839	4,467,484	1,458,851	918,154	17,314	395,319	201,324
1990	7,220,800	5,235,344	85,780	5,321,124	562,502	5,524	4,764,146	1,467,142	989,512	18,173	397,346	205,682
1991	7,269,283	5,228,424	59,974	5,288,398	577,885	13,521	4,724,034	1,485,476	1,059,773	18,187	399,686	205,854
1992	7,732,401	5,476,922	117,263	5,594,185	592,943	26,985	5,028,227	1,504,040	1,200,134	19,303	400,570	204,409
1993	8,059,334	5,812,108	83,942	5,896,050	641,443	20,500	5,275,107	1,544,458	1,239,769	20,107	400,820	207,988
1994	8,549,848	6,180,269	141,252	6,321,521	687,354	38,230	5,672,397	1,609,636	1,267,815	21,311	401,200	213,758
1995	8,798,877	6,313,489	28,821	6,342,310	700,970	53,553	5,694,893	1,751,977	1,352,007	21,735	404,828	216,727
1996	9,415,991	6,656,649	169,432	6,826,081	737,510	47,422	6,135,993	1,853,633	1,426,365	23,229	405,361	224,699
1997	9,923,745	7,047,874	145,381	7,193,255	777,609	50,272	6,465,918	2,007,892	1,449,935	24,489	405,240	228,340
1998	10,451,477	7,538,734	99,435	7,638,169	822,976	67,361	6,882,554	2,110,081	1,458,842	25,777	405,451	232,754
1999	10,719,463	7,884,931	67,967	7,952,898	844,021	90,459	7,199,336	2,034,698	1,485,429	26,402	406,015	232,531
2000	11,188,796	8,066,933	115,678	8,182,611	853,250	108,844	7,438,205	2,185,891	1,564,700	27,635	404,875	234,823
2001	11,504,154	8,380,599	98,862	8,479,461	893,222	122,553	7,708,792	2,129,978	1,665,384	28,512	403,480	230,044
2002	11,636,070	8,630,117	60,827	8,690,944	915,979	134,861	7,909,826	1,939,065	1,787,179	28,809	403,899	225,390
2003	11,976,737	8,806,156	120,575	8,926,731	939,084	133,833	8,121,480	1,991,450	1,863,807	29,648	403,961	222,771
2004	12,696,412	9,411,926	228,521	9,640,447	1,025,602	111,260	8,726,105	2,030,703	1,939,604	31,303	405,592	226,365
2005	13,271,557	10,163,894	91,015	10,254,909	1,119,090	71,188	9,207,007	1,966,259	2,098,291	32,590	407,224	229,726
2006	14,347,375	11,077,688	98,622	11,176,310	1,196,800	49,110	10,028,620	2,154,831	2,163,924	35,073	409,074	235,305
2007	15,185,816	11,541,776	217,564	11,759,340	1,250,052	29,767	10,539,055	2,281,581	2,365,180	36,908	411,451	239,867
2008	16,056,424	11,883,597	330,318	12,213,915	1,298,293	31,708	10,947,330	2,518,153	2,590,941	38,858	413,206	240,779
2009	15,801,543	11,433,473	204,075	11,637,548	1,248,265	38,957	10,428,240	2,462,181	2,911,122	37,942	416,463	229,701
2010	16,200,644	11,773,257	141,143	11,914,400	1,287,225	15,027	10,642,202	2,422,951	3,135,491	38,928	416,172	229,888
2011	17,649,650	12,924,694	350,466	13,275,160	1,258,404	-66,713	11,950,043	2,685,381	3,014,226	42,294	417,308	234,162
2012	18,206,136	13,667,846	191,900	13,859,746	1,339,536	-128,481	12,391,729	2,811,240	3,003,167	43,557	417,983	237,210
2013	17,835,242	12,925,877	543,697	13,469,574	1,450,185	-92,714	11,926,675	2,756,936	3,151,631	42,495	419,699	231,860
2014	17,976,266	13,010,059	268,688	13,278,747	1,454,059	-87,527	11,737,161	3,045,963	3,193,142	43,051	417,561	231,289
2015	18,469,834	13,341,918	24,290	13,366,208	1,474,027	-31,151	11,861,030	3,226,446	3,382,358	44,462	415,407	230,870
2016	18,439,857	13,159,476	180,122	13,339,598	1,460,685	-48,338	11,830,575	3,174,272	3,435,010	44,560	413,818	226,945
2017	18,475,146	12,949,872	132,793	13,082,665	1,448,194	-19,581	11,614,890	3,311,701	3,548,555	45,022	410,356	224,505
2018	19,253,836	13,612,897	191,283	13,804,180	1,513,661	-21,277	12,269,242	3,314,185	3,670,409	47,304	407,021	224,381
2019	19,460,292	13,644,200	115,419	13,759,619	1,520,023	-6,795	12,232,801	3,402,226	3,825,265	48,088	404,683	221,706
2020	20,856,018	13,615,614	241,084	13,856,698	1,520,154	19,741	12,356,285	3,355,938	5,143,795	51,961	401,375	212,316
2021	22,397,168	14,067,808	496,769	14,564,577	1,564,596	26,860	13,026,841	3,697,029	5,673,298	56,157	398,832	217,286
2022	22,566,174	15,032,334	584,514	15,616,848	1,728,962	-4,068	13,883,818	3,914,032	4,768,324	56,918	396,466	226,370

Personal Income and Employment by Area: Philadelphia-Camden-Wilmington, PA-NJ-DE-MD

(Thousands of dollars, except as noted.)

Year	Personal income, total	Derivation of personal income								Per capita personal income (dollars)	Population (persons)	Total employment
		Earnings by place of work			Less: Contributions for government social insurance	Plus: Adjustment for residence	Equals: Net earnings by place of residence	Plus: Dividends, interest, and rent	Plus: Personal current transfer receipts			
		Nonfarm	Farm	Total								
1970	24,520,198	20,039,390	94,448	20,133,838	1,436,557	52,200	18,749,481	3,683,033	2,087,684	4,599	5,331,133	2,424,294
1971	26,125,091	21,114,400	99,205	21,213,605	1,571,650	73,436	19,715,391	3,944,720	2,464,980	4,872	5,362,194	2,392,220
1972	28,339,983	22,923,197	91,533	23,014,730	1,793,297	124,808	21,346,241	4,212,154	2,781,588	5,293	5,353,850	2,424,493
1973	30,621,832	24,856,753	135,537	24,992,290	2,243,235	189,927	22,938,982	4,588,136	3,094,714	5,758	5,317,951	2,467,445
1974	33,305,265	26,643,145	135,103	26,778,248	2,492,914	247,132	24,532,466	5,113,733	3,659,066	6,289	5,295,959	2,453,221
1975	35,981,127	28,016,022	110,152	28,126,174	2,557,693	280,537	25,849,018	5,441,504	4,690,605	6,804	5,288,609	2,376,788
1976	39,176,435	30,459,484	139,511	30,598,995	2,831,890	360,665	28,127,770	5,850,128	5,198,537	7,418	5,280,969	2,398,310
1977	42,605,446	33,095,270	132,403	33,227,673	3,069,436	435,113	30,593,350	6,433,671	5,578,425	8,093	5,264,778	2,415,937
1978	46,787,916	36,643,060	134,332	36,777,392	3,490,984	514,103	33,800,511	7,055,916	5,931,489	8,916	5,247,420	2,480,533
1979	51,534,450	40,225,755	136,126	40,361,881	3,982,608	594,235	36,973,508	7,895,638	6,665,304	9,819	5,248,348	2,531,977
1980	57,107,204	43,529,772	89,436	43,619,208	4,330,334	732,389	40,021,263	9,521,073	7,564,868	10,890	5,244,018	2,533,311
1981	63,154,961	47,034,778	127,745	47,162,523	5,003,327	845,587	43,004,783	11,628,431	8,521,747	12,029	5,250,278	2,530,893
1982	68,255,814	49,701,183	151,116	49,852,299	5,378,387	904,056	45,377,968	13,391,982	9,485,864	12,984	5,257,004	2,524,306
1983	72,960,440	53,427,724	143,538	53,571,262	5,875,092	979,185	48,675,355	14,104,442	10,180,643	13,866	5,261,664	2,558,593
1984	79,378,086	58,523,873	202,459	58,726,332	6,681,102	1,101,664	53,146,894	15,734,966	10,496,226	15,036	5,279,124	2,645,844
1985	85,502,061	63,363,634	225,204	63,588,838	7,331,153	1,180,665	57,438,350	16,997,724	11,065,987	16,149	5,294,461	2,722,101
1986	90,937,917	67,783,561	214,907	67,998,468	7,908,084	1,311,575	61,401,959	17,859,158	11,676,800	17,044	5,335,416	2,785,227
1987	97,152,607	73,863,745	199,920	74,063,665	8,538,491	1,444,385	66,969,559	18,187,045	11,996,003	18,047	5,383,434	2,876,967
1988	105,830,420	80,579,558	182,308	80,761,866	9,540,574	1,573,396	72,794,688	20,298,277	12,737,455	19,521	5,421,382	2,951,624
1989	114,493,678	85,840,356	185,138	86,025,494	10,048,583	1,639,604	77,616,515	23,130,690	13,746,473	21,068	5,434,490	2,987,983
1990	121,247,509	90,232,511	213,732	90,446,243	10,567,223	1,710,198	81,589,218	24,849,777	14,808,514	22,267	5,445,186	2,986,306
1991	125,483,800	92,022,458	204,036	92,226,494	10,899,355	1,907,443	83,234,582	25,036,602	17,212,616	22,899	5,479,918	2,912,895
1992	132,123,433	97,329,071	225,644	97,554,715	11,453,320	1,999,852	88,101,247	25,242,784	18,779,402	24,007	5,503,640	2,891,738
1993	136,762,059	100,649,048	239,650	100,888,698	11,911,185	2,122,342	91,099,855	25,920,626	19,741,578	24,717	5,533,081	2,910,168
1994	141,374,386	104,213,364	244,090	104,457,454	12,570,444	2,228,945	94,115,955	27,013,268	20,245,163	25,416	5,562,336	2,922,050
1995	148,762,683	108,636,644	233,869	108,870,513	13,031,443	2,405,513	98,244,583	29,209,633	21,308,467	26,630	5,586,177	2,963,541
1996	156,694,291	114,018,430	281,357	114,299,787	13,469,802	2,372,665	103,202,650	30,910,535	22,581,106	27,970	5,602,154	2,998,593
1997	165,281,881	120,802,405	273,455	121,075,860	14,146,652	2,637,368	109,566,576	32,760,959	22,954,346	29,433	5,615,600	3,061,561
1998	177,107,548	130,407,357	277,968	130,685,325	15,018,450	2,650,191	118,317,066	35,452,123	23,338,359	31,402	5,640,015	3,127,485
1999	185,089,697	138,410,317	259,226	138,669,543	15,724,565	2,663,679	125,608,657	35,203,319	24,277,721	32,671	5,665,210	3,179,438
2000	200,239,969	149,121,941	306,785	149,428,726	16,672,815	2,996,110	135,752,021	38,337,407	26,150,541	35,179	5,691,968	3,250,559
2001	209,690,619	157,464,714	269,347	157,734,061	17,235,301	3,121,758	143,620,518	38,209,895	27,860,206	36,698	5,713,954	3,267,912
2002	214,288,483	162,038,056	265,988	162,304,044	17,766,296	3,212,327	147,750,075	36,672,823	29,865,585	37,310	5,743,383	3,266,690
2003	222,089,546	168,553,598	272,878	168,826,476	18,383,180	3,303,499	153,746,795	37,422,141	30,920,610	38,465	5,773,864	3,280,121
2004	234,858,037	179,752,093	318,461	180,070,554	19,426,335	3,569,769	164,213,988	39,075,193	31,568,856	40,461	5,804,535	3,324,064
2005	243,168,534	185,114,438	298,643	185,413,081	20,281,343	3,754,187	168,885,925	40,341,921	33,940,688	41,716	5,829,139	3,384,591
2006	257,772,414	193,468,063	285,452	193,753,515	21,474,416	4,049,471	176,328,570	45,845,628	35,598,216	44,018	5,856,125	3,436,652
2007	273,356,420	203,116,373	149,947	203,266,320	22,480,019	4,452,547	185,238,848	49,973,679	38,143,893	46,472	5,882,126	3,488,522
2008	280,540,550	203,658,980	174,113	203,833,093	23,232,276	4,837,359	185,438,176	52,481,263	42,621,111	47,494	5,906,917	3,501,109
2009	275,824,313	200,546,364	232,818	200,779,182	22,887,172	4,660,155	182,552,165	46,761,043	46,511,105	46,423	5,941,539	3,415,612
2010	287,819,509	208,338,362	226,958	208,565,320	23,228,996	5,036,991	190,373,315	46,421,402	51,024,792	48,175	5,974,469	3,410,318
2011	303,956,054	217,504,543	254,740	217,759,283	21,308,010	5,307,180	201,758,453	50,605,593	51,592,008	50,546	6,013,427	3,451,637
2012	318,151,947	226,650,992	359,274	227,010,266	21,946,081	5,838,121	210,902,306	55,591,235	51,658,406	52,609	6,047,506	3,476,814
2013	320,360,917	234,235,609	533,859	234,769,468	25,511,484	5,991,242	215,249,226	52,499,086	52,612,605	52,736	6,074,788	3,525,828
2014	332,785,937	240,702,492	560,375	241,262,867	26,392,363	6,503,640	221,374,144	56,468,816	54,942,977	54,499	6,106,258	3,585,855
2015	347,132,408	250,414,012	514,838	250,928,850	27,457,843	6,609,638	230,080,645	59,300,382	57,751,381	56,629	6,129,946	3,646,351
2016	360,525,766	259,412,154	453,212	259,865,366	28,097,433	6,887,263	238,655,196	61,244,746	60,625,824	58,589	6,153,468	3,728,461
2017	367,463,723	263,937,146	521,627	264,458,773	29,392,728	6,841,565	241,907,610	64,092,554	61,463,559	59,467	6,179,246	3,784,101
2018	386,607,449	272,948,202	379,745	273,327,947	30,353,299	7,479,160	250,453,808	70,555,329	65,598,312	62,282	6,207,400	3,848,572
2019	397,282,338	280,361,329	491,250	280,852,579	31,468,446	7,889,205	257,273,338	72,341,308	67,667,692	63,779	6,229,011	3,870,743
2020	422,834,425	280,298,275	470,705	280,768,980	31,486,200	7,669,635	256,952,415	75,267,738	90,614,272	67,745	6,241,540	3,710,046
2021	449,045,229	297,225,717	444,897	297,670,614	33,528,698	8,318,213	272,460,129	81,020,828	95,564,272	71,809	6,253,320	3,865,306
2022	457,424,000	316,662,005	440,661	317,102,666	36,686,193	8,409,750	288,826,223	85,851,256	82,746,521	73,291	6,241,164	4,070,548

Personal Income and Employment by Area: Phoenix-Mesa-Chandler, AZ

(Thousands of dollars, except as noted.)

		Derivation of personal income										
		Earnings by place of work										
Year	Personal income, total	Nonfarm	Farm	Total	Less: Contributions for government social insurance	Plus: Adjustment for residence	Equals: Net earnings by place of residence	Plus: Dividends, interest, and rent	Plus: Personal current transfer receipts	Per capita personal income (dollars)	Population (persons)	Total employment
1970	4,435,397	3,376,315	105,153	3,481,468	230,632	-21,339	3,229,497	869,987	335,913	4,225	1,049,680	456,574
1971	5,038,059	3,818,694	120,929	3,939,623	272,161	-21,368	3,646,094	991,866	400,099	4,579	1,100,219	478,419
1972	5,785,408	4,458,900	98,528	4,557,428	335,218	-14,476	4,207,734	1,117,667	460,007	4,970	1,163,970	522,280
1973	6,707,040	5,203,336	106,777	5,310,113	448,512	-11,443	4,850,158	1,298,017	558,865	5,419	1,237,668	574,470
1974	7,613,878	5,681,015	247,112	5,928,127	506,663	-19,760	5,401,704	1,525,580	686,594	5,848	1,301,957	592,448
1975	8,141,145	5,864,612	94,831	5,959,443	515,861	-28,218	5,415,364	1,737,879	987,902	6,086	1,337,680	573,360
1976	9,126,107	6,605,949	206,113	6,812,062	585,353	-38,357	6,188,352	1,876,238	1,061,517	6,679	1,366,423	603,064
1977	10,352,142	7,674,347	159,414	7,833,761	686,978	-39,000	7,107,783	2,119,572	1,124,787	7,306	1,416,931	654,968
1978	12,273,363	9,255,747	162,453	9,418,200	851,039	-36,532	8,530,629	2,482,221	1,260,513	8,313	1,476,485	728,998
1979	14,595,961	11,111,150	246,899	11,358,049	1,067,111	-42,081	10,248,857	2,910,284	1,436,820	9,439	1,546,348	792,672
1980	16,901,906	12,533,395	296,437	12,829,832	1,214,376	-54,931	11,560,525	3,607,698	1,733,683	10,484	1,612,182	820,853
1981	19,319,131	14,067,071	256,213	14,323,284	1,466,097	-51,903	12,805,284	4,468,071	2,045,776	11,645	1,658,988	843,575
1982	20,629,952	14,737,498	222,721	14,960,219	1,559,860	-42,589	13,357,770	5,000,586	2,271,596	12,074	1,708,649	847,957
1983	22,915,847	16,351,347	175,169	16,526,516	1,751,677	-30,908	14,743,931	5,688,947	2,482,969	13,007	1,761,819	895,053
1984	26,119,207	18,829,845	320,170	19,150,015	2,069,986	-33,099	17,046,930	6,393,602	2,678,675	14,215	1,837,457	988,892
1985	29,404,268	21,334,931	288,071	21,623,002	2,383,883	-41,013	19,198,106	7,280,246	2,925,916	15,220	1,931,978	1,074,363
1986	32,296,807	23,604,280	286,319	23,890,599	2,650,089	-44,240	21,196,270	7,861,792	3,238,745	16,042	2,013,320	1,130,847
1987	34,796,297	25,591,638	356,798	25,948,436	2,847,742	-36,320	23,064,374	8,198,846	3,533,077	16,549	2,102,571	1,175,415
1988	37,770,277	27,914,751	389,911	28,304,662	3,196,896	-50,403	25,057,363	8,834,107	3,878,807	17,465	2,162,647	1,224,682
1989	40,517,219	29,020,120	423,994	29,444,114	3,409,779	-15,279	26,019,056	10,026,805	4,471,358	18,271	2,217,530	1,247,064
1990	42,459,680	30,593,481	384,406	30,977,887	3,695,289	-12,219	27,270,379	10,267,252	4,922,049	18,878	2,249,116	1,266,338
1991	44,469,460	32,272,730	443,627	32,716,357	3,916,461	-4,641	28,795,255	10,190,186	5,484,019	19,174	2,319,206	1,263,249
1992	47,305,376	34,772,605	386,057	35,158,662	4,180,070	2,848	30,981,440	10,095,491	6,228,445	19,721	2,398,760	1,271,798
1993	50,654,537	37,487,249	422,391	37,909,640	4,508,566	13,764	33,414,838	10,542,676	6,697,023	20,328	2,491,818	1,328,795
1994	55,850,839	41,527,630	367,401	41,895,031	4,998,511	11,949	36,908,469	11,805,252	7,137,118	21,370	2,613,502	1,416,403
1995	61,571,188	45,740,134	406,849	46,146,983	5,289,086	-22,678	40,835,219	13,100,868	7,635,101	22,438	2,744,046	1,508,585
1996	67,376,089	50,860,346	443,806	51,304,152	5,996,757	-56,114	45,251,281	14,008,127	8,116,681	23,593	2,855,711	1,614,248
1997	73,811,348	55,763,048	422,315	56,185,363	6,482,785	-38,212	49,664,366	15,679,499	8,467,483	24,905	2,963,714	1,702,231
1998	81,144,061	62,364,632	455,635	62,820,267	7,128,742	-33,934	55,657,591	16,765,028	8,721,442	26,392	3,074,532	1,791,395
1999	86,389,270	67,092,192	443,376	67,535,568	7,661,580	-15,848	59,858,140	17,243,690	9,287,440	27,181	3,178,349	1,857,012
2000	94,608,262	74,076,763	361,990	74,438,753	8,419,870	-2,490	66,016,393	18,734,565	9,857,304	28,901	3,273,477	1,929,164
2001	97,797,511	76,025,167	348,160	76,373,327	8,754,785	75,431	67,693,973	18,934,164	11,169,374	29,074	3,363,736	1,952,759
2002	101,420,106	78,157,355	332,554	78,489,909	9,001,650	121,559	69,609,818	19,336,812	12,473,476	29,376	3,452,470	1,963,848
2003	107,267,836	81,811,893	374,421	82,186,314	9,295,506	175,317	73,066,125	20,581,645	13,620,066	30,333	3,536,388	2,015,178
2004	117,911,829	90,599,158	534,923	91,134,081	10,140,015	227,624	81,221,690	21,655,100	15,035,039	32,417	3,637,332	2,104,060
2005	130,916,460	100,898,978	474,740	101,373,718	11,181,850	261,959	90,453,827	23,788,215	16,674,418	34,683	3,774,696	2,245,169
2006	146,141,903	112,864,940	382,042	113,246,982	12,289,453	305,496	101,263,025	26,642,413	18,236,465	37,336	3,914,212	2,363,617
2007	153,933,545	117,234,171	424,484	117,658,655	12,966,649	400,360	105,092,366	29,017,550	19,823,629	38,310	4,018,128	2,425,687
2008	154,032,233	113,939,643	361,376	114,301,019	12,966,052	527,665	101,862,632	28,860,256	23,309,345	37,511	4,106,372	2,378,759
2009	144,533,225	104,510,259	214,933	104,725,192	12,239,195	508,847	92,994,844	25,378,719	26,159,662	34,797	4,153,609	2,246,740
2010	147,394,422	104,730,354	260,587	104,990,941	12,358,270	537,074	93,169,745	25,394,653	28,830,024	35,092	4,200,238	2,209,922
2011	155,637,518	109,597,660	488,444	110,086,104	11,481,999	563,854	99,167,959	27,647,259	28,822,300	36,767	4,233,021	2,264,679
2012	163,691,299	115,515,771	444,946	115,960,717	11,956,002	594,107	104,598,822	30,216,604	28,875,873	38,129	4,293,086	2,311,203
2013	167,844,870	121,180,548	631,709	121,812,257	14,105,420	631,817	108,338,654	29,588,255	29,917,961	38,590	4,349,413	2,375,863
2014	177,095,953	127,290,694	561,843	127,852,537	14,653,863	655,941	113,854,615	31,857,404	31,383,934	40,090	4,417,491	2,441,677
2015	187,753,244	134,592,832	547,427	135,140,259	15,534,439	656,731	120,262,551	34,681,818	32,808,875	41,828	4,488,678	2,529,496
2016	197,151,926	141,415,069	642,601	142,057,670	16,240,297	642,498	126,459,871	36,295,448	34,396,607	43,196	4,564,173	2,612,755
2017	209,485,781	149,822,737	575,794	150,398,531	17,191,926	662,706	133,869,311	38,868,380	36,748,090	45,249	4,629,645	2,693,850
2018	223,543,531	160,856,198	449,078	161,305,276	18,528,178	694,570	143,471,668	41,488,923	38,582,940	47,562	4,700,060	2,791,017
2019	240,612,139	172,534,648	532,290	173,066,938	19,873,313	722,109	153,915,734	45,403,761	41,292,644	50,332	4,780,473	2,859,233
2020	266,602,063	182,465,790	359,230	182,825,020	21,061,207	643,503	162,407,316	47,288,048	56,906,699	54,747	4,869,678	2,861,046
2021	294,187,028	200,764,281	329,592	201,093,873	23,023,801	643,469	178,713,541	52,806,211	62,667,276	59,518	4,942,837	2,996,012
2022	310,170,134	219,721,977	452,887	220,174,864	25,407,616	643,798	195,411,046	59,533,906	55,225,182	61,840	5,015,678	3,155,580

Personal Income and Employment by Area: Pine Bluff, AR

(Thousands of dollars, except as noted.)

Year	Personal income, total	Derivation of personal income									Per capita personal income (dollars)	Population (persons)	Total employment
		Earnings by place of work			Less: Contributions for government social insurance	Plus: Adjustment for residence	Equals: Net earnings by place of residence	Plus: Dividends, interest, and rent	Plus: Personal current transfer receipts				
		Nonfarm	Farm	Total									
1970	290,916	216,093	19,611	235,704	16,562	1,788	220,930	35,845	34,141	2,784	104,477	38,872
1971	320,454	233,791	24,064	257,855	18,270	1,696	241,281	39,906	39,267	3,090	103,719	39,197
1972	347,493	255,891	24,640	280,531	21,138	1,531	260,924	43,541	43,028	3,313	104,888	39,993
1973	405,124	285,991	44,097	330,088	27,314	1,070	303,844	49,656	51,624	3,887	104,231	41,117
1974	434,033	316,994	27,289	344,283	31,299	113	313,097	58,518	62,418	4,124	105,251	42,161
1975	476,783	332,287	34,207	366,494	31,913	-1,420	333,161	64,977	78,645	4,526	105,335	40,227
1976	535,406	374,787	39,947	414,734	36,522	-1,184	377,028	71,360	87,018	5,047	106,074	40,529
1977	592,237	423,222	39,313	462,535	41,774	-1,271	419,490	80,641	92,106	5,555	106,613	42,336
1978	679,727	504,132	48,248	552,380	50,778	-11,840	489,762	89,213	100,752	6,264	108,520	45,097
1979	758,622	587,653	44,581	632,234	61,539	-24,914	545,781	99,930	112,911	6,862	110,555	46,194
1980	826,097	657,337	14,601	671,938	68,113	-33,603	570,222	123,733	132,142	7,377	111,988	46,894
1981	908,759	661,580	39,133	700,713	73,591	-22,534	604,588	151,569	152,602	8,122	111,883	44,628
1982	919,412	646,749	23,206	669,955	74,269	-14,987	580,699	174,768	163,945	8,318	110,538	42,054
1983	965,322	691,675	11,379	703,054	80,028	-15,621	607,405	181,074	176,843	8,779	109,954	42,484
1984	1,050,782	745,001	28,861	773,862	89,511	-16,917	667,434	200,946	182,402	9,591	109,561	42,993
1985	1,100,685	783,931	26,203	810,134	95,465	-19,881	694,788	214,844	191,053	10,108	108,892	43,590
1986	1,183,722	882,991	23,889	906,880	108,926	-37,279	760,675	223,385	199,662	10,916	108,437	45,357
1987	1,206,566	872,370	39,024	911,394	105,889	-24,161	781,344	218,463	206,759	11,105	108,653	44,835
1988	1,308,853	933,750	66,385	1,000,135	119,358	-26,497	854,280	239,767	214,806	12,056	108,561	46,386
1989	1,364,000	968,517	42,115	1,010,632	125,893	-28,507	856,232	268,282	239,486	12,631	107,985	47,039
1990	1,426,899	1,038,584	34,870	1,073,454	137,678	-35,547	900,229	268,454	258,216	13,341	106,958	47,603
1991	1,465,028	1,027,682	46,134	1,073,816	132,871	-22,336	918,609	264,369	282,050	13,658	107,267	47,185
1992	1,575,015	1,099,015	66,146	1,165,161	139,970	-21,556	1,003,635	257,563	313,817	14,639	107,590	47,356
1993	1,637,900	1,146,494	52,152	1,198,646	146,765	-20,790	1,031,091	279,852	326,957	15,267	107,282	48,353
1994	1,710,195	1,174,682	83,601	1,258,283	150,940	-15,787	1,091,556	274,473	344,166	15,866	107,791	47,473
1995	1,771,298	1,227,698	54,941	1,282,639	157,250	-14,774	1,110,615	292,224	368,459	16,444	107,714	48,926
1996	1,856,929	1,254,948	94,248	1,349,196	159,871	-11,388	1,177,937	301,725	377,267	17,241	107,707	49,406
1997	1,901,690	1,300,372	83,386	1,383,758	165,901	-9,281	1,208,576	301,823	391,291	17,654	107,720	49,381
1998	1,986,528	1,366,548	76,277	1,442,825	172,916	-8,088	1,261,821	318,521	406,186	18,490	107,440	49,260
1999	2,021,839	1,410,344	84,910	1,495,254	177,056	-7,323	1,310,875	305,402	405,562	18,853	107,241	49,241
2000	2,106,151	1,487,956	73,583	1,561,539	184,671	-8,032	1,368,836	311,085	426,230	19,650	107,184	49,436
2001	2,191,330	1,520,876	86,656	1,607,532	188,925	-3,058	1,415,549	309,069	466,712	20,583	106,464	49,489
2002	2,247,467	1,566,228	52,075	1,618,303	193,491	-1,512	1,423,300	315,393	508,774	21,210	105,965	48,577
2003	2,380,048	1,635,879	114,982	1,750,861	200,270	-7,799	1,542,792	308,030	529,226	22,567	105,465	48,950
2004	2,499,561	1,735,825	131,864	1,867,689	210,942	-37,510	1,619,237	313,515	566,809	23,882	104,665	49,673
2005	2,511,164	1,776,121	94,666	1,870,787	215,141	-55,873	1,599,773	317,964	593,427	24,165	103,917	49,427
2006	2,554,455	1,833,264	67,729	1,900,993	225,450	-83,149	1,592,394	320,363	641,698	24,771	103,121	49,189
2007	2,676,860	1,825,899	93,705	1,919,604	226,746	-51,459	1,641,399	351,448	684,013	26,264	101,921	48,350
2008	2,734,403	1,835,894	88,118	1,924,012	232,574	-75,768	1,615,670	367,369	751,364	26,992	101,305	47,893
2009	2,743,014	1,848,829	58,638	1,907,467	236,870	-98,186	1,572,411	356,800	813,803	27,268	100,593	47,579
2010	2,790,954	1,913,702	47,601	1,961,303	244,396	-128,441	1,588,466	341,479	861,009	27,874	100,128	47,234
2011	2,857,788	1,924,809	55,028	1,979,837	221,564	-120,737	1,637,536	358,923	861,329	28,810	99,196	47,228
2012	2,896,207	1,957,905	95,159	2,053,064	222,771	-167,649	1,662,644	373,849	859,714	29,644	97,701	46,572
2013	2,937,349	1,881,549	181,994	2,063,543	240,527	-110,482	1,712,534	356,952	867,863	30,544	96,167	45,138
2014	2,946,001	1,869,147	125,121	1,994,268	243,549	-88,699	1,662,020	373,853	910,128	30,884	95,390	43,939
2015	2,933,742	1,839,542	82,058	1,921,600	240,921	-76,832	1,603,847	380,181	949,714	31,002	94,630	43,821
2016	2,922,519	1,850,775	68,771	1,919,546	241,490	-110,905	1,567,151	371,706	983,662	31,376	93,144	43,546
2017	2,994,787	1,883,868	89,960	1,973,828	247,396	-107,846	1,618,586	378,646	997,555	32,648	91,730	42,925
2018	3,019,105	1,908,510	76,360	1,984,870	250,868	-119,017	1,614,985	378,825	1,025,295	33,452	90,251	42,836
2019	3,077,312	1,936,912	57,653	1,994,565	255,019	-138,093	1,601,453	405,536	1,070,323	34,586	88,976	42,230
2020	3,263,583	1,976,847	60,592	2,037,439	264,151	-174,729	1,598,559	391,316	1,273,708	37,396	87,272	41,343
2021	3,506,890	2,060,251	154,241	2,214,492	272,982	-195,839	1,745,671	374,173	1,387,046	40,641	86,290	41,414
2022	3,429,629	2,135,017	155,670	2,290,687	288,324	-233,778	1,768,585	390,172	1,270,872	40,525	84,629	41,848

Personal Income and Employment by Area: Pittsburgh, PA

(Thousands of dollars, except as noted.)

Year	Personal income, total	Derivation of personal income								Per capita personal income (dollars)	Population (persons)	Total employment
		Earnings by place of work			Less: Contributions for government social insurance	Plus: Adjustment for residence	Equals: Net earnings by place of residence	Plus: Dividends, interest, and rent	Plus: Personal current transfer receipts			
		Nonfarm	Farm	Total								
1970	11,286,375	9,279,300	33,266	9,312,566	683,635	-29,634	8,599,297	1,521,282	1,165,796	4,091	2,758,743	1,132,359
1971	11,887,371	9,662,772	35,548	9,698,320	738,906	-37,685	8,921,729	1,598,328	1,367,314	4,306	2,760,937	1,113,813
1972	12,858,851	10,479,485	41,854	10,521,339	840,895	-45,876	9,634,568	1,688,684	1,535,599	4,673	2,751,873	1,124,028
1973	14,023,848	11,530,303	40,406	11,570,709	1,065,963	-57,855	10,446,891	1,859,448	1,717,509	5,137	2,730,057	1,154,111
1974	15,575,362	12,762,748	43,833	12,806,581	1,226,950	-85,046	11,494,585	2,108,740	1,972,037	5,762	2,703,028	1,167,040
1975	17,206,793	13,822,385	46,381	13,868,766	1,299,014	-100,947	12,468,805	2,289,266	2,448,722	6,371	2,700,715	1,159,949
1976	18,750,712	15,035,208	57,588	15,092,796	1,434,009	-105,426	13,553,361	2,459,345	2,738,006	6,960	2,693,955	1,169,981
1977	20,644,417	16,679,938	59,236	16,739,174	1,585,810	-128,573	15,024,791	2,723,794	2,895,832	7,693	2,683,597	1,185,498
1978	22,691,978	18,459,573	53,682	18,513,255	1,802,874	-153,678	16,556,703	3,008,296	3,126,979	8,484	2,674,747	1,210,116
1979	25,140,290	20,459,137	59,775	20,518,912	2,070,691	-183,553	18,264,668	3,385,695	3,489,927	9,453	2,659,625	1,231,366
1980	27,602,253	21,660,418	42,172	21,702,590	2,199,143	-191,313	19,312,134	4,225,252	4,064,867	10,430	2,646,406	1,214,171
1981	30,394,028	23,249,238	62,251	23,311,489	2,531,332	-204,533	20,575,624	5,255,415	4,562,989	11,554	2,630,712	1,200,978
1982	31,994,295	23,083,568	55,200	23,138,768	2,558,140	-97,502	20,483,126	6,117,626	5,393,543	12,210	2,620,312	1,156,673
1983	32,717,405	23,151,437	34,791	23,186,228	2,589,793	-43,873	20,552,562	6,327,320	5,837,523	12,551	2,606,777	1,121,342
1984	34,701,580	24,628,553	66,774	24,695,327	2,854,867	-26,397	21,814,063	7,017,455	5,870,062	13,440	2,581,947	1,133,457
1985	36,083,972	25,570,865	63,081	25,633,946	3,002,045	-8,046	22,623,855	7,429,325	6,030,792	14,191	2,542,677	1,144,718
1986	37,188,257	26,206,318	54,693	26,261,011	3,099,254	2,867	23,164,624	7,646,439	6,377,194	14,777	2,516,600	1,149,933
1987	38,560,333	27,752,365	50,953	27,803,318	3,232,771	10,858	24,581,405	7,452,688	6,526,240	15,456	2,494,837	1,176,201
1988	41,917,256	30,422,119	44,317	30,466,436	3,578,101	14,111	26,902,446	8,201,519	6,813,291	16,903	2,479,863	1,207,101
1989	44,941,998	32,247,720	56,804	32,304,524	3,754,299	16,778	28,567,003	9,250,962	7,124,033	18,196	2,469,921	1,228,910
1990	48,111,039	34,315,014	85,280	34,400,294	4,036,295	-5,653	30,358,346	9,875,991	7,876,702	19,481	2,469,681	1,257,869
1991	50,388,807	35,744,233	64,794	35,809,027	4,255,383	-36,916	31,516,728	9,879,642	8,992,437	20,343	2,476,980	1,250,192
1992	52,920,952	38,344,335	79,522	38,423,857	4,546,032	-84,786	33,793,039	9,678,394	9,449,519	21,287	2,486,034	1,259,326
1993	54,693,130	39,813,557	61,947	39,875,504	4,796,859	-121,255	34,957,390	9,732,169	10,003,571	21,957	2,490,949	1,267,305
1994	56,422,719	41,306,138	39,116	41,345,254	5,068,509	-138,297	36,138,448	10,036,465	10,247,806	22,687	2,486,989	1,282,644
1995	58,611,021	42,510,302	23,790	42,534,092	5,224,775	-159,045	37,150,272	10,783,217	10,677,532	23,633	2,480,098	1,296,271
1996	61,197,033	43,998,179	42,879	44,041,058	5,299,995	-184,908	38,556,155	11,402,984	11,237,894	24,764	2,471,209	1,303,923
1997	64,562,327	46,611,419	11,972	46,623,391	5,543,863	-214,747	40,864,781	12,256,614	11,440,932	26,243	2,460,208	1,320,252
1998	67,089,936	48,872,672	20,934	48,893,606	5,728,629	-243,632	42,921,345	12,702,777	11,465,814	27,386	2,449,747	1,332,351
1999	70,301,363	52,483,838	18,895	52,502,733	6,057,608	-311,466	46,133,659	12,274,889	11,892,815	28,830	2,438,518	1,354,381
2000	74,537,379	55,449,575	44,158	55,493,733	6,299,083	-353,546	48,841,104	13,278,916	12,417,359	30,695	2,428,303	1,380,946
2001	76,671,870	57,173,836	21,415	57,195,251	6,521,994	-432,315	50,240,942	13,246,301	13,184,627	31,716	2,417,480	1,386,079
2002	77,612,021	58,174,766	23,048	58,197,814	6,629,702	-477,051	51,091,061	12,690,452	13,830,508	32,226	2,408,348	1,377,904
2003	79,166,676	59,097,705	55,197	59,152,902	6,694,024	-481,417	51,977,461	12,807,799	14,381,416	32,970	2,401,168	1,364,794
2004	82,251,591	61,959,845	53,471	62,013,316	6,961,952	-528,360	54,523,004	12,875,509	14,853,078	34,428	2,389,107	1,372,741
2005	84,986,369	64,098,135	36,997	64,135,132	7,281,673	-543,097	56,310,362	12,735,550	15,940,457	35,792	2,374,483	1,378,014
2006	89,902,766	66,869,399	50,046	66,919,445	7,673,194	-629,498	58,616,753	14,462,905	16,823,108	38,029	2,364,039	1,389,175
2007	94,677,376	69,389,637	35,495	69,425,132	7,935,593	-613,220	60,876,319	15,913,294	17,887,763	40,136	2,358,914	1,410,002
2008	99,192,841	71,928,007	34,357	71,962,364	8,231,777	-615,354	63,115,233	16,559,989	19,517,619	42,088	2,356,802	1,414,784
2009	96,836,520	69,821,133	30,205	69,851,338	8,136,341	-471,775	61,243,222	14,984,434	20,608,864	41,112	2,355,432	1,385,483
2010	100,859,102	73,170,188	46,650	73,216,838	8,435,988	-503,008	64,277,842	14,702,608	21,878,652	42,763	2,358,574	1,390,567
2011	106,258,222	76,829,701	59,771	76,889,472	7,923,399	-583,734	68,382,339	16,141,921	21,733,962	44,872	2,368,043	1,413,964
2012	109,682,807	78,841,652	85,730	78,927,382	8,130,220	-534,074	70,263,088	17,698,688	21,721,031	46,200	2,374,103	1,432,379
2013	110,506,423	82,019,389	59,638	82,079,027	9,439,903	-536,425	72,102,699	16,597,215	21,806,509	46,441	2,379,483	1,440,765
2014	114,259,084	84,364,258	73,652	84,437,910	9,692,971	-549,287	74,195,652	17,684,552	22,378,880	47,970	2,381,872	1,449,400
2015	118,797,289	88,229,931	33,296	88,263,227	10,088,313	-702,587	77,472,327	18,204,425	23,120,537	49,927	2,379,439	1,458,996
2016	120,442,926	88,448,730	15,492	88,464,222	10,135,474	-736,795	77,591,953	18,730,256	24,120,717	50,652	2,377,835	1,463,729
2017	125,775,006	93,296,950	52,154	93,349,104	10,760,642	-863,883	81,724,579	19,902,041	24,148,386	53,021	2,372,173	1,477,171
2018	133,076,743	98,156,744	10,905	98,167,649	11,206,083	-912,939	86,048,627	21,402,865	25,625,251	56,109	2,371,737	1,496,389
2019	136,401,937	100,306,171	56,800	100,362,971	11,578,989	-996,992	87,786,990	22,385,219	26,229,728	57,515	2,371,584	1,494,094
2020	145,500,657	98,530,024	37,468	98,567,492	11,299,441	-968,735	86,299,316	22,780,349	36,420,992	61,414	2,369,166	1,415,717
2021	154,855,254	104,313,953	56,166	104,370,119	11,950,430	-1,154,508	91,265,181	25,816,995	37,773,078	65,473	2,365,176	1,449,415
2022	154,556,344	109,428,037	38,970	109,467,007	12,861,163	-1,159,610	95,446,234	27,465,312	31,644,798	65,792	2,349,172	1,499,454

Personal Income and Employment by Area: Pittsfield, MA

(Thousands of dollars, except as noted.)

Year	Personal income, total	Derivation of personal income: Earnings by place of work: Nonfarm	Farm	Total	Less: Contributions for government social insurance	Plus: Adjustment for residence	Equals: Net earnings by place of residence	Plus: Dividends, interest, and rent	Plus: Personal current transfer receipts	Per capita personal income (dollars)	Population (persons)	Total employment
1970	617,044	483,166	3,850	487,016	32,373	-3,355	451,288	97,099	68,657	4,117	149,893	66,119
1971	657,388	510,589	3,674	514,263	35,381	-2,942	475,940	102,987	78,461	4,354	150,987	65,091
1972	706,423	550,362	3,487	553,849	40,377	-2,114	511,358	110,296	84,769	4,745	148,869	65,585
1973	779,029	615,450	3,547	618,997	52,376	-1,649	564,972	118,250	95,807	5,208	149,573	69,449
1974	845,894	665,072	3,067	668,139	58,309	-613	609,217	128,383	108,294	5,653	149,649	70,334
1975	906,579	678,703	3,696	682,399	57,405	2,048	627,042	133,712	145,825	6,093	148,788	67,804
1976	958,249	716,704	3,568	720,272	61,743	5,004	663,533	141,123	153,593	6,547	146,360	66,846
1977	1,018,502	758,234	3,476	761,710	65,540	8,290	704,460	154,669	159,373	7,033	144,826	67,029
1978	1,119,412	840,858	4,563	845,421	75,018	11,558	781,961	168,554	168,897	7,649	146,354	68,925
1979	1,235,703	919,454	4,285	923,739	85,047	16,074	854,766	188,762	192,175	8,496	145,437	71,249
1980	1,378,606	993,177	4,098	997,275	91,459	20,510	926,326	232,801	219,479	9,502	145,081	71,264
1981	1,519,562	1,071,558	3,527	1,075,085	106,361	17,275	985,999	284,049	249,514	10,507	144,629	70,426
1982	1,649,138	1,132,450	4,247	1,136,697	114,762	12,738	1,034,673	340,322	274,143	11,600	142,162	69,487
1983	1,757,820	1,214,423	5,004	1,219,427	124,006	8,175	1,103,596	359,098	295,126	12,382	141,969	69,795
1984	1,946,220	1,360,789	6,718	1,367,507	142,937	2,695	1,227,265	407,931	311,024	13,728	141,767	72,759
1985	2,065,312	1,468,209	6,393	1,474,602	154,863	-4,547	1,315,192	425,747	324,373	14,654	140,938	74,546
1986	2,206,429	1,583,822	7,153	1,590,975	169,895	-11,783	1,409,297	457,813	339,319	15,716	140,396	77,067
1987	2,317,103	1,691,754	5,607	1,697,361	178,957	-19,259	1,499,145	467,802	350,156	16,519	140,268	76,319
1988	2,507,654	1,823,597	4,308	1,827,905	196,152	-28,564	1,603,189	525,622	378,843	17,939	139,787	78,504
1989	2,694,675	1,921,883	4,253	1,926,136	207,654	-41,245	1,677,237	598,639	418,799	19,277	139,790	79,087
1990	2,773,245	1,952,357	4,723	1,957,080	206,803	-50,866	1,699,411	612,988	460,846	19,891	139,423	77,748
1991	2,800,241	1,884,720	4,606	1,889,326	203,878	-44,005	1,641,443	630,749	528,049	20,195	138,661	73,552
1992	2,826,054	1,947,641	6,006	1,953,647	208,414	-38,662	1,706,571	572,630	546,853	20,507	137,809	73,706
1993	2,937,238	1,999,234	3,839	2,003,073	216,245	-35,854	1,750,974	622,439	563,825	21,418	137,139	75,102
1994	3,038,487	2,051,924	3,836	2,055,760	222,327	-31,104	1,802,329	639,709	596,449	22,150	137,176	75,643
1995	3,163,488	2,126,956	2,251	2,129,207	231,994	-29,002	1,868,211	668,611	626,666	23,111	136,885	75,632
1996	3,343,974	2,241,361	3,080	2,244,441	239,526	-25,780	1,979,135	721,230	643,609	24,470	136,657	76,886
1997	3,500,975	2,372,122	3,455	2,375,577	251,705	-24,135	2,099,737	735,198	666,040	25,629	136,602	77,231
1998	3,666,091	2,485,609	3,980	2,489,589	262,025	-18,764	2,208,800	801,307	655,984	27,004	135,763	78,323
1999	3,830,135	2,648,390	4,693	2,653,083	272,067	-13,474	2,367,542	783,310	679,283	28,324	135,227	79,056
2000	4,084,396	2,804,649	4,787	2,809,436	284,489	-3,008	2,521,939	855,192	707,265	30,307	134,769	79,393
2001	4,194,613	2,842,878	3,854	2,846,732	296,753	-8,362	2,541,617	884,519	768,477	31,320	133,928	79,964
2002	4,260,048	2,985,494	3,471	2,988,965	312,897	-24,233	2,651,835	781,857	826,356	31,904	133,529	80,215
2003	4,268,474	2,970,527	3,381	2,973,908	310,840	-26,016	2,637,052	750,628	880,794	31,992	133,423	79,899
2004	4,559,607	3,162,220	5,350	3,167,570	340,713	-32,587	2,794,270	844,623	920,714	34,263	133,076	80,033
2005	4,699,608	3,299,137	3,717	3,302,854	363,473	-40,980	2,898,401	810,395	990,812	35,452	132,563	81,563
2006	4,905,537	3,427,218	1,414	3,428,632	374,589	-48,353	3,005,690	855,806	1,044,041	37,170	131,977	82,230
2007	5,113,607	3,500,140	834	3,500,974	384,553	-54,014	3,062,407	969,097	1,082,103	38,774	131,883	83,314
2008	5,357,207	3,531,975	1,899	3,533,874	391,830	-62,981	3,079,063	1,062,451	1,215,693	40,779	131,372	83,437
2009	5,275,171	3,436,914	2,765	3,439,679	381,490	-67,451	2,990,738	968,273	1,316,160	40,187	131,264	81,385
2010	5,393,754	3,525,530	3,650	3,529,180	378,938	-65,832	3,084,410	925,040	1,384,304	41,040	131,427	80,928
2011	5,651,268	3,640,007	3,520	3,643,527	355,028	-70,444	3,218,055	1,031,380	1,401,833	43,105	131,106	81,163
2012	5,831,873	3,712,457	7,898	3,720,355	361,136	-73,011	3,286,208	1,111,769	1,433,896	44,417	131,297	82,429
2013	5,807,805	3,752,770	7,654	3,760,424	408,541	-73,587	3,278,296	1,084,584	1,444,925	44,353	130,946	83,429
2014	6,094,984	3,861,994	2,424	3,864,418	423,122	-69,422	3,371,874	1,232,157	1,490,953	46,612	130,759	84,001
2015	6,432,625	4,029,385	-664	4,028,721	433,989	-69,224	3,525,508	1,304,331	1,602,786	49,406	130,199	86,256
2016	6,584,919	4,148,293	-2,795	4,145,498	448,466	-73,715	3,623,317	1,300,305	1,661,297	50,712	129,850	85,654
2017	6,756,230	4,232,120	-966	4,231,154	460,603	-67,369	3,703,182	1,366,665	1,686,383	52,131	129,601	85,831
2018	7,030,940	4,373,249	-1,753	4,371,496	477,705	-70,224	3,823,567	1,441,555	1,765,818	54,231	129,648	85,860
2019	7,252,884	4,471,193	1,872	4,473,065	488,324	-58,906	3,925,835	1,516,741	1,810,308	56,172	129,119	84,836
2020	7,870,500	4,438,394	210	4,438,604	482,957	-53,100	3,902,547	1,554,487	2,413,466	61,119	128,774	78,370
2021	8,288,857	4,677,348	304	4,677,652	517,197	-47,955	4,112,500	1,578,506	2,597,851	64,444	128,621	81,251
2022	8,279,881	4,976,787	2,460	4,979,247	550,397	-50,289	4,378,561	1,649,868	2,251,452	64,758	127,859	85,015

Personal Income and Employment by Area: Pocatello, ID

(Thousands of dollars, except as noted.)

Year	Personal income, total	Derivation of personal income: Earnings by place of work: Nonfarm	Farm	Total	Less: Contributions for government social insurance	Plus: Adjustment for residence	Equals: Net earnings by place of residence	Plus: Dividends, interest, and rent	Plus: Personal current transfer receipts	Per capita personal income (dollars)	Population (persons)	Total employment
1970	203,057	155,677	10,335	166,012	12,903	3,645	156,754	28,588	17,715	3,553	57,149	25,264
1971	222,187	169,033	10,121	179,154	14,174	3,378	168,358	32,657	21,172	3,829	58,032	25,643
1972	251,464	189,932	14,414	204,346	16,589	4,003	191,760	35,867	23,837	4,243	59,267	26,383
1973	286,795	218,148	18,992	237,140	22,016	4,428	219,552	40,378	26,865	4,806	59,678	28,206
1974	330,492	252,898	22,026	274,924	26,429	4,432	252,927	46,444	31,121	5,384	61,389	29,701
1975	374,512	292,376	13,566	305,942	29,681	3,850	280,111	55,371	39,030	5,965	62,788	31,294
1976	437,143	352,034	14,348	366,382	36,253	4,323	334,452	59,748	42,943	6,630	65,932	33,799
1977	481,350	394,315	9,160	403,475	40,959	5,078	367,594	67,491	46,265	6,993	68,838	35,710
1978	544,278	439,262	14,774	454,036	46,095	7,862	415,803	76,645	51,830	7,715	70,546	36,773
1979	594,256	477,865	12,783	490,648	52,351	9,900	448,197	86,292	59,767	8,302	71,582	36,807
1980	646,584	507,297	15,995	523,292	55,988	10,799	478,103	96,939	71,542	8,916	72,516	35,440
1981	708,260	539,324	25,044	564,368	64,045	15,176	515,499	113,048	79,713	9,645	73,434	34,976
1982	746,314	554,870	18,374	573,244	68,358	18,433	523,319	133,241	89,754	10,083	74,016	34,132
1983	806,799	580,681	32,297	612,978	71,505	25,231	566,704	144,459	95,636	10,860	74,293	33,992
1984	838,699	608,123	23,290	631,413	78,210	29,820	583,023	156,045	99,631	11,301	74,217	34,514
1985	899,474	651,010	22,682	673,692	85,165	33,109	621,636	170,922	106,916	12,109	74,284	34,916
1986	894,347	625,327	26,690	652,017	82,884	40,315	609,448	172,563	112,336	12,045	74,251	33,031
1987	917,575	636,866	32,700	669,566	81,816	49,314	637,064	165,953	114,558	12,512	73,338	32,985
1988	953,053	671,236	28,279	699,515	91,552	52,797	660,760	170,539	121,754	13,106	72,718	34,401
1989	1,027,740	711,151	39,228	750,379	98,851	54,780	706,308	188,126	133,306	14,078	73,002	34,940
1990	1,091,907	749,076	53,436	802,512	108,467	62,382	756,427	191,157	144,323	14,894	73,312	35,462
1991	1,147,834	788,004	36,236	824,240	114,663	79,368	788,945	198,344	160,545	15,404	74,517	36,230
1992	1,247,071	858,749	46,415	905,164	120,908	76,257	860,513	204,356	182,202	16,292	76,544	37,488
1993	1,341,924	932,013	50,599	982,612	131,273	75,316	926,655	221,231	194,038	17,145	78,268	39,239
1994	1,396,763	982,827	38,754	1,021,581	137,719	72,453	956,315	236,245	204,203	17,426	80,153	40,991
1995	1,471,871	1,015,731	43,379	1,059,110	142,745	72,238	988,603	260,784	222,484	18,099	81,323	41,626
1996	1,554,954	1,081,870	50,502	1,132,372	148,976	65,330	1,048,726	272,373	233,855	19,028	81,721	43,451
1997	1,596,638	1,125,001	28,607	1,153,608	153,205	67,567	1,067,970	287,441	241,227	19,397	82,315	44,125
1998	1,682,235	1,206,136	33,213	1,239,349	159,450	66,116	1,146,015	292,627	243,593	20,356	82,642	45,342
1999	1,736,557	1,266,425	46,713	1,313,138	163,775	49,167	1,198,530	284,350	253,677	20,885	83,150	46,228
2000	1,813,120	1,323,110	51,085	1,374,195	170,225	47,363	1,251,333	292,612	269,175	21,789	83,212	47,657
2001	1,884,096	1,351,902	35,714	1,387,616	173,600	66,025	1,280,041	299,998	304,057	22,505	83,718	47,949
2002	1,941,428	1,350,045	53,321	1,403,366	173,125	70,207	1,300,448	307,853	333,127	23,151	83,858	47,256
2003	1,999,820	1,402,632	33,764	1,436,396	179,209	68,304	1,325,491	326,590	347,739	23,920	83,605	47,934
2004	2,139,919	1,506,923	50,898	1,557,821	192,679	65,872	1,431,014	332,949	375,956	25,395	84,266	49,501
2005	2,215,313	1,579,110	42,079	1,621,189	204,931	66,928	1,483,186	333,401	398,726	26,110	84,845	50,751
2006	2,373,407	1,651,159	52,468	1,703,627	215,335	80,065	1,568,357	371,970	433,080	27,580	86,055	51,729
2007	2,497,108	1,711,018	67,678	1,778,696	223,221	83,838	1,639,313	393,890	463,905	28,745	86,870	52,540
2008	2,580,981	1,737,234	53,544	1,790,778	227,750	88,881	1,651,909	397,612	531,460	29,272	88,173	51,215
2009	2,551,049	1,667,060	49,119	1,716,179	223,436	108,795	1,601,538	376,613	572,898	28,465	89,622	49,342
2010	2,633,405	1,690,709	53,856	1,744,565	234,190	121,107	1,631,482	368,984	632,939	28,980	90,869	48,335
2011	2,769,471	1,719,337	81,893	1,801,230	215,064	137,358	1,723,524	401,505	644,442	30,338	91,288	48,694
2012	2,848,064	1,750,760	80,291	1,831,051	217,514	150,006	1,763,543	434,148	650,373	31,182	91,338	48,559
2013	2,887,895	1,795,549	76,327	1,871,876	239,456	162,073	1,794,493	431,802	661,600	31,772	90,893	49,031
2014	2,955,319	1,853,811	49,312	1,903,123	249,282	159,806	1,813,647	458,643	683,029	32,547	90,801	49,803
2015	3,122,488	1,938,736	57,478	1,996,214	255,949	166,328	1,906,593	497,215	718,680	34,198	91,306	50,663
2016	3,189,396	1,986,688	48,954	2,035,642	263,728	184,799	1,956,713	489,189	743,494	34,807	91,632	51,082
2017	3,361,393	2,085,052	31,237	2,116,289	277,300	206,904	2,045,893	540,932	774,568	36,443	92,237	52,004
2018	3,487,802	2,164,380	50,542	2,214,922	284,891	217,435	2,147,466	526,961	813,375	37,360	93,357	52,645
2019	3,684,319	2,255,364	66,983	2,322,347	294,383	233,907	2,261,871	570,434	852,014	39,091	94,251	53,516
2020	4,071,830	2,379,675	88,129	2,467,804	315,498	251,048	2,403,354	611,932	1,056,544	42,795	95,147	53,099
2021	4,432,208	2,560,260	46,049	2,606,309	330,784	266,587	2,542,112	648,714	1,241,382	46,021	96,308	54,733
2022	4,632,407	2,739,578	85,338	2,824,916	361,188	286,403	2,750,131	723,544	1,158,732	47,470	97,585	57,233

Personal Income and Employment by Area: Portland-South Portland, ME

(Thousands of dollars, except as noted.)

Year	Personal income, total	Derivation of personal income: Earnings by place of work: Nonfarm	Farm	Total	Less: Contributions for government social insurance	Plus: Adjustment for residence	Equals: Net earnings by place of residence	Plus: Dividends, interest, and rent	Plus: Personal current transfer receipts	Per capita personal income (dollars)	Population (persons)	Total employment
1970	1,309,394	1,052,479	7,804	1,060,283	71,698	-38,473	950,112	239,994	119,288	3,985	328,590	156,769
1971	1,412,610	1,119,076	7,885	1,126,961	78,837	-36,951	1,011,173	260,636	140,801	4,202	336,169	155,953
1972	1,564,546	1,247,512	8,971	1,256,483	92,402	-42,343	1,121,738	284,116	158,692	4,562	342,955	160,994
1973	1,715,429	1,352,873	14,673	1,367,546	114,173	-39,605	1,213,768	312,092	189,569	4,908	349,490	165,759
1974	1,876,732	1,458,545	12,171	1,470,716	127,325	-50,650	1,292,741	353,833	230,158	5,270	356,106	169,317
1975	2,075,896	1,583,433	10,744	1,594,177	135,312	-66,038	1,392,827	387,620	295,449	5,752	360,891	170,259
1976	2,336,245	1,809,000	17,917	1,826,917	157,854	-75,808	1,593,255	419,222	323,768	6,397	365,186	177,404
1977	2,572,894	2,004,274	8,929	2,013,203	175,222	-84,894	1,753,087	474,479	345,328	6,906	372,562	184,124
1978	2,882,269	2,264,861	10,650	2,275,511	204,215	-95,892	1,975,404	536,078	370,787	7,628	377,860	193,643
1979	3,193,158	2,515,682	6,276	2,521,958	234,416	-104,731	2,182,811	591,991	418,356	8,334	383,159	200,253
1980	3,620,994	2,807,558	4,152	2,811,710	260,393	-117,323	2,433,994	701,878	485,122	9,387	385,753	204,838
1981	4,015,477	3,087,550	6,089	3,093,639	305,905	-169,384	2,618,350	841,604	555,523	10,268	391,072	207,150
1982	4,434,600	3,355,873	8,144	3,364,017	338,426	-192,715	2,832,876	996,269	605,455	11,244	394,395	210,235
1983	4,810,737	3,656,001	2,920	3,658,921	377,092	-191,734	3,090,095	1,068,214	652,428	12,049	399,275	217,658
1984	5,378,422	4,093,914	9,110	4,103,024	438,249	-191,245	3,473,530	1,215,615	689,277	13,265	405,463	228,798
1985	5,912,864	4,507,243	6,880	4,514,123	484,748	-170,169	3,859,206	1,318,051	735,607	14,359	411,789	239,590
1986	6,526,759	5,016,674	9,923	5,026,597	547,026	-164,003	4,315,568	1,443,323	767,868	15,615	417,991	254,199
1987	7,117,002	5,565,047	8,278	5,573,325	606,622	-161,697	4,805,006	1,522,239	789,757	16,752	424,840	265,537
1988	7,956,777	6,252,052	7,575	6,259,627	694,910	-183,844	5,380,873	1,736,463	839,441	18,349	433,634	281,206
1989	8,615,762	6,711,790	5,378	6,717,168	738,713	-212,618	5,765,837	1,947,095	902,830	19,637	438,759	287,046
1990	9,003,629	6,951,046	13,093	6,964,139	807,287	-223,226	5,933,626	2,063,251	1,006,752	20,334	442,790	285,041
1991	9,117,340	6,885,007	10,943	6,895,950	807,394	-180,000	5,908,556	2,052,070	1,156,714	20,469	445,414	273,772
1992	9,548,920	7,195,091	15,223	7,210,314	854,237	-153,002	6,203,075	2,072,928	1,272,917	21,367	446,901	274,413
1993	9,890,647	7,382,640	12,704	7,395,344	895,274	-95,209	6,404,861	2,143,853	1,341,933	21,997	449,643	276,688
1994	10,375,537	7,727,257	10,031	7,737,288	956,241	-48,463	6,732,584	2,240,760	1,402,193	22,869	453,695	283,211
1995	10,966,934	8,008,107	11,513	8,019,620	997,819	6,300	7,028,101	2,455,112	1,483,721	23,970	457,522	285,360
1996	11,671,680	8,405,806	10,943	8,416,749	1,035,159	59,434	7,441,024	2,640,482	1,590,174	25,161	463,883	290,659
1997	12,508,521	9,010,082	9,895	9,019,977	1,106,313	89,294	8,002,958	2,838,731	1,666,832	26,604	470,167	299,375
1998	13,486,835	9,724,590	11,029	9,735,619	1,179,976	145,922	8,701,565	3,075,946	1,709,324	28,367	475,444	307,580
1999	14,216,813	10,519,756	11,685	10,531,441	1,256,114	192,173	9,467,500	2,980,578	1,768,735	29,498	481,966	313,419
2000	15,343,504	11,227,090	15,799	11,242,889	1,315,947	302,248	10,229,190	3,215,968	1,898,346	31,366	489,179	323,073
2001	16,301,347	11,969,046	14,888	11,983,934	1,376,874	286,447	10,893,507	3,356,934	2,050,906	32,934	494,975	329,579
2002	16,735,136	12,448,096	14,484	12,462,580	1,391,857	259,110	11,329,833	3,217,405	2,187,898	33,458	500,178	330,406
2003	17,656,580	13,075,126	14,401	13,089,527	1,446,160	197,948	11,841,315	3,444,762	2,370,503	34,973	504,858	335,314
2004	18,774,883	13,959,699	14,523	13,974,222	1,539,684	170,238	12,604,776	3,648,651	2,521,456	36,927	508,428	343,206
2005	19,111,832	14,128,754	11,028	14,139,782	1,571,883	186,482	12,754,381	3,623,976	2,733,475	37,453	510,287	343,177
2006	20,261,441	14,932,136	10,704	14,942,840	1,673,029	204,177	13,473,988	3,989,706	2,797,747	39,681	510,614	348,302
2007	21,024,291	15,367,138	9,300	15,376,438	1,753,437	190,808	13,813,809	4,208,838	3,001,644	41,042	512,265	353,985
2008	21,906,360	15,671,738	19,729	15,691,467	1,805,265	180,588	14,066,790	4,342,126	3,497,444	42,604	514,191	353,548
2009	21,684,249	15,430,672	23,744	15,454,416	1,766,965	214,271	13,901,722	3,998,521	3,784,006	42,128	514,728	343,982
2010	22,359,636	15,936,951	32,781	15,969,732	1,817,954	300,517	14,452,295	4,027,875	3,879,466	43,489	514,139	342,258
2011	23,451,123	16,258,777	29,569	16,288,346	1,667,704	390,982	15,011,624	4,415,974	4,023,525	45,339	517,237	345,585
2012	24,061,595	16,605,195	32,327	16,637,522	1,724,455	445,322	15,358,389	4,682,187	4,021,019	46,293	519,765	347,962
2013	24,210,829	16,862,178	23,794	16,885,972	2,010,123	516,158	15,392,007	4,672,867	4,145,955	46,286	523,073	351,279
2014	25,112,929	17,446,372	21,604	17,467,976	2,059,916	599,855	16,007,915	4,812,782	4,292,232	47,558	528,051	355,939
2015	26,375,861	18,292,782	17,442	18,310,224	2,186,419	612,285	16,736,090	5,160,793	4,478,978	49,687	530,845	362,246
2016	27,644,709	19,049,171	16,065	19,065,236	2,268,849	636,443	17,432,830	5,592,709	4,619,170	51,674	534,979	369,464
2017	29,080,726	20,008,500	17,330	20,025,830	2,369,836	644,108	18,300,102	5,978,556	4,802,068	53,956	538,968	376,369
2018	30,595,797	21,062,887	12,863	21,075,750	2,513,217	669,263	19,231,796	6,263,104	5,100,897	56,288	543,562	383,047
2019	32,330,074	22,101,972	18,499	22,120,471	2,629,968	717,561	20,208,064	6,707,935	5,414,075	58,957	548,370	384,188
2020	35,077,770	23,000,332	16,468	23,016,800	2,724,735	769,894	21,061,959	6,818,756	7,197,055	63,483	552,550	369,900
2021	38,651,017	25,567,821	17,266	25,585,087	3,050,906	866,228	23,400,409	7,524,907	7,725,701	69,217	558,405	388,780
2022	40,428,120	27,568,435	23,544	27,591,979	3,318,103	794,761	25,068,637	8,150,260	7,209,223	71,990	561,576	403,480

Personal Income and Employment by Area: Portland-Vancouver-Hillsboro, OR-WA

(Thousands of dollars, except as noted.)

Year	Personal income, total	Derivation of personal income: Earnings by place of work: Nonfarm	Earnings by place of work: Farm	Earnings by place of work: Total	Less: Contributions for government social insurance	Plus: Adjustment for residence	Equals: Net earnings by place of residence	Plus: Dividends, interest, and rent	Plus: Personal current transfer receipts	Per capita personal income (dollars)	Population (persons)	Total employment
1970	4,839,750	3,841,363	48,010	3,889,373	294,374	9,352	3,604,351	807,901	427,498	4,460	1,085,025	497,091
1971	5,289,170	4,160,169	44,528	4,204,697	328,026	23,091	3,899,762	892,268	497,140	4,785	1,105,374	506,310
1972	5,892,337	4,690,577	48,379	4,738,956	392,279	37,872	4,384,549	968,100	539,688	5,195	1,134,259	535,293
1973	6,599,173	5,270,140	83,122	5,353,262	510,759	47,463	4,889,966	1,075,874	633,333	5,700	1,157,768	564,082
1974	7,470,277	5,904,154	79,239	5,983,393	586,768	58,077	5,454,702	1,248,745	766,830	6,359	1,174,809	583,002
1975	8,291,936	6,364,377	72,248	6,436,625	616,976	99,017	5,918,666	1,397,285	975,985	6,953	1,192,510	587,075
1976	9,287,115	7,220,112	70,781	7,290,893	712,908	125,697	6,703,682	1,518,155	1,065,278	7,656	1,213,090	609,841
1977	10,335,263	8,167,539	71,689	8,239,228	813,974	78,467	7,503,721	1,698,889	1,132,653	8,319	1,242,430	640,432
1978	11,888,345	9,536,300	69,748	9,606,048	977,647	48,857	8,677,258	1,979,454	1,231,633	9,322	1,275,246	683,210
1979	13,496,217	10,906,532	82,997	10,989,529	1,162,884	14,792	9,841,437	2,284,684	1,370,096	10,284	1,312,315	719,013
1980	15,117,261	11,935,285	81,851	12,017,136	1,272,567	3,955	10,748,524	2,760,290	1,608,447	11,225	1,346,705	728,447
1981	16,530,877	12,643,346	83,103	12,726,449	1,436,597	14,146	11,303,998	3,365,907	1,860,972	12,115	1,364,523	717,025
1982	17,170,565	12,717,462	69,321	12,786,783	1,470,701	40,716	11,356,798	3,697,025	2,116,742	12,503	1,373,347	694,891
1983	18,137,118	13,260,740	74,090	13,334,830	1,550,685	61,243	11,845,388	3,992,941	2,298,789	13,229	1,371,007	703,207
1984	19,770,381	14,616,848	109,744	14,726,592	1,768,828	58,169	13,015,933	4,391,441	2,363,007	14,323	1,380,339	734,223
1985	20,842,229	15,482,959	109,246	15,592,205	1,885,163	50,850	13,757,892	4,631,882	2,452,455	14,979	1,391,424	754,432
1986	22,103,675	16,557,928	158,946	16,716,874	2,010,221	51,015	14,757,668	4,833,118	2,512,889	15,679	1,409,733	775,492
1987	23,272,623	17,724,844	150,209	17,875,053	2,121,464	49,291	15,802,880	4,867,155	2,602,588	16,352	1,423,238	803,521
1988	25,596,351	19,732,690	182,506	19,915,196	2,435,516	49,649	17,529,329	5,317,287	2,749,735	17,602	1,454,141	845,832
1989	28,319,465	21,597,097	187,842	21,784,939	2,663,638	57,593	19,178,894	6,122,204	3,018,367	19,042	1,487,217	883,562
1990	31,084,849	23,954,711	240,900	24,195,611	3,033,477	55,643	21,217,777	6,597,378	3,269,694	20,238	1,535,965	918,239
1991	32,844,316	25,387,312	267,345	25,654,657	3,253,596	64,719	22,465,780	6,745,978	3,632,558	20,725	1,584,767	929,685
1992	35,216,676	27,456,074	246,867	27,702,941	3,492,382	59,318	24,269,877	6,911,260	4,035,539	21,662	1,625,751	941,423
1993	37,806,332	29,485,790	249,269	29,735,059	3,752,649	49,986	26,032,396	7,466,259	4,307,677	22,643	1,669,701	969,806
1994	40,759,072	31,747,442	230,689	31,978,131	4,077,627	42,763	27,943,267	8,368,352	4,447,453	23,861	1,708,216	1,022,108
1995	44,234,857	34,294,787	238,680	34,533,467	4,428,385	5,812	30,110,894	9,240,856	4,883,107	25,288	1,749,224	1,065,398
1996	48,245,598	37,666,234	268,174	37,934,408	4,895,457	-31,434	33,007,517	10,022,531	5,215,550	26,847	1,797,066	1,112,001
1997	51,852,622	40,966,216	318,191	41,284,407	5,236,441	-68,052	35,979,914	10,514,098	5,358,610	28,183	1,839,867	1,160,405
1998	54,916,305	43,727,458	319,646	44,047,104	5,546,839	-74,085	38,426,180	11,060,270	5,429,855	29,283	1,875,365	1,188,161
1999	56,933,284	46,061,977	327,765	46,389,742	5,773,690	-75,570	40,540,482	10,522,718	5,870,084	29,866	1,906,262	1,203,732
2000	62,431,805	50,806,441	298,757	51,105,198	6,332,901	-126,097	44,646,200	11,445,058	6,340,547	32,268	1,934,792	1,230,760
2001	63,565,533	51,119,521	327,285	51,446,806	6,315,077	-93,420	45,038,309	11,373,506	7,153,718	32,248	1,971,152	1,230,201
2002	63,847,823	51,070,870	320,698	51,391,568	6,321,772	-57,133	45,012,663	10,962,201	7,872,959	31,877	2,002,918	1,213,424
2003	66,003,568	52,492,925	405,955	52,898,880	6,502,375	-8,924	46,387,581	11,559,224	8,056,763	32,609	2,024,115	1,216,510
2004	70,050,867	56,067,628	423,329	56,490,957	6,989,256	5,541	49,507,242	12,322,461	8,221,164	34,350	2,039,297	1,248,878
2005	73,860,249	59,244,428	432,555	59,676,983	7,340,211	-9,657	52,327,115	12,875,715	8,657,419	35,727	2,067,325	1,289,802
2006	80,719,567	64,048,023	488,079	64,536,102	7,857,271	-36,977	56,641,854	14,775,109	9,302,604	38,380	2,103,164	1,330,477
2007	85,424,672	67,074,020	474,614	67,548,634	8,216,560	-549	59,331,525	16,020,960	10,072,187	39,959	2,137,828	1,368,315
2008	90,256,177	68,156,459	515,105	68,671,564	8,345,746	132,468	60,458,286	17,953,536	11,844,355	41,538	2,172,853	1,367,935
2009	86,334,545	64,295,062	466,236	64,761,298	8,027,117	292,492	57,026,673	15,716,716	13,591,156	39,123	2,206,737	1,310,510
2010	88,505,362	65,662,610	407,628	66,070,238	8,281,406	463,522	58,252,354	15,408,638	14,844,370	39,646	2,232,383	1,306,844
2011	94,311,867	69,050,595	467,981	69,518,576	7,730,032	376,339	62,164,883	17,217,456	14,929,528	41,660	2,263,852	1,333,660
2012	100,368,199	73,604,586	531,356	74,135,942	8,136,625	330,200	66,329,517	19,154,689	14,883,993	43,824	2,290,274	1,358,072
2013	101,559,620	76,470,157	466,901	76,937,058	9,585,584	320,286	67,671,760	18,499,937	15,387,923	43,895	2,313,673	1,389,373
2014	108,554,639	80,659,296	397,265	81,056,561	10,148,867	429,645	71,337,339	20,470,917	16,746,383	46,243	2,347,475	1,433,646
2015	116,717,024	86,336,136	483,555	86,819,691	10,758,980	437,700	76,498,411	22,591,888	17,626,725	48,916	2,386,057	1,481,298
2016	122,490,579	90,778,068	449,749	91,227,817	11,217,912	298,707	80,308,612	23,909,977	18,271,990	50,367	2,431,944	1,524,248
2017	130,352,553	96,856,196	388,017	97,244,213	12,059,450	226,987	85,411,750	26,192,765	18,748,038	52,962	2,461,234	1,570,646
2018	139,580,730	103,217,111	380,144	103,597,255	12,589,778	313,343	91,320,820	28,462,797	19,797,113	56,285	2,479,889	1,606,178
2019	146,230,869	108,765,464	353,978	109,119,442	13,247,370	288,462	96,160,534	29,071,365	20,998,970	58,544	2,497,793	1,618,047
2020	157,502,510	111,531,124	410,078	111,941,202	13,445,149	464,499	98,960,552	29,421,657	29,120,301	62,550	2,518,007	1,552,438
2021	172,141,831	122,415,222	447,495	122,862,717	15,203,003	479,183	108,138,897	32,101,865	31,901,069	68,356	2,518,310	1,592,807
2022	174,245,501	129,580,918	417,841	129,998,759	16,522,492	268,311	113,744,578	33,482,672	27,018,251	69,435	2,509,489	1,671,108

Personal Income and Employment by Area: Port St. Lucie, FL

(Thousands of dollars, except as noted.)

		Derivation of personal income										
		Earnings by place of work										
Year	Personal income, total	Nonfarm	Farm	Total	Less: Contributions for government social insurance	Plus: Adjustment for residence	Equals: Net earnings by place of residence	Plus: Dividends, interest, and rent	Plus: Personal current transfer receipts	Per capita personal income (dollars)	Population (persons)	Total employment
1970	314,908	185,400	23,641	209,041	12,412	309	196,938	82,937	35,033	3,949	79,741	33,285
1971	365,479	209,249	28,337	237,586	14,601	2,417	225,402	96,936	43,141	4,321	84,589	35,253
1972	441,651	257,116	34,881	291,997	18,903	2,425	275,519	113,292	52,840	4,901	90,118	39,752
1973	539,533	318,856	34,460	353,316	26,816	3,947	330,447	141,545	67,541	5,239	102,977	44,659
1974	618,281	355,871	35,234	391,105	31,474	4,798	364,429	171,150	82,702	5,482	112,792	46,293
1975	692,720	380,117	38,997	419,114	33,146	5,579	391,547	194,063	107,110	5,883	117,754	46,049
1976	790,994	434,172	46,111	480,283	37,833	7,740	450,190	219,681	121,123	6,482	122,024	48,072
1977	910,728	489,023	58,524	547,547	43,123	11,867	516,291	257,575	136,862	7,175	126,939	51,647
1978	1,086,736	579,065	77,889	656,954	51,937	16,306	621,323	310,262	155,151	8,113	133,944	56,962
1979	1,304,712	704,186	80,958	785,144	66,063	17,067	736,148	382,251	186,313	9,111	143,206	62,851
1980	1,665,380	882,979	122,384	1,005,363	83,903	2,941	924,401	513,141	227,838	10,830	153,770	68,854
1981	1,928,275	979,152	85,659	1,064,811	99,992	20,592	985,411	672,742	270,122	11,773	163,782	71,320
1982	2,137,443	1,051,361	98,310	1,149,671	111,108	31,735	1,070,298	750,514	316,631	12,312	173,600	74,297
1983	2,409,867	1,140,439	154,046	1,294,485	119,742	56,745	1,231,488	823,641	354,738	13,284	181,413	77,623
1984	2,628,604	1,236,869	101,719	1,338,588	132,984	90,490	1,296,094	945,364	387,146	13,844	189,879	81,858
1985	2,944,346	1,345,705	110,120	1,455,825	148,160	118,861	1,426,526	1,084,639	433,181	14,887	197,784	86,119
1986	3,270,017	1,508,008	110,034	1,618,042	170,297	139,868	1,587,613	1,201,078	481,326	15,800	206,964	90,815
1987	3,611,307	1,724,234	135,300	1,859,534	192,185	159,502	1,826,851	1,260,992	523,464	16,578	217,839	93,920
1988	4,251,026	1,941,389	220,566	2,161,955	223,813	187,039	2,125,181	1,533,686	592,159	18,674	227,640	101,218
1989	4,866,463	2,141,027	167,524	2,308,551	252,123	208,584	2,265,012	1,913,028	688,423	20,342	239,233	107,262
1990	5,340,271	2,277,859	124,563	2,402,422	264,565	237,932	2,375,789	2,191,625	772,857	20,967	254,702	109,748
1991	5,555,684	2,342,531	149,173	2,491,704	273,643	248,702	2,466,763	2,201,412	887,509	21,113	263,143	108,584
1992	5,824,327	2,530,054	106,874	2,636,928	292,540	267,351	2,611,739	2,178,397	1,034,191	21,594	269,716	108,447
1993	6,171,301	2,685,556	103,939	2,789,495	308,989	280,618	2,761,124	2,290,470	1,119,707	22,260	277,235	111,244
1994	6,500,261	2,805,913	88,625	2,894,538	330,635	304,064	2,867,967	2,424,761	1,207,533	22,807	285,006	113,621
1995	7,129,640	2,959,179	97,094	3,056,273	349,116	324,949	3,032,106	2,788,174	1,309,360	24,540	290,527	117,523
1996	7,620,058	3,141,218	59,515	3,200,733	365,916	363,205	3,198,022	3,019,122	1,402,914	25,575	297,947	122,505
1997	8,125,511	3,307,848	61,224	3,369,072	386,018	394,662	3,377,716	3,262,416	1,485,379	26,649	304,912	126,227
1998	8,809,567	3,523,315	105,598	3,628,913	407,982	446,781	3,667,712	3,593,783	1,548,072	28,310	311,185	133,060
1999	9,200,335	3,777,610	89,817	3,867,427	430,797	496,449	3,933,079	3,657,322	1,609,934	29,085	316,323	136,633
2000	9,870,076	4,024,672	83,733	4,108,405	458,233	567,652	4,217,824	3,931,446	1,720,806	30,765	320,819	141,761
2001	10,729,893	4,525,801	67,306	4,593,107	507,141	725,168	4,811,134	4,068,606	1,850,153	32,682	328,315	143,578
2002	11,062,052	4,916,421	66,535	4,982,956	547,949	883,352	5,318,359	3,761,999	1,981,694	32,656	338,741	148,127
2003	11,850,462	5,266,641	51,771	5,318,412	590,250	1,080,102	5,808,264	3,934,280	2,107,918	33,712	351,522	155,144
2004	13,388,222	5,910,705	64,093	5,974,798	665,454	1,196,238	6,505,582	4,579,605	2,303,035	36,354	368,277	166,983
2005	14,788,404	6,555,302	102,016	6,657,318	749,404	1,514,942	7,422,856	4,980,003	2,385,545	38,524	383,877	179,578
2006	16,214,668	6,956,322	95,861	7,052,183	819,166	1,665,566	7,898,583	5,748,509	2,567,576	40,838	397,053	187,527
2007	17,053,602	7,133,340	68,162	7,201,502	858,543	1,794,999	8,137,958	6,165,993	2,749,651	41,553	410,402	189,634
2008	17,374,069	6,712,961	62,694	6,775,655	845,905	1,899,166	7,828,916	6,420,473	3,124,680	41,613	417,520	183,486
2009	16,103,500	6,456,788	62,799	6,519,587	816,638	1,775,030	7,477,979	5,208,498	3,417,023	38,355	419,850	175,816
2010	16,623,037	6,716,118	69,968	6,786,086	820,796	1,498,171	7,463,461	5,452,266	3,707,310	39,112	425,008	176,754
2011	17,663,846	6,844,442	81,518	6,925,960	755,013	1,622,646	7,793,593	6,004,610	3,865,643	41,328	427,403	179,270
2012	19,291,040	7,076,796	106,253	7,183,049	787,036	2,186,417	8,582,430	6,863,680	3,844,930	44,833	430,287	181,956
2013	18,871,122	7,189,063	99,439	7,288,502	900,476	2,294,243	8,682,269	6,186,282	4,002,571	43,479	434,026	185,834
2014	20,514,711	7,593,773	96,744	7,690,517	948,892	2,372,749	9,114,374	7,171,646	4,228,691	46,628	439,965	194,076
2015	21,771,657	8,120,938	125,137	8,246,075	1,003,948	2,463,280	9,705,407	7,557,193	4,509,057	48,513	448,782	202,466
2016	23,278,099	8,468,193	91,350	8,559,543	1,052,703	2,962,351	10,469,191	8,072,172	4,736,736	50,727	458,889	210,071
2017	24,904,378	8,886,895	110,676	8,997,571	1,106,160	3,133,456	11,024,867	8,873,716	5,005,795	53,368	466,658	217,773
2018	26,183,961	9,421,469	68,669	9,490,138	1,186,390	3,218,491	11,522,239	9,423,989	5,237,733	55,268	473,761	226,353
2019	27,935,085	10,010,937	82,045	10,092,982	1,279,722	3,541,617	12,354,877	9,964,254	5,615,954	58,070	481,058	230,509
2020	30,547,400	10,488,590	67,469	10,556,059	1,351,356	3,616,124	12,820,827	10,840,153	6,886,420	62,331	490,086	235,753
2021	34,114,216	11,616,958	52,804	11,669,762	1,462,928	4,514,120	14,720,954	11,505,456	7,887,806	67,616	504,532	249,824
2022	36,657,864	12,703,118	56,019	12,759,137	1,633,873	5,831,817	16,957,081	12,458,988	7,241,795	70,400	520,710	262,914

Personal Income and Employment by Area: Poughkeepsie-Newburgh-Middletown, NY

(Thousands of dollars, except as noted.)

Year	Personal income, total	Derivation of personal income: Earnings by place of work: Nonfarm	Farm	Total	Less: Contributions for government social insurance	Plus: Adjustment for residence	Equals: Net earnings by place of residence	Plus: Dividends, interest, and rent	Plus: Personal current transfer receipts	Per capita personal income (dollars)	Population (persons)	Total employment
1970	1,928,321	1,486,152	23,361	1,509,513	111,073	64,522	1,462,962	309,887	155,472	4,319	446,438	186,898
1971	2,134,783	1,617,582	21,928	1,639,510	124,703	91,649	1,606,456	340,092	188,235	4,672	456,961	189,327
1972	2,357,479	1,774,960	18,441	1,793,401	143,246	122,935	1,773,090	374,687	209,702	5,130	459,527	192,493
1973	2,610,794	1,941,257	23,993	1,965,250	180,420	164,138	1,948,968	415,400	246,426	5,570	468,716	201,165
1974	2,872,515	2,089,271	21,904	2,111,175	199,764	204,484	2,115,895	463,282	293,338	6,043	475,356	203,257
1975	3,165,617	2,201,825	25,336	2,227,161	207,727	251,725	2,271,159	505,336	389,122	6,550	483,292	199,854
1976	3,397,625	2,325,464	24,807	2,350,271	224,775	304,987	2,430,483	528,605	438,537	7,026	483,589	199,394
1977	3,705,209	2,521,948	27,258	2,549,206	243,325	360,164	2,666,045	573,952	465,212	7,564	489,832	203,486
1978	4,119,419	2,812,798	27,527	2,840,325	277,283	435,227	2,998,269	622,850	498,300	8,306	495,984	212,224
1979	4,623,630	3,142,042	34,441	3,176,483	320,495	511,560	3,367,548	716,284	539,798	9,209	502,051	221,762
1980	5,209,876	3,409,977	38,475	3,448,452	345,202	623,051	3,726,301	854,671	628,904	10,299	505,849	222,410
1981	5,909,099	3,796,800	34,259	3,831,059	407,158	727,497	4,151,398	1,031,533	726,168	11,594	509,660	225,577
1982	6,567,920	4,207,339	30,928	4,238,267	453,901	789,831	4,574,197	1,192,774	800,949	12,784	513,751	230,042
1983	7,119,357	4,588,576	20,595	4,609,171	499,453	863,291	4,973,009	1,293,674	852,674	13,711	519,246	233,972
1984	7,959,627	5,188,965	29,679	5,218,644	576,101	962,456	5,604,999	1,471,361	883,267	15,129	526,116	244,050
1985	8,606,746	5,659,848	29,055	5,688,903	637,186	1,058,279	6,109,996	1,568,669	928,081	16,182	531,875	254,676
1986	9,250,581	6,089,985	32,591	6,122,576	694,576	1,176,496	6,604,496	1,656,793	989,292	17,185	538,304	261,524
1987	9,820,559	6,519,953	40,387	6,560,340	735,400	1,272,072	7,097,012	1,714,881	1,008,666	17,925	547,857	264,793
1988	10,640,966	7,078,278	39,338	7,117,616	820,862	1,399,174	7,695,928	1,861,755	1,083,283	19,081	557,662	275,305
1989	11,584,791	7,564,069	45,439	7,609,508	864,832	1,432,133	8,176,809	2,203,376	1,204,606	20,602	562,322	278,982
1990	12,232,431	7,965,816	38,809	8,004,625	876,976	1,570,627	8,698,276	2,217,433	1,316,722	21,497	569,041	279,509
1991	12,603,795	8,080,868	43,793	8,124,661	908,731	1,658,055	8,873,985	2,271,465	1,458,345	21,958	573,990	273,759
1992	13,104,591	8,353,793	34,810	8,388,603	925,403	1,735,858	9,199,058	2,233,448	1,672,085	22,578	580,407	273,282
1993	13,290,421	8,279,103	54,614	8,333,717	921,386	1,899,743	9,312,074	2,214,047	1,764,300	22,735	584,584	269,630
1994	13,503,613	8,196,111	39,039	8,235,150	922,593	2,051,293	9,363,850	2,287,617	1,852,146	23,059	585,604	272,756
1995	14,166,906	8,451,127	33,473	8,484,600	949,931	2,185,870	9,720,539	2,475,518	1,970,849	24,012	589,989	270,432
1996	14,828,603	8,767,281	28,072	8,795,353	971,608	2,375,895	10,199,640	2,562,001	2,066,962	24,923	594,986	274,599
1997	15,704,189	9,044,074	19,648	9,063,722	986,979	2,798,718	10,875,461	2,719,001	2,109,727	26,183	599,795	277,738
1998	16,634,274	9,608,351	34,191	9,642,542	1,044,416	2,867,628	11,465,754	2,854,425	2,314,095	27,450	605,983	282,874
1999	17,724,380	10,562,886	45,595	10,608,481	1,105,679	2,981,416	12,484,218	2,854,963	2,385,199	28,857	614,216	293,769
2000	19,045,933	11,217,283	56,059	11,273,342	1,177,748	3,406,863	13,502,457	3,038,230	2,505,246	30,532	623,806	301,872
2001	19,954,396	11,863,871	53,380	11,917,251	1,275,439	3,599,254	14,241,066	3,018,935	2,694,395	31,554	632,386	303,862
2002	20,272,131	12,274,433	32,880	12,307,313	1,332,615	3,677,915	14,652,613	2,701,279	2,918,239	31,642	640,675	308,083
2003	21,224,272	12,882,604	34,707	12,917,311	1,409,212	3,782,169	15,290,268	2,898,965	3,035,039	32,677	649,508	313,043
2004	22,338,611	13,516,987	34,523	13,551,510	1,485,615	3,992,431	16,058,326	2,956,430	3,323,855	34,064	655,793	320,343
2005	23,336,227	14,043,030	34,048	14,077,078	1,556,415	4,175,032	16,695,695	3,242,584	3,397,948	35,418	658,884	325,163
2006	24,716,728	14,632,097	34,915	14,667,012	1,629,805	4,593,479	17,630,686	3,486,014	3,600,028	37,358	661,620	327,930
2007	26,227,773	15,147,548	29,007	15,176,555	1,667,493	5,015,667	18,524,729	3,881,228	3,821,816	39,513	663,783	331,559
2008	27,365,294	15,532,050	51,778	15,583,828	1,737,908	4,979,826	18,825,746	4,233,535	4,306,013	41,060	666,468	332,469
2009	26,994,743	15,684,050	46,814	15,730,864	1,743,091	4,273,577	18,261,350	3,965,902	4,767,491	40,353	668,966	325,672
2010	27,641,183	16,139,903	58,425	16,198,328	1,770,122	4,139,762	18,567,968	3,934,199	5,139,016	41,155	671,628	323,891
2011	28,855,559	16,458,152	52,986	16,511,138	1,627,851	4,394,762	19,278,049	4,311,723	5,265,787	42,775	674,594	328,538
2012	29,741,658	16,808,620	68,737	16,877,357	1,647,492	4,634,214	19,864,079	4,544,554	5,333,025	44,067	674,920	328,587
2013	30,104,587	17,087,842	66,878	17,154,720	1,887,813	4,829,916	20,096,823	4,597,982	5,409,782	44,493	676,621	332,271
2014	30,823,520	17,353,782	54,739	17,408,521	1,956,205	4,895,988	20,348,304	4,794,381	5,680,835	45,474	677,831	336,427
2015	32,259,127	17,953,410	45,042	17,998,452	2,035,475	5,148,580	21,111,557	5,141,680	6,005,890	47,471	679,560	342,374
2016	33,051,560	18,328,400	45,224	18,373,624	2,078,548	5,284,285	21,579,361	5,321,829	6,150,370	48,436	682,370	343,389
2017	34,660,606	19,191,426	52,194	19,243,620	2,184,200	5,292,798	22,352,218	5,739,408	6,568,980	50,472	686,729	347,990
2018	35,718,121	20,065,084	42,200	20,107,284	2,251,340	5,666,057	23,522,001	5,710,825	6,485,295	51,652	691,510	354,604
2019	38,020,172	20,975,339	58,082	21,033,421	2,351,620	6,205,593	24,887,394	6,148,581	6,984,197	54,614	696,160	358,166
2020	41,056,934	20,997,439	54,015	21,051,454	2,353,555	6,466,298	25,164,197	6,210,972	9,681,765	58,949	696,486	339,994
2021	43,355,490	22,586,990	51,639	22,638,629	2,569,583	6,481,689	26,550,735	6,761,030	10,043,725	61,669	703,036	353,226
2022	43,974,041	23,861,976	66,793	23,928,769	2,785,937	7,559,315	28,702,147	6,865,232	8,406,662	62,509	703,486	370,127

Personal Income and Employment by Area: Prescott Valley-Prescott, AZ

(Thousands of dollars, except as noted.)

Year	Personal income, total	Derivation of personal income: Earnings by place of work: Nonfarm	Farm	Total	Less: Contributions for government social insurance	Plus: Adjustment for residence	Equals: Net earnings by place of residence	Plus: Dividends, interest, and rent	Plus: Personal current transfer receipts	Per capita personal income (dollars)	Population (persons)	Total employment
1970	144,363	80,740	2,618	83,358	5,139	2,433	80,652	44,292	19,419	3,843	37,570	12,550
1971	171,295	95,709	3,448	99,157	6,313	4,200	97,044	50,845	23,406	4,240	40,403	13,909
1972	203,467	114,316	5,913	120,229	7,929	6,226	118,526	57,461	27,480	4,535	44,864	15,086
1973	241,208	134,784	8,017	142,801	10,487	8,490	140,804	68,156	32,248	5,030	47,951	16,708
1974	263,506	148,131	552	148,683	12,164	8,397	144,916	80,726	37,864	5,246	50,233	17,382
1975	299,669	159,161	7,979	167,140	12,876	8,034	162,298	89,212	48,159	5,970	50,194	17,370
1976	332,974	184,318	2,119	186,437	14,689	7,212	178,960	98,264	55,750	5,973	55,746	18,441
1977	384,717	212,962	4,211	217,173	17,527	8,112	207,758	114,748	62,211	6,440	59,742	20,271
1978	449,804	238,570	7,945	246,515	19,845	14,422	241,092	137,416	71,296	7,211	62,377	21,755
1979	517,177	276,862	1,932	278,794	24,174	17,305	271,925	163,655	81,597	7,855	65,842	23,433
1980	618,085	313,072	5,298	318,370	28,012	19,000	309,358	208,040	100,687	8,996	68,705	24,767
1981	712,409	344,130	1,853	345,983	33,682	21,001	333,302	258,610	120,497	10,050	70,883	25,230
1982	759,416	347,549	3,847	351,396	35,049	22,031	338,378	283,068	137,970	10,261	74,009	25,227
1983	841,080	384,232	4,085	388,317	39,454	26,930	375,793	314,756	150,531	10,956	76,769	26,696
1984	945,679	420,851	6,213	427,064	44,122	35,143	418,085	363,143	164,451	11,875	79,633	28,552
1985	1,066,117	476,148	1,593	477,741	51,314	41,622	468,049	417,529	180,539	12,900	82,642	31,802
1986	1,185,773	533,455	3,059	536,514	57,507	49,878	528,885	458,115	198,773	13,320	89,025	34,400
1987	1,265,241	583,022	2,537	585,559	62,972	55,901	578,488	465,471	221,282	13,487	93,811	36,621
1988	1,407,583	640,432	327	640,759	72,277	63,402	631,884	527,251	248,448	14,148	99,493	38,956
1989	1,542,495	671,762	3,236	674,998	81,399	69,192	662,791	599,984	279,720	14,882	103,651	40,422
1990	1,657,643	728,783	5,446	734,229	89,827	77,789	722,191	621,324	314,128	15,233	108,818	42,267
1991	1,774,785	806,902	5,430	812,332	98,982	82,414	795,764	626,724	352,297	15,690	113,119	44,202
1992	1,914,709	902,200	6,620	908,820	110,219	91,511	890,112	626,607	397,990	16,168	118,427	46,644
1993	2,079,901	1,003,163	2,783	1,005,946	123,138	99,291	982,099	668,634	429,168	16,617	125,164	49,463
1994	2,368,886	1,158,743	-296	1,158,447	141,596	109,155	1,126,006	776,348	466,532	17,948	131,986	55,718
1995	2,525,938	1,227,366	-765	1,226,601	145,686	122,775	1,203,690	813,570	508,678	18,055	139,901	57,666
1996	2,741,613	1,318,743	4,724	1,323,467	158,302	136,751	1,301,916	890,148	549,549	18,725	146,414	60,672
1997	2,962,945	1,470,415	6,124	1,476,539	171,423	150,082	1,455,198	930,752	576,995	19,503	151,924	64,787
1998	3,241,490	1,570,217	12,707	1,582,924	182,163	168,148	1,568,909	1,045,387	627,194	20,557	157,686	67,473
1999	3,406,373	1,671,013	24,213	1,695,226	193,466	184,979	1,686,739	1,057,191	662,443	20,905	162,943	66,576
2000	3,645,510	1,769,977	17,673	1,787,650	206,659	206,654	1,787,645	1,137,162	720,703	21,621	168,608	69,991
2001	3,894,641	1,905,268	23,894	1,929,162	223,293	210,728	1,916,597	1,180,476	797,568	22,560	172,636	76,403
2002	4,047,972	2,054,672	10,577	2,065,249	241,830	209,383	2,032,802	1,132,161	883,009	22,823	177,362	78,540
2003	4,318,609	2,209,968	14,393	2,224,361	257,362	213,684	2,180,683	1,187,717	950,209	23,717	182,090	80,740
2004	4,782,507	2,418,167	16,076	2,434,243	282,188	225,280	2,377,335	1,339,097	1,066,075	25,463	187,822	84,764
2005	5,327,146	2,696,733	16,577	2,713,310	318,265	239,561	2,634,606	1,520,303	1,172,237	27,259	195,424	90,798
2006	5,844,312	3,018,043	11,775	3,029,818	359,787	255,948	2,925,979	1,600,349	1,317,984	28,637	204,082	95,890
2007	6,294,205	3,147,599	9,802	3,157,401	382,883	268,289	3,042,807	1,813,837	1,437,561	30,149	208,773	98,498
2008	6,517,185	3,143,984	8,090	3,152,074	391,410	263,928	3,024,592	1,868,291	1,624,302	30,856	211,211	95,086
2009	6,214,018	2,912,480	2,022	2,914,502	373,968	233,696	2,774,230	1,626,241	1,813,547	29,426	211,172	89,449
2010	6,166,361	2,802,690	2,550	2,805,240	369,518	224,840	2,660,562	1,562,770	1,943,029	29,236	210,916	87,126
2011	6,433,249	2,789,403	7,590	2,796,993	338,383	229,654	2,688,264	1,737,118	2,007,867	30,531	210,711	87,059
2012	6,583,075	2,862,145	7,126	2,869,271	347,412	228,408	2,750,267	1,761,319	2,071,489	31,141	211,394	88,282
2013	6,908,898	3,036,185	7,702	3,043,887	405,113	219,991	2,858,765	1,858,176	2,191,957	32,352	213,557	90,089
2014	7,421,700	3,266,069	7,180	3,273,249	425,991	224,229	3,071,487	2,040,047	2,310,166	34,267	216,582	92,455
2015	7,819,352	3,457,920	10,594	3,468,514	450,505	235,601	3,253,610	2,109,224	2,456,518	35,641	219,393	94,900
2016	8,209,084	3,674,410	10,340	3,684,750	481,970	239,249	3,442,029	2,169,392	2,597,663	36,834	222,867	97,396
2017	8,839,071	3,915,884	10,151	3,926,035	515,643	256,981	3,667,373	2,368,913	2,802,785	39,094	226,100	99,065
2018	9,362,371	4,141,974	11,652	4,153,626	559,831	273,489	3,867,284	2,510,712	2,984,375	40,738	229,820	102,184
2019	9,960,799	4,247,854	7,842	4,255,696	585,220	287,731	3,958,207	2,778,393	3,224,199	42,739	233,062	102,158
2020	11,138,173	4,533,070	14,184	4,547,254	631,093	290,231	4,206,392	2,902,577	4,029,204	46,954	237,216	102,647
2021	12,125,489	4,929,370	13,875	4,943,245	683,092	320,496	4,580,649	3,148,329	4,396,511	50,065	242,193	107,358
2022	12,739,608	5,435,438	16,733	5,452,171	754,332	359,046	5,056,885	3,546,739	4,135,984	51,747	246,191	112,493

Personal Income and Employment by Area: Providence-Warwick, RI-MA

(Thousands of dollars, except as noted.)

Year	Personal income, total	Derivation of personal income								Per capita personal income (dollars)	Population (persons)	Total employment
		Earnings by place of work			Less: Contributions for government social insurance	Plus: Adjustment for residence	Equals: Net earnings by place of residence	Plus: Dividends, interest, and rent	Plus: Personal current transfer receipts			
		Nonfarm	Farm	Total								
1970	5,814,992	4,387,300	16,934	4,404,234	328,715	188,818	4,264,337	921,850	628,805	4,165	1,396,129	629,664
1971	6,202,171	4,612,057	15,023	4,627,080	358,216	211,732	4,480,596	979,264	742,311	4,389	1,413,149	623,177
1972	6,770,032	5,073,636	14,154	5,087,790	411,755	235,873	4,911,908	1,046,956	811,168	4,734	1,430,040	639,853
1973	7,284,619	5,452,140	12,997	5,465,137	514,209	271,749	5,222,677	1,142,054	919,888	5,068	1,437,274	652,677
1974	7,710,883	5,598,805	13,930	5,612,735	553,187	319,367	5,378,915	1,247,976	1,083,992	5,459	1,412,609	640,670
1975	8,369,663	5,793,686	14,558	5,808,244	556,877	350,698	5,602,065	1,334,317	1,433,281	5,952	1,406,082	615,617
1976	9,182,532	6,499,990	15,516	6,515,506	636,881	392,095	6,270,720	1,427,191	1,484,621	6,486	1,415,810	641,578
1977	10,070,327	7,158,790	14,737	7,173,527	701,293	456,438	6,928,672	1,587,021	1,554,634	7,082	1,422,032	665,492
1978	11,091,486	7,962,515	19,317	7,981,832	803,514	526,850	7,705,168	1,734,397	1,651,921	7,780	1,425,662	687,471
1979	12,330,221	8,834,566	17,291	8,851,857	921,195	611,522	8,542,184	1,938,955	1,849,082	8,622	1,430,055	699,681
1980	13,801,218	9,541,656	18,875	9,560,531	996,188	720,575	9,284,918	2,377,590	2,138,710	9,691	1,424,092	699,678
1981	15,277,257	10,257,155	23,193	10,280,348	1,140,405	803,131	9,943,074	2,897,501	2,436,682	10,684	1,429,942	696,826
1982	16,508,588	10,809,823	42,156	10,851,979	1,215,934	881,739	10,517,784	3,324,947	2,665,857	11,534	1,431,288	687,087
1983	17,880,273	11,763,581	54,607	11,818,188	1,337,787	988,956	11,469,357	3,579,166	2,831,750	12,467	1,434,222	697,303
1984	19,689,952	13,050,642	54,689	13,105,331	1,540,711	1,143,170	12,707,790	4,053,001	2,929,161	13,656	1,441,812	730,198
1985	21,226,508	14,203,849	60,588	14,264,437	1,660,354	1,250,734	13,854,817	4,265,449	3,106,242	14,622	1,451,669	752,699
1986	22,763,530	15,389,867	65,343	15,455,210	1,810,674	1,337,555	14,982,091	4,527,255	3,254,184	15,565	1,462,482	774,732
1987	24,298,115	16,656,773	60,720	16,717,493	1,943,190	1,514,026	16,288,329	4,652,253	3,357,533	16,429	1,478,976	783,574
1988	26,789,067	18,364,247	60,575	18,424,822	2,170,331	1,679,706	17,934,197	5,243,666	3,611,204	17,936	1,493,594	804,366
1989	28,900,572	19,391,205	50,346	19,441,551	2,266,866	1,764,485	18,939,170	5,969,140	3,992,262	19,219	1,503,781	805,887
1990	29,804,303	19,749,929	47,613	19,797,542	2,389,123	1,874,500	19,282,919	6,068,585	4,452,799	19,696	1,513,216	786,517
1991	30,179,242	19,451,557	50,386	19,501,943	2,411,286	1,865,165	18,955,822	5,896,289	5,327,131	19,865	1,519,234	749,079
1992	31,552,296	20,678,158	45,545	20,723,703	2,560,911	1,936,178	20,098,970	5,885,718	5,567,608	20,725	1,522,392	760,306
1993	32,866,277	21,616,178	46,008	21,662,186	2,707,000	1,976,073	20,931,259	6,025,246	5,909,772	21,508	1,528,117	772,176
1994	34,074,328	22,536,267	40,456	22,576,723	2,849,013	2,135,055	21,862,765	6,200,242	6,011,321	22,241	1,532,065	778,499
1995	35,840,187	23,541,977	40,440	23,582,417	2,957,763	2,220,465	22,845,119	6,653,224	6,341,844	23,336	1,535,833	784,811
1996	37,203,828	24,425,830	44,400	24,470,230	3,032,165	2,315,182	23,753,247	6,965,351	6,485,230	24,132	1,541,702	791,039
1997	39,339,515	25,725,074	35,823	25,760,897	3,177,135	2,607,517	25,191,279	7,325,697	6,822,539	25,398	1,548,897	802,598
1998	41,735,253	27,522,364	30,321	27,552,685	3,349,029	2,886,316	27,089,972	7,745,256	6,900,025	26,782	1,558,350	815,590
1999	43,786,877	29,390,292	31,357	29,421,649	3,514,350	3,148,297	29,055,596	7,566,549	7,164,732	27,861	1,571,610	832,845
2000	47,262,106	31,618,439	35,429	31,653,868	3,732,495	3,665,617	31,586,990	8,205,692	7,469,424	29,798	1,586,085	855,161
2001	50,067,833	33,350,990	35,881	33,386,871	3,911,308	3,849,012	33,324,575	8,447,801	8,295,457	31,382	1,595,424	855,796
2002	51,912,095	34,942,889	43,677	34,986,566	4,050,851	3,817,241	34,752,956	8,355,132	8,804,007	32,269	1,608,716	859,079
2003	54,204,386	36,662,630	43,247	36,705,877	4,251,166	3,870,357	36,325,068	8,746,009	9,133,309	33,509	1,617,623	865,524
2004	56,668,321	38,555,032	46,633	38,601,665	4,499,496	4,226,508	38,328,677	8,690,220	9,649,424	34,968	1,620,567	877,824
2005	58,049,947	39,703,392	41,878	39,745,270	4,699,891	4,196,192	39,241,571	8,641,836	10,166,540	35,981	1,613,353	883,463
2006	61,169,028	41,750,822	43,371	41,794,193	4,942,157	4,367,602	41,219,638	9,364,343	10,585,047	38,050	1,607,583	889,723
2007	63,778,348	42,504,290	40,844	42,545,134	5,061,812	4,595,260	42,078,582	10,327,955	11,371,811	39,797	1,602,603	898,458
2008	65,830,007	42,856,711	49,885	42,906,596	5,149,180	4,414,368	42,171,784	10,873,416	12,784,807	41,106	1,601,459	886,215
2009	64,250,635	41,160,550	47,608	41,208,158	5,040,260	4,077,530	40,245,428	10,016,180	13,989,027	40,132	1,600,970	855,308
2010	67,263,684	43,660,603	44,943	43,705,546	5,159,456	3,909,702	42,455,792	9,979,275	14,828,617	41,924	1,604,429	852,056
2011	69,788,004	44,733,800	34,352	44,768,152	4,804,168	4,176,031	44,140,015	10,720,710	14,927,279	43,360	1,609,513	860,561
2012	72,071,368	46,317,553	41,118	46,358,671	4,922,944	4,441,014	45,876,741	11,323,744	14,870,883	44,556	1,617,546	865,526
2013	72,423,214	47,392,851	38,401	47,431,252	5,643,366	4,475,402	46,263,288	11,090,745	15,069,181	44,578	1,624,636	881,089
2014	75,159,581	49,043,204	38,059	49,081,263	5,888,198	4,338,607	47,531,672	11,712,395	15,915,514	46,012	1,633,482	898,577
2015	78,296,496	50,994,185	31,746	51,025,931	6,129,143	4,557,505	49,454,293	12,279,911	16,562,292	47,714	1,640,944	919,808
2016	79,775,319	51,638,380	22,910	51,661,290	6,296,349	5,016,239	50,381,180	12,547,408	16,846,731	48,395	1,648,427	930,413
2017	83,287,560	53,777,352	30,942	53,808,294	6,544,002	5,401,536	52,665,828	13,389,978	17,231,754	50,312	1,655,425	940,778
2018	86,781,641	55,879,972	23,709	55,903,681	6,800,382	5,925,160	55,028,459	13,960,926	17,792,256	52,061	1,666,909	955,587
2019	91,936,586	58,210,085	24,835	58,234,920	7,035,387	7,246,596	58,446,129	14,980,164	18,510,293	55,010	1,671,265	957,170
2020	99,548,107	58,795,549	24,423	58,819,972	7,036,762	7,487,940	59,271,150	14,871,541	25,405,416	59,500	1,673,082	905,472
2021	106,948,445	63,727,937	29,432	63,757,369	7,640,100	7,852,807	63,970,076	16,170,229	26,808,140	63,778	1,676,880	943,918
2022	106,698,497	67,484,406	33,547	67,517,953	8,161,297	7,967,243	67,323,899	16,785,106	22,589,492	63,746	1,673,802	985,379

Personal Income and Employment by Area: Provo-Orem, UT

(Thousands of dollars, except as noted.)

Year	Personal income, total	Derivation of personal income: Earnings by place of work								Per capita personal income (dollars)	Population (persons)	Total employment
		Nonfarm	Farm	Total	Less: Contributions for government social insurance	Plus: Adjustment for residence	Equals: Net earnings by place of residence	Plus: Dividends, interest, and rent	Plus: Personal current transfer receipts			
1970	398,439	296,737	9,575	306,312	20,247	24,775	310,840	52,323	35,276	2,774	143,630	52,365
1971	442,217	324,740	9,460	334,200	22,891	28,744	340,053	59,468	42,696	2,936	150,643	54,182
1972	512,139	381,335	7,560	388,895	28,013	34,594	395,476	67,824	48,839	3,204	159,828	58,707
1973	589,542	435,843	17,429	453,272	37,403	39,989	455,858	75,966	57,718	3,523	167,341	63,657
1974	663,155	490,487	12,655	503,142	43,894	46,645	505,893	89,473	67,789	3,802	174,411	66,614
1975	737,418	536,507	8,587	545,094	47,786	54,792	552,100	99,527	85,791	4,112	179,319	66,238
1976	859,244	630,401	10,408	640,809	55,472	68,045	653,382	112,959	92,903	4,639	185,213	70,264
1977	992,780	735,778	8,495	744,273	64,506	81,958	761,725	130,406	100,649	5,060	196,202	75,348
1978	1,147,489	854,554	6,739	861,293	77,072	92,833	877,054	155,641	114,794	5,610	204,554	80,873
1979	1,317,683	986,055	10,277	996,332	94,196	101,583	1,003,719	182,496	131,468	6,108	215,721	84,123
1980	1,467,622	1,071,011	7,749	1,078,760	102,125	113,441	1,090,076	219,348	158,198	6,510	225,440	83,779
1981	1,644,437	1,190,030	6,033	1,196,063	122,784	128,500	1,201,779	259,201	183,457	7,084	232,150	84,370
1982	1,732,159	1,188,833	7,346	1,196,179	122,681	144,660	1,218,158	296,562	217,439	7,266	238,395	85,064
1983	1,848,308	1,251,552	8,125	1,259,677	128,847	153,627	1,284,457	329,627	234,224	7,593	243,424	87,034
1984	2,049,278	1,404,257	9,736	1,413,993	147,731	171,106	1,437,368	369,298	242,612	8,294	247,068	92,533
1985	2,191,786	1,500,322	10,980	1,511,302	160,485	185,636	1,536,453	396,978	258,355	8,740	250,774	95,049
1986	2,316,406	1,591,324	9,930	1,601,254	170,807	182,401	1,612,848	419,052	284,506	9,147	253,249	97,302
1987	2,446,058	1,656,233	14,360	1,670,593	177,161	180,691	1,674,123	430,255	341,680	9,547	256,199	101,692
1988	2,697,134	1,892,175	22,414	1,914,589	214,749	178,669	1,878,509	465,194	353,431	10,373	260,016	110,799
1989	2,959,391	2,084,605	21,389	2,105,994	241,905	186,129	2,050,218	519,388	389,785	11,119	266,166	117,040
1990	3,275,023	2,390,593	23,080	2,413,673	285,763	191,350	2,319,260	530,755	425,008	12,098	270,713	125,706
1991	3,606,106	2,664,385	28,856	2,693,241	324,901	199,076	2,567,416	568,607	470,083	12,927	278,950	131,672
1992	3,918,334	2,915,232	31,985	2,947,217	351,576	220,403	2,816,044	580,603	521,687	13,514	289,947	133,739
1993	4,262,220	3,161,303	27,338	3,188,641	381,571	240,549	3,047,619	645,441	569,160	14,113	302,004	138,561
1994	4,677,264	3,505,538	23,570	3,529,108	427,534	263,012	3,364,586	729,164	583,514	14,852	314,918	151,987
1995	5,160,076	3,889,150	19,596	3,908,746	480,668	279,192	3,707,270	826,104	626,702	15,867	325,204	161,158
1996	5,664,494	4,250,640	23,519	4,274,159	512,061	312,503	4,074,601	924,634	665,259	16,775	337,667	172,108
1997	6,014,237	4,517,010	25,750	4,542,760	537,910	354,429	4,359,279	973,267	681,691	17,288	347,876	180,366
1998	6,602,005	4,990,322	33,302	5,023,624	587,400	383,775	4,819,999	1,064,444	717,562	18,278	361,197	188,543
1999	7,014,020	5,354,072	26,234	5,380,306	627,607	411,993	5,164,692	1,090,791	758,537	18,972	369,707	195,570
2000	7,589,100	5,732,323	29,655	5,761,978	674,154	447,895	5,535,719	1,233,054	820,327	19,967	380,079	203,516
2001	7,983,740	5,957,027	27,541	5,984,568	700,341	505,179	5,789,406	1,279,155	915,179	20,260	394,059	207,244
2002	8,245,548	6,046,795	19,923	6,066,718	713,712	544,170	5,897,176	1,331,404	1,016,968	20,326	405,672	208,370
2003	8,646,101	6,284,011	29,499	6,313,510	749,268	585,107	6,149,349	1,409,798	1,086,954	20,845	414,780	211,329
2004	9,385,239	6,967,586	43,390	7,010,976	829,681	691,937	6,873,232	1,357,010	1,154,997	22,082	425,023	222,607
2005	10,500,668	7,581,894	44,372	7,626,266	904,614	826,750	7,548,402	1,685,886	1,266,380	23,886	439,623	236,233
2006	11,831,501	8,514,260	24,526	8,538,786	995,987	1,065,014	8,607,813	1,860,429	1,363,259	25,863	457,471	250,783
2007	13,280,840	9,250,674	46,905	9,297,579	1,085,633	1,284,047	9,495,993	2,283,278	1,501,569	27,716	479,181	268,043
2008	14,247,877	9,386,810	30,210	9,417,020	1,105,556	1,499,137	9,810,601	2,634,187	1,803,089	28,631	497,639	268,391
2009	13,606,165	8,853,780	28,695	8,882,475	1,059,221	1,512,588	9,335,842	2,279,707	1,990,616	26,419	515,010	262,151
2010	13,924,550	8,866,424	46,201	8,912,625	1,067,115	1,633,924	9,479,434	2,212,062	2,233,054	26,247	530,529	259,787
2011	15,071,132	9,457,829	71,179	9,529,008	1,020,019	1,733,372	10,242,361	2,523,477	2,305,294	27,789	542,349	269,372
2012	16,378,560	10,394,630	79,457	10,474,087	1,097,404	1,870,062	11,246,745	2,854,142	2,277,673	29,647	552,446	278,460
2013	17,234,389	11,380,709	86,173	11,466,882	1,336,561	1,829,598	11,959,919	2,924,957	2,349,513	30,494	565,166	289,896
2014	18,643,526	12,292,547	93,507	12,386,054	1,427,107	2,004,793	12,963,740	3,271,797	2,407,989	32,375	575,858	301,325
2015	20,477,341	13,658,323	75,910	13,734,233	1,539,566	2,041,911	14,236,578	3,686,205	2,554,558	34,752	589,239	317,125
2016	22,202,045	14,826,797	46,029	14,872,826	1,649,725	2,282,830	15,505,931	4,017,351	2,678,763	36,471	608,760	334,956
2017	23,758,235	15,963,115	37,263	16,000,378	1,782,514	2,487,534	16,705,398	4,292,589	2,760,248	37,904	626,808	351,359
2018	25,565,416	17,514,903	45,034	17,559,937	1,928,110	2,431,659	18,063,486	4,558,318	2,943,612	39,765	642,919	371,507
2019	28,667,005	19,579,361	35,348	19,614,709	2,086,550	2,798,234	20,326,393	5,098,458	3,242,154	43,551	658,240	379,310
2020	31,827,127	21,131,557	41,763	21,173,320	2,288,773	3,086,691	21,971,238	5,576,666	4,279,223	47,125	675,377	393,191
2021	35,628,827	22,783,440	60,487	22,843,927	2,508,370	3,637,815	23,973,372	6,295,831	5,359,624	51,044	697,998	422,479
2022	38,417,936	24,879,263	72,471	24,951,734	2,794,416	4,662,328	26,819,646	7,148,714	4,449,576	53,731	715,001	450,100

Personal Income and Employment by Area: Pueblo, CO

(Thousands of dollars, except as noted.)

Year	Personal income, total	Derivation of personal income: Earnings by place of work: Nonfarm	Farm	Total	Less: Contributions for government social insurance	Plus: Adjustment for residence	Equals: Net earnings by place of residence	Plus: Dividends, interest, and rent	Plus: Personal current transfer receipts	Per capita personal income (dollars)	Population (persons)	Total employment
1970	417,116	326,012	2,799	328,811	18,433	-8,376	302,002	66,804	48,310	3,518	118,574	46,458
1971	460,152	355,264	2,040	357,304	20,388	-8,401	328,515	74,775	56,862	3,811	120,746	46,902
1972	510,393	397,917	3,621	401,538	24,406	-8,818	368,314	80,827	61,252	4,182	122,032	49,018
1973	579,201	456,895	3,679	460,574	33,443	-11,671	415,460	92,241	71,500	4,646	124,680	51,840
1974	647,868	507,264	3,556	510,820	38,730	-13,356	458,734	107,065	82,069	5,199	124,611	52,526
1975	715,356	542,635	5,049	547,684	41,357	-12,245	494,082	121,682	99,592	5,649	126,644	51,414
1976	775,126	588,483	5,562	594,045	46,026	-12,147	535,872	128,438	110,816	6,168	125,675	52,192
1977	830,738	630,970	3,157	634,127	50,559	-11,326	572,242	138,996	119,500	6,665	124,638	51,961
1978	920,575	702,864	2,408	705,272	58,442	-12,419	634,411	155,054	131,110	7,426	123,963	53,178
1979	1,027,464	788,450	2,784	791,234	68,723	-14,219	708,292	173,275	145,897	8,162	125,884	54,608
1980	1,126,012	828,401	3,717	832,118	72,490	-13,702	745,926	207,787	172,299	8,936	126,012	53,070
1981	1,249,825	892,401	6,589	898,990	83,788	-13,956	801,246	245,112	203,467	9,930	125,863	51,665
1982	1,281,063	853,858	4,088	857,946	81,074	-10,318	766,554	276,350	238,159	10,224	125,299	49,099
1983	1,302,308	806,536	6,344	812,880	76,284	-4,752	731,844	302,436	268,028	10,357	125,737	47,022
1984	1,379,957	847,337	6,076	853,413	83,176	-2,331	767,906	335,401	276,650	11,112	124,183	47,903
1985	1,454,657	894,266	4,593	898,859	89,995	-305	808,559	364,667	281,431	11,745	123,851	48,921
1986	1,515,627	922,944	6,196	929,140	93,809	1,317	836,648	380,586	298,393	12,212	124,111	49,175
1987	1,533,653	922,410	7,908	930,318	92,412	2,829	840,735	375,844	317,074	12,337	124,312	48,884
1988	1,623,342	990,693	8,405	999,098	105,236	3,311	897,173	387,052	339,117	13,118	123,745	51,235
1989	1,738,628	1,066,164	7,117	1,073,281	117,186	1,438	957,533	411,618	369,477	14,062	123,639	52,619
1990	1,821,654	1,135,879	5,452	1,141,331	126,029	887	1,016,189	412,261	393,204	14,794	123,134	55,119
1991	1,909,799	1,180,490	4,628	1,185,118	135,039	3,787	1,053,866	407,341	448,592	15,471	123,447	54,874
1992	2,029,468	1,254,031	5,394	1,259,425	141,534	9,535	1,127,426	396,329	505,713	16,316	124,387	55,461
1993	2,148,911	1,329,059	7,188	1,336,247	153,975	13,802	1,196,074	409,210	543,627	16,968	126,644	56,530
1994	2,305,216	1,451,207	2,425	1,453,632	168,608	17,458	1,302,482	430,603	572,131	17,899	128,787	59,435
1995	2,518,227	1,541,813	-547	1,541,266	178,535	21,745	1,384,476	475,238	658,513	19,243	130,865	61,533
1996	2,632,663	1,618,536	186	1,618,722	187,794	28,498	1,459,426	511,551	661,686	19,841	132,686	64,066
1997	2,824,769	1,770,986	-37	1,770,949	201,946	32,531	1,601,534	542,506	680,729	20,957	134,792	66,762
1998	3,004,517	1,892,900	-404	1,892,496	200,751	41,659	1,733,404	574,836	696,277	21,821	137,690	69,410
1999	3,166,391	2,012,041	-716	2,011,325	207,082	52,081	1,856,324	559,295	750,772	22,587	140,184	70,034
2000	3,366,705	2,136,113	1,152	2,137,265	215,151	68,075	1,990,189	589,121	787,395	23,743	141,800	70,788
2001	3,488,551	2,192,809	5,526	2,198,335	232,050	68,325	2,034,610	600,859	853,082	24,224	144,014	71,286
2002	3,607,187	2,264,334	-2,720	2,261,614	249,482	62,922	2,075,054	591,740	940,393	24,616	146,537	70,849
2003	3,735,220	2,329,596	495	2,330,091	255,651	61,583	2,136,023	620,522	978,675	25,254	147,907	70,865
2004	3,861,585	2,487,009	10,088	2,497,097	277,177	57,523	2,277,443	561,308	1,022,834	25,977	148,654	70,866
2005	3,963,703	2,524,834	7,649	2,532,483	285,772	67,924	2,314,635	549,864	1,099,204	26,456	149,825	71,956
2006	4,146,884	2,649,035	4,128	2,653,163	300,261	73,377	2,426,279	566,158	1,154,447	27,277	152,026	73,455
2007	4,469,638	2,806,442	9,821	2,816,263	322,519	60,466	2,554,210	695,571	1,219,857	28,814	155,121	75,883
2008	4,478,476	2,863,486	2,592	2,866,078	334,448	54,484	2,586,114	765,969	1,126,393	28,571	156,748	76,133
2009	4,511,154	2,847,398	2,661	2,850,059	332,089	29,700	2,547,670	729,653	1,233,831	28,579	157,846	74,756
2010	4,677,139	2,906,266	6,386	2,912,652	337,928	24,333	2,599,057	711,742	1,366,340	29,348	159,368	74,419
2011	4,865,919	3,017,275	13,596	3,030,871	323,726	7,190	2,714,335	741,316	1,410,268	30,404	160,044	75,213
2012	4,990,375	3,108,056	6,343	3,114,399	333,410	-1,306	2,779,683	782,391	1,428,301	31,099	160,465	75,112
2013	5,082,812	3,145,394	8,394	3,153,788	368,894	13,206	2,798,100	806,984	1,477,728	31,636	160,666	75,171
2014	5,347,467	3,315,419	9,879	3,325,298	392,665	-20	2,932,613	820,703	1,594,151	33,241	160,872	76,209
2015	5,613,207	3,437,550	10,732	3,448,282	412,512	-1,258	3,034,512	863,567	1,715,128	34,564	162,401	77,382
2016	5,791,897	3,556,056	6,304	3,562,360	426,950	-1,523	3,133,887	888,733	1,769,277	35,307	164,042	78,680
2017	5,980,659	3,703,675	5,034	3,708,709	447,010	-9,449	3,252,250	935,841	1,792,568	36,162	165,387	80,215
2018	6,326,419	3,891,463	6,820	3,898,283	471,096	-8,601	3,418,586	964,771	1,943,062	38,008	166,450	81,121
2019	6,596,712	4,080,469	7,422	4,087,891	496,991	-16,072	3,574,828	1,007,697	2,014,187	39,467	167,146	81,729
2020	7,281,133	4,271,346	7,213	4,278,559	522,743	-12,406	3,743,410	1,037,742	2,499,981	43,256	168,325	81,557
2021	7,938,790	4,457,980	14,041	4,472,021	538,427	-141	3,933,453	1,140,938	2,864,399	46,883	169,332	83,197
2022	8,003,899	4,731,525	743	4,732,268	591,286	-3,013	4,137,969	1,229,916	2,636,014	47,208	169,544	85,922

Personal Income and Employment by Area: Punta Gorda, FL

(Thousands of dollars, except as noted.)

Year	Personal income, total	Derivation of personal income								Per capita personal income (dollars)	Population (persons)	Total employment
		Earnings by place of work			Less: Contributions for government social insurance	Plus: Adjustment for residence	Equals: Net earnings by place of residence	Plus: Dividends, interest, and rent	Plus: Personal current transfer receipts			
		Nonfarm	Farm	Total								
1970	104,816	49,972	1,445	51,417	3,282	620	48,755	36,936	19,125	3,747	27,977	8,072
1971	123,756	58,030	1,667	59,697	4,050	515	56,162	44,343	23,251	4,119	30,046	8,996
1972	154,008	77,599	1,915	79,514	5,624	111	74,001	51,720	28,287	4,759	32,364	10,711
1973	187,787	92,696	1,975	94,671	7,591	1,067	88,147	64,473	35,167	5,107	36,771	12,355
1974	215,874	99,322	2,118	101,440	8,688	1,889	94,641	79,150	42,083	5,206	41,468	12,512
1975	241,617	101,005	2,556	103,561	8,787	2,458	97,232	92,273	52,112	5,517	43,796	12,707
1976	278,804	118,785	3,428	122,213	10,214	2,477	114,476	105,099	59,229	6,294	44,299	13,487
1977	330,545	142,985	3,963	146,948	12,511	2,404	136,841	124,680	69,024	7,024	47,062	15,343
1978	400,771	176,874	5,226	182,100	15,797	2,346	168,649	152,129	79,993	7,867	50,945	17,656
1979	470,291	196,875	6,258	203,133	18,416	4,865	189,582	184,557	96,152	8,505	55,299	18,195
1980	580,479	232,381	8,615	240,996	22,005	6,091	225,082	234,413	120,984	9,761	59,472	19,577
1981	694,583	269,592	4,781	274,373	27,682	8,673	255,364	290,964	148,255	10,953	63,412	21,295
1982	748,502	271,497	6,998	278,495	29,458	13,486	262,523	311,696	174,283	11,014	67,961	21,403
1983	846,021	307,113	9,099	316,212	33,087	17,190	300,315	355,545	190,161	11,828	71,524	22,702
1984	983,453	343,816	6,478	350,294	37,893	23,147	335,548	441,340	206,565	12,909	76,183	24,000
1985	1,116,272	384,272	6,489	390,761	43,555	28,703	375,909	510,154	230,209	13,801	80,886	26,318
1986	1,243,338	435,209	6,475	441,684	50,794	32,368	423,258	565,841	254,239	14,444	86,079	28,995
1987	1,364,712	502,491	6,934	509,425	57,694	39,263	490,994	598,309	275,409	14,875	91,745	30,055
1988	1,573,567	588,677	12,578	601,255	69,739	44,164	575,680	688,955	308,932	16,181	97,247	32,981
1989	1,871,026	666,924	10,764	677,688	81,958	49,725	645,455	863,004	362,567	17,982	104,050	36,229
1990	2,023,054	725,921	10,902	736,823	87,588	57,216	706,451	910,224	406,379	17,932	112,821	38,654
1991	2,098,325	756,163	16,356	772,519	92,120	63,282	743,681	894,137	460,507	17,811	117,813	39,216
1992	2,222,228	825,403	13,367	838,770	100,349	67,226	805,647	887,914	528,667	18,387	120,861	39,827
1993	2,344,657	879,405	13,998	893,403	106,622	74,031	860,812	909,842	574,003	18,888	124,134	41,205
1994	2,524,798	938,938	11,591	950,529	116,547	80,676	914,658	978,022	632,118	19,813	127,434	43,349
1995	2,702,081	990,033	11,731	1,001,764	123,536	92,570	970,798	1,049,064	682,219	20,669	130,731	44,270
1996	2,872,871	1,067,133	8,462	1,075,595	130,437	95,327	1,040,485	1,110,658	721,728	21,668	132,587	46,679
1997	3,092,300	1,110,758	10,933	1,121,691	135,545	110,127	1,096,273	1,243,261	752,766	22,913	134,959	48,085
1998	3,323,738	1,217,075	15,711	1,232,786	145,467	122,938	1,210,257	1,322,884	790,597	24,155	137,598	51,813
1999	3,456,826	1,340,430	13,276	1,353,706	156,780	135,489	1,332,415	1,304,060	820,351	24,649	140,240	54,226
2000	3,724,005	1,464,363	13,559	1,477,922	168,378	152,818	1,462,362	1,390,953	870,690	26,176	142,266	56,385
2001	3,918,592	1,616,115	8,565	1,624,680	186,097	177,542	1,616,125	1,359,225	943,242	26,783	146,311	55,287
2002	3,970,107	1,694,326	10,724	1,705,050	195,682	228,817	1,738,185	1,237,150	994,772	26,446	150,123	54,855
2003	4,162,618	1,768,196	11,914	1,780,110	204,344	282,646	1,858,412	1,258,236	1,045,970	27,165	153,235	55,225
2004	4,534,951	1,899,063	13,732	1,912,795	225,673	278,862	1,965,984	1,400,660	1,168,307	28,747	157,755	57,451
2005	4,794,651	2,052,741	23,393	2,076,134	248,078	356,053	2,184,109	1,453,606	1,156,936	30,881	155,262	59,929
2006	5,133,557	2,219,733	30,769	2,250,502	281,478	388,357	2,357,381	1,523,071	1,253,105	32,677	157,099	64,679
2007	5,353,155	2,174,283	21,552	2,195,835	281,293	394,326	2,308,868	1,708,849	1,335,438	33,511	159,742	64,360
2008	5,330,375	2,062,546	24,513	2,087,059	277,646	302,366	2,111,779	1,721,209	1,497,387	33,218	160,467	61,789
2009	5,050,645	1,945,196	32,596	1,977,792	269,610	263,614	1,971,796	1,445,736	1,633,113	31,640	159,629	59,493
2010	5,186,569	2,024,442	42,947	2,067,389	277,008	192,107	1,982,488	1,453,067	1,751,014	32,464	159,762	59,636
2011	5,380,929	2,084,857	44,142	2,128,999	260,830	152,510	2,020,679	1,555,178	1,805,072	33,790	159,248	60,938
2012	5,619,410	2,169,373	63,328	2,232,701	273,886	156,673	2,115,488	1,649,964	1,853,958	34,774	161,596	61,882
2013	5,730,459	2,241,693	46,940	2,288,633	316,048	180,740	2,153,325	1,658,014	1,919,120	35,159	162,986	63,472
2014	6,119,101	2,328,702	40,121	2,368,823	328,283	211,157	2,251,697	1,831,551	2,035,853	36,909	165,789	65,571
2015	6,556,103	2,498,538	42,238	2,540,776	345,978	240,009	2,434,807	1,934,778	2,186,518	38,669	169,546	68,126
2016	6,962,398	2,638,021	29,617	2,667,638	366,712	285,316	2,586,242	2,081,654	2,294,502	39,947	174,293	69,760
2017	7,295,387	2,759,596	32,438	2,792,034	387,796	248,099	2,652,337	2,230,577	2,412,473	41,088	177,556	71,335
2018	7,687,884	2,909,570	17,380	2,926,950	418,306	312,473	2,821,117	2,320,833	2,545,934	42,694	180,069	73,791
2019	8,387,816	3,109,392	20,068	3,129,460	453,073	393,842	3,070,229	2,583,073	2,734,514	45,638	183,791	75,069
2020	9,103,928	3,228,294	20,500	3,248,794	480,312	358,908	3,127,390	2,702,360	3,274,178	48,422	188,013	76,301
2021	10,288,088	3,666,927	15,743	3,682,670	527,559	392,648	3,547,759	3,023,500	3,716,829	52,777	194,934	80,229
2022	10,786,996	4,021,032	16,158	4,037,190	590,330	507,144	3,954,004	3,273,985	3,559,007	53,227	202,661	84,868

Personal Income and Employment by Area: Racine, WI

(Thousands of dollars, except as noted.)

Year	Personal income, total	Derivation of personal income: Earnings by place of work								Per capita personal income (dollars)	Population (persons)	Total employment
		Nonfarm	Farm	Total	Less: Contributions for government social insurance	Plus: Adjustment for residence	Equals: Net earnings by place of residence	Plus: Dividends, interest, and rent	Plus: Personal current transfer receipts			
1970	704,171	506,929	8,788	515,717	36,912	60,994	539,799	105,212	59,160	4,121	170,861	65,523
1971	745,366	529,734	10,607	540,341	40,077	62,059	562,323	111,939	71,104	4,375	170,371	64,391
1972	825,049	594,902	9,099	604,001	47,589	68,011	624,423	118,702	81,924	4,845	170,296	67,536
1973	922,302	676,807	12,091	688,898	62,908	74,842	700,832	129,699	91,771	5,405	170,642	72,370
1974	1,030,446	757,626	9,860	767,486	73,325	81,340	775,501	146,323	108,622	6,001	171,715	74,830
1975	1,137,080	821,882	17,565	839,447	77,691	77,814	839,570	163,119	134,391	6,539	173,903	74,659
1976	1,243,957	919,871	14,053	933,924	88,352	80,262	925,834	172,374	145,749	7,221	172,264	76,731
1977	1,373,950	1,021,698	24,379	1,046,077	97,927	86,166	1,034,316	186,725	152,909	8,009	171,543	78,866
1978	1,546,280	1,163,971	18,325	1,182,296	115,034	102,986	1,170,248	208,053	167,979	9,002	171,762	81,566
1979	1,733,549	1,302,854	17,773	1,320,627	133,883	126,128	1,312,872	231,276	189,401	10,063	172,266	84,225
1980	1,887,640	1,353,485	16,142	1,369,627	138,305	142,501	1,373,823	281,405	232,412	10,913	172,979	81,694
1981	2,048,378	1,424,138	16,407	1,440,545	156,343	148,378	1,432,580	348,103	267,695	11,912	171,952	79,864
1982	2,097,887	1,379,544	9,325	1,388,869	152,944	167,329	1,403,254	386,332	308,301	12,263	171,080	76,027
1983	2,191,869	1,428,010	-897	1,427,113	157,879	175,635	1,444,869	417,453	329,547	12,913	169,741	75,330
1984	2,410,671	1,590,188	11,588	1,601,776	180,511	191,179	1,612,444	469,112	329,115	14,212	169,619	79,329
1985	2,498,444	1,634,236	11,683	1,645,919	186,383	202,396	1,661,932	486,744	349,768	14,673	170,270	78,935
1986	2,629,736	1,754,803	13,822	1,768,625	199,841	199,294	1,768,078	498,075	363,583	15,500	169,655	80,809
1987	2,777,215	1,867,970	17,342	1,885,312	208,179	230,885	1,908,018	500,366	368,831	16,319	170,181	82,839
1988	3,011,618	2,021,541	15,401	2,036,942	233,497	265,388	2,068,833	562,836	379,949	17,516	171,934	85,849
1989	3,238,473	2,193,274	14,220	2,207,494	253,176	265,602	2,219,920	607,765	410,788	18,649	173,657	87,306
1990	3,452,583	2,342,401	11,249	2,353,650	281,741	296,198	2,368,107	643,588	440,888	19,671	175,518	89,786
1991	3,623,983	2,443,140	12,447	2,455,587	296,607	304,695	2,463,675	679,485	480,823	20,373	177,885	89,881
1992	3,804,976	2,558,130	26,826	2,584,956	306,654	356,286	2,634,588	653,689	516,699	21,109	180,251	89,115
1993	4,001,477	2,680,610	22,638	2,703,248	322,586	409,737	2,790,399	681,893	529,185	22,013	181,776	90,045
1994	4,237,322	2,807,911	23,509	2,831,420	342,972	462,697	2,951,145	748,631	537,546	23,112	183,338	91,293
1995	4,429,822	2,856,324	21,941	2,878,265	351,129	514,228	3,041,364	822,847	565,611	23,970	184,808	93,148
1996	4,652,266	2,989,572	19,427	3,008,999	363,022	537,673	3,183,650	884,094	584,522	25,058	185,658	94,284
1997	4,979,157	3,246,982	16,886	3,263,868	389,886	572,974	3,446,956	932,652	599,549	26,681	186,621	94,788
1998	5,216,258	3,376,647	15,408	3,392,055	404,201	620,311	3,608,165	1,001,650	606,443	27,792	187,689	95,393
1999	5,271,667	3,510,978	15,001	3,525,979	422,203	574,742	3,678,518	962,314	630,835	27,987	188,361	94,131
2000	5,548,621	3,543,314	15,088	3,558,402	420,600	704,630	3,842,432	1,017,240	688,949	29,373	188,904	94,602
2001	5,870,501	3,716,244	18,496	3,734,740	427,265	756,319	4,063,794	1,039,848	766,859	31,053	189,047	95,781
2002	6,021,735	3,831,067	17,449	3,848,516	438,170	778,543	4,188,889	1,013,477	819,369	31,721	189,833	94,911
2003	6,208,839	3,937,438	24,694	3,962,132	453,134	799,321	4,308,319	1,054,565	845,955	32,533	190,845	94,960
2004	6,489,608	4,107,731	25,366	4,133,097	474,308	842,583	4,501,372	1,131,381	856,855	33,834	191,808	96,435
2005	6,572,184	4,187,951	19,095	4,207,046	487,295	886,025	4,605,776	1,042,807	923,601	34,009	193,251	97,072
2006	6,938,729	4,313,030	26,281	4,339,311	504,907	964,962	4,799,366	1,163,735	975,628	35,782	193,915	97,227
2007	7,221,503	4,437,620	28,288	4,465,908	518,133	989,802	4,937,577	1,225,998	1,057,928	37,149	194,395	97,383
2008	7,677,306	4,476,485	24,621	4,501,106	527,950	1,057,794	5,030,950	1,450,762	1,195,594	39,425	194,730	96,571
2009	7,340,898	4,264,259	23,388	4,287,647	505,210	968,010	4,750,447	1,180,218	1,410,233	37,621	195,130	92,189
2010	7,412,709	4,357,158	19,248	4,376,406	516,762	884,097	4,743,741	1,163,709	1,505,259	37,926	195,450	91,768
2011	7,760,832	4,577,319	24,537	4,601,856	486,504	919,210	5,034,562	1,270,790	1,455,480	39,775	195,120	93,333
2012	8,076,812	4,744,648	19,663	4,764,311	503,286	861,014	5,122,039	1,470,259	1,484,514	41,424	194,980	94,218
2013	7,915,149	4,741,552	20,703	4,762,255	567,795	906,973	5,101,433	1,290,722	1,522,994	40,541	195,240	93,407
2014	8,219,343	4,883,168	11,443	4,894,611	583,698	885,945	5,196,858	1,440,192	1,582,293	42,035	195,535	94,839
2015	8,670,357	4,974,742	15,111	4,989,853	595,294	995,364	5,389,923	1,634,848	1,645,586	44,326	195,606	95,298
2016	8,688,488	4,972,067	12,940	4,985,007	599,979	1,041,691	5,426,719	1,586,569	1,675,200	44,337	195,963	94,613
2017	9,189,274	5,129,049	11,026	5,140,075	626,994	1,094,319	5,607,400	1,823,895	1,757,979	46,588	197,245	95,099
2018	9,599,959	5,395,719	12,009	5,407,728	650,561	1,096,312	5,853,479	1,897,832	1,848,648	48,550	197,734	96,769
2019	9,865,010	5,501,084	12,950	5,514,034	667,948	1,151,589	5,997,675	1,936,162	1,931,173	49,886	197,753	96,317
2020	10,459,744	5,567,374	18,633	5,586,007	683,280	1,149,635	6,052,362	1,981,255	2,426,127	52,951	197,536	92,139
2021	11,134,131	5,881,260	24,557	5,905,817	717,613	1,177,342	6,365,546	2,012,261	2,756,324	56,680	196,439	95,585
2022	11,275,643	6,236,361	25,954	6,262,315	781,896	1,232,382	6,712,801	2,138,578	2,424,264	57,574	195,846	99,496

Personal Income and Employment by Area: Raleigh-Cary, NC

(Thousands of dollars, except as noted.)

Year	Personal income, total	Derivation of personal income: Earnings by place of work: Nonfarm	Farm	Total	Less: Contributions for government social insurance	Plus: Adjustment for residence	Equals: Net earnings by place of residence	Plus: Dividends, interest, and rent	Plus: Personal current transfer receipts	Per capita personal income (dollars)	Population (persons)	Total employment
1970	1,196,842	956,524	50,778	1,007,302	63,442	18,228	962,088	156,372	78,382	3,750	319,135	165,563
1971	1,319,245	1,047,907	48,736	1,096,643	71,831	26,250	1,051,062	175,796	92,387	4,014	328,641	168,259
1972	1,494,638	1,190,116	59,681	1,249,797	86,153	30,301	1,193,945	197,306	103,387	4,425	337,793	177,550
1973	1,701,509	1,363,857	71,393	1,435,250	114,504	33,354	1,354,100	227,690	119,719	4,904	346,989	188,533
1974	1,932,923	1,524,338	86,463	1,610,801	133,023	40,186	1,517,964	266,592	148,367	5,419	356,680	195,217
1975	2,156,884	1,647,284	95,251	1,742,535	142,702	54,489	1,654,322	299,696	202,866	5,945	362,809	190,837
1976	2,383,131	1,834,193	89,164	1,923,357	162,059	64,763	1,826,061	331,124	225,946	6,461	368,858	197,595
1977	2,638,378	2,062,310	64,738	2,127,048	180,758	79,323	2,025,613	374,585	238,180	6,994	377,230	205,674
1978	3,014,777	2,361,147	92,034	2,453,181	214,033	90,108	2,329,256	426,671	258,850	7,830	385,013	214,810
1979	3,416,980	2,755,899	40,794	2,796,693	260,627	94,582	2,630,648	488,940	297,392	8,686	393,407	229,255
1980	3,893,205	3,074,966	45,642	3,120,608	293,787	104,576	2,931,397	605,398	356,410	9,629	404,305	233,851
1981	4,387,698	3,345,694	75,283	3,420,977	344,406	146,172	3,222,743	747,852	417,103	10,650	411,982	236,605
1982	4,811,361	3,628,274	74,247	3,702,521	380,184	178,684	3,501,021	852,952	457,388	11,461	419,800	239,666
1983	5,414,287	4,145,100	47,984	4,193,084	438,319	201,859	3,956,624	958,259	499,404	12,551	431,398	252,652
1984	6,353,118	4,872,431	81,770	4,954,201	523,564	248,566	4,679,203	1,139,046	534,869	14,177	448,113	273,343
1985	7,274,348	5,655,921	82,595	5,738,516	616,390	295,483	5,417,609	1,280,263	576,476	15,552	467,729	294,465
1986	7,973,464	6,235,133	49,645	6,284,778	691,844	346,665	5,939,599	1,415,508	618,357	16,502	483,172	307,223
1987	8,677,754	6,770,978	69,832	6,840,810	736,800	433,633	6,537,643	1,491,163	648,948	17,549	494,491	320,160
1988	9,655,685	7,441,720	96,170	7,537,890	834,329	490,429	7,193,990	1,751,587	710,108	18,888	511,200	336,952
1989	10,694,919	8,061,082	107,346	8,168,428	901,823	591,684	7,858,289	2,030,327	806,303	20,281	527,344	350,715
1990	11,574,407	8,706,809	137,296	8,844,105	998,559	672,128	8,517,674	2,156,995	899,738	21,088	548,874	361,542
1991	12,304,891	9,065,403	151,425	9,216,828	1,054,473	863,943	9,026,298	2,250,963	1,027,630	21,659	568,119	361,975
1992	13,598,198	10,090,907	154,988	10,245,895	1,153,124	1,002,967	10,095,738	2,347,292	1,155,168	23,097	588,751	373,756
1993	14,807,463	10,998,081	162,058	11,160,139	1,253,742	1,067,189	10,973,586	2,548,332	1,285,545	24,172	612,576	394,846
1994	16,021,387	11,932,341	160,415	12,092,756	1,380,843	1,131,981	11,843,894	2,831,535	1,345,958	25,106	638,140	413,368
1995	17,514,398	12,882,755	140,888	13,023,643	1,491,560	1,294,903	12,826,986	3,162,962	1,524,450	26,285	666,317	433,235
1996	19,174,111	14,087,067	148,754	14,235,821	1,623,545	1,405,852	14,018,128	3,519,556	1,636,427	27,609	694,496	456,366
1997	21,269,865	15,545,165	197,289	15,742,454	1,794,732	1,653,957	15,601,679	3,935,103	1,733,083	29,479	721,528	484,256
1998	23,292,321	17,204,704	166,502	17,371,206	1,986,008	1,827,947	17,213,145	4,261,576	1,817,600	31,053	750,079	512,369
1999	24,918,959	18,540,217	160,949	18,701,166	2,154,115	2,114,083	18,661,134	4,336,977	1,920,848	32,080	776,786	520,966
2000	27,486,203	20,275,147	209,874	20,485,021	2,356,853	2,645,880	20,774,048	4,644,499	2,067,656	34,180	804,157	539,376
2001	29,570,054	22,063,839	191,043	22,254,882	2,512,142	2,667,455	22,410,195	4,784,964	2,374,895	35,494	833,100	548,246
2002	30,220,191	22,560,928	77,004	22,637,932	2,563,013	2,812,972	22,887,891	4,684,615	2,647,685	35,176	859,117	551,509
2003	31,494,856	23,222,372	67,838	23,290,210	2,695,361	3,102,389	23,697,238	4,971,323	2,826,295	35,655	883,333	559,712
2004	33,664,504	24,670,602	113,599	24,784,201	2,838,272	3,233,221	25,179,150	5,450,931	3,034,423	37,014	909,510	578,163
2005	36,499,946	26,069,515	112,573	26,182,088	3,039,263	3,601,190	26,744,015	6,367,301	3,388,630	38,636	944,725	605,926
2006	40,887,886	28,827,279	96,574	28,923,853	3,306,297	4,239,230	29,856,786	7,287,574	3,743,526	41,334	989,219	640,319
2007	44,542,538	30,764,013	87,940	30,851,953	3,570,657	5,077,212	32,358,508	8,086,360	4,097,670	43,058	1,034,476	677,928
2008	47,966,646	32,340,844	122,045	32,462,889	3,695,233	5,432,405	34,200,061	8,903,006	4,863,579	44,531	1,077,163	684,042
2009	46,953,674	31,237,318	131,376	31,368,694	3,608,092	5,813,568	33,574,170	7,839,936	5,539,568	42,298	1,110,061	665,877
2010	49,383,598	32,840,919	101,708	32,942,627	3,735,616	6,208,501	35,415,512	7,887,989	6,080,097	43,418	1,137,404	666,824
2011	51,026,136	33,607,252	105,709	33,712,961	3,511,929	5,640,915	35,841,947	8,876,428	6,307,761	43,897	1,162,399	688,319
2012	54,237,210	35,936,087	135,177	36,071,264	3,678,770	5,914,029	38,306,523	9,508,741	6,421,946	45,647	1,188,200	708,464
2013	54,881,483	37,421,567	152,849	37,574,416	4,396,786	5,704,129	38,881,759	9,431,779	6,567,945	45,207	1,213,995	728,449
2014	58,851,211	40,152,896	179,595	40,332,491	4,705,296	5,823,203	41,450,398	10,500,922	6,899,891	47,391	1,241,826	757,587
2015	63,217,157	43,463,650	132,011	43,595,661	5,074,690	5,563,723	44,084,694	11,671,715	7,460,748	49,706	1,271,821	792,584
2016	66,307,479	46,211,511	127,960	46,339,471	5,332,704	5,471,133	46,477,900	11,976,527	7,853,052	50,824	1,304,639	819,514
2017	69,767,578	48,812,971	147,866	48,960,837	5,594,950	5,631,055	48,996,942	12,520,284	8,250,352	52,254	1,335,169	845,448
2018	75,886,669	53,215,109	76,552	53,291,661	5,987,639	5,789,263	53,093,285	14,029,748	8,763,636	55,686	1,362,754	876,580
2019	80,390,832	56,861,668	95,270	56,956,938	6,401,682	5,945,952	56,501,208	14,571,776	9,317,848	57,751	1,392,028	898,096
2020	86,983,113	58,770,703	91,358	58,862,061	6,623,089	7,213,266	59,452,238	14,894,192	12,636,683	61,360	1,417,587	888,889
2021	99,342,718	66,137,671	108,706	66,246,377	7,349,091	8,030,260	66,927,546	17,599,169	14,816,003	68,443	1,451,468	943,255
2022	104,836,070	72,850,752	74,154	72,924,906	8,281,036	8,314,847	72,958,717	19,297,461	12,579,892	70,628	1,484,338	1,006,993

Personal Income and Employment by Area: Rapid City, SD

(Thousands of dollars, except as noted.)

Year	Personal income, total	Derivation of personal income								Per capita personal income (dollars)	Population (persons)	Total employment
		Earnings by place of work			Less: Contributions for government social insurance	Plus: Adjustment for residence	Equals: Net earnings by place of residence	Plus: Dividends, interest, and rent	Plus: Personal current transfer receipts			
		Nonfarm	Farm	Total								
1970	305,237	226,933	11,269	238,202	14,722	4,327	227,807	55,565	21,865	3,967	76,937	35,664
1971	344,417	260,749	12,141	272,890	17,510	2,262	257,642	61,675	25,100	4,318	79,755	37,216
1972	395,778	301,530	17,098	318,628	20,682	1,684	299,630	68,263	27,885	4,761	83,137	38,899
1973	450,713	335,864	29,965	365,829	26,026	1,197	341,000	78,846	30,867	5,432	82,974	41,287
1974	479,649	364,340	13,461	377,801	29,359	2,409	350,851	92,040	36,758	5,690	84,294	41,369
1975	534,878	398,045	18,232	416,277	32,905	2,700	386,072	103,219	45,587	6,314	84,712	41,788
1976	586,845	446,731	9,936	456,667	37,005	3,237	422,899	113,355	50,591	6,622	88,627	43,688
1977	648,548	492,706	9,770	502,476	39,414	4,113	467,175	128,763	52,610	7,112	91,191	45,964
1978	751,742	567,136	16,874	584,010	45,770	5,390	543,630	151,326	56,786	8,066	93,202	49,087
1979	835,788	625,921	19,598	645,519	53,525	6,818	598,812	170,866	66,110	8,855	94,383	50,346
1980	885,967	643,135	12,282	655,417	55,014	8,163	608,566	199,276	78,125	9,712	91,221	49,245
1981	970,698	681,852	13,936	695,788	61,790	8,685	642,683	236,071	91,944	10,598	91,590	48,349
1982	1,046,073	728,667	10,857	739,524	66,547	5,668	678,645	263,784	103,644	11,279	92,747	49,034
1983	1,118,428	796,320	11,132	807,452	74,212	3,474	736,714	268,310	113,404	11,877	94,169	51,325
1984	1,238,341	888,405	18,574	906,979	84,649	1,123	823,453	294,719	120,169	12,783	96,877	55,026
1985	1,284,280	928,852	6,333	935,185	91,342	-17	843,826	310,788	129,666	13,021	98,629	55,217
1986	1,357,135	977,848	15,034	992,882	99,589	-1,583	891,710	326,401	139,024	13,572	99,995	56,510
1987	1,437,695	1,053,675	10,497	1,064,172	108,803	-3,509	951,860	340,457	145,378	14,035	102,435	60,173
1988	1,520,357	1,121,379	5,123	1,126,502	119,877	-4,586	1,002,039	364,204	154,114	14,757	103,024	59,607
1989	1,632,274	1,191,356	9,540	1,200,896	129,067	-5,472	1,066,357	393,891	172,026	15,930	102,466	61,282
1990	1,765,765	1,297,735	14,369	1,312,104	148,118	-15,251	1,148,735	430,087	186,943	17,034	103,659	64,145
1991	1,871,488	1,380,701	7,404	1,388,105	159,234	-15,813	1,213,058	455,807	202,623	17,602	106,323	65,817
1992	2,009,802	1,471,616	13,457	1,485,073	168,942	-14,192	1,301,939	484,329	223,534	18,546	108,367	67,104
1993	2,113,763	1,548,205	19,607	1,567,812	177,028	-14,449	1,376,335	496,700	240,728	19,269	109,697	68,805
1994	2,192,659	1,600,893	5,490	1,606,383	184,396	-12,445	1,409,542	521,174	261,943	19,875	110,321	71,173
1995	2,322,556	1,654,369	15,129	1,669,498	189,534	-13,158	1,466,806	568,716	287,034	20,884	111,213	71,566
1996	2,393,598	1,682,246	5,442	1,687,688	193,690	-12,700	1,481,298	605,333	306,967	21,565	110,994	71,855
1997	2,509,717	1,746,542	10,420	1,756,962	201,554	-15,107	1,540,301	649,571	319,845	22,648	110,815	72,511
1998	2,704,600	1,879,063	14,471	1,893,534	215,096	-18,786	1,659,652	711,381	333,567	24,315	111,230	74,810
1999	2,854,676	1,990,365	27,707	2,018,072	231,146	-24,085	1,762,841	741,232	350,603	25,479	112,041	77,340
2000	3,013,282	2,078,958	28,449	2,107,407	243,466	-26,858	1,837,083	796,445	379,754	26,637	113,124	79,582
2001	3,254,765	2,275,022	30,571	2,305,593	259,876	-31,796	2,013,921	819,036	421,808	28,470	114,324	78,241
2002	3,408,081	2,426,192	13,416	2,439,608	274,290	-37,374	2,127,944	827,801	452,336	29,552	115,323	78,830
2003	3,618,280	2,556,471	42,824	2,599,295	288,486	-41,293	2,269,516	877,015	471,749	31,276	115,690	79,345
2004	3,911,170	2,732,728	35,384	2,768,112	303,722	-44,919	2,419,471	985,971	505,728	33,251	117,624	80,956
2005	4,109,024	2,844,831	48,921	2,893,752	312,459	-39,355	2,541,938	1,023,909	543,177	34,767	118,188	81,854
2006	4,278,444	2,939,555	8,906	2,948,461	330,038	-39,735	2,578,688	1,110,179	589,577	35,809	119,479	82,880
2007	4,556,401	3,046,583	18,421	3,065,004	345,477	-39,081	2,680,446	1,232,118	643,837	37,690	120,890	84,511
2008	4,810,338	3,166,452	35,035	3,201,487	362,498	-46,177	2,792,812	1,268,293	749,233	39,090	123,059	85,831
2009	4,823,060	3,216,898	5,922	3,222,820	367,400	-55,579	2,799,841	1,223,398	799,821	38,535	125,159	85,154
2010	5,118,475	3,380,404	13,232	3,393,636	384,033	-49,113	2,960,490	1,263,109	894,876	40,423	126,622	85,000
2011	5,335,382	3,499,763	48,366	3,548,129	355,177	-69,144	3,123,808	1,287,233	924,341	41,881	127,393	86,513
2012	5,660,432	3,645,277	38,008	3,683,285	368,688	-64,526	3,250,071	1,473,749	936,612	43,837	129,125	87,244
2013	5,605,394	3,733,727	20,512	3,754,239	424,753	-60,214	3,269,272	1,364,253	971,869	42,811	130,935	88,309
2014	6,073,994	3,933,281	73,898	4,007,179	446,787	-48,312	3,512,080	1,534,744	1,027,170	45,883	132,379	89,629
2015	6,186,557	4,060,416	20,960	4,081,376	459,482	-61,127	3,560,767	1,533,254	1,092,536	46,669	132,563	89,757
2016	6,374,572	4,150,419	10,013	4,160,432	473,294	-92,855	3,594,283	1,625,234	1,155,055	47,683	133,687	90,771
2017	6,604,301	4,286,108	8,562	4,294,670	495,925	-87,971	3,710,774	1,677,748	1,215,779	48,826	135,263	92,449
2018	6,907,991	4,429,406	29,918	4,459,324	514,096	-77,428	3,867,800	1,752,318	1,287,873	50,568	136,609	93,667
2019	7,321,789	4,692,177	-27,707	4,664,470	545,620	-62,173	4,056,677	1,884,096	1,381,016	52,926	138,339	93,860
2020	8,066,351	5,004,773	48,799	5,053,572	589,181	-85,813	4,378,578	1,942,852	1,744,921	57,839	139,463	93,201
2021	9,036,610	5,464,152	13,761	5,477,913	639,735	-124,572	4,713,606	2,302,306	2,020,698	63,583	142,124	97,961
2022	9,552,475	5,853,125	39,872	5,892,997	691,125	-141,682	5,060,190	2,612,984	1,879,301	65,807	145,159	101,905

Personal Income and Employment by Area: Reading, PA

(Thousands of dollars, except as noted.)

Year	Personal income, total	Derivation of personal income: Earnings by place of work: Nonfarm	Farm	Total	Less: Contributions for government social insurance	Plus: Adjustment for residence	Equals: Net earnings by place of residence	Plus: Dividends, interest, and rent	Plus: Personal current transfer receipts	Per capita personal income (dollars)	Population (persons)	Total employment
1970	1,252,791	1,027,771	18,618	1,046,389	79,002	4,950	972,337	165,861	114,593	4,221	296,772	146,430
1971	1,332,288	1,086,941	13,346	1,100,287	86,780	9,547	1,023,054	176,031	133,203	4,449	299,474	145,699
1972	1,478,467	1,201,563	20,067	1,221,630	100,840	18,095	1,138,885	189,007	150,575	4,914	300,891	148,292
1973	1,645,877	1,340,100	23,025	1,363,125	129,077	29,047	1,263,095	213,654	169,128	5,396	305,011	154,355
1974	1,811,050	1,442,564	21,103	1,463,667	143,747	42,512	1,362,432	243,787	204,831	5,924	305,720	155,151
1975	1,956,345	1,485,548	19,342	1,504,890	144,415	56,246	1,416,721	268,965	270,659	6,375	306,891	149,308
1976	2,169,731	1,654,554	25,018	1,679,572	163,067	66,675	1,583,180	293,008	293,543	7,034	308,452	153,056
1977	2,415,498	1,852,844	23,147	1,875,991	181,730	81,997	1,776,258	331,538	307,702	7,877	306,642	156,627
1978	2,698,350	2,080,827	22,645	2,103,472	209,603	104,298	1,998,167	367,848	332,335	8,729	309,110	161,553
1979	3,024,151	2,320,728	25,717	2,346,445	241,628	129,276	2,234,093	420,080	369,978	9,691	312,055	164,360
1980	3,367,378	2,493,025	23,303	2,516,328	260,503	156,543	2,412,368	522,288	432,722	10,758	313,016	165,898
1981	3,727,218	2,713,378	34,842	2,748,220	303,546	153,436	2,598,110	641,248	487,860	11,854	314,414	165,448
1982	3,977,802	2,809,421	34,229	2,843,650	319,571	154,913	2,678,992	737,275	561,535	12,644	314,597	163,637
1983	4,283,884	3,041,658	40,381	3,082,039	349,732	147,328	2,879,635	798,167	606,082	13,592	315,184	164,855
1984	4,664,850	3,374,686	62,824	3,437,510	405,486	142,924	3,174,948	884,962	604,940	14,683	317,711	171,552
1985	4,900,370	3,520,221	53,764	3,573,985	427,431	151,455	3,298,009	954,807	647,554	15,405	318,105	172,691
1986	5,148,822	3,706,100	51,486	3,757,586	449,792	153,178	3,460,972	1,001,978	685,872	16,070	320,394	173,929
1987	5,446,663	4,002,755	60,684	4,063,439	479,089	153,774	3,738,124	1,006,338	702,201	16,817	323,871	179,717
1988	5,911,599	4,387,905	48,387	4,436,292	534,326	152,741	4,054,707	1,112,553	744,339	18,024	327,977	184,644
1989	6,532,418	4,830,076	63,531	4,893,607	575,104	130,818	4,449,321	1,288,148	794,949	19,562	333,938	189,338
1990	6,746,715	4,984,826	68,319	5,053,145	597,324	127,069	4,582,890	1,288,145	875,680	19,972	337,812	190,057
1991	7,000,924	5,060,132	63,660	5,123,792	610,832	153,938	4,666,898	1,313,393	1,020,633	20,432	342,637	185,735
1992	7,500,659	5,488,015	84,278	5,572,293	654,974	170,897	5,088,216	1,317,104	1,095,339	21,675	346,050	186,648
1993	7,854,448	5,786,372	72,384	5,858,756	704,888	194,990	5,348,858	1,365,522	1,140,068	22,429	350,186	188,584
1994	8,235,567	6,126,077	81,336	6,207,413	753,245	209,160	5,663,328	1,406,495	1,165,744	23,258	354,092	190,821
1995	8,597,523	6,304,713	60,382	6,365,095	772,717	246,626	5,839,004	1,536,682	1,221,837	24,070	357,193	194,899
1996	9,028,187	6,505,984	69,451	6,575,435	777,716	301,052	6,098,771	1,626,931	1,302,485	25,052	360,380	197,093
1997	9,427,600	6,777,448	61,859	6,839,307	808,392	358,448	6,389,363	1,701,784	1,336,453	25,919	363,739	202,003
1998	9,877,187	6,994,905	67,093	7,061,998	828,932	438,373	6,671,439	1,833,211	1,372,537	26,907	367,082	206,229
1999	10,297,582	7,300,423	65,566	7,365,989	848,998	519,846	7,036,837	1,807,378	1,453,367	27,761	370,942	211,470
2000	11,034,443	7,700,150	87,715	7,787,865	884,909	611,914	7,514,870	1,964,336	1,555,237	29,461	374,546	215,764
2001	11,526,446	7,982,919	90,747	8,073,666	917,155	687,551	7,844,062	1,972,650	1,709,734	30,535	377,487	207,227
2002	11,864,028	8,189,825	65,369	8,255,194	930,855	737,408	8,061,747	1,947,072	1,855,209	31,112	381,338	204,713
2003	12,235,189	8,315,234	88,151	8,403,385	936,739	872,531	8,339,177	1,974,920	1,921,092	31,710	385,846	202,718
2004	12,677,303	8,628,096	104,833	8,732,929	970,335	952,716	8,715,310	1,943,491	2,018,502	32,435	390,848	206,368
2005	13,318,485	9,014,418	92,141	9,106,559	1,021,269	1,087,136	9,172,426	1,935,898	2,210,161	33,638	395,933	210,059
2006	14,184,079	9,611,000	68,349	9,679,349	1,104,411	1,049,576	9,624,514	2,192,246	2,367,319	35,298	401,834	216,495
2007	14,848,645	9,964,139	42,472	10,006,611	1,138,430	1,064,882	9,933,063	2,434,939	2,480,643	36,643	405,223	219,163
2008	15,366,523	9,967,837	55,440	10,023,277	1,153,987	1,090,346	9,959,636	2,590,366	2,816,521	37,687	407,737	217,937
2009	15,009,880	9,607,701	43,223	9,650,924	1,126,357	998,028	9,522,595	2,317,766	3,169,519	36,618	409,904	210,367
2010	15,755,571	10,064,886	63,409	10,128,295	1,164,716	1,102,174	10,065,753	2,272,476	3,417,342	38,221	412,228	211,633
2011	16,546,969	10,539,798	82,398	10,622,196	1,089,229	1,124,633	10,657,600	2,450,701	3,438,668	39,972	413,969	214,241
2012	17,198,318	10,748,843	103,247	10,852,090	1,110,158	1,122,174	10,864,106	2,865,717	3,468,495	41,416	415,253	215,262
2013	17,097,777	10,937,358	168,476	11,105,834	1,270,136	1,134,545	10,970,243	2,607,564	3,519,970	41,058	416,433	216,765
2014	17,748,738	11,337,651	192,970	11,530,621	1,325,802	1,143,163	11,347,982	2,779,379	3,621,377	42,476	417,854	219,863
2015	18,552,909	11,937,802	157,268	12,095,070	1,392,091	1,148,878	11,851,857	2,895,671	3,805,381	44,257	419,206	222,711
2016	18,952,701	12,189,681	101,868	12,291,549	1,423,109	1,135,328	12,003,768	2,938,964	4,009,969	45,054	420,670	224,682
2017	19,579,563	12,556,240	145,490	12,701,730	1,487,277	1,221,368	12,435,821	3,082,731	4,061,011	46,271	423,146	225,492
2018	20,564,574	13,147,370	109,342	13,256,712	1,545,256	1,263,735	12,975,191	3,255,104	4,334,279	48,187	426,762	228,804
2019	21,337,786	13,645,706	127,696	13,773,402	1,603,134	1,359,345	13,529,613	3,340,568	4,467,605	49,913	427,498	230,189
2020	23,325,136	13,594,992	110,118	13,705,110	1,576,116	1,554,162	13,683,156	3,335,113	6,306,867	54,418	428,631	216,728
2021	25,051,044	14,291,840	141,079	14,432,919	1,651,886	1,859,072	14,640,105	3,806,527	6,604,412	58,311	429,612	222,509
2022	25,051,661	15,007,686	162,804	15,170,490	1,789,220	2,142,320	15,523,590	4,027,285	5,500,786	58,199	430,449	232,511

Personal Income and Employment by Area: Richmond, VA

(Thousands of dollars, except as noted.)

Year	Personal income, total	Derivation of personal income: Earnings by place of work: Nonfarm	Farm	Total	Less: Contributions for government social insurance	Plus: Adjustment for residence	Equals: Net earnings by place of residence	Plus: Dividends, interest, and rent	Plus: Personal current transfer receipts	Per capita personal income (dollars)	Population (persons)	Total employment
1970	2,862,934	2,475,763	16,284	2,492,047	156,883	-92,903	2,242,261	426,816	193,857	4,039	708,825	361,751
1971	3,158,755	2,697,671	14,636	2,712,307	178,024	-79,490	2,454,793	469,854	234,108	4,386	720,110	366,836
1972	3,466,454	2,969,675	19,577	2,989,252	205,160	-102,413	2,681,679	511,686	273,089	4,798	722,416	375,894
1973	3,881,541	3,339,203	30,127	3,369,330	265,801	-126,906	2,976,623	583,577	321,341	5,304	731,854	398,527
1974	4,357,241	3,730,653	29,263	3,759,916	307,218	-146,908	3,305,790	676,658	374,793	5,905	737,863	414,830
1975	4,859,527	4,048,121	24,163	4,072,284	327,487	-102,290	3,642,507	739,837	477,183	6,496	748,113	411,112
1976	5,352,273	4,478,872	20,978	4,499,850	370,384	-111,907	4,017,559	807,444	527,270	7,027	761,694	421,702
1977	5,939,863	4,988,488	9,831	4,998,319	410,861	-113,285	4,474,173	900,986	564,704	7,661	775,341	435,210
1978	6,731,174	5,656,680	27,368	5,684,048	474,052	-133,486	5,076,510	1,034,375	620,289	8,598	782,838	454,670
1979	7,602,541	6,349,238	1,113	6,350,351	556,469	-107,557	5,686,325	1,206,564	709,652	9,605	791,541	467,884
1980	8,545,139	6,998,786	-10,109	6,988,677	616,815	-142,107	6,229,755	1,467,477	847,907	10,706	798,178	469,329
1981	9,594,760	7,671,974	26,049	7,698,023	724,540	-154,562	6,818,921	1,795,373	980,466	11,907	805,811	467,355
1982	10,362,375	8,184,612	10,440	8,195,052	783,847	-158,161	7,253,044	2,035,565	1,073,766	12,767	811,647	465,820
1983	11,143,736	8,804,549	-6,012	8,798,537	860,424	-154,758	7,783,355	2,203,169	1,157,212	13,625	817,894	471,915
1984	12,252,244	9,622,070	36,998	9,659,068	966,673	-154,597	8,537,798	2,486,771	1,227,675	14,864	824,309	485,891
1985	13,223,901	10,460,337	20,019	10,480,356	1,078,633	-161,569	9,240,154	2,669,539	1,314,208	15,864	833,587	505,836
1986	14,222,885	11,291,283	21,223	11,312,506	1,204,120	-169,601	9,938,785	2,884,415	1,399,685	16,823	845,461	526,172
1987	15,506,486	12,511,021	26,060	12,537,081	1,322,795	-188,609	11,025,677	3,020,790	1,460,019	18,005	861,242	552,292
1988	17,121,820	13,773,724	43,817	13,817,541	1,497,589	-206,315	12,113,637	3,439,563	1,568,620	19,532	876,601	564,443
1989	18,724,457	14,823,199	53,551	14,876,750	1,619,932	-216,993	13,039,825	3,969,278	1,715,354	21,024	890,604	578,890
1990	19,707,903	15,473,376	58,684	15,532,060	1,707,738	-222,511	13,601,811	4,260,914	1,845,178	21,736	906,684	585,331
1991	20,185,582	15,878,500	46,419	15,924,919	1,771,727	-248,587	13,904,605	4,248,631	2,032,346	21,932	920,370	574,522
1992	21,368,683	16,808,529	52,477	16,861,006	1,862,883	-282,417	14,715,706	4,366,276	2,286,701	22,800	937,231	574,986
1993	22,385,567	17,558,579	38,529	17,597,108	1,951,785	-327,349	15,317,974	4,620,533	2,447,060	23,527	951,484	582,854
1994	23,679,571	18,599,840	58,274	18,658,114	2,057,544	-382,704	16,217,866	4,920,959	2,540,746	24,542	964,850	600,918
1995	24,844,422	19,506,042	55,513	19,561,555	2,154,176	-432,149	16,975,230	5,115,267	2,753,925	25,419	977,397	616,799
1996	26,062,813	20,471,622	72,974	20,544,596	2,245,708	-466,779	17,832,109	5,324,361	2,906,343	26,347	989,199	627,762
1997	27,859,558	22,073,549	42,629	22,116,178	2,402,986	-546,129	19,167,063	5,694,497	2,997,998	27,777	1,002,966	646,047
1998	29,779,639	23,670,440	26,423	23,696,863	2,539,594	-575,205	20,582,064	6,125,847	3,071,728	29,311	1,015,983	656,552
1999	31,255,533	25,250,131	25,712	25,275,843	2,715,142	-631,587	21,929,114	6,110,866	3,215,553	30,335	1,030,337	672,006
2000	33,721,367	27,153,665	44,582	27,198,247	2,872,468	-699,321	23,626,458	6,657,862	3,437,047	32,317	1,043,450	688,877
2001	36,085,571	29,180,787	26,268	29,207,055	3,095,473	-708,777	25,402,805	6,869,553	3,813,213	34,196	1,055,256	693,624
2002	36,931,256	29,803,521	24,925	29,828,446	3,197,197	-674,249	25,957,000	6,982,922	3,991,334	34,567	1,068,409	694,974
2003	38,749,739	30,897,403	28,860	30,926,263	3,307,696	-631,147	26,987,420	7,499,392	4,262,927	35,811	1,082,054	696,704
2004	41,063,835	33,026,971	38,849	33,065,820	3,578,240	-648,457	28,839,123	7,767,575	4,457,137	37,374	1,098,719	711,906
2005	43,781,142	35,210,478	33,932	35,244,410	3,832,604	-662,479	30,749,327	8,174,374	4,857,441	39,217	1,116,391	730,867
2006	46,841,675	36,897,940	20,098	36,918,038	4,048,232	-614,601	32,255,205	9,267,827	5,318,643	41,180	1,137,479	746,201
2007	49,389,825	38,811,283	19,692	38,830,975	4,254,151	-601,118	33,975,706	9,705,713	5,708,406	42,810	1,153,700	764,525
2008	51,333,970	39,309,765	37,332	39,347,097	4,359,380	-532,311	34,455,406	10,296,107	6,582,457	43,950	1,168,018	764,231
2009	49,174,645	37,621,284	40,019	37,661,303	4,233,500	-486,602	32,941,201	9,050,370	7,183,074	41,697	1,179,342	741,649
2010	50,800,458	38,910,563	24,092	38,934,655	4,325,136	-452,888	34,156,631	8,841,491	7,802,336	42,736	1,188,710	737,798
2011	53,969,937	40,486,656	72,656	40,559,312	4,005,670	-458,155	36,095,487	9,786,214	8,088,236	45,020	1,198,793	750,921
2012	57,161,344	42,427,295	82,043	42,509,338	4,164,462	-477,685	37,867,191	11,121,738	8,172,415	47,083	1,214,052	763,934
2013	57,309,265	43,844,847	90,145	43,934,992	4,909,942	-470,138	38,554,912	10,228,129	8,526,224	46,709	1,226,940	776,184
2014	60,041,009	45,732,859	45,931	45,778,790	5,087,859	-499,948	40,190,983	10,922,162	8,927,864	48,392	1,240,714	789,681
2015	63,474,721	48,371,649	25,109	48,396,758	5,379,838	-625,664	42,391,256	11,732,781	9,350,684	50,627	1,253,770	814,578
2016	65,404,993	49,477,957	13,475	49,491,432	5,499,859	-567,332	43,424,241	12,256,950	9,723,802	51,617	1,267,111	831,772
2017	68,633,164	51,695,815	31,400	51,727,215	5,782,459	-596,930	45,347,826	13,108,431	10,176,907	53,636	1,279,604	848,546
2018	70,993,770	53,057,645	12,230	53,069,875	5,962,913	-576,857	46,530,105	13,756,812	10,706,853	54,922	1,292,638	861,965
2019	75,419,387	55,542,519	32,765	55,575,284	6,235,918	-606,646	48,732,720	15,311,481	11,375,186	57,772	1,305,456	871,841
2020	80,711,156	56,386,117	21,957	56,408,074	6,381,226	-658,842	49,368,006	15,991,268	15,351,882	61,305	1,316,556	854,873
2021	87,442,936	61,062,561	58,467	61,121,028	6,879,994	-684,407	53,556,627	16,648,096	17,238,213	65,915	1,326,596	883,847
2022	91,339,123	66,149,967	61,197	66,211,164	7,580,075	-825,000	57,806,089	17,853,644	15,679,390	68,205	1,339,182	924,600

Personal Income and Employment by Area: Riverside-San Bernardino-Ontario, CA

(Thousands of dollars, except as noted.)

Year	Personal income, total	Derivation of personal income: Earnings by place of work: Nonfarm	Farm	Total	Less: Contributions for government social insurance	Plus: Adjustment for residence	Equals: Net earnings by place of residence	Plus: Dividends, interest, and rent	Plus: Personal current transfer receipts	Per capita personal income (dollars)	Population (persons)	Total employment
1970	4,910,718	3,135,466	112,771	3,248,237	204,697	439,194	3,482,734	856,272	571,712	4,294	1,143,539	418,790
1971	5,326,325	3,341,866	94,990	3,436,856	225,316	540,962	3,752,502	927,001	646,822	4,548	1,171,161	422,980
1972	5,948,005	3,683,519	144,267	3,827,786	260,583	672,950	4,240,153	1,006,723	701,129	5,001	1,189,476	436,775
1973	6,614,417	4,046,761	168,227	4,214,988	323,838	809,591	4,700,741	1,123,933	789,743	5,502	1,202,185	458,353
1974	7,425,733	4,414,477	167,136	4,581,613	364,732	958,866	5,175,747	1,286,663	963,323	6,038	1,229,743	468,665
1975	8,414,136	4,779,190	224,490	5,003,680	389,832	1,129,521	5,743,369	1,445,689	1,225,078	6,739	1,248,571	473,347
1976	9,506,530	5,383,473	257,788	5,641,261	442,192	1,334,345	6,533,414	1,589,439	1,383,677	7,412	1,282,517	491,513
1977	10,697,117	6,088,613	259,954	6,348,567	510,694	1,568,986	7,406,859	1,783,419	1,506,839	7,938	1,347,627	524,096
1978	12,367,023	7,121,761	255,381	7,377,142	610,948	1,870,814	8,637,008	2,077,828	1,652,187	8,614	1,435,733	566,072
1979	14,019,963	8,080,842	197,276	8,278,118	725,753	2,197,277	9,749,642	2,412,217	1,858,104	9,366	1,496,847	596,581
1980	16,173,034	8,889,079	263,796	9,152,875	780,376	2,592,939	10,965,438	2,972,241	2,235,355	10,285	1,572,429	609,845
1981	18,554,971	9,768,364	284,213	10,052,577	929,185	3,121,272	12,244,664	3,601,136	2,709,171	11,410	1,626,183	618,273
1982	20,048,897	10,207,063	335,822	10,542,885	992,886	3,488,818	13,038,817	4,017,468	2,992,612	11,887	1,686,602	618,248
1983	22,056,315	11,154,689	389,914	11,544,603	1,111,544	3,966,401	14,399,460	4,462,996	3,193,859	12,651	1,743,463	645,466
1984	24,831,207	12,688,834	434,226	13,123,060	1,310,782	4,639,709	16,451,987	4,987,711	3,391,509	13,711	1,811,019	685,286
1985	27,749,370	14,311,988	459,539	14,771,527	1,503,117	5,346,532	18,614,942	5,409,858	3,724,570	14,621	1,897,927	736,046
1986	30,846,509	16,059,254	519,696	16,578,950	1,708,433	6,067,605	20,938,122	5,829,748	4,078,639	15,459	1,995,378	781,634
1987	34,106,429	18,165,339	513,690	18,679,029	1,935,780	6,976,851	23,720,100	6,036,252	4,350,077	16,071	2,122,256	829,482
1988	38,061,489	20,304,888	586,423	20,891,311	2,242,076	7,903,555	26,552,790	6,694,762	4,813,937	16,788	2,267,166	889,223
1989	42,622,066	22,371,229	558,642	22,929,871	2,509,048	8,860,607	29,281,430	7,978,999	5,361,637	17,486	2,437,479	947,954
1990	47,163,106	24,489,966	610,184	25,100,150	2,724,088	10,424,343	32,800,405	8,351,388	6,011,313	17,930	2,630,471	1,003,046
1991	48,936,495	25,989,035	527,988	26,517,023	2,894,892	9,989,314	33,611,445	8,499,476	6,825,574	17,866	2,739,150	1,037,939
1992	51,241,754	27,686,170	530,221	28,216,391	3,054,213	9,716,436	34,878,614	8,451,775	7,911,365	18,162	2,821,341	1,035,249
1993	52,590,481	28,276,224	516,656	28,792,880	3,138,414	9,773,034	35,427,500	8,656,273	8,506,708	18,359	2,864,517	1,039,281
1994	54,061,369	29,562,571	562,443	30,125,014	3,293,135	9,565,778	36,397,657	8,931,668	8,732,044	18,607	2,905,505	1,065,322
1995	56,045,221	30,907,941	550,028	31,457,969	3,397,410	9,400,045	37,460,604	9,372,370	9,212,247	19,000	2,949,807	1,099,819
1996	58,694,305	32,522,674	668,841	33,191,515	3,466,710	9,275,386	39,000,191	9,956,329	9,737,785	19,628	2,990,316	1,132,225
1997	62,029,662	34,886,249	558,232	35,444,481	3,667,079	10,054,415	41,831,817	10,351,721	9,846,124	20,389	3,042,372	1,168,111
1998	67,446,948	38,830,759	741,612	39,572,371	4,005,391	10,395,776	45,962,756	11,055,355	10,428,837	21,700	3,108,220	1,244,588
1999	71,643,363	42,456,017	697,651	43,153,668	4,384,883	10,516,676	49,285,461	11,393,798	10,964,104	22,462	3,189,513	1,311,728
2000	77,036,598	46,390,367	449,493	46,839,860	4,760,005	11,266,356	53,346,211	12,178,518	11,511,869	23,508	3,277,022	1,355,540
2001	82,826,202	49,756,930	584,207	50,341,137	5,368,291	11,956,884	56,929,730	13,120,162	12,776,310	24,524	3,377,365	1,402,821
2002	87,574,813	53,826,359	502,791	54,329,150	5,904,644	12,470,849	60,895,355	12,933,832	13,745,626	25,115	3,486,938	1,458,808
2003	94,510,919	58,499,422	616,241	59,115,663	6,504,497	13,207,431	65,818,597	13,922,463	14,769,859	26,124	3,617,771	1,517,865
2004	102,460,153	65,652,579	743,363	66,395,942	7,565,705	14,036,601	72,866,838	13,916,117	15,677,198	27,282	3,755,607	1,611,456
2005	110,131,984	71,458,651	655,895	72,114,546	8,207,490	14,888,118	78,795,174	14,687,994	16,648,816	28,416	3,875,709	1,698,907
2006	118,971,034	76,906,871	465,485	77,372,356	8,501,716	16,025,627	84,896,267	15,991,702	18,083,065	29,843	3,986,510	1,766,286
2007	124,893,160	78,281,303	713,118	78,994,421	8,460,872	16,867,361	87,400,910	18,017,761	19,474,489	30,706	4,067,344	1,799,648
2008	126,738,009	75,988,449	611,869	76,600,318	8,356,649	16,462,222	84,705,891	19,550,109	22,482,009	30,811	4,113,447	1,747,924
2009	124,035,144	71,827,242	391,559	72,218,801	8,009,376	16,043,987	80,253,412	18,800,723	24,981,009	29,811	4,160,685	1,666,033
2010	128,203,659	73,514,878	480,369	73,995,247	7,957,264	15,726,744	81,764,727	18,629,893	27,809,039	30,231	4,240,739	1,638,750
2011	135,565,456	77,544,582	682,539	78,227,121	7,574,038	16,801,069	87,454,152	20,029,027	28,082,277	31,628	4,286,191	1,678,301
2012	138,531,853	79,626,191	600,419	80,226,610	7,746,585	17,218,222	89,698,247	20,421,069	28,412,537	32,076	4,318,845	1,727,717
2013	142,397,519	82,941,358	640,867	83,582,225	8,982,529	17,472,760	92,072,456	20,907,956	29,417,107	32,763	4,346,320	1,788,249
2014	149,581,603	87,551,992	810,178	88,362,170	9,565,555	17,464,242	96,260,857	22,112,700	31,208,046	34,115	4,384,684	1,868,328
2015	158,856,017	94,721,999	734,837	95,456,836	10,286,464	16,911,304	102,081,676	23,187,981	33,586,360	35,917	4,422,911	1,944,599
2016	166,450,541	99,168,139	627,390	99,795,529	10,779,158	18,653,276	107,669,647	23,970,093	34,810,801	37,275	4,465,521	1,993,220
2017	172,482,928	104,311,682	696,275	105,007,957	11,376,838	19,274,907	112,906,026	25,016,601	34,560,301	38,229	4,511,846	2,052,304
2018	180,509,249	109,973,683	525,076	110,498,759	12,183,278	20,356,762	118,672,243	25,562,184	36,274,822	39,671	4,550,170	2,121,923
2019	192,796,729	116,773,616	596,037	117,369,653	13,041,651	22,335,635	126,663,637	27,195,171	38,937,921	42,127	4,576,562	2,169,139
2020	217,299,804	121,296,133	634,398	121,930,531	13,647,229	23,016,916	131,300,218	27,752,243	58,247,343	47,177	4,606,086	2,150,070
2021	234,961,141	134,315,850	536,536	134,852,386	15,102,472	22,055,572	141,805,486	29,614,899	63,540,756	50,572	4,646,060	2,261,277
2022	235,277,628	143,347,181	598,507	143,945,688	16,555,501	26,024,704	153,414,891	31,072,748	50,789,989	50,407	4,667,558	2,393,652

Personal Income and Employment by Area: Roanoke, VA

(Thousands of dollars, except as noted.)

Year	Personal income, total	Derivation of personal income									Per capita personal income (dollars)	Population (persons)	Total employment
		Earnings by place of work			Less: Contributions for government social insurance	Plus: Adjustment for residence	Equals: Net earnings by place of residence	Plus: Dividends, interest, and rent	Plus: Personal current transfer receipts				
		Nonfarm	Farm	Total									
1970	858,818	730,643	5,166	735,809	51,639	-17,093	667,077	114,101	77,640	3,708	231,596	113,547
1971	938,685	794,236	5,124	799,360	57,676	-19,726	721,958	126,245	90,482	3,938	238,357	115,420
1972	1,036,415	884,884	6,865	891,749	67,325	-28,058	796,366	138,359	101,690	4,257	243,439	120,323
1973	1,166,816	1,001,613	8,755	1,010,368	86,635	-34,251	889,482	158,871	118,463	4,702	248,131	128,106
1974	1,295,167	1,094,586	10,001	1,104,587	97,675	-37,637	969,275	185,867	140,025	5,153	251,318	131,119
1975	1,423,222	1,160,547	7,237	1,167,784	100,252	-27,964	1,039,568	202,276	181,378	5,616	253,423	128,335
1976	1,582,041	1,297,444	6,213	1,303,657	114,726	-25,349	1,163,582	219,675	198,784	6,190	255,587	131,459
1977	1,735,818	1,426,642	5,681	1,432,323	127,564	-22,541	1,282,218	239,864	213,736	6,711	258,644	135,493
1978	1,970,463	1,610,288	7,666	1,617,954	145,076	-9,154	1,463,724	268,415	238,324	7,578	260,021	140,517
1979	2,152,456	1,764,198	6,158	1,770,356	165,451	-27,549	1,577,356	308,601	266,499	8,220	261,869	141,562
1980	2,371,938	1,901,839	148	1,901,987	178,693	-46,885	1,676,409	382,981	312,548	9,105	260,501	140,251
1981	2,616,863	2,047,711	3,461	2,051,172	207,136	-51,690	1,792,346	469,135	355,382	10,000	261,693	138,411
1982	2,778,370	2,126,898	1,017	2,127,915	220,821	-57,125	1,849,969	542,497	385,904	10,615	261,751	138,094
1983	3,020,977	2,330,508	4,006	2,334,514	245,691	-62,051	2,026,772	579,651	414,554	11,545	261,672	140,118
1984	3,385,543	2,621,925	7,535	2,629,460	286,004	-73,820	2,269,636	683,244	432,663	12,890	262,643	146,364
1985	3,652,041	2,858,005	8,502	2,866,507	317,600	-85,205	2,463,702	725,590	462,749	13,875	263,208	152,702
1986	3,875,457	3,038,603	10,437	3,049,040	348,615	-90,241	2,610,184	772,777	492,496	14,700	263,645	155,869
1987	4,120,595	3,278,186	12,646	3,290,832	371,674	-98,532	2,820,626	786,475	513,494	15,548	265,026	160,150
1988	4,371,777	3,434,023	15,906	3,449,929	399,155	-106,690	2,944,084	892,016	535,677	16,447	265,805	159,825
1989	4,751,158	3,664,584	21,315	3,685,899	425,194	-121,032	3,139,673	1,028,523	582,962	17,811	266,749	164,203
1990	5,025,179	3,904,116	25,411	3,929,527	457,682	-140,300	3,331,545	1,066,941	626,693	18,650	269,440	166,966
1991	5,167,701	4,008,534	22,642	4,031,176	474,463	-151,806	3,404,907	1,079,752	683,042	18,936	272,906	164,617
1992	5,448,127	4,287,022	22,515	4,309,537	499,944	-174,329	3,635,264	1,058,876	753,987	19,887	273,951	166,401
1993	5,732,681	4,549,155	17,606	4,566,761	530,207	-198,509	3,838,045	1,102,414	792,222	20,722	276,643	169,750
1994	6,013,912	4,758,678	18,740	4,777,418	551,815	-221,263	4,004,340	1,160,406	849,166	21,542	279,176	175,063
1995	6,322,895	4,994,027	14,725	5,008,752	582,236	-247,484	4,179,032	1,241,106	902,757	22,506	280,938	179,737
1996	6,626,181	5,196,877	12,302	5,209,179	601,512	-268,955	4,338,712	1,345,200	942,269	23,421	282,915	183,486
1997	6,911,692	5,426,825	6,988	5,433,813	625,354	-288,335	4,520,124	1,420,516	971,052	24,286	284,593	183,985
1998	7,373,361	5,873,925	9,714	5,883,639	664,502	-329,381	4,889,756	1,474,973	1,008,632	25,802	285,762	191,061
1999	7,634,915	6,136,355	4,443	6,140,798	693,661	-357,139	5,089,998	1,492,430	1,052,487	26,585	287,193	190,906
2000	8,017,260	6,391,352	9,930	6,401,282	713,014	-395,257	5,293,011	1,606,429	1,117,820	27,770	288,699	194,558
2001	8,491,236	6,754,335	7,297	6,761,632	756,393	-410,301	5,594,938	1,668,029	1,228,269	29,326	289,547	191,045
2002	8,757,473	6,976,994	2,424	6,979,418	785,650	-423,425	5,770,343	1,679,377	1,307,753	30,150	290,466	188,705
2003	8,982,945	7,139,058	-3,557	7,135,501	802,039	-433,953	5,899,509	1,688,925	1,394,511	30,755	292,082	187,373
2004	9,429,734	7,520,225	9,460	7,529,685	852,944	-464,981	6,211,760	1,738,172	1,479,802	32,102	293,745	190,308
2005	9,756,710	7,803,834	9,866	7,813,700	896,518	-491,533	6,425,649	1,728,314	1,602,747	32,917	296,405	194,974
2006	10,236,326	8,142,750	33	8,142,783	949,984	-519,961	6,672,838	1,812,939	1,750,549	34,129	299,930	200,016
2007	10,933,035	8,532,822	3,361	8,536,183	992,396	-548,416	6,995,371	2,062,475	1,875,189	36,100	302,858	202,745
2008	11,473,034	8,783,021	7,424	8,790,445	1,027,378	-577,702	7,185,365	2,184,636	2,103,033	37,543	305,596	201,275
2009	11,293,378	8,639,681	4,361	8,644,042	1,017,841	-567,886	7,058,315	1,951,414	2,283,649	36,689	307,816	193,945
2010	11,528,868	8,688,611	8,027	8,696,638	1,016,462	-552,235	7,127,941	1,950,448	2,450,479	37,354	308,634	190,542
2011	11,964,228	8,899,097	18,566	8,917,663	939,255	-580,247	7,398,161	2,073,561	2,492,506	38,678	309,333	192,046
2012	12,595,592	9,221,557	19,748	9,241,305	968,708	-598,264	7,674,333	2,368,255	2,553,004	40,521	310,843	193,642
2013	12,392,947	9,313,686	16,419	9,330,105	1,113,227	-595,383	7,621,495	2,142,441	2,629,011	39,670	312,402	194,142
2014	12,781,342	9,457,501	17,911	9,475,412	1,131,136	-608,124	7,736,152	2,298,204	2,746,986	40,778	313,438	195,909
2015	13,394,497	9,944,057	3,393	9,947,450	1,181,123	-655,326	8,111,001	2,429,320	2,854,176	42,655	314,023	196,531
2016	13,480,489	9,851,975	-3,998	9,847,977	1,177,892	-628,717	8,041,368	2,480,865	2,958,256	42,984	313,616	197,127
2017	13,757,321	9,896,183	1,380	9,897,563	1,196,015	-619,576	8,081,972	2,614,896	3,060,453	43,813	314,002	196,785
2018	14,230,948	10,168,052	-7,550	10,160,502	1,234,384	-638,756	8,287,362	2,754,872	3,188,714	45,273	314,339	198,435
2019	14,625,996	10,397,483	-1,829	10,395,654	1,268,553	-655,530	8,471,571	2,802,747	3,351,678	46,442	314,933	198,285
2020	15,688,604	10,611,655	-3,738	10,607,917	1,296,788	-671,474	8,639,655	2,798,441	4,250,508	49,773	315,205	193,366
2021	16,843,005	11,197,125	-1,289	11,195,836	1,374,857	-699,758	9,121,221	2,943,968	4,777,816	53,519	314,712	198,114
2022	17,364,939	11,988,227	-3,467	11,984,760	1,491,736	-753,468	9,739,556	3,173,232	4,452,151	55,243	314,340	205,209

Personal Income and Employment by Area: Rochester, MN

(Thousands of dollars, except as noted.)

Year	Personal income, total	Derivation of personal income: Earnings by place of work: Nonfarm	Farm	Total	Less: Contributions for government social insurance	Plus: Adjustment for residence	Equals: Net earnings by place of residence	Plus: Dividends, interest, and rent	Plus: Personal current transfer receipts	Per capita personal income (dollars)	Population (persons)	Total employment
1970	531,247	386,908	54,160	441,068	26,598	-3,571	410,899	79,110	41,238	3,888	136,645	61,810
1971	566,507	415,324	51,141	466,465	29,647	-4,464	432,354	86,631	47,522	4,105	138,020	62,584
1972	625,050	457,361	61,672	519,033	34,157	-5,673	479,203	93,502	52,345	4,478	139,574	66,413
1973	741,615	516,543	108,372	624,915	44,716	-7,622	572,577	107,062	61,976	5,288	140,244	70,682
1974	782,079	562,304	81,076	643,380	50,508	-8,512	584,360	123,485	74,234	5,529	141,439	72,619
1975	865,503	633,726	68,272	701,998	55,511	-11,901	634,586	142,159	88,758	6,088	142,168	73,701
1976	944,395	719,060	52,250	771,310	64,229	-14,830	692,251	154,826	97,318	6,563	143,886	76,699
1977	1,098,729	802,415	106,467	908,882	71,851	-18,514	818,517	176,384	103,828	7,551	145,499	78,691
1978	1,238,530	929,187	112,323	1,041,510	86,719	-25,225	929,566	195,132	113,832	8,484	145,983	81,851
1979	1,331,676	1,037,311	72,670	1,109,981	100,475	-28,452	981,054	220,822	129,800	9,015	147,713	84,728
1980	1,488,144	1,142,203	64,120	1,206,323	110,485	-32,394	1,063,444	269,221	155,479	10,024	148,456	86,430
1981	1,654,195	1,237,975	70,431	1,308,406	128,063	-33,592	1,146,751	326,421	181,023	11,045	149,775	86,334
1982	1,833,479	1,343,421	74,810	1,418,231	143,134	-38,412	1,236,685	395,415	201,379	12,188	150,427	86,370
1983	1,890,073	1,449,568	-5,787	1,443,781	156,269	-42,342	1,245,170	423,255	221,648	12,441	151,922	88,143
1984	2,199,083	1,637,710	89,078	1,726,788	181,227	-50,056	1,495,505	464,906	238,672	14,361	153,128	91,755
1985	2,306,708	1,735,272	77,798	1,813,070	195,256	-54,814	1,563,000	489,856	253,852	14,912	154,688	92,865
1986	2,424,908	1,816,262	107,005	1,923,267	209,000	-57,444	1,656,823	502,069	266,016	15,665	154,797	92,206
1987	2,567,360	1,934,281	146,085	2,080,366	220,219	-64,215	1,795,932	495,906	275,522	16,513	155,475	94,618
1988	2,674,767	2,102,498	87,019	2,189,517	247,634	-72,277	1,869,606	512,813	292,348	16,838	158,849	98,326
1989	2,988,644	2,292,336	135,285	2,427,621	269,737	-81,994	2,075,890	590,949	321,805	18,564	160,993	101,567
1990	3,191,806	2,506,340	126,270	2,632,610	296,815	-93,328	2,242,467	607,445	341,894	19,530	163,427	104,645
1991	3,318,812	2,650,254	96,584	2,746,838	318,121	-96,462	2,332,255	621,696	364,861	19,973	166,169	106,918
1992	3,526,841	2,838,454	76,200	2,914,654	337,124	-99,931	2,477,599	654,290	394,952	20,973	168,159	108,570
1993	3,581,154	2,959,484	41,748	3,001,232	352,450	-102,613	2,546,169	623,439	411,546	20,902	171,334	110,560
1994	3,753,029	3,023,006	101,797	3,124,803	364,228	-100,983	2,659,592	653,826	439,611	21,761	172,466	110,937
1995	3,894,550	3,114,067	49,006	3,163,073	375,712	-100,557	2,686,804	735,253	472,493	22,546	172,741	113,113
1996	4,228,858	3,346,391	107,306	3,453,697	400,010	-107,489	2,946,198	782,481	500,179	24,281	174,161	114,704
1997	4,427,364	3,569,824	68,056	3,637,880	426,904	-118,813	3,092,163	825,112	510,089	25,120	176,251	118,626
1998	4,905,263	3,982,545	100,032	4,082,577	470,099	-137,135	3,475,343	909,878	520,042	27,329	179,488	123,856
1999	5,227,090	4,325,049	77,950	4,402,999	510,888	-154,195	3,737,916	930,567	558,607	28,642	182,498	127,906
2000	5,561,602	4,585,413	57,502	4,642,915	539,296	-163,877	3,939,742	1,016,925	604,935	29,970	185,573	131,560
2001	6,023,098	5,004,801	40,062	5,044,863	573,397	-178,629	4,292,837	1,050,970	679,291	32,071	187,803	132,985
2002	6,275,047	5,283,688	20,489	5,304,177	601,915	-187,586	4,514,676	1,015,491	744,880	32,915	190,646	134,143
2003	6,706,772	5,652,475	52,125	5,704,600	647,623	-210,180	4,846,797	1,061,308	798,667	34,738	193,067	136,823
2004	6,982,287	5,932,495	116,898	6,049,393	676,690	-211,980	5,160,723	976,848	844,716	35,752	195,300	138,416
2005	7,037,396	5,975,420	143,913	6,119,333	694,585	-212,351	5,212,397	947,278	877,721	35,689	197,188	139,860
2006	7,426,949	6,214,941	101,987	6,316,928	733,676	-201,253	5,381,999	1,088,619	956,331	37,179	199,763	141,767
2007	7,903,398	6,502,531	121,448	6,623,979	766,947	-197,145	5,659,887	1,207,593	1,035,918	39,168	201,782	143,685
2008	8,331,191	6,671,152	157,882	6,829,034	792,503	-186,666	5,849,865	1,320,421	1,160,905	40,803	204,181	142,482
2009	8,281,165	6,682,076	69,550	6,751,626	800,075	-215,902	5,735,649	1,269,662	1,275,854	40,181	206,097	139,761
2010	8,832,380	7,110,566	136,567	7,247,133	830,156	-186,499	6,230,478	1,215,344	1,386,558	42,606	207,304	138,051
2011	9,194,714	7,053,376	249,585	7,302,961	734,875	-180,364	6,387,722	1,411,055	1,395,937	44,018	208,887	139,582
2012	9,677,136	7,391,991	306,119	7,698,110	764,558	-186,222	6,747,330	1,532,283	1,397,523	46,016	210,299	142,443
2013	9,793,355	7,589,037	338,297	7,927,334	901,830	-201,221	6,824,283	1,526,206	1,442,866	46,063	212,606	144,400
2014	10,072,451	7,788,345	197,191	7,985,536	918,429	-202,980	6,864,127	1,673,045	1,535,279	47,042	214,116	145,276
2015	10,504,508	8,142,584	150,974	8,293,558	952,672	-227,043	7,113,843	1,765,301	1,625,364	48,689	215,745	147,839
2016	10,800,605	8,452,577	78,062	8,530,639	991,764	-239,465	7,299,410	1,813,081	1,688,114	49,448	218,425	149,367
2017	11,311,991	8,837,866	96,884	8,934,750	1,039,690	-280,074	7,614,986	1,946,471	1,750,534	51,283	220,579	150,519
2018	11,921,585	9,502,205	61,858	9,564,063	1,128,124	-349,001	8,086,938	1,967,381	1,867,266	53,545	222,645	153,028
2019	12,328,967	9,818,529	23,794	9,842,323	1,162,162	-373,136	8,307,025	2,076,001	1,945,941	54,806	224,956	154,254
2020	13,347,766	10,006,888	175,737	10,182,625	1,186,165	-435,962	8,560,498	2,154,035	2,633,233	58,916	226,557	150,136
2021	14,478,522	10,673,003	204,923	10,877,926	1,254,108	-368,413	9,255,405	2,293,233	2,929,884	63,670	227,401	154,604
2022	14,825,423	11,236,047	263,284	11,499,331	1,341,151	-378,588	9,779,592	2,517,199	2,528,632	65,003	228,073	158,240

Personal Income and Employment by Area: Rochester, NY

(Thousands of dollars, except as noted.)

		Derivation of personal income										
		Earnings by place of work										
Year	Personal income, total	Nonfarm	Farm	Total	Less: Contributions for government social insurance	Plus: Adjustment for residence	Equals: Net earnings by place of residence	Plus: Dividends, interest, and rent	Plus: Personal current transfer receipts	Per capita personal income (dollars)	Population (persons)	Total employment
1970	4,543,716	3,774,719	64,553	3,839,272	276,964	-46,065	3,516,243	656,574	370,899	4,623	982,845	439,999
1971	4,870,129	4,012,962	61,581	4,074,543	304,319	-49,932	3,720,292	695,348	454,489	4,927	988,371	440,497
1972	5,244,349	4,371,248	41,128	4,412,376	352,229	-51,695	4,008,452	741,030	494,867	5,292	991,017	447,820
1973	5,757,009	4,798,117	72,803	4,870,920	448,781	-54,291	4,367,848	832,100	557,061	5,808	991,293	464,379
1974	6,304,031	5,220,989	84,056	5,305,045	507,725	-58,456	4,738,864	941,762	623,405	6,373	989,197	475,220
1975	6,814,001	5,484,338	65,112	5,549,450	521,206	-61,152	4,967,092	1,008,879	838,030	6,839	996,288	464,343
1976	7,260,204	5,896,373	57,078	5,953,451	572,254	-61,683	5,319,514	1,061,870	878,820	7,280	997,313	468,201
1977	7,870,948	6,424,789	60,062	6,484,851	622,054	-71,141	5,791,656	1,162,967	916,325	7,874	999,583	477,239
1978	8,531,744	7,045,322	66,337	7,111,659	698,906	-75,168	6,337,585	1,224,560	969,599	8,569	995,677	489,129
1979	9,465,528	7,842,783	80,471	7,923,254	805,638	-81,155	7,036,461	1,386,060	1,043,007	9,502	996,204	501,248
1980	10,651,060	8,648,149	68,504	8,716,653	886,640	-88,518	7,741,495	1,677,118	1,232,447	10,713	994,186	499,705
1981	11,937,853	9,561,796	83,508	9,645,304	1,041,775	-96,816	8,506,713	2,046,435	1,384,705	11,958	998,299	504,102
1982	13,005,796	10,302,710	71,042	10,373,752	1,137,881	-124,035	9,111,836	2,359,976	1,533,984	12,954	1,003,975	508,477
1983	13,612,090	10,651,487	35,353	10,686,840	1,181,442	-130,530	9,374,868	2,554,093	1,683,129	13,518	1,006,962	504,266
1984	14,892,614	11,624,049	57,621	11,681,670	1,312,840	-149,789	10,219,041	2,884,606	1,788,967	14,851	1,002,789	522,629
1985	15,982,681	12,620,376	69,579	12,689,955	1,444,272	-183,241	11,062,442	3,025,266	1,894,973	15,941	1,002,633	541,363
1986	16,834,692	13,303,278	83,299	13,386,577	1,549,087	-201,120	11,636,370	3,153,543	2,044,779	16,779	1,003,295	549,723
1987	17,403,989	13,877,368	100,828	13,978,196	1,589,925	-224,320	12,163,951	3,144,245	2,095,793	17,350	1,003,095	552,418
1988	18,940,036	15,185,577	102,315	15,287,892	1,774,322	-256,855	13,256,715	3,408,379	2,274,942	18,757	1,009,766	575,050
1989	20,763,806	16,269,777	107,259	16,377,036	1,881,934	-288,626	14,206,476	4,088,968	2,468,362	20,363	1,019,683	585,517
1990	21,600,921	16,873,844	103,722	16,977,566	1,870,985	-344,381	14,762,200	4,129,563	2,709,158	21,015	1,027,880	589,401
1991	22,489,828	17,603,528	92,143	17,695,671	1,998,597	-364,028	15,333,046	4,140,308	3,016,474	21,703	1,036,248	591,189
1992	23,546,129	18,490,932	101,400	18,592,332	2,061,092	-376,912	16,154,328	4,008,230	3,383,571	22,468	1,047,976	592,760
1993	24,161,700	19,004,638	110,352	19,114,990	2,131,981	-401,766	16,581,243	3,988,341	3,592,116	22,897	1,055,228	601,469
1994	24,849,088	19,484,024	91,886	19,575,910	2,216,694	-416,834	16,942,382	4,073,082	3,833,624	23,501	1,057,376	607,597
1995	25,984,191	20,253,521	73,772	20,327,293	2,297,160	-449,681	17,580,452	4,364,114	4,039,625	24,561	1,057,933	606,742
1996	26,904,280	20,802,572	92,886	20,895,458	2,341,806	-416,963	18,136,689	4,551,432	4,216,159	25,389	1,059,684	607,448
1997	28,126,713	21,652,744	89,680	21,742,424	2,402,551	-429,860	18,910,013	4,978,377	4,238,323	26,535	1,060,003	611,491
1998	29,427,566	22,507,752	98,589	22,606,341	2,452,560	-467,404	19,686,377	5,243,468	4,497,721	27,768	1,059,773	617,789
1999	30,513,953	23,653,099	128,573	23,781,672	2,509,413	-466,870	20,805,389	5,028,384	4,680,180	28,778	1,060,310	627,638
2000	32,095,457	24,824,504	131,775	24,956,279	2,603,917	-460,815	21,891,547	5,284,683	4,919,227	30,095	1,066,482	637,905
2001	32,661,826	25,305,511	150,023	25,455,534	2,730,345	-482,769	22,242,420	5,191,367	5,228,039	30,576	1,068,215	629,922
2002	32,888,219	25,513,285	114,681	25,627,966	2,773,387	-481,947	22,372,632	4,866,708	5,648,879	30,726	1,070,355	618,405
2003	33,468,819	26,190,517	144,017	26,334,534	2,854,750	-480,940	22,998,844	4,662,024	5,807,951	31,223	1,071,918	618,059
2004	34,673,784	27,032,586	151,554	27,184,140	2,966,679	-457,015	23,760,446	4,701,967	6,211,371	32,330	1,072,494	622,365
2005	35,288,749	27,518,955	121,159	27,640,114	3,082,770	-454,261	24,103,083	4,801,692	6,383,974	32,967	1,070,418	628,593
2006	36,660,848	28,446,973	132,263	28,579,236	3,201,792	-403,404	24,974,040	4,934,713	6,752,095	34,251	1,070,370	627,488
2007	38,627,659	29,530,855	248,587	29,779,442	3,295,214	-373,115	26,111,113	5,419,397	7,097,149	36,032	1,072,040	634,330
2008	40,896,753	30,224,435	291,941	30,516,376	3,404,132	-369,562	26,742,682	6,173,870	7,980,201	38,033	1,075,302	636,154
2009	41,131,515	30,285,978	164,295	30,450,273	3,363,756	-390,986	26,695,531	5,735,842	8,700,142	38,157	1,077,941	622,604
2010	42,786,903	31,582,440	271,013	31,853,453	3,429,028	-361,684	28,062,741	5,466,713	9,257,449	39,598	1,080,527	620,720
2011	44,746,344	32,553,752	301,580	32,855,332	3,190,010	-376,106	29,289,216	6,071,679	9,385,449	41,264	1,084,399	629,239
2012	46,559,915	33,612,914	306,379	33,919,293	3,254,509	-341,001	30,323,783	6,792,908	9,443,224	42,848	1,086,625	632,115
2013	46,294,174	34,019,431	352,926	34,372,357	3,738,989	-313,746	30,319,622	6,409,276	9,565,276	42,506	1,089,109	634,846
2014	46,994,478	33,892,563	304,478	34,197,041	3,842,084	-233,731	30,121,226	6,945,933	9,927,319	43,127	1,089,687	638,637
2015	49,273,823	35,526,145	196,449	35,722,594	4,022,749	-244,871	31,454,974	7,390,274	10,428,575	45,252	1,088,882	644,271
2016	49,970,367	35,791,965	192,885	35,984,850	4,075,205	-273,385	31,636,260	7,689,897	10,644,210	45,918	1,088,253	648,587
2017	52,456,438	36,996,789	257,195	37,253,984	4,214,364	-257,064	32,782,556	8,324,508	11,349,374	48,183	1,088,691	651,030
2018	53,772,103	38,104,537	145,599	38,250,136	4,296,952	-240,589	33,712,595	8,898,826	11,160,682	49,277	1,091,227	658,661
2019	55,911,219	39,238,814	228,104	39,466,918	4,428,632	-188,385	34,849,901	9,005,808	12,055,510	51,262	1,090,696	658,158
2020	60,524,128	39,268,316	253,527	39,521,843	4,419,806	-213,198	34,888,839	9,154,268	16,481,021	55,630	1,087,983	618,565
2021	63,398,598	41,334,603	283,514	41,618,117	4,738,356	-154,288	36,725,473	9,423,556	17,249,569	58,358	1,086,382	631,924
2022	62,600,574	43,510,329	324,290	43,834,619	5,124,336	-183,403	38,526,880	9,558,136	14,515,558	57,902	1,081,152	658,165

Personal Income and Employment by Area: Rockford, IL

(Thousands of dollars, except as noted.)

Year	Personal income, total	Derivation of personal income: Earnings by place of work: Nonfarm	Farm	Total	Less: Contributions for government social insurance	Plus: Adjustment for residence	Equals: Net earnings by place of residence	Plus: Dividends, interest, and rent	Plus: Personal current transfer receipts	Per capita personal income (dollars)	Population (persons)	Total employment
1970	1,156,998	1,035,712	7,477	1,043,189	70,694	-47,053	925,442	150,923	80,633	4,259	271,661	127,617
1971	1,222,779	1,076,529	10,151	1,086,680	75,477	-49,191	962,012	160,534	100,233	4,510	271,149	123,947
1972	1,345,050	1,195,710	10,445	1,206,155	89,405	-54,089	1,062,661	172,444	109,945	4,961	271,136	129,119
1973	1,512,261	1,355,735	17,225	1,372,960	117,718	-61,946	1,193,296	193,662	125,303	5,535	273,201	137,581
1974	1,646,252	1,469,984	7,638	1,477,622	132,750	-64,978	1,279,894	220,675	145,683	5,992	274,734	139,257
1975	1,767,024	1,503,986	20,025	1,524,011	130,653	-64,179	1,329,179	244,670	193,175	6,443	274,255	133,933
1976	1,951,534	1,678,631	14,558	1,693,189	148,983	-67,732	1,476,474	262,294	212,766	7,132	273,627	136,512
1977	2,143,587	1,865,124	12,755	1,877,879	167,649	-73,687	1,636,543	288,163	218,881	7,831	273,731	140,705
1978	2,407,127	2,148,911	12,304	2,161,215	200,479	-97,243	1,863,493	321,729	221,905	8,719	276,063	147,308
1979	2,666,842	2,377,406	18,108	2,395,514	228,962	-107,646	2,058,906	361,786	246,150	9,629	276,951	150,437
1980	2,875,498	2,457,490	-577	2,456,913	233,655	-111,107	2,112,151	449,178	314,169	10,276	279,829	144,840
1981	3,192,697	2,645,891	16,659	2,662,550	268,965	-115,980	2,277,605	555,125	359,967	11,378	280,591	144,654
1982	3,293,762	2,565,655	12,458	2,578,113	262,571	-91,201	2,224,341	645,100	424,321	11,809	278,911	137,928
1983	3,409,626	2,657,579	-11,555	2,646,024	274,372	-90,827	2,280,825	683,949	444,852	12,293	277,354	136,046
1984	3,810,149	3,013,873	24,062	3,037,935	324,914	-112,051	2,600,970	778,424	430,755	13,754	277,028	143,578
1985	4,031,755	3,215,941	40,072	3,256,013	353,131	-125,638	2,777,244	799,417	455,094	14,470	278,623	147,717
1986	4,257,834	3,440,924	30,056	3,470,980	377,817	-144,736	2,948,427	828,494	480,913	15,281	278,638	151,509
1987	4,463,648	3,651,401	27,066	3,678,467	393,105	-148,015	3,137,347	821,195	505,106	15,996	279,051	154,960
1988	4,884,695	4,080,969	15,656	4,096,625	449,313	-169,655	3,477,657	880,302	526,736	17,460	279,763	161,185
1989	5,223,157	4,249,693	28,887	4,278,580	468,941	-162,768	3,646,871	1,009,499	566,787	18,551	281,563	163,402
1990	5,406,822	4,428,040	30,072	4,458,112	476,477	-165,565	3,816,070	973,291	617,461	18,991	284,702	167,347
1991	5,502,967	4,449,379	12,533	4,461,912	489,174	-128,105	3,844,633	979,428	678,906	18,983	289,895	165,457
1992	5,931,852	4,692,422	21,945	4,714,367	506,653	-108,370	4,099,344	1,043,657	788,851	20,156	294,298	165,482
1993	6,165,549	4,892,878	12,180	4,905,058	536,299	-100,567	4,268,192	1,067,939	829,418	20,649	298,582	168,660
1994	6,636,535	5,368,671	27,611	5,396,282	594,036	-123,354	4,678,892	1,123,340	834,303	21,963	302,172	175,923
1995	7,098,539	5,736,995	18,000	5,754,995	632,099	-119,336	5,003,560	1,199,441	895,538	23,223	305,671	184,417
1996	7,445,757	5,931,013	42,600	5,973,613	646,241	-115,225	5,212,147	1,290,460	943,150	24,046	309,644	186,765
1997	7,776,255	6,155,794	28,260	6,184,054	666,793	-99,952	5,417,309	1,387,715	971,231	24,897	312,342	188,652
1998	8,178,991	6,476,377	27,894	6,504,271	694,598	-107,003	5,702,670	1,457,912	1,018,409	25,963	315,025	191,098
1999	8,476,237	6,770,719	20,107	6,790,826	714,536	-76,077	6,000,213	1,434,060	1,041,964	26,689	317,596	192,185
2000	8,856,046	6,994,786	23,148	7,017,934	726,990	-66,529	6,224,415	1,525,639	1,105,992	27,586	321,033	194,248
2001	8,994,195	7,022,150	18,446	7,040,596	744,069	-12,509	6,284,018	1,471,549	1,238,628	27,826	323,229	190,203
2002	9,227,431	7,225,150	10,301	7,235,451	762,671	14,243	6,487,023	1,388,506	1,351,902	28,327	325,747	188,475
2003	9,491,083	7,311,071	10,102	7,321,173	777,183	58,407	6,602,397	1,460,407	1,428,279	28,807	329,472	187,319
2004	9,744,074	7,504,165	27,058	7,531,223	812,479	122,461	6,841,205	1,402,585	1,500,284	29,329	332,230	189,278
2005	10,150,491	7,805,077	10,541	7,815,618	873,448	190,702	7,132,872	1,374,568	1,643,051	30,219	335,903	189,260
2006	10,965,004	8,311,957	9,331	8,321,288	921,977	282,704	7,682,015	1,550,012	1,732,977	32,136	341,202	192,542
2007	11,618,576	8,634,888	34,035	8,668,923	955,081	357,209	8,071,051	1,626,398	1,921,127	33,434	347,503	196,281
2008	11,915,307	8,587,169	31,970	8,619,139	950,936	395,534	8,063,737	1,688,685	2,162,885	34,050	349,937	193,044
2009	11,542,306	7,922,103	2,585	7,924,688	875,055	353,026	7,402,659	1,646,845	2,492,802	33,000	349,766	180,378
2010	11,787,735	8,054,218	5,123	8,059,341	894,361	301,549	7,466,529	1,615,964	2,705,242	33,747	349,293	178,733
2011	12,229,434	8,439,739	58,460	8,498,199	855,391	277,447	7,920,255	1,740,384	2,568,795	35,109	348,330	182,052
2012	12,508,095	8,728,416	14,684	8,743,100	896,362	259,599	8,106,337	1,843,237	2,558,521	36,065	346,820	183,934
2013	12,787,942	8,860,715	83,138	8,943,853	1,013,945	310,987	8,240,895	1,862,041	2,685,006	36,946	346,129	183,172
2014	13,043,445	9,164,549	19,576	9,184,125	1,034,472	262,895	8,412,548	1,926,340	2,704,557	37,887	344,269	186,125
2015	13,557,459	9,515,261	-16,025	9,499,236	1,051,282	271,617	8,719,571	1,952,943	2,884,945	39,524	343,015	187,489
2016	13,602,188	9,505,029	6,682	9,511,711	1,062,513	274,237	8,723,435	1,961,713	2,917,040	39,732	342,349	186,261
2017	14,147,110	9,816,530	6,986	9,823,516	1,096,976	315,485	9,042,025	2,092,255	3,012,830	41,467	341,163	183,476
2018	14,717,213	10,397,295	12,121	10,409,416	1,169,688	257,952	9,497,680	2,123,436	3,096,097	43,237	340,385	187,424
2019	14,906,664	10,453,532	2,788	10,456,320	1,181,085	272,889	9,548,124	2,166,188	3,192,352	43,898	339,575	185,095
2020	15,944,439	10,033,613	18,408	10,052,021	1,137,952	376,273	9,290,342	2,171,795	4,482,302	47,136	338,262	173,666
2021	17,290,611	10,585,931	53,175	10,639,106	1,187,324	423,647	9,875,429	2,404,240	5,010,942	51,344	336,758	177,838
2022	17,037,544	11,317,474	63,208	11,380,682	1,324,586	401,489	10,457,585	2,523,648	4,056,311	50,806	335,342	187,544

Personal Income and Employment by Area: Rocky Mount, NC

(Thousands of dollars, except as noted.)

Year	Personal income, total	Derivation of personal income: Earnings by place of work: Nonfarm	Farm	Total	Less: Contributions for government social insurance	Plus: Adjustment for residence	Equals: Net earnings by place of residence	Plus: Dividends, interest, and rent	Plus: Personal current transfer receipts	Per capita personal income (dollars)	Population (persons)	Total employment
1970	333,106	242,455	32,529	274,984	17,855	4,101	261,230	39,404	32,472	2,986	111,571	53,924
1971	364,218	272,178	28,080	300,258	20,676	4,257	283,839	43,190	37,189	3,243	112,296	54,910
1972	421,041	317,025	36,223	353,248	25,068	3,000	331,180	48,555	41,306	3,707	113,571	58,004
1973	492,168	369,709	52,346	422,055	33,369	582	389,268	55,678	47,222	4,278	115,045	61,874
1974	553,096	414,334	56,786	471,120	39,137	359	432,342	63,533	57,221	4,752	116,381	63,125
1975	595,696	434,918	53,180	488,098	40,477	125	447,746	70,136	77,814	5,040	118,189	60,327
1976	673,334	500,034	61,036	561,070	47,479	-2,738	510,853	77,751	84,730	5,629	119,609	62,983
1977	715,562	554,134	37,517	591,651	52,255	-4,172	535,224	88,615	91,723	5,894	121,414	64,333
1978	808,523	623,600	53,060	676,660	60,064	-7,143	609,453	99,633	99,437	6,605	122,406	65,387
1979	855,423	689,839	13,722	703,561	68,664	-7,809	627,088	113,119	115,216	6,941	123,247	66,769
1980	948,688	740,481	15,654	756,135	73,744	-8,992	673,399	138,225	137,064	7,684	123,463	65,511
1981	1,106,123	829,235	51,760	880,995	88,646	-13,378	778,971	169,534	157,618	8,893	124,388	66,742
1982	1,183,207	864,496	57,823	922,319	93,013	-14,710	814,596	193,421	175,190	9,426	125,524	64,937
1983	1,260,984	955,638	34,109	989,747	103,210	-18,240	868,297	204,143	188,544	9,970	126,478	66,048
1984	1,421,526	1,064,211	66,167	1,130,378	118,052	-24,708	987,618	234,600	199,308	11,183	127,115	68,538
1985	1,515,882	1,145,223	62,735	1,207,958	129,135	-28,253	1,050,570	252,720	212,592	11,769	128,799	69,053
1986	1,606,909	1,256,602	47,421	1,304,023	144,462	-39,821	1,119,740	265,358	221,811	12,377	129,830	71,452
1987	1,712,850	1,357,616	60,304	1,417,920	153,734	-51,489	1,212,697	270,592	229,561	13,064	131,116	71,862
1988	1,893,493	1,501,142	81,572	1,582,714	174,782	-63,524	1,344,408	302,747	246,338	14,364	131,826	75,005
1989	2,039,726	1,582,409	82,267	1,664,676	184,173	-71,766	1,408,737	358,980	272,009	15,411	132,358	76,775
1990	2,125,400	1,645,906	96,111	1,742,017	196,221	-90,294	1,455,502	365,678	304,220	15,901	133,668	76,391
1991	2,211,544	1,719,375	96,229	1,815,604	207,524	-111,281	1,496,799	368,539	346,206	16,405	134,810	76,478
1992	2,350,302	1,829,863	90,608	1,920,471	218,040	-110,446	1,591,985	373,909	384,408	17,294	135,899	77,279
1993	2,483,794	1,909,455	94,901	2,004,356	228,571	-103,069	1,672,716	393,709	417,369	18,096	137,253	77,560
1994	2,603,061	1,997,106	109,109	2,106,215	241,277	-102,528	1,762,410	409,268	431,383	18,728	138,990	77,617
1995	2,763,288	2,106,980	112,631	2,219,611	254,933	-127,072	1,837,606	441,807	483,875	19,666	140,508	80,590
1996	2,980,841	2,185,720	117,978	2,303,698	261,394	-77,236	1,965,068	486,107	529,666	21,056	141,570	81,061
1997	3,186,945	2,282,622	148,423	2,431,045	270,265	-36,202	2,124,578	511,898	550,469	22,316	142,807	79,237
1998	3,288,502	2,357,162	127,184	2,484,346	279,931	-35,943	2,168,472	552,584	567,446	23,012	142,903	78,718
1999	3,348,214	2,439,149	70,097	2,509,246	290,405	-28,264	2,190,577	538,917	618,720	23,360	143,333	78,734
2000	3,508,255	2,529,017	122,546	2,651,563	301,371	-37,893	2,312,299	567,119	628,837	24,509	143,139	79,541
2001	3,676,924	2,636,071	112,087	2,748,158	310,330	-26,009	2,411,819	572,869	692,236	25,528	144,034	78,749
2002	3,660,126	2,632,163	48,510	2,680,673	310,147	-8,815	2,361,711	546,442	751,973	25,295	144,698	77,720
2003	3,764,030	2,691,482	50,122	2,741,604	322,819	7,629	2,426,414	557,290	780,326	25,872	145,487	76,803
2004	3,960,232	2,805,019	77,509	2,882,528	332,811	32	2,549,749	581,871	828,612	27,064	146,326	77,372
2005	4,104,997	2,848,575	107,448	2,956,023	343,101	13,634	2,626,556	579,417	899,024	27,920	147,027	77,496
2006	4,305,484	2,975,730	82,469	3,058,199	357,476	22,102	2,722,825	613,320	969,339	29,041	148,256	79,872
2007	4,537,743	3,065,839	63,414	3,129,253	372,719	56,057	2,812,591	699,371	1,025,781	30,324	149,644	81,592
2008	4,801,977	3,088,564	79,840	3,168,404	377,213	66,681	2,857,872	771,116	1,172,989	31,772	151,138	80,082
2009	4,810,791	2,993,732	89,868	3,083,600	366,963	52,284	2,768,921	748,732	1,293,138	31,706	151,729	76,107
2010	4,847,835	3,032,427	70,673	3,103,100	367,217	83,314	2,819,197	672,754	1,355,884	31,818	152,362	74,964
2011	4,943,013	3,002,469	69,333	3,071,802	335,408	80,091	2,816,485	743,638	1,382,890	32,614	151,561	76,708
2012	5,089,559	3,098,616	75,642	3,174,258	340,290	67,700	2,901,668	761,041	1,426,850	33,833	150,433	74,493
2013	4,974,497	3,011,152	91,073	3,102,225	378,271	51,861	2,775,815	765,866	1,432,816	33,337	149,217	73,883
2014	5,173,895	3,081,318	113,085	3,194,403	386,885	69,115	2,876,633	813,644	1,483,618	34,901	148,247	73,845
2015	5,266,543	3,184,677	81,621	3,266,298	400,750	51,220	2,916,768	841,142	1,508,633	35,940	146,536	74,077
2016	5,315,326	3,164,000	86,216	3,250,216	397,241	83,350	2,936,325	846,749	1,532,252	36,384	146,089	74,139
2017	5,467,477	3,178,127	107,588	3,285,715	399,210	115,622	3,002,127	896,382	1,568,968	37,593	145,439	73,565
2018	5,665,397	3,336,616	47,992	3,384,608	412,033	125,471	3,098,046	938,781	1,628,570	39,195	144,544	74,427
2019	5,961,651	3,468,476	72,345	3,540,821	427,257	140,960	3,254,524	1,025,153	1,681,974	41,439	143,867	74,418
2020	6,406,906	3,478,629	66,800	3,545,429	433,706	168,405	3,280,128	1,029,996	2,096,782	44,516	143,925	71,845
2021	6,884,728	3,759,766	99,075	3,858,841	465,212	129,866	3,523,495	961,484	2,399,749	47,945	143,597	74,092
2022	6,959,320	4,065,127	73,957	4,139,084	512,364	143,552	3,770,272	1,043,924	2,145,124	48,298	144,090	76,609

Personal Income and Employment by Area: Rome, GA

(Thousands of dollars, except as noted.)

Year	Personal income, total	Derivation of personal income: Earnings by place of work: Nonfarm	Farm	Total	Less: Contributions for government social insurance	Plus: Adjustment for residence	Equals: Net earnings by place of residence	Plus: Dividends, interest, and rent	Plus: Personal current transfer receipts	Per capita personal income (dollars)	Population (persons)	Total employment
1970	249,840	213,913	1,300	215,213	14,268	-1,910	199,035	28,791	22,014	3,374	74,051	34,937
1971	272,366	231,703	1,480	233,183	16,110	-2,657	214,416	32,193	25,757	3,596	75,747	35,869
1972	304,137	261,379	1,752	263,131	19,108	-4,167	239,856	35,731	28,550	3,988	76,267	37,626
1973	343,221	296,170	2,816	298,986	24,839	-4,241	269,906	40,048	33,267	4,448	77,161	39,299
1974	378,749	322,845	1,544	324,389	28,021	-5,082	291,286	45,896	41,567	4,857	77,988	39,874
1975	403,089	325,740	1,467	327,207	27,711	-5,296	294,200	51,935	56,954	5,108	78,917	37,308
1976	447,558	367,645	1,443	369,088	31,912	-6,161	331,015	56,565	59,978	5,630	79,499	38,135
1977	489,905	404,988	1,192	406,180	35,013	-6,494	364,673	62,561	62,671	6,084	80,526	38,921
1978	533,718	441,624	1,222	442,846	39,348	-5,707	397,791	68,932	66,995	6,655	80,194	39,774
1979	592,748	488,966	3,957	492,923	45,262	-7,307	440,354	77,585	74,809	7,450	79,565	40,267
1980	654,493	521,924	925	522,849	48,203	-6,347	468,299	96,602	89,592	8,196	79,860	39,476
1981	718,078	555,272	2,734	558,006	54,995	-6,744	496,267	118,535	103,276	8,982	79,948	39,772
1982	747,614	563,932	4,178	568,110	56,719	-10,482	500,909	132,077	114,628	9,357	79,897	38,189
1983	801,081	604,816	1,948	606,764	61,168	-12,451	533,145	144,902	123,034	10,119	79,163	37,795
1984	869,274	655,564	2,528	658,092	68,094	-11,108	578,890	160,227	130,157	10,972	79,223	39,730
1985	924,809	700,726	1,250	701,976	74,220	-10,795	616,961	168,733	139,115	11,630	79,520	40,092
1986	999,748	761,145	583	761,728	81,288	-12,066	668,374	183,864	147,510	12,528	79,804	41,120
1987	1,073,272	828,892	-317	828,575	87,534	-13,544	727,497	191,542	154,233	13,369	80,281	42,515
1988	1,157,482	888,941	2,433	891,374	96,776	-14,024	780,574	206,982	169,926	14,282	81,046	43,653
1989	1,240,000	937,347	3,481	940,828	102,938	-15,783	822,107	237,479	180,414	15,254	81,290	44,055
1990	1,328,966	1,009,357	3,517	1,012,874	110,076	-23,092	879,706	250,012	199,248	16,310	81,483	44,628
1991	1,406,050	1,070,441	4,878	1,075,319	118,413	-33,187	923,719	256,315	226,016	17,090	82,274	44,515
1992	1,510,766	1,165,599	6,001	1,171,600	126,865	-42,110	1,002,625	258,130	250,011	18,180	83,100	45,569
1993	1,568,302	1,206,685	5,358	1,212,043	131,717	-43,000	1,037,326	263,893	267,083	18,649	84,094	47,211
1994	1,669,500	1,293,448	6,647	1,300,095	142,393	-51,271	1,106,431	280,748	282,321	19,662	84,911	49,360
1995	1,725,974	1,301,422	5,181	1,306,603	143,174	-43,610	1,119,819	303,322	302,833	20,055	86,063	49,299
1996	1,837,512	1,378,724	7,193	1,385,917	149,583	-49,917	1,186,417	330,890	320,205	21,106	87,061	49,613
1997	1,904,441	1,420,160	6,980	1,427,140	151,216	-47,639	1,228,285	347,913	328,243	21,644	87,991	50,251
1998	1,980,615	1,467,168	7,916	1,475,084	156,805	-40,163	1,278,116	362,852	339,647	22,296	88,833	49,963
1999	2,077,593	1,569,848	7,629	1,577,477	164,849	-41,232	1,371,396	343,308	362,889	23,172	89,659	49,836
2000	2,167,853	1,598,953	6,026	1,604,979	168,078	-34,627	1,402,274	380,682	384,897	23,865	90,837	50,348
2001	2,290,194	1,705,546	9,422	1,714,968	179,471	-62,607	1,472,890	392,235	425,069	25,117	91,181	50,251
2002	2,378,898	1,786,695	4,626	1,791,321	187,829	-82,763	1,520,729	382,092	476,077	25,691	92,597	50,114
2003	2,464,283	1,866,235	6,325	1,872,560	194,552	-99,383	1,578,625	409,932	475,726	26,345	93,539	50,562
2004	2,605,901	2,012,561	10,612	2,023,173	215,896	-125,703	1,681,574	394,903	529,424	27,718	94,014	51,689
2005	2,618,966	1,929,822	11,973	1,941,795	208,929	-103,132	1,629,734	418,345	570,887	27,763	94,332	51,412
2006	2,707,574	2,038,043	5,496	2,043,539	221,054	-138,356	1,684,129	428,906	594,539	28,451	95,165	52,715
2007	2,797,872	2,032,042	10,244	2,042,286	219,155	-135,202	1,687,929	487,817	622,126	29,356	95,308	52,351
2008	2,863,471	2,053,494	11,410	2,064,904	233,870	-148,294	1,682,740	507,679	673,052	29,852	95,922	51,524
2009	2,827,367	2,045,584	9,894	2,055,478	230,585	-190,186	1,634,707	449,357	743,303	29,335	96,383	49,701
2010	2,915,389	2,089,463	6,918	2,096,381	236,142	-206,528	1,653,711	449,628	812,050	30,231	96,437	49,378
2011	3,000,248	2,107,021	4,130	2,111,151	211,487	-222,160	1,677,504	469,055	853,689	31,195	96,178	49,149
2012	3,026,934	2,162,286	16,427	2,178,713	218,281	-235,523	1,724,909	463,574	838,451	31,547	95,950	49,229
2013	3,049,994	2,212,838	18,229	2,231,067	250,996	-233,819	1,746,252	450,565	853,177	31,802	95,907	49,429
2014	3,200,587	2,307,446	19,988	2,327,434	258,767	-231,456	1,837,211	477,550	885,826	33,374	95,900	50,604
2015	3,343,263	2,401,843	20,193	2,422,036	267,403	-233,656	1,920,977	516,438	905,848	34,748	96,214	51,184
2016	3,435,330	2,440,956	11,787	2,452,743	272,960	-232,600	1,947,183	556,773	931,374	35,514	96,732	51,858
2017	3,524,634	2,502,487	13,818	2,516,305	279,476	-213,458	2,023,371	548,109	953,154	36,165	97,461	52,956
2018	3,665,617	2,582,835	8,093	2,590,928	292,784	-199,288	2,098,856	566,701	1,000,060	37,439	97,909	53,224
2019	3,807,930	2,626,465	8,302	2,634,767	301,964	-188,689	2,144,114	613,424	1,050,392	38,728	98,324	53,255
2020	4,036,097	2,610,354	4,551	2,614,905	304,603	-200,721	2,109,581	581,688	1,344,828	40,944	98,575	51,953
2021	4,363,897	2,817,465	9,300	2,826,765	332,141	-225,819	2,268,805	638,803	1,456,289	44,304	98,499	54,063
2022	4,388,071	2,997,425	14,886	3,012,311	359,871	-234,833	2,417,607	670,261	1,300,203	44,126	99,443	55,906

Personal Income and Employment by Area: Sacramento-Roseville-Folsom, CA

(Thousands of dollars, except as noted.)

Year	Personal income, total	Derivation of personal income: Earnings by place of work								Per capita personal income (dollars)	Population (persons)	Total employment
		Nonfarm	Farm	Total	Less: Contributions for government social insurance	Plus: Adjustment for residence	Equals: Net earnings by place of residence	Plus: Dividends, interest, and rent	Plus: Personal current transfer receipts			
1970	4,056,127	3,019,145	78,526	3,097,671	167,543	46,767	2,976,895	667,330	411,902	4,761	852,036	360,459
1971	4,462,068	3,312,958	79,496	3,392,454	189,765	46,656	3,249,345	745,796	466,927	5,093	876,053	368,520
1972	4,928,736	3,674,421	99,494	3,773,915	223,152	48,815	3,599,578	824,161	504,997	5,460	902,647	385,583
1973	5,445,749	4,031,560	137,550	4,169,110	277,364	53,004	3,944,750	942,008	558,991	6,012	905,830	400,639
1974	6,137,885	4,441,915	192,552	4,634,467	315,137	59,040	4,378,370	1,092,913	666,602	6,619	927,304	417,125
1975	6,886,120	4,928,191	162,706	5,090,897	347,042	73,596	4,817,451	1,233,363	835,306	7,257	948,850	431,998
1976	7,619,961	5,541,048	109,773	5,650,821	401,160	77,921	5,327,582	1,358,501	933,878	7,847	971,060	450,281
1977	8,521,066	6,224,320	134,273	6,358,593	461,389	86,478	5,983,682	1,527,523	1,009,861	8,521	1,000,056	471,705
1978	9,760,416	7,156,718	141,698	7,298,416	547,397	103,593	6,854,612	1,785,780	1,120,024	9,378	1,040,724	504,114
1979	11,064,099	8,108,914	160,588	8,269,502	656,579	107,234	7,720,157	2,060,800	1,283,142	10,326	1,071,481	532,619
1980	12,431,345	8,744,342	214,973	8,959,315	690,972	132,075	8,400,418	2,490,761	1,540,166	11,230	1,106,955	544,041
1981	13,758,233	9,487,978	150,893	9,638,871	817,934	117,513	8,938,450	2,966,370	1,853,413	12,139	1,133,346	557,728
1982	14,768,437	10,104,581	117,568	10,222,149	889,275	124,855	9,457,729	3,283,293	2,027,415	12,638	1,168,540	565,530
1983	15,973,972	10,974,796	70,342	11,045,138	1,005,026	131,656	10,171,768	3,652,748	2,149,456	13,379	1,193,993	586,240
1984	17,899,515	12,445,247	159,386	12,604,633	1,184,438	135,814	11,556,009	4,070,375	2,273,131	14,691	1,218,388	613,520
1985	19,818,671	13,983,584	158,081	14,141,665	1,353,674	131,066	12,919,057	4,421,892	2,477,722	15,845	1,250,764	649,028
1986	21,639,012	15,511,373	154,651	15,666,024	1,529,413	132,797	14,269,408	4,685,312	2,684,292	16,838	1,285,092	678,664
1987	23,397,271	17,127,656	194,126	17,321,782	1,701,695	130,664	15,750,751	4,805,476	2,841,044	17,575	1,331,264	718,562
1988	25,565,044	18,839,745	194,123	19,033,868	1,947,474	140,321	17,226,715	5,240,788	3,097,541	18,540	1,378,887	756,390
1989	28,313,165	20,683,946	199,257	20,883,203	2,153,381	123,653	18,853,475	6,031,670	3,428,020	19,820	1,428,491	791,265
1990	31,024,578	22,952,847	219,420	23,172,267	2,372,660	117,914	20,917,521	6,276,448	3,830,609	20,391	1,521,462	837,598
1991	32,913,681	24,411,529	189,703	24,601,232	2,541,216	75,526	22,135,542	6,501,080	4,277,059	21,004	1,566,994	846,203
1992	34,850,641	25,780,556	192,455	25,973,011	2,668,907	20,321	23,324,425	6,556,006	4,970,210	21,900	1,591,373	838,258
1993	35,731,488	26,310,906	236,163	26,547,069	2,739,299	38,692	23,846,462	6,666,624	5,218,402	22,220	1,608,074	837,172
1994	37,761,604	28,056,083	232,174	28,288,257	2,921,374	-8,253	25,358,630	7,090,896	5,312,078	23,289	1,621,444	870,499
1995	40,291,071	29,820,984	215,440	30,036,424	3,057,859	-79,255	26,899,310	7,784,164	5,607,597	24,492	1,645,098	886,610
1996	42,195,181	31,183,514	236,265	31,419,779	3,130,865	-98,637	28,190,277	8,094,018	5,910,886	25,228	1,672,583	914,825
1997	44,847,810	33,521,185	224,093	33,745,278	3,325,745	-160,274	30,259,259	8,630,409	5,958,142	26,373	1,700,488	938,908
1998	48,309,319	36,574,979	198,079	36,773,058	3,593,508	-187,080	32,992,470	8,996,130	6,320,719	27,895	1,731,847	973,971
1999	52,043,546	39,828,950	273,415	40,102,365	3,921,445	-166,246	36,014,674	9,347,885	6,680,987	29,449	1,767,237	1,017,726
2000	56,774,638	44,126,618	233,133	44,359,751	4,286,203	-145,306	39,928,242	9,858,248	6,988,148	31,403	1,807,949	1,041,891
2001	62,032,565	48,812,679	203,317	49,015,996	4,839,635	-176,967	43,999,394	10,227,916	7,805,255	33,238	1,866,310	1,084,938
2002	64,534,545	51,416,952	202,967	51,619,919	5,162,298	-190,443	46,267,178	9,961,843	8,305,524	33,550	1,923,508	1,099,759
2003	68,434,608	54,334,193	218,002	54,552,195	5,525,250	-184,125	48,842,820	10,806,506	8,785,282	34,729	1,970,542	1,124,077
2004	72,545,312	57,923,535	253,363	58,176,898	6,066,792	-287,581	51,822,525	11,389,208	9,333,579	36,116	2,008,663	1,157,416
2005	75,722,695	60,969,583	233,953	61,203,536	6,417,650	-377,030	54,408,856	11,429,127	9,884,712	37,213	2,034,850	1,191,438
2006	80,514,751	64,137,858	214,515	64,352,373	6,541,898	-363,002	57,447,473	12,254,963	10,812,315	39,125	2,057,885	1,214,204
2007	84,139,826	65,626,374	318,775	65,945,149	6,551,592	-326,957	59,066,600	13,499,146	11,574,080	40,409	2,082,217	1,232,552
2008	87,071,361	65,657,368	339,263	65,996,631	6,639,951	-282,083	59,074,597	14,840,503	13,156,261	41,299	2,108,310	1,209,029
2009	85,564,714	63,099,988	402,534	63,502,522	6,437,524	-152,895	56,912,103	14,014,407	14,638,204	40,121	2,132,657	1,162,373
2010	87,891,943	63,812,512	299,670	64,112,182	6,356,134	-29,337	57,726,711	13,786,905	16,378,327	40,802	2,154,127	1,136,572
2011	92,398,939	66,308,271	340,647	66,648,918	5,957,602	23,324	60,714,640	15,152,489	16,531,810	42,471	2,175,562	1,139,392
2012	96,097,050	68,762,796	443,720	69,206,516	6,160,162	186,139	63,232,493	16,062,995	16,801,562	43,779	2,195,051	1,176,108
2013	99,198,076	71,833,253	487,756	72,321,009	7,144,431	221,435	65,398,013	16,152,393	17,647,670	44,734	2,217,490	1,211,576
2014	104,932,300	75,353,655	458,874	75,812,529	7,505,369	210,332	68,517,492	17,380,143	19,034,665	46,743	2,244,867	1,241,758
2015	112,107,678	80,255,037	475,125	80,730,162	7,940,542	392,391	73,182,011	18,219,365	20,706,302	49,286	2,274,649	1,278,955
2016	116,821,648	83,491,787	417,947	83,909,734	8,310,748	512,344	76,111,330	19,046,242	21,664,076	50,659	2,306,062	1,309,336
2017	121,840,785	87,523,787	420,665	87,944,452	8,736,662	674,797	79,882,587	20,383,142	21,575,056	52,134	2,337,065	1,337,175
2018	127,927,397	92,172,296	331,596	92,503,892	9,312,091	690,458	83,882,259	21,305,367	22,739,771	54,155	2,362,237	1,378,677
2019	135,140,859	96,836,520	316,721	97,153,241	9,852,766	612,487	87,912,962	23,005,291	24,222,606	56,660	2,385,124	1,395,516
2020	148,099,855	100,180,978	350,887	100,531,865	10,226,967	478,597	90,783,495	23,263,366	34,052,994	61,712	2,399,865	1,364,214
2021	160,571,732	108,258,128	342,274	108,600,402	11,049,621	385,811	97,936,592	25,702,270	36,932,870	66,696	2,407,524	1,412,828
2022	161,774,262	114,875,835	332,752	115,208,587	12,065,151	218,765	103,362,201	27,108,183	31,303,878	66,940	2,416,702	1,486,316

Personal Income and Employment by Area: Saginaw, MI

(Thousands of dollars, except as noted.)

Year	Personal income, total	Derivation of personal income: Earnings by place of work: Nonfarm	Earnings by place of work: Farm	Earnings by place of work: Total	Less: Contributions for government social insurance	Plus: Adjustment for residence	Equals: Net earnings by place of residence	Plus: Dividends, interest, and rent	Plus: Personal current transfer receipts	Per capita personal income (dollars)	Population (persons)	Total employment
1970	833,147	725,462	9,119	734,581	51,926	-38,394	644,261	112,392	76,494	3,781	220,370	84,309
1971	967,531	865,612	7,978	873,590	63,632	-52,762	757,196	120,325	90,010	4,335	223,170	89,057
1972	1,073,395	964,157	11,033	975,190	75,246	-58,727	841,217	129,388	102,790	4,790	224,074	92,541
1973	1,201,599	1,086,788	19,860	1,106,648	98,608	-66,015	942,025	141,516	118,058	5,336	225,199	96,459
1974	1,268,242	1,084,061	39,378	1,123,439	101,700	-56,915	964,824	159,063	144,355	5,614	225,920	95,113
1975	1,373,369	1,157,164	19,777	1,176,941	106,544	-58,140	1,012,257	177,262	183,850	6,084	225,723	92,153
1976	1,569,810	1,393,476	13,623	1,407,099	130,291	-84,150	1,192,658	190,532	186,620	6,942	226,118	96,864
1977	1,756,811	1,595,456	14,954	1,610,410	148,983	-110,293	1,351,134	213,583	192,094	7,744	226,861	100,874
1978	1,949,817	1,794,530	14,664	1,809,194	172,866	-129,099	1,507,229	232,162	210,426	8,585	227,115	104,515
1979	2,106,610	1,915,839	16,481	1,932,320	190,933	-140,635	1,600,752	259,708	246,150	9,291	226,732	105,175
1980	2,230,257	1,868,510	19,111	1,887,621	183,724	-133,175	1,570,722	308,753	350,782	9,809	227,373	98,304
1981	2,374,497	2,017,804	14,596	2,032,400	214,908	-156,920	1,660,572	367,164	346,761	10,594	224,132	98,329
1982	2,375,030	1,902,316	3,440	1,905,756	205,352	-137,680	1,562,724	417,579	394,727	10,750	220,925	91,223
1983	2,530,246	2,058,947	-1,869	2,057,078	227,716	-162,989	1,666,373	451,238	412,635	11,618	217,784	91,228
1984	2,755,800	2,273,797	10,295	2,284,092	260,828	-199,036	1,824,228	506,037	425,535	12,717	216,710	94,924
1985	2,938,005	2,492,114	8,707	2,500,821	291,692	-243,514	1,965,615	534,854	437,536	13,663	215,040	98,880
1986	3,017,952	2,556,163	2,888	2,559,051	300,357	-256,911	2,001,783	555,180	460,989	14,039	214,972	99,967
1987	3,072,282	2,634,909	16,687	2,651,596	304,617	-292,725	2,054,254	546,111	471,917	14,350	214,098	103,044
1988	3,225,246	2,801,764	13,870	2,815,634	332,057	-329,793	2,153,784	579,338	492,124	15,105	213,522	105,620
1989	3,418,814	2,910,020	23,482	2,933,502	345,747	-357,693	2,230,062	652,105	536,647	16,103	212,303	107,071
1990	3,521,532	2,976,864	15,114	2,991,978	358,915	-352,085	2,280,978	655,053	585,501	16,605	212,071	106,622
1991	3,624,292	3,057,343	14,911	3,072,254	373,654	-368,169	2,330,431	646,971	646,890	17,065	212,384	105,668
1992	3,796,093	3,233,318	13,108	3,246,426	388,938	-394,114	2,463,374	651,498	681,221	17,871	212,421	107,274
1993	3,987,777	3,377,601	16,127	3,393,728	412,583	-407,990	2,573,155	684,250	730,372	18,796	212,165	107,006
1994	4,225,286	3,624,150	1,699	3,625,849	446,685	-445,374	2,733,790	748,069	743,427	19,906	212,262	109,557
1995	4,406,494	3,737,765	11,843	3,749,608	460,296	-432,932	2,856,380	784,331	765,783	20,778	212,076	112,965
1996	4,604,002	3,901,180	7,989	3,909,169	466,412	-439,928	3,002,829	813,124	788,049	21,724	211,927	115,285
1997	4,815,746	4,059,224	6,680	4,065,904	481,095	-441,197	3,143,612	822,247	849,887	22,780	211,406	116,361
1998	4,934,203	4,223,787	2,212	4,225,999	491,016	-492,135	3,242,848	840,688	850,667	23,403	210,839	114,873
1999	5,168,684	4,510,783	19,876	4,530,659	518,341	-572,911	3,439,407	799,829	929,448	24,566	210,400	116,817
2000	5,415,441	4,680,876	8,449	4,689,325	530,035	-550,231	3,609,059	840,737	965,645	25,800	209,899	118,358
2001	5,374,045	4,595,219	-1,232	4,593,987	540,393	-559,351	3,494,243	819,059	1,060,743	25,657	209,460	117,341
2002	5,294,006	4,535,402	14,350	4,549,752	530,920	-549,085	3,469,747	726,050	1,098,209	25,291	209,323	114,778
2003	5,393,951	4,635,812	12,267	4,648,079	538,434	-580,037	3,529,608	713,319	1,151,024	25,839	208,755	114,387
2004	5,573,684	4,652,270	18,459	4,670,729	546,432	-525,074	3,599,223	778,961	1,195,500	26,734	208,489	113,428
2005	5,587,498	4,621,921	17,680	4,639,601	548,612	-549,677	3,541,312	782,832	1,263,354	26,945	207,368	112,824
2006	5,685,532	4,724,664	23,581	4,748,245	576,737	-570,267	3,601,241	762,996	1,321,295	27,624	205,822	111,711
2007	5,807,333	4,617,087	28,002	4,645,089	566,794	-546,703	3,531,592	833,452	1,442,289	28,587	203,144	110,931
2008	5,951,275	4,441,763	34,967	4,476,730	550,821	-496,889	3,429,020	906,220	1,616,035	29,467	201,966	106,903
2009	5,893,230	4,350,419	12,035	4,362,454	543,624	-543,684	3,275,146	847,328	1,770,756	29,344	200,835	103,077
2010	6,105,095	4,481,271	14,060	4,495,331	547,971	-546,265	3,401,095	809,594	1,894,406	30,545	199,871	102,850
2011	6,345,941	4,683,273	44,170	4,727,443	509,213	-632,144	3,586,086	885,257	1,874,598	31,901	198,928	106,087
2012	6,394,626	4,739,589	46,152	4,785,741	518,302	-647,426	3,620,013	903,970	1,870,643	32,230	198,409	106,827
2013	6,481,708	4,798,228	55,077	4,853,305	593,645	-644,021	3,615,639	934,557	1,931,512	32,926	196,859	107,243
2014	6,601,245	4,895,299	13,035	4,908,334	606,703	-685,197	3,616,434	985,788	1,999,023	33,798	195,317	107,380
2015	6,842,665	5,009,202	10,666	5,019,868	617,043	-683,651	3,719,174	1,005,845	2,117,646	35,384	193,385	107,873
2016	6,995,594	5,186,298	4,072	5,190,370	636,184	-735,779	3,818,407	1,027,586	2,149,601	36,315	192,638	108,048
2017	7,112,736	5,350,717	4,523	5,355,240	653,152	-794,721	3,907,367	1,056,446	2,148,923	37,044	192,006	107,488
2018	7,542,602	5,606,246	4,870	5,611,116	691,480	-701,392	4,218,244	1,091,259	2,233,099	39,522	190,844	108,142
2019	7,779,936	5,745,284	4,879	5,750,163	703,509	-699,559	4,347,095	1,102,119	2,330,722	40,842	190,488	107,192
2020	8,673,982	5,677,909	38,659	5,716,568	692,872	-629,452	4,394,244	1,154,638	3,125,100	45,686	189,860	99,694
2021	9,209,795	6,135,056	55,937	6,190,993	740,577	-700,204	4,750,212	1,181,626	3,277,957	48,577	189,590	102,403
2022	8,983,295	6,458,495	39,374	6,497,869	807,826	-771,750	4,918,293	1,269,875	2,795,127	47,700	188,330	106,286

Personal Income and Employment by Area: St. Cloud, MN

(Thousands of dollars, except as noted.)

Year	Personal income, total	Derivation of personal income: Earnings by place of work: Nonfarm	Farm	Total	Less: Contributions for government social insurance	Plus: Adjustment for residence	Equals: Net earnings by place of residence	Plus: Dividends, interest, and rent	Plus: Personal current transfer receipts	Per capita personal income (dollars)	Population (persons)	Total employment
1970	357,436	258,985	33,599	292,584	17,712	-2,265	272,607	50,671	34,158	3,061	116,762	45,611
1971	386,589	281,632	29,727	311,359	19,811	-900	290,648	55,791	40,150	3,249	118,978	46,936
1972	426,393	309,563	34,216	343,779	22,669	883	321,993	60,241	44,159	3,563	119,660	49,580
1973	503,680	351,670	60,194	411,864	29,713	1,753	383,904	68,432	51,344	4,130	121,957	53,110
1974	556,113	402,792	48,200	450,992	35,883	894	416,003	79,044	61,066	4,497	123,661	55,774
1975	609,861	447,005	35,997	483,002	38,868	-169	443,965	90,991	74,905	4,829	126,283	56,483
1976	671,498	498,887	29,564	528,451	44,340	553	484,664	100,148	86,686	5,268	127,477	57,890
1977	763,536	549,214	54,897	604,111	48,945	1,835	557,001	115,303	91,232	5,874	129,994	59,900
1978	852,919	632,903	48,700	681,603	58,620	1,617	624,600	130,054	98,265	6,504	131,145	62,454
1979	961,478	730,534	42,507	773,041	70,525	-575	701,941	148,757	110,780	7,261	132,420	66,254
1980	1,066,054	797,952	29,890	827,842	76,943	-2,327	748,572	184,136	133,346	7,969	133,782	67,330
1981	1,201,037	882,347	42,718	925,065	91,716	-10,459	822,890	223,754	154,393	8,883	135,211	67,644
1982	1,300,722	926,627	45,042	971,669	98,108	-14,993	858,568	268,198	173,956	9,556	136,115	67,216
1983	1,354,708	987,690	6,554	994,244	105,252	-17,157	871,835	293,360	189,513	9,885	137,048	68,777
1984	1,533,375	1,093,977	49,024	1,143,001	118,888	-16,492	1,007,621	324,493	201,261	11,108	138,037	71,557
1985	1,628,295	1,156,771	58,156	1,214,927	127,546	-16,302	1,071,079	344,558	212,658	11,682	139,387	73,891
1986	1,753,004	1,263,620	69,841	1,333,461	142,823	-22,147	1,168,491	364,512	220,001	12,442	140,892	77,336
1987	1,858,352	1,373,562	70,479	1,444,041	155,225	-28,693	1,260,123	370,348	227,881	13,058	142,314	81,199
1988	1,980,223	1,520,001	46,186	1,566,187	178,235	-39,393	1,348,559	392,273	239,391	13,669	144,873	85,778
1989	2,195,571	1,656,907	89,932	1,746,839	194,523	-48,594	1,503,722	427,418	264,431	14,927	147,087	89,177
1990	2,328,989	1,764,780	86,059	1,850,839	208,383	-57,778	1,584,678	463,193	281,118	15,519	150,078	90,903
1991	2,416,038	1,866,203	54,334	1,920,537	223,180	-62,850	1,634,507	476,127	305,404	15,915	151,812	93,550
1992	2,606,362	2,039,064	64,252	2,103,316	240,982	-65,160	1,797,174	479,505	329,683	16,987	153,430	95,350
1993	2,713,157	2,168,034	43,475	2,211,509	258,124	-72,862	1,880,523	487,345	345,289	17,449	155,495	97,771
1994	2,869,252	2,296,169	59,763	2,355,932	276,656	-72,780	2,006,496	501,825	360,931	18,245	157,264	100,598
1995	3,010,115	2,416,425	24,637	2,441,062	290,978	-80,986	2,069,098	555,155	385,862	18,905	159,224	105,687
1996	3,267,334	2,579,640	80,604	2,660,244	306,917	-84,797	2,268,530	588,007	410,797	20,349	160,563	108,022
1997	3,381,929	2,704,388	40,355	2,744,743	321,415	-88,058	2,335,270	626,294	420,365	20,846	162,234	107,758
1998	3,790,820	3,054,756	88,684	3,143,440	361,069	-121,432	2,660,939	689,572	440,309	23,206	163,352	110,718
1999	3,967,260	3,181,294	86,353	3,267,647	375,872	-82,309	2,809,466	694,637	463,157	23,977	165,463	112,488
2000	4,254,058	3,400,899	69,031	3,469,930	398,395	-75,326	2,996,209	757,434	500,415	25,301	168,139	115,436
2001	4,583,738	3,648,912	67,566	3,716,478	422,741	-58,756	3,234,981	785,242	563,515	26,870	170,587	119,810
2002	4,808,806	3,863,366	64,211	3,927,577	445,309	-61,094	3,421,174	768,744	618,888	27,777	173,123	121,271
2003	5,045,584	3,985,392	103,589	4,088,981	463,200	-58,389	3,567,392	822,441	655,751	28,805	175,161	120,862
2004	5,313,350	4,227,263	150,726	4,377,989	492,018	-32,170	3,853,801	763,311	696,238	30,043	176,860	123,416
2005	5,458,199	4,351,920	150,900	4,502,820	512,369	-41,108	3,949,343	767,940	740,916	30,455	179,222	125,142
2006	5,730,336	4,533,189	138,561	4,671,750	546,724	-71,664	4,053,362	850,178	826,796	31,507	181,873	127,620
2007	6,082,924	4,759,334	136,040	4,895,374	573,389	-122,759	4,199,226	962,355	921,343	32,952	184,598	130,262
2008	6,452,580	4,863,323	226,249	5,089,572	590,234	-158,333	4,341,005	1,031,248	1,080,327	34,597	186,507	129,561
2009	6,263,520	4,793,662	112,482	4,906,144	585,109	-264,905	4,056,130	1,012,099	1,195,291	33,296	188,114	126,353
2010	6,507,943	4,889,115	171,209	5,060,324	589,726	-245,290	4,225,308	951,816	1,330,819	34,404	189,161	126,062
2011	7,015,654	5,169,450	212,514	5,381,964	556,622	-268,290	4,557,052	1,094,661	1,363,941	36,975	189,739	128,912
2012	7,343,572	5,396,264	291,203	5,687,467	582,603	-272,183	4,832,681	1,169,801	1,341,090	38,666	189,925	130,840
2013	7,551,402	5,639,541	260,765	5,900,306	688,468	-262,510	4,949,328	1,212,336	1,389,738	39,614	190,624	132,670
2014	7,983,686	6,001,764	291,450	6,293,214	712,168	-319,086	5,261,960	1,248,177	1,473,549	41,606	191,888	134,291
2015	8,215,477	6,245,730	221,975	6,467,705	738,509	-392,945	5,336,251	1,345,407	1,533,819	42,371	193,894	136,335
2016	8,290,835	6,403,566	114,003	6,517,569	763,669	-437,501	5,316,399	1,375,280	1,599,156	42,506	195,051	137,158
2017	8,735,718	6,698,386	156,754	6,855,140	798,258	-454,832	5,602,050	1,462,871	1,670,797	44,460	196,484	137,969
2018	9,118,206	6,960,812	126,853	7,087,665	833,882	-462,178	5,791,605	1,538,758	1,787,843	46,046	198,025	138,455
2019	9,518,191	7,235,751	76,373	7,312,124	863,402	-493,844	5,954,878	1,681,286	1,882,027	47,803	199,111	139,168
2020	10,629,959	7,440,450	198,415	7,638,865	885,725	-443,806	6,309,334	1,818,969	2,501,656	53,197	199,824	133,351
2021	11,464,169	8,045,190	199,731	8,244,921	937,688	-380,963	6,926,270	1,751,153	2,786,746	57,138	200,640	135,430
2022	11,760,956	8,654,721	285,743	8,940,464	1,028,107	-416,399	7,495,958	1,900,354	2,364,644	58,261	201,868	139,901

Personal Income and Employment by Area: St. George, UT

(Thousands of dollars, except as noted.)

Year	Personal income, total	Derivation of personal income: Earnings by place of work: Nonfarm	Farm	Total	Less: Contributions for government social insurance	Plus: Adjustment for residence	Equals: Net earnings by place of residence	Plus: Dividends, interest, and rent	Plus: Personal current transfer receipts	Per capita personal income (dollars)	Population (persons)	Total employment
1970	40,890	27,300	2,048	29,348	1,684	869	28,533	7,736	4,621	2,940	13,907	4,819
1971	45,422	29,763	1,736	31,499	1,903	1,201	30,797	9,085	5,540	3,021	15,037	5,015
1972	52,409	34,658	1,700	36,358	2,345	1,355	35,368	10,605	6,436	3,376	15,526	5,512
1973	60,744	39,214	2,851	42,065	3,041	1,644	40,668	12,223	7,853	3,709	16,379	5,916
1974	66,587	42,128	1,988	44,116	3,364	2,033	42,785	14,497	9,305	3,680	18,092	5,985
1975	77,215	47,779	1,533	49,312	3,693	2,425	48,044	17,358	11,813	4,173	18,504	6,192
1976	92,191	58,536	1,635	60,171	4,506	2,859	58,524	20,139	13,528	4,645	19,846	6,898
1977	107,325	67,768	1,709	69,477	5,261	3,545	67,761	24,032	15,532	5,141	20,877	7,443
1978	129,654	80,468	1,976	82,444	6,373	4,487	80,558	30,826	18,270	5,805	22,335	8,170
1979	155,818	98,170	2,130	100,300	8,500	5,158	96,958	37,240	21,620	6,487	24,019	9,054
1980	178,567	106,873	1,285	108,158	9,509	6,030	104,679	47,369	26,519	6,744	26,478	9,442
1981	198,250	113,099	611	113,710	11,006	6,553	109,257	56,138	32,855	7,063	28,070	9,582
1982	215,552	119,667	250	119,917	11,822	6,654	114,749	63,126	37,677	7,314	29,472	9,772
1983	243,081	136,435	-19	136,416	13,208	6,853	130,061	70,131	42,889	7,851	30,963	10,358
1984	295,909	173,570	228	173,798	16,853	6,874	163,819	84,406	47,684	9,017	32,816	11,851
1985	341,432	206,233	321	206,554	20,649	6,329	192,234	94,566	54,632	9,548	35,761	13,471
1986	391,912	239,819	578	240,397	24,226	5,958	222,129	107,355	62,428	9,921	39,503	14,907
1987	431,861	260,181	51	260,232	26,301	6,592	240,523	118,665	72,673	10,095	42,781	16,230
1988	473,845	281,832	811	282,643	30,569	7,710	259,784	133,527	80,534	10,618	44,627	17,503
1989	534,674	311,485	1,128	312,613	35,775	8,658	285,496	157,784	91,394	11,438	46,744	18,975
1990	614,006	377,613	1,938	379,551	43,608	8,727	344,670	163,900	105,436	12,484	49,183	21,258
1991	700,370	441,530	638	442,168	51,360	7,258	398,066	177,784	124,520	13,262	52,811	22,774
1992	777,254	488,031	1,521	489,552	56,973	8,970	441,549	192,254	143,451	13,794	56,349	24,084
1993	907,876	574,127	1,774	575,901	67,564	9,462	517,799	222,486	167,591	14,968	60,656	27,249
1994	1,052,348	697,198	203	697,401	83,211	7,888	622,078	248,940	181,330	15,826	66,493	33,162
1995	1,168,659	773,408	-872	772,536	93,859	9,211	687,888	274,083	206,688	16,173	72,261	35,711
1996	1,302,077	853,687	-1,000	852,687	101,009	12,264	763,942	307,434	230,701	16,769	77,647	38,801
1997	1,404,978	914,889	-480	914,409	106,487	15,588	823,510	328,872	252,596	17,235	81,520	40,701
1998	1,529,781	990,887	-318	990,569	115,943	17,986	892,612	368,632	268,537	18,032	84,837	42,689
1999	1,622,252	1,055,570	-688	1,054,882	123,208	21,451	953,125	381,727	287,400	18,424	88,049	44,820
2000	1,736,758	1,100,294	-631	1,099,663	131,496	24,824	992,991	423,093	320,674	19,042	91,206	47,299
2001	1,903,802	1,225,603	713	1,226,316	145,862	24,976	1,105,430	442,379	355,993	20,143	94,512	50,066
2002	2,002,349	1,328,009	-2,018	1,325,991	160,865	24,731	1,189,857	419,992	392,500	20,170	99,274	52,664
2003	2,180,860	1,458,196	61	1,458,257	178,251	25,617	1,305,623	446,783	428,454	20,932	104,188	55,711
2004	2,469,295	1,674,989	1,123	1,676,112	208,004	26,280	1,494,388	488,759	486,148	22,406	110,207	61,675
2005	2,840,612	1,934,407	882	1,935,289	242,188	26,452	1,719,553	580,241	540,818	23,871	119,000	67,943
2006	3,206,975	2,239,383	-1,593	2,237,790	274,678	25,795	1,988,907	627,436	590,632	25,292	126,796	73,426
2007	3,476,009	2,317,648	-4,421	2,313,227	288,382	26,427	2,051,272	767,401	657,336	26,278	132,277	77,264
2008	3,592,044	2,206,820	-4,292	2,202,528	281,357	30,299	1,951,470	879,429	761,145	26,499	135,552	75,467
2009	3,490,506	2,014,502	-3,104	2,011,398	263,807	33,903	1,781,494	843,889	865,123	25,462	137,088	71,648
2010	3,627,168	2,028,293	-2,757	2,025,536	262,735	37,187	1,799,988	880,317	946,863	26,218	138,344	70,272
2011	3,795,930	2,106,732	-206	2,106,526	250,227	41,248	1,897,547	922,774	975,609	26,919	141,015	72,104
2012	4,053,908	2,248,162	-516	2,247,646	262,636	48,833	2,033,843	1,025,114	994,951	28,208	143,713	74,752
2013	4,302,407	2,472,146	2,235	2,474,381	314,867	53,527	2,213,041	1,049,357	1,040,009	29,397	146,357	77,944
2014	4,655,126	2,686,697	3,094	2,689,791	340,244	51,368	2,400,915	1,155,866	1,098,345	30,986	150,235	82,064
2015	5,052,394	2,903,058	2,362	2,905,420	357,234	50,718	2,598,904	1,269,313	1,184,177	32,898	153,578	85,546
2016	5,522,216	3,220,207	-215	3,219,992	394,303	46,316	2,872,005	1,389,158	1,261,053	34,953	157,988	90,722
2017	6,133,159	3,550,942	-2,058	3,548,884	427,250	42,747	3,164,381	1,629,871	1,338,907	37,324	164,324	94,683
2018	6,805,916	4,031,832	-1,793	4,030,039	470,857	32,725	3,591,907	1,755,768	1,458,241	40,070	169,851	100,838
2019	7,423,326	4,346,046	-791	4,345,255	501,629	35,581	3,879,207	1,924,979	1,619,140	42,324	175,393	103,381
2020	8,255,866	4,652,586	282	4,652,868	553,974	33,406	4,132,300	2,116,997	2,006,569	45,360	182,009	108,403
2021	9,463,674	5,141,608	2,039	5,143,647	611,777	33,070	4,564,940	2,512,424	2,386,310	49,425	191,476	117,403
2022	10,031,391	5,615,408	4,444	5,619,852	679,990	32,997	4,972,859	2,867,625	2,190,907	50,746	197,680	124,640

Personal Income and Employment by Area: St. Joseph, MO-KS

(Thousands of dollars, except as noted.)

Year	Personal income, total	Derivation of personal income: Earnings by place of work: Nonfarm	Earnings by place of work: Farm	Earnings by place of work: Total	Less: Contributions for government social insurance	Plus: Adjustment for residence	Equals: Net earnings by place of residence	Plus: Dividends, interest, and rent	Plus: Personal current transfer receipts	Per capita personal income (dollars)	Population (persons)	Total employment
1970	413,434	288,499	28,192	316,691	19,881	3,501	300,311	65,563	47,560	3,581	115,462	49,904
1971	446,250	310,367	27,784	338,151	22,133	4,880	320,898	70,775	54,577	3,812	117,065	50,202
1972	488,578	333,766	37,538	371,304	24,893	6,155	352,566	76,404	59,608	4,122	118,538	50,712
1973	543,724	359,429	53,986	413,415	31,136	7,793	390,072	84,689	68,963	4,597	118,278	51,864
1974	569,972	390,077	31,642	421,719	35,070	8,081	394,730	96,190	79,052	4,827	118,091	52,490
1975	625,486	419,929	30,026	449,955	36,835	11,366	424,486	105,131	95,869	5,259	118,925	52,020
1976	676,430	475,341	15,865	491,206	42,255	12,388	461,339	111,996	103,095	5,645	119,830	53,138
1977	747,067	518,123	25,614	543,737	46,062	15,909	513,584	124,890	108,593	6,221	120,097	53,528
1978	825,459	568,154	35,404	603,558	52,061	20,676	572,173	137,472	115,814	6,880	119,976	54,529
1979	923,058	624,010	45,851	669,861	59,164	25,409	636,106	155,951	131,001	7,718	119,604	55,845
1980	1,001,071	683,798	7,578	691,376	64,792	25,566	652,150	192,539	156,382	8,395	119,251	56,082
1981	1,135,576	729,394	37,359	766,753	74,086	27,895	720,562	236,020	178,994	9,576	118,583	55,596
1982	1,216,307	772,982	20,054	793,036	80,240	25,565	738,361	283,199	194,747	10,322	117,842	55,548
1983	1,255,842	804,379	-5,093	799,286	83,608	26,891	742,569	304,550	208,723	10,680	117,584	56,265
1984	1,369,244	871,392	9,717	881,109	92,793	26,492	814,808	334,586	219,850	11,667	117,358	57,192
1985	1,459,404	908,627	47,897	956,524	98,336	27,991	886,179	343,271	229,954	12,500	116,748	57,089
1986	1,496,960	939,828	34,300	974,128	101,853	28,907	901,182	352,073	243,705	12,849	116,500	56,485
1987	1,530,057	987,650	30,352	1,018,002	106,092	28,768	940,678	342,541	246,838	13,176	116,125	56,308
1988	1,602,372	1,071,267	16,741	1,088,008	119,703	26,188	994,493	356,617	251,262	13,899	115,289	57,352
1989	1,736,923	1,156,207	19,612	1,175,819	130,067	22,633	1,068,385	392,077	276,461	14,984	115,917	59,405
1990	1,778,120	1,203,202	25,060	1,228,262	137,542	16,373	1,107,093	381,505	289,522	15,328	116,008	60,198
1991	1,872,180	1,249,225	22,232	1,271,457	145,062	16,440	1,142,835	394,494	334,851	16,066	116,534	59,704
1992	1,976,176	1,306,180	38,199	1,344,379	149,136	22,601	1,217,844	402,352	355,980	16,836	117,377	59,547
1993	2,029,566	1,358,948	15,992	1,374,940	156,546	22,107	1,240,501	406,365	382,700	17,177	118,153	60,305
1994	2,147,361	1,433,949	41,352	1,475,301	166,286	27,220	1,336,235	413,654	397,472	18,180	118,119	60,738
1995	2,205,740	1,507,543	9,551	1,517,094	174,647	28,859	1,371,306	416,798	417,636	18,549	118,915	62,607
1996	2,346,221	1,541,726	62,340	1,604,066	176,031	35,364	1,463,399	445,677	437,145	19,685	119,187	62,179
1997	2,484,654	1,662,989	55,857	1,718,846	187,013	35,586	1,567,419	479,696	437,539	20,703	120,013	63,975
1998	2,577,758	1,774,970	35,275	1,810,245	198,625	36,940	1,648,560	480,230	448,968	21,305	120,992	65,446
1999	2,706,256	1,914,542	15,250	1,929,792	211,669	39,721	1,757,844	470,675	477,737	22,253	121,611	67,135
2000	2,907,535	2,048,987	26,881	2,075,868	224,002	43,873	1,895,739	498,225	513,571	23,431	124,091	68,339
2001	2,958,174	2,056,804	19,830	2,076,634	229,766	51,586	1,898,454	499,228	560,492	23,869	123,936	68,251
2002	3,018,659	2,141,588	-1,702	2,139,886	238,479	50,102	1,951,509	470,600	596,550	24,365	123,894	67,738
2003	3,102,840	2,189,630	11,348	2,200,978	244,889	45,737	2,001,826	485,530	615,484	25,038	123,923	68,097
2004	3,303,170	2,346,810	70,649	2,417,459	259,009	39,959	2,198,409	456,643	648,118	26,775	123,366	69,049
2005	3,389,867	2,434,892	44,856	2,479,748	273,134	31,009	2,237,623	458,609	693,635	27,452	123,484	69,540
2006	3,562,311	2,623,871	30,964	2,654,835	297,019	-3,831	2,353,985	476,011	732,315	28,677	124,222	71,481
2007	3,751,550	2,723,562	60,450	2,784,012	314,517	-32,432	2,437,063	539,368	775,119	29,897	125,483	74,534
2008	4,012,565	2,849,726	66,114	2,915,840	329,442	-58,311	2,528,087	618,471	866,007	31,826	126,077	75,025
2009	3,995,460	2,811,910	77,526	2,889,436	325,257	-123,992	2,440,187	610,913	944,360	31,460	127,001	73,074
2010	3,974,377	2,841,994	36,286	2,878,280	323,826	-124,913	2,429,541	549,054	995,782	31,235	127,240	70,875
2011	4,226,844	2,916,810	84,316	3,001,126	299,270	-104,260	2,597,596	616,718	1,012,530	33,138	127,554	70,967
2012	4,345,914	3,121,402	44,680	3,166,082	311,519	-175,837	2,678,726	643,781	1,023,407	34,049	127,636	71,404
2013	4,431,429	3,198,341	117,526	3,315,867	359,330	-185,418	2,771,119	640,512	1,019,798	34,827	127,243	72,281
2014	4,477,033	3,237,307	78,644	3,315,951	368,507	-197,428	2,750,016	678,891	1,048,126	35,325	126,740	71,996
2015	4,527,110	3,305,798	10,125	3,315,923	383,073	-203,206	2,729,644	700,390	1,097,076	35,907	126,078	72,700
2016	4,584,015	3,353,877	41,851	3,395,728	389,514	-231,476	2,774,738	706,637	1,102,640	36,440	125,795	73,325
2017	4,709,082	3,476,490	39,946	3,516,436	403,657	-267,823	2,844,956	718,225	1,145,901	37,565	125,357	72,848
2018	4,751,374	3,541,196	23,354	3,564,550	413,028	-254,780	2,896,742	671,316	1,183,316	38,084	124,760	72,713
2019	4,943,525	3,659,327	60,466	3,719,793	433,385	-276,892	3,009,516	694,523	1,239,486	40,503	122,054	72,197
2020	5,286,528	3,748,536	75,920	3,824,456	451,772	-333,133	3,039,551	726,692	1,520,285	43,464	121,631	70,736
2021	5,608,149	3,879,636	94,802	3,974,438	458,760	-364,089	3,151,589	768,130	1,688,430	46,420	120,814	70,986
2022	5,623,069	4,027,805	58,737	4,086,542	486,978	-358,057	3,241,507	842,385	1,539,177	46,980	119,690	71,507

Personal Income and Employment by Area: St. Louis, MO-IL

(Thousands of dollars, except as noted.)

Year	Personal income, total	Derivation of personal income: Earnings by place of work: Nonfarm	Farm	Total	Less: Contributions for government social insurance	Plus: Adjustment for residence	Equals: Net earnings by place of residence	Plus: Dividends, interest, and rent	Plus: Personal current transfer receipts	Per capita personal income (dollars)	Population (persons)	Total employment
1970	11,000,702	9,006,214	63,227	9,069,441	597,235	-15,927	8,456,279	1,662,650	881,773	4,365	2,520,475	1,119,503
1971	11,736,076	9,519,993	68,615	9,588,608	652,043	-17,253	8,919,312	1,772,811	1,043,953	4,668	2,514,268	1,108,632
1972	12,587,409	10,229,514	82,504	10,312,018	737,233	-19,706	9,555,079	1,899,282	1,133,048	5,023	2,506,053	1,120,309
1973	13,688,693	11,063,790	167,605	11,231,395	922,267	-42,015	10,267,113	2,095,321	1,326,259	5,489	2,493,703	1,155,750
1974	14,864,310	11,889,861	139,496	12,029,357	1,025,821	-65,160	10,938,376	2,385,057	1,540,877	5,986	2,483,293	1,165,071
1975	16,147,882	12,567,195	174,401	12,741,596	1,065,530	-78,602	11,597,464	2,586,215	1,964,203	6,503	2,483,274	1,144,591
1976	17,633,355	13,984,487	114,400	14,098,887	1,205,364	-129,380	12,764,143	2,777,740	2,091,472	7,101	2,483,161	1,174,761
1977	19,445,715	15,599,210	117,394	15,716,604	1,348,283	-177,931	14,190,390	3,089,157	2,166,168	7,852	2,476,457	1,208,780
1978	21,572,058	17,457,800	120,904	17,578,704	1,558,154	-230,083	15,790,467	3,432,529	2,349,062	8,699	2,479,899	1,251,667
1979	23,850,085	19,248,226	155,522	19,403,748	1,777,353	-285,212	17,341,183	3,873,992	2,634,910	9,599	2,484,555	1,285,355
1980	26,148,126	20,404,036	27,574	20,431,610	1,870,047	-315,297	18,246,266	4,671,917	3,229,943	10,514	2,486,989	1,260,871
1981	29,000,916	22,140,569	109,614	22,250,183	2,175,703	-385,480	19,689,000	5,757,954	3,553,962	11,659	2,487,360	1,257,134
1982	31,225,150	23,225,143	44,461	23,269,604	2,326,902	-374,710	20,567,992	6,798,664	3,858,494	12,583	2,481,504	1,247,588
1983	33,512,526	24,998,758	-17,801	24,980,957	2,531,847	-367,839	22,081,271	7,271,787	4,159,468	13,487	2,484,786	1,260,590
1984	36,907,698	27,687,282	77,105	27,764,387	2,894,145	-391,324	24,478,918	8,098,954	4,329,826	14,781	2,496,966	1,314,730
1985	39,335,767	29,680,497	26,835	29,707,332	3,167,919	-393,375	26,146,038	8,631,461	4,558,268	15,648	2,513,864	1,347,519
1986	41,571,900	31,499,199	67,476	31,566,675	3,395,482	-398,472	27,772,721	9,067,667	4,731,512	16,438	2,529,039	1,385,583
1987	43,710,686	33,522,476	101,578	33,624,054	3,567,501	-390,140	29,666,413	9,175,335	4,868,938	17,184	2,543,754	1,403,758
1988	46,841,436	35,977,104	77,380	36,054,484	3,937,046	-386,681	31,730,757	10,004,938	5,105,741	18,349	2,552,771	1,427,738
1989	50,086,263	38,095,922	207,195	38,303,117	4,186,353	-389,975	33,726,789	10,828,365	5,531,109	19,604	2,554,879	1,452,169
1990	52,804,282	39,840,607	125,746	39,966,353	4,493,631	-371,476	35,101,246	11,697,514	6,005,522	20,586	2,565,020	1,464,298
1991	54,119,172	40,335,399	77,097	40,412,496	4,633,512	-368,334	35,410,650	11,880,515	6,828,007	20,982	2,579,363	1,442,695
1992	57,151,472	42,531,335	181,608	42,712,943	4,825,152	-374,638	37,513,153	12,250,994	7,387,325	22,063	2,590,410	1,439,015
1993	59,486,640	44,105,797	130,440	44,236,237	5,027,815	-386,503	38,821,919	12,836,541	7,828,180	22,827	2,605,968	1,468,529
1994	62,657,659	46,599,541	147,419	46,746,960	5,400,715	-422,911	40,923,334	13,590,196	8,144,129	23,945	2,616,756	1,496,005
1995	66,383,316	49,464,297	47,068	49,511,365	5,725,922	-455,454	43,329,989	14,434,197	8,619,130	25,246	2,629,433	1,529,685
1996	69,504,899	51,836,192	178,404	52,014,596	5,942,880	-492,103	45,579,613	15,081,204	8,844,082	26,326	2,640,161	1,555,249
1997	73,812,888	55,200,184	166,447	55,366,631	6,303,331	-532,696	48,530,604	16,109,877	9,172,407	27,842	2,651,165	1,579,818
1998	77,596,205	58,030,430	135,961	58,166,391	6,597,976	-555,125	51,013,290	17,117,549	9,465,366	29,204	2,657,031	1,603,406
1999	80,157,881	61,207,796	103,792	61,311,588	6,892,404	-603,846	53,815,338	16,525,255	9,817,288	30,062	2,666,413	1,620,760
2000	85,361,444	64,946,486	150,002	65,096,488	7,250,091	-652,147	57,194,250	17,752,215	10,414,979	31,865	2,678,822	1,642,704
2001	88,080,555	67,091,732	155,461	67,247,193	7,427,797	-667,647	59,151,749	17,575,020	11,353,786	32,742	2,690,131	1,641,921
2002	90,582,071	69,385,307	71,296	69,456,603	7,635,893	-684,948	61,135,762	17,449,147	11,997,162	33,547	2,700,121	1,638,346
2003	93,657,767	71,180,654	187,941	71,368,595	7,868,617	-702,791	62,797,187	18,420,436	12,440,144	34,547	2,711,031	1,641,149
2004	97,366,191	73,997,909	355,535	74,353,444	8,113,208	-700,239	65,539,997	18,833,147	12,993,047	35,772	2,721,868	1,648,808
2005	101,360,021	76,841,589	178,865	77,020,454	8,488,553	-708,108	67,823,793	19,570,945	13,965,283	37,124	2,730,316	1,669,548
2006	107,922,900	80,687,188	175,935	80,863,123	8,940,248	-707,424	71,215,451	21,960,298	14,747,151	39,327	2,744,265	1,690,670
2007	112,191,495	83,120,047	184,380	83,304,427	9,295,760	-665,598	73,343,069	22,983,026	15,865,400	40,714	2,755,581	1,714,146
2008	118,607,414	86,947,426	307,660	87,255,086	9,793,896	-695,089	76,766,101	24,138,285	17,703,028	42,853	2,767,776	1,714,079
2009	114,564,157	84,160,916	218,499	84,379,415	9,379,919	-482,609	74,516,887	20,846,970	19,200,300	41,219	2,779,404	1,660,438
2010	118,793,433	85,775,269	263,482	86,038,751	9,396,946	-264,733	76,377,072	21,855,088	20,561,273	42,571	2,790,459	1,644,562
2011	123,032,766	87,983,690	388,961	88,372,651	8,677,718	-240,684	79,454,249	22,946,003	20,632,514	43,983	2,797,300	1,664,108
2012	129,973,588	90,909,832	209,754	91,119,586	8,899,930	-342,814	81,876,842	27,292,722	20,804,024	46,411	2,800,463	1,667,836
2013	128,685,932	92,870,453	436,651	93,307,104	10,311,120	-346,938	82,649,046	24,623,205	21,413,681	45,880	2,804,822	1,686,349
2014	133,111,264	94,454,120	172,152	94,626,272	10,592,991	-373,553	83,659,728	27,358,093	22,093,443	47,365	2,810,317	1,703,016
2015	138,052,310	97,941,001	-48,569	97,892,432	11,103,377	-389,247	86,399,808	28,252,949	23,399,553	49,025	2,815,929	1,733,548
2016	142,888,213	100,403,305	85,793	100,489,098	11,310,488	-418,087	88,760,523	30,206,091	23,921,599	50,748	2,815,619	1,755,628
2017	145,518,445	103,946,931	106,726	104,053,657	11,696,245	-433,691	91,923,721	29,055,774	24,538,950	51,653	2,817,214	1,772,444
2018	153,890,870	107,847,304	136,837	107,984,141	12,209,716	-491,109	95,283,316	33,159,146	25,448,408	54,637	2,816,606	1,792,309
2019	159,900,281	112,171,164	98,068	112,269,232	12,716,775	-577,390	98,975,067	34,322,889	26,602,325	56,751	2,817,594	1,790,759
2020	172,494,640	114,543,080	194,060	114,737,140	13,052,471	-611,487	101,073,182	37,241,478	34,179,980	61,190	2,819,023	1,736,681
2021	188,008,727	121,470,304	447,027	121,917,331	13,581,468	-672,738	107,663,125	42,616,387	37,729,215	66,848	2,812,477	1,786,658
2022	195,247,695	129,322,818	472,286	129,795,104	14,784,043	-747,971	114,263,090	47,727,549	33,257,056	69,698	2,801,319	1,858,091

Personal Income and Employment by Area: Salem, OR

(Thousands of dollars, except as noted.)

Year	Personal income, total	Derivation of personal income: Earnings by place of work: Nonfarm	Farm	Total	Less: Contributions for government social insurance	Plus: Adjustment for residence	Equals: Net earnings by place of residence	Plus: Dividends, interest, and rent	Plus: Personal current transfer receipts	Per capita personal income (dollars)	Population (persons)	Total employment
1970	707,190	497,430	23,467	520,897	36,554	8,890	493,233	138,172	75,785	3,769	187,645	76,935
1971	783,788	551,053	23,671	574,724	42,020	11,900	544,604	152,032	87,152	4,058	193,158	78,983
1972	875,726	623,246	21,463	644,709	50,028	16,462	611,143	167,036	97,547	4,445	197,027	82,993
1973	1,010,102	700,872	48,661	749,533	64,980	22,016	706,569	189,186	114,347	5,061	199,576	88,074
1974	1,156,016	786,042	55,197	841,239	75,685	28,500	794,054	220,482	141,480	5,590	206,796	91,136
1975	1,293,023	869,591	43,561	913,152	81,630	33,280	864,802	254,670	173,551	6,115	211,453	93,710
1976	1,486,085	1,014,105	49,548	1,063,653	95,898	42,857	1,010,612	282,866	192,607	6,796	218,659	99,232
1977	1,674,490	1,154,268	43,377	1,197,645	110,810	53,904	1,140,739	325,096	208,655	7,330	228,455	106,818
1978	1,914,276	1,329,344	38,807	1,368,151	131,790	71,191	1,307,552	376,137	230,587	8,075	237,065	113,216
1979	2,193,662	1,498,602	43,798	1,542,400	154,503	113,832	1,501,729	431,153	260,780	9,005	243,606	118,107
1980	2,452,891	1,579,499	60,347	1,639,846	164,441	143,393	1,618,798	520,546	313,547	9,778	250,849	117,287
1981	2,631,400	1,663,400	54,163	1,717,563	185,419	110,829	1,642,973	625,888	362,539	10,354	254,150	115,262
1982	2,710,226	1,646,286	49,451	1,695,737	185,816	105,304	1,615,225	690,232	404,769	10,635	254,850	111,166
1983	2,868,975	1,727,168	43,087	1,770,255	194,488	104,292	1,680,059	752,607	436,309	11,233	255,400	113,893
1984	3,075,253	1,872,442	53,676	1,926,118	216,849	104,844	1,814,113	810,271	450,869	11,987	256,540	117,372
1985	3,262,413	2,011,294	58,153	2,069,447	235,002	97,362	1,931,807	851,958	478,648	12,633	258,250	121,772
1986	3,444,394	2,134,365	88,334	2,222,699	249,493	93,138	2,066,344	881,186	496,864	13,225	260,438	125,261
1987	3,624,146	2,320,091	88,904	2,408,995	267,136	86,404	2,228,263	876,776	519,107	13,778	263,037	132,049
1988	3,976,333	2,561,451	142,866	2,704,317	310,080	88,211	2,482,448	936,929	556,956	14,824	268,239	137,126
1989	4,375,065	2,830,347	126,180	2,956,527	343,335	85,297	2,698,489	1,059,991	616,585	15,991	273,600	141,107
1990	4,735,866	3,135,137	141,187	3,276,324	386,738	75,760	2,965,346	1,097,267	673,253	16,922	279,862	146,094
1991	5,053,661	3,357,825	156,888	3,514,713	418,866	75,571	3,171,418	1,144,218	738,025	17,596	287,202	147,147
1992	5,399,760	3,631,579	167,302	3,798,881	448,813	81,060	3,431,128	1,153,766	814,866	18,302	295,039	149,319
1993	5,765,590	3,884,549	165,973	4,050,522	478,794	91,775	3,663,503	1,222,199	879,888	19,015	303,205	154,522
1994	6,194,791	4,240,353	167,168	4,407,521	525,098	105,599	3,988,022	1,295,810	910,959	19,943	310,626	161,451
1995	6,614,012	4,446,719	145,375	4,592,094	555,452	133,999	4,170,641	1,428,321	1,015,050	20,822	317,638	165,842
1996	7,119,164	4,769,686	195,494	4,965,180	600,873	166,841	4,531,148	1,506,150	1,081,866	21,942	324,457	172,393
1997	7,403,788	4,934,337	208,048	5,142,385	622,115	199,517	4,719,787	1,566,225	1,117,776	22,322	331,688	176,546
1998	7,855,493	5,285,780	203,888	5,489,668	661,176	215,218	5,043,710	1,611,458	1,200,325	23,223	338,269	178,362
1999	8,228,696	5,641,810	226,326	5,868,136	697,332	221,906	5,392,710	1,512,554	1,323,432	23,922	343,985	181,037
2000	8,618,035	5,955,241	179,144	6,134,385	733,103	269,546	5,670,828	1,606,597	1,340,610	24,764	348,007	183,466
2001	8,727,720	5,918,597	202,573	6,121,170	722,960	242,202	5,640,412	1,589,192	1,498,116	24,824	351,581	182,319
2002	8,847,107	6,181,283	179,206	6,360,489	761,689	180,570	5,779,370	1,495,182	1,572,555	24,805	356,668	184,085
2003	9,241,764	6,420,341	236,602	6,656,943	794,868	114,751	5,976,826	1,630,921	1,634,017	25,645	360,377	187,799
2004	9,609,102	6,674,251	248,585	6,922,836	839,762	105,080	6,188,154	1,708,169	1,712,779	26,420	363,708	192,330
2005	10,121,576	7,116,406	257,363	7,373,769	898,094	85,377	6,561,052	1,724,008	1,836,516	27,501	368,046	197,813
2006	11,112,208	7,759,503	316,085	8,075,588	971,855	69,740	7,173,473	1,955,445	1,983,290	29,687	374,317	202,458
2007	11,523,403	7,955,757	299,765	8,255,522	1,013,189	33,235	7,275,568	2,092,351	2,155,484	30,344	379,755	207,324
2008	12,198,627	8,199,622	303,331	8,502,953	1,042,676	-72,197	7,388,080	2,253,384	2,557,163	31,761	384,075	205,721
2009	12,028,637	7,958,287	268,293	8,226,580	1,014,787	-181,091	7,030,702	2,118,574	2,879,361	30,976	388,323	198,202
2010	12,272,246	8,141,046	257,947	8,398,993	1,033,540	-299,812	7,065,641	2,060,322	3,146,283	31,353	391,421	195,935
2011	12,667,483	8,202,822	266,975	8,469,797	921,068	-251,334	7,297,395	2,145,068	3,225,020	32,178	393,663	194,652
2012	13,077,956	8,430,260	295,778	8,726,038	948,691	-189,424	7,587,923	2,297,400	3,192,633	33,068	395,490	194,169
2013	13,315,038	8,764,904	302,389	9,067,293	1,115,177	-208,261	7,743,855	2,262,324	3,308,859	33,523	397,189	197,453
2014	14,222,335	9,341,999	255,029	9,597,028	1,199,242	-286,001	8,111,785	2,420,071	3,690,479	35,464	401,032	204,300
2015	15,249,400	10,003,052	303,785	10,306,837	1,266,397	-283,806	8,756,634	2,537,249	3,955,517	37,496	406,691	209,752
2016	16,076,374	10,698,146	304,749	11,002,895	1,340,159	-301,754	9,360,982	2,665,418	4,049,974	38,704	415,364	214,960
2017	16,974,424	11,433,041	252,806	11,685,847	1,448,253	-293,028	9,944,566	2,880,876	4,148,982	40,173	422,531	221,661
2018	17,989,976	12,333,388	250,729	12,584,117	1,527,154	-417,354	10,639,609	2,948,563	4,401,804	42,028	428,043	227,887
2019	19,065,148	13,150,708	239,405	13,390,113	1,614,972	-465,147	11,309,994	3,088,054	4,667,100	44,256	430,794	228,665
2020	21,034,264	13,854,398	269,590	14,123,988	1,696,695	-671,185	11,756,108	3,254,896	6,023,260	48,434	434,289	225,231
2021	23,134,310	15,217,398	290,727	15,508,125	1,966,003	-820,286	12,721,836	3,597,175	6,815,299	52,920	437,159	234,389
2022	23,381,750	16,284,943	277,017	16,561,960	2,154,207	-869,885	13,537,868	3,718,909	6,124,973	53,589	436,317	242,257

Personal Income and Employment by Area: Salinas, CA

(Thousands of dollars, except as noted.)

Year	Personal income, total	Derivation of personal income: Earnings by place of work: Nonfarm	Farm	Total	Less: Contributions for government social insurance	Plus: Adjustment for residence	Equals: Net earnings by place of residence	Plus: Dividends, interest, and rent	Plus: Personal current transfer receipts	Per capita personal income (dollars)	Population (persons)	Total employment
1970	1,364,273	908,393	109,573	1,017,966	59,309	-5,039	953,618	318,375	92,280	5,496	248,235	134,519
1971	1,537,357	1,026,264	131,596	1,157,860	70,447	-6,561	1,080,852	350,977	105,528	6,083	252,730	140,268
1972	1,643,539	1,078,857	166,158	1,245,015	76,423	-7,441	1,161,151	366,542	115,846	6,467	254,140	136,674
1973	1,839,849	1,205,691	195,923	1,401,614	94,561	-9,913	1,297,140	412,540	130,169	7,208	255,261	144,582
1974	2,050,129	1,301,198	253,541	1,554,739	106,099	-12,791	1,435,849	460,329	153,951	7,779	263,534	147,280
1975	2,188,715	1,419,258	209,655	1,628,913	117,505	-15,952	1,495,456	495,044	198,215	8,077	270,976	150,780
1976	2,290,452	1,493,285	201,272	1,694,557	125,970	-15,459	1,553,128	519,021	218,303	8,300	275,942	148,250
1977	2,521,308	1,652,411	220,800	1,873,211	140,822	-16,524	1,715,865	576,585	228,858	8,955	281,545	154,161
1978	2,899,743	1,857,164	299,584	2,156,748	158,856	-15,010	1,982,882	666,541	250,320	10,206	284,129	158,622
1979	3,122,405	2,016,145	273,706	2,289,851	179,633	-17,501	2,092,717	752,841	276,847	10,884	286,882	162,099
1980	3,503,564	2,145,504	343,054	2,488,558	186,003	-12,708	2,289,847	879,646	334,071	11,982	292,406	160,320
1981	4,029,253	2,365,806	427,400	2,793,206	221,643	-2,554	2,569,009	1,072,661	387,583	13,445	299,677	161,159
1982	4,268,949	2,537,836	432,145	2,969,981	239,698	-4,451	2,725,832	1,142,625	400,492	13,940	306,241	161,196
1983	4,759,792	2,720,079	634,627	3,354,706	264,688	1,956	3,091,974	1,233,611	434,207	15,173	313,698	164,668
1984	5,106,047	3,006,222	558,396	3,564,618	304,397	5,627	3,265,848	1,385,433	454,766	15,884	321,458	170,038
1985	5,403,609	3,306,951	482,151	3,789,102	338,804	102	3,450,400	1,462,379	490,830	16,469	328,102	175,384
1986	5,841,918	3,586,025	572,946	4,158,971	371,761	1,492	3,788,702	1,523,669	529,547	17,394	335,849	176,778
1987	6,221,996	3,910,850	614,300	4,525,150	409,511	4,394	4,120,033	1,557,428	544,535	18,232	341,268	183,254
1988	6,589,541	4,202,186	558,487	4,760,673	460,039	13,453	4,314,087	1,687,776	587,678	19,048	345,947	190,927
1989	6,958,442	4,411,361	490,591	4,901,952	489,844	21,186	4,433,294	1,879,092	646,056	19,889	349,872	194,992
1990	7,391,774	4,715,713	541,806	5,257,519	529,597	24,555	4,752,477	1,920,393	718,904	20,674	357,535	200,058
1991	7,569,474	4,952,300	414,620	5,366,920	561,913	29,166	4,834,173	1,935,219	800,082	20,749	364,805	200,838
1992	8,212,961	5,274,926	607,943	5,882,869	598,204	31,581	5,316,246	1,972,854	923,861	22,086	371,860	195,598
1993	8,352,642	5,137,732	779,971	5,917,703	582,567	51,624	5,386,760	1,991,046	974,836	22,514	371,002	191,239
1994	8,372,338	5,092,900	765,365	5,858,265	572,436	73,055	5,358,884	2,027,933	985,521	23,761	352,363	183,917
1995	8,913,802	5,298,408	888,082	6,186,490	585,085	99,359	5,700,764	2,178,887	1,034,151	25,075	355,486	187,617
1996	9,242,257	5,615,374	717,944	6,333,318	598,841	120,498	5,854,975	2,300,494	1,086,788	25,516	362,215	195,179
1997	9,900,834	5,939,085	980,677	6,919,762	622,192	149,070	6,446,640	2,346,659	1,107,535	26,277	376,794	197,557
1998	10,777,176	6,463,260	1,063,161	7,526,421	659,478	178,068	7,045,011	2,557,228	1,174,937	27,784	387,889	208,782
1999	11,518,420	7,069,718	1,111,316	8,181,034	722,519	221,690	7,680,205	2,598,732	1,239,483	29,067	396,267	218,234
2000	12,681,237	7,660,250	1,377,199	9,037,449	776,463	360,279	8,621,265	2,775,089	1,284,883	31,468	402,990	218,487
2001	12,874,760	8,100,201	1,101,554	9,201,755	876,017	262,067	8,587,805	2,881,624	1,405,331	31,627	407,082	217,510
2002	13,026,559	8,493,660	1,206,888	9,700,548	931,453	192,875	8,961,970	2,551,693	1,512,896	31,852	408,977	221,134
2003	13,657,256	8,926,444	1,335,421	10,261,865	998,133	160,144	9,423,876	2,649,769	1,583,611	33,333	409,725	223,698
2004	14,034,779	9,153,609	1,102,866	10,256,475	1,077,434	156,263	9,335,304	3,048,654	1,650,821	34,337	408,731	222,461
2005	14,526,578	9,494,396	1,182,709	10,677,105	1,106,595	130,265	9,700,775	3,103,040	1,722,763	35,856	405,139	221,524
2006	15,699,663	10,062,011	1,213,932	11,275,943	1,127,062	162,051	10,310,932	3,541,994	1,846,737	39,070	401,831	219,481
2007	16,344,825	10,470,891	1,115,578	11,586,469	1,148,104	173,197	10,611,562	3,794,856	1,938,407	40,621	402,376	224,442
2008	16,417,496	10,567,539	963,254	11,530,793	1,180,359	91,623	10,442,057	3,782,488	2,192,951	40,435	406,022	223,756
2009	16,449,126	10,377,614	1,484,475	11,862,089	1,172,648	14,631	10,704,072	3,337,624	2,407,430	40,094	410,263	217,035
2010	17,079,631	10,951,975	1,337,979	12,289,954	1,182,569	-23,443	11,083,942	3,332,651	2,663,038	41,004	416,532	220,162
2011	17,462,059	11,150,025	1,139,979	12,290,004	1,098,796	-35,104	11,156,104	3,604,728	2,701,227	41,452	421,259	221,090
2012	18,256,300	11,439,994	1,374,120	12,814,114	1,135,186	-97,831	11,581,097	3,957,242	2,717,961	42,873	425,824	225,863
2013	19,005,460	11,675,212	2,149,295	13,824,507	1,298,464	-132,179	12,393,864	3,779,495	2,832,101	44,355	428,490	230,837
2014	19,989,436	12,244,615	2,148,060	14,392,675	1,350,091	-120,297	12,922,287	4,065,330	3,001,819	46,374	431,044	238,925
2015	21,593,394	13,087,216	2,580,084	15,667,300	1,416,260	-129,442	14,121,598	4,266,865	3,204,931	49,757	433,979	244,411
2016	22,267,892	13,770,622	2,165,581	15,936,203	1,502,758	-107,261	14,326,184	4,600,911	3,340,797	50,839	438,004	248,805
2017	22,772,964	14,381,688	2,151,928	16,533,616	1,572,574	-89,586	14,871,456	4,564,960	3,336,548	51,861	439,112	250,364
2018	23,001,148	14,983,513	1,511,884	16,495,397	1,639,045	-101,735	14,754,617	4,739,122	3,507,409	52,346	439,404	256,957
2019	24,421,471	15,800,693	1,673,332	17,474,025	1,736,384	-12,787	15,724,854	4,947,781	3,748,836	55,483	440,163	257,996
2020	26,398,134	15,789,985	1,718,520	17,508,505	1,713,287	-16,827	15,778,391	4,892,065	5,727,678	60,216	438,390	245,890
2021	28,333,347	17,166,350	1,408,165	18,574,515	1,841,720	69,059	16,801,854	5,427,529	6,103,964	64,799	437,249	252,498
2022	28,189,179	18,145,044	1,517,452	19,662,496	2,042,447	36,584	17,656,633	5,728,852	4,803,694	65,123	432,858	267,130

Personal Income and Employment by Area: Salisbury, MD-DE

(Thousands of dollars, except as noted.)

Year	Personal income, total	Derivation of personal income								Per capita personal income (dollars)	Population (persons)	Total employment
		Earnings by place of work			Less: Contributions for government social insurance	Plus: Adjustment for residence	Equals: Net earnings by place of residence	Plus: Dividends, interest, and rent	Plus: Personal current transfer receipts			
		Nonfarm	Farm	Total								
1970	658,152	486,145	39,134	525,279	33,261	7,876	499,894	95,352	62,906	3,681	178,804	92,457
1971	711,893	526,723	34,025	560,748	37,313	9,158	532,593	105,311	73,989	3,858	184,503	94,642
1972	806,771	594,576	50,343	644,919	44,245	8,497	609,171	116,941	80,659	4,316	186,939	99,270
1973	954,731	665,628	108,938	774,566	57,552	7,754	724,768	136,066	93,897	4,998	191,029	102,800
1974	986,538	718,379	51,919	770,298	64,473	8,269	714,094	158,241	114,203	5,034	195,957	101,927
1975	1,127,097	762,703	102,351	865,054	67,220	8,557	806,391	172,061	148,645	5,637	199,933	99,153
1976	1,214,565	846,600	83,284	929,884	75,284	9,219	863,819	188,973	161,773	5,961	203,759	100,183
1977	1,284,161	910,541	55,376	965,917	81,243	10,762	895,436	212,180	176,545	6,210	206,805	101,923
1978	1,431,621	1,036,920	55,028	1,091,948	94,793	5,284	1,002,439	236,443	192,739	6,846	209,113	107,617
1979	1,550,019	1,119,731	42,052	1,161,783	107,333	1,835	1,056,285	270,303	223,431	7,311	212,004	108,124
1980	1,686,765	1,189,237	2,748	1,191,985	114,582	-2,116	1,075,287	340,508	270,970	7,927	212,780	106,381
1981	1,899,368	1,265,302	39,464	1,304,766	131,338	-3,226	1,170,202	414,838	314,328	8,918	212,984	107,068
1982	2,099,405	1,351,180	71,747	1,422,927	142,762	-4,274	1,275,891	481,698	341,816	9,834	213,485	108,398
1983	2,298,828	1,524,082	62,937	1,587,019	162,602	-9,357	1,415,060	514,320	369,448	10,642	216,011	116,348
1984	2,612,955	1,710,511	128,482	1,838,993	187,167	-7,875	1,643,951	576,291	392,713	11,856	220,383	121,778
1985	2,865,372	1,898,715	135,396	2,034,111	210,083	-8,010	1,816,018	624,588	424,766	12,731	225,063	127,936
1986	3,194,525	2,083,972	213,375	2,297,347	232,978	-1,797	2,062,572	682,617	449,336	13,914	229,583	132,093
1987	3,427,015	2,303,173	168,265	2,471,438	253,922	5,930	2,223,446	716,947	486,622	14,704	233,065	137,270
1988	3,780,911	2,493,068	239,183	2,732,251	284,727	17,149	2,464,673	786,072	530,166	15,852	238,509	141,970
1989	4,110,644	2,640,770	261,186	2,901,956	304,720	29,539	2,626,775	907,635	576,234	16,944	242,598	143,143
1990	4,290,926	2,848,500	168,364	3,016,864	326,820	42,834	2,732,878	914,059	643,989	17,327	247,645	146,525
1991	4,555,422	2,965,262	157,351	3,122,613	343,089	58,931	2,838,455	989,977	726,990	17,917	254,246	145,358
1992	4,776,085	3,115,036	134,066	3,249,102	356,748	75,917	2,968,271	1,000,145	807,669	18,318	260,733	145,227
1993	4,970,552	3,243,376	135,303	3,378,679	375,201	92,658	3,096,136	1,010,957	863,459	18,557	267,853	147,101
1994	5,321,991	3,437,550	144,446	3,581,996	402,858	112,107	3,291,245	1,101,325	929,421	19,380	274,618	150,301
1995	5,669,942	3,614,769	113,580	3,728,349	423,941	133,694	3,438,102	1,208,363	1,023,477	20,146	281,441	157,221
1996	6,124,163	3,780,624	166,396	3,947,020	437,628	156,437	3,665,829	1,317,154	1,141,180	21,223	288,563	160,039
1997	6,471,763	4,025,886	135,267	4,161,153	460,761	174,254	3,874,646	1,417,935	1,179,182	21,955	294,772	164,110
1998	7,052,784	4,384,856	176,501	4,561,357	487,942	204,393	4,277,808	1,500,780	1,274,196	23,406	301,328	166,774
1999	7,582,280	4,795,480	179,994	4,975,474	514,594	237,388	4,698,268	1,523,449	1,360,563	24,659	307,487	171,319
2000	8,190,308	5,181,591	170,416	5,352,007	540,312	273,448	5,085,143	1,649,240	1,455,925	26,105	313,744	176,762
2001	8,899,812	5,565,061	261,579	5,826,640	577,153	307,465	5,556,952	1,724,176	1,618,684	27,888	319,128	179,323
2002	9,155,850	5,844,722	90,620	5,935,342	610,717	344,033	5,668,658	1,741,840	1,745,352	28,166	325,063	182,884
2003	9,831,394	6,266,569	204,688	6,471,257	649,932	378,383	6,199,708	1,749,140	1,882,546	29,599	332,157	184,900
2004	10,908,441	6,950,962	305,439	7,256,401	716,681	423,090	6,962,810	1,919,795	2,025,836	32,223	338,528	191,811
2005	11,464,878	7,255,778	321,271	7,577,049	775,802	468,954	7,270,201	1,984,261	2,210,416	33,164	345,704	197,585
2006	12,082,603	7,648,887	227,080	7,875,967	834,212	508,566	7,550,321	2,169,736	2,362,546	34,148	353,828	203,075
2007	12,766,090	7,727,800	230,370	7,958,170	869,593	557,761	7,646,338	2,542,016	2,577,736	35,371	360,918	205,881
2008	13,523,655	7,742,717	275,173	8,017,890	888,423	589,420	7,718,887	2,850,663	2,954,105	36,872	366,772	203,772
2009	13,261,944	7,420,396	292,806	7,713,202	877,736	589,027	7,424,493	2,608,281	3,229,170	35,789	370,558	198,300
2010	13,567,096	7,547,248	261,360	7,808,608	904,123	591,853	7,496,338	2,582,315	3,488,443	36,205	374,734	197,107
2011	14,260,654	7,730,604	230,493	7,961,097	814,312	623,482	7,770,267	2,878,822	3,611,565	37,745	377,818	196,541
2012	14,786,537	8,040,164	285,322	8,325,486	847,854	645,491	8,123,123	2,947,907	3,715,507	38,859	380,517	199,149
2013	15,487,928	8,543,182	493,964	9,037,146	982,268	642,672	8,697,550	2,909,280	3,881,098	40,380	383,555	201,875
2014	16,356,947	8,906,564	513,794	9,420,358	1,034,009	659,321	9,045,670	3,179,793	4,131,484	42,216	387,460	206,022
2015	17,648,005	9,827,710	491,578	10,319,288	1,107,763	674,407	9,885,932	3,383,360	4,378,713	45,030	391,913	210,639
2016	17,895,029	9,925,354	369,344	10,294,698	1,140,979	678,297	9,832,016	3,468,198	4,594,815	45,081	396,952	215,327
2017	18,731,726	10,007,562	553,552	10,561,114	1,182,951	696,126	10,074,289	3,814,620	4,842,817	46,584	402,105	219,477
2018	19,644,229	10,617,422	396,170	11,013,592	1,249,592	724,005	10,488,005	4,012,139	5,144,085	48,158	407,913	224,204
2019	20,590,691	11,059,375	378,286	11,437,661	1,308,006	749,201	10,878,856	4,260,248	5,451,587	49,786	413,585	225,407
2020	21,820,386	11,237,218	95,979	11,333,197	1,357,246	778,431	10,754,382	4,313,621	6,752,383	52,014	419,510	218,995
2021	24,514,953	12,546,843	388,888	12,935,731	1,503,243	782,519	12,215,007	4,809,035	7,490,911	57,038	429,801	233,161
2022	25,874,829	13,633,557	854,625	14,488,182	1,662,568	796,125	13,621,739	5,121,117	7,131,973	58,936	439,032	243,806

Personal Income and Employment by Area: Salt Lake City, UT

(Thousands of dollars, except as noted.)

Year	Personal income, total	Derivation of personal income								Per capita personal income (dollars)	Population (persons)	Total employment
		Earnings by place of work			Less: Contributions for government social insurance	Plus: Adjustment for residence	Equals: Net earnings by place of residence	Plus: Dividends, interest, and rent	Plus: Personal current transfer receipts			
		Nonfarm	Farm	Total								
1970	1,887,139	1,625,670	6,530	1,632,200	109,178	-61,575	1,461,447	282,894	142,798	3,908	482,939	228,004
1971	2,096,973	1,785,767	6,465	1,792,232	124,888	-54,279	1,613,065	317,060	166,848	4,203	498,890	235,582
1972	2,340,137	2,008,657	8,087	2,016,744	147,664	-73,160	1,795,920	353,522	190,695	4,585	510,409	248,748
1973	2,596,645	2,259,655	11,838	2,271,493	192,936	-88,875	1,989,682	386,153	220,810	4,955	524,033	265,327
1974	2,930,323	2,561,674	7,010	2,568,684	225,365	-108,929	2,234,390	446,637	249,296	5,463	536,395	278,466
1975	3,277,475	2,825,191	5,609	2,830,800	244,183	-119,688	2,466,929	492,684	317,862	5,942	551,569	282,198
1976	3,687,002	3,212,485	6,480	3,218,965	282,242	-137,783	2,798,940	544,888	343,174	6,471	569,758	295,659
1977	4,174,375	3,682,801	4,582	3,687,383	323,489	-167,761	3,196,133	610,506	367,736	7,115	586,735	312,954
1978	4,790,945	4,255,876	4,779	4,260,655	381,656	-207,657	3,671,342	713,905	405,698	7,906	605,964	333,838
1979	5,365,143	4,790,583	5,104	4,795,687	452,551	-245,076	4,098,060	808,563	458,520	8,572	625,894	346,245
1980	6,010,203	5,311,974	3,846	5,315,820	505,939	-295,099	4,514,782	956,530	538,891	9,243	650,232	350,072
1981	6,777,312	5,926,180	3,152	5,929,332	608,290	-323,929	4,997,113	1,147,447	632,752	10,127	669,210	353,355
1982	7,370,652	6,341,284	-435	6,340,849	662,047	-354,269	5,324,533	1,319,517	726,602	10,763	684,802	359,618
1983	7,938,214	6,850,557	3,928	6,854,485	720,356	-436,077	5,698,052	1,457,372	782,790	11,333	700,444	367,055
1984	8,737,314	7,590,719	4,728	7,595,447	819,857	-485,244	6,290,346	1,639,784	807,184	12,256	712,930	388,686
1985	9,319,320	8,078,911	4,001	8,082,912	883,267	-521,418	6,678,227	1,761,716	879,377	12,928	720,877	403,373
1986	9,771,537	8,452,917	4,672	8,457,589	928,001	-557,301	6,972,287	1,851,415	947,835	13,386	729,985	409,417
1987	10,216,604	8,920,379	3,937	8,924,316	972,698	-633,092	7,318,526	1,909,562	988,516	13,882	735,973	423,933
1988	10,845,715	9,483,961	9,538	9,493,499	1,079,208	-678,064	7,736,227	2,075,819	1,033,669	14,627	741,463	438,149
1989	11,541,705	10,081,428	9,004	10,090,432	1,166,002	-728,361	8,196,069	2,200,741	1,144,895	15,478	745,687	451,777
1990	12,458,999	10,985,013	12,261	10,997,274	1,314,893	-881,417	8,800,964	2,402,290	1,255,745	16,467	756,611	470,479
1991	13,284,754	11,829,034	8,911	11,837,945	1,434,865	-999,305	9,403,775	2,491,308	1,389,671	17,069	778,307	481,251
1992	14,290,610	12,948,213	11,970	12,960,183	1,557,242	-1,188,871	10,214,070	2,555,213	1,521,327	17,813	802,260	489,997
1993	15,327,403	14,057,428	14,575	14,072,003	1,697,018	-1,348,789	11,026,196	2,678,343	1,622,864	18,542	826,621	518,184
1994	16,622,898	15,340,434	9,681	15,350,115	1,863,865	-1,494,530	11,991,720	2,980,604	1,650,574	19,588	848,617	547,370
1995	18,150,495	16,617,738	8,896	16,626,634	2,023,177	-1,641,756	12,961,701	3,409,191	1,779,603	20,950	866,353	571,123
1996	19,792,587	18,097,994	6,920	18,104,914	2,154,586	-1,848,172	14,102,156	3,819,508	1,870,923	22,379	884,440	602,150
1997	21,464,493	19,840,938	6,029	19,846,967	2,331,286	-2,093,772	15,421,909	4,107,141	1,935,443	23,727	904,628	624,849
1998	22,810,545	21,294,628	5,275	21,299,903	2,485,051	-2,325,586	16,489,266	4,316,312	2,004,967	24,870	917,191	645,322
1999	24,130,263	22,929,698	8,830	22,938,528	2,633,050	-2,563,981	17,741,497	4,279,435	2,109,331	25,969	929,195	656,570
2000	25,920,230	24,534,035	7,820	24,541,855	2,823,963	-2,756,536	18,961,356	4,694,979	2,263,895	27,500	942,537	677,903
2001	26,444,813	24,901,793	10,222	24,912,015	2,922,942	-2,901,974	19,087,099	4,884,664	2,473,050	27,718	954,081	680,542
2002	27,138,768	25,188,203	4,000	25,192,203	2,974,157	-2,931,409	19,286,637	5,147,842	2,704,289	28,177	963,150	674,069
2003	27,792,467	25,632,152	4,572	25,636,724	3,049,980	-2,963,202	19,623,542	5,312,149	2,856,776	28,609	971,454	671,944
2004	29,407,221	27,426,235	5,526	27,431,761	3,289,098	-3,255,366	20,887,297	5,514,023	3,005,901	29,945	982,034	685,598
2005	32,157,909	29,814,242	5,217	29,819,459	3,567,502	-3,599,921	22,652,036	6,232,054	3,273,819	32,248	997,221	712,947
2006	36,005,791	33,436,987	7,883	33,444,870	3,868,522	-4,112,966	25,463,382	6,951,669	3,590,740	35,359	1,018,281	745,172
2007	38,561,857	36,064,433	6,125	36,070,558	4,171,737	-4,749,573	27,149,248	7,540,926	3,871,683	37,167	1,037,540	781,686
2008	40,026,842	36,669,110	6,977	36,676,087	4,252,958	-5,020,539	27,402,590	8,129,416	4,494,836	37,924	1,055,462	787,797
2009	38,095,059	35,216,902	9,043	35,225,945	4,136,860	-5,101,936	25,987,149	7,118,297	4,989,613	35,470	1,074,013	761,062
2010	38,977,234	35,781,458	10,016	35,791,474	4,183,205	-5,321,753	26,286,516	7,171,427	5,519,291	35,696	1,091,930	756,962
2011	41,995,024	37,987,110	13,809	38,000,919	3,965,411	-5,727,260	28,308,248	7,946,862	5,739,914	37,864	1,109,089	776,318
2012	44,703,269	41,045,094	13,567	41,058,661	4,203,559	-6,307,739	30,547,363	8,496,353	5,659,553	39,632	1,127,952	797,536
2013	45,941,324	42,992,071	14,746	43,006,817	4,980,447	-6,520,461	31,505,909	8,566,519	5,868,896	40,082	1,146,171	820,419
2014	48,326,293	44,950,287	13,748	44,964,035	5,215,030	-6,707,539	33,041,466	9,245,354	6,039,473	41,677	1,159,550	839,581
2015	52,109,220	48,017,622	25,272	48,042,894	5,452,900	-7,124,403	35,465,591	10,273,620	6,370,009	44,347	1,175,028	866,867
2016	54,746,380	50,739,067	10,492	50,749,559	5,720,052	-7,758,886	37,270,621	10,858,543	6,617,216	45,734	1,197,061	897,483
2017	57,880,438	53,425,157	8,214	53,433,371	6,026,524	-8,245,388	39,161,459	11,934,014	6,784,965	47,502	1,218,488	920,670
2018	61,741,758	57,065,207	6,726	57,071,933	6,290,654	-8,736,984	42,044,295	12,516,358	7,181,105	50,006	1,234,679	949,062
2019	65,157,872	60,801,975	4,771	60,806,746	6,684,384	-9,883,617	44,238,745	13,130,963	7,788,164	52,187	1,248,555	963,205
2020	71,070,374	65,209,957	8,176	65,218,133	7,174,498	-10,594,583	47,449,052	13,480,993	10,140,329	56,393	1,260,259	968,016
2021	78,849,046	72,016,233	10,785	72,027,018	7,834,578	-12,340,449	51,851,991	15,032,229	11,964,826	62,421	1,263,174	1,012,736
2022	82,409,551	78,116,751	17,372	78,134,123	8,674,793	-14,373,900	55,085,430	16,916,252	10,407,869	65,085	1,266,191	1,064,471

Personal Income and Employment by Area: San Angelo, TX

(Thousands of dollars, except as noted.)

Year	Personal income, total	Derivation of personal income: Earnings by place of work: Nonfarm	Farm	Total	Less: Contributions for government social insurance	Plus: Adjustment for residence	Equals: Net earnings by place of residence	Plus: Dividends, interest, and rent	Plus: Personal current transfer receipts	Per capita personal income (dollars)	Population (persons)	Total employment
1970	279,657	203,272	13,069	216,341	12,315	-78	203,948	51,598	24,111	3,808	73,447	34,237
1971	300,382	223,995	8,250	232,245	14,096	-607	217,542	55,147	27,693	3,984	75,391	35,132
1972	329,940	244,593	10,616	255,209	16,007	-996	238,206	61,027	30,707	4,415	74,729	36,047
1973	372,036	274,812	13,786	288,598	20,621	-1,573	266,404	69,080	36,552	4,834	76,964	37,958
1974	404,445	302,879	5,960	308,839	23,558	-2,069	283,212	78,459	42,774	5,188	77,963	38,637
1975	464,538	343,420	7,420	350,840	26,372	-1,011	323,457	89,799	51,282	5,827	79,721	39,796
1976	527,215	390,256	14,956	405,212	30,282	-3,341	371,589	98,838	56,788	6,518	80,892	41,412
1977	581,037	439,513	7,280	446,793	34,558	-4,938	407,297	113,071	60,669	7,120	81,609	43,847
1978	667,253	511,967	5,343	517,310	41,029	-5,902	470,379	129,544	67,330	8,028	83,120	46,600
1979	738,652	570,720	3,706	574,426	48,419	-7,018	518,989	143,289	76,374	8,647	85,419	47,552
1980	846,560	646,757	-3,790	642,967	55,377	-9,166	578,424	180,313	87,823	9,626	87,944	49,257
1981	1,020,422	744,462	18,692	763,154	68,761	-9,463	684,930	235,835	99,657	11,342	89,968	51,870
1982	1,145,147	824,207	15,109	839,316	78,456	-9,127	751,733	281,476	111,938	12,204	93,833	54,203
1983	1,232,848	868,843	21,000	889,843	82,176	-9,103	798,564	309,724	124,560	12,621	97,684	54,312
1984	1,320,388	912,725	22,538	935,263	88,298	-6,645	840,320	345,679	134,389	13,267	99,525	55,022
1985	1,346,337	938,897	-14,160	924,737	92,429	-5,111	827,197	373,078	146,062	13,480	99,875	55,045
1986	1,383,128	953,077	2,329	955,406	93,451	-5,840	856,115	368,120	158,893	13,738	100,677	53,685
1987	1,400,725	963,815	10,991	974,806	93,990	-4,739	876,077	357,387	167,261	13,899	100,781	55,343
1988	1,479,236	1,013,857	7,887	1,021,744	101,844	-2,542	917,358	379,327	182,551	14,542	101,725	55,977
1989	1,570,737	1,033,453	6,856	1,040,309	105,878	-701	933,730	433,845	203,162	15,275	102,830	55,760
1990	1,631,819	1,086,110	16,656	1,102,766	109,839	2,865	995,792	417,060	218,967	16,100	101,355	55,721
1991	1,690,549	1,151,655	8,294	1,159,949	119,500	3,163	1,043,612	413,539	233,398	16,707	101,188	56,653
1992	1,790,621	1,219,004	13,038	1,232,042	125,856	2,527	1,108,713	412,458	269,450	17,445	102,646	56,824
1993	1,888,771	1,299,584	14,229	1,313,813	134,179	2,140	1,181,774	423,233	283,764	18,264	103,413	58,090
1994	1,959,594	1,332,346	18,144	1,350,490	139,351	2,840	1,213,979	447,896	297,719	18,709	104,741	59,041
1995	2,086,126	1,411,577	10,275	1,421,852	147,497	2,619	1,276,974	481,628	327,524	19,835	105,174	61,055
1996	2,161,494	1,452,991	3,875	1,456,866	150,703	3,079	1,309,242	501,326	350,926	20,379	106,063	62,274
1997	2,283,279	1,540,325	8,279	1,548,604	157,160	6,146	1,397,590	517,443	368,246	21,397	106,710	62,503
1998	2,422,997	1,675,155	3,384	1,678,539	168,264	5,101	1,515,376	534,559	373,062	22,588	107,267	63,494
1999	2,484,135	1,706,082	17,906	1,723,988	171,868	5,044	1,557,164	538,765	388,206	23,197	107,089	63,302
2000	2,606,205	1,762,090	12,771	1,774,861	176,810	7,374	1,605,425	596,642	404,138	24,312	107,199	64,431
2001	2,881,137	1,986,411	34,840	2,021,251	192,506	5,028	1,833,773	611,613	435,751	26,942	106,937	64,719
2002	2,934,753	2,045,902	22,159	2,068,061	197,590	-760	1,869,711	590,108	474,934	27,413	107,058	64,742
2003	3,084,743	2,109,500	37,751	2,147,251	208,029	-95	1,939,127	638,537	507,079	28,752	107,287	64,428
2004	3,138,728	2,156,017	34,323	2,190,340	217,009	-554	1,972,777	635,056	530,895	29,161	107,634	63,655
2005	3,377,336	2,269,198	38,419	2,307,617	224,966	3,443	2,086,094	714,021	577,221	31,334	107,785	64,073
2006	3,540,609	2,426,883	18,216	2,445,099	232,294	10,335	2,223,140	708,363	609,106	32,513	108,898	65,265
2007	3,723,517	2,463,144	33,247	2,496,391	241,332	22,214	2,277,273	776,825	669,419	34,023	109,441	65,973
2008	4,324,162	2,779,424	-1,226	2,778,198	261,060	38,906	2,556,044	1,035,026	733,092	39,176	110,379	66,905
2009	4,031,333	2,663,244	14,334	2,677,578	264,129	17,145	2,430,594	812,046	788,693	36,115	111,626	66,948
2010	4,293,182	2,790,286	34,573	2,824,859	275,765	10,467	2,559,561	870,474	863,147	37,849	113,430	67,524
2011	4,545,705	2,843,450	33,589	2,877,039	256,127	30,533	2,651,445	1,007,797	886,463	39,684	114,548	68,275
2012	4,808,425	3,010,496	15,669	3,026,165	270,132	13,806	2,769,839	1,162,504	876,082	41,407	116,125	70,407
2013	4,949,717	3,130,437	35,135	3,165,572	315,121	8,401	2,858,852	1,187,368	903,497	42,090	117,599	72,415
2014	5,449,137	3,432,530	25,513	3,458,043	337,920	10,381	3,130,504	1,378,582	940,051	45,658	119,346	73,690
2015	5,223,858	3,315,955	33,083	3,349,038	339,896	4,181	3,013,323	1,204,942	1,005,593	43,342	120,527	74,411
2016	5,051,969	3,197,873	12,264	3,210,137	336,836	-15,380	2,857,921	1,122,959	1,071,089	41,844	120,733	73,693
2017	5,357,339	3,377,625	13,674	3,391,299	354,298	-9,283	3,027,718	1,236,137	1,093,484	44,407	120,641	73,447
2018	5,887,399	3,677,588	16,243	3,693,831	378,666	-728	3,314,437	1,427,427	1,145,535	48,558	121,245	74,458
2019	6,348,344	4,056,198	21,301	4,077,499	401,590	5,278	3,681,187	1,473,136	1,194,021	51,868	122,395	74,273
2020	6,917,248	4,241,523	32,520	4,274,043	417,654	-1,017	3,855,372	1,545,837	1,516,039	56,198	123,086	72,807
2021	7,458,392	4,404,320	27,341	4,431,661	418,657	3,314	4,016,318	1,689,873	1,752,201	61,053	122,163	74,468
2022	7,710,404	4,697,148	26,096	4,723,244	457,296	11,216	4,277,164	1,845,373	1,587,867	63,284	121,839	77,788

Personal Income and Employment by Area: San Antonio-New Braunfels, TX

(Thousands of dollars, except as noted.)

Year	Personal income, total	Derivation of personal income: Earnings by place of work: Nonfarm	Farm	Total	Less: Contributions for government social insurance	Plus: Adjustment for residence	Equals: Net earnings by place of residence	Plus: Dividends, interest, and rent	Plus: Personal current transfer receipts	Per capita personal income (dollars)	Population (persons)	Total employment
1970	3,684,643	2,808,085	33,294	2,841,379	159,637	-2,265	2,679,477	731,642	273,524	3,847	957,715	421,654
1971	4,105,585	3,137,631	20,888	3,158,519	186,884	-3,174	2,968,461	817,555	319,569	4,157	987,523	433,674
1972	4,520,504	3,451,810	35,480	3,487,290	213,133	-5,444	3,268,713	891,805	359,986	4,481	1,008,844	443,581
1973	5,041,111	3,811,954	64,331	3,876,285	266,226	-7,895	3,602,164	1,001,863	437,084	4,852	1,038,887	462,283
1974	5,562,333	4,159,699	47,989	4,207,688	302,457	-2,549	3,902,682	1,133,577	526,074	5,271	1,055,225	467,397
1975	6,080,004	4,450,355	47,328	4,497,683	326,809	11,658	4,182,532	1,229,972	667,500	5,712	1,064,486	461,538
1976	6,675,840	4,925,366	40,937	4,966,303	369,354	22,298	4,619,247	1,328,332	728,261	6,161	1,083,489	475,281
1977	7,294,609	5,433,993	20,951	5,454,944	409,680	3,287	5,048,551	1,476,700	769,358	6,598	1,105,551	493,057
1978	8,225,297	6,147,597	12,971	6,160,568	475,334	-3,858	5,681,376	1,695,356	848,565	7,319	1,123,898	515,788
1979	9,307,726	6,954,727	18,472	6,973,199	566,623	2,683	6,409,259	1,920,365	978,102	8,174	1,138,722	535,097
1980	10,654,603	7,921,124	-20,539	7,900,585	654,032	7,779	7,254,332	2,268,845	1,131,426	9,169	1,161,968	557,276
1981	12,190,606	9,017,941	12,971	9,030,912	797,533	22,431	8,255,810	2,662,778	1,272,018	10,269	1,187,117	575,836
1982	13,479,088	9,808,557	11,466	9,820,023	881,171	17,696	8,956,548	3,112,133	1,410,407	11,029	1,222,136	594,500
1983	14,774,527	10,655,606	39,080	10,694,686	976,871	13,015	9,730,830	3,500,224	1,543,473	11,782	1,254,044	611,333
1984	16,553,561	11,970,928	45,086	12,016,014	1,122,939	9,729	10,902,804	3,972,037	1,678,720	12,893	1,283,925	646,427
1985	18,196,112	13,143,116	6,805	13,149,921	1,253,018	11,498	11,908,401	4,496,356	1,791,355	13,812	1,317,439	676,534
1986	19,203,488	13,868,942	12,769	13,881,711	1,318,806	6,446	12,569,351	4,697,841	1,936,296	14,155	1,356,676	685,123
1987	19,579,955	14,195,585	12,077	14,207,662	1,340,468	4,256	12,871,450	4,639,423	2,069,082	14,107	1,387,997	702,912
1988	20,810,170	15,147,620	4,503	15,152,123	1,479,625	3,852	13,676,350	4,923,480	2,210,340	14,923	1,394,458	706,182
1989	22,050,706	15,717,375	31,683	15,749,058	1,567,485	6,649	14,188,222	5,343,064	2,519,420	15,736	1,401,286	713,903
1990	23,220,198	16,526,592	49,940	16,576,532	1,641,022	11,226	14,946,736	5,428,554	2,844,908	16,458	1,410,902	723,234
1991	24,437,135	17,484,395	47,919	17,532,314	1,782,766	15,707	15,765,255	5,547,755	3,124,125	17,041	1,434,060	736,292
1992	26,596,323	19,065,737	71,050	19,136,787	1,937,420	24,978	17,224,345	5,720,168	3,651,810	18,150	1,465,365	752,583
1993	28,263,731	20,432,597	84,225	20,516,822	2,082,417	34,023	18,468,428	5,960,543	3,834,760	18,864	1,498,269	780,913
1994	30,276,685	21,965,642	70,316	22,035,958	2,252,551	38,147	19,821,554	6,322,105	4,133,026	19,722	1,535,185	813,191
1995	32,536,166	23,445,175	61,379	23,506,554	2,412,350	47,951	21,142,155	6,889,750	4,504,261	20,723	1,570,083	847,156
1996	34,328,532	24,775,742	31,257	24,806,999	2,528,201	70,634	22,349,432	7,134,978	4,844,122	21,463	1,599,427	872,230
1997	36,990,555	26,490,210	69,316	26,559,526	2,710,987	91,674	23,940,213	7,956,822	5,093,520	22,712	1,628,676	908,164
1998	39,885,322	28,941,233	60,288	29,001,521	2,918,263	133,187	26,216,445	8,428,029	5,240,848	24,030	1,659,847	931,942
1999	42,370,425	31,240,513	76,901	31,317,414	3,125,547	164,899	28,356,766	8,621,915	5,391,744	25,086	1,689,009	954,739
2000	46,361,467	34,520,529	62,957	34,583,486	3,353,732	212,225	31,441,979	9,211,367	5,708,121	26,954	1,720,003	980,454
2001	48,807,305	36,502,963	71,646	36,574,609	3,536,335	264,991	33,303,265	9,258,694	6,245,346	27,920	1,748,123	993,949
2002	50,434,015	37,763,952	101,298	37,865,250	3,663,442	283,921	34,485,729	9,167,311	6,780,975	28,268	1,784,153	1,004,361
2003	53,484,745	39,851,894	115,110	39,967,004	3,907,946	365,358	36,424,416	9,698,516	7,361,813	29,454	1,815,846	1,010,906
2004	56,018,555	41,776,974	111,531	41,888,505	4,140,632	499,318	38,247,191	9,931,710	7,839,654	30,156	1,857,602	1,028,536
2005	60,128,345	44,052,098	93,905	44,146,003	4,375,313	568,863	40,339,553	11,051,542	8,737,250	31,708	1,896,328	1,064,986
2006	65,640,997	48,044,708	58,826	48,103,534	4,699,329	775,734	44,179,939	11,990,652	9,470,406	33,553	1,956,361	1,110,224
2007	69,943,209	50,165,384	54,549	50,219,933	4,988,347	973,155	46,204,741	13,251,335	10,487,133	34,771	2,011,543	1,153,185
2008	75,594,464	52,801,841	-15,995	52,785,846	5,197,773	1,221,798	48,809,871	14,851,658	11,932,935	36,674	2,061,275	1,178,850
2009	73,792,399	51,596,031	-18,228	51,577,803	5,303,680	1,038,993	47,313,116	13,380,953	13,098,330	35,045	2,105,672	1,171,318
2010	78,690,471	54,217,566	-2,183	54,215,383	5,572,184	920,974	49,564,173	14,518,734	14,607,564	36,557	2,152,542	1,179,848
2011	85,743,494	57,575,292	-636	57,574,656	5,208,253	901,131	53,267,534	17,237,104	15,238,856	39,125	2,191,507	1,206,057
2012	88,800,011	60,287,604	16,727	60,304,331	5,466,825	960,316	55,797,822	17,729,245	15,272,944	39,774	2,232,588	1,236,729
2013	92,645,531	64,057,616	51,531	64,109,147	6,440,237	866,365	58,535,275	18,302,728	15,807,528	40,750	2,273,519	1,270,770
2014	100,226,300	69,518,038	24,518	69,542,556	6,871,499	1,003,980	63,675,037	19,852,864	16,698,399	43,198	2,320,172	1,313,102
2015	103,519,661	71,182,011	75,713	71,257,724	7,294,496	967,022	64,930,250	20,719,554	17,869,857	43,712	2,368,219	1,356,244
2016	105,273,227	73,821,692	-16,981	73,804,711	7,688,285	893,952	67,010,378	19,643,679	18,619,170	43,637	2,412,468	1,407,429
2017	111,676,821	78,316,523	-17,512	78,299,011	8,150,051	952,219	71,101,179	21,428,025	19,147,617	45,480	2,455,494	1,451,713
2018	119,243,694	83,346,484	-35,062	83,311,422	8,510,374	1,060,821	75,861,869	23,200,340	20,181,485	47,816	2,493,824	1,491,511
2019	121,994,851	84,138,003	-44,239	84,093,764	8,834,151	1,099,518	76,359,131	24,171,562	21,464,158	48,243	2,528,761	1,512,910
2020	128,842,799	83,574,173	-31,137	83,543,036	9,051,593	1,034,933	75,526,376	24,768,336	28,548,087	50,165	2,568,358	1,486,822
2021	141,862,427	89,634,307	-21,287	89,613,020	9,609,145	1,090,940	81,094,815	27,425,324	33,342,288	54,459	2,604,931	1,551,560
2022	146,521,514	97,291,694	-101,150	97,190,544	10,524,610	1,206,428	87,872,362	29,554,229	29,094,923	55,180	2,655,342	1,638,281

Personal Income and Employment by Area: San Diego-Chula Vista-Carlsbad, CA

(Thousands of dollars, except as noted.)

Year	Personal income, total	Derivation of personal income								Per capita personal income (dollars)	Population (persons)	Total employment
		Earnings by place of work			Less: Contributions for government social insurance	Plus: Adjustment for residence	Equals: Net earnings by place of residence	Plus: Dividends, interest, and rent	Plus: Personal current transfer receipts			
		Nonfarm	Farm	Total								
1970	7,021,079	5,197,882	55,543	5,253,425	330,158	-31,761	4,891,506	1,593,087	536,486	5,140	1,365,976	647,900
1971	7,542,007	5,552,875	53,571	5,606,446	366,432	-34,848	5,205,166	1,712,595	624,246	5,418	1,391,925	649,466
1972	8,389,601	6,185,140	66,676	6,251,816	421,658	-39,672	5,790,486	1,901,618	697,497	5,854	1,433,126	672,285
1973	9,259,626	6,782,180	93,067	6,875,247	513,822	-42,635	6,318,790	2,140,191	800,645	6,175	1,499,594	707,773
1974	10,346,671	7,432,299	90,285	7,522,584	582,505	-36,744	6,903,335	2,458,996	984,340	6,716	1,540,667	738,023
1975	11,572,053	8,121,710	127,474	8,249,184	641,270	-28,094	7,579,820	2,721,783	1,270,450	7,157	1,616,907	755,698
1976	12,917,968	9,111,012	140,674	9,251,686	733,932	-11,769	8,505,985	2,970,690	1,441,293	7,863	1,642,781	786,899
1977	14,430,966	10,243,704	145,540	10,389,244	841,360	-24,610	9,523,274	3,350,314	1,557,378	8,412	1,715,527	837,772
1978	16,558,724	11,843,665	121,391	11,965,056	989,270	-15,953	10,959,833	3,898,085	1,700,806	9,327	1,775,410	901,275
1979	18,774,001	13,466,406	115,005	13,581,411	1,184,792	6,180	12,402,799	4,458,564	1,912,638	10,272	1,827,602	951,199
1980	21,685,978	15,231,915	130,630	15,362,545	1,306,937	12,741	14,068,349	5,357,053	2,260,576	11,562	1,875,620	988,237
1981	24,698,953	16,898,694	136,921	17,035,615	1,565,281	138,157	15,608,491	6,383,375	2,707,087	12,817	1,927,018	994,581
1982	26,757,854	18,157,216	146,039	18,303,255	1,707,103	146,070	16,742,222	7,024,013	2,991,619	13,566	1,972,354	1,001,945
1983	28,912,657	19,592,410	152,031	19,744,441	1,907,010	174,796	18,012,227	7,687,625	3,212,805	14,326	2,018,133	1,036,404
1984	32,379,386	22,291,784	166,620	22,458,404	2,257,329	179,666	20,380,741	8,613,671	3,384,974	15,669	2,066,419	1,099,543
1985	35,556,806	24,746,996	197,066	24,944,062	2,543,992	198,416	22,598,486	9,292,115	3,666,205	16,724	2,126,090	1,160,801
1986	38,759,351	27,301,007	230,526	27,531,533	2,850,882	225,645	24,906,296	9,864,833	3,988,222	17,643	2,196,834	1,215,030
1987	41,708,359	30,029,243	212,305	30,241,548	3,155,298	262,122	27,348,372	10,124,476	4,235,511	18,331	2,275,309	1,277,030
1988	45,984,919	33,402,677	182,362	33,585,039	3,636,499	291,390	30,239,930	11,142,483	4,602,506	19,450	2,364,284	1,349,526
1989	49,948,206	35,620,581	230,526	35,851,107	3,928,187	333,883	32,256,803	12,650,230	5,041,173	20,434	2,444,380	1,396,314
1990	52,758,991	37,736,038	298,772	38,034,810	4,155,899	377,878	34,256,789	12,950,391	5,551,811	21,000	2,512,365	1,426,402
1991	55,086,852	39,699,075	241,204	39,940,279	4,392,161	334,774	35,882,892	13,045,771	6,158,189	21,576	2,553,122	1,436,665
1992	57,793,795	41,538,542	197,911	41,736,453	4,583,742	328,248	37,480,959	13,322,686	6,990,150	22,287	2,593,126	1,406,200
1993	59,109,878	42,104,423	211,031	42,315,454	4,665,573	312,453	37,962,334	13,760,612	7,386,932	22,737	2,599,776	1,402,948
1994	60,830,019	43,361,620	224,569	43,586,189	4,840,970	288,938	39,034,157	14,236,382	7,559,480	23,265	2,614,685	1,408,463
1995	63,598,316	44,858,354	246,325	45,104,679	4,934,866	281,857	40,451,670	15,186,226	7,960,420	24,240	2,623,697	1,440,496
1996	67,787,222	48,108,712	281,483	48,390,195	5,143,278	269,236	43,516,153	15,930,601	8,340,468	25,565	2,651,549	1,479,423
1997	72,194,802	52,055,833	320,278	52,376,111	5,532,467	249,861	47,093,505	16,637,223	8,464,074	26,812	2,692,600	1,521,768
1998	79,975,393	58,525,799	352,838	58,878,637	6,097,149	241,128	53,022,616	18,154,059	8,798,718	29,223	2,736,720	1,608,669
1999	86,904,668	65,104,996	360,400	65,465,396	6,743,671	182,201	58,903,926	18,735,183	9,265,559	31,153	2,789,593	1,656,003
2000	95,225,126	72,297,291	359,299	72,656,590	7,495,956	138,277	65,298,911	20,243,358	9,682,857	33,680	2,827,366	1,696,594
2001	98,120,504	74,783,608	347,415	75,131,023	7,944,179	-75,720	67,111,124	20,361,193	10,648,187	34,192	2,869,672	1,713,767
2002	102,400,239	79,037,047	362,119	79,399,166	8,476,942	-341,325	70,580,899	20,576,681	11,242,659	35,306	2,900,355	1,749,452
2003	108,141,089	84,401,920	400,846	84,802,766	9,097,397	-557,988	75,147,381	21,148,468	11,845,240	37,102	2,914,702	1,782,091
2004	116,704,322	92,161,574	446,448	92,608,022	10,110,815	-791,220	81,705,987	22,574,194	12,424,141	39,831	2,930,007	1,812,975
2005	121,815,272	96,643,489	465,617	97,109,106	10,563,821	-976,622	85,568,663	23,172,296	13,074,313	41,457	2,938,375	1,837,278
2006	128,126,344	101,194,233	418,804	101,613,037	10,796,590	-1,207,701	89,608,746	24,461,424	14,056,174	43,473	2,947,289	1,861,429
2007	131,979,831	102,237,768	401,462	102,639,230	10,870,267	-1,526,976	90,241,987	26,834,331	14,903,513	44,352	2,975,742	1,890,299
2008	135,317,499	101,896,179	460,284	102,356,463	11,159,808	-1,931,679	89,264,976	29,027,336	17,025,187	44,776	3,022,116	1,882,613
2009	131,278,107	98,354,202	532,776	98,886,978	10,940,457	-1,998,189	85,948,332	26,579,276	18,750,499	42,884	3,061,203	1,821,920
2010	136,161,972	101,389,340	587,220	101,976,560	11,097,150	-2,077,699	88,801,711	26,407,312	20,952,949	43,889	3,102,436	1,804,100
2011	144,475,867	105,785,207	510,636	106,295,843	10,446,370	-2,192,718	93,656,755	29,518,195	21,300,917	46,113	3,133,069	1,828,219
2012	151,092,176	111,189,454	626,979	111,816,433	10,836,580	-2,249,094	98,730,759	30,899,792	21,461,625	47,700	3,167,554	1,877,275
2013	155,648,494	116,354,073	517,105	116,871,178	12,579,258	-2,216,817	102,075,103	31,143,879	22,429,512	48,645	3,199,707	1,920,848
2014	164,691,400	122,010,429	536,250	122,546,679	13,187,232	-2,251,027	107,108,420	33,589,885	23,993,095	50,915	3,234,658	1,973,022
2015	174,081,824	128,460,168	604,672	129,064,840	13,794,788	-2,299,059	112,970,993	35,276,946	25,833,885	53,357	3,262,566	2,029,948
2016	180,838,809	133,446,431	519,669	133,966,100	14,267,111	-2,414,866	117,284,123	36,881,055	26,673,631	55,074	3,283,586	2,083,422
2017	187,630,531	139,219,193	550,547	139,769,740	14,909,104	-2,466,574	122,394,062	38,739,091	26,497,378	56,969	3,293,575	2,118,892
2018	194,949,226	144,805,372	413,214	145,218,586	15,637,294	-2,529,510	127,051,782	40,020,052	27,877,392	59,014	3,303,463	2,148,460
2019	204,586,175	150,518,071	488,832	151,006,903	16,357,600	-2,577,515	132,071,788	42,757,355	29,757,032	62,034	3,297,959	2,158,023
2020	222,600,097	153,713,391	482,699	154,196,090	16,687,301	-2,644,949	134,863,840	43,731,219	44,005,038	67,536	3,296,045	2,053,902
2021	240,216,669	167,022,747	415,567	167,438,314	18,205,002	-2,914,082	146,319,230	47,426,879	46,470,560	73,350	3,274,954	2,136,842
2022	243,506,541	177,724,092	490,452	178,214,544	19,946,508	-3,233,554	155,034,482	50,596,618	37,875,441	74,326	3,276,208	2,270,595

Personal Income and Employment by Area: San Francisco-Oakland-Berkeley, CA

(Thousands of dollars, except as noted.)

Year	Personal income, total	Derivation of personal income: Earnings by place of work: Nonfarm	Farm	Total	Less: Contributions for government social insurance	Plus: Adjustment for residence	Equals: Net earnings by place of residence	Plus: Dividends, interest, and rent	Plus: Personal current transfer receipts	Per capita personal income (dollars)	Population (persons)	Total employment
1970	17,758,252	14,344,577	54,040	14,398,617	916,727	-490,495	12,991,395	3,279,499	1,487,358	5,713	3,108,460	1,559,634
1971	18,922,324	15,107,827	50,566	15,158,393	993,263	-478,952	13,686,178	3,531,384	1,704,762	6,066	3,119,247	1,528,383
1972	20,547,981	16,463,802	63,355	16,527,157	1,140,417	-500,443	14,886,297	3,835,355	1,826,329	6,555	3,134,632	1,561,571
1973	22,058,296	17,686,918	67,268	17,754,186	1,417,530	-524,958	15,811,698	4,234,443	2,012,155	7,011	3,146,217	1,614,085
1974	24,304,358	19,257,861	72,533	19,330,394	1,598,743	-570,040	17,161,611	4,810,231	2,332,516	7,710	3,152,349	1,648,391
1975	26,876,119	21,067,667	78,432	21,146,099	1,712,018	-633,633	18,800,448	5,188,400	2,887,271	8,510	3,158,346	1,670,337
1976	29,450,851	23,293,131	72,610	23,365,741	1,922,349	-729,849	20,713,543	5,577,687	3,159,621	9,241	3,187,017	1,693,226
1977	32,224,427	25,722,822	63,551	25,786,373	2,145,087	-877,371	22,763,915	6,141,226	3,319,286	10,072	3,199,300	1,733,826
1978	36,044,414	29,064,238	78,859	29,143,097	2,482,258	-1,037,572	25,623,267	6,906,482	3,514,665	11,216	3,213,638	1,817,444
1979	40,239,885	32,491,677	103,502	32,595,179	2,914,715	-1,162,758	28,517,706	7,864,726	3,857,453	12,472	3,226,421	1,895,178
1980	45,561,201	36,128,140	116,289	36,244,429	3,211,117	-1,360,286	31,673,026	9,515,602	4,372,573	13,972	3,260,930	1,955,758
1981	51,359,401	39,683,581	110,412	39,793,993	3,831,802	-1,415,484	34,546,707	11,792,073	5,020,621	15,583	3,295,803	1,971,802
1982	55,029,108	42,154,077	116,698	42,270,775	4,167,479	-1,377,655	36,725,641	12,856,206	5,447,261	16,505	3,333,995	1,960,504
1983	59,932,497	45,840,294	118,991	45,959,285	4,611,921	-1,304,199	40,043,165	14,086,563	5,802,769	17,700	3,386,080	1,996,122
1984	66,261,505	50,547,490	117,042	50,664,532	5,280,746	-1,296,720	44,087,066	16,173,077	6,001,362	19,329	3,428,080	2,066,961
1985	71,061,613	54,432,869	123,645	54,556,514	5,767,651	-1,292,156	47,496,707	17,174,031	6,390,875	20,423	3,479,465	2,120,828
1986	75,632,108	58,894,918	129,897	59,024,815	6,313,809	-1,542,347	51,168,659	17,663,521	6,799,928	21,463	3,523,866	2,168,002
1987	79,596,120	62,997,206	135,832	63,133,038	6,741,661	-1,517,760	54,873,617	17,661,376	7,061,127	22,365	3,558,999	2,224,223
1988	87,416,688	69,140,538	133,159	69,273,697	7,561,469	-1,496,250	60,215,978	19,670,418	7,530,292	24,259	3,603,440	2,310,192
1989	93,511,005	72,588,296	136,327	72,724,623	8,042,499	-1,647,205	63,034,919	22,193,568	8,282,518	25,571	3,656,981	2,351,774
1990	99,029,301	76,827,714	145,811	76,973,525	8,475,271	-1,647,022	66,851,232	23,163,903	9,014,166	26,623	3,719,675	2,399,266
1991	103,656,852	81,079,411	114,587	81,193,998	8,973,128	-1,772,324	70,448,546	23,421,691	9,786,615	27,566	3,760,370	2,388,786
1992	109,559,544	85,745,583	130,332	85,875,915	9,415,352	-1,628,458	74,832,105	23,597,381	11,130,058	28,789	3,805,588	2,347,136
1993	113,767,434	88,617,212	133,073	88,750,285	9,715,926	-1,592,355	77,442,004	24,681,621	11,643,809	29,630	3,839,619	2,358,677
1994	118,005,798	91,758,127	141,876	91,900,003	10,124,732	-1,545,241	80,230,030	25,964,054	11,811,714	30,572	3,859,905	2,385,264
1995	126,275,514	97,177,962	120,170	97,298,132	10,561,012	-1,293,394	85,443,726	28,470,990	12,360,798	32,513	3,883,894	2,436,826
1996	136,615,635	104,260,168	128,917	104,389,085	11,038,955	-186,488	93,163,642	30,629,415	12,822,578	34,822	3,923,208	2,492,590
1997	144,888,171	112,099,461	192,729	112,292,190	11,815,241	284,037	100,760,986	31,255,326	12,871,859	36,352	3,985,694	2,550,128
1998	160,542,827	124,195,303	181,331	124,376,634	12,843,879	874,651	112,407,406	34,588,682	13,546,739	39,687	4,045,185	2,639,817
1999	176,390,393	137,455,287	193,137	137,648,424	14,147,782	2,761,491	126,262,133	36,086,745	14,041,515	43,131	4,089,620	2,697,881
2000	202,862,415	160,621,125	207,119	160,828,244	16,333,959	3,790,105	148,284,390	40,029,371	14,548,654	49,049	4,135,875	2,770,316
2001	206,723,086	165,694,576	218,358	165,912,934	16,944,742	892,730	149,860,922	40,898,230	15,963,934	49,517	4,174,788	2,747,283
2002	200,541,146	161,497,639	208,288	161,705,927	16,722,427	-527,827	144,455,673	38,661,732	17,423,741	48,224	4,158,544	2,679,873
2003	203,208,359	163,457,865	230,808	163,688,673	17,035,130	-1,065,851	145,587,692	39,460,946	18,159,721	49,014	4,145,965	2,653,510
2004	214,206,207	171,163,757	190,011	171,353,768	18,208,495	-1,082,938	152,062,335	43,273,336	18,870,536	51,823	4,133,400	2,659,331
2005	227,083,386	179,562,100	178,991	179,741,091	18,875,954	-1,881,701	158,983,436	48,355,740	19,744,210	54,879	4,137,858	2,682,575
2006	247,495,287	190,420,268	177,038	190,597,306	19,396,831	-1,778,908	169,421,567	56,896,205	21,177,515	59,656	4,148,724	2,728,937
2007	259,267,257	197,726,945	166,139	197,893,084	19,946,180	-989,074	176,957,830	59,992,867	22,316,560	61,972	4,183,637	2,785,064
2008	264,709,737	198,041,213	162,472	198,203,685	20,577,254	-503,770	177,122,661	62,453,305	25,133,771	62,374	4,243,932	2,785,592
2009	253,419,028	192,444,351	162,878	192,607,229	19,971,802	-756,138	171,879,289	53,706,943	27,832,796	58,896	4,302,830	2,687,693
2010	262,865,368	198,938,878	163,016	199,101,894	19,949,550	1,371,550	180,523,894	51,715,708	30,625,766	60,501	4,344,808	2,663,461
2011	283,773,466	209,273,461	180,477	209,453,938	18,681,073	2,960,625	193,733,490	59,506,168	30,533,808	64,480	4,400,957	2,715,292
2012	307,619,886	231,406,418	194,366	231,600,784	20,157,124	-2,238,606	209,205,054	67,783,282	30,631,550	68,904	4,464,478	2,836,137
2013	314,423,764	241,417,114	196,290	241,613,404	24,152,026	-277,982	217,183,396	65,353,578	31,886,790	69,370	4,532,579	2,942,929
2014	339,037,036	256,115,887	230,081	256,345,968	25,824,404	2,899,418	233,420,982	71,557,443	34,058,611	73,673	4,601,942	3,059,369
2015	371,467,709	276,492,861	221,488	276,714,349	27,736,565	4,391,865	253,369,649	81,372,447	36,725,613	79,560	4,669,035	3,184,061
2016	395,017,424	296,746,068	190,801	296,936,869	29,384,393	1,122,655	268,675,131	88,101,600	38,240,693	83,812	4,713,129	3,278,570
2017	424,593,748	319,248,265	219,429	319,467,694	31,421,648	1,069,855	289,115,901	97,393,481	38,084,366	89,560	4,740,862	3,340,119
2018	456,742,977	341,305,618	152,520	341,458,138	33,662,487	1,749,972	309,545,623	107,142,623	40,054,731	95,972	4,759,142	3,408,519
2019	475,010,141	363,159,216	200,034	363,359,250	35,895,844	386,698	327,850,104	104,634,776	42,525,261	99,758	4,761,624	3,408,916
2020	511,104,969	378,941,601	239,537	379,181,138	36,691,120	-1,003,388	341,486,630	105,615,361	64,002,978	107,815	4,740,552	3,192,147
2021	574,297,320	432,570,643	216,565	432,787,208	40,968,751	-1,118,753	390,699,704	118,068,022	65,529,594	124,398	4,616,610	3,274,556
2022	566,659,155	430,557,859	290,861	430,848,720	43,238,546	-2,048,283	385,561,891	126,888,407	54,208,857	123,736	4,579,599	3,469,922

Personal Income and Employment by Area: San Jose-Sunnyvale-Santa Clara, CA

(Thousands of dollars, except as noted.)

Year	Personal income, total	Derivation of personal income: Earnings by place of work: Nonfarm	Farm	Total	Less: Contributions for government social insurance	Plus: Adjustment for residence	Equals: Net earnings by place of residence	Plus: Dividends, interest, and rent	Plus: Personal current transfer receipts	Per capita personal income (dollars)	Population (persons)	Total employment
1970	5,534,127	4,215,123	48,867	4,263,990	284,661	369,993	4,349,322	778,460	406,345	5,079	1,089,674	465,696
1971	5,956,579	4,512,419	51,593	4,564,012	314,276	359,172	4,608,908	865,550	482,121	5,322	1,119,155	468,263
1972	6,610,349	5,105,259	57,898	5,163,157	377,334	345,027	5,130,850	958,148	521,351	5,709	1,157,841	500,625
1973	7,382,556	5,842,144	78,728	5,920,872	500,555	312,063	5,732,380	1,077,020	573,156	6,238	1,183,576	544,854
1974	8,276,698	6,583,684	81,853	6,665,537	579,590	275,225	6,361,172	1,242,730	672,796	6,986	1,184,823	576,125
1975	9,188,573	7,128,079	82,909	7,210,988	611,469	307,357	6,906,876	1,385,904	895,793	7,571	1,213,688	578,145
1976	10,249,199	8,144,218	68,233	8,212,451	715,209	283,406	7,780,648	1,501,242	967,309	8,342	1,228,572	616,284
1977	11,480,890	9,395,211	82,006	9,477,217	844,061	198,177	8,831,333	1,654,395	995,162	9,153	1,254,396	654,919
1978	13,179,444	11,023,393	83,357	11,106,750	1,020,884	120,313	10,206,179	1,909,494	1,063,771	10,264	1,284,003	708,398
1979	15,252,038	13,075,768	94,626	13,170,394	1,267,871	-7,988	11,894,535	2,217,327	1,140,176	11,771	1,295,698	770,291
1980	17,608,202	14,989,183	104,694	15,093,877	1,427,082	-122,071	13,544,724	2,740,605	1,322,873	13,272	1,326,709	814,696
1981	19,976,929	16,953,841	84,949	17,038,790	1,745,222	-297,037	14,996,531	3,428,049	1,552,349	14,791	1,350,627	832,437
1982	21,888,688	18,880,173	95,526	18,975,699	1,986,212	-553,198	16,436,289	3,786,292	1,666,107	15,954	1,371,955	848,645
1983	24,169,406	21,260,706	99,450	21,360,156	2,288,892	-899,858	18,171,406	4,212,600	1,785,400	17,242	1,401,776	879,267
1984	26,982,665	24,142,733	118,983	24,261,716	2,709,798	-1,290,765	20,261,153	4,902,684	1,818,828	18,933	1,425,185	936,276
1985	28,677,666	25,858,401	125,325	25,983,726	2,923,564	-1,628,498	21,431,664	5,273,485	1,972,517	19,779	1,449,912	949,532
1986	29,794,175	26,940,110	141,408	27,081,518	3,055,230	-1,756,278	22,270,010	5,397,242	2,126,923	20,385	1,461,582	947,268
1987	31,555,963	29,223,076	148,800	29,371,876	3,286,046	-2,187,548	23,898,282	5,444,980	2,212,701	21,314	1,480,543	978,952
1988	34,643,583	32,562,121	141,139	32,703,260	3,759,631	-2,680,069	26,263,560	6,010,029	2,369,994	22,994	1,506,608	1,023,025
1989	37,194,771	34,670,071	138,039	34,808,110	3,986,593	-3,006,249	27,815,268	6,754,312	2,625,191	24,243	1,534,258	1,036,067
1990	39,063,500	36,884,217	126,958	37,011,175	4,221,001	-3,843,936	28,946,238	7,232,185	2,885,077	25,446	1,535,142	1,052,577
1991	40,707,461	38,446,217	112,918	38,559,135	4,432,029	-3,919,521	30,207,585	7,324,809	3,175,067	26,255	1,550,447	1,040,251
1992	43,727,991	41,359,128	120,834	41,479,962	4,679,201	-4,238,479	32,562,282	7,460,858	3,704,851	27,849	1,570,207	1,017,714
1993	44,579,116	42,028,294	155,773	42,184,067	4,811,069	-4,526,487	32,846,511	7,843,946	3,888,659	28,060	1,588,680	1,023,035
1994	46,426,499	43,900,717	169,310	44,070,027	5,087,957	-4,941,200	34,040,870	8,470,723	3,914,906	28,978	1,602,152	1,036,627
1995	51,147,928	48,574,157	197,267	48,771,424	5,549,180	-5,606,237	37,616,007	9,434,774	4,097,147	31,523	1,622,579	1,075,809
1996	55,626,821	54,086,068	178,138	54,264,206	6,102,632	-7,212,730	40,948,844	10,373,789	4,304,188	33,655	1,652,864	1,131,518
1997	60,921,285	61,240,640	193,098	61,433,738	6,802,807	-8,603,956	46,026,975	10,584,638	4,309,672	36,174	1,684,121	1,175,557
1998	65,941,934	66,855,801	197,634	67,053,435	7,335,512	-9,951,158	49,766,765	11,655,370	4,519,799	38,607	1,708,031	1,221,008
1999	74,168,698	78,376,188	222,136	78,598,324	8,430,548	-12,965,383	57,202,393	12,240,307	4,725,998	43,047	1,722,965	1,226,104
2000	92,521,253	100,391,771	323,462	100,715,233	10,304,020	-16,684,824	73,726,389	13,859,443	4,935,421	53,212	1,738,728	1,283,119
2001	88,166,433	90,192,228	249,237	90,441,465	9,439,742	-13,060,106	67,941,617	14,769,907	5,454,909	50,591	1,742,726	1,245,499
2002	82,605,037	81,402,231	221,752	81,623,983	8,586,835	-10,862,825	62,174,323	14,166,598	6,264,116	47,904	1,724,404	1,151,599
2003	83,212,625	80,505,965	229,493	80,735,458	8,524,817	-10,315,342	61,895,299	14,789,925	6,527,401	48,413	1,718,790	1,111,268
2004	85,677,609	83,360,536	242,543	83,603,079	9,029,102	-10,729,775	63,844,202	15,282,396	6,551,011	49,870	1,718,016	1,110,178
2005	90,327,674	85,963,186	230,636	86,193,822	9,239,199	-10,458,950	66,495,673	16,977,546	6,854,455	52,214	1,729,959	1,120,365
2006	99,275,802	93,087,472	224,689	93,312,161	9,681,939	-11,369,231	72,260,991	19,588,802	7,426,009	56,882	1,745,283	1,146,725
2007	107,717,763	100,445,360	203,451	100,648,811	10,197,649	-12,764,520	77,686,642	22,129,606	7,901,515	60,992	1,766,098	1,183,447
2008	108,066,644	99,668,921	175,517	99,844,438	10,495,485	-12,420,994	76,927,959	22,056,146	9,082,539	60,197	1,795,231	1,186,386
2009	102,245,924	94,483,244	241,385	94,724,629	10,087,298	-11,078,859	73,558,472	18,421,729	10,265,723	56,192	1,819,573	1,130,464
2010	110,729,633	103,328,833	229,953	103,558,786	10,536,016	-12,581,909	80,440,861	18,957,931	11,330,841	60,111	1,842,072	1,126,572
2011	121,259,254	112,491,343	196,445	112,687,788	9,999,580	-14,900,921	87,787,287	22,227,530	11,244,437	64,821	1,870,668	1,159,911
2012	134,235,407	118,113,878	246,334	118,360,212	10,452,224	-10,486,370	97,421,618	25,611,924	11,201,865	70,679	1,899,220	1,206,129
2013	136,360,932	125,387,589	290,269	125,677,858	12,880,391	-13,410,783	99,386,684	25,420,840	11,553,408	70,632	1,930,576	1,254,579
2014	148,809,515	137,378,162	303,617	137,681,779	14,043,715	-16,626,585	107,011,479	29,480,668	12,317,368	75,972	1,958,735	1,300,024
2015	164,046,558	152,966,965	353,142	153,320,107	15,362,184	-19,883,435	118,074,488	32,712,416	13,259,654	82,603	1,985,975	1,358,651
2016	177,759,101	162,889,438	286,857	163,176,295	16,105,193	-18,321,048	128,750,054	35,312,346	13,696,701	88,801	2,001,778	1,395,016
2017	193,230,025	177,562,013	280,488	177,842,501	17,408,528	-19,739,878	140,694,095	38,991,560	13,544,370	96,174	2,009,163	1,424,906
2018	210,975,411	194,881,877	216,416	195,098,293	18,862,463	-21,378,728	154,857,102	41,959,821	14,158,488	104,834	2,012,463	1,459,381
2019	221,954,180	204,061,347	207,832	204,269,179	19,758,558	-22,649,032	161,861,589	44,969,538	15,123,053	110,618	2,006,501	1,466,924
2020	244,542,323	220,831,427	217,972	221,049,399	20,842,065	-24,282,709	175,924,625	46,005,942	22,611,756	122,544	1,995,547	1,399,362
2021	276,855,483	254,535,246	183,191	254,718,437	23,431,404	-27,627,773	203,659,260	49,809,982	23,386,241	141,739	1,953,270	1,433,312
2022	274,331,332	250,083,282	209,859	250,293,141	24,474,283	-24,453,016	201,365,842	53,632,698	19,332,792	141,516	1,938,524	1,522,502

Personal Income and Employment by Area: San Luis Obispo-Paso Robles, CA

(Thousands of dollars, except as noted.)

		Derivation of personal income										
		Earnings by place of work										
Year	Personal income, total	Nonfarm	Farm	Total	Less: Contributions for government social insurance	Plus: Adjustment for residence	Equals: Net earnings by place of residence	Plus: Dividends, interest, and rent	Plus: Personal current transfer receipts	Per capita personal income (dollars)	Population (persons)	Total employment
1970	410,874	250,223	17,638	267,861	14,935	13,385	266,311	88,796	55,767	3,866	106,280	38,922
1971	455,874	282,363	17,908	300,271	17,428	13,938	296,781	98,500	60,593	4,171	109,301	40,811
1972	513,809	321,221	23,147	344,368	21,113	14,896	338,151	110,387	65,271	4,449	115,484	43,478
1973	581,196	358,830	27,270	386,100	26,863	17,791	377,028	130,047	74,121	4,850	119,843	45,667
1974	673,901	399,905	40,083	439,988	31,041	21,526	430,473	152,011	91,417	5,368	125,535	48,387
1975	767,457	451,386	33,698	485,084	34,418	27,141	477,807	176,413	113,237	6,069	126,456	50,574
1976	874,841	522,678	33,850	556,528	40,031	32,959	549,456	195,569	129,816	6,516	134,260	53,644
1977	975,928	585,484	27,105	612,589	45,708	41,666	608,547	225,112	142,269	7,040	138,635	56,552
1978	1,152,991	695,073	44,864	739,937	55,958	47,902	731,881	264,676	156,434	7,902	145,914	60,728
1979	1,312,378	792,040	41,414	833,454	67,457	59,134	825,131	311,904	175,343	8,700	150,850	65,290
1980	1,487,385	843,427	45,673	889,100	70,113	72,362	891,349	389,388	206,648	9,487	156,786	66,956
1981	1,671,514	925,234	49,536	974,770	85,267	66,813	956,316	471,429	243,769	10,325	161,886	68,339
1982	1,795,502	958,879	62,286	1,021,165	90,931	74,490	1,004,724	525,567	265,211	10,780	166,563	68,574
1983	2,167,812	1,280,798	68,083	1,348,881	127,760	49,927	1,271,048	614,774	281,990	12,650	171,365	75,005
1984	2,380,254	1,412,144	53,564	1,465,708	144,599	68,057	1,389,166	685,841	305,247	13,405	177,566	79,834
1985	2,551,135	1,480,246	53,258	1,533,504	149,855	88,468	1,472,117	745,234	333,784	13,771	185,248	84,089
1986	2,777,390	1,626,663	72,418	1,699,081	165,384	94,957	1,628,654	789,536	359,200	14,428	192,497	87,984
1987	3,005,305	1,829,764	84,857	1,914,621	186,139	93,763	1,822,245	805,086	377,974	15,076	199,345	92,685
1988	3,309,864	2,022,158	88,696	2,110,854	212,600	102,754	2,001,008	902,846	406,010	16,204	204,261	98,930
1989	3,661,992	2,181,670	91,975	2,273,645	234,621	107,789	2,146,813	1,068,923	446,256	17,167	213,314	103,273
1990	3,832,943	2,346,773	72,761	2,419,534	250,092	111,320	2,280,762	1,069,163	483,018	17,560	218,276	106,051
1991	4,014,762	2,489,432	47,156	2,536,588	264,916	123,747	2,395,419	1,092,131	527,212	18,258	219,895	110,470
1992	4,245,676	2,637,813	63,697	2,701,510	279,130	129,695	2,552,075	1,096,526	597,075	19,138	221,848	110,178
1993	4,396,812	2,697,296	77,927	2,775,223	284,869	134,940	2,625,294	1,135,588	635,930	19,684	223,370	109,848
1994	4,565,415	2,795,346	70,575	2,865,921	297,402	142,581	2,711,100	1,196,293	658,022	20,181	226,228	112,959
1995	4,827,176	2,974,326	74,240	3,048,566	311,092	150,667	2,888,141	1,249,050	689,985	21,045	229,370	116,952
1996	5,199,126	3,215,172	76,942	3,292,114	324,625	159,140	3,126,629	1,341,613	730,884	22,316	232,976	120,730
1997	5,584,747	3,501,976	125,149	3,627,125	348,348	173,190	3,451,967	1,384,031	748,749	23,604	236,601	125,634
1998	6,024,568	3,822,562	101,266	3,923,828	374,399	189,506	3,738,935	1,500,291	785,342	25,100	240,020	131,952
1999	6,402,356	4,105,521	108,469	4,213,990	403,465	209,896	4,020,421	1,565,515	816,420	26,295	243,480	137,881
2000	6,937,188	4,388,050	165,767	4,553,817	432,236	249,840	4,371,421	1,700,580	865,187	27,991	247,839	138,477
2001	7,629,514	4,903,034	130,152	5,033,186	490,281	266,238	4,809,143	1,869,731	950,640	30,341	251,462	140,627
2002	7,917,931	5,249,891	131,548	5,381,439	531,506	278,876	5,128,809	1,786,927	1,002,195	31,286	253,083	144,122
2003	8,246,374	5,482,435	132,924	5,615,359	560,954	316,805	5,371,210	1,836,031	1,039,133	32,380	254,674	144,120
2004	8,771,515	5,878,861	122,344	6,001,205	621,941	352,168	5,731,432	1,962,864	1,077,219	34,151	256,842	146,486
2005	9,138,390	6,083,672	124,991	6,208,663	652,664	396,083	5,952,082	2,038,259	1,148,049	35,336	258,615	149,347
2006	9,832,504	6,419,938	123,622	6,543,560	666,316	434,584	6,311,828	2,284,604	1,236,072	37,745	260,498	152,478
2007	10,414,683	6,586,794	123,087	6,709,881	675,691	489,804	6,523,994	2,584,162	1,306,527	39,634	262,770	156,730
2008	10,522,162	6,580,755	81,882	6,662,637	692,327	525,661	6,495,971	2,530,681	1,495,510	39,504	266,358	154,611
2009	10,463,289	6,447,318	136,214	6,583,532	682,774	499,827	6,400,585	2,428,864	1,633,840	39,021	268,145	149,192
2010	10,809,063	6,679,382	167,778	6,847,160	683,025	499,351	6,663,486	2,353,396	1,792,181	40,064	269,798	147,767
2011	11,443,277	6,948,274	161,319	7,109,593	647,616	512,189	6,974,166	2,659,135	1,809,976	42,219	271,044	151,001
2012	11,971,219	7,211,333	275,406	7,486,739	666,037	533,735	7,354,437	2,785,887	1,830,895	43,666	274,152	155,732
2013	12,342,485	7,551,878	316,045	7,867,923	774,872	533,333	7,626,384	2,814,370	1,901,731	44,771	275,681	159,348
2014	13,091,879	7,892,120	303,205	8,195,325	817,215	563,222	7,941,332	3,098,406	2,052,141	47,054	278,231	164,637
2015	13,980,423	8,434,180	310,601	8,744,781	866,856	595,971	8,473,896	3,306,972	2,199,555	49,914	280,088	169,364
2016	14,406,406	8,677,057	255,838	8,932,895	892,397	600,410	8,640,908	3,467,523	2,297,975	51,118	281,825	169,801
2017	15,144,287	9,145,425	236,443	9,381,868	943,745	638,762	9,076,885	3,729,135	2,338,267	53,626	282,406	172,932
2018	15,708,604	9,655,220	189,863	9,845,083	1,007,988	654,632	9,491,727	3,753,313	2,463,564	55,473	283,176	175,338
2019	16,665,789	10,207,998	162,430	10,370,428	1,073,257	672,063	9,969,234	4,042,937	2,653,618	58,963	282,646	175,039
2020	17,765,128	10,178,548	173,369	10,351,917	1,066,173	719,744	10,005,488	4,103,877	3,655,763	63,024	281,879	165,625
2021	19,192,484	11,089,787	170,407	11,260,194	1,161,920	760,127	10,858,401	4,447,809	3,886,274	68,717	279,298	172,018
2022	19,162,980	11,405,434	154,125	11,559,559	1,245,714	784,068	11,097,913	4,727,440	3,337,627	67,951	282,013	179,692

Personal Income and Employment by Area: Santa Cruz-Watsonville, CA

(Thousands of dollars, except as noted.)

Year	Personal income, total	Derivation of personal income: Earnings by place of work: Nonfarm	Farm	Total	Less: Contributions for government social insurance	Plus: Adjustment for residence	Equals: Net earnings by place of residence	Plus: Dividends, interest, and rent	Plus: Personal current transfer receipts	Per capita personal income (dollars)	Population (persons)	Total employment
1970	558,375	311,740	19,379	331,119	20,780	47,906	358,245	129,153	70,977	4,475	124,788	49,358
1971	623,329	338,430	21,178	359,608	23,013	59,872	396,467	143,587	83,275	4,799	129,886	50,838
1972	707,795	384,651	24,048	408,699	27,479	74,952	456,172	159,149	92,474	4,989	141,878	55,131
1973	820,147	435,469	35,687	471,156	35,479	94,099	529,776	180,893	109,478	5,643	145,347	58,086
1974	937,464	484,551	35,625	520,176	40,742	117,270	596,704	210,309	130,451	6,257	149,828	61,601
1975	1,063,053	531,506	31,297	562,803	43,402	146,286	665,687	236,587	160,779	6,702	158,622	64,137
1976	1,217,157	622,603	36,258	658,861	50,905	174,909	782,865	259,135	175,157	7,244	168,026	68,940
1977	1,397,624	724,164	43,947	768,111	61,098	211,965	918,978	293,199	185,447	7,980	175,132	73,750
1978	1,611,473	839,356	50,910	890,266	72,490	256,893	1,074,669	336,234	200,570	9,216	174,865	77,918
1979	1,837,539	929,807	62,176	991,983	84,499	323,095	1,230,579	388,979	217,981	9,984	184,041	81,923
1980	2,137,179	1,036,844	65,159	1,102,003	92,240	392,587	1,402,350	482,119	252,710	11,290	189,305	84,798
1981	2,423,733	1,146,481	77,394	1,223,875	111,055	427,150	1,539,970	595,482	288,281	12,520	193,590	87,088
1982	2,593,549	1,215,440	80,138	1,295,578	120,503	465,163	1,640,238	647,198	306,113	13,142	197,353	87,797
1983	2,919,166	1,383,343	127,879	1,511,222	138,701	503,257	1,875,778	716,348	327,040	14,457	201,921	93,297
1984	3,234,512	1,570,778	129,453	1,700,231	164,062	556,295	2,092,464	802,911	339,137	15,704	205,964	97,417
1985	3,432,447	1,696,925	98,634	1,795,559	180,272	590,728	2,206,015	860,414	366,018	16,180	212,143	102,627
1986	3,682,206	1,850,595	135,321	1,985,916	198,743	605,165	2,392,338	899,695	390,173	16,995	216,661	103,042
1987	3,934,416	2,063,958	152,067	2,216,025	222,579	640,708	2,634,154	898,285	401,977	17,787	221,202	108,605
1988	4,322,252	2,334,269	160,563	2,494,832	261,690	685,327	2,918,469	980,869	422,914	19,150	225,700	117,109
1989	4,586,161	2,431,467	154,686	2,586,153	278,669	722,516	3,030,000	1,075,196	480,965	19,814	231,463	119,693
1990	4,982,088	2,736,409	187,277	2,923,686	309,712	748,190	3,362,164	1,109,494	510,430	21,697	229,616	125,068
1991	5,185,505	2,935,028	174,555	3,109,583	337,218	772,217	3,544,582	1,111,972	528,951	22,552	229,935	129,334
1992	5,534,753	3,121,225	214,771	3,335,996	357,756	822,740	3,800,980	1,124,906	608,867	23,763	232,912	126,162
1993	5,747,171	3,185,084	225,216	3,410,300	363,592	852,348	3,899,056	1,200,001	648,114	24,416	235,386	128,059
1994	5,970,796	3,308,486	211,314	3,519,800	377,774	889,950	4,031,976	1,292,091	646,729	25,118	237,714	129,313
1995	6,372,002	3,519,154	214,646	3,733,800	395,564	988,306	4,326,542	1,371,115	674,345	26,625	239,324	133,854
1996	6,858,932	3,761,809	227,894	3,989,703	406,366	1,110,516	4,693,853	1,471,047	694,032	28,440	241,168	136,690
1997	7,273,999	4,000,069	239,582	4,239,651	423,064	1,285,058	5,101,645	1,468,818	703,536	29,648	245,344	136,897
1998	7,869,531	4,395,922	215,350	4,611,272	453,680	1,423,765	5,581,357	1,571,662	716,512	31,367	250,889	145,249
1999	8,683,079	4,687,851	372,744	5,060,595	486,462	1,732,596	6,306,729	1,630,766	745,584	34,230	253,667	146,085
2000	10,053,726	5,491,706	294,745	5,786,451	554,320	2,267,192	7,499,323	1,788,847	765,556	39,298	255,835	145,981
2001	10,142,071	5,878,369	263,618	6,141,987	597,266	1,903,049	7,447,770	1,850,471	843,830	39,611	256,045	145,357
2002	9,924,226	5,920,588	241,746	6,162,334	596,147	1,620,389	7,186,576	1,823,409	914,241	38,990	254,531	143,457
2003	10,014,837	5,918,803	290,370	6,209,173	602,788	1,573,661	7,180,046	1,871,813	962,978	39,581	253,021	141,687
2004	10,365,570	5,962,972	309,416	6,272,388	636,128	1,653,013	7,289,273	2,087,162	989,135	41,075	252,356	141,555
2005	10,411,179	6,031,426	289,588	6,321,014	651,800	1,630,099	7,299,313	2,069,779	1,042,087	41,417	251,377	140,937
2006	10,987,816	6,319,281	248,399	6,567,680	664,774	1,610,719	7,513,625	2,357,818	1,116,373	43,669	251,616	142,048
2007	11,564,815	6,400,636	275,199	6,675,835	666,875	1,663,957	7,672,917	2,693,402	1,198,496	45,656	253,304	145,223
2008	11,970,815	6,397,628	281,650	6,679,278	676,889	1,662,430	7,664,819	2,931,834	1,374,162	46,666	256,520	142,695
2009	11,780,483	6,658,487	377,616	7,036,103	690,192	1,546,339	7,892,250	2,345,942	1,542,291	45,308	260,009	139,000
2010	12,854,613	7,650,227	398,668	8,048,895	706,758	1,615,976	8,958,113	2,188,616	1,707,884	48,843	263,182	138,368
2011	13,060,271	7,335,819	359,469	7,695,288	640,004	1,773,824	8,829,108	2,526,111	1,705,052	49,290	264,968	138,209
2012	13,782,878	7,283,461	413,721	7,697,182	636,818	2,056,375	9,116,739	2,939,461	1,726,678	51,725	266,467	140,231
2013	14,052,964	7,660,270	442,134	8,102,404	748,549	2,136,300	9,490,155	2,760,159	1,802,650	52,252	268,946	144,615
2014	14,653,925	7,988,140	433,294	8,421,434	788,157	2,085,798	9,719,075	2,985,596	1,949,254	54,072	271,009	149,199
2015	15,572,810	8,214,978	433,050	8,648,028	822,606	2,472,983	10,298,405	3,163,701	2,110,704	56,902	273,677	153,532
2016	16,070,715	8,384,064	393,819	8,777,883	861,873	2,549,700	10,465,710	3,411,468	2,193,537	58,504	274,694	154,848
2017	17,075,441	8,684,395	398,405	9,082,800	898,816	2,942,621	11,126,605	3,756,025	2,192,811	62,065	275,121	155,289
2018	17,767,743	9,088,910	306,151	9,395,061	942,779	3,203,279	11,655,561	3,795,715	2,316,467	64,845	274,005	156,731
2019	18,933,052	9,749,301	356,126	10,105,427	1,006,970	3,221,524	12,319,981	4,129,389	2,483,682	69,302	273,196	155,529
2020	21,176,826	9,581,157	374,284	9,955,441	1,000,572	4,143,439	13,098,308	4,353,282	3,725,236	78,299	270,462	146,408
2021	23,183,258	10,152,352	314,163	10,466,515	1,067,155	4,999,791	14,399,151	4,911,489	3,872,618	88,997	260,495	149,001
2022	22,832,350	10,641,607	315,046	10,956,653	1,174,430	4,602,006	14,384,229	5,268,437	3,179,684	86,365	264,370	156,569

Personal Income and Employment by Area: Santa Fe, NM

(Thousands of dollars, except as noted.)

Year	Personal income, total	Derivation of personal income: Earnings by place of work: Nonfarm	Farm	Total	Less: Contributions for government social insurance	Plus: Adjustment for residence	Equals: Net earnings by place of residence	Plus: Dividends, interest, and rent	Plus: Personal current transfer receipts	Per capita personal income (dollars)	Population (persons)	Total employment
1970	206,513	138,862	1,931	140,793	7,853	11,240	144,180	43,510	18,823	3,753	55,026	22,514
1971	230,769	157,567	1,472	159,039	9,362	10,996	160,673	48,906	21,190	4,058	56,874	24,070
1972	263,733	181,577	1,202	182,779	11,241	13,834	185,372	55,306	23,055	4,452	59,243	26,263
1973	298,254	206,172	2,590	208,762	14,970	15,722	209,514	62,235	26,505	4,870	61,246	28,068
1974	342,090	233,644	3,170	236,814	17,567	17,806	237,053	72,880	32,157	5,406	63,278	29,166
1975	384,068	259,740	2,160	261,900	19,143	21,688	264,445	79,169	40,454	5,825	65,930	29,184
1976	435,599	294,860	1,583	296,443	21,533	26,792	301,702	89,860	44,037	6,305	69,090	30,690
1977	493,716	338,586	1,087	339,673	25,169	31,800	346,304	101,742	45,670	6,895	71,604	33,009
1978	575,018	393,001	2,639	395,640	30,115	36,578	402,103	121,592	51,323	7,913	72,669	35,227
1979	642,804	432,145	2,461	434,606	34,969	41,637	441,274	142,393	59,137	8,531	75,353	36,981
1980	725,236	478,778	533	479,311	39,903	45,468	484,876	169,328	71,032	9,559	75,872	37,378
1981	834,911	532,646	557	533,203	47,544	54,661	540,320	214,303	80,288	10,812	77,222	38,104
1982	943,243	584,071	1,011	585,082	53,555	62,007	593,534	263,783	85,926	11,773	80,118	40,035
1983	1,040,712	657,184	-385	656,799	60,722	68,843	664,920	285,309	90,483	12,653	82,250	42,732
1984	1,159,009	731,894	1,292	733,186	68,491	81,771	746,466	315,539	97,004	13,780	84,106	44,481
1985	1,286,946	797,634	3,175	800,809	76,060	96,780	821,529	360,236	105,181	15,021	85,676	46,724
1986	1,403,204	887,304	1,874	889,178	85,081	100,773	904,870	384,715	113,619	15,743	89,134	48,864
1987	1,475,280	928,245	1,061	929,306	88,325	118,810	959,791	392,914	122,575	15,980	92,323	50,998
1988	1,594,421	995,549	2,567	998,116	101,408	118,115	1,014,823	446,741	132,857	16,871	94,507	54,052
1989	1,752,121	1,096,266	1,094	1,097,360	113,377	128,567	1,112,550	489,122	150,449	18,070	96,962	56,683
1990	1,901,082	1,207,432	2,134	1,209,566	132,417	131,170	1,208,319	529,131	163,632	19,090	99,587	58,372
1991	2,061,305	1,349,144	4,009	1,353,153	149,872	115,583	1,318,864	562,756	179,685	20,103	102,536	63,309
1992	2,262,158	1,482,232	3,207	1,485,439	162,909	138,794	1,461,324	599,371	201,463	21,335	106,030	65,129
1993	2,484,136	1,653,323	2,611	1,655,934	180,393	121,509	1,597,050	663,631	223,455	22,598	109,927	68,364
1994	2,691,392	1,763,895	3,931	1,767,826	197,198	131,254	1,701,882	750,616	238,894	23,620	113,944	70,827
1995	2,988,842	1,910,188	2,885	1,913,073	214,154	133,337	1,832,256	888,594	267,992	25,230	118,462	75,227
1996	3,139,154	1,949,078	3,345	1,952,423	219,167	131,795	1,865,051	979,027	295,076	25,937	121,031	75,777
1997	3,314,745	2,085,409	2,042	2,087,451	231,305	128,474	1,984,620	1,021,447	308,678	26,695	124,172	77,163
1998	3,581,263	2,221,322	3,024	2,224,346	247,340	160,937	2,137,943	1,119,777	323,543	28,433	125,956	78,737
1999	3,648,919	2,273,784	6,992	2,280,776	257,759	181,995	2,205,012	1,091,598	352,309	28,515	127,966	79,221
2000	4,074,139	2,530,467	5,937	2,536,404	274,923	210,149	2,471,630	1,223,231	379,278	31,409	129,713	81,236
2001	4,370,617	2,740,275	7,524	2,747,799	297,072	214,435	2,665,162	1,287,510	417,945	33,349	131,057	84,055
2002	4,545,132	2,951,687	6,378	2,958,065	318,122	226,383	2,866,326	1,216,489	462,317	34,032	133,555	85,366
2003	4,685,661	3,007,980	4,901	3,012,881	328,127	259,700	2,944,454	1,247,556	493,651	34,654	135,213	87,919
2004	4,951,825	3,137,676	4,454	3,142,130	343,537	239,261	3,037,854	1,381,593	532,378	36,306	136,391	90,107
2005	5,305,935	3,320,197	5,147	3,325,344	363,636	223,658	3,185,366	1,543,451	577,118	38,558	137,610	93,148
2006	5,816,465	3,592,460	9,255	3,601,715	397,026	193,809	3,398,498	1,783,504	634,463	41,910	138,786	94,700
2007	6,169,515	3,843,855	3,213	3,847,068	429,286	111,830	3,529,612	1,941,957	697,946	44,002	140,210	98,072
2008	6,435,013	3,959,216	6,592	3,965,808	450,761	70,506	3,585,553	2,030,587	818,873	45,412	141,704	98,101
2009	6,259,866	3,789,014	4,198	3,793,212	432,142	129,072	3,490,142	1,858,376	911,348	43,713	143,205	93,944
2010	6,310,882	3,809,487	2,045	3,811,532	431,105	167,880	3,548,307	1,753,689	1,008,886	43,645	144,596	92,500
2011	6,667,956	3,858,783	1,837	3,860,620	388,572	179,771	3,651,819	1,981,875	1,034,262	45,598	146,234	92,419
2012	6,959,861	3,898,288	781	3,899,069	394,041	248,244	3,753,272	2,155,034	1,051,555	47,210	147,424	91,823
2013	6,924,313	3,987,838	-580	3,987,258	459,979	224,271	3,751,550	2,072,063	1,100,700	46,633	148,486	92,803
2014	7,516,930	4,027,092	-650	4,026,442	469,616	252,181	3,809,007	2,495,027	1,212,896	50,413	149,108	93,262
2015	7,635,669	4,121,037	944	4,121,981	498,474	245,568	3,869,075	2,466,179	1,300,415	51,000	149,720	94,439
2016	8,076,895	4,116,375	934	4,117,309	499,988	375,975	3,993,296	2,719,604	1,363,995	53,593	150,708	94,533
2017	8,212,995	4,121,822	-1,884	4,119,938	503,687	426,886	4,043,137	2,771,877	1,397,981	54,097	151,821	93,648
2018	8,725,165	4,256,234	-2,183	4,254,051	522,022	461,797	4,193,826	3,027,449	1,503,890	57,191	152,563	94,232
2019	9,352,460	4,482,732	-881	4,481,851	548,313	504,808	4,438,346	3,304,621	1,609,493	60,852	153,693	94,318
2020	9,783,768	4,403,339	-1,845	4,401,494	547,751	578,531	4,432,274	3,235,852	2,115,642	63,104	155,041	88,032
2021	11,335,203	5,006,224	-1,805	5,004,419	611,257	547,227	4,940,389	4,008,860	2,385,954	72,940	155,404	91,475
2022	11,635,970	5,311,035	-3,400	5,307,635	661,727	654,009	5,299,917	4,165,084	2,170,969	74,751	155,664	95,312

Personal Income and Employment by Area: Santa Maria-Santa Barbara, CA

(Thousands of dollars, except as noted.)

Year	Personal income, total	Derivation of personal income: Earnings by place of work: Nonfarm	Farm	Total	Less: Contributions for government social insurance	Plus: Adjustment for residence	Equals: Net earnings by place of residence	Plus: Dividends, interest, and rent	Plus: Personal current transfer receipts	Per capita personal income (dollars)	Population (persons)	Total employment
1970	1,338,257	919,747	35,407	955,154	57,246	-5,141	892,767	338,219	107,271	5,044	265,291	116,626
1971	1,429,790	971,262	38,675	1,009,937	62,188	-4,287	943,462	364,294	122,034	5,297	269,930	117,818
1972	1,570,222	1,058,954	53,455	1,112,409	70,796	-3,337	1,038,276	396,865	135,081	5,670	276,957	121,263
1973	1,743,627	1,173,238	66,679	1,239,917	89,602	-4,758	1,145,557	445,275	152,795	6,285	277,414	129,723
1974	1,920,803	1,274,843	69,400	1,344,243	100,943	-6,187	1,237,113	503,815	179,875	6,899	278,431	134,399
1975	2,119,517	1,404,119	68,732	1,472,851	109,221	-8,321	1,355,309	542,625	221,583	7,499	282,626	138,012
1976	2,347,422	1,584,603	68,134	1,652,737	124,281	-11,050	1,517,406	585,336	244,680	8,206	286,075	141,699
1977	2,583,164	1,757,286	74,682	1,831,968	142,677	-16,131	1,673,160	651,148	258,856	8,896	290,381	149,056
1978	2,951,811	2,036,819	80,906	2,117,725	169,472	-20,552	1,927,701	748,797	275,313	9,993	295,397	160,992
1979	3,315,142	2,277,681	94,856	2,372,537	201,658	-26,716	2,144,163	867,445	303,534	11,222	295,423	168,561
1980	3,777,589	2,499,834	132,061	2,631,895	218,153	-35,381	2,378,361	1,047,769	351,459	12,584	300,191	168,218
1981	4,298,415	2,748,752	123,347	2,872,099	261,865	-40,516	2,569,718	1,311,230	417,467	14,066	305,588	171,396
1982	4,646,166	2,946,588	149,116	3,095,704	288,350	-51,437	2,755,917	1,438,756	451,493	14,841	313,073	172,644
1983	5,039,726	3,205,696	170,756	3,376,452	318,987	-48,541	3,008,924	1,549,947	480,855	15,637	322,294	176,829
1984	5,657,590	3,725,344	133,162	3,858,506	386,737	-76,545	3,395,224	1,759,249	503,117	17,189	329,133	185,802
1985	6,099,114	4,089,207	134,969	4,224,176	429,226	-95,055	3,699,895	1,860,134	539,085	18,014	338,569	192,555
1986	6,495,333	4,405,664	154,335	4,559,999	465,482	-103,463	3,991,054	1,926,952	577,327	18,792	345,651	197,339
1987	6,827,841	4,688,973	180,566	4,869,539	492,097	-99,101	4,278,341	1,947,002	602,498	19,396	352,021	200,745
1988	7,417,245	5,060,178	204,678	5,264,856	545,355	-108,219	4,611,282	2,161,665	644,298	20,846	355,810	207,750
1989	8,014,861	5,397,950	217,498	5,615,448	589,949	-124,673	4,900,826	2,408,416	705,619	21,917	365,695	212,536
1990	8,302,980	5,604,470	239,916	5,844,386	616,109	-136,186	5,092,091	2,434,613	776,276	22,406	370,565	214,939
1991	8,782,827	6,032,922	205,414	6,238,336	661,552	-152,820	5,423,964	2,502,146	856,717	23,426	374,910	220,855
1992	9,125,722	6,224,176	170,978	6,395,154	675,919	-158,000	5,561,235	2,600,746	963,741	24,142	378,003	214,252
1993	9,318,781	6,252,664	239,029	6,491,693	679,767	-160,829	5,651,097	2,644,992	1,022,692	24,519	380,064	215,117
1994	9,635,415	6,250,292	219,509	6,469,801	690,897	-169,619	5,609,285	2,985,403	1,040,727	25,077	384,226	216,284
1995	9,842,131	6,376,221	276,876	6,653,097	699,213	-182,304	5,771,580	2,977,567	1,092,984	25,592	384,582	221,933
1996	10,288,012	6,622,239	281,121	6,903,360	707,206	-194,728	6,001,426	3,142,471	1,144,115	26,645	386,108	225,153
1997	10,566,060	6,948,609	330,822	7,279,431	737,196	-219,875	6,322,360	3,078,812	1,164,888	27,003	391,290	226,970
1998	11,511,682	7,535,112	317,224	7,852,336	782,421	-241,034	6,828,881	3,474,973	1,207,828	29,163	394,738	235,910
1999	12,192,921	7,934,433	350,133	8,284,566	828,788	-267,400	7,188,378	3,741,319	1,263,224	30,720	396,906	239,821
2000	13,259,118	8,820,933	388,110	9,209,043	925,442	-324,259	7,959,342	3,970,002	1,329,774	33,149	399,990	244,170
2001	13,640,290	9,276,103	303,980	9,580,083	984,906	-353,493	8,241,684	3,955,455	1,443,151	33,833	403,164	243,235
2002	13,609,982	9,637,949	346,250	9,984,199	1,035,381	-375,920	8,572,898	3,519,611	1,517,473	33,590	405,178	244,528
2003	14,327,198	10,244,041	381,318	10,625,359	1,116,067	-431,624	9,077,668	3,666,503	1,583,027	35,218	406,810	248,296
2004	15,951,134	11,167,811	376,224	11,544,035	1,239,799	-485,780	9,818,456	4,485,030	1,647,648	39,165	407,284	250,720
2005	16,797,952	11,727,994	411,762	12,139,756	1,295,423	-546,896	10,297,437	4,772,190	1,728,325	41,163	408,079	253,190
2006	18,047,808	12,033,790	405,403	12,439,193	1,289,146	-582,182	10,567,865	5,617,714	1,862,229	44,226	408,085	253,265
2007	18,582,421	12,398,793	395,171	12,793,964	1,312,785	-646,078	10,835,101	5,787,126	1,960,194	45,186	411,243	258,291
2008	18,729,230	12,577,495	399,574	12,977,069	1,358,060	-693,288	10,925,721	5,584,201	2,219,308	45,037	415,859	258,116
2009	18,463,488	12,529,882	663,647	13,193,529	1,357,193	-667,105	11,169,231	4,884,681	2,409,576	43,923	420,356	249,792
2010	19,159,070	13,052,969	577,465	13,630,434	1,347,248	-662,618	11,620,568	4,905,476	2,633,026	45,155	424,292	245,781
2011	20,369,091	13,540,318	501,854	14,042,172	1,272,677	-697,255	12,072,240	5,630,329	2,666,522	47,840	425,775	250,771
2012	21,509,851	14,086,431	639,025	14,725,456	1,322,765	-739,820	12,662,871	6,171,682	2,675,298	49,987	430,311	256,882
2013	21,378,868	14,277,416	796,841	15,074,257	1,499,471	-723,019	12,851,767	5,745,389	2,781,712	49,091	435,492	260,916
2014	22,648,262	14,857,692	837,660	15,695,352	1,570,320	-755,099	13,369,933	6,304,518	2,973,811	51,447	440,227	269,536
2015	24,099,747	15,764,243	938,744	16,702,987	1,649,094	-824,638	14,229,255	6,691,838	3,178,654	54,318	443,677	273,876
2016	24,476,667	15,985,051	830,010	16,815,061	1,684,541	-801,887	14,328,633	6,852,141	3,295,893	54,873	446,061	274,768
2017	25,499,526	16,777,658	888,054	17,665,712	1,765,370	-849,026	15,051,316	7,138,636	3,309,574	57,012	447,267	276,094
2018	26,706,505	17,754,806	686,069	18,440,875	1,857,350	-881,865	15,701,660	7,557,945	3,446,900	59,649	447,724	281,320
2019	27,936,118	18,267,546	748,612	19,016,158	1,945,146	-910,310	16,160,702	8,075,452	3,699,964	62,306	448,368	284,445
2020	30,839,511	19,262,094	831,681	20,093,775	2,034,363	-959,548	17,099,864	8,384,973	5,354,674	68,801	448,244	282,952
2021	33,642,845	21,200,425	741,350	21,941,775	2,224,476	-1,001,331	18,715,968	9,157,333	5,769,544	76,910	437,434	292,616
2022	33,607,554	21,663,244	785,534	22,448,778	2,390,938	-1,058,019	18,999,821	9,828,861	4,778,872	75,720	443,837	306,028

Personal Income and Employment by Area: Santa Rosa-Petaluma, CA

(Thousands of dollars, except as noted.)

Year	Personal income, total	Derivation of personal income: Earnings by place of work: Nonfarm	Farm	Total	Less: Contributions for government social insurance	Plus: Adjustment for residence	Equals: Net earnings by place of residence	Plus: Dividends, interest, and rent	Plus: Personal current transfer receipts	Per capita personal income (dollars)	Population (persons)	Total employment
1970	957,026	508,418	24,485	532,903	32,136	136,914	637,681	203,063	116,282	4,646	206,003	74,003
1971	1,063,234	564,137	18,145	582,282	37,082	160,204	705,404	226,888	130,942	5,006	212,402	76,798
1972	1,205,719	643,504	25,319	668,823	44,342	186,463	810,944	254,154	140,621	5,380	224,091	82,982
1973	1,370,646	730,719	33,869	764,588	57,607	212,227	919,208	292,662	158,776	5,760	237,957	88,869
1974	1,552,265	813,707	27,524	841,231	66,380	246,577	1,021,428	339,694	191,143	6,387	243,028	93,352
1975	1,773,564	899,385	29,681	929,066	71,589	286,827	1,144,304	384,132	245,128	7,003	253,255	96,964
1976	2,023,175	1,053,365	33,457	1,086,822	84,482	323,872	1,326,212	423,641	273,322	7,703	262,654	103,354
1977	2,289,555	1,196,930	41,600	1,238,530	97,929	371,928	1,512,529	482,121	294,905	8,381	273,175	109,903
1978	2,664,526	1,421,880	46,255	1,468,135	119,024	436,620	1,785,731	559,454	319,341	9,467	281,442	118,796
1979	3,043,284	1,639,325	45,489	1,684,814	145,084	493,544	2,033,274	649,975	360,035	10,427	291,859	127,676
1980	3,478,953	1,798,627	39,817	1,838,444	156,982	579,299	2,260,761	798,772	419,420	11,536	301,586	133,637
1981	3,963,032	1,980,612	67,446	2,048,058	188,696	640,176	2,499,538	969,458	494,036	12,842	308,609	137,159
1982	4,234,235	2,100,006	57,548	2,157,554	204,122	690,400	2,643,832	1,060,896	529,507	13,458	314,636	138,573
1983	4,652,064	2,343,445	42,214	2,385,659	231,616	741,749	2,895,792	1,198,607	557,665	14,466	321,580	145,902
1984	5,212,957	2,725,524	54,957	2,780,481	280,949	804,132	3,303,664	1,329,202	580,091	15,948	326,863	155,144
1985	5,665,220	2,997,409	58,263	3,055,672	313,966	853,688	3,595,394	1,446,270	623,556	16,893	335,355	161,324
1986	6,125,807	3,292,610	60,464	3,353,074	347,162	918,852	3,924,764	1,528,588	672,455	17,742	345,270	166,384
1987	6,543,821	3,629,302	72,134	3,701,436	384,317	966,815	4,283,934	1,556,576	703,311	18,376	356,111	174,046
1988	7,203,747	4,032,568	81,747	4,114,315	439,938	1,039,378	4,713,755	1,732,981	757,011	19,581	367,893	186,395
1989	8,048,187	4,410,114	110,172	4,520,286	489,567	1,115,310	5,146,029	2,064,129	838,029	21,144	380,633	193,548
1990	8,676,716	4,841,062	101,673	4,942,735	535,389	1,261,228	5,668,574	2,102,623	905,519	22,220	390,495	204,435
1991	9,077,887	5,140,837	117,482	5,258,319	575,025	1,239,784	5,923,078	2,155,052	999,757	22,812	397,937	207,198
1992	9,580,028	5,475,542	112,314	5,587,856	604,671	1,250,062	6,233,247	2,210,115	1,136,666	23,646	405,151	207,086
1993	10,049,111	5,751,934	93,382	5,845,316	633,729	1,312,207	6,523,794	2,332,118	1,193,199	24,469	410,687	210,765
1994	10,537,214	6,079,918	93,567	6,173,485	668,508	1,356,787	6,861,764	2,443,707	1,231,743	25,321	416,152	218,474
1995	11,002,739	6,280,805	82,049	6,362,854	687,577	1,384,980	7,060,257	2,649,010	1,293,472	26,055	422,286	221,033
1996	11,851,662	6,840,345	108,322	6,948,667	722,347	1,392,784	7,619,104	2,874,488	1,358,070	27,665	428,399	232,015
1997	12,790,613	7,621,946	168,525	7,790,471	796,448	1,508,679	8,502,702	2,910,637	1,377,274	29,260	437,141	242,030
1998	13,855,106	8,588,576	132,986	8,721,562	877,951	1,525,461	9,369,072	3,053,514	1,432,520	31,072	445,901	254,209
1999	14,718,093	9,331,035	123,983	9,455,018	956,400	1,543,551	10,042,169	3,189,667	1,486,257	32,460	453,421	263,310
2000	16,754,368	10,601,529	191,064	10,792,593	1,089,290	2,008,982	11,712,285	3,486,614	1,555,469	36,389	460,421	267,725
2001	17,723,548	11,566,905	176,014	11,742,919	1,194,289	1,855,405	12,404,035	3,607,422	1,712,091	38,091	465,293	272,782
2002	17,729,515	11,890,827	166,697	12,057,524	1,232,055	1,702,846	12,528,315	3,381,191	1,820,009	38,104	465,298	272,289
2003	17,971,179	11,916,413	113,682	12,030,095	1,254,336	1,699,035	12,474,794	3,569,477	1,926,908	38,524	466,489	268,461
2004	18,142,667	12,218,603	136,566	12,355,169	1,348,270	1,549,714	12,556,613	3,589,545	1,996,509	38,865	466,809	271,429
2005	18,648,121	12,477,425	199,841	12,677,266	1,391,670	1,514,038	12,799,634	3,742,553	2,105,934	40,023	465,938	271,470
2006	19,893,406	13,021,539	118,571	13,140,110	1,406,059	1,490,720	13,224,771	4,370,107	2,298,528	42,764	465,188	274,371
2007	20,589,228	13,224,650	136,976	13,361,626	1,415,721	1,492,301	13,438,206	4,713,540	2,437,482	44,055	467,356	279,983
2008	20,444,281	13,035,933	103,543	13,139,476	1,433,969	1,244,022	12,949,529	4,723,189	2,771,563	43,214	473,091	276,215
2009	19,922,331	12,510,300	188,739	12,699,039	1,368,382	1,396,629	12,727,286	4,121,957	3,073,088	41,550	479,479	262,783
2010	20,748,776	13,263,685	132,423	13,396,108	1,384,220	1,166,739	13,178,627	4,167,704	3,402,445	42,813	484,635	260,151
2011	21,654,619	13,610,548	120,470	13,731,018	1,292,548	1,170,915	13,609,385	4,620,291	3,424,943	44,462	487,034	263,457
2012	22,636,604	13,617,334	318,030	13,935,364	1,286,120	1,551,630	14,200,874	4,970,921	3,464,809	46,251	489,428	267,009
2013	23,447,713	14,280,985	329,682	14,610,667	1,514,290	1,760,684	14,857,061	5,016,818	3,573,834	47,527	493,352	277,062
2014	24,800,332	15,202,078	365,136	15,567,214	1,614,657	1,443,481	15,396,038	5,514,100	3,890,194	49,836	497,635	288,651
2015	26,783,825	16,472,007	286,033	16,758,040	1,739,184	1,597,817	16,616,673	5,953,926	4,213,226	53,594	499,752	296,761
2016	27,836,308	17,118,604	228,791	17,347,395	1,812,671	1,699,202	17,233,926	6,189,665	4,412,717	55,513	501,437	299,273
2017	28,988,972	17,763,284	244,256	18,007,540	1,896,100	1,711,726	17,823,166	6,734,806	4,431,000	57,858	501,038	303,613
2018	30,283,557	18,804,937	206,207	19,011,144	2,037,414	1,493,662	18,467,392	7,190,390	4,625,775	61,066	495,914	309,064
2019	32,300,805	19,775,613	176,377	19,951,990	2,151,679	2,001,156	19,801,467	7,587,302	4,912,036	65,804	490,867	304,939
2020	35,091,038	19,906,715	201,538	20,108,253	2,154,601	2,496,462	20,450,114	7,651,583	6,989,341	71,866	488,281	289,663
2021	38,047,053	21,681,305	228,402	21,909,707	2,323,429	2,636,120	22,222,398	8,514,690	7,309,965	78,558	484,315	296,133
2022	37,598,558	22,706,213	192,033	22,898,246	2,534,476	1,913,617	22,277,387	9,106,544	6,214,627	77,900	482,650	312,145

Personal Income and Employment by Area: Savannah, GA

(Thousands of dollars, except as noted.)

		Derivation of personal income										
		Earnings by place of work										
Year	Personal income, total	Nonfarm	Farm	Total	Less: Contributions for government social insurance	Plus: Adjustment for residence	Equals: Net earnings by place of residence	Plus: Dividends, interest, and rent	Plus: Personal current transfer receipts	Per capita personal income (dollars)	Population (persons)	Total employment
1970	745,764	614,061	3,000	617,061	39,518	-8,341	569,202	107,281	69,281	3,608	206,709	96,506
1971	790,868	638,493	3,745	642,238	42,696	-6,742	592,800	113,677	84,391	3,891	203,279	94,486
1972	844,303	684,288	3,687	687,975	48,026	-5,898	634,051	115,795	94,457	4,133	204,260	93,250
1973	923,475	748,569	5,257	753,826	60,968	-3,909	688,949	124,682	109,844	4,509	204,809	96,053
1974	1,020,920	812,730	5,277	818,007	68,884	-2,323	746,800	141,300	132,820	4,982	204,936	96,696
1975	1,192,441	931,552	4,551	936,103	76,871	-6,142	853,090	173,038	166,313	5,612	212,479	100,738
1976	1,356,515	1,039,889	3,848	1,043,737	87,331	32,875	989,281	186,220	181,014	6,204	218,664	103,097
1977	1,512,469	1,149,844	2,004	1,151,848	96,166	61,432	1,117,114	206,717	188,638	6,730	224,727	104,468
1978	1,713,715	1,300,239	6,907	1,307,146	111,123	77,737	1,273,760	235,764	204,191	7,580	226,093	108,230
1979	1,871,653	1,407,150	8,823	1,415,973	125,085	90,134	1,381,022	261,672	228,959	8,158	229,430	108,522
1980	2,109,122	1,553,612	2,042	1,555,654	138,005	95,705	1,513,354	324,614	271,154	9,103	231,691	109,966
1981	2,416,253	1,723,166	8,243	1,731,409	164,800	138,435	1,705,044	402,055	309,154	10,277	235,102	112,942
1982	2,616,652	1,853,501	10,972	1,864,473	182,852	142,180	1,823,801	457,326	335,525	10,943	239,114	114,351
1983	2,792,384	1,976,952	9,157	1,986,109	197,362	133,255	1,922,002	500,335	370,047	11,618	240,354	114,335
1984	3,046,998	2,169,922	7,643	2,177,565	223,190	132,201	2,086,576	567,792	392,630	12,567	242,463	118,390
1985	3,282,148	2,358,033	5,621	2,363,654	247,098	133,296	2,249,852	614,817	417,479	13,418	244,606	122,010
1986	3,543,454	2,614,577	4,027	2,618,604	277,737	100,385	2,441,252	659,160	443,042	14,325	247,365	126,772
1987	3,760,302	2,785,345	4,794	2,790,139	292,431	107,918	2,605,626	688,047	466,629	14,968	251,216	130,214
1988	4,036,494	2,982,046	5,151	2,987,197	323,056	100,449	2,764,590	777,796	494,108	15,888	254,061	134,151
1989	4,380,967	3,181,316	6,282	3,187,598	347,578	76,530	2,916,550	916,552	547,865	17,148	255,475	137,367
1990	4,649,944	3,488,236	4,147	3,492,383	380,909	-32,187	3,079,287	968,695	601,962	17,942	259,160	142,254
1991	4,862,211	3,532,700	5,417	3,538,117	388,471	25,720	3,175,366	1,010,882	675,963	18,509	262,690	138,590
1992	5,284,927	3,831,893	6,243	3,838,136	414,262	93,096	3,516,970	1,023,524	744,433	19,731	267,853	143,404
1993	5,495,645	4,014,389	3,211	4,017,600	433,637	34,611	3,618,574	1,075,425	801,646	20,139	272,886	145,860
1994	5,843,668	4,219,185	5,350	4,224,535	463,607	22,443	3,783,371	1,200,176	860,121	21,052	277,581	150,429
1995	6,184,823	4,448,800	2,922	4,451,722	487,444	29,381	3,993,659	1,272,376	918,788	22,000	281,126	155,080
1996	6,559,993	4,747,715	3,820	4,751,535	518,847	-10,484	4,222,204	1,371,687	966,102	23,141	283,480	158,374
1997	6,799,670	4,867,313	3,409	4,870,722	531,790	-17,129	4,321,803	1,497,781	980,086	23,717	286,697	162,397
1998	7,369,154	5,308,230	1,265	5,309,495	576,323	-15,775	4,717,397	1,666,625	985,132	25,548	288,441	164,741
1999	7,655,833	5,634,636	4,163	5,638,799	606,506	-50,602	4,981,691	1,635,505	1,038,637	26,253	291,618	167,970
2000	8,080,650	5,886,203	4,140	5,890,343	630,315	-22,750	5,237,278	1,741,018	1,102,354	27,511	293,721	172,243
2001	8,276,251	6,035,552	6,424	6,041,976	642,025	-8,315	5,391,636	1,695,919	1,188,696	27,854	297,133	172,488
2002	8,636,662	6,232,781	4,950	6,237,731	664,783	20,531	5,593,479	1,698,965	1,344,218	28,632	301,644	173,532
2003	9,175,506	6,614,805	6,940	6,621,745	698,307	72,154	5,995,592	1,829,361	1,350,553	30,125	304,585	177,604
2004	9,798,347	7,127,301	7,311	7,134,612	771,208	73,966	6,437,370	1,932,416	1,428,561	31,551	310,553	183,250
2005	10,457,594	7,576,778	8,603	7,585,381	815,683	192,382	6,962,080	1,970,274	1,525,240	33,249	314,528	190,495
2006	11,307,778	8,211,181	9,412	8,220,593	885,775	183,233	7,518,051	2,172,023	1,617,704	35,110	322,065	198,110
2007	12,135,537	8,629,674	8,668	8,638,342	925,820	258,313	7,970,835	2,434,016	1,730,686	36,781	329,943	207,493
2008	12,681,706	8,768,043	7,902	8,775,945	980,228	401,276	8,196,993	2,497,967	1,986,746	37,835	335,185	205,681
2009	12,687,293	8,710,890	7,039	8,717,929	969,035	361,114	8,110,008	2,399,616	2,177,669	36,880	344,017	198,546
2010	13,231,568	8,872,193	7,677	8,879,870	985,177	512,543	8,407,236	2,396,079	2,428,253	37,928	348,859	196,866
2011	14,198,691	9,186,239	6,492	9,192,731	909,701	541,317	8,824,347	2,805,436	2,568,908	39,814	356,630	200,430
2012	14,423,444	9,535,249	10,334	9,545,583	947,266	493,323	9,091,640	2,825,867	2,505,937	39,662	363,657	203,230
2013	14,582,618	9,920,512	9,501	9,930,013	1,110,206	448,052	9,267,859	2,725,977	2,588,782	39,637	367,900	208,580
2014	15,301,729	10,434,282	7,544	10,441,826	1,158,233	346,211	9,629,804	2,926,077	2,745,848	40,805	374,999	214,858
2015	16,143,053	11,129,537	12,108	11,141,645	1,230,693	284,186	10,195,138	3,088,325	2,859,590	42,199	382,547	223,255
2016	16,461,275	11,349,505	12,029	11,361,534	1,249,580	207,171	10,319,125	3,178,206	2,963,944	42,326	388,917	227,871
2017	17,326,286	11,870,462	16,279	11,886,741	1,305,345	192,290	10,773,686	3,490,828	3,061,772	44,069	393,161	234,216
2018	18,176,603	12,730,373	11,118	12,741,491	1,413,757	58,475	11,386,209	3,578,002	3,212,392	45,749	397,311	242,065
2019	18,695,354	13,037,568	11,283	13,048,851	1,459,969	53,857	11,642,739	3,642,788	3,409,827	46,467	402,340	246,827
2020	20,400,054	13,210,946	15,034	13,225,980	1,485,375	86,620	11,827,225	3,847,340	4,725,489	50,339	405,257	243,501
2021	22,650,778	14,722,747	15,965	14,738,712	1,655,278	29,880	13,113,314	4,384,607	5,152,857	55,331	409,365	258,912
2022	23,170,701	16,053,705	12,603	16,066,308	1,842,835	-123,074	14,100,399	4,586,577	4,483,725	55,383	418,373	271,240

Personal Income and Employment by Area: Scranton—Wilkes-Barre, PA

(Thousands of dollars, except as noted.)

Year	Personal income, total	Derivation of personal income: Earnings by place of work: Nonfarm	Farm	Total	Less: Contributions for government social insurance	Plus: Adjustment for residence	Equals: Net earnings by place of residence	Plus: Dividends, interest, and rent	Plus: Personal current transfer receipts	Per capita personal income (dollars)	Population (persons)	Total employment
1970	2,147,763	1,639,360	5,903	1,645,263	123,705	45,680	1,567,238	275,347	305,178	3,602	596,204	255,288
1971	2,344,677	1,753,755	6,397	1,760,152	137,169	44,112	1,667,095	299,011	378,571	3,901	601,087	253,153
1972	2,590,425	1,930,929	5,327	1,936,256	156,322	42,974	1,822,908	324,211	443,306	4,272	606,331	258,007
1973	2,870,429	2,132,743	6,904	2,139,647	197,262	42,932	1,985,317	370,410	514,702	4,737	605,941	266,382
1974	3,082,235	2,229,467	6,496	2,235,963	213,816	44,955	2,067,102	424,184	590,949	5,083	606,407	260,623
1975	3,361,969	2,349,313	10,455	2,359,768	218,479	40,726	2,182,015	458,819	721,135	5,529	608,007	251,998
1976	3,649,913	2,567,537	10,704	2,578,241	243,952	37,345	2,371,634	489,134	789,145	6,045	603,751	251,764
1977	3,986,753	2,831,788	14,436	2,846,224	267,387	34,840	2,613,677	544,290	828,786	6,598	604,269	254,824
1978	4,399,963	3,175,778	11,739	3,187,517	306,458	36,478	2,917,537	597,577	884,849	7,290	603,524	261,329
1979	4,858,084	3,441,042	15,603	3,456,645	342,349	32,312	3,146,608	663,376	1,048,100	8,075	601,656	265,502
1980	5,244,378	3,561,643	14,502	3,576,145	360,355	32,482	3,248,272	820,123	1,175,983	8,784	597,021	259,934
1981	5,734,701	3,790,638	16,908	3,807,546	411,740	34,446	3,430,252	1,004,162	1,300,287	9,651	594,227	257,840
1982	6,201,956	3,957,695	13,128	3,970,823	435,352	32,154	3,567,625	1,198,667	1,435,664	10,492	591,104	252,572
1983	6,595,701	4,191,476	12,266	4,203,742	464,791	34,712	3,773,663	1,271,719	1,550,319	11,222	587,760	252,296
1984	6,963,084	4,439,219	19,731	4,458,950	509,762	51,157	4,000,345	1,395,611	1,567,128	11,919	584,185	254,756
1985	7,391,223	4,733,455	20,804	4,754,259	550,505	49,125	4,252,879	1,531,641	1,606,703	12,749	579,742	259,357
1986	7,752,215	5,005,375	18,539	5,023,914	585,002	40,548	4,479,460	1,602,650	1,670,105	13,402	578,457	263,798
1987	8,088,105	5,380,313	17,082	5,397,395	622,977	46,287	4,820,705	1,576,425	1,690,975	14,040	576,085	269,274
1988	8,709,301	5,874,494	12,117	5,886,611	695,418	34,776	5,225,969	1,720,503	1,762,829	15,122	575,917	278,326
1989	9,458,071	6,351,552	17,620	6,369,172	742,280	25,387	5,652,279	1,973,621	1,832,171	16,424	575,871	283,746
1990	9,948,052	6,709,686	19,382	6,729,068	785,703	27,539	5,970,904	2,012,662	1,964,486	17,268	576,090	288,238
1991	10,361,906	6,884,143	14,794	6,898,937	818,685	6,901	6,087,153	2,021,329	2,253,424	17,921	578,212	284,245
1992	10,842,948	7,361,071	24,814	7,385,885	874,744	-44,622	6,466,519	1,994,872	2,381,557	18,707	579,606	285,358
1993	11,158,795	7,672,302	19,231	7,691,533	930,333	-80,230	6,680,970	1,980,999	2,496,826	19,228	580,330	286,290
1994	11,559,748	8,015,042	15,462	8,030,504	986,339	-72,646	6,971,519	2,063,477	2,524,752	19,972	578,788	289,245
1995	12,063,845	8,343,793	8,860	8,352,653	1,025,320	-92,245	7,235,088	2,228,876	2,599,881	20,909	576,980	293,803
1996	12,564,186	8,551,079	14,813	8,565,892	1,026,042	-68,427	7,471,423	2,365,608	2,727,155	21,893	573,886	294,639
1997	13,109,227	8,982,449	10,638	8,993,087	1,064,932	-76,031	7,852,124	2,480,147	2,776,956	23,024	569,384	297,412
1998	13,576,516	9,296,379	13,069	9,309,448	1,088,726	-60,332	8,160,390	2,619,204	2,796,922	23,978	566,216	296,660
1999	14,063,621	9,804,808	11,454	9,816,262	1,128,448	-62,592	8,625,222	2,538,520	2,899,879	24,973	563,157	300,626
2000	14,995,996	10,501,260	19,556	10,520,816	1,187,472	-52,929	9,280,415	2,720,349	2,995,232	26,784	559,879	308,211
2001	15,564,663	10,948,909	12,887	10,961,796	1,243,868	-49,040	9,668,888	2,706,654	3,189,121	27,920	557,476	306,843
2002	15,776,449	11,118,787	11,892	11,130,679	1,258,975	-3,267	9,868,437	2,564,587	3,343,425	28,390	555,702	301,407
2003	16,127,675	11,364,506	19,604	11,384,110	1,283,790	22,485	10,122,805	2,566,635	3,438,235	29,034	555,483	301,888
2004	16,853,404	11,899,441	16,163	11,915,604	1,345,851	66,841	10,636,594	2,593,131	3,623,679	30,339	555,495	304,760
2005	17,329,667	12,244,348	13,293	12,257,641	1,422,289	119,731	10,955,083	2,523,742	3,850,842	31,132	556,652	308,370
2006	18,041,587	12,592,252	15,535	12,607,787	1,481,276	173,987	11,300,498	2,679,066	4,062,023	32,354	557,626	311,526
2007	19,038,983	12,984,861	11,445	12,996,306	1,528,181	234,343	11,702,468	3,039,151	4,297,364	33,996	560,032	316,219
2008	19,926,640	13,143,172	14,663	13,157,835	1,560,870	280,446	11,877,411	3,281,751	4,767,478	35,485	561,548	316,872
2009	19,870,401	12,943,468	16,697	12,960,165	1,555,124	268,928	11,673,969	3,025,454	5,170,978	35,298	562,933	309,012
2010	20,467,969	13,373,978	18,916	13,392,894	1,593,855	270,837	12,069,876	2,946,857	5,451,236	36,282	564,139	308,778
2011	21,172,051	13,777,662	19,351	13,797,013	1,483,573	247,579	12,561,019	3,109,011	5,502,021	37,436	565,553	311,686
2012	21,515,785	13,943,178	32,444	13,975,622	1,498,910	215,319	12,692,031	3,365,491	5,458,263	37,945	567,030	312,989
2013	21,357,392	14,275,785	21,258	14,297,043	1,718,434	153,235	12,731,844	3,182,866	5,442,682	37,717	566,254	315,602
2014	21,986,982	14,726,840	20,292	14,747,132	1,779,599	139,619	13,107,152	3,322,191	5,557,639	38,823	566,341	319,406
2015	22,807,313	15,242,591	5,464	15,248,055	1,839,479	131,688	13,540,264	3,473,225	5,793,824	40,341	565,361	321,129
2016	23,392,255	15,480,670	868	15,481,538	1,878,723	124,478	13,727,293	3,643,758	6,021,204	41,431	564,606	323,569
2017	23,885,261	15,944,081	3,016	15,947,097	1,968,110	127,141	14,106,128	3,680,790	6,098,343	42,185	566,208	324,406
2018	24,961,557	16,508,661	-3,863	16,504,798	2,025,093	135,320	14,615,025	3,873,950	6,472,582	44,020	567,044	325,907
2019	25,752,951	16,891,973	2,589	16,894,562	2,076,076	177,455	14,995,941	4,090,477	6,666,533	45,420	567,002	324,734
2020	28,276,500	16,963,592	-1,081	16,962,511	2,075,199	168,667	15,055,979	4,264,854	8,955,667	49,892	566,750	310,738
2021	30,087,612	18,081,782	2,317	18,084,099	2,206,560	136,323	16,013,862	4,481,595	9,592,155	52,976	567,946	319,659
2022	29,708,544	19,223,923	-2,970	19,220,953	2,402,018	117,880	16,936,815	4,798,247	7,973,482	52,304	567,998	335,628

Personal Income and Employment by Area: Seattle-Tacoma-Bellevue, WA

(Thousands of dollars, except as noted.)

		Derivation of personal income										
		Earnings by place of work										
Year	Personal income, total	Nonfarm	Farm	Total	Less: Contributions for government social insurance	Plus: Adjustment for residence	Equals: Net earnings by place of residence	Plus: Dividends, interest, and rent	Plus: Personal current transfer receipts	Per capita personal income (dollars)	Population (persons)	Total employment
1970	8,731,054	7,010,889	26,946	7,037,835	559,723	18,717	6,496,829	1,472,418	761,807	4,758	1,834,990	824,119
1971	8,942,817	7,011,821	28,446	7,040,267	580,348	14,736	6,474,655	1,569,989	898,173	4,873	1,835,190	786,245
1972	9,425,134	7,460,267	33,366	7,493,633	653,159	9,385	6,849,859	1,637,838	937,437	5,219	1,806,099	789,860
1973	10,474,443	8,405,539	49,155	8,454,694	840,240	386	7,614,840	1,814,212	1,045,391	5,816	1,800,981	834,401
1974	11,829,739	9,434,527	47,977	9,482,504	969,872	19,750	8,532,382	2,095,568	1,201,789	6,450	1,833,981	869,673
1975	13,418,533	10,562,573	50,176	10,612,749	1,076,303	64,080	9,600,526	2,324,517	1,493,490	7,190	1,866,276	887,648
1976	14,884,770	11,826,526	51,174	11,877,700	1,233,342	99,984	10,744,342	2,517,491	1,622,937	7,891	1,886,242	919,384
1977	16,563,011	13,425,500	54,295	13,479,795	1,428,946	51,537	12,102,386	2,796,774	1,663,851	8,641	1,916,683	968,408
1978	19,374,731	16,003,912	49,467	16,053,379	1,756,897	29,335	14,325,817	3,250,009	1,798,905	9,829	1,971,129	1,046,539
1979	22,581,520	18,823,493	56,541	18,880,034	2,138,583	110,838	16,852,289	3,759,453	1,969,778	11,112	2,032,131	1,123,231
1980	25,838,412	21,064,163	44,721	21,108,884	2,359,828	106,492	18,855,548	4,586,908	2,395,956	12,270	2,105,824	1,159,283
1981	28,834,220	23,169,342	55,977	23,225,319	2,781,762	-30,272	20,413,285	5,602,429	2,818,506	13,401	2,151,691	1,167,540
1982	30,885,433	24,269,417	47,955	24,317,372	2,960,991	-15,123	21,341,258	6,383,843	3,160,332	14,181	2,177,909	1,160,929
1983	32,569,877	25,224,672	54,058	25,278,730	3,113,281	-18,794	22,146,655	6,932,025	3,491,197	14,885	2,188,099	1,179,085
1984	35,087,649	27,286,909	55,652	27,342,561	3,469,223	-65,902	23,807,436	7,660,182	3,620,031	15,834	2,216,022	1,236,653
1985	37,998,183	29,686,537	62,125	29,748,662	3,803,822	-116,746	25,828,094	8,293,737	3,876,352	16,828	2,258,026	1,290,615
1986	40,947,216	32,448,010	70,168	32,518,178	4,169,389	-193,404	28,155,385	8,663,527	4,128,304	17,795	2,301,024	1,346,586
1987	43,602,408	35,065,262	75,522	35,140,784	4,481,173	-265,029	30,394,582	8,846,178	4,361,648	18,505	2,356,263	1,422,816
1988	48,184,151	38,848,802	77,155	38,925,957	5,073,601	-299,246	33,553,110	9,798,825	4,832,216	19,858	2,426,393	1,505,432
1989	53,382,975	42,791,792	91,413	42,883,205	5,572,026	-361,987	36,949,192	11,109,556	5,324,227	21,411	2,493,214	1,587,002
1990	58,860,184	47,565,802	94,275	47,660,077	6,338,120	-580,054	40,741,903	12,267,520	5,850,761	22,825	2,578,807	1,653,020
1991	62,630,649	50,799,730	89,714	50,889,444	6,838,633	-638,777	43,412,034	12,658,177	6,560,438	23,808	2,630,705	1,661,101
1992	67,370,212	55,510,917	117,051	55,627,968	7,472,266	-799,040	47,356,662	12,846,572	7,166,978	25,037	2,690,858	1,669,827
1993	69,990,135	57,287,857	110,486	57,398,343	7,697,910	-969,695	48,730,738	13,604,950	7,654,447	25,541	2,740,325	1,687,223
1994	73,428,582	59,550,610	105,935	59,656,545	8,113,599	-1,029,263	50,513,683	14,880,740	8,034,159	26,469	2,774,159	1,728,057
1995	77,889,001	62,510,103	95,132	62,605,235	8,532,251	-1,110,019	52,962,965	16,379,947	8,546,089	27,673	2,814,630	1,750,246
1996	84,029,365	67,638,554	100,263	67,738,817	9,072,702	-1,231,685	57,434,430	17,690,027	8,904,908	29,414	2,856,795	1,807,825
1997	91,353,305	74,960,322	91,990	75,052,312	9,785,287	-1,661,519	63,605,506	18,522,697	9,225,102	31,306	2,918,071	1,887,996
1998	102,208,532	85,258,298	116,424	85,374,722	10,957,785	-2,005,132	72,411,805	20,242,976	9,553,751	34,312	2,978,761	1,957,069
1999	110,632,350	94,339,843	121,948	94,461,791	11,578,130	-2,152,778	80,730,883	19,817,415	10,084,052	36,637	3,019,651	1,997,050
2000	117,877,598	100,503,322	91,384	100,594,706	12,561,324	-2,602,948	85,430,434	21,848,242	10,598,922	38,621	3,052,187	2,050,200
2001	120,111,274	101,280,065	107,779	101,387,844	12,097,161	-2,664,862	86,625,821	21,544,133	11,941,320	38,834	3,092,927	2,040,022
2002	121,615,328	101,738,634	91,796	101,830,430	12,149,141	-2,665,360	87,015,929	21,712,769	12,886,630	39,000	3,118,302	1,999,834
2003	125,236,051	103,886,678	132,567	104,019,245	12,591,179	-2,710,359	88,717,707	23,149,964	13,368,380	39,973	3,133,021	2,002,091
2004	135,472,788	108,797,795	113,454	108,911,249	13,325,643	-2,819,270	92,766,336	29,440,806	13,265,646	42,885	3,158,967	2,040,914
2005	139,782,327	115,179,834	104,813	115,284,647	14,132,216	-2,992,962	98,159,469	27,733,896	13,888,962	43,706	3,198,265	2,098,996
2006	153,905,359	125,058,616	92,010	125,150,626	15,119,994	-3,143,370	106,887,262	32,227,654	14,790,443	47,253	3,257,081	2,169,783
2007	167,135,846	134,306,479	90,724	134,397,203	15,999,718	-3,521,811	114,875,674	36,298,072	15,962,100	50,579	3,304,467	2,252,497
2008	173,921,094	137,097,644	107,756	137,205,400	16,320,398	-3,578,895	117,306,107	38,125,168	18,489,819	51,839	3,355,042	2,272,359
2009	163,445,528	129,326,072	113,942	129,440,014	15,937,092	-3,435,619	110,067,303	32,262,347	21,115,878	47,864	3,414,797	2,182,609
2010	167,148,855	131,832,130	108,842	131,940,972	16,361,875	-3,213,777	112,365,320	31,333,589	23,449,946	48,456	3,449,507	2,154,729
2011	178,581,070	139,604,410	120,353	139,724,763	15,446,854	-3,176,452	121,101,457	34,364,147	23,115,466	50,948	3,505,162	2,190,282
2012	195,759,329	151,249,863	125,862	151,375,725	16,081,663	-3,211,249	132,082,813	40,699,505	22,977,011	54,971	3,561,158	2,258,685
2013	201,053,010	159,811,015	125,327	159,936,342	19,028,664	-3,173,958	137,733,720	39,897,996	23,421,294	55,606	3,615,685	2,313,185
2014	218,671,343	169,693,377	139,153	169,832,530	20,044,882	-3,242,188	146,545,460	46,746,203	25,379,680	59,429	3,679,543	2,380,273
2015	232,424,749	178,791,682	199,128	178,990,810	21,241,186	-3,400,067	154,349,557	52,221,238	25,853,954	62,060	3,745,182	2,454,123
2016	247,180,380	189,866,951	129,219	189,996,170	22,267,912	-3,608,852	164,119,406	55,829,284	27,231,690	64,639	3,824,014	2,526,949
2017	265,119,073	204,543,220	150,747	204,693,967	24,024,284	-3,764,871	176,904,812	60,316,811	27,897,450	68,086	3,893,869	2,602,538
2018	284,639,784	223,413,865	123,845	223,537,710	25,566,492	-4,131,507	193,839,711	61,829,283	28,970,790	72,181	3,943,414	2,667,012
2019	305,909,569	237,987,228	157,753	238,144,981	26,721,675	-4,927,538	206,495,768	68,670,246	30,743,555	76,777	3,984,400	2,701,937
2020	329,387,153	247,955,227	189,608	248,144,835	27,926,217	-5,131,541	215,087,077	70,379,815	43,920,261	81,785	4,027,487	2,598,455
2021	362,243,577	273,082,778	197,836	273,280,614	29,915,986	-5,319,985	238,044,643	76,521,038	47,677,896	90,194	4,016,274	2,666,250
2022	371,608,223	290,512,487	235,272	290,747,759	32,840,945	-5,759,683	252,147,131	80,795,210	38,665,882	92,113	4,034,248	2,818,702

Personal Income and Employment by Area: Sebastian-Vero Beach, FL

(Thousands of dollars, except as noted.)

Year	Personal income, total	Derivation of personal income: Earnings by place of work: Nonfarm	Farm	Total	Less: Contributions for government social insurance	Plus: Adjustment for residence	Equals: Net earnings by place of residence	Plus: Dividends, interest, and rent	Plus: Personal current transfer receipts	Per capita personal income (dollars)	Population (persons)	Total employment
1970	147,387	85,590	5,816	91,406	5,485	-396	85,525	44,173	17,689	4,072	36,192	15,206
1971	173,674	100,446	8,454	108,900	6,783	-1,543	100,574	51,617	21,483	4,617	37,617	16,339
1972	209,071	123,376	12,145	135,521	8,814	-2,677	124,030	59,839	25,202	5,153	40,570	18,541
1973	250,946	151,902	12,463	164,365	12,477	-4,264	147,624	73,026	30,296	5,747	43,668	21,051
1974	281,597	162,102	14,098	176,200	14,028	-4,152	158,020	87,514	36,063	6,146	45,818	21,271
1975	304,978	169,386	12,033	181,419	14,352	-4,354	162,713	96,337	45,928	6,453	47,259	21,020
1976	350,589	196,505	12,234	208,739	16,601	-5,952	186,186	112,204	52,199	7,277	48,176	22,091
1977	404,668	221,991	15,598	237,589	19,349	-6,589	211,651	134,092	58,925	8,016	50,485	23,515
1978	486,509	264,691	20,580	285,271	23,668	-8,358	253,245	166,600	66,664	9,126	53,309	25,884
1979	576,409	304,667	21,828	326,495	28,335	-7,975	290,185	205,063	81,161	9,953	57,912	27,380
1980	699,570	335,779	34,903	370,682	30,950	-4,152	335,580	263,702	100,288	11,520	60,728	28,130
1981	844,296	396,955	24,184	421,139	39,720	-8,402	373,017	350,176	121,103	13,203	63,946	29,823
1982	886,675	388,328	26,785	415,113	40,811	-2,699	371,603	365,672	149,400	13,136	67,499	30,005
1983	994,683	416,631	47,608	464,239	43,849	-1,117	419,273	408,473	166,937	14,125	70,419	31,067
1984	1,135,501	480,384	43,885	524,269	51,911	-5,586	466,772	487,433	181,296	15,388	73,792	33,139
1985	1,292,172	534,884	55,544	590,428	59,593	-7,141	523,694	568,847	199,631	17,029	75,879	35,176
1986	1,429,737	610,458	56,815	667,273	69,320	-7,272	590,681	618,238	220,818	18,149	78,776	37,595
1987	1,584,399	683,276	74,750	758,026	76,745	-5,526	675,755	670,073	238,571	19,519	81,171	37,686
1988	1,854,534	769,114	113,426	882,540	89,616	-8,204	784,720	812,039	257,775	22,108	83,885	41,082
1989	2,077,878	885,334	88,911	974,245	105,386	-14,947	853,912	928,311	295,655	23,736	87,542	43,275
1990	2,297,724	943,785	63,267	1,007,052	109,888	-14,212	882,952	1,092,950	321,822	25,218	91,115	44,005
1991	2,433,471	921,811	75,091	996,902	109,894	-3,166	883,842	1,196,814	352,815	26,001	93,593	43,445
1992	2,560,498	987,513	61,340	1,048,853	116,950	1,397	933,300	1,221,861	405,337	26,665	96,023	42,812
1993	2,660,992	1,041,154	54,148	1,095,302	122,579	4,788	977,511	1,254,360	429,121	27,274	97,566	43,672
1994	2,847,793	1,118,441	49,310	1,167,751	133,668	2,018	1,036,101	1,345,832	465,860	28,518	99,858	45,180
1995	3,138,995	1,193,591	46,581	1,240,172	142,418	2,726	1,100,480	1,544,239	494,276	30,796	101,929	47,392
1996	3,365,472	1,304,404	32,527	1,336,931	152,074	-2,054	1,182,803	1,655,779	526,890	32,491	103,583	49,354
1997	3,609,334	1,373,159	30,739	1,403,898	160,700	-836	1,242,362	1,813,270	553,702	33,957	106,291	51,903
1998	3,917,190	1,476,135	48,551	1,524,686	170,949	-1,541	1,352,196	1,986,890	578,104	35,950	108,961	53,805
1999	4,088,064	1,633,856	39,142	1,672,998	185,502	-5,614	1,481,882	2,010,545	595,637	36,732	111,294	54,638
2000	4,376,520	1,729,519	42,819	1,772,338	194,832	3,310	1,580,816	2,160,386	635,318	38,620	113,323	55,510
2001	4,871,691	1,910,348	35,762	1,946,110	210,965	69,343	1,804,488	2,381,156	686,047	42,195	115,456	58,381
2002	5,005,151	1,994,631	41,096	2,035,727	220,356	123,330	1,938,701	2,329,347	737,103	42,365	118,144	59,595
2003	5,294,503	2,174,006	35,791	2,209,797	242,297	154,547	2,122,047	2,394,444	778,012	43,956	120,450	63,544
2004	6,130,178	2,309,282	41,961	2,351,243	262,479	236,017	2,324,781	2,956,625	848,772	49,041	125,001	65,717
2005	6,800,337	2,498,926	59,615	2,558,541	286,464	372,346	2,644,423	3,293,994	861,920	53,146	127,955	68,830
2006	7,796,765	2,742,325	60,917	2,803,242	318,640	480,322	2,964,924	3,907,322	924,519	59,308	131,463	72,591
2007	8,112,492	2,849,111	42,217	2,891,328	332,009	487,322	3,046,641	4,076,534	989,317	60,287	134,564	73,482
2008	8,320,980	2,777,645	36,216	2,813,861	331,859	521,470	3,003,472	4,198,826	1,118,682	61,059	136,277	71,666
2009	7,125,400	2,538,340	43,683	2,582,023	315,323	475,254	2,741,954	3,147,826	1,235,620	52,004	137,016	68,431
2010	7,326,166	2,526,209	48,723	2,574,932	310,024	372,415	2,637,323	3,356,333	1,332,510	52,998	138,234	67,964
2011	8,023,131	2,567,177	52,450	2,619,627	285,560	489,669	2,823,736	3,812,519	1,386,876	57,762	138,901	69,281
2012	8,492,697	2,726,788	61,931	2,788,719	301,865	563,506	3,050,360	4,039,490	1,402,847	60,614	140,111	70,303
2013	8,496,773	2,750,345	65,358	2,815,703	344,959	713,210	3,183,954	3,869,036	1,443,783	60,102	141,372	71,332
2014	9,324,498	2,994,781	64,621	3,059,402	371,195	705,097	3,393,304	4,398,314	1,532,880	64,867	143,749	73,884
2015	9,860,224	3,186,261	76,329	3,262,590	390,219	778,586	3,650,957	4,545,054	1,664,213	67,278	146,560	76,313
2016	10,528,721	3,313,151	58,200	3,371,351	406,327	949,916	3,914,940	4,861,015	1,752,766	70,156	150,076	77,700
2017	11,301,905	3,461,232	64,772	3,526,004	426,465	938,026	4,037,565	5,409,644	1,854,696	73,948	152,836	80,357
2018	12,417,377	3,657,921	30,935	3,688,856	461,485	1,109,853	4,337,224	6,107,287	1,972,866	79,919	155,374	83,112
2019	13,216,852	3,887,297	48,716	3,936,013	496,264	1,126,293	4,566,042	6,512,985	2,137,825	83,721	157,868	83,605
2020	13,975,880	4,043,967	40,231	4,084,198	522,033	1,134,804	4,696,969	6,683,931	2,594,980	87,110	160,439	83,551
2021	16,301,881	4,541,266	32,449	4,573,715	567,180	1,474,951	5,481,486	7,881,703	2,938,692	99,515	163,814	87,389
2022	17,613,769	5,097,771	27,174	5,124,945	644,432	1,817,241	6,297,754	8,539,658	2,776,357	105,250	167,352	92,532

Personal Income and Employment by Area: Sebring-Avon Park, FL

(Thousands of dollars, except as noted.)

Year	Personal income, total	Derivation of personal income: Earnings by place of work: Nonfarm	Farm	Total	Less: Contributions for government social insurance	Plus: Adjustment for residence	Equals: Net earnings by place of residence	Plus: Dividends, interest, and rent	Plus: Personal current transfer receipts	Per capita personal income (dollars)	Population (persons)	Total employment
1970	103,745	51,193	14,987	66,180	3,500	859	63,539	25,359	14,847	3,470	29,898	10,437
1971	117,865	57,785	16,873	74,658	4,108	828	71,378	28,555	17,932	3,691	31,931	10,970
1972	132,818	63,355	19,949	83,304	4,775	747	79,276	32,241	21,301	3,917	33,912	11,766
1973	155,727	75,313	20,943	96,256	6,415	408	90,249	39,105	26,373	4,333	35,937	12,899
1974	174,908	86,401	19,001	105,402	7,790	40	97,652	45,967	31,289	4,370	40,025	13,681
1975	198,890	93,321	21,470	114,791	8,307	156	106,640	52,585	39,665	4,843	41,070	13,811
1976	221,719	102,630	25,706	128,336	9,181	-203	118,952	57,953	44,814	5,332	41,584	13,930
1977	253,442	114,837	32,067	146,904	10,338	-742	135,824	67,448	50,170	6,040	41,962	14,676
1978	304,020	135,417	43,977	179,394	12,224	-1,582	165,588	81,705	56,727	6,975	43,588	16,021
1979	348,553	153,261	45,732	198,993	14,574	-2,589	181,830	98,755	67,968	7,606	45,828	16,722
1980	421,561	172,302	61,071	233,373	16,722	-3,072	213,579	125,269	82,713	8,764	48,102	17,930
1981	458,426	191,640	41,125	232,765	20,064	-6,964	205,737	153,375	99,314	9,111	50,315	18,584
1982	513,001	198,387	45,893	244,280	21,532	-6,801	215,947	180,529	116,525	9,811	52,286	19,097
1983	582,409	223,785	66,188	289,973	24,163	-7,743	258,067	197,748	126,594	10,852	53,670	20,205
1984	637,851	255,553	48,537	304,090	28,196	-8,196	267,698	233,538	136,615	11,465	55,636	21,386
1985	717,019	288,219	54,179	342,398	32,660	-9,160	300,578	263,740	152,701	12,468	57,508	22,542
1986	791,946	320,022	55,851	375,873	37,136	-9,564	329,173	293,821	168,952	13,338	59,375	23,609
1987	847,712	348,498	62,912	411,410	39,969	-7,259	364,182	300,462	183,068	13,647	62,119	23,712
1988	965,194	383,325	100,182	483,507	46,334	-6,786	430,387	333,591	201,216	15,005	64,325	24,811
1989	1,066,831	419,852	75,559	495,411	52,743	-5,239	437,429	395,710	233,692	16,083	66,334	25,945
1990	1,127,168	452,357	65,763	518,120	55,550	-3,616	458,954	408,709	259,505	16,280	69,238	27,382
1991	1,182,080	479,665	78,212	557,877	59,257	-4,010	494,610	399,263	288,207	16,506	71,614	28,117
1992	1,237,429	512,127	67,731	579,858	63,165	-3,217	513,476	393,083	330,870	16,770	73,790	28,451
1993	1,301,162	543,816	70,537	614,353	67,327	-3,109	543,917	399,598	357,647	17,053	76,301	28,985
1994	1,383,081	583,705	65,487	649,192	73,382	-2,252	573,558	414,145	395,378	17,569	78,724	30,386
1995	1,466,193	606,837	70,553	677,390	76,868	-177	600,345	445,112	420,736	18,148	80,792	30,952
1996	1,525,159	625,373	54,005	679,378	77,797	2,639	604,220	475,643	445,296	18,439	82,713	31,677
1997	1,584,447	659,145	55,855	715,000	81,298	5,128	638,830	482,979	462,638	18,788	84,334	32,801
1998	1,690,625	669,075	97,468	766,543	82,955	8,590	692,178	517,807	480,640	19,762	85,551	34,156
1999	1,720,811	702,483	98,878	801,361	85,495	10,967	726,833	494,967	499,011	19,870	86,604	35,518
2000	1,791,095	730,839	75,426	806,265	87,531	16,817	735,551	527,893	527,651	20,489	87,417	32,853
2001	1,899,216	809,782	56,153	865,935	99,525	20,202	786,612	539,880	572,724	21,458	88,510	32,571
2002	1,997,559	885,394	61,361	946,755	109,023	20,904	858,636	528,982	609,941	22,210	89,939	34,133
2003	2,080,326	950,530	50,745	1,001,275	116,570	23,538	908,243	532,904	639,179	22,875	90,943	35,969
2004	2,194,599	1,030,564	55,630	1,086,194	127,531	33,097	991,760	516,783	686,056	23,578	93,079	36,150
2005	2,348,652	1,100,271	79,797	1,180,068	140,003	41,730	1,081,795	534,180	732,677	24,564	95,614	37,339
2006	2,543,347	1,174,695	103,238	1,277,933	153,672	51,400	1,175,661	585,230	782,456	26,009	97,788	38,629
2007	2,692,180	1,198,411	77,063	1,275,474	161,044	56,175	1,170,605	692,916	828,659	27,187	99,023	40,080
2008	2,745,715	1,151,603	79,835	1,231,438	159,982	63,321	1,134,777	701,293	909,645	27,576	99,568	38,870
2009	2,742,365	1,147,353	94,739	1,242,092	161,650	55,673	1,136,115	618,722	987,528	27,713	98,956	37,759
2010	2,864,231	1,171,337	100,273	1,271,610	163,253	58,941	1,167,298	648,354	1,048,579	29,075	98,513	37,513
2011	2,929,306	1,193,107	96,300	1,289,407	152,541	59,103	1,195,969	661,239	1,072,098	29,929	97,875	37,771
2012	2,959,768	1,201,742	127,804	1,329,546	155,031	64,609	1,239,124	645,056	1,075,588	30,471	97,134	38,021
2013	2,914,628	1,206,332	105,112	1,311,444	172,503	66,709	1,205,650	611,780	1,097,198	30,197	96,521	37,532
2014	2,993,333	1,215,010	107,170	1,322,180	174,541	71,023	1,218,662	634,347	1,140,324	31,006	96,541	38,226
2015	3,132,361	1,270,946	118,600	1,389,546	180,772	73,627	1,282,401	643,166	1,206,794	32,100	97,582	38,834
2016	3,219,434	1,330,671	81,215	1,411,886	190,798	78,166	1,299,254	686,750	1,233,430	32,557	98,886	39,595
2017	3,373,319	1,391,802	89,462	1,481,264	199,662	83,912	1,365,514	722,056	1,285,749	33,702	100,094	40,486
2018	3,414,167	1,439,413	58,059	1,497,472	210,147	92,302	1,379,627	700,131	1,334,409	34,077	100,189	40,735
2019	3,626,700	1,500,363	70,679	1,571,042	222,482	100,717	1,449,277	772,847	1,404,576	35,886	101,061	40,894
2020	3,923,391	1,529,607	60,544	1,590,151	230,766	110,246	1,469,631	766,268	1,687,492	38,713	101,345	40,183
2021	4,306,675	1,650,425	53,956	1,704,381	244,406	120,341	1,580,316	800,014	1,926,345	41,693	103,295	40,258
2022	4,419,585	1,829,677	52,210	1,881,887	276,555	123,939	1,729,271	873,905	1,816,409	41,845	105,618	42,380

Personal Income and Employment by Area: Sheboygan, WI

(Thousands of dollars, except as noted.)

Year	Personal income, total	Derivation of personal income: Earnings by place of work								Per capita personal income (dollars)	Population (persons)	Total employment
		Nonfarm	Farm	Total	Less: Contributions for government social insurance	Plus: Adjustment for residence	Equals: Net earnings by place of residence	Plus: Dividends, interest, and rent	Plus: Personal current transfer receipts			
1970	381,796	297,865	11,237	309,102	22,448	-363	286,291	63,572	31,933	3,947	96,726	44,180
1971	406,232	312,983	11,680	324,663	24,438	908	301,133	68,592	36,507	4,184	97,081	44,145
1972	450,864	350,540	12,363	362,903	28,890	2,693	336,706	73,776	40,382	4,622	97,541	45,544
1973	498,159	387,255	14,081	401,336	36,779	5,105	369,662	82,037	46,460	5,042	98,803	47,761
1974	550,696	423,289	13,011	436,300	42,015	7,650	401,935	93,348	55,413	5,509	99,963	48,662
1975	596,734	437,391	17,304	454,695	42,067	9,005	421,633	102,789	72,312	5,945	100,372	47,393
1976	670,106	503,690	17,416	521,106	49,220	11,811	483,697	109,892	76,517	6,711	99,858	49,028
1977	755,393	572,442	22,151	594,593	55,830	14,434	553,197	122,138	80,058	7,517	100,495	51,286
1978	848,398	654,404	18,225	672,629	65,778	18,432	625,283	134,477	88,638	8,460	100,282	53,344
1979	960,569	739,436	22,579	762,015	77,325	23,533	708,223	150,475	101,871	9,536	100,727	55,367
1980	1,053,535	774,657	22,940	797,597	80,593	24,894	741,898	184,716	126,921	10,441	100,907	54,206
1981	1,153,187	837,311	16,912	854,223	93,101	20,687	781,809	227,789	143,589	11,468	100,554	54,019
1982	1,187,755	837,283	14,448	851,731	93,595	18,039	776,175	246,577	165,003	11,787	100,770	52,305
1983	1,239,943	883,067	2,021	885,088	98,920	14,921	801,089	263,407	175,447	12,326	100,592	51,763
1984	1,371,536	994,065	9,803	1,003,868	114,462	10,049	899,455	294,304	177,777	13,572	101,060	54,410
1985	1,422,943	1,025,862	12,451	1,038,313	118,610	7,287	926,990	308,291	187,662	14,085	101,028	54,488
1986	1,496,681	1,089,659	17,831	1,107,490	125,483	2,563	984,570	319,188	192,923	14,819	100,995	54,967
1987	1,570,097	1,165,242	21,558	1,186,800	131,329	-284	1,055,187	318,973	195,937	15,492	101,347	56,142
1988	1,691,323	1,281,860	10,271	1,292,131	148,829	-8,487	1,134,815	351,210	205,298	16,579	102,018	58,606
1989	1,850,242	1,386,232	28,321	1,414,553	160,340	-17,981	1,236,232	390,261	223,749	17,958	103,032	60,778
1990	1,920,135	1,442,748	22,717	1,465,465	172,766	-22,067	1,270,632	407,362	242,141	18,439	104,137	62,116
1991	1,975,971	1,490,765	17,541	1,508,306	180,485	-21,099	1,306,722	405,961	263,288	18,870	104,714	62,581
1992	2,143,661	1,626,472	22,572	1,649,044	194,812	-23,077	1,431,155	431,697	280,809	20,295	105,627	63,543
1993	2,280,457	1,766,222	16,296	1,782,518	213,150	-27,446	1,541,922	450,313	288,222	21,367	106,729	65,899
1994	2,441,275	1,909,135	20,155	1,929,290	232,315	-27,939	1,669,036	481,683	290,556	22,585	108,093	68,711
1995	2,575,190	1,983,885	15,082	1,998,967	242,258	-27,598	1,729,111	537,789	308,290	23,481	109,672	70,153
1996	2,684,829	2,051,025	25,566	2,076,591	249,267	-24,007	1,803,317	557,958	323,554	24,245	110,737	69,931
1997	2,785,387	2,149,203	18,727	2,167,930	259,090	-19,296	1,889,544	566,201	329,642	24,973	111,536	70,790
1998	2,999,135	2,302,110	29,778	2,331,888	276,405	-19,762	2,035,721	623,484	339,930	26,784	111,973	72,156
1999	3,130,542	2,491,032	29,928	2,520,960	299,463	-27,958	2,193,539	587,313	349,690	27,929	112,088	74,285
2000	3,332,967	2,653,717	21,716	2,675,433	314,356	-30,651	2,330,426	632,737	369,804	29,564	112,739	76,014
2001	3,438,119	2,713,160	29,747	2,742,907	315,950	-29,111	2,397,846	632,222	408,051	30,420	113,023	72,890
2002	3,572,756	2,858,148	28,949	2,887,097	326,223	-32,937	2,527,937	604,690	440,129	31,547	113,251	71,841
2003	3,634,586	2,912,985	33,783	2,946,768	336,057	-36,359	2,574,352	607,597	452,637	32,042	113,433	71,917
2004	3,841,969	3,123,007	33,762	3,156,769	360,987	-34,823	2,760,959	616,782	464,228	33,751	113,832	72,937
2005	3,893,818	3,149,236	28,221	3,177,457	369,689	-40,484	2,767,284	630,568	495,966	34,021	114,454	75,069
2006	4,059,028	3,235,724	24,592	3,260,316	381,157	-32,827	2,846,332	683,841	528,855	35,365	114,775	75,481
2007	4,274,094	3,340,816	43,446	3,384,262	392,626	-37,047	2,954,589	746,393	573,112	37,109	115,178	75,980
2008	4,577,797	3,445,119	48,965	3,494,084	404,745	-28,523	3,060,816	870,572	646,409	39,583	115,652	75,546
2009	4,483,080	3,367,418	31,368	3,398,786	393,431	-41,059	2,964,296	755,353	763,431	38,794	115,562	71,266
2010	4,481,478	3,341,302	45,786	3,387,088	395,544	-44,584	2,946,960	725,642	808,876	38,771	115,587	69,984
2011	4,723,257	3,400,908	68,745	3,469,653	363,713	-43,740	3,062,200	887,584	773,473	40,879	115,541	69,979
2012	5,005,259	3,583,916	73,575	3,657,491	378,293	-64,405	3,214,793	1,016,410	774,056	43,386	115,367	70,313
2013	4,920,140	3,670,341	72,000	3,742,341	435,990	-88,060	3,218,291	913,861	787,988	42,575	115,565	71,760
2014	5,134,229	3,803,040	76,680	3,879,720	452,727	-98,198	3,328,795	984,985	820,449	44,213	116,126	73,200
2015	5,351,641	3,973,428	59,805	4,033,233	464,553	-96,398	3,472,282	1,017,415	861,944	45,893	116,611	73,432
2016	5,424,468	4,137,491	39,810	4,177,301	481,395	-115,169	3,580,737	963,792	879,939	46,478	116,710	73,746
2017	5,725,472	4,321,020	37,653	4,358,673	502,835	-123,746	3,732,092	1,068,178	925,202	48,928	117,019	74,502
2018	6,005,261	4,528,625	33,623	4,562,248	523,639	-136,368	3,902,241	1,115,934	987,086	51,168	117,363	75,354
2019	6,115,738	4,550,955	36,201	4,587,156	535,822	-137,470	3,913,864	1,168,658	1,033,216	51,959	117,703	75,338
2020	6,487,359	4,577,507	48,123	4,625,630	542,657	-141,626	3,941,347	1,232,773	1,313,239	54,964	118,030	72,195
2021	6,922,115	4,687,454	49,648	4,737,102	558,162	-133,655	4,045,285	1,387,938	1,488,892	58,813	117,697	73,564
2022	7,112,794	5,038,078	45,115	5,083,193	612,161	-156,715	4,314,317	1,494,769	1,303,708	60,359	117,841	76,280

Personal Income and Employment by Area: Sherman-Denison, TX

(Thousands of dollars, except as noted.)

Year	Personal income, total	Derivation of personal income: Earnings by place of work: Nonfarm	Farm	Total	Less: Contributions for government social insurance	Plus: Adjustment for residence	Equals: Net earnings by place of residence	Plus: Dividends, interest, and rent	Plus: Personal current transfer receipts	Per capita personal income (dollars)	Population (persons)	Total employment
1970	287,412	230,159	1,806	231,965	15,720	-4,417	211,828	45,942	29,642	3,478	82,644	38,706
1971	281,123	218,099	2,094	220,193	15,732	-2,774	201,687	44,657	34,779	3,482	80,725	35,761
1972	309,089	240,745	4,397	245,142	18,457	-3,840	222,845	48,338	37,906	4,015	76,977	36,851
1973	350,654	266,832	9,335	276,167	23,650	-3,723	248,794	56,489	45,371	4,544	77,168	37,720
1974	388,371	299,154	-1,537	297,617	27,275	-3,273	267,069	67,981	53,321	4,905	79,176	38,648
1975	423,246	307,599	-1,624	305,975	27,180	-667	278,128	75,740	69,378	5,146	82,243	36,797
1976	475,796	345,489	7,204	352,693	30,962	-343	321,388	80,472	73,936	5,658	84,093	37,567
1977	529,118	397,084	-981	396,103	35,971	-643	359,489	89,133	80,496	6,292	84,089	39,578
1978	622,806	479,226	2,139	481,365	44,532	-2,783	434,050	99,349	89,407	7,346	84,776	42,554
1979	730,647	574,360	6,745	581,105	55,802	-4,159	521,144	111,027	98,476	8,350	87,500	45,113
1980	822,683	627,836	1,175	629,011	61,252	-1,051	566,708	140,847	115,128	9,129	90,118	44,931
1981	917,869	683,663	798	684,461	71,476	-80	612,905	171,613	133,351	10,071	91,140	45,027
1982	996,327	698,393	2,306	700,699	74,483	4,055	630,271	214,204	151,852	10,847	91,857	44,236
1983	1,086,395	752,624	5,191	757,815	79,010	4,385	683,190	237,529	165,676	11,737	92,562	44,445
1984	1,193,783	828,377	6,602	834,979	89,718	6,753	752,014	268,052	173,717	12,737	93,722	45,965
1985	1,293,103	885,112	9,291	894,403	96,420	8,897	806,880	301,928	184,295	13,636	94,827	47,323
1986	1,344,454	931,768	561	932,329	101,066	6,687	837,950	309,161	197,343	13,891	96,787	47,263
1987	1,355,058	948,109	-1,165	946,944	102,795	6,101	850,250	298,374	206,434	14,157	95,717	48,538
1988	1,415,135	1,008,909	-1,424	1,007,485	112,486	4,602	899,601	301,545	213,989	14,858	95,246	48,810
1989	1,466,253	1,022,459	-1,238	1,021,221	114,886	6,441	912,776	327,476	226,001	15,354	95,499	48,602
1990	1,531,896	1,083,358	919	1,084,277	118,312	6,552	972,517	310,257	249,122	16,105	95,120	49,556
1991	1,578,846	1,118,317	2,127	1,120,444	124,164	5,175	1,001,455	308,589	268,802	16,416	96,178	49,176
1992	1,634,603	1,141,896	6,504	1,148,400	125,335	9,429	1,032,494	296,615	305,494	16,962	96,370	48,581
1993	1,684,568	1,184,670	1,366	1,186,036	131,527	11,957	1,066,466	294,985	323,117	17,282	97,474	48,917
1994	1,766,270	1,237,192	5,219	1,242,411	138,242	13,164	1,117,333	308,497	340,440	17,867	98,857	50,201
1995	1,874,839	1,305,599	-1,279	1,304,320	146,903	14,440	1,171,857	331,217	371,765	18,684	100,342	52,249
1996	2,006,234	1,390,397	1,164	1,391,561	155,227	19,235	1,255,569	354,315	396,350	19,479	102,993	53,694
1997	2,159,276	1,507,357	2,126	1,509,483	164,401	26,088	1,371,170	373,621	414,485	20,541	105,122	56,132
1998	2,284,829	1,602,126	784	1,602,910	173,428	36,867	1,466,349	390,949	427,531	21,350	107,020	55,290
1999	2,408,856	1,702,202	6,374	1,708,576	183,024	39,696	1,565,248	400,128	443,480	22,065	109,173	56,291
2000	2,607,347	1,842,324	1,090	1,843,414	194,649	47,105	1,695,870	440,839	470,638	23,503	110,939	57,537
2001	2,720,225	1,856,417	-563	1,855,854	197,317	90,182	1,748,719	459,387	512,119	24,216	112,330	59,963
2002	2,777,437	1,846,464	4,953	1,851,417	194,691	120,379	1,777,105	444,146	556,186	24,527	113,239	59,733
2003	2,892,647	1,892,431	10,437	1,902,868	204,093	133,315	1,832,090	469,023	591,534	25,281	114,421	60,178
2004	3,037,586	1,937,943	13,290	1,951,233	211,335	203,580	1,943,478	477,761	616,347	26,414	114,998	60,293
2005	3,199,308	2,001,084	6,251	2,007,335	219,584	244,603	2,032,354	493,667	673,287	27,660	115,666	61,004
2006	3,460,767	2,141,648	4,242	2,145,890	227,876	303,996	2,222,010	518,130	720,627	29,535	117,174	62,164
2007	3,726,519	2,187,486	8,327	2,195,813	234,155	364,305	2,325,963	614,500	786,056	31,492	118,331	63,172
2008	3,996,131	2,221,750	-903	2,220,847	239,160	416,015	2,397,702	728,861	869,568	33,628	118,834	63,211
2009	3,863,195	2,182,019	-7,045	2,174,974	241,598	321,207	2,254,583	659,389	949,223	32,175	120,069	62,371
2010	3,991,751	2,270,126	-3,893	2,266,233	252,052	286,066	2,300,247	657,833	1,033,671	32,995	120,981	61,559
2011	4,201,717	2,366,670	2,810	2,369,480	232,200	301,233	2,438,513	699,115	1,064,089	34,672	121,185	62,923
2012	4,390,960	2,446,526	6,206	2,452,732	238,179	359,360	2,573,913	752,777	1,064,270	36,163	121,422	63,217
2013	4,485,524	2,561,233	4,033	2,565,266	280,405	334,348	2,619,209	748,215	1,118,100	36,845	121,742	64,745
2014	4,738,625	2,605,454	-6,055	2,599,399	287,181	439,063	2,751,281	811,672	1,175,672	38,595	122,778	66,190
2015	4,906,151	2,658,392	5,679	2,664,071	297,041	489,866	2,856,896	810,850	1,238,405	39,374	124,603	67,265
2016	5,166,497	2,699,494	-10,558	2,688,936	307,768	594,597	2,975,765	892,261	1,298,471	40,679	127,007	67,999
2017	5,369,622	2,858,052	-19,693	2,838,359	326,876	652,953	3,164,436	881,498	1,323,688	41,451	129,542	69,639
2018	5,720,450	3,020,249	-28,555	2,991,694	341,958	714,588	3,364,324	957,862	1,398,264	43,341	131,987	71,626
2019	6,088,113	3,147,692	-19,057	3,128,635	354,960	864,385	3,638,060	968,950	1,481,103	45,402	134,094	72,160
2020	6,650,503	3,287,016	-15,827	3,271,189	378,689	906,644	3,799,144	977,180	1,874,179	48,865	136,100	72,929
2021	7,378,993	3,589,376	-17,038	3,572,338	407,442	974,919	4,139,815	1,109,883	2,129,295	52,873	139,561	75,831
2022	7,642,205	3,664,069	-46,096	3,617,973	429,102	1,308,009	4,496,880	1,190,249	1,955,076	53,393	143,131	77,044

Personal Income and Employment by Area: Shreveport-Bossier City, LA

(Thousands of dollars, except as noted.)

Year	Personal income, total	Derivation of personal income: Earnings by place of work: Nonfarm	Earnings by place of work: Farm	Earnings by place of work: Total	Less: Contributions for government social insurance	Plus: Adjustment for residence	Equals: Net earnings by place of residence	Plus: Dividends, interest, and rent	Plus: Personal current transfer receipts	Per capita personal income (dollars)	Population (persons)	Total employment
1970	1,131,644	881,090	19,462	900,552	56,573	-5,473	838,506	187,919	105,219	3,552	318,633	137,728
1971	1,227,149	956,925	22,462	979,387	63,004	-12,613	903,770	200,994	122,385	3,804	322,578	139,810
1972	1,330,991	1,045,345	26,187	1,071,532	71,899	-19,024	980,609	215,480	134,902	4,072	326,844	142,301
1973	1,470,334	1,161,802	30,442	1,192,244	91,319	-26,884	1,074,041	243,777	152,516	4,467	329,175	149,308
1974	1,664,748	1,322,492	16,689	1,339,181	107,395	-37,006	1,194,780	294,792	175,176	5,012	332,185	155,649
1975	1,867,893	1,477,876	15,768	1,493,644	118,895	-46,249	1,328,500	325,273	214,120	5,499	339,670	159,226
1976	2,054,622	1,638,804	24,638	1,663,442	134,705	-55,130	1,473,607	344,953	236,062	5,957	344,880	163,180
1977	2,282,591	1,846,295	25,542	1,871,837	150,189	-64,910	1,656,738	376,627	249,226	6,573	347,270	168,483
1978	2,572,536	2,099,674	21,881	2,121,555	173,908	-83,383	1,864,264	435,858	272,414	7,340	350,493	173,533
1979	2,893,789	2,369,242	34,140	2,403,382	204,362	-103,916	2,095,104	490,721	307,964	8,165	354,406	177,031
1980	3,297,298	2,661,096	12,696	2,673,792	229,297	-125,729	2,318,766	609,350	369,182	9,155	360,154	181,594
1981	3,798,587	3,080,495	14,263	3,094,758	284,268	-183,299	2,627,191	756,382	415,014	10,419	364,582	189,295
1982	4,103,060	3,203,514	8,157	3,211,671	300,178	-144,657	2,766,836	861,804	474,420	11,077	370,428	190,425
1983	4,363,430	3,320,641	12,812	3,333,453	310,345	-143,930	2,879,178	961,119	523,133	11,673	373,804	188,971
1984	4,727,961	3,609,411	15,844	3,625,255	348,968	-152,875	3,123,412	1,057,564	546,985	12,590	375,545	194,903
1985	4,992,728	3,736,572	16,512	3,753,084	365,110	-148,045	3,239,929	1,151,170	601,629	13,179	378,841	195,586
1986	5,041,541	3,675,212	21,884	3,697,096	354,338	-135,404	3,207,354	1,168,827	665,360	13,226	381,189	185,707
1987	5,114,183	3,756,310	29,294	3,785,604	355,006	-126,700	3,303,898	1,133,447	676,838	13,583	376,505	182,242
1988	5,314,173	3,878,669	29,240	3,907,909	381,855	-120,782	3,405,272	1,192,740	716,161	14,341	370,557	180,613
1989	5,549,514	4,001,257	24,463	4,025,720	396,052	-107,932	3,521,736	1,246,901	780,877	15,155	366,185	178,734
1990	5,904,564	4,204,696	20,811	4,225,507	426,755	-94,853	3,703,899	1,349,896	850,769	16,431	359,355	179,458
1991	6,109,876	4,304,520	14,021	4,318,541	450,191	-90,523	3,777,827	1,358,764	973,285	17,032	358,735	179,349
1992	6,575,097	4,656,290	15,294	4,671,584	482,828	-116,466	4,072,290	1,389,961	1,112,846	18,194	361,390	182,259
1993	6,987,456	4,930,157	14,076	4,944,233	515,660	-153,864	4,274,709	1,460,378	1,252,369	19,168	364,541	188,128
1994	7,352,441	5,230,657	16,844	5,247,501	556,480	-180,797	4,510,224	1,516,092	1,326,125	20,068	366,379	191,696
1995	7,626,525	5,456,226	11,789	5,468,015	580,975	-220,694	4,666,346	1,624,238	1,335,941	20,635	369,593	198,717
1996	7,868,168	5,647,400	16,756	5,664,156	598,106	-235,942	4,830,108	1,686,146	1,351,914	21,189	371,337	201,411
1997	8,199,839	5,915,833	11,864	5,927,697	623,475	-259,545	5,044,677	1,780,277	1,374,885	21,926	373,985	205,253
1998	8,562,907	6,180,383	6,030	6,186,413	655,405	-281,098	5,249,910	1,890,569	1,422,428	22,962	372,924	207,956
1999	8,802,098	6,449,530	16,648	6,466,178	675,044	-287,202	5,503,932	1,818,435	1,479,731	23,497	374,607	210,083
2000	9,339,104	6,854,220	14,104	6,868,324	703,129	-298,218	5,866,977	1,954,851	1,517,276	24,828	376,150	211,708
2001	10,329,230	7,715,095	16,531	7,731,626	756,503	-316,731	6,658,392	1,951,132	1,719,706	27,453	376,250	211,573
2002	10,613,726	7,970,921	12,676	7,983,597	777,266	-323,482	6,882,849	1,898,896	1,831,981	28,185	376,578	208,942
2003	10,945,133	8,192,890	21,276	8,214,166	803,280	-345,523	7,065,363	2,001,584	1,878,186	29,024	377,109	211,975
2004	11,299,240	8,383,332	25,532	8,408,864	840,007	-384,216	7,184,641	2,040,055	2,074,544	29,692	380,550	216,237
2005	12,383,324	9,012,766	16,482	9,029,248	879,573	-402,777	7,746,898	2,421,438	2,214,988	32,324	383,099	223,298
2006	13,289,196	9,649,914	20,481	9,670,395	941,002	-439,750	8,289,643	2,649,895	2,349,658	34,117	389,521	228,152
2007	13,617,255	9,786,928	18,707	9,805,635	969,865	-444,232	8,391,538	2,745,280	2,480,437	34,896	390,221	233,288
2008	15,654,312	11,090,742	-14,809	11,075,933	1,046,111	-460,575	9,569,247	3,269,117	2,815,948	39,897	392,367	237,251
2009	14,929,499	10,453,176	-118	10,453,058	1,024,684	-413,855	9,014,519	2,934,393	2,980,587	37,811	394,845	234,081
2010	15,998,696	11,287,324	3,484	11,290,808	1,082,664	-416,306	9,791,838	3,059,245	3,147,613	40,001	399,962	237,001
2011	16,464,030	11,104,579	4,191	11,108,770	995,738	-439,545	9,673,487	3,611,780	3,178,763	40,754	403,981	242,542
2012	16,860,360	11,161,767	12,786	11,174,553	995,263	-372,876	9,806,414	3,790,747	3,263,199	41,363	407,615	243,209
2013	16,918,999	11,553,137	19,511	11,572,648	1,123,939	-305,885	10,142,824	3,396,392	3,379,783	41,625	406,463	240,790
2014	17,486,708	12,044,674	4,709	12,049,383	1,162,209	-296,253	10,590,921	3,526,025	3,369,762	43,196	404,826	241,588
2015	17,330,899	11,513,304	-4,918	11,508,386	1,166,755	-305,697	10,035,934	3,527,776	3,767,189	42,859	404,366	242,802
2016	17,048,869	11,198,434	-13,190	11,185,244	1,163,806	-312,215	9,709,223	3,351,333	3,988,313	42,379	402,296	241,744
2017	17,320,672	11,397,385	-9,394	11,387,991	1,191,613	-345,197	9,851,181	3,383,248	4,086,243	43,235	400,620	238,433
2018	18,332,649	11,886,713	-14,838	11,871,875	1,251,555	-341,289	10,279,031	3,816,457	4,237,161	46,080	397,844	239,032
2019	18,597,853	12,091,393	-12,229	12,079,164	1,267,142	-331,051	10,480,971	3,725,182	4,391,700	47,031	395,441	237,569
2020	20,501,496	12,139,643	-17,349	12,122,294	1,286,228	-314,656	10,521,410	4,299,012	5,681,074	52,235	392,483	228,331
2021	21,544,662	13,021,965	-10,198	13,011,767	1,360,524	-359,264	11,291,979	3,996,105	6,256,578	55,374	389,077	236,416
2022	21,514,093	13,683,552	-25,497	13,658,055	1,471,557	-381,544	11,804,954	4,135,492	5,573,647	55,858	385,154	244,377

Personal Income and Employment by Area: Sierra Vista-Douglas, AZ

(Thousands of dollars, except as noted.)

Year	Personal income, total	Derivation of personal income: Earnings by place of work: Nonfarm	Farm	Total	Less: Contributions for government social insurance	Plus: Adjustment for residence	Equals: Net earnings by place of residence	Plus: Dividends, interest, and rent	Plus: Personal current transfer receipts	Per capita personal income (dollars)	Population (persons)	Total employment
1970	258,346	203,119	6,493	209,612	11,329	-5,870	192,413	49,208	16,725	4,116	62,770	26,150
1971	310,805	244,189	9,400	253,589	14,297	-7,278	232,014	59,060	19,731	4,629	67,149	28,259
1972	350,963	271,112	11,193	282,305	16,344	-6,178	259,783	68,456	22,724	4,947	70,938	29,255
1973	393,750	297,934	14,483	312,417	19,246	-5,914	287,257	78,582	27,911	5,281	74,558	30,088
1974	422,424	317,600	13,649	331,249	21,768	-6,334	303,147	85,896	33,381	5,546	76,165	30,429
1975	444,691	322,041	13,448	335,489	22,551	-6,672	306,266	91,726	46,699	5,781	76,922	29,245
1976	486,415	344,990	21,298	366,288	24,075	-6,629	335,584	98,275	52,556	6,161	78,946	29,568
1977	527,949	381,694	11,603	393,297	26,597	-7,110	359,590	112,587	55,772	6,543	80,688	30,807
1978	598,871	426,557	16,333	442,890	30,254	-7,242	405,394	131,060	62,417	7,201	83,160	32,605
1979	644,364	453,440	10,252	463,692	33,640	-3,221	426,831	146,169	71,364	7,469	86,268	32,952
1980	729,878	506,074	8,623	514,697	38,656	-997	475,044	171,709	83,125	8,470	86,172	34,124
1981	811,002	551,094	11,386	562,480	45,082	-1,438	515,960	196,181	98,861	9,212	88,036	33,576
1982	858,984	566,938	13,785	580,723	46,391	-1,852	532,480	216,537	109,967	9,720	88,373	33,110
1983	938,160	612,771	18,706	631,477	52,544	-2,729	576,204	241,092	120,864	10,556	88,872	33,925
1984	1,032,848	683,141	14,677	697,818	59,650	-4,676	633,492	267,863	131,493	11,358	90,937	35,381
1985	1,084,814	712,871	10,723	723,594	65,788	-4,600	653,206	291,953	139,655	11,896	91,192	36,956
1986	1,151,728	748,877	16,665	765,542	70,853	-4,564	690,125	312,499	149,104	12,240	94,093	38,102
1987	1,223,957	799,353	18,986	818,339	75,676	-7,681	734,982	325,990	162,985	12,659	96,690	38,917
1988	1,293,491	830,427	30,623	861,050	83,964	-7,841	769,245	346,503	177,743	13,430	96,316	39,320
1989	1,357,291	858,318	19,773	878,091	91,079	-8,955	778,057	374,353	204,881	13,914	97,551	39,979
1990	1,439,193	921,108	18,913	940,021	100,320	-13,217	826,484	386,431	226,278	14,698	97,918	40,361
1991	1,528,039	977,710	19,896	997,606	107,427	-13,326	876,853	395,256	255,930	15,426	99,058	39,034
1992	1,653,535	1,057,205	28,782	1,085,987	118,798	-13,602	953,587	407,803	292,145	16,299	101,453	40,872
1993	1,717,827	1,079,140	26,738	1,105,878	123,757	-10,149	971,972	429,760	316,095	16,454	104,403	42,304
1994	1,812,731	1,138,452	9,385	1,147,837	130,616	-7,220	1,010,001	465,428	337,302	16,581	109,323	44,449
1995	1,884,229	1,156,136	6,900	1,163,036	129,596	-4,111	1,029,329	496,010	358,890	16,752	112,480	44,987
1996	1,983,259	1,192,173	23,873	1,216,046	136,244	-1,090	1,078,712	524,238	380,309	17,570	112,880	46,281
1997	2,061,796	1,245,208	30,516	1,275,724	141,091	644	1,135,277	525,447	401,072	17,943	114,907	47,434
1998	2,203,149	1,318,984	27,370	1,346,354	148,438	3,413	1,201,329	581,908	419,912	18,978	116,091	47,790
1999	2,284,612	1,352,495	34,101	1,386,596	152,316	8,593	1,242,873	594,615	447,124	19,605	116,530	48,312
2000	2,443,893	1,467,725	38,279	1,506,004	164,773	9,765	1,350,996	630,110	462,787	20,688	118,132	50,495
2001	2,635,942	1,586,948	46,986	1,633,934	176,006	-242	1,457,686	650,506	527,750	22,188	118,798	50,753
2002	2,786,758	1,707,565	33,459	1,741,024	190,215	-5,019	1,545,790	650,947	590,021	23,253	119,847	50,601
2003	3,042,203	1,905,276	34,941	1,940,217	207,720	-8,867	1,723,630	665,369	653,204	25,218	120,638	52,390
2004	3,258,198	1,994,886	42,930	2,037,816	223,480	-11,359	1,802,977	731,065	724,156	26,439	123,234	53,550
2005	3,524,250	2,174,748	68,506	2,243,254	246,287	-17,744	1,979,223	745,984	799,043	28,018	125,786	55,627
2006	3,736,653	2,330,870	34,821	2,365,691	263,925	-15,099	2,086,667	774,402	875,584	29,367	127,241	56,567
2007	4,026,415	2,475,246	46,176	2,521,422	283,954	-16,248	2,221,220	853,287	951,908	31,406	128,206	58,187
2008	4,266,312	2,616,245	23,613	2,639,858	304,999	-20,961	2,313,898	868,932	1,083,482	33,066	129,023	57,355
2009	4,452,307	2,715,294	27,653	2,742,947	319,693	-42,189	2,381,065	828,636	1,242,606	34,227	130,081	56,700
2010	4,569,454	2,824,671	31,677	2,856,348	334,215	-60,039	2,462,094	810,001	1,297,359	34,678	131,767	56,554
2011	4,703,524	2,855,146	54,486	2,909,632	306,756	-71,873	2,531,003	888,603	1,283,918	35,407	132,842	56,152
2012	4,550,122	2,725,135	40,415	2,765,550	297,648	-76,100	2,391,802	896,736	1,261,584	34,581	131,580	54,893
2013	4,440,383	2,600,666	76,396	2,677,062	319,727	-74,475	2,282,860	856,392	1,301,131	34,436	128,947	53,145
2014	4,473,661	2,559,058	39,591	2,598,649	313,080	-68,421	2,217,148	870,595	1,385,918	35,360	126,519	52,284
2015	4,599,560	2,584,729	55,124	2,639,853	317,677	-66,287	2,255,889	903,650	1,440,021	36,659	125,470	51,800
2016	4,632,411	2,589,299	53,846	2,643,145	317,840	-69,110	2,256,195	876,551	1,499,665	37,190	124,559	51,221
2017	4,807,685	2,683,916	18,689	2,702,605	329,505	-68,454	2,304,646	903,613	1,599,426	38,920	123,528	51,099
2018	4,947,982	2,752,877	15,498	2,768,375	341,956	-66,630	2,359,789	910,779	1,677,414	39,635	124,838	51,349
2019	5,173,741	2,841,571	30,987	2,872,558	356,909	-67,042	2,448,607	935,708	1,789,426	41,293	125,292	51,635
2020	5,878,777	3,161,298	24,918	3,186,216	398,638	-90,387	2,697,191	952,993	2,228,593	46,835	125,522	52,679
2021	6,218,395	3,163,147	25,658	3,188,805	401,548	-71,613	2,715,644	952,334	2,550,417	49,445	125,763	52,612
2022	6,307,666	3,291,463	48,275	3,339,738	423,161	-70,779	2,845,798	1,008,047	2,453,821	50,195	125,663	52,748

Personal Income and Employment by Area: Sioux City, IA-NE-SD

(Thousands of dollars, except as noted.)

Year	Personal income, total	Derivation of personal income: Earnings by place of work: Nonfarm	Farm	Total	Less: Contributions for government social insurance	Plus: Adjustment for residence	Equals: Net earnings by place of residence	Plus: Dividends, interest, and rent	Plus: Personal current transfer receipts	Per capita personal income (dollars)	Population (persons)	Total employment
1970	511,135	383,935	31,097	415,032	28,171	-5,701	381,160	77,452	52,523	3,827	133,570	62,944
1971	552,277	411,504	35,639	447,143	31,188	-6,278	409,677	84,676	57,924	4,083	135,267	63,389
1972	622,395	451,339	58,828	510,167	35,879	-7,561	466,727	92,777	62,891	4,597	135,402	65,276
1973	728,633	505,631	101,339	606,970	46,705	-8,959	551,306	105,108	72,219	5,356	136,036	69,291
1974	751,860	572,157	42,645	614,802	55,117	-12,830	546,855	120,629	84,376	5,520	136,216	71,552
1975	855,059	638,710	54,749	693,459	60,158	-16,050	617,251	134,576	103,232	6,213	137,619	71,954
1976	913,414	721,083	20,132	741,215	68,028	-19,069	654,118	145,779	113,517	6,566	139,120	72,967
1977	1,005,333	765,071	45,556	810,627	71,444	-20,346	718,837	164,443	122,053	7,195	139,721	72,459
1978	1,125,403	845,073	69,929	915,002	81,640	-25,546	807,816	178,984	138,603	8,166	137,819	73,684
1979	1,184,992	899,152	47,816	946,968	90,826	-24,330	831,812	197,214	155,966	8,668	136,704	72,757
1980	1,255,724	959,210	2,668	961,878	96,411	-25,693	839,774	238,321	177,629	9,253	135,714	71,639
1981	1,463,731	1,053,882	60,805	1,114,687	112,599	-32,758	969,330	296,173	198,228	10,752	136,130	71,563
1982	1,480,579	1,044,444	21,214	1,065,658	113,160	-30,971	921,527	338,191	220,861	10,944	135,287	68,961
1983	1,517,631	1,101,228	-16,015	1,085,213	118,591	-31,478	935,144	346,602	235,885	11,291	134,406	69,727
1984	1,637,203	1,157,287	23,260	1,180,547	126,916	-31,593	1,022,038	369,045	246,120	12,201	134,189	71,918
1985	1,721,649	1,202,078	42,165	1,244,243	134,880	-33,013	1,076,350	381,631	263,668	12,952	132,924	71,400
1986	1,764,488	1,241,311	41,999	1,283,310	143,077	-34,197	1,106,036	384,445	274,007	13,442	131,262	71,903
1987	1,880,991	1,337,363	79,111	1,416,474	154,562	-35,734	1,226,178	374,876	279,937	14,472	129,973	73,614
1988	1,975,120	1,434,334	61,730	1,496,064	170,671	-38,387	1,287,006	395,168	292,946	15,092	130,875	75,613
1989	2,106,271	1,538,333	76,006	1,614,339	183,258	-41,729	1,389,352	412,668	304,251	16,103	130,798	79,074
1990	2,258,549	1,624,723	90,348	1,715,071	199,347	-45,798	1,469,926	461,197	327,426	17,153	131,671	81,161
1991	2,332,844	1,684,133	82,117	1,766,250	209,223	-51,518	1,505,509	474,454	352,881	17,525	133,113	80,106
1992	2,544,607	1,865,029	108,099	1,973,128	228,946	-62,682	1,681,500	485,685	377,422	18,919	134,501	82,066
1993	2,615,368	1,980,387	71,247	2,051,634	243,389	-68,850	1,739,395	487,788	388,185	19,171	136,425	85,320
1994	2,809,945	2,151,257	101,654	2,252,911	266,708	-80,074	1,906,129	500,853	402,963	20,358	138,024	88,757
1995	3,005,109	2,345,448	61,708	2,407,156	291,223	-95,878	2,020,055	562,009	423,045	21,509	139,713	92,652
1996	3,303,670	2,509,461	148,987	2,658,448	300,369	-107,993	2,250,086	610,729	442,855	23,410	141,120	94,291
1997	3,359,474	2,595,488	101,436	2,696,924	317,322	-113,220	2,266,382	643,348	449,744	23,751	141,447	95,102
1998	3,569,114	2,791,950	84,484	2,876,434	336,991	-129,103	2,410,340	707,146	451,628	25,138	141,981	94,340
1999	3,632,387	2,886,420	69,368	2,955,788	345,615	-133,246	2,476,927	685,302	470,158	25,423	142,877	94,810
2000	3,800,710	2,999,534	65,544	3,065,078	356,081	-138,648	2,570,349	724,907	505,454	26,598	142,892	94,186
2001	3,916,806	3,032,657	70,160	3,102,817	359,372	-130,790	2,612,655	767,106	537,045	27,546	142,193	94,796
2002	3,975,229	3,034,881	61,354	3,096,235	357,244	-113,515	2,625,476	757,223	592,530	28,031	141,815	92,185
2003	4,092,503	3,118,450	95,372	3,213,822	367,075	-105,690	2,741,057	764,677	586,769	28,948	141,374	90,931
2004	4,421,975	3,409,958	141,488	3,551,446	386,297	-112,752	3,052,397	764,716	604,862	31,331	141,136	89,781
2005	4,740,467	3,676,467	130,444	3,806,911	410,200	-97,239	3,299,472	793,513	647,482	33,894	139,860	90,205
2006	5,003,894	3,888,640	65,604	3,954,244	426,578	-80,290	3,447,376	846,705	709,813	35,650	140,363	91,236
2007	5,504,095	4,194,890	115,480	4,310,370	459,138	-81,096	3,770,136	983,972	749,987	39,114	140,721	94,079
2008	6,049,843	4,592,484	177,682	4,770,166	498,276	-83,971	4,187,919	1,015,317	846,607	42,816	141,298	95,335
2009	5,655,941	4,241,645	140,642	4,382,287	477,887	-49,873	3,854,527	913,056	888,358	39,650	142,645	93,624
2010	5,885,636	4,379,556	141,588	4,521,144	480,937	-49,371	3,990,836	936,137	958,663	40,867	144,019	92,751
2011	5,802,731	4,096,368	245,111	4,341,479	422,684	-33,937	3,884,858	952,383	965,490	40,084	144,766	92,770
2012	5,943,391	4,127,847	169,094	4,296,941	422,725	-20,022	3,854,194	1,118,986	970,211	41,048	144,791	93,338
2013	5,862,830	4,217,217	213,121	4,430,338	493,546	-38,623	3,898,169	971,907	992,754	40,389	145,158	95,073
2014	6,145,415	4,481,554	108,296	4,589,850	520,575	-66,749	4,002,526	1,102,985	1,039,904	42,208	145,600	96,643
2015	6,548,409	4,829,121	130,253	4,959,374	552,591	-94,771	4,312,012	1,136,104	1,100,293	44,784	146,222	97,697
2016	6,652,063	5,002,988	79,324	5,082,312	588,447	-137,735	4,356,130	1,156,634	1,139,299	45,322	146,772	96,973
2017	6,727,891	4,836,495	75,904	4,912,399	560,485	-28,315	4,323,599	1,274,157	1,130,135	45,897	146,587	94,836
2018	7,152,526	5,053,161	94,390	5,147,551	585,120	-34,271	4,528,160	1,395,693	1,228,673	48,443	147,648	96,186
2019	7,640,303	5,315,373	95,171	5,410,544	615,898	-8,750	4,785,896	1,555,437	1,298,970	51,202	149,220	95,738
2020	8,015,261	5,455,748	123,756	5,579,504	656,728	-7,914	4,914,862	1,439,952	1,660,447	53,474	149,891	92,925
2021	8,586,624	5,803,823	269,294	6,073,117	687,499	-17,353	5,368,265	1,387,075	1,831,284	57,441	149,486	95,519
2022	8,868,923	6,223,671	275,118	6,498,789	742,101	-26,511	5,730,177	1,522,379	1,616,367	59,427	149,240	98,766

Personal Income and Employment by Area: Sioux Falls, SD

(Thousands of dollars, except as noted.)

Year	Personal income, total	Derivation of personal income: Earnings by place of work: Nonfarm	Farm	Total	Less: Contributions for government social insurance	Plus: Adjustment for residence	Equals: Net earnings by place of residence	Plus: Dividends, interest, and rent	Plus: Personal current transfer receipts	Per capita personal income (dollars)	Population (persons)	Total employment
1970	464,373	345,033	37,216	382,249	23,339	-3,952	354,958	68,819	40,596	3,740	124,171	60,271
1971	508,717	372,189	44,678	416,867	25,680	-3,979	387,208	74,776	46,733	4,067	125,075	60,995
1972	576,394	406,967	68,995	475,962	29,026	-4,130	442,806	81,583	52,005	4,571	126,094	61,395
1973	690,876	470,628	110,766	581,394	39,254	-4,514	537,626	92,948	60,302	5,443	126,920	65,595
1974	748,516	533,493	84,047	617,540	45,948	-4,921	566,671	110,909	70,936	5,847	128,011	67,350
1975	834,582	587,571	91,591	679,162	49,977	-4,611	624,574	124,846	85,162	6,468	129,032	68,274
1976	879,337	677,670	34,355	712,025	57,694	-4,679	649,652	136,837	92,848	6,710	131,050	71,764
1977	1,003,511	762,078	55,482	817,560	63,196	-5,282	749,082	156,347	98,082	7,550	132,916	75,138
1978	1,175,124	886,224	86,077	972,301	75,500	-5,994	890,807	177,855	106,462	8,804	133,481	79,276
1979	1,294,758	979,601	89,002	1,068,603	89,215	-5,635	973,753	200,714	120,291	9,569	135,312	80,201
1980	1,359,989	1,045,472	22,147	1,067,619	95,428	-5,236	966,955	251,983	141,051	9,771	139,185	79,520
1981	1,573,317	1,123,309	81,250	1,204,559	109,346	-7,776	1,087,437	319,935	165,945	11,307	139,142	78,983
1982	1,639,722	1,177,308	36,974	1,214,282	116,631	-9,103	1,088,548	366,174	185,000	11,650	140,747	79,169
1983	1,740,690	1,287,535	19,856	1,307,391	128,284	-11,861	1,167,246	374,553	198,891	12,169	143,042	82,261
1984	1,933,945	1,408,896	55,064	1,463,960	143,639	-14,298	1,306,023	417,315	210,607	13,239	146,081	86,170
1985	2,051,149	1,480,644	82,031	1,562,675	155,526	-16,146	1,391,003	433,538	226,608	13,866	147,929	88,138
1986	2,145,263	1,568,979	73,364	1,642,343	169,658	-18,092	1,454,593	451,075	239,595	14,515	147,796	89,382
1987	2,270,017	1,660,434	111,179	1,771,613	181,315	-20,091	1,570,207	451,312	248,498	15,269	148,672	93,682
1988	2,468,390	1,816,639	121,128	1,937,767	203,012	-23,973	1,710,782	492,748	264,860	16,297	151,460	97,090
1989	2,658,050	1,986,552	86,492	2,073,044	223,377	-26,575	1,823,092	550,048	284,910	17,460	152,240	100,812
1990	2,934,606	2,220,258	102,230	2,322,488	263,350	-30,347	2,028,791	601,351	304,464	19,038	154,148	105,115
1991	3,113,362	2,393,099	100,859	2,493,958	286,243	-32,946	2,174,769	611,729	326,864	19,839	156,928	109,696
1992	3,368,715	2,593,646	139,119	2,732,765	305,621	-37,754	2,389,390	625,167	354,158	20,956	160,753	113,135
1993	3,504,847	2,752,666	71,005	2,823,671	322,597	-42,413	2,458,661	674,103	372,083	21,360	164,088	116,256
1994	3,886,831	2,995,324	189,709	3,185,033	353,167	-48,651	2,783,215	712,250	391,366	23,138	167,987	122,281
1995	4,039,968	3,169,342	66,490	3,235,832	372,509	-53,059	2,810,264	806,616	423,088	23,667	170,698	125,850
1996	4,437,477	3,347,992	222,166	3,570,158	392,470	-59,131	3,118,557	868,794	450,126	25,509	173,960	129,330
1997	4,612,133	3,560,297	147,579	3,707,876	417,714	-69,368	3,220,794	922,147	469,192	26,242	175,756	132,805
1998	5,025,664	3,917,372	150,347	4,067,719	454,263	-82,034	3,531,422	1,007,554	486,688	28,082	178,964	136,890
1999	5,355,039	4,287,949	98,540	4,386,489	499,913	-96,576	3,790,000	1,055,176	509,863	29,240	183,138	142,582
2000	5,774,940	4,577,829	121,896	4,699,725	535,022	-111,921	4,052,782	1,166,758	555,400	30,667	188,310	147,233
2001	5,969,923	4,727,662	87,506	4,815,168	552,358	-118,847	4,143,963	1,223,622	602,338	31,143	191,693	148,941
2002	6,194,762	5,005,363	58,991	5,064,354	579,411	-129,314	4,355,629	1,186,580	652,553	31,859	194,442	150,767
2003	6,568,261	5,261,471	118,971	5,380,442	610,642	-133,960	4,635,840	1,253,878	678,543	33,204	197,813	152,572
2004	7,115,815	5,632,175	183,062	5,815,237	643,158	-141,097	5,030,982	1,353,670	731,163	35,170	202,328	155,872
2005	7,771,725	6,128,594	117,698	6,246,292	681,135	-150,559	5,414,598	1,549,702	807,425	37,616	206,605	160,493
2006	8,692,976	6,841,195	104,951	6,946,146	750,126	-155,677	6,040,343	1,757,453	895,180	41,087	211,576	165,729
2007	9,512,942	7,366,654	165,928	7,532,582	808,420	-156,719	6,567,443	1,989,124	956,375	43,850	216,943	171,394
2008	10,250,294	7,729,914	214,429	7,944,343	850,903	-164,569	6,928,871	2,202,849	1,118,574	46,196	221,887	175,338
2009	10,115,969	7,770,415	259,236	8,029,651	849,519	-159,438	7,020,694	1,913,928	1,181,347	44,778	225,913	173,747
2010	10,642,421	8,076,732	228,128	8,304,860	871,169	-151,410	7,282,281	2,072,058	1,288,082	46,435	229,191	174,129
2011	10,998,070	8,055,425	429,030	8,484,455	790,716	-160,991	7,532,748	2,146,758	1,318,564	47,283	232,601	177,695
2012	11,721,163	8,861,344	201,443	9,062,787	850,428	-165,596	8,046,763	2,346,077	1,328,323	49,275	237,872	181,820
2013	11,570,259	8,848,414	223,658	9,072,072	981,890	-157,575	7,932,607	2,249,956	1,387,696	47,611	243,014	185,861
2014	12,605,327	9,764,385	90,880	9,855,265	1,061,964	-159,525	8,633,776	2,484,926	1,486,625	50,875	247,771	190,944
2015	13,656,488	10,512,003	99,080	10,611,083	1,118,729	-178,509	9,313,845	2,763,508	1,579,135	54,178	252,066	194,240
2016	14,180,686	10,868,412	91,912	10,960,324	1,159,410	-183,343	9,617,571	2,912,127	1,650,988	55,137	257,191	197,446
2017	14,858,028	11,375,804	88,844	11,464,648	1,219,553	-196,164	10,048,931	3,067,896	1,741,201	56,479	263,071	200,599
2018	15,641,782	11,987,854	147,599	12,135,453	1,275,686	-210,959	10,648,808	3,140,784	1,852,190	58,529	267,250	205,462
2019	17,130,035	13,169,365	191,295	13,360,660	1,386,805	-235,522	11,738,333	3,409,270	1,982,432	62,777	272,871	208,398
2020	18,499,235	13,781,664	261,927	14,043,591	1,485,791	-257,168	12,300,632	3,583,770	2,614,833	66,620	277,681	207,428
2021	20,353,603	14,706,837	405,435	15,112,272	1,579,390	-258,884	13,273,998	4,057,034	3,022,571	72,093	282,325	216,010
2022	21,639,890	15,814,526	480,440	16,294,966	1,712,399	-257,553	14,325,014	4,623,283	2,691,593	74,725	289,592	225,187

Personal Income and Employment by Area: South Bend-Mishawaka, IN-MI

(Thousands of dollars, except as noted.)

Year	Personal income, total	Derivation of personal income: Earnings by place of work: Nonfarm	Farm	Total	Less: Contributions for government social insurance	Plus: Adjustment for residence	Equals: Net earnings by place of residence	Plus: Dividends, interest, and rent	Plus: Personal current transfer receipts	Per capita personal income (dollars)	Population (persons)	Total employment
1970	1,110,466	852,197	7,575	859,772	57,910	62,403	864,265	156,667	89,534	3,855	288,051	115,959
1971	1,185,112	883,810	9,614	893,424	62,256	73,020	904,188	169,200	111,724	4,122	287,489	113,550
1972	1,320,268	993,533	13,150	1,006,683	74,400	90,577	1,022,860	180,535	116,873	4,558	289,656	118,965
1973	1,473,106	1,104,983	23,862	1,128,845	95,536	102,991	1,136,300	200,717	136,089	5,089	289,459	125,314
1974	1,585,458	1,189,067	15,973	1,205,040	106,729	96,462	1,194,773	229,099	161,586	5,496	288,497	126,842
1975	1,714,007	1,236,664	32,921	1,269,585	109,135	95,523	1,255,973	255,539	202,495	5,945	288,309	123,186
1976	1,879,499	1,370,286	25,181	1,395,467	122,910	124,590	1,397,147	270,170	212,182	6,546	287,124	125,452
1977	2,070,331	1,522,377	14,792	1,537,169	137,336	150,918	1,550,751	297,846	221,734	7,188	288,007	129,758
1978	2,311,819	1,699,477	23,147	1,722,624	158,574	176,095	1,740,145	331,025	240,649	7,967	290,181	134,190
1979	2,527,035	1,861,451	19,796	1,881,247	179,831	181,961	1,883,377	368,498	275,160	8,665	291,639	135,847
1980	2,733,362	1,931,582	5,766	1,937,348	184,702	174,208	1,926,854	460,976	345,532	9,394	290,984	130,558
1981	3,000,626	2,069,665	8,387	2,078,052	213,252	176,335	2,041,135	570,104	389,387	10,354	289,810	129,347
1982	3,133,286	2,122,056	8,766	2,130,822	222,222	177,371	2,085,971	616,354	430,961	10,889	287,735	126,263
1983	3,338,616	2,236,100	2,936	2,239,036	235,260	215,140	2,218,916	658,592	461,108	11,648	286,626	127,770
1984	3,692,045	2,501,646	20,435	2,522,081	269,474	233,466	2,486,073	729,725	476,247	12,810	288,222	135,669
1985	3,871,528	2,630,419	14,099	2,644,518	288,088	238,778	2,595,208	772,381	503,939	13,379	289,373	137,736
1986	4,109,157	2,800,494	24,678	2,825,172	307,980	259,326	2,776,518	799,532	533,107	14,198	289,411	141,018
1987	4,362,095	3,036,124	36,483	3,072,607	329,889	274,517	3,017,235	799,575	545,285	14,992	290,952	146,392
1988	4,639,951	3,254,332	19,540	3,273,872	365,772	282,831	3,190,931	868,397	580,623	15,849	292,757	149,826
1989	4,941,029	3,407,194	41,183	3,448,377	384,834	276,024	3,339,567	974,884	626,578	16,722	295,488	151,731
1990	5,134,830	3,556,091	42,019	3,598,110	413,197	250,927	3,435,840	1,013,815	685,175	17,278	297,187	153,679
1991	5,271,087	3,665,861	25,953	3,691,814	432,885	244,338	3,503,267	1,011,810	756,010	17,646	298,719	153,036
1992	5,670,004	3,938,136	35,995	3,974,131	461,097	281,559	3,794,593	1,023,009	852,402	18,843	300,909	155,304
1993	6,022,188	4,202,048	30,101	4,232,149	494,335	294,547	4,032,361	1,095,837	893,990	19,764	304,704	158,330
1994	6,400,803	4,475,499	29,192	4,504,691	537,634	335,861	4,302,918	1,165,493	932,392	20,835	307,216	163,946
1995	6,711,057	4,722,084	18,038	4,740,122	571,582	334,369	4,502,909	1,257,571	950,577	21,644	310,072	168,659
1996	7,006,282	4,893,172	29,566	4,922,738	584,743	332,780	4,670,775	1,335,488	1,000,019	22,447	312,119	169,345
1997	7,365,054	5,130,739	31,633	5,162,372	613,749	328,736	4,877,359	1,453,909	1,033,786	23,487	313,574	172,747
1998	7,946,010	5,581,979	18,760	5,600,739	649,269	331,248	5,282,718	1,618,482	1,044,810	25,261	314,556	175,639
1999	8,262,906	5,928,923	10,354	5,939,277	680,285	369,586	5,628,578	1,534,676	1,099,652	26,165	315,804	175,066
2000	8,617,632	6,141,967	22,101	6,164,068	698,806	362,941	5,828,203	1,628,354	1,161,075	27,186	316,991	177,109
2001	8,855,614	6,285,732	24,146	6,309,878	702,018	319,976	5,927,836	1,646,022	1,281,756	27,945	316,897	174,081
2002	9,100,022	6,467,441	10,590	6,478,031	723,632	366,020	6,120,419	1,634,585	1,345,018	28,736	316,678	172,070
2003	9,251,513	6,629,525	28,580	6,658,105	751,048	389,217	6,296,274	1,562,664	1,392,575	29,227	316,545	171,684
2004	9,752,090	6,967,028	58,013	7,025,041	791,126	527,331	6,761,246	1,530,045	1,460,799	30,780	316,831	173,844
2005	10,077,245	7,086,527	36,731	7,123,258	817,466	620,287	6,926,079	1,580,841	1,570,325	31,767	317,221	174,433
2006	10,663,852	7,374,404	32,196	7,406,600	850,091	687,127	7,243,636	1,729,523	1,690,693	33,558	317,778	175,054
2007	11,053,693	7,529,758	39,863	7,569,621	874,918	710,205	7,404,908	1,870,662	1,778,123	34,687	318,668	176,311
2008	11,258,796	7,594,470	30,214	7,624,684	899,185	566,997	7,292,496	1,920,859	2,045,441	35,187	319,966	173,665
2009	10,614,597	7,106,098	23,718	7,129,816	849,503	329,034	6,609,347	1,755,806	2,249,444	33,255	319,189	164,723
2010	10,975,186	7,216,246	42,822	7,259,068	844,377	403,895	6,818,586	1,762,161	2,394,439	34,397	319,072	163,948
2011	11,643,975	7,601,627	103,575	7,705,202	779,038	382,574	7,308,738	1,958,903	2,376,334	36,492	319,082	166,844
2012	12,090,351	7,856,901	55,853	7,912,754	799,056	448,931	7,562,629	2,100,334	2,427,388	37,942	318,655	165,805
2013	12,250,993	7,959,745	105,229	8,064,974	910,034	618,642	7,773,582	2,033,559	2,443,852	38,384	319,170	165,621
2014	12,800,273	8,294,565	39,238	8,333,803	945,165	703,875	8,092,513	2,125,767	2,581,993	39,987	320,108	168,237
2015	13,591,241	8,785,663	8,172	8,793,835	995,246	799,840	8,598,429	2,308,085	2,684,727	42,399	320,556	171,836
2016	13,758,011	8,950,625	13,940	8,964,565	1,018,551	770,970	8,716,984	2,298,652	2,742,375	42,712	322,111	175,384
2017	14,381,640	9,215,486	14,186	9,229,672	1,048,961	1,077,507	9,258,218	2,319,668	2,803,754	44,579	322,611	176,648
2018	15,063,319	9,583,391	12,961	9,596,352	1,093,213	1,094,340	9,597,479	2,555,082	2,910,758	46,534	323,707	179,121
2019	15,239,459	9,901,345	4,250	9,905,595	1,139,114	826,340	9,592,821	2,571,384	3,075,254	46,944	324,629	179,644
2020	16,247,633	9,759,923	46,986	9,806,909	1,157,592	816,788	9,466,105	2,713,641	4,067,887	50,113	324,222	169,218
2021	17,882,752	10,488,398	84,114	10,572,512	1,238,737	1,156,725	10,490,500	2,888,790	4,503,462	55,221	323,842	172,122
2022	18,256,374	11,209,834	59,890	11,269,724	1,323,085	1,265,253	11,211,892	3,135,771	3,908,711	56,410	323,637	177,318

Personal Income and Employment by Area: Spartanburg, SC

(Thousands of dollars, except as noted.)

Year	Personal income, total	Derivation of personal income: Earnings by place of work: Nonfarm	Farm	Total	Less: Contributions for government social insurance	Plus: Adjustment for residence	Equals: Net earnings by place of residence	Plus: Dividends, interest, and rent	Plus: Personal current transfer receipts	Per capita personal income (dollars)	Population (persons)	Total employment
1970	566,837	516,874	6,507	523,381	37,423	-26,026	459,932	58,619	48,286	3,252	174,326	83,175
1971	622,872	566,365	8,011	574,376	42,498	-28,556	503,322	64,999	54,551	3,500	177,982	84,940
1972	695,481	638,602	3,692	642,294	50,073	-30,100	562,121	72,199	61,161	3,785	183,764	89,198
1973	794,660	728,108	8,138	736,246	65,247	-32,636	638,363	83,359	72,938	4,247	187,100	94,452
1974	883,530	795,287	7,978	803,265	74,005	-33,364	695,896	96,710	90,924	4,657	189,728	96,138
1975	959,058	829,557	13,355	842,912	74,707	-42,324	725,881	106,111	127,066	5,001	191,765	92,460
1976	1,075,500	958,591	5,896	964,487	88,522	-47,684	828,281	115,966	131,253	5,634	190,899	97,991
1977	1,166,873	1,040,171	3,969	1,044,140	96,333	-48,389	899,418	129,891	137,564	5,968	195,534	99,015
1978	1,320,389	1,184,251	4,892	1,189,143	112,886	-53,379	1,022,878	147,350	150,161	6,690	197,354	102,990
1979	1,481,885	1,320,268	5,494	1,325,762	129,627	-55,111	1,141,024	167,421	173,440	7,426	199,543	105,426
1980	1,676,501	1,461,980	2,585	1,464,565	143,157	-63,248	1,258,160	208,937	209,404	8,229	203,734	106,595
1981	1,864,568	1,581,841	5,094	1,586,935	165,495	-63,288	1,358,152	259,826	246,590	9,055	205,912	106,328
1982	1,954,841	1,611,550	-1,105	1,610,445	171,296	-62,898	1,376,251	301,811	276,779	9,423	207,456	103,733
1983	2,122,710	1,746,133	386	1,746,519	188,518	-65,002	1,492,999	337,135	292,576	10,169	208,734	104,526
1984	2,371,730	1,965,904	11,664	1,977,568	218,878	-72,177	1,686,513	380,596	304,621	11,202	211,721	109,669
1985	2,519,308	2,084,371	-2,035	2,082,336	234,834	-65,475	1,782,027	409,516	327,765	11,719	214,981	111,376
1986	2,685,191	2,211,765	1,283	2,213,048	255,088	-55,086	1,902,874	438,417	343,900	12,433	215,980	112,786
1987	2,894,725	2,415,620	5,273	2,420,893	274,174	-56,495	2,090,224	452,274	352,227	13,280	217,970	116,549
1988	3,182,455	2,662,074	9,315	2,671,389	310,588	-54,513	2,306,288	502,437	373,730	14,404	220,938	122,528
1989	3,432,772	2,839,718	7,503	2,847,221	335,025	-51,592	2,460,604	554,073	418,095	15,283	224,609	127,410
1990	3,690,515	3,010,691	4,531	3,015,222	362,462	-39,759	2,613,001	615,344	462,170	16,216	227,580	129,388
1991	3,845,180	3,104,013	8,156	3,112,169	378,431	-55,180	2,678,558	638,261	528,361	16,661	230,786	126,259
1992	4,055,199	3,377,179	8,763	3,385,942	407,325	-153,571	2,825,046	650,476	579,677	17,388	233,214	128,557
1993	4,335,014	3,596,991	10,557	3,607,548	438,367	-136,742	3,032,439	685,735	616,840	18,428	235,243	131,893
1994	4,577,415	3,811,776	9,682	3,821,458	470,696	-175,590	3,175,172	740,113	662,130	19,227	238,070	137,055
1995	4,875,362	4,091,995	7,606	4,099,601	506,573	-208,358	3,384,670	778,420	712,272	20,220	241,114	141,714
1996	5,145,457	4,253,851	3,761	4,257,612	516,995	-196,646	3,543,971	836,294	765,192	21,059	244,333	143,819
1997	5,428,838	4,477,905	5,216	4,483,121	542,306	-222,307	3,718,508	912,901	797,429	21,994	246,830	146,229
1998	5,668,130	4,713,178	5,988	4,719,166	573,159	-279,881	3,866,126	967,946	834,058	22,742	249,231	147,172
1999	5,981,590	4,949,475	8,195	4,957,670	593,562	-226,639	4,137,469	951,932	892,189	23,747	251,886	146,993
2000	6,387,173	5,187,313	8,739	5,196,052	619,130	-216,327	4,360,595	1,060,901	965,677	25,103	254,443	148,302
2001	6,557,817	5,276,675	6,017	5,282,692	642,025	-219,775	4,420,892	1,052,822	1,084,103	25,570	256,469	146,802
2002	6,770,470	5,438,940	5,374	5,444,314	660,872	-252,050	4,531,392	1,063,403	1,175,675	26,195	258,467	144,913
2003	6,900,652	5,579,411	9,305	5,588,716	676,877	-246,389	4,665,450	1,005,514	1,229,688	26,518	260,223	145,129
2004	7,289,671	5,898,711	64	5,898,775	706,930	-348,279	4,843,566	1,133,045	1,313,060	27,841	261,828	145,447
2005	7,697,918	6,076,848	7,550	6,084,398	728,401	-347,439	5,008,558	1,276,370	1,412,990	29,106	264,481	146,728
2006	8,297,066	6,522,773	8,093	6,530,866	793,903	-433,184	5,303,779	1,459,793	1,533,494	30,856	268,898	150,515
2007	8,833,422	6,824,726	10,576	6,835,302	824,434	-497,318	5,513,550	1,683,578	1,636,294	32,213	274,215	154,690
2008	9,380,050	6,971,554	16,860	6,988,414	855,894	-476,685	5,655,835	1,844,648	1,879,567	33,539	279,673	154,905
2009	8,855,749	6,424,940	20,784	6,445,724	809,912	-418,287	5,217,525	1,538,222	2,100,002	31,255	283,335	145,028
2010	9,123,398	6,681,380	23,600	6,704,980	821,693	-476,919	5,406,368	1,478,204	2,238,826	32,031	284,831	143,691
2011	9,680,088	6,910,452	11,795	6,922,247	767,089	-494,598	5,660,560	1,794,967	2,224,561	33,789	286,489	148,568
2012	10,366,740	7,303,266	9,471	7,312,737	789,097	-549,970	5,973,670	2,147,766	2,245,304	35,890	288,847	151,289
2013	10,135,861	7,608,827	8,326	7,617,153	922,846	-670,171	6,024,136	1,825,831	2,285,894	34,787	291,370	157,125
2014	11,077,972	8,104,147	2,576	8,106,723	971,268	-708,617	6,426,838	2,216,000	2,435,134	37,650	294,238	161,706
2015	11,685,542	8,613,828	2,930	8,616,758	1,022,737	-706,344	6,887,677	2,239,464	2,558,401	39,198	298,115	165,631
2016	12,291,075	9,028,128	142	9,028,270	1,074,079	-727,359	7,226,832	2,441,587	2,622,656	40,605	302,696	171,776
2017	12,715,383	9,529,966	952	9,530,918	1,138,642	-814,977	7,577,299	2,432,461	2,705,623	41,155	308,960	180,042
2018	13,299,177	9,902,483	759	9,903,242	1,194,412	-752,969	7,955,861	2,501,450	2,841,866	41,980	316,801	186,960
2019	14,370,251	10,586,459	2,367	10,588,826	1,283,457	-935,366	8,370,003	2,974,584	3,025,664	44,504	322,898	193,552
2020	15,719,115	10,880,675	4,604	10,885,279	1,307,715	-1,041,713	8,535,851	3,265,182	3,918,082	47,726	329,365	193,669
2021	17,514,836	11,907,465	6,390	11,913,855	1,405,332	-974,178	9,534,345	3,608,816	4,371,675	52,220	335,406	200,726
2022	18,197,864	12,543,680	1,155	12,544,835	1,524,905	-702,213	10,317,717	3,984,762	3,895,385	52,621	345,831	206,044

Personal Income and Employment by Area: Spokane-Spokane Valley, WA

(Thousands of dollars, except as noted.)

		Derivation of personal income										
		Earnings by place of work										
Year	Personal income, total	Nonfarm	Farm	Total	Less: Contributions for government social insurance	Plus: Adjustment for residence	Equals: Net earnings by place of residence	Plus: Dividends, interest, and rent	Plus: Personal current transfer receipts	Per capita personal income (dollars)	Population (persons)	Total employment
1970	1,184,758	895,712	22,736	918,448	72,854	-17,256	828,338	215,971	140,449	3,865	306,565	127,418
1971	1,294,936	972,904	22,333	995,237	82,214	-15,070	897,953	237,260	159,723	4,118	314,430	128,704
1972	1,430,942	1,078,410	30,130	1,108,540	95,662	-14,616	998,262	257,584	175,096	4,500	317,980	133,288
1973	1,580,338	1,191,263	41,548	1,232,811	121,733	-18,395	1,092,683	287,755	199,900	4,877	324,007	138,443
1974	1,812,252	1,344,446	66,430	1,410,876	141,053	-21,993	1,247,830	331,600	232,822	5,479	330,783	144,970
1975	2,006,155	1,462,467	59,653	1,522,120	150,858	-21,665	1,349,597	374,817	281,741	6,014	333,588	143,744
1976	2,243,050	1,686,757	43,453	1,730,210	177,723	-23,067	1,529,420	404,582	309,048	6,610	339,340	151,795
1977	2,486,700	1,899,871	32,965	1,932,836	201,345	-24,056	1,707,435	455,272	323,993	7,211	344,835	158,454
1978	2,841,255	2,208,247	33,330	2,241,577	240,388	-27,615	1,973,574	519,189	348,492	8,022	354,185	168,612
1979	3,212,696	2,472,966	46,218	2,519,184	278,397	-11,334	2,229,453	588,976	394,267	8,879	361,816	173,480
1980	3,599,982	2,686,064	40,014	2,726,078	302,242	-13,998	2,409,838	709,053	481,091	9,675	372,077	174,942
1981	3,942,254	2,898,243	42,700	2,940,943	349,440	-45,306	2,546,197	848,366	547,691	10,474	376,396	173,684
1982	4,135,501	2,937,250	31,619	2,968,869	359,476	-51,376	2,558,017	964,876	612,608	10,957	377,416	170,721
1983	4,470,982	3,151,279	50,530	3,201,809	392,373	-57,814	2,751,622	1,066,392	652,968	11,802	378,843	176,242
1984	4,754,254	3,372,581	36,973	3,409,554	436,935	-65,900	2,906,719	1,162,407	685,128	12,387	383,806	182,515
1985	4,940,542	3,458,191	28,540	3,486,731	452,547	-67,801	2,966,383	1,234,034	740,125	12,792	386,231	184,753
1986	5,146,968	3,603,536	45,164	3,648,700	476,317	-74,814	3,097,569	1,269,889	779,510	13,363	385,174	188,059
1987	5,318,813	3,807,399	17,595	3,824,994	498,322	-82,708	3,243,964	1,255,560	819,289	13,830	384,587	194,082
1988	5,652,093	4,061,740	32,005	4,093,745	549,091	-93,448	3,451,206	1,311,080	889,807	14,707	384,313	198,812
1989	6,144,561	4,311,155	36,654	4,347,809	582,597	-100,736	3,664,476	1,512,297	967,788	15,890	386,686	202,480
1990	6,596,568	4,743,625	29,609	4,773,234	647,160	-108,127	4,017,947	1,511,500	1,067,121	16,737	394,130	210,111
1991	7,172,170	5,155,891	23,757	5,179,648	705,429	-114,253	4,359,966	1,590,226	1,221,978	17,730	404,533	216,279
1992	7,750,563	5,645,598	32,354	5,677,952	768,019	-130,347	4,779,586	1,626,396	1,344,581	18,619	416,279	221,675
1993	8,234,567	6,044,865	37,865	6,082,730	828,175	-141,734	5,112,821	1,700,293	1,421,453	19,263	427,479	226,076
1994	8,717,293	6,434,877	23,141	6,458,018	886,073	-160,246	5,411,699	1,830,711	1,474,883	20,050	434,767	238,917
1995	9,069,778	6,633,991	31,894	6,665,885	915,306	-175,404	5,575,175	1,935,858	1,558,745	20,518	442,045	242,093
1996	9,521,271	6,942,776	33,836	6,976,612	933,025	-195,396	5,848,191	2,055,123	1,617,957	21,323	446,520	246,800
1997	10,064,630	7,349,912	25,115	7,375,027	948,795	-215,947	6,210,285	2,173,294	1,681,051	22,410	449,120	250,811
1998	10,681,322	7,920,493	24,148	7,944,641	1,003,519	-245,488	6,695,634	2,251,964	1,733,724	23,598	452,646	254,209
1999	11,077,206	8,346,376	19,788	8,366,164	1,020,137	-268,480	7,077,547	2,142,394	1,857,265	24,348	454,950	256,620
2000	11,957,555	9,052,245	25,967	9,078,212	1,118,101	-247,239	7,712,872	2,288,811	1,955,872	26,051	459,013	263,728
2001	12,055,719	8,969,493	22,667	8,992,160	1,130,481	-235,798	7,625,881	2,253,693	2,176,145	26,031	463,126	264,211
2002	12,357,822	9,170,080	32,099	9,202,179	1,151,892	-231,706	7,818,581	2,249,718	2,289,523	26,437	467,441	262,253
2003	12,828,102	9,510,196	48,388	9,558,584	1,205,792	-241,553	8,111,239	2,324,293	2,392,570	27,219	471,299	266,192
2004	13,476,927	10,102,539	32,731	10,135,270	1,291,458	-247,055	8,596,757	2,419,969	2,460,201	28,296	476,290	271,443
2005	14,017,617	10,688,179	21,784	10,709,963	1,382,500	-234,816	9,092,647	2,283,727	2,641,243	29,079	482,051	279,170
2006	15,101,009	11,397,511	14,877	11,412,388	1,466,973	-207,521	9,737,894	2,511,242	2,851,873	30,826	489,883	289,108
2007	16,350,912	12,070,316	19,484	12,089,800	1,534,578	-214,569	10,340,653	2,914,399	3,095,860	32,754	499,209	298,268
2008	17,501,233	12,440,835	11,638	12,452,473	1,566,812	-236,227	10,649,434	3,324,888	3,526,911	34,611	505,661	298,279
2009	17,256,853	12,030,185	19,467	12,049,652	1,564,961	-274,821	10,209,870	3,108,957	3,938,026	33,719	511,783	287,160
2010	17,657,966	12,228,657	33,192	12,261,849	1,586,104	-288,603	10,387,142	2,950,384	4,320,440	34,231	515,850	281,110
2011	18,357,886	12,583,697	43,213	12,626,910	1,483,775	-336,988	10,806,147	3,244,221	4,307,518	35,415	518,363	282,158
2012	19,039,225	13,129,798	32,838	13,162,636	1,511,362	-437,093	11,214,181	3,501,427	4,323,617	36,500	521,620	287,327
2013	19,229,600	13,535,453	37,585	13,573,038	1,747,619	-404,171	11,421,248	3,419,072	4,389,280	36,592	525,507	291,945
2014	20,253,451	14,004,878	16,074	14,020,952	1,812,078	-423,170	11,785,704	3,620,846	4,846,901	38,107	531,493	297,159
2015	21,199,369	14,671,779	56,902	14,728,681	1,900,275	-421,180	12,407,226	3,854,162	4,937,981	39,359	538,609	301,624
2016	22,138,436	15,339,711	36,342	15,376,053	1,958,548	-472,767	12,944,738	3,962,027	5,231,671	40,347	548,704	308,125
2017	23,346,888	16,202,073	54,043	16,256,116	2,093,423	-473,836	13,688,857	4,240,237	5,417,794	41,760	559,074	314,876
2018	24,800,408	17,263,372	42,043	17,305,415	2,192,957	-520,598	14,591,860	4,517,898	5,690,650	43,597	568,856	323,333
2019	26,187,803	18,257,230	63,009	18,320,239	2,263,183	-633,737	15,423,319	4,709,582	6,054,902	45,190	579,510	328,175
2020	28,549,171	18,944,173	89,085	19,033,258	2,385,540	-686,406	15,961,312	4,754,914	7,832,945	48,577	587,712	321,200
2021	31,957,979	21,127,951	93,575	21,221,526	2,594,771	-748,576	17,878,179	5,296,594	8,783,206	53,887	593,051	337,681
2022	32,060,359	22,505,358	98,776	22,604,134	2,837,122	-952,687	18,814,325	5,558,352	7,687,682	53,620	597,919	351,999

Personal Income and Employment by Area: Springfield, IL

(Thousands of dollars, except as noted.)

Year	Personal income, total	Derivation of personal income: Earnings by place of work: Nonfarm	Farm	Total	Less: Contributions for government social insurance	Plus: Adjustment for residence	Equals: Net earnings by place of residence	Plus: Dividends, interest, and rent	Plus: Personal current transfer receipts	Per capita personal income (dollars)	Population (persons)	Total employment
1970	793,627	656,376	24,255	680,631	38,683	-26,656	615,292	119,402	58,933	4,619	171,806	90,195
1971	888,773	736,448	30,181	766,629	44,476	-32,655	689,498	130,509	68,766	5,064	175,525	92,866
1972	966,057	793,177	34,982	828,159	49,801	-35,992	742,366	145,256	78,435	5,472	176,557	93,833
1973	1,076,590	856,215	58,475	914,690	61,209	-39,450	814,031	167,768	94,791	6,028	178,605	96,418
1974	1,199,367	953,354	61,155	1,014,509	70,797	-46,115	897,597	192,624	109,146	6,681	179,531	99,017
1975	1,350,941	1,045,381	80,270	1,125,651	77,368	-51,543	996,740	213,598	140,603	7,344	183,947	100,341
1976	1,444,065	1,140,058	59,592	1,199,650	86,496	-53,686	1,059,468	228,825	155,772	7,707	187,362	101,727
1977	1,550,499	1,219,356	65,617	1,284,973	93,099	-56,355	1,135,519	252,450	162,530	8,229	188,410	103,960
1978	1,706,750	1,367,710	50,614	1,418,324	107,116	-64,825	1,246,383	283,411	176,956	9,086	187,846	107,229
1979	1,826,805	1,435,609	54,873	1,490,482	116,210	-66,032	1,308,240	322,643	195,922	9,744	187,471	106,604
1980	1,966,664	1,517,872	23,097	1,540,969	119,965	-73,244	1,347,760	383,120	235,784	10,473	187,780	103,610
1981	2,193,510	1,626,163	60,846	1,687,009	138,179	-85,139	1,463,691	455,048	274,771	11,699	187,489	102,830
1982	2,372,454	1,725,218	39,850	1,765,068	147,959	-90,741	1,526,368	548,688	297,398	12,698	186,844	103,591
1983	2,458,655	1,817,016	-1,026	1,815,990	156,440	-96,226	1,563,324	577,446	317,885	13,105	187,611	104,656
1984	2,686,820	1,957,808	42,698	2,000,506	173,027	-103,870	1,723,609	631,672	331,539	14,311	187,747	106,763
1985	2,823,354	2,079,115	44,712	2,123,827	188,037	-114,270	1,821,520	653,036	348,798	15,010	188,104	110,181
1986	3,027,384	2,287,758	38,283	2,326,041	208,804	-134,868	1,982,369	683,662	361,353	16,162	187,316	115,910
1987	3,217,824	2,502,139	43,335	2,545,474	228,130	-154,131	2,163,213	681,003	373,608	17,153	187,591	117,958
1988	3,409,316	2,711,348	13,684	2,725,032	256,930	-171,380	2,296,722	722,268	390,326	18,085	188,519	120,710
1989	3,722,876	2,857,275	57,818	2,915,093	272,203	-174,211	2,468,679	838,882	415,315	19,703	188,954	122,213
1990	3,943,146	3,139,570	43,726	3,183,296	295,291	-196,675	2,691,330	800,438	451,378	20,773	189,818	125,747
1991	4,065,650	3,245,981	26,475	3,272,456	314,841	-210,657	2,746,958	834,449	484,243	21,115	192,544	125,206
1992	4,349,327	3,481,695	54,624	3,536,319	335,406	-239,654	2,961,259	844,950	543,118	22,236	195,599	126,634
1993	4,499,091	3,628,128	31,549	3,659,677	352,480	-253,649	3,053,548	880,995	564,548	22,664	198,516	125,314
1994	4,765,147	3,843,519	62,712	3,906,231	381,047	-268,845	3,256,339	930,407	578,401	23,692	201,132	128,409
1995	4,963,503	3,984,542	11,303	3,995,845	395,248	-278,543	3,322,054	1,017,797	623,652	24,621	201,598	130,309
1996	5,261,431	4,162,744	74,866	4,237,610	411,567	-296,002	3,530,041	1,079,453	651,937	26,031	202,123	131,736
1997	5,415,192	4,258,226	69,524	4,327,750	419,173	-309,533	3,599,044	1,146,404	669,744	26,823	201,884	131,819
1998	5,674,797	4,527,711	42,744	4,570,455	443,131	-333,563	3,793,761	1,208,804	672,232	28,132	201,722	133,299
1999	5,851,796	4,766,846	31,247	4,798,093	456,392	-355,477	3,986,224	1,184,843	680,729	29,063	201,347	134,275
2000	6,230,960	5,049,641	57,576	5,107,217	471,726	-380,836	4,254,655	1,248,801	727,504	30,903	201,628	137,874
2001	6,476,593	5,319,527	60,375	5,379,902	489,799	-430,041	4,460,062	1,239,068	777,463	31,995	202,427	137,075
2002	6,604,430	5,493,514	43,683	5,537,197	510,221	-449,292	4,577,684	1,201,462	825,284	32,489	203,281	134,996
2003	6,620,708	5,367,536	73,460	5,440,996	506,951	-425,407	4,508,638	1,245,374	866,696	32,470	203,901	131,008
2004	6,716,493	5,428,686	127,750	5,556,436	518,566	-423,193	4,614,677	1,192,724	909,092	32,839	204,526	130,508
2005	6,799,717	5,571,800	61,896	5,633,696	549,743	-425,734	4,658,219	1,155,509	985,989	33,171	204,988	130,881
2006	7,003,808	5,662,663	78,718	5,741,381	557,784	-410,073	4,773,524	1,212,161	1,018,123	34,018	205,887	130,289
2007	7,326,966	5,761,944	139,130	5,901,074	577,768	-380,920	4,942,386	1,267,415	1,117,165	35,435	206,771	130,148
2008	7,674,403	5,867,971	173,661	6,041,632	596,600	-360,513	5,084,519	1,352,787	1,237,097	36,919	207,874	128,937
2009	7,835,246	5,961,230	110,419	6,071,649	602,715	-367,670	5,101,264	1,369,918	1,364,064	37,507	208,900	127,556
2010	8,217,608	6,306,380	81,971	6,388,351	630,106	-389,922	5,368,323	1,348,517	1,500,768	39,034	210,526	127,801
2011	8,563,626	6,430,964	166,105	6,597,069	581,974	-377,591	5,637,504	1,455,906	1,470,216	40,384	212,055	129,079
2012	8,594,354	6,439,545	73,600	6,513,145	588,795	-381,639	5,542,711	1,565,784	1,485,859	40,412	212,667	127,811
2013	8,858,933	6,509,187	257,889	6,767,076	659,435	-366,491	5,741,150	1,575,027	1,542,756	41,679	212,550	126,365
2014	9,035,010	6,727,933	114,411	6,842,344	684,158	-396,510	5,761,676	1,673,909	1,599,425	42,460	212,788	128,104
2015	9,210,432	6,980,783	8,360	6,989,143	709,918	-483,214	5,796,011	1,707,264	1,707,157	43,324	212,596	129,809
2016	9,346,506	6,918,680	85,701	7,004,381	715,258	-478,563	5,810,560	1,805,530	1,730,416	44,085	212,010	129,809
2017	9,542,547	7,034,363	68,570	7,102,933	731,475	-488,199	5,883,259	1,859,188	1,800,100	45,183	211,199	128,820
2018	9,845,123	7,305,956	94,050	7,400,006	765,875	-515,976	6,118,155	1,853,175	1,873,793	46,871	210,048	128,811
2019	10,194,290	7,525,118	48,138	7,573,256	783,641	-508,310	6,281,305	1,950,473	1,962,512	48,717	209,255	127,044
2020	10,883,897	7,485,882	103,305	7,589,187	782,257	-487,364	6,319,566	1,907,398	2,656,933	52,228	208,393	119,520
2021	12,005,280	8,062,595	230,042	8,292,637	837,104	-579,471	6,876,062	2,153,277	2,975,941	57,827	207,606	123,896
2022	11,816,017	8,315,482	272,384	8,587,866	912,566	-598,560	7,076,740	2,245,109	2,494,168	57,178	206,655	129,611

Personal Income and Employment by Area: Springfield, MA

(Thousands of dollars, except as noted.)

Year	Personal income, total	Derivation of personal income: Earnings by place of work: Nonfarm	Farm	Total	Less: Contributions for government social insurance	Plus: Adjustment for residence	Equals: Net earnings by place of residence	Plus: Dividends, interest, and rent	Plus: Personal current transfer receipts	Per capita personal income (dollars)	Population (persons)	Total employment
1970	2,598,516	1,951,156	20,986	1,972,142	124,331	70,552	1,918,363	406,183	273,970	4,039	643,415	274,474
1971	2,755,646	2,042,120	18,353	2,060,473	134,063	74,540	2,000,950	428,168	326,528	4,271	645,128	271,255
1972	2,973,876	2,210,686	15,481	2,226,167	151,956	88,762	2,162,973	453,636	357,267	4,560	652,132	275,364
1973	3,256,953	2,424,583	19,408	2,443,991	190,976	107,481	2,360,496	493,088	403,369	4,963	656,295	284,944
1974	3,507,118	2,551,927	23,802	2,575,729	208,782	128,900	2,495,847	533,784	477,487	5,338	657,043	286,605
1975	3,824,038	2,627,904	19,738	2,647,642	207,090	144,953	2,585,505	566,104	672,429	5,825	656,518	274,948
1976	4,077,563	2,860,313	22,796	2,883,109	230,162	164,007	2,816,954	597,622	662,987	6,249	652,469	277,007
1977	4,452,720	3,155,301	22,254	3,177,555	254,971	189,425	3,112,009	654,552	686,159	6,852	649,816	285,430
1978	4,921,985	3,522,930	24,942	3,547,872	293,523	227,910	3,482,259	714,232	725,494	7,605	647,233	297,553
1979	5,498,528	3,916,028	19,962	3,935,990	339,479	278,867	3,875,378	804,797	818,353	8,497	647,146	305,592
1980	6,155,577	4,236,269	23,818	4,260,087	367,261	334,624	4,227,450	992,475	935,652	9,515	646,917	309,531
1981	6,763,869	4,533,458	26,239	4,559,697	421,165	367,293	4,505,825	1,194,725	1,063,319	10,430	648,504	306,177
1982	7,337,801	4,752,451	23,508	4,775,959	448,476	385,597	4,713,080	1,437,462	1,187,259	11,400	643,685	301,572
1983	7,845,677	5,134,422	28,058	5,162,480	490,601	403,280	5,075,159	1,490,104	1,280,414	12,159	645,245	305,712
1984	8,678,510	5,707,498	35,516	5,743,014	564,129	444,997	5,623,882	1,704,434	1,350,194	13,419	646,716	319,012
1985	9,275,360	6,157,716	34,603	6,192,319	610,550	483,517	6,065,286	1,793,231	1,416,843	14,334	647,091	327,316
1986	9,947,218	6,666,508	37,019	6,703,527	674,402	525,364	6,554,489	1,892,602	1,500,127	15,341	648,422	337,566
1987	10,777,669	7,388,898	38,498	7,427,396	737,151	565,975	7,256,220	1,963,070	1,558,379	16,418	656,473	343,255
1988	11,806,229	8,136,052	45,342	8,181,394	828,040	603,011	7,956,365	2,168,619	1,681,245	17,755	664,946	354,198
1989	12,771,549	8,512,304	37,340	8,549,644	865,488	632,688	8,316,844	2,525,002	1,929,703	19,008	671,887	353,783
1990	12,960,514	8,611,795	40,247	8,652,042	866,167	652,670	8,438,545	2,386,872	2,135,097	19,228	674,056	347,021
1991	13,220,641	8,521,131	36,948	8,558,079	873,506	652,038	8,336,611	2,355,160	2,528,870	19,628	673,564	332,245
1992	13,567,840	8,899,669	34,916	8,934,585	903,097	665,046	8,696,534	2,280,120	2,591,186	20,151	673,324	334,543
1993	13,929,031	9,156,048	30,862	9,186,910	934,508	677,975	8,930,377	2,342,112	2,656,542	20,666	674,002	335,707
1994	14,547,559	9,559,066	30,819	9,589,885	979,618	683,343	9,293,610	2,424,102	2,829,847	21,543	675,266	339,478
1995	15,186,367	9,791,823	29,705	9,821,528	1,015,222	703,245	9,509,551	2,694,691	2,982,125	22,487	675,336	340,279
1996	15,830,286	10,264,152	31,431	10,295,583	1,045,277	731,886	9,982,192	2,810,378	3,037,716	23,453	674,981	343,624
1997	16,546,503	10,760,288	32,565	10,792,853	1,096,410	789,742	10,486,185	2,900,568	3,159,750	24,474	676,079	348,420
1998	17,144,066	11,236,000	22,297	11,258,297	1,136,991	858,066	10,979,372	2,989,262	3,175,432	25,321	677,062	353,947
1999	17,837,783	11,854,074	25,137	11,879,211	1,178,393	915,954	11,616,772	2,919,670	3,301,341	26,286	678,597	359,754
2000	19,027,910	12,648,890	32,579	12,681,469	1,243,174	1,021,022	12,459,317	3,087,613	3,480,980	27,967	680,368	368,019
2001	20,174,379	13,569,032	26,043	13,595,075	1,341,297	1,016,622	13,270,400	3,092,953	3,811,026	29,641	680,632	370,842
2002	20,676,726	14,036,247	27,531	14,063,778	1,383,006	963,605	13,644,377	2,868,680	4,163,669	30,229	684,002	368,544
2003	21,322,897	14,444,846	25,857	14,470,703	1,417,851	948,593	14,001,445	2,874,497	4,446,955	31,032	687,131	366,375
2004	22,107,186	15,107,213	30,641	15,137,854	1,519,060	997,478	14,616,272	2,817,785	4,673,129	32,145	687,735	369,097
2005	22,900,627	15,535,754	31,382	15,567,136	1,606,079	1,017,571	14,978,628	2,802,616	5,119,383	33,266	688,409	369,611
2006	23,913,563	16,022,177	26,099	16,048,276	1,645,730	1,022,064	15,424,610	3,152,859	5,336,094	34,693	689,284	370,140
2007	25,064,597	16,517,868	26,350	16,544,218	1,696,694	1,086,414	15,933,938	3,605,546	5,525,113	36,333	689,853	375,638
2008	26,285,896	16,946,660	23,348	16,970,008	1,755,425	1,031,691	16,246,274	3,754,579	6,285,043	38,027	691,239	375,393
2009	26,545,353	16,734,068	22,113	16,756,181	1,738,921	1,020,370	16,037,630	3,640,148	6,867,575	38,356	692,079	365,042
2010	27,277,976	17,262,458	24,699	17,287,157	1,748,577	1,109,045	16,647,625	3,455,761	7,174,590	39,248	695,022	364,504
2011	28,625,557	17,854,619	13,088	17,867,707	1,643,142	1,246,032	17,470,597	3,888,538	7,266,422	40,984	698,452	367,445
2012	29,920,271	18,733,574	22,053	18,755,627	1,711,790	1,318,611	18,362,448	4,159,482	7,398,341	42,751	699,874	378,277
2013	30,241,379	19,057,159	31,178	19,088,337	1,943,174	1,381,119	18,526,282	4,253,132	7,461,965	43,132	701,142	383,446
2014	31,180,586	19,556,976	20,276	19,577,252	2,016,576	1,402,821	18,963,497	4,488,710	7,728,379	44,340	703,209	387,042
2015	32,955,438	20,350,869	15,746	20,366,615	2,058,178	1,482,156	19,790,593	4,793,801	8,371,044	46,906	702,585	399,358
2016	33,656,899	20,762,768	7,570	20,770,338	2,116,961	1,461,649	20,115,026	4,841,751	8,700,122	47,942	702,030	404,487
2017	34,535,108	21,412,359	19,062	21,431,421	2,197,212	1,499,653	20,733,862	5,048,077	8,753,169	49,236	701,422	407,929
2018	35,993,950	22,227,164	22,072	22,249,236	2,298,302	1,585,439	21,536,373	5,268,185	9,189,392	51,249	702,334	410,761
2019	37,447,000	23,209,075	37,348	23,246,423	2,382,922	1,614,195	22,477,696	5,582,411	9,386,893	53,472	700,308	411,724
2020	40,413,254	22,810,582	30,652	22,841,234	2,369,692	1,625,895	22,097,437	5,545,782	12,770,035	59,263	681,929	387,011
2021	42,228,979	23,832,923	32,734	23,865,657	2,527,484	1,689,005	23,027,178	5,601,815	13,599,986	60,597	696,880	402,434
2022	41,991,803	25,050,991	26,227	25,077,218	2,637,027	1,830,649	24,270,840	5,856,141	11,864,822	60,461	694,523	417,833

Personal Income and Employment by Area: Springfield, MO

(Thousands of dollars, except as noted.)

Year	Personal income, total	Derivation of personal income: Earnings by place of work: Nonfarm	Farm	Total	Less: Contributions for government social insurance	Plus: Adjustment for residence	Equals: Net earnings by place of residence	Plus: Dividends, interest, and rent	Plus: Personal current transfer receipts	Per capita personal income (dollars)	Population (persons)	Total employment
1970	701,954	555,435	16,899	572,334	38,236	-15,082	519,016	105,513	77,425	3,332	210,653	97,284
1971	769,880	606,699	17,126	623,825	42,946	-15,894	564,985	117,001	87,894	3,531	218,024	100,075
1972	865,244	684,061	22,901	706,962	50,738	-17,390	638,834	129,024	97,386	3,832	225,777	105,645
1973	977,830	766,252	35,536	801,788	65,543	-19,137	717,108	146,627	114,095	4,227	231,356	110,471
1974	1,062,911	825,668	21,499	847,167	72,837	-19,867	754,463	171,956	136,492	4,513	235,542	109,821
1975	1,175,914	875,606	25,039	900,645	75,374	-20,151	805,120	193,452	177,342	4,971	236,572	107,489
1976	1,332,580	1,014,050	30,991	1,045,041	88,263	-23,170	933,608	212,752	186,220	5,527	241,105	113,331
1977	1,480,066	1,142,472	24,874	1,167,346	99,859	-25,850	1,041,637	243,208	195,221	5,988	247,152	119,130
1978	1,692,043	1,313,407	35,266	1,348,673	118,477	-29,785	1,200,411	276,568	215,064	6,689	252,970	125,953
1979	1,890,822	1,468,989	27,809	1,496,798	137,093	-33,317	1,326,388	319,614	244,820	7,384	256,053	130,864
1980	2,141,937	1,604,901	29,827	1,634,728	149,283	-39,351	1,446,094	399,222	296,621	8,252	259,555	131,378
1981	2,397,612	1,742,939	47,968	1,790,907	174,136	-44,574	1,572,197	485,268	340,147	9,183	261,087	132,649
1982	2,589,572	1,859,877	21,229	1,881,106	189,951	-46,624	1,644,531	577,809	367,232	9,872	262,312	134,650
1983	2,810,000	2,024,641	14,861	2,039,502	206,065	-50,694	1,782,743	628,899	398,358	10,528	266,915	139,611
1984	3,128,084	2,264,931	19,031	2,283,962	236,219	-58,790	1,988,953	724,273	414,858	11,516	271,631	147,471
1985	3,345,986	2,430,795	19,928	2,450,723	258,740	-64,467	2,127,516	771,576	446,894	12,084	276,883	153,042
1986	3,595,279	2,633,717	21,354	2,655,071	282,259	-70,456	2,302,356	814,093	478,830	12,780	281,312	158,763
1987	3,785,432	2,821,909	18,293	2,840,202	297,371	-73,435	2,469,396	814,390	501,646	13,188	287,040	161,311
1988	4,063,976	3,034,576	21,912	3,056,488	329,702	-78,990	2,647,796	883,433	532,747	13,937	291,591	168,214
1989	4,419,896	3,268,638	40,960	3,309,598	357,176	-84,973	2,867,449	968,057	584,390	14,992	294,823	172,646
1990	4,673,459	3,465,471	33,517	3,498,988	390,862	-92,317	3,015,809	1,011,437	646,213	15,560	300,354	177,682
1991	5,041,768	3,716,714	24,062	3,740,776	422,924	-104,684	3,213,168	1,073,783	754,817	16,419	307,066	179,784
1992	5,491,752	4,082,276	19,502	4,101,778	459,246	-118,839	3,523,693	1,150,488	817,571	17,458	314,578	184,602
1993	5,917,387	4,414,247	16,398	4,430,645	497,638	-120,786	3,812,221	1,209,066	896,100	18,294	323,461	194,731
1994	6,388,359	4,794,406	2,814	4,797,220	545,151	-124,912	4,127,157	1,329,390	931,812	19,190	332,908	204,646
1995	6,759,684	5,101,160	76	5,101,236	578,148	-135,449	4,387,639	1,362,619	1,009,426	19,826	340,951	211,443
1996	7,152,788	5,380,337	700	5,381,037	601,224	-147,850	4,631,963	1,439,792	1,081,033	20,653	346,324	215,750
1997	7,581,508	5,660,716	3,120	5,663,836	628,278	-161,621	4,873,937	1,554,666	1,152,905	21,495	352,705	221,150
1998	8,086,973	6,080,850	7,992	6,088,842	668,763	-161,160	5,258,919	1,644,005	1,184,049	22,560	358,461	224,809
1999	8,467,119	6,541,190	-3,519	6,537,671	711,621	-169,978	5,656,072	1,574,988	1,236,059	23,269	363,882	229,377
2000	8,913,564	6,790,875	-2,352	6,788,523	739,911	-180,791	5,867,821	1,703,995	1,341,748	24,096	369,920	234,283
2001	9,691,044	7,387,151	8,422	7,395,573	789,160	-173,953	6,432,460	1,744,976	1,513,608	25,828	375,215	235,317
2002	10,085,837	7,767,933	7,153	7,775,086	823,451	-165,864	6,785,771	1,651,203	1,648,863	26,505	380,529	237,004
2003	10,713,413	8,209,963	20,469	8,230,432	870,720	-161,298	7,198,414	1,761,914	1,753,085	27,680	387,040	241,497
2004	11,413,506	8,825,582	64,496	8,890,078	925,701	-181,345	7,783,032	1,732,292	1,898,182	28,920	394,660	246,954
2005	12,046,066	9,358,861	48,475	9,407,336	995,189	-188,264	8,223,883	1,773,107	2,049,076	29,900	402,883	256,337
2006	12,696,181	9,730,770	22,636	9,753,406	1,052,141	-191,011	8,510,254	1,997,551	2,188,376	30,685	413,765	263,626
2007	13,296,008	9,906,228	6,244	9,912,472	1,099,758	-183,538	8,629,176	2,307,017	2,359,815	31,423	423,127	270,231
2008	14,106,186	9,938,091	14,151	9,952,242	1,131,101	-156,855	8,664,286	2,749,737	2,692,163	32,859	429,289	267,392
2009	13,813,567	9,803,489	-15,238	9,788,251	1,100,622	-197,623	8,490,006	2,377,433	2,946,128	31,812	434,220	258,961
2010	14,066,063	9,915,436	558	9,915,994	1,097,393	-164,949	8,653,652	2,268,023	3,144,388	32,159	437,391	254,751
2011	14,556,537	10,021,024	21,644	10,042,668	1,016,661	-166,190	8,859,817	2,429,169	3,267,551	33,034	440,656	258,558
2012	15,271,547	10,509,739	-4,235	10,505,504	1,053,953	-183,674	9,267,877	2,647,123	3,356,547	34,338	444,738	263,495
2013	15,405,253	10,844,274	1,884	10,846,158	1,224,416	-193,554	9,428,188	2,546,245	3,430,820	34,309	449,014	266,174
2014	16,125,208	11,273,302	73,300	11,346,602	1,283,878	-209,158	9,853,566	2,710,956	3,560,686	35,651	452,305	271,231
2015	17,034,454	11,969,226	25,923	11,995,149	1,368,040	-228,207	10,398,902	2,912,875	3,722,677	37,315	456,506	276,340
2016	17,403,763	12,221,073	-9,716	12,211,357	1,395,963	-256,325	10,559,069	3,009,074	3,835,620	37,915	459,020	278,746
2017	18,271,809	12,789,203	-3,746	12,785,457	1,453,192	-254,550	11,077,715	3,223,489	3,970,605	39,431	463,387	282,955
2018	19,100,203	13,443,115	6,106	13,449,221	1,538,483	-286,909	11,623,829	3,339,661	4,136,713	40,834	467,748	288,410
2019	20,101,065	14,145,632	-161	14,145,471	1,623,707	-372,518	12,149,246	3,602,482	4,349,337	42,575	472,138	290,556
2020	21,704,756	14,501,458	8,573	14,510,031	1,694,867	-439,235	12,375,929	3,900,160	5,428,667	45,566	476,340	288,698
2021	23,230,273	15,803,922	-1,181	15,802,741	1,805,571	-467,704	13,529,466	3,624,515	6,076,292	48,226	481,699	300,280
2022	24,125,631	17,113,309	24,383	17,137,692	1,982,407	-504,357	14,650,928	4,025,974	5,448,729	49,533	487,061	313,802

Personal Income and Employment by Area: Springfield, OH

(Thousands of dollars, except as noted.)

Year	Personal income, total	Derivation of personal income: Earnings by place of work: Nonfarm	Farm	Total	Less: Contributions for government social insurance	Plus: Adjustment for residence	Equals: Net earnings by place of residence	Plus: Dividends, interest, and rent	Plus: Personal current transfer receipts	Per capita personal income (dollars)	Population (persons)	Total employment
1970	624,985	400,905	8,847	409,752	26,066	109,962	493,648	84,677	46,660	3,965	157,639	55,081
1971	701,759	462,524	8,279	470,803	31,270	111,595	551,128	94,620	56,011	4,386	160,007	57,561
1972	735,920	484,167	7,107	491,274	34,671	116,064	572,667	100,481	62,772	4,661	157,903	57,769
1973	802,916	530,319	13,268	543,587	43,832	120,777	620,532	109,245	73,139	5,102	157,377	59,907
1974	860,916	553,163	17,001	570,164	47,645	127,197	649,716	121,058	90,142	5,525	155,828	59,056
1975	916,174	554,517	23,663	578,180	46,403	134,405	666,182	134,128	115,864	5,924	154,645	55,640
1976	989,647	605,349	18,344	623,693	51,447	143,196	715,442	142,575	131,630	6,522	151,748	56,507
1977	1,079,820	680,408	13,125	693,533	58,395	154,529	789,667	158,063	132,090	7,163	150,753	58,103
1978	1,192,800	768,492	13,498	781,990	68,507	165,316	878,799	175,560	138,441	7,916	150,681	60,630
1979	1,306,652	836,865	17,051	853,916	77,425	178,009	954,500	195,138	157,014	8,665	150,789	61,472
1980	1,415,585	864,123	12,589	876,712	78,966	196,323	994,069	229,989	191,527	9,428	150,149	59,719
1981	1,479,809	888,972	946	889,918	86,067	182,324	986,175	269,490	224,144	9,901	149,463	58,312
1982	1,525,589	856,688	3,414	860,102	83,835	188,219	964,486	297,753	263,350	10,321	147,821	54,398
1983	1,612,632	927,370	-3,750	923,620	92,758	189,132	1,019,994	313,018	279,620	10,960	147,142	54,481
1984	1,799,733	1,077,698	12,321	1,090,019	110,922	195,511	1,174,608	343,460	281,665	12,235	147,100	57,693
1985	1,902,982	1,143,469	17,380	1,160,849	120,282	199,632	1,240,199	362,119	300,664	12,939	147,075	59,175
1986	2,002,120	1,227,097	12,845	1,239,942	132,919	198,814	1,305,837	377,084	319,199	13,583	147,403	60,508
1987	2,069,485	1,299,395	16,410	1,315,805	142,395	194,092	1,367,502	373,110	328,873	14,029	147,514	62,208
1988	2,259,262	1,455,756	23,751	1,479,507	165,889	195,611	1,509,229	400,493	349,540	15,266	147,992	63,505
1989	2,384,641	1,498,221	28,153	1,526,374	173,317	205,501	1,558,558	455,048	371,035	16,143	147,720	65,358
1990	2,520,693	1,534,793	26,221	1,561,014	180,739	249,723	1,629,998	474,178	416,517	17,078	147,596	65,336
1991	2,598,569	1,574,084	13,086	1,587,170	190,487	260,969	1,657,652	491,925	448,992	17,588	147,747	64,309
1992	2,748,246	1,708,571	32,470	1,741,041	206,264	240,157	1,774,934	482,907	490,405	18,622	147,584	64,709
1993	2,836,902	1,757,296	20,648	1,777,944	214,469	281,668	1,845,143	483,541	508,218	19,241	147,442	64,554
1994	2,974,570	1,840,584	21,952	1,862,536	225,275	309,166	1,946,427	504,810	523,333	20,186	147,355	65,631
1995	3,125,965	1,916,494	25,776	1,942,270	236,632	339,080	2,044,718	533,541	547,706	21,223	147,289	67,425
1996	3,227,193	1,942,099	23,535	1,965,634	234,640	363,133	2,094,127	558,539	574,527	21,936	147,116	67,183
1997	3,411,991	2,039,770	32,666	2,072,436	238,006	392,247	2,226,677	592,178	593,136	23,327	146,268	67,932
1998	3,584,314	2,242,249	17,576	2,259,825	249,202	338,266	2,348,889	624,402	611,023	24,594	145,742	70,742
1999	3,653,243	2,340,199	10,372	2,350,571	258,742	335,583	2,427,412	605,428	620,403	25,167	145,159	71,410
2000	3,786,151	2,360,232	15,167	2,375,399	252,890	390,869	2,513,378	607,546	665,227	26,183	144,605	72,418
2001	3,837,634	2,362,953	22,811	2,385,764	263,449	394,476	2,516,791	601,238	719,605	26,687	143,803	68,606
2002	3,823,705	2,286,009	16,517	2,302,526	248,826	429,534	2,483,234	578,926	761,545	26,696	143,229	66,994
2003	3,890,508	2,262,006	20,271	2,282,277	249,797	461,251	2,493,731	590,730	806,047	27,445	141,758	66,259
2004	3,963,385	2,290,841	38,501	2,329,342	260,135	500,004	2,569,211	554,095	840,079	28,034	141,380	65,550
2005	4,032,736	2,326,381	34,950	2,361,331	267,364	523,843	2,617,810	534,993	879,933	28,527	141,367	65,003
2006	4,182,877	2,440,036	37,045	2,477,081	282,072	515,256	2,710,265	559,333	913,279	29,736	140,668	65,341
2007	4,298,306	2,437,497	36,426	2,473,923	282,540	519,308	2,710,691	614,576	973,039	30,740	139,829	65,334
2008	4,419,800	2,502,468	27,867	2,530,335	296,253	463,346	2,697,428	644,868	1,077,504	31,705	139,404	64,853
2009	4,394,667	2,434,951	30,216	2,465,167	294,084	415,962	2,587,045	621,784	1,185,838	31,667	138,778	62,362
2010	4,453,523	2,433,192	24,434	2,457,626	287,452	422,178	2,592,352	610,678	1,250,493	32,196	138,326	61,100
2011	4,674,123	2,545,071	34,616	2,579,687	273,480	401,475	2,707,682	669,233	1,297,208	33,848	138,093	62,235
2012	4,706,857	2,602,610	17,285	2,619,895	277,034	421,945	2,764,806	673,093	1,268,958	34,186	137,684	62,297
2013	4,767,909	2,661,063	36,461	2,697,524	304,683	393,063	2,785,904	675,434	1,306,571	34,705	137,382	62,746
2014	4,882,176	2,697,953	13,502	2,711,455	308,936	416,312	2,818,831	702,211	1,361,134	35,564	137,279	63,208
2015	4,989,480	2,727,936	1,789	2,729,725	312,110	457,526	2,875,141	720,592	1,393,747	36,436	136,937	62,538
2016	5,064,544	2,760,155	7,697	2,767,852	322,953	467,014	2,911,913	734,608	1,418,023	37,201	136,140	61,657
2017	5,235,117	2,890,230	13,997	2,904,227	346,645	478,848	3,036,430	749,431	1,449,256	38,441	136,185	62,106
2018	5,367,720	2,956,270	19,272	2,975,542	350,130	490,379	3,115,791	769,619	1,482,310	39,335	136,462	62,097
2019	5,572,427	3,025,969	3,532	3,029,501	361,972	551,728	3,219,257	809,270	1,543,900	40,887	136,290	61,885
2020	6,025,189	3,021,482	36,945	3,058,427	367,260	572,080	3,263,247	792,156	1,969,786	44,342	135,879	59,432
2021	6,426,844	3,244,016	49,162	3,293,178	392,138	551,912	3,452,952	819,295	2,154,597	47,344	135,747	61,029
2022	6,357,462	3,406,307	38,204	3,444,511	428,589	549,942	3,565,864	880,764	1,910,834	47,151	134,831	63,245

Personal Income and Employment by Area: State College, PA

(Thousands of dollars, except as noted.)

Year	Personal income, total	Derivation of personal income: Earnings by place of work: Nonfarm	Farm	Total	Less: Contributions for government social insurance	Plus: Adjustment for residence	Equals: Net earnings by place of residence	Plus: Dividends, interest, and rent	Plus: Personal current transfer receipts	Per capita personal income (dollars)	Population (persons)	Total employment
1970	311,381	273,733	3,052	276,785	18,156	-16,982	241,647	44,711	25,023	3,130	99,495	40,640
1971	338,460	298,151	2,130	300,281	20,603	-19,595	260,083	49,439	28,938	3,342	101,263	41,670
1972	377,376	328,554	2,779	331,333	23,205	-19,625	288,503	55,616	33,257	3,630	103,971	43,904
1973	428,240	368,886	4,835	373,721	29,201	-19,128	325,392	64,283	38,565	4,077	105,034	46,470
1974	475,413	406,481	5,993	412,474	33,778	-22,228	356,468	73,036	45,909	4,404	107,957	47,629
1975	530,466	437,745	4,983	442,728	35,719	-22,626	384,383	83,170	62,913	4,933	107,533	47,752
1976	591,914	490,628	6,455	497,083	41,155	-25,474	430,454	91,650	69,810	5,379	110,048	50,025
1977	658,606	551,484	5,645	557,129	46,198	-29,616	481,315	103,454	73,837	5,832	112,939	51,750
1978	725,643	610,308	3,635	613,943	52,860	-31,860	529,223	116,136	80,284	6,519	111,315	53,267
1979	819,574	683,709	8,034	691,743	61,587	-36,696	593,460	133,094	93,020	7,288	112,459	55,133
1980	909,738	736,592	8,177	744,769	67,291	-41,526	635,952	161,355	112,431	8,041	113,131	56,510
1981	993,200	784,453	9,782	794,235	77,473	-38,351	678,411	193,077	121,712	8,683	114,390	55,794
1982	1,076,427	839,029	7,119	846,148	83,543	-43,274	719,331	222,601	134,495	9,384	114,706	55,674
1983	1,170,932	908,436	3,508	911,944	91,290	-50,043	770,611	248,368	151,953	10,077	116,203	56,956
1984	1,275,014	1,006,173	10,481	1,016,654	105,992	-58,040	852,622	272,895	149,497	11,050	115,390	59,461
1985	1,349,744	1,063,136	9,944	1,073,080	114,232	-60,784	898,064	292,584	159,096	11,579	116,567	60,583
1986	1,434,000	1,140,065	7,686	1,147,751	124,853	-65,640	957,258	314,333	162,409	12,184	117,697	63,132
1987	1,550,966	1,258,169	9,246	1,267,415	136,804	-77,711	1,052,900	323,999	174,067	12,982	119,468	66,110
1988	1,723,106	1,406,658	13,392	1,420,050	159,195	-88,348	1,172,507	360,732	189,867	14,303	120,473	68,862
1989	1,931,952	1,577,695	16,006	1,593,701	174,932	-110,922	1,307,847	420,373	203,732	15,829	122,049	71,931
1990	2,049,748	1,688,862	12,166	1,701,028	188,123	-121,009	1,391,896	433,660	224,192	16,368	125,231	74,221
1991	2,188,658	1,807,604	5,159	1,812,763	203,344	-133,048	1,476,371	458,499	253,788	17,299	126,518	75,902
1992	2,324,516	1,918,670	16,831	1,935,501	213,881	-138,637	1,582,983	467,323	274,210	18,177	127,881	76,642
1993	2,395,477	1,988,224	9,622	1,997,846	223,710	-143,493	1,630,643	477,609	287,225	18,437	129,930	78,826
1994	2,526,396	2,106,336	11,365	2,117,701	238,159	-148,807	1,730,735	513,384	282,277	19,308	130,847	80,708
1995	2,650,935	2,202,699	4,197	2,206,896	249,105	-162,343	1,795,448	554,641	300,846	20,090	131,951	84,000
1996	2,808,385	2,307,483	15,646	2,323,129	254,588	-176,022	1,892,519	591,419	324,447	20,942	134,102	85,877
1997	2,971,246	2,467,545	8,575	2,476,120	271,755	-194,192	2,010,173	620,432	340,641	22,034	134,849	87,914
1998	3,125,738	2,592,692	16,798	2,609,490	278,451	-208,142	2,122,897	643,580	359,261	23,213	134,657	90,593
1999	3,285,664	2,751,243	12,424	2,763,667	291,205	-229,928	2,242,534	676,850	366,280	24,282	135,315	93,184
2000	3,448,218	2,919,438	18,923	2,938,361	306,020	-256,951	2,375,390	677,311	395,517	25,361	135,965	95,959
2001	3,651,147	3,121,884	13,825	3,135,709	318,608	-294,912	2,522,189	683,279	445,679	26,531	137,620	97,495
2002	3,829,686	3,354,604	8,285	3,362,889	339,019	-342,172	2,681,698	666,892	481,096	27,195	140,821	100,679
2003	3,997,453	3,467,537	16,072	3,483,609	343,309	-362,795	2,777,505	722,047	497,901	27,969	142,926	100,897
2004	4,275,932	3,727,077	20,947	3,748,024	364,486	-422,019	2,961,519	792,170	522,243	29,645	144,238	103,013
2005	4,525,293	4,036,132	15,575	4,051,707	392,987	-474,428	3,184,292	789,044	551,957	31,092	145,543	104,577
2006	4,683,624	4,194,719	13,000	4,207,719	410,923	-537,872	3,258,924	829,274	595,426	31,490	148,734	106,043
2007	4,883,723	4,326,286	17,653	4,343,939	426,157	-597,450	3,320,332	916,222	647,169	32,667	149,498	107,665
2008	5,176,577	4,511,267	10,686	4,521,953	443,817	-643,271	3,434,865	987,408	754,304	34,136	151,645	108,931
2009	5,229,393	4,505,317	3,845	4,509,162	449,594	-629,009	3,430,559	985,084	813,750	34,167	153,052	108,936
2010	5,516,890	4,725,330	16,091	4,741,421	466,473	-665,826	3,609,122	1,021,166	886,602	35,787	154,160	108,905
2011	5,816,855	4,921,967	24,893	4,946,860	433,669	-704,986	3,808,205	1,104,296	904,354	37,601	154,698	111,127
2012	6,014,820	5,039,297	29,699	5,068,996	440,697	-706,714	3,921,585	1,203,827	889,408	38,765	155,163	111,231
2013	6,262,001	5,358,918	30,475	5,389,393	517,163	-732,831	4,139,399	1,201,793	920,809	39,821	157,255	113,093
2014	6,535,354	5,636,400	38,477	5,674,877	546,019	-784,342	4,344,516	1,229,851	960,987	41,268	158,365	114,234
2015	6,614,240	5,705,458	17,563	5,723,021	562,390	-810,755	4,349,876	1,260,592	1,003,772	41,635	158,863	115,402
2016	6,876,576	5,882,514	13,030	5,895,544	576,209	-854,882	4,464,453	1,368,448	1,043,675	42,939	160,149	117,483
2017	7,193,446	6,155,460	28,089	6,183,549	613,498	-887,462	4,682,589	1,445,568	1,065,289	44,940	160,067	118,800
2018	7,393,049	6,289,458	14,033	6,303,491	626,032	-911,320	4,766,139	1,491,987	1,134,923	46,187	160,067	116,429
2019	7,652,240	6,377,428	30,063	6,407,491	646,710	-879,870	4,880,911	1,569,973	1,201,356	48,145	158,940	114,741
2020	8,216,113	6,500,519	25,006	6,525,525	657,113	-917,866	4,950,546	1,660,300	1,605,267	52,013	157,962	112,439
2021	8,706,362	6,804,335	32,077	6,836,412	691,929	-931,055	5,213,428	1,751,887	1,741,047	55,107	157,990	111,942
2022	8,663,589	7,039,645	34,558	7,074,203	741,698	-944,344	5,388,161	1,808,209	1,467,219	54,686	158,425	115,964

Personal Income and Employment by Area: Staunton, VA

(Thousands of dollars, except as noted.)

Year	Personal income, total	Derivation of personal income: Earnings by place of work: Nonfarm	Farm	Total	Less: Contributions for government social insurance	Plus: Adjustment for residence	Equals: Net earnings by place of residence	Plus: Dividends, interest, and rent	Plus: Personal current transfer receipts	Per capita personal income (dollars)	Population (persons)	Total employment
1970	298,781	258,450	6,640	265,090	16,761	-8,534	239,795	38,419	20,567	3,488	85,665	41,054
1971	315,732	268,852	6,450	275,302	18,116	-8,684	248,502	42,696	24,534	3,600	87,707	40,415
1972	346,385	294,291	8,144	302,435	21,001	-10,247	271,187	47,384	27,814	3,916	88,454	41,457
1973	392,997	331,105	13,216	344,321	27,310	-11,942	305,069	54,404	33,524	4,461	88,087	43,253
1974	434,939	369,435	9,811	379,246	31,707	-14,974	332,565	62,467	39,907	4,890	88,941	45,156
1975	468,654	378,060	9,283	387,343	31,546	-12,881	342,916	69,658	56,080	5,200	90,122	42,447
1976	519,353	427,717	7,125	434,842	36,294	-14,820	383,728	76,531	59,094	5,750	90,316	44,035
1977	571,105	475,350	1,262	476,612	40,483	-16,042	420,087	85,705	65,313	6,308	90,541	45,245
1978	629,926	522,859	1,061	523,920	45,569	-15,611	462,740	96,678	70,508	6,949	90,646	46,008
1979	698,865	572,543	2,405	574,948	51,953	-11,666	511,329	106,053	81,483	7,689	90,886	46,584
1980	775,283	637,445	971	638,416	58,333	-26,470	553,613	125,076	96,594	8,517	91,031	47,059
1981	857,825	684,397	-160	684,237	67,467	-27,600	589,170	154,605	114,050	9,395	91,309	47,007
1982	910,870	689,957	161	690,118	69,050	-17,642	603,426	180,177	127,267	9,933	91,701	45,701
1983	983,394	731,014	1,047	732,061	73,617	-9,640	648,804	196,338	138,252	10,709	91,828	45,092
1984	1,105,128	807,518	12,191	819,709	83,645	-9,462	726,602	233,045	145,481	12,043	91,764	46,741
1985	1,169,361	842,040	14,542	856,582	88,637	-5,221	762,724	249,817	156,820	12,732	91,846	47,500
1986	1,254,643	894,406	19,478	913,884	96,820	2,176	819,240	268,443	166,960	13,597	92,272	48,454
1987	1,345,276	980,786	17,277	998,063	105,404	5,919	898,578	273,460	173,238	14,352	93,737	51,201
1988	1,470,208	1,073,224	23,989	1,097,213	118,561	12,056	990,708	299,015	180,485	15,473	95,015	52,603
1989	1,607,874	1,135,215	32,172	1,167,387	126,230	22,545	1,063,702	350,361	193,811	16,657	96,527	53,093
1990	1,707,723	1,196,910	35,524	1,232,434	135,108	31,047	1,128,373	370,732	208,618	17,409	98,096	54,582
1991	1,738,388	1,203,780	32,799	1,236,579	136,997	37,309	1,136,891	371,000	230,497	17,540	99,110	53,191
1992	1,828,004	1,261,113	35,482	1,296,595	142,180	44,043	1,198,458	369,126	260,420	18,268	100,067	52,582
1993	1,910,894	1,325,462	32,834	1,358,296	149,081	50,017	1,259,232	378,650	273,012	18,889	101,163	53,648
1994	2,003,764	1,387,261	36,185	1,423,446	155,086	54,859	1,323,219	393,676	286,869	19,594	102,263	54,075
1995	2,096,039	1,421,494	32,039	1,453,533	158,982	59,518	1,354,069	431,183	310,787	20,213	103,697	54,791
1996	2,201,846	1,490,984	32,012	1,522,996	165,164	61,534	1,419,366	456,298	326,182	20,971	104,994	56,133
1997	2,326,538	1,615,870	15,239	1,631,109	177,963	63,009	1,516,155	472,580	337,803	21,951	105,988	58,271
1998	2,500,103	1,742,386	20,070	1,762,456	186,774	73,082	1,648,764	499,925	351,414	23,392	106,879	59,935
1999	2,545,889	1,770,773	16,349	1,787,122	191,532	85,112	1,680,702	495,425	369,762	23,540	108,150	60,837
2000	2,713,979	1,860,722	26,909	1,887,631	198,440	95,503	1,784,694	533,455	395,830	24,869	109,129	61,784
2001	2,773,640	1,844,689	35,872	1,880,561	210,409	118,321	1,788,473	541,698	443,469	25,306	109,602	60,313
2002	2,838,247	1,905,521	20,867	1,926,388	216,880	143,491	1,852,999	511,432	473,816	25,700	110,436	59,699
2003	2,993,214	1,983,518	8,114	1,991,632	223,591	174,565	1,942,606	544,330	506,278	26,833	111,549	59,784
2004	3,305,476	2,227,782	30,201	2,257,983	243,203	175,457	2,190,237	579,583	535,656	29,317	112,751	61,592
2005	3,408,283	2,270,693	39,723	2,310,416	256,684	198,860	2,252,592	568,412	587,279	29,875	114,085	63,085
2006	3,560,369	2,295,256	16,250	2,311,506	264,607	249,645	2,296,544	614,751	649,074	30,624	116,262	63,738
2007	3,938,314	2,518,203	21,765	2,539,968	282,064	283,869	2,541,773	710,625	685,916	33,458	117,708	64,902
2008	4,155,843	2,634,972	16,129	2,651,101	296,264	293,644	2,648,481	738,449	768,913	35,094	118,420	64,776
2009	4,152,060	2,588,012	13,580	2,601,592	293,511	306,760	2,614,841	700,829	836,390	35,011	118,593	62,261
2010	4,233,896	2,629,752	26,670	2,656,422	293,315	309,065	2,672,172	671,067	890,657	35,775	118,347	61,241
2011	4,319,420	2,559,917	43,242	2,603,159	266,995	336,704	2,672,868	724,229	922,323	36,323	118,916	61,545
2012	4,369,979	2,544,796	34,363	2,579,159	269,383	352,797	2,662,573	789,867	917,539	36,809	118,719	61,972
2013	4,433,847	2,623,819	51,110	2,674,929	315,225	354,450	2,714,154	770,953	948,740	37,107	119,487	62,637
2014	4,609,737	2,706,544	60,720	2,767,264	323,024	348,040	2,792,280	818,230	999,227	38,424	119,971	63,199
2015	4,764,038	2,798,950	49,638	2,848,588	333,146	357,419	2,872,861	852,206	1,038,971	39,489	120,642	64,146
2016	4,882,099	2,848,521	25,604	2,874,125	341,772	374,130	2,906,483	902,369	1,073,247	40,165	121,550	65,230
2017	5,083,837	2,943,030	38,671	2,981,701	357,222	389,614	3,014,093	951,961	1,117,783	41,424	122,727	65,079
2018	5,272,600	3,081,501	25,713	3,107,214	374,029	404,748	3,137,933	962,930	1,171,737	42,586	123,812	65,899
2019	5,569,929	3,190,204	23,341	3,213,545	389,945	459,936	3,283,536	1,042,438	1,243,955	44,736	124,506	66,480
2020	5,964,424	3,268,594	1,690	3,270,284	403,607	427,491	3,294,168	1,109,366	1,560,890	47,467	125,654	65,219
2021	6,451,559	3,467,955	53,681	3,521,636	430,086	502,204	3,593,754	1,088,945	1,768,860	51,192	126,027	66,503
2022	6,707,675	3,768,955	132,265	3,901,220	473,889	512,701	3,940,032	1,144,265	1,623,378	52,910	126,776	69,647

Personal Income and Employment by Area: Stockton, CA

(Thousands of dollars, except as noted.)

Year	Personal income, total	Derivation of personal income: Earnings by place of work: Nonfarm	Farm	Total	Less: Contributions for government social insurance	Plus: Adjustment for residence	Equals: Net earnings by place of residence	Plus: Dividends, interest, and rent	Plus: Personal current transfer receipts	Per capita personal income (dollars)	Population (persons)	Total employment
1970	1,278,250	900,345	103,228	1,003,573	56,978	-12,632	933,963	192,386	151,901	4,385	291,488	125,639
1971	1,390,528	983,384	104,415	1,087,799	64,433	-12,392	1,010,974	211,696	167,858	4,695	296,167	127,686
1972	1,528,236	1,075,883	123,592	1,199,475	74,314	-10,252	1,114,909	231,936	181,391	5,090	300,221	132,230
1973	1,704,543	1,175,239	167,599	1,342,838	93,705	-9,771	1,239,362	263,967	201,214	5,609	303,896	135,549
1974	1,936,888	1,307,453	209,817	1,517,270	108,102	-10,577	1,398,591	301,505	236,792	6,316	306,658	139,715
1975	2,130,146	1,419,692	190,228	1,609,920	114,391	-12,728	1,482,801	341,834	305,511	6,877	309,750	141,773
1976	2,320,183	1,578,559	171,009	1,749,568	130,539	-10,572	1,608,457	365,596	346,130	7,304	317,671	144,612
1977	2,556,555	1,742,951	186,272	1,929,223	147,382	-8,841	1,773,000	406,789	376,766	7,968	320,840	147,548
1978	2,868,968	1,993,874	171,395	2,165,269	171,671	-5,743	1,987,855	465,357	415,756	8,624	332,685	153,412
1979	3,245,372	2,235,724	212,841	2,448,565	203,261	-6,497	2,238,807	536,212	470,353	9,591	338,384	162,770
1980	3,692,042	2,398,775	287,853	2,686,628	215,941	-840	2,469,847	660,485	561,710	10,540	350,304	165,174
1981	4,074,063	2,624,958	212,959	2,837,917	257,384	18,131	2,598,664	808,473	666,926	11,271	361,462	167,276
1982	4,345,740	2,755,500	187,057	2,942,557	275,474	35,927	2,703,010	891,754	750,976	11,636	373,479	167,744
1983	4,581,048	2,892,580	123,438	3,016,018	293,830	67,792	2,789,980	976,166	814,902	11,877	385,721	169,304
1984	5,147,670	3,239,905	201,377	3,441,282	341,175	97,843	3,197,950	1,088,264	861,456	12,910	398,731	176,594
1985	5,581,037	3,526,682	203,962	3,730,644	375,824	130,603	3,485,423	1,161,303	934,311	13,415	416,042	181,855
1986	6,024,869	3,857,793	197,371	4,055,164	415,127	161,831	3,801,868	1,222,959	1,000,042	13,986	430,786	186,320
1987	6,537,738	4,226,092	297,989	4,524,081	455,068	198,732	4,267,745	1,224,980	1,045,013	14,668	445,726	195,501
1988	7,075,501	4,552,682	347,160	4,899,842	510,396	246,418	4,635,864	1,308,932	1,130,705	15,478	457,138	205,322
1989	7,661,053	4,871,224	317,769	5,188,993	549,747	302,129	4,941,375	1,484,333	1,235,345	16,410	466,863	209,243
1990	8,145,851	5,199,586	297,728	5,497,314	583,569	356,913	5,270,658	1,506,112	1,369,081	16,826	484,131	214,261
1991	8,548,667	5,477,326	261,403	5,738,729	622,224	376,352	5,492,857	1,528,520	1,527,290	17,351	492,694	216,618
1992	9,144,624	5,723,020	327,706	6,050,726	642,485	424,885	5,833,126	1,521,526	1,789,972	18,279	500,278	212,460
1993	9,536,166	5,943,726	374,500	6,318,226	668,946	452,432	6,101,712	1,566,029	1,868,425	18,832	506,385	214,476
1994	9,896,072	6,198,071	377,300	6,575,371	697,511	474,603	6,352,463	1,651,231	1,892,378	19,320	512,212	220,269
1995	10,220,541	6,312,788	351,001	6,663,789	704,740	546,338	6,505,387	1,737,921	1,977,233	19,734	517,923	224,933
1996	10,793,569	6,546,643	421,581	6,968,224	708,979	624,645	6,883,890	1,832,770	2,076,909	20,573	524,657	228,643
1997	11,485,151	7,121,856	449,033	7,570,889	759,186	700,851	7,512,554	1,904,701	2,067,896	21,592	531,908	233,118
1998	12,209,769	7,604,021	375,012	7,979,033	791,859	833,945	8,021,119	1,971,267	2,217,383	22,600	540,257	238,983
1999	13,053,550	8,134,641	406,711	8,541,352	851,232	990,100	8,680,220	2,049,054	2,324,276	23,630	552,424	249,510
2000	14,217,941	8,887,001	382,967	9,269,968	919,591	1,284,022	9,634,399	2,186,800	2,396,742	25,037	567,885	254,521
2001	15,503,288	9,894,834	423,307	10,318,141	1,061,648	1,305,521	10,562,014	2,226,733	2,714,541	26,223	591,207	260,519
2002	16,207,947	10,529,318	417,847	10,947,165	1,145,542	1,332,915	11,134,538	2,162,745	2,910,664	26,612	609,041	266,763
2003	17,311,544	11,270,835	505,506	11,776,341	1,243,337	1,412,588	11,945,592	2,250,448	3,115,504	27,620	626,778	274,432
2004	18,460,590	12,062,755	572,192	12,634,947	1,372,970	1,592,402	12,854,379	2,315,575	3,290,636	28,715	642,898	279,729
2005	19,508,041	12,731,064	582,890	13,313,954	1,439,229	1,836,554	13,711,279	2,351,364	3,445,398	29,693	656,985	283,432
2006	20,601,739	13,246,680	441,107	13,687,787	1,449,876	2,036,786	14,274,697	2,611,969	3,715,073	31,082	662,812	287,117
2007	21,354,780	13,177,197	597,740	13,774,937	1,448,660	2,103,630	14,429,907	2,961,780	3,963,093	31,964	668,080	293,369
2008	21,496,351	12,920,299	533,823	13,454,122	1,461,391	1,951,723	13,944,454	3,103,399	4,448,498	32,003	671,692	287,006
2009	21,657,011	12,904,151	564,522	13,468,673	1,450,058	1,829,118	13,847,733	2,876,280	4,932,998	31,955	677,736	275,703
2010	22,406,240	13,431,750	453,829	13,885,579	1,431,595	1,654,372	14,108,356	2,755,506	5,542,378	32,597	687,381	268,654
2011	22,918,431	13,324,759	561,792	13,886,551	1,316,994	1,761,526	14,331,083	3,018,196	5,569,152	32,947	695,611	269,952
2012	23,605,656	13,455,436	929,246	14,384,682	1,337,590	1,690,423	14,737,515	3,193,332	5,674,809	33,631	701,892	276,821
2013	24,541,217	13,906,286	1,054,615	14,960,901	1,541,977	2,052,225	15,471,149	3,189,415	5,880,653	34,791	705,382	285,249
2014	25,983,911	14,407,735	1,154,235	15,561,970	1,603,600	2,134,721	16,093,091	3,517,928	6,372,892	36,290	716,006	294,194
2015	27,994,154	15,822,018	987,550	16,809,568	1,738,476	2,147,142	17,218,234	3,784,509	6,991,411	38,463	727,828	310,215
2016	29,427,807	16,563,553	884,676	17,448,229	1,834,808	2,723,828	18,337,249	3,895,134	7,195,424	39,777	739,814	319,425
2017	30,735,741	17,641,056	899,296	18,540,352	1,948,564	3,016,410	19,608,198	4,104,304	7,023,239	40,888	751,714	330,628
2018	32,261,357	18,596,688	732,606	19,329,294	2,070,452	3,443,075	20,701,917	4,152,802	7,406,638	42,320	762,314	339,726
2019	34,952,093	19,639,353	738,714	20,378,067	2,206,176	4,341,698	22,513,589	4,476,716	7,961,788	45,239	772,611	345,455
2020	40,056,124	20,828,224	726,187	21,554,411	2,342,608	4,786,721	23,998,524	4,573,119	11,484,481	51,317	780,558	346,508
2021	43,999,624	23,179,577	730,220	23,909,797	2,594,153	5,259,721	26,575,365	4,970,066	12,454,193	55,827	788,140	361,661
2022	42,979,635	24,739,830	680,010	25,419,840	2,871,881	4,873,987	27,421,946	5,297,790	10,259,899	54,183	793,229	384,431

Personal Income and Employment by Area: Sumter, SC

(Thousands of dollars, except as noted.)

Year	Personal income, total	Derivation of personal income: Earnings by place of work: Nonfarm	Farm	Total	Less: Contributions for government social insurance	Plus: Adjustment for residence	Equals: Net earnings by place of residence	Plus: Dividends, interest, and rent	Plus: Personal current transfer receipts	Per capita personal income (dollars)	Population (persons)	Total employment
1970	288,705	225,589	15,939	241,528	14,834	-10,893	215,801	47,311	25,593	2,740	105,380	45,884
1971	312,582	245,695	13,734	259,429	17,074	-9,707	232,648	50,204	29,730	2,899	107,811	46,270
1972	350,446	273,851	16,753	290,604	19,509	-9,678	261,417	55,546	33,483	3,170	110,535	46,598
1973	385,022	298,268	16,734	315,002	23,639	-8,736	282,627	62,218	40,177	3,526	109,200	47,704
1974	437,226	318,084	30,941	349,025	26,378	-5,921	316,726	69,162	51,338	4,002	109,260	47,196
1975	476,829	344,569	23,334	367,903	28,848	-6,487	332,568	77,433	66,828	4,266	111,779	46,882
1976	520,996	383,638	19,032	402,670	33,196	-4,086	365,388	82,548	73,060	4,628	112,566	47,015
1977	563,567	420,271	14,060	434,331	36,218	-2,462	395,651	92,434	75,482	4,957	113,702	47,979
1978	639,625	478,950	12,711	491,661	41,782	-1,990	447,889	108,308	83,428	5,593	114,367	49,636
1979	707,084	519,501	18,167	537,668	47,197	1,158	491,629	119,329	96,126	6,117	115,598	50,160
1980	768,190	561,696	-1,706	559,990	50,495	4,176	513,671	137,261	117,258	6,607	116,269	49,762
1981	855,825	608,059	10,207	618,266	58,553	4,836	564,549	157,281	133,995	7,244	118,139	49,981
1982	926,971	652,736	12,842	665,578	62,761	1,394	604,211	179,010	143,750	7,745	119,679	49,371
1983	998,771	707,881	6,815	714,696	69,721	3,648	648,623	194,765	155,383	8,301	120,324	50,323
1984	1,128,638	781,005	36,227	817,232	79,417	5,512	743,327	220,184	165,127	9,236	122,199	51,971
1985	1,203,066	842,688	25,702	868,390	86,925	4,639	786,104	238,298	178,664	9,703	123,987	52,701
1986	1,258,571	890,474	12,029	902,503	94,334	9,409	817,578	252,912	188,081	10,014	125,682	52,902
1987	1,347,387	952,577	24,969	977,546	100,499	12,300	889,347	266,358	191,682	10,598	127,135	53,931
1988	1,448,462	1,025,790	30,820	1,056,610	113,096	14,455	957,969	286,725	203,768	11,322	127,935	55,362
1989	1,583,187	1,087,280	31,196	1,118,476	122,577	19,875	1,015,774	327,025	240,388	12,144	130,370	56,381
1990	1,735,847	1,180,770	23,291	1,204,061	136,028	61,496	1,129,529	344,142	262,176	13,375	129,782	58,796
1991	1,792,935	1,195,550	33,893	1,229,443	140,446	39,863	1,128,860	357,850	306,225	13,633	131,510	57,361
1992	1,922,704	1,268,101	32,679	1,300,780	148,668	59,705	1,211,817	367,493	343,394	14,541	132,230	58,068
1993	1,998,823	1,355,115	18,475	1,373,590	161,091	28,702	1,241,201	394,508	363,114	14,847	134,631	60,504
1994	2,137,132	1,404,308	39,330	1,443,638	167,870	44,387	1,320,155	414,677	402,300	15,788	135,364	61,224
1995	2,240,971	1,488,793	28,422	1,517,215	177,565	36,423	1,376,073	440,482	424,416	16,467	136,090	63,353
1996	2,367,058	1,547,455	50,829	1,598,284	182,040	36,113	1,452,357	461,980	452,721	17,249	137,229	63,925
1997	2,490,396	1,646,370	39,435	1,685,805	192,783	33,060	1,526,082	488,494	475,820	18,147	137,231	65,254
1998	2,596,189	1,732,622	17,562	1,750,184	203,929	25,635	1,571,890	523,316	500,983	18,899	137,375	66,005
1999	2,701,877	1,793,258	23,129	1,816,387	209,343	53,319	1,660,363	515,142	526,372	19,711	137,074	66,359
2000	2,840,055	1,893,833	30,833	1,924,666	220,620	34,414	1,738,460	540,804	560,791	20,681	137,330	67,459
2001	2,929,315	1,906,551	49,985	1,956,536	226,029	44,034	1,774,541	533,909	620,865	21,302	137,516	65,436
2002	3,059,205	1,994,984	12,566	2,007,550	235,780	46,266	1,818,036	561,562	679,607	22,092	138,474	65,234
2003	3,203,597	2,095,902	30,570	2,126,472	246,481	51,298	1,931,289	562,122	710,186	23,145	138,417	64,934
2004	3,402,445	2,210,595	46,053	2,256,648	261,331	59,297	2,054,614	570,623	777,208	24,352	139,721	66,039
2005	3,518,284	2,269,364	43,408	2,312,772	267,859	72,799	2,117,712	568,558	832,014	25,143	139,929	66,575
2006	3,698,373	2,364,121	28,162	2,392,283	286,214	87,716	2,193,785	616,534	888,054	26,408	140,047	66,592
2007	3,861,761	2,429,870	26,924	2,456,794	293,667	102,332	2,265,459	655,983	940,319	27,532	140,264	66,980
2008	4,009,355	2,402,673	23,001	2,425,674	294,126	112,741	2,244,289	699,814	1,065,252	28,367	141,338	65,286
2009	3,954,605	2,330,683	20,677	2,351,360	288,951	94,259	2,156,668	647,005	1,150,932	27,860	141,946	62,295
2010	4,090,427	2,418,620	19,681	2,438,301	298,536	63,211	2,202,976	646,743	1,240,708	28,711	142,470	62,156
2011	4,303,288	2,551,191	21,785	2,572,976	284,731	40,072	2,328,317	728,334	1,246,637	30,392	141,595	64,219
2012	4,538,447	2,796,534	49,113	2,845,647	307,364	-5,276	2,533,007	750,475	1,254,965	32,074	141,501	65,001
2013	4,568,172	2,831,556	77,742	2,909,298	346,151	-12,439	2,550,708	724,641	1,292,823	32,399	140,999	65,033
2014	4,701,480	2,914,341	13,535	2,927,876	354,559	-9,905	2,563,412	779,666	1,358,402	33,447	140,564	65,597
2015	4,801,859	2,943,696	18,567	2,962,263	360,202	2,287	2,604,348	775,674	1,421,837	34,393	139,619	66,173
2016	4,921,123	2,993,668	19,335	3,013,003	367,263	3,734	2,649,474	816,867	1,454,782	35,293	139,438	65,571
2017	5,050,704	3,117,896	25,004	3,142,900	383,472	1,974	2,761,402	807,156	1,482,146	36,535	138,244	66,380
2018	5,219,884	3,251,393	7,778	3,259,171	401,841	-1,721	2,855,609	819,022	1,545,253	37,944	137,567	67,605
2019	5,365,055	3,335,246	6,208	3,341,454	411,978	7,882	2,937,358	805,751	1,621,946	39,049	137,393	67,267
2020	5,778,966	3,408,678	8,672	3,417,350	422,323	-5,995	2,989,032	815,765	1,974,169	42,396	136,309	66,668
2021	6,300,157	3,666,877	47,424	3,714,301	450,735	-2,608	3,260,958	817,522	2,221,677	46,391	135,806	68,404
2022	6,245,402	3,796,232	27,280	3,823,512	480,975	14,943	3,357,480	849,593	2,038,329	46,288	134,925	69,416

Personal Income and Employment by Area: Syracuse, NY

(Thousands of dollars, except as noted.)

Year	Personal income, total	Derivation of personal income: Earnings by place of work: Nonfarm	Farm	Total	Less: Contributions for government social insurance	Plus: Adjustment for residence	Equals: Net earnings by place of residence	Plus: Dividends, interest, and rent	Plus: Personal current transfer receipts	Per capita personal income (dollars)	Population (persons)	Total employment
1970	2,562,246	2,134,132	25,826	2,159,958	159,044	-33,036	1,967,878	340,052	254,316	4,019	637,540	270,461
1971	2,778,329	2,306,288	24,874	2,331,162	177,611	-38,056	2,115,495	363,062	299,772	4,341	640,019	274,853
1972	2,988,887	2,511,740	22,314	2,534,054	203,519	-42,388	2,288,147	387,583	313,157	4,657	641,826	278,450
1973	3,249,712	2,745,827	28,770	2,774,597	257,308	-45,379	2,471,910	429,851	347,951	5,059	642,407	289,236
1974	3,554,107	2,981,044	26,392	3,007,436	287,568	-51,434	2,668,434	483,366	402,307	5,527	642,995	294,880
1975	3,809,864	3,033,376	21,614	3,054,990	287,290	-49,100	2,718,600	530,198	561,066	5,897	646,105	283,301
1976	4,082,945	3,304,762	22,888	3,327,650	320,529	-54,277	2,952,844	555,628	574,473	6,305	647,543	286,493
1977	4,481,088	3,685,085	16,810	3,701,895	355,778	-64,346	3,281,771	609,125	590,192	6,924	647,200	295,258
1978	4,896,592	4,067,724	24,111	4,091,835	402,548	-69,348	3,619,939	645,953	630,700	7,570	646,806	304,167
1979	5,464,243	4,573,614	31,021	4,604,635	468,697	-82,013	4,053,925	727,520	682,798	8,476	644,646	311,104
1980	6,098,541	4,961,922	31,312	4,993,234	507,669	-88,758	4,396,807	896,009	805,725	9,488	642,764	307,311
1981	6,708,471	5,373,948	35,167	5,409,115	586,156	-106,136	4,716,823	1,085,010	906,638	10,470	640,720	308,076
1982	7,330,243	5,798,723	28,946	5,827,669	637,151	-127,880	5,062,638	1,248,904	1,018,701	11,446	640,442	308,937
1983	7,945,109	6,324,443	21,258	6,345,701	698,934	-151,038	5,495,729	1,374,036	1,075,344	12,357	642,984	314,098
1984	8,856,653	7,123,028	30,728	7,153,756	805,381	-177,606	6,170,769	1,544,393	1,141,491	13,700	646,469	327,908
1985	9,443,525	7,686,438	34,666	7,721,104	878,188	-200,342	6,642,574	1,596,417	1,204,534	14,520	650,383	340,140
1986	9,962,856	8,096,865	40,575	8,137,440	935,677	-208,608	6,993,155	1,683,188	1,286,513	15,360	648,635	346,353
1987	10,240,136	8,367,092	43,463	8,410,555	957,853	-210,060	7,242,642	1,685,213	1,312,281	15,834	646,725	348,298
1988	11,019,791	9,056,761	33,579	9,090,340	1,056,380	-228,915	7,805,045	1,815,929	1,398,817	16,970	649,352	359,990
1989	12,106,544	9,786,475	46,201	9,832,676	1,126,183	-257,955	8,448,538	2,138,444	1,519,562	18,488	654,842	367,410
1990	12,789,928	10,350,434	47,141	10,397,575	1,142,373	-297,707	8,957,495	2,174,488	1,657,945	19,335	661,505	374,714
1991	13,071,305	10,456,521	39,919	10,496,440	1,182,353	-302,545	9,011,542	2,214,395	1,845,368	19,638	665,618	368,948
1992	13,793,087	11,070,719	38,854	11,109,573	1,228,735	-324,647	9,556,191	2,173,587	2,063,309	20,633	668,488	367,160
1993	14,069,710	11,240,892	49,706	11,290,598	1,254,904	-333,319	9,702,375	2,208,705	2,158,630	20,990	670,309	367,707
1994	14,400,172	11,466,575	39,718	11,506,293	1,295,586	-342,938	9,867,769	2,255,178	2,277,225	21,573	667,499	369,006
1995	14,852,316	11,663,818	27,362	11,691,180	1,319,060	-359,649	10,012,471	2,414,407	2,425,438	22,355	664,389	365,912
1996	15,172,441	11,828,229	41,231	11,869,460	1,316,544	-391,843	10,161,073	2,482,358	2,529,010	22,975	660,384	367,025
1997	15,776,203	12,292,180	24,415	12,316,595	1,350,626	-389,595	10,576,374	2,668,669	2,531,160	24,077	655,229	366,983
1998	16,530,515	12,783,876	47,366	12,831,242	1,386,050	-366,844	11,078,348	2,760,746	2,691,421	25,373	651,499	366,462
1999	17,258,208	13,574,521	54,396	13,628,917	1,431,954	-385,205	11,811,758	2,723,711	2,722,739	26,539	650,297	374,195
2000	18,200,155	14,260,420	59,220	14,319,640	1,496,406	-362,613	12,460,621	2,866,804	2,872,730	28,002	649,961	378,485
2001	18,274,826	14,330,667	72,027	14,402,694	1,565,740	-371,287	12,465,667	2,732,026	3,077,133	28,085	650,697	376,302
2002	18,695,124	14,828,071	48,830	14,876,901	1,635,287	-394,455	12,847,159	2,556,535	3,291,430	28,663	652,241	371,459
2003	19,409,355	15,313,556	54,638	15,368,194	1,692,009	-399,526	13,276,659	2,681,450	3,451,246	29,628	655,091	372,364
2004	20,249,431	16,097,082	68,326	16,165,408	1,766,704	-367,405	14,031,299	2,567,986	3,650,146	30,861	656,149	375,378
2005	20,791,068	16,484,529	66,203	16,550,732	1,838,493	-389,770	14,322,469	2,683,173	3,785,426	31,741	655,021	379,601
2006	21,743,238	17,219,043	52,102	17,271,145	1,912,877	-416,946	14,941,322	2,807,136	3,994,780	33,180	655,321	380,467
2007	23,066,901	18,053,918	89,678	18,143,596	1,987,409	-428,518	15,727,669	3,171,791	4,167,441	35,152	656,209	386,624
2008	24,075,251	18,275,503	92,099	18,367,602	2,047,324	-404,594	15,915,684	3,519,358	4,640,209	36,538	658,913	386,943
2009	24,378,179	18,316,104	46,807	18,362,911	2,029,288	-375,125	15,958,498	3,297,852	5,121,829	36,889	660,857	377,832
2010	25,179,737	18,835,421	82,648	18,918,069	2,051,579	-325,188	16,541,302	3,149,126	5,489,309	37,949	663,515	373,992
2011	26,109,920	19,112,405	103,986	19,216,391	1,878,936	-332,929	17,004,526	3,485,597	5,619,797	39,294	664,478	377,100
2012	26,927,013	19,742,461	95,274	19,837,735	1,922,739	-322,853	17,592,143	3,702,955	5,631,915	40,523	664,482	379,081
2013	27,014,706	20,058,725	125,407	20,184,132	2,202,612	-296,320	17,685,200	3,610,772	5,718,734	40,505	666,945	380,073
2014	27,720,441	20,399,965	138,103	20,538,068	2,280,696	-280,294	17,977,078	3,842,354	5,901,009	41,572	666,806	381,203
2015	28,985,467	21,147,278	80,635	21,227,913	2,367,970	-285,116	18,574,827	4,183,765	6,226,875	43,533	665,829	382,321
2016	29,387,322	21,457,340	62,323	21,519,663	2,409,783	-298,949	18,810,931	4,260,607	6,315,784	44,264	663,914	383,335
2017	30,828,342	22,382,599	95,621	22,478,220	2,510,009	-346,285	19,621,926	4,494,930	6,711,486	46,554	662,203	382,388
2018	31,846,451	23,444,914	67,361	23,512,275	2,585,243	-361,316	20,565,716	4,665,674	6,615,061	48,030	663,047	387,243
2019	33,168,698	24,102,164	118,866	24,221,030	2,659,139	-370,356	21,191,535	4,862,311	7,114,852	50,054	662,656	388,244
2020	36,312,633	24,471,666	105,043	24,576,709	2,656,965	-369,361	21,550,383	4,970,704	9,791,546	55,046	659,683	365,261
2021	38,206,198	25,893,347	122,425	26,015,772	2,886,448	-356,127	22,773,197	5,312,173	10,120,828	58,098	657,615	373,064
2022	37,633,655	27,054,586	190,131	27,244,717	3,115,397	-385,348	23,743,972	5,397,074	8,492,609	57,576	653,633	388,377

Personal Income and Employment by Area: Tallahassee, FL

(Thousands of dollars, except as noted.)

Year	Personal income, total	Derivation of personal income								Per capita personal income (dollars)	Population (persons)	Total employment
		Earnings by place of work			Less: Contributions for government social insurance	Plus: Adjustment for residence	Equals: Net earnings by place of residence	Plus: Dividends, interest, and rent	Plus: Personal current transfer receipts			
		Nonfarm	Farm	Total								
1970	491,814	399,417	18,424	417,841	23,566	-13,928	380,347	75,481	35,986	3,107	158,300	68,040
1971	567,235	463,338	17,662	481,000	28,966	-15,277	436,757	87,983	42,495	3,438	165,004	71,779
1972	669,418	551,421	16,968	568,389	35,850	-17,809	514,730	103,944	50,744	3,855	173,644	77,730
1973	785,602	645,787	20,466	666,253	48,662	-19,745	597,846	125,713	62,043	4,329	181,470	83,485
1974	884,309	717,696	18,682	736,378	56,903	-20,902	658,573	149,911	75,825	4,673	189,245	86,579
1975	977,884	779,457	17,403	796,860	62,054	-21,220	713,586	166,058	98,240	5,229	186,999	87,284
1976	1,063,676	845,362	18,407	863,769	70,559	-21,125	772,085	181,158	110,433	5,612	189,529	88,025
1977	1,160,438	924,104	12,405	936,509	78,583	-20,235	837,691	200,799	121,948	5,960	194,690	90,724
1978	1,304,352	1,037,771	16,526	1,054,297	92,922	-21,553	939,822	230,728	133,802	6,519	200,091	94,497
1979	1,485,629	1,178,811	20,378	1,199,189	111,764	-23,534	1,063,891	266,047	155,691	7,279	204,111	99,612
1980	1,705,169	1,322,513	19,914	1,342,427	122,191	-24,934	1,195,302	323,208	186,659	7,999	213,167	104,810
1981	1,931,577	1,482,934	15,531	1,498,465	148,207	-26,752	1,323,506	394,139	213,932	8,870	217,765	107,359
1982	2,106,884	1,593,554	23,265	1,616,819	162,314	-30,299	1,424,206	448,818	233,860	9,508	221,584	108,947
1983	2,329,007	1,755,153	24,597	1,779,750	177,507	-32,848	1,569,395	502,272	257,340	10,343	225,185	112,794
1984	2,550,855	1,928,535	26,125	1,954,660	198,603	-34,805	1,721,252	554,578	275,025	11,120	229,399	117,358
1985	2,770,289	2,104,870	26,093	2,130,963	219,344	-38,678	1,872,941	599,256	298,092	11,884	233,106	123,662
1986	3,076,243	2,365,868	29,076	2,394,944	250,568	-43,390	2,100,986	659,342	315,915	13,044	235,840	131,759
1987	3,353,746	2,614,843	29,532	2,644,375	270,086	-50,974	2,323,315	694,842	335,589	13,914	241,026	135,906
1988	3,734,319	2,933,807	34,484	2,968,291	316,602	-55,746	2,595,943	770,309	368,067	15,134	246,756	143,371
1989	4,165,904	3,211,390	39,370	3,250,760	345,898	-62,431	2,842,431	898,876	424,597	16,419	253,724	150,382
1990	4,540,585	3,523,250	37,538	3,560,788	374,654	-68,203	3,117,931	956,364	466,290	17,384	261,192	156,015
1991	4,834,574	3,762,671	47,278	3,809,949	401,890	-75,814	3,332,245	973,956	528,373	17,806	271,509	158,565
1992	5,130,769	4,020,962	47,474	4,068,436	429,303	-81,776	3,557,357	969,980	603,432	18,588	276,025	161,167
1993	5,470,992	4,295,830	47,845	4,343,675	453,609	-88,104	3,801,962	1,028,078	640,952	19,236	284,421	166,471
1994	5,831,309	4,590,133	45,320	4,635,453	489,181	-98,756	4,047,516	1,103,595	680,198	19,922	292,713	172,345
1995	6,332,398	4,924,978	46,894	4,971,872	523,726	-107,498	4,340,648	1,250,821	740,929	21,210	298,563	179,081
1996	6,669,704	5,211,643	44,556	5,256,199	551,491	-117,510	4,587,198	1,310,939	771,567	22,016	302,943	181,936
1997	7,018,388	5,495,050	53,182	5,548,232	583,043	-127,289	4,837,900	1,375,388	805,100	22,756	308,414	188,091
1998	7,561,911	5,948,879	54,853	6,003,732	629,147	-144,063	5,230,522	1,493,450	837,939	24,184	312,685	191,646
1999	7,993,556	6,376,036	58,579	6,434,615	673,917	-159,105	5,601,593	1,511,928	880,035	25,230	316,825	195,883
2000	8,414,598	6,705,268	55,660	6,760,928	707,286	-169,503	5,884,139	1,594,433	936,026	26,186	321,336	201,044
2001	9,035,083	7,226,567	59,649	7,286,216	755,723	-184,527	6,345,966	1,651,946	1,037,171	27,853	324,386	204,473
2002	9,280,577	7,450,352	53,594	7,503,946	781,085	-194,888	6,527,973	1,614,688	1,137,916	28,300	327,940	198,344
2003	9,698,120	7,696,262	44,772	7,741,034	805,777	-206,483	6,728,774	1,748,162	1,221,184	29,011	334,289	200,992
2004	10,300,911	8,126,676	48,904	8,175,580	854,413	-214,824	7,106,343	1,920,142	1,274,426	30,370	339,179	205,902
2005	10,911,242	8,531,982	48,919	8,580,901	902,905	-231,271	7,446,725	2,071,367	1,393,150	31,695	344,257	212,087
2006	11,431,634	8,912,619	49,515	8,962,134	954,668	-250,389	7,757,077	2,221,168	1,453,389	32,608	350,580	216,900
2007	11,998,844	9,285,719	38,400	9,324,119	1,001,027	-266,815	8,056,277	2,367,252	1,575,315	33,577	357,357	220,387
2008	12,286,776	9,319,367	44,874	9,364,241	1,015,299	-286,766	8,062,176	2,400,939	1,823,661	34,013	361,238	217,751
2009	12,124,303	9,098,132	39,166	9,137,298	999,783	-260,420	7,877,095	2,292,921	1,954,287	33,246	364,690	210,695
2010	12,793,448	9,272,453	45,117	9,317,570	1,002,386	-264,434	8,050,750	2,559,973	2,182,725	34,649	369,235	209,419
2011	13,479,239	9,310,968	39,299	9,350,267	894,029	-250,627	8,205,611	2,981,026	2,292,602	36,361	370,711	211,123
2012	13,352,304	9,588,426	55,299	9,643,725	918,713	-242,567	8,482,445	2,637,463	2,232,396	35,673	374,295	210,404
2013	13,059,743	9,503,126	52,058	9,555,184	1,042,630	-228,260	8,284,294	2,461,038	2,314,411	35,127	371,787	211,738
2014	13,731,806	9,898,177	59,518	9,957,695	1,092,287	-234,255	8,631,153	2,644,302	2,456,351	36,764	373,517	217,290
2015	14,205,240	10,166,022	69,356	10,235,378	1,119,080	-240,597	8,875,701	2,733,444	2,596,095	37,848	375,326	219,421
2016	14,725,366	10,504,952	52,229	10,557,181	1,157,248	-248,842	9,151,091	2,888,760	2,685,515	39,168	375,951	223,618
2017	15,433,218	10,982,429	61,598	11,044,027	1,216,383	-257,692	9,569,952	3,049,110	2,814,156	40,621	379,935	227,680
2018	16,210,788	11,495,396	56,637	11,552,033	1,279,473	-285,690	9,986,870	3,186,161	3,037,757	42,590	380,627	235,304
2019	17,078,135	12,039,333	86,973	12,126,306	1,357,310	-304,047	10,464,949	3,402,012	3,211,174	44,586	383,035	238,166
2020	18,307,705	12,339,039	136,387	12,475,426	1,408,604	-319,879	10,746,943	3,435,480	4,125,282	47,474	385,635	234,985
2021	20,211,955	13,419,155	325,590	13,744,745	1,516,805	-380,776	11,847,164	3,552,415	4,812,376	52,041	388,385	243,187
2022	20,471,919	14,465,599	207,355	14,672,954	1,666,206	-388,308	12,618,440	3,681,899	4,171,580	52,359	390,992	254,083

Personal Income and Employment by Area: Tampa-St. Petersburg-Clearwater, FL

(Thousands of dollars, except as noted.)

Year	Personal income, total	Derivation of personal income: Earnings by place of work			Derivation of personal income					Per capita personal income (dollars)	Population (persons)	Total employment
		Nonfarm	Farm	Total	Less: Contributions for government social insurance	Plus: Adjustment for residence	Equals: Net earnings by place of residence	Plus: Dividends, interest, and rent	Plus: Personal current transfer receipts			
1970	4,329,776	2,829,055	43,720	2,872,775	186,697	25,929	2,712,007	1,063,264	554,505	3,875	1,117,227	439,739
1971	4,872,882	3,171,668	50,731	3,222,399	217,856	28,540	3,033,083	1,184,145	655,654	4,127	1,180,716	460,528
1972	5,671,208	3,768,453	64,599	3,833,052	271,412	32,708	3,594,348	1,316,842	760,018	4,530	1,251,917	509,052
1973	6,638,176	4,446,246	72,983	4,519,229	369,372	42,299	4,192,156	1,525,278	920,742	4,978	1,333,538	565,986
1974	7,488,493	4,931,707	65,798	4,997,505	427,349	48,861	4,619,017	1,786,106	1,083,370	5,370	1,394,490	581,774
1975	8,233,437	5,176,323	78,963	5,255,286	438,549	52,743	4,869,480	1,986,268	1,377,689	5,774	1,425,848	564,107
1976	8,950,891	5,602,729	84,829	5,687,558	481,335	55,520	5,261,743	2,169,230	1,519,918	6,163	1,452,426	567,011
1977	10,169,956	6,410,543	91,282	6,501,825	544,288	65,375	6,022,912	2,478,619	1,668,425	6,880	1,478,254	597,815
1978	11,705,963	7,455,204	102,214	7,557,418	649,760	74,814	6,982,472	2,871,616	1,851,875	7,713	1,517,764	644,879
1979	13,482,811	8,565,514	103,451	8,668,965	783,780	86,492	7,971,677	3,377,135	2,133,999	8,569	1,573,352	679,429
1980	15,926,398	9,767,227	137,091	9,904,318	903,469	97,561	9,098,410	4,293,108	2,534,880	9,789	1,626,975	717,538
1981	18,401,947	11,000,672	113,744	11,114,416	1,099,800	92,195	10,106,811	5,339,780	2,955,356	10,970	1,677,405	753,441
1982	19,998,255	11,799,994	159,858	11,959,852	1,223,135	70,923	10,807,640	5,847,016	3,343,599	11,608	1,722,726	776,167
1983	22,293,172	13,342,460	199,741	13,542,201	1,389,413	44,329	12,197,117	6,461,720	3,634,335	12,564	1,774,374	821,026
1984	24,822,375	15,127,525	161,407	15,288,932	1,623,627	19,202	13,684,507	7,342,635	3,795,233	13,596	1,825,777	883,678
1985	27,115,725	16,665,179	152,397	16,817,576	1,820,009	-1,719	14,995,848	8,039,128	4,080,749	14,446	1,877,018	932,733
1986	29,216,547	18,123,147	159,092	18,282,239	2,026,789	-29,924	16,225,526	8,606,281	4,384,740	15,189	1,923,591	969,125
1987	30,972,659	19,790,203	152,513	19,942,716	2,189,286	-56,128	17,697,302	8,649,608	4,625,749	15,745	1,967,197	983,589
1988	33,811,978	21,736,261	191,645	21,927,906	2,476,426	-89,113	19,362,367	9,446,408	5,003,203	16,859	2,005,545	1,029,281
1989	37,581,126	23,331,506	194,477	23,525,983	2,694,959	-109,553	20,721,471	11,254,366	5,605,289	18,428	2,039,321	1,052,726
1990	39,448,016	24,859,946	174,027	25,033,973	2,834,593	-158,490	22,040,890	11,360,463	6,046,663	18,985	2,077,857	1,074,649
1991	40,617,998	25,780,658	196,034	25,976,692	2,967,958	-172,166	22,836,568	11,109,393	6,672,037	19,241	2,110,974	1,060,636
1992	42,668,815	27,741,661	198,060	27,939,721	3,181,097	-233,452	24,525,172	10,629,236	7,514,407	19,983	2,135,204	1,062,769
1993	45,338,364	29,507,125	193,303	29,700,428	3,365,923	-211,116	26,123,389	11,167,577	8,047,398	20,952	2,163,912	1,093,939
1994	47,568,820	31,624,671	175,092	31,799,763	3,642,029	-241,576	27,916,158	11,113,947	8,538,715	21,678	2,194,294	1,137,326
1995	51,207,949	33,788,107	184,475	33,972,582	3,880,883	-170,942	29,920,757	12,194,563	9,092,629	23,004	2,226,036	1,178,494
1996	54,297,198	36,349,360	169,905	36,519,265	4,126,779	-424,151	31,968,335	12,793,564	9,535,299	24,063	2,256,460	1,230,493
1997	57,909,408	38,881,308	192,798	39,074,106	4,419,311	-540,281	34,114,514	13,967,214	9,827,680	25,208	2,297,251	1,275,654
1998	62,155,966	42,638,751	242,665	42,881,416	4,787,704	-770,629	37,323,083	14,902,902	9,929,981	26,599	2,336,822	1,341,749
1999	64,902,188	46,213,437	235,916	46,449,353	5,155,467	-1,131,354	40,162,532	14,543,548	10,196,108	27,395	2,369,105	1,396,874
2000	70,253,479	50,083,888	238,821	50,322,709	5,519,213	-1,000,016	43,803,480	15,749,296	10,700,703	29,223	2,404,013	1,447,354
2001	72,777,802	51,638,492	258,564	51,897,056	5,747,132	-876,395	45,273,529	15,937,144	11,567,129	29,778	2,444,015	1,413,290
2002	75,378,840	54,216,484	261,523	54,478,007	6,030,111	-762,290	47,685,606	15,331,703	12,361,531	30,304	2,487,445	1,442,066
2003	79,479,440	56,965,269	227,947	57,193,216	6,301,439	-614,261	50,277,516	16,129,088	13,072,836	31,419	2,529,652	1,453,475
2004	85,293,416	61,432,503	235,820	61,668,323	6,811,211	-456,846	54,400,266	16,911,555	13,981,595	32,960	2,587,771	1,507,183
2005	91,639,254	65,834,783	272,654	66,107,437	7,331,555	-240,521	58,535,361	18,053,369	15,050,524	34,560	2,651,580	1,557,452
2006	97,812,925	69,209,124	277,779	69,486,903	7,834,511	-8,269	61,644,123	19,953,100	16,215,702	36,228	2,699,935	1,591,046
2007	101,879,331	70,685,191	244,229	70,929,420	8,074,131	199,554	63,054,843	21,495,303	17,329,185	37,363	2,726,780	1,608,928
2008	103,574,466	69,697,889	243,196	69,941,085	8,092,859	409,799	62,258,025	21,811,377	19,505,064	37,705	2,746,981	1,553,827
2009	101,113,559	67,244,734	248,460	67,493,194	7,931,790	407,341	59,968,745	19,987,610	21,157,204	36,583	2,763,937	1,484,491
2010	108,031,423	69,197,266	233,771	69,431,037	7,985,307	449,786	61,895,516	22,922,462	23,213,445	38,760	2,787,185	1,464,398
2011	115,286,858	71,290,627	200,024	71,490,651	7,366,753	497,675	64,621,573	26,473,663	24,191,622	41,067	2,807,290	1,485,050
2012	114,437,275	74,228,550	230,180	74,458,730	7,766,574	518,978	67,211,134	23,465,274	23,760,867	40,399	2,832,694	1,516,838
2013	114,342,523	76,055,043	231,620	76,286,663	9,001,916	569,279	67,854,026	22,027,471	24,461,026	39,917	2,864,523	1,558,637
2014	120,762,743	79,501,358	240,065	79,741,423	9,389,496	608,701	70,960,628	24,007,161	25,794,954	41,555	2,906,119	1,604,907
2015	127,546,542	84,131,979	297,930	84,429,909	9,866,981	630,108	75,193,036	25,091,878	27,261,628	43,131	2,957,181	1,664,587
2016	132,102,968	87,764,050	254,458	88,018,508	10,287,943	665,465	78,396,030	25,684,407	28,022,531	43,783	3,017,229	1,709,391
2017	140,156,920	91,583,671	274,309	91,857,980	10,710,324	754,047	81,901,703	28,897,558	29,357,659	45,658	3,069,701	1,773,282
2018	148,028,961	97,157,894	179,421	97,337,315	11,405,838	872,273	86,803,750	30,632,504	30,592,707	47,569	3,111,847	1,836,333
2019	157,465,192	103,109,474	208,982	103,318,456	12,245,694	819,385	91,892,147	33,078,077	32,494,968	50,033	3,147,199	1,875,014
2020	170,936,894	107,065,597	230,490	107,296,087	12,833,834	793,998	95,256,251	34,856,974	40,823,669	53,629	3,187,378	1,878,396
2021	188,955,026	119,433,158	202,789	119,635,947	13,903,606	900,316	106,632,657	36,205,655	46,116,714	58,517	3,229,077	1,976,914
2022	197,743,202	131,522,713	201,318	131,724,031	15,543,925	1,035,643	117,215,749	39,019,186	41,508,267	60,091	3,290,730	2,090,107

Personal Income and Employment by Area: Terre Haute, IN

(Thousands of dollars, except as noted.)

Year	Personal income, total	Derivation of personal income: Earnings by place of work: Nonfarm	Earnings by place of work: Farm	Earnings by place of work: Total	Less: Contributions for government social insurance	Plus: Adjustment for residence	Equals: Net earnings by place of residence	Plus: Dividends, interest, and rent	Plus: Personal current transfer receipts	Per capita personal income (dollars)	Population (persons)	Total employment
1970	653,691	503,201	14,322	517,523	34,687	8,056	490,892	92,717	70,082	3,438	190,158	76,765
1971	702,476	519,156	24,693	543,849	36,946	10,937	517,840	101,780	82,856	3,660	191,959	76,358
1972	748,050	549,121	21,875	570,996	41,038	15,752	545,710	109,319	93,021	3,901	191,761	76,688
1973	866,059	608,985	51,816	660,801	52,098	17,828	626,531	125,278	114,250	4,532	191,111	78,777
1974	924,277	661,564	29,612	691,176	59,637	18,969	650,508	143,974	129,795	4,908	188,332	79,911
1975	1,032,187	707,494	48,717	756,211	62,918	20,316	713,609	164,108	154,470	5,474	188,562	78,500
1976	1,133,593	789,503	47,552	837,055	70,842	24,587	790,800	177,141	165,652	5,981	189,548	79,775
1977	1,238,866	881,000	34,530	915,530	78,649	27,561	864,442	200,179	174,245	6,499	190,634	81,931
1978	1,374,573	994,060	33,198	1,027,258	90,920	28,764	965,102	221,717	187,754	7,206	190,751	84,461
1979	1,524,001	1,113,755	27,185	1,140,940	105,288	26,253	1,061,905	247,944	214,152	7,996	190,605	87,282
1980	1,667,911	1,186,127	15,116	1,201,243	112,343	23,284	1,112,184	303,561	252,166	8,650	192,825	86,418
1981	1,794,923	1,232,112	9,960	1,242,072	125,794	25,528	1,141,806	367,732	285,385	9,354	191,884	83,190
1982	1,874,012	1,239,913	8,811	1,248,724	129,316	24,584	1,143,992	414,809	315,211	9,796	191,309	80,299
1983	1,928,926	1,267,024	-14,550	1,252,474	131,738	28,967	1,149,703	438,630	340,593	10,154	189,960	79,148
1984	2,093,462	1,359,543	22,643	1,382,186	144,782	33,225	1,270,629	471,620	351,213	11,088	188,797	80,356
1985	2,180,943	1,415,774	21,368	1,437,142	153,752	38,626	1,322,016	492,840	366,087	11,613	187,797	80,815
1986	2,271,618	1,484,194	17,962	1,502,156	161,784	43,828	1,384,200	507,956	379,462	12,197	186,249	81,270
1987	2,333,831	1,553,047	17,581	1,570,628	166,941	47,520	1,451,207	497,517	385,107	12,636	184,704	82,193
1988	2,433,089	1,625,109	7,305	1,632,414	181,628	51,531	1,502,317	530,100	400,672	13,248	183,654	83,212
1989	2,663,938	1,734,824	32,417	1,767,241	195,809	55,331	1,626,763	599,858	437,317	14,579	182,724	85,387
1990	2,793,503	1,855,189	24,945	1,880,134	214,094	54,479	1,720,519	609,167	463,817	15,347	182,018	87,578
1991	2,915,219	1,977,628	-629	1,976,999	231,881	52,333	1,797,451	617,529	500,239	15,973	182,508	88,827
1992	3,149,816	2,134,922	41,749	2,176,671	247,725	54,499	1,983,445	603,634	562,737	17,131	183,863	90,986
1993	3,273,821	2,231,280	34,810	2,266,090	260,999	55,009	2,060,100	620,470	593,251	17,644	185,548	93,098
1994	3,411,135	2,322,626	35,255	2,357,881	275,553	58,505	2,140,833	648,390	621,912	18,340	185,997	94,999
1995	3,524,531	2,400,412	14,737	2,415,149	287,164	61,075	2,189,060	705,412	630,059	18,832	187,153	96,947
1996	3,631,082	2,420,964	34,323	2,455,287	287,175	62,638	2,230,750	736,217	664,115	19,296	188,174	96,041
1997	3,734,071	2,474,141	32,002	2,506,143	293,114	67,667	2,280,696	768,989	684,386	19,820	188,395	94,695
1998	3,969,147	2,653,325	15,904	2,669,229	306,919	68,211	2,430,521	823,098	715,528	21,082	188,270	94,792
1999	4,096,362	2,797,743	22,088	2,819,831	319,911	68,665	2,568,585	772,869	754,908	21,733	188,488	95,514
2000	4,289,231	2,890,175	35,436	2,925,611	327,745	72,570	2,670,436	828,228	790,567	22,811	188,034	96,655
2001	4,462,116	2,998,160	39,895	3,038,055	334,255	71,178	2,774,978	817,029	870,109	23,773	187,699	94,380
2002	4,545,554	3,122,913	12,367	3,135,280	349,051	64,698	2,850,927	779,175	915,452	24,265	187,329	93,388
2003	4,724,150	3,246,468	49,757	3,296,225	367,730	57,674	2,986,169	793,415	944,566	25,135	187,953	94,153
2004	4,877,372	3,348,154	76,261	3,424,415	381,911	60,071	3,102,575	776,914	997,883	26,018	187,461	94,528
2005	4,924,840	3,412,319	39,843	3,452,162	398,547	60,707	3,114,322	729,532	1,080,986	26,192	188,030	94,313
2006	5,136,458	3,548,771	22,416	3,571,187	413,392	57,675	3,215,470	764,304	1,156,684	27,162	189,106	94,763
2007	5,311,684	3,621,309	57,524	3,678,833	428,308	51,543	3,302,068	814,148	1,195,468	28,039	189,436	95,639
2008	5,656,380	3,721,911	65,968	3,787,879	441,618	40,737	3,386,998	908,503	1,360,879	29,856	189,455	94,347
2009	5,588,791	3,607,826	56,269	3,664,095	433,734	32,104	3,262,465	855,566	1,470,760	29,490	189,516	92,008
2010	5,818,477	3,763,255	72,101	3,835,356	442,486	15,950	3,408,820	850,132	1,559,525	30,701	189,519	91,515
2011	5,986,802	3,788,471	111,028	3,899,499	397,440	24,020	3,526,079	895,580	1,565,143	31,597	189,475	91,645
2012	6,112,360	3,884,189	52,134	3,936,323	408,956	23,907	3,551,274	941,449	1,619,637	32,266	189,436	92,172
2013	6,183,643	3,896,636	177,142	4,073,778	465,411	29,231	3,637,598	931,227	1,614,818	32,734	188,905	91,978
2014	6,303,264	3,971,292	49,737	4,021,029	473,651	37,193	3,584,571	986,497	1,732,196	33,527	188,007	92,008
2015	6,354,708	3,995,663	-15,112	3,980,551	480,158	61,446	3,561,839	1,000,769	1,792,100	33,967	187,085	91,547
2016	6,512,590	4,016,530	30,693	4,047,223	483,376	82,470	3,646,317	1,001,657	1,864,616	34,854	186,855	91,899
2017	6,756,501	4,132,505	22,915	4,155,420	499,812	81,645	3,737,253	1,107,999	1,911,249	36,248	186,395	91,883
2018	6,903,753	4,217,046	25,632	4,242,678	511,492	94,855	3,826,041	1,089,033	1,988,679	37,080	186,185	91,778
2019	7,088,017	4,351,773	16,136	4,367,909	531,124	82,303	3,919,088	1,083,842	2,085,087	38,196	185,570	90,859
2020	7,730,509	4,417,738	72,335	4,490,073	550,888	88,387	4,027,572	1,124,679	2,578,258	41,804	184,921	87,387
2021	8,446,200	4,693,825	130,933	4,824,758	578,243	103,460	4,349,975	1,185,802	2,910,423	45,615	185,161	88,583
2022	8,464,087	4,951,151	112,913	5,064,064	611,279	117,128	4,569,913	1,266,695	2,627,479	45,783	184,875	90,471

Personal Income and Employment by Area: Texarkana, TX-AR

(Thousands of dollars, except as noted.)

Year	Personal income, total	Derivation of personal income: Earnings by place of work: Nonfarm	Farm	Total	Less: Contributions for government social insurance	Plus: Adjustment for residence	Equals: Net earnings by place of residence	Plus: Dividends, interest, and rent	Plus: Personal current transfer receipts	Per capita personal income (dollars)	Population (persons)	Total employment
1970	376,236	324,456	11,436	335,892	18,697	-30,211	286,984	51,358	37,894	3,317	113,411	51,614
1971	401,204	335,787	9,817	345,604	19,670	-25,701	300,233	57,175	43,796	3,480	115,276	49,646
1972	451,345	374,221	13,100	387,321	22,977	-24,287	340,057	62,409	48,879	3,912	115,364	50,603
1973	500,642	405,085	17,198	422,283	28,914	-23,440	369,929	72,073	58,640	4,343	115,273	51,600
1974	557,896	441,474	16,765	458,239	32,689	-24,158	401,392	85,270	71,234	4,789	116,487	51,969
1975	612,547	469,308	10,204	479,512	33,445	-22,501	423,566	99,646	89,335	5,088	120,390	50,601
1976	688,992	528,222	11,390	539,612	38,716	-21,025	479,871	111,578	97,543	5,657	121,802	52,595
1977	758,960	583,833	9,404	593,237	43,510	-20,212	529,515	126,787	102,658	6,177	122,871	54,507
1978	853,414	659,800	10,235	670,035	51,017	-19,814	599,204	141,250	112,960	6,903	123,622	56,842
1979	975,049	770,277	21,406	791,683	63,966	-38,888	688,829	157,677	128,543	7,698	126,658	59,580
1980	1,060,581	799,347	6,746	806,093	64,733	-21,466	719,894	191,322	149,365	8,328	127,351	57,931
1981	1,189,095	876,037	11,872	887,909	75,730	-22,120	790,059	229,475	169,561	9,265	128,345	57,646
1982	1,280,521	937,625	10,523	948,148	82,646	-29,627	835,875	260,496	184,150	9,901	129,332	58,212
1983	1,375,177	1,003,663	7,881	1,011,544	92,070	-32,327	887,147	286,634	201,396	10,461	131,460	59,156
1984	1,523,810	1,110,664	21,099	1,131,763	105,168	-34,762	991,833	320,314	211,663	11,527	132,198	61,554
1985	1,617,022	1,172,824	16,009	1,188,833	114,106	-36,865	1,037,862	353,274	225,886	12,132	133,288	62,566
1986	1,666,550	1,203,071	21,265	1,224,336	118,805	-37,898	1,067,633	361,929	236,988	12,471	133,636	61,580
1987	1,701,443	1,242,492	19,495	1,261,987	122,375	-39,534	1,100,078	355,824	245,541	12,708	133,889	62,892
1988	1,778,922	1,290,326	31,411	1,321,737	133,327	-37,107	1,151,303	367,540	260,079	13,212	134,645	62,821
1989	1,904,448	1,373,138	34,858	1,407,996	144,821	-44,990	1,218,185	402,161	284,102	14,234	133,795	64,410
1990	2,016,516	1,487,624	29,284	1,516,908	161,228	-60,790	1,294,890	405,791	315,835	14,993	134,497	67,025
1991	2,106,572	1,533,055	32,544	1,565,599	168,451	-35,251	1,361,897	395,409	349,266	15,575	135,250	66,542
1992	2,217,180	1,577,584	32,928	1,610,512	173,066	-21,248	1,416,198	398,921	402,061	16,283	136,162	65,220
1993	2,294,466	1,634,262	32,845	1,667,107	179,675	-16,031	1,471,401	406,515	416,550	16,675	137,598	66,853
1994	2,405,736	1,689,673	36,552	1,726,225	188,344	-10,861	1,527,020	429,278	449,438	17,307	139,004	67,344
1995	2,540,119	1,767,390	32,753	1,800,143	196,884	-4,707	1,598,552	460,096	481,471	18,163	139,853	69,282
1996	2,674,174	1,844,765	40,961	1,885,726	202,969	-100	1,682,657	487,835	503,682	18,918	141,353	70,753
1997	2,824,844	1,960,556	49,125	2,009,681	213,779	5,639	1,801,541	498,135	525,168	19,908	141,893	71,877
1998	2,912,277	2,013,867	38,110	2,051,977	217,318	15,959	1,850,618	527,257	534,402	20,463	142,322	71,041
1999	3,041,436	2,128,799	51,551	2,180,350	228,119	9,228	1,961,459	541,363	538,614	21,261	143,051	72,551
2000	3,191,693	2,221,786	44,351	2,266,137	237,032	9,507	2,038,612	592,668	560,413	22,288	143,205	73,713
2001	3,385,564	2,330,750	51,415	2,382,165	245,137	6,839	2,143,867	627,024	614,673	23,695	142,882	73,705
2002	3,470,372	2,433,133	39,633	2,472,766	255,254	-4,728	2,212,784	598,065	659,523	24,243	143,149	73,434
2003	3,561,039	2,532,861	54,742	2,587,603	269,573	-12,805	2,305,225	556,720	699,094	24,801	143,582	73,159
2004	3,775,934	2,648,843	68,917	2,717,760	284,433	-23,870	2,409,457	622,025	744,452	26,222	143,996	73,879
2005	3,931,344	2,799,737	38,868	2,838,605	300,248	-35,276	2,503,081	623,843	804,420	27,200	144,534	75,734
2006	4,115,193	2,941,341	26,621	2,967,962	316,046	-43,772	2,608,144	641,020	866,029	28,176	146,051	76,838
2007	4,388,292	3,052,950	43,531	3,096,481	335,032	-60,203	2,701,246	744,942	942,104	30,001	146,273	78,664
2008	4,611,071	3,189,012	11,864	3,200,876	355,911	-96,016	2,748,949	811,608	1,050,514	31,263	147,495	80,176
2009	4,613,567	3,199,320	868	3,200,188	361,260	-114,064	2,724,864	764,885	1,123,818	31,017	148,743	78,627
2010	4,810,190	3,287,101	9,109	3,296,210	368,478	-81,191	2,846,541	745,997	1,217,652	32,216	149,310	77,898
2011	5,012,364	3,356,873	9,979	3,366,852	336,091	-81,560	2,949,201	829,201	1,233,962	33,555	149,378	78,988
2012	5,092,008	3,366,060	19,952	3,386,012	337,931	-92,913	2,955,168	904,430	1,232,410	34,094	149,352	78,652
2013	4,945,679	3,224,492	40,077	3,264,569	365,393	-76,999	2,822,177	849,617	1,273,885	33,163	149,132	77,555
2014	5,051,724	3,242,866	46,628	3,289,494	370,493	-73,397	2,845,604	872,938	1,333,182	33,963	148,741	77,450
2015	5,246,387	3,378,783	43,161	3,421,944	388,915	-90,405	2,942,624	906,590	1,397,173	35,294	148,650	78,452
2016	5,333,589	3,454,824	21,652	3,476,476	399,502	-95,918	2,981,056	897,388	1,455,145	35,829	148,864	79,256
2017	5,470,260	3,525,734	20,402	3,546,136	408,629	-91,455	3,046,052	939,903	1,484,305	36,773	148,756	78,803
2018	5,583,893	3,571,715	15,479	3,587,194	414,330	-92,205	3,080,659	957,915	1,545,319	37,604	148,491	79,193
2019	5,722,224	3,665,142	14,242	3,679,384	426,462	-99,418	3,153,504	957,871	1,610,849	38,696	147,875	79,494
2020	6,283,896	3,700,527	21,676	3,722,203	440,118	-89,680	3,192,405	1,076,404	2,015,087	42,609	147,478	77,406
2021	6,785,179	3,845,357	29,249	3,874,606	453,314	-85,164	3,336,128	1,185,013	2,264,038	46,238	146,744	79,727
2022	6,803,929	4,025,078	31,085	4,056,163	480,979	-84,765	3,490,419	1,265,328	2,048,182	46,472	146,408	81,015

Personal Income and Employment by Area: The Villages, FL

(Thousands of dollars, except as noted.)

Year	Personal income, total	Derivation of personal income: Earnings by place of work: Nonfarm	Farm	Total	Less: Contributions for government social insurance	Plus: Adjustment for residence	Equals: Net earnings by place of residence	Plus: Dividends, interest, and rent	Plus: Personal current transfer receipts	Per capita personal income (dollars)	Population (persons)	Total employment
1970	39,947	25,114	3,231	28,345	2,089	1,295	27,551	6,161	6,235	2,669	14,967	4,545
1971	45,938	27,459	4,346	31,805	2,296	2,017	31,526	7,111	7,301	2,908	15,797	4,724
1972	54,241	30,437	5,783	36,220	2,573	3,120	36,767	8,313	9,161	3,051	17,780	5,092
1973	65,269	34,882	7,313	42,195	3,208	4,628	43,615	10,346	11,308	3,410	19,143	5,413
1974	72,053	37,386	6,521	43,907	3,671	5,946	46,182	12,183	13,688	3,523	20,453	5,460
1975	82,166	40,682	7,113	47,795	3,978	6,857	50,674	13,848	17,644	3,913	20,999	5,497
1976	90,468	43,529	7,752	51,281	4,320	8,259	55,220	14,984	20,264	4,102	22,056	5,668
1977	100,157	47,597	7,901	55,498	4,774	10,174	60,898	16,960	22,299	4,487	22,324	5,961
1978	118,028	55,776	9,951	65,727	5,571	12,393	72,549	21,504	23,975	5,169	22,835	6,565
1979	139,104	62,836	12,223	75,059	6,433	14,668	83,294	26,783	29,027	5,966	23,318	6,841
1980	160,386	68,177	10,541	78,718	7,014	18,367	90,071	35,182	35,133	6,563	24,439	6,802
1981	178,079	74,787	7,351	82,138	8,335	19,519	93,322	43,431	41,326	7,105	25,063	6,847
1982	197,788	82,967	9,983	92,950	9,516	19,660	103,094	47,748	46,946	7,660	25,822	6,869
1983	222,046	93,219	11,107	104,326	10,554	20,701	114,473	55,365	52,208	8,355	26,577	7,337
1984	244,730	103,933	9,452	113,385	12,037	23,965	125,313	63,512	55,905	8,944	27,362	7,732
1985	266,993	115,350	7,785	123,135	13,666	26,096	135,565	69,778	61,650	9,430	28,313	8,285
1986	288,702	121,570	8,230	129,800	14,984	29,877	144,693	76,285	67,724	9,881	29,217	8,497
1987	310,149	129,283	6,940	136,223	15,473	35,048	155,798	78,757	75,594	10,418	29,771	8,769
1988	340,257	140,682	9,304	149,986	17,524	39,445	171,907	83,151	85,199	11,281	30,161	9,022
1989	374,096	150,876	11,156	162,032	18,905	43,411	186,538	98,503	89,055	12,072	30,990	9,138
1990	391,807	152,270	10,551	162,821	18,910	46,841	190,752	102,657	98,398	12,289	31,882	9,144
1991	413,210	157,377	14,012	171,389	19,854	45,923	197,458	105,033	110,719	12,574	32,863	9,069
1992	447,427	169,549	16,043	185,592	21,429	48,245	212,408	104,332	130,687	13,236	33,804	9,142
1993	469,507	178,680	14,259	192,939	22,370	51,166	221,735	105,432	142,340	13,506	34,764	9,427
1994	501,936	190,402	11,644	202,046	24,207	53,339	231,178	112,813	157,945	13,885	36,149	9,665
1995	549,357	217,251	8,772	226,023	26,926	50,469	249,566	122,656	177,135	14,291	38,441	10,357
1996	611,086	256,038	7,118	263,156	30,351	45,150	277,955	136,920	196,211	14,254	42,871	11,189
1997	655,895	277,926	9,589	287,515	32,739	45,362	300,138	141,348	214,409	14,072	46,611	11,587
1998	712,439	293,558	9,831	303,389	34,565	49,007	317,831	161,750	232,858	14,609	48,767	12,004
1999	776,950	320,990	13,398	334,388	37,458	49,039	345,969	162,277	268,704	15,021	51,725	12,199
2000	830,524	339,359	13,361	352,720	39,668	49,136	362,188	168,076	300,260	15,455	53,738	12,646
2001	977,220	420,278	14,965	435,243	47,494	52,539	440,288	173,619	363,313	17,515	55,793	14,060
2002	1,084,814	464,955	9,671	474,626	51,980	52,220	474,866	199,710	410,238	18,220	59,539	15,461
2003	1,232,950	577,883	11,124	589,007	63,623	33,019	558,403	229,293	445,254	19,907	61,934	18,140
2004	1,436,777	620,609	11,472	632,081	69,828	88,755	651,008	286,266	499,503	22,291	64,456	20,022
2005	1,685,940	764,640	13,757	778,397	85,997	96,408	788,808	312,666	584,466	24,342	69,261	24,039
2006	1,977,931	896,803	13,215	910,018	121,894	98,099	886,223	376,045	715,663	25,956	76,202	26,589
2007	2,138,856	959,746	10,101	969,847	133,642	46,256	882,461	431,639	824,756	26,052	82,101	27,723
2008	2,394,523	976,762	8,629	985,391	144,947	45,945	886,389	507,636	1,000,498	27,704	86,433	28,378
2009	2,597,065	1,037,035	8,228	1,045,263	156,550	16,928	905,641	507,201	1,184,223	28,652	90,643	29,326
2010	2,852,007	1,120,190	9,278	1,129,468	168,174	-23,006	938,288	598,903	1,314,816	30,292	94,149	30,828
2011	3,328,737	1,247,686	7,604	1,255,290	171,789	-30,035	1,053,466	810,267	1,465,004	34,211	97,300	32,746
2012	3,831,196	1,312,060	16,299	1,328,359	184,086	43,686	1,187,959	1,078,064	1,565,173	38,160	100,399	34,450
2013	4,102,343	1,409,839	10,794	1,420,633	220,102	40,350	1,240,881	1,199,894	1,661,568	39,081	104,970	37,058
2014	4,381,179	1,452,097	20,489	1,472,586	231,688	-42,309	1,198,589	1,353,080	1,829,510	39,974	109,601	39,049
2015	4,773,556	1,504,130	26,989	1,531,119	244,964	-63,362	1,222,793	1,541,313	2,009,450	41,987	113,691	40,398
2016	5,253,535	1,608,116	12,779	1,620,895	265,677	11,316	1,366,534	1,740,730	2,146,271	44,571	117,868	41,571
2017	5,688,056	1,754,445	16,217	1,770,662	291,184	-12,693	1,466,785	1,987,949	2,233,322	47,359	120,106	42,962
2018	6,193,965	1,907,478	17,474	1,924,952	323,877	-44,482	1,556,593	2,248,603	2,388,769	50,248	123,269	45,180
2019	6,972,854	2,143,009	10,651	2,153,660	361,981	-48,093	1,743,586	2,603,777	2,625,491	55,014	126,746	47,287
2020	7,768,479	2,371,153	12,850	2,384,003	399,104	41,718	2,026,617	2,739,949	3,001,913	59,621	130,298	49,083
2021	9,241,610	2,850,356	11,811	2,862,167	448,606	146,159	2,559,720	3,319,297	3,362,593	68,524	134,867	53,603
2022	10,035,455	3,292,656	17,846	3,310,502	522,776	302,883	3,090,609	3,622,362	3,322,484	69,224	144,970	57,552

Personal Income and Employment by Area: Toledo, OH

(Thousands of dollars, except as noted.)

Year	Personal income, total	Derivation of personal income								Per capita personal income (dollars)	Population (persons)	Total employment
		Earnings by place of work			Less: Contributions for government social insurance	Plus: Adjustment for residence	Equals: Net earnings by place of residence	Plus: Dividends, interest, and rent	Plus: Personal current transfer receipts			
		Nonfarm	Farm	Total								
1970	2,752,283	2,323,449	29,546	2,352,995	154,911	-61,386	2,136,698	391,699	223,886	4,269	644,655	291,261
1971	2,968,326	2,495,874	27,904	2,523,778	171,935	-59,755	2,292,088	419,655	256,583	4,556	651,449	292,004
1972	3,241,470	2,739,924	33,584	2,773,508	199,092	-62,109	2,512,307	447,993	281,170	4,935	656,834	297,549
1973	3,603,057	3,059,490	45,143	3,104,633	258,404	-68,866	2,777,363	498,949	326,745	5,462	659,712	310,566
1974	3,905,198	3,248,763	52,723	3,301,486	284,880	-71,852	2,944,754	564,898	395,546	5,899	662,010	309,862
1975	4,205,670	3,379,160	60,487	3,439,647	288,571	-70,700	3,080,376	602,686	522,608	6,364	660,803	300,346
1976	4,651,150	3,829,359	49,261	3,878,620	335,669	-89,235	3,453,716	644,447	552,987	7,110	654,162	307,168
1977	5,088,417	4,226,374	39,278	4,265,652	373,200	-103,289	3,789,163	711,751	587,503	7,782	653,870	313,528
1978	5,567,498	4,676,612	25,207	4,701,819	425,189	-118,562	4,158,068	787,051	622,379	8,544	651,604	322,150
1979	6,113,152	5,080,786	36,463	5,117,249	476,874	-136,376	4,503,999	890,942	718,211	9,321	655,820	327,504
1980	6,690,827	5,269,455	47,754	5,317,209	488,723	-148,706	4,679,780	1,072,039	939,008	10,180	657,260	317,149
1981	7,220,774	5,626,034	5,628	5,631,662	557,751	-154,708	4,919,203	1,287,630	1,013,941	10,989	657,064	313,612
1982	7,591,310	5,771,809	11,609	5,783,418	580,385	-166,967	5,036,066	1,424,048	1,131,196	11,595	654,713	305,112
1983	8,081,781	6,163,434	-9,182	6,154,252	629,989	-184,722	5,339,541	1,542,964	1,199,276	12,403	651,596	307,372
1984	8,954,771	6,911,545	57,009	6,968,554	723,831	-236,128	6,008,595	1,707,732	1,238,444	13,773	650,161	321,537
1985	9,544,044	7,476,757	42,318	7,519,075	796,351	-274,427	6,448,297	1,790,436	1,305,311	14,690	649,694	329,481
1986	9,980,838	7,833,403	35,361	7,868,764	856,466	-278,888	6,733,410	1,860,276	1,387,152	15,311	651,883	338,843
1987	10,406,943	8,242,692	41,843	8,284,535	897,806	-296,039	7,090,690	1,870,961	1,445,292	15,943	652,747	346,688
1988	11,095,116	8,840,128	53,211	8,893,339	994,468	-325,758	7,573,113	2,010,044	1,511,959	16,889	656,932	356,764
1989	11,849,274	9,302,697	71,513	9,374,210	1,051,787	-345,031	7,977,392	2,270,153	1,601,729	18,073	655,641	361,652
1990	12,326,712	9,565,086	91,021	9,656,107	1,095,444	-319,087	8,241,576	2,296,672	1,788,464	18,828	654,687	359,713
1991	12,432,847	9,564,685	80,967	9,645,652	1,125,650	-305,708	8,214,294	2,276,976	1,941,577	18,991	654,667	353,137
1992	13,248,943	10,279,434	86,270	10,365,704	1,203,457	-355,088	8,807,159	2,315,064	2,126,720	20,203	655,794	355,344
1993	13,756,262	10,785,833	77,405	10,863,238	1,274,631	-425,946	9,162,661	2,392,064	2,201,537	20,976	655,822	363,287
1994	14,452,123	11,496,742	87,665	11,584,407	1,375,223	-529,597	9,679,587	2,484,638	2,287,898	22,029	656,047	377,917
1995	15,110,468	11,914,384	68,727	11,983,111	1,436,497	-546,953	9,999,661	2,680,324	2,430,483	23,007	656,770	383,433
1996	15,684,016	12,316,019	94,236	12,410,255	1,474,108	-597,217	10,338,930	2,851,948	2,493,138	23,875	656,920	389,937
1997	16,472,489	12,915,786	116,456	13,032,242	1,502,530	-635,468	10,894,244	3,025,815	2,552,430	25,014	658,539	394,322
1998	17,161,693	13,541,745	80,836	13,622,581	1,520,381	-681,201	11,420,999	3,159,661	2,581,033	26,027	659,390	398,139
1999	17,651,045	14,317,351	54,677	14,372,028	1,602,041	-749,441	12,020,546	2,994,381	2,636,118	26,769	659,388	404,460
2000	18,353,873	14,747,853	72,482	14,820,335	1,593,538	-752,620	12,474,177	3,108,645	2,771,051	27,843	659,190	409,267
2001	18,999,927	15,270,832	59,514	15,330,346	1,658,263	-764,144	12,907,939	3,104,830	2,987,158	28,786	660,052	407,705
2002	19,355,906	15,565,986	28,287	15,594,273	1,663,068	-744,673	13,186,532	2,963,449	3,205,925	29,338	659,750	398,927
2003	19,927,430	16,003,545	53,803	16,057,348	1,731,275	-752,244	13,573,829	3,018,365	3,335,236	30,178	660,335	395,975
2004	20,342,246	16,392,342	94,331	16,486,673	1,809,077	-753,650	13,923,946	2,933,457	3,484,843	30,833	659,745	399,044
2005	20,757,586	16,654,038	91,602	16,745,640	1,851,560	-758,276	14,135,804	2,917,140	3,704,642	31,525	658,448	399,722
2006	21,848,933	17,361,792	92,167	17,453,959	1,921,423	-781,645	14,750,891	3,191,019	3,907,023	33,295	656,222	402,026
2007	22,720,439	17,722,204	83,296	17,805,500	1,954,251	-774,197	15,077,052	3,495,644	4,147,743	34,674	655,257	401,819
2008	23,203,837	17,585,216	72,157	17,657,373	1,964,574	-721,315	14,971,484	3,581,658	4,650,695	35,506	653,518	392,073
2009	22,573,607	16,625,208	99,934	16,725,142	1,880,372	-673,082	14,171,688	3,258,377	5,143,542	34,610	652,232	371,435
2010	23,270,243	17,102,305	78,841	17,181,146	1,894,377	-689,269	14,597,500	3,277,804	5,394,939	35,718	651,502	369,913
2011	24,498,851	17,826,365	155,040	17,981,405	1,797,186	-762,654	15,421,565	3,565,664	5,511,622	37,645	650,793	376,354
2012	24,967,822	18,377,434	120,943	18,498,377	1,847,509	-809,086	15,841,782	3,765,117	5,360,923	38,419	649,883	379,183
2013	25,275,093	18,887,953	169,651	19,057,604	2,041,679	-802,778	16,213,147	3,594,316	5,467,630	38,884	650,011	382,456
2014	26,382,664	19,675,446	85,208	19,760,654	2,127,762	-865,002	16,767,890	3,875,392	5,739,382	40,631	649,325	387,689
2015	27,414,546	20,503,052	32,886	20,535,938	2,199,341	-927,455	17,409,142	4,076,468	5,928,936	42,269	648,575	393,382
2016	28,024,349	21,067,876	39,580	21,107,456	2,308,460	-964,574	17,834,422	4,175,455	6,014,472	43,206	648,629	397,045
2017	28,558,483	21,317,724	36,099	21,353,823	2,388,806	-930,608	18,034,409	4,362,936	6,161,138	44,069	648,038	395,247
2018	29,768,756	22,350,563	61,832	22,412,395	2,460,689	-987,903	18,963,803	4,493,188	6,311,765	45,986	647,337	399,048
2019	30,781,380	22,978,469	55,911	23,034,380	2,562,821	-1,037,374	19,434,185	4,735,802	6,611,393	47,592	646,770	398,649
2020	32,865,944	22,675,558	86,423	22,761,981	2,541,078	-964,147	19,256,756	4,748,081	8,861,107	50,875	646,012	378,253
2021	34,821,629	23,899,402	139,289	24,038,691	2,676,599	-1,009,305	20,352,787	5,045,125	9,423,717	54,212	642,320	388,902
2022	34,890,088	25,161,911	103,330	25,265,241	2,910,497	-1,091,714	21,263,030	5,433,673	8,193,385	54,483	640,384	404,551

Personal Income and Employment by Area: Topeka, KS

(Thousands of dollars, except as noted.)

Year	Personal income, total	Derivation of personal income: Earnings by place of work: Nonfarm	Farm	Total	Less: Contributions for government social insurance	Plus: Adjustment for residence	Equals: Net earnings by place of residence	Plus: Dividends, interest, and rent	Plus: Personal current transfer receipts	Per capita personal income (dollars)	Population (persons)	Total employment
1970	802,172	641,190	11,624	652,814	48,295	-8,105	596,414	133,384	72,374	4,058	197,701	95,350
1971	886,240	700,964	17,642	718,606	54,401	-7,652	656,553	145,447	84,240	4,459	198,772	96,314
1972	984,741	776,891	26,766	803,657	63,058	-8,167	732,432	159,529	92,780	4,855	202,849	98,653
1973	1,089,232	858,242	32,617	890,859	79,969	-5,194	805,696	175,202	108,334	5,378	202,528	102,182
1974	1,139,465	883,697	24,742	908,439	86,911	-1,049	820,479	193,419	125,567	5,869	194,147	100,477
1975	1,246,682	951,373	16,367	967,740	91,905	1,275	877,110	213,133	156,439	6,389	195,125	100,810
1976	1,368,024	1,054,648	7,967	1,062,615	103,140	5,138	964,613	229,716	173,695	6,921	197,659	102,988
1977	1,541,924	1,187,906	17,253	1,205,159	115,875	10,168	1,099,452	255,591	186,881	7,748	199,010	106,791
1978	1,718,465	1,334,487	8,779	1,343,266	133,652	16,830	1,226,444	285,700	206,321	8,577	200,351	110,694
1979	1,889,022	1,471,723	3,293	1,475,016	153,257	19,644	1,341,403	321,304	226,315	9,368	201,651	112,914
1980	2,098,428	1,588,924	-23,286	1,565,638	165,791	24,637	1,424,484	399,980	273,964	10,281	204,099	113,888
1981	2,382,657	1,719,443	14,567	1,734,010	192,745	22,485	1,563,750	505,143	313,764	11,657	204,404	113,415
1982	2,547,130	1,798,372	7,732	1,806,104	207,240	21,900	1,620,764	587,554	338,812	12,433	204,869	111,566
1983	2,665,598	1,914,482	-10,998	1,903,484	219,580	17,381	1,701,285	606,318	357,995	12,964	205,608	112,196
1984	2,899,564	2,096,098	4,394	2,100,492	245,738	15,547	1,870,301	664,770	364,493	14,075	206,005	116,313
1985	3,095,293	2,206,756	52,017	2,258,773	262,712	4,519	2,000,580	707,739	386,974	15,076	205,319	116,597
1986	3,219,662	2,330,572	24,206	2,354,778	277,956	-515	2,076,307	745,507	397,848	15,644	205,805	117,515
1987	3,336,663	2,451,489	19,201	2,470,690	287,955	-1,702	2,181,033	748,657	406,973	16,093	207,337	123,311
1988	3,556,646	2,630,043	10,724	2,640,767	321,777	-4,298	2,314,692	810,442	431,512	16,916	210,255	125,741
1989	3,724,403	2,760,234	11,434	2,771,668	338,488	-9,774	2,423,406	831,732	469,265	17,753	209,794	127,498
1990	3,891,447	2,885,320	27,169	2,912,489	366,941	-11,625	2,533,923	850,997	506,527	18,478	210,598	128,053
1991	4,004,318	2,972,900	8,296	2,981,196	380,200	-11,591	2,589,405	869,543	545,370	18,846	212,479	127,916
1992	4,256,933	3,140,681	50,149	3,190,830	397,766	-11,515	2,781,549	869,986	605,398	19,891	214,014	128,684
1993	4,444,766	3,332,287	9,926	3,342,213	422,498	-15,385	2,904,330	898,325	642,111	20,554	216,252	131,257
1994	4,688,970	3,519,283	25,671	3,544,954	450,037	-15,459	3,079,458	948,424	661,088	21,451	218,593	133,525
1995	4,875,718	3,645,931	321	3,646,252	458,509	-16,570	3,171,173	1,003,928	700,617	22,159	220,036	137,625
1996	5,146,169	3,788,233	54,404	3,842,637	471,844	-15,567	3,355,226	1,062,163	728,780	23,260	221,246	139,732
1997	5,327,925	3,905,728	24,545	3,930,273	486,893	-5,402	3,437,978	1,119,468	770,479	23,966	222,316	139,357
1998	5,644,136	4,172,144	8,265	4,180,409	514,282	-8,139	3,657,988	1,192,365	793,783	25,247	223,555	142,312
1999	5,795,237	4,349,440	-5,895	4,343,545	534,266	-3,881	3,805,398	1,154,258	835,581	25,898	223,772	142,676
2000	6,134,553	4,560,052	-11,832	4,548,220	558,151	1,377	3,991,446	1,244,789	898,318	27,282	224,859	145,358
2001	6,500,741	4,871,643	13,557	4,885,200	592,396	-52	4,292,752	1,220,876	987,113	28,881	225,090	147,052
2002	6,623,923	4,956,195	-9,387	4,946,808	603,666	8,555	4,351,697	1,203,178	1,069,048	29,393	225,355	144,107
2003	6,737,132	4,938,071	10,880	4,948,951	606,463	18,981	4,361,469	1,252,848	1,122,815	29,790	226,153	142,490
2004	6,932,498	5,120,512	46,668	5,167,180	626,169	27,477	4,568,488	1,186,320	1,177,690	30,519	227,155	141,381
2005	7,113,903	5,259,124	16,704	5,275,828	646,183	37,918	4,667,563	1,211,514	1,234,826	31,173	228,208	141,141
2006	7,456,974	5,384,257	-4,772	5,379,485	657,985	63,889	4,785,389	1,355,055	1,316,530	32,588	228,825	140,009
2007	7,981,509	5,686,325	14,095	5,700,420	687,857	68,802	5,081,365	1,478,315	1,421,829	34,698	230,025	143,459
2008	8,458,716	5,929,067	18,923	5,947,990	709,882	84,683	5,322,791	1,556,622	1,579,303	36,575	231,272	144,200
2009	8,508,403	5,951,721	36,769	5,988,490	716,315	20,261	5,292,436	1,499,621	1,716,346	36,588	232,548	141,295
2010	8,595,833	6,072,734	-26	6,072,708	731,071	-26,075	5,315,562	1,458,149	1,822,122	36,685	234,314	141,077
2011	9,030,841	6,268,222	49,399	6,317,621	664,544	-73,309	5,579,768	1,558,108	1,892,965	38,436	234,956	142,105
2012	9,146,749	6,430,350	39,820	6,470,170	681,527	-123,597	5,665,046	1,588,959	1,892,744	38,943	234,873	142,191
2013	9,141,917	6,566,863	59,612	6,626,475	783,607	-166,438	5,676,430	1,539,159	1,926,328	38,981	234,522	143,434
2014	9,459,754	6,802,344	11,534	6,813,878	810,015	-166,945	5,836,918	1,631,798	1,991,038	40,321	234,613	145,203
2015	9,620,873	6,951,479	-4,883	6,946,596	831,737	-181,896	5,932,963	1,631,717	2,056,193	41,006	234,623	144,936
2016	9,879,600	7,129,217	6,947	7,136,164	843,604	-191,212	6,101,348	1,670,411	2,107,841	42,141	234,442	145,271
2017	10,120,173	7,244,727	11,193	7,255,920	860,717	-183,535	6,211,668	1,713,231	2,195,274	43,166	234,449	144,362
2018	10,607,224	7,572,938	44,019	7,616,957	907,287	-194,755	6,514,915	1,805,066	2,287,243	45,366	233,814	144,430
2019	10,868,788	7,667,292	45,619	7,712,911	925,643	-161,318	6,625,950	1,850,949	2,391,889	46,517	233,650	142,999
2020	11,672,973	7,898,359	79,191	7,977,550	970,961	-172,224	6,834,365	1,867,694	2,970,914	50,122	232,890	139,509
2021	12,443,023	8,347,472	113,273	8,460,745	1,032,193	-184,840	7,243,712	1,940,961	3,258,350	53,456	232,771	142,829
2022	12,632,271	8,996,086	-20,683	8,975,403	1,123,358	-207,191	7,644,854	2,053,577	2,933,840	54,500	231,783	147,746

Personal Income and Employment by Area: Trenton-Princeton, NJ

(Thousands of dollars, except as noted.)

Year	Personal income, total	Derivation of personal income								Per capita personal income (dollars)	Population (persons)	Total employment
		Earnings by place of work			Less: Contributions for government social insurance	Plus: Adjustment for residence	Equals: Net earnings by place of residence	Plus: Dividends, interest, and rent	Plus: Personal current transfer receipts			
		Nonfarm	Farm	Total								
1970	1,502,265	1,256,172	2,577	1,258,749	92,246	-13,057	1,153,446	237,973	110,846	4,924	305,091	153,757
1971	1,651,657	1,381,007	2,044	1,383,051	104,148	-22,573	1,256,330	261,181	134,146	5,351	308,680	153,733
1972	1,837,479	1,559,066	1,821	1,560,887	122,826	-37,860	1,400,201	287,152	150,126	5,842	314,505	161,814
1973	2,029,946	1,736,255	3,496	1,739,751	157,306	-39,270	1,543,175	314,842	171,929	6,440	315,209	166,704
1974	2,223,435	1,880,696	4,524	1,885,220	175,024	-39,310	1,670,886	350,596	201,953	7,011	317,113	169,496
1975	2,382,116	1,951,765	2,056	1,953,821	178,513	-26,107	1,749,201	368,233	264,682	7,550	315,506	163,246
1976	2,597,306	2,141,369	2,226	2,143,595	198,903	-34,758	1,909,934	398,059	289,313	8,298	313,004	166,848
1977	2,825,891	2,351,959	3,160	2,355,119	218,087	-60,324	2,076,708	440,765	308,418	9,074	311,427	169,701
1978	3,093,629	2,612,657	2,722	2,615,379	250,069	-92,598	2,272,712	486,366	334,551	9,923	311,764	175,837
1979	3,379,262	2,858,924	2,358	2,861,282	283,633	-121,920	2,455,729	546,897	376,636	10,901	309,998	180,281
1980	3,748,672	3,117,300	1,841	3,119,141	305,453	-165,310	2,648,378	661,837	438,457	12,179	307,796	182,263
1981	4,141,300	3,400,388	3,817	3,404,205	355,908	-206,494	2,841,803	818,255	481,242	13,492	306,944	182,845
1982	4,504,790	3,608,605	2,934	3,611,539	377,898	-229,663	3,003,978	965,905	534,907	14,632	307,882	181,854
1983	4,825,546	3,946,798	4,158	3,950,956	426,389	-279,165	3,245,402	1,007,377	572,767	15,514	311,052	185,431
1984	5,335,238	4,422,836	5,850	4,428,686	499,334	-337,844	3,591,508	1,146,569	597,161	17,151	311,067	194,000
1985	5,756,055	4,832,232	6,502	4,838,734	551,095	-388,126	3,899,513	1,226,354	630,188	18,324	314,133	199,290
1986	6,201,688	5,306,210	6,626	5,312,836	613,135	-449,881	4,249,820	1,292,133	659,735	19,468	318,557	207,145
1987	6,697,606	5,830,784	7,909	5,838,693	667,363	-506,716	4,664,614	1,348,491	684,501	20,782	322,280	212,933
1988	7,482,175	6,530,639	7,184	6,537,823	764,226	-580,149	5,193,448	1,561,860	726,867	22,940	326,162	218,832
1989	8,148,393	6,914,960	6,396	6,921,356	800,305	-663,732	5,457,319	1,906,798	784,276	24,976	326,246	219,559
1990	8,697,892	7,384,609	4,926	7,389,535	829,957	-711,777	5,847,801	1,989,756	860,335	26,642	326,477	219,736
1991	8,880,365	7,666,994	3,058	7,670,052	880,122	-912,431	5,877,499	2,017,106	985,760	27,017	328,694	216,604
1992	9,512,570	8,180,550	1,990	8,182,540	931,848	-866,984	6,383,708	2,000,041	1,128,821	28,767	330,674	217,454
1993	9,685,020	8,403,830	2,576	8,406,406	953,228	-945,918	6,507,260	1,978,314	1,199,446	29,059	333,292	219,615
1994	10,016,227	8,722,040	3,174	8,725,214	1,006,864	-1,012,916	6,705,434	2,100,034	1,210,759	29,879	335,229	220,293
1995	10,492,308	8,990,131	1,973	8,992,104	1,044,279	-1,052,076	6,895,749	2,303,919	1,292,640	31,091	337,476	222,501
1996	11,025,828	9,214,761	2,899	9,217,660	1,070,017	-866,524	7,281,119	2,417,469	1,327,240	32,511	339,146	220,840
1997	11,658,282	9,970,281	1,436	9,971,717	1,145,286	-1,110,449	7,715,982	2,584,583	1,357,717	34,213	340,755	224,588
1998	12,470,664	10,435,513	1,245	10,436,758	1,186,776	-965,290	8,284,692	2,822,210	1,363,762	36,251	344,013	225,414
1999	13,066,904	10,986,530	1,293	10,987,823	1,245,560	-912,577	8,829,686	2,819,808	1,417,410	37,502	348,435	228,946
2000	14,434,318	12,190,977	3,850	12,194,827	1,363,901	-1,016,691	9,814,235	3,102,527	1,517,556	41,069	351,465	242,173
2001	15,837,519	13,660,988	2,799	13,663,787	1,480,163	-1,126,802	11,056,822	3,082,254	1,698,443	44,762	353,816	247,570
2002	16,348,214	14,217,747	3,857	14,221,604	1,531,178	-1,292,102	11,398,324	3,069,298	1,880,592	45,930	355,935	249,462
2003	16,822,568	14,716,420	4,108	14,720,528	1,573,109	-1,303,143	11,844,276	3,149,289	1,829,003	46,896	358,724	252,641
2004	17,060,035	15,324,418	5,913	15,330,331	1,633,418	-1,520,847	12,176,066	3,073,915	1,810,054	47,225	361,248	257,992
2005	17,413,243	15,598,173	4,952	15,603,125	1,703,350	-1,517,765	12,382,010	3,115,410	1,915,823	48,101	362,015	259,723
2006	18,607,635	16,414,080	5,219	16,419,299	1,803,025	-1,607,652	13,008,622	3,504,971	2,094,042	51,283	362,840	265,426
2007	19,575,020	16,829,445	4,756	16,834,201	1,883,997	-1,278,112	13,672,092	3,700,319	2,202,609	53,913	363,088	264,779
2008	20,223,014	17,763,711	3,814	17,767,525	1,991,295	-1,884,772	13,891,458	3,842,065	2,489,491	55,540	364,119	265,798
2009	19,057,355	17,145,060	3,338	17,148,398	1,924,825	-2,307,367	12,916,206	3,399,723	2,741,426	52,156	365,388	259,115
2010	19,451,396	17,675,597	3,355	17,678,952	1,984,910	-2,531,535	13,162,507	3,320,935	2,967,954	52,829	368,192	260,106
2011	20,537,134	18,241,692	6,588	18,248,280	1,835,719	-2,555,016	13,857,545	3,674,515	3,005,074	55,537	369,792	262,911
2012	21,519,905	18,966,673	8,144	18,974,817	1,894,969	-2,576,971	14,502,877	4,048,794	2,968,234	57,702	372,950	263,969
2013	21,128,676	19,793,801	8,471	19,802,272	2,223,560	-3,241,281	14,337,431	3,765,639	3,025,606	56,222	375,805	267,432
2014	22,502,381	20,387,613	5,893	20,393,506	2,290,182	-3,005,749	15,097,575	4,258,238	3,146,568	59,651	377,236	272,642
2015	22,826,259	20,705,989	6,689	20,712,678	2,341,301	-3,184,095	15,187,282	4,406,361	3,232,616	60,323	378,400	276,246
2016	23,339,279	21,493,612	4,907	21,498,519	2,402,106	-3,722,796	15,373,617	4,647,239	3,318,423	61,418	380,010	282,908
2017	24,076,932	21,827,245	5,566	21,832,811	2,485,798	-3,433,529	15,913,484	4,822,898	3,340,550	62,938	382,551	283,643
2018	25,257,430	23,105,574	4,307	23,109,881	2,578,029	-3,774,331	16,757,521	5,033,182	3,466,727	65,643	384,767	290,308
2019	26,838,906	25,308,744	9,412	25,318,156	2,766,988	-4,797,199	17,753,969	5,449,659	3,635,278	69,523	386,045	296,554
2020	28,137,302	25,745,405	7,254	25,752,659	2,836,298	-4,821,906	18,094,455	5,224,981	4,817,866	72,811	386,441	286,729
2021	29,799,059	27,500,794	7,666	27,508,460	3,074,302	-5,439,682	18,994,476	5,477,197	5,327,386	77,984	382,116	296,247
2022	30,209,069	29,173,277	7,488	29,180,765	3,351,483	-5,756,130	20,073,152	5,719,195	4,416,722	79,354	380,688	311,485

Personal Income and Employment by Area: Tucson, AZ

(Thousands of dollars, except as noted.)

Year	Personal income, total	Derivation of personal income: Earnings by place of work: Nonfarm	Farm	Total	Less: Contributions for government social insurance	Plus: Adjustment for residence	Equals: Net earnings by place of residence	Plus: Dividends, interest, and rent	Plus: Personal current transfer receipts	Per capita personal income (dollars)	Population (persons)	Total employment
1970	1,450,771	1,025,196	9,121	1,034,317	69,598	14,248	978,967	344,831	126,973	4,076	355,962	144,257
1971	1,674,034	1,188,318	8,350	1,196,668	83,587	16,944	1,130,025	391,000	153,009	4,402	380,255	153,910
1972	1,905,022	1,363,766	12,649	1,376,415	100,346	15,682	1,291,751	437,269	176,002	4,675	407,515	165,820
1973	2,167,818	1,551,236	21,896	1,573,132	129,373	23,267	1,467,026	490,888	209,904	5,058	428,558	177,412
1974	2,420,702	1,708,320	16,922	1,725,242	148,097	26,991	1,604,136	566,011	250,555	5,455	443,741	181,576
1975	2,651,180	1,800,181	14,095	1,814,276	156,145	26,964	1,685,095	630,129	335,956	5,767	459,738	180,791
1976	2,900,858	1,967,561	18,384	1,985,945	171,550	32,580	1,846,975	675,058	378,825	6,151	471,596	185,903
1977	3,209,600	2,195,387	11,834	2,207,221	191,389	35,536	2,051,368	756,391	401,841	6,638	483,484	193,919
1978	3,687,707	2,514,099	15,924	2,530,023	223,517	33,891	2,340,397	887,159	460,151	7,410	497,687	206,946
1979	4,324,010	3,005,810	16,282	3,022,092	280,713	43,094	2,784,473	1,030,108	509,429	8,262	523,341	224,813
1980	4,980,562	3,390,573	16,831	3,407,404	322,646	38,753	3,123,511	1,253,964	603,087	9,296	535,780	234,354
1981	5,776,565	3,836,259	14,326	3,850,585	392,153	78,362	3,536,794	1,534,322	705,449	10,453	552,627	240,604
1982	6,162,806	4,024,506	13,593	4,038,099	419,400	59,936	3,678,635	1,701,820	782,351	10,850	568,004	245,297
1983	6,720,500	4,366,338	14,128	4,380,466	462,151	45,170	3,963,485	1,907,078	849,937	11,544	582,172	253,316
1984	7,372,071	4,842,774	33,960	4,876,734	529,159	45,672	4,393,247	2,079,334	899,490	12,451	592,087	271,828
1985	8,079,995	5,325,158	25,642	5,350,800	589,883	48,139	4,809,056	2,306,007	964,932	13,408	602,647	291,177
1986	8,768,610	5,818,120	29,159	5,847,279	646,842	57,629	5,258,066	2,464,847	1,045,697	14,107	621,586	302,631
1987	9,236,185	6,169,748	27,872	6,197,620	679,503	63,858	5,581,975	2,509,788	1,144,422	14,422	640,419	308,273
1988	9,921,227	6,559,895	31,163	6,591,058	749,448	95,324	5,936,934	2,732,718	1,251,575	15,107	656,727	318,154
1989	10,650,714	6,717,781	24,366	6,742,147	789,961	90,360	6,042,546	3,167,490	1,440,678	16,035	664,200	318,020
1990	10,995,090	6,884,706	26,634	6,911,340	830,958	116,028	6,196,410	3,197,611	1,601,069	16,439	668,844	318,925
1991	11,651,391	7,437,719	23,808	7,461,527	906,588	110,716	6,665,655	3,215,892	1,769,844	17,139	679,813	323,434
1992	12,313,700	7,956,384	20,226	7,976,610	964,708	114,383	7,126,285	3,193,678	1,993,737	17,639	698,091	328,018
1993	13,422,791	8,653,599	28,241	8,681,840	1,044,439	105,292	7,742,693	3,521,014	2,159,084	18,653	719,598	343,969
1994	14,521,488	9,548,676	14,876	9,563,552	1,160,188	93,514	8,496,878	3,727,297	2,297,313	19,489	745,112	367,152
1995	15,486,628	10,082,827	12,521	10,095,348	1,180,975	108,447	9,022,820	4,023,566	2,440,242	20,159	768,212	381,587
1996	16,465,967	10,657,629	18,087	10,675,716	1,278,928	135,529	9,532,317	4,344,682	2,588,968	21,011	783,685	389,883
1997	17,381,072	11,332,721	18,217	11,350,938	1,338,365	116,161	10,128,734	4,552,912	2,699,426	21,767	798,521	399,857
1998	18,789,640	12,335,536	14,682	12,350,218	1,440,035	108,184	11,018,367	4,996,724	2,774,549	23,101	813,386	416,075
1999	19,802,263	13,201,066	21,400	13,222,466	1,551,573	96,845	11,767,738	5,091,174	2,943,351	23,890	828,905	425,172
2000	21,110,933	14,173,700	14,964	14,188,664	1,651,400	89,262	12,626,526	5,392,447	3,091,960	24,894	848,019	441,662
2001	22,916,059	15,572,638	10,975	15,583,613	1,737,877	82,066	13,927,802	5,487,641	3,500,616	26,669	859,280	436,864
2002	23,463,511	16,240,526	17,307	16,257,833	1,810,869	54,170	14,501,134	5,062,661	3,899,716	26,838	874,267	437,032
2003	24,749,941	17,117,261	22,216	17,139,477	1,881,208	28,416	15,286,685	5,216,109	4,247,147	27,938	885,893	441,798
2004	26,191,181	17,809,101	29,526	17,838,627	1,985,778	-3,093	15,849,756	5,729,738	4,611,687	29,058	901,342	458,630
2005	28,284,249	18,884,138	32,638	18,916,776	2,128,578	-15,259	16,772,939	6,449,496	5,061,814	30,734	920,298	473,246
2006	30,951,918	20,690,556	27,530	20,718,086	2,303,817	-62,414	18,351,855	7,083,559	5,516,504	32,895	940,930	491,378
2007	32,745,785	21,823,339	16,820	21,840,159	2,448,716	-79,960	19,311,483	7,472,798	5,961,504	34,258	955,869	504,635
2008	34,780,689	22,327,044	18,751	22,345,795	2,556,117	-83,517	19,706,161	8,179,238	6,895,290	35,939	967,778	500,686
2009	33,064,732	21,365,172	36,380	21,401,552	2,487,234	-44,217	18,870,101	6,647,372	7,547,259	33,892	975,580	481,965
2010	33,460,566	21,505,997	39,220	21,545,217	2,511,151	-20,377	19,013,689	6,345,366	8,101,511	34,099	981,270	476,916
2011	34,860,323	21,797,870	57,634	21,855,504	2,300,914	25,080	19,579,670	7,228,469	8,052,184	35,334	986,581	477,591
2012	35,943,639	22,598,470	51,453	22,649,923	2,347,649	55,279	20,357,553	7,548,194	8,037,892	36,316	989,750	484,481
2013	36,280,681	23,148,328	48,031	23,196,359	2,690,370	101,196	20,607,185	7,379,164	8,294,332	36,562	992,319	489,788
2014	37,353,042	23,272,857	39,212	23,312,069	2,721,249	118,544	20,709,364	7,836,032	8,807,646	37,432	997,883	495,706
2015	38,619,993	23,593,832	39,721	23,633,553	2,775,978	129,069	20,986,644	8,368,468	9,264,881	38,571	1,001,271	500,005
2016	40,011,788	24,449,507	43,093	24,492,600	2,866,422	111,686	21,737,864	8,533,424	9,740,500	39,723	1,007,258	507,163
2017	42,607,513	26,128,276	37,428	26,165,704	3,044,748	101,982	23,222,938	9,009,965	10,374,610	41,950	1,015,666	517,567
2018	44,699,660	27,390,485	32,440	27,422,925	3,231,313	123,527	24,315,139	9,507,874	10,876,647	43,624	1,024,650	524,861
2019	47,059,014	28,690,564	30,447	28,721,011	3,409,492	95,526	25,407,045	10,043,666	11,608,303	45,490	1,034,482	530,638
2020	51,841,647	30,013,053	30,836	30,043,889	3,591,603	146,552	26,598,838	10,057,735	15,185,074	49,601	1,045,175	523,221
2021	55,627,320	31,382,638	32,651	31,415,289	3,771,843	144,787	27,788,233	10,991,333	16,847,754	53,034	1,048,895	536,459
2022	57,601,036	33,692,038	38,815	33,730,853	4,077,594	161,286	29,814,545	12,203,656	15,582,835	54,464	1,057,597	557,893

Personal Income and Employment by Area: Tulsa, OK

(Thousands of dollars, except as noted.)

Year	Personal income, total	Derivation of personal income: Earnings by place of work: Nonfarm	Farm	Total	Less: Contributions for government social insurance	Plus: Adjustment for residence	Equals: Net earnings by place of residence	Plus: Dividends, interest, and rent	Plus: Personal current transfer receipts	Per capita personal income (dollars)	Population (persons)	Total employment
1970	2,244,876	1,803,417	17,819	1,821,236	118,059	-13,643	1,689,534	344,994	210,348	3,916	573,235	253,693
1971	2,423,024	1,923,488	15,964	1,939,452	129,622	-11,000	1,798,830	380,481	243,713	4,162	582,203	255,389
1972	2,660,683	2,136,833	21,145	2,157,978	151,577	-12,550	1,993,851	400,704	266,128	4,494	592,055	270,578
1973	3,010,374	2,427,869	25,672	2,453,541	201,071	-12,440	2,240,030	465,639	304,705	5,000	602,108	286,825
1974	3,535,154	2,854,603	28,731	2,883,334	242,127	-8,842	2,632,365	545,238	357,551	5,777	611,968	301,297
1975	4,037,412	3,226,449	26,245	3,252,694	267,329	10,306	2,995,671	600,416	441,325	6,457	625,290	309,562
1976	4,496,483	3,619,842	27,581	3,647,423	307,343	19,613	3,359,693	651,137	485,653	7,043	638,395	324,739
1977	5,048,189	4,114,867	17,591	4,132,458	347,292	18,843	3,804,009	723,181	520,999	7,746	651,741	336,418
1978	5,741,100	4,735,201	5,321	4,740,522	412,300	16,667	4,344,889	837,483	558,728	8,645	664,120	356,285
1979	6,570,554	5,463,555	16,969	5,480,524	494,812	-27,859	4,957,853	968,971	643,730	9,522	690,017	372,697
1980	7,756,185	6,414,764	11,648	6,426,412	582,946	-43,751	5,799,715	1,209,354	747,116	10,837	715,729	396,414
1981	9,013,856	7,407,097	22,929	7,430,026	724,104	-57,943	6,647,979	1,514,198	851,679	12,335	730,726	416,102
1982	9,855,110	7,928,027	16,706	7,944,733	799,460	-57,708	7,087,565	1,786,774	980,771	13,056	754,809	420,399
1983	10,029,681	7,890,947	14,600	7,905,547	792,124	-47,832	7,065,591	1,879,311	1,084,779	12,979	772,780	406,405
1984	10,733,802	8,413,935	12,368	8,426,303	856,524	-36,843	7,532,936	2,084,389	1,116,477	13,859	774,500	416,659
1985	11,343,964	8,838,843	10,333	8,849,176	913,651	-45,139	7,890,386	2,264,707	1,188,871	14,671	773,203	421,361
1986	11,529,580	8,970,166	21,113	8,991,279	946,414	-49,220	7,995,645	2,259,716	1,274,219	14,862	775,798	409,752
1987	11,537,982	8,981,797	16,105	8,997,902	945,958	-44,968	8,006,976	2,199,870	1,331,136	14,971	770,713	411,356
1988	12,127,776	9,463,547	26,063	9,489,610	1,040,902	-51,303	8,397,405	2,323,617	1,406,754	15,986	758,652	413,701
1989	12,964,227	10,149,835	29,269	10,179,104	1,117,270	-79,229	8,982,605	2,471,523	1,510,099	17,118	757,345	418,975
1990	13,915,903	10,829,567	13,894	10,843,461	1,237,234	-48,716	9,557,511	2,734,289	1,624,103	18,236	763,119	430,763
1991	14,447,184	11,276,525	30,254	11,306,779	1,316,608	-50,808	9,939,363	2,734,890	1,772,931	18,647	774,765	437,718
1992	15,230,906	11,861,419	31,082	11,892,501	1,371,429	-67,034	10,454,038	2,793,418	1,983,450	19,384	785,755	438,214
1993	15,809,640	12,381,108	29,253	12,410,361	1,438,718	-88,452	10,883,191	2,809,775	2,116,674	19,883	795,139	444,889
1994	16,516,914	12,845,782	35,297	12,881,079	1,515,283	-101,367	11,264,429	3,026,876	2,225,609	20,634	800,473	453,942
1995	17,450,732	13,413,972	9,776	13,423,748	1,580,280	-111,073	11,732,395	3,300,625	2,417,712	21,658	805,725	466,011
1996	18,623,978	14,313,567	13,657	14,327,224	1,654,860	-125,433	12,546,931	3,527,589	2,549,458	22,816	816,284	481,882
1997	19,976,354	15,542,980	16,410	15,559,390	1,772,424	-167,194	13,619,772	3,659,236	2,697,346	24,086	829,391	499,806
1998	21,538,151	16,834,592	-13,913	16,820,679	1,913,669	-194,604	14,712,406	4,089,437	2,736,308	25,548	843,057	523,100
1999	21,832,432	16,922,920	7,294	16,930,214	1,948,747	-176,024	14,805,443	4,160,962	2,866,027	25,546	854,631	522,394
2000	23,683,685	18,137,745	119	18,137,864	2,060,399	-205,246	15,872,219	4,794,023	3,017,443	27,500	861,237	533,529
2001	24,014,369	18,244,880	5,015	18,249,895	2,166,703	-250,250	15,832,942	4,879,716	3,301,711	27,679	867,602	537,484
2002	24,315,475	18,388,734	29,055	18,417,789	2,208,965	-265,908	15,942,916	4,863,214	3,509,345	27,794	874,844	530,202
2003	24,909,436	18,601,076	-72	18,601,004	2,186,196	-233,729	16,181,079	4,960,103	3,768,254	28,384	877,577	516,797
2004	28,311,255	21,654,398	38,102	21,692,500	2,379,204	-241,963	19,071,333	5,272,429	3,967,493	32,245	878,004	520,224
2005	31,936,953	24,365,179	53,824	24,419,003	2,555,312	-269,271	21,594,420	6,051,745	4,290,788	36,174	882,861	535,397
2006	36,578,422	27,999,344	26,381	28,025,725	2,739,429	-345,306	24,940,990	6,928,662	4,708,770	40,915	894,011	552,741
2007	37,653,776	27,918,475	32,734	27,951,209	2,869,481	-325,991	24,755,737	7,824,177	5,073,862	41,540	906,441	567,326
2008	43,204,352	32,173,689	8,374	32,182,063	2,999,928	-299,690	28,882,445	8,601,259	5,720,648	47,139	916,525	577,830
2009	37,604,576	27,144,091	-7,233	27,136,858	2,863,253	-246,486	24,027,119	7,442,245	6,135,212	40,443	929,824	559,652
2010	39,374,835	28,263,460	18,337	28,281,797	2,887,581	-88,673	25,305,543	7,453,231	6,616,061	41,883	940,111	550,917
2011	44,072,274	31,766,446	41,425	31,807,871	2,823,845	-59,232	28,924,794	8,462,745	6,684,735	46,534	947,092	556,583
2012	48,821,301	35,180,376	70,617	35,250,993	3,033,841	-4,644	32,212,508	9,765,135	6,843,658	51,128	954,892	570,622
2013	53,993,433	41,230,870	23,571	41,254,441	3,525,161	29,934	37,759,214	9,262,983	6,971,236	55,929	965,395	579,118
2014	57,480,107	43,967,151	82,690	44,049,841	3,626,301	46,336	40,469,876	9,762,305	7,247,926	59,015	973,986	588,148
2015	52,824,918	39,113,564	45,718	39,159,282	3,621,544	40,755	35,578,493	9,710,299	7,536,126	53,544	986,572	597,099
2016	46,868,941	33,202,393	-6,926	33,195,467	3,467,731	22,000	29,749,736	9,261,368	7,857,837	47,087	995,361	598,994
2017	50,382,860	35,926,044	-14,443	35,911,601	3,626,840	24,567	32,309,328	9,884,675	8,188,857	50,433	998,996	601,844
2018	54,099,751	38,639,815	-20,699	38,619,116	3,859,410	-55,269	34,704,437	10,884,487	8,510,827	53,979	1,002,232	609,752
2019	55,817,024	39,408,481	-28,042	39,380,439	4,000,329	-23,073	35,357,037	11,289,737	9,170,250	55,346	1,008,509	610,669
2020	56,847,209	38,080,688	-23,456	38,057,232	4,015,874	35,735	34,077,093	11,120,760	11,649,356	55,882	1,017,272	597,397
2021	62,386,980	41,135,270	-13,656	41,121,614	4,202,042	39,126	36,958,698	12,203,241	13,225,041	60,830	1,025,597	613,019
2022	64,754,579	44,869,349	-86,076	44,783,273	4,560,635	6,891	40,229,529	12,599,761	11,925,289	62,618	1,034,123	639,991

Personal Income and Employment by Area: Tuscaloosa, AL

(Thousands of dollars, except as noted.)

Year	Personal income, total	Derivation of personal income: Earnings by place of work								Per capita personal income (dollars)	Population (persons)	Total employment
		Nonfarm	Farm	Total	Less: Contributions for government social insurance	Plus: Adjustment for residence	Equals: Net earnings by place of residence	Plus: Dividends, interest, and rent	Plus: Personal current transfer receipts			
1970	440,221	336,422	11,095	347,517	24,954	7,298	329,861	54,718	55,642	2,699	163,093	60,582
1971	499,561	380,275	14,656	394,931	28,958	7,720	373,693	62,657	63,211	3,012	165,840	62,424
1972	556,955	425,194	16,784	441,978	34,040	8,921	416,859	70,070	70,026	3,296	168,991	65,284
1973	625,697	476,633	23,734	500,367	43,920	10,706	467,153	79,330	79,214	3,647	171,555	67,884
1974	698,610	535,932	13,631	549,563	50,753	12,689	511,499	92,995	94,116	4,017	173,902	68,411
1975	785,971	585,431	13,830	599,261	55,165	13,527	557,623	107,342	121,006	4,490	175,046	68,143
1976	866,249	647,984	17,124	665,108	62,348	15,180	617,940	117,226	131,083	4,880	177,513	69,796
1977	980,659	753,104	11,752	764,856	70,989	15,497	709,364	131,755	139,540	5,473	179,189	71,958
1978	1,104,865	835,738	21,917	857,655	79,234	19,227	797,648	153,724	153,493	6,042	182,855	72,331
1979	1,228,547	920,384	24,228	944,612	90,159	21,636	876,089	176,267	176,191	6,670	184,180	73,456
1980	1,308,907	961,702	4,054	965,756	97,115	19,971	888,612	211,582	208,713	7,036	186,019	72,927
1981	1,465,116	1,045,443	11,926	1,057,369	114,334	29,703	972,738	256,280	236,098	7,827	187,181	73,141
1982	1,567,906	1,104,627	8,375	1,113,002	123,820	26,773	1,015,955	290,278	261,673	8,445	185,653	72,070
1983	1,683,387	1,176,722	3,880	1,180,602	130,657	36,637	1,086,582	311,850	284,955	9,039	186,235	72,423
1984	1,861,735	1,310,817	12,179	1,322,996	147,091	34,848	1,210,753	348,094	302,888	9,963	186,871	74,609
1985	2,016,787	1,412,045	16,562	1,428,607	158,230	36,850	1,307,227	380,069	329,491	10,682	188,807	75,907
1986	2,116,608	1,484,046	18,163	1,502,209	167,936	41,193	1,375,466	395,868	345,274	11,085	190,938	78,597
1987	2,273,518	1,625,938	21,496	1,647,434	179,030	50,168	1,518,572	402,593	352,353	11,789	192,851	81,651
1988	2,423,361	1,718,253	30,732	1,748,985	199,391	65,285	1,614,879	440,639	367,843	12,487	194,077	85,163
1989	2,681,406	1,851,729	31,379	1,883,108	213,655	73,792	1,743,245	517,958	420,203	13,717	195,478	87,573
1990	2,924,694	2,042,138	36,963	2,079,101	237,441	71,400	1,913,060	539,122	472,512	14,810	197,482	91,479
1991	3,076,442	2,129,108	43,153	2,172,261	247,743	73,523	1,998,041	559,915	518,486	15,363	200,247	91,363
1992	3,308,055	2,267,118	42,368	2,309,486	258,889	93,072	2,143,669	567,585	596,801	16,453	201,056	92,219
1993	3,497,428	2,417,154	43,444	2,460,598	278,952	92,442	2,274,088	588,595	634,745	17,247	202,790	96,113
1994	3,712,642	2,558,140	32,948	2,591,088	297,602	91,466	2,384,952	640,342	687,348	18,163	204,405	98,006
1995	3,930,261	2,690,850	24,382	2,715,232	314,910	87,008	2,487,330	703,304	739,627	18,927	207,659	100,331
1996	4,072,550	2,779,216	28,957	2,808,173	323,956	85,727	2,569,944	723,973	778,633	19,570	208,097	102,706
1997	4,292,132	2,949,939	37,163	2,987,102	344,599	75,305	2,717,808	754,364	819,960	20,453	209,857	105,915
1998	4,564,558	3,156,754	52,379	3,209,133	363,825	71,085	2,916,393	820,255	827,910	21,596	211,366	108,113
1999	4,806,882	3,365,817	74,616	3,440,433	386,079	63,632	3,117,986	816,968	871,928	22,628	212,433	108,935
2000	4,986,099	3,450,213	55,390	3,505,603	395,865	60,875	3,170,613	885,085	930,401	23,257	214,391	109,643
2001	5,149,469	3,597,841	64,051	3,661,892	415,376	47,279	3,293,795	895,261	960,413	23,889	215,558	110,885
2002	5,321,981	3,734,006	54,648	3,788,654	429,532	31,657	3,390,779	897,626	1,033,576	24,609	216,258	111,526
2003	5,563,529	3,871,989	76,670	3,948,659	443,810	15,781	3,520,630	967,026	1,075,873	25,618	217,173	112,066
2004	5,867,751	4,113,018	92,283	4,205,301	466,961	7,495	3,745,835	986,672	1,135,244	26,819	218,791	114,915
2005	6,319,960	4,500,691	91,987	4,592,678	511,718	-70,196	4,010,764	1,093,545	1,215,651	28,440	222,220	118,558
2006	6,713,732	4,836,808	67,092	4,903,900	551,447	-131,998	4,220,455	1,204,182	1,289,095	29,537	227,299	123,811
2007	7,075,852	5,010,360	57,956	5,068,316	578,164	-167,759	4,322,393	1,330,965	1,422,494	30,746	230,142	127,130
2008	7,360,130	5,088,202	50,294	5,138,496	600,425	-224,302	4,313,769	1,465,985	1,580,376	31,499	233,663	126,950
2009	7,369,678	4,948,292	54,879	5,003,171	582,583	-223,092	4,197,496	1,441,786	1,730,396	30,989	237,813	122,017
2010	7,576,165	5,181,312	49,563	5,230,875	612,337	-289,648	4,328,890	1,369,006	1,878,269	31,590	239,830	121,780
2011	7,842,005	5,420,027	29,932	5,449,959	567,493	-300,287	4,582,179	1,373,956	1,885,870	32,388	242,130	123,857
2012	8,105,613	5,578,660	40,679	5,619,339	584,724	-308,095	4,726,520	1,522,522	1,856,571	33,009	245,561	126,973
2013	8,227,878	5,727,325	120,968	5,848,293	677,730	-283,736	4,886,827	1,444,012	1,897,039	33,028	249,115	128,351
2014	8,476,153	5,962,207	64,899	6,027,106	703,737	-329,959	4,993,410	1,508,550	1,974,193	33,469	253,251	132,779
2015	8,763,586	6,103,180	72,414	6,175,594	720,236	-365,760	5,089,598	1,557,733	2,116,255	34,113	256,895	136,445
2016	8,873,097	6,144,565	48,493	6,193,058	720,172	-328,053	5,144,833	1,575,873	2,152,391	34,178	259,612	137,227
2017	9,236,263	6,377,677	64,930	6,442,607	753,799	-374,625	5,314,183	1,737,689	2,184,391	35,256	261,980	139,639
2018	9,525,489	6,680,710	40,151	6,720,861	798,076	-388,845	5,533,940	1,727,500	2,264,049	36,094	263,910	142,415
2019	9,994,088	7,032,020	34,562	7,066,582	837,837	-450,865	5,777,880	1,835,682	2,380,526	37,421	267,072	145,564
2020	10,696,457	7,049,463	30,808	7,080,271	850,880	-432,908	5,796,483	1,923,265	2,976,709	39,192	272,926	139,873
2021	11,403,317	7,310,735	51,064	7,361,799	885,928	-351,360	6,124,511	1,965,499	3,313,307	41,225	276,612	143,845
2022	11,474,265	7,664,726	43,060	7,707,786	951,144	-322,274	6,434,368	2,093,267	2,946,630	41,350	277,494	148,589

Personal Income and Employment by Area: Twin Falls, ID

(Thousands of dollars, except as noted.)

Year	Personal income, total	Derivation of personal income: Earnings by place of work: Nonfarm	Farm	Total	Less: Contributions for government social insurance	Plus: Adjustment for residence	Equals: Net earnings by place of residence	Plus: Dividends, interest, and rent	Plus: Personal current transfer receipts	Per capita personal income (dollars)	Population (persons)	Total employment
1970	193,857	115,179	34,956	150,135	8,618	749	142,266	32,921	18,670	3,692	52,509	25,303
1971	211,160	129,014	31,599	160,613	9,944	503	151,172	38,242	21,746	3,858	54,740	26,097
1972	244,241	143,728	44,508	188,236	11,512	819	177,543	41,913	24,785	4,305	56,740	26,921
1973	294,627	165,615	66,283	231,898	15,569	675	217,004	50,013	27,610	5,083	57,963	28,605
1974	360,419	195,209	92,805	288,014	18,974	195	269,235	58,740	32,444	6,030	59,768	30,370
1975	362,205	220,594	51,866	272,460	21,121	304	251,643	71,284	39,278	5,836	62,064	30,726
1976	383,853	249,634	41,282	290,916	24,143	255	267,028	73,680	43,145	6,122	62,700	32,480
1977	396,498	269,712	23,877	293,589	26,075	10	267,524	82,134	46,840	6,181	64,150	32,734
1978	450,350	308,982	28,809	337,791	30,090	-232	307,469	91,448	51,433	6,974	64,574	34,350
1979	498,774	349,981	23,720	373,701	36,079	-533	337,089	102,425	59,260	7,538	66,164	35,211
1980	584,110	371,461	52,978	424,439	38,634	251	386,056	127,377	70,677	8,592	67,983	34,801
1981	631,790	397,495	43,280	440,775	44,291	-2,075	394,409	155,817	81,564	9,187	68,769	34,410
1982	671,180	407,721	33,756	441,477	46,503	-2,588	392,386	186,869	91,925	9,635	69,657	33,845
1983	731,111	422,340	62,983	485,323	47,872	-2,292	435,159	196,601	99,351	10,316	70,873	34,040
1984	775,020	451,752	68,248	520,000	53,109	-2,610	464,281	207,124	103,615	10,964	70,686	34,048
1985	802,999	468,455	61,441	529,896	56,154	-3,281	470,461	221,612	110,926	11,475	69,977	33,630
1986	822,066	473,307	74,412	547,719	57,528	-2,942	487,249	218,457	116,360	11,857	69,333	33,517
1987	857,164	498,344	91,852	590,196	59,632	-2,383	528,181	209,169	119,814	12,516	68,487	34,073
1988	918,870	542,806	100,834	643,640	67,509	-1,125	575,006	214,549	129,315	13,435	68,393	35,116
1989	1,010,134	583,130	125,034	708,164	73,652	-497	634,015	237,885	138,234	14,789	68,305	35,955
1990	1,076,646	652,200	123,022	775,222	86,797	-1,520	686,905	241,804	147,937	15,596	69,033	38,157
1991	1,112,416	690,400	107,339	797,739	93,621	-789	703,329	247,260	161,827	15,760	70,584	38,905
1992	1,192,327	741,576	120,756	862,332	98,571	5	763,766	246,890	181,671	16,573	71,944	39,444
1993	1,305,723	799,106	163,535	962,641	106,760	959	856,840	258,108	190,775	17,789	73,402	40,806
1994	1,372,569	879,124	134,369	1,013,493	117,827	1,139	896,805	272,222	203,542	18,212	75,368	42,697
1995	1,475,460	925,342	148,083	1,073,425	124,249	1,672	950,848	302,233	222,379	19,264	76,590	44,397
1996	1,597,591	990,257	176,995	1,167,252	129,090	1,985	1,040,147	320,690	236,754	20,406	78,292	45,773
1997	1,648,529	1,027,697	161,088	1,188,785	133,314	2,615	1,058,086	343,900	246,543	20,685	79,696	47,072
1998	1,774,896	1,095,773	201,757	1,297,530	139,914	3,354	1,160,970	361,750	252,176	21,925	80,953	48,520
1999	1,815,022	1,153,765	192,924	1,346,689	144,148	5,521	1,208,062	341,978	264,982	22,155	81,923	48,686
2000	1,885,138	1,196,888	176,775	1,373,663	149,785	7,448	1,231,326	367,928	285,884	22,753	82,853	50,294
2001	2,013,283	1,233,672	223,721	1,457,393	154,733	6,684	1,309,344	385,465	318,474	24,217	83,135	50,131
2002	2,031,404	1,323,141	182,174	1,505,315	166,726	2,273	1,340,862	347,950	342,592	24,125	84,203	51,767
2003	2,088,418	1,371,210	162,569	1,533,779	176,327	-754	1,356,698	373,730	357,990	24,266	86,063	52,237
2004	2,286,430	1,433,001	267,508	1,700,509	184,030	637	1,517,116	387,108	382,206	26,089	87,640	52,724
2005	2,391,522	1,525,037	243,493	1,768,530	198,282	-392	1,569,856	410,086	411,580	26,725	89,487	54,866
2006	2,550,101	1,683,708	201,261	1,884,969	219,578	-4,539	1,660,852	436,502	452,747	27,693	92,085	56,596
2007	2,785,717	1,739,500	331,289	2,070,789	231,977	-5,800	1,833,012	467,318	485,387	29,538	94,310	57,880
2008	2,889,495	1,768,795	292,871	2,061,666	241,223	-10,847	1,809,596	514,491	565,408	29,986	96,360	58,309
2009	2,764,625	1,770,656	151,682	1,922,338	241,545	-13,891	1,666,902	484,761	612,962	28,122	98,310	56,666
2010	2,949,889	1,801,431	249,825	2,051,256	251,369	-13,275	1,786,612	473,348	689,929	29,494	100,017	55,505
2011	3,140,157	1,829,100	330,001	2,159,101	228,584	-11,425	1,919,092	525,908	695,157	31,156	100,789	56,052
2012	3,290,196	1,930,419	367,749	2,298,168	239,215	-13,027	2,045,926	553,832	690,438	32,436	101,437	56,349
2013	3,458,302	2,069,456	417,081	2,486,537	274,865	-12,808	2,198,864	560,461	698,977	33,536	103,122	58,182
2014	3,666,393	2,153,891	496,459	2,650,350	287,793	-19,261	2,343,296	585,271	737,826	35,077	104,523	60,215
2015	3,803,022	2,314,276	415,007	2,729,283	299,383	-28,116	2,401,784	635,502	765,736	35,882	105,988	61,340
2016	3,909,722	2,402,072	410,377	2,812,449	312,595	-26,264	2,473,590	656,274	779,858	36,143	108,175	62,369
2017	4,056,750	2,564,972	357,090	2,922,062	332,131	-26,882	2,563,049	689,215	804,486	36,785	110,282	64,401
2018	4,204,615	2,702,663	321,068	3,023,731	344,555	-36,149	2,643,027	706,238	855,350	37,724	111,458	65,299
2019	4,463,948	2,822,005	404,423	3,226,428	354,770	-45,875	2,825,783	721,810	916,355	39,510	112,983	66,080
2020	4,941,124	2,983,571	449,361	3,432,932	382,381	-41,483	3,009,068	789,238	1,142,818	43,105	114,629	66,077
2021	5,429,755	3,291,814	363,702	3,655,516	412,160	-49,779	3,193,577	865,894	1,370,284	46,368	117,102	68,981
2022	5,748,672	3,552,095	479,180	4,031,275	456,548	-54,801	3,519,926	968,602	1,260,144	48,305	119,007	71,197

Personal Income and Employment by Area: Tyler, TX

(Thousands of dollars, except as noted.)

Year	Personal income, total	Derivation of personal income: Earnings by place of work: Nonfarm	Earnings by place of work: Farm	Earnings by place of work: Total	Less: Contributions for government social insurance	Plus: Adjustment for residence	Equals: Net earnings by place of residence	Plus: Dividends, interest, and rent	Plus: Personal current transfer receipts	Per capita personal income (dollars)	Population (persons)	Total employment
1970	351,219	290,251	2,119	292,370	19,129	-11,052	262,189	57,001	32,029	3,606	97,390	46,609
1971	386,169	316,918	3,785	320,703	21,431	-11,836	287,436	62,202	36,531	3,868	99,839	47,754
1972	438,298	367,053	3,343	370,396	26,074	-15,331	328,991	68,563	40,744	4,223	103,794	51,083
1973	500,311	415,053	8,045	423,098	34,373	-17,516	371,209	79,832	49,270	4,731	105,758	53,832
1974	570,348	464,251	8,027	472,278	39,172	-19,167	413,939	96,360	60,049	5,244	108,766	54,925
1975	637,891	506,514	3,205	509,719	41,468	-19,647	448,604	112,470	76,817	5,713	111,662	55,398
1976	733,407	589,520	7,480	597,000	48,693	-21,915	526,392	123,450	83,565	6,419	114,264	57,952
1977	841,790	694,847	5,332	700,179	57,449	-29,051	613,679	139,771	88,340	7,187	117,127	62,480
1978	973,776	810,559	3,889	814,448	68,508	-34,505	711,435	163,351	98,990	8,070	120,667	66,707
1979	1,127,383	936,018	10,433	946,451	83,063	-41,602	821,786	192,670	112,927	8,954	125,905	70,277
1980	1,284,265	1,027,624	10,260	1,037,884	91,630	-42,998	903,256	245,444	135,565	9,931	129,316	71,788
1981	1,494,254	1,178,122	11,480	1,189,602	113,283	-47,603	1,028,716	313,950	151,588	11,258	132,734	75,129
1982	1,702,337	1,303,250	17,550	1,320,800	128,982	-54,379	1,137,439	393,066	171,832	12,394	137,348	79,688
1983	1,856,489	1,411,313	23,739	1,435,052	139,100	-60,783	1,235,169	429,715	191,605	13,144	141,243	81,358
1984	2,032,347	1,567,583	21,554	1,589,137	160,465	-70,804	1,357,868	470,570	203,909	14,013	145,030	85,052
1985	2,149,408	1,629,148	8,798	1,637,946	169,055	-69,845	1,399,046	526,480	223,882	14,428	148,975	85,608
1986	2,220,171	1,657,042	18,574	1,675,616	170,825	-69,145	1,435,646	533,679	250,846	14,649	151,554	82,811
1987	2,229,350	1,657,258	18,204	1,675,462	168,973	-70,102	1,436,387	522,542	270,421	14,629	152,388	84,446
1988	2,332,746	1,707,916	12,720	1,720,636	179,711	-67,633	1,473,292	571,161	288,293	15,330	152,164	84,113
1989	2,467,029	1,764,444	16,008	1,780,452	187,529	-70,734	1,522,189	632,593	312,247	16,351	150,876	84,412
1990	2,605,429	1,876,359	14,867	1,891,226	195,386	-73,280	1,622,560	634,154	348,715	17,192	151,550	85,724
1991	2,711,868	1,970,747	12,758	1,983,505	211,493	-86,143	1,685,869	644,481	381,518	17,643	153,705	87,981
1992	2,879,798	2,131,086	13,160	2,144,246	225,167	-99,811	1,819,268	619,722	440,808	18,539	155,336	88,955
1993	3,041,224	2,274,492	14,024	2,288,516	240,888	-115,983	1,931,645	640,024	469,555	19,161	158,717	91,518
1994	3,187,415	2,379,674	13,799	2,393,473	254,151	-125,837	2,013,485	673,241	500,689	19,810	160,898	94,519
1995	3,402,779	2,507,993	14,219	2,522,212	267,755	-134,456	2,120,001	741,785	540,993	20,820	163,440	97,351
1996	3,623,418	2,693,197	12,463	2,705,660	283,333	-148,191	2,274,136	761,448	587,834	21,816	166,087	99,975
1997	3,895,284	2,959,420	22,403	2,981,823	305,022	-166,899	2,509,902	767,150	618,232	23,113	168,531	104,160
1998	4,208,427	3,200,704	27,999	3,228,703	328,140	-194,383	2,706,180	859,672	642,575	24,606	171,033	105,989
1999	4,375,265	3,368,536	34,136	3,402,672	342,995	-215,012	2,844,665	874,536	656,064	25,326	172,758	107,091
2000	4,780,465	3,693,998	28,594	3,722,592	365,009	-242,641	3,114,942	967,007	698,516	27,215	175,658	110,519
2001	5,064,844	3,931,127	35,625	3,966,752	387,295	-241,597	3,337,860	962,330	764,654	28,480	177,836	112,428
2002	5,232,529	4,069,560	38,184	4,107,744	399,023	-246,641	3,462,080	938,347	832,102	28,892	181,107	113,276
2003	5,520,488	4,249,497	34,177	4,283,674	424,752	-248,834	3,610,088	1,007,361	903,039	29,961	184,254	115,188
2004	5,873,494	4,644,941	30,755	4,675,696	463,975	-296,094	3,915,627	1,010,020	947,847	31,359	187,300	118,640
2005	6,597,118	5,175,793	32,763	5,208,556	500,152	-334,688	4,373,716	1,177,438	1,045,964	34,475	191,362	123,109
2006	7,260,083	5,712,194	25,925	5,738,119	532,183	-352,468	4,853,468	1,289,564	1,117,051	37,018	196,124	127,124
2007	7,413,265	5,684,277	19,517	5,703,794	551,035	-319,289	4,833,470	1,355,690	1,224,105	37,075	199,953	130,699
2008	8,834,757	6,720,771	15,480	6,736,251	600,960	-325,569	5,809,722	1,648,418	1,376,617	43,465	203,263	134,233
2009	8,171,517	6,113,764	19,146	6,132,910	590,572	-299,119	5,243,219	1,431,248	1,497,050	39,455	207,111	131,422
2010	9,048,854	6,782,135	21,318	6,803,453	619,631	-290,838	5,892,984	1,534,308	1,621,562	43,014	210,371	132,285
2011	10,208,244	7,718,788	17,299	7,736,087	577,244	-262,089	6,896,754	1,636,394	1,675,096	48,020	212,584	133,587
2012	10,323,150	7,751,253	27,128	7,778,381	588,453	-257,671	6,932,257	1,720,301	1,670,592	48,130	214,483	136,174
2013	10,698,334	8,152,733	14,574	8,167,307	683,937	-265,790	7,217,580	1,728,907	1,751,847	49,529	216,002	139,370
2014	11,245,076	8,552,529	12,192	8,564,721	713,246	-290,068	7,561,407	1,849,202	1,834,467	51,344	219,016	141,748
2015	10,424,631	7,654,273	15,618	7,669,891	719,397	-314,399	6,636,095	1,862,714	1,925,822	47,038	221,620	145,258
2016	10,270,070	7,471,101	9,671	7,480,772	736,754	-355,086	6,388,932	1,861,639	2,019,499	45,813	224,176	148,203
2017	11,732,570	8,769,131	9,350	8,778,481	795,906	-371,557	7,611,018	2,067,398	2,054,154	51,919	225,978	149,723
2018	12,617,393	9,509,055	6,814	9,515,869	832,931	-383,142	8,299,796	2,150,874	2,166,723	55,219	228,497	151,071
2019	12,811,058	9,601,656	1,730	9,603,386	863,798	-409,701	8,329,887	2,198,117	2,283,054	55,373	231,360	151,605
2020	12,986,025	8,960,051	4,386	8,964,437	873,685	-445,829	7,644,923	2,417,163	2,923,939	55,450	234,195	151,946
2021	14,955,757	10,301,932	5,378	10,307,310	914,354	-499,838	8,893,118	2,735,837	3,326,802	63,074	237,114	158,385
2022	16,156,522	11,810,677	-6,195	11,804,482	1,021,299	-551,952	10,231,231	2,955,954	2,969,337	66,784	241,922	166,153

Personal Income and Employment by Area: Urban Honolulu, HI

(Thousands of dollars, except as noted.)

Year	Personal income, total	Derivation of personal income: Earnings by place of work								Per capita personal income (dollars)	Population (persons)	Total employment
		Nonfarm	Farm	Total	Less: Contributions for government social insurance	Plus: Adjustment for residence	Equals: Net earnings by place of residence	Plus: Dividends, interest, and rent	Plus: Personal current transfer receipts			
1970	3,634,964	2,958,005	33,864	2,991,869	183,236	4,733	2,813,366	661,296	160,302	5,828	623,756	366,968
1971	3,926,337	3,153,668	32,321	3,185,989	203,001	5,034	2,988,022	728,002	210,313	6,202	633,043	367,494
1972	4,327,655	3,480,364	32,143	3,512,507	236,141	4,610	3,280,976	797,331	249,348	6,509	664,830	381,276
1973	4,791,314	3,870,404	31,032	3,901,436	300,444	4,394	3,605,386	905,061	280,867	7,007	683,772	398,757
1974	5,274,604	4,217,804	39,362	4,257,166	343,985	4,307	3,917,488	1,024,565	332,551	7,556	698,033	407,738
1975	5,821,193	4,616,636	40,096	4,656,732	380,298	6,294	4,282,728	1,105,665	432,800	8,224	707,866	415,990
1976	6,281,530	4,969,816	41,097	5,010,913	413,473	6,456	4,603,896	1,168,788	508,846	8,762	716,911	417,620
1977	6,771,327	5,354,178	47,097	5,401,275	442,424	6,313	4,965,164	1,270,914	535,249	9,213	734,962	418,536
1978	7,496,119	5,921,228	40,954	5,962,182	502,998	5,023	5,464,207	1,460,740	571,172	10,123	740,505	431,484
1979	8,373,566	6,641,373	43,531	6,684,904	589,044	4,651	6,100,511	1,643,999	629,056	11,114	753,428	454,142
1980	9,425,648	7,372,805	63,826	7,436,631	653,607	4,972	6,787,996	1,919,265	718,387	12,340	763,820	467,461
1981	10,308,336	7,950,314	45,816	7,996,130	750,841	4,969	7,250,258	2,217,388	840,690	13,430	767,573	461,302
1982	10,886,978	8,445,216	50,452	8,495,668	787,253	4,615	7,713,030	2,269,346	904,602	14,028	776,075	457,679
1983	11,854,809	9,068,558	72,563	9,141,121	865,649	4,652	8,280,124	2,584,868	989,817	15,023	789,097	463,241
1984	12,743,337	9,716,997	51,884	9,768,881	946,084	3,616	8,826,413	2,868,590	1,048,334	15,973	797,791	467,189
1985	13,544,474	10,353,793	55,720	10,409,513	1,027,509	4,982	9,386,986	3,049,688	1,107,800	16,840	804,294	477,011
1986	14,293,368	11,032,179	59,639	11,091,818	1,119,586	5,650	9,977,882	3,167,185	1,148,301	17,636	810,444	486,861
1987	15,183,700	11,922,435	58,526	11,980,961	1,220,266	6,027	10,766,722	3,227,731	1,189,247	18,552	818,447	509,161
1988	16,642,308	13,159,375	75,279	13,234,654	1,393,147	6,226	11,847,733	3,519,651	1,274,924	20,195	824,072	525,017
1989	18,415,533	14,449,342	68,648	14,517,990	1,530,993	10,499	12,997,496	4,005,191	1,412,846	22,152	831,337	540,855
1990	20,037,018	15,941,554	76,424	16,017,978	1,760,667	12,384	14,269,695	4,242,127	1,525,196	23,895	838,534	558,346
1991	21,121,509	16,853,115	67,200	16,920,315	1,883,622	10,653	15,047,346	4,411,078	1,663,085	24,834	850,510	569,711
1992	22,655,743	18,039,436	52,140	18,091,576	2,010,280	6,749	16,088,045	4,690,612	1,877,086	26,223	863,959	570,015
1993	23,374,634	18,380,701	76,253	18,456,954	2,044,634	5,563	16,417,883	4,888,596	2,068,155	26,857	870,348	566,606
1994	23,836,238	18,465,352	64,023	18,529,375	2,070,316	1,789	16,460,848	5,133,171	2,242,219	27,130	878,591	560,810
1995	24,313,163	18,404,319	71,016	18,475,335	2,060,576	-2,183	16,412,576	5,371,007	2,529,580	27,585	881,399	556,670
1996	24,240,372	18,332,011	66,664	18,398,675	2,055,206	-4,021	16,339,448	5,316,499	2,584,425	27,439	883,443	553,469
1997	24,990,036	18,850,953	66,597	18,917,550	2,085,664	-7,107	16,824,779	5,551,939	2,613,318	28,183	886,711	550,825
1998	25,315,931	19,029,970	71,789	19,101,759	2,108,546	-9,105	16,984,108	5,689,807	2,642,016	28,544	886,909	551,211
1999	25,979,221	19,589,857	90,061	19,679,918	2,144,039	-9,383	17,526,496	5,707,481	2,745,244	29,559	878,906	546,376
2000	27,403,301	20,687,415	83,373	20,770,788	2,249,280	-11,563	18,509,945	5,975,704	2,917,652	31,260	876,629	552,871
2001	28,517,410	21,777,581	78,931	21,856,512	2,372,021	-12,269	19,472,222	5,891,411	3,153,777	32,305	882,755	549,294
2002	29,909,676	23,071,385	87,049	23,158,434	2,506,757	-12,346	20,639,331	5,876,721	3,393,624	33,589	890,473	551,417
2003	31,225,086	24,431,963	89,139	24,521,102	2,686,872	-12,802	21,821,428	5,910,580	3,493,078	34,915	894,311	561,497
2004	33,288,785	26,076,230	74,937	26,151,167	2,819,130	-13,430	23,318,607	6,266,146	3,704,032	36,662	907,997	575,802
2005	35,529,404	27,804,152	68,106	27,872,258	2,999,909	-11,565	24,860,784	6,669,012	3,999,608	38,695	918,181	587,504
2006	37,941,381	29,380,377	66,160	29,446,537	3,241,412	-10,527	26,194,598	7,525,551	4,221,232	40,931	926,954	602,414
2007	39,940,512	30,384,382	66,109	30,450,491	3,386,768	-8,540	27,055,183	8,270,689	4,614,640	43,163	925,335	614,631
2008	41,991,888	31,168,457	91,710	31,260,167	3,466,032	-8,653	27,785,482	8,859,620	5,346,786	44,975	933,680	613,189
2009	42,217,847	31,138,401	112,486	31,250,887	3,470,875	-16,761	27,763,251	8,800,721	5,653,875	44,761	943,177	598,467
2010	43,034,473	31,880,295	107,836	31,988,131	3,658,537	-21,645	28,307,949	8,415,030	6,311,494	44,945	957,482	595,767
2011	45,036,398	33,105,912	111,092	33,217,004	3,484,509	-30,539	29,701,956	8,784,420	6,550,022	46,267	973,408	603,580
2012	46,379,847	34,416,421	111,359	34,527,780	3,603,607	-35,913	30,888,260	9,023,307	6,468,280	46,893	989,064	613,440
2013	46,853,344	35,455,460	104,118	35,559,578	4,195,759	-41,991	31,321,828	8,830,256	6,701,260	46,750	1,002,219	625,445
2014	49,166,352	36,735,854	89,511	36,825,365	4,227,521	-44,987	32,552,857	9,434,820	7,178,675	48,743	1,008,682	634,617
2015	51,195,028	38,421,143	96,979	38,518,122	4,412,109	-47,656	34,058,357	9,668,576	7,468,095	50,316	1,017,472	648,010
2016	53,039,739	39,679,164	83,874	39,763,038	4,502,864	-50,713	35,209,461	10,081,866	7,748,412	51,805	1,023,837	657,796
2017	54,939,450	40,987,844	96,848	41,084,692	4,657,814	-51,340	36,375,538	10,547,010	8,016,902	53,723	1,022,650	659,037
2018	55,814,960	42,003,414	80,048	42,083,462	4,781,908	-50,729	37,250,825	10,416,590	8,147,545	54,633	1,021,634	658,341
2019	57,828,675	43,134,518	69,943	43,204,461	4,937,566	-50,319	38,216,576	11,104,679	8,507,420	56,762	1,018,784	644,819
2020	61,014,686	41,325,315	84,895	41,410,210	4,770,319	-53,193	36,586,698	11,773,269	12,654,719	60,273	1,012,305	584,173
2021	64,493,233	44,111,503	84,307	44,195,810	5,077,885	-48,876	39,069,049	11,959,346	13,464,838	64,193	1,004,673	607,535
2022	64,652,972	46,220,382	85,333	46,305,715	5,445,807	-50,238	40,809,670	12,618,041	11,225,261	64,936	995,638	635,342

Personal Income and Employment by Area: Utica-Rome, NY

(Thousands of dollars, except as noted.)

Year	Personal income, total	Derivation of personal income								Per capita personal income (dollars)	Population (persons)	Total employment
		Earnings by place of work			Less: Contributions for government social insurance	Plus: Adjustment for residence	Equals: Net earnings by place of residence	Plus: Dividends, interest, and rent	Plus: Personal current transfer receipts			
		Nonfarm	Farm	Total								
1970	1,324,477	1,060,561	20,517	1,081,078	77,266	-17,388	986,424	197,977	140,076	3,880	341,324	144,349
1971	1,413,713	1,110,302	20,540	1,130,842	83,159	-14,307	1,033,376	212,658	167,679	4,110	343,966	142,378
1972	1,494,219	1,165,518	19,851	1,185,369	91,493	-11,875	1,082,001	226,384	185,834	4,340	344,262	140,209
1973	1,617,724	1,262,975	22,213	1,285,188	113,937	-10,573	1,160,678	250,631	206,415	4,775	338,821	143,694
1974	1,736,217	1,333,690	18,273	1,351,963	124,340	-7,833	1,219,790	279,230	237,197	5,185	334,835	143,415
1975	1,880,517	1,387,031	14,400	1,401,431	127,841	-6,472	1,267,118	304,745	308,654	5,645	333,120	138,881
1976	1,992,681	1,471,966	16,023	1,487,989	138,815	-4,516	1,344,658	322,204	325,819	6,040	329,897	137,590
1977	2,119,146	1,562,799	10,130	1,572,929	147,764	-832	1,424,333	353,200	341,613	6,482	326,942	137,404
1978	2,301,630	1,719,066	14,066	1,733,132	166,510	797	1,567,419	377,472	356,739	7,070	325,540	141,015
1979	2,512,464	1,869,017	18,552	1,887,569	187,576	4,447	1,704,440	421,203	386,821	7,762	323,689	143,203
1980	2,802,148	2,016,424	18,482	2,034,906	201,409	7,642	1,841,139	511,151	449,858	8,751	320,223	142,202
1981	3,100,804	2,182,220	18,208	2,200,428	230,838	9,522	1,979,112	608,822	512,870	9,696	319,790	141,590
1982	3,374,817	2,310,389	18,059	2,328,448	243,903	9,457	2,094,002	700,877	579,938	10,553	319,788	140,336
1983	3,571,750	2,435,840	14,724	2,450,564	259,401	11,393	2,202,556	741,515	627,679	11,149	320,361	139,924
1984	3,922,807	2,705,873	19,088	2,724,961	294,788	8,611	2,438,784	831,245	652,778	12,255	320,097	144,968
1985	4,119,858	2,841,386	24,378	2,865,764	315,513	10,654	2,560,905	868,482	690,471	12,900	319,368	145,991
1986	4,316,024	2,983,477	29,378	3,012,855	336,839	9,648	2,685,664	903,057	727,303	13,617	316,950	148,023
1987	4,491,078	3,158,965	32,302	3,191,267	351,925	8,327	2,847,669	903,070	740,339	14,203	316,211	147,894
1988	4,786,466	3,419,559	25,449	3,445,008	389,858	5,051	3,060,201	939,520	786,745	15,179	315,341	152,786
1989	5,150,050	3,587,671	34,895	3,622,566	407,575	3,896	3,218,887	1,091,961	839,202	16,293	316,088	154,516
1990	5,437,833	3,799,410	35,831	3,835,241	414,060	1,375	3,422,556	1,111,146	904,131	17,150	317,074	156,491
1991	5,565,230	3,854,658	25,501	3,880,159	431,328	7,682	3,456,513	1,117,630	991,087	17,424	319,408	153,350
1992	5,886,061	4,080,340	32,105	4,112,445	449,332	6,365	3,669,478	1,105,206	1,111,377	18,370	320,421	154,175
1993	6,033,839	4,174,443	31,784	4,206,227	464,490	8,887	3,750,624	1,124,143	1,159,072	18,879	319,608	154,382
1994	6,172,591	4,263,976	31,234	4,295,210	481,799	9,837	3,823,248	1,127,148	1,222,195	19,411	318,002	156,706
1995	6,267,502	4,271,405	22,195	4,293,600	486,686	17,729	3,824,643	1,159,057	1,283,802	20,124	311,447	154,290
1996	6,323,076	4,270,347	37,531	4,307,878	480,426	22,893	3,850,345	1,162,936	1,309,795	20,684	305,700	151,768
1997	6,586,813	4,455,754	15,591	4,471,345	494,000	22,983	4,000,328	1,257,052	1,329,433	21,762	302,681	151,824
1998	6,877,132	4,609,564	35,382	4,644,946	504,636	24,773	4,165,083	1,276,883	1,435,166	22,877	300,619	153,524
1999	7,197,202	4,961,830	40,618	5,002,448	526,643	26,403	4,502,208	1,256,137	1,438,857	24,001	299,874	157,955
2000	7,524,855	5,229,804	36,211	5,266,015	553,834	22,753	4,734,934	1,299,254	1,490,667	25,117	299,597	160,777
2001	7,551,377	5,181,478	60,450	5,241,928	574,142	27,091	4,694,877	1,257,577	1,598,923	25,296	298,521	157,591
2002	7,587,894	5,299,492	44,138	5,343,630	592,778	34,952	4,785,804	1,102,898	1,699,192	25,459	298,049	156,720
2003	7,825,715	5,476,960	50,818	5,527,778	612,884	34,271	4,949,165	1,093,961	1,782,589	26,232	298,323	156,388
2004	8,230,328	5,729,312	61,490	5,790,802	642,373	37,880	5,186,309	1,152,482	1,891,537	27,527	298,986	157,197
2005	8,437,041	5,888,189	61,122	5,949,311	669,225	40,519	5,320,605	1,150,932	1,965,504	28,258	298,574	157,629
2006	8,858,752	6,286,160	47,565	6,333,725	713,891	39,866	5,659,700	1,136,006	2,063,046	29,702	298,258	158,784
2007	9,440,633	6,658,544	44,743	6,703,287	744,133	37,704	5,996,858	1,294,306	2,149,469	31,592	298,831	160,037
2008	9,930,990	6,752,994	47,668	6,800,662	765,834	39,303	6,074,131	1,460,298	2,396,561	33,227	298,886	160,582
2009	10,162,926	6,847,471	23,935	6,871,406	765,133	52,724	6,158,997	1,381,066	2,622,863	33,990	299,000	157,601
2010	10,559,775	7,056,874	45,638	7,102,512	777,422	75,877	6,400,967	1,360,802	2,798,006	35,280	299,316	157,005
2011	10,809,310	7,057,338	64,769	7,122,107	707,754	100,840	6,515,193	1,446,039	2,848,078	36,142	299,083	155,905
2012	11,009,559	7,133,778	58,444	7,192,222	712,108	128,669	6,608,783	1,552,602	2,848,174	36,840	298,847	154,973
2013	11,105,980	7,292,321	77,634	7,369,955	817,625	155,651	6,707,981	1,515,881	2,882,118	37,211	298,458	154,531
2014	11,141,723	7,193,595	78,270	7,271,865	825,858	171,222	6,617,229	1,584,705	2,939,789	37,441	297,583	154,476
2015	11,452,787	7,346,250	37,238	7,383,488	848,118	177,287	6,712,657	1,649,659	3,090,471	38,708	295,877	154,346
2016	11,637,826	7,489,093	33,014	7,522,107	868,005	173,073	6,827,175	1,681,376	3,129,275	39,443	295,057	155,359
2017	12,248,120	7,840,137	44,684	7,884,821	907,158	183,110	7,160,773	1,760,321	3,327,026	41,549	294,784	155,800
2018	12,540,727	8,174,341	32,885	8,207,226	931,244	193,792	7,469,774	1,825,514	3,245,439	42,631	294,167	156,388
2019	13,161,062	8,489,628	55,842	8,545,470	967,209	200,314	7,778,575	1,908,870	3,473,617	44,930	292,926	156,234
2020	14,354,894	8,485,924	57,191	8,543,115	968,418	207,370	7,782,067	2,000,917	4,571,910	49,228	291,599	146,558
2021	15,142,915	9,087,895	67,873	9,155,768	1,052,655	214,720	8,317,833	2,009,369	4,815,713	52,213	290,024	149,033
2022	14,768,800	9,448,335	86,258	9,534,593	1,127,396	234,698	8,641,895	2,013,385	4,113,520	51,162	288,668	152,578

Personal Income and Employment by Area: Valdosta, GA

(Thousands of dollars, except as noted.)

Year	Personal income, total	Derivation of personal income: Earnings by place of work: Nonfarm	Farm	Total	Less: Contributions for government social insurance	Plus: Adjustment for residence	Equals: Net earnings by place of residence	Plus: Dividends, interest, and rent	Plus: Personal current transfer receipts	Per capita personal income (dollars)	Population (persons)	Total employment
1970	245,043	179,555	19,547	199,102	11,387	-1,267	186,448	35,476	23,119	3,210	76,347	33,764
1971	271,673	197,873	21,745	219,618	13,112	-1,302	205,204	38,712	27,757	3,427	79,276	34,576
1972	304,782	223,945	23,089	247,034	15,309	-1,041	230,684	43,079	31,019	3,710	82,156	35,735
1973	336,050	244,220	27,018	271,238	18,758	-545	251,935	49,130	34,985	4,008	83,842	36,556
1974	374,522	263,142	32,732	295,874	21,127	-196	274,551	55,542	44,429	4,385	85,407	36,861
1975	389,535	267,730	25,892	293,622	21,582	711	272,751	61,894	54,890	4,555	85,511	35,575
1976	435,959	310,168	22,508	332,676	25,533	688	307,831	68,346	59,782	5,013	86,971	37,112
1977	464,895	345,112	6,920	352,032	28,215	1,545	325,362	76,658	62,875	5,242	88,679	38,149
1978	544,037	396,919	19,856	416,775	32,940	1,966	385,801	89,972	68,264	6,147	88,498	39,447
1979	600,907	440,089	16,711	456,800	38,008	2,005	420,797	101,175	78,935	6,641	90,486	40,040
1980	644,056	463,966	7,118	471,084	40,379	2,458	433,163	117,034	93,859	7,046	91,402	39,351
1981	731,258	510,249	16,829	527,078	47,574	1,699	481,203	139,132	110,923	7,937	92,131	40,149
1982	801,994	547,477	28,295	575,772	51,781	384	524,375	160,989	116,630	8,640	92,821	40,795
1983	853,570	594,023	15,095	609,118	56,949	1,019	553,188	173,891	126,491	9,054	94,274	42,007
1984	948,686	657,591	25,259	682,850	64,715	2,242	620,377	190,211	138,098	9,936	95,477	43,709
1985	1,019,228	711,373	25,615	736,988	71,622	1,608	666,974	203,585	148,669	10,602	96,133	44,826
1986	1,066,344	752,303	19,569	771,872	77,044	2,038	696,866	210,787	158,691	10,987	97,055	45,440
1987	1,147,594	799,885	32,496	832,381	81,333	4,833	755,881	222,228	169,485	11,727	97,863	46,586
1988	1,244,786	873,399	36,353	909,752	92,507	4,044	821,289	241,856	181,641	12,736	97,741	48,109
1989	1,357,629	945,522	37,295	982,817	100,863	-1,799	880,155	275,737	201,737	13,779	98,530	49,838
1990	1,427,681	989,328	37,252	1,026,580	106,271	-3,936	916,373	288,001	223,307	14,320	99,699	50,334
1991	1,518,019	1,039,801	45,082	1,084,883	113,106	-7,760	964,017	298,884	255,118	14,986	101,299	50,477
1992	1,626,471	1,118,863	48,259	1,167,122	120,951	-8,310	1,037,861	307,236	281,374	15,803	102,922	51,055
1993	1,721,105	1,187,933	40,102	1,228,035	129,100	-9,363	1,089,572	333,464	298,069	16,104	106,877	53,803
1994	1,845,285	1,260,115	52,868	1,312,983	137,631	-8,475	1,166,877	357,768	320,640	16,888	109,267	54,857
1995	2,008,986	1,368,451	59,701	1,428,152	147,906	-8,883	1,271,363	396,335	341,288	18,037	111,381	57,874
1996	2,117,983	1,454,549	49,757	1,504,306	155,630	-9,563	1,339,113	422,051	356,819	18,658	113,514	59,607
1997	2,243,195	1,553,060	49,694	1,602,754	164,051	-11,524	1,427,179	450,334	365,682	19,437	115,406	60,998
1998	2,384,632	1,678,265	37,090	1,715,355	174,843	-13,551	1,526,961	478,883	378,788	20,400	116,892	62,374
1999	2,488,668	1,749,804	55,911	1,805,715	180,918	-12,963	1,611,834	471,122	405,712	20,988	118,574	63,144
2000	2,606,294	1,797,444	57,645	1,855,089	185,144	-14,860	1,655,085	516,246	434,963	21,768	119,729	63,736
2001	2,713,031	1,875,355	56,674	1,932,029	193,453	-20,987	1,717,589	525,414	470,028	22,658	119,736	64,125
2002	2,877,108	2,022,662	46,192	2,068,854	208,853	-33,092	1,826,909	517,447	532,752	23,718	121,305	65,782
2003	3,011,939	2,145,361	68,695	2,214,056	218,611	-40,712	1,954,733	524,855	532,351	24,718	121,850	66,976
2004	3,151,285	2,245,754	55,037	2,300,791	237,098	-41,347	2,022,346	551,240	577,699	25,335	124,387	69,018
2005	3,338,441	2,383,481	65,486	2,448,967	249,067	-46,910	2,152,990	564,397	621,054	26,409	126,411	70,740
2006	3,450,209	2,464,642	51,267	2,515,909	263,696	-53,087	2,199,126	585,750	665,333	26,679	129,323	72,165
2007	3,642,289	2,544,567	50,252	2,594,819	269,984	-66,826	2,258,009	671,706	712,574	27,796	131,036	74,151
2008	3,867,834	2,637,431	59,804	2,697,235	296,967	-77,493	2,322,775	740,609	804,450	28,670	134,907	74,899
2009	3,911,912	2,617,963	55,121	2,673,084	294,855	-91,986	2,286,243	741,575	884,094	28,392	137,780	72,868
2010	4,080,357	2,685,498	35,893	2,721,391	300,393	-87,471	2,333,527	779,533	967,297	29,132	140,064	72,146
2011	4,273,597	2,691,736	64,012	2,755,748	270,418	-86,111	2,399,219	857,829	1,016,549	30,090	142,027	70,957
2012	4,277,354	2,790,054	49,296	2,839,350	281,842	-97,761	2,459,747	811,791	1,005,816	29,674	144,146	72,159
2013	4,324,439	2,914,217	46,154	2,960,371	321,631	-89,249	2,549,491	744,670	1,030,278	30,246	142,976	73,411
2014	4,515,014	3,032,214	39,242	3,071,456	333,759	-94,020	2,643,677	791,541	1,079,796	31,470	143,470	74,820
2015	4,664,931	3,123,228	37,798	3,161,026	341,328	-93,333	2,726,365	822,594	1,115,972	32,535	143,380	76,013
2016	4,811,622	3,191,168	31,007	3,222,175	348,072	-100,308	2,773,795	886,685	1,151,142	33,305	144,470	76,535
2017	5,000,076	3,327,890	39,835	3,367,725	362,152	-104,044	2,901,529	912,368	1,186,179	34,396	145,368	77,677
2018	5,222,064	3,530,355	23,275	3,553,630	389,960	-114,040	3,049,630	922,032	1,250,402	35,742	146,103	78,424
2019	5,417,191	3,634,301	33,723	3,668,024	404,616	-117,359	3,146,049	945,171	1,325,971	36,725	147,507	79,285
2020	5,971,754	3,675,525	53,208	3,728,733	417,194	-98,232	3,213,307	1,000,555	1,757,892	40,260	148,329	78,959
2021	6,423,544	3,928,354	44,105	3,972,459	442,814	-105,452	3,424,193	1,012,242	1,987,109	43,123	148,959	80,691
2022	6,363,970	4,087,057	40,420	4,127,477	472,210	-92,917	3,562,350	1,055,908	1,745,712	42,469	149,849	83,066

Personal Income and Employment by Area: Vallejo, CA

(Thousands of dollars, except as noted.)

Year	Personal income, total	Derivation of personal income: Earnings by place of work: Nonfarm	Farm	Total	Less: Contributions for government social insurance	Plus: Adjustment for residence	Equals: Net earnings by place of residence	Plus: Dividends, interest, and rent	Plus: Personal current transfer receipts	Per capita personal income (dollars)	Population (persons)	Total employment
1970	786,126	668,126	24,217	692,343	33,888	-113,252	545,203	173,084	67,839	4,538	173,238	77,595
1971	873,836	725,687	25,921	751,608	39,139	-108,009	604,460	191,340	78,036	4,896	178,481	77,695
1972	959,760	763,445	32,944	796,389	43,222	-84,029	669,138	206,576	84,046	5,295	181,259	76,710
1973	1,061,626	809,775	44,398	854,173	50,016	-64,012	740,145	227,516	93,965	5,794	183,223	77,022
1974	1,215,018	900,535	62,197	962,732	56,781	-57,824	848,127	254,051	112,840	6,482	187,439	80,026
1975	1,381,732	1,031,723	47,257	1,078,980	66,472	-60,827	951,681	290,793	139,258	7,214	191,535	83,585
1976	1,522,717	1,131,899	34,330	1,166,229	74,662	-40,221	1,051,346	314,590	156,781	7,692	197,971	85,184
1977	1,709,435	1,249,162	38,937	1,288,099	83,672	-13,849	1,190,578	346,660	172,197	8,350	204,713	87,746
1978	1,964,146	1,419,020	36,523	1,455,543	96,036	10,729	1,370,236	403,397	190,513	9,195	213,619	91,583
1979	2,210,116	1,530,739	41,130	1,571,869	111,544	82,226	1,542,551	448,961	218,604	9,847	224,455	94,584
1980	2,529,847	1,610,260	77,487	1,687,747	118,844	184,347	1,753,250	516,530	260,067	10,654	237,456	98,216
1981	2,844,465	1,796,582	41,290	1,837,872	142,319	234,035	1,929,588	605,380	309,497	11,563	246,003	100,008
1982	3,126,205	1,971,178	25,536	1,996,714	157,831	278,444	2,117,327	671,178	337,700	12,291	254,348	101,168
1983	3,451,862	2,176,364	21,415	2,197,779	184,630	331,938	2,345,087	748,441	358,334	13,257	260,386	103,847
1984	3,830,380	2,377,463	37,790	2,415,253	210,800	437,176	2,641,629	812,025	376,726	14,486	264,416	107,070
1985	4,257,242	2,630,390	42,855	2,673,245	241,095	524,413	2,956,563	884,476	416,203	15,673	271,634	111,397
1986	4,652,920	2,831,161	34,113	2,865,274	267,820	666,890	3,264,344	934,059	454,517	16,406	283,617	115,639
1987	5,028,100	3,009,140	50,884	3,060,024	288,555	817,772	3,589,241	957,736	481,123	16,939	296,835	119,521
1988	5,503,387	3,248,685	53,296	3,301,981	326,793	948,077	3,923,265	1,052,053	528,069	17,750	310,048	125,976
1989	6,100,945	3,518,273	67,131	3,585,404	361,330	1,098,706	4,322,780	1,192,643	585,522	18,710	326,074	131,381
1990	6,822,823	3,796,702	48,216	3,844,918	394,409	1,486,615	4,937,124	1,232,503	653,196	19,865	343,463	136,860
1991	7,098,642	3,888,819	49,734	3,938,553	412,107	1,591,718	5,118,164	1,247,117	733,361	20,047	354,104	137,031
1992	7,488,055	4,184,805	41,478	4,226,283	444,779	1,593,732	5,375,236	1,268,195	844,624	20,805	359,919	137,870
1993	7,763,300	4,338,413	44,964	4,383,377	463,885	1,638,898	5,558,390	1,325,401	879,509	21,313	364,251	139,183
1994	7,791,836	4,153,291	52,911	4,206,202	456,410	1,785,206	5,534,998	1,365,294	891,544	21,285	366,072	141,061
1995	8,000,336	4,156,411	29,342	4,185,753	450,192	1,872,123	5,607,684	1,450,617	942,035	21,895	365,395	139,996
1996	8,322,521	4,246,464	55,611	4,302,075	449,134	1,946,414	5,799,355	1,529,810	993,356	22,640	367,608	141,128
1997	8,825,097	4,483,694	36,132	4,519,826	468,093	2,207,501	6,259,234	1,563,352	1,002,511	23,731	371,881	143,144
1998	9,434,128	4,810,758	34,332	4,845,090	497,230	2,388,106	6,735,966	1,635,698	1,062,464	24,915	378,657	146,801
1999	10,120,204	5,231,496	46,471	5,277,967	539,582	2,546,205	7,284,590	1,688,083	1,147,531	26,106	387,657	152,966
2000	11,212,226	5,902,411	39,735	5,942,146	606,221	2,909,957	8,245,882	1,772,683	1,193,661	28,244	396,974	157,624
2001	12,201,783	6,711,916	47,541	6,759,457	703,326	2,946,240	9,002,371	1,883,578	1,315,834	30,187	404,209	167,983
2002	12,626,862	7,120,482	62,943	7,183,425	754,455	2,887,935	9,316,905	1,882,507	1,427,450	30,931	408,226	172,009
2003	13,109,172	7,531,975	63,035	7,595,010	815,017	2,813,439	9,593,432	1,985,677	1,530,063	32,098	408,409	175,905
2004	13,492,729	7,845,665	66,225	7,911,890	889,120	2,876,454	9,899,224	1,976,465	1,617,040	32,965	409,301	177,453
2005	13,872,723	8,120,611	80,881	8,201,492	929,252	2,875,179	10,147,419	1,989,012	1,736,292	33,987	408,181	179,245
2006	14,607,783	8,502,852	75,857	8,578,709	942,690	3,010,361	10,646,380	2,052,558	1,908,845	35,768	408,402	180,478
2007	15,280,148	8,779,822	95,876	8,875,698	944,551	3,030,056	10,961,203	2,288,480	2,030,465	37,429	408,243	181,317
2008	15,542,686	9,025,265	121,779	9,147,044	981,152	2,601,163	10,767,055	2,451,015	2,324,616	38,004	408,972	178,981
2009	15,393,099	9,220,663	101,687	9,322,350	1,001,505	2,094,921	10,415,766	2,378,908	2,598,425	37,518	410,290	174,326
2010	15,593,551	9,430,234	83,411	9,513,645	1,003,886	1,864,586	10,374,345	2,310,959	2,908,247	37,656	414,102	171,996
2011	16,111,580	9,470,976	99,397	9,570,373	924,225	2,025,824	10,671,972	2,498,950	2,940,658	38,635	417,025	169,805
2012	16,405,087	9,797,376	138,278	9,935,654	952,906	1,879,562	10,862,310	2,584,984	2,957,793	38,975	420,918	173,407
2013	17,030,120	10,265,276	145,102	10,410,378	1,109,908	1,985,659	11,286,129	2,624,041	3,119,950	40,025	425,491	178,368
2014	17,772,699	10,647,296	148,016	10,795,312	1,157,687	1,988,469	11,626,094	2,807,634	3,338,971	41,195	431,431	182,187
2015	19,027,697	11,127,085	154,555	11,281,640	1,216,738	2,389,212	12,454,114	2,923,884	3,649,699	43,597	436,450	187,951
2016	20,112,104	11,763,828	125,086	11,888,914	1,287,356	2,594,161	13,195,719	3,058,812	3,857,573	45,447	442,544	194,199
2017	20,892,491	12,348,435	105,927	12,454,362	1,351,728	2,709,517	13,812,151	3,201,816	3,878,524	46,644	447,909	198,841
2018	21,899,263	13,064,001	95,622	13,159,623	1,446,750	2,791,827	14,504,700	3,312,231	4,082,332	48,566	450,921	203,988
2019	23,350,113	13,797,199	79,128	13,876,327	1,532,445	3,176,987	15,520,869	3,431,061	4,398,183	51,540	453,051	204,620
2020	25,816,822	13,886,752	80,581	13,967,333	1,536,698	3,407,094	15,837,729	3,604,589	6,374,504	57,029	452,698	196,389
2021	26,963,798	13,819,952	94,200	13,914,152	1,562,703	4,063,272	16,414,721	3,703,633	6,845,444	59,873	450,350	199,182
2022	26,149,679	14,468,863	92,488	14,561,351	1,687,620	3,757,048	16,630,779	3,884,662	5,634,238	58,273	448,747	209,267

Personal Income and Employment by Area: Victoria, TX

(Thousands of dollars, except as noted.)

Year	Personal income, total	Earnings by place of work: Nonfarm	Farm	Total	Less: Contributions for government social insurance	Plus: Adjustment for residence	Equals: Net earnings by place of residence	Plus: Dividends, interest, and rent	Plus: Personal current transfer receipts	Per capita personal income (dollars)	Population (persons)	Total employment
1970	192,895	137,332	5,536	142,868	8,455	14,345	148,758	29,456	14,681	3,286	58,707	22,879
1971	212,966	154,479	2,694	157,173	9,867	15,898	163,204	32,801	16,961	3,570	59,656	24,144
1972	244,654	178,442	6,459	184,901	12,060	16,009	188,850	36,717	19,087	4,075	60,041	25,600
1973	272,284	193,907	10,068	203,975	15,270	18,287	206,992	41,829	23,463	4,422	61,570	26,406
1974	317,507	225,297	8,577	233,874	18,457	23,422	238,839	49,890	28,778	5,088	62,400	27,270
1975	370,669	264,375	6,762	271,137	21,345	27,103	276,895	57,988	35,786	5,789	64,032	28,572
1976	420,630	307,943	3,980	311,923	24,951	31,407	318,379	63,089	39,162	6,429	65,422	30,041
1977	469,067	347,441	-664	346,777	28,383	36,532	354,926	71,154	42,987	7,040	66,629	31,787
1978	549,409	414,129	-118	414,011	34,835	40,646	419,822	81,190	48,397	7,976	68,884	34,333
1979	642,996	471,868	10,476	482,344	41,645	53,094	493,793	93,838	55,365	8,966	71,718	35,474
1980	745,690	551,285	-5,627	545,658	49,406	61,193	557,445	121,678	66,567	9,996	74,599	37,678
1981	912,564	690,581	4,127	694,708	66,595	47,037	675,150	160,618	76,796	11,886	76,778	42,135
1982	1,001,952	731,251	-1,881	729,370	72,563	51,840	708,647	205,781	87,524	12,569	79,719	42,578
1983	1,008,145	702,531	-1,652	700,879	68,468	56,873	689,284	219,423	99,438	12,460	80,912	40,499
1984	1,081,234	749,603	-1,332	748,271	75,429	54,728	727,570	250,820	102,844	13,300	81,297	41,815
1985	1,135,504	772,260	-3,108	769,152	79,155	60,693	750,690	275,923	108,891	13,900	81,693	42,553
1986	1,115,294	725,579	-1,442	724,137	73,158	67,330	718,309	273,940	123,045	13,543	82,351	40,072
1987	1,107,083	711,764	1,204	712,968	70,983	67,750	709,735	266,346	131,002	13,649	81,112	40,743
1988	1,149,060	740,005	-1,215	738,790	76,486	70,353	732,657	279,254	137,149	14,333	80,171	40,664
1989	1,237,882	773,116	999	774,115	80,873	81,445	774,687	311,220	151,975	15,558	79,568	40,838
1990	1,354,609	838,447	3,144	841,591	85,927	93,017	848,681	340,880	165,048	16,815	80,560	41,598
1991	1,435,580	907,566	8,144	915,710	95,634	87,571	907,647	340,929	187,004	17,552	81,791	43,505
1992	1,537,602	954,385	5,790	960,175	99,325	105,461	966,311	352,051	219,240	18,458	83,304	43,216
1993	1,612,749	996,377	5,748	1,002,125	103,446	112,899	1,011,578	369,474	231,697	19,060	84,614	44,707
1994	1,664,789	1,062,588	11,512	1,074,100	111,089	116,730	1,079,741	333,374	251,674	19,381	85,899	45,882
1995	1,777,122	1,104,289	8,849	1,113,138	115,541	133,223	1,130,820	373,007	273,295	20,473	86,805	46,454
1996	1,886,417	1,176,643	-8,717	1,167,926	121,381	154,777	1,201,322	393,435	291,660	21,463	87,891	47,280
1997	1,970,878	1,252,358	1,174	1,253,532	128,314	131,455	1,256,673	410,214	303,991	22,238	88,626	48,767
1998	2,140,579	1,382,813	-8,938	1,373,875	138,921	146,342	1,381,296	452,496	306,787	23,783	90,004	49,732
1999	2,216,488	1,411,915	13,270	1,425,185	141,770	150,462	1,433,877	459,073	323,538	24,417	90,775	49,907
2000	2,409,595	1,574,579	5,872	1,580,451	154,011	161,108	1,587,548	482,758	339,289	26,495	90,944	51,226
2001	2,591,369	1,732,070	2,103	1,734,173	166,877	142,688	1,709,984	511,776	369,609	28,318	91,511	51,590
2002	2,597,812	1,771,570	2,542	1,774,112	170,490	121,837	1,725,459	473,572	398,781	28,353	91,624	51,459
2003	2,651,526	1,750,349	18,578	1,768,927	173,322	106,777	1,702,382	519,773	429,371	28,881	91,809	50,723
2004	2,758,833	1,829,242	19,596	1,848,838	181,866	97,346	1,764,318	543,771	450,744	30,056	91,789	50,881
2005	2,981,976	2,000,068	16,971	2,017,039	195,628	94,286	1,915,697	577,558	488,721	32,582	91,523	52,341
2006	3,232,489	2,254,770	13,467	2,268,237	212,565	66,428	2,122,100	590,155	520,234	35,270	91,649	54,222
2007	3,302,069	2,248,063	3,736	2,251,799	220,017	68,896	2,100,678	631,484	569,907	35,736	92,403	55,483
2008	3,606,393	2,486,994	-22,047	2,464,947	233,374	50,585	2,282,158	695,069	629,166	38,809	92,926	56,268
2009	3,270,177	2,191,691	-23,729	2,167,962	220,300	46,346	1,994,008	589,938	686,231	34,866	93,792	53,858
2010	3,480,253	2,358,201	-13,501	2,344,700	233,811	51,523	2,162,412	574,920	742,921	36,996	94,072	53,889
2011	3,767,708	2,528,501	-16,040	2,512,461	220,872	43,616	2,335,205	659,852	772,651	39,821	94,616	54,881
2012	4,095,310	2,771,741	-13,489	2,758,252	240,455	1,485	2,519,282	809,467	766,561	42,583	96,173	57,447
2013	4,338,796	2,989,609	4,050	2,993,659	289,553	-23,859	2,680,247	872,854	785,695	44,676	97,118	59,189
2014	4,636,943	3,112,624	2,544	3,115,168	301,261	-22,903	2,791,004	1,016,256	829,683	47,314	98,004	59,782
2015	4,509,126	2,919,222	3,607	2,922,829	296,783	26,664	2,652,710	959,903	896,513	45,560	98,972	59,896
2016	4,186,850	2,619,557	-8,334	2,611,223	279,004	75,938	2,408,157	834,826	943,867	42,234	99,135	57,421
2017	4,409,000	2,644,701	-5,767	2,638,934	285,195	81,100	2,434,839	1,006,811	967,350	44,700	98,636	57,590
2018	4,690,451	2,786,779	-8,896	2,777,883	298,346	111,849	2,591,386	1,092,709	1,006,356	47,691	98,350	58,389
2019	5,103,203	3,092,475	-2,670	3,089,805	313,295	169,483	2,945,993	1,105,430	1,051,780	51,844	98,434	57,859
2020	5,255,058	2,846,728	-1,275	2,845,453	298,332	232,296	2,779,417	1,121,389	1,354,252	53,446	98,324	55,040
2021	5,627,167	2,991,457	2,534	2,993,991	304,941	230,818	2,919,868	1,158,514	1,548,785	57,395	98,043	55,989
2022	5,784,212	3,262,959	-26,301	3,236,658	336,794	235,437	3,135,301	1,255,161	1,393,750	58,905	98,196	58,281

Personal Income and Employment by Area: Vineland-Bridgeton, NJ

(Thousands of dollars, except as noted.)

Year	Personal income, total	Derivation of personal income: Earnings by place of work: Nonfarm	Farm	Total	Less: Contributions for government social insurance	Plus: Adjustment for residence	Equals: Net earnings by place of residence	Plus: Dividends, interest, and rent	Plus: Personal current transfer receipts	Per capita personal income (dollars)	Population (persons)	Total employment
1970	484,498	403,917	13,534	417,451	32,316	-7,091	378,044	54,022	52,432	3,961	122,309	58,153
1971	525,214	436,580	11,888	448,468	36,077	-9,770	402,621	59,956	62,637	4,143	126,773	58,260
1972	577,162	483,794	11,364	495,158	41,580	-15,010	438,568	66,635	71,959	4,473	129,031	60,730
1973	639,905	539,214	15,511	554,725	52,807	-19,435	482,483	76,995	80,427	4,894	130,746	62,667
1974	693,446	569,549	16,967	586,516	58,025	-22,032	506,459	87,503	99,484	5,202	133,306	61,865
1975	741,572	588,557	12,184	600,741	57,976	-27,571	515,194	93,345	133,033	5,520	134,350	58,858
1976	814,288	656,021	13,483	669,504	65,587	-34,083	569,834	100,486	143,968	6,016	135,359	60,950
1977	883,666	721,598	10,309	731,907	72,390	-37,815	621,702	111,782	150,182	6,537	135,184	61,741
1978	974,644	797,603	16,199	813,802	82,460	-37,034	694,308	120,413	159,923	7,240	134,615	62,802
1979	1,053,528	859,076	14,331	873,407	91,655	-39,914	741,838	132,023	179,667	7,864	133,966	63,029
1980	1,160,223	930,866	10,718	941,584	99,041	-48,923	793,620	161,610	204,993	8,718	133,088	64,876
1981	1,285,399	987,809	15,914	1,003,723	112,078	-40,414	851,231	196,835	237,333	9,612	133,726	63,534
1982	1,387,379	1,018,669	18,554	1,037,223	115,731	-21,940	899,552	225,769	262,058	10,393	133,494	61,162
1983	1,482,196	1,067,533	21,825	1,089,358	124,197	-13,436	951,725	248,035	282,436	11,187	132,497	61,559
1984	1,589,792	1,127,441	20,777	1,148,218	136,595	4,636	1,016,259	273,270	300,263	11,852	134,138	60,966
1985	1,691,974	1,196,725	22,782	1,219,507	144,627	17,146	1,092,026	290,933	309,015	12,525	135,083	61,704
1986	1,808,145	1,314,468	23,603	1,338,071	160,475	-4,859	1,172,737	311,023	324,385	13,325	135,700	63,622
1987	1,922,950	1,436,793	26,414	1,463,207	174,087	-19,104	1,270,016	317,687	335,247	14,140	135,995	65,766
1988	2,106,695	1,580,646	29,398	1,610,044	195,349	-14,684	1,400,011	347,322	359,362	15,426	136,569	67,638
1989	2,309,080	1,684,014	30,139	1,714,153	205,544	-15,063	1,493,546	423,659	391,875	16,747	137,881	68,023
1990	2,471,728	1,766,771	32,104	1,798,875	208,842	5,960	1,595,993	443,874	431,861	17,864	138,366	68,415
1991	2,557,179	1,799,297	33,009	1,832,306	217,177	-8,213	1,606,916	449,342	500,921	18,200	140,503	66,700
1992	2,739,894	1,902,369	38,743	1,941,112	227,537	2,177	1,715,752	437,710	586,432	19,306	141,921	67,268
1993	2,815,224	1,948,757	45,932	1,994,689	232,762	9,289	1,771,216	442,875	601,133	19,641	143,334	65,632
1994	2,877,308	2,035,465	50,870	2,086,335	245,727	-3,880	1,836,728	444,010	596,570	19,906	144,544	66,357
1995	2,959,197	2,121,108	49,193	2,170,301	255,416	-59,915	1,854,970	478,859	625,368	20,432	144,829	67,555
1996	3,032,968	2,194,100	49,380	2,243,480	263,686	-75,045	1,904,749	493,298	634,921	20,855	145,430	68,018
1997	3,195,906	2,321,683	44,188	2,365,871	272,780	-70,490	2,022,601	530,923	642,382	21,918	145,811	68,540
1998	3,276,497	2,397,366	50,612	2,447,978	278,371	-81,618	2,087,989	550,465	638,043	22,453	145,924	68,962
1999	3,363,873	2,459,441	34,542	2,493,983	281,849	-46,881	2,165,253	535,768	662,852	22,994	146,293	69,065
2000	3,491,502	2,565,271	52,183	2,617,454	296,482	-72,413	2,248,559	549,479	693,464	23,871	146,263	70,953
2001	3,682,951	2,709,981	43,670	2,753,651	312,103	-65,386	2,376,162	543,497	763,292	25,148	146,451	71,167
2002	3,884,999	2,820,676	47,241	2,867,917	320,768	-78,350	2,468,799	547,431	868,769	26,376	147,294	71,225
2003	4,010,433	2,977,545	48,463	3,026,008	333,957	-107,570	2,584,481	565,448	860,504	27,018	148,437	72,418
2004	4,115,716	3,173,244	51,537	3,224,781	358,941	-135,771	2,730,069	538,942	846,705	27,468	149,837	74,741
2005	4,261,225	3,312,195	52,635	3,364,830	384,270	-157,167	2,823,393	504,085	933,747	28,030	152,022	77,030
2006	4,486,755	3,400,277	70,231	3,470,508	396,622	-109,025	2,964,861	500,700	1,021,194	29,254	153,371	76,976
2007	4,656,162	3,473,600	78,791	3,552,391	417,160	-117,373	3,017,858	571,037	1,067,267	30,139	154,489	76,639
2008	4,912,405	3,547,515	73,969	3,621,484	431,433	-137,151	3,052,900	668,469	1,191,036	31,543	155,738	76,082
2009	5,042,804	3,562,188	71,274	3,633,462	431,709	-156,139	3,045,614	655,937	1,341,253	32,216	156,531	74,701
2010	5,183,595	3,585,402	67,510	3,652,912	434,126	-146,063	3,072,723	640,043	1,470,829	33,049	156,845	73,817
2011	5,328,370	3,599,881	61,849	3,661,730	398,036	-142,142	3,121,552	704,887	1,501,931	33,740	157,926	73,479
2012	5,267,750	3,647,368	75,687	3,723,055	400,680	-236,898	3,085,477	706,623	1,475,650	33,239	158,482	73,242
2013	5,261,857	3,679,207	72,361	3,751,568	450,286	-198,536	3,102,746	674,308	1,484,803	33,252	158,240	73,811
2014	5,412,547	3,841,518	74,773	3,916,291	466,662	-279,741	3,169,888	692,474	1,550,185	34,055	158,937	74,285
2015	5,578,016	3,938,179	95,827	4,034,006	479,153	-292,781	3,262,072	724,830	1,591,114	35,232	158,321	74,523
2016	5,617,449	4,027,669	97,831	4,125,500	488,445	-371,725	3,265,330	715,643	1,636,476	35,684	157,420	75,673
2017	5,759,043	4,078,039	91,575	4,169,614	501,011	-333,019	3,335,584	762,429	1,661,030	36,866	156,217	75,491
2018	5,885,069	4,194,614	77,738	4,272,352	510,785	-362,885	3,398,682	778,818	1,707,569	37,720	156,020	75,696
2019	6,207,251	4,351,634	111,163	4,462,797	525,794	-334,062	3,602,941	831,412	1,772,898	39,945	155,394	76,000
2020	6,762,503	4,461,202	105,957	4,567,159	542,121	-409,661	3,615,377	815,921	2,331,205	44,000	153,692	73,375
2021	7,311,328	4,749,584	103,010	4,852,594	582,713	-425,166	3,844,715	828,289	2,638,324	48,073	152,089	76,538
2022	7,082,126	5,076,940	88,088	5,165,028	645,684	-513,173	4,006,171	850,914	2,225,041	46,791	151,356	80,190

Personal Income and Employment by Area: Virginia Beach-Norfolk-Newport News, VA-NC

(Thousands of dollars, except as noted.)

Year	Personal income, total	Derivation of personal income								Per capita personal income (dollars)	Population (persons)	Total employment
		Earnings by place of work			Less: Contributions for government social insurance	Plus: Adjustment for residence	Equals: Net earnings by place of residence	Plus: Dividends, interest, and rent	Plus: Personal current transfer receipts			
		Nonfarm	Farm	Total								
1970	4,717,332	3,802,409	28,878	3,831,287	219,937	-13,039	3,598,311	855,029	263,992	4,172	1,130,821	546,412
1971	5,157,723	4,160,778	17,209	4,177,987	252,796	-20,469	3,904,722	931,396	321,605	4,508	1,144,167	547,321
1972	5,704,623	4,626,218	37,647	4,663,865	292,825	-60,970	4,310,070	1,019,143	375,410	4,979	1,145,801	560,080
1973	6,341,993	5,125,610	59,219	5,184,829	359,525	-72,044	4,753,260	1,146,977	441,756	5,426	1,168,734	584,867
1974	7,048,655	5,665,151	45,995	5,711,146	415,193	-85,825	5,210,128	1,314,371	524,156	5,928	1,188,968	601,684
1975	7,559,947	5,980,651	45,184	6,025,835	448,963	-73,870	5,503,002	1,403,999	652,946	6,314	1,197,355	589,178
1976	8,213,302	6,519,688	42,706	6,562,394	501,926	-89,979	5,970,489	1,517,713	725,100	6,787	1,210,115	600,205
1977	9,060,108	7,207,215	26,427	7,233,642	558,562	-95,555	6,579,525	1,706,766	773,817	7,373	1,228,881	621,766
1978	10,220,829	8,077,966	28,746	8,106,712	625,840	-106,497	7,374,375	1,998,093	848,361	8,229	1,242,103	649,304
1979	11,209,285	8,791,905	301	8,792,206	710,903	-63,460	8,017,843	2,220,371	971,071	9,032	1,241,050	657,258
1980	12,694,930	9,792,439	-1,219	9,791,220	782,848	-79,516	8,928,856	2,600,422	1,165,652	10,169	1,248,449	667,544
1981	14,452,055	11,042,047	43,762	11,085,809	939,593	-81,803	10,064,413	3,050,394	1,337,248	11,354	1,272,873	674,533
1982	15,799,986	12,047,761	25,879	12,073,640	1,027,303	-97,983	10,948,354	3,420,868	1,430,764	12,336	1,280,758	680,514
1983	17,039,250	13,078,311	-4,069	13,074,242	1,169,341	-92,022	11,812,879	3,686,145	1,540,226	12,987	1,312,039	700,314
1984	18,790,681	14,414,021	47,864	14,461,885	1,333,106	-86,276	13,042,503	4,116,096	1,632,082	14,032	1,339,096	732,757
1985	20,234,603	15,646,425	34,705	15,681,130	1,493,381	-79,699	14,108,050	4,391,868	1,734,685	14,974	1,351,325	765,404
1986	21,755,438	16,886,388	48,131	16,934,519	1,672,537	-68,589	15,193,393	4,726,346	1,835,699	15,715	1,384,380	794,220
1987	23,176,334	18,128,483	52,152	18,180,635	1,806,268	-57,886	16,316,481	4,947,314	1,912,539	16,280	1,423,567	828,446
1988	24,935,876	19,371,311	72,825	19,444,136	2,008,077	-31,429	17,404,630	5,482,078	2,049,168	17,191	1,450,558	845,212
1989	26,634,172	20,284,188	76,921	20,361,109	2,134,751	-5,937	18,220,421	6,090,964	2,322,787	18,146	1,467,780	859,772
1990	27,965,027	21,350,698	100,040	21,450,738	2,283,906	-933	19,165,899	6,284,454	2,514,674	18,748	1,491,662	871,907
1991	29,313,241	22,306,030	87,706	22,393,736	2,416,749	5,314	19,982,301	6,502,953	2,827,987	19,487	1,504,214	861,548
1992	31,063,199	23,579,294	90,672	23,669,966	2,561,320	12,737	21,121,383	6,775,910	3,165,906	20,203	1,537,519	866,056
1993	32,330,080	24,316,541	75,469	24,392,010	2,659,484	26,143	21,758,669	7,182,184	3,389,227	20,740	1,558,836	874,111
1994	33,562,400	25,044,906	103,296	25,148,202	2,764,436	38,509	22,422,275	7,523,934	3,616,191	21,393	1,568,850	877,644
1995	34,848,754	25,650,893	85,388	25,736,281	2,818,690	55,471	22,973,062	7,968,552	3,907,140	22,101	1,576,820	893,421
1996	36,336,456	26,620,374	100,363	26,720,737	2,925,343	72,444	23,867,838	8,313,989	4,154,629	22,930	1,584,656	908,774
1997	38,260,384	28,014,211	63,498	28,077,709	3,075,676	97,512	25,099,545	8,885,486	4,275,353	24,060	1,590,181	923,287
1998	40,417,125	29,768,442	49,787	29,818,229	3,234,876	113,798	26,697,151	9,358,357	4,361,617	25,412	1,590,459	936,593
1999	42,332,056	31,420,208	31,975	31,452,183	3,413,083	137,681	28,176,781	9,531,998	4,623,277	26,438	1,601,182	946,312
2000	45,290,981	33,520,125	64,045	33,584,170	3,588,064	168,550	30,164,656	10,205,798	4,920,527	28,001	1,617,490	966,195
2001	47,513,185	35,558,479	54,599	35,613,078	3,814,926	149,408	31,947,560	10,115,994	5,449,631	29,217	1,626,238	969,615
2002	50,118,141	37,772,704	62,434	37,835,138	4,065,417	115,855	33,885,576	10,460,933	5,771,632	30,538	1,641,177	980,600
2003	53,682,011	40,627,447	89,745	40,717,192	4,343,297	42,776	36,416,671	11,031,326	6,234,014	32,540	1,649,748	991,542
2004	57,286,072	43,872,368	86,894	43,959,262	4,696,029	56,904	39,320,137	11,358,225	6,607,710	34,164	1,676,784	1,012,247
2005	59,941,621	45,880,768	122,776	46,003,544	4,952,050	41,059	41,092,553	11,589,328	7,259,740	35,593	1,684,092	1,027,651
2006	63,775,957	48,324,170	101,524	48,425,694	5,282,970	28,223	43,170,947	12,723,294	7,881,716	37,480	1,701,595	1,040,738
2007	66,751,035	50,196,316	77,364	50,273,680	5,489,468	-12,934	44,771,278	13,628,033	8,351,724	39,258	1,700,315	1,056,025
2008	68,372,273	50,340,653	79,757	50,420,410	5,598,561	-10,758	44,811,091	14,057,996	9,503,186	40,229	1,699,574	1,048,091
2009	67,610,566	49,483,464	78,263	49,561,727	5,586,774	-48,543	43,926,410	13,476,610	10,207,546	39,644	1,705,438	1,014,440
2010	69,421,096	50,364,387	36,215	50,400,602	5,680,618	-20,127	44,699,857	13,426,949	11,294,290	40,417	1,717,604	1,004,011
2011	72,239,766	51,077,992	91,987	51,169,979	5,208,835	7,568	45,968,712	14,487,599	11,783,455	41,853	1,726,032	1,005,792
2012	74,525,696	52,565,362	99,270	52,664,632	5,372,915	-7,455	47,284,262	15,324,741	11,916,693	42,849	1,739,260	1,009,929
2013	74,118,721	53,010,203	101,751	53,111,954	6,116,524	-42,295	46,953,135	14,764,272	12,401,314	42,382	1,748,819	1,017,863
2014	76,680,904	54,642,269	54,928	54,697,197	6,295,786	-27,645	48,373,766	15,378,321	12,928,817	43,551	1,760,700	1,025,903
2015	79,699,610	56,718,162	22,451	56,740,613	6,569,146	5,344	50,176,811	15,995,737	13,527,062	45,068	1,768,411	1,043,370
2016	81,830,822	57,907,021	30,874	57,937,895	6,683,243	-102,171	51,152,481	16,660,341	14,018,000	46,137	1,773,651	1,068,498
2017	84,217,611	59,270,814	62,930	59,333,744	6,915,878	-91,004	52,326,862	17,343,117	14,547,632	47,362	1,778,159	1,080,348
2018	84,706,216	59,240,277	36,374	59,276,651	6,941,300	-10,150	52,325,201	17,094,039	15,286,976	47,486	1,783,825	1,075,652
2019	88,040,196	61,379,472	77,729	61,457,201	7,188,322	-60,386	54,208,493	17,605,661	16,226,042	49,114	1,792,551	1,073,868
2020	94,166,804	62,679,224	48,366	62,727,590	7,389,405	-103,948	55,234,237	17,456,229	21,476,338	52,283	1,801,090	1,052,358
2021	102,373,414	67,342,110	109,554	67,451,664	7,900,545	-140,911	59,410,208	18,591,455	24,371,751	56,699	1,805,562	1,086,085
2022	104,566,574	71,278,993	87,042	71,366,035	8,475,559	-164,755	62,725,721	19,633,609	22,207,244	57,873	1,806,840	1,120,669

Personal Income and Employment by Area: Visalia, CA

(Thousands of dollars, except as noted.)

Year	Personal income, total	Derivation of personal income								Per capita personal income (dollars)	Population (persons)	Total employment
		Earnings by place of work			Less: Contributions for government social insurance	Plus: Adjustment for residence	Equals: Net earnings by place of residence	Plus: Dividends, interest, and rent	Plus: Personal current transfer receipts			
		Nonfarm	Farm	Total								
1970	699,055	410,591	113,102	523,693	27,938	1,858	497,613	97,445	103,997	3,695	189,191	81,225
1971	759,398	446,047	118,462	564,509	31,161	4,700	538,048	106,076	115,274	3,912	194,103	83,183
1972	861,181	505,311	143,143	648,454	37,201	7,775	619,028	118,886	123,267	4,357	197,643	89,111
1973	1,020,924	566,337	211,175	777,512	47,547	11,363	741,328	140,922	138,674	5,059	201,805	91,598
1974	1,185,031	648,329	253,948	902,277	56,373	14,459	860,363	160,357	164,311	5,736	206,589	97,440
1975	1,262,161	714,896	194,072	908,968	59,288	21,780	871,460	183,453	207,248	5,922	213,115	99,934
1976	1,413,389	824,027	204,721	1,028,748	69,111	26,081	985,718	197,010	230,661	6,450	219,123	102,675
1977	1,555,218	915,051	222,287	1,137,338	78,662	32,469	1,091,145	220,503	243,570	6,884	225,906	106,394
1978	1,774,904	1,052,271	246,952	1,299,223	91,196	38,648	1,246,675	255,512	272,717	7,610	233,220	109,228
1979	2,100,850	1,204,960	351,225	1,556,185	108,994	50,324	1,497,515	301,617	301,718	8,751	240,074	117,964
1980	2,325,361	1,285,930	361,928	1,647,858	115,101	60,098	1,592,855	373,047	359,459	9,398	247,426	119,326
1981	2,447,085	1,375,354	265,166	1,640,520	136,230	61,089	1,565,379	451,216	430,490	9,646	253,694	119,692
1982	2,638,507	1,425,669	327,810	1,753,479	143,597	63,921	1,673,803	505,475	459,229	10,158	259,759	117,129
1983	2,713,309	1,552,814	208,208	1,761,022	159,089	64,313	1,666,246	558,016	489,047	10,161	267,034	121,911
1984	2,980,925	1,681,661	259,756	1,941,417	177,839	70,674	1,834,252	616,696	529,977	10,909	273,255	120,368
1985	3,151,158	1,786,509	249,829	2,036,338	190,837	73,833	1,919,334	639,781	592,043	11,254	280,000	122,160
1986	3,368,741	1,949,924	260,994	2,210,918	212,024	74,431	2,073,325	656,691	638,725	11,788	285,767	125,690
1987	3,711,424	2,106,553	422,426	2,528,979	228,316	83,172	2,383,835	668,348	659,241	12,721	291,752	128,885
1988	3,975,591	2,259,473	433,579	2,693,052	254,392	99,515	2,538,175	728,498	708,918	13,338	298,075	133,959
1989	4,237,036	2,433,210	375,302	2,808,512	278,996	115,458	2,644,974	811,037	781,025	13,917	304,451	137,419
1990	4,685,090	2,717,905	437,819	3,155,724	306,040	125,083	2,974,767	836,488	873,835	14,918	314,062	140,864
1991	4,811,690	2,837,075	311,785	3,148,860	319,523	135,047	2,964,384	854,777	992,529	14,864	323,705	141,436
1992	5,354,554	3,097,244	510,977	3,608,221	350,019	125,590	3,383,792	830,657	1,140,105	16,130	331,956	146,844
1993	5,501,760	3,194,774	458,402	3,653,176	360,441	133,508	3,426,243	875,991	1,199,526	16,217	339,253	150,060
1994	5,766,801	3,386,870	495,073	3,881,943	377,809	134,560	3,638,694	909,034	1,219,073	16,683	345,668	153,457
1995	5,889,479	3,523,729	413,330	3,937,059	386,456	138,778	3,689,381	935,262	1,264,836	16,918	348,127	155,994
1996	6,345,020	3,669,333	628,641	4,297,974	385,374	141,640	4,054,240	967,653	1,323,127	18,091	350,732	158,687
1997	6,458,182	3,747,098	654,039	4,401,137	391,212	141,737	4,151,662	999,856	1,306,664	18,195	354,946	158,454
1998	6,907,420	4,109,319	656,977	4,766,296	414,688	140,557	4,492,165	1,035,019	1,380,236	19,195	359,854	165,685
1999	7,178,263	4,313,745	642,330	4,956,075	437,788	143,212	4,661,499	1,044,491	1,472,273	19,682	364,708	169,627
2000	7,383,689	4,601,963	528,037	5,130,000	470,265	151,558	4,811,293	1,080,644	1,491,752	20,030	368,627	172,135
2001	8,054,064	4,890,120	742,896	5,633,016	534,088	194,836	5,293,764	1,090,259	1,670,041	21,583	373,171	168,668
2002	8,286,627	5,251,587	497,989	5,749,576	585,581	254,886	5,418,881	1,080,580	1,787,166	21,832	379,568	175,322
2003	8,989,578	5,597,766	597,166	6,194,932	629,376	328,732	5,894,288	1,172,714	1,922,576	23,125	388,743	174,985
2004	9,924,459	5,875,210	1,092,666	6,967,876	686,557	405,919	6,687,238	1,190,106	2,047,115	24,922	398,226	173,728
2005	10,446,401	6,205,635	1,206,895	7,412,530	735,422	455,937	7,133,045	1,179,604	2,133,752	25,606	407,970	177,779
2006	10,786,304	6,865,722	561,259	7,426,981	772,014	508,507	7,163,474	1,319,813	2,303,017	25,996	414,921	182,703
2007	12,273,479	7,183,879	1,252,487	8,436,366	790,443	593,274	8,239,197	1,541,107	2,493,175	29,074	422,140	189,089
2008	12,294,116	7,190,271	916,540	8,106,811	813,928	680,038	7,972,921	1,552,751	2,768,444	28,639	429,283	188,448
2009	12,121,968	7,126,367	570,888	7,697,255	808,048	640,673	7,529,880	1,535,701	3,056,387	27,740	436,987	182,836
2010	13,340,455	7,660,682	904,965	8,565,647	810,675	655,674	8,410,646	1,525,390	3,404,419	30,109	443,066	183,329
2011	14,153,502	7,865,363	1,312,663	9,178,026	762,955	680,615	9,095,686	1,644,696	3,413,120	31,644	447,277	184,774
2012	14,166,005	7,574,111	1,347,858	8,921,969	752,893	706,188	8,875,264	1,830,433	3,460,308	31,434	450,656	183,676
2013	14,527,758	7,840,444	1,502,513	9,342,957	864,364	677,904	9,156,497	1,765,832	3,605,429	32,017	453,758	190,333
2014	15,981,107	8,149,237	2,238,631	10,387,868	893,724	724,993	10,219,137	1,907,376	3,854,594	34,983	456,831	192,798
2015	16,328,948	8,755,099	1,544,685	10,299,784	949,675	697,487	10,047,596	2,060,097	4,221,255	35,556	459,243	200,358
2016	17,149,047	9,418,453	1,466,492	10,884,945	1,032,097	765,755	10,618,603	2,165,827	4,364,617	37,125	461,926	205,204
2017	17,681,249	9,653,864	1,792,986	11,446,850	1,064,556	861,804	11,244,098	2,195,139	4,242,012	37,983	465,503	206,885
2018	17,824,523	9,980,859	1,457,160	11,438,019	1,107,467	836,800	11,167,352	2,223,119	4,434,052	38,070	468,208	210,143
2019	18,728,754	10,404,086	1,501,359	11,905,445	1,176,793	918,641	11,647,293	2,337,901	4,743,560	39,834	470,173	211,922
2020	21,572,811	10,880,543	1,638,106	12,518,649	1,221,343	1,011,598	12,308,904	2,438,937	6,824,970	45,523	473,891	206,147
2021	23,191,982	11,598,455	1,590,995	13,189,450	1,308,234	1,085,679	12,966,895	2,554,830	7,670,257	48,626	476,946	214,257
2022	22,585,661	12,540,493	1,620,597	14,161,090	1,472,417	1,022,674	13,711,347	2,649,255	6,225,059	47,295	477,544	229,572

Personal Income and Employment by Area: Waco, TX

(Thousands of dollars, except as noted.)

Year	Personal income, total	Derivation of personal income: Earnings by place of work: Nonfarm	Farm	Total	Less: Contributions for government social insurance	Plus: Adjustment for residence	Equals: Net earnings by place of residence	Plus: Dividends, interest, and rent	Plus: Personal current transfer receipts	Per capita personal income (dollars)	Population (persons)	Total employment
1970	556,788	421,624	11,223	432,847	26,930	1,428	407,345	86,733	62,710	3,374	165,008	72,540
1971	604,157	455,737	9,907	465,644	29,812	1,120	436,952	95,878	71,327	3,608	167,456	73,644
1972	668,055	507,739	9,600	517,339	34,736	907	483,510	105,689	78,856	3,907	170,979	77,099
1973	761,836	563,169	28,280	591,449	44,501	489	547,437	120,794	93,605	4,380	173,928	79,469
1974	828,262	617,405	6,428	623,833	50,124	185	573,894	141,911	112,457	4,678	177,057	80,372
1975	934,111	669,292	12,442	681,734	52,795	310	629,249	164,773	140,089	5,302	176,185	79,429
1976	1,049,382	773,660	12,136	785,796	61,837	-972	722,987	177,920	148,475	5,834	179,868	83,034
1977	1,133,212	847,726	194	847,920	68,812	-1,575	777,533	198,232	157,447	6,250	181,301	85,832
1978	1,284,680	970,655	2,092	972,747	80,694	-2,014	890,039	221,252	173,389	7,000	183,520	88,769
1979	1,431,111	1,085,036	2,361	1,087,397	95,001	-4,345	988,051	247,647	195,413	7,672	186,539	90,348
1980	1,617,683	1,195,746	-661	1,195,085	105,683	-5,599	1,083,803	307,683	226,197	8,540	189,416	92,112
1981	1,818,470	1,317,972	12,322	1,330,294	126,025	-9,249	1,195,020	370,397	253,053	9,485	191,717	93,873
1982	2,002,906	1,407,335	6,866	1,414,201	135,902	-7,916	1,270,383	455,938	276,585	10,326	193,961	94,587
1983	2,194,432	1,539,032	7,796	1,546,828	148,539	-6,674	1,391,615	503,321	299,496	11,101	197,671	96,325
1984	2,407,561	1,690,499	22,318	1,712,817	167,904	-9,820	1,535,093	559,651	312,817	12,049	199,820	100,053
1985	2,575,609	1,783,022	29,299	1,812,321	179,818	-12,354	1,620,149	620,818	334,642	12,801	201,204	101,927
1986	2,653,780	1,824,159	25,818	1,849,977	182,776	-17,300	1,649,901	641,901	361,978	12,973	204,568	100,542
1987	2,642,497	1,792,364	30,248	1,822,612	178,822	-18,166	1,625,624	635,100	381,773	12,921	204,519	101,805
1988	2,746,607	1,893,556	27,381	1,920,937	195,827	-19,777	1,705,333	638,286	402,988	13,441	204,348	103,130
1989	2,892,952	1,958,589	33,052	1,991,641	206,703	-21,540	1,763,398	697,620	431,934	14,077	205,516	103,364
1990	3,048,596	2,098,466	24,028	2,122,494	216,081	-19,173	1,887,240	685,047	476,309	14,694	207,477	104,832
1991	3,228,609	2,236,682	36,439	2,273,121	235,256	-23,614	2,014,251	692,475	521,883	15,409	209,531	107,920
1992	3,399,134	2,394,686	33,751	2,428,437	250,109	-29,044	2,149,284	659,366	590,484	16,088	211,278	109,069
1993	3,607,855	2,581,587	40,623	2,622,210	269,179	-31,655	2,321,376	664,195	622,284	16,828	214,400	112,112
1994	3,857,339	2,796,847	46,152	2,842,999	295,041	-33,603	2,514,355	683,189	659,795	17,623	218,877	115,322
1995	4,130,352	3,013,308	30,004	3,043,312	319,809	-38,197	2,685,306	744,302	700,744	18,679	221,128	119,892
1996	4,305,386	3,147,003	6,873	3,153,876	331,015	-36,693	2,786,168	781,513	737,705	19,178	224,497	121,857
1997	4,573,580	3,371,454	27,792	3,399,246	350,842	-38,400	3,010,004	799,306	764,270	20,187	226,561	124,685
1998	4,823,804	3,592,665	6,001	3,598,666	371,044	-41,010	3,186,612	859,503	777,689	21,115	228,450	126,949
1999	5,065,257	3,819,677	22,805	3,842,482	394,309	-43,412	3,404,761	860,729	799,767	22,011	230,120	129,275
2000	5,262,154	3,907,251	14,886	3,922,137	399,654	-37,797	3,484,686	926,355	851,113	22,634	232,489	130,926
2001	5,514,509	4,075,820	4,333	4,080,153	414,449	-58,924	3,606,780	978,739	928,990	23,629	233,379	130,991
2002	5,677,675	4,252,706	17,972	4,270,678	431,522	-82,711	3,756,445	908,446	1,012,784	24,195	234,661	131,511
2003	6,033,716	4,534,822	34,529	4,569,351	467,646	-115,449	3,986,256	963,281	1,084,179	25,477	236,830	133,445
2004	6,217,398	4,737,531	41,396	4,778,927	487,851	-130,438	4,160,638	928,651	1,128,109	25,969	239,419	135,177
2005	6,546,135	4,929,704	32,276	4,961,980	511,600	-154,695	4,295,685	1,021,625	1,228,825	27,187	240,784	137,130
2006	6,829,047	5,133,670	22,651	5,156,321	526,273	-173,269	4,456,779	1,071,134	1,301,134	28,173	242,397	138,960
2007	7,151,953	5,284,163	22,215	5,306,378	550,285	-190,451	4,565,642	1,163,497	1,422,814	29,257	244,453	141,944
2008	7,509,330	5,401,377	-1,076	5,400,301	566,115	-207,912	4,626,274	1,293,365	1,589,691	30,435	246,735	142,372
2009	7,566,153	5,464,099	-16,101	5,447,998	585,703	-215,313	4,646,982	1,208,635	1,710,536	30,332	249,441	141,711
2010	8,003,582	5,740,354	10,026	5,750,380	612,978	-220,643	4,916,759	1,215,156	1,871,667	31,532	253,821	141,540
2011	8,372,270	5,857,718	5,549	5,863,267	552,430	-218,038	5,092,799	1,352,159	1,927,312	32,728	255,812	142,741
2012	8,696,293	6,085,593	19,283	6,104,876	572,787	-225,196	5,306,893	1,473,682	1,915,718	33,819	257,142	144,444
2013	8,867,108	6,292,240	31,878	6,324,118	664,737	-221,211	5,438,170	1,470,143	1,958,795	34,238	258,986	147,140
2014	9,306,092	6,599,068	27,242	6,626,310	692,356	-210,192	5,723,762	1,539,781	2,042,549	35,686	260,780	149,926
2015	9,792,236	6,913,782	57,195	6,970,977	733,228	-219,799	6,017,950	1,593,222	2,181,064	37,209	263,166	152,215
2016	10,058,347	7,206,901	12,690	7,219,591	779,321	-251,826	6,188,444	1,592,450	2,277,453	37,895	265,424	156,955
2017	10,581,610	7,578,916	-7,266	7,571,650	823,920	-262,314	6,485,416	1,764,345	2,331,849	39,242	269,651	160,314
2018	11,096,098	7,970,482	-17,226	7,953,256	856,642	-278,134	6,818,480	1,832,694	2,444,924	40,764	272,201	163,248
2019	11,483,855	8,185,685	-10,944	8,174,741	875,266	-266,439	7,033,036	1,879,642	2,571,177	41,725	275,230	163,085
2020	12,625,536	8,568,368	5,194	8,573,562	926,841	-301,246	7,345,475	1,992,657	3,287,404	45,394	278,131	162,095
2021	13,902,414	9,220,105	6,878	9,226,983	992,608	-317,029	7,917,346	2,205,467	3,779,601	49,508	280,813	171,183
2022	14,137,044	9,849,584	-27,361	9,822,223	1,076,026	-344,156	8,402,041	2,365,670	3,369,333	49,798	283,885	178,473

Personal Income and Employment by Area: Walla Walla, WA

(Thousands of dollars, except as noted.)

Year	Personal income, total	Derivation of personal income								Per capita personal income (dollars)	Population (persons)	Total employment
		Earnings by place of work			Less: Contributions for government social insurance	Plus: Adjustment for residence	Equals: Net earnings by place of residence	Plus: Dividends, interest, and rent	Plus: Personal current transfer receipts			
		Nonfarm	Farm	Total								
1970	167,281	111,220	17,077	128,297	8,394	-5,392	114,511	33,591	19,179	3,970	42,141	19,265
1971	177,567	121,025	13,618	134,643	9,539	-6,217	118,887	37,207	21,473	4,205	42,231	19,364
1972	203,075	131,242	24,523	155,765	10,859	-5,819	139,087	40,897	23,091	4,766	42,608	19,569
1973	243,267	142,297	46,898	189,195	13,638	-5,481	170,076	47,149	26,042	5,715	42,564	20,255
1974	262,600	159,905	41,245	201,150	16,001	-6,072	179,077	52,772	30,751	6,127	42,861	21,202
1975	294,532	180,126	41,380	221,506	18,048	-5,912	197,546	59,933	37,053	6,627	44,445	21,936
1976	322,380	213,134	35,915	249,049	22,047	-8,931	218,071	64,228	40,081	7,177	44,921	23,293
1977	343,326	234,196	25,398	259,594	24,463	-8,246	226,885	73,590	42,851	7,611	45,112	22,820
1978	390,730	268,224	32,239	300,463	29,126	-9,235	262,102	81,699	46,929	8,644	45,202	23,383
1979	446,006	333,156	28,430	361,586	38,448	-22,776	300,362	92,308	53,336	9,627	46,327	25,736
1980	507,349	355,106	41,993	397,099	41,001	-22,692	333,406	110,955	62,988	10,674	47,530	25,359
1981	548,979	366,555	37,548	404,103	45,028	-12,562	346,513	133,118	69,348	11,480	47,820	25,186
1982	562,107	376,154	25,243	401,397	46,321	-16,323	338,753	148,186	75,168	11,530	48,751	24,993
1983	614,900	398,907	44,759	443,666	50,164	-22,082	371,420	162,799	80,681	12,542	49,028	25,342
1984	637,215	425,248	38,706	463,954	55,472	-29,323	379,159	172,362	85,694	13,076	48,732	25,644
1985	639,721	425,563	26,473	452,036	56,012	-30,290	365,734	180,740	93,247	13,229	48,357	25,504
1986	654,838	424,641	38,990	463,631	56,468	-31,667	375,496	181,142	98,200	13,626	48,058	25,097
1987	650,993	429,811	37,866	467,677	57,113	-33,617	376,947	171,514	102,532	13,693	47,542	24,516
1988	672,217	456,661	35,953	492,614	62,833	-38,674	391,107	171,486	109,624	14,218	47,278	24,810
1989	718,788	488,903	27,560	516,463	66,941	-44,933	404,589	196,450	117,749	14,923	48,166	25,244
1990	759,310	515,647	44,711	560,358	72,485	-48,119	439,754	192,535	127,021	15,645	48,534	26,281
1991	804,850	551,554	38,163	589,717	77,420	-52,118	460,179	199,938	144,733	16,049	50,151	26,205
1992	867,451	608,099	36,648	644,747	84,901	-56,726	503,120	204,532	159,799	17,008	51,002	26,961
1993	932,237	644,675	59,835	704,510	90,786	-58,884	554,840	210,855	166,542	17,803	52,364	27,721
1994	961,407	687,341	44,414	731,755	96,525	-59,193	576,037	214,454	170,916	18,055	53,250	28,830
1995	995,591	700,996	43,945	744,941	99,448	-60,481	585,012	230,285	180,294	18,524	53,747	29,230
1996	1,085,476	729,055	83,578	812,633	100,724	-64,065	647,844	246,369	191,263	20,060	54,111	29,580
1997	1,098,358	753,366	61,019	814,385	100,416	-64,483	649,486	253,117	195,755	20,194	54,389	29,994
1998	1,174,193	798,648	78,191	876,839	104,784	-64,377	707,678	258,030	208,485	21,519	54,566	30,029
1999	1,200,608	825,604	80,504	906,108	105,861	-64,447	735,800	245,402	219,406	21,907	54,806	30,136
2000	1,324,017	874,076	138,254	1,012,330	114,259	-69,042	829,029	260,444	234,544	23,995	55,178	30,960
2001	1,380,591	924,245	131,367	1,055,612	120,929	-74,690	859,993	268,132	252,466	25,069	55,072	31,490
2002	1,369,966	965,797	102,900	1,068,697	125,579	-75,400	867,718	239,554	262,694	24,610	55,666	31,743
2003	1,452,097	1,012,529	134,541	1,147,070	132,305	-82,273	932,492	246,551	273,054	25,880	56,108	32,160
2004	1,514,387	1,066,878	112,397	1,179,275	139,090	-78,753	961,432	266,101	286,854	26,731	56,652	32,019
2005	1,554,370	1,105,697	102,880	1,208,577	142,114	-77,063	989,400	260,801	304,169	27,477	56,569	31,928
2006	1,622,697	1,143,865	101,833	1,245,698	148,675	-78,766	1,018,257	279,341	325,099	28,616	56,705	32,235
2007	1,776,774	1,204,364	109,447	1,313,811	157,061	-75,030	1,081,720	344,542	350,512	31,259	56,840	32,613
2008	1,952,785	1,270,219	127,853	1,398,072	167,429	-76,298	1,154,345	405,443	392,997	34,071	57,315	33,935
2009	1,941,312	1,291,347	125,217	1,416,564	173,783	-86,748	1,156,033	359,887	425,392	33,412	58,103	33,659
2010	2,013,921	1,346,761	136,910	1,483,671	180,933	-99,741	1,202,997	344,586	466,338	34,166	58,945	33,862
2011	2,110,750	1,361,042	162,714	1,523,756	165,931	-102,826	1,254,999	387,065	468,686	35,413	59,604	33,714
2012	2,186,171	1,397,717	186,003	1,583,720	167,338	-123,789	1,292,593	420,187	473,391	36,671	59,616	34,100
2013	2,241,246	1,434,503	195,540	1,630,043	188,454	-137,791	1,303,798	453,616	483,832	37,489	59,784	34,752
2014	2,302,784	1,482,992	149,364	1,632,356	198,338	-145,549	1,288,469	479,820	534,495	38,336	60,069	35,328
2015	2,417,384	1,507,014	229,039	1,736,053	202,370	-139,360	1,394,323	482,145	540,916	39,878	60,619	35,100
2016	2,465,553	1,575,813	194,168	1,769,981	209,925	-153,634	1,406,422	490,736	568,395	40,493	60,888	35,499
2017	2,576,057	1,638,482	178,231	1,816,713	220,729	-150,272	1,445,712	545,096	585,249	41,825	61,592	35,559
2018	2,681,609	1,732,603	138,865	1,871,468	228,178	-162,277	1,481,013	581,406	619,190	43,381	61,815	36,286
2019	2,857,603	1,803,383	164,313	1,967,696	232,056	-161,620	1,574,020	630,362	653,221	45,919	62,231	36,787
2020	3,103,954	1,906,132	185,385	2,091,517	249,907	-186,385	1,655,225	635,498	813,231	49,569	62,619	36,365
2021	3,412,296	2,057,229	167,806	2,225,035	263,700	-174,261	1,787,074	698,981	926,241	54,897	62,158	37,515
2022	3,430,905	2,189,313	186,914	2,376,227	296,453	-210,159	1,869,615	732,662	828,628	55,436	61,890	38,849

Personal Income and Employment by Area: Warner Robins, GA

(Thousands of dollars, except as noted.)

Year	Personal income, total	Derivation of personal income: Earnings by place of work: Nonfarm	Farm	Total	Less: Contributions for government social insurance	Plus: Adjustment for residence	Equals: Net earnings by place of residence	Plus: Dividends, interest, and rent	Plus: Personal current transfer receipts	Per capita personal income (dollars)	Population (persons)	Total employment
1970	338,120	397,096	6,019	403,115	13,117	-129,878	260,120	61,999	16,001	4,243	79,693	46,612
1971	376,740	434,312	8,950	443,262	14,717	-141,270	287,275	69,800	19,665	4,542	82,942	45,923
1972	402,475	458,394	8,450	466,844	16,113	-143,761	306,970	73,167	22,338	4,746	84,796	45,165
1973	446,804	488,021	14,238	502,259	19,547	-142,898	339,814	81,187	25,803	5,212	85,726	45,730
1974	499,174	531,785	13,220	545,005	23,543	-146,507	374,955	91,785	32,434	5,670	88,037	46,789
1975	544,840	569,080	11,439	580,519	27,005	-152,390	401,124	100,999	42,717	6,064	89,845	46,327
1976	580,490	596,208	11,747	607,955	29,359	-153,475	425,121	106,180	49,189	6,371	91,111	45,885
1977	642,961	670,262	7,806	678,068	32,694	-172,667	472,707	119,691	50,563	6,978	92,141	46,706
1978	709,445	711,942	10,584	722,526	35,557	-171,542	515,427	139,071	54,947	7,567	93,751	47,661
1979	772,628	754,157	13,165	767,322	39,970	-169,767	557,585	151,921	63,122	8,079	95,630	47,369
1980	844,397	790,369	6,376	796,745	44,107	-157,505	595,133	173,709	75,555	8,692	97,150	48,505
1981	958,554	898,980	8,955	907,935	51,867	-188,577	667,491	203,603	87,460	9,727	98,541	48,212
1982	1,056,773	969,368	13,468	982,836	56,737	-196,630	729,469	233,221	94,083	10,652	99,205	49,001
1983	1,150,467	1,039,995	8,507	1,048,502	70,424	-189,666	788,412	257,598	104,457	11,480	100,214	49,858
1984	1,255,150	1,104,878	13,047	1,117,925	76,379	-183,983	857,563	284,193	113,394	12,474	100,621	50,819
1985	1,354,768	1,183,016	11,513	1,194,529	89,036	-179,067	926,426	303,866	124,476	13,255	102,209	53,102
1986	1,447,279	1,224,876	11,172	1,236,048	97,479	-148,906	989,663	324,921	132,695	13,944	103,789	55,891
1987	1,517,149	1,239,899	9,674	1,249,573	102,213	-110,449	1,036,911	340,385	139,853	14,377	105,529	56,165
1988	1,647,821	1,321,509	15,562	1,337,071	115,331	-99,259	1,122,481	373,091	152,249	15,255	108,016	56,994
1989	1,787,826	1,417,800	12,160	1,429,960	128,113	-98,772	1,203,075	417,484	167,267	16,350	109,350	58,737
1990	1,933,014	1,495,184	14,624	1,509,808	139,376	-51,564	1,318,868	427,203	186,943	17,427	110,920	59,384
1991	2,019,703	1,521,881	23,163	1,545,044	145,436	-26,718	1,372,890	431,791	215,022	17,928	112,658	57,733
1992	2,163,780	1,646,506	21,668	1,668,174	157,943	-34,151	1,476,080	443,632	244,068	18,798	115,104	59,815
1993	2,274,004	1,696,683	22,861	1,719,544	166,393	-15,343	1,537,808	475,777	260,419	19,342	117,566	61,219
1994	2,369,301	1,741,635	25,591	1,767,226	173,876	9,927	1,603,277	488,953	277,071	19,625	120,728	63,745
1995	2,539,686	1,850,192	26,155	1,876,347	185,236	10,218	1,701,329	539,384	298,973	20,790	122,157	64,981
1996	2,659,050	2,010,903	19,439	2,030,342	201,628	-67,410	1,761,304	571,187	326,559	21,351	124,542	66,642
1997	2,829,682	2,072,685	26,910	2,099,595	209,028	-6,002	1,884,565	607,455	337,662	22,172	127,625	66,472
1998	3,003,400	2,219,785	16,665	2,236,450	221,200	-11,532	2,003,718	646,538	353,144	23,086	130,098	66,900
1999	3,204,878	2,381,998	30,381	2,412,379	236,659	-8,958	2,166,762	658,551	379,565	24,176	132,564	69,607
2000	3,382,362	2,549,062	23,349	2,572,411	253,750	-49,834	2,268,827	705,040	408,495	25,024	135,165	71,651
2001	3,625,199	2,652,388	22,203	2,674,591	269,898	-65,406	2,339,287	825,930	459,982	26,366	137,495	72,479
2002	3,898,222	2,904,345	13,002	2,917,347	296,159	-105,856	2,515,332	863,242	519,648	27,694	140,759	74,713
2003	4,162,108	3,113,067	22,264	3,135,331	314,470	-127,729	2,693,132	926,844	542,132	28,905	143,991	76,635
2004	4,356,392	3,294,355	23,995	3,318,350	341,855	-101,571	2,874,924	881,669	599,799	29,328	148,541	78,889
2005	4,643,720	3,530,131	30,846	3,560,977	363,747	-149,427	3,047,803	918,341	677,576	30,762	150,957	81,312
2006	4,938,595	3,758,012	29,327	3,787,339	392,961	-144,111	3,250,267	950,248	738,080	31,967	154,488	84,883
2007	5,226,084	3,922,456	36,726	3,959,182	409,732	-210,296	3,339,154	1,069,199	817,731	32,902	158,840	87,892
2008	5,474,388	3,994,454	25,258	4,019,712	438,443	-181,597	3,399,672	1,117,914	956,802	33,763	162,144	87,679
2009	5,624,154	4,104,824	15,187	4,120,011	452,355	-168,158	3,499,498	1,088,864	1,035,792	34,109	164,890	87,911
2010	5,853,914	4,258,808	15,431	4,274,239	470,019	-199,772	3,604,448	1,098,730	1,150,736	34,719	168,609	88,125
2011	6,201,253	4,373,823	27,696	4,401,519	429,660	-206,377	3,765,482	1,227,222	1,208,549	36,043	172,052	89,969
2012	6,278,816	4,421,059	23,907	4,444,966	439,125	-150,336	3,855,505	1,206,088	1,217,223	35,983	174,492	90,150
2013	6,309,718	4,427,714	26,736	4,454,450	494,287	-91,924	3,868,239	1,183,549	1,257,930	35,850	176,001	90,858
2014	6,551,427	4,529,952	26,573	4,556,525	504,368	-46,578	4,005,579	1,219,087	1,326,761	36,920	177,448	91,031
2015	6,857,876	4,633,638	30,948	4,664,586	513,080	32,098	4,183,604	1,277,957	1,396,315	38,434	178,433	92,167
2016	7,016,276	4,758,423	32,843	4,791,266	522,256	-12,545	4,256,465	1,311,767	1,448,044	38,799	180,835	93,175
2017	7,313,669	4,921,587	31,408	4,952,995	539,193	9,708	4,423,510	1,386,178	1,503,981	40,011	182,792	95,913
2018	7,608,251	5,149,902	10,631	5,160,533	573,431	10,565	4,597,667	1,415,412	1,595,172	40,932	185,876	98,957
2019	7,971,551	5,436,265	22,811	5,459,076	612,743	-29,096	4,817,237	1,450,955	1,703,359	42,205	188,877	102,460
2020	8,627,391	5,568,826	28,637	5,597,463	637,308	-25,519	4,934,636	1,468,106	2,224,649	44,845	192,383	102,587
2021	9,490,041	5,971,446	22,244	5,993,690	679,684	-9,079	5,304,927	1,535,802	2,649,312	48,567	195,401	107,220
2022	9,409,804	6,230,519	25,383	6,255,902	718,821	15,621	5,552,702	1,591,932	2,265,170	47,478	198,193	110,293

Personal Income and Employment by Area: Washington-Arlington-Alexandria, DC-VA-MD-WV

(Thousands of dollars, except as noted.)

		Derivation of personal income										
		Earnings by place of work										
Year	Personal income, total	Nonfarm	Farm	Total	Less: Contributions for government social insurance	Plus: Adjustment for residence	Equals: Net earnings by place of residence	Plus: Dividends, interest, and rent	Plus: Personal current transfer receipts	Per capita personal income (dollars)	Population (persons)	Total employment
1970	18,481,942	15,152,883	54,235	15,207,118	705,067	-21,351	14,480,700	3,250,636	750,606	5,806	3,183,440	1,638,981
1971	20,703,541	16,924,538	51,135	16,975,673	809,560	-155,776	16,010,337	3,776,660	916,544	6,395	3,237,369	1,679,935
1972	22,693,173	18,642,918	60,775	18,703,693	948,203	-263,620	17,491,870	4,131,349	1,069,954	6,862	3,307,166	1,731,273
1973	24,759,771	20,433,138	76,056	20,509,194	1,197,275	-370,878	18,941,041	4,560,635	1,258,095	7,442	3,327,206	1,789,171
1974	26,869,832	22,075,927	69,554	22,145,481	1,352,989	-500,528	20,291,964	5,083,754	1,494,114	8,047	3,338,988	1,823,470
1975	29,358,584	24,101,686	70,991	24,172,677	1,488,160	-677,455	22,007,062	5,483,787	1,867,735	8,725	3,364,990	1,840,711
1976	31,963,218	26,466,010	63,052	26,529,062	1,663,497	-838,672	24,026,893	5,936,068	2,000,257	9,445	3,384,227	1,871,962
1977	34,767,798	28,875,833	52,598	28,928,431	1,804,571	-1,013,051	26,110,809	6,550,683	2,106,306	10,249	3,392,257	1,922,797
1978	38,575,566	31,998,364	80,543	32,078,907	2,037,736	-1,267,071	28,774,100	7,526,364	2,275,102	11,273	3,421,832	2,003,451
1979	42,347,302	35,333,813	71,038	35,404,851	2,377,544	-1,630,060	31,397,247	8,377,534	2,572,521	12,350	3,428,946	2,064,330
1980	47,341,345	39,193,275	38,460	39,231,735	2,688,709	-1,968,057	34,574,969	9,779,762	2,986,614	13,709	3,453,214	2,099,925
1981	52,621,553	43,069,811	48,586	43,118,397	3,215,137	-2,152,991	37,750,269	11,421,073	3,450,211	14,985	3,511,581	2,121,920
1982	57,232,488	46,187,423	49,964	46,237,387	3,517,808	-2,218,720	40,500,859	12,879,180	3,852,449	16,104	3,553,959	2,123,655
1983	61,712,012	50,331,045	34,551	50,365,596	4,172,136	-2,290,976	43,902,484	13,657,264	4,152,264	17,111	3,606,471	2,188,981
1984	68,942,910	56,453,054	61,619	56,514,673	4,864,301	-2,530,523	49,119,849	15,347,245	4,475,816	18,718	3,683,200	2,322,616
1985	75,327,911	62,418,623	62,901	62,481,524	5,662,630	-2,757,101	54,061,793	16,581,064	4,685,054	20,015	3,763,593	2,452,806
1986	81,848,680	68,299,964	51,425	68,351,389	6,458,019	-2,779,176	59,114,194	17,796,250	4,938,236	21,219	3,857,401	2,582,005
1987	88,652,030	74,928,673	94,825	75,023,498	7,157,353	-2,999,868	64,866,277	18,612,040	5,173,713	22,393	3,958,850	2,717,476
1988	98,514,412	83,541,341	101,162	83,642,503	8,223,031	-3,289,607	72,129,865	20,816,497	5,568,050	24,282	4,057,116	2,826,967
1989	106,780,190	89,681,387	109,963	89,791,350	9,015,096	-3,499,930	77,276,324	23,551,803	5,952,063	25,835	4,133,239	2,902,144
1990	112,759,068	94,348,503	138,503	94,487,006	9,668,192	-3,563,999	81,254,815	24,982,565	6,521,688	26,941	4,185,342	2,934,616
1991	117,802,958	97,992,466	119,457	98,111,923	10,129,299	-3,531,112	84,451,512	26,063,529	7,287,917	27,736	4,247,235	2,868,521
1992	124,658,877	103,965,994	128,971	104,094,965	10,733,254	-3,706,315	89,655,396	26,751,407	8,252,074	28,909	4,312,067	2,855,896
1993	130,982,185	108,845,087	109,923	108,955,010	11,279,670	-3,942,385	93,732,955	28,447,428	8,801,802	29,945	4,374,165	2,902,152
1994	137,526,323	113,948,438	101,707	114,050,145	12,029,403	-4,194,077	97,826,665	30,447,428	9,252,230	31,015	4,434,176	2,938,404
1995	143,687,539	118,266,196	69,170	118,335,366	12,536,019	-4,245,338	101,554,009	32,396,854	9,736,676	32,013	4,488,385	2,989,498
1996	150,768,501	123,875,947	102,470	123,978,417	13,132,003	-4,534,914	106,311,500	33,997,459	10,459,542	33,142	4,549,151	3,035,499
1997	159,960,611	132,294,448	65,871	132,360,319	14,094,140	-4,985,614	113,280,565	35,968,950	10,711,096	34,665	4,614,434	3,103,078
1998	173,388,247	144,571,029	75,296	144,646,325	15,113,473	-5,299,571	124,233,281	37,743,317	11,411,649	37,011	4,684,826	3,176,675
1999	187,341,399	157,849,275	58,800	157,908,075	16,430,681	-5,003,730	136,473,664	38,861,374	12,006,361	39,225	4,776,083	3,262,572
2000	206,585,090	175,137,624	103,556	175,241,180	17,971,619	-5,824,200	151,445,361	42,280,330	12,859,399	42,368	4,875,923	3,409,145
2001	218,222,384	186,652,055	60,643	186,712,698	19,321,639	-6,363,499	161,027,560	43,091,038	14,103,786	43,793	4,982,993	3,471,970
2002	224,089,929	192,876,374	55,331	192,931,705	20,096,864	-6,779,347	166,055,494	42,725,813	15,308,622	44,211	5,068,667	3,508,529
2003	235,724,531	203,997,728	39,810	204,037,538	21,159,100	-7,576,874	175,301,564	44,125,544	16,297,423	45,883	5,137,498	3,562,163
2004	254,097,900	222,665,689	52,952	222,718,641	23,028,261	-8,526,901	191,163,479	45,852,079	17,082,342	48,745	5,212,772	3,659,563
2005	271,103,886	236,745,121	35,103	236,780,224	24,470,903	-9,847,838	202,461,483	50,150,374	18,492,029	51,281	5,286,683	3,744,958
2006	286,705,995	246,929,349	-4,428	246,924,921	25,936,377	-10,148,239	210,840,305	56,329,937	19,535,753	53,769	5,332,180	3,810,676
2007	301,049,375	256,418,864	-11,948	256,406,916	27,127,386	-10,959,016	218,320,514	61,582,391	21,146,470	55,891	5,386,334	3,884,476
2008	315,503,808	265,054,692	36,093	265,090,785	28,497,802	-10,810,879	225,782,104	64,992,619	24,729,085	57,801	5,458,415	3,901,424
2009	313,926,738	268,050,835	46,486	268,097,321	29,030,122	-10,232,663	228,834,536	58,659,187	26,433,015	56,449	5,561,253	3,861,069
2010	331,551,958	283,686,556	39,187	283,725,743	30,320,934	-10,325,533	243,079,276	58,767,549	29,705,133	58,370	5,680,206	3,878,950
2011	354,659,229	296,791,237	74,771	296,866,008	27,899,391	-10,020,189	258,946,428	64,626,398	31,086,403	61,241	5,791,182	3,946,241
2012	366,715,385	303,100,750	130,913	303,231,663	28,693,583	-9,029,449	265,508,631	69,987,502	31,219,252	62,210	5,894,831	3,996,882
2013	362,359,068	303,157,130	147,017	303,304,147	33,040,819	-8,375,050	261,888,278	67,785,689	32,685,101	60,533	5,986,151	4,052,919
2014	376,299,159	311,452,047	103,328	311,555,375	33,920,696	-8,084,064	269,550,615	72,388,452	34,360,092	62,073	6,062,230	4,106,525
2015	395,316,712	326,438,580	36,542	326,475,122	35,509,569	-8,115,977	282,849,576	76,073,435	36,393,701	64,476	6,131,237	4,198,597
2016	409,954,943	337,929,048	26,937	337,955,985	36,465,755	-8,377,694	293,112,536	78,478,048	38,364,359	66,189	6,193,671	4,288,850
2017	425,200,818	349,081,853	86,337	349,168,190	38,059,941	-8,708,621	302,399,628	83,210,539	39,590,651	67,897	6,262,402	4,353,238
2018	443,108,260	362,340,734	38,446	362,379,180	39,788,613	-9,007,554	313,583,013	87,834,098	41,691,149	70,255	6,307,186	4,437,262
2019	458,806,299	374,394,134	125,554	374,519,688	41,207,882	-10,289,361	323,022,445	91,485,007	44,298,847	72,199	6,354,713	4,455,545
2020	478,395,666	379,822,322	73,311	379,895,633	42,075,687	-10,999,123	326,820,823	88,551,640	63,023,203	75,141	6,366,679	4,330,281
2021	516,328,343	405,685,080	83,382	405,768,462	44,563,745	-11,301,116	349,903,601	97,241,378	69,183,364	81,121	6,364,907	4,451,799
2022	529,083,813	427,455,651	84,841	427,540,492	47,642,419	-12,888,898	367,009,175	103,594,719	58,479,919	83,010	6,373,756	4,631,043

Personal Income and Employment by Area: Waterloo-Cedar Falls, IA

(Thousands of dollars, except as noted.)

		Derivation of personal income										
		Earnings by place of work										
Year	Personal income, total	Nonfarm	Farm	Total	Less: Contributions for government social insurance	Plus: Adjustment for residence	Equals: Net earnings by place of residence	Plus: Dividends, interest, and rent	Plus: Personal current transfer receipts	Per capita personal income (dollars)	Population (persons)	Total employment
1970	631,415	496,061	35,859	531,920	37,991	-21,117	472,812	100,737	57,866	3,717	169,857	76,398
1971	669,022	528,899	31,473	560,372	42,010	-23,504	494,858	109,180	64,984	3,929	170,283	75,817
1972	750,312	598,609	41,420	640,029	50,161	-27,391	562,477	118,889	68,946	4,424	169,595	77,925
1973	875,548	686,373	75,857	762,230	66,689	-33,698	661,843	134,288	79,417	5,146	170,158	83,267
1974	962,897	778,027	57,856	835,883	78,109	-39,889	717,885	152,724	92,288	5,658	170,178	85,777
1975	1,071,099	848,307	57,985	906,292	83,427	-43,798	779,067	172,278	119,754	6,264	170,987	85,435
1976	1,145,694	931,895	30,969	962,864	93,158	-47,159	822,547	188,543	134,604	6,660	172,038	86,484
1977	1,324,233	1,095,686	43,267	1,138,953	109,026	-60,399	969,528	214,651	140,054	7,664	172,797	91,066
1978	1,465,258	1,196,354	63,010	1,259,364	123,198	-67,283	1,068,883	240,315	156,060	8,401	174,425	92,582
1979	1,631,745	1,367,338	44,440	1,411,778	146,711	-82,044	1,183,023	273,955	174,767	9,330	174,893	95,443
1980	1,798,703	1,482,169	25,363	1,507,532	157,952	-91,002	1,258,578	332,571	207,554	10,152	177,172	95,288
1981	1,991,655	1,591,253	43,789	1,635,042	180,524	-98,235	1,356,283	404,109	231,263	11,261	176,866	93,456
1982	2,010,249	1,526,437	21,280	1,547,717	175,724	-89,730	1,282,263	451,954	276,032	11,458	175,444	88,697
1983	2,024,164	1,495,488	7,816	1,503,304	172,475	-82,639	1,248,190	475,551	300,423	11,640	173,893	86,524
1984	2,132,462	1,537,846	43,108	1,580,954	182,588	-83,309	1,315,057	517,790	299,615	12,428	171,586	85,792
1985	2,122,585	1,487,405	54,212	1,541,617	177,760	-75,214	1,288,643	518,246	315,696	12,707	167,036	82,930
1986	2,103,779	1,435,407	64,674	1,500,081	174,139	-65,159	1,260,783	514,472	328,524	12,968	162,232	80,235
1987	2,205,906	1,583,943	73,411	1,657,354	189,558	-80,814	1,386,982	491,209	327,715	13,878	158,953	82,491
1988	2,311,052	1,734,101	37,231	1,771,332	214,527	-94,259	1,462,546	509,653	338,853	14,698	157,238	85,872
1989	2,510,496	1,862,570	49,619	1,912,189	228,634	-104,546	1,579,009	566,587	364,900	15,881	158,077	88,775
1990	2,656,091	1,975,942	77,466	2,053,408	247,888	-113,194	1,692,326	569,648	394,117	16,702	159,026	91,900
1991	2,734,593	2,049,012	60,370	2,109,382	258,477	-114,774	1,736,131	576,669	421,793	17,039	160,489	93,283
1992	2,934,971	2,207,451	97,406	2,304,857	276,257	-125,233	1,903,367	575,692	455,912	18,200	161,261	94,400
1993	2,983,202	2,304,823	37,991	2,342,814	290,568	-129,605	1,922,641	576,572	483,989	18,392	162,204	95,937
1994	3,197,552	2,436,477	101,977	2,538,454	310,239	-134,712	2,093,503	599,531	504,518	19,689	162,400	96,870
1995	3,355,227	2,514,548	96,559	2,611,107	321,199	-136,956	2,152,952	670,122	532,153	20,665	162,363	99,104
1996	3,539,850	2,590,608	137,663	2,728,271	314,415	-142,065	2,271,791	711,640	556,419	21,716	163,010	100,755
1997	3,764,094	2,800,781	133,009	2,933,790	351,772	-156,766	2,425,252	771,400	567,442	23,106	162,902	103,664
1998	3,890,799	2,923,632	94,253	3,017,885	362,878	-159,969	2,495,038	801,028	594,733	23,820	163,342	105,588
1999	3,879,808	2,929,520	68,012	2,997,532	360,657	-155,316	2,481,559	782,971	615,278	23,727	163,516	104,942
2000	4,136,216	3,113,872	79,850	3,193,722	379,427	-172,992	2,641,303	845,487	649,426	25,267	163,699	106,241
2001	4,246,835	3,222,353	71,601	3,293,954	391,863	-187,299	2,714,792	820,669	711,374	25,960	163,590	104,894
2002	4,408,516	3,324,174	69,946	3,394,120	401,448	-200,718	2,791,954	838,499	778,063	27,107	162,634	104,572
2003	4,480,985	3,433,470	48,325	3,481,795	420,019	-212,310	2,849,466	850,558	780,961	27,594	162,388	104,473
2004	4,830,760	3,728,156	134,205	3,862,361	448,673	-232,601	3,181,087	841,949	807,724	29,674	162,793	106,240
2005	4,962,509	3,871,218	115,908	3,987,126	466,795	-249,120	3,271,211	839,732	851,566	30,396	163,260	107,312
2006	5,226,882	4,041,058	78,427	4,119,485	485,440	-265,214	3,368,831	929,850	928,201	31,876	163,976	108,751
2007	5,534,995	4,251,341	109,346	4,360,687	513,073	-290,872	3,556,742	1,003,867	974,386	33,686	164,310	110,708
2008	5,889,924	4,468,021	106,624	4,574,645	543,758	-305,329	3,725,558	1,082,941	1,081,425	35,541	165,724	111,079
2009	5,896,851	4,507,811	69,260	4,577,071	548,157	-318,814	3,710,100	1,041,062	1,145,689	35,263	167,225	110,045
2010	6,039,650	4,608,739	89,541	4,698,280	562,672	-331,519	3,804,089	1,014,904	1,220,657	35,966	167,926	109,773
2011	6,479,355	4,773,301	220,905	4,994,206	529,454	-361,316	4,103,436	1,115,203	1,260,716	38,461	168,467	111,903
2012	6,764,925	5,078,185	178,682	5,256,867	552,883	-394,754	4,309,230	1,211,117	1,244,578	40,064	168,853	113,815
2013	6,757,834	5,134,867	209,701	5,344,568	626,000	-402,530	4,316,038	1,171,176	1,270,620	39,773	169,909	114,452
2014	6,942,363	5,293,796	108,791	5,402,587	635,702	-397,174	4,369,711	1,234,774	1,337,878	40,711	170,526	114,674
2015	7,086,017	5,306,502	101,589	5,408,091	627,565	-400,310	4,380,216	1,296,212	1,409,589	41,449	170,956	113,805
2016	7,090,677	5,325,715	54,762	5,380,477	648,268	-391,890	4,340,319	1,307,817	1,442,541	41,641	170,282	113,028
2017	7,280,776	5,495,099	58,068	5,553,167	673,884	-408,819	4,470,464	1,370,417	1,439,895	42,960	169,479	112,675
2018	7,701,516	5,746,068	69,678	5,815,746	712,725	-430,939	4,672,082	1,466,280	1,563,154	45,542	169,107	114,095
2019	7,795,562	5,791,730	51,635	5,843,365	725,258	-428,439	4,689,668	1,473,527	1,632,367	46,256	168,532	112,819
2020	8,445,592	5,889,762	42,355	5,932,117	754,567	-424,129	4,753,421	1,614,387	2,077,784	50,161	168,371	108,952
2021	9,070,630	6,249,985	224,764	6,474,749	790,340	-435,160	5,249,249	1,629,003	2,192,378	53,960	168,099	111,291
2022	9,275,410	6,622,576	271,536	6,894,112	852,024	-462,735	5,579,353	1,743,381	1,952,676	55,247	167,889	113,867

Personal Income and Employment by Area: Watertown-Fort Drum, NY

(Thousands of dollars, except as noted.)

Year	Personal income, total	Derivation of personal income: Earnings by place of work: Nonfarm	Farm	Total	Less: Contributions for government social insurance	Plus: Adjustment for residence	Equals: Net earnings by place of residence	Plus: Dividends, interest, and rent	Plus: Personal current transfer receipts	Per capita personal income (dollars)	Population (persons)	Total employment
1970	313,911	233,051	13,226	246,277	17,886	1,332	229,723	45,347	38,841	3,535	88,789	36,388
1971	337,120	246,280	12,704	258,984	19,170	1,792	241,606	48,706	46,808	3,758	89,719	36,058
1972	354,161	258,045	12,596	270,641	21,020	1,164	250,785	52,350	51,026	3,902	90,773	36,058
1973	380,658	276,641	13,293	289,934	25,710	778	265,002	59,177	56,479	4,215	90,310	37,049
1974	412,204	297,281	10,516	307,797	28,471	-117	279,209	65,940	67,055	4,606	89,485	36,947
1975	450,975	315,477	7,626	323,103	29,592	-2,074	291,437	71,618	87,920	4,998	90,235	36,272
1976	480,436	336,374	10,448	346,822	32,046	-2,902	311,874	74,391	94,171	5,309	90,488	35,746
1977	507,630	360,887	5,744	366,631	34,443	-3,299	328,889	82,069	96,672	5,635	90,089	36,188
1978	560,769	406,740	10,688	417,428	39,685	-4,915	372,828	86,264	101,677	6,255	89,651	37,470
1979	617,785	453,821	11,220	465,041	45,747	-7,239	412,055	98,170	107,560	6,929	89,161	38,283
1980	686,874	493,802	8,382	502,184	49,402	-9,568	443,214	117,759	125,901	7,799	88,071	37,483
1981	749,060	527,057	7,048	534,105	55,388	-10,967	467,750	139,175	142,135	8,552	87,585	36,896
1982	823,587	555,255	9,497	564,752	58,787	-11,729	494,236	166,355	162,996	9,434	87,302	36,595
1983	880,258	597,922	7,740	605,662	63,922	-12,830	528,910	172,235	179,113	10,064	87,465	37,306
1984	975,140	674,029	9,639	683,668	73,089	-15,071	595,508	191,557	188,075	11,069	88,094	38,570
1985	1,057,466	741,730	12,640	754,370	81,387	-19,426	653,557	205,907	198,002	11,888	88,954	40,370
1986	1,168,001	841,825	15,534	857,359	92,370	-27,313	737,676	227,212	203,113	12,831	91,032	43,661
1987	1,371,349	1,059,911	17,406	1,077,317	114,820	-50,359	912,138	257,233	201,978	14,232	96,360	49,930
1988	1,580,328	1,280,260	12,875	1,293,135	143,014	-73,745	1,076,376	291,780	212,172	15,231	103,758	56,273
1989	1,786,827	1,422,493	19,483	1,441,976	156,679	-79,354	1,205,943	349,484	231,400	16,313	109,534	60,292
1990	1,852,474	1,457,107	20,830	1,477,937	156,051	-78,196	1,243,690	357,654	251,130	16,607	111,549	59,814
1991	1,947,838	1,515,191	13,645	1,528,836	165,526	-73,752	1,289,558	374,050	284,230	17,251	112,911	58,880
1992	2,055,381	1,573,569	18,860	1,592,429	172,555	-71,297	1,348,577	382,500	324,304	17,957	114,463	58,311
1993	2,058,726	1,555,290	17,626	1,572,916	173,235	-66,142	1,333,539	383,722	341,465	17,922	114,874	57,273
1994	2,118,101	1,599,431	15,834	1,615,265	177,783	-65,807	1,371,675	393,643	352,783	18,114	116,932	58,543
1995	2,200,713	1,643,327	9,650	1,652,977	180,459	-65,656	1,406,862	422,735	371,116	19,077	115,361	58,586
1996	2,259,396	1,672,858	20,720	1,693,578	182,095	-63,452	1,448,031	428,662	382,703	19,718	114,585	58,639
1997	2,328,076	1,733,861	8,033	1,741,894	186,017	-61,775	1,494,102	446,667	387,307	20,592	113,055	58,879
1998	2,451,584	1,813,967	8,916	1,822,883	193,052	-62,540	1,567,291	480,488	403,805	21,783	112,546	59,089
1999	2,563,712	1,904,832	8,920	1,913,752	197,763	-60,417	1,655,572	484,342	423,798	22,874	112,081	60,291
2000	2,707,940	2,010,563	7,663	2,018,226	207,851	-60,007	1,750,368	513,799	443,773	24,223	111,790	61,119
2001	2,706,673	2,014,208	11,694	2,025,902	217,321	-69,501	1,739,080	491,992	475,601	24,292	111,422	60,488
2002	2,871,121	2,121,724	15,459	2,137,183	230,272	-76,652	1,830,259	526,320	514,542	25,840	111,112	60,317
2003	3,057,596	2,279,655	24,788	2,304,443	245,371	-99,140	1,959,932	564,290	533,374	27,734	110,246	60,813
2004	3,256,210	2,451,544	37,821	2,489,365	267,014	-119,332	2,103,019	586,716	566,475	29,622	109,924	62,676
2005	3,564,755	2,779,805	38,357	2,818,162	303,099	-169,103	2,345,960	628,274	590,521	31,411	113,486	65,951
2006	3,866,393	3,155,038	26,096	3,181,134	346,432	-259,935	2,574,767	677,591	614,035	34,020	113,650	69,034
2007	4,123,861	3,315,963	39,747	3,355,710	360,598	-263,991	2,731,121	747,833	644,907	35,841	115,059	69,724
2008	4,399,009	3,521,050	42,701	3,563,751	385,638	-316,299	2,861,814	814,473	722,722	38,241	115,033	71,122
2009	4,606,452	3,682,804	20,789	3,703,593	404,658	-334,675	2,964,260	852,617	789,575	40,048	115,023	70,866
2010	4,897,213	3,926,069	43,370	3,969,439	430,359	-339,246	3,199,834	845,148	852,231	41,922	116,816	72,440
2011	5,119,638	4,028,530	66,913	4,095,443	406,413	-393,665	3,295,365	944,651	879,622	43,072	118,863	72,645
2012	5,164,248	3,962,237	57,278	4,019,515	401,964	-352,899	3,264,652	1,024,650	874,946	42,234	122,278	71,378
2013	4,988,114	3,879,974	82,385	3,962,359	433,672	-344,224	3,184,463	896,407	907,244	41,092	121,389	70,577
2014	5,029,567	3,844,508	92,370	3,936,878	436,679	-315,631	3,184,568	917,075	927,924	41,315	121,738	69,582
2015	5,023,544	3,832,272	54,734	3,887,006	437,109	-317,636	3,132,261	905,080	986,203	41,531	120,958	68,751
2016	4,964,138	3,756,780	48,024	3,804,804	424,974	-306,708	3,073,122	876,921	1,014,095	41,923	118,410	67,181
2017	5,128,599	3,827,065	60,359	3,887,424	435,924	-298,392	3,153,108	896,953	1,078,538	42,928	119,470	67,361
2018	5,181,000	3,902,214	47,365	3,949,579	439,387	-304,921	3,205,271	908,596	1,067,133	43,528	119,026	67,612
2019	5,358,938	4,010,353	67,312	4,077,665	450,648	-322,111	3,304,906	901,696	1,152,336	45,567	117,606	67,191
2020	5,843,908	4,088,758	73,855	4,162,613	460,378	-332,423	3,369,812	905,358	1,568,738	50,260	116,273	64,440
2021	6,160,986	4,370,512	83,986	4,454,498	496,260	-345,384	3,612,854	870,666	1,677,466	52,354	117,680	67,004
2022	6,035,804	4,550,936	109,045	4,659,981	529,685	-355,668	3,774,628	858,670	1,402,506	51,749	116,637	68,517

Personal Income and Employment by Area: Wausau-Weston, WI

(Thousands of dollars, except as noted.)

Year	Personal income, total	Derivation of personal income: Earnings by place of work: Nonfarm	Farm	Total	Less: Contributions for government social insurance	Plus: Adjustment for residence	Equals: Net earnings by place of residence	Plus: Dividends, interest, and rent	Plus: Personal current transfer receipts	Per capita personal income (dollars)	Population (persons)	Total employment
1970	411,673	307,289	23,893	331,182	22,788	4,261	312,655	58,886	40,132	3,390	121,446	52,112
1971	447,005	331,704	24,057	355,761	25,502	5,001	335,260	64,719	47,026	3,616	123,617	52,398
1972	497,510	373,750	26,134	399,884	30,245	5,386	375,025	70,683	51,802	3,984	124,883	54,119
1973	561,761	425,903	31,214	457,117	39,418	5,784	423,483	79,608	58,670	4,416	127,199	56,761
1974	613,657	464,007	26,107	490,114	44,612	7,113	452,615	90,376	70,666	4,775	128,508	57,435
1975	688,679	509,418	29,275	538,693	47,804	7,337	498,226	101,290	89,163	5,292	130,132	58,433
1976	779,425	588,074	33,081	621,155	56,052	8,392	573,495	108,577	97,353	5,997	129,960	61,056
1977	894,121	681,200	45,546	726,746	64,847	8,899	670,798	120,689	102,634	6,741	132,641	65,098
1978	1,007,038	769,325	51,591	820,916	75,194	10,533	756,255	136,378	114,405	7,493	134,393	67,794
1979	1,121,153	839,052	64,338	903,390	85,392	12,320	830,318	155,254	135,581	8,225	136,311	68,779
1980	1,224,747	876,721	62,869	939,590	88,910	14,661	865,341	191,172	168,234	8,883	137,878	67,340
1981	1,320,937	935,142	52,483	987,625	101,264	15,019	901,380	233,427	186,130	9,588	137,765	66,972
1982	1,383,993	949,866	48,426	998,292	103,791	19,056	913,557	261,232	209,204	10,054	137,655	65,879
1983	1,460,133	1,026,489	25,444	1,051,933	111,684	21,350	961,599	274,840	223,694	10,613	137,581	67,290
1984	1,590,958	1,101,504	42,458	1,143,962	122,329	24,688	1,046,321	313,020	231,617	11,483	138,554	68,697
1985	1,689,152	1,176,490	41,395	1,217,885	131,884	24,729	1,110,730	333,337	245,085	12,199	138,467	69,516
1986	1,790,709	1,256,410	47,572	1,303,982	140,749	26,516	1,189,749	353,804	247,156	12,944	138,345	70,891
1987	1,888,995	1,357,563	56,617	1,414,180	150,215	27,589	1,291,554	346,877	250,564	13,597	138,930	72,862
1988	2,006,134	1,479,792	44,422	1,524,214	169,741	29,671	1,384,144	364,402	257,588	14,332	139,971	75,021
1989	2,218,750	1,590,360	82,261	1,672,621	183,707	30,553	1,519,467	414,983	284,300	15,726	141,090	77,168
1990	2,376,440	1,737,860	74,973	1,812,833	208,609	33,083	1,637,307	434,732	304,401	16,640	142,813	80,062
1991	2,485,323	1,845,521	50,002	1,895,523	223,362	33,495	1,705,656	444,880	334,787	17,207	144,437	82,412
1992	2,684,280	2,005,766	58,283	2,064,049	239,760	37,700	1,861,989	460,734	361,557	18,354	146,253	84,331
1993	2,827,833	2,136,238	45,669	2,181,907	255,770	37,036	1,963,173	485,763	378,897	19,079	148,214	85,503
1994	2,990,621	2,276,375	52,948	2,329,323	275,519	37,616	2,091,420	506,171	393,030	20,031	149,301	87,925
1995	3,150,839	2,401,505	34,381	2,435,886	291,555	33,586	2,177,917	551,807	421,115	20,952	150,386	90,429
1996	3,361,109	2,536,428	57,875	2,594,303	305,803	30,733	2,319,233	604,880	436,996	22,181	151,530	92,147
1997	3,577,881	2,734,087	30,697	2,764,784	327,190	27,571	2,465,165	658,622	454,094	23,429	152,713	94,632
1998	3,818,325	2,875,876	54,511	2,930,387	339,900	35,163	2,625,650	728,577	464,098	24,825	153,809	97,397
1999	3,971,520	3,063,866	49,157	3,113,023	362,009	34,361	2,785,375	703,475	482,670	25,656	154,797	99,768
2000	4,233,358	3,273,967	29,690	3,303,657	380,668	31,207	2,954,196	761,028	518,134	27,195	155,665	101,578
2001	4,457,414	3,450,502	51,446	3,501,948	395,734	10,137	3,116,351	763,718	577,345	28,572	156,007	102,152
2002	4,613,387	3,632,338	42,586	3,674,924	413,691	469	3,261,702	729,988	621,697	29,475	156,521	102,921
2003	4,783,060	3,753,816	61,974	3,815,790	428,600	16,370	3,403,560	744,876	634,624	30,479	156,932	102,829
2004	4,972,563	3,961,204	70,587	4,031,791	454,087	-2,947	3,574,757	733,608	664,198	31,568	157,521	104,625
2005	5,188,561	4,159,872	57,779	4,217,651	479,945	-8,241	3,729,465	744,220	714,876	32,723	158,560	106,908
2006	5,408,302	4,323,870	41,914	4,365,784	501,917	-14,457	3,849,410	797,209	761,683	33,808	159,973	107,438
2007	5,680,893	4,453,589	71,552	4,525,141	520,040	-39,663	3,965,438	888,502	826,953	35,275	161,045	108,696
2008	5,966,238	4,533,572	65,751	4,599,323	534,262	-11,256	4,053,805	963,008	949,425	36,799	162,130	107,710
2009	6,013,506	4,371,112	24,042	4,395,154	515,922	108,525	3,987,757	925,070	1,100,679	36,978	162,626	102,890
2010	6,032,729	4,371,273	63,433	4,434,706	516,109	28,232	3,946,829	904,631	1,181,269	37,029	162,919	100,813
2011	6,349,397	4,544,150	110,667	4,654,817	480,976	65,636	4,239,477	971,206	1,138,714	38,893	163,251	101,770
2012	6,631,770	4,729,485	110,750	4,840,235	498,230	106,380	4,448,385	1,028,795	1,154,590	40,536	163,601	101,491
2013	6,679,549	4,838,310	129,168	4,967,478	574,289	87,746	4,480,935	1,039,143	1,159,471	40,669	164,240	103,006
2014	6,966,094	5,036,400	163,015	5,199,415	596,789	85,808	4,688,434	1,071,177	1,206,483	42,316	164,622	105,000
2015	7,247,631	5,213,908	128,021	5,341,929	615,337	78,515	4,805,107	1,173,117	1,269,407	43,956	164,883	106,070
2016	7,402,838	5,288,547	94,584	5,383,131	621,030	162,322	4,924,423	1,192,139	1,286,276	44,880	164,948	106,030
2017	7,668,054	5,493,068	106,415	5,599,483	647,895	129,494	5,081,082	1,240,846	1,346,126	46,316	165,559	106,551
2018	8,046,416	5,795,317	87,401	5,882,718	672,772	138,722	5,348,668	1,278,496	1,419,252	48,541	165,764	107,480
2019	8,424,252	5,987,720	112,980	6,100,700	696,917	171,667	5,575,450	1,351,897	1,496,905	50,684	166,210	107,299
2020	8,925,032	6,068,254	147,429	6,215,683	708,580	170,614	5,677,717	1,362,603	1,884,712	53,612	166,476	103,654
2021	9,634,360	6,410,762	136,524	6,547,286	744,624	195,297	5,997,959	1,502,787	2,133,614	57,969	166,199	105,690
2022	9,775,425	6,783,644	149,991	6,933,635	807,903	184,807	6,310,539	1,601,575	1,863,311	58,770	166,334	108,874

Personal Income and Employment by Area: Weirton-Steubenville, WV-OH

(Thousands of dollars, except as noted.)

Year	Personal income, total	Derivation of personal income: Earnings by place of work: Nonfarm	Farm	Total	Less: Contributions for government social insurance	Plus: Adjustment for residence	Equals: Net earnings by place of residence	Plus: Dividends, interest, and rent	Plus: Personal current transfer receipts	Per capita personal income (dollars)	Population (persons)	Total employment
1970	603,659	559,411	947	560,358	41,075	-43,339	475,944	69,924	57,791	3,626	166,471	67,336
1971	655,277	607,649	1,121	608,770	46,459	-50,591	511,720	75,349	68,208	3,920	167,161	68,528
1972	714,183	665,855	1,194	667,049	53,066	-56,403	557,580	80,090	76,513	4,301	166,032	68,997
1973	767,566	710,436	1,697	712,133	66,289	-58,488	587,356	89,130	91,080	4,622	166,066	70,056
1974	879,832	820,599	1,973	822,572	79,983	-71,107	671,482	103,506	104,844	5,346	164,593	71,072
1975	961,462	872,396	1,547	873,943	85,142	-72,638	716,163	117,557	127,742	5,793	165,977	69,428
1976	1,080,647	1,004,027	1,375	1,005,402	98,476	-92,584	814,342	126,079	140,226	6,563	164,666	71,679
1977	1,179,504	1,088,456	1,262	1,089,718	106,240	-96,473	887,005	139,717	152,782	7,202	163,770	71,144
1978	1,271,763	1,161,052	1,474	1,162,526	116,877	-98,125	947,524	152,799	171,440	7,857	161,867	70,906
1979	1,419,607	1,302,284	1,753	1,304,037	135,487	-113,633	1,054,917	171,384	193,306	8,785	161,602	72,151
1980	1,527,627	1,334,690	1,901	1,336,591	139,169	-121,663	1,075,759	213,590	238,278	9,352	163,345	68,618
1981	1,644,423	1,380,663	1,807	1,382,470	154,031	-110,106	1,118,333	259,199	266,891	10,181	161,525	66,467
1982	1,639,567	1,292,762	2,234	1,294,996	148,079	-104,287	1,042,630	289,022	307,915	10,216	160,486	60,765
1983	1,618,160	1,222,736	717	1,223,453	141,218	-95,555	986,680	307,077	324,403	10,312	156,918	57,943
1984	1,712,175	1,278,264	438	1,278,702	151,493	-101,123	1,026,086	345,901	340,188	11,072	154,644	58,635
1985	1,733,191	1,267,767	1,224	1,268,991	151,475	-92,300	1,025,216	349,233	358,742	11,404	151,981	57,275
1986	1,821,122	1,357,102	375	1,357,477	167,499	-101,260	1,088,718	361,592	370,812	12,211	149,132	58,845
1987	1,856,830	1,399,105	324	1,399,429	170,958	-100,782	1,127,689	346,994	382,147	12,651	146,776	59,897
1988	1,955,034	1,500,832	-1,417	1,499,415	190,199	-112,010	1,197,206	360,808	397,020	13,464	145,205	60,005
1989	2,098,860	1,618,251	748	1,618,999	207,340	-124,689	1,286,970	400,900	410,990	14,588	143,873	61,112
1990	2,224,659	1,681,031	757	1,681,788	218,628	-112,185	1,350,975	426,905	446,779	15,637	142,270	62,123
1991	2,222,132	1,619,569	-1,147	1,618,422	214,424	-71,622	1,332,376	403,885	485,871	15,666	141,845	60,857
1992	2,340,786	1,729,900	2,438	1,732,338	223,164	-102,326	1,406,848	398,979	534,959	16,600	141,012	60,156
1993	2,400,283	1,752,906	1,689	1,754,595	238,794	-72,376	1,443,425	391,478	565,380	17,059	140,704	59,913
1994	2,498,672	1,814,775	2,781	1,817,556	245,634	-69,362	1,502,560	402,994	593,118	17,848	140,001	60,141
1995	2,547,141	1,796,315	1,328	1,797,643	249,019	-33,271	1,515,353	414,906	616,882	18,253	139,547	60,826
1996	2,631,265	1,829,905	449	1,830,354	252,899	-36,657	1,540,798	441,476	648,991	19,029	138,275	60,868
1997	2,650,955	1,746,627	1,456	1,748,083	236,953	-4,439	1,506,691	476,494	667,770	19,404	136,619	59,452
1998	2,794,617	1,875,068	1,891	1,876,959	254,449	-9,807	1,612,703	504,795	677,119	20,751	134,675	61,710
1999	2,827,946	1,879,832	2,141	1,881,973	251,557	17,306	1,647,722	480,961	699,263	21,219	133,276	60,934
2000	2,979,538	1,984,652	3,796	1,988,448	268,538	23,208	1,743,118	508,069	728,351	22,627	131,681	60,717
2001	3,154,158	2,049,360	4,316	2,053,676	268,160	62,751	1,848,267	509,809	796,082	24,133	130,701	60,250
2002	3,237,913	2,122,833	4,485	2,127,318	271,517	67,723	1,923,524	478,611	835,778	24,955	129,750	60,338
2003	3,250,033	2,119,477	3,564	2,123,041	276,519	83,437	1,929,959	460,906	859,168	25,167	129,141	59,547
2004	3,345,023	2,112,113	3,125	2,115,238	275,950	146,865	1,986,153	485,475	873,395	26,084	128,241	58,167
2005	3,355,312	2,118,041	1,994	2,120,035	279,267	182,137	2,022,905	439,577	892,830	26,324	127,464	58,049
2006	3,519,574	2,163,419	1,664	2,165,083	273,806	242,358	2,133,635	438,920	947,019	27,862	126,321	57,501
2007	3,678,137	2,228,534	1,180	2,229,714	275,018	237,899	2,192,595	505,732	979,810	29,370	125,236	57,963
2008	3,874,779	2,392,009	-1,069	2,390,940	294,880	160,887	2,256,947	539,432	1,078,400	31,008	124,959	58,239
2009	3,782,706	2,182,514	-156	2,182,358	274,886	202,492	2,109,964	502,383	1,170,359	30,326	124,734	54,819
2010	3,860,366	2,107,830	-390	2,107,440	262,053	304,856	2,150,243	489,453	1,220,670	31,040	124,366	52,807
2011	4,068,381	2,188,827	-171	2,188,656	245,327	362,770	2,306,099	536,376	1,225,906	32,891	123,694	52,893
2012	4,135,211	2,216,516	171	2,216,687	246,545	388,036	2,358,178	557,745	1,219,288	33,605	123,053	52,508
2013	4,162,751	2,200,291	-1,694	2,198,597	268,397	443,176	2,373,376	540,876	1,248,499	33,928	122,692	52,109
2014	4,295,593	2,229,756	-3,030	2,226,726	275,693	461,526	2,412,559	570,835	1,312,199	35,144	122,228	51,811
2015	4,403,430	2,245,872	-4,244	2,241,628	277,351	484,283	2,448,560	592,257	1,362,613	36,226	121,555	51,339
2016	4,345,280	2,245,179	-5,083	2,240,096	283,742	425,035	2,381,389	576,032	1,387,859	36,131	120,265	50,336
2017	4,510,752	2,310,718	-5,459	2,305,259	295,409	484,625	2,494,475	605,900	1,410,377	37,819	119,271	49,558
2018	4,692,963	2,392,817	-5,195	2,387,622	303,381	512,605	2,596,846	646,485	1,449,632	39,668	118,307	49,642
2019	4,852,580	2,450,780	-5,408	2,445,372	310,042	526,980	2,662,310	688,143	1,502,127	41,271	117,578	49,601
2020	5,145,724	2,388,450	-4,171	2,384,279	308,114	503,062	2,579,227	680,475	1,886,022	44,101	116,680	47,388
2021	5,500,460	2,530,643	-4,085	2,526,558	323,357	532,672	2,735,873	732,159	2,032,428	47,495	115,811	48,732
2022	5,451,907	2,684,094	-7,637	2,676,457	350,207	489,633	2,815,883	826,545	1,809,479	47,725	114,235	50,245

Personal Income and Employment by Area: Wenatchee, WA

(Thousands of dollars, except as noted.)

Year	Personal income, total	Derivation of personal income								Per capita personal income (dollars)	Population (persons)	Total employment
		Earnings by place of work			Less: Contributions for government social insurance	Plus: Adjustment for residence	Equals: Net earnings by place of residence	Plus: Dividends, interest, and rent	Plus: Personal current transfer receipts			
		Nonfarm	Farm	Total								
1970	233,154	158,823	19,635	178,458	12,977	-166	165,315	41,612	26,227	4,026	57,905	28,819
1971	266,510	170,446	36,117	206,563	14,632	-175	191,756	45,048	29,706	4,581	58,182	28,335
1972	284,714	182,550	37,258	219,808	16,352	298	203,754	48,961	31,999	4,906	58,036	28,518
1973	329,056	202,945	53,433	256,378	21,005	1,100	236,473	56,723	35,860	5,642	58,318	29,659
1974	369,509	228,690	57,772	286,462	24,447	1,148	263,163	64,136	42,210	6,207	59,531	31,056
1975	432,793	260,413	72,111	332,524	27,982	1,110	305,652	75,039	52,102	7,122	60,767	32,893
1976	464,732	308,579	52,827	361,406	33,902	-102	327,402	80,329	57,001	7,442	62,443	35,350
1977	522,482	353,189	54,629	407,818	39,188	-206	368,424	91,784	62,274	8,121	64,337	36,078
1978	580,874	387,544	59,826	447,370	43,600	3,773	407,543	105,791	67,540	8,857	65,586	36,913
1979	630,339	423,119	52,683	475,802	48,920	4,434	431,316	122,188	76,835	9,511	66,273	38,625
1980	707,932	442,319	67,814	510,133	51,477	5,284	463,940	149,171	94,821	10,474	67,591	38,992
1981	762,868	473,188	59,802	532,990	58,946	5,318	479,362	179,343	104,163	11,055	69,004	39,690
1982	814,945	488,827	62,204	551,031	62,109	5,850	494,772	202,198	117,975	11,705	69,622	39,743
1983	894,651	530,011	72,443	602,454	68,509	6,583	540,528	226,605	127,518	12,604	70,983	41,521
1984	963,000	578,274	72,225	650,499	77,530	5,218	578,187	249,105	135,708	13,296	72,428	42,260
1985	990,057	609,131	47,732	656,863	82,939	5,973	579,897	262,533	147,627	13,454	73,586	42,158
1986	1,058,885	629,815	84,637	714,452	85,979	8,430	636,903	266,081	155,901	14,337	73,859	41,969
1987	1,146,755	667,198	133,123	800,321	90,570	9,218	718,969	265,281	162,505	15,447	74,236	43,915
1988	1,134,088	716,588	59,442	776,030	99,539	10,850	687,341	274,257	172,490	14,921	76,006	44,589
1989	1,249,537	760,485	87,670	848,155	107,927	12,672	752,900	307,949	188,688	16,122	77,504	45,586
1990	1,332,401	824,485	84,403	908,888	119,201	16,328	806,015	317,723	208,663	16,895	78,865	48,257
1991	1,488,329	908,940	125,219	1,034,159	131,365	17,755	920,549	333,553	234,227	18,325	81,220	48,854
1992	1,628,491	990,816	154,948	1,145,764	142,013	20,502	1,024,253	343,445	260,793	19,487	83,570	48,476
1993	1,726,129	1,069,658	142,267	1,211,925	153,062	22,937	1,081,800	368,156	276,173	20,065	86,027	49,733
1994	1,804,501	1,144,770	114,513	1,259,283	164,070	24,287	1,119,500	390,198	294,803	20,331	88,755	52,796
1995	1,878,223	1,165,647	113,796	1,279,443	167,817	26,691	1,138,317	429,406	310,500	20,488	91,676	53,327
1996	2,037,613	1,225,759	166,444	1,392,203	170,726	29,290	1,250,767	456,195	330,651	21,796	93,486	53,993
1997	2,117,577	1,318,402	121,829	1,440,231	174,799	32,519	1,297,951	479,379	340,247	22,263	95,118	54,720
1998	2,234,992	1,405,478	128,181	1,533,659	182,381	37,588	1,388,866	484,764	361,362	23,084	96,819	55,168
1999	2,260,354	1,464,189	106,281	1,570,470	186,028	41,421	1,425,863	451,179	383,312	22,986	98,336	56,072
2000	2,407,106	1,525,601	131,549	1,657,150	198,835	43,132	1,501,447	485,292	420,367	24,235	99,322	56,928
2001	2,486,125	1,603,814	101,423	1,705,237	207,156	42,775	1,540,856	480,105	465,164	25,021	99,361	56,354
2002	2,542,802	1,682,687	120,857	1,803,544	217,513	40,004	1,626,035	434,713	482,054	25,483	99,786	56,613
2003	2,665,552	1,729,826	148,603	1,878,429	225,081	39,066	1,692,414	463,235	509,903	26,482	100,654	57,199
2004	2,811,026	1,826,962	170,496	1,997,458	241,660	38,593	1,794,391	493,700	522,935	27,568	101,968	58,760
2005	2,899,325	1,928,215	136,618	2,064,833	258,998	38,758	1,844,593	492,082	562,650	28,048	103,369	60,975
2006	3,088,616	2,045,625	135,491	2,181,116	274,671	37,928	1,944,373	537,331	606,912	29,389	105,094	62,333
2007	3,348,251	2,155,910	134,537	2,290,447	288,976	39,964	2,041,435	649,486	657,330	31,375	106,717	63,791
2008	3,677,362	2,232,962	157,992	2,390,954	301,507	43,187	2,132,634	800,596	744,132	34,041	108,029	64,601
2009	3,667,774	2,198,066	171,172	2,369,238	308,475	48,537	2,109,300	736,035	822,439	33,461	109,614	63,721
2010	3,747,402	2,215,231	185,020	2,400,251	311,149	54,494	2,143,596	704,680	899,126	33,674	111,284	62,784
2011	3,983,346	2,258,987	237,082	2,496,069	293,624	63,251	2,265,696	811,948	905,702	35,566	112,000	63,195
2012	4,303,032	2,404,617	269,865	2,674,482	300,184	78,090	2,452,388	932,559	918,085	38,117	112,891	64,481
2013	4,367,710	2,548,026	252,373	2,800,399	347,627	88,086	2,540,858	892,215	934,637	38,505	113,433	65,700
2014	4,645,995	2,689,102	218,748	2,907,850	372,047	95,399	2,631,202	983,794	1,030,999	40,645	114,307	67,539
2015	4,922,221	2,841,099	294,349	3,135,448	391,347	99,315	2,843,416	1,033,209	1,045,596	42,399	116,094	69,041
2016	5,192,017	2,923,311	294,513	3,217,824	399,114	106,274	2,924,984	1,155,672	1,111,361	44,085	117,774	69,823
2017	5,455,270	3,135,003	278,691	3,413,694	429,873	112,947	3,096,768	1,223,410	1,135,092	45,867	118,937	70,921
2018	5,680,522	3,341,104	191,912	3,533,016	444,287	123,721	3,212,450	1,282,724	1,185,348	47,338	119,998	72,781
2019	5,973,141	3,496,783	192,938	3,689,721	447,742	131,924	3,373,903	1,329,437	1,269,801	49,252	121,276	73,185
2020	6,564,347	3,604,136	257,563	3,861,699	469,338	144,863	3,537,224	1,368,584	1,658,539	53,692	122,259	69,405
2021	7,141,770	3,943,036	215,886	4,158,922	504,458	154,589	3,809,053	1,430,035	1,902,682	57,775	123,613	72,422
2022	7,180,643	4,209,545	218,167	4,427,712	563,814	167,571	4,031,469	1,511,034	1,638,140	57,853	124,118	75,332

Personal Income and Employment by Area: Wheeling, WV-OH

(Thousands of dollars, except as noted.)

Year	Personal income, total	Derivation of personal income: Earnings by place of work: Nonfarm	Farm	Total	Less: Contributions for government social insurance	Plus: Adjustment for residence	Equals: Net earnings by place of residence	Plus: Dividends, interest, and rent	Plus: Personal current transfer receipts	Per capita personal income (dollars)	Population (persons)	Total employment
1970	644,855	513,841	1,901	515,742	38,769	7,056	484,029	91,851	68,975	3,532	182,552	74,553
1971	688,713	541,975	2,345	544,320	42,239	7,153	509,234	98,826	80,653	3,699	186,174	74,644
1972	748,314	588,226	2,802	591,028	47,447	7,826	551,407	106,257	90,650	4,027	185,831	74,658
1973	817,931	641,793	3,185	644,978	60,044	7,197	592,131	118,050	107,750	4,416	185,230	76,692
1974	893,606	689,250	1,677	690,927	67,207	9,685	633,405	135,031	125,170	4,851	184,209	77,111
1975	992,231	756,596	2,702	759,298	71,683	4,363	691,978	147,633	152,620	5,360	185,114	76,968
1976	1,112,204	857,184	2,585	859,769	82,833	4,085	781,021	161,441	169,742	5,966	186,432	78,256
1977	1,232,362	957,365	1,932	959,297	92,719	2,979	869,557	180,780	182,025	6,637	185,683	79,725
1978	1,348,998	1,051,647	1,367	1,053,014	104,981	-842	947,191	197,318	204,489	7,282	185,256	81,408
1979	1,499,468	1,153,813	1,076	1,154,889	118,437	8,055	1,044,507	219,041	235,920	8,042	186,463	81,667
1980	1,620,837	1,175,054	732	1,175,786	121,537	16,009	1,070,258	275,303	275,276	8,745	185,340	78,635
1981	1,766,766	1,244,445	385	1,244,830	137,959	10,742	1,117,613	342,557	306,596	9,594	184,158	76,299
1982	1,848,505	1,255,148	-252	1,254,896	142,592	2,643	1,114,947	386,256	347,302	10,138	182,331	74,012
1983	1,882,609	1,218,777	-1,025	1,217,752	139,547	8,871	1,087,076	416,219	379,314	10,456	180,057	71,069
1984	1,982,557	1,275,937	501	1,276,438	148,814	14,913	1,142,537	451,938	388,082	11,215	176,777	70,504
1985	2,023,545	1,282,802	2,314	1,285,116	150,783	9,515	1,143,848	471,121	408,576	11,691	173,087	69,315
1986	2,064,501	1,296,187	1,747	1,297,934	156,896	7,945	1,148,983	489,633	425,885	12,236	168,724	68,607
1987	2,128,492	1,380,057	1,010	1,381,067	167,850	6,938	1,220,155	474,590	433,747	12,810	166,158	70,059
1988	2,221,506	1,456,222	-1,577	1,454,645	183,796	-7,541	1,263,308	503,464	454,734	13,567	163,741	71,434
1989	2,375,476	1,533,260	1,392	1,534,652	195,465	-7,099	1,332,088	564,659	478,729	14,694	161,663	71,939
1990	2,495,417	1,618,363	1,314	1,619,677	208,013	-2,194	1,409,470	577,929	508,018	15,698	158,961	72,385
1991	2,571,710	1,662,334	-2,791	1,659,543	219,889	-8,943	1,430,711	586,713	554,286	16,248	158,283	72,525
1992	2,728,591	1,731,967	2,101	1,734,068	230,546	20,565	1,524,087	585,696	618,808	17,212	158,525	71,690
1993	2,781,891	1,783,497	1,332	1,784,829	245,159	7,187	1,546,857	583,865	651,169	17,557	158,445	72,312
1994	2,902,248	1,887,290	1,625	1,888,915	258,848	3,300	1,633,367	601,883	666,998	18,375	157,944	74,195
1995	2,974,209	1,926,768	557	1,927,325	266,974	-9,016	1,651,335	635,170	687,704	19,004	156,502	75,761
1996	3,117,560	1,991,736	-1,726	1,990,010	274,725	8,480	1,723,765	668,595	725,200	19,812	157,354	76,900
1997	3,235,036	2,073,520	-1,875	2,071,645	279,854	1,465	1,793,256	699,963	741,817	20,724	156,100	77,888
1998	3,441,826	2,185,962	-531	2,185,431	293,377	12,240	1,904,294	746,258	791,274	22,125	155,562	79,973
1999	3,491,041	2,276,282	-490	2,275,792	303,703	9,921	1,982,010	708,088	800,943	22,635	154,230	79,789
2000	3,605,774	2,337,320	4,851	2,342,171	315,287	9,341	2,036,225	746,557	822,992	23,580	152,914	80,874
2001	3,988,193	2,657,847	4,463	2,662,310	325,937	5,833	2,342,206	743,181	902,806	26,285	151,728	79,685
2002	4,094,195	2,746,926	2,062	2,748,988	329,276	10,502	2,430,214	708,224	955,757	27,035	151,442	79,957
2003	4,168,909	2,836,624	190	2,836,814	347,271	7,474	2,497,017	695,991	975,901	27,670	150,666	79,040
2004	4,296,077	2,971,775	7,657	2,979,432	361,175	-23	2,618,234	680,340	997,503	28,605	150,186	80,119
2005	4,401,488	3,107,435	5,921	3,113,356	378,118	-9,545	2,725,693	656,688	1,019,107	29,454	149,438	81,066
2006	4,636,086	3,256,980	543	3,257,523	383,043	-11,409	2,863,071	697,913	1,075,102	31,071	149,208	81,519
2007	4,843,676	3,352,999	-3,484	3,349,515	380,587	3,056	2,971,984	750,979	1,120,713	32,568	148,727	81,871
2008	5,116,149	3,470,142	-6,871	3,463,271	390,377	11,574	3,084,468	822,988	1,208,693	34,552	148,073	81,922
2009	4,899,562	3,284,781	-7,715	3,277,066	386,345	-42,904	2,847,817	748,733	1,303,012	33,125	147,910	80,136
2010	4,872,505	3,234,172	-7,428	3,226,744	382,100	-73,781	2,770,863	744,629	1,357,013	32,933	147,951	80,110
2011	5,094,799	3,333,818	-5,132	3,328,686	352,248	-81,844	2,894,594	842,994	1,357,211	34,538	147,513	80,514
2012	5,258,604	3,510,754	-7,999	3,502,755	368,677	-123,077	3,011,001	878,133	1,369,470	35,777	146,984	81,079
2013	5,369,632	3,742,556	-6,658	3,735,898	432,757	-182,919	3,120,222	871,285	1,378,125	36,629	146,594	82,122
2014	5,658,310	3,926,561	-7,266	3,919,295	459,365	-207,232	3,252,698	950,504	1,455,108	38,805	145,814	82,797
2015	5,794,480	3,917,382	-7,386	3,909,996	457,202	-198,820	3,253,974	1,035,208	1,505,298	39,906	145,202	81,555
2016	5,852,104	3,932,027	-10,012	3,922,015	465,247	-199,075	3,257,693	1,037,628	1,556,783	40,595	144,158	80,436
2017	6,387,937	4,537,358	-10,960	4,526,398	530,156	-248,002	3,748,240	1,054,410	1,585,287	44,768	142,691	81,598
2018	6,778,079	4,980,050	-11,300	4,968,750	577,249	-355,684	4,035,817	1,129,710	1,612,552	47,857	141,633	83,140
2019	6,666,202	4,607,818	-12,183	4,595,635	540,781	-284,778	3,770,076	1,233,895	1,662,231	47,349	140,788	80,308
2020	6,592,701	3,976,259	-11,045	3,965,214	494,955	-196,255	3,274,004	1,216,297	2,102,400	47,389	139,118	73,948
2021	7,173,400	4,164,949	-11,188	4,153,761	513,891	-193,017	3,446,853	1,447,028	2,279,519	51,988	137,981	75,476
2022	7,271,949	4,344,282	-16,311	4,327,971	543,220	-191,513	3,593,238	1,658,147	2,020,564	53,193	136,708	77,362

Personal Income and Employment by Area: Wichita, KS

(Thousands of dollars, except as noted.)

Year	Personal income, total	Derivation of personal income: Earnings by place of work: Nonfarm	Farm	Total	Less: Contributions for government social insurance	Plus: Adjustment for residence	Equals: Net earnings by place of residence	Plus: Dividends, interest, and rent	Plus: Personal current transfer receipts	Per capita personal income (dollars)	Population (persons)	Total employment
1970	1,776,848	1,451,620	33,365	1,484,985	103,735	-17,700	1,363,550	250,597	162,701	4,053	438,446	206,956
1971	1,873,355	1,498,412	44,554	1,542,966	110,486	-17,818	1,414,662	271,333	187,360	4,324	433,262	201,993
1972	2,076,670	1,691,790	58,031	1,749,821	131,990	-22,757	1,595,074	292,509	189,087	4,849	428,292	212,251
1973	2,321,707	1,883,462	95,684	1,979,146	168,894	-26,339	1,783,913	322,307	215,487	5,402	429,805	223,754
1974	2,617,259	2,152,667	70,199	2,222,866	199,837	-32,652	1,990,377	383,446	243,436	5,994	436,657	234,657
1975	2,954,200	2,416,610	58,092	2,474,702	220,748	-34,685	2,219,269	435,066	299,865	6,694	441,314	237,793
1976	3,248,650	2,701,244	32,602	2,733,846	251,238	-41,412	2,441,196	469,454	338,000	7,247	448,305	246,887
1977	3,508,085	2,921,928	26,651	2,948,579	276,122	-44,609	2,627,848	518,052	362,185	7,776	451,139	250,539
1978	3,993,959	3,375,604	18,552	3,394,156	330,903	-54,213	3,009,040	593,860	391,059	8,781	454,833	263,131
1979	4,606,686	3,944,521	34,523	3,979,044	402,460	-68,752	3,507,832	672,648	426,206	9,965	462,285	278,289
1980	5,222,100	4,408,241	-1,951	4,406,290	437,939	-80,419	3,887,932	826,219	507,949	11,125	469,410	283,198
1981	5,913,965	4,874,676	10,740	4,885,416	516,287	-84,249	4,284,880	1,033,152	595,933	12,403	476,819	286,820
1982	6,303,133	4,930,365	42,279	4,972,644	534,639	-80,693	4,357,312	1,234,390	711,431	13,102	481,070	275,345
1983	6,475,364	5,051,379	18,495	5,069,874	548,174	-77,162	4,444,538	1,275,223	755,603	13,465	480,917	276,537
1984	7,083,230	5,571,825	41,481	5,613,306	620,989	-84,690	4,907,627	1,408,963	766,640	14,636	483,964	287,520
1985	7,381,796	5,790,497	14,778	5,805,275	655,212	-83,912	5,066,151	1,510,709	804,936	15,137	487,650	288,009
1986	7,864,030	6,190,701	55,441	6,246,142	699,423	-91,661	5,455,058	1,559,836	849,136	16,048	490,026	288,028
1987	8,196,259	6,552,890	53,199	6,606,089	729,655	-93,395	5,783,039	1,539,735	873,485	16,536	495,657	298,136
1988	8,743,655	6,941,720	65,068	7,006,788	799,355	-96,945	6,110,488	1,700,942	932,225	17,445	501,201	303,078
1989	9,314,418	7,375,274	53,405	7,428,679	844,586	-101,465	6,482,628	1,797,577	1,034,213	18,338	507,922	310,011
1990	9,923,048	7,844,667	57,415	7,902,082	950,745	-104,148	6,847,189	1,947,771	1,128,088	19,375	512,164	315,938
1991	10,468,825	8,206,306	44,730	8,251,036	1,010,522	-112,881	7,127,633	2,102,303	1,238,889	20,149	519,559	321,194
1992	11,204,441	8,879,848	72,437	8,952,285	1,083,488	-125,750	7,743,047	2,091,725	1,369,669	21,151	529,727	323,115
1993	11,638,755	9,123,534	62,293	9,185,827	1,108,076	-126,668	7,951,083	2,223,709	1,463,963	21,703	536,264	324,933
1994	11,902,635	9,335,265	72,868	9,408,133	1,170,795	-128,864	8,108,474	2,276,644	1,517,517	22,050	539,797	328,341
1995	12,640,116	9,884,907	28,976	9,913,883	1,236,172	-138,547	8,539,164	2,505,108	1,595,844	23,261	543,401	335,285
1996	13,590,503	10,630,223	62,662	10,692,885	1,337,480	-152,315	9,203,090	2,737,201	1,650,212	24,756	548,981	344,401
1997	14,786,416	11,598,119	102,561	11,700,680	1,463,545	-174,330	10,062,805	2,993,352	1,730,259	26,579	556,313	356,914
1998	15,686,447	12,448,474	40,711	12,489,185	1,575,659	-196,240	10,717,286	3,254,039	1,715,122	27,719	565,914	367,762
1999	15,804,566	12,571,991	46,311	12,618,302	1,589,165	-198,121	10,831,016	3,191,375	1,782,175	27,730	569,949	365,827
2000	16,506,502	12,910,660	35,725	12,946,385	1,624,039	-200,352	11,121,994	3,406,382	1,978,126	28,846	572,226	365,971
2001	17,605,237	13,782,017	3,329	13,785,346	1,602,388	-221,405	11,961,553	3,458,369	2,185,315	30,594	575,446	370,228
2002	17,672,867	13,830,700	12,717	13,843,417	1,617,645	-225,948	11,999,824	3,285,436	2,387,607	30,457	580,247	364,218
2003	17,760,192	13,690,905	87,093	13,777,998	1,621,136	-229,693	11,927,169	3,305,370	2,527,653	30,507	582,168	359,001
2004	18,583,330	14,206,416	135,513	14,341,929	1,710,379	-237,613	12,393,937	3,608,245	2,581,148	31,790	584,565	361,957
2005	19,356,717	14,498,768	114,052	14,612,820	1,812,296	-258,587	12,541,937	4,104,288	2,710,492	32,918	588,021	366,815
2006	21,796,757	15,917,352	143,781	16,061,133	1,940,896	-279,962	13,840,275	5,059,221	2,897,261	36,733	593,382	374,628
2007	23,074,734	16,602,514	100,123	16,702,637	2,009,400	-291,022	14,402,215	5,556,428	3,116,091	38,406	600,805	385,589
2008	25,750,762	18,140,953	169,552	18,310,505	2,100,666	-322,173	15,887,666	6,316,085	3,547,011	42,266	609,250	392,672
2009	24,493,203	17,087,965	137,761	17,225,726	2,002,728	-280,130	14,942,868	5,566,369	3,983,966	39,548	619,330	379,190
2010	24,325,343	17,769,338	139,622	17,908,960	2,026,545	-236,701	15,645,714	4,435,982	4,243,647	38,983	624,001	371,901
2011	27,238,184	19,299,780	108,508	19,408,288	1,879,619	-223,856	17,304,813	5,658,491	4,274,880	43,518	625,899	372,714
2012	28,616,777	19,796,340	174,269	19,970,609	1,916,061	-175,410	17,879,138	6,570,553	4,167,086	45,483	629,172	376,532
2013	29,014,185	20,559,890	212,957	20,772,847	2,231,858	-148,281	18,392,708	6,392,388	4,229,089	45,920	631,841	382,376
2014	30,346,714	20,918,268	91,955	21,010,223	2,293,411	-123,034	18,593,778	7,374,593	4,378,343	47,811	634,729	386,984
2015	29,549,302	20,987,339	51,312	21,038,651	2,373,366	-128,396	18,536,889	6,492,023	4,520,390	46,320	637,932	392,292
2016	29,146,462	20,793,568	53,712	20,847,280	2,342,867	-114,881	18,389,532	6,076,077	4,680,853	45,498	640,603	394,757
2017	30,462,319	21,455,409	25,304	21,480,713	2,388,746	-101,233	18,990,734	6,646,061	4,825,524	47,530	640,908	392,363
2018	31,549,918	21,756,127	51,076	21,807,203	2,484,970	-104,069	19,218,164	7,258,326	5,073,428	49,182	641,487	396,360
2019	32,858,441	23,163,617	72,040	23,235,657	2,631,475	-158,615	20,445,567	7,036,717	5,376,157	50,963	644,752	401,627
2020	33,832,824	22,733,018	129,868	22,862,886	2,636,575	-95,776	20,130,535	6,511,172	7,191,117	52,170	648,516	388,098
2021	36,395,542	23,216,138	195,515	23,411,653	2,783,449	-107,080	20,521,124	8,051,151	7,823,267	56,110	648,652	400,363
2022	37,809,727	25,435,771	39,824	25,475,595	3,071,031	-164,542	22,240,022	8,756,588	6,813,117	58,165	650,039	416,168

Personal Income and Employment by Area: Wichita Falls, TX

(Thousands of dollars, except as noted.)

Year	Personal income, total	Derivation of personal income: Earnings by place of work: Nonfarm	Farm	Total	Less: Contributions for government social insurance	Plus: Adjustment for residence	Equals: Net earnings by place of residence	Plus: Dividends, interest, and rent	Plus: Personal current transfer receipts	Per capita personal income (dollars)	Population (persons)	Total employment
1970	574,667	443,324	4,504	447,828	25,967	-1,777	420,084	114,736	39,847	4,271	134,547	68,460
1971	645,432	500,386	5,309	505,695	30,869	-2,709	472,117	127,973	45,342	4,749	135,914	71,202
1972	674,171	521,053	5,494	526,547	32,823	-3,506	490,218	133,516	50,437	5,023	134,213	69,547
1973	750,253	570,747	12,043	582,790	40,178	-4,519	538,093	151,913	60,247	5,651	132,776	72,373
1974	842,465	639,305	17,915	657,220	47,369	-7,062	602,789	169,968	69,708	6,207	135,739	74,009
1975	906,418	683,863	13,239	697,102	51,542	-7,940	637,620	184,172	84,626	6,662	136,058	73,601
1976	1,004,485	773,977	11,610	785,587	59,718	-10,336	715,533	197,127	91,825	7,226	139,008	76,059
1977	1,068,280	829,237	6,475	835,712	64,364	-12,142	759,206	211,847	97,227	7,719	138,389	77,471
1978	1,196,734	936,713	2,831	939,544	73,381	-15,515	850,648	239,678	106,408	8,724	137,175	79,811
1979	1,343,033	1,047,148	9,006	1,056,154	86,157	-18,588	951,409	271,829	119,795	9,776	137,384	82,264
1980	1,481,526	1,150,728	-1,816	1,148,912	96,220	-23,307	1,029,385	316,740	135,401	10,698	138,486	84,353
1981	1,734,448	1,331,489	11,081	1,342,570	119,850	-26,159	1,196,561	386,493	151,394	12,362	140,309	88,921
1982	1,833,997	1,366,420	13,655	1,380,075	126,246	-24,315	1,229,514	433,966	170,517	12,840	142,833	88,337
1983	1,906,966	1,379,536	19,283	1,398,819	127,419	-22,135	1,249,265	469,620	188,081	13,232	144,114	85,451
1984	2,049,189	1,469,723	25,273	1,494,996	140,483	-22,099	1,332,414	518,607	198,168	14,210	144,209	86,935
1985	2,113,275	1,507,748	12,272	1,520,020	146,573	-21,035	1,352,412	550,939	209,924	14,628	144,471	87,027
1986	2,121,704	1,481,865	22,374	1,504,239	144,488	-19,074	1,340,677	549,287	231,740	14,648	144,842	82,505
1987	2,121,141	1,475,651	23,056	1,498,707	142,864	-17,068	1,338,775	539,723	242,643	14,892	142,433	81,957
1988	2,214,492	1,531,750	28,040	1,559,790	155,736	-16,545	1,387,509	568,215	258,768	15,663	141,380	81,928
1989	2,293,376	1,593,471	23,736	1,617,207	163,580	-14,779	1,438,848	578,552	275,976	16,271	140,953	81,822
1990	2,415,383	1,657,109	42,191	1,699,300	167,912	-22,164	1,509,224	606,776	299,383	17,215	140,303	81,730
1991	2,401,746	1,625,834	30,069	1,655,903	170,542	-20,373	1,464,988	608,661	328,097	17,270	139,070	79,063
1992	2,526,742	1,711,388	37,065	1,748,453	177,837	-20,887	1,549,729	599,438	377,575	18,206	138,786	78,932
1993	2,654,738	1,830,116	24,050	1,854,166	190,835	-23,536	1,639,795	616,685	398,258	18,774	141,403	82,583
1994	2,781,329	1,908,678	24,431	1,933,109	199,539	-25,947	1,707,623	651,893	421,813	19,317	143,986	84,658
1995	2,989,143	2,043,573	21,702	2,065,275	213,215	-29,808	1,822,252	714,053	452,838	20,232	147,740	87,085
1996	3,121,792	2,135,914	21,286	2,157,200	219,448	-30,997	1,906,755	735,203	479,834	20,651	151,170	88,384
1997	3,300,975	2,307,832	22,113	2,329,945	230,927	-31,631	2,067,387	732,135	501,453	21,791	151,480	89,491
1998	3,445,760	2,392,894	33,661	2,426,555	236,405	-30,952	2,159,198	783,999	502,563	22,789	151,206	89,655
1999	3,596,082	2,478,662	43,077	2,521,739	245,182	-30,721	2,245,836	830,875	519,371	23,756	151,374	88,964
2000	3,767,975	2,599,690	34,176	2,633,866	254,535	-32,188	2,347,143	872,466	548,366	24,814	151,847	90,930
2001	4,031,615	2,798,140	41,788	2,839,928	271,760	-30,946	2,537,222	900,475	593,918	26,740	150,770	90,627
2002	4,194,974	2,941,725	41,821	2,983,546	284,088	-28,177	2,671,281	883,984	639,709	27,782	150,995	89,770
2003	4,359,971	3,030,881	50,286	3,081,167	296,643	-22,197	2,762,327	915,239	682,405	28,933	150,694	89,026
2004	4,413,847	3,090,582	48,280	3,138,862	305,059	-15,656	2,818,147	873,061	722,639	29,032	152,033	87,369
2005	4,656,089	3,264,611	33,878	3,298,489	316,049	-6,014	2,976,426	907,808	771,855	30,804	151,152	85,765
2006	5,194,196	3,672,978	17,472	3,690,450	343,367	6,785	3,353,868	1,025,033	815,295	34,263	151,596	90,069
2007	5,291,243	3,651,018	12,758	3,663,776	353,989	18,372	3,328,159	1,072,220	890,864	35,125	150,641	90,385
2008	6,109,317	4,312,532	10,811	4,323,343	384,683	32,053	3,970,713	1,158,860	979,744	40,651	150,287	91,461
2009	5,535,334	3,779,174	-9,787	3,769,387	369,947	24,345	3,423,785	1,043,519	1,068,030	36,714	150,768	89,312
2010	5,793,445	3,954,581	-4,814	3,949,767	378,198	24,407	3,595,976	1,041,125	1,156,344	38,201	151,657	88,561
2011	6,423,833	4,404,504	2,058	4,406,562	350,351	21,726	4,077,937	1,160,447	1,185,449	42,731	150,333	87,265
2012	6,466,048	4,344,980	9,927	4,354,907	353,368	17,164	4,018,703	1,262,027	1,185,318	42,798	151,082	89,244
2013	6,572,460	4,494,289	31,689	4,525,978	399,938	14,190	4,140,230	1,200,240	1,231,990	43,379	151,512	89,005
2014	6,558,826	4,333,380	43,012	4,376,392	397,732	19,443	3,998,103	1,269,589	1,291,134	43,658	150,231	87,732
2015	6,181,088	3,932,337	35,743	3,968,080	393,068	16,050	3,591,062	1,230,263	1,359,763	41,740	148,086	88,215
2016	6,069,422	3,817,235	11,991	3,829,226	398,296	8,169	3,439,099	1,202,624	1,427,699	41,027	147,939	89,018
2017	6,289,408	3,858,460	5,158	3,863,618	410,796	11,864	3,464,686	1,368,413	1,456,309	42,443	148,185	89,520
2018	6,544,049	4,019,542	4,424	4,023,966	427,404	18,504	3,615,066	1,406,155	1,522,828	44,230	147,955	89,515
2019	6,752,625	4,156,494	6,732	4,163,226	445,394	14,775	3,732,607	1,426,456	1,593,562	45,697	147,771	88,962
2020	7,097,432	4,114,030	27,339	4,141,369	446,142	9,893	3,705,120	1,401,200	1,991,112	47,843	148,348	86,370
2021												
2022	7,585,540	4,312,869	13,759	4,326,628	465,754	5,217	3,866,091	1,462,869	2,256,580	50,905	149,013	87,061

Personal Income and Employment by Area: Williamsport, PA

(Thousands of dollars, except as noted.)

Year	Personal income, total	Derivation of personal income: Earnings by place of work: Nonfarm	Farm	Total	Less: Contributions for government social insurance	Plus: Adjustment for residence	Equals: Net earnings by place of residence	Plus: Dividends, interest, and rent	Plus: Personal current transfer receipts	Per capita personal income (dollars)	Population (persons)	Total employment
1970	411,949	351,224	3,655	354,879	26,745	-13,976	314,158	52,234	45,557	3,628	113,547	53,041
1971	436,332	367,561	2,763	370,324	28,974	-13,610	327,740	55,742	52,850	3,780	115,429	52,143
1972	480,933	406,612	2,080	408,692	33,627	-14,728	360,337	60,870	59,726	4,166	115,443	53,343
1973	538,407	459,906	5,231	465,137	43,423	-16,014	405,700	66,742	65,965	4,620	116,542	56,253
1974	592,531	497,016	6,364	503,380	48,661	-16,777	437,942	74,980	79,609	5,049	117,354	56,294
1975	644,690	521,412	5,317	526,729	49,365	-18,253	459,111	81,543	104,036	5,464	117,985	54,271
1976	709,786	577,654	6,010	583,664	55,905	-19,285	508,474	88,387	112,925	5,980	118,684	55,204
1977	776,113	634,961	5,930	640,891	61,927	-21,450	557,514	98,915	119,684	6,581	117,927	55,790
1978	865,105	719,522	4,877	724,399	71,902	-23,586	628,911	108,817	127,377	7,314	118,274	58,649
1979	947,124	779,232	8,306	787,538	80,034	-24,934	682,570	120,395	144,159	7,920	119,588	58,472
1980	1,026,741	808,711	6,340	815,051	82,731	-25,952	706,368	148,741	171,632	8,681	118,271	56,384
1981	1,125,978	862,723	10,760	873,483	94,270	-28,932	750,281	183,343	192,354	9,586	117,455	55,670
1982	1,187,245	882,320	9,655	891,975	98,007	-31,737	762,231	209,290	215,724	10,117	117,354	54,240
1983	1,227,100	889,632	1,486	891,118	99,398	-29,676	762,044	227,881	237,175	10,481	117,083	52,384
1984	1,323,686	974,344	9,562	983,906	113,145	-34,373	836,388	255,359	231,939	11,350	116,627	54,551
1985	1,393,114	1,029,434	9,553	1,038,987	120,571	-39,253	879,163	272,924	241,027	12,032	115,787	54,780
1986	1,481,922	1,109,139	7,883	1,117,022	130,133	-43,541	943,348	284,910	253,664	12,818	115,613	56,188
1987	1,587,429	1,222,379	7,793	1,230,172	141,692	-51,736	1,036,744	291,813	258,872	13,597	116,750	59,376
1988	1,722,204	1,343,730	8,936	1,352,666	158,859	-56,349	1,137,458	310,268	274,478	14,625	117,756	61,254
1989	1,862,802	1,415,164	11,994	1,427,158	164,131	-60,026	1,203,001	365,430	294,371	15,697	118,673	61,947
1990	1,918,597	1,444,061	12,709	1,456,770	169,624	-64,469	1,222,677	373,433	322,487	16,139	118,876	62,293
1991	2,001,907	1,482,365	6,141	1,488,506	175,516	-62,223	1,250,767	382,953	368,187	16,673	120,068	61,029
1992	2,106,170	1,562,554	17,758	1,580,312	184,990	-61,199	1,334,123	379,511	392,536	17,363	121,303	61,727
1993	2,186,437	1,610,893	17,926	1,628,819	194,211	-55,592	1,379,016	393,380	414,041	17,901	122,141	61,763
1994	2,225,914	1,649,704	15,949	1,665,653	203,888	-52,708	1,409,057	401,381	415,476	18,204	122,273	62,543
1995	2,315,850	1,714,145	7,926	1,722,071	209,749	-51,247	1,461,075	419,369	435,406	19,010	121,825	63,196
1996	2,418,336	1,771,052	15,708	1,786,760	212,016	-52,855	1,521,889	438,216	458,231	19,931	121,333	64,164
1997	2,521,360	1,848,837	6,787	1,855,624	218,869	-50,187	1,586,568	464,514	470,278	20,841	120,983	64,890
1998	2,623,281	1,930,779	8,671	1,939,450	225,633	-49,482	1,664,335	495,442	463,504	21,754	120,590	64,892
1999	2,672,376	2,000,829	6,927	2,007,756	232,440	-49,405	1,725,911	469,605	476,860	22,236	120,182	65,414
2000	2,817,598	2,103,358	11,429	2,114,787	242,868	-52,915	1,819,004	495,192	503,402	23,509	119,851	67,284
2001	2,984,998	2,240,528	9,165	2,249,693	254,040	-56,614	1,939,039	503,520	542,439	25,099	118,930	68,014
2002	3,059,693	2,245,111	6,740	2,251,851	251,961	-46,758	1,953,132	527,413	579,148	25,854	118,344	66,926
2003	3,157,419	2,302,247	15,160	2,317,407	257,147	-42,820	2,017,440	533,663	606,316	26,733	118,108	66,629
2004	3,266,211	2,418,597	22,634	2,441,231	269,689	-47,780	2,123,762	509,099	633,350	27,701	117,911	67,245
2005	3,319,974	2,489,963	19,168	2,509,131	282,056	-51,620	2,175,455	468,066	676,453	28,248	117,530	67,179
2006	3,407,040	2,524,099	16,436	2,540,535	290,503	-50,796	2,199,236	499,943	707,861	29,124	116,983	67,403
2007	3,574,276	2,599,204	14,914	2,614,118	298,468	-51,266	2,264,384	552,515	757,377	30,674	116,524	67,918
2008	3,739,049	2,621,079	10,253	2,631,332	304,509	-42,862	2,283,961	606,758	848,330	32,192	116,147	67,882
2009	3,765,534	2,569,237	6,603	2,575,840	303,288	-39,316	2,233,236	597,047	935,251	32,439	116,081	66,142
2010	3,950,598	2,757,514	11,481	2,768,995	322,322	-48,417	2,398,256	571,413	980,929	33,988	116,236	67,166
2011	4,297,085	3,065,442	16,724	3,082,166	320,110	-91,580	2,670,476	645,548	981,061	36,773	116,853	69,895
2012	4,395,401	3,186,194	20,234	3,206,428	331,939	-136,472	2,738,017	668,593	988,791	37,431	117,428	71,050
2013	4,413,498	3,222,749	20,593	3,243,342	375,159	-135,072	2,733,111	668,957	1,011,430	37,754	116,900	70,482
2014	4,546,304	3,318,171	24,376	3,342,547	391,594	-157,646	2,793,307	703,737	1,049,260	38,961	116,688	71,309
2015	4,617,405	3,353,713	12,965	3,366,678	397,561	-155,405	2,813,712	696,957	1,106,736	39,777	116,083	70,731
2016	4,544,941	3,136,003	9,793	3,145,796	375,903	-75,612	2,694,281	694,897	1,155,763	39,358	115,476	68,119
2017	4,667,863	3,255,583	18,822	3,274,405	397,054	-95,696	2,781,655	723,829	1,162,379	40,681	114,742	68,124
2018	4,864,441	3,377,382	11,150	3,388,532	410,888	-96,805	2,880,839	750,017	1,233,585	42,354	114,853	68,411
2019	5,025,478	3,451,850	21,577	3,473,427	419,096	-86,993	2,967,338	775,560	1,282,580	43,954	114,336	67,715
2020	5,482,453	3,409,336	14,912	3,424,248	413,355	-103,152	2,907,741	808,319	1,766,393	48,046	114,108	64,375
2021	5,762,711	3,554,742	22,078	3,576,820	429,611	-121,395	3,025,814	836,125	1,900,772	50,730	113,595	64,802
2022	5,640,409	3,778,973	22,590	3,801,563	468,374	-159,980	3,173,209	889,159	1,578,041	49,869	113,104	66,940

Personal Income and Employment by Area: Wilmington, NC

(Thousands of dollars, except as noted.)

Year	Personal income, total	Derivation of personal income: Earnings by place of work: Nonfarm	Farm	Total	Less: Contributions for government social insurance	Plus: Adjustment for residence	Equals: Net earnings by place of residence	Plus: Dividends, interest, and rent	Plus: Personal current transfer receipts	Per capita personal income (dollars)	Population (persons)	Total employment
1970	327,087	262,927	10,504	273,431	18,307	-1,770	253,354	45,048	28,685	3,212	101,837	47,452
1971	358,922	289,002	9,525	298,527	20,660	-4,025	273,842	50,661	34,419	3,400	105,562	47,676
1972	417,525	339,820	9,578	349,398	25,410	-2,614	321,374	57,205	38,946	3,795	110,029	50,224
1973	479,995	394,734	11,934	406,668	34,045	-3,468	369,155	65,634	45,206	4,220	113,741	54,092
1974	530,365	424,060	10,382	434,442	38,188	1,414	397,668	76,758	55,939	4,552	116,500	54,463
1975	583,584	448,144	8,833	456,977	39,491	4,698	422,184	85,565	75,835	4,912	118,805	52,367
1976	652,765	501,693	8,679	510,372	44,899	7,349	472,822	94,667	85,276	5,414	120,568	54,105
1977	722,594	553,591	8,893	562,484	49,170	11,104	524,418	107,027	91,149	5,891	122,652	55,642
1978	811,457	624,292	10,567	634,859	56,948	12,665	590,576	123,819	97,062	6,645	122,115	57,773
1979	925,876	704,492	12,207	716,699	66,690	16,143	666,152	146,609	113,115	7,510	123,292	60,898
1980	1,051,554	778,317	13,609	791,926	73,770	18,189	736,345	180,078	135,131	8,329	126,245	61,704
1981	1,156,316	831,804	16,534	848,338	84,945	16,815	780,208	218,646	157,462	9,040	127,918	61,913
1982	1,230,632	868,767	12,260	881,027	90,921	20,893	810,999	242,567	177,066	9,438	130,392	61,420
1983	1,341,514	944,746	5,842	950,588	98,899	26,108	877,797	269,213	194,504	10,176	131,827	62,633
1984	1,492,691	1,050,486	10,013	1,060,499	111,780	25,947	974,666	313,522	204,503	11,147	133,911	66,887
1985	1,642,128	1,168,555	5,880	1,174,435	126,377	20,784	1,068,842	351,929	221,357	12,039	136,404	70,397
1986	1,825,226	1,328,929	5,593	1,334,522	146,475	5,907	1,193,954	388,230	243,042	13,087	139,471	74,836
1987	1,957,171	1,413,855	13,524	1,427,379	153,212	1,410	1,275,577	420,350	261,244	13,767	142,160	75,940
1988	2,162,040	1,558,529	12,586	1,571,115	174,670	-6,021	1,390,424	484,620	286,996	15,017	143,969	79,824
1989	2,352,936	1,703,585	13,925	1,717,510	191,848	-18,390	1,507,272	520,874	324,790	16,091	146,223	82,275
1990	2,576,657	1,828,866	18,259	1,847,125	211,041	-31,033	1,605,051	614,083	357,523	17,152	150,226	85,684
1991	2,786,918	1,937,471	27,367	1,964,838	226,428	-7,093	1,731,317	644,473	411,128	17,914	155,570	86,116
1992	3,019,716	2,122,050	30,177	2,152,227	244,476	-12,896	1,894,855	663,588	461,273	18,885	159,904	88,808
1993	3,269,388	2,274,752	32,573	2,307,325	262,179	-3,556	2,041,590	716,038	511,760	19,708	165,895	91,851
1994	3,581,499	2,477,209	32,810	2,510,019	290,621	2,373	2,221,771	828,732	530,996	20,794	172,233	96,120
1995	3,907,891	2,672,866	33,719	2,706,585	314,665	-1,584	2,390,336	915,906	601,649	21,814	179,144	101,327
1996	4,249,172	2,907,650	42,791	2,950,441	340,402	-23,304	2,586,735	1,008,784	653,653	22,907	185,496	106,945
1997	4,576,065	3,111,332	47,948	3,159,280	365,011	-39,774	2,754,495	1,136,081	685,489	23,940	191,148	113,067
1998	4,890,140	3,396,446	17,142	3,413,588	397,169	-66,585	2,949,834	1,219,271	721,035	24,882	196,533	116,103
1999	5,172,830	3,700,005	13,963	3,713,968	434,866	-90,038	3,189,064	1,219,579	764,187	25,953	199,312	119,821
2000	5,526,739	3,912,102	31,963	3,944,065	455,695	-93,222	3,395,148	1,316,716	814,875	27,347	202,099	121,732
2001	5,809,939	4,102,376	38,975	4,141,351	467,159	-83,662	3,590,530	1,304,734	914,675	28,204	205,996	125,064
2002	5,923,017	4,198,565	17,323	4,215,888	477,596	-90,605	3,647,687	1,275,904	999,426	28,129	210,563	127,091
2003	6,243,997	4,386,762	11,742	4,398,504	508,635	-57,548	3,832,321	1,365,165	1,046,511	29,058	214,877	130,235
2004	6,880,048	4,797,381	29,561	4,826,942	548,509	-50,650	4,227,783	1,524,803	1,127,462	30,922	222,498	136,560
2005	7,544,229	5,310,982	42,782	5,353,764	613,012	-78,672	4,662,080	1,666,671	1,215,478	32,674	230,897	144,084
2006	8,219,034	5,826,097	28,277	5,854,374	661,513	-148,516	5,044,345	1,863,355	1,311,334	34,494	238,272	150,846
2007	8,670,041	6,159,616	41,230	6,200,846	711,605	-235,234	5,254,007	2,011,004	1,405,030	35,603	243,520	158,070
2008	9,005,003	6,159,238	52,179	6,211,417	717,671	-190,298	5,303,448	2,114,425	1,587,130	36,272	248,260	156,513
2009	8,660,020	5,886,188	52,020	5,938,208	699,238	-257,253	4,981,717	1,904,044	1,774,259	34,391	251,814	149,468
2010	8,792,156	5,893,325	58,578	5,951,903	698,849	-219,171	5,033,883	1,860,533	1,897,740	34,424	255,407	147,615
2011	9,196,446	5,953,672	43,211	5,996,883	652,249	-185,532	5,159,102	2,063,668	1,973,676	35,694	257,649	151,000
2012	9,402,417	5,942,157	48,752	5,990,909	654,272	-133,438	5,203,199	2,173,472	2,025,746	36,158	260,038	152,668
2013	9,684,445	6,228,342	64,640	6,292,982	777,112	-131,989	5,383,881	2,203,168	2,097,396	36,725	263,702	156,284
2014	10,489,348	6,714,945	74,400	6,789,345	831,688	-105,663	5,851,994	2,443,164	2,194,190	39,352	266,550	161,785
2015	11,073,246	7,098,004	70,015	7,168,019	872,823	-168,731	6,126,465	2,603,988	2,342,793	40,987	270,164	166,298
2016	11,598,249	7,606,245	63,060	7,669,305	918,018	-345,644	6,405,643	2,760,453	2,432,153	42,128	275,310	172,684
2017	12,061,690	7,992,992	76,567	8,069,559	954,213	-373,294	6,742,052	2,768,834	2,550,804	43,132	279,645	174,053
2018	12,947,890	8,456,230	40,683	8,496,913	997,860	-435,845	7,063,208	3,172,511	2,712,171	45,736	283,102	182,167
2019	13,805,942	9,119,679	54,815	9,174,494	1,066,075	-566,387	7,542,032	3,387,987	2,875,923	48,577	284,206	187,485
2020	14,988,245	9,749,622	51,675	9,801,297	1,139,018	-716,808	7,945,471	3,388,856	3,653,918	52,233	286,949	185,760
2021	16,904,731	10,974,682	69,949	11,044,631	1,267,151	-755,448	9,022,032	3,731,847	4,150,852	57,695	293,002	195,966
2022	17,596,212	12,120,007	59,024	12,179,031	1,424,052	-1,021,097	9,733,882	4,107,939	3,754,391	58,526	300,658	207,600

Personal Income and Employment by Area: Winchester, VA-WV

(Thousands of dollars, except as noted.)

Year	Personal income, total	Derivation of personal income: Earnings by place of work: Nonfarm	Farm	Total	Less: Contributions for government social insurance	Plus: Adjustment for residence	Equals: Net earnings by place of residence	Plus: Dividends, interest, and rent	Plus: Personal current transfer receipts	Per capita personal income (dollars)	Population (persons)	Total employment
1970	180,907	142,653	2,873	145,526	9,607	4,385	140,304	24,386	16,217	3,255	55,578	27,231
1971	201,808	159,930	3,377	163,307	11,196	3,162	155,273	27,556	18,979	3,497	57,715	28,508
1972	223,153	177,058	4,151	181,209	13,030	3,024	171,203	30,811	21,139	3,835	58,191	29,150
1973	257,504	205,821	7,724	213,545	17,494	671	196,722	36,443	24,339	4,335	59,398	30,736
1974	291,957	234,272	9,152	243,424	20,715	-2,491	220,218	42,880	28,859	4,742	61,566	31,775
1975	308,011	245,694	6,299	251,993	21,065	-8,880	222,048	47,421	38,542	4,890	62,987	30,639
1976	346,187	284,745	4,398	289,143	24,797	-12,325	252,021	52,561	41,605	5,408	64,015	32,116
1977	386,363	321,706	4,078	325,784	28,167	-15,916	281,701	60,186	44,476	5,867	65,849	33,218
1978	445,347	370,638	12,744	383,382	33,036	-21,491	328,855	68,272	48,220	6,557	67,918	35,126
1979	487,704	406,503	13,121	419,624	37,630	-26,975	355,019	76,712	55,973	7,055	69,124	35,530
1980	530,437	438,929	3,881	442,810	40,757	-28,961	373,092	90,581	66,764	7,639	69,435	35,358
1981	598,890	478,298	5,750	484,048	47,696	-26,003	410,349	111,713	76,828	8,540	70,125	35,469
1982	644,260	499,261	5,584	504,845	50,636	-24,221	429,988	127,712	86,560	9,088	70,891	34,837
1983	700,683	541,218	3,724	544,942	55,310	-22,554	467,078	140,551	93,054	9,832	71,263	35,582
1984	793,965	608,208	7,330	615,538	63,192	-19,880	532,466	163,811	97,688	11,043	71,897	36,973
1985	873,772	672,410	4,858	677,268	71,095	-16,887	589,286	179,873	104,613	12,042	72,562	38,962
1986	978,703	761,663	11,008	772,671	82,865	-17,291	672,515	195,260	110,928	13,257	73,828	41,228
1987	1,081,492	856,376	12,518	868,894	92,881	-14,353	761,660	204,611	115,221	14,209	76,112	44,617
1988	1,205,861	945,609	10,723	956,332	104,281	-5,150	846,901	232,723	126,237	15,319	78,717	46,300
1989	1,337,456	1,019,989	8,936	1,028,925	114,052	7,307	922,180	276,789	138,487	16,419	81,456	48,563
1990	1,424,273	1,062,092	9,248	1,071,340	121,434	28,167	978,073	292,816	153,384	16,763	84,964	50,045
1991	1,458,613	1,073,662	12,241	1,085,903	124,789	25,577	986,691	298,971	172,951	16,769	86,981	49,180
1992	1,559,686	1,163,882	11,307	1,175,189	134,340	16,407	1,057,256	302,671	199,759	17,592	88,657	50,686
1993	1,661,442	1,250,540	9,805	1,260,345	144,157	15,888	1,132,076	321,231	208,135	18,328	90,652	52,047
1994	1,782,659	1,348,831	9,572	1,358,403	154,482	15,929	1,219,850	341,882	220,927	19,200	92,848	53,821
1995	1,909,819	1,421,658	12,342	1,434,000	162,475	17,048	1,288,573	380,891	240,355	20,167	94,698	55,672
1996	2,041,635	1,528,577	6,923	1,535,500	172,339	19,457	1,382,618	401,181	257,836	21,161	96,479	57,680
1997	2,140,619	1,607,588	5,293	1,612,881	180,788	29,352	1,461,445	410,020	269,154	21,798	98,202	58,997
1998	2,353,957	1,751,439	4,980	1,756,419	193,755	58,628	1,621,292	450,240	282,425	23,552	99,949	61,402
1999	2,494,629	1,870,105	5,780	1,875,885	206,152	80,868	1,750,601	446,462	297,566	24,595	101,429	62,096
2000	2,741,143	2,040,046	3,974	2,044,020	221,530	101,987	1,924,477	492,660	324,006	26,452	103,626	64,579
2001	2,955,680	2,136,668	6,181	2,142,849	238,480	160,566	2,064,935	524,844	365,901	27,818	106,252	65,186
2002	3,058,259	2,268,741	-2,326	2,266,415	254,636	152,652	2,164,431	498,437	395,391	28,072	108,945	66,069
2003	3,260,982	2,372,922	-3,110	2,369,812	265,310	212,189	2,316,691	521,426	422,865	29,256	111,464	66,413
2004	3,573,722	2,571,164	5,019	2,576,183	286,424	281,298	2,571,057	560,345	442,320	31,243	114,383	68,919
2005	3,898,163	2,823,288	-996	2,822,292	315,491	336,016	2,842,817	572,146	483,200	33,078	117,847	72,145
2006	4,222,825	2,977,318	-10,067	2,967,251	335,549	410,112	3,041,814	648,176	532,835	34,833	121,229	74,461
2007	4,399,016	3,012,226	-14,389	2,997,837	340,605	436,698	3,093,930	740,389	564,697	35,515	123,863	75,093
2008	4,613,370	2,970,232	-4,033	2,966,199	342,405	504,990	3,128,784	813,444	671,142	36,693	125,728	73,717
2009	4,515,830	2,906,036	-3,189	2,902,847	339,191	482,155	3,045,811	740,697	729,322	35,465	127,333	70,838
2010	4,722,929	3,032,945	-2,107	3,030,838	351,288	496,015	3,175,565	753,235	794,129	36,709	128,659	70,848
2011	5,003,099	3,174,078	1,925	3,176,003	328,311	519,847	3,367,539	830,246	805,314	38,469	130,055	73,098
2012	5,218,211	3,300,656	10,583	3,311,239	339,073	516,422	3,488,588	903,600	826,023	39,802	131,104	73,907
2013	5,254,644	3,416,810	2,512	3,419,322	399,853	462,803	3,482,272	907,930	864,442	39,640	132,559	75,363
2014	5,431,772	3,581,224	195	3,581,419	415,241	420,203	3,586,381	929,676	915,715	40,564	133,905	77,870
2015	5,750,768	3,766,706	-4,229	3,762,477	435,701	458,983	3,785,759	991,745	973,264	42,672	134,766	79,125
2016	6,067,086	3,885,863	-4,409	3,881,454	450,872	554,830	3,985,412	1,062,310	1,019,364	44,491	136,366	80,223
2017	6,368,572	4,086,071	3,368	4,089,439	477,213	561,981	4,174,207	1,125,032	1,069,333	45,907	138,728	81,778
2018	6,610,867	4,264,829	-7,367	4,257,462	497,979	579,608	4,339,091	1,142,142	1,129,634	47,101	140,355	83,294
2019	7,032,912	4,520,917	-5,881	4,515,036	527,607	622,319	4,609,748	1,217,617	1,205,547	49,691	141,533	83,928
2020	7,597,175	4,788,663	-6,818	4,781,845	564,307	567,629	4,785,167	1,241,593	1,570,415	53,138	142,971	84,928
2021	8,401,730	5,193,833	-5,351	5,188,482	611,661	573,696	5,150,517	1,434,386	1,816,827	57,743	145,503	88,038
2022	8,743,726	5,587,795	3,735	5,591,530	667,308	654,509	5,578,731	1,541,030	1,623,965	59,702	146,455	91,905

Personal Income and Employment by Area: Winston-Salem, NC

(Thousands of dollars, except as noted.)

Year	Personal income, total	Derivation of personal income: Earnings by place of work: Nonfarm	Farm	Total	Less: Contributions for government social insurance	Plus: Adjustment for residence	Equals: Net earnings by place of residence	Plus: Dividends, interest, and rent	Plus: Personal current transfer receipts	Per capita personal income (dollars)	Population (persons)	Total employment
1970	1,446,372	1,148,746	28,572	1,177,318	80,499	61,225	1,158,044	184,906	103,422	3,814	379,270	176,320
1971	1,574,441	1,243,206	30,541	1,273,747	90,286	67,666	1,251,127	200,669	122,645	4,055	388,244	178,777
1972	1,762,561	1,409,698	29,508	1,439,206	107,273	73,272	1,405,205	219,881	137,475	4,436	397,369	186,455
1973	1,992,434	1,604,394	45,796	1,650,190	140,746	75,694	1,585,138	248,772	158,524	4,947	402,778	197,084
1974	2,206,700	1,762,240	47,581	1,809,821	160,546	79,911	1,729,186	286,528	190,986	5,417	407,337	199,954
1975	2,410,149	1,880,544	43,895	1,924,439	168,190	78,456	1,834,705	310,567	264,877	5,855	411,650	193,474
1976	2,694,649	2,135,171	46,596	2,181,767	194,757	83,590	2,070,600	344,257	279,792	6,469	416,569	201,477
1977	2,991,631	2,398,943	40,238	2,439,181	217,575	87,865	2,309,471	388,543	293,617	7,085	422,231	210,239
1978	3,342,886	2,680,546	49,795	2,730,341	250,523	109,931	2,589,749	438,791	314,346	7,773	430,074	217,753
1979	3,701,446	2,983,833	33,880	3,017,713	290,181	120,419	2,847,951	494,060	359,435	8,453	437,876	224,330
1980	4,148,682	3,268,258	28,126	3,296,384	318,797	133,703	3,111,290	611,655	425,737	9,333	444,515	224,907
1981	4,693,191	3,605,381	54,839	3,660,220	377,432	154,884	3,437,672	767,362	488,157	10,446	449,284	228,321
1982	4,997,137	3,751,384	43,157	3,794,541	394,636	172,720	3,572,625	879,195	545,317	11,011	453,824	225,398
1983	5,414,792	4,073,725	24,697	4,098,422	430,034	208,519	3,876,907	949,698	588,187	11,839	457,356	229,151
1984	6,086,893	4,550,799	40,275	4,591,074	492,124	250,576	4,349,526	1,119,192	618,175	13,168	462,248	242,002
1985	6,609,272	4,961,656	40,881	5,002,537	543,113	268,365	4,727,789	1,217,330	664,153	14,118	468,149	251,201
1986	7,087,305	5,309,801	19,179	5,328,980	592,672	303,357	5,039,665	1,315,882	731,758	15,029	471,586	258,786
1987	7,673,424	5,820,736	22,124	5,842,860	637,994	352,325	5,557,191	1,378,518	737,715	16,014	479,157	268,061
1988	8,503,120	6,406,198	35,284	6,441,482	723,843	392,089	6,109,728	1,596,598	796,794	17,631	482,283	278,597
1989	9,190,856	6,772,581	42,576	6,815,157	763,721	440,164	6,491,600	1,811,469	887,787	18,935	485,397	281,675
1990	9,611,774	6,841,277	60,153	6,901,430	795,950	481,702	6,587,182	2,053,395	971,197	19,615	490,034	288,314
1991	9,844,390	6,995,841	70,763	7,066,604	823,929	464,187	6,706,862	2,036,920	1,100,608	19,829	496,463	283,093
1992	10,481,245	7,530,157	72,156	7,602,313	876,944	497,022	7,222,391	2,049,316	1,209,538	20,832	503,138	286,803
1993	11,064,569	7,896,906	63,196	7,960,102	931,081	570,766	7,599,787	2,138,866	1,325,916	21,608	512,062	294,537
1994	11,690,940	8,417,939	64,387	8,482,326	998,429	585,080	8,068,977	2,240,661	1,381,302	22,403	521,836	300,829
1995	12,565,029	8,883,846	48,271	8,932,117	1,057,656	679,315	8,553,776	2,466,457	1,544,796	23,677	530,693	308,135
1996	13,296,955	9,223,572	65,218	9,288,790	1,091,949	750,008	8,946,849	2,672,247	1,677,859	24,592	540,712	314,617
1997	14,120,205	9,876,386	56,926	9,933,312	1,158,296	771,186	9,546,202	2,822,219	1,751,784	25,693	549,576	320,761
1998	15,034,859	10,484,897	63,776	10,548,673	1,231,355	768,032	10,085,350	3,140,759	1,808,750	26,973	557,410	326,706
1999	15,493,960	10,892,914	69,651	10,962,565	1,278,363	827,643	10,511,845	3,072,431	1,909,684	27,475	563,928	330,837
2000	16,399,024	11,525,513	63,207	11,588,720	1,351,416	827,812	11,065,116	3,267,182	2,066,726	28,709	571,210	336,834
2001	16,825,530	11,790,250	61,806	11,852,056	1,371,367	853,007	11,333,696	3,202,273	2,289,561	29,101	578,186	328,671
2002	17,099,433	11,965,936	29,792	11,995,728	1,384,999	879,441	11,490,170	3,130,859	2,478,404	29,264	584,321	324,825
2003	17,716,640	12,334,064	36,492	12,370,556	1,451,028	922,710	11,842,238	3,254,889	2,619,513	30,081	588,964	323,778
2004	18,953,817	13,003,700	63,455	13,067,155	1,504,734	1,010,996	12,573,417	3,531,568	2,848,832	31,868	594,765	327,516
2005	19,694,106	13,435,581	70,567	13,506,148	1,580,714	1,097,359	13,022,793	3,594,073	3,077,240	32,671	602,805	334,160
2006	20,998,746	14,153,075	60,864	14,213,939	1,635,481	1,158,319	13,736,777	3,864,805	3,397,164	34,228	613,494	340,046
2007	21,998,036	14,525,803	58,802	14,584,605	1,696,538	1,238,889	14,126,956	4,205,684	3,665,396	35,306	623,068	345,787
2008	23,042,869	14,866,317	66,071	14,932,388	1,722,917	1,262,796	14,472,267	4,444,956	4,125,646	36,450	632,186	342,335
2009	22,303,900	14,384,381	57,912	14,442,293	1,685,776	1,112,541	13,869,058	3,819,367	4,615,475	34,976	637,688	329,502
2010	22,898,088	14,985,101	52,139	15,037,240	1,723,361	1,104,785	14,418,664	3,589,778	4,889,646	35,713	641,171	325,622
2011	23,186,726	14,625,630	37,533	14,663,163	1,583,579	1,118,020	14,197,604	3,996,163	4,992,959	36,007	643,949	328,716
2012	24,060,274	15,273,006	65,499	15,338,505	1,625,785	1,264,022	14,976,742	4,059,650	5,023,882	37,231	646,238	332,561
2013	23,855,710	15,217,294	73,814	15,291,108	1,868,890	1,385,957	14,808,175	3,912,753	5,134,782	36,752	649,106	335,613
2014	25,477,382	16,316,311	88,811	16,405,122	1,997,967	1,320,681	15,727,836	4,393,228	5,356,318	39,065	652,182	341,325
2015	26,555,095	16,964,527	84,224	17,048,751	2,073,870	1,351,674	16,326,555	4,577,594	5,650,946	40,547	654,916	346,891
2016	27,158,516	17,258,403	58,460	17,316,863	2,098,426	1,484,130	16,702,567	4,647,109	5,808,840	41,182	659,470	351,984
2017	28,552,603	18,199,009	70,110	18,269,119	2,185,853	1,532,437	17,615,703	4,923,536	6,013,364	42,957	664,684	354,511
2018	29,241,257	18,608,942	20,457	18,629,399	2,226,111	1,525,565	17,928,853	4,976,006	6,336,398	43,732	668,646	360,898
2019	30,850,364	19,601,948	32,465	19,634,413	2,343,126	1,517,272	18,808,559	5,369,890	6,671,915	45,827	673,189	365,771
2020	32,938,093	19,923,415	26,473	19,949,888	2,394,913	1,548,103	19,103,078	5,440,143	8,394,872	48,648	677,068	356,641
2021	36,310,881	21,676,912	55,790	21,732,702	2,583,823	1,612,596	20,761,475	5,895,065	9,654,341	53,204	682,479	370,331
2022	37,404,549	23,497,398	74,540	23,571,938	2,835,699	1,639,224	22,375,463	6,470,315	8,558,771	54,330	688,471	383,952

Personal Income and Employment by Area: Worcester, MA-CT

(Thousands of dollars, except as noted.)

Year	Personal income, total	Derivation of personal income: Earnings by place of work: Nonfarm	Farm	Total	Less: Contributions for government social insurance	Plus: Adjustment for residence	Equals: Net earnings by place of residence	Plus: Dividends, interest, and rent	Plus: Personal current transfer receipts	Per capita personal income (dollars)	Population (persons)	Total employment
1970	2,936,952	2,187,578	17,410	2,204,988	144,579	166,498	2,226,907	413,891	296,154	4,059	723,625	303,453
1971	3,122,407	2,276,258	17,035	2,293,293	155,062	192,965	2,331,196	435,877	355,334	4,280	729,613	299,766
1972	3,394,252	2,470,779	18,892	2,489,671	177,513	229,145	2,541,303	460,909	392,040	4,646	730,558	305,815
1973	3,761,499	2,759,923	23,340	2,783,263	228,772	266,797	2,821,288	503,462	436,749	5,113	735,701	320,736
1974	4,086,860	2,952,112	15,189	2,967,301	253,560	307,987	3,021,728	557,552	507,580	5,562	734,725	323,556
1975	4,428,904	3,016,742	15,877	3,032,619	249,893	341,857	3,124,583	588,729	715,592	6,040	733,288	309,349
1976	4,814,796	3,343,304	18,528	3,361,832	284,544	389,465	3,466,753	626,623	721,420	6,588	730,817	317,500
1977	5,248,947	3,632,445	16,555	3,649,000	311,374	478,967	3,816,593	688,081	744,273	7,184	730,608	324,246
1978	5,857,676	4,072,032	24,527	4,096,559	359,606	568,781	4,305,734	744,637	807,305	7,918	739,765	337,775
1979	6,536,570	4,515,531	20,310	4,535,841	417,250	681,121	4,799,712	825,698	911,160	8,816	741,446	348,159
1980	7,372,319	4,900,305	16,516	4,916,821	452,368	828,289	5,292,742	1,020,735	1,058,842	9,969	739,491	348,593
1981	8,210,803	5,360,624	20,046	5,380,670	523,478	906,595	5,763,787	1,242,412	1,204,604	11,079	741,103	347,686
1982	8,882,153	5,596,273	31,330	5,627,603	554,140	1,011,321	6,084,784	1,486,236	1,311,133	11,965	742,351	341,024
1983	9,509,004	5,944,602	27,918	5,972,520	596,891	1,147,366	6,522,995	1,612,246	1,373,763	12,825	741,465	343,763
1984	10,715,977	6,776,412	34,314	6,810,726	701,484	1,306,531	7,415,773	1,866,304	1,433,900	14,299	749,409	361,994
1985	11,565,273	7,403,902	29,516	7,433,418	772,509	1,433,828	8,094,737	1,961,439	1,509,097	15,264	757,692	374,819
1986	12,552,753	8,173,489	34,556	8,208,045	863,506	1,502,969	8,847,508	2,110,304	1,594,941	16,392	765,781	390,359
1987	13,640,965	9,132,808	29,315	9,162,123	950,689	1,593,017	9,804,451	2,190,671	1,645,843	17,532	778,071	397,657
1988	14,992,810	10,123,267	26,989	10,150,256	1,070,261	1,722,078	10,802,073	2,441,253	1,749,484	18,905	793,074	413,617
1989	15,944,994	10,582,805	25,262	10,608,067	1,110,465	1,769,635	11,267,237	2,702,062	1,975,695	19,728	808,224	410,592
1990	16,450,106	10,644,295	32,529	10,676,824	1,100,796	1,879,490	11,455,518	2,767,160	2,227,428	20,224	813,391	400,251
1991	16,576,408	10,577,781	32,476	10,610,257	1,110,664	1,805,909	11,305,502	2,738,305	2,532,601	20,402	812,492	382,147
1992	17,303,858	11,250,624	39,186	11,289,810	1,166,011	1,830,541	11,954,340	2,671,187	2,678,331	21,280	813,137	391,834
1993	17,912,608	11,880,588	36,463	11,917,051	1,240,207	1,730,714	12,407,558	2,750,662	2,754,388	21,909	817,597	401,887
1994	18,866,270	12,630,125	33,435	12,663,560	1,323,092	1,768,404	13,108,872	2,842,500	2,914,898	22,931	822,735	411,296
1995	19,737,161	12,978,514	23,408	13,001,922	1,367,829	1,980,201	13,614,294	3,034,822	3,088,045	23,905	825,647	415,200
1996	20,874,802	13,722,182	31,154	13,753,336	1,426,927	2,099,020	14,425,429	3,262,641	3,186,732	25,146	830,128	420,409
1997	22,355,842	14,575,797	31,150	14,606,947	1,506,638	2,548,721	15,649,030	3,416,511	3,290,301	26,717	836,766	429,799
1998	23,615,579	15,576,351	28,875	15,605,226	1,598,779	2,729,868	16,736,315	3,550,953	3,328,311	27,968	844,368	437,985
1999	24,955,397	16,376,252	37,620	16,413,872	1,661,956	3,259,443	18,011,359	3,516,820	3,427,218	29,245	853,319	442,402
2000	27,779,983	18,438,815	39,066	18,477,881	1,857,030	3,704,862	20,325,713	3,825,082	3,629,188	32,239	861,697	454,078
2001	28,815,177	18,979,911	30,865	19,010,776	1,926,871	3,869,118	20,953,023	3,916,541	3,945,613	33,080	871,081	457,330
2002	28,880,171	19,206,564	26,613	19,233,177	1,941,907	3,801,634	21,092,904	3,481,296	4,305,971	32,834	879,568	455,346
2003	29,944,220	19,920,994	28,808	19,949,802	2,000,310	3,877,904	21,827,396	3,573,643	4,543,181	33,754	887,129	457,338
2004	31,536,878	20,874,575	33,100	20,907,675	2,158,533	4,336,606	23,085,748	3,720,649	4,730,481	35,348	892,171	463,766
2005	32,727,514	21,352,535	26,614	21,379,149	2,256,162	4,810,887	23,933,874	3,749,200	5,044,440	36,490	896,901	467,583
2006	34,777,571	22,295,259	20,230	22,315,489	2,333,861	5,262,375	25,244,003	4,217,066	5,316,502	38,551	902,123	472,686
2007	36,717,121	22,970,252	21,099	22,991,351	2,397,664	5,747,750	26,341,437	4,776,641	5,599,043	40,548	905,524	478,940
2008	38,333,696	23,363,720	36,034	23,399,754	2,451,393	5,894,871	26,843,232	5,102,993	6,387,471	42,184	908,735	477,361
2009	37,833,070	22,768,258	29,377	22,797,635	2,397,314	5,605,703	26,006,024	4,772,665	7,054,381	41,422	913,363	464,195
2010	39,302,924	23,861,172	34,175	23,895,347	2,434,703	5,715,461	27,176,105	4,659,080	7,467,739	42,734	919,702	461,432
2011	41,251,892	25,122,646	34,388	25,157,034	2,313,871	5,779,363	28,622,526	5,164,207	7,465,159	44,537	926,241	469,325
2012	42,770,430	25,828,610	41,085	25,869,695	2,361,281	6,141,258	29,649,672	5,589,380	7,531,378	45,896	931,896	473,670
2013	42,720,485	26,385,516	37,017	26,422,533	2,728,467	5,755,760	29,449,826	5,685,169	7,585,490	45,516	938,589	485,062
2014	44,146,113	27,069,983	20,240	27,090,223	2,835,222	6,070,643	30,325,644	5,980,102	7,840,367	46,678	945,756	493,027
2015	46,304,659	28,168,856	14,489	28,183,345	2,902,583	6,366,054	31,646,816	6,247,514	8,410,329	48,668	951,448	509,489
2016	47,775,242	29,033,133	5,889	29,039,022	3,003,721	6,680,295	32,715,596	6,359,415	8,700,231	49,957	956,319	515,869
2017	49,395,670	30,358,761	13,645	30,372,406	3,150,678	6,570,738	33,792,466	6,790,882	8,812,322	51,179	965,148	524,666
2018	51,356,666	31,510,695	8,814	31,519,509	3,278,753	6,863,037	35,103,793	6,991,373	9,261,500	52,828	972,147	531,663
2019	53,974,847	32,882,103	29,047	32,911,150	3,400,889	7,530,331	37,040,592	7,326,827	9,607,428	55,314	975,790	531,263
2020	58,553,768	33,277,555	15,216	33,292,771	3,446,578	7,498,256	37,344,449	7,402,860	13,806,459	59,994	975,998	507,721
2021	61,810,788	35,405,590	15,281	35,420,871	3,748,538	7,960,590	39,632,923	7,683,807	14,494,058	63,142	978,913	527,391
2022	62,213,783	37,600,098	35,461	37,635,559	3,968,746	8,345,482	42,012,295	8,063,525	12,137,963	63,475	980,137	550,499

Personal Income and Employment by Area: Yakima, WA

(Thousands of dollars, except as noted.)

Year	Personal income, total	Derivation of personal income: Earnings by place of work: Nonfarm	Farm	Total	Less: Contributions for government social insurance	Plus: Adjustment for residence	Equals: Net earnings by place of residence	Plus: Dividends, interest, and rent	Plus: Personal current transfer receipts	Per capita personal income (dollars)	Population (persons)	Total employment
1970	514,992	329,853	45,375	375,228	27,791	8,438	355,875	83,553	75,564	3,537	145,600	63,707
1971	569,171	354,361	64,535	418,896	31,102	7,792	395,586	90,713	82,872	3,845	148,017	62,448
1972	629,237	389,841	76,739	466,580	35,780	8,699	439,499	98,973	90,765	4,180	150,541	64,284
1973	731,091	436,456	114,457	550,913	46,136	10,848	515,625	115,668	99,798	4,845	150,902	67,149
1974	839,680	494,599	137,963	632,562	53,685	13,765	592,642	131,246	115,792	5,409	155,229	69,450
1975	970,992	564,133	151,451	715,584	60,611	20,803	675,776	155,746	139,470	6,099	159,209	72,488
1976	1,016,332	647,718	101,320	749,038	72,029	23,159	700,168	165,139	151,025	6,271	162,074	77,178
1977	1,096,377	710,924	80,806	791,730	79,686	34,101	746,145	188,106	162,126	6,677	164,202	76,262
1978	1,291,969	814,489	134,548	949,037	92,894	44,234	900,377	215,769	175,823	7,763	166,436	78,991
1979	1,436,273	916,956	117,398	1,034,354	107,704	56,288	982,938	249,718	203,617	8,499	168,987	82,216
1980	1,572,947	973,163	116,390	1,089,553	114,788	58,548	1,033,313	295,904	243,730	9,086	173,118	82,688
1981	1,736,049	1,038,836	125,848	1,164,684	131,870	79,250	1,112,064	353,241	270,744	9,908	175,218	82,751
1982	1,828,085	1,057,033	133,228	1,190,261	135,778	69,674	1,124,157	398,927	305,001	10,338	176,825	81,334
1983	1,937,802	1,125,227	141,956	1,267,183	146,168	59,628	1,180,643	432,032	325,127	10,811	179,248	84,131
1984	2,080,888	1,194,894	177,018	1,371,912	161,293	48,837	1,259,456	472,388	349,044	11,547	180,209	84,048
1985	2,117,671	1,226,055	129,882	1,355,937	168,027	52,015	1,239,925	497,778	379,968	11,679	181,321	83,388
1986	2,253,319	1,271,311	195,348	1,466,659	175,992	53,260	1,343,927	512,015	397,377	12,452	180,961	84,095
1987	2,405,319	1,369,906	254,204	1,624,110	190,656	52,657	1,486,111	506,425	412,783	13,237	181,707	92,689
1988	2,483,072	1,469,506	211,266	1,680,772	210,961	55,506	1,525,317	516,859	440,896	13,389	185,454	96,178
1989	2,768,597	1,582,525	285,068	1,867,593	229,564	56,452	1,694,481	586,285	487,831	14,760	187,574	99,415
1990	3,030,700	1,747,375	266,181	2,013,556	257,487	63,279	1,819,348	666,906	544,446	15,997	189,454	101,956
1991	3,236,930	1,888,794	356,699	2,245,493	280,226	40,239	2,005,506	619,181	612,243	16,693	193,904	101,599
1992	3,520,486	2,072,349	382,568	2,454,917	307,326	40,115	2,187,706	642,003	690,777	17,692	198,983	102,197
1993	3,712,852	2,190,600	395,175	2,585,775	323,782	41,249	2,303,242	672,399	737,211	18,177	204,266	103,901
1994	3,867,745	2,333,425	358,599	2,692,024	341,767	42,844	2,393,101	719,288	755,356	18,509	208,963	108,409
1995	3,997,025	2,378,550	352,389	2,730,939	351,871	37,895	2,416,963	756,287	823,775	18,801	212,601	109,268
1996	4,262,440	2,472,624	427,577	2,900,201	352,463	33,638	2,581,376	817,746	863,318	19,830	214,951	111,266
1997	4,386,299	2,621,429	352,730	2,974,159	357,630	30,979	2,647,508	856,538	882,253	20,195	217,201	112,404
1998	4,644,659	2,819,617	407,412	3,227,029	376,463	25,926	2,876,492	873,216	894,951	21,136	219,748	112,073
1999	4,695,430	2,918,366	338,218	3,256,584	382,616	23,479	2,897,447	846,999	950,984	21,191	221,573	112,619
2000	4,963,246	3,037,836	409,241	3,447,077	405,275	19,221	3,061,023	888,060	1,014,163	22,295	222,615	112,920
2001	5,064,694	3,138,952	342,906	3,481,858	420,188	21,241	3,082,911	856,985	1,124,798	22,736	222,757	112,685
2002	5,139,594	3,252,625	366,692	3,619,317	434,530	23,905	3,208,692	780,764	1,150,138	23,006	223,402	112,735
2003	5,498,973	3,410,794	447,849	3,858,643	454,771	22,140	3,426,012	857,531	1,215,430	24,422	225,161	114,191
2004	5,752,626	3,559,780	520,944	4,080,724	479,337	22,215	3,623,602	877,657	1,251,367	25,311	227,280	113,224
2005	5,833,190	3,682,439	449,586	4,132,025	507,614	20,051	3,644,462	859,250	1,329,478	25,520	228,570	114,929
2006	6,084,124	3,860,576	412,924	4,273,500	531,457	13,621	3,755,664	915,530	1,412,930	26,382	230,617	117,780
2007	6,677,960	4,064,103	536,815	4,600,918	555,417	13,481	4,058,982	1,089,108	1,529,870	28,694	232,733	118,537
2008	7,284,822	4,280,764	548,973	4,829,737	593,555	9,003	4,245,185	1,300,687	1,738,950	30,963	235,272	121,723
2009	7,268,551	4,332,334	503,729	4,836,063	615,281	13,704	4,234,486	1,132,947	1,901,118	30,336	239,604	120,009
2010	7,717,357	4,479,626	613,090	5,092,716	631,158	20,430	4,481,988	1,127,960	2,107,409	31,582	244,360	119,126
2011	8,181,394	4,556,876	787,672	5,344,548	589,837	29,364	4,784,075	1,270,370	2,126,949	33,196	246,457	120,042
2012	8,636,030	4,789,431	851,398	5,640,829	609,655	14,095	5,045,269	1,458,071	2,132,690	34,953	247,072	124,853
2013	8,670,916	4,873,401	868,625	5,742,026	683,998	10,135	5,068,163	1,472,459	2,130,294	34,984	247,853	125,391
2014	9,110,645	5,009,860	907,093	5,916,953	720,244	9,812	5,206,521	1,498,315	2,405,809	36,639	248,660	127,317
2015	9,394,226	5,143,124	1,047,437	6,190,561	743,554	17,639	5,464,646	1,575,359	2,354,221	37,574	250,020	128,600
2016	9,625,867	5,357,166	1,007,058	6,364,224	763,600	18,524	5,619,148	1,493,834	2,512,885	38,171	252,180	130,545
2017	9,944,161	5,697,846	952,087	6,649,933	817,320	22,343	5,854,956	1,559,009	2,530,196	39,279	253,166	131,989
2018	10,321,507	6,077,954	711,291	6,789,245	840,403	22,979	5,971,821	1,721,712	2,627,974	40,569	254,420	134,356
2019	10,903,120	6,310,381	864,406	7,174,787	843,243	31,403	6,362,947	1,759,151	2,781,022	42,621	255,815	136,754
2020	11,807,373	6,540,579	963,665	7,504,244	901,832	34,294	6,636,706	1,661,837	3,508,830	45,996	256,702	131,740
2021	12,739,226	6,692,267	871,802	7,564,069	928,466	38,815	6,674,418	1,855,563	4,209,245	49,637	256,647	135,828
2022	12,661,318	7,099,784	1,012,246	8,112,030	1,052,748	42,711	7,101,993	1,962,603	3,596,722	49,266	257,001	141,277

Personal Income and Employment by Area: York-Hanover, PA

(Thousands of dollars, except as noted.)

Year	Personal income, total	Derivation of personal income: Earnings by place of work: Nonfarm	Farm	Total	Less: Contributions for government social insurance	Plus: Adjustment for residence	Equals: Net earnings by place of residence	Plus: Dividends, interest, and rent	Plus: Personal current transfer receipts	Per capita personal income (dollars)	Population (persons)	Total employment
1970	1,206,079	1,063,173	9,208	1,072,381	78,376	-31,911	962,094	153,738	90,247	4,411	273,427	139,933
1971	1,279,619	1,100,094	2,949	1,103,043	83,738	-12,199	1,007,106	168,431	104,082	4,587	278,991	137,875
1972	1,425,322	1,215,586	5,097	1,220,683	98,313	4,561	1,126,931	183,687	114,704	5,043	282,646	142,624
1973	1,589,893	1,330,118	14,619	1,344,737	123,335	29,057	1,250,459	209,367	130,067	5,557	286,122	147,199
1974	1,742,726	1,402,195	15,927	1,418,122	133,836	63,257	1,347,543	239,490	155,693	6,036	288,739	146,547
1975	1,899,048	1,455,589	13,416	1,469,005	133,920	88,997	1,424,082	267,599	207,367	6,486	292,808	140,987
1976	2,116,001	1,616,229	19,089	1,635,318	152,229	122,404	1,605,493	285,542	224,966	7,123	297,047	144,496
1977	2,360,782	1,804,018	15,226	1,819,244	170,638	160,373	1,808,979	317,269	234,534	7,852	300,642	148,395
1978	2,683,469	2,069,032	11,914	2,080,946	201,666	204,194	2,083,474	351,589	248,406	8,783	305,545	154,993
1979	3,034,812	2,313,487	22,491	2,335,978	233,864	253,654	2,355,768	400,669	278,375	9,780	310,297	160,882
1980	3,396,172	2,500,700	10,514	2,511,214	254,619	316,783	2,573,378	494,896	327,898	10,830	313,599	161,194
1981	3,725,506	2,693,415	19,911	2,713,326	293,384	323,098	2,743,040	603,596	378,870	11,817	315,266	159,431
1982	3,938,946	2,740,164	16,675	2,756,839	300,531	321,702	2,778,010	709,897	451,039	12,466	315,972	155,440
1983	4,122,553	2,843,039	2,225	2,845,264	317,874	349,470	2,876,860	759,253	486,440	13,041	316,125	154,109
1984	4,520,293	3,161,299	24,713	3,186,012	370,748	376,851	3,192,115	849,413	478,765	14,144	319,582	161,378
1985	4,826,501	3,384,335	20,956	3,405,291	400,799	388,545	3,393,037	922,792	510,672	15,076	320,150	165,404
1986	5,112,374	3,560,217	19,619	3,579,836	422,196	429,750	3,587,390	981,725	543,259	15,874	322,055	169,374
1987	5,443,030	3,888,224	19,581	3,907,805	455,349	439,617	3,892,073	991,691	559,266	16,700	325,922	176,386
1988	5,942,848	4,312,767	8,427	4,321,194	513,368	458,476	4,266,302	1,074,759	601,787	17,957	330,944	184,414
1989	6,450,366	4,585,005	20,529	4,605,534	535,964	473,422	4,542,992	1,253,277	654,097	19,194	336,068	188,133
1990	6,771,551	4,843,410	26,711	4,870,121	568,238	486,389	4,788,272	1,263,293	719,986	19,869	340,810	191,073
1991	7,085,853	5,018,191	13,380	5,031,571	594,222	520,292	4,957,641	1,303,362	824,850	20,467	346,209	188,389
1992	7,514,896	5,315,529	37,621	5,353,150	626,641	584,710	5,311,219	1,312,567	891,110	21,407	351,046	188,825
1993	7,906,189	5,519,147	24,733	5,543,880	665,167	639,199	5,517,912	1,455,602	932,675	22,199	356,156	190,523
1994	8,109,868	5,734,614	23,343	5,757,957	706,628	713,539	5,764,868	1,392,646	952,354	22,459	361,092	193,790
1995	8,551,455	6,020,193	11,880	6,032,073	739,982	770,955	6,063,046	1,479,221	1,009,188	23,365	365,997	198,685
1996	8,998,636	6,245,612	35,026	6,280,638	751,965	832,075	6,360,748	1,552,429	1,085,459	24,335	369,781	201,286
1997	9,452,097	6,592,550	12,813	6,605,363	783,392	866,812	6,688,783	1,638,253	1,125,061	25,361	372,706	204,054
1998	9,953,749	6,814,862	16,013	6,830,875	804,427	997,092	7,023,540	1,749,000	1,181,209	26,486	375,810	200,364
1999	10,333,135	7,116,768	9,134	7,125,902	833,167	1,093,718	7,386,453	1,699,100	1,247,582	27,271	378,905	204,405
2000	11,115,107	7,608,911	35,757	7,644,668	878,531	1,141,244	7,907,381	1,860,966	1,346,760	29,041	382,743	210,164
2001	11,517,422	7,800,016	26,391	7,826,407	894,576	1,222,233	8,154,064	1,863,513	1,499,845	29,855	385,773	211,514
2002	11,801,026	7,996,746	10,855	8,007,601	910,639	1,353,339	8,450,301	1,722,851	1,627,874	30,283	389,692	211,137
2003	12,481,816	8,380,772	65,403	8,446,175	942,957	1,445,201	8,948,419	1,796,692	1,736,705	31,592	395,093	211,658
2004	13,767,043	9,250,245	64,880	9,315,125	1,011,609	1,692,682	9,996,198	1,959,010	1,811,835	34,297	401,403	217,005
2005	14,759,849	10,064,422	44,220	10,108,642	1,106,972	1,821,301	10,822,971	1,936,411	2,000,467	36,082	409,066	223,488
2006	15,175,402	9,872,670	27,044	9,899,714	1,127,785	2,102,796	10,874,725	2,135,259	2,165,418	36,301	418,043	226,836
2007	16,597,310	10,678,110	39,815	10,717,925	1,179,421	2,280,643	11,819,147	2,463,774	2,314,389	39,060	424,919	231,793
2008	18,000,730	11,454,437	42,940	11,497,377	1,227,497	2,400,827	12,670,707	2,659,021	2,671,002	41,921	429,399	232,143
2009	17,470,248	10,612,091	30,101	10,642,192	1,184,961	2,428,070	11,885,301	2,585,799	2,999,148	40,345	433,022	223,013
2010	17,711,030	10,770,967	32,063	10,803,030	1,215,556	2,335,023	11,922,497	2,538,361	3,250,172	40,662	435,566	221,985
2011	18,140,075	10,870,866	36,219	10,907,085	1,130,520	2,389,709	12,166,274	2,700,133	3,273,668	41,465	437,481	224,721
2012	18,323,453	10,789,409	51,479	10,840,888	1,130,586	2,361,334	12,071,636	2,933,117	3,318,700	41,751	438,872	225,938
2013	18,407,771	10,956,693	55,017	11,011,710	1,298,586	2,397,259	12,110,383	2,878,759	3,418,629	41,745	440,954	227,242
2014	18,883,072	11,150,981	45,523	11,196,504	1,327,099	2,460,366	12,329,771	2,994,620	3,558,681	42,613	443,127	229,573
2015	19,659,932	11,642,268	18,293	11,660,561	1,383,038	2,590,990	12,868,513	3,027,743	3,763,676	44,177	445,022	231,735
2016	20,366,771	12,033,777	906	12,034,683	1,435,787	2,688,013	13,286,909	3,086,947	3,992,915	45,488	447,735	235,662
2017	21,220,698	12,661,906	24,240	12,686,146	1,526,411	2,748,492	13,908,227	3,253,595	4,058,876	47,130	450,261	237,733
2018	22,224,898	13,145,965	2,497	13,148,462	1,575,412	2,852,392	14,425,442	3,443,419	4,356,037	49,020	453,380	240,504
2019	23,055,083	13,572,888	30,675	13,603,563	1,627,262	3,025,459	15,001,760	3,511,725	4,541,598	50,680	454,912	240,670
2020	24,841,690	13,452,741	8,844	13,461,585	1,601,311	3,146,908	15,007,182	3,575,600	6,258,908	54,395	456,692	230,113
2021	26,472,413	14,302,666	54,994	14,357,660	1,713,015	3,212,559	15,857,204	3,845,229	6,769,980	57,656	459,148	239,174
2022	26,428,495	15,234,627	32,385	15,267,012	1,874,787	3,290,279	16,682,504	4,072,791	5,673,200	57,321	461,058	250,052

Personal Income and Employment by Area: Youngstown-Warren-Boardman, OH-PA

(Thousands of dollars, except as noted.)

Year	Personal income, total	Derivation of personal income: Earnings by place of work: Nonfarm	Farm	Total	Less: Contributions for government social insurance	Plus: Adjustment for residence	Equals: Net earnings by place of residence	Plus: Dividends, interest, and rent	Plus: Personal current transfer receipts	Per capita personal income (dollars)	Population (persons)	Total employment
1970	2,586,501	2,238,856	8,172	2,247,028	154,468	-36,575	2,055,985	302,231	228,285	3,886	665,569	279,196
1971	2,757,559	2,363,330	7,656	2,370,986	167,755	-39,449	2,163,782	325,056	268,721	4,111	670,741	276,899
1972	3,046,740	2,635,873	8,730	2,644,603	197,250	-46,526	2,400,827	345,972	299,941	4,472	681,278	282,795
1973	3,438,961	3,016,279	14,941	3,031,220	263,301	-55,104	2,712,815	385,235	340,911	5,143	668,722	296,124
1974	3,758,820	3,251,298	15,570	3,266,868	294,955	-62,409	2,909,504	439,851	409,465	5,569	675,013	299,829
1975	3,976,949	3,292,945	17,575	3,310,520	292,039	-59,492	2,958,989	479,999	537,961	6,005	662,274	285,651
1976	4,373,755	3,629,637	20,754	3,650,391	325,744	-68,030	3,256,617	516,562	600,576	6,560	666,754	288,266
1977	4,840,148	4,063,895	17,270	4,081,165	366,240	-76,033	3,638,892	574,078	627,178	7,252	667,417	294,002
1978	5,315,357	4,472,435	12,833	4,485,268	416,924	-76,424	3,991,920	637,191	686,246	7,994	664,956	298,304
1979	5,857,498	4,905,322	13,963	4,919,285	474,007	-79,687	4,365,591	718,078	773,829	8,899	658,231	301,663
1980	6,367,333	5,035,540	8,081	5,043,621	481,906	-76,512	4,485,203	910,431	971,699	9,668	658,600	291,643
1981	6,945,653	5,379,300	12,046	5,391,346	552,630	-84,079	4,754,637	1,121,337	1,069,679	10,637	652,946	286,983
1982	6,932,232	4,925,211	9,375	4,934,586	509,401	-37,514	4,387,671	1,247,340	1,297,221	10,673	649,503	264,325
1983	7,240,270	5,124,635	1,050	5,125,685	538,677	-37,507	4,549,501	1,334,909	1,355,860	11,233	644,566	259,259
1984	7,859,275	5,649,422	17,182	5,666,604	611,158	-40,685	5,014,761	1,491,820	1,352,694	12,333	637,279	267,611
1985	8,213,297	5,885,405	19,729	5,905,134	645,437	-38,678	5,221,019	1,569,836	1,422,442	13,007	631,445	270,681
1986	8,449,527	5,982,789	16,567	5,999,356	667,063	-23,532	5,308,761	1,625,620	1,515,146	13,515	625,219	275,735
1987	8,612,327	6,135,992	22,379	6,158,371	684,228	-15,349	5,458,794	1,572,542	1,580,991	13,909	619,212	280,875
1988	9,353,781	6,773,995	29,579	6,803,574	774,133	-33,250	5,996,191	1,711,522	1,646,068	15,191	615,749	288,063
1989	10,050,014	7,234,872	35,429	7,270,301	835,787	-37,698	6,396,816	1,895,885	1,757,313	16,340	615,048	293,661
1990	10,430,456	7,383,589	33,616	7,417,205	870,440	-28,187	6,518,578	1,919,127	1,992,751	16,988	613,980	294,927
1991	10,710,312	7,555,122	19,772	7,574,894	915,359	-39,668	6,619,867	1,963,050	2,127,395	17,402	615,462	294,326
1992	11,268,588	7,973,450	38,592	8,012,042	955,716	-39,863	7,016,463	1,949,214	2,302,911	18,243	617,681	292,356
1993	11,601,371	8,251,065	25,312	8,276,377	1,010,518	-25,296	7,240,563	1,964,952	2,395,856	18,762	618,328	293,654
1994	12,178,389	8,745,285	26,268	8,771,553	1,081,259	-24,416	7,665,878	2,048,832	2,463,679	19,730	617,253	299,990
1995	12,687,344	8,991,516	21,431	9,012,947	1,121,229	4,143	7,895,861	2,205,238	2,586,245	20,610	615,595	309,477
1996	13,100,315	9,181,409	29,310	9,210,719	1,129,411	35,741	8,117,049	2,300,727	2,682,539	21,323	614,369	311,996
1997	13,687,513	9,564,928	22,530	9,587,458	1,139,754	42,072	8,489,776	2,450,425	2,747,312	22,369	611,902	315,429
1998	14,106,175	9,764,781	24,828	9,789,609	1,133,977	85,026	8,740,658	2,577,332	2,788,185	23,152	609,286	315,929
1999	14,413,786	10,137,844	21,532	10,159,376	1,166,572	91,035	9,083,839	2,470,937	2,859,010	23,786	605,978	317,483
2000	14,924,039	10,362,565	25,020	10,387,585	1,155,371	115,228	9,347,442	2,548,426	3,028,171	24,781	602,227	318,418
2001	15,477,690	10,683,630	18,625	10,702,255	1,190,590	158,201	9,669,866	2,534,097	3,273,727	25,834	599,116	311,150
2002	15,718,173	10,929,064	9,881	10,938,945	1,195,915	169,163	9,912,193	2,374,481	3,431,499	26,419	594,958	305,453
2003	16,260,742	11,311,692	17,732	11,329,424	1,246,991	191,171	10,273,604	2,421,540	3,565,598	27,467	592,016	302,593
2004	16,683,634	11,638,499	25,413	11,663,912	1,303,833	238,196	10,598,275	2,391,845	3,693,514	28,350	588,478	301,804
2005	17,107,081	11,906,922	18,231	11,925,153	1,351,222	261,910	10,835,841	2,365,879	3,905,361	29,282	584,222	303,521
2006	18,028,275	12,560,333	15,097	12,575,430	1,424,648	262,175	11,412,957	2,556,541	4,058,777	31,061	580,420	302,817
2007	18,461,316	12,391,226	30,345	12,421,571	1,415,159	311,136	11,317,548	2,879,808	4,263,960	32,076	575,543	301,453
2008	18,999,076	12,227,194	17,892	12,245,086	1,414,533	362,267	11,192,820	3,048,174	4,758,082	33,276	570,952	295,987
2009	18,066,344	11,071,594	11,652	11,083,246	1,319,808	377,015	10,140,453	2,709,971	5,215,920	31,798	568,156	280,915
2010	18,604,643	11,554,170	25,746	11,579,916	1,352,983	343,155	10,570,088	2,669,615	5,364,940	32,930	564,978	281,010
2011	19,736,441	12,324,682	53,122	12,377,804	1,295,767	348,102	11,430,139	2,861,499	5,444,803	35,029	563,424	285,244
2012	20,023,784	12,529,921	43,137	12,573,058	1,309,343	382,688	11,646,403	3,023,145	5,354,236	35,722	560,540	287,335
2013	20,073,880	12,559,651	53,811	12,613,462	1,428,408	437,988	11,623,042	2,965,116	5,485,722	35,923	558,798	287,532
2014	20,606,109	12,734,047	44,934	12,778,981	1,453,233	479,555	11,805,303	3,096,349	5,704,457	37,000	556,915	287,963
2015	21,115,377	13,029,571	14,408	13,043,979	1,486,165	486,795	12,044,609	3,203,418	5,867,350	38,143	553,591	287,961
2016	21,212,766	12,958,587	3,276	12,961,863	1,510,551	477,194	11,928,506	3,257,053	6,027,207	38,564	550,063	288,231
2017	21,635,950	13,117,164	14,232	13,131,396	1,558,125	511,384	12,084,655	3,439,741	6,111,554	39,518	547,497	284,356
2018	22,304,670	13,454,690	13,432	13,468,122	1,591,129	566,668	12,443,661	3,550,370	6,310,639	40,924	545,030	284,947
2019	22,737,714	13,436,742	11,702	13,448,444	1,605,783	658,852	12,501,513	3,674,302	6,561,899	41,907	542,582	280,258
2020	24,567,800	13,272,124	18,287	13,290,411	1,594,467	722,807	12,418,751	3,672,404	8,476,645	45,478	540,211	266,608
2021	26,163,931	14,138,051	43,098	14,181,149	1,686,742	776,866	13,271,273	3,826,974	9,065,684	48,647	537,837	273,235
2022	26,049,221	14,997,156	26,458	15,023,614	1,846,269	740,670	13,918,015	4,129,445	8,001,761	48,645	535,499	282,448

Personal Income and Employment by Area: Yuba City, CA

(Thousands of dollars, except as noted.)

Year	Personal income, total	Derivation of personal income: Earnings by place of work: Nonfarm	Farm	Total	Less: Contributions for government social insurance	Plus: Adjustment for residence	Equals: Net earnings by place of residence	Plus: Dividends, interest, and rent	Plus: Personal current transfer receipts	Per capita personal income (dollars)	Population (persons)	Total employment
1970	381,992	247,601	45,848	293,449	17,043	-1,081	275,325	67,151	39,516	4,385	87,104	38,704
1971	416,455	269,274	52,357	321,631	19,232	-1,053	301,346	71,329	43,780	4,714	88,345	39,301
1972	453,626	290,533	63,161	353,694	21,250	-1,525	330,919	76,324	46,383	5,184	87,505	39,903
1973	511,582	304,200	96,542	400,742	24,323	-2,038	374,381	85,213	51,988	5,686	89,980	39,333
1974	589,712	336,569	125,115	461,684	27,903	-3,630	430,151	95,524	64,037	6,455	91,363	40,753
1975	639,526	374,793	111,918	486,711	31,194	-4,492	451,025	110,054	78,447	6,889	92,830	42,061
1976	647,325	410,241	71,770	482,011	35,046	-5,656	441,309	116,543	89,473	6,744	95,979	42,261
1977	729,495	447,835	99,000	546,835	38,607	-6,366	501,862	128,930	98,703	7,524	96,962	42,971
1978	800,278	504,366	85,799	590,165	43,672	-6,830	539,663	149,769	110,846	8,139	98,325	44,298
1979	894,176	559,315	95,175	654,490	49,749	-6,324	598,417	170,621	125,138	8,887	100,611	45,882
1980	1,012,644	601,249	121,553	722,802	52,199	-7,344	663,259	198,256	151,129	9,890	102,388	45,871
1981	1,100,874	641,567	119,557	761,124	60,425	-8,748	691,951	231,216	177,707	10,603	103,831	45,667
1982	1,118,676	665,971	75,625	741,596	62,819	-6,008	672,769	251,093	194,814	10,513	106,405	45,349
1983	1,151,436	691,779	41,179	732,958	66,645	692	667,005	270,998	213,433	10,614	108,483	45,038
1984	1,306,084	741,008	100,198	841,206	73,967	10,438	777,677	299,669	228,738	11,977	109,052	45,505
1985	1,411,634	779,330	127,016	906,346	79,025	22,850	850,171	313,806	247,657	12,726	110,929	46,019
1986	1,471,876	842,915	94,718	937,633	86,561	32,406	883,478	323,653	264,745	13,112	112,256	46,253
1987	1,578,538	899,183	123,432	1,022,615	93,710	44,673	973,578	330,494	274,466	13,780	114,554	48,049
1988	1,683,315	979,189	106,519	1,085,708	106,289	55,869	1,035,288	350,443	297,584	14,398	116,916	50,737
1989	1,842,718	1,056,469	105,023	1,161,492	116,786	69,504	1,114,210	399,220	329,288	15,393	119,714	53,653
1990	1,937,568	1,120,634	79,553	1,200,187	123,512	89,210	1,165,885	405,897	365,786	15,689	123,499	54,925
1991	2,113,491	1,191,846	121,389	1,313,235	133,488	89,124	1,268,871	430,710	413,910	16,684	126,677	56,571
1992	2,259,074	1,246,224	135,722	1,381,946	139,558	93,742	1,336,130	442,805	480,139	17,393	129,886	56,076
1993	2,328,102	1,271,636	151,036	1,422,672	142,812	96,344	1,376,204	448,150	503,748	17,644	131,950	56,416
1994	2,428,422	1,325,659	173,133	1,498,792	147,653	105,572	1,456,711	464,031	507,680	18,053	134,518	57,920
1995	2,522,299	1,380,505	160,978	1,541,483	151,059	115,902	1,506,326	484,189	531,784	18,639	135,323	59,036
1996	2,618,248	1,422,083	160,395	1,582,478	151,366	126,390	1,557,502	505,931	554,815	19,229	136,160	60,320
1997	2,725,959	1,527,763	139,784	1,667,547	157,720	142,043	1,651,870	518,640	555,449	19,981	136,425	60,517
1998	2,882,284	1,647,110	101,503	1,748,613	164,775	161,126	1,744,964	543,176	594,144	21,036	137,016	61,798
1999	3,136,539	1,759,555	199,079	1,958,634	177,675	182,379	1,963,338	539,909	633,292	22,713	138,097	63,347
2000	3,268,216	1,863,093	169,554	2,032,647	187,549	212,581	2,057,679	562,944	647,593	23,417	139,564	63,301
2001	3,366,151	1,984,893	125,132	2,110,025	212,204	222,767	2,120,588	529,087	716,476	23,808	141,387	61,499
2002	3,542,534	2,117,540	116,146	2,233,686	228,898	251,056	2,255,844	517,827	768,863	24,556	144,262	62,408
2003	3,809,670	2,262,251	152,882	2,415,133	245,945	282,394	2,451,582	536,144	821,944	25,845	147,404	62,577
2004	4,094,896	2,393,047	158,332	2,551,379	269,600	371,819	2,653,598	586,431	854,867	27,258	150,226	63,902
2005	4,338,516	2,496,331	121,052	2,617,383	281,632	507,168	2,842,919	615,263	880,334	27,982	155,049	64,652
2006	4,734,508	2,674,374	139,515	2,813,889	292,456	606,183	3,127,616	651,290	955,602	29,520	160,384	66,170
2007	5,128,326	2,809,762	160,200	2,969,962	300,439	671,330	3,340,853	762,222	1,025,251	31,324	163,720	67,739
2008	5,398,625	2,793,420	262,136	3,055,556	304,857	722,497	3,473,196	768,138	1,157,291	32,595	165,628	65,445
2009	5,451,088	2,812,132	353,534	3,165,666	310,642	581,452	3,436,476	748,028	1,266,584	32,843	165,973	63,428
2010	5,535,689	2,918,591	275,579	3,194,170	308,809	537,894	3,423,255	711,584	1,400,850	33,109	167,196	62,527
2011	5,696,512	2,953,065	288,906	3,241,971	289,853	547,434	3,499,552	767,556	1,429,404	34,010	167,497	62,566
2012	5,697,583	3,011,683	231,049	3,242,732	299,279	509,202	3,452,655	802,962	1,441,966	33,931	167,918	63,967
2013	5,941,020	3,099,485	322,486	3,421,971	341,144	529,775	3,610,602	834,618	1,495,800	35,158	168,982	65,437
2014	6,065,415	3,247,586	167,240	3,414,826	355,918	540,694	3,599,602	860,914	1,604,899	35,648	170,146	66,807
2015	6,525,298	3,428,746	196,194	3,624,940	372,479	612,661	3,865,122	912,984	1,747,192	38,020	171,626	68,645
2016	6,756,795	3,588,861	229,435	3,818,296	393,458	579,125	4,003,963	936,708	1,816,124	38,938	173,529	69,849
2017	6,904,034	3,763,717	231,178	3,994,895	413,494	599,066	4,180,467	944,981	1,778,586	39,212	176,069	71,511
2018	7,277,180	3,945,354	212,626	4,157,980	435,649	684,448	4,406,779	1,000,461	1,869,940	40,978	177,586	73,202
2019	7,679,863	4,164,481	183,256	4,347,737	463,625	746,789	4,630,901	1,028,617	2,020,345	42,717	179,785	74,916
2020	8,672,580	4,405,395	218,229	4,623,624	490,858	733,162	4,865,928	1,022,020	2,784,632	47,794	181,458	75,340
2021	9,368,079	4,714,725	201,665	4,916,390	523,511	826,610	5,219,489	1,034,159	3,114,431	51,401	182,254	76,672
2022	9,186,797	4,929,187	196,236	5,125,423	567,879	929,112	5,486,656	1,064,450	2,635,691	50,252	182,813	79,899

Personal Income and Employment by Area: Yuma, AZ

(Thousands of dollars, except as noted.)

Year	Personal income, total	Derivation of personal income: Earnings by place of work: Nonfarm	Farm	Total	Less: Contributions for government social insurance	Plus: Adjustment for residence	Equals: Net earnings by place of residence	Plus: Dividends, interest, and rent	Plus: Personal current transfer receipts	Per capita personal income (dollars)	Population (persons)	Total employment
1970	235,094	166,029	29,515	195,544	11,394	-7,832	176,318	42,539	16,237	3,828	61,415	29,730
1971	272,044	197,321	27,253	224,574	14,114	-8,281	202,179	50,514	19,351	4,195	64,853	31,172
1972	296,854	210,699	34,364	245,063	15,579	-9,060	220,424	54,072	22,358	4,421	67,150	31,018
1973	323,703	231,159	30,905	262,064	18,851	-9,420	233,793	62,827	27,083	4,713	68,685	31,328
1974	414,496	261,191	82,162	343,353	22,284	-11,295	309,774	72,681	32,041	5,806	71,396	32,675
1975	432,086	297,812	49,068	346,880	25,142	-14,734	307,004	82,298	42,784	6,223	69,434	33,614
1976	485,479	335,643	57,368	393,011	28,944	-16,513	347,554	88,321	49,604	6,348	76,476	35,033
1977	520,645	362,899	61,665	424,564	31,563	-20,921	372,080	96,629	51,936	6,553	79,454	36,573
1978	580,758	410,261	64,781	475,042	36,149	-28,224	410,669	112,713	57,376	7,198	80,680	38,692
1979	703,023	474,938	105,570	580,508	44,524	-33,164	502,820	131,633	68,570	8,418	83,512	39,541
1980	792,151	520,044	117,724	637,768	49,114	-37,484	551,170	155,721	85,260	8,668	91,393	40,634
1981	863,605	555,336	106,873	662,209	56,585	-22,536	583,088	178,363	102,154	9,404	91,834	40,844
1982	903,903	563,940	104,043	667,983	57,259	-20,977	589,747	202,431	111,725	9,628	93,878	40,449
1983	865,612	554,421	68,863	623,284	57,148	-17,587	548,549	207,424	109,639	10,302	84,027	38,578
1984	978,070	627,396	88,653	716,049	66,181	-18,540	631,328	235,203	111,539	11,456	85,373	40,324
1985	1,084,136	668,738	130,208	798,946	71,816	-17,213	709,917	260,388	113,831	12,380	87,572	41,031
1986	1,144,127	737,509	88,883	826,392	80,405	-14,977	731,010	284,183	128,934	12,642	90,505	42,571
1987	1,291,146	800,117	163,863	963,980	87,571	-12,610	863,799	285,997	141,350	13,931	92,684	45,954
1988	1,436,064	864,850	236,865	1,101,715	98,423	-8,111	995,181	287,890	152,993	14,795	97,064	48,117
1989	1,472,284	918,771	160,598	1,079,369	109,005	-988	969,376	311,110	191,798	14,241	103,380	50,231
1990	1,533,120	971,705	137,633	1,109,338	118,748	2,223	992,813	322,801	217,506	14,187	108,063	50,626
1991	1,689,522	1,070,171	171,190	1,241,361	130,802	-7,047	1,103,512	334,581	251,429	15,089	111,967	53,294
1992	1,816,980	1,151,568	162,719	1,314,287	141,263	-4,433	1,168,591	341,192	307,197	15,312	118,660	54,781
1993	1,978,124	1,201,331	245,996	1,447,327	148,331	-5,198	1,293,798	350,079	334,247	15,839	124,892	55,460
1994	2,011,869	1,284,795	153,413	1,438,208	157,771	-8,876	1,271,561	384,016	356,292	15,721	127,975	57,080
1995	2,352,350	1,355,256	376,898	1,732,154	158,176	-11,050	1,562,928	410,940	378,482	17,851	131,776	59,415
1996	2,269,575	1,421,267	196,477	1,617,744	169,677	-12,589	1,435,478	434,730	399,367	16,536	137,248	63,061
1997	2,442,498	1,546,450	216,401	1,762,851	179,788	-16,118	1,566,945	458,940	416,613	16,974	143,896	63,462
1998	2,685,918	1,633,708	324,637	1,958,345	187,860	-15,317	1,755,168	487,188	443,562	18,018	149,065	66,554
1999	2,717,675	1,692,126	258,433	1,950,559	194,492	-12,692	1,743,375	496,375	477,925	17,458	155,665	66,938
2000	2,880,300	1,772,768	307,903	2,080,671	202,805	-12,719	1,865,147	522,541	492,612	17,937	160,576	67,936
2001	3,053,420	1,935,107	237,813	2,172,920	226,046	-826	1,946,048	545,840	561,532	18,747	162,873	70,656
2002	3,345,607	2,071,998	324,370	2,396,368	247,026	2,507	2,151,849	566,520	627,238	20,228	165,398	72,786
2003	3,631,403	2,377,437	217,181	2,594,618	271,883	4,741	2,327,476	617,557	686,370	21,615	168,003	74,551
2004	4,068,299	2,645,005	324,288	2,969,293	301,464	4,328	2,672,157	659,157	736,985	23,540	172,824	78,519
2005	4,329,980	2,810,777	319,080	3,129,857	324,418	8,334	2,813,773	709,636	806,571	24,215	178,816	80,810
2006	4,570,227	3,084,188	225,494	3,309,682	351,543	13,202	2,971,341	725,878	873,008	24,859	183,848	83,778
2007	4,928,751	3,218,642	293,505	3,512,147	378,713	16,264	3,149,698	831,936	947,117	26,307	187,357	85,117
2008	5,107,955	3,294,326	187,890	3,482,216	395,870	21,080	3,107,426	881,561	1,118,968	26,715	191,202	83,670
2009	5,190,038	3,206,468	188,850	3,395,318	391,384	17,755	3,021,689	899,912	1,268,437	26,792	193,714	79,964
2010	5,470,351	3,271,779	311,061	3,582,840	400,525	23,132	3,205,447	871,169	1,393,735	27,791	196,839	79,896
2011	5,748,504	3,365,282	457,085	3,822,367	369,947	26,668	3,479,088	891,623	1,377,793	28,558	201,291	80,990
2012	5,650,702	3,439,170	270,774	3,709,944	378,881	33,924	3,364,987	925,632	1,360,083	28,301	199,666	82,396
2013	5,953,494	3,505,958	464,740	3,970,698	431,240	41,568	3,581,026	984,547	1,387,921	30,017	198,339	83,069
2014	5,909,409	3,616,297	283,713	3,900,010	440,049	44,266	3,504,227	958,649	1,446,533	29,745	198,670	83,664
2015	6,342,206	3,787,606	472,049	4,259,655	459,806	51,283	3,851,132	981,784	1,509,290	31,949	198,510	85,800
2016	6,579,054	3,891,289	513,104	4,404,393	473,708	49,758	3,980,443	1,013,226	1,585,385	33,033	199,165	88,202
2017	6,958,895	4,142,921	529,938	4,672,859	511,193	52,315	4,213,981	1,060,570	1,684,344	34,809	199,915	87,395
2018	7,073,441	4,384,565	342,278	4,726,843	545,697	51,860	4,233,006	1,069,462	1,770,973	35,266	200,572	89,407
2019	7,474,646	4,479,825	512,519	4,992,344	560,035	53,494	4,485,803	1,083,868	1,904,975	36,985	202,099	90,238
2020	8,626,323	4,815,733	304,004	5,119,737	608,782	58,273	4,569,228	1,092,194	2,964,901	42,177	204,528	89,391
2021	9,133,418	5,122,198	237,493	5,359,691	658,632	62,075	4,763,134	1,218,283	3,152,001	44,285	206,241	91,687
2022	9,313,549	5,659,876	347,302	6,007,178	724,268	66,269	5,349,179	1,328,792	2,635,578	44,811	207,842	95,822

PART B

GROSS DOMESTIC PRODUCT (GDP) BY REGION, STATE, AND AREA

PART B: GROSS DOMESTIC PRODUCT (GDP) BY REGION, STATE, AND AREA

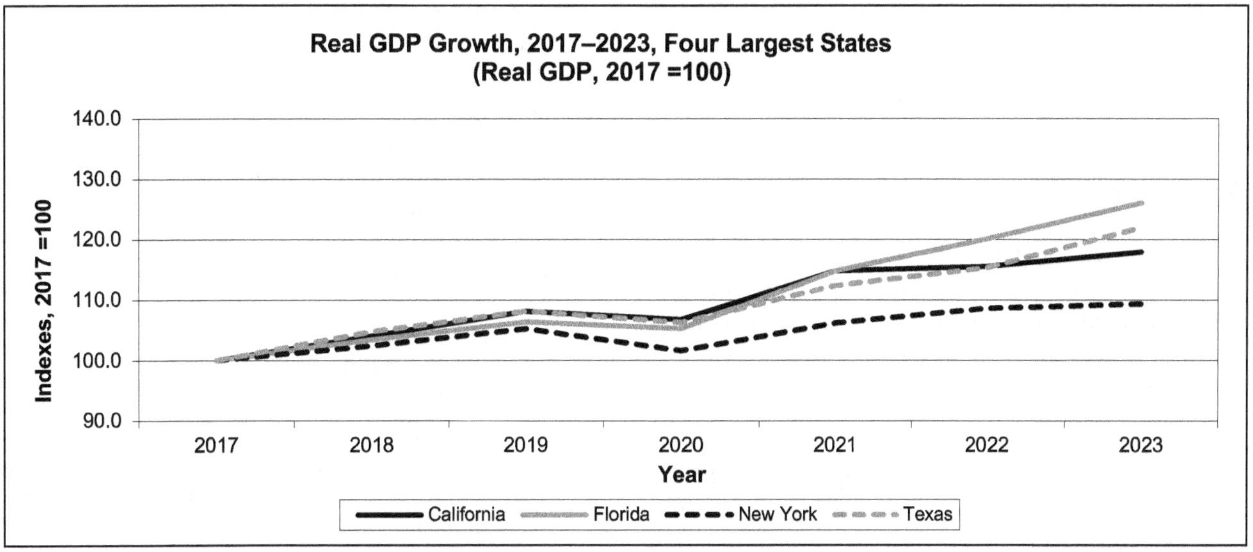

HIGHLIGHTS

- GDP increased in every state except for one in 2023. The nationwide GDP rose 2.5 percent. North Dakota had the largest increase in GDP (5.9 percent), followed by Texas (5.7 percent), and Wyoming (5.4 percent). Delaware was the only state with a decrease in GDP in 2023 (-1.2 percent).

- The three states with the largest GDP in 2023 were California ($3.2 trillion), Texas ($2.0 trillion), and New York ($1.8 trillion). Together, those three states produced 31.5 percent of the total U.S. GDP in 2023. The states with the lowest GDP were Vermont ($35.1 billion), Wyoming ($39.3 billion), and Alaska ($53.0 billion).

- GDP rose in 279 of the 384 metropolitan statistical areas (MSAs) in 2022. Kokomo, IN, experienced the largest growth in GDP among all MSAs from 2021 to 2022 at 10.1 percent. Greeley, CO, experienced a decline in GDP of -8.8 percent, which was the highest in the nation in 2022.

- New York-Newark-Jersey City, NY-NJ-PA, which had the largest GDP among all MSAs, comprised 9.5 percent of the total U.S. metropolitan portion of GDP in 2022, followed by Los Angeles-Long Beach-Anaheim, CA, with 5.4 percent of the total GDP from all MSAs.

PART B NOTES AND DEFINITIONS: GROSS DOMESTIC PRODUCT (GDP) BY REGION, STATE, AND AREA

Source: U.S. Department of Commerce, Bureau of Economic Analysis (BEA), https://www.bea.gov.

The following definitions are from the BEA. In a following section, further detail and explanation of the concepts is provided.

BEA definitions

Definitions. GDP by state is the state counterpart of the nation's gross domestic product (GDP), the BEA's featured and most comprehensive measure of U.S. economic activity. GDP by state is derived as the sum of the GDP originating in all the industries in a state.

The statistics of real GDP by state are prepared in chained (1997 or 2017) dollars. Real GDP by state is an inflation–adjusted measure of each state's gross product that is based on national prices for the goods and services produced within that state. The statistics of real GDP by state and of quantity indexes with a reference year of 2017 were derived by applying national chain–type price indexes to the current–dollar values of GDP by state for the 64 detailed NAICS–based industries for 1997 forward.

The chain–type index formula that is used in the national accounts is then used to calculate the values of total real GDP by state and of real GDP by state at more aggregated industry levels. Real GDP by state may reflect a substantial volume of output that is sold to other states and countries. To the extent that a state's output is produced and sold in national markets at relatively uniform prices (or sold locally at national prices), real GDP by state captures the differences across states that reflect the relative differences in the mix of goods and services that the states produce. However, real GDP by state does not capture geographic differences in the prices of goods and services that are produced and sold locally.

Relation of GDP by state to U.S. Gross Domestic Product (GDP). An industry's GDP by state, or its value added, in practice, is calculated as the sum of incomes earned by labor and capital and the costs incurred in the production of goods and services. That is, it includes the wages and salaries that workers earn, the income earned by individual or joint entrepreneurs as well as by corporations, and business taxes such as sales, property, and federal excise taxes—that count as a business expense.

GDP is calculated as the sum of what consumers, businesses, and government spend on final goods and services, plus investment and net foreign trade. In theory, incomes earned should equal what is spent, but due to different data sources, income earned, usually referred to as gross domestic income (GDI), does not always equal what is spent (GDP). The difference is referred to as the "statistical discrepancy."

Starting with the 2004 comprehensive revision, BEA's annual industry accounts and its GDP–by–state accounts allocate the statistical discrepancy across all private–sector industries. Therefore, the GDP–by–state statistics are now conceptually more similar to the GDP statistics in the national accounts than they had been in the past.

U.S. real GDP by state for the advance year, 2023, may differ from the Annual Industry Accounts' GDP by industry and, hence NIPA (national income and product accounts) GDP, because of different sources and vintages of data used to estimate GDP by state and NIPA GDP. For the revised years of 1997–2022, U.S. GDP by state is nearly identical to GDP by industry except for small differences resulting from GDP by state's exclusion of overseas Federal military and civilian activity (because it cannot be attributed to a particular state). The statistics of GDP by industry are from the 2023 annual update of the NIPAs, released in September 2023. However, because of revisions since September 2023, GDP in the NIPAs may differ from U.S. GDP by state.

BEA's national, international, regional, and industry statistics; the Survey of Current Business; and BEA news releases are available without charge on BEA's Web site at www.bea.gov. By visiting the site, you can also subscribe to receive free e–mail summaries of BEA releases and announcements.

Further notes

The value of an industry's GDP is equal to the market value of its gross output (which consists of sales or receipts and other operating income, taxes on production and imports, and inventory change) minus the value of its intermediate inputs (which consist of energy, raw materials, semifinished goods, and services that are purchased from domestic industries or foreign sources). In concept, this definition is equal to the sum of labor and property-type income earned in that industry in the production of GDP, plus commodity taxes. Property-type income is the sum of corporate profits, proprietors' income, rental income of persons, net interest, capital consumption allowances, business transfer payments, and the current surplus of government enterprises less subsidies.

In practice, GDP by state, like GDP by industry, is measured using the incomes data rather than data on gross output and intermediate inputs, which are not available on a sufficiently detailed and timely basis.

Therefore, the value of GDP by state is defined as the sum of labor and property-type incomes originating in each of 63 industries in that state, plus commodity taxes, and plus the allocated value of the statistical discrepancy between national GDP and national gross national income.

Chained-dollar estimates. The effect of the "chained-dollar" deflation procedure that BEA uses is to combine the real, inflation-adjusted, quantity changes in output between two adjacent time periods for individual products and industries using, as weights for the individual products, their average prices in those two periods. The estimates for successive time periods are then "chained" each to the previous one to provide a continuous index of real quantities that is not distorted by using prices from a single base year.

GDP by state is now calculated on a North American Industry Classification System (NAICS) basis back through 1997. Data for earlier years, beginning with 1977, were calculated on the Standard Industrial Classification (SIC) basis. According to BEA (in a "Cautionary note" on the Web site, dated June 7, 2007), "There is a discontinuity in the GDP by state time series at 1997, where the data change from SIC industry definitions to NAICS industry definitions. This discontinuity results from many sources, including differences in source data and different estimation methodologies. In addition, the NAICS-based GDP by state estimates are consistent with U.S. gross domestic product (GDP) while the SIC-based GDP by state estimates are consistent with U.S. gross domestic income (GDI). This data discontinuity may affect both the levels and the growth rates of the GDP by state estimates. Users of the GDP by state estimates are strongly cautioned against appending the two data series in an attempt to construct a single time series of GDP by state estimates for 1963 to 2006."

Patterns of Economic Change nevertheless provides SIC-based data for 1980 to 1997 for those who require information about states' economic growth before 1997.

Gross Domestic Product by Region and State

(Millions of chained 1997 or 2017 dollars; index numbers)

Year	United States	New England	Mideast	Great Lakes	Plains	Southeast	Southwest	Rocky Mountain	Far West	Alabama	Alaska	Arizona	Arkansas
VALUE													
Chained 1997 Dollars													
1980	4,908,867	1,012,776	854,483	344,295	976,312	481,736	143,449	824,862	64,582	22,440	55,561	34,773	599,507
1981	5,042,118	1,028,056	861,593	355,679	1,008,512	508,762	148,620	851,427	65,771	25,866	57,106	36,018	619,243
1982	4,977,350	1,020,670	822,244	346,904	997,979	510,378	147,222	849,741	64,134	26,543	55,763	35,055	619,420
1983	5,120,074	1,055,252	849,428	349,664	1,037,194	509,902	148,939	874,727	67,305	25,822	58,950	36,179	641,585
1984	5,485,271	1,120,588	916,372	376,210	1,116,483	541,315	156,456	936,298	70,481	26,854	65,288	39,015	693,095
1985	5,704,145	1,158,560	946,668	386,662	1,166,972	564,578	160,383	979,706	73,801	29,834	69,447	39,403	728,599
1986	5,826,832	1,192,646	962,229	388,432	1,203,514	555,866	158,252	1,010,168	74,558	24,957	73,546	40,177	756,166
1987	6,076,695	1,253,511	988,285	401,771	1,265,154	556,371	160,106	1,071,727	78,659	29,525	76,600	41,566	802,816
1988	6,398,624	1,327,678	1,035,997	416,799	1,330,988	586,844	166,009	1,131,172	82,508	27,843	80,258	43,158	848,273
1989	6,540,047	1,340,174	1,057,952	427,444	1,361,603	598,852	169,205	1,177,017	82,408	28,986	80,971	44,012	880,307
1990	6,638,210	1,351,182	1,062,296	433,341	1,382,836	614,113	174,758	1,218,168	83,766	28,772	81,606	44,496	906,103
1991	6,627,809	1,330,568	1,057,697	438,079	1,397,392	625,303	179,276	1,207,739	86,116	25,821	81,946	46,498	893,112
1992	6,828,525	1,353,418	1,106,985	457,254	1,449,519	654,652	189,490	1,218,219	89,814	26,151	90,282	49,260	891,631
1993	6,967,716	1,366,936	1,133,832	459,352	1,498,996	681,390	201,103	1,225,572	91,168	26,048	94,916	50,756	888,070
1994	7,288,327	1,395,466	1,207,063	490,357	1,587,062	723,716	214,348	1,255,607	94,803	26,188	104,104	53,641	904,778
1995	7,539,096	1,426,803	1,235,447	505,631	1,651,779	759,372	226,604	1,300,697	98,024	27,609	112,020	55,836	940,599
1996	7,871,721	1,475,796	1,283,159	532,340	1,720,686	805,125	239,357	1,363,152	101,379	27,271	120,869	58,346	978,300
1997	8,284,432	1,535,947	1,345,334	558,791	1,802,254	866,050	253,743	1,443,206	104,805	27,581	129,279	60,333	1,037,091
Chained 2017 Dollars													
1997[1]	12,370,299	689,814	2,438,053	2,012,225	820,782	2,734,720	1,217,039	368,387	2,043,143	154,700	41,071	180,294	87,180
1998[1]	12,924,876	717,954	2,502,639	2,082,507	847,988	2,866,446	1,296,678	394,624	2,168,491	160,396	40,264	197,492	89,905
1999[1]	13,543,774	750,272	2,614,465	2,163,842	872,881	3,001,079	1,356,476	418,719	2,319,360	166,532	39,783	214,294	94,757
2000[1]	14,096,033	803,965	2,713,232	2,223,891	910,543	3,072,356	1,404,916	447,008	2,469,130	168,695	38,428	224,729	95,510
2001[1]	14,230,726	815,552	2,771,542	2,203,149	910,419	3,118,857	1,446,382	453,119	2,463,451	168,448	40,014	230,886	95,529
2002[1]	14,472,712	819,334	2,784,056	2,243,919	930,799	3,195,087	1,480,278	459,319	2,514,957	172,430	41,905	238,257	98,557
2003[1]	14,877,312	837,234	2,829,746	2,296,971	965,432	3,312,052	1,510,597	467,704	2,609,836	178,040	41,235	253,743	102,948
2004[1]	15,449,757	871,834	2,907,955	2,363,124	1,002,490	3,473,549	1,592,176	484,374	2,705,895	189,914	42,880	264,990	108,582
2005[1]	15,987,957	889,361	2,976,619	2,408,650	1,032,697	3,634,910	1,648,724	511,144	2,835,775	197,247	44,407	283,806	112,451
2006[1]	16,433,148	914,341	3,029,492	2,425,980	1,047,758	3,726,097	1,754,562	533,205	2,947,202	199,924	47,546	296,424	114,890
2007[1]	16,762,445	936,060	3,077,937	2,450,467	1,071,800	3,752,274	1,832,803	555,985	3,026,963	202,026	50,127	306,612	114,027
2008[1]	16,781,485	941,279	3,089,355	2,403,346	1,092,076	3,738,925	1,833,233	563,306	3,056,662	200,967	49,927	302,278	113,628
2009[1]	16,349,110	920,013	3,092,498	2,284,892	1,064,276	3,611,268	1,808,210	549,727	2,948,080	194,192	54,952	277,412	109,833
2010[1]	16,789,750	948,885	3,194,703	2,368,842	1,096,010	3,695,420	1,851,649	557,538	3,010,546	199,455	53,652	282,253	113,001
2011[1]	17,052,410	954,795	3,219,507	2,421,624	1,120,460	3,716,013	1,912,614	567,498	3,066,026	201,373	54,046	290,411	115,242
2012[1]	17,442,759	968,580	3,301,294	2,463,334	1,149,894	3,762,626	1,996,352	574,358	3,148,430	203,676	57,087	297,077	116,616
2013[1]	17,812,167	968,967	3,334,509	2,505,982	1,167,912	3,828,030	2,075,731	594,721	3,249,258	206,963	54,628	298,860	119,843
2014[1]	18,261,714	982,746	3,395,873	2,569,255	1,202,107	3,902,765	2,140,042	617,618	3,360,531	206,070	53,303	301,721	121,409
2015[1]	18,799,622	1,013,588	3,465,391	2,606,192	1,227,189	4,011,954	2,229,860	641,499	3,516,768	208,950	53,681	308,583	121,533
2016[1]	19,141,672	1,023,574	3,518,585	2,632,447	1,237,736	4,102,067	2,235,959	655,673	3,629,300	212,863	53,464	319,008	123,035
2017[1]	19,612,102	1,039,545	3,572,774	2,669,538	1,250,759	4,210,089	2,286,161	681,310	3,797,441	216,616	53,551	333,099	123,883
2018[1]	20,193,896	1,062,478	3,647,342	2,722,152	1,274,026	4,315,633	2,385,042	712,372	3,956,948	220,809	52,480	346,398	126,371
2019[1]	20,692,087	1,084,356	3,715,335	2,754,724	1,287,231	4,414,689	2,462,458	746,392	4,108,526	224,945	52,325	359,646	127,216
2020[1]	20,234,074	1,055,848	3,582,053	2,649,400	1,264,481	4,338,850	2,423,336	744,870	4,048,650	222,081	50,345	362,604	128,061
2021[1]	21,407,692	1,116,078	3,741,298	2,788,919	1,320,363	4,611,710	2,557,666	794,824	4,342,903	231,893	51,022	390,805	135,569
2022[1]	21,822,037	1,140,308	3,814,224	2,825,277	1,335,232	4,735,643	2,620,457	812,969	4,385,658	235,807	50,315	403,474	137,356
2023[1]	22,376,906	1,160,814	3,862,617	2,859,300	1,369,260	4,883,069	2,754,851	836,706	4,497,211	241,753	53,006	414,273	140,785
QUANTITY INDEX													
1997=100													
1980	59.3	56.6	65.9	63.5	61.6	54.2	55.6	56.5	57.2	61.6	81.4	43.0	57.6
1981	60.9	58.0	66.9	64.0	63.7	56.0	58.7	58.6	59.0	62.8	93.8	44.2	59.7
1982	60.1	58.6	66.5	61.1	62.1	55.4	58.9	58.0	58.9	61.2	96.2	43.1	58.1
1983	61.8	61.7	68.7	63.1	62.6	57.6	58.9	58.7	60.6	64.2	93.6	45.6	60.0
1984	66.2	67.3	73.0	68.1	67.3	61.9	62.5	61.7	64.9	67.3	97.4	50.5	64.7
1985	68.9	71.2	75.4	70.4	69.2	64.8	65.2	63.2	67.9	70.4	108.2	53.7	65.3
1986	70.3	74.7	77.6	71.5	69.5	66.8	64.2	62.4	70.0	71.1	90.5	56.9	66.6
1987	73.4	80.0	81.6	73.5	71.9	70.2	64.2	63.1	74.3	75.1	107.0	59.3	68.9
1988	77.2	85.0	86.4	77.0	74.6	73.9	67.8	65.4	78.4	78.7	101.0	62.1	71.5
1989	78.9	85.9	87.3	78.6	76.5	75.6	69.1	66.7	81.6	78.6	105.1	62.6	72.9
1990	80.1	84.5	88.0	79.0	77.6	76.7	70.9	68.9	84.4	79.9	104.3	63.1	73.8
1991	80.0	82.3	86.6	78.6	78.4	77.5	72.2	70.7	83.7	82.2	93.6	63.4	77.1
1992	82.4	83.7	88.1	82.3	81.8	80.4	75.6	74.7	84.4	85.7	94.8	69.8	81.6
1993	84.1	83.8	89.0	84.3	82.2	83.2	78.7	79.3	84.9	87.0	94.4	73.4	84.1
1994	88.0	86.8	90.9	89.7	87.8	88.1	83.6	84.5	87.0	90.5	94.9	80.5	88.9
1995	91.0	90.5	92.9	91.8	90.5	91.7	87.7	89.3	90.1	93.5	100.1	86.6	92.5
1996	95.0	94.4	96.1	95.4	95.3	95.5	93.0	94.3	94.5	96.7	98.9	93.5	96.7
1997	100.0	100.0	100.0	100.0	100.0	100.0	100.0	100.0	100.0	100.0	100.0	100.0	100.0

Gross Domestic Product by Region and State—Continued

(Millions of chained 1997 or 2017 dollars; index numbers)

Year	United States	New England	Mideast	Great Lakes	Plains	Southeast	Southwest	Rocky Mountain	Far West	Alabama	Alaska	Arizona	Arkansas
2017 = 100													
1997[1]	63.1	66.4	68.2	75.4	65.6	65.0	53.2	54.1	53.8	71.4	76.7	54.1	70.4
1998[1]	65.9	69.1	70.0	78.0	67.8	68.1	56.7	57.9	57.1	74.0	75.2	59.3	72.6
1999[1]	69.1	72.2	73.2	81.1	69.8	71.3	59.3	61.5	61.1	76.9	74.3	64.3	76.5
2000[1]	71.9	77.3	75.9	83.3	72.8	73.0	61.5	65.6	65.0	77.9	71.8	67.5	77.1
2001[1]	72.6	78.5	77.6	82.5	72.8	74.1	63.3	66.5	64.9	77.8	74.7	69.3	77.1
2002[1]	73.8	78.8	77.9	84.1	74.4	75.9	64.8	67.4	66.2	79.6	78.3	71.5	79.6
2003[1]	75.9	80.5	79.2	86.0	77.2	78.7	66.1	68.6	68.7	82.2	77.0	76.2	83.1
2004[1]	78.8	83.9	81.4	88.5	80.2	82.5	69.6	71.1	71.3	87.7	80.1	79.6	87.6
2005[1]	81.5	85.6	83.3	90.2	82.6	86.3	72.1	75.0	74.7	91.1	82.9	85.2	90.8
2006[1]	83.8	88.0	84.8	90.9	83.8	88.5	76.7	78.3	77.6	92.3	88.8	89.0	92.7
2007[1]	85.5	90.0	86.2	91.8	85.7	89.1	80.2	81.6	79.7	93.3	93.6	92.0	92.0
2008[1]	85.6	90.5	86.5	90.0	87.3	88.8	80.2	82.7	80.5	92.8	93.2	90.7	91.7
2009[1]	83.4	88.5	86.6	85.6	85.1	85.8	79.1	80.7	77.6	89.6	102.6	83.3	88.7
2010[1]	85.6	91.3	89.4	88.7	87.6	87.8	81.0	81.8	79.3	92.1	100.2	84.7	91.2
2011[1]	86.9	91.8	90.1	90.7	89.6	88.3	83.7	83.3	80.7	93.0	100.9	87.2	93.0
2012[1]	88.9	93.2	92.4	92.3	91.9	89.4	87.3	84.3	82.9	94.0	106.6	89.2	94.1
2013[1]	90.8	93.2	93.3	93.9	93.4	90.9	90.8	87.3	85.6	95.5	102.0	89.7	96.7
2014[1]	93.1	94.5	95.0	96.2	96.1	92.7	93.6	90.7	88.5	95.1	99.5	90.6	98.0
2015[1]	95.9	97.5	97.0	97.6	98.1	95.3	97.5	94.2	92.6	96.5	100.2	92.6	98.1
2016[1]	97.6	98.5	98.5	98.6	99.0	97.4	97.8	96.2	95.6	98.3	99.8	95.8	99.3
2017[1]	100.0	100.0	100.0	100.0	100.0	100.0	100.0	100.0	100.0	100.0	100.0	100.0	100.0
2018[1]	103.0	102.2	102.1	102.0	101.9	102.5	104.3	104.6	104.2	101.9	98.0	104.0	102.0
2019[1]	105.5	104.3	104.0	103.2	102.9	104.9	107.7	109.6	108.2	103.8	97.7	108.0	102.7
2020[1]	103.2	101.6	100.3	99.2	101.1	103.1	106.0	109.3	106.6	102.5	94.0	108.9	103.4
2021[1]	109.2	107.4	104.7	104.5	105.6	109.5	111.9	116.7	114.4	107.1	95.3	117.3	109.4
2022[1]	111.3	109.7	106.8	105.8	106.8	112.5	114.6	119.3	115.5	108.9	94.0	121.1	110.9
2023[1]	114.1	111.7	108.1	107.1	109.5	116.0	120.5	122.8	118.4	111.6	99.0	124.4	113.6

1 = NAICS basis, not continuous with previous years, which are based on the SIC.

Gross Domestic Product by Region and State—Continued

(Millions of chained 1997 or 2017 dollars; index numbers)

Year	California	Colorado	Connecticut	Delaware	District of Columbia	Florida	Georgia	Hawaii	Idaho	Illinois	Indiana	Iowa	Kansas	Kentucky
VALUE														
Chained 1997 Dollars														
1980	70,410	78,644	16,126	45,655	186,914	102,952	26,760	16,415	258,832	102,247	56,387	49,642	63,053	98,826
1981	73,467	80,480	16,456	44,856	195,993	107,314	26,654	16,493	262,248	103,494	58,097	51,081	64,756	101,477
1982	74,962	82,538	16,640	43,539	200,772	108,942	26,867	15,824	253,052	97,816	54,248	50,638	62,456	97,626
1983	75,947	86,663	17,959	43,965	212,495	116,030	27,932	16,597	255,786	100,129	52,043	50,956	62,542	96,515
1984	80,299	94,619	19,290	44,880	230,407	127,323	28,979	16,892	274,171	109,229	54,893	53,241	67,270	102,251
1985	82,357	99,671	20,492	45,563	242,870	136,869	29,973	17,274	282,224	111,327	56,009	55,267	69,294	104,078
1986	81,845	104,258	21,068	45,848	253,651	144,853	30,989	16,937	288,439	113,098	55,262	55,466	68,323	103,870
1987	83,322	112,210	22,563	47,149	270,018	152,163	32,376	17,350	297,698	117,397	56,536	57,350	70,822	104,284
1988	85,880	119,047	23,599	49,206	286,786	158,946	34,587	18,284	314,485	123,242	59,479	58,843	75,562	108,142
1989	86,898	120,607	25,312	50,146	297,215	162,167	36,643	19,453	320,572	127,701	61,636	59,286	77,233	108,117
1990	88,933	121,176	25,887	51,175	304,324	165,062	39,176	20,161	324,012	128,197	63,460	60,672	78,206	110,272
1991	90,780	118,216	26,930	50,241	305,979	167,209	39,756	20,593	323,641	128,215	63,818	61,275	78,908	110,055
1992	97,058	119,832	27,178	50,598	317,416	176,731	40,834	22,022	336,296	136,439	66,862	63,062	83,288	102,935
1993	103,457	118,315	26,946	51,310	329,410	184,789	40,152	23,940	343,470	140,645	66,913	63,516	85,810	105,296
1994	110,529	121,002	28,750	51,290	345,550	198,125	40,062	25,845	364,916	149,157	72,503	66,732	91,063	114,156
1995	116,821	128,538	29,941	49,889	358,419	209,292	39,552	27,996	374,858	153,785	74,568	67,531	94,259	120,333
1996	123,144	131,913	30,503	49,232	376,851	223,307	39,132	28,927	389,704	160,020	78,834	70,361	97,781	121,489
1997	133,204	140,280	31,450	49,702	393,075	235,200	39,064	30,312	408,048	167,366	83,113	74,147	103,621	126,003
Chained 2017 Dollars														
1997 [1]	1,441,226	189,446	205,965	51,267	86,535	603,989	351,184	60,620	38,816	619,326	244,848	120,233	108,793	155,770
1998 [1]	1,538,612	206,449	212,255	56,487	88,108	634,032	377,706	58,946	40,879	639,643	260,550	121,031	112,626	160,810
1999 [1]	1,655,439	221,041	218,860	60,866	92,097	664,152	404,465	59,612	44,822	663,858	268,864	123,683	115,486	165,762
2000 [1]	1,784,321	238,739	233,874	63,389	92,764	693,837	417,714	60,746	49,793	687,111	278,990	129,323	118,841	161,101
2001 [1]	1,784,568	242,650	236,338	65,725	96,185	714,638	422,732	60,446	48,695	688,404	273,884	128,078	119,474	161,316
2002 [1]	1,821,510	243,702	234,307	63,703	99,015	746,253	427,330	62,355	49,841	692,398	280,723	131,035	121,051	165,435
2003 [1]	1,895,288	246,017	236,719	64,317	100,969	781,834	439,075	65,624	51,543	703,549	293,045	137,477	123,487	170,482
2004 [1]	1,956,746	250,069	252,681	67,736	106,547	833,947	461,245	69,332	55,137	726,139	303,820	149,063	124,793	175,345
2005 [1]	2,042,141	261,993	258,204	66,381	108,884	883,165	480,838	72,942	59,332	741,249	306,345	153,627	129,588	182,018
2006 [1]	2,120,435	268,191	269,479	68,412	108,848	909,299	487,525	74,893	60,739	759,826	312,526	155,705	136,136	186,333
2007 [1]	2,168,940	278,734	278,485	68,132	112,288	922,288	492,239	76,434	61,812	769,572	322,662	162,838	143,587	185,790
2008 [1]	2,192,332	281,803	277,793	65,771	116,214	891,767	481,860	76,830	63,878	759,095	322,384	160,469	147,265	186,516
2009 [1]	2,110,679	275,659	265,531	69,186	115,646	840,481	464,017	74,119	61,276	740,794	299,789	156,737	141,903	178,113
2010 [1]	2,153,853	279,386	266,773	68,292	120,393	851,956	471,588	76,130	62,626	755,391	320,732	161,593	143,870	186,721
2011 [1]	2,192,887	283,964	261,556	71,104	122,636	849,395	481,215	77,174	62,704	772,226	321,533	164,559	147,837	188,390
2012 [1]	2,255,437	289,340	263,650	70,562	123,568	857,861	489,027	78,694	62,007	790,723	323,876	170,924	150,077	192,060
2013 [1]	2,340,335	301,484	258,911	68,657	124,095	880,184	499,900	80,535	64,770	795,435	333,207	171,069	150,703	196,698
2014 [1]	2,428,676	315,399	260,606	73,962	126,884	905,649	517,512	81,305	66,785	811,490	343,828	180,310	154,110	196,796
2015 [1]	2,545,980	330,526	268,870	76,211	129,110	945,929	540,109	83,858	67,791	825,425	341,205	185,989	158,603	199,487
2016 [1]	2,623,712	337,685	268,196	71,941	132,218	978,990	561,718	85,670	70,443	826,405	348,439	186,730	164,644	201,007
2017 [1]	2,740,550	350,209	273,875	69,556	134,299	1,014,867	583,543	87,436	72,935	832,827	357,536	187,125	166,274	203,564
2018 [1]	2,850,970	365,205	274,583	70,856	138,057	1,050,434	600,935	88,836	77,652	851,517	368,763	189,245	169,797	205,940
2019 [1]	2,962,792	383,596	274,219	74,597	138,867	1,079,271	620,792	88,945	81,261	857,985	371,045	188,318	170,352	211,740
2020 [1]	2,925,147	380,922	258,625	72,550	137,762	1,068,378	602,322	79,593	82,819	810,210	359,185	187,137	168,541	206,289
2021 [1]	3,146,185	406,962	268,847	74,437	142,676	1,164,778	639,236	84,122	87,993	852,749	384,051	198,471	172,840	214,565
2022 [1]	3,167,461	416,114	276,669	75,173	144,030	1,218,430	655,827	85,211	91,684	864,171	396,009	197,846	174,795	217,568
2023 [1]	3,233,151	428,040	282,479	74,263	145,493	1,279,119	661,115	86,888	94,914	875,569	401,472	200,442	182,350	225,235
QUANTITY INDEX														
1997=100														
1980	57.8	52.9	56.1	51.3	91.9	47.6	43.8	68.5	54.2	63.4	61.1	67.8	67.0	60.8
1981	59.7	55.2	57.4	52.3	90.3	49.9	45.6	68.2	54.4	64.3	61.8	69.9	68.9	62.5
1982	59.7	56.3	58.8	52.9	87.6	51.1	46.3	68.8	52.2	62.0	58.4	65.3	68.3	60.3
1983	61.9	57.0	61.8	57.1	88.5	54.1	49.3	71.5	54.8	62.7	59.8	62.6	68.7	60.4
1984	66.8	60.3	67.5	61.3	90.3	58.6	54.1	74.2	55.7	67.2	65.3	66.0	71.8	64.9
1985	70.3	61.8	71.1	65.2	91.7	61.8	58.2	76.7	57.0	69.2	66.5	67.4	74.5	66.9
1986	72.9	61.4	74.3	67.0	92.2	64.5	61.6	79.3	55.9	70.7	67.6	66.5	74.8	65.9
1987	77.4	62.6	80.0	71.7	94.9	68.7	64.7	82.9	57.2	73.0	70.1	68.0	77.3	68.3
1988	81.8	64.5	84.9	75.0	99.0	73.0	67.6	88.5	60.3	77.1	73.6	71.6	79.4	72.9
1989	84.9	65.2	86.0	80.5	100.9	75.6	68.9	93.8	64.2	78.6	76.3	74.2	80.0	74.5
1990	87.4	66.8	86.4	82.3	103.0	77.4	70.2	100.3	66.5	79.4	76.6	76.4	81.8	75.5
1991	86.1	68.2	84.3	85.6	101.1	77.8	71.1	101.8	67.9	79.3	76.6	76.8	82.6	76.2
1992	86.0	72.9	85.4	86.4	101.8	80.8	75.1	104.5	72.7	82.4	81.5	80.4	85.1	80.4
1993	85.6	77.7	84.3	85.7	103.2	83.8	78.6	102.8	79.0	84.2	84.0	80.5	85.7	82.8
1994	87.2	83.0	86.3	91.4	103.2	87.9	84.2	102.6	85.3	89.4	89.1	87.2	90.0	87.9
1995	90.7	87.7	91.6	95.2	100.4	91.2	89.0	101.2	92.4	91.9	91.9	89.7	91.1	91.0
1996	94.3	92.4	94.0	97.0	99.1	95.9	94.9	100.2	95.4	95.5	95.6	94.9	94.9	94.4
1997	100.0	100.0	100.0	100.0	100.0	100.0	100.0	100.0	100.0	100.0	100.0	100.0	100.0	100.0

Gross Domestic Product by Region and State—Continued

(Millions of chained 1997 or 2017 dollars; index numbers)

Year	California	Colorado	Connecticut	Delaware	District of Columbia	Florida	Georgia	Hawaii	Idaho	Illinois	Indiana	Iowa	Kansas	Kentucky
2017 = 100														
1997[1]	52.6	54.1	75.2	73.7	64.4	59.5	60.2	69.3	53.2	74.4	68.5	64.3	65.4	76.5
1998[1]	56.1	59.0	77.5	81.2	65.6	62.5	64.7	67.4	56.0	76.8	72.9	64.7	67.7	79.0
1999[1]	60.4	63.1	79.9	87.5	68.6	65.4	69.3	68.2	61.5	79.7	75.2	66.1	69.5	81.4
2000[1]	65.1	68.2	85.4	91.1	69.1	68.4	71.6	69.5	68.3	82.5	78.0	69.1	71.5	79.1
2001[1]	65.1	69.3	86.3	94.5	71.6	70.4	72.4	69.1	66.8	82.7	76.6	68.4	71.9	79.2
2002[1]	66.5	69.6	85.6	91.6	73.7	73.5	73.2	71.3	68.3	83.1	78.5	70.0	72.8	81.3
2003[1]	69.2	70.2	86.4	92.5	75.2	77.0	75.2	75.1	70.7	84.5	82.0	73.5	74.3	83.7
2004[1]	71.4	71.4	92.3	97.4	79.3	82.2	79.0	79.3	75.6	87.2	85.0	79.7	75.1	86.1
2005[1]	74.5	74.8	94.3	95.4	81.1	87.0	82.4	83.4	81.3	89.0	85.7	82.1	77.9	89.4
2006[1]	77.4	76.6	98.4	98.4	81.0	89.6	83.5	85.7	83.3	91.2	87.4	83.2	81.9	91.5
2007[1]	79.1	79.6	101.7	98.0	83.6	90.9	84.4	87.4	84.7	92.4	90.2	87.0	86.4	91.3
2008[1]	80.0	80.5	101.4	94.6	86.5	87.9	82.6	87.9	87.6	91.1	90.2	85.8	88.6	91.6
2009[1]	77.0	78.7	97.0	99.5	86.1	82.8	79.5	84.8	84.0	88.9	83.8	83.8	85.3	87.5
2010[1]	78.6	79.8	97.4	98.2	89.6	83.9	80.8	87.1	85.9	90.7	89.7	86.4	86.5	91.7
2011[1]	80.0	81.1	95.5	102.2	91.3	83.7	82.5	88.3	86.0	92.7	89.9	87.9	88.9	92.5
2012[1]	82.3	82.6	96.3	101.4	92.0	84.5	83.8	90.0	85.0	94.9	90.6	91.3	90.3	94.3
2013[1]	85.4	86.1	94.5	98.7	92.4	86.7	85.7	92.1	88.8	95.5	93.2	91.4	90.6	96.6
2014[1]	88.6	90.1	95.2	106.3	94.5	89.2	88.7	93.0	91.6	97.4	96.2	96.4	92.7	96.7
2015[1]	92.9	94.4	98.2	109.6	96.1	93.2	92.6	95.9	92.9	99.1	95.4	99.4	95.4	98.0
2016[1]	95.7	96.4	97.9	103.4	98.5	96.5	96.3	98.0	96.6	99.2	97.5	99.8	99.0	98.7
2017[1]	100.0	100.0	100.0	100.0	100.0	100.0	100.0	100.0	100.0	100.0	100.0	100.0	100.0	100.0
2018[1]	104.0	104.3	100.3	101.9	102.8	103.5	103.0	101.6	106.5	102.2	103.1	101.1	102.1	101.2
2019[1]	108.1	109.5	100.1	107.2	103.4	106.3	106.4	101.7	111.4	103.0	103.8	100.6	102.5	104.0
2020[1]	106.7	108.8	94.4	104.3	102.6	105.3	103.2	91.0	113.6	97.3	100.5	100.0	101.4	101.3
2021[1]	114.8	116.2	98.2	107.0	106.2	114.8	109.5	96.2	120.6	102.4	107.4	106.1	103.9	105.4
2022[1]	115.6	118.8	101.0	108.1	107.2	120.1	112.4	97.5	125.7	103.8	110.8	105.7	105.1	106.9
2023[1]	118.0	122.2	103.1	106.8	108.3	126.0	113.3	99.4	130.1	105.1	112.3	107.1	109.7	110.6

1 = NAICS basis, not continuous with previous years, which are based on the SIC.

Gross Domestic Product by Region and State—Continued

(Millions of chained 1997 or 2017 dollars; index numbers)

Year	Louisiana	Maine	Maryland	Massachusetts	Michigan	Minnesota	Mississippi	Missouri	Montana	Nebraska	Nevada	New Hampshire	New Jersey
VALUE													
Chained 1997 Dollars													
1980	19,252	93,518	130,465	190,628	87,377	36,032	95,522	15,018	31,159	22,324	16,236	165,044	24,597
1981	19,384	95,346	133,647	190,543	89,820	37,270	96,740	15,606	32,929	23,256	16,905	169,389	24,949
1982	19,610	94,470	134,243	178,645	88,444	36,090	95,532	14,916	32,135	22,994	17,246	169,773	24,540
1983	20,471	99,052	142,103	190,879	91,405	36,857	98,611	14,932	31,360	23,738	18,344	181,669	24,951
1984	21,917	105,743	155,335	206,385	100,958	39,379	107,071	15,023	33,716	24,833	20,558	196,143	26,158
1985	22,858	111,803	164,593	215,019	104,958	40,474	108,667	14,635	34,881	25,888	22,435	206,429	27,135
1986	23,880	117,037	172,628	218,860	105,789	40,569	111,652	14,521	34,264	27,351	23,933	216,138	26,881
1987	25,426	123,260	183,712	221,362	110,916	43,229	116,060	14,624	34,351	29,144	26,669	230,997	26,932
1988	27,344	131,777	194,619	230,563	115,398	44,252	121,171	14,497	36,304	31,701	28,319	248,031	27,464
1989	27,882	134,612	195,609	234,224	118,868	44,669	123,688	15,089	37,389	34,125	28,278	251,515	28,056
1990	27,644	136,165	189,730	229,534	120,078	44,853	122,285	15,355	39,011	36,891	27,259	253,360	28,714
1991	26,836	133,662	183,996	225,576	120,067	45,841	124,167	15,739	40,250	37,713	27,411	252,718	31,980
1992	27,176	134,748	186,430	235,241	126,777	48,317	127,857	16,566	42,242	40,564	28,486	256,965	33,855
1993	27,337	137,003	187,751	242,175	127,068	50,440	128,278	17,285	42,385	43,994	28,832	259,805	37,463
1994	28,058	142,086	196,432	263,500	134,715	53,852	137,379	17,932	45,807	48,267	30,113	265,388	42,030
1995	28,769	144,424	203,189	264,125	138,724	56,528	144,371	18,036	46,556	51,081	32,379	271,764	42,733
1996	29,627	147,889	214,299	273,563	147,643	58,230	150,268	18,342	49,276	55,725	34,858	283,608	44,605
1997	30,775	154,783	226,880	286,408	156,650	59,875	158,308	18,932	50,308	59,467	36,935	292,671	48,683
Chained 2017 Dollars													
1997 [1]	202,387	46,325	237,589	322,390	423,460	225,480	88,384	243,724	30,145	73,974	97,209	51,027	454,064
1998 [1]	209,357	48,139	248,663	335,504	431,274	237,724	90,960	249,234	31,456	75,750	102,779	54,955	461,237
1999 [1]	213,475	50,620	258,913	353,838	457,638	247,005	93,598	256,290	31,633	77,421	110,091	56,913	477,828
2000 [1]	206,556	52,959	269,301	382,600	467,654	263,346	93,957	262,665	32,514	80,268	114,810	60,743	503,902
2001 [1]	210,535	54,066	281,054	388,181	453,302	263,519	93,516	260,381	32,690	82,268	116,267	61,719	509,632
2002 [1]	214,856	55,407	290,400	388,452	465,788	268,983	94,562	264,998	33,664	83,433	120,180	63,474	517,752
2003 [1]	223,576	56,882	297,691	397,070	477,085	280,797	98,762	271,971	35,250	88,311	125,905	66,119	529,816
2004 [1]	234,621	58,935	311,505	407,886	485,083	293,754	101,370	279,128	36,950	90,608	139,373	68,428	536,174
2005 [1]	249,561	59,590	325,645	417,076	493,796	301,761	103,692	285,342	38,849	94,556	150,681	69,556	546,358
2006 [1]	247,140	59,986	329,874	426,926	483,764	302,273	105,880	286,558	40,055	97,323	156,298	71,425	555,211
2007 [1]	234,216	60,033	331,764	440,374	482,935	304,208	107,714	288,321	42,058	99,781	157,734	71,944	560,824
2008 [1]	237,062	59,845	338,165	447,527	455,257	309,290	109,434	297,882	42,049	99,860	152,746	71,196	573,203
2009 [1]	241,869	58,772	336,286	441,308	416,297	296,875	105,360	289,567	40,938	99,986	140,304	70,499	546,362
2010 [1]	253,467	59,959	352,623	462,331	441,272	308,092	106,712	295,986	42,470	103,941	142,614	72,950	554,764
2011 [1]	241,236	59,430	360,156	472,664	453,989	315,213	106,491	292,984	43,532	109,734	144,341	73,465	548,479
2012 [1]	242,417	59,182	361,562	483,286	463,303	321,054	108,647	296,514	44,329	109,686	142,986	74,083	560,730
2013 [1]	236,482	59,014	364,633	486,992	472,780	329,775	109,033	302,026	45,115	111,382	144,549	75,503	570,952
2014 [1]	243,043	59,590	370,344	496,251	479,535	338,624	109,300	303,618	46,167	115,652	145,304	76,836	570,696
2015 [1]	239,584	60,563	378,746	514,399	490,619	345,456	109,402	308,010	47,766	119,641	151,056	79,319	581,415
2016 [1]	235,554	62,037	391,951	521,663	500,160	350,604	109,911	308,423	47,190	121,303	156,007	80,736	587,050
2017 [1]	239,831	63,001	399,715	530,129	505,102	354,722	110,281	311,274	48,471	123,220	163,199	81,180	590,087
2018 [1]	245,220	64,806	402,481	549,262	516,843	364,800	110,175	314,182	49,455	125,543	168,639	82,270	606,892
2019 [1]	246,361	66,351	402,346	566,706	517,845	368,689	110,538	320,881	50,319	127,482	175,771	84,031	617,111
2020 [1]	228,825	67,421	388,532	556,196	502,484	358,127	109,894	315,276	50,160	126,891	165,794	83,182	595,973
2021 [1]	234,014	70,870	405,905	591,912	531,500	374,733	114,199	330,118	52,952	133,496	181,103	89,890	629,011
2022 [1]	231,262	72,414	412,283	604,358	539,898	379,112	114,153	336,626	53,983	137,078	187,226	90,151	646,731
2023 [1]	238,196	73,781	420,997	615,148	547,772	383,619	114,950	344,115	55,193	144,183	192,216	91,255	656,480
QUANTITY INDEX													
1997=100													
1980	78.4	62.6	60.4	57.5	66.6	55.8	60.2	60.3	79.3	61.9	37.5	44.0	56.4
1981	80.5	63.0	61.6	58.9	66.5	57.3	62.2	61.1	82.4	65.5	39.1	45.8	57.9
1982	77.5	63.7	61.0	59.2	62.4	56.5	60.3	60.3	78.8	63.9	38.7	46.7	58.0
1983	76.6	66.5	64.0	62.6	66.6	58.4	61.6	62.3	78.9	62.3	39.9	49.7	62.1
1984	81.1	71.2	68.3	68.5	72.1	64.4	65.8	67.6	79.4	67.0	41.8	55.7	67.0
1985	82.6	74.3	72.2	72.5	75.1	67.0	67.6	68.6	77.3	69.3	43.5	60.7	70.5
1986	82.4	77.6	75.6	76.1	76.4	67.5	67.8	70.5	76.7	68.1	46.0	64.8	73.9
1987	82.8	82.6	79.6	81.0	77.3	70.8	72.2	73.3	77.2	68.3	49.0	72.2	78.9
1988	85.8	88.9	85.1	85.8	80.5	73.7	73.9	76.5	76.6	72.2	53.3	76.7	84.7
1989	85.8	90.6	87.0	86.2	81.8	75.9	74.6	78.1	79.7	74.3	57.4	76.6	85.9
1990	87.5	89.8	88.0	83.6	80.1	76.7	74.9	77.2	81.1	77.5	62.0	73.8	86.6
1991	87.3	87.2	86.4	81.1	78.8	76.6	76.6	78.4	83.1	80.0	63.4	74.2	86.3
1992	81.7	88.3	87.1	82.2	82.1	80.9	80.7	80.8	87.5	84.0	68.2	77.1	87.8
1993	83.6	88.8	88.5	82.8	84.6	81.1	84.2	81.0	91.3	84.3	74.0	78.1	88.8
1994	90.6	91.2	91.8	86.6	92.0	86.0	89.9	86.8	94.7	91.1	81.2	81.5	90.7
1995	95.5	93.5	93.3	89.6	92.2	88.6	94.4	91.2	95.3	92.5	85.9	87.7	92.9
1996	96.4	96.3	95.5	94.5	95.5	94.3	97.3	94.9	96.9	97.9	93.7	94.4	96.9
1997	100.0	100.0	100.0	100.0	100.0	100.0	100.0	100.0	100.0	100.0	100.0	100.0	100.0

Gross Domestic Product by Region and State—Continued

(Millions of chained 1997 or 2017 dollars; index numbers)

Year	Louisiana	Maine	Maryland	Massachusetts	Michigan	Minnesota	Mississippi	Missouri	Montana	Nebraska	Nevada	New Hampshire	New Jersey
2017 = 100													
1997 [1]	84.4	73.5	59.4	60.8	83.8	63.6	80.1	78.3	62.2	60.0	59.6	62.9	76.9
1998 [1]	87.3	76.4	62.2	63.3	85.4	67.0	82.5	80.1	64.9	61.5	63.0	67.7	78.2
1999 [1]	89.0	80.3	64.8	66.7	90.6	69.6	84.9	82.3	65.3	62.8	67.5	70.1	81.0
2000 [1]	86.1	84.1	67.4	72.2	92.6	74.2	85.2	84.4	67.1	65.1	70.4	74.8	85.4
2001 [1]	87.8	85.8	70.3	73.2	89.7	74.3	84.8	83.7	67.4	66.8	71.2	76.0	86.4
2002 [1]	89.6	87.9	72.7	73.3	92.2	75.8	85.7	85.1	69.5	67.7	73.6	78.2	87.7
2003 [1]	93.2	90.3	74.5	74.9	94.5	79.2	89.6	87.4	72.7	71.7	77.1	81.4	89.8
2004 [1]	97.8	93.5	77.9	76.9	96.0	82.8	91.9	89.7	76.2	73.5	85.4	84.3	90.9
2005 [1]	104.1	94.6	81.5	78.7	97.8	85.1	94.0	91.7	80.2	76.7	92.3	85.7	92.6
2006 [1]	103.0	95.2	82.5	80.5	95.8	85.2	96.0	92.1	82.6	79.0	95.8	88.0	94.1
2007 [1]	97.7	95.3	83.0	83.1	95.6	85.8	97.7	92.6	86.8	81.0	96.7	88.6	95.0
2008 [1]	98.8	95.0	84.6	84.4	90.1	87.2	99.2	95.7	86.8	81.0	93.6	87.7	97.1
2009 [1]	100.9	93.3	84.1	83.2	82.4	83.7	95.5	93.0	84.5	81.1	86.0	86.8	92.6
2010 [1]	105.7	95.2	88.2	87.2	87.4	86.9	96.8	95.1	87.6	84.4	87.4	89.9	94.0
2011 [1]	100.6	94.3	90.1	89.2	89.9	88.9	96.6	94.1	89.8	89.1	88.4	90.5	92.9
2012 [1]	101.1	93.9	90.5	91.2	91.7	90.5	98.5	95.3	91.5	89.0	87.6	91.3	95.0
2013 [1]	98.6	93.7	91.2	91.9	93.6	93.0	98.9	97.0	93.1	90.4	88.6	93.0	96.8
2014 [1]	101.3	94.6	92.7	93.6	94.9	95.5	99.1	97.5	95.2	93.9	89.0	94.7	96.7
2015 [1]	99.9	96.1	94.8	97.0	97.1	97.4	99.2	99.0	98.5	97.1	92.6	97.7	98.5
2016 [1]	98.2	98.5	98.1	98.4	99.0	98.8	99.7	99.1	97.4	98.4	95.6	99.5	99.5
2017 [1]	100.0	100.0	100.0	100.0	100.0	100.0	100.0	100.0	100.0	100.0	100.0	100.0	100.0
2018 [1]	102.2	102.9	100.7	103.6	102.3	102.8	99.9	100.9	102.0	101.9	103.3	101.3	102.8
2019 [1]	102.7	105.3	100.7	106.9	102.5	103.9	100.2	103.1	103.8	103.5	107.7	103.5	104.6
2020 [1]	95.4	107.0	97.2	104.9	99.5	101.0	99.6	101.3	103.5	103.0	101.6	102.5	101.0
2021 [1]	97.6	112.5	101.5	111.7	105.2	105.6	103.6	106.1	109.2	108.3	111.0	110.7	106.6
2022 [1]	96.4	114.9	103.1	114.0	106.9	106.9	103.5	108.1	111.4	111.2	114.7	111.1	109.6
2023 [1]	99.3	117.1	105.3	116.0	108.4	108.1	104.2	110.6	113.9	117.0	117.8	112.4	111.3

1 = NAICS basis, not continuous with previous years, which are based on the SIC.

Gross Domestic Product by Region and State—Continued

(Millions of chained 1997 or 2017 dollars; index numbers)

Year	New Mexico	New York	North Carolina	North Dakota	Ohio	Oklahoma	Oregon	Pennsylvania	Rhode Island	South Carolina	South Dakota	Tennessee
VALUE												
Chained 1997 Dollars												
1980	461,419	110,120	12,243	211,743	61,673	53,343	231,709	18,167	48,649	11,511	80,420	339,794
1981	469,897	113,991	14,085	213,962	65,276	51,928	232,708	18,609	50,326	12,201	82,680	361,250
1982	473,335	111,615	13,545	203,226	67,173	49,176	223,811	18,553	49,457	11,849	80,817	362,556
1983	483,340	117,269	13,282	211,442	63,976	49,722	229,968	19,086	52,632	11,778	85,226	362,005
1984	512,501	127,347	13,588	229,868	66,997	52,794	242,572	20,422	57,695	12,694	91,426	383,084
1985	526,285	135,374	13,668	238,150	68,101	54,080	248,495	21,754	59,771	13,174	94,918	400,230
1986	539,859	140,634	12,743	240,299	64,580	55,144	253,122	22,862	62,607	13,346	97,962	391,309
1987	562,846	147,274	13,074	247,287	63,487	56,988	266,991	23,871	67,198	13,623	104,884	389,772
1988	595,326	155,811	12,023	256,727	66,540	60,568	279,975	25,528	70,664	13,733	109,796	413,114
1989	594,267	160,953	12,733	262,187	66,722	62,292	284,585	26,214	72,984	13,961	110,896	423,660
1990	595,908	161,998	13,161	264,948	67,083	64,881	288,955	25,937	75,344	14,696	110,321	437,292
1991	577,446	162,239	13,118	263,064	67,424	65,969	289,708	25,005	76,010	15,411	114,266	444,358
1992	585,395	171,223	14,176	275,324	69,025	68,519	298,366	25,370	78,505	16,279	123,167	461,816
1993	588,213	176,678	13,987	277,702	70,761	72,548	303,021	25,653	81,301	17,208	128,543	478,420
1994	596,435	189,755	15,045	294,384	72,406	76,924	311,576	25,882	85,856	18,141	136,301	505,162
1995	608,937	199,056	15,325	304,834	73,889	81,919	321,832	26,552	89,046	18,520	140,814	530,666
1996	634,107	206,757	16,508	315,189	77,538	93,489	330,321	27,006	91,716	19,410	145,391	562,108
1997	664,679	221,259	16,501	332,476	81,106	100,363	342,662	28,717	96,465	19,765	152,687	606,982
Chained 2017 Dollars												
1997[1]	67,993	1,085,934	340,580	22,695	501,214	111,865	124,841	521,712	43,435	144,973	27,116	226,833
1998[1]	67,718	1,112,324	351,978	23,971	518,604	114,928	130,425	534,934	45,381	150,733	28,772	240,963
1999[1]	71,421	1,172,150	372,030	24,070	530,746	116,968	133,762	552,164	46,831	157,646	30,038	248,458
2000[1]	72,734	1,217,036	384,115	24,990	541,006	121,170	145,094	566,251	49,114	161,880	32,125	251,030
2001[1]	72,996	1,240,755	387,434	25,330	534,612	125,696	144,487	577,678	49,705	162,837	32,397	250,311
2002[1]	75,346	1,228,581	393,686	26,592	546,688	127,930	147,433	583,507	51,284	167,333	35,776	258,542
2003[1]	78,767	1,236,563	404,583	28,327	557,025	130,148	154,445	598,810	52,933	174,271	36,142	267,589
2004[1]	85,751	1,269,433	420,579	28,636	572,309	134,607	163,046	614,957	55,161	177,169	37,617	281,564
2005[1]	86,296	1,301,438	442,306	29,629	584,868	140,360	168,734	626,290	55,886	183,268	39,331	289,064
2006[1]	88,555	1,339,569	470,664	30,911	582,638	149,367	177,222	626,590	57,416	187,386	39,962	295,668
2007[1]	89,392	1,353,799	477,921	32,529	585,403	152,880	180,724	649,638	56,231	193,387	41,646	294,820
2008[1]	89,013	1,328,096	492,689	35,030	580,389	158,988	184,843	665,148	54,977	192,497	43,279	298,527
2009[1]	90,829	1,379,505	473,611	35,971	550,982	156,857	176,952	645,207	54,482	184,081	44,256	287,309
2010[1]	90,721	1,431,624	482,030	38,697	563,816	158,086	180,738	666,806	56,051	188,777	44,811	292,687
2011[1]	90,552	1,440,347	484,200	43,300	580,251	163,859	185,959	676,468	56,027	193,221	47,630	301,509
2012[1]	90,762	1,496,280	488,127	53,327	586,541	172,016	187,352	689,007	56,487	195,406	48,654	311,754
2013[1]	90,104	1,501,818	497,457	54,691	603,057	176,087	189,610	704,195	57,037	200,147	48,610	318,348
2014[1]	92,621	1,535,376	509,782	60,193	624,973	186,574	195,808	718,692	57,603	206,078	49,641	323,880
2015[1]	93,504	1,565,835	525,229	58,695	633,275	193,793	205,582	734,145	58,388	213,212	50,861	335,461
2016[1]	93,044	1,590,568	536,309	54,756	638,158	190,094	214,769	744,847	58,630	220,559	51,264	343,545
2017[1]	93,210	1,624,801	546,810	56,530	652,188	192,539	225,535	754,318	58,772	224,938	51,615	355,418
2018[1]	96,077	1,665,187	556,574	58,516	656,212	196,031	234,308	763,855	58,740	231,663	51,938	362,364
2019[1]	100,446	1,709,751	568,476	59,142	674,123	199,462	239,911	772,530	59,867	237,511	52,360	370,088
2020[1]	97,512	1,650,567	564,794	55,699	654,586	190,752	237,670	736,471	58,155	233,712	52,692	366,555
2021[1]	99,572	1,724,472	597,316	55,401	686,206	193,518	250,099	764,602	60,777	244,854	55,140	396,576
2022[1]	101,315	1,763,525	609,058	54,799	689,681	191,583	254,708	772,336	62,191	250,873	54,959	412,101
2023[1]	105,463	1,775,714	625,682	58,015	698,217	201,659	260,111	789,502	63,173	259,930	56,309	425,410
QUANTITY INDEX												
1997=100												
1980	50.5	69.4	49.8	74.2	63.7	76.0	53.2	67.6	63.3	50.4	58.2	52.7
1981	51.2	70.7	51.5	85.4	64.4	80.5	51.7	67.9	64.8	52.2	61.7	54.2
1982	50.4	71.2	50.4	82.1	61.1	82.8	49.0	65.3	64.6	51.3	60.0	52.9
1983	51.3	72.7	53.0	80.5	63.6	78.9	49.5	67.1	66.5	54.6	59.6	55.8
1984	53.7	77.1	57.6	82.3	69.1	82.6	52.6	70.8	71.1	59.8	64.2	59.9
1985	55.7	79.2	61.2	82.8	71.6	84.0	53.9	72.5	75.8	62.0	66.7	62.2
1986	55.2	81.2	63.6	77.2	72.3	79.6	54.9	73.9	79.6	64.9	67.5	64.2
1987	55.3	84.7	66.6	79.2	74.4	78.3	56.8	77.9	83.1	69.7	68.9	68.7
1988	56.4	89.6	70.4	72.9	77.2	82.0	60.3	81.7	88.9	73.3	69.5	71.9
1989	57.6	89.4	72.7	77.2	78.9	82.3	62.1	83.1	91.3	75.7	70.6	72.6
1990	59.0	89.7	73.2	79.8	79.7	82.7	64.6	84.3	90.3	78.1	74.4	72.3
1991	65.7	86.9	73.3	79.5	79.1	83.1	65.7	84.5	87.1	78.8	78.0	74.8
1992	69.5	88.1	77.4	85.9	82.8	85.1	68.3	87.1	88.3	81.4	82.4	80.7
1993	77.0	88.5	79.9	84.8	83.5	87.2	72.3	88.4	89.3	84.3	87.1	84.2
1994	86.3	89.7	85.8	91.2	88.5	89.3	76.6	90.9	90.1	89.0	91.8	89.3
1995	87.8	91.6	90.0	92.9	91.7	91.1	81.6	93.9	92.5	92.3	93.7	92.2
1996	91.6	95.4	93.4	100.0	94.8	95.6	93.2	96.4	94.0	95.1	98.2	95.2
1997	100.0	100.0	100.0	100.0	100.0	100.0	100.0	100.0	100.0	100.0	100.0	100.0

Gross Domestic Product by Region and State—Continued

(Millions of chained 1997 or 2017 dollars; index numbers)

Year	New Mexico	New York	North Carolina	North Dakota	Ohio	Oklahoma	Oregon	Pennsylvania	Rhode Island	South Carolina	South Dakota	Tennessee
2017 = 100												
1997[1]	72.9	66.8	62.3	40.1	76.9	58.1	55.4	69.2	73.9	64.5	52.5	63.8
1998[1]	72.7	68.5	64.4	42.4	79.5	59.7	57.8	70.9	77.2	67.0	55.7	67.8
1999[1]	76.6	72.1	68.0	42.6	81.4	60.8	59.3	73.2	79.7	70.1	58.2	69.9
2000[1]	78.0	74.9	70.2	44.2	83.0	62.9	64.3	75.1	83.6	72.0	62.2	70.6
2001[1]	78.3	76.4	70.9	44.8	82.0	65.3	64.1	76.6	84.6	72.4	62.8	70.4
2002[1]	80.8	75.6	72.0	47.0	83.8	66.4	65.4	77.4	87.3	74.4	69.3	72.7
2003[1]	84.5	76.1	74.0	50.1	85.4	67.6	68.5	79.4	90.1	77.5	70.0	75.3
2004[1]	92.0	78.1	76.9	50.7	87.8	69.9	72.3	81.5	93.9	78.8	72.9	79.2
2005[1]	92.6	80.1	80.9	52.4	89.7	72.9	74.8	83.0	95.1	81.5	76.2	81.3
2006[1]	95.0	82.4	86.1	54.7	89.3	77.6	78.6	83.1	97.7	83.3	77.4	83.2
2007[1]	95.9	83.3	87.4	57.5	89.8	79.4	80.1	86.1	95.7	86.0	80.7	83.0
2008[1]	95.5	81.7	90.1	62.0	89.0	82.6	82.0	88.2	93.5	85.6	83.8	84.0
2009[1]	97.4	84.9	86.6	63.6	84.5	81.5	78.5	85.5	92.7	81.8	85.7	80.8
2010[1]	97.3	88.1	88.2	68.5	86.5	82.1	80.1	88.4	95.4	83.9	86.8	82.4
2011[1]	97.1	88.6	88.6	76.6	89.0	85.1	82.5	89.7	95.3	85.9	92.3	84.8
2012[1]	97.4	92.1	89.3	94.3	89.9	89.3	83.1	91.3	96.1	86.9	94.3	87.7
2013[1]	96.7	92.4	91.0	96.7	92.5	91.5	84.1	93.4	97.0	89.0	94.2	89.6
2014[1]	99.4	94.5	93.2	106.5	95.8	96.9	86.8	95.3	98.0	91.6	96.2	91.1
2015[1]	100.3	96.4	96.1	103.8	97.1	100.7	91.2	97.3	99.3	94.8	98.5	94.4
2016[1]	99.8	97.9	98.1	96.9	97.8	98.7	95.2	98.7	99.8	98.1	99.3	96.7
2017[1]	100.0	100.0	100.0	100.0	100.0	100.0	100.0	100.0	100.0	100.0	100.0	100.0
2018[1]	103.1	102.5	101.8	103.5	100.6	101.8	103.9	101.3	99.9	103.0	100.6	102.0
2019[1]	107.8	105.2	104.0	104.6	103.4	103.6	106.4	102.4	101.9	105.6	101.4	104.1
2020[1]	104.6	101.6	103.3	98.5	100.4	99.1	105.4	97.6	99.0	103.9	102.1	103.1
2021[1]	106.8	106.1	109.2	98.0	105.2	100.5	110.9	101.4	103.4	108.9	106.8	111.6
2022[1]	108.7	108.5	111.4	96.9	105.7	99.5	112.9	102.4	105.8	111.5	106.5	115.9
2023[1]	113.1	109.3	114.4	102.6	107.1	104.7	115.3	104.7	107.5	115.6	109.1	119.7

1 = NAICS basis, not continuous with previous years, which are based on the SIC.

Gross Domestic Product by Region and State—Continued

(Millions of chained 1997 or 2017 dollars; index numbers)

Year	Texas	Utah	Vermont	Virginia	Washington	West Virginia	Wisconsin	Wyoming
VALUE								
Chained 1997 Dollars								
1980	27,127	8,540	115,633	100,522	29,233	91,254	13,547	271,111
1981	28,129	8,814	119,300	103,616	28,878	91,533	14,013	277,668
1982	27,956	8,777	119,714	103,652	28,069	89,641	13,124	280,768
1983	28,917	9,130	125,223	105,339	27,319	91,390	12,431	295,605
1984	31,159	9,590	133,820	109,176	28,766	96,922	13,028	322,249
1985	32,938	10,153	140,418	110,215	29,085	100,204	13,191	341,303
1986	32,467	10,597	147,618	115,190	28,673	101,810	12,581	358,010
1987	32,682	11,522	156,426	120,393	28,734	104,770	12,272	383,298
1988	34,413	12,521	164,558	127,672	30,865	111,180	13,050	407,276
1989	34,827	13,091	170,267	134,180	30,816	113,430	13,019	411,580
1990	36,697	13,313	173,022	141,946	31,349	115,638	13,673	404,914
1991	38,105	12,952	172,407	145,050	31,986	117,167	14,118	394,303
1992	39,564	13,562	175,795	150,245	32,880	123,617	14,327	400,774
1993	41,509	13,755	180,782	154,090	33,836	128,390	14,785	401,601
1994	44,958	14,178	188,082	159,470	35,963	135,190	15,105	415,642
1995	48,212	14,211	193,402	160,183	36,902	138,010	15,539	433,600
1996	52,980	14,839	201,703	169,162	37,750	144,558	15,968	452,476
1997	55,212	15,521	210,361	179,640	38,570	151,035	16,084	479,107
Chained 2017 Dollars								
1997[1]	860,047	86,284	21,372	319,993	281,522	60,365	222,979	24,258
1998[1]	920,060	91,313	22,267	338,932	299,817	61,726	232,087	24,805
1999[1]	957,247	95,207	23,562	356,392	322,722	63,692	242,026	25,867
2000[1]	989,905	98,649	24,845	372,914	325,858	63,365	248,572	26,614
2001[1]	1,020,517	100,244	25,682	386,445	317,861	63,600	252,942	28,338
2002[1]	1,042,584	102,828	26,523	390,242	321,977	64,466	257,967	28,901
2003[1]	1,052,132	104,829	27,548	404,522	327,645	65,107	265,746	29,807
2004[1]	1,111,189	111,319	28,989	421,744	335,449	66,078	275,412	30,780
2005[1]	1,143,413	118,430	29,283	442,090	358,396	67,889	282,066	32,463
2006[1]	1,225,147	127,539	29,421	451,263	372,145	68,900	287,147	36,656
2007[1]	1,288,829	133,800	29,297	457,569	394,222	69,374	289,855	39,505
2008[1]	1,287,192	133,663	30,169	462,035	401,093	70,967	286,205	41,641
2009[1]	1,285,560	130,959	29,566	460,075	390,814	70,887	277,279	40,600
2010[1]	1,323,059	133,739	30,891	475,699	403,471	71,824	287,653	39,136
2011[1]	1,370,175	138,301	31,664	479,571	411,576	73,175	293,664	38,930
2012[1]	1,438,354	140,623	31,898	483,041	426,447	73,125	299,008	38,085
2013[1]	1,511,807	145,027	31,495	488,741	439,472	73,949	301,551	38,409
2014[1]	1,559,636	150,076	31,848	488,919	456,187	74,111	309,426	39,287
2015[1]	1,634,127	155,432	32,043	498,944	476,715	74,261	315,688	40,064
2016[1]	1,633,863	162,528	32,313	505,108	495,725	73,513	319,272	37,854
2017[1]	1,667,313	172,075	32,589	515,167	527,169	75,172	321,887	37,620
2018[1]	1,746,543	182,106	32,828	527,768	561,786	77,407	328,832	37,977
2019[1]	1,802,913	192,699	33,208	541,070	588,930	76,787	333,699	38,558
2020[1]	1,772,186	194,754	32,307	533,828	590,401	73,953	322,973	36,181
2021[1]	1,873,473	209,975	33,861	562,888	630,820	75,521	334,517	36,930
2022[1]	1,924,008	213,898	34,609	576,964	641,144	76,526	335,689	37,294
2023[1]	2,032,933	219,181	35,074	590,802	672,125	80,136	336,461	39,322
QUANTITY INDEX								
1997=100								
1980	56.0	49.1	55.0	55.0	56.0	75.8	60.4	84.2
1981	59.5	50.9	56.8	56.7	57.7	74.9	60.6	87.1
1982	59.7	50.6	56.6	56.9	57.7	72.8	59.4	81.6
1983	59.6	52.4	58.8	59.5	58.6	70.8	60.5	77.3
1984	63.1	56.4	61.8	63.6	60.8	74.6	64.2	81.0
1985	65.9	59.7	65.4	66.8	61.4	75.4	66.3	82.0
1986	64.5	58.8	68.3	70.2	64.1	74.3	67.4	78.2
1987	64.2	59.2	74.2	74.4	67.0	74.5	69.4	76.3
1988	68.1	62.3	80.7	78.2	71.1	80.0	73.6	81.1
1989	69.8	63.1	84.3	80.9	74.7	79.9	75.1	80.9
1990	72.0	66.5	85.8	82.3	79.0	81.3	76.6	85.0
1991	73.2	69.0	83.5	82.0	80.7	82.9	77.6	87.8
1992	76.1	71.7	87.4	83.6	83.6	85.2	81.8	89.1
1993	78.8	75.2	88.6	85.9	85.8	87.7	85.0	91.9
1994	83.2	81.4	91.3	89.4	88.8	93.2	89.5	93.9
1995	87.4	87.3	91.6	91.9	89.2	95.7	91.4	96.6
1996	92.6	96.0	95.6	95.9	94.2	97.9	95.7	99.3
1997	100.0	100.0	100.0	100.0	100.0	100.0	100.0	100.0

Gross Domestic Product by Region and State—Continued

(Millions of chained 1997 or 2017 dollars; index numbers)

Year	Texas	Utah	Vermont	Virginia	Washington	West Virginia	Wisconsin	Wyoming
2017 = 100								
1997 [1]	51.6	50.1	65.6	62.1	53.4	80.3	69.3	64.5
1998 [1]	55.2	53.1	68.3	65.8	56.9	82.1	72.1	65.9
1999 [1]	57.4	55.3	72.3	69.2	61.2	84.7	75.2	68.8
2000 [1]	59.4	57.3	76.2	72.4	61.8	84.3	77.2	70.7
2001 [1]	61.2	58.3	78.8	75.0	60.3	84.6	78.6	75.3
2002 [1]	62.5	59.8	81.4	75.8	61.1	85.8	80.1	76.8
2003 [1]	63.1	60.9	84.5	78.5	62.2	86.6	82.6	79.2
2004 [1]	66.6	64.7	89.0	81.9	63.6	87.9	85.6	81.8
2005 [1]	68.6	68.8	89.9	85.8	68.0	90.3	87.6	86.3
2006 [1]	73.5	74.1	90.3	87.6	70.6	91.7	89.2	97.4
2007 [1]	77.3	77.8	89.9	88.8	74.8	92.3	90.0	105.0
2008 [1]	77.2	77.7	92.6	89.7	76.1	94.4	88.9	110.7
2009 [1]	77.1	76.1	90.7	89.3	74.1	94.3	86.1	107.9
2010 [1]	79.4	77.7	94.8	92.3	76.5	95.5	89.4	104.0
2011 [1]	82.2	80.4	97.2	93.1	78.1	97.3	91.2	103.5
2012 [1]	86.3	81.7	97.9	93.8	80.9	97.3	92.9	101.2
2013 [1]	90.7	84.3	96.6	94.9	83.4	98.4	93.7	102.1
2014 [1]	93.5	87.2	97.7	94.9	86.5	98.6	96.1	104.4
2015 [1]	98.0	90.3	98.3	96.9	90.4	98.8	98.1	106.5
2016 [1]	98.0	94.5	99.2	98.0	94.0	97.8	99.2	100.6
2017 [1]	100.0	100.0	100.0	100.0	100.0	100.0	100.0	100.0
2018 [1]	104.8	105.8	100.7	102.4	106.6	103.0	102.2	100.9
2019 [1]	108.1	112.0	101.9	105.0	111.7	102.1	103.7	102.5
2020 [1]	106.3	113.2	99.1	103.6	112.0	98.4	100.3	96.2
2021 [1]	112.4	122.0	103.9	109.3	119.7	100.5	103.9	98.2
2022 [1]	115.4	124.3	106.2	112.0	121.6	101.8	104.3	99.1
2023 [1]	121.9	127.4	107.6	114.7	127.5	106.6	104.5	104.5

1 = NAICS basis, not continuous with previous years, which are based on the SIC.

Gross Domestic Product by Metropolitan Statistical Area

(Millions of chained 2017 dollars.)

Metropolitan Statistical Area	2017	2018	2019	2020	2021	2022
Abilene, TX	6,827	7,141	7,427	7,354	7,574	7,895
Akron, OH	36,425	36,883	37,471	36,099	37,510	37,703
Albany, GA	5,694	5,702	5,840	5,798	6,069	6,096
Albany-Lebanon, OR	4,506	4,802	4,921	4,789	4,893	4,997
Albany-Schenectady-Troy, NY	61,024	61,119	64,250	62,574	66,760	68,359
Albuquerque, NM	41,881	42,671	43,914	43,195	45,286	46,218
Alexandria, LA	6,082	6,161	6,147	6,021	6,128	6,018
Allentown-Bethlehem-Easton, PA-NJ	44,541	44,765	46,551	44,682	46,291	46,645
Altoona, PA	5,850	5,945	6,081	5,916	6,114	6,106
Amarillo, TX	13,044	13,439	13,721	13,809	14,318	14,333
Ames, IA	6,445	6,563	6,654	6,569	6,852	6,825
Anchorage, AK	25,843	26,030	25,950	25,374	26,090	26,077
Ann Arbor, MI	24,040	24,650	25,481	24,988	26,314	26,781
Anniston-Oxford, AL	4,244	4,343	4,555	4,461	4,625	4,608
Appleton, WI	13,810	14,242	14,583	13,938	14,309	14,196
Asheville, NC	19,858	20,528	21,417	20,263	21,458	22,107
Athens-Clarke County, GA	9,980	10,331	10,264	9,827	10,365	10,604
Atlanta-Sandy Springs-Alpharetta, GA	398,209	413,029	429,946	414,750	442,449	455,333
Atlantic City-Hammonton, NJ	13,522	13,616	13,792	12,986	14,018	14,200
Auburn-Opelika, AL	6,139	6,112	6,342	6,187	6,561	6,861
Augusta-Richmond County, GA-SC	27,076	27,500	27,974	27,766	28,260	28,398
Austin-Round Rock-Georgetown, TX	141,103	149,307	158,684	163,075	180,241	193,632
Bakersfield, CA	43,812	43,894	45,414	45,440	45,334	43,822
Baltimore-Columbia-Towson, MD	198,332	200,410	201,675	194,651	204,205	208,025
Bangor, ME	6,361	6,600	6,762	6,783	7,004	7,141
Barnstable Town, MA	12,765	13,042	13,537	12,655	13,491	13,772
Baton Rouge, LA	52,326	55,749	54,607	50,510	51,157	51,649
Battle Creek, MI	6,451	6,467	6,412	6,372	6,913	6,985
Bay City, MI	3,540	3,632	3,536	3,550	3,841	3,851
Beaumont-Port Arthur, TX	24,454	25,657	25,099	21,737	22,261	21,847
Beckley, WV	3,990	4,065	4,185	3,918	4,023	4,237
Bellingham, WA	11,651	12,558	13,655	14,158	14,284	13,584
Bend, OR	9,524	9,882	10,464	10,479	11,520	11,781
Billings, MT	10,234	10,294	10,047	9,851	10,489	10,149
Binghamton, NY	10,763	10,788	11,025	10,410	10,716	10,773
Birmingham-Hoover, AL	60,646	61,853	62,865	62,129	65,261	66,209
Bismarck, ND	7,657	7,518	7,453	7,152	7,388	7,257
Blacksburg-Christiansburg, VA	7,016	7,365	7,264	7,053	7,599	7,911
Bloomington, IL	14,477	14,531	14,906	12,328	12,368	12,402
Bloomington, IN	7,407	7,670	7,588	7,283	7,517	7,784
Bloomsburg-Berwick, PA	4,410	4,391	4,502	4,285	4,464	4,557
Boise City, ID	32,267	34,798	36,495	37,045	40,145	42,279
Boston-Cambridge-Newton, MA-NH	433,844	451,336	467,520	460,535	492,999	504,105
Boulder, CO	26,256	27,219	29,676	29,149	31,165	32,366
Bowling Green, KY	7,184	7,131	7,484	7,422	7,933	8,338
Bremerton-Silverdale-Port Orchard, WA	11,973	12,263	12,397	12,734	13,081	13,212
Bridgeport-Stamford-Norwalk, CT	91,838	90,875	88,934	83,856	87,236	90,361
Brownsville-Harlingen, TX	10,734	10,950	11,200	10,913	11,660	12,033
Brunswick, GA	4,535	4,698	4,616	4,508	4,810	4,907
Buffalo-Cheektowaga, NY	66,331	66,983	68,812	66,832	69,329	71,301
Burlington, NC	6,088	6,125	6,296	6,302	6,675	6,675
Burlington-South Burlington, VT	13,704	13,933	14,193	13,681	14,582	15,014
California-Lexington Park, MD	7,354	7,392	7,536	7,860	7,844	7,672
Canton-Massillon, OH	18,122	17,881	18,192	17,171	18,082	18,083
Cape Coral-Fort Myers, FL	31,284	32,565	33,089	33,048	35,789	37,490
Cape Girardeau, MO-IL	4,327	4,421	4,430	4,281	4,422	4,417
Carbondale-Marion, IL	5,593	5,745	5,739	5,491	5,561	5,773
Carson City, NV	3,397	3,474	3,695	3,507	3,582	3,628
Casper, WY	5,595	5,920	5,678	5,070	5,002	4,989
Cedar Rapids, IA	18,323	18,658	18,308	17,879	18,847	18,854
Chambersburg-Waynesboro, PA	6,302	6,400	6,239	5,948	6,101	6,162
Champaign-Urbana, IL	11,567	11,476	11,608	11,410	11,818	12,085
Charleston, WV	12,812	13,533	12,864	12,063	12,392	12,567
Charleston-North Charleston, SC	41,713	43,398	45,108	44,302	46,533	48,651
Charlotte-Concord-Gastonia, NC-SC	168,120	171,576	177,258	179,456	190,504	194,262
Charlottesville, VA	13,408	13,679	13,744	13,189	14,345	14,820
Chattanooga, TN-GA	29,616	29,878	30,328	30,204	32,135	34,003
Cheyenne, WY	5,429	5,727	6,009	5,664	5,986	5,847
Chicago-Naperville-Elgin, IL-IN-WI	674,568	691,186	697,334	659,808	696,360	705,659
Chico, CA	9,181	9,273	9,448	8,879	9,070	9,107
Cincinnati, OH-KY-IN	145,242	145,312	152,467	149,379	155,513	157,024
Clarksville, TN-KY	12,303	12,436	12,616	12,692	13,491	13,632
Cleveland, TN	4,678	4,720	4,722	4,867	5,103	5,189

Gross Domestic Product by Metropolitan Statistical Area—Continued

(Millions of chained 2017 dollars.)

Metropolitan Statistical Area	2017	2018	2019	2020	2021	2022
Cleveland-Elyria, OH	128,645	130,645	133,967	129,098	135,547	138,260
Coeur d'Alene, ID	6,046	6,423	6,575	6,884	7,661	7,949
College Station-Bryan, TX	12,462	12,997	13,580	13,564	14,174	14,510
Colorado Springs, CO	35,087	36,242	37,712	38,855	40,926	41,331
Columbia, MO	9,958	10,020	10,423	10,111	10,610	10,612
Columbia, SC	41,010	41,652	42,417	42,244	44,430	45,543
Columbus, GA-AL	14,601	14,627	14,870	14,715	14,919	14,452
Columbus, IN	6,367	6,846	6,780	6,283	6,539	6,997
Columbus, OH	129,945	131,538	135,607	134,048	143,198	144,464
Corpus Christi, TX	21,073	21,759	22,343	21,358	22,092	21,042
Corvallis, OR	4,319	4,519	4,602	4,518	4,722	4,770
Crestview-Fort Walton Beach-Destin, FL	14,386	14,991	15,862	16,298	17,870	18,346
Cumberland, MD-WV	3,790	3,853	3,867	3,733	3,746	3,663
Dallas-Fort Worth-Arlington, TX	483,732	506,220	525,852	519,283	560,290	592,452
Dalton, GA	6,886	6,844	6,878	6,670	7,035	7,268
Danville, IL	3,203	3,211	3,201	3,045	3,156	3,226
Daphne-Fairhope-Foley, AL	7,383	7,759	8,149	8,102	8,739	8,924
Davenport-Moline-Rock Island, IA-IL	21,555	21,409	21,588	21,148	21,649	21,599
Dayton-Kettering, OH	42,547	43,183	44,586	43,929	45,493	45,837
Decatur, AL	6,090	6,217	6,171	6,297	6,433	6,597
Decatur, IL	6,950	6,753	6,477	6,304	6,871	7,021
Deltona-Daytona Beach-Ormond Beach, FL	20,582	21,186	21,618	21,845	23,013	23,588
Denver-Aurora-Lakewood, CO	202,210	211,193	222,302	223,271	239,402	249,653
Des Moines-West Des Moines, IA	51,811	51,930	53,816	55,169	58,996	57,783
Detroit-Warren-Dearborn, MI	256,207	261,548	261,186	250,061	264,723	269,532
Dothan, AL	6,356	6,409	6,542	6,593	6,849	6,716
Dover, DE	7,633	7,813	8,384	8,001	8,255	8,312
Dubuque, IA	6,390	6,379	6,624	6,772	7,049	6,866
Duluth, MN-WI	13,555	13,868	14,152	13,420	13,889	13,821
Durham-Chapel Hill, NC	46,431	48,727	50,044	51,329	54,380	56,137
East Stroudsburg, PA	7,597	7,669	8,263	7,897	8,360	8,326
Eau Claire, WI	8,950	9,145	9,337	8,846	9,138	9,189
El Centro, CA	8,039	8,001	8,286	8,640	8,201	8,518
Elizabethtown-Fort Knox, KY	5,939	5,878	6,049	5,968	6,323	6,411
Elkhart-Goshen, IN	16,442	16,608	16,065	15,662	18,721	20,013
Elmira, NY	3,691	3,742	3,743	3,525	3,633	3,638
El Paso, TX	30,410	31,352	32,635	32,606	34,498	34,910
Enid, OK	2,849	2,806	2,796	2,632	2,774	2,708
Erie, PA	11,500	11,600	11,677	10,980	11,164	11,189
Eugene-Springfield, OR	15,867	16,302	16,364	16,258	17,376	17,551
Evansville, IN-KY	17,861	18,372	19,412	18,468	20,100	19,589
Fairbanks, AK	5,766	5,667	5,669	5,462	5,646	5,532
Fargo, ND-MN	14,963	15,070	15,405	14,904	15,637	15,647
Farmington, NM	5,757	5,571	5,623	5,198	5,138	5,171
Fayetteville, NC	20,430	20,637	21,117	21,157	21,991	21,818
Fayetteville-Springdale-Rogers, AR	26,265	27,043	27,666	28,797	31,427	32,339
Flagstaff, AZ	7,898	7,901	7,675	6,954	7,484	7,697
Flint, MI	15,932	16,336	16,614	15,314	15,694	15,583
Florence, SC	9,628	9,651	9,847	9,613	9,919	9,903
Florence-Muscle Shoals, AL	5,105	5,215	5,217	5,157	5,306	5,408
Fond du Lac, WI	5,100	5,214	5,279	5,021	5,151	5,174
Fort Collins, CO	18,594	19,480	20,426	20,432	21,886	22,240
Fort Smith, AR-OK	9,253	9,477	9,627	9,528	9,841	10,014
Fort Wayne, IN	22,445	23,295	23,463	21,765	23,327	24,292
Fresno, CA	42,569	43,779	44,985	44,299	45,813	45,388
Gadsden, AL	3,096	3,131	3,067	2,836	2,901	2,924
Gainesville, FL	14,484	14,965	15,335	15,386	16,326	16,690
Gainesville, GA	10,518	11,029	11,295	11,587	12,134	12,921
Gettysburg, PA	4,038	3,939	3,856	3,657	3,774	3,692
Glens Falls, NY	6,115	6,111	6,492	6,375	6,675	6,721
Goldsboro, NC	4,894	4,870	4,868	4,745	4,947	4,951
Grand Forks, ND-MN	5,409	5,431	5,474	5,323	5,442	5,369
Grand Island, NE	4,050	4,106	4,123	4,078	4,450	4,402
Grand Junction, CO	6,404	6,686	6,825	6,635	6,886	6,893
Grand Rapids-Kentwood, MI	58,891	60,850	61,034	60,202	64,352	65,941
Grants Pass, OR	2,650	2,765	2,947	2,898	3,050	3,056
Great Falls, MT	3,716	3,765	3,720	3,680	3,781	3,857
Greeley, CO	18,534	20,593	21,723	19,737	20,179	18,411
Green Bay, WI	20,005	20,648	20,745	20,181	20,604	20,815
Greensboro-High Point, NC	41,216	41,410	41,098	39,588	41,004	41,406
Greenville, NC	9,658	9,399	9,294	8,990	9,243	9,399
Greenville-Anderson, SC	43,799	45,521	46,232	45,146	47,174	48,530

Gross Domestic Product by Metropolitan Statistical Area—Continued

(Millions of chained 2017 dollars.)

Metropolitan Statistical Area	2017	2018	2019	2020	2021	2022
Gulfport-Biloxi, MS	17,330	16,998	17,453	17,818	18,617	18,726
Hagerstown-Martinsburg, MD-WV	11,327	11,664	11,465	10,919	11,598	11,561
Hammond, LA	4,086	4,096	4,339	4,223	4,382	4,299
Hanford-Corcoran, CA	6,443	6,337	6,454	6,551	6,592	6,608
Harrisburg-Carlisle, PA	38,685	39,392	40,623	38,618	40,605	40,958
Harrisonburg, VA	7,665	7,860	7,985	7,590	8,205	8,693
Hartford-East Hartford-Middletown, CT	100,617	100,888	101,368	93,965	97,901	100,979
Hattiesburg, MS	6,262	6,249	6,148	6,055	6,488	6,537
Hickory-Lenoir-Morganton, NC	15,103	14,924	14,772	14,428	14,896	15,130
Hilton Head Island-Bluffton, SC	8,877	9,319	9,661	9,965	10,392	10,488
Hinesville, GA	3,791	3,833	3,849	3,757	4,070	4,007
Homosassa Springs, FL	3,704	3,890	4,147	4,209	4,460	4,615
Hot Springs, AR	3,297	3,379	3,433	3,396	3,489	3,499
Houma-Thibodaux, LA	9,241	9,580	9,539	8,952	8,821	8,814
Houston-The Woodlands-Sugar Land, TX	470,676	491,167	484,359	476,639	500,984	513,276
Huntington-Ashland, WV-KY-OH	14,670	15,382	15,631	14,396	14,701	14,598
Huntsville, AL	27,521	28,602	30,151	30,667	32,307	33,486
Idaho Falls, ID	7,362	8,111	8,950	9,009	9,137	9,287
Indianapolis-Carmel-Anderson, IN	135,882	140,736	144,384	142,339	151,510	156,533
Iowa City, IA	10,820	10,919	10,828	10,363	10,663	10,766
Ithaca, NY	6,140	6,185	6,298	5,770	6,004	6,333
Jackson, MI	5,987	6,320	6,547	6,367	6,878	6,765
Jackson, MS	27,650	27,641	27,544	27,364	28,383	28,663
Jackson, TN	8,258	8,289	8,395	8,284	8,840	8,846
Jacksonville, FL	80,342	82,994	86,378	87,857	94,323	99,473
Jacksonville, NC	8,335	8,413	8,566	8,670	9,099	9,039
Janesville-Beloit, WI	6,936	7,301	7,510	7,467	7,688	7,784
Jefferson City, MO	7,594	7,670	8,095	7,874	7,720	8,054
Johnson City, TN	7,312	7,446	7,652	7,690	8,242	8,360
Johnstown, PA	4,693	4,697	4,682	4,616	4,627	4,607
Jonesboro, AR	5,106	5,235	5,409	5,458	5,937	5,799
Joplin, MO	7,559	7,656	7,581	7,269	7,600	7,724
Kahului-Wailuku-Lahaina, HI	9,606	10,184	10,408	8,559	9,460	9,693
Kalamazoo-Portage, MI	13,679	14,547	14,956	15,060	16,058	16,353
Kankakee, IL	5,941	6,333	6,262	6,140	6,679	6,877
Kansas City, MO-KS	133,754	136,391	139,725	137,218	141,666	145,950
Kennewick-Richland, WA	14,688	15,221	15,745	15,403	16,192	16,208
Killeen-Temple, TX	18,367	18,496	18,835	19,167	19,967	20,163
Kingsport-Bristol, TN-VA	13,293	13,680	13,317	13,289	14,304	14,831
Kingston, NY	7,234	7,327	7,630	7,197	7,429	7,659
Knoxville, TN	43,011	44,070	44,952	45,119	48,680	50,422
Kokomo, IN	4,279	4,392	4,387	4,135	4,498	4,951
La Crosse-Onalaska, WI-MN	7,963	8,099	8,213	7,905	8,136	8,117
Lafayette, LA	21,116	22,042	21,835	20,926	21,203	21,023
Lafayette-West Lafayette, IN	11,077	11,728	11,805	11,107	11,486	12,090
Lake Charles, LA	16,643	16,398	16,835	13,626	14,249	13,299
Lake Havasu City-Kingman, AZ	5,323	5,437	5,639	5,774	6,269	6,257
Lakeland-Winter Haven, FL	25,742	26,450	27,403	28,204	29,828	30,524
Lancaster, PA	28,780	29,307	29,549	28,302	29,559	29,969
Lansing-East Lansing, MI	25,570	26,064	26,363	26,157	27,549	28,450
Laredo, TX	11,313	10,859	11,389	11,017	11,381	11,680
Las Cruces, NM	7,305	7,448	7,720	7,421	7,869	7,902
Las Vegas-Henderson-Paradise, NV	116,332	122,721	128,047	117,202	129,198	135,989
Lawrence, KS	4,988	5,123	5,148	5,029	5,179	5,220
Lawton, OK	5,192	5,144	5,233	5,098	5,282	5,188
Lebanon, PA	5,750	5,825	5,827	5,657	6,021	6,130
Lewiston, ID-WA	2,619	2,610	2,756	2,795	2,927	2,979
Lewiston-Auburn, ME	4,503	4,703	4,811	5,018	5,045	4,976
Lexington-Fayette, KY	28,671	29,465	30,025	28,847	29,679	30,453
Lima, OH	7,712	8,163	7,724	7,584	8,364	8,257
Lincoln, NE	19,552	19,940	20,346	20,246	20,905	21,669
Little Rock-North Little Rock-Conway, AR	36,515	37,072	37,428	37,666	39,147	39,781
Logan, UT-ID	5,666	6,169	6,315	6,365	6,791	6,809
Longview, TX	14,585	15,385	15,223	14,448	14,959	15,441
Longview, WA	4,700	4,908	5,232	5,302	5,473	5,449
Los Angeles-Long Beach-Anaheim, CA	965,280	991,254	1,024,822	981,305	1,042,007	1,060,496
Louisville/Jefferson County, KY-IN	70,802	71,638	74,329	72,916	76,189	77,453
Lubbock, TX	13,660	14,001	14,377	14,473	14,956	15,090
Lynchburg, VA	10,061	10,501	10,495	10,064	10,465	10,492
Macon-Bibb County, GA	10,846	11,031	10,873	10,132	10,715	10,723
Madera, CA	6,024	6,028	6,244	6,240	6,411	6,140
Madison, WI	47,413	49,253	50,639	49,424	52,099	53,016
Manchester-Nashua, NH	25,959	26,455	27,030	26,988	29,685	30,016

Gross Domestic Product by Metropolitan Statistical Area—Continued

(Millions of chained 2017 dollars.)

Metropolitan Statistical Area	2017	2018	2019	2020	2021	2022
Manhattan, KS	7,190	7,105	6,861	6,860	7,098	7,081
Mankato, MN	5,562	5,647	5,622	5,401	5,561	5,643
Mansfield, OH	4,544	4,591	4,596	4,414	4,599	4,582
McAllen-Edinburg-Mission, TX	20,721	21,185	21,796	21,421	22,496	22,818
Medford, OR	9,088	9,237	9,383	9,382	10,015	10,021
Memphis, TN-MS-AR	75,342	75,977	76,608	75,771	79,424	79,072
Merced, CA	9,137	9,153	9,229	9,095	9,236	9,252
Miami-Fort Lauderdale-Pompano Beach, FL	346,956	359,853	365,640	353,477	390,533	409,478
Michigan City-La Porte, IN	4,106	4,231	4,121	3,990	4,198	4,178
Midland, MI	5,482	5,521	5,351	5,689	5,840	5,978
Midland, TX	21,889	27,561	33,734	31,464	31,009	30,539
Milwaukee-Waukesha, WI	99,281	100,842	102,445	98,378	102,631	103,660
Minneapolis-St. Paul-Bloomington, MN-WI	257,849	265,735	269,647	261,229	273,794	277,602
Missoula, MT	5,531	5,598	5,759	5,743	6,374	6,517
Mobile, AL	20,576	20,913	21,226	21,416	22,277	22,790
Modesto, CA	22,192	22,810	23,294	22,611	23,527	23,458
Monroe, LA	8,331	8,468	8,204	7,970	7,972	8,113
Monroe, MI	6,000	5,881	5,928	5,598	5,738	5,708
Montgomery, AL	18,162	18,181	18,294	17,874	18,385	18,846
Morgantown, WV	7,847	7,913	7,662	7,594	7,919	7,928
Morristown, TN	5,112	5,073	5,198	5,204	5,553	5,674
Mount Vernon-Anacortes, WA	6,537	6,636	6,670	6,679	6,731	6,469
Muncie, IN	4,030	4,096	4,128	4,029	4,164	4,320
Muskegon, MI	5,987	6,085	6,119	5,902	6,155	6,230
Myrtle Beach-Conway-North Myrtle Beach, SC-NC	17,916	18,300	18,661	18,943	20,127	20,938
Napa, CA	10,997	11,047	10,988	10,387	11,381	11,317
Naples-Marco Island, FL	18,972	19,604	20,295	20,239	22,807	23,677
Nashville-Davidson--Murfreesboro--Franklin, TN	130,549	134,556	139,495	138,393	153,009	162,595
New Bern, NC	5,397	5,283	5,486	5,334	5,605	5,492
New Haven-Milford, CT	49,699	50,711	51,494	49,996	52,017	52,660
New Orleans-Metairie, LA	78,225	78,131	79,367	72,861	75,212	73,998
New York-Newark-Jersey City, NY-NJ-PA	1,714,074	1,766,287	1,803,715	1,740,098	1,823,942	1,870,253
Niles, MI	7,684	7,498	7,329	7,508	7,480	7,380
North Port-Sarasota-Bradenton, FL	34,412	36,196	37,668	37,803	40,234	41,804
Norwich-New London, CT	18,943	19,248	19,210	17,958	18,262	18,792
Ocala, FL	9,764	10,173	10,292	10,699	11,457	11,683
Ocean City, NJ	5,399	5,417	5,335	5,221	5,557	5,466
Odessa, TX	10,478	12,491	13,040	10,955	10,606	11,364
Ogden-Clearfield, UT	27,304	28,783	30,088	30,862	32,136	32,288
Oklahoma City, OK	74,419	77,047	78,353	75,889	76,593	76,111
Olympia-Lacey-Tumwater, WA	12,907	13,735	14,061	13,747	14,725	15,180
Omaha-Council Bluffs, NE-IA	64,330	65,707	66,512	65,479	68,300	72,582
Orlando-Kissimmee-Sanford, FL	136,223	141,200	146,135	140,067	156,475	165,757
Oshkosh-Neenah, WI	10,257	10,516	10,856	10,684	10,899	10,844
Owensboro, KY	5,845	5,743	5,739	5,602	5,614	5,619
Oxnard-Thousand Oaks-Ventura, CA	50,166	50,754	51,640	51,145	52,907	52,689
Palm Bay-Melbourne-Titusville, FL	24,133	25,245	26,348	26,588	29,191	30,082
Panama City, FL	8,391	8,573	8,658	8,771	9,502	9,794
Parkersburg-Vienna, WV	3,610	3,680	3,538	3,515	3,673	3,645
Pensacola-Ferry Pass-Brent, FL	20,211	20,440	20,848	20,884	22,330	22,766
Peoria, IL	21,778	22,341	21,513	20,060	20,928	22,042
Philadelphia-Camden-Wilmington, PA-NJ-DE-MD	425,374	432,303	436,749	419,663	437,550	444,999
Phoenix-Mesa-Chandler, AZ	246,068	257,410	269,600	272,794	296,340	308,215
Pine Bluff, AR	3,510	3,437	3,396	3,209	3,391	3,311
Pittsburgh, PA	150,698	154,324	155,925	147,494	152,965	153,330
Pittsfield, MA	7,025	7,118	6,998	6,766	6,897	6,928
Pocatello, ID	3,169	3,223	3,294	3,351	3,374	3,550
Portland-South Portland, ME	31,325	32,448	33,035	33,897	36,340	37,517
Portland-Vancouver-Hillsboro, OR-WA	155,832	162,730	166,879	165,138	174,790	177,818
Port St. Lucie, FL	16,744	17,315	17,465	18,443	19,126	20,002
Poughkeepsie-Newburgh-Middletown, NY	32,062	32,620	34,273	33,253	34,788	35,904
Prescott Valley-Prescott, AZ	7,229	7,346	7,388	7,451	8,087	8,092
Providence-Warwick, RI-MA	84,628	84,717	86,513	83,975	88,229	89,464
Provo-Orem, UT	25,475	27,586	30,110	31,474	34,030	35,294
Pueblo, CO	5,972	6,176	6,417	6,179	6,616	6,511
Punta Gorda, FL	5,181	5,364	5,659	5,984	6,235	6,476
Racine, WI	8,169	8,308	8,287	8,326	8,431	8,389
Raleigh-Cary, NC	84,942	89,495	92,342	92,736	100,643	104,168
Rapid City, SD	6,286	6,389	6,515	6,676	6,908	7,039
Reading, PA	20,118	20,374	20,313	19,601	20,082	20,099
Redding, CA	8,147	7,890	8,350	8,134	8,173	8,126
Reno, NV	29,361	28,776	29,840	30,088	32,927	33,593

Gross Domestic Product by Metropolitan Statistical Area—Continued

(Millions of chained 2017 dollars.)

Metropolitan Statistical Area	2017	2018	2019	2020	2021	2022
Richmond, VA	84,501	86,528	88,498	86,961	91,241	93,615
Riverside-San Bernardino-Ontario, CA	171,203	177,211	184,662	182,563	193,690	195,808
Roanoke, VA	15,919	16,184	16,073	15,737	16,634	16,911
Rochester, MN	13,102	13,556	13,848	13,673	14,129	14,230
Rochester, NY	61,031	61,353	63,573	60,832	63,207	64,230
Rockford, IL	15,827	16,254	16,161	14,490	14,905	15,371
Rocky Mount, NC	7,017	6,669	6,361	6,457	6,724	6,743
Rome, GA	4,173	4,149	4,087	3,920	4,138	4,189
Sacramento-Roseville-Folsom, CA	131,157	136,934	141,690	138,496	146,941	149,614
Saginaw, MI	8,199	8,460	8,430	8,248	8,783	8,855
St. Cloud, MN	10,581	10,676	10,581	10,400	10,532	10,660
St. George, UT	6,235	6,620	6,886	7,219	7,853	7,945
St. Joseph, MO-KS	6,081	5,960	5,978	5,852	5,854	5,693
St. Louis, MO-IL	164,415	166,574	169,262	165,804	175,042	178,657
Salem, OR	17,086	18,040	18,592	18,550	19,730	20,221
Salinas, CA	25,923	26,771	27,426	26,964	27,192	26,729
Salisbury, MD-DE	21,115	21,628	22,495	21,578	23,200	23,830
Salt Lake City, UT	91,954	97,160	102,823	102,523	111,487	113,077
San Angelo, TX	6,334	6,669	7,302	7,317	7,351	7,373
San Antonio-New Braunfels, TX	118,926	124,532	128,536	127,094	134,073	140,363
San Diego-Chula Vista-Carlsbad, CA	224,768	230,519	236,250	232,702	250,064	257,341
San Francisco-Oakland-Berkeley, CA	526,583	560,553	590,718	591,150	655,887	654,731
San Jose-Sunnyvale-Santa Clara, CA	282,663	304,610	320,853	341,921	388,071	385,011
San Luis Obispo-Paso Robles, CA	16,780	17,201	17,239	16,943	17,484	17,762
Santa Cruz-Watsonville, CA	13,942	14,364	15,340	15,222	16,385	16,408
Santa Fe, NM	6,941	7,089	7,138	6,699	7,328	7,477
Santa Maria-Santa Barbara, CA	27,474	28,505	28,901	29,367	31,365	31,147
Santa Rosa-Petaluma, CA	28,854	30,213	30,422	29,522	31,391	31,369
Savannah, GA	21,178	21,468	22,165	21,701	23,648	24,500
Scranton--Wilkes-Barre, PA	26,659	26,779	27,148	25,902	26,797	26,657
Seattle-Tacoma-Bellevue, WA	368,193	395,709	417,985	419,746	451,641	462,255
Sebastian-Vero Beach, FL	6,355	6,669	6,828	6,938	7,895	7,901
Sebring-Avon Park, FL	2,482	2,420	2,564	2,453	2,513	2,666
Sheboygan, WI	7,029	7,126	6,986	6,835	6,975	6,778
Sherman-Denison, TX	4,703	4,971	4,990	4,874	5,225	5,326
Shreveport-Bossier City, LA	20,078	20,687	21,298	20,071	20,807	20,576
Sierra Vista-Douglas, AZ	4,585	4,590	4,693	4,987	4,879	4,855
Sioux City, IA-NE-SD	8,106	8,464	8,537	8,466	9,092	9,095
Sioux Falls, SD	22,155	21,889	22,771	21,967	23,096	22,604
South Bend-Mishawaka, IN-MI	14,675	15,341	15,712	14,794	15,521	16,095
Spartanburg, SC	14,977	15,366	16,119	15,727	16,501	16,727
Spokane-Spokane Valley, WA	25,480	26,765	27,522	27,716	29,995	30,011
Springfield, IL	11,297	11,624	11,677	10,904	11,545	11,742
Springfield, MA	32,560	32,901	33,540	32,648	33,685	33,750
Springfield, MO	19,678	20,072	20,718	20,332	21,816	22,233
Springfield, OH	4,661	4,621	4,703	4,467	4,650	4,670
State College, PA	8,878	8,807	8,867	8,528	8,799	8,928
Staunton, VA	5,064	5,135	5,150	4,920	5,140	5,295
Stockton, CA	29,142	30,300	31,217	30,957	33,356	32,624
Sumter, SC	4,688	4,839	4,932	4,774	4,935	4,837
Syracuse, NY	39,834	39,856	41,019	39,843	40,906	41,061
Tallahassee, FL	17,109	17,171	17,533	17,234	18,306	19,154
Tampa-St. Petersburg-Clearwater, FL	152,661	158,044	163,322	165,493	179,027	187,734
Terre Haute, IN	7,518	7,493	7,463	7,347	7,869	8,046
Texarkana, TX-AR	5,454	5,422	5,427	5,403	5,498	5,501
The Villages, FL	3,208	3,393	3,770	3,830	4,464	4,811
Toledo, OH	35,348	35,982	37,279	34,835	37,442	36,663
Topeka, KS	11,518	11,853	11,634	11,813	12,180	12,288
Trenton-Princeton, NJ	32,454	33,564	37,150	37,990	40,960	42,924
Tucson, AZ	42,331	43,891	45,086	44,978	47,066	47,960
Tulsa, OK	51,637	53,150	53,148	50,271	52,192	51,031
Tuscaloosa, AL	11,193	11,223	11,853	11,246	11,281	11,090
Twin Falls, ID	4,698	4,881	4,987	5,130	5,330	5,445
Tyler, TX	10,501	11,028	11,422	11,144	11,616	12,001
Urban Honolulu, HI	65,758	66,030	65,648	59,886	62,532	63,072
Utica-Rome, NY	12,412	12,589	12,948	12,608	12,745	12,814
Valdosta, GA	5,414	5,518	5,708	5,726	5,926	5,844
Vallejo, CA	22,725	25,847	29,785	30,145	30,524	28,736
Victoria, TX	4,563	4,866	4,746	4,568	4,774	4,867
Vineland-Bridgeton, NJ	6,268	6,440	6,441	6,184	6,427	6,476
Virginia Beach-Norfolk-Newport News, VA-NC	94,945	93,852	94,854	94,096	98,382	100,255
Visalia, CA	17,427	17,686	18,502	18,133	18,291	18,098
Waco, TX	12,733	13,262	13,080	12,627	13,318	13,739

Gross Domestic Product by Metropolitan Statistical Area—Continued

(Millions of chained 2017 dollars.)

Metropolitan Statistical Area	2017	2018	2019	2020	2021	2022
Walla Walla, WA	3,407	3,452	3,469	3,238	3,306	3,417
Warner Robins, GA	7,641	7,760	8,024	7,990	8,285	8,405
Washington-Arlington-Alexandria, DC-VA-MD-WV	528,925	542,396	551,770	543,129	569,554	580,496
Waterloo-Cedar Falls, IA	9,420	9,586	9,506	9,493	10,151	9,914
Watertown-Fort Drum, NY	6,422	6,376	6,362	6,162	6,334	6,341
Wausau-Weston, WI	9,712	9,907	10,362	9,820	10,112	10,046
Weirton-Steubenville, WV-OH	5,268	5,308	5,438	5,503	5,379	5,096
Wenatchee, WA	6,354	6,436	6,484	6,407	6,669	6,804
Wheeling, WV-OH	9,583	9,651	9,628	9,263	8,864	8,488
Wichita, KS	35,871	35,829	36,501	35,122	36,020	37,145
Wichita Falls, TX	5,924	6,052	6,268	6,150	6,170	6,302
Williamsport, PA	5,836	5,801	5,767	5,611	5,664	5,556
Wilmington, NC	14,062	14,487	15,181	15,191	16,553	17,015
Winchester, VA-WV	6,865	7,003	7,193	7,275	7,666	7,678
Winston-Salem, NC	34,908	34,182	34,802	32,388	34,269	35,091
Worcester, MA-CT	47,239	48,100	48,943	47,842	50,144	51,133
Yakima, WA	9,986	10,546	10,696	10,523	10,676	10,477
York-Hanover, PA	21,304	21,335	21,554	20,545	21,095	21,185
Youngstown-Warren-Boardman, OH-PA	20,570	20,514	20,930	19,772	20,399	20,599
Yuba City, CA	6,342	6,680	6,781	6,740	7,015	7,016
Yuma, AZ	7,543	7,522	7,748	7,516	7,659	8,138

Quantity Indexes for Real GDP by Metropolitan Area

(2017 = 100.0)

Metropolitan Statistical Area	2017	2018	2019	2020	2021	2022
Abilene, TX	100.0	104.6	108.8	107.7	110.9	115.6
Akron, OH	100.0	101.3	102.9	99.1	103.0	103.5
Albany, GA	100.0	100.2	102.6	101.8	106.6	107.1
Albany-Lebanon, OR	100.0	106.6	109.2	106.3	108.6	110.9
Albany-Schenectady-Troy, NY	100.0	100.2	105.3	102.5	109.4	112.0
Albuquerque, NM	100.0	101.9	104.9	103.1	108.1	110.4
Alexandria, LA	100.0	101.3	101.1	99.0	100.8	99.0
Allentown-Bethlehem-Easton, PA-NJ	100.0	100.5	104.5	100.3	103.9	104.7
Altoona, PA	100.0	101.6	104.0	101.1	104.5	104.4
Amarillo, TX	100.0	103.0	105.2	105.9	109.8	109.9
Ames, IA	100.0	101.8	103.2	101.9	106.3	105.9
Anchorage, AK	100.0	100.7	100.4	98.2	101.0	100.9
Ann Arbor, MI	100.0	102.5	106.0	103.9	109.5	111.4
Anniston-Oxford, AL	100.0	102.3	107.3	105.1	109.0	108.6
Appleton, WI	100.0	103.1	105.6	100.9	103.6	102.8
Asheville, NC	100.0	103.4	107.9	102.0	108.1	111.3
Athens-Clarke County, GA	100.0	103.5	102.8	98.5	103.9	106.3
Atlanta-Sandy Springs-Alpharetta, GA	100.0	103.7	108.0	104.2	111.1	114.3
Atlantic City-Hammonton, NJ	100.0	100.7	102.0	96.0	103.7	105.0
Auburn-Opelika, AL	100.0	99.6	103.3	100.8	106.9	111.8
Augusta-Richmond County, GA-SC	100.0	101.6	103.3	102.5	104.4	104.9
Austin-Round Rock-Georgetown, TX	100.0	105.8	112.5	115.6	127.7	137.2
Bakersfield, CA	100.0	100.2	103.7	103.7	103.5	100.0
Baltimore-Columbia-Towson, MD	100.0	101.0	101.7	98.1	103.0	104.9
Bangor, ME	100.0	103.8	106.3	106.6	110.1	112.3
Barnstable Town, MA	100.0	102.2	106.1	99.1	105.7	107.9
Baton Rouge, LA	100.0	106.5	104.4	96.5	97.8	98.7
Battle Creek, MI	100.0	100.3	99.4	98.8	107.2	108.3
Bay City, MI	100.0	102.6	99.9	100.3	108.5	108.8
Beaumont-Port Arthur, TX	100.0	104.9	102.6	88.9	91.0	89.3
Beckley, WV	100.0	101.9	104.9	98.2	100.8	106.2
Bellingham, WA	100.0	107.8	117.2	121.5	122.6	116.6
Bend, OR	100.0	103.8	109.9	110.0	121.0	123.7
Billings, MT	100.0	100.6	98.2	96.3	102.5	99.2
Binghamton, NY	100.0	100.2	102.4	96.7	99.6	100.1
Birmingham-Hoover, AL	100.0	102.0	103.7	102.4	107.6	109.2
Bismarck, ND	100.0	98.2	97.3	93.4	96.5	94.8
Blacksburg-Christiansburg, VA	100.0	105.0	103.5	100.5	108.3	112.8
Bloomington, IL	100.0	100.4	103.0	85.2	85.4	85.7
Bloomington, IN	100.0	103.6	102.5	98.3	101.5	105.1
Bloomsburg-Berwick, PA	100.0	99.6	102.1	97.2	101.2	103.3
Boise City, ID	100.0	107.8	113.1	114.8	124.4	131.0
Boston-Cambridge-Newton, MA-NH	100.0	104.0	107.8	106.2	113.6	116.2
Boulder, CO	100.0	103.7	113.0	111.0	118.7	123.3
Bowling Green, KY	100.0	99.3	104.2	103.3	110.4	116.1
Bremerton-Silverdale-Port Orchard, WA	100.0	102.4	103.5	106.4	109.3	110.3
Bridgeport-Stamford-Norwalk, CT	100.0	99.0	96.8	91.3	95.0	98.4
Brownsville-Harlingen, TX	100.0	102.0	104.3	101.7	108.6	112.1
Brunswick, GA	100.0	103.6	101.8	99.4	106.1	108.2
Buffalo-Cheektowaga, NY	100.0	101.0	103.7	100.8	104.5	107.5
Burlington, NC	100.0	100.6	103.4	103.5	109.6	109.6
Burlington-South Burlington, VT	100.0	101.7	103.6	99.8	106.4	109.6
California-Lexington Park, MD	100.0	100.5	102.5	106.9	106.7	104.3
Canton-Massillon, OH	100.0	98.7	100.4	94.8	99.8	99.8
Cape Coral-Fort Myers, FL	100.0	104.1	105.8	105.6	114.4	119.8
Cape Girardeau, MO-IL	100.0	102.2	102.4	99.0	102.2	102.1
Carbondale-Marion, IL	100.0	102.7	102.6	98.2	99.4	103.2
Carson City, NV	100.0	102.3	108.7	103.2	105.4	106.8
Casper, WY	100.0	105.8	101.5	90.6	89.4	89.2
Cedar Rapids, IA	100.0	101.8	99.9	97.6	102.9	102.9
Chambersburg-Waynesboro, PA	100.0	101.6	99.0	94.4	96.8	97.8
Champaign-Urbana, IL	100.0	99.2	100.3	98.6	102.2	104.5
Charleston, WV	100.0	105.6	100.4	94.2	96.7	98.1
Charleston-North Charleston, SC	100.0	104.0	108.1	106.2	111.6	116.6
Charlotte-Concord-Gastonia, NC-SC	100.0	102.1	105.4	106.7	113.3	115.6
Charlottesville, VA	100.0	102.0	102.5	98.4	107.0	110.5
Chattanooga, TN-GA	100.0	100.9	102.4	102.0	108.5	114.8
Cheyenne, WY	100.0	105.5	110.7	104.3	110.3	107.7
Chicago-Naperville-Elgin, IL-IN-WI	100.0	102.5	103.4	97.8	103.2	104.6
Chico, CA	100.0	101.0	102.9	96.7	98.8	99.2
Cincinnati, OH-KY-IN	100.0	100.0	105.0	102.8	107.1	108.1
Clarksville, TN-KY	100.0	101.1	102.5	103.2	109.7	110.8
Cleveland, TN	100.0	100.9	100.9	104.0	109.1	110.9

Quantity Indexes for Real GDP by Metropolitan Area—Continued

(2017 = 100.0)

Metropolitan Statistical Area	2017	2018	2019	2020	2021	2022
Cleveland-Elyria, OH	100.0	101.6	104.1	100.4	105.4	107.5
Coeur d'Alene, ID	100.0	106.2	108.8	113.9	126.7	131.5
College Station-Bryan, TX	100.0	104.3	109.0	108.8	113.7	116.4
Colorado Springs, CO	100.0	103.3	107.5	110.7	116.6	117.8
Columbia, MO	100.0	100.6	104.7	101.5	106.6	106.6
Columbia, SC	100.0	101.6	103.4	103.0	108.3	111.1
Columbus, GA-AL	100.0	100.2	101.8	100.8	102.2	99.0
Columbus, IN	100.0	107.5	106.5	98.7	102.7	109.9
Columbus, OH	100.0	101.2	104.4	103.2	110.2	111.2
Corpus Christi, TX	100.0	103.3	106.0	101.4	104.8	99.9
Corvallis, OR	100.0	104.6	106.5	104.6	109.3	110.4
Crestview-Fort Walton Beach-Destin, FL	100.0	104.2	110.3	113.3	124.2	127.5
Cumberland, MD-WV	100.0	101.7	102.0	98.5	98.8	96.7
Dallas-Fort Worth-Arlington, TX	100.0	104.6	108.7	107.3	115.8	122.5
Dalton, GA	100.0	99.4	99.9	96.9	102.2	105.6
Danville, IL	100.0	100.2	99.9	95.1	98.5	100.7
Daphne-Fairhope-Foley, AL	100.0	105.1	110.4	109.7	118.4	120.9
Davenport-Moline-Rock Island, IA-IL	100.0	99.3	100.2	98.1	100.4	100.2
Dayton-Kettering, OH	100.0	101.5	104.8	103.2	106.9	107.7
Decatur, AL	100.0	102.1	101.3	103.4	105.6	108.3
Decatur, IL	100.0	97.2	93.2	90.7	98.9	101.0
Deltona-Daytona Beach-Ormond Beach, FL	100.0	102.9	105.0	106.1	111.8	114.6
Denver-Aurora-Lakewood, CO	100.0	104.4	109.9	110.4	118.4	123.5
Des Moines-West Des Moines, IA	100.0	100.2	103.9	106.5	113.9	111.5
Detroit-Warren-Dearborn, MI	100.0	102.1	101.9	97.6	103.3	105.2
Dothan, AL	100.0	100.8	102.9	103.7	107.8	105.7
Dover, DE	100.0	102.4	109.8	104.8	108.1	108.9
Dubuque, IA	100.0	99.8	103.7	106.0	110.3	107.5
Duluth, MN-WI	100.0	102.3	104.4	99.0	102.5	102.0
Durham-Chapel Hill, NC	100.0	104.9	107.8	110.5	117.1	120.9
East Stroudsburg, PA	100.0	100.9	108.8	103.9	110.0	109.6
Eau Claire, WI	100.0	102.2	104.3	98.8	102.1	102.7
El Centro, CA	100.0	99.5	103.1	107.5	102.0	106.0
Elizabethtown-Fort Knox, KY	100.0	99.0	101.9	100.5	106.5	107.9
Elkhart-Goshen, IN	100.0	101.0	97.7	95.3	113.9	121.7
Elmira, NY	100.0	101.4	101.4	95.5	98.4	98.6
El Paso, TX	100.0	103.1	107.3	107.2	113.4	114.8
Enid, OK	100.0	98.5	98.1	92.4	97.4	95.0
Erie, PA	100.0	100.9	101.5	95.5	97.1	97.3
Eugene-Springfield, OR	100.0	102.7	103.1	102.5	109.5	110.6
Evansville, IN-KY	100.0	102.9	108.7	103.4	112.5	109.7
Fairbanks, AK	100.0	98.3	98.3	94.7	97.9	96.0
Fargo, ND-MN	100.0	100.7	103.0	99.6	104.5	104.6
Farmington, NM	100.0	96.8	97.7	90.3	89.2	89.8
Fayetteville, NC	100.0	101.0	103.4	103.6	107.6	106.8
Fayetteville-Springdale-Rogers, AR	100.0	103.0	105.3	109.6	119.7	123.1
Flagstaff, AZ	100.0	100.0	97.2	88.0	94.7	97.4
Flint, MI	100.0	102.5	104.3	96.1	98.5	97.8
Florence, SC	100.0	100.2	102.3	99.8	103.0	102.9
Florence-Muscle Shoals, AL	100.0	102.2	102.2	101.0	103.9	105.9
Fond du Lac, WI	100.0	102.2	103.5	98.4	101.0	101.4
Fort Collins, CO	100.0	104.8	109.9	109.9	117.7	119.6
Fort Smith, AR-OK	100.0	102.4	104.0	103.0	106.4	108.2
Fort Wayne, IN	100.0	103.8	104.5	97.0	103.9	108.2
Fresno, CA	100.0	102.8	105.7	104.1	107.6	106.6
Gadsden, AL	100.0	101.1	99.1	91.6	93.7	94.5
Gainesville, FL	100.0	103.3	105.9	106.2	112.7	115.2
Gainesville, GA	100.0	104.9	107.4	110.2	115.4	122.8
Gettysburg, PA	100.0	97.5	95.5	90.6	93.4	91.4
Glens Falls, NY	100.0	99.9	106.2	104.2	109.2	109.9
Goldsboro, NC	100.0	99.5	99.5	97.0	101.1	101.2
Grand Forks, ND-MN	100.0	100.4	101.2	98.4	100.6	99.2
Grand Island, NE	100.0	101.4	101.8	100.7	109.9	108.7
Grand Junction, CO	100.0	104.4	106.6	103.6	107.5	107.6
Grand Rapids-Kentwood, MI	100.0	103.3	103.6	102.2	109.3	112.0
Grants Pass, OR	100.0	104.3	111.2	109.4	115.1	115.3
Great Falls, MT	100.0	101.3	100.1	99.0	101.7	103.8
Greeley, CO	100.0	111.1	117.2	106.5	108.9	99.3
Green Bay, WI	100.0	103.2	103.7	100.9	103.0	104.0
Greensboro-High Point, NC	100.0	100.5	99.7	96.1	99.5	100.5
Greenville, NC	100.0	97.3	96.2	93.1	95.7	97.3
Greenville-Anderson, SC	100.0	103.9	105.6	103.1	107.7	110.8

Quantity Indexes for Real GDP by Metropolitan Area—Continued

(2017 = 100.0)

Metropolitan Statistical Area	2017	2018	2019	2020	2021	2022
Gulfport-Biloxi, MS	100.0	98.1	100.7	102.8	107.4	108.1
Hagerstown-Martinsburg, MD-WV	100.0	103.0	101.2	96.4	102.4	102.1
Hammond, LA	100.0	100.2	106.2	103.3	107.2	105.2
Hanford-Corcoran, CA	100.0	98.3	100.2	101.7	102.3	102.6
Harrisburg-Carlisle, PA	100.0	101.8	105.0	99.8	105.0	105.9
Harrisonburg, VA	100.0	102.5	104.2	99.0	107.0	113.4
Hartford-East Hartford-Middletown, CT	100.0	100.3	100.7	93.4	97.3	100.4
Hattiesburg, MS	100.0	99.8	98.2	96.7	103.6	104.4
Hickory-Lenoir-Morganton, NC	100.0	98.8	97.8	95.5	98.6	100.2
Hilton Head Island-Bluffton, SC	100.0	105.0	108.8	112.3	117.1	118.2
Hinesville, GA	100.0	101.1	101.5	99.1	107.4	105.7
Homosassa Springs, FL	100.0	105.0	112.0	113.6	120.4	124.6
Hot Springs, AR	100.0	102.5	104.1	103.0	105.8	106.1
Houma-Thibodaux, LA	100.0	103.7	103.2	96.9	95.5	95.4
Houston-The Woodlands-Sugar Land, TX	100.0	104.4	102.9	101.3	106.4	109.1
Huntington-Ashland, WV-KY-OH	100.0	104.9	106.6	98.1	100.2	99.5
Huntsville, AL	100.0	103.9	109.6	111.4	117.4	121.7
Idaho Falls, ID	100.0	110.2	121.6	122.4	124.1	126.1
Indianapolis-Carmel-Anderson, IN	100.0	103.6	106.3	104.8	111.5	115.2
Iowa City, IA	100.0	100.9	100.1	95.8	98.5	99.5
Ithaca, NY	100.0	100.7	102.6	94.0	97.8	103.1
Jackson, MI	100.0	105.6	109.4	106.3	114.9	113.0
Jackson, MS	100.0	100.0	99.6	99.0	102.7	103.7
Jackson, TN	100.0	100.4	101.7	100.3	107.0	107.1
Jacksonville, FL	100.0	103.3	107.5	109.4	117.4	123.8
Jacksonville, NC	100.0	100.9	102.8	104.0	109.2	108.4
Janesville-Beloit, WI	100.0	105.3	108.3	107.7	110.8	112.2
Jefferson City, MO	100.0	101.0	106.6	103.7	101.7	106.1
Johnson City, TN	100.0	101.8	104.7	105.2	112.7	114.3
Johnstown, PA	100.0	100.1	99.8	98.4	98.6	98.2
Jonesboro, AR	100.0	102.5	105.9	106.9	116.3	113.6
Joplin, MO	100.0	101.3	100.3	96.2	100.5	102.2
Kahului-Wailuku-Lahaina, HI	100.0	106.0	108.3	89.1	98.5	100.9
Kalamazoo-Portage, MI	100.0	106.3	109.3	110.1	117.4	119.6
Kankakee, IL	100.0	106.6	105.4	103.4	112.4	115.8
Kansas City, MO-KS	100.0	102.0	104.5	102.6	105.9	109.1
Kennewick-Richland, WA	100.0	103.6	107.2	104.9	110.2	110.3
Killeen-Temple, TX	100.0	100.7	102.5	104.4	108.7	109.8
Kingsport-Bristol, TN-VA	100.0	102.9	100.2	100.0	107.6	111.6
Kingston, NY	100.0	101.3	105.5	99.5	102.7	105.9
Knoxville, TN	100.0	102.5	104.5	104.9	113.2	117.2
Kokomo, IN	100.0	102.6	102.5	96.6	105.1	115.7
La Crosse-Onalaska, WI-MN	100.0	101.7	103.1	99.3	102.2	101.9
Lafayette, LA	100.0	104.4	103.4	99.1	100.4	99.6
Lafayette-West Lafayette, IN	100.0	105.9	106.6	100.3	103.7	109.1
Lake Charles, LA	100.0	98.5	101.2	81.9	85.6	79.9
Lake Havasu City-Kingman, AZ	100.0	102.1	105.9	108.5	117.8	117.5
Lakeland-Winter Haven, FL	100.0	102.7	106.5	109.6	115.9	118.6
Lancaster, PA	100.0	101.8	102.7	98.3	102.7	104.1
Lansing-East Lansing, MI	100.0	101.9	103.1	102.3	107.7	111.3
Laredo, TX	100.0	96.0	100.7	97.4	100.6	103.2
Las Cruces, NM	100.0	101.9	105.7	101.6	107.7	108.2
Las Vegas-Henderson-Paradise, NV	100.0	105.5	110.1	100.7	111.1	116.9
Lawrence, KS	100.0	102.7	103.2	100.8	103.8	104.7
Lawton, OK	100.0	99.1	100.8	98.2	101.7	99.9
Lebanon, PA	100.0	101.3	101.3	98.4	104.7	106.6
Lewiston, ID-WA	100.0	99.7	105.3	106.7	111.8	113.8
Lewiston-Auburn, ME	100.0	104.4	106.8	111.4	112.0	110.5
Lexington-Fayette, KY	100.0	102.8	104.7	100.6	103.5	106.2
Lima, OH	100.0	105.9	100.2	98.3	108.5	107.1
Lincoln, NE	100.0	102.0	104.1	103.6	106.9	110.8
Little Rock-North Little Rock-Conway, AR	100.0	101.5	102.5	103.2	107.2	108.9
Logan, UT-ID	100.0	108.9	111.5	112.3	119.9	120.2
Longview, TX	100.0	105.5	104.4	99.1	102.6	105.9
Longview, WA	100.0	104.4	111.3	112.8	116.5	115.9
Los Angeles-Long Beach-Anaheim, CA	100.0	102.7	106.2	101.7	107.9	109.9
Louisville/Jefferson County, KY-IN	100.0	101.2	105.0	103.0	107.6	109.4
Lubbock, TX	100.0	102.5	105.3	106.0	109.5	110.5
Lynchburg, VA	100.0	104.4	104.3	100.0	104.0	104.3
Macon-Bibb County, GA	100.0	101.7	100.2	93.4	98.8	98.9
Madera, CA	100.0	100.1	103.7	103.6	106.4	101.9
Madison, WI	100.0	103.9	106.8	104.2	109.9	111.8

Quantity Indexes for Real GDP by Metropolitan Area—Continued

(2017 = 100.0)

Metropolitan Statistical Area	2017	2018	2019	2020	2021	2022
Manchester-Nashua, NH	100.0	101.9	104.1	104.0	114.4	115.6
Manhattan, KS	100.0	98.8	95.4	95.4	98.7	98.5
Mankato, MN	100.0	101.5	101.1	97.1	100.0	101.5
Mansfield, OH	100.0	101.0	101.1	97.1	101.2	100.8
McAllen-Edinburg-Mission, TX	100.0	102.2	105.2	103.4	108.6	110.1
Medford, OR	100.0	101.6	103.2	103.2	110.2	110.3
Memphis, TN-MS-AR	100.0	100.8	101.7	100.6	105.4	105.0
Merced, CA	100.0	100.2	101.0	99.5	101.1	101.3
Miami-Fort Lauderdale-Pompano Beach, FL	100.0	103.7	105.4	101.9	112.6	118.0
Michigan City-La Porte, IN	100.0	103.1	100.4	97.2	102.2	101.8
Midland, MI	100.0	100.7	97.6	103.8	106.5	109.0
Midland, TX	100.0	125.9	154.1	143.7	141.7	139.5
Milwaukee-Waukesha, WI	100.0	101.6	103.2	99.1	103.4	104.4
Minneapolis-St. Paul-Bloomington, MN-WI	100.0	103.1	104.6	101.3	106.2	107.7
Missoula, MT	100.0	101.2	104.1	103.8	115.2	117.8
Mobile, AL	100.0	101.6	103.2	104.1	108.3	110.8
Modesto, CA	100.0	102.8	105.0	101.9	106.0	105.7
Monroe, LA	100.0	101.6	98.5	95.7	95.7	97.4
Monroe, MI	100.0	98.0	98.8	93.3	95.6	95.1
Montgomery, AL	100.0	100.1	100.7	98.4	101.2	103.8
Morgantown, WV	100.0	100.8	97.6	96.8	100.9	101.0
Morristown, TN	100.0	99.2	101.7	101.8	108.6	111.0
Mount Vernon-Anacortes, WA	100.0	101.5	102.0	102.2	103.0	99.0
Muncie, IN	100.0	101.6	102.4	100.0	103.3	107.2
Muskegon, MI	100.0	101.6	102.2	98.6	102.8	104.1
Myrtle Beach-Conway-North Myrtle Beach, SC-NC	100.0	102.1	104.2	105.7	112.3	116.9
Napa, CA	100.0	100.5	99.9	94.5	103.5	102.9
Naples-Marco Island, FL	100.0	103.3	107.0	106.7	120.2	124.8
Nashville-Davidson--Murfreesboro--Franklin, TN	100.0	103.1	106.9	106.0	117.2	124.5
New Bern, NC	100.0	97.9	101.6	98.8	103.9	101.8
New Haven-Milford, CT	100.0	102.0	103.6	100.6	104.7	106.0
New Orleans-Metairie, LA	100.0	99.9	101.5	93.1	96.1	94.6
New York-Newark-Jersey City, NY-NJ-PA	100.0	103.0	105.2	101.5	106.4	109.1
Niles, MI	100.0	97.6	95.4	97.7	97.3	96.0
North Port-Sarasota-Bradenton, FL	100.0	105.2	109.5	109.9	116.9	121.5
Norwich-New London, CT	100.0	101.6	101.4	94.8	96.4	99.2
Ocala, FL	100.0	104.2	105.4	109.6	117.3	119.7
Ocean City, NJ	100.0	100.3	98.8	96.7	102.9	101.3
Odessa, TX	100.0	119.2	124.5	104.5	101.2	108.4
Ogden-Clearfield, UT	100.0	105.4	110.2	113.0	117.7	118.3
Oklahoma City, OK	100.0	103.5	105.3	102.0	102.9	102.3
Olympia-Lacey-Tumwater, WA	100.0	106.4	108.9	106.5	114.1	117.6
Omaha-Council Bluffs, NE-IA	100.0	102.1	103.4	101.8	106.2	112.8
Orlando-Kissimmee-Sanford, FL	100.0	103.7	107.3	102.8	114.9	121.7
Oshkosh-Neenah, WI	100.0	102.5	105.8	104.2	106.3	105.7
Owensboro, KY	100.0	98.3	98.2	95.9	96.1	96.1
Oxnard-Thousand Oaks-Ventura, CA	100.0	101.2	102.9	102.0	105.5	105.0
Palm Bay-Melbourne-Titusville, FL	100.0	104.6	109.2	110.2	121.0	124.7
Panama City, FL	100.0	102.2	103.2	104.5	113.2	116.7
Parkersburg-Vienna, WV	100.0	101.9	98.0	97.3	101.7	100.9
Pensacola-Ferry Pass-Brent, FL	100.0	101.1	103.2	103.3	110.5	112.6
Peoria, IL	100.0	102.6	98.8	92.1	96.1	101.2
Philadelphia-Camden-Wilmington, PA-NJ-DE-MD	100.0	101.6	102.7	98.7	102.9	104.6
Phoenix-Mesa-Chandler, AZ	100.0	104.6	109.6	110.9	120.4	125.3
Pine Bluff, AR	100.0	97.9	96.7	91.4	96.6	94.3
Pittsburgh, PA	100.0	102.4	103.5	97.9	101.5	101.7
Pittsfield, MA	100.0	101.3	99.6	96.3	98.2	98.6
Pocatello, ID	100.0	101.7	103.9	105.8	106.5	112.0
Portland-South Portland, ME	100.0	103.6	105.5	108.2	116.0	119.8
Portland-Vancouver-Hillsboro, OR-WA	100.0	104.4	107.1	106.0	112.2	114.1
Port St. Lucie, FL	100.0	103.4	104.3	110.1	114.2	119.5
Poughkeepsie-Newburgh-Middletown, NY	100.0	101.7	106.9	103.7	108.5	112.0
Prescott Valley-Prescott, AZ	100.0	101.6	102.2	103.1	111.9	111.9
Providence-Warwick, RI-MA	100.0	100.1	102.2	99.2	104.3	105.7
Provo-Orem, UT	100.0	108.3	118.2	123.5	133.6	138.5
Pueblo, CO	100.0	103.4	107.5	103.5	110.8	109.0
Punta Gorda, FL	100.0	103.5	109.2	115.5	120.3	125.0
Racine, WI	100.0	101.7	101.4	101.9	103.2	102.7
Raleigh-Cary, NC	100.0	105.4	108.7	109.2	118.5	122.6
Rapid City, SD	100.0	101.7	103.6	106.2	109.9	112.0
Reading, PA	100.0	101.3	101.0	97.4	99.8	99.9
Redding, CA	100.0	96.8	102.5	99.8	100.3	99.7
Reno, NV	100.0	98.0	101.6	102.5	112.1	114.4

Quantity Indexes for Real GDP by Metropolitan Area—Continued

(2017 = 100.0)

Metropolitan Statistical Area	2017	2018	2019	2020	2021	2022
Richmond, VA	100.0	102.4	104.7	102.9	108.0	110.8
Riverside-San Bernardino-Ontario, CA	100.0	103.5	107.9	106.6	113.1	114.4
Roanoke, VA	100.0	101.7	101.0	98.9	104.5	106.2
Rochester, MN	100.0	103.5	105.7	104.4	107.8	108.6
Rochester, NY	100.0	100.5	104.2	99.7	103.6	105.2
Rockford, IL	100.0	102.7	102.1	91.6	94.2	97.1
Rocky Mount, NC	100.0	95.0	90.7	92.0	95.8	96.1
Rome, GA	100.0	99.4	97.9	93.9	99.2	100.4
Sacramento-Roseville-Folsom, CA	100.0	104.4	108.0	105.6	112.0	114.1
Saginaw, MI	100.0	103.2	102.8	100.6	107.1	108.0
St. Cloud, MN	100.0	100.9	100.0	98.3	99.5	100.7
St. George, UT	100.0	106.2	110.5	115.8	126.0	127.4
St. Joseph, MO-KS	100.0	98.0	98.3	96.2	96.3	93.6
St. Louis, MO-IL	100.0	101.3	102.9	100.8	106.5	108.7
Salem, OR	100.0	105.6	108.8	108.6	115.5	118.4
Salinas, CA	100.0	103.3	105.8	104.0	104.9	103.1
Salisbury, MD-DE	100.0	102.4	106.5	102.2	109.9	112.9
Salt Lake City, UT	100.0	105.7	111.8	111.5	121.2	123.0
San Angelo, TX	100.0	105.3	115.3	115.5	116.1	116.4
San Antonio-New Braunfels, TX	100.0	104.7	108.1	106.9	112.7	118.0
San Diego-Chula Vista-Carlsbad, CA	100.0	102.6	105.1	103.5	111.3	114.5
San Francisco-Oakland-Berkeley, CA	100.0	106.5	112.2	112.3	124.6	124.3
San Jose-Sunnyvale-Santa Clara, CA	100.0	107.8	113.5	121.0	137.3	136.2
San Luis Obispo-Paso Robles, CA	100.0	102.5	102.7	101.0	104.2	105.9
Santa Cruz-Watsonville, CA	100.0	103.0	110.0	109.2	117.5	117.7
Santa Fe, NM	100.0	102.1	102.8	96.5	105.6	107.7
Santa Maria-Santa Barbara, CA	100.0	103.8	105.2	106.9	114.2	113.4
Santa Rosa-Petaluma, CA	100.0	104.7	105.4	102.3	108.8	108.7
Savannah, GA	100.0	101.4	104.7	102.5	111.7	115.7
Scranton--Wilkes-Barre, PA	100.0	100.5	101.8	97.2	100.5	100.0
Seattle-Tacoma-Bellevue, WA	100.0	107.5	113.5	114.0	122.7	125.5
Sebastian-Vero Beach, FL	100.0	104.9	107.4	109.2	124.2	124.3
Sebring-Avon Park, FL	100.0	97.5	103.3	98.8	101.3	107.4
Sheboygan, WI	100.0	101.4	99.4	97.2	99.2	96.4
Sherman-Denison, TX	100.0	105.7	106.1	103.6	111.1	113.2
Shreveport-Bossier City, LA	100.0	103.0	106.1	100.0	103.6	102.5
Sierra Vista-Douglas, AZ	100.0	100.1	102.4	108.8	106.4	105.9
Sioux City, IA-NE-SD	100.0	104.4	105.3	104.4	112.2	112.2
Sioux Falls, SD	100.0	98.8	102.8	99.2	104.2	102.0
South Bend-Mishawaka, IN-MI	100.0	104.5	107.1	100.8	105.8	109.7
Spartanburg, SC	100.0	102.6	107.6	105.0	110.2	111.7
Spokane-Spokane Valley, WA	100.0	105.0	108.0	108.8	117.7	117.8
Springfield, IL	100.0	102.9	103.4	96.5	102.2	103.9
Springfield, MA	100.0	101.0	103.0	100.3	103.5	103.7
Springfield, MO	100.0	102.0	105.3	103.3	110.9	113.0
Springfield, OH	100.0	99.1	100.9	95.8	99.8	100.2
State College, PA	100.0	99.2	99.9	96.1	99.1	100.6
Staunton, VA	100.0	101.4	101.7	97.1	101.5	104.6
Stockton, CA	100.0	104.0	107.1	106.2	114.5	112.0
Sumter, SC	100.0	103.2	105.2	101.8	105.3	103.2
Syracuse, NY	100.0	100.1	103.0	100.0	102.7	103.1
Tallahassee, FL	100.0	100.4	102.5	100.7	107.0	112.0
Tampa-St. Petersburg-Clearwater, FL	100.0	103.5	107.0	108.4	117.3	123.0
Terre Haute, IN	100.0	99.7	99.3	97.7	104.7	107.0
Texarkana, TX-AR	100.0	99.4	99.5	99.1	100.8	100.9
The Villages, FL	100.0	105.8	117.5	119.4	139.1	149.9
Toledo, OH	100.0	101.8	105.5	98.5	105.9	103.7
Topeka, KS	100.0	102.9	101.0	102.6	105.7	106.7
Trenton-Princeton, NJ	100.0	103.4	114.5	117.1	126.2	132.3
Tucson, AZ	100.0	103.7	106.5	106.3	111.2	113.3
Tulsa, OK	100.0	102.9	102.9	97.4	101.1	98.8
Tuscaloosa, AL	100.0	100.3	105.9	100.5	100.8	99.1
Twin Falls, ID	100.0	103.9	106.2	109.2	113.4	115.9
Tyler, TX	100.0	105.0	108.8	106.1	110.6	114.3
Urban Honolulu, HI	100.0	100.4	99.8	91.1	95.1	95.9
Utica-Rome, NY	100.0	101.4	104.3	101.6	102.7	103.2
Valdosta, GA	100.0	101.9	105.4	105.8	109.5	107.9
Vallejo, CA	100.0	113.7	131.1	132.7	134.3	126.5
Victoria, TX	100.0	106.6	104.0	100.1	104.6	106.7
Vineland-Bridgeton, NJ	100.0	102.7	102.8	98.7	102.5	103.3
Virginia Beach-Norfolk-Newport News, VA-NC	100.0	98.8	99.9	99.1	103.6	105.6
Visalia, CA	100.0	101.5	106.2	104.1	105.0	103.9
Waco, TX	100.0	104.2	102.7	99.2	104.6	107.9

Quantity Indexes for Real GDP by Metropolitan Area—Continued

(2017 = 100.0)

Metropolitan Statistical Area	2017	2018	2019	2020	2021	2022
Walla Walla, WA	100.0	101.3	101.8	95.0	97.0	100.3
Warner Robins, GA	100.0	101.5	105.0	104.6	108.4	110.0
Washington-Arlington-Alexandria, DC-VA-MD-WV	100.0	102.5	104.3	102.7	107.7	109.8
Waterloo-Cedar Falls, IA	100.0	101.8	100.9	100.8	107.8	105.2
Watertown-Fort Drum, NY	100.0	99.3	99.1	96.0	98.6	98.7
Wausau-Weston, WI	100.0	102.0	106.7	101.1	104.1	103.4
Weirton-Steubenville, WV-OH	100.0	100.8	103.2	104.5	102.1	96.7
Wenatchee, WA	100.0	101.3	102.0	100.8	105.0	107.1
Wheeling, WV-OH	100.0	100.7	100.5	96.7	92.5	88.6
Wichita, KS	100.0	99.9	101.8	97.9	100.4	103.6
Wichita Falls, TX	100.0	102.2	105.8	103.8	104.2	106.4
Williamsport, PA	100.0	99.4	98.8	96.1	97.0	95.2
Wilmington, NC	100.0	103.0	108.0	108.0	117.7	121.0
Winchester, VA-WV	100.0	102.0	104.8	106.0	111.7	111.8
Winston-Salem, NC	100.0	97.9	99.7	92.8	98.2	100.5
Worcester, MA-CT	100.0	101.8	103.6	101.3	106.1	108.2
Yakima, WA	100.0	105.6	107.1	105.4	106.9	104.9
York-Hanover, PA	100.0	100.1	101.2	96.4	99.0	99.4
Youngstown-Warren-Boardman, OH-PA	100.0	99.7	101.8	96.1	99.2	100.1
Yuba City, CA	100.0	105.3	106.9	106.3	110.6	110.6
Yuma, AZ	100.0	99.7	102.7	99.6	101.5	107.9

PART C

INCOME AND POVERTY BY STATE

PART C: INCOME AND POVERTY BY STATE

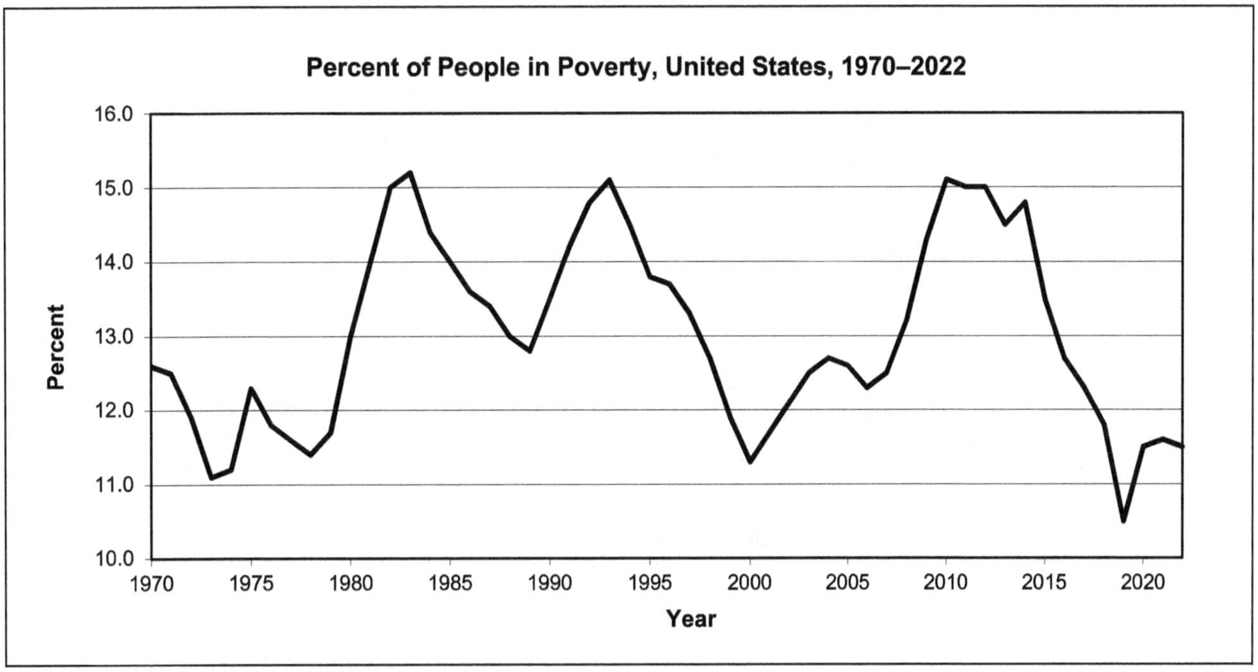

HIGHLIGHTS

- The percent of people in poverty in the United States decreased slightly from 11.6 percent in 2021 to 11.5 percent in 2022.
- The median household income in the United States decreased 2.3 percent to $74,580 in 2022. This was the third year in a row that median household income declined.
- In 2022, Maryland had the highest median household income at $108,200 (in 2022 dollars), followed by the District of Columbia ($101,700), Utah ($95,800), Massachusetts ($93,550), and New Jersey ($92,340). Mississippi and West Virginia had the lowest median household incomes at $48,610 and $52,460 respectively.
- The South was the region with the highest poverty rate among U.S. regions, with 13.2 percent of the population living in poverty in 2022, followed by the Northeast at 10.8 percent, West at 10.7 percent, and Midwest at 9.8 percent.

PART C NOTES AND DEFINITIONS: MEDIAN HOUSEHOLD INCOME AND POVERTY

Source: U.S. Department of Commerce, Bureau of the Census, https://www.census.gov.

These data are derived from the Current Population Survey (CPS), which is also the source of the widely followed monthly report on the civilian labor force, employment, and unemployment. In March of each year (with some data also collected in February and April), the households in this survey are asked additional questions concerning earnings and other income in the previous year. This additional information, informally known as the "March Supplement," is now formally known as the Current Population Survey Annual Social and Economic Supplement (CPS-ASEC). It was previously called the Annual Demographic Supplement.

The population represented by the income and poverty survey is the civilian noninstitutional population of the United States. It includes members of the armed forces in the United States living off post or with their families on post but excludes all other members of the armed forces. This is slightly different from the population base for the civilian employment and unemployment data, which excludes all armed forces households. As it is a survey of households, homeless persons are not included.

Definitions

A *household* consists of all persons who occupy a housing unit. A household includes the related family members and all the unrelated persons, if any (such as lodgers, foster children, wards, or employees), who share the housing unit. A person living alone in a housing unit or a group of unrelated persons sharing a housing unit as partners is also counted as a household. The count of households excludes group quarters.

Earnings includes all income from work, including wages, salaries, armed forces pay, commissions, tips, piece-rate payments, and cash bonuses, before deductions such as taxes, bonds, pensions, and union dues. This category also includes net income from farm and nonfarm self-employment. Wage and salary supplements that are paid directly by the employer, such as the employer share of Social Security taxes and the cost of employer-provided health insurance, are not included.

Income, in the official definition used in the survey, is money income, including *earnings* from work as defined above; unemployment compensation; workers' compensation; Social Security; Supplemental Security Income; cash public assistance (welfare payments); veterans' payments; survivor benefits; disability benefits; pension or retirement income; interest income; dividends (but not capital gains); rents, royalties, and payments from estates or trusts; educational assistance, such as scholarships or grants; child support; alimony; financial assistance from outside of the household; and other cash income regularly received, such as foster child payments, military family allotments, and foreign government pensions. Receipts not counted as income include capital gains or losses, withdrawals of bank deposits, money borrowed, tax refunds, gifts, and lump-sum inheritances or insurance payments.

Median income is the amount of income that divides a ranked income distribution into two equal groups, with half of the households having incomes above the median, and half having incomes below the median.

Historical income figures are shown in constant *2022 dollars*. All constant-dollar figures are converted from current-dollar values using the *CPI-U-RS* (the Consumer Price Index, All Urban, Research Series), compiled by the Bureau of Labor Statistics, which measures changes in prices for past periods using the methodologies of the current CPI-U.

The *number of people below poverty level,* or the number of poor people, is the number of people with family or individual incomes below a specified level representing the estimated cost of a minimum standard of living. These minimum levels vary by size and composition of family and are known as *poverty thresholds*. These poverty thresholds have been adjusted each year for price increases, using the percent change in the Consumer Price Index for All Urban Consumers (CPI-U).

The *poverty rate* for a demographic group is the number of poor people in that group expressed as a percentage of the total number of people in the group.

The data in this chapter were derived from the "Historical Income Tables" and "Historical Poverty Tables," which are available on the Census Web site.

A different set of estimates of median household income and poverty for states and smaller geographic units is also available. It is based on a different, more comprehensive Census survey, the American Community Survey (ACS); it is more precise but less timely, and it does not provide the historical record that is available in the CPS-ASEC data presented here. (The median household income data by state are available even farther back than shown here; they begin in 1984.) Further information on ACS and small-area statistics and on other research in measuring poverty can be found in the report referenced above and other reports posted on the Census Web site, under the subjects "Income" and "Poverty."

Median Household Income by State

(2022 CPI-U-RS adjusted dollars)

State	1990	1991	1992	1993	1994	1995	1996	1997	1998	1999	2000	2001	2002	2003	2004	2005	2006	2007
United States	61,500	59,710	59,210	58,920	59,550	61,440	62,350	63,640	65,980	67,650	67,470	66,360	65,820	65,860	65,760	66,780	67,520	68,610
Alabama	47,970	48,250	49,880	47,310	50,200	46,860	53,230	54,930	61,530	60,260	56,920	55,250	58,360	56,640	54,330	53,550	53,170	57,660
Alaska	80,710	80,490	80,790	80,970	83,740	86,470	92,720	82,540	86,010	85,430	84,920	90,140	81,910	78,810	81,670	80,570	79,030	86,040
Arizona	60,020	60,920	56,740	57,540	57,760	55,650	55,580	56,310	62,930	61,500	63,930	67,110	61,670	62,590	65,040	65,220	65,360	64,490
Arkansas	46,800	46,450	46,160	43,450	47,190	46,550	47,650	44,990	46,940	49,340	47,720	52,390	50,270	48,660	51,890	52,840	51,910	55,720
California	68,370	66,720	67,460	64,260	65,210	66,730	68,180	68,270	69,450	72,520	75,230	74,270	73,630	74,960	73,010	74,610	77,490	76,120
Colorado	63,120	62,430	62,790	65,050	69,830	73,400	71,940	74,350	79,060	80,080	77,520	77,620	74,960	75,930	75,480	72,720	78,020	83,510
Connecticut	79,830	83,540	78,940	74,530	75,850	72,560	73,990	75,650	78,910	84,100	80,620	83,830	82,860	83,570	81,730	81,930	87,420	87,610
Delaware	63,270	64,580	68,960	68,020	66,210	62,980	69,050	74,010	70,340	77,510	80,930	77,950	77,060	74,530	71,270	73,860	73,460	74,560
District of Columbia	56,260	59,230	58,460	51,500	55,590	55,440	56,160	54,790	56,730	64,280	66,240	64,690	60,640	68,490	64,450	64,860	67,910	69,360
Florida	54,810	54,010	52,860	53,850	54,070	53,630	53,830	55,820	59,230	59,560	62,440	57,230	59,020	59,250	60,120	61,970	63,990	62,550
Georgia	56,610	53,930	55,660	59,720	58,080	61,480	57,090	63,050	65,600	65,540	67,330	66,910	66,650	64,520	60,790	66,200	69,120	66,440
Hawaii	79,940	73,820	81,400	80,460	77,990	77,260	73,380	70,400	69,270	73,980	82,830	74,550	73,420	78,810	83,420	85,890	84,710	87,440
Idaho	51,970	51,760	53,550	58,490	58,210	58,920	60,970	57,450	62,230	59,510	60,440	60,090	58,540	64,420	65,790	63,680	64,740	67,180
Illinois	66,840	63,190	60,980	61,970	64,750	68,650	69,480	71,000	73,260	77,010	74,020	72,550	66,290	68,650	68,340	69,770	68,180	71,710
Indiana	55,310	53,690	55,140	55,590	51,420	60,200	61,740	66,880	67,410	67,880	65,660	63,450	63,710	64,500	62,790	61,170	63,610	64,810
Iowa	56,050	56,590	55,550	54,060	61,060	64,040	58,340	58,100	62,810	68,320	65,870	64,390	63,710	62,920	64,360	67,030	67,420	66,800
Kansas	61,450	58,060	58,650	56,150	52,280	54,710	57,240	62,720	62,290	62,080	65,980	65,080	66,150	67,250	60,910	60,580	63,810	66,240
Kentucky	50,900	47,100	45,390	45,980	49,090	53,750	56,940	57,530	61,510	56,080	58,270	60,400	57,060	56,160	52,820	52,900	55,310	53,890
Louisiana	46,020	50,140	49,170	49,630	47,390	50,390	53,160	57,200	53,840	54,280	49,360	52,360	52,780	50,940	54,030	53,680	51,110	56,430
Maine	56,410	55,230	57,240	51,750	55,960	61,050	60,950	56,360	60,470	64,600	59,880	57,530	57,200	56,430	61,300	63,320	63,940	65,420
Maryland	79,810	73,230	71,910	75,330	72,350	74,000	77,280	80,290	84,860	86,780	87,630	84,120	87,550	79,540	84,700	87,230	89,190	89,640
Massachusetts	74,450	70,780	70,270	69,910	74,750	69,550	69,380	72,270	71,850	73,150	75,130	82,110	77,380	77,470	77,160	80,750	77,510	79,850
Michigan	61,490	63,650	62,370	61,600	65,120	65,680	68,910	66,630	70,960	76,610	73,130	70,790	66,300	68,450	62,680	66,210	68,150	67,430
Minnesota	64,630	58,420	59,880	63,530	62,100	68,400	72,010	73,200	81,320	78,190	87,170	82,780	84,780	80,310	83,220	78,150	78,740	79,300
Mississippi	41,440	38,600	39,760	41,850	46,880	47,850	46,860	49,010	49,410	53,990	55,110	47,400	47,930	49,760	51,550	47,390	48,660	50,920
Missouri	56,140	55,350	52,880	54,100	55,720	62,790	60,190	62,870	68,210	68,790	72,470	64,960	66,390	66,540	62,500	61,970	62,450	62,840
Montana	48,010	49,200	51,270	49,920	51,000	50,050	50,390	50,240	53,580	51,590	52,670	50,480	54,070	51,860	50,370	53,790	57,580	59,630
Nebraska	56,450	58,560	58,080	58,480	58,680	59,370	59,750	59,660	61,780	64,210	67,090	68,530	66,420	66,860	64,950	69,080	67,440	67,160
Nevada	65,770	65,280	61,670	67,550	66,210	65,060	67,700	66,820	67,450	68,920	73,530	71,350	69,780	68,700	70,020	69,490	73,240	73,830
New Hampshire	83,810	71,410	76,220	71,600	65,050	70,630	69,230	70,510	76,280	76,560	81,830	80,660	85,860	84,490	84,270	82,140	86,810	92,300
New Jersey	79,560	79,370	75,380	76,390	78,040	79,200	83,390	82,590	84,540	82,670	80,990	81,350	84,690	85,210	81,990	91,350	95,340	82,640
New Mexico	51,430	52,600	49,980	50,470	49,660	46,860	44,070	51,740	53,520	54,150	56,390	52,050	55,030	53,370	58,680	56,140	56,070	60,580
New York	64,880	63,010	60,020	59,780	58,880	59,550	62,210	61,570	63,450	66,470	65,470	66,180	65,140	65,060	66,230	68,010	67,550	66,850
North Carolina	54,080	53,220	53,680	54,360	55,580	57,660	62,540	61,640	60,810	61,930	61,570	59,970	56,670	56,680	59,680	60,620	55,750	59,430
North Dakota	51,890	51,310	52,110	53,030	52,190	52,450	55,280	54,450	51,420	54,300	57,840	56,250	56,190	61,440	58,170	60,820	57,500	64,470
Ohio	61,640	59,040	60,700	59,010	58,800	63,000	59,850	62,140	66,040	65,640	69,030	65,660	66,250	66,170	63,860	63,720	64,300	67,060
Oklahoma	50,080	50,460	48,870	49,530	49,820	47,440	48,200	53,920	57,220	54,330	52,110	55,960	56,590	54,590	58,760	54,270	54,410	59,030
Oregon	60,140	59,830	61,710	62,500	58,060	65,590	62,350	64,060	66,280	67,520	68,290	64,860	64,880	63,310	60,810	63,660	65,970	68,610
Pennsylvania	59,570	60,180	57,760	58,460	59,190	62,250	61,310	64,520	66,200	62,760	67,770	68,360	65,960	65,280	65,420	66,740	67,910	66,160
Rhode Island	65,660	61,110	58,820	63,200	58,930	63,760	64,970	59,850	69,030	71,010	67,810	71,850	65,840	67,980	71,100	71,330	75,280	74,040
South Carolina	59,020	54,430	53,300	49,140	55,090	52,420	60,900	58,930	56,440	60,610	60,370	59,300	58,690	58,500	57,390	57,990	55,500	60,390
South Dakota	50,470	48,830	50,750	52,310	54,880	53,330	51,870	51,070	55,630	59,560	58,610	62,340	58,780	60,090	60,970	62,200	63,640	63,400
Tennessee	46,400	48,460	47,000	47,340	52,860	52,320	54,090	52,690	57,840	60,710	54,790	56,230	57,470	57,050	56,470	56,800	57,010	56,270
Texas	57,980	54,960	54,030	54,180	56,770	57,770	58,100	60,320	60,710	64,310	62,040	64,210	62,320	59,710	61,400	59,710	60,670	62,900
Utah	61,910	55,520	66,200	67,500	65,920	65,780	65,070	73,570	75,160	76,550	76,410	74,400	74,280	74,920	75,460	79,010	76,530	73,110
Vermont	63,870	57,780	63,310	58,590	66,080	60,990	56,840	60,290	66,800	69,120	63,620	64,110	66,740	65,770	70,200	73,090	72,820	64,730
Virginia	72,040	71,620	73,830	68,720	69,490	65,310	68,880	73,880	73,560	75,950	75,780	78,950	77,030	83,290	75,860	74,840	80,020	80,800
Washington	65,950	67,320	65,520	67,250	61,890	64,130	64,430	76,640	80,460	75,590	68,330	66,770	70,130	72,230	74,050	73,010	76,660	79,330
West Virginia	45,470	45,870	39,180	42,290	43,490	44,860	44,350	47,280	45,310	48,700	47,260	46,630	45,570	49,810	49,500	52,540	53,820	57,490
Wisconsin	63,080	61,700	64,380	59,910	65,320	73,850	70,270	68,100	70,120	75,910	72,450	71,260	71,250	70,350	67,830	64,360	72,410	70,040
Wyoming	60,510	57,570	58,390	55,530	61,170	56,850	54,380	57,480	59,810	61,920	63,680	62,420	61,720	64,700	67,340	64,460	65,900	66,580

Median Household Income by State—Continued

(2022 CPI-U-RS adjusted dollars)

State	2008	2009[1]	2010	2011	2012	2013[2]	2013[3]	2014	2015	2016	2017	2017[4]	2018	2019	2020	2021	2022
United States	66,280	65,850	64,300	63,350	63,350	63,720	65,740	64,900	68,410	70,840	72,370	72,090	73,030	78,250	76,660	76,330	74,580
Alabama	58,600	52,890	53,420	53,900	53,970	50,770	58,050	51,140	53,880	56,660	60,270	59,980	57,720	64,010	61,650	61,390	59,910
Alaska	84,310	81,490	75,490	72,690	79,030	75,000	88,910	81,800	90,920	90,860	85,170	91,960	79,450	89,290	84,260	87,490	89,740
Arizona	61,810	60,510	61,200	61,540	58,410	62,080	64,540	59,580	63,250	68,510	72,080	70,390	71,990	80,500	75,620	76,370	73,450
Arkansas	52,160	48,330	50,350	52,270	48,450	48,970	48,310	54,340	51,810	55,080	57,580	58,660	57,540	62,120	57,240	54,760	53,980
California	75,120	74,260	70,840	67,540	70,800	70,580	74,580	73,170	77,030	79,960	82,260	82,580	81,480	88,960	87,530	87,960	85,300
Colorado	80,290	73,990	78,600	74,200	71,090	77,740	83,310	73,710	80,610	84,670	87,460	88,420	84,420	82,580	94,440	91,610	89,930
Connecticut	85,220	85,790	86,120	82,790	79,770	83,150	85,010	84,870	88,230	91,100	85,820	87,620	84,160	99,420	89,540	87,300	90,730
Delaware	66,800	68,940	72,050	69,180	60,810	64,060	66,360	69,580	69,910	69,650	73,480	76,600	75,140	84,510	78,930	74,070	80,750
District of Columbia	73,240	70,300	74,290	69,930	81,010	74,440	73,680	82,590	84,820	85,170	98,320	95,840	99,110	106,100	99,440	97,740	101,700
Florida	59,100	60,360	57,500	57,090	57,210	58,750	59,540	55,810	59,100	61,400	63,300	62,600	63,160	66,480	65,110	64,410	65,370
Georgia	60,910	57,330	57,570	58,190	59,750	58,200	57,650	59,940	61,450	64,230	67,230	68,370	64,520	64,500	66,810	66,310	67,730
Hawaii	81,060	73,620	77,700	74,730	69,860	75,340	78,800	86,150	78,090	86,550	86,760	86,780	92,590	100,200	91,110	88,630	91,010
Idaho	62,480	61,880	61,400	60,070	59,500	63,510	59,460	64,640	62,490	67,870	70,990	70,160	67,880	75,160	75,220	82,940	72,580
Illinois	70,160	69,940	66,200	64,090	64,240	70,170	66,170	66,430	73,130	73,650	76,180	77,790	81,080	84,740	83,790	85,460	78,020
Indiana	61,290	58,610	60,210	56,250	57,310	62,020	60,670	58,130	62,930	67,310	69,420	69,290	69,230	75,960	75,310	75,690	70,030
Iowa	66,060	67,100	63,960	63,560	66,360	67,300	73,800	69,930	73,660	70,900	74,850	74,840	79,430	75,240	77,570	78,100	76,320
Kansas	63,080	59,150	60,100	58,410	62,090	63,160	58,670	64,650	66,410	68,160	68,240	67,090	73,900	83,320	82,380	81,930	73,040
Kentucky	54,210	56,440	53,640	50,440	51,020	51,720	55,060	51,750	51,310	54,440	60,550	58,570	63,060	63,400	63,980	59,980	55,880
Louisiana	52,130	60,100	51,280	51,460	48,530	48,610	56,950	51,290	55,590	50,630	51,770	51,370	57,760	58,890	57,700	61,690	58,330
Maine	62,220	62,840	62,550	62,890	61,040	61,490	67,420	62,550	61,440	61,020	60,920	62,870	67,810	75,800	71,800	76,710	75,160
Maryland	83,940	84,910	83,780	87,170	89,200	80,060	85,080	92,130	89,090	88,500	95,610	96,800	99,660	108,900	106,900	105,000	108,200
Massachusetts	79,470	78,540	79,520	80,130	79,040	77,240	76,710	76,390	82,150	86,710	86,350	89,900	99,800	99,900	98,980	93,340	93,550
Michigan	65,600	60,840	60,390	61,860	62,100	59,870	69,400	62,910	65,610	68,500	68,040	66,510	69,870	73,030	72,590	69,540	68,990
Minnesota	72,370	74,200	68,280	73,180	76,730	74,720	78,910	81,340	83,200	84,250	84,800	82,510	83,010	92,740	88,770	86,740	90,390
Mississippi	48,020	46,400	49,800	52,010	45,500	50,120	39,670	42,970	48,460	49,310	51,220	51,030	49,450	51,010	50,880	50,290	48,610
Missouri	60,660	64,510	59,790	57,930	61,790	61,720	56,800	68,500	71,660	66,010	67,080	66,660	71,350	69,020	70,090	68,570	71,520
Montana	56,520	53,490	53,870	50,980	55,980	54,140	53,000	61,810	62,210	68,480	69,670	67,690	66,670	68,560	63,960	70,090	72,980
Nebraska	66,840	65,610	68,510	70,390	64,810	65,970	70,690	68,790	73,200	71,240	70,300	70,260	78,110	83,230	81,440	84,220	78,360
Nevada	72,130	68,040	66,810	59,540	58,770	55,660	63,600	60,330	62,960	66,510	66,680	68,440	71,510	80,760	68,950	69,380	72,330
New Hampshire	87,190	84,840	86,950	83,380	84,210	87,500	84,770	88,780	91,600	91,500	88,200	89,180	94,020	98,980	100,200	95,800	84,970
New Jersey	86,040	85,690	82,170	78,900	82,810	75,790	78,210	78,920	82,750	82,150	86,070	84,000	85,740	99,920	96,430	95,490	92,340
New Mexico	55,470	57,600	58,900	53,130	53,920	51,680	49,280	56,470	54,620	58,130	56,430	53,770	55,810	60,500	57,380	57,650	56,420
New York	66,480	66,430	64,960	64,090	59,200	66,050	61,300	65,690	70,210	73,720	73,630	72,570	77,760	81,840	77,400	78,630	75,910
North Carolina	56,560	55,440	57,200	57,210	51,600	50,550	56,850	56,590	61,490	64,510	59,360	58,420	61,690	69,660	68,120	67,820	65,070
North Dakota	65,390	66,240	66,560	71,330	69,240	64,880	72,570	73,460	69,500	72,210	70,610	70,950	76,870	79,760	72,270	74,280	78,720
Ohio	61,840	60,690	59,880	56,510	55,100	56,920	62,260	60,050	64,520	64,770	70,480	71,560	71,240	73,650	68,060	67,600	67,520
Oklahoma	60,750	60,690	56,250	61,330	60,110	53,710	56,630	57,090	56,990	61,120	64,860	61,180	62,920	67,650	59,150	64,800	63,440
Oregon	68,150	64,950	66,030	65,210	64,290	69,080	60,110	71,220	73,640	70,950	76,180	73,690	79,950	84,760	86,630	88,260	86,780
Pennsylvania	67,720	63,720	63,050	63,170	64,450	66,190	67,670	66,740	73,100	73,170	74,490	72,260	74,580	80,390	79,800	78,310	72,210
Rhode Island	70,150	68,300	67,370	62,060	69,610	70,920	69,100	70,920	67,430	73,830	78,280	77,120	71,970	79,900	90,380	80,850	80,650
South Carolina	55,540	54,370	54,410	50,730	55,130	53,670	53,440	54,350	56,120	65,200	64,820	64,310	66,400	70,650	68,020	67,440	61,770
South Dakota	67,980	60,620	59,180	59,770	61,360	66,800	65,530	64,170	66,660	68,930	67,090	67,110	68,730	73,190	79,120	79,680	67,180
Tennessee	52,310	53,600	50,360	53,510	53,390	52,140	53,200	52,880	57,290	61,610	65,140	65,210	64,800	64,500	61,970	67,030	65,380
Texas	61,250	62,800	61,680	62,080	64,480	65,050	63,070	65,170	68,360	69,770	69,920	70,860	69,100	76,820	77,110	72,680	74,640
Utah	82,390	77,370	73,990	70,230	72,440	77,250	74,890	76,670	80,200	80,970	84,100	82,290	89,080	96,270	94,680	94,510	95,800
Vermont	66,810	69,210	72,980	65,640	69,010	67,280	80,370	73,430	72,020	73,000	75,240	75,090	80,990	84,630	75,810	82,040	72,190
Virginia	81,670	80,030	78,780	79,250	80,250	82,960	80,850	80,020	74,430	79,730	84,060	83,500	89,180	92,610	92,670	86,550	85,170
Washington	74,610	79,890	73,290	71,950	77,220	73,740	78,420	71,450	81,400	84,360	88,930	84,360	92,150	93,910	91,710	94,510	89,430
West Virginia	50,060	53,560	55,820	52,930	54,080	49,370	52,840	47,840	51,840	53,220	53,520	55,370	58,460	61,170	58,580	50,500	52,460
Wisconsin	67,460	67,780	65,710	65,890	65,910	67,790	63,460	70,250	67,090	71,770	74,820	74,850	72,390	76,720	75,980	75,420	73,330
Wyoming	70,270	69,410	68,120	68,990	71,410	68,330	82,740	67,360	73,750	69,390	68,200	70,200	72,290	74,190	73,780	76,620	73,090

[1]Beginning with 2009 income data, the Census Bureau expanded the upper income interval used to calculate medians and Gini indexes to $250,000 or more. Medians falling in the upper open-ended interval are plugged with "$250,000." Before 2009, the upper open-ended interval was $100,000 and a plug of "$100,000" was used.

[2]The 2014 CPS ASEC included redesigned questions for income and health insurance coverage. All of the approximately 98,000 addresses were eligible to receive the redesigned set of health insurance coverage questions. The redesigned income questions were implemented to a subsample of the 98,000 addresses using a probability split panel design. Approximately 68,000 addresses were eligible to receive a set of income questions similar to those used in the 2013 CPS ASEC and the remaining 30,000 addresses were eligible to receive the redesigned income questions. The source of these 2013 estimates is the portion of the CPS ASEC sample which received the income questions consistent with the 2013 CPS ASEC, approximately 68,000 addresses.

[3]The source of these 2013 estimates is the portion of the CPS ASEC sample which received the redesigned income questions, approximately 30,000 addresses.

[4]Estimates reflect the implementation of an updated data processing system, allowing users to evaluate the impact, and should be used to make comparisons to 2018 and subsequent years.

Historical Poverty Rates by State

(Percent of population.)

State	2000	2001	2002	2003	2004	2005	2006	2007	2008	2009	2010	2011	2012	2013[1]	2013[2]	2014	2015	2016	2017	2017[3]	2018	2019	2020	2021	2022
United States..........	11.3	11.7	12.1	12.5	12.7	12.6	12.3	12.5	13.2	14.3	15.1	15.0	15.0	14.5	14.8	14.8	13.5	12.7	12.3	12.3	11.8	10.5	11.5	11.6	11.5
Alabama................	13.3	15.9	14.5	15.0	16.9	16.7	14.3	14.5	14.3	16.6	17.2	15.4	16.2	16.7	18.5	17.8	16.3	16.2	15.0	15.3	16.0	12.9	14.9	15.9	13.6
Alaska....................	7.6	8.5	8.8	9.6	9.1	10.0	8.9	7.6	8.2	11.7	12.5	11.7	10.0	10.9	9.7	11.9	9.2	12.6	14.4	12.1	13.1	10.2	13.4	11.4	9.6
Arizona..................	11.7	14.6	13.5	13.5	14.4	15.2	14.4	14.3	18.0	21.2	18.8	17.2	19.0	20.2	17.8	21.2	17.2	16.1	13.2	13.6	12.8	9.9	10.9	12.6	12.7
Arkansas................	16.5	17.8	19.8	17.8	15.1	13.8	17.7	13.8	15.3	18.9	15.3	18.7	20.1	17.1	13.9	18.4	16.1	16.0	14.8	14.9	15.9	14.1	14.1	16.8	16.6
California................	12.7	12.6	13.1	13.1	13.2	13.2	12.2	12.7	14.6	15.3	16.3	16.9	15.9	14.9	15.1	15.8	13.9	13.9	12.4	12.1	11.9	10.1	11.1	11.9	11.2
Colorado................	9.8	8.7	9.8	9.7	10.0	11.4	9.7	9.8	11.0	12.3	12.3	13.2	11.9	10.6	10.7	12.3	9.9	8.5	7.7	8.9	9.1	9.3	9.5	7.9	8.1
Connecticut...........	7.7	7.3	8.3	8.1	10.1	9.3	8.0	8.9	8.1	8.4	8.6	10.1	10.3	11.3	10.9	8.6	9.1	9.8	10.9	10.6	10.2	8.3	11.2	8.0	10.2
Delaware................	8.4	6.7	9.1	7.3	9.0	9.2	9.3	9.3	9.6	12.3	12.2	13.7	13.5	14.0	11.2	11.0	11.1	11.6	9.2	8.8	7.4	6.5	10.5	11.7	9.3
D.C........................	15.2	18.2	17.0	16.8	17.0	21.3	18.3	18.0	16.5	17.9	19.5	19.9	18.4	21.3	23.2	19.0	16.6	16.3	13.6	13.9	14.7	12.5	16.8	14.0	13.4
Florida...................	11.0	12.7	12.6	12.7	11.6	11.1	11.5	12.5	13.1	14.6	16.0	14.9	15.3	14.9	14.8	16.7	16.2	13.0	13.7	13.4	13.7	11.5	13.3	12.6	13.5
Georgia..................	12.1	12.9	11.2	11.9	13.0	14.4	12.6	13.6	15.5	18.4	18.8	18.4	18.1	16.3	18.5	16.8	18.1	15.4	13.3	13.1	14.8	12.1	13.3	14.0	11.7
Hawaii....................	8.9	11.4	11.3	9.3	8.6	8.6	9.2	7.5	9.9	12.5	12.4	12.1	13.8	11.1	10.6	10.8	10.9	9.3	10.3	10.6	9.2	8.4	10.9	10.9	8.8
Idaho......................	12.5	11.5	11.3	10.2	9.9	9.9	9.5	9.9	12.2	13.7	13.8	15.7	14.4	12.9	12.4	12.4	12.3	11.1	11.7	11.5	11.5	7.1	9.1	9.3	8.2
Illinois....................	10.7	10.1	12.8	12.6	12.3	11.5	10.6	10.0	12.3	13.2	14.1	14.2	12.6	13.3	13.6	13.7	10.9	12.1	10.9	11.5	10.3	9.3	8.0	10.7	9.5
Indiana...................	8.5	8.5	9.1	9.9	11.6	12.6	10.6	11.8	14.3	16.1	16.3	15.6	15.2	11.6	16.5	14.6	13.5	11.8	11.4	11.7	11.6	10.1	12.1	10.4	10.4
Iowa.......................	8.3	7.4	9.2	8.9	10.9	11.3	10.3	8.9	9.5	10.7	10.3	10.4	10.3	10.8	13.2	10.3	10.4	9.8	9.1	7.5	8.9	9.5	9.2	9.7	9.4
Kansas....................	8.0	10.1	10.1	10.8	11.4	12.5	12.8	11.7	12.7	13.7	14.5	14.3	14.0	13.2	11.4	12.1	14.2	11.2	14.7	14.3	7.5	9.5	9.3	7.1	10.5
Kentucky................	12.6	12.6	14.2	14.4	17.8	14.8	16.8	15.5	17.1	17.0	17.7	16.0	17.9	20.0	22.0	20.0	19.5	15.2	14.4	13.5	15.7	13.6	13.9	16.2	17.1
Louisiana................	17.2	16.2	17.5	17.0	16.8	18.3	17.0	16.1	18.2	14.3	21.5	21.1	21.1	19.2	21.2	23.1	18.6	20.2	21.4	20.5	19.0	17.9	15.5	18.4	16.9
Maine.....................	10.1	10.3	13.4	11.6	11.6	12.6	10.2	10.9	12.0	11.4	12.6	13.4	12.8	12.3	11.4	14.6	12.3	12.7	12.0	12.4	11.6	10.4	8.0	9.1	9.6
Maryland................	7.4	7.2	7.4	8.6	9.9	9.7	8.4	8.8	8.7	9.6	10.9	9.3	9.9	10.3	10.5	9.8	9.6	7.1	7.8	7.6	8.0	7.0	9.4	7.7	8.6
Massachusetts.......	9.8	8.9	10.0	10.3	9.3	10.1	12.0	11.2	11.3	10.8	10.9	10.6	11.3	11.9	12.1	13.6	11.5	9.6	10.6	11.2	8.7	7.5	8.4	7.6	9.6
Michigan................	9.9	9.4	11.6	11.4	13.3	12.0	13.3	10.8	13.0	14.0	15.7	15.0	13.7	14.5	12.7	14.8	12.8	11.1	12.7	11.5	10.5	10.2	11.2	11.7	12.1
Minnesota...............	5.7	7.4	6.5	7.4	7.0	8.1	8.2	9.3	9.9	11.1	10.8	10.0	10.0	12.0	11.0	8.3	7.8	8.7	9.2	8.5	7.9	5.7	8.5	6.9	7.6
Mississippi.............	14.9	19.3	18.4	16.0	18.7	20.1	20.6	22.6	18.1	23.1	22.5	17.4	22.0	22.5	19.1	22.1	19.1	21.1	18.3	18.5	19.6	19.2	17.6	17.4	18.4
Missouri..................	9.2	9.7	9.9	10.7	12.2	11.6	11.4	12.8	13.3	15.5	15.0	15.4	15.2	13.7	17.5	10.4	9.8	13.0	11.1	11.4	12.4	9.4	10.7	12.3	11.4
Montana..................	14.1	13.3	13.5	15.1	14.2	13.8	13.5	13.0	12.9	13.5	14.5	16.5	13.4	14.5	10.5	12.0	11.9	11.7	9.7	10.3	10.3	9.7	10.9	10.7	10.4
Nebraska................	8.6	9.4	10.6	9.8	9.5	9.5	10.2	9.9	10.6	9.9	10.2	10.2	12.2	11.0	10.5	11.8	10.3	9.6	10.4	11.5	10.5	8.7	8.3	8.1	7.9
Nevada...................	8.8	7.1	8.9	10.9	10.9	10.6	9.5	9.7	10.8	13.0	16.6	15.5	15.8	17.4	14.5	17.0	13.0	10.1	13.7	13.2	13.0	10.4	12.9	12.8	12.0
New Hampshire......	4.5	6.5	5.8	5.8	5.5	5.6	5.4	5.8	7.0	7.8	6.5	7.6	8.1	9.0	5.5	7.2	7.3	6.4	6.6	7.2	6.1	3.7	6.2	6.9	8.3
New Jersey............	7.3	8.1	7.9	8.6	8.0	6.8	8.8	8.7	9.2	9.3	11.1	11.4	9.3	11.1	9.9	11.3	11.2	9.4	8.6	9.9	8.2	6.3	8.2	7.6	8.7
New Mexico...........	17.5	18.0	17.9	18.1	16.5	17.9	16.9	14.0	19.3	19.3	18.3	22.2	20.4	21.7	25.8	20.0	19.7	17.8	18.6	19.7	16.6	15.3	16.6	18.0	20.2
New York................	13.9	14.2	14.0	14.3	15.0	14.5	14.0	14.5	14.2	15.8	16.0	16.0	17.2	14.5	17.3	14.0	14.2	11.9	13.4	12.7	11.1	12.5	11.8	12.5	12.7
North Carolina........	12.5	12.5	14.3	15.7	14.6	13.1	13.8	15.5	13.9	16.9	17.4	15.4	17.2	18.6	14.7	17.1	15.3	13.6	14.5	15.2	13.1	12.7	13.8	11.8	14.2
North Dakota..........	10.4	13.8	11.6	9.7	9.7	11.2	11.4	9.3	11.8	10.9	12.6	9.9	11.4	9.9	13.2	9.7	10.7	11.1	11.3	12.4	9.7	8.1	10.7	8.5	9.7
Ohio.......................	10.0	10.5	9.8	10.9	11.6	12.3	12.1	12.8	13.7	13.3	15.4	15.1	15.4	13.7	14.9	15.6	13.6	13.7	12.7	12.9	11.9	12.4	12.7	11.6	9.9
Oklahoma...............	14.9	15.1	14.1	12.8	10.8	15.6	15.2	13.4	13.6	12.9	16.3	13.9	18.0	14.0	21.2	17.3	14.2	14.6	12.6	12.8	13.4	10.8	15.5	15.1	16.9
Oregon...................	10.9	11.8	10.9	12.5	11.8	12.0	11.8	12.8	10.6	13.4	14.3	14.4	13.5	15.1	14.0	14.4	11.9	11.8	10.2	11.5	9.7	8.1	9.4	9.2	9.9
Pennsylvania..........	8.6	9.6	9.5	10.5	11.4	11.2	11.3	10.4	11.0	11.1	12.2	12.6	13.9	12.4	11.2	12.5	12.3	11.1	11.2	10.9	11.8	8.7	10.7	10.8	10.9
Rhode Island..........	10.2	9.6	11.0	11.5	11.5	12.1	10.5	9.5	12.7	13.0	14.0	13.4	13.6	13.5	9.3	11.3	11.8	11.4	12.2	11.3	8.9	9.2	8.5	9.4	8.4
South Carolina.......	11.1	15.1	14.3	12.7	14.9	15.0	11.2	14.1	14.0	13.7	16.9	19.0	16.7	15.9	19.3	16.5	14.3	14.1	15.6	15.2	12.8	15.1	13.4	13.7	12.9
South Dakota.........	10.7	8.4	11.5	12.7	13.5	11.8	10.7	9.4	13.1	14.1	13.6	14.5	12.8	10.3	13.3	12.8	13.9	14.5	10.4	10.7	10.6	10.6	11.6	8.4	9.1
Tennessee.............	13.5	14.1	14.8	14.0	15.9	14.9	14.9	14.8	15.0	16.5	16.7	16.3	18.6	18.1	15.5	17.3	14.7	14.9	11.5	11.3	12.0	13.1	13.1	10.6	10.5
Texas......................	15.5	14.9	15.6	17.0	16.5	16.2	16.4	16.5	15.9	17.3	18.4	17.4	17.0	16.8	16.9	16.4	14.7	13.8	13.4	13.2	13.7	11.1	14.0	13.5	13.5
Utah.......................	7.6	10.5	9.9	9.1	10.1	9.2	9.3	9.6	7.6	9.7	10.0	11.0	11.0	8.3	12.2	10.2	9.3	8.6	8.6	8.7	6.9	7.3	7.4	7.9	6.0
Vermont.................	10.0	9.7	9.9	8.5	7.8	7.6	7.8	9.9	9.0	9.4	10.8	11.6	11.2	8.7	6.8	9.3	10.7	9.6	10.2	8.6	9.7	8.6	8.6	7.5	9.0
Virginia..................	8.3	8.0	9.9	10.0	9.4	9.2	8.6	8.6	10.3	10.7	10.7	11.4	10.6	10.4	9.8	10.2	10.9	11.4	10.3	10.5	9.8	8.8	7.8	9.8	8.3
Washington............	10.8	10.7	11.0	12.6	11.4	10.2	8.0	10.2	10.4	11.7	11.6	12.5	11.6	12.0	12.2	12.0	11.4	11.0	9.9	10.9	8.6	7.0	8.2	7.7	9.0
West Virginia..........	14.7	16.4	16.8	17.4	14.2	15.4	15.3	14.8	14.5	15.8	16.8	17.5	16.7	17.3	19.8	20.6	14.5	18.0	17.3	17.1	15.9	13.9	14.2	16.9	15.5
Wisconsin...............	9.3	7.9	8.6	9.8	12.4	10.2	10.1	11.0	9.8	10.8	10.1	13.1	11.4	11.0	13.5	10.9	11.4	10.7	9.5	9.2	8.6	8.4	8.0	9.3	6.6
Wyoming.................	10.8	8.7	9.0	9.8	10.0	10.6	10.0	10.9	10.1	9.2	9.6	10.7	9.6	11.8	11.4	9.7	9.8	10.9	12.4	13.0	9.5	9.2	9.7	9.4	7.1

[1]The source of these 2013 estimates is the portion of the CPS ASEC sample that received the income questions consistent with the 2013 CPS ASEC, approximately 68,000 addresses.
[2]The 2014 CPS ASEC included redesigned questions for income and health insurance coverage. All of the approximately 98,000 addresses were eligible to receive the redesigned set of health insurance coverage questions. The redesigned income questions were implemented to a subsample of the 98,000 addresses using a probability split panel design. Approximately 68,000 addresses were eligible to receive a set of income questions similar to those used in the 2013 CPS ASEC, and the remaining 30,000 addresses were eligible to receive the redesigned income questions. The source of these 2013 estimates is the portion of the CPS ASEC sample that received the redesigned income questions, approximately 30,000 addresses.
[3]Estimates reflect the implementation of an updated processing system and should be used to make comparisons to 2018 and subsequent years.

Historical Poverty Rates by Region

(Numbers in thousands, percent.)

Year	All Regions		Northeast		Midwest		South		West	
	Below Poverty		Below Poverty		Below Poverty		Below Poverty		Below Poverty	
	Number	Percent	Number	Percent	Number	Percent	Number	Percent	Number	Percent
1959	39,490	22.4	...	...	...	...	19,116	35.4	...	...
1960	39,851	22.2	...	...	...	...	...	...	...	...
1969	24,147	12.1	4,108	8.6	5,424	9.6	11,090	17.9	3,525	10.4
1970	25,420	12.6	...	...	...	...	11,480	18.5	...	...
1971	25,560	12.5	4,512	9.3	5,764	10.3	11,180	17.5	4,101	11.4
1972	24,460	11.9	4,266	8.7	5,258	9.3	10,930	16.9	4,008	11.1
1973	22,970	11.1	4,207	8.6	4,864	8.6	10,060	15.3	3,841	10.5
1974	23,370	11.2	4,473	9.3	4,990	8.8	10,760	16.1	4,036	10.7
1975	25,880	12.3	4,904	10.2	5,459	9.7	11,060	16.2	4,454	11.7
1976	24,980	11.8	4,949	10.2	5,657	9.9	10,350	15.2	4,015	10.5
1977	24,720	11.6	4,956	10.2	5,589	9.8	10,250	14.8	3,927	10.1
1978	24,500	11.4	5,050	10.4	5,192	9.1	10,260	14.7	4,000	10.0
1979	26,070	11.7	5,029	10.4	5,594	9.7	10,630	15.0	4,095	10.0
1980	29,270	13.0	5,369	11.1	6,592	11.4	12,360	16.5	4,958	11.4
1981	31,820	14.0	5,815	11.9	7,142	12.3	13,260	17.4	5,609	12.7
1982	34,400	15.0	6,364	13.0	7,772	13.3	13,970	18.1	6,296	14.1
1983	35,300	15.2	6,561	13.4	8,536	14.6	13,480	17.2	6,684	14.7
1984	33,700	14.4	6,531	13.2	8,303	14.1	12,790	16.2	6,074	13.1
1985	33,060	14.0	5,751	11.6	8,191	13.9	12,920	16.0	6,201	13.0
1986	32,370	13.6	5,211	10.5	7,641	13.0	13,110	16.1	6,412	13.2
1987	32,220	13.4	5,476	11.0	7,499	12.7	13,290	16.1	6,285	12.6
1988	31,750	13.0	5,089	10.1	6,804	11.4	13,530	16.1	6,322	12.7
1989	31,530	12.8	5,061	10.0	7,043	11.9	12,940	15.4	6,481	12.5
1990	33,590	13.5	5,794	11.4	7,458	12.4	13,460	15.8	6,877	13.0
1991	35,710	14.2	6,177	12.2	7,989	13.2	13,780	16.0	7,759	14.3
1992	38,010	14.8	6,414	12.6	8,060	13.3	15,200	17.1	8,343	14.8
1993	39,270	15.1	6,839	13.3	8,172	13.4	15,380	17.1	8,879	15.6
1994	38,060	14.5	6,597	12.9	7,965	13.0	14,730	16.1	8,768	15.3
1995	36,430	13.8	6,445	12.5	6,785	11.0	14,460	15.7	8,736	14.9
1996	36,530	13.7	6,558	12.7	6,654	10.7	14,100	15.1	9,219	15.4
1997	35,570	13.3	6,474	12.6	6,493	10.4	13,750	14.6	8,858	14.6
1998	34,480	12.7	6,357	12.3	6,501	10.3	12,990	13.7	8,625	14.0
1999	32,790	11.9	5,814	11.0	6,250	9.8	12,740	13.2	7,982	12.7
2000	31,580	11.3	5,474	10.3	5,916	9.3	12,710	12.8	7,485	11.8
2001	32,910	11.7	5,687	10.7	5,966	9.4	13,520	13.5	7,739	12.1
2002	34,570	12.1	5,871	10.9	6,616	10.3	14,020	13.8	8,064	12.4
2003	35,860	12.5	6,052	11.3	6,932	10.7	14,550	14.1	8,329	12.6
2004	37,040	12.7	6,260	11.6	7,545	11.7	14,820	14.1	8,419	12.5
2005	36,950	12.6	6,103	11.3	7,419	11.4	14,850	14.0	8,573	12.6
2006	36,460	12.3	6,222	11.5	7,324	11.2	14,880	13.8	8,032	11.6
2007	37,280	12.5	6,166	11.4	7,237	11.1	15,500	14.2	8,372	12.0
2008	39,830	13.2	6,295	11.6	8,120	12.4	15,860	14.3	9,552	13.5
2009	43,570	14.3	6,650	12.2	8,768	13.3	17,610	15.7	10,540	14.8
2010	46,340	15.1	7,038	12.9	9,216	14.0	19,120	16.8	10,970	15.3
2011	46,250	15.0	7,208	13.1	9,221	14.0	18,380	16.0	11,440	15.8
2012	46,500	15.0	7,490	13.6	8,851	13.3	19,110	16.5	11,050	15.1
2013	45,320	14.5	7,046	12.7	8,590	12.9	18,870	16.1	10,810	14.7
2014	46,660	14.8	7,020	12.6	8,714	13.0	19,530	16.5	11,390	15.2
2015	43,120	13.5	6,891	12.4	7,849	11.7	18,310	15.3	10,080	13.3
2016	40,620	12.7	5,969	10.8	7,809	11.7	17,030	14.1	9,810	12.8
2017	39,560	12.3	6,347	11.3	7,571	11.2	16,470	13.5	9,172	11.9
2018	38,150	11.8	5,682	10.3	7,005	10.4	16,760	13.6	8,701	11.2
2019	33,980	10.5	5,177	9.4	6,518	9.7	14,850	12.0	7,443	9.5
2020	37,550	11.5	5,734	10.2	6,906	10.1	16,650	13.3	8,254	10.6
2021	37,930	11.6	5,664	10.1	7,043	10.4	16,630	13.2	8,592	11.0
2022	37,920	11.5	6,083	10.8	6,648	9.8	16,830	13.2	8,364	10.7

PART D

CONSUMER SPENDING AND PRICES BY REGION, STATE, AND AREA

PART D: CONSUMER SPENDING AND PRICES BY REGION, STATE, AND AREA

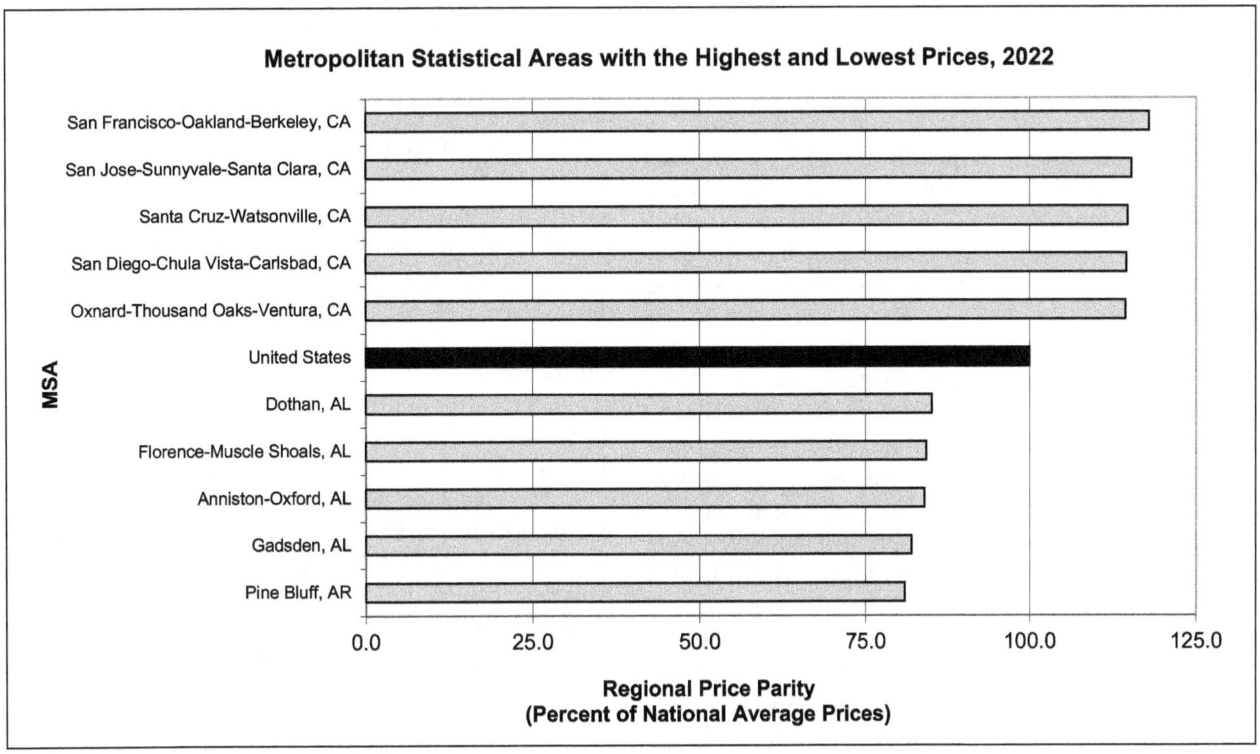

HIGHLIGHTS

- The MSAs with the highest regional price parities (RPP) in 2022 were: San Francisco-Oakland-Berkeley, CA (117.9), San Jose-Sunnyvale-Santa Clara, CA (115.3), Santa Cruz-Watsonville, CA (114.7), San Diego-Chula Vista-Carlsbad, CA (114.5), and Oxnard-Thousand Oaks-Ventura, CA (114.4). The MSAs with the lowest RPPs were: Pine Bluff, AR (80.9), Gadsden, AL (81.9), Anniston-Oxford, AL (83.9), and Florence-Muscle Shoals, AL (84.2).

- New England was the region with the highest total per capita consumption expenditure ($61,033) in 2022, and the Southwest had the lowest per capita consumption expenditure ($48,329).

- Among all the states, Washington, D.C., had the highest total per capita consumption expenditure in 2022 ($85,732). It also had the highest per capita expenditures on groceries ($7,217), housing and utilities ($14,959), and health care ($12,239). The national averages were $52,542 total, $4,181 on groceries, $9,161 on housing and utilities, and $8,331 on health care.

- Residents of Hawaii spent the second most on groceries ($5,322), and residents of Colorado spent the second most on housing and utilities ($11,466) in 2022. Residents of Oklahoma spent the least on groceries ($3,198), and residents of Mississippi spent the least on housing and utilities ($6,436).

- Per person health care spending was second highest in Alaska ($11,813) and was lowest in Utah ($6,213) in 2022.

- We see the impact of post-pandemic inflation on grocery prices reflected in the increase in per capita spending on groceries from 2019 to 2022. U.S. per capita spending on groceries increased 27.6 percent in this period.

PART D NOTES AND DEFINITIONS: CONSUMER SPENDING AND PRICES BY REGION, STATE, AND AREA

Source: U.S. Department of Commerce, Bureau of Economic Analysis (BEA), https://www.bea.gov.

The following definitions are from the BEA.

BEA definitions

Personal Consumption Expenditures (PCE) includes a measure of consumer spending on goods and services among households in the U.S. The PCE is used as a mechanism to gauge how much earned income of households is being spent on current consumption for various goods and services.

Data are sourced from several statistical reports. These reports come from various government agencies, administrative and regulatory agencies, and other private organizations. PCE utilizes data sourced for other agencies and organizations that measure the goods and services purchased by households and nonprofit institutions serving households (NPISHs) who are resident in the United States.

PCE estimates are not derived from a dedicated sample, but rather are based on statistical reports from various government agencies, administrative and regulatory agency reports, and reports from private organizations, such as trade associations. The sample represents households and nonprofit institutions serving households. The sample also includes expenditures of the institutionalized population, domestic military personnel living on post, federal military and civilian personnel stationed abroad regardless of the length of their assignments, and U.S. citizens who are employees of U.S. businesses working abroad for less than one year and whose usual residence is in the United States. Also included are expenditures by those who died during the year.

Excluded from PCE are expenditures of students, temporary workers, and foreign nationals residing in the United States who are employees of international organizations and other countries.

Regional price parities (RPPs) are price indexes that measure geographic price level differences for one period in time within the United States. For example, if the RPP for Washington, DC, is 120, prices in Washington are on average 20 percent higher than the U.S. average. An RPP is a weighted average of the price level of goods and services for the average consumer in one geographic region compared to all other regions in the United States. The U.S. Bureau of Economic Analysis (BEA) estimates of real personal consumption and real personal income consist of their respective current-dollar estimates adjusted by the RPPs and converted to constant dollars using the U.S. personal consumption expenditures (PCE) price index.

Limitations

The RPPs use mainly price- and expenditure-related survey data that are collected or published by U.S. federal agencies. These include the Consumer Price Index (CPI) survey data from the U.S. Bureau of Labor Statistics (BLS) and the Public Use Microdata Sample (PUMS) from the American Community Survey (ACS) published by the U.S. Census Bureau. As of 2021, they also include BEA's PCE by state series. These distinct data sources are estimated at different geographic scales and must be reconciled to a common unit. We allocate each series down to the county level using either housing unit or income shares as the distributional assumption.

The CPI survey was not designed for place-to-place comparisons, which can lead to volatility in the results, especially across areas that have few observations or where sampling sizes are unevenly distributed. In past estimates, the CPI results were averaged over 5 years, but as of 2021, the RPPs use annual results. Regional price levels for selected CPI items with extreme volatility, particularly in medical and education services, will be substituted with national price levels. Both BEA and BLS are looking for alternative data sources for these categories.

Per Capita Personal Consumption Expenditures by Region and State: Total

(Dollars.)

State	2000	2001	2002	2003	2004	2005	2006	2007	2008	2009	2010	2011
United States	23,983	24,823	25,550	26,682	28,114	29,674	31,092	32,356	33,049	32,243	33,164	34,309
New England	28,358	29,622	30,674	32,296	34,149	36,048	37,727	39,018	39,956	39,354	40,396	41,530
Mideast	25,705	26,744	27,704	29,166	30,829	32,652	34,308	35,787	36,811	36,250	37,400	38,535
Great Lakes	23,433	24,220	24,937	25,959	27,201	28,502	29,595	30,691	31,377	30,782	31,809	32,942
Plains	23,746	24,634	25,403	26,550	27,907	29,162	30,337	31,425	32,411	31,819	32,773	34,067
Southeast	22,543	23,253	23,869	24,881	26,246	27,728	29,148	30,261	30,698	29,901	30,764	31,821
Southwest	22,211	23,018	23,501	24,373	25,571	27,122	28,313	29,448	30,080	29,323	30,212	31,449
Rocky Mountain	23,608	24,365	24,911	25,888	27,291	28,718	30,129	31,511	32,007	30,941	31,466	32,592
Far West	24,920	25,714	26,488	27,642	29,242	31,023	32,747	34,358	35,062	33,717	34,518	35,680
Alabama	20,158	20,868	21,700	22,673	23,932	25,303	26,245	27,160	27,555	26,958	27,635	28,422
Alaska	27,243	28,599	30,252	31,704	33,138	35,017	35,947	37,656	38,911	38,871	39,968	41,449
Arizona	23,528	24,135	24,770	25,926	27,487	29,116	30,529	31,513	31,456	30,090	30,689	31,580
Arkansas	18,878	19,615	20,268	21,208	22,293	23,574	24,523	25,472	26,147	25,712	26,513	27,559
California	24,843	25,721	26,525	27,670	29,284	31,119	32,926	34,659	35,379	33,919	34,777	35,971
Colorado	27,049	27,861	28,236	29,233	30,702	32,131	33,483	34,856	35,436	34,335	34,871	36,108
Connecticut	29,575	30,664	31,654	33,023	34,916	36,902	38,715	40,184	41,165	40,137	40,978	41,987
Delaware	27,103	28,267	29,357	30,820	32,468	34,191	35,312	36,992	37,327	36,558	37,503	38,830
D.C.	39,504	40,644	42,493	45,139	48,380	51,135	53,689	55,910	57,545	55,364	57,127	58,259
Florida	25,688	26,452	26,836	27,874	29,483	31,222	33,085	34,302	34,522	33,263	34,139	35,383
Georgia	22,937	23,600	24,126	25,126	26,254	27,684	28,615	29,635	29,683	28,587	29,170	30,203
Hawaii	25,006	25,717	26,358	27,809	29,259	31,273	33,048	34,497	35,574	34,879	35,173	35,945
Idaho	20,106	20,694	21,197	22,151	23,293	24,687	26,100	27,270	27,290	26,145	26,609	27,453
Illinois	25,055	25,799	26,462	27,533	28,884	30,453	31,912	33,372	34,024	33,156	34,161	35,290
Indiana	21,856	22,548	23,206	24,145	25,580	26,874	27,752	28,595	29,149	28,558	29,371	30,370
Iowa	21,604	22,313	22,833	23,980	25,369	26,625	27,856	28,819	29,761	29,602	30,456	31,734
Kansas	22,758	23,568	24,075	25,168	26,534	27,885	29,408	30,830	31,579	30,648	31,143	32,250
Kentucky	20,645	21,277	21,975	22,889	24,086	25,299	26,382	27,048	27,754	27,576	28,392	29,278
Louisiana	19,489	20,261	20,937	22,027	23,127	24,059	27,026	28,207	29,037	28,740	29,578	30,548
Maine	24,190	25,390	26,648	27,957	29,456	30,997	32,245	33,294	34,194	34,300	35,592	36,889
Maryland	26,332	27,462	28,323	29,591	31,273	33,194	34,982	36,354	37,207	36,548	37,406	38,455
Massachusetts	29,603	30,997	32,001	33,795	35,818	37,797	39,588	40,715	41,751	41,046	42,160	43,322
Michigan	23,073	23,808	24,535	25,387	26,479	27,539	28,423	29,334	30,327	29,912	31,173	32,380
Minnesota	26,969	27,929	28,872	30,127	31,699	32,806	33,983	34,805	35,809	35,010	36,025	37,339
Mississippi	17,649	18,451	19,261	20,163	21,252	22,374	23,804	24,819	25,510	25,091	25,986	26,892
Missouri	23,557	24,458	25,317	26,336	27,392	28,594	29,419	30,560	31,588	30,989	31,960	33,117
Montana	21,413	22,432	23,568	24,797	26,293	27,928	29,551	31,259	32,496	31,485	33,123	34,476
Nebraska	22,603	23,451	24,029	25,241	26,816	28,226	29,560	30,767	31,772	31,007	32,246	33,762
Nevada	25,190	25,744	26,379	27,384	29,017	30,786	32,125	33,101	33,106	31,132	31,625	32,781
New Hampshire	27,887	29,144	30,327	32,139	33,900	35,741	37,294	39,040	39,545	39,300	40,511	41,545
New Jersey	28,193	29,466	30,708	32,338	34,080	35,947	37,750	39,189	40,170	39,123	40,043	40,789
New Mexico	19,971	20,703	21,310	22,292	23,533	25,022	26,344	27,502	28,471	27,866	28,465	29,514
New York	24,536	25,420	26,282	27,657	29,350	31,331	33,138	34,774	35,849	35,509	36,723	38,014
North Carolina	22,462	22,948	23,299	24,167	25,399	26,822	27,851	28,953	29,283	28,469	29,345	30,356
North Dakota	21,446	22,705	23,806	25,103	26,461	28,053	29,670	31,270	32,599	33,073	34,383	37,306
Ohio	22,914	23,795	24,551	25,607	26,680	27,894	28,793	29,841	30,314	29,795	30,782	31,961
Oklahoma	19,516	20,335	20,796	21,807	22,845	24,387	25,666	26,843	27,817	27,008	27,938	29,179
Oregon	23,612	24,217	24,853	25,816	27,456	28,979	30,430	31,593	31,897	30,958	31,718	32,654
Pennsylvania	24,801	25,856	26,760	28,267	29,739	31,201	32,456	33,722	34,787	34,343	35,654	36,832
Rhode Island	24,122	25,189	26,320	27,981	29,375	31,105	32,520	33,846	34,434	34,118	34,690	35,569
South Carolina	21,305	21,945	22,591	23,526	24,904	26,362	27,490	28,740	29,323	28,588	29,678	30,726
South Dakota	20,478	21,386	22,270	23,503	24,997	26,610	28,171	29,197	30,415	30,309	31,811	32,751
Tennessee	22,102	22,577	23,201	24,018	25,215	26,499	27,592	28,709	29,062	28,370	29,336	30,434
Texas	22,526	23,377	23,808	24,570	25,690	27,215	28,314	29,473	30,200	29,593	30,573	31,908
Utah	20,027	20,586	21,222	22,025	23,398	24,734	26,129	27,456	27,808	26,763	26,919	27,777
Vermont	25,541	26,934	28,064	29,590	31,301	33,059	34,444	35,819	36,976	36,954	38,121	39,856
Virginia	24,772	25,688	26,744	28,112	29,888	31,765	33,267	34,647	35,537	34,817	35,834	36,761
Washington	25,767	26,227	26,895	28,174	29,696	31,270	32,914	34,389	35,397	34,437	35,123	36,277
West Virginia	19,401	20,210	21,000	21,847	23,097	24,258	25,238	26,240	27,267	27,627	28,720	29,997
Wisconsin	23,235	24,124	24,937	26,184	27,585	28,907	30,197	31,169	31,956	31,480	32,465	33,535

Per Capita Personal Consumption Expenditures by Region and State: Total—Continued

(Dollars.)

State	2012	2013	2014	2015	2016	2017	2018	2019	2020	2021	2022
United States	35,144	35,955	37,192	38,211	39,236	40,691	42,413	43,659	42,853	48,318	52,542
New England	42,287	43,192	44,487	45,767	46,919	48,684	50,516	51,758	50,711	56,522	61,033
Mideast	39,323	40,216	41,550	42,497	43,538	45,005	46,940	48,343	46,801	52,278	57,134
Great Lakes	33,812	34,621	35,750	36,751	37,845	39,247	40,756	41,730	41,019	45,921	49,906
Plains	34,988	35,652	36,659	37,433	38,338	39,521	40,937	41,764	40,798	45,444	49,162
Southeast	32,546	33,255	34,408	35,381	36,276	37,517	39,006	40,135	39,751	45,002	48,758
Southwest	32,330	33,181	34,468	35,250	35,964	37,319	38,758	39,762	39,526	44,673	48,329
Rocky Mountain	33,268	34,282	35,732	36,747	37,951	39,541	41,269	42,754	42,514	48,497	53,075
Far West	36,713	37,590	38,975	40,391	41,780	43,685	46,008	47,837	46,622	53,299	58,466
Alabama	28,920	29,594	30,365	31,130	32,005	33,020	34,053	35,345	34,878	39,174	42,391
Alaska	42,455	42,914	44,251	45,018	45,703	47,074	48,904	50,140	47,762	53,982	59,179
Arizona	32,261	33,037	34,068	34,963	35,827	37,651	39,285	40,519	40,605	46,023	50,123
Arkansas	28,227	28,820	29,915	30,759	31,828	32,785	34,151	34,722	34,979	39,231	42,245
California	37,112	37,970	39,399	40,952	42,472	44,443	46,948	49,004	47,720	54,838	60,272
Colorado	36,572	37,798	39,447	40,878	42,285	44,281	46,115	48,067	47,355	54,126	59,371
Connecticut	42,958	43,904	45,491	46,696	47,588	49,084	50,888	51,713	51,237	56,371	60,413
Delaware	39,308	39,938	41,310	41,892	42,563	43,879	45,782	46,730	45,032	50,700	54,532
D.C.	59,099	60,427	62,088	63,388	64,561	66,501	69,871	72,117	69,929	79,105	85,732
Florida	36,295	37,064	38,593	39,913	40,682	42,102	44,005	45,273	44,655	51,038	55,516
Georgia	30,881	31,764	33,086	34,034	35,012	36,470	37,967	39,074	38,419	43,681	47,406
Hawaii	36,670	37,772	38,715	39,543	40,231	42,047	43,813	45,835	44,038	49,543	54,655
Idaho	28,109	29,207	30,167	30,573	31,610	32,724	33,973	34,643	34,689	39,639	43,508
Illinois	36,008	36,749	38,009	39,175	40,351	41,749	43,625	44,665	43,902	49,429	54,341
Indiana	31,369	31,915	32,872	33,611	34,627	36,173	37,593	38,310	38,193	42,565	46,579
Iowa	32,499	33,094	34,155	34,610	35,631	36,790	37,817	38,615	37,898	42,247	45,455
Kansas	32,799	33,224	34,094	34,839	35,643	36,710	37,966	38,971	38,541	42,438	46,069
Kentucky	29,859	30,453	31,279	32,339	33,301	34,456	35,940	36,704	36,486	41,027	44,193
Louisiana	31,288	32,050	32,991	33,707	34,426	35,577	36,862	37,830	37,393	42,115	45,178
Maine	37,030	37,869	38,457	39,645	41,399	43,245	45,253	46,310	46,170	51,730	55,789
Maryland	39,069	39,616	40,557	41,324	42,125	43,147	44,612	45,295	43,670	48,549	52,651
Massachusetts	44,088	44,949	46,336	47,725	49,061	50,990	52,863	54,409	52,701	59,267	64,214
Michigan	33,397	34,338	35,628	36,755	38,081	39,450	40,991	42,040	41,154	46,019	49,482
Minnesota	38,170	39,029	40,107	41,017	42,026	43,524	45,231	45,893	43,668	48,846	52,849
Mississippi	27,446	28,018	28,763	29,488	30,195	30,952	31,767	32,368	32,751	36,681	39,678
Missouri	34,100	34,668	35,565	36,446	37,331	38,477	39,942	40,742	40,251	44,827	48,613
Montana	35,272	36,104	37,529	38,021	38,364	39,685	41,576	42,555	42,067	48,015	51,913
Nebraska	34,613	35,118	36,174	36,886	37,865	38,869	39,995	40,872	40,371	45,469	49,522
Nevada	33,398	34,264	35,371	36,284	37,334	39,008	40,610	41,723	40,581	46,176	50,922
New Hampshire	42,586	43,632	44,330	45,941	46,880	49,084	50,571	51,826	51,357	56,507	60,828
New Jersey	41,742	42,463	43,685	44,533	45,607	46,736	48,411	50,009	48,875	55,472	60,082
New Mexico	29,950	30,456	31,620	32,292	32,896	33,853	35,349	35,705	35,031	39,950	43,336
New York	38,847	39,977	41,736	42,749	43,996	45,811	47,925	49,614	47,813	53,354	58,571
North Carolina	31,226	31,996	33,144	34,154	35,028	36,372	37,769	39,066	39,063	44,287	47,834
North Dakota	40,360	41,855	43,307	43,358	43,099	43,083	44,511	45,787	45,008	49,209	52,631
Ohio	32,988	33,966	34,939	35,898	36,834	38,164	39,380	40,364	39,700	44,215	47,768
Oklahoma	29,898	30,561	31,579	31,787	32,267	33,224	34,621	35,108	34,747	38,889	42,046
Oregon	33,247	34,050	35,437	36,853	37,857	39,694	41,613	42,776	42,277	47,649	52,159
Pennsylvania	37,515	38,298	39,200	40,187	41,003	42,352	44,338	45,489	44,184	48,874	53,703
Rhode Island	35,785	36,792	38,081	39,037	39,826	41,044	42,598	43,673	43,199	48,711	52,820
South Carolina	31,114	31,960	33,050	33,927	34,947	35,995	37,178	38,340	38,134	42,930	46,220
South Dakota	33,929	34,566	35,484	36,505	37,560	38,776	40,368	41,346	41,284	45,944	48,997
Tennessee	31,037	31,462	32,483	33,227	34,300	35,610	36,770	38,004	37,751	42,741	46,280
Texas	32,894	33,814	35,204	36,040	36,749	38,066	39,450	40,509	40,235	45,460	49,082
Utah	28,727	29,418	30,720	31,671	33,023	34,424	36,280	37,734	38,228	43,850	48,189
Vermont	40,771	41,462	42,775	43,236	43,655	44,891	47,255	48,187	47,168	51,197	55,743
Virginia	37,422	37,935	38,807	39,389	40,164	41,093	42,644	43,669	42,913	48,003	52,057
Washington	37,192	38,217	39,582	40,656	41,937	43,736	45,821	47,202	46,208	52,155	56,567
West Virginia	30,767	31,406	32,156	33,121	34,297	35,123	36,710	37,645	37,395	41,273	44,460
Wisconsin	34,032	34,729	35,815	36,631	37,578	39,054	40,432	41,453	40,430	45,491	49,284

Per Capita Personal Consumption Expenditures by Region and State: Groceries

(Dollars.)

State	2000	2001	2002	2003	2004	2005	2006	2007	2008	2009	2010	2011
United States	1,916	1,979	1,999	2,067	2,160	2,261	2,347	2,448	2,529	2,520	2,543	2,628
New England	2,184	2,285	2,337	2,384	2,523	2,623	2,719	2,825	2,917	2,920	2,956	3,064
Mideast	1,872	1,944	1,979	2,070	2,152	2,272	2,359	2,456	2,551	2,546	2,598	2,667
Great Lakes	1,877	1,934	1,959	2,020	2,107	2,169	2,239	2,328	2,399	2,400	2,418	2,505
Plains	1,887	1,952	1,988	2,042	2,124	2,212	2,262	2,352	2,451	2,481	2,504	2,594
Southeast	1,949	1,996	1,990	2,041	2,135	2,236	2,317	2,401	2,490	2,506	2,527	2,606
Southwest	1,778	1,835	1,825	1,891	2,001	2,116	2,202	2,292	2,373	2,363	2,383	2,474
Rocky Mountain	1,967	2,034	2,023	2,119	2,234	2,346	2,436	2,580	2,651	2,634	2,606	2,678
Far West	1,961	2,038	2,088	2,170	2,259	2,372	2,489	2,631	2,691	2,613	2,631	2,726
Alabama	1,872	1,968	2,019	2,074	2,138	2,196	2,216	2,262	2,336	2,348	2,352	2,419
Alaska	2,606	2,666	2,766	2,922	3,048	3,202	3,338	3,523	3,717	3,693	3,712	3,834
Arizona	1,829	1,887	1,910	2,004	2,175	2,329	2,456	2,564	2,616	2,544	2,551	2,573
Arkansas	1,610	1,649	1,644	1,696	1,751	1,809	1,835	1,917	1,993	2,060	2,091	2,186
California	1,875	1,959	2,014	2,086	2,152	2,256	2,362	2,512	2,564	2,472	2,495	2,590
Colorado	2,063	2,162	2,128	2,221	2,326	2,455	2,476	2,598	2,705	2,715	2,695	2,782
Connecticut	2,120	2,234	2,299	2,360	2,463	2,573	2,667	2,781	2,840	2,807	2,852	2,960
Delaware	2,164	2,262	2,335	2,425	2,528	2,622	2,730	2,815	2,883	2,862	2,881	2,905
D.C.	2,965	3,140	3,184	3,427	3,673	3,753	3,946	4,046	4,302	4,373	4,479	4,582
Florida	2,144	2,206	2,136	2,201	2,332	2,449	2,542	2,616	2,694	2,679	2,681	2,762
Georgia	1,926	1,963	1,975	2,019	2,108	2,200	2,255	2,331	2,384	2,417	2,449	2,560
Hawaii	2,356	2,423	2,427	2,465	2,582	2,748	2,877	3,010	3,125	3,253	3,282	3,382
Idaho	1,968	2,010	2,007	2,134	2,220	2,318	2,470	2,605	2,583	2,553	2,498	2,560
Illinois	1,765	1,819	1,848	1,934	2,052	2,138	2,264	2,378	2,399	2,354	2,355	2,429
Indiana	1,910	1,932	1,936	1,993	2,117	2,216	2,271	2,322	2,408	2,419	2,409	2,472
Iowa	1,776	1,832	1,847	1,907	2,013	2,105	2,199	2,310	2,412	2,436	2,466	2,574
Kansas	1,960	2,013	2,010	2,109	2,183	2,363	2,461	2,596	2,671	2,644	2,640	2,746
Kentucky	1,921	1,970	1,993	2,067	2,196	2,285	2,353	2,441	2,566	2,650	2,668	2,753
Louisiana	1,851	1,881	1,881	1,961	2,022	2,064	2,304	2,375	2,454	2,487	2,458	2,534
Maine	2,188	2,279	2,317	2,377	2,472	2,594	2,689	2,791	2,900	3,000	3,046	3,089
Maryland	1,992	2,056	2,055	2,114	2,204	2,300	2,400	2,495	2,556	2,551	2,595	2,669
Massachusetts	2,211	2,310	2,361	2,388	2,563	2,660	2,761	2,864	2,957	2,950	2,974	3,101
Michigan	1,982	2,050	2,071	2,105	2,188	2,200	2,224	2,292	2,370	2,417	2,455	2,532
Minnesota	2,071	2,172	2,221	2,244	2,274	2,306	2,321	2,352	2,450	2,478	2,513	2,619
Mississippi	1,717	1,767	1,769	1,839	1,937	2,038	2,169	2,172	2,276	2,331	2,367	2,445
Missouri	1,789	1,830	1,889	1,939	2,031	2,129	2,151	2,252	2,364	2,429	2,465	2,528
Montana	1,984	2,020	2,106	2,234	2,347	2,465	2,634	2,842	2,954	2,950	2,935	3,048
Nebraska	1,840	1,893	1,899	1,947	2,095	2,166	2,236	2,374	2,470	2,457	2,440	2,493
Nevada	2,145	2,200	2,168	2,266	2,409	2,463	2,612	2,711	2,754	2,669	2,634	2,708
New Hampshire	2,423	2,512	2,553	2,630	2,787	2,825	2,896	2,981	3,100	3,111	3,172	3,279
New Jersey	2,174	2,279	2,333	2,426	2,548	2,643	2,724	2,839	2,916	2,873	2,915	2,973
New Mexico	1,768	1,790	1,775	1,864	1,956	2,073	2,215	2,346	2,445	2,443	2,424	2,513
New York	1,626	1,699	1,738	1,799	1,887	2,047	2,121	2,201	2,287	2,301	2,377	2,467
North Carolina	1,991	2,018	2,015	2,029	2,076	2,192	2,223	2,343	2,421	2,369	2,388	2,414
North Dakota	1,840	1,911	1,984	2,074	2,181	2,239	2,331	2,389	2,489	2,554	2,566	2,689
Ohio	1,844	1,922	1,974	2,055	2,077	2,118	2,144	2,238	2,355	2,363	2,411	2,537
Oklahoma	1,540	1,565	1,544	1,590	1,645	1,736	1,799	1,884	1,973	2,006	2,019	2,088
Oregon	2,102	2,182	2,237	2,338	2,525	2,628	2,793	2,936	2,987	2,921	2,937	3,026
Pennsylvania	1,923	1,968	1,994	2,137	2,166	2,258	2,351	2,465	2,596	2,586	2,606	2,651
Rhode Island	1,904	1,991	2,030	2,083	2,169	2,282	2,382	2,501	2,554	2,544	2,566	2,618
South Carolina	1,959	1,989	1,961	1,984	2,120	2,283	2,318	2,398	2,540	2,574	2,624	2,669
South Dakota	1,731	1,827	1,873	1,946	2,075	2,179	2,245	2,317	2,402	2,464	2,489	2,603
Tennessee	1,808	1,849	1,847	1,887	1,955	2,040	2,135	2,284	2,394	2,482	2,528	2,653
Texas	1,806	1,870	1,853	1,913	2,017	2,124	2,198	2,279	2,365	2,364	2,391	2,504
Utah	1,755	1,789	1,774	1,847	2,003	2,081	2,217	2,370	2,409	2,351	2,325	2,369
Vermont	2,257	2,373	2,434	2,514	2,627	2,747	2,851	2,980	3,195	3,313	3,387	3,508
Virginia	1,979	2,024	2,077	2,128	2,215	2,329	2,431	2,518	2,619	2,614	2,654	2,735
Washington	2,160	2,207	2,259	2,383	2,519	2,689	2,813	2,918	3,010	2,954	2,964	3,062
West Virginia	1,811	1,822	1,842	1,879	1,975	2,056	2,155	2,253	2,401	2,478	2,524	2,607
Wisconsin	1,973	2,009	2,002	2,023	2,140	2,233	2,372	2,471	2,529	2,527	2,523	2,606
Wyoming	2,064	2,115	2,119	2,226	2,331	2,481	2,673	2,896	3,007	2,955	2,901	2,950

Per Capita Personal Consumption Expenditures by Region and State: Groceries—Continued

(Dollars.)

State	2012	2013	2014	2015	2016	2017	2018	2019	2020	2021	2022
United States	2,692	2,748	2,852	2,927	2,989	3,094	3,179	3,276	3,609	3,878	4,181
New England	3,146	3,213	3,330	3,399	3,497	3,643	3,716	3,826	4,190	4,460	4,727
Mideast	2,718	2,772	2,876	2,920	2,959	3,066	3,144	3,245	3,536	3,807	4,129
Great Lakes	2,565	2,619	2,708	2,796	2,891	3,031	3,103	3,188	3,470	3,726	4,020
Plains	2,661	2,687	2,744	2,796	2,876	2,948	3,025	3,091	3,373	3,601	3,867
Southeast	2,671	2,726	2,821	2,892	2,962	3,054	3,144	3,251	3,591	3,865	4,149
Southwest	2,549	2,601	2,715	2,770	2,818	2,913	2,992	3,044	3,404	3,627	3,906
Rocky Mountain	2,758	2,815	2,968	3,050	3,176	3,264	3,338	3,439	3,766	3,985	4,355
Far West	2,787	2,861	2,984	3,108	3,132	3,234	3,343	3,477	3,874	4,205	4,559
Alabama	2,447	2,463	2,534	2,594	2,668	2,725	2,816	2,906	3,196	3,495	3,708
Alaska	3,860	3,821	3,858	3,836	3,784	3,798	3,892	3,983	4,233	4,351	4,641
Arizona	2,589	2,619	2,755	2,821	2,848	3,023	3,087	3,105	3,438	3,591	3,836
Arkansas	2,240	2,298	2,397	2,473	2,543	2,639	2,678	2,705	3,023	3,288	3,461
California	2,659	2,732	2,867	3,019	3,058	3,157	3,266	3,410	3,801	4,160	4,534
Colorado	2,886	2,963	3,135	3,266	3,430	3,581	3,653	3,787	4,193	4,394	4,781
Connecticut	3,029	3,099	3,235	3,310	3,380	3,487	3,491	3,543	3,895	4,124	4,341
Delaware	2,914	3,008	3,088	3,119	3,126	3,185	3,293	3,322	3,691	3,924	4,173
D.C.	4,724	4,854	5,084	5,350	5,332	5,539	5,659	5,838	6,133	6,675	7,217
Florida	2,809	2,900	3,017	3,128	3,202	3,294	3,420	3,563	3,887	4,216	4,565
Georgia	2,644	2,720	2,865	2,930	2,966	3,128	3,205	3,292	3,631	3,941	4,248
Hawaii	3,363	3,441	3,502	3,531	3,618	3,776	3,969	4,171	4,526	4,898	5,322
Idaho	2,670	2,761	2,924	2,919	3,084	3,038	3,058	3,099	3,333	3,504	3,747
Illinois	2,445	2,491	2,567	2,647	2,714	2,827	2,926	3,059	3,371	3,677	3,999
Indiana	2,522	2,594	2,681	2,797	2,919	3,035	3,073	3,129	3,412	3,603	3,909
Iowa	2,660	2,685	2,767	2,832	2,913	2,955	3,034	3,113	3,414	3,656	3,938
Kansas	2,780	2,832	2,936	3,039	3,144	3,251	3,337	3,439	3,780	4,051	4,381
Kentucky	2,825	2,833	2,942	3,053	3,182	3,318	3,369	3,403	3,711	3,895	4,086
Louisiana	2,598	2,654	2,736	2,835	2,900	2,961	3,024	3,086	3,382	3,678	3,880
Maine	3,175	3,254	3,395	3,434	3,540	3,691	3,842	4,027	4,491	4,824	5,151
Maryland	2,671	2,697	2,763	2,773	2,811	2,874	2,923	2,964	3,231	3,446	3,721
Massachusetts	3,188	3,241	3,358	3,432	3,539	3,713	3,782	3,905	4,248	4,554	4,789
Michigan	2,602	2,638	2,741	2,823	2,959	3,120	3,173	3,255	3,490	3,832	4,074
Minnesota	2,716	2,719	2,708	2,733	2,803	2,887	2,978	3,025	3,267	3,461	3,657
Mississippi	2,490	2,535	2,622	2,688	2,746	2,833	2,922	3,020	3,340	3,597	3,897
Missouri	2,569	2,583	2,640	2,679	2,761	2,843	2,929	3,024	3,323	3,564	3,853
Montana	3,146	3,176	3,319	3,383	3,408	3,453	3,588	3,674	3,964	4,299	4,775
Nebraska	2,545	2,583	2,727	2,819	2,913	2,981	3,016	3,033	3,302	3,520	3,845
Nevada	2,751	2,833	2,987	3,103	3,131	3,282	3,362	3,455	3,772	4,066	4,444
New Hampshire	3,386	3,494	3,563	3,584	3,721	3,882	3,981	4,113	4,547	4,707	5,190
New Jersey	2,987	3,023	3,113	3,179	3,209	3,287	3,355	3,487	3,813	4,074	4,280
New Mexico	2,553	2,617	2,738	2,858	2,934	2,991	3,097	3,128	3,455	3,740	3,962
New York	2,539	2,618	2,756	2,781	2,812	2,962	3,062	3,174	3,478	3,778	4,119
North Carolina	2,571	2,662	2,753	2,822	2,880	2,967	3,061	3,237	3,685	3,883	4,163
North Dakota	2,885	3,030	3,046	3,028	3,033	3,049	3,079	3,087	3,303	3,512	3,676
Ohio	2,642	2,723	2,838	2,949	3,050	3,219	3,288	3,356	3,661	3,861	4,106
Oklahoma	2,121	2,157	2,222	2,259	2,301	2,376	2,463	2,487	2,747	2,962	3,198
Oregon	3,089	3,164	3,288	3,377	3,357	3,430	3,540	3,673	4,106	4,406	4,784
Pennsylvania	2,715	2,750	2,822	2,885	2,944	3,023	3,083	3,172	3,426	3,676	4,066
Rhode Island	2,667	2,761	2,894	2,994	3,118	3,247	3,377	3,470	3,797	4,125	4,342
South Carolina	2,677	2,780	2,909	2,960	3,063	3,081	3,192	3,279	3,653	3,929	4,203
South Dakota	2,639	2,661	2,745	2,819	2,885	2,872	2,905	2,891	3,131	3,338	3,592
Tennessee	2,675	2,624	2,634	2,574	2,574	2,573	2,636	2,710	3,022	3,229	3,427
Texas	2,601	2,660	2,775	2,824	2,875	2,955	3,035	3,100	3,481	3,717	4,014
Utah	2,391	2,404	2,527	2,576	2,657	2,715	2,802	2,880	3,134	3,368	3,755
Vermont	3,596	3,647	3,690	3,771	3,785	3,835	4,025	4,122	4,483	4,593	4,957
Virginia	2,809	2,819	2,872	2,942	3,049	3,189	3,255	3,344	3,686	3,949	4,258
Washington	3,107	3,193	3,255	3,280	3,240	3,352	3,453	3,546	4,003	4,232	4,460
West Virginia	2,624	2,684	2,730	2,772	2,898	2,977	3,086	3,200	3,513	3,790	4,132
Wisconsin	2,666	2,691	2,739	2,773	2,815	2,944	3,030	3,089	3,331	3,524	3,927
Wyoming	2,990	3,049	3,174	3,259	3,344	3,486	3,596	3,730	4,093	4,418	4,777

Per Capita Personal Consumption Expenditures by Region and State: Housing and Utilities

(Dollars.)

State	2000	2001	2002	2003	2004	2005	2006	2007	2008	2009	2010	2011
United States	4,248	4,518	4,622	4,795	5,009	5,347	5,583	5,841	6,158	6,194	6,296	6,360
New England	4,625	4,935	5,067	5,283	5,535	5,937	6,274	6,532	6,870	7,063	7,157	7,260
Mideast	4,512	4,817	4,953	5,165	5,412	5,801	6,039	6,310	6,705	6,832	6,963	7,028
Great Lakes	3,951	4,228	4,325	4,524	4,720	5,067	5,206	5,421	5,640	5,621	5,736	5,744
Plains	3,798	4,059	4,114	4,286	4,487	4,801	5,027	5,129	5,431	5,381	5,498	5,619
Southeast	4,101	4,356	4,457	4,606	4,803	5,106	5,365	5,673	5,926	5,933	6,028	6,076
Southwest	3,959	4,188	4,252	4,392	4,570	4,864	5,083	5,285	5,538	5,533	5,695	5,785
Rocky Mountain	4,321	4,574	4,684	4,826	5,059	5,371	5,559	5,765	6,047	6,114	6,120	6,386
Far West	4,738	5,013	5,136	5,296	5,539	5,905	6,194	6,528	7,012	7,066	7,120	7,157
Alabama	3,435	3,670	3,780	3,894	4,084	4,347	4,573	4,790	5,015	5,062	5,143	5,187
Alaska	4,544	4,817	4,991	5,158	5,381	5,736	5,548	5,841	5,986	6,351	6,675	6,793
Arizona	4,727	4,985	5,140	5,255	5,434	5,692	5,864	6,093	6,417	6,329	6,391	6,449
Arkansas	3,235	3,454	3,517	3,651	3,781	4,058	4,269	4,420	4,648	4,606	4,731	4,823
California	4,800	5,080	5,194	5,359	5,613	6,002	6,298	6,626	7,146	7,195	7,264	7,281
Colorado	4,930	5,197	5,306	5,493	5,778	6,131	6,387	6,569	6,969	6,982	6,996	7,383
Connecticut	4,751	5,071	5,202	5,416	5,662	6,041	6,404	6,689	7,262	7,507	7,516	7,458
Delaware	4,673	4,969	5,125	5,276	5,481	5,833	6,101	6,747	6,778	6,898	6,819	7,144
D.C.	5,452	5,811	5,957	6,246	6,611	7,029	7,847	8,108	8,634	8,650	9,599	9,663
Florida	5,264	5,549	5,683	5,828	6,030	6,383	6,833	7,236	7,524	7,371	7,407	7,461
Georgia	4,104	4,349	4,420	4,584	4,764	5,069	5,187	5,461	5,640	5,611	5,617	5,636
Hawaii	4,832	5,111	5,234	5,385	5,574	5,980	6,398	6,911	7,535	7,592	7,445	7,381
Idaho	3,941	4,165	4,289	4,361	4,540	4,804	4,990	5,254	5,307	5,275	5,187	5,250
Illinois	4,208	4,506	4,547	4,777	4,981	5,345	5,479	5,817	6,037	6,048	6,165	6,219
Indiana	3,699	3,949	4,039	4,208	4,379	4,718	4,811	4,971	5,219	5,154	5,263	5,258
Iowa	3,569	3,815	3,837	4,031	4,221	4,502	4,685	4,719	4,885	5,039	5,080	5,266
Kansas	3,636	3,887	3,942	4,069	4,273	4,569	4,673	4,847	5,170	5,153	5,202	5,434
Kentucky	3,294	3,517	3,611	3,730	3,924	4,198	4,278	4,414	4,696	4,764	4,884	4,838
Louisiana	3,196	3,412	3,410	3,549	3,689	3,907	4,189	4,521	4,896	5,063	5,177	5,198
Maine	4,128	4,403	4,563	4,705	4,922	5,291	5,434	5,604	5,867	6,232	6,485	6,783
Maryland	4,953	5,259	5,354	5,570	5,802	6,223	6,618	6,958	7,494	7,660	7,637	7,790
Massachusetts	4,710	5,027	5,155	5,383	5,655	6,063	6,449	6,566	6,935	7,076	7,188	7,335
Michigan	4,022	4,306	4,487	4,685	4,909	5,267	5,362	5,619	5,876	5,814	5,977	5,884
Minnesota	4,419	4,714	4,784	5,018	5,265	5,653	6,007	6,025	6,469	6,332	6,353	6,349
Mississippi	3,103	3,322	3,398	3,527	3,699	3,948	4,148	4,479	4,671	4,690	4,733	4,775
Missouri	3,705	3,958	4,006	4,155	4,331	4,612	4,772	4,975	5,211	5,122	5,360	5,421
Montana	3,421	3,659	3,761	3,874	4,080	4,417	4,623	4,797	5,076	4,978	5,679	5,895
Nebraska	3,482	3,726	3,801	3,931	4,113	4,409	4,663	4,698	4,965	4,881	5,086	5,402
Nevada	5,101	5,320	5,459	5,590	5,767	6,158	6,397	6,902	7,144	7,033	6,956	6,931
New Hampshire	4,830	5,135	5,267	5,485	5,734	6,201	6,474	7,224	7,064	7,158	7,330	7,385
New Jersey	5,228	5,574	5,737	5,998	6,301	6,729	6,977	7,295	7,849	7,802	7,932	7,824
New Mexico	3,584	3,827	3,911	4,044	4,218	4,503	4,763	4,961	5,212	5,281	5,315	5,574
New York	4,390	4,685	4,823	5,029	5,274	5,692	5,944	6,199	6,554	6,779	6,892	7,021
North Carolina	3,871	4,103	4,180	4,330	4,533	4,813	4,976	5,181	5,397	5,483	5,638	5,711
North Dakota	3,135	3,357	3,419	3,553	3,737	4,034	4,326	4,657	4,919	4,988	4,848	5,523
Ohio	3,721	3,984	4,066	4,248	4,431	4,750	4,956	5,060	5,232	5,215	5,277	5,303
Oklahoma	3,348	3,577	3,634	3,786	3,950	4,241	4,430	4,607	4,742	4,751	4,977	5,127
Oregon	4,243	4,498	4,655	4,795	5,045	5,299	5,522	5,795	6,056	6,219	6,280	6,383
Pennsylvania	3,964	4,248	4,378	4,561	4,772	5,077	5,189	5,397	5,694	5,778	5,978	5,998
Rhode Island	4,142	4,423	4,542	4,785	4,988	5,398	5,772	6,100	6,288	6,493	6,472	6,545
South Carolina	3,755	3,991	4,097	4,227	4,432	4,698	4,861	5,228	5,473	5,591	5,822	5,974
South Dakota	3,180	3,401	3,470	3,594	3,782	4,076	4,429	4,297	4,686	4,611	5,005	4,854
Tennessee	3,687	3,924	4,004	4,131	4,296	4,557	4,766	5,082	5,281	5,338	5,402	5,508
Texas	3,902	4,122	4,159	4,302	4,479	4,779	5,009	5,206	5,458	5,467	5,657	5,732
Utah	3,809	4,037	4,143	4,257	4,439	4,692	4,793	5,007	5,260	5,372	5,225	5,374
Vermont	4,499	4,806	4,957	5,147	5,419	5,802	5,956	6,535	6,671	6,920	6,988	7,291
Virginia	4,703	4,992	5,126	5,326	5,564	5,911	6,202	6,619	6,955	7,031	7,218	7,179
Washington	4,548	4,816	4,961	5,110	5,321	5,606	5,941	6,243	6,762	6,815	6,847	6,995
West Virginia	3,058	3,281	3,418	3,562	3,755	4,035	4,163	4,374	4,615	4,703	4,854	4,960
Wisconsin	3,995	4,270	4,383	4,584	4,767	5,120	5,273	5,422	5,638	5,679	5,816	5,873
Wyoming	3,967	4,248	4,360	4,495	4,722	5,088	5,078	5,403	5,454	6,354	6,052	6,465

Per Capita Personal Consumption Expenditures by Region and State: Housing and Utilities—Continued

(Dollars.)

State	2012	2013	2014	2015	2016	2017	2018	2019	2020	2021	2022
United States	6,409	6,585	6,722	6,824	6,995	7,195	7,486	7,737	8,072	8,526	9,161
New England	7,359	7,560	7,662	7,851	7,950	8,214	8,634	8,814	9,466	9,877	10,671
Mideast	7,110	7,309	7,467	7,530	7,673	7,846	8,157	8,368	8,822	9,369	10,121
Great Lakes	5,819	6,009	6,123	6,168	6,333	6,498	6,746	6,883	7,066	7,433	7,941
Plains	5,758	5,939	6,061	6,145	6,278	6,439	6,675	6,870	6,935	7,278	7,763
Southeast	6,093	6,227	6,350	6,470	6,606	6,756	7,017	7,285	7,596	7,976	8,533
Southwest	5,768	5,937	6,098	6,206	6,375	6,504	6,750	6,991	7,346	7,813	8,420
Rocky Mountain	6,345	6,631	6,820	6,908	7,167	7,385	7,663	8,100	8,168	8,932	9,695
Far West	7,221	7,397	7,543	7,686	7,961	8,337	8,710	9,082	9,550	10,099	10,883
Alabama	5,221	5,317	5,334	5,388	5,525	5,582	5,744	6,129	6,173	6,543	7,082
Alaska	7,034	7,153	7,245	7,148	7,422	7,554	7,846	7,811	7,817	8,538	9,189
Arizona	6,520	6,620	6,525	6,655	6,848	7,059	7,311	7,541	8,163	8,760	9,580
Arkansas	4,803	4,907	5,116	5,210	5,316	5,194	5,621	5,561	5,817	6,224	6,670
California	7,365	7,543	7,698	7,836	8,123	8,490	8,878	9,272	9,792	10,427	11,262
Colorado	7,245	7,606	7,786	8,122	8,430	8,753	9,011	9,635	9,572	10,587	11,466
Connecticut	7,771	7,856	8,066	8,241	8,181	8,211	8,761	8,853	9,499	9,804	10,518
Delaware	7,085	7,080	7,536	7,314	7,463	7,644	8,256	8,408	8,325	9,004	9,567
D.C.	9,734	10,014	10,541	10,386	10,337	10,603	11,054	11,282	12,048	13,755	14,959
Florida	7,476	7,537	7,674	7,859	8,023	8,254	8,565	8,916	9,507	9,894	10,526
Georgia	5,655	5,736	5,844	5,934	6,137	6,286	6,539	6,838	7,062	7,515	8,082
Hawaii	7,490	8,162	8,172	8,313	8,350	8,670	8,762	9,324	9,815	10,187	11,057
Idaho	5,301	5,768	5,785	5,542	5,732	5,862	6,243	6,536	6,806	7,504	8,254
Illinois	6,272	6,397	6,583	6,686	6,849	7,001	7,289	7,390	7,672	8,006	8,540
Indiana	5,316	5,555	5,680	5,717	5,748	5,961	6,312	6,316	6,560	6,781	7,213
Iowa	5,379	5,527	5,764	5,643	5,926	6,150	6,243	6,445	6,364	6,762	7,206
Kansas	5,473	5,591	5,625	5,688	5,860	6,064	6,228	6,475	6,714	6,652	7,068
Kentucky	4,929	5,162	5,159	5,316	5,363	5,438	5,781	5,908	6,040	6,299	6,696
Louisiana	5,302	5,495	5,527	5,569	5,733	5,814	6,042	6,259	6,266	6,522	6,946
Maine	6,603	6,813	6,351	6,626	7,192	7,315	7,758	7,496	8,296	8,731	9,415
Maryland	7,790	8,097	8,170	8,187	8,314	8,399	8,746	8,940	9,097	9,596	10,206
Massachusetts	7,349	7,630	7,815	7,979	8,185	8,514	8,938	9,269	9,906	10,433	11,315
Michigan	6,025	6,227	6,327	6,283	6,569	6,688	6,925	7,195	7,416	7,768	8,343
Minnesota	6,539	6,765	6,898	7,059	7,179	7,399	7,644	7,917	7,706	8,506	9,126
Mississippi	4,741	4,906	5,004	5,155	5,182	5,233	5,459	5,463	5,741	5,986	6,436
Missouri	5,498	5,728	5,796	5,900	5,928	6,048	6,389	6,495	6,750	6,902	7,330
Montana	5,742	5,995	6,535	6,354	6,241	6,587	7,008	7,189	7,163	7,913	8,488
Nebraska	5,419	5,451	5,714	5,865	5,947	6,050	6,310	6,505	6,667	7,083	7,631
Nevada	6,845	6,804	6,674	6,748	6,854	7,210	7,470	7,927	8,391	8,676	9,418
New Hampshire	7,706	7,884	7,630	8,205	7,953	8,797	8,584	8,777	9,298	9,375	9,971
New Jersey	8,039	8,209	8,330	8,291	8,504	8,587	8,934	9,171	9,507	10,158	10,928
New Mexico	5,512	5,616	5,795	5,722	5,841	6,018	6,182	6,345	6,598	6,956	7,529
New York	7,065	7,235	7,462	7,502	7,691	7,892	8,194	8,448	9,156	9,767	10,666
North Carolina	5,699	5,853	6,040	6,152	6,194	6,476	6,616	6,867	7,140	7,483	7,994
North Dakota	6,216	6,409	6,571	6,681	7,036	6,609	6,766	6,951	7,311	6,889	7,214
Ohio	5,365	5,637	5,673	5,745	5,901	6,036	6,254	6,371	6,524	6,926	7,412
Oklahoma	5,102	5,286	5,458	5,376	5,540	5,609	5,886	5,957	6,080	6,471	6,897
Oregon	6,454	6,554	6,700	6,929	7,132	7,594	7,916	8,160	8,406	8,721	9,319
Pennsylvania	6,092	6,311	6,379	6,600	6,635	6,860	7,106	7,242	7,558	7,896	8,469
Rhode Island	6,496	6,761	6,951	6,912	6,859	7,009	7,445	7,542	8,185	8,911	9,875
South Carolina	5,909	6,025	6,199	6,397	6,547	6,656	6,895	7,273	7,597	7,893	8,441
South Dakota	5,349	5,522	5,458	5,545	5,706	6,022	6,217	6,317	6,322	6,710	7,095
Tennessee	5,531	5,626	5,735	5,820	5,994	6,150	6,290	6,706	6,881	7,320	7,903
Texas	5,698	5,888	6,108	6,251	6,418	6,530	6,774	7,045	7,371	7,823	8,402
Utah	5,471	5,552	5,651	5,651	5,935	6,061	6,288	6,653	6,833	7,404	8,105
Vermont	7,434	7,362	7,746	7,668	7,542	7,668	8,572	8,647	9,515	9,437	10,109
Virginia	7,180	7,474	7,603	7,627	7,676	7,777	8,113	8,238	8,511	9,025	9,619
Washington	6,975	7,180	7,421	7,598	7,972	8,400	8,840	9,144	9,525	9,909	10,565
West Virginia	4,966	5,131	5,260	5,352	5,667	5,486	5,849	5,855	6,186	6,241	6,619
Wisconsin	5,935	6,025	6,153	6,181	6,314	6,601	6,731	6,915	6,821	7,394	7,875
Wyoming	6,530	6,709	7,301	6,919	7,493	7,314	7,557	7,555	7,943	7,785	8,284

Per Capita Personal Consumption Expenditures by Region and State: Health Care

(Dollars.)

State	2000	2001	2002	2003	2004	2005	2006	2007	2008	2009	2010	2011
United States	3,255	3,497	3,765	3,978	4,231	4,469	4,665	4,907	5,115	5,322	5,493	5,635
New England	4,062	4,369	4,710	5,020	5,345	5,642	5,958	6,319	6,628	6,906	7,122	7,255
Mideast	3,727	3,991	4,292	4,554	4,846	5,090	5,322	5,581	5,793	6,007	6,205	6,342
Great Lakes	3,259	3,510	3,788	4,008	4,294	4,568	4,801	5,069	5,256	5,491	5,717	5,884
Plains	3,432	3,715	4,003	4,214	4,454	4,707	4,871	5,166	5,407	5,605	5,776	5,943
Southeast	3,116	3,352	3,602	3,783	4,017	4,222	4,401	4,596	4,738	4,919	5,049	5,161
Southwest	2,835	3,086	3,354	3,529	3,723	3,955	4,069	4,254	4,475	4,672	4,833	4,944
Rocky Mountain	2,761	3,011	3,280	3,455	3,710	3,882	4,042	4,285	4,467	4,656	4,800	4,921
Far West	3,059	3,243	3,473	3,693	3,941	4,195	4,408	4,685	4,970	5,195	5,364	5,554
Alabama	3,078	3,270	3,543	3,690	3,902	4,162	4,279	4,414	4,499	4,625	4,712	4,785
Alaska	3,716	4,308	4,798	5,089	5,342	5,789	6,023	6,521	6,972	7,288	7,632	7,978
Arizona	2,683	2,872	3,137	3,404	3,618	3,905	4,016	4,185	4,390	4,564	4,737	4,816
Arkansas	2,882	3,150	3,409	3,579	3,778	4,009	4,110	4,306	4,473	4,609	4,679	4,769
California	3,039	3,191	3,405	3,629	3,873	4,127	4,355	4,615	4,906	5,134	5,310	5,520
Colorado	3,006	3,294	3,603	3,784	4,081	4,178	4,331	4,604	4,778	4,972	5,101	5,158
Connecticut	4,019	4,314	4,630	4,829	5,128	5,355	5,518	5,760	6,061	6,325	6,528	6,710
Delaware	3,488	3,815	4,137	4,503	4,870	5,233	5,421	5,747	6,065	6,276	6,667	6,939
D.C.	5,727	5,980	6,505	6,798	7,281	7,764	7,998	8,346	8,725	8,981	9,185	9,531
Florida	3,388	3,649	3,936	4,107	4,332	4,509	4,720	4,949	5,127	5,335	5,490	5,581
Georgia	3,010	3,164	3,360	3,535	3,731	3,925	4,012	4,139	4,184	4,319	4,386	4,476
Hawaii	3,349	3,540	3,667	3,870	4,066	4,379	4,531	4,787	5,020	5,180	5,175	5,227
Idaho	2,522	2,747	2,992	3,141	3,295	3,507	3,710	3,982	4,091	4,284	4,456	4,702
Illinois	3,260	3,496	3,742	3,927	4,158	4,420	4,641	4,961	5,116	5,301	5,532	5,668
Indiana	3,138	3,367	3,645	3,876	4,212	4,432	4,675	4,972	5,087	5,419	5,578	5,788
Iowa	3,172	3,406	3,649	3,815	4,035	4,275	4,465	4,681	4,881	5,039	5,211	5,352
Kansas	3,164	3,452	3,651	3,838	4,088	4,325	4,527	4,811	5,027	5,179	5,298	5,461
Kentucky	3,173	3,445	3,716	3,853	4,064	4,322	4,511	4,670	4,775	4,997	5,126	5,275
Louisiana	3,024	3,269	3,532	3,728	3,975	4,110	4,456	4,664	4,857	5,079	5,200	5,280
Maine	3,548	3,828	4,144	4,378	4,738	5,039	5,303	5,609	5,881	6,103	6,324	6,592
Maryland	3,422	3,718	4,010	4,258	4,559	4,831	5,053	5,346	5,629	5,845	6,019	6,180
Massachusetts	4,425	4,758	5,119	5,503	5,841	6,161	6,557	7,001	7,321	7,587	7,793	7,851
Michigan	3,138	3,296	3,520	3,724	3,990	4,277	4,532	4,806	5,032	5,234	5,490	5,683
Minnesota	3,981	4,230	4,610	4,812	5,083	5,329	5,540	5,802	5,938	6,191	6,384	6,534
Mississippi	2,850	3,091	3,360	3,550	3,853	3,995	4,270	4,578	4,772	4,867	5,043	5,190
Missouri	3,309	3,621	3,887	4,133	4,333	4,549	4,575	4,967	5,304	5,469	5,603	5,766
Montana	3,018	3,301	3,565	3,751	3,962	4,281	4,450	4,664	4,915	5,193	5,451	5,645
Nebraska	3,188	3,504	3,772	3,992	4,268	4,605	4,883	5,106	5,364	5,513	5,736	5,880
Nevada	2,609	2,849	3,117	3,258	3,497	3,645	3,778	4,042	4,219	4,275	4,363	4,511
New Hampshire	3,432	3,716	4,089	4,429	4,783	5,149	5,565	5,982	6,315	6,741	7,030	7,189
New Jersey	3,551	3,758	4,107	4,358	4,606	4,821	5,008	5,277	5,532	5,727	5,814	5,875
New Mexico	2,630	2,815	3,007	3,129	3,379	3,722	3,832	4,087	4,453	4,722	4,916	5,009
New York	3,923	4,187	4,482	4,769	5,061	5,262	5,508	5,745	5,894	6,156	6,338	6,423
North Carolina	3,066	3,315	3,508	3,719	3,972	4,154	4,351	4,476	4,600	4,785	4,914	5,074
North Dakota	3,382	3,745	4,033	4,233	4,509	4,803	5,032	5,347	5,665	6,070	6,304	6,678
Ohio	3,334	3,669	3,980	4,209	4,519	4,829	5,028	5,207	5,393	5,640	5,849	6,007
Oklahoma	2,848	3,071	3,298	3,612	3,798	4,108	4,267	4,495	4,740	4,789	4,918	5,101
Oregon	2,947	3,214	3,476	3,651	3,959	4,236	4,450	4,733	4,918	5,116	5,318	5,443
Pennsylvania	3,597	3,887	4,158	4,391	4,695	4,998	5,247	5,509	5,739	5,887	6,182	6,418
Rhode Island	3,733	3,976	4,256	4,507	4,834	5,114	5,393	5,680	5,962	6,190	6,379	6,523
South Carolina	2,901	3,171	3,404	3,554	3,765	3,978	4,144	4,345	4,535	4,691	4,862	4,942
South Dakota	3,314	3,609	3,977	4,234	4,496	4,931	5,259	5,535	5,893	6,209	6,524	6,807
Tennessee	3,267	3,506	3,737	3,916	4,198	4,450	4,597	4,781	4,846	4,990	5,152	5,242
Texas	2,888	3,165	3,447	3,581	3,767	3,964	4,072	4,249	4,459	4,678	4,838	4,947
Utah	2,299	2,472	2,685	2,858	3,110	3,325	3,461	3,630	3,845	4,003	4,081	4,214
Vermont	3,440	3,766	4,155	4,556	4,792	5,122	5,466	5,760	6,052	6,388	6,629	6,851
Virginia	2,836	3,049	3,313	3,530	3,775	4,018	4,182	4,453	4,682	4,901	5,033	5,199
Washington	3,261	3,522	3,809	4,058	4,319	4,567	4,739	5,091	5,440	5,729	5,889	6,029
West Virginia	3,460	3,734	4,003	4,214	4,501	4,762	4,899	5,161	5,364	5,702	5,832	6,002
Wisconsin	3,455	3,767	4,144	4,446	4,782	5,047	5,322	5,608	5,881	6,148	6,417	6,586
Wyoming	2,867	3,138	3,413	3,596	3,865	4,192	4,428	4,767	4,972	5,126	5,454	5,643

Per Capita Personal Consumption Expenditures by Region and State: Health Care—Continued

(Dollars.)

State	2012	2013	2014	2015	2016	2017	2018	2019	2020	2021	2022
United States	5,794	5,884	6,093	6,400	6,673	6,874	7,137	7,477	7,103	7,923	8,331
New England	7,355	7,433	7,630	7,952	8,298	8,458	8,687	9,047	8,565	9,427	9,777
Mideast	6,461	6,584	6,820	7,092	7,440	7,679	8,034	8,448	8,132	8,893	9,384
Great Lakes	6,094	6,173	6,386	6,651	6,945	7,128	7,347	7,715	7,273	8,049	8,543
Plains	6,120	6,222	6,408	6,721	7,036	7,211	7,506	7,810	7,383	8,183	8,581
Southeast	5,327	5,387	5,575	5,863	6,116	6,291	6,498	6,795	6,471	7,347	7,733
Southwest	5,080	5,110	5,286	5,552	5,721	5,860	6,007	6,266	5,958	6,663	6,961
Rocky Mountain	5,047	5,155	5,388	5,678	5,911	6,122	6,383	6,602	6,218	6,873	7,286
Far West	5,736	5,895	6,150	6,590	6,870	7,165	7,557	7,980	7,562	8,525	8,959
Alabama	4,963	5,080	5,195	5,452	5,710	5,816	5,957	6,259	5,987	6,678	7,032
Alaska	8,232	8,292	8,644	9,007	9,318	9,688	10,222	10,761	9,755	10,877	11,813
Arizona	4,942	5,011	5,121	5,358	5,614	5,890	6,148	6,435	6,285	6,935	7,188
Arkansas	4,922	4,939	5,152	5,462	5,865	6,137	6,269	6,597	6,314	6,974	7,482
California	5,706	5,902	6,163	6,637	6,940	7,291	7,743	8,212	7,829	8,870	9,335
Colorado	5,241	5,368	5,639	6,009	6,250	6,463	6,755	7,016	6,568	7,304	7,695
Connecticut	6,840	6,974	7,171	7,361	7,677	7,819	8,085	8,409	8,084	8,852	9,243
Delaware	7,087	7,323	7,652	7,989	8,142	8,447	8,777	9,066	8,539	9,463	10,301
D.C.	9,622	9,648	9,791	10,203	10,399	10,402	10,650	10,982	10,547	11,755	12,239
Florida	5,769	5,765	5,984	6,270	6,442	6,623	6,920	7,206	6,785	7,753	8,174
Georgia	4,670	4,844	5,015	5,342	5,612	5,755	5,984	6,355	6,110	6,913	7,260
Hawaii	5,289	5,429	5,635	5,988	6,164	6,491	6,845	7,312	7,170	7,780	8,189
Idaho	4,862	4,959	5,158	5,389	5,561	5,727	5,897	6,036	5,721	6,393	6,882
Illinois	5,801	5,901	6,133	6,336	6,653	6,824	7,064	7,344	7,067	7,799	8,362
Indiana	6,209	6,132	6,340	6,596	6,987	7,278	7,577	7,983	7,662	8,598	9,437
Iowa	5,469	5,577	5,816	6,153	6,399	6,513	6,691	7,015	6,705	7,417	7,761
Kansas	5,671	5,684	5,750	5,948	6,130	6,325	6,645	6,971	6,684	7,376	7,807
Kentucky	5,356	5,497	5,714	6,074	6,384	6,605	6,896	7,177	6,872	8,028	8,559
Louisiana	5,329	5,446	5,758	6,045	6,366	6,661	6,849	7,205	7,193	8,304	8,739
Maine	6,672	6,711	6,905	7,364	7,777	8,119	8,475	8,802	8,254	8,881	9,222
Maryland	6,251	6,263	6,480	6,790	7,016	7,196	7,380	7,551	7,186	7,843	8,166
Massachusetts	7,941	7,971	8,176	8,550	8,936	9,068	9,239	9,637	9,101	10,141	10,491
Michigan	5,848	5,894	6,050	6,372	6,641	6,778	6,950	7,264	6,778	7,470	7,765
Minnesota	6,658	6,857	7,105	7,362	7,729	7,863	8,257	8,397	7,762	8,663	8,976
Mississippi	5,360	5,376	5,524	5,753	6,059	6,161	6,155	6,390	6,222	6,909	7,174
Missouri	6,015	6,044	6,167	6,527	6,840	7,023	7,245	7,565	7,164	7,892	8,323
Montana	5,861	6,115	6,294	6,660	6,959	7,237	7,608	7,947	7,508	8,275	8,519
Nebraska	6,017	6,081	6,261	6,592	6,981	7,215	7,451	7,817	7,481	8,396	8,908
Nevada	4,636	4,801	5,077	5,289	5,647	5,810	6,028	6,200	5,783	6,441	6,703
New Hampshire	7,241	7,315	7,421	7,688	7,945	8,157	8,540	8,825	8,250	8,971	9,231
New Jersey	6,127	6,211	6,476	6,816	7,203	7,417	7,608	7,994	7,646	8,415	8,929
New Mexico	5,143	5,193	5,436	5,745	5,898	6,019	6,180	6,403	6,101	6,985	7,304
New York	6,483	6,658	6,911	7,118	7,533	7,848	8,274	8,909	8,718	9,597	10,124
North Carolina	5,274	5,241	5,388	5,713	5,973	6,140	6,364	6,626	6,181	7,228	7,481
North Dakota	6,798	7,096	7,420	7,901	8,274	8,535	8,809	9,501	9,059	10,066	10,494
Ohio	6,310	6,480	6,711	6,972	7,249	7,454	7,664	8,144	7,539	8,322	8,770
Oklahoma	5,242	5,340	5,584	5,805	6,005	6,232	6,474	6,675	6,326	7,043	7,627
Oregon	5,552	5,692	6,055	6,577	6,846	6,999	7,227	7,613	7,171	7,971	8,372
Pennsylvania	6,556	6,672	6,866	7,163	7,457	7,630	8,077	8,301	7,864	8,468	8,944
Rhode Island	6,545	6,663	6,930	7,244	7,476	7,497	7,573	7,925	7,484	8,145	8,452
South Carolina	4,979	5,008	5,173	5,377	5,601	5,688	5,778	6,010	5,702	6,432	6,677
South Dakota	7,020	7,192	7,513	7,939	8,377	8,676	9,302	9,893	9,513	10,416	10,881
Tennessee	5,407	5,529	5,656	5,949	6,224	6,484	6,526	6,702	6,488	7,160	7,535
Texas	5,085	5,095	5,272	5,548	5,694	5,789	5,895	6,158	5,817	6,522	6,793
Utah	4,358	4,385	4,569	4,725	4,954	5,143	5,377	5,538	5,231	5,710	6,213
Vermont	7,125	7,373	7,526	7,845	8,124	8,400	8,714	9,072	8,598	9,258	9,683
Virginia	5,378	5,430	5,607	5,802	6,021	6,102	6,326	6,697	6,290	7,052	7,566
Washington	6,269	6,251	6,400	6,733	6,885	7,008	7,253	7,561	6,991	7,847	8,186
West Virginia	6,352	6,520	6,819	7,300	7,835	8,254	8,539	9,014	8,713	9,573	10,030
Wisconsin	6,615	6,696	6,932	7,248	7,456	7,573	7,754	8,132	7,585	8,395	8,766
Wyoming	5,815	5,937	6,286	6,575	6,855	7,257	7,498	7,724	7,496	8,148	8,373

Regional Price Parities by Metropolitan Statistical Area

(Percent of U.S. Price Level; U.S. Average Price = 100.0)

Metropolitan Statistical Area	2008	2009	2010	2011	2012	2013	2014	2015	2016	2017	2018	2019	2020	2021	2022
United States	100.0	100.0	100.0	100.0	100.0	100.0	100.0	100.0	100.0	100.0	100.0	100.0	100.0	100.0	100.0
United States (Nonmetropolitan Portion)	86.5	86.9	88.7	88.5	88.7	89.0	88.9	88.7	87.9	87.6	89.2	89.4	88.3	88.8	88.6
Abilene, TX	92.1	89.4	92.9	92.5	94.1	92.5	94.6	92.9	93.3	93.8	92.3	92.4	90.4	91.8	91.7
Akron, OH	92.5	95.2	93.3	94.1	95.5	95.2	95.0	95.6	95.3	95.4	94.3	94.7	93.5	93.5	92.1
Albany, GA	86.5	85.6	87.2	87.7	87.4	88.1	88.4	88.0	89.3	87.3	86.5	84.2	83.9	89.3	86.4
Albany-Lebanon, OR	99.4	100.0	97.0	96.2	96.6	96.9	98.8	98.8	98.9	98.9	103.3	103.0	102.5	101.9	104.6
Albany-Schenectady-Troy, NY	102.7	102.2	99.9	100.8	99.5	101.7	99.4	100.8	101.2	100.7	99.8	99.7	99.1	99.1	96.6
Albuquerque, NM	97.0	99.0	97.4	100.4	99.6	98.3	98.5	96.8	96.6	98.1	93.9	95.1	94.2	92.2	93.4
Alexandria, LA	89.7	86.1	89.0	87.0	90.3	91.5	90.8	90.3	92.1	90.5	87.5	89.1	87.4	89.3	86.2
Allentown-Bethlehem-Easton, PA-NJ	101.1	102.5	101.2	99.9	100.0	100.8	99.6	101.0	101.2	101.7	99.2	99.2	99.7	98.1	98.0
Altoona, PA	94.0	91.9	93.9	93.5	92.3	92.8	89.4	92.6	91.6	91.2	91.3	90.8	89.7	89.2	89.0
Amarillo, TX	95.8	93.5	94.9	96.4	96.1	96.4	96.3	97.0	97.2	96.2	93.2	94.1	94.5	93.6	91.8
Ames, IA	82.4	90.0	93.0	91.7	92.4	94.6	93.0	90.1	88.9	89.9	93.9	96.0	93.4	91.5	88.5
Anchorage, AK	106.5	111.9	106.3	106.8	107.2	106.5	104.9	105.7	108.1	107.8	106.4	104.8	103.2	106.6	103.1
Ann Arbor, MI	103.6	101.3	101.1	100.4	100.9	100.2	102.5	100.2	98.3	98.5	99.2	100.6	98.5	99.4	97.7
Anniston-Oxford, AL	88.2	83.4	88.8	90.9	90.7	90.4	89.7	91.1	90.8	88.6	85.2	87.6	85.8	83.7	83.9
Appleton, WI	97.2	94.7	95.2	94.3	94.6	95.3	94.5	93.4	93.0	92.1	93.5	93.7	92.3	93.3	91.8
Asheville, NC	93.3	91.3	92.8	93.4	94.2	94.1	94.4	93.1	95.3	93.8	93.0	94.1	93.2	94.7	94.8
Athens-Clarke County, GA	94.2	94.3	94.6	94.4	93.3	93.4	93.4	92.8	93.7	93.8	90.6	90.7	90.3	94.4	93.6
Atlanta-Sandy Springs-Alpharetta, GA	98.1	95.0	98.2	96.5	99.1	98.2	98.4	98.0	98.4	99.4	98.2	98.1	98.8	99.1	98.8
Atlantic City-Hammonton, NJ	109.8	107.0	106.9	105.6	105.4	102.2	101.5	103.3	102.4	97.8	99.7	97.2	100.7	97.0	98.6
Auburn-Opelika, AL	90.3	88.4	89.3	92.1	91.0	91.0	91.3	88.7	90.2	89.6	88.9	90.7	89.2	89.6	88.7
Augusta-Richmond County, GA-SC	91.0	90.5	92.2	93.6	93.4	93.2	92.5	93.2	93.6	92.4	91.4	90.3	89.7	91.9	92.0
Austin-Round Rock-Georgetown, TX	99.5	98.8	99.6	100.3	100.9	100.7	101.3	101.5	102.5	101.8	99.1	99.3	101.2	100.1	98.8
Bakersfield, CA	96.9	100.3	98.2	100.4	101.1	99.7	99.6	97.7	96.5	98.4	101.8	101.2	100.3	100.9	104.5
Baltimore-Columbia-Towson, MD	106.5	109.6	106.3	108.8	106.5	106.8	105.7	106.0	106.1	107.6	105.2	103.9	105.3	105.0	102.4
Bangor, ME	94.1	92.3	96.7	94.0	96.4	99.6	92.2	92.9	93.5	94.7	94.0	96.6	97.5	96.7	96.8
Barnstable Town, MA	103.0	103.0	105.4	99.5	101.0	100.1	104.7	105.9	105.9	105.9	101.1	105.2	101.3	101.2	109.1
Baton Rouge, LA	93.1	91.7	93.3	94.6	94.2	94.8	94.7	94.6	95.6	94.0	92.8	92.8	93.2	93.2	92.5
Battle Creek, MI	94.7	94.5	92.3	92.7	94.2	93.4	94.1	91.8	91.9	91.0	92.0	91.8	90.7	90.3	89.3
Bay City, MI	94.2	93.9	92.5	92.7	93.2	93.4	92.9	91.1	92.1	89.4	92.7	92.4	88.7	91.4	88.0
Beaumont-Port Arthur, TX	93.4	91.4	92.6	94.7	93.3	94.4	94.5	92.7	94.7	92.4	91.6	92.3	90.2	93.1	91.3
Beckley, WV	83.4	78.2	84.8	84.0	83.6	87.2	87.5	87.5	83.2	84.8	86.2	86.3	83.5	89.3	88.3
Bellingham, WA	96.1	102.3	99.7	103.2	102.0	100.3	101.0	101.1	98.6	100.8	104.4	104.2	103.4	104.6	105.9
Bend, OR	100.5	99.4	97.0	96.4	96.6	97.1	99.3	102.2	100.6	102.7	103.6	103.9	104.3	102.8	108.0
Billings, MT	94.9	95.8	95.0	96.8	98.0	96.3	97.1	96.8	94.8	97.1	94.2	95.7	92.2	92.4	91.7
Binghamton, NY	97.3	97.3	98.1	97.7	95.0	96.0	95.0	96.1	96.2	97.9	96.0	94.1	97.0	94.4	92.0
Birmingham-Hoover, AL	93.1	92.0	93.6	94.9	94.2	94.6	93.7	93.6	94.5	93.4	90.4	91.3	91.8	90.8	91.2
Bismarck, ND	90.1	92.1	88.8	89.8	95.3	96.0	96.9	93.8	96.1	91.1	91.5	94.3	92.8	94.1	91.1
Blacksburg-Christiansburg, VA	87.8	87.3	90.0	90.4	88.5	91.9	91.8	91.5	88.4	89.0	91.6	91.0	91.0	92.1	93.1
Bloomington, IL	97.0	95.9	97.5	95.6	96.4	95.3	95.7	94.7	93.9	92.9	94.3	95.0	92.7	92.8	92.4
Bloomington, IN	94.3	96.6	95.0	95.5	94.2	94.2	95.0	94.3	95.5	93.6	93.7	94.5	93.4	93.9	93.0
Bloomsburg-Berwick, PA	94.6	93.7	93.7	92.6	92.3	93.8	92.3	93.8	94.6	94.0	93.2	91.6	91.4	89.4	89.1
Boise City, ID	95.2	97.7	95.5	97.0	96.7	96.4	95.9	94.9	93.1	95.8	93.6	95.7	93.6	93.8	94.2
Boston-Cambridge-Newton, MA-NH	107.9	106.6	106.1	106.6	105.9	104.3	105.7	106.1	110.1	108.9	110.1	109.7	112.4	109.8	112.0
Boulder, CO	108.5	105.5	104.5	107.1	107.5	105.9	106.3	106.9	105.6	105.3	101.6	105.4	101.6	101.0	99.9
Bowling Green, KY	86.6	84.7	88.4	87.7	88.6	89.9	89.3	88.9	87.3	87.9	87.9	88.9	89.5	88.6	89.3
Bremerton-Silverdale-Port Orchard, WA	107.0	105.8	103.3	103.9	103.6	103.1	104.7	104.9	107.1	107.9	107.3	105.7	105.3	103.6	108.8
Bridgeport-Stamford-Norwalk, CT	117.2	117.9	113.4	114.3	114.0	115.1	115.4	113.8	114.0	111.8	107.4	106.2	108.8	106.1	109.8
Brownsville-Harlingen, TX	85.0	86.1	87.0	89.5	89.2	87.6	87.9	88.3	89.5	88.0	85.2	87.7	85.1	87.9	85.4
Brunswick, GA	88.2	86.3	89.6	88.7	89.9	89.7	90.9	89.5	89.2	89.4	91.7	86.8	89.0	90.1	91.6
Buffalo-Cheektowaga, NY	97.3	98.0	96.4	96.3	96.2	97.4	95.0	97.9	97.6	97.3	95.5	94.8	94.3	94.9	93.9
Burlington, NC	92.5	91.8	92.4	93.4	93.3	93.8	92.7	93.2	92.2	92.2	91.4	90.5	89.7	89.4	92.3
Burlington-South Burlington, VT	103.3	105.0	102.2	102.1	102.8	103.4	99.6	103.0	102.3	103.8	102.2	104.5	105.0	102.5	106.5
California-Lexington Park, MD	98.0	95.2	98.3	99.8	99.0	100.0	99.7	100.1	99.5	94.8	98.1	96.3	98.1	96.5	99.8
Canton-Massillon, OH	93.4	92.1	92.7	91.3	92.2	92.0	92.0	91.2	90.4	90.3	90.8	91.0	88.9	89.7	88.7
Cape Coral-Fort Myers, FL	99.9	97.0	97.3	97.7	97.8	97.9	98.5	99.1	101.0	99.4	99.3	97.9	98.1	100.0	101.7
Cape Girardeau, MO-IL	81.3	83.0	87.9	87.0	88.6	89.5	88.2	86.4	86.2	85.2	87.8	90.1	88.9	88.5	86.3
Carbondale-Marion, IL	81.1	84.9	86.0	88.5	88.1	86.8	87.1	86.8	85.9	82.7	87.8	88.7	87.5	86.4	86.7
Carson City, NV	99.9	95.5	97.5	97.4	95.2	96.4	97.5	99.2	96.1	97.8	94.8	98.6	94.8	94.1	94.5
Casper, WY	92.3	97.1	95.5	97.9	99.2	99.3	98.1	95.2	97.6	98.2	95.3	93.3	93.4	91.4	92.1
Cedar Rapids, IA	93.0	93.5	93.6	92.8	93.8	89.7	92.6	92.5	91.3	91.7	92.4	92.1	91.4	92.0	90.0
Chambersburg-Waynesboro, PA	98.1	97.9	96.5	96.3	95.5	97.3	95.1	96.3	96.2	98.1	96.2	94.6	94.3	94.9	93.9
Champaign-Urbana, IL	97.4	96.7	95.6	94.8	94.6	95.0	94.9	94.0	94.4	92.8	93.4	94.3	92.1	93.2	91.3
Charleston, WV	89.8	88.7	90.7	92.8	92.3	90.9	91.4	91.2	91.5	89.6	90.3	89.1	86.8	91.0	88.6
Charleston-North Charleston, SC	97.4	97.3	97.7	99.4	100.3	99.6	99.8	100.0	99.7	99.2	98.3	98.2	98.1	99.2	99.1
Charlotte-Concord-Gastonia, NC-SC	95.3	94.0	95.6	95.7	96.1	95.9	96.3	96.2	96.9	96.2	95.5	94.5	94.2	96.6	96.9
Charlottesville, VA	99.7	98.6	100.5	100.6	98.8	100.7	99.8	100.0	100.3	99.9	98.2	95.8	98.2	100.5	97.6
Chattanooga, TN-GA	92.2	91.6	93.7	93.6	94.4	93.4	93.4	93.6	93.7	94.1	89.4	91.3	90.1	90.0	92.5
Cheyenne, WY	95.6	99.5	96.8	100.2	99.2	98.0	99.8	96.4	97.9	98.7	93.6	96.4	91.8	92.9	94.1
Chicago-Naperville-Elgin, IL-IN-WI	105.3	106.3	105.9	106.8	105.1	104.2	103.1	102.6	103.7	105.2	104.1	102.6	104.3	105.4	105.7
Chico, CA	99.4	102.2	100.7	102.1	103.5	100.4	99.8	98.4	97.0	100.8	104.3	102.3	101.7	102.5	104.3

Regional Price Parities by Metropolitan Statistical Area—Continued

(Percent of U.S. Price Level; U.S. Average Price = 100.0)

Metropolitan Statistical Area	2008	2009	2010	2011	2012	2013	2014	2015	2016	2017	2018	2019	2020	2021	2022
Cincinnati, OH-KY-IN	97.0	96.5	94.7	93.2	93.4	93.8	92.9	91.8	93.6	93.8	94.3	94.9	93.9	94.1	93.5
Clarksville, TN-KY	90.5	90.0	91.3	93.8	92.9	92.8	92.3	92.4	93.6	92.1	88.6	89.5	88.8	90.4	91.1
Cleveland, TN	87.9	86.6	87.2	86.7	89.3	90.1	89.2	88.1	88.6	85.2	88.2	86.7	86.8	87.7	89.2
Cleveland-Elyria, OH	92.8	96.4	94.4	95.0	95.2	96.5	96.3	95.7	95.7	95.5	94.7	94.3	93.5	93.9	93.1
Coeur d'Alene, ID	98.2	95.1	93.2	94.3	94.9	96.5	96.2	96.7	97.5	97.6	94.0	90.6	93.0	93.7	93.7
College Station-Bryan, TX	95.1	94.2	95.7	95.5	96.4	95.2	95.4	95.9	96.4	94.7	94.7	94.4	95.2	95.0	92.6
Colorado Springs, CO	98.0	101.5	99.1	102.5	102.2	101.3	101.0	99.7	98.9	101.9	97.9	100.3	98.6	96.6	96.8
Columbia, MO	93.6	93.5	93.1	92.0	93.5	92.6	92.9	91.6	91.3	91.1	91.6	92.5	91.2	89.5	88.0
Columbia, SC	93.5	92.3	94.1	95.2	94.4	94.7	94.1	94.6	94.6	93.6	92.4	91.1	89.9	93.3	93.6
Columbus, GA-AL	88.4	87.3	90.7	91.5	90.1	90.4	91.0	91.2	90.4	89.6	88.3	87.9	86.3	88.9	89.5
Columbus, IN	84.0	86.1	90.6	89.0	90.5	88.8	90.4	87.7	88.0	87.4	94.0	93.8	91.4	91.7	90.2
Columbus, OH	96.6	96.0	96.0	94.1	95.4	95.5	95.3	94.6	94.6	93.6	95.2	95.6	94.4	94.8	94.0
Corpus Christi, TX	96.2	92.8	95.8	95.1	95.5	97.2	96.6	96.2	97.4	96.8	93.9	95.0	95.0	94.7	93.6
Corvallis, OR	99.4	100.0	97.0	96.2	96.6	96.9	98.8	98.8	98.9	98.9	103.3	103.0	102.5	101.9	106.1
Crestview-Fort Walton Beach-Destin, FL	95.8	94.2	96.0	97.0	97.9	96.7	97.3	97.2	96.8	95.6	96.2	95.9	94.9	96.8	97.9
Cumberland, MD-WV	90.8	90.1	90.2	91.2	92.9	90.6	93.4	91.4	91.8	89.9	88.8	88.9	88.1	91.2	86.9
Dallas-Fort Worth-Arlington, TX	101.2	101.5	101.3	100.2	100.7	101.0	100.2	99.0	97.9	99.5	101.0	103.4	104.6	104.1	103.5
Dalton, GA	89.2	85.1	89.2	87.4	88.5	87.8	89.0	88.6	87.6	85.4	88.8	87.7	84.3	90.7	90.6
Danville, IL	81.0	83.5	87.7	86.7	87.6	86.4	87.3	86.0	84.3	84.0	87.8	86.9	86.6	87.9	87.8
Daphne-Fairhope-Foley, AL	95.2	94.5	96.6	93.4	95.8	94.2	94.1	93.5	94.8	95.7	91.5	94.6	90.8	92.0	91.1
Davenport-Moline-Rock Island, IA-IL	94.9	93.3	94.1	92.0	93.3	93.2	92.5	91.5	90.8	91.1	92.0	92.1	91.8	91.4	88.9
Dayton-Kettering, OH	96.1	94.7	94.3	93.2	93.1	93.6	93.5	92.7	92.8	91.8	92.8	92.5	91.8	92.2	91.4
Decatur, AL	89.8	85.2	88.8	90.5	88.2	90.7	87.3	90.2	89.2	89.0	87.2	84.4	87.2	86.1	87.2
Decatur, IL	91.1	91.8	89.5	91.6	93.1	89.7	90.3	88.9	89.0	86.0	89.8	89.5	88.3	89.4	87.3
Deltona-Daytona Beach-Ormond Beach, FL	98.6	96.6	96.1	97.9	97.5	97.1	97.6	98.2	98.2	98.2	97.1	95.8	96.7	97.8	98.8
Denver-Aurora-Lakewood, CO	105.8	103.3	101.9	105.0	105.1	104.9	104.8	105.1	105.2	104.3	102.4	104.4	109.5	109.2	107.4
Des Moines-West Des Moines, IA	95.2	97.2	95.4	94.5	95.5	95.8	96.0	94.7	94.7	93.9	95.6	95.7	93.9	93.4	92.1
Detroit-Warren-Dearborn, MI	100.6	100.2	99.4	98.5	97.9	98.4	98.7	96.8	96.2	95.8	97.2	98.4	98.3	96.3	96.1
Dothan, AL	86.7	85.6	87.7	88.0	88.5	89.0	88.1	87.3	88.3	86.4	85.0	85.8	86.5	86.0	85.0
Dover, DE	96.7	98.0	98.4	98.2	97.3	97.7	98.6	97.4	100.3	96.7	94.9	95.3	93.8	95.9	95.1
Dubuque, IA	93.5	92.7	91.8	91.4	91.9	92.5	92.8	91.4	91.3	91.5	90.5	90.0	89.9	88.2	86.4
Duluth, MN-WI	88.8	92.5	88.9	90.6	90.4	88.0	89.0	90.0	88.1	86.0	90.5	90.0	83.1	88.8	88.6
Durham-Chapel Hill, NC	96.3	95.3	96.4	96.9	96.1	96.7	97.0	96.9	96.5	96.2	95.4	94.4	94.3	96.0	96.6
East Stroudsburg, PA	101.9	100.4	100.6	98.6	96.7	100.6	100.3	97.9	97.0	101.5	98.2	100.5	98.4	97.6	94.3
Eau Claire, WI	96.7	94.4	94.5	94.4	94.8	93.6	94.1	92.4	91.7	91.1	93.1	92.7	92.2	91.8	91.1
El Centro, CA	95.3	96.3	95.2	94.8	94.0	94.3	91.8	94.5	95.7	96.0	92.8	96.4	96.8	95.6	100.1
Elizabethtown-Fort Knox, KY	90.0	88.2	90.6	92.0	88.8	89.7	90.4	89.2	88.9	87.3	87.3	89.0	88.0	87.6	88.9
Elkhart-Goshen, IN	96.7	94.2	92.9	93.6	92.7	91.3	92.2	92.2	90.2	91.0	92.4	91.4	91.1	87.6	91.5
Elmira, NY	95.9	97.0	96.5	97.9	94.5	99.0	97.8	97.8	95.4	97.8	96.1	95.9	95.4	94.7	92.7
El Paso, TX	92.4	92.6	94.5	95.7	95.6	94.7	94.1	94.0	95.2	94.7	91.5	91.6	92.8	92.9	91.2
Enid, OK	(NA)	(NA)	(NA)	(NA)	(NA)	89.9	89.6	90.6	92.1	91.7	88.0	86.1	86.7	86.9	85.5
Erie, PA	96.5	93.6	94.7	94.0	95.3	96.3	93.9	94.7	95.5	96.7	94.6	94.0	92.8	91.9	90.7
Eugene-Springfield, OR	96.3	100.0	97.8	100.9	100.5	99.1	98.6	97.7	97.9	99.6	102.2	101.6	100.6	100.7	104.6
Evansville, IN-KY	93.4	94.0	92.5	92.2	92.4	91.3	91.2	90.3	90.5	90.4	89.7	91.2	89.5	90.1	88.8
Fairbanks, AK	104.7	102.8	102.2	102.7	98.0	97.7	101.3	100.6	100.4	103.9	104.6	103.1	99.4	104.5	98.6
Fargo, ND-MN	97.4	95.0	95.4	94.4	96.0	95.4	92.7	94.6	95.5	93.8	93.1	95.1	92.6	92.6	87.9
Farmington, NM	95.1	91.1	91.0	90.6	94.8	90.1	94.8	95.4	95.1	97.1	92.1	92.1	89.2	89.3	88.4
Fayetteville, NC	91.2	89.7	91.8	92.8	92.7	92.7	92.8	92.0	91.1	90.3	90.8	89.2	88.8	91.6	91.4
Fayetteville-Springdale-Rogers, AR	92.6	91.6	92.4	93.8	94.3	93.8	93.4	93.5	94.3	93.4	90.8	91.7	92.7	93.0	90.7
Flagstaff, AZ	99.8	100.2	98.4	95.2	99.2	100.5	98.6	102.3	97.7	101.0	97.3	99.4	97.0	95.6	95.5
Flint, MI	96.0	95.0	94.7	93.2	93.1	93.4	93.2	91.7	90.7	89.5	91.7	92.1	89.8	88.9	90.7
Florence, SC	84.4	85.2	87.3	88.6	89.6	88.7	88.4	89.9	89.4	88.7	88.1	87.7	86.3	90.5	88.2
Florence-Muscle Shoals, AL	83.2	84.2	87.9	85.9	88.6	85.3	87.0	86.3	85.9	86.7	84.0	81.9	82.8	85.4	84.2
Fond du Lac, WI	83.4	85.9	88.8	87.7	91.0	91.2	90.1	89.7	88.3	87.2	92.3	92.9	91.2	92.1	89.4
Fort Collins, CO	97.2	103.1	101.3	103.3	104.7	103.2	103.1	101.7	101.3	104.3	100.9	102.2	98.5	97.7	98.2
Fort Smith, AR-OK	90.2	87.9	89.5	89.5	89.4	89.6	90.7	88.5	88.8	88.7	86.0	87.7	86.9	87.5	85.6
Fort Wayne, IN	93.8	92.3	92.8	92.2	92.4	93.0	92.1	91.3	92.2	90.7	91.8	92.3	90.0	91.9	92.7
Fresno, CA	97.1	101.0	98.9	101.2	100.6	99.3	98.9	97.6	96.7	98.2	102.6	102.6	101.2	101.5	105.2
Gadsden, AL	86.5	88.3	87.6	88.8	87.6	88.5	89.3	88.2	88.7	87.3	86.0	86.2	85.1	84.4	81.9
Gainesville, FL	97.1	97.3	96.5	97.0	95.8	96.0	96.9	96.1	95.9	96.1	96.0	94.0	92.7	95.8	96.4
Gainesville, GA	92.4	89.2	92.9	93.1	92.7	92.8	93.0	92.2	91.3	92.0	94.5	92.4	94.5	94.0	96.9
Gettysburg, PA	98.5	97.9	98.2	96.5	95.1	97.5	96.1	97.7	99.4	98.1	96.6	96.6	96.5	95.3	95.5
Glens Falls, NY	98.7	100.5	98.9	97.4	97.4	100.1	94.2	98.1	97.1	97.8	95.5	95.8	95.1	95.5	92.4
Goldsboro, NC	90.5	90.1	91.1	91.8	89.9	92.8	91.1	91.8	94.1	91.2	90.5	89.6	85.6	90.0	89.7
Grand Forks, ND-MN	95.7	92.4	93.4	92.2	89.7	93.8	92.2	93.4	92.3	91.0	91.7	94.2	91.4	90.0	86.8
Grand Island, NE	81.8	82.3	88.1	89.3	85.0	87.1	83.4	87.4	87.8	83.3	88.2	90.0	90.6	89.1	86.5
Grand Junction, CO	103.8	98.9	97.6	99.7	97.6	96.4	98.9	98.6	98.9	99.5	94.0	98.5	95.2	92.2	93.8
Grand Rapids-Kentwood, MI	96.3	96.3	95.5	94.6	94.9	95.9	95.3	93.7	94.6	92.4	94.1	95.9	94.5	96.4	94.2
Grants Pass, OR	96.2	94.7	93.9	94.4	96.1	95.3	94.6	96.3	96.2	96.1	99.9	100.2	95.0	98.8	102.8
Great Falls, MT	85.2	89.2	85.0	91.8	92.3	91.9	92.1	90.1	88.0	90.1	91.8	88.8	86.9	86.9	91.3
Greeley, CO	101.1	99.5	98.8	99.2	100.7	100.9	101.3	100.5	100.1	99.7	97.9	100.7	97.4	95.3	94.9
Green Bay, WI	94.7	94.5	95.2	93.0	92.9	93.6	92.8	91.3	92.1	91.4	93.4	92.3	92.1	92.2	90.5

Regional Price Parities by Metropolitan Statistical Area—Continued

(Percent of U.S. Price Level; U.S. Average Price = 100.0)

Metropolitan Statistical Area	2008	2009	2010	2011	2012	2013	2014	2015	2016	2017	2018	2019	2020	2021	2022
Greensboro-High Point, NC	92.5	91.1	92.8	93.7	93.4	93.3	93.8	93.7	92.7	92.4	92.2	90.3	89.4	92.8	92.7
Greenville, NC	89.9	88.4	91.8	92.0	92.6	91.6	91.5	90.0	92.3	91.0	87.8	89.4	87.5	89.5	88.5
Greenville-Anderson, SC	91.3	91.0	93.1	93.3	93.2	92.9	92.6	93.4	93.7	93.0	91.7	90.8	90.3	93.5	93.2
Gulfport-Biloxi, MS	95.3	91.4	93.3	94.0	94.3	92.8	94.2	91.3	92.5	91.9	87.3	89.2	89.3	88.9	88.9
Hagerstown-Martinsburg, MD-WV	100.2	100.8	97.0	100.1	99.4	100.1	99.4	100.8	99.7	98.6	94.0	93.3	93.1	95.3	93.5
Hammond, LA	88.5	86.7	90.9	88.9	86.5	87.6	86.7	88.5	87.7	87.7	88.7	89.1	87.0	88.8	89.4
Hanford-Corcoran, CA	100.8	97.9	95.8	99.7	96.1	95.7	94.6	99.0	97.1	96.0	101.7	98.1	99.8	98.5	102.4
Harrisburg-Carlisle, PA	99.1	99.7	98.3	97.7	97.0	98.9	95.7	98.7	98.2	99.4	97.7	96.8	96.1	97.3	95.9
Harrisonburg, VA	92.0	90.8	92.8	91.4	92.3	92.3	92.7	91.8	91.3	90.5	93.4	92.7	90.4	94.0	95.0
Hartford-East Hartford-Middletown, CT	104.7	104.9	103.0	102.4	102.5	102.1	100.8	103.3	103.0	103.6	102.4	102.8	103.9	101.8	104.9
Hattiesburg, MS	88.9	84.6	87.9	89.3	89.1	89.4	88.7	88.5	87.9	87.9	88.4	87.8	85.2	88.3	89.0
Hickory-Lenoir-Morganton, NC	90.0	90.3	90.8	92.3	90.9	89.5	91.2	89.5	90.9	90.8	88.6	87.0	87.0	89.1	89.8
Hilton Head Island-Bluffton, SC	95.0	92.5	95.8	92.9	93.5	95.6	94.8	95.2	95.9	92.1	95.9	97.8	93.6	99.1	99.3
Hinesville, GA	90.5	86.0	91.3	92.1	90.6	92.8	92.0	89.7	91.8	90.0	93.7	93.4	89.7	93.6	94.5
Homosassa Springs, FL	90.3	91.7	90.9	90.3	92.7	91.8	92.0	91.6	90.1	88.6	93.9	90.9	89.9	93.7	94.8
Hot Springs, AR	86.6	84.8	86.7	88.8	88.1	87.4	85.2	86.0	88.4	85.7	85.7	86.2	87.3	88.7	85.9
Houma-Thibodaux, LA	90.4	89.2	94.4	94.3	95.1	95.7	93.9	94.2	95.1	94.0	89.8	90.9	92.1	88.4	88.5
Houston-The Woodlands-Sugar Land, TX	99.4	100.5	101.0	98.6	100.0	101.0	102.1	103.0	102.3	99.9	101.7	101.3	100.0	99.5	98.8
Huntington-Ashland, WV-KY-OH	88.1	87.8	88.1	91.1	89.6	89.2	90.4	90.0	90.5	88.8	88.3	87.2	86.9	88.7	88.5
Huntsville, AL	92.1	91.1	92.5	93.8	94.0	93.6	92.7	92.6	93.5	94.0	89.8	91.2	90.7	91.4	92.7
Idaho Falls, ID	95.3	93.9	91.2	93.7	93.2	91.8	87.9	95.0	95.4	95.5	90.8	92.0	91.0	90.4	90.9
Indianapolis-Carmel-Anderson, IN	96.6	96.1	96.0	94.4	94.9	95.7	94.7	94.3	94.2	93.3	94.7	95.2	93.6	94.8	93.7
Iowa City, IA	95.8	95.1	97.3	96.3	96.5	97.2	97.7	95.1	95.5	94.7	94.9	95.8	95.7	93.0	91.3
Ithaca, NY	100.4	102.6	100.3	101.7	102.0	99.9	100.0	103.5	102.2	105.0	101.5	103.9	101.3	102.3	98.7
Jackson, MI	96.8	93.1	92.4	94.0	93.5	91.4	93.3	91.1	93.0	91.3	93.0	93.2	92.1	93.5	91.3
Jackson, MS	91.9	91.4	93.6	93.4	93.3	93.3	93.0	93.2	93.9	92.9	89.0	88.7	89.0	88.7	90.4
Jackson, TN	86.1	82.7	85.3	85.8	87.5	85.1	87.0	87.2	85.9	85.9	84.2	84.3	83.9	85.2	86.8
Jacksonville, FL	99.6	97.8	98.6	99.1	98.9	98.2	99.2	99.2	99.3	98.7	97.0	96.0	96.4	98.7	98.5
Jacksonville, NC	93.9	94.3	96.1	97.6	95.5	93.7	94.2	93.0	93.7	92.9	90.9	90.2	88.4	89.5	92.6
Janesville-Beloit, WI	94.6	94.7	96.3	94.8	95.0	94.4	95.4	92.8	92.8	92.5	93.9	94.1	91.5	93.0	91.7
Jefferson City, MO	81.4	84.7	87.8	87.5	90.0	88.4	86.9	86.8	85.9	82.6	89.3	91.2	89.1	88.2	87.1
Johnson City, TN	91.6	89.9	90.6	91.8	93.4	89.7	91.5	91.5	91.6	90.0	86.4	89.2	88.5	87.0	87.5
Johnstown, PA	90.8	91.1	90.6	88.9	86.9	88.6	89.2	88.6	88.7	90.8	89.3	87.1	87.5	86.1	87.4
Jonesboro, AR	84.2	81.8	83.9	85.3	85.8	85.0	85.5	85.5	84.8	85.5	84.7	85.4	85.5	86.7	86.2
Joplin, MO	91.6	90.2	90.0	90.1	90.6	90.7	90.5	90.1	89.0	88.0	87.8	89.6	88.3	88.0	85.0
Kahului-Wailuku-Lahaina, HI	107.6	101.1	103.9	104.9	102.7	107.2	102.8	109.0	102.9	104.8	109.1	109.3	111.4	111.1	108.4
Kalamazoo-Portage, MI	97.5	97.7	95.6	93.8	95.4	96.6	96.3	93.2	96.4	93.4	94.9	94.1	95.3	93.0	94.6
Kankakee, IL	99.4	98.2	99.2	100.0	99.2	98.5	97.7	96.5	97.6	98.3	93.5	94.3	90.5	91.8	92.0
Kansas City, MO-KS	93.0	94.9	95.9	96.5	96.8	95.8	97.1	98.6	97.2	96.8	94.3	95.0	95.1	93.6	92.1
Kennewick-Richland, WA	94.1	98.1	96.3	101.1	99.3	98.2	98.7	97.7	97.2	98.6	101.1	102.4	99.7	100.5	104.4
Killeen-Temple, TX	94.4	91.9	94.2	95.3	94.1	95.1	95.2	94.6	95.1	94.2	92.0	91.9	92.0	93.4	91.6
Kingsport-Bristol, TN-VA	89.5	88.3	87.9	89.8	89.9	88.5	88.3	89.2	88.9	88.8	85.1	86.6	83.5	85.5	86.2
Kingston, NY	107.4	104.4	102.9	101.6	102.1	103.6	102.5	102.6	101.3	103.0	100.9	101.8	101.7	100.0	99.4
Knoxville, TN	92.1	91.6	93.3	94.0	94.9	93.5	93.1	92.9	93.9	93.4	89.0	90.9	89.5	90.1	91.3
Kokomo, IN	92.4	91.9	92.8	89.0	90.7	92.1	91.4	89.0	87.8	87.6	89.1	90.2	88.4	90.6	86.7
La Crosse-Onalaska, WI-MN	96.0	97.4	96.0	94.6	94.5	93.4	96.4	94.4	94.7	93.1	94.6	93.9	89.5	94.8	91.1
Lafayette, LA	89.0	89.0	90.0	91.3	92.6	91.0	93.6	92.4	92.8	91.8	90.4	89.9	90.3	90.9	89.7
Lafayette-West Lafayette, IN	91.7	93.4	93.2	91.6	93.8	94.1	92.9	92.2	91.2	91.3	92.5	93.1	90.8	92.3	91.9
Lake Charles, LA	91.0	87.7	89.6	91.4	91.1	91.4	91.0	91.6	91.8	92.4	89.4	89.9	91.3	90.4	89.5
Lake Havasu City-Kingman, AZ	93.8	97.3	94.6	94.7	95.5	95.0	92.3	92.2	93.0	93.7	89.8	88.4	87.7	89.3	92.8
Lakeland-Winter Haven, FL	96.9	95.4	95.5	97.0	96.1	95.2	96.0	96.7	96.4	95.9	94.5	93.6	93.2	96.1	96.2
Lancaster, PA	100.3	100.2	98.2	97.3	97.8	99.5	97.5	99.5	99.5	101.1	98.1	97.1	97.8	96.9	96.6
Lansing-East Lansing, MI	96.6	96.0	97.2	94.3	95.3	95.9	95.4	92.9	94.1	93.3	94.2	94.8	93.5	93.8	93.8
Laredo, TX	91.5	90.0	90.9	92.0	92.4	91.6	93.3	94.0	93.6	90.6	90.6	90.7	91.7	89.6	90.3
Las Cruces, NM	92.1	93.9	93.0	94.9	94.8	94.8	93.7	92.8	90.7	92.7	87.8	91.3	87.4	86.1	86.9
Las Vegas-Henderson-Paradise, NV	101.6	104.2	101.4	103.0	102.3	100.2	99.6	98.8	97.5	100.2	96.3	99.0	97.8	95.4	96.5
Lawrence, KS	98.2	97.8	97.6	96.0	96.0	96.2	96.6	93.2	94.2	94.3	94.4	92.3	94.1	92.8	92.4
Lawton, OK	86.8	87.7	89.1	91.3	90.9	92.0	93.2	90.9	92.3	89.8	87.2	87.2	85.7	87.0	85.3
Lebanon, PA	99.1	98.3	96.5	93.2	95.7	94.1	95.9	95.9	96.5	98.1	96.6	94.7	94.9	95.8	93.0
Lewiston, ID-WA	94.0	93.6	93.7	94.1	88.3	91.4	91.6	92.7	91.5	89.8	87.7	89.6	86.0	86.8	85.2
Lewiston-Auburn, ME	97.9	103.5	99.2	98.9	98.8	95.2	92.9	97.3	96.7	96.0	99.4	96.4	99.7	93.8	101.4
Lexington-Fayette, KY	95.0	93.6	94.2	95.0	96.2	95.0	95.1	95.1	95.1	94.8	91.3	92.5	91.6	92.1	91.2
Lima, OH	92.9	90.9	92.7	89.8	91.4	90.8	91.6	89.2	88.6	87.4	89.0	89.8	89.3	88.7	89.4
Lincoln, NE	95.0	95.1	95.0	93.4	93.9	94.6	94.8	94.1	93.3	93.6	94.5	95.2	95.3	93.2	92.0
Little Rock-North Little Rock-Conway, AR	92.8	91.4	93.6	93.7	93.7	93.9	93.7	93.5	94.3	93.4	90.3	90.5	90.6	91.6	89.2
Logan, UT-ID	95.8	93.6	93.6	91.8	92.5	92.8	94.2	96.6	94.7	95.3	92.1	92.3	91.3	91.9	92.7
Longview, TX	92.2	91.0	92.6	93.2	94.3	93.1	93.4	93.6	94.2	92.1	90.8	92.1	92.4	92.5	86.9
Longview, WA	98.3	95.3	95.6	95.5	92.5	95.7	95.2	97.6	96.9	97.3	99.4	98.4	100.0	98.8	101.5
Los Angeles-Long Beach-Anaheim, CA	113.3	112.1	112.4	111.4	112.0	112.4	112.1	113.3	111.2	110.2	111.3	110.8	113.9	114.1	113.1
Louisville/Jefferson County, KY-IN	93.4	92.5	94.5	94.6	95.2	95.5	95.6	94.8	95.4	94.8	91.8	91.5	91.8	91.8	92.3
Lubbock, TX	95.5	94.0	96.0	95.7	95.7	96.0	95.6	96.7	96.5	95.5	92.4	93.3	94.7	93.8	91.8
Lynchburg, VA	90.1	87.9	89.2	92.6	91.0	92.7	91.3	93.1	91.6	91.6	89.5	89.0	88.0	91.1	91.0
Macon-Bibb County, GA	91.3	89.2	89.5	90.8	90.1	89.5	88.0	89.7	89.8	89.8	88.6	87.0	85.2	87.3	90.4

Regional Price Parities by Metropolitan Statistical Area—Continued

(Percent of U.S. Price Level; U.S. Average Price = 100.0)

Metropolitan Statistical Area	2008	2009	2010	2011	2012	2013	2014	2015	2016	2017	2018	2019	2020	2021	2022
Madera, CA	97.9	100.7	96.0	96.5	98.8	95.5	95.7	96.1	92.8	97.5	100.7	98.1	94.1	100.0	103.1
Madison, WI	98.2	98.7	98.8	96.9	97.4	97.8	98.2	96.0	96.0	95.6	98.2	98.0	95.8	96.6	95.3
Manchester-Nashua, NH	109.2	104.4	104.4	104.7	104.1	102.0	104.3	104.9	108.0	107.3	103.4	104.2	104.8	102.1	108.0
Manhattan, KS	85.8	88.5	93.1	92.6	94.6	94.9	94.8	91.6	89.6	90.8	93.8	93.1	91.8	90.7	89.8
Mankato, MN	85.1	88.7	92.8	86.3	94.5	94.2	89.5	92.2	88.8	89.4	94.8	94.9	91.4	88.3	89.1
Mansfield, OH	92.4	89.5	90.9	90.7	91.0	87.7	89.1	88.9	89.2	87.7	85.7	89.2	88.9	88.2	87.7
McAllen-Edinburg-Mission, TX	86.8	86.3	87.7	88.0	89.1	88.2	89.1	89.4	89.8	89.3	86.8	86.8	88.1	87.3	86.9
Medford, OR	97.4	99.5	98.7	102.0	100.9	97.2	98.3	98.7	98.0	100.0	102.7	99.9	101.9	102.2	105.7
Memphis, TN-MS-AR	94.2	92.8	94.7	95.0	95.1	94.8	94.6	94.3	95.3	94.3	89.6	91.4	90.5	90.4	91.8
Merced, CA	94.2	98.3	96.7	98.4	98.6	98.1	96.0	95.7	95.3	98.2	101.2	101.3	98.7	100.3	103.0
Miami-Fort Lauderdale-Pompano Beach, FL	106.5	106.0	105.3	106.7	107.4	106.7	105.8	107.3	107.9	108.3	109.5	108.7	109.4	110.0	111.5
Michigan City-La Porte, IN	83.7	87.5	88.9	89.0	88.9	89.8	90.3	87.6	87.2	84.7	91.6	89.9	91.8	90.7	88.5
Midland, MI	94.2	93.9	92.5	92.7	93.2	93.4	92.9	91.1	92.1	89.4	92.7	92.4	88.7	91.4	88.0
Midland, TX	96.5	96.2	98.5	101.1	100.3	101.5	103.2	104.2	102.6	100.6	99.8	100.5	95.9	97.8	96.0
Milwaukee-Waukesha, WI	98.0	99.1	97.8	96.3	97.7	97.1	97.1	97.8	99.1	100.8	95.9	97.5	95.7	95.5	94.9
Minneapolis-St. Paul-Bloomington, MN-WI	102.9	104.9	102.3	102.5	101.2	102.0	103.5	102.8	102.4	102.2	104.7	102.8	102.5	103.5	102.9
Missoula, MT	98.0	96.8	97.1	97.9	93.9	95.0	96.0	95.7	95.8	97.9	92.7	95.8	93.8	94.6	90.2
Mobile, AL	90.0	89.3	89.8	91.6	92.6	91.8	93.2	91.1	91.9	91.8	87.5	88.1	87.1	87.7	87.3
Modesto, CA	98.7	102.5	100.3	101.8	102.1	100.6	99.2	98.6	97.7	99.8	104.6	104.7	103.2	103.0	106.0
Monroe, LA	86.8	84.7	89.0	88.0	86.8	87.3	88.4	85.5	86.5	87.5	86.8	86.1	83.5	86.8	87.0
Monroe, MI	96.2	96.4	97.6	98.2	94.1	95.4	96.7	95.5	92.9	93.4	95.3	93.6	93.5	91.9	93.1
Montgomery, AL	91.3	90.7	92.3	91.1	93.3	91.4	90.7	90.6	93.1	92.8	88.4	88.8	87.6	88.5	89.6
Morgantown, WV	89.4	87.4	92.7	93.8	91.7	93.0	89.9	95.8	94.4	90.2	94.1	91.6	91.9	95.8	92.5
Morristown, TN	86.1	82.4	86.4	87.9	88.4	88.2	86.6	87.0	85.4	86.6	85.9	86.8	84.1	84.3	87.7
Mount Vernon-Anacortes, WA	103.1	101.2	100.0	100.0	98.7	98.8	96.9	101.4	101.5	101.8	104.1	101.8	102.1	100.4	105.7
Muncie, IN	93.9	91.4	91.7	91.3	90.6	92.1	90.0	88.3	88.6	89.0	90.9	88.4	87.2	88.9	88.1
Muskegon, MI	93.2	93.9	93.6	91.4	90.8	90.7	92.7	87.3	90.4	89.9	91.7	93.4	93.4	91.9	91.7
Myrtle Beach-Conway-North Myrtle Beach, SC-NC	94.2	93.4	94.0	94.6	94.4	93.0	94.0	93.5	94.9	93.4	92.2	92.2	92.6	94.8	94.3
Napa, CA	115.1	115.0	112.6	111.8	111.6	113.0	114.8	115.2	117.6	121.4	116.0	112.6	112.0	112.5	112.9
Naples-Marco Island, FL	104.3	101.5	102.2	99.9	101.6	101.4	101.3	102.7	103.7	104.3	100.7	100.7	99.1	102.2	102.5
Nashville-Davidson--Murfreesboro--Franklin, TN	95.8	95.3	96.7	97.1	97.4	97.6	97.3	97.3	99.4	98.6	94.0	95.8	96.0	95.3	96.6
New Bern, NC	86.7	86.9	87.1	89.3	90.7	90.4	88.4	91.4	89.1	85.8	89.2	89.1	88.2	91.1	91.0
New Haven-Milford, CT	114.0	114.0	108.8	111.2	110.4	110.0	109.7	109.1	108.6	108.7	103.2	103.2	103.7	101.3	105.4
New Orleans-Metairie, LA	97.9	96.0	97.2	97.6	97.8	97.7	97.5	96.9	98.3	97.1	93.9	94.9	95.7	94.3	93.6
New York-Newark-Jersey City, NY-NJ-PA	113.4	114.9	113.5	114.7	113.9	113.4	113.3	113.2	113.7	113.5	114.6	114.9	115.5	114.9	113.0
Niles, MI	94.3	91.7	92.5	92.0	91.3	90.7	92.0	91.1	91.3	89.6	89.1	87.4	90.3	91.9	87.9
North Port-Sarasota-Bradenton, FL	101.3	100.3	100.1	100.3	100.9	99.8	101.1	101.1	101.5	102.2	101.0	100.0	99.6	99.3	101.4
Norwich-New London, CT	104.7	105.1	102.2	102.2	102.1	102.4	98.4	102.3	103.0	102.6	102.0	102.8	102.5	100.0	104.0
Ocala, FL	96.3	95.3	94.1	95.1	94.8	93.5	93.9	93.3	94.8	94.4	93.3	91.9	91.2	93.8	94.1
Ocean City, NJ	113.2	107.5	112.6	107.2	102.8	101.4	105.1	103.5	103.1	107.0	102.5	98.3	102.1	94.2	103.2
Odessa, TX	96.4	94.1	96.2	98.6	97.9	99.9	101.2	99.3	99.0	98.4	96.9	98.0	99.2	96.4	94.2
Ogden-Clearfield, UT	95.1	99.1	97.6	100.0	100.4	98.1	98.4	95.7	96.2	97.5	95.8	97.7	95.4	93.7	94.2
Oklahoma City, OK	92.8	91.6	94.0	94.2	94.8	94.7	95.1	94.3	94.8	94.4	92.1	91.9	92.7	92.5	91.4
Olympia-Lacey-Tumwater, WA	105.4	104.1	102.8	104.9	101.3	101.9	104.7	104.0	106.0	107.5	105.0	104.6	101.8	103.5	107.4
Omaha-Council Bluffs, NE-IA	96.1	96.3	95.9	94.3	95.8	95.2	95.6	94.2	94.7	94.1	94.3	95.0	95.1	93.8	92.1
Orlando-Kissimmee-Sanford, FL	101.3	99.4	99.7	100.3	99.9	99.7	100.2	100.2	100.8	100.5	98.9	98.2	98.4	99.8	100.4
Oshkosh-Neenah, WI	97.2	94.7	95.2	94.3	94.5	95.2	93.3	93.1	93.1	92.0	92.3	92.5	92.6	92.5	91.2
Owensboro, KY	88.5	88.1	89.8	91.5	93.5	92.1	91.9	92.1	91.9	93.4	88.0	89.3	89.1	87.5	88.3
Oxnard-Thousand Oaks-Ventura, CA	109.5	110.4	109.3	109.6	110.4	111.2	113.1	113.1	111.1	108.1	114.1	112.5	111.4	111.5	114.4
Palm Bay-Melbourne-Titusville, FL	99.9	97.1	98.5	98.6	98.0	97.0	98.9	99.6	98.8	99.4	98.3	96.6	96.8	98.9	99.3
Panama City, FL	98.2	95.8	97.3	98.4	97.1	94.4	95.4	95.1	95.6	94.5	94.3	94.6	94.6	96.8	97.5
Parkersburg-Vienna, WV	87.0	86.3	87.0	88.5	91.6	91.7	90.6	92.6	92.7	91.3	89.7	88.1	86.2	89.7	87.2
Pensacola-Ferry Pass-Brent, FL	96.4	95.2	96.1	98.7	97.3	96.2	96.9	97.2	97.4	96.6	95.3	94.0	93.3	95.7	95.5
Peoria, IL	93.1	93.4	92.4	91.7	92.4	92.4	93.2	92.0	90.2	89.2	91.5	92.0	89.9	90.1	89.8
Philadelphia-Camden-Wilmington, PA-NJ-DE-MD	106.6	107.8	106.4	105.3	103.8	101.8	102.4	102.3	102.6	104.0	103.2	103.7	102.3	99.2	100.7
Phoenix-Mesa-Chandler, AZ	105.7	105.4	102.7	100.3	98.7	99.5	99.1	98.7	100.4	98.9	99.6	100.0	102.8	99.1	103.7
Pine Bluff, AR	85.5	85.6	87.4	86.7	88.1	87.9	86.7	85.6	87.4	84.6	82.9	84.5	84.0	87.3	80.9
Pittsburgh, PA	92.2	93.0	94.6	95.0	95.7	94.5	94.5	95.1	94.0	95.0	95.6	95.6	95.6	94.9	93.9
Pittsfield, MA	99.8	99.4	98.7	95.4	97.9	96.2	96.9	100.7	100.6	100.8	100.5	99.2	99.5	95.9	100.4
Pocatello, ID	94.1	89.2	90.3	88.0	91.1	91.7	89.6	94.6	89.0	92.1	89.1	87.9	89.0	88.5	87.4
Portland-South Portland, ME	102.6	103.3	101.1	98.7	101.3	103.1	94.6	100.0	102.4	102.3	101.9	97.5	102.6	101.8	104.9
Portland-Vancouver-Hillsboro, OR-WA	98.9	102.2	101.3	101.8	104.3	103.0	102.1	103.7	101.5	103.7	107.3	106.5	105.8	105.4	108.8
Port St. Lucie, FL	101.1	98.6	98.8	98.9	99.1	98.4	99.8	99.7	100.5	99.3	99.0	94.4	98.6	98.5	98.3
Poughkeepsie-Newburgh-Middletown, NY	(NA)	(NA)	(NA)	(NA)	(NA)	(NA)	(NA)	(NA)	110.0	109.6	110.8	112.0	109.6	110.4	110.0
Prescott Valley-Prescott, AZ	103.0	98.8	97.8	97.8	96.6	97.8	96.4	100.3	98.6	99.6	93.6	95.9	93.2	94.0	92.7
Providence-Warwick, RI-MA	103.9	104.0	102.0	101.4	100.4	101.6	100.6	102.4	102.0	103.1	101.5	101.8	101.7	101.2	103.9
Provo-Orem, UT	97.1	102.3	98.9	100.9	100.4	99.9	98.1	97.8	97.0	99.2	96.6	98.2	94.8	95.8	94.8
Pueblo, CO	91.3	95.0	93.5	96.2	96.2	94.3	92.1	92.6	93.1	94.3	90.9	92.6	90.2	90.7	90.5
Punta Gorda, FL	97.5	95.2	96.9	96.6	97.9	95.5	96.8	97.8	98.7	98.8	97.2	95.7	98.9	96.2	96.0
Racine, WI	96.7	96.7	94.9	93.5	94.5	95.1	95.4	96.7	94.6	98.5	93.6	94.2	93.9	92.1	90.8

Regional Price Parities by Metropolitan Statistical Area—Continued

(Percent of U.S. Price Level; U.S. Average Price = 100.0)

Metropolitan Statistical Area	2008	2009	2010	2011	2012	2013	2014	2015	2016	2017	2018	2019	2020	2021	2022
Raleigh-Cary, NC	97.0	95.9	97.1	98.2	98.0	97.9	98.4	98.2	99.2	98.4	96.9	95.6	95.4	97.6	98.4
Rapid City, SD	91.5	91.2	93.0	87.6	94.7	93.6	91.9	90.0	90.1	89.5	92.0	92.5	94.3	91.9	90.7
Reading, PA	99.1	99.4	98.2	97.7	97.8	99.9	97.4	98.2	98.8	99.1	98.3	97.4	96.0	96.0	96.3
Redding, CA	97.3	101.0	99.8	101.6	102.3	98.1	99.9	97.9	96.3	99.0	102.8	102.2	99.5	99.3	103.8
Reno, NV	101.4	103.9	101.6	103.4	103.4	101.3	100.1	99.4	98.4	100.8	97.8	100.3	98.6	97.2	98.3
Richmond, VA	98.1	97.4	98.5	99.4	98.6	98.3	98.5	98.9	99.3	97.8	97.1	95.2	95.9	98.0	97.7
Riverside-San Bernardino-Ontario, CA	106.4	106.1	105.1	104.5	104.4	105.6	107.1	107.1	105.5	102.7	105.9	105.5	104.2	105.5	106.4
Roanoke, VA	92.3	92.1	94.2	91.3	93.1	93.1	93.1	91.8	92.0	91.2	91.9	91.1	90.2	93.7	92.4
Rochester, MN	95.3	95.6	91.3	93.7	94.5	94.0	96.0	93.7	93.0	92.9	93.1	94.8	96.9	92.0	92.1
Rochester, NY	101.0	100.9	99.1	98.3	98.5	99.6	98.1	99.9	99.9	100.9	98.9	97.9	97.4	97.6	95.2
Rockford, IL	96.8	96.7	93.2	93.8	93.9	93.2	93.4	92.6	93.4	91.0	91.0	92.8	91.7	93.1	90.6
Rocky Mount, NC	88.7	88.5	89.7	91.2	89.1	89.8	89.1	90.7	87.8	89.9	86.2	84.0	83.9	87.7	87.8
Rome, GA	87.9	85.6	88.2	86.6	86.2	87.3	88.0	88.2	88.3	85.9	88.7	87.9	86.3	90.9	91.0
Sacramento-Roseville-Folsom, CA	101.3	105.1	102.7	104.9	104.9	103.2	103.0	101.2	101.0	103.5	109.0	107.5	106.9	106.3	109.9
Saginaw, MI	93.5	92.7	92.2	92.5	90.9	92.3	90.5	90.3	90.7	89.5	90.9	90.1	88.9	90.9	87.0
St. Cloud, MN	97.4	92.8	94.9	93.9	95.2	95.3	94.6	93.5	93.8	90.6	93.1	94.7	91.6	87.5	91.9
St. George, UT	98.6	93.7	94.5	93.9	96.4	95.1	94.3	98.3	99.2	99.1	94.7	95.4	95.9	94.2	94.8
St. Joseph, MO-KS	92.6	92.7	91.4	90.3	91.0	92.0	90.2	90.0	88.8	88.2	89.7	88.7	87.9	88.9	87.2
St. Louis, MO-IL	91.1	93.3	97.0	96.3	94.5	95.6	96.9	94.6	94.5	95.6	94.4	95.1	95.2	96.2	96.7
Salem, OR	94.3	98.9	98.7	98.1	101.0	99.3	97.7	99.0	97.1	99.1	102.4	101.9	100.9	101.9	104.8
Salinas, CA	104.6	107.7	106.8	109.4	110.1	108.9	106.5	106.0	104.7	107.7	112.2	111.5	110.3	109.3	113.1
Salisbury, MD-DE	93.5	91.0	94.0	92.3	91.7	94.0	95.5	93.6	90.1	90.3	95.0	92.4	90.8	93.9	95.2
Salt Lake City, UT	98.5	102.0	99.2	102.7	102.2	100.9	100.3	99.1	98.3	100.5	97.8	99.6	97.3	96.2	95.7
San Angelo, TX	91.5	93.2	92.9	93.9	96.0	95.2	96.7	97.4	96.3	95.1	94.2	93.7	95.0	91.8	92.7
San Antonio-New Braunfels, TX	96.1	95.1	96.3	96.6	97.4	97.4	97.7	97.4	98.2	97.2	95.6	95.7	96.8	96.3	95.1
San Diego-Chula Vista-Carlsbad, CA	113.9	114.6	113.2	114.1	112.8	111.7	110.9	112.3	113.6	112.2	112.5	113.4	115.1	115.1	114.5
San Francisco-Oakland-Berkeley, CA	119.0	115.1	113.8	112.4	112.5	112.9	114.0	115.7	116.2	121.5	122.2	119.6	119.4	120.0	117.9
San Jose-Sunnyvale-Santa Clara, CA	119.2	115.8	113.9	112.7	113.4	114.1	115.6	117.1	117.6	122.7	114.6	113.0	113.4	111.6	115.3
San Luis Obispo-Paso Robles, CA	105.1	109.2	106.4	109.7	107.2	106.6	106.0	105.3	104.9	108.2	111.4	110.2	111.2	108.6	112.6
Santa Cruz-Watsonville, CA	119.7	113.8	113.8	111.7	112.3	111.4	113.7	115.2	115.0	120.7	111.4	110.8	111.6	109.1	114.7
Santa Fe, NM	98.0	102.0	100.1	103.2	102.1	100.1	101.6	98.7	98.4	98.7	96.2	96.9	96.6	93.3	94.9
Santa Maria-Santa Barbara, CA	107.5	110.8	108.0	110.6	110.0	106.6	107.5	106.0	106.5	108.7	112.9	110.9	111.9	111.8	113.9
Santa Rosa-Petaluma, CA	118.0	113.3	113.6	110.4	112.3	111.5	113.2	114.5	114.9	120.2	113.2	111.5	111.6	109.9	112.5
Savannah, GA	95.7	94.9	96.2	97.8	97.9	96.3	96.5	96.1	97.1	96.3	95.2	94.2	92.4	95.4	96.3
Scranton--Wilkes-Barre, PA	95.2	96.1	94.2	94.8	94.0	94.7	91.6	95.5	94.9	95.2	92.9	92.9	93.1	93.1	91.9
Seattle-Tacoma-Bellevue, WA	109.1	108.5	106.3	106.0	105.3	105.2	107.4	107.9	110.2	112.7	110.3	112.4	112.9	114.5	113.7
Sebastian-Vero Beach, FL	93.4	90.4	94.9	92.0	92.9	94.9	93.0	91.8	94.2	92.1	94.1	94.3	95.2	98.1	95.4
Sebring-Avon Park, FL	88.3	88.6	90.0	89.4	89.1	90.6	88.9	89.3	89.2	88.3	90.2	90.0	88.2	89.8	90.2
Sheboygan, WI	95.8	95.2	94.8	95.9	93.1	94.5	93.3	93.3	93.4	93.0	92.0	92.5	93.2	93.2	89.6
Sherman-Denison, TX	91.4	91.8	94.8	93.2	94.2	93.3	94.3	93.3	95.4	95.3	92.6	92.3	92.4	92.9	92.6
Shreveport-Bossier City, LA	90.9	90.0	90.5	93.5	93.4	92.0	94.1	93.2	92.7	90.6	89.9	89.8	88.9	90.5	88.9
Sierra Vista-Douglas, AZ	93.8	93.1	91.8	92.2	93.5	92.5	92.4	94.2	93.0	93.9	89.6	91.0	88.5	87.8	88.2
Sioux City, IA-NE-SD	90.9	90.4	92.1	90.3	91.0	90.6	90.2	89.6	90.1	89.4	91.4	92.3	90.6	90.2	87.8
Sioux Falls, SD	95.1	93.3	96.0	93.9	94.4	94.3	94.8	93.5	93.8	91.6	95.2	95.5	94.1	93.2	90.2
South Bend-Mishawaka, IN-MI	92.5	93.3	92.9	92.3	90.5	92.3	92.0	90.6	91.4	88.6	91.8	92.0	91.5	91.6	92.2
Spartanburg, SC	92.4	91.7	91.0	93.0	92.8	91.6	93.2	92.7	94.1	93.1	90.1	90.0	89.1	92.6	91.6
Spokane-Spokane Valley, WA	95.2	98.1	96.7	97.0	97.9	97.5	96.6	96.1	96.0	97.0	100.3	99.5	98.5	98.7	102.7
Springfield, IL	95.1	93.7	93.6	92.0	93.3	93.4	92.9	92.2	92.4	90.7	93.0	91.7	90.9	91.5	89.6
Springfield, MA	99.8	102.7	98.4	98.5	98.4	100.9	98.9	101.0	99.7	100.1	98.6	97.7	100.2	97.8	99.5
Springfield, MO	91.8	92.2	92.1	90.5	90.8	91.5	89.9	90.4	89.6	88.3	89.8	90.2	88.5	89.1	86.9
Springfield, OH	92.1	93.2	92.1	92.0	91.9	90.9	92.1	90.5	90.6	88.9	90.5	91.5	89.3	86.8	88.7
State College, PA	99.3	99.0	99.4	98.3	96.8	99.0	97.2	99.5	101.5	102.1	98.0	97.0	98.0	95.5	96.5
Staunton, VA	89.4	85.7	88.2	87.8	90.1	90.6	91.1	91.4	83.9	89.1	92.4	89.5	87.6	92.8	91.5
Stockton, CA	100.2	104.5	101.5	103.7	103.8	102.2	102.3	100.2	99.8	101.6	106.1	105.8	105.2	104.6	108.5
Sumter, SC	88.4	86.1	89.1	91.0	88.6	89.5	88.4	88.5	86.2	89.1	87.6	85.9	81.4	86.4	88.4
Syracuse, NY	98.7	98.6	98.1	98.0	95.8	97.0	96.0	99.5	99.1	99.0	97.6	95.3	96.0	96.3	93.4
Tallahassee, FL	96.0	94.6	95.6	97.1	97.2	95.9	96.3	96.1	97.3	97.0	93.9	93.2	91.1	94.9	94.5
Tampa-St. Petersburg-Clearwater, FL	103.2	103.3	101.3	100.1	100.2	101.3	101.3	100.9	97.1	96.9	95.3	96.5	101.3	98.9	99.7
Terre Haute, IN	88.2	88.5	90.8	89.0	88.7	89.9	89.6	87.2	87.0	87.2	89.4	89.3	87.2	87.1	86.9
Texarkana, TX-AR	88.6	86.7	88.3	90.2	89.7	88.6	89.3	90.0	90.3	88.4	87.1	87.7	87.7	87.9	85.2
The Villages, FL	90.3	91.7	90.9	90.3	93.0	93.3	93.1	93.7	93.8	91.4	93.3	94.3	92.0	96.0	91.4
Toledo, OH	94.8	93.0	93.4	92.9	92.4	92.3	93.1	91.8	92.1	91.3	92.4	92.6	90.6	90.2	90.2
Topeka, KS	91.5	92.7	93.1	92.1	91.6	91.7	92.5	90.4	90.0	89.2	91.8	90.9	90.2	89.3	87.8
Trenton-Princeton, NJ	104.5	110.3	107.2	107.2	108.6	109.0	110.5	108.6	108.9	109.9	103.8	104.4	104.2	101.9	100.8
Tucson, AZ	97.1	100.4	98.9	100.1	100.6	98.9	98.5	97.4	96.6	97.6	94.8	95.3	94.0	92.9	93.8
Tulsa, OK	92.8	92.0	93.3	93.8	94.1	94.3	94.3	94.4	94.6	93.8	91.2	91.1	91.7	91.7	90.5
Tuscaloosa, AL	89.7	89.1	90.3	89.5	90.6	90.1	90.6	89.5	90.9	92.4	85.8	88.6	87.0	88.0	87.0
Twin Falls, ID	(NA)	(NA)	(NA)	(NA)	(NA)	(NA)	(NA)	93.9	94.1	94.8	89.3	90.3	87.9	89.8	90.9
Tyler, TX	95.9	95.3	97.3	96.7	95.8	97.6	95.4	96.7	96.9	95.2	93.5	94.5	95.4	94.6	92.3
Urban Honolulu, HI	111.8	117.4	112.2	113.0	112.3	115.7	114.6	114.0	113.3	113.5	112.7	113.1	115.5	114.0	112.9
Utica-Rome, NY	96.0	96.1	95.3	94.3	93.6	95.8	94.5	96.9	95.5	95.6	95.0	93.1	93.5	92.5	89.6
Valdosta, GA	88.8	85.8	88.3	85.6	88.6	87.4	88.1	86.4	87.2	86.0	87.0	87.4	85.0	88.2	89.8
Vallejo, CA	116.7	113.6	111.8	109.5	109.7	110.2	110.7	112.6	112.9	117.5	110.6	109.3	110.5	109.4	112.6

Regional Price Parities by Metropolitan Statistical Area—Continued

(Percent of U.S. Price Level; U.S. Average Price = 100.0)

Metropolitan Statistical Area	2008	2009	2010	2011	2012	2013	2014	2015	2016	2017	2018	2019	2020	2021	2022
Victoria, TX	93.8	92.5	92.2	95.4	94.5	95.9	95.9	96.1	97.5	94.8	93.6	93.4	95.4	91.8	91.2
Vineland-Bridgeton, NJ	103.1	103.4	101.9	103.9	102.7	99.0	100.0	99.0	97.3	96.3	98.2	98.2	96.6	96.5	92.8
Virginia Beach-Norfolk-Newport News, VA-NC	99.9	99.0	100.7	101.2	100.0	99.6	100.0	100.1	100.9	99.0	97.9	95.6	95.5	97.9	98.0
Visalia, CA	94.8	98.1	96.4	98.4	98.7	97.0	97.1	95.5	94.5	96.4	100.5	99.7	98.8	98.9	102.4
Waco, TX	93.9	92.5	93.2	93.7	95.4	93.6	94.7	95.1	94.7	93.9	92.2	92.5	93.7	94.5	93.4
Walla Walla, WA	95.8	95.0	94.3	94.3	95.1	95.3	98.4	99.9	96.3	99.8	99.6	100.8	95.0	99.1	100.7
Warner Robins, GA	92.1	90.2	90.2	93.4	94.3	93.2	92.2	92.4	93.0	93.5	92.5	90.0	92.0	92.0	92.7
Washington-Arlington-Alexandria, DC-VA-MD-WV	114.6	114.8	114.3	113.4	111.6	113.9	113.6	113.7	112.1	109.7	111.2	109.7	111.4	111.5	111.3
Waterloo-Cedar Falls, IA	90.5	90.9	92.4	90.5	91.0	92.4	92.3	90.5	90.6	90.2	91.2	92.9	91.1	89.1	87.9
Watertown-Fort Drum, NY	93.7	97.2	97.1	99.2	98.8	97.4	97.3	97.4	98.6	98.5	96.7	95.3	90.8	93.8	93.8
Wausau-Weston, WI	92.8	93.3	93.6	92.5	93.1	92.1	88.8	91.4	90.1	89.9	91.2	91.8	89.4	89.8	90.5
Weirton-Steubenville, WV-OH	88.1	89.5	89.1	86.5	88.7	89.2	88.8	88.1	88.0	86.2	86.9	87.5	86.7	89.2	89.1
Wenatchee, WA	98.0	98.4	94.7	97.4	97.0	97.8	97.3	98.6	97.7	101.4	102.2	104.2	102.3	103.1	103.2
Wheeling, WV-OH	87.3	87.8	89.5	88.7	90.4	90.5	90.8	90.5	91.0	89.4	87.1	87.6	86.9	89.4	89.2
Wichita, KS	94.2	93.7	93.4	92.5	92.5	93.4	92.6	91.7	92.2	91.2	91.2	92.4	92.2	91.0	89.2
Wichita Falls, TX	93.5	90.8	91.8	94.1	93.9	93.2	94.4	93.6	92.9	91.8	88.6	89.7	92.6	90.8	88.7
Williamsport, PA	95.1	91.6	92.3	93.4	93.0	95.1	94.1	95.2	95.4	96.1	94.6	92.4	93.6	91.4	89.7
Wilmington, NC	93.5	92.5	94.8	95.0	97.6	96.1	97.7	95.2	96.5	95.6	96.0	95.2	94.2	97.6	97.0
Winchester, VA-WV	91.0	89.7	93.6	94.1	94.5	96.5	93.4	95.4	94.7	92.9	95.9	94.5	94.3	97.4	96.0
Winston-Salem, NC	91.8	90.6	91.9	93.2	92.6	92.5	93.1	92.9	93.0	91.6	90.8	89.4	89.5	91.6	92.4
Worcester, MA-CT	104.1	103.2	102.5	103.3	102.4	101.5	102.2	101.5	105.5	104.0	101.0	100.8	101.3	100.1	105.1
Yakima, WA	92.9	96.3	95.5	98.0	97.1	96.9	96.7	94.4	94.3	94.7	97.4	96.9	96.2	97.7	101.0
York-Hanover, PA	99.2	100.1	98.4	95.9	96.6	99.0	97.7	98.5	98.1	100.3	97.7	96.6	97.7	96.6	95.6
Youngstown-Warren-Boardman, OH-PA	91.6	91.5	90.8	88.8	90.8	90.3	90.2	89.8	89.0	88.1	88.5	89.3	86.0	87.0	86.6
Yuba City, CA	97.8	100.8	98.1	102.2	102.2	100.4	98.6	97.8	97.6	98.0	103.6	102.8	101.9	101.5	102.7
Yuma, AZ	92.4	98.1	96.3	95.8	93.8	94.3	93.1	95.0	92.7	93.2	90.3	90.4	88.7	89.3	86.1

NOTE: Regional Price Parities are not available for Enid, OK prior to 2013, Twin Falls, ID prior to 2015, and Poughkeepsie-Newburgh-Middletown, NY prior to 2016.

APPENDIX

Metropolitan Statistical Areas, Metropolitan Divisions, and Components

Core based statistical area (CBSA)	State/ County FIPS code	Title and Geographic Components
10180		Abilene, TX
10180	48059	Callahan County
10180	48253	Jones County
10180	48441	Taylor County
10420		Akron, OH
10420	39133	Portage County
10420	39153	Summit County
10500		Albany, GA
10500	13095	Dougherty County
10500	13177	Lee County
10500	13273	Terrell County
10500	13321	Worth County
10540		Albany-Lebanon, OR
10540	41043	Linn County
10580		Albany-Schenectady-Troy, NY
10580	36001	Albany County
10580	36083	Rensselaer County
10580	36091	Saratoga County
10580	36093	Schenectady County
10580	36095	Schoharie County
10740		Albuquerque, NM
10740	35001	Bernalillo County
10740	35043	Sandoval County
10740	35057	Torrance County
10740	35061	Valencia County
10780		Alexandria, LA
10780	22043	Grant Parish
10780	22079	Rapides Parish
10900		Allentown-Bethlehem-Easton, PA-NJ
10900	34041	Warren County, NJ
10900	42025	Carbon County, PA
10900	42077	Lehigh County, PA
10900	42095	Northampton County, PA
11020		Altoona, PA
11020	42013	Blair County
11100		Amarillo, TX
11100	48011	Armstrong County
11100	48065	Carson County
11100	48359	Oldham County
11100	48375	Potter County
11100	48381	Randall County
11180		Ames, IA
11180	19015	Boone County
11180	19169	Story County
11260		Anchorage, AK
11260	02020	Anchorage Municipality
11260	02170	Matanuska-Susitna Borough
11460		Ann Arbor, MI
11460	26161	Washtenaw County
11500		Anniston-Oxford, AL
11500	01015	Calhoun County
11540		Appleton, WI
11540	55015	Calumet County
11540	55087	Outagamie County
11700		Asheville, NC
11700	37021	Buncombe County
11700	37087	Haywood County
11700	37089	Henderson County
11700	37115	Madison County
12020		Athens-Clarke County, GA
12020	13059	Clarke County
12020	13195	Madison County
12020	13219	Oconee County
12020	13221	Oglethorpe County
12060		Atlanta-Sandy Springs-Alpharetta, GA
12060	13013	Barrow County
12060	13015	Bartow County
12060	13035	Butts County
12060	13045	Carroll County
12060	13057	Cherokee County
12060	13063	Clayton County
12060	13067	Cobb County
12060	13077	Coweta County
12060	13085	Dawson County
12060	13089	DeKalb County
12060	13097	Douglas County
12060	13113	Fayette County
12060	13117	Forsyth County
12060	13121	Fulton County
12060	13135	Gwinnett County
12060	13143	Haralson County
12060	13149	Heard County
12060	13151	Henry County
12060	13159	Jasper County
12060	13171	Lamar County
12060	13199	Meriwether County
12060	13211	Morgan County
12060	13217	Newton County
12060	13223	Paulding County
12060	13227	Pickens County
12060	13231	Pike County
12060	13247	Rockdale County
12060	13255	Spalding County
12060	13297	Walton County
12100		Atlantic City-Hammonton, NJ
12100	34001	Atlantic County
12220		Auburn-Opelika, AL
12220	01081	Lee County
12260		Augusta-Richmond County, GA-SC
12260	13033	Burke County
12260	13073	Columbia County
12260	13181	Lincoln County
12260	13189	McDuffie County
12260	13245	Richmond County
12260	45003	Aiken County
12260	45037	Edgefield County
12420		Austin-Round Rock-Georgetown, TX
12420	48021	Bastrop County
12420	48055	Caldwell County
12420	48209	Hays County
12420	48453	Travis County
12420	48491	Williamson County
12540		Bakersfield, CA
12540	06029	Kern County
12580		Baltimore-Columbia-Towson, MD
12580	24003	Anne Arundel County
12580	24005	Baltimore County
12580	24013	Carroll County
12580	24025	Harford County
12580	24027	Howard County
12580	24035	Queen Anne's County
12580	24510	Baltimore city
12620		Bangor, ME
12620	23019	Penobscot County
12700		Barnstable Town, MA
12700	25001	Barnstable County
12940		Baton Rouge, LA
12940	22005	Ascension Parish
12940	22007	Assumption Parish
12940	22033	East Baton Rouge Parish
12940	22037	East Feliciana Parish
12940	22047	Iberville Parish
12940	22063	Livingston Parish
12940	22077	Pointe Coupee Parish
12940	22091	St. Helena Parish
12940	22121	West Baton Rouge Parish
12940	22125	West Feliciana Parish
12980		Battle Creek, MI
12980	26025	Calhoun County
13020		Bay City, MI

Metropolitan Statistical Areas, Metropolitan Divisions, and Components—*Continued*

Core based statistical area (CBSA)	State/ County FIPS code	Title and Geographic Components
13020	26017	Bay County
13140		Beaumont-Port Arthur, TX
13140	48199	Hardin County
13140	48245	Jefferson County
13140	48361	Orange County
13220		Beckley, WV
13220	54019	Fayette County
13220	54081	Raleigh County
13380		Bellingham, WA
13380	53073	Whatcom County
13460		Bend, OR
13460	41017	Deschutes County
13740		Billings, MT
13740	30009	Carbon County
13740	30095	Stillwater County
13740	30111	Yellowstone County
13780		Binghamton, NY
13780	36007	Broome County
13780	36107	Tioga County
13820		Birmingham-Hoover, AL
13820	01007	Bibb County
13820	01009	Blount County
13820	01021	Chilton County
13820	01073	Jefferson County
13820	01115	St. Clair County
13820	01117	Shelby County
13900		Bismarck, ND
13900	38015	Burleigh County
13900	38059	Morton County
13900	38065	Oliver County
13980		Blacksburg-Christiansburg, VA
13980	51071	Giles County
13980	51155	Pulaski County
13980	51933	Montgomery + Radford
14010		Bloomington, IL
14010	17113	McLean County
14020		Bloomington, IN
14020	18105	Monroe County
14020	18119	Owen County
14100		Bloomsburg-Berwick, PA
14100	42037	Columbia County
14100	42093	Montour County
14260		Boise City, ID
14260	16001	Ada County
14260	16015	Boise County
14260	16027	Canyon County
14260	16045	Gem County
14260	16073	Owyhee County
14460		Boston-Cambridge-Newton, MA-NH
14460		Boston, MA Div 14454
14460	25021	Norfolk County
14460	25023	Plymouth County
14460	25025	Suffolk County
14460		Cambridge-Newton-Framingham, MA Div 15764
14460	25009	Essex County
14460	25017	Middlesex County
14460		Rockingham County-Strafford County, NH Div 40484
14460	33015	Rockingham County
14460	33017	Strafford County
14500		Boulder, CO
14500	08013	Boulder County
14540		Bowling Green, KY
14540	21003	Allen County
14540	21031	Butler County
14540	21061	Edmonson County
14540	21227	Warren County
14740		Bremerton-Silverdale-Port Orchard, WA
14740	53035	Kitsap County
14860		Bridgeport-Stamford-Norwalk, CT
14860	09001	Fairfield County
15180		Brownsville-Harlingen, TX
15180	48061	Cameron County
15260		Brunswick, GA
15260	13025	Brantley County
15260	13127	Glynn County
15260	13191	McIntosh County
15380		Buffalo-Cheektowaga, NY
15380	36029	Erie County
15380	36063	Niagara County
15500		Burlington, NC
15500	37001	Alamance County
15540		Burlington-South Burlington, VT
15540	50007	Chittenden County
15540	50011	Franklin County
15540	50013	Grand Isle County
15680		California-Lexington Park, MD
15680	24037	St. Mary's County
15940		Canton-Massillon, OH
15940	39019	Carroll County
15940	39151	Stark County
15980		Cape Coral-Fort Myers, FL
15980	12071	Lee County
16020		Cape Girardeau, MO-IL
16020	17003	Alexander County, IL
16020	29017	Bollinger County, MO
16020	29031	Cape Girardeau County, MO
16060		Carbondale-Marion, IL
16060	17077	Jackson County
16060	17087	Johnson County
16060	17199	Williamson County
16180		Carson City, NV
16180	32510	Carson City
16220		Casper, WY
16220	56025	Natrona County
16300		Cedar Rapids, IA
16300	19011	Benton County
16300	19105	Jones County
16300	19113	Linn County
16540		Chambersburg-Waynesboro, PA
16540	42055	Franklin County
16580		Champaign-Urbana, IL
16580	17019	Champaign County
16580	17147	Piatt County
16620		Charleston, WV
16620	54005	Boone County
16620	54015	Clay County
16620	54035	Jackson County
16620	54039	Kanawha County
16620	54043	Lincoln County
16700		Charleston-North Charleston, SC
16700	45015	Berkeley County
16700	45019	Charleston County
16700	45035	Dorchester County
16740		Charlotte-Concord-Gastonia, NC-SC
16740	37007	Anson County, NC
16740	37025	Cabarrus County, NC
16740	37071	Gaston County, NC
16740	37097	Iredell County, NC
16740	37109	Lincoln County, NC
16740	37119	Mecklenburg County, NC
16740	37159	Rowan County, NC
16740	37179	Union County, NC
16740	45023	Chester County, SC
16740	45057	Lancaster County, SC
16740	45091	York County, SC
16820		Charlottesville, VA
16820	51065	Fluvanna County
16820	51079	Greene County
16820	51125	Nelson County
16820	51901	Albemarle + Charlottesville
16860		Chattanooga, TN-GA
16860	13047	Catoosa County, GA
16860	13083	Dade County, GA
16860	13295	Walker County, GA
16860	47065	Hamilton County, TN
16860	47115	Marion County, TN
16860	47153	Sequatchie County, TN
16940		Cheyenne, WY
16940	56021	Laramie County
16980		Chicago-Naperville-Elgin, IL-IN-WI
16980		Chicago-Naperville-Evanston, IL Div 16984
16980	17031	Cook County
16980	17043	DuPage County
16980	17063	Grundy County
16980	17111	McHenry County
16980	17197	Will County
16980		Elgin, IL Div 20994
16980	17037	DeKalb County
16980	17089	Kane County
16980	17093	Kendall County
16980		Gary, IN Div 23844
16980	18073	Jasper County
16980	18089	Lake County
16980	18111	Newton County
16980	18127	Porter County
16980		Lake County-Kenosha County, IL-WI Div 29404

Metropolitan Statistical Areas, Metropolitan Divisions, and Components—*Continued*

Core based statistical area (CBSA)	State/ County FIPS code	Title and Geographic Components
16980	17097	Lake County, IL
16980	55059	Kenosha County, WI
17020		Chico, CA
17020	06007	Butte County
17140		Cincinnati, OH-KY-IN
17140	18029	Dearborn County, IN
17140	18047	Franklin County, IN
17140	18115	Ohio County, IN
17140	18161	Union County, IN
17140	21015	Boone County, KY
17140	21023	Bracken County, KY
17140	21037	Campbell County, KY
17140	21077	Gallatin County, KY
17140	21081	Grant County, KY
17140	21117	Kenton County, KY
17140	21191	Pendleton County, KY
17140	39015	Brown County, OH
17140	39017	Butler County, OH
17140	39025	Clermont County, OH
17140	39061	Hamilton County, OH
17140	39165	Warren County, OH
17300		Clarksville, TN-KY
17300	21047	Christian County, KY
17300	21221	Trigg County, KY
17300	47125	Montgomery County, TN
17300	47161	Stewart County, TN
17420		Cleveland, TN
17420	47011	Bradley County
17420	47139	Polk County
17460		Cleveland-Elyria, OH
17460	39035	Cuyahoga County
17460	39055	Geauga County
17460	39085	Lake County
17460	39093	Lorain County
17460	39103	Medina County
17660		Coeur d'Alene, ID
17660	16055	Kootenai County
17780		College Station-Bryan, TX
17780	48041	Brazos County
17780	48051	Burleson County
17780	48395	Robertson County
17820		Colorado Springs, CO
17820	08041	El Paso County
17820	08119	Teller County
17860		Columbia, MO
17860	29019	Boone County
17860	29053	Cooper County
17860	29089	Howard County
17900		Columbia, SC
17900	45017	Calhoun County
17900	45039	Fairfield County
17900	45055	Kershaw County
17900	45063	Lexington County
17900	45079	Richland County
17900	45081	Saluda County
17980		Columbus, GA-AL
17980	01113	Russell County, AL
17980	13053	Chattahoochee County, GA
17980	13145	Harris County, GA
17980	13197	Marion County, GA
17980	13215	Muscogee County, GA
17980	13259	Stewart County, GA
17980	13263	Talbot County, GA
18020		Columbus, IN
18020	18005	Bartholomew County
18140		Columbus, OH
18140	39041	Delaware County
18140	39045	Fairfield County
18140	39049	Franklin County
18140	39073	Hocking County
18140	39089	Licking County
18140	39097	Madison County
18140	39117	Morrow County
18140	39127	Perry County
18140	39129	Pickaway County
18140	39159	Union County
18580		Corpus Christi, TX
18580	48355	Nueces County
18580	48409	San Patricio County
18700		Corvallis, OR
18700	41003	Benton County
18880		Crestview-Fort Walton Beach-Destin, FL
18880	12091	Okaloosa County
18880	12131	Walton County
19060		Cumberland, MD-WV
19060	24001	Allegany County, MD
19060	54057	Mineral County, WV
19100		Dallas-Fort Worth-Arlington, TX
19100		Dallas-Plano-Irving, TX Div 19124
19100	48085	Collin County
19100	48113	Dallas County
19100	48121	Denton County
19100	48139	Ellis County
19100	48231	Hunt County
19100	48257	Kaufman County
19100	48397	Rockwall County
19100		Fort Worth-Arlington-Grapevine, TX Div 23104
19100	48251	Johnson County
19100	48367	Parker County
19100	48439	Tarrant County
19100	48497	Wise County
19140		Dalton, GA
19140	13213	Murray County
19140	13313	Whitfield County
19180		Danville, IL
19180	17183	Vermilion County
19300		Daphne-Fairhope-Foley, AL
19300	01003	Baldwin County
19340		Davenport-Moline-Rock Island, IA-IL
19340	17073	Henry County, IL
19340	17131	Mercer County, IL
19340	17161	Rock Island County, IL
19340	19163	Scott County, IA
19380		Dayton-Kettering, OH
19380	39057	Greene County
19380	39109	Miami County
19380	39113	Montgomery County
19460		Decatur, AL
19460	01079	Lawrence County
19460	01103	Morgan County
19500		Decatur, IL
19500	17115	Macon County
19660		Deltona-Daytona Beach-Ormond Beach, FL
19660	12035	Flagler County
19660	12127	Volusia County
19740		Denver-Aurora-Lakewood, CO
19740	08001	Adams County
19740	08005	Arapahoe County
19740	08014	Broomfield County
19740	08019	Clear Creek County
19740	08031	Denver County
19740	08035	Douglas County
19740	08039	Elbert County
19740	08047	Gilpin County
19740	08059	Jefferson County
19740	08093	Park County
19780		Des Moines-West Des Moines, IA
19780	19049	Dallas County
19780	19077	Guthrie County
19780	19099	Jasper County
19780	19121	Madison County
19780	19153	Polk County
19780	19181	Warren County
19820		Detroit-Warren-Dearborn, MI
19820		Detroit-Dearborn-Livonia, MI Div 19804
19820	26163	Wayne County
19820		Warren-Troy-Farmington Hills, MI 47664
19820	26087	Lapeer County
19820	26093	Livingston County
19820	26099	Macomb County
19820	26125	Oakland County
19820	26147	St. Clair County
20020		Dothan, AL
20020	01061	Geneva County
20020	01067	Henry County
20020	01069	Houston County
20100		Dover, DE
20100	10001	Kent County
20220		Dubuque, IA
20220	19061	Dubuque County
20260		Duluth, MN-WI
20260	27017	Carlton County, MN
20260	27075	Lake County, MN
20260	27137	St. Louis County, MN
20260	55031	Douglas County, WI
20500		Durham-Chapel Hill, NC

Metropolitan Statistical Areas, Metropolitan Divisions, and Components—*Continued*

Core based statistical area (CBSA)	State/ County FIPS code	Title and Geographic Components
20500	37037	Chatham County
20500	37063	Durham County
20500	37077	Granville County
20500	37135	Orange County
20500	37145	Person County
20700		East Stroudsburg, PA
20700	42089	Monroe County
20740		Eau Claire, WI
20740	55017	Chippewa County
20740	55035	Eau Claire County
20940		El Centro, CA
20940	06025	Imperial County
21060		Elizabethtown-Fort Knox, KY
21060	21093	Hardin County
21060	21123	Larue County
21060	21163	Meade County
21140		Elkhart-Goshen, IN
21140	18039	Elkhart County
21300		Elmira, NY
21300	36015	Chemung County
21340		El Paso, TX
21340	48141	El Paso County
21340	48229	Hudspeth County
21420		Enid, OK
21420	40047	Garfield County
21500		Erie, PA
21500	42049	Erie County
21660		Eugene-Springfield, OR
21660	41039	Lane County
21780		Evansville, IN-KY
21780	18129	Posey County, IN
21780	18163	Vanderburgh County, IN
21780	18173	Warrick County, IN
21780	21101	Henderson County, KY
21820		Fairbanks, AK
21820	02090	Fairbanks North Star Borough
22020		Fargo, ND-MN
22020	27027	Clay County, MN
22020	38017	Cass County, ND
22140		Farmington, NM
22140	35045	San Juan County
22180		Fayetteville, NC
22180	37051	Cumberland County
22180	37085	Harnett County
22180	37093	Hoke County
22220		Fayetteville-Springdale-Rogers, AR-MO
22220	05007	Benton County, AR
22220	05087	Madison County, AR
22220	05143	Washington County, AR
22380		Flagstaff, AZ
22380	04005	Coconino County
22420		Flint, MI
22420	26049	Genesee County
22500		Florence, SC
22500	45031	Darlington County
22500	45041	Florence County
22520		Florence-Muscle Shoals, AL
22520	01033	Colbert County
22520	01077	Lauderdale County
22540		Fond du Lac, WI
22540	55039	Fond du Lac County
22660		Fort Collins, CO
22660	08069	Larimer County
22900		Fort Smith, AR-OK
22900	05033	Crawford County, AR
22900	05047	Franklin County, AR
22900	05131	Sebastian County, AR
22900	40135	Sequoyah County, OK
23060		Fort Wayne, IN
23060	18003	Allen County
23060	18183	Whitley County
23420		Fresno, CA
23420	06019	Fresno County
23460		Gadsden, AL
23460	01055	Etowah County
23540		Gainesville, FL
23540	12001	Alachua County
23540	12041	Gilchrist County
23540	12075	Levy County
23580		Gainesville, GA
23580	13139	Hall County
23900		Gettysburg, PA
23900	42001	Adams County
24020		Glens Falls, NY
24020	36113	Warren County
24020	36115	Washington County
24140		Goldsboro, NC
24140	37191	Wayne County
24220		Grand Forks, ND-MN
24220	27119	Polk County, MN
24220	38035	Grand Forks County, ND
24260		Grand Island, NE
24260	31079	Hall County
24260	31093	Howard County
24260	31121	Merrick County
24300		Grand Junction, CO
24300	08077	Mesa County
24340		Grand Rapids-Kentwood, MI
24340	26067	Ionia County
24340	26081	Kent County
24340	26117	Montcalm County
24340	26139	Ottawa County
24420		Grants Pass, OR
24420	41033	Josephine County
24500		Great Falls, MT
24500	30013	Cascade County
24540		Greeley, CO
24540	08123	Weld County
24580		Green Bay, WI
24580	55009	Brown County
24580	55061	Kewaunee County
24580	55083	Oconto County
24660		Greensboro-High Point, NC
24660	37081	Guilford County
24660	37151	Randolph County
24660	37157	Rockingham County
24780		Greenville, NC
24780	37147	Pitt County
24860		Greenville-Anderson, SC
24860	45007	Anderson County
24860	45045	Greenville County
24860	45059	Laurens County
24860	45077	Pickens County
25060		Gulfport-Biloxi, MS
25060	28045	Hancock County
25060	28047	Harrison County
25060	28059	Jackson County
25060	28131	Stone County
25180		Hagerstown-Martinsburg, MD-WV
25180	24043	Washington County, MD
25180	54003	Berkeley County, WV
25180	54065	Morgan County, WV
25220		Hammond, LA
25220	22105	Tangipahoa Parish
25260		Hanford-Corcoran, CA
25260	06031	Kings County
25420		Harrisburg-Carlisle, PA
25420	42041	Cumberland County
25420	42043	Dauphin County
25420	42099	Perry County
25500		Harrisonburg, VA
25500	51947	Rockingham + Harrisonburg, VA
25540		Hartford-East Hartford-Middletown, CT
25540	09003	Hartford County
25540	09007	Middlesex County
25540	09013	Tolland County
25620		Hattiesburg, MS
25620	28031	Covington County
25620	28035	Forrest County
25620	28073	Lamar County
25620	28111	Perry County
25860		Hickory-Lenoir-Morganton, NC
25860	37003	Alexander County
25860	37023	Burke County
25860	37027	Caldwell County
25860	37035	Catawba County
25940		Hilton Head Island-Bluffton, SC
25940	45013	Beaufort County
25940	45053	Jasper County
25980		Hinesville, GA
25980	13179	Liberty County
25980	13183	Long County
26140		Homosassa Springs, FL
26140	12017	Citrus County
26300		Hot Springs, AR
26300	05051	Garland County

Metropolitan Statistical Areas, Metropolitan Divisions, and Components—*Continued*

Core based statistical area (CBSA)	State/ County FIPS code	Title and Geographic Components
26380		Houma-Thibodaux, LA
26380	22057	Lafourche Parish
26380	22109	Terrebonne Parish
26420		Houston-The Woodlands-Sugar Land, TX
26420	48015	Austin County
26420	48039	Brazoria County
26420	48071	Chambers County
26420	48157	Fort Bend County
26420	48167	Galveston County
26420	48201	Harris County
26420	48291	Liberty County
26420	48339	Montgomery County
26420	48473	Waller County
26580		Huntington-Ashland, WV-KY-OH
26580	21019	Boyd County, KY
26580	21043	Carter County, KY
26580	21089	Greenup County, KY
26580	39087	Lawrence County, OH
26580	54011	Cabell County, WV
26580	54079	Putnam County, WV
26580	54099	Wayne County, WV
26620		Huntsville, AL
26620	01083	Limestone County
26620	01089	Madison County
26820		Idaho Falls, ID
26820	16019	Bonneville County
26820	16023	Butte County
26820	16051	Jefferson County
26900		Indianapolis-Carmel-Anderson, IN
26900	18011	Boone County
26900	18013	Brown County
26900	18057	Hamilton County
26900	18059	Hancock County
26900	18063	Hendricks County
26900	18081	Johnson County
26900	18095	Madison County
26900	18097	Marion County
26900	18109	Morgan County
26900	18133	Putnam County
26900	18145	Shelby County
26980		Iowa City, IA
26980	19103	Johnson County
26980	19183	Washington County
27060		Ithaca, NY
27060	36109	Tompkins County
27100		Jackson, MI
27100	26075	Jackson County
27140		Jackson, MS
27140	28029	Copiah County
27140	28049	Hinds County
27140	28051	Holmes County
27140	28089	Madison County
27140	28121	Rankin County
27140	28127	Simpson County
27140	28163	Yazoo County
27180		Jackson, TN
27180	47023	Chester County
27180	47033	Crockett County
27180	47053	Gibson County
27180	47113	Madison County
27260		Jacksonville, FL
27260	12003	Baker County
27260	12019	Clay County
27260	12031	Duval County
27260	12089	Nassau County
27260	12109	St. Johns County
27340		Jacksonville, NC
27340	37133	Onslow County
27500		Janesville-Beloit, WI
27500	55105	Rock County
27620		Jefferson City, MO
27620	29027	Callaway County
27620	29051	Cole County
27620	29135	Moniteau County
27620	29151	Osage County
27740		Johnson City, TN
27740	47019	Carter County
27740	47171	Unicoi County
27740	47179	Washington County
27780		Johnstown, PA
27780	42021	Cambria County
27860		Jonesboro, AR
27860	05031	Craighead County
27860	05111	Poinsett County
27900		Joplin, MO
27900	29097	Jasper County
27900	29145	Newton County
27980		Kahului-Wailuku-Lahaina, HI
27980	15009	Maui County
28020		Kalamazoo-Portage, MI
28020	26077	Kalamazoo County
28100		Kankakee, IL
28100	17091	Kankakee County
28140		Kansas City, MO-KS
28140	20091	Johnson County, KS
28140	20103	Leavenworth County, KS
28140	20107	Linn County, KS
28140	20121	Miami County, KS
28140	20209	Wyandotte County, KS
28140	29013	Bates County, MO
28140	29025	Caldwell County, MO
28140	29037	Cass County, MO
28140	29047	Clay County, MO
28140	29049	Clinton County, MO
28140	29095	Jackson County, MO
28140	29107	Lafayette County, MO
28140	29165	Platte County, MO
28140	29177	Ray County, MO
28420		Kennewick-Richland, WA
28420	53005	Benton County
28420	53021	Franklin County
28660		Killeen-Temple, TX
28660	48027	Bell County
28660	48099	Coryell County
28660	48281	Lampasas County
28700		Kingsport-Bristol, TN-VA
28700	47073	Hawkins County, TN
28700	47163	Sullivan County, TN
28700	51169	Scott County, VA
28700	51953	Washington + Bristol, VA
28740		Kingston, NY
28740	36111	Ulster County
28940		Knoxville, TN
28940	47001	Anderson County
28940	47009	Blount County
28940	47013	Campbell County
28940	47093	Knox County
28940	47105	Loudon County
28940	47129	Morgan County
28940	47145	Roane County
28940	47173	Union County
29020		Kokomo, IN
29020	18067	Howard County
29100		La Crosse-Onalaska, WI-MN
29100	27055	Houston County, MN
29100	55063	La Crosse County, WI
29180		Lafayette, LA
29180	22001	Acadia Parish
29180	22045	Iberia Parish
29180	22055	Lafayette Parish
29180	22099	St. Martin Parish
29180	22113	Vermilion Parish
29200		Lafayette-West Lafayette, IN
29200	18007	Benton County
29200	18015	Carroll County
29200	18157	Tippecanoe County
29200	18171	Warren County
29340		Lake Charles, LA
29340	22019	Calcasieu Parish
29340	22023	Cameron Parish
29420		Lake Havasu City-Kingman, AZ
29420	04015	Mohave County
29460		Lakeland-Winter Haven, FL
29460	12105	Polk County
29540		Lancaster, PA
29540	42071	Lancaster County
29620		Lansing-East Lansing, MI
29620	26037	Clinton County
29620	26045	Eaton County
29620	26065	Ingham County
29620	26155	Shiawassee County
29700		Laredo, TX
29700	48479	Webb County
29740		Las Cruces, NM
29740	35013	Doña Ana County
29820		Las Vegas-Henderson-Paradise, NV

Metropolitan Statistical Areas, Metropolitan Divisions, and Components—*Continued*

Core based statistical area (CBSA)	State/ County FIPS code	Title and Geographic Components
29820	32003	Clark County
29940		Lawrence, KS
29940	20045	Douglas County
30020		Lawton, OK
30020	40031	Comanche County
30020	40033	Cotton County
30140		Lebanon, PA
30140	42075	Lebanon County
30300		Lewiston, ID-WA
30300	16069	Nez Perce County, ID
30300	53003	Asotin County, WA
30340		Lewiston-Auburn, ME
30340	23001	Androscoggin County
30460		Lexington-Fayette, KY
30460	21017	Bourbon County
30460	21049	Clark County
30460	21067	Fayette County
30460	21113	Jessamine County
30460	21209	Scott County
30460	21239	Woodford County
30620		Lima, OH
30620	39003	Allen County
30700		Lincoln, NE
30700	31109	Lancaster County
30700	31159	Seward County
30780		Little Rock-North Little Rock-Conway, AR
30780	05045	Faulkner County
30780	05053	Grant County
30780	05085	Lonoke County
30780	05105	Perry County
30780	05119	Pulaski County
30780	05125	Saline County
30860		Logan, UT-ID
30860	16041	Franklin County, ID
30860	49005	Cache County, UT
30980		Longview, TX
30980	48183	Gregg County
30980	48203	Harrison County
30980	48401	Rusk County
30980	48459	Upshur County
31020		Longview, WA
31020	53015	Cowlitz County
31080		Los Angeles-Long Beach-Anaheim, CA
31080		Anaheim-Santa Ana-Irvine, CA Div 11244
31080	06059	Orange County
31080		Los Angeles-Long Beach-Glendale, CA Div 31084
31080	06037	Los Angeles County
31140		Louisville/Jefferson County, KY-IN
31140	18019	Clark County, IN
31140	18043	Floyd County, IN
31140	18061	Harrison County, IN
31140	18175	Washington County, IN
31140	21029	Bullitt County, KY
31140	21103	Henry County, KY
31140	21111	Jefferson County, KY
31140	21185	Oldham County, KY
31140	21211	Shelby County, KY
31140	21215	Spencer County, KY
31180		Lubbock, TX
31180	48107	Crosby County
31180	48303	Lubbock County
31180	48305	Lynn County
31340		Lynchburg, VA
31340	51009	Amherst County
31340	51011	Appomattox County
31340	51909	Bedford County
31340	51911	Campbell + Lynchburg, VA
31420		Macon-Bibb County, GA
31420	13021	Bibb County
31420	13079	Crawford County
31420	13169	Jones County
31420	13207	Monroe County
31420	13289	Twiggs County
31460		Madera, CA
31460	06039	Madera County
31540		Madison, WI
31540	55021	Columbia County
31540	55025	Dane County
31540	55045	Green County
31540	55049	Iowa County
31700		Manchester-Nashua, NH
31700	33011	Hillsborough County
31740		Manhattan, KS
31740	20061	Geary County
31740	20149	Pottawatomie County
31740	20161	Riley County
31860		Mankato, MN
31860	27013	Blue Earth County
31860	27103	Nicollet County
31900		Mansfield, OH
31900	39139	Richland County
32580		McAllen-Edinburg-Mission, TX
32580	48215	Hidalgo County
32780		Medford, OR
32780	41029	Jackson County
32820		Memphis, TN-MS-AR
32820	05035	Crittenden County, AR
32820	28033	DeSoto County, MS
32820	28093	Marshall County, MS
32820	28137	Tate County, MS
32820	28143	Tunica County, MS
32820	47047	Fayette County, TN
32820	47157	Shelby County, TN
32820	47167	Tipton County, TN
32900		Merced, CA
32900	06047	Merced County
33100		Miami-Fort Lauderdale-Pompano Beach, FL
33100		Fort Lauderdale-Pompano Beach-Sunrise, FL Div 22744
33100	12011	Broward County
33100		Miami-Miami Beach-Kendall, FL Div 33124
33100	12086	Miami-Dade County
33100		West Palm Beach-Boca Raton-Boynton Beach, FL Div 48424
33100	12099	Palm Beach County
33140		Michigan City-La Porte, IN
33140	18091	LaPorte County
33220		Midland, MI
33220	26111	Midland County
33260		Midland, TX
33260	48317	Martin County
33260	48329	Midland County
33340		Milwaukee-Waukesha, WI
33340	55079	Milwaukee County
33340	55089	Ozaukee County
33340	55131	Washington County
33340	55133	Waukesha County
33460		Minneapolis-St. Paul-Bloomington, MN-WI
33460	27003	Anoka County, MN
33460	27019	Carver County, MN
33460	27025	Chisago County, MN
33460	27037	Dakota County, MN
33460	27053	Hennepin County, MN
33460	27059	Isanti County, MN
33460	27079	Le Sueur County, MN
33460	27095	Mille Lacs County, MN
33460	27123	Ramsey County, MN
33460	27139	Scott County, MN
33460	27141	Sherburne County, MN
33460	27163	Washington County, MN
33460	27171	Wright County, MN
33460	55093	Pierce County, WI
33460	55109	St. Croix County, WI
33540		Missoula, MT
33540	30063	Missoula County
33660		Mobile, AL
33660	01097	Mobile County
33660	01129	Washington County
33700		Modesto, CA
33700	06099	Stanislaus County
33740		Monroe, LA
33740	22067	Morehouse Parish
33740	22073	Ouachita Parish
33740	22111	Union Parish
33780		Monroe, MI
33780	26115	Monroe County
33860		Montgomery, AL
33860	01001	Autauga County
33860	01051	Elmore County
33860	01085	Lowndes County
33860	01101	Montgomery County
34060		Morgantown, WV
34060	54061	Monongalia County
34060	54077	Preston County
34100		Morristown, TN
34100	47057	Grainger County
34100	47063	Hamblen County
34100	47089	Jefferson County

Metropolitan Statistical Areas, Metropolitan Divisions, and Components—*Continued*

Core based statistical area (CBSA)	State/ County FIPS code	Title and Geographic Components
34580		Mount Vernon-Anacortes, WA
34580	53057	Skagit County
34620		Muncie, IN
34620	18035	Delaware County
34740		Muskegon, MI
34740	26121	Muskegon County
34820		Myrtle Beach-Conway-North Myrtle Beach, SC-NC
34820	37019	Brunswick County, NC
34820	45051	Horry County, SC
34900		Napa, CA
34900	06055	Napa County
34940		Naples-Marco Island, FL
34940	12021	Collier County
34980		Nashville-Davidson—Murfreesboro—Franklin, TN
34980	47015	Cannon County
34980	47021	Cheatham County
34980	47037	Davidson County
34980	47043	Dickson County
34980	47111	Macon County
34980	47119	Maury County
34980	47147	Robertson County
34980	47149	Rutherford County
34980	47159	Smith County
34980	47165	Sumner County
34980	47169	Trousdale County
34980	47187	Williamson County
34980	47189	Wilson County
35100		New Bern, NC
35100	37049	Craven County
35100	37103	Jones County
35100	37137	Pamlico County
35300		New Haven-Milford, CT
35300	09009	New Haven County
35380		New Orleans-Metairie, LA
35380	22051	Jefferson Parish
35380	22071	Orleans Parish
35380	22075	Plaquemines Parish
35380	22087	St. Bernard Parish
35380	22089	St. Charles Parish
35380	22093	St. James Parish
35380	22095	St. John the Baptist Parish
35380	22103	St. Tammany Parish
35620		New York-Newark-Jersey City, NY-NJ-PA
35620		Nassau County-Suffolk County, NY Div 35004
35620	36059	Nassau County
35620	36103	Suffolk County
35620		Newark, NJ-PA Div 35084
35620	34013	Essex County, NJ
35620	34019	Hunterdon County, NJ
35620	34027	Morris County, NJ
35620	34037	Sussex County, NJ
35620	34039	Union County, NJ
35620	42103	Pike County, PA
35620		New Brunswick-Lakewood, NJ Div 35154
35620	34023	Middlesex County
35620	34025	Monmouth County
35620	34029	Ocean County
35620	34035	Somerset County
35620		New York-Jersey City-White Plains, NY-NJ Div 35614
35620	34003	Bergen County, NJ
35620	34017	Hudson County, NJ
35620	34031	Passaic County, NJ
35620	36005	Bronx County, NY
35620	36047	Kings County, NY
35620	36061	New York County, NY
35620	36079	Putnam County, NY
35620	36081	Queens County, NY
35620	36085	Richmond County, NY
35620	36087	Rockland County, NY
35620	36119	Westchester County, NY
35660		Niles-Benton Harbor, MI
35660	26021	Berrien County
35840		North Port-Sarasota-Bradenton, FL
35840	12081	Manatee County
35840	12115	Sarasota County
35980		Norwich-New London, CT
35980	09011	New London County
36100		Ocala, FL
36100	12083	Marion County
36140		Ocean City, NJ
36140	34009	Cape May County
36220		Odessa, TX
36220	48135	Ector County
36260		Ogden-Clearfield, UT
36260	49003	Box Elder County
36260	49011	Davis County
36260	49029	Morgan County
36260	49057	Weber County
36420		Oklahoma City, OK
36420	40017	Canadian County
36420	40027	Cleveland County
36420	40051	Grady County
36420	40081	Lincoln County
36420	40083	Logan County
36420	40087	McClain County
36420	40109	Oklahoma County
36500		Olympia-Lacey-Tumwater, WA
36500	53067	Thurston County
36540		Omaha-Council Bluffs, NE-IA
36540	19085	Harrison County, IA
36540	19129	Mills County, IA
36540	19155	Pottawattamie County, IA
36540	31025	Cass County, NE
36540	31055	Douglas County, NE
36540	31153	Sarpy County, NE
36540	31155	Saunders County, NE
36540	31177	Washington County, NE
36740		Orlando-Kissimmee-Sanford, FL
36740	12069	Lake County
36740	12095	Orange County
36740	12097	Osceola County
36740	12117	Seminole County
36780		Oshkosh-Neenah, WI
36780	55139	Winnebago County
36980		Owensboro, KY
36980	21059	Daviess County
36980	21091	Hancock County
36980	21149	McLean County
37100		Oxnard-Thousand Oaks-Ventura, CA
37100	06111	Ventura County
37340		Palm Bay-Melbourne-Titusville, FL
37340	12009	Brevard County
37460		Panama City, FL
37460	12005	Bay County
37620		Parkersburg-Vienna, WV
37620	54105	Wirt County
37620	54107	Wood County
37860		Pensacola-Ferry Pass-Brent, FL
37860	12033	Escambia County
37860	12113	Santa Rosa County
37900		Peoria, IL
37900	17057	Fulton County
37900	17123	Marshall County
37900	17143	Peoria County
37900	17175	Stark County
37900	17179	Tazewell County
37900	17203	Woodford County
37980		Philadelphia-Camden-Wilmington, PA-NJ-DE-MD
37980		Camden, NJ Div 15804
37980	34005	Burlington County, NJ
37980	34007	Camden County, NJ
37980	34015	Gloucester County, NJ
37980		Montgomery County-Bucks County-Chester County, PA Div 33874
37980	42017	Bucks County, PA
37980	42029	Chester County, PA
37980	42091	Montgomery County, PA
37980		Philadelphia, PA Div 37964
37980	42045	Delaware County, PA
37980	42101	Philadelphia County, PA
37980		Wilmington, DE-MD-NJ Div 48864
37980	10003	New Castle County, DE
37980	24015	Cecil County, MD
37980	34033	Salem County, NJ
38060		Phoenix-Mesa-Chandler, AZ
38060	04013	Maricopa County
38060	04021	Pinal County
38220		Pine Bluff, AR
38220	05025	Cleveland County
38220	05069	Jefferson County
38220	05079	Lincoln County
38300		Pittsburgh, PA
38300	42003	Allegheny County
38300	42005	Armstrong County
38300	42007	Beaver County
38300	42019	Butler County
38300	42051	Fayette County

Metropolitan Statistical Areas, Metropolitan Divisions, and Components—*Continued*

Core based statistical area (CBSA)	State/ County FIPS code	Title and Geographic Components
38300	42125	Washington County
38300	42129	Westmoreland County
38340		Pittsfield, MA
38340	25003	Berkshire County
38540		Pocatello, ID
38540	16005	Bannock County
38540	16077	Power County
38860		Portland-South Portland, ME
38860	23005	Cumberland County
38860	23023	Sagadahoc County
38860	23031	York County
38900		Portland-Vancouver-Hillsboro, OR-WA
38900	41005	Clackamas County, OR
38900	41009	Columbia County, OR
38900	41051	Multnomah County, OR
38900	41067	Washington County, OR
38900	41071	Yamhill County, OR
38900	53011	Clark County, WA
38900	53059	Skamania County, WA
38940		Port St. Lucie, FL
38940	12085	Martin County
38940	12111	St. Lucie County
39100		Poughkeepsie-Newburgh-Middletown, NY
39100	36027	Dutchess County
39100	36071	Orange County
39140		Prescott Valley-Prescott, AZ
39140	04025	Yavapai County
39300		Providence-Warwick, RI-MA
39300	25005	Bristol County, MA
39300	44001	Bristol County, RI
39300	44003	Kent County, RI
39300	44005	Newport County, RI
39300	44007	Providence County, RI
39300	44009	Washington County, RI
39340		Provo-Orem, UT
39340	49023	Juab County
39340	49049	Utah County
39380		Pueblo, CO
39380	08101	Pueblo County
39460		Punta Gorda, FL
39460	12015	Charlotte County
39540		Racine, WI
39540	55101	Racine County
39580		Raleigh-Cary, NC
39580	37069	Franklin County
39580	37101	Johnston County
39580	37183	Wake County
39660		Rapid City, SD
39660	46093	Meade County
39660	46103	Pennington County
39740		Reading, PA
39740	42011	Berks County
39820		Redding, CA
39820	06089	Shasta County
39900		Reno, NV
39900	32029	Storey County
39900	32031	Washoe County
40060		Richmond, VA
40060	51007	Amelia County
40060	51036	Charles City County
40060	51041	Chesterfield County
40060	51075	Goochland County
40060	51085	Hanover County
40060	51087	Henrico County
40060	51097	King and Queen County
40060	51101	King William County
40060	51127	New Kent County
40060	51145	Powhatan County
40060	51183	Sussex County
40060	51760	Richmond city
40060	51918	Dinwiddie, Colonial Heights + Petersburg, VA
40060	51941	Prince George + Hopewell, VA
40140		Riverside-San Bernardino-Ontario, CA
40140	06065	Riverside County
40140	06071	San Bernardino County
40220		Roanoke, VA
40220	51023	Botetourt County
40220	51045	Craig County
40220	51067	Franklin County
40220	51770	Roanoke city
40220	51944	Roanoke + Salem, VA
40340		Rochester, MN
40340	27039	Dodge County
40340	27045	Fillmore County
40340	27109	Olmsted County
40340	27157	Wabasha County
40380		Rochester, NY
40380	36051	Livingston County
40380	36055	Monroe County
40380	36069	Ontario County
40380	36073	Orleans County
40380	36117	Wayne County
40380	36123	Yates County
40420		Rockford, IL
40420	17007	Boone County
40420	17201	Winnebago County
40580		Rocky Mount, NC
40580	37065	Edgecombe County
40580	37127	Nash County
40660		Rome, GA
40660	13115	Floyd County
40900		Sacramento—Roseville—Folsom, CA
40900	06017	El Dorado County
40900	06061	Placer County
40900	06067	Sacramento County
40900	06113	Yolo County
40980		Saginaw, MI
40980	26145	Saginaw County
41060		St. Cloud, MN
41060	27009	Benton County
41060	27145	Stearns County
41100		St. George, UT
41100	49053	Washington County
41140		St. Joseph, MO-KS
41140	20043	Doniphan County, KS
41140	29003	Andrew County, MO
41140	29021	Buchanan County, MO
41140	29063	DeKalb County, MO
41180		St. Louis, MO-IL
41180	17005	Bond County, IL
41180	17013	Calhoun County, IL
41180	17027	Clinton County, IL
41180	17083	Jersey County, IL
41180	17117	Macoupin County, IL
41180	17119	Madison County, IL
41180	17133	Monroe County, IL
41180	17163	St. Clair County, IL
41180	29055	Crawford County + Sullivan, MO
41180	29071	Franklin County, MO
41180	29099	Jefferson County, MO
41180	29113	Lincoln County, MO
41180	29183	St. Charles County, MO
41180	29189	St. Louis County, MO
41180	29219	Warren County, MO
41180	29510	St. Louis city, MO
41420		Salem, OR
41420	41047	Marion County
41420	41053	Polk County
41500		Salinas, CA
41500	06053	Monterey County
41540		Salisbury, MD-DE
41540	10005	Sussex County, DE
41540	24039	Somerset County, MD
41540	24045	Wicomico County, MD
41540	24047	Worcester County, MD
41620		Salt Lake City, UT
41620	49035	Salt Lake County
41620	49045	Tooele County
41660		San Angelo, TX
41660	48235	Irion County
41660	48431	Sterling County
41660	48451	Tom Green County
41700		San Antonio-New Braunfels, TX
41700	48013	Atascosa County
41700	48019	Bandera County
41700	48029	Bexar County
41700	48091	Comal County
41700	48187	Guadalupe County
41700	48259	Kendall County
41700	48325	Medina County
41700	48493	Wilson County
41740		San Diego-Chula Vista-Carlsbad, CA
41740	06073	San Diego County
41860		San Francisco-Oakland-Berkeley, CA
41860		Oakland-Berkeley-Livermore, CA Div 36084
41860	06001	Alameda County

Metropolitan Statistical Areas, Metropolitan Divisions, and Components—*Continued*

Core based statistical area (CBSA)	State/ County FIPS code	Title and Geographic Components
41860	06013	Contra Costa County
41860		San Francisco-San Mateo-Redwood City, CA Div 41884
41860	06075	San Francisco County
41860	06081	San Mateo County
41860		San Rafael, CA Div 42034
41860	06041	Marin County
41940		San Jose-Sunnyvale-Santa Clara, CA
41940	06069	San Benito County
41940	06085	Santa Clara County
42020		San Luis Obispo-Paso Robles, CA
42020	06079	San Luis Obispo County
42100		Santa Cruz-Watsonville, CA
42100	06087	Santa Cruz County
42140		Santa Fe, NM
42140	35049	Santa Fe County
42200		Santa Maria-Santa Barbara, CA
42200	06083	Santa Barbara County
42220		Santa Rosa-Petaluma, CA
42220	06097	Sonoma County
42340		Savannah, GA
42340	13029	Bryan County
42340	13051	Chatham County
42340	13103	Effingham County
42540		Scranton—Wilkes-Barre, PA
42540	42069	Lackawanna County
42540	42079	Luzerne County
42540	42131	Wyoming County
42660		Seattle-Tacoma-Bellevue, WA
42660		Seattle-Bellevue-Kent, WA Div 42644
42660	53033	King County
42660	53061	Snohomish County
42660		Tacoma-Lakewood, WA Div 45104
42660	53053	Pierce County
42680		Sebastian-Vero Beach, FL
42680	12061	Indian River County
42700		Sebring-Avon Park, FL
42700	12055	Highlands County
43100		Sheboygan, WI
43100	55117	Sheboygan County
43300		Sherman-Denison, TX
43300	48181	Grayson County
43340		Shreveport-Bossier City, LA
43340	22015	Bossier Parish
43340	22017	Caddo Parish
43340	22031	De Soto Parish
43420		Sierra Vista-Douglas, AZ
43420	04003	Cochise County
43580		Sioux City, IA-NE-SD
43580	19193	Woodbury County, IA
43580	31043	Dakota County, NE
43580	31051	Dixon County, NE
43580	46127	Union County, SD
43620		Sioux Falls, SD
43620	46083	Lincoln County
43620	46087	McCook County
43620	46099	Minnehaha County
43620	46125	Turner County
43780		South Bend-Mishawaka, IN-MI
43780	18141	St. Joseph County, IN
43780	26027	Cass County, MI
43900		Spartanburg, SC
43900	45083	Spartanburg County
44060		Spokane-Spokane Valley, WA
44060	53063	Spokane County
44060	53065	Stevens County
44100		Springfield, IL
44100	17129	Menard County
44100	17167	Sangamon County
44140		Springfield, MA
44140	25011	Franklin County
44140	25013	Hampden County
44140	25015	Hampshire County
44180		Springfield, MO
44180	29043	Christian County
44180	29059	Dallas County
44180	29077	Greene County
44180	29167	Polk County
44180	29225	Webster County
44220		Springfield, OH
44220	39023	Clark County
44300		State College, PA
44300	42027	Centre County
44420		Staunton, VA

Core based statistical area (CBSA)	State/ County FIPS code	Title and Geographic Components
44420	51907	Augusta County + Staunton + Waynesboro, VA
44700		Stockton, CA
44700	06077	San Joaquin County
44940		Sumter, SC
44940	45027	Clarendon County
44940	45085	Sumter County
45060		Syracuse, NY
45060	36053	Madison County
45060	36067	Onondaga County
45060	36075	Oswego County
45220		Tallahassee, FL
45220	12039	Gadsden County
45220	12065	Jefferson County
45220	12073	Leon County
45220	12129	Wakulla County
45300		Tampa-St. Petersburg-Clearwater, FL
45300	12053	Hernando County
45300	12057	Hillsborough County
45300	12101	Pasco County
45300	12103	Pinellas County
45460		Terre Haute, IN
45460	18021	Clay County
45460	18121	Parke County
45460	18153	Sullivan County
45460	18165	Vermillion County
45460	18167	Vigo County
45500		Texarkana, TX-AR
45500	05081	Little River County, AR
45500	05091	Miller County, AR
45500	48037	Bowie County, TX
45540		The Villages, FL
45540	12119	Sumter County
45780		Toledo, OH
45780	39051	Fulton County
45780	39095	Lucas County
45780	39123	Ottawa County
45780	39173	Wood County
45820		Topeka, KS
45820	20085	Jackson County
45820	20087	Jefferson County
45820	20139	Osage County
45820	20177	Shawnee County
45820	20197	Wabaunsee County
45940		Trenton-Princeton, NJ
45940	34021	Mercer County
46060		Tucson, AZ
46060	04019	Pima County
46140		Tulsa, OK
46140	40037	Creek County
46140	40111	Okmulgee County
46140	40113	Osage County
46140	40117	Pawnee County
46140	40131	Rogers County
46140	40143	Tulsa County
46140	40145	Wagoner County
46220		Tuscaloosa, AL
46220	01063	Greene County
46220	01065	Hale County
46220	01107	Pickens County
46220	01125	Tuscaloosa County
46300		Twin Falls, ID
46300	16053	Jerome County
46300	16083	Twin Falls County
46340		Tyler, TX
46340	48423	Smith County
46520		Urban Honolulu, HI
46520	15003	Honolulu County
46540		Utica-Rome, NY
46540	36043	Herkimer County
46540	36065	Oneida County
46660		Valdosta, GA
46660	13027	Brooks County
46660	13101	Echols County
46660	13173	Lanier County
46660	13185	Lowndes County
46700		Vallejo, CA
46700	06095	Solano County
47020		Victoria, TX
47020	48175	Goliad County
47020	48469	Victoria County
47220		Vineland-Bridgeton, NJ
47220	34011	Cumberland County
47260		Virginia Beach-Norfolk-Newport News, VA-NC

Metropolitan Statistical Areas, Metropolitan Divisions, and Components—*Continued*

Core based statistical area (CBSA)	State/ County FIPS code	Title and Geographic Components
47260	37029	Camden County, NC
47260	37053	Currituck County, NC
47260	37073	Gates County, NC
47260	51073	Gloucester County, VA
47260	51093	Isle of Wight County, VA
47260	51115	Mathews County, VA
47260	51175	Southampton County, VA
47260	51550	Chesapeake city, VA
47260	51650	Hampton city, VA
47260	51700	Newport News city, VA
47260	51710	Norfolk city, VA
47260	51735	Poquoson city, VA
47260	51740	Portsmouth city, VA
47260	51800	Suffolk city, VA
47260	51810	Virginia Beach city, VA
47260	51931	James City County + Williamsburg, VA
47300		Visalia, CA
47300	06107	Tulare County
47380		Waco, TX
47380	48145	Falls County
47380	48309	McLennan County
47460		Walla Walla, WA
47460	53071	Walla Walla County
47580		Warner Robins, GA
47580	13153	Houston County
47580	13225	Peach County
47900		Washington-Arlington-Alexandria, DC-VA-MD-WV
47900		Frederick-Gaithersburg-Rockville, MD Div 23224
47900	24021	Frederick County, MD
47900	24031	Montgomery County, MD
47900		Washington-Arlington-Alexandria, DC-VA-MD-WV Div 47894
47900	11001	District of Columbia, DC
47900	24009	Calvert County, MD
47900	24017	Charles County, MD
47900	24033	Prince George's County, MD
47900	51013	Arlington County, VA
47900	51043	Clarke County, VA
47900	51047	Culpeper County, VA
47900	51061	Fauquier County, VA
47900	51107	Loudoun County, VA
47900	51113	Madison County, VA
47900	51157	Rappahannock County, VA
47900	51179	Stafford County, VA
47900	51187	Warren County, VA
47900	51510	Alexandria city, VA
47900	51919	Fairfax County + Fairfax + Falls Church, VA
47900	51942	Prince William County + Manassas + Manassas Park, VA
47900	51951	Spotsylvania County + Fredericksburg, VA
47900	54037	Jefferson County, WV
47940		Waterloo-Cedar Falls, IA
47940	19013	Black Hawk County
47940	19017	Bremer County
47940	19075	Grundy County
48060		Watertown-Fort Drum, NY
48060	36045	Jefferson County
48140		Wausau-Weston, WI
48140	55069	Lincoln County
48140	55073	Marathon County
48260		Weirton-Steubenville, WV-OH
48260	39081	Jefferson County, OH
48260	54009	Brooke County, WV
48260	54029	Hancock County, WV
48300		Wenatchee, WA
48300	53007	Chelan County
48300	53017	Douglas County
48540		Wheeling, WV-OH
48540	39013	Belmont County, OH
48540	54051	Marshall County, WV
48540	54069	Ohio County, WV
48620		Wichita, KS
48620	20015	Butler County
48620	20079	Harvey County
48620	20173	Sedgwick County
48620	20191	Sumner County
48660		Wichita Falls, TX
48660	48009	Archer County
48660	48077	Clay County
48660	48485	Wichita County
48700		Williamsport, PA
48700	42081	Lycoming County
48900		Wilmington, NC
48900	37129	New Hanover County
48900	37141	Pender County
49020		Winchester, VA-WV
49020	51921	Frederick County + Winchester, VA
49020	54027	Hampshire County, WV
49180		Winston-Salem, NC
49180	37057	Davidson County
49180	37059	Davie County
49180	37067	Forsyth County
49180	37169	Stokes County
49180	37197	Yadkin County
49340		Worcester, MA-CT
49340	09015	Windham County, CT
49340	25027	Worcester County, MA
49420		Yakima, WA
49420	53077	Yakima County
49620		York-Hanover, PA
49620	42133	York County
49660		Youngstown-Warren-Boardman, OH-PA
49660	39099	Mahoning County, OH
49660	39155	Trumbull County, OH
49660	42085	Mercer County, PA
49700		Yuba City, CA
49700	06101	Sutter County
49700	06115	Yuba County
49740		Yuma, AZ
49740	04027	Yuma County

www.ingramcontent.com/pod-product-compliance
Lightning Source LLC
LaVergne TN
LVHW082021200926
848481LV00010B/2898
9798892050425